AMERICAN
HISTORICAL
ASSOCIATION

DIRECTORY

OF HISTORY DEPARTMENTS,
HISTORICAL ORGANIZATIONS,
AND HISTORIANS

45th EDITION 2019-20

Editor: Liz Townsend

© American Historical Association, 2019
ISBN 978-0-87229-099-0

Copies of the *Directory of History Departments, Historical Organizations, and Historians*
may be obtained from:

Oxford University Press
2001 Evans Road
Cary NC 27513

Phone: 800.451.7556
Fax: 919.677.1303
Email: orders.us@oup.com
Web page: http://historians.org/booklets
Member discounts: http://historians.org/memberpubs

About the *Directory* . . .

With this edition, the annual *Directory of History Departments, Historical Organizations, and Historians* enters its 45th year as the primary reference tool on the history profession. Both the print and online versions provide information about almost 700 history programs and historical organizations and about 23,000 historians and history specialists. The searchable online version is available at http://historians.org/directorysearch.

The schools and organizations in this print version appear in three parts—with separate sections for history departments in the United States and Canada, followed by a section on historical organizations. The department listings provide a basic snapshot of activities and personnel as of fall 2019, including contact information, tuition, enrollment data, and faculty. In addition to basic contact information and listings of professional staff, the historical organizations also provide extensive information on their collections, programs, publications, and fellowships and other awards.

In the back you will find the Guide to Historians. This index (which starts on page 553) includes the names of all listed faculty members and organization staff and their affiliated institution(s). In addition, it includes the names, affiliations, interests, and email addresses of American Historical Association members as of August 9, 2019. It adds information on many thousands of historians who are employed in departments outside of history, or in other historical organizations and private activities that are not listed in the *Directory*. Please note that we only list detailed information for those members who have authorized their inclusion in the print *Directory*.

All the departments and organizations listed here have direct access to their information online, allowing them to update their information for the print edition and throughout the year. **Because the departments themselves provide the information for the *Directory*, they bear primary responsibility for the decision to be included and for the content of their entries.** The *Directory* staff reviews the information for completeness and edits the entries to conform to style (for instance, faculty specializations do not generally include the word "history," which should be assumed).

In addition to offering the most up-to-date information, the online *Directory* database also allows searches for historians across a wide range of characteristics (such as school of degree and specialization) and permits department chairs, student advisors, and others to compare departments across metrics such as tuition, highest degree, and faculty size. This opens up the rich array of information in the *Directory* to a variety of uses.

We extend particular thanks to the many people who made this *Directory* possible, especially the department chairs, assistants, and AHA members who provided information. We welcome any comments or suggestions about how the *Directory* might be made more useful and comprehensive. Comments can be directed by email to ltownsend@historians.org.

Liz Townsend
Directory Editor and AHA Manager,
Data Administration and Integrity

Table of Contents

US Departments

A a

B b

C c

Canadian Departments

Historical Organizations

US Departments

Adelphi University

Dept. of History, 1 South Ave., Garden City, NY 11530. 516.877.4790. Fax 516.877.4797. Email: ereno@adelphi.edu. Website: https://history.adelphi.edu/.

Adelphi's history department engages students in what is one of the most intellectual of pursuits. Our program requires history majors to become critical thinkers, perfect their skills in reading and writing, use their imagination to visualize past events and outcomes, and form strong opinions.

Chair: Edward Reno
Degrees Offered: BA
Academic Year System: Semester
Areas of Specialization: Europe, US, Africa, East Asia
Tuition (per academic year): $38470
Enrollment 2018-19:
   Undergraduate Majors: 75
   Degrees in History: 10 BA
Addresses:
   Admissions: http://admissions.adelphi.edu/
   Financial Aid: http://ecampus.adelphi.edu/sfs/

Full-time Faculty

Chande, Abdin (PhD, McGill 1992; assoc. prof.) Africa, Islam, Indian Ocean; chande@adelphi.edu

Christofferson, Michael (PhD, Columbia 1998; prof.) modern Europe, modern France, French intellectual; mchristofferson@adelphi.edu

Darling, Marsha J. (PhD, Duke 1982; prof.; dir., Center for African, Black, and Caribbean Studies) African American, women; darling@adelphi.edu

Haas, Martin R. (PhD, Rutgers 1974; assoc. prof.) US diplomatic, Progressive Era; haas@adelphi.edu

LaCombe, Michael A. (PhD, NYU 2006; assoc. prof.) early America/American Revolution, food, Native American; lacombe@adelphi.edu

Reno, Edward Andrew, III (PhD, Columbia 2011; asst. prof. and chair) medieval, canon law, church; ereno@adelphi.edu

Zaccarini, M. Cristina (PhD, SUNY, Stony Brook 1998; assoc. prof.) spiritualism and spirituality, Sino-American relations, women and medicine; zaccarini@adelphi.edu

Ziomek, Kirsten Laurie (PhD, California, Santa Barbara 2011; assoc. prof.) modern Japan, East Asia, imperialism and visual culture; kziomek@adelphi.edu

Joint/Cross Appointments

Rudolph, Nicole C. (PhD, NYU 2005; assoc. prof.; Languages, Literatures and Cultures) women, France, urban; nrudolph@adelphi.edu

Nondepartmental Historians

Rosenberg, Daniel (PhD, Grad. Center, CUNY 1985; dir., General Studies, Univ. Coll.) American labor, slavery and Civil War, American economic; rosenber@adelphi.edu

Retired/Emeritus Faculty

Baltimore, Lester B. (PhD, Missouri, Columbia 1968; assoc. prof. emeritus; assoc. provost, Acad. Affairs) Civil War and Reconstruction, American radical; baltimor@adelphi.edu

Starkey, Armstrong M., III (PhD, Illinois, Urbana-Champaign 1968; prof. emeritus) Tudor-Stuart England, early modern Europe, Scotland; starkey@adelphi.edu

Agnes Scott College

Dept. of History, 141 E. College Ave., Decatur, GA 30030-3797. 404.471.6239. Fax 404.471.5336. Email: ymanes@agnesscott.edu. Website: http://www.agnesscott.edu/history/.

By offering courses on different regions of the world and on different eras in history, and by emphasizing diversity within cultures, history courses seek to deepen each student's understanding of human experience in its multiple facets. Agnes Scott's history faculty members bring an international perspective to their work and students also have ample opportunities to pursue mentored research and experiential learning.

Chair: Yael Manes
Degrees Offered: BA
Academic Year System: Semester
Areas of Specialization: Africa and African diaspora, Asia, Europe, Middle East, US, women and gender
Tuition (per academic year): $42360
Enrollment 2018-19:
   Undergraduate Majors: 30
   Degrees in History: 13 BA
Addresses:
   Admissions: http://www.agnesscott.edu/admission/
   Financial Aid: http://www.agnesscott.edu/admission/financial-aid/

Full-time Faculty

Bailony, Reem (PhD, UCLA 2015; asst. prof.) Middle East, early modern Ottoman Empire; rbailony@agnesscott.edu

Blaich, Kristian B. (PhD, Emory 2001; Kirk Scholar) modern Europe, modern Germany, transnational identity; kblaich@agnesscott.edu

Cain, Mary Cathryn (PhD, Emory 2001; assoc. prof.) US, US women, African American; mcain@agnesscott.edu

Manes, Yael (PhD, Cornell 2010; assoc. prof. and chair) early modern gender studies; ymanes@agnesscott.edu

Morris, Robin M. (PhD, Yale 2011; assoc. prof.) 20th-century US, US South, women; rmorris@agnesscott.edu

Twagira, Benjamin E. (PhD, Boston Univ. 2018; asst. prof.) Africa, urban; btwagira@agnesscott.edu

Wu, Shu-chin (PhD, Wisconsin, Madison 2005; assoc. prof.) China, East Asia; swu@agnesscott.edu

Retired/Emeritus Faculty

Kennedy, Katharine D. (PhD, Stanford 1982; prof. emerita) modern Europe, Germany, European women; kkennedy@agnesscott.edu

University of Alabama at Birmingham

Dept. of History, 1401 University Blvd., Heritage Hall 360, Birmingham, AL 35294-1152. 205.934.5634. Fax 205.934.8360. Email: melanied@uab.edu. Website: https://www.uab.edu/cas/history/.

Alternate Address: 1720 2nd Ave. S., HHB 360, Birmingham, AL 35294-1152

We offer undergraduate and graduate courses leading to the BA and MA in History. The department is dedicated to our students, and we offer programs, opportunities, and guidance to aid in their success.

Chair: Jonathan Wiesen
Director of Graduate Studies: Andrew W. Keitt
Director of Undergraduate Studies: Walter D. Ward
Degrees Offered: BA,MA
Academic Year System: Semester
Areas of Specialization: US, Europe, Asia, Latin America, Germany, late antiquity
Undergraduate Tuition (per academic year):
  In-State: $8568
  Out-of-State: $19704
Graduate Tuition (per academic year):
  In-State: $8100
  Out-of-State: $18540
Enrollment 2018-19:
  Undergraduate Majors: 132
  New Graduate Students: 6
  Full-time Graduate Students: 5
  Part-time Graduate Students: 11
  Degrees in History: 24 BA, 5 MA
Undergraduate Addresses:
  Admissions: http://www.uab.edu/students/undergraduate-admissions/
  Financial Aid: http://www.uab.edu/students/paying-for-uab
Graduate Addresses:
  Admissions: http://www.uab.edu/graduate/
  Financial Aid: http://www.uab.edu/cas/history/

Full-time Faculty

Baer, Andrew Scott (PhD, Northwestern 2015; asst. prof.) US, African American, urban; abaer@uab.edu
Doss, Harriet E. Amos (PhD, Emory 1976; assoc. prof.) Middle Period US, Old US South, historical editing; hadoss@uab.edu
Keitt, Andrew W. (PhD, California, Berkeley 1998; assoc. prof. and dir., grad. studies) early modern Europe, European cultural and intellectual, Iberian world; akeitt@uab.edu
King, Pamela Sterne (MA, Alabama 1977; teaching asst. prof.) US South, historical preservation; pamking@uab.edu
Liber, George O. (PhD, Columbia 1986; prof.) Soviet Union, imperial Russia, eastern Europe; gliber@uab.edu
Millard, Andre J. (PhD, Emory 1981; prof.) American technology, popular culture, American studies; amillard@uab.edu
Miller, Stephen J. (PhD, UCLA 1999; assoc. prof.) French Revolution, modern France, comparative revolutions; sjmiller@uab.edu
Murray, Pamela S. (PhD, Tulane 1990; prof.) Latin America, national period, Colombia; pmurray@uab.edu
Steele, Brian D. (PhD, North Carolina, Chapel Hill 2003; assoc. prof.) early Republic US; bdsteele@uab.edu
Van Sant, John E. (PhD, Oregon 1996; assoc. prof.) East Asia, modern Japan, US-Japanese relations; jvansant@uab.edu
Ward, Walter David (PhD, UCLA 2008; assoc. prof. and dir., undergrad. studies) late antiquity, Rome and Greece, Hellenistic-Roman Near East archaeology; wdward@uab.edu
Wiesen, Jonathan (PhD, Brown 1998; prof. and chair) modern Europe, Germany; jwiesen@uab.edu

Retired/Emeritus Faculty

Conley, Carolyn A. (PhD, Duke 1984; prof. emerita) British political and social, British Empire, crime/violence social; cconley@uab.edu
Davis, Colin J. (PhD, SUNY, Binghamton 1989; prof. emeritus) US labor, US social, comparative labor movements; cjdavis@uab.edu
Lesnick, Daniel R. (PhD, Rochester 1976; assoc. prof. emeritus) medieval Europe, Renaissance, ancient Greece and Rome
McConnell, Michael N. (PhD, William and Mary 1983; assoc. prof. emeritus) colonial America, ethnohistory; mcconnel@uab.edu
McWilliams, Tennant S. (PhD, Georgia 1973; prof. and dean emeritus) late 19th- and 20th-century US, recent US South, US foreign affairs; tsm@uab.edu
Penick, James L., Jr. (PhD, California, Berkeley 1962; prof. emeritus) late 19th- and 20th-century US
Tent, James F. (PhD, Wisconsin, Madison 1973; prof. and Univ. scholar emeritus) modern Europe, Germany, Cold War; jtent@uab.edu
Webb, Samuel L., Jr. (PhD, Arkansas 1991; assoc. prof. emeritus) US since Reconstruction, New South and southern politics, US constitutional and legal

University of Alabama in Huntsville

Dept. of History, 301 Sparkman Dr., 409 Roberts Hall, Huntsville, AL 35899. 256.824.6310. Fax 256.824.6477. Email: warings@uah.edu. Website: https://www.uah.edu/ahs/departments/history.

The history faculty wants to help you learn about the past and prepare you for the future. We are dedicated to excellence in research and teaching, and strive to create a range of classes and programs to meet your interests.

Chair: Stephen P. Waring
Degrees Offered: BA,MA
Academic Year System: Semester
Areas of Specialization: 20th century, Europe, US, women
Undergraduate Tuition (per academic year):
  In-State: $9730
  Out-of-State: $22126
Graduate Tuition (per academic year):
  In-State: $10632
  Out-of-State: $24430
Enrollment 2018-19:
  Undergraduate Majors: 42
  New Graduate Students: 9
  Full-time Graduate Students: 14
  Part-time Graduate Students: 7
  Degrees in History: 14 BA, 5 MA
Addresses:
  Admissions: http://www.uah.edu/admissions/
  Financial Aid: http://www.uah.edu/financial-aid/

Full-time Faculty

Baun, Dylan (PhD, Arizona 2015; asst. prof.) modern Middle East and Islamic world, youth cultures, street politics; dylan.baun@uah.edu
Gandila, Andrei (PhD, Florida 2013; asst. prof.) Rome, Roman archaeology, late antiquity; andrei.gandila@uah.edu

Johnson, Molly Wilkinson (PhD, Illinois, Urbana-Champaign 2003; assoc. prof.) modern Europe, Germany, women; johnsomw@uah.edu

Pacino, Nicole L. (PhD, California, Santa Barbara 2013; asst. prof.) Latin America, science and medicine, gender studies; nicole.pacino@uah.edu

Sears, Christine E. (PhD, Delaware 2007; assoc. prof.) Atlantic world, early Republic US, slavery; christine.sears@uah.edu

Waring, Stephen P. (PhD, Iowa 1988; prof. and chair) modern US, US intellectual, US technology; warings@uah.edu

Retired/Emeritus Faculty

Boucher, Philip P. (PhD, Connecticut 1974; dist. prof. emeritus) early modern Europe, colonial expansion, Caribbean; boucherp@uah.edu

Dunar, Andrew J. (PhD, Southern California 1981; prof. emeritus) 20th-century US, US diplomatic, oral; dunara@uah.edu

Ellis, Jack D. (PhD, Tulane 1967; prof. emeritus) 19th- and 20th-century Europe, modern France, social history of medicine; jellis1789@comcast.net

Gerberding, Richard A. (PhD, Oxford 1982; prof. emeritus) ancient, medieval; gerberdingr@uah.edu

Severn, John K. (PhD, Florida State 1975; prof. emeritus and assoc. provost) French Revolution and Napoleon, 19th-century Europe, modern France; severnj@uah.edu

Shields, Johanna N. (PhD, Alabama 1972; prof. emeritus) US social and cultural, early Republic, Old US South; shieldsj@uah.edu

White, Carolyn W. (PhD, Duke 1974; prof. emeritus) Britain, historiography, modern Europe

White, John C. (PhD, Duke 1964; prof. emeritus) modern France, Age of Reason, administrative

Williams, Lee E., II (PhD, Mississippi State 1975; prof. emeritus) 20th-century US, African American, modern US South; willial@uah.edu

University of Alabama at Tuscaloosa

Dept. of History, PO Box 870212, 202 ten Hoor Hall, 305 Marrs Spring Rd., Tuscaloosa, AL 35487-0212. 205.348.7100. Fax 205.348.0670. Email: history@ua.edu; scott076@ua.edu. Website: https://history.ua.edu/.

The History Department is a vital part of the research, instructional, and outreach missions of The University of Alabama.

Chair: Joshua Rothman
Director of Graduate Studies: Daniel Riches
Director of Undergraduate Studies: Margaret Peacock
Degrees Offered: BA, MA, PhD
Academic Year System: Semester
Areas of Specialization: US, US South, military, religion, race, gender and women, Latin America, modern Europe
Tuition (per academic year):
  In-State: $10780
  Out-of-State: $29230
Enrollment 2018-19:
  Undergraduate Majors: 400
  New Graduate Students: 15
  Full-time Graduate Students: 50
  Degrees in History: 125 BA, 14 MA, 3 PhD
Undergraduate Addresses:
  Admissions: https://gobama.ua.edu/
  Financial Aid: http://financialaid.ua.edu/

Graduate Addresses:
  Admissions: http://graduate.ua.edu/prospects/application/
  Financial Aid: http://financialaid.ua.edu/

Full-time Faculty

Abruzzo, Margaret N. (PhD, Notre Dame 2005; assoc. prof.) colonial and early modern US; mabruzzo@ua.edu

Beeler, John F. (PhD, Illinois, Urbana-Champaign 1991; prof.) naval and military, modern Britain and Empire/Commonwealth, modern Europe; jbeeler@tenhoor.as.ua.edu

Beito, David T. (PhD, Wisconsin, Madison 1986; prof.) US social; dbeito@bama.ua.edu

Brock, Julia (PhD, California, Santa Barbara 2013; asst. prof.) public, modern US South; jbrock2@ua.edu

Bunker, Steven B. (PhD, Texas Christian 2006; assoc. prof.) Latin America; sbunker@bama.ua.edu

Cappello, Lawrence (PhD, Graduate Center, CUNY 2017; asst. prof.) US legal and constitutional; lcappello@ua.edu

Cribelli, C. Teresa (PhD, Johns Hopkins 2009; assoc. prof.) Latin America; ctcribelli@bama.ua.edu

Frederickson, Kari (PhD, Rutgers 1996; prof.) US South; kfrederi@as.ua.edu

Giggie, John Michael (PhD, Princeton 1998; assoc. prof.; dir., Summersell Center for the Study of the South) African American; jmgiggie@bama.ua.edu

Gordon, Lesley J. (PhD, Georgia 1995; prof. and Charles G. Summersell Chair) US South, American Civil War; ljgordon1@ua.edu

Green, Sharony A. (PhD, Illinois, Urbana-Champaign 2013; asst. prof.) African American; sagreen1@ua.edu

Grout, Holly L. (PhD, Wisconsin-Madison 2009; assoc. prof.) modern European cultural and intellectual; hlgrout@bama.ua.edu

Huebner, Andrew J. (PhD, Brown 2004; assoc. prof.) 20th-century US intellectual and cultural; ahuebner@bama.ua.edu

Kaufman, Lucy M. (PhD, Yale 2014; asst. prof.) early modern Britain, popular politics and power, religious and national identity; lmkaufman@ua.edu

Kopelson, Heather Miyano (PhD, Iowa 2008; assoc. prof.) Atlantic world race and gender, early American religion; hmkopelson@bama.ua.edu

Lindquist-Dorr, Lisa J. (PhD, Virginia 2000; assoc. prof.) 20th-century US South, women; ldorr@bama.ua.edu

Luo, Di (PhD, Ohio State 2015; asst. prof.) Asia; dluo10@ua.edu

Mixson, James David (PhD, Notre Dame 2002; assoc. prof.) medieval religious, intellectual, manuscript studies; jmixson@ua.edu

Peacock, Margaret E. (PhD, Texas, Austin 2009; assoc. prof. and undergrad. program dir.) Russia and Soviet Union, Cold War, semiotics and visual culture; mepeacock@ua.edu

Peterson, Erik L. (PhD, Notre Dame 2010; asst. prof.) history and philosophy of science; elpeterson@ua.edu

Ponce Vazquez, Juan Jose (PhD, Pennsylvania 2011; asst. prof.) colonial Latin America; jponcevasquez@ua.edu

Riches, Daniel L. (PhD, Chicago 2007; assoc. prof. and grad. dir.) European military and diplomatic; dlriches@ua.edu

Rothman, Joshua D. (PhD, Virginia 2000; prof. and chair) US slavery, American South; jrothman@bama.ua.edu

Selesky, Harold E. (PhD, Yale 1984; assoc. prof.) US military, colonial and revolutionary America; hselesky@tenhoor.as.ua.edu

Shaw, Jenny (PhD, NYU 2009; assoc. prof.) Atlantic world race and labor, American religious rituals and practices; jenny.shaw@ua.edu

Steinbock-Pratt, Sarah (PhD, Texas, Austin 2013; asst. prof.) US and
world, diplomatic; sksteinbockpratt@ua.edu
Wasserman, Janek (PhD, Washington, St. Louis 2010; assoc. prof.)
modern Europe; iwasserman@bama.ua.edu

Retired/Emeritus Faculty

Clayton, Lawrence A. (PhD, Tulane 1972; prof. emeritus) colonial
Latin America, Andean nations, US-Latin American relations
lclayton@simplecom.net
Freyer, Tony (PhD, Indiana 1975; Univ. Research Prof. emeritus;
Law Sch.) US legal and constitutional; tfreyer@law.ua.edu
Jones, Howard (PhD, Indiana 1973; Univ. Research Prof. emeritus)
recent US, American international relations, Vietnam; hjones@
tenhoor.as.ua.edu
Kohl, Lawrence F. (PhD, Michigan 1980; assoc. prof. emeritus) US
1815-77, Civil War; lfkohl@bama.ua.edu
McClure, George William (PhD, Michigan 1981; prof. emeritus)
Renaissance and Reformation Europe, medieval; gmcclure@
ua.edu
Mendle, Michael J. (PhD, Washington, St. Louis 1977; prof.
emeritus) Tudor-Stuart England, British political thought;
mmendle@bama.ua.edu
Rable, George C. (PhD, Louisiana State 1978; Charles E.
Summersell Chair emeritus) US South; grable@ua.edu
Ultee, Maarten (PhD, Johns Hopkins 1975; prof. emeritus)
Wiggins, Sarah W. (PhD, Louisiana State 1965; prof. emeritus
and ed., Alabama Review) Reconstruction South, Alabama;
swiggins@dbtech.net

Recently Awarded PhDs

Hughes, Kevin L. "The Promise and Perils of Reconstruction:
Augusta, Georgia, 1865-86"
Privette, Lindsay R. "'Fighting Johnnies, Fevers, and Mosquitoes':
A Medical History of the Vicksburg Campaign"

Albion College

*Dept. of History, 611 E. Porter St., Albion, MI 49224-5013.
517.629.0396. Fax 517.629.0556. Email: dkanter@albion.edu.
Website: http://www.albion.edu/academics/departments/
history.*

*The History Department at Albion College seeks to foster creative
and analytical thinkers who are interested in questions of how
human societies change over time. Faculty members have been
selected for their ability to help you work through critical historical
issues and experience those issues firsthand through relevant off-
campus opportunities, internships, and compelling research.*

Chair: Deborah Kanter
Degrees Offered: BA
Academic Year System: Semester
Areas of Specialization: US, Europe, Latin America, Asia, race and
gender
Tuition (per academic year): $45070
Enrollment 2018-19:
Undergraduate Majors: 38
Degrees in History: 9 BA
Addresses:
Admissions: http://www.albion.edu/admission
Financial Aid: http://www.albion.edu/admission/scholarships-
and-financial-aid

Full-time Faculty

Brade, Laura Elizabeth (PhD, North Carolina, Chapel Hill 2017; asst.
prof.) modern Europe, eastern Europe, Holocaust
Dick, Wesley A. (PhD, Washington 1973; prof.) US, 20th-century
social and cultural, environmental; wdick@albion.edu
Ho, Joseph W. (PhD, Michigan 2017; asst. prof.) East Asia, modern
China, visual culture
Kanter, Deborah (PhD, Virginia 1993; prof. and chair) Latin
America, Mexico, Chicano; dkanter@albion.edu
Sacks, Marcy S. (PhD, California, Berkeley 1999; prof.) US, African
American, race relations; msacks@albion.edu

Nondepartmental Historians

Franzen, Trisha (PhD, New Mexico 1990; prof.; Women and Gender
Studies) modern US women and sexuality; tfranzen@albion.edu
Yoshii, Midori (PhD, Boston Univ. 2003; assoc. prof.; International
Studies) US-East Asian relations, modern Japan, US foreign
policy; myoshii@albion.edu

Retired/Emeritus Faculty

Cocks, Geoffrey C. (PhD, UCLA 1975; prof. emeritus) modern
Germany, recent Europe and European film, psychohistory and
psychiatry; gcocks@albion.edu

Visiting Faculty

Riedel, Christopher Tolin (PhD, Boston Coll. 2015; vis. asst. prof.)
medieval Europe, religion, Western-Islamic relations

Albright College

*Dept. of History, PO Box 15234, Reading, PA 19612-5234.
610.921.7810. Fax 610.921.7683. Email: pturning@albright.edu.
Website: https://www.albright.edu/academic/undergraduate-
programs/history/.*

*The History Department is committed to expanding the
intellectual and cultural dimensions of concentrators as well
as non-concentrators. The department's goals are to introduce
students to the discipline of history, prepare students to be
effective and clear communicators, prepare students for future
studies and careers in a variety of fields, and prepare students for
a lifetime of critical engagement with their worlds.*

Chair: Patricia Turning
Degrees Offered: BA
Academic Year System: Semester
Areas of Specialization: America, Europe, Asia
Tuition (per academic year): $44206
Enrollment 2018-19:
Undergraduate Majors: 95
Degrees in History: 24 BA
Addresses:
Admissions: http://www.albright.edu/admit/home
Financial Aid: http://www.albright.edu/admit/home/home/
financial-aid

Full-time Faculty

de Syon, Guillaume P. (PhD, Boston Univ. 1994; prof.) modern
Germany and France, technology, popular culture; gdesyon@
albright.edu
Fletcher, Kami L. (PhD, Morgan State 2013; assoc. prof.) modern
America, African American
Palshikar, Shreeyash S. (PhD, Chicago 2009; asst. prof.) South Asia,
world, magic; spalshikar@albright.edu

Pankratz, John R. (PhD, Cornell 1988; prof.) America, ecological, Africa; jpankratz@albright.edu

Turning, Patricia (PhD, California, Davis 2007; assoc. prof. and chair) medieval Europe, early modern Europe, crime and punishment, urban; pturning@albright.edu

Joint/Cross Appointments

Aquino, Hilary C. (PhD, SUNY, Stony Brook 2004; asst. prof.; Sch. of Professional Studies) America, medicine, women; haquino@albright.edu

Retired/Emeritus Faculty

Fahy, Barbara M. (PhD, Temple 1975; prof. emeritus) medieval, Renaissance, Reformation; bfahy@albright.edu

Alfred University

Div. of Human Studies, One Saxon Dr., Alfred, NY 14802. 607.871.2217. Fax 607.871.2097. Email: saxtonmj@alfred. edu. Website: https://www.alfred.edu/academics/undergrad-majors-minors/history.cfm.

Alfred University's history program offers students a challenging and unique perspective because the faculty emphasize interdisciplinary and global learning. Small classes enable students to engage with teachers and peers in lively discussions. Faculty members take pride in their active involvement in writing books and articles and participating in conferences around the world.

Chair: Emrys Westacott
Degrees Offered: BA
Academic Year System: Semester
Areas of Specialization: America, Europe, Middle East, intellectual and cultural, gender and sexuality
Tuition (per academic year): $32494
Enrollment 2018-19:
Undergraduate Majors: 60
Degrees in History: 10 BA
Addresses:
Admissions: http://www.alfred.edu/admissions/
Financial Aid: http://www.alfred.edu/finaid/

Full-time Faculty

Ostrower, Gary B. (PhD, Rochester 1970; prof.) US diplomatic, 20th-century political; ostrower@alfred.edu

Szymanski, Mallory (PhD, Florida 2017; asst. prof.) US and transatlantic, women; gender studies; szymanski@alfred.edu

Joint/Cross Appointments

Singer, Sandra L. (PhD, Wisconsin-Madison 1992; prof.; Modern Languages) fsinger@alfred.edu

Visiting Faculty

Kless, Andrew Hoyt (ABD, Rochester; vis. lect.) Europe

Allegheny College

Dept. of History, 520 N. Main St., Box 27, Meadville, PA 16335-3999. 814.332.4342. Fax 814.332.2710. Email: lriggle@allegheny.edu. Website: https://sites.allegheny.edu/history/.

We treat history as an interpretive endeavor, investigating from various points of view the ways in which individuals and social groups have sought to order and understand their world across time. As a department, we strive to provide wisdom in particular historical fields, and to assist our students in the development of conceptual skills, critical analysis, research competence, writing fluency, and sophistication in the uses and abuses of knowledge.

Chair: Judson Herrman
Degrees Offered: BA
Academic Year System: Semester
Areas of Specialization: US, Europe, Latin America, Asia, Middle East
Tuition (per academic year): $48760
Enrollment 2018-19:
Undergraduate Majors: 53
Degrees in History: 24 BA
Addresses:
Admissions: http://sites.allegheny.edu/admissions
Financial Aid: http://sites.allegheny.edu/finaid/

Full-time Faculty

Binnington, Ian (PhD, Illinois, Urbana-Champaign 2004; registrar; assoc. dean; and assoc. prof.) 19th-century America, American South, Civil War and Reconstruction; ibinning@allegheny.edu

Haywood, Elisabeth Kalé (PhD, Stanford 2001; assoc. prof.) Latin America, colonial Mexico, ecclesiastical; khaywood@allegheny.edu

Keysor, Angela Miller (PhD, Iowa 2013; asst. prof.) colonial and revolutionary America, women, medicine and law; akeysor@allegheny.edu

Miller, Brian JK (PhD, Iowa 2015; asst. prof.) modern Turkey and Germany, Middle East and North Africa, migration and transnational; bmiller2@allegheny.edu

Pinnow, Kenneth M. (PhD, Columbia 1998; prof.) Tsarist and Soviet Russia, medicine, modern Europe; kpinnow@allegheny.edu

Ribeiro, Alyssa (PhD, Pittsburgh 2013; asst. prof.) 20th-century America, urban, race/ethnicity/gender; aribeiro@allegheny.edu

Wu, Guo (PhD, SUNY, Albany 2006; assoc. prof.) modern China, intellectual, film; gwu@allegheny.edu

Joint/Cross Appointments

Herrman, Judson (PhD, Harvard 1999; prof.; chair, Classical Studies) ancient Greece; jherrman@allegheny.edu

Part-time Faculty

Jackson, Patrick D. (PhD, Vanderbilt 2012; vis. asst. prof. and National Fellowships Advisor) early 20th-century America, religious; pjackson@allegheny.edu

Orttung, Robin (ABD, Boston Univ.; instr.) ancient Rome; rorttung@allegheny.edu

Retired/Emeritus Faculty

Clayton, Bruce L. (PhD, Duke 1966; prof. emeritus) American intellectual, biography, US South; bclayton39@yahoo.com

Helmreich, Jonathan E. (PhD, Princeton 1961; prof. emeritus) 19th- and 20th-century Europe, Low Countries, 19th- and 20th-century diplomatic; jhelmrei@allegheny.edu

Lyons, Stephen M. (PhD, Brown 1980; prof. emeritus) medieval Europe, Crusades, chivalry; slyons@allegheny.edu

Shapiro, Barry M. (PhD, UCLA 1989; prof. emeritus) 18th-century Europe, French Revolution, psychohistory; bshapiro@allegheny.edu

Treckel, Paula A. (PhD, Syracuse 1978; prof. emerita) colonial America, women, fashion; ptreckel@allegheny.edu

Turk, Richard W. (PhD, Tufts 1962; prof. emeritus) American diplomatic, naval and maritime, America 1865-1920; rturk@allegheny.edu

Alma College

Dept. of History, 614 W. Superior St., Alma, MI 48801-1599.
989.463.7111. Fax 989.463.7277. Email: bulipi@alma.edu.
Website: https://www.alma.edu/academics/history/.

Alma's history program offers courses on Africa, Asia, the
Americas, and Europe. Subject matter spans an extensive range
of time periods and cultures, addressing special topics like the
history of public health, religion, immigration and ethnicity,
foreign policy, the American Constitution and law. Thanks to the
breadth of topics and flexible course sequencing, many history
majors also choose to double major in related subjects.

Chair: Liping Bu
Degrees Offered: BA
Academic Year System: Semester
Areas of Specialization: US, Europe, Africa, East Asia, Latin
America
Tuition (per academic year): $41000
Enrollment 2018-19:
Undergraduate Majors: 25
Degrees in History: 10 BA
Addresses:
Admissions: http://www.alma.edu/admissions/
Financial Aid: http://www.alma.edu/admissions/financial-aid/

Adjunct Faculty

Wise, Keith (PhD, American 1997; instr.) ancient Mediterranean;
kwise@edzone.net

Full-time Faculty

Bu, Liping (PhD, Carnegie Mellon 1995; prof. and chair) 20th-
century America, US foreign relations, modern China/East Asia;
bulipi@alma.edu
Furlong, Patrick J. (PhD, California, Santa Barbara 1987; prof.)
South Africa, modern Europe, fascism; furlong@alma.edu
Olbertson, Kristin A. (JD,PhD, Michigan 2005; assoc. prof.) legal,
US; olbertson@alma.edu
Wasserman-Soler, Daniel I. (PhD, Virginia 2012; assoc. prof.) early
modern Europe, Spain and Spanish Empire; wasserman@alma.
edu

Joint/Cross Appointments

Peterson, Benjamin (PhD, Illinois, Chicago 2016; vis. asst. prof.;
Political Science) American history and politics; petersonbl@
alma.edu

Retired/Emeritus Faculty

Lorenz, Edward C. (PhD, Chicago 1978; prof. emeritus; Political
Science) US social policy, US political, Latin America; lorenz@
alma.edu
Yavenditti, Michael J. (PhD, California, Berkeley 1970; prof.
emeritus) US racial and ethnic minorities, Latin America, Russia
and Soviet Union; yavendit@alma.edu

American International College

Dept. of History, 1000 State St., Springfield, MA 01109-3184.
413.205.3281. Fax 413.205.3943. Email: thomas.maulucci@aic.
edu. Website: https://www.aic.edu/school-of-business-arts-
and-sciences/program/history/.

The history program at AIC provides undergraduate students with
a comprehensive overview of the fields of American, world, and
Western history. Upper-level electives focus on subjects like African
American history, modern diplomatic and military history, the
history of political thought, and the American radical tradition.
Students intending to teach history in secondary schools are
strongly encouraged to major in History/Education.

Chair: Thomas W. Maulucci Jr.
Degrees Offered: BA
Academic Year System: Semester
Areas of Specialization: America, Europe, world
Tuition (per academic year): $36930
Enrollment 2018-19:
Undergraduate Majors: 9
Degrees in History: 4 BA
Addresses:
Admissions: http://www.aic.edu/admissions/
Financial Aid: http://www.aic.edu/financialaid

Adjunct Faculty

Agnitti, Allen (JD, Northeastern Sch. Law; adj.) US, legal; allen.
agnitti@aic.edu
Rogers, Amelia (MA, Urbino, Italy 1966; adj.) ancient
Mediterranean; amelia.rogers@aic.edu
Sternberg, Robert (MEd, Concordia, Can. 1977; adj.) Holocaust
studies, Judaic studies; robert.sternberg@aic.edu

Full-time Faculty

Jones, Gary (PhD, Lehigh 1997; assoc. prof.) modern America,
labor; gary.jones@aic.edu
Maulucci, Thomas W. (PhD, Yale 1998; prof. and chair) 20th-
century Europe, international relations, modern Germany;
thomas.maulucci@aic.edu

Nondepartmental Historians

Walsh, Julie A. (PhD, Connecticut 1995; assoc. prof.; Political
Science) political thought; julie.walsh@aic.edu

Retired/Emeritus Faculty

Horsnell, Margaret E. (PhD, Minnesota 1967; prof. emeritus)
revolutionary and early Republic America

American University

Dept. of History, 4400 Massachusetts Ave. NW, Washington,
DC 20016-8038. 202.885.2401 Email: history@american.edu.
Website: https://www.american.edu/cas/history/.

American University is a private, doctoral institution in a
residential neighborhood of Washington, DC. Our department
encourages interdisciplinary study, individually designed
programs, and close contact between faculty and students. The
outstanding faculty in our department are dedicated to teaching,
scholarship, and helping students use the matchless resources in
the nation's capital.

Chair: Eric Lohr
Director of Graduate Studies: Gautham Rao
Director of Undergraduate Studies: April Shelford and Pedram
Partovi
Degrees Offered: BA,MA,PhD
Academic Year System: Semester
Areas of Specialization: America, Europe, public, Russia, Jewish
Undergraduate Tuition (per academic year): $26170
Graduate Tuition (per academic year): $31662

Enrollment 2018-19:
  Undergraduate Majors: 120
  New Graduate Students: 25
  Full-time Graduate Students: 44
  Part-time Graduate Students: 25
  Degrees in History: 62 BA, 22 MA, 6 PhD
Addresses:
  Admissions: http://www.american.edu/admissions/
  Financial Aid: http://www.american.edu/financialaid/

Full-time Faculty

Beers, Laura D. (PhD, Harvard 2007; assoc. prof.) modern British political and cultural; beers@american.edu

Brenner, Michael (PhD, Columbia 1994; prof. and Seymour and Lillian Abensohn Chair and dir., Center for Israel Studies) Israel and Jewish; mbrenner@american.edu

Curtin, Mary Ellen (PhD, Duke 1992; assoc. prof.; Critical Race, Gender, Cultural Studies Collaborative) African American, social, women; curtin@american.edu

Demshuk, Andrew T. (PhD, Illinois, Urbana-Champaign 2010; assoc. prof.) Germany, modern Europe; demshuk@american.edu

Fedyashin, Anton (PhD, Georgetown 2007; assoc. prof. and dir., Carmel Inst. of Russian Culture & Hist.) Russia and Europe, Cold War, geopolitics; fedyashi@american.edu

Findlay, Eileen J. (PhD, Wisconsin, Madison 1995; prof.; Critical Race, Gender, Cultural Studies Collaborative) Latin America and Caribbean, race, gender; efindla@american.edu

Friedman, Max Paul (PhD, California, Berkeley 2000; prof.; Sch. of International Service) 20th-century US foreign relations; friedman@american.edu

Giandrea, Mary Frances (PhD, Boston Coll. 1997; sr. professorial lect.) medieval Europe, Britain, early Christianity; giandrea@american.edu

Haulman, Kate (PhD, Cornell 2002; assoc. prof.) early America, women/gender/sexuality, cultural; haulman@american.edu

Jacobs, Justin Matthew (PhD, California, San Diego 2011; assoc. prof.) premodern China, modern Japan, Asia; jjacobs@american.edu

Kendi, Ibram X. (PhD, Temple 2010; prof. and dir., Antiracist Research and Policy Center; Sch. of International Service) African American studies, racism

Kerr, Daniel R. (PhD, Case Western Reserve 2005; assoc. prof. and dir., Public History Prog.) public, US, urban; kerr@american.edu

Kraut, Alan (PhD, Cornell 1975; Univ. Prof.; Sch. of International Studies, Public Health Prog.) US immigration and ethnicity, medicine, Civil War and American South; akraut@american.edu

Kuznick, Peter J. (PhD, Rutgers 1984; prof. and dir., Nuclear Studies Inst.) US cultural, science, 20th-century US; kuznick@american.edu

Leff, Lisa Moses (PhD, Chicago 2000; acting dean of academic affairs) Europe 1789-present, modern Jewish; leff@american.edu

Lichtman, Allan J. (PhD, Harvard 1973; Dist. Prof.; Justice, Law & Criminology) quantitative methods, American political, late 19th- and 20th-century US; lichtman@american.edu

Lohr, Eric J. (PhD, Harvard 1999; prof.; Susan Carmel Lehrman Chair, Russian Hist. and Culture; and chair) Russia, World War I, Russian Revolution; elohr@american.edu

Nadell, Pamela S. (PhD, Ohio State 1982; prof. and Patrick Clendenen Chair and chair, Critical Race, Gender and Cultural Studies.) American Jewish, women and gender; pnadell@american.edu

Partovi, Pedram (PhD, Chicago 2010; assoc. prof. and dir., undergrad. studies) Iran, Middle East; partovi@american.edu

Rao, Gautham (PhD, Chicago 2008; assoc. prof. and dir., grad. studies) early America, legal; grao@american.edu

Runstedtler, Theresa E. (PhD, Yale 2007; assoc. prof.; chair, Critical Race, Gender, and Cultural Studies) African American, African diaspora, US transnational/imperial; runstedt@american.edu

Rymsza-Pawlowlska, Malgorzata Joanna (PhD, Brown 2012; asst. prof.) public, cultural, modern America; rymszapa@american.edu

Shelford, April G. (PhD, Princeton 1997; assoc. prof. and dir., undergrad. studies) early modern Europe, religion and culture; shelfor@american.edu

Stockreiter, Elke E. (PhD, SOAS, London 2008; assoc. prof.) Africa, Islamic studies, modern Middle East; estockre@american.edu

Thompson, Elizabeth F. (PhD, Columbia 1995; prof.; Sch. of International Service) Middle East, political movements, constitutions; eft@american.edu

Vester, Katharina (PhD, Ruhr, Bochum 2007; assoc. prof.; American Studies) cultural studies, foodscapes, gender and sexuality; vester@american.edu

Retired/Emeritus Faculty

Breitman, Richard (PhD, Harvard 1975; prof. emeritus) modern Germany, Europe since 1914, European social and political; rbreit@american.edu

Brown, Roger H. (PhD, Harvard 1960; prof. emeritus) colonial/revolutionary/early Republic America, early political parties; rbrown9@aol.com

Klein, Ira (PhD, Columbia 1968; assoc. prof. emeritus) European diplomatic, modern India, modern Britain and British Empire; iklein@american.edu

Malloy, James A., Jr. (PhD, Ohio State 1965; prof. emeritus) imperial Russia, eastern Europe; malloyjimm@aol.com

Reagon, Bernice Johnson (PhD, Howard 1975; dist. prof. emeritus) African American, African American culture; breagon@aol.com

Recently Awarded PhDs

Kaplan, Anna F. "Left by the Wayside: Memories and Postmemories of the Integration of the University of Mississippi"

Amherst College

Dept. of History, Chapin 11, AC#2254, Amherst, MA 01002-5000. 413.542.2229. Fax 413.542.2727. Email:history@amherst.edu. Website: http://www.amherst.edu/academiclife/departments/history.

The department comprises scholars whose work and teaching connects different regions of the world and integrates multiple topics into a common disciplinary endeavor. Courses in the department seek to stimulate independent and creative thought. We encourage majors and non-majors who take our courses to construct programs of study that transcend national boundaries and group identities and that broaden their own conceptual frameworks for understanding the past and the present.

Chair: Hilary J. Moss
Degrees Offered: BA
Academic Year System: Semester
Areas of Specialization: Europe, Americas, Asia, Africa, science
Tuition (per academic year): $72950
Enrollment 2018-19:
  Undergraduate Majors: 108
  Degrees in History: 39 BA
Addresses:
  Admissions: http://www.amherst.edu/admission
  Financial Aid: http://www.amherst.edu/admission/financial_a

Full-time Faculty

Boucher, Ellen R. (PhD, Columbia 2008; assoc. prof.) modern Britain, British Empire, childhood; eboucher@amherst.edu

Cho, Jun Hee (PhD, Columbia 2013; asst. prof.) medieval Europe, economic, early modern Europe; jcho@amherst.edu

Epstein, Catherine A. (PhD, Harvard 1998; prof.) 20th-century Europe, modern Germany; cepstein@amherst.edu

Gordon, Adi (PhD, Hebrew, Jerusalem 2009; assoc. prof.) modern Jewish, European intellectual; agordon@amherst.edu

Lopez, Rick A. (PhD, Yale 2001; prof.) Latin America social and cultural, nation formation, environmental; ralopez@amherst.edu

Melillo, Edward Dallam (PhD, Yale 2006; assoc. prof.) global environmental, 19th-century US, modern Latin America; emelillo@amherst.edu

Redding, Sean (PhD, Yale 1987; prof.) South Africa, Africa; sredding@amherst.edu

Walker, Vanessa (PhD, Wisconsin-Madison 2011; asst. prof.) US foreign relations, human rights, US-Latin American relations; vwalker@amherst.edu

Joint/Cross Appointments

Couvares, Francis G. (PhD, Michigan 1980; prof.; American Studies) 19th- and 20th-century US social and cultural; fgcouvares@amherst.edu

Glebov, Sergey (PhD, Rutgers 2004; assoc. prof.; Smith Coll.) Russia, Eurasia, Soviet Union; sglebov@amherst.edu

Maxey, Trent Elliott (PhD, Cornell 2005; prof.; Asian Languages and Civilizations) modern, intellectual, Japan; tmaxey@amherst.edu

Moss, Hilary J. (PhD, Brandeis 2004; prof. and chair; Black Studies) African American, 19th-century US, American education; hmoss@amherst.edu

Qiao, Zhijian (PhD, Stanford 2017; asst. prof.; Asian Languages and Civilizations) Chinese empires, mercantilism in premodern China, capitalism; gqiao@amherst.edu

Ringer, Monica M. (PhD, UCLA 1998; prof.; Asian Languages and Civilizations) modern Middle East, Iran, Ottoman Empire; mmringer@amherst.edu

Sen, Dwaipayan (PhD, Chicago 2012; asst. prof.; Asian Languages and Civilizations) modern South Asia, political and social, Bengal; dsen@amherst.edu

Part-time Faculty

Servos, John W. (PhD, Johns Hopkins 1979; prof.) science, medicine and technology; jwservos@amherst.edu

Retired/Emeritus Faculty

Bezucha, Robert J. (PhD, Michigan 1968; prof. emeritus) modern European social and cultural; rjbezucha@amherst.edu

Campbell, Mavis C. (PhD, London 1971; prof. emeritus) Caribbean, Central America, comparative slavery

Czap, Peter, Jr. (PhD, Cornell 1959; prof. emeritus) Russia, historical demography, 19th-century social; pczap@amherst.edu

Dennerline, Jerry P. (PhD, Yale 1973; prof. emeritus) China, East Asia; jpdennerline@amherst.edu

Levin, N. Gordon (PhD, Harvard 1967; prof. emeritus) American diplomatic, American studies, Israel

Moore, Ray A. (PhD, Michigan 1968; prof. emeritus) Japan, East Asia; ramoore@amherst.edu

Saxton, Martha (PhD, Columbia 1989; prof. emeritus) 18th- and 19th-century American women; msaxton@amherst.edu

Sweeney, Kevin M. (PhD, Yale 1986; prof. emeritus) colonial America, material culture; kmsweeney@amherst.edu

Andrews University

Dept. of History and Political Science, Buller Hall 126, 8488 E. Campus Circle Dr., Berrien Springs, MI 49104-0010. 269.471.3292. Fax 269.471.3112. Email: history@andrews.edu. Website: https://www.andrews.edu/cas/history/.

The Department of History and Political Science offers majors in history, political science, and social studies.

Chair: Stephanie A. Carpenter
Degrees Offered: BA,BS
Academic Year System: Semester
Areas of Specialization: 20th-century US, church, comparative/international/US politics/political philosophy/public policy, modern Europe, race/class/gender
Tuition (per academic year): $28272
Enrollment 2018-19:
  Undergraduate Majors: 38
  Degrees in History: 3 BA
Addresses:
  Admissions: http://www.andrews.edu/undergrad/
  Financial Aid: https://www.andrews.edu/future/financing/

Full-time Faculty

Carpenter, Stephanie A. (PhD, Iowa State 1998; prof. and chair) 20th-century America, rural life, women; carpenter@andrews.edu

Markovic, John Jovan (PhD, Bowling Green State 1990; prof.) Soviet Union and modern Europe, Church and Jewish-Christian relations, emergent Christianity; jjmarko@andrews.edu

Myers, Marcella J. (PhD, Western Michigan 2009; assoc. prof.) comparative politics, political institutions, public policy; marcellm@andrews.edu

Wood, Gary V. (PhD, Claremont Grad. 2001; assoc. prof.) political theory, international relations, American foreign policy; gwood@andrews.edu

Retired/Emeritus Faculty

Strayer, Brian E. (PhD, Iowa 1987; prof. emeritus) 18th-century France, modern England, Reformation; bstrayer@andrews.edu

Appalachian State University

Dept. of History, PO Box 32072, Boone, NC 28608-2072. 828.262.2282. Fax 828.262.4976. Email: goffjr@appstate.edu. Website: https://history.appstate.edu/.

The History Department at Appalachian State provides students with knowledge of their own cultural tradition and an appreciation of other cultures and societies of the past. It promotes an appreciation of the complexity of human affairs and the difficulties involved in interpreting them. The Department offers a broad curriculum in local, national, regional, and world history which encourages history majors to develop a comparative approach to human problems.

Chair: James R. Goff Jr.
Director of Graduate Studies: Judkin Browning
Director of Undergraduate Studies: Jason White
Degrees Offered: BA,BS,MA
Academic Year System: Semester
Areas of Specialization: US, modern and medieval Europe, public, environmental, US South and Appalachian culture

Undergraduate Tuition (per academic year):
  In-State: $7652
  Out-of-State: $22459
Graduate Tuition (per academic year):
  In-State: $7961
  Out-of-State: $21393
Enrollment 2018-19:
  Undergraduate Majors: 325
  New Graduate Students: 12
  Full-time Graduate Students: 26
  Part-time Graduate Students: 6
  Degrees in History: 18 BA, 58 BS, 12 MA
Undergraduate Addresses:
  Admissions: http://admissions.appstate.edu/
  Financial Aid: http://financialaid.appstate.edu/
Graduate Addresses:
  Admissions and Financial Aid: http://www.graduate.appstate.edu/

Full-time Faculty

Behrend-Martinez, Edward J. (PhD, Illinois, Chicago 2002; prof.) early modern Europe, Spain, women and gender; behrendmarte@appstate.edu

Behrent, Michael C. (PhD, NYU 2006; assoc. prof.) modern France; behrentmc@appstate.edu

Billheimer, Jonathan D. (MA, East Tennessee State 1998; lect.) world civilization; billheimerjd@appstate.edu

Bortz, Jeffrey L. (PhD, UCLA 1984; prof.) Latin America, Mexico; bortzjl@appstate.edu

Browning, Judkin (PhD, Georgia 2006; prof. and dir., grad. studies) US military, Civil War; browningjj@appstate.edu

Burns, Andrea A. (PhD, Minnesota 2008; assoc. prof.) public, recent US; burnsaa@appstate.edu

Caldwell, Craig H., III (PhD, Princeton 2007; assoc. prof.) ancient; caldwellch@appstate.edu

Campbell, Karl E. (PhD, North Carolina, Chapel Hill 1995; assoc. prof.) North Carolina, recent US; campbllke@appstate.edu

Carey, Anthony Gene (PhD, Emory 1992; prof.) US South; careyag@appstate.edu

Chauvin, Kenneth (MA, Appalachian State 1991; lect.) early Europe; chauvinkm@appstate.edu

Deathridge, Kristen Baldwin (PhD, Middle Tennessee State 2012; assoc. prof.) historic preservation, public; baldwindeathridgekd@appstate.edu

Fredette, Allison Dorothy (PhD, Florida 2014; asst. prof.) American Civil War, women; fredettead@appstate.edu

Getz, Lynne M. (PhD, Washington 1989; prof.) 20th-century US, intellectual, cultural resources; getzlm@appstate.edu

Goff, James R., Jr. (PhD, Arkansas 1987; prof. and chair) American religious, New US South; goffjr@appstate.edu

Horst, Rene D. Harder (PhD, Indiana 1998; prof.) Latin America, Southern Cone; horstrh@appstate.edu

Hudnall, Amy C. (MA, Appalachian State 2001; lect.) world civilization; hudnallac@appstate.edu

Isaenko, Anatoly (PhD, Moscow State 1976; prof.) Soviet Union, Central Asia, ethnicity; isaenkoa@appstate.edu

Kitunda, Jeremiah Mutio (PhD, Wisconsin, Madison 2003; assoc. prof.) Africa, environmental; kitundajm@appstate.edu

Krenn, Michael L. (PhD, Rutgers 1985; prof.) US diplomatic; krennml@appstate.edu

Lentz, Ralph E. (MA, Appalachian State 1998; lect.) world civilization; lentzre@appstate.edu

Morris, Jennifer (MA, Wake Forest 2011; lect.) history education; morrisjf1@appstate.edu

Pegelow Kaplan, Thomas (PhD, North Carolina, Chapel Hill 2004; Dist. Prof.) modern Europe; thomaspegelowkaplan@appstate.edu

Phipps, Sheila (PhD, William and Mary 1998; prof.) women, colonial, early Republic; phippssr@appstate.edu

Relyea, Scott (PhD, Chicago 2010; asst. prof.) China; relyeas@appstate.edu

Silver, Timothy H. (PhD, William and Mary 1985; prof.) colonial America, environmental; silverth@appstate.edu

Specht, Neva Jean (PhD, Delaware 1997; prof.) early Republic, material culture; spechtnj@appstate.edu

Stewart, Bruce E. (PhD, Georgia 2007; assoc. prof.) Appalachia, US South; stewartbe1@appstate.edu

Stone, Christopher (PhD, Indiana 2009; lect.) American film and music

Turner, Michael (DPhil, Oxford 1991; Dist. Prof.) British studies; turnermj@appstate.edu

Valante, Mary A. (PhD, Penn State 1998; prof.) medieval, Ireland; valantema@appstate.edu

Wade, Michael G. (PhD, Louisiana, Lafayette 1978; prof.) recent US, oral, civil rights; wademg@appstate.edu

White, Jason Cameron (PhD, Brown 2008; assoc. prof. and asst. chair) early modern Europe, Britain; whitejc3@appstate.edu

Part-time Faculty

Cox, Donald (MDiv, Trinity Episcopal School for Ministry 1996; adj. lect.; First-Year Seminar) coxda@appstate.edu

Ingerick, Ryan Eric (MA, Appalachian State 2017; adj. lect.) world; ingerickre@appstate.edu

Kellam, James Patrick (MA, Appalachian State 2017; adj. lect.) America

Maney, Paul (MA, Appalachian State 1995; adj. instr.) world civilization; maneyp@appstate.edu

McDaniel, Layne (PhD, Emory 1997; lect.) American education, women; mcdanielml1@appstate.edu

Turner, Catherine (MA, Rochester 1992; lect.) America; turnerce@appstate.edu

University of Arizona

Dept. of History, 415 César Chávez Bldg., PO Box 210023, Tucson, AZ 85721-0023. 520.621.1586. Fax 520.621.2422. Email: afutrell@email.arizona.edu. Website: https://history.arizona.edu/.

For over 100 years, the UA Department of History has been dedicated to understanding the human past, tracing the deep temporal roots of contemporary phenomena and working to make sense of the human experience through better comprehension of patterns of past behavior. We invite our students, majors and non-majors, to explore the creation of human identities through many and varied historical narratives, to test and support interpretations through the use of evidence, and to strengthen their habits of research, analysis, and communication. Our Latin American history program has been ranked in the top 10 and we received the AHA Equity Award in 2011. We offer graduate training to MA and PhD students in five major fields. We share cross-listed courses and affiliated faculty across campus.

Chair: Alison Futrell
Director of Graduate Studies: David Ortiz
Director of Undergraduate Studies: Jeremy Vetter
Degrees Offered: BA, MA, PhD

Academic Year System: Semester
Areas of Specialization: Latin America, late medieval and Reformation, US, Middle East, early and modern Europe
Undergraduate Tuition (per academic year):
In-State: $12600
Out-of-State: $36600
Graduate Tuition (per academic year):
In-State: $13271
Out-of-State: $33398
Enrollment 2018-19:
Undergraduate Majors: 245
New Graduate Students: 4
Full-time Graduate Students: 51
Part-time Graduate Students: 1
Degrees in History: 107 BA, 10 MA, 14 PhD
Online-Only Courses: 30%
Undergraduate Addresses:
Admissions: http://admissions.arizona.edu
Financial Aid: http://financialaid.arizona.edu/
Graduate Addresses:
Admissions: http://grad.arizona.edu/admissions
Financial Aid: http://financialaid.arizona.edu/

Adjunct Faculty

Berry, Michelle K. (PhD, Arizona, 2005; adj. faculty; Gender & Women's Studies) US West, environmental; mkberry@email.arizona.edu

DuMontier, Benjamin (PhD, Arizona, 2018; adj. faculty) Latin America; bjohnd@email.arizona.edu

Kashanipour, Ryan Amir (PhD, Arizona, 2011; adj. faculty) colonial-era Mesoamerica

Pierce, Mary (PhD, Arizona, 2015; adj. faculty; Africana Studies) Britain; piercem@email.arizona.edu

Zenger, Robin (PhD, Arizona, 2015; adj. faculty) US, Latin America; rzenger@email.arizona.edu

Full-time Faculty

Bauschatz, John (PhD, Duke 2005; assoc. prof.; Classics and Religious Studies) ancient world, Greece, Rome; jbausch1@email.arizona.edu

Beezley, William H. (PhD, Nebraska 1968; prof.) post-independence Mexico; beezley@u.arizona.edu

Crane, Susan A. (PhD, Chicago 1992; assoc. prof.) modern Europe, Germany, cultural and intellectual; scrane@u.arizona.edu

Darling, Linda T. (PhD, Chicago 1990; prof.) Ottoman, Middle East; ldarling@u.arizona.edu

Eaton, Richard M. (PhD, Wisconsin-Madison 1972; prof.) South Asia; reaton@u.arizona.edu

Futrell, Alison (PhD, California, Berkeley 1992; assoc. prof. and head) Rome; afutrell@u.arizona.edu

Garcia, Juan Ramon (PhD, Notre Dame 1977; prof.) US, Mexican American; jugarcia@u.arizona.edu

Gibbs, David N. (PhD, MIT 1989; prof.) American foreign policy, Africa; dgibbs@u.arizona.edu

Gosner, Kevin M. (PhD, Pennsylvania 1984; assoc. prof.) colonial Mexico; kgosner@u.arizona.edu

Hemphill, Katie (PhD, Johns Hopkins 2014; asst. prof.) 19th-century US, US South, gender; khemphill@email.arizona.edu

Johnstone, Steven (PhD, Chicago 1989; prof.) ancient Greece; sjohnsto@u.arizona.edu

Lanza, Fabio (PhD, Columbia 2004; prof.; East Asian Studies) modern China; flanza@email.arizona.edu

Lotz-Heumann, Ute (PhD, Humboldt, Berlin 1999; Heiko A. Oberman Prof.) medieval and early modern Europe; ulotzh@email.arizona.edu

McQuirter, Marya A. (PhD, Michigan 2000; dir., public hist. collaborative; UA Libraries) mmcquirter@email.arizona.edu

Milliman, Paul (PhD, Cornell 2007; assoc. prof.) medieval and early modern Europe; milliman@email.arizona.edu

Morrissey, Katherine G. (PhD, Yale 1990; assoc. prof.) American West, cultural, environmental; kmorriss@u.arizona.edu

Ortiz, David, Jr. (PhD, California, San Diego 1995; assoc. prof. and dir., grad. studies) modern Europe; davido@u.arizona.edu

Perez, Erika (PhD, UCLA 2010; assoc. prof.) US West, gender, early California; erikaperez@email.arizona.edu

Pieper Mooney, Jadwiga E. (PhD, Rutgers 2000; assoc. prof.) modern Latin America, Chile, women and gender; jadwiga@email.arizona.edu

Senseney, John (PhD, California, Santa Barbara 2002; assoc. prof.; Art History) ancient Rome and Greece; jsenseney@email.arizona.edu

Steptoe, Tyina (PhD, Wisconsin, Madison 2008; assoc. prof.) 20th-century US, race and ethnicity, gender; tsteptoe@email.arizona.edu

Tabili, Laura E. (PhD, Rutgers 1988; prof.) Britain, modern Europe; tabili@u.arizona.edu

Vetter, Jeremy (PhD, Pennsylvania 2005; assoc. prof. and dir., undergrad. studies) US environmental, science, West; jvetter@email.arizona.edu

Weiner, Douglas R. (PhD, Columbia 1984; prof.) modern Russia, USSR, global environment; dweiner@u.arizona.edu

Nondepartmental Historians

Brescia, Michael M. (PhD, Arizona 2000; curator, ethnohistory, Arizona State Museum) Mexico, colonial and early national; brescia@email.arizona.edu

Clancy-Smith, Julia A. (PhD, UCLA 1988; Regent's Prof.; Middle Eastern and North African Studies) North Africa, colonialism, gender; juliac@email.arizona.edu

Coronado Guel, Luis Edgardo, Sr. (PhD, Arizona 2016; dir., SBS Mexico Initiatives) Mexico; luisguel@email.arizona.edu

González de Bustamante, Celeste (PhD, Arizona 2005; assoc. prof.; Journalism) media in Latin America; celesteg@email.arizona.edu

Graizbord, David I. (PhD, Michigan 2000; assoc. prof.; Arizona Center for Judaic Studies) medieval and early modern Jewish; dlgraizb@email.arizona.edu

Mutchler, J. C. (PhD, Yale 2002; retired assoc. prof.; assoc. research historian, Southwest Center) US West, environmental, public; mutchler@email.arizona.edu

Otero, Lydia R. (PhD, Arizona 2003; assoc. prof.; Mexican American Studies) Mexico culture, public, gender, urbanization; lotero@email.arizona.edu

Ribak, Gil (PhD, Wisconsin, Madison 2007; asst. prof.; Judaic Studies) modern Jewish; gribak@email.arizona.edu

Schlachet, Joshua (PhD, Columbia 2017; asst. prof.; East Asian Studies) Japan, early modern and modern; jschlachet@email.arizona.edu

Smith, Charles D., Jr. (PhD, Michigan 1968; prof. emeritus; Near Eastern Studies) Middle East; cdsmith@u.arizona.edu

Stephan, Rob (PhD, Stanford 2014; lect.; Classics) Roman archaeology, classics; rstephan@email.arizona.edu

Retired/Emeritus Faculty

Anderson, Karen S. (PhD, Washington 1975; prof. emeritus) karena@u.arizona.edu

Bernstein, Alan Edgar (PhD, Columbia 1972; prof. emeritus) medieval, intellectual, religious; aebern@u.arizona.edu

Bernstein, Gail Lee (PhD, Harvard 1968; prof. emeritus) Japan; glbernst@u.arizona.edu

Cosgrove, Richard A. (PhD, California, Riverside 1967; prof. emeritus) modern Britain; rcosgrov@u.arizona.edu

Guy, Donna J. (PhD, Indiana 1973; prof. emeritus) Latin America, Argentina; dguy@earthlink.net

Karant-Nunn, Susan C. (PhD, Indiana 1971; prof. emeritus) medieval, Renaissance and Reformation; karantnu@u.arizona.edu

Marietta, Jack (PhD, Stanford 1968; assoc. prof. emeritus) jack-marietta@ns.arizona.edu

Martinez, Oscar (PhD, UCLA 1975; prof. emeritus) Latin America, Chicano; oscar-martinez@ns.arizona.edu

Nichols, Roger L. (PhD, Wisconsin, Madison 1964; prof. emeritus) American West and Europe; nichols@u.arizona.edu

Rebel, Hermann (PhD, California, Berkeley 1976; assoc. prof. emeritus) Habsburg Austria, European socioeconomic; hrebel@u.arizona.edu

Schaller, Michael R. (PhD, Michigan 1974; prof. emeritus) US diplomatic, recent US; schaller@u.arizona.edu

Recently Awarded PhDs

Carminati, Lucia "Bur Sa'id/Port Said, 1859-1914: Migration, Urbanization, and Empire in an Egyptian and Mediterranean Port City"

Howard, Sarah E. "A Comic Truth: Rius, the Mexican Counterculture, and the Non-Official Foundational Fiction"

Huntley, Allison D. "The Children of the Cosmic Race: The Planning and Celebration of the 1968 Cultural Olympics in Mexico City"

Johnson, Tai E. "The Shifting Nature of Food, Water, and Public Health on the Hopi Indian Reservation since 1930"

Macias, Marco A. "Imagining Villa: An Examination of Francisco 'Pancho' Villa through Popular Culture and Collective Memory, 1910-2015"

Uluisik, Secil "Empire, Province, and Power: Chorbadzhi Networks in the Ottoman Empire, 1790s-1850s"

Arizona State University

School of Historical, Philosophy & Religious Studies, 975 S. Myrtle Ave., Tempe, AZ 85287-4302. 480.965.5778. Fax 480.965.0310. Email: history@asu.edu. Website: https://shprs.asu.edu/.

The 40-plus historians who make up the Faculty of History within the School of Historical, Philosophical and Religious Studies preside over one of the largest and strongest undergraduate history programs in the country, covering the full range of topics, periods and regions in world history. It continues to operate a vibrant graduate program, with its traditional area strengths in North American, Europe, Asia, and Latin America, as well as offering preparation in topical areas.

Chair: Richard Amesbury
Director of Graduate Studies: Aaron Moore
Director of Undergraduate Studies: Alexander Avina
Degrees Offered: BA,BAEd,MA,MAEd,PhD
Academic Year System: Semester
Areas of Specialization: North America, public, Europe, East Asia/Southeast Asia
Undergraduate Tuition (per academic year):
  In-State: $11338
  Out-of-State: $24503
Graduate Tuition (per academic year):
  In-State: $12608
  Out-of-State: $28800
Enrollment 2018-19:
  Undergraduate Majors: 1002

New Graduate Students: 64
Full-time Graduate Students: 147
Degrees in History: 181 BA, 10 MA, 11 PhD
Undergraduate Addresses:
  Admissions: http://students.asu.edu/apply
  Financial Aid: http://students.asu.edu/financialaid
Graduate Addresses:
  Admissions and Financial Aid: http://graduate.asu.edu/

Adjunct Faculty

Stout, Joseph A., Jr. (PhD, Oklahoma State 1971; adj. prof.) American Southwest, Mexico and Latin America, US military

Affiliated Faculty

Escobar, Edward J. (PhD, California, Riverside 1983; assoc. prof.; Transborder Chicana/o Latina/o Studies) Chicano/a studies; edward.escobar@asu.edu

Leong, Karen J. (PhD, California, Berkeley 1999; assoc. prof.; Women & Gender Studies) women; karen.leong@asu.edu

Pyne, Stephen J. (PhD, Texas, Austin 1976; prof.; Sch. Life Sciences) ecology; stephen.pyne@asu.edu

Full-time Faculty

Aviña, Alexander (PhD, Southern California 2009; assoc. prof. and dir., undergrad. studies) Latin America, activism and social movements; alexander.avina@asu.edu

Barker, Hannah (PhD, Columbia 2014; asst. prof.) medieval; hannah.barker@asu.edu

Barnes, Andrew E. (PhD, Princeton 1983; assoc. prof.) early modern Europe, modern Africa; andrew.barnes@asu.edu

Barth, Jonathan E. (PhD, George Mason 2014; asst. prof.) early American Republic; jonathan.barth@asu.edu

Benkert, Volker (DPhil, Potsdam 2016; asst. prof.) Communist East Germany; volker.benkert@asu.edu

Cichopek-Gajraj, Anna (PhD, Michigan 2008; asst. prof.) modern eastern Europe, modern Jewish, social and comparative; anna.cichopek-gajraj@asu.edu

Critchlow, Donald Thomas (PhD, California, Berkeley 1978; prof.) political science, US; donald.critchlow@asu.edu

Davis, Thomas J. (PhD, Columbia 1974; JD, SUNY, Buffalo 1993; prof.) US, legal, economic; tjdavis@asu.edu

El Hamel, Chouki (PhD, Paris 1993; prof.) Africa; chouki.elhamel@asu.edu

Escobar, Gayle Gullett (PhD, California, Riverside 1982; assoc. prof.) US, women; gayle.gullett@asu.edu

Fixico, Donald L. (PhD, Oklahoma 1980; Dist. Found. Prof.) American Indian, American West, 20th-century US; donald.fixico@asu.edu

Gray, Susan E. (PhD, Chicago 1985; assoc. prof.) early 19th-century US and women; segray@asu.edu

Green, Monica H. (PhD, Princeton 1985; prof.) women's health care, medieval Europe, women in science; monica.green@asu.edu

Harper, Tobias Joel (PhD, Columbia 2014; asst. prof.) modern Britain; tobias.harper@asu.edu

Harris, Lauren McArthur (PhD, Michigan 2008; asst. prof.) history education, world; lauren.harris.1@asu.edu

Hirt, Paul W. (PhD, Arizona 1991; assoc. prof.) 20th-century US, US West, environmental; paul.hirt@asu.edu

Holian, Anna (PhD, Chicago 2004; assoc. prof.; Jewish Studies) Jewish studies, Europe, political; anna.holian@asu.edu

Jones, Christopher F. (PhD, Pennsylvania 2009; asst. prof.) environmental, business; cjones36@asu.edu

Longley, Kyle (PhD, Kentucky 1994; Snell Family Dean's Dist. Prof.) US international relations, 20th-century US; kyle.longley@asu.edu

Manchester, Laurie (PhD, Columbia 1995; assoc. prof.) modern Europe, cultural, Russia; laurie.manchester@asu.edu

Moore, Aaron Stephen (PhD, Cornell 2006; asst. prof. and dir., grad. studies) modern Japan, Asian studies; aaron.s.moore@asu.edu

O'Donnell, Catherine (PhD, Michigan 1998; assoc. prof.) America, revolutionary and early national, colonial; codonnell@asu.edu

Osburn, Katherine (PhD, Denver 1993; assoc. prof.) North American Indian, US environment, US; katherine.osburn@asu.edu

Rush, James R. (PhD, Yale 1977; assoc. prof.) Southeast Asia; james.rush@asu.edu

Saikia, Yasmin (PhD, Wisconsin, Madison 1999; prof.) South Asia, Islam, women and gender; yasmin.saikia@asu.edu

Schermerhorn, Calvin (PhD, Virginia 2008; assoc. prof.) 18th- to 19th-century US, African American, slavery; j.schermerhorn@asu.edu

Tebeau, Mark T. (PhD, Carnegie Mellon 1997; assoc. prof.) environmental, public, digital humanities; mark.tebeau@asu.edu

Thompson, Victoria E. (PhD, Pennsylvania 1993; assoc. prof.) modern Europe, cultural, France; victoria.thompson@asu.edu

Tirosh-Samuelson, Hava (PhD, Jerusalem 1978; prof.) Jewish studies, European intellectual; hava.samuelson@asu.edu

Retired/Emeritus Faculty

Adelson, Roger (PhD, Washington, St. Louis 1972; prof. emeritus) modern Britain, British Empire, modern Middle East; adelsonr@asu.edu

Barlow, Richard (PhD, Pennsylvania 1957; prof. emeritus) Europe and Britain

Batalden, Stephen K. (PhD, Minnesota 1975; prof. emeritus) modern Russia, Balkans; stephen.batalden@asu.edu

Burg, B. Richard (PhD, Colorado, Boulder 1967; prof. emeritus) 18th-century Royal Navy courts martial, US sailing and Navy courts martial

Dellheim, Charles (PhD, Yale 1979; prof. emeritus) modern Britain, 19th-century Europe; dellheim@bu.edu

Giffin, Frederick (PhD, Emory 1965; prof. emeritus) Russia and Soviet Union

Gratton, Brian (PhD, Boston Univ. 1980; prof. emeritus) 20th-century US social, immigration; brian@asu.edu

Hubbard, Paul G. (PhD, Illinois, Urbana-Champaign 1949; prof. emeritus) Civil War and Reconstruction

Iverson, Peter J. (PhD, Wisconsin, Madison 1975; Regents' prof. emeritus) American Indian, US West; peter.iverson@asu.edu

Kleinfeld, Gerald R. (PhD, NYU 1961; prof. emeritus) modern Europe and Germany

Lavrin, Asuncion A. (PhD, Harvard 1963; prof. emeritus) colonial Latin America, Mexico, women; lavrind@aol.com

Mackinnon, Stephen R. (PhD, California, Davis 1971; prof. emeritus) modern China; stephen.mackinnon@asu.edu

Phillips, William W. (PhD, Missouri, Columbia 1958; prof. emeritus) US and Progressive era

Smith, L. Christian (PhD, Illinois, Urbana-Champaign 1972; assoc. prof. emeritus) US cultural, popular culture

Smith, Ronald D. (PhD, Southern California 1964; prof. emeritus) Europe

Stoner, K. Lynn (PhD, Indiana 1982; assoc. prof. emeritus) Latin America; lynn.stoner@asu.edu

Tambs, Lewis (PhD, California, Santa Barbara 1967; prof. emeritus) Latin America

Thornton, Sybil (PhD, Cambridge 1990; assoc. prof. emeritus) premodern Japan; sybil.thornton@asu.edu

VanderMeer, Phillip (PhD, Illinois, Urbana-Champaign 1976; assoc. prof. emeritus) US political, Gilded Age and Progressive Era, community; p.vander.meer@asu.edu

Warnicke, Retha M. (PhD, Harvard 1969; prof. emeritus) Tudor-Stuart England; retha.warnicke@asu.edu

Weiner, Gordon (PhD, Pennsylvania 1970; prof. emeritus) early modern Europe, demography, economics

Recently Awarded PhDs

Bridgewater, Devon Leal "El Comité Nacional de Repatriación: Mexican Management of the Conational Exodus and the National Repatriation Committee, 1932-34"

Dingatantrige Perera, Judith I. "From Exclusion to State Violence: The Transformation of Immigrant Detention in the United States"

Groat, Bridget Lee "The Changing Tides of Bristol Bay: Salmon, Sovereignty, and Alaska Natives"

Kirk, Tyler "Life after GULAG: Identity and Community Building in Far North, 1953-2010"

Romero, Jacqueline Elizabeth "By the Labors of Our Hands and the Sweat of Our Brows: The Institutional and Community Role of the Sisters of Charity in Midwestern Catholicism, 1812-60"

Vale, Catherine M. "From State Exposition Building to Science Center: Ideals of Progress in Los Angeles, 1913-98"

Vicknair, Alexandra Katherine "A Tale of Two Parks: Nature Tourism, Visual Rhetoric, and the Power of Place: A Comparative History of Yosemite National Park and Mineral King, California"

University of Arkansas at Fayetteville

Dept. of History, 416 N. Campus Dr., Old Main Bldg., Rm. 416, Fayetteville, AR 72701. 479.575.3001. Fax 479.575.2775. Email: jgiganti@uark.edu. Website: https://fulbright.uark.edu/departments/history/.

The faculty of the Department of History range widely across the discipline, in a variety of geographies and cultures, from the ancient to the post-modern world, with teaching and research emphases in political, social, diplomatic, cultural, intellectual, and environmental history. The doctoral program of the history department ranked third among doctoral-granting universities in the nation in terms of graduate student placement in academic jobs.

Chair: James Gigantino II
Director of Graduate Studies: Todd Cleveland
Director of Undergraduate Studies: Alessandro Brogi
Degrees Offered: BA, MA, PhD
Academic Year System: Semester
Areas of Specialization: US, Europe and Asia, Middle East, Latin America, Africa
Undergraduate Tuition (per academic year):
In-State: $9130
Out-of-State: $25168
Graduate Tuition (per academic year):
In-State: $11482
Out-of-State: $28700
Enrollment 2018-19:
Undergraduate Majors: 274
New Graduate Students: 8
Full-time Graduate Students: 64
Part-time Graduate Students: 30
Degrees in History: 73 BA, 6 MA, 5 PhD

Undergraduate Addresses:
Admissions: http://admissions.uark.edu/
Financial Aid: http://finaid.uark.edu/
Graduate Addresses:
Admissions: http://graduate-and-international.uark.edu
Financial Aid: https://fulbright.uark.edu/departments/history/

Full-time Faculty

Antov, Nikolay (PhD, Chicago 2011; assoc. prof.) Ottoman Empire, Islamic civilizations; antov@uark.edu

Austin, Shawn Michael (PhD, New Mexico 2014; asst. prof.) colonial Latin America, South America; saustin1@uark.edu

Banton, Caree Ann Marie (PhD, Vanderbilt 2013; assoc. prof.) Atlantic world and Caribbean, 19th-century America, Africa and African diaspora; cabanton@uark.edu

Brogi, Alessandro (PhD, Ohio 1998; PhD, Studi di Firenze, Italy 1993; prof. and dir., undergrad. studies) US foreign relations, international relations; abrogi@uark.edu

Cleveland, Todd C. (PhD, Minnesota 2008; assoc. prof. and dir., grad. studies) Africa, African diaspora; tcclevel@uark.edu

Coon, Lynda L. (PhD, Virginia 1990; prof. and dean, Honors Coll.) medieval Europe; llcoon@uark.edu

Dominguez, Freddy C. (PhD, Princeton 2011; asst. prof.) early modern Europe; fcdoming@uark.edu

Gigantino, James John, II (PhD, Georgia 2010; prof. and chair) colonial America, revolutionary America, slavery; jgiganti@uark.edu

Gordon, Joel (PhD, Michigan 1987; prof.) modern Middle East; joelg@uark.edu

Hammond, Kelly (PhD, Georgetown 2015; asst. prof.) modern China, modern Japan; kah018@uark.edu

Hare, J. Laurence (PhD, North Carolina, Chapel Hill 2007; assoc. prof. and dir., international studies) 19th- and 20th-century Germany, early modern and modern Europe, global; lhare@uark.edu

Muntz, Charles E. (PhD, Duke 2008; assoc. prof.) ancient; cmuntz@uark.edu

Pepitone, Ren (PhD, Johns Hopkins 2015; asst. prof.) modern Britain; pepitone@uark.edu

Pierce, Michael Cain (PhD, Ohio State 1999; assoc. prof.) modern US, US labor; mpierce@uark.edu

Robinson, Charles F., II (PhD, Houston 1998; prof. and vice chancellor, student affairs) African American, US; cfrobins@uark.edu

Rodriguez, Sarah Katherine Manning (PhD, Pennsylvania 2015; asst. prof.) antebellum America; skrodrig@uark.edu

Rosales, Steven (PhD, California, Irvine 2007; assoc. prof.) Chicano/Latino studies, 20th-century US, gender and sexuality; rosales@uark.edu

Sloan, Kathryn A. (PhD, Kansas 2002; prof. and dir., Humanities; Fine Arts & Humanities) Latin America; ksloan@uark.edu

Sonn, Richard D. (PhD, California, Berkeley 1981; prof.) modern France, modern Europe, social/cultural/intellectual; rsonn@uark.edu

Starks, Tricia (PhD, Ohio State 2000; prof.) Russia, medicine; tstarks@uark.edu

Sutherland, Daniel E. (PhD, Wayne State 1976; Dist. Prof.) Civil War, military, Reconstruction; dsutherl@uark.edu

West, Elliott (PhD, Colorado, Boulder 1971; Dist. Prof.) American West, American Indian; ewest@uark.edu

Whayne, Jeannie M. (PhD, California, San Diego 1989; Univ. prof.) American South, Arkansas; jwhayne@uark.edu

White, Calvin, Jr. (PhD, Mississippi 2007; assoc. prof. and assoc. dean) African American, colonial Africa, American religion; calvinwh@uark.edu

Williams, Patrick G. (PhD, Columbia 1996; prof.) 19th-century US, American South; pgwillia@uark.edu

Woods, Randall Bennett (PhD, Texas, Austin 1972; Cooper Dist. Prof.) US diplomatic, 20th-century US; rwoods@uark.edu

Retired/Emeritus Faculty

Bukey, Evan B. (PhD, Ohio State 1969; prof. emeritus) modern Germany, 19th- and 20th-century Europe; ebukey@uark.edu

Edwards, David Wayne (PhD, Kansas State 1967; assoc. prof. emeritus) Russia; dedwards@uark.edu

Engels, Donald (PhD, Pennsylvania 1976; prof. emeritus) ancient Greece and Rome

Finlay, Robert (PhD, Chicago 1973; prof. emeritus) Renaissance and Reformation, early modern Europe; rfinlay@uark.edu

Markham, Elizabeth (PhD, Cambridge 1980; prof. emerita) medieval Japan, music/religion/culture; markham@uark.edu

McMath, Robert C., Jr. (PhD, North Carolina, Chapel Hill 1972; prof. emeritus) US political, US South; bmcmath@uark.edu

Sloan, David A. (PhD, California, Santa Barbara 1969; assoc. prof. emeritus) colonial America, American Revolution, early national; dsloan@uark.edu

Tsai, Shih-Shan Henry (PhD, Oregon 1970; prof. emeritus) China, Chinese immigration to US; htsai@uark.edu

Tucker, William F. (PhD, Indiana 1971; assoc. prof. emeritus) Islam, Middle East; wtucker@uark.edu

Wolpert, Rembrandt (PhD, Cambridge 1975; prof. emeritus) Sinology and Tang China, music/religion/culture, Chinese performing arts 600-1300; wolpert@uark.edu

Recently Awarded PhDs

Elkin, Daniel "Zona Libre: San Diego and the Transnational Politics of Growth"

Grove, Jama McMurtery "The Farmers' Federation: Regional Racial Mythologies as Agricultural Capital"

Hall, Natalie A. "The Spatial Agency of the Catacombs: An Analysis of the Interventions of Damasus I (366-84)"

Martin, Anne Marie "Death among the Palmettos: Changes in Burial Law and Practice in Charleston, South Carolina, between the Revolution and 1850"

McMillan, Rebekah "'The Healing Hand Laid on a Great Wound': The Elberfeld System and the Transformation of Poverty in Germany, Britain, and the United States"

Rosenbaum, Bethany Henry "Promise and Practice: Toward an Expansive, Integrated, Collaborative Narrative on American Indians in the National Park Service"

Walker, David Blaine "The Importance of Being Great: British Perceptions of Imperial Decline, c. 1870-1914"

University of Arkansas at Little Rock

Dept. of History, 2801 S. University Ave., Little Rock, AR 72204-1099. 501.569.3236. Fax 501.569.3059. Email: jcporter@ualr.edu. Website: https://ualr.edu/history/.

We offer a BA in History, a BA in History/Secondary Education, an MA in Public History, and a minor in Geography. Our History of Civilization and US Survey courses are an important element of the UA Little Rock Core required of almost all students, helping them to improve their knowledge of the past and their skills at analytical thinking, coherent argument, and clarity of expression.

Chair: Jess Porter
Director of Graduate Studies: Barclay Key
Degrees Offered: BA, MA

Academic Year System: Semester
Areas of Specialization: Arkansas, US, Europe, world, public
Undergraduate Tuition (per academic year):
  In-State: $8633
  Out-of-State: $20888
Graduate Tuition (per academic year):
  In-State: $5595
  Out-of-State: $11445
Enrollment 2018-19:
  Undergraduate Majors: 90
  New Graduate Students: 12
  Full-time Graduate Students: 30
  Part-time Graduate Students: 5
  Degrees in History: 27 BA, 7 MA
  Students in Undergraduate Courses: 1200
  Students in Undergraduate Intro Courses: 900
  Online-Only Courses: 20%
Undergraduate Addresses:
  Admissions: http://ualr.edu/admissions/
  Financial Aid: http://ualr.edu/financialaid/
Graduate Addresses:
  Admissions: http://ualr.edu/gradschool/graduate-application/
  Financial Aid: http://ualr.edu/financialaid/

Adjunct Faculty

Stricklin, David (PhD, Tulane 1996; adj.) public, oral
Worthen, Shana (PhD, Toronto 2006; adj.) technology, medieval; ssworthen@ualr.edu

Full-time Faculty

Anson, Edward M. IV (PhD, Virginia 1975; prof.) ancient Greece, Rome; emanson@ualr.edu
Baldwin, Deborah J. (PhD, Chicago 1979; prof.) Latin America; djbaldwin@ualr.edu
Heil, Michael W. (PhD, Columbia 2013; asst. prof.) medieval Europe, legal; mwheil@ualr.edu
Key, Barclay (PhD, Florida 2007; assoc. prof. and dir., grad. studies) US South, African American, Arkansas; btkey@ualr.edu
Kirk, John A. (PhD, Newcastle, UK 1997; Donaghey dist. prof.) US, US South, African American; jakirk@ualr.edu
Lewis, Johanna M. (PhD, William and Mary 1991; prof.) public, material culture, colonial North America; jmlewis@ualr.edu
Mann, Kristin Dutcher (PhD, Northern Arizona 2002; prof.) colonial Mexico, social studies secondary education; kdmann@ualr.edu
Mitchell, Brian K. (PhD, New Orleans 2013; asst. prof.) US; bkmitchell@ualr.edu
Porter, Jess (PhD, Oklahoma State 2007; assoc. prof. and chair; Geography) geography; jcporter@ualr.edu
Romney, Charles W. (PhD, UCLA 1996; assoc. prof.) public, modern US, Africa in world; cwromney@ualr.edu
Ross, James D., Jr. (PhD, Auburn 2004; assoc. prof.) Arkansas, social studies secondary education, labor; jdross@ualr.edu
Yeaw, Katrina Elizabeth Anderson (PhD, Georgetown 2018; asst. prof.) Middle East

Retired/Emeritus Faculty

Bilsky, Lester J. (PhD, Washington 1971; prof. emeritus) East Asia
Bolton, S. Charles (PhD, Wisconsin, Madison 1973; prof. emeritus) colonial North America, early national US, US religion; scbolton@ualr.edu
Bowlus, Charles R. (PhD, Massachusetts 1973; prof. emeritus) medieval Europe, environmental; crbowlus@ualr.edu
Kaiser, Thomas E. (PhD, Harvard 1976; prof. emeritus) France, early modern Europe; tekaiser@ualr.edu
Moneyhon, Carl H. (PhD, Chicago 1973; prof. emeritus) US South, Civil War and Reconstruction; chmoneyhon@ualr.edu

Ross, Frances M. (MA, Arkansas 1963; asst. prof. emeritus) women, oral, Arkansas; fmross@ualr.edu
Sherrill, Peter T. (PhD, Vanderbilt 1970; prof. emeritus) England, British Empire, Canada; ptsherrill@ualr.edu
Smith, Harold T. (PhD, Nevada 1972; prof. emeritus) US diplomatic, Russia
Vinikas, Vincent A. (PhD, Columbia 1983; prof. emeritus) US, social, Native American; vxvinikas@ualr.edu
Williams, Leroy T. (PhD, Toledo 1977; prof. emeritus) Afro-American, labor; drlee629@aol.com

Visiting Faculty

Cieslak, Marta (PhD, SUNY, Buffalo 2014; vis. asst. prof.) transatlantic, East-Central Europe and US; mxcieslak@ualr.edu

Arkansas State University

Dept. of History, PO Box 1690, State University, AR 72467-1690. 870.972.3046. Fax 870.972.2880. Email: jcastro@astate. edu. Website: https://www.astate.edu/college/liberal-arts/ departments/history/.

Arkansas State University educates leaders, enhances intellectual growth, and enriches lives. The department offers the BA and MA in history, the BSE and the MSE for social science majors; minors in US and European history and African American studies; and a certificate in Digital Humanities.

Chair: J. Justin Castro
Director of Graduate Studies: Erik Gilbert
Director of Undergraduate Studies: Gary Edwards
Degrees Offered: BA, BSE, MA, MSE
Academic Year System: Semester
Areas of Specialization: US, social science, global, public, heritage studies
Undergraduate Tuition (per academic year):
  In-State: $5040
  Out-of-State: $10080
Graduate Tuition (per academic year):
  In-State: $4806
  Out-of-State: $9612
Enrollment 2018-19:
  Undergraduate Majors: 180
  New Graduate Students: 8
  Full-time Graduate Students: 25
  Degrees in History: 20 BA, 11 BSE, 10 MA
Undergraduate Addresses:
  Admissions: http://www.astate.edu/info/admissions/
  Financial Aid: http://www.astate.edu/a/finaid/
Graduate Addresses:
  Admissions: http://www.astate.edu/info/admissions/graduate/
  Financial Aid: http://www.astate.edu/a/finaid/

Full-time Faculty

Buford, Kellie Wilson (PhD, Nebraska 2014; asst. prof.) social science education, military, gender; kbuford@astate.edu
Castro, J. Justin (PhD, Oklahoma 2013; assoc. prof. and chair) Latin America, Mexico, technology; jcastro@astate.edu
Davis, Andrea Rebecca (PhD, California, San Diego 2014; asst. prof.; dir., digital humanities program) modern Europe, digital humanities; andavis@astate.edu
Edwards, Gary T. (PhD, Memphis 2004; assoc. prof. and dir., undergrad. studies) US South, Civil War and Reconstruction, Arkansas; gedwards@astate.edu
Gilbert, Erik O. (PhD, Boston Univ. 1996; prof. and dir., grad. studies) Africa, global, Indian Ocean; egilbert@astate.edu

Hronek, Pamela (PhD, Arizona State 1985; assoc. prof.) social and cultural, recent US, US environmental; phronek@astate.edu

Hu, Aiqun (PhD, Northeastern 2007; assoc. prof.) China, East Asia, global; aiqunhu@astate.edu

Jones-Branch, Cherisse Renee (PhD, Ohio State 2003; prof.) women, African American; crjones@astate.edu

Key, Joseph P. (PhD, Arkansas 2001; assoc. prof.) Native American, early America; jkey@astate.edu

Maynard, William (PhD, Durham, UK 1973; assoc. prof.) England, Great Britain, military; wmaynard@astate.edu

McNamee, Heather (MA, Arkansas State 2010; instr.) US South, African American, social studies education; hmcnamee@astate.edu

Salo, Edward (PhD, Middle Tennessee State 2009; asst. prof.; Heritage Studies) historic preservation; esalo@astate.edu

Sydorenko, Alexander (PhD, Illinois, Urbana-Champaign 1974; prof.) imperial Russia, Soviet Union; asydorenko@astate.edu

Wilkerson-Freeman, Sarah L. (PhD, North Carolina, Chapel Hill 1995; prof.) 20th-century US, women, public; sarahwf@astate.edu

Joint/Cross Appointments

Banta, Brady (PhD, Louisiana State 1981; assoc. prof.; asst. dir., Heritage Studies and archivist) public; bbanta@astate.edu

Hogue, Gina (PhD, Memphis 1997; assoc. prof.; assoc. dean, Coll. of Liberal Arts and Communication) social science education, US diplomatic; ghogue@astate.edu

Umansky, Lauri (PhD, Brown 1994; prof.; dir., Heritage Studies PhD Program) heritage studies, women, disability studies; lumansky@astate.edu

Retired/Emeritus Faculty

Anderson, Robin L. (PhD, California, Davis 1976; prof. emeritus) Latin America, medicine

Ball, Larry D., Sr. (PhD, Colorado, Boulder 1970; prof. emeritus) American West, philosophy of history, military

Beineke, John A. (EdD, Ball State 1977; prof. emeritus; Teacher Education) social science education, recent US; jbeineke@astate.edu

Dougan, Michael B. (PhD, Emory 1970; prof. emeritus) Arkansas and South, constitutional, Civil War and Reconstruction

Greenwald, W. James, Jr. (PhD, North Carolina, Chapel Hill 1972; assoc. prof. emeritus) Germany, European intellectual

Milner, Clyde A., II (PhD, Yale 1979; prof. emeritus) American West, heritage studies

O'Connor, Carol A. (PhD, Yale 1976; prof. emeritus) 20th-century US

Pobst, Phyllis E. (PhD, Toronto 1992; assoc. prof. emeritus) medieval and Renaissance Europe; ppobst@astate.edu

Arkansas Tech University

Dept. of History and Political Science, 407 W. Q St., Witherspoon 255, Russellville, AR 72801-2222. 479.968.0265. Fax 479.356.2189. Email: hps@atu.edu; dblanks@atu.edu. Website: https://www.atu.edu/history/.

We want to see you succeed in your college career. The department has several organizations which are geared toward giving students more of an opportunity for detailed study and involvement in campus life. It also has a Nationally Recognized Social Studies Teacher Education Program, as awarded by the National Council for the Social Studies.

Chair: David Blanks
Director of Graduate Studies: Peter Dykema

Degrees Offered: BA,MA
Academic Year System: Semester
Areas of Specialization: US, modern Europe, Arkansas, US South, world
Undergraduate Tuition (per academic year):
In-State: $7494
Out-of-State: $13489
Graduate Tuition (per academic year):
In-State: $6480
Out-of-State: $11664
Enrollment 2018-19:
Undergraduate Majors: 70
New Graduate Students: 8
Full-time Graduate Students: 16
Part-time Graduate Students: 10
Degrees in History: 35 AA, 18 BA, 9 MA
Undergraduate Addresses:
Admissions: http://www.atu.edu/futurestudents.php
Financial Aid: http://www.atu.edu/finaid/
Graduate Addresses:
Admissions: http://www.atu.edu/gradcollege/
Financial Aid: http://www.atu.edu/finaid/

Adjunct Faculty

Cullen, David (PhD, North Texas 1992; adj.) US labor; dcullen@atu.edu

Rowley, John D. (MA, Arkansas Tech 2012; adj.) America, Arkansas

Tubbs, Melanie (OMS, Arkansas Tech 2004; adj.) US, world

White, Stephen (MA, 2006; adj.) US

Full-time Faculty

Blanks, David R. (PhD, Ohio State 1991; prof. and chair) world, big history, medieval Europe; dblanks@atu.edu

Dykema, Peter (PhD, Arizona 1998; prof. and dir., grad. studies) Europe 1300-1648, religion; pdykema@atu.edu

Jenkins, Ellen J. (PhD, North Texas 1992; prof.) England, World War I, modern Europe; ejenkins@atu.edu

Jones, Kelly E. (PhD, Arkansas 2014; asst. prof.) 19th-century America, African American

McArthur, Aaron J. (PhD, Nevada, Las Vegas 2012; assoc. prof.) public, American West; amcarthur2@atu.edu

Michna, Gregory (PhD, West Virginia 2016; asst. prof.) early America; gmichna@atu.edu

Moses, James L. (PhD, Tulane 1997; prof.) modern America, American constitutional, African American; jmoses@atu.edu

Pearson, Jeffrey V. (PhD, New Mexico 2011; assoc. prof.) American West, Native American; jpearson9@atu.edu

Tarver, H. Micheal (PhD, Bowling Green State 1995; prof.) Latin America, world, 19th-century US; mtarver@atu.edu

Woods, Jeffrey (PhD, Ohio 2000; prof.) modern America, American diplomatic; jwoods@atu.edu

Yi, Guolin (PhD, Wayne State 2013; asst. prof.) China, East Asia; gyi@atu.edu

Assumption College

Dept. of History, 500 Salisbury St., Worcester, MA 01609-1296. 508.767.7377. Fax 508.756.7382. Email: slewando@assumption.edu. Website: https://www.assumption.edu/undergraduate/history.

When you study history at Assumption College you'll gather the many threads of the past and follow them through to the modern day. Through careful analysis, you'll determine where we come from—and where we're headed.

Chair: Irina Mukhina
Degrees Offered: BA
Academic Year System: Semester
Areas of Specialization: Europe, US, Latin America, elementary and secondary education
Tuition (per academic year): $41516
Enrollment 2018-19:
Undergraduate Majors: 50
Degrees in History: 23 BA
Addresses:
Admissions: https://www.assumption.edu/admissions/home
Financial Aid: https://www.assumption.edu/admissions/financial-aid

Full-time Faculty

Borsch, Stuart James (PhD, Columbia 2002; assoc. prof.) Middle East, Islam; sborsch@assumption.edu

Choquette, Leslie P. (PhD, Harvard 1988; prof.) European social and economic, France and French literature, women; lchoquet@assumption.edu

Cohen, David A. (ABD, Yale; lect.) medieval Europe and Spain, Islam, Middle East

Keyes, Carl Robert (PhD, Johns Hopkins 2007; assoc. prof.) colonial America, early modern Atlantic world; ckeyes@assumption.edu

Kisatsky, Deborah L. (PhD, Connecticut 2001; assoc. prof.) US diplomacy; dkisatsk@assumption.edu

Lazar, Lance (PhD, Harvard 1998; assoc. prof.) early modern Europe; llazar@assumption.edu

Mukhina, Irina A. (PhD, Boston Coll. 2006; assoc. prof. and chair) Russia, eastern Europe, gender studies; imukhina@assumption.edu

Wheatland, Thomas P. (PhD, Boston Coll. 2002; assoc. prof.) modern European intellectual; twheatland@assumption.edu

Part-time Faculty

Knowlton, B. C. (PhD, Boston Coll. 1998) linguistic turn

Lynch, Shawn M. (PhD, Boston Coll. 2006; lect.) free speech in Massachusetts 1915-45, 20th-century US political; slynch@assumption.edu

Auburn University

Dept. of History, 310 Thach Hall, Auburn, AL 36849-5207. 334.844.4360. Fax 334.844.6673. Website: https://cla.auburn.edu/history/.

The department is a vibrant community of scholars with a keen interest in research, teaching, and public outreach. History students learn about the past and its relevance to the present, how to ask and answer complex questions, and how to communicate research results in oral and written forms. Alumni are successfully engaged in a wide range of careers, well prepared by their time at Auburn to excel in an ever-changing world with the knowledge and skills to interrogate past and present alike.

Chair: David Lucsko
Director of Graduate Studies: Jennifer Brooks
Director of Undergraduate Studies: W. Matthew Malczycki
Degrees Offered: BA,MA,PhD,Cert. (public hist.; archival studies)
Academic Year System: Semester
Areas of Specialization: US South, technology, Europe since 1500, public history and archives
Undergraduate Tuition (per academic year):
In-State: $9852
Out-of-State: $26364

Graduate Tuition (per academic year):
In-State: $9858
Out-of-State: $26382
Enrollment 2018-19:
Undergraduate Majors: 150
New Graduate Students: 13
Full-time Graduate Students: 51
Part-time Graduate Students: 9
Degrees in History: 78 BA, 8 MA, 5 PhD
Undergraduate Addresses:
Admissions: http://www.auburn.edu/admissions
Financial Aid: http://www.auburn.edu/finaid
Graduate Addresses:
Admissions: http://www.grad.auburn.edu
Financial Aid: http://cla.auburn.edu/history/

Full-time Faculty

Beckwith, Guy (PhD, California, Santa Barbara 1978; assoc. prof.) technology, European intellectual; beckwgv@auburn.edu

Bian, Morris L. (PhD, Washington 1998; prof.) East Asia, modern China; bianmor@auburn.edu

Blair, Melissa Estes (PhD, Virginia 2008; asst. prof.) US women/gender/sexuality; mab0122@auburn.edu

Bohanan, Donna J. (PhD, Emory 1982; prof.) early modern France, social; bohandj@auburn.edu

Braund, Kathryn H. (PhD, Florida State 1986; prof.) colonial America, Native American; braunkh@auburn.edu

Brooks, Jennifer E. (PhD, Tennessee, Knoxville 1997; assoc. prof. and dir., grad. studies) US South, recent US, labor; jebrooks@auburn.edu

Carter, David (PhD, Duke 2000; assoc. prof.) New US South, civil rights; cartedc@auburn.edu

Craig, Kate Melissa (PhD, UCLA 2015; asst. prof.) medieval Europe; kmc0088@auburn.edu

Ferguson, Christopher John (PhD, Indiana 2008; asst. prof.) modern Britain and Europe; cjf0006@auburn.edu

Giblin, Daniel F. (PhD, North Carolina, Chapel Hill 2016; instr.) military

Giustino, Cathleen M. (PhD, Chicago 1997; prof.) modern central Europe; giustcm@auburn.edu

Hamilton, Sarah R. (PhD, Michigan 2013; asst. prof.) environmental, modern Spain; srhamilton@auburn.edu

Hebert, Keith S. (PhD, Auburn 2007; asst. prof.) public, US South; heberks@auburn.edu

Henning, Lori (PhD, Texas A&M 2015; instr.) technology, military

Israel, Charles Alan (PhD, Rice 2001; assoc. prof. and assoc. dean, Acad. Affairs) US South, US, religion; israeca@auburn.edu

Jortner, Adam (PhD, Virginia 2009; assoc. prof.) early Republic US, religion; ajj0008@auburn.edu

Kennington, Kelly Marie (PhD, Duke 2009; asst. prof.) legal and constitutional, slavery, Old South; kennington@auburn.edu

Kingston, Ralph (PhD, Univ. Coll. London 2002; assoc. prof.) revolutionary era Europe; rfk0001@auburn.edu

Kozuh, Michael (PhD, Chicago 2006; assoc. prof.) ancient; mgk0001@auburn.edu

Laney, Monique (PhD, Kansas 2009; asst. prof.) US technology in global context, immigration/popular culture/Cold War; laney@auburn.edu

Lucsko, David N. (PhD, MIT 2005; assoc. prof. and chair) technology; dnl0006@auburn.edu

Malczycki, W. Matt (PhD, Utah 2006; assoc. prof. and dir., undergrad. studies) Middle East, Islam; malczycki@auburn.edu

McLean, Eden Knudsen (PhD, Yale 2010; asst. prof.) modern Europe, modern Italy, modern imperialism; ekmclean@auburn.edu

Meyer, Alan D. (PhD, Delaware 2009; asst. prof.) technology, aviation; adm0027@auburn.edu

Mishra, Rupali Raj (PhD, Princeton 2011; asst. prof.) Tudor-Stuart England, early modern Europe, Mughal India; rrm0009@auburn.edu

Noe, Kenneth W. (PhD, Illinois, Urbana-Champaign 1990; prof.) Civil War and Reconstruction, Appalachia; noekenn@auburn.edu

Ray, Daren E. (PhD, Virginia 2014; asst. prof.) Africa, East Africa; dzr0033@auburn.edu

Sheftall, Mark D. (PhD, Duke 2002; assoc. prof.) war and society, modern Britain/British Empire, modern Europe; mds0020@auburn.edu

Sippial, Tiffany Anise (PhD, New Mexico 2007; assoc. prof. and dir., Honors Coll.) Latin America; tat0004@auburn.edu

Retired/Emeritus Faculty

Biggs, Lindy B. (PhD, MIT 1987; assoc. prof. emeritus) technology, urban, American social; biggslb@auburn.edu

Crocker, Ruth C. (PhD, Purdue 1982; prof. emeritus) Progressive Era, women; crockrc@auburn.edu

Cronenberg, Allen T. (PhD, Stanford 1970; assoc. prof. emeritus) modern Germany, 19th-century Europe

Essah, Patience (PhD, UCLA 1985; assoc. prof. emeritus) African American, US, Africa; essahpa@auburn.edu

Flynt, Wayne (PhD, Florida State 1965; prof. emeritus) US since 1876, New US South; henkewi@duc.auburn.edu

Gerber, Larry G. (PhD, California, Berkeley 1979; prof. emeritus) US, 20th century; gerbelg@auburn.edu

Hall, Hines H. (PhD, Vanderbilt 1971; prof. emeritus) modern Europe; hallhin@auburn.edu

Hansen, James Roger (PhD, Ohio State 1981; prof. emeritus) science and technology, aerospace, sport; hansejr@auburn.edu

Harrell, David E. (PhD, Vanderbilt 1962; prof. emeritus) US, religious; harrede@auburn.edu

Jakeman, Robert J. (PhD, Auburn 1988; assoc. prof. emeritus) US, archives; jakemrj@auburn.edu

Kicklighter, Joseph A. (PhD, Emory 1973; prof. emeritus) medieval; kicklja@auburn.edu

Lakwete, Angela (PhD, Delaware 1997; assoc. prof. emeritus) technology, southern industrialization; lakwean@auburn.edu

Melancon, Michael S. (PhD, Indiana 1984; prof. emeritus) Russia, Soviet Union; melanms@auburn.edu

Szechi, Daniel (DPhil, Oxford 1983; prof. emeritus) early modern Britain; daniel.szechi@manchester.ac.uk

Trimble, William F. (PhD, Colorado, Boulder 1974; prof. emeritus) technology, diplomatic, naval; trimbwf@auburn.edu

Recently Awarded PhDs

Bishop, Christopher M. "Methodism and the Rise of the Southern Middle Class, 1866-94"

Colvin, Alex "The Sehoy Legacy: Kinship, Gender, and Race in a Tensaw Community"

Colvin, Perry A. "The Lord of the Air: Winston Churchill and the Rise of the Technocratic British State, 1917-22"

Derbes, Brett Josef "Prisoners Make War: The Production of Military Supplies with Inmate Labor at Confederate State Penitentiaries during the Civil War"

Marini, Angelica "Southern by Birth, Queer by the Grace of God: Southern Sexualities and Regional Identity, 1920-70"

Mohr, John "Wallace's Long Shadow: Technology, Politics, and Industry in the American South"

Pequignot, Jennifer Lynn "Why a Diamond Means Forever: The Creation of the Diamond Engagement Ring Tradition in the United States, 1939-96"

Augsburg University

Dept. of History, 2211 Riverside Ave. S., Minneapolis, MN 55454. 612.330.1665. Fax 612.330.1649. Email: lansing@augsburg.edu. Website: https://www.augsburg.edu/history/.

Augsburg's mission is to educate students to be informed citizens, thoughtful stewards, critical thinkers, and responsible leaders. This is what we teach our students in the Department of History.

Chair: Michael J. Lansing
Degrees Offered: BA
Academic Year System: Semester
Areas of Specialization: environmental, US civil rights, Islam, religion, women and gender, medieval, diplomacy and European politics, world
Tuition (per academic year): $39295
Enrollment 2018-19:
  Undergraduate Majors: 45
  Degrees in History: 13 BA
Addresses:
  Admissions: http://www.augsburg.edu/admissions/
  Financial Aid: http://www.augsburg.edu/studentfinancial/

Full-time Faculty

Adamo, Phillip C. (PhD, Ohio State 2000; prof.) medieval, religion, ancient; adamo@augsburg.edu

deVries, Jacqueline R. (PhD, Illinois, Urbana-Champaign 1997; prof.) modern Britain, modern Europe, women and gender; devries@augsburg.edu

Green, William D. (PhD, Minnesota 1976; prof.) African American, legal, Minnesota; greenb@augsburg.edu

Lansing, Michael J. (PhD, Minnesota 2003; assoc. prof. and chair) North American West and Midwest, environmental, political; lansing@augsburg.edu

Zaman, Maheen (PhD, Columbia 2014; asst. prof.) Islam, South Asia, world; zamanm@augsburg.edu

Part-time Faculty

Lorenz-Meyer, Martin (PhD, Kansas 2004; lect.) US diplomatic, World War II, Cold War; lorenz@augsburg.edu

Retired/Emeritus Faculty

Nelson, Richard C. (PhD, Minnesota 1975; prof. emeritus) ancient Near East, Greece and Rome; nelson@augsburg.edu

Augusta University

Dept. of History, Anthropology, and Philosophy, Summerville Campus, Allgood Hall E222, 1120 15th St., Augusta, GA 30912. 706.737.1709. Fax 706.729.2177. Email: hap@augusta.edu. Website: https://www.augusta.edu/pamplin/hist-anth-phil/.

We offer a dynamic curriculum where students can choose from a wide array of courses about US, European, and world history; historical archaeology and cultural anthropology; and contemporary and historical philosophy. Our faculty are devoted teachers and talented researchers, who hail from top-ranked graduate programs across the US and Canada. The department's mission is to create critical thinkers, writers, and researchers.

Chair: Andrew Goss
Degrees Offered: BA
Academic Year System: Semester
Areas of Specialization: US, Europe, Asia, Latin America, military

Tuition (per academic year):
In-State: $6892
Out-of-State: $22270
Enrollment 2018-19:
Undergraduate Majors: 85
Degrees in History: 19 BA
Addresses:
Admissions: http://www.augusta.edu/admissions
Financial Aid: http://www.augusta.edu/finaid

Full-time Faculty

Bishku, Michael B. (PhD, NYU 1981; prof.) Middle East, Africa; mbishku@augusta.edu

Caldwell, Lee Ann (PhD, Georgia 1986; prof.; historian-in-residence; and dir., Center Georgia Hist.) Georgia, US, American women; lcaldwel@augusta.edu

Catris, Sandrine Emmanuelle (PhD, Indiana 2015; asst. prof.) China, Asia; scatris@augusta.edu

Chiero, Heather J. (PhD, Texas Christian 2005; assoc. prof.) Latin America; hchiero@augusta.edu

Goss, Andrew (PhD, Michigan 2004; prof. and chair) Indonesia, Asia, science; angoss@augusta.edu

Green, Elna C. (PhD, Tulane 1992; prof. and dean, Pamplin Coll.) US South, women; elngreen@augusta.edu

Hayes, John (PhD, Georgia 2007; assoc. prof.) US South, religion in American South; jhayes22@augusta.edu

McClelland-Nugent, Ruth E. (PhD, Dalhousie 2000; assoc. prof.) Atlantic world; rmcclel1@augusta.edu

Pinheiro, Holly Anthony, Jr. (PhD, Iowa 2017; asst. prof.) African American, military

Turner, Wendy J. (PhD, UCLA 2000; prof.) medieval world, Britain; wturner1@augusta.edu

van Tuyll, Hubert P. (PhD, Texas A&M 1986; prof.) military, modern Europe, Russia; hvantuyl@augusta.edu

Joint/Cross Appointments

Bloodworth, William (PhD, Texas, Austin 1972; prof.; American Culture) American West, American literature; wbloodwo@augusta.edu

Retired/Emeritus Faculty

Clark, Charles W., III (PhD, Colorado, Boulder 1979; prof. and dean emeritus) medieval and early modern, witchcraft, science

Fissel, Mark Charles (PhD, California, Berkeley 1983; prof. emeritus) Tudor-Stuart England, European military, military revolution; mfissel@augusta.edu

Searles, Michael N. (MA, Howard; asst. prof. emeritus) African American, US West; cowboymike@augusta.edu

Augustana College

Dept. of History, 639 38th St., Rock Island, IL 61201-2296. 309.794.7679. Email: lendolcalder@augustana.edu; ellafly@augustana.edu. Website: https://www.augustana.edu/academics/areas-of-study/history.

Augustana offers a major and minor in history and a major in History Education. Newly designed Compass Points allow students to focus on one of four areas: History Communication, Information Analytics, Nations & Global Politics, and Social Justice. Faculty are affiliated with Asian Studies, Environmental Studies, Latin American Studies, Africana Studies, and Women's, Gender & Sexuality Studies, and have been at the forefront of the scholarship of teaching and learning in history.

Chair: Lendol Calder
Degrees Offered: BA
Academic Year System: Semester
Areas of Specialization: US, early modern and modern Europe, Asia, Latin America, history education, gender
Tuition (per academic year): $42135
Enrollment 2018-19:
Undergraduate Majors: 54
Degrees in History: 17 BA
Students in Undergraduate Courses: 758
Students in Undergraduate Intro Courses: 497
Addresses:
Admissions: http://www.augustana.edu/admissions
Financial Aid: http://www.augustana.edu/admissions/financial-assistance

Full-time Faculty

Calder, Lendol G. (PhD, Chicago 1993; prof. and chair) modern US, history teaching and learning; lendolcalder@augustana.edu

Ellis, David L. (PhD, Chicago 2002; prof.) modern Europe, Germany, religion; davidellis@augustana.edu

Hammond, Lauren (PhD, Texas, Austin 2014; asst. prof.; Latin American Studies) Latin America, African diaspora; laurenhammond@augustana.edu

Lawrence, Elizabeth (PhD, Columbia 2014; asst. prof.) Asia, history and heritage, material culture; elizabethlawrence@augustana.edu

Leech, Brian J. (PhD, Wisconsin-Madison 2012; assoc. prof.) modern US, environmental, labor; brianleech@augustana.edu

Simonsen, Jane E (PhD, Iowa 2001; prof.; Women's, Gender & Sexuality Studies) 19th-century US, gender, women; janesimonsen@augustana.edu

Nondepartmental Historians

Blanck, Dag (PhD, Uppsala, Sweden 1997; asst. prof.; dir., Swenson Swedish Immigration Research Center) US immigration, Scandinavia; dagblanck@augustana.edu

Kramer, Emil A. (PhD, Cincinnati 1999; prof.; Classics) ancient Greece and Rome; emilkramer@augustana.edu

Part-time Faculty

Kolp, John (PhD, Iowa 1988; asst. prof.) US; johnkolp@augustana.edu

Retired/Emeritus Faculty

Brown, Thomas A. (PhD, Duke 1970; prof. emeritus) Latin America; tombrown@augustana.edu

Symons, Van J. (PhD, Brown 1975; prof. emeritus) China, Japan; vansymons@augustana.edu

Austin College

Dept. of History, 900 N. Grand Ave., Sherman, TX 75090-4440. 903.813.2361. Fax 903.813.2368. Email: htooley@austincollege.edu. Website: https://www.austincollege.edu/academics/majors-and-minors/history/.

The Austin College Department of History plays an integral role in the liberal arts curriculum of the college. The mission of the department is to provide students with an analytical basis, encompassing multiple areas and time frames, for judgment and perspective on the past.

Chair: T. Hunt Tooley
Degrees Offered: BA
Academic Year System: 4-1-4

Areas of Specialization: US, Europe, Latin America, Southwest and Latin American studies, women
Tuition (per academic year): $41155
Enrollment 2018-19:
  Undergraduate Majors: 43
  Degrees in History: 18 BA
Addresses:
  Admissions: http://www.austincollege.edu/admission/
  Financial Aid: http://www.austincollege.edu/financial-aid/

Full-time Faculty

Cummins, Victoria H. (PhD, Tulane 1979; Pate Prof.) colonial Mexico, Latin America, US women; vcummins@austincollege.edu
Grober, Max C. (PhD, California, Berkeley 1990; prof. and dean, Humanities) early modern Europe, intellectual; mgrober@austincollege.edu
Harcourt, Felix A. (PhD, George Washington 2014; asst. prof.) modern US, interwar, New Deal; fharcourt@austincollege.edu
Tooley, T. Hunt (PhD, Virginia 1986; prof. and chair) modern Europe, central Europe, 20th-century world; htooley@austincollege.edu
Wolnisty, Claire Marie (PhD, Kansas 2016; asst. prof.) 19th-century US, US South, expansion, Western Hemisphere; cwolnisty@austincollege.edu

Nondepartmental Historians

Bucher, Henry Hale, Jr. (PhD, Wisconsin, Madison 1977; assoc. prof. emeritus; Coll. chaplain emeritus) Africa, precolonial Gabon; hbucher@austincollege.edu

Retired/Emeritus Faculty

Cummins, Light T. (PhD, Tulane 1977; prof. emeritus) American Revolution, Spanish borderlands, Texas; lcummins@austincollege.edu
Page, Oscar C. (PhD, Kentucky 1967; prof. emeritus and Coll. pres. emeritus) opage@austincollege.edu

Austin Community College

Dept. of History, 5930 Middle Fiskville Rd., Austin, TX 78752-4390. 512.223.3385. Fax 512.223.3414. Email: apurcell@austincc.edu. Website: https://sites.austincc.edu/history/.

Historians broaden our understanding of our world by objectively viewing civilizations and our own national and state heritage. Students choosing to major in history typically follow the pathway through the History Program at Austin Community College, then transfer to a bachelor's degree program at a four-year institution.

Chair: Allan R. Purcell
Degrees Offered: AA
Academic Year System: Semester
Areas of Specialization: US, Texas, African American, Mexican American, Western civilization
Tuition (per academic year):
  In-State: $1860
  Out-of-State: $6720
Enrollment 2018-19:
  Students in Program: 425
  Degrees in History: 16 AA
Addresses:
  Admissions: http://www.austincc.edu/apply-and-register
  Financial Aid: http://www.austincc.edu/tuition-and-financial-aid

Full-time Faculty

Addis, Cameron Clark (PhD, Texas, Austin 2000; prof.) revolutionary and Jeffersonian America, popular historiography, American West; caddis@austincc.edu
Bell, Harris E. (MA, Prairie View A&M 1979; prof.) African American; hbell@austincc.edu
Bonafont, Melissa N. (PhD, California, Irvine 1996; prof.) US, Gilded Age and Progressive era, modern Europe; mbonafon@austincc.edu
Bucco, Jack A. (PhD, Bowling Green State 2002; prof.) US, economic, Latin America; jbucco@austincc.edu
Diaz-Miranda, Mariano (PhD, Texas, Austin 1988; prof.) Latin America, 19th-century Brazil and Cuba, Mexican American/Chicano; marianod@austincc.edu
Goines, L. Patrick (MA, Texas, Austin 1985; prof.) US, American Indian; pgoines@austincc.edu
Haney, David Paul (PhD, Texas, Austin 1998; assoc. prof.) US, 20th-century society and culture, intellectual; dhaney@austincc.edu
Hayes, Roland C. (MA, Michigan State 1971; prof.) African American; rhayes@austincc.edu
Lauderback, David Marcus (PhD, Texas, Austin 2004; prof.) US diplomatic, Cold War, African American sports; dlauderb@austincc.edu
Purcell, Allan R. (PhD, Texas, Austin 1981; prof. and chair) US, Civil War, military; apurcell@austincc.edu
Rebhorn, Marlette (PhD, Texas, Austin 1971; prof.) Cold War, American diplomacy, film; mrebhorn@austincc.edu
Summers, Suzanne L. (PhD, Texas, Austin 1996; prof.) US economic and business; smcfadde@austincc.edu
Thomas, Teresa M. (PhD, Texas, Austin 2001; prof.) US legal and urban, Civil War and Reconstruction, national period; tmthomas@austincc.edu
Tijerina, Andres (PhD, Texas, Austin 1977; prof.) US, Great Plains and borderlands, Chicano/Latino; andrest@austincc.edu
VanSandt, Zoe Irene (MEd, Texas State 1996; prof.) US social, women; vansandt@austincc.edu

Retired/Emeritus Faculty

Boeke, Kristine E. (MA, Notre Dame 1998; assoc. prof. emeritus) 20th-century cultural and intellectual, ethnic studies, 1960s; kboeke@austincc.edu
Griffin, Roger A. (PhD, Texas, Austin 1973; prof. emeritus) US, Texas, Western civilization; rgriffin1@austin.rr.com
Hughes, L. Patrick (MA, Texas, Austin 1975; prof. emeritus) US, Texas, 20th century; lpatrick@austincc.edu
Kent, H. Ren, Jr. (PhD, Texas, Austin 1967; prof. emeritus) US diplomatic, 20th century, American West; renk@austincc.edu
Lain, Bobby D. (PhD, Texas, Austin 1974; prof. emeritus) US West, social, military; bdlain@cvtv.net
Montgomery, William E. (PhD, Texas, Austin 1974; prof. emeritus) African American, South, West; bmontgom@austincc.edu
Murray, Sean Collins (PhD, SUNY, Buffalo 1975; prof. emeritus) colonial America; smurray@austincc.edu
Willoughby, Larry (MA, West Texas A&M 1979; prof. emeritus) civil rights, 20th century, Texas; jlw@austincc.edu

Austin Peay State University

Dept. of History and Philosophy, Harned Hall, Rm. 340, Clarksville, TN 37044-0001. 931.221.7924. Fax 931.221.7917. Email: suttc@apsu.edu. Website: https://www.apsu.edu/history-and-philosophy/.

With offerings on campus and online during the regular academic year and over breaks, the department offers students the flexibility to complete not only general degree requirements but entire programs of study at their own pace and in a way that fits into their schedule. With a faculty made up of scholars recognized not only regionally but nationally as well, students have the chance to learn from and work with experts in their fields.

Chair: Cameron M. Sutt
Director of Graduate Studies: David R. Snyder
Degrees Offered: BA,BS,MA
Academic Year System: Semester
Areas of Specialization: colonial New England and American Revolution, US South, recent America, Europe, military
Undergraduate Tuition (per academic year):
In-State: $7168
Out-of-State: $21664
Graduate Tuition (per academic year):
In-State: $7654
Out-of-State: $19282
Enrollment 2018-19:
Undergraduate Majors: 225
New Graduate Students: 21
Full-time Graduate Students: 15
Part-time Graduate Students: 10
Degrees in History: 30 MA
Addresses:
Admissions: http://www.apsu.edu/admissions
Financial Aid: http://www.apsu.edu/financialaid

Adjunct Faculty

Briggs, Pamela R. (MA, Austin Peay State 1986; adj.) briggsp@apsu.edu
Broggie, Matthew D. (MA, Austin Peay State 2015; adj.) broggiem@apsu.edu
Campbell, Daniel (MA, Austin Peay State 2013; adj.) campbelld@apsu.edu
Compton, Aaron (MA, Austin Peay State 2009; adj.) military; comptona@apsu.edu
Culver, Gregory (PhD, Southern Illinois, Carbondale 2000; instr.) US South; culverg@apsu.edu
Demetrides, Sara (MA, Evergreen State 2006; adj.) demetridess@apsu.edu
Drummond, Benjamin (MA, Austin Peay State 2004; instr.) drummondb@apsu.edu
Esing, Christopher (PhD, Kentucky 2014; instr.) esingc@apsu.edu
Gillis, Gregory R. (MA, Southeast Missouri State 1984; instr.) America; gillisg@apsu.edu
Jones, Ashley (MA, East Tennessee State 2016; adj.) jonesa@apsu.edu
Kruk, William K. (MA, Murray State 2005; instr.) America; krukw@apsu.edu
Maurer, Daniel (MA, East Tennessee State 2010; instr.) maurerd@apsu.edu
Moure, Frank (MA, Austin Peay State 2014; adj.) mouref@apsu.edu
O'Brien, John J. (PhD, St. Louis 2017; instr.) America, public; obrienj@apsu.edu
Parker, William (MA, Austin Peay State 2008; instr.) parkerw@apsu.edu
Pigg, Jimmy J. (MA, Western Kentucky 2002; instr.) America; piggj@apsu.edu
Poppendorf, Alexandria (MA, Austin Peay State 2016; instr.) poppendorfa@apsu.edu
Ross, Robert (MA, Austin Peay State 2011; adj.) rossr@apsu.edu

Scott, Jonathan G. (MA, Villanova 1999; instr.) America, world, military; scottj@apsu.edu

Full-time Faculty

Banerjee, Somaditya (PhD, British Columbia 2013; asst. prof.) science, modern Asia; banerjees@apsu.edu
Butts, Michele T. (PhD, New Mexico 1992; prof.) American Indian and West, Latin America; buttsmt@apsu.edu
Cross, C. Wallace (PhD, Vanderbilt 1983; prof.) England, American Civil War, British Empire; crossw@apsu.edu
Dzanic, Dzavid (PhD, Harvard 2016; asst. prof.) modern Europe, Mediterranean; dzanicd@apsu.edu
Frentzos, Christos G. (PhD, Houston 2004; assoc. prof.) US diplomatic and military, 20th-century US political; frentzosc@apsu.edu
Hammond, Gregory S. (PhD, Texas, Austin 2004; assoc. prof.) Latin America; hammondg@apsu.edu
Pesely, George E. (PhD, California, Berkeley 1983; prof.) ancient Greece and Rome, late antiquity; peselyg@apsu.edu
Rands, David C. (PhD, Southern California 2011; assoc. prof.) modern Japan, Asia, urban; randsd@apsu.edu
Snyder, David R. (PhD, Nebraska 2002; prof. and dir., grad. studies) military, modern Europe, Holocaust; snyderdr@apsu.edu
Steinberg, John W. (PhD, Ohio State 1990; prof.) Russia, eastern Europe, military and Holocaust; steinbergj@apsu.edu
Sutt, Cameron M. (PhD, Cambridge 2008; assoc. prof. and chair) medieval Europe and Middle East; suttc@apsu.edu
Tanner, Kevin, Jr. (PhD, SUNY, Binghamton 2008; assoc. prof.) America; tannerk@apsu.edu
Thompson, Antonio Scott (PhD, Kentucky 2006; assoc. prof.) US diplomatic, modern Germany, military; thompsonas@apsu.edu
Uffelman, Minoa D. (PhD, Mississippi 2003; assoc. prof.) America, US South, gender; uffelmanm@apsu.edu
Wesley, Timothy Leon (PhD, Penn State 2010; assoc. prof.) politics and religion, Civil War era; wesleyt@apsu.edu
Zieren, Gregory R. (PhD, Delaware 1982; prof.) Gilded Age, US economic, oral and military; ziereng@apsu.edu

Retired/Emeritus Faculty

Akerman, Hugh (MA, Florida 1955; assoc. prof. emeritus)
Browder, Dewey A. (PhD, Louisiana State 1987; prof. emeritus) modern Europe and Germany, Holocaust, military; browderd@apsu.edu
Gildrie, Richard P. (PhD, Virginia 1971; prof. emeritus) colonial America, American Revolution, intellectual; gildrier@apsu.edu
Hughes, C. Alvin (PhD, Ohio 1982; prof. emeritus) 20th-century US, Africa and Afro-American, US social; hughesc@apsu.edu
Muir, Malcolm, Jr. (PhD, Ohio State 1976; prof. emeritus) military
Winn, Thomas H. (EdD, Ball State 1974; prof. emeritus) early Republic, US South, Tennessee

Azusa Pacific University

Dept. of History and Political Science, 901 E. Alosta Ave., PO Box 7000, Azusa, CA 91702-7000. 626.815.3843. Fax 626.815.3868. Email: historyps@apu.edu. Website: https://www.apu.edu/clas/historypolisci/.

The Department of History and Political Science offers undergraduate degree programs in political science, history, international relations and social science, and preparation for a teaching credential in social science; provides general education in history and political science courses consistent with the outcomes of a liberal arts education; and prepares students for graduate study, law school, or success in their chosen careers.

Chair: Daniel Palm
Degrees Offered: BA
Academic Year System: Semester
Areas of Specialization: US, Europe, Latin America, medieval, American intellectual
Tuition (per academic year): $39640
Enrollment 2018-19:
 Undergraduate Majors: 37
 Degrees in History: 13 BA
 Students in Undergraduate Courses: 1000
 Students in Undergraduate Intro Courses: 745
Addresses:
 Admissions: http://www.apu.edu/admissions/
 Financial Aid: http://www.apu.edu/undergraduate-admissions/financialaid/

Full-time Faculty

Flannery, Christopher (PhD, Claremont Grad. 1980; prof.) political science, American foreign relations, Shakespeare's politics; cflannery@apu.edu

Gutierrez, Veronica A. (PhD, UCLA 2012; assoc. prof.) Latin America; vgutierrez@apu.edu

Hale, Bradley R. (PhD, Connecticut 2005; assoc. prof. and dir., Humanities) world, modern Europe, 1968; bhale@apu.edu

Hume, Doug (JD, Pepperdine 1997; asst. prof.) pre-law, constitutional law, legal studies; dhume@apu.edu

King, Joshua (PhD, Baylor 2016; asst. prof.) modern political thought, American political thought, international relations theory

Lambert, David E. (PhD, Claremont Grad. 2008; asst. prof.) political science, America; dlambert@apu.edu

Lamkin, Bryan J. (PhD, California, Riverside 1997; prof.) America, Irish-American immigration; blamkin@apu.edu

Mazza, Edmund J. (PhD, Grad. Center, CUNY 2004; prof.) world, medieval Europe; emazza@apu.edu

Palm, Daniel (PhD, Claremont Grad. 1991; prof. and chair) political science, American foreign affairs, Asia; dpalm@apu.edu

Schrum, Ethan (PhD, Pennsylvania 2009; asst. prof.) America, intellectual, US foreign affairs; eschrum@apu.edu

Sellers, Abbylin (PhD, Claremont Grad. 2012; assoc. prof.) American politics, public policy; asellers@apu.edu

Walsh, Jennifer (PhD, Claremont Grad. 2000; prof. and dean, Coll. of Liberal Arts and Sciences) three-strikes laws, law, government; jwalsh@apu.edu

Weeks, David L. (PhD, Loyola, Chicago 1991; prof. and dean, Honors Coll.) political science, law; dweeks@apu.edu

Part-time Faculty

Harrington, Wade (MA, California State, Fullerton 2006; lect.) jharrington@apu.edu

Plummer, Brian (PhD, Claremont Grad. 2011; lect.) America; bplummer@apu.edu

Baldwin Wallace University

Dept. of History, 275 Eastland Rd., 50 Seminary St., Berea, OH 44017-2088. 440.826.2076. Fax 440.826.3264. Email: igesink@bw.edu; blennox@bw.edu. Website: https://www.bw.edu/academics/undergraduate/history/.

The department offers three types of degrees: History BA, Public History BA, and Applied History BS as well as a teaching license in integrated social studies. The Public History major is intensively experiential including a required completion of an internship. Much of the coursework takes place in archives and local museums. The Applied History major is the first program of its kind in Ohio. It is designed for people who have a passion for history but want a career in the corporate world. BW offers hands-on learning and real-world projects like historical cemetery documentation, exploration of local archives for unique independent research, and collaboration with archivists and other professionals. The history professors at BW bring impressive academic and scholarly credentials to the classroom. Whether you are fascinated with US, East Asian, Russian, Middle Eastern or the entire world, our faculty will help you explore your interests. All programs are fully accredited.

Chair: Indira Falk Gesink
Degrees Offered: BA,BS
Academic Year System: Semester
Areas of Specialization: US, Europe, Russia, Asia, Middle East, medieval/ancient
Tuition (per academic year): $33530
Enrollment 2018-19:
 Undergraduate Majors: 70
 Degrees in History: 24 BA
Addresses:
 Admissions: https://www.bw.edu/undergraduate-admission/
 Financial Aid: https://www.bw.edu/financial-aid/

Adjunct Faculty

Boaz, Rachael E. (PhD, Kent State 2009; lect. III) modern Europe, Weimar and Nazi Germany, science and environmental; rboaz@bw.edu

Rand, Tamara S. (PhD, Akron 2013; lect. II) Middle Ages through 20th-century Europe, Black Death, women, quantitative research methods; trand@bw.edu

Uthup, Thomas (PhD, Binghamton, SUNY 1996; lect. III) Africa; tuthup@bw.edu

Full-time Faculty

Gesink, Indira Falk (PhD, Washington, St. Louis 2000; prof. and chair; dir., Middle East and North Africa Minor) modern Middle East and Islamic world, historiography and gender studies; igesink@bw.edu

Mays, Nicholas S. (ABD, Kent State; asst. prof.; First Year Experience) modern US, African American, urban, hip-hop and black freedom struggle; nmays@bw.edu

Mieyal, Timothy J. (ABD, Kent State; asst. prof.) Civil Rights Movement, African American, modern US social and cultural, Vietnam; tmieyal@bw.edu

Montgomery, Robert W. (PhD, Indiana 1995; prof.) Russia, East Asia, native Asian peoples of Siberia; rmontgom@bw.edu

Nalmpantis, Kyriakos (PhD, Kent State 2010; asst. prof.) Greece and Rome, Europe, Latin America, modern Balkans; knalmpan@bw.edu

Siry, Steven E. (PhD, Cincinnati 1986; prof.) colonial America, American Revolution, Jefferson-Jacksonian America, US Civil War, US to 1877, World War I and II, war; ssiry@bw.edu

Joint/Cross Appointments

Peppers, Kieth (MA, Cleveland State 2010; Univ. archivist) public, archive and museum management, curatorship, geocaching; kpeppers@bw.edu

Ball State University

Dept. of History, Burkhardt Bldg. 200, Muncie, IN 47306-0480. 765.285.8700. Fax 765.285.5612. Email: history@bsu.edu; aalves@bsu.edu. Website: https://www.bsu.edu/academics/ collegesanddepartments/history.

Our department has exceptional teachers who have received several honors and recognition and have a wide range of research interest. Our curricula will challenge you to think differently about cultures, places, and events in history. You will also benefit from personal attention in our classrooms, as we have small class sizes. In addition, you can do research with us the day you step foot at Ball State.

Chair: Abel Alves
Director of Graduate Studies: Daniel P. Ingram
Degrees Offered: BA,BS,MA
Academic Year System: Semester
Areas of Specialization: public, digital, teacher education
Undergraduate Tuition (per academic year):
  In-State: $10016
  Out-of-State: $26588
Graduate Tuition (per academic year):
  In-State: $9506
  Out-of-State: $22448
Enrollment 2018-19:
  Undergraduate Majors: 319
  Full-time Graduate Students: 16
  Part-time Graduate Students: 9
  Degrees in History: 10 BA, 38 BS, 5 MA
Undergraduate Addresses:
  Admissions: http://cms.bsu.edu/admissions
  Financial Aid: http://cms.bsu.edu/admissions/ scholarshipsandfinancialaid/
Graduate Addresses:
  Admissions: http://cms.bsu.edu/academics/ collegesanddepartments/gradschool/
  Financial Aid: http://cms.bsu.edu/admissions/ scholarshipsandfinancialaid/

Adjunct Faculty

Bosworth, Amy K. (PhD, Purdue 2008; asst. teaching prof.) world, medieval and Carolingian, hagiography; akbosworth@bsu.edu

Felker-Kantor, Max (PhD, Southern California 2014; vis. asst. prof.) African American, urban, carceral state; mfelkerkanto@bsu.edu

Hall, Robert G. (PhD, Vanderbilt 1991; teaching prof.) modern Britain and world, reading; rghall@bsu.edu

Krzemienski, Edward (PhD, Purdue 2015; assoc. teaching prof.) world and 20th century US, sports, military; krzemienski@bsu. edu

McBride Scheurer, Heather (MA, Auburn 2015; asst. teaching prof.) public, World War II, cultural property; hrscheurer@bsu.edu

Parkinson, John Scott (PhD, Miami, Ohio 1998; asst. teaching prof.) early America, US Civil War, imperial and Third Reich Germany; sparkins@bsu.edu

Stewart, Dorshell (EdD, Indiana 2012; asst. teaching prof.) curriculum studies, teacher education; dmstewart@bsu.edu

Wood, Tara S. (PhD, Arizona State 2008; MLS, Indiana 2017; asst. teaching prof.; Distance and Online Learning) early modern England, early modern women, history of the book; tswood@ bsu.edu

Full-time Faculty

Alves, Abel A. (PhD, Massachusetts Amherst 1990; prof. and chair) early modern global studies, animal studies, deep history; aalves@bsu.edu

Chen, Shiau-Yun (PhD, Cornell 2019; asst. prof.; Women's and Gender Studies) Ming China, women, East Asia; schen5@bsu. edu

Connolly, James J. (PhD, Brandeis 1995; prof. and dir., Center for Middletown Studies) late 19th- and 20th-century US, political/ urban/ethnic; jconnoll@bsu.edu

DeSilva, Jennifer Mara (PhD, Toronto 2007; assoc. prof.) late medieval and early modern Europe, Renaissance and Reformation, papacy; jmdesilva@bsu.edu

Dmitriev, Sviatoslav (PhD, Harvard 2001; assoc. prof.) ancient Greece and Rome, ancient social and administrative; dmitriev@ bsu.edu

Drake Brown, Sarah (PhD, Indiana 2004; assoc. prof.; dir., History/ Social Studies Education) history/civic education, curriculum studies, teacher education; sedrakebrown@bsu.edu

Etcheson, Nicole (PhD, Indiana 1991; prof. and Alexander M. Bracken Chair) sectional crisis, Civil War and Reconstruction, Indiana; netcheson@bsu.edu

Geelhoed, E. Bruce (PhD, Ball State 1975; prof.) recent America, 20th-century business; bgeelhoed@bsu.edu

Hall, Kenneth R. (PhD, Michigan 1975; prof.) South and Southeast Asia, China and Japan, Indian Ocean; khall2@bsu.edu

Ingram, Daniel P. (PhD, William and Mary 2008; assoc. prof. and dir., MA Program) colonial and revolutionary America, Native Americans; dpingram@bsu.edu

Johnson, Emily Suzanne (PhD, Yale 2014; asst. prof.) US women, women's studies, religion and politics; esjohnson2@bsu.edu

Malone, Carolyn A. (PhD, Rochester 1991; assoc. prof.) modern Europe, modern Britain, modern European women; camalone@ bsu.edu

Morris, Ronald V. (PhD, Purdue 1997; prof.) elementary social studies education, museum studies, digital; rvmorris@bsu.edu

Reuther, Jessica Catherine (PhD, Emory 2016; asst. prof.) Africa, France and its empire, law and colonialism; jcreuther@bsu.edu

Seefeldt, Douglas (PhD, Arizona State 2001; assoc. prof.) digital, American West, public memory; wdseefeldt@bsu.edu

Smith, Kevin E. (PhD, Yale 1990; prof. and assoc. dean) US diplomatic, international relations, World War II; ksmith@bsu. edu

Stephan, Scott M. (PhD, Indiana 2002; assoc. prof.) 19th-century US, US South, social and cultural; sstephan@bsu.edu

Suppe, Frederick C. (PhD, Minnesota 1981; assoc. prof.) Celtic, medieval Europe, Wales; fsuppe@bsu.edu

Thompson, Christopher S. (PhD, NYU 1997; prof.) modern and postcolonial France, European social and cultural, sports; cthompso@bsu.edu

Zhuk, Sergei I. (PhD, Johns Hopkins 2002; prof.) Russia/Ukraine/ eastern Europe, Cold War and American-Russian relations, comparative religion and popular culture; sizhuk@bsu.edu

Bard College

Historical Studies Program, PO Box 5000, Annandale On Hudson, NY 12504. 845.758.6822. Fax 845.758.7628. Email: culp@bard. edu. Website: http://historicalstudies.bard.edu/.

The Historical Studies Program focuses primarily, but not exclusively, on political, social, economic, and cultural aspects of history. The program encourages students to examine history

through the prism of other relevant disciplines and different forms of expression. The program also introduces students to a variety of methodological perspectives used in historical research and to philosophical assumptions about men, women, and society that underlie these perspectives.

Chair: Robert J. Culp
Degrees Offered: BA
Academic Year System: Semester
Areas of Specialization: US and Latin America, Europe and Atlantic world, Russia and Soviet Union, Asia, Middle East and Africa
Tuition (per academic year): $69787
Enrollment 2018-19:
Undergraduate Majors: 72
Degrees in History: 22 BA
Addresses:
Admissions: http://www.bard.edu/admission/
Financial Aid: http://www.bard.edu/financialaid/

Full-time Faculty

Aldous, Richard (PhD, Cambridge 1993; Eugene Meyer Prof.) 19th- and 20th-century Britain, international relations, Anglo-American relations; raldous@bard.edu

Armstead, Myra B. Young (PhD, Chicago 1987; prof.) 19th-century US social, urban, African American; armstead@bard.edu

Cheta, Omar (PhD, NYU 2013; asst. prof.; Middle Eastern Studies) Middle East and Islamic, economic, legal; cheta@bard.edu

Crouch, Christian Ayne (PhD, NYU 2007; assoc. prof.) colonial/early national/antebellum America, Atlantic; crouch@bard.edu

Culp, Robert J. (PhD, Cornell 1999; assoc. prof. and chair) China, modern Japan, Asian studies; culp@bard.edu

Estruth, Jeannette Alden (PhD, NYU 2018; asst. prof.) US

Ewing, Tabetha (PhD, Princeton 2005; assoc. prof.) 17th- and 18th-century France, French intellectual, French Caribbean; ewing@bard.edu

Kuznitz, Cecile E. (PhD, Stanford 2000; assoc. prof.) Jewish, Jewish studies; kuznitz@bard.edu

McMeekin, Sean A. (PhD, California, Berkeley 2000; assoc. prof.; Russian and Eurasian Studies) diplomatic, Russia, Ottoman; mcmeekin@bard.edu

Moynahan, Gregory B. (PhD, California, Berkeley 1999; assoc. prof.) modern Germany and Europe, European intellectual, science and technology; moynahan@bard.edu

Rodriguez, Miles Vincent (PhD, Harvard 2010; asst. prof.) Latin America, Mexico; rodriguez@bard.edu

Stroup, Alice (PhD, Oxford 1978; prof.) early modern science and medicine, 17th-century France, cultural and intellectual; stroup@bard.edu

Thompson, Drew Anthony (PhD, Minnesota 2013; asst. prof.; Africana Studies) Africa, decolonization, visual culture

Part-time Faculty

Botstein, Leon (PhD, Harvard 1985; prof.) 19th- and 20th-century Europe, music, modern European intellectual; botstein@bard.edu

Lagemann, Ellen Condliffe (PhD, Columbia 1978; prof.) education, social policy, American social; lagemann@bard.edu

Perlmann, Joel (PhD, Harvard 1980; Levy Inst. research prof.) US social, education, immigration; perlmann@bard.edu

Urban-Mead, Wendy E. (PhD, Columbia 2004; asst. prof.; Master of Arts in Teaching Prog.) Africa, Germany, religion; wum@bard.edu

Barnard College, Columbia University

Dept. of History, 3009 Broadway, New York, NY 10027-6598. 212.854.2159. Email: srios@barnard.edu. Website: http://history.barnard.edu/.

Since its founding in 1889, Barnard has been a distinguished leader in higher education, offering a rigorous liberal arts foundation to young women whose curiosity, drive, and exuberance set them apart. Ours is a diverse intellectual community in a unique learning environment that provides the best of all worlds: small, intimate classes in a collaborative liberal arts setting dedicated to the advancement of women with the vast resources of Columbia University just steps away.

Chair: Dorothy Ko
Degrees Offered: BA
Academic Year System: Semester
Areas of Specialization: US, Latin America, Europe, China and India, Africa
Tuition (per academic year): $53252
Enrollment 2018-19:
Undergraduate Majors: 164
Degrees in History: 55 BA
Addresses:
Admissions: http://barnard.edu/admissions
Financial Aid: http://barnard.edu/finaid

Adjunct Faculty

Woloch, Nancy (PhD, Indiana 1968; research scholar) American cultural, social, women; nw49@columbia.edu

Full-time Faculty

Baics, Gergely (PhD, Northwestern 2009; assoc. prof.) American urban; gbaics@barnard.edu

Carnes, Mark C. (PhD, Columbia 1982; prof.) American social, gender, modern America; mc422@columbia.edu

George, Abosede A. (PhD, Stanford 2006; assoc. prof.) Africa; ageorge@barnard.edu

Kaye, Joel B. (PhD, Pennsylvania 1991; prof.) medieval, European intellectual/economic/science; jkaye@barnard.edu

Ko, Dorothy (PhD, Stanford 1989; prof. and chair) China, gender; dko@barnard.edu

Lipman, Andrew C. (PhD, Pennsylvania 2010; asst. prof.) early America, Atlantic world, frontiers/borderlands; alipman@barnard.edu

McCaughey, Robert A. (PhD, Harvard 1970; prof.) American intellectual, higher education, maritime; ram31@columbia.edu

Milanich, Nara (PhD, Yale 2002; prof.) modern Latin America, social, family and gender; nmilanich@barnard.edu

Moya, Jose C. (PhD, Rutgers 1988; prof.) Latin America, social/cultural/intellectual; jmoya@barnard.edu

Nadasen, Premilla (PhD, Columbia 1999; prof.) America, women and gender; pnadasen@barnard.edu

Naylor, Celia E. (PhD, Duke 2001; assoc. prof.) African American; cnaylor@barnard.edu

Rao, Anupama P. (PhD, Michigan 1999; assoc. prof.) India, gender; arao@barnard.edu

Tiersten, Lisa S. (PhD, Yale 1991; prof.) modern European cultural and social; ltiersten@barnard.edu

Valenze, Deborah M. (PhD, Brandeis 1982; prof.) early modern and modern European social and cultural; dvalenze@barnard.edu

Wennerlind, Carl (PhD, Texas, Austin 1999; prof.) early modern and modern British political economy, intellectual and economic; cwennerl@barnard.edu

Retired/Emeritus Faculty

Rosenberg, Rosalind Navin (PhD, Stanford 1974; prof. emerita) American social, women, legal; rrosenberg@barnard.edu
Sloan, Herbert E. (PhD, Columbia 1988; sr. scholar) colonial America, revolutionary America, constitutional; hsloan@barnard.edu

Bates College

Dept. of History, 4 Andrews Rd., Lewiston, ME 04240. 207.786.6462. Fax 207.786.8333. Email: jhall2@bates.edu. Website: https://www.bates.edu/history/.

The members of the History Department at Bates College offer widely differing views of the history of a broad variety of peoples, yet they agree that the study of the past provides meaning in the present and informed choices for the future. We seek to acquaint students with a broad range of approaches to historical methodology and familiarize them with the ways in which historians have thought and written.

Chair: Joseph Hall
Degrees Offered: BA,BS
Academic Year System: Semester
Areas of Specialization: Africa, East Asia, Europe, Latin America, US
Comprehensive Fee: $71388
Enrollment 2018-19:
  Undergraduate Majors: 73
  Degrees in History: 22 BA
Addresses:
  Admissions: http://www.bates.edu/admission/
  Financial Aid: http://www.bates.edu/admission/student-financial-services/

Full-time Faculty

Baker, Andrew David (PhD, Harvard 2017; asst. prof.) US, African American, 19th century; abaker2@bates.edu
Chaney, Wesley B. (PhD, Stanford 2016; asst. prof.) East Asia, China; wchaney@bates.edu
Hall, Joseph M., Jr. (PhD, Wisconsin-Madison 2001; assoc. prof. and chair) early America, Native American; jhall2@bates.edu
Melvin, Karen (PhD, California, Berkeley 2005; prof.) Latin America, early modern world, religious; kmelvin@bates.edu
Otim, Patrick William (PhD, Wisconsin, Madison 2016; asst. prof.) Africa, East Africa; potim@bates.edu
Shaw, Caroline Emily (PhD, California, Berkeley 2010; assoc. prof.) modern Europe, Britain and Ireland, diplomatic and international; cshaw@bates.edu

Retired/Emeritus Faculty

Creighton, Margaret S. (PhD, Boston Univ. 1985; prof. emeritus) 19th-century US, social, gender; mcreight@bates.edu
Grafflin, Dennis (PhD, Harvard 1980; prof. emeritus) China; dgraffli@bates.edu
Jensen, Hilmar L. (PhD, Cornell 1997; assoc. prof. emeritus) 20th-century US, African American; hjensen@bates.edu
Jones, Michael E. (PhD, Texas, Austin 1985; prof. emeritus) medieval Europe, Roman Empire; mjones@bates.edu

Visiting Faculty

Bigelow, Gerald F. (PhD, Cambridge 1984; vis. assoc. prof.) North Atlantic, archaeology, historical ecology; gbigelow@bates.edu
Cwiek, Brian E. (PhD, Indiana 2019; lect.) China, East Asia, Central Asia; bcwiek@bates.edu
Essame, Jeanne (PhD, Wisconsin, Madison 2019; vis. asst. prof.) Haiti, US since 1900, African diaspora; jessame@bates.edu
Kazyulina, Regina (PhD, Northeastern 2018; lect.) eastern Europe, modern Europe, world; rkazyuli@bates.edu

Baylor University

Dept. of History, 1 Bear Pl., #97306, Waco, TX 76798-7306. 254.710.2667. Fax 254.710.2551. Email: barry_hankins@baylor.edu. Website: https://www.baylor.edu/History/.

The Department of History prides itself on maintaining relatively small classes to facilitate a close cooperative relationship between students and faculty members. Such an environment fosters a positive learning experience by encouraging intellectual exchange.

Chair: Barry G. Hankins
Director of Graduate Studies: Joseph Stubenrauch
Director of Undergraduate Studies: Julie K. deGraffenried
Degrees Offered: BA,MA,PhD
Academic Year System: Semester
Areas of Specialization: modern Europe, US, Latin America, East Asia, Africa, Middle East
Undergraduate Tuition (per academic year): $42842
Graduate Tuition (per academic year): $32130
Enrollment 2018-19:
  Undergraduate Majors: 117
  New Graduate Students: 6
  Full-time Graduate Students: 21
  Degrees in History: 26 BA, 4 MA, 4 PhD
Undergraduate Addresses:
  Admissions: http://www.baylor.edu/admissions/
  Financial Aid: http://www.baylor.edu/admissions/index.php?id=871964
Graduate Addresses:
  Admissions and Financial Aid: http://www.baylor.edu/graduate/

Full-time Faculty

Barish, Daniel (PhD, Princeton 2017; asst. prof.) East Asia; daniel_barish@baylor.edu
Barr, Beth Allison (PhD, North Carolina, Chapel Hill 2004; assoc. prof.) women and medieval; beth_barr@baylor.edu
Coffman, Elesha (PhD, Duke 2008; asst. prof.) US intellectual and religious; elesha_coffman@baylor.edu
deGraffenried, Julie K. (PhD, Texas, Austin 2009; assoc. prof. and dir., undergrad. studies) Russia; julie_degraffenried@baylor.edu
Elder, Robert (PhD, Emory 2011; asst. prof.) US South; robert_elder@baylor.edu
Gawrych, George W. (PhD, Michigan 1980; prof.) Middle East, Islamic world; george_gawrych@baylor.edu
Hamilton, Jeffrey S. (PhD, Emory 1982; prof.) medieval, Britain; jeffrey_hamilton@baylor.edu
Hankins, Barry G. (PhD, Kansas State 1990; prof. and chair) US religion; barry_hankins@baylor.edu
Hendon, David W. (PhD, Emory 1976; prof.) Germany, modern Europe; david_hendon@baylor.edu
Hill, Bracy V., II (PhD, Baylor 2010; sr. lect.) world; bracy_hill@baylor.edu

Jenkins, Philip (PhD, Cambridge 1978; dist. prof.) global Christianity, US; philip_jenkins@baylor.edu

Kellison, Kimberly R. (PhD, South Carolina 1997; assoc. prof.) US South, Civil War and Reconstruction; kimberly_kellison@baylor.edu

Kidd, Thomas S. (PhD, Notre Dame 2001; dist. prof. and James Vardaman Prof.) early America, American religion; thomas_kidd@baylor.edu

Morera, Luis X. (PhD, Minnesota 2009; sr. lect.) world; luis_morera@baylor.edu

Mougoue, Jacqueline-Bethel Tchouta (PhD, Purdue 2013; assoc. prof.) Africa; jb_mougoue@baylor.edu

Parrish, T. Michael (PhD, Texas, Austin 1991; Linden G. Bowers Prof.) Civil War, Texas, public; michael_parrish@baylor.edu

Poor, Lauren Renee Miller (PhD, Indiana 2015; lect.) world; lauren_poor@baylor.edu

Rust, Eric C. (PhD, Texas, Austin 1987; prof.) Renaissance, early modern Europe, maritime; eric_rust@baylor.edu

Smith, David A. (PhD, Missouri, Columbia 2000; sr. lect.) US; david_a_smith@baylor.edu

SoRelle, James M. (PhD, Kent State 1980; prof.) urban, African American, recent US; james_sorelle@baylor.edu

Stubenrauch, Joseph (PhD, Indiana 2011; assoc. prof. and dir., grad. studies) modern Britain; joseph_stubenrauch@baylor.edu

Supplee, Joan E. (PhD, Texas, Austin 1988; Ralph L. and Bessie Mae Lynn Prof.) Latin America; joan_supplee@baylor.edu

Sweet, Julie Anne (PhD, Kentucky 2002; prof.) early America, Native American, public; julie_sweet@baylor.edu

Turpin, Andrea L. (PhD, Notre Dame 2011; assoc. prof.) US women; andrea_turpin@baylor.edu

Watkins, Daniel James (PhD, Ohio State 2014; asst. prof.) early modern Europe; daniel_watkins@baylor.edu

Wingerd, Zachary D. (PhD, Texas, Arlington 2008; sr. lect.) world, US; zachary_wingerd@baylor.edu

Joint/Cross Appointments

Jones, Kenneth R. (PhD, California, Berkeley 2006; assoc. prof.; Classics) ancient; k_r_jones@baylor.edu

Sloan, Stephen M. (PhD, Arizona State 2003; assoc. prof.; dir., Inst. for Oral Hist.) 20th-century US public, American West; stephen_sloan@baylor.edu

Retired/Emeritus Faculty

Daniel, Wallace L., Jr. (PhD, North Carolina, Chapel Hill 1973; prof. emeritus) Soviet, east European studies; wallace_daniel@baylor.edu

Hull, Gary W. (PhD, Maryland, Coll. Park 1968; prof. emeritus) American intellectual, historiography; gary_hull@baylor.edu

Longfellow, David L. (PhD, Johns Hopkins 1980; assoc. prof. emeritus) French Revolution and Napoleon, European intellectual; david_longfellow@baylor.edu

Mungello, D. E. (PhD, California, Berkeley 1973; prof. emeritus) China, Japan, early modern Sino-Western; d_e_mungello@baylor.edu

Spain, Rufus B. (PhD, Vanderbilt 1961; prof. emeritus) US social and cultural; rufus_spain@baylor.edu

Wallace, Patricia (PhD, Texas, Austin 1975; prof. emeritus) US diplomatic, women; patricia_wallace@baylor.edu

Recently Awarded PhDs

Butler, Ryan "'Give an Account of Thy Stewardship': How 'Vital Religion' Forged Anti-Slavery and Empire in the British World, 1772-1846"

Gutacker, Paul "Remembering the Old Faith in the New Nation: American Protestants and the Christian Past, 1780-1865"

Bellevue College

Dept. of History, Div. of Social Science, 3000 Landerholm Cir. SE, Bellevue, WA 98007. 425.564.2331. Fax 425.564.3108. Website: https://www.bellevuecollege.edu/hist/.

The Department of History at Bellevue College offers courses that prepare students to investigate the lives, choices, limitations, and patterns of the past.

Chair: Sabrina Sanchez
Degrees Offered: AA
Academic Year System: Quarter
Areas of Specialization: US, world, Latin America, military, Pacific Northwest
Tuition (per academic year):
In-State: $5747
Out-of-State: $13046
Enrollment 2018-19:
Students in Program: 2073
Addresses:
Admissions: http://www.bellevuecollege.edu/admissions
Financial Aid: http://www.bellevuecollege.edu/fa

Adjunct Faculty

Atchison, Devon H. (PhD, Boston Univ. 2007; adj.) US survey, women; devon.atchison@bellevuecollege.edu

Doan, Robert A. (PhD, Temple 1998; adj.) US survey, modern Europe, immigration; rdoan@bellevuecollege.edu

Ma, Chiemi (MA, California State, Dominguez Hills 2005; adj.) ancient world, US survey; chiemi.ma@bellevuecollege.edu

Ricar, Sondra L. (PhD, California, Santa Cruz 1995; adj.) world, Russia, US; sondra.ricar@bellevuecollege.edu

Full-time Faculty

Casserly, Brian G. (PhD, Washington 2007; assoc. prof.) US survey, Pacific Northwest, military; brian.casserly@bellevuecollege.edu

Pulido, Michael P. (PhD, Marquette 2017; asst. prof.) Europe, Middle East and North Africa, world; michael.pulido@bellevuecollege.edu

Sanchez, Sabrina (PhD, California, Santa Cruz 2013; assoc. prof. and chair) Latin America, US survey, ancient world; s.sanchez@bellevuecollege.edu

Retired/Emeritus Faculty

Perry, Thornton A (MA, Ohio State 1969; prof. emeritus) US survey, European Enlightenment, sports; tperry@bellevuecollege.edu

Belmont University

Dept. of History, 1900 Belmont Blvd., Nashville, TN 37212-3757. 615.460.6251. Fax 615.460.6697. Email: brenda.jackson@belmont.edu. Website: http://www.belmont.edu/history/.

As part of Belmont University's common core, historical reflection strengthens students' understanding of the variety of human ideas, cultural perspectives and conceptual frameworks which make up the interdependent world in which we live.

Chair: Brenda Jackson-Abernathy
Degrees Offered: BA,BS
Academic Year System: Semester
Areas of Specialization: US, early and modern Europe, world
Tuition (per academic year): $35650

Enrollment 2018-19:
    Undergraduate Majors: 40
    Degrees in History: 8 BA, 6 BS
Addresses:
    Admissions: http://www.belmont.edu/admissions/
    Financial Aid: http://www.belmont.edu/sfs/

Full-time Faculty

Bisson, Cynthia S. (PhD, Ohio State 1989; asst. prof.) 19th-century France, early modern Europe, modern Japan; cynthia.bisson@belmont.edu

Bisson, Douglas R. (PhD, Ohio State 1987; prof.) early modern Britain, medieval Europe, economic; douglas.bisson@belmont.edu

Jackson-Abernathy, Brenda K. (PhD, Washington State 2002; prof. and chair) 19th-century US, American West, American women; brenda.jackson@belmont.edu

Kuryla, Peter A. (PhD, Vanderbilt 2006; assoc. prof.) 20th-century US, intellectual; peter.kuryla@belmont.edu

Schafer, Daniel E. (PhD, Michigan 1995; prof.) Russia, Central Asia, nationalism and ethnic identity; daniel.schafer@belmont.edu

Beloit College

Dept. of History, 700 College St., Beloit, WI 53511. 608.363.2000. Fax 608.363.2384. Email: joycee@beloit.edu. Website: https://www.beloit.edu/history/.

Reading and writing are the primary tools of historical inquiry, and some historians also evaluate oral and material sources as they set out to discover the past. The history major at Beloit emphasizes that these skills are at the heart of what it means to think critically about past and present, about our own society and those that are foreign to us, as well as about what distinguishes our own cultural or individual perspective.

Chair: Ellen Joyce
Degrees Offered: BA
Academic Year System: Semester
Areas of Specialization: North America, modern and medieval Europe, East Asia, Atlantic world
Tuition (per academic year): $48236
Enrollment 2018-19:
    Undergraduate Majors: 40
    Degrees in History: 10 BA
Addresses:
    Admissions: https://www.beloit.edu/prospective/
    Financial Aid: http://www.beloit.edu/financialaid/

Full-time Faculty

Brueckenhaus, Daniel (PhD, Yale 2011; assoc. prof.) modern Europe; brueckenhausd@beloit.edu

Johnston, Katherine (PhD, Columbia 2016; asst. prof.) Atlantic world, early America, Caribbean; johnstonkm@beloit.edu

Joyce, Ellen E. (PhD, Toronto 2001; assoc. prof. and chair) medieval Europe, early modern Europe, digital; joycee@beloit.edu

LaFleur, Robert Andre (PhD, Chicago 1996; prof.; Anthropology) East Asia, anthropology; lafleur@beloit.edu

McKenzie, Beatrice L. (PhD, Oregon 2006; prof.) modern US, immigration; mckenzie@beloit.edu

Nondepartmental Historians

Burwell, Fred (BA, Beloit 1986; instr.; Archives) burwellf@beloit.edu

Retired/Emeritus Faculty

Hodge, Bob (PhD, Michigan State 1968; prof. emeritus) recent America, Latin America, Australia; hodgeb@beloit.edu

Bemidji State University

History Program, Dept. of Humanities, 1500 Birchmont Dr. NE, #23, Bemidji, MN 56601-2699. 218.755.4124. Fax 218.744.2822. Email: daniel.guentchev@bemidjistate.edu; brendan.mcmanus@bemidjistate.edu. Website: https://www.bemidjistate.edu/academics/departments/humanities/history/.

The BSU History Program emphasizes writing and oral communication skills, analytical skills, and research skills to interpret both why and how major events in the world's past occurred.

Chair: Daniel Guentchev
Degrees Offered: BA,BS
Academic Year System: Semester
Areas of Specialization: world, Europe, US
Tuition (per academic year): $6840
Enrollment 2018-19:
    Undergraduate Majors: 26
    Degrees in History: 5 BA
Addresses:
    Admissions: http://www.bemidjistate.edu/admissions/undergraduate/
    Financial Aid: http://www.bemidjistate.edu/mybsu/finances/aid/

Full-time Faculty

Allosso, Dan (PhD, Massachusetts Amherst 2017; asst. prof.) US environmental and agricultural, world, South America; daniel.allosso@bemidjistate.edu

Ellis, John P. (PhD, Purdue 2010; assoc. prof.) US, early modern Europe; john.ellis@bemidjistate.edu

McManus, Brendan J. (PhD, Syracuse 1991; assoc. prof.) medieval Europe, Roman and European legal, European political thought; brendan.mcmanus@bemidjistate.edu

Bentley University

Dept. of History, 175 Forest St., Waltham, MA 02452-4705. 781.891.3157. Fax 781.891.2896. Email: bandrews@bentley.edu. Website: https://www.bentley.edu/academics/undergraduate-programs/history.

In our History major, your studies will take you everywhere from colonial America to the former Soviet Union to the medieval West. But you won't spend your time exclusively in the past; through a broad range of business courses, you'll also explore how your knowledge is relevant to today's world. It's all designed to make sure you leave here with top-notch skills in critical thinking, data analysis, and communication.

Chair: Bridie Andrews
Degrees Offered: BA
Academic Year System: Semester
Areas of Specialization: business and economic, globalization, US, Europe, religion
Tuition (per academic year): $48180

Enrollment 2018-19:
Undergraduate Majors: 1
Degrees in History: 1 BA
Addresses:
Admissions: http://www.bentley.edu/undergraduate
Financial Aid: http://www.bentley.edu/offices/
financial-assistance

Full-time Faculty

Andrews, Bridie (PhD, Cambridge 1996; assoc. prof. and chair) East Asian and Chinese medicine, science, colonialism; bandrews@bentley.edu

Beneke, Chris (PhD, Northwestern 2001; prof.) American religion, early national US, sports; cbeneke@bentley.edu

Choi, Sung-Eun (PhD, California, Los Angeles 2007; asst. prof.) modern Europe, North Africa, empire and decolonization; schoi@bentley.edu

Jhala, Angma D. (PhD, Oxford 2006; assoc. prof.) South Asia, women; ajhala@bentley.edu

Putney, Clifford W. (PhD, Brandeis 1995; assoc. prof.) modern US; cputney@bentley.edu

Stern, Marc J. (PhD, SUNY, Stony Brook 1986; prof.) business and economic, technology, US labor; mstern@bentley.edu

Trofimov, Leonid T. (PhD, Illinois, Chicago 2004; sr. lect.) Russia and Soviet Union, Cold War, media; ltrofimov@bentley.edu

Veeser, Cyrus (PhD, Columbia 1997; prof.) modern US, US diplomatic, Latin America and Caribbean; cveeser@bentley.edu

Part-time Faculty

Albanese, David (PhD, Northeastern 2015; adj. prof.) Cold War espionage and international politics, modern Russia and Soviet Union, nationalism; dalbanese@bentley.edu

Alpert, Jennifer S. (PhD, Boston Univ. 2004; adj. prof.) American cultural, American medical, 19th-century US; jalpert@bentley.edu

Beardsley, Thomas R. (PhD, Leicester, UK 2005; adj. prof.) US, labor, British and Western civilization; tbeardsley@bentley.edu

Hermanson, John (MA, Yale 1964; adj. prof.) art and society; jhermanson@bentley.edu

Kierdorf, Doug C. (PhD, Boston Univ. 2012; adj. prof.) medieval Europe/Ireland/Greece, Western civilization, Renaissance and Reformation; dkierdorf@bentley.edu

Rosenberg, Mark (MA, Brandeis 1995; adj. prof.) Middle East, modern Europe; mrosenberg@bentley.edu

Retired/Emeritus Faculty

Tolpin, Martha (PhD, Harvard 1972; assoc. prof. emeritus) modern Europe, intellectual, gender; mtolpin@bentley.edu

Berea College

Dept. of History, CPO 2135, Berea, KY 40404. 859.985.3939. Fax 859.985.3642. Email: guthmanj@berea.edu. Website: https://www.berea.edu/his/.

The department requires that majors have a breadth of competence in the history of various areas of the world, and that they have an ability to research carefully, using a variety of methods. Considerable attention is given to the philosophy of history and the various points of view with which scholars have approached the study of the past. Berea is the only one of America's top colleges that awards every enrolled student a no-tuition promise.

Chair: Joshua Guthman
Degrees Offered: BA
Academic Year System: Semester
Areas of Specialization: America, Asia, Europe, global
Tuition: None
Enrollment 2018-19:
Undergraduate Majors: 20
Degrees in History: 6 BA
Addresses:
Admissions: http://www.berea.edu/admissions/
Financial Aid: http://www.berea.edu/student-financial-aid/

Adjunct Faculty

Groppo, Martha Johanna (PhD, Princeton 2019; adj.) modern Europe, global; groppom@berea.edu

Full-time Faculty

Bates, Rebecca J. (PhD, Kentucky 2007; assoc. prof.) modern Britain, modern Europe, gender; rebecca_bates@berea.edu

Berry, Chad T. (PhD, Indiana 1995; prof.; academic vice pres. and dean, Faculty) Appalachia, American social and cultural, south Africa; chad_berry@berea.edu

Cahill, Richard Andrew (PhD, California, Santa Barbara 1996; assoc. prof. and dir., International Education Center) Islam, Middle East; richard_cahill@berea.edu

Foster, Robert W. (PhD, Harvard 1997; prof.) East Asia, Asian philosophies and religions; robert_foster@berea.edu

Guthman, Joshua (PhD, North Carolina, Chapel Hill 2008; assoc. prof. and chair) intersection of religion and emotion; joshua_guthman@berea.edu

Mack, Dwayne Anthony (PhD, Washington State 2002; assoc. prof.) African American, public; dwayne_mack@berea.edu

Joint/Cross Appointments

Sergent, Tyler (PhD, Roskilde 2009; assoc. prof.; General Studies) medieval, religion; tyler_sergent@berea.edu

Nondepartmental Historians

Carlevale, John (PhD, Boston Univ. 1999; asst. prof.; Classics) john_carlevale@berea.edu

Miller, Christopher (MA, Delaware 1990; Coll. curator) christopher_miller@berea.edu

Retired/Emeritus Faculty

Drake, Richard B. (PhD, Emory 1957; prof. emeritus) Reconstruction, East Asia, Appalachia

McKinney, Gordon B. (PhD, Northwestern 1971; prof. emeritus) Appalachia, US South; gordon_mckinney@berea.edu

Nelson, Paul David (PhD, Duke 1969; prof. emeritus) America, Latin America, historiography; david_nelson@berea.edu

Perkins, Alfred (PhD, Harvard 1965; prof. emeritus) modern Europe, France, European imperialism; alperk@earthlink.net

Berry College

Dept. of History, PO Box 5010, Mount Berry, GA 30149-5010. 706.236.2222. Fax 706.236.2205. Email: dfox@berry.edu; jatkins@berry.edu. Website: https://www.berry.edu/academics/majors/history.

The major requires students to complete one survey course in U.S. history, two in world history, and eight electives on specialized topics as well as a senior capstone writing course on the Meaning and Method of History. The Department's new "History PLUS" program pairs the History major with directed study in one of eight different fields: Technology, the Environment, Global Issues, Justice, the Public, Writing, Gender, or Enterprise.

Chair: Jonathan Atkins
Degrees Offered: BA
Academic Year System: Semester
Areas of Specialization: US, Europe, Latin America, Africa
Tuition (per academic year): $35176
Enrollment 2018-19:
  Undergraduate Majors: 41
  Degrees in History: 12 BA
  Students in Undergraduate Courses: 530
  Students in Undergraduate Intro Courses: 383
Addresses:
  Admissions: http://berry.edu/admission/
  Financial Aid: http://berry.edu/aid/

Full-time Faculty

Atkins, Jonathan M. (PhD, Michigan 1991; prof. and chair) US 1763-1877, US South, Britain; jatkins@berry.edu
Hoyt, Jennifer Tamara (PhD, Texas, Austin 2012; asst. prof.) Latin America, urbanization, environment; jhoyt@berry.edu
Marvin, Laurence W. (PhD, Illinois, Urbana-Champaign 1997; prof.) medieval, Europe to 1600, military; lmarvin@berry.edu
Snider, Christy Jo (PhD, Purdue 2000; assoc. prof.) 20th-century US, women, diplomatic; csnider@berry.edu
Stanard, Matthew G. (PhD, Indiana, Bloomington 2006; prof.) modern Europe, modern Africa, imperialism; mstanard@berry.edu

Binghamton University, State University of New York

Dept. of History, PO Box 6000, Binghamton, NY 13902-6000. 607.777.2625. Fax 607.777.2896. Email: hdehaan@binghamton.edu. Website: https://www.binghamton.edu/history/.

We offer an outstanding undergraduate program with hundreds of courses spanning the globe from the ancient world to the present. Our highly-rated graduate program offers both MA and PhD degrees in several major fields, including those that center on the United States, Europe, Asia, Latin America, and the Ottoman Empire. Our faculty members are routinely recognized for the excellence of their scholarship, teaching and service.

Chair: Heather DeHaan
Director of Graduate Studies: Fa-ti Fan
Degrees Offered: BA, MA, PhD
Academic Year System: Semester
Areas of Specialization: US, Europe, women/gender/sexuality, East Asia, Ottoman
Undergraduate Tuition (per academic year):
  In-State: $6470
  Out-of-State: $21550
Graduate Tuition (per academic year):
  In-State: $10870
  Out-of-State: $22210
Enrollment 2018-19:
  Undergraduate Majors: 279
  New Graduate Students: 17
  Full-time Graduate Students: 56
  Part-time Graduate Students: 5
  Degrees in History: 96 BA, 12 MA, 7 PhD
Undergraduate Addresses:
  Admissions: http://www.binghamton.edu/admissions/
  Financial Aid: http://www.binghamton.edu/financial-aid/

Graduate Addresses:
  Admissions: http://www.binghamton.edu/grad-school/prospective-students/
  Financial Aid: http://history.binghamton.edu

Affiliated Faculty

Arkush, Alan (PhD, Brandeis 1988; assoc. prof.; Judaic Studies) modern Jewish intellectual; arkjustbb@aol.com
Danon, Dina (PhD, Stanford 2012; asst. prof.; Judaic Studies) Sephardic Jewry, modern Jewish; ddanon@binghamton.edu
Kim, Sonja (PhD, UCLA 2008; asst. prof.; Asian and Asian American Studies) Korea, gender and empire in East Asia, medicine; skim@binghamton.edu
Laats, Adam (PhD, Wisconsin, Madison 2006; assoc. prof.; Graduate Sch. of Education) Protestant fundamentalism and education, US; alaats@binghamton.edu
Marasigan, Cynthia (PhD, Michigan 2010; asst. prof.; Asian and Asian American Studies) Asian American, post-1865 US, comparative colonialisms; cmarasig@binghamton.edu
Roth, Benita (PhD, UCLA 1998; assoc. prof.; Sociology) gender, race/ethnicity/class, social theory; broth@binghamton.edu
Tomich, Dale W. (PhD, Wisconsin, Madison 1976; prof.; Sociology) world system, political economy, Caribbean; dtomich@binghamton.edu
West, Michael (PhD, Harvard 1990; assoc. prof.; Sociology, Africana Studies) African diaspora, Africa, social; mwest@binghamton.edu

Full-time Faculty

Andrade, Nathanael J. (PhD, Michigan 2009; asst. prof.) ancient, Roman and later Roman Syria, Roman Empire and late antiquity; nandrade@binghamton.edu
Appelbaum, Nancy P. (PhD, Wisconsin-Madison 1997; prof.) modern Latin America; nappel@binghamton.edu
Baltacioglu-Brammer, Ayse (PhD, Ohio State 2016; asst. prof.) early modern Ottoman, Middle East, Shi'ism; abaltaci@binghamton.edu
Brown, Howard G. (DPhil, Oxford 1990; prof.) early modern Europe, France; hgbrown@binghamton.edu
Camiscioli, Elisa (PhD, Chicago 2000; assoc. prof.) 19th- and 20th-century Europe, France, comparative and gender; ecamis@binghamton.edu
Casteen, Elizabeth Ingeborg (PhD, Northwestern 2009; assoc. prof.) medieval and early modern Europe, high and late medieval cultural and religious, women and sexuality in medieval Europe; ecasteen@binghamton.edu
DeHaan, Heather D. (PhD, Toronto 2005; assoc. prof. and chair) Russia and Soviet Union, east central Europe, urban; hdehaan@binghamton.edu
Dey, Arnab (PhD, Chicago 2012; assoc. prof.) South Asia, India; adey@binghamton.edu
Fan, Fa-Ti (PhD, Wisconsin, Madison 1999; assoc. prof. and dir., grad. studies) modern empire, modern China, science and technology; ffan@binghamton.edu
Kutcher, Gerald J. (PhD, Cambridge 2002; prof.) science and medicine; gkutcher@binghamton.edu
Leja, Meg (PhD, Princeton 2015; asst. prof.) late antique and medieval world, history of the body and medicine
Mackenney, Richard S. (PhD, Cambridge 1982; prof.) Italian Renaissance, early modern Venice, Shakespeare; rmackenn@binghamton.edu
Norwood, Dael A. (PhD, Princeton 2012; asst. prof.) US politics of commerce and capitalism, American imperialism, 19th-century US; dnorwood@binghamton.edu

Ortiz, Stephen R. (PhD, Florida 2004; assoc. prof.) 20th-century US, political, military; sortiz@binghamton.edu

Parkinson, Robert (PhD, Virginia 2005; asst. prof.) revolution/military/race/nationalism, early Republic race; rparkins@binghamton.edu

Quataert, Jean H. (PhD, UCLA 1974; prof.) women, Germany, social and labor; profquat@binghamton.edu

Schull, Kent F. (PhD, UCLA 2007; asst. prof.) Middle East, Ottoman Empire; kschull@binghamton.edu

Skopyk, Bradley (PhD, York, Can. 2010; asst. prof.) colonial Latin America, environmental; bskopyk@binghamton.edu

Sommerville, Diane Miller (PhD, Rutgers 1995; assoc. prof.) 19th-century US South, Civil War America, US women/gender/sexuality; sommervi@binghamton.edu

Wall, Wendy L. (PhD, Stanford 1998; assoc. prof.) 20th-century US; wwall@binghamton.edu

Wang, Yi (PhD, Chicago 2013; asst. prof.) East Asia and Inner Asia, social and cultural; wangy@binghamton.edu

Welland, Heather (PhD, Chicago 2011; asst. prof.) early modern Britain, British Empire, Atlantic world; hwelland@binghamton.edu

Wheeler, Leigh Ann (PhD, Minnesota 1998; assoc. prof.) US women, sexuality, law; lwheeler@binghamton.edu

Joint/Cross Appointments

Bailey, Anne C. (PhD, Pennsylvania 1998; assoc. prof.; Africana Studies) African American, Africa, African diaspora; abailey@binghamton.edu

Chaffee, John W. (PhD, Chicago 1979; dist. service prof.; Asian and Asian American Studies) East Asia, early China; chaffee@binghamton.edu

Dunwoody, Sean F. (PhD, Chicago 2012; asst. prof.; Medieval Studies) early modern Europe, early modern Germany, religion; sdunwood@binghamton.edu

Karp, Jonathan (PhD, Columbia 1999; assoc. prof.; Judaic Studies) Jewish, early modern and modern Europ; jkarp@binghamton.edu

Retired/Emeritus Faculty

Abou-El-Haj, Rifaat Ali (PhD, Princeton 1963; prof. emeritus) Near East, Europe; rasultani@aol.com

Bix, Herbert P. (PhD, Harvard 1972; prof. emeritus) 20th-century Japan, Japan-US relations, monarchial studies; hbix@binghamton.edu

Dublin, Thomas (PhD, Columbia 1975; Bartle dist. prof. emeritus) US labor and social; tdublin@binghamton.edu

Dubofsky, Melvyn (PhD, Rochester 1960; dist. prof. emeritus) US labor and social; dubof@binghamton.edu

Kadish, Gerald E. (PhD, Chicago 1964; dist. teaching prof. emeritus) ancient, Egypt; kadishg@binghamton.edu

Lopez, Adalberto (PhD, Harvard 1972; assoc. prof. emeritus) Hispanic America, Spain

Oggins, Robin S. (PhD, Chicago 1967; assoc. prof. emeritus) medieval, England

Sklar, Kathryn Kish (PhD, Michigan 1969; Dist. Bartle Prof. emeritus; co-dir., Center for Hist. Study of Women and Gender and co-dir., Center for Teaching of American Hist.) US women, social movements, comparative; kksklar@binghamton.edu

Biola University

Dept. of History, 13800 Biola Ave., La Mirada, CA 90639-0001. 562.944.0351. Fax 562.903.4562. Email: carolyn.kemp@biola.edu; alicia.dewey@biola.edu. Website: https://www.biola.edu/history-department.

In recognition of both the dignity and depravity of humankind, our aim is to develop historical insight into the diversity of civilizations, based upon our acknowledgement of God's providence, the dependability of his promises and his redemptive purpose on earth. Through the rigors of our discipline, we prepare our students to obey the Greatest Commandment and Great Commission through their lives and vocations. We aspire to prepare students for careers in education, public service, publishing, museum or archival work, library science, the law, ministry and business.

Chair: Alicia Dewey
Degrees Offered: BA
Academic Year System: Semester
Areas of Specialization: Asian civilization, African civilization, European civilization, civilizations of Americas
Tuition (per academic year): $34498
Enrollment 2018-19:
  Undergraduate Majors: 60
  Degrees in History: 11 BA
Addresses:
  Admissions: http://biola.edu/undergrad
  Financial Aid: http://biola.edu/finaid

Full-time Faculty

Christensen, Daniel Eric (PhD, California, Riverside 2004; assoc. prof.) early modern Europe, Germany, world theory; daniel.christensen@biola.edu

Dewey, Alicia M. (PhD, Southern Methodist 2007; JD, Southern Methodist 2005; assoc. prof. and chair) US/Mexico borderlands, American West, environmental/irrigation and water rights; alicia.dewey@biola.edu

Lim, Susan C. (PhD, UCLA 2006; assoc. prof.) America, colonial America; susan.lim@biola.edu

Rood, Judith M. (PhD, Chicago 1993; prof.) Middle East and Islamic, international relations; judith.rood@biola.edu

Wamagatta, Evanson N. (PhD, West Virginia 2001; assoc. prof.) Africa, missionary work past and present; evanson.wamagatta@biola.edu

Part-time Faculty

Jimenez, Mike (PhD, Fuller Theological Seminary) mike.jimenez@biola.edu

Lind, Mary Ann (PhD, Colorado, Boulder 1985) maryann.lind@biola.edu

Mills Robbins, Ruth Ann (PhD, Southern California 2010) 10th- and 11th-century abbots; ruth.mill-robbins@biola.edu

Riggin, Lisa (PhD, California, Riverside 2006) US; lisa.riggin@biola.edu

Rood, Paul (MA, Claremont Grad. 1976; lect.; Political Science) political science; paul.rood@biola.edu

Birmingham-Southern College

Dept. of History, BSC Box 549031, 900 Arkadelphia Rd., Birmingham, AL 35254. 205.226.4860. Fax 205.226.3089. Email: whustwit@bsc.edu. Website: https://www.bsc.edu/academics/history/.

If you study history at BSC, you'll find professors that are outstanding in their fields and deeply committed to teaching; you'll be on a great path for a number of careers; you'll find plenty of opportunities for internships; you can use our unique January Exploration Term to check out a subject that's new for you; and you'll tackle a research paper as part of the senior research symposium capstone under the guidance of a professor and present your findings at a senior conference.

Chair: Will Hustwit
Degrees Offered: BA
Academic Year System: 3-1-3
Areas of Specialization: US, American South, modern Europe and Russia, East Asia, Latin America
Tuition (per academic year): $17650
Enrollment 2018-19:
   Undergraduate Majors: 30
   Degrees in History: 12 BA
Addresses:
   Admissions: http://www.bsc.edu/admission/
   Financial Aid: http://www.bsc.edu/fp/

Full-time Faculty

Hustwit, William P. (PhD, Mississippi 2008; assoc. prof. and chair) 20th-century US, civil rights, Latin America; whustwit@bsc.edu

Law, Randall D. (PhD, Georgetown 2001; prof.) Russia, modern Europe, terrorism; rlaw@bsc.edu

Lester, V. Markham (DPhil, Oxford 1991; W. Michael Atchison Prof.) Britain, Middle East, US constitutional; mlester@bsc.edu

Levey, Matthew A. (PhD, Chicago 1991; prof.) East Asia, comparative intellectual, World War II and memory; mlevey@bsc.edu

Ott, Victoria E. (PhD, Tennessee, Knoxville 2003; James A. Wood Prof.) 19th-century US, Civil War, women; vott@bsc.edu

Schantz, Mark S. (PhD, Emory 1991; prof.) 19th-century US, Civil War; mschantz@bsc.edu

Retired/Emeritus Faculty

Fraley, J. David, Jr. (PhD, Duke 1971; prof. emeritus) modern Germany

Hubbs, Guy W. (PhD, Alabama 1999; prof. emeritus) 19th-century US; ghubbs@bsc.edu

Nicholas, William E., III (PhD, Tulane 1970; prof. emeritus) recent US, US diplomatic, Latin America

Stayer, Samuel N. (PhD, Duke 1970; prof. emeritus) 19th-century US

Bloomsburg University

Dept. of History, 400 E. Second St., Old Science Hall, Bloomsburg, PA 17815-1301. 570.389.4156. Fax 570.389.4946. Email: joast@bloomu.edu. Website: https://www.bloomu.edu/history.

Bloomsburg's Department of History delivers a great course of studies where students and faculty work together in pursuit of excellence. The department provides scholarships for outstanding students; in fact, no major at Bloomsburg University offers more scholarships and fellowships than does the history department. The department is dedicated to honing students' intellectual skills and fostering their love of learning, while providing a solid grounding in American, European, and world history.

Chair: Jennifer Oast
Degrees Offered: BA
Academic Year System: Semester
Areas of Specialization: US, Europe, Asia, Middle East, Latin America
Tuition (per academic year):
   In-State: $7492
   Out-of-State: $18730

Enrollment 2018-19:
   Undergraduate Majors: 140
   Degrees in History: 40 BA
Addresses:
   Admissions: http://www.bloomu.edu/admissions
   Financial Aid: http://www.bloomu.edu/aid

Full-time Faculty

Davis, Jeffrey A. (PhD, Washington State 1996; prof.) early national US, Civil War, Pennsylvania; jdavis@bloomu.edu

Ford, Nancy Gentile (PhD, Temple 1994; prof.) US social-military, recent America, ethnic studies; nford@bloomu.edu

Hickey, Michael C. (PhD, Northern Illinois 1993; prof.) Russia and Soviet Union, modern Europe, Jewish; mhickey@bloomu.edu

Hudon, William V. (PhD, Chicago 1987; prof.) Renaissance and Reformation, Italy, church; whudon@bloomu.edu

Karsner, Douglas G. (PhD, Temple 1993; assoc. prof.) US business and economic, urban, American foreign relations; dkarsner@bloomu.edu

Long, Jeff E. (PhD, Hawai'i, Manoa 2000; assoc. prof.) modern Japan, militarism, East Asia; jlon2@bloomu.edu

Oast, Jennifer B. (PhD, William and Mary 2008; assoc. prof. and chair) colonial America, American War of Independence, comparative slave societies; joast@bloomu.edu

Saracoglu, M. Safa (PhD, Ohio State 2007; prof.) modern Middle East, world, eastern Europe; msaracog@bloomu.edu

Stallbaumer-Beishline, Lisa M. (PhD, Wisconsin, Madison 1995; assoc. prof.) 19th- and 20th-century Europe, modern Germany, Holocaust; lstallba@bloomu.edu

Boise State University

Dept. of History, 1910 University Dr., MailStop 1925, Boise, ID 83725-1925. 208.426.1255. Email: bsuhistory@boisestate.edu. Website: https://www.boisestate.edu/history/.

The department boasts award-winning researchers and teachers, and participates in the mission of the College of Arts & Sciences to engage in and serve the Boise community, the treasure valley, and the state of Idaho. At the graduate level, we offer an MA in history as well as a Master of Applied Historical Research degree. At the undergraduate level, we offer a BA in history, a BA in history and secondary education, and a BA in history and secondary education with a social science emphasis.

Chair: Nick Miller
Director of Graduate Studies: David Walker
Degrees Offered: BA, MA, MAHR
Academic Year System: Semester
Areas of Specialization: Americas, Europe, public, women, regional
Undergraduate Tuition (per academic year):
   In-State: $7326
   Out-of-State: $22642
Graduate Tuition (per academic year):
   In-State: $8754
   Out-of-State: $24070
Enrollment 2018-19:
   Undergraduate Majors: 252
   New Graduate Students: 6
   Full-time Graduate Students: 59
   Part-time Graduate Students: 10
   Degrees in History: 59 BA, 5 MA, PhD

Undergraduate Addresses:
Admissions: http://admissions.boisestate.edu/
Financial Aid: http://financialaid.boisestate.edu/
Graduate Addresses:
Admissions: http://graduatecollege.boisestate.edu/
Financial Aid: http://financialaid.boisestate.edu/

Adjunct Faculty

Felton, Ann (MA, Boise State; adj.) US, Western civilizations; annfelton@boisestate.edu
Schroeder, Carole (MA, Boise State; adj.) Asia, Europe; caroleschroeder@boisestate.edu
Sermon, Suzanne (PhD, New Mexico; adj.) US; suzannesermon@boisestate.edu
Stevens, Jennifer A. (PhD, California, Davis 2008; adj.) US environmental/urban

Affiliated Faculty

Madsen-Brooks, Leslie (PhD, California, Davis 2006; assoc. prof.; dir., IDEA Shop and assoc. dir., Center for Teaching and Learning) US, public, gender studies; lesliemadsen-brooks@boisestate.edu

Full-time Faculty

Bieter, John (PhD, Boston Coll. 2004; prof.) secondary education, US, immigration; johnbieter@boisestate.edu
Brady, Lisa M. (PhD, Kansas 2003; prof.) US, global environmental; lisabrady@boisestate.edu
Gill, Jill K. (PhD, Pennsylvania 1996; prof.) US, social/political/religion/race; jgill@boisestate.edu
Hadley, Erik J. (PhD, SUNY, Buffalo 2006; lect.) early modern Europe; erikhadley@boisestate.edu
Huntley, Katherine V. (PhD, Leicester 2010; asst. prof.) ancient, medieval; kvhuntley@boisestate.edu
Klein, Joanne M. (PhD, Rice 1992; prof.) modern European comparative; jklein@boisestate.edu
Krohn, Raymond James (PhD, Purdue 2010; lect.) US, world; raymondkrohn@boisestate.edu
Lubamersky, Lynn T. (PhD, Indiana 1998; assoc. prof.) early modern Europe, family, women; llubame@boisestate.edu
McClain, Lisa R. (PhD, Texas, Austin 2000; prof.) Renaissance and Reformation Europe, gender, religion; lmcclain@boisestate.edu
Meftahi, Ida (PhD, Toronto 2013; asst. prof.) modern Iran cultural; idameftahi@boisestate.edu
Miller, Nicholas (PhD, Indiana 1991; prof. and chair) eastern Europe; nmiller@boisestate.edu
Walker, David Mckinley (PhD, George Washington 2004; asst. prof. and dir., grad. studies) US, military, diplomatic; davidwalker2@boisestate.edu
Ysursa, John M. (PhD, California, Riverside 1996; dir., Basque Studies Consortium) modern Europe, world; johnysursa@boisestate.edu

Retired/Emeritus Faculty

Barbour, Barton (PhD, New Mexico 1993; prof. emeritus) colonial to 19th-century America, US West; bbarbour@boisestate.edu
Buhler, Peter (PhD, California, San Diego 1975; prof. emeritus) Africa, India, comparative religions; pbuhler@boisestate.edu
Fletcher, Allan W. (PhD, Washington 1970; prof. emeritus) England, modern Europe; afletch@boisestate.edu
Lundy, Phoebe (MS, Drake 1966; prof. emeritus) Russia, Europe, women's studies
Odahl, Charles Matson (PhD, California, San Diego 1976; prof. emeritus) ancient, early Christian, medieval; codahl@boisestate.edu

Schackel, Sandra (PhD, New Mexico 1988; prof. emeritus) US, Idaho; sschack@boisestate.edu
Vinz, Warren L. (PhD, Utah 1968; prof. emeritus) American religious, early modern Europe, Reformation; wvinz@aol.com
Zirinsky, Michael P. (PhD, North Carolina, Chapel Hill 1976; prof. emeritus) modern France, Middle East, modern Germany; mzirins@boisestate.edu

Boston College

Dept. of History, 140 Commonwealth Ave., Stokes Hall South, Floor 3, Chestnut Hill, MA 02467-3806. 617.552.2267. Fax 617.552.2478. Email: sarah.ross@bc.edu. Website: https://www.bc.edu/bc-web/schools/mcas/departments/history.html.

At BC, our distinguished faculty members are active participants in the scholarly community, and they share their passion for innovative research through teaching and mentorship. The wealth of historical resources in the Boston area means that our students not only benefit from working closely with the faculty, but also from having access to world-class libraries, cultural institutions, and some of the oldest historical sites in the United States.

Chair: Sarah G. Ross
Director of Graduate Studies: Devin O. Pendas
Director of Undergraduate Studies: Arissa H. Oh
Degrees Offered: BA,MA,MAT,PhD
Academic Year System: Semester
Areas of Specialization: medieval/early modern/modern Europe, US, Latin America, South Asia, Britain/Ireland/Boston
Undergraduate Tuition (per academic year): $56780
Graduate Tuition (per academic year): $30600
Enrollment 2018-19:
Undergraduate Majors: 240
New Graduate Students: 11
Full-time Graduate Students: 42
Part-time Graduate Students: 1
Degrees in History: 79 BA, 5 MA, 3 PhD
Undergraduate Addresses:
Admissions: http://www.bc.edu/admission/undergrad/
Financial Aid: http://www.bc.edu/offices/stserv/financial/finaid/
Graduate Addresses:
Admissions and Financial Aid: http://www.bc.edu/schools/gsas/admissions.html

Full-time Faculty

Bourg, Julian Edward (PhD, California, Berkeley 2001; assoc. prof.) modern European intellectual and cultural; julian.bourg.1@bc.edu
Braude, Benjamin (PhD, Harvard 1978; assoc. prof.) Middle East; braude@bc.edu
Cronin, James E. (PhD, Brandeis 1977; prof.) British labor, European labor; croninj@bc.edu
Eaton, Nicole M. (PhD, California, Berkeley 2013; asst. prof.) revolution in Königsberg-Kaliningrad; nicole.eaton.2@bc.edu
Fleming, Robin (PhD, California, Santa Barbara 1984; prof.) medieval; robin.fleming@bc.edu
Gallagher, Charles R., SJ (PhD, Marquette 1998; assoc. prof.) American Catholic; gallagch@bc.edu
Ismay, Penelope Gwynn (PhD, California, Berkeley 2010; assoc. prof.) 18th-century Britain; penelope.ismay@bc.edu
Jacobs, Seth S. (PhD, Northwestern 2000; prof.) 20th-century US foreign policy, America, international politics; jacobssd@bc.edu

Johnson, Marilynn S. (PhD, NYU 1990; prof.) US social, urban, American West; johnsohi@bc.edu

Kenny, Kevin (PhD, Columbia 1994; prof.) US immigration, US labor, global migration; kevin.kenny@bc.edu

Kent, Stacie A. (PhD, Chicago 2015; asst. prof.; International Studies) globalization; stacie.kent@bc.edu

Lal, Priya (PhD, NYU 2011; assoc. prof.) postcolonial Africa; priya.lal@bc.edu

Leahy, William P., SJ (PhD, Stanford 1986; assoc. prof. and Univ. pres.) US social and religious 1861-present; leahy@bc.edu

Lyerly, Cynthia Lynn (PhD, Rice 1995; assoc. prof.) US women, US South, American religion; lyerly@bc.edu

Maney, Patrick J. (PhD, Maryland, Coll. Park 1976; prof.) 20th-century US political; patrick.maney@bc.edu

Matus, Zachary A. (PhD, Harvard 2010; assoc. prof.) medieval Europe, religion; matusz@bc.edu

Miller, Karen K. (PhD, California, Santa Barbara 1986; asst. prof. of practice of history) African American; millerkj@bc.edu

Mo, Yajun (PhD, California, Santa Cruz 2011; asst. prof.) Chinese tourism and travel culture; yajun.mo@bc.edu

O'Neill, Kevin (PhD, Brown 1979; assoc. prof.) early modern and modern Ireland; kevin.oneill@bc.edu

O'Toole, James M. (PhD, Boston Coll. 1987; prof.) American religion; otoolejb@bc.edu

Oh, Arissa (PhD, Chicago 2008; assoc. prof. and dir., undergrad. studies) America, Korean immigration; arissa.oh@bc.edu

Parthasarathi, Prasannan (PhD, Harvard 1992; prof.) Southeast Asia, India; parthasa@bc.edu

Pendas, Devin Owen (PhD, Chicago 2000; assoc. prof. and dir., grad. studies) modern Germany; pendas@bc.edu

Picone, María de los Ángeles (PhD, Emory 2019; asst. prof.) modern Latin America; piconemb@bc.edu

Quigley, David (PhD, NYU 1997; prof.; Univ. provost; and dean of faculties) US political and cultural; quigleyda@bc.edu

Rafferty, Oliver P., SJ (DPhil, Oxford 1996; prof.) modern Ireland, church; oliver.rafferty@bc.edu

Reinburg, Virginia (PhD, Princeton 1985; assoc. prof.) early modern Europe, religious; reinburg@bc.edu

Richardson, Heather Cox (PhD, Harvard 1992; prof.) 19th-century US; heather.richardson@bc.edu

Rogers, Alan (PhD, California, Santa Barbara 1968; prof.) American Revolution, American constitutional and legal; rogersa@bc.edu

Ross, Sarah Gwyneth (PhD, Northwestern 2006; prof. and chair) early modern Europe, women; sarah.ross.1@bc.edu

Sajdi, Dana (PhD, Columbia 2002; assoc. prof.) Middle East; sajdi@bc.edu

Savage, Robert J. (PhD, Boston Coll. 1993; assoc. prof. of practice of history) modern Ireland; savager@bc.edu

Sellers-Garcia, Sylvia M. (PhD, California, Berkeley 2009; assoc. prof.) colonial Latin America; sylvia.sellers-garcia@bc.edu

Seraphim, Franziska (PhD, Columbia 2001; assoc. prof.) modern Japan; seraphim@bc.edu

Stanwood, Owen C. (PhD, Northwestern 2005; assoc. prof.) Atlantic world; owen.stanwood@bc.edu

Summers, Martin (PhD, Rutgers 1997; assoc. prof.) African American intellectual and cultural, African diaspora, gender and masculinity; summermb@bc.edu

Valencius, Conevery Bolton (PhD, Harvard 1998; prof.) US, environmental, science; conevery.valencius@bc.edu

Zhang, Ling (PhD, Cambridge 2008; assoc. prof.) modern China, environmental; ling.zhang.2@bc.edu

Retired/Emeritus Faculty

Gelfand, Mark I. (PhD, Columbia 1972; assoc. prof. emeritus) contemporary American political, 20th-century America, presidency; mark.gelfand@bc.edu

Levenson, Deborah T. (PhD, NYU 1988; prof. emeritus) Latin America, Guatemalan social and cultural; levensod@bc.edu

Northrup, David A. (PhD, UCLA 1974; prof. emeritus) Africa, black Atlantic; david.northrup@bc.edu

Rosser, John (PhD, Rutgers 1972; assoc. prof. emeritus) Byzantine Europe, medieval Slavic, archaeology; rosserj@bc.edu

Spagnoli, Paul G. (PhD, Harvard 1974; assoc. prof. emeritus) modern European social and economic, France 1789-1914; paul.spagnoli@bc.edu

Taylor, Frank (PhD, Geneva 1976; assoc. prof. emeritus) African American, Caribbean; taylorfa@bc.edu

Weiler, Peter (PhD, Harvard 1969; prof. emeritus) modern Britain; weiler@bc.edu

Wu, Silas (PhD, Columbia 1967; prof. emeritus) China; wu@bc.edu

Recently Awarded PhDs

Delvaux, Matthew "Consuming Violence: Slaving and Slaveries in the Viking World and Beyond"

Kelly, Joanna Louise "The Transformation of Evangelical Christian Media, 1950s-90s"

Morton, John Davis "To Settle the Frontier on Sober Principles: Power, Faith, and Nationality in the New England/Maritime Borderlands"

Trutor, Clayton "'Carpetbaggers': Professional Sports Team Relocations and the Making of Sunbelt and Rust Belt Cities, 1946-97"

Boston University

Dept. of History, 226 Bay State Rd., Boston, MA 02215. 617.353.2551. Fax 617.353.2556. Email: history@bu.edu. Website: http://www.bu.edu/history/.

The Department of History offers strong programs in African, American, and European history as well as in the history of the Atlantic world. Among the department's thematic and methodological strengths are political, cultural, intellectual, environmental, transnational, and diplomatic history.

Chair: James McCann
Director of Graduate Studies: Sarah Phillips
Director of Undergraduate Studies: Andrew Robichaud
Degrees Offered: BA, MA, PhD
Academic Year System: Semester
Areas of Specialization: modern Europe, US, Africa, cultural and intellectual
Tuition (per academic year): $54720
Enrollment 2018-19:
  Undergraduate Majors: 129
  New Graduate Students: 4
  Full-time Graduate Students: 31
  Part-time Graduate Students: 3
  Degrees in History: 50 BA, 2 MA, 3 PhD
Undergraduate Addresses:
  Admissions: http://www.bu.edu/admissions/
  Financial Aid: http://www.bu.edu/finaid/
Graduate Addresses:
  Admissions: http://www.bu.edu/info/admissions-overview/graduate-admissions/
  Financial Aid: http://www.bu.edu/finaid/

Full-time Faculty

Anderson, Betty S. (PhD, UCLA 1997; prof.) Middle East, North Africa; banderso@bu.edu

Austin, Paula (PhD, Graduate Center, CUNY 2015; asst. prof; African American Studies) African American, social and intellectual

Backman, Clifford R. (PhD, UCLA 1989; assoc. prof.) medieval; cbackman@bu.edu

Blower, Brooke L. (PhD, Princeton 2005; assoc. prof.) US cultural; bblower@bu.edu

Capper, Charles H. (PhD, California, Berkeley 1984; prof.) US intellectual and cultural; capper@bu.edu

Chernock, Arianne J. (PhD, California, Berkeley 2004; assoc. prof.) modern Britain; chernock@bu.edu

David, Andrew Nicholas (PhD, Boston Univ. 2018; lect.) 20th-century US, American political development, international relations; andavid@bu.edu

Dellheim, Charles (PhD, Yale 1979; prof.) modern European cultural, modern Britain; dellheim@bu.edu

Ferleger, Louis A. (PhD, Temple 1978; prof.) US economic; ferleger@bu.edu

Haberkern, Phillip Nelson (PhD, Virginia 2009; assoc. prof.) early modern Europe; phaberke@bu.edu

Heywood, Linda M. (PhD, Columbia 1984; prof.) Africa, African diaspora, African American; heywood@bu.edu

Johnson, James H., Jr. (PhD, Chicago 1988; prof.) modern European intellectual; jhj@bu.edu

McCann, James C. (PhD, Michigan State 1984; prof. and chair) East Africa, environmental; mccann@bu.edu

McConville, Brendan (PhD, Brown 1992; prof.) early America; bmcconv@bu.edu

Menegon, Eugenio (PhD, California, Berkeley 2002; assoc. prof.) China, world; emenegon@bu.edu

Nolan, Cathal J. (PhD, Toronto 1989; assoc. prof.) American foreign policy, diplomatic; cnolan@bu.edu

Payaslian, Simon (PhD, UCLA 2003; PhD, Wayne State 1992; assoc. prof.) Armenian studies; payas@bu.edu

Peri, Alexis Jean (PhD, California, Berkeley 2011; assoc. prof.) modern Russia and eastern Europe; alexisp4@bu.edu

Phillips, Sarah T. (PhD, Boston Univ. 2004; assoc. prof. and dir., grad. studies) 20th-century America; sarahphi@bu.edu

Richardson, Ronald K. (PhD, SUNY, Binghamton 1983; assoc. prof.) African American, racial thought; hdarodius@aol.com

Roberts, Jon H. (PhD, Harvard 1980; prof.) US intellectual, Anglo-American religion, science; roberts1@bu.edu

Robichaud, Andrew (PhD, Stanford 2015; asst. prof. and dir., undergrad. studies) environmental, US; andrewr1@bu.edu

Russell, Edmund P., III (PhD, Michigan 1993; prof.) environmental, technology, US; edruss@bu.edu

Schmidt, James (PhD, MIT 1974; prof.) European intellectual; jschmidt@bu.edu

Schulman, Bruce J. (PhD, Stanford 1987; prof.) 20th-century America; bjschulm@bu.edu

Siegel, Benjamin (PhD, Harvard 2014; asst. prof.) modern South Asia; siegelb@bu.edu

Silber, Nina (PhD, California, Berkeley 1989; prof.) 19th-century America; nsilber@bu.edu

Thornton, John K. (PhD, UCLA 1979; prof.) Africa, Atlantic, world; jkthorn@bu.edu

Westling, Jon (PhD, Reed 1964; prof.) medieval; westling@bu.edu

Wylie, Diana S. (PhD, Yale 1984; prof.) South Africa; dwylie@bu.edu

Zatlin, Jonathan R. (PhD, California, Berkeley 2000; assoc. prof.) modern Europe, Germany; jzatlin@bu.edu

Joint/Cross Appointments

Chehabi, Houchang E. (PhD, Yale 1986; prof.; International Relations) Central Asia; chehabi@bu.edu

Goldstein, Erik (PhD, Cambridge 1984; prof.; International Relations) international, Britain and British Empire; goldstee@bu.edu

Klepper, Deeana C. (PhD, Northwestern 1995; assoc. prof.; Religion) medieval; dklepper@bu.edu

Lukes, Igor (PhD, Fletcher Sch., Tufts 1985; prof.; International Relations) eastern Europe; lukes@bu.edu

Mayers, David A. (PhD, Chicago 1979; prof.; Political Science) American foreign policy, international relations; dmayers@bu.edu

Rubin, Jeffrey W. (PhD, Harvard 1991; assoc. prof.; Inst. on Culture, Religion, and World Affairs) Latin America; jwr@bu.edu

Retired/Emeritus Faculty

Keylor, William R. (PhD, Columbia 1971; prof. emeritus) modern Europe, modern France, international relations; wrkeylor@bu.edu

Recently Awarded PhDs

David, Andrew Nicholas "Fighting for National Security: Building the National Security State in the Eisenhower and Kennedy Administrations"

Havstad, Lilly Anne "'To Live a Better Life': The Making of a Mozambican Middle Class"

Kinslow, Krista "Contesting the Centennial: Politics and Culture at the 1876 World's Fair"

Bowdoin College

Dept. of History, 9900 College Station, Brunswick, ME 04011-8499. 207.725.3291. Email: rbanks@bowdoin.edu. Website: https://www.bowdoin.edu/history/.

Bowdoin College's rich history combines with the exceptional resources of an elite liberal arts college to offer students an exciting atmosphere for the study of history.

Chair: David Gordon
Degrees Offered: BA
Academic Year System: Semester
Areas of Specialization: US, Europe, East and South Asia, Africa, Latin America
Tuition (per academic year): $51344
Enrollment 2018-19:
 Undergraduate Majors: 76
 Degrees in History: 37 BA
Addresses:
 Admissions: http://www.bowdoin.edu/admissions/
 Financial Aid: http://www.bowdoin.edu/studentaid/

Full-time Faculty

Cikota, Javier (PhD, California, Berkeley 2017; asst. prof.) Latin America, state formation, borderlands; jcikota@bowdoin.edu

Denery, Dallas G., II (PhD, California, Berkeley 1999; prof.) medieval intellectual and cultural; ddenery@bowdoin.edu

Gordon, David Malcolm (PhD, Princeton 2000; prof. and chair) Africa, environmental; dgordon@bowdoin.edu

Hecht, David K. (PhD, Yale 2005; assoc. prof.) 20th-century US, Cold War, science; dhecht@bowdoin.edu

Herrlinger, Page (PhD, California, Berkeley 1996; assoc. prof.) late imperial Russia, Soviet, late modern Europe; pherrlin@bowdoin.edu

McMahon, Sarah F. (PhD, Brandeis 1982; assoc. prof.) colonial and early national America, family/community/gender, environmental; smcmahon@bowdoin.edu

Mohandesi, Salar (PhD, Pennsylvania 2017; asst. prof.) modern Europe; smohande@bowdoin.edu

Rael, Patrick J. (PhD, California, Berkeley 1995; prof.) 19th-century America, African American, multiethnic; prael@bowdoin.edu

Roberts, Meghan (PhD, Northwestern 2011; assoc. prof.) early modern Europe, Enlightenment, France; mroberts@bowdoin.edu

Roberts, Strother E. (PhD, Northwestern 2011; asst. prof.) early America, environmental; seroberts@bowdoin.edu

Joint/Cross Appointments

Chiang, Connie Y. (PhD, Washington 2002; prof.; Environmental Studies) US West, social, environmental; cchiang@bowdoin.edu

Christmas, Sakura (PhD, Harvard 2015; asst. prof.; Asian Studies) Japan; schristm@bowdoin.edu

Klingle, Matthew W. (PhD, Washington 2001; assoc. prof.; Environmental Studies) urban, environmental, 20th-century America; mklingle@bowdoin.edu

Purnell, Brian (PhD, NYU 2006; assoc. prof.; Africana Studies) bpurnell@bowdoin.edu

Sturman, Rachel L. (PhD, California, Davis 2001; assoc. prof.; Asian Studies) South Asia; rsturman@bowdoin.edu

Zuo, Ya Leah (PhD, Princeton 2011; assoc. prof.; Asian Studies) middle period and early modern China; lzuo@bowdoin.edu

Nondepartmental Historians

Nerdahl, Michael D. (PhD, Wisconsin, Madison; lect.; Classics) mnerdahl@bowdoin.edu

Pearlman, Jill (PhD, Chicago; sr. lect.; Environmental Studies) jpearlma@bowdoin.edu

Sobak, Robert (PhD, Princeton; assoc. prof.; Classics) rsobak@bowdoin.edu

Part-time Faculty

Jebari, Idriss (DPhil, Oxford; Andrew W. Mellon Postdoc. Fellow) Middle East; ijebari@bowdoin.edu

Bowie State University

Dept. of History and Government, 14000 Jericho Park Rd., Martin Luther King Bldg., Rm. 0205, Bowie, MD 20715. 301.860.3600. Fax 301.860.3619. Email: dorobertson@bowiestate.edu. Website: https://www.bowiestate.edu/academics-research/colleges/college-arts-sciences/departments/.

When you study and major in history and government at Bowie State University, with concentration in either history or government, you will have the opportunity to experience the responsibilities and rewards of combining theory with practice that will prepare students for leadership positions in the public or private sector.

Chair: Diarra O. Robertson
Degrees Offered: BA,BS
Academic Year System: Semester
Areas of Specialization: US, African American, Africa, Europe, women's studies
Tuition (per academic year):
  In-State: $4222
  Out-of-State: $9568
Enrollment 2018-19:
  Undergraduate Majors: 95
  Degrees in History: 20 BA

Addresses:
  Admissions: http://www.bowiestate.edu/admissions-financial-aid/undergraduate-admissions/
  Financial Aid: http://www.bowiestate.edu/admissions-financial-aid/financial-aid/

Full-time Faculty

Arah, Benjamin (PhD, Howard 2001; prof.) government, philosophy, women's studies; barah@bowiestate.edu

Bell, Karen Cook (PhD, Howard 2008; assoc. prof.) African American, 19th-century US, intellectual, women's studies; kcookbell@bowiestate.edu

Birt, Robert (PhD, Vanderbilt 1984; asst. prof.) philosophy; rbirt@bowiestate.edu

Brown, Tamara L. (PhD, Howard 2004; assoc. prof.) African American, women's studies, cultural, popular culture, African diaspora; tlbrown@bowiestate.edu

Cole, Festus (PhD, SOAS, London 1994; asst. prof.) Africa; fcole@bowiestate.edu

Davidson, Roger A. Jr (PhD, Howard 2000; assoc. prof.) African American, military and naval, diplomatic, 19th-century US; rdavidson@bowiestate.edu

Fenyo, Mario D. (PhD, American 1969; prof.) early and modern Europe, US-African relations; mfenyo@bowiestate.edu

Jackson, Weldon (PhD, Harvard 1978; prof.) American government, constitutional law; wjackson@bowiestate.edu

Lewis, William B. (PhD, Howard 1981; prof.) contemporary Africa; wlewis@bowiestate.edu

Miller, M. Sammye (PhD, Catholic 1977; prof.) antebellum South, African American; smiller@bowiestate.edu

Mills, Frederick (PhD, American 1985; prof.) philosophy; fmills@bowiestate.edu

Reddy, Sumanth (PhD, Kansas State 2011; asst. prof.) geography; sreddy@bowiestate.edu

Reed, David Leon (PhD, Morgan State 2010; asst. prof.) dreed@bowiestate.edu

Robertson, Diarra Osei (PhD, Howard 2005; assoc. prof. and chair) political science, black politics; dorobertson@bowiestate.edu

Shook, John R. (PhD, SUNY, Buffalo 1994; lect.) American philosophy/pragmatism, philosophy of mind, science and naturalism; jrshook@bowiestate.edu

Sochan, George (PhD, Loyola, Chicago 1995; prof.) Europe, Britain; gsochan@bowiestate.edu

Walker, Carmen V. (PhD, Clark Atlanta 2007; assoc. prof.) public policy, US constitutional law, American government, women's studies; cwalker@bowiestate.edu

Bowling Green State University

Dept. of History, 128 Williams Hall, Bowling Green, OH 43403-0220. 419.372.2030. Fax 419.372.7208. Email: history@bgsu.edu. Website: https://www.bgsu.edu/arts-and-sciences/history.html.

The department's faculty maintains areas of specialty in a number of geographic regions, including North America and the United States, Latin America, Europe, Asia, and Africa. Transcending these geographic categories, however, the faculty collectively possesses areas of expertise in a number of thematic areas that cross traditional boundaries, allowing our students the opportunity to become truly global, comparative, and interdisciplinary historians.

Chair: Amilcar E. Challu
Director of Graduate Studies: Benjamin P. Greene

Degrees Offered: BA,MA
Academic Year System: Semester
Areas of Specialization: world, US since 1750, Atlantic world, Europe, public
Undergraduate Tuition (per academic year):
In-State: $9096
Out-of-State: $16632
Graduate Tuition (per academic year):
In-State: $10168
Out-of-State: $17704
Enrollment 2018-19:
Undergraduate Majors: 103
New Graduate Students: 10
Full-time Graduate Students: 22
Part-time Graduate Students: 8
Degrees in History: 25 BA, 13 MA
Students in Undergraduate Courses: 2227
Students in Undergraduate Intro Courses: 1291
Online-Only Courses: 25%
Undergraduate Addresses:
Admissions: http://www.bgsu.edu/admissions.html
Financial Aid: https://www.bgsu.edu/financial-aid.html
Graduate Addresses:
Admissions: http://www.bgsu.edu/graduate.html
Financial Aid: https://www.bgsu.edu/financial-aid.html

Adjunct Faculty

Carver, Michael M. (PhD, Bowling Green State 2011; instr.) modern America, modern Europe; mcarver@bgsu.edu

Green, Shirley L. (PhD, Bowling Green State 2011; instr.; dir., Toledo Police Museum) African American, American Revolution, early America, public; shirllg@bgsu.edu

Hartlerode, Holly A. (MA, Toledo 2002; instr.; curator, Wood County Historical Center and Museum) public; curator@woodcountyhistory.org

McLochlin, Dustin (PhD, Bowling Green State 2014; instr.; curator, Rutherford B. Hayes Presidential Center) modern America, public; DMcLochlin@rbhayes.org

Schrag, Steven D. (PhD, Toledo 2015; instr.) modern Europe, world; sschrag@bgsu.edu

Full-time Faculty

Barr, Kara E. (PhD, Ohio State 2014; instr.) early modern Europe, modern world; kebarr@bgsu.edu

Brooks, Michael E. (PhD, Toledo 2009; lect.) modern America, Ohio, modern world, European expansion; mebrook@bgsu.edu

Challu, Amilcar E. (PhD, Harvard 2007; assoc. prof. and chair) Latin America, Mexico, economic; achallu@bgsu.edu

Forsyth, Douglas J. (PhD, Princeton 1987; assoc. prof.) comparative modern European political and economic, modern Italy; dougfor@bgsu.edu

Greene, Benjamin P. (PhD, Stanford 2004; assoc. prof. and dir., grad. studies) 20th-century US, US foreign relations, international; greeneb@bgsu.edu

Grunden, Walter Eugene (PhD, California, Santa Barbara 1998; assoc. prof.) Japan, modern Asia, science; wgrund@bgsu.edu

Herndon, Ruth Wallis (PhD, American 1992; prof.) colonial America, family, welfare; rwhernd@bgsu.edu

Jackson, Nicole Maelyn (PhD, Ohio State 2012; asst. prof.) African diaspora, African American, 20th-century US; nmjacks@bgsu.edu

Mancuso, Rebecca (PhD, McGill 1999; assoc. prof.) Canada, immigration, local, public; rmancus@bgsu.edu

Martin, Scott C. (PhD, Pittsburgh 1990; prof.) 19th-century US, drugs and alcohol; smartin@bgsu.edu

Nwauwa, Apollos O. (PhD, Dalhousie 1993; prof.) modern Africa; nwauwa@bgsu.edu

Schocket, Andrew M. (PhD, William and Mary 2001; prof.; American Culture Studies) American Revolution, early Republic, memory; aschock@bgsu.edu

Stark, Casey M. (PhD, Wisconsin, Madison 2014; instr.) ancient Rome, classical world, gender, religion; starkcm@bgsu.edu

Joint/Cross Appointments

Sweetser, Michelle (MSI, Michigan 2003; asst. prof.; head librarian, Center for Archival Collections) archival administration

Retired/Emeritus Faculty

Ashcraft-Eason, Lillian (PhD, William and Mary 1975; prof. emeritus) Afro-American, women; lashcra@bgsu.edu

Daly, Lawrence J. (PhD, Loyola, Chicago 1965; prof. emeritus) Bible, ancient Greece, Roman Republic and Empire; ldaly@bgsu.edu

Forse, James H. (PhD, Illinois, Urbana-Champaign 1967; prof. emeritus) medieval, early modern English theater; jforse@bgsu.edu

Hess, Gary R. (PhD, Virginia 1965; prof. emeritus) American diplomatic; ghess@bgsu.edu

Knox, Thomas R. (PhD, Yale 1969; prof. emeritus) Britain; tknox@bgsu.edu

Rock, William R. (PhD, Duke 1956; prof. emeritus) European diplomatic

Rowney, Don K. (PhD, Indiana 1964; prof. emeritus) Russia, Soviet Union; drowney@bgsu.edu

Seavoy, Ronald E. (PhD, Michigan 1969; prof. emeritus) US business, political economy, famine; rseavoy@bgsu.edu

Skaggs, David C., Jr. (PhD, Georgetown 1966; prof. emeritus) colonial and revolutionary America, American military; dskaggs@bgsu.edu

Thomas, Jack Ray (PhD, Ohio State 1962; prof. emeritus) Latin America; tomjack@bgsu.edu

Weinberg, David H. (PhD, Wisconsin, Madison 1971; prof. emeritus) European social and intellectual, modern Jewish; davidweinberg@wayne.edu

Brandeis University

Dept. of History, MailStop 036, 415 South St., Waltham, MA 02453-9110. 781.736.2270. Fax 781.736.2273. Email: delorenz@brandeis.edu. Website: https://www.brandeis.edu/history/.

Despite its relatively small size, the Department of History offers Brandeis students a comprehensive education in the study of the past, both on the undergraduate and on the graduate level. Indeed, its PhD program has consistently received high marks in national surveys and rankings, and can boast an outstanding placement record.

Chair: Michael Willrich
Director of Graduate Studies: Paul Jankowski
Director of Undergraduate Studies: Govind Sreenivasan
Degrees Offered: BA,MA,PhD
Academic Year System: Semester
Areas of Specialization: early modern and modern Europe, America, transnational
Undergraduate Tuition (per academic year): $55130
Graduate Tuition (per academic year): $51940
Enrollment 2018-19:
Undergraduate Majors: 111
New Graduate Students: 7

Full-time Graduate Students: 29
Degrees in History: 32 BA, 3 MA, 2 PhD
Undergraduate Addresses:
Admissions: http://www.brandeis.edu/admissions/
Financial Aid: http://www.brandeis.edu/sfs/
Graduate Addresses:
Admissions and Financial Aid: http://www.brandeis.edu/gsas/

Affiliated Faculty

Donahue, Brian (PhD, Brandeis 1994; assoc. prof.; American Studies) environmental studies; bdonahue@brandeis.edu

Freeze, ChaeRan (PhD, Brandeis; assoc. prof.; Near Eastern & Judaic Studies) eastern European Jewish; cfreeze@brandeis.edu

Hansen, Karen V. (PhD, California, Berkeley 1989; prof.; Sociology) feminist theory, sociology of family and gender, historical sociology; khansen@brandeis.edu

Jockusch, Laura (PhD, NYU 2007; asst. prof.; Near Eastern and Judaic Studies) modern Jewish, Holocaust studies; jockusch@brandeis.edu

Kryder, Daniel (PhD, New Sch. 1995; assoc. prof.; Politics) American political development; kryder@brandeis.edu

Ray, Carina E. (PhD, Cornell 2007; assoc. prof.; African and Afro-American Studies) Africa and black Atlantic, West Africa; cer15@brandeis.edu

Reinharz, Jehuda (PhD, Brandeis 1972; prof.; Tauber Inst./Near Eastern & Judaic Studies) modern Jewish; jreinhar@brandeis.edu

Sarna, Jonathan D. (PhD, Yale 1979; Braun Prof.; Near Eastern and Judaic Studies) American Jewish; sarna@brandeis.edu

Sheppard, Eugene R. (PhD, UCLA 2001; assoc. prof.; Near Eastern & Judaic Studies) modern Jewish history and thought; sheppard@brandeis.edu

Williams, Chad Louis (PhD, Princeton 2004; assoc. prof.; African and Afro-American Studies) African American and modern US African American military and intellectual, World War I; chadw@brandeis.edu

Full-time Faculty

Childs, Greg L. (PhD, NYU 2012; asst. prof.) African diaspora, Latin America and Caribbean, African American; gchilds@brandeis.edu

Cooper, Abigail J. (PhD, Pennsylvania 2015; asst. prof.) 19th-century America, religious and cultural, American South/African American/slavery; abcooper@brandeis.edu

Freeze, Gregory L. (PhD, Columbia 1972; Beinfield Prof.) Russia and Germany, social and religious; freeze@brandeis.edu

Hang, Xing (PhD, California, Berkeley 2010; asst. prof.) East Asia; xinghang@brandeis.edu

Hulliung, Mark (PhD, Harvard 1973; Koret Prof.) intellectual/cultural/political, Europe and America; hulliung@brandeis.edu

Jankowski, Paul (DPhil, Oxford 1987; Ginger Prof. and dir., grad. studies) modern Europe, France; jankowski@brandeis.edu

Kapelle, William E. (PhD, Massachusetts Amherst 1975; assoc. prof.) medieval; wkapelle@brandeis.edu

Kelikian, Alice A. (PhD, Oxford 1978; assoc. prof.) modern, social institutions; kelikian@brandeis.edu

Sohrabi, Naghmeh (PhD, Harvard 2005; asst. prof.; Crown Center for Middle East Studies) cultural and political; sohrabi@brandeis.edu

Sreenivasan, Govind (PhD, Harvard 1995; assoc. prof. and dir., undergrad. studies) early modern Europe, Germany; sreenivasan@brandeis.edu

Weiss Muller, Hannah (PhD, Princeton 2010; asst. prof.) Britain, British Empire; mullerh@brandeis.edu

Willrich, Michael (PhD, Chicago 1997; Leff Prof. and chair) American social and legal; willrich@brandeis.edu

Retired/Emeritus Faculty

Antler, Joyce (PhD, SUNY, Stony Brook 1977; Lane Prof. emeritus) American women, social; antler@brandeis.edu

Arrom, Silvia M. (PhD, Stanford 1978; prof. emeritus) Latin America, women, social; arrom@brandeis.edu

Fischer, David Hackett (PhD, Johns Hopkins 1962; Univ. Prof. emeritus) modern social institutions; fischer@brandeis.edu

Polonsky, Antony (DPhil, Oxford 1968; Abramson Prof. emeritus) eastern European Jewish, Holocaust studies; polonsky@brandeis.edu

Schrecker, John E. (PhD, Harvard 1968; prof. emeritus) East Asia; schrecker@brandeis.edu

Sundiata, Ibrahim K. (PhD, Northwestern 1972; prof. emeritus) African social, slavery and African diaspora, Afro-Brazil; sundiata@brandeis.edu

Vanger, Milton I. (PhD, Harvard 1958; prof. emeritus) Latin America

Recently Awarded PhDs

Cohen, David "Harvesting Green: Capitalism and Environmental Stewardship in the Great North Woods"

Gudefin, Geraldine "The Civil and Religious Worlds of Marriage and Divorce: Russian Jewish Immigrants in France and the United States, 1881-1939"

Brigham Young University

Dept. of History, 2130 JFSB, Provo, UT 84602-4446. 801.422.4335. Fax 801.422.0275. Email: hist_sec@byu.edu. Website: http://history.byu.edu/.

The mission of Brigham Young University—founded, supported, and guided by The Church of Jesus Christ of Latter-day Saints—is to assist individuals in their quest for perfection and eternal life. That assistance should provide a period of intensive learning in a stimulating setting where a commitment to excellence is expected and the full realization of human potential is pursued.

Chair: Brian Q. Cannon
Degrees Offered: BA,BS
Academic Year System: Semester
Areas of Specialization: family, secondary teaching, America, Europe
Tuition:
Latter-day Saint $5,790
Non-Latter-day Saint $11,580
Enrollment 2018-19:
Undergraduate Majors: 447
Degrees in History: 89 BA, 22 BS
Addresses:
Admissions: https://admissions.byu.edu/
Financial Aid: https://financialaid.byu.edu/

Full-time Faculty

Anderson, Stewart Hurst (PhD, SUNY, Binghamton 2012; asst. prof.) modern Europe; stewart_anderson@byu.edu

Auman, Karen E. (PhD, NYU 2014; asst. prof.) Atlantic world; kauman@byu.edu

Buckley, Jay H. (PhD, Nebraska 2001; assoc. prof.) American West, Native American, 19th-century US; jay_buckley@byu.edu

Cannon, Brian Q. (PhD, Wisconsin-Madison 1992; prof. and chair) 20th-century America, agricultural; brian_cannon@byu.edu

Carter, Karen E. (PhD, Georgetown 2006; assoc. prof.) early modern France, Europe, European religious; karen_carter@byu.edu

Choate, Mark I. (PhD, Yale 2002; assoc. prof.) modern Italy, European culture and politics, colonialism and migration; mark_choate@byu.edu

Crandell, Jill N. (MA, Brigham Young 2010; asst. teaching prof.) family, midwestern genealogy; jill_crandell@byu.edu

de Schweinitz, Rebecca L. (PhD, Virginia 2004; assoc. prof.) US children, women and gender, civil rights; rld@byu.edu

Dursteler, Eric R (PhD, Brown 2000; prof.) late medieval Italy, Mediterranean; eric_dursteler@byu.edu

Fluhman, J. Spencer (PhD, Wisconsin-Madison 2006; assoc. prof.) 19th-century US, religious, US West; fluhman@byu.edu

Garcia, Ignacio M. (PhD, Arizona 1995; prof.) Chicano studies; ignacio_garcia@byu.edu

Hadfield, Leslie (PhD, Michigan State 2010; assoc. prof.) Africa, South Africa, black comparative; leslie_hadfield@byu.edu

Hardy, Jeffrey S. (PhD, Princeton 2011; assoc. prof.) Russia, eastern Europe; jeff_hardy@byu.edu

Harline, Craig (PhD, Rutgers 1986; prof.) Renaissance and Reformation; craig_harline@byu.edu

Harris, Amy B. (PhD, California, Berkeley 2006; assoc. prof.) Britain, women and gender, family; amy_harris@byu.edu

Hodson, Christopher G. (PhD, Northwestern 2004; assoc. prof.) colonial America, Atlantic; chris_hodson@byu.edu

Isom-Verhaaren, Christine (PhD, Chicago 1997; asst. prof.) Ottoman; cisom-verhaaren@byu.edu

Johns, Andrew L. (PhD, California, Santa Barbara 2000; assoc. prof.) US foreign relations, 20th-century US; andrew_johns@byu.edu

Kerry, Paul E. (PhD, Oxford 1998; assoc. prof.) German studies, Jewish studies, intellectual; paul_kerry@byu.edu

Kesler Lund, Alisa (PhD, Michigan State 2012; asst. prof.) curriculum, teaching and educational policy; alisa.keslerlund@byu.edu

Kimball, Richard Ian (PhD, Purdue 1999; assoc. prof.) social, sports and leisure, US; richard_kimball@byu.edu

Larsen, Kirk W. (PhD, Harvard 2000; assoc. prof.) modern East Asia, Korea

Madsen, Grant (PhD, Chicago 2011; asst. prof.) US political, US economic; gmadsen@byu.edu

Mason, Matthew E. (PhD, Maryland, Coll. Park 2002; prof.) US slavery, political, early Republic; matthew_mason@byu.edu

Miller, Shawn W. (PhD, Columbia 1997; assoc. prof.) Latin America, Brazil, environmental; shawn_miller@byu.edu

Nokes, Jeffery D. (PhD, Utah 2005; assoc. prof.) pedagogy, teaching, historical literacy; jeff_nokes@byu.edu

Pulsipher, Jenny Hale (PhD, Brandeis 1999; assoc. prof.) colonial America, Native American; jenny_pulsipher@byu.edu

Rensink, Brenden W. (PhD, Nebraska 2010; assoc. prof.) American West, borderlands, Native America; bwrensink@byu.edu

Rugh, Susan S. (PhD, Chicago 1993; prof.) US, travel, rural; susan_rugh@byu.edu

Ryskamp, George (JD, Brigham Young 1979; prof.) Hispanic family; george_ryskamp@byu.edu

Shumway, Jeffrey M. (PhD, Arizona 1999; assoc. prof.) Latin America, Argentina; jshumway@byu.edu

Skabelund, Aaron H. (PhD, Columbia 2004; assoc. prof.) Japan, East Asian languages and culture; aaron_skabelund@byu.edu

Stratford, Edward P. (PhD, Chicago 2009; assoc. prof.) ancient Near East, Old Assyria; edward_stratford@byu.edu

Underwood, Grant (PhD, UCLA 1989; prof.) American religious, Christianity, Mormon; gru2@byu.edu

Ward, Evan R. (PhD, Georgia 2001; assoc. prof.) Mexico, Spanish Caribbean, Latin America; evan_ward@byu.edu

Retired/Emeritus Faculty

Addy, George M. (PhD, Duke 1957; prof. emeritus) colonial Latin America, Spain, Enlightenment

Alexander, Thomas G. (PhD, California, Berkeley 1965; prof. emeritus) late 19th- and early 20th-century US, western Mormon; thomas_alexander@byu.edu

Allen, James B. (PhD, Southern California 1963; prof. emeritus) US, American West, Mormon

Bohac, Rodney D. (PhD, Illinois, Urbana-Champaign 1982; assoc. prof. emeritus) Russia, rural Europe; rodney_bohac@byu.edu

Britsch, R. Lanier (PhD, Claremont Grad. 1967; prof. emeritus) Asian religions, missiology; lanny@byu.edu

Brown, Kendall Walker (PhD, Duke 1979; prof. emeritus) Latin America; kwb3@byu.edu

Daynes, Kathryn M. (PhD, Indiana 1991; assoc. prof. emeritus) American family, 19th-century social; kathryn_daynes@byu.edu

Fox, Frank W. (PhD, Stanford 1973; prof. emeritus) modern US, US cultural; frank_fox@byu.edu

Gowans, Frederick R. (PhD, Brigham Young 1972; prof. emeritus) American West

Grandstaff, Mark R. (PhD, Wisconsin, Madison 1992; assoc. prof. emeritus) Cold War America, US military, US foreign relations; mark_grandstaff@byu.edu

Green, Arnold H. (PhD, UCLA 1973; prof. emeritus) modern Near East; arnold_green@byu.edu

Hamblin, William (PhD, Michigan 1985; prof. emeritus) Near East studies; william_hamblin@byu.edu

Harreld, Donald J. (PhD, Minnesota 2000; assoc. prof. emeritus) early modern Europe, economic, world 1450-1770; donald_harreld@byu.edu

Haslam, Gerald M. (PhD, Brigham Young 1981; assoc. prof. emeritus) family, European community and family; gerald_haslam@byu.edu

Hill, Marvin S. (PhD, Chicago 1968; prof. emeritus) US intellectual and social

Holmes, Blair R. (PhD, Colorado, Boulder 1972; assoc. prof. emeritus) eastern Europe, central Europe, European social; blair_holmes@byu.edu

Hyer, Paul V. (PhD, California, Berkeley 1960; prof. emeritus) modern China, China border areas

Jensen, De Lamar (PhD, Columbia 1957; prof. emeritus) Renaissance and Reformation, early modern intellectual and diplomatic, European expansion

Montgomery, David C. (PhD, Indiana 1971; prof. emeritus) Central Asia, Middle East, aviation

Pixton, Paul B. (PhD, Iowa 1972; prof. emeritus) medieval Europe; paul_pixton@byu.edu

Pratt, David H. (PhD, Nebraska 1975; prof. emeritus) Britain, modern England

Richards, Mary Stovall (PhD, Chicago 1983; assoc. prof. emeritus) family, 19th-century US South, 20th-century US southern novelists; mary_richards@byu.edu

Thorp, Malcolm R. (PhD, Wisconsin, Madison 1972; prof. emeritus) Tudor-Stuart England, modern Britain; malcolm_thorp@byu.edu

Tobler, Douglas F. (PhD, Kansas 1967; prof. emeritus) modern Germany, European intellectual

Westover, V. Robert (PhD, Arizona State 1979; asst. prof. emeritus) family; robert_westover@byu.edu

York, Neil L. (PhD, California, Santa Barbara 1978; prof. emeritus) colonial, technology, American Revolution; neil_york@byu.edu

Brooklyn College, City University of New York

Dept. of History, 2900 Bedford Ave., Brooklyn, NY 11210-2889. 718.951.5303. Fax 718.951.4504. Email: sengupta@brooklyn. cuny.edu; lgreenfield@brooklyn.cuny.edu. Website: http://www. brooklyn.cuny.edu/web/academics/schools/socialsciences/ undergraduate/history.php.

A degree in history means that you've learned which ideals, systems and structures benefited mankind and which ones didn't, and that can ease your entry into almost any field, such as government, education and business. Our Department of History faculty, which includes Pulitzer Prize winners and finalists, will work closely with you to advise you on the myriad opportunities awaiting you.

Chair: Gunja SenGupta
Director of Graduate Studies: Christopher Ebert
Degrees Offered: BA,MA
Academic Year System: Semester
Areas of Specialization: US, Europe, Asia, Latin America, Middle East
Undergraduate Tuition (per academic year):
   In-State: $6530
   Out-of-State: $17400
Graduate Tuition (per academic year):
   In-State: $10450
   Out-of-State: $19320
Enrollment 2018-19:
   Undergraduate Majors: 165
   New Graduate Students: 15
   Part-time Graduate Students: 40
   Degrees in History: 45 BA, 10 MA, PhD
Undergraduate Addresses:
   Admissions: http://www.brooklyn.cuny.edu/web/ admissions.php
   Financial Aid: http://www.brooklyn.cuny.edu/web/about/ offices/financial.php
Graduate Addresses:
   Admissions: http://www.brooklyn.cuny.edu/web/admissions/ graduate.php
   Financial Aid: http://www.brooklyn.cuny.edu/web/about/ offices/financial.php

Full-time Faculty

Banerjee, Swapna M. (PhD, Temple 1998; assoc. prof.) modern South Asia, colonialism, gender and family; banerjee@brooklyn. cuny.edu

Carp, Benjamin L. (PhD, Virginia 2004; assoc. prof.) early America, American Revolution; BCarp@brooklyn.cuny.edu

Ebert, Christopher C. (PhD, Columbia 2004; assoc. prof. and dir., grad. studies) Latin America, Atlantic world; cebert@brooklyn. cuny.edu

Fishman, Louis (PhD, Chicago 2007; asst. prof.) Middle East; lfishman@brooklyn.cuny.edu

Ibrahim, Bilal (PhD, McGill 2013; asst. prof.) Islamic intellectual, ancient Greek thought, Islamic law and society; bibrahim@ brooklyn.cuny.edu

Johnson, Robert D. (PhD, Harvard 1993; prof.) 20th-century US, foreign relations; kcjohnson9@gmail.com

Mancia, Lauren E. (PhD, Yale 2013; asst. prof.) medieval Europe, medieval and early modern Christianity, emotions; laurenmancia@brooklyn.cuny.edu

Meyer, Andrew S. (PhD, Harvard 1999; prof.) Chinese civilization, East Asian religions; ameyer@brooklyn.cuny.edu

Napoli, Philip (PhD, Columbia 1998; assoc. prof.) US social, immigration, public; pnapoli@brooklyn.cuny.edu

O'Keeffe, Brigid M. (PhD, NYU 2008; assoc. prof.) imperial Russia, Soviet Union, modern Europe; bokeeffe@brooklyn.cuny.edu

Rawson, Michael J. (PhD, Wisconsin, Madison 2005; assoc. prof.) environmental, US social/cultural/urban; mrawson@brooklyn. cuny.edu

Remy, Steven P. (PhD, Ohio 2000; prof.) 20th-century central and eastern Europe, political/international/intellectual; sremy@ brooklyn.cuny.edu

SenGupta, Gunja (PhD, Tulane 1991; prof. and chair) African American, Civil War and Reconstruction; sengupta@brooklyn. cuny.edu

Stern, Karen B. (PhD, Brown 2006; assoc. prof.) Jewish, ancient; kstern@brooklyn.cuny.edu

Troyansky, David G. (PhD, Brandeis 1983; prof.) early modern and modern Europe, France; troyansky@brooklyn.cuny.edu

Warren, Christian S. (PhD, Brandeis 1997; assoc. prof.) American public health and medicine; cwarren@brooklyn.cuny.edu

Wills, Jocelyn (PhD, Texas A&M 1998; prof.) American economic and social, comparative industrialization, failure studies; jwills@ brooklyn.cuny.edu

Retired/Emeritus Faculty

Gallagher, Philip F. (PhD, Notre Dame 1970; prof. emeritus) medieval religious, monastic; philipg@brooklyn.cuny.edu

King, Margaret L. (PhD, Stanford 1972; prof. emeritus) Italian Renaissance, European intellectual; marglking@gmail.com

Brown University

Dept. of History, 79 Brown St., Providence, RI 02912-9114. 401.863.2131. Fax 401.863.1040. Email: history@brown.edu. Website: https://www.brown.edu/academics/history/.

The Brown History Department: Research, teaching, and public outreach devoted to the study of humanity's vast and diverse past. We are a community of scholars and students committed to the values and ethics of rigorous education in the humanities.

Chair: Robert Self
Director of Graduate Studies: Linford Fisher
Director of Undergraduate Studies: Naoko Shibusawa
Degrees Offered: BA,MA,MAT,PhD
Academic Year System: Semester
Areas of Specialization: US, Asia, Europe, Latin America, Africa
Tuition (per academic year): $57112
Enrollment 2018-19:
   Undergraduate Majors: 219
   New Graduate Students: 10
   Full-time Graduate Students: 62
   Degrees in History: 78 BA, 16 MA, 7 PhD
Undergraduate Addresses:
   Admissions: http://www.brown.edu/admission
   Financial Aid: http://www.brown.edu/about/administration/ financial-aid/
Graduate Addresses:
   Admissions: http://www.brown.edu/academics/gradschool/ apply
   Financial Aid: http://www.brown.edu/academics/gradschool/ financing-support

Adjunct Faculty

Bushnell, Amy Turner (PhD, Florida 1978; adj. assoc. prof.) colonial Latin America, Spanish Florida, indigenous Americas up to 1900; Amy_Bushnell@Brown.edu

Greene, Jack P. (PhD, Duke 1956; adj. prof.) early America; Jack_Greene@Brown.edu

Meisel, Joseph S. (PhD, Columbia 1999; adj. assoc. prof. and deputy provost) modern Britain; Joseph_Meisel@Brown.edu

Revill, Joel (PhD, Duke 2006; adj. asst. prof. and asst. dean, Faculty) modern France, intellectual; Joel_Revill@Brown.edu

Rojanski, Rachel (PhD, Tel Aviv 1996; adj. prof.; Judaic Studies) modern Jewish history and culture, American Jewish, Israel and Yiddish culture; Rachel_Rojanski@Brown.edu

Full-time Faculty

Ahmed, Faiz (PhD, California, Berkeley 2013; assoc. prof.) modern Middle East and Islamicate world, legal and constitutional, Afghanistan/Ottoman Empire/Turkey; Faiz_Ahmed@Brown.edu

Bartov, Omer (DPhil, Oxford 1983; prof.) modern Germany, Holocaust and genocide, eastern Europe and Israel-Palestine; Omer_Bartov@Brown.edu

Brokaw, Cynthia J. (PhD, Harvard 1984; prof.) late imperial China; Cynthia_Brokaw@Brown.edu

Case, Holly A. (PhD, Stanford 2004; assoc. prof.) international history of 19th-/20th-century Europe, minorities and contested territory, ideas

Chudacoff, Howard P. (PhD, Chicago 1969; prof.) American urban, American social, American cultural and sports; Howard_Chudacoff@Brown.edu

Conant, Jonathan P. (PhD, Harvard 2004; assoc. prof.) late antiquity, medieval Europe, early Islam; Jonathan_Conant@Brown.edu

Cook, Harold J. (PhD, Michigan 1981; prof.) early modern, medicine and science, Dutch Golden Age; Harold_Cook@Brown.edu

Cope, R. Douglas (PhD, Wisconsin, Madison 1987; assoc. prof.) colonial Latin America; Robert_Cope@Brown.edu

Doumani, Beshara B. (PhD, Georgetown 1990; prof.) early modern and modern Middle East, Islamic law and society, Palestinian social; bdoumani@brown.edu

Fisher, Linford D. (PhD, Harvard 2008; assoc. prof. and dir., grad. studies) colonial America, Native America, American religion and slavery; Linford_Fisher@Brown.edu

Gluck, Mary (PhD, Columbia 1977; prof.) 19th- and 20th-century European intellectual; Mary_Gluck@Brown.edu

Green, James N. (PhD, UCLA 1996; prof.) modern Brazil, gender and sexuality; James_Green@Brown.edu

Harris, Tim J. (PhD, Cambridge 1985; prof.) early modern England, Scotland and Ireland; Tim_Harris@Brown.edu

Hein, Benjamin P. (PhD, Stanford 2018; asst. prof.) modern Europe, Atlantic world, social; benjamin_hein@brown.edu

Hu-DeHart, Evelyn (PhD, Texas, Austin 1976; prof.) Latin America/Caribbean, Mexican Revolution, US-Mexico borderlands; Evelyn_Hu-Dehart@Brown.edu

Jacobs, Nancy J. (PhD, Indiana 1995; prof.) southern Africa, African environmental, science in Africa; Nancy_Jacobs@Brown.edu

Johnson, Jennifer (PhD, Princeton 2010; assoc. prof.) modern Africa, North Africa, nationalism/decolonization/public health; Jennifer_Johnson1@Brown.edu

Lambe, Jennifer Lynn (PhD, Yale 2014; assoc. prof.) modern Latin America and Caribbean, psychiatry, Cuba; Jennifer_Lambe@Brown.edu

Mumford, Jeremy Ravi (PhD, Yale 2005; asst. prof.) colonial Latin America, Atlantic World, comparative Native American; Jeremy_Mumford@Brown.edu

Nedostup, Rebecca (PhD, Columbia 2001; assoc. prof.) modern China; Rebecca_Nedostup@Brown.edu

Nummedal, Tara E. (PhD, Stanford 2001; prof.) early modern Europe; Tara_Nummedal@Brown.edu

Owens, Emily A. (PhD, Harvard 2015; asst. prof.) African American women, slavery studies, sexuality

Pollock, Ethan M. (PhD, California, Berkeley 2000; assoc. prof.) late modern Europe, Russia; Ethan_Pollock@Brown.edu

Remensnyder, Amy G. (PhD, California, Berkeley 1992; prof.) medieval European cultural and religious, medieval Mediterranean, medieval Iberia; Amy_Remensnyder@Brown.edu

Richards, Joan L. (PhD, Harvard 1980; prof. and dir., Sci. and Technology Studies Prog.) science; Joan_Richards@Brown.edu

Rieppel, Lukas (PhD, Harvard 2012; asst. prof.) science, capitalism, US cultural; Lukas_Rieppel@Brown.edu

Rockman, Seth E. (PhD, California, Davis 1999; assoc. prof.) early Republic US; Seth_Rockman@Brown.edu

Rodriguez, Daniel Arturo (PhD, NYU 2013; asst. prof.) 19th- and 20th-century Cuba, public health and medicine; Daniel_Rodriguez@Brown.edu

Sacks, Kenneth (PhD, California, Berkeley 1976; prof.) ancient Greek intellectual, American transcendentalism; Kenneth_Sacks@Brown.edu

Self, Robert O. (PhD, Washington 1998; Mary Ann Lippitt Prof. and chair) 20th-century US; Robert_Self@Brown.edu

Shibusawa, Naoko (PhD, Northwestern 1998; assoc. prof. and dir., undergrad. studies) US empire, US cultural, Asian American; Naoko_Shibusawa@Brown.edu

Smith, Kerry (PhD, Harvard 1994; assoc. prof.) modern Japan; Kerry_Smith@Brown.edu

Vorenberg, Michael (PhD, Harvard 1995; assoc. prof.) 19th-century US, Civil War and Reconstruction, legal; Michael_Vorenberg@Brown.edu

Zamindar, Vazira F.-Y. (PhD, Columbia 2003; assoc. prof.) modern South Asia; Vazira_F-Y_Zamindar@Brown.edu

Joint/Cross Appointments

Bashir, Shahzad (PhD, Yale 1998; Aga Khan Prof.; Religious Studies) Iran and Central and South Asia 1300-1800 CE, Islam, Persia, historiographical theory, temporality, corporeality; shahzad_bashir@brown.edu

Bodel, John P. (PhD, Michigan 1984; prof.; Classics) ancient; John_Bodel@Brown.edu

Castiglione, Caroline F. (PhD, Harvard 1995; prof.; Italian Studies) early modern Europe, Italy, politics and society; Caroline_Castiglione@Brown.edu

Demuth, Bathsheba (PhD, California, Berkeley 2016; asst. prof.; Inst. at Brown for Environment and Society) environmental, Russia, US/Native American; bathsheba_demuth@brown.edu

Hamlin, Francoise N. (PhD, Yale 2004; assoc. prof.; Africana Studies) US, African American; Francoise_Hamlin@Brown.edu

Lander, Brian George (PhD, Columbia 2015; asst. prof.; Inst. at Brown for Environment and Soc.) Chinese history and archaeology, environmental, world

Lubar, Steven D. (PhD, Chicago 1983; prof.; American Studies) public, material culture studies, museums and memorials; Steven_Lubar@Brown.edu

Mitter, Sreemati (PhD, Harvard 2014; asst. prof.; Watson Inst.) modern Middle East, Palestine, economic

Oliver, Graham J. (DPhil, Oxford 1995; prof.; Classics) Greece, epigraphy, ancient economy; Graham_Oliver@Brown.edu

Safier, Neil F. (PhD, Johns Hopkins 2004; assoc. prof.; dir., John Carter Brown Library) early modern Europe and colonial Latin

America, Amazonia, comparative imperial history and history of science; Neil_Safier@Brown.edu

Steffes, Tracy L. (PhD, Chicago 2007; assoc. prof.; Education) 20th-century US, education; Tracy_Steffes@Brown.edu

Steinberg, Michael P. (PhD, Chicago 1985; prof.; Music and German Studies) modern European cultural and intellectual, German Jewish, music and opera; Michael_Steinberg@Brown.edu

Teller, Adam (PhD, Hebrew Univ., Jerusalem 1997; prof.; Judaic Studies) Jews in Polish-Lithuanian commonwealth, early modern Jewish, Jewish economic; Adam_Teller@Brown.edu

Nondepartmental Historians

Meckel, Richard (PhD, Michigan 1981; prof.; American Studies) medicine and public health, childhood and youth, immigration; Richard_Meckel@Brown.edu

Spoehr, Luther W. (PhD, Stanford 1975; sr. lect.; Education) American higher education, American school reform, history teaching; Luther_Spoehr@Brown.edu

Retired/Emeritus Faculty

Akarli, Engin D. (PhD, Princeton 1976; prof. emeritus) modern Middle East; Engin_Akarli@Brown.edu

Buhle, Mari Jo (PhD, Wisconsin, Madison 1974; prof. emeritus) American women, American culture; Mari_Buhle@Brown.edu

Buhle, Paul M. (PhD, Wisconsin, Madison 1975; prof. emeritus) American oral, social; Paul_Buhle@Brown.edu

Graubard, Stephen R. (PhD, Harvard 1952; prof. emeritus) 19th- and 20th-century Europe; stephengraubard@aol.com

Grieder, Jerome B. (PhD, Harvard 1963; prof. emeritus) modern Chinese intellectual and social; Jerome_Grieder@Brown.edu

Kaestle, Carl F. (PhD, Harvard 1971; prof. emeritus) American education; Carl_Kaestle@Brown.edu

Litchfield, R. Burr (PhD, Princeton 1965; prof. emeritus) 18th- and 19th-century Europe, social and demographic, France and Italy; Robert_Litchfield@Brown.edu

McClain, James L. (PhD, Yale 1979; prof. emeritus) premodern Japan; James_McClain@Brown.edu

Molho, Anthony (PhD, Case Western Reserve 1965; prof. emeritus) medieval, early modern, Italy; Anthony_Molho@Brown.edu

Neu, Charles E. (PhD, Harvard 1964; prof. emeritus) American foreign relations, Vietnam War; Charles_Neu@Brown.edu

Patterson, James T. (PhD, Harvard 1964; prof. emeritus) modern US, social welfare, race relations; James_Patterson@Brown.edu

Raaflaub, Kurt (PhD, Basel 1970; Other, Free, Berlin 1979; prof. emeritus) Greece and Rome, classics, comparative ancient world; Kurt_Raaflaub@Brown.edu

Rich, Norman (PhD, California, Berkeley 1949; prof. emeritus) Germany

Williams, Lea E. (PhD, Harvard 1956; prof. emeritus) China, Southeast Asia, maritime; Lea_Williams@Brown.edu

Wood, Gordon S. (PhD, Harvard 1964; prof. emeritus) colonial America, American Revolution, early Republic; Gordon_Wood@Brown.edu

Recently Awarded PhDs

Ani, Filip Metro Anchidim "Communities of Destruction: A Biography of the Jewish-Romanian-Ukrainian Borderlands"

Ayanna, Amiri "Ethics, Devotion, and Everyday Life: Literature by Women in Germany's Long 15th Century"

Caldis, Sam "Brothers, Colleagues, and Power in Imperial Rome"

Carroll, Charles "Gender and the Making of the University of Paris, 1150-1300"

Housman, Talya "'To Plunder All under the Petty-coate': Prosecuting Sexual Crime and Gendered Violence in The English Revolution"

Kerner, Amy K. "A Fragile Inheritance: The Fate of Yiddish in Argentina, 1930-70"

Medhi, Abhilash "Frontier Capitalism, Infrastructure Expansion and the Forging of British India's Northwestern and Northeastern Borderlands, 1840-1930"

Tanzer, Frances Anne "Performing Vienna: Jewish Presence and Absence in Post-Nazi Central Europe"

Bryant University

Dept. of History and Social Science, 1150 Douglas Pike, Smithfield, RI 02917. 401.232.6585. Fax 401.232.6585. Email: mbryant@bryant.edu. Website: https://departments.bryant.edu/history-and-social-sciences/.

The faculty and students within our multidisciplinary department advance the study and practice of history and the social sciences through teaching, research, and outreach. Our research generates knowledge rooted in historical and social scientific approaches to the study of the human condition.

Chair: John Dietrich
Degrees Offered: BA
Academic Year System: Semester
Areas of Specialization: 20th-century US social and cultural, world, science and technology, World War II, Latin America
Tuition (per academic year): $36872
Enrollment 2018-19:
  Undergraduate Majors: 7
  Degrees in History: 2 BA
Addresses:
  Admissions: http://www.bryant.edu/admissions/
  Financial Aid: http://www.bryant.edu/admissions/cost-and-financial-aid/

Full-time Faculty

Bobroff, Ronald P. (PhD, Duke 2000; assoc. prof.) modern Russia; modern diplomatic and international; ronbobroff@hotmail.com

Bryant, Michael Scott (PhD, Ohio State 2001; prof. and history coord.) Holocaust and law, German legal, comparative legal; mbryant@bryant.edu

Daly, Kathleen (PhD, Boston Univ. 2015; lect.) American history/studies, visual culture, gender; kdaly1@bryant.edu

Joseph, Antoine (PhD, Chicago 1976; prof.) US and European labor and economic, comparative, historical sociology; ajoseph@bryant.edu

Litoff, Judy Barrett (PhD, Maine 1975; prof.) 20th-century US, US social, women; jlitoff@bryant.edu

Lokken, Paul (PhD, Florida 2000; assoc. prof.) Latin America, African diaspora, race and ethnicity; plokken@bryant.edu

Martin, Bradford D. (PhD, Boston Univ. 2000; prof.) US cultural/political/intellectual, popular culture, American studies; bmartin@bryant.edu

Pearson, Jeremy D. (PhD, Tennessee, Knoxville 2017; lect.) medieval Europe; jpearson3@bryant.edu

Bryn Mawr College

Dept. of History, 101 N. Merion Ave., Bryn Mawr, PA 19010-2899. 610.526.5332. Fax 610.526.7479. Email: phealy@brynmawr.edu. Website: https://www.brynmawr.edu/history/.

History at Bryn Mawr is about questioning and explaining how the past has been constructed, understood, and made into what we call "history." You'll find that our teaching emphasizes interpretation over factual narration, and that we offer students many approaches to reading, researching, and thinking about the past.

Chair: Madhavi Kale
Degrees Offered: BA
Academic Year System: Semester
Areas of Specialization: Britain, imperial
Tuition (per academic year): $65000
Enrollment 2018-19:
  Undergraduate Majors: 24
  Degrees in History: 14 BA
Addresses:
  Admissions: http://www.brynmawr.edu/admissions/
  Financial Aid: http://www.brynmawr.edu/sfs/

Full-time Faculty

Gallup-Diaz, Ignacio J. (PhD, Princeton 1999; assoc. prof.) early modern Atlantic world, indigenous peoples, colonial Latin and British America; igallupd@brynmawr.edu

Kale, Madhavi (PhD, Pennsylvania 1992; prof. and chair) British Empire, race, gender; mkale@brynmawr.edu

Kurimay, Anita A. (PhD, Rutgers 2012; asst. prof.) modern Europe, women and gender, sexuality; akurimay@brynmawr.edu

Truitt, Elly (PhD, Harvard 2007; assoc. prof.) medieval, science and medicine; etruitt@brynmawr.edu

Ullman, Sharon R. (PhD, California, Berkeley 1990; prof.) modern US, gender, cultural studies; sullman@brynmawr.edu

Joint/Cross Appointments

Ngalamulume, Kalala J. (PhD, Michigan State 1996; assoc. prof.; Africana Studies) West Africa, health and medicine, urban and colonial; kngalamu@brynmawr.edu

Bucknell University

Dept. of History, 1 Dent Dr., 62A Coleman Hall, Lewisburg, PA 17837. 570.577.1123. Email: history@bucknell.edu. Website: https://www.bucknell.edu/history.

At Bucknell, history majors develop their own focus for their program of study in close collaboration with their departmental adviser. Students are encouraged to choose courses that reflect their particular interests and shape their own methodologies, foci, questions, and answers.

Chair: John Enyeart
Degrees Offered: BA
Academic Year System: Semester
Areas of Specialization: America/Europe/non-Western/Middle East, intellectual, political/economic/labor, social, science and medicine
Tuition (per academic year): $57882
Enrollment 2018-19:
  Undergraduate Majors: 72
  Degrees in History: 31 BA
Addresses:
  Admissions: https://www.bucknell.edu/admissions.html
  Financial Aid: https://www.bucknell.edu/FinancialAid

Full-time Faculty

Baghoolizadeh, Beeta (PhD, Pennsylvania 2018; asst. prof.; Africana Studies) modern Middle East, photography, slavery; bb038@bucknell.edu

Barba, Paul (PhD, California, Santa Barbara 2016; asst. prof.) Texas and Southwest, Mexico, black studies and Caribbean

Campbell, Claire (PhD, Western Ontario 2001; assoc. prof.) environmental, North America, Canada; cec036@bucknell.edu

Del Testa, David W. (PhD, California, Davis 2001; assoc. prof.) modern Europe, Southeast Asia, political; ddeltest@bucknell.edu

Dosemeci, Mehmet (PhD, Columbia 2009; asst. prof.) Middle East, Europe, intellectual and social movements; md053@bucknell.edu

Enyeart, John P. (PhD, Colorado, Boulder 2002; assoc. prof. and chair) American political, economic, labor and immigration; jenyeart@bucknell.edu

Fourshey, C. Cymone (PhD, UCLA 2001; assoc. prof.) Tanzanian agricultural, hospitality; ccf014@bucknell.edu

Goodale, James A. (PhD, UCLA 1995; assoc. prof.) early modern Europe, Russia, medieval; jgoodale@bucknell.edu

Kosmin, Jennifer Frances (PhD, North Carolina, Chapel Hill 2014; asst. prof.) medicine, early modern Italy, women and gender; jennifer.kosmin@bucknell.edu

Sheftall, Mark D. (PhD, Duke 2002; assoc. prof.) British Empire, military; mds037@bucknell.edu

Thomson, Jennifer (PhD, Harvard 2013; asst. prof.) environmental, medicine, 20th-century US; j.thomson@bucknell.edu

Tlusty, B. Ann (PhD, Maryland, Coll. Park 1994; prof.) central and eastern Europe, social; tlusty@bucknell.edu

Nondepartmental Historians

Orr, James J. (PhD, Stanford 1996; assoc. prof.; East Asian Studies) modern Japan, national identity; jamesorr@bucknell.edu

Retired/Emeritus Faculty

Kirkland, John D., Jr. (PhD, Duke 1965; prof. emeritus) European intellectual, critical theory, political-philosophical thought; kirkland@bucknell.edu

Neuman, Mark D. (PhD, California, Berkeley 1967; prof. emeritus) 19th- and 20th-century Britain; mneuman@bucknell.edu

Patrick, Leslie C. (PhD, California, Santa Cruz 1989; assoc. prof. emeritus) African American, colonial, 18th- and 19th-century American social; lpatrick@bucknell.edu

Verbrugge, Martha H. (PhD, Harvard 1978; prof. emeritus) science and medicine; verbrgge@bucknell.edu

Waller, Richard D. (PhD, Cambridge 1979; assoc. prof. emeritus) international relations, East Africa, imperialism and colonialism; rwaller@bucknell.edu

Butler University

Dept. of History and Anthropology, 4600 Sunset Ave., Indianapolis, IN 46208. 317.940.9230. Fax 317.940.8815. Email: amarnol1@butler.edu. Website: https://www.butler.edu/history-anthropology.

Butler has the only undergraduate department in the United States that integrates cultural anthropology and history in its curricula, connecting common topics, research methods, and theories, much like graduate studies do. Our students learn to think critically and write effectively.

Chair: Elise Edwards
Degrees Offered: BA,MA
Academic Year System: Semester
Areas of Specialization: 18th- to 20th-century US, medieval to modern Europe, East Asia, Latin America, cultural geography
Undergraduate Tuition (per academic year): $38900
Graduate Tuition (per academic year): $9720
Enrollment 2018-19:
  Undergraduate Majors: 61
  New Graduate Students: 3
  Full-time Graduate Students: 2
  Part-time Graduate Students: 3
  Degrees in History: 13 BA
Undergraduate Addresses:
  Admissions: http://www.butler.edu/admission/
  Financial Aid: http://www.butler.edu/admission/financial/
Graduate Addresses:
  Admissions: https://www.butler.edu/admission/graduate-application-process
  Financial Aid: https://www.butler.edu/financial-aid/graduate-students-financial-aid

Full-time Faculty

Bigelow, Bruce L. (PhD, Syracuse 1978; prof.) Indiana and Midwest historical geography, historical geography of American expansionism and imperialism; bbigelow@butler.edu
Cornell, John S. (PhD, Yale 1990; assoc. prof.) modern European cultural and intellectual, Germany; jcornell@butler.edu
Deno, Vivian E. (PhD, California, Irvine 2002; assoc. prof.) African American, 20th-century cultural and social, labor and class studies; vdeno@butler.edu
Hanson, Paul R. (PhD, California, Berkeley 1981; prof.) Europe, French Revolution, modern China; phanson@butler.edu
Hunter, Antwain Kenton (PhD, Penn State 2015; asst. prof.) 18th- and 19th-century US, colonial and antebellum America, American Revolution; ahunter1@butler.edu
Paradis, Thomas (PhD, Illinois, Urbana-Champaign 1997; prof.; faculty dir., Assessment and Accreditation) urban and cultural geography, downtown redevelopment, historic preservation; tparadis@butler.edu
Scarlett, Zachary (PhD, Northeastern 2013; asst. prof.) modern China, Maoist politics and culture, global 1960s; zscarlet@butler.edu
Sluis, Ageeth (PhD, Arizona 2006; assoc. prof.) Latin America, gender; asluis@butler.edu
Swanson, Scott G. (PhD, Cornell 1988; assoc. prof.) medieval, early modern Europe; sswanson@butler.edu

Cabrini University

Dept. of History and Political Science, 610 King of Prussia Rd., Radnor, PA 19087-3698. 610.902.8182. Fax 610.902.8285. Email: mace@cabrini.edu. Website: https://www.cabrini.edu/about/departments/academic-departments.

The History and Political Science Department offers majors in American studies, black studies, history, and political science that lead to careers in business, government, law, teaching, and archival professions.

Chair: Darryl Mace
Degrees Offered: BA
Academic Year System: Semester
Areas of Specialization: US, popular culture, sports, African American, political
Tuition (per academic year): $30588
Enrollment 2018-19:
  Undergraduate Majors: 80
  Degrees in History: 15 BA
Addresses:
  Admissions: http://www.cabrini.edu/admissions
  Financial Aid: http://www.cabrini.edu/financialaid

Full-time Faculty

Fitzgerald, Joseph R. (PhD, Temple 2005; asst. prof.) black studies, civil rights/black power movements, Africa; jrf723@cabrini.edu
Hedtke, James R. (PhD, Temple 1997; prof.) US presidency, Constitution, Civil War; james.r.hedtke@cabrini.edu
Mace, Darryl C. (PhD, Temple 2007; prof. and chair) 20th-century US, race and gender, African Americans; mace@cabrini.edu
Smith, Courtney Michelle (PhD, Lehigh 2009; prof.) American popular culture, colonial America, sports; cms392@cabrini.edu
Watterson, Nancy (PhD, Pennsylvania; assoc. prof.) folklore and folklife, ethnography, arts; nlw724@cabrini.edu

Retired/Emeritus Faculty

Girard, Jolyon P. (PhD, Maryland, Coll. Park 1973; prof. emeritus) US diplomatic, military, Latin America; jgirard@cabrini.edu

University of California, Berkeley

Dept. of History, 3229 Dwinelle Hall, MC#2550, Berkeley, CA 94720-2550. 510.642.1971. Fax 510.643.5323. Email: history@berkeley.edu. Website: https://history.berkeley.edu/.

The Department of History is one of the largest and most distinguished units in UC Berkeley's College of Letters and Science. The Department's faculty ranges across virtually all of the major geographical and chronological fields recognized by the discipline.

Chair: Peter Zinoman
Director of Graduate Studies: Susanna Elm
Degrees Offered: BA,MA,PhD
Academic Year System: Semester
Areas of Specialization: Africa, ancient Greece and Rome, Asia, Byzantine, Jewish, Latin America, medieval, Middle East, North America, science
Undergraduate Tuition (per academic year):
  In-State: $11502
  Out-of-State: $39098
Graduate Tuition (per academic year):
  In-State: $11502
  Out-of-State: $26604
Enrollment 2018-19:
  Undergraduate Majors: 360
  New Graduate Students: 26
  Full-time Graduate Students: 175
  Degrees in History: 172 BA, 26 MA, 25 PhD
Undergraduate Addresses:
  Admissions: http://admissions.berkeley.edu/
  Financial Aid: http://financialaid.berkeley.edu/
Graduate Addresses:
  Admissions: http://history.berkeley.edu
  Financial Aid: http://financialaid.berkeley.edu/

Affiliated Faculty

Frick, David (PhD, Yale 1983; prof.; Slavic Languages and Literature) early modern eastern Europe, Poland, Lithuania; frick@berkeley.edu

Gottreich, Emily R. (PhD, Harvard 1999; assoc. prof.; vice chair, Center for Middle Eastern Studies) Middle Eastern studies; emilyrg@berkeley.edu

Holo, Joshua David (PhD, Chicago 2001; assoc. prof.; dean, Hebrew Union Coll., Los Angeles) Jewish studies; jholo@huc.edu

Lieberman, David (PhD, London 1980; prof.; Boalt Sch. Law) legal; dlieb@law.berkeley.edu

Merchant, Carolyn (PhD, Wisconsin, Madison 1967; prof. emerita; Environmental Science, Policy, and Management) environmental, philosophy and ethics; merchant@nature.berkeley.edu

Ocker, Christopher M. (PhD, Princeton Theological Seminary 1991; prof.; Grad. Theological Union) Christianity, late medieval and early modern central Europe; ocker@sfts.edu

Paperno, Irina (PhD, Stanford 1984; prof.; Slavic Languages and Literatures) 19th- and 20th-century Russian intellectual/cultural/literary; ipaperno@berkeley.edu

Porter, Dorothy E. (PhD, Univ. Coll., London 1984; prof.; California, San Francisco) science and medicine; dporter@itsa.ucsf.edu

Scheiber, Harry N. (PhD, Cornell 1962; prof.; Boalt Sch. Law) America since 1607, legal and constitutional; scheiber@uclink.berkeley.edu

Watkins, Elizabeth (PhD, Harvard 1996; assoc. prof.; Science, Tech., and Society Center) sex hormones and aging, gender and medicine, popularization of science and medicine; watkinse@dahsm.ucsf.edu

Full-time Faculty

Bakhle, Janaki (PhD, Columbia 2002; assoc. prof.) Intellectual history of religion, politics and modern India; jbakhle@berkeley.edu

Barshay, Andrew E. (PhD, California, Berkeley 1986; Dr. C. F. Koo & Cecilia Koo Chair; East Asian Studies) modern Japan; abars@berkeley.edu

Carson, Cathryn L. (PhD, Harvard 1995; Thomas M. Siebel Presidential Chair) science, physics, technology, philosophy; clcarson@berkeley.edu

Chowning, Margaret (PhD, Stanford 1985; prof.) Latin America, Mexico, socioeconomics; chowning@berkeley.edu

Connelly, John (PhD, Harvard 1994; prof.) late modern Europe, Czechoslovakia, East Germany and Poland; jfconnel@berkeley.edu

Dandelet, Thomas (PhD, California, Berkeley 1995; prof.) early modern Europe, Spanish Empire, Italy, Mediterranean; tdandelet@berkeley.edu

DeLay, Brian (PhD, Harvard 2004; assoc. prof.) US and the world, American West, US-Mexico borderlands, Native American history, international arms trade; delay@berkeley.edu

Dirks, Nicholas B. (PhD, Chicago 1981; prof.) modern South Asia; ndirks@berkeley.edu

Eder, Sandra (PhD, Johns Hopkins 2011; asst. prof.) gender and sexuality, medicine; s.eder@berkeley.edu

Efron, John (PhD, Columbia 1991; Koret Prof., Jewish Hist.) modern Jewish, German Jewry cultural and social; efron@berkeley.edu

Elm, Susanna K. (DPhil, Oxford 1987; Sidney H. Ehrman Prof. and dir., grad. studies) early Christianity, later Roman Empire; elm@berkeley.edu

Frede, Victoria (PhD, California, Berkeley 2002; assoc. prof.) imperial Russia; vfrede@berkeley.edu

Hall, Bruce S. (PhD, Illinois, Urbana-Champaign 2005; assoc. prof.) Africa, Muslim world, Muslim intellectual; bruce.hall@berkeley.edu

Henkin, David (PhD, California, Berkeley 1995; prof.) US, urban, cultural; marhevka@berkeley.edu

Herman, Rebecca (PhD, California, Berkeley 2014; asst. prof.) modern Latin America/Brazil/Argentina/Cuba/Panama, US-Latin American relations, Latin America in world; rebeccaherman@berkeley.edu

Hesse, Carla A. (PhD, Princeton 1986; Peder Sather Prof.) Old Regime and revolutionary France; chesse@berkeley.edu

Hoffmann, Stefan-Ludwig (PhD, Bielefeld 1999; assoc. prof.) late modern Europe and Germany, transnational; slhoffmann@berkeley.edu

Jones-Rogers, Stephanie E. (PhD, Rutgers 2012; asst. prof.) African American, slavery, women and gender; sejr@berkeley.edu

Kaicker, Abhishek (PhD, Columbia 2014; asst. prof.) early modern and modern South Asia, Mughal Empire politics and culture, 20th-century world; kaicker@berkeley.edu

Kanogo, Tabitha (PhD, Nairobi 1981; prof.) colonial Kenya, African women, East Africa; kanogo@berkeley.edu

Katz, Ethan B. (PhD, Wisconsin, Madison 2009; assoc. prof.) modern Jewish, modern France and its empire, North Africa, religion and secularism in modern world, Jewish-Muslim relations, collective memory, Jews in colonial societies, transnational, citizenship; ebkatz@berkeley.edu

Koziol, Geoffrey (PhD, Stanford 1982; prof.) medieval Europe; gkoz@berkeley.edu

Mackil, Emily M. (PhD, Princeton 2003; assoc. prof.) ancient Greece; emackil@berkeley.edu

Martin, Waldo Emerson, Jr. (PhD, California, Berkeley 1980; Alexander F. & May T. Morrison Prof., American Hist. and Citizenship) America since 1607, Afro-American, social and cultural; wmartin@berkeley.edu

Mavroudi, Maria (PhD, Harvard 1998; prof.) Byzantine studies; mavroudi@berkeley.edu

Mazzotti, Massimo (PhD, Edinburgh 2000; assoc. prof.) 16th- to 20th-century mathematics, science and Catholic Church, Enlightenment science and technology; mazzotti@berkeley.edu

McLennan, Rebecca (PhD, Columbia 1999; assoc. prof.) America since 1607, US social/political/labor, crime and punishment; mclennan@berkeley.edu

Miller, Maureen C. (PhD, Harvard 1989; prof.) medieval; mcmiller@berkeley.edu

Noreña, Carlos F. (PhD, Pennsylvania 2001; assoc. prof.) ancient Rome; norena@berkeley.edu

Nylan, Michael (PhD, Princeton 1982; prof.) East Asia, premodern China; mnylan@berkeley.edu

Ogle, Vanessa (PhD, Harvard 2011; assoc. prof.) modern Europe, global and globalization, political economy

Philliou, Christine May (PhD, Princeton 2004; assoc. prof.) Ottoman Empire, modern Turkey and Greece; philliou@berkeley.edu

Rosenthal, Caitlin (PhD, Harvard 2012; asst. prof.) political economy of slavery, US social and economic, capitalism; crosenthal@berkeley.edu

Sargent, Daniel J. (PhD, Harvard 2008; assoc. prof.) America, US foreign relations, global and international; daniel.sargent@berkeley.edu

Schneider, Elena Andrea (PhD, Princeton 2011; asst. prof.) Atlantic world 1400-1888, Cuba and Carribbean, colonial Latin America; eschneider@berkeley.edu

Shagan, Ethan H. (PhD, Princeton 2000; prof.) Britain, early modern Europe; shagan@berkeley.edu

Sheehan, Jonathan L. (PhD, California, Berkeley 1999; prof.) early modern Europe; sheehan@berkeley.edu

Stahl, Ronit Y. (PhD, Michigan 2014; asst. prof.) American social, politics, law, religion, military, medicine; rystahl@berkeley.edu

Tackett, Nicolas O. (PhD, Columbia 2006; assoc. prof.) China; tackett@berkeley.edu

Vernon, James (PhD, Manchester, UK 1991; prof.) modern Britain; jvernon@berkeley.edu

Yeh, Wen-hsin (PhD, California, Berkeley 1984; Richard H. and Laurie C. Morrison Chair) modern China, social and cultural; sha@berkeley.edu

Zinoman, Peter B. (PhD, Cornell 1995; prof. and chair) Southeast Asia, Vietnam; pzinoman@berkeley.edu

Joint/Cross Appointments

Angelova, Diliana (PhD, Harvard 2005; assoc. prof.; Hist. of Art) early Christian and Byzantine art, art and society in late antiquity; angelova@berkeley.edu

Brilliant, Mark R. (PhD, Stanford 2002; assoc. prof.; American Studies) 20th-century US, comparative civil rights, American West; mbrill@berkeley.edu

Penningroth, Dylan C. (PhD, Johns Hopkins 2000; prof.; Law) African American, US socio-legal; dcap@law.berkeley.edu

Part-time Faculty

Astourian, Stephan (PhD, UCLA 1996; adj. assoc. prof.) Armenian and Caucasian studies; astour@berkeley.edu

Recently Awarded PhDs

Ganor, Sheer "In Scattered Formation, Displacement, Alignment, and the German-Jewish Diaspora"

Hall, Aaron Roy "Claiming the Founding: Slavery and Constitutional History in Antebellum America"

Johnson, Eric McCurdy "Revolutionary Lives: Ideals and the Everyday for Russian Radicals in the 1870s"

Lewandoski, Julia "Real Properties: Imperial Treaties, Land Surveys, and Indigenous Territories in North America"

Lund-Montaño, Camilo E. "Out of Order: Radical Lawyers and Social Movements in the Cold War"

Madej-Krupitski, Urszula "Mapping Jewish Poland: Leisure Travel and Identity in the Interwar Period"

Makleff, Ron M. "Ceremonial Bureaucracy in the Unstable Archive: Paper, Pomp, and Political Legitimacy in the Low Countries, c. 1300-1600"

Nelson, Robert G. "The People's Capital: The Politics of Working-Class Wealth in the Gilded Age"

Nguyen, Cindy A. "Reading & Misreading: The Social Life of Libraries, Print Culture, and Colonial Control in Vietnam, 1865-57"

Novoa, Natalie N. "'A Home Away from Home': Recreation Centers and Black Community Development in the Bay Area, 1920-60"

Pattison, Joel S "Trade and Religious Boundaries in the Medieval Maghreb: Genoese Merchants, Their Products, and Islamic Law"

Shannon, Kerry Seiji "Cleanliness and Civilization: Public Health and the Making of Modern Japan and Korea, 1870-1910"

Tang, Jonathan Ming-En "A Stable Society in the Midst of Strife: Hunan Province and 'Warlord' China, 1912-28"

Waits, Hannah R. "Missionary-Minded: American Evangelicals and Power in a Postcolonial World"

Watson, Jesse "Paperwork before Paper: Law and Materiality in China's Early Empires, 221 BCE-220 CE"

Wright, Eloise "Re-Writing Dali: Literati and Local Identity in Dali, Yunnan, 1253-1675"

University of California, Davis

Dept. of History, 1 Shields Ave., Davis, CA 95616. 530.752.9825. Fax 530.752.5301. Email: lyyang@ucdavis.edu. Website: https:// history.ucdavis.edu/.

With a firm foundation in US and Latin American history, we have developed increasing strength in the history of the Middle East, South Asia, and Africa, along with robust programs in environmental history, gender history, the history of migrations, and the history of capitalism. Our faculty are deeply committed to their pedagogical and research mission as a service to the citizens of the Central Valley and the state of California.

Chair: Sally McKee
Director of Graduate Studies: Lorena Oropeza
Director of Undergraduate Studies: Gregory Downs
Degrees Offered: BA,MA,PhD
Academic Year System: Quarter
Areas of Specialization: US social/cultural/environmental, early modern and modern Europe, Asia and Africa, Latin America, crosscultural women and gender
Undergraduate Tuition (per academic year):
  In-State: $13896
  Out-of-State: $36780
Graduate Tuition (per academic year):
  In-State: $13109
  Out-of-State: $28211
Enrollment 2018-19:
  Undergraduate Majors: 321
  New Graduate Students: 9
  Full-time Graduate Students: 52
  Degrees in History: 125 BA, 6 MA, 5 PhD
  Students in Undergraduate Courses: 6167
  Students in Undergraduate Intro Courses: 1082
Undergraduate Addresses:
  Admissions: http://admissions.ucdavis.edu/
  Financial Aid: http://financialaid.ucdavis.edu/
Graduate Addresses:
  Admissions: http://gradstudies.ucdavis.edu/
  Financial Aid: http://gradstudies.ucdavis.edu/ssupport/

Full-time Faculty

Anooshahr, Ali (PhD, UCLA 2005; prof.) Islamic empires, Middle East, South Asia; aanooshahr@ucdavis.edu

Biale, David (PhD, UCLA 1977; prof. and Emmanuel Ringelblum Chair) Jewish intellectual and cultural, modern European intellectual and cultural, sexuality; dbiale@ucdavis.edu

Bossler, Beverly (PhD, California, Berkeley 1991; prof.) 10th- to 14th-century Chinese social and intellectual, Chinese women and family; bjbossler@ucdavis.edu

Campbell, Ian Wylie (PhD, Michigan 2011; assoc. prof.) Russian Empire and 19th-century Europe, comparative colonialisms and Central Asia, intellectual and cultural histories of imperialism; iwcampbell@ucdavis.edu

Chiang, Howard Hsueh-Hao (PhD, Princeton 2012; assoc. prof.) modern China, science and medicine, gender/sexuality/body; hhchiang@ucdavis.edu

Davis, Diana (PhD, California, Berkeley 2001; prof.) environmental, Middle East and North Africa, medicine and health; geovet@ucdavis.edu

Decker, Corrie R. (PhD, California, Berkeley 2007; assoc. prof.) 20th-century East Africa, education/girlhood/adolescence; crdecker@ucdavis.edu

Dickinson, Edward R. (PhD, California, Berkeley 1991; prof.) 20th-century European cultural and political, welfare state; erdickinson@ucdavis.edu

Downs, Gregory P. (PhD, Pennsylvania 2006; prof. and dir., undergrad. studies) 19th-century/Civil War era US, African American, political; gdowns@ucdavis.edu

El Shakry, Omnia (PhD, Princeton 2002; prof.) modern Middle East, colonialism, modern European intellectual; oselshakry@ucdavis.edu

Fahrenthold, Stacy D. (PhD, Northeastern 2014; asst. prof.) Middle East, labor migration, displacement/refugees, border studies, disasporas within and from the Middle East; sfahrenthold@ucdavis.edu

Hartigan-O'Connor, Ellen (PhD, Michigan 2003; assoc. prof.) 18th- and early 19th-century America, American women, social/cultural/economic; eoconnor@ucdavis.edu

Javers, Quinn Doyle (PhD, Stanford 2012; asst. prof.) late imperial and modern China, social and legal; qdjavers@ucdavis.edu

Jean-Baptiste, Rachel (PhD, Stanford 2005; assoc. prof.) gender, Central Africa, colonialism; rjeanbaptiste@ucdavis.edu

Kelman, Ari (PhD, Brown 1998; prof.) America, environmental; akelman@ucdavis.edu

Kim, Kyu Hyun (PhD, Harvard 1997; assoc. prof.) modern Japanese social and intellectual, China and Japan; kyukim@ucdavis.edu

Leroy, Justin (PhD, New York Univ. 2014; asst. prof.) African American, Atlantic, 19th-century US; jleroy@ucdavis.edu

Materson, Lisa G. (PhD, UCLA 2000; assoc. prof.) American women, African American, late 19th- and 20th-century US political; lgmaterson@ucdavis.edu

McKee, Sally (PhD, Toronto 1993; prof. and chair) late medieval, Mediterranean, ethnicity; sjmckee@ucdavis.edu

Miller, Susan Gilson (PhD, Michigan 1976; prof.) Sephardic Jewry, North Africa and Mediterranean; sgmiller@ucdavis.edu

Olmsted, Kathryn S. (PhD, California, Davis 1993; prof.) 20th-century US, political and cultural; ksolmsted@ucdavis.edu

Oropeza, Lorena (PhD, Cornell 1995; assoc. prof. and dir., grad. studies) 19th- and 20th-century Mexico and America, US foreign policy; lboropeza@ucdavis.edu

Perez Melendez, Jose Juan (PhD, Chicago 2016; asst. prof.) Brazil; jjperdez@ucdavis.edu

Rauchway, Eric (PhD, Stanford 1996; prof.) Progressive-era political and cultural; earauchway@ucdavis.edu

Resendez, Andres (PhD, Chicago 1997; prof.) Mexico, US Southwest, social; aresendez@ucdavis.edu

Saler, Michael T. (PhD, Stanford 1992; prof.) modern Europe, cultural and intellectual, 19th- and 20th-century Britain; mtsaler@ucdavis.edu

Schlotterbeck, Marian E. (PhD, Yale 2013; assoc. prof.) modern Latin America, Chile, social movements; mschlotterbeck@ucdavis.edu

Sen, Sudipta (PhD, Chicago 1994; prof.) late medieval and early colonial India, modern India, British Empire; ssen@ucdavis.edu

Smolenski, John J. (PhD, Pennsylvania 2001; assoc. prof.) colonial North America, cultural, religion; jsmolenski@ucdavis.edu

St. John, Rachel C. (PhD, Stanford 2005; assoc. prof.) US, transnational borderlands, North American West; rcstjohn@ucdavis.edu

Sterling-Harris, A. Katie (PhD, Johns Hopkins 2001; assoc. prof.) Spain and Portugal, Mexico and Central America, early modern Europe; akharris@ucdavis.edu

Stolzenberg, Daniel (PhD, Stanford 2003; assoc. prof.) early modern European intellectual, science, Italy; dstolz@ucdavis.edu

Stuart, Kathy (PhD, Yale 1993; assoc. prof.) early modern Europe, early modern Germany, social and cultural; kestuart@ucdavis.edu

Tezcan, Baki (PhD, Princeton 2001; assoc. prof.) medieval and early modern Middle East, making of premodern ethnic and racial identities, political ethics; btezcan@ucdavis.edu

Tsu, Cecilia M. (PhD, Stanford 2006; assoc. prof.) Asian American, California and West, agricultural; cmtsu@ucdavis.edu

Walker, Charles F. (PhD, Chicago 1992; prof.) modern Spanish America, Andes, social movements; cfwalker@ucdavis.edu

Warren, Louis S. (PhD, Yale 1993; prof. and W. Turrentine Jackson Chair) American West, California, environmental; lswarren@ucdavis.edu

Zientek, Adam Derek (PhD, Stanford 2012; asst. prof.) modern France and World War I, drugs and alcohol, medicine; azientek@ucdavis.edu

Retired/Emeritus Faculty

Borgen, Robert (PhD, Michigan 1978; prof. emeritus) early Japanese cultural/religion/literature, Sino-Japanese relations; rborgen@ucdavis.edu

Brody, David (PhD, Harvard 1958; prof. emeritus) emergence of modern America, labor, recent US

Cadden, Joan (PhD, Indiana 1971; prof. emeritus) medieval Europe, early science and medicine, sexuality; jcadden@ucdavis.edu

Crummey, Robert O. (PhD, Chicago 1964; prof. emeritus) 16th- and 17th-century Russia; rocrummey@ucdavis.edu

Hagen, William W. (PhD, Chicago 1971; prof. emeritus) modern Germany and east central Europe; wwhagen@ucdavis.edu

Holloway, Thomas H. (PhD, Wisconsin-Madison 1974; prof. emeritus) Latin America, Brazil, social; thholloway@ucdavis.edu

Landau, Norma B. (PhD, California, Berkeley 1974; prof. emeritus) 18th- and 19th-century England; nblandau@ucdavis.edu

Mann, Susan Louise (PhD, Stanford 1972; prof. emeritus) late imperial China, social and economic, women; slmann@ucdavis.edu

Margadant, Ted W. (PhD, Harvard 1972; prof. emeritus) 19th- and 20th-century France; twmargadant@ucdavis.edu

Metcalf, Barbara (PhD, California, Berkeley 1974; prof. emerita) Islamic, South Asia; bdmetcalf@ucdavis.edu

Price, Don C. (PhD, Harvard 1968; prof. emeritus) Chinese intellectual, 20th-century China; dcprice@ucdavis.edu

Rosen, Ruth E. (PhD, California, Berkeley 1976; prof. emeritus) women and family, American social and cultural; rerosen@ucdavis.edu

Schwab, Richard N. (PhD, Harvard 1954; prof. emeritus) early modern Europe, Enlightenment; rnschwab@ucdavis.edu

Spyridakis, Stylianos (PhD, UCLA 1966; prof. emeritus) ancient; svspyridakis@ucdavis.edu

Taylor, Alan S. (PhD, Brandeis 1986; prof. emeritus) early America, American West, colonial/revolutionary/early national America; astaylor@ucdavis.edu

Walker, Clarence E. (PhD, California, Berkeley 1976; prof. emeritus) American black 1450-present, 19th-century social and political; cewalker@ucdavis.edu

Willis, F. Roy (PhD, Stanford 1959; prof. emeritus) contemporary France, 20th-century Europe

Recently Awarded PhDs

Dries, Mark Pierre "Mercurial Colonialism: Indigenous Andeans and Spanish Power in Colonial Huancavelica, Peru"

Egli, Rebecca A. "The World of Our Dreams: Agricultural Explorers and the Promise of American Science, 1890-1945"

Judge, Rajbir Singh "Occult Intrigue: Sikhs, Anti-Colonial Resistance and the Theosophical Society"

Layton, Brandon "Children of Two Fires: Adoption, Diplomacy, and Change among the Choctaws and Chickasaws"

Lin, Zoe Shan "The Fractured Ricebowl: Food Dearth, Bureaucratic Infighting, and the State in Southern Song China, 1127-1279"

Tavolacci, Laura "Agriculture as Redemption: The Evangelical Building Blocks of Development"

University of California, Irvine

Dept. of History, 200 Murray Krieger Hall, Irvine, CA 92697-3275. 949.824.6521. Fax 949.824.2865. Email: history@uci.edu. Website: https://www.humanities.uci.edu/history/.

Our strong undergraduate program offers opportunities for internships, overseas study, and advanced research. Our small, high-quality graduate program combines emphases in specific regions of the world (America and Latin America, Asia, Europe, Middle East, and Africa) and specific thematic specialties (gender and sexuality; medicine and science; slavery, race, diaspora; empire and colonialism; environment).

Chair: Heidi Tinsman
Director of Graduate Studies: Houri Berberian
Director of Undergraduate Studies: Renee Raphael
Degrees Offered: BA,MA,PhD
Academic Year System: Quarter
Areas of Specialization: world, US, gender, Asia/Europe/Middle East/Africa, Latin America and Caribbean
Undergraduate Tuition (per academic year):
   In-State: $15035
   Out-of-State: $41717
Graduate Tuition (per academic year):
   In-State: $16985
   Out-of-State: $32087
Enrollment 2018-19:
   Undergraduate Majors: 175
   New Graduate Students: 6
   Full-time Graduate Students: 75
   Part-time Graduate Students: 3
   Degrees in History: 72 BA, 6 MA, 8 PhD
Undergraduate Addresses:
   Admissions: http://www.admissions.uci.edu/
   Financial Aid: http://www.ofas.uci.edu/
Graduate Addresses:
   Admissions: http://www.humanities.uci.edu/history/
   Financial Aid: http://www.ofas.uci.edu/

Affiliated Faculty

Brodbeck, David (PhD, Pennsylvania 1984; prof.; Music) Central European music, Anglo American popular music; david. brodbeck@uci.edu

Casavantes Bradford, Anita (PhD, California, San Diego 2010; assoc. prof.; Chicano-Latino Studies) cultural, race and ethnicity citizenship/immigration status/nationality; acasavan@uci.edu

Cole, Simon (PhD, Cornell 1998; prof.; Criminology, Law, and Society) science and technology, law, criminal justice; scole@uci.edu

Fujita-Rony, Dorothy P. (PhD, Yale 1996; assoc. prof.; Asian American Studies) US; dfr@uci.edu

Gilbertson-Thompson, Nicole (PhD, California, Irvine 2007; site dir., UCI Hist. Project) history education research and pedagogy, modern Europe, world; gilbertn@uci.edu

Gillman, Howard (PhD, UCLA 1988; prof. and chancellor; Political Science, Law, Criminology, Law and Society) constitutional law/history/theory/politics, Supreme Court politics, American political development; chancellor@uci.edu

Patel, Alka (PhD, Harvard 2000; assoc. prof.; Art History) art and architecture of South Asia/Iran/Central Asia/al-Andalus, early modern Andalusian/Islamicate diaspora in New World; alka. patel@uci.edu

Swain, Amanda Jeanne (PhD, Washington 2013; assoc. dir., UCI Humanities Commons) Soviet Union and late imperial Russia, east central Europe, theories of culture in Europe; ajswain@uci. edu

Thuma, Emily (PhD, NYU; asst. prof.; Gender & Sexuality Studies) 20th-century US gender/race/sexuality, feminist studies and queer studies, social movements and state; ethuma@uci.edu

Wu, Judy Tzu-Chun (PhD, Stanford 1998; prof.; Asian American Studies) Asian American, comparative racialization and immigration, empire and decolonization; j.wu@uci.edu

Full-time Faculty

Baum, Emily L. (PhD, California, San Diego 2013; assoc. prof.) modern China, psychology and medicine, insanity; emily. baum@uci.edu

Berberian, Houri (PhD, UCLA 1997; prof. and dir., grad. studies) Middle East, world, women; houri.berberian@uci.edu

Block, Sharon (PhD, Princeton 1995; prof.) early America, sexuality, gender; sblock@uci.edu

Borucki, Alex F. (PhD, Emory 2011; assoc. prof.) African diaspora and early modern Atlantic world, slave trade, colonial Latin America and black narratives; aborucki@uci.edu

Chaturvedi, Vinayak (PhD, Cambridge 2001; assoc. prof.) South Asia, social and intellectual; vinayak@uci.edu

Chen, Yong (PhD, Cornell 1993; prof.) Asian American, Pacific Rim, US race and ethnicity; y3chen@uci.edu

Coller, Ian (PhD, Melbourne 2006; assoc. prof.) Europe and Muslim world, Napoleonic Europe and French Revolution, Revolutionary age global; i.coller@uci.edu

Daryaee, Touraj (PhD, UCLA 1999; prof.) ancient and medieval Iran; tdaryaee@uci.edu

Farmer, Sarah B. (PhD, California, Berkeley 1992; assoc. prof.) 20th-century European cultural; sfarmer@uci.edu

Fedman, David (PhD, Stanford 2015; asst. prof.) modern and early modern Japan, modern Korea, global environmental; dfedman@uci.edu

Guo, Qitao (PhD, California, Berkeley 1994; prof.) Ming-Qing China; guoq@uci.edu

Haynes, Douglas M. (PhD, California, Berkeley 1992; prof.) modern Britain; dhaynes@uci.edu

Highsmith, Andrew Robert (PhD, Michigan 2009; assoc. prof.) US since 1865, cities and suburbs in American life, urban policy

Igler, David B. (PhD, California, Berkeley 1997; prof.) US environmental, American West, Pacific; digler@uci.edu

Imada, Adria L. (PhD, NYU 2003; assoc. prof.) indigenous and Pacific Islands studies, race/gender/medicine, visual studies; aimada@uci.edu

James, Winston (PhD, London Sch. Econ. 1993; prof.) Caribbean, African American, African diaspora; wjames@uci.edu

Lehmann, Matthias B. (PhD, Freie, Berlin 2002; prof. and Teller Family Chair) early modern and modern Jewish, Sephardic studies; m.lehmann@uci.edu

Levine, Mark A. (PhD, NYU 1999; prof.) modern Middle East, Islamic studies, empire and globalization; mlevine@uci.edu

Malczewski, Joan (PhD, Columbia 2002; assoc. prof.) philanthropy and education, US

McLoughlin, Nancy A. (PhD, California, Santa Barbara 2005; assoc. prof.) late medieval Europe, intellectual, gender; nmclough@uci.edu

Millward, Jessica (PhD, UCLA 2003; assoc. prof.) US slavery, African American studies, women and gender; millward@uci.edu

Mitchell, Laura J. (PhD, UCLA 2001; assoc. prof.) Africa, colonial, social; mitchell@uci.edu

Morrissey, Susan K. (PhD, California, Berkeley 1993; prof.) Russia and world, political violence and terrorism, suicide; susan.morrissey@uci.edu

O'Toole, Rachel Sarah (PhD, North Carolina, Chapel Hill 2001; assoc. prof.) colonial Latin America, Andes, African diaspora; rotoole@uci.edu

Perlman, Allison J. (PhD, Texas, Austin 2007; assoc. prof.; Film and Media Studies) broadcasting and American social movements, media law/policy/activism, popular memory; aperlman@uci.edu

Philip, Kavita Sara (PhD, Cornell 1996; assoc. prof.) science and technology, environment, gender; kphilip@uci.edu

Raphael, Renee J. (PhD, Princeton 2009; assoc. prof. and dir., undergrad. studies) early modern science and technology, science/religion/visual culture, Renaissance and early modern Italian book; renee.raphael@uci.edu

Robertson, James MacEwan (PhD, NYU, 2014; asst. prof.) eastern European and Balkans intellectual and cultural, political, economic and aesthetic philosophies, modernism and discourses of modernity, global socialism, imagined geographies, urban history and theory; jamesmr1@uci.edu

Rosas, Ana E. (PhD, Southern California 2006; assoc. prof.; Chicano/Latino Studies) Chicano/a, immigration, gender; arosas1@uci.edu

Schields, Chelsea Angela (PhD, Graduate Center, CUNY 2017; asst. prof.) modern Europe, Caribbean, decolonization, gender and sexuality, race, global; cschield@uci.edu

Seed, Patricia (PhD, Wisconsin, Madison 1980; prof.) Spanish and Portuguese overseas, cartography, world; seed5@uci.edu

Tinsman, Heidi E. (PhD, Yale 1996; prof. and chair) Latin America, Chile, gender and sexuality; hetinsma@uci.edu

Topik, Steven C. (PhD, Texas, Austin 1978; prof.) world commodities and coffee, Latin America, Brazil; sctopik@uci.edu

Wasserstrom, Jeffrey N. (PhD, California, Berkeley 1989; Chancellor's Prof.) modern China, cultural, urban; jwassers@uci.edu

Part-time Faculty

Duncan, Robert H. (PhD, California, Irvine 2001; lect.) Latin America

McKenna, Joseph (PhD, Fordham 1987; lect.) religion; mckenna@uci.edu

Ragsdale, Kathryn (PhD, Chicago 1991; lect.) Japan; kragsdal@uci.edu

Retired/Emeritus Faculty

Chenut, Helen Harden (PhD, Paris VII 1988; lect. emeritus) European social movements, feminism/socialism/political rights; hchenut@uci.edu

Fahs, Alice (PhD, NYU 1993; prof. emeritus) US intellectual and cultural; afahs@uci.edu

Frank, Richard I. (PhD, California, Berkeley 1965; assoc. prof. emeritus) Roman Empire, political, literature; rifrank@uci.edu

Given, James B. (PhD, Stanford 1976; prof. emeritus) medieval social and political; jbgiven@uci.edu

Hill, Lamar M. (PhD, London 1968; prof. emeritus) Tudor-Stuart Britain, legal administration, English and Continental Reformations; lmhill@uci.edu

Hufbauer, Karl (PhD, California, Berkeley 1970; prof. emeritus) physical sciences since 1600; hufbauer@uci.edu

Jacobson, Jon S. (PhD, California, Berkeley 1966; prof. emeritus) 20th-century European international, Germany; jsjacobs@uci.edu

Mally, Lynn (PhD, California, Berkeley 1985; prof. emeritus) Soviet Union; lmally@uci.edu

Moeller, Robert G. (PhD, California, Berkeley 1980; prof. emeritus) modern Germany, European women, social; rgmoelle@uci.edu

Nelson, Keith L. (PhD, California, Berkeley 1965; Edward A. Dickson Prof. emeritus) American foreign relations, Cold War, war and society; klnelson@uci.edu

Olin, Spencer C. (PhD, Claremont Graduate 1964; prof. emeritus) recent American social/economic/political, California and American West; scolin@uci.edu

Rodriguez, Jaime E. (PhD, Texas, Austin 1970; prof. emeritus) Latin America, political culture, Atlantic revolutions; jerodrig@uci.edu

Rosenberg, Emily S. (PhD, SUNY, Stony Brook 1973; prof. emeritus) US and world; e.rosenberg@uci.edu

Ruiz, Vicki L. (PhD, Stanford 1982; dist. prof. emeritus; Chicano/Latino Studies) 20th-century US, Chicana/o studies, Latina, oral narratives, gender studies, labor, California and West; vruiz@uci.edu

Salinger, Sharon V. (PhD, UCLA 1980; prof. emeritus) colonial America, social, labor and economic; salinger@uci.edu

Tackett, Timothy N. (PhD, Stanford 1973; prof. emeritus) Old Regime France, French Revolution, socio-cultural and religious; ttackett@uci.edu

Thorne, Tanis C. (PhD, UCLA 1987; lect. emeritus) Native American, California Indian; tcthorne@uci.edu

Walthall, Anne (PhD, Chicago 1979; prof. emeritus) East Asia, Japan, women; walthall@uci.edu

Wiener, Jon (PhD, Harvard 1973; prof. emeritus) US since 1945; wiener@uci.edu

Recently Awarded PhDs

Combs, Matthew Tyler "Camphor, a Plastic History: China, Taiwan, and Celluloid, 1868-1937"

Goodale, Sif Ida "Nordby, Sønderho, and Marstal: Global Maritime Communities in the Late 19th and Early 20th Centuries"

Olomi, Ali Ahmad "Becoming Muslim: Homeland, Identity, and the Making of Perso-Islamic World"

Pascoe, Stephen "Contesting Concessions: Infrastructure, Imperialism, and the Struggle for Sovereignty in Syria, 1908-46"

Rad, Assal "The State of Resistance: National Identity Formation In Modern Iran"

University of California, Los Angeles

Dept. of History, 6265 Bunche Hall, Box 951473, Los Angeles, CA 90095-1473. 310.825.4601. Fax 310.206.9630. Email: info@history.ucla.edu. Website: https://history.ucla.edu/.

The goal of the UCLA History Department is to provide cross-temporal and cross-cultural perspectives and to bring historical knowledge, depth, and context to our students and to the broader public with whom we constantly interact. That mission informs our scholarship and our teaching and it calls us to engage with our students beyond the classroom and with the public beyond the university.

Chair: Carla G. Pestana

Director of Graduate Studies: Peter J. Hudson
Degrees Offered: BA,MA,CPhil,PhD
Academic Year System: Quarter
Areas of Specialization: Africa, Asia, US, Europe, Latin America
Undergraduate Tuition (per academic year):
In-State: $15940
Out-of-State: $44932
Graduate Tuition (per academic year):
In-State: $16948
Out-of-State: $32050
Enrollment 2018-19:
Undergraduate Majors: 712
New Graduate Students: 10
Full-time Graduate Students: 98
Degrees in History: 299 BA, 9 MA, 19 PhD
Undergraduate Addresses:
Admissions: http://www.ucla.edu/admission/undergraduate-admission
Financial Aid: http://www.ucla.edu/admission/affordability
Graduate Addresses:
Admissions: http://www.ucla.edu/admission/graduate-admission
Financial Aid: http://www.ucla.edu/admission/affordability

Adjunct Faculty

Alexander, Amir (PhD, Stanford 1996; adj. assoc. prof.) science, mathematics and cultural context; amiralex@ucla.edu
Corey, Mary F. (PhD, UCLA 1996; sr. continuing lect.) US; mcorey@ucla.edu
Langdon, John S. (PhD, UCLA 1978; continuing lect.) late antiquity, Byzantium; jlangdon@ucla.edu

Full-time Faculty

Apter, Andrew (PhD, Yale 1987; prof.) West Africa, African diaspora, anthropology; aapter@history.ucla.edu
Aron, Stephen (PhD, California, Berkeley 1990; prof.) colonial America, early Republic, American West; saron@history.ucla.edu
Aslanian, Sebouh David (PhD, Columbia 2007; assoc. prof. and Richard Hovannisian Chair) Armenian diaspora; saslanian@history.ucla.edu
Avila, Eric R. (PhD, California, Berkeley 1997; prof.) post-WWII US urban; eavila@ucla.edu
Baldwin, Peter (PhD, Harvard 1986; prof.) modern Europe; pbaldwin@history.ucla.edu
Brown, Scot D. (PhD, Cornell 1999; assoc. prof.) African American studies; sbrown@history.ucla.edu
de Chadarevian, Soraya (PhD, Konstanz 1988; prof.) science; chadarevian@history.ucla.edu
Derby, Robin (PhD, Chicago 1998; assoc. prof.) Latin American studies; derby@history.ucla.edu
Ford, Caroline C. (PhD, Chicago 1987; prof. and Peter Reill Chair) modern France, Europe; cford@history.ucla.edu
Frank, Stephen (PhD, Brown 1987; assoc. prof.) Russia, European social, peasant studies; frank@history.ucla.edu
Gelvin, James L. (PhD, Harvard 1992; prof.) modern Near East; gelvin@history.ucla.edu
Goldberg, Jessica L. (PhD, Columbia 2005; assoc. prof.) medieval; goldberg@history.ucla.edu
Goldman, Andrea S. (PhD, California, Berkeley 2005; assoc. prof.) modern China; goldman@history.ucla.edu
Green, Nile (PhD, London 2002; prof. and Ibn Khaldun Chair) South Asia, Islamic studies; green@history.ucla.edu
Higbie, Frank Tobias (PhD, Illinois, Urbana-Champaign 2000; prof.) US, working-class and immigrant intellectuals; higbie@history.ucla.edu

Hirano, Katsuya (PhD, Chicago 2004; assoc. prof.) modern Japan; hirano@history.ucla.edu
Hudson, Peter James (PhD, NYU 2007; assoc. prof. and dir., grad. studies) African American; pjhudson@ucla.edu
Jacob, Margaret C. (PhD, Cornell 1968; prof. emeritus) early modern Europe, history and sociology of science; mjacob@history.ucla.edu
Jacoby, Russell (PhD, Rochester 1974; prof.-in-residence) 20th-century European and American intellectual, education; rjacoby@history.ucla.edu
Kelley, Robin D. G. (PhD, UCLA 1987; prof. and Gary B. Nash Chair) 20th-century America, African American activists and artists; rdkelley@history.ucla.edu
Lal, Vinay (PhD, Chicago 1992; prof.) South Asia, Indian social/political/cultural/literary; vlal@history.ucla.edu
Lydon, Ghislaine E. (PhD, Michigan State 2000; assoc. prof.) 19th- and 20th-century western Africa; lydon@history.ucla.edu
Lytle Hernandez, Kelly (PhD, UCLA 2002; prof.) 20th-century US borderlands; hernandez@history.ucla.edu
Madley, Benjamin (PhD, Yale 2009; assoc. prof.) American Indian; madley@history.ucla.edu
Marino, Katherine Marie (PhD, Stanford 2013; asst. prof.) women, gender and sexuality, Latin America and US; kmarino@history.ucla.edu
Marotti, William (PhD, Chicago 2001; assoc. prof.) Japan, modern; marotti@history.ucla.edu
Matsumoto, Valerie J. (PhD, Stanford 1985; prof. and Aratani Chair, Japanese American Incarceration, Redress and Community) Japanese American, 20th-century US, women; matsumot@history.ucla.edu
McClendon, Muriel C. (PhD, Stanford 1990; assoc. prof.) Britain 1485-present; mcclendo@history.ucla.edu
Meranze, Michael (PhD, California, Berkeley 1987; prof.) US, US intellectual and legal, early America; meranze@history.ucla.edu
Morony, Michael G. (PhD, UCLA 1972; prof.) Near East; morony@history.ucla.edu
Myers, David N. (PhD, Columbia 1991; prof. and Kahn Chair) modern Jewish intellectual and cultural; myers@history.ucla.edu
Nasiali, Minayo Anne (PhD, Michigan 2010; assoc. prof.) modern France, Empire, welfare state; mnasiali@history.ucla.edu
Norberg, Kathryn (PhD, Yale 1978; assoc. prof.) European women, early modern France; knorberg@ucla.edu
Perez-Montesinos, Fernando (PhD, Georgetown 2015; asst. prof.) modern Mexico, modern Latin American indigenous people, Latin American social and environmental; fperez@history.ucla.edu
Pestana, Carla G. (PhD, UCLA 1987; prof.; Joyce Appleby Chair; and dept. chair) colonial America, British Atlantic world, Carribean; cgpestana@history.ucla.edu
Phillips, David D. (PhD, Michigan 2000; prof.) ancient Greece; phillips@history.ucla.edu
Porter, Theodore M. (PhD, Princeton 1981; prof.) science, statistics; tporter@history.ucla.edu
Reiff, Janice L. (PhD, Washington 1981; prof.) 20th-century US, quantitative methods; jreiff@ucla.edu
Robinson, Geoffrey B. (PhD, Cornell 1992; prof.) Southeast Asia, Balinese and Indonesian political, human rights in Southeast Asia; robinson@history.ucla.edu
Ruiz, Teofilo F. (PhD, Princeton 1974; prof. and Wellman Chair) medieval, Spain; tfruiz@history.ucla.edu
Salman, Michael A. (PhD, Stanford 1993; assoc. prof.) US, comparative slavery and emancipation, Philippines; salman@history.ucla.edu

Silverman, Debora Leah (PhD, Princeton 1983; prof. and Pres. Chair) 19th-century Europe, cultural and intellectual, France; silverma@history.ucla.edu

Stacey, Peter (PhD, Cambridge 2000; assoc. prof.) early modern Europe, Italian Renaissance; pstacey@history.ucla.edu

Stein, Sarah A. (PhD, Stanford 1999; prof. and Maurice Amado Chair) modern Jewish; sstein@history.ucla.edu

Stevenson, Brenda E. (PhD, Yale 1991; prof. and Nickoll Family Chair) US, African American, US South; stevenso@history.ucla.edu

Subrahmanyam, Sanjay (PhD, Delhi 1987; prof. and Irving and Jean Stone Chair) South Asia, India; subrahma@history.ucla.edu

Summerhill, William, III (PhD, Stanford 1995; prof. and Burns Chair) Brazil, economic; wrs@history.ucla.edu

Terraciano, Kevin (PhD, UCLA 1994; prof.) colonial Latin America; terra@history.ucla.edu

Terrall, Mary (PhD, UCLA 1987; prof.) science, gender, Enlightenment; terrall@history.ucla.edu

Tutino, Stefania (PhD, Scuola Normale Superiore 2003; prof.) Europe, religion; tutino@history.ucla.edu

Urdank, Albion Mier (PhD, Columbia 1983; assoc. prof.) 18th- to 20th-century British economic and social; aurdank@history.ucla.edu

von Glahn, Richard (PhD, Yale 1983; prof.) China; vonglahn@history.ucla.edu

Waugh, Joan (PhD, UCLA 1993; prof.) US social, Civil War, philanthropy; jwaugh@history.ucla.edu

Waugh, Scott L. (PhD, London 1975; prof.; exec. vice chancellor; and provost) medieval England; scottw@college.ucla.edu

Wong, R. Bin (PhD, Harvard 1984; prof.) modern China, world; wong@history.ucla.edu

Worger, William H. (PhD, Yale 1982; prof.) African social and economic, southern Africa, comparative; worger@history.ucla.edu

Yeager, Mary A. (PhD, Johns Hopkins 1973; prof.) US economic; yeager@ucla.edu

Yirush, Craig Bryan (PhD, Johns Hopkins 2004; assoc. prof.) colonial America; yirush@history.ucla.edu

Joint/Cross Appointments

Bell, Stephen (PhD, Toronto 1991; prof.; Geography) sbell@geog.ucla.edu

Braslow, Joel (PhD, UCLA 1994; MD, Loma Linda 1984; prof.-in-residence; Psychiatry and Biobehavioral Science) medicine; jbraslow@ucla.edu

Duncan, John (PhD, Washington 1988; prof.; East Asian Languages and Cultures) Korea; duncan@humnet.ucla.edu

Finch, Aisha K. (PhD, NYU 2007; assoc. prof.; Gender, African American Studies) US, gender, African American; akfinch@ucla.edu

Pagden, Anthony (PhD, Oxford 1980; prof.; Political Science) Europe; pagden@ucla.edu

Traweek, Sharon (PhD, California, Santa Cruz 1982; assoc. prof.; Center for Women's Studies) modern physics, anthropology of science; traweek@history.ucla.edu

Yoo, David K. (PhD, Yale 1994; prof.; vice provost) US, Asian American Studies; dkyoo@ucla.edu

Retired/Emeritus Faculty

Alpers, Edward A. (PhD, London 1966; prof. emeritus) eastern Africa, African diaspora, Indian Ocean; alpers@history.ucla.edu

Anderson, Perry (BA, Oxford 1959; prof. emeritus) modern Europe, Marxism; fanderso@ucla.edu

Bartchy, S. Scott (PhD, Harvard 1971; sr. lect. emeritus) religious, early Christian, New Testament; bartchy@history.ucla.edu

Berend, Ivan (PhD, Budapest 1958; prof. emeritus) modern European economic; iberend@history.ucla.edu

Bernhardt, Kathryn (PhD, Stanford 1984; prof. emeritus) late imperial and modern China, women's studies; bernhard@history.ucla.edu

Bloch, Ruth (PhD, California, Berkeley 1980; prof. emeritus) US, early American intellectual, religious; bloch@history.ucla.edu

Bolle, Kees W. (PhD, Chicago 1961; prof. emeritus) religion; kbolle@gwi.net

Brenner, Robert P. (PhD, Princeton 1970; prof. emeritus) England, early modern European social and economic, social theory; brenner@history.ucla.edu

Buccellati, Giorgio (PhD, Chicago 1965; prof. emeritus) ancient Near East; buccella@ucla.edu

Chambers, Mortimer (PhD, Harvard 1954; prof. emeritus) ancient Greece; chambers@history.ucla.edu

Copenhaver, Brian P. (PhD, Kansas 1970; prof. emeritus) brianc@college.ucla.edu

Dallek, Robert (PhD, Columbia 1964; prof. emeritus) US; rdallek@ucla.edu

DuBois, Ellen C. (PhD, Northwestern 1978; prof. emeritus) US women; edubois@ucla.edu

Ehret, Christopher (PhD, Northwestern 1968; prof. emeritus) Africa, early southern and eastern Africa, linguistics; ehret@history.ucla.edu

Elman, Benjamin A. (PhD, Pennsylvania 1980; prof. emeritus) Chinese intellectual; elman@history.ucla.edu

Frank, Robert G., Jr. (PhD, Harvard 1971; prof. emeritus) biological sciences, medicine; rfrankj@ucla.edu

Friedlander, Saul (PhD, Geneva, Switzerland 1963; prof. and 1939 Club Chair emeritus) modern Germany, Nazi Germany, modern Jewish; friedlan@history.ucla.edu

Geary, Patrick J. (PhD, Yale 1974; prof. emeritus) early medieval France, social and cultural; geary@ucla.edu

Getty, J. Arch (PhD, Boston Coll. 1979; prof. emeritus) Russia; getty@ucla.edu

Ginzburg, Carlo (OPhD, Pisa, Italy 1961; prof. emeritus) Italian Renaissance, early modern Europe; ginzburg@history.ucla.edu

Gomez-Quinones, Juan (PhD, UCLA 1972; prof. emeritus) Chicano, Latin American intellectual, social change and nationalism; quinones@history.ucla.edu

Hill, Robert A. (MS, West Indies 1976; prof. emeritus) 20th-century African American; rhill@history.ucla.edu

Hines, Thomas S., Jr. (PhD, Wisconsin, Madison 1971; prof. emeritus) US urban architectural and cultural; hines@history.ucla.edu

Hovannisian, Richard G. (PhD, UCLA 1966; prof. emeritus) Armenia, post-World War I Soviet-Turkish-Armenian relations, Armenian Republic 1918-20; hovannis@history.ucla.edu

Howe, Daniel Walker (PhD, California, Berkeley 1966; prof. emeritus) US; howe@history.ucla.edu

Huang, Philip C. (PhD, Washington 1966; prof. emeritus) modern and contemporary China; huang@history.ucla.edu

Hunt, Lynn A. (PhD, Stanford 1973; prof. emeritus) early modern Europe, France, late modern Europe since 1789; lhunt@history.ucla.edu

Jacoby, Sanford (PhD, California, Berkeley 1981; prof. emeritus) 20th-century US business, economic and labor; sanford.jacoby@anderson.ucla.edu

Keddie, Nikki R. (PhD, California, Berkeley 1955; prof. emeritus) Near East, social, political; keddie@history.ucla.edu

Krekic, Barisa (PhD, Serbian Acad. 1954; prof. emeritus) eastern Europe, Middle Ages Balkan Slavs, Byzantine; bkrekic4@hotmail.com

Laslett, John H. M. (DPhil, Oxford 1962; prof. emeritus) US, comparative Euro-American socialism and radical, labor; laslett@history.ucla.edu

Lauerhass, Ludwig, Jr. (PhD, UCLA 1972; lect. emeritus; librarian, Univ. Research Library and Latin American Center) Latin America, Brazil since 1889, nationalism; lauerhas@ucla.edu

Loewenberg, Peter J. (PhD, California, Berkeley 1966; prof. emeritus) modern Germany and Austria, European cultural and intellectual, psychohistory; peterl@ucla.edu

Marsot, Afaf (DPhil, Oxford 1963; prof. emeritus) modern Near East; amarsot@ucla.edu

Martines, Lauro R. (PhD, Harvard 1960; prof. emeritus) Italian Renaissance; martines@history.ucla.edu

Mellor, Ronald J. (PhD, Princeton 1967; prof. emeritus) ancient, Hellenistic Greece, Rome; mellor@history.ucla.edu

Moya, Jose C. (PhD, Rutgers 1988; prof. emeritus) 19th-century Latin America; moya@history.ucla.edu

Nash, Gary Baring (PhD, Princeton 1964; prof. emeritus) colonial American social, American Indian; gnash@ucla.edu

Notehelfer, Fred G. (PhD, Princeton 1968; prof. emeritus) Japan, modern social and intellectual, borrowed ideas and institutions in traditional societies; notehelf@history.ucla.edu

O'Brien, Patricia (PhD, Columbia 1973; prof. emeritus) modern France, Europe; pobrien@college.ucla.edu

Ooms, Herman (PhD, Chicago 1973; prof. emeritus) premodern Japan; ooms@history.ucla.edu

Posnansky, Merrick (PhD, Nottingham, UK 1956; prof. emeritus) African prehistory and archaeology; merrick@history.ucla.edu

Reill, Peter H. (PhD, Northwestern 1969; prof. emeritus) modern Europe, intellectual, Germany; reill@humnet.ucla.edu

Rouse, Richard H. (PhD, Cornell 1963; prof. emeritus) medieval, intellectual and literary, paleography; rouse@history.ucla.edu

Sabean, David Warren (PhD, Wisconsin-Madison 1969; prof. emeritus) European social and cultural, 16th and 19th centuries; dsabean@history.ucla.edu

Symcox, Geoffrey W. (PhD, UCLA 1967; prof. emeritus) modern Europe, France and Italy 1500-1800, early modern European war and society; symcox@history.ucla.edu

Weiss, Richard (PhD, Columbia 1966; prof. emeritus) 20th-century US social and intellectual, Great Depression; rweiss@history.ucla.edu

Wilkie, James W. (PhD, California, Berkeley 1966; prof. emeritus) Latin America, 20th-century quantitative and oral, Mexico/Bolivia/Costa Rica/Venezuela; wilkie@ucla.edu

Wise, M. Norton (PhD, Princeton 1977; PhD, Washington State 1967; prof. emeritus) science, physics, culture; nortonw@history.ucla.edu

Wohl, Robert A. (PhD, Princeton 1963; prof. emeritus) modern Europe, modern European cities cultural, late 19th- and 20th-century social thought and movements; rwohl@ucla.edu

Recently Awarded PhDs

Ballor, Grace "Agents of Integration: Multinational Firms and the European Union"

Casper, Michael "Strangers and Sojourners: The Politics of Jewish Belonging in Lithuania, 1914-40"

Degani, Arnon Yehuda "Both Arab and Israeli: The Subordinate Integration of Palestinian Arabs into Israeli Society, 1948-67"

Deriev, Denis Alexander "Augustus the Machiavellian Prince: Pareto's Theory of Elites and the Changing Models of Honor Acquisition and Conflict Resolution in the Early Roman Empire"

DeSanto, Ingrid "Righteous Citizens: The Lynching of Johan and Cornelis DeWitt,The Hague, Collective Violence, and the Myth of Tolerance in the Dutch Golden Age, 1650-72"

Katin, William Maurice "A Re-Assessment of Aryanization of Large Jewish Companies in Hitler's Reich, 1933-35: The Role of Conservative, Non-Nazi Businessmen"

Lewis, Pauline Lucy "Wired Ottomans: A Sociotechnical History of the Telegraph and the Modern Ottoman Empire, 1855-1911"

McCollum, Jonathan Claymore "The Anti-Colonial Empire: Ottoman Mobilization and Resistance in the Italo-Turkish War, 1911-12"

McCullough, Patrick G. "Apocalypse and Difference: Rereading Cultural Boundaries in Early Christian Texts"

Naqvi, Naveena "Writing the Inter-Imperial World in Afghan North India, c. 1774-1857"

Schneider, Winter Rae "Free of Everything Save Independence: Property, Personhood and the Archive in 19th-Century Haiti"

Woodhouse, Adam J. "Liberty and Empire in Florentine Renaissance Republicanism: from Salutati to Machiavelli"

University of California, Riverside

Dept. of History, 1212 HMNSS Bldg., 900 University Ave., Riverside, CA 92521-0204. 951.827.5401. Fax 951.827.5299. Email: history@ucr.edu. Website: https://history.ucr.edu/.

The UC Riverside History department is a dynamic department that is deeply committed to undergraduate and graduate training. We seek to produce highly qualified professional historians with exceptionally strong research and teaching skills, a breadth of historical knowledge, and an understanding of the variety of methods and approaches that historians employ.

Chair: Thomas Cogswell
Director of Graduate Studies: Steven Hackel
Director of Undergraduate Studies: James Brennan
Degrees Offered: BA,MA,PhD
Academic Year System: Quarter
Areas of Specialization: America since 1607, ancient Mediterranean and early modern/modern Europe, Native American, Latin America, public
Undergraduate Tuition (per academic year):
  In-State: $14799
  Out-of-State: $37677
Graduate Tuition (per academic year):
  In-State: $16198
  Out-of-State: $31300
Enrollment 2018-19:
  Undergraduate Majors: 437
  New Graduate Students: 12
  Full-time Graduate Students: 60
  Degrees in History: 180 BA, 10 MA, 12 PhD
Undergraduate Addresses:
  Admissions: http://admissions.ucr.edu/
  Financial Aid: http://finaid.ucr.edu/
Graduate Addresses:
  Admissions: http://history.ucr.edu/graduate/admissions.html
  Financial Aid: https://history.ucr.edu/financial-information

Full-time Faculty

Adelusi-Adeluyi, Ademide (PhD, NYU 2015; asst. prof.) Africa, urban, historical cartography; ademide.adelusi-adeluyi@ucr.edu

Asaka, Megan (PhD, Yale 2014; asst. prof.) Asian American, public; megan.asaka@ucr.edu

Benjamin, Jody (PhD, Harvard 2016; asst. prof.) West Africa; jody.benjamin@ucr.edu

Brennan, James P. (PhD, Harvard 1988; prof. and dir., undergrad. studies) 20th-century Argentina and Brazil, modern Latin America; james.brennan@ucr.edu

Chia, Lucille (PhD, Columbia 1996; prof.) traditional China, social and cultural; lucille.chia@ucr.edu

Cogswell, Thomas (PhD, Washington, St. Louis 1983; prof. and chair) early modern England; thomas.cogswell@ucr.edu

Dubcovsky, Alejandra (PhD, California, Berkeley 2011; assoc. prof.) early America, American Indians, Spanish borderlands; alejandra.dubcovsky@ucr.edu

Eacott, Jonathan P. (PhD, Michigan 2008; assoc. prof.) Britain 1750-1990, early America, colonialism; jonathan.eacott@ucr.edu

Goldberg, Ann E. (PhD, UCLA 1992; prof.) modern Europe, gender and cultural, Germany; ann.goldberg@ucr.edu

Gorecki, Piotr S. (PhD, Chicago 1988; prof.) medieval Europe, Poland and eastern Europe, European legal and economic; piotr.gorecki@ucr.edu

Graninger, C. Denver (PhD, Cornell 2006; assoc. prof.) ancient Greece and Rome, material culture; charles.graninger@ucr.edu

Gudis, Catherine (PhD, Yale 1999; assoc. prof.) American studies, consumer culture, public history and preservation; catherine.gudis@ucr.edu

Hackel, Steven W. (PhD, Cornell 1994; prof. and dir., grad. studies) American West, colonial America, American Indian; shackel@ucr.edu

Haskell, Alexander B. (PhD, Johns Hopkins 2005; assoc. prof.) early America; alexander.haskell@ucr.edu

Head, Randolph C. (PhD, Virginia 1992; prof.) early modern Europe, Switzerland, archives; randolph.head@ucr.edu

Hughes, Jennifer S. (PhD, Grad. Theological Union 2005; assoc. prof.) religions, Latin America; jennifer.hughes@ucr.edu

Kugel, Rebecca (PhD, UCLA 1986; assoc. prof.) US social, American Indian; rebecca.kugel@ucr.edu

Lehmann, Philipp N. (PhD, Harvard 2014; asst. prof.) environmental, science and technology, modern Europe and Africa; philipp.lehmann@ucr.edu

Lentacker, Antoine (PhD, Yale 2016; asst. prof.) modern Europe, science/medicine/technology, media studies; antoine.lentacker@ucr.edu

Levy, Juliette (PhD, UCLA 2003; assoc. prof.) modern Mexico, Latin America, economic; juliette.levy@ucr.edu

Lloyd, Brian D. (PhD, Michigan 1991; assoc. prof.) American cultural and intellectual, American radicalism; brian.lloyd@ucr.edu

McGarry, Molly K. (PhD, NYU 1999; assoc. prof.) 19th-century US, sexuality, social movements; molly.mcgarry@ucr.edu

McPherson, Natasha L. (PhD, Emory 2011; asst. prof.) African American, black family and community development, women's influence on identity politics and citizenship rights; natasha.mcpherson@ucr.edu

Michels, Georg B. (PhD, Harvard 1991; prof.) imperial Russia, eastern Europe, religion; georg.michels@ucr.edu

Patch, Robert W. (PhD, Princeton 1979; prof.) Mexico, Central America; robert.patch@ucr.edu

Salzman, Michele R. (PhD, Bryn Mawr 1981; prof.) ancient Greece and Rome, late antiquity, social and religious; michele.salzman@ucr.edu

Simmons, Dana J. (PhD, Chicago 2004; assoc. prof.) modern France, modern Europe, science and technology; dana.simmons@ucr.edu

Tomoff, Kiril (PhD, Chicago 2001; prof.) Russia and Soviet Union, modern Europe, music; kiril.tomoff@ucr.edu

Trafzer, Clifford E. (PhD, Oklahoma State 1973; Dist. Prof. and Rupert Costo Chair) Native American social and cultural, American West, oral traditions; clifford.trafzer@ucr.edu

Weber, Devra (PhD, UCLA 1986; assoc. prof.) 20th-century US, labor, Mexicans in US; devra.weber@ucr.edu

Zarinebaf, Fariba (PhD, Chicago 1991; prof.) Ottoman Empire, social, Middle East; fariba.zarinebaf@ucr.edu

Joint/Cross Appointments

Biggs, David A. (PhD, Washington 2004; prof.; Sch. Public Policy) Southeast Asia, Vietnam, environmental; david.biggs@ucr.edu

Part-time Faculty

Chrissanthos, Stefan G. (PhD, Southern California 1999; lect.) ancient Greece and Rome; stefan.chrissanthos@ucr.edu

Retired/Emeritus Faculty

Barkin, Kenneth David (PhD, Brown 1966; prof. emeritus) recent Europe, modern Germany, material culture; kenneth.barkin@ucr.edu

Burgess, Larry E. (PhD, Claremont Grad. 1972; adj. prof. emeritus; A. K. Smiley Library) local, archival management; admin@aksmiley.org

Cortes, Carlos E. (PhD, New Mexico 1969; prof. emeritus) Latin America, Mexican American, mass media; carlos.cortes@ucr.edu

Franklin, V. P. (PhD, Chicago 1975; Dist. Prof. and President's Chair emeritus) African American, education; vp.franklin@ucr.edu

Kea, Ray A. (PhD, London 1974; prof. emeritus) West Africa, Gold Coast and Asante; ray.kea@ucr.edu

Kent, Dale V. (PhD, London 1971; prof. emeritus) Renaissance, social, Florence; dale.kent@ucr.edu

Ransom, Roger L. (PhD, Washington 1963; prof. emeritus) US Civil War, economic, world; roger.ransom@ucr.edu

Ravitch, Norman (PhD, Princeton 1962; prof. emeritus) 18th-century Europe, French Revolution, French Catholicism

Thompson, Mack E. (PhD, Brown 1955; prof. emeritus) early America

Tobey, Ronald C. (PhD, Cornell 1969; prof. emeritus) science/technology/intellectual, 19th- and 20th-century US; ronald.tobey@ucr.edu

Wall, Irwin M. (PhD, Columbia 1968; prof. emeritus) recent Europe, modern France, socialism; irwin.wall@ucr.edu

Wetherell, Charles (PhD, New Hampshire 1980; prof. emeritus) American social, family, quantitative methods; charles.wetherell@ucr.edu

Recently Awarded PhDs

Thornton, Jennifer "A Home on the Range: Murray's Dude Ranch and the Making of Los Angeles's Black Urban District"

Vargas, Daisy "Race, Religion, and the Law in the US-Mexico Borderlands"

University of California, San Diego

Dept. of History, H&SS Bldg., Rm. 5016, 9500 Gilman Dr., La Jolla, CA 92093-0104. 858.534.1996. Fax 858.534.7283. Email: history@ucsd.edu. Website: http://history.ucsd.edu/.

At the undergraduate level, we emphasize the traditional humanistic skills of critical reading, good writing, and analysis of historical texts, and allow majors to take a broad range of courses across regional and temporal boundaries. At the graduate level, our PhD students focus on one of our areas of specialization for their dissertation research, but also pick two minor fields that provide greater breadth to their training.

Chair: Edward Watts
Director of Graduate Studies: Rachel Klein
Director of Undergraduate Studies: G. Mark Hendrickson
Degrees Offered: BA,MA,CPhil,PhD
Academic Year System: Quarter
Areas of Specialization: ancient, East Asia, Europe, Latin America, science, Middle East, US
Undergraduate Tuition (per academic year):
In-State: $14429
Out-of-State: $28992
Graduate Tuition (per academic year):
In-State: $17006
Out-of-State: $32108
Enrollment 2018-19:
Undergraduate Majors: 228
New Graduate Students: 15
Full-time Graduate Students: 87
Degrees in History: 49 BA, 4 MA, 18 PhD
Undergraduate Addresses:
Admissions: http://www.ucsd.edu/admissions/
Financial Aid: https://students.ucsd.edu/finances/financial-aid/
Graduate Addresses:
Admissions: https://history.ucsd.edu/graduate/prospective
Financial Aid: https://students.ucsd.edu/finances/financial-aid/

Adjunct Faculty

Bridges, Amy (PhD, Chicago 1980; adj. prof.) US urban; abridges@weber.ucsd.edu
Drake, Paul W. (PhD, Stanford 1971; adj. prof.) Latin America; pdrake@ucsd.edu

Full-time Faculty

Alvarez, Luis A. (PhD, Texas, Austin 2001; assoc. prof.) 20th-century American economic and political; luisalvarez@ucsd.edu
Balberg, Mira (PhD, Stanford 2011; prof. and endowed chair) ancient Jewish civilization, Judaism in Roman Syria-Palestine in late antiquity; mbalberg@ucsd.edu
Biess, Frank P. (PhD, Brown 2000; prof.) Germany, modern Europe; fbiess@ucsd.edu
Caciola, Nancy A. (PhD, Michigan 1994; prof.) medieval Europe, European women, Christianity; ncaciola@ucsd.edu
Cowan, Benjamin Arthur (PhD, UCLA 2010; assoc. prof.) right-wing radicalism/morality/sexuality, 20th-century imperialism, Cold War Brazil; bacowan@ucsd.edu
Demetriou, Denise (PhD, Johns Hopkins 2005; assoc. prof. and Gerry and Jeannie Ranglas Endowed Chair) archaic and classical Greece; dedemetriou@ucsd.edu
Devereux, Andrew (PhD, Johns Hopkins 2011; asst. prof.) medieval and early modern Mediterranean; adevereux@ucsd.edu
Edelman, Robert (PhD, Columbia 1973; prof.) Russia, neo-Marxist thought, European agricultural; redelman@ucsd.edu
Edington, Claire (PhD, Columbia 2013; asst. prof.) medicine and public health; cedington@ucsd.edu
Gallant, Thomas W. (PhD, Cambridge 1982; prof. and Nicholas Family Endowed Chair) modern Greek rural society and culture, banditry/piracy/violence, masculinity and gender; tgallant@ucsd.edu
Gere, Catherina (PhD, Cambridge 2002; prof.) biological science and medicine; cgere@ucsd.edu
Gerth, Karl (PhD, Harvard 2000; prof. and Hwei-Chih and Julia Hsiu Chair) contemporary implications of Chinese consumerism; kgerth@ucsd.edu
Golan, Tal (PhD, California, Berkeley 1997; assoc. prof.) modern science, relations between science/technology/law; tgolan@ucsd.edu

Graham, Jessica L. (PhD, Chicago 2010; assoc. prof.) African American, transnational orientation of US history; jlgraham@ucsd.edu
Hanna, Mark G. (PhD, Harvard 2006; assoc. prof.) early America and Atlantic world; m1hanna@ucsd.edu
Hendrickson, Mark G. (PhD, California, Santa Barbara 2004; assoc. prof. and dir., undergrad. studies) US labor, capitalism; ghendrickson@ucsd.edu
Henry, Todd A. (PhD, UCLA 2006; assoc. prof.) modern Korea, Korea 1910-45; tahenry@ucsd.edu
Hertz, Deborah (PhD, Minnesota 1979; prof. and Herman Wouk Prof.) modern Jewish, European women, modern Germany; dhertz@ucsd.edu
Hunefeldt, Christine (PhD, Bonn 1982; prof.) Latin America and Andes, life of women, indigenous populations and slaves; chunefeldt@ucsd.edu
Kayali, Hasan (PhD, Harvard 1988; assoc. prof.) modern Middle East and Islamic studies, late Ottoman Empire politics and ideology; hkayali@ucsd.edu
Klein, Rachel N. (PhD, Yale 1979; assoc. prof. and dir., grad. studies) early national and 19th-century US cultural; rklein@ucsd.edu
Kwak, Nancy H. (PhD, Columbia 2006; assoc. prof.) cities, urban planning, housing policy; nhkwak@ucsd.edu
Lu, Weijing (PhD, California, Davis 2001; assoc. prof.) Chinese women and gender, late imperial social; w1lu@ucsd.edu
Man, Simeon (PhD, Yale 2012; asst. prof.) Asian American, transnational US, politics of race and empire; siman@ucsd.edu
Matsumura, Wendy Y. (PhD, NYU 2007; asst. prof.) modern Japan, Japanese empire; wmatsumura@ucsd.edu
Murillo, Dana Velasco (PhD, UCLA 2009; assoc. prof.) intersections of colonialism with gender and ethnicity, identity formation in early Latin America; dvmurillo@ucsd.edu
Muscolino, Micah S. (PhD, Harvard 2006; prof. and Paul G. Pickowicz Endowed Chair) modern Chinese environmental; mmuscolino@ucsd.edu
Patterson, Patrick Hyder (PhD, Michigan 2001; assoc. prof.) 19th- and 20th-century eastern Europe and Balkans, cultural and political, nationalism and ethnicity; patrickpatterson@ucsd.edu
Plant, Rebecca Jo (PhD, Johns Hopkins 2001; assoc. prof.) 20th-century US, women and gender, popular culture and psychological professions; rplant@ucsd.edu
Prestholdt, Jeremy G. (PhD, Northwestern 2003; prof.) Africa, East African economic, international trade and indigenous cultures; jprestholdt@ucsd.edu
Provence, Michael (PhD, Chicago 2001; prof.) modern Middle East, colonial and postcolonial Arab world; mprovence@ucsd.edu
Radcliff, Pamela B. (PhD, Columbia 1990; prof.) 19th- and 20th-century Spanish politics/culture/labor reform, post-1800 France and Italy; pradcliff@ucsd.edu
Schneewind, Sarah (PhD, Columbia 1999; prof. and vice chair, acad. affairs) premodern China, late imperial; sschneewind@ucsd.edu
Shafir, Nir (PhD, UCLA 2016; asst. prof.) late medieval and early modern Middle East, intellectual and cultural, intersections of knowledge production; nshafir@ucsd.edu
Strasser, Ulrike (PhD, Minnesota 1997; prof.) early modern central Europe, early modern religion and politics, gender and sexuality; ustrasser@ucsd.edu
Vitz, Matthew (PhD, NYU 2010; assoc. prof.) modern Mexico; mvitz@ucsd.edu
Watts, Edward Jay (PhD, Yale 2002; prof.; Alkiviadis Vassiladis Endowed Chair; and chair) early Byzantine Empire intellectual and religious; ewatts@ucsd.edu

Widener, Daniel (PhD, NYU 2003; assoc. prof.) African American, California, expressive culture/race/ethnicity and political radicalism; dwidener@ucsd.edu

Retired/Emeritus Faculty

Cahill, Suzanne E. (PhD, California, Berkeley 1982; adj. prof. emeritus) medieval China, Tao, Taoists saints, research on women in medieval China

Chodorow, Stanley (PhD, Cornell 1968; prof. emeritus) medieval, legal and constitutional, political theory; schodorow@ucsd.edu

Esherick, Joseph W. (PhD, California, Berkeley 1971; prof. emeritus) modern China; jesherick@ucsd.edu

Fujitani, Takashi (PhD, California, Berkeley 1986; prof. emeritus) modern Japan, modern and contemporary Japanese cultural, military culture; tfujitani@ucsd.edu

Goodblatt, David M. (PhD, Brown 1972; dist. prof. emeritus) Jewish, Judaism in antiquity, pre-Islamic Middle East; dgoodblatt@ucsd.edu

Gutierrez, David G. (PhD, Stanford 1988; prof. emeritus) Chicano, American Southwest, comparative immigration; dggutierrez@ucsd.edu

Hu, Ping C. (lect. WSOE and prof. emeritus)

Hughes, Judith M. (PhD, Harvard 1970; prof. emeritus) modern European diplomatic and political, Britain, psychoanalysis; jhughes@ucsd.edu

Jackson, Gabriel (PhD, Toulouse, France 1952; prof. emeritus) Spain, Spanish Civil War; history@ucsd.edu

Luft, David S. (PhD, Harvard 1972; prof. emeritus) modern Germany and Austria, modern European intellectual; history@ucsd.edu

Metzger, Thomas A. (PhD, Harvard 1967; prof. emeritus) premodern Chinese institutional and intellectual; history@ucsd.edu

Monteon, Michael P. (PhD, Harvard 1974; prof. emeritus) Latin American political economic, Chile; mmonteon@ucsd.edu

Mosshammer, Alden A. (PhD, Brown 1971; prof. emeritus) ancient Greece, Rome, early Christianity; amosshammer@ucsd.edu

Parrish, Michael E. (PhD, Yale 1968; dist. prof. emeritus) US legal and constitutional, post-Progressive era American political reform trends; mparrish@ucsd.edu

Pickowicz, Paul G. (PhD, Wisconsin, Madison 1973; dist. prof. emeritus) 20th-century China, Chinese rural studies, Chinese cinema and society; bikewei@ucsd.edu

Propp, William H. C. (PhD, Harvard 1985; prof. emeritus) ancient Near East civilizations and languages, biblical and Judaic studies; wpropp@ucsd.edu

Reynolds, Edward (PhD, London 1972; prof. emeritus) Africa, West African economic, missionary; ereynolds@ucsd.edu

Ringrose, David R. (PhD, Wisconsin, Madison 1966; prof. emeritus) early modern Europe, European economic, Spain; dringrose@ucsd.edu

Rudwick, Martin J. S. (PhD, Cambridge 1958; prof. emeritus) earth and life sciences; mjsr100@cam.ac.uk

Truant, Cynthia M. (PhD, Chicago 1978; prof. emeritus) European and French labor, European women and gender studies, French social and cultural 1650-1850; ctruant@ucsd.edu

Van Young, Eric J. (PhD, California, Berkeley 1978; Dist. Prof. emeritus) colonial Latin America, Mexico; evanyoung@ucsd.edu

Westman, Robert S. (PhD, Michigan 1971; prof. emeritus) early modern science cultural, Copernican question and occult philosophies of nature; rwestman@ucsd.edu

Recently Awarded PhDs

Abreu, Johnathan "Frontiers beyond Abolition: Fugitive Slave Communities and Resistance in Marahao and Para, Brazil, 1860-1950"

Carmona Zabala, Juan "State Expansion and Economic Integration: A Transnational History of Oriental Tobacco in Greece and Germany, 1880-1941"

Dryer, Theodora "Designing Certainty: The Rise of Algorithmic Computing in an Age of Anxiety"

Dunai, Suzanne "Food Politics in Postwar Spain: Everyday Life during the Early Franco Dictatorship, 1939-52"

Egan, Nancy Elizabeth "Infrastructure, State Formation, and Social Change in Bolivia at the Start of the 20th Century"

Flach, Kate L "Tell It Like It Is: Television and Social Change, 1960-80"

Idol, David H. "Betting on the Farm: Rural Economic and Environmental History of Greece, 1860-1900"

Kim, Young-Hyun "Popular Politics of Social Emancipation in Bolivia from the 1930s to the Present: Indigeneity, Revolution, and the State"

Leal, Jorge N. "Aquí y Allá: ¡Yo Voy a Existir! Young Latina/o Ingenuity, Sounds, and Solidarity in Late 20th-Century Los Ángeles, 1980-97"

Morales Fontanilla, Manuel Antonio "Impossible Roads: Cycling Landscapes and Cultural Representation in Colombia, 1930-58"

West, Cameo Lyn S. "Antebellum Inc., Hollywood, and the Construction of Southern Identity, 1920-40"

University of California, Santa Barbara

Dept. of History, HSSB 4001, Santa Barbara, CA 93106-9410. 805.893.5681. Fax 805.893.7671. Email: rappaport@ucsb.edu. Website: https://www.history.ucsb.edu/.

The department offers a BA in history and in history of public policy. It also offers graduate program training across a broad spectrum of time periods, geographically defined and topical areas of specialization, and methodological approaches.

Chair: Erika Rappaport
Director of Graduate Studies: Salim Yaqub
Degrees Offered: BA, MA, PhD
Academic Year System: Quarter
Areas of Specialization: US, ancient/medieval/early modern/modern Europe, public, East Asia, Middle East/Africa
Undergraduate Tuition (per academic year):
  In-State: $14472
  Out-of-State: $43464
Graduate Tuition (per academic year):
  In-State: $13584
  Out-of-State: $28686
Enrollment 2018-19:
  Undergraduate Majors: 442
  New Graduate Students: 13
  Full-time Graduate Students: 86
  Degrees in History: 121 BA, 2 MA, 3 PhD
Undergraduate Addresses:
  Admissions: http://admissions.sa.ucsb.edu/
  Financial Aid: http://www.finaid.ucsb.edu/
Graduate Addresses:
  Admissions: http://www.history.ucsb.edu/academics/graduate/
  Financial Aid: http://www.finaid.ucsb.edu/

Affiliated Faculty

Afary, Janet (PhD, Michigan 1991; prof.; Religious Studies) 19th- to 20th-century Iran, Middle Eastern religion/politics/society, Middle Eastern gender and sexuality; afary@religion.ucsb.edu

Aldana, Gerardo V. (PhD, Harvard 2001; asst. prof.; Chicana and Chicano Studies) premodern Latin America, astronomy, imperialism; gvaldana@chicst.ucsb.edu

Armbruster-Sandoval, Ralph (PhD, California, Riverside; assoc. prof.; Chicano/a Studies) social movements, Los Angeles urban studies, racial studies; armbrust@chicst.ucsb.edu

Blankholm, Joseph (PhD, Columbia; asst. prof.; Religious Studies) American religion; blankholm@religion.ucsb.edu

Bloom, Peter (PhD, UCLA 1997; assoc. prof.; Film and Media Studies) French and Francophone media, early cinema; pblom@filmandmedia.ucsb.edu

Boris, Eileen (PhD, Brown 1981; Hull Prof.; Feminist Studies) US women; boris@femst.ucsb.edu

Busto, Rudy (PhD, California, Berkeley; assoc. prof.; Religious Studies) religion in North America, religion through lens of race and ethnicity; rude@religion.ucsb.edu

Daniel, G. Reginald (PhD, UCLA; prof.; Sociology) race and ethnic relations, multiracial identity, cultural formation and change rdaniel@soc.ucsb.edu

Elison, William (PhD, Chicago 2007; asst. prof.; Religious Studies) South Asian religions, religion and media, visual culture; welison@religion.ucsb.edu

Erickson, Brice (PhD, Texas, Austin 2000; asst. prof.; Classics) archaic and classical Greek archaeology; berickson@classics.ucsb.edu

Fogu, Claudio (PhD, UCLA 1995; asst. prof.; French and Italian) modern and contemporary Italy; cfogu@french-ital.ucsb.edu

Fruhstuck, Sabine (PhD, Vienna 1996; prof.; East Asian Languages and Cultural Studies) modern Japanese cultural studies; fruhstuck@eastasian.ucsb.edu

Garcia, Mario T. (PhD, California, San Diego 1975; prof.; Chicana and Chicano Studies) Chicano; garcia@history.ucsb.edu

Hecht, Richard D. (PhD, UCLA 1976; prof.; Religious Studies) religious; ariel@religion.ucsb.edu

Johnson, Gaye (PhD, Minnesota; assoc. prof.; Black Studies) US cultural; gtjohnson@blackstudies.ucsb.edu

Kaplan, Cynthia (PhD, Columbia 1981; prof.; Political Science) comparative politics, Russian/Tatar/Baltic/Kazakh politics, ethnicity/political behavior/public opinion; kaplan@polsci.ucsb.edu

Lipsitz, George (PhD, Wisconsin, Madison 1979; prof.; Black Studies) 20th-century US, urban culture, social movements; glipsitz@blackstudies.ucsb.edu

MacLean, Rose (PhD, Princeton 2012; asst. prof.; Classics) ancient; maclean@classics.ucsb.edu

Malhotra, Anshu (PhD, SOAS, London; Kundan Kaur Kapany Prof.; Global Studies) gender histories, cultural studies, autobiography studies and histories of South Asia; anshumalhotra@ucsb.edu

McAuley, Christopher (PhD, Michigan; assoc. prof.; Black Studies) northern and southern African politics, world systems theory, intellectual; mcauley@blackstudies.ucsb.edu

Miller-Young, Mireille L. (PhD, NYU 2009; assoc. prof.; Feminist Studies) black cultural studies; mmilleryoung@femst.ucsb.edu

Morstein-Marx, Robert (PhD, California, Berkeley 1987; assoc. prof.; Classics) ancient Mediterranean; morstein@classics.ucsb.edu

Moser, Claudia (PhD, Brown; asst. prof.; Hist. of Art and Architecture) medieval art; moser@arthistory.ucsb.edu

Rupp, Leila J. (PhD, Bryn Mawr 1976; prof.; Feminist Studies) women's movements, sexuality, gay and lesbian; lrupp@femst.ucsb.edu

Salton-Cox, Glyn (PhD, Yale 2013; asst. prof.; English) Marxism, queer theory, mid-20th-century literature and culture, 19th- and 20th-century intellectual, comparative urbanisms; saltoncox@english.ucsb.edu

Smith, Stuart Tyson (PhD, UCLA; prof.; Anthropology) archaeology of Egypt and Nubia, ethnicity and imperialism; stsmith@anth.ucsb.edu

Sorkin, Jenni (PhD, Yale 2010; assoc. prof.; Hist. of Art and Architecture) material culture, craft, gender and artistic labor, quee culture and theory; jsorkin@arthistory.ucsb.edu

Stewart, Jeffrey (PhD, Yale 1979; prof.; Black Studies) Harlem Renaissance; jstewart@blackstudies.ucsb.edu

Taves, Ann (PhD, Chicago 1983; prof.; Religious Studies) Catholicism, US; taves@religion.ucsb.edu

Thomas, Christine (PhD, Harvard; assoc. prof.; Religious Studies) early Christianity, Roman empire religions; thomas@religion.ucsb.edu

Tsouna, Voula (PhD, Paris X; prof.; Philosophy) ancient philosophy; vtsouna@philosophy.ucsb.edu

Walker, David (PhD, Yale; asst. prof.; Religious Studies) 19th-century US religion; dwalker@religion.ucsb.edu

Welter, Volker (PhD, Edinburgh; prof.; Hist. of Art and Architecture) modern architecture; welter@arthistory.ucsb.edu

Zhao, Xiaojian (PhD, California, Berkeley 1993; assoc. prof.; Asian American Studies) Asian American; xiaojian@asamst.ucsb.edu

Full-time Faculty

Alagona, Peter S. (PhD, UCLA 2006; asst. prof.) endangered species and biodiversity; alagona@history.ucsb.edu

Barbieri-Low, Anthony J. (PhD, Princeton 2001; assoc. prof.) premodern China; barbieri-low@history.ucsb.edu

Bergstrom, Randolph E. (PhD, Columbia 1988; assoc. prof.) US social policy; bergstro@history.ucsb.edu

Bernstein, Hilary J. (PhD, Princeton 1996; assoc. prof.) Renaissance; bernstein@history.ucsb.edu

Blumenthal, Debra G. (PhD, Toronto 2000; assoc. prof.) medieval; blumenthal@history.ucsb.edu

Bouley, Bradford Albert (PhD, Stanford 2012; asst. prof.) early modern Europe, religion and science; bouley@history.ucsb.edu

Brooks, James F. (PhD, California, Davis 1995; prof.; Anthropology) borderlands, comparative slavery, ethnohistorical methods and theories; jbrooks@history.ucsb.edu

Castillo-Munoz, Veronica (PhD, California, Irvine 2009; asst. prof.) 20th-century Mexican gender and labor, Latin American agrarian reform, regional; castillomunoz@history.ucsb.edu

Chattopadhyaya, Utathya (PhD, Illinois, Urbana-Champaign 2018; asst. prof.) modern South Asia

Chavez-Garcia, Miroslava (PhD, UCLA 1998; prof.) Chicano/a and Latino/a, race and juvenile justice, Spanish borderlands; mchavezgarcia@history.ucsb.edu

Chikowero, Moses (PhD, Dalhousie 2008; asst. prof.) African social and economic, music/African identities/power; chikowero@history.ucsb.edu

Cobo Betancourt, Juan Fernando (PhD, Cambridge 2015; asst. prof.) colonial Latin America; jcobo@history.ucsb.edu

Covo, Manuel (PhD, EHESS, France 2013; asst. prof.) modern Europe, Age of Revolution in Atlantic world, French Empire; mcovo@history.ucsb.edu

DePalma Digeser, Elizabeth (PhD, California, Santa Barbara 1996; prof.) ancient Rome and late antiquity; edepalma@history.ucsb.edu

Edgar, Adrienne (PhD, California, Berkeley 1999; assoc. prof.) modern Russia and the Soviet Union, Central Asia; edgar@history.ucsb.edu

Farmer, Sharon A. (PhD, Harvard 1983; prof.) medieval; farmer@history.ucsb.edu

Hancock, Mary E. (PhD, Pennsylvania 1990; prof.) modern India, public memory, gender; hancock@anth.ucsb.edu

Jacobson, Lisa S. (PhD, UCLA 1997; assoc. prof.) US cultural; jacobson@history.ucsb.edu

Kalman, Laura (PhD, Yale 1982; prof.) 20th-century US; kalman@history.ucsb.edu

Keel, Terence (PhD, Harvard 2012; asst. prof.; Black Studies) race/science and medicine, relationship between religion and science, African American intellectual; tkeel@blackstudies.ucsb.edu

Lansing, Carol L. (PhD, Michigan 1984; prof.) medieval Europe; lansing@history.ucsb.edu

Laurent-Perrault, Evelyne (PhD, NYU 2015; asst. prof.) Latin America; elaurentperrault@history.ucsb.edu

Lee, John W. I. (PhD, Cornell 1999; assoc. prof.) ancient Greece; jwilee@history.ucsb.edu

Lichtenstein, Nelson N. (PhD, California, Berkeley 1974; prof.) US labor, 20th-century US; nelson@history.ucsb.edu

Majewski, John D. (PhD, UCLA 1994; prof.) 19th-century US, Civil War, political economy; majewski@history.ucsb.edu

Marcuse, Harold (PhD, Michigan 1992; prof.) modern Germany; marcuse@history.ucsb.edu

McCray, Patrick (PhD, Arizona 1996; prof.) science; pmccray@history.ucsb.edu

McDonald, Kate (PhD, California, San Diego 2011; asst. prof.) modern Japan; kmcdonald@history.ucsb.edu

Mendez, S. Cecilia (PhD, SUNY, Stony Brook 1996; assoc. prof.) Latin America; mendez@history.ucsb.edu

Miescher, Stephan F. (PhD, Northwestern 1997; assoc. prof.) Africa; miescher@history.ucsb.edu

O'Connor, Alice M. (PhD, Johns Hopkins 1991; prof.) US public policy; aoconnor@history.ucsb.edu

Perrone, Giuliana (PhD, California, Berkeley 2015; asst. prof.) North American slavery, legal, Civil War and Reconstruction; gperrone@history.ucsb.edu

Plane, Ann Marie (PhD, Brandeis 1994; prof.) colonial America; plane@history.ucsb.edu

Rappaport, Erika D. (PhD, Rutgers 1993; prof. and chair) modern Britain; rappaport@history.ucsb.edu

Roberts, Luke S. (PhD, Princeton 1991; prof.) Japan; lukerobt@history.ucsb.edu

Sabra, Adam A. (PhD, Princeton 1998; prof.) premodern Middle East, Cairo social and cultural, legal; asabra@history.ucsb.edu

Seikaly, Sherene R. (PhD, NYU 2007; assoc. prof.) modern Middle East, Israel/Palestine; sseikaly@history.ucsb.edu

Sonnino, Paul M. (PhD, UCLA 1964; prof.) early modern Europe; sonnino@history.ucsb.edu

Spickard, Paul (PhD, California, Berkeley 1983; prof.) Asian American; spickard@history.ucsb.edu

Yaqub, Salim C. (PhD, Yale 1999; assoc. prof. and dir., grad. studies) US foreign relations; syaqub@history.ucsb.edu

Zheng, Xiaowei (PhD, California, San Diego 2009; assoc. prof.) comparative revolution, constitutionalism in China; zheng@history.ucsb.edu

Retired/Emeritus Faculty

Brownlee, W. Elliot (PhD, Wisconsin, Madison 1969; prof. emeritus) American economic; brownlee@history.ucsb.edu

Chen, Chi-yun (PhD, Harvard 1967; prof. emeritus) ancient China

Cline, Sarah (PhD, UCLA 1981; research prof. emeritus) Mexico; cline@history.ucsb.edu

Cohen, Patricia Cline (PhD, California, Berkeley 1977; prof. emeritus) women, social; pcohen@history.ucsb.edu

Daniels, Douglas (PhD, California, Berkeley 1975; prof. emeritus) America, Afro-American; daniels@blackstudies.ucsb.edu

De Hart, Jane S. (PhD, Duke 1966; prof. emeritus) modern US, women, public policy; dehart@history.ucsb.edu

Drake, Harold A. (PhD, Wisconsin, Madison 1970; prof. emeritus) Rome; drake@history.ucsb.edu

Dutra, Francis A. (PhD, NYU 1968; prof. emeritus) Brazil and Portugal; dutra@history.ucsb.edu

Friesen, Abraham (PhD, Stanford 1967; prof. emeritus) Renaissance and Reformation

Frost, Frank (PhD, UCLA 1961; prof. emeritus)

Furner, Mary O. (PhD, Northwestern 1972; prof. emeritus) US public policy; furner@history.ucsb.edu

Gallagher, Nancy (PhD, UCLA 1977; prof. emeritus) Middle East; gallagher@history.ucsb.edu

Glickstein, Jonathan A. (PhD, Yale 1989; prof. emeritus) US intellectual

Hasegawa, Tsuyoshi (PhD, Washington 1969; prof. emeritus) Russia; hasegawa@history.ucsb.edu

Humphreys, R. Stephen (PhD, Michigan 1969; prof. emeritus) Middle East; humphreys@history.ucsb.edu

Lindemann, Albert S. (PhD, Harvard 1968; prof. emeritus) modern European socialism; lindeman@history.ucsb.edu

McGee, J. Sears (PhD, Yale 1971; prof. emeritus) Tudor-Stuart England; jsmcgee@history.ucsb.edu

Nash, Roderick W. (PhD, Wisconsin, Madison 1964; prof. emeritus) American intellectual and popular culture

Oglesby, Richard E. (PhD, Northwestern 1962; prof. emeritus) American West

Rock, David P. (PhD, Cambridge 1971; prof. emeritus) Latin America, Argentina; rock@history.ucsb.edu

Russell, Jeffrey B. (PhD, Emory 1960; prof. emeritus) medieval Europe

Talbott, John E. (PhD, Stanford 1966; prof. emeritus) modern Europe, war and society; talbott@history.ucsb.edu

Recently Awarded PhDs

Baillargeon, David "'A Burmese Wonderland': British World Mining and the Making of Colonial Burma"

Frei, Cheryl "Shaping and Contesting the Past: Monuments, Memory, and Identity in Buenos Aires, 1811-Present"

He, Fang "'Golden Lilies' across the Pacific: Bodies and the Paradoxes of US Inclusion in Enforcing the Chinese Exclusion Laws"

Hooton, Laura Kaye Fleisch "Co-Opting the Border: The Dream of African American Integration via Baja California"

Moore, Laura "From Enslaved to Free Consumers: African Americans' Struggle for Consumer Autonomy and Purchasing Power in the Civil War and Reconstruction South"

Stephens, Christopher "Defining the Monster: The Social Science and Rhetoric of Neo-Marxist Theories of Imperialism in the United States and Latin America, 1945-73"

Thompson, William Keene "Iconoclasm and Religious Identity Formation in Tudor England"

Tyrrell, Brian Patrick "Bred for the Races: Thoroughbred Breeding and Heredity"

Walker, Dustin "Unleashing the Financial Sector: Home Loan Deregulation and the Savings and Loan Crisis, 1966-89"

University of California, Santa Cruz

Dept. of History, 1156 High St., Santa Cruz, CA 95064-1077. 831.459.3701. Fax 831.502.7287. Email: history@ucsc.edu. Website: https://history.ucsc.edu/.

The UCSC History Department is known for the strength of its undergraduate program. The campus has recognized the excellence of the department's teaching by conferring distinguished teaching awards on multiple members of our faculty. The graduate program in history at UCSC emphasizes an interdisciplinary and cross-cultural approach to historical studies, encouraging innovative thinking about global historical processes.

Chair: Matt O'Hara
Director of Graduate Studies: Marc Matera
Director of Undergraduate Studies: Catherine Jones
Degrees Offered: BA, MA, PhD
Academic Year System: Quarter
Areas of Specialization: Europe, Asia, world, Americas
Undergraduate Tuition (per academic year):
  In-State: $14025
  Out-of-State: $42039
Graduate Tuition (per academic year):
  In-State: $18468
  Out-of-State: $15102
Enrollment 2018-19:
  Undergraduate Majors: 208
  New Graduate Students: 12
  Full-time Graduate Students: 38
  Part-time Graduate Students: 1
  Degrees in History: 170 BA, 2 MA, 4 PhD
Undergraduate Addresses:
  Admissions: http://admissions.ucsc.edu
  Financial Aid: http://financialaid.ucsc.edu/
Graduate Addresses:
  Admissions: http://graddiv.ucsc.edu
  Financial Aid: http://financialaid.ucsc.edu/

Full-time Faculty

Anthony, David H., III (PhD, Wisconsin, Madison 1983; assoc. prof.) Africa, African American, African diasporic studies; danthony@ucsc.edu

Aso, Noriko (PhD, Chicago 1997; assoc. prof.) modern Japanese social and cultural, women, Korea; naso@ucsc.edu

Breen, Ben (PhD, Texas, Austin 2015; asst. prof.) Atlantic, early modern Iberia; bebreen@ucsc.edu

Brundage, David (PhD, UCLA 1982; prof.) American immigration, US labor and social, modern Ireland; brundage@ucsc.edu

Christy, Alan S. (PhD, Chicago 1997; assoc. prof.) early modern and modern Japan, social sciences; achristy@ucsc.edu

Delgado, Grace Peña (PhD, UCLA 2000; assoc. prof.) Chicano/a, Mexico-US-Canadian borderlands, Latino/a studies; gpdelgad@ucsc.edu

Derr, Jennifer L. (PhD, Stanford 2009; asst. prof.) colonial and postcolonial Middle East, Egypt, agricultural and environmental; jderr@ucsc.edu

Deutsch, Nathaniel (PhD, Chicago 1995; prof.) religions, Judaism; ndeutsch@ucsc.edu

Diaz, Maria Elena (PhD, Texas, Austin 1992; assoc. prof.) colonial Caribbean and Latin America, social and cultural, slavery; mediaz@ucsc.edu

Frank, Dana (PhD, Yale 1988; prof.) US social and economic, women, labor and working class; dlfrank@ucsc.edu

Haas, Lisbeth (PhD, California, Irvine 1985; prof.) US cultural and social, US Southwest, colonial Americas; lhaas@ucsc.edu

Heckman, Alma (PhD, UCLA 2015; asst. prof.) Sephardic, European Jewish; aheckman@ucsc.edu

Hedrick, Charles W., Jr. (PhD, Pennsylvania 1984; prof.) Greece and Rome, epigraphy, historiography; hedrick@ucsc.edu

Hershatter, Gail (PhD, Stanford 1982; prof.) modern Chinese social and cultural, labor, gender; gbhers@ucsc.edu

Honig, Emily (PhD, Stanford 1982; prof.) modern Chinese gender/sexuality/ethnicity; ehonig@ucsc.edu

Hu, Minghui (PhD, UCLA 2004; assoc. prof.) late imperial China; mhu@ucsc.edu

Jones, Catherine A. (PhD, Johns Hopkins 2007; assoc. prof. and dir., undergrad. studies) US Civil War and Reconstruction, slavery and emancipation; catjones@ucsc.edu

Lonetree, Amy J. (PhD, California, Berkeley 2002; assoc. prof.) indigenous, museum studies, commemoration and public memory; lonetree@ucsc.edu

Matera, Marc (PhD, Rutgers 2008; asst. prof. and dir., grad. studies) Britain and British Empire, modern Europe, Atlantic world; mmatera@ucsc.edu

O'Hara, Matt (PhD, California, San Diego 2003; prof. and chair) modern Latin America and Mexico, late colonial Latin America, religion/spirituality/ritual; mdohara@ucsc.edu

O'Malley, Gregory E. (PhD, Johns Hopkins 2006; assoc. prof.) colonial British America and Caribbean, Atlantic world, slavery and slave trade; gomalley@ucsc.edu

Peterson, Maya Karin (PhD, Harvard 2011; asst. prof.) Russia and Soviet Union, environmental; mkpeters@ucsc.edu

Polecritti, Cynthia L. (PhD, California, Berkeley 1988; assoc. prof.) medieval/Renaissance/modern Italy, Mediterranean, urban and cultural; clpolecr@ucsc.edu

Porter, Eric (PhD, Michigan 1997; prof.) black cultural and intellectual, US cultural, critical ethnic studies; ecporter@ucsc.edu

Shaikh, Juned (PhD, Washington 2011; asst. prof.) modern South Asian social and cultural, urban, labor; jmshaikh@ucsc.edu

Sullivan, Elaine (PhD, Johns Hopkins 2008; asst. prof.) Pharaonic period Egypt, Greek and Roman Egypt, digital humanities; easulliv@ucsc.edu

Westerkamp, Marilyn J. (PhD, Pennsylvania 1984; prof.) British America, American Revolution, early national US; mjw@ucsc.edu

Yang, Alice (PhD, Stanford 1994; assoc. prof.) historical memory, Asian American, gender; ayang@ucsc.edu

Part-time Faculty

Lasar, Matthew (PhD, Claremont Grad. 1997; lect.) US and international telecommunications, political, social and economic; mlasar@ucsc.edu

Lynn, Jennifer (PhD, Columbia 1995; lect.) later Roman republic and principate, Homeric epic, lives of women in ancient world; jklynn@ucsc.edu

Thompson, Bruce A. (PhD, Stanford 1987; lect.) European and Jewish intellectual and cultural, France; brucet@ucsc.edu

Retired/Emeritus Faculty

Beecher, Jonathan F. (PhD, Harvard 1968; prof. emeritus) France, European intellectual, Russian intellectual; jbeecher@ucsc.edu

Burke, Edmund, III (PhD, Princeton 1970; prof. emeritus) modern Middle East and North Africa, world; eburke@ucsc.edu

Castillo, Pedro (PhD, California, Santa Barbara 1979; prof. emeritus) Chicano/a history and culture, American social and urban, California race/class/gender; pcastle@ucsc.edu

Hamel, Gildas (PhD, California, Santa Cruz 1983; lect. emeritus) Judaism and Christianity; gweltaz@ucsc.edu

Kenez, Peter (PhD, Harvard 1967; prof. emeritus) Russia, 20th century, eastern Europe; kenez@ucsc.edu

Levine, Bruce C. (PhD, Rochester 1980; prof. emeritus) Civil War, 19th-century US economic and social; blevine@ucsc.edu

Miles, Gary B. (PhD, Yale 1971; prof. emeritus) historiography, Greek and Roman cultural and institutional, Greek and Latin literature; miles@ucsc.edu

Sharp, Buchanan (PhD, California, Berkeley 1971; prof. emeritus) England; bsharp@ucsc.edu

Sweet, David Graham (PhD, Wisconsin, Madison 1974; prof. emeritus) colonial and modern Latin America, Southeast Asia, world; dgsweet@ucsc.edu

Traugott, Mark (PhD, California, Berkeley 1976; prof. emeritus) 19th-century France, French revolutions and social movements, social and economic; traugott@ucsc.edu

Recently Awarded PhDs

Brzycki, Melissa A. "Inventing the Socialist Child in China, 1949-66"

Conrad, Nickolas "Leaving the Church: Studies of Apostasy within the Catholic Church in 19th-Century France"

Gao, Xiaofei "Maritime Manchuria: Empire, State, and Laborers 1905-99"

Hart, Amy "Life after Community: The Communitarian Women Who Transformed 19th-Century American Society"

MacGiollabhui, Muiris "Carrying the Green Bough: An Atlantic History of the United Irishmen, 1795-1830"

Montgomery, Stephanie "Gender, Criminality, and the Prison in China, 1928-53"

Williams, Samantha "'That Was Our Home, and It Needs to Be Remembered': Erasing and Reclaiming the History of the Stewart Indian School"

California Institute of Technology

Div. of the Humanities and Social Science, 1200 E. California Blvd., MC 228-77, Pasadena, CA 91125. 626.395.4065. Fax 626.405.9841. Email: jlr@hss.caltech.edu. Website: http://www.hss.caltech.edu/.

The Division of the Humanities and Social Sciences is focused on understanding the human experience, from the evolution of culture and institutions to social, political, and economic behavior, from the products of the imagination to the conceptual underpinnings of science.

Chair: Jean-Laurent Rosenthal
Degrees Offered: BS
Academic Year System: Quarter
Areas of Specialization: quantitative social science, social, economic, science, cultural
Tuition (per academic year): $52242
Enrollment 2018-19:
  Undergraduate Majors: 3
  Degrees in History: BA, 3 BS
Addresses:
  Admissions: http://www.admissions.caltech.edu/
  Financial Aid: http://www.finaid.caltech.edu/

Full-time Faculty

Brown, Warren C. (PhD, UCLA 1997; prof.) medieval; wcb@hss.caltech.edu

Buchwald, Jed Z. (PhD, Harvard 1974; Dreyfuss Prof.) 19th- and early 20th-century physics; buchwald@hss.caltech.edu

Dennison, Tracy (PhD, Cambridge 2004; prof.) Russia, early modern literature and intellectual; tkd@hss.caltech.edu

Dykstra, Maura D. (PhD, UCLA 2014; asst. prof.) China, legal and economic, late imperial institutional; maura@caltech.edu

Feingold, Mordechai (DPhil, Oxford 1976; Van Nuys Page Prof.) early modern, science; feingold@hss.caltech.edu

Hoffman, Philip T. (PhD, Yale 1979; Axline Prof.) early modern European economic and social, France, political economy; pth@hss.caltech.edu

Kormos-Buchwald, Diana (PhD, Harvard 1990; Abbey Prof.) 19th- and 20th-century physical sciences, philosophy of 19th- and 20th-century physical sciences; diana_buchwald@caltech.edu

Kousser, J. Morgan (PhD, Yale 1971; prof., Social Science) quantitative methods, US South, US legal and constitutional; kousser@hss.caltech.edu

Rosenthal, Jean-Laurent (PhD, California Inst. of Technology 1988; Axline Prof. and chair) social science, economic; jlr@hss.caltech.edu

Wey-Gomez, Nicolas (PhD, Johns Hopkins 1996; prof.) exploration, early modern Atlantic, literature; nweygome@hss.caltech.edu

Wiggins, Danielle L. (PhD, Emory 2018; asst. prof.) 20th-century African American, urban/metropolitan, capitalism, crime and crime control; dwiggins@caltech.edu

Retired/Emeritus Faculty

Brewer, John (PhD, Cambridge 1973; prof. emeritus) early modern British literature, early modern Europe, consumerism; jbrewer@caltech.edu

Kevles, Daniel J. (PhD, Princeton 1964; prof. emeritus) science, US 1945-present, US social and cultural; kevles@hss.caltech.edu

Rosenstone, Robert Allan (PhD, UCLA 1966; prof. emeritus) cultural, modern, film and history; rr@hss.caltech.edu

California Polytechnic State University

Dept. of History, Faculty Office Bldg. 47, 1 Grand Ave., San Luis Obispo, CA 93407-0324. 805.756.2543. Fax 805.756.5055. Email: hist@calpoly.edu. Website: https://history.calpoly.edu/.

All courses offered in the History Department seek to examine the issues of race, gender, class, and cultural diversity. A degree in history is excellent preparation for students interested in a teaching career, the legal profession, or advanced work in the discipline. Students wishing to become business executives, administrators, and public servants profit immensely by gaining the methodological skills of the historian. Historians learn to gather, synthesize, analyze, and interpret evidence; they become skilled in presenting their conclusions to a general audience in a lucid and logical manner.

Chair: Kathleen S. Murphy
Director of Graduate Studies: Andrew Morris
Degrees Offered: BA,MA
Academic Year System: Quarter
Areas of Specialization: US, Asia, comparative, Europe, Latin America

Undergraduate Tuition (per academic year):
  In-State: $8523
  Out-of-State: $12491
Graduate Tuition (per academic year):
  In-State: $9789
  Out-of-State: $13787
Enrollment 2018-19:
  Undergraduate Majors: 247
  New Graduate Students: 6
  Full-time Graduate Students: 10
  Part-time Graduate Students: 2
  Degrees in History: 76 BA, 15 MA, PhD
Undergraduate Addresses:
  Admissions: http://admissions.calpoly.edu/
  Financial Aid: http://financialaid.calpoly.edu/
Graduate Addresses:
  Admissions: http://admissions.calpoly.edu/applicants/graduate/
  Financial Aid: http://financialaid.calpoly.edu/

Full-time Faculty

Al-Nakib, Farah (PhD, Sch. of Oriental and African Studies, London 2011; asst. prof.) Middle East, North America

Beaton, Brian W. (PhD, Toronto 2012; assoc. prof.) information, intellectual, science and technology studies; brbeaton@calpoly.edu

Bridger, Sarah (PhD, Columbia 2011; assoc. prof.) 20th-century US, science; sbridger@calpoly.edu

Call, Lewis (PhD, California, Irvine 1996; prof.) modern Europe, intellectual; lcall@calpoly.edu

Firpo, Christina E. (PhD, UCLA 2006; prof.) Southeast Asia; cfirpo@calpoly.edu

Hiltpold, Paul J. (PhD, Texas, Austin 1981; prof.) Spain and Renaissance; philtpol@calpoly.edu

Hopper, Matthew S. (PhD, UCLA 2006; prof.) Africa, Middle East; mshopper@calpoly.edu

Loberg, Molly J. (PhD, Princeton 2006; prof.) modern Europe, Germany, cultural and urban; mjloberg@calpoly.edu

Morris, Andrew D. (PhD, California, San Diego 1998; prof. and dir., grad. studies) modern China, East Asia; admorris@calpoly.edu

Murphy, Kathleen Susan (PhD, Johns Hopkins 2007; prof. and chair) science, British Atlantic, colonial America; ksmurphy@calpoly.edu

Onate-Madrazo, Andrea (PhD, Princeton 2016; asst. prof.) Latin America; aonatema@calpoly.edu

Orth, Joel Jason (PhD, Iowa State 2004; assoc. prof.) US environmental, agricultural and rural, history-social science teacher preparation; jorth@calpoly.edu

Reid, Anne M. (PhD, Southern California 2014; asst. prof.) US borderlands, California; anreid@calpoly.edu

Tejani, James (PhD, Columbia 2009; asst. prof.) 19th-century US, American West; jtejani@calpoly.edu

Trice, Tom R. (PhD, Illinois, Urbana-Champaign 1998; assoc. prof.) Russia, eastern Europe; ttrice@calpoly.edu

Part-time Faculty

Bodemer, Margaret (PhD, Hawai'i, Manoa 2010; lect.) Southeast Asia; mbodemer@calpoly.edu

Domber, Gregory F. (PhD, George Washington 2008; lect.) 19th- and 20th-century America, Cold War international; gdomber@calpoly.edu

Hall, Roger (PhD, Bowling Green State 1993; lect.) US; rhall05@calpoly.edu

Jones, Cameron David (PhD, Ohio State 2013; lect.) Latin America; cjones81@calpoly.edu

Linn, Jason (PhD, California, Santa Barbara 2014; lect.) world, ancient Greece and Rome; jalinn@calpoly.edu

Perry, Nathan W. (PhD, California, Santa Barbara 2012; lect.) early modern Europe, Western civilization, world; naperry@calpoly.edu

Wilson, Jonathan (MS, Illinois State 1988; lect.) US; jdwilson@calpoly.edu

Retired/Emeritus Faculty

Barnes, Timothy M. (PhD, New Mexico 1970; prof. emeritus) colonial America; tbarnes@calpoly.edu

Cotkin, George B. (PhD, Ohio State 1978; prof. emeritus) US intellectual and cultural; gcotkin@calpoly.edu

Foroohar, Manzar (PhD, UCLA 1984; prof. emeritus) Latin America, Middle East; mforooha@calpoly.edu

Harlan, David Craig (PhD, California, Irvine 1979; prof. emeritus) philosophy of history; charlan@calpoly.edu

Krieger, Daniel E. (PhD, California, Davis 1973; prof. emeritus) modern Europe; dkrieger@calpoly.edu

Oriji, John N. (PhD, Rutgers 1977; prof. emeritus) modern world, Africa; joriji@calpoly.edu

Snetsinger, John G. (PhD, Stanford 1969; prof. emeritus) US diplomatic, recent US; jsnetsin@calpoly.edu

California State University, Bakersfield

Dept. of History, 9001 Stockdale Hwy, Bakersfield, CA 93311-1022. 661.654.3079. Fax 661.654.6906. Email: jstenehjem@csub.edu. Website: https://www.csub.edu/History/.

As one of the oldest of the liberal arts, the study of history emphasizes the importance of reading widely and deeply in the sources of human civilization and develops in its students the skills of thoughtful analysis of evidence and effective communication. The department offers BA and MA degrees in history. The department also offers a program of study leading to a California Teaching Credential in Social Science, as well as a minor in history.

Chair: Miriam Raub Vivian
Director of Graduate Studies: Douglas W. Dodd
Degrees Offered: BA,MA
Academic Year System: Semester
Areas of Specialization: US, Europe/ancient Mediterranean, Middle East/Africa, Asia, Latin America
Undergraduate Tuition (per academic year):
  In-State: $7422
  Out-of-State: $16926
Graduate Tuition (per academic year):
  In-State: $8856
  Out-of-State: $15984
Enrollment 2018-19:
  Undergraduate Majors: 130
  New Graduate Students: 8
  Full-time Graduate Students: 3
  Part-time Graduate Students: 15
  Degrees in History: 35 BA, 5 MA, PhD
Addresses:
  Admissions: http://www.csub.edu/admissions/
  Financial Aid: http://www.csub.edu/finaid/

Full-time Faculty

Allen, Stephen D. (PhD, Rutgers 2013; asst. prof.) modern Latin America and Mexico, revolution in Latin America, masculinity and boxing; sallen13@csub.edu

Dhada, Mustafah (DPhil, Oxford 1987; prof.) Africa, Islamic world, decolonization; mdhada@csub.edu

Dodd, Douglas W. (PhD, California, Santa Barbara 2000; prof. and dir., grad. studies) US West, environmental, public; ddodd@csub.edu

Mulry, Kate Luce (PhD, NYU 2014; asst. prof.) colonial America, Atlantic world and early modern England, science/medicine/environmental; kmulry@csub.edu

Murphy, Cliona (PhD, SUNY, Binghamton 1986; prof.) modern Europe/Ireland/Britain, women and gender, Mexican-European connections; cmurphy@csub.edu

Rodriquez, Alicia E. (PhD, California, Santa Barbara 1998; prof.) American South, race relations, 19th-century US; arodriquez@csub.edu

Tang, Christopher (PhD, Cornell 2016; asst. prof.) modern China, Cold War; ctang3@csub.edu

Vivian, Miriam Raub (PhD, California, Santa Barbara 1987; prof. and chair) late Roman Empire, ancient Mediterranean, early medieval Europe; mvivian@csub.edu

Wempe, Sean Andrew (PhD, Emory 2015; asst. prof.) modern Europe, modern Germany, imperialism, internationalism; swempe@csub.edu

Retired/Emeritus Faculty

Dolkart, Ron (PhD, UCLA 1969; prof. emeritus) Latin America

George, James H., Jr. (PhD, Wisconsin, Madison 1970; prof. emeritus) US diplomatic; jgeorge@csub.edu

Harrie, Jeanne E. (PhD, California, Riverside 1975; prof. emerita) early modern Europe, medieval; jharrie@csub.edu

Litzinger, Charles A. (PhD, California, Davis 1983; prof. emeritus) modern China, East Asia

Maynard, John A. (PhD, Southern California 1988; prof. emeritus) California

Orliski, Constance I. (PhD, Southern California 1998; retired assoc. prof.) modern China, Japan

Rink, Oliver A. (PhD, Southern California 1976; prof. emeritus) US, colonial

Stanley, Jerry (PhD, Arizona 1973; prof. emeritus) California, American West, Native American

California State University, Channel Islands

Dept. of History, One University Dr., Camarillo, CA 93012-8599. 805.437.3517. Fax 805.437.2012. Email: amanda.sanchez@csuci.edu. Website: https://history.csuci.edu/.

An emphasis of the program is to examine events from local and global perspectives. In this regard, a defining aspect of the History Program consists of a cutting-edge series of courses that emphasize the United States' relationship with the Pacific Rim, encompassing the Americas, the Pacific Islands, and Asia.

Chair: Frank P. Barajas
Degrees Offered: BA
Academic Year System: Semester
Areas of Specialization: North America, world
Tuition (per academic year):
In-State: $6802
Out-of-State: $17707
Enrollment 2018-19:
Undergraduate Majors: 189
Degrees in History: 37 BA

Addresses:
Admissions: http://www.csuci.edu/admissions/
Financial Aid: http://www.csuci.edu/financialaid/

Full-time Faculty

Barajas, Frank P. (PhD, Claremont Grad. 2001; prof. and chair) 20th-century US, California, Chicana/o studies; frank.barajas@csuci.edu

Buschmann, Rainer F. (PhD, Hawai'i, Manoa 1999; prof.) ocean and Pacific islands, world, Europe; rainer.buschmann@csuci.edu

Francois, Marie E. (PhD, Arizona 1998; prof.) Mexico, Latin America, women's studies; marie.francois@csuci.edu

Meriwether, James H. (PhD, UCLA 1995; prof.) 20th-century US, America in world, African American; james.meriwether@csuci.edu

Mitchell, Robin (PhD, California, Berkeley 2010; asst. prof.) France, gender, race; robin.mitchell@csuci.edu

Nolde, Lance (PhD, Hawai'i, Manoa 2014; asst. prof.) Southeast Asia, world; lance.nolde741@csuci.edu

Ornelas-Higdon, Julia (PhD, Southern California 2014; asst. prof.) 19th-century US, California and West, race and ethnicity; julia.ornelas-higdon@csuci.edu

Reynoso, Jacqueline (PhD, Cornell 2017; asst. prof.) American Revolution, colonial America; jacqueline.reynoso@csuci.edu

California State University, Chico

Dept. of History, 400 W. First St., Chico, CA 95929-0735. 530.898.5366. Fax 530.898.6925. Email: histstudent@csuchico.edu. Website: https://www.csuchico.edu/hist/.

he department offers programs at both the undergraduate and graduate levels. Undergraduate students who wish to major in history choose from the Social Science Pre-Credential Option, for those who intend to pursue a career in teaching middle or high school, and the General History Option. At the graduate level, the department offers an MA in history designed for students who aspire to teach at a community college, enter a doctoral program, or simply seek advanced study in the discipline. The department also offers a certificate program in Public History.

Chair: Stephen E. Lewis
Director of Graduate Studies: Robert Tinkler
Degrees Offered: BA,MA,Cert.
Academic Year System: Semester
Areas of Specialization: US, Europe, Latin America, Middle East, East Asia
Undergraduate Tuition (per academic year):
In-State: $7806
Out-of-State: $19752
Graduate Tuition (per academic year):
In-State: $9020
Out-of-State: $18546
Enrollment 2018-19:
Undergraduate Majors: 208
New Graduate Students: 5
Full-time Graduate Students: 12
Part-time Graduate Students: 3
Degrees in History: 72 BA, 5 MA, PhD
Undergraduate Addresses:
Admissions: http://www.csuchico.edu/admissions/
Financial Aid: http://www.csuchico.edu/fa/

Graduate Addresses:
Admissions: https://www.csuchico.edu/graduatestudies/
prospective-students/apply/graduate-admissions.shtml
Financial Aid: http://www.csuchico.edu/fa/

Full-time Faculty

DeForest, Dallas (PhD, Ohio State 2013; asst. prof.) ancient,
Byzantine; ddeforest@csuchico.edu

Easton, Laird M. (PhD, Stanford 1991; prof.) modern Europe,
European cultural and intellectual, modern Germany; leaston@
csuchico.edu

Green, Susan M. (PhD, Minnesota 1997; assoc. prof.) Chicano,
American studies; sgreen@csuchico.edu

Lee, Sinwoo (PhD, UCLA 2015; asst. prof.) East Asia, modern Korea;
slee143@csuchico.edu

Lewis, Stephen E. (PhD, California, San Diego 1997; prof. and chair)
Mexico, Latin America; slewis2@csuchico.edu

Livingston, Jeffery C. (PhD, Toledo 1989; prof.) US diplomatic,
20th-century America; jlivingston@csuchico.edu

Magliari, Michael F. (PhD, California, Davis 1992; prof.) California,
American agriculture, US West; mmagliari@csuchico.edu

Matray, James I. (PhD, Virginia 1977; prof.) US diplomatic, recent
US, East Asia; jmatray@csuchico.edu

Nice, Jason A. (PhD, York, UK 2004; assoc. prof.) early modern
Europe, Britain; jnice@csuchico.edu

Tinkler, Robert S. (PhD, North Carolina, Chapel Hill 2000; prof.
and dir., grad. studies) early 19th-century US, Civil War and
Reconstruction, American South; rtinkler@csuchico.edu

Transchel, Kate (PhD, North Carolina, Chapel Hill 1996; prof.)
Russia, eastern Europe, European women; ktranschel@csuchico.
edu

Wade, Alisa J. (PhD, Graduate Center, CUNY 2016; asst. prof.) early
America, women and gender

Yousefi, Najm al-Din (PhD, Virginia Tech 2009; assoc. prof.) Middle
East, science; nyousefi@csuchico.edu

Part-time Faculty

Archer, Robert D. (MA, California State, Chico 1992; lect.) US,
American studies; rarcher@csuchico.edu

Averbeck, Robin Marie (PhD, California, Davis 2013; lect.) 20th
century US, liberalism; rmaverbeck@csuchico.edu

Benedict, Jerrad (MA, California State, Chico 2016; lect.) US, Latin
America; jbenedict4@csuchico.edu

Nissen, Karen J. (MA, California, Davis 1987; lect.) European
intellectual, Germany, US; knissen@csuchico.edu

Pedeva-Fazlic, Desislava (MA, California State, Chico 2002; lect.)
US, modern Europe; dpedeva@csuchico.edu

Schwaller, Shawn W. (PhD, Claremont Graduate 2015; lect.)
California and American West, race and ethnic relations;
sschwaller@csuchico.edu

Sistrunk, Timothy G. (PhD, Kansas 1995; lect.) medieval Europe,
environmental; tsistrunk@csuchico.edu

Thomson, Rodney (MA, California State, Chico 2017; lect.) Middle
East, 20th-century US; rthomson2@csuchico.edu

Zelnik, Eran (PhD, ezelnik@csuchico.edu 2016; lect.) colonial US,
early Republic, social, cultural; ezelnik@csuchico.edu

Retired/Emeritus Faculty

Cottrell, Robert Charles (PhD, Oklahoma 1983; prof. emeritus)
20th-century America, intellectual; bcottrell@csuchico.edu

Emmerich, Lisa E. (PhD, Maryland, Coll. Park 1987; prof. emeritus)
Native American, women; lemmerich@csuchico.edu

California State University, Dominguez Hills

*Dept. of History, 1000 E. Victoria St., LCH A342, Carson, CA 90747.
310.243.3328. Email: cmonty@csudh.edu; rrubio14@csudh.edu.
Website: https://www.csudh.edu/history/.*

*The CSUDH History Department offers an undergraduate major
and minor in history. It provides history subject matter content
for teachers in Liberal Studies and a subject matter preparation
program for aspiring secondary school social science teachers,
completion of which satisfies the California Teacher Credentialing
Commission's subject matter competency requirement. It also
provides a solid foundation for students interested in graduate
and/or professional training.*

Chair: Christopher Monty
Degrees Offered: BA
Academic Year System: Semester
Areas of Specialization: California, Native American and
environmental, colonial to present US, Latin America and
Mexico, Europe/Russian Empire/Soviet Union
Tuition (per academic year):
In-State: $6418
Out-of-State: $15346
Enrollment 2018-19:
Undergraduate Majors: 165
Degrees in History: 32 BA
Students in Undergraduate Courses: 1825
Students in Undergraduate Intro Courses: 1189
Addresses:
Admissions: https://www.csudh.edu/future-students/
Financial Aid: https://www.csudh.edu/financial-aid/

Full-time Faculty

Fawver, Kate M. (PhD, California, Riverside 2002; prof.) early
America, US social and economic, demographic and family;
kfawver@csudh.edu

Jeffers, Joshua Jack (PhD, Purdue 2014; asst. prof.) Native
American, borderlands, environmental, intellectual, colonial
studies; jojeffers@csudh.edu

Johnson, Andrea S. (PhD, Missouri, Columbia 2006; assoc. prof.)
anjohnson@csudh.edu

Monty, Christopher Sullivan (PhD, UCLA 2004; prof. and chair)
Soviet Union, modern Europe, history and theory; cmonty@
csudh.edu

Murillo, Bianca (PhD, California, Santa Barbara 2009; assoc. prof.)
modern Africa, African social and economic, colonialism;
biancaannamurillo@gmail.com

Namala, Doris (PhD, UCLA 2002; lect.) colonial Mexico, indigenous
peoples, Nahuatl studies; dnamala@csudh.edu

Talamante, Laura R. E. (PhD, UCLA 2003; prof.) French Revolution
and early modern Europe, women, 18th-century novel and
women's writing; ltalamante@csudh.edu

Part-time Faculty

Alvarez, Thomas A. (PhD, Michigan 2007; lect.) Gilded Age and
Progressive Era, African American, US labor and class; talvarez@
csudh.edu

Archibald, Ryan (PhD, Washington 2019; lect.) US race/nation/
empire, 20th-century US social and cultural, comparative
colonialism

Desrochers, Michael (PhD, UCLA 1978; instr.) world; mdesrochers@csudh.edu

Griffey, Trevor (PhD, Washington 2011; lect.) 20th-century US empire, 20th-century US law/society/justice, US labor and public

O'Mara, William Edward IV (PhD, California, Irvine 2017; lect.) Middle East, European intellectual, evolution and sexuality; womaraiv@csudh.edu

Resnick, Kirsten (MA, California, Santa Barbara 1994; lect.) American survey, history teaching, women; kresnick@csudh.edu

Yoon, Sun-Hee (PhD, Washington 2009; instr.) early modern East Asia; syoon@csudh.edu

Retired/Emeritus Faculty

Cortes, Enrique (PhD, Southern California 1974; prof. emeritus)

Garber, Marilyn (PhD, UCLA 1967; prof. emeritus) US legal

Grenier, Judson (PhD, UCLA 1965; prof. emeritus) California, 19th-century US, education; jgrenier@csudh.edu

Hata, Donald Teruo, Jr. (PhD, Southern California 1970; prof. emeritus) Japanese Americans, history teaching; dhata@csudh.edu

Hollander, Nancy Caro (PhD, UCLA 1974; prof. emeritus) Latin America, women, film as history

Holter, Howard R. (PhD, Wisconsin, Madison 1967; prof. emeritus) modern Europe, world; hholter@csudh.edu

Jeffers, James S. (PhD, California, Irvine 1988; prof. emeritus) early Christianity, Roman Empire, Western religions; jjeffers@csudh.edu

Loeb, Lynne (PhD, Southern California 1997; assoc. prof. emeritus) 19th- and 20th-century US, social, gender; lloeb@csudh.edu

MacPhee, Donald A. (PhD, California, Berkeley 1959; prof. emeritus)

Pomerantz, Linda (PhD, UCLA 1970; prof. emeritus) China; lpomerantz@csudh.edu

Stricker, Frank (PhD, Princeton 1974; prof. emeritus) fstricker@csudh.edu

Udeze, Clement Okafor (MA, Minnesota 1967; asst. prof. emeritus) cudeze@csudh.edu

California State University, East Bay

Dept. of History, 25800 Carlos Bee Blvd., Hayward, CA 94542-3045. 510.885.3207. Fax 510.885.4791. Email: linda.ivey@csueastbay.edu. Website: http://www.csueastbay.edu/history.

The department offers both the BA and MA in history. Our faculty includes specialists in US, European, Latin American, and East Asian History, and the History of California and the US West.

Chair: Linda L. Ivey
Director of Graduate Studies: Kevin Kaatz
Degrees Offered: BA,MA
Academic Year System: Semester
Areas of Specialization: US, California/West, Europe, Asia, Latin America
Undergraduate Tuition (per academic year):
  In-State: $6453
  Out-of-State: $17631
Graduate Tuition (per academic year):
  In-State: $7719
  Out-of-State: $18879

Enrollment 2018-19:
  Undergraduate Majors: 160
  New Graduate Students: 16
  Full-time Graduate Students: 18
  Part-time Graduate Students: 20
  Degrees in History: 47 BA, 5 MA, PhD
Addresses:
  Admissions: http://www20.csueastbay.edu/prospective/
  Financial Aid: http://www20.csueastbay.edu/prospective/cost-and-financial-aid/

Full-time Faculty

Alexander, Anna Rose (PhD, Arizona 2012; asst. prof.) Latin America, environment, sustainability; anna.alexander@csueastbay.edu

Ford, Bridget (PhD, California, Davis 2002; prof.) New Republic, Civil War, American cultural and religious; bridget.ford@csueastbay.edu

Fozdar, Vahid J. (PhD, California, Berkeley 2001; assoc. prof.) modern South Asia, modern colonialism, Middle East; vahid.fozdar@csueastbay.edu

Garcia, Richard A. (PhD, California, Irvine 1980; prof.) Mexican American, California, US intellectual; richard.garcia@csueastbay.edu

Ivey, Linda (PhD, Georgetown 2003; prof. and chair) environmental, race/ethnicity/immigration, California; linda.ivey@csueastbay.edu

Kaatz, Kevin Warren (PhD, Macquarie, Australia 2004; asst. prof. and dir., grad. studies) digital, ancient world; kevin.kaatz@csueastbay.edu

McGuire, Elizabeth A. (PhD, California, Berkeley 2010; asst. prof.) globalization, Soviet Union, China; elizabeth.mcguire@csueastbay.edu

Phelps, Robert A. (PhD, California, Riverside 1996; assoc. prof.) California, US West, US urban; robert.phelps@csueastbay.edu

Weiss, Jessica (PhD, California, Berkeley 1994; prof.) recent US, women, family; jessica.weiss@csueastbay.edu

Part-time Faculty

Baldwin, Roger (MA, California, Berkeley 1989; lect.) US; roger.baldwin@csueastbay.edu

Brueck, Gregory J. (PhD, California, Davis 2012; lect.) American West; gregory.brueck@csueastbay.edu

Francois, Samantha Yates (PhD, California, Davis 2003; lect.) US, women; samantha.francois@csueastbay.edu

Houlihan, Lynn (MA, California State, East Bay 2012; lect.) nursing

Irwin, Mary Ann (MA, San Francisco State 1995; lect.) California, gender; maryann.irwin@csueastbay.edu

Kim, Richard J. (PhD, California, Berkeley 2005; lect.) modern Europe, world; richard.kim@csueastbay.edu

Klein, Benjamin F. (PhD, Brown 2002; lect.) early modern England, modern American cultural; bkklein@lmi.net

Pare, Karen L. (MA, Rutgers; lect.) US women

Park, Nancy (PhD, Harvard 1993; lect.) China; nancy.park@csueastbay.edu

Robinson, Daniel (PhD, Graduate Theological Union 2015; lect.) ancient world, early Christianity; daniel.robinson@csueastbay.edu

Retired/Emeritus Faculty

Andrews, Dee E. (PhD, Pennsylvania 1986; prof. emeritus) early America, social and cultural; dee.andrews@csueastbay.edu

Thompson, Nancy M. (PhD, Stanford 1994; prof. emeritus) medieval Europe, world civilizations; nancy.thompson@csueastbay.edu

California State University, Fresno

Dept. of History, 5340 N. Campus Dr., M/S SS21, Fresno, CA 93740-8019. 559.278.2153. Fax 559.278.5321 Email: ekytle@ csufresno.edu. Website: http://fresnostate.edu/socialsciences/ historydept/.

The Department of History at California State University, Fresno offers a variety of programs, including a BA, a history minor, and an MA with two different options: Traditional Track and Teaching Option, and a Jewish Studies Certificate.

Chair: Ethan Kytle
Director of Graduate Studies: Bradley Jones
Degrees Offered: BA,MA
Academic Year System: Semester
Areas of Specialization: US, Europe, Latin America, women and gender, world and Middle East
Undergraduate Tuition (per academic year):
In-State: $6589
Out-of-State: $11341
Graduate Tuition (per academic year):
In-State: $8023
Out-of-State: $12775
Enrollment 2018-19:
Undergraduate Majors: 337
New Graduate Students: 41
Full-time Graduate Students: 49
Part-time Graduate Students: 7
Degrees in History: 78 BA, 10 MA
Addresses:
Admissions: http://www.fresnostate.edu/home/admissions/
Financial Aid: http://www.fresnostate.edu/studentaffairs/ financialaid/

Full-time Faculty

Arvanigian, Mark E. (PhD, Durham, UK 2000; prof.) England, medieval Europe; marvanig@csufresno.edu
Cady, Daniel J. (PhD, Claremont Grad. 2005; assoc. prof.) American West and South, California; dcady@csufresno.edu
Clune, Lori A. (PhD, California, Davis 2010; prof.) 20th-century US, Cold War; lclune@csufresno.edu
DenBeste, Michelle D. (PhD, Southern Illinois, Carbondale 1997; prof.) world, Russia, women; mdenbest@csufresno.edu
Fields, Jill S. (PhD, Southern California 1997; prof.) 20th-century US, women; jfields@csufresno.edu
Guzman, Romeo (PhD, Columbia 2017; asst. prof.) Mexico; romeog@csufresno.edu
Jones, Brad A. (PhD, Glasgow 2006; prof. and dir., grad. studies) colonial America, British Atlantic world; brajones@csufresno. edu
Jordine, Melissa R. (PhD, Southern Illinois, Carbondale 1998; prof.) world, Europe, military; mjordine@csufresno.edu
Kytle, Ethan J. (PhD, North Carolina, Chapel Hill 2004; prof. and chair) 18th- and 19th-century US; ekytle@csufresno.edu
Lopez, Maritere (PhD, SUNY, Buffalo 2003; assoc. prof.) Renaissance and Reformation, world; mariterel@csufresno.edu
Roberts, Kathleen Blain (PhD, North Carolina, Chapel Hill 2005; prof.) modern US, women; broberts@csufresno.edu
Shatz, Julia Rivkind (PhD, California, Berkeley 2018; asst. prof.) Middle East, empire, childhood; jshatz@csufresno.edu
Skuban, William E. (PhD, California, Davis 2000; prof.) Latin America, US-Latin American relations; weskuban@csufresno. edu

Joint/Cross Appointments

Lopes, Maria-Aparecida (PhD, El Colegio de México 1999; prof.; Chicano and Latin American Studies) Latin America; mlopes@ csufresno.edu
Reese, De Anna J. (PhD, Missouri, Columbia 2004; prof.; Africana Studies) African American, women, modern US; dreese@ csufresno.edu

Retired/Emeritus Faculty

Simba, Malik (PhD, Minnesota 1977; prof. emeritus) modern US, Africa and African American; maliks@csufresno.edu

California State University, Fullerton

Dept. of History, PO Box 6846, Fullerton, CA 92834-6846. 657.278.3474. Fax 657.278.2101. Website: http://hss.fullerton. edu/history/.

Alternate Address: 800 N. State College Blvd., Fullerton, CA 92834

CSUF offers a BA, minor, and MA in history. The History Department provides academic advisement for these courses of study, as well as the Credential Program (also known as the "History Social Science Subject Matter Preparation Program"). Our undergraduate and graduate students are encouraged to participate in our Internship Program and become involved in our Center for Oral and Public History.

Chair: Jasamin Rostam-Kolayi
Director of Graduate Studies: Stephen Neufeld
Degrees Offered: BA,MA
Academic Year System: Semester
Areas of Specialization: America, Europe, world
Undergraduate Tuition (per academic year):
In-State: $6186
Out-of-State: $16236
Graduate Tuition (per academic year):
In-State: $7452
Out-of-State: $17268
Enrollment 2018-19:
Undergraduate Majors: 450
New Graduate Students: 50
Full-time Graduate Students: 100
Degrees in History: 120 BA, 25 MA
Undergraduate Addresses:
Admissions: http://www.fullerton.edu/admissions.aspx
Financial Aid: http://www.fullerton.edu/financialaid/
Graduate Addresses:
Admissions: http://fullerton.edu/admissions/ ProspectiveStudent/admissions_graduate.asp
Financial Aid: http://hss.fullerton.edu/history/

Full-time Faculty

Brown-Coronel, Margie (PhD, California, Irvine 2011; asst. prof.) US; mbrown-coronel@fullerton.edu
Brunelle, Gayle K. (PhD, Emory 1988; prof.) early modern Europe; gbrunelle@fullerton.edu
Burgtorf, Jochen (PhD, Heinrich-Heine, Duesseldorf, Germany 2001; prof.) medieval Europe, papacy, Crusades; jburgtorf@ fullerton.edu
Burlingham, Kate (PhD, Rutgers 2011; asssoc. prof.) US and world; kburlingham@fullerton.edu
Cawthra, Benjamin (PhD, Washington, St. Louis 2007; prof.) US cultural, public; bcawthra@fullerton.edu

Dennehy, Kristine (PhD, UCLA 2002; prof.) Japan; kdennehy@fullerton.edu

Fitch, Nancy E. (PhD, UCLA 1985; prof.) modern Europe; nfitch@fullerton.edu

Fousekis, Natalie M. (PhD, North Carolina, Chapel Hill 2000; prof. and dir., Center for Oral and Public Hist.) post-1945 US; nfousekis@fullerton.edu

Granata, Cora (PhD, North Carolina, Chapel Hill 2001; prof.) modern Germany, Europe; cgranata@fullerton.edu

Guia-Conca, Aitana (PhD, York, Can. 2012; assoc. prof.) modern Europe, Mediterranean; aguia@fullerton.edu

Janssen, Volker (PhD, California, San Diego 2005; prof.) California; vjanssen@fullerton.edu

Markley, Jonathan Bruce (PhD, Macquarie, Australia 2005; assoc. prof.) ancient China, Rome; jmarkley@fullerton.edu

McLain, Robert (PhD, Illinois, Urbana-Champaign 2002; prof.) modern Britain, British empire; rmclain@fullerton.edu

Mikhail, Maged S. (PhD, UCLA 2004; prof.) world 500-1500; mmikhail@fullerton.edu

Moore-Pewu, Jamila (PhD, California, Davis 2015; asst. prof.) digital, African diaspora, US; jmoorepewu@fullerton.edu

Neufeld, Stephen B. (PhD, Arizona 2009; prof. and dir., grad. studies) modern Mexico; sneufeld@fullerton.edu

O'Connor, Stephen (PhD, Columbia 2011; assoc. prof.) ancient Greece, military; soconnor@fullerton.edu

Rostam-Kolayi, Jasamin (PhD, UCLA 2000; prof. and chair) modern Middle East; jrostam@fullerton.edu

Stern, Jessica R. (PhD, Johns Hopkins 2007; prof.) colonial America; jessicastern@fullerton.edu

Sun, Laichen (PhD, Michigan 2000; prof.) Southeast Asia; ssun@fullerton.edu

Tran, Lisa (PhD, UCLA 2005; prof.) China, gender, law; lisatran@fullerton.edu

Varzally, Allison (PhD, UCLA 2002; prof.) California, US; avarzally@fullerton.edu

Zacair, Philippe (PhD, Paris, Sorbonne 1999; assoc. prof.) colonial Latin America; pzacair@fullerton.edu

Part-time Faculty

Chrissanthos, Stefan G. (PhD, Southern California 1999; lect.) Greece and Rome; schrissanthos@fullerton.edu

Christensen, Daniel Eric (PhD, California, Riverside 2004; lect.) modern Europe; dchristensen@fullerton.edu

Essington, Amy (PhD, Claremont Grad. 2013; lect.) US; aessington@fullerton.edu

Fogleman, Andrew M. (PhD, Southern California 2011; lect.) medieval Europe; afogleman@fullerton.edu

Freeman, David (PhD, Texas A&M 2000; lect.) modern Europe; dafreeman@fullerton.edu

Giacumakis, George (PhD, Brandeis 1963; prof. emeritus) Mediterranean and Middle East; ggiacumakis@fullerton.edu

Hall, David R. (PhD, California, Santa Barbara 2004; lect.) US; dhall@fullerton.edu

Myers, William A. (PhD, California, Riverside 1997; lect.) US; wmyers@fullerton.edu

Papandreu, Dimitri (PhD, California, Santa Cruz 2005; lect.) modern Europe; dpapandreu@fullerton.edu

Reemes, Dana (CPhil, UCLA; lect.) ancient Near East; dreemes@fullerton.edu

Rietveld, Ronald D. (PhD, Illinois, Urbana-Champaign 1967; prof. emeritus) American religious, Middle Period, Civil War and Reconstruction; rrietveld@fullerton.edu

Riggin, Lisa (PhD, California, Riverside 2006; lect.) US; lriggin@fullerton.edu

Seager, Michael Allen (PhD, California, Riverside 2009; lect.) US; mseager@fullerton.edu

Smith, Steven L. (PhD, California, Santa Barbara 2010; lect.) modern Europe, Middle East; stevensmith@fullerton.edu

Thompson, Jennifer (PhD, UCLA 1999; lect.) world; jethompson@fullerton.edu

Tippeconnic, Eric (PhD, New Mexico 2016; lect.) US and world; etippeconnic@fullerton.edu

Walia, Mark K. (PhD, California, Riverside 2001; lect.) Britain; mwalia@fullerton.edu

Retired/Emeritus Faculty

Bellot, Leland J. (PhD, Texas, Austin 1967; prof. emeritus) modern Britain, First British Empire, family; lbellot@fullerton.edu

Crabbs, Jack A., Jr. (PhD, Chicago 1971; prof. emeritus) historiography, Islamic civilization, modern Middle East; jcrabbs@fullerton.edu

De Graaf, Lawrence B. (PhD, UCLA 1962; prof. emeritus) community and local, public, Western black; ldegraaf@fullerton.edu

Feldman, Robert S. (PhD, Indiana 1967; prof. emeritus) Russian military, Russian Revolution, 20th-century Russia; rfeldman@fullerton.edu

Frazee, Charles A. (PhD, Indiana 1965; prof. emeritus) Balkans, east Mediterranean Byzantine, church; cfrazee@sbcglobal.net

Haddad, William W. (PhD, Ohio State 1970; prof. emeritus) Middle East, Japan; whaddad@fullerton.edu

Hansen, Arthur A. (PhD, California, Santa Barbara 1972; prof. emeritus) Japanese American, American oral and cultural radicalism; ahansen@fullerton.edu

Kupper, Samuel Y. (PhD, Michigan 1972; assoc. prof. emeritus) revolutionary China 1900–49, traditional Chinese legal, Peoples' Republic of China's utilization of Western legal systems; skupper@fullerton.edu

Pivar, David J. (PhD, Pennsylvania 1965; prof. emeritus) US, US social, economic; pivar@fullerton.edu

Putnam, Jackson K. (PhD, Stanford 1964; prof. emeritus) US westward movement, California, aging; jputnam@fullerton.edu

Shumway, Gary L. (PhD, Southern California 1969; prof. emeritus) westward movement, modern West, oral; gshumway@fullerton.edu

Toy, Ernest W. (MA, Southern California 1954; assoc. prof. emeritus) Britain; etoy@fullerton.edu

Van Deventer, David E. (PhD, Case Western Reserve 1969; prof. emeritus) early America to 1789, methodology; dvandeventer@fullerton.edu

Woodard, Nelson E. (PhD, Wisconsin, Madison 1970; assoc. prof. emeritus) US diplomatic, 20th-century US; nwoodard@fullerton.edu

Woodward, James F. (PhD, Denver 1972; prof. emeritus) science; jwoodward@fullerton.edu

Zinberg, Cecile (PhD, Chicago 1968; prof. emeritus) Tudor-Stuart England, European ecclesiastical, European historiography; czinberg@fullerton.edu

California State University, Long Beach

Dept. of History, 1250 Bellflower Blvd., Long Beach, CA 90840-1601. 562.985.4431. Fax 562.985.5431. Email: david.shafer@csulb.edu. Website: http://www.cla.csulb.edu/departments/history/.

We are a vibrant community of students, staff and faculty. We offer the BA and MA degrees in History, as well as the History minor. We are also the home of other degree-granting programs in Jewish Studies and Middle Eastern Studies.

Chair: David Shafer
Director of Graduate Studies: Caitlin Murdock
Degrees Offered: BA, MA
Academic Year System: Semester
Areas of Specialization: US/Europe/world, Latin America, Africa and Middle East, Asia, ancient and medieval
Undergraduate Tuition (per academic year):
In-State: $6452
Out-of-State: $9672
Graduate Tuition (per academic year):
In-State: $7718
Out-of-State: $13847
Teacher credential: $7328
Enrollment 2018-19:
Undergraduate Majors: 550
New Graduate Students: 15
Full-time Graduate Students: 60
Degrees in History: 99 BA, 14 MA
Addresses:
Admissions: http://www.csulb.edu/depts/enrollment/admissions/
Financial Aid: http://www.csulb.edu/depts/enrollment/financial_aid/

Full-time Faculty

Berquist Soule, Emily K. (PhD, Texas, Austin 2007; prof.) colonial Latin America, Peru; emily.berquist@csulb.edu

Cleary, Patricia A. (PhD, Northwestern 1989; prof.) colonial and early national America, women; patricia.cleary@csulb.edu

Curtis, Kenneth R. (PhD, Wisconsin-Madison 1989; prof.; Liberal Studies) Africa, Third World comparative; kenneth.curtis@csulb.edu

Dabel, Jane E. (PhD, UCLA 2000; prof.) 19th-century US, African American, women; jane.dabel@csulb.edu

Hawk, Angela S. (PhD, California, Irvine 2011; instr.) US, world; angela.hawk@csulb.edu

Igmen, Ali F. (PhD, Washington 2004; prof. and undergrad. advisor, Oral Hist. Program) Central Asia, Soviet Union, Turkic diaspora; ali.igmen@csulb.edu

Jenks, Andrew Leslie (PhD, Stanford 2002; prof.) Russia, Soviet Union; andrew.jenks@csulb.edu

Kelleher, Marie A. (PhD, Kansas 2003; prof.) Middle Ages, medieval Spain, women; m.kelleher@csulb.edu

Kuo, Margaret (PhD, UCLA 2003; prof.) modern China; margaret.kuo@csulb.edu

Lawler, Jeff (MA, California State, Long Beach 1998; lect.) US; jeffrey.lawler@csulb.edu

Li, Guotong (PhD, California, Davis 2007; prof.) imperial China; guotong.li@csulb.edu

Luhr, Eileen S. (PhD, California, Irvine 2004; assoc. prof.) US, culture, institutional; eileen.luhr@csulb.edu

Mizelle, Brett (PhD, Minnesota 2000; prof.; American Studies) early national US, social and cultural; brett.mizelle@csulb.edu

Murdock, Caitlin E. (PhD, Stanford 2003; prof. and dir., grad. studies) central and eastern Europe, borderlands; c.murdock@csulb.edu

Piña, Ulices (PhD, California, San Diego 2017; asst. prof.) modern Latin America, Mexico; ulices.pina@csulb.edu

Ponce de Leon, Charles Leonard (PhD, Rutgers 1992; prof.) US cultural and intellectual; charles.poncedeleon@csulb.edu

Quam-Wickham, Nancy L. (PhD, California, Berkeley 1994; prof.) US West, California, labor; nancy.quam-wickham@csulb.edu

Sayegh, Sharlene (PhD, California, Irvine 2004; lect.) 18th-century Britain, world, methodology and theory; sharlene.sayegh@csulb.edu

Schrank, Sarah (PhD, California, San Diego 2002; prof.) US urban, women; sarah.schrank@csulb.edu

Shafer, David (PhD, London 1994; prof. and chair) French social and cultural; david.shafer@csulb.edu

Sheridan, David Allen (PhD, Southern California 2007; lect.) Britain, women and gender, arts; david.sheridan@csulb.edu

Smith, Sean W. (MA, California State, Long Beach 1998; instr.) US, digital; sean.smith@csulb.edu

Takeuchi, Michiko (PhD, UCLA 2010; prof.) women and feminism(s) in Northeast Asia, sexuality, Japan-US relations; michiko.takeuchi@csulb.edu

Wilford, F. Hugh (PhD, Exeter 1991; prof.) US institutional; hugh.wilford@csulb.edu

Joint/Cross Appointments

Blutinger, Jeffrey C. (PhD, UCLA 2003; prof.; Jewish Studies) 18th-century European intellectual, Jewish, religion; jeffrey.blutinger@csulb.edu

Kaminsky, Arnold P. (PhD, UCLA 1976; prof.; Asian Studies) India, Southeast Asia, British Empire and Commonwealth; arnold.kaminsky@csulb.edu

Retired/Emeritus Faculty

Abrahamse, Dorothy de F. (PhD, Michigan 1967; prof. emerita) Byzantine, medieval Europe; dabraham@csulb.edu

Alkana, Linda Kelly (PhD, California, Irvine 1985; lect. emeritus) European intellectual, women, recent US; linda.alkana@csulb.edu

Berk, Stephen E. (PhD, Iowa 1971; prof. emeritus) American religious and cultural, social criticism, recent US; sberk@csulb.edu

Bernstein, David A. (PhD, Rutgers 1969; prof. emeritus) US since World War II, sports, methodology; dbernste@csulb.edu

Black, Paul V. (PhD, Wisconsin, Madison 1972; prof. emeritus) business, quantitative methods, recent US; pvblack@csulb.edu

Cerillo, Augustus, Jr. (PhD, Northwestern 1969; prof. emeritus) Progressive Era and early 20th-century US, American religious; acerillo@vanguard.edu

Collins, Keith E. (PhD, California, San Diego 1975; prof. emeritus) Civil War and Reconstruction, US South, urban; keith.collins@csulb.edu

Gluck, Sherna (MA, UCLA 1959; lect. emeritus) oral, women, recent US; sbgluck@csulb.edu

Gosselin, Edward A. (PhD, Columbia 1973; prof. emeritus) late medieval and early modern Europe, science, didactics; egosseli@csulb.edu

Gunns, Albert F. (PhD, Washington 1972; prof. emeritus) 20th-century US, World War II, modernization; agunns@csulb.edu

Polakoff, Keith I. (PhD, Northwestern 1968; prof. emeritus) 19th-century US, American political parties; kip@csulb.edu

Schwartz, Donald (PhD, NYU 1977; prof. emeritus) modern Europe, recent US; don.schwartz@csulb.edu

Springer, Arnold R. (PhD, UCLA 1971; prof. emeritus) imperial Russia, local, methodology; ulanbator@venice-ca.com

Weber, William A. (PhD, Chicago 1970; prof. emeritus) modern Europe, social history of music; william.weber@csulb.edu

California State University, Los Angeles

Dept. of History, 5151 State University Dr., Los Angeles, CA 90032-8223. 323.343.2020. Fax 323.343.6431. Email: history@calstatela.edu. Website: http://www.calstatela.edu/academic/history/.

The Cal State L.A. History Department faculty believes that historical perspective is fundamental to understanding the world in which we live. To that end, the department offers a great variety of courses to both majors and non-majors that explore both past and contemporary societies and their peoples.

Chair: Mark Wild
Director of Graduate Studies: Birte Pfleger
Degrees Offered: BA,MA
Academic Year System: Semester
Areas of Specialization: US, world, Latin America, Europe, Africa/Asia/Middle East
Undergraduate Tuition (per academic year):
   In-State: $6764
   Out-of-State: $16248
Graduate Tuition (per academic year):
   In-State: $8198
   Out-of-State: $17568
Enrollment 2018-19:
   Undergraduate Majors: 231
   New Graduate Students: 28
   Full-time Graduate Students: 24
   Part-time Graduate Students: 24
   Degrees in History: 50 BA, 12 MA
Undergraduate Addresses:
   Admissions: http://www.calstatela.edu/admissions
   Financial Aid: http://www.calstatela.edu/financialaid
Graduate Addresses:
   Admissions: http://www.calstatela.edu/graduateadmissions
   Financial Aid: http://www.calstatela.edu/financialaid

Full-time Faculty

Chatterjee, Choi (PhD, Indiana 1995; prof.) modern Europe, Russia; cchatte@calstatela.edu

Doran, Timothy (PhD, California, Berkeley 2011; asst. prof.) ancient Greece and Rome, world, historical deomography and sociobiology; tdoran@calstatela.edu

Endy, Christopher (PhD, North Carolina, Chapel Hill 2000; prof.) 20th-century US, international relations; cendy@calstatela.edu

Ford, Eileen Mary (PhD, Illinois, Urbana-Champaign 2007; assoc. prof.) Mexico, Latin America, childhood; eford@calstatela.edu

Koos, Cheryl A. (PhD, Southern California 1996; prof.) modern Europe, France; ckoos@calstatela.edu

Lee, M. Kittiya (PhD, Johns Hopkins 2006; assoc. prof.) colonial Latin America, Brazil, ethnography; klee40@calstatela.edu

Mahoney, Lynn (PhD, Rutgers 1999; prof.) US social, gender and women's studies, US race and ethnicity; Lynn.Mahoney@calstatela.edu

Matin-asgari, Afshin (PhD, UCLA 1993; prof.) Middle East, religion; amatina@calstatela.edu

Ochoa, Enrique C. (PhD, UCLA 1993; prof.; Latin American Studies) Mexico, Latin America; eochoa3@calstatela.edu

Pfleger, Birte B. (PhD, California, Irvine 2003; prof. and dir., grad. studies) early US, social; bpflege@calstatela.edu

Pugach, Sara E. (PhD, Chicago 2001; prof.) Africa, world, Germany; spugach@calstatela.edu

Schoepflin, Rennie B. (PhD, Wisconsin, Madison 1995; prof.) US, intellectual, science/medicine/religion; rschoep@calstatela.edu

Vergara, Angela (PhD, California, San Diego 2002; prof.) Latin America, labor; avergar@calstatela.edu

Wells, Scott (PhD, NYU 2003; prof.) medieval Europe, intellectual, Germany; swells2@calstatela.edu

Wild, H. Mark (PhD, California, San Diego 2000; prof. and chair) US, urban, religion; mwild@calstatela.edu

Yao, Ping (PhD, Illinois, Urbana-Champaign 1997; prof.) Asia, China, women and gender; pyao@calstatela.edu

Yeakey, Lamont H. (PhD, Columbia 1979; assoc. prof.) 19th- and 20th-century US, social and intellectual, Afro-American and US South; lyeakey@calstatela.edu

Part-time Faculty

Alvarez, Thomas A. (PhD, Michigan 2007; lect.) US, race, politics; talavar10@calstatela.edu

Beirich, Gregory S. (PhD, Fordham 1999; lect.) world civilization, medieval Europe; gbeiric@calstatela.edu

Callejas, Karla (EdD, Southern California 2016; lect.) pedagogy, US; Karla.Callejas4@calstatela.edu

Cardona, Cynthia (PhD, California, Irvine 2015; lect.) Europe, France, gender; ccardon7@calstatela.edu

Cohen, Julie T. (PhD, California, Irvine 2009; lect.) California, US West, women and gender; Julie.Cohen6@calstatela.edu

Cupchoy, Lani (PhD, California, Irvine 2015; lect.) US, Chicana/o and Latina/o studies; lcupcho@calstatela.edu

Curren, Jennifer (MA, Southern California; lect.) world civilization, US; jcurren@calstatela.edu

Dennis, Dawn Amber (PhD, Claremont Graduate 2011; lect.) US, pan-African studies, archival studies; ddennis3@calstatela.edu

Donovan, John T. (PhD, Marquette 2000; lect.) 20th-century US, diplomatic, religion; jdonova@calstatela.edu

Guillow, Lawrence (PhD, Arizona State 1996; lect.) US, California, Southwest; lguillo@calstatela.edu

Hortua, Giovanni (PhD, California, Irvine 2013; lect.) Latin America, US, critical theory; ghortua@calstatela.edu

Paynich, Timothy John (ABD, California, Riverside 1991; lect.) Russia, Europe, military; tpaynic@calstatela.edu

Sater Foss, M. Nichole (PhD, California, Santa Barbara 2014; lect.) US, women and gender; msaterf@calstatela.edu

Retired/Emeritus Faculty

Allswang, John M. (PhD, Pittsburgh 1967; prof. emeritus) 20th-century US, political, social; allswang@adelphia.net

Balderrama, Francisco (PhD, UCLA 1978; prof. emeritus) California, Southwest, Chicano; fbalder@calstatela.edu

Burns, Richard Dean (PhD, Illinois, Urbana-Champaign 1960; prof. emeritus) 19th- and 20th-century US, diplomatic; rdburns@earthlink.net

Burstein, Stanley M. (PhD, UCLA 1972; prof. emeritus) ancient Near East, Greece, Rome; sburste@calstatela.edu

Crecelius, Daniel (PhD, Princeton 1967; prof. emeritus) Near East, Islamic; dcrecel@calstatela.edu

Harding, Timothy F. (PhD, Stanford 1973; prof. emeritus) Latin America, Brazil, Cuba

Heyn, Udo (PhD, Wisconsin, Madison 1969; prof. emeritus) European social and intellectual, economic, war and peace issues; uheyn@calstatela.edu

Leung, Yuen-Sang (PhD, California, Santa Barbara 1980; prof. emeritus) modern China, Chinese immigration, US-Chinese relations; yuensleung@cuhk.edu.hk

Pincus, Arnold (MA, Brooklyn, CUNY 1952; asst. prof. emeritus) Renaissance and Reformation, 17th- and 18th-century Europe

Rabitoy, Neil (PhD, Pennsylvania 1972; prof. emeritus) South Asia, British Empire

Schiesl, Martin J. (PhD, SUNY, Buffalo 1972; prof. emeritus) 19th- and 20th-century US, urban, California and Los Angeles; mschies@calstatela.edu

Smith, Arthur L., Jr. (PhD, Southern California 1956; prof. emeritus) 19th- and 20th-century Europe, Germany; arthursmith@cox.net

Srole, Carole (PhD, UCLA 1984; prof. emeritus) 19th- and 20th-century US, social and labor, family and women; csrole@calstatela.edu

Taiz, Lillian K. (PhD, California, Davis 1994; prof. emeritus) 19th-century US, social, cultural; ltaiz@calstatela.edu

California State University, Northridge

Dept. of History, Sierra Tower 612, 18111 Nordhoff St., Northridge, CA 91330-8250. 818.677.3566. Fax 818.677.3614. Email: kelly. winkleblack.shea@csun.edu. Website: https://www.csun.edu/ social-behavioral-sciences/history.

The History Department combines teaching and research at the highest levels.

Chair: Susan Fitzpatrick Behrens
Degrees Offered: BA,MA
Academic Year System: Semester
Areas of Specialization: US, local and urban archival, California, Europe, Third World
Undergraduate Tuition (per academic year):
   In-State: $6870
   Out-of-State: $9325
Graduate Tuition (per academic year):
   In-State: $8304
   Out-of-State: $11689
Enrollment 2018-19:
   Undergraduate Majors: 326
   New Graduate Students: 21
   Full-time Graduate Students: 15
   Part-time Graduate Students: 21
   Degrees in History: 115 BA, 10 MA, PhD
Addresses:
   Admissions: http://www.csun.edu/admissions-records
   Financial Aid: http://www.csun.edu/financialaid

Full-time Faculty

Auerbach, Jeffrey A. (PhD, Yale 1995; prof.) Britain, imperialism, world; jeffrey.auerbach@csun.edu

Broussard, Joyce L. (PhD, Southern California 1998; prof.) US women and gender; joyce.broussard@csun.edu

Devine, Thomas W. (PhD, North Carolina, Chapel Hill 2000; prof.) 20th-century US; tom.devine@csun.edu

Fitzpatrick Behrens, Susan R. (PhD, California, San Diego 2001; prof. and chair) Central and South America, indigenous peoples, religion; susan.fitzpatrick@csun.edu

Goldner, Erik (PhD, Columbia 2008; assoc. prof.) early modern Europe; erik.goldner@csun.edu

Horowitz, Richard S. (PhD, Harvard 1998; prof.) China, Japan; richard.s.horowitz@csun.edu

Howes, Rachel T. (PhD, California, Santa Barbara 2003; assoc. prof.) Islamic world, Middle East, world; rachel.howes@csun.edu

Juarez-Dappe, Patricia I. (PhD, UCLA 2002; prof.) Latin America, Argentina, economic and social; patricia.juarezdappe@csun.edu

Kaja, Jeffrey D. (PhD, Michigan 2011; asst. prof.) colonial America, early US; jeffrey.kaja@csun.edu

Kim, Jessica Michelle (PhD, Southern California 2012; asst. prof.) California and West, borderlands, public; jessica.kim@csun.edu

Neirick, Miriam Beth (PhD, California, Berkeley 2007; assoc. prof.) Russia, Soviet Union; miriam.neirick@csun.edu

Nuno, John Paul A. (PhD, Texas, El Paso 2010; asst. prof.) colonial America, early US, American Indian; johnpaul.nuno@csun.edu

O'Sullivan, Donal B. (PhD, Catholic, Eichstatt, Germany 2001; prof.) Russia, Soviet Union, international relations; donal.osullivan@csun.edu

Oliver, Clementine (PhD, California, Berkeley 2000; prof.) medieval Europe; coliver@csun.edu

Sides, Josh A. (PhD, UCLA 1999; Whitsett Prof.) California; jsides@csun.edu

Retired/Emeritus Faculty

Broesamle, John J. (PhD, Columbia 1969; prof. emeritus) 20th-century US political, social

Camp, Richard L. (PhD, Columbia 1965; prof. emeritus) Europe, women; richard.camp@csun.edu

Chen, Joseph T. (PhD, California, Berkeley 1964; prof. emeritus) China

Davis, Ronald L. F. (PhD, Missouri-Columbia 1974; prof. emeritus) US economic, labor, Civil War; ronald.davis@csun.edu

Dirrim, Allen W. (PhD, Indiana 1959; prof. emeritus) population, early modern Europe, US

Keller, Ralph A. (PhD, Wisconsin, Madison 1969; prof. emeritus) American church, slavery, US

Koistinen, Paul A. (PhD, California, Berkeley 1964; prof. emeritus) US economic, sociological, political

Maddux, Thomas R. (PhD, Michigan 1969; prof. emeritus) US, diplomatic, foreign affairs; thomas.maddux@csun.edu

Meyer, Michael (PhD, UCLA 1970; prof. emeritus) Germany, anti-Semitism, cultural; michael.meyer@csun.edu

Morse, Darrell P. (PhD, California, Berkeley 1962; prof. emeritus) France, science

Muller, Alexander V. (PhD, Washington 1973; prof. emeritus) Russia, modern Europe, Byzantine

Nava, Julian (PhD, Harvard 1955; prof. emeritus) US, Latin America, Mexico

Ovnick, Merry A. (PhD, UCLA 2000; assoc. prof. emeritus) US urban, Los Angeles; merry.ovnick@csun.edu

Resovich, Thomas (PhD, Wisconsin, Madison 1966; prof. emeritus) modern Europe, 20th-century Germany and France

Shaw, Ezel Kural (PhD, Harvard 1975; prof. emeritus) Byzantine, Middle East, Europe

Soffer, Reba N. (PhD, Radcliffe 1962; prof. emeritus) England, European social and intellectual, philosophy of history; rsoffer@csun.edu

Vatai, Frank L. (PhD, SUNY, Binghamton 1982; assoc. prof. emeritus) ancient, European intellectual; frank.vatai@csun.edu

Wood, David L. (PhD, Utah 1972; prof. emeritus) Latin America, frontier, American Indian

California State University, Sacramento

Dept. of History, 3080 Tahoe Hall, 6000 J St., Sacramento, CA 95819-6059. 916.278.6206. Fax 916.278.7476. Email: history@csus.edu. Website: https://www.csus.edu/college/arts-letters/history/.

The PhD program in Public History is a joint program with the University of California at Santa Barbara.

Chair: Jeffrey K. Wilson

Director of Graduate Studies: Nikolaos Lazaridis; Anne Lindsay (public hist.)

Degrees Offered: BA,MA,PhD

Academic Year System: Semester

Areas of Specialization: US, public, California, American West, world

Undergraduate Tuition (per academic year):
In-State: $6900
Out-of-State: $12480

Graduate Tuition (per academic year):
In-State: $8166
Out-of-State: $11514

Enrollment 2018-19:
Undergraduate Majors: 452
New Graduate Students: 30
Full-time Graduate Students: 33
Part-time Graduate Students: 46
Degrees in History: 112 BA, 22 MA
Students in Undergraduate Courses: 9593
Students in Undergraduate Intro Courses: 5239

Undergraduate Addresses:
Admissions: http://www.csus.edu/admissions/
Financial Aid: http://www.csus.edu/faid/

Graduate Addresses:
Admissions: http://www.csus.edu/gradstudies/FutureStudents/GraduateAdmissions/
Financial Aid: http://www.csus.edu/faid/

Full-time Faculty

Atamaz-Topcu, Serpil (PhD, Arizona 2010; asst. prof.) Middle East, Ottoman Empire, women; atamaztopcu@csus.edu

Austin, Paula (PhD, Graduate Center, CUNY 2015; asst. prof.) African American, US; paula.austin@csus.edu

Burke, Chloe S. (PhD, Michigan 2005; assoc. prof.) US cultural; cburke@csus.edu

Castaneda, Chris J. (PhD, Houston 1990; prof.) US economic, public; cjc@csus.edu

Cohen, Aaron J. (PhD, Johns Hopkins 1998; prof.) Russia; cohenaj@csus.edu

Dym, Jeffrey A. (PhD, Hawai'i, Manoa 1998; prof.) Japan, film; dym@csus.edu

Ettinger, Patrick W. (PhD, Indiana 2000; prof.) American West, immigration, oral; ettinger@csus.edu

Gaston, Jessie (PhD, UCLA 1984; prof.) Africa, African American, ethnic studies; gaston@csus.edu

Gregory, Candace (PhD, Yale 2003; prof.) medieval Europe; cgregory@csus.edu

Kluchin, Rebecca M. (PhD, Carnegie Mellon 2004; prof.) US, women, health care policy; rkluchin@csus.edu

Lagos, Katerina G. (PhD, Oxford 2005; prof.) modern Greece, Europe; klagos@csus.edu

Lazaridis, Nikolaos (DPhil, Oxford 2006; prof. and dir., grad. studies) ancient Greece, Rome, Egypt; lazaridi@saclink.csus.edu

Lindsay, Anne M. (PhD, California, Riverside 2010; asst. prof. and dir., grad. studies) public, colonial US; anne.lindsay@csus.edu

Lindsay, Brendan Charles (PhD, California, Riverside 2007; asst. prof.) California, Native American; brendan.lindsay@csus.edu

Numark, Mitch (PhD, UCLA 2006; assoc. prof.) modern Britain and British Empire, South Asia, Jewish; mnumark@saclink.csus.edu

Ocegueda, Mark Anthony (PhD, California, Irvine 2017; asst. prof.) US, Mexican American, public; ocegueda@csus.edu

Palermo, Joseph A. (PhD, Cornell 1998; prof.) US, 20th-century politics; jpalermo@csus.edu

Schneider, Khal R. (PhD, California, Berkeley 2006; assoc. prof.) American Indian, California, American West; schneider@csus.edu

Siegel, Mona L. (PhD, Wisconsin, Madison 1996; prof.) modern Europe, France; msiegel@csus.edu

Simpson, Lee M. A. (PhD, California, Riverside 1996; prof.) public, urban; lsimpson@csus.edu

Vann, Michael G. (PhD, California, Santa Cruz 1999; prof.) world, French colonial empires; mikevann@csus.edu

Wilson, Jeffrey K. (PhD, Michigan 2002; prof. and chair) modern Europe, Germany, European environmental; jkwilson@csus.edu

Part-time Faculty

Lupo, Michael Scott (PhD, Nevada, Reno 2002; lect.) US, cultural; sac69485@csus.edu

Reed, Loretta G. (PhD, California, Davis 2000; lect.) ancient, women; lreed@csus.edu

Retired/Emeritus Faculty

Chambers, Henry E. (PhD, Indiana 1968; prof. emeritus) ancient Near East, Greece and Rome, Middle East; hchamber@csus.edu

Craft, George S., Jr. (PhD, Stanford 1970; prof. emeritus) modern Europe, modern France; gcraft@csus.edu

Donaldson, Robert C. (PhD, Michigan 1954; prof. emeritus) modern Europe

Garosi, Frank J. (PhD, Minnesota 1965; prof. emeritus) 18th-century Europe, French Revolution and Napoleon, European warfare; garosi@saclink.csus.edu

Goodart, Margaret M. (PhD, California, Davis 1975; prof. emeritus) US, US women, Civil War; goodartm@saclink.csus.edu

Kornweibel, Richard (PhD, California, Santa Barbara 1971; prof. emeritus) Latin America; kornweibelr@saclink.csus.edu

Long, Robert E. (PhD, Wisconsin, Madison 1969; prof. emeritus) recent US; relong@csus.edu

Lower, Richard C. (PhD, California, Berkeley 1969; prof. emeritus) early 20th-century US; rclower@csus.edu

Moon, S. Joan (PhD, Wayne State 1968; prof. emeritus) modern Europe, European women; joanmoon@csus.edu

Moore, Shirley Ann (PhD, California, Berkeley 1989; prof. emeritus) US, African American; smoore@csus.edu

Mullin, Michael (PhD, California, Berkeley 1968; prof. emeritus) colonial America, American Revolution, social

Pitti, Joseph A. (PhD, New Mexico 1975; prof. emeritus) US, California; japitti@saclink.csus.edu

Roberts, Charles E. (PhD, Oregon 1975; prof. emeritus) American Indian; cerobts@saclink.csus.edu

Tobey, Jerry L. (PhD, Brandeis 1964; prof. emeritus) European intellectual, early Christianity; wuff@saclink.csus.edu

Von Den Steinen, Karl (PhD, UCLA 1969; prof. emeritus) Britain, military; karl@csus.edu

Williamson, Arthur H. (PhD, Washington, St. Louis 1974; prof. emeritus) European intellectual, Britain; williamsonah@csus.edu

California State University, San Bernardino

Dept. of History, 5500 University Pkwy, San Bernardino, CA 92407-2397. 909.537.5524. Fax 909.537.7645. Email: pcrosson@csusb.edu; tjones@csusb.edu. Website: https://csbs.csusb.edu/history.

The Department of History is part of the College of Social and Behavioral Sciences and offers three undergraduate majors, a history minor, and participates in the MA Social Sciences program. The department is committed to excellent instruction and high levels of research.

Chair: Tiffany Jones
Degrees Offered: BA
Academic Year System: Quarter
Areas of Specialization: US, Africa, Europe, Latin America, Asia
Tuition (per academic year):
In-State: $6567
Out-of-State: add $248 per unit
Enrollment 2018-19:
Undergraduate Majors: 316
Degrees in History: 78 BA
Addresses:
Admissions: http://admissions.csusb.edu/
Financial Aid: http://finaid.csusb.edu/

Full-time Faculty

Barber, Cary Michael (PhD, Ohio State 2016; asst. prof.) ancient; barberc@wfu.edu
Huacuja Alonso, Isabel (PhD, Texas, Austin 2015; asst. prof.) South Asia, media studies; iha@csusb.edu
Johnson, Diana (PhD, California, Davis 2107; asst. prof.) 20th-century US race and ethnicity; dekjohnson@ucdavis.edu
Jones, Tiffany F. (PhD, Queen's, Can. 2004; prof. and chair) Africa, health and disease, madness; tjones@csusb.edu
Keating, Ryan W. (PhD, Fordham 2013; assoc. prof.) Civil War and Reconstruction; rkeating@csusb.edu
Liszka, Kate (PhD, Pennsylvania 2012; asst. prof.; Near Eastern Languages and Civilizations) Egyptology, ancient Egyptian and Nubian interactions, archaeology; kate.liszka@csusb.edu
Long, Thomas E. (PhD, California, Riverside 2006; prof.) public, Native American, US; tlong@csusb.edu
Murray, Jeremy Andrew (PhD, California, San Diego 2011; assoc. prof.) 20th-century China; jmurray@csusb.edu
Pytell, Timothy E. (PhD, NYU 2002; prof.) modern Europe; tpytell@csusb.edu
Robinson, Marc Arsell (PhD, Washington State 2012; asst. prof.) African American; marc.robinson@csusb.edu
Samuelson, Richard A. (PhD, Virginia 2000; assoc. prof.) US; rsamuels@csusb.edu
Yaghoubian, David N. (PhD, California, Berkeley 2000; prof.) Middle East, Islam; dny@csusb.edu

Retired/Emeritus Faculty

Blackey, Robert A. (PhD, NYU 1968; prof. emeritus) Britain, early modern Europe, revolutions; rblackey@csusb.edu
Fields, Lanny B. (PhD, Indiana 1972; prof. emeritus) China and Japan, Asia, Russia
Hanson, Joyce A. (PhD, Connecticut 1997; prof. emeritus) US, African American, women; jahanson@csusb.edu
McAfee, Ward M. (PhD, Stanford 1965; prof. emeritus) US, world religious, historiography; wmcafee@csusb.edu
Persell, S. Michael (PhD, Stanford 1969; prof. emeritus) modern Europe, France, North Africa
Riggs, Cheryl (PhD, California, Santa Barbara 1989; prof. emeritus) medieval Europe, Greece, Rome; criggs@csusb.edu
Santoni, Pedro M. (PhD, Colegio de Mexico 1987; prof. emeritus) Mexico, Latin America; psantoni@csusb.edu
Schofield, Kent M. (PhD, California, Riverside 1966; prof. emeritus) US, family, military

California State University, San Marcos

Dept. of History, 333 S. Twin Oak Valley Rd., San Marcos, CA 92096-0001. 760.750.4152. Fax 760.750.3190. Email: history@csusm.edu. Website: https://www.csusm.edu/history/.

Our department consists of faculty who are committed to excellence in teaching, research, and serving the university and the wider community.

Chair: Carmen Nava
Degrees Offered: BA,MA
Academic Year System: Semester
Areas of Specialization: US, world, social and cultural, gender, film and media
Undergraduate Tuition (per academic year):
In-State: $7702
Out-of-State: $14400
Graduate Tuition (per academic year):
In-State: $9136
Out-of-State: $15666
Enrollment 2018-19:
Undergraduate Majors: 241
Degrees in History: 67 BA, 7 MA
Undergraduate Addresses:
Admissions: http://www.csusm.edu/admissions
Financial Aid: http://www.csusm.edu/finaid/
Graduate Addresses:
Admissions: http://www.csusm.edu/gsr/graduatestudies/
Financial Aid: http://www.csusm.edu/finaid/

Adjunct Faculty

Bechtol, Jonathan (MA, California State, San Marcos 2010; adj.) jbechtol@csusm.edu
Elwood, Ann (PhD, California, San Diego 1989; adj. lect.) Europe, women; aelwood@csusm.edu
Garcia, Octavio Delgadillo (PhD, Arizona 2015; adj. instr.) African population in Central America; ogarcia@csusm.edu
Henderson, Michael (adj. lect.) mhenderson@csusm.edu
McGuire, Melissa M. (MA, Southern Illinois, Edwardsville 2002; adj. lect.) America, Western civilization; mmcguire@csusm.edu
Miller, Robert David (PhD, California, Riverside 2011; adj. lect.) romiller@csusm.edu
Strathman, Andy (PhD, California, San Diego 2005; adj. lect.) America, California, environmental issues; astrathm@csusm.edu

Full-time Faculty

Al-Marashi, Ibrahim (DPhil, Oxford 2004; assoc. prof.) Univ. of Oxford; ialmarashi@csusm.edu
Charles, Jeffrey (PhD, Johns Hopkins 1987; assoc. prof.) US urban, social and cultural, sports; jcharles@csusm.edu
Engen, Darel Tai (PhD, UCLA 1996; assoc. prof.) ancient world, Greece and Rome; dengen@csusm.edu
Hijar, Katherine (PhD, Johns Hopkins 2008; asst. prof.) America, social and cultural, women/gender/urban; khijar@csusm.edu
Kang, S. Deborah (PhD, California, Berkeley 2005; assoc. prof.) US West and borderlands, immigration, legal; dkang@csusm.edu
Mekenye, Reuben (PhD, UCLA 1996; assoc. prof.) southern Africa, modern Africa; rmekenye@csusm.edu
Nava, Carmen (PhD, UCLA 1995; prof. and chair) Latin America/Brazil, Chicano/a, gender; cnava@csusm.edu

Quinney, Kimber M. (PhD, California, Santa Barbara 2003; asst. prof.) America, international relations, modern Europe; kquinney@csusm.edu

Seleski, Patricia S. (PhD, Stanford 1989; prof.) modern Europe, British Isles, international studies; pseleski@csusm.edu

Sepinwall, Alyssa Goldstein (PhD, Stanford 1998; prof.) world, France, Jewish studies; sepinwal@csusm.edu

Watts, Jill M. (PhD, UCLA 1989; prof.) 20th-century America, social and cultural, African American; jwatts@csusm.edu

Xiao, Zhiwei (PhD, California, San Diego 1994; prof.) Asia, modern China, Chinese cinema; zxiao@csusm.edu

Zaldivar, Antonio M. (PhD, UCLA 2014; asst. prof.) azaldivar@csusm.edu

Retired/Emeritus Faculty

Gundersen, Joan R. (PhD, Notre Dame 1972; prof. emeritus) colonial America, women's studies, religion

Lombard, Anne S. (PhD, UCLA 1998; prof. emeritus) colonial America, gender, law; alombard@csusm.edu

California State University, Stanislaus

Dept. of History, One University Circle, Turlock, CA 95382. 209.667.3238. Fax 209.667.3132. Email: pgarone@csustan.edu; aandrade@csustan.edu. Website: https://www.csustan.edu/history.

How did we get where we are today? What caused past events? What differences did individuals make? If these and other questions intrigue you, history has the answers-or, more specifically, a choice of answers. Stanislaus State offers you the chance to study the varieties of history, explore your own favorite corners of the past, and effectively communicate what you've discovered.

Chair: Philip Garone
Director of Graduate Studies: Brandon Wolfe-Hunnicutt
Degrees Offered: BA,MA
Academic Year System: Semester
Areas of Specialization: US, Europe, Asia, Latin America, Middle East
Undergraduate Tuition (per academic year):
 In-State: $7076
 Out-of-State: add $396 per unit
Graduate Tuition (per academic year):
 In-State: $8509
 Out-of-State: add $396 per unit
Enrollment 2018-19:
 Undergraduate Majors: 186
 New Graduate Students: 8
 Full-time Graduate Students: 18
 Degrees in History: 45 BA, 5 MA
Undergraduate Addresses:
 Admissions: http://www.csustan.edu/admissions
 Financial Aid: http://www.csustan.edu/financial-aid-scholarships
Graduate Addresses:
 Admissions: http://www.csustan.edu/grad
 Financial Aid: http://www.csustan.edu/financial-aid-scholarships

Full-time Faculty

Carroll, Bret Evan (PhD, Cornell 1991; prof.) early national and antebellum US, US gender and masculinity, US religious and family; bcarroll@csustan.edu

Garone, Philip F. (PhD, California, Davis 2006; prof. and chair) environmental history and ecology, California, US West, US since Civil War; pgarone@csustan.edu

Strauss, Paul (PhD, Nebraska, Lincoln 2016; asst. prof.) German Reformation, early modern Europe, Renaissance; pstrauss@csustan.edu

Wang, Shuo (PhD, Michigan State 2002; prof.) East Asia, modern China, gender and ethnicity; swang@csustan.edu

Weikart, Richard C. (PhD, Iowa 1994; prof.) modern Europe, modern Germany, European intellectual; rweikart@csustan.edu

Wolfe-Hunnicutt, Brandon (PhD, Stanford 2011; assoc. prof. and dir., grad. studies) US diplomatic, Middle East; bwolfehunnicutt@csustan.edu

Retired/Emeritus Faculty

Grant, Curtis R. (PhD, Stanford 1968; prof. emeritus) early national US, antebellum US, American religious

Oppenheim, Samuel A. (PhD, Indiana 1972; prof. emeritus) modern Russia, modern Europe, Jewish and Holocaust; soppenheim@csustan.edu

Regalado, Samuel O. (PhD, Washington State 1987; prof. emeritus) US, Latin America/East Asia, US ethnic/immigration/sport/legal; sregalado@csustan.edu

Royer, Katherine A. (PhD, Stanford 2001; prof. emerita) medieval and early modern Europe, Britain and empire, legal and disease; kroyer@csustan.edu

Sanchez-Walker, Marjorie (PhD, Washington State 1999; prof. emerita) Latin America, comparative world women, 19th- and 20th-century Middle East; mwalker@csustan.edu

Taniguchi, Nancy J. (PhD, Utah 1985; prof. emerita) post-Civil War US, California, US legal; ntaniguchi@csustan.edu

California University of Pennsylvania

Dept. of History, Politics, Society & Law, 250 University Ave., Box 6, California, PA 15419-1394. 724.938.4054. Fax 724.938.5942. Email: slaven@calu.edu; speer@calu.edu. Website: https://www.calu.edu/academics/undergraduate/bachelors/history/.

Our history program encourages literate, critical thinking by students who work with faculty engaged in diverse, broadly based scholarship

Chair: Michael Slaven
Degrees Offered: BA
Academic Year System: Semester
Areas of Specialization: US social, African American and contemporary, western European social, public, medieval
Tuition (per academic year):
 In-State: $7492
 Out-of-State: $11238
Enrollment 2018-19:
 Undergraduate Majors: 56
 Degrees in History: 8 BA
 Students in Undergraduate Courses: 1125
 Students in Undergraduate Intro Courses: 624

Addresses:

Admissions: http://www.calu.edu/prospective/undergraduate-admissions/

Financial Aid: http://www.calu.edu/tuition-and-aid/

Full-time Faculty

Confer, Clarissa W. (PhD, Penn State 1997; asst. prof.) 19th-century social, Civil War, Native American; confer_c@calu.edu

Crawford, Paul F. (PhD, Wisconsin, Madison 1998; asst. prof.) ancient and medieval studies; crawford_p@calu.edu

Edmonds, Kelton R. (PhD, Missouri, Columbia 2005; asst. prof.) 20th-century US, African American and black studies; edmonds_k@calu.edu

Madden, Sean C. (DA, Carnegie Mellon 1988; prof.) US social, US constitutional, sport; madden@calu.edu

Slaven, Michael D. (PhD, West Virginia 1993; prof. and chair) early modern France and European cultural, contemporary European cultural; slaven@calu.edu

Smith, Craig A. (PhD, Missouri, Kansas City 2003; asst. prof.) constitutional, secondary education; smith_c@calu.edu

Tuennerman, Laura A. (PhD, Minnesota 1997; prof.) public, US cultural and social, women; tuennerman@calu.edu

Retired/Emeritus Faculty

Bauman, John F. (PhD, Rutgers 1969; prof. emeritus) urban, African American, modern America

Edwards, Frank T. (PhD, Catholic 1969; prof. emeritus) foreign relations, military

Folmar, J. K. (PhD, Alabama 1968; prof. emeritus) US transportation, Civil War and Reconstruction, local and Pennsylvania

Calvin College

Dept. of History, Hiemenga Hall 481, 1845 Knollcrest Cir. SE, Grand Rapids, MI 49546. 616.526.6394. Fax 616.526.8799. Email: history@calvin.edu. Website: https://calvin.edu/academics/departments-programs/history/.

We study the past to understand humanity's place in the world, to remember those who came before us, and to help us live more wisely in our own time.

Chair: Kristin Kobes Du Mez
Degrees Offered: BA
Academic Year System: 4-1-4
Areas of Specialization: US cultural/religious/intellectual, ancient/medieval/early modern Europe, Roman and Near Eastern archaeology, Mediterranean world and modern Middle East, women and gender
Tuition (per academic year): $34600
Enrollment 2018-19:
Undergraduate Majors: 70
Degrees in History: 20 BA
Addresses:
Admissions: http://calvin.edu/admissions/
Financial Aid: https://calvin.edu/offices-services/financial-aid/

Adjunct Faculty

Cunigan, Nicholas (PhD, Kansas 2017; adj. prof.) environmental, indigenous peoples, early modern Atlantic; njcunigan@calvin.edu

Full-time Faculty

Du Mez, Kristin Kobes (PhD, Notre Dame 2004; prof. and chair) US religious, US women, modern America; kkd3@calvin.edu

Howard, Douglas A. (PhD, Indiana 1987; prof.) Ottoman, Middle East, India; dhoward@calvin.edu

Katerberg, William H. (PhD, Queen's, Can. 1995; prof.; dean; and dir., Mellema Prog. in Western American Studies) North American West, Canada, US cultural; wkaterbe@calvin.edu

Rohl, Darrell (PhD, Durham 2014; asst. prof.; Archaeology) Roman and late antique archaeology, frontiers and borderlands, digital humanities; dr33@calvin.edu

van Liere, Frans A. (PhD, Groningen, Netherlands 1995; prof.) medieval Europe, Jewish-Christian relations; fvliere@calvin.edu

van Liere, Katherine (PhD, Princeton 1995; prof.) Renaissance and Reformation, early modern Europe, Spain; kvliere@calvin.edu

Van Vugt, William E. (PhD, London Sch. Econ. 1986; prof.) Britain, US economic, US social; wvanvugt@calvin.edu

Washington, Eric M. (PhD, Michigan State 2010; assoc. prof.) African American, South Africa, African diaspora; emw23@calvin.edu

Part-time Faculty

Maag, Karin Y. (PhD, St. Andrews 1994; prof. and dir., Meeter Center for Calvin Studies) Reformation, France, European social; kmaag@calvin.edu

Staggs, Stephen Thomas (PhD, Western Michigan 2014; instr.) history and social studies education, colonial North America, early modern Europe, Low Countries, ethnohistory, pedagogy; sts2@calvin.edu

Retired/Emeritus Faculty

Bolt, Robert (PhD, Michigan State 1963; prof. emeritus) recent US, Michigan

Bratt, James D. (PhD, Yale 1978; prof. emeritus) US intellectual, US religious; jbratt@calvin.edu

Bult, Conrad J. (MLS, Michigan 1965; asst. dir. emeritus, Coll. Library) US; cbult@calvin.edu

Carpenter, Joel A. (PhD, Johns Hopkins 1984; prof. emeritus and dir., Nagel Inst. for Study of World Christianity) US religious; jcarpent@calvin.edu

De Vries, Bert (PhD, Brandeis 1967; prof. emeritus) Near East, Greece and Rome, archaeology; dvrb@calvin.edu

Diephouse, David J. (PhD, Princeton 1974; prof. emeritus) modern Europe, Germany; ddiephou@calvin.edu

Miller, Daniel R. (PhD, North Carolina, Chapel Hill 1987; prof. emeritus) Latin America, US political, US West; mill@calvin.edu

Schoone-Jongen, Robert P. (PhD, Delaware 2007; assoc. prof. emeritus) 19th-century US, US religious, secondary education; rps2@calvin.edu

Wells, Ronald (PhD, Boston Univ. 1967; prof. emeritus) American social, Canada; well@calvin.edu

Cameron University

Dept. of Social Sciences, 2800 W. Gore Blvd., South Shepler 632, Lawton, OK 73505-6377. 580.581.2499. Fax 580.581.2941. Email: lancej@cameron.edu. Website: http://www.cameron.edu/socialsciences.

Our department includes bachelor's degree programs in history, political science, sociology, social studies education, and criminal justice, plus minors in history, political science, sociology, criminal justice, pre-law, humanities, and geography.

Chair: Robert L. Janda
Degrees Offered: AAS,BA,BS
Academic Year System: Semester

Areas of Specialization: 19th-century US/Texas/Native American/Oklahoma, early modern Europe, American military, world and modern Europe, American social

Undergraduate Tuition (per academic year):

In-State: $3816

Out-of-State: $9396

Enrollment 2018-19:

Undergraduate Majors: 64

Degrees in History: 9 BA

Undergraduate Addresses:

Admissions: http://www.cameron.edu/admissions

Financial Aid: http://www.cameron.edu/financial_aid

Full-time Faculty

Catterall, W. Douglas (PhD, Minnesota, Twin Cities 1998; prof.) Atlantic world trading networks, early modern Europe, Atlantic world; dougc@cameron.edu

Childs, Travis Madison (ABD, Texas Tech; instr.) Texas, 19th-century US, American West; tchilds@cameron.edu

Janda, Lance (PhD, Oklahoma 1998; prof. and chair) American military, women in military, US since 1945; lancej@cameron.edu

Janda, Sarah Eppler (PhD, Oklahoma 2002; prof.) 20th-century Native American, American women, US since 1945; sjanda@cameron.edu

Campbell University

Dept. of History, Criminal Justice, Political Science, PO Box 356, Buies Creek, NC 27506. 910.893.1480. Fax 910.814.4311. Email: martinj@campbell.edu. Website: https://cas.campbell.edu/academic-programs/history/.

The mission of the History, Criminal Justice, and Political Science Department is to guide students toward growth in their base of knowledge in political science, history, criminal justice, and the social sciences in general, that they may have the opportunity to walk wisely, guided by the foundational purpose of this University-a Christian perspective toward faith and learning.

Chair: James I. Martin Sr.

Degrees Offered: BA

Academic Year System: Semester

Areas of Specialization: Europe, US, international studies, social studies education

Tuition (per academic year): $32380

Enrollment 2018-19:

Undergraduate Majors: 33

Degrees in History: 8 BA

Addresses:

Admissions: http://www.campbell.edu/admissions/

Financial Aid: http://www.campbell.edu/admissions/financialaid/

Adjunct Faculty

Davis-Doyle, Jennifer M. (PhD, North Carolina State 2013; adj. prof.) Western civilization, North Carolina; davisj@campbell.edu

Slattery, Michael G. (MA, South Florida 1990; adj. prof.) government, national security, Western civilization; sealsrest@earthlink.net

Full-time Faculty

Johnson, Lloyd (PhD, South Carolina 1995; prof. and dir., Historical Studies) colonial America, African American and Africa, social; johnson@campbell.edu

Martin, James I., Sr. (PhD, Emory 1990; prof. and chair) area studies, modern Europe, social studies education; martinj@campbell.edu

McNair, Bruce G. (PhD, Duke 1991; assoc. prof.) Renaissance and Reformation, early modern, Western civilization; mcnair@campbell.edu

Mercogliano, Salvatore R. (PhD, Alabama 2004; assoc. prof.) maritime, military; mercoglianos@campbell.edu

Stanke, Jaclyn (PhD, Emory 2001; assoc. prof.) modern US diplomatic, 20th-century US, Russia and Soviet Union; stanke@campbell.edu

Joint/Cross Appointments

Alexander-Davey, Ethan (PhD, Wisconsin-Madison 2013; asst. prof.; Political Science) political theory, constitutional development; alexander-davey@campbell.edu

Mero, John C. (PhD, Syracuse 2008; assoc. prof.; Political Science) American government, public administration, public policy; meroj@campbell.edu

Thornton, David W. (PhD, South Carolina 1993; assoc. prof.; dir., Political Science) international relations, Western civilization; thornton@campbell.edu

Canisius College

Dept. of History, 2001 Main St., Buffalo, NY 14208-1098. 716.888.2690. Fax 716.888.2688. Email: devereud@canisius. edu. Website: https://www.canisius.edu/academics/programs/history.

The history program at Canisius College is challenging and comprehensive, and prepares graduates for a broad scope of careers including law, business, journalism, public policy, the military, and museum studies. The history program provides an excellent foundation for graduate studies.

Chair: David Devereux

Degrees Offered: BA

Academic Year System: Semester

Areas of Specialization: US, Europe, Africa/Asia/Middle East, Latin America

Tuition (per academic year): $33282

Enrollment 2018-19:

Undergraduate Majors: 40

Degrees in History: 12 BA

Addresses:

Admissions: http://www.canisius.edu/admissions/

Financial Aid: http://www.canisius.edu/admissions/financial-aid/

Adjunct Faculty

Barker, Ray C. (PhD, SUNY, Buffalo 2003; adj. prof.) modern Europe; barker@canisius.edu

Dierenfield, Kate M. (PhD, Virginia 2001; adj. prof.) US, public policy, civil rights movement; dierenfk@wehle.canisius.edu

Gallimore, Mark K. (PhD, Lehigh 2010; adj. prof.) 20th century, military, technology; gallimom@canisius.edu

Slavin, Bridgette (PhD, Sydney 2009; adj. prof.) medieval, Ireland; slavinb@canisius.edu

Full-time Faculty

Bailey, Richard A. (PhD, Kentucky 2006; assoc. prof.) early America; bailey22@canisius.edu

De La Pedraja Toman, Rene A. (PhD, Chicago 1977; prof.) Latin America, business, military; delapedr@canisius.edu

Devereux, David R. (PhD, London 1988; assoc. prof. and chair) Asia, modern Africa, Middle East; devereud@canisius.edu

Dierenfield, Bruce J. (PhD, Virginia 1981; prof.) recent US, public policy, civil rights movement; dierenfb@canisius.edu

Gibert, Julie S. (PhD, North Carolina, Chapel Hill 1988; assoc. prof.) modern Britain, European social; gibert@canisius.edu

Jones, Larry Eugene (PhD, Wisconsin, Madison 1970; prof.) modern Europe, Germany, intellectual; jones@canisius.edu

Maddox, Steven M. (PhD, Toronto 2008; assoc. prof.) modern Russia, modern eastern Europe, postwar Europe; maddoxs@canisius.edu

Rosenbloom, Nancy J. (PhD, Rochester 1981; prof.) American social, women, film; rosenbln@canisius.edu

Retired/Emeritus Faculty

Costello, David R. (PhD, Virginia 1970; prof. emeritus) Russia, 20th-century eastern Europe, 20th-century Europe; costello@canisius.edu

Sharrow, Walter B. (PhD, Rochester 1965; prof. emeritus) US constitutional, 19th-century US; sharrow@canisius.edu

Starr, Daniel P. (PhD, Rutgers 1967; assoc. prof. emeritus) 20th-century US, sports; starr@canisius.edu

Capital University

Dept. of History, 1 College and Main, Columbus, OH 43209-2394. 614.236.6324. Fax 614.236.6916. Email: acarlson@capital.edu. Website: https://www.capital.edu/history/.

History is the study of the record of the human past. At Capital, students acquire knowledge of a wide range of historical eras and then develop the analytical ability to assess and synthesize historical data and historical interpretations.

Chair: Andrew J. Carlson
Degrees Offered: BA
Academic Year System: Semester
Areas of Specialization: US, ancient/medieval/modern Europe, China, Africa, Russia
Tuition (per academic year): $31990
Enrollment 2018-19:
  Undergraduate Majors: 51
  Degrees in History: 12 BA
Addresses:
  Admissions: http://www.capital.edu/Admission/
  Financial Aid: http://www.capital.edu/finaid/

Full-time Faculty

Bowman, Denvy A. (PhD, North Carolina, Chapel Hill 1987; prof. and former Univ. pres.) ancient; dbowman@capital.edu

Carlson, Andrew J. (PhD, Brown 1993; prof. and chair) US, Africa; acarlson@capital.edu

George, Eva (PhD, Maryland, Coll. Park 2004; assoc. prof.) US women, African American; egeorge@capital.edu

Pantsov, Alexander V. (PhD, Russian Acad. Sciences 1983; prof.) 20th-century Europe, China, Russia; apantsov@capital.edu

Retired/Emeritus Faculty

Burke, James (PhD, Ohio State 1969; prof. emeritus) modern Europe, Russia, Ohio

Jebsen, Henry, Jr. (PhD, Cincinnati 1971; prof. emeritus) 20th-century US, sports; hjebsen@capital.edu

Maroukis, Thomas C. (PhD, Boston Univ. 1974; prof. emeritus) Africa, American Indian; tmarouki@capital.edu

Mayer, David N. (PhD, Virginia 1988; prof. emeritus) US constitutional; dmayer@law.capital.edu

Slocum, Kay B. (PhD, Kent State 1987; prof. emeritus) ancient/medieval/Renaissance Europe; kslocum@capital.edu

Tellier, Cassandra L. (PhD, Ohio State 1984; prof. emeritus) art, museum studies; ctellier@capital.edu

Carleton College

Dept. of History, 1 N. College St., Northfield, MN 55057. 507.222.4217. Fax 507.222.7900. Email: nlambert@carleton.edu; syoon@carleton.edu. Website: https://www.carleton.edu/history/.

Range across the world's cultures and civilizations with our diverse faculty. Develop exhibitions and outreach programs on historical topics. Pursue your interests and develop your analytical skills in a rich array of courses and research experiences.

Chair: Seungjoo Yoon
Degrees Offered: BA
Academic Year System: Trimestermester
Areas of Specialization: US, medieval/early modern/modern Europe, Latin America/Atlantic world, Central/East/South Asia, African diaspora
Tuition (per academic year): $56778
Enrollment 2018-19:
  Undergraduate Majors: 51
  Degrees in History: 20 BA
  Students in Undergraduate Courses: 1002
  Students in Undergraduate Intro Courses: 400
Addresses:
  Admissions: http://apps.carleton.edu/admissions/
  Financial Aid: http://apps.carleton.edu/campus/sfs/

Full-time Faculty

Fisher, Andrew B. (PhD, California, San Diego 2002; prof.) Latin America, social culture, slavery; afisher@carleton.edu

Igra, Annette R. (PhD, Rutgers 1996; prof.) US women, US social and social welfare; aigra@carleton.edu

Khalid, Adeeb (PhD, Wisconsin, Madison 1993; prof.) Russia, Central Asia, Middle East; akhalid@carleton.edu

Khalid, Amna (PhD, St. Antonys Coll., Oxford 2008; assoc. prof.) India and South Asia, disease/medicine/pilgrimage, colonial expansion and empire; amkhalid@carleton.edu

Mason, Austin (PhD, Boston Coll. 2012; lect.; asst. dir., Center for Digital Humanities) medieval studies, digital humanities, Britain and Anglo-Saxons; amason@carleton.edu

McCoy, Meredith Leigh (PhD, North Carolina, Chapel Hill 2019; asst. prof.) American Indian, American studies, education; mmccoy@carleton.edu

Morse, Victoria M. (PhD, California, Berkeley 1996; prof.) Italy and medieval Europe, cartography, geography; vmorse@carleton.edu

North, William L. (PhD, California, Berkeley 1998; prof.) medieval Europe, Byzantium, late antiquity; wnorth@carleton.edu

Ottaway, Susannah R. (PhD, Brown 1998; prof.) early modern Europe, Enlightenment, England; sottaway@carleton.edu

Tompkins, David G. (PhD, Columbia 2004; assoc. prof.) modern Europe and Germany, east central Europe, central European music; dtompkin@carleton.edu

Vrtis, George H. (PhD, Georgetown 2005; assoc. prof.) US environmental, environmental and technology studies; gvrtis@carleton.edu

Williams, Harry McKinley (PhD, Brown 1988; prof.) African American, 20th-century America; hwilliam@carleton.edu

Willis, Thabiti (PhD, Emory 2008; assoc. prof.) Africa; jcwillis@carleton.edu

Yoon, Seungjoo (PhD, Harvard 1999; assoc. prof. and chair) modern China and East Asia; syoon@carleton.edu

Zabin, Serena R. (PhD, Rutgers 2000; prof.) colonial America, early modern Atlantic world, Age of Revolutions; szabin@carleton.edu

Retired/Emeritus Faculty

Bonner, Robert E. (PhD, Minnesota 1968; prof. emeritus) England, historiography, modern Europe; rbonner@carleton.edu

Clark, Clifford E. (PhD, Harvard 1968; prof. emeritus) American social and intellectual, American architecture and material culture, American studies; cclark@carleton.edu

Jeffrey, Kirk, Jr. (PhD, Stanford 1972; prof. emeritus) modern US, business and technology; kirkjeffrey@icloud.com

Niles, Philip (PhD, Toronto 1968; prof. emeritus) medieval and Renaissance, social, medieval England

Weiner, Carl D. (MA, Columbia 1959; prof. emeritus) early modern and modern France, French Revolution, Marxism; cweiner@carleton.edu

Woehrlin, William F. (PhD, Harvard 1961; prof. emeritus) Russia and Soviet Union, comparative revolutions; wwoehrli@carleton.edu

Visiting Faculty

McGrath, Elena C. (PhD, Wisconsin, Madison 2017; vis. asst. prof.) Latin America, revolutionary movements/gender/natural resources, Andes; emcgrath@carleton.edu

Steward, Tyran Kai (PhD, Ohio State 2013; postdoc. fellow) African American, 20th-century US race relations/black politics/popular culture, American political and social; tsteward@carleton.edu

Carnegie Mellon University

Dept. of History, 240 Baker Hall, 5000 Forbes Ave., Pittsburgh, PA 15213. 412.268.2880. Fax 412.268.1019. Email: dh44@andrew.cmu.edu. Website: https://www.cmu.edu/dietrich/history/.

We offer three degree programs which focus on connections between past and present and on how historical knowledge facilitates understanding of social, cultural, and policy change.

Chair: Donna Harsch
Director of Graduate Studies: Nico Slate
Director of Undergraduate Studies: Steven Schlossman
Degrees Offered: BA,BS,MA,PhD
Academic Year System: Semester
Areas of Specialization: women and family, global studies, ethics and public policy, African and African American, science/technology/environment
Undergraduate Tuition (per academic year): $55816
Graduate Tuition (per academic year): $45330
Enrollment 2018-19:
Undergraduate Majors: 63
New Graduate Students: 8
Full-time Graduate Students: 11
Part-time Graduate Students: 1
Degrees in History: 19 BA, 7 BS, 2 MS, 4 PhD
Undergraduate Addresses:
Admissions: http://admission.enrollment.cmu.edu/
Financial Aid: http://admission.enrollment.cmu.edu/pages/financial-aid

Graduate Addresses:
Admissions: https://www.cmu.edu/dietrich/history/graduate/admissions/
Financial Aid: https://www.cmu.edu/dietrich/history/

Full-time Faculty

Aronson, Jay David (PhD, Minnesota 2003; prof.) science and technology; aronson@andrew.cmu.edu

Creasman, Allyson F. (PhD, Virginia 2002; assoc. prof.) early modern Germany, Reformation; allysonc@andrew.cmu.edu

Eisenberg, Laurie Zittrain (PhD, Michigan 1990; teaching prof.) Middle East, Arab-Israel conflict and peace process; le3a@andrew.cmu.edu

Eiss, Paul (PhD, Michigan 2000; assoc. prof.) anthropology and history, Yucatan Mexico, Latin America; pke@andrew.cmu.edu

Fields-Black, Edda L. (PhD, Pennsylvania 2001; assoc. prof.) Africa, labor, women; fieldsblack@cmu.edu

Goldman, Wendy Z. (PhD, Pennsylvania 1987; Paul Mellon Dist. Prof.) Russia and Soviet Union, social and political; goldman@andrew.cmu.edu

Grama, Emanuela (PhD, Michigan 2010; asst. prof.) 20th-century central and eastern Europe, anthropology and history; egrama@andrew.cmu.edu

Harsch, Donna T. (PhD, Yale 1987; prof. and chair) modern Europe, Germany, women; dh44@andrew.cmu.edu

Laemmli, Whitney (PhD, Pennsylvania 2016; asst. prof.) 20th-century US technology

Law, Ricky W. (PhD, North Carolina, Chapel Hill 2012; assoc. prof.) Europe, East Asia, global and comparative; rlaw@andrew.cmu.edu

Lynch, Katherine A. (PhD, Harvard 1976; prof.) modern European family and population, French social, methods; kl18@andrew.cmu.edu

Phillips, Christopher J. (PhD, Harvard 2011; asst. prof.) 20th-century US, science, education; cjp1@cmu.edu

Russell, Edmund P., III (PhD, Michigan 1993; prof.) 19th- and 20th-century US environment and technology; edmundr@andrew.cmu.edu

Sandage, Scott A. (PhD, Rutgers 1995; assoc. prof.) cultural, 19th-century America; sandage@andrew.cmu.edu

Schlossman, Steven (PhD, Columbia 1976; prof. and dir., undergrad. studies) criminal justice, education, sport and society; sls+@andrew.cmu.edu

Slate, Nico (PhD, Harvard 2009; prof. and dir., grad. studies) 20th-century US and South Asia; nslate@andrew.cmu.edu

Soluri, John (PhD, Michigan 1998; assoc. prof.) Latin America, environmental, business; jsoluri@andrew.cmu.edu

Tarr, Joel A. (PhD, Northwestern 1963; Richard S. Caliguiri Univ. Prof.) urban, environmental, policy; jt03@andrew.cmu.edu

Tetrault, Lisa M. (PhD, Wisconsin, Madison 2004; assoc. prof.) US women, social movements and memory; tetrault@andrew.cmu.edu

Theriault, Noah (PhD, Wisconsin, Madison 2013; asst. prof.) political ecology, indigeneity, Southeast Asia; noaht@andrew.cmu.edu

Trotter, Joe William, Jr. (PhD, Minnesota 1980; Giant Eagle Prof.; dir., Center for African American Urban Studies and the Econ.) US, urban and labor, African American; trotter@andrew.cmu.edu

Weiner, Benno Ryan (PhD, Columbia 2012; asst. prof.) Qing and 20th-century China, Tibet and Inner Asia; bweiner@andrew.cmu.edu

Retired/Emeritus Faculty

Acker, Caroline J. (PhD, California, San Francisco 1993; prof. emeritus) medicine, drugs, policy; acker@andrew.cmu.edu

Fenton, Edwin (PhD, Harvard 1958; prof. emeritus) social studies education, curriculum development; ef19@andrew.cmu.edu

Maddox, Richard (PhD, Stanford 1986; prof. emeritus) anthropology, Hispanic world, ritual and politics; maddox@andrew.cmu.edu

Miller, David W. (PhD, Chicago 1968; prof. emeritus) modern Britain and Ireland, computer applications, religion; dwmiller@cmu.edu

Modell, John (PhD, Columbia 1969; prof. emeritus) comparative education, history and sociology of social sciences; exigent@andrew.cmu.edu

Resnick, Daniel P. (PhD, Harvard 1962; prof. emeritus) education, policy, modern Europe; dr0q@andrew.cmu.edu

Schachter, Judith (PhD, Minnesota 1978; prof. emeritus) cultural anthropology, kinship and ritual studies, field methods; jm1e@andrew.cmu.edu

Sutton, Donald S. (PhD, Cambridge 1971; prof. emeritus) modern and early modern China, Taiwan, religion and ethnicity; ds27@andrew.cmu.edu

Recently Awarded PhDs

Busch, David "The Civic Revolution on Campus: Student Activism and the Politics of Service Learning"

Grunewald, Susan "German Prisoners of War in the Soviet Union: Life, Law, and Memory, 1941-56"

Hauser, Mark "All the Comforts of Hell: Doughboys and American Mass Culture in the First World War"

Vaughn-Roberson, Clayton "Fascism with a Jim Crow Face: The National Negro Congress and the Global Popular Front"

Winters, Dawn M. "'The Ladies Are Coming!' A New History of Antebellum Temperance, Women's Rights, and Political Activism"

Carroll University

Dept. of History, Political Science, and Religious Studies, 100 N. East Ave., Waukesha, WI 53186-5593. 262.951.3007. Email: lgoren@carrollu.edu. Website: https://www.carrollu.edu/academics/arts-sciences/history.

At Carroll University, we focus on understanding why individuals, groups and societies lived (and died) in particular ways. Our classes teach you to analyze and interpret decisions, events and cultures from the past. We also use lessons of history to evaluate contemporary issues.

Chair: Lilly Goren
Degrees Offered: BA
Academic Year System: Semester
Areas of Specialization: European social and cultural, 19th- and 20th-century US, comparative, global, intellectual
Tuition (per academic year): $30403
Enrollment 2018-19:
  Undergraduate Majors: 38
  Degrees in History: 5 BA
Addresses:
  Admissions: http://www.carrollu.edu/prospective
  Financial Aid: http://www.carrollu.edu/prospective/financial-aid/undergraduate

Adjunct Faculty

Larsen, Andrew E. (PhD, Wisconsin, Madison 1998; adj.) medieval Europe, English literature; alarsen@carrollu.edu

Malcolm, Allison (PhD, Illinois, Chicago 2011; adj. lect.) 19th-century US; amalcom@carrollu.edu

Full-time Faculty

Byler, Charles A. (PhD, Yale 1990; prof. and dean, Humanities and Social Sciences) American diplomatic and military, 20th-century US; cbyler@carrollu.edu

Hendrix, Scott (PhD, Tennessee, Knoxville 2007; assoc. prof.) medieval, intellectual, Renaissance and Reformation; shendrix@carrollu.edu

Markwyn, Abigail M. (PhD, Wisconsin, Madison 2006; assoc. prof.) pre-1900 US, Latin America; amarkwyn@carrollu.edu

Redding, Kimberly A. (PhD, North Carolina, Chapel Hill 2001; assoc. prof.) modern Germany, social, modern world; redding@carrollu.edu

Retired/Emeritus Faculty

Rempe, Paul L. (PhD, SUNY, Stony Brook 1976; assoc. prof. emeritus) Britain and Ireland, modern Europe; prempe@carrollu.edu

Case Western Reserve University

Dept. of History, 11201 Euclid Ave., Mather House 106, Cleveland, OH 44106-7107. 216.368.2380. Fax 216.368.4681. Email: history@case.edu. Website: https://history.case.edu/.

Our department has a long and prestigious tradition that stretches back to the origins of Western Reserve University in 1826. Today, our faculty specialize in a range of thematic and regional subjects. We have a strong tradition in the study of social, cultural, legal, policy, and political history.

Chair: Kenneth Ledford
Director of Graduate Studies: Daniel A. Cohen
Director of Undergraduate Studies: Peter A. Shulman
Degrees Offered: BA,MA,PhD
Academic Year System: Semester
Areas of Specialization: America, science/technology/environment/medicine, social history and policy
Undergraduate Tuition (per academic year): $50450
Graduate Tuition (per academic year): $46524
Enrollment 2018-19:
  Undergraduate Majors: 30
  New Graduate Students: 2
  Full-time Graduate Students: 20
  Part-time Graduate Students: 1
  Degrees in History: 11 BA, 2 MA, 5 PhD
Undergraduate Addresses:
  Admissions: http://admission.case.edu/
  Financial Aid: http://case.edu/financialaid/
Graduate Addresses:
  Admissions: http://www.case.edu/gradstudies/
  Financial Aid: http://case.edu/financialaid/

Affiliated Faculty

Daniel, Vicki (PhD, Wisconsin-Madison 2017; SAGES Fellow) science, body; vicki.daniel@case.edu

Dawson, Virginia (PhD, Case Western Reserve 1983; adj. assoc. prof.) science, technology, business; vpd@historyenterprises.com

Jim, Bernard L. (PhD, Case Western Reserve 2006; SAGES Fellow and lect.) 19th- and 20th-century US, American science and technology, gender and methodology; bernard.jim@case.edu

Milne, Andrea Elizabeth (PhD, California, Irvine 2017; SAGES Fellow) medicine, women; andrea.milne@case.edu

Murnane, M. Susan (PhD, Case Western Reserve 2005; adj. instr.) income tax reform in 1920s, bankruptcy; susan.murnane@case.edu

Princehouse, Patricia (PhD, Harvard 2003; sr. research assoc.) science, evolutionary biology; patricia.princehouse@case.edu

Full-time Faculty

Broich, John E. (PhD, Stanford 2005; assoc. prof.) Britain, British Empire, environmental and public health; john.broich@case.edu

Cohen, Daniel A. (PhD, Brandeis 1989; assoc. prof. and dir., grad. studies) colonial America, US cultural; daniel.a.cohen@case.edu

Dasgupta, Ananya (PhD, Pennsylvania 2013; asst. prof.) modern South Asia; ananya.dasgupta@case.edu

Flores, John H. (PhD, Illinois, Chicago 2009; assoc. prof.) Mexican American, immigration, labor; john.flores@case.edu

Geller, Jay Howard (PhD, Yale 2001; Rosenthal Prof.) Jewish, modern Europe, modern Germany; jay.geller@case.edu

Ledford, Kenneth F. (PhD, Johns Hopkins 1989; assoc. prof. and chair) modern Germany, modern Europe, European legal; kenneth.ledford@case.edu

Rothman, Aviva Tova (PhD, Princeton 2012; asst. prof.) science, early modern Europe, intellectual; aviva.rothman@case.edu

Sadowsky, Jonathan Hal (PhD, Johns Hopkins 1993; Castele Prof.) medical, Africa, comparative; jonathan.sadowsky@case.edu

Sentilles, Renee M. (PhD, William and Mary 1997; assoc. prof.) American women, American studies and US cultural, children's studies; renee.sentilles@case.edu

Shulman, Peter Adam (PhD, MIT 2007; assoc. prof. and dir., undergrad. studies) science/technology/American politics, environmental and energy, US foreign relations; peter.shulman@case.edu

Steinberg, Ted L. (PhD, Brandeis 1989; Davee Prof.) US, environmental/social/legal; theodore.steinberg@case.edu

Vinson, Ben, III (PhD, Columbia 1998; provost and Hiram C. Haydn Prof.) colonial Latin America, African diaspora, Mexico; ben.vinson@case.edu

Weiss, Gillian L. (PhD, Stanford 2002; assoc. prof.) early modern France, Mediterranean, comparative slaveries; gillian.weiss@case.edu

Joint/Cross Appointments

Grabowski, John J. (PhD, Case Western Reserve 1977; Krieger-Mueller Assoc. Prof.; research dir., Western Reserve Hist. Soc.) archival administration, ethnic, urban; john.grabowski@case.edu

Sternberg, Rachel (PhD, Bryn Mawr 1998; assoc. prof.; Classics) classical antiquity, cultural; rachel.sternberg@case.edu

Part-time Faculty

Todd, Elizabeth K. (PhD, Ohio State 1993; lect.) medieval world, Reformation Europe; elizabeth.todd@case.edu

Retired/Emeritus Faculty

Berger, Molly W. (PhD, Case Western Reserve 1997; assoc. dean emeritus) technology, US cultural, 19th and 20th centuries; molly.berger@case.edu

Hammack, David C. (PhD, Columbia 1973; Haydn Prof. emeritus) American social and urban, economic, civil society and philanthropy; david.hammack@case.edu

Levin, Miriam R. (PhD, Massachusetts Amherst 1980; prof. emeritus) industrial societies and cultures, modern France, women in science; miriam.levin@case.edu

Pursell, Carroll (PhD, California, Berkeley 1962; prof. emeritus) technology

Rocke, Alan J. (PhD, Wisconsin, Madison 1975; Bourne Prof. emeritus) science, science/technology/society; alan.rocke@case.edu

Centenary College of Louisiana

Dept. of History and Political Science, 2911 Centenary Blvd., Magale Library, Shreveport, LA 71104. 318.869.5166. Fax 318.869.5004. Email: cfulwider@centenary.edu. Website: https://www.centenary.edu/academics/departments-schools/history-and-political-science/.

The courses offered by the History Department are designed to make an essential contribution to a liberal education by providing the general student with a comprehensive and integrated knowledge of human history; to provide the training necessary for more advanced study in history; and to provide practical knowledge of historical and political developments.

Chair: Chad Fulwider
Degrees Offered: BA
Academic Year System: Semester
Areas of Specialization: modern Europe, 20th-century America, US South
Tuition (per academic year): $35430
Enrollment 2018-19:
  Undergraduate Majors: 18
  Degrees in History: 4 BA
  Students in Undergraduate Intro Courses: 100
Addresses:
  Admissions: http://www.centenary.edu/admission
  Financial Aid: http://www.centenary.edu/fa

Full-time Faculty

Bailey, John W., Jr. (MA, Oregon 1977; lect.) diplomatic, early America; jbailey2@centenary.edu

Fulwider, Chad R. (PhD, Emory 2008; assoc. prof. and chair) 20th-century Europe, Germany; cfulwider@centenary.edu

Lechner, Zachary James (PhD, Temple 2012; asst. prof.) US South; zlechner@centenary.edu

Retired/Emeritus Faculty

Hancock, Alton O. (PhD, Emory 1962; prof. emeritus) 16th-century Europe, Reformation; aohancock@charter.net

Shepherd, Sam C., Jr. (PhD, Wisconsin, Madison 1980; prof. emeritus) 20th-century America, US South; sshepher@centenary.edu

University of Central Arkansas

Dept. of History, 201 Donaghey Ave., Irby 105, Conway, AR 72035-4935. 501.450.3158. Fax 501.450.5617. Email: wendyc@uca.edu; judyh@uca.edu. Website: https://uca.edu/history/.

Students say our faculty is the reason to study history at UCA. Our award-winning professors offer useful and diverse classes, and the faculty collectively dedicates its time beyond the classroom to help with departmental and honors theses, internships, conference presentations, service-learning, and social events.

Chair: Wendy Lucas
Director of Graduate Studies: Mike Rosenow
Degrees Offered: BA,BS,BSE,MA
Academic Year System: Semester
Areas of Specialization: US, Europe, world

Undergraduate Tuition (per academic year):
  In-State: $6867
  Out-of-State: $12085
Graduate Tuition (per academic year):
  In-State: $6093
  Out-of-State: $10900
Enrollment 2018-19:
  Undergraduate Majors: 161
  New Graduate Students: 3
  Full-time Graduate Students: 14
  Part-time Graduate Students: 2
  Degrees in History: 7 BA, 2 BS, 1 MA
Undergraduate Addresses:
  Admissions: http://uca.edu/admissions/
  Financial Aid: http://uca.edu/financialaid/
Graduate Addresses:
  Admissions: http://uca.edu/graduateschool/
  Financial Aid: http://uca.edu/financialaid/

Full-time Faculty

Anderson, Hillary (PhD, Texas A&M 2018; asst. prof.) sports, social studies education; handerson7@uca.edu

Barnes, Kenneth C. (PhD, Duke 1985; prof.) European social and intellectual, Germany; kennethb@uca.edu

Craun, Christopher Carl (PhD, St. Andrews, Scotland 2006; asst. prof.) medieval, Byzantine, ancient; craunc@uca.edu

Epps, Kristen K. (PhD, Kansas 2010; assoc. prof. and co-dir., African/African American Studies) Civil War, slavery; kkepps@uca.edu

Foster, Buckley T. (PhD, Mississippi State 2003; lect. 2) 19th-century US; bfoster@uca.edu

Jones, Donald G. (PhD, Kansas 1994; assoc. prof.) 20th-century Europe; donj@uca.edu

Kithinji, Michael Mwenda (PhD, Bowling Green State 2009; assoc. prof. and co-dir., African/African American Studies) Africa; mkithinji@uca.edu

Little, Kimberly S. (PhD, Wisconsin, Madison 1998; lect. 2 and internship coord.) 20th-century America, urban, environment; klittle@uca.edu

Lucas, Wendy E. (PhD, California, Riverside 2004; prof. and chair) early America, women, native Americans; wendyc@uca.edu

Matkin-Rawn, Story L. (PhD, Wisconsin, Madison 2007; assoc. prof.) African American, South, Arkansas; slmatkinrawn@uca.edu

O'Hara, David A. (PhD, McGill 2001; assoc. prof.) Tudor-Stuart Britain, Ireland; dohara@uca.edu

Pauly, Roger A., Jr. (PhD, Delaware 2000; assoc. prof.) modern Britain, imperialism, 19th-century anthropology; rpauly@uca.edu

Rosenow, Michael (PhD, Illinois, Urbana-Champaign 2008; assoc. prof. and dir., grad. studies) US Gilded Age and Progressive Era; mrosenow@uca.edu

Rushing, Tracie (MA, Central Arkansas 2010; lect.) trushing@uca.edu

Scribner, Vaughn Paul (PhD, Kansas 2013; asst. prof.) colonial America; vscribner@uca.edu

Smith, Zachary Philip (PhD, North Carolina, Chapel Hill 2015; asst. prof.) China

Toudji, Sonia (PhD, Arkansas 2012; assoc. prof.) Arkansas, early America, Native Americans; stoudji@uca.edu

Welky, David B. (PhD, Purdue 2001; prof.) 20th-century America; dwelky@uca.edu

Central Connecticut State University

Dept. of History, 216 Ebenezer Bassett Hall, 1615 Stanley St., New Britain, CT 06050. 860.832.2800. Fax 860.832.2804. Email: HistoryDept@ccsu.edu. Website: https://www.ccsu.edu/history/.

The department offers the MA in history, as well as the MA in public history. Central to the department's mission is our secondary education program leading to teacher certification.

Chair: John D. Tully
Director of Graduate Studies: Louise Blakeney Williams
Degrees Offered: BA,BS,MA
Academic Year System: Semester
Areas of Specialization: public, US, Europe, comparative world
Undergraduate Tuition (per academic year):
  In-State: $10848
  Out-of-State: $23084
Graduate Tuition (per academic year):
  In-State: $11835
  Out-of-State: $24178
Enrollment 2018-19:
  Undergraduate Majors: 214
  New Graduate Students: 16
  Full-time Graduate Students: 37
  Part-time Graduate Students: 24
  Degrees in History: 97 BA, 46 BS, 10 Cert.
Undergraduate Addresses:
  Admissions: http://www.ccsu.edu/undergradadmission/
  Financial Aid: http://www.ccsu.edu/financialaid/
Graduate Addresses:
  Admissions: http://www.ccsu.edu/grad/admission/
  Financial Aid: http://www.ccsu.edu/financialaid/

Full-time Faculty

Bergman, Jay A. (PhD, Yale 1977; prof.) Russia; bergmanj@ccsu.edu

Biskupski, M. B. B. (PhD, Yale 1981; Prof. Stanislaus A. Blejwas Endowed Chair) east central Europe; biskupskim@ccsu.edu

Broyld, Daniel J. (PhD, Howard 2011; asst. prof.) public, African American, Atlantic world; d.broyld@ccsu.edu

Coronado, Juan (PhD, Texas Tech 2013; asst. prof.) US, Latinx, Puerto Rico; jdcoronado@ccsu.edu

Emeagwali, Gloria (PhD, Ahmadu Bello, Nigeria 1985; prof.) precolonial West Africa, ancient Northeast Africa, world; emeagwali@ccsu.edu

Glaser, Leah Suzanne (PhD, Arizona State 2002; assoc. prof.) public, 20th-century US, American West; glaserles@ccsu.edu

Hermes, Katherine A. (PhD, Yale 1995; JD, Duke 1992; prof.) early America and Atlantic world, American legal and constitutional, Native American; hermesk@ccsu.edu

Jones, Mark A. (PhD, Columbia 2001; prof.) Japan and East Asia, childhood, middle class; jonesm@ccsu.edu

Mahony, Mary Ann (PhD, Yale 1996; prof.) Latin American social and economic, agrarian exports, historical memory; mahonym@ccsu.edu

McGrath, Kate E. (PhD, Emory 2007; assoc. prof.) medieval Europe, cultural, gender; mcgrathkae@ccsu.edu

Prescott, Heather Munro (PhD, Cornell 1992; CSU Prof.) recent US, social and women, medicine; prescott@ccsu.edu

Sunshine, Glenn S. (PhD, Wisconsin, Madison 1992; prof.) early modern, medieval Europe, church; sunshineg@ccsu.edu

Tully, John D. (PhD, Ohio State 2004; prof. and chair) social studies education, American foreign relations, modern US; tullyj@ccsu.edu

Vedeler, Harold Torger (PhD, Yale 2006; asst. prof.) ancient Mesopotamia and Israel, Greece, Rome and Egypt; vedelerhat@ccsu.edu

Warshauer, Matthew S. (PhD, St. Louis 1997; prof.) early Republic, Jacksonian era, 19th-century politics; warshauerm@ccsu.edu

Williams, Louise B. (PhD, Columbia 1992; prof. and dir., grad. studies) Britain, imperialism, European intellectual; williamsl@ccsu.edu

Wolff, Robert S. (PhD, Minnesota 1998; prof.) Civil War and Reconstruction, US economic and social, education; wolffr@ccsu.edu

Part-time Faculty

Armstrong, Stephen A. (MA, Central Connecticut State; adj.) Russia, 20th-century America; armstrong@ccsu.edu

Byczkiewicz, Romuald K. (MA, Connecticut 1997) 18th- and 20th-century Europe, central and eastern Europe, Holocaust and genocide; byczkiewiczr@ccsu.edu

Chauvin, Thomas N. (MS, Central Connecticut State) world, teacher certification; chauvinthn@mail.ccsu.edu

DeVita, George A., Jr. (MA, Hartford) social studies, secondary education, teacher certification; devitag@ccsu.edu

Mann, William (MA, Wesleyan; adj.) LGBT, popular biography; williammann@ccsu.edu

Maravel, Alexandra C. Esq. (JD, Columbia 1977; adj.) US, legal, international trade; maravela@ccsu.edu

McGrath, Stephen (MA, Trinity Coll., Conn. 1976; adj.) US; mcgraths@ccsu.edu

Mitchell, Virginia R. (PhD, Rochester 2002; adj.) Germany, French and European cultural; mitchellv@ccsu.edu

Moylan, Thomas (MS, Central Connecticut State; adj.) social studies; moylantom@ccsu.edu

Mueller, John H. (MA, Connecticut 1999; adj.) Germany, Western civilization, US; muellerj@mail.ccsu.edu

Norton, Phyllis (MS, Central Connecticut State 1983; student teacher supervisor) pnorton@ccsu.edu

Ratliff, Thomas (MA, Central Connecticut State 1994; adj.) US, early America, Connecticut; ratliftt@ccsu.edu

Richards, Holly (MA, Central Connecticut State; adj.) modern Europe; richardsh@ccsu.edu

Rogers, Donald W. (PhD, Wisconsin-Madison 1983; adj.) US, US legal and constitutional, Progressive Era; rogersd@ccsu.edu

Russo, Daniel G. (PhD, Connecticut 1995; adj.) medieval and ancient, medieval England, early European urban; russod@ccsu.edu

Scopino, A. J., Jr. (PhD, Connecticut 1993; adj.) American social and religious; scopinoa@ccsu.edu

Retired/Emeritus Faculty

Brown, H. Haines (PhD, Michigan State 1968; assoc. prof. emeritus) world, feudal Europe; BrownH@mail.ccsu.edu

Enck, Henry S. (PhD, Cincinnati 1968; assoc. prof. emeritus) US

Hommon, William S. (PhD, Pennsylvania 1973; prof. emeritus) Europe; hommonbill@comcast.net

Kapetanopoulos, Elias (PhD, Yale 1964; prof. emeritus) ancient Greece, Rome, Near East; kapetanopoulos@mail.ccsu.edu

Mezvinsky, Norton H. (PhD, Wisconsin, Madison 1959; CSU Prof. emeritus) US 1880-1933, modern Middle East, US immigration; mezvinskyn@ccsu.edu

Rommel, John G., Jr. (PhD, Columbia 1966; prof. emeritus) US

Sanford, Donald G. (PhD, Michigan 1971; assoc. prof. emeritus) European intellectual, Germany

Visiting Faculty

Marino, Kelly (PhD, SUNY, Binghamton 2016; vis. asst. prof.) US, Latin America, women; kmarino@ccsu.edu

University of Central Florida

Dept. of History, 12796 Aquarius Agora Dr., TCH 319, Orlando, FL 32816-1350. 407.823.2225. Fax 407.823.3184. Email: history@ucf.edu. Website: https://history.cah.ucf.edu/.

The History Department at the University of Central Florida offers students an excellent opportunity to cultivate analytical, reading, and writing skills while enhancing their knowledge of history and its role in today's society.

Chair: Peter L. Larson
Director of Graduate Studies: Amelia Lyons
Degrees Offered: BA,MA
Academic Year System: Semester
Areas of Specialization: America, Asia, Europe, Latin America, women's studies, Africana studies, Judaic studies
Undergraduate Tuition (per academic year):
  In-State: $5094
  Out-of-State: $17973
Graduate Tuition (per academic year):
  In-State: $6654
  Out-of-State: $21493
Enrollment 2018-19:
  Undergraduate Majors: 412
  New Graduate Students: 20
  Full-time Graduate Students: 31
  Part-time Graduate Students: 38
  Degrees in History: 153 BA, 12 MA
Undergraduate Addresses:
  Admissions: http://www.ucf.edu/admissions/
  Financial Aid: http://finaid.ucf.edu/
Graduate Addresses:
  Admissions: http://history.cah.ucf.edu/
  Financial Aid: http://finaid.ucf.edu/

Full-time Faculty

Adams, Michelle (MA, Northeastern Illinois 1999; assoc. instr.) 19th-century US, women, social; Michelle.Adams@ucf.edu

Beiler, Rosalind J. (PhD, Pennsylvania 1994; assoc. prof. and interim dir., Public Hist.) early America, Atlantic, early modern Germany; rosalind.beiler@ucf.edu

Bowen, Wayne H. (PhD, Northwestern 1996; prof.) Europe, Spain; Wayne.Bowen@ucf.edu

Cassanello, Robert V. (PhD, Florida State 2000; assoc. prof.) Florida, Gilded Age and Progressive era, race and gender; Robert.Cassanello@ucf.edu

Cheong, Caroline (PhD, Pennsylvania 2016; asst. prof.) modern Latin America, historic preservation; Caroline.Cheong@ucf.edu

Clark, James C. (PhD, Florida 1998; assoc. lect.) US South, Florida, presidential; James.Clark@ucf.edu

Dandrow, Edward M. (PhD, Chicago 2009; asst. prof.) ancient, comparative, historiography; edward.dandrow@ucf.edu

Darty, Amy (MA, Central Florida 2003; assoc. instr.) US; Amy.Darty@ucf.edu

Duffy, Alicia (MA, Memphis 2001; instr.) alicia.duffy@ucf.edu

Earley-Spadoni, Tiffany (PhD, Johns Hopkins 2015; asst. prof.) ancient Near East, digital, landscape archaeology; Tiffany.Earley-Spadoni@ucf.edu

Farless, Patricia L. (ABD, Florida; assoc. instr.) US, women; Patricia.Farless@ucf.edu

Fernandez, Jose B. (PhD, Florida State 1973; prof.) Latin America; Jose.Fernandez@ucf.edu

Foster, Amy E. (PhD, Auburn 2005; assoc. prof.) US space, science and technology; Amy.Foster@ucf.edu

French, Scot A. (PhD, Virginia 2000; assoc. prof.) digital, African American, US South; scot.french@ucf.edu

Gannon, Barbara A. (PhD, Penn State 2005; assoc. prof.) US military, 19th-century African American, US foreign policy; Barbara.Gannon@ucf.edu

Gordon, Fon L. (PhD, Arkansas 1988; assoc. prof.) African American, women; Fon.Gordon@ucf.edu

Hanson, Kenneth (PhD, Texas, Austin 1991; assoc. prof. and coord., Judaic Studies) Kenneth.Hanson@ucf.edu

Hardy, Duncan (DPhil, Oxford 2015; asst. prof.) medieval society and civilization, early modern, Renaissance and Reformation; Duncan.Hardy@ucf.edu

Head, David (PhD, SUNY, Buffalo 2010; lect.) American Revolution, early American Republic, Atlantic world; David.Head@ucf.edu

Larson, Peter L. (PhD, Rutgers 2004; assoc. prof. and interim chair) England, medieval Europe, law; Peter.Larson@ucf.edu

Lester, Connie L. (PhD, Tennessee, Knoxville 1998; assoc. prof.; dir., RICHES; and ed., Florida Historical Quarterly) US South, Gilded Age and Progressive Era, agricultural and environmental; Connie.Lester@ucf.edu

Lyons, Amelia H. (PhD, California, Irvine 2004; assoc. prof. and dir., grad. studies) France, French colonial, modern Europe; Amelia.Lyons@ucf.edu

Martinez Fernandez, Luis (PhD, Duke 1990; prof.) Latin America, Caribbean, Cuba and Puerto Rico; Luis.MartinezFernandez@ucf.edu

Murphree, Daniel S. (PhD, Florida State 2001; assoc. prof. and asst. ed., Florida Historical Quarterly) Florida, French and Spanish borderlands, Native American studies; daniel.murphree@ucf.edu

O'Shea, Deirdre Patricia (MA, Central Florida 2003; assoc. instr.) World War II, Civil War and Reconstruction, Quakers; Deirdre.OShea@ucf.edu

Ozoglu, Hakan (PhD, Ohio State 1997; prof. and dir., Middle Eastern Studies) Middle East, Islamic, Turkish studies; hakan@ucf.edu

Pelli, Moshe (PhD, Dropsie 1967; Abe and Tess Wise Endowed Prof.) Moshe.Pelli@ucf.edu

Pineda, Yovanna (PhD, UCLA 2002; assoc. prof.) early Latin America, modern Latin America; Yovanna.Pineda@ucf.edu

Rutkow, Eric (PhD, Yale 2017; asst. prof.) Eric.Rutkow@ucf.edu

Sacher, John M. (PhD, Louisiana State 1999; assoc. prof.) Civil War and Reconstruction, US South, 19th-century politics; john.sacher@ucf.edu

Snyder, Amanda J. (PhD, Florida International 2013; lect.) Atlantic piracy 1560-1692, comparative English and Spanish New World; amanda.snyder@ucf.edu

Solonari, Vladimir (PhD, Moscow State 1986; assoc. prof.) Russia, eastern Europe, Holocaust; Vladimir.Solonari@ucf.edu

Walker, Ezekiel (PhD, Michigan State 1998; assoc. prof.) Africa, African American; Ezekiel.Walker@ucf.edu

Walters, Lori C. (PhD, Florida State 1998; asst. prof.) public, US space, US 1939-60; lcwalter@ist.ucf.edu

Zhang, Hong (PhD, Arizona 1996; assoc. prof.) Asia, US foreign relations, Chinese civilization; Hong.Zhang@ucf.edu

Central Michigan University

Dept. of History, 1201 South Washington, Powers Hall 106, Mount Pleasant, MI 48859. 989.774.3374. Fax 989.774.1156. Email: history@cmich.edu. Website: https://www.cmich.edu/colleges/class/History/.

The department offers a joint PhD in association with major international universities in Germany, France, and Scotland.

Chair: Gregory A. Smith
Director of Graduate Studies: Kathleen G. Donohue
Director of Undergraduate Studies: Tara M. McCarthy
Degrees Offered: BA,BS,MA,MA/PhD,PhD
Academic Year System: Semester
Areas of Specialization: US, Europe, Latin America, Africa, East Asia
Undergraduate Tuition (per academic year):
  In-State: $12510
  Out-of-State: $23670
Graduate Tuition (per academic year):
  In-State: $10350
  In-state PhD $12222
  Out-of-State: $15300
  Out-of-state PhD $16920
Enrollment 2018-19:
  Undergraduate Majors: 241
  New Graduate Students: 13
  Full-time Graduate Students: 14
  Part-time Graduate Students: 20
  Degrees in History: 59 BA, 5 MA, 3 PhD
Addresses:
  Admissions: https://www.applycmich.edu/
  Financial Aid: https://www.cmich.edu/ess/OSFA/

Full-time Faculty

Cassidy, Michelle (PhD, Michigan 2016; asst. prof.) Native American; cassi2m@cmich.edu

Demas, Lane (PhD, California, Irvine 2008; assoc. prof. and ed., Michigan Historical Review) African American, sports; demas1lt@cmich.edu

Donohue, Kathleen G. (PhD, Virginia 1994; prof. and dir., grad. studies) America, 20th century; donoh1k@cmich.edu

Euler, Carrie E. (PhD, Johns Hopkins 2004; assoc. prof.) medieval; euler1ce@cmich.edu

Fremion, Brittany Bayless (PhD, Purdue 2012; asst. prof.) environmental, public; fremi1b@cmich.edu

Getahun, Solomon Addis (PhD, Michigan State 2005; assoc. prof.) sub-Saharan Africa; getah1sa@cmich.edu

Hall, Mitchell K. (PhD, Kentucky 1987; prof.) America, Cold War/Vietnam era; hall1mk@cmich.edu

Harsanyi, Doina P. (PhD, North Carolina, Chapel Hill 2000; prof.) modern Europe, French Revolution; harsa1dp@cmich.edu

Johnson, Eric A. (PhD, Pennsylvania 1976; prof.) modern Europe, Germany and quantitative social; johns1ea@cmich.edu

Liu, Jennifer (PhD, California, Irvine 2010; asst. prof.) East Asia, China, world; liu3j@cmich.edu

Martin, Jay (PhD, Bowling Green State 1995; asst. prof. and dir., Museum of Cultural and Natural Hist.) public, maritime; marti6jc@cmich.edu

McCarthy, Tara M. (PhD, Rochester 2005; assoc. prof. and dir., undergrad. studies) America, post-1870 women and gender; mccar1tm@cmich.edu

O'Neil, Timothy M. (PhD, Wayne State 1999; assoc. prof.) modern Europe; oneil1tm@cmich.edu

Smith, Gregory A. (PhD, Harvard 2005; assoc. prof. and chair) ancient Mediterranean world; smith5ga@cmich.edu

Tobin, Catherine (PhD, Notre Dame 1987; lect.) US social, immigration, women; tobin1c@cmich.edu

Truitt, Jonathan G. (PhD, Tulane 2009; assoc. prof.) Latin America, world; truit1jg@cmich.edu

Wehrman, Andrew M. (PhD, Northwestern 2011; asst. prof.) colonial through early Republic US; wehrm1am@cmich.edu

Retired/Emeritus Faculty

Benjamin, Thomas L. (PhD, Michigan State 1981; prof. emeritus) Latin America, Mexico, Atlantic world; benja1t@cmich.edu

Dealing, James R. (PhD, Northwestern 1974; asst. prof. emeritus) Africa; j.dealing@cmich.edu

Federspiel, Michael (MA, Central Michigan 1986; lect. emeritus) teaching methods; feder1mr@cmich.edu

Macleod, David (PhD, Wisconsin, Madison 1973; prof. emeritus) America, 19th- and early 20th-century social; macle1d@cmich.edu

Ramirez-Shkwegnaabi, Benjamin (PhD, Wisconsin, Madison 1987; assoc. prof. emeritus) Native America; ramir1b@cmich.edu

Ranft, Patricia (PhD, West Virginia 1981; prof. emeritus) medieval, women; patricia.ranft@cmich.edu

Robertson, John F. (PhD, Pennsylvania 1981; prof. emeritus) ancient Near East, Islamic Middle East; rober1j@cmich.edu

Rutherford, David E. (PhD, Michigan 1988; prof. emeritus) early modern Europe, Renaissance and Reformation; ruthe1de@cmich.edu

Scherer, Stephen (PhD, Ohio State 1969; prof. emeritus) modern Europe, Russia and eastern Europe, historiography; scher1s@cmich.edu

Schmiechen, James A. (PhD, Illinois, Urbana-Champaign 1975; prof. emeritus) 19th-century Britain, social space; james.schmiechen@cmich.edu

Thavenet, Dennis (PhD, Nebraska 1967; prof. emeritus) Jacksonian America; d.thavenet@cmich.edu

Recently Awarded PhDs

Moler, Dale R. "Televiewpoints: Consumption and the Cold War in American and British Television Culture, 1945-55"

Reynolds, Earl Wesley III "Nova Romana Caledonia in Brittania: A Cultural History of Scottish Jacobite Pageantry"

Zayas-Gonzalez, Carlos Hugo A. "The Concept of Knowledge and Jesuit Science: Magic, Religion, and Science in Colonial Americas"

University of Central Missouri

School of Communication, History, and Interdisciplinary Studies, Wood Bldg., Rm. 136, Warrensburg, MO 6409. 660.544.4404. Fax 660.543.4535. Email: jtaylor01@ucmo.edu. Website: http://www.ucmo.edu/hist-anth/.

Interpreting and comprehending the past is challenging, but it can help us navigate the rapidly-changing world with greater success. The History program's goal is to provide a broad understanding of the causes and effects of our past across multiple cultures and peoples, in order to accurately read the present. You will build fundamental critical-thinking, research, and communication skills while expanding your cultural literacy and coming to understand better the world in which we live today. This major is for students who wish to work in museums and archives, state and federal government, law, journalism, teaching, or the business world.

Chair: Art Rennels

Director of Graduate Studies: Micah Alpaugh
Director of Undergraduate Studies: Jon E. Taylor
Degrees Offered: BA,BS,BSE,MA
Academic Year System: Semester
Areas of Specialization: America, Europe, Far East, public, social studies education
Undergraduate Tuition (per academic year):
In-State: $5116
Out-of-State: $10231
Graduate Tuition (per academic year):
In-State: $4973
Out-of-State: $9945
Enrollment 2018-19:
Undergraduate Majors: 165
New Graduate Students: 6
Full-time Graduate Students: 24
Degrees in History: 5 BA, 11 BS, 3 MA, 25 BSE
Undergraduate Addresses:
Admissions: http://www.ucmo.edu/undergrad/
Financial Aid: http://www.ucmo.edu/sfs/
Graduate Addresses:
Admissions and Financial Aid: http://www.ucmo.edu/graduate.cfm

Full-time Faculty

Alpaugh, Micah (PhD, California, Irvine 2010; assoc. prof. and dir., grad. prog.) modern France, French empire, Atlantic world; alpaugh@ucmo.edu

Cannon, Jessica A. (PhD, Rice 2010; assoc. prof.) US South, Civil War, 19th-century US; jacannon@ucmo.edu

Crews, Daniel A. (PhD, Auburn 1984; prof.) Spain, early modern Europe, Latin America; crews@ucmo.edu

Gillis, Delia (PhD, Missouri, Columbia 1996; prof. and dir., Africana Studies) African American, South Africa, Missouri; dgillis@ucmo.edu

Goldstein, Thomas William (PhD, North Carolina, Chapel Hill 2010; asst. prof.) 20th-century Germany, Cold War Europe, Russia/Soviet Union

Kim, Chong (Sean) Bum (PhD, Harvard 2004; assoc. prof.) East Asia, Korea, religion; ckim@ucmo.edu

Nygren, Joshua (PhD, Kansas 2015; asst. prof.) 20th-century US, environmental; nygren@ucmo.edu

Sundberg, Sara B. (PhD, Louisiana State 2001; prof.) early America, social, women; ssundberg@ucmo.edu

Taylor, Jon E. (PhD, Missouri, Columbia 2004; prof. and BA/BS undergrad. coord.) public, historic preservation, 20th-century US; jtaylor01@ucmo.edu

Retired/Emeritus Faculty

Ashman, Patricia Shaw (PhD, St. Louis 1968; prof. emeritus) Great Britain, women

Foley, William E. (PhD, Missouri, Columbia 1967; prof. emeritus) early America, Missouri, American West; foleyw@charter.net

Heming, Carol P. (PhD, Missouri, Columbia 2000; prof. emeritus) German Reformation, modern Germany, women; heming@ucmo.edu

Johnson, Yvonne J. (PhD, Texas, Dallas 1992; prof. emeritus) African American, Africa, US South

McCandless, Perry G. (PhD, Missouri, Columbia 1953; prof. emeritus) 19th-century America, Missouri

Rice, C. David (PhD, Emory 1973; prof. emeritus) 18th-century Europe, East Asia; rice@ucmo.edu

Rowe, Mary Ellen (PhD, Washington 1988; prof. emeritus) Native American, medieval Europe, ancient Rome and Greece; rowe@ucmo.edu

Sylwester, H. James (PhD, Kansas 1969; prof. emeritus) diplomacy, social studies education

Twomey, Alfred E. (EdD, Northern Colorado 1962; prof. emeritus) 19th- and 20th-century Europe, modern Germany

Viscusi, Peter L. (PhD, Delaware 1973; prof. emeritus) Greece and Rome

University of Central Oklahoma

Dept. of History and Geography, 100 N. University Dr., Box 182, Edmond, OK 73034-0182. 405.974.5592. Email: klacher@uco.edu; amartucci@uco.edu. Website: https://www.uco.edu/cla/departments/history-geography/.

The faculty of the University of Central Oklahoma's Department of History and Geography represent an active and interdisciplinary group of scholars, particularly student-centered, whose expertise ranges broadly across thematic, chronological, and geographical areas. The mission of the department is to provide transformative learning experiences in geography, history, history education, and museum studies.

Chair: Katrina Lacher
Director of Graduate Studies: Patricia Loughlin
Director of Undergraduate Studies: Andrew Magnusson
Degrees Offered: BA, BAEd, MA
Academic Year System: Semester
Undergraduate Tuition (per academic year):
   In-State: $5990
   Out-of-State: $14700
Graduate Tuition (per academic year):
   In-State: $5963
   Out-of-State: $13199
Enrollment 2018-19:
   Undergraduate Majors: 246
   New Graduate Students: 16
   Full-time Graduate Students: 36
   Part-time Graduate Students: 7
   Degrees in History: 28 BA, 14 BAEd, 20 MA
Undergraduate Addresses:
   Admissions and Financial Aid: https://www.uco.edu/admissions-aid/
Graduate Addresses:
   Admissions: http://www.uco.edu/graduate/admissions/
   Financial Aid: http://www.uco.edu/graduate/financial/

Full-time Faculty

Adamiak, Stanley (PhD, Nebraska 1994; prof.) US, military; sadamiak@uco.edu

Churchill, Lindsey Blake (PhD, Florida State 2010; assoc. prof.) Latin America, Cold War, revolution; lchurchill@uco.edu

Diaz Montejo, Maria (PhD, SUNY, Albany 2016; lect.) anthropology; mdiazmontejo@uco.edu

Goulding, Marc C. (PhD, NYU 2012; assoc. prof.) African diaspora, empires and anti-imperialism, anticolonial nationalism; mgoulding@uco.edu

Huneke, Erik Georg (PhD, Michigan 2013; asst. prof.) modern Germany and Europe, world, gender and sexuality; ehuneke@uco.edu

Janzen, Mark Ryan (PhD, Texas A&M 2010; assoc. prof.) museum studies, museum practice, technology; mjanzen@uco.edu

Lacher, Katrina (PhD, Oklahoma 2011; assoc. prof. and chair) environmental, 20th-century US; klacher@uco.edu

Li, Xiao-Bing (PhD, Carnegie Mellon 1991; prof.) 20th-century Asia, US, diplomatic; bli@uco.edu

Loughlin, Patricia (PhD, Oklahoma State 2000; prof. and grad. advisor) American West, American Indian, women; ploughlin@uco.edu

Magnusson, Andrew (PhD, California, Santa Barbara 2014; prof. and grad. advisor) Islamic, modern Middle East, religious violence; amagnusson@uco.edu

Olmstead, Justin Quinn (PhD, Sheffield 2013; assoc. prof.) history education, World War I, diplomatic; jolmstead@uco.edu

Panther, Natalie B. (PhD, Oklahoma State 2013; asst. prof.) American Indian, US West, public; npanther@uco.edu

Sheetz-Nguyen, Jessica Ann (PhD, Marquette 1999; prof.) Britain and Europe, women, world; jsheetznguyen@uco.edu

Springer, Michael M. (PhD, St. Andrews 2005; prof.) medieval Europe, early modern Europe; mspringer@uco.edu

Joint/Cross Appointments

Musgrove, Margaret (PhD, North Carolina, Chapel Hill 1991; prof.; Humanities) ancient Greece, ancient Rome; mmusgrove2@uco.edu

Part-time Faculty

Caffee, Cheryl Ann (MA, Central Oklahoma 2016; instr.) US; ccaffee@uco.edu

Dudley, Leigh (MA, Central Oklahoma 2013; instr.) US; ldudley2@uco.edu

Fox, Carrie (MA, Central Oklahoma 2002; instr.) US; cfox@uco.edu

Ham, Herbert (MA, Central Oklahoma 1999; instr.) US; hham@uco.edu

Karl, Erin (MA, Central Oklahoma 2008; instr.) US; ekarl@uco.edu

Lynch, Jennifer (MA, Central Oklahoma 2016; instr.) US; jlynch3@uco.edu

McAllister, Stuart (MA, Oklahoma State 2007; instr.) US; smcallister2@uco.edu

St. Clare, Dawn (PhD, Oklahoma 2016; instr.) interdisciplinary studies; lstclare@uco.edu

Retired/Emeritus Faculty

Baker, James F. (PhD, Tulane 1971; prof. emeritus) Latin America, World War II, 20th-century American diplomatic; jbaker@uco.edu

Brown, Kenny L. (PhD, Oklahoma State 1985; prof. emeritus) American West, Oklahoma, 20th-century US; kebrown@uco.edu

Plaks, Jeff (PhD, Northern Illinois 1998; prof. emeritus) Europe, Russia; jplaks@uco.edu

Webb, David D. (PhD, Oklahoma 1978; prof. emeritus) 20th-century America; dwebb@uco.edu

Central Washington University

Dept. of History, Language & Literature Bldg. 100, 400 E. University Way, Ellensburg, WA 98926-7553. 509.963.1655. Email: history@cwu.edu. Website: http://www.cwu.edu/history/.

The history department seeks to convey historical knowledge and historical modes of understanding to the student population and citizens of Washington State.

Chair: Roxanne Easley
Director of Graduate Studies: Jason Knirck
Degrees Offered: BA, MA
Academic Year System: Quarter
Areas of Specialization: colonial and modern US, US local and regional, modern eastern and western Europe, Latin America, East Asia and Africa

Undergraduate Tuition (per academic year):
In-State: $8072
Out-of-State: $23053
Graduate Tuition (per academic year):
In-State: $11116
Out-of-State: $23485
Enrollment 2018-19:
Undergraduate Majors: 146
New Graduate Students: 6
Full-time Graduate Students: 13
Part-time Graduate Students: 1
Degrees in History: 39 BA, 5 MA
Undergraduate Addresses:
Admissions: http://www.cwu.edu/admissions/
Financial Aid: http://www.cwu.edu/financial-aid/
Graduate Addresses:
Admissions: http://www.cwu.edu/masters/
Financial Aid: http://www.cwu.edu/financial-aid/

Full-time Faculty

Ahn, Chong Eun (PhD, Washington 2013; assoc. prof.) modern China; ahnc@cwu.edu

Dormady, Jason H. (PhD, California, Santa Barbara 2007; assoc. prof.) modern Mexico, Latin America, US borderlands; dormadyj@cwu.edu

Easley, Roxanne I. (PhD, Oregon 1997; prof. and chair) Russia, eastern Europe, medieval and Renaissance Europe; easleyr@cwu.edu

Ferrell, Lacy Spotswood (PhD, Wisconsin-Madison 2013; assoc. prof.) Africa; ferrelll@cwu.edu

Herman, Daniel J. (PhD, California, Berkeley 1995; prof. and dir., grad. studies) pre-1877 US, cultural, Native American; hermand@cwu.edu

Knirck, Jason K. (PhD, Washington State 2000; prof.) modern Europe, Ireland; knirckj@cwu.edu

Levine, Marilyn A. (PhD, Chicago 1985; prof.) Asia, Southeast Asia; levinem@cwu.edu

Moore, Stephen T. (PhD, William and Mary 2000; prof.) Pacific Northwest, US foreign policy, social studies education; moorest@cwu.edu

Morgan, Marjorie (PhD, Tulane 1988; prof.) 19th-century Britain, social and cultural; mmorgan@cwu.edu

Retired/Emeritus Faculty

Blair, Karen J. (PhD, SUNY, Buffalo 1976; prof. emeritus) US, social, women; blairk@cwu.edu

Heckart, Beverly A. (PhD, Washington, St. Louis 1968; prof. emeritus) Europe, Germany, social and economic; heckartb@cwu.edu

Richards, Kent D. (PhD, Wisconsin, Madison 1966; prof. emeritus) American West, Pacific Northwest; richardsk@cwu.edu

Chapman University

Dept. of History, One University Dr. RO 130, Orange, CA 92866-1099. 714.997.6641. Email: bay@chapman.edu. Website: https://www.chapman.edu/wilkinson/history/.

History is our collective memory, an understanding of our heritage, of who we are and how we came to be. The history major not only provides students with the knowledge and tools of history, but also provides a sense of roots, as well as a broader perspective on the diverse regions and peoples of the world.

Chair: Alexander Bay
Director of Graduate Studies: Gregory A. Daddis

Director of Undergraduate Studies: Alexander Bay
Degrees Offered: BA,MA
Academic Year System: Semester
Areas of Specialization: Europe and US, war and society, Holocaust, East Asia and Africa, US social and cultural, women and gender, social justice
Undergraduate Tuition (per academic year): $54540
Graduate Tuition (per academic year): $16420
Enrollment 2018-19:
Undergraduate Majors: 68
New Graduate Students: 10
Full-time Graduate Students: 13
Part-time Graduate Students: 12
Degrees in History: 23 BA, 5 MA
Undergraduate Addresses:
Admissions: http://www.chapman.edu/admission
Financial Aid: http://www.chapman.edu/finaid
Graduate Addresses:
Admissions: http://www.chapman.edu/war-and-society
Financial Aid: http://www.chapman.edu/finaid

Full-time Faculty

Bay, Alexander R. (PhD, Stanford 2006; assoc. prof.; chair; and dir., undergrad. studies) modern Japan, East Asian medicine and science; bay@chapman.edu

Cumiford, William (PhD, Texas Tech 1977; assoc. prof.) Latin America, US, modern Europe; cumiford@chapman.edu

Daddis, Gregory A. (PhD, North Carolina, Chapel Hill 2009; assoc. prof. and dir., grad. studies) American military, Vietnam War, war and society; daddis@chapman.edu

Keene, Jennifer D. (PhD, Carnegie Mellon 1991; prof.) 20th-century US, World War I, war and society; keene@chapman.edu

Klein, Shira (PhD, NYU 2012; asst. prof.) Jewish, modern Europe; sklein@chapman.edu

Mosely, Erin (ABD, Harvard; asst. prof.) Africa; mosely@chapman.edu

Slayton, Robert A. (PhD, Northwestern 1982; prof.) 20th-century US, African American; slayton@chapman.edu

Threat, Charissa J. (PhD, Iowa 2008; asst. prof.) threat@chapman.edu

Joint/Cross Appointments

Harran, Marilyn J. (PhD, Stanford 1979; prof.; Religion) Reformation, Holocaust, Western religions; harran@chapman.edu

Remy, Jana C. (PhD, California, Irvine 2012; assoc. dir., Digital Scholarship) environmental, digital humanities, disability studies and medicine; remy@chapman.edu

Part-time Faculty

Cecil, Patrick William (PhD, Alabama 2015) Western civilization, US, geography; pcecil@chapman.edu

Farrington, Brenda (MA, California State, Fullerton 1991) US; farringt@chapman.edu

Fouser, David C. (PhD, California, Irvine 2016) Britain, Europe; fouser@chapman.edu

Fraga, Mike (MA, UCLA 1980) Chicano studies; fraga@chapman.edu

Gunther, Vanessa Ann (PhD, California, Riverside 2001) US; vagunthe@chapman.edu

Koerber, Jeffrey P. (PhD, Clark 2015; asst. prof.) Holocaust, Soviet Union; koerber@chapman.edu

McClure, Daniel R. (PhD, California, Irvine 2013) 20th-century US economic, African American and African diaspora, world and popular culture; dmcclure@chapman.edu

O'Mara, William Edward IV (PhD, California, Irvine 2017) Middle East; womaraiv@chapman.edu

Reins, Thomas D. (PhD, Claremont Grad. 1981) Asia; reins@fullerton.edu

College of Charleston

Dept. of History, 165 Calhoun St., Maybank Hall, 202, Charleston, SC 29424. 843.953.5711. Fax 843.953.6349. Email: spenceca@cofc.edu. Website: http://history.cofc.edu/.

The Department of History at the College of Charleston is committed to providing an education that gives a mature understanding and appreciation of the global past (its cultures, politics, and societies), to prepare students to engage the present, and ultimately to shape the future. Our curriculum will hold students' attentions and allow them the opportunity to develop critical reading and sophisticated writing skills. Ultimately, our goal is to graduate interesting, analytical thinkers, ready to address the challenges of the 21st century. Our undergraduate and graduate History programs support the mission of the School of Humanities and Social Science to "prepare students to be independent, engaged, lifelong learners who write with confidence, speak with clarity, solve complex problems, and act as responsible citizens." The master's program is joint with The Citadel.

Chair: Phyllis G. Jestice
Director of Graduate Studies: Jason Coy
Degrees Offered: BA,MA
Academic Year System: Semester
Areas of Specialization: US, Asia/Africa/Latin America, modern Europe, premodern Europe
Undergraduate Tuition (per academic year):
In-State: $13268
Out-of-State: $33278
Graduate Tuition (per academic year):
In-State: $13658
Out-of-State: $14120
Enrollment 2018-19:
Undergraduate Majors: 182
New Graduate Students: 14
Full-time Graduate Students: 30
Part-time Graduate Students: 10
Degrees in History: 65 BA, 14 MA
Undergraduate Addresses:
Admissions: http://admissions.cofc.edu/
Financial Aid: http://finaid.cofc.edu/
Graduate Addresses:
Admissions: http://gradschool.cofc.edu
Financial Aid: http://finaid.cofc.edu/

Adjunct Faculty

Crosby, Heather (MA, Citadel; adj.) crosbyhe@cofc.edu
Crout, Robert Rhodes (PhD, Georgia 1977; adj.) croutr@cofc.edu
Davis, C. Earl, Jr. (MA, South Carolina 1977; adj.) Europe; davisce@cofc.edu
Halvorson, Kristin D. (MA, Chicago 2003; adj.) Egyptology; halvorsonkd@cofc.edu
Lary, John Draughon (PhD, Indiana 2011; adj.) immigration/nationalism/ethnicity, postwar Brussels; laryjd@cofc.edu
Luquer, Karone (MA, SUNY, Stony Brook 2008; adj.) luquerk@cofc.edu
Phillips, Susan (MA, Charleston 2003; adj.) American popular culture; phillipss@cofc.edu

Schaffer, Benjamin (MA, New Hampshire 2018; adj.) British Atlantic world; schafferbc@cofc.edu
Smith, Hayden R. (PhD, Georgia 2012; adj.) American rice culture, agroecology; smithhr1@cofc.edu
Stockton, Robert P. (MA, South Carolina 1979; adj.) Charleston history and architecture; stocktonr@cofc.edu
van Meer, Elisabeth (PhD, Minnesota 2006; adj.) modern Europe, science and technology; vanmeerb@cofc.edu
Vincent, James W. (PhD, Duke 1990; adj.) late medieval England; vincentj@cofc.edu

Full-time Faculty

Bodek, Richard H. (PhD, Michigan 1990; prof.) modern Germany, Europe since 1870; bodekr@cofc.edu
Boucher, Christophe (PhD, Kansas 2001; assoc. prof.) Native American, US West; boucherc@cofc.edu
Covert, Lisa Pinley (PhD, Yale 2010; assoc. prof.) modern Latin America; covertl@cofc.edu
Coy, Jason Philip (PhD, UCLA 2001; prof. and dir., grad. studies) early modern Germany; coyj@cofc.edu
Cropper, John S. (PhD, Chicago 2019; asst. prof.) modern Africa; cropperjs@cofc.edu
Delay, Cara (PhD, Brandeis 2002; prof.) European women and gender; delayc@cofc.edu
Domby, Adam H (PhD, North Carolina, Chapel Hill 2015; asst. prof.) Civil War; dombyah@cofc.edu
Donaldson, Rachel Clare (PhD, Vanderbilt 2011; asst. prof.) public, US labor; donaldsonrc@cofc.edu
Eaves, Shannon Camille (PhD, North Carolina, Chapel Hill 2015; asst. prof.) African American; eavessc@cofc.edu
Gigova, Irina (PhD, Illinois, Urbana-Champaign 2005; assoc. prof.) modern Europe; gigovai@cofc.edu
Gordanier, Amy (PhD, UCLA 2019; asst. prof.) modern China; gordanieraw@cofc.edu
Ingram, Tammy (PhD, Yale 2007; assoc. prof.) modern US South, Progressive Era; ingramt@cofc.edu
Jestice, Phyllis G. (PhD, Stanford 1989; prof. and chair) medieval Europe; jesticepg@cofc.edu
Mikati, Rana (PhD, Chicago 2013; asst. prof.) early Islam; mikatir@cofc.edu
Piccione, Peter A. (PhD, Chicago 1990; assoc. prof.) comparative ancient Near East, Egypt; piccionep@cofc.edu
Poole, W. Scott (PhD, Mississippi 2001; prof.) popular culture; poolews@cofc.edu
Slater, Sandra D. (PhD, Kentucky 2009; assoc. prof.) US colonial; slaters@cofc.edu
Steere-Williams, Jacob (PhD, Minnesota 2011; assoc. prof.) ecology of disease/history of medicine, colonial and imperial, modern Britain; steerewilliamsj@cofc.edu

Nondepartmental Historians

Alwine, Andrew (PhD, Florida 2010; assoc. prof.; Classics) ancient Greece, classical philology; alwineat@cofc.edu
Crabtree, Mari N. (PhD, Cornell 2014; asst. prof.; African American Studies) African American; crabtreemn@cofc.edu
Ganaway, Bryan F. (PhD, Illinois, Urbana-Champaign 2002; academic advisor; Honors Coll.) modern Europe; ganawayb@cofc.edu
Gerrish, Jennifer L. (PhD, Pennsylvania 2012; asst. prof.; Classics) classical studies, ancient Rome
McCandless, Amy Thompson (PhD, Wisconsin, Madison 1972; prof.; dean, Grad. Sch.) women, Tudor-Stuart England, US southern women's higher education; mccandlessa@cofc.edu

Rabin, Shari Lisa (PhD, Yale 2015; asst. prof.; Jewish Studies)
American Judaism; rabinsl@cofc.edu
Shanes, Joshua M. (PhD, Wisconsin, Madison 2002; asst. prof.;
Jewish Studies) modern European Jewish; shanesj@cofc.edu
Slucki, David S. (PhD, Monash 2010; asst. prof.; Jewish Studies)
Jews in modern world; sluckds@cofc.edu

Retired/Emeritus Faculty

Clark, Malcolm C. (PhD, Georgetown 1970; prof. emeritus) US
diplomatic
Coates, Timothy J. (PhD, Minnesota 1993; prof. emeritus) Latin
America, Portuguese Empire; coatest@cofc.edu
Drago, Edmund L. (PhD, California, Berkeley 1975; prof. emeritus)
19th-century US, US South, African American; dragoe@cofc.edu
Hopkins, George W. (PhD, North Carolina, Chapel Hill 1976; prof.
emeritus) urban planning; hopkinsg@cofc.edu
Olejniczak, William (PhD, Duke 1983; prof. emeritus)
Enlightenment and French Revolution, France, European Union;
olejniczakb@cofc.edu
Powers, Bernard E., Jr. (PhD, Northwestern 1982; prof. emeritus)
US, African American; powersb@cofc.edu

Visiting Faculty

Koopman, Nicole (PhD, St. Louis 2019; vis. asst. prof.) medieval
Europe; koopmannm@cofc.edu
Krajewski, Heidi Marie (PhD, Tulane 2017; vis. asst. prof.) modern
Latin America; krajewskih@cofc.edu
Piercy, Jeremy (PhD, Edinburgh 2018; vis. asst. prof.) Europe;
piercyjl@cofc.edu
Veeder, Stacy Renee (PhD, SUNY, Albany 2018; vis. asst. prof.)
modern France; veedersr@cofc.edu

Charleston Southern University

*Dept. of History, 9200 University Blvd., Charleston, SC 29423-
8087. 843.863.7133. Fax 843.863.7971. Email: jkuykendall@
csuniv.edu. Website: https://www.charlestonsouthern.edu/
academics/college-of-humanities-and-social-sciences/history/.*

*The Department of History and Political Science seeks to develop
students' skills in critical thinking, interdisciplinary research, and
oral and written communication through historical study and
political investigation. These skills are necessary foundations
for professional employment, graduate study, and informed
participation in the global community.*

Chair: John Edward Kuykendall
Degrees Offered: BA
Academic Year System: Semester
Areas of Specialization: US South, modern US, modern Europe,
modern East Asia
Tuition (per academic year): $25500
Enrollment 2018-19:
Undergraduate Majors: 26
Degrees in History: 9 BA
Addresses:
Admissions: http://www.csuniv.edu/admissions
Financial Aid: http://www.csuniv.edu/admissions/tuition/
financialaid

Full-time Faculty

Kuykendall, John E. (PhD, South Carolina 2002; prof. and chair)
Germany, modern Europe; jkuykendall@csuniv.edu

Martin, Nathan J. (PhD, Nebraska 2008; assoc. prof.) medieval,
early modern England; nmartin@csuniv.edu
Miller, Brian S (PhD, Mississippi 2006; prof.) US South, modern US;
bmiller@csuniv.edu
Park, Haeseong (PhD, Purdue 2015; asst. prof.) modern East Asia,
gender studies; hpark@csuniv.edu
Williams, Mark Kenneth (PhD, Tennessee, Knoxville 2003; assoc.
prof.) US diplomatic, US South, modern US; mkwilliams@csuniv.
edu

Chestnut Hill College

*Dept. of History, 9601 Germantown Ave., Philadelphia, PA 19118-
2693. 215.248.7184. Fax 215.248.7056. Email: lcoons@chc.edu.
Website: https://www.chc.edu/academics/undergraduate/
history.*

*As a history major and graduate of Chestnut Hill, your classroom
study will be paired with incomparable real-world experiences
both in and around the College. Through courses that go beyond
just a traditional study of the past, CHC students leave as problem
solvers, prepared to change the world through their knowledge
and critical thinking skills.*

Chair: Lorraine Coons
Degrees Offered: BA
Academic Year System: Semester
Areas of Specialization: early/modern European social/cultural/
intellectual, US Gilded Age and Progressive Era, 20th-century
US, global, women, medicine
Tuition (per academic year): $35950
Enrollment 2018-19:
Undergraduate Majors: 16
Degrees in History: 5 BA
Students in Undergraduate Courses: 264
Students in Undergraduate Intro Courses: 79
Addresses:
Admissions: https://www.chc.edu/undergraduate-admissions
Financial Aid: https://www.chc.edu/financial-services

Adjunct Faculty

Buehner, Henry (PhD, Temple 2014; instr.) American legal/
political/social 1600-1800; buehnerh@chc.edu
Caldwell, Holly (PhD, Delaware 2016; instr.) Latin America,
medicine; caldwellh@chc.edu
Craig, John Paul (MA, Temple; instr.) African American; craigj@chc.
edu
Lawson, J. Kime (MA, Georgia 2002; instr.) American social,
political, religious; lawsonk@chc.edu
Miller, Gerald Adam, Jr. (MA, Arcadia 1987; instr.) American
political and social, Vietnam; millerg@chc.edu
Varias, Alexander (PhD, NYU 1986; asst. prof.) early and modern
Europe, intellectual and cultural, film, travel and tourism;
alexander.varias@villanova.edu
Walker, William T. (PhD, South Carolina 1983; prof.) modern Britain,
political and religious; wwalker@chc.edu

Full-time Faculty

Contosta, David R. (PhD, Miami, Ohio 1973; prof.) US urban/social/
intellectual/political 1865-present; contostad@yahoo.com
Coons, Lorraine (PhD, NYU 1985; prof. and chair) modern Europe,
social and cultural, women; lcoons@chc.edu

University of Chicago

Graduate Dept. of History, 1126 E. 59th St., Chicago, IL 60637-1554. 773.702.8397. Fax 773.702.7550. Email: history@uchicago.edu. Website: https://history.uchicago.edu/.

We are a community of scholars engaged in cutting-edge research. Our expertise spans many centuries and continents: Africa to Asia, Europe and the Americas, ancient Greece and Rome to Byzantium, and modern nation-states around the globe. We bring different approaches, methodologies, and analytical paradigms to these various places and eras, but share a firm belief that rigorous historical analysis can give us a better understanding of our place in time.

Chair: Adrian Johns, interim
Director of Graduate Studies: Paul Cheney
Degrees Offered: BA, MA, PhD
Academic Year System: Quarter
Areas of Specialization: US, Europe, Latin America, East and South Asia, intellectual
Undergraduate Tuition (per academic year): $55425
Graduate Tuition (per academic year): $57996
Enrollment 2018-19:
Undergraduate Majors: 179
New Graduate Students: 12
Full-time Graduate Students: 159
Degrees in History: 62 BA, 10 MA, 22 PhD
Undergraduate Addresses:
Admissions: http://collegeadmissions.uchicago.edu/
Financial Aid: http://collegeadmissions.uchicago.edu/costs
Graduate Addresses:
Admissions: http://grad.uchicago.edu/admissions
Financial Aid: http://gradadmissions.uchicago.edu/funding/

Full-time Faculty

Albritton Jonsson, Fredrik L. (PhD, Chicago 2005; assoc. prof.) Britain; fljonsso@uchicago.edu

Alitto, Guy S. (PhD, Harvard 1975; assoc. prof.) modern Chinese intellectual and social, Chinese local, Chinese communist movement; galitto@uchicago.edu

Andrews, Margaret (PhD, Pennsylvania 2015; asst. prof.) Rome; margaretandrews@uchicago.edu

Auslander, Leora (PhD, Brown 1988; Arthur and Joann Rasmussen Prof.) modern European social; lausland@uchicago.edu

Belew, Kathleen K. (PhD, Yale 2011; asst. prof.) 20th-century US, violence, militarization; belew@uchicago.edu

Borges, Dain E. (PhD, Stanford 1986; assoc. prof.) Latin America, Brazil; dborges@uchicago.edu

Boyer, John W. (PhD, Chicago 1975; Martin A. Ryerson Dist. Service Prof. and Coll. dean) 19th- and 20th-century European intellectual and political, Austria 1867-1955, World War I origins and meaning; jwboyer@uchicago.edu

Bradley, Mark Philip (PhD, Harvard 1996; Bernadotte E. Schmitt Prof.) international, Southeast Asia; mbradley@uchicago.edu

Briones, Matthew Manuel (PhD, Harvard 2005; assoc. prof.) Asian/Pacific Islander American, African American; brio@uchicago.edu

Burns, Susan L. (PhD, Chicago 1994; prof.) Japan; slburns@uchicago.edu

Chakrabarty, Dipesh (PhD, Australian National 1984; Lawrence A. Kimpton Dist. Service Prof.) modern Indian cultural and social, Bengal; dchakrab@uchicago.edu

Cheney, Paul B. (PhD, Columbia 2002; prof. and dir., grad. studies) Enlightenment, French Revolution, Old Regime Europe; cheney@uchicago.edu

Cumings, Bruce (PhD, Columbia 1975; Gustavus F. and Ann M. Swift Dist. Service Prof.) international, East Asian political economy; rufus88@uchicago.edu

Dailey, Jane (PhD, Princeton 1995; assoc. prof.) 19th- and 20th-century US, American South; dailey@uchicago.edu

Fischer, Brodwyn M. (PhD, Harvard 1999; prof.) Brazil; bmf@uchicago.edu

Fulton Brown, Rachel L. (PhD, Columbia 1994; assoc. prof.) Christianity, medieval European culture, social and religious; rfulton@uchicago.edu

Gilburd, Eleonory (PhD, California, Berkeley 2010; asst. prof.) Russia and Soviet Union, modern Europe; egilburd@uchicago.edu

Goff, Alice M. (PhD, California, Berkeley 2015; asst. prof.) 19th-century German cultural and intellectual, Vormärz Prussia, museums/collections/material culture; agoff@uchicago.edu

Goldstein, Jan E. (PhD, Columbia 1978; Norman and Edna Freehling Prof.) 19th- and 20th-century European intellectual, modern France, psychiatry and psychoanalysis; jegoldst@uchicago.edu

Green, Adam Paul (PhD, Yale 1998; assoc. prof.) African American, US cultural; apgreen@uchicago.edu

Gutierrez, Ramon A. (PhD, Wisconsin, Madison 1980; Preston and Sterling Morton Dist. Service Prof.) Chicano/a, Spanish borderlands, colonial Latin America; rgutierrez@uchicago.edu

Hall, Jonathan M. (PhD, Cambridge 1993; Phyllis F. Horton Dist. Service Prof.) ancient Greece, ancient Greek ethnicity; jhall@uchicago.edu

Hillis, Faith C. (PhD, Yale 2009; assoc. prof.) modern Russia, Ukraine, modern Europe; hillis@uchicago.edu

Holt, Thomas C. (PhD, Yale 1973; James Westfall Thompson Prof.) 19th-century US southern political, Reconstruction, Caribbean; tholt@uchicago.edu

Jenkins, Destin K. (PhD, Stanford 2016; Neubauer Family Asst. Prof.) 20th-century US, African American, urban studies, race and inequality, capitalism; destin@uchicago.edu

Johns, Adrian D. S. (PhD, Cambridge 1992; Allan Grant Maclear Prof. and interim chair) early modern science, book; johns@uchicago.edu

Ketelaar, James E. (PhD, Chicago 1987; prof.) Japanese nationalism and religion, premodern and modern; jketelaa@uchicago.edu

Kouri, Emilio (PhD, Harvard 1996; prof.) Latin America, Mexico, agrarian; kouri@uchicago.edu

Kruer, Matthew (PhD, Pennsylvania 2015; asst. prof.) early America, Native American popular politics, colonial violence; kruer@uchicago.edu

Levy, Jonathan Ira (PhD, Chicago 2008; prof.) US; jlevy@uchicago.edu

Lippert, Amy K. (PhD, California, Berkeley 2009; asst. prof.) 19th-century US; lippert@uchicago.edu

Lyon, Jonathan Reed (PhD, Notre Dame 2005; assoc. prof.) medieval politics and society, medieval nobility, Holy Roman Empire; jlyon@uchicago.edu

Osborn, Emily L. (PhD, Stanford 2000; assoc. prof.) Africa; eosborn1@uchicago.edu

Palmer, Ada L. (PhD, Harvard 2009; assoc. prof.) early modern Europe; adapalmer@uchicago.edu

Payne, Richard E., III (PhD, Princeton 2009; assoc. prof.) Persia and Islamic, Sasanian Empire, late antiquity; repayne@uchicago.edu

Pincus, Steven C. (PhD, Harvard 1990; Thomas E. Donnelly Prof.) Britain; spincus@uchicago.edu

Pomeranz, Kenneth L. (PhD, Yale 1988; Univ. Prof.) modern China, world, social and economic; kpomeranz1@uchicago.edu

Ransmeier, Johanna Sirera (PhD, Yale 2008; assoc. prof.) modern China, Chinese legal, crime; jsransmeier@uchicago.edu

Richards, Robert J. (PhD, Chicago 1978; Morris Fishbein Distinguished Prof.) science, visual perception, idea of social science; r-richards@uchicago.edu

Rossi, Michael (PhD, MIT 2011; asst. prof.) medicine and the body, perception and visual culture, social science; michaelrossi@uchicago.edu

Sparrow, James T. (PhD, Brown 2002; assoc. prof.) 20th-century US, state/culture/society, technology; jts@uchicago.edu

Stanley, Amy Dru (PhD, Yale 1990; assoc. prof.) US, gender, legal and intellectual; adstanle@uchicago.edu

Tenorio, Mauricio (PhD, Stanford 1993; Samuel N. Harper Prof.) Latin America, Mexico, cultural; tenoriom@uchicago.edu

Woods, John E. (PhD, Princeton 1974; prof.) Iran and central Asia, premodern Islamic Middle Eastern state formation and economic; j-woods@uchicago.edu

Zahra, Tara (PhD, Michigan 2005; Homer J. Livingston Prof.) modern central and eastern Europe; tzahra@uchicago.edu

Joint/Cross Appointments

Ando, Clifford (PhD, Michigan 1996; David B. and Clara E. Stern Prof.; Classics) Roman imperial; cando@uchicago.edu

Bresson, Alain (PhD, Franche-Comté, Besançon 1977; prof.; Classics) ancient world; abresson@uchicago.edu

Eyferth, Jacob (PhD, Leiden, Netherlands 2000; assoc. prof.; East Asian Languages and Civilizations) 20th-century China; eyferth@uchicago.edu

Fleischer, Cornell H. (PhD, Princeton 1982; Kanunî Süleuman Prof.; Near Eastern Languages and Civilizations) Ottoman, medieval and early modern Islamic social and cultural, comparative studies of early modern societies; c-fleischer@uchicago.edu

Hevia, James L. (PhD, Chicago 1986; prof.; The Coll.) modern China, British Empire, imperialism and colonialism; jhevia@uchicago.edu

Nirenberg, David (PhD, Princeton 1992; Deborah R. and Edgar D. Jannotta Prof. and exec. vice provost; Comm. on Social Thought and The Coll.) medieval Europe; nirenberg@uchicago.edu

Retired/Emeritus Faculty

Austen, Ralph A. (PhD, Harvard 1966; prof. emeritus) African economic, comparative slavery and slave trade, colonialism and imperialism; wwb3@uchicago.edu

Conzen, Kathleen Neils (PhD, Wisconsin-Madison 1972; Thomas E. Donnelley Prof. emeritus) American urban, social, 19th century; k-conzen@uchicago.edu

Cook, Edward M., Jr. (PhD, Johns Hopkins 1972; assoc. prof. emeritus) colonial and revolutionary America, social, 18th-century Britain; ecook@uchicago.edu

Duara, Prasenjit (PhD, Harvard 1983; prof. emeritus) China, nationalism and nationalist movements

Fasolt, Constantin (PhD, Columbia 1981; Karl J. Weintraub Prof. emeritus) political/social/legal thought in Germany and Europe 1300-1700; icon@uchicago.edu

Fitzpatrick, Sheila (DPhil, Oxford 1969; Bernadotte E. Schmitt Dist. Service Prof. emeritus) Soviet Russia; sf13@uchicago.edu

Geyer, Michael E. (DPhil, Albert-Ludwigs, Freiburg 1976; Samuel N. Harper Prof. emeritus) contemporary Europe; mgeyer@uchicago.edu

Gray, Hanna H. (PhD, Radcliffe 1957; Harry Pratt Judson Dist. Service Prof. emeritus) Renaissance intellectual; h-gray@uchicago.edu

Harootunian, Harry D. (PhD, Michigan 1957; Max Palevsky Prof. emeritus) cultural, Japan; hh3@nyu.edu

Harris, Neil (PhD, Harvard 1965; Preston and Sterling Morton Prof. emeritus) modern American cultural, technology and communications, architecture and design arts; nh16@uchicago.edu

Inden, Ronald B. (PhD, Chicago 1972; prof. emeritus) South Asia, Bengali literature and institutions; rbinden@uchicago.edu

Kaegi, Walter E. (PhD, Harvard 1965; prof. emeritus) late Roman and Byzantine political/social/military/religious structure, historiography; kwal@uchicago.edu

Kirshner, Julius (PhD, Columbia 1970; prof. emeritus) Middle Ages and Renaissance Italy; jkir@uchicago.edu

Najita, Tetsuo (PhD, Harvard 1965; Robert S. Ingersoll Dist. Service Prof. emeritus) Japan, 18th-century Tokugawa political thought structure, modern Japanese political thought; t-najita@uchicago.edu

Saville, Julie (PhD, Yale 1986; assoc. prof. emeritus) African American and Caribbean, slavery and emancipation; jsaville@uchicago.edu

Sewell, William H. (PhD, California, Berkeley 1971; Frank P. Hixon Dist. Service Prof. emeritus) French social and cultural; wsewell@uchicago.edu

Stansell, Christine (PhD, Yale 1980; Stein-Freiler Dist. Service Prof. emeritus) 19th- and 20th-century women, urban, human rights; stansell@uchicago.edu

Suny, Ronald Grigor (PhD, Columbia 1968; prof. emeritus) comparative politics, Russia; rgsuny@uchicago.edu

Swerdlow, Noel (PhD, Yale 1968; prof. emeritus) ancient to 17th-century exact sciences; nms@oddjob.uchicago.edu

Wasserstein, Bernard M. J. (DPhil, Oxford 2001; Harriet & Ulrich E. Meyer Prof. emeritus) modern Jewish, modern Middle East, 20th-century European politics and diplomacy; bmjw@uchicago.edu

Recently Awarded PhDs

Anduiza Pimentel, Marcel Sebastian "From Pacific Gateway to Tourist City: Mobility, Revolution, and the Development of the Mexican Seaside, Acapulco, Mexico, 1849-1970"

Ballan, Mohamad "The Scribe of the Alhambra: Lisan al-Din ibn al-Khatib, Sovereignty and History in Nasrid Granada"

Cropper, John S. "The People's Energy: The History of Charcoal Production and Forest Access in Senegal, 1900-2014"

Del Rio, Richard "The Mass Transformation of Retail Pharmacy and the Development of a Modern Illicit Narcotics Market, 1870-1930"

Dingley, Zebulon York "Kinship, Capital, and the Occult on the South Coast of Kenya"

Fransee, Emily "Without Distinction: Gender and Political Rights in the French Empire, 1943-76"

Fretwell, Elizabeth "Tailoring Benin: Material Culture and Artisan Production in Urban West Africa"

Genova, Aimee Michelle "Strategies of Resistance: Cretan Archaeology and Political Networks during the Late 19th and Early 20th Century"

Grimaldi, Carmine "Structuring Vision: A History of Videotape"

Henry, Phillip "Experimental Futures and Impossible Professions: Psychoanalysis, Education, and Politics in Interwar Vienna, 1918-38"

Jo, Kyuhyun "The Rise of the South Korean Left, the Death of Unitary Socialism, and the Origins of the Korean War, 1945-47"

Kahle, Trish "The Graveyard Shift: Mining Democracy in an Age of Energy Crisis, 1963-81"

Kim, Taeju "Security State, Moral Realism and Post-Conflict Resolution: The Politics of Memory and Apologies in Japan"

Kunze, Savitri Maya "The Periphery of Rights and Membership in the Interwar American Imaginary"

Leonard, Zachary "Against 'Anomaly': India Reformism and the Politics of Colonial Dissent"

McQuinn, Ilana R. "The Symbolic Image of Central Europe: Jewish Experiences in Postwar Czechoslovak and Polish Culture, 1945-75"

Montgomery, Kirsty A. "'Floating Bridges,' 'Knotty Points,' and 'Boroughmonger Tools': Malthus, Extra-Parliamentary Politics, and the Debates on Emigration, 1798-1834"

Niermeier-Dohoney, Justin "A Vital Matter: Alchemy, Cornucopianism, and Agricultural Improvement in 17th-Century England"

Parker, Kai Perry "Faith without Hope: Black Protestants, Chicago, and the Critique of Progress, 1914-68"

Rowe, Adam Lynd "The Paradox of Union: Republicans and the American Polity in the Civil War Era"

Scott, Lisa "Assembly, Dissent, and Political Cohesion: Bohemian Institutional Development in the 15th Century"

Sequin, Caroline "Prostitution and the Policing of Race in the French Atlantic, 1848-1947"

Todd, Christopher Patrick "The Slave's Money: Bondage, Freedom and Social Change in Jamaica, 1776-1838"

Tschinkel, Erika "The Just Enemy in a Time of Terror and Conflict"

Christopher Newport University

Dept. of History, 1 Ave. of the Arts, Newport News, VA 23606-3072. 757.594.7159. Fax 757.594.8771. Email: nancy.wilson@cnu.edu. Website: http://cnu.edu/academics/departments/history/.

In the History Department we pride ourselves on maintaining high standards while remaining committed to working closely with our students to help them achieve their academic and career goals.

Chair: Andrew J. Falk
Degrees Offered: BA
Academic Year System: Semester
Areas of Specialization: Africa and Middle East, East Asia, Europe, Latin America, US
Tuition (per academic year):
   In-State: $25574
   Out-of-State: $39440
Enrollment 2018-19:
   Undergraduate Majors: 178
   Degrees in History: 50 BA, 11 MAT
Addresses:
   Admissions: http://cnu.edu/admission/
   Financial Aid: http://cnu.edu/financialaid/

Adjunct Faculty

Outlaw, Alain C. (MA, Florida State 1978; lect.) historical archaeology; aoutlaw@cnu.edu

Stokes, Brian (MA, Rutgers 1997; lect.) America; brian.stokes@cnu.edu

Full-time Faculty

Allison, James Robert, III (PhD, Virginia 2013; asst. prof.) modern America, environmental and energy, American West; james.allison@cnu.edu

Black, Sara (PhD, Rutgers 2016; asst. prof.) modern Europe, global and comparative; sara.black@cnu.edu

Cartwright, Charlotte (PhD, Liverpool 2012; lect.) ancient and early medieval; charlotte.cartwright@cnu.edu

Connell, William F. (PhD, Tulane 2003; prof.) Latin America, world civilizations; wconnell@cnu.edu

Falk, Andrew J. (PhD, Texas, Austin 2003; assoc. prof. and chair) US diplomatic; falk@cnu.edu

Hamilton, Phillip F. (PhD, Washington, St. Louis 1995; prof.) 19th-century US, American South, slavery; phamilt@cnu.edu

Harshman, Deirdre Ruscitti (PhD, Illinois, Urbana-Champaign 2018; asst. prof.) Russia, Soviet Union; deirdre.harshman@cnu.edu

Hyland, John O. (PhD, Chicago 2005; assoc. prof.) ancient and medieval Europe; john.hyland@cnu.edu

Puaca, Brian M. (PhD, North Carolina, Chapel Hill 2005; assoc. prof.) contemporary Europe; bpuaca@cnu.edu

Puaca, Laura Micheletti (PhD, North Carolina, Chapel Hill 2007; assoc. prof.) America, women and gender; laura.puaca@cnu.edu

Santoro, Anthony R. (PhD, Rutgers 1978; dist. prof.) ancient Egypt, Byzantine Empire, Nazi state and Holocaust; santoro@cnu.edu

Sellars, Nigel Anthony (PhD, Oklahoma 1994; assoc. prof.) 20th-century America, American social, labor and intellectual; nsellers@cnu.edu

Shuck-Hall, Sheri Marie (PhD, Auburn 2000; assoc. prof.) Native American, early colonial; sheri.shuckhall@cnu.edu

Stenner, David (PhD, California, Davis 2015; asst. prof.) Middle East studies, Africa; david.stenner@cnu.edu

Wood, Elizabeth J. (PhD, William and Mary 2018; lect.) 19th-century US, US South, African American, women and gender, methods teaching-social studies; elizabeth.wood@cnu.edu

Xu, Xiaoqun (PhD, Columbia 1993; prof.) Asian civilization, China and Japan, world civilizations; xxu@cnu.edu

Part-time Faculty

Harshman, Matthew James (MA, Illinois, Urbana-Champaign 2013; instr.) America, Caribbean; matthew.harshman@cnu.edu

Retired/Emeritus Faculty

Bostick, Theodore P. (PhD, Illinois, Urbana-Champaign 1970; prof. emeritus) England, Renaissance and Reformation, ancient; tbostick@cnu.edu

Duskin, J. Eric (PhD, Michigan 1993; prof. emeritus) Russia, Soviet Union, Central Asia; eduskin@cnu.edu

Mazzarella, Mario D. (PhD, American 1977; prof. emeritus) 19th- and 20th-century Europe, modern Germany, world civilizations; mazz@cnu.edu

Morris, James M. (PhD, Cincinnati 1969; prof. emeritus) American military, American utopianism, Civil War; mjames792@aol.com

Saunders, Robert M. (PhD, Virginia 1967; prof. emeritus) 20th-century America, American presidency, Virginia; saunders@cnu.edu

Sishagne, Shumet (PhD, Illinois, Urbana-Champaign 1991; prof. emeritus) Africa, Middle East; sishagne@cnu.edu

University of Cincinnati

Dept. of History, 360 McMicken Hall, PO Box 210373, Cincinnati, OH 45221-0373. 513.556.2144. Fax 513.556.7901. Email: maura.oconnor@uc.edu. Website: https://www.artsci.uc.edu/departments/history.html.

The Department of History at the University of Cincinnati strives for excellence in learning the past, reassessing the present, and developing skills for each student's future.

Chair: Maura O'Connor
Director of Graduate Studies: Sigrun Haude
Director of Undergraduate Studies: Erika Gasser
Degrees Offered: BA, MA, PhD

Academic Year System: Semester
Areas of Specialization: US, modern Europe, Britain, transnational
Undergraduate Tuition (per academic year):
In-State: $11000
Out-of-State: $26334
Graduate Tuition (per academic year):
In-State: $14468
Out-of-State: $26210
Enrollment 2018-19:
Undergraduate Majors: 146
New Graduate Students: 14
Full-time Graduate Students: 27
Part-time Graduate Students: 1
Degrees in History: 33 BA, 8 MA
Students in Undergraduate Courses: 2219
Students in Undergraduate Intro Courses: 863
Online-Only Courses: 6%
Undergraduate Addresses:
Admissions: https://admissions.uc.edu/apply.html
Financial Aid: https://financialaid.uc.edu/
Graduate Addresses:
Admissions: https://grad.uc.edu/admissions.html
Financial Aid: https://financialaid.uc.edu/gradstudents.html

Full-time Faculty

Campos, Isaac P. (PhD, Harvard 2006; assoc. prof.) Latin America; camposip@ucmail.uc.edu

Durrill, Wayne K. (PhD, North Carolina, Chapel Hill 1987; prof.) 19th-century US, US South, Civil War; wayne.durrill@uc.edu

Frierson, Elizabeth B. (PhD, Princeton 1996; assoc. prof.) Middle East, Ottoman Empire; elizabeth.frierson@uc.edu

Gasser, Erika (PhD, Michigan 2007; assoc. prof. and dir., undergrad. studies) early America, colonial, women

Haude, Sigrun (PhD, Arizona 1993; assoc. prof. and dir., grad. prog.) continental Europe, Reformation; sigrun.haude@uc.edu

Haug, Robert J. (PhD, Michigan 2010; educator asst. prof.) early Islam, Middle East and Central Asia; haugrt@ucmail.uc.edu

Karr, Susan Longfield (PhD, Chicago 2009; asst. prof. and dir., undergrad. advising) early 16th-century European social/political/legal/intellectual; karrsn@ucmail.uc.edu

Krupar, Jason N. (PhD, Case Western Reserve 2000; assoc. prof.) technology and science policy, engineering, Manhattan Project, Cold War technology; kruparjn@ucmail.uc.edu

Kwan, Man Bun (PhD, Stanford 1990; assoc. prof.) modern China, urban; kwanmb@uc.edu

Lause, Mark A. (PhD, Illinois, Chicago 1985; prof.) America before 1877, labor; mark.lause@uc.edu

Leavitt-Alcantara, Brianna N. (PhD, California, Berkeley 2009; assoc. prof.) colonial Latin America; leavitba@ucmail.uc.edu

McGee, Holly Y. (PhD, Wisconsin-Madison 2011; asst. prof.) African American, 20th century; holly.mcgee@uc.edu

O'Connor, Maura (PhD, California, Berkeley 1992; assoc. prof. and chair) modern Britain, modern Europe, cultural; oconnoma@ucmail.uc.edu

Paik, Shailaja D. (PhD, Warwick, UK 2007; asst. prof.) South Asia, women; shailaja.paik@uc.edu

Phillips, Christopher (PhD, Georgia 1992; prof.) Civil War and Reconstruction, 19th-century US South; christopher.phillips@uc.edu

Porter, Stephen R. (PhD, Chicago 2009; asst. prof.) US political and legal; stephen.porter@uc.edu

Sorrels, Katherine (PhD, Pittsburgh 2009; asst. prof.) modern Europe, Jewish, intellectual and cultural; katherine.sorrels@uc.edu

Stradling, David S. (PhD, Wisconsin, Madison 1996; prof.) US urban, environment, technology; david.stradling@uc.edu

Sunderland, Willard (PhD, Indiana 1997; assoc. prof.) Russia, Europe, world; willard.sunderland@uc.edu

Teslow, Tracy L. (PhD, Chicago 2002; assoc. prof.) 20th-century US, public, race; tracy.teslow@uc.edu

Wingo, Rebecca S. (PhD, Nebraska 2015; asst. prof.; dir., Public History) digital, public, American and indigenous West, women and gender studies; wingora@ucmail.uc.edu

Zalar, Jeffrey T. (PhD, Georgetown 2003; asst. prof. and Conway Chair, Catholic Studies) modern Germany, religion, culture; jeffrey.zalar@uc.edu

Joint/Cross Appointments

Raider, Mark A. (PhD, Brandeis 1996; prof.; Judaic Studies) modern Jewish; raiderma@uc.mail.uc.edu

Van Minnen, Peter (PhD, Leuven, Belgium 1997; asst. prof.; Classics) papyrology; peter.vanminnen@uc.edu

Nondepartmental Historians

Bowman, Steven B. (PhD, Ohio State 1974; prof.; Judaic Studies) Byzantine, Middle East; steven.bowman@uc.edu

Douglass, John E. (PhD, Missouri, Columbia 1984; assoc. prof.; UC Blue Ash Coll.) 17th- and 18th-century colonial British North America, early American legal; john.douglass@uc.edu

Forest, Timothy Steven (PhD, Texas, Austin 2008; asst. prof.; UC Blue Ash Coll.) modern Europe/British Empire/Scotland, identity, comparative empire

Ghebre-Ab, Habtu (PhD, Miami, Ohio 1990; assoc. prof.; Clermont Coll.) modern Africa, Middle East, modern Europe; habtu.ghebre-ab@uc.edu

Gioielli, Robert R. (PhD, Cincinnati 2008; asst. prof.; UC Blue Ash Coll.) 20th century, urban/environmental/social, African American

Hartman, Janine C. (PhD, Illinois, Chicago 1986; assoc. prof.; A & S Coll.) modern Europe, French intellectual; janine.hartman@uc.edu

Kornbluh, Andrea T. (PhD, Cincinnati 1988; prof.; UC Blue Ash Coll.) American women, urban, social; andrea.kornbluh@uc.edu

Lambert, Margo M. (PhD, Georgetown 2007; asst. prof.; UC Blue Ash Coll.) 18th-century America, religion, intellectual

McNay, John T. (PhD, Temple 1997; prof.; UC Blue Ash Coll.) US foreign relations/military; john.mcnay@uc.edu

Norman, Matthew (PhD, Illinois, Urbana-Champaign 2006; asst. prof.; UC Blue Ash Coll.) 19th-century American politics, Civil War and Lincoln; matthew.norman@uc.edu

Sigler, Krista L. (PhD, Cincinnati 2009; assoc. prof.; chair, UC Blue Ash Coll.) 19th- and 20th-century Russia, cultural, aristocracy; krista.sigler@uc.edu

Takougang, Joseph (PhD, Illinois, Chicago 1985; assoc. prof.; Africana Studies) Africa, modern Europe; joseph.takougang@uc.edu

Westheider, James E. (PhD, Cincinnati 1993; asst. prof.; Clermont West Woods Academic Center) African American, race, Vietnam War; james.westheider@uc.edu

Retired/Emeritus Faculty

Alexander, John K. (PhD, Chicago 1973; prof. emeritus) American Revolution, 18th-century US urban, media; john.k.alexander@uc.edu

Brackett, John K. (PhD, California, Berkeley 1986; assoc. prof. emeritus) Renaissance Italy, social

Casey-Leininger, Charles F. (PhD, Cincinnati 1993; assoc. prof. emeritus) fair housing, neighborhood; caseylcf@ucmail.uc.edu

Daniels, Roger (PhD, UCLA 1961; prof. emeritus) US social and economic, immigration; roger.daniels@uc.edu

Kafker, Frank A. (PhD, Columbia 1961; prof. emeritus) Europe 1715-1815, European intellectual, France; fkafker@msn.com

Laux, James M. (PhD, Northwestern 1957; prof. emeritus) modern France, European economic; jlaux@mpinet.net

Lewis, Gene D. (PhD, Illinois, Urbana-Champaign 1957; prof. emeritus) Jeffersonian-Jacksonian America, US historiography; gene.lewis@uc.edu

Ramusack, Barbara N. (PhD, Michigan 1969; Charles Phelps Taft prof. emeritus) modern South Asia, Asian women; barbara.ramusack@uc.edu

Sakmyster, Thomas L. (PhD, Indiana 1971; Walter C. Langsam Prof. emeritus) modern eastern Europe, European diplomatic, film; tom.sakmyster@uc.edu

Smith, Hilda L. (PhD, Chicago 1975; prof. emeritus) women, Britain; hilda.smith@uc.edu

Twinam, Ann (PhD, Yale 1976; prof. emeritus) colonial Spanish America, Spain, family; ann.twinam@uc.edu

The Citadel

Dept. of History, 171 Moultrie St., Charleston, SC 29409-6360. 843.953.5073. Email: vmusheff@citadel.edu. Website: http://www.citadel.edu/root/history.

Our department is a community of faculty, students and staff who share a passion for the study of the past and enjoy sharing that enthusiasm through classes, discussions, lectures, and other activities. We believe that an understanding of the past, and the ways in which it has shaped the present, is vital to the education of productive citizens and thoughtful, principled leaders. The master's program is joint with the College of Charleston.

Chair: Joelle Neulander
Director of Graduate Studies: Keith N. Knapp
Degrees Offered: BA,MA
Academic Year System: Semester
Areas of Specialization: Europe, America, diplomatic and military, non-Western world
Undergraduate Tuition (per academic year):
In-State: $23409
Out-of-State: $42210
Graduate Tuition (per academic year):
In-State: $9450
Out-of-State: $15570
Enrollment 2018-19:
Undergraduate Majors: 100
New Graduate Students: 10
Undergraduate Addresses:
Admissions: http://www.citadel.edu/root/cadet-admissions
Financial Aid: http://www.citadel.edu/root/finaid
Graduate Addresses:
Admissions: http://www.citadel.edu/root/graduatecollege-apply
Financial Aid: http://www.citadel.edu/root/finaid

Full-time Faculty

Aguirre, Nancy (PhD, Texas, El Paso 2012; asst. prof.) Latin America, Mexico; naguirre@citadel.edu

Boughan, Kurt M. (PhD, Iowa 2006; assoc. prof.) early modern Europe; kurt.boughan@citadel.edu

Giblin, Daniel F. (PhD, North Carolina, Chapel Hill 2016; asst. prof.) Russia/Soviet Union, military

Grenier, Katherine H. (PhD, Virginia 1990; prof.) Britain, modern Europe; grenierk@citadel.edu

Johstono, Paul (PhD, Duke 2012; asst. prof.) military; pjohston@citadel.edu

Knapp, Keith N. (PhD, California, Berkeley 1997; prof. and dir., grad. studies) East Asia, premodern China; keith.knapp@citadel.edu

Maddox, Melanie C. (PhD, St. Andrews, Scotland 2010; asst. prof.) medieval British Isles; mmaddox@citadel.edu

Mushal, Amanda R. (PhD, Virginia 2010; assoc. prof.) antebellum South; amanda.mushal@citadel.edu

Neulander, Joelle (PhD, Iowa 2001; prof. and chair) modern France, Africa; neulanderj@citadel.edu

Preston, David L (PhD, William and Mary 2002; prof.) early America; david.preston@citadel.edu

Sinisi, Kyle S. (PhD, Kansas State 1997; prof.) 19th-century US, military; sinisik@citadel.edu

Taylor, Kerry W. (PhD, North Carolina, Chapel Hill 2007; assoc. prof.) US social and labor, oral; kerry.taylor@citadel.edu

Wright, Christopher James (PhD, California, Santa Barbara 2006; assoc. prof.) Middle East, Islamic world; christopher.wright@citadel.edu

Retired/Emeritus Faculty

Addington, Larry H. (PhD, Duke 1962; prof. emeritus) military; larrya103@aol.com

Barrett, Michael B. (PhD, Massachusetts Amherst 1977; prof. emeritus) modern Germany, Europe, World War I

Bishop, Jane C. (PhD, Columbia 1980; assoc. prof. emeritus) ancient, medieval, Byzantine; bishopj@citadel.edu

Gordon, John W., Jr. (PhD, Duke 1974; prof. emeritus) American Revolution, military; gordonjw@tecom.usmc.mil

Harris, William L. (PhD, Vanderbilt 1968; prof. emeritus) Latin America

Moore, Jamie W. (PhD, North Carolina, Chapel Hill 1970; prof. emeritus) diplomatic, modern America; moorej@cchat.com

Nichols, William G. (PhD, Alabama 1970; prof. emeritus) Europe, Russia, military

Tyler, Lyon Gardiner, Jr. (PhD, Duke 1967; prof. emeritus) constitutional, 20th-century America

White, David H., Jr. (PhD, Tulane 1974; prof. emeritus) 20th-century US

Claremont Graduate University

Dept. of History, 831 N. Dartmouth Ave., Claremont, CA 91711-6163. 909.621.8612. Fax 909.607.9587. Email: joshua.goode@cgu.edu. Website: https://www.cgu.edu/departments/history/.

Coordinated by the core faculty of the Graduate University, the faculty in history draws on the combined faculties of The Claremont Colleges with a resulting staff equivalent to that of a much larger university. Yet, because of the unique organization of the Graduate University, the history faculty can emphasize individual instruction and frequent advising and mentoring.

Chair: Joshua Goode
Degrees Offered: MA,PhD
Academic Year System: Semester
Areas of Specialization: US, American studies, European studies, intellectual/social/cultural, archival studies
Tuition (per academic year): $44328
Enrollment 2018-19:
New Graduate Students: 9
Full-time Graduate Students: 52
Part-time Graduate Students: 4
Degrees in History: 1 MA, 3 PhD

Addresses:
Admissions: https://www.cgu.edu/admissions/
Financial Aid: https://www.cgu.edu/admissions/cost-aid/

Adjunct Faculty

Jones, William D. (PhD, Claremont Graduate 1992; adj. prof.) modern Europe, intellectual; joneswmd@gmail.com

Full-time Faculty

Brodie, Janet Farrell (PhD, Chicago 1982; prof.) 19th- and 20th-century US social and cultural, US women, Cold War; janet.brodie@cgu.edu

Ferrell, Lori Anne (PhD, Yale 1991; prof.) early modern literature, Reformation, archival studies; lori.ferrell@cgu.edu

Goode, Joshua S. (PhD, UCLA 1999; assoc. prof. and chair) 19th- and 20th-century Europe, genocide and racial thought, museums and commemoration; joshua.goode@cgu.edu

Perkins, Linda (PhD, Illinois, Urbana-Champaign 1978; assoc. Univ. Prof. and dir., Applied Women's Studies) women, African American higher education; linda.perkins@cgu.edu

Poblete, JoAnna U. (PhD, UCLA 2006; assoc. prof.) 20th-century US, colonialism/imperialism, comparative; joanna.poblete@cgu.edu

Part-time Faculty

Lewis, Daniel (PhD, California, Riverside 1997; assoc. research prof.) archival studies, science

Retired/Emeritus Faculty

Dawidoff, Robert (PhD, Cornell 1975; prof. emeritus) American intellectual and cultural, gay and lesbian; robert.dawidoff@cgu.edu

Claremont McKenna College

Dept. of History, 850 Columbia Ave., Claremont, CA 91711-6420. 909.607.2835. Fax 909.621.8419. Email: sbjornlie@cmc.edu; bstokes@cmc.edu. Website: https://www.cmc.edu/history.

Faculty of Claremont McKenna College offer undergraduate courses open to other Claremont Colleges and Claremont Graduate University.

Chair: Shane Bjornlie
Degrees Offered: BA
Academic Year System: Semester
Areas of Specialization: Americas, Asia, Europe, Middle East, ancient world
Tuition (per academic year): $65245
Enrollment 2018-19:
Undergraduate Majors: 51
Degrees in History: 12 BA
Students in Undergraduate Courses: 669
Undergraduate Addresses:
Admissions: http://www.cmc.edu/admission
Financial Aid: http://www.cmc.edu/financial-aid

Full-time Faculty

Bjornlie, Shane (PhD, Princeton 2006; assoc. prof. and chair) Rome, late antique; shane.bjornlie@cmc.edu

Cody, Lisa Forman (PhD, California, Berkeley 1993; assoc. prof.) Britain, France; lisa.cody@cmc.edu

Ferguson, Heather Lynn (PhD, California, Berkeley 2009; assoc. prof.) Middle Eastern studies, comparative empires; heather.ferguson@claremontmckenna.edu

Geismer, Lily (PhD, Michigan 2010; assoc. prof.) modern US; lgeismer@cmc.edu

Hamburg, Gary M. (PhD, Stanford 1978; prof.) Russian studies, intellectual, Europe since 1750; gary.hamburg@cmc.edu

Kumar, Nita (PhD, Chicago 1984; prof.) modern South Asia, South Asian anthropological and cultural study, historiography; nkumar@cmc.edu

Livesay, Daniel (PhD, Michigan 2010; assoc. prof.) early America, race and slavery in Atlantic, Caribbean; dlivesay@cmc.edu

Lower, Wendy Morgan (PhD, American 1999; prof.) Holocaust studies, east central Europe, women; wlower@cmc.edu

Park, Albert L. (PhD, Chicago 2007; assoc. prof.) East Asia, Korea; albert.park@cmc.edu

Petropoulos, Jonathan (PhD, Harvard 1990; prof.) National Socialism, WWII art looting, European aristocracy, Holocaust; jpetropoulos@cmc.edu

Sarzynski, Sarah R. (PhD, Maryland, Coll. Park 2008; asst. prof.) Latin American studies, Portuguese language, modern Brazil; ssarzynski@cmc.edu

Selig, Diana M. (PhD, California, Berkeley 2001; assoc. prof.) modern US, race/ethnicity/gender, social science; dselig@cmc.edu

Venit-Shelton, Tamara (PhD, Stanford 2008; assoc. prof.) American West, 19th-century US, race and ethnicity; tvenit@cmc.edu

Wang, Chelsea Zi (PhD, Columbia 2017; asst. prof.) premodern China, social and cultural, premodern Japan; cwang@cmc.edu

Part-time Faculty

Mestaz, James (PhD, Illinois, Chicago 2016; postdoctoral fellow) modern Latin America, Mexico, Latinx studies; jmestaz@cmc.edu

Retired/Emeritus Faculty

Rosenbaum, Arthur L. (PhD, Yale 1971; assoc. prof. emeritus) modern China, contemporary Asia, premodern China; arthur.rosenbaum@cmc.edu

Clarion University of Pennsylvania

History Program, Dept. of Social Sciences, 840 Wood St., Clarion, PA 16214. 814.393.2357. Fax 814.393.2550. Email: mrobinson@clarion.edu. Website: http://www.clarion.edu/academics/colleges-and-schools/college-of-arts-and-sciences/social-sciences/.

History studies the human past. History studies the causes and effects of change through an examination of social, political, economic, cultural, and intellectual developments. The department's goal is to help students view issues from a variety of perspectives.

Chair: Martha Robinson
Degrees Offered: BA,BSEd
Academic Year System: Semester
Areas of Specialization: US, ancient/medieval/modern Europe, Latin America
Undergraduate Tuition (per academic year):
In-State: $10470
Out-of-State: $14090
Enrollment 2018-19:
Undergraduate Majors: 45
Degrees in History: 12 BA
Addresses:
Admissions: http://www.clarion.edu/admissions/
Financial Aid: http://www.clarion.edu/tuition-and-financial-aid/

Adjunct Faculty

Diamond, Jeffrey M. (PhD, Sch. Oriental and African Studies, London 2002; adj.) jdiamond@clarion.edu

Full-time Faculty

Robinson, Martha K. (PhD, Southern California 2005; assoc. prof. and chair) colonial North America, medicine and health, American Indian; mrobinson@clarion.edu

Sanko, Marc A. (PhD, West Virginia 2018; assoc. prof.) msanko@clarion.edu

Nondepartmental Historians

Maccaferri, James T. (PhD, UCLA 1983; assoc. prof.; Library Science) Ottoman Empire, Middle East since 1500, Balkans; jmaccaferri@clarion.edu

Retired/Emeritus Faculty

Day, Anne L. (PhD, St. Louis 1965; prof. emeritus) US diplomatic, recent diplomatic relations, science and technology; aday@clarion.edu

Duffy, Edward G. (PhD, Penn State 1969; prof. emeritus) Latin America

Dunn, Brian R. (PhD, Bryn Mawr 1987; prof. emeritus) Tudor-Stuart England, early modern France, modern Germany; bdunn@clarion.edu

Frakes, Robert M. (PhD, California, Santa Barbara 1991; prof. emeritus) ancient Mediterranean, late antiquity, 19th-century Europe; rfrakes@clarion.edu

Kennedy, Cynthia M. (PhD, Maryland, Coll. Park 1999; prof. emeritus) early Republic US, Civil War, women; ckennedy@clarion.edu

Larue, George M. (PhD, Boston Univ. 1989; prof. emeritus) Africa, Islam, slavery; larue@clarion.edu

Piott, Steven L. (PhD, Missouri, Columbia 1978; prof. emeritus) US Gilded Age-Progressive Era, labor, recent US; piott@clarion.edu

Smaby, Beverly P. (PhD, Pennsylvania 1986; prof. emeritus) colonial America, women, religion; bsmaby@clarion.edu

Swecker, Zoe A. (PhD, Chicago 1960; prof. emeritus) Russia, Reformation, Renaissance

Van Meter, Suzanne (PhD, Indiana 1977; prof. emeritus) African American, early Republic, American diplomatic; svanmeter@clarion.edu

Clark University

Dept. of History, 950 Main St., Worcester, MA 01610-1477. 508.793.7288. Fax 508.793.8816. Email: history@clarku.edu. Website: http://www2.clarku.edu/departments/history/.

Clark's History Department, while small, is of unusually high quality, activity, and visibility in the field. Programs of study are available for both undergraduate and graduate students.

Chair: Nina Kushner
Director of Graduate Studies: Wim Klooster
Degrees Offered: BA,MA,PhD
Academic Year System: Semester
Areas of Specialization: America, Europe, Asia, Holocaust and genocide studies, Atlantic world
Tuition (per academic year): $45380
Enrollment 2018-19:
  Undergraduate Majors: 55
  New Graduate Students: 7
  Full-time Graduate Students: 17
  Degrees in History: 17 BA, 4 MA, 2 PhD

Undergraduate Addresses:
  Admissions: http://www.clarku.edu/undergraduate-admissions/
  Financial Aid: http://www.clarku.edu/financial-aid-and-scholarships
Graduate Addresses:
  Admissions: http://www.clarku.edu/graduate-admissions/
  Financial Aid: http://www.clarku.edu/financial-aid/graduate/

Full-time Faculty

Akcam, Taner (PhD, Hanover, Germany 1996; prof.) Turkish nationalism and Armenian genocide; takcam@clarku.edu

Greenwood, Janette Thomas (PhD, Virginia 1991; prof.) American social, African American, US South; jgreenwood@clarku.edu

Imber, Elizabeth E. (PhD, Johns Hopkins 2018; asst. prof.) modern Jewish, 19th- and 20th-century Jewish, British imperial; eimber@clarku.edu

Klooster, Willem (PhD, Leiden, Netherlands 1995; prof. and dir., grad. studies) Atlantic world, early modern Europe, Caribbean; wklooster@clarku.edu

Kuehne, Thomas (PhD, Tübingen, Germany 1994; prof.) modern Europe, Holocaust; tkuehne@clarku.edu

Kushner, Nina J. (PhD, Columbia 2005; assoc. prof. and chair) early modern Europe, France, sexuality; nkushner@clarku.edu

Little, Douglas J. (PhD, Cornell 1978; prof.) 20th-century America, American diplomatic; dlittle@clarku.edu

Lu, Lex Jing (PhD, Syracuse 2016; asst. prof.) modern East Asia, gender studies, beauty/fashion/masculinity; JingLu@clarku.edu

McCoy, Drew R. (PhD, Virginia 1976; prof.) early America, US intellectual and political; dmccoy@clarku.edu

Power-Greene, Ousmane K. (PhD, Massachusetts 2007; assoc. prof.) African American, African diaspora; opowergreene@clarku.edu

Richter, Amy G. (PhD, NYU 2000; assoc. prof.) US women, US urban, 19th-century America; arichter@clarku.edu

Retired/Emeritus Faculty

Borg, Daniel R. (PhD, Yale 1963; prof. emeritus) Germany, modern Europe, totalitarianism

Lucas, Paul (PhD, Princeton 1963; prof. emeritus) England and France before 1800, European intellectual 1650-1945

Recently Awarded PhDs

Allar, Kimberly "Education in Violence: Training Guards in Nazi Concentration Camps and Killing Centers"

Poliec, Mihai "A Dangerous Proximity: The Civilian Complicity during the Holocaust in Romania's Borderlands, 1941-44"

Cleveland State University

Dept. of History, 1860 E. 22nd St., Rhodes Tower, Cleveland, OH 44115. 216.687.3920. Fax 216.687.5592. Email: history@csuohio.edu. Website: https://www.csuohio.edu/class/history/history.

Alternate Address: 2121 Euclid Ave., Rhodes Tower 1315, Cleveland, OH 44115

We are dedicated to providing our students with hands-on opportunities for learning and furthering their interest in history. Through projects like research papers, designing online exhibits, and internships, studying history at CSU will give you the opportunity to prepare for the future by making the past come alive.

Chair: Tom Humphrey
Director of Graduate Studies: Rob Shelton

Director of Undergraduate Studies: Kelly Wrenhaven
Degrees Offered: BA,MA
Academic Year System: Semester
Areas of Specialization: US social, US race and immigration, US public, Africa, China, Middle East, sexuality, European peace/war/fascism
Undergraduate Tuition (per academic year):
In-State: $9636
Out-of-State: $12878
Graduate Tuition (per academic year):
In-State: $9565
Out-of-State: $17980
Enrollment 2018-19:
Undergraduate Majors: 189
New Graduate Students: 26
Full-time Graduate Students: 100
Part-time Graduate Students: 16
Degrees in History: 15 BA, 11 MA
Undergraduate Addresses:
Admissions: http://www.csuohio.edu/engagecsu/
Financial Aid: http://www.csuohio.edu/financial-aid/
Graduate Addresses:
Admissions: http://www.csuohio.edu/graduate-admissions/
Financial Aid: http://www.csuohio.edu/financial-aid/

Full-time Faculty

Cole, Mark B. (PhD, Florida 2011; Coll. assoc. lect.) modern Europe, Germany; m.b.cole@csuohio.edu
Conerly, Gregory (PhD, Iowa 1997; assoc. prof.) American studies, African American; g.conerly@csuohio.edu
Cory, Stephen Charles (PhD, California, Santa Barbara 2002; prof.) early modern Islamic world, religious studies, modern Middle East; s.cory@csuohio.edu
Hinnershitz, Stephanie Dawn (PhD, Maryland, Coll. Park 2013; asst. prof.) 20th-century US; s.hinnershitz@csuohio.edu
Humphrey, Thomas J. (PhD, Northern Illinois 1996; assoc. prof. and chair) colonial and revolutionary America; tom.humphrey@csuohio.edu
Kang, Wenqing (PhD, California, Santa Cruz 2006; assoc. prof.) Asia, gender and sexuality; w.kang@csuohio.edu
Lehfeldt, Elizabeth A. (PhD, Indiana 1996; prof.) early modern Europe, women, Spain; e.lehfeldt@csuohio.edu
Owino, Meshack (PhD, Rice 2004; assoc. prof.) modern Africa, modern African democracy and human rights, origin and nature of African states; m.owino@csuohio.edu
Rose, Shelley E. (PhD, SUNY, Binghamton 2010; assoc. prof.) modern Germany, world, social studies and geography; shelley.rose@csuohio.edu
Shelton, Robert S. (PhD, Rice 2000; assoc. prof. and dir., grad. studies) 19th-century America, Civil War and Reconstruction; r.s.shelton@csuohio.edu
Sola, Jose O. (PhD, Connecticut 2004; assoc. prof.) modern Latin America, colonialism and imperialism, popular culture; j.sola@csuohio.edu
Sotiropoulos, Karen (PhD, Grad. Center, CUNY 2000; assoc. prof.) African American, American cultural, gender and feminist; k.sotiropoulos@csuohio.edu
Souther, J. Mark (PhD, Tulane 2002; prof.) 20th-century US urban and public, tourism; m.souther@csuohio.edu
Wertheimer, Laura Anne (PhD, California, Santa Barbara 2000; assoc. prof. and dir., Classical and Medieval Studies and Liberal Studies) medieval Europe, ancient Mediterranean, medieval Latin; l.wertheimer@csuohio.edu

Retired/Emeritus Faculty

Adams, David Wallace (EdD, Indiana 1975; prof. emeritus) Native American studies, US, American West; d.adams@csuohio.edu
Borchert, James A. (PhD, Maryland, Coll. Park 1976; prof. emeritus) US urban, African American, social and public; jamesborchert@netscape.net
Goldberg, David J. (PhD, Columbia 1984; prof. emeritus) American labor and immigration, social movements, early 20th-century America; d.goldberg@csuohio.edu
Hartshorne, Thomas L. (PhD, Wisconsin, Madison 1965; assoc. prof. emeritus) recent America, American cultural and intellectual; t.hartshorne@csuohio.edu
Makela, Lee A. (PhD, Stanford 1973; assoc. prof. emeritus) East Asian studies; l.makela@csuohio.edu
Manning, Roger B. (PhD, Georgetown 1961; prof. emeritus) Tudor-Stuart England, Europe; r.manning@csuohio.edu
Mastboom, Joyce M. (PhD, Brandeis 1990; assoc. prof. emeritus) early modern Europe, social, economic; j.mastboom@csuohio.edu
Ramos, Donald (PhD, Florida 1972; prof. emeritus) Latin America, Brazil, family; d.ramos@csuohio.edu
Wheeler, Robert A. (PhD, Brown 1972; assoc. prof. emeritus) colonial American family, Western Reserve; r.wheeler@csuohio.edu

Coastal Carolina University

Dept. of History, PO Box 261954, Conway, SC 29528-6054. 843.349.2472. Fax 843.349.2847. Email: bpalmer@coastal.edu. Website: https://www.coastal.edu/history/.

Explore the Atlantic world, women and gender, medicine and science, war and society, transregional and global, digital history and culture. Learn the skillset of numerous professional and academic fields: research, analysis, writing, and global awareness.

Chair: Brandon Palmer
Director of Graduate Studies: Shari Orisich
Degrees Offered: BA,MALS
Academic Year System: Semester
Areas of Specialization: US, Europe, African diaspora, cultural heritage, war and society
Undergraduate Tuition (per academic year):
In-State: $11640
Out-of-State: $27394
Graduate Tuition (per academic year):
In-State: $10764
Out-of-State: $20484
Enrollment 2018-19:
Undergraduate Majors: 104
New Graduate Students: 8
Full-time Graduate Students: 7
Part-time Graduate Students: 4
Degrees in History: 38 BA, 3 MALS
Online-Only Courses: 15%
Undergraduate Addresses:
Admissions: https://www.coastal.edu/admissions/
Financial Aid: https://www.coastal.edu/financialaid/
Graduate Addresses:
Admissions: http://www.coastal.edu/academics/graduatestudies/applynow/
Financial Aid: https://www.coastal.edu/financialaid/

Full-time Faculty

Barnes, Aneilya K. (PhD, Arkansas 2007; assoc. prof.) ancient world, early Middle Ages; abarnes@coastal.edu

Brian, Amanda M. (PhD, Illinois, Urbana-Champaign 2009; assoc. prof. and dir., MALS Prog.) modern Europe, cultural, childhood and youth; abrian@coastal.edu

Castillo, Thomas A. (PhD, Maryland, Coll. Park 2011; asst. prof.) labor, social, US; tcastillo@coastal.edu

Clary, Mary Kate Stringer (PhD, Middle Tennessee State 2013; asst. prof.) public, museum studies, Europe; mclary@coastal.edu

Cromwell, Alisha Marie (PhD, Georgia 2017; asst. prof.) scromwell@coastal.edu

Glaze, Florence Eliza (PhD, Duke 2000; prof.) medieval and Renaissance Europe, science and medicine; fglaze@coastal.edu

Gunn, Christopher (PhD, Florida State 2014; asst. prof.) Turkey, Caucasus; cgunn@coastal.edu

Hassett, Matthew J. (MA, North Carolina, Wilmington 2007; lect.) Western civilization, US; mhassett@coastal.edu

Hourigan, Richard R., III (PhD, Alabama 2010; lect.) US, New South, tourism; rhouriga@coastal.edu

Kent, Larry J. (MA, Villanova 1989; sr. instr.) US, Western civilization; lkent@coastal.edu

Kokomoor, Kevin (PhD, Florida State 2014; lect.) slavery, Native American; kkokomoor@coastal.edu

McDonough, Matthew (PhD, Kansas State 2011; lect.) American military, Atlantic piracy; mmcdonoug@coastal.edu

Morehouse, Maggi M. (PhD, California, Berkeley 2001; Burroughs Dist. Prof.) American South, African American, diaspora and migration; morehouse@coastal.edu

Nance, Brian Kenneth (PhD, North Carolina, Chapel Hill 1991; prof.; dir., COHFA Graduate Study) early modern Europe, cultural and intellectual, medicine; brian@coastal.edu

Navin, John J. (PhD, Brandeis 1997; prof.) colonial America, early Republic US; jnavin@coastal.edu

Orisich, Shari M. (PhD, Maryland, Coll. Park 2013; asst. prof. and dir., grad. studies) crime/urban, youth/class; sorisich@coastal.edu

Palmer, Brandon (PhD, Hawai'i, Mânoa 2005; prof. and chair) East Asia, Japan, Korea; bpalmer@coastal.edu

Searfoss, Renee C. (PhD, Purdue 2013; lect.) rsearfoss@coastal.edu

Whalen, Philip (PhD, California, Santa Cruz 2000; prof.) interwar France, Burgundy; pwhalen@coastal.edu

Part-time Faculty

Berler, Anne (PhD, North Carolina, Chapel Hill 2013; adj. faculty and academic advisor) aberler@coastal.edu

Dembiczak, Angela (MA, La Salle 2010; adj. faculty and acad. coaching specialist; Provost's Office) Renaissance Europe, central and eastern Europe; ajdembic@coastal.edu

McKee, Elizabeth (MA, Duquesne 2015; teaching assoc. and coord., SC History Day) elmckee@coastal.edu

Roper, John H. (PhD, North Carolina, Chapel Hill 1977; teaching assoc.) jroper@coastal.edu

Retired/Emeritus Faculty

Farsolas, James J. (PhD, South Carolina 1973; prof. emeritus) Russia and Soviet Union, eastern Europe, Balkans; farsolas@coastal.edu

Henderson, James D. (PhD, Texas Christian 1972; prof. emeritus) modern Latin America, international studies

Oliver, Robert (MA, Clemson 1997; prof. emeritus) US; roliver@coastal.edu

Prince, Eldred E. 'Wink', Jr. (PhD, South Carolina 1993; prof. emeritus) New US South, 20th-century US, business; prince@coastal.edu

Talbert, Roy, Jr. (PhD, Vanderbilt 1971; prof. emeritus) talbert@coastal.edu

Townsend, Kenneth W. (PhD, North Carolina, Chapel Hill 1991; prof. emeritus) 20th-century US, American frontier; ken@coastal.edu

Coe College

Dept. of History, 1220 First Ave. NE, Cedar Rapids, IA 52402-5092. 319.399.8000. Fax 319.399.8557. Email: bkeenan@coe.edu. Website: https://www.coe.edu/academics/majors-areas-study/history.

In the Coe History Department, you get the opportunity to study history broadly, while also focusing on your specific interests. The classes are small and lively, with plenty of opportunities to know your professors and peers. You'll learn to read and you'll learn to think.

Chair: Bethany S. Keenan
Degrees Offered: BA
Academic Year System: Semester
Areas of Specialization: America, Asia, Europe, ancient world
Tuition (per academic year): $43700
Enrollment 2018-19:
    Undergraduate Majors: 45
    Degrees in History: 10 BA
Addresses:
    Admissions: http://www.coe.edu/admission
    Financial Aid: http://www.coe.edu/admission/financialaid

Full-time Faculty

Arnold, Brie Swenson (PhD, Minnesota 2008; assoc. prof.) early US, women and gender, Civil War; barnold@coe.edu

Buckaloo, Derek N. (PhD, Emory 2002; William R. and Winifred Shuttleworth Prof.) US, Vietnam War, diplomatic; dbuckalo@coe.edu

Keenan, Bethany S. (PhD, North Carolina, Chapel Hill 2009; assoc. prof. and chair) modern Europe, France, culture and national identity; bkeenan@coe.edu

Nordmann, David A. (PhD, Indiana 2001; Henrietta Arnold Assoc. Prof.) East Asia, modern Japan, Korea; dnordman@coe.edu

Ziskowski, Angela (PhD, Bryn Mawr 2011; assoc. prof.) archaic and classical Greece, ancient Corinth, identity; aziskowski@coe.edu

Retired/Emeritus Faculty

Burke, Edmund M. (PhD, Tufts 1972; prof. emeritus) classical and Macedonian Greece, Philip II and Alexander, Roman Republic

Carroll, Rosemary F. (PhD, Rutgers 1968; JD, Iowa 1983; Henry and Margaret Haegg Dist. Prof. emeritus and attorney) US women, US legal, Latin America

Janus, Glenn A. (PhD, Ohio State 1971; Henrietta Arnold Prof. emeritus) Russia and eastern Europe, modern Europe, Catholicism; gjanus@coe.edu

Lisio, Donald J. (PhD, Wisconsin, Madison 1965; Henrietta Arnold Prof. emeritus) recent America, US social and intellectual

Phifer, James R. (PhD, Colorado, Boulder 1975; prof. emeritus and Coll. Pres. emeritus) Tudor-Stuart England, English constitutional and legal, British Empire; jphifer@coe.edu

Colby College

Dept. of History, 5320 Mayflower Hill, Waterville, ME 04901-8853. 207.859.5320. Fax 207.859.5340. Email: jpturner@colby.edu; tvdevent@colby.edu. Website: http://www.colby.edu/historydept/.

When you study history at Colby, you're signing on for an intellectually rigorous and rewarding experience. Working alongside our accomplished faculty, you'll examine the diversity of human experience by studying the evolution of your culture and others around the world.

Chair: John Turner
Degrees Offered: BA
Academic Year System: 2 semesters and January program
Areas of Specialization: North America/Europe/USSR, China/Japan/Korea, Africa, comparative world, Islamic world
Comprehensive Fee: $72,000
Enrollment 2018-19:
 Undergraduate Majors: 88
 Degrees in History: 24 BA
Addresses:
 Admissions: http://www.colby.edu/admission/
 Financial Aid: http://www.colby.edu/admission/

Full-time Faculty

Duff, Sarah Emily (PhD, Birkbeck Coll., London 2011; asst. prof.) world, Africa; seduff@colby.edu

Josephson, Paul (PhD, MIT 1986; prof.) Russia, science and technology; paul.josephson@colby.edu

Scheck, Raffael M. (PhD, Brandeis 1993; prof.) modern Europe, Germany; raffael.scheck@colby.edu

Taylor, Larissa Juliet (PhD, Brown 1990; prof.) late medieval, Reformation Europe; larissa.taylor@colby.edu

Turner, John P. (PhD, Michigan 2001; assoc. prof. and chair) Islamic world; john.turner@colby.edu

Van Der Meer, Arnout H.C. (PhD, Rutgers 2014; asst. prof.) comparative world, Southeast Asia, Indonesia; arnout.van.der.meer@colby.edu

Weisbrot, Robert S. (PhD, Harvard 1980; prof.) 20th-century America, African American; robert.weisbrot@colby.edu

Nondepartmental Historians

Fallaw, Ben W. (PhD, Chicago 1995; prof.; Latin American Studies) Mexico and modern Latin America; ben.fallaw@colby.edu

Fleming, James Rodger (PhD, Princeton 1988; prof.; Science and Tech. Studies) science and technology; james.fleming@colby.edu

Part-time Faculty

Jacobson, Danae Ann (PhD, Notre Dame 2019; faculty fellow) 19th-century America

Reardon, Erik (PhD, Maine 2016; faculty fellow) colonial America, environmental; erik.reardon@colby.edu

Retired/Emeritus Faculty

Leonard, Elizabeth D. (PhD, California, Riverside 1992; prof. emeritus) Civil War and Reconstruction, 19th-century America, American women; elizabeth.leonard@colby.edu

Roisman, Joseph (PhD, Washington 1981; prof. emeritus; Classics) ancient; joseph.roisman@colby.edu

Visiting Faculty

Parker, Lauren (PhD, Stanford 2019; vis. instr.) modern China; lauren.parker@colby.edu

Shmagin, Viktor (PhD, California, Santa Barbara 2016; vis. asst. prof.) East Asia; viktor.e.shmagin@gmail.com

Colgate University

Dept. of History, 13 Oak Dr., 330 Alumni Hall, Hamilton, NY 13346-1398. 315.228.7511. Fax 315.228.7098. Email rnemes@colgate.edu. Website: https://www.colgate.edu/academics/departments-programs/department-history.

While it is important for our society to have an understanding of history, the process of studying history is also an excellent way to train your mind. Exposure to rigorous historical method and clear narrative style develops conceptual skills, research competence, writing fluency, and sensitivity to the uses and abuses of language and historical knowledge.

Chair: Robert Nemes
Degrees Offered: BA
Academic Year System: Semester
Areas of Specialization: US, Europe, East Asia, Latin America, Africa
Tuition (per academic year): $55530
Enrollment 2018-19:
 Undergraduate Majors: 98
 Degrees in History: 37 BA
Addresses:
 Admissions: http://www.colgate.edu/admission-financial-aid
 Financial Aid: http://www.colgate.edu/admission-financial-aid/financial-aid

Full-time Faculty

Banner-Haley, Charles Pete (PhD, SUNY, Binghamton 1980; prof.) Afro-American, recent US; cbannerhaley@colgate.edu

Barrera, Antonio (PhD, California, Davis 1999; assoc. prof.) Atlantic world, science, Spain; abarrera@colgate.edu

Bouk, Dan (PhD, Princeton 2009; assoc. prof.) US, science, capitalism; dbouk@colgate.edu

Cooper, Alan Ralph (PhD, Harvard 1998; assoc. prof.) medieval Europe; acooper@colgate.edu

Douglas, R.M. M. (PhD, Brown 1996; prof.) modern Britain, Ireland, 20th-century Europe; rdouglas@colgate.edu

Etefa, Tsega (PhD, Hamburg, Germany 2006; assoc. prof.) Africa; tetefa@colgate.edu

Hall, Ryan C. (PhD, Yale 2015; asst. prof.; Native American Studies) US, Native American, transnational; rhall@colgate.edu

Harsin, Jill (PhD, Iowa 1981; prof. and Christian A. Johnson Endeavor Chair) modern France, social, French Revolution; jharsin@colgate.edu

Hodges, Graham R. (PhD, NYU 1982; George Dorland Langdon Jr. Prof.) early America, New York, labor; ghodges@colgate.edu

Karn, Alexander M. (PhD, Claremont Grad. 2006; asst. prof.) modern Europe; akarn@colgate.edu

Khan, Noor-aiman Iftikhar (PhD, Chicago 2006; assoc. prof.) Middle East; nikhan@colgate.edu

Mercado, Monica L. (PhD, Chicago 2014; asst. prof.) US women/gender/sexuality, religion in American culture, girlhood/childhood studies; mmercado@colgate.edu

Nemes, Robert (PhD, Columbia 1999; assoc. prof. and chair) modern central Europe, Germany; rnemes@colgate.edu

Robinson, David M. (PhD, Princeton 1995; prof.) China, Japan, Korea; drobinson@colgate.edu

Roller, Heather Flynn (PhD, Stanford 2010; assoc. prof.) Latin America, colonialism, Native American; hroller@colgate.edu

Rotter, Andrew Jon (PhD, Stanford 1981; Charles A. Dana Prof.) US diplomatic, recent US; arotter@colgate.edu

Stevens, Carol B. (PhD, Michigan 1985; prof.) Russia, Siberia; kstevens@colgate.edu

Tomlinson, Tristan (PhD, SUNY, Stony Brook 2014; sr. lect.) 18th-Century Britain, Atlantic world, population and governance; ttomlinson@colgate.edu

Retired/Emeritus Faculty

Dudden, Faye E. (PhD, Rochester 1981; prof. emerita) 19th-century US, social, women; fdudden@colgate.edu

Moore, Brian L. (PhD, West Indies 1974; John D. and Catherine T. MacArthur Prof. emeritus) Caribbean; blmoore@colgate.edu

University of Colorado Boulder

Dept. of History, 234 UCB, 204 Hellems Bldg., Boulder, CO 80309-0234. 303.492.6683. Fax 303.492.1868. Email: history@ colorado.edu. Website: https://www.colorado.edu/history/.

With more than 30 full-time faculty covering a range of fields from the colonial and modern Americas to African, Asian, and European studies, the CU Boulder History Department encourages students with a passion for learning and an interest in the past to check out one of the many courses offered every semester.

Chair: Paul Sutter
Director of Graduate Studies: Thomas Andrews
Director of Undergraduate Studies: Phoebe S. K. Young
Degrees Offered: BA,MA,PhD
Academic Year System: Semester
Areas of Specialization: medieval/early modern/modern Europe, US diplomatic/environmental/intellectual/cultural, US West, Native American, Japan/China/India/Southeast Asia, imperialism/nationalism/decolonization
Undergraduate Tuition (per academic year):
  In-State: $28750
  Out-of-State: $53504
  International: $59312
Graduate Tuition (per academic year):
  In-State: $15046
  Out-of-State: $33946
Enrollment 2018-19:
  Undergraduate Majors: 371
  New Graduate Students: 10
  Full-time Graduate Students: 45
  Degrees in History: 140 BA, 4 MA, 3 PhD
  Students in Undergraduate Courses: 5940
  Students in Undergraduate Intro Courses: 4451
Undergraduate Addresses:
  Admissions: http://www.colorado.edu/admissions
  Financial Aid: http://www.colorado.edu/admissions/cost
Graduate Addresses:
  Admissions: http://www.colorado.edu/admissions/graduate/ programs/history
  Financial Aid: http://www.colorado.edu/graduateschool/ funding

Adjunct Faculty

Wood, Peter H. (PhD, Harvard 1972; adj. prof.) African American, ethnohistory, US South; peter.wood@colorado.edu

Full-time Faculty

Anderson, Virginia D. (PhD, Harvard 1984; prof.) colonial America; virginia.anderson@colorado.edu

Andrews, Thomas G. (PhD, Wisconsin, Madison 2003; prof. and dir., grad. studies) US since 1865, environmental; thomas.andrews@ colorado.edu

Ciarlo, David M. (PhD, Wisconsin-Madison 2003; assoc. prof.) modern Germany; david.ciarlo@colorado.edu

Dauverd, Celine (PhD, UCLA 2007; assoc. prof.) early modern Europe, Mediterranean; celine.dauverd@colorado.edu

Fenn, Elizabeth (PhD, Yale 1999; Dist. prof.) pre-1865 US, Native Americans; elizabeth.fenn@colorado.edu

Ferry, Robert J. (PhD, Minnesota 1980; assoc. prof.) Latin America; robert.ferry@colorado.edu

Gautam, Sanjay (PhD, Chicago 2005; assoc. prof.) South Asia; sanjay.gautam@colorado.edu

Gerber, Matthew Dean (PhD, California, Berkeley 2004; assoc. prof.) early modern Europe, France, family; matthew.gerber@ colorado.edu

Hammer, Paul E. J. (PhD, Selwyn Coll., Cambridge 1991; prof.) early modern England; paul.hammer@colorado.edu

Hanna, Martha T. (PhD, Georgetown 1989; prof.) modern France; martha.hanna@colorado.edu

Kadia, Miriam Kingsberg (PhD, California, Berkeley 2009; assoc. prof.) Japan, China, political economy; miriam.kingsberg@ colorado.edu

Kent, Susan Kingsley (PhD, Brandeis 1984; prof.) 19th- and 20th-century Britain, Europe, gender; susan.kent@colorado.edu

Kim, Kwangmin (PhD, California, Berkeley 2008; assoc. prof.) China, East Asia; kwangmin.kim@colorado.edu

Lim, Sungyun (PhD, California, Berkeley 2011; assoc. prof.) modern Japan, Korea, family and gender; sungyun.lim@colorado.edu

Limerick, Patricia Nelson (PhD, Yale 1980; prof.) American West; patricia.limerick@colorado.edu

Lovejoy, Henry B. (PhD, California, Los Angeles 2012; asst. prof.) West Africa, African diaspora, Atlantic world; hlovejoy@ colorado.edu

Mendoza Gutierrez, Natalie (PhD, California, Berkeley 2016; asst. prof.) history pedagogy, US Latinx; natalie.mendozagutierrez@ colorado.edu

Mukherjee, Mithi (PhD, Chicago 2001; assoc. prof.) South Asia; mukherjm@colorado.edu

Osborne, Myles Gregory (PhD, Harvard 2008; assoc. prof.) sub-Saharan Africa; myles.osborne@colorado.edu

Pittenger, Mark A. (PhD, Michigan 1984; prof.) US intellectual and cultural; mark.pittenger@colorado.edu

Sachs, Honor R. (PhD, Wisconsin, Madison 2006; asst. prof.) early America, slavery, gender, law; Honor.Sachs@colorado.edu

Sutter, Paul S. (PhD, Kansas 1997; prof. and chair) US, environmental, science and technology; paul.sutter@colorado.edu

Wei, William (PhD, Michigan 1978; prof.) China, Asian American; william.wei@colorado.edu

Weston, Timothy B. (PhD, California, Berkeley 1995; assoc. prof.) China, intellectual; timothy.b.weston@colorado.edu

Willis, John M. (PhD, NYU 2007; assoc. prof.) Middle East; jwillis@ colorado.edu

Yonemoto, Marcia A. (PhD, California, Berkeley 1995; prof.) Japan, intellectual; yonemoto@colorado.edu

Young, Phoebe S. K. (PhD, California, San Diego 1999; assoc. prof. and dir., undergrad. studies) US since 1877, US women, Mexico; phoebe.young@colorado.edu

Zeiler, Thomas W. (PhD, Massachusetts Amherst 1989; prof. and dir., International Affairs) US diplomatic, recent US; thomas. zeiler@colorado.edu

Joint/Cross Appointments

Chester, Lucy (PhD, Yale 2002; assoc. prof.; International Affairs) South Asia, British Empire; chester@colorado.edu

Gutmann, Myron P. (PhD, Princeton 1976; prof.; Inst. of Behavioral Science) Europe, American West demographic and environmental; myron.gutmann@colorado.edu

Kalisman, Hilary Falb (PhD, California, Berkeley 2015; asst. prof.; Jewish Studies) Israel/Palestine, broader Middle East, education, colonialism, state and nation; Hilary.Kalisman@colorado.edu

Shneer, David (PhD, California, Berkeley 2001; prof.; Jewish Studies, Religious Studies) Jewish, eastern Europe, media; david.shneer@colorado.edu

Part-time Faculty

Hulden, Vilja (PhD, Arizona 2011; instr.) US labor; vilja.hulden@colorado.edu

Paradis, David H. (PhD, Emory 1998; sr. instr.) medieval, England, early modern Europe; david.paradis@colorado.edu

Retired/Emeritus Faculty

Anderson, Fred (PhD, Harvard 1981; prof. emeritus) American Revolution, early national; fred.anderson@colorado.edu

Chambers, Lee (PhD, Michigan 1977; prof. emeritus) American women, 19th-century social and cultural; chambers@colorado.edu

Christensen, Carl C. (PhD, Ohio State 1965; prof. emeritus) Renaissance and Reformation

Engel, Barbara A. (PhD, Columbia 1974; Dist. Prof. emeritus) Russia, European women, Soviet Union; barbara.engel@colorado.edu

Gross, David L. (PhD, Wisconsin-Madison 1969; prof. emeritus) European intellectual; david.l.gross@colorado.edu

Hohlfelder, Bob (PhD, Indiana 1966; prof. emeritus) ancient, early Byzantine; robert.hohlfelder@colorado.edu

Jankowski, James P. (PhD, Michigan 1967; prof. emeritus) Middle East; jankowsk@colorado.edu

Lebra, Joyce C. (PhD, Radcliffe 1958; prof. emeritus) Japan, India; joycelebra@gmail.com

Main, Gloria L. (PhD, Columbia 1972; prof. emeritus) colonial America; gloria.main@colorado.edu

McIntosh, Marjorie K. (PhD, Harvard 1967; Dist. Prof. emeritus) Tudor-Stuart England; marjorie.mcintosh@colorado.edu

Phillips, George H. (PhD, UCLA 1973; assoc. prof. emeritus) American Indian, Southwest

Ruestow, Edward G. (PhD, Indiana 1970; prof. emeritus) 17th- and 18th-century Europe, science; edward.ruestow@colorado.edu

Schulzinger, Robert D. (PhD, Yale 1971; prof. emeritus) US diplomatic; schulzin@colorado.edu

Recently Awarded PhDs

Driver, Beau "The Worker: Walter Wykoff and His Experiment in Reality"

Gavison, Sarah J. F. "What Should We Do with the Jews? The Soviet Union, the United States, Jewish Refugees in Postwar Europe, and the Creation of Israel"

Grego, Caroline "Hurricane of the New South: Disruption, Dispossession, and the Great Sea Island Storm of 1893"

Colorado College

Dept. of History, 208C Palmer Hall, 14 E. Cache La Poudre St., Colorado Springs, CO 80903. 719.389.6523. Fax 719.389.6524. Email: jpopiel@coloradocollege.edu. Website: https://www.coloradocollege.edu/academics/dept/history/.

The History Department cultivates in our students a passion for and a critical understanding of the past while developing their intellectual, analytical, and rhetorical abilities.

Chair: Bryan Rommel-Ruiz
Degrees Offered: BA,MSE
Academic Year System: Eight blocks of 3.5 weeks each
Areas of Specialization: US West and Southwest, European cultural and social, Latin America, Islamic world and Asia
Tuition (per academic year): $57612
Enrollment 2018-19:
  Undergraduate Majors: 58
  Degrees in History: 28 BA
Addresses:
  Admissions: http://www.coloradocollege.edu/admission/
  Financial Aid: http://www.coloradocollege.edu/admission/financialaid/

Full-time Faculty

Adler, Paul K. (PhD, Georgetown 2014; asst. prof.) US and the world, social movements, international political economy/development; padler@coloradocollege.edu

Kohout, Amy (PhD, Cornell 2015; asst. prof.) 19th-century US, US West, environmental; akohout@coloradocollege.edu

Mehta, Purvi (PhD, Michigan 2013; asst. prof.) South Asia, caste, gender; pmehta@coloradocollege.edu

Murphy, Jane H. (PhD, Princeton 2006; assoc. prof.) Islamic world, science; jmurphy@coloradocollege.edu

Neel, Carol L. (PhD, Cornell 1981; prof.) Middle Ages, women and family, history of the book; cneel@coloradocollege.edu

Ragan, Bryant T., Jr. (PhD, California, Berkeley 1988; prof.) early modern Europe, gender, sexuality; bragan@coloradocollege.edu

Ratchford, Jamal (PhD, Purdue 2011; asst. prof.) African American, sports; jratchford@coloradocollege.edu

Rommel-Ruiz, Bryan (PhD, Michigan 1999; prof. and chair) early America, Atlantic world, African American; bruiz@coloradocollege.edu

Sanchez, Danielle (PhD, Texas, Austin 2015; asst. prof.) 20th-century Africa, colonialism, popular culture; dsanchez@coloradocollege.edu

Smith, Jake Patrick (PhD, Chicago 2017; asst. prof.) 20th-century Europe; jpsmith@coloradocollege.edu

Williams, John R. (PhD, California, Berkeley 2005; assoc. prof.) China, popular culture, world; jwilliams@coloradocollege.edu

Retired/Emeritus Faculty

Ashley, Susan A. (PhD, Columbia 1973; prof. emeritus) modern Europe, France, Italy; sashley@coloradocollege.edu

Blasenheim, Peter L. (PhD, Stanford 1982; prof. emeritus) Latin America, Africa; pblasenheim@coloradocollege.edu

Monroy, Douglas (PhD, UCLA 1978; prof. emeritus) US Southwest/Mexican American, 20th-century US, California; dmonroy@coloradocollege.edu

University of Colorado Colorado Springs

Dept. of History, 1420 Austin Bluffs Pkwy., Room 2048, Colorado Springs, CO 80918. 719.255.4069. Fax 719.255.4068. Email: cjimenez@uccs.edu; ismith2@uccs.edu. Website: https://www.uccs.edu/history/.

The Department of History is a community of scholars who seek to understand the past and strive to introduce students to the process of historical thinking.

Chair: Christina Jimenez
Director of Graduate Studies: Roger Martinez
Director of Undergraduate Studies: Carole Woodall
Degrees Offered: BA,MA
Academic Year System: Semester
Areas of Specialization: 18th- to 20th-century US/Southwest/ borderlands, medieval, India and Asian studies, modern Germany, Middle Eastern studies
Undergraduate Tuition (per academic year):
  In-State: $6688
  Out-of-State: $17768
Graduate Tuition (per academic year):
  In-State: $8882
  Out-of-State: $17432
Enrollment 2018-19:
  Undergraduate Majors: 235
  New Graduate Students: 19
  Full-time Graduate Students: 45
  Part-time Graduate Students: 15
  Degrees in History: 60 BA, 18 MA
Undergraduate Addresses:
  Admissions: https://www.uccs.edu/admissions/
  Financial Aid: https://www.uccs.edu/finaid/
Graduate Addresses:
  Admissions: https://www.uccs.edu/history/graduate
  Financial Aid: https://www.uccs.edu/finaid/

Full-time Faculty

Christiansen, Samantha M. R. (PhD, Northeastern 2012; asst. prof.) Asian subcontinent; schrist3@uccs.edu
Duvick, Brian (PhD, Chicago 1992; assoc. prof.) later Greece, early medieval; bduvick@uccs.edu
Forrest, Bernice E. (PhD, Tulane 1983; assoc. prof.) Native American, African American, US literature; bguillau@uccs.edu
Harvey, Paul William (PhD, California, Berkeley 1992; prof.) 20th-century US, cultural, US South; pharvey@uccs.edu
Headle, Barbara A. (MA, California State, Northridge; sr. instr.) US West, environmental; bheadle@uccs.edu
Jimenez, Christina M. (PhD, California, San Diego 2001; assoc. prof. and chair) American Southwest, Chicano/a, Latin America; cjimenez@uccs.edu
Martinez, Roger Louis (PhD, Texas, Austin 2008; assoc. prof. and dir., grad. studies) medieval
Sackett, Robert E. (PhD, Washington, St. Louis 1980; prof.) modern Germany, popular culture, nationalism; rsackett@uccs.edu
Wei, Yang (PhD, Harvard 2012; asst. prof.) Asian studies; ywei@uccs.edu
Woodall, G. Carole (PhD, NYU 2008; assoc. prof. and dir., undergrad. studies) Middle Eastern studies; gwoodall@uccs.edu

Part-time Faculty

Davis-Witherow, Leah (MA, Colorado, Colorado Springs 1997; instr.) Colorado; ldavis2@uccs.edu
Myers, Janet (MA, Colorado, Colorado Springs; sr. instr.) medieval, Renaissance; kpmyers@adelphia.net
Sartin, Roy Jo (MA, Colorado, Colorado Springs; instr.) antiquities; rsartin@uccs.edu

Retired/Emeritus Faculty

Bender, Norman J. (PhD, Colorado, Boulder 1971; prof. emeritus) 19th-century America, US military
Hill, Christopher V. (PhD, Virginia 1987; prof. emeritus) India, Asia, environmental; chill@uccs.edu
Wunderli, Richard M. (PhD, California, Berkeley 1975; prof. emeritus) medieval Europe, Tudor-Stuart England, London; rwunderl@uccs.edu

University of Colorado Denver

Dept. of History, Campus Box 182, PO Box 173364, Denver, CO 80217-3364. 303.315.1795. Fax 303.315.1780. Email: chris.agee@ucdenver.edu; tabitha.fitzpatrick@ucdenver.edu. Website: https://clas.ucdenver.edu/history/.

The special responsibility of historical studies is to help individuals and communities understand the past. History courses integrate many branches of knowledge, cutting across the lines of the social sciences and the humanities, and even the natural sciences. Identifying forces of stability and processes of change, history students develop research, writing and analytical skills, which serve them well beyond their university years.

Chair: Christopher Agee
Director of Graduate Studies: Ryan Crewe
Director of Undergraduate Studies: Bill Wagner
Degrees Offered: BA,MA
Academic Year System: Semester
Areas of Specialization: US, Europe, global, public
Undergraduate Tuition (per academic year):
  In-State: $7536
  Out-of-State: $22416
Graduate Tuition (per academic year):
  In-State: $11006
  Out-of-State: $28212
Enrollment 2018-19:
  Undergraduate Majors: 158
  New Graduate Students: 18
  Full-time Graduate Students: 17
  Part-time Graduate Students: 55
  Degrees in History: 35 BA, 18 MA
Undergraduate Addresses:
  Admissions: http://www.ucdenver.edu/admissions/ BACHELORS/
  Financial Aid: http://www.ucdenver.edu/student-services/ resources/CostsAndFinancing/
Graduate Addresses:
  Admissions: http://www.ucdenver.edu/academics/colleges/ Graduate-School/
  Financial Aid: http://www.ucdenver.edu/student-services/ resources/CostsAndFinancing/

Full-time Faculty

Agee, Christopher L. (PhD, California, Berkeley 2005; assoc. prof. and chair) modern US, urban; chris.agee@ucdenver.edu

Crewe, Ryan D. (PhD, Yale 2009; asst. prof. and grad. advisor) Mexico, colonial Latin America, Pacific world; ryan.crewe@ ucdenver.edu

Fell, James E., Jr. (PhD, Colorado, Boulder 1975; sr. instr.) US social, economic, cultural; james.fell@ucdenver.edu

Finkelstein, Gabriel W. (PhD, Princeton 1996; assoc. prof.) Germany, Europe, science; gabriel.finkelstein@ucdenver.edu

Hunt, Rebecca A. (PhD, Colorado, Boulder 1999; sr. instr.) US West, museum studies, public; rebecca.hunt@ucdenver.edu

Kozakowski, Michael (PhD, Chicago 2014; instr.) modern Europe, migration; michael.kozakowski@ucdenver.edu

Laird, Pamela W. (PhD, Boston Univ. 1992; prof.) US social and intellectual, business and technology, public; pamela.laird@ ucdenver.edu

Levine-Clark, Marjorie (PhD, Iowa 1997; assoc. prof.) modern Britain, women/gender/sexuality, health and welfare; marjorie. levine-clark@ucdenver.edu

Noel, Thomas J. (PhD, Colorado, Boulder 1978; prof.) Colorado, American West, public; tom.noel@ucdenver.edu

Smith, Richard Dean (PhD, Colorado, Boulder 1996; sr. instr.) early modern Europe; richard.smith@ucdenver.edu

Stahl, Dale J. (PhD, Columbia 2014; asst. prof.) modern Middle East, global environment; dale.stahl@ucdenver.edu

Wagner, William E. (PhD, California, Berkeley 2011; asst. prof. and undergrad. advisor) 19th-century US, American West, social and cultural; william.wagner@ucdenver.edu

Whitesides, Greg G (PhD, California, Santa Barbara 2004; sr. instr.) US, science, world; john.whitesides@colorado.edu

Yokota, Kariann A. (PhD, UCLA 2002; assoc. prof.) early US, transnational and ethnic studies, Pacific; kariann.yokota@ ucdenver.edu

Part-time Faculty

Sundberg, Christine (MA, Colorado Denver; instr.) modern Africa, globalization; christine.sundberg@ucdenver.edu

Retired/Emeritus Faculty

Conroy, Mary E. Schaeffer (PhD, Indiana 1964; prof. emeritus) Russia; mary.conroy@ucdenver.edu

Pletsch, Carl (PhD, Chicago 1977; assoc. prof. emeritus) modern Europe, European intellectual, 20th-century world; carl. pletsch@ucdenver.edu

Rich, Myra L. (PhD, Yale 1966; assoc. prof. emeritus) colonial America, early national US, women and family; myra.rich@ ucdenver.edu

Whiteside, James B. (PhD, Colorado, Boulder 1986; assoc. prof. emeritus) 19th- and 20th-century US, American West, public; jamesb.whiteside@comcast.net

Colorado State University

Dept. of History, 1776 Campus Delivery, Fort Collins, CO 80523-1776. 970.491.6334. Fax 970.491.2941. Email: robert. gudmestad@colostate.edu. Website: https://history.colostate. edu/.

Students have the opportunity to take courses that bring history to life in unique and engaging ways. The History faculty at CSU are continually introducing innovative elements into coursework, so students are engaged with the past in a variety of ways.

Chair: Robert Gudmestad
Director of Graduate Studies: Debbie Yalen
Director of Undergraduate Studies: Ann Little
Degrees Offered: BA,MA

Academic Year System: Semester
Areas of Specialization: US West, environmental, digital, public, gender
Undergraduate Tuition (per academic year):
  In-State: $11466
  Out-of-State: $27326
Graduate Tuition (per academic year):
  In-State: $10214
  Out-of-State: $25040
Enrollment 2018-19:
  Undergraduate Majors: 729
  New Graduate Students: 12
  Full-time Graduate Students: 23
  Part-time Graduate Students: 2
  Degrees in History: 115 BA, 20 MA
  Students in Undergraduate Courses: 5667
  Students in Undergraduate Intro Courses: 4144
  Online-Only Courses: 4%
Undergraduate Addresses:
  Admissions: http://admissions.colostate.edu
  Financial Aid: https://financialaid.colostate.edu
Graduate Addresses:
  Admissions and Financial Aid: http://graduateschool.colostate. edu

Full-time Faculty

Archambeau, Nicole A. (PhD, California, Santa Barbara 2009; asst. prof.) medieval Europe; nicole.archambeau@colostate.edu

Carr Childers, Leisl Ann (PhD, Nevada, Las Vegas 2011; asst. prof.) public, environmental, American West, digital; leisl.carr_ childers@colostate.edu

Cauvin, Thomas (PhD, European Univ. Inst. 2012; asst. prof.) public; thomas.cauvin@colostate.edu

Childers, Michael Wayne (PhD, Nevada, Las Vegas 2010; asst. prof.) environmental, American West; michael.childers@colostate.edu

Gudmestad, Robert (PhD, Louisiana State 1999; prof. and chair) US South; robert.gudmestad@colostate.edu

Jackson, Jessica Barbata (PhD, California, Santa Cruz 2017; asst. prof.) social studies teaching; jessica.jackson@colostate.edu

Jones, Elizabeth Bright (PhD, Minnesota 2000; prof.) European social and women; elizabeth.jones@colostate.edu

Lindsay, James E. (PhD, Wisconsin, Madison 1994; prof.) Middle East; james.lindsay@colostate.edu

Little, Ann M. (PhD, Pennsylvania 1996; prof. and dir., undergrad. studies) colonial America, women and gender, northeastern borderlands; amlittle@colostate.edu

Long, Kelly Ann (PhD, Colorado, Boulder 1998; assoc. prof.) American intellectual, American-East Asian relations; kelly. long@colostate.edu

Margolf, Diane C. (PhD, Yale 1990; prof.) early modern Europe; diane.margolf@colostate.edu

Orsi, Jared P. (PhD, Wisconsin-Madison 1999; prof.) US borderlands and Mexico; jared.orsi@colostate.edu

Payne, Sarah Ruth (PhD, New Mexico 2010; asst. prof.) environment, gender, US West; sarah.payne@colostate.edu

Sunseri, Thaddeus (PhD, Minnesota 1993; prof.) Africa; thaddeus. sunseri@colostate.edu

Xiang, Hongyan (PhD, Penn State 2014; asst. prof.) modern East Asia; hongyan.xiang@colostate.edu

Yalen, Deborah H. (PhD, California, Berkeley 2007; assoc. prof. and dir., grad. studies) Russia, modern Jewish; deborah.yalen@ colostate.edu

Yarrington, Douglas K. (PhD, Texas, Austin 1992; assoc. prof.) Latin America; doug.yarrington@colostate.edu

Part-time Faculty

Alexander, Ruth M. (PhD, Cornell 1990; prof.) 20th-century US, American women; ruth.alexander@colostate.edu

Retired/Emeritus Faculty

Enssle, Manfred J. (PhD, Colorado, Boulder 1970; prof. emeritus) contemporary Europe, European intellectual, Germany; manfred.enssle@colostate.edu

Griswold, William J. (PhD, UCLA 1966; prof. emeritus) Islamic, Near East; william.griswold@colostate.edu

Hansen, James E., II (PhD, Denver 1968; prof. emeritus) US intellectual, Colorado, agriculture; james.hansen@colostate.edu

Knight, Thomas J. (PhD, Texas, Austin 1967; prof. emeritus) European diplomatic and intellectual, world; thomas.knight@colostate.edu

McComb, David G. (PhD, Texas, Austin 1968; prof. emeritus) sports, world; david.mccomb@colostate.edu

Rock, Kenneth W. (PhD, Stanford 1969; prof. emeritus) central and eastern Europe, European diplomatic, immigration; kenneth.rock@colostate.edu

Tyler, Daniel (PhD, New Mexico 1970; prof. emeritus) US Southwest, US West, Colorado; rockydan@aol.com

Weisser, Henry G. (PhD, Columbia 1965; prof. emeritus) Britain, Ireland; henry.weisser@colostate.edu

Worrall, Arthur J. (PhD, Indiana 1969; prof. emeritus) colonial America; arthur.worrall@colostate.edu

Colorado State University-Pueblo

Dept. of History, Political Science, Philosophy, and Geography, 2200 Bonforte Blvd., Pueblo, CO 81001-4901. 719.549.2156. Fax 719.549.2705. Email: lorraine.blase@csupueblo.edu. Website: https://www.csupueblo.edu/college-of-humanities-and-social-sciences/.

The History undergraduate program at CSU-Pueblo offers a rigorous curriculum, emphasizing knowledge, communication, critical reasoning, research, and on-the-job experience.

Chair: Grant Weller
Degrees Offered: BA,BS
Academic Year System: Semester
Areas of Specialization: ancient Mediterranean, legal studies, American religion, American food, military, US West and Southwest
Tuition (per academic year):
  In-State: $8605
  Western Undergraduate Exchange: $12907
  Out-of-State: $19658
Enrollment 2018-19:
  Undergraduate Majors: 72
Addresses:
  Admissions: https://www.csupueblo.edu/admissions
  Financial Aid: https://www.csupueblo.edu/student-financial-services

Full-time Faculty

Gaughan, Judy E. (PhD, California, Berkeley 1999; assoc. prof.) ancient Greece and Rome, legal, women; judy.gaughan@csupueblo.edu

Harris, Matthew L. (PhD, Syracuse 2004; prof.) early America, race and religion, legal and constitutional; matt.harris@csupueblo.edu

Rees, Jonathan (PhD, Wisconsin-Madison 1997; prof.) labor, business, 20th-century US; jonathan.rees@csupueblo.edu

Weller, Grant Thomas (PhD, Temple 2008; assoc. prof. and chair) modern military, Russia, modern world; grant.weller@csupueblo.edu

Columbia University

Center for History and Ethics of Public Health, 722 W. 168th St., 9th Floor, New York, NY 10032. 212.305.1307. Fax 212.342.1986. Email: nnn4@columbia.edu. Website: https://www.mailman.columbia.edu/research/center-history-and-ethics-public-health.

The only center of its kind in the nation and the only program in a school of public health endowed by the National Endowment for the Humanities, the Center for the History & Ethics of Public Health relies on historical methods and ethical analysis to investigate critical public health issues.

Chair: David Rosner and Ronald Bayer
Degrees Offered: MPH,MS,PhD
Academic Year System: Semester
Areas of Specialization: public health/medicine/health policy, environmental and occupational disease and tobacco, immigration, aging policy, ethics
Tuition (per academic year): $48036
Enrollment 2018-19:
  New Graduate Students: 2
  Full-time Graduate Students: 10
  Degrees in History: 1 PhD
Addresses:
  Admissions: http://www.mailman.columbia.edu/become-student/apply
  Financial Aid: http://www.mailman.columbia.edu/become-student/apply/financial-aid

Affiliated Faculty

Blackmar, Elizabeth (PhD, Harvard 1981; prof.; History) US social and urban; eb16@columbia.edu

Connelly, Matthew J. (PhD, Yale 1997; prof.; History) international, global; mjc96@columbia.edu

Jones, Matthew L. (PhD, Harvard 2000; prof.; History) science and technology, information technologies; mj340@columbia.edu

Roberts, Samuel K., Jr. (PhD, Princeton 2002; assoc. prof.; History) postemancipation African American social movements, class formations, urban political economy tuberculosis race disease; skr2001@columbia.edu

Full-time Faculty

Bayer, Ronald (PhD, Chicago 1976; prof. and co-dir.) public health policy, public health ethics, HIV and AIDS; rb8@columbia.edu

Chowkwanyun, Merlin (PhD, Pennsylvania 2014; asst. prof.) public health and health policy, racial inequality, urban and social movements; mc2028@cumc.columbia.edu

Colgrove, James (PhD, Columbia 2004; prof.) public health policy, vaccination; jc988@columbia.edu

Rosner, David (PhD, Harvard 1978; prof. and co-dir.) public health and 9/11, occupational and environmental, hospitals; dr289@columbia.edu

Sivaramakrishnan, Kavita (PhD, Jawaharlal Nehru, India 2004; asst. prof.) 20th-century South Asian medicine, international and global health, aging and epidemics; ks2890@columbia.edu

Joint/Cross Appointments

Markowitz, Gerald E. (PhD, Wisconsin, Madison 1971; adj. prof.; John Jay, CUNY and Grad. Center, CUNY) occupational and environmental health; gmarkowitz@jjay.cuny.edu

Oppenheimer, Gerald (PhD, Chicago 1976; prof.; Health and Nutrition Sciences, Brooklyn, CUNY) epidemiology, public health policy, health care financing; go10@columbia.edu

Recently Awarded PhDs

Johns, David "Adopting and De-adopting Public Health Policies: Science and the Politics of Evidence-Informed Decision-Making"

Columbia University

Dept. of History, 1180 Amsterdam Ave., Mail Code 2527, New York, NY 10027. 212.854.2413. Fax 212.851.5963. Email: history@columbia.edu. Website: https://history.columbia.edu/.

The Department of History at Columbia University is one of the leading centers of historical scholarship in the world. Our faculty of approximately 50 faculty members—together with colleagues in the Department of History at Barnard College, and historians in other affiliated departments in the University—studies all aspects of human history, from ancient to contemporary societies, across the entire globe.

Chair: Adam Kosto
Director of Graduate Studies: Natasha Lightfoot
Director of Undergraduate Studies: Neslihan Senocak
Degrees Offered: BA,MA,MPhil,PhD
Academic Year System: Semester
Areas of Specialization: Americas, Europe, Asia, Africa, Middle East
Undergraduate Tuition (per academic year): $59430
  Sch. General Studies: $65,592
Graduate Tuition (per academic year): $48390
Enrollment 2018-19:
  Undergraduate Majors: 430
  New Graduate Students: 23
  Full-time Graduate Students: 148
  Degrees in History: 91 BA, 20 MA, 19 PhD
Undergraduate Addresses:
  Admissions: http://undergrad.admissions.columbia.edu/
  Financial Aid: http://cc-seas.financialaid.columbia.edu/
Graduate Addresses:
  Admissions: http://gsas.columbia.edu/admissions
  Financial Aid: http://gsas.columbia.edu/financial-aid

Affiliated Faculty

Awn, Peter J. (PhD, Harvard 1978; prof.; Religion) comparative religion, Islamic; pja3@columbia.edu
Barkan, Elazar (PhD, Brandeis 1988; prof.; Sch. International and Public Affairs) US, crime, human rights; eb2302@columbia.edu
Cameron, Euan K. (PhD, Oxford 1982; prof.; Union Theological Sem., Religion) Reformation; ecameron@uts.columbia.edu
Delbanco, Andrew (PhD, Harvard 1980; prof.; English) colonial America; ad19@columbia.edu
Diouf, Mamadou (PhD, Paris 1981; prof.; Middle East and Asian Languages and Cultures) Africa; md2573@columbia.edu
Dye, Alan (PhD, Illinois, Urbana-Champaign 1991; assoc. prof.; Barnard, Columbia, Economics) US and Latin American economic; ad245@columbia.edu
Erickson, Ansley T. (PhD, Columbia 2010; asst. prof.; Teachers Coll., Columbia) erickson@tc.columbia.edu
Force, Pierre (PhD, Paris 1987; prof.; French and Romance Philology) Europe, intellectual; pf3@columbia.edu
Hymes, Robert P. (PhD, Pennsylvania 1979; prof.; East Asian Languages and Cultures) Middle Period social, China; hymes@columbia.edu

John, Richard R. (PhD, Harvard 1989; prof.; Sch. Journalism) journalism; rrj2115@columbia.edu
Lean, Eugenia Y. (PhD, UCLA 2001; assoc. prof.; East Asian Languages & Cultures) modern China; eyl2006@columbia.edu
Li, Feng (PhD, Chicago 2000; prof.; East Asian Languages and Cultures) early China; fl123@columbia.edu
Lilla, Mark (PhD, Harvard 1990; prof.; Religion) early modern Europe, political philosophy; mlilla@columbia.edu
Lomnitz, Claudio (PhD, Stanford 1987; prof.; Anthropology) anthropology, Latina/o studies; cl2510@columbia.edu
Lurie, David Barnett (PhD, Columbia 2001; assoc. prof.; East Asian Languages and Cultures) Japan; dbl11@columbia.edu
Pflugfelder, Gregory M. (PhD, Stanford 1996; assoc. prof.; East Asian Languages and Cultures) East Asia; gmp12@columbia.edu
Saada, Emmanuelle M. (PhD, EHESS, France 2001; assoc. prof.; dir., Center for French and Francophone Studies) sociology of colonization; es2593@columbia.edu
Tuttle, Gray (PhD, Harvard 2002; assoc. prof.; East Asian Languages and Cultures) Tibet; gwt2102@columbia.edu
Weiman, David F. (PhD, Stanford 1984; prof.; Barnard, Columbia, Economics) US economic; dfw5@columbia.edu

Full-time Faculty

Ahmed, Manan (PhD, Chicago 2008; assoc. prof.) South Asia; ma3179@columbia.edu
Amar, Tarik Cyril (PhD, Princeton 2006; assoc. prof.) Soviet Union; tca2109@columbia.edu
Armstrong, Charles K. (PhD, Chicago 1994; prof.) Korea; cra10@columbia.edu
Billows, Richard A. (PhD, California, Berkeley 1985; prof.) ancient Greece; rab4@columbia.edu
Blackmar, Elizabeth (PhD, Harvard 1981; prof.) American social, American women; eb16@columbia.edu
Blake, Casey N. (PhD, Rochester 1987; prof.) US intellectual and cultural, American studies; cb460@columbia.edu
Brown, Christopher L. (DPhil, Oxford 1994; prof.) early British Empire, slavery, Atlantic world; clb2140@columbia.edu
Carlebach, Elisheva (PhD, Columbia 1986; prof. and vice chair) early modern Jewish; ec607@columbia.edu
Chamberlin, Paul T. (PhD, Ohio State 2009; assoc. prof.) 20th-century international, US foreign relations, Middle East; ptc2121@columbia.edu
Chauncey, George (PhD, Yale 1989; prof.) modern US gender/sexuality/city, American LGBTQ; george.chauncey@columbia.edu
Coleman, Charly (PhD, Stanford 2005; assoc. prof.) selfhood, religion; cc3472@columbia.edu
Connelly, Matthew J. (PhD, Yale 1997; prof.) modern Europe and international; mjc96@columbia.edu
de Grazia, Victoria (PhD, Columbia 1976; prof.) modern western Europe, Italy; vd19@columbia.edu
Elshakry, Marwa S. (PhD, Princeton 2003; assoc. prof.) Middle East, science/technology/medicine; me2335@columbia.edu
Evtuhov, Catherine (PhD, California, Berkeley 1991; prof.) imperial Russia, ideas/culture/religion; ce2308@columbia.edu
Farber, Hannah A. (PhD, California, Berkeley 2014; asst. prof.) colonial North America, early American Republic, Atlantic world; hannah.farber@columbia.edu
Fields, Barbara J. (PhD, Yale 1978; prof.) US South, 19th-century American social
Gluck, Carol N. (PhD, Columbia 1977; prof.) Meiji Japan; cg9@columbia.edu
Guridy, Frank A. (PhD, Michigan 2002; assoc. prof.) African American and African diaspora studies, urban and sport; fg2368@columbia.edu

Hallett, Hilary (PhD, Grad. Center, CUNY 2005; assoc. prof.) American studies; hah2117@columbia.edu

Howell, Martha C. (PhD, Columbia 1979; Miriam Champion Prof.) early modern Europe; mch4@columbia.edu

Jackson, Kenneth T. (PhD, Chicago 1966; prof.) American urban and social, development of transportation; ktj1@columbia.edu

Jacoby, Karl H. (PhD, Yale 1997; prof.) Great Plains and borderlands, US; kj2305@columbia.edu

Jones, Matthew L. (PhD, Harvard 2000; prof.) early modern European intellectual; mj340@columbia.edu

Khalidi, Rashid I. (PhD, Oxford 1974; prof.) Middle East; rik2101@columbia.edu

Kobrin, Rebecca (PhD, Pennsylvania 2002; assoc. prof.) American Jewish; rk2351@columbia.edu

Kosto, Adam J. (PhD, Harvard 1996; prof. and chair) medieval; ajkosto@columbia.edu

Lightfoot, Natasha J. (PhD, NYU 2007; assoc. prof. and dir., grad. studies) African American, Caribbean; nlightfoot@columbia.edu

Mann, Gregory (PhD, Northwestern 2000; prof.) Francophone Africa; gm522@columbia.edu

Mazower, Mark (DPhil, Oxford 1988; prof.) Balkans, modern Greece; mm2669@columbia.edu

Mazurek, Malgorzata (PhD, Warsaw 2008; assoc. prof.) Polish studies, east central Europe, intellectual history of development; mm4293@columbia.edu

McCurry, Stephanie (PhD, SUNY, Binghamton 1988; prof.) 19th-century America, US South; sm4041@columbia.edu

Ngai, Mae M. (PhD, Columbia 1998; prof.) US, immigration; mn53@columbia.edu

Nguyen, Lien-Hang Thi (PhD, Yale 2008; assoc. prof.) US-Southeast Asian relations, global Cold War, Vietnam War; ln2358@columbia.edu

Pedersen, Susan (PhD, Harvard 1989; prof.) modern Britain; sp2216@columbia.edu

Piccato, Pablo A. (PhD, Texas, Austin 1997; prof.) Latin America; pp143@columbia.edu

Pizzigoni, Caterina L. (PhD, London 2002; assoc. prof.) Latin America; cp2313@columbia.edu

Ramgopal, Sailakshmi (PhD, Chicago 2016; asst. prof.) Rome; sr3658@columbia.edu

Schama, Simon (MA, Cambridge 1969; Univ. Prof.) early modern Europe, Dutch art; sms53@columbia.edu

Sen, Ahmet Tunc (PhD, Chicago 2016; asst. prof.) Ottoman; ats2171@columbia.edu

Senocak, Neslihan (PhD, Bilkent, Turkey 2002; assoc. prof. and dir., undergrad. studies) medieval Europe; nsenocak@columbia.edu

Smith, Pamela H. (PhD, Johns Hopkins 1990; prof. and dir., Center for Science and Soc.) early modern Europe; ps2270@columbia.edu

Stanislawski, Michael F. (PhD, Harvard 1979; prof.) eastern European Jewish; mfs3@columbia.edu

Steingart, Alma (PhD, MIT 2013; asst. prof.) as2475@columbia.edu

Stephanson, Anders (PhD, Columbia 1986; prof.) 20th-century US, postwar US foreign policy; ags8@columbia.edu

Stephens, Rhiannon (PhD, Northwestern 2007; assoc. prof.) East/Central Africa, gender/kinship/poverty; rs3169@columbia.edu

Tooze, J. Adam (PhD, London Sch. Econ. 1996; prof.) modern Germany; adam.tooze@columbia.edu

Van De Mieroop, Marc (PhD, Yale 1983; prof.) ancient Near East; mv1@columbia.edu

Winter, Emma L. (PhD, Cambridge 2005; asst. prof.) 18th- and 19th-century Britain and Europe; ew2176@columbia.edu

Zelin, Madeleine (PhD, California, Berkeley 1979; prof.) modern China, social, economic; mhz1@columbia.edu

Joint/Cross Appointments

Coatsworth, John H. (PhD, Wisconsin, Madison 1972; prof. and provost; International Affairs) Latin America; jhc2125@columbia.edu

Katznelson, Ira (PhD, Cambridge 1969; prof.; Political Science) American politics and race relations; iik1@columbia.edu

Robcis, Camille (PhD, Cornell 2007; assoc. prof.; French and Romance Philology) modern France, cultural and intellectual, critical theory; car2129@columbia.edu

Roberts, Samuel K., Jr. (PhD, Princeton 2002; assoc. prof.; Sociomedical Sciences) African American; skr2001@columbia.edu

Rosner, David (PhD, Harvard 1978; prof.; Public Health) public health; dr289@columbia.edu

Rothman, David J. (PhD, Harvard 1964; prof.; Medicine) American social; djr5@columbia.edu

Schwartz, Seth R. (PhD, Columbia 1985; prof.; Classics) srs166@columbia.edu

Somerville, Robert (PhD, Yale 1968; prof.; Religion) medieval canon law, church through Reformation; somervil@columbia.edu

Retired/Emeritus Faculty

Berghahn, Volker R. (PhD, London 1966; prof. emeritus) modern western Europe, Germany; vrb7@columbia.edu

Bulliet, Richard W. (PhD, Harvard 1967; prof. emeritus) medieval and modern Middle East; rwb3@columbia.edu

Bushman, Richard L. (PhD, Harvard 1961; prof. emeritus) American Revolution; rlb7@columbia.edu

Bynum, Caroline W. (PhD, Harvard 1969; Univ. Prof. emerita) medieval Europe; cwb4@columbia.edu

Deak, Istvan (PhD, Columbia 1964; prof. emeritus) 19th- and 20th-century Europe, Habsburg monarchy and east central Europe; id1@columbia.edu

Dirks, Nicholas B. (PhD, Chicago 1981; prof. emeritus) modern South Asia, historical anthropology

Foner, Eric (PhD, Columbia 1969; prof. emeritus) Civil War and Reconstruction, slavery, 19th-century America; ef17@columbia.edu

Goren, Arthur (PhD, Columbia 1966; prof. emeritus) US, Jewish; aag3@columbia.edu

Graff, Henry F. (PhD, Columbia 1949; prof. emeritus) US, social, political; hfg1@columbia.edu

Kessler-Harris, Alice (PhD, Rutgers 1968; prof. emerita) 20th-century US, women; ak571@columbia.edu

Klein, Herbert S. (PhD, Chicago 1963; prof. emeritus) Latin America; hsk1@columbia.edu

Leach, William R. (PhD, Rochester 1976; prof. emeritus) modern American cultural; wrl3@columbia.edu

Malefakis, Edward E. (PhD, Columbia 1965; prof. emeritus) Spain, 19th- and 20th-century southern European comparative; eem1@columbia.edu

Paxton, Robert O. (PhD, Harvard 1963; prof. emeritus) 19th- and 20th-century France, Europe since 1815; rop1@columbia.edu

Stepan, Nancy L. (PhD, UCLA 1971; prof. emerita) science and medicine; nls1@columbia.edu

Woloch, Isser (PhD, Princeton 1965; prof. emeritus) 18th- to mid-19th-century western Europe, French social, French Revolution; iw6@columbia.edu

Wortman, Richard (PhD, Chicago 1966; prof. emeritus) 19th-century Russia; rsw3@columbia.edu

Wright, Marcia (PhD, London 1966; prof. emerita) eastern and southern Africa; mw32@columbia.edu

Recently Awarded PhDs

Alcenat, Westenley "'Children of Africa, Shall be Haytians': Prince Saunders, Revolutionary Transnationalism, and the Foundations of Black Emigration"

Bhattacharyya, Tania "Bombay, 1839-1932: Empire, Space, and Belonging in an Indian Ocean Port City"

Buljina, Harun "Empire, Nation, and the Islamic World: Bosnian Muslim Reformists between the Habsburg and Ottoman Empires, 1901-14"

Elmer, Hannah "Alive Enough: Reanimating the Dead in Central Europe, 1200-1545"

Ferguson, Susanna "Tracing Tarbuya: Women, Education, and Childrearing in Lebanon and Egypt, 1860-1939"

Gonzalez Le Saux, Marianne "The Rule of Lawyers: Legal Profession, Politics, and the Social in Chile, 1925-89"

Kaplan, Abram "The Myth of Greek Algebra: Progress and Community in Early Modern Mathematics"

Kressel, Daniel Gunnar "Technicians of the Spirit: Post-Fascist Technocratic Authoritarianism in Spain, Argentina, and Chile, 1945-88"

Marcus, David "In Socialism's Twilight: Michael Walzer and the Politics of the Long New Left"

Mulder, Nicholas Jan Thomas "The Economic Weapon: Interwar Internationalism and the Rise of Sanctions, 1914-45"

Murphy, AJ "Management Expertise in the Cold War US Military"

Neubauer, Jack Maren "Adopted by the World: China and the Rise of Global Intimacy"

Newman, Rachel Grace "Transnational Ambitions: Student Migrants and the Making of a National Future in 20th-Century Mexico"

Shinnar, Shulamit "Illness, Healing, and the Contours of Religious Community: Jewsish Medical Culture in Late Antiquity, 200-600 CE"

Vendell, Dominic "Scribes and the Vocation of Politics in the Maratha Empire, 1708-1818"

Yee, Ethan Leong "The Burden of Forgiveness: Franciscans' Impact on Penitential Practices in the 13th Century"

Zakar, Adrien "The Disembodied Eye: Technologies of Surveillance and the Logistics of Perception in the Ottoman Empire and Syria, 1900-30"

Zarate, Arthur "The Making of a Muslim Reformer: Muhammad al-Ghazáli (1917-96) and Islam in Postcolonial Egypt, 1947-67"

Columbus State University

Dept. of History and Geography, 4225 University Ave., Yancey Center at One Arsenal, Suite 340, Columbus, GA 31907-5645. 706.507.8350. Fax 706.507.8362. Email: history_geographydept@columbusstate.edu. Website: https://history.columbusstate.edu/

Located on the RiverPark campus in uptown Columbus, Georgia, the department houses faculty with expertise in Latin American, African American, Islamic, military and international, Native American, early and modern European, religious, and United States history.

Chair: Doug Tompson
Director of Graduate Studies: Ryan Lynch
Degrees Offered: BA,MA
Academic Year System: Semester
Areas of Specialization: US, Latin America, Asia, Islamic, international

Undergraduate Tuition (per academic year):
In-State: $5857
Out-of-State: $15990
Graduate Tuition (per academic year):
In-State: $5458
Out-of-State: $16268
Enrollment 2018-19:
Undergraduate Majors: 100
New Graduate Students: 3
Full-time Graduate Students: 9
Degrees in History: 21 BA
Undergraduate Addresses:
Admissions: http://academics.columbusstate.edu/catalogs/current/admission/undergraduate/
Financial Aid: http://finaid.columbusstate.edu
Graduate Addresses:
Admissions: http://academics.columbusstate.edu/catalogs/current/admission/graduate/graduate.php
Financial Aid: http://finaid.columbusstate.edu

Full-time Faculty

Banks, Bryan Andrew (PhD, Florida State 2014; asst. prof.) early modern and modern Europe, comparative revolutions, religious studies; banks_bryan@columbusstate.edu

Bowman, Sarah K. (PhD, Yale 2015; asst. prof.) US South, American cultural and US 1865-1945, memory; bowman_sarah@columbusstate.edu

Crosswell, Daniel K. R. (PhD, Kansas State 1986; Col. Richard R. Hallock Dist. Univ. Chair) military, Europe and world, intellectual; crosswell_daniel@columbusstate.edu

Ellisor, John (PhD, Tennessee, Knoxville 1996; assoc. prof.) early US, Native American, race and ethnicity; ellisor_john@columbusstate.edu

Huff, Brad (PhD, Florida State 2012; asst. prof.) GIS, spatial data analysis, cultural geography; huff_brad@columbusstate.edu

Lynch, Ryan Joseph (DPhil, Oxford 2016; asst. prof. and dir., grad. studies) medieval and classical Islamic, early Islamic conquests, Umayyad and early 'Abbasid dynasties and Arabic historiography; lynch_ryanj@columbusstate.edu

Rees, Amanda (PhD, Kansas 1998; prof.) community and cultural geography, tourism, stand alone geographers; rees_amanda@columbusstate.edu

Sprayberry, Gary (PhD, Alabama 2003; assoc. prof.) African American, American social and cultural, US since 1865; sprayberry_gary@columbusstate.edu

Tompson, Doug (PhD, Florida 2001; assoc. prof. and chair) Latin America, race and ethnicity, state and nation; tompson_doug@columbusstate.edu

Part-time Faculty

Baird, Andrew T. (ABD, Auburn; part-time faculty) US space program; baird_andrew@columbustate.edu

Barber, Stephen P. (PhD, Auburn 2011; part-time faculty) US; barber_stephen@columbusstate.edu

Cope, Don (MA, Auburn; prof. emeritus) military, US Civil War; cope_don@columbusstate.edu

Luck, Patrick F. (PhD, Johns Hopkins 2012; part-time faculty) US, African American; luck_patrick@columbustate.ed

Melton, Maurice K. (PhD, Emory 1978; part-time faculty) African American, US South; melton_maurice@columbusstate.edu

Schulz, Zachary W. (PhD, Purdue 2018; part-time faculty) schulz_zachary@columbusstate.edu

Seymour, Jeffery (MA, Jacksonville State; part-time faculty) US Civil War, naval; seymour_jeffery@columbusstate.edu

Stokes, Kimberly (MEd, Columbus State 2005; part-time faculty) stokes_kimberly@columbusstate.edu

Turner, Andrew A. (MA, Auburn 2013; part-time faculty) GIS, spatial data analysis; turner_andrew@columbusstate.edu

Retired/Emeritus Faculty

Causey, Virginia E. (PhD, Emory 1983; prof. emeritus) Georgia, oral; causey_virginia@columbusstate.edu

Lloyd, Craig (PhD, Iowa 1970; prof. emeritus) craiglloyd40@hotmail.com

Lupold, John S. (PhD, South Carolina 1970; prof. emeritus) lupold_john@columbusstate.edu

Murzyn, John S. (PhD, NYU 1969; prof. emeritus)

Myers, John (PhD, Florida State 1974; prof. emeritus) myers_jack@columbusstate.edu

Rodgers, Hugh I. (PhD, Texas, Austin 1968; prof. emeritus) h_slrodgers@knology.net

Wadkins, Mary Jane (MA, Auburn; assoc. prof. emeritus) mjwadkins@hotmail.com

Concordia College

Dept. of History, 901 S. Eighth St., Moorhead, MN 56562. 218.299.3501. Fax 218.299.4552. Email: chapman@cord. edu. Website: https://www.concordiacollege.edu/academics/ programs-of-study/history/.

If you hope to compete and contribute in a complex global society, you must be thoughtfully engaged in understanding the cultures and histories of diverse people and places. Concordia's history program builds your global competence for thriving in any career calling.

Chair: Richard M. Chapman
Degrees Offered: BA
Academic Year System: Semester
Areas of Specialization: US, East Asia, world, Europe
Tuition (per academic year): $39650
Enrollment 2018-19:
  Undergraduate Majors: 22
  Degrees in History: 5 BA
Addresses:
  Admissions: http://www.concordiacollege.edu/admission-aid/
  Financial Aid: https://www.concordiacollege.edu/admission-aid/tuition-aid/

Full-time Faculty

Arnold, W. Vincent (PhD, Miami, Ohio 1990; prof.) modern Germany, modern Italy, imperial and 20th-century Russia; arnold@cord.edu

Bender, John Elijah (PhD, California, Santa Barbara 2017; asst. prof.) premodern Japan, environmental, East Asia; bender@cord.edu

Chapman, Richard M. (PhD, Minnesota 1993; prof. and chair) US, social welfare and religion, African American, Latin America chapman@cord.edu

Lintelman, Joy K. (PhD, Minnesota 1991; prof.) immigration and ethnic, US women, food; lintelma@cord.edu

Wentling, Sonja P. (PhD, Kent State 2002; assoc. prof.) US foreign relations, 20th-century world, Middle East; wentling@cord.edu

Retired/Emeritus Faculty

Drache, Hiram (PhD, North Dakota 1963; prof. emeritus and hist.-in-residence) drache@cord.edu

Engelhardt, Carroll L. (PhD, Iowa 1969; prof. emeritus) American thought and culture, European thought and culture, modern England; cengelha@cord.edu

Sandgren, David P. (PhD, Wisconsin, Madison 1976; prof. emeritus) Africa, world, global issues; sandgren@cord.edu

Concord University

History Program, Dept. of Humanities, 1000 Vermillion St., Athens, WV 24712. 304.384.5352. Fax 304.384.6091 Email: humanities@concord.edu. Website: https://www.concord.edu/ humanities.

History is the study of the past. It shapes the present and sets the course for the future. The study of history enables students to gain a greater understanding of the people, events, and trends that have influenced the present, and provides the knowledge, skills, and attitudes to solve contemporary problems. The Program in History prepares students for graduate school in history and closely related disciplines, and a wide variety of careers in schools, colleges, and universities, museums, archives, and libraries, federal, state, and local government, law, tourism, and consulting.

Chair: Jonathan Berkey
Degrees Offered: BA
Academic Year System: Semester
Areas of Specialization: American Civil War, international affairs, science
Tuition (per academic year):
  In-State: $8050
  Out-of-State: $17702
Enrollment 2018-19:
  Undergraduate Majors: 34
  Degrees in History: 11 BA
  Students in Undergraduate Courses: 596
  Students in Undergraduate Intro Courses: 485
  Online-Only Courses: 37%
Addresses:
  Admissions: https://www.concord.edu/Admissions.aspx
  Financial Aid: https://www.concord.edu/Financial-Aid.aspx

Full-time Faculty

Berkey, Jonathan M. (PhD, Penn State 2003; prof. and chair) US Civil War, US South; berkeyj@concord.edu

Lilly, R. Keith (MA, Virginia Tech 1996; instr.) rklilly@concord.edu

Manzione, Joseph A. (PhD, Michigan 1992; prof.) international affairs, science; manzionej@concord.edu

McKenna, Thomas J. (PhD, Yale 2004; prof.; interim dean, Coll. of Fine Arts, Humanities, and Social Sci.) tjmckenna@concord.edu

University of Connecticut at Storrs

Dept. of History, Wood Hall, Unit 4103, 241 Glenbrook Rd., Storrs Mansfield, CT 06269-4103. 860.486.3722. Fax 860.486.0641. Email: history@uconn.edu. Website: https://history.uconn.edu/.

Learning about history at UConn, through taking just a few courses or completing a major or a graduate degree, contributes to the richness of a university education and fosters critical habits of thinking, speaking, and writing, valuable in any walk of life.

Chair: Mark Healey
Director of Graduate Studies: Nancy Shoemaker
Director of Undergraduate Studies: Peter Baldwin
Degrees Offered: BA,MA,PhD
Academic Year System: Semester

Areas of Specialization: early US, modern US, medieval Europe, modern Europe, Latin American and Caribbean studies

Undergraduate Tuition (per academic year):
In-State: $13798
New England Regional: $22816
Out-of-State: $36466

Graduate Tuition (per academic year):
In-State: $16300
New England Regional: $27196
Out-of-State: $38212

Enrollment 2018-19:
Undergraduate Majors: 207
New Graduate Students: 6
Full-time Graduate Students: 42
Part-time Graduate Students: 6
Degrees in History: 98 BA, 1 MA, 5 PhD

Undergraduate Addresses:
Admissions: http://admissions.uconn.edu/
Financial Aid: http://financialaid.uconn.edu/

Graduate Addresses:
Admissions and Financial Aid: http://grad.uconn.edu/

Affiliated Faculty

Miller, Stuart (PhD, NYU 1980; prof.; Literatures, Cultures, and Languages) ancient Near East, Greco-Roman Palestine, Jewish; stuart.miller@uconn.edu

Scheinfeldt, Tom (DPhil, Oxford 2003; assoc. prof.; dir., Digital Humanities/Digital Media Center) digital humanities, scholarly open source software; tom.scheinfeldt@uconn.edu

Full-time Faculty

Amador, Emma Balbina (PhD, Michigan 2015; asst. prof.; El Instituto) Latin American/Caribbean/Latino/a; emma.amador@uconn.edu

Azimi, Fakhreddin (PhD, Oxford 1985; prof.) modern Middle East, Iran; fakhreddin.azimi@uconn.edu

Baldwin, Peter C. (PhD, Brown 1997; prof. and dir., undergrad. studies) American urban, American social and cultural; peter.baldwin@uconn.edu

Blatt, Joel R. (PhD, Rochester 1977; assoc. prof.; Stamford) French political and diplomatic, Europe 1914-45; joel.blatt@uconn.edu

Canning, Paul M. (PhD, Washington 1979; assoc. prof.; Hartford) modern Britain, modern Ireland; paul.canning@uconn.edu

Chang, Jason Oliver (PhD, California, Berkeley 2010; asst. prof.; Asian and Asian American Studies Inst.) Asian American, Lati America, comparative ethnic studies/diaspora/migration/transnationalism; jason.o.chang@uconn.edu

Clark, Christopher F. (PhD, Harvard 1982; prof.) early America, social and rural; c.clark@uconn.edu

Costigliola, Frank C. (PhD, Cornell 1973; prof.) US foreign relations, cultural relations; frank.costigliola@uconn.edu

Cygan, Mary E. (PhD, Northwestern 1989; assoc. prof.; Stamford) immigration; mary.cygan@uconn.edu

Dayton, Cornelia H. (PhD, Princeton 1986; assoc. prof.) colonial, women and gender, US law; cornelia.dayton@uconn.edu

Dintenfass, Michael (PhD, Columbia 1985; assoc. prof.) Europe; michael.dintenfass@uconn.edu

Dudden, Alexis (PhD, Chicago 1998; prof.) modern Japan, Korea; alexis.dudden@uconn.edu

Gabriel, Dexter J. (PhD, SUNY, Stony Brook 2016; asst. prof.; Inst. of Africana Studies) dexter.gabriel@uconn.edu

Gouwens, Kenneth (PhD, Stanford 1991; prof.) Renaissance, intellectual and cultural; kenneth.gouwens@uconn.edu

Healey, Mark Alan (PhD, Duke 2000; assoc. prof. and chair) modern Latin America, Argentina urban/environmental/political; mark.healey@uconn.edu

Kane, Brendan M. (PhD, Princeton 2004; assoc. prof.) early modern Ireland and England; brendan.kane@uconn.edu

Lambe, Ariel Mae (PhD, Columbia 2014; asst. prof.) Latin America; ariel.lambe@uconn.edu

Lansing, Charles B. IV (PhD, Yale 2004; assoc. prof.) modern Germany since 1870; charles.lansing@uconn.edu

McAlhany, Joseph (PhD, Columbia 2003; assoc. prof.) Roman intellectual, translation, medieval Latin; joseph.mcalhany@uconn.edu

McElya, Micki (PhD, NYU 2003; prof.) American studies, US; micki.mcelya@uconn.edu

McKenzie, Matthew G. (PhD, New Hampshire 2003; asst. prof.; Avery Point) maritime, American studies; matthew.mckenzie@uconn.edu

Meyer, Judith P. (PhD, Iowa 1977; assoc. prof.; Waterbury) Renaissance and Reformation, early modern France; judith.p.meyer@uconn.edu

Newport, Melanie Diane (PhD, Temple 2016; asst. prof.; Hartford) carceral state/jails, recent US; melanie.newport@uconn.edu

Ogbar, Jeffrey Ogbonna (PhD, Indiana 1997; prof.) 20th-century US, African American; jeffrey.ogbar@uconn.edu

Olson, Sherri (PhD, Toronto 1988; prof.) medieval, social; sherri.olson@uconn.edu

Omara-Otunnu, Amii (PhD, Oxford 1985; assoc. prof.) Africa; amii.omara-otunnu@uconn.edu

Overmyer-Velazquez, Mark (PhD, Yale 2002; prof.; dir., UConn Hartford Regional Campus) modern Mexico, transnational migration, US Latino/a; mark.velazquez@uconn.edu

Pappademos, Melina (PhD, NYU 2004; assoc. prof.; dir., Africana Studies Inst.) 20th-century African diaspora, Cuba; melina.pappademos@uconn.edu

Roe, Shirley A. (PhD, Harvard 1976; prof.) science, 17th- and 18th-century European intellectual; shirley.roe@uconn.edu

Rozwadowski, Helen M. (PhD, Pennsylvania 1996; assoc. prof.; Avery Point) maritime, science, environmental; helen.rozwadowski@uconn.edu

Salazar Rey, Ricardo Raul (PhD, Harvard 2014; asst. prof.; Stamford) Atlantic slavery, imperial Spain; ricardo.salazar-rey@uconn.edu

Schafer, Sylvia (PhD, California, Berkeley 1992; assoc. prof.) modern Europe, France, feminist theory; sylvia.schafer@uconn.edu

Shoemaker, Nancy L. (PhD, Minnesota 1991; prof. and dir., grad. studies) American Indian; nancy.shoemaker@uconn.edu

Silverstein, Sara (PhD, Yale 2016; asst. prof.; Human Rights) modern Europe, international movements and social policy; sara.silverstein@uconn.edu

Simpson, Bradley R. (PhD, Northwestern 2003; assoc. prof.) post-WWII US-Indonesian relations; bradley.simpson@uconn.edu

Sinha, Manisha (PhD, Columbia 1994; Draper Chair) African Americans and abolition movement; manisha.sinha@uconn.edu

Tran, Nu-Anh (PhD, California, Berkeley 2015; asst. prof.; Asian and Asian American Studies Inst.) Vietnam War, Southeast Asia; nu-anh.tran@uconn.edu

Vernal, Fiona (PhD, Yale 2003; assoc. prof.) 19th-century Africa, South Africa; fiona.vernal@uconn.edu

Watson, Janet S. K. (PhD, Stanford 1996; assoc. prof.) 20th-century European cultural, modern Britain, gender; janet.watson@uconn.edu

Woodward, Walter W. (PhD, Connecticut 2001; assoc. prof.; Hartford; Connecticut State Historian) early America; walter.woodward@uconn.edu

Zarrow, Peter G. (PhD, Columbia 1987; prof.) Chinese and comparative political thought; peter.zarrow@uconn.edu

Zatsepine, Victor (PhD, British Columbia 2007; asst. prof.) China, Russia; victor.zatsepine@uconn.edu

Retired/Emeritus Faculty

Asher, Robert (PhD, Minnesota 1971; prof. emeritus) labor and social developments, technology

Brown, Richard D. (PhD, Harvard 1966; prof. emeritus) colonial, revolutionary, preindustrial social and cultural; richard.d.brown@uconn.edu

Buckley, Roger Norman (PhD, McGill 1975; prof. emeritus) colonial Latin America, Caribbean, colonial British military; roger.buckley@uconn.edu

Collier, Christopher (PhD, Columbia 1964; prof. emeritus) colonial, Connecticut; ccollier@mindspring.com

Coons, Ronald E. (PhD, Harvard 1966; prof. emeritus) 19th-century Europe, Habsburg monarchy; ronald.coons@uconn.edu

Cox, Marvin R. (PhD, Yale 1965; assoc. prof. emeritus) modern France; marvin.cox@uconn.edu

Davis, John A. (PhD, Oxford 1975; prof. emeritus) Italy since 1700, comparative European social and economic since 1750; john.davis@uconn.edu

Dickerman, Edmund (PhD, Brown 1965; prof. emeritus) Renaissance and Reformation

Goodheart, Lawrence B. (PhD, Connecticut 1979; prof. emeritus) 19th-century US social and intellectual; lawrence.goodheart@uconn.edu

Goodwin, Paul B., Jr. (PhD, Massachusetts 1971; prof. emeritus) modern Latin America, Argentina, Britain in Latin America; paul.goodwin@uconn.edu

Gross, Robert A. (PhD, Columbia 1976; Draper Prof. emeritus) transcendentalism and society, history of the book

Kupperman, Karen Ordahl (PhD, Cambridge 1978; prof. emeritus) early America; karen.kupperman@uconn.edu

Langer, Lawrence N. (PhD, Chicago 1972; assoc. prof. emeritus) medieval Russia; lawrence.langer@uconn.edu

Mast, Herman W., III (PhD, Illinois, Urbana-Champaign 1970; retired assoc. prof.) modern China, Chinese thought

Newmyer, R. Kent (PhD, Nebraska 1959; prof. emeritus) early national period, constitutional and legal; k.newmyer@uconn.edu

Paterson, Thomas G. (PhD, California, Berkeley 1968; prof. emeritus) foreign relations, Cold War, post-World War II US

Phillips, Kim T. (PhD, California, Berkeley 1968; assoc. prof. emeritus) 19th-century US political and social; kim.phillips@uconn.edu

Reed, Howard (PhD, Princeton 1951; prof. emeritus) modern Middle East, Turkey; howard.reed@uconn.edu

Silvestrini, Blanca G. (PhD, SUNY, Albany 1973; prof. emeritus) modern Latin America, Caribbean, social; blanca.silvestrini@uconn.edu

Spalding, Karen (PhD, California, Berkeley 1968; prof. emeritus) colonial Latin America, Andean area; karen.spalding@uconn.edu

Walker, Anita (PhD, Harvard 1970; prof. emeritus) ancient Near East; anita.walker@uconn.edu

Waller, Altina L. (PhD, Massachusetts Amherst 1980; prof. emeritus) 19th-century US social and cultural, family, community; altina.waller@uconn.edu

Wang, Guanhua (PhD, Michigan State 1995; assoc. prof. emeritus) 20th-century Chinese social and cultural, popular movements, communication; g.wang@uconn.edu

Ward, Allen M. (PhD, Princeton 1968; prof. emeritus) ancient Greece and Rome; allen.ward@uconn.edu

Wehrle, Edmund S. (PhD, Chicago 1962; prof. emeritus) European imperialism, modern Asia

Recently Awarded PhDs

Bogert-Winkler, Hilary "Prayerful Protest and Clandestine Conformity Alternative Liturgies and the Book of Common Prayer in Interregnum England"

Deavila, Orlando "City of Rights vs. City of Patrimony: Heritage Tourism, Popular Politics, and Race in the Remaking of Cartagena, Colombia, 1943-84"

Guariglia, Matthew "Learning to Police: Knowledge, Power, and Law Enforcement in Multiracial New York City, 1880-1920"

Loiselle, Aimee "The Norma Rae Phenomenon: Crystal Lee Sutton, the Global Labor Force, and a Pop Icon"

Sopcak-Joseph, Amy "Fashioning American Women: Godey's Lady's Book, Female Consumers, and Periodical Publishing in the 19th Century"

Connecticut College

Dept. of History, 270 Mohegan Ave., Box 5552, New London, CT 06320-4196. 860.439.2248. Fax 860.439.5332. Email: lgar@conncoll.edu. Website: https://www.conncoll.edu/academics/majors-departments-programs/departments/history/.

The history department is the most international department on campus. Our faculty members teach and conduct research on Europe, Africa, East Asia, South Asia, Latin America, the Caribbean, Central Asia, Russia, the United States, and numerous transnational and global themes.

Chair: Leo J. Garofalo
Degrees Offered: BA
Academic Year System: Semester
Areas of Specialization: global, Africa, Asia, Europe, Latin America, US
Tuition (per academic year): $67440
Enrollment 2018-19:
 Undergraduate Majors: 79
 Degrees in History: 20 BA
Addresses:
 Admissions: http://www.conncoll.edu/admission
 Financial Aid: http://www.conncoll.edu/admission

Full-time Faculty

Ballah, Henryatta (PhD, Ohio State 2012; asst. prof.) 19th- and 20th-century Africa, French and English colonialism, youth/women and labor/social movements; hballah@conncoll.edu

Canton, David A. (PhD, Temple 2001; assoc. prof.) African American, 20th-century US; dacan@conncoll.edu

Chhabria, Sheetal (PhD, Columbia 2012; assoc. prof.) South Asia, urbanization; sheetal.chhabria@conncoll.edu

Downs, James T., Jr. (PhD, Columbia 2005; prof.) 19th-century US, Civil War, African American; james.downs@conncoll.edu

Forster, Marc R. (PhD, Harvard 1989; prof.) early modern Europe, Reformation, Germany; mrfor@conncoll.edu

Garofalo, Leo J. (PhD, Wisconsin, Madison 2001; assoc. prof. and chair) Latin America; lgar@conncoll.edu

Kane, Eileen Mary (PhD, Princeton 2005; assoc. prof.) 19th- and 20th-century Europe, Russia, Islam; ekane2@conncoll.edu

Paxton, Frederick S. (PhD, California, Berkeley 1985; prof.) medieval Europe; fspax@conncoll.edu

Queen, Sarah A. (PhD, Harvard 1991; prof.) early China, Confucianism, Chinese intellectual; saque@conncoll.edu

Stock, Catherine McNicol (PhD, Yale 1988; prof.) modern America, American West, Native American; cmsto@conncoll.edu

Part-time Faculty

Accardi, Dean (PhD, Texas, Austin 2014; asst. prof.) South Asia, Islam; daccardi@conncoll.edu

Cornell College

Dept. of History, 600 First St. W, Mount Vernon, IA 52314-1098. 319.895.4205. Fax 319.895.4473. Email: plucas@cornellcollege.edu; mherder@cornellcollege.edu. Website: https://www.cornellcollege.edu/history/.

Our focus is on the history of Western civilization, particularly European and US history, with occasional courses available in Islamic, Asian, and Latin American history.

Chair: Phil Lucas
Degrees Offered: BA,BSS
Academic Year System: Eight single-course terms
Areas of Specialization: early to modern US, early to modern Europe
Tuition (per academic year): $39675
Enrollment 2018-19:
  Undergraduate Majors: 33
  Degrees in History: 7 BA
Addresses:
  Admissions: http://www.cornellcollege.edu/admissions/
  Financial Aid: http://www.cornellcollege.edu/financial-assistance/

Full-time Faculty

Herder, Michelle M. (PhD, Yale 2003; assoc. prof.) medieval and early modern Europe, religion, social and gender; mherder@cornellcollege.edu

Lucas, M. Philip (PhD, Cornell 1983; prof. and chair) Jacksonian America, colonial America, Civil War; plucas@cornellcollege.edu

Stewart, Catherine Aileen (PhD, SUNY, Stony Brook 1999; prof.) 19th- and 20th-century US, social and cultural, African American; cstewart@cornellcollege.edu

Retired/Emeritus Faculty

Givens, Robert D. (PhD, California, Berkeley 1975; prof. emeritus) modern Russia, modern European diplomatic; rgivens@cornellcollege.edu

Cornell University

Dept. of History, 450 McGraw Hall, Ithaca, NY 14853-4601. 607.255.8862. Fax 607.255.0469. Email: tl14@cornell.edu. Website: https://history.cornell.edu/.

The department is committed to pursuing excellence in historical scholarship and teaching across many different time periods and research interests. Our outstanding faculty and students also specialize in a wide array of historical issues and themes that transcend particular regions and periods.

Chair: Tamara Loos
Director of Graduate Studies: Raymond Craib
Director of Undergraduate Studies: Russell Rickford
Degrees Offered: BA,MA,PhD
Academic Year System: Semester

Areas of Specialization: North and Latin America, Africa, medieval and modern Europe, premodern and modern East and Southeast Asia, premodern Islamic and modern Middle East
Undergraduate Tuition (per academic year): $56550
Graduate Tuition (per academic year): $29500
Enrollment 2018-19:
  Undergraduate Majors: 150
  New Graduate Students: 10
  Full-time Graduate Students: 56
  Degrees in History: 52 BA, 7 MA, 5 PhD
Undergraduate Addresses:
  Admissions: http://www.cornell.edu/admissions
  Financial Aid: http://www.finaid.cornell.edu
Graduate Addresses:
  Admissions: http://www.cornell.edu/admissions/#graduate
  Financial Aid: http://www.gradschool.cornell.edu/costs-and-funding

Full-time Faculty

Baptist, Edward E. (PhD, Pennsylvania 1997; prof.) US political, 19th-century America, US South; eeb36@cornell.edu

Bassi Arevalo, Ernesto (PhD, California, Irvine 2012; assoc. prof.) colonial Latin America, Caribbean, Atlantic world; eb577@cornell.edu

Byfield, Judith A. (PhD, Columbia 1993; prof.) Africa/African diaspora, West Africa/Caribbean, gender and labor; jab632@cornell.edu

Chang, Derek S. (PhD, Duke 2002; assoc. prof.) Asian American, 19th-century US; dsc37@cornell.edu

Craib, Raymond B. (PhD, Yale 2001; prof. and dir., grad. studies) Latin America, social, cultural; rbc23@cornell.edu

Dear, Peter R. (PhD, Princeton 1984; prof.) science, scientific revolution; prd3@cornell.edu

Du, Yue (PhD, New York Univ. 2017; asst. prof.) modern Chinese legal/political/social, gender

Falk, Oren (PhD, Toronto 2002; assoc. prof.) medieval, cultural, Norse; of24@cornell.edu

Florea, Cristina (PhD, Princeton 2016; asst. prof.) 19th- and 20th-century eastern and central Europe.

Friedland, Paul (PhD, California, Berkeley 1995; prof.) early modern France, French Revolution cultural, political and intellectual; paf67@cornell.edu

Garcia, Maria Cristina (PhD, Texas, Austin 1990; prof.) comparative migrations, US Latino/a, folklore; mcg20@cornell.edu

Ghosh, Durba (PhD, California, Berkeley 2000; prof.) modern South Asia, British Empire, gender and sexuality; dg256@cornell.edu

Glickman, Lawrence B. (PhD, California, Berkeley 1992; prof.) US cultural/labor/political, consumer society, Gilded Age and Progressive era; lbg49@cornell.edu

Greene, Sandra E. (PhD, Northwestern 1981; prof.) Africa, Ghana, social/cultural/religious; seg6@cornell.edu

Hinrichs, TJ (PhD, Harvard 2003; assoc. prof.) Chinese medical and religious; th289@cornell.edu

Kohler-Hausmann, Julilly (PhD, Illinois, Urbana-Champaign 2010; assoc. prof.) postwar US, political and social; jkh224@cornell.edu

Litvak, Olga (PhD, Columbia 1999; prof.) Jewish intellectual and political, modern Europe and imperial Russia, ideas

Loos, Tamara L. (PhD, Cornell 1999; prof. and chair) Southeast Asia, Thailand, gender/social/legal; tl14@cornell.edu

Minawi, Mostafa (PhD, NYU 2011; assoc. prof.) modern Middle East, Ottoman, Mediterranean and North African imperial; mm2492@cornell.edu

Parmenter, Jon (PhD, Michigan 1999; assoc. prof.) Native American, Iroquois, early America; jwp35@cornell.edu

Rebillard, Eric (PhD, Paris 1993; prof.; Classics) Rome; er97@cornell.edu

Rickford, Russell John (PhD, Columbia 2009; assoc. prof. and dir., undergrad. studies) Pan Africanism/black nationalism/radicalism, transnational blackness, African American political culture; rr447@cornell.edu

Roebuck, Kristin (PhD, Columbia 2015; asst. prof.) modern Japan, body, medicine and law; kar79@cornell.edu

Sachs, Aaron (PhD, Yale 2004; prof.) US cultural and intellectual; as475@cornell.edu

Strauss, Barry S. (PhD, Yale 1979; prof.) ancient Greece and Rome, military; bss4@cornell.edu

Tagliacozzo, Eric (PhD, Yale 1999; prof.) modern Southeast Asia, economic, religious; et54@cornell.edu

Travers, Thomas Robert (PhD, Cambridge 2001; assoc. prof.) British imperial; trt5@cornell.edu

Verhoeven, Claudia (PhD, UCLA 2004; assoc. prof.) modern Russia and Europe, cultural, political violence; cv89@cornell.edu

Vider, Stephen Joshua (PhD, Harvard 2013; asst. prof.) public, gender and sexuality, LGBTQ+ studies, US social/political/cultural

Washington, Margaret (PhD, California, Davis 1980; prof.) African American cultural/intellectual/religious, gender, American South; mw26@cornell.edu

Weil, Rachel J. (PhD, Princeton 1991; prof.) early modern English political and cultural, gender; rjw5@cornell.edu

Joint/Cross Appointments

Altschuler, Glenn (PhD, Cornell 1976; dean; Continuing Education) popular culture, Jewish American, politics; gca1@cornell.edu

Bensel, Richard F. (PhD, Cornell 1978; prof.; Government) American political; rfb2@cornell.edu

DeVault, Ileen A. (PhD, Yale 1985; prof.; Industrial & Labor Relations) American social, labor and working class, gender and women; iad1@cornell.edu

Fahmy, Ziad A. (PhD, Arizona 2007; assoc. prof.; Near Eastern Studies) modern Middle East, Egypt and Arab world; zaf3@cornell.edu

Formichi, Chiara (PhD, SOAS London 2009; assoc. prof.; Asian Studies) Islam as lived religion and political ideology, 20th-century Indonesia and Southeast Asia; cf398@cornell.edu

Hyman, Louis R. (PhD, Harvard 2007; assoc. prof.; Labor Relations, Law, and History) capitalism, labor and business, consumption; lrh62@cornell.edu

Kline, Ronald R. (PhD, Wisconsin, Madison 1983; prof.; Science & Tech. Studies) US technology and engineering; rkline@ee.cornell.edu

Martinez-Matsuda, Veronica (PhD, Texas, Austin 2009; asst. prof.; Labor Relations, Law, and History) American social and cultural, immigration and migration, labor and working class; vm248@cornell.edu

Powers, David S. (PhD, Princeton 1979; prof.; Near Eastern Studies) premodern Islamic; dsp4@cornell.edu

Pritchard, Sara B. (PhD, Stanford 2001; assoc. prof.; Science & Tech. Studies) technology, environmental, 20th-century France/French Empire; sbp65@cornell.edu

Rana, Aziz (PhD, Harvard 2007; prof.; Law Sch.) American political and constitutional thought, comparative colonial and postcolonial, citizenship and immigration; ar643@cornell.edu

Sakai, Naoki (PhD, Chicago 1983; prof.; Asian Studies) early modern and modern Japan, intellectual and cultural; ns32@cornell.edu

Salvatore, Nick (PhD, California, Berkeley 1977; prof.; American Studies and Industrial and Labor Relations) American labor and social; nas4@cornell.edu

Seth, Suman (PhD, Princeton 2003; prof.; Science & Tech. Studies) physical sciences, 19th and 20th century, gender and science; ss536@cornell.edu

Taylor, Keith W. (PhD, Michigan 1976; prof.; Asian Studies) Southeast Asia, Vietnam; kwt3@cornell.edu

Traverso, Enzo (PhD, EHESS, France 1989; prof.; Romance Studies) contemporary social and cultural, European intellectual, political; vt225@cornell.edu

Retired/Emeritus Faculty

Baugh, Daniel A. (PhD, Cambridge 1961; prof. emeritus) modern English political/social/economic 1688-1918, European maritime 1600-1800; dab3@cornell.edu

Blumin, Stuart M. (PhD, Pennsylvania 1968; prof. emeritus) American social/cultural/demographic, American urban; smb5@cornell.edu

Caron, Vicki (PhD, Columbia 1983; prof. emeritus) modern European Jewish; vc21@cornell.edu

Chen, Jian (PhD, Southern Illinois, Carbondale 1990; prof. emeritus) Sino-American relations, China; jc585@cornell.edu

Cochran, Sherman Gilbert (PhD, Yale 1975; prof. emeritus) modern China, social/economic/cultural; sgc11@cornell.edu

Hull, Isabel V. (PhD, Yale 1978; prof. emeritus) Germany 1700-1945; ivh1@cornell.edu

Hyams, Paul R. (PhD, Oxford 1968; prof. emeritus) medieval, legal, political; prh3@cornell.edu

John, James J. (PhD, Notre Dame 1959; prof. emeritus) medieval intellectual, Latin paleography; jjj2@cornell.edu

Kaplan, Steven (PhD, Yale 1974; prof. emeritus) France 1500-present, comparative European social/food/work; slk8@cornell.edu

Koschmann, J. Victor (PhD, Chicago 1980; prof. emeritus) modern Japan, Japanese intellectual and cultural; jvk1@cornell.edu

LaCapra, Dominick C. (PhD, Harvard 1970; prof. emeritus) modern European intellectual and cultural; dcl3@cornell.edu

LaFeber, Walter F. (PhD, Wisconsin, Madison 1959; prof. emeritus) America, US foreign policy 1750-present; wfl3@cornell.edu

Moore, R. Laurence (PhD, Yale 1968; prof. emeritus) American intellectual, cultural, religious; rlm8@cornell.edu

Najemy, John M. (PhD, Harvard 1972; prof. emeritus) late medieval and Renaissance Italy, Florence; jmn4@cornell.edu

Norton, Mary Beth (PhD, Harvard 1969; prof. emeritus) early America, women and gender; mbn1@cornell.edu

Peterson, Charles A. (PhD, Washington 1966; prof. emeritus) T'ang-Sung Chinese political/military/administrative/foreign relations; cap4@cornell.edu

Polenberg, Richard (PhD, Columbia 1964; prof. emeritus) modern American political and social 1930-present; rp19@cornell.edu

Tierney, Brian (PhD, Pembroke Coll., Cambridge 1952; Bryce and Edith M. Bowman Prof. emeritus) medieval; bt20@cornell.edu

Weiss, John H. (PhD, Harvard 1977; assoc. prof. emeritus) modern European social and political, postwar political culture, French education; jhw4@cornell.edu

Recently Awarded PhDs

Chen, Shiau-Yun "Legitimating and Constraining Womanly Violence in Ming China, 1368-1644"

Harvey, Kyle Edmund "Prepositional Geographies: Rebellion, Railroads, and the Transandean, 1830s-1910s"

Katungi, Candace "Pioneering Race Women: Black Women's Activism in the Antebellum North, 1830-50"

Minarchek, Matthew "Militarized Ecologies: Violence, Science, and the Creation of Sumatra's Leuser Ecosystem (Indonesia)"

Reeder, Matt "Categorical Kingdoms: Innovations in Ethnic Labeling and Visions of Communal States in Early Modern Siam"

Rutledge, Brian "The Elsewhere Department: Black Readers in the Making of South Africa's Mass Media, 1932-65"

Savala, Joshua "Beyond Patriotic Phobias: Connections, Class, and State Formation in the Peruvian-Chilean Pacific World"

Siddiqui, Osama "A Science of Society: The Rise of Urdu Economic Thought in Colonial India"

Covenant College

Dept. of History and Politics, 14049 Scenic Hwy., Lookout Mountain, GA 30750-4100. 706.419.1626. Fax 706.820.2165. Email: morton@covenant.edu. Website: https://www.covenant. edu/academics/undergrad/history.

The Department of History & Politics believes that historical thinking is an essential feature of faithful living. In our classes, we aim to help cultivate in students the skills, knowledge, and virtues necessary for thinking historically.

Chair: Paul J. Morton
Degrees Offered: BA
Academic Year System: Semester
Areas of Specialization: US, modern Europe, world, religious, international relations
Tuition (per academic year): $34660
Enrollment 2018-19:
    Undergraduate Majors: 42
    Degrees in History: 15 BA
    Students in Undergraduate Courses: 563
    Students in Undergraduate Intro Courses: 14
Addresses:
    Admissions: http://www.covenant.edu/admissions/undergrad
    Financial Aid: http://www.covenant.edu/admissions/
        undergrad/costs

Full-time Faculty

Follett, Richard R. (PhD, Washington, St. Louis 1996; prof.) modern Europe, modern Britain, European intellectual; follett@covenant.edu

Green, Jay D. (PhD, Kent State 1998; prof.) US religious and cultural, historiography, world; jdgreen@covenant.edu

Horne, Cale (PhD, Georgia 2010; assoc. prof.) international relations, comparative politics, political science; cale.horne@covenant.edu

Jackson, Alicia K. (PhD, Mississippi 2004; assoc. prof.) late 19th- and 20th-century US, South, Africa; ajackson@covenant.edu

Morton, Paul J. (PhD, Southern California 1996; prof. and dean, academic progs.) US, North American environmental, US diplomatic; morton@covenant.edu

Nondepartmental Historians

Dennison, William D. (PhD, Michigan State 1992; prof.; Interdisciplinary Studies) German intellectual; dennison@covenant.edu

Stewart, Kenneth J. (PhD, Edinburgh 1992; prof.; Biblical and Theological Studies) Renaissance and Reformation, Christianity and Christian thought; kstewart@covenant.edu

Creighton University

Dept. of History, 2500 California Plaza, Humanities 216, Omaha, NE 68178-0103. 402.280.2884. Fax 402.280.1454. Email: history@creighton.edu. Website: http://www.creighton.edu/ ccas/history/.

The Department of History at Creighton University is a vibrant community of experienced and productive faculty members and talented and ambitious students. Our courses cover the world and invite students to immerse themselves in virtually every time period of human history. Beyond the curriculum, we offer opportunities for undergraduate research, internships, study abroad, presentation and publication, fellowships, and more.

Chair: Michael Hawkins
Degrees Offered: BA
Academic Year System: Semester
Areas of Specialization: US, Europe, Latin America, Asia, Middle East, and Africa
Tuition (per academic year): $39630
Enrollment 2018-19:
    Undergraduate Majors: 37
    Degrees in History: 19 BA, 1 BS
Addresses:
    Admissions: http://www.creighton.edu/admissions/
    Financial Aid: http://www.creighton.edu/financialaid/

Full-time Faculty

Appleford, Simon (PhD, Illinois, Urbana-Champaign 2014; asst. prof.) digital humanities, US; simonappleford@creighton.edu

Calvert, John (PhD, McGill 1994; prof.) Middle East; johncalvert@creighton.edu

Dugan, Eileen T. (PhD, Ohio State 1987; assoc. prof.) Renaissance and Reformation, British Isles, medieval science and mathematics; etdugan@creighton.edu

Eastman, Scott B. (PhD, California, Irvine 2006; assoc. prof.) Atlantic world, nationalism, Latin America; seastman@creighton.edu

Elliot-Meisel, Elizabeth B. (PhD, Duke 1992; assoc. prof.) US diplomacy, US Constitution, Canada; elmeis@creighton.edu

Fryer, Heather E. (PhD, Boston Coll. 2001; assoc. prof.) modern US, US social and gender, American West; heatherfryer@creighton.edu

Hawkins, Michael (PhD, Northern Illinois 2009; assoc. prof. and chair) Southeast Asia, imperialism, modern China; michaelhawkins@creighton.edu

Hogan, Andrew J. (PhD, Pennsylvania 2013; asst. prof.) science and medicine; andrewhogan@creighton.edu

Leavelle, Tracy Neal (PhD, Arizona State 2001; assoc. prof.) colonial and early America, Native American, religion; tracy.leavelle@creighton.edu

McEwen, Britta Isabelle (PhD, UCLA 2003; assoc. prof.) modern Europe, US culture; brittamcewen@creighton.edu

Sundberg, Adam (PhD, Kansas 2015; asst. prof.) environmental studies, digital humanities; adamsundberg@creighton.edu

Williams, Ogechukwu Ezekwem (PhD, Texas, Austin 2017; asst. prof.) Africa; ogechukwuwilliams@creighton.edu

Retired/Emeritus Faculty

Super, Richard R. (PhD, Arizona State 1975; assoc. prof. emeritus) Latin America, inter-American relations, Americas; super@creighton.edu

University of the Cumberlands

Dept. of History and Political Science, 6557 College Station Dr., Williamsburg, KY 40769. 606.539.4270. Fax 606.539.4175. Email: nathan.coleman@ucumberlands.edu. Website: https:// www.ucumberlands.edu/academics/undergraduate/majors-minors/history.

Whatever your reasons for wanting to earn a history degree, you'll have opportunities to explore them as you choose courses that cover everything from the great cultures of ancient times to 21st-century America. As a history major, you'll be able to investigate other areas of history that will help you make connections and draw conclusions based on what you learn.

Chair: Nathan Coleman
Degrees Offered: BA,BS,BSEd
Academic Year System: Semester
Areas of Specialization: social and intellectual to 1860, American constitutional, early modern Europe, modern Britain
Tuition (per academic year): $23000
Enrollment 2018-19:
   Undergraduate Majors: 39
   Degrees in History: 2 BA, 5 BS, 2 BSEd
Addresses:
   Admissions: http://www.ucumberlands.edu/admissions/
   Financial Aid: http://www.ucumberlands.edu/admissions/aid/

Adjunct Faculty

Pilant, Charles A. (PhD, Marquette 1989; prof.) America since 1877, China and Japan, Africa and Arab world; al.pilant@ ucumberlands.edu

Full-time Faculty

Carmical, Oline, Jr. (PhD, Kentucky 1975; prof.) America to 1877, American constitutional, early America; oline.carmical@ ucumberlands.edu
Coleman, Aaron Nathan (PhD, Kentucky 2008; assoc. prof. and chair) American Revolution, constitutional, US; nathan. coleman@ucumberlands.edu
Hicks, D. Bruce (PhD, Emory 1987; assoc. prof.; Political Science) US politics, political theory; bruce.hicks@ucumberlands.edu
Smith, Melvin Charles (PhD, Auburn 2000; assoc. prof.) world civilizations, modern Europe, Britain; chuck.smith@ ucumberlands.edu

University of Dallas

Dept. of History, 1845 E. Northgate Dr., Irving, TX 75062-4736. 972.721.5390. Fax 972.265.5760. Email: kallen@udallas. edu; shanssen@udallas.edu. Website: https://udallas.edu/ constantin/academics/programs/history/.

History is a subject particularly appropriate to the University of Dallas, which defines its purpose in terms of the renewal of the Western heritage of liberal learning and the recovery of the Christian intellectual tradition. History provides a unique bridge between the two.

Chair: Susan Hanssen
Degrees Offered: BA
Academic Year System: Semester
Areas of Specialization: ancient/medieval/modern Europe, colonial America, 19th- and 20th-century America, American Catholic, Latin America

Tuition (per academic year): $33360
Enrollment 2018-19:
   Undergraduate Majors: 41
   Degrees in History: 18 BA
Addresses:
   Admissions: http://www.udallas.edu/admissions/
   Financial Aid: http://www.udallas.edu/offices/finaid/

Adjunct Faculty

Ansiaux, Robert R. (PhD, Texas, Arlington 2006; adj. prof.) world, Western and American civilization; ransiaux@udallas.edu

Full-time Faculty

Atto, William J. (PhD, Arkansas 2000; assoc. prof.) 19th-century America, American military, American West; atto@udallas.edu
Gibson, Kelly (PhD, Harvard 2011; assoc. prof.) Europe c. 300-c. 1400, Middle East c. 500-c. 1500, archaeology; kgibson@udallas. edu
Hanssen, Susan E. (PhD, Rice 2002; assoc. prof. and chair) American intellectual, American South, British Empire; shanssen@udallas.edu
Jodziewicz, Thomas W. (PhD, William and Mary 1974; prof.) colonial America, American Catholic; tjodz@udallas.edu
Petersen, Mark Jeffrey (DPhil, Oxford 2014; asst. prof.) Latin America; mpetersen@udallas.edu
Sullivan, Charles R. (PhD, Columbia 1992; assoc. prof.) modern Europe, early modern France, Scottish Enlightenment; sullivan@ udallas.edu
Swietek, Francis R. (PhD, Illinois, Urbana-Champaign 1978; assoc. prof.) medieval, ancient, church; swietek@udallas.edu

Dartmouth College

Dept. of History, 6107 Carson Hall, Hanover, NH 03755-3506. 603.646.2545. Fax 603.646.3353. Email: gail.m.patten@ dartmouth.edu; robert.e.bonner@dartmouth.edu. Website: https://history.dartmouth.edu/.

Founded in 1894, the History Department has long offered one of the most popular majors and course selections in the undergraduate College. While relatively few students come to Dartmouth intending to concentrate in History, the stimulating experience they have in the History courses they encounter translates into healthy enrollments and a major that consistently hovers among the most popular at Dartmouth.

Chair: Robert E. Bonner
Degrees Offered: BA
Academic Year System: Quarter
Areas of Specialization: America, Europe, South and East Asia, Latin America, Middle East
Tuition (per academic year): $55605
Enrollment 2018-19:
   Undergraduate Majors: 76
   Degrees in History: 16 BA
Addresses:
   Admissions: http://admissions.dartmouth.edu/
   Financial Aid: http://admissions.dartmouth.edu/financial-aid/

Full-time Faculty

Bonner, Robert E. (PhD, Yale 1997; prof. and chair) 19th-century US; robert.bonner@dartmouth.edu
Butler, Leslie A. (PhD, Yale 1997; assoc. prof.) US intellectual and cultural; leslie.butler@dartmouth.edu
Crossley, Pamela Kyle (PhD, Yale 1983; Collis Prof.) China, Central Asia, East Asian intellectual; pamela.crossley@dartmouth.edu

Delmont, Matthew (PhD, Brown 2008; prof.) African American; matthew.delmont@dartmouth.edu

Ericson, Steven J. (PhD, Harvard 1985; assoc. prof.) Japan, East Asia; steven.ericson@dartmouth.edu

Estabrook, Carl B. (PhD, Brown 1990; assoc. prof.) early modern England, modern Britain; carl.estabrook@dartmouth.edu

Gaposchkin, Cecilia (PhD, California, Berkeley 2001; prof.) medieval and Renaissance; m.c.gaposchkin@dartmouth.edu

Greenberg, Udi (PhD, Hebrew, Jerusalem 2010; assoc. prof.) modern Germany, modern European intellectual and cultural; udi.greenberg@dartmouth.edu

Haynes, Douglas E. (PhD, Pennsylvania 1982; prof.) South Asia; douglas.haynes@dartmouth.edu

Johnson, Rashauna (PhD, NYU 2010; assoc. prof.) African diaspora, US South and Caribbean; rashauna.r.johnson@dartmouth.edu

Link, Stefan J. (PhD, Harvard 2012; asst. prof.) economic; stefan.j.link@dartmouth.edu

McMahon, Darrin M. (PhD, Yale 1998; prof.) modern European cultural and intellectual, Old Regime Europe, French Revolution; darrin.mcmahon@dartmouth.edu

Miller, Edward (PhD, Harvard 2004; assoc. prof.) US foreign relations; edward.miller@dartmouth.edu

Miller, Jennifer Michelle (PhD, Wisconsin-Madison 2012; asst. prof.) US foreign relations, US and world; jennifer.m.miller@dartmouth.edu

Moreton, Bethany E. (PhD, Yale 2006; prof.) capitalism, gender and sexuality, religion; bethany.e.moreton@dartmouth.edu

Musselwhite, Paul P. (PhD, William and Mary 2011; assoc. prof.) early North America; paul.p.musselwhite@dartmouth.edu

Nikpour, Golnar S. (PhD, Columbia 2015; asst. prof.) Middle East and Iranian studies; golnar.nikpour@dartmouth.edu

Orleck, Annelise (PhD, NYU 1989; prof.) late 19th- and 20th-century US political, women; annelise.orleck@dartmouth.edu

Petruccelli, David (PhD, Yale 2015; asst. prof.) modern Europe; david.petruccelli@dartmouth.edu

Rabig, Julia A. (PhD, Pennsylvania 2007; asst. prof.) African American, urban; julia.rabig@dartmouth.edu

Sackeyfio-Lenoch, Naaborko (PhD, Wisconsin, Madison 2008; assoc. prof.) West Africa, 20th-century Ghana; naaborko.sackeyfio@dartmouth.edu

Simons, Walter P. (PhD, Belgium, Ghent 1985; prof.) medieval Europe; walter.p.simons@dartmouth.edu

Suh, Soyoung (PhD, UCLA 2007; assoc. prof.; Asian and Middle Eastern Languages and Literatures) Korea, East Asian science/technology/medicine; soyoung.suh@dartmouth.edu

Voekel, Pamela (PhD, Texas, Austin 1997; assoc. prof.) capitalism, imperialism and colonialism, Latin America and Caribbean; pamela.voekel@dartmouth.edu

Joint/Cross Appointments

Calloway, Colin G. (PhD, Leeds, UK 1974; prof.; Native American Studies) Native American; colin.calloway@dartmouth.edu

Garcia, Matthew John (PhD, Claremont Grad. 1997; prof.; Latin American, Latino and Caribbean Studies) Latinx labor and immigration, rural-to-urban studies; matthew.garcia@dartmouth.edu

Part-time Faculty

Koop, Allen V. (PhD, Pennsylvania 1975; prof.) 20th-century Europe; allen.koop@dartmouth.edu

Melendez-Badillo, Jorell Alexander (PhD, Connecticut 2018; Mellon Faculty Fellow) Latin America; jorell.a.melendez-badillo@dartmouth.edu

Retired/Emeritus Faculty

Daniell, Jere R., II (PhD, Harvard 1964; prof. emeritus) colonial America, American Revolution; jere.daniell@dartmouth.edu

Darrow, Margaret (PhD, Rutgers 1982; prof. emerita) modern France; margaret.darrow@dartmouth.edu

Ermarth, H. Michael (PhD, Chicago 1973; prof. emeritus) Germany, 19th- and 20th-century Europe; michael.ermarth@dartmouth.edu

Garthwaite, Gene R. (PhD, UCLA 1968; prof. emeritus) Middle East; gene.garthwaite@dartmouth.edu

Kremer, Richard (PhD, Harvard 1984; assoc. prof. emeritus) science; richard.kremer@dartmouth.edu

Lagomarsino, P. David (PhD, Cambridge 1974; assoc. prof. emeritus) early modern Europe; david.lagomarsino@dartmouth.edu

Navarro-Aranguren, Marysa (PhD, Columbia 1964; prof. emerita) Latin America; marysa.navarro@dartmouth.edu

Nelson, J. Bruce (PhD, California, Berkeley 1982; prof. emeritus) labor, 20th-century America; bruce.nelson@dartmouth.edu

Spitzer, Leo (PhD, Wisconsin, Madison 1969; prof. emeritus) Africa, comparative Third World; leo.spitzer@dartmouth.edu

Whelan, Heide W. (PhD, Chicago 1973; prof. emerita) Russia, Soviet Union; heide.w.whelan@dartmouth.edu

Wright, James E. (PhD, Wisconsin, Madison 1969; prof. emeritus) 19th- and 20th-century US political, American frontier; james.e.wright@dartmouth.edu

Davidson College

Dept. of History, PO Box 7128, Davidson, NC 28035-7128. 704.894.2986. Fax 704.894.3066. Email: miguasco@davidson. edu. Website: https://www.davidson.edu/academic-departments/history.

The History Department exposes students to the richness, diversity, and complexities of human history during various periods and in different geographic regions.

Chair: Jane Mangan
Degrees Offered: BA
Academic Year System: Semester
Areas of Specialization: America, Latin America, Europe and Britain, Middle East, East and South Asia
Tuition (per academic year): $60119
Enrollment 2018-19:
Undergraduate Majors: 80
Degrees in History: 27 BA
Addresses:
Admissions and Financial Aid: http://www.davidson.edu/admission-and-financial-aid

Full-time Faculty

Aldridge, Daniel W., III (PhD, Emory 1998; prof.) African American, America, cultural and intellectual; daaldridge@davidson.edu

Berkey, Jonathan P. (PhD, Princeton 1989; prof.) Islamic civilization, Middle East; joberkey@davidson.edu

Dietz, Vivien E. (PhD, Princeton 1990; prof.) Britain, gender; vidietz@davidson.edu

Guasco, Michael J. (PhD, William and Mary 2000; prof.) early America, Atlantic world; miguasco@davidson.edu

Kabala, Jakub J. (PhD, Harvard 2014; asst. prof.) medieval Europe, eastern Europe, digital studies; kukabala@davidson.edu

Mangan, Jane E. (PhD, Duke 1999; prof. and chair) Latin America, gender; jamangan@davidson.edu

McQuinn, Ilana R. (PhD, Chicago 2019; asst. prof.) eastern Europe, Jewish, cultural; ilmcquinn@davidson.edu

Mortensen, Dáša Pejchar (PhD, North Carolina, Chapel Hill 2016; asst. prof.) East Asia; damortensen@davidson.edu

Stremlau, Rose (PhD, North Carolina, Chapel Hill 2006; asst. prof.) 19th-century US, women, Native American

Tilburg, Patricia A. (PhD, UCLA 2002; assoc. prof.) France, gender, modern Europe; patilburg@davidson.edu

Waheed, Sarah F. (PhD, Tufts 2011; asst. prof.) India; sawaheed@davidson.edu

Wertheimer, John (PhD, Princeton 1992; prof.) 20th-century US, legal; jowertheimer@davidson.edu

Wiemers, Alice (PhD, Johns Hopkins 2012; asst. prof.) 20th-century Ghana, sub-Saharan Africa; alwiemers@davidson.edu

Joint/Cross Appointments

Krentz, Peter M. (PhD, Yale 1979; prof.; Classics) ancient Greece and Rome; pekrentz@davidson.edu

Retired/Emeritus Faculty

Barnes, Robin Bruce (PhD, Virginia 1980; prof. emeritus) Reformation, early modern Europe; robarnes@davidson.edu

Edmondson, C. Earl (PhD, Duke 1966; prof. emeritus) modern Europe, Austria, Russia; eaedmondson@davidson.edu

Levering, Ralph B. (PhD, Princeton 1972; prof. emeritus) US diplomatic, public opinion; ralevering@davidson.edu

McMillen, Sally G. (PhD, Duke 1985; prof. emeritus) US South, women; samcmillen@davidson.edu

Thomas, I. Job (PhD, Michigan 1979; prof. emeritus) South Asia, art; jothomas@davidson.edu

Williams, Robert C. (PhD, Harvard 1966; prof. emeritus) Russia, modern European intellectual; bob03harmony@yahoo.com

Zimmermann, T. C. Price (PhD, Harvard 1964; prof. emeritus) Italian Renaissance; tczimmerman@aol.com

University of Dayton

Dept. of History, Jessie Phillips Humanities Bldg., 300 College Park, Dayton, OH 45469-1540. 937.229.2848. Fax 937.229.2816. Email: jsantamarina1@udayton.edu. Website: https://udayton.edu/artssciences/academics/history/

The Department of History offers students a challenging yet flexible program of study that emphasizes both the distinctiveness and the utility of the historian's craft. Our program is distinctive in that all history courses focus not only on the past's exciting events and developments, but also on the manner in which historians gather their evidence and reach their conclusions. A history background can provide important advantages in analyzing contemporary events and trends. Whether in business or in service, good solutions today depend on a clear understanding of yesterday. By learning from the past, we can improve the future. Even in daily life, history not only informs but instructs. The skills of the historian—critical thinking and the ability to conduct documentary research—can influence the way we read a newspaper, shop for a car, trace our family lineage, or evaluate the performance of our institutions.

Chair: Juan C. Santamarina
Degrees Offered: BA
Academic Year System: Semester
Areas of Specialization: US/Europe/Asia/Middle East/Latin America/Africa, comparative and foreign relations, science and technology, business and economic, women and gender
Tuition (per academic year): $44100

Enrollment 2018-19:
  Undergraduate Majors: 85
  Degrees in History: 20 BA
  Students in Undergraduate Courses: 4000
  Students in Undergraduate Intro Courses: 2300
  Online-Only Courses: 5%
Addresses:
  Admissions: https://www.udayton.edu/apply/undergraduate/
  Financial Aid: https://udayton.edu/affordability/undergraduate/financial-aid/index.php

Full-time Faculty

Agnew, Christopher Stephen (PhD, Washington 2006; assoc. prof. and dir., Univ. Honors Prog.) Asia; cagnew1@udayton.edu

Amin, Julius A. (PhD, Texas Tech 1988; prof. and Alumni Chair in Humanities) African American, Africa, recent US; jamin1@udayton.edu

Bartley, Karen (PhD, Kent State 1999; asst. prof.) kbartley1@udayton.edu

Borbonus, Dorian (PhD, Pennsylvania 2006; asst. prof.) ancient; borbondo@notes.udayton.edu

Carlson, Marybeth (PhD, Wisconsin-Madison 1993; assoc. prof.; dir., International Studies) early modern Europe, European social and cultural; mcarlson1@udayton.edu

Carter, Michael S. (PhD, Southern California 2006; assoc. prof.) religious; carterms@notes.udayton.edu

Daly Bednarek, Janet R. (PhD, Pittsburgh 1987; prof.) US urban, aviation, city planning; jbednarek1@udayton.edu

Darrow, David W. (PhD, Iowa 1996; assoc. prof.) imperial Russia, Soviet Union, European intellectual; david.darrow@notes.udayton.edu

Fleischmann, Ellen L. (PhD, Georgetown 1996; prof.) Middle East, women and gender, mission and missionaries in Arab lands; efleischmann1@udayton.edu

Heitmann, John A. (PhD, Johns Hopkins 1983; prof. and Alumni Chair in Humanities) science, technology, environmental; john.heitmann@notes.udayton.edu

Hume, Laura Hunt (PhD, Cincinnati 1993; assoc. prof. and dir., Pre-Law) early modern England, medieval Europe; lhume1@udayton.edu

Jaffe, Tracey Lynn (PhD, Pittsburgh 2009; lect.) women and Catholicism; tjaffe1@udayton.edu

Merithew, Caroline W. (PhD, Illinois, Urbana-Champaign 2000; asst. prof.) labor, social, women; caroline.merithew@notes.udayton.edu

Roy, Haimanti (PhD, Cincinnati 2006; asst. prof.) citizenship and migration; hroy1@udayton.edu

Sanderson, Mary (PhD, Vanderbilt 2010; lect.) msanderson1@udayton.edu

Santamarina, Juan C. (PhD, Rutgers 1995; assoc. prof. and chair) Cuba and Caribbean, Latin American business and economic, US diplomatic; santamar@udayton.edu

Sextro, Laura Elizabeth (PhD, California, Irvine 2011; lect.) imperialism and colonialism; lsextro1@udayton.edu

Sutherland, Bobbi Sue (PhD, Yale 2009; asst. prof.) medieval Europe, cuisine and food, social; bsutherland1@udayton.edu

Trollinger, William V., Jr. (PhD, Wisconsin, Madison 1984; prof. and dir., Core) US religious, social, contemporary America; trolliwv@notes.udayton.edu

Uhlman, James Todd (PhD, Rutgers 2007; lect.) juhlman1@udayton.edu

Washington, Versalle F. (PhD, Ohio State 1995; lect.)

Part-time Faculty

Bieber, Jason Parker (PhD, Florida State 2016; adj.) World War I/military, Europe/Germany, world; jbieber1@udayton.edu

Jones, Linda (JD, Toledo 1980; lect.) linda.jones@notes.udayton.edu

West, Scott (MA, Akron 1992; lect.; Roesch Library) scott.west@notes.udayton.edu

Retired/Emeritus Faculty

Alexander, Roberta S. (PhD, Chicago 1974; Dist. Service Prof. emeritus) Civil War and Reconstruction, US legal and constitutional, historiography

Cadegan, Una M. (PhD, Pennsylvania 1987; retired assoc. prof.) American studies, American Catholic; una.cadegan@notes.udayton.edu

Eid, Leroy V. (PhD, St. John's, NY 1961; prof. emeritus) American Indian, Ireland; leroy.eid@notes.udayton.edu

Flockerzie, Lawrence J. (PhD, Indiana 1987; assoc. prof. emeritus) modern Europe, central and eastern Europe, diplomatic; lflockerzie1@udayton.edu

Morman, Paul J. (PhD, Penn State 1973; prof. emeritus) early modern Europe; paul.morman@notes.udayton.edu

Palermo, Patrick F. (PhD, SUNY, Binghamton 1973; prof. emeritus) American political culture, Progressive era

University of Delaware

Dept. of History, 236 John Munroe Hall, 46 W. Delaware Ave., Newark, DE 19716-2547. 302.831.2371. Fax 302.831.1538. Email: dtobias@udel.edu. Website: https://www.history.udel.edu/.

Welcome to the History Department where you can explore the past and shape your future. We offer outstanding programs for students, including the History and History Education majors and internationally recognized graduate programs.

Chair: Alison Parker
Director of Graduate Studies: Owen White
Director of Undergraduate Studies: Darryl Flaherty
Degrees Offered: BA,MA,PhD
Academic Year System: Semester
Areas of Specialization: America, material culture, industrialization/capitalism/technology/environment, museum studies, Europe in transnational perspective
Undergraduate Tuition (per academic year):
In-State: $12730
Out-of-State: $34160
Graduate Tuition (per academic year): $34164
Enrollment 2018-19:
Undergraduate Majors: 302
New Graduate Students: 10
Full-time Graduate Students: 52
Degrees in History: 78 BA, 6 MA, 2 PhD
Students in Undergraduate Courses: 5574
Students in Undergraduate Intro Courses: 2787
Online-Only Courses: 8%
Undergraduate Addresses:
Admissions: http://www.udel.edu/admissions/
Financial Aid: http://www.udel.edu/finaid/
Graduate Addresses:
Admissions and Financial Aid: http://grad.udel.edu/

Full-time Faculty

Alchon, Guy (PhD, Iowa 1982; assoc. prof.) 20th-century US, political economy; galchon@udel.edu

Anishanslin, Zara (PhD, Delaware 2009; assoc. prof.) colonial America, Atlantic world, material culture; zma@udel.edu

Bernstein, John Andrew (PhD, Harvard 1970; prof.) European intellectual; johnbern@udel.edu

Brophy, James M. (PhD, Indiana 1991; Francis H. Squire Prof.) modern Germany; jbrophy@udel.edu

Buckley, Eve E. (PhD, Pennsylvania 2006; assoc. prof.) Latin America, environmental, science and medicine; ebuckley@udel.edu

Cruz, Jesus (PhD, California, San Diego 1992; prof.) Iberia, 19th-century Europe, modern Latin America; jesus@udel.edu

Davis, Rebecca L. (PhD, Yale 2006; assoc. prof.) 19th- and 20th-century US, social, religious; rldavis@udel.edu

Duggan, Lawrence G. J. (PhD, Harvard 1971; prof.) Renaissance and Reformation, medieval church; lgjd@udel.edu

Flaherty, Darryl (PhD, Columbia 2001; assoc. prof. and dir., undergrad. studies) Japan, modern political and social, law and social change; flaherty@udel.edu

Garrison, J. Ritchie (PhD, Pennsylvania 1985; prof.) American material culture, American social, agriculture; jrg@udel.edu

Grier, Katherine C. (PhD, Delaware 1988; prof. and dir., museum studies) museum studies, American material culture, public; kcgrier@udel.edu

Heyrman, Christine Leigh (PhD, Yale 1977; Grimble Prof.) early America, social and economic, religious; cheyrman@udel.edu

Joyce, Barry Alan (PhD, California, Riverside 1995; prof.) social studies education, ethnic studies, US West; bjoyce@udel.edu

Kim, Hannah (PhD, Delaware 2011; assoc. prof.) social studies education, Asian American; hkim@udel.edu

Matthee, Rudi (PhD, UCLA 1991; Munroe Prof.) Iran, Middle East; matthee@udel.edu

McLeod, Mark W. (PhD, UCLA 1988; assoc. prof.) modern Vietnam, Southeast Asia, world; mwm@udel.edu

Mohun, Arwen Palmer (PhD, Case Western Reserve 1992; Henry Clay Reed Prof.) technology; mohun@udel.edu

Montano, John P. (PhD, Harvard 1987; prof.) early modern Ireland and Britain; jpmon@udel.edu

Norwood, Dael A. (PhD, Princeton 2012; asst. prof.) early US Republic, political economy, capitalism; dnorwood@udel.edu

Ott, Cindy (PhD, Pennsylvania 2002; assoc. prof.) American food/environment/culture, museum studies; cott@udel.edu

Parker, Alison M. (PhD, Johns Hopkins 1993; prof. and chair) US women, race, legal and constitutional; aparker@udel.edu

Rawat, Ramnarayan S. (PhD, Delhi 2006; assoc. prof.) South Asia, colonialism and nationalism, identity politics; rawat@udel.edu

Russ, Jonathan S. (PhD, Delaware 1996; assoc. prof.) US business, 20th-century US; jruss@udel.edu

Shearer, David R. (PhD, Pennsylvania 1988; Thomas Muncy Keith Prof.) Soviet Union, history and sociology of technology, modern Europe; dshearer@udel.edu

Sidebotham, Steven (PhD, Michigan 1981; prof.) classical archaeology, Greece and Rome; ses@udel.edu

Suisman, David (PhD, Columbia 2002; assoc. prof. and coord., Hagley Program) US popular culture, senses, US business and consumption; dsuisman@udel.edu

Virdi, Jaipreet (PhD, Toronto 2014; asst. prof.) disability, medicine, business; jvirdi@udel.edu

Wang, Yuanchong (PhD, Cornell 2014; assoc. prof.) China since 1600, 17th- to 19th-century China and Korea, China-Korea-Japan trilateral relations; ychwang@udel.edu

White, Owen C. (DPhil, Oxford 1996; assoc. prof. and dir., grad. studies) modern France, French colonial empire, world; owhite@udel.edu

Joint/Cross Appointments

Ford, Tanisha C. (PhD, Indiana 2011; assoc. prof.; Africana Studies) 20th-century US/African diaspora, gender/sexuality/black feminist studies, fashion/beauty culture/body politics; tcford@udel.edu

Foreman, P. Gabrielle (PhD, California, Berkeley 1993; Ned Allen Prof.; English, Africana Studies) African American studies, 19th-century literary history and culture; gforeman@udel.edu

Gill, Tiffany M. (PhD, Rutgers 2003; Cochran Scholar; Africana Studies) 20th-century African American, business and economic, women; tgill@udel.edu

Grubb, Farley (PhD, Chicago 1984; prof.; Economics) colonial American economy, educational and monetary development 1650-1830; grubbf@lerner.udel.edu

Hicks, Cheryl D. (PhD, Princeton 1999; assoc. prof.; Africana Studies) 19th- and 20th-cetury African American and America, urban/gender/civil rights; cdhicks@udel.edu

Maloba, Wunyabari O. (PhD, Stanford 1988; prof.; Africana Studies) modern Africa, Kenya; maloba@udel.edu

Rise, Eric W. (PhD, Florida 1992; assoc. prof.; Criminal Justice) US constitutional and legal; erise@udel.edu

Van Horn, Jennifer (PhD, Virginia 2009; asst. prof.; Art History) early American art and material culture; jvanhorn@udel.edu

Retired/Emeritus Faculty

Allmendinger, David F., Jr. (PhD, Wisconsin, Madison 1968; prof. emeritus) American social and cultural, 19th-century US; dfa@udel.edu

Basalla, George (PhD, Harvard 1963; prof. emeritus) science and technology, social; basalla@udel.edu

Beer, John J. (PhD, Illinois, Urbana-Champaign 1956; assoc. prof. emeritus) science and technology; johnbeer@udel.edu

Boylan, Anne M. (PhD, Wisconsin-Madison 1973; prof. emerita) women, US social; aboylan@udel.edu

Callahan, Daniel F. (PhD, Wisconsin, Madison 1968; prof. emeritus) medieval Europe; dfcao@udel.edu

Callahan, Raymond A., Jr. (PhD, Harvard 1967; prof. emeritus) 20th-century Britain, military; rac@udel.edu

Curtis, James C. (PhD, Northwestern 1967; prof. emeritus) material culture, visual, documentary photography; jcurtis@udel.edu

Hoffecker, Carol E. (PhD, Harvard 1967; Richards Prof. emerita) American urban, women, Delaware

Hurt, John J. (PhD, North Carolina, Chapel Hill 1970; prof. emeritus) 17th- and 18th-century France, military; hurt@udel.edu

Johnson, Howard B. (DPhil, Oxford 1970; Squire Prof. emeritus) Caribbean; howardj@udel.edu

Kolchin, Peter (PhD, Johns Hopkins 1970; Reed Prof. emeritus) 19th-century US, US South, slavery; pkolchin@udel.edu

Lukashevich, Stephen (PhD, California, Berkeley 1961; prof. emeritus) modern Russia

Matson, Cathy (PhD, Columbia 1985; Richards Prof. emerita) colonial America, early Republic, economic; cmatson@udel.edu

May, Gary (PhD, UCLA 1974; prof. emeritus) 20th-century US, presidential, US diplomatic; garymay@udel.edu

Pong, David B. (PhD, SOAS, London 1969; prof. emeritus) modern East Asia, modern China, Chinese institutions; dpong@udel.edu

Pulliam, William (PhD, Illinois, Urbana-Champaign 1968; assoc. prof. emeritus) social studies education, curriculum development; wpulliam@udel.edu

Strasser, Susan M. (PhD, SUNY, Stony Brook 1977; Richards Prof. emerita) 19th- and 20th-century America, daily life, business; strasser@udel.edu

Tolles, Bryant (PhD, Boston Univ. 1970; prof. emeritus) museum studies, 19th-century American social and cultural, New England; bftolles@udel.edu

Wolters, Raymond (PhD, California, Berkeley 1967; Keith Prof. emeritus) 20th-century US, race relations; wolters@udel.edu

Recently Awarded PhDs

Appelhans, Jeffery R. "Catholics in Early American Civil Society and the Public Sphere"

Kraft, Jesse "The Circulation of Foreign Coinage in the United States: An American Response, c.1750-1857"

Denison University

Dept. of History, 100 W. College St., Granville, OH 43023. 740.587.6251. Email: araizal@denison.edu. Website: https://denison.edu/academics/history.

The Department of History seeks to develop in its students an appreciation for the richness, diversity and complexities of human history. In the course of their studies, students are exposed to a wide range of different historical periods and geographic regions, including courses on the history of America, Latin America, Europe, Africa, the Middle East, and Asia.

Chair: Lauren Araiza
Degrees Offered: BA
Academic Year System: Semester
Areas of Specialization: US, Europe, world
Tuition (per academic year): $52620
Enrollment 2018-19:
  Undergraduate Majors: 71
  Degrees in History: 29 BA
Addresses:
  Admissions: http://denison.edu/admissions
  Financial Aid: http://denison.edu/campus/student-finances

Full-time Faculty

Araiza, Lauren (PhD, California, Berkeley 2006; assoc. prof. and chair) modern US, African American; araizal@denison.edu

Davis, Adam J. (PhD, Princeton 2001; assoc. prof.) medieval Europe, church, charity; davisaj@denison.edu

Dollard, Catherine L. (PhD, North Carolina, Chapel Hill 1999; assoc. prof.) modern Europe, Germany, European women; dollard@denison.edu

Proctor, Frank Trey, III (PhD, Emory 2003; assoc. prof.) Latin America, Atlantic world and comparative slavery; proctorf@denison.edu

Snay, Mitchell (PhD, Brandeis 1984; prof.) 19th-century US, US South, intellectual; snay@denison.edu

Spierling, Karen E. (PhD, Wisconsin, Madison 2001; assoc. prof.) early modern Europe; spierlingk@denison.edu

Tague, Joanna Teresa (PhD, California, Davis 2012; asst. prof.) Africa, refugee settlement, development and borderlands; taguej@denison.edu

Threlkeld, Megan S. (PhD, Iowa 2008; assoc. prof.) US women and gender, US foreign relations; threlkeldm@denison.edu

Yang, Shao-yun (PhD, California, Berkeley 2014; asst. prof.) medieval China, intellectual, ethnocultural identities; yangs@denison.edu

Young, Adrian Michael (PhD, Princeton 2016; asst. prof.) modern Europe, British Empire, science; younga@denison.edu

Yousef, Hoda A (PhD, Georgetown 2011; asst. prof.) literacy studies, gender studies; yousefh@denison.edu

Visiting Faculty

Hempson, Leslie (PhD, Michigan 2018; vis. asst. prof.) modern South Asia, economic life, inequality; hempsonl@denison.edu

Sachs, Miranda Rogow (PhD, Yale 2017; vis. asst. prof.) modern Europe, France, childhood; sachsm@denison.edu

University of Denver

Dept. of History, 2000 E. Asbury Ave., Denver, CO 80208-0930. 303.871.2347. Fax 303.871.2957. Email: history@du.edu. Website: https://www.du.edu/ahss/history/.

At the University of Denver, there's no one-size-fits-all approach to the study of history. Our students take courses rooted in a variety of different geographical areas and periods. You'll be inspired to explore all the facets of the past that have shaped our world, and focus on an area of interest that will help you shape your future.

Chair: Carol Helstosky
Degrees Offered: BA
Academic Year System: Quarter
Areas of Specialization: US, Europe, Asia, Latin America, Middle East
Tuition (per academic year): $45232
Enrollment 2018-19:
  Undergraduate Majors: 85
  Degrees in History: 28 BA
Addresses:
  Admissions: http://www.du.edu/apply/admission/
  Financial Aid: http://www.du.edu/financialaid/undergraduate/

Full-time Faculty

Campbell, Elizabeth (PhD, NYU 2002; assoc. prof.) modern Europe, France, cultural; ecampbell@du.edu

Escobedo, Elizabeth R. (PhD, Washington 2004; assoc. prof.) modern US, Latino, women; elizabeth.escobedo@du.edu

Gibbs, Michael H. (PhD, California, Berkeley 1990; assoc. prof.) Japan, social, cultural; mgibbs@du.edu

Goodfriend, Joyce D. (PhD, UCLA 1975; prof.) colonial America, immigration, women; jgoodfri@du.edu

Helstosky, Carol F. (PhD, Rutgers 1996; assoc. prof. and chair) modern Europe, Italy, history of food; chelstos@du.edu

Ioris, Rafael Rossotto (PhD, Emory 2009; assoc. prof.) Latin America, economic, social; rafael.ioris@du.edu

Kreider, Jodie A. (PhD, Arizona 2004; lect.) modern Europe, Britain, gender; jkreide2@du.edu

Melleno, Daniel F. (PhD, California, Berkeley 2014; asst. prof.) ancient, medieval; daniel.melleno@du.edu

Philpott, William P. (PhD, Wisconsin-Madison 2002; assoc. prof.) US, environmental; william.philpott@du.edu

Schulten, Susan (PhD, Pennsylvania 1995; prof.) America, 20th century, 19th century; sschulte@du.edu

Sciarcon, Jonathan I. (PhD, California, Santa Barbara 2010; assoc. prof.) Jewish, Middle East; jonathan.sciarcon@du.edu

Smith, Hilary A. (PhD, Pennsylvania 2008; assoc. prof.) China, medicine, science; hilary.smith@du.edu

Tague, Ingrid H. (PhD, Brown 1997; prof.) early modern Europe, Great Britain, women; itague@du.edu

Retired/Emeritus Faculty

Golas, Peter J. (PhD, Harvard 1972; prof. emeritus) China; pgolas@du.edu

Pulman, Michael (PhD, California, Berkeley 1964; assoc. prof. emeritus)

DePaul University

Dept. of History, 2320 N. Kenmore Ave., Schmitt Academic Center, Ste. 420, Chicago, IL 60614-3298. 773.325.7470. Fax 773.325.4764. Email: history@depaul.edu. Website: http://las.depaul.edu/academics/history/.

Our department offers a full, rich curriculum in undergraduate and graduate education. More than 30 full and part-time outstanding faculty offer day and night courses on the Lincoln Park and Loop campuses, as well as online.

Chair: John Burton
Director of Graduate Studies: Scott Bucking
Director of Undergraduate Studies: Kerry Ross
Degrees Offered: BA,MA
Academic Year System: Quarter
Areas of Specialization: Europe, US, Latin America, Islamic, Africa
Undergraduate Tuition (per academic year): $39369
Graduate Tuition (per academic year): $16800
Enrollment 2018-19:
  Undergraduate Majors: 122
  New Graduate Students: 8
  Full-time Graduate Students: 20
  Part-time Graduate Students: 20
  Degrees in History: 36 BA, 6 MA
  Students in Undergraduate Courses: 1415
  Students in Undergraduate Intro Courses: 1255
  Online-Only Courses: 4%
Addresses:
  Admissions and Financial Aid: https://www.depaul.edu/admission-and-aid/

Full-time Faculty

Agyepong, Tera (JD,PhD, Northwestern 2013; asst. prof.) race/gender/law, criminal/juvenile justice; tagyepon@depaul.edu

Beiriger, Eugene E. (PhD, Illinois, Chicago 1992; assoc. prof.) 19th- and 20th-century Britain and Europe; ebeirige@depaul.edu

Boeck, Brian J. (PhD, Harvard 2002; assoc. prof.) pre-modern Russia; bboeck@depaul.edu

Bucking, Scott J. (PhD, Cambridge 1998; assoc. prof. and grad. dir.) ancient; sbucking@depaul.edu

Burton, John (PhD, William and Mary 1996; assoc. prof. and chair) colonial, higher education, Bahamas; jburton@depaul.edu

Doody, Colleen P. (PhD, Virginia 2005; assoc. prof. and assoc. chair) 20th-century US, urban, labor; cdoody@depaul.edu

Krainz, Thomas A. (PhD, Colorado, Boulder 2000; assoc. prof.) America West, Gilded Age and Progressive Era; tkrainz@depaul.edu

Maguire, Matthew W (PhD, Harvard 1999; assoc. prof.) modern European political philosophy and philosophy of religion, Enlightenment, Belle Époque; mmaguir3@depaul.edu

Mazumder, Rajit K. (PhD, SOAS, London 2001; assoc. prof.) modern South Asia; rmazumde@depaul.edu

Mockaitis, Thomas R. (PhD, Wisconsin, Madison 1988; prof.) modern Britain and Ireland; tmockait@depaul.edu

Mora-Torres, Juan T. (PhD, Chicago 1991; assoc. prof.) Latin America; jmorator@depaul.edu

Otunnu, Ogenga (PhD, York, Can. 1997; assoc. prof.) modern Africa; ootunnu@depaul.edu

Ross, Kerry L. (PhD, Columbia 2006; assoc. prof. and dir., undergrad. prog.) Japan; kross9@depaul.edu

Schaposchnik, Ana E. (PhD, Wisconsin, Madison 2007; assoc. prof.) colonial Latin America, Jewish studies; aschapos@depaul.edu

Schultz, Warren C. (PhD, Chicago 1995; prof.) Islamic, Middle East; wschultz@depaul.edu

Scott, Karen (PhD, California, Berkeley 1989; assoc. prof. and dir., undergrad advising) medieval, Renaissance; kscott@depaul.edu

Sigel, Lisa Z. (PhD, Carnegie Mellon 1996; prof.) Europe; lsigel@depaul.edu

Storey, Margaret M. (PhD, Emory 1999; prof.) Civil War, Reconstruction, US South; mstorey@depaul.edu

Tikoff, Valentina K. (PhD, Indiana 2000; assoc. prof.) early modern Europe, Spain, European women; vtikoff@depaul.edu

Tyson, Amy Marie (PhD, Minnesota 2006; assoc. prof.) public, oral, 19th- and 20th-century American social and cultural; atyson2@depaul.edu

Woesthoff, Julia M. (PhD, Michigan State 2004; assoc. prof.) modern Germany; jwoestho@depaul.edu

Retired/Emeritus Faculty

Croak, Thomas M. CM (DA, Carnegie Mellon 1978; JD, DePaul 1991; assoc. prof. emeritus) American social; tcroak@depaul.edu

Erlebacher, Albert (PhD, Wisconsin, Madison 1965; prof. emeritus) Civil War to present; aerlebac@depaul.edu

Garfield, Robert (PhD, Northwestern 1971; assoc. prof. emeritus) Africa; rgarfiel@depaul.edu

Goffman, Daniel (PhD, Chicago 1985; prof. emeritus) Middle East, Ottoman; dgoffman@depaul.edu

Krokar, James P. (PhD, Indiana 1980; assoc. prof. emeritus) eastern Europe; jkrokar@depaul.edu

Lindsey, Howard Odell (PhD, Michigan 1993; asst. prof. emeritus) African American, Africa, US; hlindsey@depaul.edu

Masud-Piloto, Felix R. (PhD, Florida State 1985; prof. emeritus) Latin America and US since 1865; fmasud-p@depaul.edu

Meister, Richard J. (PhD, Notre Dame 1967; prof. emeritus) American urban; rmeister@depaul.edu

Sippel, Cornelius, III (PhD, Michigan 1961; assoc. prof. emeritus) France, Russia; csippel@depaul.edu

Udovic, Edward R. CM (PhD, Catholic 1997; prof. emeritus) modern French religious; eudovic@depaul.edu

DePauw University

Dept. of History, 7 E. Larabee St., Greencastle, IN 46135-0037. 765.658.4587. Fax 765.658.1044. Email: dgellman@depauw.edu. Website: https://www.depauw.edu/academics/departments-programs/history/.

History coursework encourages students to think critically, argue logically and examine the values of their society and those of other societies. History students develop research, analytical, writing, oral communication and problem-solving skills that prepare them for a range of occupations, for graduate and professional schools and for the responsibilities of informed citizenship.

Chair: David Gellman
Degrees Offered: BA
Academic Year System: Semester
Areas of Specialization: Africa, East Asia, Europe, Middle East, US and Latin America
Tuition (per academic year): $48860
Enrollment 2018-19:
 Undergraduate Majors: 45
 Degrees in History: 12 BA

Addresses:
 Admissions: http://www.depauw.edu/admission/
 Financial Aid: http://www.depauw.edu/admission/financial-aid/

Full-time Faculty

Adler, Ayden (PhD, Rochester 2007; OPhD, Rochester 1999; prof.) American art and culture, power/privilege/diversity in historiography, economic history of the arts; aydenadler@depauw.edu

Bruggemann, Julia C. (PhD, Georgetown 1999; prof.) Europe, Germany, women; jbruggemann@depauw.edu

Chiang, Yung-chen (PhD, Harvard 1986; prof.) East Asia, modern China, US-East Asian relations; ychiang@depauw.edu

Dewey, Robert F., Jr. (PhD, Oxford 2003; assoc. prof.) modern Britain, modern Europe, British Empire and Pacific Islands; rdewey@depauw.edu

Dixon-Fyle, M. Samuel (PhD, London 1976; prof. emeritus) 20th-century Africa, colonialism, nationalist movements; macdixon@depauw.edu

Fancy, Nahyan (PhD, Notre Dame 2007; assoc. prof.) Middle East, science and medicine; nahyanfancy@depauw.edu

Gellman, David N. (PhD, Northwestern 1997; prof. and chair) colonial North America, early national US, abolition; dgellman@depauw.edu

Magaya, Aldrin Tinashe (PhD, Iowa 2018; asst. prof.) Africa

Rowley, Sarah B. (PhD, Indiana 2015; asst. prof.) 20th-century US, women/gender/sexuality

Whitehead, Barbara J. (PhD, Bryn Mawr 1992; prof.) modern France, Europe, Mediterranean; whitehea@depauw.edu

Retired/Emeritus Faculty

Baughman, John J. (PhD, Michigan 1953; prof. emeritus) modern France, Europe, modern Mediterranean

Clifford, Roderick A. (PhD, Johns Hopkins 1970; prof. emeritus) modern Britain, modern Europe, Ireland; clifford@depauw.edu

Dittmer, John (PhD, Indiana 1971; prof. emeritus) 20th-century US, Afro-American, US South; rip@depauw.edu

Schlotterbeck, John T. (PhD, Johns Hopkins 1980; prof. emeritus) colonial, 19th-century US, American Indian; jschlot@depauw.edu

Steinson, Barbara J. (PhD, Michigan 1977; prof. emeritus) 20th-century US, women, legal; steinson@depauw.edu

University of Detroit Mercy

Dept. of History, 4001 W. McNichols Rd., Detroit, MI 48221-3038. 313.993.1121. Fax 313.993.1166. Email: sumnergd@udmercy.edu. Website: http://liberalarts.udmercy.edu/academics/his/.

The legacy of our past paves the way to creating our future. Uncover new perspectives and insights from ancient civilizations. Understand the struggles and strengths that have shaped the United States. We'll teach you how to research the past like a history detective, develop your analytical skills and your writing-three skills in top demand by today's employers.

Chair: Gregory Sumner and Roy E. Finkenbine
Degrees Offered: BA
Academic Year System: Semester
Areas of Specialization: Europe, US, African American, Latino/a, cross-cultural, museum studies
Tuition (per academic year): $28000
Enrollment 2018-19:
 Undergraduate Majors: 19
 Degrees in History: 5 BA

Students in Undergraduate Courses: 592
Students in Undergraduate Intro Courses: 490
Addresses:
Admissions: http://www.udmercy.edu/apply/
Financial Aid: http://www.udmercy.edu/apply/financial-aid/

Adjunct Faculty

Grant, Ken A. (PhD, Lutheran Sch. of Theology 2009; adj.) medieval Europe, church, religious studies; grantka@udmercy.edu
Klug, Thomas (PhD, Wayne State 1993; adj.) world civilization, modern Detroit; klugta@udmercy.edu

Affiliated Faculty

Presbey, Gail (PhD, Fordham 1989; prof.; Philosophy) modern Latin America, Latino/a, social justice studies; presbegm@udmercy.edu

Full-time Faculty

Finkenbine, Roy E. (PhD, Bowling Green State 1982; prof. and chair) African American, 19th-century US, Africa; finkenre@udmercy.edu
Kroupa, Daniel (MA, Michigan State 1997; lect.) 19th-century US, museum studies; kroupadr@udmercy.edu
Robinson-Dunn, Diane (PhD, SUNY, Stony Brook 1999; assoc. prof.) modern Europe, gender, Middle East; robinsod@udmercy.edu
Sumner, Gregory D. (PhD, Indiana 1992; JD, Michigan 1980; prof. and chair) 20th-century US politics and society, World War II, American popular culture; sumnergd@udmercy.edu

Retired/Emeritus Faculty

Stever, Sarah N. (PhD, Michigan 1976; retired assoc. prof.) Italian Renaissance, art history and architecture; steversn@udmercy.edu

Dickinson College

Dept. of History, PO Box 1773, Carlisle, PA 17013-2896. 717.245.1521. Fax 717.245.1479. Email: brownmad@dickinson.edu. Website: https://www.dickinson.edu/homepage/100/history.

The Department of History exemplifies Dickinson in the way it covers the world beyond our shores: Students may study the regional histories of Africa, East Asia, Europe, Latin America and the Middle East, or they may explore the diversity of American history.

Chair: Christopher Bilodeau
Degrees Offered: BA
Academic Year System: Semester
Areas of Specialization: Africa/Middle East/Asia, America, Europe, Latin America, science and environment
Tuition (per academic year): $56498
Enrollment 2018-19:
Undergraduate Majors: 42
Degrees in History: 18 BA
Addresses:
Admissions: http://www.dickinson.edu/homepage/287/admissions
Financial Aid: http://www.dickinson.edu/info/20081/financial_aid/1112/how_to_apply

Full-time Faculty

Ball, Jeremy R. (PhD, UCLA 2003; assoc. prof.) west central and southern Africa; ballj@dickinson.edu

Bilodeau, Christopher J. (PhD, Cornell 2006; assoc. prof. and chair) early US; bilodeac@dickinson.edu
Borges, Marcelo J. (PhD, Rutgers 1997; prof.) Latin America, comparative immigration; borges@dickinson.edu
Burgin, Say (PhD, Leeds 2013; asst. prof.) 20th-century US, African American, gender; burgins@dickinson.edu
Commins, David (PhD, Michigan 1985; Benjamin Rush Chair and prof.) modern Middle East, South Asia; commins@dickinson.edu
Pawley, Emily J. (PhD, Pennsylvania 2009; asst. prof.) America, 19th century, environmental; pawleye@dickinson.edu
Pinsker, Matthew (DPhil, Oxford 1995; prof. and Pohanka Chair) US political, Civil War era, Abraham Lincoln; pinskerm@dickinson.edu
Qualls, Karl D. (PhD, Georgetown 1998; prof. and John B. Parsons Chair) modern Russia and central Europe, urban; quallsk@dickinson.edu
Sweeney, Regina M. (PhD, California, Berkeley 1992; assoc. prof.) modern Europe, French cultural and women; sweeneyr@dickinson.edu
Weinberger, Stephen (PhD, Wisconsin, Madison 1969; Robert Coleman Prof.) medieval and Renaissance, women, film; weinberg@dickinson.edu
Weissman, Neil (PhD, Princeton 1976; prof. and interim Coll. pres.) Russia, East Asia, comparative civilization; weissmne@dickinson.edu
Young, W. Evan (PhD, Princeton 2015; asst. prof.) Asia, science; youngw@dickinson.edu

Joint/Cross Appointments

Strand, David (PhD, Columbia 1980; prof.; Political Science) 20th-century China; strand@dickinson.edu

Retired/Emeritus Faculty

Fitts, Leon (PhD, Ohio State 1971; prof. emeritus) Roman-Britain archaeology, classical studies; fitts@dickinson.edu
Garrett, Clarke W. (PhD, Wisconsin, Madison 1961; prof. emeritus) France, historiography, popular culture
Jarvis, Charles A. (PhD, Missouri, Columbia 1970; prof. emeritus) US diplomatic, 19th-century US, Afro-American; jarvisc@dickinson.edu
Osborne, John M. (PhD, Stanford 1979; assoc. prof. emeritus) England, 19th-century sports; osborne@dickinson.edu
Rhyne, George N. (PhD, North Carolina, Chapel Hill 1968; prof. emeritus) Russia, 20th-century Europe, European diplomatic; rhyne@dickinson.edu

Drexel University

Dept. of History, 3250-60 Chestnut St., 3025 MacAlister Hall, Philadelphia, PA 19104. 215.895.2463. Fax 215.895.6614. Email: history@drexel.edu. Website: https://drexel.edu/coas/academics/departments-centers/history/.

In the Department of History at Drexel University, our students learn through experience, from full-time co-op positions in archives, museums and other sites, to conducting and presenting original research, to visiting sites of historical significance. The department has particular strengths in the History of Science, Technology and the Environment, and in Global History.

Chair: Scott Knowles
Director of Undergraduate Studies: Jonathan Seitz
Degrees Offered: BA
Academic Year System: Quarter
Areas of Specialization: science/technology/environment, transnational/global

Tuition (per academic year): $33000
Enrollment 2018-19:
   Undergraduate Majors: 24
   Degrees in History: 6 BA
Addresses:
   Admissions: http://drexel.edu/undergrad
   Financial Aid: http://drexel.edu/undergrad/financing/overview

Affiliated Faculty

Remer, Rosalind (PhD, UCLA 1991; vice provost; exec. dir., Lenfest Center for Cultural Partnerships) book, early American economic and business, public history and museum planning; rosalind.remer@drexel.edu

Full-time Faculty

Ackert, Lloyd Thomas, Jr. (PhD, Johns Hopkins 2004; teaching prof.) Russian science, biology, ecology; lta24@drexel.edu

Bhattacharyya, Debjani (PhD, Emory 2014; asst. prof.) South Asia, urban environmental, transnational; db893@drexel.edu

Knowles, Scott Gabriel (PhD, Johns Hopkins 2003; prof. and chair) science and technology, risk and disaster, Philadelphia; sgk23@drexel.edu

Miller, Jonson W. (PhD, Virginia Tech 2007; assoc. teaching prof.) science and technology, military; jwm54@drexel.edu

Rocha, Gabriel de Avilez (PhD, NYU 2016; asst. prof.) environmental, Atlantic world and global, slavery and capitalism; gabriel.a.rocha@drexel.edu

Saraiva, Tiago (PhD, Autónoma de Madrid 2004; assoc. prof.) science, technology, environmental; tfs37@drexel.edu

Seitz, Jonathan W. (PhD, Wisconsin, Madison 2006; teaching prof.) religion/science/medicine/witchcraft, early Europe and Italy; jwseitz@drexel.edu

Slaton, Amy (PhD, Pennsylvania 1995; prof.) labor and technology, standards, materials science; slatonae@drexel.edu

Steen, Kathryn (PhD, Delaware 1995; assoc. prof.) technology, industrialization; steen@drexel.edu

Stevens, Donald Fithian (PhD, Chicago 1984; assoc. prof.) Latin America, Mexico; stevens@drexel.edu

Young, Alden Harrington (PhD, Princeton 2013; asst. prof.) modern Africa, Middle East, postcolonial Africa; ahy24@drexel.edu

Retired/Emeritus Faculty

Brose, Eric Dorn (PhD, Ohio State 1978; prof. emeritus) modern Europe, military, science and technology; broseed@drexel.edu

Rosen, Richard L. (PhD, Case Western Reserve 1971; assoc. prof. emeritus) science, Italian science, modern Europe; rosenrl@drexel.edu

Smith, Cecil O., Jr. (PhD, Harvard 1959; assoc. prof. emeritus) modern Europe, France, technology

Sullivan, Michael J. (PhD, Virginia 1969; prof. emeritus) international relations, developing nations; sullivmj@drexel.edu

Zaller, Robert (PhD, Washington, St. Louis 1968; prof. emeritus) 17th-century England, early modern Europe; zallerrm@drexel.edu

Duke University

Dept. of History, Box 90719, 226 Classroom Bldg., Durham, NC 27708. 919.684.2343. Fax 919.681.7670. Email: jamie.hardy@duke.edu. Website: https://history.duke.edu/.

Duke's History Department ranks among the top 15 programs in the country. We regard the creation of knowledge as one of the fundamental missions of a research university. Our faculty and students work at the cutting edge of research in their fields and collaborate with colleagues across disciplines and around the world to address society's biggest challenge.

Chair: Sumathi Ramaswamy
Director of Graduate Studies: Phil Stern
Director of Undergraduate Studies: Malachi Hacohen
Degrees Offered: BA, MA, PhD
Academic Year System: Semester
Areas of Specialization: North America, Latin America and Caribbean, Africa, Asia, Europe
Undergraduate Tuition (per academic year): $55960
Graduate Tuition (per academic year): $51480
Enrollment 2018-19:
   Undergraduate Majors: 145
   New Graduate Students: 12
   Full-time Graduate Students: 58
   Degrees in History: 42 BA 5 MA, 7 PhD
Undergraduate Addresses:
   Admissions: http://admissions.duke.edu/
   Financial Aid: http://financialaid.duke.edu/
Graduate Addresses:
   Admissions: http://gradschool.duke.edu/
   Financial Aid: http://gradschool.duke.edu/financial_support/

Adjunct Faculty

Duffy, Eve M. (PhD, North Carolina, Chapel Hill 2002; adj. asst. prof.) German cultural and social; eve.duffy@duke.edu

Jakubs, Deborah (PhD, Stanford 1986; adj. assoc. prof.) Latin American social; jakubs@duke.edu

Morrow, Mary Jane (PhD, Duke 1999; adj. asst. prof.) Roman Empire, early Christianity, medieval Europe; oscar@duke.edu

Roberts, James S. (PhD, Iowa 1979; adj. prof.) modern European social and labor; jroberts@mail01.adm.duke.edu

Troost, Kristina (PhD, Harvard 1990; adj. asst. prof.) East Asian languages; kristina.troost@duke.edu

Wilson, Gerald L. (PhD, North Carolina, Chapel Hill 1974; adj. assoc. prof.) 19th- and 20th-century US; gerald.wilson@duke.edu

Full-time Faculty

Balleisen, Edward J. (PhD, Yale 1995; prof.) 19th-century US; eballeis@duke.edu

Barnes, Nicole E. (PhD, California, Irvine 2012; asst. prof.) modern China; neb18@duke.edu

Barr, Juliana (PhD, Wisconsin-Madison 1999; assoc. prof.) early America; juliana.barr@duke.edu

Boenker, Dirk (PhD, Johns Hopkins 2002; assoc. prof.) military; db48@duke.edu

Chappel, James G. (PhD, Columbia 2012; asst. prof.) post-1945 Europe, transnational Europe; jgc@duke.edu

Deutsch, Sarah J. (PhD, Yale 1985; prof. and assoc. chair) American social, American women; sdeutsch@duke.edu

Duara, Prasenjit (PhD, Harvard 1983; prof.) Asia; prasenjit.duara@duke.edu

Edwards, Laura F. (PhD, North Carolina, Chapel Hill 1991; prof.) legal, US women; ledwards@duke.edu

Ewald, Janet J. (PhD, Wisconsin, Madison 1982; assoc. prof.) Africa; jewald@duke.edu

French, John D. (PhD, Yale 1985; prof.) Latin America and Caribbean, Brazil; jdfrench@duke.edu

Gaspar, David Barry (PhD, Johns Hopkins 1974; prof.) colonial North America and Caribbean, Atlantic; dgaspar@duke.edu

Glymph, Thavolia (PhD, Purdue 1994; prof.) 19th-century US South; thavolia@duke.edu

Hacohen, Malachi Haim (PhD, Columbia 1993; prof. and dir., undergrad. studies) modern Europe, intellectual; mhacohen@duke.edu

Humphreys, Margaret (PhD, Harvard 1983; prof.) medicine; meh@duke.edu

Huston, Reeve (PhD, Yale 1994; assoc. prof.) 19th-century US, political and labor, agriculture; reeve.huston@duke.edu

Krylova, Anna (PhD, Johns Hopkins 2000; assoc. prof.) eastern Europe, Soviet Russia; krylova@duke.edu

Lentz-Smith, Adriane D. (PhD, Yale 2005; assoc. prof.) 20th-century Afro-American social and political; adl16@duke.edu

MacLean, Nancy (PhD, Wisconsin-Madison 1989; prof.) US, US women; nm71@duke.edu

Malegam, Jehangir Yezdi (PhD, Stanford 2006; assoc. prof.) medieval Europe; jehangir.malegam@duke.edu

Martin, John Jeffries (PhD, Harvard 1982; prof.) early modern Europe; john.j.martin@duke.edu

Mazumdar, Sucheta (PhD, UCLA 1984; assoc. prof.) modern China; skmmaz@duke.edu

Mestyan, Adam (PhD, Central European 2011; asst. prof.) Islamic Muslim world; adam.mestyan@duke.edu

Miller, Martin A. (PhD, Chicago 1967; prof.) imperial Russia; mmiller@duke.edu

Neuschel, Kristen B. (PhD, Brown 1982; assoc. prof.) early modern Europe; kneusche@duke.edu

Olcott, Jocelyn H. (PhD, Yale 2000; assoc. prof.) Latin America, 20th-century gender, labor; olcott@duke.edu

Partner, Simon (PhD, Columbia 1997; prof.) modern Japan; spartner@duke.edu

Ramaswamy, Sumathi (PhD, California, Berkeley 1992; prof. and chair) South Asia; sr76@duke.edu

Robisheaux, Thomas (PhD, Virginia 1981; prof.) early modern Europe; trobish@duke.edu

Rosenberg, Gabriel N. (PhD, Brown 2011; asst. prof.; Women's Studies) industrialization of US agriculture; gnr3@duke.edu

Sigal, Pete (PhD, UCLA 1995; prof.) colonial Latin America; psigal@duke.edu

Stern, Philip J. (PhD, Columbia 2004; assoc. prof. and dir., grad. studies) British Empire; ps91@duke.edu

Thorne, Susan E. (PhD, Michigan 1990; assoc. prof.) Great Britain; sthorne@duke.edu

Joint/Cross Appointments

Baker, Jeffrey (PhD, Duke 1993; asst. clinical prof.; Pediatrics) medicine; jeffrey.baker@duke.edu

Boatwright, Mary T. (PhD, Michigan 1980; prof.; Classical Studies) Rome; tboat@duke.edu

Dubois, Laurent M. (PhD, Michigan 1998; prof.; Romance Studies) 18th- and 19th-century French Caribbean; laurent.dubois@duke.edu

Hassan, Mona (PhD, Princeton 2008; asst. prof.; Islamic Studies and Religion) emotions, religious images; mona.hassan@duke.edu

Hasso, Frances (PhD, Michigan 1997; assoc. prof.; Sociology) frances.hasso@duke.edu

Korstad, Robert R. (PhD, North Carolina, Chapel Hill 1987; prof.; Public Policy) US, social policy; rkorstad@duke.edu

Peck, Gunther W. (PhD, Yale 1995; assoc. prof.; Public Policy) US West; peckgw@duke.edu

Petroski, Henry (PhD, Illinois, Urbana-Champaign 1968; Aleksander S. Vesic Prof.; Civil Engineering) hp@egr.duke.edu

Silverblatt, Irene (PhD, Michigan 1981; assoc. prof.; Cultural Anthropology) isilver@duke.edu

Sosin, Joshua (PhD, Duke 2000; assoc. prof.; Classical Studies) joshua.sosin@duke.edu

Starn, Orin (PhD, Stanford 1989; prof.; Cultural Anthropology) sports and society; ostarn@duke.edu

Tuna, Mustafa O. (PhD, Princeton 2009; asst. prof.; Slavic and Eurasian Studies) Islam in Central Eurasia; mustafa.tuna@duke.edu

Zanalda, Giovanni (PhD, Johns Hopkins 2008; asst. research prof.; Social Science Research Inst.) giovanni.zanalda@duke.edu

Retired/Emeritus Faculty

Chafe, William H. (PhD, Columbia 1971; Alice Mary Baldwin Prof. emeritus) 20th-century US, oral, social; william.chafe@duke.edu

English, Peter (PhD, Duke 1975; prof. emeritus) medicine; penglish@duke.edu

Herrup, Cynthia B. (PhD, Northwestern 1982; prof. emeritus) England, early modern Europe; cherrup@acpub.duke.edu

Koonz, Claudia Ann (PhD, Rutgers 1969; prof. emeritus) women, Weimar and Nazi Germany; ckoonz@duke.edu

Mauskopf, Seymour (PhD, Princeton 1966; prof. emeritus) science; shmaus@duke.edu

Nathans, Sydney H. (PhD, Johns Hopkins 1969; assoc. prof. emeritus) early national US; snathans@duke.edu

Reddy, William M. (PhD, Chicago 1974; prof. emeritus) 19th-century Europe, social and economic, labor; wmr@duke.edu

Roland, Alex F. (PhD, Duke 1974; prof. emeritus) military, technology; aroland@duke.edu

Shatzmiller, Joseph (PhD, Aix-en-Provence, France 1967; prof. emeritus) Judaic studies, medieval; joshatz@duke.edu

Thompson, John Herd (PhD, Queen's, Can. 1975; prof. emeritus) 19th- and 20th-century Canada; jthompso@duke.edu

Wood, Peter H. (PhD, Harvard 1972; prof. emeritus) colonial and revolutionary America; pwood@duke.edu

Young, Charles R. (PhD, Cornell 1954; prof. emeritus) medieval

Visiting Faculty

Dubois, Katharine Brophy (PhD, Michigan 2001; vis. asst. prof.) medieval social and cultural; kbd6@duke.edu

Freeman, John Rich (PhD, Pennsylvania 1991; vis. asst. prof.) jrf15@duke.edu

Kaiwar, Vasant (PhD, UCLA 1989; vis. asst. prof.) South Asia; vkaiwar@duke.edu

Recently Awarded PhDs

Bobadilla, Eladio B. "One People without Borders: The Lost Roots of the Immigrants' Rights Movement, 1954-2006"

Cashwell, Meggan Farish "Rethinking Violence, Legal Culture, and Community in New York City, 1785-1827"

Cooper, Mandy L. "Cultures of Emotion: Families, Friends, and the Making of the United States"

Garriott, Caroline "Coloring the Sacred: Art and Devotion in Colonial Peru and Brazil"

Goldsmith, William Dixon "Kids, the New Cash Crop: The Promise and Limits of Educating for Economic Development in the New South, 1960-2000"

Malitoris, Jessica "The Promise of Marriage Consent: Family Politics, the United Nations, and Women's Rights in the US, 1947-67"

Romine, David "Into the Mainstream and Oblivion: Julian Mayfield's Black Tradition, 1948-84"

Rytilahti, Stephanie "Taking the Moral Ground: Protestants, Feminists, and Gay Equality in North Carolina, 1970-80"

Duquesne University

Dept. of History, 603 College Hall, 600 Forbes Ave., Pittsburgh, PA 15282-1704. 412.396.6470. Fax 412.396.1439 Email: history@duq.edu. Website: https://www.duq.edu/academics/schools/liberal-arts/departments-and-programs/history

Our History and Public History programs provide students with a challenging education and equips them with skills that they—and employers—will find invaluable: to think critically, to write with authority, and to understand broadly.

Chair: John C. Mitcham
Director of Graduate Studies: Philipp Stelzel
Director of Undergraduate Studies: Jotham Parsons
Degrees Offered: BA,MA
Academic Year System: Semester
Areas of Specialization: US, early modern and modern Europe, world, public
Undergraduate Tuition (per academic year): $39992
Graduate Tuition (per academic year): $19650
Enrollment 2018-19:
  Undergraduate Majors: 98
  New Graduate Students: 14
  Full-time Graduate Students: 31
  Part-time Graduate Students: 3
  Degrees in History: 20 BA, 17 MA
Undergraduate Addresses:
  Admissions: http://www.duq.edu/admissions-and-aid
  Financial Aid: http://www.duq.edu/admissions-and-aid/financial-aid
Graduate Addresses:
  Admissions: http://www.duq.edu/admissions-and-aid/graduate-admissions
  Financial Aid: http://www.duq.edu/admissions-and-aid/financial-aid

Adjunct Faculty

Butko, Brian (MA, Duquesne; adj. prof.) public, historical editing; butkob@duq.edu

Csorba, Mrea (PhD, Pittsburgh 1997; adj. asst. prof.) ancient Chinese art, archaeology, western art and architecture; csorba@duq.edu

Cymbala, Amy (PhD, Pittsburgh 2016; adj. prof.) Renaissance, early modern art, women; cymbalaa@duq.edu

Davis, Adam W. (MA, Pittsburgh 2004; adj. prof.) science; davisa1@duq.edu

Gillen, Amanda (MA, Duquesne; adj. prof.) public, museums; gillena@duq.edu

Grimes, Richard (PhD, West Virginia 2006; adj. prof.) colonial America, early Republic, native; grimesr1@duq.edu

Hier, Charles B. (PhD, Pittsburgh 2003; adj. prof.) Soviet Union, US, world; hierc@duq.edu

Hudson-Richards, Julia Anne (PhD, Arizona 2008; adj. prof.) modern Spain, Europe, world; hudsonrichardsj@duq.edu

Lorenz, Christine (OMS, California, Santa Barbara 1997; adj. prof.) art, fine art, photography; lorenzc@duq.edu

Maharaja, Gita (EdD, Duquesne 2009; adj. prof.) India, UK; maharaja@duq.edu

Marcinizyn, John (PhD, Pittsburgh; adj. asst. prof.) music composition, music theory; marcinizynj@duq.edu

Oliver, Megan (MA, Duquesne 2016; adj. prof.) modern Europe, world; oliverm2@duq.edu

Rodrigues, Robert (MA,MEd, Duquesne; adj. prof.) Vietnam, US, world; rodriguesr@duq.edu

Steinmetz, Charles Edwin, Jr. (PhD, West Virginia 2012; adj. prof.) modern Africa, England, world; steinmetzc@duq.edu

Trimarchi, Carolyn (MA, Indiana, Pa. 2004; adj. prof.) geography, social; trimarchic@duq.edu

White, Thomas (MA, Duquesne 1999; adj. prof.) archival studies, US, public; whitet@duq.edu

Full-time Faculty

Chapdelaine, Robin P. (PhD, Rutgers 2014; asst. prof.; Center for African Studies) Africa and international studies, women and gender, child trafficking and human rights; chapdelainer@duq.edu

Dwyer, John Joseph (PhD, Illinois, Urbana-Champaign 1998; assoc. prof.) modern Latin America and Mexico, international, environmental; dwyer@duq.edu

Gray, Stephanie (PhD, South Carolina 2019; asst. prof.) 20th-century US, public, cultural

Li, Jing (PhD, Rice 1995; assoc. prof.) China, East Asia, US-China relations; lij@duq.edu

Mitcham, John Calvin (PhD, Alabama 2012; assoc. prof. and chair) British Empire, global, military and diplomatic; mitchamj@duq.edu

Parsons, Jotham W. (PhD, Johns Hopkins 1997; assoc. prof. and undergrad. dir.) early modern and medieval Europe, France, political institutions; parsonsj@duq.edu

Simpson, Andrew T. (PhD, Carnegie Mellon 2013; asst. prof.) contemporary US, politics and history of US healthcare; simpson4@duq.edu

Stelzel, Philipp J. (PhD, North Carolina, Chapel Hill 2010; asst. prof. and grad. dir.) modern Europe, Germany, international; stelzelp@duq.edu

Taylor, Jennifer Whitmer (PhD, South Carolina 2017; asst. prof.) 19th- and 20th-century US, public, gender; taylorj8@duq.edu

Retired/Emeritus Faculty

Mayer, Holly A. (PhD, William and Mary 1990; prof. emerita) colonial America, American Revolution, military and diplomatic; mayer@duq.edu

Rishel, Joseph (PhD, Pittsburgh; prof. emeritus) US; rishelj@duq.edu

Earlham College

Dept. of History, 801 National Rd. W., Richmond, IN 47374. 765.983.1525. Fax 765.983.1304. Email: tomh@earlham.edu. Website: https://earlham.edu/history/.

History requires active inquiry into the human past. By delving into the past, students gain a better understanding of the present, training them for citizenship and for a life of thoughtful action. At Earlham, the study of history includes the use of museums, extensive electronic media, and our Quaker archives.

Chair: Thomas Hamm
Degrees Offered: BA
Academic Year System: Semester
Areas of Specialization: US, East Asia, Europe, Latin America, Africa
Tuition (per academic year): $43500
Enrollment 2018-19:
  Undergraduate Majors: 29
  Degrees in History: 6 BA

Addresses:

Admissions: http://www.earlham.edu/admissions
Financial Aid: https://www.earlham.edu/financial-aid

Full-time Faculty

Murphy, Ryan Patrick (PhD, Minnesota 2010; assoc. prof.) US labor, US women, sexuality; murphry@earlham.edu

Passman, Elana M. (PhD, North Carolina, Chapel Hill 2009; assoc. prof.) Europe, France, Germany; passman@earlham.edu

Schlabach, Elizabeth S. (PhD, St. Louis 2008; assoc. prof.) African American, US urban; schlabe@earlham.edu

Joint/Cross Appointments

Hamm, Thomas D. (PhD, Indiana 1985; prof. and chair; Coll. Archives and Special Collections) 19th-century US, Quaker, British; tomh@earlham.edu

Nondepartmental Historians

Swanger, Joanna B. (PhD, Texas, Austin 1999; prof.; Peace and Global Studies) Latin America, peace studies; swangjo@earlham.edu

Retired/Emeritus Faculty

Boanes, Phyllis (ABD, Northwestern; prof. emeritus) Africa, African American; phyllisb@earlham.edu

Shrock, Alice Almond (PhD, North Carolina, Chapel Hill 1974; prof. emeritus) recent US, women, museum studies; alices@earlham.edu

Shrock, Randall (PhD, North Carolina, Chapel Hill 1980; prof. emeritus) colonial America, early Republic, Quaker; randalls@earlham.edu

Yates, Charles (PhD, Princeton 1987; prof. emeritus) Japan, East Asia; yatesch@earlham.edu

Visiting Faculty

Song, Womai Ignatius (PhD, Howard 2015; asst. prof.; African and African American Studies) Africa, African diaspora; songwo@earlham.edu

East Carolina University

Dept. of History, A-316 Brewster Bldg, Greenville, NC 27858-4353. 252.328.6155. Fax 252.328.6774. Email: history@ecu.edu. Website: https://history.ecu.edu/.

The Department is home to over 20 full-time professors whose strengths include US, European, public, military, Atlantic world, and maritime history. The Department offers courses in the full range of international areas.

Chair: Christopher A. Oakley
Director of Graduate Studies: Jennifer F. McKinnon
Director of Undergraduate Studies: Timothy Jenks
Degrees Offered: BA,MA
Academic Year System: Semester
Areas of Specialization: US, Europe, maritime, Atlantic world, public
Undergraduate Tuition (per academic year):
In-State: $7188
Out-of-State: $23464
Graduate Tuition (per academic year):
In-State: $7485
Out-of-State: $20634

Enrollment 2018-19:

Undergraduate Majors: 241
New Graduate Students: 11
Full-time Graduate Students: 63
Part-time Graduate Students: 2
Degrees in History: 51 BA, 18 MA
Students in Undergraduate Courses: 1158
Students in Undergraduate Intro Courses: 716

Undergraduate Addresses:

Admissions: http://www.ecu.edu/admissions/
Financial Aid: http://www.ecu.edu/cs-acad/financial/

Graduate Addresses:

Admissions: http://www.ecu.edu/cs-acad/gradschool/index.cfm
Financial Aid: http://www.ecu.edu/cs-acad/financial/

Full-time Faculty

Bennett, Todd (PhD, Georgia 2001; assoc. prof.) 20th-century US, US foreign relations, US cultural; bennettm@ecu.edu

Dennard, David C. (PhD, Northwestern 1983; assoc. prof.) African American, US, Old US South; dennardd@ecu.edu

Dudley, Wade G. (PhD, Alabama 1999; teaching prof.) military and naval, North Carolina, US to 1877; dudleyw@ecu.edu

Gross, Michael B. (PhD, Brown 1997; assoc. prof.) modern Germany; grossm@ecu.edu

Harris, Lynn B. (PhD, South Carolina 2002; assoc. prof.) maritime archaeology; harrisly@ecu.edu

Hernandez, Richard L. (PhD, Stanford 2002; assoc. prof.) Russia; hernandezr@ecu.edu

Jenks, Timothy D. (PhD, Toronto 2000; assoc. prof. and dir., undergrad. studies) Britain; jenkst@ecu.edu

McKinnon, Jennifer F. (PhD, Florida State 2010; assoc. prof. and dir., grad. studies) maritime archaeology; mckinnonje@ecu.edu

Oakley, Christopher Arris (PhD, Tennessee, Knoxville 2002; assoc. prof. and chair) North Carolina; oakleyc@ecu.edu

Palmer, Michael A. (PhD, Temple 1981; prof.) early national, maritime, US foreign relations; palmerm@ecu.edu

Parkerson, Donald H. (PhD, Illinois, Chicago 1983; prof.) American economic, quantitative methods, urban; parkersond@ecu.edu

Prokopowicz, Gerald J. (PhD, Harvard 1994; prof.) public, Civil War; prokopowiczg@ecu.edu

Reid, Jonathan A. (PhD, Arizona 2001; assoc. prof.) Europe, Renaissance, Reformation; reidj@ecu.edu

Richards, Nathan T. (PhD, Flinders 2003; assoc. prof.) maritime archaeology; richardsn@ecu.edu

Romer, Frank (PhD, Stanford; prof.) ancient, Greek and Roman geography and mapping; romerf@ecu.edu

Russell, Mona L. (PhD, Georgetown 1998; assoc. prof.) Middle East; russellm@ecu.edu

Stewart, David J. (PhD, Texas A&M; assoc. prof.) maritime archaeology; stewartda@ecu.edu

Thompson, Angela T. (PhD, Texas, Austin 1989; asst. prof.) Latin America; thompsona@ecu.edu

Tucker, John A. (PhD, Columbia 1990; prof.) Asia; tuckerjo@ecu.edu

Vance, Shannon H. (PhD, Michigan State 2009; teaching asst. prof.) African, African diaspora, imperialism, world; vances18@ecu.edu

Zipf, Karin L. (PhD, Georgia 2000; prof.) US women; zipfk@ecu.edu

Retired/Emeritus Faculty

Babits, Lawrence E. (PhD, Brown 1981; prof. emeritus) US, nautical archaeology, military; babitsl@ecu.edu

Calhoun, Charles W. (PhD, Columbia 1977; prof. emeritus) 19th-century US, Gilded Age, US foreign relations; calhounc@ecu.edu

Collins, Donald (PhD, Georgia 1975; assoc. prof. emeritus) US; collinsd@ecu.edu

Ferrell, Henry C., Jr. (PhD, Virginia 1964; prof. emeritus) 20th-century US, New Deal; ferrellh@ecu.edu

Papalas, Anthony J. (PhD, Chicago 1969; prof. emeritus) ancient, Greece and Rome, maritime; papalasa@ecu.edu

Rodgers, Bradley A. (PhD, Union Inst. 1993; prof. emeritus) maritime, nautical archaeology; rodgersb@ecu.edu

Swanson, Carl E. (PhD, Western Ontario 1979; assoc. prof. emeritus) colonial America, maritime; swansonc@ecu.edu

Wilburn, Kenneth E. (DPhil, Oxford 1983; prof. emeritus) Africa, modern Europe, business and economic; wilburnk@ecu.edu

Eastern Connecticut State University

Dept. of History, 83 Windham St., Willimantic, CT 06226-2295. 860.465.4594. Fax 860.465.0650. Email: meznarj@easternct. edu. Website: http://www.easternct.edu/history/.

The History major provides students with an understanding of the historical background of modern society, politics, economics, and culture, while also offering opportunities to cultivate research and writing skills.

Chair: Jamel Ostwald
Degrees Offered: BA
Academic Year System: Semester
Areas of Specialization: US, ancient, early modern and modern Europe, East Asia, Latin America
Tuition (per academic year):
   In-State: $4285
   Out-of-State: $13866
Enrollment 2018-19:
   Undergraduate Majors: 152
   Degrees in History: 49 BA
Addresses:
   Admissions: http://www.easternct.edu/admissions/
   Financial Aid: http://www.easternct.edu/finaid/

Full-time Faculty

Balcerski, Thomas J. (PhD, Cornell 2014; asst. prof.) antebellum US, political, manhood; balcerskit@easternct.edu

Carenen, Caitlin Elisabeth (PhD, Emory 2008; prof.) US diplomatic, American religious, terrorism; carenenc@easternct.edu

Davis, Bradley Camp (PhD, Washington 2008; assoc. prof.) East Asia, comparative colonialism; davisbrad@easternct.edu

Frye, David (PhD, Duke 1992; prof.) ancient Rome, medieval Europe; fryed@easternct.edu

Jaroszynska-Kirchmann, Anna D. (PhD, Minnesota 1997; prof.) recent US, immigration and ethnic; kirchmanna@easternct.edu

Kamola, Stefan (PhD, Washington 2013; asst. prof.) Middle East, Central Asia; kamolas@easternct.edu

Meznar, Joan E. (PhD, Texas, Austin 1986; prof.) Brazil, Latin America; meznarj@easternct.edu

Moore, Scott O. (PhD, Maryland, Coll. Park 2015; asst. prof.) modern Europe, central Europe, Habsburg monarchy; mooresc@easternct.edu

Ostwald, Jamel M. (PhD, Ohio State 2002; prof. and chair) early modern Europe, military; ostwaldj@easternct.edu

Tucker, Barbara M. (PhD, California, Davis 1974; prof.) New England studies, Jacksonian Era, colonial America; tuckerb@easternct.edu

Part-time Faculty

Eves, Jamie (PhD, Connecticut 2005; instr.) US environmental, New England, public; evesj@easternct.edu

Retired/Emeritus Faculty

Higginbotham, Ann R. (PhD, Indiana 1985; prof. emeritus) adoption and social policy, 19th-century illegitimacy; higginbotham@easternct.edu

Pocock, Emil (PhD, Indiana 1984; prof. emeritus) American studies, frontier, early Republic; pocock@easternct.edu

Eastern Illinois University

Dept. of History, Coleman Hall, 600 Lincoln Ave., Charleston, IL 61920-3099. 217.581.3310. Email: seelder@eiu.edu. Website: https://www.eiu.edu/history/.

The Department of History at EIU offers over 60 courses, ranging from sweeping surveys of long periods to tightly focused seminars on specific topics and countries. Core courses provide grounding in American and World History as well as the tools to research, write, and present focused subjects.

Chair: Sace Elder
Director of Graduate Studies: Lee Patterson
Degrees Offered: BA,MA
Academic Year System: Semester
Areas of Specialization: US, Europe, East Asia, Middle East
Undergraduate Tuition (per academic year):
   In-State and Border States: $9060
   Out-of-State: $11340
Graduate Tuition (per academic year):
   In-State: $6743
   Out-of-State: $16183
Enrollment 2018-19:
   Undergraduate Majors: 4
   New Graduate Students: 15
   Full-time Graduate Students: 12
   Part-time Graduate Students: 18
   Degrees in History: 39 BA, 17 MA
   Students in Undergraduate Courses: 487
   Students in Undergraduate Intro Courses: 258
   Online-Only Courses: 7%
Undergraduate Addresses:
   Admissions: http://www.eiu.edu/admissions.php
   Financial Aid: http://www.eiu.edu/finaid/
Graduate Addresses:
   Admissions: http://www.eiu.edu/graduate/aboutadmissions.php
   Financial Aid: http://www.eiu.edu/graduate/students_assistantships.php

Full-time Faculty

Dries, Mark Pierre (PhD, California, Davis 2018; instr.) Latin America, colonial, Andes

Elder, Sace E. (PhD, Illinois, Urbana-Champaign 2002; prof. and chair) modern Germany, Europe, crime, violence, children and childhood; seelder@eiu.edu

Farnia, Navid (PhD, Ohio State 2019; instr.) African American history and studies, 20th-century US, race and racism, empire

Hardeman, Martin J. (PhD, Chicago 1992; assoc. prof.) 19th-century US, African American, Civil War and Reconstruction; mjhardeman@eiu.edu

Kammerling, Joy (PhD, Illinois, Chicago 1994; assoc. prof.) Renaissance and Reformation, early modern Europe; jmkammerling@eiu.edu

Key, Newton E. (PhD, Cornell 1989; prof.) Britain, early modern Europe; nekey@eiu.edu

Laughlin-Schultz, Bonnie Ellen (PhD, Indiana 2010; assoc. prof.) 19th-century US, women and gender; blaughlinschul@eiu.edu

Lee, Jinhee (PhD, Illinois, Urbana-Champaign 2004; assoc. prof.) modern East Asia; jlee@eiu.edu

Mann, Brian (PhD, Texas, Austin 2011; instr.) modern Middle East, Iran

Patterson, Lee E. (PhD, Missouri–Columbia 2003; prof. and dir., grad. studies) ancient Greece and Rome, classical studies; lepatterson2@eiu.edu

Smith, David K. (PhD, Pennsylvania 1995; prof.) 17th- and 18th-century France, economic, science; dksmith@eiu.edu

Voss-Hubbard, Mark (PhD, Massachusetts Amherst 1997; assoc. prof.) antebellum US, US Civil War; mvosshubbard@eiu.edu

Wehrle, Edmund F. (PhD, Maryland, Coll. Park 1998; prof.) US foreign policy, labor; efwehrle@eiu.edu

Young, Bailey K. (PhD, Pennsylvania 1975; prof.) medieval, France, archaeology; bkyoung@eiu.edu

Part-time Faculty

Shelton, Anita (PhD, Washington 1986; prof. and interim dean, Coll. of Arts and Humanities) eastern Europe, Russia, modern Europe; ashelton@eiu.edu

Retired/Emeritus Faculty

Barnhart, Terry A. (PhD, Miami, Ohio 1989; prof. emeritus) 19th- and 20th-century US social and cultural, interpretation; tabarnhart@eiu.edu

Beck, Roger B. (PhD, Indiana 1987; prof. emeritus) Africa, South Africa, world; rbbeck@eiu.edu

Curry, Lynne (PhD, Illinois, Urbana-Champaign 1995; prof. emeritus) US women, 20th-century US, constitutional and legal; lecurry@eiu.edu

Foy, Charles R. (PhD, Rutgers 2008; prof. emeritus) Atlantic world, early America, African American; crfoy@eiu.edu

Small, Nora Pat (PhD, Boston Univ. 1994; prof. emeritus) American architecture, historic preservation, 19th-century US social and cultural; npsmall@eiu.edu

Eastern Kentucky University

Dept. of History, Philosophy, & Religious Studies, 323 Keith Bldg., 521 Lancaster Ave., Richmond, KY 40475-3102. 859.622.1287. Fax 859.622.1357. Email: john.bowes@eku.edu. Website: https://hpr.eku.edu/.

Our program is very personalized and can offer you small class sizes, a wide variety of history courses offered regularly, active student organizations, opportunity to gain "hands on" professional experience through course-related research and our internship program, and nationally and internationally recognized and published professors.

Chair: John Bowes
Director of Graduate Studies: Bradford Wood
Degrees Offered: BA,MA
Academic Year System: Semester
Areas of Specialization: US, Kentucky/South/Appalachia, Europe, social, religion

Undergraduate Tuition (per academic year):
In-State: $7320
Out-of-State: $16464
Graduate Tuition (per academic year):
In-State: $5280
Out-of-State: $9240
Enrollment 2018-19:
Undergraduate Majors: 138
New Graduate Students: 6
Full-time Graduate Students: 20
Part-time Graduate Students: 12
Degrees in History: 47 BA, 8 MA
Undergraduate Addresses:
Admissions: http://admissions.eku.edu/
Financial Aid: http://finaid.eku.edu/
Graduate Addresses:
Admissions: http://gradschool.eku.edu/
Financial Aid: http://finaid.eku.edu/

Full-time Faculty

Anyanwu, Ogechi (PhD, Bowling Green State 2006; prof.) Africa; ogechi.anyanwu@eku.edu

Blaylock, David W. (PhD, Ohio State 1992; assoc. prof.) East Asia, Japan; david.blaylock@eku.edu

Bowes, John P. (PhD, UCLA 2003; prof. and chair) Native American, US; john.bowes@eku.edu

Dupont, Carolyn R. (PhD, Kentucky 2003; assoc. prof.) 20th-century US, religion; carolyn.dupont@eku.edu

Hartch, Todd F. (PhD, Yale 2000; prof.) Latin America, Mexico; todd.hartch@eku.edu

Jay, Jacqueline (PhD, Chicago 2008; assoc. prof.) ancient Egypt; jackie.jay@eku.edu

Lowry, John S. (PhD, Yale 1999; assoc. prof.) modern Germany, Europe; john.lowry@eku.edu

Lynn, Joshua A. (PhD, North Carolina, Chapel Hill 2015; asst. prof.) 19th-century US, politics and culture, gender/race/sexuality; joshua.lynn@eku.edu

Smit, Timothy J. (PhD, Minnesota 2009; asst. prof.) medieval Europe; tim.smit@eku.edu

Spock, Jennifer B. (PhD, Yale 1999; prof.) Russia, eastern Europe; jennifer.spock@eku.edu

Stearn, Catherine L. (PhD, Rutgers 2007; assoc. prof.) early modern Europe; catherine.stearn@eku.edu

Weise, Robert S. (PhD, Virginia 1995; prof.) US South, Appalachia; rob.weise@eku.edu

Wood, Bradford James (PhD, Johns Hopkins 1999; prof. and dir., grad. studies) colonial and revolutionary America; brad.wood@eku.edu

Yazdani, Mina (PhD, Toronto 2010; assoc. prof.) Islamic world, Iran, modern Middle East; mina.yazdani@eku.edu

Part-time Faculty

Huch, Ronald K. (PhD, Michigan 1971; retired prof.) modern Europe, 19th-century England; ron.huch@eku.edu

Retired/Emeritus Faculty

Appleton, Thomas H., Jr. (PhD, Kentucky 1981; prof. emeritus) Kentucky, US since 1877; tom.appleton@eku.edu

Campbell, George (PhD, Georgia 1972; assoc. prof. emeritus) America

Chase, Lawrence J. (PhD, Notre Dame 1973; prof. emeritus) modern Europe, France; larry.chase@eku.edu

Coe, Stephen H. (PhD, American 1968; assoc. prof. emeritus) colonial and revolutionary America

Dunston-Coleman, Aingred G. (PhD, Duke 1981; assoc. prof. emeritus) 20th-century US, African American; a.dunston@eku.edu

Ellis, William E. (PhD, Kentucky 1974; prof. emeritus) 20th-century America, Kentucky, oral; william.ellis@eku.edu

Everman, Henry E. (PhD, Louisiana State 1970; prof. emeritus) 20th-century US, world civilization; hank.everman@eku.edu

Forderhase, Nancy K. K. (PhD, Missouri, Columbia 1971; prof. emeritus) US diplomatic, women

Forderhase, R. E. (PhD, Missouri, Columbia 1968; prof. emeritus) 19th-century America, South

Klatte, Mary Ellen (EdD, Kentucky 1981; assoc. prof. emeritus) women, education, world; maryellen.klatte@eku.edu

Lewis, L. Michael (MA, Notre Dame 1966; prof. emeritus) Middle East; m.lewis@eku.edu

MacLaren, Bruce (PhD, Wisconsin, Madison 1978; prof. emeritus) science; bruce.maclaren@eku.edu

Mutersbaugh, Bert M. (PhD, Missouri, Columbia 1973; assoc. prof. emeritus) American frontier

Nelson, Kenneth Ross (PhD, Georgia 1972; prof. emeritus) world, early modern Europe

Roitman, Joel M. (PhD, Cincinnati 1981; assoc. prof. emeritus) 20th-century US, Progressive Era; joel.roitman@eku.edu

Sefton, David S. (PhD, Michigan State 1975; prof. emeritus) medieval Europe, England; david.sefton@eku.edu

Taylor, Christiane Diehl (PhD, Minnesota 1997; prof. emeritus) US Gilded Age, Progressive Era, business and economic; chris.taylor@eku.edu

Eastern Michigan University

Dept. of History and Philosophy, 701 Pray-Harrold, Ypsilanti, MI 48197-2234. 734.487.1018. Email: jegge@emich.edu; jesse.kauffman@emich.edu. Website: http://www.emich.edu/history/.

Our mission is to increase historical knowledge and understanding and to prepare our students for lives of learning, citizenship, and professional success. We offer major, minor, and Master's programs in History, major programs for Social Studies for Secondary Education, major and minor programs in Religious Studies, and a Master's program in Social Science.

Chair: James Egge; Section **Chair:** Jesse Kauffman
Director of Graduate Studies: John McCurdy
Degrees Offered: BA,MA
Academic Year System: Semester
Areas of Specialization: US, modern Europe, world, religious studies, military
Undergraduate Tuition (per academic year): $9926
Graduate Tuition (per academic year):
  In-State: $13500
  Out-of-State: $24030
Enrollment 2018-19:
  Undergraduate Majors: 251
  New Graduate Students: 20
  Full-time Graduate Students: 10
  Part-time Graduate Students: 30
  Degrees in History: 51 BA, 14 MA
Undergraduate Addresses:
  Admissions: http://www.emich.edu/admissions/
  Financial Aid: http://www.emich.edu/finaid/
Graduate Addresses:
  Admissions: http://www.emich.edu/graduate/prospective_students/admissions/requirements.php
  Financial Aid: http://www.emich.edu/historyphilosophy/history/scholarships/graduate.php

Full-time Faculty

Bavery, Ashley Johnson (PhD, Northwestern 2015; asst. prof.) 20th-century US, urban, immigration; abavery@emich.edu

Delph, Ronald K. (PhD, Michigan 1987; prof.) medieval Europe, early modern Europe, European women; rdelph@emich.edu

Egge, James (PhD, Chicago 1998; prof. and head) religion, South Asia, Buddhism; jegge@emich.edu

Engwenyu, Joseph (ABD, Dalhousie; instr.) Africa, world, African women; jengwenyu@emich.edu

Higbee, Mark D. (PhD, Columbia 1995; prof.) African American, scholarship of teaching, constitutional; mhigbee@emich.edu

Kauffman, Jesse C. (PhD, Stanford 2008; assoc. prof. and section chair) modern Germany and eastern Europe, military, Europe; jesse.kauffman@emich.edu

Long, Roger D. (PhD, UCLA 1985; prof.) Britain and British Empire, South and Southeast Asia, Canada; rlong@emich.edu

McCurdy, John Gilbert (PhD, Washington, St. Louis 2004; prof. and dir., grad. studies) colonial and revolutionary America, sexuality, gender; jmccurdy@emich.edu

Murphy, Mary-Elizabeth B. (PhD, Maryland, Coll. Park 2012; assoc. prof.) US women, African American women, diversity; mmurph54@emich.edu

Nation, Richard F. (PhD, Michigan 1995; prof.) 19th-century US, environmental, intellectual; rnation@emich.edu

Ramold, Steven J. (PhD, Nebraska 1999; prof.) Civil War and Reconstruction, military, World War II; sramold@emich.edu

Rogers, Rick M. (PhD, Michigan 1997; lect.) religion, early Christianity; rrogers@emich.edu

Schmitz, Philip C. (PhD, Michigan 1990; prof.) ancient Near East, religion, Phoenicians; pschmitz@emich.edu

Strasma, Mary Grace (PhD, Minnesota 2010; assoc. prof.) Latin America, Mexico, Latin American women; mstrasma@emich.edu

Wegner, John M. (PhD, Bowling Green State 1992; lect.) US Gilded Age and Progressive Era, Ohio, historic preservation; jwegner@emich.edu

Whitters, Mark (PhD, Catholic 1999; lect.) Jewish-Christian origins, Graeco-Roman world, early Islam; mwhitters@emich.edu

Eastern Washington University

Dept. of History, 103 Patterson Hall, Cheney, WA 99004-2424. 509.359.2337. Fax 509.359.4275. Email: vburnett@ewu.edu. Website: https://www.ewu.edu/css/history/.

History provides knowledge for unlocking all other realms of human development. The study of history provides a solid foundation not only for history and social studies education majors, but for careers in law, business, government, international relations, journalism, library services and museums, to name but a few.

Chair: Michael Conlin and Liping Zhu
Director of Graduate Studies: Joseph Lenti
Director of Undergraduate Studies: Ann Le Bar
Degrees Offered: BA,BAE,MA
Academic Year System: Quarter
Areas of Specialization: US, public, Latin America
Undergraduate Tuition (per academic year):
  In-State: $6378
  Out-of-State: $23499

Graduate Tuition (per academic year):
   In-State: $11439
   Out-of-State: $26568
Enrollment 2018-19:
   Undergraduate Majors: 120
   New Graduate Students: 8
   Full-time Graduate Students: 18
   Part-time Graduate Students: 2
   Degrees in History: 30 BA, 8 MA
Undergraduate Addresses:
   Admissions: http://www.ewu.edu/undergrad
   Financial Aid: http://www.ewu.edu/admissions/financial-aid
Graduate Addresses:
   Admissions: https://www2.ewu.edu/grad
   Financial Aid: http://www.ewu.edu/admissions/financial-aid

Adjunct Faculty

Selmanovic, Amir (PhD, Washington State 2015; lect.) Soviet Union, modern Europe, imperialism; aselmanovic29@ewu.edu

Full-time Faculty

Bazemore, Georgia B. (PhD, Chicago 1998; assoc. prof.) ancient Greece and Rome, archaeology, linguistics; gbazemore@ewu.edu

Collins, John Michael (PhD, Virginia 2013; sr. lect.) Great Britain, British Empire; jcollins2@ewu.edu

Conlin, Michael F. (PhD, Illinois, Urbana-Champaign 1999; prof. and chair) antebellum and Civil War America, science; mconlin@ewu.edu

Dean, Robert (PhD, Arizona 1995; prof.) 20th-century US, culture, gender; rdean@ewu.edu

Le Bar, Ann C. (PhD, University of Washington 1993; prof. and undergrad. advisor) early modern Europe, cultural and intellectual, Germany; alebar@ewu.edu

Lenti, Joseph Umberto (PhD, New Mexico 2011; assoc. prof. and grad. advisor) Latin America, world; jlenti@ewu.edu

Slack, Edward, Jr. (PhD, Hawaii 1997; prof.) China, East Asia, world; eslack@ewu.edu

Tyler, Jacki Hedlund (PhD, Washington State 2015; asst. prof.) race and gender studies, public, history education; jtyler5@ewu.edu

Youngs, J. William T., Jr. (PhD, California, Berkeley 1970; prof.) US, American wilderness, early America; jyoungs@ewu.edu

Zhu, Liping (PhD, New Mexico 1994; prof. and co-chair) US, American West, Asian Americans; lzhu@ewu.edu

Joint/Cross Appointments

Cebula, Larry (PhD, William and Mary 2000; prof. and asst. state archivist) public, Pacific Northwest, Native American; lcebula@ewu.edu

Martinez, Nydia A. (PhD, New Mexico 2015; asst. prof.) Latin America, Chicano, Mexico; nmartinez9@ewu.edu

Retired/Emeritus Faculty

Donley, Richard (ABD, Humboldt State; prof. emeritus) Civil War and Reconstruction

Green, Michael K. (PhD, Idaho 1968; prof. emeritus) public, US diplomacy, Pacific Northwest

Hodgman, Laura S. (PhD, Illinois, Urbana-Champaign 1993; prof. emeritus) Russia, modern Europe, LGBTQ; lhodgman@ewu.edu

Huttenmaier, Kathleen (MA, Eastern Washington 1987; retired sr. lect.) women, social studies education; khuttenmaier@ewu.edu

Innes, John S. (PhD, Texas, Austin 1970; assoc. prof. emeritus) Latin America, Spain, Western civilization

Kieswetter, James K. (PhD, Colorado, Boulder 1968; prof. emeritus) France, 19th- and 20th-century Europe, military; jkieswetter@ewu.edu

Lauritsen, Frederick M. (PhD, Minnesota 1973; prof. emeritus) ancient, Near East, Greece and Rome; flauritsen@mail.ewu.edu

Nichols, Claude W. (PhD, Oregon 1959; prof. emeritus) American West, Pacific Northwest

Seedorf, Martin F. (PhD, Washington 1974; prof. emeritus) Britain, Ireland, modern European diplomacy; mseedorf@mail.ewu.edu

Wong, H. T. (MA, UCLA 1965; prof. emeritus) East Asia

East Tennessee State University

Dept. of History, Box 70672, Johnson City, TN 37614-0672. 423.439.4222. Fax 423.439.5373. Email: burgessw@etsu.edu; woodringk@etsu.edu. Website: https://www.etsu.edu/cas/history/.

The Department of History offers a wide array of courses in the history of Asia, Africa, Europe, Latin America, and the United States designed to acquaint students with the complexities of today's multicultural "global village" and to deepen their understanding of the events, opinions, ideas, and facts they will need to make informed political, social, and personal judgments throughout their lives.

Chair: William D. Burgess Jr.
Director of Graduate Studies: Brian Maxson
Degrees Offered: BA,MA
Academic Year System: Semester
Areas of Specialization: US, modern Europe, world civilization, military
Undergraduate Tuition (per academic year):
   In-State: $4572
   Out-of-State: $13704
Graduate Tuition (per academic year):
   In-State: $5280
   Out-of-State: $12840
Enrollment 2018-19:
   Undergraduate Majors: 189
   New Graduate Students: 20
   Full-time Graduate Students: 47
   Part-time Graduate Students: 10
   Degrees in History: 35 BA, 21 MA
Undergraduate Addresses:
   Admissions: http://admissions.etsu.edu/
   Financial Aid: http://www.etsu.edu/finaid/
Graduate Addresses:
   Admissions: http://www.etsu.edu/gradstud/
   Financial Aid: http://www.etsu.edu/finaid/

Full-time Faculty

Al-Imad, Leila S. (PhD, NYU 1985; assoc. prof.) Middle East, women, religion; alimad@etsu.edu

Antkiewicz, Henry J. (PhD, Ohio State 1976; prof.) Russia and eastern Europe, Far East, Third World; antkiewh@etsu.edu

Burgess, William D. (PhD, Wisconsin, Madison 1985; prof. and chair) ancient, medieval, historiography; burgessw@etsu.edu

Carter, Daryl Anthony (PhD, Memphis 2011; asst. prof.) US, 20th-century US political; carterda@etsu.edu

Drinkard-Hawkshawe, Dorothy Lee (PhD, Catholic 1974; prof. and dir., African/African American Studies Prog.) US, Civil War and Reconstruction, African American; drinkard@etsu.edu

Fritz, Stephen G. (PhD, Illinois, Urbana-Champaign 1980; prof.) Germany, modern Europe, military; fritzs@etsu.edu

Lee, Tommy David, II (PhD, Tennessee, Knoxville 2001; asst. prof.) Tennessee; leet@etsu.edu

Maxson, Brian Jeffrey (PhD, Northwestern 2008; asst. prof. and asst. dean, Sch. of Graduate Studies) early modern Europe; maxson@etsu.edu

Mayo-Bobee, Dinah (PhD, Massachusetts Amherst 2007; asst. prof.) early America; mayobobee@etsu.edu

Nash, Steven E. (PhD, Georgia 2009; asst. prof.) 19th-century America; nashse@etsu.edu

Newcomer, Daniel (PhD, Texas Christian 2000; asst. prof.) Latin America, modern Mexico, historiography; newcomer@etsu.edu

Rankin, John M. (PhD, McMaster 2010; asst. prof.) French/British colonialism; rankinj@etsu.edu

Slap, Andrew L. (PhD, Penn State 2002; assoc. prof.) Civil War and Reconstruction, US political and social; slap@etsu.edu

Watson, Elwood D. (PhD, Maine 1999; prof.) 20th-century America, women and gender, African American; watson@etsu.edu

Nondepartmental Historians

Tedesco, Marie (PhD, Georgia State 1978; instr.; archivist, Archives of Appalachia) economic, social, women; tedescom@etsu.edu

Retired/Emeritus Faculty

Baxter, Colin F. (PhD, Georgia 1965; prof. emeritus) Britain, military, historiography; baxterc@etsu.edu

Essin, Emmett M., III (PhD, Texas Christian 1968; prof. emeritus) 20th-century America, American frontier, military; essine@etsu.edu

McKee, James W., Jr. (PhD, Mississippi State 1966; prof. emeritus) Civil War, US, US South

Odom, James L. (PhD, Georgia 1968; prof. emeritus) Latin America; odomj@etsu.edu

Page, Melvin E. (PhD, Michigan State 1977; prof. emeritus) Africa, world civilization, methodology; pagem@etsu.edu

Royalty, Dale M. (PhD, Kentucky 1971; prof. emeritus) early Republic, Jacksonian America; royalty@etsu.edu

Rushing, Allen (MA, Tennessee Tech 1965; prof. emeritus) Renaissance and Reformation, world civilization; rushinga@etsu.edu

Schmitt, Dale J. (PhD, Kansas 1970; prof. emeritus) colonial and revolutionary America; schmittd@etsu.edu

Elmhurst College

Dept. of History, 190 Prospect Ave., Elmhurst, IL 60126. 630.617.3073. Fax 630.617.3799. Email: robb@elmhurst.edu. Website: https://www.elmhurst.edu/academics/departments/history/.

Students of history at Elmhurst don't just learn who won which battles; they learn to evaluate information, research and write compellingly, and assess competing arguments. The major consists of at least seven history courses, including a senior thesis. History majors can, and should, chose courses from a wide variety of historical periods and areas.

Chair: Robert Butler
Degrees Offered: BA,BS
Academic Year System: two semesters with optional January term
Areas of Specialization: Europe, US, women, identity/memory/culture, disability and civil rights
Tuition (per academic year): $32720
Enrollment 2018-19:
  Undergraduate Majors: 80
  Degrees in History: 32 BA, 2 BS

Addresses:
  Admissions: https://www.elmhurst.edu/admission/
  Financial Aid: https://www.elmhurst.edu/admission/financial-aid/

Adjunct Faculty

Bates, Edward (PhD, Northern Illinois 2016; adj.) edward.bates@elmhurst.edu

Johnson, Andrew (MAT, Aurora; adj.) andrew.johnson@elmhurst.edu

Long, Robert L. (PhD, California, San Diego 2014; adj.) robert.long@elmhurst.edu

McCormick, Nicholas J. (PhD, Illinois, Chicago 2017; adj.) nick.mccormick@elmhurst.edu

Piorkowski, Thomas (MA, Roosevelt; adj.) thomas.piorkowski@elmhurst.edu

Reynolds, Amber Thomas (PhD, Edinburgh 2018; adj.) amber.thomas@elmhurst.edu

Soybel, Phyllis L. (PhD, Illinois, Chicago 1997; adj.) soybelp@elmhurst.edu

Steward, Journey Lynne (ABD, Northern Illinois; adj.) journey.steward@elmhurst.edu

Full-time Faculty

Benjamin, Karen A. (PhD, Wisconsin, Madison 2006; asst. prof.) 20th-century US, US race relations, urban and suburban, US South; karen.benjamin@elmhurst.edu

Butler, Robert W. (PhD, Ohio State 1989; prof. and chair) modern Britain, modern Europe, intellectual and cultural; robb@elmhurst.edu

Elon University

Dept. of History and Geography, Campus Box 2335, Elon, NC 27244. 336.278.6434. Fax 336.278.2849. Email: cirons@elon.edu. Website: https://www.elon.edu/u/academics/arts-and-sciences/history-geography/.

Our department offers majors in history and art history, as well as minors in history, geography, geographic information systems, and art history. Our faculty consists of scholar-mentors who work closely with students in the classroom, on research projects, and through internships.

Chair: Charles F. Irons
Degrees Offered: BA
Academic Year System: Semester
Areas of Specialization: US, Africa, Europe, Latin America/Caribbean, China
Tuition (per academic year): $36082
Enrollment 2018-19:
  Undergraduate Majors: 70
  Degrees in History: 20 BA
Addresses:
  Admissions: https://www.elon.edu/u/admissions/undergraduate/
  Financial Aid: https://www.elon.edu/u/admissions/undergraduate/financial-aid/

Full-time Faculty

Bin-Kasim, Waseem-Ahmed (PhD, Washington, St. Louis 2019; asst. prof.) 20th-century Africa, cities, environmental; wbinkasim@gmail.com

Bissett, James (PhD, Duke 1989; prof.) US since 1865, US social; bissett@elon.edu

Carignan, Michael Ian (PhD, Michigan State 2001; assoc. prof.) cultural and intellectual, modern Europe, Britain; mcarignan@elon.edu

Chang, Hui-hua (PhD, Indiana 2003; assoc. prof.) ancient, medicine, women; hchang@elon.edu

Clare, Rod (PhD, Duke 2001; assoc. prof.) modern US, women, Canada-US; rclare@elon.edu

Ellis, Clyde (PhD, Oklahoma State 1993; prof.) Native American, 20th-century US; ellisrc@elon.edu

Festle, Mary Jo (PhD, North Carolina, Chapel Hill 2003; prof.) 20th-century US, gender and sexuality, teaching and learning; festle@elon.edu

Gatti, Evan (PhD, North Carolina, Chapel Hill 2005; assoc. prof.) medieval Europe, religious art and ritual, museums and exhibitions; egatti@elon.edu

Irons, Charles F. (PhD, Virginia 2003; prof. and chair) 19th-century US, US South, race and religion, history and memory; cirons@elon.edu

Marshall, David J. (PhD, Kentucky 2013; asst. prof.) migration and displacement, geographies of children and youth, Middle Eastern geography; dmarshall@elon.edu

Matthews, Michael A. (PhD, Arizona 2008; assoc. prof.) modern Latin America, modern Mexico; mmatthews6@elon.edu

Ringelberg, Kirstin (PhD, North Carolina, Chapel Hill 2000; prof.) modern and contemporary art historiography, US/France/Japan, gender and sexuality; kringelberg@elon.edu

Sinn, Andrea A. (PhD, LMU, Munich 2012; asst. prof.) modern Germany, Holocaust, Jewish studies; asinn@elon.edu

Xiao, Honglin (PhD, Georgia 2003; assoc. prof.) geographic information systems, Asian geography, physical geography; hxiao@elon.edu

Joint/Cross Appointments

Felten, Peter G. (PhD, Texas, Austin 1995; prof.; asst. provost) 20th-century US, history teaching and learning; pfelten@elon.edu

Johnson, Amy M. (PhD, Duke 2008; assoc. prof.; Core Curriculum) early colonial Caribbean, slavery and resistance, pre-colonial West Africa; ajohnson60@elon.edu

Kirk, Ryan (PhD, Minnesota 2008; assoc. prof.; Environmental Studies) geographic information systems, natural resource management, Appalachian studies; rkirk2@elon.edu

Retired/Emeritus Faculty

Crowe, David M., Jr. (PhD, Georgia 1974; prof. emeritus) international criminal law, eastern Europe, East Asia; crowed@elon.edu

Digre, Brian (PhD, George Washington 1987; prof. emeritus) modern Africa, modern Middle East; digreb@elon.edu

Midgette, Nancy Smith (PhD, Georgia 1984; prof. emerita) US South, science, Civil War; midgette@elon.edu

Troxler, Carole Watterson (PhD, North Carolina, Chapel Hill 1974; prof. emerita) Britain, 18th-century Atlantic world, Loyalist studies; troxlerc@elon.edu

Troxler, George (PhD, North Carolina, Chapel Hill 1970; prof. emeritus and univ. historian) colonial and revolutionary America, US state and local; troxlerg@elon.edu

Visiting Faculty

Mehas, Shayna Rene (PhD, Arizona 2016; asst. prof.) colonial Latin America, pre-colonial and colonial Mexico and Andes, Atlantic world, gender and religion; smehas@elon.edu

Emory University

Dept. of History, 561 S. Kilgo Cir. NE, Bowden Hall, Suite 221, Atlanta, GA 30322-1120. 404.727.6555. Fax 404.727.4959. Email: history@emory.edu. Website: http://history.emory.edu/.

Since developing our graduate program more than 60 years ago, we have diversified substantially both with respect to faculty research foci and graduate and undergraduate program development. Our undergraduate major now offers concentrations both in geographic areas and in thematic areas, and our graduate program was also recently revised so as to encourage students to develop their own unique course of study.

Chair: Joseph Crespino
Director of Graduate Studies: Jason Morgan Ward
Director of Undergraduate Studies: Matthew Payne
Degrees Offered: BA,PhD
Academic Year System: Semester
Areas of Specialization: Africa and Asia, ancient/early modern/modern Europe, Jewish, Latin America, US
Undergraduate Tuition (per academic year): $53070
Graduate Tuition (per academic year): $54722
Enrollment 2018-19:
 Undergraduate Majors: 123
 New Graduate Students: 7
 Full-time Graduate Students: 51
 Degrees in History: 69 BA, 7 MA, 4 PhD
Undergraduate Addresses:
 Admissions: http://apply.emory.edu/
 Financial Aid: http://apply.emory.edu/apply/financing.php
Graduate Addresses:
 Admissions: http://www.gs.emory.edu/admissions/
 Financial Aid: http://www.gs.emory.edu/admissions/

Affiliated Faculty

Anderson, Carol (PhD, Ohio State 1995; assoc. prof.; African American Studies) human rights, racial quality; carol.anderson@emory.edu

Ashmore, Susan Youngblood (PhD, Auburn 1999; assoc. prof.; Oxford Coll.) 20th-century US South; sashmor@emory.edu

Carlson, Leonard A. (PhD, Stanford 1977; assoc. prof.; Economics) US South, US economic; econlac@emory.edu

Creekmore, Marion, Jr. (PhD, Tulane 1968; Dist. Vis. Prof.; Political Science) South Asia, public policy, nongovernmental organizations; mcreekm@emory.edu

Dudziak, Mary L. (PhD, Yale 1992; prof.; Law Sch.) US legal; mary.dudziak@emory.edu

Goodstein, Elizabeth S. (PhD, California, Berkeley 1996; assoc. prof.; Grad. Inst. Liberal Arts) French literature and culture of modernity, Germany and Austria; egoodst@emory.edu

Jackson, Lawrence (PhD, Stanford 1997; prof.; African American Studies; English) lpjacks@emory.edu

Karnes, Kevin C. (PhD, Brandeis 2001; assoc. prof.; Music) musicology, music; kkarnes@emory.edu

Klehr, Harvey (PhD, North Carolina, Chapel Hill 1971; Dobbs Prof.; Political Science) American political; hklehr@ps.emory.edu

Kushner, Howard I. (PhD, Cornell 1970; Nat C. Robertson Prof.; Grad. Inst. Liberal Arts) medicine and disease; hkushne@emory.edu

Lal, Ruby (PhD, Oxford 2000; assoc. prof.; Middle Eastern and South Asian Studies) South Asia; rlal2@emory.edu

Lipstadt, Deborah E. (PhD, Brandeis 1976; Dorot Prof.; Religion) Judaic studies, Holocaust; dlipsta@emory.edu

Margariti, Roxani Eleni (PhD, Princeton 2002; assoc. prof.; Middle Eastern Studies) Middle Eastern social and economic, maritime history and archaeology, material culture and urban studies; rmargar@emory.edu

Newby, Gordon D. (PhD, Brandeis 1966; prof.; Middle Eastern and South Asian Studies) Judeo-Islamic studies; gdnewby@emory.edu

Price, Polly (JD, Harvard 1989; prof.; Emory Law Sch.) American legal, legal methods, torts; pprice@emory.edu

Ruskola, Teemu (BA, Stanford 1990; prof.; Law Sch.) contracts and business associations, comparative law, Chinese law; teemu.ruskola@emory.edu

Scully, Pamela (PhD, Michigan 1993; prof.; Women's, Gender and Sexuality Studies and African Studies) South Africa, comparative gender and women; pamela.scully@emory.edu

Strom, Jonathan (PhD, Chicago 1996; assoc. prof.; Grad. Div. of Religion) early modern clergy; jstrom@emory.edu

Tullos, Allen E. (PhD, Yale 1985; prof.; co-dir., Emory Center for Digital Scholarship) critical regionalism, American music, US South; allen.tullos@emory.edu

Full-time Faculty

Allitt, Patrick N. (PhD, California, Berkeley 1986; Cahoon Family Prof.) 20th-century America, intellectual; pallitt@emory.edu

Amdur, Kathryn E. (PhD, Stanford 1978; assoc. prof.) modern European labor and social; kamdur@emory.edu

Andrade, Tonio A. (PhD, Yale 2001; prof.) modern China; tandrad@emory.edu

Chira, Adriana (PhD, Michigan 2016; asst. prof.) Atlantic world, Cuban race/slavery/emancipation; adriana.chira@emory.edu

Crais, Clifton C. (PhD, Johns Hopkins 1988; prof.) Africa, cross-cultural; ccrais@emory.edu

Crespino, Joseph H. (PhD, Stanford 2002; prof. and chair) modern American political, modern US South; jcrespi@emory.edu

Eckert, Astrid M. (PhD, Free Berlin 2003; assoc. prof.) modern Germany; aeckert@emory.edu

Evans-Grubbs, Judith A. (PhD, Stanford 1987; Betty Gage Holland Prof.) Roman law and family, imperial and late antique Rome; jevansg@emory.edu

Goldstein, Eric L. (PhD, Michigan 2000; assoc. prof.) 19th- and 20th-century American Jewish; egoldst@emory.edu

LaChance, Daniel (PhD, Minnesota 2011; asst. prof.) post-WWII US crime and punishment; dlachance@emory.edu

Lesser, Jeffrey (PhD, NYU 1989; Samuel Candler Dobbs Prof.) modern Latin America and Brazil, immigration, ethnicity and national identity; jlesser@emory.edu

Melton, James V. H. (PhD, Chicago 1982; prof.) early modern Europe, Germany; jmelt01@emory.edu

Miller, Judith A. (PhD, Duke 1987; assoc. prof.) 18th- and 19th-century France, French Revolution; histjam@emory.edu

Odem, Mary E. (PhD, California, Berkeley 1989; assoc. prof.) modern US, immigration/Latinos in US, women and gender; modem@emory.edu

Pandey, Gyanendra (PhD, Oxford 1975; Arts and Sciences Dist. Prof.) colonial and postcolonial, subaltern studies and South Asia, 19th- and 20th-century US; gpande2@emory.edu

Patterson, Cynthia B. (PhD, Pennsylvania 1976; prof.) ancient Greece, women in antiquity; cpatt01@emory.edu

Payne, Matthew John, III (PhD, Chicago 1995; assoc. prof. and dir., undergrad. studies) Russia and Soviet Union, Central Asia; mpayn01@emory.edu

Peterson, Dawn (PhD, NYU 2011; asst. prof.) 18th- and 19th-century North America; dawn.peterson@emory.edu

Prude, Jonathan D. (PhD, Harvard 1976; assoc. prof.) American social and labor; histjp@emory.edu

Ravina, Mark (PhD, Stanford 1991; prof.) early modern and modern Japan and East Asia; histmr@emory.edu

Rogers, Thomas D. (PhD, Duke 2005; assoc. prof.) modern Latin America, Brazilian labor and environmental; tomrogers@emory.edu

Sasson, Tehila (PhD, California, Berkeley 2015; asst. prof.) humanitarianism and capitalism in Britain and world; tehila.sasson@emory.edu

Schainker, Ellie (PhD, Pennsylvania 2010; asst. prof.; Jewish Studies) modern European Jewish, eastern Europe; ellie.schainker@emory.edu

Stein, Kenneth W. (PhD, Michigan 1976; Schatten Prof.) modern Arab world, modern Israel; kstein@emory.edu

Strocchia, Sharon T. (PhD, California, Berkeley 1981; prof.) Renaissance Italy, early modern women, early modern medicine; sstrocc@emory.edu

Vick, Brian E. (PhD, Yale 1997; prof.) 19th-century Germany; bvick@emory.edu

Ward, Jason Morgan (PhD, Yale 2008; prof. and dir., grad. studies) African American, American South; jmward4@emory.edu

Yannakakis, Yanna P. (PhD, Pennsylvania 2003; assoc. prof.) colonial Latin America, Mexico, ethnohistory; yanna.yannakakis@emory.edu

Nondepartmental Historians

Hochman, Steven H. (PhD, Virginia 1987; adj. asst. prof.; dir., Research, Carter Center) Age of Jefferson, American presidency; steven.hochman@emory.edu

Spornick, Charles D. G. (PhD, Notre Dame 1988; collection management leader; Woodruff Library) medieval; libeds@emory.edu

Wainwright, Philip (PhD, Stanford 1994; vice provost; Global Strategy) Britain; global@emory.edu

Zainaldin, Jamil S. (PhD, Chicago 1976; pres., Georgia Humanities Council) law, philanthropy; jz@georgiahumanities.org

Retired/Emeritus Faculty

Adamson, Walter Luiz (PhD, Brandeis 1976; Dobbs Prof. emeritus) European intellectual; wadamso@emory.edu

Burns, Thomas S. (PhD, Michigan 1974; Dobbs Prof. emeritus) late ancient and early medieval; histsb@emory.edu

Davis, Leroy (PhD, Kent State 1990; assoc. prof. emeritus) African American studies; ldavi04@emory.edu

Eltis, David (PhD, Rochester 1979; Woodruff Prof. emeritus) Atlantic world; deltis@emory.edu

Hyatt, Irwin T., Jr. (PhD, Harvard 1969; assoc. prof. emeritus) modern China, US-East Asian relations

Juricek, John T. (PhD, Chicago 1970; assoc. prof. emeritus) colonial America, American Indian; jjurice@emory.edu

Mann, Kristin (PhD, Stanford 1977; prof. emeritus) Africa, black Atlantic; histkm@emory.edu

Roark, James L. (PhD, Stanford 1973; Dobbs Prof. emeritus) US South, 19th-century America; jlroark@emory.edu

Silliman, Robert H. (PhD, Princeton 1967; assoc. prof. emeritus) science, intellectual; rsillim@emory.edu

Smith, Robert A. (PhD, Yale 1955; prof. emeritus) 18th-century England

Socolow, Susan M. (PhD, Columbia 1973; Dobbs Prof. emeritus) Latin America; socolow@emory.edu

Unfug, Douglas A. (PhD, Yale 1960; assoc. prof. emeritus) modern Germany; dunfug@emory.edu

White, Stephen D. (PhD, Harvard 1972; Asa G. Candler Prof. emeritus) medieval France, medieval and early modern Britain; stephen.d.white@emory.edu

Recently Awarded PhDs

Blank, Johanne "Southern Women, Feminist Health: Place, Politics, and Priorities in Five Feminist Women's Health Organizations in the Southeastern US, 1970-95"

Britt, Andrew Graham "'I'll Samba Someplace Else': Constructing Identity and Neighborhood in São Paulo, 1930s-80s"

Brown, Christopher David "Envisioning a City through Soccer in the Brazilian Amazon: Manaus, 1896-2016"

Casias, Cassandra "Bishops and Other Men's Wives in the Later Roman Empire"

Kreklau, Claudia "'Eat as the King Eats': Making the Middle Class through Food, Foodways, and Food Discourses in 19th-Century Germany"

Meert, Abigail "Suffering, Struggle, and the Politics of Legitimacy in Uganda, 1962-96"

Picone, María de los Ángeles "Landscaping Patagonia: A Spatial History of Nation-Making in the Northern Patagonian Andes, 1895-1945"

Woodard, Stefanie Marie "The Latecomers: Ethnic German Resettlers and Their Integration into West Germany, 1970-90"

Emporia State University

Dept. of Social Sciences, Box 32, 1 Kellogg Cir., Emporia, KS 66801. 620.341.5566. Fax 620.341.5143. Email: mjohns38@emporia.edu; msmith3@emporia.edu. Website: https://www.emporia.edu/socsci/.

Our department houses the disciplines of geography, history, philosophy, and political science, and the Social Sciences Secondary Education Program. Undergraduate students can pursue a variety of degrees or minors; we also offer an online master's degree in history.

Chair: Michael Smith
Director of Graduate Studies: Amanda Miracle
Degrees Offered: BA,BS,BSE,MA
Academic Year System: Semester
Areas of Specialization: America, Europe, teaching social sciences, ethnic and gender studies, war and society
Undergraduate Tuition (per academic year):
In-State: $6608
Out-of-State: $20788
Graduate Tuition (per academic year):
In-State: $8878
Out-of-State: $19918
Enrollment 2018-19:
Undergraduate Majors: 40
New Graduate Students: 10
Full-time Graduate Students: 25
Part-time Graduate Students: 10
Degrees in History: 5 BA, 5 BS, 5 MA
Online-Only Courses: 50%
Undergraduate Addresses:
Admissions: http://www.emporia.edu/admissions/
Financial Aid: http://www.emporia.edu/finaid/
Graduate Addresses:
Admissions: http://www.emporia.edu/grad/
Financial Aid: https://www.emporia.edu/grad/financial/

Full-time Faculty

Johnson, Maire N. (PhD, Toronto 2010; asst. prof.) Celtic Ireland, world to 1550

Lovett, Christopher C. (PhD, Kansas State 1989; prof.) Russia and Soviet Union, Germany, military; clovett@emporia.edu

Miracle, Amanda Lea (PhD, Bowling Green State 2008; assoc. prof. and dir., grad. studies) early America, women; amiracle@emporia.edu

Schneider, Gregory L. (PhD, Illinois, Chicago 1996; prof.) 20th-century US, diplomatic, political; gschneid@emporia.edu

Retired/Emeritus Faculty

Dicks, Samuel E. (PhD, Oklahoma 1966; prof. emeritus) medieval, ancient, historiography; dickssam@emporia.edu

O'Brien, Patrick G. (PhD, Wayne State 1968; prof. emeritus) recent US, reform movements, archival

Pennington, Loren E. (PhD, Michigan 1962; prof. emeritus) colonial America, England, archives management

Smith, Karen Manners (PhD, Massachusetts 1990; prof. emeritus) US women, 19th-century US, immigration; ksmith@emporia.edu

Thierer, Joyce M. (PhD, Kansas State 1994; prof. emeritus) public, agricultural, women; jthierer@emporia.edu

Torrey, Glenn E. (PhD, Oregon 1960; prof. emeritus) eastern and central Europe, modern Germany, World War I

University of Evansville

Dept. of History, 1800 Lincoln Ave., Olmsted Hall, Rm. 345, Evansville, IN 47722. 812.488.2963. Fax 812.488.2430. Email: km283@evansville.edu; jm224@evansville.edu. Website: https://www.evansville.edu/majors/history/.

The Department of History at the University of Evansville nurtures high academic standards. Faculty deliver a rigorous, challenging education balanced with one-on-one support and mentoring from faculty.

Chair: James MacLeod
Degrees Offered: BA
Academic Year System: Semester
Areas of Specialization: early and modern America, US foreign policy, medieval and modern Britain and Europe, ancient Rome and Greece, gender
Tuition (per academic year): $35300
Enrollment 2018-19:
Undergraduate Majors: 21
Degrees in History: 12 BA
Addresses:
Admissions: http://www.evansville.edu/admission/
Financial Aid: http://www.evansville.edu/tuitionandaid/

Full-time Faculty

Byrne, Daniel (PhD, Georgetown 2003; assoc. prof.) US since 1850, foreign policy; db89@evansville.edu

Gahan, Daniel (PhD, Kansas 1985; prof.) US to 1850, Europe 1700-1850, Ireland; dg23@evansville.edu

MacLeod, James L. (PhD, Edinburgh 1993; prof. and chair) modern Britain, Europe; jm224@evansville.edu

Parks, Annette (PhD, Emory 2000; prof.) medieval, England, gender and women's studies; ap3@evansville.edu

Nondepartmental Historians

Kaiser, Alan (PhD, Boston Univ.; assoc. prof.; Archaeology) Roman archaeology; ak58@evansville.edu

Thomas, Patrick M. (PhD, North Carolina, Chapel Hill; assoc. prof.; Archaeology) Greek Bronze Age and Early Iron Age ceramics; pt4@evansville.edu

Visiting Faculty

Murphy, Kevin A. (PhD, SUNY, Binghamton 2015; vis. asst. prof.) US, women/gender/sexuality, race and Latin America; km421@evansville.edu

Fairfield University

Dept. of History, 1073 N. Benson Rd., Fairfield, CT 06824-5195. 203.254.4000. Fax 203.254.5513. Email: pbehre@fairfield.edu. Website: https://www.fairfield.edu/undergraduate/academics/schools-and-colleges/.

The Department of History at Fairfield University is dedicated to teaching its students to understand today's world through the study of the past. We examine and record the daily lives, conflicts, cultures, relationships, work, beliefs, and morals of people throughout time.

Chair: Patricia Behre
Degrees Offered: BA
Academic Year System: Semester
Areas of Specialization: US, Europe, Russia, East and South Asia, Islamic world
Tuition (per academic year): $49080
Enrollment 2018-19:
Undergraduate Majors: 26
Degrees in History: 10 BA
Students in Undergraduate Intro Courses: 676
Addresses:
Admissions: http://www.fairfield.edu/undergraduate/visit-and-apply/
Financial Aid: http://www.fairfield.edu/undergraduate/financial-aid-and-tuition/

Adjunct Faculty

Palmer, Louise Y. (PhD, Yale 1998; asst. prof.) science, medicine; lpalmer1@fairfield.edu
Rutter, Nick (PhD, Yale 2013; asst. prof.) Cold War, modern Germany, modern Russia; nrutter@fairfield.edu

Full-time Faculty

Abbott, William M. (PhD, Oxford 1982; assoc. prof.) Britain, Tudor-Stuart England, British Empire; wmabbott@fairfield.edu
Adair, Jennifer (PhD, NYU 2013; asst. prof.) Latin America; jadair@fairfield.edu
Behre, Patricia E. (PhD, Yale 1991; assoc. prof. and chair) early modern Europe, France, Jewish-Christian relations; pbehre@fairfield.edu
Bucki, Cecelia (PhD, Pittsburgh 1991; prof.) US social and labor, 20th-century US, New Deal; cbucki@fairfield.edu
Greenwald, Richard A. (PhD, NYU 1998; prof. and dean; Coll. of Arts & Sciences) American economic/political/labor/urban; rgreenwald@fairfield.edu
Hohl, Elizabeth (PhD, Union Inst. 2010; asst. prof. of the practice) 19th-century US, women, African American; ehohl@fairfield.edu
King, Shannon (PhD, SUNY, Binghamton 2006; assoc. prof.) African American, urban, 20th century
Lawrence, Anna M. (PhD, Michigan 2004; assoc. prof.) colonial and revolutionary America, religious, women and gender; alawrence3@fairfield.edu

Li, Danke (PhD, Michigan 1999; prof.) modern China and Japan, East Asia, women in China; dli@fairfield.edu
Marsans-Sakly, Silvia (PhD, NYU 2010; asst. prof.) Islamic world, Middle East; smarsans-sakly@fairfield.edu
McFadden, David W. (PhD, California, Berkeley 1990; prof.) US foreign relations, Russia and former Soviet Union, 20th-century US; dmcfadden@fairfield.edu
Purushotham, Sunil (PhD, Cambridge 2013; asst. prof.) South Asia, decolonization, modern imperialism; spurushotham@fairfield.edu
Rosenfeld, Gavriel D. (PhD, UCLA 1996; prof.) modern Germany, collective memory, 20th-century Europe; grosenfeld@fairfield.edu
Ruffini, Giovanni R. (PhD, Columbia 2005; prof.) Roman late antiquity, Greco-Roman Egypt, Christian Nubia; gruffini@fairfield.edu

University of Florida

Dept. of History, PO Box 117320, 025 Keene-Flint Hall, Gainesville, FL 32611-7320. 352.392.0271. Fax 352.392.6927. Email: edale@ufl.edu. Website: https://history.ufl.edu/.

History at UF starts with a creative and dynamic faculty, a community scholars engaged in a broad range of scholarship and teaching. Our faculty's work reaches audiences in nearly every corner of the globe-and right here in Gainesville, Florida.

Chair: Elizabeth Dale
Director of Graduate Studies: Michelle Campos
Degrees Offered: BA,MA,PhD
Academic Year System: Semester
Areas of Specialization: US, Latin America, Europe, Africa
Undergraduate Tuition (per academic year):
In-State: $5010
Out-of-State: $22832
Graduate Tuition (per academic year):
In-State: $9482
Out-of-State: $22526
Enrollment 2018-19:
Undergraduate Majors: 350
New Graduate Students: 10
Full-time Graduate Students: 75
Part-time Graduate Students: 26
Degrees in History: 135 BA, 6 MA, 14 PhD
Undergraduate Addresses:
Admissions: http://www.admissions.ufl.edu/
Financial Aid: http://www.sfa.ufl.edu/
Graduate Addresses:
Admissions: http://history.ufl.edu/graduate-studies/prospective-students/
Financial Aid: http://history.ufl.edu/graduate-studies/prospective-students/financial-issues/

Adjunct Faculty

Tegeder, David (PhD, Florida 1997; asst. prof.) US, 20th century, US South; dtegeder@ufl.edu

Full-time Faculty

Adams, Sean Patrick (PhD, Wisconsin, Madison 1999; prof.) 19th-century US, industrialization, energy; spadams@ufl.edu
Adler, Jeffrey S. (PhD, Harvard 1986; prof.; Criminology) US urban, crime; jadler@ufl.edu

Campos, Michelle U. (PhD, Stanford 2003; assoc. prof. and grad. coord.) modern Middle East; mcampos@ufl.edu

Caputo, Nina (PhD, California, Berkeley 1999; assoc. prof.) medieval Jewish, religion; ncaputo@ufl.edu

Curta, Florin (PhD, Western Michigan 1998; prof.) medieval, Mediterranean; fcurta@ufl.edu

Dale, Elizabeth (PhD, Chicago 1995; prof. and chair) US legal, constitutional; edale@ufl.edu

Davis, Jack E. (PhD, Brandeis 1994; prof.) Florida, US South, environmental; davisjac@ufl.edu

Effros, Bonnie (PhD, UCLA 1994; prof.; dir., Center for Humanities and Public Sphere) medieval Europe; beffros@ufl.edu

Esenwein, George R. (PhD, London 1987; assoc. prof.) modern Spain, political, Spanish Civil War; gesenwei@ufl.edu

Finkel, Stuart D. (PhD, Stanford 2001; assoc. prof.) modern Russia, Europe; sfinkel@ufl.edu

Freifeld, Alice (PhD, California, Berkeley 1992; assoc. prof.) Hungary, eastern Europe; freifeld@ufl.edu

Gallman, J. Matthew (PhD, Brandeis 1986; prof.) 19th-century US, Civil War, gender; gallmanm@ufl.edu

Geggus, David P. (PhD, York, UK 1979; prof.) Caribbean, slavery; dgeggus@ufl.edu

Guerra, Lillian (PhD, Wisconsin, Madison 2000; assoc. prof.) 19th- and 20th-century Caribbean, nationalisms, Cuban Revolution; lillian.guerra@ufl.edu

Harland-Jacobs, Jessica L. (PhD, Duke 2000; assoc. prof.) British Empire; harlandj@ufl.edu

Hart, Mitchell (PhD, UCLA 1994; prof.) European and American Jewish; hartm@ufl.edu

Jacobs, Matthew F. (PhD, North Carolina, Chapel Hill 2002; assoc. prof.) US foreign relations, world, Middle East; mjacobs@ufl.edu

Kroen, Sheryl T. (PhD, California, Berkeley 1992; assoc. prof.) France, modern Europe; stkroen@ufl.edu

Kwolek-Folland, Angel (PhD, Minnesota 1987; prof. and assoc. provost) US women, business; akf@aa.ufl.edu

Link, William A. (PhD, Virginia 1981; Milbauer Prof.) US South; linkwa@ufl.edu

Needell, Jeffrey D. (PhD, Stanford 1982; prof.) modern Latin America, Brazil; jneedell@ufl.edu

Newman, Louise M. (PhD, Brown 1992; assoc. prof.) US, gender, cultural; lnewman@ufl.edu

Noll, Steven G. (PhD, Florida 1991; sr. lect.) US social, institutional; nolls@ufl.edu

Ortiz, Paul A. (PhD, Duke 2000; assoc. prof.; dir., Samuel Proctor Oral Hist. Prog.) oral; portiz@ufl.edu

Pearlman, Lauren (PhD, Yale 2013; asst. prof.; African American Studies) African American, post-World War II America; lpearlman@ufl.edu

Sensbach, Jon F. (PhD, Duke 1992; prof.) colonial America, religion; jsensbach@ufl.edu

Spillane, Joseph F. (PhD, Carnegie Mellon 1994; assoc. prof. and assoc. dean; Student Affairs) legal; spillane@ufl.edu

Vrana, Heather A. (PhD, Indiana 2013; asst. prof.) modern Latin America; hvrana@ufl.edu

White, Luise S. (PhD, Cambridge 1986; prof.) East Africa, historiography, oral; lswhite@ufl.edu

Wise, Benjamin E. (PhD, Rice 2008; asst. prof.) modern US, South, cultural; benwise@ufl.edu

Joint/Cross Appointments

Goda, Norman J. W. (PhD, North Carolina, Chapel Hill 1991; Norman and Irma Braman Chair; Center for Jewish Studies) Holocaust studies; goda@ufl.edu

O'Brien, Susan Marie (PhD, Wisconsin-Madison 2000; assoc. prof.; African Studies) Africa, women's studies, religion; smobrien@ufl.edu

Smocovitis, Vassiliki B. (PhD, Cornell 1988; assoc. prof.; Zoology) science, 20th-century US; bsmocovi@ufl.edu

Nondepartmental Historians

Cusick, James (PhD, Florida 1993; curator; P.K. Yonge Library of Florida History) colonial Florida; jgcusick@ufl.edu

Hackett, David G. (PhD, Emory 1987; assoc. prof.; Religion) US religious; dhackett@ufl.edu

Leedy, Todd H. (PhD, Florida 2000; lect.; assoc. dir., Center for African Studies) contemporary Africa; tleedy@ufl.edu

Terzian, Sevan (PhD, Indiana 2000; assoc. prof.; Education) US education; sterzian@coe.ufl.edu

Travis, Trysh (PhD, Yale 1998; assoc. prof.; Center for Women's Studies) US cultural, women; ttravis@ufl.edu

Retired/Emeritus Faculty

Altman, Ida (PhD, Johns Hopkins 1981; prof. emeritus) colonial Latin America, Caribbean, Mexico; ialtman@ufl.edu

Bergmann, Peter E. (PhD, California, Berkeley 1983; sr. lect. emeritus) Germany, modern European intellectual; bergmann@ufl.edu

Chalmers, David (PhD, Rochester 1955; Dist. Service Prof. emeritus) US intellectual, social movements; chi@ufl.edu

Colburn, David R. (PhD, North Carolina, Chapel Hill 1971; prof. emeritus; dir., Askew Inst.) 20th-century US, race relations, political; colburn@ufl.edu

Davis, R. Hunt, Jr. (PhD, Wisconsin, Madison 1969; prof. emeritus) Africa, southern Africa; hdavis@ufl.edu

Giles, Geoffrey J. (PhD, Cambridge 1975; assoc. prof. emeritus) Germany, higher education, alcohol; ggiles@ufl.edu

Gregory, Frederick (PhD, Harvard 1973; prof. emeritus) science, Germany; fgregory@ufl.edu

Hatch, Robert A. (PhD, Wisconsin, Madison 1978; assoc. prof. emeritus) science, 16th-century France; ufhatch@ufl.edu

Macleod, Murdo J. (PhD, Florida 1962; prof. emeritus) colonial Mexico; macleodmurd@hotmail.com

McKnight, Stephen A. (PhD, Emory 1972; prof. emeritus) European cultural and intellectual; smcknigh@ufl.edu

Pleasants, Julian Mciver (PhD, North Carolina, Chapel Hill 1971; prof. emeritus) 20th-century US; jpleasan@history.ufl.edu

Sommerville, C. John (PhD, Iowa 1970; prof. emeritus) Tudor-Stuart England; jsommerv@ufl.edu

Thurner, Mark W. (PhD, Wisconsin, Madison 1993; prof. emeritus) modern Latin America, Peru, anthropology; mthurner@ufl.edu

Turner, Eldon R. (PhD, Kansas 1973; prof. emeritus) colonial America, cultural and intellectual; eturner@ufl.edu

Recently Awarded PhDs

Aubert, Aurelia M. "Empires of Liberty: Achille Murat, a Napoleonic Prince in the American South"

deNoyelles, Adrienne "The Lung Block: Tuberculosis and Contested Spaces in Progressive-Era New York"

Donaldson, Anthony J. "Waiting Is Not an Option: The Quest for Black Political Power in North Carolina, 1963-81"

Foreman, Nicholas "The Calorie of Progress: Food and Culture in the Lower Mississippi Valley, 1760-1860"

Kozik, Bryan D. "Building a Cosmopolitan Episcopacy in Reformations Central Europe: Johannes Dantiscus's Pursuit of Reform across Latin Christendom, 1518-48"

Mellis, Johanna "Negotiation through Sport: Navigating Everyday Life in Communist Hungary, 1948-89"

Simmons, Matthew F. "Revolt in the Fields: Building the Southern Tenant Farmers' Union in the Old Southwest"

Tepperman, Alexander "Strange Bedfellows: Convict Culture in the First Era of Mass Imprisonment, 1919-40"

Florida Atlantic University

Dept. of History, 777 Glades Rd., Boca Raton, FL 33431-0991. 561.297.3840. Fax 561.297.2704. Email: bplowe@fau.edu. Website: http://www.fau.edu/artsandletters/history/.

The Department of History includes highly recognized authors of scholarly books, essays and articles in American, European, Asian and Latin American history. Several faculty members have received teaching awards, and maintain a record of admirable service to the community and the profession.

Chair: Benno P. Lowe
Director of Graduate Studies: Douglas Kanter
Director of Undergraduate Studies: Eric Hanne
Degrees Offered: BA,MA,Cert.
Academic Year System: Semester
Areas of Specialization: 19th- and 20th-century US, modern Europe, Florida, Latin America
Undergraduate Tuition (per academic year):
  In-State: $4848
  Out-of-State: $17280
Graduate Tuition (per academic year):
  In-State: $6660
  Out-of-State: $18450
Enrollment 2018-19:
  Undergraduate Majors: 176
  New Graduate Students: 10
  Full-time Graduate Students: 11
  Part-time Graduate Students: 18
  Degrees in History: 46 BA, 9 MA
Undergraduate Addresses:
  Admissions: http://fau.edu/admissions/
  Financial Aid: http://fau.edu/finaid/
Graduate Addresses:
  Admissions: http://www.fau.edu/graduate/
  Financial Aid: http://fau.edu/finaid/

Adjunct Faculty

Dunne, Brian Thomas (PhD, Florida Atlantic 2011; adj.) 18th- and 19th-century US, intellectual; bdunne1@fau.edu
Jones, Daniel A. (MA, Florida Atlantic 2015; JD, Alabama 2003; adj.) US constitutional, early Republic US; djones89@fau.edu
Krzeminski, Stephen (MA, Florida Atlantic 2019; adj.) world civilization, modern Europe; skrzeminski2013@fau.edu
McGeary, Stephen (MA, West Chester 2016; adj.) African American, historical writing; smcgeary2018@fau.edu
Perrott, Claire (MA, Arizona 2016; adj.) Latin America, cultural and environmental
Rosenkranz, Susan A. (PhD, Florida International 2013; adj.) world civilization, 19th-century Europe; srosenk@fau.edu

Affiliated Faculty

Pratt, Edward E. (PhD, Virginia 1990; prof. and dean; Undergrad. Studies) Japan; epratt2@fau.edu

Full-time Faculty

Bennett, Evan P. (PhD, William and Mary 2005; assoc. prof.) US, Florida, American South; ebennett@fau.edu
Breslow, Boyd (PhD, Ohio State 1968; assoc. prof.) Greece and Rome, medieval, England; breslow@fau.edu
Dalin, Miriam R. (PhD, Columbia 1994; prof.) American Jewish, Zionism, Sephardic studies; msanua@fau.edu

Dunlea, Claudia (PhD, Hamburg, Germany 2003; sr. instr.) modern Europe; cdunlea@fau.edu
Ely, Christopher David (PhD, Brown 1997; assoc. prof.; Harriet L. Wilkes Honors Coll.) modern Russia, European cultural; cely@fau.edu
Engle, Stephen D. (PhD, Florida State 1989; prof.) 19th-century America, Civil War and Reconstruction, US South; engle@fau.edu
Finucane, Adrian (PhD, Harvard 2010; asst. prof.) Atlantic world, early America, law/religion/society; afinucane@fau.edu
Ganson, Barbara A. (PhD, Texas, Austin 1994; prof.) Latin America, aviation; bganson@fau.edu
Hanne, Eric J. (PhD, Michigan 1998; assoc. prof. and dir., undergrad. studies) Islamic, numismatics; ehanne@fau.edu
Holloway, Kenneth William (PhD, Pennsylvania 2002; assoc. prof.) China, Japan; khollow4@fau.edu
Kanter, Douglas (PhD, Chicago 2006; assoc. prof. and dir., grad. studies) modern Britain, Ireland; dkanter1@fau.edu
Kollander, Patricia A. (PhD, Brown 1992; prof.) modern Germany, Russia, European diplomatic; kollande@fau.edu
Lowe, Ben (PhD, Georgetown 1990; prof. and chair) early modern Europe, Tudor-Stuart England, intellectual; bplowe@fau.edu
McGetchin, Douglas T. (PhD, California, San Diego 2002; assoc. prof.) world, modern Germany; dmcgetch@fau.edu
Mitton, Steven Heath (PhD, Louisiana State 2005; instr.) 19th-century US, world, economic; smitton@fau.edu
Norman, Sandra L. (PhD, Brown 1988; assoc. prof.) public, material culture, environmental; norman@fau.edu
Rose, Mark H. (PhD, Ohio State 1973; prof.) 20th-century US, urban, business and public policy; mrose@fau.edu
Shannon, Kelly J. (PhD, Temple 2010; asst. prof.) 20th-century US, US foreign relations, international; shannonk@fau.edu
Sharples, Jason T. (PhD, Princeton 2010; asst. prof.) colonial America, early Republic, Atlantic slavery; jsharples@fau.edu
Strain, Christopher B. (PhD, California, Berkeley 2000; prof.; Harriet L. Wilkes Honors Coll.) American studies, African American, ethnic studies; cstrain@fau.edu

Retired/Emeritus Faculty

Derfler, Leslie (PhD, Columbia 1962; prof. emeritus) France, socialism, 20th-century Europe; derflerl@fau.edu
Kersey, Harry A., Jr. (PhD, Illinois, Urbana-Champaign 1965; prof. emeritus) US, American Indian, Florida; kersey@fau.edu

Visiting Faculty

Davis, Christopher Anderson (PhD, Florida International 2018; vis. instr.) Caribbean, African American, Africa diaspora, race and identity; christopherdavis@fau.edu

Florida Gulf Coast University

Dept. of Social Sciences, 10501 FGCU Blvd. S., Merwin Hall, Fort Myers, FL 33965-6565. 239.590.7417. Fax 239.590.7445. Email: dwoncheck@fgcu.edu. Website: https://www.fgcu.edu/cas/departments/socialsciences/historyba/.

To change the future, one must understand the past. A degree in history helps us to understand how people and societies behave and their motivations for their actions. From this fundamental basis, we can understand change and how the society came to be. It also sparks a moral understanding of a society's motivations, which is essential for good citizenship.

Chair: Alison Elgart
Director of Graduate Studies: Elizabeth Bouldin
Director of Undergraduate Studies: Melodie Eichbauer

Degrees Offered: BA,MA
Academic Year System: Semester
Areas of Specialization: US, Latin America and Caribbean, medieval and modern Europe, world, public
Undergraduate Tuition (per academic year):
  In-State: $4900
  Out-of-State: $20130
Graduate Tuition (per academic year):
  In-State: $6725
  Out-of-State: $23415
Enrollment 2018-19:
  Degrees in History: 110 BA
Undergraduate Addresses:
  Admissions: https://www2.fgcu.edu/admissions.asp
  Financial Aid: https://www2.fgcu.edu/FinancialAid/Undergraduate/
Graduate Addresses:
  Admissions: https://www2.fgcu.edu/graduate/
  Financial Aid: https://www2.fgcu.edu/FinancialAid/Graduate/

Full-time Faculty

Bartrop, Paul (PhD, Monash, Australia 1989; prof.; dir., Center for Judaic, Holocaust & Genocide Studies) Holocaust, genocide studies, modern Jewish; pbartrop@fgcu.edu

Bouldin, Elizabeth (PhD, Emory 2012; asst. prof. and grad. prog. leader) early modern Britain, British Atlantic world, women and religion; ebouldin@fgcu.edu

Carlson, Erik D. (PhD, Texas Tech 1996; assoc. prof.) public, 20th-century America, US military; ecarlson@fgcu.edu

Cole, Michael S. (PhD, Florida 2003; asst. prof.) colonial Latin America, conquest of Mexico, witchcraft; mcole@fgcu.edu

Davey, Frances E. (PhD, Delaware 2011; asst. prof.) US social and cultural, women and gender; fdavey@fgcu.edu

Eichbauer, Melodie Harris (PhD, Catholic 2010; assoc. prof. and undergrad. prog. leader) medieval Europe, legal and ecclesiastical, medieval religious culture; meichbauer@fgcu.edu

Epple, Michael J. (PhD, Akron 2001; asst. prof.) early America, US foreign relations, Cold War; mepple@fgcu.edu

Fortney, Jeffrey (PhD, Oklahoma 2014; asst. prof.) antebellum US South, Native American, African American; jfortney@fgcu.edu

Rohrer, Scott R. (PhD, Northwestern 2006; instr.) post-1945 US, modern East Asia, comparative military occupations; srohrer@fgcu.edu

Steineker, Rowan (PhD, Oklahoma 2016; asst. prof.) American West, digital humanities, modern Florida; rsteineker@fgcu.edu

Strahorn, Eric A. (PhD, Iowa 1997; assoc. prof.) colonial and postcolonial India, modern and imperial Britain, environmental; estraho@fgcu.edu

Straussberger, John Fredrick, III (PhD, Columbia 2015; asst. prof.) Africa, migration, decolonization; jstraussberger@fgcu.edu

Florida International University

Dept. of History, 11200 SW 8th St., DM 397, Miami, FL 33199. 305.348.2328. Fax 305.348.3561. Email: uribev@fiu.edu. Website: https://history.fiu.edu/.

FIU is a public research university located in Miami, Florida. The History Department is part of the Steven J. Green School of International and Public Affairs, an independent unit.

Chair: Victor M. Uribe-Uran
Director of Graduate Studies: Okezi Otovo
Director of Undergraduate Studies: Tovah Bender
Degrees Offered: BA,MA,PhD

Academic Year System: Semester
Areas of Specialization: Atlantic, Latin America, US, Europe
Undergraduate Tuition (per academic year):
  In-State: $7330
  Out-of-State: $22209
Graduate Tuition (per academic year):
  In-State: $15552
  Out-of-State: $33696
Enrollment 2018-19:
  Undergraduate Majors: 194
  New Graduate Students: 18
  Full-time Graduate Students: 38
  Part-time Graduate Students: 19
  Degrees in History: 57 BA, 5 MA, 5 PhD
Undergraduate Addresses:
  Admissions: https://www.fiu.edu/admissions/
  Financial Aid: https://www.fiu.edu/admissions/costs-and-aid/
Graduate Addresses:
  Admissions: http://gradschool.fiu.edu/admissions/
  Financial Aid: http://gradschool.fiu.edu/students/funding/

Adjunct Faculty

Holbrook, Joseph W. (PhD, Florida International 2013; adj.) modern Latin America, religion, social movements; jholbroo@fiu.edu

Luca, Francis X. (PhD, Florida International 2004; adj.) Latin America, US, colonial; lucaf@fiu.edu

Messersmith, Eric T. (PhD, Miami 2002; adj.) Asia/Japan/China, US-Japan relations, culture/economy/politics; messerse@fiu.edu

Sordo, Emma M. (PhD, Miami 2000; adj.) Latin America; sordoe@fiu.edu

Affiliated Faculty

Bidegain, Ana Maria (PhD, Catholic, Louvain 1979; prof.; Religious Studies) Latin America, Colombian studies, Christianity; bidegain@fiu.edu

Heine, Steven (PhD, Temple 1980; prof.; Religious Studies) Japanese intellectual, medieval Japan, Buddhism; heines@fiu.edu

Revell, Keith D. (PhD, Virginia 1994; assoc. prof.; Public Administration) modern America, urban, public policy; revellk@fiu.edu

Full-time Faculty

Abi-Hamad, Saad G. (PhD, Texas, Austin 2007; instr.) modern Middle East and Egypt, British colonialism, social thought; sabihama@fiu.edu

Adler, Jessica L. (PhD, Columbia 2013; asst. prof.) modern America, health care, military; adlerj@fiu.edu

Bender, Tovah L. (PhD, Minnesota 2009; instr. and dir., undergrad. studies) premodern Europe, Italy; tbender@fiu.edu

Bustamante, Michael (PhD, Yale 2016; asst. prof.) modern Cuba, US Latinos and memory, migration and revolution; Michael.Bustamante@fiu.edu

Capo, Julio C., Jr. (PhD, Florida International 2011; assoc. prof.; Wolfsonian Public Humanities Laboratory) America, transnational, gender, queer, migration, Latin America; Julio.capo@fiu.edu

Cornelius, Alexandra (PhD, Washington, St. Louis 2006; instr.) race/science/gender studies, US and Third World political movements; acdiallo@fiu.edu

Davies, Gwyn (PhD, Univ. Coll. London 2001; assoc. prof.) ancient, Rome, military; daviesg@fiu.edu

Friedman, Rebecca (PhD, Michigan 2000; assoc. prof.) Russia and Soviet Union, eastern Europe, women; friedmar@fiu.edu

Gibbs, Jenna M. (PhD, UCLA 2008; assoc. prof.) early US, Europe, Atlantic; jgibbs@fiu.edu

Johnson, Sherry (PhD, Florida 1995; prof.) Latin America, Cuba, environmental and social; johnsons@fiu.edu

Lipartito, Kenneth J. (PhD, Johns Hopkins 1986; prof.) American economic, business, 20th-century US; lipark@fiu.edu

Marshall, Amy Bliss (PhD, Brown 2013; asst. prof.) 20th-century Asia and Japan, social/cultural/media, gender and rural studies; ammarsha@fiu.edu

Mas, Catherine (PhD, Yale 2019; asst. prof.) America, medicine, science, ethnic relations, anthropology, comparative; catherine. mas@fiu.edu

Morcillo, Aurora G. (PhD, New Mexico 1995; prof.) modern Spain, women, sexuality and right-wing politics; morcillo@fiu.edu

Otovo, Okezi T. (PhD, Georgetown 2009; assoc. prof. and dir., grad. studies) Brazil, Latin America; okezi.otovo@fiu.edu

Peterson, Terrence Gordon (PhD, Wisconsin-Madison 2015; asst. prof.) modern Europe and France, colonialism, Algeria; Terrence. Peterson@fiu.edu

Premo, Bianca (PhD, North Carolina, Chapel Hill 2001; prof.) colonial Latin America, family and childhood, Andean region; premob@fiu.edu

Rowan, Jeremy D. (PhD, Louisiana State 2003; sr. lect.) modern western Europe, Britain, business; rowanj@fiu.edu

Royles, Dan (PhD, Temple 2014; asst. prof.) modern America, African American, social movements; droyles@fiu.edu

Terry-Roisin, Elizabeth Ashcroft (PhD, California, Berkeley 2015; asst. prof.) Europe, Spain, Italy, early modern, religion, ethni relations; elizabeth.terry@fiu.edu

Uribe-Uran, Victor M. (PhD, Pittsburgh 1993; prof. and chair) Colombia/Mexico/Latin America, social and legal; uribev@fiu. edu

Verna, Chantalle F. (PhD, Michigan State 2005; assoc. prof.) modern America, US foreign policy, Caribbean; verna@fiu.edu

Wood, Kirsten E. (PhD, Pennsylvania 1998; assoc. prof.) early America, American South, women; woodk@fiu.edu

Nondepartmental Historians

Breslin, Thomas Aloysius (PhD, Virginia 1972; prof.; Politics and International Relations) Chinese diplomatic, US diplomatic; breslint@fiu.edu

Retired/Emeritus Faculty

Cook, Noble David (PhD, Texas, Austin 1973; prof. emeritus) colonial Spanish America, early modern Spain, ethnohistory; cookn@fiu.edu

Kahan, Alan (PhD, Chicago 1987; prof. emeritus) modern Europe, intellectual, political; kahana@fiu.edu

Kaminsky, Howard M. (PhD, Chicago 1952; prof. emeritus) medieval; kaminsky@fiu.edu

Peterson, Joyce S. (PhD, Wisconsin, Madison 1976; assoc. prof. emeritus) labor, US social, women; petersoj@fiu.edu

Pyron, Darden A. (PhD, Virginia 1975; prof. emeritus) Civil War and Reconstruction, American cultural and intellectual; pyrond@fiu. edu

Rock, Howard B. (PhD, NYU 1974; prof. emeritus) colonial America, American Revolution, American West; rockh@fiu.edu

Szuchman, Mark D. (PhD, Texas, Austin 1976; prof. emeritus) Latin America and Argentina, urban and social, politics and family; mark.szuchman@gmail.com

Recently Awarded PhDs

Alzate, Adrian "Traitors and Citizens: Rebellion, Political Crimes, and the Law in Colombia and Mexico, 1870s-1910s"

Davis, Christopher Anderson "Problems with Race Crossing: How Atlantic Intellectuals Attempt to Construct Race and Identity in the 20th-Century British West Indies"

Pelegrin Taboada, Ricardo "For Liberty and Fatherland: Cuban Lawyers, Society, and Political Culture, 1860s-1930s"

Perdue, Doyle "Mexicanization of the Compañia Minera de Cananea, 1971-1990: A Cultural History"

Silva, Rene "Pennsylvania's Loyalists and Disaffected in the Age of Revolution: Defining the Terrain of Reintegration, 1765-1800"

Florida State University

Dept. of History, 401 Bellamy Bldg., 113 Collegiate Loop, Tallahassee, FL 32306-2200. 850.644.5888. Fax 850.644.6402. Email: methompson@fsu.edu; jnetter@fsu.edu. Website: https://history.fsu.edu/.

The Department of History at Florida State University is among the very best history departments in the southeastern United States, with a lengthy tradition of scholarly excellence and academic achievement.

Chair: Edward G. Gray
Director of Graduate Studies: Suzanne M. Sinke
Director of Undergraduate Studies: Claudia Liebeskind
Degrees Offered: BA,BS,MA,MS,PhD
Academic Year System: Semester
Areas of Specialization: US, modern Europe, Latin America/ Middle East/Asia/Atlantic world, public/STEM, war and society
Undergraduate Tuition (per academic year):
  In-State: $2522
  Out-of-State: $14077
Graduate Tuition (per academic year):
  In-State: $7263
  Out-of-State: $18087
Enrollment 2018-19:
  Undergraduate Majors: 361
  New Graduate Students: 17
  Full-time Graduate Students: 48
  Part-time Graduate Students: 37
  Degrees in History: 13 MA, 1 MS, 10 PhD
Undergraduate Addresses:
  Admissions: http://admissions.fsu.edu/
  Financial Aid: http://financialaid.fsu.edu/
Graduate Addresses:
  Admissions: http://admissions.fsu.edu/graduate/
  Financial Aid: http://www.gradstudies.fsu.edu//Funding-Awards

Full-time Faculty

Blaufarb, Rafe (PhD, Michigan 1996; prof.) revolutionary/ Napoleonic France, military, legal; rblaufarb@fsu.edu

Creswell, Michael H. (PhD, Chicago 1997; assoc. prof.) contemporary Europe/modern France, Cold War, military; mcreswell@fsu.edu

Culver, Annika A. (PhD, Chicago 2007; assoc. prof.) East Asia, modern Japanese intellectual; aculver@fsu.edu

Dodds, Ben (PhD, Durham 2002; assoc. prof.) medieval Europe, peasants and rural society, modern Spain; bdodds@fsu.edu

Doel, Ronald E. (PhD, Princeton 1990; assoc. prof.) science and technology, environmental, Arctic; rdoel@fsu.edu

Frank, Andrew K. (PhD, Florida 1998; prof.) Native American, US South/Florida, early America; afrank@fsu.edu

Gellately, Robert J. (PhD, London 1974; prof.) modern Germany, modern Russia, Holocaust; rgellately@fsu.edu

Grant, Jonathan A. (PhD, Wisconsin-Madison 1995; prof.) Russia, Central Asia; jgrant@fsu.edu

Gray, Edward G. (PhD, Brown 1996; prof. and chair) colonial America, Native American; egray@fsu.edu

Hanley, Will (PhD, Princeton 2007; assoc. prof.) Middle East, empire, legal; whanley@fsu.edu

Harper, Kristine C. (PhD, Oregon State 2003; prof.) science and technology, women and science, environment and Cold War; kcharper@fsu.edu

Herrera, Robinson A. (PhD, UCLA 1997; assoc. prof.) colonial Latin America, Central America; rherrera@fsu.edu

Hicks, Anasa Samantha (PhD, NYU 2017; asst. prof.) 20th-century Cuba, Hispanic Caribbean, labor studies; ahicks@fsu.edu

Jones, Maxine D. (PhD, Florida State 1982; prof.) 19th-century US, African American; mjones@fsu.edu

Koslow, Jennifer L. (PhD, UCLA 2001; assoc. prof.) public, urban and women, Gilded Age and Progressive Era; jkoslow@fsu.edu

Liebeskind, Claudia (PhD, London 1995; assoc. prof. and dir., undergrad. studies) South Asia, Islam, medicine; cliebeskind@fsu.edu

McClive, Cathy (PhD, Warwick 2004; assoc. prof.) early modern France/French Revolution, medicine, gender; cmcclive@fsu.edu

Mooney, Katherine (PhD, Yale 2012; asst. prof.) US South; kmooney@fsu.edu

Ozok Gundogan, Nilay (PhD, SUNY, Binghamton 2011; asst. prof.) Middle East, Ottoman Empire

Palmer, James A. (PhD, Washington, St Louis 2015; asst. prof.) medieval Europe, Italian communes, Italian Renaissance; japalmer@fsu.edu

Piehler, G. Kurt (PhD, Rutgers 1990; assoc. prof.) World War II, American military, war/society/oral; kpiehler@fsu.edu

Scholz, Maximilian Miguel (PhD, Yale 2016; asst. prof.) Reformation/religion, migration and exiles, early modern Europe; mscholz@fsu.edu

Sinke, Suzanne M. (PhD, Minnesota 1993; assoc. prof. and dir., grad. studies) migration, gender, US history in comparative perspective; ssinke@fsu.edu

Stoltzfus, Nathan A. (PhD, Harvard 1993; prof.) modern Germany, modern Europe, Holocaust/political violence/resistance; nstoltzfus@fsu.edu

Upchurch, Charles (PhD, Rutgers 2003; assoc. prof.) modern Britain, British Empire and Atlantic world, gender and sexuality; cupchurch@fsu.edu

Williamson, George S. (PhD, Yale 1996; assoc. prof.) 19th-century Germany, European religious, European cultural and intellectual; gwilliamson@fsu.edu

Wood, Laurie (PhD, Texas, Austin 2013; asst. prof.) early modern France, Atlantic world, Indian Ocean/empire/legal

Recently Awarded PhDs

Moriyama, Takahito "Empire of Direct Mail: Media, Fundraising, and Conservative Political Consultants"

Patterson, Sarah Elizabeth "The Few, the Proud: Gender and the Marine Corps Body"

Soash, Richard "Tempered Inclusion: Syrian-Lebanese and Armenian Immigrants and Progressive Era Policy Making, 1894-1924"

Whitehurst, John Robert "Diagnosing the Planet: Medical Activism in the Nuclear Age"

Fordham University

Dept. of History, 441 E. Fordham Rd., Dealy Hall, 6th Fl, Bronx, NY 10458-5159. 718.817.3925. Fax 718.817.4680. Email: historydept@fordham.edu. Website: https://www.fordham.edu/history.

Our department explores world history from the medieval through the present period, stressing a diverse, student-oriented education.

Chair: David Hamlin

Director of Graduate Studies: Grace Shen

Degrees Offered: BA, MA, PhD

Academic Year System: Semester

Areas of Specialization: medieval Europe, early modern and modern Europe, US, Latin America, gender (MA only)

Undergraduate Tuition (per academic year): $51285

Graduate Tuition (per academic year): $35664

Enrollment 2018-19:
Undergraduate Majors: 203
New Graduate Students: 11
Full-time Graduate Students: 52
Degrees in History: 73 BA, 6 MA, 5 PhD

Undergraduate Addresses:
Admissions: http://www.fordham.edu/info/20063/undergraduate_admission
Financial Aid: http://www.fordham.edu/info/20069/undergraduate_financial_aid

Graduate Addresses:
Admissions: http://www.fordham.edu/info/20064/graduate_admission
Financial Aid: http://www.fordham.edu/info/20787/graduate_financial_aid

Adjunct Faculty

Krukofsky, Howard C. (PhD, Columbia 1966; adj. asst. prof.) modern America; c.howardkrukofsky@hunter.edu

Full-time Faculty

Acosta, Sal (PhD, Arizona 2010; assoc. prof.) US Latino; sacosta3@fordham.edu

Alcenat, Westenley (PhD, Columbia 2019; asst. prof.) African American; walcenat@fordham.edu

Armstrong-Price, Amanda (PhD, California, Berkeley 2015; asst. prof.) aarmstrongprice@fordham.edu

Ben Atar, Doron (PhD, Columbia 1990; prof.; Lincoln Center) revolutionary and early national US, early American foreign politics, psychohistory; benatar@fordham.edu

Bristow, Edward (PhD, Yale 1970; prof.; Lincoln Center) modern Europe, modern Britain; ebristow@fordham.edu

Bruce, Scott G. (PhD, Princeton 2000; prof.) sbruce3@fordham.edu

Cimbala, Paul A. (PhD, Emory 1983; prof.) US South, Civil War and Reconstruction; cimbala@fordham.edu

Cornell, Saul A. (PhD, Pennsylvania 1989; prof. and Paul B. Guenther Chair) constitutional, revolutionary and early Republic, public policy; scornell1@fordham.edu

Dietrich, Christopher R. W. (PhD, Texas, Austin 2012; assoc. prof.) 20th-century America, foreign relations; cdietrich2@fordham.edu

Gherini, Claire E. (PhD, Johns Hopkins 2016; asst. prof.) early North America, trans-Atlantic, gender

Goldberg, Barry (PhD, Columbia 1979; assoc. prof.; Lincoln Center) US, labor, race and ethnicity; bgoldberg@fordham.edu

Hamlin, David (PhD, Brown 2002; assoc. prof. and chair) modern Germany; hamlin@fordham.edu

Iyer, Samantha Gayathri (PhD, California, Berkeley 2014; asst. prof.) modern US, international political economy; siyer1@fordham.edu

Kowaleski, Maryanne (PhD, Toronto 1982; Fitzpatrick Dist. Prof.) medieval social and economic, England, gender; kowaleski@fordham.edu

Lindo-Fuentes, Hector (PhD, Chicago 1984; prof.; Lincoln Center) Latin America, economy and education; hlindo@aol.com

Maginn, Christopher Robert (PhD, National, Ireland, Galway 2003; assoc. prof.; Lincoln Center) medieval and early modern Ireland; maginn@fordham.edu

Marme, Michael (PhD, California, Berkeley 1987; asst. prof.; Lincoln Center) East Asia, China, social; marme@fordham.edu

Miki, Yuko (PhD, NYU 2010; assoc. prof.; Lincoln Center) 19th-century Brazil, Latin America; ymiki1@fordham.edu

Mueller, Wolfgang P. (PhD, Syracuse 1991; DPhil, Augsburg 1998; prof.) canon law, later medieval church; wpmueller2@gmail.com

Myers, W. David (PhD, Yale 1991; prof.) Renaissance and Reformation, early modern Germany; dmyers@fordham.edu

Patriarca, Silvana (PhD, Johns Hopkins 1992; prof.) modern Italy, European social and cultural; patriarca@fordham.edu

Paul, Nicholas Lithgow (PhD, Cambridge 2005; assoc. prof.) Crusades, medieval political and cultural; npaul@fordham.edu

Penry, Sarah Elizabeth (PhD, Miami 1996; asst. prof.) colonial Latin America, gender and ethnicity; spenry@fordham.edu

Rigogne, Thierry (PhD, Princeton 2005; assoc. prof.) early modern France; rigogne@fordham.edu

Shen, Grace Yen (PhD, Harvard 2007; assoc. prof. and dir., grad. studies) modern East Asia; gshen1@fordham.edu

Siddiqi, Asif A. (PhD, Carnegie Mellon 2004; prof.) science and technology; siddiqi@fordham.edu

Soyer, Daniel (PhD, NYU 1994; prof.) US urban and ethnic, Jewish; soyer@fordham.edu

Stoll, Steven (PhD, Yale 1994; assoc. prof.) North American environmental; stoll@fordham.edu

Swinth, Kirsten N. (PhD, Yale 1995; assoc. prof.) American cultural, gender; swinth@fordham.edu

Teter, Magda (PhD, Columbia 2000; prof. and Shvidler Prof.) medieval and early modern Jewish, early modern eastern Europe; mteter@fordham.edu

Turan, Ebru (PhD, Chicago 2006; asst. prof.) Ottoman Empire; turan@fordham.edu

Wabuda, Susan (PhD, Cambridge 1992; assoc. prof.) early modern England; wabuda@fordham.edu

Wakeman, Rosemary (PhD, California, Davis 1985; prof.; Lincoln Center) modern France, European city; rwakeman@fordham.edu

Nondepartmental Historians

Anderson, R. Bentley, SJ (PhD, Boston Coll. 2001; assoc. prof.; African American Studies) race and religion

Idris, Amir (PhD, Queen's, Can. 2000; asst. prof.; African American Studies) idris@fordham.edu

Naison, Mark D. (PhD, Columbia 1976; prof.; African American Studies) Afro-American, American social; naison@fordham.edu

Penella, Robert (PhD, Harvard 1971; prof.; Classical Languages) Latin historiography, Rome, imperial Greek prose; rpenella@fordham.edu

Retired/Emeritus Faculty

Crane, Elaine Forman (PhD, NYU 1977; prof. emeritus) colonial and revolutionary America, American gender roles; ecrane@fordham.edu

Gyug, Richard F. (PhD, Toronto 1984; prof. emeritus) medieval Spain and Italy, liturgy, culture; gyug@fordham.edu

Himmelberg, Robert F. (PhD, Penn State 1963; prof. emeritus) late 19th- and 20th-century America; himmelberg@fordham.edu

Jones, Robert F. (PhD, Notre Dame 1967; prof. emeritus) early national America; rfjones51@verizon.net

McCarthy, John (PhD, Columbia 1969; prof. emeritus) modern Europe, 19th- and 20th-century Britain and Ireland, conservative political thought; jmccarthy@fordham.edu

O'Callaghan, Joseph F. (PhD, Fordham 1957; prof. emeritus) medieval political institutions, medieval Spain; clonmeen@optonline.net

Rosenthal, Bernice Glatzer (PhD, California, Berkeley 1970; prof. emeritus) Russia, European intellectual; rosenthal@fordham.edu

Wines, Roger A. (PhD, Columbia 1961; prof. emeritus) modern Germany; pegrogwines@optonline.net

Recently Awarded PhDs

Barsotti, Edoardo Marcello "At the 'Roots' of Italian Identity: 'Race' and 'Nation' in the Italian Risorgimento, 1796-1870"

De Paola, Stephanie Lauren "Sexual Violence, Interracial Relations, and Racism during the Allied Occupation of Italy: History and the Politics of Memory"

Howard, Jacquelyne Thoni "Families on the Borderlands: Marriage and Kinship in Lower French Louisiana, 1700-95"

Kelly, Christine Anne "Singing Out between Tradition and Rebellion: Folk Music, Folk Womanhood, and American Feminism in an Era of Social Change, 1954-85"

Liberman Cuenca, Esther "The Making of Borough Customary Law in Medieval Britain"

Fort Hays State University

Dept. of History, 600 Park St., Hays, KS 67601-4099. 785.628.4248. Fax 785.628.4086. Email: degoodlett@fhsu.edu; history@fhsu.edu. Website: https://www.fhsu.edu/history/.

The Department of History at Fort Hays State University emphasizes a world-view of human development and prepares students for the world beyond college.

Chair: David E. Goodlett
Director of Graduate Studies: Kimberly E. Perez
Degrees Offered: BA, MA
Academic Year System: Semester
Areas of Specialization: world civilization, Europe, Latin America, intellectual and cultural, science and technology, American Southwest, American Indian, US
Undergraduate Tuition (per academic year):
  In-State: $4220
  Out-of-State: $12275
Graduate Tuition (per academic year):
  In-State: $4350
  Out-of-State: $10976
Enrollment 2018-19:
  Undergraduate Majors: 69
  New Graduate Students: 50
  Full-time Graduate Students: 34
  Degrees in History: 5 BA, 4 MA
Undergraduate Addresses:
  Admissions: http://www.fhsu.edu/admissions/
  Financial Aid: http://www.fhsu.edu/admissions/scholarships-and-costs/
Graduate Addresses:
  Admissions and Financial Aid: http://www.fhsu.edu/gradschl/

Full-time Faculty

Goodlett, David E. (PhD, Illinois, Chicago 1990; assoc. prof. and chair) eastern Europe, Russia, Europe; dgoodlet@fhsu.edu

Macias, Marco A. (PhD, Arizona 2018; asst. prof.) Latin American studies, US, political science; m_macias2@fhsu.edu

Marquess, Hollie A. (MA, Fort Hays State 2009; instr.) colonial to present America, women's/gender studies, late 19th- to early 20th-century sexuality; hahailey@fhsu.edu

McClure, Daniel R. (PhD, California, Irvine 2013; asst. prof.) 20th-century US, capitalism, popular culture, world, international studies, historical theory and methods; drmcclure2@fhsu.edu

Nienkamp, Paul (PhD, Iowa State 2008; assoc. prof.) science and technology, American political, intellectual and cultural; pknienkamp@fhsu.edu

Perez, Kim E. (PhD, Oklahoma 2007; assoc. prof. and dir., grad. studies) science, environmental, intellectual and cultural; kperez@fhsu.edu

Winchester, Juti A. (PhD, Northern Arizona 1999; asst. prof.) public, US West, Indian; jawinchester@fhsu.edu

Retired/Emeritus Faculty

Busch, Allan, Jr. (PhD, Kansas 1971; prof. emeritus) England, early US

Caulfield, Norman E. (PhD, Houston 1990; prof. emeritus) Mexico, Latin America, 19th-century US; ncaulfie@fhsu.edu

Forsythe, James L. (PhD, New Mexico 1971; prof. emeritus) US South, Civil War, recent US; jforsyth@fhsu.edu

Liston, Ann E. (PhD, Ohio State 1972; assoc. prof. emeritus) US diplomatic, early Republic America

Schmeller, Helmut J. (PhD, Kansas State 1975; prof. emeritus) modern Europe, Germany, European social and intellectual

Smith, Wilda M. (PhD, Illinois, Urbana-Champaign 1960; prof. emeritus) US constitutional, Middle East, women

Wilson, Raymond (PhD, New Mexico 1977; prof. emeritus) American Indian, US West

Framingham State University

Dept. of History, May Hall, Framingham, MA 01701-9101. 508.626.4800. Fax 508.626.4022. Email: ghalfond@ framingham.edu. Website: https://www.framingham.edu/ academics/colleges/arts-and-humanities/history/.

The Department of History is a community of accomplished teacher-scholars committed to preparing students for successful lives and careers in the 21st century through a program that values academic rigor and excellence in a liberal arts education and fosters responsible citizenship and ethical behavior.

Chair: Gregory I. Halfond
Degrees Offered: BA
Academic Year System: Semester
Areas of Specialization: America, Europe, world, social and economic, museum studies
Undergraduate Tuition (per academic year):
In-State: $8000
Out-of-State: $10000
Enrollment 2018-19:
Undergraduate Majors: 92
Degrees in History: 12 BA
Addresses:
Admissions: http://www.framingham.edu/admissions/
Financial Aid: http://www.framingham.edu/admissions/ financial-aid/

Full-time Faculty

Adelman, Joseph M. (PhD, Johns Hopkins 2010; assoc. prof.) North America, business, media; jadelman@framingham.edu

Adelman, Sarah Mulhall (PhD, Johns Hopkins 2010; assoc. prof.) 19th- and early 20th-century US social and economic, childhood, women; sadelman1@framingham.edu

Allen, Richard B. (PhD, Illinois, Urbana-Champaign 1983; prof.) Indian Ocean, Africa, comparative slavery; rallen1@framingham.edu

Bihler, Lori G. (PhD, Sussex, UK 2005; assoc. prof.) Jewish, Germany, genocide; lbihler@framingham.edu

Bollettino, Maria Alessandra (PhD, Texas, Austin 2009; assoc. prof.) early and colonial America, Atlantic world, race and gender; mbollettino@framingham.edu

Halfond, Gregory Isaac (PhD, Minnesota 2007; prof. and chair) late antiquity, early medieval Europe, church; ghalfond@ framingham.edu

Huibregtse, Jon R. (PhD, Akron 1995; prof.) modern America, labor, China; jhuibregtse@framingham.edu

Papaioannou, Stefan Sotiris (PhD, Maryland, Coll. Park 2012; assoc. prof.) modern Europe, Balkans, Middle East; spapaioannou@ framingham.edu

Sheridan, Bridgette A. (PhD, Boston Coll. 2002; prof.) modern Europe, gender, France; bsheridan@framingham.edu

Retired/Emeritus Faculty

Barron, Gloria J. (PhD, Tufts 1971; prof. emerita) New Deal, 20th-century US

Harrington, Joseph F., Jr. (PhD, Georgetown 1971; prof. emeritus) Romanian-American relations, 20th-century European diplomatic; jharrington@framingham.edu

Nutting, P. Bradley (PhD, North Carolina, Chapel Hill 1972; prof. emeritus) colonial and revolutionary America, religion; pnutting@framingham.edu

Racheotes, Nicholas S. (PhD, Boston Coll. 1975; prof. emeritus) Russia, Balkans, modern intellectual; nracheotes@framingham.edu

Roberts, Roberta A. (MA, Fordham 1965; asst. prof. emerita) ancient and medieval, intellectual, historical research and writing

Francis Marion University

Dept. of History, PO Box 100547, Florence, SC 29502-0547. 843.661.1374. Fax 843.661.1155. Email: vkaufman@fmarion.edu. Website: https://www.fmarion.edu/history/.

In collaboration with the History faculty, students can design special courses tailored to their needs and interests. Through the study of History, students gain a better understanding of contemporary events, a knowledge of people in various times and places, critical thinking skills, and the ability to express themselves effectively in oral and written communication.

Chair: Scott Kaufman
Degrees Offered: BA,BS
Academic Year System: Semester
Areas of Specialization: US, Europe, Latin America, Asia, public history and archaeology
Tuition (per academic year):
In-State: $11160
Out-of-State: $21544
Enrollment 2018-19:
Undergraduate Majors: 46
Degrees in History: 2 BA, 9 BS

Addresses:

Admissions: http://www.fmarion.edu/fmuadmissions
Financial Aid: http://www.fmarion.edu/enrollment/
financialassistance

Full-time Faculty

Barton, Christopher (PhD, Temple 2014; asst. prof.) archaeology, US survey, African American; cbarton@fmarion.edu

Bolt, William (PhD, Tennessee, Knoxville 2010; assoc. prof.) US survey, colonial and revolutionary America, age of Jackson; wbolt@fmarion.edu

Eskridge-Kosmach, Elena (PhD, Belarusian State 1985; assoc. prof.) Russia, modern Europe, Europe survey; aeskridgekosmach@fmarion.edu

Johnson, Erica R. (PhD, Florida State 2012; asst. prof.) Europe, Latin America, Caribbean; ejohnson@fmarion.edu

Kaufman, V. Scott (PhD, Ohio 1998; prof. and chair) US diplomatic, US military, environmental; vkaufman@fmarion.edu

Kennedy, Christopher M. (PhD, Univ. Coll., Cork, Ireland 2003; prof. and vice pres., student life) Ireland, Britain, British Empire; ckennedy@fmarion.edu

Kirby, Jason (PHD, Georgia, 2018; asst. prof. and coord., secondary ed. program in Social Studies) modern US, war and society, civil rights, Cold War-era social and political; jason.kirby@fmarion.edu

Nagata, Mary Louise (PhD, Hawai`i, Manoa 1996; prof.) Asia, Japan, China; mnagata@fmarion.edu

Venters, Louis (PhD, South Carolina 2010; assoc. prof.) South Carolina, African American, US survey; lventers@fmarion.edu

Part-time Faculty

Britton, John A. (PhD, Tulane 1971; prof. emeritus) Latin America, Mexico, historiography; jbritton@fmarion.edu

Retired/Emeritus Faculty

Campbell, Jacqueline Glass (PhD, Duke 2000; prof. emeritus) US Civil War, Old South, US survey; jcampbell@fmarion.edu

Chapman, Richard N. (PhD, Yale 1976; prof. emeritus) US economic, modern US, US survey; rchapman@fmarion.edu

de Montluzin, E. Lorraine (PhD, Duke 1974; prof. emeritus) Britain, Europe, press; edemontluzin@fmarion.edu

Nelson, Larry E. (PhD, Duke 1975; prof. emeritus) US West, US Civil War, historiography

Franklin & Marshall College

Dept. of History, PO Box 3003, Lancaster, PA 17604-3003. 717.358.4047. Fax 717.358.4518. Email: richard.reitan@fandm. edu. Website: https://www.fandm.edu/history.

Meet the future with an understanding of the past. Through its course offerings, individual interactions with students, and advising, the History Department aims to foster an understanding of history and historical processes.

Chair: Richard Reitan
Degrees Offered: BA
Academic Year System: Semester
Areas of Specialization: US and Europe, Africa, Asia, Latin America, Islamic world
Tuition (per academic year): $56450
Enrollment 2018-19:

Undergraduate Majors: 56
Degrees in History: 24 BA

Addresses:

Admissions: http://www.fandm.edu/admission
Financial Aid: http://www.fandm.edu/financialaid

Full-time Faculty

Anthony, Douglas A. (PhD, Northwestern 1996; assoc. prof.) Africa, modern Nigeria; douglas.anthony@fandm.edu

Gosse, Van E. (PhD, Rutgers 1992; prof.) 20th-century US, African American, global Cold War; van.gosse@fandm.edu

Hoffman, Matthew (PhD, California, Berkeley 2000; assoc. prof.; Judaic Studies) Jewish; matthew.hoffman@fandm.edu

McRee, Ben R. (PhD, Indiana 1987; prof.) medieval Europe, England, urban; ben.mcree@fandm.edu

Mitchell, Maria D. (PhD, Boston Univ. 1995; prof.) modern Europe, Germany, religion; maria.mitchell@fandm.edu

Pearson, Edward A. (PhD, Wisconsin, Madison 1992; assoc. prof.) colonial and revolutionary America, African American, Atlantic world; tpearson@fandm.edu

Reitan, Richard M. (PhD, Chicago 2002; assoc. prof. and chair) East Asia; rreitan@fandm.edu

Schrader, Abby (PhD, Pennsylvania 1996; prof.) Russia, women and gender; abby.schrader@fandm.edu

Shelton, Laura M. (PhD, Arizona 2004; assoc. prof.) colonial Latin America, Mexico, gender; laura.shelton@fandm.edu

Stevenson, Louise L. (PhD, Boston Univ. 1981; prof.; American Studies) 19th century US intellectual and cultural, Lincoln and Civil War, women and gender; louise.stevenson@fandm.edu

Yilmaz, Seçil (PhD, Graduate Center, CUNY 2016; asst. prof.) Middle East, Islamic studies, women and gender; syilmaz@fandm.edu

Nondepartmental Historians

Deslippe, Dennis A. (PhD, Iowa 1994; prof.; American Studies; Women's, Gender & Sexuality Studies) America, labor, women and gender; dennis.deslippe@fandm.edu

Schuyler, David (PhD, Columbia 1979; Shadek Prof.; American Studies) US urban and cultural; david.schuyler@fandm.edu

Strick, James E. (PhD, Princeton 1997; assoc. prof.; Science, Tech. and Soc.) biology and medicine, environmental, microbiology and evolution; james.strick@fandm.edu

Part-time Faculty

Kaliss, Gregory (PhD, North Carolina, Chapel Hill 2008; adj. asst. prof.) modern US, sports, race; gkaliss@fandm.edu

Retired/Emeritus Faculty

Joseph, John (PhD, Princeton 1957; prof. emeritus) Middle East; john.joseph@fandm.edu

Visiting Faculty

Hamza, Ibrahim (PhD, York, Can. 2009; vis. asst. prof.) Africa, Nigeria; ihamza@fandm.edu

Oelze, Micah J. (PhD, Florida Internatonal 2016; vis. asst. prof.) Latin America, Atlantic, Brazil; moelze@fandm.edu

Frostburg State University

Dept. of History, Dunkle Hall 107, Frostburg, MD 21532-2303. 301.687.7496. Fax 301.687.3099. Email: sboniece@frostburg. edu. Website: https://www.frostburg.edu/departments/history/.

The Department of History offers a strong liberal arts education including an in-depth study of the history of a broad spectrum of geographical regions and cultural traditions supported by a solid grounding in historical research methods.

Chair: Sally A. Boniece

Degrees Offered: BA,BS
Academic Year System: Semester
Areas of Specialization: Europe, US, Africa, Latin America, Asia
Tuition (per academic year):
In-State: $6700
Out-of-State: $20800
Enrollment 2018-19:
Undergraduate Majors: 25
Degrees in History: 5 BS
Addresses:
Admissions: http://www.frostburg.edu/admiss/
Financial Aid: http://www.frostburg.edu/ungrad/faid/

Full-time Faculty

Abbay, Alemseged (PhD, California, Berkeley 1996; prof.) Africa, Middle East, African American; aabbay@frostburg.edu

Boniece, Sally A. (PhD, Indiana 1995; prof. and chair) Russia, modern Europe, women; sboniece@frostburg.edu

Ma, Haiyun (PhD, Georgetown 2007; assoc. prof.) Islam in China, China, Asia; hma@frostburg.edu

McConnell, Eleanor H. (PhD, Iowa 2008; assoc. prof.) early America, legal and economic, Atlantic world; ehmcconnell@frostburg.edu

Wood, Gregory John (PhD, Pittsburgh 2006; assoc. prof.; dir., Honors Program) modern US, labor, social; gwood@frostburg.edu

Retired/Emeritus Faculty

Adams, Elizabeth C. (PhD, West Virginia 1976; prof. emeritus) ancient, modern Europe, women

Charney, Paul J. (PhD, Texas, Austin 1989; assoc. prof. emeritus) Latin America; pcharney@frostburg.edu

Clulee, Nicholas H. (PhD, Chicago 1973; prof. emeritus) medieval and early modern Europe, science; nclulee@frostburg.edu

Dean, David M. (PhD, Texas, Austin 1972; prof. emeritus) 19th-century America, American West; ddean@frostburg.edu

Kershaw, Gordon E. (PhD, Pennsylvania 1971; prof. emeritus) colonial America, modern Britain, Ireland

McGovern, Constance (PhD, Massachusetts Amherst 1976; prof. emeritus) US women, social, colonial

Furman University

Dept. of History, 3300 Poinsett Hwy., Furman Hall, Suite 200, Greenville, SC 29613-0443. 864.294.2182. Fax 864.294.2295. Email: lilah.westmoreland@furman.edu. Website: http://www2.furman.edu/academics/history/.

The goal of the History Department at Furman University is to increase a student's understanding of the present through a critical examination of the past. With a firm foundation in the liberal arts, our program exposes students to a wide range of geographical regions and time periods, civilizations, and cultures.

Chair: Lane J. Harris
Degrees Offered: BA
Academic Year System: Semester
Areas of Specialization: US, Europe, Asia, Latin America, Africa, Middle East
Tuition (per academic year): $50464
Addresses:
Admissions: http://www.furman.edu/Admission/engagefurman/
Financial Aid: http://www.furman.edu/admission/EngageFurman/FinancialInformation/

Full-time Faculty

Barrington, John P. T. (PhD, William and Mary 1997; prof.) colonial North America; john.barrington@furman.edu

Benson, T. Lloyd (PhD, Virginia 1990; Walter Kenneth Mattison Prof.) US before 1860, Civil War; lloyd.benson@furman.edu

Ching, Erik K. (PhD, California, Santa Barbara 1997; prof.) modern Latin America, Africa; erik.ching@furman.edu

Day, Carolyn Anne (PhD, Tulane 2010; assoc. prof.) modern Britain, medicine, gender; carolyn.day@furman.edu

Fehler, Timothy G. (PhD, Wisconsin, Madison 1995; prof.) early modern Europe, England; timothy.fehler@furman.edu

Hamed-Troyansky, Vladimir (PhD, Stanford 2018; asst. prof.) Middle East; vladimir.hamed-troyansky@furman.edu

Hansen, Jason D. (PhD, Illinois, Urbana-Champaign 2010; assoc. prof.) modern Germany, nationalism; jason.hansen@furman.edu

Harris, Lane J. (PhD, Illinois, Urbana-Champaign 2012; assoc. prof. and chair) China, state-building, communications; lane.harris@furman.edu

Kanagawa, Nadia (PhD, Southern California 2019; instr.) Japan; nadia.kanagawa@furman.edu

Nair, Savita (PhD, Pennsylvania 2001; prof.; Asian Studies) South Asia, British Empire and emigration; savita.nair@furman.edu

O'Neill, Stephen (PhD, Virginia 1994; prof.) US South, South Carolina, 20th-century US; steve.oneill@furman.edu

Spear, David S. (PhD, California, Santa Barbara 1982; William E. Leverette Jr. Prof.) medieval Europe, ancient; david.spear@furman.edu

Strobel, Marian E. (PhD, Duke 1975; William Montgomery Burnett Prof.) recent US, women, social; marian.strobel@furman.edu

Part-time Faculty

Tollison, Courtney L. (PhD, South Carolina 2003; Dist. Univ. Public Hist. and Scholar) modern US, civil rights, oral; courtney.tollison@furman.edu

George Fox University

Dept. of History, 414 N. Meridian St. #6244, Newberg, OR 97132-2697. 503.554.2678. Fax 503.554.3899. Email: potto@georgefox.edu. Website: https://www.georgefox.edu/academics/undergrad/departments/history/.

The History Program is dedicated to helping our majors become thoughtful, mature Christian thinkers who can contribute to their world in a variety of professions.

Chair: Paul Otto
Degrees Offered: BA
Academic Year System: Semester
Areas of Specialization: US, Europe, peace studies, church
Tuition (per academic year): $35016
Enrollment 2018-19:
Undergraduate Majors: 51
Degrees in History: 12 BA
Addresses:
Admissions: http://www.georgefox.edu/admission/
Financial Aid: http://www.georgefox.edu/college-admissions/scholarships/

Full-time Faculty

Corning, Caitlin (PhD, Leeds 1996; prof.) ancient and medieval, England, church; ccorning@georgefox.edu

Irish, Kerry Eugene (PhD, Washington 1994; prof.) modern US; kirish@georgefox.edu

Otto, Paul (PhD, Indiana 1995; prof. and chair) early America, southern Africa; potto@georgefox.edu

Weinert, Mark (PhD, Vanderbilt 1993; assoc. prof.) Europe, England, church; mweinert@georgefox.edu

Nondepartmental Historians

Hall, Mark (PhD, Virginia 1993; Herbert Hoover Dist. Prof.; Political Science) American political theory; mhall@georgefox.edu

Thomas, Rachel C. (MA, William and Mary; instr.; archivist, George Fox Univ. & Northwest Yearly Meeting of Friends) rthomas@georgefox.edu

Retired/Emeritus Faculty

Beebe, Ralph (PhD, Oregon 1972; prof. emeritus) US, peace studies; rbeebe@georgefox.edu

George Mason University

Dept. of History and Art Hist., 4400 University Dr., MSN 3G1, Fairfax, VA 22030. 703.993.1250. Fax 703.993.1251. Email: bplatt1@gmu.edu. Website: https://historyarthistory.gmu.edu/.

While maintaining a reputation for excellence in the traditional academic pursuits of teaching and research, the Department of History and Art History undertakes three additional and distinctive missions: we make use of digital media to preserve and present the past in new ways; we approach the past from an essentially multidisciplinary perspective; and we seek to engage the broader public in a discussion about the past.

Chair: Brian W. Platt

Director of Graduate Studies: Zachary Schrag (MA); Sam Lebovic (PhD)

Degrees Offered: BA,MA,PhD,Cert. (digital public humanities)

Academic Year System: Semester

Areas of Specialization: US, Europe, Latin America, Africa, Middle East

Undergraduate Tuition (per academic year):
In-State: $10675
Out-of-State: $30230

Graduate Tuition (per academic year):
In-State: $11340
Out-of-State: $26800

Enrollment 2018-19:
Undergraduate Majors: 270
New Graduate Students: 64
Full-time Graduate Students: 52
Part-time Graduate Students: 93
Degrees in History: 92 BA, 15 MA, 3 PhD

Undergraduate Addresses:
Admissions: http://admissions.gmu.edu/
Financial Aid: http://financialaid.gmu.edu/

Graduate Addresses:
Admissions: http://chss.gmu.edu/admissions/
Financial Aid: http://financialaid.gmu.edu/

Full-time Faculty

Barnes, Steven A. (PhD, Stanford 2003; assoc. prof.) 20th-century Europe, Russia; sbarnes3@gmu.edu

Bristol, Joan (PhD, Pennsylvania 2001; assoc. prof.) colonial Latin America, African diaspora; jbristol@gmu.edu

Carton, Benedict (PhD, Yale 1996; assoc. prof.) sub-Saharan Africa, southern Africa, comparative colonial frontiers; bcarton1@gmu.edu

Chang, Michael G. (PhD, California, San Diego 2001; assoc. prof.) modern China; mchang5@gmu.edu

Collins, Samuel W. (PhD, California, Berkeley 2005; assoc. prof.) medieval Europe; scolline@gmu.edu

Copelman, Dina M. (PhD, Princeton 1985; assoc. prof.) Britain, women, cultural studies; dcopelma@gmu.edu

DeCaroli, Robert (PhD, UCLA 1999; assoc. prof.; dir., Art Hist.) South and Southeast Asian art; rdecarol@gmu.edu

Elzey, Christopher (PhD, Purdue 2004; term asst. prof.) Western civilization, sports; celzey@gmu.edu

Genetin-Pilawa, C. Joseph (PhD, Michigan State 2008; asst. prof.) 19th century, indigenous, public; cgenetin@gmu.edu

Greet, Michele (PhD, NYU 2004; assoc. prof.) 20th-century Andean art, Latin American artists in Europe; mgreet@gmu.edu

Gregg, Christopher (PhD, North Carolina, Chapel Hill 2000; term asst. prof.; Art Hist.) classical archaeology, Roman imperial architecture and sculpture; cgregg@gmu.edu

Hamdani, Sumaiya A. (PhD, Princeton 1995; assoc. prof.) Islamic, women, modern Middle East; shamdani@gmu.edu

Hamner, Christopher Heald (PhD, North Carolina, Chapel Hill 2004; assoc. prof.) US military; chamner@gmu.edu

Ho, Angela (PhD, Michigan; asst. prof.; Art Hist.) Renaissance art, Baroque art; aho5@gmu.edu

Hooper, Jane (PhD, Emory 2010; asst. prof.) history and trade in early modern Madagascar, transatlantic and Indian Ocean slave trades, precolonial African state-building; jhooper3@gmu.edu

Karush, Matthew B. (PhD, Chicago 1997; prof.) Latin America, Argentina; mkarush@gmu.edu

Kelly, Mills (PhD, George Washington 1996; prof.) Czechoslovakia, 20th-century Europe, eastern Europe; tkelly7@gmu.edu

Kierner, Cynthia A. (PhD, Virginia 1986; prof.) early America, US to 1850; ckierner@gmu.edu

Lair, Meredith H. (PhD, Penn State 2004; assoc. prof.) US military, Vietnam; mlair@gmu.edu

Landsberg, Alison (PhD, Chicago 1996; assoc. prof.) US film and culture; alandsb1@gmu.edu

Lebovic, Sam (PhD, Chicago 2011; asst. prof. and PhD dir.) 20th-century US, 19th-century US, global; slebovic@gmu.edu

Manuel-Scott, Wendi N. (PhD, Howard 2003; asst. prof.) Caribbean, African diaspora; wmanuels@gmu.edu

McCord, Theodore B. (PhD, American 1991; term asst. prof.) Virginia, US; tmccord@gmu.edu

McGuire, Heather (PhD, Virginia Commonwealth 2010; term asst. prof.) modern and contemporary art; hmcguir@gmu.edu

Mullen, Lincoln (PhD, Brandeis 2014; assoc. prof.) US, American religions, digital; lmullen@gmu.edu

O'Malley, Michael H. (PhD, California, Berkeley 1988; prof.) 19th-century US social and cultural; momalle3@gmu.edu

Orens, John R. (PhD, Columbia 1976; term prof.) modern Europe, intellectual; jorens@gmu.edu

Otis, Jessica Marie (PhD, Virginia 2014; asst. prof.) Europe, early modern Britain, science and math, digital; jotis2@gmu.edu

Park, Sun-Young (PhD, Harvard 2014; asst. prof.) 19th-century Europe, French cultural, architectural and urban; spark53@gmu.edu

Platt, Brian W. (PhD, Illinois, Urbana-Champaign 1998; assoc. prof. and chair) Japan, China, early modern; bplatt1@gmu.edu

Richards, Yevette (PhD, Yale 1994; assoc. prof.) women, African American, labor; yjordan@gmu.edu

Ritterhouse, Jennifer L. (PhD, North Carolina, Chapel Hill 1999; assoc. prof.) 20th-century US, women and gender, children and childhood; jritterh@gmu.edu

Robertson, Stephen M. (PhD, Rutgers 1998; prof.; dir., Roy Rosenzweig Center for Hist. and New Media) digital, sexual violence, US; srober30@gmu.edu

Schrag, Zachary M. (PhD, Columbia 2002; prof. and dir., grad. program and MA) 20th-century US; zschrag@gmu.edu

Schulman, Vanessa (PhD, California, Irvine 2010; asst. prof.) 19th- and 20th-century US visual culture, technology; vschulma@gmu.edu

Schulze, Susan E. (PhD, St. Louis 2006; term asst. prof.) medieval Europe; sschulze@gmu.edu

Scully, Randolph F. (PhD, Pennsylvania 2002; assoc. prof.) colonial and revolutionary America, religion; rscully@gmu.edu

Sherwin, Martin J. (PhD, UCLA 1971; Univ. Prof.) Vietnam and Cold War; msherwin@gmu.edu

Smith, Suzanne E. (PhD, Yale 1996; prof.) African American studies, 20th-century cultural, film studies; smisuze@gmu.edu

Stearns, Peter N. (PhD, Harvard 1963; Univ. Prof. and provost emeritus) social and world; pstearns@gmu.edu

Takats, Sean P. (PhD, Michigan 2005; assoc. prof.) French cultural, 18th century; stakats@gmu.edu

Williamson, Jacquelyn C. (PhD, Johns Hopkins 2009; asst. prof.) ancient Egypt, gender, religion; jwilli98@gmu.edu

Yilmaz, Huseyin (PhD, Harvard 2005; asst. prof.) Ottoman Empire, Middle Eastt; hyilmaz@gmu.edu

Zagarri, Rosemarie (PhD, Yale 1984; Univ. Prof.) colonial and revolutionary America, political, cultural; rzagarri@gmu.edu

Retired/Emeritus Faculty

Bakhash, Shaul (PhD, Oxford 1972; Robinson Prof. emeritus) modern Near East, Iran, Persian Gulf; sbakhash@gmu.edu

Butler, Larry (PhD, Pennsylvania 1989; prof. emeritus; Art Hist.) medieval, Islamic, architecture

Censer, Jack R. (PhD, Johns Hopkins 1973; prof. emeritus) France, Europe, social and intellectual

Censer, Jane T. (PhD, Johns Hopkins 1980; retired prof.) US social, family, US South; jcense1@gmu.edu

Henriques, Peter R. (PhD, Virginia 1971; prof. emeritus)

Holt, Mack P. (PhD, Emory 1982; prof. emeritus) early modern France, Renaissance, Reformation; mholt@gmu.edu

Horton, Lois (PhD, Brandeis 1977; prof. emeritus) race, civil rights

Lytton, Randolph H. (PhD, Penn State 1973; assoc. prof. emeritus) classical Greece and Rome, Alexander the Great

Mattusch, Carol (PhD, North Carolina, Chapel Hill 1975; Mathy Prof. emeritus) classical art and archaeology, rediscovery of antiquity

Petrik, Paula (PhD, SUNY, Binghamton 1982; prof. emeritus) 19th-century America, women's rights, history and new media

Todd, Ellen Wiley (PhD, Stanford 1987; assoc. prof. emeritus) US

Wade, Rex A. (PhD, Nebraska 1963; Univ. Prof. emeritus) Russian Revolution, Russian political and cultural

Recently Awarded PhDs

Beasley, Gretchen "Creating Identity, Defining Culture, Building Nations: An Examination of Material Culture and Exchange between the Polish-Lithuanian Commonwealth and Ottoman Empire, 1562-1795"

Bradshaw, Kellie Kahrmann "Reality, Expectations, and Fears: Women Shop Assistants in London, 1890-1914"

Bush, Erin N. "Marked for Reform: Race and Rehabilition of Virginia's Wayward Girls, 1910-42"

Francavilla, Lisa "Markets and Masculinity: Pursuing Wealth, Power, and American 'Manliness' in the China Trade"

Gonzaba, Eric N. "Because the Night: Nightlife and Remaking the Gay Male World, 1970-2000"

Regan, Amanda "Shaping Up: Physical Culture Initiatives for Women in the United States, 1900-65"

Schneider, Benjamin "Murder and the American Soldier, 1942-45"

Georgetown University

Dept. of History, 3700 O St. NW, Box 571035 - ICC 600, Washington, DC 20057-1035. 202.687.6061. Fax 202.687.7245. Email: alc284@georgetown.edu. Website: https://history.georgetown.edu/.

The Department of History at Georgetown University is a collegial community of undergraduate majors, graduate students, alumni, and more than 40 full-time faculty members. Our faculty is broadly international in its range of skills and interests and we are known as a leader in global, transregional, and comparative history.

Chair: Bryan McCann
Director of Graduate Studies: Jordan Sand (PhD); James Millward (MA)
Director of Undergraduate Studies: Amy Leonard
Degrees Offered: BA, MA, PhD
Academic Year System: Semester
Areas of Specialization: US and Atlantic world, Middle East/Latin America/Asia/Africa, Russia and east central Europe, late medieval/early modern/modern Europe, environmental and transregional
Undergraduate Tuition (per academic year): $51720
Graduate Tuition (per academic year): $35910
Enrollment 2018-19:
Undergraduate Majors: 138
New Graduate Students: 10
Full-time Graduate Students: 82
Degrees in History: 43 BA, 15 MA, 12 PhD
Undergraduate Addresses:
Admissions: http://uadmissions.georgetown.edu/
Financial Aid: http://uadmissions.georgetown.edu/financial_aid/
Graduate Addresses:
Admissions: https://grad.georgetown.edu/admissions/programs/history#
Financial Aid: https://grad.georgetown.edu/financial-support#

Adjunct Faculty

Gettig, Eric (PhD, Georgetown 2017; adj.) Latin America; etg22@georgetown.edu

Martin, Kevin W. (PhD, Georgetown 2005; adj.) Middle East/North Africa

Wall, Michael C. (PhD, Georgetown 2002; adj. prof.) US-East Asian relations, modern China, world and global; wallm@georgetown.edu

Zimmers, Stefan (PhD, Georgetown 2007; adj. prof.) medieval Europe; zimmerss@georgetown.edu

Affiliated Faculty

Balzer, Harley D. (PhD, Pennsylvania 1980; assoc. prof.; Government) Russian politics, social, science and technology; balzerh@georgetown.edu

Daniels, Mario (PhD, Tuebingen 2007; DAAD vis. asst. prof.; BMW Center for German and European History) economic/social/business, science and technology, national security; md1367@georgetown.edu

Ernst, Daniel R. (PhD, Princeton 1989; JD, Chicago 1983; prof.; Law) US legal; ernst@law.georgetown.edu

Kim, Christine (PhD, Harvard 2004; lect.; Sch. of Foreign Service) modern Korea, colonial modernity, empire studies; cjk25@georgetown.edu

Sassoon, Joseph (PhD, St. Antony's Coll., Oxford 1981; assoc. prof.; Sch. of Foreign Service) modern Arab world, Middle East economic; js824@georgetown.edu

Full-time Faculty

Abi-Mershed, Osama W. (PhD, Georgetown 2003; assoc. prof.; dir., Center for Contemporary Arab Studies; Sch. of Foreign Service) Middle East and North Africa; Osama.AbiMershed@georgetown.edu

Afinogenov, Gregory (PhD, Harvard 2016; asst. prof.) Russia; gda8@georgetown.edu

Agoston, Gabor J. (PhD, Hungarian Acad. Sciences, Budapest 1994; assoc. prof.) Ottoman Empire, Turkey, early modern military; agostong@georgetown.edu

Aksakal, Mustafa (PhD, Princeton 2003; assoc. prof.; Sch. of Foreign Service) modern Turkey, Ottoman Empire, Middle East; Mustafa.Aksakal@georgetown.edu

Astarita, Tommaso (PhD, Johns Hopkins 1988; prof.) early modern Europe, Mediterranean, Italian South; astaritt@georgetown.edu

Benedict, Carol A. (PhD, Stanford 1992; prof.; Sch. of Foreign Service) China and Pacific world, Chinese medicine and disease, consumer and material culture; benedicc@georgetown.edu

Benton-Cohen, Katherine A. (PhD, Wisconsin-Madison 2002; prof.) US, women and gender, borderlands and Immigration; kab237@georgetown.edu

Chakravarti, Ananya (PhD, Chicago 2012; assoc. prof.) South Asia, Portuguese Empire; ac1646@georgetown.edu

Chatelain, Marcia (PhD, Brown 2008; assoc. prof.) American civilization, African American, women/food/culture/community; Marcia.Chatelain@georgetown.edu

Collins, David J. (PhD, Northwestern 2004; assoc. prof.) medieval Germany; djc44@georgetown.edu

Collins, James B. (PhD, Columbia 1978; prof.) 16th- through 18th-century Europe; collinja@georgetown.edu

David-Fox, Michael (PhD, Yale 1993; prof.; Sch. of Foreign Service) modern Russia, Soviet/Russia/Eurasia; md672@georgetown.edu

de Luna, Kathryn M. (PhD, Northwestern 2008; assoc. prof.) precolonial Africa, historical linguistics; deLuna@georgetown.edu

Degroot, Dagomar (PhD, York, Can. 2014; assoc. prof.) environmental, climate and historical climatology, early modern European cultural and military; dd865@georgetown.edu

Games, Alison F. (PhD, Pennsylvania 1992; prof.) colonial America, Atlantic, migration; gamesa@georgetown.edu

Haddad, Yvonne (PhD, Hartford Sem. 1979; prof.; faculty, Center for Muslim-Christian Understanding) Middle East, 20th-century Islamic, social and intellectual; haddady@georgetown.edu

Higuchi, Toshihiro (PhD, Georgetown 2011; asst. prof.; Sch. of Foreign Service) US-East Asian relations, international, science/technology/environmental; th233@georgetown.edu

Jackson, Maurice (PhD, Georgetown 2001; assoc. prof.) African American, Atlantic, radicalism; jacksonz@georgetown.edu

Kazin, Michael (PhD, Stanford 1983; prof.) US social movements and politics, Reconstruction to present; Michael.Kazin@georgetown.edu

Langer, Erick Detlef (PhD, Stanford 1984; prof.; Sch. of Foreign Service) Latin America and Andes, social and economic, frontiers; Erik.Langer@georgetown.edu

Leonard, Amy E. (PhD, California, Berkeley 1999; assoc. prof. and dir., undergrad. studies) early modern Germany, gender, Protestant Reformation; Amy.Leonard@georgetown.edu

Manning, Chandra Miller (PhD, Harvard 2002; assoc. prof.) 19th-century US, sectionalism, Civil War/Reconstruction/baseball; cmm97@georgetown.edu

McCann, Bryan (PhD, Yale 1999; prof. and chair) Latin America, Brazil, popular music; bm85@georgetown.edu

McCartin, Joseph A. (PhD, SUNY, Binghamton 1990; prof.; dir., Kalmanovitz Inst.) 20th-century US labor, social, political; jam6@georgetown.edu

McKittrick, Meredith K. (PhD, Stanford 1995; assoc. prof.; Sch. of Foreign Service) African colonial, gender; McKittrick@georgetown.edu

McNeill, John R. (PhD, Duke 1981; Univ. Prof.; Sch. of Foreign Service) environmental, Mediterranean, Atlantic; mcneillj@georgetown.edu

Millward, James (PhD, Stanford 1993; prof. and dir., MA Progs.; Sch. of Foreign Service) intersocietal, late imperial China, Central and Inner Asia; millwarj@georgetown.edu

Moran Cruz, Jo Ann Hoeppner (PhD, Brandeis 1975; assoc. prof.) medieval and early modern, education and literacy, England moranj@georgetown.edu

Newfield, Timothy P. (PhD, McGill 2011; asst. prof.; Biology) environmental, medieval Europe, animal and human disease

Olesko, Kathryn M. (PhD, Cornell 1980; assoc. prof.; Science, Technology, and International Affairs) 17th- to 20th-century science and technology, atomic age and comparative nuclear cultures, European intellectual; Kathryn.Olesko@georgetown.edu

Painter, David S. (PhD, North Carolina, Chapel Hill 1982; assoc. prof.; Sch. of Foreign Service) US diplomatic; painterd@georgetown.edu

Pinkard, Susan K. (PhD, Chicago 1982; teaching prof.) ideas, material culture, early modern Europe; pinkards@georgetown.edu

Roshwald, Aviel I. (PhD, Harvard 1987; prof.) 19th- and 20th-century European diplomatic, ethnic politics and nationalism; Aviel.Roshwald@georgetown.edu

Rothman, Adam (PhD, Columbia 2000; prof.) early national US, slavery, Atlantic; ar44@georgetown.edu

Sand, Jordan A. (PhD, Columbia 1996; prof. and dir., PhD studies; East Asian Languages & Cultures) modern Japan, social reform, domesticity; sandj@georgetown.edu

Shedel, James P. (PhD, Rochester 1978; assoc. prof.) Habsburg Austria, Germany, central Europe; shedelj@georgetown.edu

Spendelow, Howard (PhD, Harvard 1982; assoc. prof.) China, East Asia; spendelh@georgetown.edu

Traugh, Geoffrey (ABD, NYU; full-time non-tenure-line faculty) Africa

Tucker, Judith E. (PhD, Harvard 1981; prof.) Middle East and Egypt, women, Ottoman; Judith.Tucker@georgetown.edu

Tutino, John (PhD, Texas, Austin 1976; prof.; dir., Americas Initiative; Sch. of Foreign Service) Latin America, Mexico, social/cultural/political; tutinoj@georgetown.edu

von der Goltz, Anna (PhD, Oxford 2007; assoc. prof.; Sch. of Foreign Service, Center for German & European Studies) modern, 20th-century Germany, modern Europe; Anna.Vondergoltz@georgetown.edu

Retired/Emeritus Faculty

Brown, Dorothy M. (PhD, Georgetown 1962; prof. emeritus) 20th-century America, interwar America, Progressive Era; brownd@georgetown.edu

Chickering, Roger P. (PhD, Stanford 1968; prof. emeritus) modern Germany; chickerr@georgetown.edu

Curran, R. Emmett (PhD, Yale 1974; prof. emeritus) American intellectual and religious, American immigration, US South; currane@georgetown.edu

Duncan, Richard (PhD, Ohio State 1963; prof. emeritus) US political, Civil War and Reconstruction, Middle Period US; duncanr@georgetown.edu

Dunkley, Peter (PhD, Stanford 1976; prof. emeritus) Britain, 19th century; dunkleyp@georgetown.edu

Evtuhov, Catherine (PhD, California, Berkeley 1991; prof. emeritus) imperial Russia, ideas/culture/religion, local; evtuhovc@georgetown.edu

Goldfrank, David M. (PhD, Washington 1970; prof. emeritus) medieval and early modern Russia, Russian intellectual and foreign policy, eastern Europe; goldfrad@georgetown.edu

Horvath-Peterson, Sandra (PhD, Catholic 1971; assoc. prof. emeritus) modern France, social and religious; horvaths@georgetown.edu

Johnson, Ronald M. (PhD, Illinois, Urbana-Champaign 1970; prof. emeritus) American urban, African American, US social; johnsorm@georgetown.edu

Kaminski, Andrzej (PhD, Jagellonian, Poland 1966; prof. emeritus) Soviet Union, eastern Europe; kaminska@georgetown.edu

Voll, John (PhD, Harvard 1969; prof. emeritus) world, Middle East, modern Islamic; vollj@georgetown.edu

Recently Awarded PhDs

Al-Saif, Bader Mousa "Reform Islam? The Renewal of Islamic Thought and Praxis in Modern and Contemporary Arabian Peninsula"

Alejandrino, Clark Lim "Weathering History: Storms, State and Society in South China from the Fifth Century CE"

Berry, Chelsea L. "Poisoned Relations: Medicine, Sorcery, and Poison Trials in the Contested Atlantic, 1680-1850"

Brew, Gregory Ralph "Mandarins, Paladins, and Pahlavis: the International Energy System, the United States, and the Dual Integration of Oil in Iran, 1925-64"

Cornwell, Graham H. "Sweetening the Pot: A History of Tea and Sugar in Morocco, 1850-1960"

Dannies, Kate "Breadwinner Soldiers: Gender, Warfare, and Sovereignty in the Ottoman First World War"

Horn, Oliver Lawrence "From Model to Menace: US Foreign Aid, Development, and Drugs in Cold War Colombia, 1956-78"

Kates, Adrienne "The Persistence of Maya Autonomy: Global Capitalism, Tropical Environments, and the Limits of the Mexican State, 1880-1950"

Mellor, Robynne "The Cold War Underground: An Environmental History of Uranium Mining in the United States, Candaa and the Soviet Union, 1945-91"

Porta, Earnest "Morocco in the Early Atlantic World"

Raykhlina, Yelizaveta "Russian Literary Marketplace: Periodicals, Social Identity, and Publishing for the Middle Stratum in Imperial Russia, 1825-65"

Shi, Yue "The Seven Rivers: Emipre and Economy in the Russo-Qing Central Asian Frontier, 1860s-1910s"

George Washington University

Dept. of History, 801 22nd St. NW, Phillips 335, Washington, DC 20052. 202.994.6230. Fax 202.994.6231. Email: history@gwu.edu. Website: https://history.columbian.gwu.edu/.

Located in the heart of Washington, DC, the George Washington University History Department is an intellectual community of faculty, graduate students, undergraduates, and many associates and friends.

Chair: Katrin Schultheiss
Director of Graduate Studies: David Silverman

Director of Undergraduate Studies: Steven Brady
Degrees Offered: BA,MA,MPhil,PhD
Academic Year System: Semester
Areas of Specialization: early and modern America, Middle East, Europe, Cold War, East Asia, Africa
Undergraduate Tuition (per academic year): $55230
Graduate Tuition (per academic year): $31861
Enrollment 2018-19:
  Undergraduate Majors: 170
  New Graduate Students: 14
  Full-time Graduate Students: 55
  Part-time Graduate Students: 12
  Degrees in History: 50 BA, 8 MA, 6 PhD
Undergraduate Addresses:
  Admissions and Financial Aid: https://www.gwu.edu/undergraduate-admissions
Graduate Addresses:
  Admissions and Financial Aid: https://columbian.gwu.edu/prospective-students

Full-time Faculty

Agnew, Hugh L. (PhD, Stanford 1981; prof.) eastern Europe; agnew@gwu.edu

Alonso, Paula (DPhil, Oxford 1992; assoc. prof.; History and International Affairs) modern Latin America, Argentina; palonso@gwu.edu

Anbinder, Tyler G. (PhD, Columbia 1990; prof.) Civil War-era America, immigration; anbinder@gwu.edu

Arnesen, Eric (PhD, Yale 1986; prof.) modern America, US labor; arnesen@gwu.edu

Atkin, Muriel A. (PhD, Yale 1976; prof.) Russia, Tajikistan, Iran; matkin@gwu.edu

Becker, William H. (PhD, Johns Hopkins 1969; prof.) business, business-government relations; whbecker@gwu.edu

Berkowitz, Edward D. (PhD, Northwestern 1976; prof.) US, social policy; ber@gwu.edu

Blyden, Nemata (PhD, Yale 1998; assoc. prof.) Africa; nemata@gwu.edu

Brazinsky, Gregg A. (PhD, Cornell 2002; assoc. prof.) US-East Asian relations; brazinsk@gwu.edu

Brunsman, Denver A. (PhD, Princeton 2004; asst. prof.) American Revolution and early Republic; brunsman@gwu.edu

Chapman, Erin D. (PhD, Yale 2006; asst. prof.) African American, gender; echapman@gwu.edu

Cline, Diane Harris (PhD, Princeton 1991; assoc. prof.; Classical and Near Eastern Literatures and Civlizations) ancient Greece and Rome, digital; drcline@gwu.edu

Cline, Eric H. (PhD, Pennsylvania 1991; prof.; Classical and Near Eastern Languages and Civilizations) ancient, classics, anthropology; ehcline@gwu.edu

Cottrol, Robert J. (PhD, Yale 1978; prof.; Law Sch.) legal, race, comparative; bcottrol@law.gwu.edu

Harrison, Hope M. (PhD, Columbia 1993; assoc. prof.) Cold War, Russian foreign policy, Russian and eastern European politics; hopeharr@gwu.edu

Hershberg, James G. (PhD, Tufts 1989; prof.) US diplomatic, Cold War; jhershb@gwu.edu

Hiltebeitel, Alf (PhD, Chicago 1973; prof.; Religion) religion; beitel@gwu.edu

Hopkins, Benjamin D. (PhD, Cambridge 2006; assoc. prof.) world, South Asia, Afghanistan; bhopkins@gwu.edu

Joselit, Jenna Weissman (PhD, Columbia 1981; Charles E. Smith Prof.; dir., Judaic Studies Prog.) American Jewish; joselit@gwu.edu

Kennedy, Dane K. (PhD, California, Berkeley 1981; Elmer Louis Kayser Prof.) modern Britain, imperialism; dkennedy@gwu.edu

Khoury, Dina R. (PhD, Georgetown 1987; prof.) Middle East; dikhy@gwu.edu

Kim, Jisoo Monica (PhD, Columbia 2010; assoc. prof.) Korea, gender; jsk10@gwu.edu

Klemek, Christopher (PhD, Pennsylvania 2004; assoc. prof.) US and comparative urban; klemek@gwu.edu

Krug, Jessica A. (PhD, Wisconsin-Madison 2012; asst. prof.) Afro-Atlantic; jkrug@gwu.edu

Long, C. Thomas (PhD, George Washington 2005; asst. prof.) colonial, military; tomlong@gwu.edu

McCord, Edward A. (PhD, Michigan 1985; prof.) China; mccord@gwu.edu

McHale, Shawn F. (PhD, Cornell 1995; assoc. prof.) Southeast Asia, Vietnam; mchale@gwu.edu

Miller, Suzanne Mariko (PhD, Stanford 2007; asst. prof.) medieval, women; smmiller@gwu.edu

Norton, Marcy (PhD, California, Berkeley 2000; assoc. prof.) early modern Europe, Spain; mnorton@gwu.edu

Robinson, Shira N. (PhD, Stanford 2005; assoc. prof.) modern Middle East; snrobins@gwu.edu

Schultheiss, Katrin (PhD, Harvard 1994; assoc. prof. and chair) France, women, medicine; kschulth@gwu.edu

Schwartz, Daniel B. (PhD, Columbia 2007; assoc. prof.) modern Jewish, modern Europe; dbs50@gwu.edu

Silverman, David J. (PhD, Princeton 2000; prof. and dir., grad. studies) colonial, American Indian; djsilver@gwu.edu

Smith, Andrew M., II (PhD, Maryland, Coll. Park 2004; assoc. prof.; Classical and Near Eastern Languages and Civilizations) classics, ancient; amsii@gwu.edu

Spector, Ronald H. (PhD, Yale 1967; prof.) US, military, foreign policy; spector@gwu.edu

Stott, Richard (PhD, Cornell 1983; prof.) US social, urban, labor; rstott@gwu.edu

Thornton, Richard C. (PhD, Washington 1966; prof.) China, Russia, US-Soviet strategic relations; rthornto@gwu.edu

Yang, Daqing (PhD, Harvard 1996; assoc. prof.) Japan; yanghist@gwu.edu

Zimmerman, Andrew (PhD, California, San Diego 1998; prof.) Germany, colonial and imperial studies; azimmer@gwu.edu

Nondepartmental Historians

Bickford, Charlene Bangs (MA, George Washington 1969; dir. and principal investigator, First Federal Congress Proj.) early America; bickford@gwu.edu

Bowling, Kenneth R. (PhD, Wisconsin, Madison 1967; co-ed., First Federal Congress Proj.) American Revolution; kbowling@gwu.edu

Brick, Christopher E. (MA, Brown 2005; dir., Eleanor Roosevelt Papers) recent US; cbrick@gwu.edu

Retired/Emeritus Faculty

DePauw, Linda Grant (PhD, Johns Hopkins 1964; prof. emeritus) early America, American women; minervacen@aol.com

Harrison, Cynthia E. (PhD, Columbia 1982; assoc. prof. emerita) US women, public policy; harrison@gwu.edu

Herber, Charles J. (PhD, California, Berkeley 1965; assoc. prof. emeritus) Germany, Europe, Reformation; cherber@gwu.edu

Hill, Peter P. (PhD, George Washington 1966; prof. emeritus and Univ. historian) US diplomatic, early national US; pphill@gwu.edu

Kennedy, R. Emmet (PhD, Brandeis 1973; prof. emeritus) France, intellectual; ekennedy@gwu.edu

Klaren, Peter F. (PhD, UCLA 1968; prof. emeritus) Latin America; klaren@gwu.edu

Peck, Linda Levy (PhD, Yale 1973; prof. emerita) early modern Britain; llpeck@gwu.edu

Saperstein, Marc E. (PhD, Harvard 1977; Charles E. Smith Prof. emeritus) Jewish; msaper@gwu.edu

Schwoerer, Lois G. (PhD, Bryn Mawr 1956; prof. emeritus) England, Renaissance, European women; lgsch@gwu.edu

Recently Awarded PhDs

Bakhtary, Elham "Mirrors for Ulama: Kabul at the Crossroads of Reformism and Revivalism"

Densford, Kathryn Elizabeth "The Relationship between Vienna and Moravia during the Great War"

Musto, Ryan A. "Regional Fallout: The United States and Nuclear Weapon Free Zones during the Eisenhower Era"

Price, Alexa "Nostalgia, Heroism, and British Conceptions of the Historical Sailor at the Turn of the 19th Century"

Sommers, Kyla "I Believe in the City: The Black Freedom Struggle and the 1968 Civil Disturbances in Washington, DC"

University of Georgia

Dept. of History, 220 LeConte Hall, Athens, GA 30602-1602. 706.542.2053. Fax 706.542.2455. Email: history@uga.edu. Website: http://history.uga.edu/.

The department has a strong tradition of expertise in subjects ranging from early American to modern African American history, the Caribbean to the Middle East, early modern Europe to the modern US South, popular culture to foreign policy, religion to global capitalism.

Chair: Claudio Saunt
Director of Graduate Studies: Daniel Rood
Director of Undergraduate Studies: Jamie Kreiner
Degrees Offered: BA, MA, PhD
Academic Year System: Semester
Areas of Specialization: US and US South, Europe, Latin America, war and society, capitalism, public
Undergraduate Tuition (per academic year):
   In-State: $4776
   Out-of-State: $14063
Graduate Tuition (per academic year):
   In-State: $4352
   Out-of-State: $12346
Enrollment 2018-19:
   Undergraduate Majors: 255
   New Graduate Students: 19
   Full-time Graduate Students: 40
   Part-time Graduate Students: 5
   Degrees in History: 68 BA, 3 MA, 5 PhD
Undergraduate Addresses:
   Admissions: https://www.admissions.uga.edu/
   Financial Aid: http://osfa.uga.edu/
Graduate Addresses:
   Admissions: http://www.grad.uga.edu/
   Financial Aid: http://osfa.uga.edu/

Adjunct Faculty

Hamilton, Shane L. (PhD, MIT 2005; adj. prof.) supermarkets, political ecology; shamilto@uga.edu

Larson, Edward J. (PhD, Wisconsin, Madison 1984; JD, Harvard 1979; adj. prof.) science, law; edlarson@uga.edu

McMurry, Nan (PhD, Duke 1985; adj. instr. and librarian) medicine, historical bibliography; nmcmurry@uga.edu

Full-time Faculty

Berry, Stephen William, II (PhD, North Carolina, Chapel Hill 2000; assoc. prof.) Civil War; berry@uga.edu

Chamosa, Oscar (PhD, North Carolina, Chapel Hill 2003; asst. prof.) Argentine cultural, Latin American folklore, American diaspora; chamo01@uga.edu

Cleaveland, Timothy (PhD, Northwestern 1994; assoc. prof.) Africa, gender; tcleave@uga.edu

Drake, Brian (PhD, Kansas 2006; sr. lect.) America; bdrake@uga.edu

Ehlers, Benjamin (PhD, Johns Hopkins 1999; assoc. prof.) early modern Europe, Spain; behlers@uga.edu

Hahamovitch, Cindy (PhD, North Carolina, Chapel Hill 1992; Spalding Chair in History) America

Hoffer, Peter C. (PhD, Harvard 1970; research prof.) early America, legal, quantitative methods; pchoffer@uga.edu

Inscoe, John C. (PhD, North Carolina, Chapel Hill 1985; Univ. prof.) 19th-century US South, Appalachia; jinscoe@uga.edu

Jones, Kevin Michael (PhD, Michigan 2013; asst. prof.) Middle East; kevjones@uga.edu

Kreiner, Jamie (PhD, Princeton 2011; assoc. prof. and dir., undergrad. studies) late antiquity, medieval Europe; jkreiner@uga.edu

Levine, Ari Daniel (PhD, Columbia 2002; assoc. prof.) late imperial Chinese political culture; adlevine@uga.edu

Mattern, Susan P. (PhD, Yale 1995; prof.) ancient Greek and Roman social and cultural; smattern@uga.edu

Mihm, Stephen A. (PhD, NYU 2003; assoc. prof.) 19th-century America, economic and cultural; smihm@uga.edu

Morrow, John H., Jr. (PhD, Pennsylvania 1971; Franklin Prof.) modern Europe, war and society, modern Germany; jmorrow@uga.edu

Nelson, Scott Reynolds (PhD, North Carolina, Chapel Hill 1995; UGA Athletic Association Prof. in Humanities) America

Palmer, Jennifer L. (PhD, Michigan 2008; assoc. prof.) early modern France; palmerjl@uga.edu

Pollard, Miranda J. (PhD, Trinity Coll., Dublin 1990; assoc. prof.) modern Europe, women, 20th-century France; mpollard@uga.edu

Pratt, Robert A., III (PhD, Virginia 1987; prof.) 20th-century US, African American, race and ethnicity; rapratt@uga.edu

Reason, Akela (PhD, Maryland, Coll. Park 2005; assoc. prof.) 19th-century US cultural; areason@uga.edu

Roman, Reinaldo L. (PhD, UCLA 2000; assoc. prof.) modern Latin America; rroman@uga.edu

Rood, Dan B. (PhD, California, Irvine 2010; asst. prof. and dir., grad. studies) slavery in Atlantic world, antebellum US South, Latin America and Caribbean; danrood@uga.edu

Saunt, Claudio (PhD, Duke 1996; Richard B. Russell Prof. and chair) Native American, early America; csaunt@uga.edu

Short, John Phillip (PhD, Columbia 2004; assoc. prof.) modern European social and cultural; jshort@uga.edu

Soper, Steven C. (PhD, Michigan 1996; asst. prof.) modern Italy and modern Europe; ssoper@uga.edu

Willis, Kirk (PhD, Wisconsin, Madison 1982; assoc. prof.) modern Britain; kw@uga.edu

Winship, Michael P. (PhD, Cornell 1992; E. M. Coulter Prof.) early modern America and Britain, intellectual and cultural; mwinship@uga.edu

Wolf, M. Montgomery (PhD, North Carolina, Chapel Hill 2008; sr. lect.) America; mwolf@uga.edu

Yang, Timothy (PhD, Columbia 2013; asst. prof.) medicine and capitalism, modern Japan, Asian studies; timothy.yang@uga.edu

Joint/Cross Appointments

Lee, Chana Kai (PhD, UCLA 1993; assoc. prof.; Institute for African American Studies) 20th-century African American, women, recent US; chanakai@uga.edu

Morrow, Diane Batts (PhD, Georgia 1996; assoc. prof.; Inst. African American Studies) 19th-century African American, US multicultural; dbmorrow@uga.edu

Roth, Cassia Paigen (PhD, UCLA 2016; asst. prof.; Latin American and Caribbean Studies Institute) health/reproduction/sexuality, gender studies, Latin American studies; cassia.roth@uga.edu

Retired/Emeritus Faculty

Cobb, James C. (PhD, Georgia 1975; B. Phinizy Spalding Prof. emeritus) US South, US southern culture; cobby@uga.edu

Kulikoff, Allan (PhD, Brandeis 1976; Abraham Baldwin Prof. emeritus) early America, US South, slavery; kulikoff@uga.edu

Whigham, Thomas L. (PhD, Stanford 1986; prof. emeritus) Latin America; twhigham@uga.edu

Recently Awarded PhDs

Angermeier, Derrick J. "Both Hitler and Jim Crow: Lost Causes and Imagined Futures in Interwar Bavaria and the New South, 1919-39"

Kirby, Jason "Both Force and Symbol: General William C. Westmoreland and the Shifting Priorities of Cold War America"

Wall, James "Settling Down for the Long Haul: The Struggle for Freedom Rights in Southwest Georgia, 1945-95"

Washnock, Kaylynn Lee "Making Atlanta: Civil War Memory, Civic Branding, and Heritage Tourism in the New South City, 1958-96"

Windisch, Kurt W. "The Battle of a Thousand Slain: St. Clair's Defeat and the Origins of the First Constitutional Crisis in American History, 1783-92"

Georgia College and State University

Dept. of History and Geography, Campus Box 47, Milledgeville, GA 31061-0490. 478.445.5215. Fax 478.445.4009. Email: amy. mimes@gcsu.edu; aran.mackinnon@gcsu.edu. Website: https:// www.gcsu.edu/artsandsciences/history.

We seek to provide students with an understanding of the connections of past and present; intellectual curiosity and enthusiasm for learning; an ability to conduct historical, and geographical research, to examine and analyze material critically, and to communicate knowledge and ideas effectively; preparation for advanced study and professional careers in history or other occupations; and the capacity for lifelong learning and responsible participation as citizens of today's world.

Chair: Aran MacKinnon
Degrees Offered: BA
Academic Year System: Semester
Areas of Specialization: US and US South, Africa and Asia, Europe, Latin America, geography
Tuition (per academic year):
  In-State: $9346
  Out-of-State: $28060
Enrollment 2018-19:
  Undergraduate Majors: 90
  Degrees in History: 21 BA
Addresses:
  Admissions: http://www.gcsu.edu/admissions/apply
  Financial Aid: http://www.gcsu.edu/financialaid

Full-time Faculty

Auerbach, Stephen D. (PhD, Louisiana State 2001; prof.) early modern Europe; stephen.auerbach@gcsu.edu

Dean, Ashleigh (PhD, Emory 2016; asst. prof.) Asia; ashleigh.dean@gcsu.edu

Fahrer, Charles (PhD, South Carolina 2001; prof.) political geography, military geography, Middle East and North Africa; chuck.fahrer@gcsu.edu

Huddle, Mark A. (PhD, Georgia 2001; assoc. prof.) African American, popular culture; mark.huddle@gcsu.edu

MacKinnon, Aran (PhD, Inst. of Commonwealth Studies, London 1996; prof. and chair) Africa, South Africa; aran.mackinnon@gcsu.edu

Oetter, Doug R. (PhD, Oregon State 2002; prof.) geography, GIS, environmental geography; doug.oetter@gcsu.edu

Opperman, Stephanie Baker (PhD, Illinois, Chicago 2012; asst. prof.) Latin America, Mexico, immigration and public health; stephanie.opperman@gcsu.edu

Pascoe, Craig S. (PhD, Tennessee, Knoxville 1998; prof.) US, US South; craig.pascoe@gcsu.edu

Risch, William Jay (PhD, Ohio State 2001; assoc. prof.) modern Europe, Russia, Ukraine; william.risch@gcsu.edu

Rochelo, Mark (PhD, Florida Atlantic 2017; temporary lect.) Geographic Information Science, drone research; mark.rochelo@gcsu.edu

Scallet, Daniel (PhD, Washington, St. Louis 2011; temp. lect.) US, Native American, Latin America; daniel.scallet@gcsu.edu

Sumpter, Amy (PhD, Louisiana State 2008; assoc. prof.) cultural and economic geography; amy.sumpter@gcsu.edu

Wallace, Jessica Lynn (PhD, Ohio State 2014; asst. prof.) early America, Atlantic world, Native American; jessica.wallace@gcsu.edu

Welborn, James Hill, III (PhD, Georgia 2014; asst. prof.) Civil War, southern religions; james.welborn@gcsu.edu

Retired/Emeritus Faculty

Begemann, Rosemary E. (PhD, Emory 1973; prof. emeritus) England, women, modern Europe

Keber, Martha L. (PhD, Emory 1975; prof. emeritus) modern Europe

Vinson, Frank B. (PhD, Georgia 1971; prof. emeritus) US South, military

Wilson, Robert J., III (PhD, Massachusetts Amherst 1980; prof. emeritus and Univ. historian) American religion, colonial America, local; bob.wilson@gcsu.edu

Georgia Institute of Technology

Sch. of History and Sociology, 221 Bobby Dodd Way, Atlanta, GA 30332-0225. 404.894.3196. Fax 404.894.0535. Email: eschatzberg3@gatech.edu. Website: https://hsoc.gatech.edu/.

The School of History and Sociology brings the perspective of the social sciences to bear on critical issues facing the modern world, while providing a source of analysis that emphasizes both change over time and cultural comparisons on a global scale.

Chair: Eric Schatzberg
Director of Graduate Studies: William Winders
Degrees Offered: BS,MS,PhD
Academic Year System: Semester
Areas of Specialization: science, technology, medicine, industrialization, labor

Undergraduate Tuition (per academic year):
In-State: $15224
Out-of-State: $35820
Graduate Tuition (per academic year):
In-State: $18204
Out-of-State: $32484
Enrollment 2018-19:
Undergraduate Majors: 59
New Graduate Students: 6
Full-time Graduate Students: 15
Part-time Graduate Students: 9
Degrees in History: 4 BS, 1 PhD
Students in Undergraduate Courses: 1235
Students in Undergraduate Intro Courses: 876
Undergraduate Addresses:
Admissions: http://www.admission.gatech.edu
Financial Aid: http://www.finaid.gatech.edu/
Graduate Addresses:
Admissions: http://www.gradadmiss.gatech.edu
Financial Aid: http://www.finaid.gatech.edu/

Full-time Faculty

Amsterdam, Daniel (PhD, Pennsylvania 2009; asst. prof.) American urban; daniel.amsterdam@hts.gatech.edu

Bier, Laura (PhD, NYU 2006; asst. prof.) modern Middle East; laura.bier@hts.gatech.edu

Brown, Kate Pride (PhD, Vanderbilt 2015; asst. prof.) environmental sociology, political economy, globalization/transnationalism; k.p.brown@gatech.edu

Flamming, Douglas (PhD, Vanderbilt 1987; prof.) American social, US South, recent America; doug.flamming@hts.gatech.edu

Gerona, Carla (PhD, Johns Hopkins 1998; asst. prof.) Atlantic world and borderlands; carla.gerona@hts.gatech.edu

Hyde, Allen (PhD, Connecticut 2016; asst. prof.; Sociology) social stratification and inequality, urban sociology, immigration; allen.hyde@hsoc.gatech.edu

Krige, John (PhD, Sussex, UK 1979; Kranzberg Prof.) science, technology, US foreign policy; john.krige@hts.gatech.edu

Lu, Hanchao (PhD, UCLA 1991; prof.) modern China, Chinese industrialization and urbanization; hanchao.lu@hts.gatech.edu

Macrakis, Kristie (PhD, Harvard 1989; prof.) science and technology, intelligence, German science; kristie.macrakis@hts.gatech.edu

McDonald, Mary (PhD, Iowa 1995; Homer Rice Prof.) sociology of sports; mary.mcdonald@hts.gatech.edu

Michney, Todd M. (PhD, Minnesota 2004; asst. prof.) digital, African American, urban; todd.michney@hsoc.gatech.edu

Pearson, Willie, Jr. (PhD, Southern Illinois 1981; prof.; Sociology) sociology of science, education, race and ethnicity; willie.pearsonjr@hts.gatech.edu

Randolph, Sherie M. (PhD, NYU 2007; assoc. prof.) social movements, black feminist theory, gender and race; sherie.randolph@hsoc.gatech.edu

Singh, Jennifer (PhD, California, San Francisco 2010; asst. prof.; Sociology) sociology of science and technology; jennifer.singh@hts.gatech.edu

Smith, John M. (PhD, Purdue 2011; asst. prof.) sports and American society; john.smith@hts.gatech.edu

Tone, John Lawrence (PhD, Columbia 1989; prof.) Spain, Cuban military medicine; john.tone@hts.gatech.edu

Usselman, Steven W. (PhD, Delaware 1985; prof.) technology and science; steve.usselman@hsoc.gatech.edu

Vergara, German (PhD, California, Berkeley 2015; asst. prof.) Latin America, environmental, energy; german.vergara@hsoc.gatech.edu

Winders, William (PhD, Emory 2002; assoc. prof. and dir., grad. studies) social inequality, social movements, political sociology; william.winders@hts.gatech.edu

Nondepartmental Historians

Moore, Carole E. (PhD, California, Santa Barbara 1973; special asst. to vice provost) medieval, ancient; moore@gatech.edu

Retired/Emeritus Faculty

Bayor, Ronald H. (PhD, Pennsylvania 1970; prof. emeritus) American urban and ethnic; ronald.bayor@hts.gatech.edu

Brittain, James E. (PhD, Case Western Reserve 1970; prof. emeritus) science and technology

Foster, Lawrence (PhD, Chicago 1976; prof. emeritus) American social, religious; lawrence.foster@hts.gatech.edu

Giebelhaus, August W., Jr. (PhD, Delaware 1976; prof. emeritus) American economic/business/technology; gus.giebelhaus@hts.gatech.edu

Knoespel, Kenneth (PhD, Chicago 1982; prof. emeritus) Scandinavian and Russian studies, material culture, northern Europe; kenneth.knoespel@iac.gatech.edu

Nobles, Gregory H. (PhD, Michigan 1979; prof. emeritus) early America, labor, environment; gregory.nobles@gatech.edu

Reed, Germaine M. (PhD, Louisiana State 1970; assoc. prof. emeritus) Civil War and Reconstruction, biography

Schneer, Jonathan (PhD, Columbia 1978; prof. emeritus) modern Britain, labor, politics; jonathan.schneer@hts.gatech.edu

Recently Awarded PhDs

Dempsey, Ron Jr. "The Role of Engineering Technology as a Pathway for African Americans into the Field of Engineering"

Hull, Rebecca Ann Watts "Winning Real Food on Campus: The Role of Opportunity Structures, Strategic Capacity, and Identity in the Outcomes of Student Campaigns"

Georgia Southern University

Dept. of History, Statesboro Campus, PO Box 8054, Interdisciplinary Academic Bldg. #3007, Statesboro, GA 30460-8054. 912.478.4478. Fax 912.478.0377. Email: history@georgiasouthern.edu. Website: https://cah.georgiasouthern.edu/history/.

Alternate Address: Armstrong Campus, 11935 Abercorn St., Hawes Hall 110, Savannah, GA 31419-1997

Our faculty are engaging teachers and nationally and internationally known scholars in various historical fields. You will be in the classroom with award-winning teachers and scholars, taking a range of classes that satisfy just about any historical interest.

Chair: Carol Engelhardt Herringer
Director of Graduate Studies: Craig Roell
Degrees Offered: BA,MA
Academic Year System: Semester
Areas of Specialization: American South, Europe, public, military, women
Undergraduate Tuition (per academic year):
   In-State: $5464
   Out-of-State: $19280
Graduate Tuition (per academic year):
   In-State: $6636
   Out-of-State: $26500
Enrollment 2018-19:
   Undergraduate Majors: 222

New Graduate Students: 8
Full-time Graduate Students: 19
Part-time Graduate Students: 8
Degrees in History: 61 BA, 12 MA
Undergraduate Addresses:
   Admissions: http://admissions.georgiasouthern.edu/
   Financial Aid: http://em.georgiasouthern.edu/finaid/
Graduate Addresses:
   Admissions: http://cogs.georgiasouthern.edu/admission/
   Financial Aid: http://em.georgiasouthern.edu/finaid/

Full-time Faculty

Akturk, Ahmet Serdar (PhD, Arkansas 2012; asst. prof.; Statesboro) modern Middle East, identity politics in post-Ottoman Middle East; aakturk@georgiasouthern.edu

Allison, William Thomas (PhD, Bowling Green State 1995; prof.; Statesboro) US diplomatic, military; billallison@georgiasouthern.edu

Arens, Olavi (PhD, Columbia 1976; prof.; Armstrong) modern Russia and Soviet Union; oarens@georgiasouthern.edu

Batchelor, Robert Kinnaird, Jr. (PhD, UCLA 1999; prof.; Statesboro) modern Britain, British Empire; batchelo@georgiasouthern.edu

Belzer, Allison S. (PhD, Emory 2002; assoc. prof.; Armstrong) modern Europe, Italy, Great Britain; abelzer@georgiasouthern.edu

Benjamin, Michael (PhD, Drew 2007; assoc. prof.; Armstrong) African American, public, book; mbenjamin@georgiasouthern.edu

Bryant, Jonathan M. (PhD, Georgia 1992; JD, Mercer 1983; prof.; Statesboro) Georgia, US South, special collections; jbryant@georgiasouthern.edu

Burson, Jeffrey D. (PhD, George Washington 2006; assoc. prof.; Statesboro) modern France; jburson@georgiasouthern.edu

Comerford, Kathleen M. (PhD, Wisconsin, Madison 1995; prof.; Statesboro) Renaissance, Reformation; kcomerfo@georgiasouthern.edu

Curtis, Christopher M. (PhD, Emory 2002; prof.; Armstrong) early national US, legal and constitutional, Civil War and Reconstruction; ccurtis@georgiasouthern.edu

de Chantal, Julie (PhD, Massachusetts Amherst 2016; asst. prof.; Statesboro) African American; jdechantal@georgiasouthern.edu

Denmark, Lisa L. (PhD, South Carolina 2004; assoc. prof.; Statesboro) US South, Georgia, urban; ldenmark@georgiasouthern.edu

Downs, Alan Craig (PhD, North Carolina, Chapel Hill 1991; assoc. prof.; Statesboro) Civil War era, American Indian, US West; acdowns@georgiasouthern.edu

Feltman, Brian K. (PhD, Ohio State 2010; asst. prof.; Statesboro) modern Germany, military; bfeltman@georgiasouthern.edu

Gayan, Melissa Faris (MA, North Carolina, Charlotte 2003; sr. lect.; Statesboro) mfgayan@georgiasouthern.edu

Haberland, Michelle (PhD, Tulane 2001; prof.; Statesboro) labor, US women, late 19th- and early 20th-century US; mah@georgiasouthern.edu

Hall, Michael R. (PhD, Ohio 1996; prof.; Armstrong) 20th-century America, US foreign relations, Latin America; mrhall@georgiasouthern.edu

Hendricks, Christopher E. (PhD, William and Mary 1991; prof.; Armstrong) architectural, historic preservation, colonial America; chendricks@georgiasouthern.edu

Herringer, Carol Englehardt (PhD, Indiana 1997; prof. and chair; Statesboro) Victorian Britain, gender, early modern and modern Britain, decorative arts; cherringer@georgiasouthern.edu

Knoerl, T. Kurt (PhD, George Mason 2013; asst. prof.; Armstrong) public; kknoerl@georgiasouthern.edu

Lin, Mao (PhD, Georgia 2010; asst. prof.; Statesboro) US diplomatic, international relations, US-Chinese relations; mlin@georgiasouthern.edu

Nti, Kwaku (PhD, Michigan State 2011; assoc. prof.; Armstrong) postcolonial West Africa, Africa, globalization; knti@georgiasouthern.edu

O'Neill, Johnathan G. (PhD, Maryland, Coll. Park 2000; prof.; Statesboro) US constitutional, political thought; joneill@georgiasouthern.edu

Peng, Juanjuan (PhD, Johns Hopkins 2007; assoc. prof.; Statesboro) Chinese economic and business; jpeng@georgiasouthern.edu

Pirok, Alena R. (PhD, South Florida 2017; asst. prof.; Armstrong) public; apirok@georgiasouthern.edu

Rodell, Paul A. (PhD, SUNY, Buffalo 1992; prof.; Statesboro) Southeast Asia, Pacific Rim, Islamic affairs; rodell@georgiasouthern.edu

Roell, Craig H. (PhD, Texas, Austin 1986; prof. and grad. coord.; Statesboro) US business, economic, cultural; croell@georgiasouthern.edu

Sims, Anastatia (PhD, North Carolina, Chapel Hill 1985; prof.; Statesboro) US women, recent US; asims@georgiasouthern.edu

Skidmore-Hess, Cathy J. (PhD, Wisconsin, Madison 1995; assoc. prof.; Statesboro) Africa, environmental, gender; cskid@georgiasouthern.edu

Smith, Solomon Kelly (PhD, Georgia 2009; assoc. prof.; Statesboro) Revolutionary War, industrial ventures in Chesapeake; sksmith@georgiasouthern.edu

Tatlock, Jason Robert (PhD, Michigan 2006; assoc. prof.; Armstrong) Near Eastern studies, human rights, comparative religions; jtatlock@georgiasouthern.edu

Teeter, Timothy M. (PhD, Columbia 1989; assoc. prof.; Statesboro) ancient Greece and Rome, late antiquity; tmteeter@georgiasouthern.edu

Timmons-Hill, Deborah L. (ABD, Georgia State 2009; sr. lect.; Statesboro) medieval Mediterranean, Eastern religion; deborahhill@georgiasouthern.edu

Todesca, James C. (PhD, Fordham 1996; assoc. prof.; Armstrong) medieval Spain, numismatics; jtodesca@georgiasouthern.edu

Turner, Felicity M. (PhD, Duke 2010; asst. prof.; Armstrong) 19th-century America, women, legal; fturner@georgiasouthern.edu

Van Wagenen, Michael Scott (PhD, Utah 2009; assoc. prof.; Statesboro) public, US-Mexico borderlands; mvanwagenen@georgiasouthern.edu

Wang, Hongjie (PhD, Brown 2008; assoc. prof.; Armstrong) China, East Asia; hongjiewang@georgiasouthern.edu

Woods, James M. (PhD, Tulane 1983; prof.; Statesboro) Jacksonian America, early Republic, US religion; jmwoods@georgiasouthern.edu

Zeltsman, Corinna (PhD, Duke 2016; asst. prof.; Statesboro) 19th-century Mexico, print culture; czeltsman@georgiasouthern.edu

Nondepartmental Historians

Caplinger, Christopher (PhD, Vanderbilt 2003; dir., First Year Experience) caplinca@georgiasouthern.edu

Tharp, Brent W. (PhD, William and Mary 1996; dir., Georgia Southern Univ. Museum) material culture, early American social; btharp@georgiasouthern.edu

Retired/Emeritus Faculty

Barrow, Robert M. (PhD, Virginia 1967; assoc. prof. emeritus) colonial America, naval

Brogdon, Frederick W. (MA, Georgia Southern 1967; asst. prof. emeritus) US, Georgia

Egger, Vernon O. (PhD, Michigan 1983; prof. emeritus) modern Middle East, Islamic; voegger@georgiasouthern.edu

Joiner, G. Hewett, Jr. (PhD, Northwestern 1971; prof. emeritus) modern Britain, European intellectual

Moseley, C. Charlton (PhD, Georgia 1968; prof. emeritus) American West, recent US

Rogers, George A. (PhD, Illinois, Urbana-Champaign 1950; prof. emeritus) Europe, classical world

Shriver, George H. (PhD, Duke 1961; prof. emeritus) Western religious, religious dissent and heresy

Shurbutt, T. Ray (PhD, Georgia 1971; prof. emeritus) Latin America

Thomas, Charles S. (PhD, Vanderbilt 1983; prof. emeritus) modern Germany, military; cthomas@georgiasouthern.edu

Young, Alfred (PhD, Syracuse 1977; prof. emeritus) African American; ayoung@georgiasouthern.edu

Georgia State University

Dept. of History, PO Box 4117, Atlanta, GA 30302-4117. 404.413.6385. Fax 404.413.6384. Email: DGSHistory@gsu.edu. Website: https://history.gsu.edu.

As part of a public research university, our primary mission is to create and disseminate knowledge and research methods that promote the intellectual development of our students. Graduates of Georgia State's history programs will have the ability to analyze conflicting information and viewpoints, write clearly and communicate ideas, find reliable evidence for judgments about human actions and motives, and place particular events in a wider context or historical pattern.

Chair: Michelle Brattain
Director of Graduate Studies: Alex S. Cummings
Director of Undergraduate Studies: Larry B. Grubbs
Degrees Offered: BA,MA,MHP,PhD
Academic Year System: Semester
Areas of Specialization: US, Europe, world, heritage preservation, public
Undergraduate Tuition (per academic year):
 In-State: $9286
 Out-of-State: $24516
Graduate Tuition (per academic year):
 In-State: $9292
 Out-of-State: $24790
Enrollment 2018-19:
 Undergraduate Majors: 192
 New Graduate Students: 32
 Full-time Graduate Students: 51
 Part-time Graduate Students: 62
 Degrees in History: 54 BA, 4 MA, 4 PhD, 7 MHP
Undergraduate Addresses:
 Admissions: http://admissions.gsu.edu
 Financial Aid: http://sfs.gsu.edu/the-financial-aid-process/
Graduate Addresses:
 Admissions: https://graduate.gsu.edu/
 Financial Aid: http://sfs.gsu.edu/the-financial-aid-process/

Full-time Faculty

Baker, H. Robert (PhD, UCLA 2004; assoc. prof.) American legal and constitutional; robertbaker@gsu.edu

Brattain, Michelle (PhD, Rutgers 1997; assoc. prof. and chair) cultural and intellectual, labor, 20th-century US and South; mbrattain@gsu.edu

Conner, Robin (PhD, Emory 2008; lect.) women and gender, social; rconner@gsu.edu

Cummings, Alex Sayf (PhD, Columbia 2009; assoc. prof. and dir., grad. studies) cultural and intellectual, legal and constitutional, 20th century; alexcummings@gsu.edu

Davidson, Denise Z. (PhD, Pennsylvania 1997; prof.) modern France, French social and cultural, women; ddavidson2@gsu.edu

Davis, Marni (PhD, Emory 2006; assoc. prof.) US, 20th century, ethnicity and immigration; marnidavis@gsu.edu

Eskew, Glenn T. (PhD, Georgia 1993; prof.) 20th-century US, US South; gteskew@gsu.edu

Fletcher, Ian C. (PhD, Johns Hopkins 1991; assoc. prof.) modern Britain, Ireland, British Empire; icfletcher@gsu.edu

Fromherz, Allen (PhD, St. Andrews, Scotland 2006; prof.) medieval Mediterranean and Islamic world; afromherz@gsu.edu

Fuller, Harcourt T. (PhD, London Sch. of Economics 2010; assoc. prof.) African diaspora and African American, Atlantic world, economic and business; hfuller@gsu.edu

Gaffield, Julia (PhD, Duke 2012; asst. prof.) early modern Atlantic world; jgaffield@gsu.edu

Grubbs, Larry (PhD, South Carolina 2003; sr. lect. and dir., undergrad. advisement) US, imperialism; lgrubbs@gsu.edu

Marshall, Amani N. (PhD, Indiana 2007; lect.) African American, antebellum South, women and gender; amarshall@gsu.edu

McMillian, John C. (PhD, Columbia 2006; assoc. prof.) cultural and intellectual, 20th-century US; jmcmillian@gsu.edu

Nadri, Ghulam Ahmad (PhD, Leiden, Netherlands 2007; assoc. prof.) South Asia, Indian Ocean; gnadri@gsu.edu

Perry, Joe (PhD, Illinois, Urbana-Champaign 2001; assoc. prof.) modern Europe, Germany, gender; jbperry@gsu.edu

Poley, Jared (PhD, UCLA 2001; prof.) Atlantic world, cultural and intellectual, science; jpoley@gsu.edu

Reynolds, Douglas R. (PhD, Columbia 1976; prof.) East Asia; dreynolds@gsu.edu

Rolinson, Mary G. (PhD, Georgia State 2002; lect.) African diaspora, African American, political; mrolinson1@gsu.edu

Sehat, David J. (PhD, North Carolina, Chapel Hill 2007; prof.) US, 19th century, cultural and intellectual; dsehat@gsu.edu

Selwood, Jacob W. (PhD, Duke 2003; assoc. prof.) Britain; jselwood@gsu.edu

Venet, Wendy Hamand (PhD, Illinois, Urbana-Champaign 1985; prof.) 19th-century US, women; wvenet@gsu.edu

Way, John T. (PhD, Yale 2006; asst. prof.) Latin America, transnational; jway@gsu.edu

Wilding, Nick (PhD, European Univ. Inst., Fiesole, Italy 2000; prof.) early modern Europe; nwilding@gsu.edu

Wilson, Kathryn E. (PhD, Pennsylvania 1996; assoc. prof.) public; kewilson@gsu.edu

Joint/Cross Appointments

Young, Jeffrey R. (PhD, Emory 1996; lect.; dir., undergrad. honors prog.) African American, South, 18th and 19th century; jryoung@gsu.edu

Retired/Emeritus Faculty

Ali, Mohammed Hassen (PhD, London 1983; assoc. prof. emeritus) African diaspora, Islamic world; mali@gsu.edu

Crimmins, Timothy J. (PhD, Emory 1972; prof. emeritus) urban, historic preservation; tcrimmin@gsu.edu

Davis, Gerald H. (PhD, Vanderbilt 1958; prof. emeritus) 20th-century central Europe, military; ghdavis3@aol.com

Evans, Ellen L. (PhD, Columbia 1956; prof. emeritus) 19th- and 20th-century Europe, modern Germany, European intellectual; ele1730@mindspring.com

Galishoff, Stuart E. (PhD, NYU 1969; prof. emeritus) US public health, urban, recent US

Gorsuch, Edwin N. (PhD, Ohio State 1967; assoc. prof. emeritus) medieval and Renaissance, comparative; egorsuch@gsu.edu

Harrold, Frances L. (PhD, Bryn Mawr 1960; assoc. prof. emeritus) early national US, 18th-century England, Enlightenment

Hudson, Hugh D. (PhD, North Carolina, Chapel Hill 1981; prof. emeritus) 18th- to 20th-century Russia and Soviet Union; hhudson@gsu.edu

Laub, Richard (OMS, Virginia 1987; retired acad. professional) heritage preservation; rlaub@gsu.edu

Matthews, John M. (PhD, Duke 1970; assoc. prof. emeritus) US South, US 1850-1900

McCreery, David J. (PhD, Tulane 1973; prof. emeritus) Latin America; dmccreery@gsu.edu

Reed, Merl E. (PhD, Louisiana State 1957; prof. emeritus) US economic, labor, urban; fsmer@panther.gsu.edu

Reid, Donald M. (PhD, Princeton 1969; prof. emeritus) modern Middle East; hisdmr@langate.gsu.edu

Rouse, Jacqueline A. (PhD, Emory 1983; assoc. prof. emeritus) African American, women; jrouse@gsu.edu

Schwenk, Cynthia J. (PhD, Missouri, Columbia 1977; assoc. prof. emeritus) ancient; cschwenk@gsu.edu

Steffen, Charles G. (PhD, Northwestern 1977; prof. emeritus) colonial America, labor; csteffen@gsu.edu

Willen, Diane (PhD, Tufts 1972; prof. emeritus) early modern England, early modern European women; dwillen@gsu.edu

Recently Awarded PhDs

Floyd, Joseph "The Making of Mañana-Land: The American Mediterranean in the Age of Jim Crow and the United Fruit Company"

Gleason, Christopher "American Poly: A History"

Graves, Kristina Marie "'They Ought to Wear Petticoats!' Male Support of Women's Suffrage in America, 1840-1920"

Greeson, Helen Quinones "Catalan Modernism in Fin-de-Siècle Spain: Culture and Medicine"

Hand-Stephenson, Corrie "Demons of Discord: Violence and the Socio-political Growth of Colonial South Carolina and Georgia, 1690-1776"

Hoffmann, Nicolas G. "Off the Bloodied Grounds: The Civil War and the Professionalization of American Medicine"

Land, Jeremy "Boston, New York, and Philadelphia in Global Maritime Trade, 1700-75"

Patenaude, Sara "The False Promise of Individual Choice: Residential Segregation and Policy Discourse in Baltimore Public Housing, 1940-70"

Gettysburg College

Dept. of History, 300 N. Washington St., Campus Box 401, Gettysburg, PA 17325. 717.337.6565. Fax 717.337.8565. Email: shancock@gettysburg.edu. Website: https://www.gettysburg.edu/academic-programs/history/.

The study of history challenges students to explore a variety of sources as they gain a greater understanding of the past. The College's expansive history curriculum spans a wide range of periods and developments around the world.

Chair: Scott Hancock
Degrees Offered: BA
Academic Year System: Semester
Areas of Specialization: America and Latin America, Europe, East Asia, Africa, Islamic
Tuition (per academic year): $69850

Enrollment 2018-19:
Undergraduate Majors: 120
Degrees in History: 33 BA
Addresses:
Admissions: http://www.gettysburg.edu/admissions/
Financial Aid: http://www.gettysburg.edu/scholarships_aid/

Full-time Faculty

Bamba, Abou (PhD, Georgia State 2008; assoc. prof.) sub-Saharan Africa; abamba@gettysburg.edu

Birkner, Michael J. (PhD, Virginia 1981; prof.) recent US, methodology; mbirkner@gettysburg.edu

Bowman, William D. (PhD, Johns Hopkins 1990; prof.) modern Europe, modern Germany; wbowman@gettysburg.edu

Carmichael, Peter S. (PhD, Penn State 1996; prof.) Civil War, American social and cultural; pcarmich@gettysburg.edu

Hancock, Scott (PhD, New Hampshire 1999; assoc. prof. and chair) African American, early America; shancock@gettysburg.edu

Lowy, Dina (PhD, Rutgers 2000; assoc. prof.) East Asia, modern Japan; dlowy@gettysburg.edu

Samji, Karim (PhD, Michigan 2013; asst. prof.) Islamic world; ksamji@gettysburg.edu

Sanchez, Magdalena S. (PhD, Johns Hopkins 1988; prof.) women, Spain, early modern Europe; msanchez@gettysburg.edu

Shannon, Timothy J. (PhD, Northwestern 1993; prof.) early America, British Isles, Native American; tshannon@gettysburg.edu

Sommer, Barbara A. (PhD, New Mexico 2000; prof.) Latin America, colonial Brazil, Amazonia; bsommer@gettysburg.edu

Part-time Faculty

Dombrowsky, Thomas (MA, Morgan State; MA, US Army War Coll.; adj. prof.) American military; tdombrowsky@gettysburg.edu

Hartzok, Justus G. (PhD, Iowa 2009; adj. asst. prof.) modern Europe, Russia, Islamic world; jhartzok@gettysburg.edu

Isherwood, Ian (PhD, Glasgow, Scotland 2012; vis. asst. prof.; Interdisciplinary Studies) Britain, war studies; iisherwo@gettysburg.edu

Krysiek, James S. (PhD, Marquette 1988; adj. assoc. prof.) 19th-century Europe, international relations, Islamic; jkrysiek@gettysburg.edu

Ogline Titus, Jill L. (PhD, Massachusetts Amherst 2007; adj. prof.; assoc. dir., Civil War Inst.) 20th-century African American; jtitus@gettysburg.edu

Visiting Faculty

Whitcomb, Katheryn E. (PhD, Rutgers 2016; vis. asst. prof.; Classics) classical philology, classical languages; kewhitco@gettysburg.edu

Gonzaga University

Dept. of History, 502 E. Boone Ave., Spokane, WA 99258-0037. 509.313.3687. Fax 509.313.5718. Email: goeller-bloom@gonzaga.edu. Website: https://www.gonzaga.edu/college-of-arts-sciences/departments/history.

The goals of the history curriculum are to engender an informed, critical, and articulate sense of the past, an appreciation for the diversity of human experience, and an awareness of the role of tradition in shaping the present.

Chair: Kevin O'Connor
Degrees Offered: BA
Academic Year System: Semester

Areas of Specialization: Europe, classical/medieval/early modern/modern, US, Latin America, East Asia and Pacific world
Tuition (per academic year): $31730
Enrollment 2018-19:
Undergraduate Majors: 80
Degrees in History: 35 BA
Addresses:
Admissions: http://www.gonzaga.edu/Admissions/Undergraduate-Admissions/
Financial Aid: http://www.gonzaga.edu/Admissions/Undergraduate-Admissions/Scholarships/

Full-time Faculty

Chambers, Kevin C. (PhD, California, Santa Barbara 1999; assoc. prof.) Latin America, Paraguay; chambersk@gonzaga.edu

Cunningham, Eric P. (PhD, Oregon 2004; prof.) Japan, China, modern intellectual; cunningham@gonzaga.edu

De Aragon, RaGena (PhD, California, Santa Barbara 1982; prof.) medieval and Renaissance, women, Britain; dearagon@gonzaga.edu

Donnelly, Robert C. (PhD, Marquette 2004; assoc. prof.) post-1945 US, urban; donnelly@gonzaga.edu

Goldman, Andrew (PhD, North Carolina, Chapel Hill 2000; prof.) ancient Greece and Rome; goldman@gonzaga.edu

O'Connor, Kevin C. (PhD, Ohio 2000; prof. and chair) Russia and Soviet Union; oconnork@gonzaga.edu

Ostendorf, Ann (PhD, Marquette 2009; assoc. prof.) early US, cultural; ostendorf@gonzaga.edu

Schlimgen, Veta R. (PhD, Oregon 2010; assoc. prof.) American expansion/empire/Pacific world, racial and ethnic minorities, American citizenship and Constitution; schlimgen@gonzaga.edu

Joint/Cross Appointments

Arnold, Laurie (PhD, Arizona State 2005; assoc. prof.; Native American Studies) Native American; arnoldl@gonzaga.edu

Retired/Emeritus Faculty

Balzarini, Stephen E. (PhD, Washington State 1979; assoc. prof. emeritus) modern Britain, modern Europe, military; balzarini@gonzaga.edu

Carriker, Robert Charles (PhD, Oklahoma 1967; retired prof.) US frontier, Pacific Northwest; carriker@gonzaga.edu

Downey, Elizabeth A. (PhD, Denver 1971; prof. emerita) Progressive Era, Roosevelts, environment; downey@gonzaga.edu

Nitz, Theodore A. (PhD, Washington State 1999; assoc. prof. emeritus) modern Germany, modern Europe, modern Middle East; nitz@gonzaga.edu

Stackelberg, Roderick (PhD, Massachusetts 1974; prof. emeritus) modern Europe, Germany, Russia; stackelberg@gonzaga.edu

Via, Anthony P., SJ (PhD, Wisconsin, Madison 1966; prof. emeritus) medieval, Byzantine; via@gonzaga.edu

Grace College

Dept. of History and Political Science, 200 Seminary Dr., Winona Lake, IN 46590. 574.372.5100. Fax 574.372.5139. Email: jared.burkholder@grace.edu. Website: https://www.grace.edu/major/history/.

We encourage our students to think incarnationally through their shared departmental experiences, through electives in their disciplines, by engaging in applied learning, and by participating in a capstone experience.

Chair: Jared S. Burkholder
Degrees Offered: BA,BS
Academic Year System: Semester
Areas of Specialization: US, Europe, Britain, religion, public
Tuition (per academic year): $23970
Enrollment 2018-19:
  Undergraduate Majors: 40
  Degrees in History: 4 BA, 5 BS
Addresses:
  Admissions: http://www.grace.edu/admissions/
    undergraduate-admissions
  Financial Aid: http://www.grace.edu/admissions/
    undergraduate-admissions/financial-aid-scholarships

Full-time Faculty

Burkholder, Jared S. (PhD, Iowa 2007; assoc. prof. and chair)
  America, 18th-century and colonial America, religious and Islam
  burkhojs@grace.edu
Norris, Mark M. (PhD, Edinburgh 1996; prof.) Tudor England, India,
  early 20th-century American religion; norrismm@grace.edu

Retired/Emeritus Faculty

Snider, R. Wayne (MA, Indiana; prof. emeritus) modern Europe,
  world

Graduate Center of the City University of New York

*PhD Program in History, 365 Fifth Ave., Room 5114, New York,
NY 10016-4309. 212.817.8430. Email: history@gc.cuny.edu.
Website: http://gc.cuny.edu/History/.*

*The PhD Program in History at the Graduate Center, CUNY, is a
major center for research and graduate training in a wide array
of fields of historical inquiry. The program stresses training in
primary research and encourages interdisciplinary study.*

Chair: Joel Allen
Degrees Offered: PhD
Academic Year System: Semester
Areas of Specialization: US, Europe, Middle East, Latin America
Tuition (per academic year):
  In-State: $4965
  Out-of-State: $14475
Enrollment 2018-19:
  New Graduate Students: 13
  Full-time Graduate Students: 116
  Degrees in History: 3 PhD
Addresses:
  Admissions: http://www.gc.cuny.edu/Admissions/
  Financial Aid: http://www.gc.cuny.edu/fellowships/

Full-time Faculty

Akasoy, Anna (PhD, Johann Wolfgang Goethe; prof.) medieval
  Islamic, Islamic intellectual traditions, cultural and religious
  contacts in Europe; aa739@hunter.cuny.edu
Alborn, Timothy L. (PhD, Harvard 1991; assoc. prof.) Britain,
  business; timothy.alborn@lehman.cuny.edu
Allen, Joel W. (PhD, Yale 1999; assoc. prof. and chair) Roman
  Empire, Hellenistic; jallen@gc.cuny.edu
Baron, Beth (PhD, UCLA 1988; prof.) Middle East, women;
  bbaron@gc.cuny.edu
Bemporad, Elissa (PhD, Stanford 2006; assoc. prof.) Jewish life in
  interwar Soviet Union; elissa.bemporad@qc.cuny.edu

Bennett, Herman L. (PhD, Duke 1993; prof.) African American,
  Latin America; hbennett@gc.cuny.edu
Bergad, Laird W. (PhD, Pittsburgh 1980; dist. prof.) Latin America,
  Caribbean; lbergad@gc.cuny.edu
Bhagavan, Manu B. (PhD, Texas, Austin 1999; prof.) South Asia,
  comparative; manu.bhagavan@hunter.cuny.edu
Bregoli, Francesca (PhD, Pennsylvania 2007; assoc. prof.) 18th-
  century Mediterranean; francesca.bregoli@qc.cuny.edu
Burke, Martin Joseph (PhD, Michigan 1987; prof.) US; mburke1@
  gc.cuny.edu
Cook, Blanche Wiesen (PhD, Johns Hopkins 1970; Dist. Prof.)
  American women, lesbian and gay; Blanchewcook@gmail.com
Covington, Sarah Amy (PhD, Grad. Center, CUNY 2000; assoc.
  prof.) early modern Europe; sarah.covington@qc.cuny.edu
Dauben, Joseph W. (PhD, Harvard 1972; Dist. Prof.) science;
  jdauben@att.net
Davis, Simon (PhD, Exeter, UK 1994; asst. prof.) British imperialism,
  Middle East, Anglo-American relations; simon.davis@bcc.cuny.
  edu
Frangakis-Syrett, Elena (PhD, King's Coll., London 1985; prof.)
  European economic, Ottoman-Greek socioeconomic; elenafs@
  aol.com
Freeman, Joshua B. (PhD, Rutgers 1983; prof.) US, labor;
  jfreeman@gc.cuny.edu
Gordon, David M. (PhD, Brown 1978; assoc. prof.) France,
  economic; dmgordon@mindspring.net
Haj, Samira A. (PhD, UCLA 1988; assoc. prof.) Middle East, Islamic;
  samirahaj@nyc.rr.com
Herzog, Dagmar (PhD, Brown 1991; prof.) Germany, comparative
  Europe; dherzog@gc.cuny.edu
Hett, Benjamin C. (PhD, Harvard 2001; assoc. prof.) legal, Germany;
  bhett@hunter.cuny.edu
Ivison, Eric A. (PhD, Birmingham, UK 1993; assoc. prof.) Byzantine;
  eric.ivison@csi.cuny.edu
Johnson, Robert D. (PhD, Harvard 1993; prof.) US; kcjohnson9@
  gmail.com
Kavey, Allison (PhD, Johns Hopkins 2004; prof.) Renaissance and
  early modern natural philosophy, cultural and intellectual,
  gender and sexuality; akavey@jjay.cuny.edu
Kessner, Thomas (PhD, Columbia 1975; Dist. Prof.) American social;
  tkessner@gc.cuny.edu
Killen, Andreas (PhD, NYU 2000; assoc. prof.) European cultural
  and intellectual, Germany, urban; akillen@ccny.cuny.edu
Kornhauser, Anne M. (PhD, Columbia 2004; asst. prof.) US in world
  since 1914; AKornhauser@ccny.cuny.edu
LeGall, Dina (PhD, Princeton 1992; asst. prof.) Middle East, Islam;
  dinalegall@aol.com
Lewis, Mark (PhD, UCLA 2008; assoc. prof.) central Europe,
  southeastern Europe; mark.lewis@csi.cuny.edu
Lufrano, Richard (PhD, Columbia 1987; assoc. prof.) China;
  lufrano@mail.csi.cuny.edu
Markowitz, Gerald E. (PhD, Wisconsin, Madison 1971; Dist. Prof.)
  American medicine and public health; gmarkowitz@jjay.cuny.
  edu
McCarthy, Kathleen D. (PhD, Chicago 1980; prof.) American
  philanthropy; kmccarthy@gc.cuny.edu
Naddeo, Barbara Ann (PhD, Chicago 2001; assoc. prof.) Europe;
  bnaddeo@ccny.cuny.edu
Oakes, James (PhD, California, Berkeley 1981; Dist. Prof.) America;
  joakes@gc.cuny.edu
Oppenheimer, Gerald (PhD, Chicago 1976; Dist. Prof.) US
  medicine; geraldo@brooklyn.cuny.edu
Park, Hyunhee (PhD, Yale 2008; assoc. prof.) premodern China,
  premodern Islamic world; hpark@jjay.cuny.edu

Pfeifer, Michael James (PhD, Iowa 1998; assoc. prof.) America; mpfeifer@jjay.cuny.edu

Rawson, Michael J. (PhD, Wisconsin, Madison 2005; asst. prof.) America; mrawson@brooklyn.cuny.edu

Remy, Steven P. (PhD, Ohio 2000; assoc. prof.) modern Europe, Germany; sremy@brooklyn.cuny.edu

Renique, Jose Luis (PhD, Columbia 1988; assoc. prof.) Latin America; jrenique@aol.com

Reynolds, David (PhD, California, Berkeley 1979; Dist. Prof.) American literature, American Renaissance; dreynolds@gc.cuny.edu

Robertson, Andrew W. (DPhil, Oxford 1989; assoc. prof.) early national US, 19th-century politics; andrew.robertson@lehman.cuny.edu

Roldan, Mary J. (PhD, Harvard 1992; assoc. prof.) modern Latin America; mrol@hunter.cuny.edu

Rosenberg, Clifford D. (PhD, Princeton 2000; assoc. prof.) modern France, imperialism/immigration/public health; CRosenberg@ccny.cuny.edu

Rosenberg, Jonathan (PhD, Harvard 1997; assoc. prof.) US international, cultural, civil rights; jrosen8637@aol.com

Rosenblatt, Helena A. (PhD, Columbia 1994; prof.) early modern Europe; hrosenblatt@gc.cuny.edu

Rossabi, Morris (PhD, Columbia 1970; Dist. Prof.) Asia; mr63@columbia.edu

Sassi, Jonathan D. (PhD, UCLA 1996; prof.) early national US, American religion; jsassi@gc.cuny.edu

Scott, Joan Wallach (PhD, Wisconsin, Madison 1969; adj. prof.) women; jscott@gc.cuny.edu

SenGupta, Gunja (PhD, Tulane 1991; assoc. prof.; dir., Macauley Honors Coll., Brooklyn, CUNY) 19th-century US, social and cultural, African American; sengupta@brooklyn.cuny.edu

Sneeringer, Julia E. (PhD, Pennsylvania 1995; assoc. prof.) 20th-century Germany, women and gender; juliasneeringer@verizon.net

Spencer, Robyn C. (PhD, Columbia 2001; assoc. prof.) African American, recent US; robyn.spencer@lehman.cuny.edu

Torpey, John (PhD, California, Berkeley 1992; prof.; Sociology) America, sociology; jtorpey@gc.cuny.edu

Troyansky, David G. (PhD, Brandeis 1983; prof.) modern Europe, France; troyansky@brooklyn.cuny.edu

Trumbach, Randolph (PhD, Johns Hopkins 1972; prof.) modern Britain, lesbian and gay; randolph.trumbach@baruch.cuny.edu

Waldstreicher, David L. (PhD, Yale 1994; Dist. Prof.) 18th- and 19th-century US, political; dwaldstreicher@gc.cuny.edu

Wallace, Michael L. (PhD, Columbia 1973; Dist. Prof.) US urban, New York City; mawjj@aol.com

Weitz, Eric D. (PhD, Boston Univ. 1983; prof.; dean, Humanities and Arts and Dist. Prof., City Coll., NY) modern Europe, Germany, labor and international human rights and crimes against humanity; eweitz@ccny.cuny.edu

Wolin, Richard (PhD, York, Can. 1980; Dist. Prof.; Political Science and Comparative Literature) Europe; rwolin@gc.cuny.edu

Wunder, Amanda J. (PhD, Princeton 2002; assoc. prof.) early modern Spain; AWunder@gc.cuny.edu

Retired/Emeritus Faculty

Abrahamian, Ervand (PhD, Columbia 1969; dist. prof. emeritus) Iran and Middle East; ervand.abrahamian@baruch.cuny.edu

Ackerman, Evelyn B. (PhD, Harvard 1973; prof. emeritus) modern France, French social

Ascher, Abraham (PhD, Columbia 1957; Dist. Prof. emeritus) Russia; a.ascher@att.net

Besse, Susan K. (PhD, Yale 1983; assoc. prof. emeritus) Latin America, women; skbesse@earthlink.net

Brown, Joshua (PhD, Columbia 1993; prof. emeritus; exec. dir., American Social Hist. Proj., Center for Media and Learning) 19th-century US, visual culture, history and new media; jbrown@gc.cuny.edu

Cooper, Sandi E. (PhD, NYU 1967; prof. emeritus) peace studies; sandi.cooper@csi.cuny.edu

Gerber, Jane S. (PhD, Columbia 1972; prof. emeritus) Jewish, Sephardic studies; gerberjs@aol.com

Gibson, Mary S. (PhD, Indiana 1979; prof. emeritus) Italy, women; mgibson@jjay.cuny.edu

Harvey, David (PhD, St. Johns Coll., Oxford 1962; Dist. Prof. emeritus) geography, urban, social theory; dharvey@gc.cuny.edu

Himmelfarb, Gertrude (PhD, Chicago 1950; Dist. Prof. emeritus) intellectual, Europe

Kimmich, Christoph (PhD, Oxford 1964; prof. emeritus) modern Europe; ckimmich@gc.cuny.edu

Nasaw, David (PhD, Columbia 1974; Dist. Prof. emeritus) US social, cultural; dnasaw@gc.cuny.edu

Oldenburg, Veena Talwar (PhD, Illinois, Urbana-Champaign 1979; prof. emeritus) modern India, Britain, women

Pomeroy, Sarah B. (PhD, Columbia 1960; Dist. Prof. emeritus) ancient, women; sbpom@aol.com

Powers, Richard Gid (PhD, Brown 1969; prof. emeritus) America; rgpsi@earthlink.net

Roberts, Jennifer T. (PhD, Yale 1976; prof. emeritus) ancient; robertsjt@aol.com

Siraisi, Nancy G. (PhD, Grad. Center, CUNY 1970; Dist. Prof. emeritus) medieval, science and medicine; nsiraisi@verizon.net

Taylor, Clarence W. (PhD, Grad. Center, CUNY 1992; prof. emeritus) African American, labor, US; clarence.taylor@baruch.cuny.edu

Welter, Barbara (PhD, Wisconsin, Madison 1960; prof. emeritus) America, women; bwelter@hunter.cuny.edu

Recently Awarded PhDs

Ackerman, Scott "'We Are Abolitionizing the West': The Union Army and the Implementation of Federal Emancipation Policy, 1861-65"

Brooks, Emily "'A War within a War': Policing Gender and Race in New York City during World War II"

Charnoff, Deborah B. "Men Set on Fire--Algernon Sidney and John Adams: Remodeling Anglo-American Republicanism"

Chen, Michelle "'Americans All': The American Committee for Protection of Foreign Born, Immigrants' Rights, and Defending the Constitution under the Red Scare"

Cooper, Brendan "The Domino Effect: Politics, Policy, and the Consolidation of the Sugar Refining Industry in the United States, 1789-1895"

Crowder, Michael "Human Capital: The Moral and Political Economy of Northeastern Abolitionism, 1763-1833"

Reynolds, Luke A. L. "Who Owned Waterloo? Wellington's Veterans and the Battle for Relevance"

Rocklin, Mitchell "The American Whig Party and Slavery"

Stockstill, Marcella "John Babington's /Pyrotechnia/: The Natural Philosophy of a 17th-Century English Gunner, Mathematician, Alchemist, and Mechanician"

Swaidan, Jacqueline "Authority, Subordinates and Expectations of Early Modern English Privateer Captains, 1577 and 1627"

Swen, Litian "Privileges for Being Slaves: Christian Missionaries in the Early Qing Court"

Woltering, Ky N. "'A Christian World Order': Protestants, Democracy, and Christian Aid to Germany, 1945-61"

Grand Valley State University

Dept. of History, D-1-160 Mackinac Hall, Allendale, MI 49401. 616.331.3298. Fax 616.331.3285. Email: morisonw@gvsu.edu. Website: https://www.gvsu.edu/history/.

What human beings can do, might do, or ought to do makes no sense at all unless we know what they have done already. This involves the study of history.

Chair: William Morison
Degrees Offered: BA,BS
Academic Year System: Semester
Areas of Specialization: Europe, Middle East, Latin America, Africa/Asia, US social and diplomatic
Tuition (per academic year): $16053
Enrollment 2018-19:
   Undergraduate Majors: 399
   Degrees in History: 39 BA, 49 BS
Addresses:
   Admissions: https://www.gvsu.edu/admissions/
   Financial Aid: https://www.gvsu.edu/financialaid/

Adjunct Faculty

Constant, Eric (PhD, Michigan State 2016; adj.) medieval and Renaissance; constane@gvsu.edu

Duram, David (MA, Wisconsin-Eau Claire 1983; adj.) teaching of history; dduram@hpseagles.net

Hendershot, Gillian (ABD, Central Michigan 2002; adj.) early modern Europe, gender; hendersg@gvsu.edu

Peterson, Andrew C. (PhD, Hawaii, Manoa 2014; adj.) early modern Europe, colonial Southeast Asia, maritime; peteran1@gvsu.edu

Pospisek, Patrick Allan (PhD, Purdue 2013; adj.) America; pospisep@gvsu.edu

Warber, Samantha (MA, New Mexico State 2002; adj.) US, social and cultural, women; warbersa@gvsu.edu

Affiliated Faculty

Tate, Sarah (MEd, Central Michigan 2009; affiliate prof.) instruction, social studies; tatesara@gvsu.edu

Full-time Faculty

Andrews, Gordon (PhD, Western Michigan 2011; assoc. prof.) America, social studies education; andrewgo@gvsu.edu

Buckridge, Steeve O. (PhD, Ohio State 1998; prof.) Africa, Caribbean, women; buckrids@gvsu.edu

Chapman, Alice L. (PhD, Cambridge 2006; assoc. prof.) medieval Europe; chapmali@gvsu.edu

Cooley, Richard (EdD, Kansas State 2002; prof.) social studies curriculum and instruction; cooleyri@gvsu.edu

Coolidge, Grace E. (PhD, Indiana 2001; prof.) early modern Europe, Spain; coolidgg@gvsu.edu

Crouthamel, Jason P. (PhD, Indiana 2001; prof.) modern Europe, Germany; crouthaj@gvsu.edu

Daley, Matthew Lawrence (PhD, Bowling Green State 2004; assoc. prof.) Michigan, public, US; daleym@gvsu.edu

Eaton, David (PhD, Dalhousie 2008; assoc. prof.) Africa; eatond@gvsu.edu

Galbraith, Gretchen (PhD, Rutgers 1992; prof. and asst. dean; Coll. of Liberal Arts and Sciences) modern Britain, gender; galbraig@gvsu.edu

Gautreau, Abigail (PhD, Middle Tennessee State 2015; asst. prof.) public; gautreaa@gvsu.edu

Gottlieb, Gabriele (PhD, Pittsburgh 2004; assoc. prof.) colonial America, capital punishment; gottlieg@gvsu.edu

Huner, Michael Kenneth (PhD, North Carolina, Chapel Hill 2011; assoc. prof.) Latin America; hunerm@gvsu.edu

Lingwood, Chad Gilbert (PhD, Toronto 2009; assoc. prof.) Middle East; lingwoch@gvsu.edu

Montagna, Douglas S. (PhD, Northern Illinois 2000; assoc. prof.) 19th-century America, religion; montagnd@gvsu.edu

Moore, Louis Allen (PhD, California, Davis 2008; assoc. prof.) African American, civil rights, race and sports; moorelou@gvsu.edu

Morison, William (PhD, California, Santa Barbara 1998; assoc. prof. and chair) ancient Greece and Rome; morisonw@gvsu.edu

Murphy, Paul V. (PhD, Indiana 1996; prof.) 20th-century US, intellectual; murphyp@gvsu.edu

O'Neill, Sean (PhD, California, Santa Barbara 1991; prof.) American Indian, education; oneills@gvsu.edu

Salas, Nora (PhD, Michigan State 2015; asst. prof.) Latina/o, gender; salasn@gvsu.edu

Shan, Patrick Fuliang (PhD, McMaster 2003; prof.) East Asia, China; shanp@gvsu.edu

Shapiro-Shapin, Carolyn G. (PhD, Yale 1993; prof. and asst. chair) American medicine, public health; shapiroc@gvsu.edu

Shreiner, Tamara Lynn (PhD, Michigan 2009; asst. prof.) educational studies, history, social science education; shreinet@gvsu.edu

Smither, James R. (PhD, Brown 1989; prof.) France, early modern Europe, Renaissance; smitherj@gvsu.edu

Stabler, Scott L. (PhD, Arizona State 2004; prof.) social studies education, Civil War, US West; stablers@gvsu.edu

Stark, David M. (PhD, Indiana 1999; prof.) Latin America; starkd@gvsu.edu

Tripp, Steven E. (PhD, Carnegie Mellon 1990; prof.) US social, Civil War and Reconstruction; tripps@gvsu.edu

Wangdi, Yosay (PhD, Nevada, Reno 2003; prof.) South Asia, Himalayan region, environmental; wangdiy@gvsu.edu

Zwart, David E. (PhD, Western Michigan 2012; assoc. prof.) history education, 20th-century US social and cultural, world; zwartdav@gvsu.edu

Retired/Emeritus Faculty

Cole, Edward A. (PhD, California, Berkeley 1972; prof. emeritus) Russia, Soviet Union; colee@gvsu.edu

Devlin, Dennis S. (PhD, Chicago 1975; prof. emeritus) ancient, medieval, Byzantine; devlind@gvsu.edu

Goode, James F. (PhD, Indiana 1984; prof. emeritus) 20th-century US, diplomatic, Middle East; goodej@gvsu.edu

Mapes, Lynn G. (PhD, Rochester 1973; prof. emeritus) early 20th-century US, intellectual, urban; mapesl@gvsu.edu

Niemeyer, Glenn A. (PhD, Michigan State 1963; prof. emeritus) 20th-century US, economic

Preston, Joseph H. (PhD, Missouri, Columbia 1966; prof. emeritus)

Stark, Gary D. (PhD, Johns Hopkins 1974; prof. emeritus) modern Germany; starkg@gvsu.edu

Travis, Anthony R. (PhD, Michigan State 1971; prof. emeritus) 20th-century US, social, urban; travisa@gvsu.edu

Underwood, Kathleen (PhD, UCLA 1982; prof. emerita) US West, education, historical demography; underwok@gvsu.edu

Visiting Faculty

Gonzalez, Jennifer (PhD, Michigan State 2016; vis. asst. prof.) colonial Latin America; gonzalje@gvsu.edu

Lingenfelter, Scott (PhD, Illinois, Chicago 2005; vis. asst. prof.) early 20th-century Russian culture, Russo-Japanese relations; lingenfs@gvsu.edu

Terry, David D. (PhD, Western Michigan 2017; vis. asst. prof.) Spain and Medieval Mediterranean; terrydav@gvsu.edu

Grinnell College

Dept. of History, 1213 6th Ave., Mears Cottage, Grinnell, IA 50112-1670. 641.269.4628. Fax 641.269.4733. Email: purcelsj@grinnell.edu. Website: https://www.grinnell.edu/academics/majors-concentrations/history.

While the members of the history department faculty vary widely in areas of expertise and classroom styles, we share a commitment to research, teaching, and learning in a collaborative environment, where students and faculty engage together in the processes of intellectual inquiry.

Chair: Sarah Purcell
Degrees Offered: BA
Academic Year System: Semester
Areas of Specialization: US, Latin America, Europe, East Asia, Africa, Middle East
Tuition (per academic year): $54354
Enrollment 2018-19:
   Undergraduate Majors: 46
   Degrees in History: 28 BA
Addresses:
   Admissions: http://www.grinnell.edu/admission
   Financial Aid: http://www.grinnell.edu/financial-aid

Full-time Faculty

Chou, Catherine (PhD, Stanford 2016; asst. prof.) early modern Britain and Europe, Reformation studies, political theory and culture; choucath@grinnell.edu

Cohn, Edward D. (PhD, Chicago 2007; assoc. prof.) Soviet Union, Russia, modern Europe; cohned@grinnell.edu

Guenther, Michael B. (PhD, Northwestern 2008; assoc. prof.) Atlantic world, science and technology, environmental; guenthmb@grinnell.edu

Lacson, P. Albert (PhD, California, Davis 2009; assoc. prof.) early America, Native American, American West; lacson@grinnell.edu

Lewis, Carolyn Herbst (PhD, California, Santa Barbara 2007; assoc. prof.) US women, gender and sexuality, medicine; lewiscar@grinnell.edu

Luo, Weiwei (PhD, Columbia 2018; asst. prof.) China and East Asia, legal, political economy; luoweiwei@grinnell.edu

Maynard, Kelly J. (PhD, UCLA 2007; assoc. prof.; chair, European Studies) modern France, cultural and intellectual, material culture; maynardk@grinnell.edu

Prevost, Elizabeth E. (PhD, Northwestern 2006; prof.) modern Britain and empire, colonial Africa, women and gender; prevoste@grinnell.edu

Purcell, Sarah J. (PhD, Brown 1997; L. F. Parker Prof. and chair) Civil War and Reconstruction, 19th-century US, American Revolution; purcelsj@grinnell.edu

Silva, Jose Pablo (PhD, Chicago 2000; assoc. prof.) modern Latin America, labor, Chile; silvajp@grinnell.edu

Joint/Cross Appointments

Elfenbein, Caleb (PhD, California, Santa Barbara 2008; assoc. prof.; dir., Center for the Humanities; Religious Studies) Islam in America, modern Middle East, religion and modernity; elfenbei@grinnell.edu

Saba, Elias (PhD, Pennsylvania 2017; sr. lect.; Religious Studies) Islamic law, premodern Middle East, religion and society; sabaelia@grinnell.edu

Nondepartmental Historians

McKee, Christopher (MA, Michigan 1960; prof. emeritus; Library Science) social, US, British navies; mckee@grinnell.edu

Retired/Emeritus Faculty

Brown, Victoria Bissell (PhD, California, San Diego 1985; prof. emeritus) modern US, women, immigration; brownv@grinnell.edu

Drake, George A. (PhD, Chicago 1965; prof. emeritus) early modern Europe, southern Africa; drake@grinnell.edu

Hsieh, Andrew (PhD, Yale 1975; prof. emeritus) China, Japan; hsieh@grinnell.edu

Kaiser, Daniel H. (PhD, Chicago 1977; prof. emeritus) Russia, family; kaiser@grinnell.edu

Osgood, Russell K. (JD, Yale 1974; prof. emeritus) English and American legal; osgood@grinnell.edu

Smith, Don A. (PhD, Yale 1965; prof. emeritus) modern Britain, modern Europe; smithd@grinnell.edu

Grove City College

Dept. of History, 100 Campus Dr., Grove City, PA 16127-2104. 724.458.2057. Fax 724.458.3852. Email: gjharp@gcc.edu. Website: http://www.gcc.edu/Home/Academics/Arts-Letters/Majors-Departments/History.

The Department of History at Grove City College prepares students for graduate and professional study, as well as for careers in teaching, business, politics, journalism, and more.

Chair: Gillis J. Harp
Degrees Offered: BA
Academic Year System: Semester
Areas of Specialization: America, military, religious, ancient, secondary certification preparation
Tuition (per academic year): $17930
Enrollment 2018-19:
   Undergraduate Majors: 60
   Degrees in History: 15 BA
Addresses:
   Admissions: http://www.gcc.edu/futurestudents/
   Financial Aid: http://www.gcc.edu/futurestudents/financialaid/

Full-time Faculty

Baker, Elizabeth Anne (PhD, Notre Dame 2018; asst. prof.) modern Britain, India; bakerea@gcc.edu

Edwards, Jason R. (PhD, Kentucky 2003; prof.) American educational, agrarian philosophy, US South; jredwards@gcc.edu

Graham, Mark W. (PhD, Michigan State 2001; prof.) ancient, medieval, world; mwgraham@gcc.edu

Harp, Gillis J. (PhD, Virginia 1986; prof. and chair) American intellectual, American religious, American conservatism; gjharp@gcc.edu

Mitchell, Andrew J. (PhD, Ohio State 2005; assoc. prof.) early modern Spain, military; ajmitchell@gcc.edu

Gustavus Adolphus College

Dept. of History, 800 W. College Ave., Saint Peter, MN 56082-1498. 507.933.7413. Fax 507.933.7041. Email: amukamur@gustavus.edu. Website: https://gustavus.edu/history/.

The mission of the Department of History is to help students develop the capacity to think historically.

Chair: Kathleen Keller

Degrees Offered: BA
Academic Year System: Semester
Areas of Specialization: gender and social, immigration and ethnic, religion, environmental, global
Tuition (per academic year): $41140
Enrollment 2018-19:
Undergraduate Majors: 49
Degrees in History: 11 BA
Addresses:
Admissions: http://gustavus.edu/admission/
Financial Aid: http://gustavus.edu/admission/financial-aid/

Full-time Faculty

Cabrera Geserick, Marco A. (PhD, Arizona State 2013; asst. prof.) Latin America; cabrerageserick@gustavus.edu
Kaster, Gregory L. (PhD, Boston Univ. 1990; prof.) 19th-century US, US Civil War, American intellectual/political/masculinity; gkaster@gustavus.edu
Keller, Kathleen A. (PhD, Rutgers 2007; assoc. prof. and chair) modern Europe, world and comparative, modern Africa; kkeller2@gustavus.edu
Kranking, Glenn Eric (PhD, Ohio State 2009; assoc. prof.) Scandinavia, Russia, Baltic; kranking@gustavus.edu
Marinari, Maddalena (PhD, Kansas 2009; asst. prof.) 20th-century US, immigration; mmarinar@gustavus.edu
Obermiller, David Tobaru (PhD, Iowa 2006; assoc. prof.) East Asia, Japan, environmental; dobermil@gustavus.edu

Visiting Faculty

Dirks, Whitney (PhD, Ohio State 2013; vis. asst. prof.) early modern England; dirksw@gustavus.edu
Harper, Misti Nicole (PhD, Arkansas 2017; vis. asst. prof.) mnharper@gustavus.edu

Hamilton College

Dept. of History, 198 College Hill Rd., Clinton, NY 13323-1218. 315.859.4404. Fax 315.859.4649. Email: ltrivedi@hamilton. edu. Website: https://www.hamilton.edu/academics/ departments?dept=History.

Your studies will cultivate an understanding of the present that is informed by history. Expect to write extensively: Your courses will help you develop sophisticated writing and speaking skills. You also will hone an ability to think critically about complex issues and events of the past.

Chair: Lisa Trivedi
Degrees Offered: BA
Academic Year System: Semester
Areas of Specialization: modern and medieval Europe, US, Russia/Eurasia, South and East Asia, international/intellectual/ cultural
Tuition (per academic year): $60000
Enrollment 2018-19:
Undergraduate Majors: 50
Degrees in History: 18 BA
Addresses:
Admissions: http://www.hamilton.edu/admission
Financial Aid: http://www.hamilton.edu/finaid

Adjunct Faculty

Simons, Peter (PhD, Chicago 2012; lect.) US, environmental; psimons@hamilton.edu

Full-time Faculty

Ambrose, Douglas (PhD, SUNY, Binghamton 1991; prof.) early America, Old US South, American religious; dambrose@hamilton.edu
Cooley, Mackenzie Anne (PhD, Stanford 2018; asst. prof.) science, early modern Europe, colonial Latin America; mcooley@hamilton.edu
Day Moore, Celeste (PhD, Chicago 2014; asst. prof.) African American, transnational; cdmoore@hamilton.edu
Eldevik, John T. (PhD, UCLA 2001; assoc. prof.) medieval Europe, church, social; jeldevik@hamilton.edu
Grant, Kevin P. (PhD, California, Berkeley 1997; Edgar B. Graves Prof.) Great Britain and Ireland, British Empire, Africa, photography; kgrant@hamilton.edu
Isserman, Maurice (PhD, Rochester 1979; Publius Virgilius Rogers Prof.) 20th-century US, political, exploration; misserma@hamilton.edu
Keller, Shoshana (PhD, Indiana 1995; prof.) modern Russia and Soviet Union, Central Asia; skeller@hamilton.edu
Trivedi, Lisa (PhD, California, Davis 1999; prof. and chair) South Asia, cultural and social, women; ltrivedi@hamilton.edu
Wilson, Thomas A. (PhD, Chicago 1988; prof.) East Asia, Chinese cultural and religious; twilson@hamilton.edu

Retired/Emeritus Faculty

Kanipe, Esther S. (PhD, Wisconsin, Madison 1976; Marjorie and Robert W. McEwen Prof. emeritus) European social, modern France, women and family; ekanipe@hamilton.edu
Kelly, Alfred H. (PhD, Wisconsin, Madison 1975; Edgar B. Graves Prof. emeritus) European intellectual and cultural, modern Germany, science; akelly@hamilton.edu

University of Hartford

Dept. of History, 200 Bloomfield Ave., 126 Hillyer Hall, West Hartford, CT 06117. 860.768.4630. Fax 860.768.4251 Email: wgoldstei@hartford.edu. Website: https://www.hartford.edu/ history.

History courses emphasize a grasp of themes and context-the experience of people in the past rather than rote and tedious memorization. They also focus on helping students learn to write clearly and critically about primary sources and more complex historical issues. All students complete historically-based internships.

Chair: Warren Goldstein
Degrees Offered: BA
Academic Year System: Semester
Areas of Specialization: US, Europe, Middle East, Asia
Tuition (per academic year): $30618
Enrollment 2018-19:
Undergraduate Majors: 22
Degrees in History: 6 BA
Addresses:
Admissions: http://admission.hartford.edu/
Financial Aid: http://admission.hartford.edu/finaid/

Affiliated Faculty

Churchill, Robert H. (PhD, Rutgers 2001; assoc. prof.; Hillyer Coll.) American Revolution, early national US, political violence; churchill@hartford.edu
Firkatian, Mari A. (PhD, Indiana 1991; prof.; Hillyer Coll.) eastern Europe, Russia, Balkans; firkatian@hartford.edu

Patt, Avinoam (PhD, NYU 2005; assoc. prof.; Judaic Studies) modern Jewish, Holocaust, Zionism and Israel; patt@hartford.edu

Robinson, Michael F. (PhD, Wisconsin-Madison 2002; prof.; Hillyer Coll.) 19th-century US, science and exploration, popular culture; microbins@hartford.edu

Williamson, Daniel C. (PhD, Connecticut 2000; prof.; Hillyer Coll.) modern Ireland and Europe, diplomatic; dwilliams@hartford.edu

Full-time Faculty

Freund, Richard (PhD, Jewish Theological Sem. 1982; prof.; dir., Maurice Greenberg Center Jewish Studies) Biblical archeology, Jewish ethics, world religions; freund@hartford.edu

Goldstein, Warren J. (PhD, Yale 1983; prof. and chair) US social and cultural, sports, religion; wgoldstei@hartford.edu

Rosenthal, Steven (PhD, Yale 1975; prof.) Middle East, genocide, Ottoman; srosentha@hartford.edu

Walker, Rachel E. (PhD, Maryland, Coll. Park 2018; asst. prof.) US women/gender/sexuality, science, trans-Atlantic cultural and intellectual

Part-time Faculty

Davis, Bradley Camp (PhD, Washington 2008; vis. asst. prof.) modern Southeast Asia, late imperial China, comparative colonialisms; davisbrad@easternct.edu

Mueller, John H. (MA, Connecticut 1999; vis. lect.) US and Europe, military, world civilization

Hartwick College

Dept. of History, 329 Golisano Hall, 1 Hartwick Dr., Oneonta, NY 13820-4020. 607.431.4839. Fax 607.431.4351. Email: nishidam@hartwick.edu. Website: https://www.hartwick.edu/academics/academic-departments/history-department/.

The history department is participating in Hartwick College's three-year Bachelor's Degree Program for qualified students.

Chair: Mieko Nishida
Degrees Offered: BA
Academic Year System: Semester plus January term
Areas of Specialization: US, Europe, Latin America, and global
Tuition (per academic year): $45990
Enrollment 2018-19:
 Undergraduate Majors: 42
 Degrees in History: 6 BA
 Students in Undergraduate Courses: 315
 Students in Undergraduate Intro Courses: 243
Addresses:
 Admissions: http://www.hartwick.edu/admissions/
 Financial Aid: http://www.hartwick.edu/admissions/cost-aid/financial-aid/

Full-time Faculty

Burke, Kyle Bradford (PhD, Northwestern 2015; asst. prof.) modern America, global, war and empire; burkek@hartwick.edu

Lacy, Cherilyn M. (PhD, Chicago 1997; prof.) modern Europe, medicine and public health, women/gender/sexuality; lacyc@hartwick.edu

Nishida, Mieko (PhD, Johns Hopkins 1992; prof. and chair) Latin America, Brazil, social; nishidam@hartwick.edu

Retired/Emeritus Faculty

Pudelka, Leonard W. (PhD, Syracuse 1972; prof. emeritus) 19th-century US political and social, Civil War, US Whig party; pudelkal@hartwick.edu

Quinn, Edythe Ann (PhD, Tennessee, Knoxville 1994; prof. emeritus) contemporary America, civil rights movement, US environmental; quinne@hartwick.edu

Wallace, Peter G. (PhD, Oregon 1983; prof. emeritus) premodern Europe, Renaissance and Reformation Europe, nationalism and national identities; wallacep@hartwick.edu

Visiting Faculty

Anderson, Chad L. (PhD, California, Davis 2012; vis. asst. prof.) early America, Native American, environmental; andersonc2@hartwick.edu

Harvard University

Dept. of History, Robinson Hall, 35 Quincy St., Cambridge, MA 02138. 617.496.2556. Fax 617.496.3425. Email: history@fas.harvard.edu. Website: https://history.fas.harvard.edu/.

Offering programs of study for undergraduate and graduate students, the Department of History at Harvard University is home to a vibrant and dynamic community of scholars.

Chair: Evelyn Brooks Higginbotham
Director of Graduate Studies: Sidney Chalhoub
Director of Undergraduate Studies: Lisa McGirr
Degrees Offered: BA,PhD
Academic Year System: Semester
Areas of Specialization: US, ancient/medieval/early modern/modern Europe, Latin America, East and South Asia, international
Undergraduate Tuition (per academic year): $46340
Graduate Tuition (per academic year): $48008
Enrollment 2018-19:
 Undergraduate Majors: 153
 New Graduate Students: 14
 Full-time Graduate Students: 121
 Degrees in History: 50 BA, 16 PhD
Undergraduate Addresses:
 Admissions: https://college.harvard.edu/admissions
 Financial Aid: https://college.harvard.edu/financial-aid
Graduate Addresses:
 Admissions and Financial Aid: http://www.gsas.harvard.edu/

Full-time Faculty

Akyeampong, Emmanuel K. (PhD, Virginia 1993; Ellen Gurney Prof.; African and African American Studies) sub-Saharan West Africa; akyeamp@fas.harvard.edu

Amrith, Sunil (PhD, Cambridge 2004; Mehra Family Prof.) Bay of Bengal region, environmental history of water; amrith@fas.harvard.edu

Angelov, Dimiter (PhD, Harvard 2002; Dumbarton Oaks Prof.) Byzantine; dangelov@fas.harvard.edu

Armitage, David (PhD, Cambridge 1992; Lloyd C. Blankfein Prof.) early modern, intellectual, international; armitage@fas.harvard.edu

Beckert, Sven (PhD, Columbia 1995; Laird Bell Prof.) America; beckert@fas.harvard.edu

Blair, Ann (PhD, Princeton 1990; Carl H. Pforzheimer Univ. Prof.) early modern Europe; amblair@fas.harvard.edu

Bose, Sugata (PhD, Cambridge 1983; Gardiner Prof.) South Asia and Indian Ocean; sbose@fas.harvard.edu

Bsheer, Rosie (PhD, Columbia 2014; asst. prof.) modern Middle East; rbsheer@fas.harvard.edu

Chaplin, Joyce (PhD, Johns Hopkins 1986; James Duncan Phillips Prof.) colonial America; chaplin@fas.harvard.edu

Cohen, Lizabeth (PhD, California, Berkeley 1986; Howard Mumford Jones Prof.; American Studies) US social and urban, 20th century; cohen3@fas.harvard.edu

Deloria, Philip (PhD, Yale 1994; prof.) Native American, cultural, environmental; deloria@fas.harvard.edu

Elkins, Caroline M. (PhD, Harvard 2001; prof.) sub-Saharan Africa; elkins@fas.harvard.edu

Elliott, Mark C. (PhD, California, Berkeley 1993; Mark Schwartz Prof.) China, Inner Asia; elliott3@fas.harvard.edu

Faust, Drew G. (PhD, Pennsylvania 1975; Lincoln Prof. and Univ. pres. emerita) 19th-century America, Civil War; drew_faust@harvard.edu

Frank Johnson, Alison (PhD, Harvard 2001; prof.) 19th-century Germany and Habsburg empire; afrank@fas.harvard.edu

Ghosh, Arunabh (PhD, Columbia 2014; assoc. prof.) modern China; aghosh@wcfia.harvard.edu

Gordon, Andrew (PhD, Harvard 1981; Lee and Juliet Folger Fund Prof.) modern Japan; agordon@fas.harvard.edu

Gordon, Peter E. (PhD, California, Berkeley 1997; Amabel B. James Prof.) modern European intellectual; pgordon@fas.harvard.edu

Hankins, James (PhD, Columbia 1984; prof.) Renaissance and Reformation; jhankins@fas.harvard.edu

Herzog, Tamar (PhD, EHESS, France 1994; Monroe Gutman Prof.) Latin America; therzog@fas.harvard.edu

Jasanoff, Maya (PhD, Yale 2002; Coolidge Prof.) 18th- and 19th-century Britain; mjasanof@fas.harvard.edu

Johnson, Walter (PhD, Princeton 1994; Winthrop Prof.; African and African American Studies) 19th-century US, African American, US South; johnson2@fas.harvard.edu

Kafadar, Cemal (PhD, McGill 1986; Vehbi Koç Prof.) Ottoman, paleography, historiography; kafadar@fas.harvard.edu

Kloppenberg, James T. (PhD, Stanford 1980; Charles Warren Prof.) intellectual and political; jkloppen@fas.harvard.edu

Lepore, Jill (PhD, Yale 1995; David Woods Kemper '41 Prof.) early America; jill_lepore@harvard.edu

Lewis, Mary D. (PhD, NYU 2000; Robert Walton Goelet Prof.) 20th-century France and Europe; mdlewis@fas.harvard.edu

Manela, Erez (PhD, Yale 2003; prof.) international relations; manela@fas.harvard.edu

Martin, Terry D. (PhD, Chicago 1996; George F. Baker III Prof.) Russia and eastern Europe, USSR formation of national identity and government; martin11@fas.harvard.edu

McCormick, Michael (PhD, Louvain, Belgium 1979; Francis Goelet Prof.) Byzantine, early medieval, paleography

McGirr, Lisa (PhD, Columbia 1995; prof. and dir., undergrad. studies) 20th-century US social and political; lmcgirr@fas.harvard.edu

Miller, Ian J. (PhD, Columbia 2005; prof.) modern Japan; ian_miller@harvard.edu

O'Neill, Kelly (PhD, Harvard 2006; assoc. prof.) modern Russia; koneill@fas.harvard.edu

Plokhii, Serhii (PhD, Kiev, Ukraine 1990; Mykhailo S. Hrushevs'kyi Prof.) Russia and Ukraine; plokhii@fas.harvard.edu

Rothschild, Emma (MA, Oxford 1970; prof.) 18th-century economic thought; rothsch@fas.harvard.edu

Smail, Daniel L. (PhD, Michigan 1994; Frank B. Baird Jr. Prof.) medieval France, law and politics, cultural; smail@fas.harvard.edu

Szonyi, Michael (DPhil, Oxford 1995; Frank Wen-Hsiung Wu Memorial Prof.) China; szonyi@fas.harvard.edu

Weld, Kirsten A. (PhD, Yale 2010; prof.) Latin America; weld@fas.harvard.edu

Joint/Cross Appointments

Brown, Vincent Aaron (PhD, Duke 2002; Charles Warren Prof.; African and African American Studies) Atlantic slavery, British Atlantic world, Caribbean; brown8@fas.harvard.edu

Brown-Nagin, Tomiko (PhD, Duke 2002; JD, Yale Law Sch. ; Daniel P.S. Paul Prof.; Harvard Law School) constitutional, social, politics and law; tbrownnagin@law.harvard.edu

Chalhoub, Sidney (PhD, Estadual de Campinas 1989; prof. and dir., grad. studies; African and African American Studies) Brazil; chalhoub@fas.harvard.edu

de la Fuente, Alejandro (PhD, Pittsburgh 1996; JD, Havana 1985; prof.; African and African American Studies) Latin America and Caribbean, comparative slavery, race relations; delafuente@fas.harvard.edu

Dench, Emma (DPhil, Oxford 1993; McLean Prof.; Classics) ancient; dench@fas.harvard.edu

Gordon-Reed, Annette (JD, Harvard 1984; Charles Warren Prof.; Harvard Law School/Radcliffe Inst.) US, legal; agordonreed@law.harvard.edu

Higginbotham, Evelyn Brooks (PhD, Rochester 1984; Victor S. Thomas Prof. and chair; Afro-American Studies) 19th- and 20th-century US, African American, women; ebhiggin@fas.harvard.edu

Hinton, Elizabeth Kai (PhD, Columbia 2013; assoc. prof.; African and African American Studies) 20th-century US poverty and racial inequality; ehinton@fas.harvard.edu

Kamensky, Jane (PhD, Yale 1993; Jonathan Trumbull Prof.; Pforzheimer Foundation Dir., Schlesinger Library, Radcliffe Inst. fo Advanced Study) colonial America, American social and cultural; kamensky@g.harvard.edu

Kirby, William C. (PhD, Harvard 1981; Spangler Family Prof. and T. M. Chang Prof.; Harvard Business School) 20th-century China; wkirby@hbs.edu

Logevall, Fredrik (PhD, Yale 1993; Laurence D. Belfer Prof.; Harvard Kennedy School) US foreign relations

Najmabadi, Afsaneh (PhD, Manchester, UK 1984; Francis Lee Higginson Prof.; Women's Studies) Middle East, gender and modernity; najmabad@fas.harvard.edu

Rabb, Insitar (PhD, Princeton 2009; JD, Yale Law Sch. 2006; prof.; Harvard Law School) Middle East law and constitutional; irabb@law.harvard.edu

Retired/Emeritus Faculty

Bailyn, Bernard (PhD, Harvard 1953; Adams Univ. Prof. emeritus and James Duncan Phillips Prof. emeritus) America; bailyn@fas.harvard.edu

Bisson, Thomas N. (PhD, Princeton 1958; Henry Charles Lea Prof. emeritus) medieval; tnbisson@fas.harvard.edu

Blackbourn, David (PhD, Cambridge 1976; Coolidge Prof. emeritus) modern Europe, Germany; dgblackb@fas.harvard.edu

Coatsworth, John H. (PhD, Wisconsin, Madison 1972; Monroe Gutman Prof. emeritus) Latin America, economic, comparative social

Cott, Nancy F. (PhD, Brandeis 1974; Jonathan Trumbull Research Prof. emeritus) US social and women; ncott@fas.harvard.edu

Craig, Albert M. (PhD, Harvard 1959; Harvard-Yenching Prof. emeritus) modern Japan; acraig@fas.harvard.edu

Darnton, Robert C. (DPhil, Oxford 1964; Carl H. Pforzheimer Univ. Prof. emeritus) book, digital; robert_darnton@harvard.edu

Higonnet, Patrice Louis-Rene (PhD, Harvard 1964; Robert Walton Goelet Research Prof. emeritus) modern Europe, France; higonnet@fas.harvard.edu

Iriye, Akira (PhD, Harvard 1961; Charles Warren Prof. emeritus) American diplomatic, American-Asian relations, international airiye@fas.harvard.edu

Jones, Christopher P. (PhD, Harvard 1965; George Martin Lane Prof. emeritus) ancient; cjones@fas.harvard.edu

Maier, Charles S. (PhD, Harvard 1967; Leverett Saltonstall Prof. emeritus) 20th-century Europe; csmaier@fas.harvard.edu

Mottahedeh, Roy (PhD, Harvard 1969; Gurney Prof. emeritus) Islamic; mottahed@fas.harvard.edu

Ozment, Steven E. (PhD, Harvard 1967; McLean Prof. emeritus) late medieval, Reformation Europe; ozment@fas.harvard.edu

Szporluk, Roman (PhD, Stanford 1965; Mykhailo S. Hrushevs'kyi Prof. emeritus) modern Ukraine, eastern Europe; szporluk@fas.harvard.edu

Tai, Hue-Tam Ho (PhD, Harvard 1977; Kenneth T. Young Prof. emerita) Sino-Vietnamese relations; hhtai@fas.harvard.edu

Thernstrom, Stephan (PhD, Harvard 1962; Winthrop Prof. emeritus) American social and economic; thernstr@fas.harvard.edu

Ulrich, Laurel T. (PhD, New Hampshire 1980; 300th Anniversary Univ. Prof. emerita) early America, social, women; ulrich@fas.harvard.edu

Womack, John , Jr. (PhD, Harvard 1966; Robert Woods Bliss Prof. emeritus) modern Latin America; jwomack@fas.harvard.edu

Recently Awarded PhDs

Aschenbrenner, Nathanael "Imperial Alchemy: Politics and Ideologies of Eastern Empire in the 15th-Century Mediterranean"

Blackwood, Maria "Personal Experiences of Nationality and Power in Soviet Kazakhstan, 1917-53"

Clavey, Charles H. "'All Machine and No Heart': The Problem of Feification in European Social and Philosophical Thought, 1920-70"

Crowcroft, Barnaby "Decolonization in the British Empire of Protectorates, 1945-67"

Ehrlich, Joshua "The East India Company and the Politics of Knowledge, 1772-1835"

Ibarguen, Irvin "Coveted across the Continuum: The Politics of Mexican Migration in Transnational Perspective, 1940-70"

Jarquin, Mateo "A Latin American Revolution: The Sandinistas, the Cold War, and Political Change in Latin America, 1977-90"

McSpadden, James "Enemies or Colleagues? Parliamentary Culture in Interwar Europe"

Menzin, Marion "The Sugar Revolution in New England: Barbados, Massachusetts, and the Atlantic Sugar Economy in the 17th Century"

Miller, Julie "The Person in America before 1857: A History"

Pope, Andrew "Living in the Struggle: Black Power, Gay Liberation, and Women's Liberation Movements in Atlanta, 1964-96"

Spiro, Liat N "Drawing Capital: Depiction, Machine Tools, and the Political Economy of Industrial Knowledge in the Long 19th Century"

Tycko, Sonia "Captured Consent: Bound Service and Freedom of Contract in Early Modern England and English America"

Wadia, Guillaume "A Constellation of Outposts: French Intelligence in the Making of Modern Morocco, 1912-37"

Harvard University

Dept. of History of Science, Science Center 371, 1 Oxford St., Cambridge, MA 02138. 617.495.9978. Fax 617.495.3344. Email: linda_schneider@harvard.edu. Website: https://histsci.fas.harvard.edu/.

The Department of the History of Science is a lively interdisciplinary community of scholars, undergraduate and graduate students, visiting researchers, and affiliated faculty in other Harvard programs. We seek to understand the sciences, technology, and medicine in their historical, cultural, and current contexts, using history as a tool to help illuminate how knowledge of various kinds has come to be configured as it is.

Chair: Evelynn Hammonds
Director of Graduate Studies: Elizabeth Lunbeck
Director of Undergraduate Studies: Anne Harrington
Degrees Offered: BA,MA,PhD
Academic Year System: Semester
Areas of Specialization: ancient/medieval/Renaissance/ early modern science, medicine and public health, physical/ biological/human sciences, social history of science
Undergraduate Tuition (per academic year): $50420
Graduate Tuition (per academic year): $50972
Enrollment 2018-19:
   Undergraduate Majors: 128
   New Graduate Students: 8
   Full-time Graduate Students: 49
   Part-time Graduate Students: 2
   Degrees in History: 36 BA, 2 MA, 9 PhD
   Students in Undergraduate Courses: 1139
   Students in Undergraduate Intro Courses: 109
Undergraduate Addresses:
   Admissions: https://college.harvard.edu/admissions
   Financial Aid: https://college.harvard.edu/financial-aid
Graduate Addresses:
   Admissions and Financial Aid: http://www.gsas.harvard.edu/

Full-time Faculty

Alam, Eram (PhD, Pennsylvania 2016; asst. prof.) medicine, globalization, 20th-century migration and health; ealam@fas.harvard.edu

Brandt, Allan M. (PhD, Columbia 1983; prof.; Harvard Medical Sch.) American medicine and science, health and public policy, medical ethics; brandt@fas.harvard.edu

Browne, Janet (PhD, Imperial Coll., London 1978; prof.) natural, evolutionary biology, empire; jbrowne@fas.harvard.edu

Csiszar, Alex (PhD, Harvard 2010; assoc. prof.) scientific communication, physical sciences, 19th- and early 20th-century France; acsiszar@fas.harvard.edu

Galison, Peter L. (PhD, Harvard 1983; prof.; Physics) history and philosophy of 20th-century physics, instrumentation, relationship of physics to engineering; galison@fas.harvard.edu

Hammonds, Evelynn M. (PhD, Harvard 1993; prof. and chair; African and African American Studies) race in biology/medicine/ anthropology, women and gender studies; hammonds@fas.harvard.edu

Harrington, Anne (DPhil, Oxford 1985; prof. and dir., undergrad. studies) psychology and brain sciences, 18th to 20th century; aharring@fas.harvard.edu

Hersch, Matthew (PhD, Pennsylvania 2010; JD, NYU Sch. of Law 1997; asst. prof.) Cold War Era aerospace/computer/military technologies, STS, museum studies; hersch@fas.harvard.edu

Jones, David S. (MD,PhD, Harvard 2001; prof.; Harvard Medical Sch.) medicine, cardiology and cardiac therapeutics, global health/public health; dsjones@harvard.edu

Kuriyama, Shigehisa (PhD, Harvard 1986; prof.; East Asian Languages and Civilizations) East Asian science and medicine, comparative Chinese/Japanese/European medical; hkuriyam@fas.harvard.edu

Lemov, Rebecca (PhD, California, Berkeley 2000; prof.) psychology and brain sciences; rlemov@fas.harvard.edu

Lunbeck, Elizabeth (PhD, Harvard 1984; prof. in residence and dir., grad. studies) medicine/health/society, women and gender studies, psychoanalysis and Freud; lunbeck@fas.harvard.edu

Marcus, Hannah F. (PhD, Stanford 2016; asst. prof.) medicine, science, early modern Europe; hmarcus@fas.harvard.edu

Oreskes, Naomi (PhD, Stanford 1990; prof.; Earth and Planetary Sciences) earth and environmental sciences, scientific consensus and dissent; oreskes@fas.harvard.edu

Ragab, Ahmed (PhD, Ecole Pratiques des Hautes Etudes 2010; MD, Cairo 2006; assoc. prof.; Harvard Divinity Sch.) science and religion, medieval Islamic sciences, medieval and modern Middle East; ahmed_ragab@harvard.edu

Richardson, Sarah S. (PhD, Stanford 2009; prof.; Studies in Women, Gender, and Sexuality) history and philosophy of biology, race and gender in biosciences, science and technology studies; srichard@fas.harvard.edu

Roosth, Sophia (PhD, MIT 2010; assoc. prof.) 20th- and 21st-century life sciences; roosth@fas.harvard.edu

Schiefsky, Mark (PhD, Harvard 1999; prof.; Classics) ancient philosophy, ancient science, ancient medicine; mjschief@fas.harvard.edu

Seow, Victor (PhD, Harvard 2013; asst. prof.) technology, environmental, modern East Asia; seow@fas.harvard.edu

Soto Laveaga, Gabriela (PhD, California, San Diego 2001; prof.) modern Latin America, intersection of science and culture, public health; gsotolaveaga@fas.harvard.edu

Wilson, Benjamin (PhD, MIT 2014; asst. prof.) physical sciences, Cold War, nuclear weapons; btwilson@fas.harvard.edu

Retired/Emeritus Faculty

Gingerich, Owen J. (PhD, Harvard 1962; prof. emeritus) astronomy; ogingerich@cfa.harvard.edu

Graham, Loren R. (PhD, Columbia 1964; prof. emeritus) Russian science; lrg@mit.edu

Holton, Gerald (PhD, Harvard 1948; prof. emeritus) history and philosophy of science, physics of matter at high pressure, career paths of young scientists; holton@physics.harvard.edu

Mendelsohn, Everett I. (PhD, Harvard 1960; prof. emeritus) biological sciences, sociological history of science, policy-oriented science; emendels@fas.harvard.edu

Park, Katharine (PhD, Harvard 1981; prof. emerita) medieval and early modern science and medicine, women/gender/sexuality studies; park28@fas.harvard.edu

Rosenberg, Charles E. (PhD, Columbia 1961; prof. emeritus) 19th- and 20th-century medicine and disease; rosenb3@fas.harvard.edu

Shapin, Steven (PhD, Pennsylvania 1971; prof. emeritus) sociology of scientific knowledge, early modern science, taste and subjectivity; shapin@fas.harvard.edu

Recently Awarded PhDs

Fallon, Cara Kiernan "Forever Young: The Social Transformation of Aging in America since 1900"

Heintzman, Kathryn "Keeping Economies Alive: Animals, Medicine, and the Domestication of the French Empire, 1761-1814"

Inkpen, Dani Hallet "Frozen Icons: The Science and Politics of Repeat Glacier Photographs, 1887-2010"

Kennedy, Devin "Virtual Capital: Computers and the Making of Modern Finance, 1929-75"

Morar, Florin "Connected Cartographies: World Maps in Translation between China, Inner Asia, and Early Modern Europe, 1550-1650"

Rich, Miriam "Monstrous Births: Race, Gender, and Defective Reproduction in US Medical Science, 1830-1930"

Volmar, Daniel "The Computer in the Garbage Can: Air-Defense Systems in the Organization of US Nuclear Command and Control 1940-60"

Hastings College

Dept. of History, 710 N. Turner Ave., Hastings, NE 68901. 402.461.7758. Fax 402.461.7480. Email: gavent@hastings.edu. Website: https://www.hastings.edu/academics/undergraduate-majors/history/.

Don't just study history—do history! With professors actively engaged in diverse research projects and committed to classroom excellence, the Hastings College History Department helps you build a deeper understanding of the past, which impacts the present and, perhaps, your future.

Chair: Glenn Avent
Degrees Offered: BA,MAT
Academic Year System: 2-7-7
Areas of Specialization: women and gender, medieval Europe, Latin America, environmental, Russia
Tuition (per academic year): $23900
Enrollment 2018-19:
 Undergraduate Majors: 40
 Degrees in History: 10 BA, 1 MAT
Addresses:
 Admissions: http://www.hastings.edu/admissions-cost
 Financial Aid: http://www.hastings.edu/admissions-cost/cost-aid

Full-time Faculty

Avent, Glenn J. (PhD, Arizona 2004; prof. and chair) Mexico, Latin America, world civilization; gavent@hastings.edu

Babcock, Robert S. (PhD, California, Santa Barbara 1992; prof.) medieval Europe/Wales/Ireland, environmental, Russia; rbabcock@hastings.edu

Biba, Catherine (PhD, Cornell 2015; asst. prof.) US, women and gender, natural disasters; cbiba@hastings.edu

University of Hawai'i at Hilo

Dept. of History, 200 W. Kawili St., Hilo, HI 96720-4091. 808.932.7121. Fax 808.932.7098. Email: smith808@hawaii.edu. Website: https://hilo.hawaii.edu/depts/history/.

The History Department at the University of Hawai'i at Hilo provides students with an understanding of the past and its application to the present. The curriculum leading to the degree of BA in history is designed to develop broad historical knowledge, global understanding, and important skills in data analysis and communication crucial in many professional fields.

Chair: Jeffrey A. Smith
Degrees Offered: BA
Academic Year System: Semester
Areas of Specialization: East Asia, Pacific/Oceania, Europe, US, Hawai'i
Tuition (per academic year):
 In-State: $7272
 Out-of-State: $20232
Enrollment 2018-19:
 Undergraduate Majors: 45
 Degrees in History: 12 BA

Addresses:

Admissions: https://hilo.hawaii.edu/admissions/
Financial Aid: http://hilo.hawaii.edu/financialaid/

Full-time Faculty

Bitter, Michael J. (PhD, Minnesota 1999; prof.) 18th-century Anglo-Russian relations, Russian expansion; bitter@hawaii.edu

Inglis, Kerri A. (PhD, Hawai'i, Manoa 2004; prof.) disease, medicine, Hawai'i and Pacific biological and cross-cultural exchange; inglis@hawaii.edu

Mikkelson, Douglas Kent (PhD, Columbia 1992; prof.) religion, ancient; dougmikk@hawaii.edu

Qin, Yucheng (PhD, Iowa 2002; assoc. prof.) Chinese nationalism and transnationalism, Sino-American relations, Asian American; ycqin@hawaii.edu

Smith, Jeffrey Allen (PhD, California, Riverside 2006; assoc. prof. and chair) America, public, indigenous American; smith808@hawaii.edu

Retired/Emeritus Faculty

Wagner-Wright, Sandra (PhD, Hawai'i, Manoa 1986; prof. emerita) US prior to 1877, women, Hawai'i; sandraww@hawaii.edu

---

University of Hawai'i at Manoa

Dept. of History, 2530 Dole St., Sakamaki A203, Honolulu, HI 96822-2383. 808.956.8358. Fax 808.956.9600. Email: history@hawaii.edu; histch@hawaii.edu. Website: http://manoa.hawaii.edu/history/.

Our faculty members are passionate about the history that they study, write, and teach. Given our geographical location, it's not surprising that we have strong expertise in Asian, Hawaiian, Pacific and World histories as well as the American and European pasts.

Chair: Shana J. Brown
Director of Graduate Studies: Matthew Lauzon
Degrees Offered: BA, MA, PhD
Academic Year System: Semester
Areas of Specialization: East/South/Southeast Asia, Pacific/Hawai'i, world and comparative, environmental, US, Europe
Undergraduate Tuition (per academic year):
In-State: $11088
Out-of-State: $33120
Graduate Tuition (per academic year):
In-State: $15600
Out-of-State: $37080
Enrollment 2018-19:
Undergraduate Majors: 120
New Graduate Students: 7
Full-time Graduate Students: 37
Part-time Graduate Students: 4
Degrees in History: 28 BA, 1 MA, 2 PhD
Students in Undergraduate Courses: 1800
Students in Undergraduate Intro Courses: 700
Online-Only Courses: 5%
Undergraduate Addresses:
Admissions: http://manoa.hawaii.edu/admissions/
Financial Aid: http://www.hawaii.edu/fas/
Graduate Addresses:
Admissions: http://manoa.hawaii.edu/graduate/
Financial Aid: http://manoa.hawaii.edu/history/

Full-time Faculty

Andaya, Leonard Y. (PhD, Cornell 1971; prof.) Southeast Asia, Indonesia; andaya@hawaii.edu

Arista, Noelani M. (PhD, Brandeis 2009; assoc. prof.) Hawai'i, 19th-century America, Pacific world; arista@hawaii.edu

Bertz, Ned O. (PhD, Iowa 2009; assoc. prof.) South Asia; bertz@hawaii.edu

Brown, Shana J. (PhD, California, Berkeley 2003; assoc. prof. and chair) 20th-century China; shanab@hawaii.edu

Daniel, Marcus L. (PhD, Princeton 1998; assoc. prof.) early America, early national US; marcusd@hawaii.edu

Davis, Edward L. (PhD, California, Berkeley 1993; assoc. prof.) Middle China; edavis@hawaii.edu

Henriksen, Margot A. (PhD, California, Berkeley 1989; assoc. prof.) recent US, US cultural; henrikm@hawaii.edu

Hoffenberg, Peter H. (PhD, California, Berkeley 1993; assoc. prof.) modern Britain, British Empire; peterh@hawaii.edu

Jolly, Karen Louise (PhD, California, Santa Barbara 1987; prof.) medieval Europe, Christianity; kjolly@hawaii.edu

Kim, Harrison (PhD, Columbia 2010; asst. prof.) modern East Asia, modern Korea, North Korea; chk7@hawaii.edu

Kraft, James P. (PhD, Southern California 1990; prof.) US economic, business and labor; jkraft@hawaii.edu

Lanzona, Vina (PhD, Wisconsin, Madison 2000; assoc. prof.) Philippines, Southeast Asia, gender; vlanzona@hawaii.edu

Lauzon, Matt J. (PhD, Johns Hopkins 2002; assoc. prof.) European intellectual; mlauzon@hawaii.edu

Lopez Lazaro, Fabio T. (PhD, Toronto 1996; assoc. prof.) world/Latin America, medieval/early modern Europe, Arab and Islamic; fll@hawaii.edu

Matteson, C. Kieko (PhD, Yale 2008; assoc. prof.) environmental world, social, 18th- and 19th-century France; cmatteso@hawaii.edu

McNally, Mark Thomas (PhD, UCLA 1998; prof.) Tokugawa Japan, Japanese intellectual; mmcnally@hawaii.edu

Njoroge, Njoroge (PhD, NYU 2007; assoc. prof.) US, Caribbean and Latin America, race and critical theory; njoroge@hawaii.edu

Rath, Richard C. (PhD, Brandeis 2001; assoc. prof.) colonial America; rrath@hawaii.edu

Reiss, Suzanna J. (PhD, NYU 2005; assoc. prof.) US foreign relations; sreiss@hawaii.edu

Rosa, John (PhD, California, Irvine 1999; assoc. prof.) Hawaiian islands, 20th-century Hawai'i, US social and cultural; rosajohn@hawaii.edu

Schwartz, Saundra (PhD, Columbia 1998; assoc. prof.) ancient Europe, classical, gender; saundras@hawaii.edu

Stalker, Nancy K. (PhD, Stanford 2002; Sen Chair) Japan, 20th century, cultural and gender; nancy.stalker@hawaii.edu

Totani, Yuma (PhD, California, Berkeley 2005; prof.) modern Japan, World War II Pacific war crime trials; yuma.totani@hawaii.edu

Wang, Wensheng (PhD, California, Irvine 2008; assoc. prof.) Ming-Qing China, social protests, politics and culture; wensheng@hawaii.edu

Zelko, Frank S. (PhD, Kansas 2003; assoc. prof.) environmental and world; fzelko@hawaii.edu

Retired/Emeritus Faculty

Akita, George (PhD, Harvard 1960; prof. emeritus) modern Japan, Far East

Chappell, David A. (PhD, Hawai'i, Manoa 1991; prof. emeritus) Pacific Islands, world, Africa; dchappel@hawaii.edu

Choe, Yong-ho (PhD, Chicago 1971; prof. emeritus) modern Korea, East Asia, US-East Asian relations; choeyh@hawaii.edu

Farris, William Wayne (PhD, Harvard 1981; Sen Chair Prof. emeritus) traditional Japan; wfarris@hawaii.edu

Hanlon, David (PhD, Hawai'i, Mânoa 1984; prof. emeritus) Pacific Islands, ethnography; hanlon@hawaii.edu

Kang, Hugh H. W. (PhD, Washington 1964; prof. emeritus) Korean institutional, premodern Korea, East Asia; hwkang@hawaii.edu

King, Pauline N. (PhD, Hawai'i, Mânoa 1976; prof. emeritus) Hawai'i, US in Pacific; paulinek@hawaii.edu

Kwok, Daniel W. Y. (PhD, Yale 1959; prof. emeritus) Chinese thought, modern China, Asia; dkwok@hawaii.edu

Locke, Robert R. (PhD, UCLA 1965; prof. emeritus) European social and economic, modern France, modern Germany; blocke@hawaii.edu

Rapson, Richard L. (PhD, Columbia 1966; prof. emeritus) US cultural and intellectual, sexuality and private lives; rapson@hawaii.edu

Speidel, Michael P. (PhD, Freiburg, Germany 1962; prof. emeritus) Greece and Rome, ancient Near East; speidel@hawaii.edu

Stephan, John J. (PhD, London 1969; prof. emeritus) modern Japan, Japanese foreign policy, Russia in Asia; stephan@hawaii.edu

Ziegler, Herbert F. (PhD, Emory 1980; retired assoc. prof.) 20th-century Europe, modern Germany, world; hziegler@hawaii.edu

Hawai'i Pacific University

Dept. of History and International Studies, 1188 Fort St. Mall, Ste. 306, Honolulu, HI 96813. 808.544.0810. Fax 808.544.1424. Email: llierheimer@hpu.edu. Website: https://www.hpu.edu/CHSS/History/.

The Department of History and International Studies provides students with the tools to become global leaders and active and reflective citizens of the 21st century world. Through our interdisciplinary programs students develop a rational and knowledge based understanding of the past, present, and future worlds and develop critical decision making and problem solving skills required to successfully navigate and mold a rapidly changing society.

Chair: Linda Lierheimer
Director of Graduate Studies: Russell A. Hart
Degrees Offered: BA,BS,MA,Cert.
Academic Year System: Semester
Areas of Specialization: world, Asia and Pacific, military and diplomatic, modern US, Europe
Undergraduate Tuition (per academic year): $24200
Graduate Tuition (per academic year): $18000
Enrollment 2018-19:
Undergraduate Majors: 130
New Graduate Students: 26
Full-time Graduate Students: 62
Part-time Graduate Students: 56
Degrees in History: 6 BA, 5 BS, 10 MA
Undergraduate Addresses:
Admissions: https://www.hpu.edu/undergraduate-admissions/first-year/
Financial Aid: https://www.hpu.edu/financial-aid/
Graduate Addresses:
Admissions: https://www.hpu.edu/graduate-admissions/
Financial Aid: https://www.hpu.edu/financial-aid/

Adjunct Faculty

Kang, Sung Pil (PhD, Hawai'i, Mânoa 2014; instr.) US and world; skang@hpu.edu

Millett, Allan R. (PhD, Ohio State 1966; adj. prof.) US military, Korean War, military thought; amillett@hpu.edu

Full-time Faculty

Askman, Douglas Victor (PhD, UCLA 2001; assoc. prof.) early modern and modern Europe, Spain, Hawai'i; daskman@hpu.edu

Bliss, Brenden (MA, King's Coll., London 2004; instr.; Off Campus Programs) military; bbliss@hpu.edu

Corcoran, James R. (PhD, Hawai'i, Manoa 2005; asst. prof.; Military Campus Programs) Asia, military; jcorcoran@hpu.edu

Davidann, Jon Thares (PhD, Minnesota 1995; prof.) US, US-Japanese relations, world; jdavidann@hpu.edu

Gibson, Bryan R. (PhD, London Sch. of Economics 2012; asst. prof.) US foreign policy, Cold War, modern Middle East; brgibson@hpu.edu

Gilbert, Marc Jason (PhD, UCLA 1978; prof. and NEH Endowed Chair in World History) modern South and South East Asia, world; mgilbert@hpu.edu

Gough, Allison J. (PhD, Ohio State 2000; assoc. prof.) modern US, African American and Atlantic, race and gender; agough@hpu.edu

Hart, Russell A. (PhD, Ohio State 1999; prof. and dir., grad. studies) modern military, modern Europe, World War II; rhart@hpu.edu

Lierheimer, Linda (PhD, Princeton 1994; prof. and chair) Renaissance and Reformation, early modern France, European women; llierheimer@hpu.edu

Henry Ford College

History Program, Dept. of Social Sciences, 5101 Evergreen Rd., Dearborn, MI 48128-1495. 313.845.9625. Fax 313.845.9778. Email: friedman@hfcc.edu. Website: https://hss.hfcc.edu/areas-study/history.

The History Program offers courses on world civilization, from ancient to modern world history, and American history. Other specialized topics include the modern Middle East, African American history, the Roman Empire, Michigan history, the history of American wars, and women's history.

Chair: Pamela Sayre
Degrees Offered: AA
Academic Year System: Semester
Areas of Specialization: early and modern America, ancient/medieval/modern world, American military (online)
Tuition:
In-district $101.50; Out-of-district $177; Out-of-state and international $257 (per credit hour)
Enrollment 2018-19:
Students in Program: 473
Addresses:
Admissions: http://www.hfcc.edu/admissions
Financial Aid: http://www.hfcc.edu/financial-aid

Affiliated Faculty

Berryman, Thomas G. (ABD, Wayne State 1990; asst. to assoc. dean for Social Sci.; Arts & Fitness Div.) medieval Europe, early modern Europe, modern Europe; berryman@hfcc.edu

Burks, John L. (MA, Wayne State 1984; adj. prof.; Religious Studies) ancient and religious, secondary social studies education; jburks@hfcc.edu

Carson, Thomas Edward (PhD, Michigan 1972; adj. prof.; Art) art, Latin; tecarson@hfcc.edu

Gibson, John W. (MA, Wayne State 2001; Coll. archivist) Detroit 1805-12, archival management; jwgibson@hfcc.edu

Harrison, Daniel F. (MA, Oakland 1987; reference librarian) research methodology, Great Lakes maritime heritage, historical archaeology; dharrisn@hfcc.edu

Mitchell, Gary R. (MA, Wayne State 2006; adj. prof.; Computer Information Systems) 20th-century American survey, American technological, Great Depression religion and media; grmitchell1@hfcc.edu

Neher, Kathleen A. (MA, NYU 1980; adj. prof.; Paralegal Studies) Europe, post-Civil War America, dance; neher@millercanfield.com

Full-time Faculty

Friedman, Hal M. (PhD, Michigan State 1995; prof.) US national security affairs, US foreign relations, US military and naval; friedman@hfcc.edu

Plaza, Samuel Joseph (MA, Eastern Michigan 1990; prof.) antebellum South, 1950s American culture, presidential elections; sjplaza@hfcc.edu

Sayre, Pamela G. (ABD, Michigan; prof. and program chair) Rome and Byzantium, ancient and medieval Near East, Germanic; psayre@hfcc.edu

Part-time Faculty

Baydoun, Shatha (MA, Michigan 2005; adj. prof.) African studies, colonial and postcolonial Middle East; sbaydoun@hfcc.edu

Jacobson, Keith (PhD, Wayne State 2003; adj. prof.) Native American, Russia, Africa; keith2169@hotmail.com

Shepherd, Kenneth Reynolds (ABD, Wayne State; adj. prof.) early modern Europe, early America, colonial Africa; kshepherd@hfcc.edu

Retired/Emeritus Faculty

Anderson, Thomas L., Jr. (PhD, Wayne State 1991; adj. prof. emeritus) ancient, medieval, early modern; tomlanderson@sbcglobal.net

Barnhart, Rodney R. (MA, Eastern Michigan 1976; prof. emeritus) US to 1865, Progressive Era, Europe from 1800

Caruso, Virginia P. (PhD, Michigan State 1986; prof. emerita) US women, American survey, world since 1800; tuffey10@aol.com

Di Ponio, Mario (EdD, Wayne State 1972; adj. prof. emeritus) European intellectual, Renaissance and Reformation, social science methodology; mariodiponio19@gmail.com

Hackett, William H. (MA, Michigan 1961; prof. emeritus) labor and urban; pwhackett@wowway.com

Holland, Robert M. (MA, Wayne State 1972; adj. prof. emeritus) British and American diplomatic

Johns, Michael J. (MA, Detroit 1989; adj. prof. emeritus) ancient, modern Europe, modern American survey; mjohns@schoolcraft.edu

Lewandowski, Cristopher J. (MA, Eastern Michigan 2006; adj. prof. emeritus) early America, 20th-century American social, modern European military; clewandow@gmail.com

Litogot, Lynda M. (PhD, Wayne State 2017; adj. prof. emerita) early America, modern America, modern Europe; lylitogot@yahoo.com

Marietti, John P. (PhD, Wayne State 1997; adj. prof. emeritus) Europe, modern Middle East, modern Jewish

Muhammad, Devissi (PhD, Bowling Green State 2004; adj. prof. emeritus) African American, American constitutional and legal, early national US; Devissi.Muhammad@gmail.com

Osthaus, Wendy B. (MA, Oakland 1988; adj. prof. emerita) 19th-century American South, American survey; wosthaus@aol.com

Ringle, Dennis J. (MA, Eastern Michigan 1997; adj. prof. emeritus) America, naval, social; djringle@charter.net

Secrest, William L. (MA, Detroit 1977; prof. emeritus) South Asian religions, religions, interfaith dialogue; willysecrest@gmail.com

Wilkinson, William J. (MA, Eastern Michigan 1974; admin. emeritus) modern Europe, early America, modern America

Williamson, Wilbert E. (MA, Wayne State 1974; reference librarian emeritus) modern America, local, library science; billwilliamson3890@att.net

Witherspoon, Reginald (PhD, Union Grad. Sch. 1993; admin. emeritus) America, African American, urban; rwitherspoon@comcast.net

Zimmerman, Susan C. (MA, Eastern Michigan 1986; adj. prof. emerita) 20th-century America, 20th-century Europe, US women; zimmdhsmun@yahoo.com

Hillsdale College

Dept. of History, 33 E. College St., Hillsdale, MI 49242. 517.437.7341. Fax 517.437.3923. Email: mkalthoff@hillsdale.edu. Website: https://www.hillsdale.edu/majors-minors/history/.

The Hillsdale College history program is rooted in the liberal arts. This means that we teach and study history because as human beings we know it is worth doing for its own sake.

Chair: Mark A. Kalthoff
Degrees Offered: BA,BS
Academic Year System: Semester
Areas of Specialization: US, Europe, intellectual, religion/cultural/economic, military
Tuition (per academic year): $27090
Enrollment 2018-19:
  Undergraduate Majors: 120
  Degrees in History: 35 BA
  Students in Undergraduate Courses: 1350
  Students in Undergraduate Intro Courses: 760
Addresses:
  Admissions: http://www.hillsdale.edu/admissions-aid/admissions
  Financial Aid: http://www.hillsdale.edu/admissions-aid/financial-aid

Full-time Faculty

Birzer, Bradley J. (PhD, Indiana 1998; prof.) 18th- and 19th-century US, US frontier, US cultural and intellectual; bbirzer@hillsdale.edu

Calvert, Kenneth (PhD, Miami, Ohio 2000; assoc. prof.) ancient, Christianity; kcalvert@hillsdale.edu

Conner, Thomas H. (PhD, North Carolina, Chapel Hill 1983; prof.) modern Europe, 19th- and 20th-century diplomatic, France; tconner@hillsdale.edu

Gaetano, Matthew (PhD, Pennsylvania 2014; asst. prof.) Renaissance, Reformation, medieval intellectual; mgaetano@hillsdale.edu

Gamble, Richard M. (PhD, South Carolina 1992; assoc. prof.) US cultural and intellectual; rgamble@hillsdale.edu

Hart, Darryl G. (PhD, Johns Hopkins 1988; prof.) American religion, American cultural, American political; dhart@hillsdale.edu

Kalthoff, Mark A. (PhD, Indiana 1998; prof. and chair) science, US cultural and intellectual; mkalthoff@hillsdale.edu

Maas, Korey (DPhil, Oxford 2006; asst. prof.) Reformation, church, intellectual; kmaas@hillsdale.edu

Moreno, Paul (PhD, Maryland, Coll. Park 1994; prof.) US constitutional; pmoreno@hillsdale.edu

Moye, Lucy E. (PhD, Duke 1985; assoc. prof.) medieval, England; lmoye@hillsdale.edu

Rahe, Paul (PhD, Yale 1977; prof.) ancient Rome, ancient Greece, modern Europe; prahe@hillsdale.edu

Raney, David Alan (PhD, Illinois, Urbana-Champaign 2001; prof.) colonial America, founding, sectionalism and Civil War; draney@hillsdale.edu

Stewart, H. David (PhD, Ohio State 1993; assoc. prof.) early modern Europe, military; hstewart@hillsdale.edu

Strasburg, James D. (PhD, Notre Dame 2018; asst. prof.) 20th-century US, US foreign policy and economic, American Christianity; jstrasburg@hillsdale.edu

Joint/Cross Appointments

Hanson, Victor Davis (PhD, Stanford 1980; sr. fellow; Hoover Inst.; Classics) ancient, military; vhanson@hillsdale.edu

Part-time Faculty

Arnn, Larry P. (PhD, Claremont Grad. 1985; prof. and Coll. pres.) 20th-century Europe and America; larnn@hillsdale.edu

Hofstra University

Dept. of History, 301 Shapiro Family Hall, Hempstead, NY 11550. 516.463.5604. Fax 516.463.7009. Email: simon.r.doubleday@hofstra.edu. Website: https://www.hofstra.edu/academics/colleges/hclas/his/.

The Department of History at Hofstra University offers a wide variety of courses on the history of the US, Europe, Africa, Asia, Latin America and the Middle East, from ancient and medieval times to the 21st century. Through the study of history, students acquire the skills in critical analysis and communication crucial for professional success, as well as the knowledge they need as citizens.

Chair: Simon R. Doubleday
Degrees Offered: BA
Academic Year System: Semester
Areas of Specialization: US, Europe, Latin America, Asia, Middle East
Tuition (per academic year): $42900
Enrollment 2018-19:
  Undergraduate Majors: 100
  Degrees in History: 25 BA
Addresses:
  Admissions: http://www.hofstra.edu/Admission/
  Financial Aid: http://www.hofstra.edu/Admission/adm_costofattendance.html

Adjunct Faculty

Chen, Anne Hunnell (PhD, Columbia 2014; adj. asst. prof.) anne.h.chen@hofstra.edu

Di Pasqua, Federico (MA, Freie, Berlin 2015; adj. instr.) ancient Greece and Rome

Full-time Faculty

Ahr, Johan (PhD, Yale 1999; assoc. prof.) modern Europe, social, France and Germany; johan.ahr@hofstra.edu

Charnow, Sally (PhD, NYU 1999; prof.) 19th-century France; sally.charnow@hofstra.edu

Doubleday, Simon R. (PhD, Harvard 1996; prof. and chair) medieval, Spain; simon.r.doubleday@hofstra.edu

Eisenberg, Carolyn (PhD, Columbia 1971; prof.) 20th-century foreign relations, Nixon-Kissinger era, Vietnam War; carolyn.eisenberg@hofstra.edu

Elsey, Brenda (PhD, SUNY, Stony Brook 2007; assoc. prof.) Latin America, Chile, sports; brenda.elsey@hofstra.edu

Pugliese, Stanislao G. (PhD, Grad. Center, CUNY 1995; dist. prof.) Italy, 20th-century Europe, Italian American; stanislao.pugliese@hofstra.edu

Ruiz, Mario M. (PhD, Michigan 2004; assoc. prof.) Middle East, Egypt; mario.ruiz@hofstra.edu

Sims, Katrina Rochelle (PhD, Mississippi 2016; asst. prof.) US race and gender, public health and medicine; katrina.sims@hofstra.edu

Terazawa, Yuki (PhD, UCLA 2001; assoc. prof.) modern Asia, Japan, medicine and science; yuki.terazawa@hofstra.edu

Part-time Faculty

Galgano, Michael (MA, Long Island, Post 1993; adj. instr.) America

Munz, John (MA, NYU 1999; adj. instr.) 20th-century US; john.f.munz@hofstra.edu

Staudt, John (PhD, George Washington 2005; adj. asst. prof.) colonial and 20th-century American social and political; john.staudt@hofstra.edu

Retired/Emeritus Faculty

D'Innocenzo, Michael (MA, Columbia 1959; Harry Wachtel Dist. Teaching Prof. emeritus) America, revolutionary era, New York state; michael.dinnocenzo@hofstra.edu

Jeanneney, John R. (PhD, Columbia 1969; prof. emeritus) modern Europe, France

Kern, Louis J. (PhD, Rutgers 1977; prof. emeritus) 19th-century American cultural and intellectual; louis.j.kern@hofstra.edu

Moore, John C. (PhD, Johns Hopkins 1960; prof. emeritus) medieval Europe, religion

Naylor, Natalie (EdD, Columbia 1971; prof. emeritus) New York state, education

Yohn, Susan M. (PhD, NYU 1987; prof. emeritus) 19th- and 20th-century America, women and gender; susan.m.yohn@hofstra.edu

Hollins University

Dept. of History, 8015 Quadrangle Ln., Box 9722, Roanoke, VA 24020. 540.362.6352. Fax 540.362.6286. Email: pcoogan@hollins.edu. Website: https://www.hollins.edu/academics/majors-minors/history/.

Students of history do more than study the past. They learn broad, critical thinking, to look beyond what happened to why. History is not only inherently interesting, it's also good preparation for anything else you do.

Chair: Peter F. Coogan
Degrees Offered: BA
Academic Year System: Semester
Areas of Specialization: US, modern Europe and women, diplomatic
Tuition (per academic year): $38400
Enrollment 2018-19:
  Undergraduate Majors: 34
  Degrees in History: 10 BA
Addresses:
  Admissions: http://www.hollins.edu/admissions/
  Financial Aid: http://www.hollins.edu/admissions/

Full-time Faculty

Coogan, Peter F. (PhD, North Carolina, Chapel Hill 1991; assoc. prof. and chair) 20th-century US, international relations; pcoogan@hollins.edu

Florio, Christopher Michael (PhD, Princeton 2016; asst. prof.) 19th-century US, US intellectual and cultural; cflorio@hollins.edu

Nunez, Rachel M. (PhD, Stanford 2006; assoc. prof.) modern Europe, France, women; rnunez@hollins.edu

College of the Holy Cross

Dept. of History, 1 College St., Worcester, MA 01610-2395. 508.793.2465. Fax 508.793.3881. Email: mconley@holycross. edu. Website: https://www.holycross.edu/academics/ programs/history.

In recent years, the field of history has become less bound in national histories and much more comparative, thematic, and transnational. Holy Cross is leading the way among undergraduate curricula nationwide to reflect this change by approaching history through thematic clusters.

Chair: Edward T. O'Donnell
Degrees Offered: BA
Academic Year System: Semester
Areas of Specialization: US, Europe/Russia, Africa and Middle East, Asia, Latin America
Tuition (per academic year): $46550
Enrollment 2018-19:
  Undergraduate Majors: 180
  Degrees in History: 55 BA
Addresses:
  Admissions: http://www.holycross.edu/admissions-aid
  Financial Aid: http://www.holycross.edu/admissions-aid/ financial-aid

Full-time Faculty

Attreed, Lorraine C. (PhD, Harvard 1984; prof.) ancient, medieval Europe and England, Renaissance; lattreed@holycross.edu

Bazzaz, Sahar (PhD, Harvard 2002; prof.) early modern and modern Middle East, North Africa, Morocco; sbazzaz@holycross. edu

Carrasquillo, Rosa E. (PhD, Connecticut 2001; prof.) colonial and modern Latin America; rcarrasq@holycross.edu

Cary, Noel D. (PhD, California, Berkeley 1988; prof.) 20th-century Europe, modern Germany, science/music/sports; ncary@ holycross.edu

Conley, Mary A. (PhD, Boston Coll. 2000; assoc. prof.) British Empire and Ireland, gender and childhood, naval; mconley@ holycross.edu

Hooper, Cynthia V. (PhD, Princeton 2003; assoc. prof.) Soviet Union, eastern Europe, imperial Russia; chooper@holycross.edu

McBride, Theresa M. (PhD, Rutgers 1973; prof.) modern France and Italy, women, environmental; tmcbride@holycross.edu

Miller, Gwenn A. (PhD, Duke 2004; assoc. prof.) early America, ethnohistory, gender; gmiller@holycross.edu

Munochiveyi, Munya B. (PhD, Minnesota 2008; assoc. prof.) sub-Saharan Africa; mmunochi@holycross.edu

O'Donnell, Edward T. (PhD, Columbia 1995; assoc. prof. and chair) US urban, immigration, Irish in US; eodonnell@holycross.edu

Poche, Justin David (PhD, Notre Dame 2007; assoc. prof.) American religion, Catholicism; jpoche@holycross.edu

Ren, Ke (PhD, Johns Hopkins 2014; asst. prof.) modern China, modern Asia; kren@holycross.edu

Rupakheti, Sanjog (PhD, Rutgers 2012; asst. prof.) South Asian colonialism, Nepal, labor/gender/kingship/law; srupakhe@ holycross.edu

Semley, Lorelle D. (PhD, Northwestern 2002; assoc. prof.) precolonial Africa, African diaspora; lsemley@holycross.edu

Spiro, Liat N (PhD, Harvard 2019; asst. prof.) US capitalism and technology, Atlantic; lspiro@holycross.edu

West, Michael R. (PhD, Columbia 2000; assoc. prof.) African American, 20th-century US, civil rights movement; mwest@ holycross.edu

Yuhl, Stephanie E. (PhD, Duke 1998; prof.) 20th-century US social and political, US South, US women; syuhl@holycross.edu

Retired/Emeritus Faculty

Anderson, John B. (MA, Notre Dame 1959; assoc. prof. emeritus) 19th- and 20th-century US, American political; jbanders@ holycross.edu

Beales, Ross W., Jr. (PhD, California, Davis 1971; prof. emeritus) colonial and revolutionary America, family and community, historical editing; rbeales@holycross.edu

Brandfon, Robert L. (PhD, Harvard 1962; prof. emeritus) 20th-century US, New Deal, World War II

Flynn, James T. (PhD, Clark 1964; prof. emeritus) 18th- and 19th-century Russia and Poland; jflynn@holycross.edu

Green, William A., Jr. (PhD, Harvard 1962; prof. emeritus) England, modern Europe, historiography

Lapomarda, Vincent A. (PhD, Boston Univ. 1968; assoc. prof. emeritus) US diplomacy, American religious, Italian American; vlapomar@holycross.edu

Lincicome, Mark E. (PhD, Chicago 1985; assoc. prof. emeritus) modern Japan, modern Asia; mlincico@holycross.edu

O'Brien, David J. (PhD, Rochester 1965; Loyola Prof. emeritus) 20th-century US, American church, American Catholicism; dobrien@holycross.edu

Powers, James F. (PhD, Virginia 1966; prof. emeritus) medieval Europe, Spain, medieval urban; jpowers@holycross.edu

Turner, Karen Gottschang (PhD, Michigan 1983; prof. emeritus) China, Chinese legal, Vietnamese women in war; kturner@ holycross.edu

Visiting Faculty

Megowan, Erina (PhD, Georgetown 2016; vis. prof.) modern Russia, modern Europe, World War II; emegowan@holycross.edu

Thompson, Catherine L. (PhD, Connecticut 2009; vis. prof.) US, medicine; catherine.thompson@uconn.edu

Hope College

Dept. of History, PO Box 9000, 126 E. 10th St., Holland, MI 49422-9000. 616.395.7590. Fax 616.395.7447. Email: petit@hope.edu; baar@hope.edu. Website: https://hope.edu/academics/history/.

History students at Hope cultivate a deeper understanding of the past through rigorous courses with first-rate teachers. You can expect your professors to know you by name, and you can develop the best learning experience for you—whether working one-on-one with faculty on a research project based on your interests or gaining valuable workplace skills through a local internship.

Chair: Jeanne Petit
Degrees Offered: BA
Academic Year System: Semester
Areas of Specialization: US, ancient/early modern/modern Europe, Africa, East Asia, Latin America
Tuition (per academic year): $30550
Enrollment 2018-19:
  Undergraduate Majors: 37
  Degrees in History: 13 BA
Addresses:
  Admissions: http://www.hope.edu/admissions
  Financial Aid: http://www.hope.edu/offices/financial-aid/

Adjunct Faculty

Awad, Habeeb (MDiv, Michigan 1999; adj. prof.; advisor,
international students and scholars; International Education)
Model Arab League, Arabic language and culture; hawad@
hope.edu

Swierenga, Robert P. (PhD, Iowa 1965; adj.) 19th-century US,
economic; swierenga@hope.edu

Full-time Faculty

Bell, Albert A., Jr. (PhD, North Carolina, Chapel Hill 1977; prof.)
ancient Greece and Rome, classics; bell@hope.edu

Gibbs, Janis M. (PhD, Virginia 1996; assoc. prof.) Germany,
Reformation, Middle East; gibbs@hope.edu

Hagood, Jonathan D. (PhD, California, Davis 2008; asst. prof.)
Argentina, Latin America, science; hagood@hope.edu

Janes, Lauren R. H. (PhD, UCLA 2011; assoc. prof.) modern France,
Africa, global; janes@hope.edu

Johnson, Fred L., III (PhD, Kent State 1999; assoc. prof.) 19th-
century US, African American, military; johnson@hope.edu

Petit, Jeanne D. (PhD, Notre Dame 2000; assoc. prof. and chair)
modern US, women, immigration; petit@hope.edu

Tan, Wei Yu Wayne (PhD, Harvard 2015; asst. prof.) Japan; tan@
hope.edu

Tseng, Gloria S. (PhD, California, Berkeley 2002; assoc. prof.)
modern France, modern China; tseng@hope.edu

Retired/Emeritus Faculty

Baer, Marc B. (PhD, Iowa 1976; prof. emeritus) Britain, imperialism;
baer@hope.edu

Bultman, C. Baars (PhD, Michigan State 1995; prof. emeritus)
Michigan; bultmanb@hope.edu

Cohen, William (PhD, NYU 1968; prof. emeritus) US social, 19th-
century US, American South; cohen@hope.edu

Curry, Earl R. (PhD, Minnesota 1966; prof. emeritus) modern US,
Latin America, diplomatic; curry@hope.edu

Penrose, G. L. (PhD, Indiana 1975; prof. emeritus) Russia, Middle
East; penrose@hope.edu

University of Houston

*Dept. of History, 524 Agnes Arnold Hall, Houston, TX 77204-3003.
713.743.3083. Fax 713.743.3216. Email: pahoward@uh.edu.
Website: http://www.uh.edu/class/history/.*

*The Department of History celebrates the dynamic and diverse
city in which it is located and the students who call Houston home.*

Chair: Philip A. Howard
Director of Graduate Studies: Richard Mizelle
Director of Undergraduate Studies: Cihan Yüksel Muslu
Degrees Offered: BA, MA, PhD
Academic Year System: Semester
Areas of Specialization: US, Europe, Latin America, public,
Mexican American, transnational
Undergraduate Tuition (per academic year):
In-State: $9434
Out-of-State: $21794
Graduate Tuition (per academic year):
In-State: $8732
Out-of-State: $18002
Enrollment 2018-19:
Undergraduate Majors: 461
New Graduate Students: 12
Full-time Graduate Students: 40

Part-time Graduate Students: 12
Degrees in History: 100 BA, 4 MA, 8 PhD
Undergraduate Addresses:
Admissions: http://www.uh.edu/undergraduate-admissions/
Financial Aid: http://www.uh.edu/undergraduate-admissions/
cost/
Graduate Addresses:
Admissions: http://www.uh.edu/graduate-school/admissions/
Financial Aid: http://www.uh.edu/graduate-school/graduate-
funding/

Affiliated Faculty

Al-Sowayel, Dina (PhD, Rice 1999; non-tenure-track instructional
faculty; assoc. dir., Women's, Gender & Sexuality Studies) Middle
East, women; dina@chasecom.net

Behr, Thomas Chauncey (PhD, SUNY, Buffalo 2000; adj.; faculty dir.,
Liberal Studies) Europe, intellectual; thomasbehr@earthlink.net

Semendeferi, Ioanna (PhD, Minnesota 2003; asst. research/
teaching prof.; Coll. of Natural Sciences and Mathematics)
science/technology/medicine

Valier, Helen (PhD, Manchester 2001; faculty; Honors Coll.)
Western and colonial/postcolonial medicine, technology, late
19th and 20th centuries; hkvalier@uh.edu

Velez, Diana (PhD, Princeton 1977; adj.; Undergraduate Scholars)
modern Europe, Latin America and Caribbean; dvelez@uh.edu

Young, Mark E. (PhD, Texas, Austin 1997; archivist and historian;
Hilton Coll. of Hotel and Restaurant Management) hospitality
industry, public, political; markyoung@uh.edu

Full-time Faculty

Buzzanco, Robert (PhD, Ohio State 1993; prof.) US foreign
relations, European military and diplomatic, 20th-century US;
buzz@uh.edu

Chery, Tshepo Masango (PhD, Pennsylvania 2012; asst. prof.) 20th-
century southern Africa, African religion, social and political
movements; tmchery@central.uh.edu

Clavin, Matthew J. (PhD, American 2005; prof.) Haitian Revolution,
Civil War; mjclavin@uh.edu

Cong, Xiaoping (PhD, UCLA 2001; assoc. prof.) China, education,
women; mikecon@optonline.net

Decker, Hannah S. (PhD, Columbia 1971; prof.) modern Germany,
19th-century European intellectual, psychoanalysis; hsdecker@
uh.edu

Deyle, Steven H. (PhD, Columbia 1995; assoc. prof.) 19th-century
US social, political, slavery and abolition; shdeyle@uh.edu

Fishman, Sarah (PhD, Harvard 1987; prof.) modern France, social,
women; sfishman@uh.edu

Gharala, Norah Linda Andrews (PhD, Johns Hopkins 2014; asst.
prof.) colonial Mexico, Hapsburg Spain, slavery in Caribbean;
nlgharal@central.uh.edu

Goldberg, Mark Allan (PhD, Wisconsin, Madison 2011; asst. prof.)
health and healing, ethnic studies; magoldberg@uh.edu

Harwell, Debbie Z. (PhD, Houston 2012; non-tenure-track
instructional faculty) Houston, 20th-century America, US civil
rights, public; dzharwel@central.uh.edu

Hernandez, Jose Angel (PhD, Chicago 2008; assoc. prof.) Mexico,
borderlands

Holt, Frank Lee (PhD, Virginia 1984; prof.) ancient, Greece and
Rome, Middle East; fholt@uh.edu

Hopkins, Kelly Yvonne (PhD, California, Davis 2010; non-tenure-
track instructional faculty) early America, Native American;
kyhopkins@uh.edu

Horne, Gerald C. (PhD, Columbia 1984; prof.) African American,
foreign policy; ghorne@uh.edu

Howard, Philip Anthony (PhD, Indiana 1988; prof. and chair) Latin America and Caribbean; pahoward@uh.edu

Ittmann, Karl E. (PhD, Pennsylvania 1987; prof.) modern Britain; kittmann@uh.edu

Klieman, Kairn A. (PhD, UCLA 1996; assoc. prof.) Africa, linguistic methods; kklieman@uh.edu

Milanesio, Natalia (PhD, Indiana 2009; assoc. prof.) 20th-century Argentina social, nmilanesio@uh.edu

Mizelle, Richard, Jr. (PhD, Rutgers 2006; assoc. prof. and dir., grad. studies) medicine, African American, technology and environment; rmmizelle@uh.edu

Neumann, Kristina M. (PhD, Cincinnati 2015; asst. prof.) ancient Rome, digital

O'Brien, Thomas F., Jr. (PhD, Connecticut 1976; prof.) Latin America, business; tobrien@uh.edu

Patterson, Catherine F. (PhD, Chicago 1994; assoc. prof.) England, Tudor-Stuart England; cpatters@uh.edu

Perales, Monica (PhD, Stanford 2004; assoc. prof.) Chicana, borderlands; mperales3@uh.edu

Ramos, Raúl A. (PhD, Yale 1999; assoc. prof.) American West, American social and labor, Mexican American; raramos@uh.edu

Rector, Josiah J. (PhD, Wayne State 2016; asst. prof.) 20th-century America, urban, environmental; jjrector@central.uh.edu

Reed, Linda L. (PhD, Indiana 1986; assoc. prof.) African American, recent US; lreed@uh.edu

Romero, R. Todd (PhD, Boston Coll. 2004; assoc. prof.) colonial America, Native American; tromero2@uh.edu

San Miguel, Guadalupe, Jr. (PhD, Stanford 1978; prof.) Chicano education, race and ethnicity in school policy, politics of discrimination; gsanmiguel@uh.edu

Schafer, James A., Jr. (PhD, Johns Hopkins 2008; assoc. prof.) medicine, contemporary US; jschafer@uh.edu

Takriti, Abdel Razzaq (PhD, Oxford 2010; assoc. prof.) modern Arab

Tillery, Tyrone (PhD, Kent State 1981; assoc. prof.) African American, 20th-century US, urban; ttillery@mail.uh.edu

Vaughn, Sally N. (PhD, California, Santa Barbara 1978; prof.) medieval, Reformation; snvaughn@sbcglobal.net

Walther, Eric H. (PhD, Louisiana State 1988; prof.) antebellum US; ewalther@uh.edu

Wintersteen, Kristin A. (PhD, Duke 2011; asst. prof.) environmental, Latin America, public

Young, Nancy Beck (PhD, Texas, Austin 1995; prof.) 20th-century US, political; nyoung2@uh.edu

Yuksel Muslu, Cihan (PhD, Harvard 2007; assoc. prof. and dir., undergrad. studies) medieval Ottoman

Zarnow, Leandra Ruth (PhD, California, Santa Barbara 2010; asst. prof.) modern US, women; lrzarnow@central.uh.edu

Joint/Cross Appointments

Achenbaum, Andrew (PhD, Michigan 1976; prof.; Graduate Coll. of Social Work) aging; achenbaum@uh.edu

Zamora, Lois (PhD, California, Berkeley; prof.; Comparative Cultural Studies) Latin American literature; lzamora@uh.edu

Retired/Emeritus Faculty

Curry, Lawrence H., Jr. (PhD, Duke 1971; asst. prof. emeritus) modern US; lcurry@uh.edu

Hart, John Mason (PhD, UCLA 1970; prof. emeritus) Latin America, Mexico; jhart@uh.edu

Kellogg, Susan (PhD, Rochester 1980; prof. emeritus) colonial Latin America, ethnohistory, women and family; skellogg@uh.edu

Martin, James Kirby (PhD, Wisconsin, Madison 1969; prof. emeritus) colonial and revolutionary America, social, military; jmartin@uh.edu

Melosi, Martin V. (PhD, Texas, Austin 1975; prof. emeritus) US urban, environmental, public; mmelosi@uh.edu

Pratt, Joseph A. (PhD, Johns Hopkins 1976; prof. emeritus) US business; joepratt@uh.edu

Stone, Bailey S. (PhD, Princeton 1973; prof. emeritus) 17th- and 18th-century Europe, French Revolution; bsstone@mail.uh.edu

Recently Awarded PhDs

Ashton, Deanne Morgan "The Industrialization of English Brewing in the Long 19th Century"

Bettinger, Rikki "Imperial Counterparts: North Atlantic Women's Travels in the Caribbean and Mexico, 1800-60"

Jacobs, Crescida "Biography of Mabel of Belleme (1030-82)"

LaRotta, Alex "Young, Gifted, and Brown: The History of San Antonio's West Side Sound"

McDonald, Eric J. "Violent Identity: Elite Manhood and Power in Early Barbados"

Mendiola, Daniel "Contructing Imperial Spaces: The Spanish nd Mosquito Conquests of 18th-Century Central America"

Muschi, Gianncarlo "From Factory Workers to Owners: Informality, Resurseo, and Entrepreneurship in the Formation of the Peruvian Community of Patterson, New Jersey, 1960-2001"

Neil, Mallory "Curating the Nation: Gender, Class and Empire at the 1908 Franco-British Exhibition"

Rodriguez, Samantha M. "Carving Spaces for Feminism and Nationalism: Tejana Activism in the Matrix of Social Unrest, 1967-78"

Thompson, Joseph "Something Like a Failed War: Major League Baseball's Unwinnable Conflict against Drugs"

Welborn, Ty "Lone Star Crusader: Antonio Maceo Smith and he Texas Civil Rights Movement"

University of Houston-Clear Lake

History Program, 2700 Bay Area Blvd., Houston, TX 77058-1098. 281.283.3395. Fax 281.283.3408. Email: hodgesaj@uhcl.edu. Website: https://www.uhcl.edu/human-sciences-humanities/departments/liberal-arts/history/.

The University of Houston-Clear Lake is a four-year institution offering undergraduate courses and master's-level graduate courses.

Chair: Cengiz Sisman
Degrees Offered: BA, MA
Academic Year System: Semester
Areas of Specialization: US, Europe, Latin America, Middle East
Undergraduate Tuition (per academic year):
  In-State: $7310
  Out-of-State: $20578
Graduate Tuition (per academic year):
  In-State: $9524
  Out-of-State: $19046
Undergraduate Addresses:
  Admissions: http://www.uhcl.edu/admissions/
  Financial Aid: http://www.uhcl.edu/costs-aid/
Graduate Addresses:
  Admissions: http://www.uhcl.edu/admissions/apply/graduate/
  Financial Aid: http://www.uhcl.edu/costs-aid/

Full-time Faculty

Dugre, Neal T. (PhD, Northwestern 2014; asst. prof.) colonial America; dugre@uhcl.edu

Hales, Barbara (PhD, Arizona 1995; assoc. prof.) modern Europe; hales@uhcl.edu

Haworth, Daniel S. (PhD, Texas, Austin 2002; assoc. prof.) Latin America; haworth@uhcl.edu

Hodges, Adam J. (PhD, Illinois, Urbana-Champaign 2002; assoc. prof.) 20th-century US; hodgesaj@uhcl.edu

Howard, Angela Marie (PhD, Ohio State 1978; prof.) 19th-century US; howarda@uhcl.edu

Sisman, Cengiz (PhD, Harvard 2004; assoc. prof. and program dir.) Middle East; sisman@uhcl.edu

Zophy, Jonathan W. (PhD, Ohio State 1972; prof.) premodern Europe; zophy@uhcl.edu

Nondepartmental Historians

Powers, Bill (PhD, Texas A&M 1993; adj.; dir., UHCL Texas Dept. of Criminal Justice Prog.) 19th- and 20th-century US; powers@uhcl.edu

Part-time Faculty

Weller, Cecil Edward, Jr. (PhD, Texas Christian 1993; adj.) Texas; weller@uhcl.edu

University of Houston-Downtown

Dept. of History, Humanities, and Languages, 1 Main St., N-1009, Houston, TX 77002. 713.221.8014. Fax 713.221.8144. Email: caset@uhd.edu. Website: https://www.uhd.edu/academics/humanities/undergraduate-programs/history/.

The BA in history at University of Houston-Downtown develops skills in writing, research, problem-solving and cultural sensitivity which prepare them for postgraduate study as well as professional success. It is a major opportunity to gain a comprehensive understanding of the political, social, and commercial history of the United States and the world.

Chair: Austin Allen
Degrees Offered: BA,Cert.
Academic Year System: Semester
Areas of Specialization: US, Texas and US borderlands, Atlantic, military, secondary education
Tuition (per academic year):
 In-State: $6400
 Out-of-State: $16400
Enrollment 2018-19:
 Undergraduate Majors: 115
 Degrees in History: 25 BA
Addresses:
 Admissions: https://www.uhd.edu/admissions/Pages/admissions-index.aspx
 Financial Aid: https://www.uhd.edu/financial/Pages/financial-index-2.aspx

Full-time Faculty

Allen, Austin L. (PhD, Houston 2001; assoc. prof. and history coord.) antebellum US, legal and constitutional; allena@uhd.edu

Alvarez, Jose E. (PhD, Florida State 1995; assoc. prof.) 20th-century Europe, Middle East; alvarezj@uhd.edu

Case, Theresa A. (PhD, Texas, Austin 2002; assoc. prof.) labor, social, women; caset@uhd.edu

Chism, Jonathan (PhD, Rice 2014; lect.) US religious; chismj@uhd.edu

Davey, Joseph (PhD, Michigan State 2015; lect.) Africa; daveyj@uhd.edu

Gillette, Aaron K. (PhD, SUNY, Binghamton 1993; assoc. prof.) Europe, racism, eugenics; gillettea@uhd.edu

Hovsepian, Melissa (PhD, Houston 1996; lect. and advisor; Coll. of Humanities and Social Sciences) world, ancient; hovsepianm@uhd.edu

Lopez, Nancy (PhD, Rice 2002; lect.) US; lopezn@uhd.edu

Preuss, Gene B. (PhD, Texas Tech 2004; assoc. prof.) American South, education, minorities; preussg@uhd.edu

Ryden, David Beck (PhD, Minnesota 2000; prof.) British colonial America, Jamaica and Atlantic world, slavery and abolition; rydend@uhd.edu

Salinas, Salvador (PhD, Texas, Austin 2014; asst. prof.) Latin America; salinass@uhd.edu

Hunter College, City University of New York

Dept. of History, 695 Park Ave., New York, NY 10065-5024. 212.772.5480. Fax 212.772.5545. Email: history@hunter.cuny.edu. Website: http://www.hunter.cuny.edu/history/.

The History Department at Hunter College offers courses in the history of the United States, the ancient world, medieval and modern Europe, Russia, Jewish studies, the Middle East and Islamic world, Latin America, Africa, East Asia and South Asia, as well as many comparative topics in political, intellectual, and world history.

Chair: Mary Roldan
Director of Graduate Studies: Karen Kern
Degrees Offered: BA,MA
Academic Year System: Semester
Areas of Specialization: US, Europe, Asia, Latin America, Africa
Undergraduate Tuition (per academic year):
 In-State: $6330
 Out-of-State: $16800
Graduate Tuition (per academic year):
 In-State: $13370
 Out-of-State: $23400
Enrollment 2018-19:
 Undergraduate Majors: 225
 Part-time Graduate Students: 86
 Degrees in History: 58 BA
Undergraduate Addresses:
 Admissions: http://www.hunter.cuny.edu/admissions/
 Financial Aid: http://www.hunter.cuny.edu/onestop/finances/financial-aid
Graduate Addresses:
 Admissions: http://www.hunter.cuny.edu/graduateadmissions
 Financial Aid: http://www.hunter.cuny.edu/onestop/finances/financial-aid

Full-time Faculty

Belsky, Richard D. (PhD, Harvard 1997; assoc. prof.) East Asia, China; rbelsky@hunter.cuny.edu

Bhagavan, Manu B. (PhD, Texas, Austin 1999; prof.) modern South Asia, human rights, internationalism; mbhagava@hunter.cuny.edu

Contreras, Eduardo A. (PhD, Chicago 2007; assoc. prof.) comparative Latino, urban, gender; econtre@hunter.cuny.edu

Haverty-Stacke, Donna Truglio (PhD, Cornell 2003; prof.) US labor, US urban, US cultural; dhaverty@hunter.cuny.edu

Haywood, D'Weston L. (PhD, Northwestern 2013; assoc. prof.) African American; dh2036@hunter.cuny.edu

Hett, Benjamin C. (PhD, Harvard 2001; prof.) modern Europe and Germany, legal, cultural; bhett@hunter.cuny.edu

Hurewitz, Daniel (PhD, UCLA 2001; assoc. prof.) US since 1920, sexuality/gay/lesbian, US political; dhurewit@hunter.cuny.edu

Kern, Karen M. (PhD, Columbia 1999; assoc. prof. and dir., grad. studies) Middle East, Ottoman Empire, women and gender; kkern@hunter.cuny.edu

Mehilli, Elidor (PhD, Princeton 2011; asst. prof.) modern eastern central Europe, Russia and Soviet Union, modern Italy; em705@hunter.cuny.edu

Roldan, Mary J. (PhD, Harvard 1992; Dorothy Epstein Prof. and chair) Colombia, radio and violence, 20th-century culture and politics; mrol@hunter.cuny.edu

Rosenberg, Jonathan (PhD, Harvard 1997; assoc. prof.) 20th-century US, US civil rights; jonathan.rosenberg@aol.com

Rosenthal, Jill (PhD, Emory 2014; asst. prof.) Africa/Great Lakes region, humanitarian and development aid; jr3192@hunter.cuny.edu

Schor, Laura Strumingher (PhD, Rochester 1974; prof.) French women, French labor, French Jewish; lschor@hunter.cuny.edu

Vushko, Iryna (PhD, Yale 2008; asst. prof.) Russia; iv30@hunter.cuny.edu

Part-time Faculty

Asher, Florence (PhD, Grad. Center, CUNY 2006; adj. asst. prof.) US; fasher@hunter.cuny.edu

John, S. Sandor (PhD, Grad. Center, CUNY 2006; adj. assoc. prof.) Latin America; s_an@msn.com

Memegalos, Florene S. (PhD, Grad. Center, CUNY 1999; adj. assoc. prof.) early modern Europe, England; fmemegal@hunter.cuny.edu

Ranlet, Philip (PhD, Columbia 1983; adj. assoc. prof.) US, early America; pranlet@hunter.cuny.edu

Sclar, Arieh (PhD, SUNY, Stony Brook 2008; adj. asst. prof.) US; asclar@hunter.cuny.edu

University of Idaho

Dept. of History, 875 Perimeter Dr., MS 3175, Administration Bldg. 315, Moscow, ID 83844-3175. 208.885.6253. Fax 208.885.5221. Email: history@uidaho.edu. Website: https://www.uidaho.edu/class/history.

Discover a whole new world—the human past. There's no better way to know where you're going than knowing where you've been. And that's the beauty of studying history.

Chair: Ellen E. Kittell, interim
Director of Graduate Studies: Pingchao Zhu
Degrees Offered: BA,BS,MA,PhD
Academic Year System: Semester
Areas of Specialization: ancient world, premodern and modern Europe, modern Latin America, modern Asia, science/health/environment, gender studies, material culture
Undergraduate Tuition (per academic year):
  In-State: $7232
  Out-of-State: $22040
Graduate Tuition (per academic year):
  In-State: $8530
  Out-of-State: $23338
Enrollment 2018-19:
  Undergraduate Majors: 153
  New Graduate Students: 4
  Full-time Graduate Students: 7
  Part-time Graduate Students: 3
  Degrees in History: 19 BA, 21 BS, 5 MA, 2 PhD

Undergraduate Addresses:
  Admissions: https://www.uidaho.edu/admissions
  Financial Aid: https://www.uidaho.edu/financial-aid
Graduate Addresses:
  Admissions: https://www.uidaho.edu/admissions/graduate
  Financial Aid: https://www.uidaho.edu/financial-aid

Adjunct Faculty

Gosse, Johanna (PhD, Bryn Mawr 2014; asst. prof.; Art & Design) modern and contemporary art, experimental film and media, Cold War cultural; johannagosse@gmail.com

Kyong-McClain, Jeff (PhD, Illinois, Urbana-Champaign 2009; co-dir., Confucius Institute) 20th-century China; jeffkm@uidaho.edu

Smith, Bill L. (PhD, Washington State 2000; clinical prof.; prog. coord., Martin Inst. for Peace Studies and Conflict Resolution) Latin America; bills@uidaho.edu

Full-time Faculty

Fox-Amato, Matthew (PhD, Southern California 2013; asst. prof.) early America, slavery, visual culture studies; mamato@uidaho.edu

Graden, Dale T. (PhD, Connecticut 1991; prof.) Latin America, Atlantic world, comparative slavery; graden@uidaho.edu

Kittell, Ellen E. (PhD, Illinois, Urbana-Champaign 1983; prof. and interim chair) medieval Europe, Renaissance and Reformation, women and gender; kittell@uidaho.edu

Quinlan, Sean M. (PhD, Indiana 2000; prof. and interim dean) 18th-century studies, science and medicine in France and Italy, Western gender and sexuality; quinlan@uidaho.edu

Scofield, Rebecca Elena (PhD, Harvard 2015; asst. prof.) gender and sexuality, American West, cultural; rscofield@uidaho.edu

Sowards, Adam M. (PhD, Arizona State 2001; prof.) US West, environmental, science and exploration; asowards@uidaho.edu

Spence, Richard B. (PhD, California, Santa Barbara 1981; prof.) modern Russia and eastern Europe, Middle East, military; rspence@uidaho.edu

Zhu, Pingchao (PhD, Miami, Ohio 1998; prof. and dir., grad. studies) modern East Asia, US diplomatic, cultural; pzhu@uidaho.edu

Retired/Emeritus Faculty

Aiken, Katherine G. (PhD, Washington State 1980; prof. emeritus) modern America, women and labor, social and cultural; kaiken@uidaho.edu

Hackmann, Wm. Kent (PhD, Michigan 1969; prof. emeritus) Tudor-Stuart-Georgian England; hackmann@uidaho.edu

Perraud, Louis (PhD, Indiana; prof. emeritus) Latin, classical and Koine Greek, classical mythology and civilization; phantom@uidaho.edu

Schwantes, Carlos A. (PhD, Michigan 1976; prof. emeritus; St. Louis Mercantile Library Prof., Transportation Studies) 20th-century American West, labor, Pacific Northwest; cmschwantes@aol.com

Idaho State University

Dept. of History, 921 S. 8th Ave., Stop 8079, Pocatello, ID 83209-8079. 208.282.2379. Fax 208.282.4267. Email: histdept@isu.edu. Website: https://isu.edu/history/.

The History curriculum ensures that students study a range of topics and develop analytical skills in research and writing. The MA program offers students a professional master's degree in applied, digital history. This program trains students to apply sophisticated information technologies to a rigorous analysis of historical problems. The MA is offered in Pocatello, Idaho Falls, and online.

Chair: Zackery Heern
Director of Graduate Studies: Justin Dolan Stover
Degrees Offered: BA,MA
Academic Year System: Semester
Areas of Specialization: world, America, science/technology/medicine, environmental, digital
Undergraduate Tuition (per academic year):
 In-State: $7166
 Out-of-State: $21942
Graduate Tuition (per academic year):
 In-state and Western Regional Graduate Programs: $8928
 Out-of-State: $23704
Enrollment 2018-19:
 Undergraduate Majors: 68
 New Graduate Students: 4
 Full-time Graduate Students: 7
 Part-time Graduate Students: 4
 Degrees in History: 35 BA, 3 MA
Undergraduate Addresses:
 Admissions: http://www.isu.edu/future/
 Financial Aid: http://www2.isu.edu/finaid/
Graduate Addresses:
 Admissions: http://www2.isu.edu/graduate/
 Financial Aid: http://www2.isu.edu/finaid/

Full-time Faculty

Datta, Arunima (PhD, National, Singapore 2015; asst. prof.) dattarun@isu.edu

Heern, Zackery M. (PhD, Utah 2011; assoc. prof. and chair) Middle East, Islam, world; heerzack@isu.edu

Kole de Peralta, Kathleen M. (PhD, Notre Dame 2015; asst. prof.) colonial Latin America, environmental, public health; kolekath@isu.edu

Kuhlman, Erika Ann (PhD, Washington State 1995; prof.) American studies, early 20th-century women, transnational; kuhlerik@isu.edu

Marsh, Kevin R. (PhD, Washington State 2002; prof.) environmental, US West, modern US; marskevi@isu.edu

Njoku, Raphael Chijioke (PhD, Dalhousie 2003; prof.; chair, Global Studies) modern Africa, African diaspora, medicine; njokraph@isu.edu

Robey, Sarah (PhD, Temple 2017; asst. prof.) energy, US cultural, modern US; robesar5@isu.edu

Stango, Marie Elizabeth (PhD, Michigan 2016; asst. prof.) stanmari@isu.edu

Stover, Justin Dolan (PhD, Trinity Coll., Dublin 2011; assoc. prof. and dir., grad. studies) modern Ireland, modern Europe, war and nationalism; stovjust@isu.edu

Woodworth-Ney, Laura Ellen (PhD, Washington State 1996; prof.; provost; and vice pres., Academic Affairs) US West, women, Native American; woodlaur@isu.edu

Part-time Faculty

Benedict, Hope Ann (PhD, Oregon 1997; instr.) Idaho; benehope@isu.edu

Retired/Emeritus Faculty

Christelow, Allan, Jr. (PhD, Michigan 1977; prof. emeritus) Middle East/North Africa, Islamic law, transnational

Christelow, Stephanie Mooers (PhD, California, Santa Barbara 1983; prof. emerita) medieval England

Hatzenbuehler, Ronald (PhD, Kent State 1972; prof. emeritus) colonial and revolutionary America, early national, American diplomatic; hatzrona@isu.edu

Owens, J. B. (PhD, Wisconsin-Madison 1972; prof. emeritus) Renaissance and Reformation, Spain, historical GIS; owenjack@isu.edu

University of Illinois at Chicago

Dept. of History, 601 S. Morgan St., M/C 198, Chicago, IL 60607-7109. 312.996.3141. Fax 312.996.6377. Email: crboyer@uic.edu. Website: https://hist.uic.edu/.

Our faculty members are leaders in their fields, our graduate students typically go on to secure tenure-track jobs in universities and colleges throughout the nation, and our undergraduates have the freedom to explore their variety of interests while remaining grounded in the mainstream of the discipline. The Department of History is an exciting place to be.

Chair: Christopher Boyer
Director of Graduate Studies: Keely Stauter-Halsted
Director of Undergraduate Studies: Laura Hostetler
Degrees Offered: BA,BAT,MA,MAT,PhD
Academic Year System: Semester
Areas of Specialization: US, modern Europe, Russia and eastern Europe, Progressive Era, gender and women
Undergraduate Tuition (per academic year):
 In-State: $14870
 Out-of-State: $28086
Graduate Tuition (per academic year):
 In-State: $15946
 Out-of-State: $28186
Enrollment 2018-19:
 Undergraduate Majors: 174
 New Graduate Students: 9
 Full-time Graduate Students: 43
 Part-time Graduate Students: 10
 Degrees in History: 89 BA, 5 MA, 6 PhD, 85 BAT, 12 MAT
Undergraduate Addresses:
 Admissions: https://admissions.uic.edu/undergraduate
 Financial Aid: http://financialaid.uic.edu/
Graduate Addresses:
 Admissions: https://hist.uic.edu/history/programs/graduate
 Financial Aid: https://hist.uic.edu/history/programs/graduate/funding

Affiliated Faculty

Balserak, Jon (PhD, Edinburgh 2002; assoc. prof.) Reformation; J.Balserak@bristol.ac.uk

Bauer, Brian (PhD, Chicago 1990; prof.; dir., grad. studies, Anthropology) Inca; bsb@uic.edu

Englemann, Stephen (PhD, Johns Hopkins 1996; assoc. prof.; Political Science) political thought; sengelma@uic.edu

Greene, Daniel A. (PhD, Chicago 2004; guest curator, Northwestern) US immigration, modern Jewish; daniel.greene@northwestern.edu

Morruzzi, Norma (PhD, Johns Hopkins 1990; assoc. prof.; Gender and Women's Studies, Political Science) Middle East; nmorruzzi@uic.edu

Sufian, Sandy (PhD, NYU 1999; assoc. prof.; Medical Education, Sch. Medicine) medicine, Middle East; sufians@uic.edu

Full-time Faculty

Abbott, John (PhD, Illinois, Chicago 2000; sr. lect.) modern Europe; jabbot1@uic.edu

Chavez, Joaquin M. (PhD, NYU 2010; assoc. prof.) El Salvador; chavezj1@uic.edu

Daly, Jonathan W. (PhD, Harvard 1992; prof.) late imperial and Soviet Russia; daly@uic.edu

Fidelis, Malgorzata (PhD, Stanford 2006; assoc. prof.) eastern and modern Europe, Soviet Union, gender; gosia01@uic.edu

Hoppe, Kirk A. (PhD, Boston Univ. 1995; assoc. prof.) world, Africa; kahoppe1@uic.edu

Hostetler, Laura E. (PhD, Pennsylvania 1995; prof. and dir., undergrad. studies) China; hostetle@uic.edu

Hudson, Lynn M. (PhD, Indiana 1996; assoc. prof.) US West, African American, gender; hudsonlm@uic.edu

Johnston, Robert D. (PhD, Rutgers 1993; assoc. prof.) Progressive Era, America, teacher education; johnsto1@uic.edu

Jordan, Nicole T. (PhD, London Sch. Econ. 1984; assoc. prof.) modern Europe, European diplomatic; njordan@uic.edu

Levy, Richard S. (PhD, Yale 1969; prof.) modern Europe, modern Germany; rslevy@uic.edu

Mantena, Rama S. (PhD, Michigan 2002; assoc. prof.) South and Southeast Asia; rmantena@uic.edu

Peters, Julie (MAT, Illinois, Chicago 1987; clinical assoc. prof.) teacher education; jlpeters@uic.edu

Quadri, Syed Junaid (PhD, McGill 2013; asst. prof.) Islamic law, Islamic theology, Egypt; jquadri@uic.edu

Sklansky, Jeffrey (PhD, Columbia 1996; assoc. prof.) 19th-century US, social and intellectual; sklanskj@uic.edu

Stauter-Halsted, Keely D. (PhD, Michigan 1993; prof. and dir., grad. studies) eastern Europe, Poland; stauterh@uic.edu

Todd-Breland, Elizabeth S. (PhD, Chicago 2010; asst. prof.) US urban, social, African American and education; etoddbre@uic.edu

Joint/Cross Appointments

Agnani, Sunil (PhD, Columbia 2004; assoc. prof.; English) English and comparative literature; sagnani1@uic.edu

Blair, Cynthia M. (PhD, Harvard 1999; assoc. prof.; African American Studies) African American, US urban, sexuality; cmblair@uic.edu

Boyer, Christopher R. (PhD, Chicago 1997; prof.; chair; Latin American and Latino Studies) modern Mexico, environmental, social; crboyer@uic.edu

Brier, Jennifer (PhD, Rutgers 2002; assoc. prof.; dir., Gender and Women's Studies) gay and lesbian, women; jbrier@uic.edu

Goodman, Adam (PhD, Pennsylvania 2015; asst. prof.; Latin American Latino Studies) migration and immigration, borders and borderland, Latino and Latin America; asig@uic.edu

Jin, Michael (PhD, California, Santa Cruz 2013; asst. prof.; Global Asian Studies) migration and diaspora, transnational Asia and Pacific Rim world, critical race and ethnic and Asian American; mrjin@uic.edu

Keen, Ralph (PhD, Chicago 1990; prof.; Catholic Studies) Christianity; rkeen01@uic.edu

Liechty, Mark (PhD, Pennsylvania 1994; prof.; Anthropology) South Asia, consumer, world; liechty@uic.edu

McClure, Ellen (PhD, Michigan 1997; assoc. prof.; French and Francophone Studies) France; ellenmc@uic.edu

Ransby, Barbara (PhD, Michigan 1996; prof.; African American Studies) African American; bransby@uic.edu

Schultz, Kevin M. (PhD, California, Berkeley 2005; prof. and assoc. chair; Catholic Studies) 20th-century US, US religion; schultzk@uic.edu

Retired/Emeritus Faculty

Alexander, Michael C. (PhD, Toronto 1977; prof. emeritus) Rome; micalexa@uic.edu

Barahona, Renato (PhD, Princeton 1979; prof. emeritus) Spain; barahona@uic.edu

Bledstein, Burton J. (PhD, Princeton 1967; assoc. prof. emeritus) US intellectual and social thought; bjb@uic.edu

Calder, Bruce J. (PhD, Texas, Austin 1974; assoc. prof. emeritus) Latin America, Caribbean, Central America; bcalder@uic.edu

Cracraft, James E. (PhD, Oxford 1968; prof. emeritus) 17th- and 18th-century Russia; cracraft@uic.edu

D'Emilio, John A. (PhD, Columbia 1982; prof. emeritus) sexuality, social movements, post-World War II US; demilioj@uic.edu

Danzer, Gerald A. (PhD, Northwestern 1967; prof. emeritus) American historiography, teaching methods; gdanzer@uic.edu

Duis, Perry R. (PhD, Chicago 1975; prof. emeritus) US urban, Chicago; prduis@uic.edu

Fink, Leon (PhD, Rochester 1977; Dist. Prof. emeritus) US labor and immigration, Gilded Age and Progressive Era, intellectuals and social movements; leonfink@uic.edu

Fried, Richard M. (PhD, Columbia 1972; prof. emeritus) 20th-century US political, foreign policy; rmfried@uic.edu

Hoisington, William A., Jr. (PhD, Stanford 1968; prof. emeritus) 20th-century Europe, North Africa; williamh@uic.edu

Huppert, George (PhD, California, Berkeley 1962; prof. emeritus) Renaissance Europe, European historiography; huppert@uic.edu

Jordan, David Paul (PhD, Yale 1966; prof. emeritus) 18th-century European intellectual, French Revolution; dpj@uic.edu

Kaba, Lansine (PhD, Northwestern 1972; prof. emeritus) Africa; lkaba@uic.edu

Kulczycki, John J. (PhD, Columbia 1973; prof. emeritus) eastern Europe, Poland; kul@uic.edu

Levine, Susan B. (PhD, Grad. Center, CUNY 1980; prof. emeritus) US women and labor, consumer culture, public policy; slevine@uic.edu

McCloskey, Deirdre (PhD, Harvard 1970; prof. emeritus) British economic; deirdre2@uic.edu

Messer, Robert L. (PhD, California, Berkeley 1975; assoc. prof. emeritus) US diplomatic; messer@uic.edu

Nashat, Guity (PhD, Chicago 1973; assoc. prof. emeritus) Middle East; gnashat@uic.edu

Perman, Michael (PhD, Chicago 1969; prof. emeritus) American South, Civil War and Reconstruction; mperman@uic.edu

Sack, James J. (PhD, Michigan 1973; prof. emeritus) 18th- and 19th-century Britain; jsack@uic.edu

Schelbert, Leo (PhD, Columbia 1966; prof. emeritus) American immigration and European emigration; lschelbe@uic.edu

Strobel, Margaret A. (PhD, UCLA 1975; prof. emeritus) East Africa; pegs@uic.edu

Zweiniger-Bargielowska, Ina (PhD, Cambridge 1990; prof. emeritus) 20th-century Britain, women; inazb@uic.edu

Visiting Faculty

Baber, R. Jovita (PhD, Chicago 2005; vis. lect.) Latin America; jbabe@comcast.net

Davis, Cory (PhD, Illinois, Chicago 2014; vis. asst. prof.) modern US; cdavis26@uic.edu

Strickland, Peter (PhD, Illinois, Chicago 2015; vis. lect.) modern Ireland and Britain, modern Europe, gender; pstric2@uic.edu

Wilczewski, Michal Janusz (PhD, Illinois, Chicago 2017; vis. lect.) modern eastern Europe; mwilcz5@uic.edu

Recently Awarded PhDs

Ash, Jennifer Scism "Invincible Not Invisible: Black Women and Resistance at Black Colleges, 1957-2018"

Mertz, Adam Ralph "Growing Realignment"

University of Illinois at Springfield

Dept. of History, University Hall Bldg., MS 3050, 1 University Plaza, Springfield, IL 62703-5407. 217.206.7189. Fax 217.206.6217. Email: his@uis.edu. Website: https://www.uis.edu/history/.

The department encourages students to compare elements of their own culture with those of other cultures from other time periods. Students of history gain a sense of what is unique in- as well as generally characteristic of-individuals, groups, and national cultures in the present as well as the past.

Chair: David Bertaina
Degrees Offered: BA,MA
Academic Year System: Semester
Areas of Specialization: US, Europe, Asia, public, Middle East
Undergraduate Tuition (per academic year):
  In-State: $8670
  Out-of-State: $17820
Graduate Tuition (per academic year):
  In-State: $6704
  Out-of-State: $14316
Enrollment 2018-19:
  Undergraduate Majors: 76
  Full-time Graduate Students: 26
Undergraduate Addresses:
  Admissions: http://www.uis.edu/admissions/
  Financial Aid: http://www.uis.edu/financialaid/
Graduate Addresses:
  Admissions and Financial Aid: http://www.uis.edu/
    graduateeducation/

Full-time Faculty

Bailey, Heather (PhD, Minnesota 2001; assoc. prof.) modern Europe, 19th-century Russia, intellectual and cultural; hbail2@uis.edu

Barnwell, Kristi N. (PhD, Texas, Austin 2010; asst. prof.) modern Middle East; kbarn2@uis.edu

Bertaina, David (PhD, Catholic 2007; assoc. prof. and chair) comparative religion, Semitic languages, early Christianity and Islam; dbert3@uis.edu

Burlingame, Michael A. (PhD, Johns Hopkins 1971; Lynn Chair) era of Lincoln; mburl2@uis.edu

Cornell, Cecilia Stiles (PhD, Vanderbilt 1987; assoc. prof.) 20th-century US, American foreign relations; cornell.cecilia@uis.edu

Hogan, Michael J. (PhD, Iowa 1974; dist. prof.) 20th-century US political and diplomatic, Truman administration and Marshall Plan

Hunter, Devin (PhD, Loyola, Chicago 2015; asst. prof.) public, urban, 20th-century US

Kent, Holly M. (PhD, Lehigh 2010; asst. prof.) 19th-century US, US women; hkent3@uis.edu

Kosmetatou, Elizabeth (PhD, Cincinnati 1993; assoc. prof.) ancient Greece and Rome; ekosm2@uis.edu

Owen, Kenneth (DPhil, Oxford 2011; asst. prof.) colonial and revolutionary America; kowen8@uis.edu

Shapinsky, Peter D. (PhD, Michigan 2004; assoc. prof.) East Asia, maritime; pshap2@uis.edu

Retired/Emeritus Faculty

Davis, Cullom (PhD, Illinois 1969; prof. emeritus) US, Lincoln, legal studies

McGregor, Deborah (PhD, SUNY, Binghamton 1986; prof. emeritus) 19th-century US, US women, oral

McGregor, Robert K. (PhD, SUNY, Binghamton 1984; prof. emeritus) colonial and early national America, environmental; mcgregor.robert@uis.edu

Shiner, Larry (PhD, Strasbourg, France 1961; prof. emeritus) 18th- and 19th-century Europe

Siles, William H. (PhD, Massachusetts Amherst 1978; assoc. prof. emeritus) public, US westward expansion, urban; siles.william@uis.edu

University of Illinois at Urbana-Champaign

Dept. of History, 309 Gregory Hall, 810 S. Wright St., Urbana, IL 61801-3697. 217.333.1155. Fax 217.333.2297. Email: history@illinois.edu. Website: https://history.illinois.edu/.

Our goal is to foster critical understanding of our collective past and to instill our passion and curiosity in future generations. Faculty in our department focus on a truly astounding array of questions. All of our students gain impressive skills in locating and analyzing complex documents and in expressing their ideas with eloquence and conviction. They become the engaged and informed citizens so vital to our future.

Chair: Clare H. Crowston
Director of Graduate Studies: Carol Symes
Director of Undergraduate Studies: Kristin Hoganson
Degrees Offered: BA,PhD
Academic Year System: Semester
Areas of Specialization: US, Europe, Africa and Middle East, Asia and East Asia, Latin America
Undergraduate Tuition (per academic year):
  In-State: $16004
  Out-of-State: $32574
Graduate Tuition (per academic year):
  In-State: $12942
  Out-of-State: $27960
Enrollment 2018-19:
  Undergraduate Majors: 228
  New Graduate Students: 6
  Full-time Graduate Students: 84
  Degrees in History: 80 BA, 13 PhD
Undergraduate Addresses:
  Admissions: http://admissions.illinois.edu/
  Financial Aid: http://www.osfa.illinois.edu/
Graduate Addresses:
  Admissions and Financial Aid: http://www.grad.illinois.edu/
    admissions/

Adjunct Faculty

Gilbert, Daniel (PhD, Yale 2008; assoc. prof.; Sch. of Labor and Employment Relations) modern US labor and cultural; gilbertd@illinois.edu

Schneider, Dorothee (PhD, Munich, Germany 1983; teaching assoc. prof.) immigration, labor migration and Americanization; schndr@illinois.edu

Full-time Faculty

Asaka, Ikuko (PhD, Wisconsin, Madison 2010; assoc. prof.) African American, gender; iasaka@illinois.edu

Avrutin, Eugene M. (PhD, Michigan 2004; prof.) early modern and modern Jewish history and culture; eavrutin@illinois.edu

Barrett, Marsha E. (PhD, Rutgers 2014; asst. prof.) US political, policy, African American; meb@illinois.edu

Brennan, James R. (PhD, Northwestern 2002; assoc. prof.) Africa, urbanization, citizenship; jbrennan@illinois.edu

Brosseder, Claudia R. (PhD, Munich 2002; assoc. prof.) science and indigenous religion in colonial Peru, Christianity; cbrossed@illinois.edu

Burgos, Adrian, Jr. (PhD, Michigan 2000; prof.) Latino/a, African American, comparative ethnic; burgosjr@illinois.edu

Burton, Antoinette M. (PhD, Chicago 1990; Bastian Prof.) British Empire, women, colonial India; aburton@illinois.edu

Chaplin, Tamara (PhD, Rutgers 2002; assoc. prof.) 20th-century France, intellectual and cultural, gender and sexuality; tchaplin@illinois.edu

Chettiar, Teri Anne (PhD, Northwestern 2013; asst. prof.) 20th-century psychology and medicine; chettiar@illinois.edu

Crowston, Clare (PhD, Cornell 1996; prof.; Univ. Scholar; and chair) early modern Europe, gender; crowston@illinois.edu

Cuno, Kenneth M. (PhD, UCLA 1985; prof.) modern Middle East; kmcuno@illinois.edu

Davila, Jerry (PhD, Brown 1998; prof.) Brazil; jdavila@illinois.edu

Fritzsche, Peter (PhD, California, Berkeley 1986; prof.) modern Europe, 20th-century Germany; pfritzsc@illinois.edu

Fu, Poshek (PhD, Stanford 1989; prof.) modern China, film culture, Hong Kong cultural and social; poshekfu@illinois.edu

Hertzman, Marc Adam (PhD, Wisconsin, Madison 2008; assoc. prof.) Brazil; hertzman@illinois.edu

Hitchins, Keith A. (PhD, Harvard 1964; prof.) modern Europe, southeastern Europe; khitchin@illinois.edu

Hoganson, Kristin L. (PhD, Yale 1995; prof. and dir., undergrad. studies) US cultural, foreign relations; hoganson@illinois.edu

Hogarth, Rana (PhD, Yale 2012; asst. prof.) African American, medicine; rhogarth@illinois.edu

Koslofsky, Craig M. (PhD, Michigan 1994; prof.) early modern Europe 1400-1600; koslof@illinois.edu

Mathisen, Ralph W. (PhD, Wisconsin, Madison 1979; prof.) Roman Empire and late antiquity; ralphwm@illinois.edu

Morrissey, Robert Michael (PhD, Yale 2006; assoc. prof.) colonial America; rmorriss@illinois.edu

Mumford, Kevin J. (PhD, Stanford 1993; prof.) African American, gender, urban; kmumford@illinois.edu

Nobili, Mauro (PhD, Naples, Italy 2008; asst. prof.) precolonial West Africa; nobili@illinois.edu

Oberdeck, Kathryn J. (PhD, Yale 1991; assoc. prof.) US cultural, intellectual; kjo@illinois.edu

Rabin, Dana (PhD, Michigan 1996; prof.) Britain, 18th-century Europe, modern European women; drabin@illinois.edu

Randolph, John W., Jr. (PhD, California, Berkeley 1997; assoc. prof.) early Russia; jwr@illinois.edu

Reagan, Leslie J. (PhD, Wisconsin, Madison 1991; prof.) US women, medicine; lreagan@illinois.edu

Sepkoski, David (PhD, Minnesota 2002; prof.) science; sepkoski@illinois.edu

Steinberg, Mark D. (PhD, California, Berkeley 1987; prof.) imperial Russia; steinb@illinois.edu

Symes, Carol (PhD, Harvard 1999; assoc. prof. and dir., grad studies) medieval Europe, cultural; symes@illinois.edu

Todorova, Maria N. (PhD, Sofia 1977; Gutgsell Prof.) Balkans, eastern Europe; mtodorov@illinois.edu

Joint/Cross Appointments

Anderson, James D. (PhD, Illinois, Urbana-Champaign 1973; prof.; Educational Policy Studies) American education, African American; janders@illinois.edu

Barnes, Teresa A. (PhD, Zimbabwe 1994; assoc. prof.; Gender and Women's Studies) Africa, women, education; tbarnes2@illinois.edu

Bosak-Schroeder, Clara (PhD, Michigan 2015; asst. prof.; Classical Studies) Greece and Rome, classical languages; cbosak@illinois.edu

Cha-Jua, Sundiata K. (PhD, Illinois, Urbana-Champaign 1993; assoc. prof.; African American Studies) African American; schajua@illinois.edu

Chow, Kai-wing (PhD, California, Davis 1988; prof.; East Asian Languages and Cultures) Asia, premodern China; kchow1@illinois.edu

Espiritu, Augusto F. (PhD, UCLA 2000; assoc. prof.; Asian American Studies) Asian American; aespirit@illinois.edu

Loughran, Trish (PhD, Chicago 2000; assoc. prof.; English) pre-1865 American literature and culture; loughran@illinois.edu

McDuffie, Erik S. (PhD, NYU 2003; assoc. prof.; African American Studies) African American, gender, diaspora; emcduffi@illinois.edu

Ross, Richard J. (PhD, Yale 1998; prof.; Law) early US, legal; rjross@illinois.edu

Rota, Emanuel (PhD, California, Berkeley 2005; assoc. prof.; Spanish, Italian & Portuguese) modern Europe; rota@illinois.edu

Wilson, Roderick I. (PhD, Stanford 2011; asst. prof.; East Asian Languages and Cultures) modern Japan; riwilson@illinois.edu

Recently Awarded PhDs

Bamberger, Benjamin "Mountains of Discontent: Georgian Alpinism and the Limits of Soviet Equality, 1923-55"

Corrêa, Marília "Unusual Suspects: Expelled Officers and Soldiers under Military Rule in Brazil, 1964-85"

Crafts, Lydia "Mining Bodies: US Medical Experimentation in Guatemala during the 20th Century"

Eby, Beth "Building Bodies, (Un)Making Empire: Gender, Sport, and Colonialism in the United States, 1880-1930"

Harrison, Scott "The State of Belonging: Gay and Lesbian Activism in the German Democratic Republic and Beyond, 1949-89"

Marquez, John C. "Freedom's Edge: Enslaved People, Manumision, and the Law in the 18th-Century South Atlantic World"

Peralta, Christine Noelle "Medical Modernity: Rethinking the Health Work of Filipina Women under Spanish and US Colonial Rule, 1870-1948"

Riebeling, Zachary "Wounds of the Past: Trauma and German Historical Thought after 1945"

Rouphail, Robert "Essentially Cyclonic: Race, Gender, and Disaster in Modern Mauritius"

Tye, Nathan Thomas "The Ways of the Hobo: Transient Mobility and Culture in the United States, 1870s-1930s"

Illinois State University

Dept. of History, Campus Box 4420, Normal, IL 61790-4420. 309.438.5641. Fax 309.438.5607. Email: history@ilstu.edu. Website: https://history.illinoisstate.edu/.

With thirty faculty members and about 400 full-time undergraduate and graduate students, the Illinois State University History department is one of the largest in the state. We offer over 100 undergraduate and graduate courses.

Chair: Ross A. Kennedy
Director of Graduate Studies: Amy Wood
Degrees Offered: BA, BS, MA, MS
Academic Year System: Semester
Areas of Specialization: America, Europe, global, social, cultural
Undergraduate Tuition (per academic year):
  In-State: $14062
  Out-of-State: $25170

Graduate Tuition (per academic year):
In-State: $8973
Out-of-State: $16515
Enrollment 2018-19:
Undergraduate Majors: 463
New Graduate Students: 14
Full-time Graduate Students: 13
Part-time Graduate Students: 4
Degrees in History: 18 BA, 67 BS, 2 MA, 8 MS
Undergraduate Addresses:
Admissions: http://illlinoisstate.edu/admissions/
Financial Aid: http://financialaid.illinoisstate.edu/
Graduate Addresses:
Admissions: http://illinoisstated.edu/academics/graduate/
Financial Aid: http://financialaid.illinoisstate.edu/

Adjunct Faculty

Cutter, Doug (ABD, Arizona; instructional asst. prof.) Latin America; dacutte@ilstu.edu
Hollywood, Mary (MA, Illinois State 2005; instructional asst. prof.) American diversity; meholly@ilstu.edu
Jayes, Janice L. (PhD, American 1998; instructional asst. prof.) jjayes@ilstu.edu
Johnson, David B. (ABD, Illinois, Urbana-Champaign; instructional asst. prof.) 20th-century US; dbjohns@ilstu.edu
Kennedy, Larissa (MA, Massachusetts 2000; instructional asst. prof.) China; lkenned@ilstu.edu
McCarthy, Kate (PhD, Pittsburgh 1996; instructional asst. prof.) eastern Europe; kmccart@ilstu.edu
Reger, William M., IV (PhD, Illinois, Urbana-Champaign 1997; instructional asst. prof.) Russia; wmreger@ilstu.edu

Full-time Faculty

Adedze, Agbenyega Tony (PhD, UCLA 1997; assoc. prof.) Africa; adedze@ilstu.edu
Ciani, Kyle E. (PhD, Michigan State 1998; assoc. prof.) women; keciani@ilstu.edu
Clemmons, Linda M. (PhD, Illinois, Urbana-Champaign 1998; prof.) antebellum, Native American; lmclemm@ilstu.edu
Crubaugh, Anthony (PhD, Columbia 1996; assoc. prof.) 18th-century France; acrubau@ilstu.edu
Hartman, Andrew G. (PhD, George Washington 2006; prof.) history education, cultural, intellectual; ahartma@ilstu.edu
He, Qiliang (PhD, Minnesota 2006; assoc. prof.) modern Chinese cultural, gender and mass media; qhe@ilstu.edu
Hughes, Richard Lowry (PhD, Kansas 2002; assoc. prof.) history education, 20th-century America; rhughes@ilstu.edu
Jasper, Kathryn Lee (PhD, California, Berkeley 2012; assoc. prof.) kljaspe@ilstu.edu
Kennedy, Ross A. (PhD, California, Berkeley 1994; prof. and chair) US foreign relations; rkenned@ilstu.edu
Lessoff, Alan H. (PhD, Johns Hopkins 1990; prof.) Progressive Era, urban, business; ahlesso@ilstu.edu
Nassar, Issam (DA, Illinois State 1997; prof.) Middle East; irnassa@ilstu.edu
Noraian, Monica Cousins (PhD, Illinois State 2007; assoc. prof.) history education; mcnora2@ilstu.edu
Olsen, Patrice Elizabeth (PhD, Penn State 1998; assoc. prof.) Latin America; peolsen@ilstu.edu
Paehler, Katrin (PhD, American 2004; assoc. prof.) modern Germany, Holocaust; katpaehler@ilstu.edu
Pluymers, Keith D. (PhD, Southern California 2015; asst. prof.) early modern Europe; kdpluym@ilstu.edu
Reda, John E. (PhD, Illinois, Chicago 2009; assoc. prof.) colonial North America; jreda@ilstu.edu

Reed, Toure F. (PhD, Columbia 2002; prof.) African American; tfreed@ilstu.edu
Soderlund, Richard J. (PhD, Maryland, Coll. Park 1992; asst. prof.) modern Britain, European social, labor; rjsoder@ilstu.edu
Topdar, Sudipa (PhD, Michigan; asst. prof.) South Asia; stopdar@ilstu.edu
Tsouvala, Georgia (PhD, Grad. Center, CUNY 2007; assoc. prof.) ancient; gtsouva@ilstu.edu
Varga-Harris, Christine (PhD, Illinois, Urbana-Champaign 2005; assoc. prof.) Russia; cvargah@ilstu.edu
Winger, Stewart Lance (PhD, Chicago 1998; assoc. prof.) Civil War; swinger@ilstu.edu
Wood, Amy Louise (PhD, Emory 2002; prof. and dir., grad. studies) US intellectual, cultural; alwood@ilstu.edu

Part-time Faculty

Gifford, Ronald M. (PhD, Indiana 1999; instructional asst. prof.) African American; rmgiffo@ilstu.edu
Stump, Daniel H. (DA, Illinois State 2000; instructional asst. prof.) America; dhstump@ilstu.edu

Illinois Wesleyan University

Dept. of History, PO Box 2900, Bloomington, IL 61702-2900. 309.556.3118. Fax 309.556.3719. Email: rschultz@iwu.edu. Website: https://www.iwu.edu/history/.

Our students are urged to speak out in class, defending what they believe in but listening to opposing ideas with an open mind. We strive to challenge students and expand their horizons.

Chair: Robert Schultz
Degrees Offered: BA
Academic Year System: Semester
Areas of Specialization: US, Latin America, Europe, ancient Greece and Rome, East Asia
Tuition (per academic year): $49284
Enrollment 2018-19:
Undergraduate Majors: 37
Degrees in History: 6 BA
Addresses:
Admissions: http://www.iwu.edu/admissions/
Financial Aid: https://www.iwu.edu/financial-aid/

Full-time Faculty

Coles, Amanda Jo (PhD, Pennsylvania 2009; assoc. prof.) Rome, ancient religion, colonization; acoles@iwu.edu
Horwitz, Gordon J. (PhD, Harvard 1985; prof.) Germany, Holocaust, Russia; ghorwitz@iwu.edu
Lutze, Thomas D. (PhD, Wisconsin-Madison 1996; prof.) 20th-century China, Japan, Vietnam; tlutze@iwu.edu
Schultz, April R. (PhD, Minnesota 1991; prof.) US social and cultural, women, immigration and ethnicity; aschultz@iwu.edu
Schultz, Robert T. (PhD, Minnesota 1991; prof. and chair) US social and intellectual, labor, American West; rschultz@iwu.edu
Weis, W. Michael (PhD, Ohio State 1987; prof.) US foreign relations, Latin America, rock and roll; mweis@iwu.edu
Young, Michael B. (PhD, Harvard 1971; prof.) England, early modern Europe; myoung@iwu.edu

Retired/Emeritus Faculty

Bushnell, Paul E. (MA, Michigan 1957; prof. emeritus) US social and intellectual, colonial, African American; bushnell@iwu.edu

University of Indianapolis

Dept. of History and Political Science, 1400 E. Hanna Ave., Indianapolis, IN 46227-3697. 317.788.2196. Fax 317.788.3480. Email: mthakar@uindy.edu. Website: https://uindy.edu/cas/history-political-science/.

At UIndy, studying history and political science is more than just learning about the past. You'll develop a broad understanding of where we have come from so you can understand today's world and the world of tomorrow.

Chair: Milind Thakar
Director of Graduate Studies: Lawrence Sondhaus
Degrees Offered: BA,MA
Academic Year System: 4-4-1
Areas of Specialization: US, modern Europe
Undergraduate Tuition (per academic year): $25910
Graduate Tuition (per academic year): $8406
Enrollment 2018-19:
   Undergraduate Majors: 33
   Part-time Graduate Students: 8
   Degrees in History: 6 BA, 1 MA
Undergraduate Addresses:
   Admissions: http://uindy.edu/admissions-home
   Financial Aid: http://uindy.edu/financial-aid
Graduate Addresses:
   Admissions: http://uindy.edu/graduate-admissions
   Financial Aid: http://uindy.edu/financial-aid

Full-time Faculty

Albright, Laura Merrifield (PhD, Alabama 2014; asst. prof.) American politics, public administration; albrightlm@uindy.edu

Frantz, Edward O. (PhD, Wisconsin, Madison 2002; prof.; dir., Inst. for Civic Engagement and Mayoral Archives) US 1877-1920, Midwest, political; efrantz@uindy.edu

Fuller, A. James (PhD, Miami, Ohio 1995; prof.) early Republic America, Civil War and Reconstruction; afuller@uindy.edu

Martin, Chad A. (PhD, Stanford 2003; assoc. prof.) modern Britain, modern Africa, British Empire; cmartin@uindy.edu

Meigs, Samantha A. (PhD, Northwestern 1993; assoc. prof.; dir., Experience Design) early modern Europe; smeigs@uindy.edu

Root, David (PhD, Oregon 2015; JD, Indiana 2006; asst. prof.) American politics, public law; rootd@uindy.edu

Saksena, Jyotika (PhD, Georgia 2001; assoc. prof.) international political economy; jsaksena@uindy.edu

Sondhaus, Lawrence (PhD, Virginia 1986; prof. and dir., grad. studies) modern Europe, Germany and Austria, naval and military; sondhaus@uindy.edu

Thakar, Milind (PhD, Georgia 2001; assoc. prof. and chair) comparative politics, South Asia; mthakar@uindy.edu

Williams, James B. (PhD, Purdue 2009; asst. prof.) medieval Europe, Latin America; williamsjb@uindy.edu

Woodwell, Douglas (PhD, Yale 2005; assoc. prof.) international relations; woodwelld@uindy.edu

Part-time Faculty

Billings, Mathieu W. (PhD, Northern Illinois 2016; instr.) US, world; billingsm@uindy.edu

Horner, John Benjamin (MA, Indianapolis 2009; instr.) international relations, American politics

Miller, Emily G. (MA, Purdue 2003; instr.) US, world; millereg@uindy.edu

Nichols, Melvin E., Jr. (MA, Purdue 1990; instr.) world; mnichols@uindy.edu

Platt, Brian D. (MA, Indianapolis 2012; instr.) world geography

Retired/Emeritus Faculty

Guthrie, Charles C. (PhD, Indiana 1978; assoc. prof. emeritus) Africa, Latin America, world

Israel, Jerry (PhD, Rutgers 1967; prof. emeritus) US, China

Indiana State University

Dept. of History, 621 Chestnut St., Rm. 104, Terre Haute, IN 47809-0001. 812.237.2710. Fax 812.237.7713. Email: history@indstate.edu. Website: https://www.indstate.edu/cas/history.

As scholars, the History faculty are engaged in the creation of new knowledge and many have gained national recognition through their activities in research, teaching, and publishing. We are also engaged locally with the wider University community, the city of Terre Haute, and the state of Indiana with sustained support for service and outreach efforts.

Chair: Steven Stofferahn
Director of Graduate Studies: Barbara Skinner
Degrees Offered: BA,BS,MA,MS
Academic Year System: Semester
Areas of Specialization: US, Europe, Middle East, Latin America
Undergraduate Tuition (per academic year):
   In-State: $8890
   Out-of-State: $19636
Graduate Tuition (per academic year):
   In-State: $7416
   Out-of-State: $14562
Enrollment 2018-19:
   Undergraduate Majors: 43
   New Graduate Students: 9
   Full-time Graduate Students: 2
   Part-time Graduate Students: 25
   Degrees in History: 5 BA, 4 BS, 6 MA, 3 MS
Undergraduate Addresses:
   Admissions: http://www.indstate.edu/admissions
   Financial Aid: http://www2.indstate.edu/finaid/
Graduate Addresses:
   Admissions: http://www.indstate.edu/graduate/
   Financial Aid: http://www.indstate.edu/graduate/apply/costs-and-aid

Full-time Faculty

Arrington, Andrea Lynn (PhD, Emory 2007; asst. prof.) Africa, comparative women; Andrea.Arrington@indstate.edu

Chirhart, Ann S. (PhD, Emory 1997; prof.) 20th-century US, US South and African American, US women; Ann.Chirhart@indstate.edu

Clark, Daniel A. (PhD, Purdue 2001; assoc. prof.) US intellectual, cultural, education; Dan.Clark@indstate.edu

Fischer, Christopher J. (PhD, North Carolina, Chapel Hill 2003; assoc. prof.) Germany and France, European regionalism, cultural; Christopher.Fischer@indstate.edu

Foster, Anne L. (PhD, Cornell 1995; assoc. prof.) US foreign policy, Southeast Asia, imperialism; Anne.Foster@indstate.edu

Gustafson, James M. (PhD, Washington 2010; assoc. prof.; Political Science) Islamic Near East social/economic/cultural, modern Middle East, medieval Islamic social; james.gustafson@indstate.edu

Hawkins, Timothy Paul (PhD, Tulane 1999; prof.) Latin America, Central American independence, imperial Spain; Timothy.Hawkins@indstate.edu

Hunter, F. Robert (PhD, Harvard 1979; prof. emeritus) modern Middle East, classical Islam, Mediterranean world; Robert. Hunter@indstate.edu

Land, Isaac E. (PhD, Michigan 1999; prof.) Britain, Atlantic, modern Europe; Isaac.Land@indstate.edu

Nichols, David Andrew (PhD, Kentucky 2000; prof.) early America, Native American, antebellum US South; Dave.Nichols@indstate.edu

Olsen, Christopher J. (PhD, Florida 1996; prof.) antebellum and US Civil War, US South and comparative slavery, political culture; Christopher.Olsen@indstate.edu

Phillips, Lisa A. (PhD, Rutgers 2002; assoc. prof.) 20th-century US labor, African American, women; Lisa.Phillips@indstate.edu

Schneirov, Richard (PhD, Northern Illinois 1984; prof.) US labor, Gilded Age-Progressive era, social movements; Richard. Schneirov@indstate.edu

Skinner, Barbara J. (PhD, Georgetown 2001; assoc. prof. and coord., grad. studies) Russia, eastern Europe, Christianity and church; Barbara.Skinner@indstate.edu

Stanley, Kimberly (PhD, Indiana 2015; asst. prof.) African American studies, African diaspora; Kimberly.Stanley@indstate.ed

Stofferahn, Steven A. (PhD, Purdue 2003; assoc. prof. and chair) medieval and early modern Europe, ancient world, women in Europe; Steven.Stofferahn@indstate.edu

Retired/Emeritus Faculty

Clokey, Richard M. (PhD, Wisconsin, Madison 1969; prof. emeritus) American West, early national; Richard.Clokey@indstate.edu

Daily, Gary W. (ABD, Rutgers; assoc. prof. emeritus) Afro-American, American women; gdaily@isugw.indstate.edu

Giffin, William W. (PhD, Ohio State 1968; prof. emeritus) US race and nationality, Indiana; william.giffin@indstate.edu

Layton, Donald L. (PhD, Indiana 1965; prof. emeritus) Russia, communism; dlayton@isugw.indstate.edu

Mansur, Abed H. (PhD, Oregon 1964; prof. emeritus) West Asia, European diplomatic

Perez, Arvid H. (PhD, UCLA 1970; assoc. prof. emeritus) European intellectual, historiography; hiperez@yahoo.com

Pierard, Richard V. (PhD, Iowa 1964; prof. emeritus) Germany, Africa; charrichp@aol.com

Shoemaker, Rebecca S. (PhD, Indiana 1976; prof. emeritus) colonial America, civil liberties; rshoemaker@isugw.indstate.edu

Siefert, Thomas (EdD, Ball State 1970; prof. emeritus) US, diplomatic, social science education; tsiefert@isugw.indstate.edu

Indiana University

Dept. of History, Weatherly Hall, 400 N. Sunrise Dr., Bloomington, IN 47405. 812.855.7581. Fax 812.855.3378. Email: histadm@indiana.edu. Website: https://history.indiana.edu/.

Together with their colleagues across IU's College of Arts and Sciences, History's faculty members contribute to IU's international reputation a destination for students seeking a world-class liberal-arts education that prepares them to deal with the global challenges of the 21st century.

Chair: Wendy Gamber
Director of Graduate Studies: Peter Guardino
Director of Undergraduate Studies: Roberta Pergher
Degrees Offered: BA,MA,MAT,PhD
Academic Year System: Semester

Areas of Specialization: Africa, Britain, East Asia, Latin America, Middle East, Russia and eastern Europe, South Asia, US, western Europe
Undergraduate Tuition (per academic year):
In-State: $9342
Out-of-State: $34116
Graduate Tuition (per academic year):
In-State: $6918
Out-of-State: $23949
Enrollment 2018-19:
Undergraduate Majors: 225
New Graduate Students: 17
Full-time Graduate Students: 95
Degrees in History: 66 BA, 11 MA, 12 PhD
Undergraduate Addresses:
Admissions: http://admissions.indiana.edu
Financial Aid: http://studentcentral.indiana.edu/financial-aid/
Graduate Addresses:
Admissions: https://history.indiana.edu/graduate/apply.html
Financial Aid: http://history.indiana.edu

Adjunct Faculty

Andrews, Stephen Douglas (PhD, Stanford 2005; adj. prof.; managing ed., Journal of American History) 19th-century US social and intellectual, literature and popular culture, religion; standrew@indiana.edu

Bannon, Cynthia J. (PhD, Michigan 1991; prof.; Classical Studies) ancient Rome, Roman law, historiography; cbannon@indiana.edu

Barton, Keith C. (EdD, Kentucky 1994; prof.; Education) history education, curriculum, US South; kcbarton@indiana.edu

Bertoloni Meli, Domenico (PhD, Cambridge 1988; prof.; History and Philosophy of Science) medical and mathematical disciplines, Renaissance to the 19th century; dbmeli@indiana.edu

Bose, Purnima (PhD, Texas, Austin 1993; assoc. prof.; English and International Studies) modern South Asian gender/social/cultural, postcolonial theory; pbose@indiana.edu

Bowles, Brett C. (PhD, Penn State 1998; assoc. prof.; French and Italian) 20th-century France and Germany, film and media, social and political; bowlesb@indiana.edu

Caner, Daniel F. (PhD, California, Berkeley 1998; assoc. prof.; Near Eastern Languages and Cultures) late antique social and cultural, early Byzantium and early eastern Christianity, monasticism/philanthropy/hagiography; dcaner@indiana.edu

Capshew, James H. (PhD, Pennsylvania 1986; prof.; History and Philosophy of Science and Medicine) American science and universities, psychology, environmental humanities; jcapshew@indiana.edu

Christ, Matthew (PhD, Princeton 1987; prof.; chair, Classical Studies) classical Athens, legal, social and cultural; mrchrist@indiana.edu

DeWeese, Devin A. (PhD, Indiana 1985; prof.; Central Eurasian Studies) Islamic Central Asia, Islamization, Sufi traditions in Central Eurasia; deweese@indiana.edu

Frazier, Lessie Jo (PhD, Michigan 1998; assoc. prof.; Gender Studies) Latin America, political culture, gender and sexuality; frazierl@indiana.edu

Furey, Constance (PhD, Chicago 2000; assoc. prof.; Religious Studies) early modern Europe, Protestant and Catholic Reformations; cfurey@indiana.edu

Gonzalez, Luis A. (PhD, Minnesota 1998; adj. asst. prof.; librarian, Univ. Libraries) Brazil, Latin American social/legal/agrarian, library research methods; luisgonz@indiana.edu

Imhoff, Sarah (PhD, Chicago 2010; asst. prof.; Religious Studies and Borns Jewish Studies Prog.) religion, gender, American Judaism; seimhoff@indiana.edu

Johnson, Colin R. (PhD, Michigan 2003; assoc. prof.; Gender Studies) modern US, LGBT/gender/sexuality, rural social and cultural/agriculture/environment; crj2@indiana.edu

Kamp, Marianne R. (PhD, Chicago 1998; assoc. prof.; Central Eurasian Studies) 20th-century Central Asia, gender, oral; mkamp@indiana.edu

Lovelace, H. Timothy Jr (PhD, Virginia 2012; JD, Virginia 2006; asst. prof.; Law) legal, civil rights, human rights; lovelace@indiana.edu

Macekura, Stephen (PhD, Virginia 2013; assoc. prof.; International Studies) US foreign relations, international development and political economy, environmental; smacekur@indiana.edu

Mokhtarian, Jason (PhD, UCLA 2011; asst. prof.; Religious Studies) ancient Judaism, pre-Islamic Iran, late antiquity; jmokhtar@indiana.edu

Myers, Kathleen A. (PhD, Brown 1986; prof.; Spanish and Portuguese) colonial Latin America, women, chronicles; myersk@indiana.edu

Newman, William R. (PhD, Harvard 1986; Dist. Prof. and Ruth Halls Prof.; History and Philosophy of Science) Europe and America, medieval and early modern science; wnewman@indiana.edu

Oxenboell, Morten (PhD, Copenhagen 2009; asst. prof.; East Asian Languages and Cultures) medieval Japan, violence, premodern political/social; mortoxen@indiana.edu

Pinaud, Clémence (PhD, Sorbonne (Paris 1) 2013; asst. prof.; International Studies) Africa, military, women; cpinaud@indiana.edu

Raun, Toivo U. (PhD, Princeton 1969; prof.; Central Eurasian Studies) Baltic and Scandinavia, non-Russian nationalities, modern Russia and Soviet Union; raunt@indiana.edu

Sela, Ron (PhD, Indiana 2004; assoc. prof.; Central Eurasian Studies) 16th- to 19th-century Central Asia, Islamic world; rsela@indiana.edu

Vogt, Nicholas (PhD, Columbia 2012; asst. prof.; East Asian Languages and Cultures) early China, cultural/religious, ritual studies; pnvogt@indiana.edu

Weinberg, Carl R. (PhD, Yale 1995; adj. assoc. prof. and sr. lect.; Coll. of Arts and Sciences) 20th-century US social and political, US labor, evolutionism and creationism; crweinbe@indiana.edu

Full-time Faculty

Allen, Judith A. (PhD, Macquarie, Australia 1985; Walter prof.; assoc. ed., Journal of American History) 19th- and 20th-century Anglophone feminisms, sexualities and criminalities; juallen@indiana.edu

Craig, Kalani (PhD, Indiana 2013; clinical asst. prof.; co-dir., Inst. for Digital Arts & Humanities) early medieval, digital, intellectual and cultural; craigkl@indiana.edu

Deliyannis, Deborah Mauskopf (PhD, Pennsylvania 1994; prof.; ed., The Medieval Review) early medieval, intellectual and cultural, historiography/archaeology/material culture; ddeliyan@indiana.edu

Diaz, Arlene J. (PhD, Minnesota 1997; assoc. prof.) Latin America, gender, social and cultural; ardiaz@indiana.edu

Dierks, Konstantin (PhD, Brown 1999; assoc. prof.; assoc. ed., American Historical Review) early America and British Atlantic, cultural and social, globalization; kdierks@indiana.edu

Dodson, Michael S. (PhD, Cambridge 2003; assoc. prof.; dir., IU India Gateway) South Asian intellectual and cultural, British imperialism, architecture/urbanism; msdodson@indiana.edu

Drake, Janine Giordano (PhD, Illinois, Urbana-Champaign 2014; clinical asst. prof.) modern US, comparative labor/working class, cultural/intellectual; jgdrake@iu.edu

Eklof, A. Ben (PhD, Princeton 1977; prof.) modern Russia, education, politics and society; eklof@indiana.edu

Elliott, Colin (PhD, Bristol 2012; asst. prof.) ancient Rome, money/markets/connectivity, Mediterranean ecology; cpe@indiana.edu

Gamber, Wendy E. (PhD, Brandeis 1991; Byrnes Prof. and chair) 19th-century US, women and gender, social and cultural; wgamber@indiana.edu

Gould, Jeffrey L. (PhD, Yale 1988; Rudy Prof.) 20th-century Central America, social movements, documentary film; gouldj@indiana.edu

Grossberg, Michael C. (PhD, Brandeis 1979; Reahard Prof.) US legal, constitutional, social; grossber@indiana.edu

Guardino, Peter F. (PhD, Chicago 1992; prof.) Mexico, Latin America, political culture; pguardin@indiana.edu

Hanson, John (PhD, Michigan State 1989; prof.; dir., African Studies; and ed., History in Africa) western Africa, social and cultural, intellectual and religious; jhhanson@indiana.edu

Hsia, Ke-chin (PhD, Chicago 2013; lect.) modern Central Europe, Habsburg Empire, war/welfare/citizenship; khsia@indiana.edu

Ipsen, Carl D. (PhD, California, Berkeley 1992; prof.; dir., Collins Living Learning Center and dir., IU Food Project) modern Italy, population, fascism; cipsen@indiana.edu

Irvin, Benjamin H. (PhD, Brandeis 2004; assoc. prof.; editor, Journal of American History) early America and revolutionary era, US social and cultural, disability; bhirvin@indiana.edu

James, Daniel M. (PhD, London 1979; Mendel Chair) Latin American social/cultural/labor; dajames@indiana.edu

Knott, Sarah (DPhil, Oxford 1999; assoc. prof.) early America, Atlantic world, women and gender; saknott@indiana.edu

Kuromiya, Hiroaki (PhD, Princeton 1985; prof.) modern Eurasia; hkuromiy@indiana.edu

Lichtenstein, Alex (PhD, Pennsylvania 1990; prof.; ed., American Historical Review) US South, US labor, South Africa; lichtens@indiana.edu

Linenthal, Edward T. (PhD, California, Santa Barbara 1979; prof.) history and memory, American religion, 20th-century US; etl@indiana.edu

Machado, Pedro A. (PhD, SOAS, London 2005; assoc. prof.) Indian Ocean and global, social/cultural/economic, slavery/material culture/South Asian merchant networks/commodity exchange/pearling histories; pmachado@indiana.edu

Maglen, Krista (PhD, Glasgow 2002; assoc. prof.) modern Britain/Australia, medicine/immigration, animals; kmaglen@indiana.edu

McGerr, Michael E. (PhD, Yale 1984; McNutt Prof.) US social/cultural/political; mmcgerr@indiana.edu

McGraw, Jason Peter (PhD, Chicago 2006; assoc. prof.) Latin America and Caribbean, postemancipation societies, labor/race/popular culture; jpmcgraw@indiana.edu

Moyd, Michelle (PhD, Cornell 2008; assoc. prof.) East Africa, colonial, cultural and military; mimoyd@indiana.edu

Pergher, Roberta (PhD, Michigan 2007; assoc. prof. and dir., undergrad. studies) modern Italy, fascism, empire; rpergher@indiana.edu

Robinson, Eric W. (PhD, Pennsylvania 1994; prof.) archaic Greece, classical Greece, political and military; ewr@indiana.edu

Roos, Julia (PhD, Carnegie Mellon 2001; assoc. prof.) modern Europe, 20th-century Germany, gender/race/propaganda; roos@indiana.edu

Saburova, Tatiana (PhD, Omsk State Pedagogical 2006; lect.) imperial, Soviet Russia; generations/memory; photography; tsaburov@indiana.edu

Sahin, Kaya (PhD, Chicago 2007; assoc. prof.; dir., IU Eurasia Gateway) early modern Ottoman, comparative empires, Islamic intellectual; iksahin@indiana.edu

Sandweiss, Eric (PhD, California, Berkeley 1991; prof. and Carmony Chair; ed., Indiana Magazine of History) US urban, public, American and European architectural; sesandw@indiana.edu

Schlesinger, Jonathan (PhD, Harvard 2012; assoc. prof.) late imperial China, environmental, fashion and material culture; joschles@indiana.edu

Schneider, Robert A. (PhD, Michigan 1982; prof.) Old Regime France, early modern Europe, social and cultural; raschnei@indiana.edu

Shopkow, Leah (PhD, Toronto 1984; prof.) medieval intellectual and cultural, historiography, scholarship of teaching and learning; shopkowl@indiana.edu

Spang, Rebecca L. (PhD, Cornell 1993; prof.; dir., Center for 18th-Century Studies; and dir., Liberal Arts and Management) modern France, 18th- and 19th-century Europe, cultural/intellectual/economic; rlspang@indiana.edu

Wang, Fei-Hsien (PhD, Chicago 2013; asst. prof.) modern China, book, law and economic life; feihwang@indiana.edu

Wu, Ellen D. (PhD, Chicago 2006; assoc. prof.; dir., Asian American Studies) Asian American, race, immigration; wue@indiana.edu

Joint/Cross Appointments

Black, Liza (PhD, Washington 1999; asst. prof.; Native American and Indigenous Studies) 20th-century Native America, film studies, Native representations; blackli@indiana.edu

Bucur, Maria (PhD, Illinois, Urbana-Champaign 1996; prof.; Gender Studies) modern eastern Europe, gender, cultural; mbucur@indiana.edu

Caddoo, Cara (PhD, Graduate Center, CUNY 2013; assoc. prof.; Cinema and Media Studies) African American, race, film/media; ccaddoo@indiana.edu

Cullather, Nick B. (PhD, Virginia 1992; prof.; International Studies) US foreign relations, intelligence, modernization; ncullath@indiana.edu

Kenney, Padraic J. (PhD, Michigan 1992; prof.; International Studies) Poland and eastern Europe, communism and postcommunism, global; pjkenney@indiana.edu

Kriegel, Lara H. (PhD, Johns Hopkins 2000; assoc. prof.; dir. and co-ed., Victorian Studies; English) modern Britain, cultural, European empires; lkriegel@indiana.edu

Moorman, Marissa J. (PhD, Minnesota 2004; assoc. prof.; Cinema and Media Studies) southern Africa, social and cultural, gender and popular culture; moorman@indiana.edu

Myers, Amrita Chakrabarti (PhD, Rutgers 2004; Halls assoc. prof.; Gender Studies) African American, women, 18th- and 19th-century US/South/social; apmyers@indiana.edu

Nieto-Phillips, John (PhD, UCLA 1997; assoc. prof.; vice provost, Diversity and Inclusion; assoc. vice pres., Diversity, Equity and Multicultural Affairs; and ed., Chiricu Journal; Latino Studies) US/Latina/o, Mexican American, Latin America and Caribbean; jnietoph@indiana.edu

O'Bryan, Scott P. (PhD, Columbia 2000; assoc. prof.; chair, East Asian Languages and Cultures) Japan, environmental, urban; spobryan@indiana.edu

Roseman, Mark (PhD, Warwick 1987; Dist. prof. and Pat M. Glazer Chair; dir., Jewish Studies) modern Germany, Holocaust, world wars and impact; marrosem@indiana.edu

Seigel, Micol (PhD, NYU 2001; prof.; American Studies) race, policing, transnational; mseigel@indiana.edu

Williams, Jakobi (PhD, UCLA 2008; Ruth N. Halls Assoc. Prof.; African American and African Diaspora Studies) African American, modern US/race/politics, civil rights/black power/Black Panther Party; jakowill@indiana.edu

Zadoff, Mirjam (PhD, Munich 2006; assoc. prof. and Alvin H. Rosenfeld Chair; Jewish Studies) cultural and intellectual, central and eastern Europe, 19th and 20th century; mizadoff@indiana.edu

Zadoff, Noam (PhD, Hebrew, Jerusalem 2011; asst. prof.; Jewish Studies) Israel studies, Jewish intellectual and cultural; nzadoff@indiana.edu

Retired/Emeritus Faculty

Bodnar, John E. (PhD, Connecticut 1975; Chancellor's and Dist. Prof. emeritus) modern US; bodnar@indiana.edu

Brooks, George E., Jr. (PhD, Boston Univ. 1962; prof. emeritus) Africa, western Africa, world

Carmichael, Ann G. (PhD, Duke 1978; assoc. prof. emeritus) historical epidemiology, medicine; carmicha@indiana.edu

Demand, Nancy (PhD, Bryn Mawr 1978; prof. emeritus) Greece, ancient Mediterranean, ancient medicine

Diehl, James M. (PhD, California, Berkeley 1972; prof. emeritus) modern Europe and modern Germany; diehl@indiana.edu

Dwyer, Ellen (PhD, Yale 1977; prof. emeritus) US medicine, women, crime and criminal justice; dwyer@indiana.edu

Field, Arthur (PhD, Michigan 1980; assoc. prof. emeritus) Italian Renaissance, early modern intellectual; afield@indiana.edu

Friedman, Lawrence J., Jr. (PhD, UCLA 1967; prof. emeritus) American and European intellectual and cultural, American philanthropy; ljfriedm@indiana.edu

Madison, James H. (PhD, Indiana 1972; prof. emeritus) 20th-century US, World War II, Indiana; madison@indiana.edu

Martin, Phyllis (PhD, London 1970; prof. emeritus) Central Africa, social and cultural, Scotland; martinp@indiana.edu

Pace, David (PhD, Yale 1973; prof. emeritus) scholarship of teaching and learning, 19th- and 20th-century European intellectual and cultural; dpace@indiana.edu

Peterson, M. Jeanne (PhD, California, Berkeley 1972; prof. emeritus) Victorian England, gender and body, medicine and professions; petersom@indiana.edu

Rabinowitch, Alexander (PhD, Indiana 1965; prof. emeritus) Russian revolutions, Soviet-era Russia, World War II Soviet Union; arabinow@indiana.edu

Ransel, David L. (PhD, Yale 1969; prof. emeritus) modern Russia, social and cultural; ransel@indiana.edu

Riley, James C. (PhD, North Carolina, Chapel Hill 1971; Dist. Prof. emeritus) old regime Europe, health, 20th-century world; rileyj@indiana.edu

Stowe, Steven M. (PhD, SUNY, Stony Brook 1979; prof. emeritus) US South, medicine, 19th-century US social and cultural; sstowe@indiana.edu

Struve, Lynn A. (PhD, Michigan 1974; prof. emeritus) premodern Chinese political/intellectual/cultural, 17th century; struve@indiana.edu

Thelen, David P. (PhD, Wisconsin-Madison 1967; dist. prof. emeritus) US

Recently Awarded PhDs

Almy, Ruth "Law, Nation, and Migration in the Komagata Maru Incident of 1914"

Antone, Marc L. "Topographies of Power: Ethnic Conflict and Authoritarian Pluralism in 19th-Century Chiapas"

Brudney, Edward "Remaking Argentina: Labor and Citizenship during the Proceso de Reorganización Nacional"

Coleman, Rachel Elisse "'Save Our Children': Evangelicals, the Politics of Childhood, and the Rise of the Christian Right in America"

Craddock, Hannah "Fetal Attraction: Embryology, Fetal Images, and Pregnancy, 1870-1935"

Cwiek, Brian E. "Sowing the Seeds of Discontent: Agriculture, Society, and the State in Provincial Xinjiang, 1884-1955"

Esseissah, Khaled "Making a Way Out of No Way: Haratin Muslims' Initiatives to Gain Respectability in Post-Emancipation Mauritania, from 1905 to Recent Times"

Huezo, Stephanie "Resisting and Surviving: Popular Education in El Salvador and its Diaspora, 1968-2018"

Lockton, Richard "Warriors of Empire: The Image of the Scottish Highlander in British Atlantic Print Culture, 1745-83"

Ndanyi, Samson K. "'The Cinema is a Great Influence in the Life of the Modern Child': Cinema and African Child Audiences in Colonial Kenya, 1926-63"

Pease, Betsy "The Great Depression and the Making of a Suburban Nation"

Seaver, James B. "Fighting for Souvenirs: Americans and the Material Culture of World War II"

Stellwagen, Benjamin Joel "German by Association: German Subjectivity and Behavior in Interwar Moscow"

Story, Daniel Jackson "Ready to Believe: How American Business Came to Faith in Advertising"

Tarankow, Paula "Searching for Humanity: The Problem of Animal Cruelty in the Post-Civil War South"

Taylor, Jordan E. "The Page of Revolutions: Information Politics and Atlantic Networks in Revolutionary North America, 1763-1804"

Valone, T. Fielder "The Power of Grievance: Ethnic Germans, National Socialism, and the Holocaust in the 'Incorporated Territories' of Western Poland, 1939-52"

Indiana University Northwest

Dept. of History, Philosophy, Political Science, Religious Studies, 3400 Broadway, Gary, IN 46408. 219.980.6781. Fax 219.980.6579. Email: daqualls@iun.edu. Website: https://www.iun.edu/hist-phil-rel-pols/.

The study of history, philosophy, political science, and religion offers meaningful insight into how humans have gone about making decisions in the past, how they make decisions in the present, and how they should make decisions in the future.

Chair: Jonathyne W. Briggs
Degrees Offered: AA,BA
Academic Year System: Semester
Areas of Specialization: US, ancient and medieval Europe, modern western Europe, Asia, Calumet region
Tuition (per academic year):
  In-State: $6263
  Out-of-State: $17490
Addresses:
  Admissions: http://www.iun.edu/admissions/
  Financial Aid: http://www.iun.edu/financialaid/

Full-time Faculty

Anslover, Nicole L. (PhD, Kansas 2007; assoc. prof.) modern US; nanslove@iun.edu

Briggs, Jonathyne W. (PhD, Emory 2006; prof. and chair) modern Europe; jwbriggs@iun.edu

Chen-Lin, Diana (PhD, Chicago 1993; prof.) modern Asia; dchenlin@iun.edu

Parnell, David Alan (PhD, Saint Louis 2010; assoc. prof.) ancient and medieval Europe; parnelld@iun.edu

Young, Christopher J. (PhD, Illinois, Chicago 2001; prof. and dir., Center for Innovation and Scholarship in Teaching and Learning) colonial and revolutionary America; cjy@iun.edu

Nondepartmental Historians

Contreras, Raoul (PhD, UCLA 1993; assoc. prof.; Minority Studies) Chicano, Latino; rcontrer@iun.edu

McShane, Stephen G. (MA, Northern Illinois 1982; archivist curator; Calumet Regional Archives) America, Northwest Indiana, archival; smcshane@iun.edu

Retired/Emeritus Faculty

Chary, Frederick B. (PhD, Pittsburgh 1968; prof. emeritus) modern eastern Europe, Russia, Soviet Union

Cohen, Ronald D. (PhD, Minnesota 1967; prof. emeritus) 20th-century US, education, popular culture

Kern, Paul B. (PhD, Chicago 1970; prof. emeritus) modern Europe, ancient, military

Lane, James B. (PhD, Maryland, Coll. Park 1970; prof. emeritus) 20th-century US, diplomatic, urban

Indiana University of Pennsylvania

Dept. of History, 304 Humanities and Social Sciences Bldg., 981 Grant St., Indiana, PA 15705. 724.357.2284. Fax 724.357.6478. Email: rsmoore@iup.edu; dgryczuk@iup.edu. Website: https://www.iup.edu/history/.

The Department of History offers students a wide range of opportunities to learn about and practice history. Our current faculty offer classes in many different fields that span the range of recorded history.

Chair: R. Scott Moore
Degrees Offered: BA,BS,Cert.
Academic Year System: Semester
Areas of Specialization: US social, Europe, African American, public, ancient
Tuition (per academic year):
  In-State: $11304
  Out-of-State: $16348
Enrollment 2018-19:
  Undergraduate Majors: 112
  Full-time Graduate Students: 2
  Degrees in History: 13 BA, 14 BS, 2 MA
Addresses:
  Admissions: http://www.iup.edu/admissions/
  Financial Aid: http://www.iup.edu/financialaid/

Full-time Faculty

Arpaia, Paul-Marie T. (PhD, Georgetown 1999; assoc. prof.) Italy, Germany, European cultural and political; arpaia@iup.edu

Baker, Christine D. (PhD, Texas, Austin 2013; asst. prof.) medieval/modern Middle East; cbaker@iup.edu

Baumler, Alan (PhD, Illinois, Urbana-Champaign 1997; assoc. prof.; co-ed., Chinese Historical Review) China, East Asia; baumler@iup.edu

Botelho, Lynn (PhD, Cambridge 1996; prof.) early modern England and Europe, social and cultural; botelho@iup.edu

Conlin, Erin L. (PhD, Florida 2014; asst. prof. and internship coord.) public, US, oral; erin.conlin@iup.edu

Finegan, Caleb P.S. (PhD, Florida 1999; assoc. prof.) colonial Andes, Latin America, medieval Spain; cfinegan@iup.edu

Franklin-Rahkonen, Sharon (PhD, Indiana 1991; assoc. prof.) Scandinavia, Russia, East Baltic; franklin@iup.edu

Lippert, Werner D. (PhD, Vanderbilt 2005; assoc. prof.; coord., Social Studies Educ. Prog.) modern Europe, Germany, European diplomatic; lippert@iup.edu

Lu, Soo Chun (PhD, Ohio 1997; assoc. prof.) social studies education, US foreign relations; sclu@iup.edu

Mannard, Joseph G. (PhD, Maryland, Coll. Park 1989; assoc. prof.) early Republic US, religion, women; jmannard@iup.edu

Mazak-Kahne, Jeanine M. (PhD, Michigan State 2009; assoc. prof.) public, crime, Pennsylvania; jmkahne@iup.edu

Moore, R. Scott (PhD, Ohio State 2000; prof. and chair) Greece and Rome, digital, classical archaeology; rsmoore@iup.edu

Ricketts, Elizabeth (PhD, Emory 1996; asst. prof.) working-class US, women, labor; ricketts@iup.edu

Schroeder, Steven P. (PhD, Pittsburgh 2006; asst. prof.) medieval, military, US; schroder@iup.edu

Wang, Xi (PhD, Columbia 1993; prof.) African American, constitutional, Civil War and Reconstruction; wangxi@iup.edu

Whited, Tamara L. (PhD, California, Berkeley 1994; prof.) modern Europe, France, environmental; twhited@iup.edu

Indiana University–Purdue University Indianapolis

Dept. of History, 425 University Blvd., Cavanaugh Hall 504L, Indianapolis, IN 46202-5140. 317.274.3811. Fax 317.278.7800. Email: history@iupui.edu. Website: https://liberalarts.iupui.edu/history/.

We are committed to quality teaching at the undergraduate and graduate levels. The History Department's undergraduate program offers a BA to students in three standard concentrations: US, European, and African/Asian/Latin American history. The department's graduate program offers MAs in the following areas of concentration: US, public history, and European. We also offer a dual MA in History and MLS in Library Science and a dual MA in History and Philanthropic Studies.

Chair: Kevin Cramer
Director of Graduate Studies: Kevin Robbins
Director of Undergraduate Studies: Modupe Labode
Degrees Offered: BA,MA
Academic Year System: Semester
Areas of Specialization: US, Europe, public, world
Undergraduate Tuition (per academic year):
    In-State: $7620
    Out-of-State: $28080
Graduate Tuition (per academic year):
    In-State: $6249
    Out-of-State: $17239
Enrollment 2018-19:
    Undergraduate Majors: 140
    New Graduate Students: 9
    Full-time Graduate Students: 16
    Part-time Graduate Students: 16
    Degrees in History: 38 BA, 9 MA
Undergraduate Addresses:
    Admissions: http://enroll.iupui.edu/admissions/
    Financial Aid: http://www.iupui.edu/~finaid/
Graduate Addresses:
    Admissions and Financial Aid: http://liberalarts.iupui.edu/history/index.php/graduate

Affiliated Faculty

Goff, Phiip (PhD, North Carolina, Chapel Hill 1993; Chancellor's Prof.; American Studies) religion, 19th- and 20th-century US, US West; pgoff@iupui.edu

Kryder-Reid, Elizabeth (PhD, Brown 1981; prof.; Anthropology) museum studies; ekryderr@iupui.edu

Schultz, Jane E. (PhD, Michigan 1988; prof.; English) American culture, 19th-century US, women and medicine; jschult@iupui.edu

Witkowski, Gregory R. (PhD, SUNY, Buffalo 2003; assoc. prof.; Philanthropic Studies) philanthropy, modern Germany, transnationalism; gwitkows@iupui.edu

Full-time Faculty

Bodenhamer, David J. (PhD, Indiana 1977; prof.; dir., Polis Center) 19th-century US, legal and constitutional; intu100@iupui.edu

Cramer, Kevin Charles (PhD, Harvard 1998; assoc. prof. and chair) European intellectual and cultural, Germany and central Europe; kcramer@iupui.edu

Gondola, Ch. Didier (PhD, Paris-VII-Denis-Diderot, France 1993; prof.) Africa and Middle East; gondola@iupui.edu

Guiliano, Jennifer E. (PhD, Illinois, Urbana-Champaign 2010; asst. prof.) digital, America, sports; guiliano@iupui.edu

Haberski, Raymond J. (PhD, Ohio 1999; prof.; American Studies) America, intellectual; haberski@iupui.edu

Kaufman-McKivigan, John R. (PhD, Ohio State 1977; Mary O'Brien Gibson Prof.) antebellum US, Civil War and Reconstruction, Gilded Age; jmckivig@iupui.edu

Kelly, Jason M. (PhD, California, Santa Barbara 2004; assoc. prof.; dir., IUPUI Arts & Humanities Inst.) 18th-century Britain, early modern Europe; jaskelly@iupui.edu

Kostroun, Daniella J. (PhD, Duke 2000; assoc. prof.) early modern Europe, Atlantic world, women and religion; dkostrou@iupui.edu

Labode, Modupe (DPhil, Oxford 1992; assoc. prof. and dir., undergrad. prog.) African American, museum studies; mlabode@iupui.edu

Lindseth, Erik L. (PhD, Edinburgh, Scotland 1992; sr. lect.) Britain and Scotland, early modern Europe, book; elindset@iupui.edu

Monroe, Elizabeth Brand (PhD, Florida 1989; assoc. prof.) US legal and constitutional, public; emonroe@iupui.edu

Morgan, Anita (PhD, Purdue 1997; sr. lect.) antebellum US, women, Indiana; aashende@iupui.edu

Robbins, Kevin C. (PhD, Johns Hopkins 1991; assoc. prof. and dir., grad. studies) France, 19th-century art and media; krobbin1@iupui.edu

Robertson, Nancy Marie (PhD, NYU 1997; assoc. prof.) 20th-century US, women, philanthropy; nmrobert@iupui.edu

Saak, Eric Leland (PhD, Arizona 1993; prof.) medieval, Renaissance and Reformation Europe; esaak@iupui.edu

Scarpino, Philip V. (PhD, Missouri, Columbia 1983; prof. and dir., public hist.) environmental, public, oral; pscarpin@iupui.edu

Schneider, William H. (PhD, Pennsylvania 1976; prof.; dir., Medical Humanities Prog.) medicine and science, modern France, Africa; whschnei@iupui.edu

Shrum, Rebecca K. (PhD, South Carolina 2007; asst. prof.) public, material culture, colonial and early Republic America; rshrum@iupui.edu

Snodgrass, Michael D. (PhD, Texas, Austin 1998; assoc. prof.) modern Latin America; misnodgr@iupui.edu

Zhang, Xin (PhD, Chicago 1991; assoc. prof.) modern Asia, China; xzhang@iupui.edu

Nondepartmental Historians

Towne, Stephen E. (MA, Indiana 1985; assoc. univ. archivist) US Civil War, Indiana, archives; setowne@iupui.edu

White, Angela M. (PhD, Indiana 2007; philanthropic studies archivist) archives, Poland, modern Jewish; angwhite@iupui.edu

Retired/Emeritus Faculty

Barrows, Robert G. (PhD, Indiana 1977; prof. emeritus) US, Indiana; rbarrows@iupui.edu

Cooper, Sheila M. (PhD, Indiana 1985; asst. prof. emerita) Britain

Cutler, Kenneth E. (PhD, Indiana 1965; assoc. prof. emeritus) medieval; kcutler@iupui.edu

Friedman, Bernard (PhD, Indiana 1959; prof. emeritus) colonial and revolutionary America, US intellectual, American studies

Gray, Ralph D. (PhD, Illinois, Urbana-Champaign 1962; prof. emeritus) American economic, Indiana, Middle Period US; rgray@iupui.edu

Jessner, Sabine (PhD, Columbia 1963; assoc. prof. emerita) France, women

Langsam, Miriam Z. (PhD, Wisconsin, Madison 1967; prof. emerita) American intellectual, science and technology, women; mlangsam@iupui.edu

Libby, Justin H. (PhD, Michigan State 1971; assoc. prof. emeritus) US diplomatic, Japan; jhlibby@iupui.edu

Little, Monroe H., Jr. (PhD, Princeton 1977; assoc. prof. emeritus) American education; mlittle@iupui.edu

Riesterer, Berthold P. (PhD, Wayne State 1966; prof. emeritus) Germany, European intellectual; briester@iupui.edu

Sehlinger, Peter J. (PhD, Kentucky 1969; prof. emeritus) Latin America, Spain and Portugal; psehling@iupui.edu

Seldon, Mary Elisabeth (PhD, Indiana 1959; prof. emerita) Britain, public policy, social welfare

Shipps, Jan (PhD, Colorado, Boulder 1965; prof. emerita) American religious, social, community; shipps@iupui.edu

Wokeck, Marianne S. (PhD, Temple 1982; Chancellor's Prof. emeritus) colonial and revolutionary America, immigration, women; mwokeck@iupui.edu

Indiana University South Bend

Dept. of History, 1700 Mishawaka Ave., South Bend, IN 46634-7111. 574.520.4491. Fax 574.520.4538. Email: twillig@iusb.edu; vpontius@iusb.edu. Website: https://www.iusb.edu/history/.

The faculty in the History Department seek to create a stimulating and supportive environment for the study of peoples, movements, nations, and events across human history. Through a critical engagement with historical documents and interpretations, we engage in original research and model historical methods in our classes.

Chair: Timothy Willig
Degrees Offered: BA
Academic Year System: Semester
Areas of Specialization: US, Europe, Latin America, Asia
Tuition (per academic year):
  In-State: $7073
  Out-of-State: $18683
Enrollment 2018-19:
  Undergraduate Majors: 100
  Degrees in History: 12 BA
Addresses:
  Admissions: http://www.iusb.edu/admissions/
  Financial Aid: http://www.iusb.edu/finaid/

Adjunct Faculty

Novotny, Sharon K. (MA, Ball State 1974; lect.) US; snovotny@iusb.edu

Spencer, Thomas Tucker (PhD, Notre Dame 1976; adj. assoc. prof.) recent US; thspence@iusb.edu

Full-time Faculty

Froysland, Hayley (PhD, Virginia 2002; assoc. prof.) Latin America, Columbia, health; hfroysla@iusb.edu

Murphy, J. Thomas (PhD, Illinois, Urbana-Champaign 1993; prof.) American West, Civil War and Reconstruction, military; murphyjt@iusb.edu

Nashel, Jonathan (PhD, Rutgers 1994; assoc. prof.) modern US, US foreign policy, film; jnashel@iusb.edu

Shlapentokh, Dmitry V. (PhD, Chicago 1988; assoc. prof.) Russia, French Revolution, Russian Asia; dshlapen@iusb.edu

Tetzlaff, Monica Maria (PhD, Pennsylvania 1995; assoc. prof.) African American, US women; mtetzlaf@iusb.edu

Willig, Timothy David (PhD, Massachusetts Amherst 2003; assoc. prof. and chair) colonial America, Native American; twillig@iusb.edu

Zwicker, Lisa F. (PhD, California, Berkeley 2002; assoc. prof.) modern Europe, Germany; zwicker@iusb.edu

Nondepartmental Historians

Mishler, Paul C. (PhD, Boston Univ. 1988; assoc. prof.; Labor Studies) labor, social reform, 20th-century US; pmishler@iusb.edu

Retired/Emeritus Faculty

Chesnut, Glenn F. (PhD, Oxford 1971; prof. emeritus) ancient, medieval, religious; gchesnut@iusb.edu

Furlong, Patrick J. (PhD, Northwestern 1966; prof. emeritus) Indiana, early America, business; pfurlong@iusb.edu

Lamon, Lester C. (PhD, North Carolina, Chapel Hill 1971; prof. emeritus) Progressive Era, black, urban; llamon@iusb.edu

Marti, Donald B. (PhD, Wisconsin, Madison 1966; assoc. prof. emeritus) US intellectual and religious, 19th-century US, agriculture; dmarti@iusb.edu

Schreiber, Roy E. (PhD, London 1967; prof. emeritus) Britain, exploration and discovery; rschreib@iusb.edu

Tull, Charles J. (PhD, Notre Dame 1961; prof. emeritus) recent US, US diplomatic, Catholic

Indiana University Southeast

History Program, Sch. of Social Sciences, 4201 Grant Line Rd., New Albany, IN 47150-6405. 812.941.2391. Fax 812.941.2591. Email: yshen@ius.edu. Website: https://www.ius.edu/social-sciences/programs/history/.

The skills and knowledge acquired in the History major at IU Southeast prepare students for success. History sharpens your ability to think critically, argue logically, conduct research, analyze data, and communicate clearly, both orally and in writing.

Chair: Yu Shen
Degrees Offered: BA,BS,Cert.
Academic Year System: Semester
Areas of Specialization: US, Europe, Asia, Latin America, modern world
Tuition (per academic year):
  In-State: $7207
  Out-of-State: $19038

Enrollment 2018-19:
Undergraduate Majors: 49
Degrees in History: 10 BA
Addresses:
Admissions: http://www.ius.edu/admissions/
Financial Aid: http://www.ius.edu/financialaid/

Full-time Faculty

Dauer, Quinn P. (PhD, Florida International 2012; asst. prof.) Latin America, Chile and Argentina, environmental; qdauer@ius.edu
Gritter, Elizabeth (PhD, North Carolina, Chapel Hill 2010; assoc. prof.) US, civil rights, oral; egritter@ius.edu
Rennie, Robert William (PhD, Tennessee, Knoxville 2017; asst. prof.) modern Europe, modern Germany, military
Ryan, Kelly A. (PhD, Maryland, Coll. Park 2006; prof. and dean) early US, gender, sexuality; ryanka@ius.edu
Shen, Yu (PhD, Illinois, Urbana-Champaign 1995; prof. and coord.) East Asia, China, US-Asian relations; yshen@ius.edu

Retired/Emeritus Faculty

Bower, Stephanie B. (PhD, Wisconsin, Madison 1971; prof. emeritus) Latin America, family, urban; sbower@ius.edu
Findling, John E. (PhD, Texas, Austin 1971; prof. emeritus) US diplomatic, US 1877-present, sports; jfindlin@ius.edu
Thackeray, Frank W. (PhD, Temple 1977; prof. emeritus) imperial Russia, Soviet Union, modern Germany; fthacker@ius.edu

University of Iowa

Dept. of History, 280 Schaeffer Hall, Iowa City, IA 52242-1409. 319.335.2299. Email: historydept@uiowa.edu. Website: https://clas.uiowa.edu/history/.

History is the heart of a liberal arts education. Students of history develop an understanding of change-how it happens and why it happens the way it does-that enables them to engage the world they inhabit and to participate fully in civic life. Department of History courses engage the diversity of American life and bring a global consciousness that helps students to navigate the streets (and the news) from Iowa City to Berlin to Nairobi.

Chair: Landon Storrs
Director of Graduate Studies: H. Glenn Penny
Director of Undergraduate Studies: R. Tyler Priest
Degrees Offered: BA,MA,PhD
Academic Year System: Semester
Undergraduate Tuition (per academic year):
In-State: $8073
Out-of-State: $30036
Graduate Tuition (per academic year):
In-State: $10079
Out-of-State: $29026
Enrollment 2018-19:
Undergraduate Majors: 269
New Graduate Students: 9
Full-time Graduate Students: 43
Degrees in History: 48 BA, 5 MA, 5 PhD
Students in Undergraduate Courses: 3725
Students in Undergraduate Intro Courses: 2755
Online-Only Courses: 4.7%
Undergraduate Addresses:
Admissions: http://admissions.uiowa.edu/
Financial Aid: https://admissions.uiowa.edu/finances
Graduate Addresses:
Admissions: http://grad.admissions.uiowa.edu/
Financial Aid: https://grad.admissions.uiowa.edu/finances

Adjunct Faculty

Butterfield, Jo E. (PhD, Iowa 2012; adj. asst. prof.) world, human rights; jo-butterfield@uiowa.edu
Donovan, Brian E. (PhD, Iowa 2015; adj. asst. prof.) disability, US; brian-donovan@uiowa.edu
McKerley, John William (PhD, Iowa 2009; adj. asst. prof.) labor, US social, race; john-mckerley@uiowa.edu
Steck, Andrew N. (PhD, Iowa 2019; adj. asst. prof.) medieval; andrew-steck@uiowa.edu
Tucker, David V. (PhD, Iowa 1999; adj. asst. prof.) Asia, China and Japan; david-tucker@uiowa.edu

Affiliated Faculty

Ehrstine, Glenn (PhD, Texas, Austin 1995; assoc. prof.; German) medieval and early modern German literature, religion, politics; glenn-ehrstine@uiowa.edu
Gallanis, Thomas P. (PhD, Cambridge 1997; JD, Chicago Law Sch. 1990; prof.; Coll. of Law) English and continental European legal; thomas-gallanis@uiowa.edu
Mentzer, Raymond A., Jr. (PhD, Wisconsin, Madison 1973; prof.; Religious Studies) Reformation studies, early modern European religious; raymond-mentzer@uiowa.edu
Nabhan-Warren, Kristy (PhD, Indiana 2001; prof.; Religious Studies) religious studies; kristy-nabhan-warren@uiowa.edu

Full-time Faculty

Belli, Mériam (PhD, Georgetown 2005; assoc. prof.) Middle East; meriam-belli@uiowa.edu
Bond, Sarah E. (PhD, North Carolina, Chapel Hill 2011; assoc. prof.) late Rome, epigraphy and late antique law; sarah-bond@uiowa.edu
Chen, Shuang (PhD, Michigan 2009; assoc. prof.) late imperial China; shuang-chen@uiowa.edu
Cox, Jeffrey L. (PhD, Harvard 1978; prof.) modern Britain; jeffrey-cox@uiowa.edu
Espinosa, Mariola (PhD, North Carolina, Chapel Hill 2003; assoc. prof.) public health, US-Caribbean relations; mariola-espinosa@uiowa.edu
Giblin, James L. (PhD, Wisconsin, Madison 1986; prof.) Africa; james-giblin@uiowa.edu
Gordon, Colin H. (PhD, Wisconsin, Madison 1990; prof.) 20th-century US; colin-gordon@uiowa.edu
Hoenicke Moore, Michaela M. (PhD, North Carolina, Chapel Hill 1998; assoc. prof.) US in world, international relations; michaela-hoenicke-moore@uiowa.edu
Midtrod, Tom Arne (PhD, Northern Illinois 2008; assoc. prof.) early America; tom-midtrod@uiowa.edu
Moore, Michael E. (PhD, Michigan 1993; assoc. prof.) medieval; michael-e-moore@uiowa.edu
Noellert, Matthew Z. (PhD, Hong Kong Univ. of Science and Tech. 2014; asst. prof.) digital humanities, China; matthew-noellert@uiowa.edu
Park, Alyssa (PhD, Columbia 2009; assoc. prof.) modern Korea; alyssa-park@uiowa.edu
Penny, H. Glenn (PhD, Illinois, Urbana-Champaign 1999; prof. and dir., grad. studies) modern Europe; h-penny@uiowa.edu
Rand, Jacki T. (PhD, Oklahoma 1998; assoc. prof.) American Indian; jacki-rand@uiowa.edu
Storrs, Landon R. (PhD, Wisconsin, Madison 1994; prof. and chair) US women; landon-storrs@uiowa.edu
Yablon, Nick William (PhD, Chicago 2003; assoc. prof.; American Studies) 19th-century US cultural and urban, visual culture and memory; nick-yablon@uiowa.edu

Joint/Cross Appointments

Ariel, Ari (PhD, Columbia 2009; lect.; Div. of Interdisciplinary Programs) Israel-Palestine conflict, Middle East; ari-ariel@uiowa.edu

Balto, Simon Ezra (PhD, Wisconsin-Madison 2015; asst. prof.; African American Studies) African American; simon-balto@uiowa.edu

Heineman, Elizabeth D. (PhD, North Carolina, Chapel Hill 1993; prof.; Gender, Women's, and Sexuality Studies) modern European women, modern Germany; elizabeth-heineman@uiowa.edu

Howard, Ashley M. (PhD, Illinois, Urbana-Champaign 2012; asst. prof.; African American Studies) African Americans in Midwest, intersection between race/class/gender, global racial violence; ashley-howard@uiowa.edu

Moore, Rosemary L. (PhD, Michigan 2002; lect.; Classics) ancient; rosemary-moore@uiowa.edu

Murillo, Lina Maria (PhD, Texas, El Paso 2017; asst. prof.; Gender, Women's and Sexuality Studies) borderlands, reproductive freedom, race, gender, class, sexuality, Latina/o/x; lina-murillo@uiowa.edu

Ortiz Diaz, Alberto (PhD, Wisconsin-Madison 2017; asst. prof.; Global Health Studies) Latin America and Caribbean, global health studies, policing and incarceration; alberto-ortizdiaz@uiowa.edu

Priest, Tyler (PhD, Wisconsin, Madison 1996; assoc. prof. and dir., undergrad. studies; Geographical and Sustainability Sciences) environmental, public; tyler-priest@uiowa.edu

Schwalm, Leslie A. (PhD, Wisconsin, Madison 1991; prof.; Gender, Women's, and Sexuality Studies) 19th-century US, Civil War and Reconstruction, slavery; leslie-schwalm@uiowa.edu

Warren, Stephen (PhD, Indiana 2000; assoc. prof.; American Studies) American Indian histories and cultures, ethnohistorical methods; stephen-warren@uiowa.edu

Zmolek, Michael A. (PhD, York, Can. 2009; lect.; International Studies) world; michael-zmolek@uiowa.edu

Part-time Faculty

Yale, Elizabeth E. (PhD, Harvard 2008; lect.) early modern Europe, science; elizabeth-yale@uiowa.edu

Retired/Emeritus Faculty

Baynton, Douglas C. (PhD, Iowa 1993; prof. emeritus) American cultural, disability, American Sign Language; douglas-baynton@uiowa.edu

Berman, Constance H. (PhD, Wisconsin, Madison 1978; prof. emerita) medieval Europe; constance-berman@uiowa.edu

Bozeman, T. Dwight (PhD, Duke 1974; prof. emeritus) US religious; d-bozeman@uiowa.edu

Greenough, Paul R. (PhD, Chicago 1977; prof. emeritus) 20th-century India; paul-greenough@uiowa.edu

Hanley, Sarah (PhD, Iowa 1975; prof. emerita) France, politics and society, law; sarah-hanley@uiowa.edu

Hawley, Ellis W. (PhD, Wisconsin, Madison 1959; prof. emeritus) 20th-century US; ellis.hawley@mchsi.com

Kamerick, Kathleen C. (PhD, Iowa 1991; retired lect.) medieval; kathleen-kamerick@uiowa.edu

Kerber, Linda K. (PhD, Columbia 1968; prof. emerita) Federalist America, US women; linda-kerber@uiowa.edu

Pelenski, Jaroslaw (PhD, Columbia 1968; PhD, Munich, Germany 1957; prof. emeritus) early modern Russia, Soviet Union, eastern Europe

Rohrbough, Malcolm J. (PhD, Wisconsin, Madison 1963; prof. emeritus) American West; malcolm-rohrbough@uiowa.edu

Schoenbaum, David (DPhil, Oxford 1966; prof. emeritus) modern Germany, recent international relations; dlschoen@aol.com

Spitzer, Alan B. (PhD, Columbia 1955; prof. emeritus) modern France; absandmfs@yahoo.com

Steinberg, Allen (PhD, Columbia 1983; assoc. prof. emeritus) 19th-century US, social, legal; allen-steinberg@uiowa.edu

Stromquist, H. Shelton (PhD, Pittsburgh 1981; prof. emeritus) American social, labor; shelton-stromquist@uiowa.edu

Tachau, Katherine H. (PhD, Wisconsin-Madison 1981; prof. emerita) medieval intellectual; katherine-tachau@uiowa.edu

Vlastos, Stephen (PhD, California, Berkeley 1977; prof. emeritus) modern Japan; stephen-vlastos@uiowa.edu

Visiting Faculty

Bartram, Faye Lin (PhD, Iowa 2017; vis. asst. prof.) modern Europe, Soviet, France; faye-bartram@uiowa.edu

Radesky, Caroline Elizabeth (PhD, Iowa 2019; vis. asst. prof.; Gender, Women's & Sexuality Studies) sexuality, queer history, gender in US; caroline-radesky@uiowa.edu

Recently Awarded PhDs

Callahan, Noaquia "A Peculiar Exceptionalism: African American Feminist Transnational Activism, 1888-1922"

Nyanto, Salvatory Stephen "Slave Emancipation, Christian Communities, and Dissent in Western Tanzania, 1878-1960"

Radesky, Caroline Elizabeth "Feeling Historical: Same-Sex Desire and the Creation of Historical Imaginaries, 1890-1920"

Steck, Andrew N. "The Populus in Early Medieval Rome"

Weaver, Janet "Pearl McGill and the Promise of Industrial Unionism: Button Workers, the Women's Trade Union League, and the AFL "

Zheng, Aihua "Shaku Soen (1860-1919) and Rinzai Zen in Modern Japan, 1868-1919"

Iowa State University

Dept. of History, 603 Ross Hall, 527 Farm House Ln., Ames, IA 50011-1202. 515.294.7266. Fax 515.294.6390. Email: scordery@iastate.edu. Website: https://history.iastate.edu/.

The History Department at Iowa State University was established as a separate department in 1969, having been for many decades before that time a part of the joint Department of History, Political Science, and Philosophy. Since 1969, the Department has continued to offer undergraduate and graduate degrees over a variety of national, chronological, and specialized areas of historical study.

Chair: Simon Cordery
Director of Graduate Studies: Michael D. Bailey
Director of Undergraduate Studies: Brian Behnken
Degrees Offered: BA, BS, MA, PhD
Academic Year System: Semester
Areas of Specialization: agricultural and rural, technological, environmental
Undergraduate Tuition (per academic year):
  In-State: $6848
  Out-of-State: $19768
Graduate Tuition (per academic year):
  In-State: $8130
  Out-of-State: $21054
Enrollment 2018-19:
  Undergraduate Majors: 241
  New Graduate Students: 9
  Full-time Graduate Students: 32

Part-time Graduate Students: 4
Degrees in History: 45 BA, 55 BS, 5 MA, 1 PhD
Undergraduate Addresses:
Admissions: http://www.admissions.iastate.edu/
Financial Aid: http://www.admissions.iastate.edu/finance.php
Graduate Addresses:
Admissions: http://www.admissions.iastate.edu/graduate/
Financial Aid: http://history.iastate.edu/

Full-time Faculty

Adeleke, R. Tunde (PhD, Western Ontario 1985; prof.; dir., African and African American Studies Prog.) African American; tadeleke@iastate.edu

Andrews, James T. (PhD, Chicago 1994; prof.) Russia, science and technology, social and cultural; andrewsj@iastate.edu

Bailey, Michael D. (PhD, Northwestern 1998; prof. and dir., grad. studies) medieval, religion, magic and witchcraft; mdbailey@iastate.edu

Behnken, Brian D. (PhD, California, Davis 2007; assoc. prof. and dir., undergrad. studies) US Latino/a, African American, 20th-century US; bbehnken@iastate.edu

Best, Jeremy (PhD, Maryland, Coll. Park 2012; asst. prof.) modern Germany; bestja@iastate.edu

Bix, Amy S. (PhD, Johns Hopkins 1994; prof.) American technology, science, medicine; abix@iastate.edu

Bremer, Jeff R. (PhD, Kansas 2006; assoc. prof.; Curriculum and Instruction) history education, frontier, rural and agricultural; jrbremer@iastate.edu

Cordery, Simon C. E. (PhD, Texas, Austin 1995; prof. and chair) modern Britain, labor; scordery@iastate.edu

Cordery, Stacy A. (PhD, Texas, Austin 1992; prof.) 20th-century US, US women; cordery@iastate.edu

Courtwright, Julie R. (PhD, Arkansas 2007; assoc. prof.) environmental, Great Plains; jcourtw@iastate.edu

Griffiths, Paul D. (PhD, Cambridge 1992; prof.) early modern Britain; pgriff@iastate.edu

Hernandez, Bonar L. (PhD, Texas, Austin 2010; asst. prof.) modern Latin America, Guatemala; bhernand@iastate.edu

Hilliard, Kathleen M. (PhD, South Carolina 2006; assoc. prof.) 19th-century US, agricultural and rural, antebellum South/slavery; khilliar@iastate.edu

Hollander, David B. (PhD, Columbia 2002; prof.) ancient Rome, agriculture, economic; dbh8@iastate.edu

Low, Michael C. (PhD, Columbia 2015; asst. prof.) Middle East, environmental; low@iastate.edu

McDonnell, Lawrence T. (PhD, Illinois, Urbana-Champaign 2014; asst. prof.) US South, 19th-century US; lmcd@iastate.edu

Monroe, John Warne (PhD, Yale 2002; assoc. prof.) France; jmonroe@iastate.edu

Riney-Kehrberg, Pamela L. (PhD, Wisconsin-Madison 1991; prof.) US agriculture, rural, family/childhood; prinkeh@iastate.edu

Rutenberg, Amy (PhD, Maryland, Coll. Park 2013; asst. prof.) history and social sciences education, 20th-century US; arutenbe@iastate.edu

Wang, Tao (PhD, Georgetown 2012; asst. prof.) modern China, Cold War, diplomatic; twang@iastate.edu

Wolters, Timothy S. (PhD, MIT 2003; assoc. prof.) technology, naval and military; wolters@iastate.edu

Part-time Faculty

Hill, Kevin D. (PhD, Iowa State 2002; sr. lect.) agricultural; kdhill@iastate.edu

Kehrberg, Richard (MA, Wisconsin-Madison 1986; lect.) military, US; kehrberg@iastate.edu

Schneider, Wendie E. (PhD, Yale 2006; adj. assoc. prof.) British legal, China; wschneid@iastate.edu

Retired/Emeritus Faculty

Avraamides, Achilles (PhD, Minnesota 1971; assoc. prof. emeritus) ancient

Dobbs, Charles M. (PhD, Indiana 1978; prof. emeritus) US diplomatic

Dobson, John M. (PhD, Wisconsin, Madison 1966; prof. emeritus) Gilded Age

Farnham Pope, Christie A. (PhD, Chicago 1977; prof. emeritus) African American, US women, US South; cfpope@iastate.edu

Kottman, Richard N. (PhD, Vanderbilt 1958; prof. emeritus) diplomatic, 20th-century US

Marcus, Alan I (PhD, Cincinnati 1979; prof. emeritus) science, technology, medicine

McJimsey, George T. (PhD, Wisconsin, Madison 1968; prof. emeritus) Middle Period US, Civil War

Osborn, Wayne S. (PhD, Iowa 1970; asst. prof. emeritus) Latin America, peace

Plakans, Andrejs (PhD, Harvard 1969; prof. emeritus) European social, eastern Europe, quantitative methods; aplakans@iastate.edu

Rawson, Don C. (PhD, Washington 1971; prof. emeritus) Russia

Wilson, David B. (PhD, Johns Hopkins 1968; prof. emeritus) science; davidw@iastate.edu

Recently Awarded PhDs

Weber, Margaret Baker "The American Way of Farming: Agribusiness and Power in Postwar America"

Ithaca College

Dept. of History, 424 Muller Faculty Center, 953 Danby Rd., Ithaca, NY 14850-7000. 607.274.3303. Fax 607.274.5118. Email: pponce@ithaca.edu. Website: https://www.ithaca.edu/academics/school-humanities-and-sciences/history.

While firmly focused on the critical examination of our past, our department's flexible curriculum gives students the freedom to explore complementary disciplines such as anthropology, politics, and geography. Our graduates emerge with broad historical perspectives and strong writing and analytical skills that are well-suited to a variety of careers.

Chair: Pearl Ponce
Degrees Offered: BA, Cert.
Academic Year System: Semester
Areas of Specialization: US, Europe, global, non-Western, social studies teacher education
Tuition (per academic year): $42884
Enrollment 2018-19:
Undergraduate Majors: 65
Degrees in History: 24 BA
Addresses:
Admissions: http://www.ithaca.edu/admission/
Financial Aid: http://www.ithaca.edu/finaid/

Full-time Faculty

Ablard, Jonathan D. (PhD, New Mexico 2000; assoc. prof.) Latin America, health; jablard@ithaca.edu

Breuer, Karin H. (PhD, North Carolina, Chapel Hill 2002; assoc. prof.) modern Europe, Germany; kbreuer@ithaca.edu

Conger, Vivian Bruce (PhD, Cornell 1994; prof.; Humanities) early US, US women; vconger@ithaca.edu

Freitag, Jason P. (PhD, Columbia 2001; assoc. prof.) South Asia, British Empire, Islamic civilizations; jfreitag@ithaca.edu

Klemm, Matthew E. (PhD, Johns Hopkins 2007; assoc. prof.) medieval Europe, ancient/classical Europe; mklemm@ithaca.edu

Lin, Zoe Shan (PhD, California, Davis 2018; asst. prof.) East Asia, China; zslin@ithaca.edu

Ponce, Pearl T. (PhD, Harvard 2002; assoc. prof. and chair) 19th-century US political, US foreign relations; pponce@ithaca.edu

Smith, Michael B. (PhD, Indiana 2002; assoc. prof.) US and global environmental, public; mismith@ithaca.edu

Trotti, Michael Ayers (PhD, North Carolina, Chapel Hill 1999; prof.) US, 20th century, social and cultural; mtrotti@ithaca.edu

Wasyliw, Zenon V. (PhD, SUNY, Binghamton 1992; prof.) eastern Europe/USSR/Eurasia, social studies teacher education, comparative global; wasyliw@ithaca.edu

Jacksonville University

Dept. of History, Social Sciences Division, 2800 University Blvd. N., Jacksonville, FL 32211-3394. 904.256.7215. Email: jhingso@ju.edu. Website: https://www.ju.edu/history/.

When you major in History, you explore the making of today's world. Your starting point might be the distant or the near past; your focus might be the US or another region; your perspective might be political, social, military, or one of many other approaches. The end result will be a greater understanding of the past, of historical change, and of the historical context of today's global challenges.

Chair: Jesse Hingson
Degrees Offered: BA,BS
Academic Year System: Semester
Areas of Specialization: modern world, US, Latin America, Europe, Africa
Tuition (per academic year): $33930
Enrollment 2018-19:
  Undergraduate Majors: 14
  Degrees in History: 2 BA, 1 BS
Addresses:
  Admissions: http://www.ju.edu/admissions/undergraduate/
  Financial Aid: http://www.ju.edu/financialaid/

Full-time Faculty

Blanton, S. Walker, Jr. (PhD, Virginia 1969; prof.) US, US South, Civil War; sblanto@ju.edu

Hingson, Jesse (PhD, Florida International 2003; prof. and chair) Latin America, US-Latin American relations, historical methods; jhingso@ju.edu

Parcells, Ashley (PhD, Emory 2018; asst. prof.) Africa, South Africa, apartheid; aparcel@ju.edu

Unangst, Matthew (PhD, Temple 2015; asst. prof.) Europe, Germany, colonialism; munangs@ju.edu

Retired/Emeritus Faculty

Buettinger, Craig (PhD, Northwestern 1982; prof. emeritus) US South, slavery; cbuetti@ju.edu

Clarke, J. Calvitt, III (PhD, Maryland, Coll. Park 1988; prof. emeritus) 1930s diplomacy; jclarke@ju.edu

James Madison University

Dept. of History, 951 Madison Dr., MSC 2001, Harrisonburg, VA 22807. 540.568.6132. Fax 540.568.5808. Email: history@jmu.edu. Website: https://www.jmu.edu/history/.

The Department of History provides an exceptional educational experience. It introduces students to the study of history as a discipline, inculcates habits of lifelong learning and cross disciplinary perspectives among its graduates, and provides important skills designed to meet the changing needs of our students in society.

Chair: Maura E. Hametz
Director of Graduate Studies: William C. Van Norman
Degrees Offered: BA,MA
Academic Year System: Semester
Areas of Specialization: world, US, local and regional, public
Undergraduate Tuition (per academic year):
  In-State: $12016
  Out-of-State: $28416
Graduate Tuition (per academic year):
  In-State: $8730
  Out-of-State: $22158
Enrollment 2018-19:
  Undergraduate Majors: 223
  New Graduate Students: 10
  Full-time Graduate Students: 22
  Part-time Graduate Students: 2
  Degrees in History: 80 BA, 6 MA
Undergraduate Addresses:
  Admissions: http://www.jmu.edu/admissions/undergrad/
  Financial Aid: http://www.jmu.edu/finaid/
Graduate Addresses:
  Admissions and Financial Aid: http://www.jmu.edu/grad/

Full-time Faculty

Arndt, J. Chris (PhD, Florida State 1987; prof. and assoc. dean; Coll. of Arts and Letters) America, early Republic, historical methods; arndtjc@jmu.edu

Borg, Kevin L. (PhD, Delaware 2000; prof.) US public, American technology social, American automobile cultures; borgkl@jmu.edu

Brannon, Rebecca (PhD, Michigan 2007; assoc. prof.) colonial America and American Revolution, consumerism, cultural; brannorn@jmu.edu

Butt, John J. (PhD, Rutgers 1982; prof.) British history and literature; buttjj@jmu.edu

Chappell, L. Stephen (PhD, UCLA 2005; assoc. prof.) Rome and Greece, late antiquity and classics, Byzantine; chappesx@jmu.edu

Davidson, Jessica B. (PhD, Brandeis 2005; assoc. prof.) world since 1500, modern European political/social/women, Spain and Latin America; davidsjb@jmu.edu

Davis, Christian S. (PhD, Rutgers 2005; assoc. prof.) modern Europe and Germany, European colonialism, Holocaust and Genocide studies; davis2cs@jmu.edu

Dillard, P. David (PhD, Rice 1999; prof.) antebellum/Civil War/Reconstruction US South, military, Caribbean; dillarpd@jmu.edu

Fitzgerald, Timothy J. (PhD, Harvard 2009; assoc. prof.) Middle East and world, comparative empire, practice of history; fitzgetj@jmu.edu

Friss, Evan Jay (PhD, Grad. Center, CUNY 2011; asst. prof.) US, urban, public and digital; frissej@jmu.edu

Galgano, Michael J. (PhD, Vanderbilt 1971; prof.) Tudor-Stuart England, Renaissance and Reformation, research methods; galganmj@jmu.edu

Gayne, Mary K. (PhD, Cornell 2007; assoc. prof.) France, world, research methods; gaynemk@jmu.edu

Gelfand, H. Michael (PhD, Arizona 2002; assoc. prof.) recent US, North American West; gelfanhm@jmu.edu

Gubser, Michael D. (PhD, California, Berkeley 2001; prof.) intellectual, central and eastern Europe, international development; gubsermd@jmu.edu

Guerrier, Steve (PhD, Michigan 1988; prof.) US diplomatic and military, US 1929-80; guerrisw@jmu.edu

Hametz, Maura E. (PhD, Brandeis 1995; prof. and chair) modern Italy; hametzme@jmu.edu

Hanifi, Shah Mahmoud (PhD, Michigan 2001; prof.) modern Middle East, global South Asia, Afghanistan; hanifism@jmu.edu

Hardwick, Kevin R. (PhD, Maryland, Coll. Park 1996; prof.) Anglo-American constitutional thought, Atlantic world; hardwikr@jmu.edu

Herrington, Philip (PhD, Virginia 2012; asst. prof.) US, public, historic preservation; herrinpm@jmu.edu

Hu, Yongguang (PhD, SUNY, Binghamton 2011; assoc. prof.) China and Japan, East Asia, comparative world; hu2yx@jmu.edu

Hyser, Raymond M. (PhD, Florida State 1983; prof. and general education coord.) Gilded Age and Progressive Era, US, business; hyserrm@jmu.edu

King, Lamont D (PhD, Temple 1996; assoc. prof.) Africa, Africana studies, nationalism; kingld@jmu.edu

Lanier, Gabrielle M. (PhD, Delaware 1998; prof.) material culture, public, US; laniergm@jmu.edu

McCleary, Kristen L. (PhD, UCLA 2002; assoc. prof.) Latin America, world, urban cultural; mccleakl@jmu.edu

Meixsel, Richard B. (PhD, Ohio State 1993; assoc. prof. and asst. chair) military, India, US; meixserb@jmu.edu

Moore, Colleen Mary (PhD, Indiana 2013; asst. prof.) world, Russia and Soviet

Morales, Daniel (PhD, Columbia 2016; asst. prof.) Latino immigration and borderlands, Latin America, 20th century; moral3dx@jmu.edu

Mulrooney, Margaret M. (PhD, William and Mary 1996; prof.; assoc. vice provost for Univ. progs.) American studies, local and public; mulroomm@jmu.edu

Owusu-Ansah, David (PhD, Northwestern 1986; prof.; dir., Summer Prog. in Ghana; and special asst. to pres. for faculty diversity) modern Africa; owusuadx@jmu.edu

Reich, Steven A. (PhD, Northwestern 1998; prof.) African American, US South, labor; reichsa@jmu.edu

Sandman, Alison D. (PhD, Wisconsin, Madison 2001; assoc. prof.) science and religion, comparative empires, world to 1500; sandmaad@jmu.edu

Seth, Michael J. (PhD, Hawai'i, Mânoa 1994; prof.) Korea, East Asia, world; sethmj@jmu.edu

Van Norman, William C., Jr. (PhD, North Carolina, Chapel Hill 2005; assoc. prof. and grad. prog. dir.) Latin American and Caribbean history and culture, slavery and African diaspora, gender; vannorwc@jmu.edu

Westkaemper, Emily M. (PhD, Rutgers 2009; assoc. prof.) US women, advertising, research methods; westkaem@jmu.edu

Witmer, Andrew (PhD, Virginia 2008; assoc. prof.) American religious, race and religion, African American; witmerad@jmu.ed

Part-time Faculty

Allain, Michael L. (PhD, Ohio State; asst. prof.) ancient Greece and Rome; allainml@jmu.edu

Harding, Jeannie C. (MA, James Madison 2013; instr.) hardinjc@jmu.edu

Harter, Kevin L. (BA, Duke; instr.) cultural anthropology; harterkl@jmu.edu

Hartog, Joanne D. (MA, Virginia; instr.) hartogjd@jmu.edu

Kelley, Hannah R. (MA, James Madison 2004; instr.) US; kelleyhr@jmu.edu

Mooney, M. Shaun (MA, James Madison 2003; instr.) US; mooneyms@jmu.edu

Murray, Constance P. (MA, James Madison 2011; instr.) murraycp@jmu.edu

Retired/Emeritus Faculty

Bland, Sidney R. (PhD, George Washington 1972; prof. emeritus) US 1877-1919, US women; blandsr@jmu.edu

Boyd, Catherine Elaine (PhD, Georgia 1979; prof. emeritus) Germany, 20th-century Europe, European women

Boyd-Bragg, Dorothy (PhD, Temple 1972; prof. emeritus) Tudor-Stuart England

Congdon, Lee W. (PhD, Northern Illinois 1972; prof. emeritus) modern Europe, cultural and intellectual, central and eastern Europe; congdolw@jmu.edu

Hallman, Clive R. (PhD, Georgia 1987; prof. emeritus) colonial America, US South; hallmacr@jmu.edu

Lembright, Robert L. (PhD, Ohio State 1974; prof. emeritus) ancient world, Byzantine, Ottoman Empire and Turkey; lembrirl@jmu.edu

Loe, Mary Louise (PhD, Columbia 1977; prof. emeritus) Russia, Soviet Union; loeml@jmu.edu

Riley, Philip F. (PhD, Notre Dame 1971; prof. emeritus) France, 17th- and 18th-century Europe, world; rileypf@jmu.edu

Walker, Jacqueline B. (PhD, Duke 1979; prof. emeritus) Afro-American, US South, Civil War and Reconstruction; walkerjb@jmu.edu

Yoon, Chong-kun (PhD, American 1968; prof. emeritus) East and Southeast Asia, modern China, modern Japan; yoonck@jmu.edu

Visiting Faculty

Amin, Neel (PhD, California, Davis 2016; vis. asst. prof.) modern South Asia, world, modern India; aminnn@jmu.edu

John Carroll University

Dept. of History, 1 John Carroll Blvd., University Heights, OH 44118-4581. 216.397.4366. Fax 216.397.4175. Email: mberg@jcu.edu. Website: http://sites.jcu.edu/history/.

With its small classes and strong mission, John Carroll is an outstanding place to study history and other humanities. We are a dynamic department offering a wide variety of courses in African, Asian, European, Latin American, and US history.

Chair: Matthew P. Berg
Degrees Offered: BA
Academic Year System: Semester
Areas of Specialization: US, Europe, East Asia, Latin America, global
Tuition (per academic year): $41230
Enrollment 2018-19:
  Undergraduate Majors: 39
  Degrees in History: 16 BA
  Students in Undergraduate Courses: 762
  Students in Undergraduate Intro Courses: 549
  Online-Only Courses: .5%

Addresses:
Admissions: http://sites.jcu.edu/admission/
Financial Aid: http://sites.jcu.edu/aid/

Full-time Faculty

Berg, Matthew P. (PhD, Chicago 1993; prof. and chair; Peace, Justice, and Human Rights) Germany and Austria, 20th-century Europe, social democracy; mberg@jcu.edu

Gallo, Marcus T. (PhD, California, Davis 2012; asst. prof.) early America, colonial; mgallo@jcu.edu

Hessinger, Rodney J. (PhD, Temple 2000; prof.) early America, sexuality, religion; rhessinger@jcu.edu

Kilbride, Daniel (PhD, Florida 1996; prof.) 19th-century US, US South, African American; dkilbride@jcu.edu

Marsilli Cardozo, Maria N. (PhD, Emory 2002; prof.) Latin America; mmarsilli@jcu.edu

McAndrew, J. Malia (PhD, Maryland, Coll. Park 2008; assoc. prof.) modern US, women, African American; jmcandrew@jcu.edu

Murphy, Paul V. (PhD, Toronto 1996; prof.; Catholic Studies) Renaissance and Reformation, church, early modern Europe; pvmurphy@jcu.edu

Purdy, Roger W. (PhD, California, Santa Barbara 1987; assoc. prof.; East Asian Studies) Japan, East Asia, US diplomatic; rpurdy@jcu.edu

Nondepartmental Historians

Krukones, James H. (PhD, Wisconsin, Madison 1983; prof. and assoc. academic vice pres.) Russia, Soviet Union, eastern Europe; jkrukones@jcu.edu

Kugler, Anne (PhD, Michigan 1994; prof.; Coll. of Arts & Sciences) Britain and France, European society, women; akugler@jcu.edu

Part-time Faculty

Bowen, Michael D. (PhD, Florida 2006; instr.) modern America; mbowen@jcu.edu

Burkle, Aaron Scott (MS, Indiana, Pa. 2010; instr.; Geography) cultural geography; aburkle@jcu.edu

Patton, John P. (PhD, Notre Dame 1974; instr.) early modern Europe; jpatton@jcu.edu

Vourlojianis, George N. (PhD, Kent State 1994; instr.) US military; gvourlojianis@jcu.edu

Retired/Emeritus Faculty

Morton, Marian J. (PhD, Case Western Reserve 1970; prof. emerita) US, social, women; mmorton@jcu.edu

Robson, David W. (PhD, Yale 1974; prof. emeritus) early America to 1815, US constitutional; robson@jcu.edu

Johns Hopkins University

Dept. of History, 3400 N. Charles St., 301 Gilman Hall, Baltimore, MD 21218-2685. 410.516.7575. Fax 410.516.7586. Email: history@jhu.edu. Website: https://history.jhu.edu/.

The Department of History offers students the opportunity to work intensively in the classroom and with individual faculty to discover the richness and complexity of history.

Chair: Michael Kwass
Director of Graduate Studies: Angus Burgin
Director of Undergraduate Studies: Erin Rowe
Degrees Offered: BA,MA,PhD
Academic Year System: Semester
Areas of Specialization: US, Europe, Latin America, Africa, East Asia

Tuition (per academic year): $55350
Enrollment 2018-19:
Undergraduate Majors: 54
New Graduate Students: 11
Full-time Graduate Students: 78
Degrees in History: 42 BA, 12 MA, 7 PhD
Undergraduate Addresses:
Admissions: https://www.jhu.edu/admissions/undergraduate-admissions/
Financial Aid: https://www.jhu.edu/admissions/financial-aid/
Graduate Addresses:
Admissions: https://www.jhu.edu/admissions/graduate-admissions/
Financial Aid: https://www.jhu.edu/admissions/financial-aid/

Full-time Faculty

Brooks, Jeffrey P. (PhD, Stanford 1972; prof.) Russian intellectual and literary, eastern Europe, popular culture; brooksjp@jhu.edu

Burgin, Angus Robinson (PhD, Harvard 2009; assoc. prof. and dir., grad. studies) 20th-century US political/economic/capitalism; burgin@jhu.edu

Connolly, Nathan D. (PhD, Michigan 2008; assoc. prof.) 20th-century African American; nconnol2@jhu.edu

el-Leithy, Tamer M. (PhD, Princeton 2005; asst. prof.) medieval Egyptian religious conversion, gender and sexuality; tamer.elleithy@jhu.edu

Furstenberg, Francois (PhD, Johns Hopkins 2003; prof.) 18th- and 19th-century US, French Atlantic; f.furstenberg@jhu.edu

Galambos, Louis P. (PhD, Yale 1960; research prof.) US economic and political, institutional change since 1880; galambos@jhu.edu

Hindmarch-Watson, Katie A. (PhD, Johns Hopkins 2013; asst. prof.) technology and labor, gender and sexuality; katie.hw@jhu.edu

Jelavich, Peter (PhD, Princeton 1982; prof.) modern European cultural and intellectual; jelavich@jhu.edu

Johnson, Jessica Marie (PhD, Maryland, Coll. Park 2012; asst. prof.) African diaspora, slavery; jmjohnso@gmail.com

Jones, Martha S. (PhD, Columbia 2001; prof.) Atlantic world slavery and law; msjonz@jhu.edu

Kim, Yumi (PhD, Columbia 2015; asst. prof.) modern Japan; h.yumikim@jhu.edu

Kwass, Michael (PhD, Michigan 1994; prof. and chair) early modern France; kwass@jhu.edu

Larson, Pier M. (PhD, Wisconsin, Madison 1992; prof.) East Africa, Madagascar, Indian Ocean; larson@jhu.edu

Lester, Anne E. (PhD, Princeton 2003; assoc. prof.) monasticism and religion; alester5@jhu.edu

Lurtz, Casey M. (PhD, Chicago 2014; asst. prof.) 19th-century economic; lurtz@jhu.edu

Maciejko, Pawel (DPhil, Oxford 2003; assoc. prof.) 16th-19th-century European Jewry, Jewish mysticism; pmaciej1@jhu.edu

Marshall, John W. (PhD, Johns Hopkins 1990; prof.) early modern Europe, Britain and intellectual; jmarsha2@jhu.edu

Mason, Laura (PhD, Princeton 1990; sr. lect.) French Revolution, history and film; lmason@jhu.edu

Meyer-Fong, Tobie S. (PhD, Stanford 1998; prof.) East Asia, cultural and social, race/gender/nationalism; tmeyerf@jhu.edu

Morgan, Philip D. (PhD, Univ. Coll., London 1978; prof.) early America, African American, Atlantic world; pmorgan@jhu.edu

Moss, Kenneth B. (PhD, Stanford 2003; assoc. prof.) modern European Jewish, Russia; kmoss5@jhu.edu

Rowe, Erin Kathleen (PhD, Johns Hopkins 2005; assoc. prof. and dir., undergrad. studies) early modern Spain and Mediterranean, religious and political; erowe1@jhu.edu

Rowe, William T. (PhD, Columbia 1980; prof.) modern East Asia, socioeconomic, urban; wtrowe@jhu.edu

Shepard, Todd (PhD, Rutgers 2002; prof.) 20th-century France; tshep75@jhu.edu

Spiegel, Gabrielle M. (PhD, Johns Hopkins 1974; prof.) medieval, early modern Europe; spiegel@jhu.edu

Thornberry, Elizabeth (PhD, Stanford 2011; asst. prof.) South Africa, sexual violence, customary law; liz.thornberry@gmail.com

Walters, Ronald G. (PhD, California, Berkeley 1971; prof.) early US, family, Afro-American; rgw1@jhu.edu

Part-time Faculty

Hebrard, Jean M. (Other, Paris III 1974; vis. prof.) social and cultural history of slavery; jhebrard@jhu.edu

Retired/Emeritus Faculty

Berry, Sara S. (PhD, Michigan 1967; prof. emeritus) African studies, economic and social; sberry@jhu.edu

Ditz, Toby L. (PhD, Columbia 1982; prof. emeritus) 18th- and 19th-century US, comparative family; toby.ditz@jhu.edu

Forster, Robert (PhD, Johns Hopkins 1956; prof. emeritus) 18th- and 19th-century French social and economic; elbobf@aol.com

Goldthwaite, Richard (PhD, Columbia 1965; prof. emeritus) Renaissance Italian economic and social

Greene, Jack P. (PhD, Duke 1956; prof. emeritus) colonial Anglo-American 1607-1789; jack_greene@brown.edu

Johnson, Michael P. (PhD, Stanford 1973; prof. emeritus) 19th-century US, slavery and US South; vze1vntz@verizon.net

Kagan, Richard L. (PhD, Cambridge 1968; prof. emeritus) early modern Europe, Spanish and Iberian expansion; kagan@jhu.edu

Knight, Franklin W. (PhD, Wisconsin, Madison 1969; prof. emeritus) Latin American social and economic, colonial Latin America, American slave systems; fknight@jhu.edu

Lidtke, Vernon L. (PhD, California, Berkeley 1962; prof. emeritus) modern Germany, European social movements; lidtke@jhu.edu

Pocock, John G. A. (PhD, Cambridge 1952; prof. emeritus) European intellectual, history of ideas; jgap@earthlink.net

Ranum, Orest (PhD, Minnesota 1960; prof. emeritus) early modern Europe, France; pranum@compuserve.com

Ross, Dorothy (PhD, Columbia 1965; prof. emeritus) American intellectual, historiography; dottross@comcast.net

Ryan, Mary P. (PhD, California, Santa Barbara 1971; prof. emeritus) gender, class, family; mpryan@jhu.edu

Struever, Nancy (PhD, Rochester 1966; prof. emeritus) Renaissance and early modern European intellectual; n.struever@jhu.edu

Walker, Mack (PhD, Harvard 1959; prof. emeritus) European social and political, early modern Germany; erwalk@worldnet.att.net

Walkowitz, Judith R. (PhD, Rochester 1974; prof. emeritus) modern European women, Britain, Victorian cultural and social; jw27@nyu.edu

Recently Awarded PhDs

Imber, Elizabeth E. "Jewish Political Lives in the British Empire: Zionism, Nationalism, and Imperialism in Palestine, India, and South Africa, 1917-39"

Levy, Jessica Ann "Black Power, Inc.: Global American Business and the Post-Apartheid City"

Peters, Dexnell "Circulating Counterfeits: Making Money and its Meanings in the 18th-Century British Atlantic World"

Smoak, Katherine "Circulating Counterfeits: Making Money and its Meanings in the 18th-Century British Atlantic World"

Johns Hopkins University

Prog. in the History of Science, Medicine, and Technology, History of Science and Technology, 3400 N. Charles St., Gilman 301, Baltimore, MD 21218. 410.516.7501. Fax 410.516.7502. Website: https://host.jhu.edu/.

Alternate Address: Inst. of the History of Medicine, Sch. of Medicine, 1900 E. Monument St., Baltimore, MD 21205-2169

A joint program by the Department of History of Science and Technology, in the Krieger School of Arts and Sciences, and the Department of History of Medicine, in the School of Medicine.

Chair: Jeremy Greene (medicine); Sharon Kingsland, acting (science and tech.)

Director of Graduate Studies: Nathaniel Comfort (medicine); Yulia Frumer (science and tech.)

Director of Undergraduate Studies: Joris Mercelis

Degrees Offered: MA,PhD

Academic Year System: Semester

Areas of Specialization: biology, chemistry, physics, technology, medicine and public health, early modern science, technology and medicine, modern science, technology and medicine

Tuition (per academic year): $53740

Enrollment 2018-19:
New Graduate Students: 5
Full-time Graduate Students: 16
Degrees in History: 2 PhD

Addresses:
Admissions: http://host.jhu.edu/graduate/admissions/
Financial Aid: http://finaid.johnshopkins.edu/grads.html

Full-time Faculty

Comfort, Nathaniel C. (PhD, SUNY, Stony Brook 1997; prof. and dir., grad. studies) 20th-century American biomedicine, genetics, social relations of science; nccomfort@gmail.com

Fissell, Mary E. (PhD, Pennsylvania 1988; prof.) 17th- and 18th-century European health care and popular medicine, early modern gender and body; mfissell@jhmi.edu

Frumer, Yulia (PhD, Princeton 2013; assoc. prof.; Bo Jung and Soon Young Kim Prof.; and dir., grad. studies) East Asian science and technology; yfrumer@jhu.edu

Greene, Jeremy Alan (MD,PhD, Harvard 2005; prof. and dir., Hist. of Medicine) therapeutics, disease, 19th- and 20th-century American medicine; jgree115@jhmi.edu

Hanson, Marta E. (PhD, Pennsylvania 1997; assoc. prof.) late imperial Chinese medicine; mhanson4@jhmi.edu

Kargon, Robert A. (PhD, Cornell 1964; Willis K. Shepard Prof.) physics, science and social change, American science; kargon@jhu.edu

Kingsland, Sharon E. (PhD, Toronto 1981; prof. and acting chair, Hist. of Science and Tech.) biology, genetics and behavioral biology, American science; sharon@jhu.edu

Leslie, Stuart W. (PhD, Delaware 1980; prof.) technology, science-based industry, 20th-century American science; swleslie@jhu.edu

Mercelis, Joris (PhD, Ghent 2013; asst. prof. and dir., undergrad. studies) 18th- to 20th-century technology, photographic emulsion technology; jmercelis@jhu.edu

Mooney, Graham P. (PhD, Liverpool, UK 1994; assoc. prof.) 19th- and 20th-century public health, historical epidemiology, historical demography; gmooney3@jhmi.edu

O'Brien, Elizabeth (PhD, Texas, Austin 2019; asst. prof.) Mexican and Latin American medicine

Packard, Randall M. (PhD, Wisconsin, Madison 1976; William H. Welch Prof.) disease social, colonial medicine and international health, African health and healing; rpackar2@jhmi.edu

Portuondo, Maria M. (PhD, Johns Hopkins 2005; assoc. prof.) science, Latin American science and technology, Spanish science; mportuondo@jhu.edu

Principe, Lawrence (PhD, Johns Hopkins 1996; Drew Prof.; dir., Singleton Center for the Study of Premodern Europe) chemistry and alchemy, early modern science, science and religion; lmafp@jhu.edu

Ruggere, Christine A. (lect. and curator; Hist. Collection, Inst. of Hist. of Medicine) ruggere@jhmi.edu

Retired/Emeritus Faculty

Pomata, Gianna (PhD, Florence, Italy 1973; prof. emeritus) early modern European medicine, women and gender; gpomata1@jhmi.edu

Todes, Daniel P. (PhD, Pennsylvania 1981; prof. emeritus) Russian medicine and science, social relations of scientific thought, biomedical sciences; dtodes@jhmi.edu

Recently Awarded PhDs

Margolis, Emily A. "Space Travel at 1 G: Space Tourism in Cold War America"

Morefield, Heidi "Developing to Scale: Appropriate Technology and the Making of Global Health"

Raymer, Emilie "From Social Darwinism to Human Ecology: Transforming the Disciplines of Sociology, History, and Cultural Geography in the United States, 1890-1955"

Kalamazoo College

Dept. of History, 1200 Academy St., Kalamazoo, MI 49006-3295. 269.337.7053. Fax 269.337.5733. Email: bangura@kzoo.edu. Website: https://history.kzoo.edu/.

Liberal arts education equips individuals to understand and appreciate the world and to meet its challenges. The study of History contributes much to these ends, maintaining that people and society are, in important respects, the products of their past; therefore, the story of the past provides insight helpful to both personal and social development.

Chair: Joseph J. Bangura
Degrees Offered: BA
Academic Year System: Trimester
Areas of Specialization: US, Europe, Africa, East Asia, Jewish
Tuition (per academic year): $44418
Enrollment 2018-19:
  Undergraduate Majors: 30
  Degrees in History: 17 BA
Addresses:
  Admissions: http://www.kzoo.edu/admission/
  Financial Aid: http://www.kzoo.edu/admission/finaid/

Full-time Faculty

Bangura, Joseph J (PhD, Dalhousie 2006; prof. and chair) Africa, Islam, politics; bangura@kzoo.edu

Boyer Lewis, Charlene (PhD, Virginia 1997; prof.) US, 18th- and 19th-century social, women; clewis@kzoo.edu

Carroll, Christina B. (PhD, North Carolina, Chapel Hill 2015; asst. prof.) modern France, modern Middle East, history and identity in modern Europe; christina.carroll@kzoo.edu

Frost, Dennis J. (PhD, Columbia 2007; assoc. prof.) modern Japan, East Asia, sport; dennis.frost@kzoo.edu

Haus, Jeffrey (PhD, Brandeis 1997; prof.; Religion) Jewish history and religion, Jews of modern France; jhaus@kzoo.edu

Lewis, James E., Jr. (PhD, Virginia 1994; prof.) US, American Revolution, methodology; jlewis@kzoo.edu

Rojas, Rochelle (PhD, Duke 2017; asst. prof.) medieval and early modern Mediterranean, Latin America; Rochelle.Rojas-Nielsen@kzoo.edu

Joint/Cross Appointments

Brock, Lisa A. (PhD, Northwestern 1990; assoc. prof.; acad. dir., Arcus Center for Social Justice Leadership) southern Africa, Cuba, African American; lbrock@kzoo.edu

Retired/Emeritus Faculty

Barclay, David E. (PhD, Stanford 1974; prof. emeritus) modern Germany, modern France, modern Britain; david.barclay@kzoo.edu

Wickstrom, John B. (PhD, Yale 1969; prof. emeritus) late antiquity, medieval, early modern; john.wickstrom@kzoo.edu

Visiting Faculty

Elliott, Emily J. (PhD, Michigan State 2019; vis. asst. prof.) Soviet Union

University of Kansas

Dept. of History, 3650 Wescoe Hall, 1445 Jayhawk Blvd., Lawrence, KS 66045-7590. 785.864.3569. Fax 785.864.1785. Email: evelevin@ku.edu; acon@ku.edu. Website: http://history.ku.edu/.

Historians at the University of Kansas train individuals to appreciate the complexity and diversity of the human experience, to question simple explanations, to evaluate evidence in multiple forms, and to offer insightful interpretations with clarity of expression.

Chair: Eve Levin
Director of Graduate Studies: Andrew Denning
Director of Undergraduate Studies: Robert Schwaller
Degrees Offered: BA, MA, PhD
Academic Year System: Semester
Areas of Specialization: medieval, modern Europe, US, Latin America, East Asia, military
Undergraduate Tuition (per academic year):
  In-State: $8347
  Out-of-State: $21640
Graduate Tuition (per academic year):
  In-State: $7546
  Out-of-State: $17579
Enrollment 2018-19:
  Undergraduate Majors: 200
  New Graduate Students: 8
  Full-time Graduate Students: 80
  Degrees in History: 40 BA, 4 MA, 7 PhD, 27 BGS
Undergraduate Addresses:
  Admissions: https://ku.edu/admissions
  Financial Aid: http://affordability.ku.edu/financialaid/
Graduate Addresses:
  Admissions and Financial Aid: http://www.history.ku.edu/

Full-time Faculty

Bailey, Beth L. (PhD, Chicago 1986; Dist. Prof.) US gender and sexuality; blbailey@ku.edu

Brown, Marie (PhD, Pennsylvania 2012; assoc. prof.) Middle East; mgbrown@ku.edu

Corteguera, Luis (PhD, Princeton 1992; prof.) early modern Europe; lcortegu@ku.edu

Denning, Andrew (PhD, California, Davis 2011; assoc. prof. and dir., grad. studies) modern Europe, environmental; asdenning@ku.edu

Farber, David (PhD, Chicago 1985; prof.) US civil society; dfarber@ku.edu

Greene, J. Megan (PhD, Washington 1997; assoc. prof.) modern China; mgreene@ku.edu

Gregg, Sara M. (PhD, Columbia 2004; assoc. prof.) North American environmental; sgregg@ku.edu

Hagel, Jonathan C. (PhD, Brown 2012; asst. teaching specialist) jhagel@ku.edu

Isenberg, Andrew C. (PhD, Northwestern 1993; Dist. Prof.) isenberg@ku.edu

Jahanbani, Sheyda F. A. (PhD, Brown 2007; assoc. prof.) US diplomatic, international; sfaj@ku.edu

Kuznesof, Elizabeth A. (PhD, California, Berkeley 1976; prof.) Brazil, family, social and economic; kuznesof@ku.edu

Levin, Eve (PhD, Indiana 1983; prof. and chair) medieval Russia; evelevin@ku.edu

Lewis, Adrian R. (PhD, Chicago 1995; prof.) Europe, military; arl0008@ku.edu

Moran, Jeffrey P. (PhD, Harvard 1996; prof.) 20th-century US cultural and social; jefmoran@ku.edu

Rath, Eric C. (PhD, Michigan 1998; prof.) premodern Japan, East Asia; erath@ku.edu

Rosenthal, Anton (PhD, Minnesota 1990; assoc. prof.) modern Latin America, labor and urban, comparative; surreal@ku.edu

Schwaller, Robert C. (PhD, Penn State 2010; assoc. prof. and dir., undergrad. studies) Latin America; rschwaller@ku.edu

Scott, Erik R. (PhD, California, Berkeley 2011; assoc. prof.) modern Russia; scott@ku.edu

Warren, Kim D. (PhD, Stanford 2004; assoc. prof.) US women; kwarren@ku.edu

Weber, Jennifer L. (PhD, Princeton 2003; assoc. prof.) US Civil War; jlweber@ku.edu

Wood, Nathaniel David (PhD, Indiana 2004; assoc. prof.) eastern Europe; ndwood@ku.edu

Joint/Cross Appointments

Cushman, Gregory T. (PhD, Texas, Austin 2003; assoc. prof.; Environmental Studies) global environmental, Latin America, science and technology; gcushman@ku.edu

Forth, Christopher E. (PhD, SUNY, Buffalo 1994; prof.; Humanities and Western Civilization) European intellectual and cultural, gender and sexuality, modern France; ce.forth@anu.edu.au

MacGonagle, Elizabeth L. (PhD, Michigan State 2002; assoc. prof.; African and African American Studies) Africa; macgonag@ku.edu

Roediger, David Randall (PhD, Northwestern 1980; Dist. Prof.; American Studies) US labor and race; droediger@ku.edu

Vicente, Marta V. (PhD, Johns Hopkins 1998; prof.; Women's Studies) labor and women; mvicente@ku.edu

Nondepartmental Historians

Alexander, Shawn Leigh (PhD, Massachusetts 2004; asst. prof.; African and African American Studies) African American; slalexan@ku.edu

Flores, Ruben (PhD, California, Berkeley 2006; asst. prof.; American Studies) 20th-century US, Mexican American; flores@ku.edu

Hoeflich, Michael H. (PhD, Cambridge 2001; JD, Yale Law Sch. 1979; prof.; Sch. Law) British and American legal; hoeflich@ku.edu

Jelks, Randal Maurice (PhD, Michigan State 1999; Langston Hughes Prof.; American Studies) US, African American; rmjelks@ku.edu

Rosenbloom, Joshua (PhD, Stanford 1988; Economics) economic; jrosenbloom@ku.edu

Rury, John L. (PhD, Wisconsin-Madison 1982; prof.; Sch. Education) US education; jrury@ku.edu

Retired/Emeritus Faculty

Brundage, James A. (PhD, Fordham 1955; prof. emeritus) medieval; jabrun@ukans.edu

Clark, J.C.D. (PhD, Cambridge 1981; prof. emeritus) British political 1688-1832; jcdclark@ku.edu

Clark, Katherine R. P. (PhD, Johns Hopkins 1998; prof. emerita) early modern Britain; krpclark@ku.edu

Dardess, John (PhD, Columbia 1968; prof. emeritus) late imperial China; jdardess@ku.edu

DeKosky, Robert K. (PhD, Wisconsin, Madison 1972; assoc. prof. emeritus) rdekosky@ku.edu

Epstein, Steven A. (PhD, Harvard 1981; prof. emeritus) medieval; sae@ku.edu

Lewin, Thomas J. (PhD, Northwestern 1974; assoc. prof. emeritus) Africa, oral, multinational corporations; tomlewin@ku.edu

Saul, Norman E. (PhD, Columbia 1965; prof. emeritus) imperial Russia, Soviet Union, Russian political/diplomatic/socioeconomic; normsaul@ku.edu

Sivan, Hagith (PhD, Columbia 1982; prof. emerita) ancient, Rome; dinah01@ku.edu

Sweets, John F. (PhD, Duke 1972; prof. emeritus) modern Europe; exprofjfs@ku.edu

Wilson, Theodore Allen (PhD, Indiana 1966; prof. emeritus) diplomatic, military; taw@ku.edu

Worster, Donald E. (PhD, Yale 1971; Hall Dist. Prof. emeritus) North American environmental, American frontier and West; dworster@ku.edu

Recently Awarded PhDs

Bell, Sarah "Politics on the Platform: The Intersection of Women's Organizations and the Chautauqua Movement, 1874-1919"

Burks, Drew "The Persistence of Advertising Culture: Commerce and Consumers in Multi-Ethnic Galicia, 1911-21"

Gatzemeyer, Maj Garrett "Bodies for Battle: Systematic Training in the US Army's Physical Culture, 1885-1958"

Masten, Randy "From Hope to Hopeless: UN and US Peacekeeping Operations in Somalia, 1992-95"

Mizumoto-Gitter, Alex "Princes and Popes: Family Ties and the Creation of the Early Modern State"

Wells, Jon "'The Publishers Are to Blame': Manhood, Race, and the Memory of Frederick Funston"

Kansas State University

Dept. of History, 117 D Calvin Hall, 802 Mid-Campus Dr. S., Manhattan, KS 66506-1002. 785.532.6730. Fax 785.532.2045. Email: hoffice@ksu.edu. Website: https://www.k-state.edu/history/.

Our major is designed to be broad, requiring students to take classes that vary widely across time and place, but the department has particular strengths in military, agricultural/environmental, and religious history.

Chair: Michael A. Krykso
Director of Graduate Studies: Albert N. Hamscher
Degrees Offered: BA, BS, MA, PhD
Academic Year System: Semester

Areas of Specialization: US, modern Europe, military, science and technology studies, environmental and agricultural, religious, gender studies

Undergraduate Tuition (per academic year):
In-State: $8000
Out-of-State: $20903

Graduate Tuition (per academic year):
In-State: $8362
Out-of-State: $17849

Enrollment 2018-19:
Undergraduate Majors: 87
New Graduate Students: 8
Full-time Graduate Students: 33
Degrees in History: 13 BA, 10 BS, 6 MA, 4 PhD
Students in Undergraduate Courses: 2558
Students in Undergraduate Intro Courses: 1500
Online-Only Courses: 10%

Undergraduate Addresses:
Admissions: http://www.k-state.edu/admissions/
Financial Aid: http://www.k-state.edu/sfa/

Graduate Addresses:
Admissions and Financial Aid: https://www.k-state.edu/grad/

Full-time Faculty

Aley, Ginette (PhD, Iowa State 2005; instr.) 19th-century America, women, agricultural/rural; galey@ksu.edu

Brandom, Eric W. (PhD, Duke 2013; instr.) modern European intellectual, France, Atlantic world; brandom@ksu.edu

Breen, Louise A. (PhD, Connecticut 1993; assoc. prof.) colonial America, American Revolution, Puritanism; breen@ksu.edu

Defries, David J. (PhD, Ohio State 2004; asst. prof.) medieval western Europe, premodern Christianity, monasticism; ddefries@ksu.edu

Frey, Marsha L. (PhD, Ohio State 1971; prof.) European diplomacy, early modern Europe; mfrey@ksu.edu

Graff, David A. (PhD, Princeton 1995; assoc. prof.) China, Japan, military; dgraff@ksu.edu

Hamscher, Albert N. (PhD, Emory 1973; Kenneth S. Davis Prof. and dir., grad. studies) early modern France, US cemeteries; aham@ksu.edu

Krysko, Michael A. (PhD, SUNY, Stony Brook 2001; assoc. prof. and chair) US foreign relations, technology, mass media; mkrysko@ksu.edu

Lynn-Sherow, Bonnie (PhD, Northwestern 1998; assoc. prof.) environmental, American agricultural, Native American; blynn@ksu.edu

Maner, Brent E. (PhD, Illinois, Urbana-Champaign 2001; assoc. prof.) Germany, modern Europe, modern Middle East; maner@ksu.edu

McCrea, Heather L. (PhD, SUNY, Stony Brook 2002; assoc. prof.) colonial and modern Mexico, peasant studies, public health; hmccrea@ksu.edu

Morgan, M. J. (PhD, Cincinnati 2005; asst. prof.) French empire in America, Mississippi Valley, environmental; morganm@ksu.edu

Mrozek, Donald J. (PhD, Rutgers 1972; prof.) American cultural, sports, military; mrozek@ksu.edu

Orr, Andrew (PhD, Notre Dame 2007; assoc. prof.) France, military, Africa; aorr1@k-state.edu

Orr, Suzanne (PhD, Notre Dame 2010; asst. prof.) 20th-century America, immigration, gender; sorr1@ksu.edu

Oweidat, Nadia (DPhil, Oxford 2014; asst. prof.) modern Middle East, Islamic thought, religious theories; oweidat@ksu.edu

Parillo, Mark P. (PhD, Ohio State 1987; prof.) US military, diplomatic, Japan; parillo@ksu.edu

Sanders, Charles W., Jr. (PhD, Kansas State 2001; assoc. prof.) 19th-century US, American Civil War, political and military; chassan@ksu.edu

Sherow, James E. (PhD, Colorado, Boulder 1987; prof.) American West, environmental, Kansas; jsherow@ksu.edu

Tiemeyer, Phil (PhD, Texas, Austin 2007; assoc. prof.) gender and sexuality, social, US foreign relations; tiemeyerp@ksu.edu

Williams, Lou Falkner (PhD, Florida 1991; assoc. prof.) US constitutional and legal, Civil War and Reconstruction, US South; lwill@ksu.edu

Retired/Emeritus Faculty

Ferguson, Clyde R. (PhD, Duke 1960; assoc. prof. emeritus) colonial and revolutionary America

Holl, Jack M. (PhD, Cornell 1969; prof. emeritus) recent US, science and technology, social; jackholl@ksu.edu

Linder, Robert D. (PhD, Iowa 1963; dist. prof. emeritus) Renaissance and Reformation, Christianity; rdl@ksu.edu

McCulloh, John M. (PhD, California, Berkeley 1971; prof. emeritus) medieval; jmmcc@ksu.edu

Smith, Sarah Anne (ABD, Indiana; Carey Fellow emeritus) medieval Europe, magic and occult, science; arcana@ksu.edu

Zschoche, Sue (PhD, Kansas 1984; retired assoc. prof.) US, social, women; suez@ksu.edu

Recently Awarded PhDs

Gresham, Daniel T. "Reshaping the Cattle Industry: The Origin of Collaboration between Big Producers and Big Meat Packers, 1914-33"

Scott, Mack H. "From a 'Great Tree' to a New Dawn: Race, Ethnogeneisis, and Indigeneity in Southern New England"

Kean University

Dept. of History, 212 Liberty Hall Academic Center, 1000 Morris Ave., Union, NJ 07083. 908.737.1830. Fax 908.737.1835. Email: kuhist@kean.edu. Website: http://history.kean.edu/.

The Department of History is one of Kean University's oldest and most productive programs of study and has been a part of the instructional component of the institution since its inception in 1855.

Chair: Elizabeth Hyde
Degrees Offered: BA
Academic Year System: Semester
Areas of Specialization: US, Asia, Europe, Latin America, world
Tuition (per academic year):
In-State: $7754
Out-of-State: $14521

Enrollment 2018-19:
Undergraduate Majors: 264
Degrees in History: 79 BA

Addresses:
Admissions: http://www.kean.edu/undergraduate-admissions
Financial Aid: http://www.kean.edu/offices/financial-aid

Full-time Faculty

Argote-Freyre, Frank (PhD, Rutgers 2004; assoc. prof.) Latin America; fargotef@kean.edu

Bellitto, Christopher M. (PhD, Fordham 1997; prof.) classics, early church; cbellitt@kean.edu

Esposito, Frank J. (PhD, Rutgers 1976; prof.) colonial America, American Indian; fesposit@kean.edu

Gronewold, Sue (PhD, Columbia 1996; assoc. prof.) Asia; sgronewo@kean.edu

Hyde, Elizabeth (PhD, Harvard 1998; prof. and chair) early modern Europe; ehyde@kean.edu

Klein, Dennis B. (PhD, Rochester 1978; prof.) Germany and central Europe, Judaic studies; dklein@kean.edu

Kong, Xurong (PhD, Wisconsin-Madison; asst. prof.) early Chinese poetry, Chinese art, Chinese history and civilization; xkong@kean.edu

Mercantini, Jonathan (PhD, Emory 2000; acting dean, Coll. of Liberal Arts) America; jmercant@kean.edu

Nicholson, Brid (PhD, Drew 2006; assoc. prof.) labor, women, Ireland; cnichols@kean.edu

Perkiss, Abigail L. (PhD, Temple 2010; asst. prof.) civil rights and intentional integration, historical memory and monuments; aperkiss@kean.edu

Regal, Brian (PhD, Drew 2001; assoc. prof.) science and technology; bregal@kean.edu

Wetta, Frank J. (PhD, Louisiana State 1977; sr. lect.) US, military; fwetta@kean.edu

Keene State College

Dept. of History, 229 Main St., Mail Stop 1301, Keene, NH 03435-1301. 603.358.2965. Fax 603.358.2257. Email: swade@keene.edu. Website: https://www.keene.edu/academics/programs/hist/.

KSC history majors communicate ideas effectively. And perhaps most importantly, they acquire a body of knowledge and perspectives that will enable them to understand contemporary events and trends as well as understand and appreciate the myriad cultures and civilizations that make up the world community.

Chair: Susan Wade
Degrees Offered: BA,MA
Academic Year System: Semester
Areas of Specialization: war/peace/society, gender/race/class, ideas and beliefs, media and popular culture, history and archives
Tuition (per academic year):
In-State: $10410
Out-of-State: $18800
Enrollment 2018-19:
Undergraduate Majors: 90
Degrees in History: 35 BA
Addresses:
Admissions: http://www.keene.edu/admissions/
Financial Aid: http://www.keene.edu/admissions/aid/

Adjunct Faculty

Whitcomb, Thomas (PhD, London 1979; adj.) Middle East, Africa, Islam; twhitcom@keene.edu

Full-time Faculty

Crocker, Matthew H. (PhD, Massachusetts Amherst 1997; prof.) early Republic, Jacksonian era, political; mcrocker@keene.edu

Germana, Nicholas A. (PhD, Boston Coll. 2006; assoc. prof.) Europe to 1800, intellectual; ngermana@keene.edu

Knouff, Gregory T. (PhD, Rutgers 1996; prof.) colonial and revolutionary America, race, gender; gknouff@keene.edu

Wade, Susan W. (PhD, NYU 2007; assoc. prof. and chair) medieval Europe, medieval Islamic world, gender; swade@keene.edu

Warder, Graham D. (PhD, Massachusetts Amherst 2000; assoc. prof.) 19th-century US, cultural; gwarder@keene.edu

Wilson, Andrew D. (PhD, Cornell 1989; prof.; Philosophy) modern Europe, history and philosophy of science, ancient Greece; awilson@keene.edu

Retired/Emeritus Faculty

Granquist, Carl R., Jr. (PhD, Wisconsin, Madison 1967; prof. emeritus) French Revolution, modern Europe; cgranqui@keene.edu

Kennesaw State University

Dept. of History and Philosophy, 402 Bartow Ave., MD 2206, Kennesaw, GA 30144-5591. 470.578.6294. Fax 470.578.9149. Email: histphildept@kennesaw.edu. Website: https://chss.kennesaw.edu/historyphilosophy/.

Our first mission as faculty of the Department is to provide the highest quality in teaching for each of our majors and general education students. Beyond careful conveyance of salient content, departmental instruction will strongly encourage development in higher-order thinking, meaningful self-reflection, and understanding.

Chair: Alice K. Pate
Degrees Offered: BA,BS
Academic Year System: Semester
Areas of Specialization: US social and cultural, US South, Europe, Asia, Africa
Tuition (per academic year):
In-State: $3228
Out-of-State: $8855
Enrollment 2018-19:
Undergraduate Majors: 460
Degrees in History: 51 BA, 24 BS
Addresses:
Admissions: http://admissions.kennesaw.edu
Financial Aid: http://financialaid.kennesaw.edu

Full-time Faculty

Adebayo, A. G. (PhD, Obafemi Awolowo, Nigeria 1986; prof.) Africa, African American; aadebayo@kennesaw.edu

Bartlett, Stephen M. (MA, Clemson 1997; sr. lect.) world; sbartlet@kennesaw.edu

Carroll, Fred (PhD, William and Mary 2012; lect.) black print culture, black press; fcarrol4@kennesaw.edu

Churella, Albert J. (PhD, Ohio State 1994; prof.) tourism and American Southwest; achurell@kennesaw.edu

Conner, Caroline J. (PhD, Georgia State 2015; asst. prof.) history education; conne33@kennesaw.edu

DeAngelo, Angela D. (MEd, West Georgia 2000; sr. lect.) adeangel@kennesaw.edu

Dickey, Jennifer (PhD, Georgia State 2007; assoc. prof.) public; jdickey2@kennesaw.edu

Dover, Paul Marcus (PhD, Yale 2002; assoc. prof.) medieval and Renaissance Europe; pdover@kennesaw.edu

Dunagin, Amy M. (PhD, Yale 2014; asst. prof.) cultural and political; adunagin@kennesaw.edu

Gentry, Jonathan (PhD, Brown 2015; asst. prof.) 19th-century Europe; jgentr30@kennesaw.edu

Gurkas, Hakki (PhD, Purdue 2008; assoc. prof.) Middle East, Turkey; hgurkas@kennesaw.edu

Holdzkom, Marianne (PhD, Ohio State 1995; assoc. prof.) America; mholdzko@kennesaw.edu

Holliman Way, Irene (PhD, Georgia 2010; lect.) America; iway@kennesaw.edu

Hurgobin, Yoshina (PhD, Syracuse 2016; asst. prof.) labor migration, citizenship, South Asian diaspora rights and nationalism; yhurgobi@kennesaw.edu

Laaman, John Henry (PhD, Auburn 2016; lect.) modern US, comparative world, Latin American, religious, peace movements; jlaaman@kennesaw.edu

Lands, LeeAnn Bishop (PhD, Georgia Tech 2001; assoc. prof.) US urban, US South; llands@kennesaw.edu

Lebaron, Alan V. (PhD, Florida 1988; prof.) Latin America, world; alebaron@kennesaw.edu

Lewis, Catherine (PhD, Iowa 1997; prof.) American studies; clewis1@kennesaw.edu

McCandless, Jamie (PhD, Western Michigan 2015; lect.) late Middle Ages, central Europe, religious; jmccandl@kennesaw.edu

McGovern, Bryan P. (PhD, Missouri, Columbia 2003; prof.) history education; bmcgover@kennesaw.edu

Mims, La Shonda C. (PhD, Georgia 2012; asst. prof.; Interdisciplinary Studies) US, gender and women's studies; lmims4@kennesaw.edu

Oakley, Eric O. (PhD, North Carolina, Greensboro 2017; lect.) colonial America, American Revolution, early US, Pacific world, East Asia; eoakley1@kennesaw.edu

Okie, William Thomas (PhD, Georgia 2012; asst. prof.) history education; wokie1@kennesaw.edu

Parker, David B. (PhD, North Carolina, Chapel Hill 1988; prof. and asst. chair) US South, US cultural; dparker@kennesaw.edu

Pate, Alice K. (PhD, Ohio State 1995; prof. and chair) Russia; apate9@kennesaw.edu

Patton, Randall L. (PhD, Georgia 1990; prof.) Georgia, US South, recent US; rpatton@kennesaw.edu

Racel, Masako N. (PhD, Georgia State 2011; asst. prof.) world, Japan, Indo-Japanese relations; mracel@kennesaw.edu

Reidy, Joseph Jude (PhD, St. Louis 2015; lect.) premodern Mediterranean, intellectual developments, religious dissent; jjr8934@kennesaw.edu

Ronnenberg, Ryan (PhD, Wisconsin, Madison 2006; assoc. prof.) world, Africa; pryan4@kennesaw.edu

Swain, Brian Sidney (MA, Ohio State 2009; asst. prof.) ancient world; bswain3@kennesaw.edu

Traille, E. Kay (PhD, London 2006; assoc. prof.) Britain; etraille@kennesaw.edu

Vaught, Seneca D. (PhD, Bowling Green State 2006; assoc. prof.) African American; svaught3@kennesaw.edu

Vickrey, Mark (MA, Appalachian State; sr. lect.) world, America; mvickre1@kennesaw.edu

Vladimirov, Katya V. (PhD, Georgetown 1998; prof.) Russia; kvladimi@kennesaw.edu

Voogt, Pieter G. (PhD, Georgia State 1997; prof.) early modern Europe; gvoogt@kennesaw.edu

Way, Albert G. (PhD, Georgia 2008; assoc. prof.) Georgia, US South; away5@kennesaw.edu

Wills, Brian S. (PhD, Georgia 1991; prof.) Civil War; bwills2@kennesaw.edu

Wynn, Charles Taylor, Sr. (PhD, Georgia State 1989; assoc. prof.) history education; cwynn6@kennesaw.edu

Zhang, Jiayan (PhD, UCLA 2004; prof.) modern China, East Asia; jzhang@kennesaw.edu

Retired/Emeritus Faculty

Keene, Thomas H. (PhD, Emory 1974; prof. emeritus)

Nystrom, Elsa A. (PhD, Loyola, Chicago 1989; prof. emeritus) 19th- and 20th-century American cultural, minorities and ethnicity, family; enystrom@kennesaw.edu

Papageorge, Linda M. (PhD, Michigan State 1973; assoc. prof. emeritus) diplomatic, modern China, early national US; lpapageo@kennesaw.edu

Piecuch, James R. (PhD, William and Mary 2005; prof. emeritus) colonial and revolutionary America, US diplomatic; jpiecuch@kennesaw.edu

Pullen, Ann W. Ellis (PhD, Georgia State 1975; prof. emeritus) race relations, women, US South; apullen@kennesaw.edu

Reeve, Kay A. (PhD, Texas A&M 1977; prof. emeritus) American West, 20th-century America, US social and cultural; kreeve@kennesaw.edu

Roach, Samuel F., Jr. (PhD, Oklahoma 1972; prof. emeritus) US social and cultural, US South; froach@kennesaw.edu

Scott, Thomas A. (PhD, Tennessee, Knoxville 1978; prof. emeritus) US, Georgia, social and cultural; tscott@kennesaw.edu

Shealy, E. Howard (PhD, Emory 1977; prof. emeritus) England; hshealy@kennesaw.edu

Tate, James B. (MA, George Peabody 1960; assoc. prof. emeritus) Civil War, recent US

Kent State University

Dept. of History, 305 Bowman Hall, Kent, OH 44242-0001. 330.672.2882. Fax 330.672.8902. Email: kadams9@kent.edu. Website: https://www.kent.edu/history.

The department offers both major and minor programs at the undergraduate level, as well as MA and PhD programs for advanced study in history. The department's course offerings at all levels are chronologically, geographically, and topically broad. With a presence on six of Kent State's eight campuses, the department's faculty presently number two dozen and include many award-winning teachers and researchers.

Chair: Kevin Adams
Director of Graduate Studies: Mary Ann Heiss
Director of Undergraduate Studies: Matthew Crawford
Degrees Offered: BA,MA,PhD
Academic Year System: Semester
Areas of Specialization: US, Europe since 1500, science and medicine
Undergraduate Tuition (per academic year): In-State: $9816 Out-of-State: $17776
Graduate Tuition (per academic year):
In-State: $10444
Out-of-State: $17960
Enrollment 2018-19:
Undergraduate Majors: 150
New Graduate Students: 23
Full-time Graduate Students: 19
Part-time Graduate Students: 19
Degrees in History: 80 BA, 7 MA, 4 PhD
Undergraduate Addresses:
Admissions: http://www.kent.edu/admissions/undergraduate
Financial Aid: http://www.kent.edu/tuition
Graduate Addresses:
Admissions: http://www.kent.edu/graduatestudies/admissions
Financial Aid: http://www.kent.edu/tuition

Full-time Faculty

Adams, Kevin John (PhD, California, Berkeley 2004; assoc. prof. and chair) US, war and society, Gilded Age; kadams9@kent.edu

Bindas, Kenneth J. (PhD, Toledo 1988; prof.) US, cultural; kbindas@kent.edu

Crawford, Matthew J. (PhD, California, San Diego 2009; asst. prof. and undergrad. coord.) science, medicine; mcrawf11@kent.edu

Frantz (Parsons), Elaine (PhD, Johns Hopkins 1998; prof.) violence, culture, 19th-century America; eparso12@kent.edu

Gruenwald, Kim M. (PhD, Colorado, Boulder 1994; assoc. prof.) colonial America; kgruenwa@kent.edu

Hayashi, Brian M. (PhD, UCLA 1990; prof.) Asian American, immigration, intelligence; bhayashi@kent.edu

Heaphy, Leslie A. (PhD, Toledo 1995; assoc. prof.; Stark) US, sports; lheaphy@kent.edu

Heiss, Mary Ann (PhD, Ohio State 1991; assoc. prof. and grad. coord.) US, diplomatic; mheiss@kent.edu

Hudson, Leonne M. (PhD, Kent State 1990; assoc. prof.) Civil War, African American; lhudson@kent.edu

Keefer, Bradley S. (PhD, Kent State 2006; assoc. prof.; Ashtabula) US; bkeefer@kent.edu

Li, Hongshan (PhD, Missouri, Columbia 1992; prof.; Tuscarawas) China, diplomatic; hli@kent.edu

Menning, Ralph (PhD, Brown 1986; asst. prof.; Stark) modern Europe; rmenning@kent.edu

Scarnecchia, Timothy L. (PhD, Michigan 1994; assoc. prof.) Africa; tscarnec@kent.edu

Seelye, James Edward, Jr. (PhD, Toledo 2010; asst. prof.) US; jseelye@kent.edu

Smith-Pryor, Elizabeth M. (PhD, Rutgers 2001; JD, Stanford Law Sch. 1987; asst. prof.) African American; esmith1@kent.edu

Steigmann-Gall, Richard Albert (PhD, Toronto 1999; assoc. prof.) modern Germany; rsteigma@kent.edu

Strate, Shane R. (PhD, Wisconsin, Madison 2009; asst. prof.) Southeast Asia; sstrate@kent.edu

Thyret, Isolde R. (PhD, Washington 1992; assoc. prof.) medieval Europe, medieval Russia; ithyret@kent.edu

Wamsley, E. Sue (PhD, Ohio State 1998; asst. prof.; Salem) US; ewamsley@kent.edu

Nondepartmental Historians

Booth, Stephane Elise (DA, Illinois State 1983; assoc. prof.; assoc. provost) US, women; sbooth@kent.edu

Retired/Emeritus Faculty

Beer, Barrett L. (PhD, Northwestern 1965; prof. emeritus) early modern England; bbeer@kent.edu

Bittle, William G. (PhD, Kent State 1975; assoc. prof. emeritus) Britain; wbittle@kent.edu

Calkins, Kenneth R. (PhD, Chicago 1966; prof. emeritus) modern Europe, Germany; kcalk@aol.com

Ekechi, Felix K. (PhD, Wisconsin, Madison 1969; prof. emeritus) Africa; fekechi@kent.edu

Friedman, Jerome (PhD, Wisconsin, Madison 1971; prof. emeritus) Renaissance and Reformation

Hubbell, John T. (PhD, Illinois, Urbana-Champaign 1969; prof. emeritus) US, Civil War

Jameson, John R. (PhD, Toledo 1974; prof. emeritus) public, 20th-century US; jjameson@kent.edu

Kaplan, Lawrence S. (PhD, Yale 1951; Univ. prof. emeritus) early national US, diplomatic; lkaplan24@aol.com

Kenney, William H. (PhD, Pennsylvania 1966; prof. emeritus) US, colonial, music; wkenney@kent.edu

Knopf, Richard C. (PhD, Ohio State 1960; prof. emeritus) US, Ohio

LeBrun, John L. (PhD, Case Western Reserve 1975; prof. emeritus) modern America

Morris, John D. (PhD, Rochester 1970; assoc. prof. emeritus) US, Britain, modern Europe

Newman, Gerald G. (PhD, Harvard 1971; prof. emeritus) modern England

Papacosma, S. Victor (PhD, Indiana 1971; prof. emeritus) modern Europe, Balkans; spapacos@kent.edu

Patras, Louis (PhD, Ohio State 1966; prof. emeritus) modern Europe

Snyder, John W. (PhD, Minnesota 1954; prof. emeritus) ancient

Sosnowski, Thomas (PhD, Kent State 1975; assoc. prof. emeritus) France; tsosnow1@kent.edu

Swierenga, Robert P. (PhD, Iowa 1965; prof. emeritus) US, economic; swierenga@hope.edu

Wang, Yeh-chien (PhD, Harvard 1969; prof. emeritus) East Asia

Weeks, Philip (PhD, Case Western Reserve 1989; prof. emeritus) US, Native American; pweeks@kent.edu

Wilson, Glee E. (PhD, Washington 1971; assoc. prof. emeritus) ancient, Greece

Wunderlin, Clarence E., Jr. (PhD, Northern Illinois 1987; prof. emeritus) US, economic, political; cwunderl@kent.edu

Recently Awarded PhDs

Baehler, Joel Edward "Robert Martin, Citizenship, and Identity in Post-WWII Gay Rights Movement"

Cornell, Michele Curran "Gender, Love, and Duty: Patriotic Romance during the Second World War"

Demaree, David "Perceptions of Lincoln's Manhood: The Rise of Hardy 'American' Manliness in the North, 1848-63"

Goodnough, Michael Daniel "Don't Leave Me This Way: Power and Exclusion in the 1970s Health Boom"

Pride, Aaron "For Every Right with All Thy Might: William Monroe Trotter's Crusade for an Interracial Society, 1872-1919"

University of Kentucky

Dept. of History, 1715 Patterson Office Tower, Lexington, KY 40506-0027. 859.257.6861. Fax 859.323.3885. Email: petrone@uky.edu. Website: https://history.as.uky.edu/.

The Department of History of the University of Kentucky is a vibrant center of scholarship and teaching that has been training students for over 80 years.

Chair: Karen Petrone
Director of Graduate Studies: David E. Hamilton
Director of Undergraduate Studies: Erik Lars Myrup
Degrees Offered: BA, MA, PhD
Academic Year System: Semester
Areas of Specialization: US political, premodern/early modern/modern Europe, religion, women and gender, culture/ideas/society, Appalachia, US South, Africa, African American, race and gender, memory studies, Atlantic world
Undergraduate Tuition (per academic year):
  In-State: $12244
  Out-of-State: $29098
Graduate Tuition (per academic year):
  In-State: $13052
  Out-of-State: $31364
Enrollment 2018-19:
  Undergraduate Majors: 350
  New Graduate Students: 8
  Full-time Graduate Students: 40
  Degrees in History: 75 BA, 6 MA, 1 PhD
Undergraduate Addresses:
  Admissions: http://history.as.uky.edu/history-admission
  Financial Aid: http://www.uky.edu/financialaid/
Graduate Addresses:
  Admissions: https://history.as.uky.edu/admission1
  Financial Aid: https://history.as.uky.edu/funding-0

Full-time Faculty

Albisetti, James C. (PhD, Yale 1976; prof.) Germany, European intellectual, social and women; jcalbi01@uky.edu

Bobadilla, Eladio B. (PhD, Duke 2019; asst. prof.) US, Chicanx and Latinx, immigration, oral, social movements; eladio.bobadilla@uky.edu

Calvert, Jane E. (PhD, Chicago 2003; assoc. prof.) American Revolution, early Republic; jane.calvert@uky.edu

Campbell, Tracy (PhD, Duke 1988; E. Vernon Smith Prof.) 20th-century US, Kentucky; tracamp@uky.edu

Chassen-Lopez, Francie R. (PhD, Nacional Autónoma, Mexico 1986; prof.) Latin America, Mexico, gender; frclopz@uky.edu

Christianson, Eric H. (PhD, Southern California 1976; assoc. prof.) US, science and medicine; ehchri01@uky.edu

Clark, J.M.H. (PhD, Johns Hopkins 2016; asst. prof.) Atlantic slavery, Latin American studies; jmhclark@uky.edu

Curwood, Anastasia C. (PhD, Princeton 2003; assoc. prof.; African American and Africana Studies) African American, diaspora; anastasia.curwood@uky.edu

Davis, Stephen R. (PhD, Florida 2010; assoc. prof.) precolonial Africa, South Africa, digital; srda227@g.uky.edu

Firey, Abigail A. (PhD, Toronto 1995; prof.) early medieval, canon law; afire2@uky.edu

Gargola, Daniel J. (PhD, North Carolina, Chapel Hill 1988; prof.) ancient, Rome; djgarg01@uky.edu

Goan, Melanie Beals (PhD, Kentucky 1999; assoc. prof.) Kentucky, US, gender; melanie.goan@uky.edu

Hamilton, David E. (PhD, Iowa 1985; assoc. prof. and dir., grad. studies) recent US, political; dehami01@uky.edu

Harling, Philip (PhD, Princeton 1992; prof.) modern Britain; harling@uky.edu

Holden, Vanessa M. (PhD, Rutgers 2012; asst. prof.) African American, black Atlantic, Africana studies; vanessa.holden@uky.edu

Holle, Bruce F. (PhD, Michigan 1978; assoc. prof.) Europe, ancient; bholl2@uky.edu

Kern, Kathi (PhD, Pennsylvania 1989; assoc. prof.) American women and religious; kern@uky.edu

Mokros, Emily (PhD, Johns Hopkins 2016; asst. prof.) China, political culture and authority, late imperial and modern China; emily.mokros@uky.edu

Musoni, Francis (PhD, Emory 2011; assoc. prof.) Africa; francis.musoni@uky.edu

Myrup, Erik Lars (PhD, Yale 2006; assoc. prof. and dir., undergrad. studies) Atlantic world; erik.myrup@uky.edu

Newfont, Kathryn (PhD, North Carolina, Chapel Hill 2001; assoc. prof.) Appalachia, US South

Olster, David M. (PhD, Chicago 1986; prof.) Rome and Byzantine; dmolst01@uky.edu

Petrone, Karen (PhD, Michigan 1994; prof. and chair) modern Russia and Soviet, gender; petrone@uky.edu

Popkin, Jeremy D. (PhD, California, Berkeley 1977; William T. Bryan Chair Prof.) Europe 1700-1870, French Revolution, historical method and theory; popkin@uky.edu

Smith, Gerald L. (PhD, Kentucky 1988; prof.) American urban, African American; glsmit01@uky.edu

Summers, Mark W. (PhD, California, Berkeley 1980; Clark Prof.) 19th-century US; msumm2@uky.edu

Takenaka, Akiko (PhD, Yale 2004; assoc. prof.) modern Japan; a.takenaka@uky.edu

Taylor, Amy Murrell (PhD, Virginia 2001; prof.) 19th-century US South; amtaylor1@uky.edu

Taylor, Scott K. (PhD, Virginia 2001; assoc. prof.) early modern Europe; scottktaylor@uky.edu

Whitlock, Tammy C. (PhD, Rice 1998; assoc. prof.) Victorian, early Britain; hrhwhitlock@uky.edu

Joint/Cross Appointments

Clark, Claire Ducharme (PhD, Emory 2014; asst. prof.; Behavioral Science) medicine and addiction; claire.clark@uky.edu

Diaz, Monica (PhD, Indiana 2002; assoc. prof.; Hispanic Studies) international studies, social theory, Latin America and Caribbean; monica.diaz@uky.edu

Stein, Melissa N. (PhD, Rutgers 2008; assoc. prof.; Gender and Women's Studies) gender studies, race and ethnicity, women and gender, science and medicine, US African American, cultural and intellectual, sexuality, LGBT, queer studies, critical race studies; melissa.stein@uky.edu

Vivian, Daniel J. (PhD, Johns Hopkins 2011; assoc. prof.; Historic Preservation) 19th- and 20th-century US, public; daniel.vivian@uky.edu

Kenyon College

Dept. of History, Seitz House, 104 East Wiggin St., Gambier, OH 43022. 740.427.5316. Fax 740.427.5762. Email: bursonp@kenyon.edu. Website: https://www.kenyon.edu/academics/departments-programs/history/.

As historians, we shape and articulate our own narratives and understandings of historical evidence. We discern and analyze varieties of and connections among human experiences. Through departmental course offerings, the major, and participation in interdisciplinary studies, we teach students to join us in exploring the world's past.

Chair: Eliza Ablovatski
Degrees Offered: BA
Academic Year System: Semester
Areas of Specialization: Europe, US, Africa, Asia, Islamic
Tuition (per academic year): $71150
Enrollment 2018-19:
  Undergraduate Majors: 62
  Degrees in History: 22 BA
Addresses:
  Admissions and Financial Aid: http://www.kenyon.edu/admissions-aid/

Full-time Faculty

Ablovatski, Eliza (PhD, Columbia 2005; assoc. prof. and chair) central and eastern Europe, European women, European Jewish; ablovatskie@kenyon.edu

Bae, Kyoungjin (PhD, Columbia 2016; James P. Storer Prof.) Asian studies, early modern Eurasia and China, early modern Europe and Asia; baek@kenyon.edu

Bottiger, Patrick Gary (PhD, Oklahoma 2009; assoc. prof.) American Indian, pre-Civil War US, Latin America; bottigerp@kenyon.edu

Bowman, Jeffrey A. (PhD, Yale 1997; prof. and assoc. provost) medieval, France and Spain, Mediterranean; bowmanj@kenyon.edu

Coulibaly, Sylvie (PhD, Emory 2005; assoc. prof.) African American, Africa, US; coulibalys@kenyon.edu

Dunnell, Ruth (PhD, Princeton 1983; prof. emeritus) China, Inner Asia, Mongol Empire; dunnell@kenyon.edu

Gourrier, Francis, Jr. (ABD, Wisconsin-Madison; asst. prof.; American Studies) African American, civil rights/black freedom movement/Black Power, black women; gourrier@kenyon.edu

Kilic-Schubel, Nurten (PhD, Ankara, Turkey 1999; assoc. prof.) Islamic world, premodern Central Eurasia, Islamic women and gender; kilicn@kenyon.edu

Kinzer, Bruce L. (PhD, Toronto 1975; prof.) modern Britain, British Empire; kinzerb@kenyon.edu

McNair, Glenn (PhD, Emory 2001; prof.) early and modern African American, slavery/civil rights/US South, African American political and intellectual culture; mcnairg@kenyon.edu

Singer, Wendy (PhD, Virginia 1991; Roy T. Wortman Dist. prof.) India and South Asia, Indian politics, globalization and migration; singerw@kenyon.edu

Suarez-Potts, William J. (PhD, Harvard 2005; JD, Pennsylvania 1987; assoc. prof.) Latin America, Mexico, international relations/legal and labor; suarezpottsw@kenyon.edu

Volz, Stephen (PhD, Wisconsin, Madison 2006; R. Todd Ruppert assoc. prof.; dir., International Studies) southern Africa, colonialism, religion; volzs@kenyon.edu

Nondepartmental Historians

Rutkoff, Peter M. (PhD, Pennsylvania 1971; prof.; American Studies) modern America, American studies, urban education; rutkoff@kenyon.edu

Retired/Emeritus Faculty

Browning, Reed S. (PhD, Yale 1965; prof. emeritus) Britain; browninr@kenyon.edu

Scott, William B. (PhD, Wisconsin, Madison 1973; prof. emeritus) America, US South; scott@kenyon.edu

Visiting Faculty

Cantisano, Pedro (PhD, Michigan 2018; vis. asst. prof.) modern and colonial Latin America, law/human rights, environmental and rights in Americas; cantisanop@kenyon.edu

Hunt, Catalina (PhD, Ohio State 2015; vis. asst. prof.) borderland identities, migrations, gender; hunt2@kenyon.edu

Novikoff, Alex J. (PhD, Pennsylvania 2007; vis. asst. prof.) medieval, intellectual and cultural, interfaith relations and historiography; novikoff1@kenyon.edu

Kutztown University

Dept. of History, 115 Lytle Hall, PO Box 730, Kutztown, PA 19530-0730. 610.683.4385. Fax 610.683.4047. Email: arnold@kutztown.edu; manmille@kutztown.edu. Website: http://www.kutztown.edu/history.

The history department offers a BA in History and a BA in History with Paralegal degree, as well as provides core classes for the BS degree in Secondary Education. The department has designed a curriculum that prepares students for diverse careers and for advanced study at the graduate level.

Chair: Andrew Arnold
Degrees Offered: BA,BS,BSSecEd
Academic Year System: Semester
Areas of Specialization: US, Europe, non-Western/Africa/Asia/Latin America, world, social studies education
Tuition (per academic year):
In-State: $10448
Out-of-State: $12442
Enrollment 2018-19:
Undergraduate Majors: 180
Degrees in History: 21 BA, 15 BS
Addresses:
Admissions: http://www.kutztown.edu/admissions.htm
Financial Aid: http://www.kutztown.edu/financialaid

Full-time Faculty

Arnold, Andrew B. (PhD, North Carolina, Chapel Hill 2002; prof. and chair) Pennsylvania, constitutional; arnold@kutztown.edu

Delaney, John J. (PhD, SUNY, Buffalo 1995; prof.) modern Europe, Germany, Holocaust; delaney@kutztown.edu

Derr, Patricia Norred (PhD, Missouri, Columbia 1996; assoc. prof.) American cultural and religious, early America, African American; derr@kutztown.edu

Gabriel, Michael P. (PhD, Penn State 1996; prof.) colonial and revolutionary America, Civil War, public; gabriel@kutztown.edu

Gambone, Michael David (PhD, Chicago 1993; prof.) Latin America, recent US, military; gambone@kutztown.edu

Johnson, Eric F. (PhD, UCLA 2003; assoc. prof.) early modern Europe; ejohnson@kutztown.edu

Kelleher, Patricia (PhD, Wisconsin, Madison 1995; prof.) US social, immigration, urban and women; kelleher@kutztown.edu

Reynolds, Robert (PhD, Lehigh 2003; assoc. prof.) Pennsylvania German, environmental, colonial; reynolds@kutztown.edu

Rodriquez, Louis (PhD, Lehigh 1997; asst. prof.) recent US, minorities, business; rodrique@kutztown.edu

Saidi, Christine (PhD, UCLA 1996; prof.) Africa; saidi@kutztown.edu

Sanelli, Maria F. (EdD, Pacific 1998; assoc. prof.; Secondary Education) social studies education, US; msanelli@kutztown.edu

Stanley, John R. (PhD, London 2003; assoc. prof.) East Asia; stanley@kutztown.edu

Lafayette College

Dept. of History, Ramer History House, 718 Sullivan Rd., Easton, PA 18042-1768. 610.330.5167. Fax 610.330.5176. Email: barclayp@lafayette.edu. Website: https://history.lafayette.edu/.

Students taking history courses at Lafayette acquire knowledge about past events around the globe, develop analytical skills, and are taught to think both about historical specificities and about connections across time and space. The curriculum also teaches apprentice historians how to ask important questions about the past, how to research answers to those questions, and then how to communicate findings in compelling prose and clear oral presentations.

Chair: Paul Barclay
Degrees Offered: BA
Academic Year System: Semester
Areas of Specialization: global, Russia, East Asia, South Asia, Latin America, Africa, Middle East, US, premodern and modern Europe
Tuition (per academic year): $54512
Enrollment 2018-19:
Undergraduate Majors: 20
Degrees in History: 35 BA
Addresses:
Admissions: http://admissions.lafayette.edu/
Financial Aid: https://admissions.lafayette.edu/financial-aid/

Full-time Faculty

Barclay, Paul David (PhD, Minnesota 1999; prof. and head) modern Japan, East Asia; barclayp@lafayette.edu

Goshgarian, Rachel (PhD, Harvard 2008; assoc. prof.) Middle Eastern studies; goshgarr@lafayette.edu

Jackson, Donald C (PhD, Pennsylvania 1986; prof.) technology, modern US, American West; jacksond@lafayette.edu

Kanjwal, Hafsa (PhD, Michigan 2017; asst. prof.) South Asia, gender, decolonization; kanjwalh@lafayette.edu

Lee, Christopher J. (PhD, Stanford 2003; assoc. prof.) Africa; leechris@lafayette.edu

Pite, Rebekah E. (PhD, Michigan 2007; assoc. prof.) Latin America and Caribbean, women; piter@lafayette.edu

Rosen, Deborah A. (PhD, Columbia 1990; prof.) early America, legal and constitutional; rosend@lafayette.edu

Sanborn, Joshua (PhD, Chicago 1998; prof.) Russia and Soviet Union, war and society, gender; sanbornj@lafayette.edu

Weiner, Robert I. (PhD, Rutgers 1974; prof.) modern Europe, diplomatic, Jewish; weinerr@lafayette.edu

Zallen, Jeremy (PhD, Harvard 2014; asst. prof.) US, race and ethnicity, environmental; zallenj@lafayette.edu

Retired/Emeritus Faculty

Miller, Donald L. (PhD, Maryland, Coll. Park 1972; prof. emeritus) US social, urban, intellectual; millerd@lafayette.edu

Offner, Arnold A. (PhD, Indiana 1964; prof. emeritus) American diplomatic, 20th-century America; offnera@lafayette.edu

Sharpless, Richard E. (PhD, Rutgers 1975; prof. emeritus) Latin America

Lake Forest College

Dept. of History, 555 N. Sheridan Rd., Lake Forest, IL 60045-2399. 847.735.5121. Fax 847.735.6193. Email: lemahieu@mx.lakeforest.edu. Website: http://www.lakeforest.edu/academics/programs/history/.

Lake Forest College affirms that education ennobles the individual. Our curriculum engages students in the breadth of the liberal arts and the depth of traditional disciplines. We encourage students to read critically, reason analytically, communicate persuasively, and, above all, to think for themselves. We prepare our students for, and help them attain, productive and rewarding careers. We foster creative talent and independent research. We embrace cultural diversity. We honor achievement. Our faculty of distinguished scholars takes pride in its commitment to teaching. We know our students by name and prepare them to become responsible citizens of the global community. We enable students, faculty, trustees, and administrators to solve problems in a civil manner, collectively. We maintain a secure residential campus of great beauty. We enrich our curriculum with the vibrant resources of Chicago. Lake Forest College celebrates the personal growth that accompanies the quest for excellence.

Chair: D. L. LeMahieu
Degrees Offered: BA
Academic Year System: Semester
Areas of Specialization: US, Europe, Asia, ancient and medieval
Tuition (per academic year): $47064
Enrollment 2018-19:
　Undergraduate Majors: 31
　Degrees in History: 11 BA
Addresses:
　Admissions: http://www.lakeforest.edu/admissions/
　Financial Aid: http://www.lakeforest.edu/admissions/finaid/

Full-time Faculty

Batzell, Rudi E. (PhD, Harvard 2017; asst. prof.) US, economic, social; batzell@mx.lakeforest.edu

Cain, Courtney (PhD, Illinois, Urbana-Champaign 2017; asst. prof.; African American Studies) African American, US, African diaspora; cain@mx.lakeforest.edu

Chen, Shiwei (PhD, Harvard 1998; prof.) East Asia, modern China; chen@lakeforest.edu

Groeger, Cristina V. (PhD, Harvard 2017; asst. prof.) US, education, urban; groeger@mx.lakeforest.edu

LeMahieu, D. L. (PhD, Harvard 1973; prof. and chair) modern Britain, modern Europe; lemahieu@lakeforest.edu

Joint/Cross Appointments

Jones, Anna Trumbore (PhD, Columbia 2003; prof.; assoc. dean, Faculty) medieval, ancient; jones@lakeforest.edu

Roman, Emilie (PhD, Aix-Marseille; lect.; Modern Languages and Literatures) American civilization, history and memory; roman@lakeforest.edu

Part-time Faculty

Ordman, Jilana (PhD, Loyola, Chicago 2013; lect.) ancient, medieval; ordman@lakeforest.edu

Retired/Emeritus Faculty

Ebner, Michael H. (PhD, Virginia 1974; prof. emeritus) modern America, urban, social; ebner@lakeforest.edu

Gayle, Carol (MA, Columbia 1961; assoc. prof. emeritus) modern Europe, Russia; gayle@lakeforest.edu

Georges, Pericles B. (PhD, California, Berkeley 1981; assoc. prof. emeritus) ancient Greece, Rome, medieval; georges@lakeforest.edu

Rosswurm, Steven (PhD, Northern Illinois 1979; prof. emeritus) US, gender, Mexico; rosswurm@lakeforest.edu

Spadafora, David (PhD, Yale 1981; prof. emeritus) Europe, British intellectual

Visiting Faculty

Blan, Noah (PhD, Michigan 2018; vis. asst. prof.) medieval, environmental; blan@lakeforest.edu

Lamar University

Dept. of History, PO Box 10048, Beaumont, TX 77710-0048. 409.880.8511. Fax 409.880.8710. Email: mamengerink@lamar.edu. Website: https://www.lamar.edu/arts-sciences/history/.

The history department uses the exploration of the past to provide students the intellectual tools to become informed, responsible citizens. The department specializes in the fields of American, European, Asian, and African history and offers both bachelor's and master's degrees as well as a combined BA/MA fast-track program.

Chair: Mark Mengerink, interim
Director of Graduate Studies: Jeffrey Forret
Degrees Offered: BA,MA
Academic Year System: Semester
Areas of Specialization: US and Texas, world, Europe, Asia, Africa
Undergraduate Tuition (per academic year):
　In-State: $10092
　Out-of-State: $22630
Graduate Tuition (per academic year):
　In-State: $8174
　Out-of-State: $15644
Enrollment 2018-19:
　Undergraduate Majors: 65
　Full-time Graduate Students: 9
　Part-time Graduate Students: 2
　Degrees in History: 12 BA, 1 MA

Undergraduate Addresses:
Admissions: http://www.lamar.edu/admissions/
Financial Aid: http://financialaid.lamar.edu/
Graduate Addresses:
Admissions: http://graduatestudies.lamar.edu/admissions/
Financial Aid: http://financialaid.lamar.edu/

Full-time Faculty

Boone, Rebecca Ard (PhD, Rutgers 2000; prof.) early modern Europe, intellectual and cultural, Renaissance France and Italy; rebecca.boone@lamar.edu

Bryan, Jimmy L., Jr. (PhD, Southern Methodist 2006; assoc. prof.) Civil War, Texas, American West; jlbryan@lamar.edu

Carroll, John M. (PhD, Kentucky 1973; prof.) American diplomatic, sports, 20th-century US; jmcarroll1@my.lamar.edu

Chavez, Miguel M. (PhD, California, Los Angeles 2010; asst. prof.) Chicana/o, US; miguel.chavez@lamar.edu

Forret, Jeffrey Paul (PhD, Delaware 2003; prof. and dir., grad. studies) colonial America, US South; forretjp@lamar.edu

Gillis, Brendan J. (PhD, Indiana 2015; asst. prof.) British Empire, colonial North America, legal; bgillis@lamar.edu

Kibbe, Tina M. (PhD, SUNY, Buffalo 2012; instr.) US, science and medicine, US women; tkibbe@lamar.edu

Mengerink, Mark A (PhD, Toledo 2006; assoc. prof. and interim chair) modern Europe and Middle East, Nazi Germany; mamengerink@my.lamar.edu

Muzorewa, Gwinyai P. (PhD, Morgan State 2012; asst. prof.) Africa/African American studies; gmuzorewa@lamar.edu

Poston, Ken (MA, Lamar 1995; instr.) US and Texas; kposton@lamar.edu

Sato, Yasuko (PhD, Chicago 2002; asst. prof.) premodern and modern East Asia, Japan/China/Pacific theater in World War II, Cold War in East Asia; ysato@lamar.edu

Scheer, Mary L. (PhD, Texas Christian 2000; prof.) modern US, Texas, US social/women/presidents; mary.scheer@my.lamar.edu

Seratt, Jim (MA, Rowan 1995; instr.) US; serattjd@my.lamar.edu

Retired/Emeritus Faculty

Storey, John W. (PhD, Kentucky 1968; prof. emeritus) American intellectual, American religious, southern religious; storeyjw@my.lamar.edu

Thompson, Jerry Lee (PhD, Texas A&M 1996; prof. emeritus) modern Britain, modern Europe, modern US; jlthompson1@my.lamar.edu

Wooster, Ralph A. (PhD, Texas, Austin 1954; dist. prof. emeritus) Old US South, Civil War, Texas

Lander University

Dept. of History and Philosophy, 320 Stanley Ave., Greenwood, SC 29649. 864.388.8261. Fax 864.388.8890. Email: kwitherspoon@lander.edu. Website:

To understand the present—and prepare for the future—you must first know the past. At Lander, we'll take you on a journey through history and philosophy, guiding you through a rich tapestry of cultures, civilizations, movements, and ideas.

Chair: Kevin B. Witherspoon
Degrees Offered: BA,BS,BSEd
Academic Year System: Semester
Areas of Specialization: US, Europe, Korea/China/Japan, military and diplomatic
Tuition (per academic year):
In-State: $10104
Out-of-State: $19018

Enrollment 2018-19:
Undergraduate Majors: 78
Degrees in History: 16 BA, 8 BS
Addresses:
Admissions: http://www.lander.edu/sites/office-of-admissions
Financial Aid: http://www.lander.edu/sites/financial-aid-office

Full-time Faculty

Figueira, Robert C. (PhD, Cornell 1980; prof.) ancient, medieval, Renaissance Europe; figueira@lander.edu

Floyd, Michael Ryan (PhD, Alabama 2010; assoc. prof.) US since 1877, US diplomatic, secondary social studies education; mrfloyd@lander.edu

Ramsey, William Little, III (PhD, Tulane 1998; prof.) early America, frontier and borderlands, slavery; wramsey@lander.edu

Rausch, Franklin David (PhD, British Columbia 2011; assoc. prof.) Asian studies, Korea, religious; fdrausch@hotmail.com

Witherspoon, Kevin B. (PhD, Florida State 2003; prof. and chair) US since 1877, Cold War studies, sports; kwitherspoon@lander.edu

Retired/Emeritus Faculty

Cleland, Joel S. (PhD, South Carolina 1974; prof. emeritus) modern Europe, Latin America

Mufuka, N. Kenneth (PhD, Queen's, Can. 1975; prof. emeritus) Africa, India

Paquette, Jean (PhD, UCLA 1987; prof. emerita) modern Europe, Britain and British Empire, East Asia

La Salle University

Dept. of History, 1900 W. Olney Ave., Philadelphia, PA 19141-1199. 215.951.1090. Fax 215.991.3554. Email: leibiger@lasalle.edu. Website: https://www.lasalle.edu/history/.

If the past, as is often said, is a foreign country, the modern traveler needs to know something of its language, geography, and customs. Everyone and everything has a past, and close, systematic study of these pasts can yield important insights about the present and, sometimes, clues about the future.

Chair: Stuart Leibiger
Director of Graduate Studies: George B. Stow
Degrees Offered: BA,MA
Academic Year System: Semester
Areas of Specialization: America, Europe, Third World, Asia, Latin America
Undergraduate Tuition (per academic year): $30700
Graduate Tuition (per academic year): $13230
Enrollment 2018-19:
Undergraduate Majors: 51
New Graduate Students: 1
Part-time Graduate Students: 8
Degrees in History: 19 BA, 1 MA
Undergraduate Addresses:
Admissions: http://www.lasalle.edu/admission/
Financial Aid: http://www.lasalle.edu/financialaid/
Graduate Addresses:
Admissions: http://www.lasalle.edu/grad/
Financial Aid: http://www.lasalle.edu/financialaid/

Adjunct Faculty

Frassetto, Michael (PhD, Delaware 1993; adj. instr.) world; frassetto83@lasalle.edu

Kamper, Kathleen G. (ABD, Notre Dame; adj. instr.) England, Ireland, 19th-century America; kamper@lasalle.edu

McKee, Francis (MA, Villanova 1976; adj. instr.; dir., American Studies) US; mckeef@lasalle.edu

Prendergast, John A. (MA, La Salle 2013; adj. instr.) US; prendergastj1@lasalle.edu

Roessner, Patricia (MA, La Salle 2007; adj. instr.) modern America, world; roessner@lasalle.edu

Full-time Faculty

Allen, Barbara C. (PhD, Indiana 2001; assoc. prof.) modern Russia and Soviet Union; allenb@lasalle.edu

Desnoyers, Charles A. (PhD, Temple 1988; prof.) modern East Asia; desnoyer@lasalle.edu

Jallow, Baba Galleh (PhD, California, Davis 2011; asst. prof.) Africa

Jarvinen, Lisa (PhD, Syracuse 2006; assoc. prof.) modern American social and cultural, Latin America, film; jarvinen@lasalle.edu

Leibiger, Stuart (PhD, North Carolina, Chapel Hill 1995; prof. and chair) revolutionary/early national/Civil War America, US founders and presidents, US Constitution; leibiger@lasalle.edu

Sheehy, Edward J. (PhD, George Washington 1983; assoc. prof.) modern America, US maritime and military, diplomacy; sheehy@lasalle.edu

Stebbins, H. Lyman (PhD, Chicago 2009; assoc. prof.) modern Britain, British Empire, modern Middle East

Stow, George B., Jr. (PhD, Illinois, Urbana-Champaign 1972; prof. and dir., grad. studies) classical world, medieval Europe; stow@lasalle.edu

Retired/Emeritus Faculty

Rossi, John P. (PhD, Pennsylvania 1965; prof. emeritus) modern Britain and Ireland, World War II, American baseball; rossi@lasalle.edu

Ryan, Francis (EdD, Temple 1987; prof. emeritus) 19th- and 20th-century American social and intellectual, American studies; ryan@lasalle.edu

Lehigh University

Dept. of History, 9 W. Packer Ave., Bethlehem, PA 18015-3081. 610.758.3360. Fax 610.758.6554. Email: inhis@lehigh.edu. Website: http://history.cas2.lehigh.edu/.

The department, like the university as a whole, combines two models-the liberal arts college, with a strong commitment to undergraduate education, and the research institution, dedicated to the creation of new knowledge.

Chair: Scott Gordon
Director of Graduate Studies: John Savage
Degrees Offered: BA,MA,PhD
Academic Year System: Semester
Areas of Specialization: colonial America, US, Atlantic world empires, public, gender
Undergraduate Tuition (per academic year): $47920
Graduate Tuition (per academic year): $24760
Enrollment 2018-19:
  Undergraduate Majors: 20
  New Graduate Students: 3
  Full-time Graduate Students: 33
  Part-time Graduate Students: 12
  Degrees in History: 10 BA, 4 MA, 3 PhD
Undergraduate Addresses:
  Admissions: http://www4.lehigh.edu/admissions/undergrad
  Financial Aid: http://www4.lehigh.edu/admissions/undergrad/tuition

Graduate Addresses:
  Admissions and Financial Aid: https://history.cas2.lehigh.edu/content/graduate-program

Full-time Faculty

Bulman, William J. (PhD, Princeton 2010; assoc. prof.) Britain and British Empire, religion, intellectual; wib311@lehigh.edu

Cooper, Gail (PhD, California, Santa Barbara 1987; assoc. prof.) technology, Japan; gail.cooper@lehigh.edu

Duncan, Natanya (PhD, Florida 2009; asst. prof.) African American, gender, African diaspora; nad415@lehigh.edu

Essien, Kwame (PhD, Texas, Austin 2010; assoc. prof.; Africana Studies Prog.) Africa, African diaspora; kwe212@lehigh.edu

Lebovic, Nitzan (PhD, UCLA 2005; assoc. prof.) German-Jewish culture, Holocaust, intellectual; nil210@lehigh.edu

LeMaster, Michelle M. (PhD, Johns Hopkins 2002; assoc. prof.) colonial and Atlantic world, Native American, gender; mil206@lehigh.edu

Najar, Monica E. (PhD, Wisconsin, Madison 2000; assoc. prof.) revolutionary and early national US, women, American religion; mon2@lehigh.edu

Peçe, Ugur Z. (PhD, Stanford 2016; asst. prof.) Ottoman Empire, Middle East, global; uzp218@lehigh.edu

Savage, John M. (PhD, NYU 1999; assoc. prof. and dir., grad. studies) French Atlantic world, European social and cultural, law and slavery; savage@lehigh.edu

Smith, John K. (PhD, Delaware 1986; assoc. prof.) technology; jks0@lehigh.edu

Zepeda Cortes, Maria Barbara (PhD, California, San Diego 2013; asst. prof.) Latin America, imperial Spain; maz213@lehigh.edu

Retired/Emeritus Faculty

Baylor, Michael (PhD, Stanford 1971; prof. emeritus) early modern Europe, Germany, European intellectual; mgb2@lehigh.edu

Cutcliffe, Stephen H. (PhD, Lehigh 1976; prof. emeritus) American technology, environmental; shc0@lehigh.edu

Goldman, Steven (PhD, Boston Univ. 1971; prof. emeritus) science, technology, social; slg2@lehigh.edu

Phillips, C. Robert III (PhD, Brown 1974; prof. emeritus) ancient, Roman law, Roman religion; crp0@lehigh.edu

Saeger, James S. (PhD, Ohio State 1969; prof. emeritus) Latin America, imperial Spain; jss0@lehigh.edu

Scott, William Randolph (PhD, Princeton 1972; prof. emeritus) Africa, African American; wrs4@lehigh.edu

Simon, Roger D. (PhD, Wisconsin, Madison 1971; prof. emeritus) US 1870-1920, social, urban; rds2@lehigh.edu

Soderlund, Jean (PhD, Temple 1982; prof. emeritus) colonial America, African American, US women; jrsa@lehigh.edu

Lehman College, City University of New York

Dept. of History, 202 Carman Hall, 250 Bedford Park Blvd. W., Bronx, NY 10468. 718.960.8288. Fax 718.960.1104. Email: marie.marianetti@lehman.cuny.edu. Website: http://www.lehman.edu/academics/arts-humanities/history/.

Faculty members in the Department are committed to excellence in narrative and analytical historical reading and writing. They offer a variety of services to students who wish to improve their reading or writing skills, or who wish to pursue a historical problem in more depth than class time permits.

Chair: Marie Marianetti
Director of Graduate Studies: José Luis Rénique

Degrees Offered: BA,MA
Academic Year System: Semester
Areas of Specialization: US, Europe, Latin America, ancient world, Middle East
Undergraduate Tuition (per academic year):
In-State: $5430
Out-of-State: $11640
Graduate Tuition (per academic year):
In-State: $7360
Out-of-State: $12150
Enrollment 2018-19:
Undergraduate Majors: 152
New Graduate Students: 16
Full-time Graduate Students: 1
Part-time Graduate Students: 20
Degrees in History: 34 BA, 3 MA
Addresses:
Admissions: http://www.lehman.edu/admissions/
Financial Aid: http://www.lehman.edu/financial-aid/

Adjunct Faculty

Auslander, Diane P. (PhD, Grad. Center, CUNY 2010; adj. asst. prof.) medieval Europe; diane.auslander@lehman.cuny.edu
Frangos, John E. (PhD, NYU 1991; adj. asst. prof.) health care and disease, modern Europe; jefny60@verizon.net
Kagan, Marc (MA, City Coll., NY 2014; MEd, Lehman, CUNY 2006; adj. lect.) America; marc.kagan@lehman.cuny.edu
Mellen, Abigail (PhD, NYU 1991; adj. asst. prof.) 19th-century French and American intellectual; amellen@nyc.rr.com
Suchma, Philip Charles (PhD, Ohio State 2005; adj. asst. prof.) US, sports; philip.suchma@lehman.cuny.edu
Wilson, Mark B. (PhD, Graduate Center, CUNY 2017; adj. asst. prof.) ancient and medieval; mark.wilson@lehman.cuny.edu

Affiliated Faculty

Bergad, Laird W. (PhD, Pittsburgh 1980; dist. prof.; Latin American and Puerto Rican Studies) slavery, Latin America and Caribbean; lbergad@gc.cuny.edu
Levy, Teresita (PhD, Grad. Center, CUNY 2007; asst. prof.; Latin American and Puerto Rican Studies) Puerto Rico; teresita.levy@lehman.cuny.edu

Full-time Faculty

Alborn, Timothy L. (PhD, Harvard 1991; prof.; dir., Master in Liberal Arts) Britain, business, science; timothy.alborn@lehman.cuny.edu
Burke, Martin Joseph (PhD, Michigan 1987; prof.) American cultural, intellectual, religious; martin.burke@lehman.cuny.edu
Dauben, Joseph W. (PhD, Harvard 1972; dist. prof.) mathematics, science, sociology of science; jdauben@att.net
LeGall, Dina (PhD, Princeton 1992; assoc. prof.) Middle East; dinalegall@aol.com
Marianetti, Marie (PhD, Southern California 1990; assoc. prof. and chair) ancient Greece and Rome, classical mythology, classical literature; marie.marianetti@lehman.cuny.edu
Renique, Jose Luis (PhD, Columbia 1988; prof. and dir., grad. studies) Latin America, Caribbean; jrenique@aol.com
Robertson, Andrew W. (DPhil, Oxford 1989; assoc. prof.) early Republic America, political, cultural; andrew.robertson@lehman.cuny.edu
Spencer, Robyn C. (PhD, Columbia 2001; assoc. prof.) African American, recent US; robyn.spencer@lehman.cuny.edu
Tananbaum, Duane A. (PhD, Columbia 1980; prof.) American foreign relations, recent US, Vietnam War; duane.tananbaum@lehman.cuny.edu

Valentine, Robert T. (PhD, South Carolina 1997; lect.) US 1789-1876, American military; robert.valentine@lehman.cuny.edu
Wooldridge, Chuck (PhD, Princeton 2007; assoc. prof.) China, East Asia; chuck.wooldridge@lehman.cuny.edu
Wunder, Amanda J. (PhD, Princeton 2002; assoc. prof.) early modern Spain, art; ajwunder@gmail.com

Part-time Faculty

Bussan, Samuel (graduate teaching fellow) sbussan@gradcenter.cuny.edu
Calabrese, Victoria (PhD, Graduate Center, CUNY 2017; adj. asst. prof.) modern Europe, transnational; victoria.calabrese@lehman.cuny.edu
DeDe-Panken, Madeline (MA, Clark 2013; graduate teaching fellow) mdedepanken@gradcenter.cuny.edu
Keisman, Philip (MEd, Hebrew Coll. 2011; graduate teaching fellow) pkeisman@gradcenter.cuny.edu
Schmacks, Yanara (graduate teaching fellow) yschmacks@gradcenter.cuny.edu
Uva, Katharine (MPhil, Graduate Center, CUNY 2014; adj. lect.) katie.uva@gmail.com

Retired/Emeritus Faculty

Ackerman, Evelyn B. (PhD, Harvard 1973; prof. emeritus) France, medicine, modern European social and economic; eackerman7@att.net
Duberman, Martin (PhD, Harvard 1957; dist. prof. emeritus) queer, culture and politics, slavery and antislavery; martinduberman@aol.com
Judd, Jacob (PhD, NYU 1959; prof. emeritus) immigration, colonial America, New York; jjudd18@optonline.net
Zerner, Ruth (PhD, California, Berkeley 1962; assoc. prof. emerita) Holocaust and survivorship, human rights, European diplomatic; ruth.zerner@lehman.cuny.edu

Le Moyne College

Dept. of History, 1419 Salt Springs Rd., Syracuse, NY 13214-1399. 315.445.4253. Fax 315.445.4540. Email: xuy@lemoyne.edu. Website: https://www.lemoyne.edu/history.

The classrooms of Le Moyne's History Department extend from traditional lecture halls to historic sites like Gettysburg, Seneca Falls, and Fort Niagara, as well as various museums in New York City, and places around the world.

Chair: Yamin Xu
Degrees Offered: BA
Academic Year System: Semester
Areas of Specialization: early modern and modern Europe, Middle East, Americas, East Asia, Africa
Tuition (per academic year): $31260
Enrollment 2018-19:
Undergraduate Majors: 65
Degrees in History: 22 BA
Addresses:
Admissions: http://www.lemoyne.edu/Apply/Undergraduate-Admission
Financial Aid: http://www.lemoyne.edu/Apply/Financial-Aid

Full-time Faculty

Egerton, Douglas R. (PhD, Georgetown 1985; prof.) US 1789-1877, Old South; egertodr@lemoyne.edu
Erickson, Bruce A. (PhD, New Mexico 2001; assoc. prof.) colonial and modern Latin America, women and gender; ericksba@lemoyne.edu

Fought, Leigh (PhD, Houston 2000; assoc. prof.) antebellum US, slavery and African American, women; foughtlk@lemoyne.edu

Guzik, Michael A., SJ (PhD, Wisconsin-Milwaukee 2017; asst. prof.) central and eastern Europe, church; guzikma@lemoyne.edu

Langdon, John W. (PhD, Syracuse 1973; prof.) modern Europe, Cold War; langdon@lemoyne.edu

Odhiambo, Godriver (PhD, West Virginia 2010; assoc. prof.) East Africa, West Africa, African American; odhiamga@lemoyne.edu

Rine, Holly A. (PhD, New Hampshire 2004; assoc. prof.) colonial North America, European and Native American; rineha@lemoyne.edu

Scully, Robert, SJ (JD, Seton Hall 1984; prof.) early modern Europe, legal, Jesuits; scullyre@lemoyne.edu

Xu, Yamin (PhD, California, Berkeley 2002; assoc. prof. and chair) premodern and modern China and East Asia, world; xuy@lemoyne.edu

Zens, Robert (PhD, Wisconsin-Madison 2004; assoc. prof.) Middle East, Balkans, Islam and Ottoman; zensrw@lemoyne.edu

Retired/Emeritus Faculty

Bashaw, Carolyn (PhD, Georgia 1992; prof. emerita) 20th-century US, women, education; bashawct@lemoyne.edu

Blaszak, Barbara J. (PhD, SUNY, Buffalo 1978; prof. emerita) Britain, labor, modern Europe; blaszabj@lemoyne.edu

Bosch, William J., SJ (PhD, North Carolina, Chapel Hill 1966; prof. emeritus) BoschWJ@lemoyne.edu

Judge, Edward H. (PhD, Michigan 1975; prof. emeritus) Russia, 20th-century global; judge@lemoyne.edu

Telesca, William John (PhD, Fordham 1969; prof. emeritus)

Lewis & Clark College

Dept. of History, 0615 SW Palatine Hill Rd., MSC 41, Portland, OR 97219-7899. 503.768.7405. Fax 503.768.7418. Email: history@lclark.edu. Website: https://college.lclark.edu/departments/history/.

Our curriculum is global in scope, inviting students to compare the traditions of various cultures and countries. We offer sufficient depth in the history of the Americas, Europe, and Asia to allow students to develop sophisticated knowledge of these regions in the modern and premodern eras.

Chair: Maureen Healy
Degrees Offered: BA
Academic Year System: Semester
Areas of Specialization: America, Asia, Europe, Latin America
Tuition (per academic year): $52346
Enrollment 2018-19:
  Undergraduate Majors: 55
  Degrees in History: 29 BA
Addresses:
  Admissions: http://college.lclark.edu/offices/admissions/
  Financial Aid: https://www.lclark.edu/offices/financial_aid/

Full-time Faculty

Bernstein, Andrew W. (PhD, Columbia 1999; assoc. prof.) Japan, environmental; awb@lclark.edu

Campion, David A. (PhD, Virginia 2002; Dr. Robert B. Pamplin Jr. Assoc. Prof.) Britain, British Empire, India; campion@lclark.edu

Gallman, Nancy O. (PhD, California, Davis 2017; asst. prof.) Spanish borderlands, legal pluralism, early Native and African American, comparative empire; ngallman@lclark.edu

Glosser, Susan (PhD, California, Berkeley 1995; assoc. prof.) China, gender, family; sglosser@lclark.edu

Healy, Maureen (PhD, Chicago 2000; assoc. prof. and chair) modern Europe; healy@lclark.edu

Hillyer, Reiko (PhD, Columbia 2007; asst. prof.) 20th-century US; rhillyer@lclark.edu

Westervelt, Benjamin W. (PhD, Harvard 1993; assoc. prof.) medieval and early modern Europe, Catholic Reformation; bww@lclark.edu

Young, Elliott G. (PhD, Texas, Austin 1997; assoc. prof.) Latin America, borderlands, transnational; eyoung@lclark.edu

Lewis University

Dept. of History, 1 University Pkwy, Romeoville, IL 60446-2200. 815.836.5862. Fax 815.836.5068. Email: creminde@lewisu.edu. Website: https://www.lewisu.edu/academics/history/.

As a history degree student at Lewis, you will study historically significant events, ideas, persons and civilizations—and be prepared to analyze modern-day economic, social, and political happenings with deeper clarity and wisdom.

Chair: Dennis Cremin
Degrees Offered: BA
Academic Year System: Semester
Areas of Specialization: US local and regional, Europe, East Asia, Middle East, Africa
Tuition (per academic year): $33270
Enrollment 2018-19:
  Undergraduate Majors: 57
  Degrees in History: 11 BA
Addresses:
  Admissions: http://www.lewisu.edu/admissions
  Financial Aid: http://www.lewisu.edu/admissions/finaid

Adjunct Faculty

Piotrowski, Sara (MS, Illinois State 2011; MS, St. Francis 2007; adj. prof.) global history and culture, American pluralism; piotrosa@lewisu.edu

Full-time Faculty

Cremin, Dennis H. (PhD, Loyola, Chicago 1999; prof. and chair) urban, public, state and local; creminde@lewisu.edu

Hannon, Peter J., FSC (MA, Catholic 1985; MA, DePaul 1971; asst. prof.) international affairs; hannonpe@lewisu.edu

Kopp, Frederic M. (PhD, Illinois, Chicago 2001; asst. prof.) global history and culture, Germany, modern Europe; koppfr@lewisu.edu

McMahon, Eileen (PhD, Loyola, Chicago 1989; prof.) Ireland and Britain, US immigration/ethnicity/race, Irish America; mcmahoei@lewisu.edu

Schultz, Mark (PhD, Chicago 1999; prof.) African American in Jim Crow South, oral, agricultural; schultma@lewisu.edu

Tallon, James N. (PhD, Chicago 2012; assoc. prof.) Ottoman Empire, Middle East, Balkans; tallonja@lewisu.edu

Vietoris, John M., FSC (PhD, Marquette 2008; assoc. prof.) US urban, US military, modern Europe; vietorjo@lewisu.edu

Retired/Emeritus Faculty

Bacon, Ewa K. (PhD, Chicago 1975; prof. emerita) eastern Europe, global, science; baconew@lewisu.edu

Pruter, Robert (MA, Roosevelt 1976; MLS, Dominican 2000; librarian emeritus) African American music, sport, cultural; pruter@comcast.net

Liberty University

Dept. of History, 1971 University Blvd., Lynchburg, VA 24515. 434.592.4366. Email: history@liberty.edu; scsmith4@liberty.edu. Website: http://www.liberty.edu/academics/arts-sciences/history/.

Prepare for a successful career while earning your bachelor's, master's, or minor from Liberty University's Department of History. With our history and social sciences degree programs, your knowledge of these fields will be enriched as you explore exciting career options. Courses are taught from a Christian worldview by experienced professors who share your passion for history and are grounded in their faith. Interested in a career in politics, education, or communications? A degree from our Department of History will get you ready for these fields and more.

Chair: Samuel C. Smith
Director of Graduate Studies: Samuel C. Smith
Degrees Offered: BA,BS,MA
Academic Year System: Semester
Areas of Specialization: US military and diplomatic, American religion, modern Europe
Undergraduate Tuition (per academic year): $23800
Graduate Tuition (per academic year): $9810
Enrollment 2018-19:
Undergraduate Majors: 250
New Graduate Students: 15
Full-time Graduate Students: 25
Undergraduate Addresses:
Admissions: https://www.liberty.edu/admissions/
Financial Aid: https://www.liberty.edu/admissions/
Graduate Addresses:
Admissions and Financial Aid: https://www.liberty.edu/admissions/index.cfm?PID=21168

Full-time Faculty

Davis, Michael (PhD, Arkansas 2005; assoc. prof.) American political, recent US; madavis6@liberty.edu

Donald, Donna Davis (ABD, George Mason; asst. prof.) early modern Europe; ddonald@liberty.edu

Esswein, Benjamin Thomas (PhD, California, Riverside 2013; asst. prof.) early modern Europe, central and eastern Europe, Austro-Ottoman borderlands; btesswein@liberty.edu

Jones, Christopher (MA, Virginia Tech; asst. prof.) Civil War, Latin America, teaching methods; cljones5@liberty.edu

Ritchie, Robert (MA, American Military 1998; asst. prof.) geography, social science methods; rfritchie@liberty.edu

Roberts, Carey M. (PhD, South Carolina 2000; prof. and assoc. dean; Coll. of Arts and Sciences) American intellectual, early Republic; croberts@liberty.edu

Schultz, Roger (PhD, Arkansas 1989; prof. and dean; Coll. of Arts and Sciences) American religion, American Revolution; rschultz@liberty.edu

Smith, Christopher J. (PhD, Houston 2007; asst. prof.) Atlantic world revolutions, ancient Greece and Rome, American West; cjsmith19@liberty.edu

Smith, Samuel C. (PhD, South Carolina 1999; assoc. prof.; chair; and dir., grad. studies) colonial religion, American economic; scsmith4@liberty.edu

Snead, David L. (PhD, Virginia 1997; prof.) 20th-century US, American military and diplomatic; dlsnead@liberty.edu

Lincoln Memorial University

History Program, Dept. of Humanities, 6965 Cumberland Gap Pkwy., Harrogate, TN 37752. 423.869.6296. Fax 423.869.6426. Email: debra.salata@lmunet.edu. Website: https://www.lmunet.edu/academics/undergraduate/baccalaureate-degrees/bachelor-of-arts-ba/history.php.

LMU's history major will teach you to be a historian and provide you with a solid foundation for a variety of careers in teaching, historic preservation, and further study in law school and graduate school.

Chair: Joanna Neilson
Degrees Offered: BA
Academic Year System: Semester
Areas of Specialization: American Civil War, Appalachia, US frontier, Britain and Empire, ancient and medieval Europe
Tuition (per academic year): $20520
Enrollment 2018-19:
Undergraduate Majors: 19
Degrees in History: 1 BA
Addresses:
Admissions: https://www.lmunet.edu/admissions/undergraduate
Financial Aid: https://www.lmunet.edu/admissions/financial-aid

Full-time Faculty

Hess, Earl J. (PhD, Purdue 1986; assoc. prof.) Civil War, military; earl.hess@lmunet.edu

Hubbard, Charles M. (PhD, Tennessee, Knoxville 1994; prof.) Civil War, foreign affairs; charles.hubbard@lmunet.edu

Neilson, Joanna (PhD, Florida State 2005; asst. prof. and chair; Humanities) Britain, world, cultural; joanna.neilson@lmunet.edu

Salata, Debra A. (PhD, Minnesota 2003; assoc. prof. and dir., hist. prog.) medieval, ancient world, world; debra.salata@lmunet.edu

Toomey, Michael (PhD, Tennessee, Knoxville 1991; prof.) Appalachia, Tennessee, frontier; michael.toomey@lmunet.edu

Nondepartmental Historians

Booth, Teddy W., II (PhD, Tennessee, Knoxville 2011; dir., Academic Support; Academic Affairs) Renaissance Europe, Reformation Europe; teddy.booth@lmunet.edu

Harden, Michael Wayne (MA, Florida State; visitor services; Abraham Lincoln Library and Museum) michael.harden@lmunet.edu

Lynch, Michael L. (MA, Tennessee, Knoxville; dir., Abraham Lincoln Library Museum) colonial America, Revolutionary War; michael.lynch02@lmunet.edu

Smallwood, Jonathan (MA, Oklahoma 2010; museum specialist; Abraham Lincoln Library and Museum) museum studies; jonathan.smallwood@lmunet.edu

Sweet, Natalie Heather (MA, Kentucky; program coord.; Abraham Lincoln Library and Museum) natalie.sweet@lmunet.edu

Wilson, Steven (MA, Tennessee, Knoxville 1988; curator; asst. dir., Abraham Lincoln Library and Museum) Abraham Lincoln, museum studies; steven.wilson@lmunet.edu

Linfield College

Dept. of History, 900 SE Baker St., McMinnville, OR 97128-6894. 503.883.2660. Fax 503.883.2306. Email: lwadewi@linfield.edu. Website: https://www.linfield.edu/history.html.

The mission of the History Department is to teach history as a distinct form of inquiry into the human condition. Students will learn the skills of history through the study of historical methods, area studies, and research and writing.

Chair: Lissa K. Wadewitz
Degrees Offered: BA
Academic Year System: Semester
Areas of Specialization: US, Europe, Asia, Latin America, world
Tuition (per academic year): $43194
Enrollment 2018-19:
   Undergraduate Majors: 15
   Degrees in History: 11 BA
Addresses:
   Admissions: http://www.linfield.edu/admission.html
   Financial Aid: http://www.linfield.edu/admission/apply/costs.html

Adjunct Faculty

Glasco, Jeffrey D. (PhD, Arizona 2001; adj. faculty) Britain, modern Europe, world; jglasco@linfield.edu
Rutledge, Steven H. (PhD, Brown 1996; adj. prof.) ancient Rome, ancient Greece

Full-time Faculty

Bailey Glasco, Sharon (PhD, Arizona 2002; assoc. prof.) Latin America, Mexico, world urban/social/cultural; sglasco@linfield.edu
Buckingham, Peter H. (PhD, Washington State 1980; prof.) American foreign policy, Irish-America, American labor; pbucking@linfield.edu
Sagers, John H. (PhD, Washington 2001; prof.) Japan, China, East Asia; jsagers@linfield.edu
Wadewitz, Lissa K. (PhD, UCLA 2004; assoc. prof. and chair) US West, environmental, Native American; lwadewi@linfield.edu

Joint/Cross Appointments

Snyder, Stephen H. (PhD, Chicago 1975; prof.; Religious Studies) social; ssnyder@linfield.edu

Long Island University, Brooklyn Campus

Dept. of History, 1 University Plaza, Brooklyn, NY 11201-5372. 718.488.1057. Fax 718.488.1086. Email: stacey.horstmann@liu.edu. Website: http://liu.edu/Brooklyn/Academics/Liberal-Arts-Sciences/Academic-Programs/History.

The Department of History is dedicated to providing students with an education that enables them to understand their place in contemporary society by exploring how individuals, ideas, and social conflicts in the past created change and shaped our modern world. Our faculty of accomplished historians will introduce you to the histories of America, Europe, Latin America, and the Ancient world as well as economic and social issues that continue to influence the world today. In all of our courses we emphasize the importance of asking questions, analyzing evidence and evaluating conflicting interpretations.

Chair: Stacey Horstmann Gatti
Degrees Offered: BA
Academic Year System: Semester
Areas of Specialization: civilization
Tuition (per academic year): $34352

Enrollment 2018-19:
   Undergraduate Majors: 5
Addresses:
   Admissions: http://www.liu.edu/brooklyn/admissions
   Financial Aid: http://www.liu.edu/brooklyn/enrollment-services

Full-time Faculty

Agrait, Nicolas (PhD, Fordham 2003; assoc. prof.) ancient, medieval; Nicolas.Agrait@liu.edu
Dorinson, Joseph (MPhil, Columbia 1976; prof.) America, popular culture, sports; joseph.dorinson@liu.edu
Horstmann-Gatti, Stacey M. (PhD, Emory 2000; assoc. prof. and chair) America, comparative women, US South; stacey.horstmann@liu.edu
Jones, Kimberly F (PhD, UCLA 1995; assoc. prof.) Brazil, race relations, black consciousness movement; Kimberly.Jones@liu.edu
Warmund, Joram (PhD, NYU 1968; prof.) modern Europe, Germany, Holocaust; joram.warmund@liu.edu
Xia, Yafeng (PhD, Maryland, Coll. Park 2003; prof.) modern East Asia, modern China and Japan, American-East Asian relations; yafeng.xia@liu.edu

Longwood University

Dept. of History, Political Science, and Philosophy, 201 High St., Farmville, VA 23909. 434.395.2224. Fax 434.395.2200. Email: colesdj@longwood.edu. Website: http://www.longwood.edu/philpolhist/history/.

Longwood University offers prospective majors in History a rich tradition in both teaching and scholarship. Students enjoy the distinct advantage of close association with individual faculty members who not only are committed to undergraduate instruction but also are productively engaged in significant research in their fields.

Chair: David J. Coles
Degrees Offered: BA
Academic Year System: Semester
Areas of Specialization: US, public, modern Europe, world, social studies education
Tuition (per academic year):
   In-State: $24366
   Out-of-State: $40326
Enrollment 2018-19:
   Undergraduate Majors: 150
   Degrees in History: 35 BA
Addresses:
   Admissions: http://www.longwood.edu/admissions.htm
   Financial Aid: http://www.longwood.edu/tuitionaid.htm

Full-time Faculty

Cantrell, Phillip Allen, II (PhD, West Virginia 2004; assoc. prof.) Asia, Africa, world; cantrellpa@longwood.edu
Coles, David J. (PhD, Florida State 1996; prof. and chair) American Civil War, military, Old South; colesdj@longwood.edu
Fergeson, Larissa Smith (PhD, Emory 2001; prof.) African American, 20th-century US, Virginia; fergesonls@longwood.edu
Geraghty, David Alan (PhD, Virginia 2009; assoc. prof.) social studies education, early modern England, early national US; geraghtyda@longwood.edu
Holliday, William C., Jr. (PhD, Kansas 2004; assoc. prof.) Latin America, environmental, world; hollidaywc@longwood.edu
Isaac, Steven (PhD, Louisiana State 1998; prof.) medieval Europe, ancient, Islam and Middle East; isaacsw@longwood.edu

Johnson, Tai E. (PhD, Arizona 2019; asst. prof.) public, American Indian, environmental

Kravetz, Melissa Lynn (PhD, Maryland, Coll. Park 2011; assoc. prof.) modern Germany, women and gender in Europe, science and medicine; kravetzml@longwood.edu

Munson, James R. (PhD, Columbia 1992; assoc. prof.) French Revolution, European intellectual, 19th-century Europe; munsonjr@longwood.edu

Newton, Barbara Hensley (PhD, Mississippi 2013; asst. prof.) American social and intellectual, Virginia, Renaissance/Reformation; newtonbh@longwood.edu

Uryadova, Yulia (PhD, Arkansas 2012; asst. prof.) Islam, Russia, world; uryadovay@longwood.edu

Retired/Emeritus Faculty

Etheridge, Elizabeth W. (PhD, Georgia 1966; prof. emeritus) women, western, social and intellectual

Millar, Gilbert J. (PhD, Louisiana State 1974; prof. emeritus) England, medieval Europe, Renaissance and Reformation

Sneller, Maurice P., Jr. (PhD, Virginia 1960; prof. emeritus) modern US, 20th-century US, diplomatic

Welch, Deborah (PhD, Wyoming 1985; prof. emeritus) public, American Indian, American West; welchds@longwood.edu

University of Louisiana at Lafayette

Dept. of History, Geography, and Philosophy, PO Box 42531, Lafayette, LA 70504-2531. 337.482.6900. Fax 337.482.6809. Email: ritchey@louisiana.edu. Website: https://history.louisiana.edu/.

The Department of History, Geography and Philosophy is based on interdisciplinary and innovative courses in the Liberal Arts. Our different fields of studies provide our students a variety of skills to pursue their training and careers.

Chair: Chad H. Parker
Director of Graduate Studies: Richard Frankel
Director of Undergraduate Studies: Liz Skilton
Degrees Offered: BA,MA
Academic Year System: Semester
Areas of Specialization: US, Europe, Latin America, public
Undergraduate Tuition (per academic year):
　In-State: $5374
　Out-of-State: $14344
Graduate Tuition (per academic year):
　In-State: $5830
　Out-of-State: $14800
Undergraduate Addresses:
　Admissions: http://www.louisiana.edu/admissions
　Financial Aid: http://www.louisiana.edu/admissions/paying-college
Graduate Addresses:
　Admissions and Financial Aid: http://gradschool.louisiana.edu

Full-time Faculty

Carriker, Robert M. (PhD, Arizona State 1996; prof.) public; carriker@louisiana.edu

de la Garza, Andrew (PhD, Ohio State 2010; instr.) Asian military, Islamic; adelagarza@louisiana.edu

Farmer-Kaiser, Mary (PhD, Bowling Green State 2000; prof. and dean; Graduate Sch.) 19th-century women and legal; kaiser@louisiana.edu

Foster, Theodore (PhD, Northwestern 2019; asst. prof.) African American, black politics, black critical theory, racial capitalism; theodore.foster@louisiana.edu

Frankel, Richard E. (PhD, North Carolina, Chapel Hill 1999; assoc. prof. and dir., grad. studies) modern Germany; frankel@louisiana.edu

Frederick, Julia (PhD, Louisiana State 2000; asst. prof.; dir., Honors Prog.) Latin America, East Asia; julia@louisiana.edu

Hermann, Robin (PhD, Washington, St. Louis 2004; assoc. prof.) Britain; rhermann@louisiana.edu

Kellman, Jordan (PhD, Princeton 1998; prof. and dean; Coll. of Liberal Arts) early modern France, French colonial, history and philosophy of science; kellman@louisiana.edu

Martin, Michael S. (PhD, Arkansas 2003; assoc. prof.; dir., Center for Louisiana Studies) colonial and recent Louisiana, public; docmartin@louisiana.edu

Parker, Chad Hunter (PhD, Indiana 2008; assoc. prof. and head) US foreign relations, modern US; chparker@louisiana.edu

Richard, Carl J. (PhD, Vanderbilt 1988; prof.) early national US, intellectual

Runcie, Sarah Cook (PhD, Columbia 2017; asst. prof.) Africa

Rzadkiewicz, Chester M. (PhD, SUNY, Buffalo 1987; asst. prof.) modern Europe, Russia

Skilton, Liz (PhD, Tulane 2013; asst. prof. and dir., undergrad. studies) US, gender, US South; skilton@louisiana.edu

Retired/Emeritus Faculty

Baker, Vaughan B. (PhD, Southwestern Louisiana 1975; prof. emeritus) modern Europe, Germany

Brasseaux, Carl A. (PhD, Paris 1982; prof. emeritus) Louisiana, France in America

Cusimano, Richard C. (PhD, Georgia 1970; prof. emeritus) ancient and medieval Europe

Dormon, James H., Jr. (PhD, North Carolina, Chapel Hill 1966; prof. emeritus) cultural, American ethnic

Fiero, Gloria K. (PhD, Florida State 1970; prof. emeritus) Renaissance, cultural

Gentry, Judith F. (PhD, Rice 1969; prof. emeritus) economic, Civil War; jfgentry@louisiana.edu

Moore, John Robert (PhD, Duke 1962; prof. emeritus) 20th century, New Deal and after

Nicassio, Susan Vandiver (PhD, Louisiana State 1989; prof. emeritus) Italy, early modern Europe, social and cultural; svn4713@louisiana.edu

Schoonover, Thomas D. (PhD, Minnesota 1970; prof. emeritus) foreign relations

Louisiana State University

Dept. of History, 224 Himes Hall, Baton Rouge, LA 70803-3601. 225.578.4471. Email: asd@lsu.edu. Website: https://www.lsu.edu/hss/history/.

LSU's History Department has earned an outstanding reputation for both the quality of its teaching and the high standards of its scholarship. The Department is nationally and internationally recognized as a center for the study of Southern and Civil War history, but the Department is strong in other areas of US history.

Chair: Aaron Sheehan-Dean
Director of Graduate Studies: Alecia P. Long
Degrees Offered: BA,MA,PhD
Academic Year System: Semester
Areas of Specialization: US, Latin America, Britain, Europe to 1650, Europe since 1500

Undergraduate Tuition (per academic year):
  In-State: $10688
  Out-of-State: $27434
Graduate Tuition (per academic year):
  In-State: $11373
  Out-of-State: $28308
Enrollment 2018-19:
  Undergraduate Majors: 220
  New Graduate Students: 9
  Full-time Graduate Students: 51
  Part-time Graduate Students: 2
  Degrees in History: 134 BA, 2 MA, 5 PhD
Undergraduate Addresses:
  Admissions: https://www.lsu.edu/admission/
  Financial Aid: https://www.lsu.edu/financialaid/
Graduate Addresses:
  Admissions: https://www.lsu.edu/graduateschool/apply/
  Financial Aid: https://www.lsu.edu/hss/history/graduate/

Full-time Faculty

Alam, Asiya (PhD, Texas, Austin 2013; asst. prof.) South Asia; aalam@lsu.edu

Andes, Stephen J. C. (PhD, Oxford 2010; asst. prof.; International Studies) Latin America, Mexico; sandes@lsu.edu

Burstein, Andrew (PhD, Virginia 1994; Manship Prof.) revolutionary and early Republic US; aburstein@lsu.edu

Cole, Gibril R. (PhD, UCLA 2000; assoc. prof.; African and African American Studies) West Africa; gcole@lsu.edu

Dietz, Maribel (PhD, Princeton 1997; assoc. prof.) medieval, late antiquity; maribel@lsu.edu

Foster, Gaines M. (PhD, North Carolina, Chapel Hill 1982; Foster Family Prof.) New South; hyfost@lsu.edu

Gutfreund, Zevi (PhD, UCLA 2013; asst. prof.) education, US urban; zgutfreund@lsu.edu

Hardy, James D., Jr. (PhD, Pennsylvania 1961; prof.) early modern Europe

Isenberg, Nancy G. (PhD, Wisconsin, Madison 1990; T. Harry Williams Prof.) early national, gender, women; nisenberg@lsu.edu

Jacquet, Catherine O. (PhD, Illinois, Chicago 2012; asst. prof.; Women's and Gender Studies) US women and gender; cjacquet@lsu.edu

Johnson, Sherri Franks (PhD, Arizona 2004; asst. prof.) late medieval Europe, Renaissance; sfj@lsu.edu

Karch, Brendan J. (PhD, Harvard 2010; asst. prof.) central Europe; bkarch@lsu.edu

Kooi, Christine (PhD, Yale 1993; prof.) Renaissance, Reformation, early modern Netherlands; ckooi1@lsu.edu

Long, Alecia P. (PhD, Delaware 2001; assoc. prof. and dir., grad. studies) Louisiana, gender, sexuality; aplong@lsu.edu

Marchand, Suzanne Lynn (PhD, Chicago 1992; Boyd Prof.) European intellectual; smarch1@lsu.edu

Roberts, Kodi Alphonse (PhD, Chicago 2012; asst. prof.) African American; kodiroberts@lsu.edu

Ross, Steven K. (PhD, California, Berkeley 1997; assoc. prof.) ancient Greece, Rome; skross@lsu.edu

Sheehan-Dean, Aaron C. (PhD, Virginia 2003; Frey Prof. and chair) Civil War and Reconstruction; asd@lsu.edu

Shindo, Charles J. (PhD, Rochester 1992; prof.) 20th-century US, American West, Asian American; cshindo@lsu.edu

Stater, Victor L., III (PhD, Chicago 1988; prof.) Tudor-Stuart England; stater@lsu.edu

Veldman, Meredith (PhD, Northwestern 1988; assoc. prof.) modern Britain; hyveld@lsu.edu

Zanasi, Margherita (PhD, Columbia 1997; assoc. prof.) modern China; mzanasi@lsu.edu

Retired/Emeritus Faculty

Clark, Nancy (PhD, Yale 1988; prof. emeritus) Africa; nclark@lsu.edu

Cooper, William J., Jr. (PhD, Johns Hopkins 1966; Boyd Prof. emeritus) US South, 19th-century US; wcooper@lsu.edu

Hilton, Stanley (PhD, Texas, Austin 1969; DeGrummond Prof. emeritus) Latin America and Brazil, US military

Hoffman, Paul E. (PhD, Florida 1969; Murrill Prof. emeritus) colonial Latin America, southeastern borderlands, Spain; hyhoff@lsu.edu

Lindenfeld, David F. (PhD, Chicago 1973; prof. emeritus) European intellectual, Germany; hylind@lsu.edu

Lipscomb, Patrick C. (PhD, Texas, Austin 1960; assoc. prof. emeritus) Britain

Loveland, Anne C. (PhD, Cornell 1968; T. Harry Williams Prof. emeritus) US religion

Martin, Benjamin F., Jr. (PhD, North Carolina, Chapel Hill 1974; Price Prof. emeritus) modern France, 19th-century Europe; bmarti9@lsu.edu

Owen, Thomas C. (PhD, Harvard 1973; prof. emeritus) Russia

Paskoff, Paul F. (PhD, Johns Hopkins 1976; prof. emeritus) US economic; ppaskoff@lsu.edu

Roider, Karl A., Jr. (PhD, Stanford 1970; Alumni Prof. emeritus) east central Europe; kroider@lsu.edu

Royster, Charles W. (PhD, California, Berkeley 1977; Boyd Prof. emeritus) US Civil War, American Revolution, US military

Recently Awarded PhDs

Awtrey, Jonathon Derek "Jews and the Sources of Religious Freedom in Early Pennsylvania"

Gray, Audrey Lynne "The 'Happiest Corner' of London: Bethnal Green, 1550-1945 "

Halloran, Erin "Between Regulation and Repression, Tradition and Innovation: How the Royal College of Physicians of London Negotiated Its Place in the Early Modern Medical Field"

Isenhower, Zachary C. "At the Edge of Humanity: American Indian Legal Identity and the Development of American Citizenship"

Nabours, Ali Katherine "The Jeffersonian Huey Long: The Rise of Southern Socialism"

Louisiana Tech University

Dept. of History, Sch. of History & Social Sciences, PO Box 8548, Ruston, LA 71272-0034. 318.257.2872. Fax 318.257.4735. Email: history@latech.edu. Website: https://liberalarts.latech.edu/history-and-social-science/history/

Alternate Address: Railroad Ave., Ruston, LA 71270

Consistent with the missions of Louisiana Tech University and the College of Liberal Arts, the School of History and Social Sciences maintains a faculty composed of professionals who understand and value the interrelated goals of instruction, research, and community service. In the tradition of liberal arts education, our school is student-centered and is committed to teaching and advising.

Chair: Elaine Thompson
Director of Graduate Studies: Jeffery R. Hankins
Degrees Offered: BA, MA
Academic Year System: Quarter

Areas of Specialization: US, modern Europe, medieval and early modern, post-1945 world, Middle East
Undergraduate Tuition (per academic year):
In-State: $8000
Out-of-State: $15000
Graduate Tuition (per academic year):
In-State: $5468
Out-of-State: $10096
Enrollment 2018-19:
Undergraduate Majors: 65
New Graduate Students: 4
Full-time Graduate Students: 7
Part-time Graduate Students: 12
Degrees in History: 15 BA, 5 MA
Undergraduate Addresses:
Admissions: http://admissions.latech.edu/
Financial Aid: http://www.latech.edu/financial_aid/
Graduate Addresses:
Admissions and Financial Aid: https://www.latech.edu/study-with-us/graduate/admission-apply/

Full-time Faculty

Anderson, David M. (PhD, North Carolina, Chapel Hill 2002; assoc. prof.) US Gilded Age, 20th century, business/technology/labor; davida@latech.edu

Atassi, Ahmad Nazir (PhD, California, Santa Barbara 2009; asst. prof.) Middle East, Africa, religion; aatassi@latech.edu

Hankins, Jeffrey R. (PhD, Louisiana State 2003; assoc. prof. and dir., grad. studies) Britain, early modern Europe, early America; jhankins@latech.edu

McKevitt, Andrew C. (PhD, Temple 2009; assoc. prof.) US foreign relations, modern Europe, globalization; mckevitt@latech.edu

Thompson, V. Elaine (PhD, Rice 2003; assoc. prof. and coord.) US South, early America, public; elainet@latech.edu

Worsencroft, John (PhD, Temple 2017; asst. prof.) johnw@latech.edu

Retired/Emeritus Faculty

Cook, Philip C. (PhD, Georgia 1968; prof. emeritus) modern Europe, Louisiana

Gilley, B. H. (PhD, Georgia 1966; prof. emeritus) US, intellectual

Rea, Kenneth W. (PhD, Colorado, Boulder 1970; prof. emeritus) East Asia; rea@latech.edu

Webre, Stephen (PhD, Tulane 1980; McGinty Prof. emeritus) Latin America; swebre@latech.edu

University of Louisville

Dept. of History, 101 Gottschalk Hall, Louisville, KY 40292-0001. 502.852.6817. Fax 502.852.0770. Email: blake.beattie@louisville.edu. Website: http://louisville.edu/history/.

The Department of History contributes to the collective understanding of the past through teaching, service, and the scholarly and public dissemination of original research.

Chair: Blake Beattie
Director of Graduate Studies: Jennifer Westerfeld
Director of Undergraduate Studies: John McLeod
Degrees Offered: BA, MA, Cert.
Academic Year System: Semester
Areas of Specialization: US, Europe, comparative world, public
Undergraduate Tuition (per academic year):
In-State: $9466
Out-of-State: $22950

Graduate Tuition (per academic year):
In-State: $10274
Out-of-State: $21378
Enrollment 2018-19:
Undergraduate Majors: 220
New Graduate Students: 7
Full-time Graduate Students: 19
Degrees in History: 56 BA, 7 MA
Undergraduate Addresses:
Admissions: http://louisville.edu/history/undergraduate-studies
Financial Aid: http://louisville.edu/financialaid
Graduate Addresses:
Admissions: http://louisville.edu/history/graduate-studies
Financial Aid: http://louisville.edu/history/graduate-studies/funding

Affiliated Faculty

Fosl, Catherine A. (PhD, Emory 2000; assoc. prof.; Women's and Gender Studies) US, women, social movements; cfosl@louisville.edu

Full-time Faculty

Beattie, Blake R. (PhD, Toronto 1992; assoc. prof. and chair) medieval, Avignon papacy, Italy; blake.beattie@louisville.edu

Blum, Mark E. (PhD, Pennsylvania 1970; prof.) German and Austrian intellectual and cultural, modern European intellectual; mark.blum@louisville.edu

Bowman, Brad (PhD, Chicago 2013; asst. prof.) early Islamic, medieval Muslim-Christian interactions, monasticism, pilgrimage, Christian Arabic historiography; brad.bowman@lousville.edu

Crothers, A. Glenn (PhD, Florida 1997; assoc. prof.; ir. of research, Filson Hist. Soc.) antebellum US South, oral and public; glenn.crothers@louisville.edu

Devlin, Rebecca A. (PhD, Florida 2016; term asst. prof.) western Roman empire, expansion of Christianity, medieval society; rebecca.devlin@louisville.edu

Ehrick, Christine T. (PhD, UCLA 1997; assoc. prof.) Latin America, 20th century, Uruguay; ehrick@louisville.edu

Fleming, Tyler D. (PhD, Texas, Austin 2009; asst. prof.; Pan-African Studies) Africa, southern Africa, popular culture; tyler.fleming@louisville.edu

K'Meyer, Tracy E. (PhD, North Carolina, Chapel Hill 1993; prof.) 20th-century US, oral; tracyk@louisville.edu

Keeley, Theresa (PhD, Northwestern 2013; J.D., University of Pennsylvania Law School 2004; asst. prof.) US foreign relations, Central America, human rights, religion, transnational activism, law, gender; theresa.keeley@louisville.edu

Kelland, Lara L. (PhD, Illinois, Chicago 2012; asst. prof.) public, women, digital; lara.kelland@louisville.edu

Krebs, Daniel (PhD, Emory 2007; assoc. prof.) colonial America, American Revolution, military; daniel.krebs@louisville.edu

Ma, Yuxin (PhD, Minnesota 2003; assoc. prof.) East Asia, women; yuxin.ma@louisville.edu

Mackey, Thomas C. (PhD, Rice 1984; prof.) American constitutional and legal, 19th century, Civil War era; thomasmackey@louisville.edu

Massoth, Katherine Sarah (PhD, Iowa 2016; asst. prof.) Americas, US-Mexico borderlands, women and gender, Chicanx/Latinx studies; katherine.massoth@louisville.edu

McInnis, Edward C. (PhD, Michigan State 2006; asst. prof.) civilizations; ecmcin02@louisville.edu

McLeod, John E. (PhD, Toronto 1993; prof. and dir., undergrad. studies) Britain, South Asia, British Empire; john.mcleod@louisville.edu

Westerfeld, Jennifer Taylor (PhD, Chicago 2010; assoc. prof. and dir., grad. studies) Egyptology, Coptic studies, late antique social and cultural; jennifer.westerfeld@louisville.edu

Yingling, Charlton W. (PhD, South Carolina 2016; asst. prof.) Atlantic/Caribbean/Latin America, Age of Revolutions, race and slavery; charlton.yingling@louisville.edu

Retired/Emeritus Faculty

Allen, Ann T. (PhD, Columbia 1974; prof. emeritus) women, modern Germany; ann.allen@louisville.edu

Brockwell, Charles W. (PhD, Duke 1971; prof. emeritus) medieval ecclesiastical and intellectual, Renaissance, Reformation

Cumbler, John T., Jr. (PhD, Michigan 1974; prof. emeritus) US, environmental; cumbler@louisville.edu

Harrison, Benjamin T. (PhD, UCLA 1969; prof. emeritus) US, US foreign relations; ben.harrison@louisville.edu

McCarthy, Justin A., Jr. (PhD, UCLA 1978; prof. emeritus) modern Middle East, Turkey; jmc@louisville.edu

McElderry, Andrea L. (PhD, Michigan 1975; prof. emeritus) modern China, East Asia

Morrill, James R., III (PhD, North Carolina, Chapel Hill 1967; prof. emeritus) American Revolution, colonial America, US economic

Newton, Lowell W. (PhD, Tulane 1972; assoc. prof. emeritus) early modern Europe, military

Weissbach, Lee Shai (PhD, Harvard 1975; prof. emeritus) France, Jewish; weissbach@louisville.edu

Ziskind, Jonathan R. (PhD, Columbia 1967; assoc. prof. emeritus) ancient Greece, Rome, ancient Near East

Lourdes University

Dept. of History, Geography, and Political Science, 6832 Convent Blvd., Sylvania, OH 43560-4805. 419.824.3676. Fax 419.824.3526. Email: ahodge@lourdes.edu. Website: https://www.lourdes.edu/academics/history/.

The Lourdes University Department of History, Political Science, and Geography faculty offer curriculum that allows students to acquire a greater understanding of world cultures and human interaction while strengthening their critical thinking and communication skills and their global awareness. Lourdes history majors take full advantage of a wide variety of opportunities including study abroad and internships.

Chair: Adam R. Hodge
Degrees Offered: AA,BA
Academic Year System: Semester
Areas of Specialization: America, Europe, non-Western
Tuition (per academic year): $22650
Enrollment 2018-19:
   Undergraduate Majors: 12
   Degrees in History: 1 AA, 5 BA
Addresses:
   Admissions: http://www.lourdes.edu/admissions/
   Financial Aid: http://www.lourdes.edu/costs-financial-aid/

Full-time Faculty

Hodge, Adam R. (PhD, Nebraska 2013; assoc. prof. and chair) US to 1865, environmental, Native American; ahodge@lourdes.edu

Robinson, Mary Kathryn Cooney (PhD, Florida State 2003; assoc. prof.) French Revolution and Napoleon, Europe, Middle East; mrobinson@lourdes.edu

Part-time Faculty

Beggs, Alvin Dwayne (PhD, Bowling Green State 2010; asst. prof.; dir., ARCHES Program) Vietnam War, presidential/congressional relations, US military and diplomatic; abeggs@lourdes.edu

Loyola Marymount University

Dept. of History, 1 LMU Dr., Ste. 3500, Los Angeles, CA 90045-2659. 310.338.7662. Fax 310.338.6008. Email: HistoryDepartment@lmu.edu. Website: https://bellarmine.lmu.edu/history/.

A History degree gives you the unique perspective offered by studying the past and by understanding how the past is reflected and refracted in the present. The LMU History curriculum will train you to be alert, critical, and inquisitive, a careful and keen researcher and writer. Studying a broad range of places and times, you will become an informed global citizen, able to participate in public life with articulate, effective, and persuasive arguments. Your own research will demonstrate that historical interpretations are always changing, while your ability to make sense of complex problems will make you an effective decisionmaker. When you graduate, you will be prepared to follow any career you choose, armed with knowledge, skepticism, empathy, eloquence— and perspective.

Chair: Elizabeth Drummond
Degrees Offered: BA
Academic Year System: Semester
Areas of Specialization: Africa, Americas, Asia, Europe, Middle East
Tuition (per academic year): $49550
Enrollment 2018-19:
   Undergraduate Majors: 75
   Degrees in History: 15 BA
   Students in Undergraduate Courses: 1414
   Students in Undergraduate Intro Courses: 837
Addresses:
   Admissions: http://admission.lmu.edu/
   Financial Aid: http://financialaid.lmu.edu/

Full-time Faculty

Al-Qattan, Najwa (PhD, Harvard 1996; prof.) Middle East and Ottoman Empire, Islamic law, minorities; nalqatta@lmu.edu

Anzilotti, Cara (PhD, California, Santa Barbara 1994; assoc. prof.) colonial America, 18th- and 19th-century US women, women and reform; cara.anzilotti@lmu.edu

Bittel, Carla J. (PhD, Cornell 2003; assoc. prof.) 19th-century US, women and gender, science and medicine; cbittel@lmu.edu

Chen, Constance J. S. (PhD, UCLA 2000; assoc. prof.) Asian Pacific American, Asian art and transnational exchange, comparative race and gender; cchen@lmu.edu

Dempsey, Sean Thomas (PhD, Pennsylvania 2015; asst. prof.) 20th-century US, religion, Los Angeles and urban; sean.dempsey@lmu.edu

Drummond, Elizabeth A. (PhD, Georgetown 2004; assoc. prof. and chair) modern Europe, Germany and Poland, gender/nationalism/imperialism; edrummon@lmu.edu

McDonald, Kevin P. (PhD, California, Santa Cruz 2008; assoc. prof.) Atlantic world, colonial America, world; kevin.mcdonald@lmu.edu

Ochoa, Margarita R. (PhD, New Mexico 2011; assoc. prof.) Latin America, colonial Mexico, ethnohistory/women and gender/urban Indians; margarita.ochoa@lmu.edu

Perron, Anthony M. (PhD, Chicago 2003; assoc. prof.) medieval Europe, Scandinavia, canon law; aperron@lmu.edu

Raab, Nigel A. (PhD, Columbia 2002; prof.) 19th-century Russia, world, urban history and public service; nraab@lmu.edu

Rosenthal, Nicolas G. (PhD, UCLA 2005; assoc. prof.) Los Angeles, Native American, American West; ngrosen@lmu.edu

Woodson-Boulton, Amy (PhD, UCLA 2003; assoc. prof.) modern Britain and Ireland, cultural, European imperialism; awoodson@lmu.edu

Zhang, Meng (PhD, UCLA 2017; asst. prof.) East Asia, China, environmental; Meng.Zhang@lmu.edu

Part-time Faculty

Cole, Lauren Elizabeth (MA, Oregon 2000; ABD, California, San Diego; lect.) modern US; lcole14@lmu.edu

Jacoby, Alex (PhD, California, Irvine 2017; lect.)

Sadler, Jesse (PhD, UCLA 2015; lect.)

Retired/Emeritus Faculty

Grever, John H. (PhD, UCLA 1973; prof. emeritus) early modern Europe; john.grever@lmu.edu

Mahan, Terrance L., SJ (PhD, Wisconsin, Madison 1960; prof. emeritus) colonial America; tmahan@lmu.edu

Rolfs, Richard W., SJ (PhD, California, Santa Barbara 1976; prof. emeritus) modern Europe, Germany; rrolfs@lmu.edu

Tiedemann, Joseph S. (PhD, Grad. Center, CUNY 1977; prof. emeritus) early America, American Revolution; jtiedema@lmu.edu

Tritle, Lawrence A. (PhD, Chicago 1978; prof. emeritus) ancient Greece, republican and imperial Rome, war and violence in ancient world; ltritle@lmu.edu

Visiting Faculty

Anderson, Mark (PhD, Yale 2012; vis. asst. prof.; Classics & Archaeology) ancient

Loyola University Chicago

Dept. of History, Crown Center for the Humanities, 5th Fl., 1032 W. Sheridan Rd., Chicago, IL 60660. 773.508.2221. Fax 773.508.3693. Email: history@luc.edu; sschloesser@luc.edu. Website: https://www.luc.edu/history/.

The field of history has changed significantly in recent decades- and public interest in history has grown. The Department of History's curriculum reflects these changes, while maintaining Loyola's traditional strengths in medieval, modern western European, and United States history.

Chair: Stephen Schloesser
Director of Graduate Studies: Patricia Mooney-Melvin
Director of Undergraduate Studies: Tanya Stabler Miller
Degrees Offered: BA,BA/MA,MA,MA/PhD,MA/MLIS,PhD
Academic Year System: Semester
Areas of Specialization: public, US, transnational urban/social/cultural
Undergraduate Tuition (per academic year): $44130
Graduate Tuition (per academic year): $18594
Enrollment 2018-19:
  Undergraduate Majors: 188
  New Graduate Students: 15
  Full-time Graduate Students: 35
  Part-time Graduate Students: 4
  Degrees in History: 43 BA, 14 MA, 7 PhD
  Students in Undergraduate Courses: 4771

Students in Undergraduate Intro Courses: 3959
Online-Only Courses: 7%
Undergraduate Addresses:
  Admissions: https://www.luc.edu/undergrad/
  Financial Aid: https://www.luc.edu/undergrad/featurecontent/canvases/costandvalue/
Graduate Addresses:
  Admissions: https://www.luc.edu/gradschool/admission.shtml
  Financial Aid: http://www.luc.edu/gradschool/FundingGrad.Education.shtml

Full-time Faculty

Allee, Mark A. (PhD, Pennsylvania 1987; assoc. prof.) East Asia, China; mallee@luc.edu

Bucholz, Robert (DPhil, Oxford 1988; prof.) England, Tudor-Stuart; rbuchol@luc.edu

Cardoza, Anthony L. (PhD, Princeton 1975; prof.) modern Europe, Italy; acardoz@luc.edu

Dennis, David B. (PhD, UCLA 1991; prof.) contemporary Europe, intellectual and cultural; dennis@luc.edu

Donoghue, John L. (PhD, Pittsburgh 2005; assoc. prof.) colonial America, Atlantic world; jdonoghue@luc.edu

Dossey, Leslie D. (PhD, Harvard 1998; assoc. prof.) Rome, late antiquity; ldossey@luc.edu

Forth, Aidan (PhD, Stanford 2012; assoc. prof.) modern Britain, imperial, colonial; aforth@luc.edu

Fraterrigo, Elizabeth S. (PhD, Loyola, Chicago 2004; assoc. prof.) public, American social and cultural; efrater@luc.edu

Ghazzal, Zouhair A. (PhD, Paris, Sorbonne 1986; assoc. prof.) modern Islamic, Middle East; zghazza@luc.edu

Gilfoyle, Timothy J. (PhD, Columbia 1987; prof.) 19th-century US social, urban, sexuality; tgilfoy@luc.edu

Gorn, Elliott J. (PhD, Yale 1983; Joseph A. Gagliano Prof.) urban, 19th- and 20th-century US, cultural and social; egorn@luc.edu

Gross-Diaz, Theresa J. (PhD, Northwestern 1992; assoc. prof.; dir., Medieval Studies) Western civilization, medieval; tgross@luc.edu

Hajdarpasic, Edin (PhD, Michigan 2008; assoc. prof.) modern eastern Europe, nationalism, Balkans; ehajdarpasic@luc.edu

Hemenway, Betsy Jones (PhD, North Carolina, Chapel Hill 1999; sr. lect.; dir., Women's/Gender Studies) Russia, Soviet, gender; ehemenway@luc.edu

Johnson, Benjamin H. (PhD, Yale 2000; assoc. prof.) American environmental, borderlands; bjohnson25@luc.edu

Karamanski, Theodore J. (PhD, Loyola, Chicago 1980; prof.; dir., public hist. prog.) public, frontier, environment; tkarama@luc.edu

Kaufman, Suzanne K. (PhD, Rutgers 1996; assoc. prof.) modern Europe, France; skaufma@luc.edu

Khodarkovsky, Michael (PhD, Chicago 1987; prof.) Russia, Soviet Union; mkhodar@luc.edu

Manning, Christopher E. (PhD, Northwestern 2003; assoc. prof.) US, African American, oral; cmannin@luc.edu

McManamon, John M., SJ (PhD, North Carolina, Chapel Hill 1984; prof.) Renaissance, Italy; jmcmana@luc.edu

Miller, Tanya Stabler (PhD, California, Santa Barbara 2007; assoc. prof. and dir., undergrad prog.) medieval, urban, women; tstabler@luc.edu

Mooney-Melvin, Patricia (PhD, Cincinnati 1978; assoc. prof. and dir., grad. studies) US urban, public; pmooney@luc.edu

Nickerson, Michelle M. (PhD, Yale 2003; assoc. prof.) 20th-century US, women and gender, urban; mnickerson@luc.edu

O'Connor, Kelly (PhD, Loyola, Chicago 2014; instr.) US; kocon6@luc.edu

Pincince, John R. (PhD, Hawai'i, Manoa 2007; sr. lect.; dir., Asian Studies) modern South Asia, India; jpincince@luc.edu

Roberts, Kyle B. (PhD, Pennsylvania 2007; assoc. prof.; dir., Center for Textual Studies and Digital Humanities) 19th-century US religion, new media and digital humanities, public; kroberts2@luc.edu

Santamaria Balmaceda, Gema Karina (PhD, New Sch. for Social Research 2015; asst. prof.) Latin America; gsantamaria@luc.edu

Schloesser, Stephen R., SJ (PhD, Stanford 1999; prof. and chair) modern European intellectual and cultural, Roman Catholicism, France; sschloesser@luc.edu

Searcy, Kim (PhD, Indiana 2004; assoc. prof.) Africa, Islamic civilizations; ksearcy@luc.edu

Shermer, Elizabeth Tandy (PhD, California, Santa Barbara 2009; assoc. prof.) 20th-century US, capitalism, business; eshermer@luc.edu

Suszko, Marek (PhD, Illinois, Chicago 2004; sr. lect.) Poland, Russia; msuszko@luc.edu

Valussi, Elena (PhD, London 2003; sr. lect.) East Asia, China; evalussi@luc.edu

Weinreb, Alice Autumn (PhD, Michigan 2009; assoc. prof.) modern Germany, European gender, comparative colonialisms; aweinreb@luc.edu

Wilson, Andrew (PhD, Loyola, Chicago 1991; lect.) Western civilization, Ireland; awilso@luc.edu

Part-time Faculty

Biletz, Frank A. (PhD, Chicago 1995; instr.) Western civilization; fbiletz@luc.edu

Buckley, Constance R. (PhD, Loyola, Chicago 2005; instr.) American pluralism; cbuckl@luc.edu

Candeloro, Dominic (PhD, Illinois, Urbana-Champaign 1970; instr.) Italian American, US; dcandeloro@luc.edu

Lapsley, Joseph W. (PhD, Illinois, Chicago 2009; instr.) US, American pluralism; jlapsle@luc.edu

Young, Katherine A. (MS, Illinois State 1991; MLIS, Dominican 2001; instr. and Univ. archivist) archives; kyoung3@luc.edu

Retired/Emeritus Faculty

Cohen, Sheldon S. (PhD, NYU 1963; prof. emeritus) America, colonial, education; scohen@luc.edu

Erenberg, Lewis A. (PhD, Michigan 1974; prof. emeritus) American social and cultural; lerenbe@luc.edu

Galush, William J. (PhD, Minnesota 1975; prof. emeritus) American ethnic, American religious; wgalush@aol.com

Harrington, Ann M., BVM (PhD, Claremont Grad. 1977; prof. emeritus) modern Japan, China, women; aharri1@luc.edu

Hays, Jo N. (PhD, Chicago 1970; prof. emeritus) modern Britain, science; jhays@luc.edu

Hirsch, Susan E. (PhD, Michigan 1974; prof. emeritus) 19th- and 20th-century labor, women; shirsch@luc.edu

Knapp, Thomas A. (PhD, Catholic 1967; prof. emeritus) modern Europe, Germany; tknapp@luc.edu

McCaffrey, Lawrence J. (PhD, Iowa 1954; prof. emeritus) modern Europe, Ireland; ljpmcc@aol.com

Moylan, Prudence A. (PhD, Illinois, Urbana-Champaign 1975; prof. emeritus) modern Britain, women; pmoylan@luc.edu

Nolan, Janet A. (PhD, Connecticut 1986; prof. emeritus) modern Ireland; jnolan@luc.edu

Pfeffer, Paula F. (PhD, Northwestern 1980; prof. emeritus) US ethnic, urban, women; ppfeffer@luc.edu

Platt, Harold L. (PhD, Rice 1974; prof. emeritus) American legal, American urban, environment; hplatt@luc.edu

Reardon, John J. (PhD, Georgetown 1953; prof. emeritus) revolutionary and early national America; jjreardon7@aol.com

Rosenwein, Barbara H. (PhD, Chicago 1974; prof. emeritus) medieval, France; brosenw@luc.edu

Recently Awarded PhDs

Jeremie-Brink, Nathan "'Gratuitous Distribution': Distributing African American Antislavery Texts, 1773-1845"

McChesney, Meagan "Exhibiting Sovereignty: Tribal Museums in the Great Lakes Region, 1975-2010"

Loyola University Maryland

Dept. of History, 4501 N. Charles St., HU 322a, Baltimore, MD 21210-2699. 410.617.2326. Fax 410.617.2832. Website: http://www.loyola.edu/academics/history.

The History major at Loyola combines rigorous study with close interaction between students and faculty. The focus of the History department is to teach not just the "facts" of history, but the patterns and interpretations as well.

Chair: Sara Scalenghe
Degrees Offered: BA
Academic Year System: Semester
Areas of Specialization: medieval and modern Europe, US social and political, Africa and Middle East, Asia, Latin America
Tuition (per academic year): $47520
Enrollment 2018-19:
  Undergraduate Majors: 80
  Degrees in History: 16 BA
Addresses:
  Admissions: http://www.loyola.edu/admission
  Financial Aid: http://www.loyola.edu/department/financialaid/undergraduate

Full-time Faculty

Borges, Charles J., SJ (PhD, Bombay, India 1983; assoc. prof.) church, India; cborges@loyola.edu

Carey, David, Jr. (PhD, Tulane 1999; prof.) modern Latin America/crime/gender, Guatemala, Mayan; drcarey@loyola.edu

Devries, Kelly (PhD, Toronto 1987; prof.) medieval, military, technology; kdevries@loyola.edu

Diehl, Chad R. (PhD, Columbia 2012; asst. prof.) Japan, East Asia; crdiehl@loyola.edu

Edwards, Jane (ABD, Ohio State; instr.) modern Europe, intellectual; jedwards@loyola.edu

Mulcahy, Matthew B. (PhD, Minnesota 1999; prof.) colonial and revolutionary America, disasters; mmulcahy@loyola.edu

Okoh, Oghenetoja H. (PhD, NYU 2012; asst. prof.) Africa, Nigeria, Niger Delta, citizenship, nationalism, minorities; ohokoh@loyola.edu

Pegram, Thomas Ray (PhD, Brandeis 1988; prof.) US political, diplomatic, Progressive Era; tpegram@loyola.edu

Ross, Andrew Israel (PhD, Michigan 2011; asst. prof.) modern Europe, sexuality, cultural; aross1@loyola.edu

Sandler, Willeke (PhD, Duke 2012; asst. prof.) modern Germany/Nazi Germany and Holocaust, public, cultural; wsandler@loyola.edu

Scalenghe, Sara (PhD, Georgetown 2006; assoc. prof. and chair) Middle East; sscalenghe@loyola.edu

Joint/Cross Appointments

Taylor, Martha (PhD, Stanford 1993; prof.; Classics) ancient world, gender; mtaylor@loyola.edu

Walsh, Joseph (PhD, Texas, Austin 1988; prof.; Classics) ancient world; jwalsh@loyola.edu

Retired/Emeritus Faculty

Breihan, John R. (PhD, Cambridge 1977; prof. emeritus) England, historic preservation, war and society; breihan@loyola.edu

Brennan, Katherine Stern (PhD, Johns Hopkins 1982; assoc. prof. emeritus) early modern Europe, France, women; kbrennan@loyola.edu

Cheape, Charles W., III (PhD, Brandeis 1976; prof. emeritus) US business and economic; ccheape@loyola.edu

Donovan, Bill Michael (PhD, Johns Hopkins 1991; assoc. prof. emeritus) Latin America, business and economic; donovan@loyola.edu

Hughes, Steven C. (PhD, Michigan 1984; prof. emeritus) European social, police, Italy; schughes@loyola.edu

Leonard, Angela M. (PhD, George Washington 1994; assoc. prof. emeritus) American studies, African American; aleonard@loyola.edu

McCormick, P. Andrew (PhD, Georgetown 1974; prof. emeritus) Russia and Soviet Union

Schmidt, Elizabeth S. (PhD, Wisconsin, Madison 1987; prof. emeritus) Africa, women; eschmidt@loyola.edu

Schoppa, R. Keith (PhD, Michigan 1975; prof. emeritus) China, Japan, Vietnam; kschoppa@loyola.edu

Visiting Faculty

Bolaños, Isacar (PhD, Ohio State 2019; vis. asst. prof.) Middle East

Jamison, Felicia (PhD, Massachusetts Amherst 2017; vis. asst. prof.) African American

Parlopiano, Brandon T. (PhD, Catholic 2013; vis. asst. prof.) medieval

Loyola University New Orleans

Dept. of History, 6363 Charles Ave., Box 191, New Orleans, LA 70118. 504.865.3537. Fax 504.865.2010. Email: mffernan@loyno.edu. Website: http://cas.loyno.edu/history.

History at Loyola is an integral part of the university's liberal arts program. As such, it seeks to free the mind from common prejudices and faulty intellectual assumptions through a broad-based study of the human past.

Chair: Mark F. Fernandez
Degrees Offered: BA
Academic Year System: Semester
Areas of Specialization: US, Europe, Latin America, Middle East, Asia and Africa
Tuition (per academic year): $40592
Enrollment 2018-19:
Undergraduate Majors: 60
Degrees in History: 17 BA
Addresses:
Admissions: http://apply.loyno.edu/
Financial Aid: http://apply.loyno.edu/cost-of-attendance

Adjunct Faculty

Edgren, Allison (PhD, Notre Dame 2016; adj.) Middle Ages

Katz, Sara (PhD, Michigan 2019; adj.) Africa, global Islam, visual culture, Muslim-Christian relations

Full-time Faculty

Brungardt, Maurice P. (PhD, Texas, Austin 1974; prof., on leave) Colombia, Spain, Mexico; brungard@loyno.edu

Fernandez, Mark F. (PhD, William and Mary 1991; prof. and chair) colonial, early America, US South; mffernan@loyno.edu

Gerlich, Robert S., SJ (PhD, St. Louis 1987; assoc. prof.) central Europe, Germany, European intellectual; gerlich@loyno.edu

Howard, Ashley M. (PhD, Illinois, Urbana-Champaign 2012; On Leave 2019-2020) African American; ahoward2@loyno.edu

Moazami, Behrooz (PhD, New Sch. 2004; assoc. prof.) Middle East, comparative governments; bmoazami@loyno.edu

Moore, David W. (PhD, Maryland, Coll. Park 1978; assoc. prof., on leave) American studies, late 19th- and 20th-century US intellectual and cultural, Louisiana; dmoore@loyno.edu

Nystrom, Justin A. (PhD, Georgia 2004; asst. prof.) Reconstruction, US South; jnystrom@loyno.edu

Thum, Rian (PhD, Harvard 2010; asst. prof., on leave) China; thum@loyno.edu

Part-time Faculty

Buzard Boyett, Patricia M. (PhD, Southern Mississippi 2011; instr.; dir., Women's Resource Center) US, South; pbboyett@loyno.edu

Lilly, David (PhD, Louisiana State 2011) modern Britain, modern Europe, imperialism; dlilly@loyno.edu

McQueeney, Kevin G. (PhD, Rutgers 2012)

Moore, Jonathan Allen (PhD, Tulane 2016) 20th-century British Empire, whiteness/Britishness, gender/masculinity; jamoore@loyno.edu

Wallace, Rachel (PhD, Queens, Belfast 2018) rewallla@loyno.edu

Retired/Emeritus Faculty

Anderson, Nancy Fix (PhD, Tulane 1973; prof. emerita) Britain, women, India

Cook, Bernard A. (PhD, St. Louis 1970; prof. emeritus) modern Europe, Germany, Italy; cook@loyno.edu

Nicoll, Leo A., SJ (PhD, Vienna 1970; assoc. prof. emeritus) central Europe, philosophy of history; nicoll@loyno.edu

Pillar, James J., OMI (PhD, Pontifical Gregorian 1962; prof. emeritus) US, American church

Swift, Mary G., OSU (PhD, Notre Dame 1967; prof. emerita) Russia, medieval

Visiting Faculty

Hardy, Eric M. (PhD, Georgia Tech 2011; vis. asst. prof.) world civilization, environmental studies; emhardy@loyno.edu

Luther College

Dept. of History, 700 College Dr., Decorah, IA 52101-1045. 563.387.1806. Fax 563.387.1107. Email: catobr01@luther.edu. Website: https://www.luther.edu/history/.

At Luther College, you can study history from a variety of perspectives. We currently offer courses covering the history of Africa, Asia, Europe, and the United States.

Chair: Brian Caton
Degrees Offered: BA
Academic Year System: 4-1-4
Areas of Specialization: US, Europe, Africa, Asia
Tuition (per academic year): $43500
Enrollment 2018-19:
Undergraduate Majors: 50
Degrees in History: 14 BA
Addresses:
Admissions: http://www.luther.edu/admissions/
Financial Aid: http://www.luther.edu/financialaid/

Full-time Faculty

Caton, Brian P. (PhD, Pennsylvania 2003; assoc. prof. and chair) South Asia, environmental, imperialism; catobr01@luther.edu

Christman, Robert J. (PhD, Arizona 2004; assoc. prof.) early modern Europe, Germany, Renaissance and Reformation; chriro05@luther.edu

Peterson, Anna Marie (PhD, Ohio State 2013; asst. prof.) 19th- and 20th-century Europe, Scandinavia, women; petean07@luther.edu

Joint/Cross Appointments

Christman, Victoria (PhD, Arizona 2005; assoc. prof.; International Studies) early modern Europe, Low Countries, Inquisition; chrivi02@luther.edu

Mtisi, Richard (PhD, Iowa 2008; assoc. prof.; Africana Studies) 20th-century Africa, environmental; mtisri01@luther.edu

Sharp, Kelly Kean (PhD, California, Davis 2018; asst. prof.; Africana Studies) US, African American

Part-time Faculty

Crider, Destiny (PhD, Arizona State 2011; instr.) museum studies, collections management, archaeology and mesoamerica and North American Indians; cridde01@luther.edu

Retired/Emeritus Faculty

Christianson, J. R. (PhD, Minnesota 1964; prof. emeritus) science, early modern Scandinavia, Scandinavian immigration; christjr@luther.edu

Cole, Richard G. (PhD, Ohio State 1963; prof. emeritus) Renaissance and Reformation, Russia, 19th- and 20th-century Europe; coler@luther.edu

Hanson, Richard Simon (PhD, Harvard 1963; prof. emeritus) ancient; hansri01@luther.edu

Hervey, Norma J. (PhD, Minnesota 1991; prof. emeritus) economic, 19th-century US, ethnic; herveynj@luther.edu

Slind, Marvin G. (PhD, Washington State 1978; prof. emeritus) modern Europe, Scandinavian immigration; slindmar@luther.edu

Tebbenhoff, Edward H. (PhD, Minnesota 1992; assoc. prof. emeritus) early America, US social, museum studies; tebbened@luther.edu

Wilkie, Jacqueline S. (DA, Carnegie Mellon 1982; prof. emeritus) US social, women, medicine; wilkieja@luther.edu

University of Lynchburg

Dept. of History, 505 Brevard St., Lynchburg, VA 24501-3199. 434.544.8328. Fax 434.544.8487. Email: amos.n@lynchburg.edu. Website: https://www.lynchburg.edu/academics/majors-and-minors/history/.

Alternate Address: 1501 Lakeside Dr., Lynchburg, VA 24501

Our challenging major (BA) or minor in history gives you opportunities to explore all aspects of history in a friendly and supportive setting. The history program has close ties with the interdisciplinary major in International Relations and the minors in Gender Studies and Medieval and Renaissance Studies.

Chair: N. Scott Amos
Degrees Offered: BA
Academic Year System: Semester
Areas of Specialization: US, Europe, Asia, African American, Latin America
Tuition (per academic year): $38560
Enrollment 2018-19:
  Undergraduate Majors: 34
  Degrees in History: 11 BA

Addresses:
  Admissions: http://www.lynchburg.edu/undergraduate-admission
  Financial Aid: http://www.lynchburg.edu/admission/financial-aid/

Full-time Faculty

Amos, N. Scott (PhD, St. Andrews, Scotland 2003; prof. and chair) Renaissance and Reformation Europe, Tudor England, Christianity; amos.n@lynchburg.edu

Crim, Brian E. (PhD, Rutgers 2003; prof.) modern Europe, Middle East, Africa; crim@lynchburg.edu

Crutchfield, Lisa L. (PhD, William and Mary 2007; asst. prof.) early America; crutchfield_l@lynchburg.edu

Dean, Adam W. (PhD, Virginia 2010; assoc. prof.) Civil War, America, global environmental; dean.aw@lynchburg.edu

Michie, Lindsay (PhD, St. Andrews, Scotland; assoc. prof.) modern Africa, modern Europe; michie.l@lynchburg.edu

Sanders, Nichole M. (PhD, California, Irvine 2003; prof.) Latin America, women and gender, world; sanders.n@lynchburg.edu

Santos, Michael Wayne (PhD, Carnegie Mellon 1984; prof.) US, urban/labor/social, Lynchburg; santos@lynchburg.edu

Macalester College

Dept. of History, 1600 Grand Ave., Saint Paul, MN 55105-1899. 651.696.6376. Email: lsturtz@macalester.edu. Website: https://www.macalester.edu/history/.

We offer classes on individual regions of the world while emphasizing global connections among them. Courses highlight new scholarship relating to gender, race, class, ethnicity, and culture. We examine interpretive problems that historians encounter and enhance our inquiry by interacting with other fields of academic study. Students appraise the past in its own terms, communicate effectively by crafting arguments and narratives, and examine the ethical implications of our retelling the past.

Chair: Linda Sturtz
Degrees Offered: BA
Academic Year System: Semester
Areas of Specialization: North America, East Asia, Europe, Latin America, Africa
Tuition (per academic year): $56062
Enrollment 2018-19:
  Undergraduate Majors: 51
  Degrees in History: 20 BA
Addresses:
  Admissions: http://www.macalester.edu/admissions/
  Financial Aid: http://www.macalester.edu/admissions/financialaid/

Full-time Faculty

Capello, Ernesto B. (PhD, Texas, Austin 2005; prof.) Latin America, urban, cartography and visual culture; ecapello@macalester.edu

Pearson, Jessica L. (PhD, NYU 2013; asst. prof.) modern Europe, public health, decolonization; jpearso4@macalester.edu

Phillips, Katrina (PhD, Minnesota 2015; asst. prof.) US, Native American, performance; kphilli2@macalester.edu

Sturtz, Linda L. (PhD, Washington, St. Louis 1992; prof. and chair) early North America, Caribbean; lsturtz@macalester.edu

Tam, Yue-Him (PhD, Princeton 1975; prof.) China and Japan; tam@macalester.edu

Velez, Karin A. (PhD, Princeton 2008; assoc. prof.) Atlantic world, early modern empires, religious encounters; kvelez@macalester.edu

Wells, Christopher W. (PhD, Wisconsin, Madison 2004; prof.; Environmental Studies) US environment, technology, culture; wells@macalester.edu

Retired/Emeritus Faculty

El-Kati, Mahmoud (BA, Wilberforce 1960; lect. emeritus) US, Afro-American

Fisher, Jerry K. (PhD, Virginia 1974; prof. emeritus) Japan, China, communication studies; fisher@macalester.edu

Itzkowitz, David C. (PhD, Columbia 1972; prof. emeritus) Britain, modern Europe, Jewish; itzkowitz@macalester.edu

Rachleff, Peter J. (PhD, Pittsburgh 1981; prof. emeritus) US, labor, immigration; rachleff@macalester.edu

Solon, Paul D. (PhD, Brown 1970; prof. emeritus) medieval Europe, Renaissance, military; solon@macalester.edu

Stewart, James B. (PhD, Case Western Reserve 1968; prof. emeritus) 18th- and 19th-century US, political and social, comparative slavery and emancipation; stewart@macalester.edu

Weisensel, Peter R. (PhD, Minnesota 1973; prof. emeritus) Russia, Germany, empires; weisensel@macalester.edu

University of Maine

Dept. of History, 5774 Stevens Hall, Orono, ME 04469-5774. 207.581.1908. Fax 207.581.1817. Email: umhist@maine.edu; lang@maine.edu. Website: https://umaine.edu/history/.

Our daily lives are linked to everything that came before us. History courses will help you see those connections and make sense of the world.

Chair: Michael Lang
Director of Graduate Studies: Anne Knowles
Degrees Offered: BA,MA,PhD
Academic Year System: Semester
Areas of Specialization: US, Canada, Europe, environmental, labor
Undergraduate Tuition (per academic year):
In-State: $8790
New England Regional and Canadian: $14,070
Out-of-State: $28590
Graduate Tuition (per academic year):
In-State: $7902
New England Regional and Canadian: $12,636
Out-of-State: $25740
Enrollment 2018-19:
Undergraduate Majors: 100
New Graduate Students: 6
Full-time Graduate Students: 41
Part-time Graduate Students: 5
Degrees in History: 14 BA, 1 MA
Undergraduate Addresses:
Admissions: https://go.umaine.edu/
Financial Aid: https://umaine.edu/stuaid/
Graduate Addresses:
Admissions: https://umaine.edu/graduate/
Financial Aid: https://umaine.edu/stuaid/

Adjunct Faculty

O'Leary, Wayne (PhD, Maine 1981; research assoc. prof.) maritime, economic, political

Full-time Faculty

Anderson, Joel (PhD, Cornell 2015; asst. prof.) medieval, Nordic, religious; joel.anderson@maine.edu

Ferland, Jacques (PhD, McGill 1986; assoc. prof.) colonial Canada, French Canadian, native peoples; jferland@maine.edu

Freeman, Mary T. (PhD, Columbia 2018; asst. prof.) Maine, New England, slavery and emancipation; mary.t.freeman@maine.edu

Godfried, Nathan (PhD, Wisconsin, Madison 1980; prof.) 20th-century US, popular culture, labor; godfried@maine.edu

Knowles, Anne Kelly (PhD, Wisconsin-Madison 1993; prof. and dir., grad. studies) historical geography, digital humanities, Holocaust; anne.knowles@maine.edu

Lang, Michael (PhD, California, Irvine 1997; assoc. prof. and chair) modern Europe, military, international affairs; lang@maine.edu

Long, Ngo Vinh (PhD, Harvard 1978; prof.) China, Japan, Southeast Asia; vinhlong.ngo@maine.edu

McKillen, Elizabeth A. (PhD, Northwestern 1987; prof.) American diplomatic, 20th century, social; mckillen@maine.edu

Miller, Stephen M. (PhD, Connecticut 1996; prof.) Britain, Africa, colonialism; stephen.miller@maine.edu

Riordan, Liam O. (PhD, Pennsylvania 1996; prof.) colonial America, American Revolution, Latin America; riordan@maine.edu

Segal, Howard P. (PhD, Princeton 1975; prof.) American science and technology, America; segal@maine.edu

Joint/Cross Appointments

Hough, Mazie Louise (PhD, Maine 1997; assoc. prof.; Women in the Curriculum) women, social, US; hough@maine.edu

McLaughlin, Mark J. (PhD, New Brunswick 2013; asst. prof.; Canadian-American Center) Canada, environmental, labor; mark.j.mclaughlin@maine.edu

Nawaz, Asif (PhD, Kansas State 2016; asst. prof.; International Affairs) modern terrorism, political, Islamic/South Asian/Middle Eastern military history and politics, evolution of modern warfare; asif.nawaz@maine.edu

Pawling, Micah Abell (PhD, Maine 2010; asst. prof.; Native American Studies) Native American, US, Canada; micah.pawling@maine.edu

Nondepartmental Historians

Beattie, Mary E. (PhD, Maine 1984; librarian; Canadian Studies) beattie@maine.edu

Socolow, Michael J. (PhD, Georgetown 2001; assoc. prof.; Communication and Journalism) US national radio networks, media and society; michael.socolow@maine.edu

Retired/Emeritus Faculty

Baker, William J. (PhD, Cambridge 1967; prof. emeritus) modern England, Europe, sports; william.baker@maine.edu

Battick, John F. (PhD, Boston Univ. 1967; assoc. prof. emeritus) maritime, Europe, Renaissance and Reformation; jbattick@adelphia.net

Blanke, Richard D. (PhD, California, Berkeley 1970; prof. emeritus) contemporary Europe, Russia, modern Germany; blanke@maine.edu

Bregman, Jay A. (PhD, Yale 1974; prof. emeritus) ancient, intellectual, jazz; jay.bregman@umit.maine.edu

Grab, Alexander Israel (PhD, UCLA 1980; prof. emeritus) 18th- and 19th-century Europe, Middle East, modern Italy; agrab@maine.edu

Judd, Richard W. (PhD, California, Irvine 1979; prof. emeritus) Maine, US labor, environmental; rjudd@maine.edu

Nadelhaft, Jerome J. (PhD, Wisconsin, Madison 1965; prof. emeritus) colonial America, American Revolution; jjnadelhaft@verizon.net

Riess, Warren C. (PhD, New Hampshire 1987; research assoc. prof. emeritus) early America, modern America, maritime archaeology; riess@maine.edu

See, Scott W. (PhD, Maine 1984; Libra Prof. emeritus) Canada, Canadian American, US; scott.see@maine.edu

TeBrake, William H. (PhD, Texas, Austin 1975; prof. emeritus) medieval, western European environmental, European social; tebrake@maine.edu

Recently Awarded PhDs

Miller, Cody P "Environment and Resiliency in the Northern and Southern Appalachian Mountains, 1870-1930"

Soucier, Daniel S. "Navigating Wilderness and Borderland: Environment and Culture in the Northeastern Americas during the American Revolution"

Manhattan College

Dept. of History, 4513 Manhattan College Pkwy, Riverdale, NY 10471-4004. 718.862.7129. Fax 718.862.8044. Email: jennifer. edwards@manhattan.edu. Website: https://manhattan.edu/ academics/schools-and-departments/school-of-liberal-arts/. history-dept/.

Our expert faculty are the driving force of this department. They are published scholars in their respective fields. Research and hands-on learning are important parts your experience as a history major.

Chair: Jennifer C. Edwards
Degrees Offered: BA
Academic Year System: Semester
Areas of Specialization: US, modern Europe, modern Asia, Latin America, medieval Europe
Tuition (per academic year): $34000
Enrollment 2018-19:
　Undergraduate Majors: 50
　Degrees in History: 12 BA
Addresses:
　Admissions: http://manhattan.edu/admissions
　Financial Aid: https://manhattan.edu/admissions/
　　undergraduate/pay-for-college/index.php

Full-time Faculty

Arenson, Adam (PhD, Yale 2008; assoc. prof.) US West, US 1815-77, urban; adam.arenson@manhattan.edu

Crafts, Lydia (PhD, Illinois, Urbana-Champaign 2019; asst. prof.) lcrafts01@manhattan.edu

Droubie, Paul (PhD, Illinois, Urbana-Champaign 2009; asst. prof.) Asia, modern Japan, cultural and political; paul.droubie@manhattan.edu

Edwards, Jennifer C. (PhD, Illinois, Urbana-Champaign 2008; assoc. prof. and chair) medieval, religion, women and gender; jennifer.edwards@manhattan.edu

Horn, Jeff (PhD, Pennsylvania 1993; prof.) Industrial Revolution and political economy, French Revolution, science and technology; jeff.horn@manhattan.edu

Takla, Nefertiti (PhD, UCLA 2016; asst. prof.) Middle East, women and gender; ntakla01@manhattan.edu

Retired/Emeritus Faculty

Nolte, Claire E. (PhD, Columbia 1990; prof. emerita) eastern and central Europe, cultural/political/urban, women; claire.nolte@manhattan.edu

Pycior, Julie L. (PhD, Notre Dame 1979; prof. emerita) Mexican American, US ethnic and West, Latin America; julie.pycior@manhattan.edu

Manhattanville College

Dept. of History, 2900 Purchase St., Purchase, NY 10577. 914.694.2200. Email: gregory.swedberg@mville.edu. Website: https://www.mville.edu/programs/history.

Courses offered at Manhattanville span global history from ancient through contemporary eras and provide introductory level surveys through advanced seminars on the history of Asia, Africa, Europe, the Middle East, Latin America, the Caribbean, and North America. Our faculty are specialists in each of these areas whose scholarship and expertise informs their work with students.

Chair: David Gutman
Degrees Offered: BA, MALS (affiliated)
Academic Year System: Semester
Areas of Specialization: Asia, Africa, Americas, Middle East, Europe, diasporas
Tuition (per academic year): $36220
Enrollment 2018-19:
　Undergraduate Majors: 35
　Degrees in History: 10 BA
Addresses:
　Admissions: https://www.mville.edu/admissions/
　　undergraduate-admissions
　Financial Aid: https://www.mville.edu/admissions/
　　financial-aid-scholarships

Full-time Faculty

Bowling, Lawson H., III (PhD, Columbia 1990; prof.; International Studies) 20th-century US, sports, Italy; Lawson.Bowling@mville.edu

Gutman, David Edward (PhD, SUNY, Binghamton 2012; asst. prof. and chair) modern Middle East, Ottoman, Slavic world/Russia; David.Gutman@mville.edu

Mbodj, Mohamed (PhD, Paris 1978; prof.; African Studies) Africa and African American, economic, Islam; Mohamed.Mbodj@mville.edu

Morris, Colin Jeffrey (PhD, Rochester 1994; prof.; dir., American Studies) early America, intellectual and political, historic places; colin.morris@mville.edu

Swedberg, Gregory John (PhD, Rutgers 2007; assoc. prof.; Latin American Studies) Mexico/Central America, South America, women and gender; gregory.swedberg@mville.edu

Whelan, Irene M. (PhD, Wisconsin, Madison 1994; prof.; dir., Irish Studies) Britain and Ireland, modern Europe, nationalism; Irene.Whelan@mville.edu

Marquette University

Dept. of History, Sensenbrenner Hall, 202A, PO Box 1881, Milwaukee, WI 53201-1881. 414.288.7217. Fax 414.288.5099. Email: muhist@marquette.edu. Website: https://www.marquette.edu/history/.

Marquette is a Catholic and Jesuit university located in Milwaukee, Wisconsin, that offers more than 80 majors in its nationally and internationally recognized colleges and schools.

Chair: James Marten
Director of Graduate Studies: Timothy G. McMahon

Director of Undergraduate Studies: Laura E. Matthew
Degrees Offered: BA,MA,PhD
Academic Year System: Semester
Areas of Specialization: early modern and modern Europe, US
Undergraduate Tuition (per academic year): $43350
Graduate Tuition (per academic year): $21060
Enrollment 2018-19:
   Undergraduate Majors: 121
   New Graduate Students: 9
   Full-time Graduate Students: 38
   Part-time Graduate Students: 8
   Degrees in History: 30 BA, 8 MA
Undergraduate Addresses:
   Admissions: http://www.marquette.edu/explore/
   Financial Aid: http://www.marquette.edu/mucentral/
      financialaid/
Graduate Addresses:
   Admissions and Financial Aid: http://www.marquette.edu/grad/

Full-time Faculty

Avella, Steven M. (PhD, Notre Dame 1984; prof.) US religious, social, foreign relations; steven.avella@marquette.edu

Ball, Alan M. (PhD, North Carolina, Chapel Hill 1982; prof.) Russia, Soviet Union; alan.ball@marquette.edu

Donoghue, Michael E. (PhD, Connecticut 2006; assoc. prof.) US foreign relations, Latin America; michael.donoghue@marquette.edu

Efford, Alison Clark (PhD, Ohio State 2008; assoc. prof.) US, immigration; alison.efford@marquette.edu

Finn, Jennifer (PhD, Michigan 2012; PhD, Ludwig-Maximilians, Munich 2015; asst. prof.) ancient Greece and Rome, Assyria; jennifer.finn@marquette.edu

Foster, A. Kristen (PhD, Wisconsin, Madison 2001; asst. prof.) early national US, women; kristen.foster@marquette.edu

Gonzalez, Sergio M. (PhD, Wisconsin-Madison 2018; asst. prof.; Languages, Literatures, and Cultures) 20th-century US, Latinx studies, Catholicism; sergio.gonzalez@marquette.edu

Hay, Carla H. (PhD, Kentucky 1972; assoc. prof.) 18th-century Britain, women; carla.hay@marquette.edu

Knox, Lezlie S. (PhD, Notre Dame 1999; assoc. prof.) medieval Europe, women; lezlie.knox@marquette.edu

Korieh, Chima (PhD, Toronto 2003; asst. prof.) Africa; chima.korieh@marquette.edu

Marten, James A. (PhD, Texas, Austin 1986; prof. and chair) US, Civil War, children; james.marten@marquette.edu

Matthew, Laura E. (PhD, Pennsylvania 2004; assoc. prof. and dir., undergrad. studies) Latin America, Atlantic world; laura.matthew@marquette.edu

McMahon, Timothy G. (PhD, Wisconsin, Madison 2001; assoc. prof. and dir., grad. studies) modern Ireland, modern Britain; timothy.g.mcmahon@marquette.edu

Meissner, Daniel J. (PhD, Wisconsin, Madison 1996; assoc. prof.) modern China, modern Japan, Sino-American relations; daniel.meissner@marquette.edu

Mullins, John Patrick (PhD, Kentucky 2005; asst. prof.) cultural and intellectual, 17th- and 18th-century British North America; john.mullins@marquette.edu

Naylor, Phillip C. (PhD, Marquette 1980; prof.) modern Europe, Africa, Middle East and Islamic; phillip.naylor@marquette.edu

Rindfleisch, Bryan Christopher (PhD, Oklahoma 2015; asst. prof.) Native American, colonial America; bryan.c.rindfleisch@marquette.edu

Smith, Robert S. (PhD, Bowling Green State 2002; assoc. prof. and John Prof.; dir., Center for Urban Research, Teaching, and Outreach) African American, race and law; robert.smith@marquette.edu

Staudenmaier, Peter (PhD, Cornell 2010; asst. prof.) modern Germany, intellectual; peter.staudenmaier@marquette.edu

Wert, Michael J. (PhD, California, Irvine 2007; assoc. prof.) Japan; michael.wert@marquette.edu

Retired/Emeritus Faculty

Bicha, Karel D. (PhD, Minnesota 1963; prof. emeritus) US 1877-1920

Donnelly, John Patrick SJ (PhD, Wisconsin, Madison 1971; prof. emeritus) Renaissance and Reformation; john.p.donnelly@marquette.edu

Gardinier, David E. (PhD, Yale 1960; prof. emeritus) Africa, modern Europe

Hay, Robert P. (PhD, Kentucky 1967; assoc. prof. emeritus) US social/cultural/intellectual 1783-1861

Jablonsky, Thomas J. (PhD, Southern California 1978; Harry G. John Prof. emeritus) US urban, American West; thomas.jablonsky@marquette.edu

Krugler, John D. (PhD, Illinois, Urbana-Champaign 1971; prof. emeritus) colonial and revolutionary America, public; john.krugler@marquette.edu

Phayer, Michael (PhD, Munich, Germany 1968; prof. emeritus) modern Germany, modern European social

Ruff, Julius R. (PhD, North Carolina, Chapel Hill 1979; prof. emeritus) 18th-century Europe, France, criminal justice; julius.ruff@marquette.edu

Theoharis, Athan G. (PhD, Chicago 1965; prof. emeritus) 20th-century US, Truman administration, FBI

Weber, Ralph E. (PhD, Notre Dame 1956; prof. emeritus) US diplomatic, business; ralph.weber@marquette.edu

Zeps, Michael J. (PhD, Stanford 1978; assoc. prof. emeritus) 20th-century Europe, Austria; michael.zeps@marquette.edu

Zupko, Ronald E. (PhD, Wisconsin, Madison 1966; prof. emeritus) medieval economic and social, medieval England; ronald.zupko@marquette.edu

Visiting Faculty

McDaniel, David (PhD, Wisconsin, Madison 1999; vis. asst. prof.) US; david.mcdaniel@marquette.edu

Marshall University

Dept. of History, Harris Hall 116, Huntington, WV 25755. 304.696.6780. Fax 304.696.2957. Email: history@marshall.edu. Website: http://www.marshall.edu/history/.

The Department of History at Marshall University is a growing, active department of 13 full-time faculty. We welcome and encourage student interaction, emphasize reading, writing, and critical analysis skills, and promote chronological, cultural, and geographic diversity.

Chair: Greta Rensenbrink
Director of Graduate Studies: Robert Deal
Degrees Offered: BA,MA
Academic Year System: Semester
Areas of Specialization: Europe, US, Asia, world civilization, military
Undergraduate Tuition (per academic year):
   In-State: $8128
   Metro Residents: $14006
   Out-of-State: $18614

Graduate Tuition (per academic year):
In-State: $8432
Metro Residents $14948
Out-of-State: $20350

Enrollment 2018-19:
Undergraduate Majors: 82
New Graduate Students: 5
Full-time Graduate Students: 12
Part-time Graduate Students: 4
Degrees in History: 19 BA, 7 MA
Online-Only Courses: 18%

Undergraduate Addresses:
Admissions: http://www.marshall.edu/admissions/
Financial Aid: http://www.marshall.edu/sfa/

Graduate Addresses:
Admissions: http://www.marshall.edu/graduate/
Financial Aid: http://www.marshall.edu/sfa/

Full-time Faculty

Barksdale, Kevin T. (PhD, West Virginia 2005; prof.) Appalachia, US; barksdale@marshall.edu

Deal, Robert C. (PhD, Temple 2010; assoc. prof. and dir., grad. studies) America, colonial and legal; dealr@marshall.edu

Diener, Laura Michele (PhD, Ohio State 2008; assoc. prof.; dir., Women's Studies) medieval; diener@marshall.edu

Holbrook, Daniel U. (PhD, Carnegie Mellon 1999; prof.) public, technology, business; holbrook@marshall.edu

Miller, Montserrat M. (PhD, Carnegie Mellon 1994; prof.) modern European social, women, Catalunya; millerm@marshall.edu

Palmer, William G. (PhD, Maine 1981; prof.) Britain, methodology, early modern Europe; palmer@marshall.edu

Rensenbrink, Greta (PhD, Chicago 2003; assoc. prof. and chair) US, intellectual; rensenbrink@marshall.edu

Rutherford, Phillip (PhD, Penn State 2001; prof.) modern Europe, Germany; rutherfordp@marshall.edu

Tabyshalieva, Anara (PhD, Kyrgyz National, Kyrgyzstan 1985; assoc. prof.) East Asia; tabyshalieva@marshall.edu

Trowbridge, David J. (PhD, Kansas 2008; assoc. prof.) US, African American; david.trowbridge@marshall.edu

White, Christopher (PhD, Kansas 2005; prof.) Latin America, US diplomatic; whitec@marshall.edu

Williams, Kat D. (PhD, Kentucky 2001; prof.) modern America, women, sexuality; williamskath@marshall.edu

Woods, Michael Eugene (PhD, South Carolina 2012; assoc. prof.) 19th-century US political and cultural, Civil War era; woodsm@marshall.edu

Mars Hill University

Dept. of History, 100 Athletic St., Mars Hill, NC 28754. 828.689.1199. Fax 828.689.1309. Email: lcarter@mhu.edu. Website: https://www.mhu.edu/academics/majors-and-minors/history/.

The history program seeks to prepare its students for active roles in society, to train them for graduate study, and to develop and refine skills that will be useful in a variety of professions. Special importance is given to training secondary social studies teachers and to the subject-matter concentration for middle school social studies teachers.

Chair: John Gripentrog
Degrees Offered: BA
Academic Year System: Semester

Areas of Specialization: US, modern Europe, East Asia, Latin America, public
Tuition (per academic year): $25156
Enrollment 2018-19:
Undergraduate Majors: 40
Degrees in History: 10 BA
Addresses:
Admissions: http://www.mhu.edu/admissions
Financial Aid: http://www.mhu.edu/financial-aid

Full-time Faculty

Carter, Lucia (OPhD, Bologna, Italy 1998; assoc. prof.) Europe, world; lcarter@mhu.edu

Gilbert, David Walker (PhD, Wisconsin, Madison 2010; asst. prof.) African American

Gripentrog, John G. (PhD, Wisconsin, Madison 2006; assoc. prof. and chair) US political, diplomatic, East Asia; jgripentrog@mhu.edu

Smith, Phyllis L. (PhD, Arizona 1996; prof.) Latin America; psmith@mhu.edu

Retired/Emeritus Faculty

Jolley, Harley E. (PhD, Florida State 1964; prof. emeritus) US, Appalachia

Lenburg, L. James (PhD, Penn State 1973; prof. emeritus) US diplomatic, labor, East Asia; jlenburg@mhu.edu

Mary Baldwin University

Dept. of History, 201 E. Frederick St., Staunton, VA 24401. 540.887.7046. Email: atillers@marybaldwin.edu. Website: https://go.marybaldwin.edu/academics/history/.

A faculty of enthusiastic historians provides a broad but disciplined understanding of American, British, African American, and European history.

Chair: Amy Tillerson-Brown
Degrees Offered: BA
Academic Year System: Semester
Areas of Specialization: Virginia, Tudor-Stuart and modern Britain, African American, public
Tuition (per academic year): $39865
Enrollment 2018-19:
Undergraduate Majors: 71
Degrees in History: 53 BA
Addresses:
Admissions: http://www.mbc.edu/college_for_women/
Financial Aid: http://www.mbc.edu/financial_aid/

Adjunct Faculty

Franzen, Katharine G. (PhD, Virginia 1996; asst. prof.) modern Britain; kfranzen@mbc.edu

Full-time Faculty

Brooks, Clayton M. (PhD, Virginia 2005; asst. prof.) Virginia; cbrooks@mbc.edu

Cole, Mary Hill (PhD, Virginia 1985; prof.) England, Tudor-Stuart, European women; mhcole@mbc.edu

Tillerson-Brown, Amy J. (PhD, Morgan State 2006; assoc. prof. and chair) African American, US since 1877, Africa; atillers@mbc.edu

Retired/Emeritus Faculty

Alexander, Ann Field (PhD, Duke 1973; prof. emerita) Virginia, African American; aalexand@mbc.edu

Keller, Kenneth W. (PhD, Yale 1971; prof. emeritus) early national, frontier; kkeller@mbc.edu

University of Maryland, Baltimore County

Dept. of History, 1000 Hilltop Cir, Baltimore, MD 21250. 410.455.2312. Fax 410.455.1045. Email: froide@umbc.edu; ison@umbc.edu. Website: https://history.umbc.edu/.

The Department of History at UMBC is committed to guiding students to develop critical and analytical thinking skills, oral and written communication skills, and an understanding of cultural diversity. Such skills will launch them into successful careers or serve as exceptional preparation for graduate and professional schools and programs. In addition to a wide range of subject/area specialties, the MA includes a track in public history.

Chair: Amy Froide
Director of Graduate Studies: Daniel Ritschel
Director of Undergraduate Studies: Amy Froide
Degrees Offered: BA,MA
Academic Year System: Semester
Areas of Specialization: social, economic, political, gender/women's, policy, transnational, pre-modern, public
Undergraduate Tuition (per academic year):
  In-State: $8500
  Out-of-State: $23600
Graduate Tuition (per academic year):
  In-State: $11500
  Out-of-State: $19800
Enrollment 2018-19:
  Undergraduate Majors: 203
  New Graduate Students: 13
  Full-time Graduate Students: 31
  Part-time Graduate Students: 10
  Degrees in History: 83 BA, 15 MA
Undergraduate Addresses:
  Admissions: http://undergraduate.umbc.edu/
  Financial Aid: http://financialaid.umbc.edu/
Graduate Addresses:
  Admissions and Financial Aid: http://gradschool.umbc.edu/

Adjunct Faculty

Birkenmeier, John W. (PhD, Catholic 1998; adj.) medieval social and religious, Byzantine; jwbirk@umbc.edu

Oakes, Julie (PhD, Chicago 2009; adj.; Asian Studies) Japan, art, Asia; juloakes@umbc.edu

Smead, E. Howard (PhD, Maryland, Coll. Park 1979; adj. assoc. prof.) civil rights, 20th-century US; smead@umbc.edu

Full-time Faculty

Blair, Melissa F. (PhD, Delaware 2014; lect.; Universities at Shady Grove) public; mfblair@umbc.edu

Boehling, Rebecca (PhD, Wisconsin- Madison 1990; prof.) Germany, women, Holocaust; boehling@umbc.edu

Bouton, R. Terry (PhD, Duke 1996; assoc. prof.) early national US; bouton@umbc.edu

Chapin, Christy Ford (PhD, Virginia 2011; assoc. prof.) 20th-century US, political and economic, business; cchapin@umbc.edu

Froide, Amy M. (PhD, Duke 1996; prof.; chair; and dir., undergrad. studies) early modern Britain, early modern Europe, European women; froide@umbc.edu

Kars, Marjoleine (PhD, Duke 1994; assoc. prof.) early Americas, slavery, Atlantic; kars@umbc.edu

McDonough, Susan Alice (PhD, Yale 2005; assoc. prof.) medieval, Western civilization; mcdonoug@umbc.edu

Meringolo, Denise D. (PhD, George Washington 2005; assoc. prof.) 20th-century America, public, community; ddm@umbc.edu

Musgrove, George Derek (PhD, NYU 2005; assoc. prof.) 20th-century US, politics, race; derek.musgrove@umbc.edu

Nolan, Andrew S. (PhD, Illinois, Urbana-Champaign 2001; sr. lect.; program dir., Universities at Shady Grove) biology and religion; nolan@umbc.edu

Oyen, Meredith L. (PhD, Georgetown 2007; assoc. prof.) US in world, US and China, US and Asia; oyen@umbc.edu

Ritschel, Daniel (PhD, Oxford 1987; assoc. prof. and dir., grad. program) modern Britain, economic, social; ritschel@umbc.edu

Rubin, Anne Sarah (PhD, Virginia 1999; prof.) Civil War, US South, culture and nationalism; arubin@umbc.edu

Scott, Michelle R. (PhD, Cornell 2002; assoc. prof.) African American, race, ethnicity; mscott@umbc.edu

Song, Nianshen (PhD, Chicago 2013; asst. prof.) China, inter-Asian, transnational; nianshen@umbc.edu

Tatarewicz, Joseph N. (PhD, Indiana 1984; assoc. prof. emeritus) science, technology, public; tatarewicz@umbc.edu

Vaporis, Constantine N. (PhD, Princeton 1987; prof.) Japan; vaporis@umbc.edu

Zaidi, Noor (PhD, Pennsylvania 2015; asst. prof.) Middle East, women, Islam; nzaidi@umbc.edu

Retired/Emeritus Faculty

Burke, Colin B. (PhD, Washington, St. Louis 1973; assoc. prof. emeritus) education, computers; burke@umbc.edu

Cohen, Warren I. (PhD, Washington 1962; prof. emeritus) American diplomatic, American-Asian relations; wcohen@umbc.edu

Grubb, James S. (PhD, Chicago 1983; prof. emeritus) Renaissance and Reformation; grubb@umbc.edu

Herbert, Sandra (PhD, Brandeis 1968; prof. emeritus) science; herbert@umbc.edu

Jeffries, John W. (PhD, Yale 1973; prof. emeritus; dean, Coll. Arts, Humanities, and Social Sciences) recent US, American political and policy; jeffries@umbc.edu

Papadakis, Aristeides (PhD, Fordham 1968; prof. emeritus) Byzantine, medieval; papadaki@umbc.edu

Wexler, Victor G. (PhD, Columbia 1971; assoc. prof. emeritus) 18th-century European intellectual; wexler@umbc.edu

Yip, Ka-che (PhD, Columbia 1970; prof. emeritus) China, Asia; yip@umbc.edu

University of Maryland, College Park

Dept. of History, 2115 Francis Scott Key Hall, College Park, MD 20742-7315. 301.405.4265. Fax 301.314.9399. Email: history-web@umd.edu. Website: http://history.umd.edu/.

We are a large department whose distinguished faculty's expertise encompasses many areas of the globe as well as several millennia of human history.

Chair: Philip Soergel
Director of Graduate Studies: Alejandro Cañeque
Director of Undergraduate Studies: Antoine Borrut
Degrees Offered: BA,MA,PhD
Academic Year System: Semester
Areas of Specialization: US, ancient to modern Europe, Atlantic world, medieval to modern Middle East, women and gender

Undergraduate Tuition (per academic year):
In-State: $10778
Out-of-State: $36890
Graduate Tuition (per academic year):
In-State: $13158
Out-of-State: $29250
Enrollment 2018-19:
Undergraduate Majors: 324
New Graduate Students: 24
Full-time Graduate Students: 103
Degrees in History: 74 BA, 12 MA, 2 PhD
Undergraduate Addresses:
Admissions: http://www.admissions.umd.edu/
Financial Aid: http://www.financialaid.umd.edu/
Graduate Addresses:
Admissions: http://www.gradschool.umd.edu/admissions
Financial Aid: http://history.umd.edu/graduate

Adjunct Faculty

Baron, Sabrina Alcorn (PhD, Chicago 1995; asst. research prof.) 16th- and 17th-century British political; sbaron@umd.edu

Chiles, Robert (PhD, Maryland, Coll. Park 2012; lect.) US political; rchiles@umd.edu

Ho, Colleen C. (PhD, California, Santa Barbara 2013; lect.) medieval Europe, Mongols, religion; coho@umd.edu

Keane, Katarina (PhD, Maryland, Coll. Park 2009; lect.; asst. dir., Center for Global Migration Studies) US, women; kkeane@umd.edu

Rubinfien, Louisa D. (PhD, Harvard 1995; lect.) East Asia, Japan

Rush, Anne Spry (PhD, American 2004; lect.) Europe; arush1@umd.edu

Smead, E. Howard (PhD, Maryland, Coll. Park 1979) America; hsmead@umd.edu

Taddeo, Julie Anne (PhD, Rochester 1997; assoc. research prof.; dir., undergrad. internship prog.) modern British and European cultural, gender and women's studies; taddeo@umd.edu

Zhang, Dewen (PhD, SUNY, Stony Brook 2013; adj.) China, East Asia

Affiliated Faculty

Darden, Lindley (PhD, Chicago 1974; prof.; Philosophy) history and philosophy of biology; darden@umd.edu

Jones, Marian Moser (PhD, Columbia 2008; asst. prof.; Public Health) medicine and public health; moserj@umd.edu

Moses, Claire G. (PhD, George Washington 1978; prof.; Women's Studies) women, modern France; cmoses@umd.edu

Full-time Faculty

Bell, Richard J. (PhD, Harvard 2006; assoc. prof.) early and modern America; rjbell@umd.edu

Bianchini, Janna C. (PhD, Harvard 2007; assoc. prof.) medieval; jcwb@umd.edu

Bonner, Christopher James (PhD, Yale 2014; asst. prof.) African American; cjbonner@umd.edu

Borrut, Antoine (PhD, Sorbonne, Paris 2007; assoc. prof. and dir., undergrad. studies) Middle East; aborrut@umd.edu

Brewer, Holly (PhD, UCLA 1994; Burke Assoc. Prof.) US legal, cultural, intellectual; hbrewer@umd.edu

Cameron, Sarah I. (PhD, Yale 2010; assoc. prof.) Russia; scameron@umd.edu

Cañeque, Alejandro (PhD, NYU 1999; assoc. prof. and dir., grad. studies) Latin America, Atlantic world; acaneque@umd.edu

Cooperman, Bernard D. (PhD, Harvard 1976; Kaplan Assoc. Prof.) early modern Jewish; cooperma@umd.edu

Dolbilov, Mikhail (PhD, Voronezh State, Russia 1996; asst. prof.) Russian Empire; dolbilov@umd.edu

Eckstein, Arthur M. (PhD, California, Berkeley 1978; prof.) ancient Rome, Hellenic world, ancient historiography; ameckst1@umd.edu

Freund, David M. P. (PhD, Michigan 1999; assoc. prof.) modern US; dmfreund@umd.edu

Gao, James Z. (PhD, Yale 1994; assoc. prof.) China, East Asia; jzgao@umd.edu

Giovacchini, Saverio (PhD, NYU 1998; assoc. prof.) 20th-century media; saverio@umd.edu

Greene, Julie M. (PhD, Yale 1990; prof.; co-dir., Center for Global Migration Studies) US labor and working class, transnational; jmg@umd.edu

Hazkani, Shay (PhD, NYU 2016; asst. prof.; Jewish Studies) Jewish, Israel, Middle East; hazkani@umd.edu

Herf, Jeffrey C. (PhD, Brandeis 1981; Dist. Univ. Prof.) 20th-century Germany, modern European political and intellectual; jherf@umd.edu

Karamustafa, Ahmet (PhD, McGill 1987; prof.) Islamic studies; akaramus@umd.edu

Kosicki, Piotr H. (PhD, Princeton 2011; assoc. prof.) Russia; kosicki@umd.edu

Landau, Paul S. (PhD, Wisconsin, Madison 1992; assoc. prof.) southern Africa; plandau@umd.edu

Lyons, Clare A. (PhD, Yale 1996; assoc. prof.) early America, women, comparative cultural frontiers; clyons@umd.edu

Muncy, Robyn (PhD, Northwestern 1987; prof.) US women; rmuncy@umd.edu

Raianu, Mircea Constantin (PhD, Harvard 2017; asst. prof.) global capitalism, India, British Empire; mraianu@umd.edu

Rodriguez, Chantel Renee (PhD, Minnesota 2013; asst. prof.) chanrod@umd.edu

Rosemblatt, Karin A. (PhD, Wisconsin, Madison 1996; prof.) Latin America, Chile; karosemb@umd.edu

Ross, Michael A. (PhD, North Carolina, Chapel Hill 1999; JD, Duke Sch. of Law 1989; prof.) US law and society; maross@umd.edu

Rowland, Leslie S. (PhD, Rochester 1991; assoc. prof.; ed., Freedmen and Southern Soc. Proj.) US South, Civil War and Reconstruction; lrowland@umd.edu

Rozenblit, Marsha L. (PhD, Columbia 1980; Meyerhoff Prof.) modern Jewish; mrozenbl@umd.edu

Sartorius, David A. (PhD, North Carolina, Chapel Hill 2003; asst. prof.) colonial Latin America, Cuba; das@umd.edu

Sicilia, David B. (PhD, Brandeis 1991; assoc. prof.) 20th-century US, business, economic; dsicilia@umd.edu

Soergel, Philip M. (PhD, Michigan 1988; prof. and chair) medieval and early modern Europe, Reformation, Germany; psoergel@umd.edu

Villani, Stefano (PhD, Scuola Normale Superiore, Pisa, Italy 1998; assoc. prof.; dir., Miller Center for Hist. Studies) religious, early modern Europe; villani@umd.edu

Wien, Peter (PhD, Bonn 2003; prof.) modern Arab, Middle East, North Africa; pwien@umd.edu

Williams, Daryle (PhD, Stanford 1995; assoc. prof.) Brazil; daryle@umd.edu

Woods, Colleen (PhD, Michigan 2012; asst. prof.) US in world, comparative colonialisms; woodscp@umd.edu

Zeller, Thomas (PhD, Munich 1999; assoc. prof.) technology, environment; tzeller@umd.edu

Zhang, Ting (PhD, Johns Hopkins 2014; asst. prof.) China since 1600

Zilfi, Madeline C. (PhD, Chicago 1976; prof.) Middle East, Ottoman, Islamic; mzilfi@umd.edu

Joint/Cross Appointments

Barkley Brown, Elsa (PhD, Kent State 1994; assoc. prof.; Women's Studies) Afro-American and women; barkleyb@umd.edu

Lapin, Hayim (PhD, Columbia 1994; prof.; Jewish Studies) ancient Jewish, rabbinics; hlapin@umd.edu

Nondepartmental Historians

Miller, Steven F. (MA, Maryland, Coll. Park 1979; co-ed., Freedmen and Southern Soc. Proj.) US South, Civil War and Reconstruction; sfmiller@umd.edu

Retired/Emeritus Faculty

Belz, Herman (PhD, Washington 1966; prof. emeritus) American constitutional, Civil War and Reconstruction; redbelz@comcast.net

Bradbury, Miles L. (PhD, Harvard 1967; asst. prof. emeritus) colonial, religious, education; bradbuml@umd.edu

Breslow, Marvin A. (PhD, Harvard 1963; prof. emeritus) Britain, Tudor-Stuart England; mab@umd.edu

Callcott, George H. (PhD, North Carolina, Chapel Hill 1956; prof. emeritus) US South, Maryland; gcallcott@aol.com

Flack, J. Kirkpatrick (PhD, Wayne State 1968; assoc. prof. emeritus) America, social and cultural, urban; jflack@umd.edu

Foust, Clifford M., Jr. (PhD, Chicago 1957; prof. emeritus) Russia, Soviet Union; cfoust@wam.umd.edu

Friedel, Robert D. (PhD, Johns Hopkins 1977; prof. emeritus) technology; friedel@umd.edu

Gilbert, James B. (PhD, Wisconsin-Madison 1966; Dist. Univ. Prof. emeritus) America, American intellectual and cultural; gilbertj@umd.edu

Grimsted, David A. (PhD, California, Berkeley 1963; prof. emeritus) American social, Jacksonian America, film; grimsted@umd.edu

Gullickson, Gay L. (PhD, North Carolina, Chapel Hill 1978; prof. emeritus) early modern and modern France, women, modern Britain; glg@umd.edu

Harris, James F. (PhD, Wisconsin, Madison 1968; prof. emeritus) modern Europe, Germany; jharris@umd.edu

Henretta, James A. (PhD, Harvard 1968; Burke Prof. emeritus) early America, legal, political; henretta@umd.edu

Lampe, John R. (PhD, Wisconsin, Madison 1971; prof. emeritus) European economic, Balkans, business; jrlampe@umd.edu

Majeska, George P. (PhD, Indiana 1968; assoc. prof. emeritus) Byzantine, early Russia; gm5@umail.umd.edu

Mayo, Marlene J. (PhD, Columbia 1961; assoc. prof. emeritus) Japan, East Asia; mmayo@umd.edu

Michel, Sonya Alice (PhD, Brown 1986; prof. emeritus) late modern US, women; smichel@umd.edu

Moss, Alfred A., Jr. (PhD, Chicago 1977; assoc. prof. emeritus) black, social and intellectual, American church; almoss@umd.edu

Olson, Alison G. (PhD, Oxford 1956; prof. emeritus) America, colonial; alisongolson@hotmail.com

Olson, Keith W. (PhD, Wisconsin, Madison 1964; prof. emeritus) America, recent America; kwolson@umd.edu

Price, Richard (PhD, Sussex, UK 1968; prof. emeritus) Britain, labor; rnp@umd.edu

Ridgway, Whitman (PhD, Pennsylvania 1973; assoc. prof. emeritus) early national and Middle Period US; ridgway@umd.edu

Sumida, Jon (PhD, Chicago 1982; prof. emeritus) modern Europe, military; jtsumida@umd.edu

Sutherland, Donald M. G. (PhD, London 1974; prof. emeritus) modern France, French Revolution; dsutherl@umd.edu

Vaughan, Mary Kay (PhD, Wisconsin, Madison 1973; prof. emeritus) Mexico, Latin America; mkv@umd.edu

Recently Awarded PhDs

Donohue, Christopher "Eternal Recurrence in the History of the Social Sciences: From 'Social Selection' to Social Evolution and Back Again"

Holness, Lucien "Between North and South, East and West: The Antislavery Movement in Southwestern Pennsylvania"

Leininger, Derek "A Dark, Evil Enemy Within: Decline at the End of the American Century"

Morningstar, James "War without MacArthur: The Philippines, 1942-44"

Slaughter, Lt Cmdr Joseph P. "Faith in Markets: Christian Business Enterprise in the US, 1800-1850"

Stoehr, Gregory "The End of Roman Temples in Palestine"

Walker, Rachel E. "A Beautiful Mind: Faces, Beauty, and the Brain in the Anglo-Atlantic World, 1780-1870"

Wessell, Erin "Knowing Time, Knowing the World: John Dee, His Contemporaries, and the Gregorian Calendar Reform"

Zarley, Jesse "Mapuche Territoriality from the Late Spanish Empire to the Early Republic, 1793-1862"

Maryville College

Faculty of History, Div. of Humanities, 502 E. Lamar Alexander Pkwy., Anderson Hall, Suite 251, Maryville, TN 37804-5907. 865.981.8224. Fax 865.981.8010. Email: wendy.specter@maryvillecollege.edu. Website: https://www.maryvillecollege.edu/academics/programs-of-study/history/.

Maryville College history majors encounter the seemingly endless diversity of human experience, as lived through thousands of years from the ancient world to the 21st century.

Chair: Phillip M. Sherman
Degrees Offered: BA
Academic Year System: Semester and January term
Areas of Specialization: US, Europe, Africa, Asia, Latin America
Tuition (per academic year): $40218
Enrollment 2018-19:
  Undergraduate Majors: 51
  Degrees in History: 17 BA
Addresses:
  Admissions: http://www.maryvillecollege.edu/admissions/
  Financial Aid: http://www.maryvillecollege.edu/admissions/finaid/

Full-time Faculty

Astor, Aaron (PhD, Northwestern 2006; assoc. prof.) US South, African American, Civil War; aaron.astor@maryvillecollege.edu

Klingensmith, Daniel E. (PhD, Chicago 1998; assoc. prof.) modern Europe, colonialism, India; dan.klingensmith@maryvillecollege.edu

Locklin-Sofer, Nancy Lynne (PhD, Emory 2000; prof.) early modern Europe, colonial Latin America, women and gender; nancy.locklin@maryvillecollege.edu

Sofer, Douglas O. (PhD, Texas, Austin 2003; assoc. prof.) Latin America, modern African political, American hemisphere; doug.sofer@maryvillecollege.edu

Retired/Emeritus Faculty

Lewis, Wallace Leigh (PhD, Iowa 1969; prof. emeritus) modern Germany, naval, East Asia

University of Mary Washington

Dept. of History and American Studies, 1301 College Ave., Fredericksburg, VA 22401-5358. 540.654.1066. Fax 540.654.1482. Email: jbatten@umw.edu. Website: https://cas.umw.edu/historyamericanstudies/.

In their study, students gain a rigorous preparation in research and writing, a strong set of skills necessary to analyzing and communicating ideas clearly and effectively, as well as training in digital fluencies for a 21th-century world.

Chair: Claudine L. Ferrell
Degrees Offered: BA,BLS
Academic Year System: Semester
Areas of Specialization: US, Europe, East Asia, Middle East
Tuition (per academic year):
  In-State: $10968
  Out-of-State: $24814
Enrollment 2018-19:
  Undergraduate Majors: 203
  Degrees in History: 65 BA
Addresses:
  Admissions: http://admissions.umw.edu/
  Financial Aid: http://adminfinance.umw.edu/financialaid/

Full-time Faculty

Al-Tikriti, Nabil Sirri (PhD, Chicago 2004; assoc. prof.) Middle East and Islam; naltikri@umw.edu

Blakemore, Porter R. (PhD, Georgia 1978; assoc. prof.) European diplomatic, Germany, military; pblakemo@umw.edu

Devlin, Erin K. (PhD, William and Mary 2011; asst. prof.) America, public history and American memory, performance studies, labor, oral; edevlin@umw.edu

Fernsebner, Susan R. (PhD, California, San Diego 2002; prof.) East Asia, China; sfernseb@umw.edu

Ferrell, Claudine (PhD, Rice 1983; prof. and chair) African American, Vietnam, legal and constitutional, post-Civil War US, disasters; cferrell@umw.edu

Harris, Steven E. (PhD, Chicago 2003; assoc. prof.) modern Europe and Russia, urban, conspiracy theories; sharris@umw.edu

Mackintosh, Will (PhD, Michigan 2009; asst. prof.) early national US, urban, manhood in US; wmackint@umw.edu

McClurken, Jeffrey W. (PhD, Johns Hopkins 2002; prof.) 19th-century US social/cultural/gender/families, digital and technology, veterans and mental institutions; jmcclurk@umw.edu

Moon, Krystyn R. (PhD, Johns Hopkins 2002; assoc. prof.) 19th- and 20th-century US social and cultural; kmoon@umw.edu

O'Brien, Bruce R. (PhD, Yale 1990; prof.) medieval culture and translation, early medieval law, ancient Greece and Rome; bobrien@umw.edu

Poska, Allyson M. (PhD, Minnesota 1992; prof.) Spain, Latin America, women; aposka@umw.edu

Sellers, Jason R. (PhD, California, Irvine 2010; assoc. prof.) Native American, colonial, environmental; jseller4@umw.edu

Nondepartmental Historians

Preston, David (PhD, Maryland, Coll. Park 1989; ed.; James Monroe Papers) early national US; dpreston@umw.edu

Retired/Emeritus Faculty

Bourdon, Roger J. (PhD, UCLA 1965; prof. emeritus) early America, American Indian; rbourdon@umw.edu

Crawley, William B., Jr. (PhD, Virginia 1974; Dist. Prof., Rector and Visitors' Chair emeritus) 20th-century US, Old US South; wcrawley@umw.edu

Ryang, Key Sun (PhD, Columbia 1972; prof. emeritus) Asian civilization, modern Japan, China

Thomas, Glen R. (PhD, Emory; prof. emeritus) American studies

Tracy, Arthur L. (PhD, American 1975; assoc. prof. emeritus) American studies; atracy@umw.edu

Zimdars, Benjamin (PhD, Texas, Austin 1965; prof. emeritus) Latin America, Spain

University of Massachusetts Amherst

Dept. of History, 616 Herter Hall, 161 Presidents Dr., Amherst, MA 01003-9312. 413.545.1330. Fax 413.545.6137. Email: gradprogram@history.umass.edu; history@history.umass.edu. Website: https://www.umass.edu/history/.

The University of Massachusetts/Five College Graduate Program in History is a collaboration between the state's flagship research university and the history faculty at Amherst, Hampshire, Mount Holyoke, and Smith Colleges.

Chair: Brian Ogilvie; Audrey Altstadt, interim
Director of Graduate Studies: Jason Moralee
Director of Undergraduate Studies: Heidi Scott
Degrees Offered: BA,MA,PhD,Cert. (public hist.)
Academic Year System: Semester
Areas of Specialization: US, Europe, Latin America, public, global
Undergraduate Tuition (per academic year):
  In-State: $15887
  New England Regional: $13817
  Out-of-State: $34570
Graduate Tuition (per academic year):
  In-State: $11359
  New England Regional: $19223
  Out-of-State: $22767
Enrollment 2018-19:
  Undergraduate Majors: 290
  New Graduate Students: 13
  Full-time Graduate Students: 58
  Degrees in History: 86 BA, 5 MA, 3 PhD
  Students in Undergraduate Courses: 4755
  Students in Undergraduate Intro Courses: 2726
Undergraduate Addresses:
  Admissions: http://www.umass.edu/admissions/
  Financial Aid: http://www.umass.edu/umfa/
Graduate Addresses:
  Admissions: http://www.umass.edu/gradschool/admissions
  Financial Aid: http://www.umass.edu/gradschool/funding-support

Adjunct Faculty

Ben-Ur, Aviva (PhD, Brandeis 1998; assoc. prof.; Judaic and Near Eastern Studies) Eurafricans in Suriname, US ethnohistory; aben-ur@judnea.umass.edu

Berkovitz, Jay (PhD, Brandeis 1983; prof.; Judaic Studies) European Jewry, France; jrb@judnea.umass.edu

Briggs, Laura J. (PhD, Brown 1997; prof.; Women, Gender, Sexuality Studies) US women, politics of reproduction, gender and science; ljbriggs@wost.umass.edu

Cox, Robert S. (PhD, Michigan 2002; adj. asst. prof.; head, Univ. Archives and Special Collections) US, science, biology; rscox@library.umass.edu

Page, Max (PhD, Pennsylvania 1995; adj. prof.; Art) 20th-century US society and culture, urban, architecture; mpage@art.umass.edu

Shabazz, Amilcar (PhD, Houston 1996; prof.; W.E.B. Du Bois Dept. of Afro-American Studies) African educational history and public policy, Afro-Americans in Caribbean/Central and South America, African American biography

Skolnik, Jonathan (PhD, Columbia 1999; assoc. prof.; German and Scandinavian Studies) German-Jewish literature and culture, 19th- and 20th-century literature, intellectual; jskolnik@german.umass.edu

Stern, Peter (PhD, California, Berkeley 1984; adj. assoc. prof.; Library) Latin America; pstern@library.umass.edu

Sullivan, Robert (PhD, Wisconsin-Madison 1991; assoc. prof.; German and Scandinavian Studies) medieval literature; sullivan@german.umass.edu

Full-time Faculty

Altstadt, Audrey (PhD, Chicago 1983; prof. and interim chair) Soviet Union, Azerbaijan; altstadt@history.umass.edu

Appy, Christian G. (PhD, Harvard 1987; prof.) US, Vietnam, Cold War; appy@history.umass.edu

Bowman, Joye L. (PhD, UCLA 1980; prof.; assoc. dean, research and personnel) Portuguese Africa, South Africa; jbowman@history.umass.edu

Broadbridge, Anne F. (PhD, Chicago 2001; assoc. prof.) Middle East, medieval Islam; broadbridge@history.umass.edu

Bunk, Brian D. (PhD, Wisconsin, Madison 2000; sr. lect.) world; bunk@history.umass.edu

Capo, Julio C., Jr. (PhD, Florida International 2011; assoc. prof.) transnational US, Latino/a studies, Caribbean gender/sexuality/migration; capo@history.umass.edu

Chu, Richard T. (PhD, Southern California 2003; assoc. prof.) Chinese diaspora, Philippines; rtchu@history.umass.edu

Confino, Alon (PhD, California, Berkeley 1992; prof.; dir., Inst. for Holocaust, Genocide and Memory Studies) Israel, Germany and Holocaust, memory/culture/nationhood; confino@umass.edu

Cornell, Sarah E. (PhD, NYU 2008; asst. prof.) Civil War era, transnational race, slavery and emancipation

Fronc, Jennifer (PhD, Columbia 2005; assoc. prof.) Gilded Age and Progressive era, urban, labor; jfronc@history.umass.edu

Glassberg, David (PhD, Johns Hopkins 1982; prof.) public, US social and intellectual; glassberg@history.umass.edu

Gordon, Daniel L. (PhD, Chicago 1990; prof.; dir., Bachelor's Degree with Individual Concentration, Commonwealth Honors Coll.) early modern Europe, Enlightenment, legal and constitutional; dgordon@history.umass.edu

Heuer, Jennifer N. (PhD, Chicago 1998; assoc. prof.) modern Europe, France, women and gender; heuer@history.umass.edu

Higginson, John Edward (PhD, Michigan 1979; prof.) southern Africa, comparative labor; jeh@history.umass.edu

Krauthamer, Barbara (PhD, Princeton 2000; prof. and dean; Grad. School) slavery/emancipation in Indian Territory; barbarak@history.umass.edu

Lovett, Laura L. (PhD, California, Berkeley 1998; assoc. prof.) 20th-century US, women, childhood and youth; lovett@history.umass.edu

Miller, Marla R. (PhD, North Carolina, Chapel Hill 1997; prof.) public, early America, US women; mmiller@history.umass.edu

Moralee, Jason W (PhD, UCLA 2002; assoc. prof. and dir., grad. prog.) Greece, Rome, late antiquity; jmoralee@history.umass.edu

Nash, Alice (PhD, Columbia 1997; assoc. prof.) Native American, early America, women; anash@history.umass.edu

Nye, Jennifer L. (JD, Boston Coll. Law Sch. 1998; lect.; Commonwealth Honors Coll.) law and litigation, social movements, LGBT law/sex and gender discrimination; jlnye@history.umass.edu

Ogilvie, Brian W. (PhD, Chicago 1997; prof. and chair) Renaissance, early modern science, scholarship; ogilvie@history.umass.edu

Olsen, Jon Berndt (PhD, North Carolina, Chapel Hill 2004; assoc. prof.) modern Germany, public, memory and commemoration; jon@history.umass.edu

Platt, Stephen R. (PhD, Yale 2004; prof.) modern China; platt@history.umass.edu

Redman, Emily T. (PhD, California, Berkeley 2013; asst. prof.) science, 20th-century US; eredman@history.umass.edu

Redman, Samuel James (PhD, California, Berkeley 2012; assoc. prof.) heritage studies, public, 19th- and 20th-century US; sredman@history.umass.edu

Schmalzer, Sigrid (PhD, California, Santa Barbara 2004; prof.) modern China; sigrid@history.umass.edu

Schwartz, Kathryn A. (PhD, Harvard 2015; asst. prof.) modern Middle East and Ottoman, book, technology; kaschwartz@umass.edu

Scott, Heidi Victoria (PhD, Cambridge 2002; assoc. prof. and dir., undergrad. prog.) Latin American colonial, Peru and Bolivia; hvscott@history.umass.edu

Srivastava, Priyanka (PhD, Cincinnati 2012; assoc. prof.; Economics) colonial South Asia, labor social, women and gender; priyanka@history.umass.edu

Taylor, Anna Lisa (PhD, Texas, Austin 2006; assoc. prof.) medieval Europe, Christianity, animal studies; annat@history.umass.edu

Washington, Garrett L. (PhD, Purdue 2010; asst. prof.) Japan, environmental, religion; gwashington@history.umass.edu

Wolfe, Joel W. (PhD, Wisconsin, Madison 1990; prof.) Latin America, Brazil, technology; jwolfe@history.umass.edu

Young, Kevin (PhD, SUNY, Stony Brook 2013; asst. prof.) Latin America; kayoung@history.umass.edu

Joint/Cross Appointments

Donson, Andrew C. (PhD, Michigan 2000; assoc. prof.; German and Scandinavian Studies) modern Germany; adonson@german.umass.edu

Sharrow, Elizabeth A. (PhD, Minnesota; asst. prof.; Political Science) sports/policy/politics, US social policy and politics of gender; sharrow@polsci.umass.edu

Retired/Emeritus Faculty

Barton, Carlin Adele (PhD, California, Berkeley 1984; prof. emeritus) ancient Greece and Rome; cbarton@history.umass.edu

Berkman, Joyce A. (PhD, Yale 1967; prof. emeritus) modern England, 19th- and 20th-century British and American women; jberkman@history.umass.edu

Bernhard, Winfred E. (PhD, Columbia 1961; prof. emeritus) colonial New England; winbern@comcast.net

Cantor, Milton (PhD, Columbia 1954; prof. emeritus) US, intellectual/labor/constitutional; mcantor@history.umass.edu

DePillis, Mario S. (PhD, Yale 1961; prof. emeritus) American religious; depillis@history.umass.edu

Drake, Frederic (PhD, Harvard 1971; prof. emeritus) modern China; fwdrake@gmail.com

Johnston, William M. (PhD, Harvard 1965; prof. emeritus) European intellectual; william@etterlink.com.au

Jones, Robert E. (PhD, Cornell 1968; prof. emeritus) Europe, Russia; rejones@history.umass.edu

Laurie, Bruce G. (PhD, Pittsburgh 1971; prof. emeritus) American labor, American immigration; laurie@history.umass.edu

Levy, Barry J. (PhD, Pennsylvania 1976; prof. emeritus) colonial America, family; bjl@history.umass.edu

McFarland, Gerald W. (PhD, Columbia 1965; prof. emeritus) Gilded Age, Progressive era, historiography; geraldm@history.umass.edu

Minear, Richard H. (PhD, Harvard 1968; prof. emeritus) East Asia, Far Eastern languages, Japan; rhminear@history.umass.edu

Nissenbaum, Stephen (PhD, Wisconsin, Madison 1968; prof. emeritus) US shame and honor, cultural politics of Handel's Messiah; snissenbaum@history.umass.edu

Oates, Stephen B. (PhD, Texas, Austin 1969; prof. emeritus) Civil War; sboates@history.umass.edu

Owens, Larry (PhD, Rutgers 1972; prof. emeritus) science and technology, US, comparative; lowens@history.umass.edu

Pelz, Stephen E. (PhD, Harvard 1971; prof. emeritus) World War II

Rausch, Jane M. (PhD, Wisconsin-Madison 1969; prof. emerita) Latin America, Colombia, Caribbean; jrausch@history.umass.edu

Rearick, Charles (PhD, Harvard 1968; prof. emeritus) Europe 1815-70, France since 1789, 19th-century European intellectual; rearick@history.umass.edu

Richards, Leonard L. (PhD, California, Davis 1968; prof. emeritus) US to 1865, Jacksonian America, slavery and antislavery; llr@history.umass.edu

Sarti, Roland (PhD, Rutgers 1967; prof. emeritus) modern Europe, Italy; sarti@history.umass.edu

Shipley, Neal (PhD, Harvard 1967; prof. emeritus) Great Britain and modern Europe; n.shipley@comcast.net

Story, Ronald (PhD, SUNY, Stony Brook 1972; prof. emeritus) American culture and society; rstory@history.umass.edu

Swartz, Marvin (PhD, Yale 1969; prof. emeritus) Europe, World War I, British political; mswartz@history.umass.edu

Wilson, Mary Christina (DPhil, Oxford 1984; prof. emeritus) modern Middle East social and political; wilson@history.umass.edu

Recently Awarded PhDs

Fagen, Erica "Hashtag Holocaust: Negotiating Memory in the Age of Multimedia"

Fobare, Christopher J. "A Generational Divide: The Reconstruction of American Party Politics, 1865-1912"

Roblee, Mark "'Greetings, I Am an Immortal God!' Self-Deification in Late Antique Roman North Africa, Second through Fifth Centuries CE"

University of Massachusetts Boston

Dept. of History, 100 Morrissey Blvd., Boston, MA 02125-3393. 617.287.6860. Fax 617.287.6899. Email: maureen.dwyer@umb. edu. Website: https://www.umb.edu/academics/cla/history.

History: it's all about the present. Learning about people and cultures, and the debates and controversies of the past, helps us understand our world today.

Chair: Tim Hacsi
Director of Graduate Studies: Elizabeth McCahill
Degrees Offered: BA,MA
Academic Year System: Semester
Areas of Specialization: Europe, US, Atlantic and Latin America, East and Southeast Asia, science and medicine
Undergraduate Tuition (per academic year):
In-State: $13841
Out-of-State: $33640

Graduate Tuition (per academic year):
In-State: $17896
Out-of-State: $34932
Enrollment 2018-19:
Undergraduate Majors: 115
New Graduate Students: 20
Full-time Graduate Students: 30
Part-time Graduate Students: 70
Degrees in History: 45 BA, 20 MA
Undergraduate Addresses:
Admissions: http://www.umb.edu/admissions/ug
Financial Aid: http://www.umb.edu/admissions/financial_aid_scholarships
Graduate Addresses:
Admissions and Financial Aid: http://www.umb.edu/admissions/grad

Full-time Faculty

Cannato, Vincent J. (PhD, Columbia 1998; assoc. prof.) 20th-century US; vincent.cannato@umb.edu

Chu, Jonathan M. (PhD, Washington 1978; prof.) colonial and revolutionary America, legal; jonathan.chu@umb.edu

Di Scala, Spencer (PhD, Columbia 1969; prof.) modern Italy, 19th- and 20th-century Europe; spencer.discala@umb.edu

Gengenbach, Heidi (PhD, Minnesota 1999; asst. prof.) African society and environment, gender and agrarian change, food security and nutrition; heidi.gengenbach@umb.edu

Hacsi, Tim A. (PhD, Pennsylvania 1993; assoc. prof. and chair) social and public policy, poverty; tim.hacsi@umb.edu

Haroon, Sana (PhD, SOAS, London 2004; assoc. prof.; Asian Studies) Islamic culture, South Asia, Pakistan; sana.haroon@umb.edu

Hunt, David (PhD, Harvard 1969; prof.) French Revolution, Vietnam, peasant studies; david.hunt@umb.edu

John, Maria K. (PhD, Columbia 2017; asst. prof.) Native American, Aboriginal Australian, health/urban communities/activism; mkj2111@columbia.edu-

Johnson, Benjamin Daniel (PhD, Chicago 2011; asst. prof.) Mexico, Brazil and Caribbean, global trade and colonialism; benjamin.johnson@umb.edu

McCahill, Elizabeth M. (PhD, Princeton 2005; asst. prof. and dir., grad. studies) city of Rome, papal court, early 15th-century humanism; elizabeth.mccahill@umb.edu

Wang, Luman (PhD, Southern California 2014; asst. prof.; Asian Studies) late imperial and modern China, economic and business, Asia; wangluman@gmail.com

Weisser, Olivia A. (PhD, Johns Hopkins 2010; asst. prof.) medicine, early modern England, women and gender; olivia.weisser@umb.edu

Winch, Julie P. (PhD, Bryn Mawr 1982; prof.) early American republic, African American, maritime; julie.winch@umb.edu

Wollons, Roberta (PhD, Chicago 1983; prof.) US, women, education; roberta.wollons@umb.edu

Nondepartmental Historians

Smith, Judith E. (PhD, Brown 1980; prof.; American Studies) ethnicity and race, 20th-century US, social and women; judith.smith@umb.edu

Part-time Faculty

Becker, Jane S. (PhD, Boston Univ. 1993; dir., public hist.) public, 20th-century US cultural and social, material culture; jane.becker@umb.edu

Brink, Maryann E. (PhD, Brown 1988; lect. II) Western civilization, medieval; maryann.brink@umb.edu

Johnson, Thomas P. (MA, Boston Univ. 1992; lect.) Africa; thomas.johnson@umb.edu

Miller, Gary M. (PhD, Yale 1998; sr. lect.) early modern Europe; gary.miller@umb.edu

Retired/Emeritus Faculty

Ahmad, Feroz (PhD, London 1966; prof. emeritus) Middle East

Foss, Clive F. (PhD, Harvard 1973; prof. emeritus) ancient

Quitt, Martin H. (PhD, Washington, St. Louis 1970; prof. emeritus) early America; martin.quitt@umb.edu

Segal, Lester A. (PhD, Columbia 1968; prof. emeritus) early modern, Jewish; lester.segal@umb.edu

Shatz, Marshall S. (PhD, Columbia 1968; prof. emeritus) Russia; marshall.shatz@umb.edu

Smith, Woodruff D. (PhD, Chicago 1972; prof. emeritus) Germany, Africa, Atlantic; woodruff.smith@umb.edu

Smuts, R. Malcolm (PhD, Princeton 1976; prof. emeritus) early modern England; malcolm.smuts@umb.edu

Massachusetts Institute of Technology

History Faculty, Sch. of Humanities, Arts & Social Sciences, E51-255, 77 Massachusetts Ave., Cambridge, MA 02139-4307. 617.253.4965. Fax 617.253.9406. Email: history-info@mit.edu. Website: http://history.mit.edu/.

History at MIT brings together outstanding scholarship, teaching, and public engagement.

Chair: Jeffrey S. Ravel
Degrees Offered: BS,PhD
Academic Year System: Semester
Areas of Specialization: Americas, Europe, South and East Asia, Middle East and Africa, science and technology
Tuition (per academic year): $53450
Enrollment 2018-19:
New Graduate Students: 5
Undergraduate Addresses:
Admissions: http://web.mit.edu/admissions/
Financial Aid: http://web.mit.edu/admissions/graduate/
Graduate Addresses:
Admissions and Financial Aid: http://web.mit.edu/sfs/

Full-time Faculty

Aiyar, Sana (PhD, Harvard 2009; assoc. prof. and Class of 1948 Career Development Chair) South Asia and its diasporas, Indian Ocean and Burma, East Africa; aiyar@mit.edu

Broadhead, Will (PhD, London 2002; assoc. prof. and MacVicar Faculty Fellow) Roman Italy, ancient epigraphy, ancient and modern perceptions of Roman emperors; williamb@mit.edu

Capozzola, Christopher (PhD, Columbia 2002; prof.) US political, cultural, foreign relations; capozzol@mit.edu

Ekmekcioglu, Lerna (PhD, NYU 2010; McMillan-Stewart Career Development Assoc. Prof.) Middle East, Ottoman Empire, Turkey and Armenians; lerna@mit.edu

Ghachem, Malick Walid (PhD, Stanford 2002; assoc. prof.) slavery/abolition, legal, Atlantic; mghachem@mit.edu

Goldberg, Eric J. (PhD, Virginia 1998; assoc. prof.) late antiquity, early Middle Ages, Carolingian Europe; egoldber@mit.edu

Horan, Caley D. (PhD, Minnesota 2011; assoc. prof.) modern US; cdhoran@mit.edu

Khoury, Philip S. (PhD, Harvard 1980; Ford International Prof. and assoc. provost) Middle East and Islamic, social and political; khoury@mit.edu

McCants, Anne E. C. (PhD, California, Berkeley 1991; prof.; dir., Concourse) late medieval and early modern Europe, economic, demography; amccants@mit.edu

Mutongi, Kenda B. (PhD, Virginia 1996; prof.) modern Africa, urban, political economy; kmutongi@mit.edu

Nagahara, Hiromu (PhD, Harvard 2011; assoc. prof.) modern Japan, cultural; nagahara@mit.edu

Padilla, Tanalis (PhD, California, San Diego 2001; assoc. prof.) Mexico, Cuba; tanalis@mit.edu

Ravel, Jeffrey S. (PhD, California, Berkeley 1991; prof. and chair) 17th- through 19th-century Europe, France, cultural; ravel@mit.edu

Ritvo, Harriet (PhD, Harvard 1975; Arthur J. Conner Prof.) Britain, environmental, science; ritvo@mit.edu

Teng, Emma J. (PhD, Harvard 1997; T.T. and Wei Fong Chao Prof. and MacVicar Faculty Fellow) Asian American studies, gender studies, China studies; eteng@mit.edu

Wilder, Craig Steven (PhD, Columbia 1994; Barton L. Weller Prof.) US urban and intellectual; cwilder@mit.edu

Wood, Elizabeth A. (PhD, Michigan 1991; prof.) Russia and Soviet Union, gender studies; elizwood@mit.edu

Joint/Cross Appointments

Fogelson, Robert M. (PhD, Harvard 1964; prof.; Urban Studies and Planning) American urban; foge@mit.edu

Smith, Merritt Roe (PhD, Penn State 1971; Leverett Howell and William King Cutten Prof. and MacVicar Faculty Fellow; Prog. in Science, Tech., and Soc.) American technology, Industrial Revolution, technology and culture; roesmith@mit.edu

Nondepartmental Historians

Deringer, William Peter (PhD, Princeton 2012; asst. prof.; Prog. in Science, Tech., and Soc.) science and technology, economic and financial, Britain; deringer@mit.edu

Fitzgerald, Deborah K. (PhD, Pennsylvania 1985; prof.; Prog. in Science, Tech., and Soc.) agriculture and food, technology; dkfitz@mit.edu

Kaiser, David (PhD, Harvard 2000; prof.; Prog. in Science, Tech., and Soc.; Physics) modern physics, American science, science and popularization; dikaiser@mit.edu

Light, Jennifer (PhD, Harvard 1999; prof.; Hist. of Science) US, intellectual, urban; jslight@mit.edu

Mindell, David A. (PhD, MIT 1996; Frances and David Dibner Prof.; Aeronautics and Astronautics; Prog. in Science, Tech., and Soc., Engineering Systems Div.) spaceflight, automation and robotics, electronics and computing; mindell@mit.edu

Scheffler, Robin Wolfe (PhD, Yale 2014; asst. prof.; Prog. in Science, Tech., and Soc.) science, medicine, 20th-century US; rws42@mit.edu

Temin, Peter (PhD, MIT 1964; Elisha Gray II Prof. emeritus; Economics) economic; ptemin@mit.edu

Yates, JoAnne (PhD, North Carolina, Chapel Hill 1980; Sloan Dist. Prof.; Sloan Sch. Management) 19th- and 20th-century American business and technology, information systems, international private standardization; jyates@mit.edu

Part-time Faculty

Alimagham, Pouya (PhD, Michigan 2015; lect.) modern Middle East/Iran, transnational Shi'ism, revolutionary movements; ipouya@mit.edu

Pope, Andrew (PhD, Harvard 2018; lect.) African American, gender and sexuality, 20th-century US; andrewpope@fas.harvard.edu

Pugliano, Valentina (DPhil, Oxford 2013; lect.) science and medicine, global and Mediterranean, material culture studies; pugliano@mit.edu

Susmann, Natalie (PhD, Boston Univ. 2019; lect.) Greece, landscape archaeology, memory; nsusmann@mit.edu

Zimmer, Mary Erica (PhD, Boston Univ. 2019; lect.) bibliography, English book trade, media studies; ezimmer@mit.edu

Retired/Emeritus Faculty

Dower, John W. (PhD, Harvard 1972; Ford International Prof. emeritus) Japan, international relations, race and culture

Fox Keller, Evelyn (PhD, Harvard 1963; prof. emeritus) history and philosophy of science, gender and science, language and science; efkeller@mit.edu

Graham, Loren R. (PhD, Columbia 1964; prof. emeritus) science, Russia; lrg@mit.edu

Perdue, Peter C. (PhD, Harvard 1981; prof. emeritus) modern Chinese and Japanese social and economic, frontiers, world; peter.c.perdue@yale.edu

Watson, William B. (PhD, Harvard 1963; assoc. prof. emeritus) modern Spain, Spanish Civil War, Hemingway; wbwatson@mit.edu

Williams, Rosalind (PhD, Massachusetts Amherst 1978; Bern Dinner Prof. emeritus) literary, modern Britain and Europe, technological; rhwill@mit.edu

Visiting Faculty

Brown, Tristan (PhD, Columbia 2017; vis. scholar) late imperial China, legal, environmental; tristanb@mit.edu

Stewart, Jeffrey (PhD, Yale 1979; prof.) intellectual, African American, art and cultural

Williams, Rhonda Y. (PhD, Pennsylvania 1998; John L. Seigenthaler Chair) civil rights and black power, race/class/gender, urban/social movements/social justice; rhonda.williams@vanderbilt.edu

Recently Awarded PhDs

Kim, Grace "The Work of Art in the Age of Its Technoscientific Re-Enchantment: Recasting Light, Colloids, and Microbes for Art and Heritage Conservation in US and Italian Laboratories"

Labruto, Nicole "The Plantation Network: Brazilian Bioenergy Science and Sustainability in the Global South"

Mutlu, Burcu "Transnational Biopolitics and Family-Making in Secrecy: An Ethnography of Reproductive Travel from Turkey to Northern Cyprus"

Shapiro, Ryan "Bodies at War: National Security in American Controversies over Animal and Human Experimentation from WWI to the War on Terror"

University of Memphis

Dept. of History, 219 Mitchell Hall, Memphis, TN 38152-3450. 901.678.2515. Fax 901.678.2720. Email: agoudszn@memphis. edu. Website: https://www.memphis.edu/history/.

When you study history at the University of Memphis, you learn from a team of talented, award-winning scholars and teachers. You absorb the diverse, important, and fascinating lessons of the human past. And you master the necessary skills to succeed in today's economy: you think critically, research deeply, analyze complex events, and write with clarity and distinction.

Chair: Aram G. Goudsouzian
Director of Graduate Studies: Daniel L. Unowsky
Director of Undergraduate Studies: Sarah E. Potter
Degrees Offered: BA, MA, PhD
Academic Year System: Semester
Areas of Specialization: US, modern Europe, women and gender, African American, ancient Egypt

Undergraduate Tuition (per academic year):
In-State: $9317
Out-of-State: $21029
Graduate Tuition (per academic year):
In-State: $10697
Out-of-State: $19481
Enrollment 2018-19:
Undergraduate Majors: 214
New Graduate Students: 22
Full-time Graduate Students: 68
Degrees in History: 89 BA, 9 MA, 7 PhD
Undergraduate Addresses:
Admissions: http://www.memphis.edu/admissions/
Financial Aid: http://www.memphis.edu/financialaid/
Graduate Addresses:
Admissions: http://www.memphis.edu/graduateadmissions/future/apply_grad.php
Financial Aid: http://www.memphis.edu/financialaid/

Full-time Faculty

Arnold, Catherine (PhD, Yale 2017; asst. prof.) early modern Britain and Europe; crnold13@memphis.edu

Bond, Beverly Greene (PhD, Memphis 1996; assoc. prof.) 19th-century African American; bgbond@memphis.edu

Brand, Peter J. (PhD, Toronto 1998; prof.) Egyptology, ancient Near and Middle East; pbrand@memphis.edu

Coffey, Michele L. (PhD, South Carolina 2010; instr.) African American women and gender, American political, 20th-century US; mlcoffey@memphis.edu

Crawford, Charles W. (PhD, Mississippi 1968; prof.) Tennessee, oral; cwcrwfrd@memphis.edu

Daily, Andrew M. (PhD, Rutgers 2011; asst. prof.) modern France, global; amdaily@memphis.edu

Duenas-Vargas, Guiomar (PhD, Texas, Austin 1995; prof.) Latin America, Caribbean, women and gender; gduenas@memphis.edu

Eisel, Christine L. (PhD, Bowling Green State 2012; instr.) colonial America, American women; cleisel@memphis.edu

Fickle, James E. (PhD, Louisiana State 1970; prof.) American economic, labor; jfickle@memphis.edu

Goudsouzian, Aram G. (PhD, Purdue 2002; prof. and chair) 20th-century African American; agoudszn@memphis.edu

Goudsouzian, Chrystal Elaine (PhD, Memphis 2012; instr. and advisor) Egyptology; cdykes@memphis.edu

Graham, Benjamin Jon (PhD, Michigan 2014; asst. prof.) medieval Europe, Mediterranean, environmental; bjgraham@memphis.edu

Kwoba, Brian (PhD, Oxford 2017; asst. prof.) African American; bwkwoba@memphis.edu

Laumann, Dennis (PhD, UCLA 1999; assoc. prof.) sub-Saharan Africa; dlaumann@memphis.edu

Marler, Scott P. (PhD, Rice 2007; assoc. prof.) US, Atlantic world; spmarler@memphis.edu

Mole, Gregory Thomas (PhD, North Carolina, Chapel Hill 2015; instr.) early modern France and Europe, global; gmole@memphis.edu

O'Donovan, Susan E. (PhD, California, San Diego 1997; assoc. prof.) 19th-century South, slavery, emancipation; odonovan@memphis.edu

Onstine, Suzanne L. (PhD, Toronto 2001; assoc. prof.) Egyptology, Greece and Rome; sonstine@memphis.edu

Phipps, Catherine L. (PhD, Duke 2006; assoc. prof.) Asia; cphipps1@memphis.edu

Potter, Sarah E. (PhD, Chicago 2008; assoc. prof. and dir., undergrad. studies) US, gender/family/childhood; spotter1@memphis.edu

Savage, Amanda Lee Keikialoha (MA, William and Mary 2011; instr. and undergrad. advisor) early America, Native American, Pacific world; aksavage@memphis.edu

Stein, Stephen K. (PhD, Ohio State 1999; assoc. prof.) military and naval, post-Civil War US, ancient; sstein@memphis.edu

Tsacoyianis, Beverly A. (PhD, Washington, St. Louis 2014; asst. prof.) modern Middle East and Islamic, 20th-century global and comparative, science and medicine; btscynis@memphis.edu

Unowsky, Daniel L. (PhD, Columbia 2000; prof. and dir., grad. studies) modern east central Europe; dunowsky@memphis.edu

Woolner, Cookie (PhD, Michigan 2014; instr.) 20th century, women and gender

Znamenski, Andrei A. (PhD, Toledo 1997; prof.) Russia and Soviet Union, Central Asia; znmenski@memphis.edu

Retired/Emeritus Faculty

Blythe, James M. (PhD, Cornell 1987; prof. emeritus) medieval Europe, Renaissance; jmblythe@memphis.edu

Brown, Walter R. (PhD, Emory 1973; assoc. prof. emeritus) early modern Europe, France; wrbrown@memphis.edu

Caffrey, Margaret M. (PhD, Texas, Austin 1986; assoc. prof. emeritus) American women; mcaffrey@memphis.edu

Chumney, James R., Jr. (PhD, Rice 1964; assoc. prof. emeritus) US South; jchumney@memphis.edu

Crouse, Maurice A. (PhD, Northwestern 1964; prof. emeritus) colonial and revolutionary America; mcrouse@memphis.edu

Ellis, Donald W. (PhD, Kansas 1970; assoc. prof. emeritus) 20th-century Europe, modern Germany

Frankle, Robert J. (PhD, Wisconsin, Madison 1970; assoc. prof. emeritus) Tudor-Stuart England, Reformation; rfrankle@memphis.edu

Hawes, Joseph M. (PhD, Texas, Austin 1969; prof. emeritus) US, family; jhawes@memphis.edu

Hurley, F. Jack (PhD, Tulane 1971; prof. emeritus) US between the wars, technology, urban; hurleyj1@bellsouth.net

Kalin, Berkley (PhD, St. Louis 1967; assoc. prof. emeritus) American social and intellectual

Sherman, Janann M. (PhD, Rutgers 1993; prof. emeritus) 20th-century US, women; sherman@memphis.edu

Skeen, C. Edward (PhD, Ohio State 1966; prof. emeritus) early national; ceskeen@memphis.edu

Tucker, David M. (PhD, Iowa 1965; prof. emeritus) African American

Wilson, Major L. (PhD, Kansas 1964; prof. emeritus) American intellectual, US

Recently Awarded PhDs

Gray, Victoria Jackson "Mission of a Meddler: Mixed Matters of Class, Gender, and Race in Mary Church Terrell's Model of Elite Black Female Activism"

Hallsell, Troy Alan "The Overton Park Freeway Revolt: Urban Environmentalism, Historic Preservation, and Neighborhood Protection in Memphis, Tennessee, 1956-2016"

Jones, Jeffery "Benjamin O. Davis Sr., America's First Black General: The Paradox of Racial Leadership and the Military Profession"

Ringer, Andrea "Big Top Labor: Life and Labor in the Circus World"

Warkentin, Elizabeth Rose "Looking Behind the Image: An Exploration of the Relationship between Political Power and the Cult Places of Hathor in New Kingdom Egypt"

Wildberger, Isabel Machado "Marked Bodies and the Intervention of Tradition in Mobile, Alabama's Mardi Gras"

Wood, Keith Brian "Larry Finch's Memphis: Race, Basketball and the City, 1967-77"

Mercer University

Dept. of History, 1501 Mercer University Dr., Macon, GA 31207. 478.301.2910. Fax 478.301.2855. Email: scott_jt@mercer.edu. Website: http://cla.mercer.edu/history/.

History students learn to see how different forces have interacted in different contexts, how the past has shaped the present, and how today's challenges are both unique and familiar.

Chair: John Thomas Scott
Degrees Offered: BA
Academic Year System: Semester
Areas of Specialization: early Americas, American South, France, intellectual and religious
Tuition (per academic year): $36594
Enrollment 2018-19:
  Undergraduate Majors: 30
  Degrees in History: 7 BA
Addresses:
  Admissions: http://admission.mercer.edu/
  Financial Aid: http://financialaid.mercer.edu/

Full-time Faculty

Daniel, Wallace L., Jr. (PhD, North Carolina, Chapel Hill 1973; prof.) Soviet Union and post-Communist Russia, comparative revolutions, church and state in modern world; daniel_wl@mercer.edu

Dowling, Abigail P. (PhD, California, Santa Barbara 2014; asst. prof.) late antiquity, medieval, environmental; dowling_ap@mercer.edu

Gardner, Sarah E. (PhD, Emory 1996; prof.) American South, American cultural; gardner_se@mercer.edu

Good, Robert (PhD, McGill 1993; assoc. prof.) modern France, European intellectual, Africa; good_rm@mercer.edu

Harper, Matt J. Z. (PhD, North Carolina, Chapel Hill 2009; assoc. prof.) African American, US religious, Atlantic world; harper_mjz@mercer.edu

Scott, John Thomas (PhD, William and Mary 1991; prof. and chair) colonial America, US religious and intellectual; scott_jt@mercer.edu

Thompson, Douglas E. (PhD, Virginia 2003; prof.) southern race relations, US South and automobile, southern religious; thompson_d@mercer.edu

Retired/Emeritus Faculty

Cockfield, Jamie H. (PhD, Virginia 1972; prof. emeritus) Russian Empire, World War I

Klingelhofer, Eric (PhD, Johns Hopkins 1985; prof. emeritus) medieval England, early colonization, archaeology; klingelhof_e@mercer.edu

Platt, Wilfred C., Jr. (PhD, Georgia 1966; prof. emeritus) British Empire, early modern Europe

Steeples, Doug W. (PhD, North Carolina, Chapel Hill 1961; prof. emeritus) US economic, Gilded Age, US West

Messiah College

Dept. of History, 1 College Ave., Ste. 3051, Mechanicsburg, PA 17055. 717.766.2511. Fax 717.796.4790. Email: dpettegrew@messiah.edu. Website: https://www.messiah.edu/info/20212/department_of_history.

We are a vibrant and growing community of teachers and scholars who are passionate about the study of the past. In the tradition of the Christian liberal arts, the history program provides a wide range of course offerings and experiences.

Chair: David Pettegrew and Bernardo Michael
Degrees Offered: BA
Academic Year System: Semester
Areas of Specialization: America, Europe, world, public
Tuition (per academic year): $35280
Enrollment 2018-19:
Undergraduate Majors: 42
Degrees in History: 10 BA
Addresses:
Admissions: http://www.messiah.edu/admissions
Financial Aid: http://www.messiah.edu/info/21085/financial_aid

Adjunct Faculty

Snyder, Cathay L. (MA, Penn State 1995; adj. instr.) US; csnyder@messiah.edu

Full-time Faculty

Fea, John (PhD, SUNY, Stony Brook 1999; prof.) early America, cultural; jfea@messiah.edu

Huffman, Joseph P. (PhD, UCLA 1991; prof.) medieval Europe, Germany, England, social, cultural, church; jhuffman@messiah.edu

LaGrand, James B. (PhD, Indiana 1997; prof. and dir., Coll. Honors) modern US, American Indian; jlagrand@messiah.edu

Michael, Bernardo A. (PhD, Hawai'i, Manoa 2001; prof. and co-chair) Indian subcontinent, comparative Asia; bmichael@messiah.edu

Myers, Sarah (PhD, Texas Tech 2014; asst. prof.) public, oral, US, women, military; spmyers@messiah.edu

Pettegrew, David K. (PhD, Ohio State 2006; prof. and co-chair) early Christianity, church, digital, archeology, late antiquity/Byzantium; dpettegrew@messiah.edu

Wilson, Norman J. (PhD, UCLA 1994; prof.) early modern Europe, Germany, historiography; nwilson@messiah.edu

Joint/Cross Appointments

Weaver-Zercher, David L. (PhD, North Carolina, Chapel Hill 1997; prof.; chair, Biblical and Religious Studies) American religious; dzercher@messiah.edu

Retired/Emeritus Faculty

Sider, E. Morris (PhD, SUNY, Buffalo 1966; prof. emeritus) Britain, North American religious; msider@messiah.edu

Metropolitan State University

Dept. of History, 700 E. Seventh St., Saint Paul, MN 55106-5000. 651.793.1494. Fax 651.793.1446. Email: history@metrostate. edu. Website: https://www.metrostate.edu/academics/liberal-arts/history.

At Metropolitan State, history is taught in ways that are both fascinating and important to everyone. Our courses tend to balance the actions of leaders and elites with stories of the grassroots movements that have challenged those elites and advanced popular agendas.

Chair: Jeanne E. Grant
Degrees Offered: BA
Academic Year System: Semester

Areas of Specialization: modern US women, modern US politics and social movements, modern Japan, early modern and modern Europe, US legal
Tuition (per academic year):
In-State: $7491
Out-of-State: $14319
Enrollment 2018-19:
Undergraduate Majors: 90
Degrees in History: 10 BA
Addresses:
Admissions: http://www.metrostate.edu/msweb/apply/
Financial Aid: http://www.metrostate.edu/msweb/pathway/aid/

Adjunct Faculty

Chhun, Maura Elizabeth (PhD, Colorado, Boulder 2015; adj.) modern Europe, world and British Empire, 1918 flu epidemic; maura.chhun@metrostate.edu

Church, Rebecca Ellen (PhD, Iowa 2013; adj.) medieval and ancient Middle East, medieval Mediterranean, women's monasticism and religious movements; rebecca.church@metrostate.edu

Jurss, Jacob (PhD, Michigan State 2017; adj.) early US, Native American; jacob.jurss@metrostate.edu

Kurhajec, Anna L. (PhD, Illinois, Urbana-Champaign 2015; adj.) US since 1815, race and ethnicity, gender and colonialism; anna.kurhajec@metrostate.edu

Lowen, Rebecca S. (PhD, Stanford 1990; adj.) 20th-century US political, institutional, science and technology; rebecca.lowen@metrostate.edu

Marshall, Christopher (PhD, Minnesota 2014; adj.) modern Europe, modern US, 19th-century French radicalism; chris.marshall@metrostate.edu

Moerer, Andrea K. (PhD, Minnesota 2013; adj.) world/US/Mexico, Chapultepec forest; andrea.moerer@metrostate.edu

O'Toole, Tomas (PhD, Carnegie Mellon 1976; adj.) Africa, world; thomas.otoole@metrostate.edu

Rachleff, Peter J. (PhD, Pittsburgh 1981; adj.) US labor, immigration; peter.rachleff@metrostate.edu

Sayer, John W. (PhD, Minnesota 1991; JD, Houston 1970; adj.) modern US and American Indian; john.sayer@metrostate.edu

Wagstrom, Thor (PhD, Nebraska 1999; adj.) world; thor.wagstrom@metrostate.edu

Winkler-Morey, Anne (PhD, Minnesota 2001; adj.) Latin America, US diplomatic; anne.winklermorey@metrostate.edu

Zepcevski, Joline (PhD, Minnesota 2011; adj.) science and technology; joline.zepcevski@metrostate.edu

Full-time Faculty

Grant, Jeanne E. (PhD, California, Berkeley 2005; prof. and chair) late medieval/early modern/modern east central Europe, Hussite Bohemia; jeanne.grant@metrostate.edu

Laughlin, Kathleen A. (PhD, Ohio State 1993; prof.) 20th-century US women, US public policy, US social movements; kathleen.laughlin@metrostate.edu

Otsubo Sitcawich, Sumiko (PhD, Ohio State 1998; prof.) modern Japan, science/technology/medicine, women; sumiko.otsubo@metrostate.edu

Rossinow, Doug (PhD, Johns Hopkins 1994; prof.) 20th-century US politics, social movements, political culture; doug.rossinow@metrostate.edu

University of Miami

Dept. of History, PO Box 248107, Miami, FL 33124-4662. 305.284.3660. Fax 305.284.3558. Email: history@miami.edu. Website: https://history.as.miami.edu.

Alternate Address: Ashe Bldg. 619, 1252 Memorial Dr., Miami, FL 33146

Our Department is committed to pursuing excellence in historical and interdisciplinary scholarship, teaching, and service to the profession, the University, and the wider community. Our fine faculty of some 22 professors does research and teaches in many historical areas, often crossing chronological, geographic, and disciplinary boundaries.

Chair: Mary Lindemann
Director of Graduate Studies: Michael B. Miller, interim
Director of Undergraduate Studies: Karl Gunther
Degrees Offered: BA,MA,PhD
Academic Year System: Semester
Areas of Specialization: Latin America, US, Europe, China, Africa
Undergraduate Tuition (per academic year): $50400
Graduate Tuition (per academic year): $38908
Enrollment 2018-19:
Undergraduate Majors: 85
New Graduate Students: 3
Full-time Graduate Students: 16
Degrees in History: 13 BA
Addresses:
Admissions: http://welcome.miami.edu/admissions/
Financial Aid: http://www.miami.edu/ofas

Adjunct Faculty

Neu, Charles E. (PhD, Harvard 1964; prof. emeritus, Brown) American foreign relations, Vietnam War; cneu@bellsouth.net
Reill, Peter H. (PhD, Northwestern 1969; prof. emeritus, UCLA) intellectual, European Enlightenment; reill@humnet.ucla.edu

Full-time Faculty

Abaka, Edmund (PhD, York, Can. 1998; assoc. prof.; International Studies) sub-Saharan Africa, West Africa; e.abaka@miami.edu
Bachin, Robin F. (PhD, Michigan 1996; Tebeau assoc. prof.) US cultural, urban planning, sport; rbachin@miami.edu
Beck, Hermann (PhD, UCLA 1989; Professor) Modern Europe, Germany; hbeck@miami.edu
Bernath, Michael T. (PhD, Harvard 2005; Tebeau assoc. prof.) 19th-century US, Civil War, South; mbernath@miami.edu
Chatterjee, Sumita (PhD, Massachusetts 1997; lect.) India, gender; s.chatterjee@miami.edu
Elena, Eduardo D. (PhD, Princeton 2002; assoc. prof.) modern Latin America, Argentina, consumerism; edelena@miami.edu
Fraser, Max (PhD, Yale 2017; asst. prof.) US since 1865, labor, working class, popular culture; history@miami.edu
Goff, Krista (PhD, Michigan 2014; asst. prof.) modern Russia, nationalities, modern Middle East; kgoff@miami.edu
Gunther, Karl A. (PhD, Northwestern 2007; assoc. prof. and dir., undergrad. studies) early modern Europe, Britain, Reformation; k.gunther@miami.edu
Halsey, Stephen Robert (PhD, Chicago 2007; assoc. prof.) China; s.halsey@miami.edu
Heerman, Scott (PhD, Maryland, Coll. Park 2013; asst. prof.) 19th-century US, slavery and emancipation, law and society; s.heerman@miami.edu
Lindemann, Mary (PhD, Cincinnati 1980; prof. and chair) German social and cultural, medicine, gender; mlindemann@miami.edu
Lipschultz, Sybil (PhD, Pennsylvania 1987; assoc. prof.) US legal, women; slipschultz@miami.edu
Miller, Michael B. (PhD, Pennsylvania 1976; prof. and interim dir., grad. studies) Modern Europe and France, urbanism and globalization, business; mbmiller@miami.edu

Nesvig, Martin A. (PhD, Yale 2004; assoc. prof.) colonial Latin America, Mexico, Inquisition; mnesvig@miami.edu
Ramsey, Kate (PhD, Columbia 2002; assoc. prof.) Caribbean, Haiti, popular spirituality; kramsey@miami.edu
Reill, Dominique K. (PhD, Columbia 2007; assoc. prof.) modern Europe, Adriatic and Italy, nationalism; d.reill@miami.edu
Ruggiero, Guido, Jr. (PhD, UCLA 1972; prof.) Renaissance Italy, gender and sex, culture; gruggiero@miami.edu
Spivey, Donald (PhD, California, Davis 1976; prof.) US since 1865, African American, sport; dspivey@miami.edu
Thomas, Hugh M. (PhD, Yale 1988; prof.) medieval, England; h.thomas@miami.edu
White, Ashli (PhD, Columbia 2003; assoc. prof.) early America, Atlantic, colonial Caribbean; acwhite@miami.edu

Joint/Cross Appointments

Pals, Daniel L. (PhD, Chicago 1975; prof.; Religion) Europe, religious, intellectual; dpals@miami.edu

Retired/Emeritus Faculty

Bush, Gregory W. (PhD, Columbia 1983; prof. emeritus) US social and cultural; publicbush@gmail.com
Johnson, Whittington B. (PhD, Georgia 1970; prof. emeritus) US, 18th century, African American; whittjo@bellsouth.net
Martin, Janet L. B. (PhD, Chicago 1980; prof. emeritus) Russia; j.martin1@miami.edu
Stein, Steve J. (PhD, Stanford 1973; prof. emeritus) Latin America; srafael@miami.edu

Miami University

Dept. of History, 254 Upham Hall, 100 Bishop Cir., Oxford, OH 45056-1879. 513.529.5121. Fax 513.529.3224. Email: history@miamioh.edu. Website: http://miamioh.edu/cas/academics/departments/history/.

The Department of History fulfills Miami University's mission of promoting liberal learning and liberal education.

Chair: Wietse de Boer
Director of Graduate Studies: Nishani Frazier
Director of Undergraduate Studies: Amanda McVety
Degrees Offered: BA,MA
Academic Year System: Semester
Areas of Specialization: US, Europe since 1500, world
Undergraduate Tuition (per academic year):
In-State: $15378
Out-of-State: $34894
Graduate Tuition (per academic year):
In-State: $7044
Out-of-State: $15738
Enrollment 2018-19:
Undergraduate Majors: 178
New Graduate Students: 6
Full-time Graduate Students: 15
Degrees in History: 47 BA, 5 MA
Undergraduate Addresses:
Admissions: http://miamioh.edu/admission/
Financial Aid: http://miamioh.edu/finaid/
Graduate Addresses:
Admissions and Financial Aid: http://miamioh.edu/cas/academics/departments/history/academics/graduate-studies/

Adjunct Faculty

Goldy, Robert (PhD, Hebrew, Jerusalem 1987; adj. assoc. prof.) 20th-century American and European intellectual, Jewish and Christian philosophy

Kolbas, Judith (PhD, NYU 1992; adj. prof.) Central Asia, numismatics; kolbasjg@miamioh.edu

White, John H., Jr. (BA, Miami, Ohio 1958; adj. prof.; sr. hist. emeritus, Smithsonian Inst.) US transportation

Full-time Faculty

Anderson, Sheldon R. (PhD, Minnesota 1989; prof.) modern eastern Europe, Cold War, sports; anderss@miamioh.edu

Baernstein, P. Renee (PhD, Harvard 1993; prof.) early modern Europe, early modern Italy, women and family; baernspr@miamioh.edu

Carrafiello, Michael L. (PhD, Vanderbilt 1987; prof.) colonial America, Civil War; carrafml@miamioh.edu

Conn, Steven (PhD, Pennsylvania 1994; prof.) American cultural, urban, public; conns@miamioh.edu

de Boer, Wietse T. (PhD, Erasmus Univ. Rotterdam, Netherlands 1995; prof. and chair) early modern Europe, Italian cultural; deboerwt@miamioh.edu

Frazier, Nishani (PhD, Columbia 2007; assoc. prof. and dir., grad. studies) African American, 1960s and 1970s US, public; frazien@miamioh.edu

Gordon, Matthew S. (PhD, Columbia 1993; prof.) Islamic world, Middle East; gordonms@miamioh.edu

Jensen, Erik Norman (PhD, Wisconsin, Madison 2003; assoc. prof.) modern Europe, 20th-century Germany, gender and sport; jensenen@miamioh.edu

Johnson, Martin P. (PhD, Brown 1993; assoc. prof.) Lincoln, Civil War, modern Europe; johnsomp@miamioh.edu

McVety, Amanda Kay (PhD, UCLA 2006; prof. and dir., undergrad. studies) US foreign policy; mcvetyak@miamioh.edu

Norris, Stephen M. (PhD, Virginia 2002; prof.) Russia since 1800, nationalism, visual; norriss1@miamioh.edu

Offenburger, Andrew (PhD, Yale 2014; asst. prof.) American West, borderlands, comparative frontiers; offenba@miamioh.edu

Prior, Daniel G. (PhD, Indiana 2002; assoc. prof.) inner Asia, nomadic culture, oral heroic poetry; priordg@miamioh.edu

Schakenbach Regele, Lindsay (PhD, Brown 2015; asst. prof.) American economic; regelels@miamioh.edu

Spellman, Susan V. (PhD, Carnegie Mellon 2009; assoc. prof.) 19th- and 20th-century US, business, technology; spellmsv@miamioh.edu

Joint/Cross Appointments

Albarran, Elena Jackson (PhD, Arizona 2008; assoc. prof.; Latin America, Latino/a and Caribbean Studies) revolution and social movement in Latin America, world childhoods; albarrej@miamioh.edu

Brown, Tammy L. (PhD, Princeton 2007; assoc. prof.; Black World Studies) African diaspora, race/class/gender, film; browntl3@miamioh.edu

Hamlin, Kimberly A. (PhD, Texas, Austin 2007; assoc. prof.; American Studies) women and gender, science; hamlinka@miamioh.edu

Shaffer, Marguerite S. (PhD, Harvard 1994; prof.; American Studies) environmental, cultural, public; shaffems@miamioh.edu

Sheumaker, Helen (PhD, Kansas 1999; assoc. teaching prof.; American Studies) 19th-century US cultural, public, material culture; sheumahd@miamioh.edu

Nondepartmental Historians

Amador, Jose (PhD, Michigan 2008; prof.; Latin American, Latino/a and Caribbean Studies) Brazil, Spanish-speaking Caribbean, public health; amadorj@miamioh.edu

Ettouney, Osama (PhD, Minnesota 1987; prof.; Manufacturing Engineering) technology; ettounom@miamioh.edu

Kenworthy, Scott M. (PhD, Brandeis 2002; assoc. prof.; Comparative Religion) Russian and Eurasian religions, Christianity; kenwors@miamioh.edu

Meckley, Robert (PhD, Miami, Ohio 1999; vis. asst. prof.; Humanities and Creative Arts) US, American frontier; mecklerc@miamioh.edu

Neumann, Caryn E. (PhD, Ohio State 2006; lect.; Integrative Studies) 20th-century US, women, political; neumance@miamioh.edu

Robinson, Marsha R. (PhD, Ohio State 2006; vis. asst. prof.; Humanities and Creative Arts) empires and colonialism, women and gender; robins78@miamioh.edu

Rousmaniere, Kate (PhD, Columbia 1992; prof.; Educational Leadership) education; rousmak@miamioh.edu

Smith, Matthew David (PhD, Miami, Ohio 2011; vis. asst. prof.; Humanities and Creative Arts) early America, 18th- and 19th-century religion; smithmd6@miamioh.edu

Vascik, George S. (PhD, Michigan 1988; assoc. prof.; Integrative Studies) modern Germany, European economic; vascikgs@miamioh.edu

Retired/Emeritus Faculty

Baird, Jay W. (PhD, Columbia 1966; prof. emeritus) modern Germany; bairdjw@miamioh.edu

Blaisdell, Muriel L. (PhD, Harvard 1976; prof. emerita) science; blaisdml@miamioh.edu

Cayton, Mary Kupiec (PhD, Brown 1981; prof. emerita) US intellectual and cultural, US public culture; caytonmk@miamioh.edu

Chandler, D. S. (PhD, Duke 1970; prof. emeritus) Latin America, Mexico; chandlds@miamioh.edu

Ellison, Curtis W. (PhD, Minnesota 1970; prof. emeritus; dir., Colligan Hist. Proj.) US; ellisocw@miamioh.edu

Fahey, David M. (PhD, Notre Dame 1964; prof. emeritus) modern Britain, Anglo-American temperance, world; faheydm@miamioh.edu

Foster, Carrie A. (PhD, Denver 1984; prof. emerita) 20th-century America; fosterca@miamioh.edu

Frederickson, Mary E. (PhD, North Carolina, Chapel Hill 1981; prof. emerita) American women, labor, social; frederme@miamioh.edu

Goldy, Charlotte Newman (PhD, SUNY, Binghamton 1978; prof. emerita) medieval Europe, social and women, Jewish studies; goldycn@miamioh.edu

Jackson, W. Sherman (PhD, Ohio State 1969; prof. emeritus) American constitutional, law; jacksows@miamioh.edu

Kaufman, Burton I. (PhD, Rice 1966; prof. emeritus) US diplomatic; kaufmabi@miamioh.edu

Kimball, Jeffrey (PhD, Louisiana State 1969; prof. emeritus) foreign affairs, war and peace, Vietnam War; jpkimball@miamioh.edu

Liu, Wenxi (PhD, Iowa 1992; prof. emeritus) medieval English constitutional and legal; liuw@miamioh.edu

Olumwullah, Osaak (PhD, Rice 1995; assoc. prof. emeritus) Africa, environment; olumwuoa@miamioh.edu

Pan, Yihong (PhD, British Columbia 1990; prof. emerita) China's Cultural Revolution, Chinese women, Tang 618-907; pany@miamioh.edu

Schorman, Rob R. (PhD, Indiana 1998; prof. emeritus) American popular culture, advertising, business; schormr@miamioh.edu

Thurston, Robert William (PhD, Michigan 1980; prof. emeritus) Russia since Peter the Great, mass persecution, coffee; thurstrw@miamioh.edu

Winkler, Allan M. (PhD, Yale 1974; prof. emeritus) 20th-century America; winkleam@miamioh.edu

Yamauchi, Edwin M. (PhD, Brandeis 1964; prof. emeritus) ancient; yamauce@miamioh.edu

Zinsser, Judith P. (PhD, Rutgers 1993; prof. emerita) early modern Europe, European women, world; zinssejp@miamioh.edu

Visiting Faculty

Brown, William Allan Sazie (PhD, Johns Hopkins 2016; vis. asst. prof.) early modern Europe, Old Regime France; brownwa3@miamioh.edu

Duah, Manna (PhD, Temple 2019; vis. asst. prof.) Africa to AD 1800, Latin America to 1800, women in history; duahm@miamioh.edu

Miller, Anthony Joseph (PhD, Kentucky 2015; vis. asst. prof.) transnational, Cold War US/China/Soviet Union, mobility and human rights; mille932@miamioh.edu

Shaul, Hollis (PhD, Princeton 2019; vis. asst. prof.) monasticism, religious property, kingship and state-craft in high medieval Europe; shaulhe@miamioh.edu

Shriver, Cameron (PhD, Ohio State 2016; vis. asst. prof.; Myaamia Center) Native American, Miami tribe of Oklahoma; shrivecm@miamioh.edu

Silano, Francesca (PhD, Toronto 2017; vis. asst. prof.; Havighurst Center for Russian Studies) imperial Russia, Soviet Russia; silanofg@miamioh.edu

University of Michigan, Ann Arbor

Dept. of History, 1029 Tisch Hall, 435 S. State St., Ann Arbor, MI 48109-1003. 734.764.6305. Fax 734.647.4881. Email: umhistory@umich.edu. Website: https://lsa.umich.edu/history/.

What Is U-M History? Global, multidimensional, interdisciplinary. Regularly ranked among the top history departments in the nation, we combine state-of-the-art research with innovative teaching and a commitment to embrace all the diversity of the past.

Chair: Jay Cook
Director of Graduate Studies: Brian Porter-Szucs
Director of Undergraduate Studies: Stephen Berrey
Degrees Offered: BA,BS,PhD
Academic Year System: Semester
Areas of Specialization: Africa and Asia, US, Europe, Latin America and Caribbean, Middle East and Near East
Undergraduate Tuition (per academic year):
In-State: $15262
In-State Junior/Senior: $17188
Out-of-State: $49350
Out-of-State Junior/Senior: $52814
Graduate Tuition (per academic year):
In-State: $23456
Out-of-State: $47006
Enrollment 2018-19:
Undergraduate Majors: 273
New Graduate Students: 18
Full-time Graduate Students: 140
Degrees in History: 111 BA, 3 BS, 24 PhD
Undergraduate Addresses:
Admissions: http://admissions.umich.edu/
Financial Aid: http://finaid.umich.edu/

Graduate Addresses:
Admissions and financial Aid: https://lsa.umich.edu/history/graduates.html

Affiliated Faculty

Alter, George C. (PhD, Pennsylvania 1978; prof.; Inter-U. Consortium for Social and Political Research) family, demography, economic; altergc@umich.edu

Bain, Bob (PhD, Case Western Reserve 1990; assoc. prof.; Sch. of Education) teacher education in design and use of history, technology; bbain@umich.edu

Bonner, Michael (PhD, Princeton 1987; prof.; Near Eastern Studies) Islamic; mbonner@umich.edu

Forsdyke, Sara L. (PhD, Princeton 1997; prof.; Classical Studies) Greek historiography, Greek political thought and ideology, Greek law; forsdyke@umich.edu

Maiorova, Olga Yevgenyevna (PhD, Moscow State 1985; assoc. prof.; Slavic Languages and Literature) Russian language and literature; maiorova@umich.edu

Markel, Howard (MD, Johns Hopkins Sch. Medicine 1994; assoc. prof.; Hist. Center for Health Sciences) science, medicine, technology; howard@umich.edu

Mays, Devi Elizabeth (PhD, Indiana 2013; asst. prof.; Judaic Studies) Jewish

Novak, William J. (PhD, Brandeis 1991; prof.; Law Sch.) US legal/political/intellectual; wnovak@umich.edu

Rhode, Joy (PhD, Pennsylvania 2007; asst. prof.; Public Policy) democracy and expert knowledge, militarization of American state, contemporary policy analysis; joyrohde@umich.edu

Vaillant, Derek W. (PhD, Chicago 1999; prof.; Communication Studies) technology and culture; dvail@umich.edu

Wang, Zheng (PhD, California, Davis 1995; assoc. prof.; Women's Studies; Inst. for Research on Women and Gender; Chinese Studies) wangzhen@umich.edu

Wells, Jonathan Daniel (PhD, Michigan 1998; prof.; Afroamerican and African Studies and Residential Coll.) 19th-century America, social and cultural; jonwells@umich.edu

Full-time Faculty

Al-Rustom, Hakem (PhD, London Sch. of Economics 2013; asst. prof. and Alex Manoogian Prof.) Europe, historical materials, Middle East; hakemaa@umich.edu

Ballinger, Pamela L. (PhD, Johns Hopkins 1999; prof. and Fred Cuny Chair) anthropology, Balkans; pballing@umich.edu

Bonnell-Freidin, Anna (PhD, Princeton 2018; asst. prof.) ancient Rome and Mediterranean, gender and sexuality; freidin@umich.edu

Brick, Howard (PhD, Michigan 1983; prof.) 20th-century US, American intellectual and social theory, post-1865 US social movements and politics; hbrick@umich.edu

Carson, John (PhD, Princeton 1994; assoc. prof.) American intellectual, culture; jscarson@umich.edu

Cassel, Par K. (PhD, Harvard 2006; assoc. prof.) late imperial and modern China, Chinese legal and institutional, Sino-Japanese relations; cassel@umich.edu

Chang, Chun-Shu (PhD, Harvard 1964; prof.) ancient and early imperial China, early modern, Chinese historical literature; cschang@umich.edu

Chin, Rita C-K (PhD, California, Berkeley 1999; prof.) modern Europe, Germany, immigration; rchin@umich.edu

Cole, Joshua H. (PhD, California, Berkeley 1991; prof.) modern France, Europe; joshcole@umich.edu

Cole, Juan R. I. (PhD, UCLA 1984; prof.) modern Middle East, South Asian Islamic, social and cultural; jrcole@umich.edu

Cook, James W., Jr. (PhD, California, Berkeley 1996; prof. and chair) 19th-century US cultural/social/intellectual; jwcook@umich.edu

Cowles, Henry M. (PhD, Princeton 2015; asst. prof.) human sciences, US, Britain; cowles@umich.edu

de Pee, Christian (PhD, Columbia 1997; assoc. prof.) Tang-Song-Yuan China, representations of imperial power, text and writing; cdepee@umich.edu

Eley, Geoff (PhD, Sussex, UK 1974; prof.) modern Europe, Germany, nationalism and socialism; ghe@umich.edu

Fancy, Hussein (PhD, Princeton 2008; assoc. prof.) medieval Europe and North Africa, Mediterranean, religious interaction cultural/social/intellectual; fancy@umich.edu

French, Katherine L. (PhD, Minnesota 1993; prof.) medieval Europe, medieval religious, social and cultural; frenchk@umich.edu

Gaggio, Dario (PhD, Northwestern 1999; prof.) modern Europe, modern Italy, economic and cultural; dariog@umich.edu

Glover, William J. (PhD, California, Berkeley 1999; assoc. prof.) architecture, South Asian studies, South Asian urban/colonialism/postcolonialism; wglover@umich.edu

Hancock, David John (PhD, Harvard 1990; prof.) early America, economic; hancockd@umich.edu

Israel, Kali (PhD, Rutgers 1992; assoc. prof.) modern Britain, Scotland; kisrael@umich.edu

Juster, Susan (PhD, Michigan 1990; prof.) early America, women, religion; sjuster@umich.edu

Kivelson, Valerie A. (PhD, Stanford 1988; prof.) early modern Russia; vkivelso@umich.edu

Lassiter, Matthew D. (PhD, Virginia 1999; prof.) 20th-century US, social and political; mlassite@umich.edu

Lieberman, Victor B. (PhD, London 1976; prof.) Southeast Asia, premodern Burma; eurasia@umich.edu

Marwil, Jonathan L. (PhD, Michigan 1970; lect.) modern Europe, war, photography; jmarwil@umich.edu

McDonald, Terrence J. (PhD, Stanford 1979; prof.) US urban; tmcd@umich.edu

Mills, Kenneth R. (DPhil, Oxford 1992; prof.) medieval and early modern Europe, Latin America and Caribbean/African diaspora, religion/intellectual/cultural; millsken@umich.edu

Mir, Farina (PhD, Columbia 2002; assoc. prof.) colonial and modern South Asia, culture; fmir@umich.edu

Moyer, Ian S. (PhD, Chicago 2004; assoc. prof.) ancient Greece; ianmoyer@umich.edu

Northrop, Douglas T. (PhD, Stanford 1999; prof.) Central Asian social and cultural; northrop@umich.edu

Pernick, Martin S. (PhD, Columbia 1979; prof.) medicine; mpernick@umich.edu

Porter-Szucs, Brian A. (PhD, Wisconsin-Madison 1994; prof. and dir., grad. studies) eastern Europe, 19th- and 20th-century Poland; baporter@umich.edu

Selcer, Perrin (PhD, Pennsylvania 2011; asst. prof.) environmental, global, science/technology/society; pselcer@umich.edu

Simmons, LaKisha Michelle (PhD, Michigan 2009; asst. prof.; Women's Studies) US, race and ethnicity, gender studies and sexuality; kisha@umich.edu

Sinha, Mrinalini (PhD, SUNY, Stony Brook 1988; prof.) South Asia, British colonial Indian gender; sinha@umich.edu

Spooner, Matthew P. (PhD, Columbia 2015; asst. prof.) US, race and ethnicity, African diaspora; spoonerm@umich.edu

Suny, Ronald Grigor (PhD, Columbia 1968; prof.) Russia, Soviet nationalities; rgsuny@umich.edu

Tanielian, Melanie (PhD, California, Berkeley 2012; assoc. prof.) war and violence; meltan@umich.edu

Tonomura, Hitomi (PhD, Stanford 1986; prof.) premodern Japan, East Asia; tomitono@umich.edu

Young, Jason R. (PhD, California, Riverside 2002; assoc. prof.) 19th-century US, cultural; youngjr@umich.edu

Joint/Cross Appointments

Alberto, Paulina Laura (PhD, Pennsylvania 2005; assoc. prof.; Romance Languages and Literature) palberto@umich.edu

Babayan, Kathryn (PhD, Princeton 1993; assoc. prof.; Near East Studies and Armenian Studies) early modern Iran, Shi'ism and Sufism, gender and sexuality; babayan@umich.edu

Berrey, Stephen A. (PhD, Texas, Austin 2006; assoc. prof. and dir., undergrad. studies; American Culture) US, African American, African diaspora; sberrey@umich.edu

Caulfield, Sueann (PhD, NYU 1994; assoc. prof.; Residential Coll.) Latin America, women; scaul@umich.edu

Cipa, Hakki Erdem (PhD, Harvard 2007; assoc. prof.; Near Eastern Studies) early modern Middle Eastern social and political, Ottoman; ecipa@umich.edu

Countryman, Matthew Jon (PhD, Duke 1998; assoc. prof.; Prog. in American Culture) African American, American culture; mcountry@umich.edu

Dash Moore, Deborah (PhD, Columbia 1975; prof.; Frankel Center for Judaic Studies) modern US Jewish, urban; ddmoore@umich.edu

de la Cruz, Deirdre (PhD, Columbia 2006; assoc. prof.; Asian Languages and Cultures) cultural anthropology; ddelac@umich.edu

Dowd, Gregory (PhD, Princeton 1986; prof.; American Culture) American Indian; dowdg@umich.edu

Hawes, Clement (PhD, Yale 1986; prof.; English Language and Literature) 18th-century English literary study, British colonialism and postcoloniality, Ireland; cchawes@umich.edu

Hoffnung-Garskof, Jesse (PhD, Princeton 2002; prof.; American Culture) modern Latin America and Caribbean, colonial Latin America; jessehg@umich.edu

Howell, Joel D. (PhD, Pennsylvania 1987; prof.; Internal Medicine) medicine; jhowell@medmail.med.umich.edu

Johnson, Paul C. (PhD, Chicago 1997; prof.; Afroamerican and African Studies) African diasporic religion, ethnography, modern Brazil; paulcjoh@umich.edu

Kelley, Mary C. (PhD, Iowa 1974; prof.; American Culture) 19th-century American women, American intellectual and cultural, gender studies; mckelley@umich.edu

Langland, Victoria (PhD, Yale 2004; assoc. prof.; Romance Languages and Literatures) Brazil, Latin America; langland@umich.edu

Lewis, Earl (PhD, Minnesota 1984; prof.; Afroamerican and African Studies) African American studies; earlewis@umich.edu

Masuzawa, Tomoko (PhD, California, Santa Barbara 1985; prof.; Comparative Literature) religion, European intellectual; masuzawa@umich.edu

Mora, Anthony P. (PhD, Notre Dame 2002; assoc. prof.; American Culture) Latinas/os in US; apmora@umich.edu

Muehlberger, Ellen (PhD, Indiana 2008; assoc. prof.; Near Eastern Studies) religious studies; emuehlbe@umich.edu

Neis, Rachel (PhD, Harvard 2007; assoc. prof.; Judaic Studies) rabbinic literature; rneis@umich.edu

Peterson, Derek R. (PhD, Minnesota 2000; prof.; Afroamerican and African Studies) colonial East Africa; drpeters@umich.edu

Puff, Helmut (PhD, Basel, Switzerland 1992; prof.; German) early modern Europe, sexuality; puffh@umich.edu

Scott, Rebecca J. (PhD, Princeton 1982; prof.; Law) Latin America, slavery and emancipation, labor systems; rjscott@umich.edu

Shin, Ian (PhD, Columbia 2016; asst. prof.; American Culture) US social and cultural, Asian American, US in world 1850-1950; ianshin@umich.edu

Spector, Scott (PhD, Johns Hopkins 1993; prof.; German) German intellectual; spec@umich.edu

Squatriti, Paolo (PhD, Virginia 1990; prof.; Romance Languages) medieval Europe; pasqua@umich.edu

Stern, Alexandra Minna (PhD, Chicago 1999; prof.; American Culture) medicine and science, reproduction, American gender/ethics/society; amstern@umich.edu

Thompson, Heather Ann (PhD, Princeton 1995; prof.; Afroamerican and African Studies and Residential Coll.) carceral and urban, African American, labor; hthompsn@umich.edu

Thurman, Kira L. (PhD, Rochester 2013; asst. prof.; German) Europe, African diaspora, Atlantic studies; thurmank@umich.edu

Veidlinger, Jeffrey (PhD, Georgetown 1998; prof.; Judaic Studies) modern Jewish, Europe; jveidlin@umich.edu

Witgen, Michael (PhD, Washington 2004; assoc. prof.; American Culture) Native American studies; mwitgen@umich.edu

Retired/Emeritus Faculty

Blouin, Francis X., Jr. (PhD, Minnesota 1978; prof. emeritus; Info. and Library Studies, Michigan Hist. Collections) archival administration; fblouin@umich.edu

Bright, Charles C. (PhD, Yale 1971; prof. emeritus) US urban, world, comparative; cbright@umich.edu

Canning, Kathleen M. (PhD, Johns Hopkins 1988; prof. emeritus) modern Germany, European women, labor; kcanning@umich.edu

Cohen, David Wm. (PhD, London 1970; prof. emeritus) historical anthropology, pre-colonial Lakes Plateau Region; dwcohen@umich.edu

Endelman, Todd (PhD, Harvard 1976; prof. emeritus) modern Jewish; endelman@umich.edu

Fine, John V. A., Jr. (PhD, Harvard 1969; prof. emeritus) medieval and modern Balkans, Byzantine; jvafine@umich.edu

Goodman, Dena (PhD, Chicago 1982; prof. emerita; Women's Studies) French culture, gender; goodmand@umich.edu

Green, Thomas A. (PhD, Harvard 1970; JD, Harvard 1972; prof. emeritus) English and American criminal justice, British Isles c. 1000-1800; tagreen@umich.edu

Grew, Raymond (PhD, Harvard 1957; prof. emeritus) Italian political culture, French church and social change; rgrew@umich.edu

Hughes, Diane Owen (PhD, Yale 1967; assoc. prof. emeritus) medieval; dohughes@umich.edu

Karlsen, Carol F. (PhD, Yale 1980; prof. emeritus) witches after 1692, gender and representation

Linderman, Gerald (PhD, Northwestern 1971; prof. emeritus) gfl@umich.edu

Lindner, Rudi (PhD, California, Berkeley 1976; prof. emeritus) Byzantine, Turkey, astronomy; rpl@umich.edu

MacDonald, Michael (PhD, Stanford 1979; prof. emeritus) dreams and visions in England 1300-1850, popular religion and magic; mmacdon@umich.edu

Morantz-Sanchez, Regina (PhD, Columbia 1971; prof. emeritus) 20th-century gender and acculturation, Jewish family/women/medicine; reginann@umich.edu

Mrazek, Rudolf (PhD, Czechoslovak Academy, Prague 1987; prof. emeritus) modern Southeast Asia; rdlf@umich.edu

Pincus, Leslie (PhD, Chicago 1989; assoc. prof. emeritus) modern Japanese intellectual and cultural; lpincus@umich.edu

Rose, Sonya O. (PhD, Northwestern 1974; prof. emeritus) defining the nation/Britain after 1945, aftermath of war; sorose@umich.edu

Rosenberg, William G. (PhD, Harvard 1967; prof. emeritus) Russia, Soviet Union; wgr@umich.edu

Scott, Julius (PhD, Duke 1986; lect. emeritus) African American, early America, Atlantic; jsscott@umich.edu

Shy, John W. (PhD, Princeton 1961; prof. emeritus) colonial America; johnshy@umich.edu

Smith-Rosenberg, Carroll (PhD, Columbia 1968; prof. emeritus) women and sexuality, early America; csmithro@umich.edu

Steneck, Nicholas H. (PhD, Wisconsin, Madison 1970; prof. emeritus) medieval intellectual, medieval and modern science; nsteneck@umich.edu

Tentler, Thomas N. (PhD, Harvard 1961; prof. emeritus) medieval and early modern Europe; ttentler@umich.edu

Thornton, J. Mills, III (PhD, Yale 1974; prof. emeritus) US civil rights movement, US Civil War origins; jmthrntn@umich.edu

Trautmann, Thomas R. (PhD, London 1968; prof. emeritus) ancient India; ttraut@umich.edu

Van Dam, Raymond H. (PhD, Cambridge 1977; prof. emeritus) Rome, early medieval; rvandam@umich.edu

Vinovskis, Maris A. (PhD, Harvard 1975; prof. emeritus) US social, family, demography; vinovski@umich.edu

Young, Ernest P. (PhD, Harvard 1965; prof. emeritus) early 20th-century China, nationalism/reform/revolution; epyoung@umich.edu

Recently Awarded PhDs

Blan, Noah "'To See the Lion Dominating All Creatures and Beasts': Sovereignty and the Environment in Charlemagne's Empire"

Cantisano, Pedro "Rio de Janeiro on Trial: Law and Urban Reform in Modern Brazil"

Curtis, Paula R. "Inauthentic Truths: Forgery, Authority, and Economy in Medieval Japan"

Donovan, Kevin "Sovereign Scales: Frontiers of Value in East Africa"

Elliott, Harold Walker Jr. "The Unsettled State: Migration, Desegregation, and the Birth of Tribal Bureaucracy among the Lumbee Indians"

Hallock, Zachary "Locating Imperial Power: Cultural Interaction of the Romans and Italians of the Middle Republic"

Hempson, Leslie "The Social Life of Khadi: Gandhi's Experiments with the Indian Economy, 1915-60"

Johnson, Melissa "The Talk of the Town: Gossip and Watchfulness in 17th-Century Massachusetts"

Johnson, Adam Fulton "Secretsharers: Intersecting Systems of Knowledge and Ethnographic Encounters in the American Southwest, 1880-1930"

Katz, Sara "Mobilizing the Hajj in Southwest Nigeria: Pilgrims, Technologies, and State Regulation, 1914-90"

Kemmerle, Allison "The Performance of Identity in Classical Athens"

Khurana, Gurveen Kaur "Selective Visions of the Past: The Golden Temple and Its Heritage in the 20th Century"

Maccourt, Anna "Lord of the Universe Among Equals: The Challenges of Kingship in Early Historic/Early Medieval Gujarat"

Machava, Benedito "The Morality of Revolution: Urban Life, Moral Purity, and Citizenship in Socialist Mozambique, 1974-89"

Mass, Sarah Merritt "At the Heart of the City: The Battle for British Marketplaces, c. 1925-79"

Mathur, Tapsi "Known Geography: Natives in the Trans-Frontier Exploration of Colonial India"

Matsusaka, Hiroaki "Border Crossings: Anti-Imperialism and Race-Making in Transpacific Movements, 1910-51"

Maugeri, Brittany "Children Lost and Children Found: Literature, Education, and National Memory in Transitional Argentina, 1982-2000"

O'Brien, Cyrus "Redeeming Imprisonment: Religion and the Making of Mass Incarceration in Florida since 1941"

Renero-Hannan, Emanuel " In the Wake of Insurgency: Testimony and the Politics of Memory and Silence in Oaxaca"

Rutledge, Andrew James "Still No Peace Beyond the Line: Commerce and Conflict in the Anglo-Spanish Caribbean, 1710-60"

Seife, Hillina "To Stretch Forth: Ethiopia and Pan-African Practice in the 20th Century"

Shaw, Jonathan "Young at War: Violent Childhoods, Therapeutic Insurgency, and the Simba Rebellion in Eastern Congo, 1870-Present"

Silva, Ana Maria "Roots in Stone and Slavery: Permanence, Mobility, and Empire in 17th-Century Cartagena de Indias"

Smith, John S. F. "State, Community, and Ethnicity in Early Modern Thailand, 1351-1767"

Van Eynde, Joost "Bodies of the Weak: The Circulation of the Indigenous Dead in the British World, 1780-1880"

Vest, Jacques Bert "Vox Machinae: Phonographs and the Birth of Sonic Modernity, 1870-1930"

Waggoner Karchner, Kate "Riccoldo da Montecroce, Western Christendom, and Islam: Ideas of Mission, Crusade, and Polemic and their Transmission in Medieval and Early Modern Europe"

Walker, Andrew Joseph "Strains of Unity: Emancipation, Property, and the Post-Revolutionary State in Haitian Santo Domingo, 1822-44"

Whittington, Anna "Forging Soviet Citizens: Ideology, Identity, and Stability in the Soviet Union, 1930-91"

Michigan State University

Dept. of History, 256 Old Horticulture, 506 E. Circle Dr., East Lansing, MI 48824. 517.355.7500. Fax 517.353.5599. Email: history@msu.edu. Website: https://history.msu.edu/.

The Department of History at Michigan State University is a large, vibrant intellectual community. Our faculty members and graduate and undergraduate students are actively engaged in an enormous range of activities involving research, publishing, teaching, learning, and public outreach.

Chair: Lisa M. Fine
Director of Graduate Studies: Karrin Hanshew
Director of Undergraduate Studies: Emily Tabuteau
Degrees Offered: BA,MA,PhD
Academic Year System: Semester
Areas of Specialization: Africa, US, Atlantic world, Europe, Latin America and Caribbean
Undergraduate Tuition (per academic year):
  In-State: $13650
  Out-of-State: $36360
Graduate Tuition (per academic year):
  In-State: $13590
  Out-of-State: $26712
Enrollment 2018-19:
  Undergraduate Majors: 260
  New Graduate Students: 6
  Full-time Graduate Students: 65
  Degrees in History: 121 BA, 6 PhD
Undergraduate Addresses:
  Admissions: https://admissions.msu.edu
  Financial Aid: https://finaid.msu.edu
Graduate Addresses:
  Admissions: https://grad.msu.edu/apply/
  Financial Aid: https://finaid.msu.edu

Full-time Faculty

Achebe, Nwando (PhD, UCLA 2000; prof.) Africa and West Africa, African American, women's and gender studies; achebe@msu.edu

Alegi, Peter C. (PhD, Boston Univ. 2000; prof.) 20th-century contemporary, South Africa, social and urban; alegi@msu.edu

Anderson, James R. (PhD, Yale 1982; prof.) 20th-century US, US business; anders90@msu.edu

Beattie, Peter M. (PhD, Miami 1994; prof.) Latin America and Brazil; beattiep@msu.edu

Bellon, Richard (PhD, Washington 2000; assoc. prof.; Lyman Briggs Coll.) 19th century, science and medicine, US and western Europe; bellonr@msu.edu

Brockey, Liam Matthew (PhD, Brown 2002; prof.) East Asia, western Europe, religious; brockey@msu.edu

Chambers, Glenn Anthony (PhD, Howard 2006; assoc. prof.) African diaspora, Caribbean and Latin America; chamb311@msu.edu

Conroy-Krutz, Emily (PhD, Harvard 2012; assoc. prof.) 18th- and 19th-century America, American reform and religion; conroyk5@msu.edu

Dagbovie, Pero G. (PhD, Michigan State 1999; prof.) 20th-century African American; dagbovie@msu.edu

Evered, Emine Onhan (PhD, Arizona 2005; assoc. prof.) modern Islamic, Middle East and Turkey, women's and gender studies; evered@msu.edu

Fair, Laura J. (PhD, Minnesota 1994; assoc. prof.) 20th-century African cultural/social/women/gender; fairl@msu.edu

Fermaglich, Kirsten L. (PhD, NYU 2001; assoc. prof.) modern American Jewish, America; fermagli@msu.edu

Fernandez, Delia (PhD, Ohio State 2015; asst. prof.) Latina/o; dmf@msu.edu

Fine, Lisa Michelle (PhD, Wisconsin, Madison 1985; prof. and chair) American economic and social, American labor, American women; fine@msu.edu

Forner, Sean A. (PhD, Chicago 2007; assoc. prof.) 20th-century Germany and Europe, European political culture/Cold War/democracy 1945-60; saforner@msu.edu

Hanshew, Karrin M. (PhD, Chicago 2006; assoc. prof. and dir., grad. studies) modern Europe, modern Germany; hanshew@msu.edu

Harris, LaShawn D. (PhD, Howard 2007; assoc. prof.) 20th-century cultural/social/urban, women and gender, labor and working class; harri859@msu.edu

Hawthorne, Walter W., III (PhD, Stanford 1998; prof.) Africa, West Africa; walterh@msu.edu

Kaye, Noah (PhD, California, Berkeley 2012; asst. prof.) ancient; kayenoah@msu.edu

Keith, Charles P. (PhD, Yale 2008; assoc. prof.) Southeast Asia, cultural/political/religious; ckeith@msu.edu

Knupfer, Peter B. (PhD, Wisconsin-Madison 1988; assoc. prof.) 19th-century US; knupfer@msu.edu

Lu, Sidney Xu (PhD, Pennsylvania 2014; asst. prof.) Japan; slu@msu.edu

Monson, Jamie (PhD, UCLA 1991; prof.) Africa; monsonj@isp.msu.edu

Montgomery, Georgina Mary (PhD, Minnesota 2005; assoc. prof.) science, primatology; montg165@msu.edu

Murphy, Edward L. (PhD, Michigan 2006; assoc. prof.) 20th-century contemporary, Latin America, Caribbean; murph367@msu.edu

Pescador, Juan Javier (PhD, Michigan 1998; prof.) Chicano/Latino, Mexico, immigration; pescador@msu.edu

Rehberger, Dean (PhD, Utah; assoc. prof.; dir., MATRIX) rehberge@msu.edu

Segal, Ethan I. (PhD, Stanford 2003; assoc. prof.) premodern Japan; segale@msu.edu

Sleeper-Smith, Susan (PhD, Michigan 1994; prof.) early America, Native American, Great Lakes; sleepers@msu.edu

Smith, Aminda M. (PhD, Princeton 2006; assoc. prof.) modern China; amsmith@msu.edu

Stamm, Michael R. (PhD, Chicago 2006; assoc. prof.; Journalism) cultural, political; stamm@msu.edu

Summerhill, Thomas (PhD, California, San Diego 1993; assoc. prof.) 19th-century American political and social, rural; summerhi@msu.edu

Tabuteau, Emily Z. (PhD, Harvard 1975; assoc. prof. and dir., undergrad. studies) Anglo-Saxon through Stuart England, English constitutional and legal; tabuteau@msu.edu

Veit, Helen (PhD, Yale 2008; assoc. prof.) 20th-century US, science and medicine; hveit@msu.edu

Waddell, Mark (PhD, Johns Hopkins 2006; assoc. prof.) 16th- and 17th-century Europe, science and medicine; waddellm@msu.edu

Wake, Naoko (PhD, Indiana 2005; assoc. prof.) 20th-century US, gender/sexuality/medicine; wake@msu.edu

Waller, John (PhD, Univ. Coll. London 2002; assoc. prof.) science, medicine; wallerj1@msu.edu

Wheat, David (PhD, Vanderbilt 2009; assoc. prof.) Latin America; dwheat@msu.edu

Joint/Cross Appointments

Charenko, Melissa (PhD, Wisconsin, Madison 2018; asst. prof.; Lyman Briggs Coll.) charenko@msu.edu

Leon, Sharon M. (PhD, Minnesota 2004; assoc. prof.; Coll. of Arts & Letters) digital humanities; leonshar@msu.edu

Retired/Emeritus Faculty

Siegelbaum, Lewis Henry (DPhil, Oxford 1976; prof. emeritus) modern Russia, social and labor; siegelba@msu.edu

Vieth, Jane K. (PhD, Ohio State 1975; prof. emeritus) modern Britain; vieth@msu.edu

Visiting Faculty

Pauly, Matthew D. (PhD, Indiana 2005; vis. assoc. prof.) Russia, Eurasia; paulym@msu.edu

Recently Awarded PhDs

Edwards, Janelle Marlena "'... To Do Credit to My Nation, Wherever I Go': West Indian and Cape Verdean Immigrants in Southeastern New England, 1890-1940"

Elliott, Emily J. "Migrants and Muscovites: The Boundaries of Belonging in Moscow, 1971-2002"

Jackson, Ronald II "African American Athletes, Actors, Singers, Performers and the Anti-Apartheid Movement, 1948-94"

Kalbach, Harrison Levan "Historical Scientific Displays during the German Empire: The Role of Science, National Identity, and Bourgeois Culture in the Growth of the History of Science as a Discipline"

Liu, Shaonan "'The Chinese Are Coming': A History of Chinese Migrants in Nigeria"

Mercier, Sebastian T. "'The Whole Furshlugginer Operation': The Jewish Comic Book Industry, 1933-54"

Milstead, John "Afro-Mexicans and the Making of Modern Mexico: Citizenship, Race, and Capitalism in Jamiltepec, Oaxaca, 1821-1910"

Pratt, Carolyn Maria "'Type-C': Empowerment, Blame, and Gender in the Creation of a Carcinogenic Personality"

Timbs, Elizabeth H. "The Regiments: Cultural Histories of Zulu Masculinities and Gender Formation in South Africa, 1816-2018"

Tyrey, Adrienne "Divide and School : Berber Education in Morocco under the French Protectorate"

Van Wyck, Brian "Islam, Education, and the Nation: Turkish Teachers and Imams in (West) Germany, 1961-2006"

Michigan Technological University

Dept. of Social Sciences, 1400 Townsend Dr., Houghton, MI 49931-1295. 906.487.2113. Fax 906.487.2468. Email: socialsciences@mtu.edu; gmsteven@mtu.edu. Website: https://www.mtu.edu/social-sciences/.

The Department of Social Sciences at Michigan Technological University is committed to high-quality undergraduate and graduate instruction across the social sciences.

Chair: Hugh S. Gorman
Director of Graduate Studies: Chelsea Schelly
Director of Undergraduate Studies: Melissa Baird
Degrees Offered: BA,MS,PhD
Academic Year System: Semester
Areas of Specialization: environmental, technology, industrial heritage and material culture, America, global
Undergraduate Tuition (per academic year):
 In-State: $15346
 Out-of-State: $33426
Graduate Tuition (per academic year): $18126
Enrollment 2018-19:
 Undergraduate Majors: 6
 New Graduate Students: 4
 Full-time Graduate Students: 11
 Part-time Graduate Students: 4
 Degrees in History: 2 BA, 2 MS, 2 PhD
Undergraduate Addresses:
 Admissions: http://www.mtu.edu/admissions/
 Financial Aid: http://www.mtu.edu/finaid/
Graduate Addresses:
 Admissions: http://www.mtu.edu/gradschool/
 Financial Aid: http://www.mtu.edu/social-sciences/

Full-time Faculty

Baird, Melissa F. (PhD, Oregon 2009; assoc. prof. and dir., undergrad. studies) critical heritage; mfbaird@mtu.edu

Blair, Carl (PhD, Minnesota 1992; lect.) archaeology; cblair@mtu.edu

Gorman, Hugh S. (PhD, Carnegie Mellon 1996; prof. and chair) technology, environmental, policy; hsgorman@mtu.edu

LaFreniere, Donald J. (PhD, Western Ontario 2014; assoc. prof.) historical geography, spatial, GIS; djlafren@mtu.edu

Langston, Nancy (PhD, Washington 1994; prof.) environmental, environmental health and policy, Lake Superior Basin; nelangs3@mtu.edu

Robins, Jonathan E. (PhD, Rochester 2010; assoc. prof.) globalization; jrobins@mtu.edu

Rouleau, Laura Walikainen (PhD, Delaware 2014; lect.) lwrouleau@mtu.edu

Scarlett, Sarah Fayen (PhD, Wisconsin-Madison 2014; asst. prof.) sfscarle@mtu.edu

Schelly, Chelsea (PhD, Wisconsin-Madison 2013; assoc. prof. and dir., grad. studies) natural resource sociology; cschelly@mtu.edu

Sweitz, Samuel R. (PhD, Texas A&M 2005; assoc. prof.) historical archaeology, mining, industrial heritage; srsweitz@mtu.edu

Walton, Steven (PhD, Toronto 1999; assoc. prof.) science and technology; sawalton@mtu.edu

Wellstead, Adam (PhD, Alberta 2006; assoc. prof.) environmental and energy policy; awellste@mtu.edu

Part-time Faculty

MacLennan, Carol A. (PhD, California, Berkeley 1979; retired prof.) camac@mtu.edu

Seely, Bruce E. (PhD, Delaware 1982; res. prof.) bseely@mtu.edu

Recently Awarded PhDs

Medeiros, Leonor "Heritage-led Development in Postindustrial Areas: A Systemic Approach to Industrial Landscapes"

Middlebury College

Dept. of History, 14 Old Chapel Rd., Axinn Center at Starr Library, Middlebury, VT 05753. 802.443.5313. Fax 802.443.2084. Email: davis@middlebury.edu. Website: http://www.middlebury.edu/academics/hist.

Our major program is unique in structure and in depth. Students graduate from the department having learned the skills of historical analysis and writing through a variety of lecture and seminar courses, which may be national, transnational or comparative across six distinct geographical areas.

Chair: Darién J. Davis
Degrees Offered: BA
Academic Year System: Semester
Areas of Specialization: Africa, East and South Asia, Europe and Russia, Latin America, US
Tuition (per academic year): $63917
Enrollment 2018-19:
  Undergraduate Majors: 102
  Degrees in History: 31 BA
Addresses:
  Admissions: http://www.middlebury.edu/admissions
  Financial Aid: http://www.middlebury.edu/admissions/finaid

Full-time Faculty

Armanios, Febe Y. (PhD, Ohio State 2003; prof.) Middle East, Islam, gender; farmanio@middlebury.edu

Barrow, Ian J. (PhD, Chicago 1998; prof.) South Asia, world, empire; ibarrow@middlebury.edu

Bennette, Rebecca Ayako (PhD, Harvard 2002; assoc. prof.) modern Europe, Germany, religion; rbennett@middlebury.edu

Burnham, Louisa A. (PhD, Northwestern 2000; assoc. prof.) medieval, France; lburnham@middlebury.edu

Clinton, Maggie (PhD, NYU 2009; asst. prof.) modern China; mclinton@middlebury.edu

Davis, Darién J. (PhD, Tulane 1993; prof. and chair) Latin America, diasporas, Latinos in the Atlantic world; davis@middlebury.edu

Hart, William B. (PhD, Brown 1998; assoc. prof.) 17th- and 18th-century America, social, Native American; hart@middlebury.edu

Mao, Joyce (PhD, California, Berkeley 2007; asst. prof.) US, foreign relations, politics; jmao@middlebury.edu

Mitchell, Rebecca Anne (PhD, Illinois, Urbana-Champaign 2011; asst. prof.) late imperial Russia; rmitchell@middlebury.edu

Monod, Paul Kleber (PhD, Yale 1986; Hepburn Prof.) Britain, early modern Europe; monod@middlebury.edu

Morsman, Amy F. (PhD, Virginia 2004; prof.) 19th-century US, gender, US South; amorsman@middlebury.edu

Ralph, James R., Jr. (PhD, Harvard 1990; Rehnquist Prof.) 19th- and 20th-century US, African American; ralph@middlebury.edu

Tropp, Jacob A. (PhD, Minnesota 2002; prof.) Africa, environmental, world; jtropp@middlebury.edu

Ward, Max M. (PhD, NYU 2011; asst. prof.) modern Japan, modern China; maxwellw@middlebury.edu

Wyatt, Don J. (PhD, Harvard 1984; McCardell Prof.) China, intellectual; wyatt@middlebury.edu

Joint/Cross Appointments

Morse, Kathryn T. (PhD, Washington 1997; prof.; Environmental Studies) environmental, US West; kmorse@middlebury.edu

Retired/Emeritus Faculty

Clifford, Nicholas R. (PhD, Harvard 1961; College Prof. emeritus) East Asia, China; clifford@middlebury.edu

Endicott, Elizabeth (PhD, Princeton 1982; prof. emeritus) Mongolia, Sino-Mongolian and Russo-Mongolian relations; endicott@middlebury.edu

Jacobs, Travis Beal (PhD, Columbia 1971; Proctor Prof. emeritus) US; tjacobs@middlebury.edu

Lamberti, Marjorie E. (PhD, Yale 1965; Dana Prof. emeritus) Germany, Europe; lamberti@middlebury.edu

Spencer, John (PhD, Columbia 1977; African Studies Prof. emeritus) Africa

Waters, Neil L. (PhD, Hawai'i, Manoa 1978; Kawashima Prof. emeritus) Japan, East Asia; nwaters@middlebury.edu

Middle Tennessee State University

Dept. of History, Box 23, 1301 E. Main St., Murfreesboro, TN 37132-0001. 615.898.2631. Fax 615.898.4881. Email: history@mtsu.edu. Website: https://mtsu.edu/history/.

In the MTSU history department you'll find a community dedicated to good teaching, rigorous scholarship, and community service, a classroom environment that encourages critical thinking and original research, and a multitude of opportunities for hands-on experience in the study of history.

Chair: Kevin A. Leonard
Director of Graduate Studies: Ashley Riley Sousa
Director of Undergraduate Studies: Aliou Ly
Degrees Offered: BA,BS,MA,PhD
Academic Year System: Semester
Areas of Specialization: public, US, American South, Europe, global
Undergraduate Tuition (per academic year):
  In-State: $7200
  Out-of-State: $25872
Graduate Tuition (per academic year):
  In-State: $8946
  Out-of-State: $24768
Enrollment 2018-19:
  Undergraduate Majors: 228
  New Graduate Students: 25
  Full-time Graduate Students: 27
  Part-time Graduate Students: 46
  Degrees in History: 18 BA, 37 BS, 22 MA, 5 PhD
  Students in Undergraduate Courses: 7964
  Students in Undergraduate Intro Courses: 7260
Undergraduate Addresses:
  Admissions: http://mtsu.edu/how-to-apply/
  Financial Aid: http://www.mtsu.edu/financialaid/
Graduate Addresses:
  Admissions and Financial Aid: http://www.mtsu.edu/graduate/

Full-time Faculty

Bakari, Adonijah L. (PhD, Temple 1999; assoc. prof.) Africa, African American; adonijah.bakari@mtsu.edu

Baran, Emily B. (PhD, North Carolina, Chapel Hill 2011; assoc. prof.) Soviet and post-Soviet Russia, eastern Europe; Emily.Baran@mtsu.edu

Chao, Yuan-ling (PhD, UCLA 1995; prof.) China, Japan, medicine; YuanLing.Chao@mtsu.edu

Doyle, Mark E. (PhD, Boston Coll. 2006; prof.) modern Britain and British Empire; Mark.Doyle@mtsu.edu

Fialka, Andrew (PhD, Georgia 2018; asst. prof.) American Civil War, 19th- and 20th-century US, guerrilla war, digital humanities, Geographic Information Systems; Andrew.Fialka@mtsu.edu

Foley, Sean E. (PhD, Georgetown 2005; prof.) Middle East; Sean.Foley@mtsu.edu

Haas, Louis B. (PhD, Illinois, Urbana-Champaign 1990; prof.) medieval and Renaissance Europe; Louis.Haas@mtsu.edu

Hoffschwelle, Mary S. (PhD, Vanderbilt 1993; prof.) America, US South, women; Mary.Hoffschwelle@mtsu.edu

Holloway, Pippa E. (PhD, Ohio State 1999; prof.) modern US, US South; Pippa.Holloway@mtsu.edu

Kolar, Kelly A. (PhD, UCLA 2012; asst. prof.) public, archives, Soviet Union; Kelly.Kolar@mtsu.edu

Kyriakoudes, Louis M. (PhD, Vanderbilt 1997; prof.; dir., Gore Research Center) modern US, economic, US South; Louis.Kyriakoudes@mtsu.edu

Leonard, Kevin A. (PhD, California, Davis 1992; prof. and chair) modern US; Kevin.Leonard@mtsu.edu

Ly, Aliou (PhD, California, Davis 2012; assoc. prof. and undergrad. dir.) Africa, African diaspora; Aliou.Ly@mtsu.edu

Martin, Christopher Brenden (PhD, Tennessee, Knoxville 1997; prof.) public, museum studies, US South; Brenden.Martin@mtsu.edu

McCormack, Dawn (BA, Pennsylvania 1997; assoc. prof.) ancient, Egypt; Dawn.Mccormack@mtsu.edu

McCusker, Kristine M. (PhD, Indiana 2000; prof.) post-1945, ethnomusicology; Kristine.Mccusker@mtsu.edu

Myers-Shirk, Susan E. (PhD, Penn State 1994; prof.) US cultural and intellectual; Susan.Myers-Shirk@mtsu.edu

Nelson, Lynn A. (PhD, William and Mary 1998; prof.) American Revolution, environmental; Lynn.Nelson@mtsu.edu

Norkunas, Martha (PhD, Indiana 1990; prof.) public, folklore, oral; Martha.Norkunas@mtsu.edu

Polk, Andrew (PhD, Florida State 2013; asst. prof.) history education, American religion; Andrew.Polk@mtsu.edu

Pruitt, Lisa J. (PhD, Vanderbilt 1998; prof. and dir., public hist.) medical, Jacksonian America; Lisa.Pruitt@mtsu.edu

Riley Sousa, Mary Ashley (PhD, Yale 2013; assoc. prof. and grad. dir.) Native American, ethnohistory, American West; Ashley.Rileysousa@mtsu.edu

Rosenmuller, Christoph (PhD, Tulane 2003; prof.) Latin America; Christoph.Rosenmuller@mtsu.edu

Rupprecht, Nancy E. (PhD, Michigan 1982; prof.) modern Europe, Germany, European women; Nancy.Rupprecht@mtsu.edu

Sayward, Amy L. (PhD, Ohio State 1998; prof.) post-1945 US diplomatic; Amy.Sayward@mtsu.edu

Scherzer, Kenneth A. (PhD, Harvard 1982; prof.) US urban, social, quantitative; Kenneth.Scherzer@mtsu.edu

Sikes, Kathryn (PhD, William and Mary 2013; assoc. prof.) historical archaeology, colonial America, postcolonial studies; Kathryn.Sikes@mtsu.edu

Sutherland, Suzanne (PhD, Stanford 2012; assoc. prof.) early modern central Europe, early modern Italy, medieval Europe; suzanne.sutherland@mtsu.edu

Taylor-Poleskey, Molly (PhD, Stanford 2016; asst. prof.) digital, early modern Europe

Treadwell, Aaron (PhD, Howard 2017; asst. prof.) African American; Aaron.Treadwell@mtsu.edu

West, Carroll Van (PhD, William and Mary 1982; prof.; dir., Center for Historic Preservation) historic preservation, material culture; Carroll.West@mtsu.edu

Woods, Louis L. (PhD, Howard 2006; assoc. prof.) African American, economic; Louis.Woods@mtsu.edu

Nondepartmental Historians

Graham, Stacey R. (PhD, UCLA 2005; research assoc. prof.; Center for Historic Preservation) medieval, historic preservation, history education; Stacey.Graham@mtsu.edu

Retired/Emeritus Faculty

Conard, Rebecca A. (PhD, California, Santa Barbara 1984; prof. emerita) African American; Rebecca.Conard@mtsu.edu

Foster, Martha Harroun (PhD, UCLA 2000; assoc. prof. emerita) Martha.Foster@mtsu.edu

Hunt, Robert E. (PhD, Missouri, Columbia 1988; prof. emeritus) US South, Civil War and Reconstruction, US military; Robert.Hunt@mtsu.edu

Leone, Janice M. (PhD, Ohio State 1989; prof. emerita) Jan.Leone@mtsu.edu

McWatters, D. Lorne (PhD, Florida 1979; prof. emeritus) Lorne.McWatters@mtsu.edu

Rowe, David L. (PhD, Virginia 1974; prof. emeritus) David.Rowe@mtsu.edu

Recently Awarded PhDs

Beatty, Bob "'You Wanna Play in My Band, You'd Better Come to Pick': Duane Allman and American Music"

Gatson, Torren L. "The Combative Tactics of the NAACP Against Unfair Housing Laws and Practices: A Comparative Study of the Dynamic Changes in Urban and Rural Landscapes, 1920-60"

Momon, Tiffany Nicole "Constructing Traditions: Architecture, Objects, and the Higher Education Experience at Spelman College"

Reed, Marquita "'What You See is What You Get ... But That Ain't What We Want': Decolonizing African American Protest and Identity Politics through Popular Culture"

Millersville University of Pennsylvania

Dept. of History, PO Box 1002, Millersville, PA 17551-0302. 717.871.7212. Email: maggie.eichler@millersville.edu. Website: https://www.millersville.edu/history/.

Millersville is the only institution in southeastern Pennsylvania outside the Philadelphia area to grant these three advanced degrees in history: Baccalaureates in Liberal Arts and in Education, and a Master of Arts in History.

Chair: John M. McLarnon
Director of Graduate Studies: Robyn Lily Davis
Degrees Offered: BA,BSEd,MA
Academic Year System: Semester
Areas of Specialization: US political/social/cultural, modern Europe/Russia/Britain, Latin America, modern Africa, American diplomatic and military
Undergraduate Tuition (per academic year):
In-State: $12250
Out-of-State: $22220
Graduate Tuition (per academic year):
In-State: $15906
Out-of-State: $22386

Enrollment 2018-19:
  Undergraduate Majors: 181
  New Graduate Students: 4
  Full-time Graduate Students: 1
  Part-time Graduate Students: 11
  Degrees in History: 12 BA, 2 MA, 14 BSE
Undergraduate Addresses:
  Admissions: http://www.millersville.edu/admissions/
    undergrad/index.php
  Financial Aid: http://www.millersville.edu/finaid/
Graduate Addresses:
  Admissions: http://www.millersville.edu/graduate/
  Financial Aid: http://www.millersville.edu/graduate/admissions/
    financial-support.php

Adjunct Faculty

Ortmann, Susan (PhD, Penn State 2015; adj. instr.) colonial and
  revolutionary America, 19th-century Ohio River Valley and
  borderlines, 15th- to 18th-century Atlantic world; susan.
  ortmann@millersville.edu
Prushankin, Jeffery S. (PhD, Arkansas 2000; adj. asst. prof.)
  Civil War, 19th-century US, US military; jeffery.prushankin@
  millersville.edu
Spiese, Monica D. (ABD, Delaware; adj. instr.) 18th-century mid-
  Atlantic region, social and cultural; monica.spiese@millersville.
  edu

Full-time Faculty

Adyanga, Onek C. (PhD, Connecticut 2009; assoc. prof.) Africa,
  imperial and colonial, Atlantic slave trade; onek.adyanga@
  millersville.edu
Davis, Robyn Lily (PhD, Oklahoma 2009; assoc. prof. and dir., grad.
  studies) colonial and revolutionary America, early American
  science; robyn.davis@millersville.edu
Frankum, Ronald B, Jr. (PhD, Syracuse 1997; prof.) American
  foreign relations, Vietnam War, military; ronald.frankum@
  millersville.edu
Kevorkian, Tanya E. (PhD, Johns Hopkins 1997; assoc. prof.) early
  modern Germany, colonial Pennsylvania German, music social;
  tanya.kevorkian@millersville.edu
Khiterer, Victoria M. (PhD, Brandeis 2008; assoc. prof.) Russia,
  eastern Europe, Holocaust and genocide studies; victoria.
  khiterer@millersville.edu
Maxwell, Clarence V. H. (PhD, Warwick, UK 1999; asst. prof.; co-dir.,
  MDST, Atlantic World Research) African diaspora 1492-1834,
  Bermuda/Latin America/Caribbean, slavery and slave resistance;
  clarence.maxwell@millersville.edu
McLarnon, John Morrison, III (PhD, Delaware 1998; assoc. prof.
  and chair) 20th-century political, Central American political, civil
  rights; john.mclarnon@millersville.edu
Shelor, Erin J. (PhD, Kentucky 2003; assoc. prof.) Britain and Ireland
  1750-1914, modern Europe, medicine and health; erin.shelor@
  millersville.edu
Sommar, Mary E. (PhD, Syracuse 1998; asst. prof.) medieval
  Europe, Christianity, legal; mary.sommar@millersville.edu
Weis, Tracey M. (PhD, Rutgers 1992; assoc. prof.) 19th-century US,
  African American, women; tracey.weis@millersville.edu

Retired/Emeritus Faculty

Benson, Ronald M. (PhD, Notre Dame 1974; prof. emeritus)
  American business, economics, military
Bremer, Francis J. (PhD, Columbia 1972; prof. emeritus; ed.,
  Winthrop Papers) colonial and revolutionary America, Tudor-
  Stuart England; francis.bremer@millersville.edu
Clark, Linda L. (PhD, North Carolina 1968; prof. emeritus) modern
  France, modern Europe, European women

Downey, Dennis B. (PhD, Marquette 1981; prof. emeritus) America
  1876-1930, social and cultural, violence; dennis.downey@
  millersville.edu
Fischel, Jack R. (PhD, Delaware 1973; prof. emeritus) modern
  Jewish, Cold War, American intellectual and cultural; jack.
  fischel@millersville.edu
Jolly, James A. (MA, Michigan State 1960; assoc. prof. emeritus)
  America, 20th-century US, Pennsylvania
Koppel, Reynold S. (PhD, Washington 1969; prof. emeritus)
  Germany, early modern and modern Europe
Osborne, John B., Jr. (PhD, Rutgers 1971; prof. emeritus) England,
  modern Britain and British Empire, modern Europe
Suziedelis, Saulius A. (PhD, Kansas 1977; prof. emeritus) Russia,
  eastern Europe, modern Europe; ssuziedelis@millersville.edu
Tirado, Thomas C. (PhD, Temple 1978; prof. emeritus) world
  civilization, Latin America, inter-American relations; tctirado@
  millersville.edu

University of Minnesota

*Dept. of History, 1110 Heller Hall, 271 19th Ave. S., Minneapolis,
MN 55455-0406. 612.624.2800. Fax 612.624.7096. Email:
history@umn.edu. Website: https://cla.umn.edu/history.*

*By pushing the boundaries of the human story across time, space,
cultures, and media, we reveal the interconnected narrative
threads and patterns of our individual and collective lives.*

Chair: Ann Waltner
Director of Graduate Studies: Howard Louthan
Director of Undergraduate Studies: Mai Na Lee
Degrees Offered: BA,MA,PhD
Academic Year System: Semester
Areas of Specialization: Africa, Asia, comparative, Europe, US
Undergraduate Tuition (per academic year):
  In-State: $13058
  Out-of-State: $24258
Graduate Tuition (per academic year):
  In-State: $17064
  Out-of-State: $26412
Enrollment 2018-19:
  Undergraduate Majors: 320
  New Graduate Students: 12
  Full-time Graduate Students: 67
  Degrees in History: 112 BA, 3 MA, 8 PhD
Undergraduate Addresses:
  Admissions: http://twin-cities.umn.edu/admissions-aid
  Financial Aid: http://admissions.tc.umn.edu/costsaid/
Graduate Addresses:
  Admissions: https://cla.umn.edu/history/graduate
  Financial Aid: http://www.grad.umn.edu/funding_tuition/

Adjunct Faculty

Blumenthal, Susanna (PhD, Yale 2001; prof.; Law Sch.) American
  legal, 19th-century US cultural and intellectual; blume047@
  umn.edu
Coifman, Victoria Bomba (PhD, Wisconsin, Madison 1969; asst.
  prof.; African American & African Studies) comparative tropical;
  coifm@umn.edu
Kohlstedt, Sally Gregory (PhD, Illinois, Urbana-Champaign 1972;
  prof.; Prog. in the Hist. of Sci., Tech., and Medicine) science,
  nature study movement; sgk@umn.edu
Matar, Nabil (PhD, Cambridge 1976; prof.; English) modern
  Europe, cultural; matar010@umn.edu

Mayes, Keith A. (PhD, Princeton 2002; assoc. prof.; African American & African Studies) African American studies; mayes@umn.edu

Von Dassow, Eva (PhD, NYU 1997; assoc. prof.; Classics and Near Eastern Studies) ancient Near East, Egypt; vonda001@umn.edu

Full-time Faculty

Bachrach, Bernard S. (PhD, California, Berkeley 1966; prof.) medieval and Renaissance, medieval military; bachr001@umn.edu

Bashiri, Iraj (PhD, Michigan 1972; prof.) Islamic intellectual; bashi001@umn.edu

Casale, Giancarlo L. (PhD, Harvard 2004; assoc. prof.) Ottoman Empire, comparative early modern, geography and cartography; casale@umn.edu

Chambers, Sarah C. (PhD, Wisconsin-Madison 1992; prof.) colonial Latin America, women, gender; chambers@umn.edu

Chang, David A. (PhD, Wisconsin, Madison 2001; prof.) US West, African American, Indian since Civil War; dchang@umn.edu

Clark, Anna K. (PhD, Rutgers 1987; prof.) modern Europe, Britain; clark106@umn.edu

Deutsch, Tracey Ann (PhD, Wisconsin, Madison 2001; assoc. prof.) 20th-century US political/business/social; tdeutsch@umn.edu

Fischer, Kirsten (PhD, Duke 1994; assoc. prof.) colonial America, social; kfischer@umn.edu

Gallia, Andrew B. (PhD, Pennsylvania 2003; assoc. prof.; Classical and Near Eastern Studies) Rome and ancient Mediterranean; abgallia@umn.edu

Gerbner, Katharine (PhD, Harvard 2013; assoc. prof.) Atlantic world, early America, early modern; kgerbner@umn.edu

Hacker, J. David (PhD, Minnesota 1999; assoc. prof.; Minnesota Population Center) demographic, quantitative, American Civil War; hacke010@umn.edu

Hakim, Carol D. (DPhil, Oxford 1998; assoc. prof.) modern Middle East, Arab world; hakimc@umn.edu

Isaacman, Allen F. (PhD, Wisconsin, Madison 1970; Regents' Prof.) central and southern Africa; isaac001@umn.edu

Isett, Christopher M. (PhD, UCLA 1997; assoc. prof.) modern China, economic, social; isett003@umn.edu

Jones, William P. (PhD, North Carolina, Chapel Hill 2000; prof.) US, civil rights, African American; wpjones@umn.edu

Lee, Erika (PhD, California, Berkeley 1998; Regents' Prof.; dir., Immigration History Research Center) 20th-century US, Asian American, immigration, American West; erikalee@umn.edu

Lee, Mai Na M. (PhD, Wisconsin, Madison 2005; assoc. prof. and dir., undergrad. studies) Southeast Asia, Southeast Asian diaspora; mainalee@umn.edu

Lindquist, Malinda Alaine (PhD, Princeton 2004; assoc. prof.) US, African American, gender; lindqust@umn.edu

Lorcin, Patricia M. E. (PhD, Columbia 1992; prof.) modern Europe; plorcin@umn.edu

Louthan, Howard P. (PhD, Princeton 1994; prof. and dir., grad. studies; dir., Center for Austrian Studies) central Europe, Austria, religion; hlouthan@umn.edu

Lower, Michael (PhD, Cambridge 1999; prof.) medieval, early modern Europe; mlower@umn.edu

Mathieu, Sarah-Jane (PhD, Yale 2001; assoc. prof.) 20th-century American social/political/labor, African American, comparative race/ethnicity/immigration; smathieu@umn.edu

May, Elaine Tyler (PhD, UCLA 1975; Regents' Prof.; American Studies) US, US women; mayxx002@umn.edu

Maynes, MaryJo (PhD, Michigan 1977; prof.) modern Germany, European social, women; mayne001@umn.edu

McNamara, Patrick J. (PhD, Wisconsin, Madison 1999; assoc. prof.) colonial and modern Latin America, Mexico; pjm@umn.edu

Mizuno, Hiromi (PhD, UCLA 2001; assoc. prof.) modern Japan; mizuno@umn.edu

Murphy, Kevin P. (PhD, New York Univ. 2001; prof.) US urban/political/intellectual/cultural, sexuality and masculinity; kpmurphy@umn.edu

O'Brien, Jean M. (PhD, Chicago 1990; prof.) colonial America, Native American; obrie002@umn.edu

Reyerson, Kathryn L. (PhD, Yale 1974; prof.) France, medieval social, economic; reyer001@umn.edu

Ruggles, Steven (PhD, Pennsylvania 1984; Regents' Prof.; dir., Minnesota Population Center) American demographic and social; ruggles@umn.edu

Schroeter, Daniel J. (PhD, Manchester 1984; prof.) Jewish, modern Middle East and North Africa; schro800@umn.edu

Shank, J. B. (PhD, Stanford 2000; prof.; dir., Center for Early Modern Hist., Consortium of the Premodern World) early modern France, European intellectual; jbshank@umn.edu

Skaria, Ajay (PhD, Cambridge 1992; prof.; Inst. for Global Studies) South Asia; skari002@umn.edu

Stavrou, Theofanis G. (PhD, Indiana 1961; prof.; dir., Modern Greek Studies) modern Russia, Balkans, modern Greece; stavr001@umn.edu

Sterk, Andrea L. (PhD, Princeton Theological Seminary 1994; assoc. prof.) medieval Europe, religious studies; sterk@umn.edu

Waltner, Ann (PhD, California, Berkeley 1981; prof. and chair) traditional China; waltn001@umn.edu

Wang, Liping (PhD, California, San Diego 1997; assoc. prof.) modern China, social, cultural; lipin003@umn.edu

Welke, Barbara Young (PhD, Chicago 1995; prof.) 20th-century US, legal and constitutional; welke004@umn.edu

Wolfe, Thomas Cox (PhD, Michigan 1997; assoc. prof.; Inst. for Global Studies) modern Europe, contemporary Russia; wolfe023@umn.edu

Retired/Emeritus Faculty

Cohen, Gary B. (PhD, Princeton 1975; prof. emeritus) modern European social, Austria and Germany, Czechoslovakia since 1790; gcohen@umn.edu

Evans, John K. (PhD, McMaster 1974; prof. emeritus) ancient, Rome; evans002@umn.edu

Evans, Sara M. (PhD, North Carolina, Chapel Hill 1976; Regents' Prof. emeritus) 20th-century US social, American women; s-evan@umn.edu

Farmer, Edward L. (PhD, Harvard 1968; prof. emeritus) modern China, comparative early modern, world; efarmer@umn.edu

Good, David F. (PhD, Pennsylvania 1972; prof. emeritus) European economic, Austria; goodx001@umn.edu

Green, George D. (PhD, Stanford 1968; assoc. prof. emeritus) American economic and business; green007@umn.edu

Howe, John R., Jr. (PhD, Yale 1962; prof. emeritus) political, 18th- and 19th-century America; howex002@umn.edu

Kelly, Thomas (PhD, Illinois, Urbana-Champaign 1964; prof. emeritus) ancient, Greece

Kieft, David O. (PhD, California, Berkeley 1966; assoc. prof. emeritus) European diplomatic

Kopf, David (PhD, Chicago 1964; prof. emeritus) India, comparative world; kopfx001@umn.edu

Marshall, Byron K. (PhD, Stanford 1966; prof. emeritus) modern Japan, social, education; marsh004@umn.edu

May, Lary (PhD, UCLA 1976; prof. emeritus) US, film and popular culture; mayxx001@umn.edu

McCaa, Robert E., Jr. (PhD, UCLA 1978; prof. emeritus) modern Latin America, population; rmccaa@umn.edu

Menard, Russell R. (PhD, Iowa 1975; prof. emeritus) colonial America, slavery, plantation slavery; menar001@umn.edu

Munholland, J. Kim (PhD, Princeton 1964; prof. emeritus) contemporary Europe, 20th-century France; munhollandj@aol.com

Norling, Lisa A. (PhD, Rutgers 1992; assoc. prof. emeritus) American Revolution and 19th-century social, women and gender, maritime; norli001@umn.edu

Phillips, Carla Rahn (PhD, NYU 1972; prof. emeritus) early modern Europe, social and economic, Spain; phill002@umn.edu

Phillips, William D., Jr. (PhD, NYU 1971; prof. emeritus) medieval and early modern Europe, Mediterranean, Spain; phill004@umn.edu

Rudolph, Richard L. (PhD, Wisconsin, Madison 1968; prof. emeritus) modern European social and economic, central and eastern Europe; rrudolph11@comcast.net

Taylor, Romeyn (PhD, Chicago 1960; prof. emeritus) traditional China, Asian civilizations, East Asia; taylo0017@aol.com

Thayer, John A. (PhD, Wisconsin, Madison 1960; prof. emeritus) European intellectual, Italy; thaye001@umn.edu

Tracy, James D. (PhD, Princeton 1967; prof. emeritus) Renaissance and Reformation, 16th-century Europe; tracy001@umn.edu

Recently Awarded PhDs

Arnett, Jessica "Between Empires and Frontiers: Alaska Native Sovereignty and US Settler Imperialism"

Dillenburg, Elizabeth "Constructing and Contesting 'the Girlhood of Our Empire': Girls' Culture, Labor, and Mobility in 19th- and Early 20th-Century Britain, South Africa, and New Zealand"

Haker, Joseph P. "The Rock of the Republic: The Ten Commandments in American Life from World War II to the Culture Wars"

Hoyt, Andrew Douglas "And They Called Them 'Galleanisti': The Rise of the Cronaca Sovversiva and the Formation of America's Most Infamous Anarchist Faction, 1895-1912"

James, Elliot "Sithutha Isizwe ('We Carry the Nation'): Dispossession, Displacement, and the Making of the Shared Minibus Taxi in Cape Town and Johannesburg, South Africa, 1930-Present"

Kim, Jee-Yeon (Jay) "Korean War Memories"

Nelson, Matt Andrew "Relieved of These Little Chores: Agricultural Neighbor Labor, Family Labor, and Kinship in the United States, 1790-1940"

Taparata, Evan "No Asylum for Mankind: The Creation of Refugee Law and Policy in the United States, 1776-1951"

Thumbran, Janeke Deodata "The 'Coloured Question' and the University of Pretoria: Separate Development, Trusteeship, and Self Reliance, 1933-2012"

Wang, Luo "The Gothic Saints and Their Mystical Songs: Performing Sanctity in the 13th-Century Diocese of Liège"

Williams, Blair "Making Japan's National Game: Baseball, Bushido, and Discourses of National Identity, 1868-2008"

University of Minnesota

Prog. in the History of Science, Technology, and Medicine, 585 Shepherd Laboratories, 100 Union St. SE, Minneapolis, MN 55455-0231. 612.624.7069. Fax 612.301.1442. Email: hstm@umn.edu. Website: https://www.hstm.umn.edu/.

The Program in the History of Science, Technology, and Medicine integrates faculty and students from several departments and programs at the University of Minnesota. The program encourages a diversity of methodological approaches.

Chair: Mark Borrello
Director of Graduate Studies: Jennifer Alexander

Degrees Offered: MA, PhD
Academic Year System: Semester
Areas of Specialization: physical sciences, biological sciences, technology, medicine
Tuition (per academic year):
In-State: $16728
Out-of-State: $25884
Enrollment 2018-19:
New Graduate Students: 2
Full-time Graduate Students: 32
Degrees in History: 1 MA, 3 PhD
Addresses:
Admissions and Financial Aid: https://www.hstm.umn.edu/graduate-program

Full-time Faculty

Alexander, Jennifer K. (PhD, Washington 1996; assoc. prof. and dir., grad. studies) technology, modern Germany, comparative industrial cultures; alexa056@umn.edu

Boantza, Victor (PhD, Toronto 2009; asst. prof.) early modern physical sciences, Enlightenment science, scientific and chemical revolutions; vboantza@umn.edu

Borrello, Mark E. (PhD, Indiana 2002; assoc. prof. and chair) biology, evolutionary theory, genetics and ecology; borrello@umn.edu

Graber, Anna (PhD, Yale 2016; asst. prof.) early modern Russia, earth sciences; agraber@umn.edu

Gunn, Jennifer L. (PhD, Pennsylvania 1997; assoc. prof.) 19th- and 20th-century US medicine and public health, rural studies, social sciences; gunnx005@umn.edu

Janssen, Michel (PhD, Pittsburgh 1995; prof.) modern physics, relativity and quantum revolutions, Einstein; janss011@umn.edu

Jones, Susan D. (PhD, Pennsylvania 1997; prof.) biomedical sciences, ecology of disease, role of science in mediating human-animal interactions; jone0996@umn.edu

Kohlstedt, Sally Gregory (PhD, Illinois, Urbana-Champaign 1972; prof.) US natural sciences, institutional and cultural contexts for science practice, women and gender in science; sgk@umn.edu

Shackelford, Jole R. (PhD, Wisconsin-Madison 1989; asst. prof.) early modern Scandinavian science and medicine, paracelsian studies, chronobiology; shack001@umn.edu

Tobbell, Dominique A. (PhD, Pennsylvania 2008; asst. prof.) pharmaceuticals, health care policy, biomedical science and technology; dtobbell@umn.edu

Retired/Emeritus Faculty

Eyler, John M. (PhD, Wisconsin-Madison 1971; prof. emeritus) public health, disease theory, social medicine; eyler001@umn.edu

Misa, Thomas J. (PhD, Pennsylvania 1987; prof. emeritus) technology, computer processing; tmisa@umn.edu

Norberg, Arthur L. (PhD, Wisconsin-Madison 1974; prof. emeritus) science/technology/industry relations, federal government role in stimulating scientific and technological development, information processing; anorberg@umn.edu

Seidel, Robert W. (PhD, California, Berkeley 1978; prof. emeritus) 19th- and 20th-century physical sciences and related technologies; rws@umn.edu

Shapiro, Alan E. (PhD, Yale 1970; prof. emeritus) physical science, Isaac Newton, Scientific Revolution; ashapiro@physics.umn.edu

Stuewer, Roger H. (PhD, Wisconsin-Madison 1968; prof. emeritus) quantum mechanics, nuclear physics; rstuewer@physics.umn.edu

Recently Awarded PhDs

Miller, Emelin E. "Empire of Ice: Arctic Natural History and British Visions of the North, 1650-1800"

University of Minnesota Duluth

Dept. of History, 265 A.B. Anderson Hall, 1121 University Dr., Duluth, MN 55812-2496. 218.726.7253. Fax 218.726.638. Email: hist@d.umn.edu. Website: https://cla.d.umn.edu/departments/history-political-science-and-international-studies/history.

This program introduces students to major world cultures and provides experiences in the critical use of historical literature and other source materials. It offers concentrations in five geographical areas (Africa, East Asia, Europe, the Middle East and United States) and three chronological periodizations (Ancient, Pre-Modern, and Modern).

Chair: Gideon Mailer
Degrees Offered: BA
Academic Year System: Semester
Areas of Specialization: Africa, East Asia, early modern and modern Europe, Russia, US
Tuition (per academic year):
 In-State: $13140
 Out-of-State: $17486
Enrollment 2018-19:
 Undergraduate Majors: 85
 Degrees in History: 20 BA
Addresses:
 Admissions: http://www.d.umn.edu/prospective/
 Financial Aid: http://www.d.umn.edu/admissions/
  undergraduate-admissions/costs-and-aid

Full-time Faculty

Belsky, Natalie (PhD, Chicago 2014; asst. prof.) Russia; nbelsky@d.umn.edu
Fang, Qiang (PhD, SUNY, Buffalo 2006; asst. prof.) modern Japan, China, East Asia; qfang@d.umn.edu
Laderman, Scott (PhD, Minnesota 2005; prof.) 20th-century US, foreign relations, American Indian; laderman@d.umn.edu
Mailer, Gideon A. (PhD, Cambridge 2008; asst. prof. and chair) colonial America, religion, American frontiers; gamailer@d.umn.edu
Matthews, Steven Paul (PhD, Florida 2003; asst. prof.) Europe, science, Christianity; smatthew@d.umn.edu
Rop, Jeffrey (PhD, Penn State 2013; asst. prof.) Greece and Persia
Spencer, Steffan A. (PhD, Howard 2010; asst. prof.) Africa; saspence@d.umn.edu
Stanfield-Johnson, Rosemary (PhD, NYU 1993; assoc. prof.) Islam, Islamic societies, women in Islam; rstanfie@d.umn.edu

Retired/Emeritus Faculty

Hoover, Roy (PhD, Washington State 1967; prof. emeritus) fur trade, Minnesota, westward expansion
Pogorelskin, Alexis E. (PhD, Yale 1976; assoc. prof. emeritus) Russia and Soviet Union, modern Europe, modern America; apogorel@d.umn.edu
Storch, Neil T. (PhD, Wisconsin, Madison 1969; prof. emeritus) colonial America, US Catholic, US foreign relations; nstorch@d.umn.edu
Trolander, Judith Ann (PhD, Case Western Reserve 1972; prof. emeritus) US, women, urban; jtroland@d.umn.edu
Yelengi, Nkasa T. (PhD, Minnesota 1996; assoc. prof. emeritus) modern Africa, modern Europe; nyelengi@d.umn.edu

Minnesota State University, Mankato

Dept. of History, 110 Armstrong Hall, Mankato, MN 56001. 507.389.1618. Fax 507.389.5569. Email: christopher.corley@mnsu.edu. Website: https://sbs.mnsu.edu/academics/history.

The mission of the History Department at Minnesota State University, Mankato is to develop a broader, deeper understanding of the past by offering a globally oriented curriculum that introduces students to the methods and processes used by professional historians to make informed, accurate conclusions about the past.

Chair: Christopher R. Corley
Director of Graduate Studies: Lori Lahlum
Director of Undergraduate Studies: Justin Biel
Degrees Offered: BA,BS,MA,MS, Cert.
Academic Year System: Semester
Areas of Specialization: US, social and cultural, women and gender, US foreign relations, Europe, Middle East, modern Asia, Africa and Latin America
Undergraduate Tuition (per academic year):
 In-State: $7178
 Out-of-State: $15228
Graduate Tuition (per academic year): $7398
Enrollment 2018-19:
 Undergraduate Majors: 87
 New Graduate Students: 2
 Full-time Graduate Students: 8
 Part-time Graduate Students: 12
 Degrees in History: 3 BA, 8 BS, 2 MA, 3 Cert.
 Students in Undergraduate Courses: 1228
 Students in Undergraduate Intro Courses: 881
 Online-Only Courses: 10%
Undergraduate Addresses:
 Admissions: http://www.mnsu.edu/admissions/
 Financial Aid: http://www.mnsu.edu/campushub/
Graduate Addresses:
 Admissions: http://grad.mnsu.edu/
 Financial Aid: http://www.mnsu.edu/campushub/

Full-time Faculty

Biel, Justin (PhD, Minnesota 2014; asst. prof. and undergrad. coord.) Britain, Ireland, Canada, modern Empires; justin.biel@mnsu.edu
Cooley, Angela Jill (PhD, Alabama 2011; JD, George Washington; assoc. prof.) 20th-century US, civil rights, US constitution and legal; angela.cooley@mnsu.edu
Corley, Christopher R. (PhD, Purdue 2001; prof. and chair) early modern Europe, women and family; christopher.corley@mnsu.edu
Haque, Jameel (PhD, Graduate Center, CUNY 2016; asst. prof.) Middle East; jameel.haque@mnsu.edu
Lahlum, Lori Ann (PhD, Idaho 2003; prof. and grad. coord.) US West, women and gender; lori.lahlum@mnsu.edu
Loayza, Matthew (PhD, Purdue 1999; prof. and dean) US foreign policy, 20th-century US; matt.loayza@mnsu.edu
McCutchen, Chad (PhD, Texas Christian 2016; asst. prof.) Latin America; chad.mccutchen@mnsu.edu
Odinga, Agnes A. (PhD, Minnesota 2001; asst. prof.) Africa; agnes.odinga@mnsu.edu
Peng, Tao (PhD, Georgia 2002; assoc. prof.) modern Asia, Asian diplomatic, world; tao.peng@mnsu.edu

Ward, Kyle (PhD, Indiana State 2007; assoc. prof. and dir., social studies) social studies education, US; kyle.ward@mnsu.edu

Retired/Emeritus Faculty

Gorman, Kathleen L. (PhD, California, Riverside 1994; prof. emeritus) 19th-century US, Civil War; kathleen.gorman@mnsu.edu

Handke, Margaretta S. (PhD, Colorado, Boulder 1986; assoc. prof. emeritus) medieval Europe, ancient, Middle East; margaretta.handke@mnsu.edu

Witherell, Larry L. (PhD, Minnesota, Twin Cities 1992; prof. emeritus) modern Europe, Britain; larry.witherell@mnsu.edu

Minot State University

Dept. of History, 500 University Ave. W., Minot, ND 58707-2005. 701.858.3243. Fax 701.858.3132. Email: bethany.andreasen@minotstateu.edu. Website: https://www.minotstateu.edu/history/.

History at Minot State University prepares students for diverse careers in education, law, public service, consulting, and many other areas. The department offers two degrees: a BA and a BSEd, the teaching degree which leads to grade 5-12 certification.

Chair: Bethany Andreasen
Degrees Offered: BA,BS
Academic Year System: Semester
Areas of Specialization: American and European social and cultural, medieval and modern Europe, Native American, Latin America, Atlantic world
Tuition (per academic year): $7063
Enrollment 2018-19:
  Undergraduate Majors: 54
  Degrees in History: 6 BA, 5 BSEd
Addresses:
  Admissions: http://www.minotstateu.edu/enroll/
  Financial Aid: http://www.minotstateu.edu/finaid/

Adjunct Faculty

Biles, Amanda B. (MA, Central Oklahoma 2011; instr.) agricultural, legal, social; amanda.biles@minotstateu.edu

Flory, Lynsay (MA, Wichita State 2014; instr.) public, rural and regional, social; lynsay.flory@ndsu.edu

Sunwall, Christina (MA, Leicester, UK 2003; instr.) US, public; christina.sunwall@minotstateu.edu

Full-time Faculty

Andreasen, Bethany (PhD, Cornell 1987; prof. and coord.) 20th-century US, US social and cultural, women; bethany.andreasen@minotstateu.edu

Jastrzembski, Joseph C. (PhD, Chicago 1994; prof.) American West, Native American, ethnohistory; joseph.jastrzembski@minotstateu.edu

Pijning, Ernst (PhD, Johns Hopkins 1998; prof.) Latin America, Brazil, Atlantic world; ernst.pijning@minotstateu.edu

Ringrose, Daniel M. (PhD, Michigan 1995; prof.) European social, France and empire, technology; daniel.ringrose@minotstateu.edu

Singer, Mark Alan (PhD, Missouri, Columbia 2012; asst. prof.) early Middle Ages, Europe 1000-1500, religion; mark.singer@minotstateu.edu

Retired/Emeritus Faculty

Wagner, Jonathan (PhD, Wisconsin, Madison 1969; JD, Wisconsin, Madison 1982; prof. emeritus) modern Germany, Canadian German, immigration; jonathan.wagner@minotstateu.edu

University of Mississippi

Arch Dalrymple III Dept. of History, 310 Bishop Hall, PO Box 1848, University, MS 38677-1848. 662.915.7148. Fax 662.915.7033. Email: history@olemiss.edu. Website: http://history.olemiss.edu/.

The study of history explores our shared and diverse past, providing an essential context and perspective on the contemporary world. Studying history enhances a student's ability to think and reason, to communicate effectively, and to organize systematically, evaluate, and interpret information.

Chair: Noell Wilson
Director of Graduate Studies: Marc H. Lerner
Director of Undergraduate Studies: Anne Twitty
Degrees Offered: BA,MA,PhD
Academic Year System: Semester
Areas of Specialization: US, Europe, Latin America, Africa, East Asia, Middle East, Atlantic world, medieval
Tuition (per academic year):
  In-State: $8550
  Out-of-State: $24504
Enrollment 2018-19:
  Undergraduate Majors: 166
  New Graduate Students: 19
  Full-time Graduate Students: 46
  Part-time Graduate Students: 12
  Degrees in History: 46 BA, 5 MA, 5 PhD
  Students in Undergraduate Courses: 5429
  Students in Undergraduate Intro Courses: 4183
Undergraduate Addresses:
  Admissions: http://admissions.olemiss.edu/
  Financial Aid: http://finaid.olemiss.edu/
Graduate Addresses:
  Admissions and Financial Aid: http://gradschool.olemiss.edu/

Full-time Faculty

Adams, Mikaela M. (PhD, North Carolina, Chapel Hill 2012; assoc. prof.) Native America; mmadams@olemiss.edu

Cromwell, Jesse Levis (PhD, Texas, Austin 2012; assoc. prof.) colonial Latin America; cromwell@olemiss.edu

Dinius, Oliver J. (PhD, Harvard 2004; Croft assoc. prof.; Croft Inst. for International Studies) modern South America; dinius@olemiss.edu

Esposito, Chiarella (PhD, SUNY, Stony Brook 1985; assoc. prof.) Europe since 1945, France, Italy; esposito@olemiss.edu

Felber, Garrett (PhD, Michigan 2016; asst. prof.) US, race in America

Field, Lester L., Jr. (PhD, UCLA 1985; prof.) medieval; hsfield@olemiss.edu

First, Joshua J. (PhD, Michigan 2008; assoc. prof.; Croft Inst. for International Studies) 20th-century Russia; jfirst@olemiss.edu

Fleegler, Robert L. (PhD, Brown 2005; instr. assoc. prof.; Southaven/Tupelo) US since 1877; fleegler@olemiss.edu

Garrett-Scott, Shennette (PhD, Texas, Austin 2011; assoc. prof.; African American Studies) African American history and studies; mgscott@olemiss.edu

Grem, Darren E. (PhD, Georgia 2010; assoc. prof.; Center for the Study of Southern Culture) US South, southern studies

Holm, April E. (PhD, Columbia 2010; assoc. prof.) US Civil War era; aholm@olemiss.edu

Howard, Joshua H. (PhD, California, Berkeley 1998; Croft assoc. prof.; Croft Inst. for International Studies) East Asia; jhhoward@olemiss.edu

Ibrahim, Vivian (PhD, London 2008; Croft assoc. prof.; Croft Inst. for International Studies) modern Middle East; vibrahim@olemiss.edu

Kagan Guthrie, Zachary (PhD, Princeton 2014; asst. prof.) Africa, sub-Saharan Africa, colonial

Lerner, Marc H. (PhD, Columbia 2003; assoc. prof. and dir., grad. studies) early modern Europe; mlerner@olemiss.edu

Levitt, Theresa Hilary (PhD, Harvard 2002; prof.) science, France; tlevitt@olemiss.edu

Lindgren-Gibson, Alexandra S. (PhD, Northwestern 2016; asst. prof.) modern Europe

Luse, Christopher Allen (PhD, Emory 2008; instr. asst. prof.; Southaven/Tupelo) US to 1877; caluse@olemiss.edu

Marchiel, Rebecca K. (PhD, Northwestern 2014; asst. prof.) 20th-century US, urban, political

Neff, John R. (PhD, California, Riverside 1998; assoc. prof.) US Civil War era; jneff@olemiss.edu

Ownby, Ted (PhD, Johns Hopkins 1986; William F. Winter Prof.; dir., Center for the Study of Southern Culture) US South; hsownby@olemiss.edu

Payne, Eva Bernice (PhD, Harvard 2018; asst. prof.) US, gender and sexuality

Polgar, Paul J. (PhD, Grad. Center, CUNY 2013; asst. prof.) American slavery and emancipation

Rice, Melinda C. (PhD, UCLA 2007; instr. assoc. prof.; Southaven/Tupelo) Europe; mcrice1@olemiss.edu

Roll, Jarod H. (PhD, Northwestern 2006; assoc. prof.) US South, labor; jhroll@olemiss.edu

Ross, Charles Kenyatta (PhD, Ohio State 1996; prof.; dir., African American Studies) African American, sports; cross@olemiss.edu

Salau, Mohammed Bashir (PhD, York, Can. 2005; prof.) sub-Saharan Africa; bashir@olemiss.edu

Stearns, Susan Gaunt (PhD, Chicago 2011; asst. prof.) American Revolution

Stephens, Isaac Sean (PhD, California, Riverside 2008; asst. prof.) cultural and political, early modern Britain

Sullivan-Gonzalez, Douglass C. (PhD, Texas, Austin 1994; prof. and dean; McDonnell-Barksdale Honors Coll.) Latin America; dsg@olemiss.edu

Thilly, Peter Dewitt (PhD, Northwestern 2015; asst. prof.) legal culture and capitalism, modern Asia; pdthilly@olemiss.edu

Trepanier, Nicolas (PhD, Harvard 2008; assoc. prof.) Middle East, early Ottoman; ntrepani@olemiss.edu

Twitty, Anne S. (PhD, Princeton 2010; assoc. prof. and dir., undergrad. studies) American slavery, legal; atwitty@olemiss.edu

Watt, Jeffrey R. (PhD, Wisconsin, Madison 1987; prof. and Kelly Gene Cook Sr. Chair) early modern Europe; hswatt@olemiss.edu

Wilkerson, Jessica (PhD, North Carolina, Chapel Hill 2014; asst. prof.; Center for the Study of Southern Culture) US South, gender studies

Wilson, Noell H. (PhD, Harvard 2004; Croft assoc. prof. and chair) early modern Japan; nrwilson@olemiss.edu

Retired/Emeritus Faculty

Abadie, H. Dale (PhD, UCLA 1971; prof. emeritus) 19th-century Britain, British political

Eagles, Charles W. (PhD, North Carolina, Chapel Hill 1978; William F. Winter Prof. emeritus) 20th-century US; eagles@olemiss.edu

Gispen, Kees (PhD, California, Berkeley 1981; prof. emeritus; exec. dir., Croft Inst. for International Studies) Germany, social and economic; hsgispen@olemiss.edu

Haws, Robert J. (PhD, Nebraska 1973; assoc. prof. emeritus) US legal and constitutional

Landon, Michael de L. (PhD, Wisconsin, Madison 1966; prof. emeritus) Tudor-Stuart Britain, English legal

Laurenzo, Frederick E. (PhD, Illinois, Urbana-Champaign 1969; assoc. prof. emeritus) modern Britain

Metcalf, Michael F. (PhD, Stockholm 1977; prof. emeritus; assoc. provost, International Affairs) Scandinavia; mmetcalf@olemiss.edu

Namorato, Michael V. (PhD, Michigan State 1975; prof. emeritus) 20th-century US, US economic, quantitative methods; hsmvn@olemiss.edu

Owens, Harry P. (PhD, Florida State 1966; prof. emeritus) US and Civil War era

Payne, Elizabeth Anne (PhD, Illinois, Chicago 1981; prof. emerita) social and intellectual, women and religion; epayne@olemiss.edu

Payne, James F. (PhD, California, Irvine 1975; assoc. prof. emeritus) African American

Skemp, Sheila L. (PhD, Iowa 1974; Clare Leslie Marquette Prof. emeritus) colonial America, American Revolution; sskemp@olemiss.edu

Taylor, Jackson, Jr. (PhD, NYU 1970; assoc. prof. emeritus) Russia, social and intellectual

Wilson, Charles Reagan (PhD, Texas, Austin 1977; prof. emeritus; Kelly Gene Cook Sr. Chair, Center for the Study of Southern Culture) American religious, US South; crwilson@olemiss.edu

Recently Awarded PhDs

Davis, Andrew "A Balm for the Times: The Origins and Evolution of the Lost Cause in the South Carolina Lowcountry, 1830-76"

Mosvick, Nicholas "Courtroom Wars: Constitutional Battles over Conscription in the Civil War North"

Rizzi, Christine Antoinette "'My Feet Are Chained': Settler Colonialism and Mobility in the Florida Borderlands, 1812-86"

Robinson, Tom "Identity, Dissent, and the Roots of Georgia's Middle Class, 1848-65"

Rogers, Justin Isaac "Creating and Crossing Color Lines: Race and Religion among African Americans, European Americans and Chickasaw Indians in the Deep South during the 19th Century"

Smith, Laura E. "Populism and Democratization in the Presidential Election of 1832"

Mississippi State University

Dept. of History, PO Box H, Mississippi State, MS 39762-5508. 662.325.3604. Fax 662.325.1139. Email: aimarcus@history.msstate.edu. Website: https://www.history.msstate.edu/.

The Department of History, Mississippi State University, is a nationally ranked, research-extensive, PhD-granting department. Its efforts concentrate in and on the history of the United States and Europe since 1650 but the department also seeks to offer students some other aspects of the world's history.

Chair: Alan I Marcus
Director of Graduate Studies: Stephen C. Brain
Director of Undergraduate Studies: Matthew Lavine
Degrees Offered: BA, MA, PhD
Academic Year System: Semester

Areas of Specialization: science/technology/medicine, agricultural/rural/environmental, military and international affairs, race/gender/identity, US, Europe

Tuition (per academic year):
In-State: $8818
Out-of-State: $17626

Enrollment 2018-19:
Undergraduate Majors: 112
New Graduate Students: 14
Full-time Graduate Students: 52
Part-time Graduate Students: 4
Degrees in History: 34 BA, 12 MA, 4 PhD
Students in Undergraduate Courses: 4100
Students in Undergraduate Intro Courses: 3200
Online-Only Courses: 1%

Undergraduate Addresses:
Admissions: http://www.admissions.msstate.edu/
Financial Aid: http://www.admissions.msstate.edu/

Graduate Addresses:
Admissions: http://www.grad.msstate.edu/future-students/
Financial Aid: http://www.grad.msstate.edu/tuition/

Adjunct Faculty

Williams, Michael Vinson (PhD, Mississippi 2007; adj. prof.) African American studies, civil rights; mwilliams@history.msstate.edu

Full-time Faculty

Barbier, Mary Kathryn (PhD, Southern Mississippi 1998; prof.) military, US, post-1870 Europe; mkb99@msstate.edu

Bates, Toby Glenn (PhD, Mississippi 2006; assoc. prof.; Meridian) modern US, Civil War, Latin America; tgb52@msstate.edu

Brain, Stephen (PhD, California, Berkeley 2007; assoc. prof.; head, Div. Arts & Sciences, Meridian) Russia and Soviet Union, environmental, forest; scbrain@history.msstate.edu

Damms, Richard V. (PhD, Ohio State 1993; assoc. prof.; Arts & Sciences Div., Meridian) US foreign relations, Latin America, 20th-century US; rdamms@history.msstate.edu

Freeman, Stephanie (PhD, Virginia 2017; asst. prof.) US foreign relations, 20th-century US, nuclear

Giesen, James C. (PhD, Georgia 2004; assoc. prof.) agriculture, US, African American; jgiesen@history.msstate.edu

Hay, William Anthony (PhD, Virginia 2000; prof.) modern Britain, international relations, Europe 1750-present; wilhay6248@aol.com

Hersey, Mark D. (PhD, Kansas 2007; assoc. prof.) environmental and agricultural, African American, US South; mhersey@history.msstate.edu

Hui, Alexandra (PhD, UCLA 2008; assoc. prof.) modern Germany, European science and intellectual; ahui@history.msstate.edu

Lang, Andrew F. (PhD, Rice 2013; assoc. prof.) American Civil War, Reconstruction, 19th-century America; alang@history.msstate.edu

Lavine, Matthew B. (PhD, Wisconsin, Madison 2008; assoc. prof. and undergrad coord.) science and culture, American West; mlavine@history.msstate.edu

Marcus, Alan I (PhD, Cincinnati 1979; William L. Giles Dist. Prof. and head) agriculture, science and technology, medicine; aimarcus@history.msstate.edu

Marshall, Anne Elizabeth (PhD, Georgia 2004; assoc. prof.) US, women, South and Civil War; amarshall@history.msstate.edu

Messer, Peter Crozier (PhD, Rutgers 1997; assoc. prof.) colonial and revolutionary America; pmesser@history.msstate.edu

Orsini, Davide (PhD, Michigan 2015; asst. prof.) technology, modern Europe, Italy

Osman, Julia Anne (PhD, North Carolina, Chapel Hill 2010; assoc. prof.) France, military, Atlantic world; josman@history.msstate.edu

Ridner, Judy A. (PhD, William and Mary 1994; prof.) early America, frontier, immigration and ethnicity; jridner@history.msstate.edu

Robinson, Morgan Jean (PhD, Princeton 2018; asst. prof.) Africa, science, foreign affairs; mrobinson@history.msstate.edu

Scott, Jermaine (PhD, Northwestern 2019; asst. prof.) 20th-century African American, African diaspora studies, black politics, black popular culture, race and sport, postcolonial studies

Snyder, Christopher A. (PhD, Emory 1994; prof.; dean, Shackouls Honors Coll.) medieval, late Rome; cas741@msstate.edu

Soares, Leigh (PhD, Northwestern 2019; asst. prof.) African American, US South, 19th- and 20th-century US, education

Thompson, Courtney (PhD, Yale 2015; asst. prof.) US women, science, medicine

Thompson, Joseph (PhD, Virginia 2019; asst. prof.) US South, 20th-century America

Wu, Shu-hui (PhD, Free, Berlin 1993; prof.) East Asia, China, Japan; shuwu@history.msstate.edu

Zubovich, Gene (PhD, California, Berkeley 2015; asst. prof.) 19th- and 20th-century US, religion, US/world and human rights

Retired/Emeritus Faculty

Godbold, E. Stanly, Jr. (PhD, Duke 1970; prof. emeritus) US South, American religion; stjean@joimail.com

Grill, Johnpeter H. (PhD, Michigan 1975; prof. emeritus) 20th-century Europe, Germany, Russia; grillb1@bellsouth.net

Haug, C. James (PhD, Kansas 1976; prof. emeritus) 19th-century Europe, France, modern Western science and technology; ncentralmiss@yahoo.com

Jenkins, Robert L. (PhD, Mississippi State 1978; assoc. prof. emeritus) Mississippi, African American; rjenkins3874@bellsouth.net

Marszalek, John F. (PhD, Notre Dame 1968; prof. emeritus) Jacksonian America, Civil War and Reconstruction, African American; johnmarsz@yahoo.com

Middleton, Stephen (PhD, Miami, Ohio 1987; prof. emeritus) race and American law, African American, constitutional law; smiddleton@history.msstate.edu

Mitchell, Dennis J. (PhD, Mississippi 1976; prof. emeritus; Meridian) Great Britain and Empire, modern Europe, US since 1877; dmitchell@meridian.msstate.edu

Nybakken, Elizabeth (PhD, Delaware 1974; assoc. prof. emeritus) colonial and revolutionary America, women, US social and intellectual; enybakken@cox.net

Parrish, William E. (PhD, Missouri, Columbia 1955; prof. emeritus) Civil War and Reconstruction, American West, historiography; whsp@ms.metrocast.net

Scott, Roy V. (PhD, Illinois, Urbana-Champaign 1957; prof. emeritus) American economic, US 1877-1917; royvandjaneb@aol.com

Swain, Martha H. (PhD, Vanderbilt 1975; prof. emeritus) 20th-century US, southern women, Mississippi; mes6@ra.msstate.edu

Uzoigwe, Godfrey N. (DPhil, Oxford 1967; prof. emeritus) Africa, imperialism, historiography; guzoigwe@history.msstate.edu

Willman, Robert I. (PhD, Harvard 1968; assoc. prof. emeritus) England, Europe 1648-1815, ancient

Recently Awarded PhDs

Forrest, John Douglas "Containerizing Containment: Managerial Innovation, Organized Labor, and the Globalization fo the National Security Waterfront"

Hauser, Jason "Heat: A Southern History"

Hyman, Owen "The Cut and the Color Line: An Environmental History of Jim Crow in the Deep South's Forests, 1876-1965"

Murphy, Michael T. "Inhospitable in the Hospitality State: The Mississippi State Hospital and the Origins of Deinstitutionalization in the Deep South"

Plyler, Larsen B. "Fertilizing Faith: Religious Reformers and Land Grant Colleges and Universities, 1900-41"

Timmerman, Nick Andrew "The Mysterious Mounds: Indian Mounds and Contested Landscapes in the South"

Traylor-Heard, Nancy Jane "Save the Women and Children: American Democracy and Maternal and Children's Health Care in America, 1917-69"

Trzaskowski, Niklas "The Politics of Business and and the Business of Politics: H.R. Haldeman and White Collar Politics in the Post-WWII United States"

University of Missouri–Columbia

Dept. of History, 101 Read Hall, Columbia, MO 65211-7500. 573.882.2481. Fax 573.884.5151. Email: rymphc@missouri.edu; tauben@missouri.edu. Website: https://history.missouri.edu/.

The University of Missouri Department of History has a reputation for excellence, both on the MU campus and beyond.

Chair: Catherine Rymph
Director of Graduate Studies: John Frymire
Director of Undergraduate Studies: Jerritt Frank
Degrees Offered: BA,MA,PhD
Academic Year System: Semester
Areas of Specialization: America, Europe, East Asia, Latin America
Undergraduate Tuition (per academic year):
 In-State: $8606
 Out-of-State: $22336
Graduate Tuition (per academic year):
 In-State: $8031
 Out-of-State: $19531
Enrollment 2018-19:
 Undergraduate Majors: 170
 New Graduate Students: 4
 Full-time Graduate Students: 16
 Part-time Graduate Students: 17
 Degrees in History: 47 BA, 5 MA, 6 PhD
Addresses:
 Admissions: https://admissions.missouri.edu/
 Financial Aid: https://admissions.missouri.edu/financial-aid/

Adjunct Faculty

Conklin, Carli N. (PhD, Virginia 2012; adj. prof.; prof., Sch. of Law) American legal, dispute resolution; conklinc@missouri.edu

Dunkley, Daive Anthony (PhD, Warwick, UK 2009; adj. prof.; asst. prof., Black Studies) Caribbean and wider black Atlantic, history and culture of Rastafari movement; dunkleyd@missouri.edu

Kremer, Gary R. (PhD, American 1978; adj. prof.; exec. dir., State Hist. Soc. Missouri) Missouri, US social, African American; kremerg@umsystem.edu

Rost, Sean (PhD, Missouri, Columbia 2018; adj. prof.; oral historian, State Hist. Soc. of Missouri) 20th-century US, Missouri, African American, history education, public, digital humanities; rosts@shsmo.org

Trout, Dennis (PhD, Duke 1989; adj. prof.; prof., Classical Studies) history and literature in late antiquity, Latin epigraphic poetry; trout@missouri.edu

Full-time Faculty

Bowers, Kristy Wilson (PhD, Indiana 2001; asst. prof.) early modern, medicine, Spain; bowersks@missouri.edu

Carroll, Mark M. (PhD, Houston 1997; assoc. prof.) US South; carrollmm@missouri.edu

Ervin, Keona Katrice (PhD, Washington, St. Louis 2009; assoc. prof.) African American, US since 1865, Africa; ervink@missouri.edu

Fergus, Devin (PhD, Columbia 2001; prof.; Black Studies) African American, contemporary capitalism; fergusd@missouri.edu

Frank, Jerritt J. (PhD, Kansas 2008; assoc. prof. and dir., undergrad. studies) US environmental, indigenous peoples, comparative world; frankje@missouri.edu

Frymire, John M. (PhD, Arizona 2001; assoc. prof. and dir., grad. studies) Renaissance and Reformation; frymirej@missouri.edu

Huneycutt, Lois L. (PhD, California, Santa Barbara 1992; assoc. prof.) medieval women, Europe; huneycuttl@missouri.edu

Karthas, Ilyana (PhD, Brown 2006; assoc. prof.) modern European intellectual and cultural; karthasi@missouri.edu

McFarland, Victor Robert (PhD, Yale 2013; asst. prof.) US-Arab Gulf relationship, Middle East internal state politics and institutions, global natural resource and energy markets; mcfarlandv@missouri.edu

Morris, M. Michelle J. (PhD, Harvard 2005; assoc. prof.) US women, colonial era; morrismary@missouri.edu

Pasley, Jeffrey L. (PhD, Harvard 1993; prof.) early US; pasleyj@missouri.edu

Reeder, Linda (PhD, Rutgers 1995; assoc. prof.) European women; reederl@missouri.edu

Rymph, Catherine W. (PhD, Iowa 1998; prof. and chair) modern US; rymphc@missouri.edu

Sexton, Jay (DPhil, Worcester Coll., Oxford 2003; prof. and Kinder Endowed Chair; Kinder Inst. on Constitutional Democracy) global dimensions of early US history

Smale, Robert L. (PhD, Texas, Austin 2005; assoc. prof.) Latin America; smaler@missouri.edu

Smith, A. Mark, III (PhD, Wisconsin, Madison 1976; Curators' Prof.) medieval, science; smitham@missouri.edu

Sperber, Jonathan (PhD, Chicago 1980; Curators' Prof.) modern Germany; sperberj@missouri.edu

Watts, Steven A. (PhD, Missouri, Columbia 1984; prof.) American cultural and intellectual; wattss@missouri.edu

Wigger, John H. (PhD, Notre Dame 1994; prof.) pre-1865 US social and cultural; wiggerj@missouri.edu

Yang, Dominic Meng-Hsuan (PhD, British Columbia 2012; asst. prof.) East Asia, China/Taiwan/Hong Kong, diaspora; yangmeng@missouri.edu

Joint/Cross Appointments

Mseba, Admire (PhD, Iowa 2015; asst. prof.; Black Studies) Africa

Retired/Emeritus Faculty

Bienvenu, Richard T. (PhD, Harvard 1965; prof. emeritus) modern France, European intellectual; bienvenur@missouri.edu

Bullion, John L. (PhD, Texas, Austin 1977; prof. emeritus) colonial America; bullionj@missouri.edu

Burggraaff, Winfield J. (PhD, New Mexico 1967; prof. emeritus) Latin America; burggraaffw@missouri.edu

Collins, Robert M. (PhD, Johns Hopkins 1975; prof. emeritus) recent US; collinsr@missouri.edu

Flader, Susan L. (PhD, Stanford 1971; prof. emeritus) American West, American environmental; fladers@missouri.edu

Ibrahim, Abdullahi (PhD, Indiana; prof. emeritus) Africa and Islam; ibrahima@missouri.edu

King, Wilma (PhD, Indiana 1982; prof. emeritus) African American; kingw@missouri.edu

Koditschek, Theodore (PhD, Princeton 1981; prof. emeritus) modern British social; koditschekt@missouri.edu

Lankford, John (PhD, Wisconsin, Madison 1962; prof. emeritus) social history of modern science

Miller, Kerby A. (PhD, California, Berkeley 1976; Curators' Prof. emeritus) American urban, immigration; millerk@missouri.edu

Okamura, Lawrence (PhD, Michigan 1984; assoc. prof. emeritus) ancient, late antiquity, Roman frontier; okamural@missouri.edu

Whites, LeeAnn (PhD, California, Irvine 1982; prof. emeritus) Reconstruction, women; whitesl@missouri.edu

Zguta, Russ (PhD, Penn State 1967; prof. emeritus) medieval Russia; zgutar@missouri.edu

Recently Awarded PhDs

Deutsch, Christopher Robert "Democratic Beef: The Federal Government and Making the American Diet, 1945-70"

Eakin, Ardis Travis "Between the Old and the New: Friedrich Gentz, 1764-1832"

Paolella, Christopher "A Never-Ending Stream: Human Trafficking in Medieval Europe"

Rost, Sean "A Call to Citizenship: Anti-Klan Activism in Missouri, 1921-28"

Tuck, Darin "Seizing the Elephant: Kansas City and the Great Western Migration, 1840-65"

University of Missouri–Kansas City

Dept. of History, 203 Cockefair Hall, 5121 Rockhill Rd., Kansas City, MO 64110-2499. 816.235.1631. Fax 816.235.5723. Email: history@umkc.edu. Website: https://cas.umkc.edu/history/.

The UMKC History Department is dedicated to the production of cutting edge scholarship and teaching and mentoring future historians. We also actively engage with the greater Kansas City community through our Public History program and the Center for Midwestern Studies.

Chair: Diane Mutti Burke
Director of Graduate Studies: Matthew Osborn (PhD); Massimiliano Vitiello (MA)
Degrees Offered: BA, MA, PhD
Academic Year System: Semester
Areas of Specialization: Europe, America, public, women/gender/race/ethnicity
Undergraduate Tuition (per academic year):
  In-State: $8540
  Out-of-State: $21248
Graduate Tuition (per academic year):
  In-State: $8280
  Out-of-State: $19600
Enrollment 2018-19:
  Undergraduate Majors: 111
  New Graduate Students: 7
  Full-time Graduate Students: 12
  Part-time Graduate Students: 38
  Degrees in History: 35 BA, 9 MA
Addresses:
  Admissions: http://www.umkc.edu/admissions/
  Financial Aid: http://www.sfa.umkc.edu/

Affiliated Faculty

Gross, Benjamin H. (PhD, Princeton 2011; assoc. vice pres., Collections; Linda Hall Library) technology, science, museums; grossb@lindahall.org

Full-time Faculty

Bergerson, Andrew Stuart (PhD, Chicago 1998; prof.) modern Europe, modern Germany, German studies; bergersona@umkc.edu

Davis, Rebecca Miller (PhD, South Carolina 2011; assoc. teaching prof.) 20th-century America, civil rights, New South; davisrebe@umkc.edu

Enríquez, Sandra Ivette (PhD, Houston 2016; asst. prof. and dir., public hist. prog.) urban, Chicana/o, public and oral; enriquezs@umkc.edu

Freeman, David Fors (PhD, Emory 2003; assoc. prof.) early modern Europe, religious studies, German studies; freemandf@umkc.edu

Frehner, Brian W. (PhD, Oklahoma 2004; assoc. prof.) science and technology, environmental

Grieco, Viviana L. (PhD, Emory 2005; assoc. prof.) Latin America, gender, economic and social; griecov@umkc.edu

Herron, John (PhD, New Mexico 2001; prof. and assoc. dean) modern America, American West, environmental; herronj@umkc.edu

Mitchell, Linda E. (PhD, Indiana 1991; prof.) medieval Europe and Ireland, women and gender, ancient Greece and Rome; mitchelll@umkc.edu

Mutti Burke, Diane (PhD, Emory 2004; prof. and chair) US, American South and Midwest, Civil War; muttiburked@umkc.edu

Osborn, Matthew Warner (PhD, California, Davis 2007; assoc. prof. and dir., grad. studies) early America; osbornmw@umkc.edu

Vitiello, Massimiliano (PhD, Messina, Italy 2001; prof. and dir., grad. studies) ancient, late antiquity

Retired/Emeritus Faculty

Ashworth, William B. (PhD, Wisconsin-Madison 1975; assoc. prof. emeritus) science, Renaissance, astronomy; ashworthw@umkc.edu

Ebersole, Gary L. (PhD, Chicago 1981; prof. emeritus) religious studies, Japanese culture and literature; ebersoleg@umkc.edu

Falls, James S. (PhD, Mississippi State 1967; prof. emeritus) ancient, medieval England; fallsj@umkc.edu

Forman-Brunell, Miriam (PhD, Rutgers 1990; prof. emerita) US women, gender, 19th- to 20th-century social; forman-brunellm@umkc.edu

Klausner, Carla L. (PhD, Harvard 1963; prof. emerita) modern Middle East, medieval Europe, Judaic studies; klausnerc@umkc.edu

Merrill, Dennis J. (PhD, Connecticut 1986; prof. emeritus) US diplomatic, recent US, Latin America; merrilld@umkc.edu

Payne, Lynda E. (PhD, California, Davis 1997; prof. emerita) Britain, science and medicine, gender; paynel@umkc.edu

Peebles, Patrick A. (PhD, Chicago 1973; prof. emeritus) Asia, world, quantitative methods; peeblesp@umkc.edu

Potts, Louis W. (PhD, Duke 1970; prof. emeritus) early America, Missouri

Wynkoop, Mary Ann (PhD, Indiana 1992; asst. prof. emerita) modern America; wynkoopm@umkc.edu

Visiting Faculty

Moore, Lindsay Rae (PhD, George Washington 2011; vis. asst. prof.) early modern Britain; mooreiv@umkc.edu

University of Missouri–St. Louis

Dept. of History, 1 University Blvd., Saint Louis, MO 63121-4499. 314.516.5681. Fax 314.516.5781. Email: westhoffL@umsl.edu. Website: http://www.umsl.edu/~umslhistory/.

Faculty and students in the History Department ask big questions about the past to understand the present and build the future. We offer the BA, MA in History, MA in Museums, Heritage and Public History, and graduate certificates in History Education and Museums and Public History. An accelerated BA + MA is available.

Chair: Laura Westhoff
Director of Graduate Studies: Andrew Hurley
Degrees Offered: BA,BSEd,MA
Academic Year System: Semester
Areas of Specialization: US, public, museum studies, Europe, Africa
Undergraduate Tuition (per academic year):
  In-State: $8220
  Out-of-State: $21861
Graduate Tuition (per academic year):
  In-State: $8400
  Out-of-State: $20620
Enrollment 2018-19:
  Undergraduate Majors: 100
  New Graduate Students: 20
  Full-time Graduate Students: 10
  Part-time Graduate Students: 30
  Degrees in History: 30 BA, 18 MA
Undergraduate Addresses:
  Admissions: http://www.umsl.edu/admissions/undergraduate/
  Financial Aid: http://www.umsl.edu/services/finaid/
Graduate Addresses:
  Admissions: http://www.umsl.edu/gradschool/
  Financial Aid: http://www.umsl.edu/gradschool/prospective/funding-graduate-school.html

Full-time Faculty

Acsay, Peter (PhD, St. Louis 2002; assoc. teaching prof.) recent US, modern Europe; acsayp@msx.umsl.edu
Cohen, Deborah (PhD, Chicago 2001; assoc. prof.) Mexico and US, gender and labor; deborah.cohen@umsl.edu
Dowden-White, Priscilla A. (PhD, Indiana 1996; assoc. prof.) recent US, African American; padhist@umsl.edu
Fernlund, Kevin Jon (PhD, New Mexico 1992; prof.) world, US West; fernlund@umsl.edu
Hurley, Andrew (PhD, Northwestern 1988; prof. and dir., grad. studies) urban, environmental, public; ahurley@umsl.edu
Kang, Minsoo (PhD, UCLA 2004; assoc. prof.) modern Europe; kangmi@umsl.edu
Kelland, Lara L. (PhD, Illinois, Chicago 2012; E. Desmond Lee Prof.) museum studies, community
Miller, Laura (PhD, UCLA 1988; Eiichi Shibusawa-Seigo Arai Endowed Prof.) Japan studies, linguistic anthropology, gender studies; millerlau@umsl.edu
Moskowitz, Kara (PhD, Emory 2014; asst. prof.) Africa; moskowitz@umsl.edu
Westhoff, Laura M. (PhD, Washington, St. Louis 1999; assoc. prof. and chair) modern US social movements, history education, Progressive Era; westhoffl@msx.umsl.edu

Joint/Cross Appointments

Hoover, John (MA, Missouri-Columbia 1982; assoc. prof.; dir., St. Louis Mercantile Library) US West; hooverj@umsl.edu

Retired/Emeritus Faculty

Bliss, Robert M., Jr. (PhD, Wisconsin, Madison 1983; retired assoc. prof.) colonial America; rmbliss@umsl.edu
Burkholder, Mark A. (PhD, Duke 1970; Founder's Prof. emeritus) Latin America, Spanish colonial administration, Spain; burkholder@umsl.edu
Cooper, Jerry M. (PhD, Wisconsin, Madison 1971; prof. emeritus) military, US Army and National Guard, 20th-century US; cooperj@msx.umsl.edu
Fausz, J. Frederick (PhD, William and Mary 1977; assoc. prof. emeritus) Native American, colonial America; jff@umsl.edu
Finney, P. Corby (PhD, Harvard 1973; prof. emeritus) Roman Empire, late antiquity, early church; finneyp@msx.umsl.edu
Gerteis, Louis S. (PhD, Wisconsin, Madison 1969; retired Founder's Prof.) 19th-century US, slavery and emancipation, Civil War and Reconstruction; gerteis@umsl.edu
Gillingham, John R., III (PhD, California, Berkeley 1973; Founders' Prof. emeritus) European business and economic, modern Europe, modern Germany; gillingham@umsl.edu
Hause, Steven C. (PhD, Washington, St. Louis 1969; prof. emeritus) modern Europe, modern France, women; shause@wustl.edu
Hsieh, Winston (PhD, Harvard 1970; assoc. prof. emeritus) China, Asian-Pacific Rim, Chinese American ethnic; hsiehw@umsl.edu
Korr, Charles P. (PhD, UCLA 1969; prof. emeritus) 19th- and 20th-century sports, Tudor-Stuart England; cpkorr@umsl.edu
Maltby, William S. (PhD, Duke 1967; prof. emeritus) early modern Europe, Spain, Renaissance and Reformation; maltbyw@msx.umsl.edu
Mitchell, Richard H. (PhD, Wisconsin, Madison 1963; Curator's prof. emeritus) modern Japan; richardmitchell@umsl.edu
Ray, Gerda W. (PhD, California, Berkeley 1990; assoc. prof. emerita) US political and social, law and society; rayg@umsl.edu
Rounds, Jay (PhD, UCLA 1979; prof. emeritus) museum studies; roundsj@msx.umsl.edu
Rowan, Steven W. (PhD, Harvard 1970; retired Founder's Prof.) premodern Germany, medieval, German American ethnic; srowan@umsl.edu
Schwantes, Carlos A. (PhD, Michigan 1976; Founder's Prof. and St. Louis Mercantile Library Prof. emeritus) 20th-century American West, labor, Pacific Northwest; cmschwantes@aol.com
Touhill, Blanche M. (PhD, St. Louis 1962; prof. and chancellor emeritus) 19th- and 20th-century England, Ireland; touhillb@msx.umsl.edu
Works, John A., Jr. (PhD, Wisconsin, Madison 1972; assoc. prof. emeritus) Africa, West Africa, Islamic; historyworks@umsl.edu

Missouri State University

Dept. of History, 901 S. National, Strong Hall 410, Springfield, MO 65897. 417.836.5511. Fax 417.836.5523. Email: History@MissouriState.edu. Website: https://history.missouristate.edu/.

Our 22 faculty members have expertise in a wide variety of eras and areas. The blending of their research specialties and dedication to students creates a comprehensive program that provides you with both broad knowledge and excellent advising.

Chair: Kathleen A. Kennedy
Director of Graduate Studies: Dejene R. Bajalan
Degrees Offered: BA,BS,BSEd,MA,MS,MSEd,Accelerated Master's
Academic Year System: Semester
Areas of Specialization: US, world
Undergraduate Tuition (per academic year):
  In-State: $5232
  Out-of-State: $11880

Graduate Tuition (per academic year):
In-State: $6250
Out-of-State: $11524
Enrollment 2018-19:
Undergraduate Majors: 225
New Graduate Students: 27
Full-time Graduate Students: 232
Part-time Graduate Students: 46
Degrees in History: 73 BA, 36 MA, 3 MS, BSEd
Undergraduate Addresses:
Admissions: http://www.missouristate.edu/admissions/
Financial Aid: http://www.missouristate.edu/financialaid/
Graduate Addresses:
Admissions: http://graduate.missouristate.edu/
Financial Aid: http://www.missouristate.edu/financialaid/

Full-time Faculty

Ammons, Jacynda (PhD, Texas Tech 2015; instr.) African and African American studies; JacyndaAmmons@MissouriState.edu

Baggett, Holly (PhD, Delaware 1992; prof.) US women; hollybaggett@missouristate.edu

Bajalan, Djene Rhys (DPhil, Oxford 2015; asst. prof. and dir., grad. studies) Middle East; DRBajalan@MissouriState.edu

Barber, Marlin Christopher (PhD, Missouri, Columbia 2011; sr. instr.) 18th- and 19th-century America, southern African American; mcbarber@missouristate.edu

Blevins, Brooks (PhD, Auburn 1999; prof.) US, Ozarks; brblevins@missouristate.edu

Chuchiak, John F. IV (PhD, Tulane 1999; prof.) Latin America, colonial Mexico, Mayan and Mesoamerican ethnohistory; johnchuchiak@missouristate.edu

Dicke, Thomas S. (PhD, Ohio State 1988; prof.) US business; tomdicke@missouristate.edu

Elliott, Jessica Marin (PhD, California, Santa Barbara 2014; asst. prof.) medieval, gender, religion; JessicaElliott@MissouriState.edu

Gram, John R. (PhD, Southern Methodist 2012; instr.) Native American, American West, southwestern borderlands; JohnRGram@MissouriState.edu

Gutzke, David W. (PhD, Toronto 1982; dist. prof.) Britain; davidgutzke@missouristate.edu

Hornsby-Gutting, Angela Mandee (PhD, North Carolina, Chapel Hill 2003; assoc. prof.) 20th-century US, women and gender, African American; ahornsbygutting@missouristate.edu

Kennedy, Kathleen A. (PhD, California, Irvine 1992; prof. and chair) US women and gender, cultural, African American; kathleenkennedy@missouristate.edu

McIntyre, Stephen L. (PhD, Missouri-Columbia 1995; prof.) American labor, Missouri; stephenmcintyre@missouristate.edu

Mellors, Sarah (PhD, California, Irvine 2018; asst. prof.) East Asia, women, science and technology; SarahMellors@missouristate.edu

Miller, F. Thornton (PhD, Alabama 1986; prof.) US, early Republic, legal and constitutional; ftmiller@missouristate.edu

Morgan, Michelle M. (PhD, Wisconsin, Madison 2007; assoc. prof.) America, educational policy studies; michellemorgan@missouristate.edu

Neely, Jeremy (PhD, Missouri–Columbia 2004; asst. prof.) Civil War, 19th-century America, American South and West; jeremyneely@missouristate.edu

Nelson, Eric W. (DPhil, Oxford 1999; prof.) early modern Europe, France; ericnelson@missouristate.edu

Oyeniyi, Bukola (PhD, Leiden, Netherlands 2012; assoc. prof.) Africa; BukolaOyeniyi@missouristate.edu

Panzer, Sarah Jordan (PhD, Chicago 2015; asst. prof.) 20th-century continental Europe, German-Japanese relationships; SPanzer@MissouriState.edu

Troche, Julia D. (PhD, Brown 2015; asst. prof.) ancient Near East, Egyptology and Assyriology; JuliaTroche@missouristate.edu

Retired/Emeritus Faculty

Abidogun, Jamaine M. (PhD, Kansas 2000; prof. emeritus) curriculum and instruction, African and African American studies; jamaineabidogun@missouristate.edu

Adams, David B. (PhD, Texas, Austin 1971; prof. emeritus) Latin America; dba995f-sgf@missouristate.edu

Adams, Meredith L. (PhD, Texas, Austin 1971; prof. emeritus) Germany, Russia; meredithadams@missouristate.edu

Bartee, Wayne C. (PhD, Columbia 1966; prof. emeritus) Germany, Reformation, English constitutional; waynebartee@missouristate.edu

Capeci, Dominic J., Jr. (PhD, California, Riverside 1970; dist. prof. emeritus) Afro-American; dominiccapeci@missouristate.edu

Flanders, Robert (PhD, Wisconsin, Madison 1964; prof. emeritus) Jacksonian America, Ozarks regional studies

Giglio, James N. (PhD, Ohio State 1968; dist. prof. emeritus) 20th-century US; jamesgiglio@missouristate.edu

Hammond, William E. (PhD, Missouri, Columbia 1962; prof. emeritus) France, 19th-century Europe

Meyer, Duane G. (PhD, Iowa 1956; pres. emeritus and prof. emeritus) Missouri, American West

Miller, Worth R. (PhD, Oklahoma 1984; prof. emeritus) populism, Gilded Age, US South; bobmiller@missouristate.edu

Piston, William G. (PhD, South Carolina 1982; prof. emeritus) Civil War, military; williampiston@missouristate.edu

Sheng, Michael M. (PhD, York, Can. 1992; prof. emeritus) modern China, Cold War; msheng@uakron.edu

Missouri University of Science and Technology

Dept. of History and Political Science, 500 W. 14th St., Rolla, MO 65409-1260. 573.341.4801. Fax 573.341.4871. Email: hist-ps@mst.edu. Website: https://history.mst.edu/.

Missouri S&T's History and Political Science department provides students with unique opportunities and close faculty interaction. Overall, the department enjoys a long-established reputation of excellence in teaching and research.

Chair: Shannon Fogg
Degrees Offered: BA, BS
Academic Year System: Semester
Areas of Specialization: America, Missouri and US South, science and technology, military, early modern and modern Europe
Tuition (per academic year):
In-State: $7734
Out-of-State: $23850
Enrollment 2018-19:
Undergraduate Majors: 49
Degrees in History: 5 BA, 5 BS
Addresses:
Admissions: http://futurestudents.mst.edu/
Financial Aid: http://futurestudents.mst.edu/costs/

Full-time Faculty

Ahmad, Diana L. (PhD, Missouri, Columbia 1997; Curators' Dist. Teaching Prof.) American West, American Pacific, Asia; ahmadd@mst.edu

Behrendt, Andrew E. (PhD, Pittsburgh 2016; asst. teaching prof.) cultural and social, east central Europe, interwar period; behrendta@mst.edu

Bruening, Michael W. (PhD, Arizona 2002; assoc. prof.) Renaissance, Reformation, Switzerland; bruening@mst.edu

DeWitt, Petra (PhD, Missouri, Columbia 2005; asst. prof.) immigration, Missouri, historiography; dewittp@mst.edu

Fogg, Shannon (PhD, Iowa 2003; prof. and chair) modern France, French Revolution, precolonial and modern Africa; sfogg@mst.edu

Huber, Patrick J. (PhD, North Carolina, Chapel Hill 2000; prof.) American South, Missouri, modern US; huberp@mst.edu

Isaac, Tseggai (PhD, Missouri, Columbia 1991; prof.) policymaking, international relations, Africa; tseggai@mst.edu

Krolikowski, Alanna (PhD, Toronto 2013; asst. prof.) comparative politics, international relations, technology policy

McManus, John (PhD, Tennessee, Knoxville 1996; Curators' Dist. Prof.) 20th- to 21st-century US, military, social; mcmanusj@mst.edu

Meagher, Michael (PhD, Southern Illinois, Carbondale 1993; assoc. prof.) political theory, American government, American presidency; mmeagher@mst.edu

Pope, Justin James (PhD, George Washington 2014; asst. prof.) early Atlantic world, slavery, religion

Schramm, Jeff (PhD, Lehigh 2003; assoc. prof.) technology, science, modern US; schrammj@mst.edu

Sheppard, Kathleen (PhD, Oklahoma 2010; assoc. prof.) science, Western civilization, women and science; sheppardka@mst.edu

Nondepartmental Historians

Bradbury, John F., Jr. (BA, Missouri-Rolla 1974; manuscript specialist) Civil War, Missouri; jfb@mst.edu

Retired/Emeritus Faculty

Bledsoe, Wayne M. (PhD, Michigan State 1969; prof. emeritus) ancient, medieval, theories of civilization; wbledsoe@mst.edu

Eisenman, Harry J. (PhD, Case Western Reserve 1967; prof. emeritus) technology, US since 1865, technology and society; hje@mst.edu

Gragg, Larry D. (PhD, Missouri-Columbia 1978; Curators' Distinguished Teaching Prof. emeritus) colonial America, revolutionary America, Las Vegas; lgragg@mst.edu

Oster, Donald B. (PhD, Missouri, Columbia 1969; assoc. prof. emeritus) American urban, American frontier, American intellectual; donoster@mst.edu

Ridley, Jack B. (PhD, Oklahoma 1970; Dist. Teaching Prof. emeritus) 19th-century France and Britain, engineering education; ridley@mst.edu

Williams, Lance (PhD, Georgia 1970; assoc. prof. emeritus) British social since 1700, modern Britain, contemporary Europe; lancewms@mst.edu

Monmouth University

Dept. of History and Anthropology, 400 Cedar Ave., West Long Branch, NJ 07764. 732.571.3440. Fax 732.263.5320. Email: cderosa@monmouth.edu. Website: https://www.monmouth.edu/department-of-history-and-anthropology/

The disciplines of History and Anthropology focus on the study of the human experience, past and present. The Department of History and Anthropology at Monmouth University is built on the characteristics that the disciplines share and is supported by those that make each unique.

Chair: Christopher DeRosa
Director of Graduate Studies: Maryanne Rhett
Degrees Offered: BA,MA
Academic Year System: Semester
Areas of Specialization: Russia, Britain, Germany, modern Africa, US social, US military, world, African American, modern China,
Undergraduate Tuition (per academic year): $38880
Graduate Tuition (per academic year): $29568
Enrollment 2018-19:
    Undergraduate Majors: 85
    New Graduate Students: 9
    Full-time Graduate Students: 30
    Degrees in History: 25 BA, 7 MA
Undergraduate Addresses:
    Admissions: https://www.monmouth.edu/admission/undergraduate/
    Financial Aid: https://www.monmouth.edu/finaid/
Graduate Addresses:
    Admissions: https://www.monmouth.edu/graduate/
    Financial Aid: https://www.monmouth.edu/graduate/cost-and-financial-aid/

Full-time Faculty

Adekunle, Julius (PhD, Dalhousie 1993; prof.) Africa, oral; jadekunl@monmouth.edu

Brzycki, Melissa A. (PhD, California, Santa Cruz 2018; asst. prof.) Asia; mbrzycki@monmouth.edu

Campbell, Kenneth L. (PhD, Delaware 1984; prof.) Britain, medieval and early modern Europe, historiography; campbell@monmouth.edu

DeRosa, Christopher S. (PhD, Temple 2000; assoc. prof. and chair) US military, political; cderosa@monmouth.edu

Dorment, Maureen (MA, Monmouth 1992; lect.) book; mdorment@monmouth.edu

Fouad, Geoffrey (PhD, San Diego State 2016; asst. prof.) geographic information systems, remote sensing, statistical and hydrologic modeling; gfouad@monmouth.edu

Gorman, William P. (MA, Monmouth; instr.) American economic; wgorman@monmouth.edu

McKitrick, Frederick L. (PhD, Columbia 1994; assoc. prof.) modern Germany, modern France; fmckitri@monmouth.edu

Parkin, Katherine (PhD, Temple 2001; assoc. prof.) US, American women, American cultural; kparkin@monmouth.edu

Pearson, Thomas S. (PhD, North Carolina, Chapel Hill 1977; prof.) Russia, 19th-century Europe; pearson@monmouth.edu

Rhett, Maryanne A. (PhD, Washington State 2008; assoc. prof. and dir., grad. studies) world, imperialism, Middle East; mrhett@monmouth.edu

Schmelzkopf, Karen (PhD, Penn State 1985; assoc. prof.) US urban, geography; kschmelz@monmouth.edu

Veit, Richard (PhD, Pennsylvania 1997; prof.) historical archaeology; rveit@monmouth.edu

Williams, Hettie V. (PhD, Drew 2017; lect.) African American; hwilliam@monmouth.edu

Ziobro, Melissa (MA, Monmouth; instr.) mziobro@monmouth.edu

University of Montana

Dept. of History, 32 Campus Dr., Missoula, MT 59812-6264. 406.243.2231. Fax 406.243.4076. Email: robert.greene@umontana.edu. Website: http://hs.umt.edu/history/.

We strive to acquaint students with history as an analytical research discipline and to provide them with a life perspective based on actual human experience. To offset parochialism and ethnocentrism, we offer courses that deal with a rich variety of the world's civilizations, nations, and peoples.

Chair: Robert H. Greene
Director of Graduate Studies: Kyle G. Volk
Director of Undergraduate Studies: Tobin Miller Shearer
Degrees Offered: BA,MA,PhD
Academic Year System: Semester
Areas of Specialization: US, Europe, world
Undergraduate Tuition (per academic year):
  In-State: $6182
  Out-of-State: $23072
Graduate Tuition (per academic year):
  In-State: $5930
  Out-of-State: $20626
Enrollment 2018-19:
  Undergraduate Majors: 195
  New Graduate Students: 8
  Full-time Graduate Students: 13
  Part-time Graduate Students: 5
  Degrees in History: 40 BA, 7 MA, 2 PhD
Undergraduate Addresses:
  Admissions: http://admissions.umt.edu/
  Financial Aid: http://www.umt.edu/finaid/
Graduate Addresses:
  Admissions: http://www.umt.edu/grad/Apply/
  Financial Aid: http://www.umt.edu/finaid/

Affiliated Faculty

Beck, David R. M. (PhD, Illinois, Chicago 1994; prof.; Native American Studies) federal Indian policy; david.beck@mso.umt.edu

Davies, Wade (PhD, Arizona State 1998; prof.; Native American Studies) Navajo health and healing, Native American sports and games; wade.davies@mso.umt.edu

Kia, Ardeshir (PhD, Wisconsin-Madison 1988; assoc. prof.; Anthropology) Central Asia, art; ardi.kia@mso.umt.edu

Full-time Faculty

Arcenas, Claire Rydell (PhD, Stanford 2016; asst. prof.) early America, American intellectual and cultural, Atlantic world; claire.arcenas@mso.umt.edu

Drake, Richard R. (PhD, UCLA 1975; prof.) modern Italy, modern European social and intellectual, terrorism; richard.drake@umontana.edu

Eglin, John A. (PhD, Yale 1996; prof.) England and early modern Europe, cultural; john.eglin@umontana.edu

Frey, Linda S. (PhD, Ohio State 1971; prof.) early modern Europe/France/Germany, international law and international state system, French Revolution; linda.frey@umontana.edu

Greene, Robert H. (PhD, Michigan 2004; assoc. prof. and chair) imperial Russia and Soviet Union, cultural and religious; robert.greene@umontana.edu

Jabour, Anya (PhD, Rice 1995; prof.) 19th- and 20th-century US social/political/cultural, Progressive Era and New Deal women/family/gender/sexuality, American South; anya.jabour@umontana.edu

Kia, Mehrdad (PhD, Wisconsin-Madison 1986; prof.) Islamic civilization, Middle East/Central Asia/North Africa; mehrdad.kia@umontana.edu

Mayer, Michael S. (PhD, Princeton 1984; prof.) US since 1945, American law, civil rights movement; michael.mayer@mso.umt.edu

Pavilack, Jody C. (PhD, Duke 2003; assoc. prof. and dir., undergrad. studies) modern Latin America, labor, historical memory; jody.pavilack@mso.umt.edu

Schluessel, Eric Tanner (PhD, Harvard 2016; asst. prof.; Political Sci.) China and Central Asia, frontiers, legal; eric.schluessel@mso.umt.edu

Shearer, Tobin Miller (PhD, Northwestern 2008; assoc. prof. and dir., undergrad. studies; dir., African American Studies) African American, religious, civil rights movement; tobin.shearer@umontana.edu

Volk, Kyle G. (PhD, Chicago 2008; assoc. prof. and dir., grad. studies) 19th-century US political/intellectual/cultural/legal; kyle.volk@umontana.edu

Wiltse, Jeff (PhD, Brandeis 2003; prof.) 19th- and 20th-century US social and cultural, public space and public life, Montana; jeff.wiltse@mso.umt.edu

Retired/Emeritus Faculty

Clow, Richmond (PhD, New Mexico 1977; prof. emeritus) tribal resource management, politics on Montana's reservations; clowrl@mso.umt.edu

Emmons, David M. (PhD, Colorado, Boulder 1969; prof. emeritus) 19th-century US, American immigration, labor; david.emmons@umontana.edu

Farr, William E. (PhD, Washington 1971; prof. emeritus) medieval, Reformation, tribal cultures; farr@crmw.org

Flores, Dan L. (PhD, Texas A&M 1978; A. B. Hammond Prof. emeritus) American West, American environmental, Native American; dlfnewmexico@aol.com

Fritz, Harry W. (PhD, Washington, St. Louis 1971; prof. emeritus) early America, Montana, military; harry.fritz@umontana.edu

Lauren, Paul Gordon (PhD, Stanford 1974; Regents prof. emeritus) international relations, diplomacy, human rights; paul.lauren@mso.umt.edu

Lockridge, Kenneth A. (PhD, Princeton 1965; prof. emeritus) colonial and revolutionary America, family, social

Price, George (PhD, Montana 2006; lect. emeritus) African American, Native American; george.price@mso.umt.edu

Skinner, Frederick W. (PhD, Princeton 1973; prof. emeritus) Russia, development of Western city, Russian Revolution; frederick.skinner@umontana.edu

Montana State University-Bozeman

Dept. of History and Philosophy, 2-155 Wilson Hall, PO Box 172320, Bozeman, MT 59717-3440. 406.994.4395. Fax 406.994.7420. Email: history@montana.edu. Website: http://www.montana.edu/history/.

The department offers both a master's and doctoral degree in history, in three areas of specialty: environmental history; history of the American West; and the history of science, technology and society. The program offers many opportunities for students to collaborate with peers, professors, and visiting scholars.

Chair: Susan Cohen
Director of Graduate Studies: Michael Reidy
Degrees Offered: BA,MA,PhD
Academic Year System: Semester

Areas of Specialization: America, American West, environmental, science and technology, public

Undergraduate Tuition (per academic year):
In-State: $6801
Out-of-State: $21390

Graduate Tuition (per academic year):
In-State: $6120
Out-of-State: $17062

Enrollment 2018-19:
Undergraduate Majors: 167
New Graduate Students: 8
Full-time Graduate Students: 26
Part-time Graduate Students: 2
Degrees in History: 51 BA, 7 MA, 3 PhD

Undergraduate Addresses:
Admissions: http://www.montana.edu/admissions/
Financial Aid: http://www.montana.edu/wwwfa/

Graduate Addresses:
Admissions: http://www.montana.edu/wwwdg/
Financial Aid: http://www.montana.edu/wwwfa/

Adjunct Faculty

Hardy, Robin Aspasia (PhD, Montana State 2016; adj.,) modern Europe, colonialism and postcolonialism in Africa, human rights and conflict resolution; rahardy25@gmail.com

Martin, Dale (MA, Washington State 1984; adj. prof.) American West, Montana, World War I; dlmartin@montana.edu

Ore, Janet (PhD, Utah 1993; adj.) architectural, public; janet.ore@montana.edu

Snow, Bradley (PhD, Montana State, Bozeman 2012; adj. prof.) environmental, American West, 20th-century US; bdsnow@gmail.com

Full-time Faculty

Cherry, David (PhD, Ottawa 1985; prof. and assoc. dean) ancient; dcherry@montana.edu

Cohen, Susan (PhD, Harvard 2000; prof. and chair) ancient, Near Eastern archaeology, religion; scohen@montana.edu

Dunlop, Catherine T. (PhD, Yale 2010; assoc. prof.) modern France, modern Europe, African colonialism; catherine.dunlop@montana.edu

Fiege, Mark (PhD, Utah 1994; Wallace Stegner Prof.) American West, environmental, National Parks; mark.fiege@montana.edu

Greene, Maggie (PhD, California, San Diego 2013; asst. prof.) modern China; margaret.greene1@montana.edu

Hendrix-Komoto, Amanda L. (PhD, Michigan 2015; asst. prof.) American West, women; amanda.hendrixkomoto@montana.edu

LeCain, Timothy James (PhD, Delaware 1998; prof.) US technology, environment; tlecain@montana.edu

Meyer, James H. (PhD, Brown 2007; assoc. prof.) Ottoman Empire and Turkey, modern Russia; james.meyer7@montana.edu

Murphy, Mary (PhD, North Carolina, Chapel Hill 1990; prof.) women and gender, American West, labor; mmurphy@montana.edu

Reidy, Michael S. (PhD, Minnesota 1999; assoc. prof.) science, Britain, mountaineering; mreidy@montana.edu

Rydell, Robert W., II (PhD, UCLA 1980; Michael P. Malone Prof.) US intellectual and cultural, world's fairs, museums; rwrydell@montana.edu

Smith, Billy G. (PhD, UCLA 1981; prof.) colonial America, economic methodology, race and class in America; bgs@montana.edu

Todd, Molly (PhD, Wisconsin-Madison 2007; assoc. prof.) modern Latin America, human rights; molly.todd@montana.edu

Walker, Brett Laurence (PhD, Oregon 1997; prof.) Japan, environment, science; bwalker@montana.edu

Joint/Cross Appointments

Martin, James W. (PhD, New Mexico 2008; asst. prof.; Modern Languages and Literatures) Latin America, Latin American literature; jameswm@montana.edu

Schweppe, Peter (PhD, McGill 2017; asst. prof.; German Studies) Germany, postwar literature/visual culture/print

Recently Awarded PhDs

Bartos, Jeffrey "Mining for Empire: Gold, American Engineers, and Transnational Extractive Capitalism, 1889-1914"

Montclair State University

Dept. of History, 427 Dickson Hall, 1 Normal Ave., Montclair, NJ 07043. 973.655.5261. Fax 973.655.3159. Email: stricklandj@mail.montclair.edu. Website: https://www.montclair.edu/history/.

The department offers specialized study mainly in United States, European, African, Asian, and Latin American history.

Chair: Jeff Strickland
Degrees Offered: BA
Academic Year System: Semester
Areas of Specialization: America, Europe, non-Western, social studies teacher education

Tuition (per academic year):
In-State: $12455
Out-of-State: $20566

Enrollment 2018-19:
Undergraduate Majors: 245
Degrees in History: 75 BA, 2 MA

Addresses:
Admissions: http://www.montclair.edu/admissions/
Financial Aid: http://www.montclair.edu/financial-aid/

Full-time Faculty

Brizuela-Garcia, Esperanza (PhD, London 2001; assoc. prof.) Africa, 20th-century colonialism, historiography; brizuelagare@mail.montclair.edu

Carnevale, Nancy C. (PhD, Rutgers 2000; assoc. prof.) America, Italian American; carnevalen@mail.montclair.edu

Clark, Shannan Wayne (PhD, Columbia 2006; asst. prof.) 20th-century America; clarksh@mail.montclair.edu

Conway, Richard (PhD, Tulane 2009; asst. prof.) colonial/modern Latin America, Atlantic world; conwayr@mail.montclair.edu

Cray, Robert E. (PhD, SUNY, Stony Brook 1984; prof.) colonial America, US social, religion; crayr@mail.montclair.edu

Hayes, Dawn Marie (PhD, NYU 1998; prof.) medieval Europe, early modern Europe, Italy; hayesd@mail.montclair.edu

Landweber, Julia A. (PhD, Rutgers 2001; assoc. prof.) European women, early modern France; landweberj@mail.montclair.edu

Lapp, Benjamin (PhD, California, Berkeley 1991; assoc. prof.) Germany, 20th-century Europe; lappb@mail.montclair.edu

Martini, Elspeth Ann (PhD, Michigan 2013; asst. prof.) 19th-century US, comparative settler colonialism; martinie@mail.montclair.edu

Moran, Megan Catherine (PhD, Vanderbilt 2005; asst. prof.) early modern Europe, Mediterranean, gender and family; moranm@mail.montclair.edu

Nabavi, Negin (PhD, Oxford 1997; assoc. prof.) Middle East, modern Iran; nabavin@mail.montclair.edu

Olenik, J. Kenneth (PhD, Cornell 1973; prof.) modern Republic of China, Chinese political, traditional China; olenikk@mail.montclair.edu

Rashkow, Ezra (PhD, London 2008; assoc. prof.) modern South Asia, environmental; rashkowe@mail.montclair.edu

Strickland, Jeff (PhD, Florida State 2003; prof. and chair) slavery, Civil War and Reconstruction, US South; stricklandj@mail.montclair.edu

Wilson, Leslie E. (PhD, Grad. Center, CUNY 1992; prof.) US black, US urban; wilsonl@mail.montclair.edu

Woodard, James P. (PhD, Brown 2004; prof.) Latin America; woodardj@mail.montclair.edu

Retired/Emeritus Faculty

Pastor, Peter (PhD, NYU 1969; prof. emeritus) modern Russia, eastern Europe, 20th-century Europe; pastorp@mail.montclair.edu

Srebnick, Amy Gilman (PhD, SUNY, Stony Brook 1979; prof. emerita) US social, cultural, women; srebnicka@mail.montclair.edu

Morgan State University

Dept. of History and Geography, 1700 E. Coldspring Ln, Baltimore, MD 21251-0001. 443.885.3190. Fax 443.885.8227. Email: Jeremiah.Dibua@morgan.edu. Website: https://www.morgan.edu/cla/history.

The Department of History and Geography is the second-largest in the College of Liberal Arts at Morgan State, and it offers a comprehensive range of courses and degrees. Its programs prepare students for professional life by teaching them to read analytically, think critically, write persuasively, and learn comprehensively.

Chair: Jeremiah Dibua
Director of Graduate Studies: Jeremiah Dibua
Degrees Offered: BA,MA,PhD
Academic Year System: Semester
Areas of Specialization: African American, African diaspora, US social and cultural, popular culture, Africa
Undergraduate Tuition (per academic year):
In-State: $3754
Out-of-State: $8591
Graduate Tuition (per academic year):
In-State: $16254
Out-of-State: $29700
Enrollment 2018-19:
Undergraduate Majors: 46
New Graduate Students: 18
Full-time Graduate Students: 64
Part-time Graduate Students: 5
Degrees in History: 12 BA, 8 MA, 6 PhD
Undergraduate Addresses:
Admissions: http://www.morgan.edu/undergradadmissions
Financial Aid: http://www.morgan.edu/financialaid
Graduate Addresses:
Admissions and Financial Aid: http://www.morgan.edu/gradschool

Full-time Faculty

Barnes, Mark (PhD, Rutgers 2013; assoc. prof.) geography, transportation; mark.barnes@morgan.edu

Berliner, Brett (PhD, Massachusetts Amherst 1999; assoc. prof.) modern Europe; brett.berliner@morgan.edu

Blackman, Dexter Lee (PhD, Georgia State 2009; asst. prof.) African American, sports, civil rights; dexter.blackman@morgan.edu

Brewer, Herbert (PhD, Maryland, Coll. Park 2017; asst. prof.) African diaspora, US; herbert.brewer@morgan.edu

Debnam, Jewell (PhD, Michigan State 2016; asst. prof.) African American, women and gender, labor; jewell.debnam@morgan.edu

Dibua, Jeremiah (PhD, Benin, Nigeria 1988; prof.; interim chair; and dir., grad. studies) Africa, development, pan-Africanism and African diaspora identity; jeremiah.dibua@morgan.edu

Dube, Francis (PhD, Iowa 2009; assoc. prof.) Africa, environmental, health; francis.dube@morgan.edu

Hendricks, Derick Antony (PhD, Morgan State 2009; lect.) African diaspora; derick.hendricks@morgan.edu

Kumolalo, Frederick (PhD, Morgan State 2015; lect.) African diaspora, religion; Frederick.Kumolalo@morgan.edu

Ngovo, Samuel Benedict (PhD, Western Michigan 2011; lect.) Africa, African diaspora, African American; Samuel.Ngovo@morgan.edu

Noel, Linda (PhD, Maryland, Coll. Park 2006; assoc. prof.) US, immigration, urban; linda.noel@morgan.edu

Pavuk, Alexander (PhD, Delaware 2009; asst. prof.) science and religion, intellectual and cultural, US and world; alexander.pavuk@morgan.edu

Peskin, Lawrence A. (PhD, Maryland, Coll. Park 1998; prof.) colonial America, US and the world; lawrence.peskin@morgan.edu

Terry, David Taft (PhD, Howard 2002; assoc. prof. and dir., museum studies and historical preservation) African American, civil rights, museum studies; david.terry@morgan.edu

Thomas, Felicia Y. (PhD, Rutgers 2014; asst. prof.) African American, women and gender, religion; felicia.thomas@morgan.edu

Thompson, Aubrey (PhD, Howard 2002; lect.) world civilization, Caribbean; aubrey.thompson@morgan.edu

Retired/Emeritus Faculty

Newman Ham, Debra (PhD, Howard 1984; prof. emeritus) African American, public; newman.ham2@verizon.net

Phillips, Glenn O. (PhD, Howard 1976; prof. emeritus) Caribbean, Latin America; gopper.phillips@gmail.com

Recently Awarded PhDs

Barnes, Iris Leigh "Sacrificing Margaret Morgan: Slavery and Freedom through the Lens of Prigg v. Pennsylvania"

Chavis, Charles Lester Jr. "When the Unknown Becomes Known: Matthew Williams, Judge Lynch and the Politics of Racism in the Free State: 1931-32"

Price, Omar "Freedom, Faith and Education: The Formation and Legacy of Freedmen Schools in Prince George's County, Maryland, 1865-70"

Robinson, Bridgette "The Battle for Respectability: The Black Bourgeoisie's Use of Eugenic Rhetoric in Racial Uplift Politics, 1895-1940"

Sadrud-Din, Zaakira "Fighting for a Chance to Fight for Democracy: Mary Mcleod Bethune's Involvement with the Women's Army Corps during World War II"

Washington, Matthew George "'Jim Crow, Yankee Style': Civil Rights and Working-Class Pottstown, Pennsylvania, 1941-69"

Wilson, Teisha "WDAS-AM/FM: The Community's Radio Station and the Sound of Black Philadelphia, 1950-79"

Mount Holyoke College

Dept. of History, 50 College St., South Hadley, MA 01075-1450. 413.538.2377. Fax 413.538.2513. Email: history@mtholyoke. edu. Website: https://www.mtholyoke.edu/acad/history/.

Mount Holyoke College is a highly selective, nondenominational, residential, research liberal arts college for women.

Chair: Daniel Czitrom
Degrees Offered: BA
Academic Year System: Semester
Areas of Specialization: US, Africa, Europe, East Asia, Latin America
Undergraduate Tuition (per academic year): $52040
Enrollment 2018-19:
 Undergraduate Majors: 72
 Degrees in History: 24 BA
 Students in Undergraduate Courses: 706
 Students in Undergraduate Intro Courses: 212
Addresses:
 Admissions: https://www.mtholyoke.edu/admission
 Financial Aid: https://www.mtholyoke.edu/sfs

Full-time Faculty

Czitrom, Daniel J. (PhD, Wisconsin, Madison 1979; prof. and chair) US intellectual and cultural, 20th century; dczitrom@mtholyoke. edu

Fitz-Gibbon, Desmond (PhD, California, Berkeley 2011; assoc. prof.) modern Britain, modern Europe, cultural; dfitzgib@ mtholyoke.edu

Gudmundson, Lowell (PhD, Minnesota 1982; prof.) Latin America, Central America, agrarian; lgudmund@mtholyoke.edu

Hanson, Holly E. (PhD, Florida 1997; prof.) Africa, African women; hhanson@mtholyoke.edu

King, Jeremy R. (PhD, Columbia 1998; prof.) 20th-century central Europe; jking@mtholyoke.edu

Medhi, Abhilash (PhD, Brown 2019; asst. prof.) modern South Asia; amedhi@mtholyoke.edu

Morgan, Lynda J. (PhD, Virginia 1986; prof.) US, African American, US South; ljmorgan@mtholyoke.edu

Renda, Mary A. (PhD, Yale 1993; prof.) American women; mrenda@ mtholyoke.edu

Wu, Lan (PhD, Columbia 2015; asst. prof.) East Asia; lwu@ mtholyoke.edu

Retired/Emeritus Faculty

Burns, Michael (PhD, Yale 1981; prof. emeritus) modern European social, cultural; mburns@mtholyoke.edu

Ellis, Joseph J., III (PhD, Yale 1969; prof. emeritus) colonial America, US intellectual, military; jellis@mtholyoke.edu

Garrett-Goodyear, R. H. (PhD, Harvard 1974; prof. emeritus) early modern Europe, Tudor-Stuart England, legal; hgarrett@ mtholyoke.edu

Herbert, Eugenia W. (PhD, Yale 1957; prof. emeritus) Africa, colonial America, European cultural; eherbert@mtholyoke.edu

Lipman, Jonathan N. (PhD, Stanford 1981; prof. emeritus) modern East Asia, Central Asia; jlipman@mtholyoke.edu

McGinness, Frederick J. (PhD, California, Berkeley 1982; prof. emeritus) medieval Europe, Renaissance, Reformation; mcginnes@mtholyoke.edu

Schwartz, Robert M. (PhD, Michigan 1980; prof. emeritus) early modern Europe, France, social; rschwart@mtholyoke.edu

Straw, Carole E. (PhD, California, Berkeley 1979; prof. emeritus) late classical and early medieval Europe, European intellectual; cstraw@mtholyoke.edu

Visiting Faculty

Duker, Adam Asher (PhD, Notre Dame 2016; vist. asst. prof.; Jewish Studies) early modern Europe and Jewish; aduker@mtholyoke. edu

Gao, Xiaofei (PhD, California, Santa Cruz 2018; vis. lect.) modern China; xgao@mtholyoke.edu

Huezo, Stephanie (PhD, Indiana 2019; Mount Holyoke Fellow and vis. lect.) Latin America, Latina/o; shuezo@mtholyoke.edu

Mount St. Mary's University

Dept. of History, 16300 Old Emmitsburg Rd., Emmitsburg, MD 21727-7799. 301.447.5375. Fax 301.447.8396. Email: murry@ msmary.edu. Website: https://msmary.edu/academics/majors-minors/history.html.

The Department of History provides a perspective that is central to the University's liberal arts curriculum, namely, an intellectual framework for understanding the evolution of the human condition.

Chair: Greg Murry
Degrees Offered: BA
Academic Year System: Semester
Areas of Specialization: medieval Europe, Renaissance and Reformation, Italy/France/Latin America, US, religious and social
Tuition (per academic year): $53380
Enrollment 2018-19:
 Undergraduate Majors: 52
 Degrees in History: 14 BA
Addresses:
 Admissions: http://www.msmary.edu/admissions/
 Financial Aid: http://www.msmary.edu/admissions/
  financial-aid/

Full-time Faculty

Fritz, Timothy David (PhD, Florida 2014; asst. prof.) colonial America, African American, US borderlands; fritz@msmary.edu

Gianoutsos, Jamie (PhD, Johns Hopkins 2014; asst. prof.) early modern and modern Europe, England, political/intellectual/ gender; gianoutsos@msmary.edu

Johnson, Curtis D. (PhD, Minnesota 1985; prof.) 19th-century US social and religious; johnson@msmary.edu

Murry, Gregory W. (PhD, Penn State 2009; assoc. prof. and chair) early modern European political and religious, art, colonial Mexico; murry@msmary.edu

Patterson, Michelle Wick (PhD, Purdue 2003; assoc. prof.) 20th-century US, women, Native American; patterson@msmary.edu

Rupp, Teresa Pugh (PhD, Cornell 1988; prof.) ancient and medieval; rupp@msmary.edu

Strauss, Charles Thomas (PhD, Notre Dame 2012; assoc. prof.) US political and religious, US in world, global Cold War; strauss@ msmary.edu

Strauss, Elizabeth (PhD, Notre Dame 2014; asst. prof.) US political and religious, US in world, global Cold War; strauss@msmary. edu

College of Mount Saint Vincent

Dept. of History, 6301 Riverdale Ave., Riverdale, NY 10471-1093. 718.405.3306. Fax 718.405.3747. Email: daniel.opler@mountsaintvincent.edu. Website: https://www.mountsaintvincent.edu/history.

The program comprises a range of exciting, cutting-edge courses in American, European, and global history. Students will master academic skills essential to professional life, including analytical writing, information literacy, complex research methodologies, critical assessment, and public speaking.

Chair: Daniel Opler
Degrees Offered: BA
Academic Year System: Semester
Areas of Specialization: ancient/medieval, early modern Europe, US, New York City, Middle East
Tuition (per academic year): $29980
Enrollment 2018-19:
Undergraduate Majors: 37
Degrees in History: 10 BA
Addresses:
Admissions: https://mountsaintvincent.edu/admission/
Financial Aid: https://mountsaintvincent.edu/admission/financial-aid/

Full-time Faculty

Gallo, David M. (PhD, Boston Coll. 1992; assoc. prof.) 17th-century French society and culture, early modern Europe, Byzantine; david.gallo@mountsaintvincent.edu

Opler, Daniel J. (PhD, NYU 2003; assoc. prof. and chair) US, labor, urban; daniel.opler@mountsaintvincent.edu

Skelly, Joseph Morrison (PhD, Univ. Coll., Dublin 1994; prof.) international terrorism, Middle East, modern Europe; joe.skelly@mountsaintvincent.edu

Nondepartmental Historians

Aliano, David (PhD, Grad. Center, CUNY 2008; asst. prof.; Modern Languages and Literatures) modern Latin America, colonial and postcolonial, modern Italy and France; david.aliano@mountsaintvincent.edu

Retired/Emeritus Faculty

Coady, Joseph W. (PhD, St. John's, NY 1968; prof. emeritus) 20th-century US, American presidency

Muhlenberg College

Dept. of History, 2400 Chew St., Allentown, PA 18104-5586. 484.664.3323. Fax 484.664.3536. Email: giacomogambino@muhlenberg.edu. Website: https://www.muhlenberg.edu/academics/history/.

The major is designed to introduce the students to the principles of historical study, to provide them with the tools to become an effective researcher and writer, and to deepen their knowledge and understanding of the past. Significant emphasis is put on reading original texts and scholarship written by historians.

Chair: Giacomo (Jack) Gambino
Degrees Offered: BA
Academic Year System: Semester
Areas of Specialization: colonial to present US, modern Europe and Great Britain, Russia, Middle East, Latin America/Caribbean/Africa

Tuition (per academic year): $51860
Enrollment 2018-19:
Undergraduate Majors: 47
Degrees in History: 15 BA
Addresses:
Admissions: http://www.muhlenberg.edu/main/admissions/
Financial Aid: http://www.muhlenberg.edu/main/aboutus/finaid/

Full-time Faculty

Antonovich, Jacqueline (PhD, Michigan 2018; asst. prof.) 19th-century America, 20th-century America, public health; jacquelineanotovich@muhlenberg.edu

Clemens-Bruder, Susan W. (MA, Lehigh 1990; sr. lect.) 20th-century intellectual and cultural, labor, urban; clemens@muhlenberg.edu

Cragin, Thomas J. (PhD, Indiana 1997; prof.) modern France, early modern Europe; cragin@muhlenberg.edu

D'Haeseleer, Tineke (PhD, Cambridge 2012; asst. prof.) Tang dynasty China, East Asia before 1800, traditional Chinese foreign relations; tinekedhaeseleer@muhlenberg.edu

Malsberger, John W. (PhD, Temple 1980; prof.) 20th-century US economic/political/diplomatic; malsberg@muhlenberg.edu

Ouellette, Cathy Marie (PhD, Emory 2008; assoc. prof.) Latin America; couellette@muhlenberg.edu

Sanchez, Danielle (PhD, Texas, Austin 2015; asst. prof.) Africa

Stein, Mark L. (PhD, Chicago 2001; assoc. prof.) Middle East, Ottoman Empire; stein@muhlenberg.edu

Tighe, William J. (PhD, Cambridge 1984; assoc. prof.) 16th- and 17th-century England, modern Europe, Renaissance and Reformation; tighe@muhlenberg.edu

Yankaskas, Lynda K. (PhD, Brandeis 2009; asst. prof.) colonial and revolutionary America, early Republic, women and gender; lyankaskas@muhlenberg.edu

Murray State University

Dept. of History, 6B Faculty Hall, Murray, KY 42071-3341. 270.809.2231. Fax 270.809.6587. Email: msu.deptofhistory@murraystate.edu. Website: http://www.murraystate.edu/history.

As the only university in Kentucky to focus on world civilizations, we are particularly well suited to prepare you for careers in these paths. We offer a wide diversity in areas of study as we have historians specialized in every field of history.

Chair: Kathy J. Callahan
Director of Graduate Studies: David Pizzo
Degrees Offered: BA,MA
Academic Year System: Semester
Areas of Specialization: US, Europe, non-Western, religious studies
Undergraduate Tuition (per academic year):
In-State: $7392
Out-of-State: $20112
Graduate Tuition (per academic year):
In-State: $8424
Out-of-State: $23724
Enrollment 2018-19:
Undergraduate Majors: 129
New Graduate Students: 3
Full-time Graduate Students: 14
Part-time Graduate Students: 2
Degrees in History: 18 BA, 1 BS, 6 MA

Undergraduate Addresses:
  Admissions: http://www.murraystate.edu/admissions/
  Financial Aid: http://www.murraystate.edu/admissions/
    financialaid/
Graduate Addresses:
  Admissions: http://www.murraystate.edu/history
  Financial Aid: http://www.murraystate.edu/admissions/
    financialaid/

Adjunct Faculty

McLaughlin, Sean J. (PhD, Western Ontario 2009; adj.) 20th-century international relations, 20th-century France

Full-time Faculty

Belue, Ted Franklin (MA, Murray State 1985; sr. lect.) roots music, American frontier, Native American; tbelue@murraystate.edu

Bolin, James Duane (PhD, Kentucky 1988; prof.) late 19th- and early 20th-century US, Kentucky, teaching history; jbolin@murraystate.edu

Callahan, Kathy J. (PhD, Marquette 2005; assoc. prof. and chair) modern Europe, Britain, US; kcallahan@murraystate.edu

Clardy, Brian Keith (PhD, Southern Illinois, Carbondale 1999; assoc. prof.) post-1900 foreign policy, US political, social protest movements; bclardy@murraystate.edu

Gao, Jie (PhD, Western Ontario 2009; asst. prof.) Asia; selinahistory@gmail.com

Hilton, Marjorie L. (PhD, Illinois, Urbana-Champaign 2003; assoc. prof.) Russia and Soviet Union, modern Europe, comparative modern European and US gender; mhilton@murraystate.edu

Humphreys, James Scott (PhD, Mississippi State 2005; prof.) American South, US; jhumphreys@murraystate.edu

Irvin, Aaron William (PhD, California, Los Angeles 2012; asst. prof.) ancient Rome, ancient Greece, ancient Near East; airvin1@murraystate.edu

Lindner, Christine Beth (PhD, Edinburgh 2009; asst. prof.) Middle East; christinebethlindner@gmail.com

Mulligan, William H., Jr. (PhD, Clark 1982; prof.) colonial America, Ireland; wmulligan@murraystate.edu

Pizzo, David John (PhD, North Carolina, Chapel Hill 2007; asst. prof. and grad. coord.) modern Germany, modern Europe, colonial Africa; dpizzo@murraystate.edu

Rashid, Taufiq (MA, Indiana 1987; sr. lect.) world civilizations, US foreign policy, India; trashid@murraystate.edu

Rivera, Eleanor (PhD, Chicago 2015; asst. prof.) Europe; erivera@murraystate.edu

Willoughby, Urmi Engineer (PhD, California, Santa Cruz 2010; asst. prof.) America, world, women; uenginee@gmail.com

University of Nebraska, Kearney

Dept. of History, 2507 11th Ave., COPH 103, Kearney, NE 68849. 308.865.8509. Email: wellsrjd@unk.edu. Website: http://www.unk.edu/academics/history/.

The Department of History at UNK provides instruction, research, and service functions that are representative of today's world. We offer several courses of study for students including online classes and an online history master's degree program.

Chair: Jeff Wells
Director of Graduate Studies: Douglas L. Biggs
Degrees Offered: BA,BAEd,BS,MA
Academic Year System: Semester
Areas of Specialization: US, Great Plains, American West, Midwest, Native American, Europe, Latin America, South Asia, military, political, gender, agricultural, environmental, public, digital

Undergraduate Tuition (per academic year):
  In-State: $7752
  Out-of-State: $14530
Graduate Tuition (per academic year):
  In-State: $6048
  Out-of-State: $9972
Enrollment 2018-19:
  Undergraduate Majors: 112
  New Graduate Students: 67
  Full-time Graduate Students: 15
  Part-time Graduate Students: 127
  Degrees in History: 17 BA, 8 BS, 39 MA
Undergraduate Addresses:
  Admissions: http://www.unk.edu/admissions/undergraduate/
  Financial Aid: http://www.unk.edu/offices/financial_aid/
    index.php
Graduate Addresses:
  Admissions: http://www.unk.edu/academics/gradstudies/
    admissions/
  Financial Aid: http://www.unk.edu/offices/financial_aid/
    index.php

Full-time Faculty

Ailes, Mary E. (PhD, Minnesota 1997; prof.) early modern Europe, Scandinavia; ailesm@unk.edu

Barua, Pradeep (PhD, Illinois, Urbana-Champaign 1995; prof.) South Asia, developing world, military; baruap@unk.edu

Biggs, Douglas L. (PhD, Minnesota 1996; prof. and dir., grad. studies) medieval Europe, England, ancient, military; biggsdl@unk.edu

Davis, Roger (PhD, Arizona 1983; prof.) Latin America, US Gilded Age; davisr@unk.edu

Ellis, Mark Robert (PhD, Nebraska 1999; prof. and dean, grad. studies) American West, Great Plains and Nebraska, US sports; ellismr@unk.edu

Lilly, Carol S. (PhD, Yale 1990; prof.) eastern Europe, Russia; lillyc@unk.edu

Rohrer, James R. (PhD, Ohio State 1991; prof.) early/colonial America, religious; rohrerjr@unk.edu

Steinke, Christopher Joseph (PhD, New Mexico 2015; assoc. prof.) Native American, Great Plains, colonial America; steinkecj@unk.edu

Tye, Nathan Thomas (PhD, Illinois, Urbana-Champaign 2019; asst. prof.) Great Plains and Nebraska, labor, gender; tyen@unk.edu

Vail, David D. (PhD, Kansas State 2012; assoc. prof.) environmental, agricultural, science, technology, American West; vaildd@unk.edu

Van Ingen, Linda (PhD, California, Riverside 2000; prof.) 20th century US, cold war, civil rights, immigration, women; vaningenL1@unk.edu

Volpe, Vernon L. (PhD, Nebraska 1984; prof.) Civil War and Reconstruction, 19th-century US political, western exploration and expansion; volpev@unk.edu

Wells, Jeff (PhD, Texas Christian 2014; assoc. prof. and chair) US 1877-1920, political, digital; wellsrjd@unk.edu

Part-time Faculty

Alexander, Amber (MA, Nebraska, Kearney 2012; adj. and online prog. coord.) US, Nebraska, Great Plains; alexanderaj@unk.edu

White, April (MA, Nebraska, Kearney 2017; adj. and interim dir., G.W. Frank Museum of Hist. and Culture) public, US, women, gender; whiteac@unk.edu

Visiting Faculty

Homberger, Torsten (PhD, Washington State 2014; asst. prof.) modern Europe, Germany, cultural; hombergert@unk.edu

Kruger, Cole (ABD, Kansas State; lect.) US, military, 20th century, agriculture

University of Nebraska, Lincoln

Dept. of History, 612 Oldfather Hall, Lincoln, NE 68588-0327. 402.472.2414. Fax 402.472.8839. Email: jlesueur@unl.edu. Website: https://history.unl.edu/.

Our award-winning, global experts teach innovative courses on subjects that affect our world today. And we attract students ready to work hand-in-hand with them on innovative research projects that challenge the field's status quo.

Chair: James D. Le Sueur
Director of Graduate Studies: Katrina L. Jagodinsky
Director of Undergraduate Studies: Vanessa B. Gorman
Degrees Offered: BA,MA,PhD
Academic Year System: Semester
Areas of Specialization: North American West, race/ethnicity/ identity, 19th-century US, 20th-century international, Germany and central Europe
Undergraduate Tuition (per academic year):
  In-State: $5880
  Out-of-State: $18504
Graduate Tuition (per academic year):
  In-State: $5819
  Out-of-State: $16655
Enrollment 2018-19:
  Undergraduate Majors: 190
  New Graduate Students: 6
  Full-time Graduate Students: 43
  Degrees in History: 37 BA, 5 MA, 3 PhD
  Students in Undergraduate Courses: 4711
  Students in Undergraduate Intro Courses: 1991
Undergraduate Addresses:
  Admissions: http://admissions.unl.edu/
  Financial Aid: http://financialaid.unl.edu/
Graduate Addresses:
  Admissions and Financial Aid: http://www.unl.edu/gradstudies/

Full-time Faculty

Borstelmann, Tim (PhD, Duke 1990; E. N. and Katherine Thompson Prof.) modern world, US foreign relations, 20th-century US; tborstelmann2@unl.edu

Burnett, Amy Nelson (PhD, Wisconsin-Madison 1989; Paula and D. B. Varner Univ. Prof.) Renaissance and Reformation, religious; aburnett1@unl.edu

Cahan, David (PhD, Johns Hopkins 1980; Charles Bessey Prof.) premodern Jewish, early modern Europe; dcahan2@unl.edu

Coble, Parks M., Jr. (PhD, Illinois, Urbana-Champaign 1975; James L. Sellers Prof.) East Asia, modern China, Japan; pcoble1@unl.edu

Coltrain, James (PhD, Northwestern 2012; assoc. prof.) colonial America, digital, Atlantic world; jcoltrain2@unl.edu

Coope, Jessica A. (PhD, California, Berkeley 1988; assoc. prof.) medieval, Islamic; jcoope1@unl.edu

Cooper Owens, Deirdre B. (PhD, UCLA 2008; Charles and Linda Wilson Prof.; dir., Humanities in Medicine) race, gender, medicine

Der Matossian, Bedross (PhD, Columbia 2008; assoc. prof.) modern Middle East; bdermatossian2@unl.edu

Gorman, Vanessa B. (PhD, Pennsylvania 1993; prof. and dir., undergrad. studies) ancient Greece, Rome; vgorman1@unl.edu

Jacobs, Margaret D. (PhD, California, Davis 1996; Chancellor's Prof.; chair, Women's & Gender Studies) North American West, women, indigenous peoples; mjacobs3@unl.edu

Jagodinsky, Katrina L. (PhD, Arizona 2011; Susan J. Rosowski Assoc. Prof. and dir., grad. studies) North American West, legal, women and gender; kjagodinsky@unl.edu

Le Sueur, James Dean (PhD, Chicago 1996; Samuel Clark Waugh Dist. Prof. and chair) modern France, world decolonization, intellectual and cultural; jlesueur@unl.edu

Levin, Carole B. (PhD, Tufts 1976; Willa Cather Prof.) early modern England, women; clevin2@unl.edu

Mahoney, Timothy R. (PhD, Chicago 1982; prof.) US urban, 19th-century US; tmahoney1@unl.edu

Steinacher, Gerald J. (PhD, Innsbruck, Austria 1999; prof. and Hymen Rosenberg Prof.; Jewish Studies) modern Germany, Holocaust; gsteinacher2@unl.edu

Thomas, William G., III (PhD, Virginia 1995; John and Catherine Angle Prof.) digital, 19th-century US; wthomas4@unl.edu

Vazansky, Alexander (PhD, Heidelberg 2009; asst. prof.) modern Europe and Germany, German-American relations, military-civilian relations; avazansky2@unl.edu

Winkle, Kenneth J. (PhD, Wisconsin, Madison 1984; Thomas C. Sorensen Prof.) US political, social, quantitative methods; kwinkle1@unl.edu

Joint/Cross Appointments

Ari-Chachaki, Waskar T. (PhD, Georgetown 2005; assoc. prof.; Ethnic Studies) Latin America, social; wari2@unl.edu

Curry, Dawne Yvette (PhD, Michigan State 2006; assoc. prof.; Ethnic Studies) Africa, oral; dcurry2@unl.edu

Garza, James Alex (PhD, Texas Christian 2001; assoc. prof.; dir., Ethnic Studies) modern Mexico, Latin America, Latino; jgarza2@unl.edu

Huettl, Margaret (PhD, Nevada, Las Vegas 2016; asst. prof.; Ethnic Studies) Native American, North American West, colonialism and decolonization; mhuettl2@unl.edu

Jones, Jeannette Eileen (PhD, SUNY, Buffalo 2003; assoc. prof.; Ethnic Studies) American cultural and intellectual, African American, pre-colonial Africa; jjones11@unl.edu

Jones, Patrick D. (PhD, Wisconsin, Madison 2002; assoc. prof.; Ethnic Studies) African American, 20th-century US; pjones2@unl.edu

Muñoz, Laura K. (PhD, Arizona State 2006; asst. prof.; Ethnic Studies) race and gender in borderlands, Chicana/o, US and Latin American women; laura.munoz@unl.edu

Smith, Victoria A. O. (PhD, Arizona State 2002; assoc. prof.; Ethnic Studies) Native American, 19th-century US; vsmith4@unl.edu

Nondepartmental Historians

Turner, John (PhD, Duke 1965; prof.; Classics) ancient, religious; jturner2@unl.edu

Retired/Emeritus Faculty

Ambrosius, Lloyd E. (PhD, Illinois, Urbana-Champaign 1967; prof. emeritus) US foreign relations, presidency; lambrosius1@unl.edu

Berger, Patrice (PhD, Chicago 1972; prof. emeritus; dir., Honors Prog.) 17th- and 18th-century France; pberger1@unl.edu

Dorsey, Leathen (PhD, Michigan 1980; assoc. prof. emeritus) Africa; ldorsey1@unl.edu

Kleimola, Ann (PhD, Michigan 1970; prof. emeritus) eastern Europe, Russia, women; akleimola1@unl.edu

Luebke, Frederick C. (PhD, Nebraska 1966; Charles J. Mach Dist. Prof. emeritus) immigration, frontier, Nebraska; fredluebke@comcast.net

Maslowski, Peter (PhD, Ohio State 1972; prof. emeritus) US military; pmaslowski1@unl.edu

McClelland, James C. (PhD, Princeton 1970; assoc. prof. emeritus) 20th-century Russia; jmcclelland@neb.rr.com

Moulton, Gary E. (PhD, Oklahoma State 1973; prof. emeritus) US frontier, American Indian; gmoulton1@unl.edu

Rader, Benjamin G. (PhD, Maryland, Coll. Park 1964; James L. Sellers Prof. emeritus) American intellectual, sports; brader1@unl.edu

Vigil, Ralph H. (PhD, New Mexico 1969; prof. emeritus) colonial, Spanish-Mexican borderlands; rvigil2@unl.edu

Wunder, John R. (PhD, Washington 1974; prof. emeritus) US legal, American West, American Indian; jwunder1@unl.edu

Recently Awarded PhDs

Alvarez, Alyson "'Against the Good Widdow No Harme We Doe Know': Examining How English Widows Crafted Their Identities and Shaped Their Communities through Charity, 1550-1650"

Eckstrom, Mikal "Probationary Settlers and Indigenous Peoples in the American West: American Indians and American Jews, 1850-1934"

Klinetobe, Charles John "Diamond Mine: Segregation, Alabama, and the Making of the Players Who 'Saved Baseball'"

Rasmussen, Svetlana A. "Rearing the Collective: Evolution of the Soviet School Social Values and Practices, 1953-68"

University of Nebraska, Omaha

Dept. of History, 6001 Dodge St., 287 A & S Hall, Omaha, NE 68182-0213. 402.554.2593. Fax 402.554.2794. Email: history@unomaha.edu. Website: https://www.unomaha.edu/college-of-arts-and-sciences/history/.

The History Department is a critical component of a liberal arts education, as our faculty engage students in learning historical perspectives from all places and periods of time.

Chair: John Grigg
Director of Graduate Studies: Jeanne Reames
Degrees Offered: BA,BGS,BS,MA
Academic Year System: Semester
Areas of Specialization: US West and Great Plains, ancient Mediterranean, medieval and Renaissance, Native American, Middle East
Undergraduate Tuition (per academic year):
  In-State: $4722
  Out-of-State: $13932
Graduate Tuition (per academic year):
  In-State: $4415
  Out-of-State: $11624
Enrollment 2018-19:
  Undergraduate Majors: 212
  New Graduate Students: 25
  Full-time Graduate Students: 71
  Part-time Graduate Students: 56
  Degrees in History: 20 BA, 25 MA
Undergraduate Addresses:
  Admissions: http://www.unomaha.edu/admissions/
  Financial Aid: http://www.unomaha.edu/admissions/financial-support-and-scholarships/
Graduate Addresses:
  Admissions: http://www.unomaha.edu/graduate-studies/

Financial Aid: http://www.unomaha.edu/admissions/financial-support-and-scholarships/

Adjunct Faculty

Aftonomos, Anthony (PhD, Concordia, Can. 2005; adj.)

Bauer, Jeremiah (MA, Nebraska, Omaha 2010; adj.)

King, Kimberly (MA, Nebraska, Omaha 2010; adj.)

Klinetobe, Charles John (PhD, Nebraska 2018; adj.)

Knotts, Kenneth (MA, Nebraska, Omaha 2014; adj.)

Lyons-Barrett, Mary (PhD, Nebraska 2002; adj.) world civilizations, modern US; mlyonsbarrett@msn.com

Nielsen, Fredrick H. (PhD, Kansas 1997; adj.) late 19th- and early 20th-century US; fnielsen@unomaha.edu

Robertson, David (MA, UCLA 1968; adj.)

Stejskal, Sonya (MA, NYU; adj.)

Weis, Dan (MA; adj.)

Welchans, Katherine (MA, Nebraska, Omaha; adj.)

Full-time Faculty

Arbelaez, Maria S. (PhD, Miami 1995; assoc. prof.) Latin America, US Hispanic; marbelaez@unomaha.edu

Battisti, Danielle (PhD, SUNY, Buffalo 2010; asst. prof.) 20th-century US, immigration; dbattisti@unomaha.edu

Blansett, Kent (PhD, New Mexico 2011; assoc. prof.) Native American, America; kblansett@unomaha.edu

Celinscak, Mark (PhD, York, Can. 2012; asst. prof.) modern Europe, modern Britain, war and Holocaust studies; mcelinscak@unomaha.edu

Grigg, John A. (PhD, Kansas 2002; assoc. prof. and chair) early America; jgrigg@unomaha.edu

King, Charles W. (PhD, Chicago 1998; assoc. prof.) Roman Republic, Roman Empire, early Christian era; cwking@mail.unomaha.edu

Nelson, Elaine Marie (PhD, New Mexico 2011; asst. prof.) American trans-Mississippi West; emnelson@unomaha.edu

Reames, Jeanne (PhD, Penn State 1998; assoc. prof. and grad. prog. chair) ancient Greece and Macedonia; mreames@unomaha.edu

Saltamacchia, Martina (PhD, Rutgers 2013; PhD, Bocconi, Milan 2011; assoc. prof.) medieval, social and economic; msaltamacchia@unomaha.edu

Scherer, Mark (PhD, Nebraska 2002; assoc. prof.) US Midwest, legal, Nebraska; mscherer@unomaha.edu

Smith, Dennis J. (PhD, Nebraska 2001; assoc. prof.) Native American, Sioux and Assiniboine tribes; dennissmith@unomaha.edu

Wood, Sharon E. (PhD, Iowa 1994; prof.) women, 19th-century US cultural and social; swood@mail.unomaha.edu

Retired/Emeritus Faculty

Dalstrom, Harl A. (PhD, Nebraska 1965; prof. emeritus) Nebraska and Great Plains; kdalstrom@msn.com

Garver, Bruce M. (PhD, Yale 1971; prof. emeritus) modern Europe, military, transport; bgarver@unomaha.edu

Garver, Karen K. (PhD, UCLA 1974; prof. emeritus) modern France, education; kgarver@unomaha.edu

Gesick, Lorraine (PhD, Cornell 1976; prof. emeritus) lgesick@unomaha.edu

Nelson, Marian (PhD, Nebraska 1978; assoc. prof. emeritus) modern Europe, 20th-century European diplomatic, ancient

Overfield, Richard (PhD, Maryland, Coll. Park 1968; prof. emeritus) 18th- and 19th-century America, science

Petrowski, William (PhD, Wisconsin, Madison 1966; prof. emeritus) 19th-century US

Pollak, Oliver B. (PhD, UCLA 1973; prof. emeritus) modern Britain and Commonwealth, legal, American Jewish; obpomni@aol.com

Pratt, William C. (PhD, Emory 1969; prof. emeritus) 20th-century US, American social and intellectual, labor; bpratt@unomaha.edu

Simmons, Jerold (PhD, Minnesota 1971; prof. emeritus) US constitutional, film; jsimmons@unomaha.edu

Tate, Michael L. (PhD, Toledo 1974; prof. emeritus) American West, American Indian; mtate@unomaha.edu

Thompson, Tommy R. (PhD, Maryland, Coll. Park 1972; prof. emeritus) early America, US South; tthompson@unomaha.edu

Walker, Samuel E. (PhD, Ohio State 1973; prof. emeritus) civil liberties, law enforcement; swalker@unomaha.edu

Nebraska Wesleyan University

Dept. of History, 5000 St. Paul Ave., Lincoln, NE 68504-2796. 402.465.2443. Fax 402.465.2179. Email: swills@nebrwesleyan. edu. Website: https://www.nebrwesleyan.edu/academics/ majors-and-minors/history/.

Our degree in history develops students' abilities to ask incisive questions about the past, collect relevant information to answer such questions, interpret and critique sources, write effectively and insightfully about the results of their research, and engage others with the results of their learning.

Chair: Steve Wills
Degrees Offered: BA,BS
Academic Year System: Semester
Areas of Specialization: early modern and modern Europe, American Indian and West, modern US, East Asia/Japan, women
Tuition (per academic year): $25500
Enrollment 2018-19:
  Undergraduate Majors: 45
  Degrees in History: 16 BA, 20 MA
Addresses:
  Admissions: http://www.nebrwesleyan.edu/undergraduate-admissions
  Financial Aid: http://www.nebrwesleyan.edu/scholarships-and-financial-aid

Full-time Faculty

Bower, Kevin P. (PhD, Cincinnati 2003; assoc. prof.) modern US, civil rights; kbower@nebrwesleyan.edu

Hayden-Roy, Patrick M. (PhD, Stanford 1988; prof.) medieval and early modern Europe, Germany, Reformation; phr@nebrwesleyan.edu

Mathews-Benham, Sandra K. (PhD, New Mexico 1998; prof.) American West, Spanish borderlands and Mexico, American Indian; smathews@nebrwesleyan.edu

Wills, Steven (PhD, Columbia 2010; assoc. prof. and chair) East Asia, early modern Japan, modern Japan; swills@nebrwesleyan.edu

Winchell, Meghan K. (PhD, Arizona 2003; assoc. prof.) modern US, comparative women, African American; mwinchel@nebrwesleyan.edu

University of Nevada at Las Vegas

Dept. of History, 4505 S. Maryland Pkwy., Box 455020, Las Vegas, NV 89154-5020. 702.895.3349. Fax 702.895.1782. Email: andy. kirk@unlv.edu. Website: https://www.unlv.edu/history.

The UNLV History Department supplies a critical component of a liberal arts education by providing a historically informed perspective on the contemporary world and the challenges that it faces.

Chair: Andrew Kirk
Director of Graduate Studies: William J. Bauer Jr.
Degrees Offered: BA,MA,PhD
Academic Year System: Semester
Areas of Specialization: North American West, North American culture and society, European culture and society
Undergraduate Tuition (per academic year):
  In-State: $4596
  Out-of-State: $9108
Graduate Tuition (per academic year):
  In-State: $4752
  Out-of-State: $9495
Enrollment 2018-19:
  Undergraduate Majors: 143
  New Graduate Students: 9
  Full-time Graduate Students: 16
  Part-time Graduate Students: 52
  Degrees in History: 27 BA, 4 MA, 2 PhD
Undergraduate Addresses:
  Admissions: http://www.unlv.edu/admissions
  Financial Aid: http://www.unlv.edu/finaid
Graduate Addresses:
  Admissions: http://www.unlv.edu/graduatecollege/futurestudents
  Financial Aid: http://www.unlv.edu/finaid

Full-time Faculty

Alarid, Michael Joseph (PhD, Ohio State 2012; asst. prof.) borderlands, US Southwest; michael.alarid@unlv.edu

Bauer, William J., Jr. (PhD, Oklahoma 2003; prof. and dir., grad. studies) Native American; wbauer@unlv.edu

Brown, Gregory Stephen (PhD, Columbia 1997; prof.) France, Enlightenment, theater; gbrown@unlv.nevada.edu

Casas, Maria Raquel (PhD, Yale 1998; assoc. prof.) Chicano/a, gender, US Southwest; maria.casas@unlv.edu

Clemente, Deirdre (PhD, Carnegie Mellon 2010; assoc. prof.) 20th-century American cultural, material culture; deirdre.clemente@unlv.edu

Coughtry, Jay (PhD, Wisconsin, Madison 1978; assoc. prof.) colonial and early national America, US social, labor; jay.coughtry@unlv.edu

Curry, John J. IV (PhD, Ohio State 2005; assoc. prof.) Near East, Islamic; john.curry@unlv.edu

Dean, Austin L. (PhD, Ohio State 2016; asst. prof) East Asia, modern China, capitalism; austin.dean@unlv.edu

Dimas, Carlos S. (PhD, California, Riverside 2014; asst. prof.) global medical, Latin America, Caribbean; carlos.dimas@unlv.edu

Dziedziak, Caryll Batt (PhD, Nevada, Las Vegas 2010; prof. in residence) US, women, medicine; caryll.dziedziak@unlv.edu

Gallo, Marcia M. (PhD, Grad. Center, CUNY 2004; assoc. prof.) US, gender and sexuality; marcia.gallo@unlv.edu

Goodwin, Joanne L. (PhD, Michigan 1991; prof.) US women, social, policy; joanne.goodwin@unlv.edu

Green, Michael S. (PhD, Columbia 2000; assoc. prof.) Nevada, American Civil War, Abraham Lincoln; michael.green@unlv.edu

Johnson, Susan Lee (PhD, Yale 1993; Harry Reid Endowed Chair) Intermountain West, North American West borderlands, gender, race, ethnicity, indigeneity

Kirk, Andy (PhD, New Mexico 1998; prof. and chair; dir., Prog. in Public Hist.) public, US West, environmental; andy.kirk@unlv.edu

Litaker, Noria (PhD, Pennsylvania 2017; asst. prof.) modern Germany/Europe, relics/religious material culture, Reformations

McMahon, Cian T. (PhD, Carnegie Mellon 2010; assoc. prof.)
transnationalization, Ireland, immigration; cian.mcmahon@unlv.edu

Melton-Villanueva, Miriam (PhD, UCLA 2012; assoc. prof.) modern
Latin America; miriam.melton-villanueva@unlv.edu

Nelson, Elizabeth White (PhD, Yale 1995; assoc. prof.) American
cultural, Civil War and Reconstruction; elizabeth.nelson@unlv.edu

Robinson, Todd E. (PhD, Michigan 2006; assoc. prof.) African
American, social; todd.robinson@unlv.edu

Schauer, Jeff (PhD, California, Berkeley 2014; asst. prof.) modern
Britain, modern Africa, environmental sciences/policy/
management; jeff.schauer@unlv.edu

Tusan, Michelle E. (PhD, California, Berkeley 1999; prof.) Britain,
Empire, modern European women; michelle.tusan@unlv.edu

Werth, Paul W. (PhD, Michigan 1996; prof.) Russia, empire, religion;
werthp@unlv.nevada.edu

Whitney, Elspeth (PhD, Grad. Center, CUNY 1985; prof.) medieval
Europe, science and technology, European women; elspeth@
unlv.nevada.edu

Wilkinson, A.B. (PhD, California, Berkeley 2013; asst. prof.) slavery,
mixed race ideologies; AB.Wilkinson@unlv.edu

Winkelmann, Tessa Ong (PhD, Illinois, Urbana-Champaign 2015;
asst. prof.) US in world, gender and sexuality, race and ethnicity;
tessa.winkelmann@unlv.edu

Joint/Cross Appointments

Tanenhaus, David S. (PhD, Chicago 1997; prof.; William S. Boyd
School of Law) US constitutional and legal; david.tanenhaus@
unlv.edu

Nondepartmental Historians

Michel, Peter (PhD, Washington, St. Louis 1994; dir., Special
Collections; Lied Library) archives and manuscripts, public,
medieval; peter.michel@unlv.edu

Retired/Emeritus Faculty

Burns, Paul E. (PhD, Indiana 1967; prof. emeritus) modern Russia,
Russian film

Chung, Sue Fawn (PhD, California, Berkeley 1975; prof. emerita)
China, Chinese American, Chinese art; suefawn.chung@unlv.edu

Fry, Joseph A. (PhD, Virginia 1974; Dist. Prof. emeritus) US foreign
relations, US South; joseph.fry@unlv.edu

Hise, Greg (PhD, California, Berkeley 1992; prof. emeritus) urban;
hise@unlv.edu

Loader, Colin T. (PhD, UCLA 1974; prof. emeritus) Germany,
European intellectual; loaderc@unlv.nevada.edu

Mattson, Vernon E. (PhD, Kansas 1971; assoc. prof. emeritus) US
intellectual and religious, Holocaust studies

Moehring, Eugene Peter (PhD, Grad. Center, CUNY 1976; prof.
emeritus) modern US, urban, business; eugene.moehring@unlv.edu

Wright, Thomas C. (PhD, California, Berkeley 1971; Dist. Prof.
emeritus) modern Latin America; tom.wright@unlv.edu

Recently Awarded PhDs

Bohigian, Stephen Muir "Eyes on the Street: Los Angeles Police
Department Surveillance, Policing, and Crime in Black South
Central from William Parker to Rodney King"

Yamamoto, Shiori "Beyond Suffering: Intermarraige, Land, and
Meaning of Citizenships and Marital Naturalization/Expatriation
in the United States"

University of Nevada at Reno

*Dept. of History, 1664 N. Virginia St., Mail Stop 0308, Reno, NV
89557-0037. 775.784.6855. Fax 775.784.6805. Email: jenni@unr.
edu. Website: https://www.unr.edu/history.*

*We are an ambitious department at an expanding research
university. Our award-winning faculty is a diverse group of
talented scholars whose research and teaching explores
innumerable facets of human experience over millennia.*

Chair: Dennis Dworkin
Director of Graduate Studies: Linda Curcio
Degrees Offered: BA,MA,MAT,PhD
Academic Year System: Semester
Areas of Specialization: American West, Nevada, cultural,
medicine, science
Undergraduate Tuition (per academic year):
In-State: $3666
Out-of-State: $10760
Graduate Tuition (per academic year): $2570
Enrollment 2018-19:
Undergraduate Majors: 133
New Graduate Students: 20
Degrees in History: 28 BA, 3 MA, 1 MAT
Undergraduate Addresses:
Admissions: http://www.unr.edu/admissions
Financial Aid: http://www.unr.edu/financial-aid
Graduate Addresses:
Admissions: http://www.unr.edu/grad/admissions
Financial Aid: http://www.unr.edu/financial-aid

Full-time Faculty

Church, Christopher M. (PhD, California, Berkeley 2014; asst. prof.)
digital, late modern Europe, France; christopherchurch@unr.edu

Curcio-Nagy, Linda A. (PhD, Tulane 1993; assoc. prof. and dir., grad.
studies) Latin American cultural, Mexico; lindacurcio@unr.edu

de Jong, Greta E. (PhD, Penn State 1999; assoc. prof.) 20th-century
US, US social, southern and African American; gdejong@unr.edu

Dorman, Jacob S. (PhD, UCLA 2004; assoc. prof.; Core Humanities)
African American, US cultural, African diaspora religions;
jdorman@unr.edu

Dworkin, Dennis L. (PhD, Chicago 1990; prof. and chair) Britain,
modern European intellectual, cultural theory; dworkin@unr.edu

Hobson, Emily K. (PhD, Southern California 2009; asst. prof.;
Gender, Race and Identity) 20th-century US, radical social
movements, sexuality; ehobson@unr.edu

Keller, Renata N. (PhD, Texas, Austin 2012; asst. prof.) international
relations, Latin American studies

Keyes, Sarah (PhD, Southern California 2012; asst. prof.) US West,
Overland Trail

Moran, Bruce T. (PhD, UCLA 1978; prof.) early modern, science,
medicine; moran@unr.edu

Oda, Meredith A. (PhD, Chicago 2010; asst. prof.) 20th-century
Asian American; mereditho@unr.edu

Raymond, C. Elizabeth (PhD, Pennsylvania 1979; prof.) American
social, cultural, landscape; raymond@unr.edu

Shapiro, Hugh L. (PhD, Harvard 1995; assoc. prof.) China, social,
medicine; shapiro@unr.edu

Stevens, Kevin M. (PhD, Wisconsin, Madison 1992; assoc. prof.)
Renaissance, social, book; kstevens@unr.edu

Strang, Cameron B. (PhD, Texas, Austin 2013; asst. prof.) early
America, borderlands, science; cstrang@unr.edu

Tshimanga-Kashama, Charles (PhD, Paris VII, Denis Diderot 1999; assoc. prof.) colonial and postcolonial Africa, diaspora studies; ckashama@unr.edu

Walker, Barbara B. (PhD, Michigan 1994; assoc. prof.) Russia and eastern Europe, cultural; bbwalker@unr.edu

Retired/Emeritus Faculty

Casper, Scott E. (PhD, Yale 1992; prof. emeritus) 19th-century America, American cultural; casper@unr.edu

Coray, Michael (PhD, California, Santa Barbara 1973; assoc. prof. emeritus) slavery, American cultural; mcoray@unr.edu

Davies, Richard O. (PhD, Missouri, Columbia 1963; prof. emeritus) ridavies@unr.edu

Edwards, Jerome E. (PhD, Chicago 1966; prof. emeritus) American diplomatic; jedwards@unr.nevada.edu

Ferguson, Neal (PhD, Oregon 1971; assoc. prof. emeritus) Britain, military; nealf@unr.edu

Hartigan, Francis X. (PhD, Wisconsin-Madison 1970; prof. emeritus) medieval; hartigan@unr.edu

Hildreth, Martha L. (PhD, California, Riverside 1983; assoc. prof. emeritus) modern Europe, social, medicine; hildreth@unr.edu

Hulse, James W. (PhD, Stanford 1962; prof. emeritus) European intellectual, Russia; jhulse@unr.edu

Marschall, John P. (PhD, Catholic 1965; prof. emeritus) American religious; johnm@admin.unr.edu

Rowley, William Dean (PhD, Nebraska 1966; prof. emeritus) American West, environmental, Nevada; rowley@unr.nevada.edu

University of New Hampshire, Durham

Dept. of History, Horton Social Science Center, 20 Academic Way, Durham, NH 03824-3586. 603.862.1764. Fax 603.862.1502. Email: history.undergrad@unh.edu; history.grad@unh.edu. Website: https://cola.unh.edu/history.

UNH's Department of History is one of the top history departments in the country, with an internationally recognized faculty in American, European, and world and ancient history. But what really sets our faculty apart is that we love to teach. History majors at UNH take almost all of their ten required classes with tenured or tenure-track faculty.

Chair: Kurk Dorsey
Director of Graduate Studies: David Bachrach
Degrees Offered: BA,MA,PhD
Academic Year System: Semester
Areas of Specialization: early and modern America, early and modern Europe, museum studies, comparative
Undergraduate Tuition (per academic year):
 In-State: $15520
 Out-of-State: $32050
Graduate Tuition (per academic year):
 In-State: $14170
 Out-of-State: $27810
Enrollment 2018-19:
 Undergraduate Majors: 171
 New Graduate Students: 11
 Full-time Graduate Students: 38
 Part-time Graduate Students: 1
 Degrees in History: 55 BA, 11 MA, 2 PhD
Undergraduate Addresses:
 Admissions: http://admissions.unh.edu/
 Financial Aid: http://financialaid.unh.edu/

Graduate Addresses:
 Admissions: http://www.gradschool.unh.edu/apply.php
 Financial Aid: http://www.gradschool.unh.edu/grad_aid.php

Affiliated Faculty

Harris, Benjamin (PhD, Vanderbilt 1975; prof.; Psychology) psychology; bh5@unh.edu

McMahon, J. Gregory (PhD, Chicago 1988; assoc. prof.; Classics, Humanities, and Italian Studies) ancient and classical; gregory.mcmahon@unh.edu

Ross, William (PhD, American 1992; prof.; special collections librarian, Dimond Library) special collections; bill.ross@unh.edu

Full-time Faculty

Afolayan, Funso S. (PhD, Obafemi Awolowo, Nigeria 1991; assoc. prof.) Africa; funso.afolayan@unh.edu

Alexander, Kimberly S. (PhD, Boston Univ. 1999; lect.) museum studies; kimberly.alexander@unh.edu

Bachrach, David Stewart (PhD, Notre Dame 2001; prof. and dir., grad. studies) medieval Europe; david.bachrach@unh.edu

Dorsey, Kurk (PhD, Yale 1994; prof. and chair) US foreign relations, environmental; kurk.dorsey@unh.edu

Dorsey, Marion Girard (PhD, Yale 2002; assoc. prof.) Europe, diplomatic and military, US medicine; marion.girard.dorsey@unh.edu

Fitzpatrick, Ellen F. (PhD, Brandeis 1981; prof.) modern America, intellectual, Progressive Era; ellen.fitzpatrick@unh.edu

Frierson, Cathy A. (PhD, Harvard 1985; prof.) Russia; cathy.frierson@unh.edu

Golinski, Jan V. (PhD, Leeds, UK 1984; prof.) science; jan.golinski@unh.edu

Gould, Eliga H. (PhD, Johns Hopkins 1993; prof.) early America, modern Britain, Atlantic world; eliga.gould@unh.edu

Gullace, Nicoletta F. (PhD, California, Berkeley 1993; assoc. prof.) modern Britain; nfg@unh.edu

Leese, Michael Stevens (PhD, Michigan 2014; asst. prof.) ancient Greek law and economy, Athenian democracy, economic and capitalism; michael.leese@unh.edu

Lepler, Jessica M. (PhD, Brandeis 2008; assoc. prof.) early America; jessica.lepler@unh.edu

Lu, Yan (PhD, Cornell 1996; assoc. prof.) modern China, modern Japan; yan.lu@unh.edu

Meiton, Fredrik (PhD, NYU 2015; asst. prof.) Middle East; fredrik.meiton@unh.edu

Mellyn, Elizabeth Walker (PhD, Harvard 2007; assoc. prof.) early modern Europe; elizabeth.mellyn@unh.edu

Polasky, Janet L. (PhD, Stanford 1978; Presidential Prof.) early and modern Europe; janet.polasky@unh.edu

Rodriguez, Julia E. (PhD, Columbia 2000; assoc. prof.) Latin America, science and medicine; julia.rodriguez@unh.edu

Salyer, Lucy (PhD, California, Berkeley 1989; prof.) American legal; lucy.salyer@unh.edu

Sokol, Jason C. (PhD, California, Berkeley 2006; assoc. prof.) modern US; jason.sokol@unh.edu

Van Zandt, Cynthia J. (PhD, Connecticut 1998; assoc. prof.) colonial America, Native American, early modern Atlantic world; cynthia.vanzandt@unh.edu

Wolper, Ethel Sara (PhD, UCLA 1994; assoc. prof.) Islamic world; ethel.wolper@unh.edu

Recently Awarded PhDs

Coulombe, Jordan "Mules, Fuels, and Fusion: Energy, Entropy, and the Crossing of the Panamanian Transit Zone, 1848-1990"

Deily-Swearingen, Susan Neelly "Rebel Rebels: Race, Resistance, and Remembrance in the Free State of Winston"

The College of New Jersey

Dept. of History, PO Box 7718, 2000 Pennington Rd., Ewing, NJ 08628-0718. 609.771.2341. Fax 609.637.5176. Email: history@tcnj.edu. Website: https://history.tcnj.edu/.

From the local to the global, history matters. The TCNJ History Department believes that we cannot understand today's world without a deep knowledge of the past. To that end, we offer courses and research opportunities in fields from the ancient world to New Jersey history.

Chair: Cynthia Paces
Degrees Offered: BA
Academic Year System: Semester
Areas of Specialization: US and Americas, ancient world, medieval and modern Europe, East and South Asia, modern Middle East
Tuition (per academic year):
  In-State: $16571
  Out-of-State: $28286
Enrollment 2018-19:
  Undergraduate Majors: 298
  Degrees in History: 65 BA
Addresses:
  Admissions: http://admissions.tcnj.edu/
  Financial Aid: http://admissions.tcnj.edu/about-tcnj/costs-financial-aid/

Full-time Faculty

Audain, Mekala S. (PhD, Rutgers 2014; asst. prof.) 19th-century America, African American
Bender, Matthew V. (PhD, Johns Hopkins 2006; assoc. prof.) sub-Saharan Africa, agrarian and environmental; bender@tcnj.edu
Boero, Dina (PhD, Southern California 2015; asst. prof.) ancient Mediterranean
Chazelle, Celia (PhD, Yale 1985; prof.) early medieval Europe, ancient and medieval Christianity, prison history and culture; chazelle@tcnj.edu
Fisher, Christopher T. (PhD, Rutgers 2002; assoc. prof.) 20th-century American diplomacy, Cold War, US race politics; fisherc@tcnj.edu
Gross, Jo-Ann (PhD, NYU 1982; prof.) Middle East and central Eurasia, Sufism; gross@tcnj.edu
Hollander, Craig Benjamin (PhD, Johns Hopkins 2013; asst. prof.) 19th-century US, Atlantic slave trade
Kovalev, Roman K. (PhD, Minnesota 2003; assoc. prof.) Russia, premodern Eurasia, medieval; kovalev@tcnj.edu
Marino, Michael P. (PhD, Columbia 2008; assoc. prof.) social studies education, modern Europe; marino@tcnj.edu
McGreevey, Robert C. (PhD, Brandeis 2008; assoc. prof.) modern US, US and world; mcgreeve@tcnj.edu
Paces, Cynthia (PhD, Columbia 1998; prof. and chair) modern Europe; paces@tcnj.edu
Shao, Qin (PhD, Michigan State 1994; prof.) modern East China, China through the ages, city in modern China; shao@tcnj.edu

Part-time Faculty

Weinstein, Jodi L. (PhD, Yale 2007) late imperial China, modern world; weinstei@tcnj.edu

Retired/Emeritus Faculty

Crofts, Daniel W. (PhD, Yale 1968; prof. emeritus) 19th-century American South, North-South sectional conflict; crofts@tcnj.edu

Irigoin, Alejandra (PhD, London Sch. Econ. 2000; asst. prof. emeritus) Latin America, economic and global; irigoin@tcnj.edu
Knobler, Adam (PhD, Cambridge 1990; assoc. prof. emeritus) early modern Europe, popular culture; knobler@tcnj.edu
Liu, Xinru (PhD, Pennsylvania 1985; prof. emeritus) ancient India, Silk Road, world; liux@tcnj.edu

New Jersey City University

Dept. of History, 2039 Kennedy Blvd., K-505, Jersey City, NJ 07305-1597. 201.200.3251. Fax 201.200.2574. Email: rthurston2@njcu.edu. Website: https://www.njcu.edu/department/history.

Our faculty is student-centered and passionate about bringing history to life. Their specialties are as diverse as our student body, and they are sought-after experts in the discipline. They are dedicated to helping students learn, grow, and succeed.

Chair: Rosemary Fox Thurston
Degrees Offered: BA
Academic Year System: Semester
Areas of Specialization: Americas, Europe, New Jersey, 20th-century US, ethnic studies
Tuition (per academic year):
  In-State: $12051
  Out-of-State: $21573
Enrollment 2018-19:
  Undergraduate Majors: 125
  Degrees in History: 70 BA
Addresses:
  Admissions: http://www.njcu.edu/admissions/apply
  Financial Aid: http://www.njcu.edu/academics/financial-aid-scholarships

Full-time Faculty

Bragg, John Kenneth (PhD, Wisconsin, Madison 2010; assoc. prof.; Elementary and Secondary Education) Middle East, world history education, Ottoman; JBragg@njcu.edu
Chadwick, Bruce (PhD, Rutgers 1999; prof.) American studies, journalism, political science; bchadwick@njcu.edu
Martinek, Jason D. (PhD, Carnegie Mellon 2005; assoc. prof.) US, Gilded Age and Progressive Era, cultural; jmartinek@njcu.edu
Thurston, Rosemary Fox (PhD, Fordham 1991; assoc. prof. and chair) Europe, medieval, Spain; rthurston2@njcu.edu
White, Timothy R. (PhD, Columbia 2008; assoc. prof.) America, urban; twhite@njcu.edu
Zumoff, Jacob A. (PhD, London 2003; asst. prof.) US, Europe, world; jzumoff@njcu.edu

University of New Mexico

Dept. of History, MSC06 3760, 1 Univ. of New Mexico, Albuquerque, NM 87131-0001. 505.277.2451. Fax 505.277.6023. Email: history@unm.edu. Website: http://history.unm.edu/.

The Department of History at the University of New Mexico is a vibrant community of scholars, teachers, and students located in the center of the American Southwest.

Chair: Melissa Bokovoy
Director of Graduate Studies: Jason Smith
Director of Undergraduate Studies: Fred Gibbs
Degrees Offered: BA,MA,PhD
Academic Year System: Semester
Areas of Specialization: US West, Latin America, Europe, Asia, comparative women and gender

Undergraduate Tuition (per academic year):
In-State: $5418
Out-of-State: $21063

Graduate Tuition (per academic year):
In-State: $5000
Out-of-State: $16883

Enrollment 2018-19:
Undergraduate Majors: 151
Full-time Graduate Students: 30
Part-time Graduate Students: 24
Degrees in History: 57 BA, 3 MA, 3 PhD
Students in Undergraduate Courses: 1232
Students in Undergraduate Intro Courses: 474
Online-Only Courses: 1%

Undergraduate Addresses:
Admissions: http://admissions.unm.edu/
Financial Aid: http://admissions.unm.edu/costs_financial_aid/

Graduate Addresses:
Admissions and Financial Aid: http://grad.unm.edu/

Full-time Faculty

Ball, L. Durwood, Jr. (PhD, New Mexico 1994; assoc. prof.; ed., New Mexico Historical Review) western America; lball@unm.edu

Bieber, Judy (PhD, Johns Hopkins 1995; assoc. prof.) Brazil, Latin America; jbieber@unm.edu

Bokovoy, Melissa K. (PhD, Indiana 1991; prof. and chair) eastern Europe since World War II, 20th-century eastern Europe, world; mbokovoy@unm.edu

Campos, Luis (PhD, Harvard 2006; assoc. prof.) science; luiscampos@unm.edu

Connell Szasz, Margaret (PhD, New Mexico 1972; Regents prof.) American West, Native American; conszasz@unm.edu

Davis-Secord, Sarah C. (PhD, Notre Dame 2007; asst. prof.) Middle Ages; scds@unm.edu

Florvil, Tiffany Nicole (PhD, South Carolina 2013; asst. prof.) 20th-century Europe, women and gender; tflorvil@unm.edu

Garcia y Griego, L. Manuel (PhD, UCLA 1988; assoc. prof.; dir., Southwest Hispanic Research Inst.) 20th-century Mexico, 20th-century US political; mgarciay@unm.edu

Gauderman, Kimberly A. (PhD, UCLA 1998; assoc. prof.) colonial Latin America, Andes; kgaud@unm.edu

Gibbs, Fred (PhD, Wisconsin, Madison 2009; assoc. prof. and undergrad. advisor) digital humanities, medieval medicine; fwgibbs@unm.edu

Graham, Timothy C. (PhD, Cambridge 1999; Regents prof.; dir., Inst. for Medieval Studies) medieval, paleography and manuscript studies; tgraham@unm.edu

Herran Avila, Luis Alberto (PhD, New Sch. for Social Research 2017; asst. prof.) Latin America; lherranavila@unm.edu

Hutchison, Elizabeth Q. (PhD, California, Berkeley 1995; prof.) modern Latin America, Argentina, Chile; ehutch@unm.edu

Hutton, Paul (PhD, Indiana 1980; Dist. Prof.) American West, military; hutton@unm.edu

Jefferson, Robert F. Jr (PhD, Michigan 1995; assoc. prof.; dir., African Studies) African American, 20th-century US; jeffersonr@unm.edu

Monahan, Erika (PhD, Stanford 2007; asst. prof.) Russia, early modern Europe; emonahan@unm.edu

Prior, David Matthew (PhD, South Carolina 2010; asst. prof.) Civil War and Reconstruction, US diplomatic

Ray, Donna E. (PhD, New Mexico 2011; lect. III; Religious Studies) medieval, religion; donnaray@unm.edu

Richardson, Caleb W. (PhD, Stanford 2006; asst. prof.) modern British and Irish cultural; cwr@unm.edu

Ryan, Michael A. (PhD, Minnesota 2005; assoc. prof.) medieval; ryan6@unm.edu

Sanabria, Enrique A. (PhD, California, San Diego 2001; assoc. prof.) modern and early modern Iberia; sanabria@unm.edu

Smith, Jason S. (PhD, California, Berkeley 2001; prof. and dir., grad. studies) 20th-century US; jssmith@unm.edu

Spence, Taylor (PhD, Yale 2012; postdoc. teaching fellow) early America, American West, indigenous; tspence@unm.edu

Steen, Charlie R., III (PhD, UCLA 1970; prof.) early modern Europe, France; csteen@unm.edu

Truett, Samuel (PhD, Yale 1997; assoc. prof.) colonial American Southwest; truett@unm.edu

Withycombe, Shannon (PhD, Wisconsin-Madison 2010; asst. prof.) medicine; swithycombe@unm.edu

Retired/Emeritus Faculty

Berthold, Richard M. (PhD, Cornell 1971; assoc. prof. emeritus) ancient; qqduckus@unm.edu

Etulain, Richard W. (PhD, Oregon 1966; prof. emeritus) America, US West, American West literature; baldbasq@unm.edu

Hall, Linda B. (PhD, Columbia 1976; Dist. and Regents prof. emeritus) modern Mexico, US-Mexico, modern Latin America; lbhall@unm.edu

Himmerich y Valencia, Robert (PhD, UCLA 1984; assoc. prof. emeritus) colonial Latin America

Kessell, John L. (PhD, New Mexico 1969; prof. emeritus) American West, Spanish borderlands; kessell@unm.edu

McClelland, Charles (PhD, Yale 1967; prof. emeritus) modern Germany, European intellectual; cemcc@unm.edu

Porter, Jonathan (PhD, California, Berkeley 1971; prof. emeritus) modern China, East Asia, world; jporter@unm.edu

Pugach, Noel H. (PhD, Wisconsin, Madison 1967; prof. emeritus) US diplomatic; npugach@unm.edu

Reyes, Barbara (PhD, California, San Diego 2000; prof. emeritus) Chicano/a; breyes3@unm.edu

Risso, Patricia (PhD, McGill 1983; prof. emeritus) Middle East, Islamic, South Asia; prisso@unm.edu

Robbins, Richard G., Jr. (PhD, Columbia 1970; prof. emeritus) Russia; rrobbins@unm.edu

Roebuck, Janet (PhD, London 1968; prof. emeritus) England, urban; jroebuck@unm.edu

Scharff, Virginia J. (PhD, Arizona 1987; Dist. prof. emeritus) US social, women; vscharff@unm.edu

Semo, Enrique (PhD, Humboldt, Berlin 1971; prof. emeritus) colonial Latin America, Mexico

Skabelund, Donald E. (PhD, Utah 1956; prof. emeritus) science

Slaughter, Jane (PhD, New Mexico 1972; prof. emeritus) women, modern Europe, sexuality; mjane@unm.edu

Spidle, Jake W., Jr. (PhD, Stanford 1972; assoc. prof. emeritus) medicine, modern Germany; jspidle@unm.edu

Yazawa, Melvin (PhD, Johns Hopkins 1977; prof. emeritus) colonial/revolutionary/early Republic America; yazawa@unm.edu

Recently Awarded PhDs

DePond, Margaret Elena "Beach Babes: Gender and the Beach in American Culture, 1880-1940"

Mandrgoc, Stephen "Educational Policies and Hispanic Education in the Southwest"

McClellan, Guy "State of the Park: Yosemite and California, 1850-1970"

New Mexico State University

Dept. of History, MSC 3H, Las Cruces, NM 88003-8001. 575.646.4601. Email: mcioc@nmsu.edu. Website: http://history.nmsu.edu/.

Alternate Address: 1525 Stewart St., Breland Hall 239, Las Cruces, NM 88003-8001

As part of the College of Arts and Sciences, our department is comprised of 10 full-time faculty, and offers excellent undergraduate and graduate programs in a number of geographic and thematic areas.

Chair: Mark Cioc-Ortega
Director of Graduate Studies: Margaret Malamud
Degrees Offered: BA,MA
Academic Year System: Semester
Areas of Specialization: US, Europe, Latin America, Asia, public
Undergraduate Tuition (per academic year):
   In-State: $6461
   Out-of-State: $21022
Graduate Tuition (per academic year):
   In-State: $5243
   Out-of-State: $16162
Enrollment 2018-19:
   Undergraduate Majors: 112
   New Graduate Students: 22
   Full-time Graduate Students: 22
   Degrees in History: 7 MA
Undergraduate Addresses:
   Admissions: http://admissions.nmsu.edu/
   Financial Aid: http://fa.nmsu.edu/
Graduate Addresses:
   Admissions: http://gradschool.nmsu.edu/
   Financial Aid: http://fa.nmsu.edu/

Full-time Faculty

Bronstein, Jamie L. (PhD, Stanford 1996; prof.) US, 19th-century British social; jbronste@nmsu.edu
Brooks, Nathan M. (PhD, Columbia 1989; assoc. prof.) Russia, Soviet Union, modern science; nbrooks@nmsu.edu
Cioc-Ortega, Mark (PhD, California, Berkeley 1986; prof. and head) US-Mexico borderlands, public, environmental, international relations, Germany, modern Europe; mcioc@nmsu.edu
Garcia-Bryce, Inigo L. (PhD, Stanford 1999; assoc. prof.) Latin America, Peru; igarciab@nmsu.edu
Hammond, Kenneth (PhD, Harvard 1994; prof.) East Asia, China; khammond@nmsu.edu
Horodowich, Liz (PhD, Michigan 2000; assoc. prof.) medieval, modern Europe; lizh@nmsu.edu
Malamud, Margaret I. (PhD, California, Berkeley 1990; prof. and dir., grad. studies) ancient, medieval; mmalamud@nmsu.edu
Orzoff, Andrea (PhD, Stanford 2000; assoc. prof.) 20th century, central and eastern Europe; aorzoff@nmsu.edu
Tollefson, Harold (PhD, California, Santa Barbara 1987; coll. prof.) Western civilization, modern Middle East; hatollef@nmsu.edu

Part-time Faculty

Masson, Elvira (MA, Stanford 1985; coll. asst. prof.) East Asia, Korea; emasson@nmsu.edu
Pitcaithley, Dwight T. (PhD, Texas Tech 1976; coll. prof.) public history and memory, Civil War; dwightp@nmsu.edu

Retired/Emeritus Faculty

Brown, Jeffrey P. (PhD, Illinois, Urbana-Champaign 1979; assoc. prof. emeritus) US, early 19th century, public; jbrown@nmsu.edu
Brown, Jerome F. (PhD, California, Berkeley 1966; assoc. prof. emeritus) Europe, Britain
Eamon, William (PhD, Kansas 1977; prof. emeritus) science and technology, early modern Europe; weamon@nmsu.edu
Harris, Charles H., III (PhD, Texas, Austin 1968; prof. emeritus) Mexico
Hunner, Jon (PhD, New Mexico 1996; prof. emeritus) US, public, 20th-century US West; jhunner@nmsu.edu
Jensen, Joan M. (PhD, UCLA 1962; prof. emeritus) 20th-century US, women; jjensen@nmsu.edu
Matray, James I. (PhD, Virginia 1977; prof. emeritus) US diplomatic, recent US; jmatray@csuchico.edu
Sadler, Louis R. (PhD, South Carolina 1971; assoc. prof. emeritus) 20th-century Mexico; losadler@nmsu.edu
Schneider-Hector, Dietmar (PhD, Texas Tech 1990; coll. prof. emeritus) US West, environmental; dschneid@nmsu.edu

University of New Orleans

Dept. of History, Liberals Arts Bldg., Rm. 135, New Orleans, LA 70148. 504.280.6611. Fax 504.280.6883. Email: rldupont@uno.edu. Website: http://www.uno.edu/academics/colaehd/la/history/.

History has been an integral part of the undergraduate and graduate curriculum at the University of New Orleans since the University was founded.

Chair: Robert L. Dupont
Director of Graduate Studies: Robert L. Dupont
Degrees Offered: BA,MA,PhD (urban studies)
Academic Year System: Semester
Areas of Specialization: US, urban, public, military, international and global studies
Tuition (per academic year):
   In-State: $8800
   Out-of-State: $14000
Enrollment 2018-19:
   Undergraduate Majors: 85
   New Graduate Students: 16
   Full-time Graduate Students: 36
   Part-time Graduate Students: 8
   Degrees in History: 28 BA, 15 MA
Undergraduate Addresses:
   Admissions: http://www.uno.edu/admissions/
   Financial Aid: http://www.uno.edu/admissions/scholarships-awards.aspx
Graduate Addresses:
   Admissions: http://www.uno.edu/grad/
   Financial Aid: http://www.uno.edu/grad/financing-your-education/index.aspx

Full-time Faculty

Atkinson, Connie Zeanah (PhD, Liverpool 1996; assoc. prof.; dir., Midlo Center) local and regional, US cultural, popular music; c.atkinson@uno.edu
Bischof, Guenter J. (PhD, Harvard 1989; Univ. Research and Marshall Plan Prof.; dir., CenterAustria) 20th-century diplomatic and international, Austria, Central Europe; gjbischo@uno.edu

Brown, Nikki Lynn Marie (PhD, Yale 2001; assoc. prof.) 20th-century African American women, 20th-century US, World War I; nlbrown2@uno.edu

Dupont, Robert L. (PhD, Louisiana State 1999; assoc. prof.; chair; and dir., grad. studies) Progressive era, 20th-century America, Louisiana; rldupont@uno.edu

Landry, Marc D., II (PhD, Georgetown 2013; asst. prof.) central Europe, Hapsburg Empire, environmental; mdlandr1@uno.edu

Millett, Allan R. (PhD, Ohio State 1966; Ambrose Prof.; dir., Eisenhower Center for American Studies) American military; amillett@uno.edu

Mitchell, Mary Niall (PhD, NYU 2001; assoc. prof. and Tregle Prof.; Midlo Center Chair) US cultural, slavery/emancipation/Civil War, visual culture; molly.mitchell@uno.edu

Mokhiber, James P. (PhD, Johns Hopkins 2002; assoc. prof.) Africa, colonial, world; jmokhibe@uno.edu

Mosterman, Andrea Catharina (PhD, Boston Univ. 2011; asst. prof.) Atlantic, colonial America, African diaspora; amosterm@uno.edu

Retired/Emeritus Faculty

Altman, Ida (PhD, Johns Hopkins 1981; Research Prof. emeritus) Latin America, Caribbean, Latin American urban; ialtman@uno.edu

Billings, Warren M. (PhD, Northern Illinois 1968; Dist. Prof. emeritus) colonial and revolutionary America; wbilling@uno.edu

Bodet, Gerald P. (PhD, Tulane 1963; prof. emeritus) England; gbodet@uno.edu

Cassimere, Raphael, Jr. (PhD, Lehigh 1971; prof. emeritus) African American, constitutional; rcassime@uno.edu

Clark, Michael D. (PhD, North Carolina, Chapel Hill 1964; prof. emeritus) American intellectual, religious; mdclark1@uno.edu

Mueller, Gordon 'Nick' Herbert (PhD, North Carolina, Chapel Hill 1970; prof. emeritus) European diplomatic, Germany; ghmer@uno.edu

The New School

Committee on Historical Studies, 80 Fifth Ave., 5th Fl., New York, NY 10011-8002. 212.229.5376. Fax 212.229.5929. Email: history@newschool.edu. Website: https://www.newschool.edu/nssr/historical-studies/.

The department offers a BA, MA and dual-degree PhD. The PhD is Historical Studies & Anthropology, Economics, Political Science, or Sociology. This interdisciplinary program is based on the conviction that systematic historical analysis is vital to understanding processes of change; hence, its focus is both comparative and theoretically informed history.

Chair: Oz Frankel
Degrees Offered: BA,MA,PhD
Academic Year System: Semester
Areas of Specialization: history and theory, politics and political violence, capitalism, global and transnational, US and Latin America
Undergraduate Tuition (per academic year): $42000
Graduate Tuition (per academic year): $31590
Enrollment 2018-19:
New Graduate Students: 7
Full-time Graduate Students: 39
Degrees in History: 9 MA, 2 PhD

Addresses:
Admissions: https://www.newschool.edu/lang/admission/
Financial Aid: https://www.newschool.edu/lang/finances/

Affiliated Faculty

Foulkes, Julia (PhD, Massachusetts Amherst 1997; assoc. prof.; Bachelor's Prog., New Sch. for Public Engagement)) urbanization, public sphere, art; foulkesj@newschool.edu

Heathcott, Joseph E. (PhD, Indiana 2002; assoc. prof.; Urban Studies, New Sch. for Public Engagement) US social and cultural, comparative urbanism, architectural; heathcoj@newschool.edu

Potter, Claire Bond (PhD, NYU 1990; prof.; New Sch. for Public Engagement) 20th-century political culture, sex/gender/state; potterc@newschool.edu

Full-time Faculty

Abelson, Elaine S. (PhD, NYU 1986; assoc. prof.; Eugene Lang Coll.) US women and gender, urban; abelson@newschool.edu

Auricchio, Laura (PhD, Columbia 2000; assoc. prof.; chair, Humanities, New Sch. for Public Engagement) art and visual culture, women and gender, French Revolution; auricchl@newschool.edu

Finchelstein, Federico (PhD, Cornell 2006; asst. prof.) history and theory, comparative and transnational fascism, cultural; finchelf@newschool.edu

Frankel, Oz (PhD, California, Berkeley 1998; assoc. prof. and chair) media, print culture, public sphere; frankelo@newschool.edu

Hattam, Victoria C. (PhD, MIT 1987; assoc. prof.; Politics) 19th-century US labor and politics; hattamv@newschool.edu

Ikegami, Eiko (PhD, Harvard 1989; prof.; Sociology) medieval and early modern Japan, political and cultural; ikegame1@newschool.edu

Jakes, Aaron George (PhD, NYU 2015; asst. prof.) modern Middle East and South Asia, historical geography of capitalism, environmental; jakesa@newschool.edu

Ott, Julia (PhD, Yale 2007; asst. prof.) 20th-century America, financial and business, women and gender; ottj@newschool.edu

Park, Emma F. (PhD, Michigan 2017; asst. prof.) modern Africa, science and technology studies, social studies of finance, capitalism, colonialism and empire, economic anthropology; Parke@newschool.edu

Petrzela, Natalia (PhD, Stanford 2009; asst. prof.) 20th-century US, American social politics, self-help cultures; mehlmann@newschool.edu

Plotke, David (PhD, California, Berkeley 1985; assoc. prof.; Politics) 20th-century American political development; plotked@newschool.edu

Stoler, Ann Laura (PhD, Columbia 1982; Willy Brandt Prof.) colonial and postcolonial, empire and exile, Asia; stolera@newschool.edu

Varon, Jeremy P. (PhD, Cornell 1998; assoc. prof.) US, European and American cultural and intellectual, transnational; varonj@newschool.edu

Zaretsky, Eli (PhD, Maryland, Coll. Park 1978; prof.) cultural, family, psychoanalysis; zarete@newschool.edu

Retired/Emeritus Faculty

Zolberg, Vera (PhD, Chicago 1974; prof. emeritus) cultural sociology, sociology of art; zolbergv@newschool.edu

State University of New York, University at Albany

Dept. of History, 1400 Washington Ave., Social Science 145, Albany, NY 12222-0001. 518.442.5300. Fax 518.442.5301. Email: pnold@albany.edu; jenglish2@albany.edu. Website: https:// www.albany.edu/history/.

The Department of History provides students with a thorough grounding in the past, seen from both social scientific and humanistic perspectives, and in the nature of history and historical analysis.

Chair: Nadieszda Kizenko
Director of Graduate Studies: Carl Bon Tempo
Director of Undergraduate Studies: Michitake Aso
Degrees Offered: BA,CAS,MA,PhD
Academic Year System: Semester
Areas of Specialization: culture, gender, international/global/ comparative, social and economic, public policy
Undergraduate Tuition (per academic year):
 In-State: $6870
 Out-of-State: $23710
Graduate Tuition (per academic year):
 In-State: $11090
 Out-of-State: $22650
Enrollment 2018-19:
 Undergraduate Majors: 235
 New Graduate Students: 20
 Full-time Graduate Students: 48
 Part-time Graduate Students: 27
 Degrees in History: 52 BA, 5 MA
Undergraduate Addresses:
 Admissions: http://www.albany.edu/admissions/
 Financial Aid: http://www.albany.edu/studentservices/
Graduate Addresses:
 Admissions: http://www.albany.edu/graduate/graduate-admissions.php
 Financial Aid: http://www.albany.edu/studentservices/

Adjunct Faculty

Ladd, Brian K. (PhD, Yale 1986; adj. research assoc.) ladd@albany.edu

Affiliated Faculty

DeBlasi, Anthony (PhD, Harvard 1996; assoc. prof.; East Asian Studies) Middle Period China, Chinese intellectual, medieval Europe; deblasi@albany.edu

Full-time Faculty

Aso, Michitake (PhD, Wisconsin-Madison 2011; assoc. prof. and dir., undergrad. studies) global environmental, 20th-century Southeast Asia, medicine and health; maso@albany.edu
Bernard, Sheila Curran (MFA, Goddard 2010; assoc. prof.) documentary studies; sbernard@albany.edu
Bon Tempo, Carl (PhD, Virginia 2004; assoc. prof. and dir., grad. studies) 20th-century US political, public policy, immigration; cbontempo@albany.edu
Fogarty, Richard S. (PhD, California, Santa Barbara 2002; assoc. prof.) modern Europe and France, European imperialism, war and society; rfogarty@albany.edu
Francesconi, Federica (PhD, Haifa 2007; asst. prof.; dir., Judaic Studies Prog.) Jewish history and cultures, European social, women and gender studies; ffrancesconi@albany.edu

Graves, Kori A. (PhD, Wisconsin-Madison 2011; asst. prof.) 20th-century US, gender/women/marriage and family/adoption, foreign relations; kgraves@albany.edu
Hamm, Richard F. (PhD, Virginia 1987; prof.) US legal, public policy; rhamm@albany.edu
Hochfelder, David (PhD, Case Western Reserve 1999; assoc. prof.) US technology, public and business, Gilded Age and Progressive Era; dhochfelder@albany.edu
Irwin, Ryan M. (PhD, Ohio State 2010; assoc. prof.) US and world, African and Asian decolonization, 20th-century international
Kane, Maeve E. (PhD, Cornell 2014; asst. prof.) US
Kizenko, Nadieszda (PhD, Columbia 1995; prof. and chair) Russia and Soviet Union, religion, culture; kizenko@albany.edu
Korobeinikov, Dimitri (DPhil, Oxford 2004; assoc. prof.) Byzantine, Turkey; dkorobeynikov@albany.edu
Krosby, H. Peter (PhD, Columbia 1967; prof.) European diplomatic since 1871; krosby@albany.edu
Nold, Patrick (PhD, Oxford 1999; assoc. prof.) medieval, intellectual and cultural, medieval manuscripts; pnold@albany.edu
Pastore, Christopher L. (PhD, New Hampshire 2011; asst. prof.) US, environmental; cpastore@albany.edu
Schwaller, John F. (PhD, Indiana 1978; prof.) Latin America; jschwaller@albany.edu
Smith-Howard, Kendra D. (PhD, Wisconsin, Madison 2007; assoc. prof.) 20th-century US, environmental and agricultural, public policy; ksmithhoward@albany.edu
Zahavi, Gerald (PhD, Syracuse 1983; prof.) 20th-century US business and labor, local and regional, oral and media; gzahavi@albany.edu

Part-time Faculty

Bonafide, John (MA, SUNY, Albany 1998) public; john.bonafide@oprhp.state.ny.us
Campbell, Robin (PhD, SUNY, Albany 2002) public
Groft, Tammis (MA, Cooperstown Grad. Prog. 1979) public; grofttk@albanyinstitute.org
Kozakiewicz, Laurie (PhD, SUNY, Albany 2006; lect.) US, women and gender; lk0550@albany.edu
Leibo, Steven Andrew (PhD, Washington State 1982; lect.) modern Asia; leibos@sage.edu
Palmquist, David (MA, Case Western Reserve 1980) museum/ historical agency management and practice; dpalmqui@mail.nysed.gov
Sorin, Gretchen Sullivan (PhD, SUNY, Albany 2008) public; sorings@oneonta.edu

Retired/Emeritus Faculty

Ballard, Allen B. (PhD, Harvard 1962; prof. emeritus) Afro-American urban, education, public policy; aballard@albany.edu
Barker-Benfield, Graham John (PhD, UCLA 1968; prof. emeritus) US social and cultural, gender; benfield@albany.edu
Berger, Iris (PhD, Wisconsin, Madison 1973; prof. emeritus) Africa, women and gender, labor; iberger@albany.edu
Berger, Ronald M. (PhD, Wisconsin, Madison 1974; prof. emeritus) early modern Britain, imperialism, gender; rberger@albany.edu
Birn, Donald S. (PhD, Columbia 1964; assoc. prof. emeritus) peace research, British foreign policy; dbirn@albany.edu
Dykstra, Robert (PhD, Iowa 1964; prof. emeritus) US political and social, public policy, American West; dykstra39@aol.com
Hahner, June E. (PhD, Cornell 1966; prof. emerita) Brazil, Latin America, women; jhahner@albany.edu
Kendall, Richard H. (PhD, Yale 1964; assoc. prof. emeritus) US diplomatic, US constitutional
Kim, Sung Bok (PhD, Michigan State 1966; prof. emeritus) America to 1800; sbkim@albany.edu

Monfasani, John (PhD, Columbia 1973; prof. emeritus) Renaissance Italy, early modern Europe; monf@albany.edu

Solnick, Bruce B. (PhD, NYU 1960; assoc. prof. emeritus) Latin America, US-Latin American relations; bsol@albany.edu

Steen, Ivan D. (PhD, NYU 1962; assoc. prof. emeritus) US urban and social, public, public policy; oralhis@albany.edu

Wesser, Robert F. (PhD, Rochester 1961; prof. emeritus) 20th-century US political and social, public policy

White, Dan S. (PhD, Harvard 1967; prof. emeritus) modern Germany and Europe, state and society; dwhite@albany.edu

Withington, Ann F. (PhD, Yale 1983; assoc. prof. emeritus) colonial America, 19th- and 20th-century US culture

Wittner, Lawrence S. (PhD, Columbia 1967; prof. emeritus) foreign policy, recent US, peace; wittner@albany.edu

Zacek, Joseph Frederick (PhD, Illinois, Urbana-Champaign 1962; prof. emeritus) central and eastern Europe

Visiting Faculty

Wittern-Keller, Laura (PhD, SUNY, Albany 2003; vis. asst. prof.) US, film; lwittern@albany.edu

Recently Awarded PhDs

Burns, Jennifer "Black Trojans: The Grassroots Abolition Campaign of the Free Black Community in Troy, New York, before 1860"

Herman, Bryan Keith "Russian Culture and Science on the Soviet Screen: Soviet Cinematic Propaganda of the Early Cold War, 1946-53"

Moir, Nathaniel L. "Bernard Fall and Vietnamese Revolutionary Warfare in Indochina"

State University of New York, College at Brockport

Dept. of History, 350 New Campus Dr., Brockport, NY 14420-2956. 585.395.2377. Fax 585.395.2620. Email: amacpher@brockport. edu. Website: https://www.brockport.edu/academics/history/.

Brockport is a selective, nationally recognized and accredited public institution. We are the engaged SUNY campus and one of the most engaged college campuses in the country.

Chair: Anne Macpherson
Director of Graduate Studies: Carl Davila
Degrees Offered: BA,BS,MA
Academic Year System: Semester
Areas of Specialization: early and modern US, world, modern Europe
Undergraduate Tuition (per academic year):
In-State: $6864
Out-of-State: $16656
Graduate Tuition (per academic year):
In-State: $11088
Out-of-State: $22656
Enrollment 2018-19:
Undergraduate Majors: 226
New Graduate Students: 15
Full-time Graduate Students: 11
Part-time Graduate Students: 30
Degrees in History: 54 BA, 9 MA
Undergraduate Addresses:
Admissions: http://www.brockport.edu/admissions/
Financial Aid: http://www.brockport.edu/finaid/

Graduate Addresses:
Admissions: http://www.brockport.edu/graduate/programs/
Financial Aid: http://www.brockport.edu/finaid/

Full-time Faculty

Clark, Katherine Ann (PhD, Indiana 2002; assoc. prof.) medieval, religious, women; kaclark@brockport.edu

Daly, John P. (PhD, Rice 1993; assoc. prof.) US cultural and social, US South; jdaly@brockport.edu

Davila, Carl (PhD, Yale 2006; assoc. prof. and dir., grad. studies) world, Arabic studies; cdavila@brockport.edu

Kramer, Michael J. (PhD, North Carolina, Chapel Hill 2006; asst. prof.) modern US, digital, public; mkramer@brockport.edu

Leslie, W. Bruce (PhD, Johns Hopkins 1971; prof.) US since 1877, social, education; bleslie@brockport.edu

Macpherson, Anne (PhD, Wisconsin, Madison 1998; prof. and chair) Latin America, Caribbean, gender; amacpher@brockport. edu

Malik, Salahuddin (PhD, McGill 1954; prof.) modern India and Pakistan, modern Southeast Asia, Islamic; smalik@brockport. edu

Martin, Morag (PhD, California, Irvine 1999; assoc. prof.) Europe, France, commerce; mmartin@brockport.edu

Moyer, Paul B. (PhD, William and Mary 1999; prof.) colonial/revolutionary/frontier America; pmoyer@brockport.edu

Nishiyama, Takashi (PhD, Ohio State 2005; assoc. prof.) Japan, science and technology, world; tnishiya@brockport.edu

Roman, Meredith (PhD, Michigan State 2005; assoc. prof.) Russia and Soviet Union, world; mroman@brockport.edu

Spiller, James A. (PhD, Wisconsin, Madison 1999; prof.) American cultural, environmental, science and technology; jspiller@brockport.edu

Thompsell, Angela (PhD, Michigan 2009; assoc. prof.) modern Britain and British Africa, modern Africa; athompse@brockport. edu

Torre, Jose R. (PhD, SUNY, Binghamton 2002; assoc. prof.) America, early Republic, social and cultural; jrtorre@brockport.edu

Retired/Emeritus Faculty

Herlan, Ronald W. (PhD, SUNY, Buffalo 1973; assoc. prof. emeritus) world civilization, England, poverty and social welfare

Ireland, Owen S. (PhD, Pittsburgh 1966; Dist. Teaching Prof. emeritus) American Revolution, early Republic, political and women; oireland@brockport.edu

Killigrew, John W. (PhD, Indiana 1960; prof. emeritus) China, Japan, Asian communism

Kutolowski, John F. (PhD, Chicago 1966; prof. emeritus) England, modern warfare, Germany

Kutolowski, Kathleen S. (PhD, Rochester 1973; assoc. prof. emeritus) pre-1877 US, early Republic, New York state; kkutolow@brockport.edu

Lloyd, Jennifer M. (PhD, Rochester 1992; assoc. prof. emeritus) Europe, Britain, women; jlloyd@brockport.edu

O'Brien, Kenneth P. (PhD, Northwestern 1974; assoc. prof. emeritus) modern America, American film, local; kobrien@brockport.edu

Parsons, Lynn H. (PhD, Johns Hopkins 1967; prof. emeritus) early Republic, Civil War and Reconstruction; lparsons@brockport. edu

Strayer, Robert (PhD, Wisconsin 1971; prof. emeritus) world, Africa, Soviet Union; rstrayer@brockport.edu

State University of New York, University at Buffalo

Dept. of History, 546 Park Hall, Buffalo, NY 14260-4130. 716.645.2182. Fax 716.645.5954. Email: ubhistor@buffalo.edu. Website: https://arts-sciences.buffalo.edu/history.html.

We are dedicated to the belief that the critical study of the past is foundational to a sound liberal arts education. Understanding our human past makes us better citizens as it gives us the tools to effectively confront the issues facing the world today.

Chair: Erik R. Seeman
Director of Graduate Studies: Sasha D. Pack
Director of Undergraduate Studies: Camilo Trumper
Degrees Offered: BA, MA, PhD
Academic Year System: Semester
Areas of Specialization: early modern Europe, modern Europe, US, Asia, North and South Atlantic
Undergraduate Tuition (per academic year):
In-State: $6770
Out-of-State: $23270
Graduate Tuition (per academic year):
In-State: $10870
Out-of-State: $22210
Enrollment 2018-19:
Undergraduate Majors: 225
New Graduate Students: 24
Full-time Graduate Students: 54
Part-time Graduate Students: 7
Degrees in History: 69 BA, 10 MA, 5 PhD
Online-Only Courses: 3%
Undergraduate Addresses:
Admissions: http://admissions.buffalo.edu/
Financial Aid: http://financialaid.buffalo.edu/
Graduate Addresses:
Admissions: http://grad.buffalo.edu/admissions.html
Financial Aid: http://financialaid.buffalo.edu/

Full-time Faculty

Bono, James J. (PhD, Harvard 1981; assoc. prof.) science and medicine, Renaissance and early modern Europe; hischaos@buffalo.edu

Cahn, Susan K. (PhD, Minnesota 1990; prof.) 20th-century US, women, sexuality; cahn@buffalo.edu

Daum, Andreas W. (PhD, Munich, Germany 1995; prof.) modern Germany, trans-Atlantic relations, science; adaum@buffalo.edu

Dewald, Jonathan (PhD, California, Berkeley 1974; UB Dist. Prof.) France, early modern Europe; jdewald@buffalo.edu

Emberton, Carole T. (PhD, Northwestern 2006; assoc. prof.) American Civil War and Reconstruction, 19th-century US South; emberton@buffalo.edu

Herzberg, David L. (PhD, Wisconsin, Madison 2005; assoc. prof.) US, pharmaceuticals, popular culture; herzberg@buffalo.edu

Langfur, Hal (PhD, Texas, Austin 1999; assoc. prof.) Brazil, Latin America, Atlantic world; hlangfur@buffalo.edu

Liu, Yan (PhD, Harvard 2015; asst. prof.) premodern China, cultural history of medicine, materiality/body/making and circulation of knowledge

Malka, Adam C. (PhD, Wisconsin-Madison 2012; asst. prof.) US, early Republic, law and politics; adammalk@buffalo.edu

Mbah, Ndubueze Leonard (PhD, Michigan State 2013; asst. prof.) Africa, gender and masculinity, trans-Atlantic exchanges; ndubueze@buffalo.edu

McDevitt, Patrick F. (PhD, Rutgers 1999; assoc. prof.) British Empire, Britain and Ireland; mcdevitt@buffalo.edu

Muller, Dalia A. (PhD, California, Berkeley 2007; assoc. prof.) Latin America, Caribbean, Cuba and Mexico; daliamul@buffalo.edu

Nathan, Mark (PhD, UCLA 2010; asst. prof.) Korea, East Asia, religion; mnathan@buffalo.edu

Pack, Sasha David (PhD, Wisconsin, Madison 2004; assoc. prof. and dir., grad. studies) modern Europe, Spain and Portugal, modern Mediterranean; sdpack@buffalo.edu

Radford, Gail E. (PhD, Columbia 1989; prof.) 20th-century US, political; radford@buffalo.edu

Rembis, Michael A. (PhD, Arizona 2003; asst. prof.; dir., Center for Disability Studies) US, disability, social history of medicine; marembis@buffalo.edu

Schen, Claire S. (PhD, Brandeis 1995; assoc. prof.) early modern England; cschen@buffalo.edu

Seeman, Erik R. (PhD, Michigan 1995; prof. and chair) colonial America; seeman@buffalo.edu

Stapleton, Kristin (PhD, Harvard 1993; prof.) modern and republican China; kstaple@buffalo.edu

Thornton, Tamara Plakins (PhD, Yale 1987; prof.) US cultural and intellectual; thornton@buffalo.edu

Trumper, Camilo (PhD, California, Berkeley 2008; assoc. prof. and dir., undergrad. studies) Latin America, urban; ctrumper@buffalo.edu

Vardi, Liana (PhD, McGill 1985; prof.) France, culture and economics, revolution; vardi@buffalo.edu

Wolcott, Victoria W. (PhD, Michigan 1995; prof.) urban, African American; vwwolcot@buffalo.edu

Retired/Emeritus Faculty

Baker, Norman (PhD, London 1967; assoc. prof. emeritus) 18th- and 19th-century England, 20th-century sport; nbaker@buffalo.edu

Des Forges, Roger V. (PhD, Yale 1971; prof. emeritus) Chinese cultural, political, social; rvd@buffalo.edu

Frisch, Michael H. (PhD, Princeton 1967; prof. emeritus) American social and urban, oral and public, American studies; mfrisch@buffalo.edu

Gerber, David A. (PhD, Princeton 1971; UB Dist. Prof. emeritus) US social, group and personal identities; dagerber@buffalo.edu

Larkin, John A. (PhD, NYU 1966; prof. emeritus) Southeast Asia, US-Asian relations

Naylor, John F. (PhD, Harvard 1964; prof. emeritus) modern Britain; jfnaylor@buffalo.edu

Stinger, Charles L. (PhD, Stanford 1971; prof. emeritus) Renaissance and Reformation; stinger@buffalo.edu

Recently Awarded PhDs

Ding, Xiangli "Transforming Waters: A History of Hydroelectric Power in 20th-Century China"

George, Elisabeth Frances "LGBT Network Formation(s) in the Queen City and Beyond: Articulations of Identity and Community Mobilization in Southwest Missouri"

Marsland, John Charles II "'We'll Help Ourselves': The English Working-Class Struggle to Remake Itself, 1968-85"

Rhodes, Marissa Christman "Body Work: Wet Nurses, and Politics of the Breast in 18th-Century Philadelphia and London"

Schroeder, Joshua "'Building a Godly World': The Efforts to Create a Puritan Atlantic in the Early 17th Century"

Strittmatter, David "In Sites of British History: The Revival, Creation, and Unmaking of a National Narrative"

State University of New York, Buffalo State College

Dept. of History and Social Studies Ed., 1300 Elmwood Ave., Buffalo, NY 14222-1096. 716.878.5412. Fax 716.878.3882. Email: nicholad@buffalostate.edu. Website: https://history. buffalostate.edu/.

Programs in the History and Social Studies Education Department ensure both a knowledge and an understanding of the foundations of human civilization, stimulate thinking about the evolution and interaction of ideas, develop facility with written and verbal expression, increase confidence in articulating ideas, and encourage the critical awareness of self so important to an educated individual.

Chair: Andrew D. Nicholls
Director of Graduate Studies: Andrew D. Nicholls
Degrees Offered: BA,BS,MA,MS
Academic Year System: Semester
Areas of Specialization: US and Canada, Europe, museum studies, Asia, Latin America/Africa/Middle East
Undergraduate Tuition (per academic year):
  In-State: $5570
  Out-of-State: $14820
Graduate Tuition (per academic year):
  In-State: $7020
  Out-of-State: $12510
Enrollment 2018-19:
  Undergraduate Majors: 454
  New Graduate Students: 25
  Full-time Graduate Students: 96
  Degrees in History: 60 BA, 40 BS, 12 MA, 10 MS
Undergraduate Addresses:
  Admissions: http://admissions.buffalostate.edu/
  Financial Aid: http://financialaid.buffalostate.edu/
Graduate Addresses:
  Admissions: http://graduateschool.buffalostate.edu/
  Financial Aid: http://financialaid.buffalostate.edu/

Adjunct Faculty

Mancuso, Charles (MA, SUNY, Buffalo 1982; prof.) music; mancusc@buffalostate.edu
Metz, Donald (BA, SUNY, Buffalo; lect.) museums
Weekly, Nancy (MA, SUNY, Buffalo 1983; lect.) museums

Full-time Faculty

Abromeit, John (PhD, California, Berkeley 2004; assoc. prof.) European intellectual, Germany; abromejd@buffalostate.edu
Carson, David A. (PhD, Texas Christian 1983; Dist. Service Prof.) colonial and early national America, American presidents, westward expansion; carsonda@buffalostate.edu
Chesterton, Bridget M. (PhD, SUNY, Buffalo 2007; prof.) Latin America, Caribbean; chesterbm@buffalostate.edu
Conides, Cynthia (PhD, Columbia 1998; assoc. prof.) museum and archival studies, Aztec/Mayan/Incan empires; conideca@ buffalostate.edu
Ederer, Martin (PhD, SUNY, Buffalo 1993; assoc. prof.) medieval Europe, Renaissance and Reformation; ederermf@buffalostate. edu
Gradwell, Jill M. (PhD, SUNY, Buffalo 2005; prof.) social studies education; gradwejm@buffalostate.edu
Lazich, Michael C. (PhD, SUNY, Buffalo 1997; assoc. prof.) East Asia, Southeast Asia; lazichmc@buffalostate.edu

Mernitz, Kenneth S. (PhD, Missouri, Columbia 1983; assoc. prof.) US, technology, environment; mernitks@buffalostate.edu
Michaels, Albert L. (PhD, Pennsylvania 1966; prof.) Latin America, US foreign policy; michaeal@buffalostate.edu
Mitchell, William I. (PhD, Missouri, Columbia 1991; assoc. prof.) social studies education, Progressive era, 20th-century world; mitchewi@buffalostate.edu
Nicholls, Andrew D. (PhD, Guelph 1997; prof.; chair; and dir., grad. studies) Britain, Canada, World War I; nicholad@buffalostate.edu
Norman, York Allen (PhD, Georgetown 2006; assoc. prof.) Ottoman, Islamic world, early modern eastern Europe; normanya@buffalostate.edu
Orosz, Kenneth J. (PhD, SUNY, Binghamton 2003; prof.) modern Europe, Africa, imperialism; oroszkj@buffalostate.edu
Peraza, Steve (PhD, SUNY, Buffalo 2015; asst. prof.) African American, America, legal; perazas@buffalostate.edu

Part-time Faculty

Black, Scott M. (MA, SUNY, Buffalo State 2004; lect.) America
Blair, George Alexander (PhD, SUNY, Buffalo 1993; lect.) US, US labor; blairga@buffalostate.edu
Blum, Dan (MA, SUNY, Buffalo State 2002; lect.) multidisciplinary studies; blumdm@buffalostate.edu
Dobies, Eric (MS, Canisius 1999; lect.) social studies education; dobiesem@buffalostate.edu
Dunlavey, Reid (MA, SUNY, Buffalo 2006; lect.) America; dunlavrv@ buffalostate.edu
Franczyk, David (MA, Niagara 1999; lect.) modern Europe; franczda@buffalostate.edu
Golombek, Joseph (MA, Marquette 1996; MS, SUNY, Buffalo State 1994; lect.) US, Poland, Western civilization; golombj@ buffalostate.edu
Grennell, Katherine (PhD, SUNY, Buffalo 2016; Ph.D., SUNY, Buffalo 2016; lect.) 20th-century America, American popular music disability studies; grenneke@buffalostate.edu
Henry, Terrence (MA, SUNY, Buffalo State 2005; lect.) America; henrytj@buffalostate.edu
Horton, Scott (MS, SUNY, Buffalo State 1996; lect.) US, technology; hortons@buffalostate.edu
Kotlik, Ronald H. (PhD, SUNY, Buffalo 2005; lect.) American military, US immigration, Atlantic world; kotlikrh@buffalostate. edu
Leacock, Kathryn (MLS, SUNY, Buffalo 2005; lect.) museum studies; leacockh@buffalostate.edu
Lupo, Ann (MS, SUNY, Buffalo State; lect.) social studies education; lupoak@buffalostate.edu
Marcy, William L. IV (PhD, SUNY, Buffalo 2007; lect.) US diplomatic, Latin America; marcywl@buffalostate.edu
Randaccio, Susan Clark (MA, SUNY, Buffalo State 2009; MBA, Cornell 1989; lect.) modern Middle East, development studies, US diplomatic; randacsc@buffalostate.edu
Silverstrim, Karen F., Esq. (JD, Vermont Law School 2003; MA, Central Arkansas 2000; lect.) America, constitutional law, 1960s politics, genocides, environmental, world civilization; silverkf@ buffalostate.edu
Ulrich, David (MEd, Niagara 1977; lect.) America, Canada, urban studies; ulrichdl@buffalostate.edu
Wiedemer, Noelle (MA, SUNY, Buffalo 2014; lect.) photography, digital collections, exhibit design, collections management; wiedemnj@buffalostate.edu

Retired/Emeritus Faculty

Drescher, Nuala M. (PhD, Delaware 1964; Dist. Service Prof. emeritus) US, American thought, labor

Hetzner, Donald R. (EdD, SUNY, Buffalo 1970; prof. emeritus) social studies education

Lang, Henry J. (PhD, Indiana 1966; prof. emeritus) medieval Europe, classical and Byzantine, Poland

Marotta, Gary M. (PhD, NYU 1973; prof. emeritus) US diplomatic, US intellectual, historiography; marottg@buffalostate.edu

McDonnell, James R. (PhD, Wisconsin, Madison 1970; prof. emeritus) US, labor

McFarren, Allen (PhD, Ohio State 1962; prof. emeritus) social studies education

Min, Benjamin (PhD, Massachusetts Amherst 1967; prof. emeritus) Asia

Richardson, Jean (PhD, SUNY, Buffalo 1996; assoc. prof. emeritus) US, Civil War, New York state and local; richarje@buffalostate.edu

Shelton, Brenda (PhD, SUNY, Buffalo 1970; assoc. prof. emeritus) US, women, Progressive Era

Slavenas, Julius P. (PhD, Chicago 1970; prof. emeritus) Europe, Soviet Union, Germany and Baltics

Visiting Faculty

Hauser, Reine (MFA, Columbia 1983; lect.) museums; hauserr@buffalostate.edu

State University of New York, College at Geneseo

Dept. of History, Sturges 16, 1 College Cir., Geneseo, NY 14454-1401. 585.245.5374. Fax 585.245.5161. Email: behrend@geneseo.edu; mckinney@geneseo.edu. Website: https://www.geneseo.edu/history.

At SUNY Geneseo, we've designed a curriculum that reflects important practical and intellectual skills integral to the discipline of History, which are also applicable in a variety of fields.

Chair: Justin Behrend
Degrees Offered: BA
Academic Year System: Semester
Areas of Specialization: US, ancient/medieval/modern Europe, Latin America, Islamic, East Asia
Tuition (per academic year):
In-State: $5870
Out-of-State: $15320
Enrollment 2018-19:
Undergraduate Majors: 280
Degrees in History: 70 BA
Addresses:
Admissions: http://www.geneseo.edu/admissions
Financial Aid: http://www.geneseo.edu/financial_aid

Adjunct Faculty

Brubaker, Jeffrey (PhD, Birmingham 2015; adj. lect.) Byzantine studies; brubaker@geneseo.edu

Full-time Faculty

Adams, Catherine J. (PhD, Illinois, Urbana-Champaign 2004; assoc. prof.) African American, public; adamsc@geneseo.edu

Babovic, Jovana (PhD, Illinois, Urbana-Champaign 2014; asst. prof.) eastern Europe, Balkans, urban, popular culture, animal studies; babovic@geneseo.edu

Behrend, Justin J. (PhD, Northwestern 2006; assoc. prof. and chair) US, African American, US South; behrend@geneseo.edu

Crosby, Emilye J. (PhD, Indiana 1995; prof.) 20th-century US social, African American; crosby@geneseo.edu

Jones, Ryan M. (PhD, Illinois, Urbana-Champaign 2012; asst. prof.) Latin America, gender and women's studies, world/global; jonesr@geneseo.edu

Kleiman, Jordan B. (PhD, Rochester 2000; assoc. prof.) modern American political culture, environmental, technology; kleiman@geneseo.edu

Lewis-Nang'ea, Amanda E. (PhD, Michigan State 2015; Ph.D.; asst. prof.) Africa, science, East African pastoralists and wildlife conservation; lewisam@geneseo.edu

Ma, Ling (PhD, SUNY, Buffalo 2016; asst. prof.) modern China, women, gender, reproduction; mal@geneseo.edu

Mapes, Kathleen Anne (PhD, Illinois, Urbana-Champaign 2000; assoc. prof.) US from 1877, rural; mapes@geneseo.edu

Oberg, Michael L. (PhD, Syracuse 1994; prof.) colonial and revolutionary America, Native American; oberg@geneseo.edu

Seale, Yvonne (PhD, Iowa 2016; asst. prof.) European Middle Ages women/social/religion; seale@geneseo.edu

Joint/Cross Appointments

Cope, Joseph A. (PhD, Penn State 2001; prof. and assoc. provost) early modern Europe; cope@geneseo.edu

Robertson, Stacey M. (PhD, California, Santa Barbara 1994; prof. and provost) 19th-century US; robertsons@geneseo.edu

Part-time Faculty

Mapes, Mary L. (PhD, Michigan State 1998; adj. lect.) women, social welfare

Retired/Emeritus Faculty

Cook, William R. (PhD, Cornell 1971; Dist. Teaching Prof. emeritus) medieval, church, Renaissance and Reformation; cookb@geneseo.edu

Hon, Tze-Ki (PhD, Chicago 1992; prof. emeritus) modern Chinese cultural and political; hon@geneseo.edu

Somerville, James K. (PhD, Case Western Reserve 1965; assoc. prof. emeritus) colonial and revolutionary America, family, psychohistory

Stolee, Margaret K. (PhD, Duke 1982; asst. prof. emeritus) Russia, European social and intellectual; stolee@geneseo.edu

Tamarin, David (PhD, Washington 1977; assoc. prof. emeritus) Latin America, Spain; tamarin@geneseo.edu

Waddy, Helena (PhD, California, San Diego 1984; prof. emeritus) modern Germany, European social and cultural; waddy@geneseo.edu

Williams, James M. (PhD, Yale 1982; assoc. prof. emeritus) ancient Greece and Rome; williams@geneseo.edu

Visiting Faculty

Samuels, Peter S (PhD, Stanford 2014; vis. asst. prof.) modern India; samuels@geneseo.edu

State University of New York, Maritime College

Dept. of Humanities, Fort Schuyler, 6 Pennyfield Ave., Bronx, NY 10465. 718.409.7252. Fax 718.409.2873. Email: kmarkoe@sunymaritime.edu. Website: http://www.sunymaritime.edu/academics/academic-departments/humanities

SUNY Maritime College is one of six state maritime academies in the United States. Located 30 minutes from mid- town Manhattan, Maritime College educates dynamic leaders for the global maritime industry.

Chair: Karen E. Markoe

Director of Graduate Studies: Karen E. Markoe
Degrees Offered: BS,MS
Academic Year System: Semester
Areas of Specialization: US urban and social, maritime, US foreign policy
Tuition (per academic year):
  In-State: $5570
  Out-of-State: $14820
  Merchant Marine Reserve Cadets: $1,700
Addresses:
  Admissions: http://www.sunymaritime.edu/Admissions/
  Financial Aid: http://www.sunymaritime.edu/financialaid

Full-time Faculty

Allen, David B. (MA, Southern Illinois, Edwardsville 1993; asst. prof.) dallen@sunymaritime.edu

Markoe, Karen E. (PhD, Columbia 1971; dist. service prof.; chair; and dir., grad. studies) US urban and social, maritime; kmarkoe@sunymaritime.edu

Meirowitz, Mark John (PhD, Fordham 1989; asst. prof.) foreign policy, legal; mmeirowitz@sunymaritime.edu

Tassinari, Edward J. (PhD, Miami 1982; asst. prof.) US, Latin America; etassinari@sunymaritime.edu

Part-time Faculty

Malloy, Girard J. (MA, SUNY, Coll. Cortland 1993; adj. lect.) gmalloy@sunymaritime.edu

Matthews, Michael (MBA, Fordham 1981)

State University of New York at New Paltz

Dept. of History, 1 Hawk Dr., JFT 916, New Paltz, NY 12561-2440. 845.257.3545. Fax 845.257.2735. Email: morrisoh@newpaltz. edu; teckm@newpaltz.edu. Website: https://www.newpaltz. edu/history/.

We pride ourselves in the care we provide to our pupils both in the classroom and out. While many in the history faculty have received national and regional honors for their work, they are above all teachers and mentors, as evidenced by the recognition accorded to them for their work with students.

Chair: Heather Morrison
Director of Graduate Studies: Kristine Harris
Degrees Offered: BA,BS
Academic Year System: Semester
Areas of Specialization: North America, Europe, Asia, ancient, Latin America
Tuition (per academic year):
  In-State: $6470
  Out-of-State: $16320
Enrollment 2018-19:
  Undergraduate Majors: 279
  Degrees in History: 80 BA, 17 BS
Addresses:
  Admissions: http://www.newpaltz.edu/admissions/
  Financial Aid: http://www.newpaltz.edu/financialaid/

Full-time Faculty

Albi, Christopher (PhD, Texas, Austin 2009; asst. prof.) Latin American economic/legal/political, rule of law in Mexico; albic@newpaltz.edu

Bernstein, Lee (PhD, Minnesota 1997; prof.) 20th-century US, crime and punishment; bernstel@newpaltz.edu

Evans, Andrew D. (PhD, Indiana 2002; assoc. prof.) modern Germany, anthropology, science; evansa@newpaltz.edu

Gatzke, Andrea F. (PhD, Penn State 2013; asst. prof.) ancient Rome, ancient Greece, epigraphy; gatzkea@newpaltz.edu

Harris, Kristine M. (PhD, Columbia 1997; assoc. prof.) East Asia, women, film; harrisk@newpaltz.edu

Morrison, Heather Christine (PhD, Louisiana State 2005; assoc. prof. and chair) Austrian Enlightenment, early modern Europe; morrisoh@newpaltz.edu

O'Sullivan, Meg Devlin (PhD, North Carolina, Chapel Hill 2007; assoc. prof.; Women's, Gender, and Sexuality Studies) Native American, women's studies; osullivm@newpaltz.edu

Roper, Lou (PhD, Rochester 1992; SUNY Dist. Prof.) early modern colonization, early modern Britain, US South; roperl@newpaltz.edu

Scott-Childress, Reynolds J. (PhD, Maryland, Coll. Park 2004; asst. prof.) American culture, media; scottchr@newpaltz.edu

Shimada, Akira (PhD, London 2005; assoc. prof.) ancient India, Asian religions, Indian Ocean world; shimadaa@newpaltz.edu

Stapell, Hamilton Michael (PhD, California, San Diego 2004; assoc. prof.) modern Europe, post-1975 Spain; stapellh@newpaltz.edu

Vargas, Michael (PhD, Fordham 2006; assoc. prof.) medieval, religious orders; vargasm@newpaltz.edu

Part-time Faculty

Strongin, William (OMS, Harvard 1984; lect.; dir., Resnick Center for Jewish Studies) Jewish studies; strongis@newpaltz.edu

Retired/Emeritus Faculty

Hauptman, Laurence M. (PhD, NYU 1972; SUNY Dist. Prof. emeritus) American Indians, Civil War, New York state; hauptmal@newpaltz.edu

Krikun, David (PhD, Wisconsin, Madison 1971; assoc. prof. emeritus) postwar America; krikund@newpaltz.edu

Lewis, Susan Ingalls (PhD, SUNY, Binghamton 2002; prof. emeritus) American women, business, New York state; lewiss@newpaltz.edu

Roper, Donald M. (PhD, Indiana 1963; assoc. prof. emeritus) American constitutional, legal; drop@hvi.net

Sorin, Gerald (PhD, Columbia 1969; prof. emeritus) American Jewish; soring@newpaltz.edu

State University of New York, Oneonta

Dept. of History, 108 Ravine Pkwy., 61 Bacon Hall, Oneonta, NY 13820-4016. 607.436.3326. Fax 607.436.2689. Email: Matthew. Hendley@oneonta.edu; history@oneonta.edu. Website: https:// suny.oneonta.edu/history.

The SUNY Oneonta History Department offers students a rich and diverse learning experience in an intimate setting.

Chair: Matthew Hendley
Degrees Offered: BS
Academic Year System: Semester
Areas of Specialization: North America, Europe, Asia, Latin America
Tuition (per academic year):
  In-State: $8421
  Out-of-State: $18201
Enrollment 2018-19:
  Undergraduate Majors: 101
  Degrees in History: 19 BS

Addresses:
Admissions: http://suny.oneonta.edu/admissions
Financial Aid: http://suny.oneonta.edu/cost-aid

Affiliated Faculty

Ashford, Evan Howard (PhD, Massachusetts Amherst 2018; asst. prof.; Africana & Latino Studies) African American, politics, culture; evan.ashford@oneonta.edu

Full-time Faculty

Ashbaugh, William B. (PhD, Temple 2000; prof.) US foreign relations, Asia, Japan, anime; william.ashbaugh@oneonta.edu

Beal, Thomas D. (PhD, SUNY, Stony Brook 1998; asst. prof.) 19th-century America, urban and economic, New York City; thomas.beal@oneonta.edu

Freeman, Julie D. (PhD, SUNY, Buffalo 1992; asst. prof.) modern Germany, 20th-century Europe, Holocaust; julie.freeman@oneonta.edu

Goodier, Susan (PhD, SUNY, Albany 2007; lect.) New York state, women, suffrage/anti-suffrage; susan.goodier@oneonta.edu

Harder, Mette (PhD, York, UK 2009; assoc. prof.) French Revolution, France, modern Europe; mette.harder@oneonta.edu

Harper, April (PhD, St. Andrews 2003; assoc. prof.) medieval Europe, ancient world, women, sexuality; april.harper@oneonta.edu

Hendley, Matthew C. (PhD, Toronto 1998; prof. and chair) modern Britain and British Empire, Hong Kong, Canada, political culture; matthew.hendley@oneonta.edu

Leon, Miguel Angel (PhD, Columbia 1999; assoc. prof.) colonial and modern Latin America, Peru; miguel.leon@oneonta.edu

Malikov, Yuriy A. (PhD, California, Santa Barbara 2006; assoc. prof.) Russia, Central Asia, Kazakhstan; yuriy.malikov@oneonta.edu

Noorlander, Danny L. (PhD, Georgetown 2011; assoc. prof.) colonial America, Dutch Empire; danny.noorlander@oneonta.edu

Simons, William M. (DA, Carnegie Mellon 1977; prof.) US social and intellectual, ethnic, sports; william.simons@oneonta.edu

Part-time Faculty

Avitabile, Matthew (MA, SUNY, Albany 2010; adj. lect.) Europe, US; matthew.avitabile@oneonta.edu

Duerden, Tim (ABD, Temple 1996; adj. lect.) Europe, public; timothy.duerden@oneonta.edu

Friery, James (MA, SUNY, Albany; adj. lect.) US, Europe; james.friery@oneonta.edu

Ingrassia, Joseph (MA, SUNY, Oneonta; adj. lect.) US; joseph.ingrassia@oneonta.edu

Shea, Matthew (MA, SUNY, Albany; adj. lect.) US, Europe; matthew.shea@oneonta.edu

Traitor, Ann (ABD, SUNY, Albany; MA, Binghamton, SUNY; adj. lect.) Lithuania, Europe; ann.traitor@oneonta.edu

Retired/Emeritus Faculty

O'Mara, Kathleen K. (PhD, Columbia 1986; prof. emeritus) Islam, Africa, women; kathleen.omara@oneonta.edu

State University of New York at Oswego

Dept. of History, 7060 State Rte. 104, 433 Mahar Hall, Oswego, NY 13126. 315.312.2170. Fax 315.341.5444. Email: mary.mccune@oswego.edu. Website: https://www.oswego.edu/history/.

Department courses stress the importance of disciplined methods of inquiry and interpretation, as well as empathy and imagination, and are taught by widely published scholars and other seasoned historians.

Chair: Mary McCune
Degrees Offered: BA
Academic Year System: Semester
Areas of Specialization: Europe, US, world, women, digital humanities
Tuition (per academic year):
In-State: $6870
Out-of-State: $16320
Enrollment 2018-19:
Undergraduate Majors: 120
Degrees in History: 46 BA
Addresses:
Admissions: https://www.oswego.edu/admissions/undergraduate-admissions
Financial Aid: https://www.oswego.edu/financial-aid/

Full-time Faculty

Byrne, Frank J. (PhD, Ohio State 2001; prof.) 19th-century US, US Civil War, antebellum South; frank.byrne@oswego.edu

Haak, Candis L. (PhD, Toronto 2018; asst. prof.) South Asian studies; candis.haak@oswego.edu

Hernandez, Leonardo F. (PhD, Brown 1999; assoc. prof.) Latin America, colonial America; leonardo.hernandez@oswego.edu

Kay, Gwen E. (PhD, Yale 1997; prof.; assoc. dir., Honors Prog.) US social, medicine and science, women; gwen.kay@oswego.edu

Mack, Christopher J. (PhD, Grad. Center, CUNY 1999; assoc. prof.) European intellectual, Germany; christopher.mack@oswego.edu

Marshall, Kenneth E. (PhD, Michigan State 2003; assoc. prof.) 17th- and 18th-century America, African American; kenneth.marshall@oswego.edu

McCune, Mary E. (PhD, Ohio State 2000; assoc. prof. and chair) women, modern US, modern Jewish; mary.mccune@oswego.edu

Pan, Ming-te (PhD, California, Irvine 1994; assoc. prof.) China, Japan; mingte.pan@oswego.edu

Parsons, Gregory S. (PhD, Rochester 2006; asst. prof.) Western civilization, Europe; gregory.parsons@oswego.edu

Usuanlele, Uyilawa (PhD, Queen's, Can. 2010; PhD, Ibadan, Nigeria 2003; assoc. prof.) African environmental, African political economy; uyilawa.usuanlele@oswego.edu

Weyhing, Richard T. (PhD, Chicago 2012; assoc. prof.) early America, Atlantic world; richard.weyhing@oswego.edu

Yasar, Murat (PhD, Toronto 2011; asst. prof.) Middle East; murat.yasar@oswego.edu

Part-time Faculty

Deacon, David W. (PhD, Syracuse 2012; adj. prof.) modern US; david.deacon@oswego.edu

Mann, Holly Marie (MA, SUNY, Oswego 2003; adj. prof.) world; holly.mann@oswego.edu

Oakes, Karen (ABD, Boston Univ.; adj. prof.) American studies, local and regional, women; karen.oakes@oswego.edu

Retired/Emeritus Faculty

Conrad, David (PhD, SOAS, London 1981; prof. emeritus) Africa; bastigi@earthlink.net

Forbes, Geraldine M. (PhD, Illinois, Urbana-Champaign 1972; dist. teaching prof. emerita) India, Middle East, women; geraldine.forbes@oswego.edu

King, David W. (PhD, SUNY, Stony Brook 1979; prof. emeritus) European intellectual, Britain; david.king@oswego.edu

Nicholas, Karen (PhD, Brown 1972; prof. emeritus) medieval and classical Europe; karen.nicholas@oswego.edu

Wellman, Judith M. (PhD, Virginia 1974; prof. emeritus) 19th-century US, local and regional, public; judith.wellman@oswego.edu

Visiting Faculty

Blanchfield, Lyn A. (PhD, SUNY, Binghamton 2004; vis. asst. prof.) medieval Europe, early modern Europe, medieval women; lyn.blanchfield@oswego.edu

Murphy, William B. (PhD, Syracuse 2006; vis. asst. prof.) modern US, Gilded Age and Progressive era America, American politics/constitutional/legal; william.murphy@oswego.edu

State University of New York at Plattsburgh

Dept. of History, Champlain Valley Hall, 101 Broad St., Plattsburgh, NY 12901-2681. 518.564.2213. Fax 518.564.2210. Email: schaefr@plattsburgh.edu. Website: https://www.plattsburgh.edu/academics/schools/arts-sciences/history/.

History majors at SUNY Plattsburgh become part of a community of scholars that attempts to think deeply and critically about the ways history shapes our world.

Chair: Richard Schaefer
Degrees Offered: BA,BS
Academic Year System: Semester
Areas of Specialization: transnational/global, Western hemisphere, gender, migration and borderlands, culture and society
Tuition (per academic year):
  In-State: $7070
  Out-of-State: $16980
Enrollment 2018-19:
  Undergraduate Majors: 130
Addresses:
  Admissions: http://www.plattsburgh.edu/admissions/
  Financial Aid: http://www.plattsburgh.edu/studentlife/studentaccounts/

Full-time Faculty

Alexander, Ryan M. (PhD, Arizona 2011; assoc. prof.) Latin America, modern Mexico, world and comparative; ralex006@plattsburgh.edu

Beaudreau, Sylvie (PhD, York, Can. 1992; assoc. prof.) Canada, Québec, Canadian-American relations; beaudrsm@plattsburgh.edu

Carey, Vincent (PhD, SUNY, Stony Brook 1991; prof.) early modern Europe, Ireland, Tudor England; careyvp@plattsburgh.edu

Gordon, Wendy (PhD, Central Michigan/Strathclyde, UK 1999; prof.) migration, Scotland, comparative women's migration; gordonwm@plattsburgh.edu

Hornibrook, Jeff (PhD, Minnesota 1996; prof.) peasants, East Asia, China; hornibjh@plattsburgh.edu

Kroll, Gary M. (PhD, Oklahoma 2000; prof.) environmental, science; krollgm@plattsburgh.edu

Lindgren, James (PhD, William and Mary 1984; prof.) late 19th- and early 20th-century US, historic preservation and museums, US foreign policy; james.lindgren@plattsburgh.edu

Neuhaus, Jessamyn Anne (PhD, Claremont Grad. 2001; prof.) US popular culture, gender; jessamyn.neuhaus@plattsburgh.edu

Richard, Mark P. (PhD, Duke 2001; prof.) Canada and Québec, migration, modern US; richarmp@plattsburgh.edu

Schaefer, Richard (PhD, Cornell 2005; prof. and chair) religion, modern Europe, modern Germany; schaefr@plattsburgh.edu

Shemo, Connie A. (PhD, SUNY, Binghamton 2002; prof.) women and global, East Asia, medicine; connie.shemo@plattsburgh.edu

Retired/Emeritus Faculty

Rapone, Anita (PhD, NYU 1981; prof. emeritus) 20th-century US, US and Latin American women, Central America; raponeaj@plattsburgh.edu

Voss, Stuart F. (PhD, Harvard 1972; Dist. Service Prof. emeritus) Latin America, family and regionalism, Mexico; vosssf@plattsburgh.edu

State University of New York, College at Potsdam

Dept. of History, 44 Pierrepont Ave., Potsdam, NY 13676-2294. 315.267.2876. Fax 315.267.2550. Email: imais@potsdam.edu. Website: https://www.potsdam.edu/academics/AAS/depts/history.

If you enjoy the study of the past, you've found a home in the history program at SUNY Potsdam.

Chair: Shiho Imai
Degrees Offered: BA
Academic Year System: Semester
Areas of Specialization: Europe, North America, Japan, Africa
Tuition (per academic year):
  In-State: $5570
  Out-of-State: $14820
Enrollment 2018-19:
  Undergraduate Majors: 111
  Degrees in History: 45 BA
Addresses:
  Admissions: http://www.potsdam.edu/admissions/
  Financial Aid: http://www.potsdam.edu/admissions/financial/

Full-time Faculty

Baker, Thomas N. (PhD, North Carolina, Chapel Hill 1995; assoc. prof.) 19th-century US; bakertn@potsdam.edu

Clark, Geoffrey W. (PhD, Princeton 1993; prof.) Europe, cultural and intellectual; clarkgw@potsdam.edu

Fair-Schulz, Axel (PhD, SUNY, Buffalo 2004; assoc. prof.) Germany, modern Europe; fairsca@potsdam.edu

Freed, Libbie J. (PhD, Wisconsin, Madison 2006; assoc. prof.) Africa, science and technology; freedlj@potsdam.edu

Heisey, M. J. (PhD, Syracuse 1998; assoc. prof.) 20th-century America, women, labor; heiseymj@potsdam.edu

Imai, Shiho (PhD, Brown 2005; assoc. prof. and chair) Asia, Asian American; imais@potsdam.edu

McIntyre, Sheila M. (PhD, Boston Univ. 1996; assoc. prof.) early America; mcintysm@potsdam.edu

Smith, Kevin D. (PhD, Wisconsin, Madison 1999; assoc. prof.) 20th-century America, Latin America and Caribbean; smithkd@potsdam.edu

Stannish, Steven M. (PhD, Miami, Ohio 2001; assoc. prof.) ancient; stannism@potsdam.edu

Visiting Faculty

Welch, Gaylynn J. (PhD, SUNY, Binghamton 2009; vis. asst. prof.) US, women and gender; welchgj@potsdam.edu

State University of New York at Stony Brook

Dept. of History, 3rd Fl., Social and Behavioral Sciences Bldg., Stony Brook, NY 11794-4348. 631.632.7500. Fax 631.632.7367. Email: roxanne.fernandez@stonybrook.edu. Website: https:// www.stonybrook.edu/commcms/history/

Study the past. Understand the present. Make your future at Stony Brook.

Chair: Paul Gootenberg
Director of Graduate Studies: Jennifer Anderson
Director of Undergraduate Studies: Donna Rilling
Degrees Offered: BA,MA,MAT,PhD
Academic Year System: Semester
Areas of Specialization: Asia, Europe, Latin America, US, women/ gender/sexuality/reproduction
Undergraduate Tuition (per academic year):
  In-State: $11977
  Out-of-State: $27057
Graduate Tuition (per academic year):
  In-State: $15544
  Out-of-State: $26884
Enrollment 2018-19:
  Undergraduate Majors: 464
  New Graduate Students: 7
  Full-time Graduate Students: 80
  Part-time Graduate Students: 1
  Degrees in History: 113 BA, 5 MA, 11 PhD
Undergraduate Addresses:
  Admissions: http://www.stonybrook.edu/ugadmissions/
  Financial Aid: http://www.stonybrook.edu/finaid/
Graduate Addresses:
  Admissions: https://www.grad.stonybrook.edu/
  Financial Aid: http://www.stonybrook.edu/finaid/

Affiliated Faculty

Schaefer, Wolf (PhD, Bremen, Germany 1983; prof.; Technology and Society, Coll. of Engineering) science, European social and intellectual; wolf.schafer@stonybrook.edu

Full-time Faculty

Anderson, Jennifer L. (PhD, New York Univ. 2007; assoc. prof. and dir., grad. studies) early America and Atlantic; Jennifer.L.Anderson@stonybrook.edu

Backfish, Charles G. (MA, NYU 1969; lect.) social studies education; charles.backfish@stonybrook.edu

Ballan, Mohamad (PhD, Chicago 2019; asst. prof.) medieval

Barnhart, Michael A. (PhD, Harvard 1980; prof.) US foreign relations; michael.barnhart@stonybrook.edu

Beverley, Eric L. (PhD, Harvard 2007; assoc. prof.) South Asia, comparative colonialism; eric.beverley@stonybrook.edu

Chase, Robert T. (PhD, Maryland, Coll. Park 2009; asst. prof.) US, 20th century and race; robert.chase@stonybrook.edu

Cooper, Alix (PhD, Harvard 1998; assoc. prof.) early modern Europe, science and environment; mary.cooper@stonybrook.edu

Farmer, Jared (PhD, Stanford 2005; assoc. prof.) US environmental, western US cultural; jared.farmer@stonybrook.edu

Flores, Lori A. (PhD, Stanford 2011; assoc. prof.) 20th-century US, Mexican American, race/ethnicity/labor; lori.flores@stonybrook.edu

Frohman, Lawrence S. (PhD, California, Berkeley 1992; assoc. prof.) European intellectual, social studies education; lawrence.frohman@stonybrook.edu

Gootenberg, Paul E. (PhD, Chicago 1985; prof. and chair) colonial and modern Latin America, Andes, comparative economic; paul.gootenberg@stonybrook.edu

Hinely, Susan D. (PhD, Stanford 1987; lect.) modern Europe, political theory; susan.hinely@stonybrook.edu

Hong, Young-Sun (PhD, Michigan 1989; prof.) modern Germany; young-sun.hong@stonybrook.edu

Landsman, Ned C. (PhD, Pennsylvania 1979; prof.) early America and Atlantic; ned.landsman@stonybrook.edu

Larson, Brooke (PhD, Columbia 1978; prof.) Latin America, social, mining and agrarian change; brooke.larson@stonybrook.edu

Lim, Shirley (PhD, UCLA 1998; assoc. prof.) US race/ethnicity/ women, Asian American, cultural; shirley.lim@stonybrook.edu

Lipton, Sara G. (PhD, Yale 1991; prof.) medieval Europe, Jewish, women; sara.lipton@stonybrook.edu

Man-Cheong, Iona D. (PhD, Yale 1991; assoc. prof.) modern China, Japan; Iona.Man-Cheong@stonybrook.edu

Marker, Gary J. (PhD, California, Berkeley 1977; prof.) Russia, European social; gary.marker@stonybrook.edu

Masten, April F. (PhD, Rutgers 1999; assoc. prof.) 19th-century US, social, art and women; april.masten@stonybrook.edu

Mimura, Janis A. (PhD, California, Berkeley 2002; asst. prof.) modern Japan; janis.mimura@stonybrook.edu

Newman, Elizabeth Terese (PhD, Yale 2008; assoc. prof.) archaeology, ethnohistory, zooarchaeology; elizabeth.newman@stonybrook.edu

Rilling, Donna J. (PhD, Pennsylvania 1993; assoc. prof. and dir., undergrad. studies) US urban/labor/business, early national period; donna.rilling@stonybrook.edu

Sellers, Chris (PhD, Yale 1992; prof.) America, environmental, science and medicine; christopher.sellers@stonybrook.edu

Shankar, Shobana (PhD, UCLA 2003; assoc. prof.) West Africa, comparative Islamic East Africa, South Asia; shobana.shankar@stonybrook.edu

Teplitsky, Joshua (PhD, NYU 2012; asst. prof.) early modern Europe 1500-1750, German principalities 1500-1750, diaspora studies; joshua.teplitsky@stonybrook.edu

Tomes, Nancy J. (PhD, Pennsylvania 1978; prof.) US social, women; nancy.tomes@stonybrook.edu

Wilson, Kathleen (PhD, Yale 1985; prof.) modern Britain, 18th- and 19th-century cultural and social; kathleen.wilson@stonybrook.edu

Zimansky, Paul (PhD, Chicago 1980; prof.) Near Eastern languages and civilizations, history and archaeology; paul.zimansky@stonybrook.edu

Joint/Cross Appointments

Owens, Leslie (PhD, California, Riverside 1972; assoc. prof.; Africana Studies) antebellum US, black; leslie.owens@stonybrook.edu

Sanderson, Warren (PhD, Stanford 1974; prof.; Economics) economic, economic demography; warren.sanderson@stonybrook.edu

Retired/Emeritus Faculty

Bottigheimer, Karl S. (PhD, California, Berkeley 1965; prof. emeritus) early modern Europe, Britain and Ireland; Karl.Bottigheimer@stonybrook.edu

Cowan, Ruth S. (PhD, Johns Hopkins 1969; prof. emeritus) science, women; Ruth.Cowan@stonybrook.edu

Garber, Elizabeth (PhD, Case Inst. Tech. 1966; prof. emeritus) science, European social and intellectual; Elizabeth.Garber@stonybrook.edu

Goldenberg, Robert (PhD, Brown 1974; prof. emeritus) religions, Judaism; Robert.Goldenberg@stonybrook.edu

Kuisel, Richard F. (PhD, California, Berkeley 1963; prof. emeritus) modern Europe; Richard.Kuisel@stonybrook.edu

Lebovics, Herman (PhD, Yale 1966; prof. emeritus) European social and intellectual; herman.lebovics@stonybrook.edu

Lemay, Helen R. (PhD, Columbia 1972; prof. emeritus) medieval, Renaissance and Reformation; Helen.Lemay@stonybrook.edu

Miller, Wilbur R., Jr. (PhD, Columbia 1973; prof. emeritus) US social, police, Civil War and Reconstruction; wilbur.miller@stonybrook.edu

Rosenthal, Joel T. (PhD, Chicago 1963; prof. emeritus) medieval, social science; joel.rosenthal@stonybrook.edu

Roxborough, Ian (PhD, Wisconsin, Madison 1977; prof. emeritus; Sociology) sociology of war, Latin American social, modern Mexico; ian.roxborough@stonybrook.edu

Williams, John A. (PhD, Wisconsin, Madison 1963; assoc. prof. emeritus) British Empire, Africa, Commonwealth; John.Williams@stonybrook.edu

Wishnia, Judith (PhD, SUNY, Stony Brook 1978; assoc. prof. emeritus) France; Judith.Wishnia@stonybrook.edu

Recently Awarded PhDs

Black, Ashley L "The Politics of Asylum: Stability, Sovereignty, and Mexican Foreign Policy in the Caribbean Basin, 1945-59"

Conrad, Michael "Concrete Aggregate and the Building of the New York Metropolis, 1919-76"

Ehrinpreis, Andrew Bernard "Coca Nation: The Protean Politics of the Coca Leaf in Bolivia, 1900-88"

Gebhart, Brian "Ostforschung and Empire: Race, History, and Imperialism in the Kaiserreich, 1900-18"

Jones, Kelly Hacker "Needles, Herbs, and Qi: Chinese Medicine in the United States Post-World War II"

Mukherjee, Erica "The Real and Imagined Environments of the Colonial Indian Railway"

Pinto-Handler, Sergio Estuardo "The Last Emancipation: Rio de Janeiro and the Atlantic History of Slavery and Abolition, 1880-1900"

Yee, David James "Divided Landscapes in the Mexican Metropolis: Housing and Segregation in Mexico City, 1940-76"

New York University

Dept. of History, 53 Washington Sq. S., Floor 4E, New York, NY 10012-1018. 212.995.8600. Fax 212.995.4017. Email: history.dept@nyu.edu. Website: http://as.nyu.edu/history.html.

The Department of History at New York University has long been home to some of the most innovative and original scholarship in higher education. The community of students, faculty and staff in the history department is bound together in the pursuit of educational excellence and ground-breaking research.

Chair: Edward Berenson
Director of Graduate Studies: Andrew Needham
Director of Undergraduate Studies: John Shovlin
Degrees Offered: BA,BA/MA,MA,MA/PhD,MA/JD,PhD,PhD/JD,Adv. Cert.
Academic Year System: Semester
Areas of Specialization: Africa and African diaspora, East and South Asia, Europe and Atlantic world, US, Latin America and Caribbean

Undergraduate Tuition (per academic year): $47750
Graduate Tuition (per academic year): $38592
Enrollment 2018-19:
  Undergraduate Majors: 314
  New Graduate Students: 46
  Full-time Graduate Students: 157
  Degrees in History: 110 BA, 18 MA, 11 PhD
Undergraduate Addresses:
  Admissions: http://www.nyu.edu/admissions/undergraduate-admissions.html
  Financial Aid: http://www.nyu.edu/admissions/financial-aid-and-scholarships.html
Graduate Addresses:
  Admissions: http://www.nyu.edu/admissions/graduate-admissions.html
  Financial Aid: http://www.nyu.edu/admissions/financial-aid-and-scholarships.html

Affiliated Faculty

Abercrombie, Thomas A. (PhD, Chicago 1986; assoc. prof.; Anthropology) anthropology of history, colonial Andes, Spain; thomas.abercrombie@nyu.edu

Brathwaite, Kamau (PhD, Sussex 1968; prof.; Comparative Literature) Caribbean literature/culture/society, comparative literature; kb5@nyu.edu

Chazan, Robert (PhD, Columbia 1967; prof.; Hebrew and Judaic Studies) medieval Jewish, medieval polemics; rc2@nyu.edu

el-Leithy, Tamer M. (PhD, Princeton 2005; asst. prof.; Kevorkian Center) medieval Middle East and Mediterranean, Islamic law and society, religious differences; tel3@nyu.edu

Engel, David (PhD, UCLA 1979; Maurice R. and Corinne P. Greenberg Prof.; Hebrew and Judaic Studies) Jews in eastern Europe, Holocaust, Zionism and Israel; de2@nyu.edu

Fischer, Sibylle Maria (PhD, Columbia 1995; assoc. prof.; Spanish and Portuguese, Comparative Literature) Caribbean literature and culture, Spanish American independence, Haitian Revolution; sibylle.fischer@nyu.edu

Hulsebosch, Daniel (PhD, Harvard 1999; prof.; Sch. of Law) American and English legal; daniel.hulsebosch@nyu.edu

Kafka, Ben (PhD, Stanford 2004; assoc. prof.; Media, Culture, and Communication) cultural; kafka@nyu.edu

Kaplan, Marion (PhD, Columbia 1977; Skirball Prof.; Hebrew and Judaic Studies) modern Jewish, German-Jewish; marion.kaplan@nyu.edu

Klimke, Martin A. (PhD, Heidelberg 2005; assoc. prof.; NYU Abu Dhabi) US and world, US foreign affairs and transatlantic relations, Cold War; klimke@nyu.edu

Kowalzig, Barbara (DPhil, St. John's Coll., Oxford 2002; assoc. prof.; Classics) ancient Greece and Rome, sociology of music and performance; barbara.kowalzig@nyu.edu

Lerner, Barron H. (PhD, Washington 1996; prof.; Sch. of Medicine) medical ethics, medicine; barron.lerner@nyumc.org

Lockman, Zachary (PhD, Harvard 1983; prof.; Middle Eastern Studies) modern Middle East; zachary.lockman@nyu.edu

Monson, Andrew P. (PhD, Stanford 2008; assoc. prof.; Classics) Greek relations with Near East, Hellenistic kingdoms, eastern Roman Empire; andrew.monson@nyu.edu

Nelson, William E. (PhD, Harvard 1971; Judge Edward Weinfeld Prof.; Sch. of Law) colonial American legal, New York legal; william.nelson@nyu.edu

Peachin, Michael (PhD, Columbia 1983; prof.; Classics) Roman law and society; mp8@nyu.edu

Phillips-Fein, Kim (PhD, Columbia 2005; assoc. prof.; Gallatin Sch. of Individualized Study) American political, American business, American labor; kpf2@nyu.edu

Robin, Ron Theodore (PhD, California, Berkeley 1986; prof.; Social and Cultural Hist.) US; ron.robin@nyu.edu

Romig, Andrew J. (PhD, Brown 2008; asst. prof.; Gallatin Sch. of Individualized Study) medieval, Carolingian history and culture, emotion/kindness/masculinity; romig@nyu.edu

Soffer, Jonathan M. (PhD, Columbia 1992; JD, Denver 1982; prof.; chair, Technology, Culture and Society) 20th-century American political and urban; jonathan.soffer@nyu.edu

Swislocki, Mark S. (PhD, Stanford 2002; assoc. prof.; NYU Abu Dhabi) Chinese cultural, Chinese environmental, Chinese minority peoples; mark.swislocki@nyu.edu

Zhang, Zhen (PhD, Chicago; assoc. prof.; Cinema Studies) film, early cinema, Chinese-language cinemas; zz6@nyu.edu

Full-time Faculty

Appuhn, Karl R. (PhD, Northwestern 1999; assoc. prof.) early modern Europe, environmental, science/technology/medicine; appuhn@nyu.edu

Aune, Stefan (PhD, Michigan 2019; asst. prof./faculty fellow)

Baltacioglu-Brammer, Ayse (PhD, Ohio State 2016; asst. prof.; Middle Eastern and Islamic Studies) early modern Middle East, Ottoman Empire, Iran, Sunni-Shiite divide, sects and sectarianism, empire and identity formation; abb12@nyu.edu

Bedos-Rezak, Brigitte Miriam (PhD, École nationale des chartes, Paris 1977; prof.) medieval Europe; bbr2@nyu.edu

Burbank, Jane R. (PhD, Harvard 1981; prof.) modern Europe, Russia, empire; jane.burbank@nyu.edu

Cooper, Frederick (PhD, Yale 1974; prof.) Africa, empires, colonization and decolonization; fred.cooper@nyu.edu

d'Avignon, Robyn (PhD, Michigan 2015; asst. prof.) Africa, economic, anthropology

Ellis, Elizabeth N. (PhD, North Carolina, Chapel Hill 2015; asst. prof.) early America, Native American; ene1@nyu.edu

Eustace, Nicole E. (PhD, Pennsylvania 2001; prof.) 18th-century America, gender, culture and politics; nicole.eustace@nyu.edu

Ferrer, Ada (PhD, Michigan 1995; prof.) Latin America, Caribbean, Cuba; af6@nyu.edu

Geroulanos, Stefanos N. (PhD, Johns Hopkins 2007; prof.) modern European intellectual, 20th-century French and German thought, ethics; sg127@nyu.edu

Goetz, Rebecca A. (PhD, Harvard 2006; assoc. prof.) Atlantic world, religion, race and slavery; rag11@nyu.edu

Gomez, Michael A. (PhD, Chicago 1985; prof.) West Africa, African diaspora, Islam; michael.gomez@nyu.edu

Gordon, Linda (PhD, Yale 1970; Florence Kelley Prof.) 20th-century US social/political/social policy, women and gender, family; linda.gordon@nyu.edu

Goswami, Manu (PhD, Chicago 1998; assoc. prof.) modern South Asia, 19th- and 20th-century India, economic thought; manu.goswami@nyu.edu

Grandin, Greg (PhD, Yale 1999; prof.) modern Latin America; grandin@nyu.edu

Hahn, Steven H. (PhD, Yale 1979; prof.) 19th-century US, slavery and emancipation, capitalism; steven.hahn@nyu.edu

Hasegawa, Masato (PhD, Yale 2013; asst. prof.) East Asia, early modern and modern China, early modern and modern Korea; masato.hasegawa@nyu.edu

Hodes, Martha (PhD, Princeton 1991; prof.) 19th-century US, Civil War and Reconstruction, gender and sexuality; martha.hodes@nyu.edu

Homans, Jennifer (PhD, NYU 2008; Dist. Scholar in Residence) dance; jah20@nyu.edu

Ibarguen, Irvin (PhD, Harvard 2018; asst. prof.) Latino/a, migration/immigration in Americas, transnational histories; ibarguen@nyu.edu

Jütte, Daniel (PhD, Heidelberg 2010; assoc. prof.) cultural, urban, knowledge, Jewish, Germany, material culture and everyday life; daniel.juette@nyu.edu

Kim, Monica (PhD, Michigan 2011; asst. prof.) US, decolonization, transpacific Asia and Asian American; monica.kim@nyu.edu

Kotsonis, Yanni (PhD, Columbia 1994; assoc. prof.) 20th-century Russia, modern Europe, political economy; yanni.kotsonis@nyu.edu

Linkhoeva, Tatiana (PhD, California, Berkeley 2015; asst. prof.) modern Japan, intellectual, Left and Right radicalism, transnational, Soviet-Japanese-Mongolian relations; tatiana.linkhoeva@nyu.edu

Ludden, David E. (PhD, Pennsylvania 1978; prof.) South Asia, Middle East, East Asia, world, globalization, agrarian, economic development; del5@nyu.edu

Mitchell, Michele (PhD, Northwestern 1998; assoc. prof.) US and African American, African diaspora, women; michele.mitchell@nyu.edu

Montoya, Maria E. (PhD, Yale 1993; assoc. prof.) American West, labor, Latina/o; maria.montoya@nyu.edu

Needham, Andrew (PhD, Michigan 2006; assoc. prof. and dir., grad studies) US, urban and suburban, American West; andrew.needham@nyu.edu

O'Donnell, Anne (PhD, Princeton 2014; asst. prof.) Russia and Soviet Union, Soviet political

Ortolano, Guy (PhD, Northwestern 2005; assoc. prof.) modern Britain, science and technology, cultural and intellectual; ortolano@nyu.edu

Oshinsky, David M. (PhD, Brandeis 1971; prof.) medicine and public health; oshind01@nyu.edu

Pettigrew, Erin (PhD, Stanford 2014; asst. prof.) 19th- and 20th-century West Africa, histories of Islam; erin.pettigrew@nyu.edu

Romney, Susanah Shaw (PhD, Cornell 2000; asst. prof.) Atlantic, women and gender, early modern Dutch Empire, Native American and indigenous; ssr8@nyu.edu

Sammons, Jeffrey T. (PhD, North Carolina, Chapel Hill 1982; prof.) US social and cultural, African American, film and sports; jeffrey.sammons@nyu.edu

Sartori, Andrew S. (PhD, Chicago 2003; prof.) modern South Asia, British Empire, intellectual, economic thought, capitalism, social theory; asartori@nyu.edu

Schmidt, Benjamin MacDonald (PhD, Princeton 2013; clinical assoc. prof.; dir., Digital Humanities) data visualization, machine learning,

Shovlin, John (PhD, Chicago 1998; assoc. prof. and dir., undergrad. studies) ancien régime European/French political and cultural, French Revolution, political economy, aristocratic culture and politics, 18th-century European international politics and international political thought; john.shovlin@nyu.edu

Smyrlis, Konstantinos (PhD, Paris I 2002; assoc. prof.) Byzantine Empire, economic, emperor and subjects; ks113@nyu.edu

Thomson, Sinclair S. (PhD, Wisconsin, Madison 1996; assoc. prof.) colonial Latin America, Andean region, peasant and Indian politics; st19@nyu.edu

Velasco, Alejandro (PhD, Duke 2009; assoc. prof.) social movements, urban culture, democratization; av48@nyu.edu

Waley-Cohen, Joanna (PhD, Yale 1987; prof.) early modern China, China and West, Chinese imperial culture; jw5@nyu.edu

Wang, Yijun (PhD, Columbia 2019; asst. prof.)

Weinstein, Barbara (PhD, Yale 1980; prof.) modern Latin America, Brazil, labor; bw52@nyu.edu

Wolff, Larry (PhD, Stanford 1984; prof.) eastern Europe, Habsburg monarchy, Enlightenment; lw59@nyu.edu

Wosh, Peter J. (PhD, NYU 1988; clinical assoc. prof.; dir., Archives/Public Hist. Prog.) archival managment, public, American Christianity; pw1@nyu.edu

Joint/Cross Appointments

Ben-Ghiat, Ruth (PhD, Brandeis 1991; prof.; Italian) modern Italian history and culture; ruth.benghiat@nyu.edu

Benite, Zvi Ben-Dor (PhD, UCLA 2000; prof.; Middle Eastern and Islamic Studies) East Asia, religion and world, Middle East; zvi@nyu.edu

Berenson, Edward G. (PhD, Rochester 1981; prof. and chair; dir., Inst. of French Studies) modern Europe, colonialism; edward.berenson@nyu.edu

Chapman, Herrick E. (PhD, California, Berkeley 1983; prof.; Inst. French Studies) modern Europe, France, economic; hc3@nyu.edu

Diner, Hasia R. (PhD, Illinois, Urbana-Champaign 1976; Steinberg Chair; Hebrew and Judaic Studies) American Jewish, American immigrant; hasia.diner@nyu.edu

Fleming, Katherine E. (PhD, California, Berkeley 1995; Alexander S. Onassis Prof.; Hellenic Studies) modern Europe, Greece, nationalism; katherine.fleming@nyu.edu

Gross, Stephen Gerard (PhD, California, Berkeley 2010; asst. prof.; European Studies) modern Europe, 19th- and 20th-century Germany, 20th-century Europe and European unification; sg152@nyu.edu

Jackson, Myles W. (PhD, Cambridge 1991; prof.; Div. of Medical Ethics) science, intellectual property and gene patenting, humans/machines/aesthetic theories; myles.jackson@nyu.edu

Karl, Rebecca E. (PhD, Duke 1995; assoc. prof.; East Asian Studies) modern China, intellectual, nationalism in Asia; rebecca.karl@nyu.edu

Kenny, Kevin (PhD, Columbia 1994; prof.; dir., Glucksman Ireland House) Irish emigration, US immigration, 19th-century US, global migration; kevin.kenny@nyu.edu

Livingston, Julie (PhD, Emory 2001; prof.; Social and Cultural Analysis) body, southern Africa, interspecies, gender, ethnography, development; jl6877@nyu.edu

Morgan, Jennifer L. (PhD, Duke 1996; prof.; Social and Cultural Analysis) early African American, comparative slavery, racial ideology; jennifer.morgan@nyu.edu

Naftali, Timothy James (PhD, Harvard 1993; clinical assoc. prof.; NYU Wagner) international affairs; timothy.naftali@nyu.edu

Peck, James (PhD, NYU 1996; adj. asst. prof.; East Asian Studies) Asia; jlp7923@nyu.edu

Pimentel, Jose Ernesto, Jr. (PhD, São Paulo 2002; vis. scholar)

Revel, Jacques (PhD, Sorbonne; Global Dist. Prof.; Inst. French Studies) early and modern European social and cultural, historiography; jr77@nyu.edu

Sennett, Richard (PhD, Harvard 1969; prof.; Sociology) urban sociology, body, art and music; richard.sennett@nyu.edu

Singh, Nikhil Pal (PhD, Yale 1995; prof.; Social and Cultural Analysis) 20th-century US race/empire/culture, black radicalism and US liberalism, US foreign policy; nikhil.singh@nyu.edu

Sugrue, Thomas J. (PhD, Harvard 1992; prof.; Social and Cultural Analysis) late 20th-century US race and politics, cities and suburbs/real estate in America, public policy and civil rights; tjs7@nyu.edu

Tchen, John Kuo Wei (PhD, NYU 1992; assoc. prof.; Social and Cultural Analysis and dir., Asian/Pacific/American Studies) interethnic and interracial relations of Asian and Americans, New York City, cross-cultural and community studies

Truxes, Thomas M. (PhD, Trinity Coll., Dublin 1985; clinical assoc. prof.; Irish Studies) early modern Ireland, Ireland and Atlantic world before 1800, early modern maritime; thomas.truxes@nyu.edu

Weimer, Lawrence D. (MA, NYU 2005; adj. asst. prof.; Archives and Public Hist. Prog.) lweimer@nyu.edu

Zimmerman, Jonathan L. (PhD, Johns Hopkins 1993; prof.; Sch. of Education) education; jlzimm@aol.com

Nondepartmental Historians

Bacopoulos-Viau, Alexandra (PhD, Cambridge 2013) modern European studies

Hajo, Cathy Moran (PhD, NYU 2006; adj. asst. prof.; Archives and Public Hist. Prog.) documentary editing, women, digital; cathy.hajo@nyu.edu

Katz, Esther (PhD, NYU 1980; assoc. prof.; dir./ed., Margaret Sanger Papers Project) US, historical editing; esther.katz@nyu.edu

Lee, Andrew H. (PhD, NYU 2012; assoc. curator) Spain 1917-41, Scottsboro case; andrew.lee@nyu.edu

Noonan, Ellen (adj. asst. prof.; Archives and Public Hist. Prog.) history education, digital media, public; men2022@nyu.edu

Voorhees, David William (PhD, New York Univ. 1988; research scholar; Jacob Leisler Papers Project) Anglo-Dutch New York and New Jersey; dwv1@nyu.edu

Retired/Emeritus Faculty

Baker, Paul (PhD, Harvard 1960; prof. emeritus) American intellectual, architecture, biography; prbaker2@aol.com

Bender, Thomas (PhD, California, Davis 1971; prof. emeritus) US, intellectuals and cities; tb1@nyu.edu

Bonomi, Patricia U. (PhD, Columbia 1970; prof. emerita) colonial America, American Revolution; pub1@nyu.edu

Harootunian, Harry D. (PhD, Michigan 1957; prof. emeritus) modern Japan; hh3@nyu.edu

Hull, Richard W. (PhD, Columbia 1968; prof. emeritus) Africa, democratization in Africa; richard.hull@nyu.edu

Johnson, Penelope D. (PhD, Yale 1979; prof. emerita) medieval, women; pdj1@nyu.edu

Kupperman, Karen Ordahl (PhD, Cambridge 1978; Silver Prof. emeritus) early modern Atlantic, American Indian; karen.kupperman@nyu.edu

Lee, John Joseph (MA, Univ. Coll., Dublin 1965; Glucksman Prof. emeritus) 19th- and 20th-century Ireland, Irish American; joe.lee@nyu.edu

Levy, Darline G. (PhD, Harvard 1968; prof. emerita) intellectual and cultural, early modern Europe, Enlightenment; darline.levy@nyu.edu

Lewis, David Levering (PhD, London Sch. of Economics 1963; Julius Silver Univ. Prof. emeritus) Africa, literature of racism, Europe in Africa and Africa in Europe; dll7@nyu.edu

Mattingly, Paul H. (PhD, Wisconsin, Madison 1968; prof. emeritus) suburbanization and urbanization, education; phm2@nyu.edu

Nolan, Mary (PhD, Columbia 1975; prof. emeritus) 20th-century Europe and America, modern Germany, European women; mn4@nyu.edu

Peirce, Leslie (PhD, Princeton 1988; prof. emeritus) early modern Ottoman, gender, comparative empires; lp50@nyu.edu

Prince, Carl E. (PhD, Rutgers 1963; prof. emeritus) American Revolution, early national America; cp2@nyu.edu

Reimers, David (PhD, Wisconsin, Madison 1961; prof. emeritus) immigration, American social and ethnic, recent America; dr5@nyu.edu

Sanchez-Albornoz, Nicolas (prof. emeritus) Spain and Latin America

Scally, Robert J. (PhD, Princeton 1967; prof. emeritus) Irish studies, modern Europe, English social; robert.scally@nyu.edu

Schult, Frederick, Jr. (PhD, NYU 1962; prof. emeritus) 19th-century American Indian policy, 19th-century American frontier, Old South industrialization; fs3@nyu.edu

Seigel, Jerrold E. (PhD, Princeton 1964; William R. Kenan Jr. Prof. emeritus) social and cultural theory, selfhood and subjectivity, relations between art and society; jes3@nyu.edu

Stehlin, Stewart A. (PhD, Yale 1965; prof. emeritus) modern Germany, European diplomatic, modern European diplomatic; stewart.stehlin@nyu.edu

Unger, Irwin (PhD, Columbia 1958; prof. emeritus) radicalism and reform, Gilded Age, economic; iu1@nyu.edu

Walkowitz, Daniel J. (PhD, Rochester 1972; prof. emeritus) US social and cultural, labor and urban; daniel.walkowitz@nyu.edu

Visiting Faculty

Wragge-Morley, Alexander (PhD, Cambridge 2012; vis. asst. prof.) science, teleology and aesthetics, science and rhetoric/literature; awm5@nyu.edu

Recently Awarded PhDs

Andersson, Anthony W. "Environmentalists with Guns: Conservation, Revolution, and Counterinsurgency in the Petén, Guatemala, 1944-96"

Blum-Ross, Natalie "Find Yourself in a Lonely Cloud"

Connolly, Emilie "Indian Trust Funds and the Routes of American Capitalism, 1795-1865"

Davidson, Ben "Freedom's Generation: American Families and the Meaning of Emancipation, 1850-1900"

Levin, Geoffrey "It Is No Secret: America and Israel's Palestinian Minority, 1949-66"

Merkel, Ian "Terms of Exchange: Brazilian Intellectuals and the Remaking of the French Social Sciences"

Nolan, Rachel "'Children for Export': A History of International Adoption from Guatemala"

Steinlight, Alexandra "The Politics of Preserving the Past: Constructing France's Wartime Archives"

Stephan, Tara D. "Representing and Regulating Women: Gender, Class, and Space in Mamluk Cairo, 1250-1517"

Urus, Arianne Sarah "Troubled Water: International Order and Conceptions of Nature in the North Atlantic Fisheries, 1701-1815"

Zivkovic, Lisa Victoria "Reconciling the European and American Approaches to Privacy Law: A Historical and Legal Analysis of Privacy Law and Data Communications Technology in the United States and Europe, 1970-2018"

Niagara University

Dept. of History, Timon Hall, 5795 Lewiston Rd., Niagara University, NY 14109. 716.286.8696. Fax 716.286.8079. Email: skw@niagara.edu. Website: https://www.niagara.edu/history/.

For more than 150 years, we have provided students with well-rounded education that has prepared them for careers in many fields, as well as for graduate and professional schools.

Chair: Stefanie K. Wichhart
Director of Graduate Studies: Mustafa Gokcek
Degrees Offered: BA,MA
Academic Year System: Semester
Areas of Specialization: America, Europe, East Asia, Middle East, public
Undergraduate Tuition (per academic year): $33000
Graduate Tuition (per academic year): $14670

Enrollment 2018-19:
Undergraduate Majors: 27
New Graduate Students: 1
Full-time Graduate Students: 2
Part-time Graduate Students: 6
Degrees in History: 12 BA, 4 MA
Undergraduate Addresses:
Admissions: http://www.niagara.edu/admissions
Financial Aid: http://www.niagara.edu/scholarships-financialaid/
Graduate Addresses:
Admissions: http://www.niagara.edu/mais/
Financial Aid: http://www.niagara.edu/scholarships-financialaid/

Full-time Faculty

Durfee, Michael Jordan (PhD, SUNY, Buffalo 2015; asst. prof.) modern US, public policy, mass incarceration; mdurfee@niagara.edu

Gokcek, Mustafa (PhD, Wisconsin, Madison 2007; assoc. prof. and dir., grad. studies) Russia, Central Asia, Middle East; gokcek@niagara.edu

Kane, Robert G., Jr. (PhD, Pennsylvania 2002; prof. and assoc. dean; Coll. of Arts & Sciences) modern Japan, US politics and diplomacy, transnationalism; rkane@niagara.edu

Risk, Shannon M. (PhD, Maine 2009; assoc. prof.) women's studies, public, borderlands and Canada; srisk@niagara.edu

Stranges, John B. (PhD, Columbia 1970; Univ. Prof.; Political Science) modern US, foreign policy; jbs@niagara.edu

Wichhart, Stefanie K. (PhD, Texas, Austin 2007; assoc. prof. and chair) modern Middle East, British Empire; skw@niagara.edu

Retired/Emeritus Faculty

Carpenter, Gerald G. (PhD, Tulane 1973; prof. emeritus) US labor; cgc@niagara.edu

Gredel-Manuele, Zdenka (PhD, SUNY, Buffalo 1969; prof. emeritus) early modern and modern Europe; zgm@niagara.edu

Visiting Faculty

Rhodes, Marissa Christman (PhD, SUNY, Buffalo 2019; vis. asst. prof.) mrhodes@niagara.edu

University of North Alabama

Dept. of History, UNA Box 5019, Florence, AL 35632-0001. 256.765.4306. Email: history@una.edu; jbaughman@una.edu. Website: https://www.una.edu/history/.

The Department of History is a dynamic department where hundreds of courses are taught by excellent faculty engaged in award-winning teaching, original research, and university service.

Chair: Matthew Schoenbachler
Director of Graduate Studies: Lynne Rieff (hist.); George Makowski (public hist.)
Degrees Offered: BA,BS,MA
Academic Year System: Semester
Areas of Specialization: US, Europe, public, Latin America, Russia, ancient Mediterranean, African American
Undergraduate Tuition (per academic year):
In-State: $9600
Out-of-State: $19200
Graduate Tuition (per academic year):
In-State: $6660
Out-of-State: $13320

Enrollment 2018-19:
  Undergraduate Majors: 150
  New Graduate Students: 12
  Full-time Graduate Students: 15
  Part-time Graduate Students: 20
  Degrees in History: 15 BA, 30 BS, 15 MA
  Students in Undergraduate Courses: 3000
  Students in Undergraduate Intro Courses: 2400
  Online-Only Courses: 25%
Undergraduate Addresses:
  Admissions: http://www.una.edu/admissions/
  Financial Aid: http://www.una.edu/financial-aid/
Graduate Addresses:
  Admissions: http://www.una.edu/graduate/
  Financial Aid: http://www.una.edu/financial-aid/

Full-time Faculty

Bernier, Julia Wallace (PhD, Massachusetts Amherst 2017; asst. prof.) African American studies; jbernier@una.edu

Bibbee, Jeffrey R. (PhD, London 2008; prof.) Britain, history education; jrbibbee@una.edu

Burton, Danny E. (PhD, Indiana 2000; prof.) science and religion, medieval, science and technology; deburton@una.edu

Dempsey, Brian (PhD, Middle Tennessee State 2009; asst. prof.) public; bdempsey@una.edu

Franklin, Sarah L. (PhD, Florida State 2006; prof.) Latin America; sfranklin@una.edu

Groetsch, Ulrich (PhD, Rutgers 2008; assoc. prof.) early modern Europe, modern Europe; ugroetsch@una.edu

Lowe, Benedict James (PhD, Edinburgh 1997; assoc. prof.) ancient, archaeology; blowe1@una.edu

Makowski, George J. (PhD, Indiana 1993; prof. and coord., grad. studies) Russia, eastern Europe, geography; gjmakowski@una.edu

Quiros, Ansley (PhD, Vanderbilt 2014; asst. prof.) US; aquiros@una.edu

Rieff, Lynne A. (PhD, Auburn 1995; prof. and coord., grad. studies) Alabama, women's studies, US South; larieff@una.edu

Schoenbachler, Matthew G. (PhD, Kentucky 1996; prof. and chair) early Republic US, colonial America; mschoenbachler@una.edu

Retired/Emeritus Faculty

Barty, Peter F. (PhD, Kentucky 1972; prof. emeritus) modern Britain, English constitutional, Africa

Osborne, Thomas R. (PhD, Connecticut 1974; prof. emeritus) modern Europe, imperialism, Middle East; trosborne@una.edu

Ott, Thomas O., III (PhD, Tennessee, Knoxville 1970; prof. emeritus) Caribbean, Latin America, World War II

North Carolina Agricultural and Technical State University

Dept. of History and Political Science, 324 Gibbs Hall, 1601 E. Market St., Greensboro, NC 27411. 336.285.2048. Fax 336.256.2111. Email: asmallwo@ncat.edu. Website: https://www.ncat.edu/cahss/departments/hist/.

The primary goals of the Department are to foster students' aspirations, to cultivate intellectual curiosity, and to prepare graduates for successful careers, graduate school and law school.

Chair: Arwin D. Smallwood
Director of Graduate Studies: Fuabeh Fonge
Degrees Offered: BA,MAT
Academic Year System: Semester

Areas of Specialization: US, African American, Africa, Native American, US South, political science
Undergraduate Tuition (per academic year):
  In-State: $5508
  Out-of-State: $16503
Graduate Tuition (per academic year):
  In-State: $3248
  Out-of-State: $18902
Enrollment 2018-19:
  Undergraduate Majors: 45
  New Graduate Students: 3
  Full-time Graduate Students: 5
  Degrees in History: 9 BA, 2 MAT
Undergraduate Addresses:
  Admissions: http://www.ncat.edu/admissions/undergraduate/
  Financial Aid: http://www.ncat.edu/admissions/financial-aid/
Graduate Addresses:
  Admissions: http://www.ncat.edu/tgc/admissions/
  Financial Aid: http://www.ncat.edu/admissions/financial-aid/

Adjunct Faculty

Beale, Sarah (MA, Duke 1990; adj. instr.) world civilization; sjbeale@ncat.edu

Farrington, Elliot (MAT, North Carolina A&T State 2013; adj. instr.) history education, US, African American; cefarrin@aggies.ncat.edu

Harris, David (MA, Indiana 1989; adj. instr.) geography; harrisda@ncat.edu

Hooker, Ernest (MAT, North Carolina A&T State 2009; adj. instr.) history education, military; edhooker@ncat.edu

McDaniel, Cecily Barker (PhD, Ohio State 2007; adj. prof.) US, African American; cmcdaniel@ncat.edu

Middleton, Shelly Ann (MA, North Carolina Central 2011; adj.) African American, US, North Carolina; samiddle@ncat.edu

Wadelington, Flora J. (MA, North Carolina Central 1980; adj.) African American, North Carolina, US; fjwadeli@ncat.edu

Woodbury, Malishai (MAT, North Carolina A&T State 1999; adj. instr.) history education, African American; woodbury@ncat.edu

Full-time Faculty

Armstrong, Ayanna (PhD, Clark Atlanta 2012; asst. prof.; Political Science) Caribbean politics; ararmst3@ncat.edu

Fonge, Fuabeh P. (PhD, Howard 1989; prof. and dir., grad. studies) Africa; fpfonge@ncat.edu

Porter, Thomas E. (PhD, Washington 1991; prof.) Russia, modern Europe; portert@ncat.edu

Rubio, Philip F. (PhD, Duke 2006; prof.) 20th-century US, African American; pfrubio@ncat.edu

Smallwood, Arwin D. (PhD, Ohio State 1997; prof. and chair) African American, Native American, early America; asmallwo@ncat.edu

Smith, Derick (MA, Fayetteville State 1994; lect.; Political Science) political science; dksmith@ncat.edu

Steele, James (PhD, Atlanta 1989; assoc. prof.; Political Science) political science; steelej@ncat.edu

Wood, James A. (PhD, North Carolina, Chapel Hill 2000; assoc. prof.; coord., MAT Program) Latin America, modern world; woodj@ncat.edu

Zhang, Yunqiu (PhD, Toronto 1997; assoc. prof.) China, East Asia; yzhang@ncat.edu

Part-time Faculty

Allen, Marcus Anthony (PhD, Morgan State 2013; lect.) African American; maallen5@ncat.edu

Carter, Daryl Anthony (PhD, Memphis 2011; adj.) African American; dacarter1@ncat.edu

Haith, Evonda (MA, North Carolina A&T State 2005; adj.) history education, world cvilization; erhaith@ncat.edu

Hicks Few, Maria L. (MPA, North Carolina, Greensboro 2000; adj.; Political Science) public affairs; mlhicks@ncat.edu

Howerton, James (MPA, North Carolina, Chapel Hill 1977; adj.; Political Science) public administration; howerton@ncat.edu

Jessup, Kesa (MA, North Carolina Central 2011; adj.) US; kcjessup@ncat.edu

McRavion, Faye (MA, North Carolina A&T State 2008; adj.; Political Science) English and African American literature; fmcravion@ncat.edu

Robinson, Brian (PhD, South Carolina 2018; lect.) African American; barobinson@ncat.edu

Torain, Corey (MAT, North Carolina A&T State 2007; adj.) history education, African American; cltorain@ncat.edu

Tracey, Ainsworth (MA, Queens, CUNY 2007; adj.) Africa, African American; altracey@ncat.edu

Wellman, Darien (MA, North Carolina Central 2016; adj,) military, world civilization; dmwellma@ncat.edu

Retired/Emeritus Faculty

Cole, Olen, Jr. (PhD, North Carolina, Chapel Hill 1987; prof. emeritus) US, African American; colen@ncat.edu

Ndege, Conchita (PhD, Howard 1991; prof. emeritus) African studies, museum studies; ndegec@ncat.edu

University of North Carolina at Chapel Hill

Dept. of History, Hamilton Hall, CB #3195, Chapel Hill, NC 27599-3195. 919.962.2115. Fax 919.962.1403. Email: history@unc.edu. Website: https://history.unc.edu/.

The Department of History at the University of North Carolina, Chapel Hill is an open learning community, dedicated to rigorous research and critical inquiry into the whole spectrum of human experiences across time and space.

Chair: Lisa A. Lindsay
Director of Graduate Studies: Sarah Shields
Director of Undergraduate Studies: Brett Whalen
Degrees Offered: BA,MA,PhD
Academic Year System: Semester
Areas of Specialization: Africa/ancient/Asia, Europe/global/Latin America, military/Russian and eastern Europe, US, women and gender
Undergraduate Tuition (per academic year):
In-State: $9018
Out-of-State: $36000
Graduate Tuition (per academic year):
In-State: $12580
Out-of-State: $30306
Enrollment 2018-19:
Undergraduate Majors: 405
New Graduate Students: 19
Full-time Graduate Students: 103
Degrees in History: 144 BA, 11 MA, 13 PhD
Students in Undergraduate Courses: 7660
Students in Undergraduate Intro Courses: 6348
Undergraduate Addresses:
Admissions: http://admissions.unc.edu/
Financial Aid: http://studentaid.unc.edu/
Graduate Addresses:
Admissions and Financial Aid: http://gradschool.unc.edu/

Adjunct Faculty

Cobb, Daniel M. (PhD, Oklahoma 2003; assoc. prof.; American Studies) 20th-century American Indian; dcobb@unc.edu

Janken, Kenneth R. (PhD, Rutgers 1991; prof.; African and Afro-American Studies) 20th-century African American; krjanken@email.unc.edu

Necochea, Raul (PhD, McGill 2009; adj. asst. prof.; Social Medicine) modern medicine global; necochea@email.unc.edu

Pitelka, Morgan (PhD, Princeton 2001; assoc. prof.; Asian Studies) Japan; mpitelka@email.unc.edu

Seidman, Rachel Filene (PhD, Yale 1995; asst. prof.; Southern Oral History/Women's Studies) US social, oral; rachel.seidman@unc.edu

Whisnant, Anne Mitchell (PhD, North Carolina 1997; adj. assoc. prof.; deputy secretary of the faculty; American Studies) North Carolina; anne_whisnant@unc.edu

Full-time Faculty

Andrews, Matthew P. (PhD, North Carolina, Chapel Hill 2008; teaching assoc. prof. and advisor) modern US; andrewsm@email.unc.edu

Auerbach, Karen (PhD, Brandeis 2009; asst. prof.) Jewish history and culture, Holocaust, Poland; kauerbach@unc.edu

Aydin, Cemil (PhD, Harvard 2002; prof.) global, modern Ottoman and Japan; history@unc.edu

Barney, William L. (PhD, Columbia 1971; prof.) 19th-century US political and social; wbarney@email.unc.edu

Brundage, W. Fitzhugh (PhD, Harvard 1988; William B. Umstead Prof.) US South; brundage@email.unc.edu

Bryant, Chad (PhD, California, Berkeley 2002; assoc. prof.) eastern and central Europe; bryantc@email.unc.edu

Bull, Marcus G. (PhD, London 1991; Mellon Dist. Prof.) medieval; mgbull@email.unc.edu

Bullard, Melissa M. (PhD, Cornell 1977; prof.) early modern Europe, European economic; mbullard@email.unc.edu

Burns, Kathryn J. (PhD, Harvard 1993; prof.) colonial Latin America; kjburns@email.unc.edu

Caddell, Joseph W. (PhD, Duke 1984; lect.) military; caddellj@email.unc.edu

Coclanis, Peter A. (PhD, Columbia 1984; Albert Newsome Prof.; assoc. provost, International Affairs) American economic and social, Southeast Asia; coclanis@unc.edu

DuVal, Kathleen (PhD, California, Davis 2001; prof.) early America; duval@email.unc.edu

Flatt, Emma J. (PhD, London 2008; asst. prof.) premodern South Asia; history@unc.edu

Gellman, Erik S. (PhD, Northwestern 2006; assoc. prof.) 19th- and 20th-century US; egellman@email.unc.edu

Glatthaar, Joseph T. (PhD, Wisconsin, Madison 1983; Alan Stephenson Prof.) Civil War-era US; jtg@unc.edu

Hagemann, Karen (PhD, Hamburg, Germany 1989; James G. Kenan Prof.) modern Europe, gender and social; hagemann@unc.edu

Jackson, Jerma A. (PhD, Rutgers 1995; assoc. prof.) African American; jaj@email.unc.edu

Jarausch, Konrad H. (PhD, Wisconsin-Madison 1969; Lurcy Prof.) 19th-century Europe; jarausch@email.unc.edu

Jarvis, Lauren V. (PhD, Stanford 2012; asst. prof.) sub-Saharan Africa, African religious, gender; ljarvis@email.unc.edu

King, Michelle T. (PhD, California, Berkeley 2007; assoc. prof.) modern China; mtking@email.unc.edu

Kramer, Lloyd S. (PhD, Cornell 1983; prof.) modern European intellectual; lkramer@email.unc.edu

La Serna, Miguel A. (PhD, California, San Diego 2008; asst. prof.) modern Latin America; laserna@email.unc.edu

Larres, Klaus W. (PhD, Cologne 1992; Richard M. Krasno Dist. Prof.) modern international and diplomatic; history@unc.edu

Lee, Wayne E. (PhD, Duke 1999; Dowd Dist. Term Prof.; chair, Curriculum in Peace, War, and Defense) military; welee@email.unc.edu

Leloudis, James L. (PhD, North Carolina, Chapel Hill 1989; prof.) North Carolina, US South, education; leloudis@email.unc.edu

Lindsay, Lisa A. (PhD, Michigan 1996; prof. and chair) West Africa, African diaspora; lalindsa@email.unc.edu

Lowery, Malinda Maynor (PhD, North Carolina, Chapel Hill 2005; assoc. prof.) Native American; mmaynor@email.unc.edu

McIntosh, Terence V. (PhD, Yale 1989; assoc. prof.) 17th- and 18th-century Germany, Reformation Germany, historical demography; terence_mcintosh@unc.edu

McNeil, Genna Rae (PhD, Chicago 1975; prof.) Afro-American; grmcneil@email.unc.edu

McReynolds, Louise (PhD, Chicago 1984; prof.) imperial Russia; louisem@email.unc.edu

Morgan, Michael Cotey (PhD, Yale 2010; asst. prof.) modern international; morgan@unc.edu

Naiden, Fred (PhD, Harvard 2000; assoc. prof.) ancient Greece; naiden@email.unc.edu

Owre, Maximilian Paul (PhD, North Carolina, Chapel Hill 2008; lect.) Europe, world, colonial; owre@email.unc.edu

Pennybacker, Susan Dabney (PhD, Cambridge 1984; Charles W. Poston Dist. Prof.) modern Britain; pennybac@email.unc.edu

Perez, Louis A., Jr. (PhD, New Mexico 1970; Carlyle Sitterson Prof.; dir., Inst. for Study of Americas) Latin America, Cuba, Iberia perez@email.unc.edu

Radding, Cynthia (PhD, California, San Diego 1990; Gussenhoven Dist. Prof.) Latin America and Mexico; radding@email.unc.edu

Raleigh, Donald J. (PhD, Indiana 1978; Jay Richard Judson Prof.) Russia; djr@email.unc.edu

Reid, Donald M. (PhD, Stanford 1981; prof.) modern France; dreid1@email.unc.edu

Sevea, Iqbal Singh (PhD, Oxford 2007; assoc. prof.) modern South Asia; isevea@email.unc.edu

Shields, Sarah D. (PhD, Chicago 1986; Bowman Gray Dist. Term Prof. and dir., grad. studies) Islamic civilization; sshields@email.unc.edu

Smith, Jay M. (PhD, Michigan 1990; prof.) early modern France 1550-1815; jaysmith@email.unc.edu

Sturkey, William M. (PhD, Ohio State 2012; asst. prof.) modern America, African American, US South; wsturkey@live.unc.edu

Sweet, John W. (PhD, Princeton 1995; assoc. prof.) early America; sweet@unc.edu

Talbert, Richard J. A. (PhD, Cambridge 1972; Kenan Jr. Prof.) ancient Rome; talbert@email.unc.edu

Tasar, Eren M. (PhD, Harvard 2010; asst. prof. and Hyde Family Found. fellow) Central Asia, global, Russia; etasar@email.unc.edu

Tsin, Michael T. (PhD, Princeton 1991; assoc. prof.) modern China; tsin@email.unc.edu

Turk, Katherine Lee (PhD, Chicago 2011; asst. prof.) US women; kturk@email.unc.edu

Waterhouse, Benjamin Cooper (PhD, Harvard 2009; assoc. prof. and assoc. chair) 20th-century US political/economic/social; waterhou@email.unc.edu

Watson, Harry L., II (PhD, Northwestern 1976; Atlanta Dist. Prof.) North Carolina, antebellum US; hwatson@email.unc.edu

Whalen, Brett Edward (PhD, Stanford 2005; assoc. prof. and dir., undergrad. studies) medieval and early modern Europe; bwhalen@email.unc.edu

Worthen, Molly C. (PhD, Yale 2011; asst. prof.) US religious and intellectual; mworthen@email.unc.edu

Joint/Cross Appointments

Burrill, Emily Susan (PhD, Stanford 2007; assoc. prof.; Women's & Gender Studies) gender, Africa; eburrill@email.unc.edu

Clegg, Claude A., III (PhD, Michigan 1995; Lyle V. Jones Dist. Prof.; African, African American, and Diaspora Studies) African diaspora, African American in US South; cclegg@email.unc.edu

Sherman, Daniel J. (PhD, Yale 1985; prof.; Art Hist.) European art 1850-1960, critical museum studies, cultural history and theory; dsherman@email.unc.edu

Retired/Emeritus Faculty

Baxter, Stephen (PhD, Cambridge 1954; prof. emeritus) England, Tudor-Stuart England, 18th century

Behrends, Frederick (PhD, North Carolina, Chapel Hill 1962; prof. emeritus) medieval Europe

Bennett, Judith M. (PhD, Toronto 1981; prof. emerita) late medieval, England, European women; judithb@usc.edu

Brooks, E. Willis (PhD, Stanford 1970; assoc. prof. emeritus) 19th-century Russia social, administrative, intellectual; ewbrooks@live.unc.edu

Browning, Christopher R. (PhD, Wisconsin, Madison 1975; Frank Porter Graham Prof. emeritus) modern Europe, Germany, Holocaust; cbrownin@email.unc.edu

Chasteen, John C. (PhD, North Carolina, Chapel Hill 1988; prof. emeritus) Latin America, Brazil; chasteen@email.unc.edu

Chojnacki, Stanley J. (PhD, California, Berkeley 1968; prof. emeritus) late medieval, Renaissance, Italy and Venice; venetian@live.unc.edu

Ferris, William R. (PhD, Pennsylvania 1969; Joel Williamson Prof. emeritus) US South, African American, folklore; wferris@email.unc.edu

Filene, Peter G. (PhD, Harvard 1965; prof. emeritus) modern American social; filene@live.unc.edu

Fletcher, W. Miles, III (PhD, Yale 1975; prof. emeritus) Asia; wmfletch@email.unc.edu

Hall, Jacquelyn Dowd (PhD, Columbia 1974; Julia Cherry Spruill Prof. emeritus; dir., Southern Oral Hist. Prog.) US women, US South; jhall@email.unc.edu

Harris, Barbara J. (PhD, Harvard 1968; prof. emeritus) Tudor-Stuart England, women and family; bharris@live.unc.edu

Kasson, John F. (PhD, Yale 1971; prof. emeritus) American cultural; jfkasson@email.unc.edu

Kessler, Lawrence D. (PhD, Chicago 1969; prof. emeritus) modern Chinese political and social, US-Chinese relations; ldk@live.unc.edu

Kohn, Richard H. (PhD, Wisconsin-Madison 1968; prof. emeritus) military; rhkohn@unc.edu

Leuchtenburg, William (PhD, Columbia 1951; prof. emeritus) recent America

Lotchin, Roger W. (PhD, Chicago 1969; prof. emeritus) modern American urban; rlotchin@email.unc.edu

Mathews, Donald G. (PhD, Duke 1962; prof. emeritus) American social, religious, US South; dgmathew@bellsouth.net

McCoy, W. James (PhD, Yale 1970; prof. emeritus) sixth to fourth centuries Greece; wjmccoy@unc.edu

McVaugh, Michael R. (PhD, Princeton 1965; prof. emeritus) science and medicine, medieval and early modern; mcvaugh@live.unc.edu

Nelson, John K. (PhD, Northwestern 1962; prof. emeritus) early America; jknelson73@bellsouth.net

Perdue, Theda (PhD, Georgia 1976; Atlanta Dist. Prof. emeritus) Native American; tperdue@live.unc.edu

Semonche, John E. (PhD, Northwestern 1962; prof. emeritus) American legal and constitutional; semche@live.unc.edu

Vargas, Zaragosa (PhD, Michigan 1984; Kenan Eminent dist. prof. emeritus) Latino, Mexican American; zvargas@email.unc.edu

Weinberg, Gerhard L. (PhD, Chicago 1951; prof. emeritus) modern Germany, Europe; gweinber@live.unc.edu

Williamson, Joel (PhD, California, Berkeley 1964; prof. emeritus) southern US race relations; annaleoww@aol.com

Visiting Faculty

Mukherjee, Erica (PhD, SUNY, Stony Brook 2019; vis. teaching asst. prof.)

Recently Awarded PhDs

Akers, Joshua Kyle "Straddling the Threshold of Two Worlds: The Culture of American Soldiers in the Vietnam War, 1965-73"

Blanton, Justin Blaine "Becoming Chiquitano: Crafting Ethnic Identity in the Amazonian Borderlands, 1561-1767"

Castillo Reyna, Angélica "Horsemanship, Nationalism, and Manly Relevance in Modern Mexico"

Farinas Borrego, Maikel "Envisioning Capitalist Alternatives: Business Leaders and the Politics of Influence in Cuba, 1920-40"

Finesurrey, Samuel "Cuba's Anglo-American Colony in Times of Revolution, 1952-61"

Gengler, Peter N. "Constructing and Leveraging 'Flight and Expulsion': Expellee Memory Politics in the Federal Republic of Germany, 1944-70"

Hebert, Joel "The Sun Never Sets: Rethinking the Politics of Late British Decolonization, 1968 to the Present"

Hillaker, Lorn Edward "Promising a Better Germany: Competing Cultural Diplomacies Between West and East Germany, 1949-73"

Levandoski, Rachel "'The Touchstone of Insanity': Perceptions of the Psychological Trauma of War within the United States, 1861-1918"

Raleigh, Peter Joseph "Narrative, History, and Kingship in Angevin England"

Stieb, Joseph "The Regime Change Consensus: Iraq in American Politics, 1990-2003"

Young, Pearl J. "Secession as a Moral Imperative: White Southerners and Evangelical Theology"

University of North Carolina at Charlotte

Dept. of History, Garinger 226, 9201 University City Blvd., Charlotte, NC 28223. 704.687.5125. Fax 704.687.1687. Email: history@uncc.edu. Website: https://history.uncc.edu/.

Our department offers students a range of programs and courses that explore the fascinating and complex history of human society while helping them develop the crucial analytic and communications skills needed for success in a wide range of careers.

Chair: Jürgen Buchenau
Director of Graduate Studies: Peter Thorsheim
Director of Undergraduate Studies: Oscar Lansen
Degrees Offered: BA,MA
Academic Year System: Semester
Areas of Specialization: social, race relations, US South, modern Europe, Latin America
Undergraduate Tuition (per academic year):
In-State: $6277
Out-of-State: $19448

Graduate Tuition (per academic year):
In-State: $6763
Out-of-State: $20050
Enrollment 2018-19:
Undergraduate Majors: 437
New Graduate Students: 19
Full-time Graduate Students: 37
Part-time Graduate Students: 15
Degrees in History: 92 BA, 16 MA; Latin American Studies: 11 BA, 13 MA
Undergraduate Addresses:
Admissions: http://www.uncc.edu/landing/admissions
Financial Aid: http://finaid.uncc.edu/
Graduate Addresses:
Admissions: http://graduateschool.uncc.edu/
Financial Aid: http://graduateschool.uncc.edu/funding

Full-time Faculty

Andres, Benny J., Jr. (PhD, New Mexico 2003; assoc. prof.) US West, Latino; bandres@uncc.edu

Buchenau, Jurgen (PhD, North Carolina, Chapel Hill 1993; prof. and chair) Latin America, Mexico, inter-American relations; jbuchenau@uncc.edu

Cameron, Christopher Alain (PhD, North Carolina, Chapel Hill 2010; assoc. prof.) slavery and abolition, colonial North America; ccamer17@uncc.edu

Cox, Karen L. (PhD, Southern Mississippi 1997; prof.) public, US South; kcox@uncc.edu

Du, Dan (PhD, Georgia 2017; asst. prof.) ddu2@uncc.edu

Dupre, Daniel (PhD, Brandeis 1990; prof.) American Revolution to Civil War; ddupre@uncc.edu

Edwards, Erika Denise (PhD, Florida International 2011; assoc. prof.) Latin America; eedwar27@uncc.edu

Ehlers, Maren Annika (PhD, Princeton 2011; assoc. prof.) Japan; mehlers@uncc.edu

Ferdinando, Peter (PhD, Florida International 2015; lect.) Atlantic world; pferdina@uncc.edu

Flint, Karen Elizabeth (PhD, UCLA 2001; assoc. prof.) sub-Saharan Africa, medicine; kflint@uncc.edu

Fratantuono, Ella (PhD, Michigan State 2016; asst. prof.) Islamic world; efratant@uncc.edu

Gibson, Shimon (PhD, Univ. Coll. London 1995; prof. of practice) S.Gibson@uncc.edu

Goldfield, David R. (PhD, Maryland, Coll. Park 1970; Bailey Prof.) US South, urban; drgoldfi@uncc.edu

Haynes, Christine S. (PhD, Chicago 2001; prof.) 19th-century Europe, France; chaynes@uncc.edu

Higham, Carol Alexander (PhD, Duke 1993; lect.) Native American; ahigham@uncc.edu

Johnson, David A. (PhD, California, Irvine 2004; assoc. prof.) South Asia, British Empire, colonial built environments; dajohns1@uncc.edu

Lansen, Oscar (PhD, Nijmegen, Netherlands 1988; teaching prof. and undergrad. coord.) Holocaust, Nazism, Dutch West Indies; oelansen@uncc.edu

Massino, Jill Marie (PhD, Indiana 2008; assoc. prof.) eastern Europe, gender; jmassino@uncc.edu

McEachnie, Robert J. (PhD, Florida 2013; lect.)

McKinley, Shepherd W. (PhD, Delaware 2003; lect.) US South, business, Reconstruction and New South; swmckinl@uncc.edu

Mixon, Gregory L. (PhD, Cincinnati 1989; prof.) African American, urban; gmixon@uncc.edu

Perry, Heather R. (PhD, Indiana 2005; assoc. prof.) 20th-century Europe, Germany, medicine; hrperry@uncc.edu

Pipkin Anderson, Amanda Cathryn (PhD, Rutgers 2007; assoc. prof.) early modern Europe, women, gender; apipkin@uncc.edu

Prasad, Ritika (PhD, UCLA 2009; assoc. prof.) South Asia, India; rprasad2@uncc.edu

Ramsey, Sonya Y. (PhD, North Carolina, Chapel Hill 2000; assoc. prof.) African American, women; sramse17@uncc.edu

Sabol, Steven O'Neal (PhD, Georgia State 1998; prof.) Soviet Union, Central Asia, Native American; sosabol@uncc.edu

Shapiro, Aaron (PhD, Chicago 2005; assoc. prof. and dir., public hist.) public; ashapi10@uncc.edu

Smail, John (PhD, Stanford 1988; prof. and dean; Univ. Coll.) early modern Britain, industrialization; jsmail@uncc.edu

Smith, John David (PhD, Kentucky 1977; Stone Prof.) Civil War and Reconstruction, US South, slavery; jdsmith4@uncc.edu

Soliz, Carmen (PhD, NYU 2014; asst. prof.) Latin American social movements, Bolivia, indigenous politics; msolizur@uncc.edu

Thorsheim, Peter (PhD, Wisconsin-Madison 2000; prof. and dir., grad. studies) modern Britain, environment, science and technology; pthorshe@uncc.edu

Wilson, Mark R. (PhD, Chicago 2002; prof.) 19th- and 20th-century US, business, political; mrwilson@uncc.edu

Retired/Emeritus Faculty

Hogue, James Keith (PhD, Princeton 1998; assoc. prof. emeritus) Civil War and Reconstruction, military; jhogue@uncc.edu

Johnson, Lyman L. (PhD, Connecticut 1974; prof. emeritus) colonial Latin America, Argentina; ljohnson@uncc.edu

Morrill, Dan L. (PhD, Emory 1966; prof. emeritus) Russia, historic preservation, historical video production; dlmorril@uncc.edu

University of North Carolina at Greensboro

Dept. of History, PO Box 26170, Greensboro, NC 27402-6170. 336.334.5992. Fax 336.334.5910. Email: history_department@ uncg.edu. Website: https://his.uncg.edu/.

The UNCG Department of History creates and disseminates knowledge of history through research, teaching, and public and professional service.

Chair: W. Greg O'Brien
Director of Graduate Studies: Richard E. Barton
Director of Undergraduate Studies: Jeffrey W. Jones
Degrees Offered: BA,MA,PhD
Academic Year System: Semester
Areas of Specialization: America, Europe, Atlantic world, museum studies
Undergraduate Tuition (per academic year):
    In-State: $7331
    Out-of-State: $22490
Graduate Tuition (per academic year):
    In-State: $7479
    Out-of-State: $21846
Enrollment 2018-19:
    Undergraduate Majors: 192
    New Graduate Students: 22
    Full-time Graduate Students: 63
    Degrees in History: 54 BA, 20 MA, 7 PhD
Undergraduate Addresses:
    Admissions: http://admissions.uncg.edu/
    Financial Aid: http://fia.uncg.edu/

Graduate Addresses:
    Admissions: http://grs.uncg.edu/
    Financial Aid: http://fia.uncg.edu/

Full-time Faculty

Anderson, James A. (PhD, Washington 1999; assoc. prof.) East Asia; jamie_anderson@uncg.edu

Barton, Richard E. (PhD, California, Santa Barbara 1997; assoc. prof. and dir., grad studies) medieval; rebarton@uncg.edu

Bender, Jill C. (PhD, Boston Coll. 2011; assoc. prof.) British Empire; jcbender@uncg.edu

Bilinkoff, Jodi E. (PhD, Princeton 1983; prof.) medieval, Renaissance and Reformation; jodi_bilinkoff@uncg.edu

Bolton, Charles C. (PhD, Duke 1989; prof.) US South, oral; ccbolton@uncg.edu

Eger, A. Asa (PhD, Chicago 2008; assoc. prof.) Islam; aaeger@uncg. edu

Elliott, Mark E. (PhD, NYU 2002; assoc. prof. and assoc. head) 19th-century US; meelliot@uncg.edu

Gatson, Torren L. (PhD, Middle Tennessee State 2018; asst. prof.) public; tlgatson@uncg.edu

Jackson, Thomas F. (PhD, Stanford 1994; assoc. prof.) 20th-century US; tjackson@uncg.edu

Jennison, Watson W., III (PhD, Virginia 2005; assoc. prof.) America, African American; wwjennis@uncg.edu

Jones, Jeffrey W. (PhD, North Carolina, Chapel Hill 1999; assoc. prof. and dir., undergrad. studies) Russia; jwjones@uncg.edu

Kriger, Colleen E. (PhD, York, Can. 1992; prof.) Africa; c_kriger@ uncg.edu

Levenstein, Lisa M. (PhD, Wisconsin-Madison 2002; assoc. prof.) women; l_levens@uncg.edu

Milteer, Warren E., Jr. (PhD, North Carolina, Chapel Hill 2014; asst. prof.) early America

Moser, Mark A. (MA, North Carolina, Greensboro; sr. lect.) America, world; mamoser@uncg.edu

O'Brien, Greg (PhD, Kentucky 1998; assoc. prof. and head) early America; wgobrien@uncg.edu

Parsons, Anne Elizabeth (PhD, Illinois, Chicago 2013; assoc. prof. and dir., public hist.) public; aeparson@uncg.edu

Rupert, Linda M. (PhD, Duke 2006; assoc. prof.) Atlantic world; lmrupert@uncg.edu

Ruzicka, Stephen Q. (PhD, Chicago 1979; prof.) ancient; sqruzick@ uncg.edu

Tolbert, Lisa C. (PhD, North Carolina, Chapel Hill 1994; assoc. prof.) 19th-century US, cultural; lctolber@uncg.edu

Recently Awarded PhDs

McCartney, Sarah E. "'O'er Mountains and Rivers': Community and Commerce in the Greenbrier River Valley in the Late 18th Century"

Michie, Ian MacDonald "Agents of Empire: Entrepreneurship and the Transformation of Virginia, 1688-1750"

Petersen, Keri T. "The North Carolina Railroad, Industrial Slavery, and the Economic Development of North Carolina"

Ross, Joseph Andrew "The Nuremberg Paradox: How the Trial of the Nazis Challenged American Support of International Human Rights Law"

Russell, Deborah D. "'This Must Be Worked Out Locally': Race, Education, and Leadership in Rockingham County, North Carolina, 1820-1970"

Ward, Monica Rose "Little Tallassee: A Creek Indian Colonial Town"

University of North Carolina Wilmington

Dept. of History, 601 S. College Rd., Wilmington, NC 28403-5957. 910.962.3656. Fax 910.962.7011. Email: masseya@uncw.edu; mollenauerl@uncw.edu. Website: https://uncw.edu/hst/.

A comprehensive, doctoral high research activity university situated in the historic port city of Wilmington, UNCW enrolls approximately 17,000 students and offers the opportunity to specialize in American, European, global, and public history at the MA level.

Chair: Lynn Wood Mollenauer
Director of Graduate Studies: W. Taylor Fain
Director of Undergraduate Studies: Nathan Crowe
Degrees Offered: BA,MA
Academic Year System: Semester
Areas of Specialization: US, Europe, global, public
Undergraduate Tuition (per academic year):
In-State: $4400
Out-of-State: $18508
Graduate Tuition (per academic year):
In-State: $4720
In-State MA Online: $7770.30
Out-of-State: $18548
Out-of-State MA Online: $28107.30
Enrollment 2018-19:
Undergraduate Majors: 140
New Graduate Students: 12
Full-time Graduate Students: 36
Degrees in History: 39 BA, 9 MA
Undergraduate Addresses:
Admissions: http://www.uncw.edu/admissions/
Financial Aid: http://www.uncw.edu/finaid/
Graduate Addresses:
Admissions: http://uncw.edu/gradschool/
Financial Aid: http://www.uncw.edu/finaid/

Full-time Faculty

Chen, Yixin (PhD, Washington, St. Louis 1995; assoc. prof.) 20th-century China; cheny@uncw.edu
Crowe, Nathan P. (PhD, Minnesota 2011; asst. prof. and dir., undergrad. studies) science; crowen@uncw.edu
Dhulipala, Venkat (PhD, Minnesota 2008; assoc. prof.) modern South Asia; dhulipalav@uncw.edu
Fain, W. Taylor, III (PhD, Virginia 2002; assoc. prof. and dir., grad. studies) America in world, international; fainwt@uncw.edu
Gisolfi, Monica Richmond (PhD, Columbia 2007; assoc. prof.) American South, environmental; gisolfim@uncw.edu
Harris, Glen Anthony (PhD, Florida State 2003; assoc. prof.) African American, US, Harlem Renaissance, Civil Rights Movement, Hollywood and black film; harrisg@uncw.edu
Hart, T. Robert (PhD, Alabama 2004; lect.) environmental, US South; hartt@uncw.edu
Houpt, David W. (PhD, Graduate Center, CUNY 2015; asst. prof.) revolutionary America, political culture, Atlantic world; houptd@uncw.edu
La Vere, David L (PhD, Texas A&M 1993; prof.) southeastern and North Carolina Indians, southern Plains; lavered@uncw.edu
Le Zotte, Jennifer K. (PhD, Virginia 2013; asst. prof.) public, modern US culture and capitalism; lezottej@uncw.edu
McFarland, Stephen L. (PhD, Texas, Austin 1981; prof.) flight, technology, Middle East; mcfarlands@uncw.edu

Mehl, Eva M. (PhD, California, Davis 2011; PhD, Alicante 2002; assoc. prof.) Latin America and Spanish Empire; mehle@uncw.edu
Mollenauer, Lynn Wood (PhD, Northwestern 1999; assoc. prof. and chair) early modern Europe; mollenauerl@uncw.edu
Seidman, Michael M. (PhD, Amsterdam 1982; prof.) modern Europe, social and individual; seidmanm@uncw.edu
Shefsiek, Kenneth P. (PhD, Georgia 2010; assoc. prof. and dir., public hist. studies) public, colonial America; shefsiekk@uncw.edu
Spaulding, Robert Mark, Jr. (PhD, Harvard 1989; prof.) Germany, European political economy, global trade; spauldingr@uncw.edu
Tanny, Jarrod (PhD, California, Berkeley 2008; assoc. prof. and Charles and Hannah Block Dist. Scholar) Russian Jewish; tannyj@uncw.edu
Townend, Paul A. (PhD, Chicago 1999; prof.; assoc. vice chancellor; and dean, undergrad. studies) modern and early Britain and Ireland; townendp@uncw.edu
Usilton, Larry W. (PhD, Mississippi State 1971; prof.) ancient and medieval Western civilization; usiltonl@uncw.edu
Zombek, Angela Marie (PhD, Florida 2012; asst. prof.) US Civil War and Reconstruction, Old US South, gender; zombeka@uncw.edu

Joint/Cross Appointments

Conser, Walter H., Jr. (PhD, Brown 1981; prof.; Philosophy and Religion) American religion; conserw@uncw.edu
Kirschke, Amy (PhD, Tulane; prof.; Art and Art History) African American art, 20th-century art, African art, contemporary; kirschkea@uncw.edu

Part-time Faculty

Amponsah, Nana Akua (PhD, Texas, Austin 2011; asst. prof.) modern Africa, African diaspora, women/gender/sexuality; amponsahn@uncw.edu
Chapman, Ryan (MA, North Carolina, Wilmington 2013; instr.) chapmanrj@uncw.edu
Ellithorpe, Corey James (PhD, North Carolina, Chapel Hill 2017; lect.) ancient
Goforth, Sean (MA, North Carolina, Wilmington 2014; instr.) goforths@uncw.edu
Gouverneur, Joseph (PhD, Sheffield 2005; instr.) religion; gouverneurj@uncw.edu
Hassett, Matthew J. (MA, North Carolina, Wilmington 2007; instr.) hassetm@uncw.edu
Johnson, Donald G. (MA, MD, North Carolina, Wilmington 1999; instr.) johnsondg@uncw.edu
Lamberton, Christine (MA, North Carolina, Wilmington; instr.) lambertonc@uncw.edu
Laursen, Christopher (PhD, British Columbia 2016; instr.) laursenc@uncw.edu

Retired/Emeritus Faculty

Berkeley, Kathleen Christine (PhD, UCLA 1980; prof. emerita) women, US social, sexuality; berkeleyk@uncw.edu
Bredbenner, Candice (PhD, Virginia 1990; assoc. prof. emerita) Progressive and interwar era; bredbennerc@uncw.edu
Fink, Carole K. (PhD, Yale 1968; prof. emerita) modern Europe, Cold War, European diplomatic; fink.24@osu.edu
Fonvielle, Chris E., Jr. (PhD, South Carolina 1994; assoc. prof. emeritus) Civil War, Lower Cape Fear; fonviellec@uncw.edu
Haley, John Hamilton (PhD, North Carolina, Chapel Hill 1981; assoc. prof. emeritus) haleyj@uncw.edu
McCaffray, Susan P. (PhD, Duke 1983; prof. emerita) Russia, Soviet Union, 19th-century Europe; mccaffrays@uncw.edu

McLaurin, Melton A. (PhD, South Carolina 1967; prof. emeritus) US labor, Populist-Progressive Era, US South; mclaurinm@uncw.edu

Pollard, Lisa (PhD, California, Berkeley 1997; prof. emerita) modern Middle East, social, Egypt; pollardl@uncw.edu

Toplin, Robert Brent (PhD, Rutgers 1968; prof. emeritus) film, US social, Latin America; toplinrb@uncw.edu

Watson, Alan D. (PhD, South Carolina 1971; prof. emeritus) colonial America, early North Carolina, US economic; watsona@uncw.edu

North Carolina State University

Dept. of History, Box 8108, Raleigh, NC 27695-8108. 919.515.2483. Fax 919.515.3886. Email: david_zonderman@ncsu.edu. Website: https://history.ncsu.edu/.

NC State's Department of History provides a stellar learning environment. Whether you've always had a passion for history or you want to hone your critical thinking, writing and research skills, explore the past and envision the future in the Department of History.

Chair: David Zonderman
Director of Graduate Studies: Brent Sirota
Director of Undergraduate Studies: William Kimler
Degrees Offered: BA,BS,MA,PhD
Academic Year System: Semester
Areas of Specialization: ancient/medieval/modern Europe, Third World, US, science and technology, public
Undergraduate Tuition (per academic year):
In-State: $9100
Out-of-State: $29220
Graduate Tuition (per academic year):
In-State: $11672
Out-of-State: $28998
Enrollment 2018-19:
Undergraduate Majors: 262
New Graduate Students: 24
Full-time Graduate Students: 63
Part-time Graduate Students: 3
Degrees in History: 64 BA, 6 BS, 14 MA
Undergraduate Addresses:
Admissions: http://www.ncsu.edu/future-students/admissions/
Financial Aid: http://financialaid.ncsu.edu/
Graduate Addresses:
Admissions: http://www.ncsu.edu/grad/admissions/
Financial Aid: http://financialaid.ncsu.edu/

Adjunct Faculty

Caddell, Joseph W. (PhD, Duke 1984; teaching asst. prof.) American military; jcaddell@ncsu.edu

Full-time Faculty

Ambaras, David Richard (PhD, Princeton 1999; prof.) Japan; david_ambaras@ncsu.edu

Bassett, Ross Knox (PhD, Princeton 1998; prof.) technology; ross_bassett@ncsu.edu

Booker, Matthew Morse (PhD, Stanford 2005; assoc. prof.) US environmental; matthew_booker@ncsu.edu

Cherry, Megan Lindsay (PhD, Yale 2012; asst. prof.) colonial and revolutionary America; megan_cherry@ncsu.edu

Duan, Xiaolin (PhD, Washington 2014; asst. prof.) China; xduan4@ncsu.edu

Freitas, Frederico Santos Soares (PhD, Stanford 2016; asst. prof.) Latin America, digital; f_freitas@ncsu.edu

Friend, Craig Thompson (PhD, Kentucky 1995; prof.) public, early Republic US; craig_friend@ncsu.edu

Gilmartin, David P. (PhD, California, Berkeley 1979; prof.) comparative imperialism, South Asia; david_gilmartin@ncsu.edu

Gordon, Tammy (PhD, Michigan State 1998; prof. and dir., public hist. program) public, US cultural; tammy_gordon@ncsu.edu

Jones, Ebony Pearl (PhD, NYU 2017; asst. prof.) slavery, Caribbean

Kasper-Marienberg, Verena (PhD, Graz, Austria 2009; asst. prof.) early modern Europe, Jewish; vikasper@ncsu.edu

Kelley, Blair (PhD, Duke 2003; assoc. prof.) African American; blmkelley@ncsu.edu

Kertesz, Judy (PhD, Harvard 2008; asst. prof.) Native American, public; jkertes@ncsu.edu

Khater, Akram F. (PhD, California, Berkeley 1993; prof.) Middle East; akram_khater@ncsu.edu

Kim, Mi Gyung (PhD, UCLA 1990; prof.) science and technology; migkim@ncsu.edu

Kimler, William (PhD, Cornell 1983; assoc. prof. and dir., undergrad. programs) biology, modern science; kimler@ncsu.edu

Lee, Susanna M., III (PhD, Virginia 2005; assoc. prof.) US, Civil War and Reconstruction, US South; susanna_lee@ncsu.edu

Luria, Keith P. (PhD, California, Berkeley 1982; prof.) early modern Europe, France, religious; keithluria@ncsu.edu

McGill, Alicia (PhD, Indiana 2012; asst. prof.) international heritage, public; aemcgill@ncsu.edu

Mell, Julie L. (PhD, North Carolina, Chapel Hill 2007; assoc. prof.) medieval, Jewish, economic; jlmell@ncsu.edu

Mellen Charron, Katherine (PhD, Yale 2005; assoc. prof.) US, southern women and gender; kmcharron@ncsu.edu

Mitchell, Nancy (PhD, Johns Hopkins 1993; prof.) US foreign relations; nancy_mitchell@ncsu.edu

Parker, S. Thomas (PhD, UCLA 1979; prof.) ancient, Rome; thomas_parker@ncsu.edu

Paulette, Tate (PhD, Chicago 2015; asst. prof.) agriculture, ancient

Rudolph, Julia E. (PhD, Columbia 1995; prof.) early modern Britain, legal, intellectual; jerudolp@ncsu.edu

Sirota, Brent Stuart (PhD, Chicago 2007; assoc. prof. and dir., grad. studies) Britain; bssirota@ncsu.edu

Strote, Noah Benezra (PhD, California, Berkeley 2011; assoc. prof.) 20th-century Europe and Germany, intellectual; nbstrote@ncsu.edu

Vincent, K. Steven (PhD, California, Berkeley 1981; prof.) modern Europe, France, intellectual; steven_vincent@ncsu.edu

Zonderman, David A. (PhD, Yale 1986; prof. and head) US, labor, public; david_zonderman@ncsu.edu

Retired/Emeritus Faculty

Banker, James R. (PhD, Rochester 1971; prof. emeritus) Europe, Renaissance, Reformation; james_banker@ncsu.edu

Crisp, James E. (PhD, Yale 1976; prof. emeritus) US, frontier, antebellum US South; james_crisp@ncsu.edu

De Grand, Alexander Joseph (PhD, Chicago 1968; prof. emeritus) 20th century, Italy, diplomatic; alex_degrand@ncsu.edu

Downs, Murray (PhD, Duke 1959; prof. emeritus) British studies; downs@unity.ncsu.edu

Harris, William C. (PhD, Alabama 1965; prof. emeritus) Civil War and Reconstruction; william_harris@ncsu.edu

Kalinga, Owen J. (PhD, London 1974; prof. emeritus) Africa; owen_kalinga@ncsu.edu

LaVopa, Anthony J. (PhD, Cornell 1976; prof. emeritus) Germany, social, intellectual; anthony_lavopa@ncsu.edu

McMurry, Linda O. (PhD, Auburn 1976; prof. emeritus) African American, US, New US South

Mulholland, James A. (PhD, Delaware 1975; assoc. prof. emeritus) US, science and technology

O'Brien, Gail W (PhD, North Carolina, Chapel Hill 1975; prof. emeritus) US, US South, social; gail_obrien@ncsu.edu

Riddle, John M. (PhD, North Carolina, Chapel Hill 1963; prof. emeritus) ancient, medieval, science; john_riddle@ncsu.edu

Sack, Ronald H. (PhD, Minnesota 1970; prof. emeritus) ancient, Near East; ronald_sack@ncsu.edu

Slatta, Richard W. (PhD, Texas, Austin 1980; prof. emeritus) Latin America, comparative frontiers; slatta@ncsu.edu

Spencer, Stephanie (PhD, Michigan 1981; prof. emeritus) art; stephanie_spencer@ncsu.edu

Surh, Gerald D. (PhD, California, Berkeley 1979; assoc. prof. emeritus) Russia, Soviet Union; surh@ncsu.edu

Sylla, Edith D. (PhD, Harvard 1971; prof. emeritus) science, medieval and early modern Europe; edith_sylla@ncsu.edu

Vickery, Kenneth P. (PhD, Yale 1978; prof. emeritus) South Africa; kpvicker@ncsu.edu

North Central College

Dept. of History, 30 N. Brainard St., Naperville, IL 60540. 630.637.5319. Fax 630.637.5610. Email: wcbarnett@noctrl.edu. Website: https://www.northcentralcollege.edu/college-arts-sciences/department-history.

Do you want to understand how political, economic, intellectual, cultural and social forces shape civilizations from age to age? Study history and broaden your understanding of specific geographical regions as you develop a deeper perspective on global events. We offer a variety of courses on the history of the United States, Europe, Asia, Latin America and Africa, as well as courses on local history, western civilization and global history.

Chair: William C. Barnett
Degrees Offered: BA
Academic Year System: Semester
Areas of Specialization: US urban and environmental, 19th- and 20th-century America, medieval and early modern Europe, East Asia, British Empire
Tuition (per academic year): $39860
Enrollment 2018-19:
  Undergraduate Majors: 58
  Degrees in History: 15 BA
Addresses:
  Admissions: http://northcentralcollege.edu/admission
  Financial Aid: http://www.northcentralcollege.edu/financial-aid

Full-time Faculty

Barnett, William C. (PhD, Wisconsin-Madison 2005; assoc. prof. and chair) 20th-century US, environmental, US West; wcbarnett@noctrl.edu

Franks, Luke A. (PhD, California, Berkeley 2009; assoc. prof.) modern East Asia; lafranks@noctrl.edu

Ilahi, Shereen F. (PhD, Texas, Austin 2008; assoc. prof. and dir., General Education) British imperialism and modern Europe; silahi@noctrl.edu

Janacek, Bruce (PhD, California, Davis 1996; prof.) medieval, early modern Europe; bnjanacek@noctrl.edu

Keating, Ann Durkin (PhD, Chicago 1984; Dr. C. Frederick Toenniges Prof.) urban, 19th-century US, local; adkeating@noctrl.edu

Joint/Cross Appointments

Hoffert, Brian (PhD, Harvard 2002; assoc. prof.; Religious Studies) East Asia; bhoffert@noctrl.edu

University of North Dakota

Dept. of History and American Indian Studies, O'Kelly Hall 208, 221 Centennial Dr., Stop 8096, Grand Forks, ND 58202-8096. 701.777.3681. Fax 701.777.4636. Email: history.und@und.edu. Website: https://arts-sciences.und.edu/academics/history/.

From the earliest days of the University of North Dakota, history faculty have played an important part in preparing students to be engaged citizens of their communities, the state, and the world. Today the department remains committed to teaching the past and developing in our students the reading, writing, and critical thinking skills necessary to contribute to an increasingly global world. Each faculty member is an active researcher in their respective fields, and bring fresh perspectives on different cultures and ideas into the classes they teach. The PhD program is joint with North Dakota State University.

Chair: Hans Broedel
Director of Graduate Studies: William Caraher
Degrees Offered: BA,MA,DA,PhD
Academic Year System: Semester
Areas of Specialization: Europe, US, northern Great Plains, world
Undergraduate Tuition (per academic year):
  In-State: $9737
  Out-of-State: $13843
Graduate Tuition (per academic year):
  In-State: $8928
  Out-of-State: $12888
Enrollment 2018-19:
  Undergraduate Majors: 69
  Full-time Graduate Students: 4
  Part-time Graduate Students: 4
  Degrees in History: 11 BA, 1 MA
  Students in Undergraduate Courses: 1897
  Students in Undergraduate Intro Courses: 1290
  Online-Only Courses: 5%
Undergraduate Addresses:
  Admissions: http://und.edu/admissions/undergraduate/
  Financial Aid: http://und.edu/admissions/financial-aid/
Graduate Addresses:
  Admissions and Financial Aid: http://graduateschool.und.edu/graduate-students/new/

Full-time Faculty

Berg Burin, Nikki (PhD, Minnesota 2007; asst. prof.) 19th-century America, women, US South and African American; nikki.berg@und.edu

Broedel, Hans Peter (PhD, Washington 1998; assoc. prof. and chair) early modern European science, witchcraft, popular culture and folklore; hans.broedel@und.edu

Burin, Eric (PhD, Illinois, Urbana-Champaign 1999; prof.) African American, US South, antebellum America; eric.burin@und.edu

Campbell, Caroline Jane (PhD, Iowa 2009; assoc. prof.) modern France, 20th-century European women and gender, nationalisms; caroline.campbell@und.edu

Caraher, William R. (PhD, Ohio State 2003; assoc. prof. and dir., grad. studies) ancient and medieval, Byzantine, ancient Christianity; william.caraher@und.edu

Mochoruk, J. D. (PhD, Manitoba 1992; prof.) Canada, northern development, British Empire and Commonwealth; james.mochoruk@und.edu

Porter, Kimberly K. (PhD, Iowa 1995; prof.) agriculture, late 19th- and 20th-century US, oral; kimberly.porter@und.edu

Prescott, Cynthia Culver (PhD, UCLA 2004; assoc. prof.) American women, US West, material culture; cynthia.prescott@und.edu

Reese, Ty M. (PhD, Toledo 1999; prof.) Atlantic world, slave trade and comparative; ty.reese@und.edu

Nondepartmental Historians

Baukol, Bard (PhD, Arizona State 2007; online instr.) English Civil War; bard.baukol@und.edu

Kelsch, Anne V. (PhD, Texas A&M 1993; assoc. prof.; prog. dir., Instructional Development) European women, European social modern Britain; anne.kelsch@und.edu

Retired/Emeritus Faculty

Berger, Albert I. (PhD, Northern Illinois 1978; prof. emeritus) 20th-century US, military, US foreign relations; albert.berger@und.edu

Beringer, Richard E. (PhD, Northwestern 1966; prof. emeritus) national period US, Civil War and Reconstruction

Handy-Marchello, Barbara (PhD, Iowa 1996; assoc. prof. emeritus) American women, trans-Mississippi West, North Dakota; barbara.handy.marchello@und.edu

Iseminger, Gordon L. (PhD, Oklahoma 1965; prof. emeritus) 19th-century Europe, Victorian England; gordon.iseminger@und.edu

Tweton, D. Jerome (PhD, Oklahoma 1959; prof. emeritus) Great Plains, Populist-Progressive Era

North Dakota State University

Dept. of History, Philos., and Religious Studies, 422 Minard Hall, PO Box 6050, Dept. 2340, Fargo, ND 58108-6050. 701.231.8654. Fax 701.231.1047. Email: ndsu.history@ndsu.edu; mark.harvey@ndsu.edu. Website: http://ndsuhprs.org/.

The department is committed to pursuing excellence in scholarship and teaching in all of its many areas of specialization. Our outstanding faculty and students specialize in a wide variety of historical, contemporary, and global themes that reflect the human condition. For all of its students, the Department of History, Philosophy, and Religious Studies promotes active learning and individual engagement, provides exciting and diverse learning opportunities, and creates personal and academic connections to last a lifetime. The PhD degree in history is offered in cooperation with the University of North Dakota.

Chair: Mark Harvey
Director of Graduate Studies: Bradley Benton
Degrees Offered: BA,BS,MA,MS,PhD
Academic Year System: Semester
Areas of Specialization: US West and Great Plains, North America, eastern and western Europe, East Asia, Mexico and Latin America
Undergraduate Tuition (per academic year):
In-State: $7957
MN: $8912
Contiguous/MSEP/WUE: $11936
Out-of-State: $11936
Graduate Tuition (per academic year):
In-State: $6498
MN: $8244
Contiguous/MSEP: $9720
Out-of-State: $9720
Enrollment 2018-19:
Undergraduate Majors: 105
New Graduate Students: 5
Full-time Graduate Students: 18

Part-time Graduate Students: 12
Degrees in History: 6 BA, 12 BS, 3 MA, 2 PhD
Undergraduate Addresses:
Admissions: https://www.ndsu.edu/admission/
Financial Aid: https://www.ndsu.edu/gradschool/
Graduate Addresses:
Admissions and Financial Aid: https://www.ndsu.edu/onestop/finaid/

Full-time Faculty

Baggett, Ashley (PhD, Louisiana State 2014; asst. prof.; Education) women's and gender studies, 19th-century US, American South; ashley.baggett@ndsu.edu

Barrett, Tracy C. (PhD, Cornell 2007; assoc. prof.) modern East Asia, China, Vietnam; tracy.barrett@ndsu.edu

Benton, Bradley T. (PhD, UCLA 2012; assoc. prof. and dir., grad. studies) Mexico, Latin America, indigenous peoples; bradley.benton@ndsu.edu

Blankenship, Anne Michele (PhD, North Carolina, Chapel Hill 2012; asst. prof.) religion and American West, immigration, trans-Pacific studies; anne.blankenship@ndsu.edu

Burt, Sean (PhD, Duke 2009; asst. prof.; English) ancient Jewish and Israelite; sean.burt@ndsu.edu

Cox, John K. (PhD, Indiana 1995; prof.) 19th- and 20th-century eastern European intellectual, Balkans, Holocaust; john.cox.1@ndsu.edu

Harvey, Mark (PhD, Wyoming 1986; prof. and head) Environmental, American West, 20th-century US; mark.harvey@ndsu.edu

Isern, Tom D. (PhD, Oklahoma State 1977; prof.) Great Plains, Canada, Australasia; isern@plainsfolk.com

Johnson, Donald F. (PhD, Northwestern 2015; asst. prof.) colonial and revolutionary America, early modern empires; donald.f.johnson@ndsu.edu

Perett, Marcela K. (PhD, Notre Dame 2009; asst. prof.) late antiquity, medieval Europe, Renaissance and Reformation; marcela.perett@ndsu.edu

Smith, Angela J. (PhD, Middle Tennessee State 2011; assoc. prof.) public, digital, 20th-century US; angela.smith.1@ndsu.edu

Northeastern Illinois University

Dept. of History, 5500 N. St. Louis Ave., Chicago, IL 60625-4699. 773.442.5630. Fax 773.442.5620. Email: C-Steinwedel@neiu.edu. Website: https://www.neiu.edu/academics/college-of-arts-and-sciences/departments/history

Our world-class faculty and students engage in the study of the historical development of a broad spectrum of human societies. We analyze historical change rather than memorizing facts. Members of the department produce award-winning research, and have been selected by the University for their teaching excellence.

Chair: Charles Steinwedel
Director of Graduate Studies: Christina Bueno
Degrees Offered: BA,MA
Academic Year System: Semester
Areas of Specialization: US, Europe, Latin America, Asia, Africa and African American
Undergraduate Tuition (per academic year):
In-State: $9698
Out-of-State: $19397

Graduate Tuition (per academic year):
In-State: $7419
Out-of-State: $14838
Enrollment 2018-19:
Undergraduate Majors: 93
New Graduate Students: 10
Part-time Graduate Students: 20
Degrees in History: 30 BA, 5 MA
Undergraduate Addresses:
Admissions: http://www.neiu.edu/future-students/
Financial Aid: http://www.neiu.edu/financial-aid/
Graduate Addresses:
Admissions: http://www.neiu.edu/graduate-college/future-students/
Financial Aid: https://www.neiu.edu/academics/college-of-arts-and-sciences/departments/department-history/master-arts-history

Adjunct Faculty

Bacino, Leo J. (PhD, Northern Illinois 1993; instr.) US political economy, foreign relations; L-Bacino@neiu.edu
Gerdow, George (MA, Loyola, Chicago 1994; instr.) Latin America, US; G-Gerdow@neiu.edu
Grossman, Richard (PhD, Chicago 1996; instr.) Latin America; R-Grossman@neiu.edu
Hoel, Nikolas (PhD, Wisconsin-Madison 2013; instr.) medieval, Byzantine, comparative hagiography; N-Hoel@neiu.edu

Full-time Faculty

Bueno, Christina M. (PhD, California, Davis 2004; assoc. prof. and dir., grad. studies) Latin America, Mexico, archaeology; C-Bueno@neiu.edu
Eisenberg, Andrew (PhD, Washington 1991; prof.) China, Japan; a-eisenberg@neiu.edu
Farzaneh, Mateo Mohammad (PhD, California, Santa Barbara 2010; asst. prof.) Islamic world, modern Middle East; m-farzaneh@neiu.edu
Miller, Patrick B. (PhD, California, Berkeley 1987; prof.) African American, 19th- and 20th-century America; P-Miller1@neiu.edu
Morgan, Francesca C. (PhD, Columbia 1998; assoc. prof.) gender and women, 19th- and 20th-century America; F-Morgan@neiu.edu
Salzmann, Joshua A. T. (PhD, Illinois, Chicago 2008; asst. prof.) modern US, urban and environmental, Chicago; J-Salzmann@neiu.edu
Steinwedel, Charles R. (PhD, Columbia 1999; assoc. prof. and chair) Russia, Soviet Union, modern Europe; C-Steinwedel@neiu.edu
Tuck, Michael W. (PhD, Northwestern 1997; assoc. prof.) Africa, medicine, slavery and Atlantic world; M-Tuck@neiu.edu

Retired/Emeritus Faculty

Mendez, J. Ignacio (PhD, California, Berkeley 1970; assoc. prof. emeritus) Latin America/Puerto Rico/Brazil/Gran Colombia, quantitative methods, inter-American relations
Riess, Steven A. (PhD, Chicago 1974; prof. emeritus) sport, US urban and ethnic, Chicago; s-riess@neiu.edu
Schiffman, Zachary S. (PhD, Chicago 1980; prof. emeritus) Renaissance and Reformation, early modern Europe, ancient; Z-Schiffman@neiu.edu
Singleton, Gregory H. (PhD, UCLA 1976; prof. emeritus) American social, intellectual, cultural; roc1940@comcast.net
Sochen, June (PhD, Northwestern 1967; prof. emeritus) US cultural, women; J-Sochen@neiu.edu
Steinberg, Salme H. (PhD, Johns Hopkins 1971; prof. emeritus) US economic and social, US business; S-Steinberg@neiu.edu

Walker, Sue Sheridan (PhD, Chicago 1966; prof. emeritus) England, legal, women

Northeastern University

Dept. of History, 249 Meserve, 360 Huntington Ave., Boston, MA 02115-5005. 617.373.2660. Fax 617.373.2661. Email: b.knipfer@northeastern.edu; k.bilas@northeastern.edu. Website: https://cssh.northeastern.edu/history/.

The History Department at Northeastern University is a national leader in undergraduate and graduate training in world history as well as in public history. The department features a highly productive faculty actively engaged in the publication of innovative research in transnational and global approaches to African, Latin American, European, Asian, and US history.

Chair: Timothy S. Brown
Degrees Offered: BA,BA/MA,BS,MA,PhD
Academic Year System: Semester
Areas of Specialization: global, public, empire, America
Undergraduate Tuition (per academic year): $39320
Graduate Tuition (per academic year): $21150
Enrollment 2018-19:
Undergraduate Majors: 115
New Graduate Students: 5
Full-time Graduate Students: 62
Part-time Graduate Students: 2
Degrees in History: 23 BA, 15 BS, 8 MA, 3 PhD
Undergraduate Addresses:
Admissions: http://www.northeastern.edu/admissions/
Financial Aid: http://www.northeastern.edu/financialaid/
Graduate Addresses:
Admissions and Financial Aid: http://www.northeastern.edu/graduate/

Full-time Faculty

Blatt, Martin Henry (PhD, Boston Univ. 1983; prof. of practice; dir., Public Hist. Prog.) public; m.blatt@northeastern.edu
Blevins, Cameron (PhD, Stanford 2015; asst. prof.) digital; c.blevins@northeastern.edu
Brown, Timothy Scott (PhD, California, Berkeley 2000; prof. and chair) modern Germany, Europe, imperialism and colonialism; ti.brown@neu.edu
Burds, Jeffrey (PhD, Yale 1990; assoc. prof.) Russia and Soviet Union; j.burds@neu.edu
Cain, Victoria (PhD, Columbia 2007; assoc. prof.) America, public; v.cain@neu.edu
Frader, Laura Levine (PhD, Rochester 1979; prof.) modern French social, women, gender; l.frader@neu.edu
Havens, T.R.H. (PhD, California, Berkeley 1965; prof.) Japanese culture; thavens@bhavens.com
Heefner, Gretchen A. (PhD, Yale 2009; assoc. prof.) US and world; g.heefner@neu.edu
Khuri-Makdisi, Ilham (PhD, Harvard 2003; assoc. prof.) Middle East, Islam, diaspora; i.khuri-makdisi@neu.edu
Luongo, Katherine A. (PhD, Michigan 2006; assoc. prof.) Africa, South Asia, world; k.luongo@neu.edu
Parsons, Christopher M. (PhD, Toronto 2011; assoc. prof.) French Atlantic, environmental; c.parsons@neu.edu
Poiger, Uta G. (PhD, Brown 1995; prof. and dean, Coll. of Social Sciences and Humanities) modern Germany, gender and sexuality, Americanization and comparative; u.poiger@neu.edu
Streets-Salter, Heather E. (PhD, Duke 1998; prof.) modern Britain, British Empire, world; h.streetssalter@neu.edu

Thai, Philip (PhD, Stanford 2013; assoc. prof.) China; p.thai@neu.edu

Walker, Louise E. (PhD, Yale 2008; assoc. prof.) Latin America; l.walker@northeastern.edu

Retired/Emeritus Faculty

Fowler, William M., Jr. (PhD, Notre Dame 1971; dist. prof. emeritus) early America, maritime, Atlantic; w.fowler@neu.edu

Freeland, Richard M. (PhD, Pennsylvania 1969; prof. emeritus) Cold War and higher education; r.freeland@neu.edu

Hall, Robert L. (PhD, Florida State 1984; assoc. prof. emeritus) African American, comparative slavery, demographic; r.hall@neu.edu

Penna, Anthony N. (DA, Carnegie Mellon 1969; prof. emeritus) America, environmental, Latin America; a.penna@neu.edu

Robinson, Harlow L. (PhD, California, Berkeley 1980; prof. emeritus; Cinema Studies) Russian culture; h.robinson@neu.edu

Robinson, Raymond H. (PhD, Harvard 1958; prof. emeritus) American historiography, US 1789-1877, US cultural; ra.robinson@neu.edu

Recently Awarded PhDs

DeCamp, David "The Elephant in the Room: Empire Animals, and Visual Culture in Interwar London"

Kazyulina, Regina "'Socially Dangerous' Women: Accommodation, Collaboration, and Retribution in Soviet Ukraine, 1941-45"

Schouteden, Olivier J-F "Impossible Indochina: Obstacles, Issues and Failures of French Colonial Exploration in Southeast Asia, 1862-1914"

Sefer, Akin "The Arsenal of Ottoman Modernity: Workers, Industry, and the State in Late Ottoman Istanbul"

Tannoury-Karam, Sana "The Making of a Leftist Milieu: Anti-Colonialism, Anti-Fascism, and the Political Engagement of Intellectuals in Mandate Lebanon, 1920-48"

Northern Arizona University

Dept. of History, PO Box 6023, Bldg. 18, Rm. 213, Flagstaff, AZ 86011-6023. 928.523.4378. Fax 928.523.1277. Email: derek.heng@nau.edu. Website: https://nau.edu/history-department/.

The Department of History serves the larger university's core values of sustainability, diversity, and global engagement. History faculty members impart these values through learner-centered education and by personal example.

Chair: Derek Heng
Director of Graduate Studies: Paul Dutton
Degrees Offered: BA, BS, BSEd, MA
Academic Year System: Semester
Areas of Specialization: US West/US-Mexican borderlands, western Europe, Indian Ocean, Atlantic world, comparative world
Undergraduate Tuition (per academic year):
  In-State: $10358
  Out-of-State: $23348
Graduate Tuition (per academic year):
  In-State: $9606
  Out-of-State: $21244
Enrollment 2018-19:
  Undergraduate Majors: 349
  New Graduate Students: 5
  Full-time Graduate Students: 23
  Degrees in History: 17 BA, 42 BS, 10 MA

Undergraduate Addresses:
  Admissions: http://nau.edu/admissions/
  Financial Aid: http://nau.edu/finaid/
Graduate Addresses:
  Admissions: http://nau.edu/gradcol/
  Financial Aid: http://nau.edu/gradcol/financing/

Full-time Faculty

Amundson, Michael A. (PhD, Nebraska 1996; prof.) American West, US Southwest, public; michael.amundson@nau.edu

Burton-Rose, Daniel J. (PhD, Princeton 2016; lect.) East Asia, religion, science; Daniel.Burton-Rose@nau.edu

Carlson, Christi (MEd, Northern Arizona 2013; sr. lect.) history/social studies secondary teacher education; christi.carlson@nau.edu

Danielson, Leilah Claire (PhD, Texas, Austin 2002; prof.) US cultural and social, diplomatic; leilah.danielson@nau.edu

Dutton, Paul V. (PhD, California, San Diego 1997; prof. and dir., grad. studies) European social reform, modern France, health; paul.dutton@nau.edu

Finger, Thomas David (PhD, Virginia 2014; asst. prof.) environmental, US and Atlantic world, economic and ecological; thomas.finger@nau.edu

Heng, Derek (PhD, Hull 2005; prof. and chair) maritime Asia, premodern Southeast Asia, economic and diplomatic; derek.heng@nau.edu

Joshi, Sanjay (PhD, Pennsylvania 1995; prof.) India, nationalism, colonial societies; sanjay.joshi@nau.edu

Kashanipour, Ryan Amir (PhD, Arizona 2011; asst. prof.) Latin America, Mexico; ryan.kashanipour@nau.edu

LaBuff, Jeremy (PhD, Pennsylvania 2010; asst. prof.) ancient Greece and Rome, gender and social; jeremy.labuff@nau.edu

Martel, Heather E. (PhD, California, Irvine 2001; assoc. prof.) US, gender, early America and Atlantic world; heather.martel@nau.edu

Meeks, Eric V. (PhD, Texas, Austin 2001; assoc. prof.) US-Mexican borderlands, race and ethnicity; eric.meeks@nau.edu

Reese, Scott Steven (PhD, Pennsylvania 1996; prof.) Islamic world, Africa, Indian Ocean, imperialism; scott.reese@nau.edu

Sargent Wood, Linda A. (PhD, Maryland, Coll. Park 2002; assoc. prof.) US cultural and intellectual, health and disabilities, history/social studies secondary teacher education; linda.sargent.wood@nau.edu

Varela-Lago, Ana M. (PhD, California, San Diego 2008; sr. lect.) modern Spain, modern Europe, modern France, world, war and memory

Wilson, Lindsay Blake (PhD, Stanford 1982; assoc. prof.) France, early modern Europe, women; lindsay.wilson@nau.edu

Joint/Cross Appointments

Ahluwalia, Sanjam (PhD, Cincinnati 2000; prof.; Women and Gender Studies) South Asia, women, social; sanjam.ahluwalia@nau.edu

Nondepartmental Historians

Haeger, John D. (PhD, Loyola, Chicago 1969; Univ. Prof. and pres. emeritus) US, economic, higher education; john.haeger@nau.edu

Ishii, Lomayumtewa C. (PhD, Northern Arizona 2001; assoc. prof.; Applied Indigenous Studies) US, US Southwest, American Indian; lomayumtew.ishii@nau.edu

Retired/Emeritus Faculty

Becher, Harvey (PhD, Missouri, Columbia 1971; prof. emeritus) science, Britain, modern Europe; harvey.becher@nau.edu

Connell, Charles W. (PhD, Rutgers 1969; prof. emeritus) medieval, Europe; charles.connell@nau.edu

Deeds, Susan M. (PhD, Arizona 1981; prof. emerita) Latin America, Mexico, borderlands; susan.deeds@nau.edu

Kitterman, David H. (PhD, Washington 1972; assoc. prof. emeritus) Germany, Russia, modern Europe; david.kitterman@nau.edu

Kosso, Cynthia (PhD, Illinois, Chicago 1993; prof. emerita) ancient Mediterranean world, archaeology, Greece and Rome

Leung, John (PhD, Brown 1982; assoc. prof. emeritus) modern Asia, China, modern Japan; john.leung@nau.edu

Lubick, George M. (PhD, Toledo 1974; prof. emeritus) environmental; george.lubick@nau.edu

McFarlane, Larry A. (PhD, Missouri, Columbia 1963; prof. emeritus) US, economic; larry.mcfarlane@nau.edu

Morley, Margaret R. (PhD, Wisconsin, Madison 1972; assoc. prof. emerita) diplomatic, women; margaret.morley@nau.edu

Nutt, Katharine F. (PhD, New Mexico 1951; prof. emeritus) Latin America

Poen, Monte (PhD, Missouri, Columbia 1967; prof. emeritus) recent America, presidency, Gilded Age; monte.poen@nau.edu

Strate, David K. (EdD, Oklahoma State 1969; prof. emeritus) American West, plains frontier, history education

Wallace, Andrew (PhD, Arizona 1968; prof. emeritus) American Southwest, Arizona, borderlands

Northern Illinois University

Dept. of History, Zulauf Hall 715, Dekalb, IL 60115-2854. 815.753.0131. Fax 815.753.6801. Email: history@niu.edu. Website: https://www.niu.edu/history/.

For students interested in a strong liberal arts education, history represents a fascinating, flexible major that permits study of the broadest possible range of human experience.

Chair: Valerie L. Garver
Director of Graduate Studies: Andy Bruno
Director of Undergraduate Studies: Kristin Huffine
Degrees Offered: BA,BS,MA,PhD
Academic Year System: Semester
Areas of Specialization: US, ancient, medieval, early modern/ modern Europe, Russia, Asia and Southeast Asian studies, Latin America and Africa
Undergraduate Tuition (per academic year): $14609
Graduate Tuition (per academic year): $11281
Enrollment 2018-19:
  Undergraduate Majors: 190
  New Graduate Students: 16
  Full-time Graduate Students: 21
  Part-time Graduate Students: 27
  Degrees in History: 43 BA, 9 BS, 5 MA, 2 PhD
Undergraduate Addresses:
  Admissions: http://www.niu.edu/Admissions/
  Financial Aid: http://www.niu.edu/fa/
Graduate Addresses:
  Admissions: http://www.niu.edu/grad/admissions/
  Financial Aid: http://www.niu.edu/grad/funding/

Full-time Faculty

Abreu, Christina Denise (PhD, Michigan 2012; assoc. prof.; dir., Center for Latino and Latin American Studies) US Latinx, Cuba, race and ethnicity; cabreu@niu.edu

Arnold, Stanley (PhD, Temple 1999; assoc. prof.) African American, civil rights, sports; sarnold@niu.edu

Atkins, E. Taylor (PhD, Illinois, Urbana-Champaign 1997; Dist. Teaching Prof.) Japan; etatkins@niu.edu

Bruno, Andy R. (PhD, Illinois, Urbana-Champaign 2011; assoc. prof. and dir., grad. studies) Russia/Soviet Union, environmental; abruno2@niu.edu

Clymer, Kenton J. (PhD, Michigan 1970; prof.) US foreign relations, US and Asia; kclymer@niu.edu

Djata, Sundiata (PhD, Illinois, Urbana-Champaign 1994; prof.) Africa and African American, Latin America and Caribbean, sports; sdjata@niu.edu

Farrell, Sean M. (PhD, Wisconsin, Madison 1996; prof.) modern Europe, British Empire, Ireland; sfarrel1@niu.edu

Fehrenbach, Heide (PhD, Rutgers 1990; prof.) visual culture, modern Europe, German-US relations; hfehrenbach@niu.edu

Fernandez, Damian (PhD, Princeton 2010; assoc. prof.) ancient, late antiquity; dfernandez@niu.edu

Feurer, Rosemary (PhD, Washington, St. Louis 1997; assoc. prof.) labor and protest movements, capitalism, public; rfeurer@niu.edu

Fogleman, Aaron Spencer (PhD, Michigan 1991; prof.) early America, Atlantic world; aaronfogleman@niu.edu

Garver, Valerie L. (PhD, Virginia 2003; prof. and chair) Early Middle Ages, Carolingian Europe, women, childhood, material culture; vgarver@niu.edu

Hall, Eric A. (PhD, Purdue 2011; assoc. prof.) African American, 20th-century US, sports; ehall4@niu.edu

Hanley, Anne G. (PhD, Stanford 1995; prof.) Latin America, Brazil, economic; ahanley@niu.edu

Hoffman, Beatrix R. (PhD, Rutgers 1996; prof.) US, medicine, legal and constitutional; beatrix@niu.edu

Huffine, Kristin L. (PhD, California, Berkeley 2006; assoc. prof. and dir., undergrad. studies) colonial Latin America; khuffine@niu.edu

Jacobsen, Trude (PhD, Queensland 2004; prof.) Southeast Asia; tjacobsen1@niu.edu

Jones, Eric Alan (PhD, California, Berkeley 2003; assoc. prof.) Southeast Asia, Indonesia; iloveroti@gmail.com

Joy, Natalie Irene (PhD, UCLA 2008; assoc. prof.) early America; njoy@niu.edu

Kuby, Emma (PhD, Cornell 2011; assoc. prof.) modern France; ekuby@niu.edu

Lind, Vera (DPhil, Christian-Albrechts, Kiel, Germany 1997; assoc. prof.) 17th- and 18th-century Europe, Germany; vlind@niu.edu

Mogren, Eric William (PhD, Michigan 1995; JD, Colorado 1985; assoc. prof.) US legal, public policy, environmental; mogren@niu.edu

Montana, Ismael M. (PhD, York, Can. 2007; assoc. prof.) Africa; montana@niu.edu

Sandberg, Brian (PhD, Illinois, Urbana-Champaign 2001; prof.) early modern France and Europe, Mediterranean, religious violence; bsandberg@niu.edu

Schmidt, Jim (PhD, Rice 1992; prof.) US law and society, childhood, 19th century; jschmidt@niu.edu

Smalley, Andrea (PhD, Northern Illinois 2005; assoc. prof.) early America, environmental, history education; asmalley@niu.edu

Joint/Cross Appointments

Littauer, Amanda H. (PhD, California, Berkeley 2006; assoc. prof.; Women, Gender, Sexuality Studies) US, women/gender/ sexuality, LGBT history and queer youth; alittauer@niu.edu

Retired/Emeritus Faculty

Burchfield, Joe D. (PhD, Johns Hopkins 1969; assoc. prof. emeritus) science; burchfield@niu.edu

Foster, Stephen (PhD, Yale 1966; prof. emeritus) colonial America; sfoster@niu.edu

Gonzales, Michael (PhD, California, Berkeley 1978; prof. emeritus) modern Latin America, social and economic, Andes region; gonzales@niu.edu

Haliczer, Stephen H. (PhD, St. Andrew's, UK 1969; prof. emeritus) Spain, early modern Europe; shaliczer@niu.edu

Kinser, Samuel C. (PhD, Cornell 1960; prof. emeritus) Renaissance and Reformation, popular culture; sakinser@aol.com

Logue, William H. (PhD, Chicago 1964; prof. emeritus) modern France, modern Europe; wlogue@mindspring.com

Parot, Joseph J. (PhD, Northern Illinois 1971; prof. emeritus) American religious, ethnic, urban

Posadas, Barbara M. (PhD, Northwestern 1976; prof. emeritus) American urban, social, women; bposadas@niu.edu

Resis, Albert (PhD, Columbia 1964; prof. emeritus) Soviet Union; resis@niu.edu

Smith, J. Harvey (PhD, Wisconsin, Madison 1972; assoc. prof. emeritus) modern France, European social and economic; hsmith@niu.edu

Spencer, Elaine G. (PhD, California, Berkeley 1969; prof. emeritus) Germany, European social and economic; espencer@niu.edu

Spencer, George W. (PhD, California, Berkeley 1967; prof. emeritus) India; gspencer@niu.edu

Wingfield, Nancy M. (PhD, Columbia 1987; prof. emeritus) Habsburg Central Europe, gender and sexuality; nmw@niu.edu

Worobec, Christine D. (PhD, Toronto 1984; prof. emeritus) modern Europe, Russia; worobec@niu.edu

Recently Awarded PhDs

Chludzinski, Katrina "Choosing Race: The Constructions of Anglo-Burman Identity, 1885-1962"

Dressler, Nicole "Morality, Convict Servitude, and the Rise of Humanitarianism in the Anglo-American World, 1718-88"

University of Northern Iowa

Dept. of History, Seerley 319, Cedar Falls, IA 50614-0701. 319.273.2097. Fax 319.273.5846. Email: jennifer.mcnabb@uni. edu. Website: https://csbs.uni.edu/history/.

Our department specializes in preparation for teaching and public history, with innovative programs that offer hands-on training through internships and field experiences, and also provides strong foundations for those who wish to do graduate work in History or pursue other professional careers.

Chair: Jennifer L. McNabb
Director of Graduate Studies: Donna Maier
Degrees Offered: BA, MA
Academic Year System: Semester
Areas of Specialization: US, Europe, Latin America, Africa, Asia
Undergraduate Tuition (per academic year):
  In-State: $7727
  Out-of-State: $18260
Graduate Tuition (per academic year):
  In-State: $9212
  Out-of-State: $19686
Enrollment 2018-19:
  Undergraduate Majors: 150
  New Graduate Students: 5
  Full-time Graduate Students: 10
  Part-time Graduate Students: 6
  Degrees in History: 35 BA, 8 MA

Undergraduate Addresses:
  Admissions: https://admissions.uni.edu/app
  Financial Aid: https://finaid.uni.edu/academic-progress
Graduate Addresses:
  Admissions and Financial Aid: https://csbs.uni.edu/history/masters-history:

Adjunct Faculty

Boruta-Sadkowski, Alicja (PhD, Michigan 1997; lect.) Russia and Soviet Union, Poland; alicja.boruta-sadkowski@uni.edu

Christopher, Chad A. (OMS, Northern Iowa 2009; lect.; teaching advisor and field experience coord.) social science; chad.christopher@uni.edu

Neymeyer, Robert J. (PhD, Iowa 1991; lect.) US diplomatic, Iowa; robert.neymeyer@uni.edu

Schaffner, Heather M. (MA, Northern Iowa 2013; lect.) humanities; schaffnh@uni.edu

Waddle, Joshua (MA, Northern Iowa 2009; lect.) public, US; flywheel@uni.edu

Full-time Faculty

Atkinson, Kenneth R. (PhD, Temple 1999; prof.) ancient and modern Middle East, world religions, Dead Sea Scrolls; kenneth.atkinson@uni.edu

Calderón, Fernando H. (PhD, Minnesota 2011; assoc. prof.) modern Latin America, post-revolutionary Mexico, urban-armed revolutionary organizations; fernando.calderon@uni.edu

Connors, Thomas G. (PhD, Illinois, Urbana-Champaign 1997; assoc. prof.) historical methods, Britain, Ireland; thomas.connors@uni.edu

Cutter, Barbara A. (PhD, Rutgers 1999; assoc. prof.) US women; barbara.cutter@uni.edu

Dise, Robert L., Jr. (PhD, Michigan 1986; assoc. prof.) ancient Greece and Rome, ancient Near East; robert.dise@uni.edu

Fenech, Louis E. (PhD, Toronto 1995; prof.) South Asia; lou.fenech@uni.edu

Goldman, Joanne A. (PhD, SUNY, Stony Brook 1988; prof.) US technology, 19th-century US; joanne.goldman@uni.edu

Hesselink, Reinier H. (PhD, Hawai'i, Manoa 1992; prof.) Japan; reinier.hesselink@uni.edu

Hettle, Wallace A. (PhD, Northwestern 1994; prof.) Civil War and Reconstruction, US South, labor; wallace.hettle@uni.edu

Holcombe, Charles W. (PhD, Michigan 1986; prof.) China, Japan; charles.holcombe@uni.edu

Machen, Emily A. (PhD, Mississippi 2006; assoc. prof.) modern Europe, European women; emily.machen@uni.edu

Maier, Donna J. E. (PhD, Northwestern 1975; prof. and dir., grad. studies) Africa, modern Near East, European imperialism; donna.maier@uni.edu

Martin, Robert F. (PhD, North Carolina, Chapel Hill 1975; prof.) US social, US South; robert.martin@uni.edu

McNabb, Jennifer Lynn (PhD, Colorado, Boulder 2003; prof. and head) England, modern Europe; Jennifer.mcnabb@uni.edu

Roberts, Brian E. (PhD, Rutgers 1995; prof.) US labor, US popular culture; brian.roberts@uni.edu

Sadkowski, Konrad (PhD, Michigan 1995; assoc. prof.) eastern Europe; konrad.sadkowski@uni.edu

Wells, Charlotte C. (PhD, Indiana 1992; assoc. prof.) Renaissance and Reformation, early modern Europe; charlotte.wells@uni.edu

Joint/Cross Appointments

Bruess, Gregory L. (PhD, Minnesota 1991; assoc. prof.; assoc. dean, Coll. of Social and Behavioral Sci.) Russia, Balkans; gregory.bruess@uni.edu

Retired/Emeritus Faculty

Johnson, John W. (PhD, Minnesota 1974; prof. emeritus) US legal and constitutional, 20th-century US; john.johnson@uni.edu

Lees, Jay T. (PhD, Tulane 1983; prof. emeritus) medieval, European intellectual, methodology; jay.lees@uni.edu

Lyftogt, Kenneth L. (MA, Northern Iowa 1989; lect. emeritus) US, humanities; ken.lyftogt@uni.edu

O'Connor, Timothy E. (PhD, Minnesota 1980; prof. emeritus) Russia, Soviet Union; tim.oconnor@uni.edu

Quirk, Charles E. (PhD, Iowa 1967; prof. emeritus) methodology

Sandstrom, Roy E. (PhD, SUNY, Buffalo 1972; assoc. prof. emeritus) France, European popular culture, Europe since 1850

Talbott, Robert D. (PhD, Illinois, Urbana-Champaign 1959; prof. emeritus) Latin America

Walker, David A. (PhD, Wisconsin, Madison 1973; prof. emeritus) US West, US economic, Native American; david.walker@uni.edu

Weisenberger, Carol A. (PhD, Texas A&M 1988; assoc. prof. emeritus) 20th-century US, US business, public policy; carol.weisenberger@uni.edu

Wohl, Harold B. (PhD, Iowa 1956; prof. emeritus) historical methods and historiography, US intellectual

Northern Kentucky University

Dept. of History and Geography, 415 Landrum Academic Center, Highland Heights, KY 41099-2205. 859.572.5461. Email: hisgeo@nku.edu. Website: https://www.nku.edu/academics/artsci/programs/undergraduate/history.html.

We are explorers, storytellers, educators, and activists who offer opportunities to engage with the forces that make us who we are as individuals and global citizens. Our goal is to provide students with foundations for fulfilling lives and careers of discovery and creativity.

Chair: Burke Miller
Director of Graduate Studies: Brian Hackett
Degrees Offered: BA,MA
Academic Year System: Semester
Areas of Specialization: US and world, Europe, public, social studies, black studies/women's and gender studies
Undergraduate Tuition (per academic year):
In-State: $8088
Out-of-State: $16176
Graduate Tuition (per academic year):
In-State: $11856
Out-of-State: $18360
Enrollment 2018-19:
Undergraduate Majors: 220
Full-time Graduate Students: 30
Degrees in History: 64 BA, 15 MA
Undergraduate Addresses:
Admissions: http://www.nku.edu/admission.html
Financial Aid: http://financialaid.nku.edu/
Graduate Addresses:
Admissions: http://gradschool.nku.edu/
Financial Aid: http://financialaid.nku.edu/

Full-time Faculty

Bailey, Rebecca J. (PhD, West Virginia 2001; assoc. prof.) Appalachia, public; baileyr4@nku.edu

Hackett, Brian (PhD, Middle Tennessee State 2009; assoc. prof. and dir., grad. studies) public, museum studies, American material culture; hackettb1@nku.edu

Jackson, Eric R. (EdD, Cincinnati 2000; assoc. prof.) African American, colonial America; jacksoner@nku.edu

Landon, William J. (PhD, Edinburgh, UK 2003; assoc. prof.) premodern Europe, Renaissance; landonw1@nku.edu

LeRoy, Francois J. (PhD, Kentucky 1997; assoc. prof.) modern US, Vietnam, France; leroy@nku.edu

Lombardi, Joseph (MA, Ohio 2002; lect.) medieval, England; lombardij2@nku.edu

Meyers, Debra A. (PhD, Rochester 1997; prof.) US women, colonial America; meyersde@nku.edu

Miller, Burke R. (PhD, Miami, Ohio 2002; assoc. prof. and chair) early American Republic, popular culture, social studies; millerbu@nku.edu

Quinn, Kathleen (ABD, Cincinnati; lect.) ancient, Byzantine, classical reception; quinnka@nku.edu

Reynolds, Jonathan T. (PhD, Boston Univ. 1995; prof.) Africa, Middle East; reynoljo@nku.edu

Tenkotte, Paul A. (PhD, Cincinnati 1989; prof.) American urban, Kentucky; tenkottep@nku.edu

Vance-Eliany, Sharon A. (PhD, Pennsylvania 2005; assoc. prof.) Middle East; vances1@nku.edu

Washington, Michael H. (EdD, Cincinnati 1984; prof.) African American; washington@nku.edu

Watkins, Andrea S. (PhD, Kentucky 1999; assoc. prof.) US South, Kentucky; watkinsan@nku.edu

Wilcox, Robert W. (PhD, NYU 1992; assoc. prof.) Latin America; wilcox@nku.edu

Retired/Emeritus Faculty

Adams, Michael C. C. (PhD, Sussex, UK 1973; Regents prof. emeritus) military, American identity; adamsm@nku.edu

Boothe, Leon E. (PhD, Illinois, Urbana-Champaign 1966; prof. emeritus) modern US, diplomatic; boothel@nku.edu

Claypool, James C. (PhD, Kentucky 1968; prof. emeritus) Kentucky, modern Europe; claypoolj@nku.edu

Desai, Tripta (PhD, Indore, India 1979; prof. emeritus) India, US, India diplomatic relations.; desai@nku.edu

Payne, David S. (PhD, Duke 1970; prof. emeritus) medieval and Renaissance Europe, Native American, Asia; payneda@nku.edu

Ramage, James A. (PhD, Kentucky 1972; Regents prof. emeritus) early national US, Civil War; ramage@nku.edu

Ryan, W. Michael (PhD, Cincinnati 1976; prof. emeritus) Great Britain, military; ryanw@nku.edu

Vitz, Robert C. (PhD, North Carolina, Chapel Hill 1971; prof. emeritus) US intellectual, modern, urban; vitz@nku.edu

Williams, Jeffrey C. (PhD, Edinburgh, UK 1972; prof. emeritus) London, women, First World War; williamsj@nku.edu

Northern Michigan University

Dept. of History, 200A Gries Hall, 1401 Presque Isle Ave., Marquette, MI 49855-5301. 906.227.2512. Fax 906.227.2229. Email: awillis@nmu.edu. Website: https://www.nmu.edu/history/.

At Northern, we strongly believe in learning by thinking and doing. With guidance from caring, engaged instructors, you will be challenged to do high-quality research, improve your communication skills, and develop an understanding of global, societal and individual factors that motivate human action-all skills desired by employers in many fields.

Chair: Alan Willis
Degrees Offered: BA,BS
Academic Year System: Semester

Areas of Specialization: Michigan, globalization, modern Europe, 19th- and 20th-century US
Tuition (per academic year):
In-State: $10729
Out-of-State: $16225
Enrollment 2018-19:
Undergraduate Majors: 65
Degrees in History: 1 BA, 16 BS
Addresses:
Admissions: http://www.nmu.edu/admissions/home
Financial Aid: http://www.nmu.edu/financialaid/home

Adjunct Faculty

Archibald, Robert (PhD, New Mexico 1975; adj. prof.) public, local; roarchib@nmu.edu
Dupras, Nickolas (DPhil, Leeds 2013; contingent asst. prof.) medieval European material culture, medieval European arms and armor, science and technology; ndupras@nmu.edu
Johnson, Kathryn R. (MA, Northern Illinois 2006; contingent instr.) US, world; kathryjo@nmu.edu
Stonehouse, Frederick (MA, Northern Michigan 1985; instr.) Great Lakes; stonef@charter.net

Full-time Faculty

DeFonso, Chet R. (PhD, Illinois, Urbana-Champaign 1990; assoc. prof.) Britain, gender, Canada; cdefonso@nmu.edu
Goodrich, Robert W. (PhD, Wisconsin, Madison 2000; prof.) modern Germany, religion, cultural; rgoodric@nmu.edu
Kendall, Keith H. (PhD, Syracuse 2003; assoc. prof.) medieval Europe, religion, intellectual; kkendall@nmu.edu
Logan, Gabe (PhD, Northern Illinois 2006; assoc. prof.) sport, teacher certification, immigration; glogan@nmu.edu
Mead, Rebecca J. (PhD, UCLA 1999; prof.) women, labor, US West; rmead@nmu.edu
Willis, Alan Scot (PhD, Syracuse 1999; prof. and chair) modern US religion, intellectual; awillis@nmu.edu

Retired/Emeritus Faculty

Magnaghi, Russell M. (PhD, St. Louis 1970; prof. emeritus) regional, Americas, Mexico; rmagnagh@nmu.edu
Maier, Clifford F. (PhD, Washington 1971; prof. emeritus) modern Germany
Nicholson, Howard Lee (PhD, Miami, Ohio 1992; prof. emeritus) history and social studies education, US, Latin America; hnichols@nmu.edu
Saari, Jon L. (PhD, Harvard 1971; prof. emeritus) Asia; jsaari@nmu.edu

University of North Florida

Dept. of History, Bldg. 9, Rm. 2501, 1 UNF Dr., Jacksonville, FL 32224-7699. 904.620.2880. Fax 904.620.1018. Email: mroberts@unf.edu; dsheffle@unf.edu. Website: https://www.unf.edu/coas/history/.

Our mission is to graduate a liberally educated person who can view the world with a historical perspective, appreciate the traditions of various cultures, understand the role of change and continuity, and have interests encompassing humanities, social sciences, fine arts, and natural sciences.

Chair: David Sheffler
Director of Graduate Studies: Chau J. Kelly
Degrees Offered: BA,MA
Academic Year System: Semester

Areas of Specialization: US, ancient/medieval/modern Europe, East and Southeast Asia, Latin America, Africa and African American
Undergraduate Tuition (per academic year):
In-State: $4205
Out-of-State: $15728
Graduate Tuition (per academic year):
In-State: $8881
Out-of-State: $18794
Enrollment 2018-19:
Undergraduate Majors: 273
New Graduate Students: 15
Full-time Graduate Students: 17
Part-time Graduate Students: 28
Degrees in History: 53 BA, 14 MA
Undergraduate Addresses:
Admissions: http://www.unf.edu/admissions/
Financial Aid: http://www.unf.edu/onestop/finaid/
Graduate Addresses:
Admissions: http://www.unf.edu/graduateschool/
Financial Aid: http://www.unf.edu/onestop/finaid/

Full-time Faculty

Bevel, Felicia (PhD, Brown 2019; asst. prof.) American studies; felicia_bevel@brown.edu
Bossy, Denise Ileana (PhD, Yale 2007; assoc. prof.) colonial America, Native American; denise.bossy@unf.edu
Bruey, Alison Jane (PhD, Yale 2007; assoc. prof.) modern and colonial Latin America, US social and political; alison.bruey@unf.edu
Closmann, Charles (PhD, Houston 2002; assoc. prof.) environmental, modern Germany; cclosman@unf.edu
Kaplan, Philip G. (PhD, Pennsylvania 1999; assoc. prof.) ancient Greece and Rome; pkaplan@unf.edu
Kelly, Chau J. (PhD, California, Davis 2011; asst. prof. and dir., grad. studies) Africa; chau.kelly@unf.edu
Rominger, Christopher James (PhD, Graduate Center, CUNY 2018; asst. prof.) chris.rominger@unf.edu
Rothschild, Norman H. (PhD, Brown 2003; prof.) China; hrothsch@unf.edu
Sheffler, David L. (PhD, Wisconsin-Madison 2005; assoc. prof. and chair) medieval; dsheffle@unf.edu

Retired/Emeritus Faculty

Clifford, Dale Lothrop (PhD, Tennessee, Knoxville 1975; assoc. prof. emerita) modern Europe, French Revolution, military; clifford@unf.edu
Courtwright, David T. (PhD, Rice 1979; Presidential Prof. emeritus) US social and legal, medicine; dcourtwr@unf.edu
Crooks, James B. (PhD, Johns Hopkins 1964; prof. emeritus) Progressive era, urban; jamesbcrooks@comcast.net
Furdell, Elizabeth Lane (PhD, Kent State 1973; prof. emerita) Britain, Tudor-Stuart England, women; efurdell@unf.edu
Leonard, Thomas M. (PhD, American 1969; prof. emeritus) US diplomatic, Latin America; tleonard@unf.edu
Prousis, Theophilus C. (PhD, Minnesota 1982; prof. emeritus) modern Europe, Russia, Middle East; tprousis@unf.edu
Schafer, Daniel L. (PhD, Minnesota 1973; prof. emeritus) US, African American, Florida; dschafer@unf.edu

Visiting Faculty

Mieczkowski, Yanek (PhD, Columbia 1995; vis. eminent scholar) America, US presidents; y.mieczkowski@unf.edu

University of North Georgia

Dept. of History, Anthropology, and Philosophy, Barnes Hall, 3rd Fl., Dahlonega, GA 30597. 706.864.1903. Fax 706.864.1873. Email: julie.scott@ung.edu; jeff.pardue@ung.edu. Website: https://ung.edu/history-anthropology-philosophy/.

The University of North Georgia is a multi-campus university with an enrollment of over 19,000 students, making it one of the largest institutions in the University System of Georgia. Federally designated as a senior military college, one of the university's signature leadership programs is its 800-member Corps of Cadets on UNG's Dahlonega Campus.

Chair: Jeff Pardue
Director of Graduate Studies: Michael Proulx
Degrees Offered: AA,BA,MA
Academic Year System: Semester
Areas of Specialization: modern Europe, Britain/Germany/Russia, Middle East/Central Eurasia, 20th-century US diplomatic/African American/women, British imperial and India, Latin America
Undergraduate Tuition (per academic year):
In-State: $6244
Out-of-State: $17294
Graduate Tuition (per academic year):
In-State: $5926
Out-of-State: $18040
Enrollment 2018-19:
Undergraduate Majors: 347
New Graduate Students: 3
Full-time Graduate Students: 17
Degrees in History: 13 AA, 37 BA, 3 MA
Undergraduate Addresses:
Admissions: https://ung.edu/landing/admissions.php
Financial Aid: https://ung.edu/financial-aid/
Graduate Addresses:
Admissions: https://ung.edu/graduate-admissions/
Financial Aid: https://ung.edu/graduate-admissions/financial-info.php

Full-time Faculty

Beall, Jonathan (PhD, Texas A&M 2014; asst. prof.; Dahlonega) military; jonathan.beall@ung.edu
Bricker, Renee Pilette (PhD, Wayne State 2010; assoc. prof.; Dahlonega) early modern Britain, early modern France, medieval Europe; renee.bricker@ung.edu
Buchbinder, Lorraine (MA, NYU; lect.; Gainesville) lorraine.buchbinder@ung.edu
Buseman, Michael (PhD, West Virginia 2013; lect.; Dahlonega) America, Appalachia; michael.buseman@ung.edu
Bush, Erin N. (PhD, George Mason 2019; asst. prof.; Dahlonega) erin.bush@ung.edu
Byers, Richard (PhD, Georgia 2003; prof.; Dahlonega) Germany; richard.byers@ung.edu
Gillespie, Deanna M. (PhD, SUNY, Binghamton 2008; prof.; Gainesville) 20th-century US, US South, African American; dee.gillespie@ung.edu
Greene, Thomas A. (PhD, Loyola, Chicago 2012; asst. prof.; Gainesville) thomas.greene@ung.edu
Guerty, Phillip Michael (PhD, Indiana 2007; assoc. prof.; Gainesville) modern Britain and empire, British India, consumer culture; phillip.guerty@ung.edu
Hightower, Victoria P. (PhD, Florida State 2011; assoc. prof.; Dahlonega) Middle East; victoria.hightower@ung.edu
Hightower, W. Patrick (MA, Florida State 2004; lect.; Dahlonega) environmental, world, US; patrick.hightower@ung.edu
Jespersen, T. Christopher (PhD, Rutgers 1991; prof.; Dahlonega) US diplomacy, China, Vietnam; christopher.jespersen@ung.edu
Justice, George W. (PhD, Georgia 2008; lect.; Oconee) American South, Georgia; george.justice@ung.edu
Kabat, Ric (PhD, Florida State 1995; prof.; Gainesville) 19th- and 20th-century US political/social/cultural, 19th- and 20th-century US South; ric.kabat@ung.edu
Kauffeldt, Jonas (PhD, Florida State 2006; assoc. prof.; Gainesville) modern Middle East, 18th century; jonas.kauffeldt@ung.edu
Kim, Sung Shin (PhD, Pennsylvania 2008; prof.; Dahlonega) China; sungshin.kim@ung.edu
Lambert, Cornelia C. (PhD, Oklahoma 2010; lect.; Gainesville) cornelia.lambert@ung.edu
Luthman, Johanna A. (PhD, Emory 2004; prof.; Gainesville) early modern Britain, women and gender, love/sex/marriage; johanna.rickman@ung.edu
May, Timothy M. (PhD, Wisconsin-Madison 2004; prof.; Dahlonega) Islamic, Russia, Mongolia; timothy.may@ung.edu
McEwan, Diane (MEd, Oglethorpe; lect.; Cumming) diane.mcewan@ung.edu
Murray, Heather (ABD, Louisiana State; sr. lect.; Gainesville) new South, Appalachia, WWII American home front; heather.murray@ung.edu
Ouzts, Clay (PhD, Florida State 1996; prof.; Gainesville and Oconee) 19th- and 20th-century US South; clay.ouzts@ung.edu
Pardue, Jeff D. (PhD, Waterloo 1996; prof. and chair; Gainesville) British Empire, modern Britain, Atlantic world; jeff.pardue@ung.edu
Proulx, Michael L. (PhD, California, Santa Barbara 2007; assoc. prof. and dir., grad. studies; Dahlonega) Mediterranean; michael.proulx@ung.edu
Rogers, Warren, Jr. (PhD, Auburn 1983; prof.; Oconee) 19th-century US, Civil War and Reconstruction, New South; warren.rogers@ung.edu
Rohrer, Katherine (PhD, Georgia 2015; asst. prof; Dahlonega) America; katherine.rohrer@ung.edu
Smith, Jennifer L. (PhD, Georgia 1997; assoc. prof.; Dahlonega) US South; jennifer.smith@ung.edu
Spike, Tamara S. (PhD, Florida State 2006; prof. and assoc. chair; Dahlonega) Latin America; tamara.spike@ung.edu
Tucker, Ann L. (PhD, South Carolina 2014; asst. prof.; Gainesville) America; ann.tucker@ung.edu
Whittemore, Barry (DA, Carnegie Mellon 1996; lect.; Dahlonega) Appalachia; barry.whittemore@ung.edu
Wisnoski, Alexander, III (PhD, Minnesota 2015; asst. prof.; Gainesville) Latin America; alexander.wisnoski@ung.edu
Wynne, Benjamin R. (PhD, Mississippi 2000; prof.; Gainesville) 19th- and 20th-century US South, Civil War; ben.wynne@ung.edu

North Greenville University

Dept. of History, 7801 N. Tigerville Rd., Tigerville, SC 29688. 864.977.7768. Fax 864.977.7021. Email: pthompson@ngu.edu. Website: https://www.ngu.edu/history.php.

As a history major at NGU, you will spend much of your time reading books, searching for information to answer questions, evaluating information and arguments, and then organizing and interpreting evidence to support your own position.

Chair: H. Paul Thompson Jr.
Degrees Offered: BA,BS

Academic Year System: Semester
Areas of Specialization: US South, African American, Europe/ Africa/Middle East, Latin America
Tuition (per academic year): $19750
Enrollment 2018-19:
Undergraduate Majors: 72
Degrees in History: 5 BA, 6 BS
Addresses:
Admissions: http://www.ngu.edu/admissions.php
Financial Aid: http://www.ngu.edu/financial-aid.php

Adjunct Faculty

Black, Kayla (MA, Charleston 2008; adj.) US South, African American; kayla.black@ngu.edu

Larson, Rachel (PhD, Emory 1996; adj.) Latin America, Europe; rachel.larson@ngu.edu

Full-time Faculty

Bell, David (MA, Furman 1988; instr.) 19th-century US, 20th-century US; david.bell@ngu.edu

Boggs, Robert (MA, Furman 1984; MDiv, Duke 1988; instr.) ancient, Europe; robert.boggs@ngu.edu

Cook, Jeffery B. (PhD, West Virginia 1998; prof.) 20th-century US; jeff.cook@ngu.edu

Payne, Brendan John (PhD, Baylor 2017; MDiv, Gordon-Conwell Theological Seminary 2012; asst. prof.) US South, Latin America, East Asia; brendan.payne@ngu.edu

Thompson, H. Paul, Jr. (PhD, Emory 2005; prof. and chair) 19th-century US, African American, US Christianity; paul.thompson@ngu.edu

Thrasher, Rosemary (MA, Clemson 1998; instr.) historical geography, American women; rosemary.thrasher@ngu.edu

Yandle, Paul (PhD, West Virginia 2006; assoc. prof.) mountain South, 19th-century African American, early modern Europe; pyandle@ngu.edu

University of North Texas

Dept. of History, 1155 Union Cir. #310650, Denton, TX 76203-5017. 940.565.2288. Fax 940.369.8838. Email: history@unt.edu. Website: http://history.unt.edu/.

History encompasses all aspects of past human endeavor; it encourages students to think broadly and to attempt to integrate all of their knowledge into a meaningful whole.

Chair: Jennifer Jensen Wallach
Director of Graduate Studies: Michael Wise
Director of Undergraduate Studies: D. Keith Mitchener and Walter Roberts
Degrees Offered: BA, MA, MS, PhD
Academic Year System: Semester
Areas of Specialization: US, Europe, military, Texas, body/place/ identity, food
Undergraduate Tuition (per academic year):
In-State: $7895
Out-of-State: $18023
Graduate Tuition (per academic year):
In-State: $7552
Out-of-State: $15148
Enrollment 2018-19:
Undergraduate Majors: 442
New Graduate Students: 19
Full-time Graduate Students: 86
Degrees in History: 150 BA, 6 MA, 1 MS, 4 PhD

Students in Undergraduate Courses: 12375
Students in Undergraduate Intro Courses: 9413
Undergraduate Addresses:
Admissions: http://admissions.unt.edu/
Financial Aid: http://financialaid.unt.edu/
Graduate Addresses:
Admissions: http://tsgs.unt.edu/future-students
Financial Aid: http://history.unt.edu/

Full-time Faculty

Beebe, Kathryne Elizabeth (DPhil, Oxford 2007; assoc. prof.) medieval Europe, digital humanities, culture/religion/everyday life; kathryne.beebe@unt.edu

Calderon, Roberto R. (PhD, UCLA 1993; assoc. prof.) 19th-/20th-century Mexican American/Texas/US, borders/migration/ diaspora, labor/political economy/politics and policy; beto@ unt.edu

Campbell, Randolph B. 'Mike' (PhD, Virginia 1966; Regents Prof.) early national US 1789-1846, local, 19th-century Texas; mike@ unt.edu

Chet, Guy (PhD, Yale 2001; prof.) colonial America, American Revolution, 17th- to 19th-century Atlantic world and military; guychet@unt.edu

Cox, Graham (PhD, Houston 2008; lect.) 20th-century US, US in world, war crimes/genocide and justice; graham.cox@unt.edu

Fuhrmann, Christopher Joseph (PhD, North Carolina, Chapel Hill 2005; assoc. prof.) ancient and classical Greece and Rome, war and society/religion, war/society/martial culture; cfuhrmann@ unt.edu

Golden, Richard M. (PhD, Johns Hopkins 1975; prof.; dir., Jewish & Israel Studies) 17th- and 18th-century Europe, early modern France; rmg@unt.edu

Hilliard, Constance Bernette (PhD, Harvard 1977; prof.) ancient Egypt and Nubia/Muslim Africa, violence, black women in America; connie@unt.edu

Imy, Kate Alison (PhD, Rutgers 2016; asst. prof.) modern Britain, colonial India, gender/war/religion; kate.imy@unt.edu

Leggiere, Michael V. (PhD, Florida State 1997; prof.) French Revolution and Napoleon, early modern and modern France, 18th-/19th-century European military/war and society/military theory and strategic thought; michael.leggiere@unt.edu

Majstorovic, Vojin (PhD, Toronto 2017; asst. prof.) modern Europe, World War II; vojin.majstorovic@unt.edu

McCaslin, Richard B. (PhD, Texas, Austin 1988; TSHA endowed prof.) early national Texas and US, 19th-century US military, American military culture; mccaslin@unt.edu

Mendiola Garcia, Sandra Celia (PhD, Rutgers 2008; assoc. prof.) modern Mexico; Latin America; sandra.mendiolagarcia@unt. edu

Mendoza, Alex (PhD, Texas Tech 2002; assoc. prof.) 19th-/20th-century US, Texas and Mexican American, US military/Civil War and Reconstruction; amendoza@unt.edu

Mierzejewski, Alfred C. (PhD, North Carolina, Chapel Hill 1985; prof.) modern Germany, 20th-century business and economic/welfare state, 19th-/20th-century European military; acmierzeje@aol.com

Mitchener, D. Keith (PhD, North Texas 2006; lect. and undergrad. advisor) US since 1865, naval; donald.mitchener@unt.edu

Moran, Rachel Louise (PhD, Penn State 2013; lect.) late 19th- and 20th-century US, social and cultural/women and gender, food and body/gender and sexuality; rachel.moran@unt.edu

Morris, Marilyn A. (PhD, London 1988; prof.) 17th- and 18th-century Britain, revolutionary Europe, gender and sexuality; mmorris@unt.edu

Moye, J. Todd (PhD, Texas, Austin 1999; assoc. prof.; dir., Oral History Prog.) late 19th- and 20th-century US social, New South, political and cultural; moye@unt.edu

Phelps, Wesley G. (PhD, Rice 2010; asst. prof.) US; wesley.phelps@unt.edu

Pomerleau, Clark A. (PhD, Arizona 2004; assoc. prof.) late 19th- and 20th-century US women and gender, gender and sexuality, religion and belief; clark.pomerleau@unt.edu

Roberts, Walter E. (PhD, Emory 2003; lect. and undergrad. advisor) late Roman Empire, Byzantine, pre-1500 Mediterranean world; walter.roberts@unt.edu

Seligmann, Gustav L., Jr. (PhD, Arizona 1967; assoc. prof.) US constitutional, American political parties and presidential elections, American military culture; gus@unt.edu

Smith, F. Todd (PhD, Tulane 1989; prof.) Southern Plains Indians, empire/indigeneity/(de)colonization, Spanish and French North America; ftsmith@unt.edu

Stockdale, Nancy L. (PhD, California, Santa Barbara 2000; assoc. prof.) Middle East and Islam, borderlands/migration/diaspora, empire/indigeneity/(de)colonization; stockdale@unt.edu

Tanner, Harold M. (PhD, Columbia 1994; prof.) 20th-century Chinese political/diplomatic/intellectual/military, US-Chinese relations, revolution and insurgency/military theory and strategic thought; htanner@unt.edu

Tomlin, J. L. (PhD, Tennessee, Knoxville 2018; lect.) early America; J.Tomlin@unt.edu

Torget, Andrew J. (PhD, Virginia 2009; asst. prof.) Old South and Texas/US-Mexican borderlands, digital scholarship, migration and diaspora; torget@unt.edu

Velikanova, Olga (PhD, St. Petersburg State 1992; assoc. prof.) Russia and 19th-/20th-century Europe, culture and everyday life, memory and representation; velikanova@unt.edu

Wallach, Jennifer Jensen (PhD, Massachusetts Amherst 2004; assoc. prof. and chair) late 19th-/20th-century US/New South/African American, culture and everyday life, food and the body; jennifer.wallach@unt.edu

Wawro, Geoffrey D. W. (PhD, Yale 1992; prof.; dir., Military Hist. Center) 19th- to 21st-century Europe, modern military/World War I/World War II/Cold War, culture of war; wawro@unt.edu

Welch, Courtney (PhD, North Texas 2010; lect.) US; mcwelch1897@yahoo.com

Wise, Michael David (PhD, Minnesota 2012; assoc. prof. and grad. advisor) late 19th-/20th-century US/American West, environment/food and the body, memory and representation; michael.wise@unt.edu

Recently Awarded PhDs

Bridges, Jennifer "Reclaiming Female Virtue: Social Hygene and Texas Reclamation Centers during WWI"

Smith, Tiffany "Uncle Sam Doesn't Want You: Military Rejection, Early Military Separation, and American Military Potential during WWII"

Truxal, Luke "The Role of Command in the Combined Bomber Offensive: Reopening a Closed Debate"

Wisely, Karen "Developing an LGBT Community in the 'Dallas Way'"

Northwestern College

Dept. of History, 101 7th St. SW, Orange City, IA 51041-1996. 712.707.7056. Fax 712.707.7247. Email: rewinn@nwciowa.edu. Website: https://www.nwciowa.edu/history/.

Study the stories of the past and you'll better understand the present—and be more adequately prepared for the future. As a history major at Northwestern, you'll learn about people: where

they've been, what they've done, how they think, and who they've influenced.

Chair: Robert Winn
Degrees Offered: BA
Academic Year System: Semester
Areas of Specialization: US, Europe, American religion, ancient and early medieval, Enlightenment Europe
Tuition (per academic year): $33510
Enrollment 2018-19:
  Undergraduate Majors: 25
  Degrees in History: 6 BA
Addresses:
  Admissions: http://www.nwciowa.edu/admissions
  Financial Aid: https://www.nwciowa.edu/financial-aid

Adjunct Faculty

Anderson, Douglas F. (PhD, Grad. Theological Union 1988; prof.) US religious, US West, Progressive Era; firth@nwciowa.edu

Full-time Faculty

Koerselman, Rebecca A. (PhD, Michigan State 2013; asst. prof.) modern American religion, women and gender; rebecca.koerselman@nwciowa.edu

Kugler, Michael James (PhD, Chicago 1994; prof.) Enlightenment Europe, intellectual, Britain; kugler@nwciowa.edu

Winn, Robert E (PhD, Catholic 2002; prof. and chair) late antiquity, medieval, classical civilization; rewinn@nwciowa.edu

Northwestern University

Dept. of History, 1881 Sheridan Rd., Harris Hall, Evanston, IL 60208-2220. 847.491.3406. Fax 847.467.1393. Email: history@northwestern.edu. Website: https://www.history.northwestern.edu/.

The History Department is composed of about 50 scholars who take a wide range of approaches to the problems revealed by studying change over time. Notable strengths include Africa and its global connections, medieval and early modern history, modern Europe, history of science/medicine/technology/environment, global history, and the history of the Americas, especially African American and indigenous history.

Chair: Laura Hein
Director of Graduate Studies: Sean Hanretta
Director of Undergraduate Studies: Gerardo Cadava
Degrees Offered: BA,PhD
Academic Year System: Quarter
Areas of Specialization: Americas, England/Europe, Asia/Middle East, Africa/Middle East, global
Undergraduate Tuition (per academic year): $75753
Graduate Tuition (per academic year): $18540
Enrollment 2018-19:
  Undergraduate Majors: 168
  New Graduate Students: 12
  Full-time Graduate Students: 90
  Degrees in History: 53 BA, 8 MA, 16 PhD
Undergraduate Addresses:
  Admissions: http://admissions.northwestern.edu/
  Financial Aid: http://admissions.northwestern.edu/tuition-aid/
Graduate Addresses:
  Admissions: http://www.tgs.northwestern.edu/admission/
  Financial Aid: http://www.tgs.northwestern.edu/funding/

Adjunct Faculty

Lightman, Harriet (PhD, Bryn Mawr 1981; adj.; head, Library Academic Liaison Services) economics, philosophy, bibliography; h-lightman@northwestern.edu

Full-time Faculty

Alder, Ken L. (PhD, Harvard 1991; prof.) science and technology, France; k-alder@northwestern.edu

Allen, Michael J. (PhD, Northwestern 2003; assoc. prof.) 20th-century US; m-allen1@northwestern.edu

Barnett, Lydia (PhD, Stanford 2011; asst. prof.) early modern Europe; lydia.barnett@northwestern.edu

Binford, Henry C. (PhD, Harvard 1973; assoc. prof.) 19th- and 20th-century US, urban, social; hcbin@northwestern.edu

Boyle, Kevin (PhD, Michigan 1990; prof.) 20th-century US; kevin.boyle@northwestern.edu

Britto, Lina M. (PhD, NYU 2013; asst. prof.) Latin America and Caribbean, 20th-century Colombia; lina.britto@northwestern.edu

Bushnell, John S. (PhD, Indiana 1977; prof.) Russia; j-bushnell@northwestern.edu

Cadava, Geraldo Lujan (PhD, Yale 2008; assoc. prof. and dir., undergrad. studies) US-Mexico borderlands; g-cadava@northwestern.edu

Carroll, Peter J. (PhD, Yale 1998; assoc. prof.) Qing and republican Chinese urban, gender and sexuality; p-carroll@northwestern.edu

Cherry, Haydon L. (PhD, Yale 2011; asst. prof.) modern Southeast Asia; haydon.cherry@northwestern.edu

Cohen, Deborah A. (PhD, California, Berkeley 1996; prof. and assoc. chair) modern Britain, Europe; deborah-cohen@northwestern.edu

Elliott, Dyan H. (PhD, Toronto 1989; prof.) medieval; d-elliott@northwestern.edu

Fitz, Caitlin A. (PhD, Yale 2010; asst. prof.) early and revolutionary America, Latin America; c-fitz@northwestern.edu

Frommer, Benjamin R. (PhD, Harvard 1999; assoc. prof.) modern eastern Europe; b-frommer@northwestern.edu

Gadsden, Brett V. (PhD, Northwestern 2006; assoc. prof.) 20th-century African American; brett.gadsden@northwestern.edu

Gillingham, Paul (DPhil, Oxford 2006; assoc. prof.) modern Latin America, 20th-century Mexico; paul.gillingham@northwestern.edu

Glassman, Jonathon (PhD, Wisconsin, Madison 1988; prof.) Africa, East Africa, comparative world; j-glassman@northwestern.edu

Hanretta, Sean A. (PhD, Wisconsin, Madison 2003; assoc. prof. and dir., grad. studies) West Africa, modern West African Islam; sean.hanretta@northwestern.edu

Harris, Leslie M. (PhD, Stanford 1995; prof.) African American, US, urban; leslie.harris@northwestern.edu

Hein, Laura E. (PhD, Wisconsin, Madison 1986; prof. and chair) Japan; l-hein@northwestern.edu

Immerwahr, Daniel (PhD, California, Berkeley 2011; asst. prof.) US in international history; daniel.immerwahr@northwestern.edu

Kiel, Doug (PhD, Wisconsin, Madison 2012; asst. prof.) Native American; doug.kiel@northwestern.edu

Kinra, Rajeev Kumar (PhD, Chicago 2008; assoc. prof.) India, South Asia, Mughal and early British periods; r-kinra@northwestern.edu

Koul, Ashish (PhD, Vanderbilt 2017; asst. prof.) Asia; ashish.koul@northwestern.edu

Lauziere, Henri (PhD, Georgetown 2008; assoc. prof.) North Africa, modern Middle East, modern Europe; h-lauziere@northwestern.edu

Liu, Tessie P. (PhD, Michigan 1987; assoc. prof.) women and gender, European social; t-liu@northwestern.edu

Macauley, Melissa (PhD, California, Berkeley 1993; assoc. prof.) China; m-macauley@northwestern.edu

Masur, Kate (PhD, Michigan 2001; assoc. prof.) US, African American, urban; kmasur@northwestern.edu

Maza, Sarah C. (PhD, Princeton 1978; prof.) French Revolution, 18th-century European intellectual; scm@northwestern.edu

Muir, Edward W., Jr. (PhD, Rutgers 1975; prof.) Renaissance and Reformation, Italy; e-muir@northwestern.edu

Pearson, Susan J. (PhD, North Carolina, Chapel Hill 2004; assoc. prof.) American cultural; sjp@northwestern.edu

Petrovsky-Shtern, Yohanan (PhD, Brandeis 2001; prof.) premodern and modern eastern Europe, Jewish; yps@northwestern.edu

Petry, Carl F. (PhD, Michigan 1974; prof.) medieval and modern Middle East, Islamic, medieval Egypt; c-petry@northwestern.edu

Ramirez, Paul F. (PhD, California, Berkeley 2010; assoc. prof.) Latin America; pramirez@northwestern.edu

Schoenbrun, David (PhD, UCLA 1990; assoc. prof.) early Africa, historical linguistics, comparative ethnography; dls@northwestern.edu

Sherry, Michael S. (PhD, Yale 1975; prof.) modern US, World War II; m-sherry@northwestern.edu

Shyovitz, David (PhD, Pennsylvania 2011; asst. prof.) medieval Jewish; davidshy@northwestern.edu

Sowerby, Scott Andrew (PhD, Harvard 2006; assoc. prof.) early modern Britain, Europe; sowerby@northwestern.edu

Stanley, Amy B. (PhD, Harvard 2007; assoc. prof.) early modern Japan; a-stanley@northwestern.edu

Stokes, Lauren Kelsey (PhD, Chicago 2016; asst. prof.) 20th-century Germany; lauren.stokes@northwestern.edu

Tilley, Helen L. (PhD, Oxford 2001; assoc. prof.) science/medicine/empire, Africa; helen.tilley@northwestern.edu

Woodhouse, Keith (PhD, Wisconsin, Madison 2010; asst. prof.) environmental, social science; keith.woodhouse@northwestern.edu

Yosmaoglu, Ipek K. (PhD, Princeton 2005; assoc. prof.) Ottoman Empire, Turkish Republic; i-yosmaoglu@northwestern.edu

Yuh, Ji-Yeon (PhD, Pennsylvania 1999; assoc. prof.) Asian Pacific American; j-yuh@northwestern.edu

Joint/Cross Appointments

Biondi, Martha (PhD, Columbia 1997; assoc. prof.; African American Studies) African American; m-biondi@northwestern.edu

Bryant, Sherwin K. (PhD, Ohio State 2003; assoc. prof.; African American Studies) African American, Latin American and Caribbean, African diaspora; s-bryant@northwestern.edu

Clayson, S. Hollis (PhD, UCLA 1984; prof.; Art Hist.) modern Europe; shc@northwestern.edu

Hine, Darlene Clark (PhD, Kent State 1975; prof.; African American Studies) African American, African diaspora, African American women; d-hine@northwestern.edu

Kieckhefer, Richard (PhD, Texas, Austin 1972; prof.; Religion) medieval religious; kieckhefer@northwestern.edu

Mokyr, Joel (PhD, Yale 1974; Robert H. Strotz Prof.; Economics) European economic; j-mokyr@northwestern.edu

Orsi, Robert Anthony (PhD, Yale 1981; prof.; Religion) American religious; r-orsi@northwestern.edu

Nondepartmental Historians

Presser, Stephen (JD, Harvard 1971; prof.; Law) American legal and constitutional; s-presser@northwestern.edu

Retired/Emeritus Faculty

Barton, Josef (PhD, Michigan 1971; assoc. prof. emeritus) American social, immigration and ethnic, 19th- and 20th-century European and Latin American peasant; j-barton@northwestern.edu

Breen, Timothy H. (PhD, Yale 1968; prof. emeritus) colonial and revolutionary America, cultural anthropology; t-breen@northwestern.edu

Hayes, Peter F. (PhD, Yale 1982; prof. emeritus) Germany, modern Europe, Holocaust; p-hayes@northwestern.edu

Joravsky, David (PhD, Columbia 1958; prof. emeritus) Russia, European intellectual, science

Lassner, Jacob (PhD, Yale 1963; prof. emeritus) medieval Near East, Jews of Islamic lands; j-lassner@northwestern.edu

Lerner, Robert E. (PhD, Princeton 1964; prof. emeritus) medieval Europe; rlerner@northwestern.edu

McLane, John R. (PhD, London 1961; prof. emeritus) India, Southeast Asia; jockmcl@northwestern.edu

Monter, William (PhD, Princeton 1963; prof. emeritus) Renaissance and Reformation, European witchcraft, Spain; monter@northwestern.edu

Owen, Alex (PhD, Sussex, UK 1987; prof. emeritus) modern Britain, social and cultural, women and gender; a-owen@northwestern.edu

Rowe, John A. (PhD, Wisconsin, Madison 1966; assoc. prof. emeritus) eastern and southern Africa, 19th- and 20th-century Buganda; ugandarowe@rowezone.com

Safford, Frank R. (PhD, Columbia 1965; prof. emeritus) Latin America, 19th-century economic and political; f-safford@northwestern.edu

Wills, Garry (PhD, Yale 1961; prof. emeritus) American cultural and political; g-wills@northwestern.edu

Recently Awarded PhDs

Akiboh, Alvita "Material Culture and Constructions of National Identity in the US Colonial Empire, 1898-1959"

Baker, Kevin T. "World Processor: Computer Modeling, the Limits to Growth, and the Birth of Sustainable Development"

Bottura, Juri "Shaping the Body of the Nation: 'Organicist Agrarianism' in 1930s Brazil"

Burns, Ryan "Potential Protestants: Catholics, Conformity, and Conversion in Early Modern Scotland, 1560-1780"

Doolan, Yuri "The First Amerasians: Mixed Race Koreans from Camptowns to America"

Eatmon, Myisha S. "Public Wrongs, Private Rights: African Americans, Private Law, and White Violence during Jim Crow"

Ernst, Bonnie "Women in the Age of Mass Incarceration: Gender, Rights, and Punishment in Michigan"

Falcone, Michael "The Rocket's Red Glare: Global Power and the Rise of American State Technology, 1940-60"

Hepworth, Mariah "'When the Bestial War Shall Rule No More': D.W. Griffith, World War I, and the Antiwar War Film"

Jiménez, Valeria P. "Brokering Modernity: The World's Fair, Mexico's Eighth Cavalry Band, and the Borderlands of New Orleans Music, 1884-1910"

Miglets, Julia Lauren "Holy Mediocrity: Saintly Matrons and the Dominicans in Late Medieval Italy"

Moy, Charlotte Elizabeth Cover "The Enclosed Renaissance: Intellectual and Spiritual Learning in Early Modern Venetian Convents"

Noddings, Timothy R. "Main Street Jesus: Small-City Revivalism, Chautauqua, and the Birth of Religious Conservatism, 1880-1930"

Sales, Joy Nicolas "Diasporic Struggle: Transnational Activism, Migration, and Anti-Imperialism in Filipino America, 1964-91"

Santana-Rivera, Melissa "Latino Migration Politics in Chicago from the 1930s to the 1970s"

Sarkisian, Aram G. "The Cross Between Hammer and Sickle: Russian Orthodox Christians in the United States, 1908-28"

Soares, Leigh "Higher Ambitions for Freedom: The Politics of Public Black Colleges in the South, 1865-1915"

Takayama, Emilie Yuki "Civilizing Japanese Bodies: A History of Self-Improvement and the Beauty Industry in the Japanese Empire 1868-1945"

Thomas, Alexandra "In Praise of Dracula: Giovanni Botero, Reason of State, and the Ottoman Empire"

Norwich University

Dept. of History and Political Science, Ainsworth Hall, 158 Harmon Dr., Northfield, VT 05663-1035. 802.485.2360. Fax 802.485.2252. Email: egray1@norwich.edu. Website: https://www.norwich.edu/programs/history.

Norwich's History program, which offers a range of classes in US, European, pre-modern (before 1648), non-Western and military history, fosters an understanding of how political, economic and cultural forces have influenced the present.

Chair: Steven Sodergren; History Program Director: Emily Gray
Degrees Offered: BA
Academic Year System: Semester
Areas of Specialization: America, Europe, military, China/Asia
Tuition (per academic year): $31550
Enrollment 2018-19:
  Undergraduate Majors: 100
  Degrees in History: 23 BA
Addresses:
  Admissions: http://www.norwich.edu/admissions/
  Financial Aid: http://www.norwich.edu/admissions/financial/

Full-time Faculty

Boonshoft, Mark (PhD, Ohio State 2015; asst. prof.) colonial America, American education, public; mboonsho@norwich.edu

Brucken, Rowland M. (PhD, Ohio State 1999; prof.) American diplomatic, modern America, world; rbrucken@norwich.edu

Gray, Emily Fisher (PhD, Pennsylvania 2004; assoc. prof. and program dir.) early modern Germany, cultural and religious; egray1@norwich.edu

Kim, Miri (PhD, California, Irvine 2014; asst. prof.) modern China, world, East Asia; mkim1@norwich.edu

McCann, Christine (PhD, California, Santa Barbara 1998; prof.) medieval Europe, Christianity, late antiquity; cmccann@norwich.edu

Pennington, Reina J. (PhD, South Carolina 2000; prof.) modern Europe, military, Russia; rpenning@norwich.edu

Sodergren, Steven E. (PhD, Kansas 2006; prof.) 19th-century America, military, Britain; ssodergr@norwich.edu

Taylor, Thomas F. (PhD, Syracuse 1981; prof.) Africa, Middle East, European expansion; ttaylor@norwich.edu

Retired/Emeritus Faculty

Lord, Gary T. (PhD, Virginia 1976; prof. emeritus) colonial and revolutionary America, Middle Period US, New England material culture; glord@norwich.edu

University of Notre Dame

Dept. of History, 219 O'Shaughnessy Hall, Notre Dame, IN 46556-0368. 574.631.7266. Fax 574.631.4717. Email: history@nd.edu. Website: https://history.nd.edu/.

Notre Dame is a distinctive place, a university steeped in tradition, faith, service, and the life of the mind. Historically, its mission has been to prepare students to engage the world as it is and to transform it. The history department thrives on and fosters this distinctive mission.

Chair: Jon T. Coleman
Director of Graduate Studies: Jaime Pensado
Director of Undergraduate Studies: James Lundberg
Degrees Offered: BA,MA,PhD
Academic Year System: Semester
Areas of Specialization: modern Europe, medieval, science and technology, US, Latin America
Tuition (per academic year): $51336
Enrollment 2018-19:
   Undergraduate Majors: 207
   New Graduate Students: 6
   Full-time Graduate Students: 56
   Degrees in History: 40 BA, 6 PhD
Undergraduate Addresses:
   Admissions: http://admissions.nd.edu
   Financial Aid: http://financialaid.nd.edu
Graduate Addresses:
   Admissions and Financial Aid: http://graduateschool.nd.edu

Adjunct Faculty

Soares, John A., Jr. (PhD, George Washington 2002; adj. asst. prof.) modern global and US; John.A.Soares.2@nd.edu

Full-time Faculty

Appleby, R. Scott (PhD, Chicago 1985; prof.) 20th-century American religious, world fundamentalism; Appleby.3@nd.edu

Beatty, Edward N. (PhD, Stanford 1996; prof.) Latin America, modern Mexico, technology; ebeatty@nd.edu

Bederman, Gail (PhD, Brown 1992; assoc. prof.) American women; Bederman.1@nd.edu

Beihammer, Alexander (PhD, Vienna 1999; prof.) Byzantine; Alexander.D.Beihammer.1@nd.edu

Burman, Thomas E. (PhD, Toronto 1991; prof.; Robert M. Conway Dir., Medieval Inst.) medieval European intellectual; tburman@nd.edu

Cai, Liang (PhD, Cornell 2007; asst. prof.) Chinese intellectual; lcai@nd.edu

Candido, Mariana P. (PhD, York, Can. 2006; assoc. prof.) slavery, identity; mcandido@nd.edu

Coleman, Jon T. (PhD, Yale 2003; asst. prof. and chair) colonial America, US environmental; jcolema2@nd.edu

Deak, John D. (PhD, Chicago 2009; asst. prof.) central Europe, Germany; jdeak@nd.edu

Dochuk, Darren T. (PhD, Notre Dame 2005; assoc. prof.) post-1920s US religion and politics; ddochuk@nd.edu

Fernandez-Armesto, Felipe (DPhil, Oxford 1977; prof.) modern Europe; Felipe.Fernandez-Armesto@nd.edu

Graff, Daniel A. (PhD, Wisconsin-Madison 2004; prof. of the practice) US, labor; Graff.4@nd.edu

Graubart, Karen B. (PhD, Massachusetts Amherst 2000; assoc. prof.) colonial Latin America; kgraubar@nd.edu

Gregory, Brad S. (PhD, Princeton 1996; assoc. prof.) early modern Europe, Reformation; bgregor3@nd.edu

Griffin, Patrick (PhD, Northwestern 1999; prof.) Irish American, early America; pgriffi4@nd.edu

Hamlin, Christopher S. (PhD, Wisconsin-Madison 1982; prof.) science, technology, medicine; chamlin@nd.edu

Hobbins, Daniel (PhD, Notre Dame 2002; assoc. prof.) high and late medieval France; dhobbins@nd.edu

Jarvis, Katie L. (PhD, Wisconsin, Madison 2014; asst. prof.) French Revolution, sociocultural; kjarvis@nd.edu

Johnson, Ian Ona (PhD, Ohio State 2016; J. P. Moran Family Asst. Prof.) military; ijohnso2@nd.edu

Kaufman, Asher (PhD, Brandeis 2000; prof.) modern Middle East; Kaufman.15@nd.edu

Koll, Elisabeth (PhD, Oxford 1998; William Payden Assoc. Prof.) modern China; ekoll@nd.edu

Lundberg, James M. (PhD, Yale 2009; asst. prof. of the practice and dir., undergrad. studies) US cultural and intellectual; jlundbe1@nd.edu

Lyandres, Semion (PhD, Stanford 1992; prof.) modern Russia; Lyandres.1@nd.edu

Martin, Alexander M. (PhD, Pennsylvania 1993; prof.) early modern, modern Europe/Russia; a.m.martin@nd.edu

McGreevy, John T. (PhD, Stanford 1992; prof.) US religious and intellectual, urban; Mcgreevy.5@nd.edu

McKenna, Rebecca Tinio (PhD, Yale 2010; asst. prof.) US cultural and economic; rtmckenna@nd.edu

Menon Shivram, Nikhil (PhD, Princeton 2017; asst. prof.) modern Asia, global economic and capitalism, empires and colonialism, political; nikhilmenon@nd.edu

Meserve, Margaret H. (PhD, London 2001; assoc. prof.) early modern Europe, Renaissance; Meserve.1@nd.edu

Miscamble, Wilson D., CSC (PhD, Notre Dame 1980; prof.) American foreign policy; wmiscamb@nd.edu

Ocobock, Paul Robert (PhD, Princeton 2010; assoc. prof.) Africa; pocobock@nd.edu

Pensado, Jaime (PhD, Chicago 2008; asst. prof. and dir., grad. studies) modern Latin America, modern Mexico; jpensado@nd.edu

Pierce, Richard B., II (PhD, Indiana 1996; assoc. prof.) African American, urban; rpierce@nd.edu

Przybyszewski, Linda C. A. (PhD, Stanford 1989; assoc. prof.) US legal, 19th-century US; Przybyszewski.1@nd.edu

Ragland, Evan R. (PhD, Indiana 2012; asst. prof.) 17th-century medicine/anatomy/experiment; eragland@nd.edu

Rapple, Rory (PhD, Cambridge 2002; assoc. prof.) Tudor England and Ireland, political thought; roryrapple220@gmail.com

Remus, Emily A. (PhD, Chicago 2014; asst. prof.) American social and cultural, capitalism; eremus@nd.edu

Shortall, Sarah Elizabeth (PhD, Harvard 2015; asst. prof.) intellectual, political, religious, Europe/global; sshortal@nd.edu

Sullivan, Robert E. (PhD, Harvard 1977; prof.) post-Reformation, European church, modern western European intellectual; Sullivan.158@nd.edu

Thomas, Julia Adeney (PhD, Chicago 1993; assoc. prof.) Japan; Thomas.165@nd.edu

Tor, Deborah G. (PhD, Harvard 2002; assoc. prof.) medieval Islamic; dtor@nd.edu

Joint/Cross Appointments

Boulton, D'Arcy Jonathan D. (PhD, Pennsylvania 1978; DPhil, Oxford 1976; concurrent assoc. prof.; professional specialist, Medieval Inst.) medieval, nobility and feudalism; Boulton.2@nd.edu

Bradley, Keith R. (PhD, Sheffield; concurrent prof.; prof., Classics) Roman Empire; Bradley.45@nd.edu

Cummings, Kathleen Sprows (PhD, Notre Dame 1999; concurrent asst. prof.; American Studies and assoc. dir., Cushwa Center) American Catholicism, gender, US Catholic; cummings.23@nd.edu

Goulding, Robert D. (PhD, Warburg Inst., London 1999; concurrent asst. prof.; Liberal Studies) Renaissance science; Goulding.2@nd.edu

Jensen, Lionel M. (PhD, California, Berkeley 1992; concurrent assoc. prof.; chair, East Asian Languages and Literatures) Chinese cultural and intellectual; ljensen@nd.edu

Rowland, Ingrid D. (PhD, Bryn Mawr 1980; prof.; Architecture) ancient Roman architecture, classical antiquity; irowland@nd.edu

Stapleford, Thomas A. (PhD, Harvard 2003; concurrent asst. prof.; Liberal Studies) early 20th-century human science; tstaplef@nd.edu

Tweed, Thomas (PhD, Stanford 1989; Harold and Martha Welch Endowed Chair; American Studies) religion in Americas, migration; ttweed@nd.edu

Retired/Emeritus Faculty

Blantz, Thomas E., CSC (PhD, Columbia 1968; prof. emeritus) US political since 1920, Gilded Age political and religious; thomas.e.blantz.1@nd.edu

Crowe, Michael (PhD, Wisconsin, Madison 1965; prof. emeritus) 19th-century life and physical sciences; Crowe.13@nd.edu

Dolan, Jay P. (PhD, Chicago 1970; prof. emeritus) US social, immigration, religious; Dolan.1@nd.edu

Gleason, J. Philip (PhD, Notre Dame 1960; prof. emeritus) US immigration, US religious, intellectual; jgleason@nd.edu

Kerby, Robert L. (PhD, Columbia 1969; assoc. prof. emeritus) national period, Civil War and Reconstruction, US military; Kerby.1@nd.edu

Kselman, Thomas A. (PhD, Michigan 1978; prof. emeritus) France, modern Europe; Kselman.1@nd.edu

Marsden, George M. (PhD, Yale 1965; prof. emeritus) US religious and intellectual; Marsden.1@nd.edu

Murray, Dian H. (PhD, Cornell 1979; prof. emeritus) China; Murray.1@nd.edu

Noble, Thomas F. X. (PhD, Michigan State 1974; prof. emeritus) medieval; Noble.8@nd.edu

Noll, Mark A. (PhD, Vanderbilt 1975; prof. emeritus) US religious; mark.noll.8@nd.edu

Nugent, Walter (PhD, Chicago 1961; prof. emeritus) US 1860-1920, frontier and US West environmental, comparative; Nugent.1@nd.edu

Turner, James (PhD, Harvard 1975; prof. emeritus) US intellectual, religious; jturner2@nd.edu

Van Engen, John H. (PhD, UCLA 1976; prof. emeritus) medieval religious and intellectual; Vanengen.1@nd.edu

Walicki, Andrzej (PhD, Warsaw 1958; prof. emeritus) Russia, eastern Europe; Waliki.1@nd.edu

Recently Awarded PhDs

Baker, Elizabeth Anne "'More Romance than Reality': Mary Carpenter, 'Native Gentlemen,' and the National Indiana Association, 1830-80"

Bonenfant-Juwong, Francis "Ever-Widening Circles: Private Voluntary Development, Colonialism, and Arab Palestinians, 1930-60"

Flanagan, Christopher "Empire Remade: Refining Empire in the American Revolution, 1774-95"

Fontenot, Garrett Andrew "In the Shadows of Empire: Canada, Louisiana, France, and the Shaping of North America, 1763-1803"

Jacobson, Danae Ann "Spiritual Geographies: How Nuns Changed the US West"

Karaulshchikov, Taras Igorevich "A History of Georgian Scientific Intelligentsia: The Case of the Nikoladze Family, 1860-1981"

Liu, Yin "Teaching the 'Secunda Lex': Deuteronomy and Church Reform at Lyon in the Age of Charlemagne"

Moralez, Felicia "From Immigrants to Citizens: Mexicans and Settlement Houses in Gary, Indiana, 1919-65"

Riddle, Jonathan D. "Prospering Body and Soul: Health Reform, Religion, and Capitalism in Antebellum America"

Sawyer, Kathryn Rose "Belief in Power: Building a National Church of Ireland, 1660-89"

Shanley, John Joseph "Catholic Freedom, Protestant Slavery? Reconsidering Anti-Catholicism in Maryland, 1688-1776"

Stanfiel, Heather Lynn "Imperial Heriatge: Empire and Commemoration in Pre-Independence Ireland"

Ulrickson, Maria Cecilia "Free People of African Descent in Santo Domingo, 1750-1844"

Valarezo-Duenas, Aurelio E. "'Para el bien universal y quietud de esta república y provincia': Political Culture, Representation and Policy Making in 17th-Century Northern Andes"

Oakland University

Dept. of History, 371 Varner Dr., Room 416 Varner Hall, Rochester, MI 48309-4485. 248.370.3510. Fax 248.370.3528. Email: naus@oakland.edu. Website: https://www.oakland.edu/history/.

The Department of History faculty guide students toward professional careers and provide opportunities to support academic preparation with field experience in the community.

Chair: James Naus
Director of Graduate Studies: Weldon C. Matthews
Degrees Offered: BA,MA
Academic Year System: Semester
Areas of Specialization: US, Europe, Africa, Asia, Latin America
Undergraduate Tuition (per academic year):
In-State: $10314
Out-of-State: $19098
Graduate Tuition (per academic year):
In-State: $13284
Out-of-State: $18486
Enrollment 2018-19:
Undergraduate Majors: 177
New Graduate Students: 4
Full-time Graduate Students: 3
Part-time Graduate Students: 4
Degrees in History: 56 BA, 3 MA
Undergraduate Addresses:
Admissions: http://www.oakland.edu/futurestudents
Financial Aid: http://www.oakland.edu/financialservices
Graduate Addresses:
Admissions: http://www.oakland.edu/grad
Financial Aid: http://www.oakland.edu/financialservices

Full-time Faculty

Bekele, Getnet (PhD, Michigan State 2005; assoc. prof.) Africa; bekele@oakland.edu

Chapman Williams, Sara E. (PhD, Georgetown 1997; assoc. prof.) early modern Europe, France; chapman@oakland.edu

Clark, Daniel J. (PhD, Duke 1989; assoc. prof.) US labor; djclark@oakland.edu

Dwyer, Erin Austin (PhD, Harvard 2012; asst. prof.) Latin America; dwyer@oakland.edu

Dykes, De Witt S., Jr. (MA, Michigan 1961; assoc. prof.) African American, US urban, family and gender; dykes@oakland.edu

Estes, Todd A. (PhD, Kentucky 1995; prof.) early national US, colonial and revolutionary America, political culture; estes@oakland.edu

Hastings, Derek K. (PhD, Chicago 2004; assoc. prof.) modern Germany; hastings@oakland.edu

Li, Yan (PhD, Northeastern 2012; asst. prof.) modern China; yanli@oakland.edu

Matthews, Weldon C. (PhD, Chicago 1998; assoc. prof. and dir., grad. studies) modern Middle East; matthews@oakland.edu

Miller, Karen A. J. (PhD, Columbia 1992; assoc. prof.) US 1877-present, diplomatic, political; kjmiller@oakland.edu

Milne, George Edward (PhD, Oklahoma 2006; assoc. prof.) colonial America, Native American; milne@oakland.edu

Moran, Sean Farrell (PhD, American 1989; assoc. prof.) modern Britain, Ireland, 19th- and 20th-century European intellectual; moran@oakland.edu

Naus, James L. (PhD, St. Louis 2011; assoc. prof. and chair) medieval Europe; naus@oakland.edu

Shesko, Elizabeth M. (PhD, Duke 2012; asst. prof.) US Civil War; shesko@oakland.edu

Wenz, Andrea Beth (PhD, Boston Coll. 2017; asst. prof.) late medieval, early modern Europe

Part-time Faculty

Greenspan, Ian G. (PhD, California, Berkeley 2006; lect.) Europe; greenspa@oakland.edu

Londo, William (PhD, Michigan 2004; lect.) Japan; londo@oakland.edu

Miles, Mary Jo (MA, Oakland 1992; lect.) US; miles@oakland.edu

Powell, Jeffrey N. (MA, Wayne State 2004; lect.) US; powell2@oakland.edu

Shelly, Cara L. (MA, Michigan 1990; lect.) US; shelly@oakland.edu

Zellers, Bruce L. (MA, Clark 1978; lect.) US; zellers@oakland.edu

Oberlin College

Dept. of History, 10 N. Professor St., Rice Hall 316, Oberlin, OH 44074-1095. 440.775.8520. Fax 440.775.6910. Email: history@oberlin.edu. Website: https://www.oberlin.edu/arts-and-sciences/departments/history.

History is one of the largest academic departments at Oberlin. Interdisciplinary by design, we engage our students in numerous subjects approached through a variety of methodologies to help them become astute observers, practiced researchers, and critical thinkers.

Chair: Leonard Smith
Degrees Offered: BA
Academic Year System: Semester
Areas of Specialization: US, Europe, East Asia and South Asia, Latin America, Middle East and North Africa
Tuition (per academic year): $55976
Enrollment 2018-19:
  Undergraduate Majors: 103
  Degrees in History: 50 BA
  Students in Undergraduate Courses: 1116
Addresses:
  Admissions: https://new.oberlin.edu/arts-and-sciences/admissions/
  Financial Aid: http://new.oberlin.edu/office/financial-aid/

Full-time Faculty

Abul-Magd, Zeinab A (PhD, Georgetown 2008; assoc. prof.) modern Middle East, Islamic law and society, Middle Eastern women and gender; zeinab.abul-magd@oberlin.edu

Bahar, Matthew Robert (PhD, Oklahoma 2012; asst. prof.) early America, Native American; mbahar@oberlin.edu

Choudhury, Rishad (PhD, Cornell 2015; asst. prof.) South Asia; rchoudhury@oberlin.edu

Koppes, Clayton R. (PhD, Kansas 1974; prof.) US political/social/diplomatic since 1900, film, sexuality; clayton.koppes@oberlin.edu

Mitchell, Pablo R. (PhD, Michigan 2000; prof.) Latino/a, US, sexuality; pablo.mitchell@oberlin.edu

Nunley, Tamika Yolanda (PhD, Virginia 2015; asst. prof.) US, African American, digital and public; tamika.nunley@oberlin.edu

Romano, Renee C. (PhD, Stanford 1996; Robert S. Danforth Prof.) US since 1945, race, historical memory; renee.romano@oberlin.edu

Sammartino, Annemarie H. (PhD, Michigan 2004; prof.) modern Central Europe and Germany, migration, urban; annemarie.sammartino@oberlin.edu

Smith, Leonard V. (PhD, Columbia 1990; Frederick B. Artz Prof. and chair) modern Europe, war and society, French Empire; lvsmith@oberlin.edu

Terrazas Williams, Danielle (PhD, Duke 2013; asst. prof.) Latin America, Mexico, Caribbean

Wurtzel, Ellen B. (PhD, Columbia 2007; assoc. prof.) medieval and early modern Europe, urban studies, legal; ellen.wurtzel@oberlin.edu

Joint/Cross Appointments

Lee, Shelley S. (PhD, Stanford 2005; assoc. prof.; Comparative American Studies) US race and culture, Asian American, urban shelley.lee@oberlin.edu

O'Dwyer, Emer Sinead (PhD, Harvard 2007; assoc. prof.; East Asian Studies) Japan and East Asia; emer.odwyer@oberlin.edu

Nondepartmental Historians

Alexis, Yveline (PhD, Massachusetts Amherst 2011; asst. prof.; Africana Studies) Caribbean, Haiti; yalexis@oberin.edu

Brooks, Pam E. (PhD, Northeastern 2000; assoc. prof.; Africana Studies) African American, women, South Africa; pam.brooks@oberlin.edu

Jaeger, Sheila (PhD, Chicago 1994; prof.; East Asian Studies) Korea; sjaeger@oberlin.edu

Wilburn, Drew (PhD, Michigan 2005; asst. prof.; Classics) Greece and Rome; Drew.Wilburn@oberlin.edu

Retired/Emeritus Faculty

Baumann, Roland M. (PhD, Penn State 1970; Coll. archivist emeritus) archives; roland.m.baumann@oberlin.edu

Colish, Marcia L. (PhD, Yale 1965; Frederick B. Artz Prof. emerita) medieval intellectual, Crusades, humanism and reform; marcia.colish@yale.edu

Fisher, Michael H. (PhD, Chicago 1978; Danforth Prof. emeritus) modern South Asia, India, British Empire; michael.fisher@oberlin.edu

Hogan, Heather (PhD, Michigan 1981; prof. emeritus) imperial/Soviet/post-Soviet Russia, Central Asia, labor; heather.hogan@oberlin.edu

Jacobson, Carl W. (PhD, Michigan 1993; adj. asst. prof. emeritus; exec. dir., Oberlin Shansi Memorial Assoc.) China; carl.jacobson@oberlin.edu

Kelley, David E. (PhD, Harvard 1986; assoc. prof. emeritus; East Asian Studies) traditional and modern China, images of Asia, Vietnam; david.e.kelley@oberlin.edu

Kornblith, Gary J. (PhD, Princeton 1983; prof. emeritus) America before 1877, industrialization, slavery and abolitionism; gary.kornblith@oberlin.edu

Lasser, Carol S. (PhD, Harvard 1981; prof. emeritus) American women and social, antislavery, Oberlin; carol.lasser@oberlin.edu

Magnus, Shulamit (PhD, Columbia 1988; prof. emeritus) ancient/medieval/modern European Jewish, memoirs, women; shulamit.magnus@oberlin.edu

Millette, James (PhD, Kings Coll., London 1964; prof. emeritus) Caribbean, antislavery and labor, constitutional; james.millette@oberlin.edu

Soucy, Robert J. (PhD, Wisconsin, Madison 1963; prof. emeritus) Europe, France, fascism

Volk, Steven S. (PhD, Columbia 1983; prof. emeritus) Latin America, museum studies, nationalism and identity; steven.volk@oberlin.edu

Visiting Faculty

Watson, Jesse (PhD, California, Berkeley 2019; vis. asst. prof.; East Asian Studies) China; jesse.d.watson@gmail.com

Occidental College

Dept. of History, 1600 Campus Rd., Los Angeles, CA 90041-3314. 323.259.2751. Fax 323.341.4977. Email: history@oxy.edu. Website: https://www.oxy.edu/academics/areas-study/history.

History is one of the most vital and comprehensive subjects in the Occidental curriculum. Our department offers a broad diversity of courses and approaches covering every time period, and cultures from all over the globe.

Chair: Alexandra Puerto
Degrees Offered: BA
Academic Year System: Semester
Areas of Specialization: Asia, Europe, Latin America, US, Middle East and Africa
Tuition (per academic year): $55980
Enrollment 2018-19:
   Undergraduate Majors: 37
   Degrees in History: 18 BA
Addresses:
   Admissions: http://www.oxy.edu/admission-aid
   Financial Aid: http://www.oxy.edu/admission-aid/financial-aid

Adjunct Faculty

Axelrod, Jeremiah Borenstein (PhD, California, Irvine 2001; adj. asst. prof.) US, California; axelrod@oxy.edu

Full-time Faculty

Ball, Erica L. (PhD, Grad. Center, CUNY 2002; prof.) African American, gender, race, popular culture; balle@oxy.edu

Day, Alexander F. (PhD, California, Santa Cruz 2007; assoc. prof.) modern China, peasant studies; aday@oxy.edu

Fett, Sharla M. (PhD, Rutgers 1995; prof.) early US; sfett@oxy.edu

Gasper, Michael E. (PhD, NYU 2004; assoc. prof.) Middle East and Africa; gasper@oxy.edu

Gelbart, Nina R. (PhD, Chicago 1974; prof.) early modern Europe, science and medicine, women; gelbart@oxy.edu

Hong, Jane H. (PhD, Harvard 2013; asst. prof.) US immigration, ethnicity; janehong@oxy.edu

Horowitz, Maryanne Cline (PhD, Wisconsin, Madison 1970; prof.) medieval, Renaissance, intellectual; horowitz@oxy.edu

Puerto, Alexandra Maria (PhD, California, Davis 2005; assoc. prof. and chair) Latin America; apuerto@oxy.edu

Sousa, Lisa M. (PhD, UCLA 1998; prof.) Latin America; lsousa@oxy.edu

Stone, Marla S. (PhD, Princeton 1990; prof.) 19th- and 20th-century Europe, comparative fascism, European cultural; mstone@oxy.edu

Nondepartmental Historians

Yin, Xiao-huang (PhD, Harvard 1991; prof.; Ethnic Studies) Asian-American relations; emyin@oxy.edu

Retired/Emeritus Faculty

Chan, Wellington (PhD, Harvard 1972; prof. emeritus) China; wkchan@oxy.edu

Cohen, Norman S. (PhD, California, Berkeley 1966; prof. emeritus) colonial and early America, Marxism; cohen@oxy.edu

Dumenil, Lynn (PhD, California, Berkeley 1981; prof. emeritus) US cultural, women, political; dumenil@oxy.edu

Harris, Brice, Jr. (PhD, Harvard 1962; prof. emeritus) Africa, Middle East; bharris@oxy.edu

Kroeber, Clifton B. (PhD, California, Berkeley 1951; prof. emeritus) Hispanic American

Rolle, Andrew F. (PhD, UCLA 1952; prof. emeritus) America

Ohio State University

Dept. of History, 106 Dulles Hall, 230 Annie and John Glenn Ave., Columbus, OH 43210-1367. 614.292.2674. Fax 614.292.2282. Email: history@osu.edu. Website: https://history.osu.edu/.

Our faculty travel the world conducting research and bring that wealth of knowledge and expertise back to the classroom. Their research topics are wide-ranging from environmental history such as the history of water to ancient history and the study of medieval monasteries. They remain excited about their teaching and research while active in the process of historical inquiry.

Chair: Scott Levi
Director of Graduate Studies: Greg Anderson
Director of Undergraduate Studies: Christopher Otter
Degrees Offered: BA,MA,PhD
Academic Year System: Semester
Areas of Specialization: Africa, African American, early and modern US, Latin America, ancient and medieval, early and modern Europe, environmental, military and diplomatic, non-Western, women/gender/sexuality
Undergraduate Tuition (per academic year):
   In-State: $10726
   Out-of-State: $30742
Graduate Tuition (per academic year):
   In-State: $12424
   Out-of-State: $36052
Enrollment 2018-19:
   Undergraduate Majors: 390
   New Graduate Students: 14
   Full-time Graduate Students: 86
   Degrees in History: 120 BA, 12 MA, 12 PhD
   Students in Undergraduate Courses: 12700
   Online-Only Courses: 20%
Undergraduate Addresses:
   Admissions: http://undergrad.osu.edu/
   Financial Aid: http://www.sfa.osu.edu/
Graduate Addresses:
   Admissions: http://gradadmissions.osu.edu/
   Financial Aid: https://history.osu.edu/graduate

Adjunct Faculty

Tzortzopoulou-Gregory, Lita (PhD, La Trobe 2008; adj. asst. prof.) Greece, ancient, archaeology; gregory.257@osu.edu

Affiliated Faculty

Adelman, Melvin L. (PhD, Illinois, Urbana-Champaign 1980; assoc. prof.; Health, Physical Education & Recreation) American sports; adelman.1@osu.edu

Arnold, Bruce Makoto (PhD, Louisiana State 2015; asst. prof.; Educational Studies) African American, modern US, military, women/gender/sexuality; arnold.1041@osu.edu

Frank, Daniel (PhD, Harvard; assoc. prof.; Near Eastern Languages and Cultures) Jewish, medieval; frank.152@osu.edu

Goings, Kenneth W. (PhD, Princeton 1977; prof.; African American and African Studies) African American, urban, US popular culture; goings.14@osu.edu

Iles Johnston, Sarah (PhD, Cornell 1987; Arts and Humanities Dist. Prof.; Classics) ancient, religious studies; johnston.2@osu.edu

Kaldellis, Anthony (PhD, Michigan 2001; prof.; Classics) Byzantium; Kaldellis.1@osu.edu

Larsen, Clark Spencer (PhD, Michigan 1980; prof.; Anthropology) anthropology; larsen.53@osu.edu

Low, John (PhD, Michigan 2011; asst. prof.; Comparative Studies, Newark) US, Native American; low.89@osu.edu

Meier, Samuel A. (PhD, Harvard 1987; prof.; Near Eastern Languages and Literatures) Hebrew and comparative Semitics; meier.3@osu.edu

Full-time Faculty

Anderson, Greg (PhD, Yale 1997; assoc. prof. and dir., grad. studies) ancient Greece; anderson.1381@osu.edu

Baker, Paula (PhD, Rutgers 1987; assoc. prof.) US political; baker.973@osu.edu

Beach, Alison Isdale (PhD, Columbia 1996; assoc. prof.) European medieval, religious, women; beach.174@osu.edu

Blake, Stanley E. (PhD, SUNY, Stony Brook 2001; assoc. prof.; Lima) Latin America, Brazil; blake.166@osu.edu

Bond, Elizabeth Andrews (PhD, California, Irvine 2014; asst. prof.) early modern Europe, modern Europe; bond.282@osu.edu

Brakke, David (PhD, Yale 1992; prof. and Joe R. Engle Chair) Christianity, religious studies, late antiquity; brakke.2@osu.edu

Breyfogle, Nicholas (PhD, Pennsylvania 1998; assoc. prof.) Russian empire; breyfogle.1@osu.edu

Brooke, John L. (PhD, Pennsylvania 1982; Humanities Dist. Prof.) early North America, global environment; brooke.10@osu.edu

Brown, Philip C. (PhD, Pennsylvania 1981; prof. and dir., grad. admissions) Japan; brown.113@osu.edu

Butler, Sara M. (PhD, Dalhousie 2001; prof. and King George III Chair) medieval, women and gender; butler.960@osu.edu

Cabanes, Bruno (PhD, Paris I-Pantheon Sorbonne 2002; prof. and Donald G. and Mary A. Dunn Chair) military, modern Europe; cabanes.2@osu.edu

Cashin, Joan E. (PhD, Harvard 1985; prof.) America, early Republic through Reconstruction; cashin.2@osu.edu

Cavender, Mary Wells (PhD, Michigan 1997; assoc. prof.; Mansfield) Russia, modern Europe, cultural and intellectual; cavender.13@osu.edu

Conklin, Alice L. (PhD, Princeton 1989; prof.; France) conklin.44@osu.edu

Curtis, Kip (PhD, Kansas 2001; assoc. prof.) environment, technology, science; curtis.457@osu.edu

Dragostinova, Theodora (PhD, Illinois, Urbana-Champaign 2005; assoc. prof.) modern eastern and western Europe; dragostinova.1@osu.edu

Duenas, Alcira (PhD, Ohio State 2001; assoc. prof.; Newark) Latin America; duenas.2@osu.edu

Eaglin, Jennifer (PhD, Michigan State 2015; asst. prof.) Latin America, alternative energy, emerging markets; eaglin.5@osu.edu

Elmore, Bartow Jerome (PhD, Virginia 2012; asst. prof.) global/American environmental, business, US South

Flores-Villalobos, Joan Victoria (PhD, NYU 2018; asst. prof.) Latin America; flores-villalobos.1@osu.edu

Genova, James E. (PhD, SUNY, Stony Brook 2000; prof.; Marion) modern Africa, modern France; genova.2@osu.edu

Goldish, Matt (PhD, Hebrew, Jerusalem; prof. and Samuel M. and Esther Melton Chair) Europe, Jewish; goldish.1@osu.edu

Gregory, Timothy E. (PhD, Michigan 1971; prof.) Byzantine, early Roman Empire; gregory.4@osu.edu

Grimsley, Mark (PhD, Ohio State 1992; assoc. prof.) American military, Civil War and Reconstruction; grimsley.1@osu.edu

Hahn, Peter L. (PhD, Vanderbilt 1987; prof. and dean; Arts & Humanities, Coll. of Arts and Sci.) US diplomatic; hahn.29@osu.edu

Harrill, J. Albert (PhD, Chicago 1993; prof.) ancient, religious studies; harrill.5@osu.edu

Hathaway, Jane (PhD, Princeton 1992; Arts & Sciences Dist. Prof.) Egypt, Middle East, world; hathaway.24@osu.edu

Helfferich, Tryntje (PhD, California, Santa Barbara 2003; assoc. prof.; Lima) medieval and early modern Europe, Tudor-Stuart Britain, medieval Islam; helfferich.1@osu.edu

Hoffmann, David L. (PhD, Columbia 1990; Arts & Sciences Dist. Prof.) Russia, Soviet Union; hoffmann.218@osu.edu

Howard, Clayton Charles (PhD, Michigan 2010; asst. prof.) urban, US, sexuality and politics; howard.1141@osu.edu

Hsieh, Meiyu (PhD, Stanford 2011; asst. prof.; Marion) China, comparative state formation and empire building, East Eurasia; hsieh.230@osu.edu

Ingersoll, Thomas Neil (PhD, UCLA 1990; assoc. prof.; Lima) US, modern Europe; ingersoll.11@osu.edu

Jeffries, Hasan Kwame (PhD, Duke 2002; assoc. prof.; Kirwan Inst. for Study of Race and Ethnicity in Americas) African American; jeffries.57@osu.edu

Judd, Robin E. (PhD, Michigan 2000; assoc. prof.) Jewish, Germany, gender; judd.18@osu.edu

Kern, Stephen (PhD, Columbia 1970; Humanities Dist. Prof.) modern European cultural and social; kern.193@osu.edu

Kobo, Ousman M. (PhD, Wisconsin, Madison 2005; assoc. prof.) West Africa; kobo.1@osu.edu

Lerner, Mitchell B. (PhD, Texas, Austin 1999; assoc. prof.; Newark) 20th-century US; lerner.26@osu.edu

Levi, Scott C. (PhD, Wisconsin-Madison 2000; prof. and chair) Central Asia, cultural anthropology; levi.18@osu.edu

McDow, Thomas F. (PhD, Yale 2008; assoc. prof.; dir., Harvey Goldberg Center) Africa, Islamic, Indian Ocean; mcdow.4@osu.edu

Murphy, Lucy E. (PhD, Northern Illinois 1995; prof.; Newark) US; murphy.500@osu.edu

Newell, Margaret E. (PhD, Virginia 1991; prof.) colonial, early US; newell.20@osu.edu

Otter, Christopher J. (PhD, Manchester, UK 2002; assoc. prof. and dir., undergrad. studies) modern Britain, modern Europe; otter.4@osu.edu

Parrott, R. Joseph (PhD, Texas, Austin 2016; asst. prof.) diplomatic, Pan-Africanism; parrott.36@osu.edu

Reed, Christopher A. (PhD, California, Berkeley 1996; assoc. prof.) China; reed.434@osu.edu

Rivers, Daniel Winunwe (PhD, Stanford 2007; assoc. prof.) lesbian/gay/bisexual/transgender, US social movements, family/gender/sexuality; rivers.91@osu.edu

Roth, Randolph A. (PhD, Yale 1981; prof.) early national and revolutionary; roth.5@osu.edu

Sessa, Kristina (PhD, California, Berkeley 2003; assoc. prof.) ancient and medieval; sessa.3@osu.edu

Shaw, Stephanie J. (PhD, Ohio State 1986; prof.) women, African American; shaw.1@osu.edu

Siegel, Jennifer (PhD, Yale 1998; prof.) modern European diplomatic and military; siegel.83@osu.edu

Sikainga, Ahmad A. (PhD, California, Santa Barbara 1986; prof.; African American and African Studies) Africa; sikainga.1@osu.edu

Smith, Stephanie J. (PhD, SUNY, Stony Brook 2002; prof.) Latin America; smith.4858@osu.edu

Soland, Birgitte (PhD, Minnesota 1993; assoc. prof.) Scandinavia, women, modern Europe; soland.1@osu.edu

Staley, David J. (PhD, Ohio State 1993; assoc. prof.; interim dir., Humanities Inst. and dir., Center for Humanities in Practice) digital, digital humanities, historical methods; staley.3@osu.edu

Stebenne, David L. (PhD, Columbia 1991; prof.) 20th-century US, legal, political; stebenne.1@osu.edu

Steigerwald, David H. (PhD, Rochester 1987; prof.) 20th-century US, US intellectual; steigerwald.2@osu.edu

Sumner, Margaret (PhD, Rutgers 2006; assoc. prof.; Marion) early US; sumner.27@osu.edu

Tanner, Heather J. (PhD, California, Santa Barbara 1993; assoc. prof.; Mansfield) medieval Europe; tanner.87@osu.edu

Van Beurden, Sarah (PhD, Pennsylvania 2009; assoc. prof.; African American & African Studies) Africa; van-beurden.1@osu.edu

White, Samuel A. (PhD, Columbia 2008; assoc. prof.) environment and technology, early modern economic, global; white.2426@osu.edu

Zhang, Ying (PhD, Michigan 2010; assoc. prof.) China; zhang.1889@osu.edu

Joint/Cross Appointments

Mansoor, Peter R. (PhD, Ohio State 1995; prof. and Raymond E. Mason Jr. Chair; Mershon Center) military, national security and policy studies; mansoor.1@osu.edu

Parker, Geoffrey (PhD, Cambridge 1968; LittD, Cambridge 1981; Andreas Dorpalen Prof.; Mershon Center) early modern Europe, European expansion, military; parker.277@osu.edu

Sreenivas, Mytheli (PhD, Pennsylvania 2001; assoc. prof.; Women's Studies) India, South Asia, women; sreenivas.2@osu.edu

Retired/Emeritus Faculty

Andrien, Kenneth J. (PhD, Duke 1977; Humanities Dist. Prof. emeritus) colonial Latin America; andrien.1@osu.edu

Bartholomew, James R. (PhD, Stanford 1972; prof. emeritus) Japan, social history of science, Japanese business; bartholomew.5@osu.edu

Benedict, Michael Les (PhD, Rice 1971; prof. emeritus) American constitutional, Civil War and Reconstruction; benedict.3@osu.edu

Beyerchen, Alan D. (PhD, California, Santa Barbara 1973; assoc. prof. emeritus) modern Germany; beyerchen.1@osu.edu

Blackford, Mansel G. (PhD, California, Berkeley 1972; prof. emeritus) American business and economic; blackford.1@osu.edu

Chang, Hao (PhD, Harvard 1966; prof. emeritus) Chinese intellectual

Childs, William R. (PhD, Texas, Austin 1982; prof. emeritus) American business; childs.1@osu.edu

Cressy, David (PhD, Cambridge 1973; prof. emeritus) early modern England, family and kinship; cressy.3@osu.edu

Dahlstrand, Frederick C. (PhD, Kansas 1977; assoc. prof. emeritus; Mansfield) US cultural and intellectual; dahlstrand.1@osu.edu

Dale, Stephen F. (PhD, California, Berkeley 1972; prof. emeritus) Muslim India, modern India, Iran and central Asia; dale.1@osu.edu

Davis, Robert C. (PhD, Johns Hopkins 1989; prof. emeritus) Italy, 17th-century Venice; davis.711@osu.edu

Dominick, Raymond H., III (PhD, North Carolina, Chapel Hill 1973; prof. emeritus) modern Germany; dominick.1@osu.edu

Findley, Carter V. (PhD, Harvard 1969; Humanities Dist. Prof. emeritus) Ottoman Empire, Turkey, modern Middle East; findley.1@osu.edu

Fink, Carole K. (PhD, Yale 1968; prof. emeritus) Europe, 20th-century international; fink.24@osu.edu

Gallay, Alan (PhD, Georgetown 1986; prof. emeritus) colonial and revolutionary America, US South, Atlantic world; gallay.1@osu.edu

Ganz, A. Harding (PhD, Ohio State 1972; assoc. prof. emeritus) European military; ganz.1@osu.edu

Garland, Martha MacMackin (PhD, Ohio State 1975; assoc. prof. emeritus; vice provost, Acad. Affairs) modern Britain; garland.1@osu.edu

Gilmore, Allison B. (PhD, Ohio State 1989; assoc. prof. emeritus) military, America, modern Japan; gilmore.24@osu.edu

Guy, Donna J. (PhD, Indiana 1973; prof. emeritus) Latin America, Argentina; guy.60@osu.edu

Hanawalt, Barbara A. (PhD, Michigan 1970; King George III Prof. emeritus) Britain, medieval social, crime; hanawalt.4@osu.edu

Hartmann, Susan M. (PhD, Missouri, Columbia 1966; prof. emeritus) women; hartmann.1@osu.edu

Hogan, Michael J. (PhD, Iowa 1974; prof. emeritus) American diplomatic, recent US; hogan.5@osu.edu

Hopkins, Richard J. (PhD, Emory 1972; assoc. prof. emeritus) America, Ohio, urban; richard_hopkins@hotmail.com

Kerr, K. Austin (PhD, Pittsburgh 1965; prof. emeritus) 20th-century America; kerr.6@osu.edu

McMahon, Robert J. (PhD, Connecticut 1977; Ralph D. Mershon Prof. emeritus) US diplomatic; mcmahon.121@osu.edu

Millett, Allan R. (PhD, Ohio State 1966; prof. emeritus) American military; millett.2@osu.edu

Murray, Williamson (PhD, Yale 1975; prof. emeritus) modern Europe, military

Robertson, Claire C. (PhD, Wisconsin, Madison 1974; prof. emeritus) Africa, women; robertson.8@osu.edu

Rogel, Carole R. (PhD, Columbia 1966; assoc. prof. emeritus) rogel.1@osu.edu

Rosenstein, Nathan S. (PhD, California, Berkeley 1982; prof. emeritus) ancient

Shiels, Richard D. (PhD, Boston Univ. 1976; assoc. prof. emeritus) America, religious; shiels.1@osu.edu

Steffel, R. Vladimir (PhD, Ohio State 1969; assoc. prof. emeritus; Marion) modern Britain; steffel.1@osu.edu

Van Kley, Dale K. (PhD, Yale 1970; prof. emeritus) France, European intellectual; vankley.1@osu.edu

Van Tine, Warren R. (PhD, Massachusetts Amherst 1972; prof. emeritus) US, labor; vantine.1@osu.edu

Zahniser, Marvin R. (PhD, California, Santa Barbara 1963; prof. emeritus) US diplomatic, early national; marzahn@wideopenwest.com

Recently Awarded PhDs

Anthony, Danielle "Intimate Invasion: Andeans and Europeans in 16th-Century Peru"

Bolaños, Isacar "Environmental Management and the Iraqi Frontier during the Late Ottoman Period, 1831-1909"

Esquivel-King, Reyna "Mexican Film Censorship and the Creation of Regime Legitimacy, 1913-45"

Kadric, Sanja "Ottoman Bosnia and Hercegovina: Islamization, Ottomanization, and Origin Myths"

Larson, Robert "The Local and Transnational Dimensions of the US Anti-Apartheid Movement"

Lopez, Delano J. "How We Became Postmodern"

McCarthy, Brendan "Going Viral in Ancient Rome: Spreading and Controlling Information in the Roman Republic"

McCutcheon, Bonnie "Spectacular Gifts: Gifts Given to Delian Apollo During the Greek Archaic Period"

Miller, Brenna Caroline "Between Faith and Nation: Defining Bosnian Muslims in Tito's Yugoslavia, 1945-80"

Niebrzydowski, Paul "Reining in the Four Horsemen: American Relief to Eastern Central Europe, 1915-23"

Perry, John "From Sea to Lake: Steamships, French Algeria, and the Mediterranean, 1830-1940"

Schultz, Ryan "Mutual Defense: Japanese Officers and National Soldiers in the Manchukuo Army, 1932-45"

Shimoda, Kyle S. T. "The 'Gateways' of the Crusader Peloponnese: Castles, Fortifications, and Feudal Exchanges in the Principality of Achaea, 1204-1432"

Tadlock, Stephen Kyle "Forging the Sword of Damocles: Memory, Mercenaries, and Monarchy on Sicily"

Torkelsen, Leif A. "'Battles Were Not Fought In Lines': Nationalism, Industrialism and Progressivism in the American Military Discourse, 1865-1918"

Torunoglu, Gulsah "Difference and Dialogue: A Comparative History of the Egyptian and Turkish Feminisms, 1880-1935"

Villanueva, Capt James "Awaiting the Allies' Return: The Guerrilla Resistance Against the Japanese in the Philippines during World War II"

Viñas-Nelson, Jessica "Debating the Future: African Americans' on Interracial Marriage"

Wood, Joshua K. E. "In the Shadow of Freedom: Race and the Building of Community in Ross County, Ohio"

Ohio University

Dept. of History, 4th Fl., Bentley Annex, Athens, OH 45701-2979. 740.593.4334. Fax 740.593.0259. Email: history.department@ ohio.edu. Website: https://www.ohio.edu/cas/history/.

Studying history propels our lives, whether for the purposes of entering an important and satisfying profession or for the more expansive incentive of revealing the human condition.

Chair: Katherine Jellison
Director of Graduate Studies: Assan Sarr
Director of Undergraduate Studies: Joshua Hill
Degrees Offered: BA,MA,PhD
Academic Year System: Semester
Areas of Specialization: US, Europe, Africa, Asia, Latin America
Undergraduate Tuition (per academic year):
  In-State: $11896
  Out-of-State: $21360
Graduate Tuition (per academic year):
  In-State: $9444
  Out-of-State: $17436
Enrollment 2018-19:
  Undergraduate Majors: 159
  New Graduate Students: 6

Full-time Graduate Students: 35
Degrees in History: 55 BA, 6 MA, 6 PhD
Students in Undergraduate Courses: 2817
Students in Undergraduate Intro Courses: 1183
Undergraduate Addresses:
  Admissions: https://www.ohio.edu/admissions/
  Financial Aid: http://www.ohio.edu/financialaid/
Graduate Addresses:
  Admissions: http://www.ohio.edu/graduate/
  Financial Aid: http://www.ohio.edu/financialaid/

Full-time Faculty

Abu-Rish, Ziad M. (PhD, UCLA 2014; asst. prof.) Middle East; abuz@ ohio.edu

Bach, Morten (PhD, Ohio 2007; assoc. lect.; Zanesville) 20th-century US, modern Southeast Asia; bach@ohio.edu

Barr-Melej, Patrick (PhD, California, Berkeley 1998; prof.) modern Latin America, cultural and political, Chile; barr-mel@ohio.edu

Brobst, Peter John (PhD, Texas, Austin 1997; assoc. prof.) British Empire, international relations; brobst@ohio.edu

Castle, David B. (PhD, Oregon 1991; asst. prof.; Eastern) Latin America, American diplomatic; castle@ohio.edu

Clouse, Michele L. (PhD, California, Davis 2004; assoc. prof.) Renaissance and Reformation; clousem@ohio.edu

Curp, T. David (PhD, Washington 1998; assoc. prof.) eastern Europe; curp@ohio.edu

Dantas, Mariana L. (PhD, Johns Hopkins 2004; assoc. prof.) African diaspora, Atlantic world; dantas@ohio.edu

Hale, Korcaighe P. (PhD, Ohio 2002; assoc. prof.; Zanesville) modern Europe; halek@ohio.edu

Hill, Joshua Benjamin (PhD, Harvard 2011; asst. prof. and dir., undergrad. studies) East Asia; hillj6@ohio.edu

Holcombe, Alec (PhD, California, Berkeley 2014; asst. prof.) Southeast Asia; holcombe@ohio.edu

Ingram, Robert G. (PhD, Virginia 2002; prof.) early modern Britain; ingramr@ohio.edu

Jellison, Katherine K. (PhD, Iowa 1991; prof. and chair) American women, social; jellison@ohio.edu

Lee, Victoria (PhD, Princeton 2014; asst. prof.) science and technology; leev@ohio.edu

Marinski, Deborah R. (PhD, Toledo 2006; assoc. prof.; Southern) Gilded Age, Progressive Era; marinski@ohio.edu

Mattson, Kevin M. (PhD, Rochester 1994; prof.) American intellectual, social; mattson@ohio.edu

Maxwell, Jaclyn L. (PhD, Princeton 2000; assoc. prof.) ancient Greece, Rome; maxwelj1@ohio.edu

Milazzo, Paul C. (PhD, Virginia 2001; assoc. prof.) American political, environmental; milazzo@ohio.edu

Miner, Steven M. (PhD, Indiana 1986; prof.) Czarist and Soviet Russia; miner@ohio.edu

Nevin, Mark David (PhD, Virginia 2010; assoc. prof.; Lancaster) recent American political; nevinm@ohio.edu

O'Keefe, John McNelis (PhD, George Washington 2012; asst. prof.; Chillicothe) early America; okeefe@ohio.edu

Pach, Chester J., Jr. (PhD, Northwestern 1981; assoc. prof.) recent American political and diplomatic; pach@ohio.edu

Sarr, Assan (PhD, Michigan State 2010; assoc. prof. and dir., grad. studies) Africa; sarr@ohio.edu

Schoen, Brian (PhD, Virginia 2004; assoc. prof.) early US, Civil War, South; schoen@ohio.edu

Shadis, Miriam T. (PhD, Duke 1994; assoc. prof.) medieval, women; shadis@ohio.edu

Trauschweizer, Ingo (PhD, Maryland, Coll. Park 2006; assoc. prof.) military and diplomatic, Germany and US; trauschw@ohio.edu

Uhalde, Kevin (PhD, Princeton 1999; assoc. prof.) medieval; uhalde@ohio.edu

Wolf, Jacqueline H. (PhD, Illinois, Chicago 1998; prof.) medicine, public health; wolfj1@ohio.edu

Zakic, Mirna (PhD, Maryland, Coll. Park 2011; assoc. prof.) modern Germany, Nazism; zakic@ohio.edu

Retired/Emeritus Faculty

Alexander, Charles C., Jr. (PhD, Texas, Austin 1962; prof. emeritus) American intellectual, sports; calexa35@peoplepc.com

Baxter, Douglas C. (PhD, Minnesota 1970; assoc. prof. emeritus) early modern Europe; baxter@ohio.edu

Booth, Alan R. (PhD, Boston Univ. 1964; prof. emeritus) Africa; boothar@gmail.com

Chastain, James G. (PhD, Oklahoma 1967; prof. emeritus) modern Germany, France; jameschastain5@yahoo.com

Eckes, Alfred E., Jr. (PhD, Texas, Austin 1969; prof. emeritus) recent American economic and diplomatic; eckes777@gmail.com

Field, Phyllis F. (PhD, Cornell 1974; assoc. prof. emeritus) Civil War and Reconstruction; field@ohio.edu

Fitzgibbon, Edward M., Jr. (PhD, Ohio State 1974; assoc. prof. emeritus) Czarist and Soviet Russia, Middle East; fitzgibb@ohio.edu

Fletcher, Marvin E. (PhD, Wisconsin, Madison 1968; prof. emeritus) American military, African American; fletcher@ohio.edu

Frederick, William H. (PhD, Hawai'i, Mânoa 1978; assoc. prof. emeritus) Southeast Asia; frederic@ohio.edu

Grow, Michael R. (PhD, George Washington 1977; assoc. prof. emeritus) Latin America; grow@ohio.edu

Hamby, Alonzo L. (PhD, Missouri, Columbia 1965; prof. emeritus) US, 20th century; hambya@ohio.edu

Harvey, Richard L. (PhD, Missouri, Columbia 1966; assoc. prof. emeritus) Tudor-Stuart England; harvey@ohio.edu

Jordan, Donald A. (PhD, Wisconsin, Madison 1967; prof. emeritus) East Asia; jordand@ohio.edu

Kaldis, William Peter (PhD, Wisconsin, Madison 1959; prof. emeritus) Balkans, Byzantine Empire; kaldis@ohio.edu

Reeves, A. Compton (PhD, Emory 1967; prof. emeritus) medieval Europe; reevesc@ohio.edu

Reiger, John F. (PhD, Northwestern 1970; prof. emeritus) American environmental; reiger@ohio.edu

Richter, Donald C. (PhD, Maryland, Coll. Park 1964; prof. emeritus) ancient, modern England; richter@ohio.edu

Whealey, Robert H. (PhD, Michigan 1963; assoc. prof. emeritus) European diplomatic, 20th century, modern Spain; whealey@ohio.edu

Recently Awarded PhDs

Givens, Seth Andrew "Cold War Capital: The United States, the Western Allies, and the Fight for Berlin, 1945-94"

Givens, Adam T. "The Busuness of Airmobility: US Army Aviation, the Helicopter Industry, and Innovation in the Cold War"

Griffith, Luke "'Green Cheese' and 'the Moon': Jimmy Carter, Ronald Reagan, and the Euromissiles"

Marchbanks, Jack R. "Pride and Protest in Letters and Song: Jazz Artists and Writers during the Civil Rights Movement, 1955-65"

Poston, Lance Edward II "Deconstructing Sodom and Gomorrah: A Historical Analysis of the Mythology of Black Homophobia"

Rattanasengchanh, Phimmasone Michael "Thai Hearts and Minds: The Public Diplomacy and Public Relations Program of the United States Information Service and Thai Ministry of Interior, 1957-79"

Ohio Wesleyan University

Dept. of History, 110 Elliott Hall, Delaware, OH 43015-2370. 740.368.3630. Fax 740.368.3653. Email: history@owu.edu. Website: https://www.owu.edu/academics/departments-programs/department-of-history/.

Ohio Wesleyan offers a broad range of US, European, Pacific Asian, and Latin American history courses. You have a great deal of creativity and flexibility in designing a program that suits your personal and historical interests, whether by taking listed courses or pursuing independent studies with individual faculty.

Chair: Barbara Terzian
Degrees Offered: BA
Academic Year System: Semester
Areas of Specialization: early and modern US, medieval and modern Europe, Latin America, Pacific Asia
Tuition (per academic year): $46870
Enrollment 2018-19:
   Undergraduate Majors: 48
   Degrees in History: 25 BA
Addresses:
   Admissions: https://www.owu.edu/admission/
   Financial Aid: https://www.owu.edu/admission/financial-aid-scholarships-tuition/

Full-time Faculty

Arnold, Ellen F. (PhD, Minnesota 2006; assoc. prof.) medieval and early modern Europe; efarnold@owu.edu

Baskes, Jeremy A. (PhD, Chicago 1993; prof.) Latin America, colonial Mexico, economic; jabaskes@owu.edu

Chen, Xiaoming (PhD, Ohio State 1995; prof.) East Asia, modern China and Japan; xmchen@owu.edu

Flamm, Michael W. (PhD, Columbia 1998; prof.) modern America, political; mwflamm@owu.edu

Gingerich, Mark P. (PhD, Wisconsin, Madison 1991; prof.) modern Europe, Germany; mpginger@owu.edu

Spall, Richard F., Jr. (PhD, Illinois, Urbana-Champaign 1985; prof.) Britain, historiography, modern Europe; rfspall@owu.edu

Terzian, Barbara A. (PhD, Ohio State 1999; JD, Ohio State 1975; assoc. prof. and chair) colonial and 19th-century America, legal; baterzia@owu.edu

Retired/Emeritus Faculty

Macias, Anna (PhD, Columbia 1965; prof. emeritus) Latin America, women, Indians of the Americas

Smith, Richard W. (PhD, Ohio State 1959; prof. emeritus) Civil War, slavery controversy, frontier; rwsmith@owu.edu

University of Oklahoma

Dept. of History, 455 W. Lindsey St., Rm. 403A, Norman, OK 73019-2004. 405.325.6002. Fax 405.325.4503. Email: jshart@ou.edu. Website: http://www.ou.edu/cas/history.

Our faculty offers courses covering all parts of the globe, from the ancient to the modern periods. We offer BA, MA, and PhD degrees. At every level, we aim to cultivate an exciting and challenging intellectual community.

Chair: James S. Hart
Director of Graduate Studies: Raphael Folsom
Director of Undergraduate Studies: Jennifer Davis-Cline
Degrees Offered: BA,MA,PhD

Academic Year System: Semester

Areas of Specialization: American West, Native American, Latin America, environmental

Undergraduate Tuition (per academic year):
In-State: $8809
Out-of-State: $2419

Graduate Tuition (per academic year):
In-State: $6243
Out-of-State: $17234

Enrollment 2018-19:
Undergraduate Majors: 188
New Graduate Students: 10
Full-time Graduate Students: 49
Degrees in History: 39 BA, 7 MA, 7 PhD

Addresses:
Admissions: http://www.ou.edu/web/admissions_aid.html
Financial Aid: http://www.ou.edu/financialaid.html

Affiliated Faculty

Harper, Kyle (PhD, Harvard 2007; prof.; sr. vice pres.; and provost; Classics & Letters) Greece and Rome, early Christianity, late antiquity and ancient law; kyleharper@ou.edu

Lifset, Robert D. (PhD, Columbia 2005; assoc. prof.; Honors) 20th-century US, political, energy and environmental; robertlifset@ou.edu

Marashi, Afshin (PhD, UCLA 2003; assoc. prof.; International and Area Studies) Iran and Islam, Middle East, international; amarashi@ou.edu

McClay, Wilfred M. (PhD, Johns Hopkins 1987; Blankenship Chair; Center for the Hist. of Liberty) liberty; wmcclay@ou.edu

Porwancher, Andrew (PhD, Cambridge 2011; asst. prof.; Classics and Letters; Inst. for American Constitutional Heritage) legal/intellectual/social; porwancher@ou.edu

Robertson, Lindsay (PhD, Virginia 1997; prof.; Law) Native American law; lrobertson@ou.edu

Schumaker, Kathryn Anne (PhD, Chicago 2013; asst. prof.; Classics and Letters; Civil Rights) legal, African American, urban; schumaker@ou.edu

Tracy, Sarah (PhD, Pennsylvania 1992; assoc. prof.; Honors) American medicine history and sociology, alcohol and drug treatment and policy, holism in modern medicine; swtracy@ou.edu

Full-time Faculty

Anderson, Gary C. (PhD, Toledo 1978; George Lynn Cross Research Prof.) American Indian, ethnohistory; gcanderson@ou.edu

Bradford, Alfred S. (PhD, Chicago 1973; John Saxon Chair) ancient Greece and Rome; abradford@ou.edu

Brosnan, Kathleen Anne (PhD, Chicago 1999; assoc. prof. and Travis Chair) US West, environmental, urban/legal/public; kbrosnan@ou.edu

Cane-Carrasco, James A. (PhD, California, Berkeley 2000; assoc. prof.) Latin America; cane@ou.edu

Chappell, David L. (PhD, Rochester 1991; Rothbaum Prof.) modern US; dchappell@ou.edu

Davis-Cline, Jennifer J. (PhD, Penn State 2004; assoc. prof. and dir., undergrad. studies) France; jennifer.j.davis@ou.edu

Faison, Elyssa (PhD, UCLA 2001; assoc. prof.) Japan; efaison@ou.edu

Folsom, Raphael B. (PhD, Yale 2007; assoc. prof. and dir., grad. studies) Latin America; raphael.folsom@ou.edu

Grinberg, Ronnie Avital (PhD, Northwestern 2010; asst. prof.) American Jewish, modern US, women and gender; grinberg@ou.edu

Griswold, Robert L. (PhD, Stanford 1979; prof.) recent US, American social; rgriswold@ou.edu

Hart, James S., Jr. (PhD, Cambridge 1984; Hudson Prof. and chair) Tudor-Stuart England, Ireland; jshart@ou.edu

Hines, Sarah Thompson (PhD, California, Berkeley 2015; asst. prof.) Latin America, Caribbean; sarahthines@ou.edu

Holguin, Sandie E. (PhD, UCLA 1994; assoc. prof.) modern European intellectual and cultural, modern Spain; sholguin@ou.edu

Holland, Jennifer Louise (PhD, Wisconsin, Madison 2013; asst. prof.) gender and women, North American West, 20th-century US; jennifer.holland@ou.edu

Hyde, Anne (PhD, California, Berkeley 1988; prof.) 19th-century North American West, Native American, race; anne.hyde@ou.edu

Keppel, Ben (PhD, UCLA 1992; prof.) 20th-century US, African American; bkeppel@ou.edu

Levenson, Alan T. (PhD, Ohio State 1990; prof. and Schusterman/Josey Chair) Jewish intellectual, literary and religious; alevenson@ou.edu

Magnusson, Roberta (PhD, California, Berkeley 1994; assoc. prof.) medieval Europe, Italy; rmagnusson@ou.edu

Malka, Adam C. (PhD, Wisconsin-Madison 2012; asst. prof.) early Republic US, North American slavery, law/politics/society acmalka@ou.edu

Metcalf, Warren (PhD, Arizona State 1995; assoc. prof.) American Indian, American West; wmetcalf@ou.edu

Norwood, Stephen H. (PhD, Columbia 1984; prof.) 20th-century US, American social and labor, Jewish and Holocaust studies; shnorwood@ou.edu

Olberding, Garret P. (PhD, Chicago 2007; assoc. prof.) ancient China; golberding@ou.edu

Saho, Bala S. K. (PhD, Michigan State 2012; assoc. prof.) Africa, 19th- and 20th-century colonialism; bsaho1@ou.edu

Schapkow, Carsten (PhD, Free, Berlin 2000; assoc. prof.) Jewish, Germany; cschapkow@ou.edu

Seidelman, Rhona (PhD, Ben Gurion 2009; asst. prof.) Israel, immigration, public health and quarantine; rds@ou.edu

Shelden, Rachel A. (PhD, Virginia 2011; assoc. prof.) 19th-century American political and cultural, US Civil War, slavery and race; rachel.shelden@ou.edu

Shepkaru, Shmuel (PhD, NYU 1997; Schusterman Prof.) late antiquity and medieval Jewish, Hebrew; shepkaru@ou.edu

Stockdale, Melissa K. (PhD, Harvard 1989; prof.) Russia and Soviet Union; mstockdale@ou.edu

Ward, Janet A. (PhD, Virginia 1993; prof. and CAS Faculty Fellow) urban studies, visual culture and memory studies, 20th-century Germany and border studies; janet.ward@ou.edu

Wickersham, Jane K. (PhD, Indiana 2004; assoc. prof.) Italy and Reformation; jwickersham@ou.edu

Wrobel, David M. (PhD, Ohio 1991; prof. and Merrick Chair; dean, Coll. of Arts and Sciences) North American West, American intellectual and cultural; David.Wrobel@ou.edu

Joint/Cross Appointments

Gross, Miriam D. (PhD, California, San Diego 2010; assoc. prof.; Sch. of International and Area Studies) modern China, Asia; mdgross@ou.edu

Retired/Emeritus Faculty

Gilje, Paul A. (PhD, Brown 1980; prof. emeritus) revolutionary and early America, maritime; pgilje@ou.edu

Lewis Phillips, Judith Schneid (PhD, Johns Hopkins 1979; prof. emeritus) modern Europe, modern Britain, British Empire; judith.s.lewis-1@ou.edu

Snell, Daniel C. (PhD, Yale 1975; prof. emeritus) ancient Near East; dcsnell@ou.edu

Recently Awarded PhDs

Dupree, James E., Jr. "Defining America at the Border: The Line Riders of the Mexican Border District, 1892-1924"

Flynt, Mette "Reborn on Skis: Winter Recreation and the Transformation of the Wasatch Front, 1915-2002"

Griffith, Bobby "Freedom Is My Business: Carl McIntire, Christian Fundamentalism, and the Rise of Modern Conservatism"

Marshall, Lindsay "Teaching Us To Forget: American History Textbooks, the Plains Wars, and Public Memory"

University of Oklahoma

Dept. of History of Science, 601 Elm St., Rm. 625, Norman, OK 73019-3106. 405.325.2213. Email: hheyck@ou.edu. Website: http://ou.edu/cas/hsci.

The University of Oklahoma helped pioneer the professional study of the history of science in American universities. You'll find opportunities here that are hard to find anywhere else, because only a few universities have a department devoted to the history of science, technology, and medicine as we do at OU.

Chair: Hunter Heyck
Director of Graduate Studies: Rienk Vermij
Director of Undergraduate Studies: Piers Hale
Degrees Offered: BA, MA, PhD
Academic Year System: Semester
Areas of Specialization: premodern science and religion, biological and social science, medicine and public health, technology/new media in history of science, modern science/popular culture
Undergraduate Tuition (per academic year):
  In-State: $12783
  Out-of-State: $28164
Graduate Tuition (per academic year):
  In-State: $8602
  Out-of-State: $19596
Enrollment 2018-19:
  Undergraduate Majors: 35
  New Graduate Students: 1
  Full-time Graduate Students: 10
  Part-time Graduate Students: 3
  Degrees in History: 8 BA, 3 PhD
  Students in Undergraduate Courses: 1179
  Students in Undergraduate Intro Courses: 310
Undergraduate Addresses:
  Admissions: http://www.ou.edu/admissions.html/
  Financial Aid: http://www.ou.edu/financialaid
Graduate Addresses:
  Admissions: http://ou.edu/gradcollege/admissions
  Financial Aid: http://ou.edu/cas/hsci/graduate-program/funding-your-graduate-education

Affiliated Faculty

Gross, Miriam D. (PhD, California, San Diego 2010; assoc. prof.; History and International & Area Studies) East Asia medicine, environment/medicine/public health in China, AIDS/endemic diseases/global environmental issues; mdgross@ou.edu

Hamerla, Ralph R. (PhD, Case Western Reserve 2000; assoc. prof.; assoc. dean, Honors Coll.) late 19th-/early 20th-century US chemistry and physics, scientific apparatus, Cold War science; rhamerla@ou.edu

Seidelman, Rhona (PhD, Ben Gurion 2009; asst. prof.; History and Schusterman Center of Judaic & Israel Studies) Israel, immigration, public health/medicine/quarantine; rds@ou.edu

Tracy, Sarah (PhD, Pennsylvania 1992; assoc. prof.; Honors Coll.) sociology of American medicine/gender and medicine, medical anthropology/food studies, psychoactive substances; swtracy@ou.edu

Full-time Faculty

Barker, Peter (PhD, SUNY, Buffalo 1975; prof.) Scientific Revolution historiography, 19th/20th-century physics and psychology, philosophy of science; barkerp@ou.edu

Crowther, Kathleen M. (PhD, Johns Hopkins 2001; assoc. prof.) early modern science and medicine, body and gender in early modern Europe, science and religion; kcrowther@ou.edu

Hale, Piers J. (DPhil, Lancaster, UK 2003; assoc. prof. and dir., undergrad. studies) science/technology/society, modern biology, biomedical and environmental ethics; phale@ou.edu

Heyck, Hunter (PhD, Johns Hopkins 1999; prof. and chair) 19th/20th-century science/science and social thought/technology, information technology and society, technology and environment; hheyck@ou.edu

Magruder, Kerry V. (PhD, Oklahoma 2000; assoc. prof.; curator, Hist. of Science Collections) 17th- and 18th-century theories of Earth, cosmology and early geology, science and religion; kmagruder@ou.edu

Moon, Suzanne Marie (PhD, Cornell 2000; assoc. prof.; ed.-in-chief, Technology & Culture) technology and 20th-century international development, Southeast Asian science and technology, environment; suzannemoon@ou.edu

Nair, Aparna (PhD, Australian National 2010; asst. prof.) medicine and public health, disability studies, colonial and postcolonial studies in India

Pandora, Katherine A. (PhD, California, San Diego 1993; assoc. prof.) science and the public, 19th- and 20th-century American science and technology, social sciences; kpandora@ou.edu

Soppelsa, Peter S. (PhD, Michigan 2009; asst. prof.; managing ed., Technology and Culture) technology, transportation and water infrastructures, urban geography and ecology; peter.soppelsa@ou.edu

Vermij, Rienk H. (PhD, Utrecht, Netherlands 1991; prof. and dir., grad. studies) Cartesian natural philosophy, Copernicanism/science/religion, early modern meteorology; rienk.vermij@ou.edu

Weldon, Stephen P. (PhD, Wisconsin, Madison 1997; assoc. prof.; bibliographer, Hist. of Science Soc.) science and religion, study of paranormal, modern biology and evolutionary psychology; spweldon@ou.edu

Retired/Emeritus Faculty

Livesey, Steven J. (PhD, UCLA 1982; prof. emeritus) medieval science, early scientific methodologies, science in medieval universities; slivesey@ou.edu

Ogilvie, Marilyn B. (PhD, Oklahoma 1973; prof. emerita) women in science; mogilvie@ou.edu

Taylor, Kenneth L. (PhD, Harvard 1968; prof. emeritus) geology, 18th-century science; ktaylor@ou.edu

Recently Awarded PhDs

Kapoor, Nathan Narain "Systematic Colonization: The Coproduction of Electrification and Colonialism in New Zealand"

Reser, Anna N. "Images of Place in American Spaceflight, 1958-74"

Stein, Blair R. "All That is Solid Melts into Air Travel: Environments, Technologies, and the Modern Nation at Trans-Canada Airlines"

Oklahoma State University

Dept. of History, 101 Murray, Stillwater, OK 74078-3054. 405.744.5679. Fax 405.744.5400. Email: michael.logan@ okstate.edu. Website: http://history.okstate.edu/.

Home to leading scholars in many fields, the department has earned a reputation for excellence in teaching, research, and scholarship.

Chair: Michael Logan
Director of Graduate Studies: Douglas Miller
Degrees Offered: BA,MA,PhD
Academic Year System: Semester
Areas of Specialization: US West/native North America, public, transnational, medicine/food/environment, gender/religion/ race
Undergraduate Tuition (per academic year):
 In-State: $5444
 Out-of-State: $14684
Graduate Tuition (per academic year):
 In-State: $5423
 Out-of-State: $16038
Enrollment 2018-19:
 Undergraduate Majors: 93
 New Graduate Students: 9
 Full-time Graduate Students: 29
 Part-time Graduate Students: 19
 Degrees in History: 32 BA, 3 MA, 8 PhD
Undergraduate Addresses:
 Admissions: https://admissions.okstate.edu/
 Financial Aid: https://admissions.okstate.edu/cost-aid/
  financial-aid/
Graduate Addresses:
 Admissions and Financial Aid: http://history.okstate.edu/
  academics/graduate/applying

Full-time Faculty

Arata, Laura J. (PhD, Washington State 2014; asst. prof.) public, US, modern East Asia; larata@okstate.edu
Belmonte, Laura A. (PhD, Virginia 1996; prof.) US foreign policy, US women, post-1945 US; laura.belmonte@okstate.edu
Boles, Richard J. (PhD, George Washington 2013; asst. prof.) race and religion, colonial and early Republic America
Carlson, Thomas A. (PhD, Princeton 2012; asst. prof.) Middle East, Christians in 15th-century Iraq
D'Andrea, David M. (PhD, Virginia 1999; assoc. prof.) early modern Italy, Venice and Veneto, charity; david.dandrea@okstate.edu
Du, Yongtao (PhD, Illinois, Urbana-Champaign 2006; asst. prof.) East Asia; yongtao.du@okstate.edu
Foss, Sarah (PhD, Indiana 2018; asst. prof.) Latin America
Graham, Emily E. (PhD, St. Andrews, Scotland 2009; asst. prof.) medieval England
Griswold, Sarah Kephart (PhD, NYU 2018; asst. prof.) France, museum studies/public
Karibo, Holly M. (PhD, Toronto 2012; asst. prof.) North American borderlands, American social and cultural, women/gender/ sexuality
Kinder, John M. (PhD, Minnesota 2007; assoc. prof.) American studies, war and society, modern US, gender, disability studies, veterans, zoos, bodies in history and culture, historical trauma; john.kinder@okstate.edu
Lavery, Jason E. (PhD, Yale 1997; prof.) early modern Europe, Germany, Scandinavia; jason.lavery@okstate.edu

Logan, Michael F. (PhD, Arizona 1994; prof. and chair) American West, urban, environmental; michael.logan@okstate.edu
Miller, Douglas K. (PhD, Oklahoma 2014; asst. prof. and dir., grad. studies) Native American, modern US; douglas.miller@okstate. edu
Murray, Jennifer M. (PhD, Auburn 2010; teaching asst. prof.)
Rimmel, Lesley A. (PhD, Pennsylvania 1995; assoc. prof.) Russia and Soviet Union, modern Europe, women; lesley.rimmel@ okstate.edu
Schauer, Matthew (PhD, Pennsylvania 2013; asst. prof.) modern Europe and Britain, global empires, anthropology; matthew. schauer@okstate.edu
Sharlach, Tonia M. (PhD, Harvard 1999; asst. prof.) ancient Near East; tonia.sharlach@okstate.edu
Wells, Brandy Thomas (PhD, Ohio State 2015; asst. prof.) African American, women
Zeide, Anna (PhD, Wisconsin, Madison 2014; clinical asst. prof.) environmental, food studies, science and medicine; zeide@ okstate.edu

Retired/Emeritus Faculty

Bryans, William S. (PhD, Wyoming 1987; prof. emeritus) public, state and local, American West; bill.bryans@okstate.edu
Byrnes, Joseph F. (PhD, Chicago 1976; prof. emeritus) modern Europe, religious studies; joseph.byrnes@okstate.edu
Huston, James L. (PhD, Illinois, Urbana-Champaign 1980; prof. emeritus) Civil War and Reconstruction, economic; james. huston@okstate.edu
Rohrs, Richard C. (PhD, Nebraska 1976; prof. emeritus) early national America, Jacksonian America; richard.rohrs@okstate. edu
Smith, Michael M. (PhD, Texas Christian 1971; prof. emeritus) Latin America, Mexico; michael.m.smith@okstate.edu

Recently Awarded PhDs

Brooks, Cecelia R. "Chisum's Pilgrimage and Others II: Questioning the Control of the Black Narrative"
McKinney, Jennifer E. "Breaking the Photographic Frame: Photographic Analysis of the Dakota Sioux and Their Uprising in 1862"

Old Dominion University

Dept. of History, 1 Old Dominion Univ., 8000 Batten Arts and Letters Bldg., Norfolk, VA 23529-0091. 757.683.3949. Fax 757.683.5644. Email: sdanders@odu.edu; ajersild@odu.edu. Website: https://www.odu.edu/historydept.

The Department of History offers both BA and MA degrees that prepare students broadly for modern careers in business, government, and teaching or graduate study in history, law, library science, business, or education. The Department's academic offerings reflect the diversity of the faculty, and students are encouraged to sample broadly the course offerings.

Chair: Austin Jersild
Director of Graduate Studies: Brett Bebber
Degrees Offered: BA,MA,Cert. (maritime)
Academic Year System: Semester
Areas of Specialization: US, international relations, military, African American
Undergraduate Tuition (per academic year):
 In-State: $11000
 Out-of-State: $31000

Graduate Tuition (per academic year):
  In-State: $16750
  Out-of-State: $41000
Enrollment 2018-19:
  Undergraduate Majors: 250
  New Graduate Students: 20
  Full-time Graduate Students: 18
  Part-time Graduate Students: 36
  Degrees in History: 49 BA, 7 MA
Undergraduate Addresses:
  Admissions: http://www.odu.edu/admission/undergraduate
  Financial Aid: http://www.odu.edu/admission/financial-aid
Graduate Addresses:
  Admissions: http://www.odu.edu/admission/graduate
  Financial Aid: http://www.odu.edu/admission/financial-aid

Full-time Faculty

Abbott, Nicholas J. (PhD, Wisconsin-Madison 2017; asst. prof.) Islamic world
Bebber, Brett M. (PhD, Arizona 2008; assoc. prof. and dir., grad. studies) modern Britain and Empire, 20th-century Europe, race and migration; bbebber@odu.edu
Carhart, Michael C. (PhD, Rutgers 1999; assoc. prof.) 18th-century Europe, intellectual and cultural, science; mcarhart@odu.edu
Del Corso, Robert Engel (MA, Naval Postgrad. Sch. 1996; lect.) Western civilization, world; rdelcors@odu.edu
Finley-Croswhite, S. Annette (PhD, Emory 1991; prof.) early modern Europe, modern Europe, Holocaust; acroswhi@odu.edu
Hailstork, Qiu Jin (PhD, Hawai'i, Manoa 1995; assoc. prof.) East Asia, China, Japan; qjin@odu.edu
Heidbrink, Ingo (PhD, Hamburg, Germany 1999; DPhil, Bremen, Germany 2004; prof.) maritime, economic, environmental; iheidbri@odu.edu
Holden, Robert H. (PhD, Chicago 1986; prof.) Latin America; rholden@odu.edu
Jersild, Austin (PhD, California, Davis 1994; prof. and chair) Russia, European intellectual; ajersild@odu.edu
Jordan, Erin Lynn (PhD, Iowa 2000; assoc. prof.) medieval, women and gender, religion; ejordan@odu.edu
Lawes, Carolyn J. (PhD, California, Davis 1992; assoc. prof.) 19th-century US social, women, religious; clawes@odu.edu
Merritt, Jane T. (PhD, Washington 1995; prof.) early America, Atlantic world, Native American; jmerritt@odu.edu
Nutzman, Megan (PhD, Chicago 2014; asst. prof.) ancient Mediterranean world, early Christianity, second temple Judaism; mnutzman@odu.edu
Orr, Timothy (PhD, Penn State 2010; assoc. prof.) military; torr@odu.edu
Weber, John W. (PhD, William and Mary 2008; assoc. prof.) America, migration, US labor; jwweber@odu.edu
Zanoni, Elizabeth Ann (PhD, Minnesota 2011; assoc. prof.) US, immigration, gender; ezanoni@odu.edu

Joint/Cross Appointments

Myrick, Bismarck (MA, Syracuse 1973; ambassador in residence; Political Science) international affairs; bmyrick@odu.edu
Whitehurst, G. William (PhD, West Virginia 1962; Kaufman Lect.; Political Science) US foreign relations, Middle East, US Congress; drbillodu@cox.net

Part-time Faculty

Rodner, William S. (PhD, Penn State 1977; adj. prof.; ed., Scotia) wrodner@odu.edu

Retired/Emeritus Faculty

Greene, Douglas G. (PhD, Chicago 1972; prof. emeritus) Britain; dgreene@odu.edu
Lees, Lorraine M. (PhD, Penn State 1976; prof. emeritus) US foreign policy and Cold War; llees@odu.edu
Pearson, Kathy L. (PhD, Emory 1990; assoc. prof. emeritus) classical and medieval Europe; kpearson@odu.edu
Stewart, Peter C. (PhD, Virginia 1967; prof. emeritus) US, American sports, Virginia; pstewart@odu.edu
Sweeney, James R. (PhD, Notre Dame 1970; assoc. prof. emeritus) Virginia, US since 1940, New South; jsweeney@odu.edu
Wilson, Harold S. (PhD, Emory 1966; prof. emeritus) Civil War and Reconstruction, US South, Progressive Era; hwilson@odu.edu

University of Oregon

Dept. of History, 1101 Kincaid St., 275 McKenzie Hall, Eugene, OR 97403-1288. 541.346.4806. Fax 541.346.4895. Email: lpinchin@uoregon.edu; bhrush@uoregon.edu. Website: https://history.uoregon.edu/.

Alternate Address: 1288 Univ. of Oregon, Eugene, OR 97403

Undergraduate history majors learn about the variety of human experience over time and, in so doing, acquire analytical and writing skills that prepare them for success in numerous areas of work and study. History graduate students become immersed in the latest scholarship and develop research projects that contribute in significant ways to an understanding of the past.

Chair: Brett Rushforth
Director of Graduate Studies: Ryan Jones
Director of Undergraduate Studies: Julie Weise
Degrees Offered: BA,BS,MA,PhD
Academic Year System: Quarter
Areas of Specialization: US, Europe, East and Southeast Asia, Latin America, Africa
Undergraduate Tuition (per academic year):
  In-State: $14044
  Out-of-State: $44764
Graduate Tuition (per academic year):
  In-State: $15910
  Out-of-State: $26899
Enrollment 2018-19:
  Undergraduate Majors: 256
  New Graduate Students: 7
  Full-time Graduate Students: 33
  Degrees in History: 56 BA, 9 BS, 4 MA, 2 PhD
  Students in Undergraduate Courses: 5014
  Students in Undergraduate Intro Courses: 1694
  Online-Only Courses: 8%
Undergraduate Addresses:
  Admissions: http://admissions.uoregon.edu/
  Financial Aid: http://financialaid.uoregon.edu/
Graduate Addresses:
  Admissions and Financial Aid: https://history.uoregon.edu/graduate/

Affiliated Faculty

Bussel, Bob (PhD, Cornell 1993; prof.; Labor Education and Research Center) bussel@uoregon.edu
Carey, Mark (PhD, California, Davis 2005; assoc. prof.; Robert D. Clark Honors Coll.) Latin America, environmental; carey@uoregon.edu

Cheney, Charise (PhD, Illinois, Urbana-Champaign 1999; assoc. prof.; Ethnic Studies) African American popular/political cultures, gender and sexuality; ccheney@uoregon.edu

Fracchia, Joseph (PhD, California, Davis 1985; prof. emeritus; Robert D. Clark Honors Coll.) German social and intellectual, history of philosophy; fracchia@uoregon.edu

Hatfield, Kevin D. (PhD, Oregon 2003; asst. prof.; Robert D. Clark Honors Coll.) American West, Basque immigration; kevhat@uoregon.edu

Howell, Ocean (PhD, California, Berkeley 2009; asst. prof.; Robert D. Clark Honors Coll.) architecture, urban planning; ohowell@uoregon.edu

Klopotek, Brian R. (PhD, Minnesota 2004; assoc. prof.; Ethnic Studies) Native American studies; klopotek@uoregon.edu

Prazniak, Roxann (PhD, California, Davis 1981; assoc. prof.; Robert D. Clark Honors Coll.) China and Eurasia, emergence of modernity, transcultural studies; prazniak@uoregon.edu

Rosenberg, Daniel B. (PhD, California, Berkeley 1996; prof.; Robert D. Clark Honors Coll.) modern European intellectual and cultural, Enlightenment; dbr@uoregon.edu

Williams, Timothy (PhD, North Carolina, Chapel Hill 2010; asst. prof.; Robert D. Clark Honors Coll.) 19th-century US, intellectual and cultural, gender and sexuality; timw@uoregon.edu

Wood, Stephanie (PhD, UCLA 1984; dir., Wired Humanities Projects) Latin America; swood@uoregon.edu

Full-time Faculty

Aguirre, Carlos (PhD, Minnesota 1996; prof.) Latin America; caguirre@uoregon.edu

Alexander, Leslie M. (PhD, Cornell 2001; assoc. prof.) early African American, African diaspora; lalexand@uoregon.edu

Asim, Ina (PhD, Würzburg, Germany 2001; assoc. prof.) late imperial China; inaasim@uoregon.edu

Austin, Curtis J. (PhD, Mississippi State 1998; assoc. prof.) US social and political, African American, civil rights; caustin@uoregon.edu

Beda, Steven (PhD, Washington 2014; asst. prof.) 20th-century US, environmental, labor; sbeda@uoregon.edu

Braun, Lindsay Frederick (PhD, Rutgers 2008; assoc. prof.) Africa; lfbraun@uoregon.edu

Dracobly, Alexander (PhD, Chicago 1996; sr. instr.) modern Europe, military, medical; dracobly@uoregon.edu

Goble, Andrew E. (PhD, Stanford 1987; prof.) East Asia, premodern Japan; platypus@uoregon.edu

Goodman, Bryna (PhD, Stanford 1990; prof.) modern China; bgoodman@uoregon.edu

Hanes, Jeffrey (PhD, California, Berkeley 1988; assoc. prof.) modern Japan; hanes@uoregon.edu

Haskett, Robert Stephen (PhD, UCLA 1985; prof.) Latin America; rhaskett@uoregon.edu

Heinz, Annelise (PhD, Stanford 2015; asst. prof.) gender, trans-Pacific

Herman, Ellen P. (PhD, Brandeis 1993; prof.; vice provost, Academic Affairs; and codir., Wayne Morse Center for Law and Politics) modern US; eherman@uoregon.edu

Hessler, Julie M. (PhD, Chicago 1996; assoc. prof.) modern Europe; hessler@uoregon.edu

Jones, Ryan T. (PhD, Columbia 2008; assoc. prof. and dir., grad. studies) Russia, Pacific, global environmental; rtj@uoregon.edu

Keller, Vera A. (PhD, Princeton 2008; assoc. prof.; Robert D. Clark Honors Coll.) alchemy and scientific experimentation, Europe, Ottoman empires; keller@uoregon.edu

Luebke, David M. (PhD, Yale 1990; prof.) Germany; dluebke@uoregon.edu

Madar, Allison (PhD, Rice 2013; asst. prof.) social/cultural histories of law in early America, Atlantic world; amadar@uoregon.edu

Mazurek, Lindsey (PhD, Duke 2016; asst. prof.) Hellenistic and Roman material culture, migration, globalization

McCole, John J. (PhD, Boston Univ. 1988; assoc. prof.) modern Europe; mccole@uoregon.edu

McNeely, Ian Farrell (PhD, Michigan 1998; prof.) modern Europe and world; imcneely@uoregon.edu

Ostler, Jeff (PhD, Iowa 1990; prof.) American West; jostler@uoregon.edu

Rushforth, Brett (PhD, California, Davis 2003; assoc. prof. and head) early and colonial America; bhrush@uoregon.edu

Sheridan, George J. (PhD, Yale 1978; assoc. prof.) France, European social and economic; gjs@uoregon.edu

Valiani, Arafaat A. (PhD, Columbia 2005; assoc. prof.) South Asia; valiani@uoregon.edu

Weise, Julie (PhD, Yale 2009; assoc. prof. and dir., undergrad. studies) 20th-century US, modern Mexico, global migration; jweise@uoregon.edu

Weisiger, Marsha L. (PhD, Wisconsin, Madison 2000; assoc. prof.) environmental, Native American, American West; weisiger@uoregon.edu

Wolverton, Lisa (PhD, Notre Dame 1997; prof.) medieval Europe; lwolvert@uoregon.edu

Zahler, Reuben C. (PhD, Chicago 2006; assoc. prof.) Latin America; rczahler@uoregon.edu

Joint/Cross Appointments

Paquette, Gabriel (PhD, Cambridge 2006; prof.; dean, Robert D. Clark Honors Coll.; International Studies) European empires, intellectual, Portugal and Spain, international relations; paquette@uoregon.edu

Retired/Emeritus Faculty

Dennis, Matthew J. (PhD, California, Berkeley 1987; prof. emeritus) early America, environment, American Indian; mjdennis@uoregon.edu

Holbo, Paul S. (PhD, Chicago 1961; prof. emeritus) US foreign relations

Kimball, R. Alan (PhD, Washington 1967; prof. emeritus) modern Russia; kimball@uoregon.edu

Maddex, Jack P., Jr. (PhD, North Carolina, Chapel Hill 1966; prof. emeritus) American South, Civil War; jmaddex@uoregon.edu

May, Glenn A. (PhD, Yale 1975; prof. emeritus) Southeast Asia, American foreign relations; gmay@uoregon.edu

McGowen, Randall E. (PhD, Illinois, Urbana-Champaign 1979; prof. emeritus) modern Britain, India; rmcgowen@uoregon.edu

Mohr, James C. (PhD, Stanford 1969; prof. emeritus) 19th-century US; jmohr@uoregon.edu

Nicols, John (PhD, UCLA 1974; prof. emeritus) ancient Greece and Rome; jnicols@uoregon.edu

Pope, Barbara C. (PhD, Columbia 1981; prof. emerita) Europe, women/gender/religion; bcpope@uoregon.edu

Pope, Daniel (PhD, Columbia 1973; prof. emeritus) American economic, modern US; dapope@uoregon.edu

Recently Awarded PhDs

Bedan, John Daniel "No Second Chances: US-Guatemala Relations in the 1960s"

Fitzgerald, Joshua Jacob "Spanish Colonial Education in Post-Conquest Mexico"

Leone, Steven "The Nature of Death: An Environmental History of Dying and Death in the Early Republic and Antebellum America"

Maxson, Hillary "Kakeibo Monogatari: Women's Consumerism and the Postwar Japanese Kitchen"

Our Lady of the Lake University

History Program, Humanities & Social Studies Dept., 411 SW 24th St., San Antonio, TX 78207-4689. 210.431.3918. Fax 210.436.4090. Email: mnagy@ollusa.edu. Website: http://www. ollusa.edu/history.

The History Program offers a new concentration in integrated digital and public history. Courses feature global/regional perspectives and incorporate values, electronic resources, and analytical thinking and writing. Degrees include Bachelor of Arts degrees in History; Social Studies/History core, and Grades 7-12 Certification in History. The Minor consists of 18 semester hours with a focus on digital and public history.

Chair: Margit Nagy, CDP
Degrees Offered: BA
Academic Year System: Semester; Trimester (Weekend Coll.)
Areas of Specialization: US, Asia, Europe, colonial Southwest/US/Latin America, digital/public
Tuition (per academic year): $27366
Enrollment 2018-19:
  Undergraduate Majors: 29
  Degrees in History: 3 BA
Addresses:
  Admissions: http://www.ollusa.edu/admissions
  Financial Aid: http://www.ollusa.edu/financialaid

Full-time Faculty

Martinez, Valerie (PhD, Texas, Austin 2016; asst. prof.) 20th-century US/Mexican American studies, US military, women's and gender studies; vamartinez@ollusa.edu
Nagy, Margit CDP (PhD, Washington 1981; prof. and chair) Asia/Japan, US social, comparative women; mnagy@ollusa.edu

Pace University

Dept. of History, 1 Pace Plaza, New York, NY 10038. 212.346.1454. Fax 212.346.1457. Email: lfaillace@pace.edu; rfrank2@pace. edu. Website: https://www.pace.edu/dyson/programs/ba-history.

Alternate Address: Dept. of Economics, History and Political Science, 861 Bedford Rd., Pleasantville, NY 10570

Our BA in History will serve you well whether you want to launch your career or pursue a graduate degree.

Chair: Ronald Frank, New York; Walter Morris, Pleasantville
Degrees Offered: BA
Academic Year System: Semester
Areas of Specialization: Latin America, US, Europe, Africa and Middle East, East Asia
Tuition (per academic year): $36732
Enrollment 2018-19:
  Undergraduate Majors: 78
  Degrees in History: 27 BA
Addresses:
  Admissions: https://www.pace.edu/admissions-and-aid
  Financial Aid: https://www.pace.edu/financial-aid

Adjunct Faculty

Courtney-Batson, Deirdre (MA, Cornell; adj. asst. prof.; Pleasantville) Europe; dcourtneybatson@pace.edu
Kaplan, Mark (PhD, Grad. Center, CUNY 1975; adj. prof.; Pleasantville) US, Europe

Moglia-Bratt, Marie (MA, Manhattan; adj. asst. prof.; Pleasantville) Europe, Russia; mmogliabratt@pace.edu

Full-time Faculty

Alberi, Mary L. (PhD, SUNY, Binghamton 1980; assoc. prof.; New York) medieval, late Rome; malberi@pace.edu
Chase, Michelle Chi (PhD, NYU 2010; asst. prof.; Pleasantville) Latin America
Frank, Ronald (PhD, Humboldt, Germany 1991; assoc. prof. and chair; New York) Japan, East Asia, Russia; rfrank2@pace.edu
Gloster Coates, Patricia (PhD, Columbia 1987; assoc. prof.; New York) Islamic and West Africa, Afro-American; pglostercoates@pace.edu
Greenberg, Daniel J. (PhD, Washington 1985; assoc. prof.; New York) modern Latin America; dgreenberg2@pace.edu
Lee, Joseph Tse-Hei (PhD, SOAS, London 2000; prof.; New York) China, Asia; jlee@pace.edu
Manasek, Jared (PhD, Columbia 2013; asst. prof.; Pleasantville) forced migration in Balkans; manasek@pace.edu
Offutt, William M. (PhD, Johns Hopkins 1987; prof.; New York) early America; billoffutt@aol.com
Reagin, Nancy R. (PhD, Johns Hopkins 1990; prof.; New York) Germany, European women, modern Europe; nreagin@aol.com
Roland, Joan G. (PhD, Columbia 1969; prof.; New York) Middle East, Jewish; jroland@pace.edu
Taylor, Durahn A. B. (PhD, Columbia 1999; asst. prof.; Pleasantville) US urban, African American; dtaylor@pace.edu
Weigold, Marilyn E. (PhD, St. John's, NY 1970; prof.; Pleasantville) US, local; mweigold@pace.edu

Retired/Emeritus Faculty

Afshari, Reza (PhD, Temple 1981; prof. emeritus; Pleasantville) Middle East, human rights; rafshari@pace.edu

Pacific Lutheran University

Dept. of History, Xavier Hall, Tacoma, WA 98447-0003. 253.535.7595. Fax 253.535.8305. Email: hamesgl@plu.edu. Website: https://www.plu.edu/history/.

Through the study of history at Pacific Lutheran University students gain an understanding and appreciation of the historical perspective. Opportunities for developing analytical and interpretative skills are provided through research and writing projects, internships, class presentations, and study tours.

Chair: Gina Hames
Degrees Offered: BA
Academic Year System: Semester
Areas of Specialization: US, Europe, Latin America, innovation and technology, Holocaust
Tuition (per academic year): $43264
Enrollment 2018-19:
  Undergraduate Majors: 47
  Degrees in History: 17 BA
Addresses:
  Admissions: http://www.plu.edu/admission/
  Financial Aid: http://www.plu.edu/financial-aid/

Full-time Faculty

Allinson, Rayne (DPhil, Oxford 2010; asst. prof.) early modern Europe, Anglo-Scottish diplomacy, biography; allinsra@plu.edu
Griech-Polelle, Beth Ann (PhD, Rutgers 1999; assoc. prof. and Kurtis R. Mayer Chair) Holocaust studies, modern Germany, modern Europe; griechba@plu.edu

Halvorson, Michael J. (PhD, Washington 2001; assoc. prof. and Benson Family Chair) business and economic, early modern Europe, Reformation; halvormj@plu.edu

Hames, Gina L. (PhD, Carnegie Mellon 1996; assoc. prof. and chair) Latin America, world, alcohol studies; hamesgl@plu.edu

Kraig, Beth M. (PhD, Washington 1987; prof.) 19th- and 20th-century US, women; kraigbm@plu.edu

Mergenthal, Rebekah M. K. (PhD, Chicago 2008; assoc. prof.) 19th-century US, American West; mergenrm@plu.edu

Retired/Emeritus Faculty

Carp, E. Wayne (PhD, California, Berkeley 1981; prof. emeritus) business and economic, adoption, social welfare; carpw@plu.edu

Ericksen, Robert P. (PhD, London Sch. Economics 1980; prof. emeritus) modern Europe, Germany, Holocaust; ericksrp@plu.edu

Nordquist, Philip A. (PhD, Washington 1964; prof. emeritus) early modern Europe, Reformation; nordqupa@plu.edu

Sobania, Neal (PhD, London 1980; prof. emeritus) Africa, African art; sobania@plu.edu

Park University

Dept. of History and Political Science, 8700 NW River Park Dr., PMB 117, Kansas City, MO 64152-3795. 816.584.6391. Email: debra.sheffer@park.edu. Website: https://www.park.edu/academics/explore-majors-programs/history/.

At Park University, our Bachelor of Arts in History degree program is designed to give students the opportunity to appreciate the diversity of human encounters through their own and other's cultures and societies as they have developed over time. Whether you want to embark on a career as a history teacher, writer, archivist, lawyer or any number of different career paths, a degree in history can prepare you to pursue your own unique career path.

Chair: Debra Sheffer
Degrees Offered: BA,BS
Academic Year System: SEM
Areas of Specialization: Europe/classical, US, public, military
Tuition (per academic year): $9576
Addresses:
   Admissions: https://www.park.edu/admissions/undergraduate-admissions/
   Financial Aid: https://www.park.edu/tuition-financial-aid/

Full-time Faculty

Sheffer, Debra (PHD, Kansas, 2009; prof. and chair) American Civil War, post-traumatic stress disorder; debra.sheffer@park.edu

Westcott, Timothy C. (PHD, Union Inst., 2002; assoc. prof.; assoc. Univ. archivist; and program coord.) utopian communities, Underground Railroad; tim.westcott@park.edu

Penn State University

Dept. of History, 108 Weaver Bldg, University Park, PA 16802-5500. 814.865.1367. Fax 814.863.7840. Email: mek31@psu.edu. Website: https://history.la.psu.edu/.

History majors at PSU benefit from an excellent faculty, sound curriculum, and small class sizes. Our graduate program focuses on only four areas of departmental strength: the United States, Latin America, early modern global, and China. Students admitted to the Department of History's graduate program is receives funding for five years.

Chair: Michael Kulikowski
Director of Graduate Studies: Gregory Smits
Degrees Offered: BA,MA,PhD
Academic Year System: Semester
Areas of Specialization: early modern global, 19th-century US, Latin America, late imperial and 20th-century China, African American/Asian/women's studies
Undergraduate Tuition (per academic year):
   In-State: $16572
   Out-of-State: $30404
Graduate Tuition (per academic year):
   In-State: $19328
   Out-of-State: $33142
Enrollment 2018-19:
   Undergraduate Majors: 186
   New Graduate Students: 8
   Full-time Graduate Students: 31
   Degrees in History: 92 BA, 3 MA, 7 PhD
Undergraduate Addresses:
   Admissions: http://admissions.psu.edu/apply/requirements
   Financial Aid: http://studentaid.psu.edu
Graduate Addresses:
   Admissions: http://gradschool.psu.edu/admissions/
   Financial Aid: http://studentaid.psu.edu/graduate-and-professional-students

Full-time Faculty

Atwill, David G. (PhD, Hawaii 1999; assoc. prof.) modern China, Islam in Asia; dga11@psu.edu

August, Andrew (PhD, Columbia 1993; assoc. prof.; Abington) modern Britain; axa24@psu.edu

Balachandran, Jyoti Gulati (PhD, UCLA 2012; asst. prof.) medieval/early modern South Asia, Islam, Indian Ocean world; jzb461@psu.edu

Baldanza, Kathlene T. (PhD, Pennsylvania 2010; assoc. prof.) Ming and Qing China, China and Vietnam; ktb3@psu.edu

Beaver, Daniel C. (PhD, Chicago 1991; assoc. prof.) early modern Britain, early modern Europe, colonial America; dxb28@psu.edu

Black, Brian (PhD, Kansas 1996; assoc. prof.; Altoona) North American landscape and environmental; bcb4@psu.edu

Brockopp, Jonathan (PhD, Yale 1995; prof.) Islamic law, religion; jeb38@psu.edu

Cahill, Cathleen D. (PhD, Chicago 2004; assoc. prof.) US, Native American, women and gender; czc335@psu.edu

Creagh, C. Dianne (PhD, SUNY, Stony Brook 2006; asst. prof.; York) information sciences and technology; cdc16@psu.edu

Davis, Amira Rose (PhD, Johns Hopkins 2016; asst. prof.) 20th-century US, African American, gender; ard51@psu.edu

DeSchaepdrijver, Sophie C. M. (PhD, Amsterdam 1990; prof.) modern Europe, Belgium, urban; scd10@psu.edu

Donovan, James M. (PhD, Syracuse 1982; assoc. prof.; Mont Alto) Europe, French social; jmd9@psu.edu

Eghigian, Greg (PhD, Chicago 1993; prof.) modern Germany, modern Europe; gae2@psu.edu

Fegley, Randall Arlin (PhD, Reading, UK 1986; asst. prof.; Berks) Africa and western Europe, human rights and conflict resolution; raf8@psu.edu

Few, Martha (PhD, Arizona 1997; prof.) Latin America, medicine, human-animal studies; mzf52@psu.edu

Gallagher, Julie A. (PhD, Massachusetts Amherst 2003; assoc. prof.; Brandywine) arts and humanities; jag63@psu.edu

Greenberg, Amy S. (PhD, Harvard 1995; prof.) 19th-century social, urban; asg5@psu.edu

Hauser, Robert (PhD, Penn State 1973; assoc. prof.; Greater Allegheny) US, modern; reh6@psu.edu

Heaney, Christopher H. (PhD, Texas, Austin 2016; asst. prof.) modern Latin America, science and indigenous peoples, Peru; cuh282@psu.edu

Henderson, Rodger C. (PhD, SUNY, Binghamton 1983; assoc. prof.; Fayette) Pennsylvania, colonial America, US; rch5@psu.edu

Hsia, Ronnie Po-chia (PhD, Yale 1982; prof.) early modern Europe and global interaction, Reformation; rxh46@psu.edu

Hudson, Benjamin T. (PhD, Oxford 1983; prof.) medieval Britain, Celtic, Viking; bth1@psu.edu

Kulikowski, Michael (PhD, Toronto 1998; prof. and head) ancient Rome; mek31@psu.edu

Kumar, Prakash (PhD, Georgia Tech 2004; assoc. prof.) South Asia; puk15@psu.edu

Lee, Jacob (PhD, California, Davis 2014; asst. prof.) early America, American West, borderlands; jul782@psu.edu

Letwin, Dan (PhD, Yale 1991; assoc. prof.) US labor, African American, late 19th- and early 20th-century US; dll8@psu.edu

Mart, Michelle A. (PhD, NYU 1993; assoc. prof.; Berks) American diplomatic, US-Israel relations; mam20@psu.edu

Mayr, Norbert J. (PhD, North Carolina, Chapel Hill 1988; assoc. prof.; Worthington-Scranton) modern Europe, Germany, 19th- and 20th-century social and political; njm5@psu.edu

McDonald, Bryan (PhD, California, Irvine 2008; assoc. prof.; Science, Tech., and Soc. Prog.) modern US, environmental and food; blm26@psu.edu

McGlade, Jacqueline (PhD, George Washington 1995; assoc. prof.; Shenango) jam838@psu.edu

McWilliams, John C. (PhD, Penn State 1986; assoc. prof.; DuBois) recent US, social, political; jcm6@psu.edu

Mendoza, Mary Elizabeth (PhD, California, Davis 2015; asst. prof.) environmental, borderlands, race in American West

Merkel-Hess, Kate (PhD, California, Irvine 2009; assoc. prof.) modern China; kxm81@psu.edu

Miller, Eugene W., Jr. (PhD, Penn State 1972; asst. prof.; Hazleton) Europe, modern Germany; ewm1@psu.edu

Morgan, Zachary R. (PhD, Brown 2001; assoc. prof.) modern Brazil, modern Latin America, African diaspora; zzm20@psu.edu

Nash, Philip (PhD, Ohio 1994; assoc. prof.; Shenango) US; pxn4@psu.edu

Ng, On-cho (PhD, Hawai'i, Manoa 1986; prof.) late imperial Chinese intellectual, Confucian hermeneutics and historiography; oxn1@psu.edu

Nordstrom, Justin Abel (PhD, Indiana 2003; asst. prof.; Hazleton) American utopianism; jan13@psu.edu

Restall, Matthew B. (PhD, UCLA 1992; prof.) colonial Latin America; mxr40@psu.edu

Rossi, John Paul (PhD, Rutgers 1988; assoc. prof.; Penn State, Erie) US foreign relations, 20th-century US, East Asia; jpr2@psu.edu

Ruth, David E. (PhD, Northwestern 1992; assoc. prof.; Abington) 20th century, US cultural and social; dxr35@psu.edu

Safran, Janina (PhD, Harvard 1994; assoc. prof.) Islamic, Ottoman, Mediterranean 1000-1500; jxs57@psu.edu

Salzer, Kathryn E. (PhD, Toronto 2009; assoc. prof.) medieval France, monastic, economic; kes30@psu.edu

Sanders, Crystal R. (PhD, Northwestern 2011; assoc. prof.) modern US, civil rights

Sandoval-Strausz, Andrew K. (PhD, Chicago 2002; assoc. prof.) urban, Latina/o, cultural landscape studies; aus1050@psu.edu

Smits, Gregory J. (PhD, Southern California 1992; prof. and dir., grad. studies) Tokugawa to modern Japan, Okinawan intellectual and cultural; gjs4@psu.edu

Snyder, Christina N. (PhD, North Carolina, Chapel Hill 2007; McCabe Greer Prof.) Native American, slavery, America to 1900; czs398@psu.edu

Stefon, Frederick J. (EdD, Penn State 1983; asst. prof.; Wilkes-Barre) US, American Indian education; fjs3@psu.edu

Stroud, Ellen (PhD, Columbia 2001; assoc. prof.) US, environmental, urban; estroud@psu.edu

Szymczak, Robert B. (PhD, Carnegie Mellon 1980; assoc. prof.; Beaver) US, diplomatic, ethnic; rxs16@psu.edu

Tounsel, Christopher (PhD, Michigan 2015; asst. prof.) Africa, nationalism, Christianity; cut70@psu.edu

Wanner, Catherine (PhD, Columbia 1996; prof.) Ukraine and eastern Europe, religion, nationalism and historiography; cew10@psu.edu

Joint/Cross Appointments

Adler, Eliyana R. (PhD, Brandeis 2003; assoc. prof.; Jewish Studies) Jewish, eastern Europe, Holocaust; era12@psu.edu

Boittin, Jennifer Anne (PhD, Yale 2005; assoc. prof.; French and Francophone Studies) modern France, French colonialism; jab808@psu.edu

Brinkmann, Tobias (PhD, Tech., Berlin 2000; assoc. prof.; Jewish Studies) migration, modern Jewish; thb10@psu.edu

Ginzberg, Lori (PhD, Yale 1985; prof.; Women's, Gender, and Sexuality Studies) US women, antebellum social and intellectual; ldg1@psu.edu

Guettel, Jens-Uwe (PhD, Yale 2007; assoc. prof.; Religious Studies) modern Europe; jug17@psu.edu

Sternfeld, Lior Betzalel (PhD, Texas, Austin 2014; asst. prof.; Jewish Studies) modern Iran, modern Middle East, Jewish; lbs18@psu.edu

Nondepartmental Historians

Bezilla, Michael (PhD, Penn State 1978; research assoc.; Public Info.) American technology, agriculture, education; mxb13@psu.edu

Dyreson, Mark (PhD, Arizona 1989; affiliate prof.; Kinesiology) late 19th- and 20th-century US, sport and American culture, American thought and culture; mxd52@psu.edu

Joyce, William L. (PhD, Michigan 1974; librarian emeritus) 19th-century publishing, American publishing; wlj2@psu.edu

McBride, David (PhD, Columbia 1981; affiliate prof.; head, African and African American Studies) African American, contemporary medicine, public; djm9@psu.edu

Stout, Leon J. (MA, Penn State 1972; assoc. librarian and Univ. archivist) American education, archival and manuscript, oral; lys2@psu.edu

Retired/Emeritus Faculty

Blair, William Alan (PhD, Penn State 1995; prof. emeritus) Civil War and Reconstruction, US South; wab120@psu.edu

Borza, Eugene N. (PhD, Chicago 1966; prof. emeritus) Greece and Macedon, Alexander the Great, historiography; borza@comcast.net

Cross, Gary S. (PhD, Wisconsin, Madison 1977; prof. emeritus) late industrial society, western Europe/England/US, society and technology; gsc2@psu.edu

Duiker, William J., III (PhD, Georgetown 1968; prof. emeritus) modern China, Vietnam, modern Southeast Asia; wjd2@psu.edu

Enteen, George M. (PhD, George Washington 1965; prof. emeritus) Russia and Soviet Union, historiography; gxe1@psu.edu

Frankforter, A. Daniel, III (PhD, Penn State 1971; prof. emeritus; Penn State, Erie) ancient and medieval; adf1@psu.edu

Frantz, John B. (PhD, Pennsylvania 1961; assoc. prof. emeritus) colonial and revolutionary America, Pennsylvania; jbf2@psu.edu

Goldschmidt, Arthur E. (PhD, Harvard 1968; prof. emeritus) Middle East, 19th- and 20th-century Egypt, Arab nationalist movements; axg2@psu.edu

Harris, Marc L. (PhD, Johns Hopkins 1984; assoc. prof. emeritus; Altoona) revolutionary and early national US; mlh6@psu.edu

Isser, Natalie K. (PhD, Pennsylvania 1962; prof. emeritus) Europe, modern France; nxi1@psu.edu

Jenkins, Philip (PhD, Cambridge 1978; prof. emeritus) early modern and modern politics and society, Celtic nations, crime and justice; jpj1@psu.edu

Knight, Isabel F. (PhD, Yale 1964; assoc. prof. emeritus) 19th- and 20th-century European intellectual; ifk@psu.edu

Landes, Joan B. (PhD, NYU 1975; prof. emeritus) feminist theory, French Revolution, 18th-century French women; jb15@psu.edu

Lodwick, Kathleen L. (PhD, Arizona 1976; prof. emeritus; Lehigh Valley) China, 19th- and 20th-century cultural; kll2@psu.edu

Maddox, Robert J. (PhD, Rutgers 1964; prof. emeritus) American diplomatic, American political, Soviet-American relations; rjm5@psu.edu

McMurry, Sally A. (PhD, Cornell 1984; prof. emeritus) Middle Period US, rural, material culture; sam9@psu.edu

Meyerhuber, Carl I., Jr. (PhD, California, San Diego 1972; assoc. prof. emeritus) history; cim1@psu.edu

Moses, Wilson J. (PhD, Brown 1975; prof. emeritus) Afro-American, 19th-century US, American social and intellectual; wjm12@psu.edu

Neely, Mark E., Jr. (PhD, Yale 1973; McCabe Greer Prof. emeritus) Civil War, US social and political; mxn10@psu.edu

Neely, Sylvia E. (PhD, Notre Dame 1980; assoc. prof. emeritus) France, modern Europe; sxn13@psu.edu

Prebish, Charles S. (PhD, Wisconsin, Madison 1971; prof. emeritus) South Asian Buddhism, early Indian and Sri Lankan Buddhism; csp1@psu.edu

Reardon, Carol (PhD, Kentucky 1987; prof. emeritus) American military, military thought; car9@psu.edu

Rebane, P. Peter (PhD, Michigan State 1969; assoc. prof. emeritus; Abington) Europe, medieval Baltic, medieval crime; ppr1@psu.edu

Roeber, Anthony G. (PhD, Brown 1977; prof. emeritus) colonial America, early modern Germany; agr2@psu.edu

Rose, Anne C. (PhD, Yale 1979; prof. emeritus) American intellectual, American religious; acr5@psu.edu

Silverman, Dan P. (PhD, Yale 1963; prof. emeritus) 19th- and 20th-century Europe, modern European social and economic, modern Germany; dps1@psu.edu

Spielvogel, Jackson J. (PhD, Ohio State 1967; assoc. prof. emeritus) Renaissance, Reformation, Nazi Germany; jxs12@psu.edu

Stephens, Bruce (PhD, Drew 1970; assoc. prof. emeritus) 19th-century American Protestantism, religion in American culture; bms3@psu.edu

Sun, E-tu Zen (PhD, Radcliffe 1949; prof. emeritus) traditional Chinese economic, Chinese social institutions, Chinese technology

Woodruff, Nan E. (PhD, Tennessee, Knoxville 1977; prof. emeritus; African American Studies) 20th-century US, political and social development, US South; new7@psu.edu

Recently Awarded PhDs

Golder, Lauren "Anarchy at Home: Creating the Anarchist Household in Late 19th-Century America"

Penn State University, Erie, The Behrend College

History Program, 170 Kochel Center, College Rd., Erie, PA 16563-1501. 814.898.6051. Fax 814.898.6032. Email: abc13@psu.edu. Website: https://behrend.psu.edu/school-of-humanities-social-sciences/academic-programs/history.

The School of Humanities and Social Science's 14:1 average faculty to student ratio in upper-division classes means that you will enjoy mentoring relationships with your professors. But because Behrend is a four-year and graduate college of Penn State, you'll also have access to the opportunities and resources of a preeminent global research university.

Chair: Amy Carney
Degrees Offered: BA
Academic Year System: Semester
Areas of Specialization: US, ancient and modern Europe, world, Latin America, anthropology
Tuition (per academic year):
In-State: $13658
Out-of-State: $20890
Enrollment 2018-19:
Undergraduate Majors: 23
Degrees in History: 6 BA
Students in Undergraduate Courses: 1100
Students in Undergraduate Intro Courses: 1000
Addresses:
Admissions: http://psbehrend.psu.edu/admissions-financial-aid
Financial Aid: http://psbehrend.psu.edu/admissions-financial-aid/financial-aid

Full-time Faculty

Bedal, Leigh-Ann (PhD, Pennsylvania 2000; assoc. prof.) anthropology, Near Eastern archaeology; lxb41@psu.edu

Beilein, Joseph, Jr. (PhD, Missouri, Columbia 2011; assoc. prof.) early US, Civil War era, guerilla warfare and gender; jmb79@psu.edu

Carney, Amy (PhD, Florida State 2010; assoc. prof. and chair) modern Europe, Germany and fascism, science; abc13@psu.edu

Cosby, Patrick H. (PhD, Florida 2011; asst. teaching prof.) Latin America; environmental, world; phc14@psu.edu

Kumhera, Glenn J. (PhD, Chicago 2005; assoc. prof.) medieval Europe, Renaissance Italy, ancient Greece and Rome; gjk19@psu.edu

Rossi, John Paul (PhD, Rutgers 1988; assoc. prof.) 20th-century US, business and economic; Vietnam; jpr2@psu.edu

University of Pennsylvania

Dept. of History, 208 College Hall, Philadelphia, PA 19104-6379. 215.898.8452. Fax 215.573.2089. Email: octaviac@sas.upenn.edu. Website: https://www.history.upenn.edu/.

Penn's graduate program trains the next generation of scholars and teachers. The department's strong commitment to undergraduate education can be seen in the prominence of the history major, one of the largest on campus, in the numerous teaching awards earned by both standing faculty and graduate students, and history's strong presence in general education.

Chair: Antonio Feros
Director of Graduate Studies: Benjamin Nathans
Director of Undergraduate Studies: Si-yen Fei
Degrees Offered: BA,MA,PhD
Academic Year System: Semester
Areas of Specialization: early/19th-/20th-century America, medieval/early modern/modern Europe, China/Japan/Korea, Africa and Middle East, colonial and modern Latin America
Undergraduate Tuition (per academic year): $43738
Graduate Tuition (per academic year): $25660
Enrollment 2018-19:
    Undergraduate Majors: 320
    New Graduate Students: 14
    Full-time Graduate Students: 81
    Degrees in History: 212 BA, 2 MA, 7 PhD
Undergraduate Addresses:
    Admissions: http://www.upenn.edu/admissions
    Financial Aid: http://www.sfs.upenn.edu
Graduate Addresses:
    Admissions: https://www.sas.upenn.edu/index.php/graduate-division/admissions
    Financial Aid: http://www.sas.upenn.edu/graduate-division/resources/financing

Adjunct Faculty

Harkavy, Ira (PhD, Pennsylvania 1979; adj. asst. prof.; vice dean, Sch. Arts and Sciences) US urban, social; harkavy@pobox.upenn.edu

Kiron, Arthur (PhD, Columbia 1999; adj. asst. prof.; curator, Judaica Collections, Van Pelt Library) Atlantic Jewish, Jewish book

Lenthall, Bruce (PhD, Pennsylvania 1999; adj. asst. prof.; dir., Center for Teaching and Learning) 20th-century US culture and media; lenthall@sas.upenn.edu

Full-time Faculty

Aguirre-Mandujano, Oscar (PhD, Washington 2018; asst. prof.)

Azuma, Eiichiro (PhD, UCLA 2001; assoc. prof.) Asian American, modern Japan; eazuma@sas.upenn.edu

Babou, Cheikh A. M. (PhD, Michigan State 2002; assoc. prof.) Islam in West Africa, Islamic education, French colonialism; cheikh@sas.upenn.edu

Bay, Mia E. (PhD, Yale 1993; prof.) African American; mbay@sas.upenn.edu

Berg, Anne Kristina (PhD, Michigan 2011; asst. prof.)

Berry, Mary F. (PhD, Michigan 1966; JD, Michigan 1970; Geraldine R. Segal Prof.) US constitutional and legal, Afro-American; mfberry@sas.upenn.edu

Breckman, Warren Glen (PhD, California, Berkeley 1993; prof.) late and early modern European intellectual; breckman@sas.upenn.edu

Brown, Kathleen M. (PhD, Wisconsin-Madison 1990; prof.) colonial America, women, race; kabrown@sas.upenn.edu

Cassanelli, Lee (PhD, Wisconsin, Madison 1973; assoc. prof.) Africa; lcassane@sas.upenn.edu

Cebul, Brent (PhD, Virginia 2014; asst. prof.) US business and political

Chase-Levenson, Alexander (PhD, Princeton 2015; asst. prof.) modern Europe, Britain and British Empire, Mediterranean; alchase@sas.upenn.edu

Dickinson, Frederick R. (PhD, Yale 1993; prof.) modern Japan, political and diplomatic; frdickin@sas.upenn.edu

Farnsworth-Alvear, Ann C. (PhD, Duke 1994; assoc. prof.) modern and colonial Latin America, women, comparative labor; farnswor@sas.upenn.edu

Fei, Si-yen (PhD, Stanford 2004; assoc. prof. and dir., undergrad. studies) China, Ming, Qing; siyen@sas.upenn.edu

Feros, Antonio (PhD, Johns Hopkins 1995; prof. and chair) political and intellectual, early modern Europe/Spain/Atlantic world; aferos@sas.upenn.edu

Ferreira, Roquinaldo (PhD, UCLA 2003; prof.) early Africa, colonial Brazil

Flandreau, Marc (PhD, EHESS, Paris 1993; prof.) credit/information/finance, international monetary system, exchange-rate regimes

Gronningsater, Sarah L. H. (PhD, Chicago 2014; asst. prof.) 18th- and 19th-century US; gronning@sas.upenn.edu

Holquist, Peter I. (PhD, Columbia 1995; assoc. prof.) 19th- and 20th-century Russia and Soviet Union; holquist@sas.upenn.edu

Kashani-Sabet, Firoozeh (PhD, Yale 1997; assoc. prof.) modern Middle East, Ottoman Empire and Iran; fks@history.upenn.edu

Kuskowski, Ada-Maria (PhD, Cornell 2013; asst. prof.) medieval, legal

Licht, Walter M. (PhD, Princeton 1977; prof.) US, labor and economic; wlicht@sas.upenn.edu

McDougall, Walter A. (PhD, Chicago 1974; Alloy-Ansin Prof.) European and US diplomatic, Western civilization, technology and international relations; wamcd@sas.upenn.edu

Moyer, Ann E. (PhD, Michigan 1987; assoc. prof. and undergrad. chair) Mediterranean world 1300-1700, Renaissance; moyer@sas.upenn.edu

Nathans, Benjamin (PhD, California, Berkeley 1995; Ronald S. Lauder Endowed Term Assoc. Prof. and dir., grad. studies) Jewish, modern Russia, modern Europe; bnathans@history.upenn.edu

Norton, Marcy (PhD, California, Berkeley 2000; assoc. prof.) colonial Latin America, Atlantic world

Offner, Amy C. (PhD, Columbia 2012; asst. prof.) 20th-century US and Latin America, transnational, capitalism and political economy; offner@sas.upenn.edu

Peiss, Kathy L. (PhD, Brown 1982; Roy F. and Jeannette P. Nichols Prof.) US women and gender, social and cultural; peiss@sas.upenn.edu

Richter, Daniel K. (PhD, Columbia 1984; prof.) colonial America, social and intellectual; drichter@history.upenn.edu

Rosenfeld, Sophia (PhD, Harvard 1996; Walter H. Annenberg Prof.) Age of Revolutions, political theory; srosenf@sas.upenn.edu

Ruderman, David B. (PhD, Hebrew, Jerusalem 1975; Joseph Meyerhoff Prof.) modern Jewish; ruderman@sas.upenn.edu

Safley, Thomas M. (PhD, Wisconsin, Madison 1980; prof.) Renaissance and Reformation, early modern Europe; tsafley@history.upenn.edu

St. George, Robert Blair (PhD, Pennsylvania 1982; assoc. prof.) folklore and folklife, early America; stgeorge@sas.upenn.edu

Teixeira, Melissa (PhD, Princeton 2016; asst. prof.)

Todd, Margo (PhD, Washington, St. Louis 1981; Walter H. Annenberg Prof.) early modern Britain, religion and culture, urban; mtodd@sas.upenn.edu

Troutt Powell, Eve M. (PhD, Harvard 1995; prof.) Islamic Middle East, modern Egyptian culture, women; troutt@sas.upenn.edu

Waldron, Arthur N. (PhD, Harvard 1981; Lauder Prof.) China, international relations; awaldron2@mac.com

Wenger, Beth S. (PhD, Yale 1992; prof.) Jewish, America, ethnic; bwenger@sas.upenn.edu

Joint/Cross Appointments

Gordon, Sarah Barringer (PhD, Princeton 1995; prof.; Law Sch.) American legal, property, gender in American legal; sgordon@law.upenn.edu

Nondepartmental Historians

Raff, Daniel (PhD, MIT 1987; assoc. prof.; Management, Wharton Sch.) American business, comparative business; raff@wharton.upenn.edu

Part-time Faculty

Chartier, Roger A. (PhD, ENS de Saint-Cloud 1969; Annenberg Vis. Prof.) early modern Europe, European culture; chartier@history.upenn.edu

Retired/Emeritus Faculty

Childers, Thomas, Jr. (PhD, Harvard 1976; Sheldon and Lucy Hackney Prof. emeritus) modern Germany; childers@sas.upenn.edu

Farriss, Nancy M. (PhD, London 1965; Walter H. Annenberg Prof. emeritus) Latin America

Feierman, Steven M. (PhD, Northwestern 1970; prof. emeritus) Africa; feierman@sas.upenn.edu

Kors, Alan C. (PhD, Harvard 1968; prof. emeritus) European intellectual; akors@sas.upenn.edu

Kuklick, Bruce (PhD, Pennsylvania 1968; Roy F. & Jeannette P. Nichols Prof. emeritus) 20th-century America, intellectual; bkuklick@sas.upenn.edu

Lees, Lynn Hollen (PhD, Harvard 1969; prof. emeritus) Britain; lhlees@history.upenn.edu

Peters, Edward M. (PhD, Yale 1967; Henry Charles Lea Prof. emeritus) medieval; empeters@sas.upenn.edu

Steinberg, Jonathan (PhD, Cambridge 1965; Walter H. Annenberg Prof. emeritus) modern western Europe; steinbej@history.upenn.edu

Zuckerman, Michael W. (PhD, Harvard 1967; prof. emeritus) American social, American political; mzuckerm@history.upenn.edu

Recently Awarded PhDs

Irvine, Tina "Reclaiming Appalachia: Mountain Reform and the Preservation of White Citizenship, 1890-1929"

Neumann, Alexis "American Incest: Kinship, Sex and Commerce in Slavery and Reconstruction"

Shibley, Natalie "Sexual Contagion: The Politics of Sexuality and Public Health in the US Military, 1941-93"

Suarez, Camille A. "How the West Was Won: Race, Citizenship, and the Colonial Roots of California, 1849-79"

Teitelman, Emma "Governing the Peripheries: The Social Reconstruction of the South and West after the American Civil War"

Yun, Seok-min "Utopia Uncovenanted: James Harrington's Commonwealth of Oceana (1656) and the Remaking of Anglo Scottish Relations"

Pepperdine University

Dept. of History, 24255 Pacific Coast Hwy., Malibu, CA 90263-4225. 310.506.4225. Fax 310.506.7307. Email: loretta.hunnicutt@pepperdine.edu. Website: https://seaver.pepperdine.edu/humanities/undergraduate/history/.

Our history major program helps students develop an understanding of the complex factors that have produced the civilization and conditions of the present century.

Chair: Sharyl Corrado
Degrees Offered: BA
Academic Year System: Semester

Areas of Specialization: America, Europe, Asia and Latin America, religion, American foreign relations
Tuition (per academic year): $55640
Enrollment 2018-19:
  Undergraduate Majors: 35
  Degrees in History: 7 BA
Addresses:
  Admissions: http://www.pepperdine.edu/admission
  Financial Aid: http://www.pepperdine.edu/admission/financialaid

Full-time Faculty

Corrado, Sharyl (PhD, Illinois, Urbana-Champaign 2010; assoc. prof. and program dir.) modern Russia, modern Europe; sharyl.corrado@pepperdine.edu

Davenport, Stewart A. (PhD, Yale 2001; assoc. prof.) early America, American religious; stewart.davenport@pepperdine.edu

Givens, Bryan Alan (PhD, UCLA 2003; assoc. prof.) Iberia and early modern Europe; bryan.givens@pepperdine.edu

Hart, Tanya (PhD, Yale 2006; asst. prof.) US women, African American, public health and medicine; tanya.hart@pepperdine.edu

Hunnicutt, Loretta Long (PhD, Georgetown 1998; assoc. prof.) women, social; loretta.hunnicutt@pepperdine.edu

Rivas, Darlene S. (PhD, Vanderbilt 1996; prof.) US foreign relations, 20th-century Latin America; darlene.rivas@pepperdine.edu

Joint/Cross Appointments

Larson, Edward J. (PhD, Wisconsin, Madison 1984; JD, Harvard 1979; Hugh and Hazel Darling Prof.; Law) law/science/technology, health care law; elarson@pepperdine.edu

Nondepartmental Historians

McAllister, Ted (PhD, Vanderbilt 1994; assoc. prof.; Sch. Public Policy) American intellectual, 20th-century America; ted.mcallister@pepperdine.edu

Reilly, Thomas H. (PhD, Washington 1997; assoc. prof.; International Studies and Languages) imperial China, modern China; thomas.reilly@pepperdine.edu

Retired/Emeritus Faculty

Baird, W. David (PhD, Oklahoma 1968; Howard A. White Prof. emeritus) American Indian, American West, methodology; david.baird@pepperdine.edu

University of Pittsburgh

Dept. of History, 3702 Posvar Hall, Pittsburgh, PA 15260. 412.648.7451. Fax 412.648.9074. Email: lep12@pitt.edu. Website: http://www.history.pitt.edu/.

The History Department at the University of Pittsburgh enjoys an international reputation. The area studies—US, East Asia, Latin America, and Europe—rank among the best programs in the nation and attract both national and international students.

Chair: Lara Putnam
Director of Graduate Studies: Michel Gobat
Director of Undergraduate Studies: Anthony Novosel and Liann Tsoukas
Degrees Offered: BA, MA, PhD
Academic Year System: Semester
Areas of Specialization: US, East Asia, Latin America, Europe, world

Undergraduate Tuition (per academic year):
In-State: $18130
Out-of-State: $31102
Graduate Tuition (per academic year):
In-State: $22846
Out-of-State: $38736
Enrollment 2018-19:
Undergraduate Majors: 220
New Graduate Students: 4
Full-time Graduate Students: 30
Degrees in History: 95 BA, 6 MA, 8 PhD
Undergraduate Addresses:
Admissions: http://www.pitt.edu/admissions
Financial Aid: http://oafa.pitt.edu/learn-about-aid/
Graduate Addresses:
Admissions and Financial Aid: http://www.history.pitt.edu/graduate

Full-time Faculty

Adal, Raja (PhD, Harvard 2009; asst. prof.) modern Japan, comparative Asia, world; raja.adal@pitt.edu

Andrews, George Reid (PhD, Wisconsin, Madison 1978; Dist. Prof. and UCIS Prof.) Latin America 1750-present, Argentina and Brazil, comparative; reid1@pitt.edu

Blain, Keisha N. (PhD, Princeton 2014; asst. prof.) 20th-century US, African American, modern African diaspora; Keisha.Blain@gmail.com

Carson, Carolyn (PhD, Carnegie Mellon 1995; sr. lect.; coord., Urban Studies Prog.) 20th-century US, urban, medicine; cjlc@pitt.edu

Frykman, Niklas (PhD, Pittsburgh 2010; asst. prof.) early America, Atlantic, slavery and abolition

Glasco, Laurence (PhD, SUNY, Buffalo 1969; assoc. prof.) American urban, race and ethnic, social structure; lag1@pitt.edu

Gobat, Michel (PhD, Chicago 1998; assoc. prof. and dir., grad. studies) Latin America, international; mgobat@pitt.edu

Gotkowitz, Laura E. S. (PhD, Chicago 1998; assoc. prof.) modern Latin America, Andes; laurag1@pitt.edu

Greenberg, Janelle (PhD, Michigan 1971; prof.) English legal, political thought, European women; janelleg@pitt.edu

Greenwald, Maurine W. (PhD, Brown 1977; assoc. prof.) 19th- and 20th-century American social, US women, American labor; greenwal@pitt.edu

Hagerty, Bernard (PhD, Pittsburgh 2000; sr. lect.) modern Europe and Great Britain; kazuo@pitt.edu

Hammond, Leslie (PhD, Pittsburgh 2001; lect.) Europe; lhammond@pitt.edu

Holstein, Diego (PhD, Hebrew, Israel 2003; assoc. prof.) world, medieval Iberia; holstein@pitt.edu

Hoock, Holger (DPhil, Oxford 2001; Amundson Prof.) Britain and Ireland 1750-1914, American Revolution and early Republic 1754-1815, military; hoock@pitt.edu

Livezeanu, Irina (PhD, Michigan 1986; assoc. prof.) eastern European political, 20th century; irina1@pitt.edu

Mostern, Ruth (PhD, California, Berkeley 2003; assoc. prof.) spatial and environmental, imperial China; rmostern@pitt.edu

Novosel, Anthony (PhD, Pittsburgh 2004; sr. lect. and undergrad. advisor) Russia, Ireland, Western civilization; pugachev@pitt.edu

Pickett, James Robert (PhD, Princeton 2015; asst. prof.) Eurasia, Soviet; pickettj@pitt.edu

Putnam, Lara E. (PhD, Michigan 2000; UCIS Prof. and chair) Latin America, Atlantic, Caribbean; lep12@pitt.edu

Rediker, Marcus (PhD, Pennsylvania 1982; Dist. Prof.) colonial American social, Atlantic; red1@pitt.edu

Roege, Pernille (PhD, Cambridge 2010; asst. prof.) France, French colonial, 18th century; per20@pitt.edu

Ruck, Rob (PhD, Pittsburgh 1983; prof.) 20th-century American labor, sports; ruck439019@aol.com

Smith, Randy Scott (PhD, Pittsburgh 2004; lect.) colonial US, Atlantic, Russia; smitty@pitt.edu

Stoner, John C. (PhD, Columbia 2001; lect.) US political and social, labor, 20th century; stonerjc@pitt.edu

Thum, Gregor (PhD, European Univ., Viadrina 2002; assoc. prof.) 19th- and 20th-century central Europe, Germany and Poland, politics and culture; thum@pitt.edu

Tsoukas, Liann E. (PhD, Indiana 1999; sr. lect. and undergrad. advisor) US, African American; lit2@pitt.edu

Warsh, Molly A. (PhD, Johns Hopkins 2009; asst. prof.) early modern empires, early Caribbean, world; warsh@pitt.edu

Webel, Mari K. (PhD, Columbia 2012; asst. prof.) Africa, global public health; mwebel@pitt.edu

Retired/Emeritus Faculty

Chase, William J. (PhD, Boston Coll. 1979; prof. emeritus) Soviet Union, Soviet urbanization, Soviet labor and political; wchase@pitt.edu

Drescher, Seymour (PhD, Wisconsin, Madison 1960; Univ. Prof. emeritus) modern Europe, slavery and antislavery, modern European cultural; syd@pitt.edu

Galpern, Allan N. (PhD, California, Berkeley 1971; assoc. prof. emeritus) early modern western Europe, religious and social; riocoa@pitt.edu

Hall, Van Beck (PhD, Wisconsin, Madison 1964; assoc. prof. emeritus) early 19th-century US, revolutionary US, US social and political; vanbeck@pitt.edu

Hsu, Cho-yun (PhD, Chicago 1962; Univ. Prof. emeritus) ancient China, Chinese American, Chinese social; hsusun@yahoo.com

Jannetta, Ann B. (PhD, Pittsburgh 1983; prof. emeritus) Japan, East Asian traditional; annj@pitt.edu

Karsten, Peter D. (PhD, Wisconsin, Madison 1968; prof. emeritus) comparative military systems, comparative legal developments, modern national security policy; pjk2@pitt.edu

Kehl, James (PhD, Pennsylvania 1954; prof. emeritus) 19th-century US, American political parties, Pennsylvania political; jak18@pitt.edu

Manning, Patrick (PhD, Wisconsin, Madison 1969; Andrew Mellon Prof. emeritus) world and Africa, Islamic, comparative tropical; pmanning@pitt.edu

Muller, Edward (PhD, Wisconsin, Madison 1972; prof. emeritus) US urban, city spatial structure, North American historical geography; ekmuller@pitt.edu

Oestreicher, Richard J. (PhD, Michigan State 1979; assoc. prof. emeritus) US labor and working class, comparative labor, US popular culture; dick@pitt.edu

Rawski, Evelyn S. (PhD, Harvard 1968; Univ. Prof. and UCIS Prof. emeritus) early modern Chinese economic, political and social development, rural China; esrx@pitt.edu

Sims, Harold D. (PhD, Florida 1968; prof. emeritus) 19th- and 20th-century Mexico, Latin American immigration, recent Central American revolutions; hdsim1@netzero.com

Smethurst, Richard (PhD, Michigan 1968; UCIS Prof. emeritus) modern Japan, Japanese military, Japanese rural and economic; rsmet@pitt.edu

Recently Awarded PhDs

Holland, Dan "Communities of Resistance: How Ordinary People Developed Creative Responses to Marginalization in Lyon and Pittsburgh, 1980-2010"

Ladson, Marcy "We Didn't Start the Fire: Natural Gas Drilling in Pennsylvania before the Marcellus Boom"

Luecke, Mirelle G. "Topsail Alley: Labor Networks and Social Conflict on the New York Waterfront in the Age of Revolution"

Olsavsky, Jesse "Fire and Sword Will Affect More Good: Runaways, Vigilance Committees and the Rise of Revolutionary Abolitionism, 1835-60"

Sherry, Bennett Gabriel "Crossing Lines: How Transnational Advocacy and Refugee Migration Shaped the UNHCR in Turkey, 1960-88"

University of Pittsburgh at Johnstown

Dept. of History, Krebs 101, 450 Schoolhouse Rd., Johnstown, PA 15904. 814.269.2990. Fax 814.269.7255. Email: rmatson@pitt.edu; wilsons@pitt.edu. Website: https://www.johnstown.pitt.edu/academics/majors-programs/social-sciences/history.

Pitt-Johnstown offers a comprehensive selection of courses and classes leading to a BA degree or minor in history. History department faculty are actively engaged as scholars in their field and serve not only as teachers in the classroom, but as mentors to their students, providing a critical link to other professionals in the field.

Chair: Robert W. Matson
Degrees Offered: BA
Academic Year System: Semester
Areas of Specialization: US, Europe, Asia
Tuition (per academic year): $24520
Enrollment 2018-19:
  Undergraduate Majors: 50
  Degrees in History: 20 BA
Addresses:
  Admissions: http://www.upj.pitt.edu/en/admissions/admissions
  Financial Aid: http://www.upj.pitt.edu/en/admissions/financial-aid

Full-time Faculty

Matson, Robert W. (PhD, Oregon 1981; prof. and chair) diplomatic, film and history, religions; rmatson@pitt.edu

Newman, Paul Douglas (PhD, Kentucky 1996; prof.) early America, American social and religious; pnewman@pitt.edu

Reist, Katherine K. (PhD, Ohio State 1983; assoc. prof.) East Asia, Vietnam, political and military; kreist@pitt.edu

Wilson, Veronica Anne (PhD, Rutgers 2002; assoc. prof.) 20th-century US, social movements, women; vwilson@pitt.edu

Pittsburg State University

Dept. of History, Philosophy, and Social Science, 1701 S. Broadway, Pittsburg, KS 66762. 620.235.4325. Fax 620.235.4338. Email: history@pittstate.edu. Website: https://www.pittstate.edu/hpss/.

Part of PSU's College of Arts and Sciences, History offers classes that attract students with interests from across campus. Our department maintains a broad selection of courses in a rigorous undergraduate program, where students have a tremendous opportunity to interact with high-quality professors. History also houses one of the few distance-friendly MA programs in the United States.

Chair: Barbara Bonnekessen

Director of Graduate Studies: Jonathan F. Dresner
Director of Undergraduate Studies: Kirstin L. Lawson
Degrees Offered: BA,BS,MA
Academic Year System: Semester
Areas of Specialization: colonial/early Republic/19th- and 20th-century US, modern Europe, Africa and Middle East, Asia, modern military
Undergraduate Tuition (per academic year):
  In-State: $5906
  Out-of-State: $15786
Graduate Tuition (per academic year):
  In-State: $6626
  Out-of-State: $15786
Enrollment 2018-19:
  Undergraduate Majors: 77
  New Graduate Students: 37
  Full-time Graduate Students: 5
  Part-time Graduate Students: 26
  Degrees in History: 5 BA, 5 BS, 7 MA
Undergraduate Addresses:
  Admissions: http://www.pittstate.edu/admission/
  Financial Aid: http://www.pittstate.edu/office/financial_aid/
Graduate Addresses:
  Admissions: http://www.pittstate.edu/office/graduate/
  Financial Aid: http://www.pittstate.edu/office/financial_aid/

Adjunct Faculty

Minton, Amanda D. (MA, Pittsburg State 2011; lect.)
Smith, Robert (MA, Pittsburg State 2014; lect.)

Full-time Faculty

Childers, Christopher (PhD, Louisiana State 2010; asst. prof.) political, early Republic US; rchilders@pittstate.edu

Daley, John L. S. (PhD, Kent State 1993; prof.) 19th-century US, Civil War, modern military; jdaley@pittstate.edu

Dresner, Jonathan F. (PhD, Harvard 2001; assoc. prof. and dir., grad. studies) 19th-century Japan, East Asia, migration; jdresner@pittstate.edu

Harmon, Stephen A. (PhD, UCLA 1988; assoc. prof.) Africa, Middle East, Southern Cone; sharmon@pittstate.edu

Lawson, Kirstin L. (PhD, Missouri, Columbia 2008; assoc. prof. and dir., undergrad. studies) Gilded Age and Progressive Era US, women, health and health care; klawson@pittstate.edu

Thompson, Michael Kyle (PhD, Edinburgh 2011; assoc. prof.) Britain, modern Europe; mkthompson@pittstate.edu

Woestman, Kelly A. (PhD, North Texas 1993; prof.) 20th-century US, Latin America; woestman@pittstate.edu

Retired/Emeritus Faculty

Fischer, Kathleen G. (MA, Pittsburg State 1987; instr. emeritus) American women, early Republic

Gupta, Surendra K. (PhD, Johns Hopkins 1970; prof. emeritus) Soviet Union, 20th-century diplomatic, modern South Asia

Schick, James B. M. (PhD, Indiana 1971; prof. emeritus) colonial America, American Revolution; jschick@pittstate.edu

Walther, Thomas R. (PhD, Oklahoma 1970; prof. emeritus) Native Americans, Kansas and American frontier, industrial and labor

Pitzer College

History Field Group, 1050 N. Mills, Claremont, CA 91711. 909.621.8218. Fax 909.621.8481. Email: harmony_orourkel@pitzer.edu. Website: https://www.pitzer.edu/academics/field-groups/history/.

At Pitzer, history invites students to understand the contours of their world—its political boundaries, its economic systems, its social structures and its cultural practices—as historical products. It pushes them to question assumptions and to approach the present through the prism of a rich and variegated past.

Chair: Harmony O'Rourke
Degrees Offered: BA
Academic Year System: Semester
Areas of Specialization: US, world, colonialism, science, Africa
Tuition (per academic year): $68500
Enrollment 2018-19:
    Undergraduate Majors: 15
    Degrees in History: 1 BA
Addresses:
    Admissions: http://pitweb.pitzer.edu/admission/
    Financial Aid: http://www.pitzer.edu/admission/financial_aid/

Full-time Faculty

Johnson, Carina L. (PhD, California, Berkeley 2000; prof.) Habsburg Empire, cultural, early modern Europe; carina_johnson@pitzer.edu

O'Rourke, Harmony Susan (PhD, Harvard 2009; assoc. prof. and convenor) Africa, gender, Islam; harmony_orourke@pitzer.edu

Wakefield, Andre (PhD, Chicago 1999; prof.) early modern Germany, science and technology, environmental; andre_wakefield@pitzer.edu

Joint/Cross Appointments

Segal, Daniel A. (PhD, Chicago 1988; prof.; Anthropology) world, schooling, theory; dan_segal@pitzer.edu

Plymouth State University

Dept. of History, Philosophy, and Social Studies Education, MSC 30, 17 High St., Plymouth, NH 03264-1595. 603.535.3071. Fax 603.535.2358. Email: jkrueckeberg@plymouth.edu. Website: https://campus.plymouth.edu/history-philosophy-social-studies/.

The BA in history serves Plymouth State students in learning about and preparing for a range of professions, sharpening skills that enhance comprehension and communication, providing academically challenging and rigorous courses, developing self-understanding and respectful awareness of diverse ways of life, and growing toward constructive citizenship in a pluralistic society.

Chair: John Krueckeberg
Degrees Offered: BA
Academic Year System: Semester
Areas of Specialization: US, New England, global, Asia
Tuition (per academic year):
    In-State: $11610
    New England Resident: $14120
    Out-of-State: $17830
Enrollment 2018-19:
    Undergraduate Majors: 36
    Degrees in History: 11 BA
Addresses:
    Admissions: http://www.plymouth.edu/admissions/
    Financial Aid: http://www.plymouth.edu/office/financial-aid/

Full-time Faculty

Blaine, Marcia Schmidt (PhD, New Hampshire 1999; prof.; interim dir., Museum of the White Mountains) early America, New Hampshire/New England/White Mountains, public; mblaine@plymouth.edu

Couser, Jonathan B. (PhD, Notre Dame 2006; contract asst. prof.) medieval Europe, Christianity; jbcouser@mail.plymouth.edu

Howarth, Whitney E. (PhD, Northeastern 2004; assoc. prof.) comparative global, India, gender; wbhowarth@plymouth.edu

Krueckeberg, John (PhD, Arizona 1997; prof. and chair) 20th-century US, Great Depression; jkrueckeberg@plymouth.edu

Li, Xiaoxiong (PhD, Johns Hopkins 1991; prof.) regional world, modern China, Southeast Asia; xli@plymouth.edu

Noel, Rebecca R. (PhD, Boston Univ. 1999; assoc. prof.) 19th-century US, cultural and intellectual; rrnoel@plymouth.edu

Part-time Faculty

Nelson, Jacqueline (MA, Norwich 2011) military, US; jenelson@plymouth.edu

Upham-Bornstein, Linda L. (PhD, New Hampshire 2009; teaching lect.) 19th-century America, legal and immigration, forest; luphambornstein@plymouth.edu

Retired/Emeritus Faculty

Allen, E. John (PhD, Brigham Young 1968; prof. emeritus) Europe, skiing

Douglas, Lawrence H. (PhD, Syracuse 1970; prof. emeritus) modern US, military

Freyhofer, Horst H. (PhD, UCLA 1979; prof. emeritus) central and eastern Europe, former Soviet Union, intellectual

Marquez-Sterling, Manuel (PhD, Havana 1955; prof. emeritus) medieval Europe, Cuba, baseball

Point Loma Nazarene University

Dept. of History and Political Science, 3900 Lomaland Dr., San Diego, CA 92106-2899. 619.849.2450. Fax 619.849.2554. Email: lindseylupo@pointloma.edu. Website: https://www.pointloma.edu/schools-departments-colleges/department-history-political-science.

Intelligent Christians can be a force for good in the world. Knowledge is responsibility: to whom much is given, much is expected. Here, the pursuit of learning and understanding is coupled with the Wesleyan emphasis on human responsibility and creativity.

Chair: Lindsey Lupo
Degrees Offered: BA
Academic Year System: Semester
Areas of Specialization: history, political science, international studies, social science
Tuition (per academic year): $28900
Enrollment 2018-19:
    Undergraduate Majors: 105
    Degrees in History: 31 BA
Addresses:
    Admissions: http://undergraduate.pointloma.edu/
    Financial Aid: http://undergraduate.pointloma.edu/tuition-value

Adjunct Faculty

Cater, Benjamin Michael (PhD, Utah 2013; adj. prof. and dean) North American West, public health, religion; bencater@pointloma.edu

Full-time Faculty

Beail, Linda (PhD, Iowa 1998; prof.) American government, political theory, feminist political theory; lindabeail@pointloma.edu

Kennedy, Rick A. (PhD, California, Santa Barbara 1987; prof.) intellectual, ancient Mediterranean, early America and California; rickkennedy@pointloma.edu

Kim, Jaeyoon (PhD, Oregon 2005; prof.) modern East Asia; jaeyoonkim@pointloma.edu

Lupo, Lindsey (PhD, California, Irvine 2007; assoc. prof. and chair) international relations, American foreign policy, comparative studies; lindseylupo@pointloma.edu

McCoy, Kelli Ann (PhD, California, San Diego 2010; asst. prof.) 20th-century US, women; kellimccoy@pointloma.edu

Williamson, Rosco (PhD, California, San Diego 2007; assoc. prof.) international politics; roscowilliamson@pointloma.edu

Wood, William (PhD, Indiana 1998; prof.) central Asia, India, Russia; billwood@pointloma.edu

Retired/Emeritus Faculty

Cordileone, Diana Reynolds (PhD, California, San Diego 1997; prof. emeritus) modern Europe intellectual and cultural; dianacordileone@pointloma.edu

Little, Dwayne L. (PhD, Cincinnati 1970; prof. emeritus) 20th-century US, San Diego and California, American social; dwaynelittle@pointloma.edu

Pomona College

Dept. of History, 550 N. Harvard Ave., Claremont, CA 91711-6337. 909.607.3075. Fax 909.621.8574. Email: GE004747@pomona.edu; tfss@pomona.edu. Website: https://www.pomona.edu/academics/departments/history.

The History Department offers an array of courses that span the globe, cross time, and take a penetrating look at social, cultural and political turning points and movements.

Chair: April J. Mayes
Degrees Offered: BA
Academic Year System: Semester
Areas of Specialization: Africa/African diaspora/Middle East, East Asia and Indian Ocean, ancient and medieval Mediterranean, Latin America and Caribbean, US
Tuition (per academic year): $50720
Enrollment 2018-19:
 Undergraduate Majors: 31
 Degrees in History: 7 BA
Addresses:
 Admissions: http://www.pomona.edu/admissions/
 Financial Aid: https://www.pomona.edu/financial-aid

Full-time Faculty

Chin, Angelina (PhD, California, Santa Cruz 2006; assoc. prof.) modern China, gender, labor; angelina.chin@pomona.edu

Chu, Pey-Yi (PhD, Princeton 2011; asst. prof.) modern Europe, Russia/USSR/Siberia

Kates, Gary (PhD, Chicago 1978; prof.) French Revolution, modern European intellectual; gary_kates@pomona.edu

Khazeni, Arash (PhD, Yale 2005; asst. prof.) Iran, Afghanistan, Central Eurasia; arash_khazeni@pomona.edu

Mayes, April J. (PhD, Michigan 2003; assoc. prof. and chair) Africa and Latin America; april_mayes@pomona.edu

Silverman, Victor I. (PhD, California, Berkeley 1990; prof.) recent US, international, labor; vsilverman@pomona.edu

Summers Sandoval, Tomas F., Jr. (PhD, California, Berkeley 2002; assoc. prof.) Chicano/a, US West; tfss@pomona.edu

Tinker Salas, Miguel Roberto (PhD, California, San Diego 1989; prof.) Latin America; mtinkersalas@pomona.edu

Traore, M. Ousmane (PhD, Paris-Sorbonne, Paris IV 2009; asst. prof.; Africana Studies) Africa; makhroufi.traore@pomona.edu

Wall, Helena M. (PhD, Harvard 1983; prof.) colonial America, social; hwall@pomona.edu

Wolf, Kenneth Baxter (PhD, Stanford 1985; prof.) medieval, Christianity; kwolf@pomona.edu

Yamashita, Samuel H. (PhD, Michigan 1981; prof.) Japan and China, East Asian intellectual, historiography; syamashita@pomona.edu

Nondepartmental Historians

Keim, Ben (PhD, Cambridge 2011; asst. prof.; Classics) ancient, Greece, Attic oratory; benjamin.keim@pomona.edu

Miller, Char (PhD, Johns Hopkins 1980; prof.; Environmental Analysis Prog.) environmental, urban history and studies, US; char.miller@pomona.edu

Palmer, Beverly (MA, California, Berkeley 1961; editor; Lucretia Mott Papers) bpalmer@pomona.edu

Retired/Emeritus Faculty

Lemelle, Sidney J. (PhD, UCLA 1986; prof. emeritus) modern Africa; sidney.lemelle@pomona.edu

Woods, Robert L., Jr. (PhD, UCLA 1974; prof. emeritus) England, early modern Europe, legal; rwoods@pomona.edu

University of Portland

Dept. of History, 5000 N. Willamette Blvd., MSC 154, Portland, OR 97203-5798. 503.943.7274. Fax 503.943.7803. Email: hancock@up.edu; mackinno@up.edu. Website: https://college.up.edu/history/.

The history program offers all the University's undergraduates the opportunity to acquire a working familiarity with the history of Western civilization, the United States, and other areas of the world, together with the institutions and structures of organized society.

Chair: Christin Hancock
Degrees Offered: BA
Academic Year System: Semester
Areas of Specialization: America, Europe, Latin America, Asia
Tuition (per academic year): $45564
Enrollment 2018-19:
 Undergraduate Majors: 37
 Degrees in History: 14 BA
 Students in Undergraduate Courses: 1200
 Students in Undergraduate Intro Courses: 700
Addresses:
 Admissions: http://www.up.edu/admissions
 Financial Aid: http://www.up.edu/finaid

Full-time Faculty

Eifler, Mark A. (PhD, California, Berkeley 1992; assoc. prof.) American frontier, Pacific Rim; eiflerm@up.edu

Els, Brian (PhD, Indiana 2004; assoc. prof.) early modern and modern Europe, Germany, child welfare; els@up.edu

Franco, Bradley (PhD, Syracuse 2010; assoc. prof.) medieval Europe, medieval and Renaissance Italy, ancient and medieval Mediterranean world; franco@up.edu

Hancock, Christin Lee (PhD, Brown 2006; assoc. prof. and chair) 19th-century to present US women, race and gender, US cultural and social; hancock@up.edu

Moentmann, Elise M. (PhD, Illinois, Urbana-Champaign 1998; assoc. prof. and assoc. provost) modern Europe, France, East Asia; moentman@up.edu

Wheeler, Arthur F., CSC (PhD, Notre Dame 1979; assoc. prof.) Britain, Ireland, modern America; wheeler@up.edu

Woodard, Blair D. (PhD, New Mexico 2010; assoc. prof.) Latin American studies, US-Latin American relations, Cuba; woodard@up.edu

Retired/Emeritus Faculty

Connelly, James T., CSC (PhD, Chicago 1977; assoc. prof. emeritus) US social, political, religious

Zimmerman, Loretta E. (PhD, Tulane 1964; prof. emeritus) American intellectual, women, reform movements

Portland State University

Dept. of History, PO Box 751, Portland, OR 97207-0751. 503.725.3917. Fax 503.725.3953. Email: hist@pdx.edu. Website: https://www.pdx.edu/history/.

The PSU Department of History encourages active engagement in historical inquiry, whether at the introductory survey level, in seminars, or in community-based learning. Active engagement requires students to learn how to master basic knowledge, ask historical questions, access and evaluate information, and communicate what they have learned in both written and oral forms. Helping students master the use of a variety of sources and tools to unlock the past is a goal of all history courses. The department houses the editorial offices of the Pacific Historical Review.

Chair: John S. Ott
Director of Graduate Studies: Brian D. Turner
Degrees Offered: BA,BS,MA
Academic Year System: Quarter
Areas of Specialization: world, public, Pacific Northwest
Undergraduate Tuition (per academic year):
In-State: $9105
Out-of-State: $27060
Graduate Tuition (per academic year):
In-State: $12993
Out-of-State: $18825
Enrollment 2018-19:
Undergraduate Majors: 209
New Graduate Students: 9
Full-time Graduate Students: 10
Part-time Graduate Students: 23
Degrees in History: 20 BA, 30 BS, 5 MA
Undergraduate Addresses:
Admissions: http://www.pdx.edu/admissions
Financial Aid: http://www.pdx.edu/finaid
Graduate Addresses:
Admissions: http://www.pdx.edu/graduate-admissions
Financial Aid: https://www.pdx.edu/scholarships/future-graduate

Adjunct Faculty

Armantrout, George L. (PhD, Michigan 1990; adj. asst. prof.; Art Hist.) ancient Mediterranean, Greece, art and archaeology; d1ga@pdx.edu

Del Mar, David P. (PhD, Oregon 1993; adj. assoc. prof.) Pacific Northwest, Oregon, family; delmard@pdx.edu

Kerns-Robison, Jennifer (PhD, Arizona 2002; adj. asst. prof.) US, women; jkk@pdx.edu

Koeneke, Rodney B. (PhD, Stanford 1997; adj. asst. prof.) modern Britain, British Empire, world; rodneyk@pdx.edu

Full-time Faculty

Barber, Katrine (PhD, Washington State 1999; assoc. prof.) Pacific Northwest, public, Native American; barberk@pdx.edu

Beyler, Richard H. (PhD, Harvard 1994; prof.) science, modern Germany; beylerr@pdx.edu

Bohling, Joseph (PhD, California, Berkeley 2012; asst. prof.) modern Europe, capitalism, international relations; jbohling@pdx.edu

Garrison, Tim Alan (PhD, Kentucky 1997; JD, Georgia 1986; prof.) US legal and constitutional, US Indian policy, US South; timgarrison@pdx.edu

Grehan, James P. (PhD, Texas, Austin 1999; assoc. prof.) Ottoman, Middle East, social and cultural; grehanjp@pdx.edu

Horowitz, David A. (PhD, Minnesota 1971; prof.) 20th-century US, American cultural, historiography

Hsu, Chia Yin (PhD, New York Univ. 2006; assoc. prof.) Russia, Eurasia; hsuc@pdx.edu

Johnson, David Alan (PhD, Pennsylvania 1977; prof.) American social and intellectual; johnsonda@pdx.edu

Luckett, Thomas M. (PhD, Princeton 1992; assoc. prof.) early modern France, French Revolution, financial; luckettt@pdx.edu

McNeur, Catherine Clare (PhD, Yale 2012; assoc. prof.) US, environmental, urban and public; catherine.mcneur@pdx.edu

Ott, John S. (PhD, Stanford 1999; prof. and chair) medieval and Renaissance Europe; ottj@pdx.edu

Robson, Laura C. (PhD, Yale 2009; assoc. prof.) modern Middle East, Israel and Palestine, religious minorities; lrobson@pdx.edu

Rodriguez, Marc Simon (PhD, Northwestern 2000; assoc. prof.; managing ed., Pacific Historical Review) Chicano/Latino, immigration; msr4@pdx.edu

Ruoff, Ken J. (PhD, Columbia 1997; prof.; dir., Center for Japanese Studies) modern Japan; ruoffk@pdx.edu

Schechter, Patricia A. (PhD, Princeton 1993; prof.) US, women; schechp@pdx.edu

Schuler, Friedrich E. (PhD, Chicago 1990; prof.) Latin America, Mexico, European-Latin American relations; schulerf@pdx.edu

Tappan, Jennifer N. (PhD, Columbia 2010; assoc. prof.) modern Africa, Uganda, health care; jtappan@pdx.edu

Turner, Brian David (PhD, North Carolina, Chapel Hill 2010; assoc. prof. and dir., grad. studies) ancient Mediterranean, Roman Empire military, Geographic Information System; brian.turner@pdx.edu

Nondepartmental Historians

Abbott, Carl (PhD, Chicago 1971; prof. emeritus; Urban Studies and Planning) US urban; abbottc@pdx.edu

Carter, Derrais (PhD, Iowa 2013; asst. prof.; Black Studies) African American, gender and sexuality studies, black cultural studies, black critical theory; derrais@pdx.edu

Davidova, Evguenia N. (PhD, Bulgarian Acad. of Sci. 1998; assoc. prof.; International Studies) 19th- and 20th-century Balkan socio-economic, southeastern European commerce/modernization/nationalism, travel and medicine in Balkans; evguenia@pdx.edu

Frink, Brenda D. (PhD, Stanford 2010; coordinating ed.; Pacific Historical Review) US West, gender and race, historical memory; brenda.frink@pdx.edu

Meir, Natan M. (PhD, Columbia 2003; assoc. prof.; Judaic Studies) modern Judaism, eastern Europe; meir@pdx.edu

Merrow, Kathleen M. (PhD, Cornell 1998; assoc. prof.; Univ. Honors Prog.) European intellectual; merrowk@pdx.edu

Smallman, Shawn C. (PhD, Yale 1995; prof.; International Studies) Brazil, military, social; smallmans@pdx.edu

Spiegel, Nina S. (PhD, Stanford 2001; asst. prof.; Judaic Studies) Israel and Judaism, public, cultural and gender; nspiegel@pdx.edu

Spielman, Loren R. (PhD, Jewish Theological Sem. 2010; asst. prof.; Judaic Studies) ancient Judaism, ancient Israel; spielman@pdx.edu

York, William H. (PhD, Johns Hopkins 2003; asst. prof.; Humanities) science, medicine, technology; why@pdx.edu

Retired/Emeritus Faculty

Belco, Victoria C. (PhD, California, Berkeley 2001; assoc. prof. emeritus) modern Europe, Italy

Benowitz, Elliot (PhD, Wisconsin, Madison 1966; assoc. prof. emeritus) central Europe

Carr, Karen E. (PhD, Michigan 1992; assoc. prof. emeritus) ancient Mediterranean

Dahl, Victor C. (PhD, California, Berkeley 1959; prof. emeritus) Latin America

Dmytryshyn, Basil (PhD, California, Berkeley 1955; prof. emeritus) Russia

Karant-Nunn, Susan C. (PhD, Indiana 1971; prof. emeritus) early modern Europe, Reformation

Lang, William L. (PhD, Delaware 1974; prof. emeritus) environmental, public

Le Guin, Charles A. (PhD, Emory 1956; prof. emeritus) early modern France

Litzenberger, Caroline J. (PhD, Cambridge 1993; assoc. prof. emeritus) early modern England, women, religion

Morris, Thomas D. (PhD, Washington 1969; prof. emeritus) US legal and constitutional

Nunn, Frederick M. (PhD, New Mexico 1963; prof. emeritus) Latin America

Reardon, Michael F. (PhD, Indiana 1965; prof. emeritus) European intellectual, historiography, modern France

Walton, Linda A. (PhD, Pennsylvania 1978; prof. emeritus) premodern China, East Asia, world

White, Charles M. (PhD, Southern California 1959; prof. emeritus) Europe, British Commonwealth, Canada

Presbyterian College

Dept. of History, 503 S. Broad St., Clinton, SC 29325. 864.833.8376. Fax 864.833.8481. Email: mnelson@presby.edu. Website: https://www.presby.edu/academics/undergraduate/academic-departments-programs/history-department/.

We pride ourselves on offering students an educational experience that places them in the center of an engaging globally based curriculum.

Chair: Michael A. Nelson
Degrees Offered: BA
Academic Year System: Semester
Areas of Specialization: medieval, modern US, modern Europe, Asia, Latin America
Tuition (per academic year): $42678
Enrollment 2018-19:
Undergraduate Majors: 70
Degrees in History: 22 BA

Addresses:
Admissions: http://www.presby.edu/admissions/
Financial Aid: http://www.presby.edu/admissions/scholarships-and-financial-aid/

Full-time Faculty

Campbell, Roy B. (PhD, Florida State 2002; prof.) modern China, India, Middle East; rbcamp@presby.edu

Harris, William James, Sr. (PhD, Cornell 2015; asst. prof.) American slavery, race and identity, antebellum American South; wjharris@presby.edu

Heiser, Richard R. (PhD, Florida State 1993; prof.) 12th-century England, English monarchy, medieval and Renaissance Europe; rrheiser@presby.edu

Nelson, Michael A. (PhD, Arkansas 1999; prof. and chair) modern America, US diplomatic and military, Cold War; mnelson@presby.edu

Sumner, Jaclyn Ann (PhD, Chicago 2014; asst. prof.) modern Mexico, colonial Latin America, Mexican immigration; jasumner@presby.edu

Wiecki, Stefan Wolfgang (PhD, Brandeis 2009; assoc. prof.) modern Germany, democratization, fascism and communism; swwiecki@presby.edu

Retired/Emeritus Faculty

Burnside, Ron (PhD, Indiana 1963; Marshall W. Brown Prof. emeritus) colonial America

Coker, Charlie (PhD, South Carolina 1973; Marshall W. Brown Prof. emeritus) modern Britain

Needham, Dave (PhD, Georgia 1970; Charles A. Dana Prof. emeritus) modern America, Progressive era

Princeton University

Dept. of History, 129 Dickinson Hall, Princeton, NJ 08544-1017. 609.258.4159. Fax 609.258.5326. Email: kwailoo@princeton.edu. Website: https://history.princeton.edu/.

The History Department offers a rich curriculum for undergraduate and graduate students, including a program in History of Science, and frequently hosts visiting research collaborators. We are a community of scholars with interests spanning social to intellectual, political to military, economic to legal history, and all parts of the globe. Chronologically, our research ranges from late antiquity to the present. Graduate students are admitted only as candidates for the PhD, but may earn an incidental MA upon successful completion of program requirements.

Chair: Keith Wailoo
Director of Graduate Studies: Michael F. Laffan (hist.); Katja Guenther (hist. of science)
Degrees Offered: BA, MA, PhD
Academic Year System: Semester
Areas of Specialization: North and South America, Asia, Europe, Africa, science
Tuition (per academic year): $51870
Enrollment 2018-19:
Undergraduate Majors: 144
New Graduate Students: 25
Full-time Graduate Students: 159
Degrees in History: 75 BA, 26 MA, 28 PhD
Undergraduate Addresses:
Admissions: http://admission.princeton.edu/
Financial Aid: https://admission.princeton.edu/cost-aid

Graduate Addresses:

Admissions: http://gradschool.princeton.edu/admission

Financial Aid: http://gradschool.princeton.edu/costs-funding

Affiliated Faculty

Best, Wallace D. (PhD, Northwestern 2000; prof.; Religion and African American Studies) religion in America; wbest@princeton.edu

Cook, Michael A. (BA, Cambridge 1964; prof.; Near Eastern Studies) Islamic; mcook@princeton.edu

Hanioglu, M. Sukru (PhD, Istanbul 1981; prof.; Near Eastern Studies) late Ottoman empire; hanioglu@princeton.edu

Haykel, Bernard (DPhil, Oxford 1997; prof.; Near Eastern Studies) Saudi Arabia, Yemen, Islamism and Islamic law; haykel@princeton.edu

Reeves, Eileen A. (PhD, Stanford 1987; prof.; Comparative Literature) early modern scientific literature; ereeves@princeton.edu

Smith, Nigel (DPhil, Oxford 1985; prof.; English) British and European literature and history 1500-1700, intellectual 1500-1700; nsmith@princeton.edu

Full-time Faculty

Adelman, Jeremy I. (DPhil, Oxford 1989; prof.) Latin America, global; adelman@princeton.edu

Barnes, Rhae Lynn (PhD, Harvard 2016; asst. prof.) American cultural, race and racism in North America, digital humanities; rlbarnes@princeton.edu

Bell, David A. (PhD, Princeton 1991; prof.) early modern Europe, France, origins of nationalism; dabell@princeton.edu

Bian, He (PhD, Harvard 2014; asst. prof.) early modern China; hbian@princeton.edu

Blaakman, Michael Albert (PhD, Yale 2016; asst. prof.) American revolutionary era; blaakman@princeton.edu

Burnett, D. Graham (PhD, Cambridge 1997; prof.) science, cartography, European expansion; dburnett@princeton.edu

Canaday, Margot (PhD, Minnesota 2004; prof.) modern US, gender and sexuality; mcanaday@princeton.edu

Candiani, Vera Silvina (PhD, California, Berkeley 2004; assoc. prof.) colonial Latin America, Mexico; candiani@princeton.edu

Cannadine, David N. (DPhil, Oxford 1975; prof.) modern Britain; dcannadi@princeton.edu

Chen, Janet Y. (PhD, Yale 2005; assoc. prof.) modern China; jychen@princeton.edu

Cherian, Divya (PhD, Columbia 2015; asst. prof.) South Asia; dcherian@princeton.edu

Colley, Linda Jane (PhD, Cambridge 1976; prof.) British political/social/cultural, British Empire, global 1650-1900; lcolley@princeton.edu

Creager, Angela N. H. (PhD, California, Berkeley 1991; prof.) 20th-century biology; creager@princeton.edu

Dlamini, Jacob S. T. (PhD, Yale 2012; asst. prof.) modern Africa; jdlamini@princeton.edu

Dweck, Yaacob H. (PhD, Pennsylvania 2008; prof.) modern Jewish; jdweck@princeton.edu

Garon, Sheldon M. (PhD, Yale 1981; prof.) modern Japan; garon@princeton.edu

Gordin, Michael D. (PhD, Harvard 2001; prof.) physical science, imperial Russia; mgordin@princeton.edu

Grafton, Anthony T. (PhD, Chicago 1975; prof.) Renaissance and Reformation; grafton@princeton.edu

Greene, Molly (PhD, Princeton 1992; prof. and assoc. chair) modern Greece and Ottoman; greene@princeton.edu

Guenther, Katja (PhD, Harvard 2009; assoc. prof. and dir., grad. studies) medicine; kguenthe@princeton.edu

Guild, Joshua Bruce (PhD, Yale 2007; assoc. prof.) African American; jguild@princeton.edu

Hubbard, Eleanor K. (PhD, Harvard 2009; asst. prof.) early modern Britain; ehubbard@princeton.edu

Hunter, Tera W. (PhD, Yale 1990; prof.) African American, women and labor, US South; thunter@princeton.edu

Isenberg, Alison E. (PhD, Pennsylvania 1995; prof.) American urban, business culture, built environment; isenber@princeton.edu

James, Harold (PhD, Cambridge 1982; prof.) modern Germany, European economic; hjames@princeton.edu

Jordan, William Chester (PhD, Princeton 1973; prof.) medieval, English constitutional; wchester@princeton.edu

Karp, Matthew J. (PhD, Pennsylvania 2011; assoc. prof.) 19th-century US, Civil War; mjkarp@princeton.edu

Kotkin, Stephen M. (PhD, California, Berkeley 1988; prof.) modern Russia, Soviet Union; kotkin@princeton.edu

Kreike, Emmanuel (PhD, Yale 1996; prof.) Africa, environmental; kreike@princeton.edu

Kruse, Kevin M. (PhD, Cornell 2000; prof.) 20th-century US; kkruse@princeton.edu

Kunzel, Regina G. (PhD, Yale 1990; prof.) modern US, gender and sexuality; rkunzel@princeton.edu

Laffan, Michael F. (PhD, Sydney 2001; prof. and dir., grad. studies) Southeast Asia; mlaffan@princeton.edu

Lew-Williams, Beth (PhD, Stanford 2011; assoc. prof.) Asian American; bethlw@princeton.edu

Lozano, Rosina A. (PhD, Southern California 2011; assoc. prof.) Mexican American, American West; rlozano@princeton.edu

Milam, Erika Lorraine (PhD, Wisconsin-Madison 2006; prof.) modern life sciences, gender and science; emilam@princeton.edu

Mintzker, Yair (PhD, Stanford 2009; prof.) early modern Europe, Germany; mintzker@princeton.edu

Mota, Isadora Moura (PhD, Brown 2017; asst. prof.) Brazil, slavery and abolition; imota@princeton.edu

Nord, Philip G. (PhD, Columbia 1982; prof.) modern France; pgnord@princeton.edu

Prakash, Gyan (PhD, Pennsylvania 1984; prof.) modern India; prakash@princeton.edu

Pravilova, Ekaterina (PhD, Inst. Russian History 1997; prof.) imperial Russia; kprav@princeton.edu

Rampling, Jennifer M. (PhD, Cambridge 2009; asst. prof.) Scientific Revolution, alchemy; rampling@princeton.edu

Reimitz, Helmut (PhD, Vienna 1999; prof.) early medieval; hreimitz@princeton.edu

Sandweiss, Martha A. (PhD, Yale 1985; prof.) American West, visual culture, public; masand@princeton.edu

Shawcross, Clare Teresa (DPhil, Oxford 2006; assoc. prof.) Byzantine; cshawcro@princeton.edu

Tannous, Jack B. (PhD, Princeton 2010; asst. prof.) late antiquity; jtannous@princeton.edu

Thompson, Emily (PhD, Princeton 1992; prof.) early 20th-century US technology; emilyt@princeton.edu

Vushko, Iryna (PhD, Yale 2008; asst. prof.) modern continental Europe, Russia

Wailoo, Keith A. (PhD, Pennsylvania 1992; prof. and chair) medicine and science, US cultural and intellectual, African American; kwailoo@princeton.edu

Warren, Wendy A. (PhD, Yale 2008; assoc. prof.) colonial America; wawarren@princeton.edu

Weiss, Max D. (PhD, Stanford 2007; assoc. prof.) modern Islamic world; maxweiss@princeton.edu

Wheatley, Natasha (PhD, Columbia 2015; asst. prof.) Europe, international, legal; nwheatley@princeton.edu

Wilentz, Sean (PhD, Yale 1980; prof.) 19th-century US; swilentz@princeton.edu

Wirzbicki, Peter J. (PhD, NYU 2012; asst. prof.) US intellectual; pw14@princeton.edu

Joint/Cross Appointments

Conlan, Thomas D. (PhD, Stanford 1998; prof.; East Asian Studies) premodern Japan; tconlan@princeton.edu

Marcon, Federico (PhD, Columbia 2007; assoc. prof.; East Asian Studies) early modern Japan; fmarcon@princeton.edu

Oualdi, M'hamed (PhD, Paris 1-Pantheon Sorbonne 2008; assoc. prof.; Near Eastern Studies) Ottoman North Africa; moualdi@princeton.edu

Peterson, Willard J. (PhD, Harvard 1970; prof.; East Asian Studies) Chinese intellectual; easwjp@princeton.edu

Rustow, Marina (PhD, Columbia 2004; prof.; Near Eastern Studies) medieval Mediterranean Jewish communities, medieval Middle East; mrustow@princeton.edu

Wen, Xin (PhD, Harvard 2017; asst. prof.; East Asian Studies) premodern China; xinwen@princeton.edu

Zelizer, Julian E. (PhD, Johns Hopkins 1996; prof.; Woodrow Wilson Sch.) 20th-century America; jzelizer@princeton.edu

Nondepartmental Historians

Carrick, Christina R. (MA, Boston Univ. 2014; asst. editor; Papers of Thomas Jefferson) American Revolution, early Republic; ccarrick@princeton.edu

Downey, Thomas M. (PhD, South Carolina 2000; sr. editor; Papers of Thomas Jefferson) American South and early Republic; tdowney@princeton.edu

Fagal, Andrew J. B. (PhD, SUNY, Binghamton 2013; asst. editor; Papers of Thomas Jefferson) early Republic US, military, political; afagal@princeton.edu

King, Martha J. (PhD, William and Mary 1992; sr. editor; Papers of Thomas Jefferson) American Revolution and early Republic; mjking@princeton.edu

McClure, James P. (PhD, Michigan 1983; general editor; Papers of Thomas Jefferson) early Republic US; mcclur@princeton.edu

Scofield, Merry Ellen (PhD, Wayne State 2014; asst. editor; Papers of Thomas Jefferson) early Republic US; mscofield@princeton.edu

Whitley, W. Bland (PhD, Florida 2003; sr. editor; Papers of Thomas Jefferson) US South, political, religion; wwhitley@princeton.edu

Recently Awarded PhDs

Anderson, Richard "The City That Worked: Machine Politics and Urban Liberalism in Chicago, 1945-63"

Andrade, Diana "The Postwar Colombian Congress: Economic Management, Women's Rights, and the Law, 1942-57"

Ayers, Elaine "Strange Beauty: Botanical Collecting, Preservation, and Display in the 19th-Century Tropics"

Buonaiuto, Zoe Rose "Jouant l'hôte à la mort: War Casualities, Cemeteries, and the Politics of French Commemoration, 1944-2004"

Collings, Andrew "The King Cannot Be Everywhere: Royal Governance and Local Society in the Reign of Louis IX"

Davis, Teresa E. "América para la humanidad: Law, Liberalism, and Empire in the South Atlantic, 1870-1939"

Fraga, Sean "Ocean Fever: Water, Trade, and the Shaping of the Terraqueous Pacific Northwest"

Funk, Kellen "The Lawyers' Code: The Transformation of American Legal Practice, 1828-1938"

Groppo, Martha Johanna "Making the Peripheral Central: Nursing, Rural Health, and the Anglo World, 1887-1939"

Kim, Allen "Rhetoric, Polemic, and Narrative: The Social Life of Political Ideas in Duvalier and Early Post-Duvalier Haiti, 1957-87"

Mack, Jessica Robin "A Campus for Mexico: Knowledge and Power in UNAM's University City"

Manners, Jane "Congress and the Problem of Legislative Discretion, 1790-1870"

Principia College

Dept. of History, 1 Maybeck Pl., Elsah, IL 62028-9799. 618.374.5684. Fax 618.374.5945. Email: peter.vanlidth@principia.edu. Website: http://www.principiacollege.edu/history.

Our program emphasizes the broad context of human events. You'll develop the ability to distinguish what is lasting and significant from what is temporary and trivial, looking beyond the boundaries of your own time and place. You'll also gain a breadth of historical knowledge while exploring in depth the topics that interest you most.

Chair: Peter van Lidth de Jeude
Degrees Offered: BA
Academic Year System: Semester
Areas of Specialization: America, Europe, methodology
Tuition (per academic year): $27980
Enrollment 2018-19:
   Undergraduate Majors: 8
   Degrees in History: 1 BA
Addresses:
   Admissions: http://www.principiacollege.edu/admissions
   Financial Aid: http://www.principiacollege.edu/finaid

Full-time Faculty

Van Lidth de Jeude, Peter C. P. (PhD, Penn State 2017; asst. prof. and chair) 20th-century Germany, methodology, early America; Peter.vanLidth@principia.edu

Providence College

Dept. of History and Classics, 1 Cunningham Sq., Providence, RI 02918-0001. 401.865.2193. Fax 401.865.1193. Email: history2@providence.edu. Website: https://history.providence.edu/.

Alternate Address: 549 River Ave., Providence, RI 02918-0001

Passionate faculty. Curious students. These are essential ingredients to the best history departments—like ours.

Chair: Edward E. Andrews
Director of Graduate Studies: Jeffrey A. Johnson
Degrees Offered: BA,MA
Academic Year System: Semester
Areas of Specialization: Europe, America, Britain, Ireland, East Asia
Undergraduate Tuition (per academic year): $46840
Graduate Tuition (per academic year): $7560
Enrollment 2018-19:
   Undergraduate Majors: 116
   New Graduate Students: 3
   Full-time Graduate Students: 9
   Part-time Graduate Students: 24
   Degrees in History: 32 BA, 16 MA

Undergraduate Addresses:
Admissions: http://www.providence.edu/admissions/
Financial Aid: http://www.providence.edu/financial-aid/
Graduate Addresses:
Admissions: https://graduate-history.providence.edu/
Financial Aid: http://www.providence.edu/financial-aid/

Full-time Faculty

Andrews, Edward E. (PhD, New Hampshire 2009; assoc. prof. and chair) early America, Atlantic world, race; eandrews@providence.edu

Breen, Patrick H. (PhD, Georgia 2005; assoc. prof.) antebellum American South, slavery, science; pbreen@providence.edu

Dowling, Matthew J. (PhD, Yale 1995; asst. prof.) modern Europe, France, Africa; mdowling@providence.edu

Erginbas, Vefa (PhD, Ohio State 2013; assoc. prof.) Islamic, Ottoman, Middle East; erginbas@providence.edu

Greene, Robin J. (PhD, Washington 2011; assoc. prof.; Classics) Greek and Latin poetry, Greek historiography, Greco-Roman Egypt; rgreene2@providence.edu

Grzebien, Thomas W., III (PhD, Notre Dame 1990; asst. prof.) medieval, Capetian and Valois France, Western civilization; grzebien@providence.edu

Holland, Karen A. (PhD, Providence 1996; asst. prof.) early modern Ireland/England/France, Irish women, Western civilization; kholland@providence.edu

Huber, Melissa (PhD, Duke 2019; asst. prof.; Classics) Roman imperial, Roman topography, epigraphy, numismatics, imperial biography, historiography,

Illuzzi, Jennifer Grana (PhD, Minnesota 2008; assoc. prof.) modern Europe, Romani studies, modern Italy; jilluzz1@providence.edu

Jaundrill, David Colin (PhD, Columbia 2009; assoc. prof.) East Asia, Japan, military; jaundrill@providence.edu

Johnson, Jeffrey Alan (PhD, Washington State 2004; prof. and dir., grad. prog.) Progressive-era America, labor, US West; j.johnson@providence.edu

Lawless, John M. (PhD, Brown 1991; asst. prof.; Classics) ancient Greece and Rome, early medieval; jlawless@providence.edu

Manchester, Margaret M. (PhD, Clark 1994; assoc. prof.) 19th- and 20th-century America and Cold War, modern Middle East, women; mmanch@providence.edu

Murphy, Sharon Ann (PhD, Virginia 2005; prof.) 19th-century American business, finance, slavery; sharon.murphy@providence.edu

O'Malley, Paul F. (PhD, Boston Univ. 1980; asst. prof.) modern Europe, Ireland, Middle East; pomalley@providence.edu

Orique, David Thomas OP (PhD, Oregon 2011; assoc. prof.) colonial and modern Latin America, Christianity and religion in Americas, Iberian Atlantic world; dorique@providence.edu

Orquiza, Alex, Jr. (PhD, Johns Hopkins 2012; asst. prof.) 20th-century America, immigration, Asian American; rorquiza@providence.edu

Rousseau, Constance M. (PhD, Toronto 1992; prof.) medieval and early modern Europe, Western civilization, women and gender; rousseau@providence.edu

Sickinger, Raymond L. (PhD, Notre Dame 1978; prof.) modern Germany and France, European folklore, 18th-century British trade; rsicking@providence.edu

Siddiqui, Osama (PhD, Cornell 2019; asst. prof.) British Empire

Smith, Steven C. (PhD, Missouri, Columbia 2013; assoc. prof. and asst. chair) revolutionary America, Federalist era, print culture in Atlantic world; ssmith32@providence.edu

Vidmar, John C. OP (OPhD, St. Thomas, Rome 1991; assoc. prof.) English Reformation, 19th-century England, Western civilization; jvidmar@providence.edu

Weimer, Adrian Chastain (PhD, Harvard 2008; assoc. prof.) colonial America, early modern Christianity; aweimer@providence.edu

Retired/Emeritus Faculty

Di Nunzio, Mario R. (PhD, Clark 1964; prof. emeritus) 19th- and 20th-century America, modern Western civilization; dinunzio@providence.edu

Grace, Richard J. (PhD, Fordham 1974; prof. emeritus) Britain and British Empire, World War II, Western civilization; rjgrace@providence.edu

McCarthy, Robert E. (PhD, Harvard 1977; prof. emeritus) 18th- and 19th-century America, historiography and documentary editing

Quinlan, Paul D. (PhD, Boston Coll. 1974; prof. emeritus) eastern Europe, Balkans, Russia; pquinlan@providence.edu

Visiting Faculty

Mulderry, Darra D. (PhD, Brandeis 2006; adj. prof.) Western intellectual, US Catholic, women religious; mulderry@providence.edu

Parrott, Christopher (PhD, Harvard 2013; vis. lect.) classical languages and literature, classical philology; parrott@providence.edu

Wales, Jonathan (PhD, St. Andrews 2017; adj. prof.) European intellectual, modern Britain, modern Germany; Jonathan.Wales@providence.edu

University of Puget Sound

Dept. of History, 1500 N. Warner, #1033, Tacoma, WA 98416-1033. 253.879.3166. Fax 253.879.3500. Email: fphillippi@pugetsound.edu. Website: https://www.pugetsound.edu/academics/departments-and-programs/undergraduate/history/.

Convinced that the study of history is an essential component of a superior education in the liberal arts and sciences, the Department of History offers a strong academic program in a number of areas within the discipline of history. Students who study history develop and sharpen their minds as they learn to think, to evaluate, to communicate, and ultimately to judge.

Chair: Nancy Bristow
Degrees Offered: BA
Academic Year System: Semester
Areas of Specialization: US, Europe, East Asia, Latin America, Africa
Tuition (per academic year): $51470
Enrollment 2018-19:
Undergraduate Majors: 51
Degrees in History: 19 BA
Students in Undergraduate Courses: 189
Students in Undergraduate Intro Courses: 106
Addresses:
Admissions: http://www.pugetsound.edu/admission/
Financial Aid: http://www.pugetsound.edu/admission/tuition-aid-scholarships/

Full-time Faculty

Bristow, Nancy K. (PhD, California, Berkeley 1989; prof. and chair) US social, 20th century, African American; nbristow@pugetsound.edu

Fry, Poppy (PhD, Harvard 2007; assoc. prof.) Africa, British Empire; pfry@pugetsound.edu

Gomez, Andrew (PhD, UCLA 2015; asst. prof.) US immigration, Latino, public and digital; andrewgomez@pugetsound.edu

Lear, John Robert (PhD, California, Berkeley 1993; prof.) 19th- and 20th-century Mexico and Latin America; lear@ups.edu

Neighbors, Jennifer M. (PhD, UCLA 2004; prof.) late imperial China, modern China and Japan; jneighbors@pugetsound.edu

Sackman, Douglas C. (PhD, California, Irvine 1997; prof.) North American West, environmental, Pacific world and Native American; dsackman@pugetsound.edu

Smith, Katherine Allen (PhD, NYU 2004; prof.) medieval Europe, cultural and religious; kasmith2@pugetsound.edu

Tromly, Benjamin K. (PhD, Harvard 2007; prof.) modern Europe, 20th-century Soviet and eastern European social/political/cultural; btromly@pugetsound.edu

Nondepartmental Historians

Barry, William D. (PhD, Michigan 1988; prof.; Classics) Greece and Rome, crowds; bbarry@pugetsound.edu

Fisher, Amy A. (PhD, Minnesota 2010; assoc. prof.; Science, Tech. and Soc.) 19th- and 20th-century science and technology; afisher@pugetsound.edu

Johnson, Kristin R. (PhD, Oregon State 2003; prof.; Science, Tech. and Soc.) science; kristinjohnson@pugetsound.edu

Orlin, Eric M. (PhD, California, Berkeley 1994; prof.; Classics) Roman social and cultural, Greece; eorlin@pugetsound.edu

Purdue University

Dept. of History, University Hall, 672 Oval Dr., West Lafayette, IN 47907-2087. 765.494.4132. Fax 765.496.1755. Email: history@purdue.edu. Website: https://www.cla.purdue.edu/academic/history/.

The Department of History at Purdue University, which offers undergraduate and graduate degrees (MA and PhD), comprises more than 30 award-winning faculty with specialties that span the globe and include a wide array of topical fields including women & gender, conflict & violence, politics, human rights, and the history of science, technology, & medicine. Within the history program, students also have opportunities to pursue honors, study abroad, complete internships and research projects, and choose from among 170 courses.

Chair: Frederick R. Davis
Director of Graduate Studies: David Atkinson
Director of Undergraduate Studies: Rebekah Klein-Pejšová
Degrees Offered: BA, MA, PhD
Academic Year System: Semester
Areas of Specialization: Europe, global, US, science, medicine, technology, political
Tuition (per academic year):
  In-State: $9992
  Out-of-State: $28794
Enrollment 2018-19:
  Undergraduate Majors: 110
  New Graduate Students: 8
  Full-time Graduate Students: 33
  Part-time Graduate Students: 4
  Degrees in History: 27 BA, 1 MA, 4 PhD
  Students in Undergraduate Courses: 5202
  Students in Undergraduate Intro Courses: 5022
Undergraduate Addresses:
  Admissions: https://admissions.purdue.edu/
  Financial Aid: https://www.purdue.edu/dfa/

Graduate Addresses:
  Admissions and Financial Aid: https://www.purdue.edu/gradschool/prospective/index.php

Full-time Faculty

Atkinson, David Christopher (PhD, Boston Univ. 2010; assoc. prof. and dir., grad. education) US foreign relations, migration and diplomatic, international; atkinsod@purdue.edu

Bhattacharya, Tithi (PhD, London 2000; assoc. prof. and dir., global studies) South Asia, class formation and colonialism, gender and Marxist theory; tbhattac@purdue.edu

Brownell, Kathryn Cramer (PhD, Boston Univ. 2011; assoc. prof.) 20th-century US political, American presidency, media; brownell@purdue.edu

Bynum, Cornelius Lyn (PhD, Virginia 2004; assoc. prof.) African American, urban and labor, US; clbynum@purdue.edu

Davis, Frederick R. (PhD, Yale 2001; R. Mark Lubbers Chair and head) science, environmental; frdavis@purdue.edu

de la Fuente, Ariel (PhD, SUNY, Stony Brook 1995; assoc. prof.) global, Latin America, literary; delafuen@purdue.edu

Foley, Vernard L. (PhD, California, Berkeley 1970; assoc. prof.) science and technology; foleyv@purdue.edu

Foray, Jennifer L. (PhD, Columbia 2006; assoc. prof.) modern Europe, imperialism, decolonization; jforay@purdue.edu

Gabin, Nancy F. (PhD, Michigan 1984; assoc. prof.) US women and gender, US labor, 20th-century US; ngabin@purdue.edu

Gallon, Kim Teresa (PhD, Pennsylvania 2009; asst. prof.) African American, African diaspora, sub-Saharan Africa; kgallon@purdue.edu

Gray, William G. (PhD, Yale 1999; assoc. prof.; international progs. liaison) modern Germany, 20th-century Europe, world economy; wggray@purdue.edu

Holden, Stacy E. (PhD, Boston Univ. 2005; assoc. prof.) modern Middle East and North Africa, US engagement with Arab world; sholden@purdue.edu

Hurt, R. Douglas (PhD, Kansas State 1975; prof.) US, American agricultural and rural, US West/Midwest/South; doughurt@purdue.edu

Jones, Trenton Cole (PhD, Johns Hopkins 2014; asst. prof.) colonial and revolutionary America, Atlantic world, cultural history of violence; colejones@purdue.edu

Klein-Pejsova, Rebekah (PhD, Columbia 2007; assoc. prof.; dir., undergrad. studies; and dir., human rights prog.) modern Jewish and East Central Europe, Jewish/state relations, comparative nationalism; rkleinpe@purdue.edu

Kline, Wendy (PhD, California, Davis 1998; Dema G. Seelye Chair) medicine, US, women; wkline@purdue.edu

Larson, John L. (PhD, Brown 1981; prof.) US, US political and early national, US business; larsonjl@purdue.edu

Marsh, Dawn G. (PhD, California, Riverside 2003; assoc. prof.; dir., Native American and indigenous studies) Native American, indigenous studies; dmarsh@purdue.edu

Mitchell, Mary X. (PhD, Pennsylvania 2016; asst. prof.) science/technology/medicine, legal, US in the world; mitch279@purdue.edu

Mitchell, Silvia Z. (PhD, Miami 2013; asst. prof.) early modern Europe, Spain and Spanish Atlantic world, women and gender; mitch131@purdue.edu

Pitts, Yvonne M. (PhD, Iowa 2006; assoc. prof.) US, US legal and constitutional, sexuality; ypitts@purdue.edu

Roberts, Randy W. (PhD, Louisiana State 1978; 150th Anniversary Prof. and Dist. Prof.) recent US, sports, Hollywood; rroberts@purdue.edu

Smith, Michael G. (PhD, Georgetown 1991; prof.) Russia, aerospace; mgsmith@purdue.edu

Tillman, Margaret Mih (PhD, California, Berkeley 2013; asst. prof.) China and East Asia, education in modern China, childhood and gender; mmtillman@purdue.edu

Vostral, Sharra L. (PhD, Washington, St. Louis 2000; assoc. prof.) gender/science/technology, health and popular culture, material culture; svostral@purdue.edu

Walton, Whitney (PhD, Wisconsin-Madison 1984; prof. and dir., hist. honors prog.) modern France, modern Europe, 19th-/20th-century cultural/social/gender/international; awhitney@purdue.edu

Zook, Melinda (PhD, Georgetown 1993; prof.; dir., cornerstone integrated liberal arts) early modern Europe, Tudor-Stuart England, political thought and culture; mzook@purdue.edu

Part-time Faculty

Bouquet, Dorothee M. (PhD, Purdue 2012; continuing lect.) Europe; dbouquet@purdue.edu

Curtis, Susan (PhD, Missouri, Columbia 1986; prof.) US intellectual and religious; curtis@purdue.edu

Farr, James R. (PhD, Northwestern 1983; prof.) Europe, early modern Europe, Renaissance; jrfarr@purdue.edu

Fleetham, Deborah L. (PhD, Rochester 2002; continuing lect.) Europe, modern Germany, religious; dfleetham@purdue.edu

Hastings, Sally Ann (PhD, Chicago 1980; assoc. prof.) Japan and East Asia, gender in modern Japan; sahnolte@purdue.edu

Retired/Emeritus Faculty

Contreni, John J., Jr. (PhD, Michigan State 1971; prof. emeritus) Europe, early medieval; contreni@purdue.edu

Cutter, Charles R. (PhD, New Mexico 1989; assoc. prof. emeritus) colonial Latin America, Spanish borderlands, Spanish colonial legal; cutter@purdue.edu

Dumett, Raymond E. (PhD, London 1966; prof. emeritus) Africa, British colonization of Africa; rdumett@purdue.edu

Hearden, Patrick J. (PhD, Wisconsin-Madison 1971; prof. emeritus) US diplomatic; phearden@purdue.edu

Ingrao, Charles W. (PhD, Brown 1974; prof. emeritus) early modern Europe, southeastern Europe; ingrao@purdue.edu

Lambert, Franklin T. (PhD, Northwestern 1990; prof. emeritus) colonial America, revolutionary era; flambert@purdue.edu

Magner, Lois N. (PhD, Wisconsin, Madison 1968; prof. emeritus) medicine and biology; magnerln@aol.com

May, Robert E. (PhD, Wisconsin, Madison 1969; prof. emeritus) US South, US military; mayr@purdue.edu

Parman, Donald L. (PhD, Oklahoma 1967; prof. emeritus) US West, American Indian; parmand@purdue.edu

Teaford, Jon C. (PhD, Wisconsin, Madison 1973; prof. emeritus) US constitutional, urban; teaford@purdue.edu

Woodman, Harold D. (PhD, Chicago 1964; Louis Martin Sears prof. emeritus) US economic, American studies; hwoodman@purdue.edu

Recently Awarded PhDs

Bishop, Wesley Reid "Creating the Commonweal: Coxey's Army of 1894, and the Path of Protest from Populism to the New Deal, 1892-1936"

Lawlor, Pádraig A. "God's Preservationists: The Championing of Conformity in Interregnum England, 1649-60"

Rieger, Maximilian J. "Destiny and the Law: The California Land Act of 1850"

Zhang, Ruisheng "A Green Revolution for China: American Engagement with China's Agricultural Modernizations, 1925-79"

Purdue University Fort Wayne

Dept. of History, 2101 E. Coliseum Blvd., Fort Wayne, IN 46805-1499. 260.481.6686. Fax 260.481.6985. Email: weinerr@pfw.edu. Website: https://www.pfw.edu/history/.

The Purdue University Fort Wayne Department of History is a community of scholars who seek to understand the past and strive to introduce students to the process of historical thinking.

Chair: Richard Weiner
Degrees Offered: BA
Academic Year System: Semester
Areas of Specialization: America, modern and medieval Europe, Latin America, eastern Europe, women
Tuition (per academic year):
In-State: $7640
Out-of-State: $18349
Enrollment 2018-19:
Undergraduate Majors: 105
Degrees in History: 19 BA
Addresses:
Admissions: https://www.pfw.edu/admissions/
Financial Aid: https://www.pfw.edu/financial-aid/

Full-time Faculty

Bauer, Deborah (PhD, UCLA 2013; asst. prof.) modern France, modern European cultural and intellectual, espionage; bauerd@pfw.edu

Dixie, Quinton (PhD, Union Theological Sem. 1999; asst. prof.) African American religious, religion and labor, hip-hop and spirituality; dixieq@pfw.edu

Erickson, Christine K. (PhD, California, Santa Barbara 1999; assoc. prof.) women, recent US; ericksoc@pfw.edu

Gates, Benton E. (PhD, Tennessee, Knoxville 1996; continuing lect.) colonial America, American religious; gatesb@pfw.edu

LaVere, Suzanne Michelle (PhD, Northwestern 2009; assoc. prof.) medieval Europe, ancient civilizations; laveres@pfw.edu

Livschiz, Ann (PhD, Stanford 2005; assoc. prof.) Russia and Soviet Union, Central Asia, gender; livschia@pfw.edu

Malanson, Jeffrey J. (PhD, Boston Coll. 2010; assoc. prof.) early American Republic, American foreign policy, colonial and revolutionary America; malansoj@pfw.edu

Ohlander, Erik (PhD, Michigan 2004; prof.) Islamic studies, religion; ohlandee@pfw.edu

Schuster, David G. (PhD, California, Santa Barbara 2006; assoc. prof.) US, Gilded Age and Progressive era, culture; schusted@pfw.edu

Weiner, Richard (PhD, California, Irvine 1999; prof. and chair) modern Mexico, political economy; weinerr@pfw.edu

Part-time Faculty

Campbell, Stanley L. (JD, Indiana 1976; assoc. faculty) US, Native American

Coles, David (PhD, Yale 1982; assoc. faculty) Islam, imperial Spain, medieval church; colesd@ctsfw.edu

MacKenzie, Cameron A. (PhD, Notre Dame 1992; assoc. faculty) England, Renaissance and Reformation, early modern Europe; mackenzc@pfw.edu

Ringle, Carter Drew (MA, Chicago 2009; assoc. faculty) ringcd01@pfw.edu

Wooley, Deanna Gayle (ABD, Indiana 2009; assoc. faculty) modern eastern Europe, cultural; wooleyd@pfw.edu

Retired/Emeritus Faculty

Bell, John P. (PhD, Tulane 1968; assoc. prof. emeritus) Latin America, US-Latin American relations, US economic; bellj@pfw.edu

Cantor, Louis (PhD, Duke 1963; prof. emeritus) Afro-American, recent US, popular culture; louiscantor@earthlink.net

Fischer, Bernd J. (PhD, California, Santa Barbara 1982; prof. emeritus) modern eastern Europe, modern western Europe, Balkans; fischer@pfw.edu

Thorn, Samuel A. (MS, Indiana 1981; assoc. faculty emeritus) US

Violette, Aurele J. (PhD, Ohio State 1971; assoc. prof. emeritus) Russia, eastern Europe, modern Europe; aviolette@verizon.net

Queens College, City University of New York

Dept. of History, 65-30 Kissena Blvd., Powdermaker 352, Flushing, NY 11367. 718.997.5350. Fax 718.997.5359. Email: kristin.celello@qc.cuny.edu. Website: https://www.qc.cuny.edu/Academics/Degrees/DSS/History/.

Courses offered by the history department acquaint students, both history and non-history majors, with the aims, methods, and results of historical research. The contemporary trend to expand the study of history beyond a national and Western framework is reflected in the offerings of the department.

Chair: Kristin Celello
Director of Graduate Studies: Grace Davie
Director of Undergraduate Studies: Aaron Freundschuh
Degrees Offered: BA,MA,MLS/MA
Academic Year System: Semester
Areas of Specialization: US, Europe, Jewish, Asia, Latin America
Undergraduate Tuition (per academic year):
   In-State: $6730
   Out-of-State: $18000
Graduate Tuition (per academic year):
   In-State: $6570
   Out-of-State: $12150
Enrollment 2018-19:
   Undergraduate Majors: 318
   Full-time Graduate Students: 5
   Part-time Graduate Students: 74
   Students in Undergraduate Courses: 4838
   Students in Undergraduate Intro Courses: 2781
Undergraduate Addresses:
   Admissions: http://www.qc.cuny.edu/admissions/undergraduate/
   Financial Aid: http://www.qc.cuny.edu/admissions/fa/
Graduate Addresses:
   Admissions: http://www.qc.cuny.edu/admissions/graduate/
   Financial Aid: http://www.qc.cuny.edu/admissions/fa/

Adjunct Faculty

McGough, Patrick (BA, SUNY, Stony Brook 1992; adj. lect.) Ireland; mcgoughs@optonline.net

Simon, Mark (MA, NYU 1980; adj. lect.)

Tilitz, Thomas (MA, Queens, CUNY 1999; adj. lect.)

Full-time Faculty

Allen, Joel W. (PhD, Yale 1999; assoc. prof.) ancient Rome, Hellenistic world; joel.allen@qc.cuny.edu

Alteras, Isaac (PhD, Grad. Center, CUNY 1971; prof.) Jewish, Israel; ialteras@aol.com

Antonova, Katherine Pickering (PhD, Columbia 2007; assoc. prof.) Russia; katherine.antonova@qc.cuny.edu

Bemporad, Elissa (PhD, Stanford 2006; assoc. prof.) eastern European Jewish; elissa.bemporad@qc.cuny.edu

Bregoli, Francesca (PhD, Pennsylvania 2007; assoc. prof.) early modern Jewish, Sephardic studies, Europe; francesca.bregoli@qc.cuny.edu

Celello, Kristin M. (PhD, Virginia 2004; assoc. prof. and chair) US women; kristin.celello@qc.cuny.edu

Conolly-Smith, Peter (PhD, Yale 1996; assoc. prof.) US, immigration, film; peter.conollysmith@qc.cuny.edu

Covington, Sarah Amy (PhD, Grad. Center, CUNY 2000; prof.) early modern Europe, Britain, Ireland; sarah.covington@qc.cuny.edu

Daniel, Evan Matthew (PhD, New Sch. 2011; lect.) US labor, Cuba; evan.daniel@qc.cuny.edu

Davie, Grace (PhD, Michigan 2005; assoc. prof. and dir., grad. studies) Africa; grace.davie@qc.cuny.edu

Frangakis-Syrett, Elena (PhD, King's Coll., London 1985; prof.) Ottoman and modern Greece; elena_frangakis-syrett@qc.cuny.edu

Franklin, Arnold (PhD, Princeton 2001; assoc. prof.) ancient and medieval Jewish; arnold.franklin@qc.cuny.edu

Freeman, Joshua B. (PhD, Rutgers 1983; Dist. Prof.) labor, modern America; jfreeman@gc.cuny.edu

Freundschuh, Aaron C. (PhD, California, Berkeley 2006; assoc. prof. and dir., undergrad. studies) France; aaron.freundschuh@qc.cuny.edu

Giardina, Carol A. (PhD, Grad. Center, CUNY 2004; assoc. prof.) US women, labor; cgia@juno.com

Matos Rodriguez, Felix V. (PhD, Columbia 1994; prof. and Univ. chancellor) Puerto Rico and Caribbean

Ort, Thomas W. (PhD, NYU 2005; assoc. prof.) Czech Republic, eastern Europe; thomas.ort@qc.cuny.edu

Placido, Sandy Isabel (PhD, Harvard 2017; asst. prof.) Caribbean; Sandy.Placido@qc.cuny.edu

Richardson, Kristina (PhD, Michigan 2008; assoc. prof.) Islam; kristina.richardson@qc.cuny.edu

Rossabi, Morris (PhD, Columbia 1970; Dist. Prof.) Far East, Mongolian Empire; morris.rossabi@qc.cuny.edu

Schlichting, Kara Murphy (PhD, Rutgers 2014; asst. prof.) US urban; kara.schlichting@qc.cuny.edu

Sneeringer, Julia E. (PhD, Pennsylvania 1995; prof.) modern Europe, Germany; juliasneeringer@verizon.net

Vellon, Peter G. (PhD, Grad. Center, CUNY 2003; assoc. prof.) immigration, Italian American; peter.vellon@qc.cuny.edu

Wintermute, Bob (PhD, Temple 2006; assoc. prof.) US military, diplomatic; b_wintermute@hotmail.com

Wolfe, Michael W. (PhD, Johns Hopkins 1986; prof. and dean, Social Sci.) France, early modern Europe; michael.wolfe@qc.cuny.edu

Joint/Cross Appointments

Cordero, Alberto (PhD, Maryland, Coll. Park 1986; assoc. prof.; Philosophy) history and philosophy of science; alberto.cordero@qc.cuny.edu

Woodfin, Warren (PhD, Illinois, Urbana-Champaign 2002; assoc. prof.; Art Hist.) Byzantine history and art

Retired/Emeritus Faculty

Della Cava, Ralph (PhD, Columbia 1968; prof. emeritus) Latin America, 19th- and 20th-century Brazil; rd79@columbia.edu

Gruder, Vivian R. (PhD, Harvard 1966; prof. emerita) France; vrgruder@att.net

McManus, Edgar J. (PhD, Columbia 1959; prof. emeritus) American constitutional and legal; edgar.mcmanus@qc.cuny.edu

O'Brien, John M. (PhD, Southern California 1964; prof. emeritus) medieval, Alexander the Great

Peterson, Jon A. (PhD, Harvard 1967; prof. emeritus) US urban, immigration and business; japhistqc@aol.com

Prall, Stuart E. (PhD, Columbia 1960; prof. emeritus) England

Rosenblum, Mark (MA, Goddard 1975; prof. emeritus) modern Middle Eastern political; mrapn@earthlink.net

Scott, Donald M. (PhD, Wisconsin, Madison 1968; prof. emeritus) US cultural; donald.scott@qc.cuny.edu

Warren, Frank A. (PhD, Brown 1962; prof. emeritus) 20th-century US; frank.warren@qc.cuny.edu

Radford University

Dept. of History, PO Box 6941, Radford, VA 24142. 540.831.5147. Fax 540.831.5294. Email: shepburn@radford.edu. Website: https://www.radford.edu/content/chbs/home/history.html.

The study of history unveils the complexity of human existence in the past and supplies insight into the present and future. History majors learn not just about the past and its relevance to today, but they also learn to think, write and speak analytically, skills that may be applied in many careers.

Chair: Sharon A. Roger Hepburn
Degrees Offered: BA,BS
Academic Year System: Semester
Areas of Specialization: American South, military, colonial and revolutionary America, Europe, African American
Tuition (per academic year):
　In-State: $10627
　Out-of-State: $22709
Enrollment 2018-19:
　Undergraduate Majors: 180
　Degrees in History: 15 BA, 25 BS
Addresses:
　Admissions: http://www.radford.edu/content/radfordcore/home/admissions.html
　Financial Aid: http://www.radford.edu/content/financial-aid/home.html

Full-time Faculty

Ament, Suzanne E. (PhD, Indiana 1996; prof.) Russia; seament@radford.edu

Cutler, Brock (PhD, California, Irvine 2011; assoc. prof.) Islamic world, environmental, North Africa; bcutler2@radford.edu

Ferrari, Mary C. (PhD, William and Mary 1992; prof.) colonial America, revolutionary America, Latin America; mferrari@radford.edu

Gingrich, Kurt A. (PhD, Wisconsin, Madison 1999; prof.) England, British Empire; kgingric@radford.edu

Montgomery, Garth N., Jr. (PhD, SUNY, Buffalo 1993; assoc. prof.) modern Europe, modern Germany; gmontgom@radford.edu

Moore, Johnny Stuart (PhD, Virginia 1990; prof.) American social and religious, medicine; jsmoore@radford.edu

Munzinger, Mark R. (PhD, Kansas 2004; prof.) medieval, ancient, eastern Europe; mmunzinge@radford.edu

Oyos, Matthew M. (PhD, Ohio State 1993; prof.) military, 20th-century US; moyos@radford.edu

Roger Hepburn, Sharon A. (PhD, SUNY, Buffalo 1995; prof. and chair) African American, Civil War; shepburn@radford.edu

Ryder, John Gregory (MA, Virginia Tech 1981; instr.) US

Straw, Richard Alan (PhD, Missouri, Columbia 1979; prof.) New US South, Appalachia; rstraw@radford.edu

Retired/Emeritus Faculty

McClellan, Charles W. (PhD, Michigan State 1978; prof. emeritus) Africa, Middle East, Third World; cmcclell@radford.edu

Ramapo College

History Convening Group, School of Humanities and Global Studies, 505 Ramapo Valley Rd., Mahwah, NJ 07430-1680. 201.684.7406. Fax 201.684.7973. Email: staranto@ramapo.edu. Website: https://www.ramapo.edu/hgs/history/.

The History major at Ramapo College offers students the opportunity to study this subject for the reasons that have made it a hallmark of an educated person: it appeals to intellectual curiosity, expands awareness of other cultures, develops the imagination and helps connect the past to contemporary concerns.

Chair: Stacie Taranto
Degrees Offered: BA
Academic Year System: Semester
Areas of Specialization: US, world
Tuition (per academic year):
　In-State: $8480
　Out-of-State: $16960
Enrollment 2018-19:
　Undergraduate Majors: 200
　Degrees in History: 35 BA
Addresses:
　Admissions: http://www.ramapo.edu/admissions/
　Financial Aid: http://www.ramapo.edu/finaid/

Full-time Faculty

Atkinson, Roark (PhD, Indiana 2005; assoc. prof.) early America, Atlantic, religion; atkinson@ramapo.edu

Colman, David M. (PhD, Iowa 2001; assoc. prof.) African American, 20th-century US; dlewisc@ramapo.edu

Elovitz, Paul (PhD, Rutgers 1969; assoc. prof.) psychohistory, modern Europe, biography; pelovitz@ramapo.edu

Gronbeck-Tedesco, John (PhD, Texas, Austin 2010; assoc. prof.; American Studies) US cultural, race and ethnicity, US foreign relations; jgronbec@ramapo.edu

Johnson, Karl Ellis (PhD, Temple 2001; assoc. prof.) African American, ethnicity and race, US foreign policy; kjohnson@ramapo.edu

Kayaalp, Pinar (PhD, Harvard 2005; assoc. prof.) Ottoman Empire, Middle Eastern women; pkayaalp@ramapo.edu

Kwak, Tae Yang (PhD, Harvard 2006; assoc. prof.) Korea, East Asia; tkwak@ramapo.edu

Mustafa, Sam A. (PhD, Tennessee, Knoxville 1999; prof.) Europe since 1700, Arabic and Middle East, Atlantic; smustafa@ramapo.edu

Rice, Stephen (PhD, Yale 1996; prof.) 19th-century US social/cultural/technology, American studies; srice@ramapo.edu

Spar, Ira (PhD, Minnesota 1972; prof.) Assyriology, Biblical archaeology, ancient law; ispar@ramapo.edu

Taranto, Stacie (PhD, Brown 2010; assoc. prof. and convener) post-1945 US, US women and gender; staranto@ramapo.edu

Urbiel, Alexander (PhD, Indiana 1996; assoc. prof.) 20th-century US social, labor, education; aurbiel@ramapo.edu

Nondepartmental Historians

Hajo, Cathy Moran (PhD, NYU 2006; dir.; Jane Addams Papers Project) US birth control clinics; chajo@ramapo.edu

Riff, Michael A. (PhD, London 1974; dir.; Center for Holocaust and Genocide Studies) 19th- and 20th-century Europe, Jews in central Europe; mriff@ramapo.edu

Retired/Emeritus Faculty

Carreras, Charles E. (PhD, North Carolina, Chapel Hill 1971; prof. emeritus) Latin America, US-Latin American relations; ccarrera@ramapo.edu

Heed, Thomas (EdD, Columbia 1975; prof. emeritus) Civil War, business, 20th-century US; theed@ramapo.edu

Visiting Faculty

Koenig, Sarah (PhD, Yale 2015; vis. asst. prof.) religion in American West; skoenig1@ramapo.edu

Randolph College

Dept. of History, 2500 Rivermont Ave., Lynchburg, VA 24503-1526. 434.947.8000. Fax 434.947.8138. Email: gsherayko@randolphcollege.edu. Website: http://www.randolphcollege.edu/history/.

The history program at Randolph College focuses not only on historical events, individuals, and institutions, but also on methodology, analysis and interpretation, and the critical examination of sources.

Chair: Gerard F. Sherayko
Degrees Offered: BA
Academic Year System: Semester
Areas of Specialization: Atlantic, US social and cultural, US South, modern Europe, East Asia
Tuition (per academic year): $37540
Enrollment 2018-19:
  Undergraduate Majors: 36
  Degrees in History: 6 BA
Addresses:
  Admissions: http://www.randolphcollege.edu/admission/
  Financial Aid: http://www.randolphcollege.edu/financialaid/

Full-time Faculty

Altan, Selda (PhD, NYU 2017; asst. prof.) modern China, Middle East and Asia, labor, empires and colonialism; saltan@randolphcollege.edu

Berry, Chelsea L. (PhD, Georgetown 2019; asst. prof.) Atlantic, early modern Caribbean, slavery; cberry@randolphcollege.edu

d'Entremont, John P. (PhD, Johns Hopkins 1981; Theodore H. Jack Prof.) 19th-century US, American social and cultural, US South; jdentremont@randolphcollege.edu

Sherayko, Gerard F. (PhD, Indiana 1996; prof. and chair) modern European cultural and social, modern Germany; gsherayko@randolphcollege.edu

Reed College

Dept. of History, 3203 SE Woodstock Blvd., Portland, OR 97202-8199. 503.777.7771. Fax 503.777.7776. Email: mamiller@reed.edu. Website: https://www.reed.edu/history/.

At Reed, history is treated as a basic component of general education. The department attempts to include in its course offerings as many periods and areas of study as student enrollment and available faculty make possible.

Chair: Mary Ashburn Miller
Degrees Offered: BA
Academic Year System: Semester
Areas of Specialization: Europe, US, Atlantic world, East Asia, Latin America
Tuition (per academic year): $58130
Enrollment 2018-19:
  Undergraduate Majors: 46
  Degrees in History: 23 BA
Addresses:
  Admissions: http://www.reed.edu/apply/index.html
  Financial Aid: http://www.reed.edu/apply/costs.html

Full-time Faculty

Breen, Michael P. (PhD, Brown 2000; prof.) late medieval to early modern Europe, old regime France and French Atlantic, social/legal/cultural; breenm@reed.edu

Dirks, Jacqueline K. (PhD, Yale 1996; prof.) American social and cultural, US women; jacqueline.dirks@reed.edu

Fix, Douglas L. (PhD, California, Berkeley 1993; prof.) modern China and Japan; dfix@reed.edu

Garrett, David T. (PhD, Columbia 2002; prof.) early modern Latin America and Iberia, intellectual and social; david.garrett@reed.edu

Howe, Joshua (PhD, Stanford 2010; asst. prof.) 20th-century US, environmental studies; jhowe@reed.edu

Lazier, Benjamin (PhD, California, Berkeley 2002; assoc. prof.) modern Europe, intellectual; lazierb@reed.edu

Miller, Mary Ashburn (PhD, Johns Hopkins 2008; assoc. prof. and chair) revolutionary-era France and Europe, modern European cultural and intellectual, migration and transnational identity; mary.miller@reed.edu

Minardi, Margot (PhD, Harvard 2007; assoc. prof.) colonial and revolutionary America, 19th-century US; margot.minardi@reed.edu

Natarajan, Radhika (PhD, California, Berkeley 2013; asst. prof.) 20th-century Britain, imperial; e.radhika@gmail.com

Smiley, Will (PhD, Cambridge 2012; asst. prof.) Ottoman Empire, Middle East, international law; william.smiley@reed.edu

Retired/Emeritus Faculty

Kierstead, Raymond F., Jr. (PhD, Northwestern 1964; prof. emeritus) early modern European social, Old Regime France, French historiography; raymond.kierstead@reed.edu

Mueller, Christine L. (PhD, Virginia 1979; prof. emeritus) early modern and modern German and Austrian institutional and cultural; cmueller@reed.edu

Sacks, David Harris (PhD, Harvard 1977; Scholz Prof. emeritus) medieval and early modern England, Atlantic world, social/cultural/intellectual; dsacks@reed.edu

Segel, Edward B. (PhD, California, Berkeley 1969; prof. emeritus) 19th- and 20th-century Europe, diplomatic, war; edward.segel@reed.edu

Visiting Faculty

Tyrrell, Brian Patrick (PhD, California, Santa Barbara 2019; vis. asst. prof.) US environmental and social, animals

University of Rhode Island

Dept. of History, 113 Washburn Hall, 80 Upper College Rd., Kingston, RI 02881. 401.874.2528. Fax 401.874.2595. Email: rodmather@uri.edu. Website: https://web.uri.edu/history/.

Our faculty is committed to education and research, taking pride in teaching our students to write persuasively, read critically, think creatively and work independently.

Chair: Ian Rod Mather
Director of Graduate Studies: Evelyn Sterne
Degrees Offered: BA,MA,ABM
Academic Year System: Semester
Areas of Specialization: US, Europe, Latin America/Asia/Middle East, archaeology and anthropology, applied and public
Undergraduate Tuition (per academic year):
   In-State: $12248
   Regional: $21,434
   Out-of-State: $28972
Graduate Tuition (per academic year):
   In-State: $13226
   Regional: $19,840
   Out-of-State: $25854
Enrollment 2018-19:
   Undergraduate Majors: 180
   New Graduate Students: 5
   Full-time Graduate Students: 12
   Part-time Graduate Students: 5
   Degrees in History: 60 BA, 5 MA
Undergraduate Addresses:
   Admissions: http://web.uri.edu/admission
   Financial Aid: http://web.uri.edu/enrollment/financial-aid
Graduate Addresses:
   Admissions: http://web.uri.edu/graduate-school/apply/
   Financial Aid: http://web.uri.edu/graduate-school/financial-support

Full-time Faculty

Buxton, Bridget A. (PhD, California, Berkeley 2003; assoc. prof.) ancient Mediterranean, archaeology; babuxton@uri.edu

DeCesare, Catherine Osborne (PhD, Providence 2000; lect.) US, urban, Rhode Island; cdecesare@uri.edu

Ferguson, Earline Rae (PhD, Indiana 1997; assoc. prof.) African American, women, diaspora; erferguson@uri.edu

George, Timothy S. (PhD, Harvard 1996; prof.) modern Japan, East Asia, environmental; tgeorge@uri.edu

Gonzales, Christian M. (PhD, California, San Diego 2010; asst. prof.) Native American, early America; cgonzal@uri.edu

Honhart, Michael W. (PhD, Duke 1972; prof.) modern Germany; honhart@uri.edu

Loomis, Erik S. (PhD, New Mexico 2008; asst. prof.) US, Civil War and Reconstruction, environmental; eloomis@uri.edu

Mather, I. Roderick (DPhil, Oxford 1996; prof. and chair) maritime, marine archaeology; rodmather@uri.edu

Nevius, Marcus P. (PhD, Ohio State 2016; asst. prof.) early African American; mpnevius@uri.edu

Reumann, Miriam G. (PhD, Brown 1998; lect.) American civilization, 20th-century US, gender and sexuality; mreumann@uri.edu

Rollo-Koster, Joelle (PhD, SUNY, Binghamton 1992; prof.) late medieval, Renaissance; joellekoster@uri.edu

Rusnock, Andrea A. (PhD, Princeton 1990; prof.) science and medicine, early modern Europe; rusnock@uri.edu

Sterne, Evelyn (PhD, Duke 1999; assoc. prof. and dir., grad. studies) 20th-century America, religion, immigration; sterne@uri.edu

Verskin, Alan (PhD, Princeton 2010; asst. prof.) premodern Islam, Middle East; verskin@uri.edu

Ward, James Mace (PhD, Stanford 2008; lect.) modern eastern Europe, World War II; jmward@uri.edu

Widell, Robert Warner, Jr. (PhD, Emory 2007; assoc. prof.) 20th-century America, African American, civil rights; professorwidell@gmail.com

Rhodes College

Dept. of History, 2000 North Pkwy., Memphis, TN 38112-1690. 901.843.3662. Fax 901.843.3727. Email: jacksonj@rhodes.edu. Website: https://www.rhodes.edu/academics/majors-minors/history.

Rhodes College is a four-year undergraduate institution with a major and minor in history, as well as an interdisciplinary major in history and international studies and a concentration in public history. The department emphasizes diverse course offerings, undergraduate research, and internship opportunities.

Chair: Jeffrey H. Jackson
Degrees Offered: BA
Academic Year System: Semester
Areas of Specialization: US, African American, Europe, East and South Asia, Latin America, Middle East, North Africa, sub-Saharan Africa, gender and sexuality, environment, medicine, public
Tuition (per academic year): $46194
Enrollment 2018-19:
   Undergraduate Majors: 54
   Degrees in History: 20 BA
Addresses:
   Admissions: http://www.rhodes.edu/admission/
   Financial Aid: http://www.rhodes.edu/finaid/

Full-time Faculty

Drompp, Michael R. (PhD, Indiana 1986; prof.) East Asia, Inner Asia; drompp@rhodes.edu

Eisenberg, Ariel (PhD, Wisconsin, Madison 2014; asst. prof.) gender and sexuality, urban, poverty; eisenberga@rhodes.edu

Huebner, Tim (PhD, Florida 1993; Sternberg Prof.) US South, 19th century, US constitutional and legal; huebner@rhodes.edu

Jackson, Jeffrey H. (PhD, Rochester 1999; prof. and chair) modern Europe, public, environmental; jacksonj@rhodes.edu

Judaken, Jonathan (PhD, California, Irvine 1997; Spence Wilson Prof.) modern Europe, cultural and intellectual; judakenj@rhodes.edu

Keller, Tait S. (PhD, Georgetown 2006; assoc. prof.) Germany, environmental, modern Europe; kellert@rhodes.edu

LaRosa, Michael J. (PhD, Miami 1995; assoc. prof.) contemporary Latin America, Colombia, church; larosa@rhodes.edu

Lee, Seok Won (PhD, Cornell 2010; assoc. prof.) modern East Asia; lees@rhodes.edu

McKinney, Charles W., Jr. (PhD, Duke 2003; assoc. prof.) 20th-century US, African American, civil rights studies; mckinneyc@rhodes.edu

Ndanyi, Samson K. (PhD, Indiana 2019; asst. prof.) Africa, world, African diaspora, cinema; ndanyis@rhodes.edu

Saxe, Robert F. (PhD, Illinois, Urbana-Champaign 2002; assoc. prof.) 20th-century US, political history, war and society; saxer@rhodes.edu

Terem, Etty (PhD, Harvard 2007; assoc. prof. and J.J. McComb Chair) Islamic law and society, modern Middle East, North Africa; tereme@rhodes.edu

Zastoupil, Lynn B. (PhD, Minnesota 1985; prof.) modern Britain, European intellectual, ancient and modern India; zastoupil@rhodes.edu

Part-time Faculty

Hughes, Charles L. (PhD, Wisconsin-Madison 2012; dir.; Memphis Center) Memphis, African American, American music and sexuality; hughesc@rhodes.edu

Retired/Emeritus Faculty

Garceau, Dee (PhD, Brown 1995; prof. emeritus) gender, US West, documentary film; garceau@rhodes.edu

Hatfield, Douglas W. (PhD, Kentucky 1969; prof. emeritus) modern Europe, Germany; hatfield@rhodes.edu

Lanier, James C. (PhD, Emory 1970; assoc. prof. emeritus) American cultural and intellectual, 20th century; lanier@rhodes.edu

Murray, Gail S. (PhD, Memphis 1991; assoc. prof. emeritus) colonial and early America, southern women, US childhood; murray@rhodes.edu

Schriber, Carolyn P. (PhD, Colorado, Boulder 1988; assoc. prof. emeritus) medieval and early modern Europe; schriber@rhodes.edu

Rice University

Dept. of History, MS 42, PO Box 1892, Houston, TX 77251-1892. 713.348.4947. Fax 713.348.5207. Email: hist@rice.edu. Website: https://history.rice.edu/.

Alternate Address: 6100 Main St., Humanities Bldg., Rm. 326, Houston, TX 77005

In the History Department, Rice students learn with accomplished scholars in small classroom settings. Our faculty enjoy teaching, and many have been recognized with awards for exceptional teaching.

Chair: Peter C. Caldwell
Director of Graduate Studies: Nathan Citino
Director of Undergraduate Studies: Lisa Balabanlilar
Degrees Offered: BA,MA,PhD
Academic Year System: Semester
Areas of Specialization: US, Atlantic, Asia, Europe, Latin America
Tuition (per academic year): $48330
Enrollment 2018-19:
   Undergraduate Majors: 91
   New Graduate Students: 5
   Full-time Graduate Students: 29
   Degrees in History: 25 BA, 3 MA, 5 PhD
Undergraduate Addresses:
   Admissions: http://admissions.rice.edu/
   Financial Aid: http://financialaid.rice.edu/
Graduate Addresses:
   Admissions and Financial Aid: https://history.rice.edu/graduate

Full-time Faculty

Balabanlilar, Lisa Ann (PhD, Ohio State 2007; assoc. prof. and dir., undergrad. studies) South Asia, eastern Islamic world; balabanlilar@rice.edu

Barlow, Tani E. (PhD, California, Davis 1985; T.T. & W.F. Chao Prof.; editor, positions: East Asia Cultures Critique) modern China, women; tb5@rice.edu

Boles, John B. (PhD, Virginia 1969; William P. Hobby Prof.) US South, US slavery, American religious; boles@rice.edu

Brinkley, Douglas G. (PhD, Georgetown 1989; Katherine Tsanoff Brown Prof. in Humanities) 20th-century US, US diplomatic; douglas.brinkley@rice.edu

Byrd, Alexander X. (PhD, Duke 2001; assoc. prof.) African diaspora, African American; axb@rice.edu

Caldwell, Peter C. (PhD, Cornell 1993; Samuel G. McCann Prof. and chair) modern Germany, comparative Europe, European intellectual; caldwell@rice.edu

Canning, Kathleen M. (PhD, Johns Hopkins 1988; Andrew Mellon Prof. and dean, Humanities) modern Germany, modern European women and gender, labor and social movements, welfare state, history of the body; kcanning@rice.edu

Citino, Nathan J. (PhD, Ohio State 1999; Barbara Kirkland Chiles Prof. and dir., grad. studies) US in world, American foreign relations, modern US and Middle East; Nathan.J.Citino@rice.edu

Cohen, G. Daniel (PhD, NYU 2000; Samuel W. and Goldye Marion Spain Assoc. Prof.) modern France, immigration; gdcohen@rice.edu

Domingues da Silva, Daniel B. (PhD, Emory 2011; asst. prof.) transatlantic slave trade, comparative slavery; domingues@rice.edu

Hall, Randal Lee (PhD, Rice 1998; prof.; editor, Journal of Southern History) US South; rh@rice.edu

Irish, Maya Soifer (PhD, Princeton 2007; assoc. prof.) medieval Europe, pre-modern Jewish-Christian relations; maya.s.irish@rice.edu

Li, Lan (PhD, MIT 2016; asst. prof.) medicine, science, East Asia; hist@rice.edu

Lopez-Alonso, Moramay (PhD, Stanford 2000; assoc. prof.) Mexico, economic, demographic; moramay@rice.edu

Maas, Michael R. (PhD, California, Berkeley 1982; William G. Twyman Chair) ancient Greece and Rome, late Roman Empire and Byzantine; maas@rice.edu

Makdisi, Ussama S. (PhD, Princeton 1997; Arab American Education Found. Prof.) modern Middle East; makdisi@rice.edu

McDaniel, W. Caleb (PhD, Johns Hopkins 2006; assoc. prof.) antebellum US; caleb.mcdaniel@rice.edu

Metcalf, Alida C. (PhD, Texas, Austin 1983; Harris Masterson Jr. Prof.) Brazil, colonial Latin America, Atlantic world; alida.c.metcalf@rice.edu

Petrick, Elizabeth R. (PhD, California, San Diego 2012; assoc. prof.) computer technology; hist@rice.edu

Pollnitz, Aysha (PhD, Cambridge 2006; assoc. prof.) early modern Britain and Europe, political thought, intellectual; aysha.pollnitz@rice.edu

Sanders, Paula A. (PhD, Princeton 1984; prof.) medieval Middle East, Islamic civilization; sanders@rice.edu

Shimizu, Sayuri Guthrie (PhD, Cornell 1992; Dunlevie Family Chair) America; sayuri.guthrie.shimizu@rice.edu

Sidbury, James (PhD, Johns Hopkins 1991; Andrew W. Mellon Dist. Prof.) US, Atlantic world; james.sidbury@rice.edu

Suarez-Potts, William J. (PhD, Harvard 2005; JD, Pennsylvania 1987; assoc. prof.) legal labor, Mexico, Latin America; william.suarez-potts@rice.edu

Ward, Kerry R. (PhD, Michigan 2002; assoc. prof.) global, Africa, Southeast Asia; kward@rice.edu

Wildenthal, Lora (PhD, Michigan 1994; prof.) modern Germany, colonialism, gender and human rights; wildenth@rice.edu

Yarbrough, Fay A. (PhD, Emory 2003; assoc. prof.) American Indian, African American, US South; fyarbrough@rice.edu

Zammito, John H. (PhD, California, Berkeley 1978; John Antony Weir Prof.) European intellectual, modern Germany; zammito@rice.edu

Nondepartmental Historians

Chao, Anne Shen (PhD, Rice 2009; adj. lect.; Humanities) modern China, Asian American oral, poverty/gender/human capability; annechao@rice.edu

Johnson, Bethany L. (PhD, Rice 2001; managing ed.; Journal of Southern History) US South; bethanyj@rice.edu

Kean, Melissa Fitzsimons (PhD, Rice 2000; Univ. historian) US South; kean@rice.edu

Taylor, Matthew D. (PhD, Rice 1992; assoc. vice provost and assoc. dean, undergrad.) recent America; ptt@rice.edu

Retired/Emeritus Faculty

Cox, Edward L. (PhD, Johns Hopkins 1977; assoc. prof. emeritus) Caribbean; ecox@rice.edu

Drew, Katherine Fischer (PhD, Cornell 1950; Lynette S. Autrey Prof. emeritus) early medieval, medieval; kdrew@rice.edu

Gruber, Ira D. (PhD, Duke 1961; Harris Masterson Jr. Prof. emeritus) colonial America, American Revolution, warfare; gruber@rice.edu

Hyman, Harold M. (PhD, Columbia 1952; William P. Hobby Prof. emeritus) constitutional and legal, Civil War and Reconstruction, urban; hyman@rice.edu

Matusow, Allen J. (PhD, Harvard 1963; William G. Twyman Prof. emeritus and research prof.; assoc. dir., Acad. Progs., James Baker III Inst. for Public Policy) recent America; matusow@rice.edu

Seed, Patricia (PhD, Wisconsin, Madison 1980; prof. emeritus) world, cartography

Smith, Richard J. (PhD, California, Davis 1972; George & Nancy Rupp Prof. emeritus) traditional Chinese culture, modern China, comparative and global; smithrj@rice.edu

Van Helden, Albert (PhD, London 1970; Lynette S. Autrey Prof. emeritus) science, technology, medicine; helden@rice.edu

Wiener, Martin J. (PhD, Harvard 1967; research prof.) modern Britain, modern European intellectual; wiener@rice.edu

Recently Awarded PhDs

Black, William "No Northern or Southern Religion: Cumberland Presbyterians and the Christian Nation, 1800-1906"

Gomez, Christina "Displaced White Women in the Civil War South"

Kennedy, Wright "Urban Mortality in the Mississippi Valley"

Khan, Suraya "The Impact of the Arab-Israeli Conflict on Arab-American Nationalism and Race Formation"

McCall, Keith Dennis "Reconstructing Race, Place, and Population Postemancipation Migrations and the Making of the Black South, 1865-1915"

Rendon-Ramos, Erika Rebecca "Between Borders: A Comparative Study of Traditional and Fronterizo Migrants, 1978-2005"

Skidmore, William Everett II "Informed Activism: Abolitionists and the Global Movement against Slavery"

University of Richmond

Dept. of History, 106 UR Dr., Richmond, VA 23173. 804.289.8332. Fax 804.287.1992. Email: jdrell@richmond.edu. Website: https:// history.richmond.edu/.

The Department of History provides a window through which students can study a wide range of human activity across the globe. The study of the past helps students understand how people construct, try to live in, and change their social, political, and symbolic worlds.

Chair: Joanna Drell
Degrees Offered: BA
Academic Year System: Semester
Areas of Specialization: US, Britain and Europe, Latin America, Middle East, Africa
Tuition (per academic year): $67590
Enrollment 2018-19:
    Undergraduate Majors: 44
    Degrees in History: 13 BA

Addresses:
    Admissions: https://www.richmond.edu/admission/
    Financial Aid: http://financialaid.richmond.edu/

Full-time Faculty

Bischof, Christopher R. (PhD, Rutgers 2014; asst. prof.) modern Europe

Brandenberger, David (PhD, Harvard 1999; prof.) Russia, Soviet Union; dbranden@richmond.edu

Drell, Joanna H. (PhD, Brown 1996; prof. and chair) medieval Europe, Italy; jdrell@richmond.edu

Holloway, Pippa E. (PhD, Ohio State 1999; Dist. Douglas Southall Freeman Chair, Fall 2020) US legal, US gender and sexuality

Kahn, Michelle (PhD, Stanford 2018; asst. prof.) modern Germany; mkahn@richmond.edu

Kenzer, Robert C. (PhD, Harvard 1982; William Binford Vest Prof.) 19th-century US, US South, US economic and social; rkenzer@richmond.edu

Loo, Tze May (PhD, Cornell 2007; assoc. prof.) East Asia; tloo@richmond.edu

Meyer, Manuella (PhD, Yale 2008; assoc. prof.) Latin America, Brazil; mmeyer@richmond.edu

Sackley, Nicole (PhD, Princeton 2004; assoc. prof.) 20th-century US, US and world; nsackley@richmond.edu

Seeley, Samantha M. (PhD, NYU 2014; asst. prof.) early America; sseeley@richmond.edu

Summers, Carol (PhD, Johns Hopkins 1991; prof.) Africa; lsummers@richmond.edu

Watts, Sydney E. (PhD, Cornell 1999; assoc. prof.) early modern France; swatts@richmond.edu

Yanikdag, Yucel (PhD, Ohio State 2002; assoc. prof.) modern Middle East, late Ottoman Empire; yyanikda@richmond.edu

Yellin, Eric S. (PhD, Princeton 2006; assoc. prof.) 20th-century US; eyellin@richmond.edu

Nondepartmental Historians

Ayers, Edward L. (PhD, Yale 1980; Tucker-Boatwright Prof.) US South; eayers@richmond.edu

Baughan, Elizabeth (PhD, California, Berkeley 2008; assoc. prof.; Classical Studies) classical archaeology; ebaughan@richmond.edu

Hayter, Julian Maxwell (PhD, Virginia 2010; assoc. prof.; Jepson Sch. of Leadership Studies) modern African American, American political development after 1945; jhayter@richmond.edu

Howard, Amy L. (PhD, William and Mary 2005; dir.; Center for Civic Engagement) 20th-century US; ahoward3@richmond.edu

Nelson, Robert K. (PhD, William and Mary 2006; assoc. dir.; Digital Scholarship Lab) 19th-century US; rnelson2@richmond.edu

Ooten, Melissa D. (PhD, William and Mary 2006; assoc. dir.; Women in Living & Learning) 20th-century US; mooten@richmond.edu

Roberts, Daniel M., Jr. (PhD, Virginia 1997; asst. prof.; Sch. Continuing Studies) Tudor-Stuart England, Reformation; droberts@richmond.edu

Schuyler, Lorraine Gates (PhD, Virginia 2001; vice pres., Planning and Policy and chief of staff; Office of Pres.) 20th-century US South; lschuyle@richmond.edu

Stevenson, Walter N. (PhD, Brown 1989; assoc. prof.; Classical Studies) Roman Republic and Empire; wstevens@richmond.edu

Winiarski, Douglas Leo (PhD, Indiana 2000; prof.; Religion) US religion; dwiniars@richmond.edu

Part-time Faculty

Checkovich, Alex (PhD, Pennsylvania 2004; instr.) US science and technology; acheckov@richmond.edu

Galgano, Robert C. (PhD, William and Mary 2003; instr.) colonial America; rgalgano@richmond.edu

Retired/Emeritus Faculty

Bak, Joan Lamaysou (PhD, Yale 1977; prof. emerita) Latin America, modern Brazil; jbak@richmond.edu

Gordon, John L., Jr. (PhD, Vanderbilt 1972; prof. emeritus) modern Britain, British Empire, Canada; jgordon@richmond.edu

Treadway, John D. (PhD, Virginia 1980; prof. emeritus) European diplomatic, eastern Europe; jtreadwa@richmond.edu

West, Hugh A. (PhD, Stanford 1980; prof. emeritus) modern European intellectual; hwest@richmond.edu

Westin, R. Barry (PhD, Duke 1966; prof. emeritus) 20th-century US, African American; bwestin@richmond.edu

Roanoke College

Dept. of History, 221 College Ln., Salem, VA 24153-3794. 540.375.4954. Fax 540.375.4935. Email: willingham@roanoke. edu. Website: https://www.roanoke.edu/history/.

Roanoke's History Department boasts as many tenured professors as some large state institutions. They teach everything from Latin American and African history to European and public history.

Chair: Robert Willingham
Degrees Offered: BA
Academic Year System: Semester
Areas of Specialization: Renaissance and Reformation, US, Britain, East Asia
Tuition (per academic year): $55952
Enrollment 2018-19:
  Undergraduate Majors: 135
  Degrees in History: 37 BA
Addresses:
  Admissions: http://roanoke.edu/Admissions.htm
  Financial Aid: http://www.roanoke.edu/admissions/ scholarships_and_financial_aid

Adjunct Faculty

Dent, Gary L. (DA, Catholic 1985; adj. assoc. prof.) colonial America, revolution, sports; dent@roanoke.edu

Long, John D. (MA, Virginia 1993; sr. lect.) modern Europe, Germany; jlong@roanoke.edu

Miller, Linda Angle (MA, North Carolina 1985; sr. lect.) US social, 19th century, archives; lmiller@roanoke.edu

Full-time Faculty

Bucher, Jesse W. (PhD, Minnesota 2010; asst. prof.) Africa; bucher@ roanoke.edu

Gibbs, Gary G. (PhD, Virginia 1990; prof.) Tudor-Stuart England, early modern Europe, South Asia; gibbs@roanoke.edu

Hakkenberg, Michael A. (PhD, California, Berkeley 1989; prof.) Renaissance and Reformation, early modern Europe, religious; hakkenbe@roanoke.edu

Hawke, Jason G. (PhD, Washington 2000; assoc. prof.) classics; hawke@roanoke.edu

Henold, Mary J. (PhD, Rochester 2003; John R. Turbyfill Prof.) women's studies, US social; henold@roanoke.edu

Leeson, Whitney A. M. (PhD, Virginia 1998; prof.) medieval France, historical anthropology, archaeology; wleeson@roanoke.edu

Miller, Mark F. (PhD, North Carolina, Chapel Hill 1979; David F. Bittle Historian of the Coll. and prof.) colonial America, American Revolution, US frontier; mmiller@roanoke.edu

Rosenthal, Gregory (PhD, SUNY, Stony Brook 2015; asst. prof.) New York state environmental

Selby, John G. (PhD, Duke 1984; John R. Turbyfill Prof.) 19th-century US, modern US; selby@roanoke.edu

Wallace Fuentes, M. Ivonne (PhD, Duke 2006; assoc. prof.) 20th-century Latin America, gender, populist politics; wallacefuentes@roanoke.edu

Willingham, Robert A. (PhD, Texas, Austin 2004; assoc. prof. and chair) modern Europe, Germany, Russia; willingham@roanoke. edu

Xu, Stella Yingzi (PhD, UCLA 2006; assoc. prof.) China, Korea, Japan; sxu@roanoke.edu

Retired/Emeritus Faculty

Millinger, Susan P. (PhD, California, Berkeley 1974; prof. emeritus) Anglo-Saxon England, medieval Europe, early world civilization; millinger@roanoke.edu

Saunders, Janice M. (PhD, Virginia Tech 1981; prof. emeritus) Africa, environmental; saunders@roanoke.edu

University of Rochester

Dept. of History, Rush Rhees 364, 755 Library Rd., Rochester, NY 14627-0070. 585.275.2053. Fax 585.756.4425. Email: history. department@rochester.edu. Website: http://www.sas.rochester. edu/his/.

The Department of History offers programs of study for both undergraduates and graduates. We are committed to teaching and scholarship and to intellectual rigor in the context of close attention to students' needs and interests.

Chair: Laura Ackerman Smoller
Director of Graduate Studies: Thomas Slaughter
Director of Undergraduate Studies: Pablo Sierra Silva
Degrees Offered: BA,MA,PhD
Academic Year System: Semester
Areas of Specialization: American cultural and intellectual, America to 1800, early modern and medieval world, Africa/ Atlantic world/slavery, East Asia and Latin America
Undergraduate Tuition (per academic year): $55040
Graduate Tuition (per academic year): $51540
Enrollment 2018-19:
  Undergraduate Majors: 47
  New Graduate Students: 5
  Full-time Graduate Students: 35
  Degrees in History: 24 BA, 5 MA, 3 PhD
Addresses:
  Admissions: http://enrollment.rochester.edu/
  Financial Aid: http://enrollment.rochester.edu/financial-aid/

Adjunct Faculty

Pierce, Morris A. (PhD, Rochester 1993; adj. prof.) m.pierce@mail. rochester.edu

Full-time Faculty

Ball, Molly C. (PhD, UCLA 2013; lect.) global; mollycball@rochester. edu

Devaney, Thomas C. (PhD, Brown 2011; assoc. prof.) medieval and early modern Mediterranean, social and cultural; thomas. devaney@rochester.edu

Fleischman, Thomas (PhD, NYU 2013; asst. prof.) tfleisch@ ur.rochester.edu

Flores, Ruben (PhD, California, Berkeley 2006; assoc. prof.) ruben. flores@rochester.edu

Ho, Dahpon D. (PhD, California, San Diego 2011; asst. prof.) early modern China, maritime, frontiers; dho2@mail.rochester.edu

Hudson, Larry E. (PhD, Keele, UK 1989; assoc. prof.) US South, African American, oral; larry.hudson@rochester.edu

Inikori, Joseph Eyitemi (PhD, Ibadan, Nigeria 1973; prof.) Africa, slavery, economics; inik@mail.rochester.edu

Jarvis, Michael J. (PhD, William and Mary 1998; assoc. prof.) early America, Atlantic world, maritime; michael.jarvis@rochester.edu

Kaeuper, Richard W. (PhD, Princeton 1967; Gladys I. & Franklin W. Clark Prof.) medieval; richard.kaeuper@rochester.edu

Lenoe, Matthew Edward (PhD, Chicago 1997; assoc. prof.) Russia, Soviet Union; matthew.lenoe@rochester.edu

Mandala, Elias C. (PhD, Minnesota 1983; prof.) Africa; elias.c.mandala@rochester.edu

Rubin, Joan Shelley (PhD, Yale 1974; Dexter Perkins Prof.) 19th- and 20th-century American intellectual, women; joan.rubin@rochester.edu

Sierra Silva, Pablo Miguel (PhD, UCLA 2013; asst. prof. and dir., undergrad. studies) Latin America; sierrapm@gmail.com

Slaughter, Thomas P. (PhD, Princeton 1983; Arthur Miller Prof. and dir., grad. studies) early America; thomas.slaughter@rochester.edu

Smoller, Laura Ackerman (PhD, Harvard 1991; prof. and chair) medieval, religion and science; laura.smoller@rochester.edu

Theobald, Brianna (PhD, Arizona State 2015; asst. prof.) US, gender, Native American

Weaver, Stewart A. (PhD, Stanford 1985; prof.) Britain, British Empire 1485-present; stewart.weaver@rochester.edu

Westbrook, Robert B. (PhD, Stanford 1980; Joseph F. Cunningham Prof.) American cultural, 20th-century America, social sciences; robert.westbrook@rochester.edu

Zhang, Elya J. (PhD, California, San Diego 2008; asst. prof.) modern China, financial; elya.zhang@gmail.com

Joint/Cross Appointments

Bakhmetyeva, Tatyana V. (PhD, Rochester 2006; assoc. prof.; Susan B. Anthony Inst. for Gender, Sexuality, and Women's Studies) tatyana.bakhmetyeva@rochester.edu

Gamm, Gerald H. (PhD, Harvard 1994; assoc. prof.; Political Science) 19th- and 20th-century America, American political and social; gerald.gamm@rochester.edu

Pedersen, Jean Elisabeth (PhD, Chicago 1993; assoc. prof.; Humanities, Eastman Sch. of Music) modern France, medicine and social sciences, women and gender; jpedersen@esm.rochester.edu

Raz, Mical (MD, Tel Aviv 2009; PhD, Tel Aviv 2007; assoc. prof.; Clinical Medicine) health policy, mental health, psychiatry; mical.raz@rochester.edu

Retired/Emeritus Faculty

Borus, Daniel H. (PhD, Virginia 1985; prof. emeritus) 19th-century American cultural and intellectual; daniel.borus@rochester.edu

Brown, Theodore M. (PhD, Princeton 1968; prof. emeritus) medicine, public health, health policy; theodore_brown@urmc.rochester.edu

Hauser, William (PhD, Yale 1969; prof. emeritus) traditional and modern Japan, Pacific war cultural, East Asian women; william.hauser@rochester.edu

Outram, Dorinda (PhD, Cambridge 1974; Gladys I. and Franklin W. Clark Prof. emeritus) 18th-century Europe, science; d.outram@rochester.edu

Walsh, David A. (PhD, Minnesota 1974; prof. emeritus) medieval studies, monasticism, archaeology; david.walsh@rochester.edu

Young, Mary E. (PhD, Cornell 1955; prof. emeritus) America, American Indian; mary.young@rochester.edu

Visiting Faculty

Greenwood, Jonathan Edward (PhD, Johns Hopkins 2015; vis. asst. prof.) jonathan.greenwood@rochester.edu

Rockhurst University

Dept. of History, 1100 Rockhurst Rd., Kansas City, MO 64110-2561. 816.501.4785. Fax 816.501.4515. Email: faith.childress@rockhurst.edu. Website: https://www.rockhurst.edu/history.

The goal of the Rockhurst Department of History is to make a difference in students' lives by increasing their understanding of the past and improving their ability to think critically, reason cogently, and communicate clearly.

Chair: Faith J. Childress
Degrees Offered: BA
Academic Year System: Semester
Areas of Specialization: US social/political/diplomatic, ancient/medieval/modern Europe, American Indian, modern Middle East and South Asia, Catholic thought and culture
Tuition (per academic year): $34000
Enrollment 2018-19:
 Undergraduate Majors: 13
 Degrees in History: 5 BA
 Students in Undergraduate Courses: 98
 Students in Undergraduate Intro Courses: 290
Addresses:
 Admissions: http://www.rockhurst.edu/admissions/
 Financial Aid: http://www.rockhurst.edu/admissions/scholarships-financial-aid/

Full-time Faculty

Childress, Faith J. (PhD, Utah 2001; prof. and chair) modern Middle East, modern South Asia; faith.childress@rockhurst.edu

Janet, Richard J. (PhD, Notre Dame 1984; prof.) modern Europe, modern Britain, Catholic; rick.janet@rockhurst.edu

Motes, Kevin Daniel (PhD, California, Riverside 2008; assoc. prof.) American Indian, early America; kd.motes@rockhurst.edu

Samonte, Cecilia Astraquillo (PhD, Michigan State 2003; assoc. prof.) modern America, women, Asia; cecilia.samonte@rockhurst.edu

Vitiello, Joanna J. Carraway (PhD, Toronto 2007; prof.) medieval Europe, law and justice; joanna.carraway@rockhurst.edu

Retired/Emeritus Faculty

Robinson, Genevieve OSB (PhD, Boston Coll. 1986; prof. emeritus) American ethnic and immigration, urban America, Vietnam War; robinsong4@mountosb.org

Roger Williams University

Dept. of History and American Studies, 1 Old Ferry Rd., Bristol, RI 02809-2921. 401.253.1040. Fax 401.254.3853. Email: sdonabed@rwu.edu. Website: https://www.rwu.edu/academics/schools-and-colleges/fshae/departments/history-american-studies.

Our talented faculty are versed in a variety of topics, teaching styles, and educational environments, and we take seriously our role in undergraduate education at Roger Williams University. From ancient Assyria or Chiapas land rights, to the American home or steampunk comic-book culture, we are ready to enhance your academic experience.

Chair: Sargon Donabed
Degrees Offered: BA
Academic Year System: Semester
Areas of Specialization: Europe, US, Middle East, Latin America, Asia
Tuition (per academic year): $31800
Enrollment 2018-19:
  Undergraduate Majors: 135
  Degrees in History: 29 BA
Addresses:
  Admissions: http://rwu.edu/admission-financial-aid
  Financial Aid: http://rwu.edu/admission-financial-aid/
    financial-aid

Adjunct Faculty

LaFauci, Joseph P. (MA, Providence 1974; adj.) modern Europe

Full-time Faculty

Allen, Aaron C. (PhD, Maryland, Coll. Park 2016; asst. prof.; American Studies) American studies, race relations; aallen@rwu.edu

Carrington-Farmer, Charlotte Victoria (PhD, Trinity Hall, Cambridge 2010; asst. prof.) early America, religious dissent; ccarrington@rwu.edu

D'Amore, Laura (PhD, Boston Univ. 2009; assoc. prof.) gender studies; ldamore@rwu.edu

Donabed, Sargon (PhD, Toronto 2009; assoc. prof. and chair) Middle East/Assyrian studies, animal studies, myth/folklore/fantasy/enchantment; sdonabed@rwu.edu

Meriwether, Jeffrey L. (PhD, Exeter, UK 2001; prof.) modern Europe, Africa, British military; jmeriwether@rwu.edu

Mulligan, Debra (PhD, Providence 1997; assoc. prof.) modern US, Japan, Rhode Island; dmulligan@rwu.edu

Quezada-Grant, Autumn Lee (PhD, Mississippi 2009; assoc. prof.) Mexico, Latin America; aquezada-grant@rwu.edu

Stevens, Jennifer L. (PhD, Michigan State 2005; assoc. prof.) American studies, popular culture, ethnic studies; jstevens@rwu.edu

Retired/Emeritus Faculty

Swanson, Michael (PhD, Case Western Reserve 1972; prof. emeritus) American studies, American urban, New England; mswanson@rwu.edu

Roosevelt University

Dept. of Humanities, 430 S. Michigan Ave., Chicago, IL 60605-1397. 312.341.2157. Fax 312.341.2156. Email: mrung@roosevelt.edu. Website: https://www.roosevelt.edu/academics/programs/bachelors-in-history-ba.

The history program at Roosevelt University is committed to providing students with an awareness of the past that fosters an informed citizenry capable of building and sustaining democratic traditions.

Chair: Margaret Rung
Director of Graduate Studies: Margaret Rung
Degrees Offered: BA,MA
Academic Year System: Semester
Areas of Specialization: US, Europe, African American, Atlantic world, labor, gender, race
Undergraduate Tuition (per academic year): $30876
Graduate Tuition (per academic year): $20858

Enrollment 2018-19:
  Undergraduate Majors: 28
  New Graduate Students: 7
  Full-time Graduate Students: 1
  Part-time Graduate Students: 14
  Degrees in History: 5 BA, 5 MA
Undergraduate Addresses:
  Admissions: https://www.roosevelt.edu/admission/undergraduate
  Financial Aid: https://www.roosevelt.edu/tuition-aid/learn-about-financial-aid-undergraduate
Graduate Addresses:
  Admissions: https://www.roosevelt.edu/admission/graduate
  Financial Aid: https://www.roosevelt.edu/tuition-aid/learn-about-financial-aid-graduate

Full-time Faculty

Chamberland, Celeste C. (PhD, California, Davis 2004; assoc. prof.) early modern Europe, England, medicine; cchamberland@roosevelt.edu

Frink, Sandra M. (PhD, Texas, Austin 2004; assoc. prof.) 19th-century US, urban; sfrink@roosevelt.edu

Rung, Margaret C. (PhD, Johns Hopkins 1993; prof.; chair; and dir., grad. studies) US political and social, New Deal; mrung@roosevelt.edu

Joint/Cross Appointments

Chulos, Chris John (PhD, Chicago 1994; prof.; assoc. dean, Coll. of Arts and Sciences) modern Europe, Russia, cinema; cchulos@roosevelt.edu

Retired/Emeritus Faculty

Headrick, Daniel R. (PhD, Princeton 1971; prof. emeritus) world, imperialism, technology; dheadric@roosevelt.edu

Kraig, Bruce Z. (PhD, Pennsylvania 1969; prof. emeritus) ancient, medieval Europe, food; bkraig@roosevelt.edu

Middleton, Charles R. (PhD, Duke 1969; pres. emeritus) Britain and Ireland 1750-1914, education, gay and lesbian; cmiddleton@roosevelt.edu

Miller, David B. (PhD, Columbia 1967; prof. emeritus) Russia, medieval Europe; dbmjjm@rcn.com

Reed, Christopher Robert (PhD, Kent State 1982; prof. emeritus) early America and Civil War, Chicago, African American; creed@roosevelt.edu

Stein, Leon (PhD, NYU 1966; prof. emeritus) modern Germany, modern European cultural, Holocaust; lstein3100@aol.com

Tallman, Ronald Duea (PhD, Maine 1971; prof. emeritus and dean emeritus; Coll. Arts and Sciences) Canada; rtallman@roosevelt.edu

Weiner, Lynn (PhD, Boston Univ. 1981; prof. emerita) women, US social and cultural; lweiner@roosevelt.edu

Rosemont College

Dept. of History, 1400 Montgomery Ave., Rosemont, PA 19010-1699. 610.527.0200. Fax 610.525.2930. Email: rleiby@rosemont.edu. Website: https://www.rosemont.edu/academics/undergraduate/majors/history/.

The history major provides students with an appreciation of the variety of world cultures. Students, through their historical studies, learn how religious, economic, social, and political institutions make one culture distinct from another, and how these institutions developed over time.

Chair: Richard A. Leiby
Degrees Offered: BA
Academic Year System: Semester
Areas of Specialization: US social and intellectual, modern Germany, 20th-century Europe, digital
Tuition (per academic year): $18900
Enrollment 2018-19:
Undergraduate Majors: 15
Degrees in History: 3 BA
Online-Only Courses: 10%
Addresses:
Admissions: http://www.rosemont.edu/admissions/undergraduate/
Financial Aid: http://www.rosemont.edu/admissions/tuition-and-aid/

Full-time Faculty

Leiby, Richard A. (PhD, Delaware 1984; prof. and chair) modern Europe, 20th-century Germany, postwar Europe; rleiby@rosemont.edu
Moravec, Michelle (PhD, UCLA 1998; assoc. prof.) 20th-century US, women social and intellectual, digital; mmoravec@rosemont.edu

Retired/Emeritus Faculty

Donagher, Richard J. (PhD, Fordham 1979; prof. emeritus) 20th-century US, US foreign policy, Pennsylvania; rdonagher@rosemont.edu

Rowan University

Dept. of History, 201 Mullica Hill Rd., Robinson Hall, Glassboro, NJ 08028. 856.256.4818. Fax 856.256.4791. Email: Lindman@rowan.edu. Website: https://academics.rowan.edu/chss/departments/history/.

The Department of History at Rowan University delivers high quality instruction and advising to both undergraduate and graduate students.

Chair: Janet Lindman
Director of Graduate Studies: Scott Morschauser
Degrees Offered: BA,MA
Academic Year System: Semester
Areas of Specialization: America, Europe, Asia, Africa, Middle East
Undergraduate Tuition (per academic year):
In-State: $14000
Out-of-State: $15786
Graduate Tuition (per academic year):
In-State: $15786
Out-of-State: $21378
Enrollment 2018-19:
Undergraduate Majors: 307
New Graduate Students: 15
Degrees in History: 43 BA, 1 MA
Undergraduate Addresses:
Admissions: https://admissions.rowan.edu/
Financial Aid: http://sites.rowan.edu/financial-aid/
Graduate Addresses:
Admissions: http://www.rowanu.com/admission
Financial Aid: http://www.rowanu.com/graduate/aid

Full-time Faculty

Blake, Corinne (PhD, Princeton 1991; assoc. prof.) Middle East, Ottoman Empire; blake@rowan.edu

Blanck, Emily V. (PhD, Emory 2004; assoc. prof.; American Studies) US, legal, America; blancke@rowan.edu
Carrigan, William D. (PhD, Emory 1999; prof.) US, economic, Civil War; carrigan@rowan.edu
Dack, Mikkel (PhD, Calgary 2016; asst. prof.) modern Europe; dack@rowan.edu
Duke Bryant, Kelly M. (PhD, Johns Hopkins 2009; assoc. prof.) Africa; duke-bryant@rowan.edu
Hague, Stephen G. (PhD, Oxford 2011; asst. prof.) Europe, Britain; hague@rowan.edu
Heinzen, James W. (PhD, Pennsylvania 1993; prof.) Russia, eastern Europe; heinzen@rowan.edu
Klapper, Melissa R. (PhD, Rutgers 2001; prof.) Progressive Era, urban, cultural; klapper@rowan.edu
Lindman, Janet M. (PhD, Minnesota 1993; prof. and chair) US women, social; lindman@rowan.edu
Manning, Jody R. (MA, Clark 2007; lect.) modern Europe, Holocaust and genocide studies; manningj@rowan.edu
Morschauser, Scott (PhD, Johns Hopkins 1987; prof. and dir., grad. studies) ancient, medieval; morschauser@rowan.edu
Rose, Chanelle Nyree (PhD, Miami 2007; assoc. prof.) African American, race, ethnicity; rosec@rowan.edu
Sharnak, Debbie Victoria (PhD, Wisconsin, Madison 2017; asst. prof.) Latin America; sharnak@rowan.edu
Wang, Edward (PhD, Syracuse 1992; prof.) East Asia, China; wangq@rowan.edu
Wiltenburg, Joy (PhD, Virginia 1984; prof.) early modern Europe, women; wiltenburg@rowan.edu

Retired/Emeritus Faculty

Kress, Lee B. (PhD, Columbia 1972; prof. emeritus) US, Latin America, military; lbkress@rowan.edu

Rutgers, The State University of New Jersey

Dept. of History, 16 Seminary Pl., Van Dyck Hall, New Brunswick, NJ 08901-1108. 848.932.7905. Fax 732.932.6763. Email: chair@history.rutgers.edu. Website: https://history.rutgers.edu/.

History happens every day, and informs who we are as individuals, as citizens, and as members of the world community. The Department of History at Rutgers University is dedicated to the close study and teaching of history from all periods and places.

Chair: Alastair J. Bellany
Director of Graduate Studies: Jennifer Mittelstadt
Director of Undergraduate Studies: Leah DeVun
Degrees Offered: BA,MA,PhD
Academic Year System: Semester
Areas of Specialization: US, Europe, women, African American, comparative
Undergraduate Tuition (per academic year):
In-State: $11999
Out-of-State: $28036
Graduate Tuition (per academic year):
In-State: $19074
Out-of-State: $31950
Enrollment 2018-19:
Undergraduate Majors: 340
New Graduate Students: 17
Full-time Graduate Students: 108
Part-time Graduate Students: 4
Degrees in History: 157 BA, 8 MA, 9 PhD

Undergraduate Addresses:
  Admissions: http://admissions.rutgers.edu/
  Financial Aid: http://newbrunswick.rutgers.edu/admissions/
  financial-aid
Graduate Addresses:
  Admissions: http://gradstudy.rutgers.edu/
  Financial Aid: http://newbrunswick.rutgers.edu/admissions/
  financial-aid

Full-time Faculty

Artun, Tuna (PhD, Princeton 2012; asst. prof.) Ottoman Empire, medieval and early modern science, late Byzantine; tuna.artun@rutgers.edu

Barragan, Yesenia (PhD, Columbia 2016; asst. prof.) Afro-Latin America and Americas, slavery, emancipation; yesenia.barragan@rutgers.edu

Bell, Rudolph M. (PhD, Grad. Center, CUNY 1969; dist. prof.) quantitative methods, European social, Renaissance Italy; rbell@history.rutgers.edu

Bellany, Alastair J. (PhD, Princeton 1995; prof. and chair) early modern Britain; bellany@history.rutgers.edu

Brown, Carolyn A. (PhD, Columbia 1985; prof.) Africa, labor; cbrown@panix.com

Clemens, Paul G.E. (PhD, Wisconsin-Madison 1974; prof.) colonial America, American constitutional; clemens@history.rutgers.edu

Cooper, Barbara M. (PhD, Boston Univ. 1992; prof.) Africa; bacooper@history.rutgers.edu

Davis, Belinda J. (PhD, Michigan 1992; prof.) modern Europe, Germany; bedavis@history.rutgers.edu

Delbourgo, James (PhD, Columbia 2003; prof.) Atlantic world, early modern science, Enlightenment; jdelbourgo@history.rutgers.edu

Devlin, Rachel Jennifer (PhD, Yale 1998; assoc. prof.) 20th-century American culture and gender; rachel.devlin@rutgers.edu

DeVun, Leah (PhD, Columbia 2004; assoc. prof. and vice chair, undergrad. education) medieval and Renaissance, science, gender and sexuality; ldevun@history.rutgers.edu

Dunbar, Erica R. Armstrong (PhD, Columbia 2000; Charles and Mary Beard Prof.) African American, women, 19th-century America; erica.dunbar@rutgers.edu

Feinberg, Melissa (PhD, Chicago 2000; prof.) modern central and eastern Europe, gender; mfeinberg@history.rutgers.edu

Foglesong, David S. (PhD, California, Berkeley 1991; prof.) American diplomatic, Soviet diplomatic; dsfoglesong@gmail.com

Fuentes, Marisa J. (PhD, California, Berkeley 2007; assoc. prof.) early African American, Caribbean, women and gender; fuentesm@womenstudies.rutgers.edu

Gross, Kali Nicole (PhD, Pennsylvania 1999; Martin Luther King Jr. Prof.) African American women, crime; kali.gross@rutgers.edu

Hanebrink, Paul A. (PhD, Chicago 2000; prof.) 20th-century eastern Europe, Habsburg Empire, 20th-century Europe; hanebrin@history.rutgers.edu

Hellbeck, Jochen (PhD, Columbia 1998; dist. prof.) Russian cultural 1700-present, illiberal subjectivities, 'New Man' in Russia and Europe; hellbeck@history.rutgers.edu

Ikeya, Chie (PhD, Cornell 2006; assoc. prof.) modern Southeast Asia, gender, colonialism; chie.ikeya@rutgers.edu

Jones, Jennifer M. (PhD, Princeton 1991; assoc. prof.) 18th-century France, early modern Europe, women; jemjones@sas.rutgers.edu

Jones, Toby C. (PhD, Stanford 2006; assoc. prof.) modern Middle East, Islamic political, technology and environment; tobycjones@yahoo.com

Kelly, Samantha L. (PhD, Northwestern 1998; prof.) medieval Europe; slkelly@history.rutgers.edu

Koven, Seth D. (PhD, Harvard 1987; G. E. Lessing Dist. Prof.) Britain, European social and cultural, women; skoven@history.rutgers.edu

Lears, Jackson (PhD, Yale 1979; dist. prof.) American cultural and intellectual; tjlears@history.rutgers.edu

Lee, Sukhee (PhD, Harvard 2009; assoc. prof.) middle period China, traditional Chinese legal thought and practice, East Asian Confucianism; sukhlee@history.rutgers.edu

Liu, Xun (PhD, Southern California 2001; assoc. prof.) modern and traditional China, religion, medicine and material life; xunliu@history.rutgers.edu

Livingston, James C. (PhD, Northern Illinois 1980; prof.) 19th- and 20th-century American economic, intellectual; jameslivingston49@hotmail.com

Markowitz, Norman (PhD, Michigan 1970; assoc. prof.) American political and radical movements; markowit@history.rutgers.edu

Masschaele, James P. (PhD, Toronto 1990; prof.) medieval Europe, England; massch@sas.rutgers.edu

Mathew, Johan (PhD, Harvard 2012; assoc. prof.) Indian Ocean, capitalism, transnational; johan.mathew@rutgers.edu

Matsuda, Matt K. (PhD, UCLA 1993; prof.) modern Europe, France; mmatsuda@echo.rutgers.edu

McCormick, Richard L. (PhD, Yale 1976; dist. prof.) US political, higher education; rlm@rutgers.edu

Mittelstadt, Jennifer L. (PhD, Michigan 2000; prof. and vice chair, grad. education) 20th-century US, politics, gender; jmittel@history.rutgers.edu

Murch, Donna (PhD, California, Berkeley 2004; assoc. prof.) African American, urban, postwar social movements; dmurch@history.rutgers.edu

O'Brassill-Kulfan, Kristin (PhD, Leicester 2016; teaching instr. and coord., public hist./internship prog.) public, 19th-century US, poverty; kristin.obrassillkulfan@rutgers.edu

Pietruska, Jamie L. (PhD, MIT 2009; assoc. prof.) 19th-century US, culture, science and technology; pietrusk@history.rutgers.edu

Reinert, Stephen W. (PhD, UCLA 1981; assoc. prof.) Byzantine, medieval Balkans, early Ottoman; sreinert@history.rutgers.edu

Roden, Donald T. (PhD, Wisconsin, Madison 1975; assoc. prof.) modern Japanese social and intellectual; donroden@aol.com

Schoen, Johanna (PhD, North Carolina, Chapel Hill 1996; prof.; co-proj. dir., Life and Death, Rutgers Center Hist. Analysis) 20th-century US, women, public health; johanna.schoen@rutgers.edu

Seijas, Tatiana (PhD, Yale 2009; assoc. prof.) Pacific world, slavery, ethnohistory; tatiana.seijas@rutgers.edu

Silver, Peter R. (PhD, Yale 2001; assoc. prof.) colonial and revolutionary North America, American Indian, Atlantic empires; peter.silver@rutgers.edu

Stephens, Julia A. (PhD, Harvard 2013; asst. prof.) South Asia, Islam, gender; julia.stephens@rutgers.edu

Surkis, Judith (PhD, Cornell 2001; assoc. prof.) France, Algeria, gender; judith.surkis@rutgers.edu

Townsend, Camilla D. (PhD, Rutgers 1995; dist. prof.) Latin America, comparative; ctownsend@history.rutgers.edu

White, Deborah Gray (PhD, Illinois, Chicago 1979; dist. prof.) US women, Afro-American; dgw@history.rutgers.edu

Joint/Cross Appointments

Butler, Kim D. (PhD, Johns Hopkins 1995; assoc. prof.; Africana Studies) comparative and global; kbutler@africana.rutgers.edu

Cobble, Dorothy Sue (PhD, Stanford 1986; dist. prof.; Labor Prog., Sch. Management and Labor Relations) labor studies, gender and women's studies; cobble@smlr.rutgers.edu

Fernandez, Lilia (PhD, California, San Diego 2005; assoc. prof.; Latino and Caribbean Studies) Latino/a, US; lilia.fernandez@rutgers.edu

Greenberg, David (PhD, Columbia 2001; prof.; Sch. of Communication and Information) US since 1900, political, media; davidgr@rutgers.edu

Lauria-Santiago, Aldo A. (PhD, Chicago 1992; prof.; Latino and Caribbean Studies) Latin America, Mexico, El Salvador; alauria@lcs.rutgers.edu

Lopez, Kathleen (PhD, Michigan 2005; assoc. prof.; Latino and Caribbean Studies) Caribbean, Latin America, diaspora studies; kmlopez@lcs.rutgers.edu

Masur, Louis P. (PhD, Princeton 1985; dist. prof.; American Studies) American cultural, Civil War, visual culture; louis.masur@rutgers.edu

Rendsburg, Gary (PhD, NYU 1980; dist. prof.; Jewish Studies) ancient Israel, ancient Near East; grends@jewishstudies.rutgers.edu

Sinkoff, Nancy (PhD, Columbia 1996; assoc. prof.; dir., Center Study of Jewish Life; Jewish Studies) early modern and modern Jewish, eastern Europe; nsinkoff@jewishstudies.rutgers.edu

Tartakoff, Paola (PhD, Columbia 2007; assoc. prof.; Jewish Studies) medieval Europe, Jews in medieval Iberia, religious and cultural; paola.tartakof@rutgers.edu

Urban, Andrew T. (PhD, Minnesota 2009; asst. prof.; American Studies) 19th-century US, immigration/labor/race, public; aturban@amerstudies.rutgers.edu

Nondepartmental Historians

Carlat, Louis E. (PhD, Johns Hopkins 1995; assoc. research prof.; ed., Edison Papers) US technology, social; carlat@taep.rutgers.edu

Collins, Theresa M. (PhD, NYU 1998; assoc. research prof.; ed., Edison Papers) 19th- and 20th-century business, cultural; theresac@taep.rutgers.edu

Israel, Paul B. (PhD, Rutgers 1989; research prof.; ed. and dir., Edison Papers) American technology and science; pisrael@taep.rutgers.edu

Jeffrey, Thomas E. (PhD, Catholic 1976; assoc. research prof. emeritus; ed., Edison Papers)) early national and antebellum America; tomjeffrey2001@yahoo.com

Weeks, Daniel (PhD, Rutgers 2012; asst. research prof.; asst. ed., Edison Papers) US social, cultural; dweeks@monmouth.edu

Retired/Emeritus Faculty

Adas, Michael P. (PhD, Wisconsin, Madison 1970; Voorhees Prof. emeritus) comparative colonialism, global; madas@scarletmail.rutgers.edu

Baily, Samuel L., III (PhD, Pennsylvania 1964; prof. emeritus) Latin America, comparative immigration; bailysj@comcast.net

Becker, Seymour (PhD, Harvard 1963; prof. emeritus) Russia, modern Europe; seymourb@nyc.rr.com

Cargill, Jack (PhD, California, Berkeley 1977; prof. emeritus) ancient Greece; jcargill@scarletmail.rutgers.edu

Chambers, John W., II (PhD, Columbia 1973; dist. prof. emeritus) 20th-century US, war and peace studies; chamber@history.rutgers.edu

Fabian, Ann V. (PhD, Yale 1982; dist. prof. emeritus) American culture; afabian@scarletmail.rutgers.edu

Galili, Ziva (PhD, Columbia 1980; dist. prof. emeritus) Russia, modern Europe; galili@scarletmail.rutgers.edu

Gardner, Lloyd C. (PhD, Wisconsin, Madison 1960; Charles and Mary Beard Prof. emeritus and Dist. Research Prof.) American diplomacy; lgardner79@gmail.com

Gillette, William (PhD, Princeton 1963; prof. emeritus) American political, Civil War and Reconstruction, New Jersey; begillet@infionline.net

Gillis, John R. (PhD, Stanford 1965; prof. emeritus) modern European social, family, global; gottgillis@cs.com

Gordon, Ann D. (PhD, Wisconsin, Madison 1975; research prof. emeritus; editor, Papers of Elizabeth Cady Stanton and Susan Anthony) 19th-century US; agordon@scarletmail.rutgers.edu

Greenberg, Douglas S. (PhD, Cornell 1973; dist. prof. emeritus) Holocaust, comparative genocide; doug.greenberg@rutgers.edu

Greven, Philip J., Jr. (PhD, Harvard 1965; prof. emeritus) colonial America, family, social and religious; pgreven@aol.com

Hall, Gwendolyn Midlo (PhD, Michigan 1970; prof. emeritus) Latin America, Caribbean; ghall1929@gmail.com

Hewitt, Nancy A. (PhD, Pennsylvania 1981; prof. emeritus) American women, 19th-century US, comparative women; nhewitt@scarletmail.rutgers.edu

Howard, Allen M. (PhD, Wisconsin, Madison 1972; prof. emeritus) Africa, urban, global; ahoward@scarletmail.rutgers.edu

Jenkins, Reese V. (PhD, Wisconsin, Madison 1966; prof. emeritus) modern science and technology; reese638@aol.com

Kaplan, Temma (PhD, Harvard 1969; dist. prof. emeritus) comparative women, Latin America, Spain; temma555@aol.com

Kelley, Donald R. (PhD, Columbia 1962; prof. emeritus) European intellectual; dkelley@scarletmail.rutgers.edu

Lawson, Steven F. (PhD, Columbia 1974; prof. emeritus) 20th-century US, post-1945 US, civil rights movement; slawson@scarletmail.rutgers.edu

Lebsock, Suzanne D. (PhD, Virginia 1977; Board of Governors Prof. emeritus) women, US South, US social; lebsock@history.rutgers.edu

Lee, Maurice D., Jr. (PhD, Princeton 1950; Margaret A. Judson Prof. emeritus) Tudor-Stuart Britain

Lenaghan, John O. (PhD, Princeton 1962; prof. emeritus) ancient Rome; lenaghan@scarletmail.rutgers.edu

Mack, Phyllis B. (PhD, Cornell 1974; prof. emeritus) early modern Europe, women; pmack@scarletmail.rutgers.edu

Morrison, Karl F. (PhD, Cornell 1961; Lessing Prof. emeritus) medieval Europe, Renaissance; ankamor@verizon.net

Reed, James W. (PhD, Harvard 1974; prof. emeritus) American social; jwr@scarletmail.rutgers.edu

Smith, Bonnie G. (PhD, Rochester 1976; Board of Governors Dist. Prof. emeritus) modern Europe, women and gender, France; bosmith@scarletmail.rutgers.edu

Triner, Gail D. (PhD, Columbia 1994; prof. emeritus) Latin America, Brazil, economic; gtriner@gmail.com

Wasserman, Mark (PhD, Chicago 1975; prof. emeritus) Latin America, Mexico; wasserm@scarletmail.rutgers.edu

Wheeler, Kenneth W. (PhD, Rochester 1964; Univ. Prof. emeritus) Europe, urban

Yans, Virginia Y. (PhD, SUNY, Buffalo 1970; prof. emeritus) US women, immigration; virginiayans@earthlink.net

Zerubavel, Yael (PhD, Pennsylvania 1980; prof. emeritus; Jewish Studies) Jewish social and cultural, modern Israel, nationalism and memory; yaelzeru@jewishstudies.rutgers.edu

Recently Awarded PhDs

Bayker, Jesse "Before Transsexuality: Transgender Lives and Practices in 19th-Century America"

Bennett, Zachary Morgan "Flowing Power: Rivers, Energy, and the Remaiking of Colonial New England"

Chakraborty, Satyasikha "The 'Faithful' Ayah in Colonial Households: Gender, Caste, and Race of South Asian Domestic Labors"

Clayman, Lillian "Life of the Party: Unions and the Making of the Moderate Republican Party in Nassau County, New York"

Esty, Kaisha "A Crusade against the Despoiler of Virtue: Black Women, Sexual Purity, and the Gendered Politics of the Negro Problem, 1839-1920"

Jeffres, Travis "We Nahuas Went Everywhere in That Land: The Mexican Indian Diaspora in the Greater Southwest, 1540-1680"

Katz, Julia "From Coolies to Colonials: Chinese Migrants in Hawai'i"

Lenhart, Michael "Gamesmanship and Sportsmanship in the Rise of American Football: From Play to Performance to Entertainment, 1869-1970"

Reynolds, Melissa Buckner "'Gentyll Reader Ye Shall Understande': Practical Books and the Making of an English Reading Public, 1400-1600"

Thurner, Lance C "The Making and Taking of 'Indian Medicine': Race, Empire, and Bioprospecting in Colonial Mexico"

Rutgers University-Camden

Dept. of History, 429 Cooper St., Camden, NJ 08102. 856.225.6080. Fax 856.225.6602. Email: lthomas2@camden. rutgers.edu; sas548@camden.rutgers.edu. Website: https:// history.camden.rutgers.edu/.

We seek to foster understanding of the historical experiences of peoples around the world, to strengthen our students' analytical and communications skills, and to prepare them for life after university.

Chair: Lorrin Thomas
Director of Graduate Studies: Andrew Shankman
Degrees Offered: BA,MA
Academic Year System: Semester
Areas of Specialization: US, Europe, women and gender, science and technology, cultural
Undergraduate Tuition (per academic year):
In-State: $13010
Out-of-State: $28520
Graduate Tuition (per academic year):
In-State: $18010
Out-of-State: $28930
Enrollment 2018-19:
Undergraduate Majors: 60
New Graduate Students: 7
Full-time Graduate Students: 10
Part-time Graduate Students: 19
Degrees in History: 22 BA, 2 MA
Addresses:
Admissions: http://admission.rutgers.edu
Financial Aid: https://financialaid.rutgers.edu/

Full-time Faculty

Epstein, Katherine C. (PhD, Ohio State 2011; assoc. prof.) US, military, US diplomatic; kce17@camden.rutgers.edu

Glasker, Wayne (PhD, Pennsylvania 1995; assoc. prof.) Afro-American, social, US; glasker@camden.rutgers.edu

Golden, Janet (PhD, Boston Univ. 1984; prof.) public, American medicine, modern US; jgolden@camden.rutgers.edu

Kapur, Nick (PhD, Harvard 2011; asst. prof.) East Asia, modern Japan, cultural; nick.kapur@rutgers.edu

Lindenmeyer, Kriste (PhD, Cincinnati 1991; Univ. prof.) women and gender, childhood studies, US social; kriste.lindenmeyer@camden.rutgers.edu

Marker, Emily (PhD, Chicago 2016; asst. prof.) modern Europe, France and Francophone Africa, empire and race; emily.marker@rutgers.edu

Marsh, Margaret S. (PhD, Rutgers 1974; Univ. Prof.) women and gender, medicine; mmarsh@camden.rutgers.edu

Mires, Charlene (PhD, Temple 1997; prof.) public, early America, material culture; cmires@camden.rutgers.edu

Mokhberi, Susan Marie (PhD, California, Los Angeles 2010; asst. prof.)

Shankman, Andrew Benjamin (PhD, Princeton 1997; prof. and dir., grad. studies) early America, American political and economic, early modern England; shankman@camden.rutgers.edu

Thomas, Lorrin Reed (PhD, Pennsylvania 2002; assoc. prof. and chair) 20th-century Latin America and US, comparative race and ethnicity, citizenship; lthomas2@camden.rutgers.edu

Woloson, Wendy (PhD, Pennsylvania 1999; assoc. prof.)

Retired/Emeritus Faculty

Bernstein, Laurie (PhD, California, Berkeley 1987; assoc. prof. emeritus) Russia, women's and gender studies, Jewish; lbernste@camden.rutgers.edu

Carlisle, Rodney P. (PhD, California, Berkeley 1965; prof. emeritus) recent America, naval, Afro-American

Dorwart, Jeffery M. (PhD, Massachusetts Amherst 1971; prof. emeritus) military, diplomatic, US 1877-1900; dorwart@camden.rutgers.edu

Gillette, Howard F. (PhD, Yale 1970; prof. emeritus) urban, urban policy; hfg@camden.rutgers.edu

Held, Joseph (PhD, Rutgers 1968; assoc. prof. emeritus) eastern Europe, modern Europe

Lees, Andrew (PhD, Harvard 1969; dist. prof. emeritus) Germany, intellectual, urban; alees@camden.rutgers.edu

Muldoon, James M. (PhD, Cornell 1965; prof. emeritus) medieval, early modern

Scranton, Philip B. (PhD, Pennsylvania 1975; Univ. Board of Governors Prof. emeritus) American economic, business, labor; scranton@camden.rutgers.edu

Verbrugghe, Gerald P. (PhD, Princeton 1971; assoc. prof. emeritus) ancient Greece, Rome, ancient historiography; verbrugg@camden.rutgers.edu

Woll, Allen L. (PhD, Wisconsin, Madison 1975; prof. emeritus) popular culture, American intellectual, modern US; awoll@camden.rutgers.edu

Rutgers University-Newark/New Jersey Institute of Technology

Federated Dept. of History, 175 University Ave., 323 Conklin Hall, Newark, NJ 07102-1814. 973.353.5410. Fax 973.353.1193. Email: history@newark.rutgers.edu. Website: http://history.newark.rutgers.edu.

Alternate Address: 331 Cullimore Hall, University Heights, Newark, NJ 07102

The department includes faculty from Rutgers University at Newark and New Jersey Institute of Technology and offers joint undergraduate and graduate degrees.

Chair: Gary D. Farney (Rutgers, Newark) and Neil M. Maher (NJIT)
Director of Graduate Studies: Timothy Stewart-Winter
Director of Undergraduate Studies: Daniel Asen
Degrees Offered: BA,MA,MAT
Academic Year System: Semester

Areas of Specialization: America, world/comparative, technology/environment/medicine/health, race, gender

Undergraduate Tuition (per academic year):
In-State: $14409
Out-of-State: $30717

Graduate Tuition (per academic year):
In-State: $15555
Out-of-State: $24861

Enrollment 2018-19:
Undergraduate Majors: 190
New Graduate Students: 15
Full-time Graduate Students: 11
Part-time Graduate Students: 22
Degrees in History: 35 BA, 10 MA

Undergraduate Addresses:
Admissions: https://admissions.newark.rutgers.edu/
Financial Aid: http://finaid.newark.rutgers.edu/

Graduate Addresses:
Admissions: http://gradstudy.rutgers.edu/apply/overview
Financial Aid: http://finaid.newark.rutgers.edu/

Full-time Faculty

Amzi-Erdogdular, Leyla (PhD, Columbia 2013; asst. prof.; Rutgers, Newark) Ottoman Empire, Middle East; leyla.amzi@rutgers.edu

Asen, Daniel (PhD, Columbia 2012; assoc. prof. and undergrad. dir.; Rutgers, Newark) China, East Asia; da467@rutgers.edu

Caplan, Karen D. (PhD, Princeton 2001; assoc. prof.; Rutgers, Newark) 19th-century Latin America, Mexico and US; kcaplan@rutgers.edu

Çelik, Zeynep (PhD, California, Berkeley 1984; dist. prof.; New Jersey Inst. Tech.) Middle East and North Africa, architectural and urban, archeology and politic; zeynep.celik@njit.edu

Chang, Kornel (PhD, Chicago 2007; assoc. prof.; Rutgers, Newark) modern US, migration and border controls, US empire and Pacific world; kchang4@rutgers.edu

Cooper, Melissa L. (PhD, Rutgers 2012; assoc. prof.; Rutgers, Newark) African American cultural and intellectual, African diaspora; melissa.cooper@rutgers.edu

Cowans, Jon (PhD, Stanford 1994; assoc. prof.; Rutgers, Newark) France, modern Europe; jonco58@aol.com

Dent, Rosanna (PhD, Pennsylvania 2017; asst. prof.; New Jersey Inst. Tech.) science and medicine, modern Latin America, feminist science studies; rdent@njit.edu

Diner, Steven J. (PhD, Chicago 1972; Univ. Prof.; Rutgers, Newark) US immigration, urban and suburban studies, Progressive Era; sdiner@rutgers.edu

Esquilin, Marta (MA, Columbia 2003; asst. prof.; Rutgers, Newark) social justice, education; marta.esquilin@rutgers.edu

Farney, Gary D. (PhD, Bryn Mawr 1999; assoc. prof. and chair; Rutgers, Newark) Roman Republic and early Empire, political culture and group identity, Roman archaeology; gfarney@rutgers.edu

Feldstein, Ruth S. (PhD, Brown 1997; prof.; Rutgers, Newark) 20th-century US culture and politics, women and gender, African American; feldst@rutgers.edu

Giloi, Eva D. (PhD, Princeton 2000; assoc. prof.; Rutgers, Newark) 19th- and 20th-century Europe, modern Germany, cultural; evagiloi@rutgers.edu

Goodman, James (PhD, Princeton 1990; dist. prof.; Rutgers, Newark) 20th-century US, race, narrative; goodmanj@rutgers.edu

Green-Mercado, Marya T. (PhD, Chicago 2012; asst. prof.; Rutgers, Newark) Islamic, early modern Spain, Mediterranean; mayte.green@rutgers.edu

Hamilton, Louis I. (PhD, Fordham 2000; prof.; New Jersey Inst. Tech.) medieval ritual and liturgy, Italian urban, church and canon law; louis.i.hamilton@njit.edu

Krasovic, Mark (PhD, Yale 2008; assoc. prof.; Rutgers, Newark) modern US, cultural and urban, public humanities; krasovic@rutgers.edu

Lefkovitz, Alison L. (PhD, Chicago 2010; assoc. prof.; New Jersey Inst. of Tech.) law, gender and sexuality, politics; alefkovi@njit.edu

Maher, Neil M. (PhD, NYU 2001; prof. and chair; New Jersey Inst. Tech.) environment, 20th-century US social and political; maher@njit.edu

Monteiro, Lyra D. (PhD, Brown 2012; asst. prof.; Rutgers, Newark) public, early US, race and ethnic identity; lyra.monteiro@rutgers.edu

Murphy, Brian Phillips (PhD, Virginia 2008; assoc. prof.; Rutgers, Newark) early Republic US, political economy, corruption and corporations; brian.phillips.murphy@rutgers.edu

Pemberton, Stephen G. (PhD, North Carolina, Chapel Hill 2001; assoc. prof.; New Jersey Inst. Tech.) medicine, biomedical science and technology; stephen.pemberton@njit.edu

Riismandel, Kyle (PhD, George Washington 2010; sr. Univ. lect.; New Jersey Inst. Tech.) 20th-century US urban and cultural, legal history of media, film history and theory; kyle.riismandel@njit.edu

Rizzo, Mary (PhD, Minnesota 2005; asst. prof.; Rutgers, Newark) public, urban studies; mary.rizzo@rutgers.edu

Satter, Beryl E. (PhD, Yale 1992; prof.; Rutgers, Newark) 20th-century US, women, urban and economic; satter@rutgers.edu

Schweizer, Karl W. (PhD, Cambridge 1976; prof.; New Jersey Inst. Tech.) British and European diplomatic, international relations, historiography; schweizer@njit.edu

Sevcenko, Liz (MA, NYU 2000; assoc. prof.) public humanities, trauma and human rights, migration

Stewart-Winter, Timothy David (PhD, Chicago 2009; assoc. prof. and grad. dir.; Rutgers, Newark) modern US, sexuality and gender, urban; timsw@rutgers.edu

Strub, Whitney (PhD, UCLA 2006; assoc. prof.; Rutgers, Newark) modern US, sexuality and law, film/culture/politics; wstrub@rutgers.edu

Tchen, John Kuo Wei (PhD, NYU 1992; prof.; Rutgers, Newark) public, Asian American, urban, race and ethnicity; jack.tchen@rutgers.edu

Tegegne, Habtamu M. (PhD, Illinois, Urbana-Champaign 2011; asst. prof.; Rutgers, Newark) Africa, Middle East, premodern agrarian societies; habtamu.tegegne@rutgers.edu

Truschke, Audrey (PhD, Columbia 2012; asst. prof.; Rutgers, Newark) India, South Asia; audrey.truschke@gmail.com

Varlik, Nühket (PhD, Chicago 2008; assoc. prof.; Rutgers, Newark) Ottoman Empire, early modern Mediterranean, medicine; varlik@rutgers.edu

Nondepartmental Historians

Snyder, Robert W. (PhD, NYU 1986; prof.; Arts, Culture and Media, Rutgers, Newark) US urban, popular culture, media studies rwsnyder@rutgers.edu

Retired/Emeritus Faculty

Golden, Peter B. (PhD, Columbia 1970; prof. emeritus; Rutgers, Newark) Eurasian Turkic nomads, Byzantine, Islamic world; pgolden@rutgers.edu

Hosford, David H. (PhD, Wisconsin, Madison 1970; prof. emeritus; Rutgers, Newark) Tudor-Stuart England, 18th-century England, early modern Europe; dhosford@andromeda.rutgers.edu

Hunczak, Taras (PhD, Vienna 1960; prof. emeritus; Rutgers, Newark) Russia, Ukraine, Poland; thunczak@andromeda.rutgers.edu

Kimball, Warren F. (PhD, Georgetown 1968; prof. emeritus; Rutgers, Newark) US foreign policy and diplomacy, Franklin Roosevelt and World War II, US 1945; wkimball@andromeda.rutgers.edu

Lurie, Jonathan (PhD, Wisconsin, Madison 1970; prof. emeritus; Rutgers, Newark) late 19th-century America, American legal; jlurie@andromeda.rutgers.edu

Merker, Irwin L. (PhD, Princeton 1958; assoc. prof. emeritus; Rutgers, Newark) ancient Greece and Rome, ancient technology

O'Connor, John E. (PhD, Grad. Center, CUNY 1973; prof. emeritus; New Jersey Inst. Tech.) film and history, colonial America; oconnor@njit.edu

Rosen, Elliot A. (PhD, NYU 1954; prof. emeritus; Rutgers, Newark) US, 20th-century economic, New Deal

Russell, Frederick H. (PhD, Johns Hopkins 1969; assoc. prof. emeritus; Rutgers, Newark) medieval; frussell@andromeda.rutgers.edu

Sher, Doris (MA, Columbia 1967; asst. prof. emeritus; New Jersey Inst. Tech.) modern European intellectual

Sher, Richard B. (PhD, Chicago 1979; dist. prof. emeritus; New Jersey Inst. Tech.) Enlightenment, technology, print culture; sher@njit.edu

Tobias, Norman (PhD, Rutgers 1969; assoc. prof. emeritus; New Jersey Inst. Tech.) ancient Greece and Rome, Byzantine; tobias@njit.edu

Wagenheim, Olga J. (PhD, Rutgers 1980; assoc. prof. emeritus; Rutgers, Newark) Puerto Rican social/cultural/women, Latin America and Caribbean

Wou, Odoric Y. K. (PhD, Columbia 1970; prof. emeritus; Rutgers, Newark) East Asia, modern China; wou@andromeda.rutgers.edu

Saginaw Valley State University

Dept. of History, Brown Hall 328, University Center, MI 48710. 989.964.4000. Fax 989.790.7656. Email: jbaesler@svsu.edu. Website: http://www.svsu.edu/history/.

At Saginaw Valley, our students experience opportunities for research, internships, and a broad education in history. Our faculty are here to teach and mentor students to become all they can be.

Chair: John Baesler
Degrees Offered: BA
Academic Year System: Semester
Areas of Specialization: Civil War, African American, 20th-century US social, US foreign relations, modern Europe, world, Asia
Tuition (per academic year):
  In-State: $7505
  Out-of-State: $18100
Enrollment 2018-19:
  Undergraduate Majors: 90
Addresses:
  Admissions: http://svsu.edu/apply/undergraduate/
  Financial Aid: http://svsu.edu/financialaid/

Full-time Faculty

Ahn, Byungil (PhD, UCLA 2011; assoc. prof.) modern China, social; bahn@svsu.edu

Baesler, John (PhD, Indiana 2009; prof. and chair) US foreign relations, cultural, technology; jbaesler@svsu.edu

Gehrke, Jules Philip (PhD, Minnesota 2006; assoc. prof.) modern England, Europe; jgehrke@svsu.edu

Jarvis, Brad D. (PhD, Minnesota 2006; assoc. prof.) early America, Native American; bjarvis@svsu.edu

Jolly, Kenneth S. (PhD, Missouri, Columbia 2002; prof.) African American, modern US; kjolly@svsu.edu

Mathur, Nameeta (PhD, West Virginia 2001; prof.) east-central Europe and Russia, postwar Europe, South Asia; nmathur@svsu.edu

Stinson, Jennifer K. (PhD, Indiana 2010; assoc. prof.) 19th-century Midwest, race; jstinson@svsu.edu

Teed, Melissa Ladd (PhD, Connecticut 1999; prof.) US women, 19th-century social, education; mteed@svsu.edu

Teed, Paul E. (PhD, Connecticut 1994; prof.) antebellum reform, Civil War, religion; pteed@svsu.edu

Saint Anselm College

Dept. of History, Campus Box 1629, 100 St. Anselm Dr., Manchester, NH 03102-1310. 603.641.7048. Email: hdubrull@anselm.edu; bsalerno@anselm.edu. Website: https://www.anselm.edu/academics/departments/history-department.

Through active research and engaged teaching and conversation, the History Department helps students develop a literate, insightful understanding of human experience. We invite students who share our commitment to historical study to join in that exhilarating, demanding, and rewarding project.

Chair: Hugh Dubrulle
Degrees Offered: BA
Academic Year System: Semester
Areas of Specialization: US, gender, medieval/early modern/modern Europe, Russia, Latin America, Asia and Africa
Tuition (per academic year): $40500
Enrollment 2018-19:
  Undergraduate Majors: 84
  Degrees in History: 24 BA
  Students in Undergraduate Courses: 839
  Students in Undergraduate Intro Courses: 557
  Online-Only Courses: 1%
Addresses:
  Admissions: https://www.anselm.edu/admission-aid
  Financial Aid: http://www.anselm.edu/financialaid

Full-time Faculty

Dubrulle, Hugh F. (PhD, California, Santa Barbara 1999; prof. and chair) modern Britain, modern Europe; hdubrull@anselm.edu

Hardin, Sarah F. (PhD, Wisconsin-Madison 2012; asst. prof.) Africa, West Africa, environment; shardin@anselm.edu

Masur, Matthew (PhD, Ohio State 2004; prof.) US, US diplomatic, Asia; mmasur@anselm.edu

Moore, Andrew S. (PhD, Florida 2000; prof.) 20th-century US, American religion, race and civil rights; amoore@anselm.edu

Pajakowski, Philip E. (PhD, Indiana 1989; prof.) Habsburg Empire, eastern Europe, modern Germany; ppajakow@anselm.edu

Perrone, Sean T. (PhD, Wisconsin, Madison 1997; prof.) early modern Europe, Spain, Atlantic world; sperrone@anselm.edu

Salerno, Beth A. (PhD, Minnesota 2000; prof.) women, antebellum America, antislavery; bsalerno@anselm.edu

Shannon, Silvia C. (PhD, Boston Univ. 1988; assoc. prof.) medieval, Renaissance and Reformation, early modern France; sshannon@anselm.edu

St. Bonaventure University

Dept. of History, 3261 W. State Rd., Saint Bonaventure, NY 14778. 716.375.2123. Fax 716.375.2005. Email: ppayne@sbu.edu. Website: https://www.sbu.edu/academics/history.

At St. Bonaventure University, history students explore the world with highly qualified professors. Our students get the best of both worlds, professors who are dedicated teachers and accomplished researchers.

Chair: Phillip G. Payne
Degrees Offered: BA
Academic Year System: Semester
Areas of Specialization: US, Europe, China, world
Tuition (per academic year): $28727
Enrollment 2018-19:
  Undergraduate Majors: 52
  Degrees in History: 22 BA
Addresses:
  Admissions and Financial Aid: http://www.sbu.edu/admission-aid

Full-time Faculty

Dalton, Chris (ABD, Arizona; lect.) China, Asia; cdalton@sbu.edu
Henning, Lori (PhD, Texas A&M 2015; asst. prof.) Europe, military, America
Payne, Phillip Gene (PhD, Ohio State 1994; prof. and chair) US, public; ppayne@sbu.edu
Pitt, Steven (PhD, Pittsburgh 2015; lect.) early America, maritime, Atlantic world; spitt@sbu.edu

Retired/Emeritus Faculty

Horowitz, Joel (PhD, California, Berkeley 1979; prof. emeritus) Latin America; jhorowit@sbu.edu
Robbins, Karen E. (PhD, Columbia 1994; prof. emeritus) US, revolutionary era, women; krobbins@sbu.edu
Schaeper, Thomas J. (PhD, Ohio State 1977; prof. emeritus) early modern Europe, France, Britain; tschaepe@sbu.edu

St. Cloud State University

Dept. of History, Stewart Hall 283, 720 Fourth Ave. S., Saint Cloud, MN 56301-4498. 320.308.3165. Fax 320.308.1516. Email: history@stcloudstate.edu. Website: https://www.stcloudstate.edu/history/.

As a History student, you will gain strong critical thinking skills allowing you to strategically solve a problem and form a solid argument. The History Department aims to offset parochialism and ethnocentrism by offering courses dealing with as many as possible of the world's civilization, nations, and peoples.

Chair: Robert W. Galler Jr.
Director of Graduate Studies: Maureen M. O'Brien
Degrees Offered: BA,BS,MA,MS
Academic Year System: Semester
Areas of Specialization: ancient/medieval/modern Europe, US, Latin America, public
Undergraduate Tuition (per academic year):
  In-State: $8656
  Out-of-State: $16948
Graduate Tuition (per academic year):
  In-State: $8570
  Out-of-State: $12444

Enrollment 2018-19:
  Undergraduate Majors: 48
  New Graduate Students: 5
  Full-time Graduate Students: 5
  Part-time Graduate Students: 10
  Degrees in History: 10 BA, 2 MA, 1 MS
Undergraduate Addresses:
  Admissions: http://www.stcloudstate.edu/scsu4u/
  Financial Aid: http://www.stcloudstate.edu/financialaid/
Graduate Addresses:
  Admissions: http://www.stcloudstate.edu/gradadmissions/
  Financial Aid: http://www.stcloudstate.edu/gradadmissions/financing-your-education/

Full-time Faculty

Eden, Jason E. (PhD, Minnesota 2006; prof.) race in America, Atlantic world; jeeden@stcloudstate.edu
Galler, Robert W., Jr. (PhD, Western Michigan 2000; prof. and chair) US, Native American, race in America, history education; rwgaller@stcloudstate.edu
Harvey, John Layton (PhD, Penn State 2003; assoc. prof.) 20th-century central and western Europe; jlharvey@stcloudstate.edu
Jaede, Mark G. (PhD, SUNY, Buffalo 2002; asst. prof.) US, Latin America, race; mgjaede@stcloudstate.edu
Kim, Marie Seong-Hak (PhD, Minnesota 1991; JD, Minnesota 1994; prof.) early modern France, Renaissance and Reformation, legal; mskim@stcloudstate.edu
Mullins, Jeffrey A. (PhD, Johns Hopkins 1997; prof.) American cultural and intellectual, American race; jamullins@stcloudstate.edu
O'Brien, Maureen M. (PhD, Western Michigan 2006; prof. and dir., grad. studies) medieval, monasticism, Jewish/Christian/Muslim relations; mmobrien@stcloudstate.edu

Retired/Emeritus Faculty

Glade, Mary E. (PhD, Colorado, Boulder 1996; asst. prof. emeritus) US social, US women, Civil War and Reconstruction; beglade@stcloudstate.edu
Hofsommer, Don L. (PhD, Oklahoma State 1973; prof. emeritus) public, Minnesota, transportation
Nayenga, Peter F. (PhD, Michigan 1976; prof. emeritus) Africa
Ness, John P. (PhD, Minnesota 1998; retired asst. prof.) Asia, world
Wingerd, Mary C. (PhD, Duke 1998; prof. emeritus) 20th-century US, public

St. John Fisher College

Dept. of History, 3690 East Ave., Rochester, NY 14618. 585.385.8244. Email: cvacca@sjfc.edu. Website: https://www.sjfc.edu/major-minors/history/.

Studying history at Fisher involves examining the issues, ideas, people, and events that gave rise to the world's major civilizations. It provides an understanding of the present by imposing order on the chaos of the past.

Chair: Carolyn Vacca
Degrees Offered: BA
Academic Year System: Semester
Areas of Specialization: 19th- and 20th-century US, modern Europe, military and strategic, public
Tuition (per academic year): $34340
Enrollment 2018-19:
  Undergraduate Majors: 67
  Degrees in History: 16 BA

Addresses:

Admissions: http://www.sjfc.edu/admissions/

Financial Aid: http://www.sjfc.edu/campus-services/
financial-aid/

Full-time Faculty

Dotolo, Frederick Henry, III (PhD, SUNY, Buffalo 2001; assoc. prof.)
Italy, diplomatic, modern Europe; fdotolo@sjfc.edu

Fouraker, Lawrence (PhD, California, Berkeley 1994; assoc. prof.)
Japan, Asia; lfouraker@sjfc.edu

Griffin, Oliver (PhD, Harvard 1998; asst. prof.) 19th- and 20th-
century Europe, modern Germany; ogriffin@sjfc.edu

Vacca, Carolyn Summers (PhD, Rochester 1998; assoc. prof. and
chair) 19th- and 20th-century America, social, women; cvacca@
sjfc.edu

Valone, Stephen J. (PhD, Rochester 1989; prof.) 19th- and 20th-
century America, US diplomatic, US political; svalone@sjfc.edu

Nondepartmental Historians

Bain, Donald E., Jr. (PhD, SUNY, Buffalo 1974; prof. and Coll. pres.)
20th-century America, US national security; dbain@sjfc.edu

Part-time Faculty

Macgregor, David (PhD, Rochester 1990; adj. asst. prof.) naval,
modern Britain; dmacgregor@sjfc.edu

Saint John's University

*Dept. of History, 8000 Utopia Pkwy., Jamaica, NY 11439.
718.990.6229. Fax 718.990.2644. Email: rustomjn@stjohns.edu.
Website: https://www.stjohns.edu/academics/schools-and-
colleges/st-johns-college-liberal-arts-and-sciences/*

*Our faculty are dedicated researchers and teachers committed
to student learning. They are recognized experts in a wide
range of fields, including US, African, African American, East
Asian, European, Latin American, Middle Eastern, and South
Asian history. Internship and service learning opportunities are
available for history majors and minors.*

Chair: Nerina Rustomji
Director of Graduate Studies: Timothy Milford
Degrees Offered: BA,BA/MA,MA,PhD
Academic Year System: Semester
Areas of Specialization: world, Americas, East Asia/Middle East/
South Asia/Africa/Europe, public, social/cultural/gender
Undergraduate Tuition (per academic year): $40680
Graduate Tuition (per academic year): $29520
Enrollment 2018-19:

Undergraduate Majors: 89

New Graduate Students: 17

Full-time Graduate Students: 25

Part-time Graduate Students: 23

Degrees in History: 17 BA, 10 MA, 1 PhD

Undergraduate Addresses:

Admissions: https://www.stjohns.edu/admission-aid/apply-st-
johns-university

Financial Aid: https://www.stjohns.edu/admission-aid/tuition-
and-financial-aid/undergraduate-aid

Graduate Addresses:

Admissions: https://www.stjohns.edu/admission-aid/graduate-
admission

Financial Aid: https://www.stjohns.edu/admission-aid/
graduate-admission/graduate-assistantships-and-fellowships

Full-time Faculty

Augustine, Dolores L. (PhD, Free, Berlin 1991; prof.) modern
Germany; augustid@stjohns.edu

Bongiorno, Joseph (PhD, Connecticut 1990; assoc. prof.) Italy,
diplomatic, America; bongiorj@stjohns.edu

Borrero, Mauricio (PhD, Indiana 1992; assoc. prof.) Russia;
borrerom@stjohns.edu

Cooper, Tracey-Anne (PhD, Boston Coll. 2005; assoc. prof.) world,
medieval; coopert@stjohns.edu

Hussain, Shahla (PhD, Tufts 2014; asst. prof.) South Asia; hussains@
stjohns.edu

Milford, Timothy A. (PhD, Harvard 1999; assoc. prof. and dir., grad.
studies) colonial America; milfordt@stjohns.edu

Miller, Ian Matthew (PhD, Harvard 2015; asst. prof.) environmental,
China; milleri1@stjohns.edu

Misevich, Philip (PhD, Emory 2009; asst. prof.) Atlantic world,
Africa, comparative slavery; misevicp@stjohns.edu

Pak, Susie J. (PhD, Cornell 2004; assoc. prof.) 20th-century US,
ethnic, gender; paks1@stjohns.edu

Quintana, Alejandro (PhD, Grad. Center, CUNY 2007; asst. prof.)
world, Latin America; quintana@stjohns.edu

Rao, John (PhD, Oxford 1977; assoc. prof.) Europe; raoj@stjohns.
edu

Rustomji, Nerina (PhD, Columbia 2003; assoc. prof. and chair)
Middle East, Islamic world; rustomjn@stjohns.edu

Schmidt Horning, Susan (PhD, Case Western Reserve 2002; assoc.
prof.) technology, 20th-century US, world; schmidts@stjohns.
edu

Szylvian, Kristin M. (PhD, Carnegie Mellon 1988; assoc. prof.;
Library & Information Science) public; szylviak@stjohns.edu

Tuchscherer, Konrad T., Jr. (PhD, London 1996; assoc. prof.) Africa;
tuchschk@stjohns.edu

Vapnek, Lara (PhD, Columbia 2000; assoc. prof.) 19th-century US,
labor, gender; vapnekl@stjohns.edu

Vause, Erika (PhD, Chicago 2012; asst. prof.) France, legal,
capitalism; vausee@stjohns.edu

Recently Awarded PhDs

Capani, Jennifer Brigette "An 'Alter Kampfer' at the Forefront of
the Holocaust: Otto Ohlendorf between Careerism and Nazi
Fundamentalism"

Saint Joseph's University

*Dept. of History, 5600 City Ave., Philadelphia, PA 19131-
1395. 610.660.1740. Fax 610.660.1918. Email: history@
sju.edu. Website: https://www.sju.edu/majors-programs/
undergraduate/majors/history-major.*

*Saint Joseph's history program encourages students to become
discerning researchers, critical thinkers, clear writers and
historically aware global citizens.*

Chair: James H. Carter
Degrees Offered: BA
Academic Year System: Semester
Areas of Specialization: medieval to modern Europe, US
political/social/cultural, Latin America, East and South Asia,
Russia and Africa
Tuition (per academic year): $44974
Enrollment 2018-19:

Undergraduate Majors: 49

Degrees in History: 17 BA

Addresses:
Admissions: http://www.sju.edu/information/apply-undergraduate-admission
Financial Aid: http://www.sju.edu/information/financial-aid

Full-time Faculty

Abbas, Amber Heather (PhD, Texas, Austin 2012; assoc. prof.) South Asia; aabbas@sju.edu

Carter, James H. (PhD, Yale 1998; prof. and chair) East Asia; jcarter@sju.edu

Chakars, Melissa (PhD, Indiana 2008; assoc. prof.) Russia, Eurasia; mchakars@sju.edu

Close, Christopher W. (PhD, Pennsylvania 2006; assoc. prof.) early modern Europe; cclose@sju.edu

Hyson, Jeffrey N. (PhD, Cornell 1999; asst. prof.) American environmental, intellectual, cultural; jhyson@sju.edu

Lewin, Alison Williams (PhD, Cornell 1991; assoc. prof.) medieval, Renaissance, Reformation; lewin@sju.edu

Miller, Randall M. (PhD, Ohio State 1971; prof.) colonial and revolutionary America, Civil War and Reconstruction, slavery; miller@sju.edu

Sibley, Katherine A. S. (PhD, California, Santa Barbara 1991; prof.) American diplomatic, 20th-century America; sibley@sju.edu

Warren, Richard A. (PhD, Chicago 1994; prof.) Latin America, Mexico; warren@sju.edu

Yates, Brian J. (PhD, Illinois, Urbana-Champaign 2009; assoc. prof.) Africa; byates@sju.edu

Part-time Faculty

Arnau, Ariel (PhD, Graduate Center, CUNY 2018; lect.) US, Latin America

Gallagher, Patrick (PhD, SUNY, Albany 2016; lect.) US, Europe

Hanson, Matthew M. (MA, Villanova 1975; lect.) US, Europe

Maher, Bernard (EdD, Widener 1999; lect.)

McInneshin, Michael T. (PhD, Minnesota 2008; lect.) Africa

Zeman, Theodore J. (PhD, Temple 2000; lect.) US, Europe

Retired/Emeritus Faculty

Keefe, Thomas M. (PhD, Loyola, Chicago 1966; assoc. prof. emeritus) France, Germany

Smith, Phillip T. (PhD, Columbia 1976; prof. emeritus) Britain, British Empire; psmith@sju.edu

St. Lawrence University

Dept. of History, 114 Piskor Hall, 23 Romoda Dr., Canton, NY 13617. 315.229.5222. Fax 315.229.5803. Email: jdegroat@stlawu.edu. Website: https://www.stlawu.edu/history.

The history department offers a wide range of courses in American, European, and non-Western history. The major or minor in history allows you to construct a program that is flexible enough to enable you to pursue your own interests and goals while at the same time developing an appreciation of the diversity of human culture.

Chair: Donna Alvah
Degrees Offered: BA
Academic Year System: Semester
Areas of Specialization: US and Europe, Africa, Asia, Latin America and Caribbean, Middle East
Tuition (per academic year): $52610
Enrollment 2018-19:
Undergraduate Majors: 64
Degrees in History: 27 BA

Addresses:
Admissions: http://www.stlawu.edu/admissions
Financial Aid: http://www.stlawu.edu/financialaid

Full-time Faculty

Alvah, Donna (PhD, California, Davis 2000; assoc. prof. and chair) 20th-century US; dalvah@stlawu.edu

Carotenuto, Matthew P. (PhD, Indiana 2006; assoc. prof.) Africa; mcarotenuto@stlawu.edu

Csete, Anne A. (PhD, SUNY, Buffalo 1995; assoc. prof.) East Asia, China, women; acsete@stlawu.edu

DeGroat, Judith A. (PhD, Rochester 1991; assoc. prof.) European social and cultural, European women's labor; jdegroat@stlawu.edu

Eissenstat, Howard L. (PhD, UCLA 2007; assoc. prof.) Middle East; heissenstat@stlawu.edu

Gabriel, Elun T. (PhD, California, Davis 2003; assoc. prof.) modern Europe, German political culture, genocide; egabriel@stlawu.edu

Jennings, Evelyn Powell (PhD, Rochester 2001; prof.) Latin America and Caribbean; ejennings@stlawu.edu

Regosin, Elizabeth (PhD, California, Irvine 1995; prof.) US, African American; eregosin@stlawu.edu

Schrems, Melissane Parm (PhD, Boston Univ. 2003; assoc. prof.) colonial America, Native American; mschrems@stlawu.edu

Smith, Mary Jane (PhD, Louisiana State 2002; assoc. prof.) southern US race and gender relations; msm1@stlawu.edu

Retired/Emeritus Faculty

Hunt, William A., Jr. (PhD, Harvard 1974; prof. emeritus) Western civilization, Britain to 1688, Renaissance Europe; whunt@stlawu.edu

Lloyd, David T. (PhD, UCLA 1978; assoc. prof. emeritus) Africa, sub-Sahara, economic; dlloyd@stlawu.edu

Visiting Faculty

Feinstein, Tamara D. N. (PhD, Wisconsin, Madison 2013; vis. asst. prof.; Caribbean & Latin American Studies) Latin America in Cold War, political violence, Peru; tfeinstein@stlawu.edu

Saint Louis University

Dept. of History, Adjoran Hall, 3800 Lindell Blvd., Saint Louis, MO 63108-3414. 314.977.2910. Fax 314.977.1603. Email: history@slu.edu. Website: https://www.slu.edu/arts-and-sciences/history/.

The Department of History has been providing a solid foundation of historical understanding to the undergraduate students of Saint Louis University for more than a century and a half.

Chair: Thomas Finan
Director of Graduate Studies: Jennifer Popiel
Director of Undergraduate Studies: Torrie Hester
Degrees Offered: BA,MA,PhD
Academic Year System: Semester
Areas of Specialization: medieval Europe, early modern Europe, modern Europe, US, world
Undergraduate Tuition (per academic year): $40100
Graduate Tuition (per academic year): $19350
Enrollment 2018-19:
Undergraduate Majors: 60
New Graduate Students: 7
Full-time Graduate Students: 45
Part-time Graduate Students: 5

Degrees in History: 17 BA, 1 MA, 3 PhD
Online-Only Courses: 5%

Undergraduate Addresses:
Admissions: http://www.slu.edu/admission/freshman/
Financial Aid: http://www.slu.edu/financial-aid

Graduate Addresses:
Admissions: http://www.slu.edu/admission/graduate
Financial Aid: http://www.slu.edu/financial-aid

Full-time Faculty

Boin, Douglas (PhD, Texas, Austin 2009; assoc. prof.) Greek and Roman history and epigraphy, religions of Roman world, late antiquity; boindr@slu.edu

Burke, Flannery (PhD, Wisconsin-Madison 2002; assoc. prof.) American West; fburke@slu.edu

Finan, Thomas J. (PhD, Catholic 2001; assoc. prof. and chair) medieval Europe, Ireland; finantj@slu.edu

Gavitt, Philip R. (PhD, Michigan 1988; prof.) early modern Europe; gavitt@slu.edu

Gilbert, Claire (PhD, UCLA 2014; asst. prof.) early modern Europe; gilbertcm@slu.edu

Glover, Lorri M. (PhD, Kentucky 1996; prof.) early America, social; lglover1@slu.edu

Hester, Torrie R. (PhD, Oregon 2008; asst. prof. and dir., undergrad. studies) American deportation policy, Gilded Age Americ thester4@slu.edu

Madden, Thomas F. (PhD, Illinois, Urbana-Champaign 1993; prof.) medieval Europe; maddentf@slu.edu

Marsili, Filippo (PhD, California, Berkeley 2011; asst. prof.) early imperial China; fmarsil1@slu.edu

Millett, Nathaniel C. (PhD, Cambridge 2002; assoc. prof.) Latin America, borderlands; nmillet1@slu.edu

Montcher, Fabien (PhD, Complutense, Madrid 2013; asst. prof.) early modern Europe, Atlantic world, intellectual

Ndege, George G. (PhD, West Virginia 1996; assoc. prof.) Africa, European colonialism; ndegego@slu.edu

Parker, Charles H., Jr. (PhD, Minnesota 1993; prof.) early modern Europe; parkerch@slu.edu

Popiel, Jennifer J. (PhD, Pennsylvania 2000; assoc. prof. and dir., grad. studies) modern France, women; popiel@slu.edu

Rozbicki, Michal (PhD, Warsaw 1984; prof.) colonial America, cultural; rozbicmj@slu.edu

Ruff, Mark Edward (PhD, Brown 1999; assoc. prof.) modern Germany; ruff@slu.edu

Schlafly, Daniel L., Jr. (PhD, Columbia 1972; prof.) Russia, modern Europe; daniel@slu.edu

Schoenig, Steven A. (PhD, Columbia 2009; assoc. prof.) medieval Europe; sschoeni@slu.edu

Siddali, Silvana R. (PhD, Harvard 1999; assoc. prof.) US Civil War era; siddalis@slu.edu

Smith, Damian J. (PhD, Birmingham 1997; prof.) medieval Europe; dsmith69@slu.edu

Treadgold, Warren T. (PhD, Harvard 1977; prof.) Byzantine Empire, Rome; treadgw@slu.edu

Joint/Cross Appointments

Thompson, Katrina Dyonne (PhD, SUNY, Stony Brook 2007; assoc. prof.; African American Studies) African American; kthomp35@slu.edu

Retired/Emeritus Faculty

Hitchcock, James F. (PhD, Princeton 1965; prof. emeritus) Reformation, religious, social and intellectual; hitchcpj@slu.edu

Kolmer, Elizabeth, ASC (PhD, St. Louis 1965; prof. emeritus) 19th-century US social; kolmere@slu.edu

Perry, Lewis C. (PhD, Cornell 1967; prof. emeritus) antebellum US, US Civil War, cultural and intellectual; perryl@slu.edu

Ruddy, T. Michael (PhD, Kent State 1973; prof. emeritus) America, US diplomatic; ruddytm@slu.edu

Sanchez, Jose M. (PhD, New Mexico 1961; prof. emeritus) recent Europe, Spain; sanchejm@slu.edu

Recently Awarded PhDs

Allington, Richard "Prayer Warriors: Crusading Piety in Rome and the Papal States, 1187-1240"

Holt, Edward "Liturgy, Ritual, and Kingship in the age of Fernando III of Castile-León (r. 1217-1252)"

Koopman, Nicole "'My Eyes Are Ever towards the Lord': The Career of Innocent V, Dominican Scholar and Pope"

Parker, Matthew E. "Accounting for the Collapse of Pisan Maritime Power amid Economic Boom in the 13th Century"

Webb, Daniel "Henry VI, Empire, and Crusade"

Western, Joseph "At the Edge of Empires: Competition and Coexistence in the Church in Byzantine Southern Italy, 868-1071"

Winston, Bryan "Mexican Corridors: Migration and Community Formation in the Central United States, 1900-50"

Saint Mary's College of California

Dept. of History, 1928 St. Mary's Rd., Moraga, CA 94556. 925.631.6279. Fax 925.631.8565. Email: ees4@stmarys-ca.edu. Website: https://www.stmarys-ca.edu/history.

Our department prepares students to engage the issues of their time by offering a program of study that emphasizes global perspectives, American diversity, gender in history, environmental history, and the challenging question of what is the common good and can it be achieved.

Chair: E. Elena Songster
Degrees Offered: BA
Academic Year System: 4-1-4
Areas of Specialization: Europe, US, Latin America, China, world
Tuition (per academic year): $50000
Enrollment 2018-19:
Undergraduate Majors: 32
Degrees in History: 12 BA
Addresses:
Admissions: http://www.stmarys-ca.edu/admissions-aid
Financial Aid: http://www.stmarys-ca.edu/admissions-aid/financial-aid

Full-time Faculty

Guarneri, Carl J. (PhD, Johns Hopkins 1979; prof.) US social and intellectual 1830-1930, comparative, American Civil War; cguarner@stmarys-ca.edu

Hilken, Charles A. (PhD, Toronto 1994; prof.) medieval and Renaissance Europe; chilken@stmarys-ca.edu

Lemke-Santangelo, Gretchen J. (PhD, Duke 1993; prof.) modern US, California women, African American; glemke@stmarys-ca.edu

Santiago, Myrna I. (PhD, California, Berkeley 1997; prof.) Latin America, environmental, labor; msantiag@stmarys-ca.edu

Soine, Aeleah H. (PhD, Minnesota 2009; assoc. prof.) modern Europe, gender, comparative; ahs3@stmarys-ca.edu

Songster, E. Elena (PhD, California, San Diego 2004; assoc. prof. and chair) modern China, environmental, Asia; ees4@stmarys-ca.edu

Part-time Faculty

Flemer, Paul A. (PhD, California, Berkeley 1989; adj. lect.) medieval and early modern Europe; pflemer@stmarys-ca.edu

Retired/Emeritus Faculty

Isetti, Ronald (PhD, California, Berkeley 1971; prof. emeritus) US, Asia, world

Roper, Katherine S. (PhD, Stanford 1968; prof. emeritus) modern Europe, early modern Europe, Germany; kroper@stmarys-ca.edu

Saint Mary's College of Maryland

Dept. of History, 18952 E. Fisher Rd., Saint Marys City, MD 20686-3001. 240.895.4392. Fax 240.895.4450. Email: cdmusgrove@smcm.edu. Website: http://www.smcm.edu/history/.

The St. Mary's History Department exposes students to the richness of the diversity in the history of the human experience throughout the world. In the course of their studies, students will develop a deeper understanding of themselves, their culture, and humanity in general.

Chair: Charles D. Musgrove
Degrees Offered: BA
Academic Year System: Semester
Areas of Specialization: US and Latin America, ancient Greece and Rome, Europe and Russia, China and Japan, Africa
Tuition (per academic year):
   In-State: $13895
   Out-of-State: $28745
Enrollment 2018-19:
   Undergraduate Majors: 90
   Degrees in History: 20 BA
Addresses:
   Admissions: http://www.smcm.edu/admissions/
   Financial Aid: http://www.smcm.edu/financialaid/

Full-time Faculty

Adams, Christine M. (PhD, Johns Hopkins 1993; prof.) modern Europe, France, family; cmadams@smcm.edu

Brodsky, Adriana Mariel (PhD, Duke 2004; prof.) Latin America, immigration; ambrodsky@smcm.edu

Dennie, Garrey M (PhD, Johns Hopkins 1996; assoc. prof.) Africa, Caribbean; gmdennie@smcm.edu

Eden, Jeffrey (PhD, Harvard 2016; asst. prof.) Russia, Central Asia; jeeden@smcm.edu

Holden, Charles J. (PhD, Penn State 1997; prof.) post-Civil War US, American thought; cjholden@smcm.edu

Malena, Sarah L. (PhD, California, San Diego 2015; asst. prof.) ancient

Musgrove, Charles D. (PhD, California, San Diego 2002; prof. and chair) China; cdmusgrove@smcm.edu

Retired/Emeritus Faculty

Hall, Linda Jones (PhD, Ohio State 1996; prof. emeritus) ancient; ljhall@smcm.edu

Hirschfield, John M. (PhD, Chicago 1957; prof. emeritus)

Savage, Gail L. (PhD, Texas, Austin 1977; prof. emeritus) modern Britain; glsavage@smcm.edu

Stevens, L. Tomlin (PhD, Ohio State 1969; prof. emeritus) colonial America, 18th- and 19th-century America; ltstevens@smcm.edu

Winnik, Herbert C. (PhD, Wisconsin, Madison 1968; prof. emeritus) hcwinnik@smcm.edu

St. Michael's College

Dept. of History, One Winooski Park, Box L, Colchester, VT 05439. 802.654.2621. Fax 802.654.2679. Email: jpurcell@smcvt.edu. Website: https://www.smcvt.edu/Academics/Majors-Minors-and-Curriculum/History.aspx.

At Saint Michael's College, students work with professional historians to bring the past to life. There is a diverse array of courses offered that focus on a variety of time periods (ancient, medieval, early modern, modern) and geographical regions (United States, Europe, Latin America, and East Asia).

Chair: Jennifer Purcell
Degrees Offered: BA
Academic Year System: Semester
Areas of Specialization: East Asia, Europe, Latin America, US
Tuition (per academic year): $43315
Enrollment 2018-19:
   Undergraduate Majors: 65
   Degrees in History: 25 BA
Addresses:
   Admissions: http://www.smcvt.edu/Admissions.aspx
   Financial Aid: http://www.smcvt.edu/Admissions/Financial-Aid-and-Tuition.aspx

Full-time Faculty

Dameron, George W. (PhD, Harvard 1983; prof.) medieval, economic/social/cultural, Italy; gdameron@smcvt.edu

Dungy, Kathryn (PhD, Duke 2000; assoc. prof.) Latin America, Caribbean, American South and slavery; kdungy@smcvt.edu

He, Rowena Xiaoqing (PhD, Toronto 2008; asst. prof.) modern China, politics, human rights; rhe@smcvt.edu

Ouellette, Susan (PhD, Massachusetts Amherst 1996; prof.) early America, women and gender, Native America; souellette@smcvt.edu

Purcell, Jennifer J. (DPhil, Sussex, UK 2008; assoc. prof. and chair) Great Britain, gender and war, gender and popular culture; jpurcell@smcvt.edu

Retired/Emeritus Faculty

Andersen, Thomas B. (PhD, Fordham 1973; assoc. prof. emeritus) medieval Europe, religious and cultural

Nicosia, Francis R. (PhD, McGill 1977; prof. emeritus) modern Europe, Germany, Holocaust

Slaybaugh, Douglas (PhD, Cornell 1981; prof. emeritus) 20th-century America, politics, social work; dslaybaugh@smcvt.edu

Wang, Ke-wen (PhD, Stanford 1985; prof. emeritus) China, Japan; kwang@smcvt.edu

Visiting Faculty

Saba, Roberto N. P. F. (PhD, Pennsylvania 2017; Henry G. Fairbanks Vis. Humanities Scholar-in-Residence) 19th- and 20th-century America, US foreign relations, transnational, imperialism, immigration, slavery and emancipation; rsaba@smcvt.edu

St. Norbert College

Dept. of History, 100 Grant St., DePere, WI 54115-2099. 920.403.3119. Fax 920.403.4086. Email: robert.kramer@snc.edu. Website: https://www.snc.edu/history/.

As a historian, you'll learn the lessons of history: to compare and contrast differing economies, societies, political systems and cultures; to identify the origins of change in the past and present; and to understand the continuities in history.

Chair: Robert Kramer
Degrees Offered: BA
Academic Year System: Semester
Areas of Specialization: US, Europe, Latin America, Africa, Middle East and East Asia
Tuition (per academic year): $33622
Enrollment 2018-19:
  Undergraduate Majors: 25
  Degrees in History: 9 BA
Addresses:
  Admissions: http://www.snc.edu/admission/
  Financial Aid: http://www.snc.edu/financialaid/

Full-time Faculty

Kramer, Robert S. (PhD, Northwestern 1991; prof. and chair) Islamic, Middle East; robert.kramer@snc.edu

Larson, Carolyne Ryan (PhD, Wisconsin-Madison 2011; asst. prof.) Latin America, culture/race/identity/indigenous peoples, public history and anthropology; carrie.larson@snc.edu

Lovano, Michael (PhD, UCLA 1996; asst. prof.) Europe, ancient Greece and Rome, medieval and Byzantine; michael.lovano@snc.edu

Patterson, Wayne K. (PhD, Pennsylvania 1977; prof.) modern East Asia, Asian-American relations, modern Korea; wayne.patterson@snc.edu

Tashjian, Victoria B. (PhD, Northwestern 1995; prof.) Africa, social and economic, women; victoria.tashjian@snc.edu

Trollinger, Abigail P. (PhD, Northwestern 2014; asst. prof.) US, immigration and ethnicity, poverty and welfare; abigail.trollinger@snc.edu

St. Olaf College

Dept. of History, 1520 St. Olaf Ave., Northfield, MN 55057-1098. 507.786.3167. Email: hahn@stolaf.edu. Website: https://wp.stolaf.edu/history/.

History at St. Olaf is a progressively sophisticated learning experience, where students gain the skills and expertise necessary to conduct their own research and produce original works of history.

Chair: Steve C. Hahn
Degrees Offered: BA
Academic Year System: Semester
Areas of Specialization: US, Africa, Europe, East Asia, Latin America
Tuition (per academic year): $49710
Enrollment 2018-19:
  Undergraduate Majors: 83
  Degrees in History: 18 BA
Addresses:
  Admissions: https://wp.stolaf.edu/admissions/
  Financial Aid: https://wp.stolaf.edu/financialaid/

Full-time Faculty

DeLaney, Jeane (PhD, Stanford 1989; assoc. prof.) Latin America, Argentina and Brazil, Cuba; delaney@stolaf.edu

Entenmann, Robert E. (PhD, Harvard 1982; prof.) China and Japan, Asian studies; entenman@stolaf.edu

Fitzgerald, Michael W. (PhD, UCLA 1986; prof.) African American, Civil War and Reconstruction, US South; fitz@stolaf.edu

Fure-Slocum, Eric J. (PhD, Iowa 2001; assoc. prof.) 20th-century US, US social/labor/urban, political; furesloc@stolaf.edu

Hahn, Steven C. (PhD, Emory 2000; prof. and chair) colonial and Native American, US South; hahn@stolaf.edu

Howe, Timothy R. (PhD, Penn State 2000; prof.) ancient Mediterranean, archaeology; howe@stolaf.edu

Iddrisu, Abdulai (PhD, Illinois, Urbana-Champaign 2009; assoc. prof.) Africa, Islam; iddrisu@stolaf.edu

Kutulas, Judy A. (PhD, UCLA 1986; prof.) 20th-century US, women, cultural; kutulas@stolaf.edu

Kuxhausen, Anna K. (PhD, Michigan 2006; assoc. prof.) Russia, modern Europe; kux@stolaf.edu

Peters, Dolores A. (PhD, Minnesota 1991; assoc. prof.) modern Europe, modern France, medicine; petersdo@stolaf.edu

Part-time Faculty

Jessup, David (ABD, Washington; instr.) Scandinavian emigration/immigration, Swedish Protestantism, Alaska and circumpolar North; jessdave@uw.edu

Retired/Emeritus Faculty

Carrington, Laurel (PhD, Cornell 1986; prof. emeritus) medieval, early modern Europe, intellectual; carringt@stolaf.edu

De Krey, Gary S. (PhD, Princeton 1978; prof. emeritus) Britain, early modern Europe; dekrey@stolaf.edu

Lovoll, Odd S. (PhD, Minnesota 1973; prof. emeritus) American immigration, ethnic, Scandinavia; lovoll@stolaf.edu

Nichol, Todd W. (OPhD, Grad. Theological Union 1988; King Olav V Prof. emeritus) Scandinavian American, modern Scandinavia, church; nicholt@stolaf.edu

Nichols, Robert L. (PhD, Washington 1972; prof. emeritus) modern Europe, Russia, East Asia; nichols@stolaf.edu

Olson, Richard A. (PhD, Minnesota 1968; assoc. prof. emeritus) ancient; olsonri@stolaf.edu

Visiting Faculty

Elias, Christopher Michael (PhD, Brown 2017; vis. asst. prof.) modern US cultural and political, gender and sexuality; christophermelias@gmail.com

Mummey, Kevin Dean (PhD, Minnesota 2013; vis. asst. prof.) medieval Europe/Mediterranean/cities, women and gender in medieval and early modern worlds; mummey1@stolaf.edu

Saint Peter's University

Dept. of History, Hilsdorf Hall, Rm. 303, 51 Glenwood Ave., Jersey City, NJ 07306. 201.761.6170. Fax 201.761.6171. Email: dgerlach@saintpeters.edu. Website: https://www.saintpeters.edu/academics/undergraduate-programs/history/.

Consonant with the mission of Saint Peter's College the Department of History seeks to develop the whole person in preparation for a lifetime of learning, leadership and service in a diverse and global society. The study of history supports the mission of the College by preparing students to participate knowledgeably in this society by exposing them to the myriad and varying cultures of the human past. The methods, content and values of the discipline of history will foster in students a spirit of inquiry and the ability to think critically. An emphasis on clarity in oral and written communications will help prepare students for success in any future endeavors.

Chair: David Gerlach
Degrees Offered: BA
Academic Year System: Semester
Areas of Specialization: US, Europe, Africa, science
Tuition (per academic year): $36386
Enrollment 2018-19:
  Undergraduate Majors: 16
  Degrees in History: 4 BA
Addresses:
  Admissions: http://www.saintpeters.edu/admission/
  Financial Aid: http://www.saintpeters.edu/enrollment-services/

Full-time Faculty

Americo, Maria (PhD, NYU 2019; asst. prof.) science in antiquity, late antiquity, Mediterranean intellectual and cultural, Islam; mamerico@saintpeters.edu

DeGruccio, Michael E. (PhD, Notre Dame 2007; assoc. prof.) 19th-century US, antebellum and Civil War eras; mdegruccio@saintpeters.edu

Gerlach, David W. (PhD, Pittsburgh 2007; assoc. prof. and chair) modern central and eastern Europe, World War II, Holocaust; dgerlach@saintpeters.edu

Johnson, John W. Jr (PhD, Rutgers, Newark 2014; asst. prof.) American Civil War, African American, civil rights; jjohnson5@saintpeters.edu

Retired/Emeritus Faculty

Gillen, Jerome J. (Ph.D., Lehigh 1972; assoc. prof. emeritus) America, colonial America, 20th century; jgillen2@saintpeters.edu

Palmegiano, Eugenia M. (PhD, Rutgers 1966; prof. emerita) modern Britain and British Empire, European women, press; epalmegiano@saintpeters.edu

Rabin, Sheila J. (PhD, Grad. Center, CUNY 1987; prof. emerita) medieval and early modern Europe, science, Middle East and Islam; srabin@saintpeters.edu

College of St. Rose

Dept. of History and Political Science, 432 Western Ave., Albany, NY 12203-1419. 518.458.5326. Fax 518.454.2862. Email: williamb@strose.edu. Website: https://www.strose.edu/history-and-political-science/.

We are a diverse interdisciplinary department of engaged scholars and teachers who prepare students for rewarding careers and meaningful lives.

Chair: Bridgett Williams-Searle
Degrees Offered: BA
Academic Year System: Semester
Areas of Specialization: 19th- and 20th-century US, labor and reform movements, US foreign relations, Latin America, Europe
Tuition (per academic year): $29820
Enrollment 2018-19:
  Undergraduate Majors: 73
  Degrees in History: 30 BA
Addresses:
  Admissions: http://www.strose.edu/admissions
  Financial Aid: http://www.strose.edu/admissions/financialaid

Full-time Faculty

Abdul-Korah, Gariba B. (PhD, Minnesota 2004; asst. prof.) Africa, African diaspora; abdulkog@strose.edu

Clansy, Benjamin (PhD, Colorado, Boulder 1992; assoc. prof.) international relations, comparative politics, political philosophy; bclansy@mail.strose.edu

DePinto, Jenise R. (PhD, SUNY, Stony Brook 2005; assoc. prof.) Europe, Britain, comparative empire; depintoj@mail.strose.edu

Faussette, Risa (PhD, SUNY, Binghamton 2002; assoc. prof.) African American, Africa, US labor; faussetr@strose.edu

Kannenberg, Lisa A. (PhD, Rutgers 1999; assoc. prof.) 20th-century US, US labor, women; kannenbl@strose.edu

Ledford, Angela (PhD, South Carolina 2006; prof.) political theory, gender and sexuality, social movements; ledforda@mail.strose.edu

Mustapha, Marda (PhD, Northern Arizona 2006; asst. prof.) mustaphm@mail.strose.edu

Straus, Ryane McAuliffe (PhD, California, Irvine 2006; prof.) US politics, race and ethnicity; strausr@mail.strose.edu

Williams-Searle, Bridgett M. (PhD, Iowa 2005; assoc. prof. and chair) colonial and early national America, Native American, gender and race relations; williamb@mail.strose.edu

University of St. Thomas

Dept. of History, 2115 Summit Ave., Mail #JRC432, Saint Paul, MN 55105-1096. 651.962.5730. Fax 651.962.5741. Email: cacory@stthomas.edu; history@stthomas.edu. Website: https://www.stthomas.edu/history/.

We are scholar-educators who take seriously our responsibility to help our students acquire the critical thinking, communication, and problem-solving skills necessary for professional and personal success. We are also committed to advancing scholarship in our research areas and to mentoring students to become successful researchers in their own right.

Chair: Catherine Cory
Degrees Offered: BA
Academic Year System: Semester
Areas of Specialization: US and Latin America, western and eastern Europe, East Asia, Middle East, Atlantic world
Tuition (per academic year): $41792
Enrollment 2018-19:
  Undergraduate Majors: 75
  Degrees in History: 21 BA
  Students in Undergraduate Courses: 1610
  Students in Undergraduate Intro Courses: 1403
Addresses:
  Admissions and Financial Aid: http://www.stthomas.edu/admissions/undergraduate/

Adjunct Faculty

Ceric, Meliha (MA, Minnesota State 2004; instr.) America; mceric@stthomas.edu

Donahue, Kelly Lynn (PhD, Minnesota 2013; adj. asst. prof.) modern Europe, modern Britain and Ireland; dona9875@stthomas.edu

Forrester, Max (ABD, Washington, St. Louis; instr.) 19th-century America, American Southwest borderlands; mforrester@stthomas.edu

Harry, Elizabeth A. (PhD, Brandeis 1999; adj. asst. prof.) modern Russia and Germany, political and social; eaharry@stthomas.edu

Lummus, Wesley (ABD, Minnesota; adj. instr.) modern Middle East, Turkey; lumm2160@stthomas.edu

Osler, Anne (PhD, Wisconsin-Madison 1995; adj. asst. prof.) America; osle6883@stthomas.edu

Schrunk, Ivancica (PhD, Minnesota 1984; adj. asst. prof.) classical area studies, archaeology; idschrunk@stthomas.edu

Schultz, Jenna M. (PhD, Wisconsin-Madison 2015; adj. asst. prof.) early modern Britain, Anglo-Scottish relations, borderland and identity studies; schu2971@stthomas.edu

Full-time Faculty

Ahmadi, Shaherzad R. (PhD, Texas, Austin 2018; asst. prof.) modern Iran, Middle East; srahmadi@stthomas.edu

Cavert, William M. (PhD, Northwestern 2011; asst. prof.) early modern Britain, urban and environmental; william.cavert@stthomas.edu

Hausmann, Stephen R. (PhD, Temple 2019; asst. prof.) 20th-century US; srhausmann@stthomas.edu

Kim, Jaymin (PhD, Michigan 2018; asst. prof.) early modern China, Chinese borderlands; kim07259@stthomas.edu

Nagy, Zsolt (PhD, North Carolina, Chapel Hill 2012; assoc. prof.) modern Europe, cultural diplomacy and international relations, transnational studies; nagy4291@stthomas.edu

Williard, David Christopher (PhD, North Carolina, Chapel Hill 2012; assoc. prof.) US Civil War and Reconstruction, US military, African American; dwilliard@stthomas.edu

Zimmerman, Kari E. (PhD, Stanford 2010; assoc. prof.) Latin America, Atlantic world; zimm2550@stthomas.edu

Retired/Emeritus Faculty

Chrislock, C. Winston (PhD, Indiana 1971; prof. emeritus) eastern Europe, US foreign policy; cwchrislock@stthomas.edu

Delehanty, William (PhD, Minnesota 1975; assoc. prof. emeritus) medieval Europe; wmdelehanty@stthomas.edu

Fitzharris, Joseph (PhD, Wisconsin, Madison 1975; prof. emeritus) US, military; jcfitzharris@stthomas.edu

Klejment, Anne (PhD, SUNY, Binghamton 1981; prof. emeritus) US, Catholic, social; amklejment@stthomas.edu

Mega, Thomas B. (PhD, Minnesota 1985; asst. prof. emeritus) US, colonial and revolutionary America, constitutional; tbmega@stthomas.edu

Wright, Scott K. (PhD, Minnesota 1973; prof. emeritus) US, intellectual, Japan; skwright@stthomas.edu

Saint Xavier University

Dept. of History and Political Science, 3700 W. 103 St., Chicago, IL 60655. 773.298.3281. Fax 773.298.3314. Email: clark@sxu.edu. Website: https://www.sxu.edu/academics/colleges_schools/cas/dept/history-political-science/.

The History and Political Science Department supports the University mission of liberal arts education in providing scholarship, academic programs and extracurricular activities to help students better understand the diverse world in which they live, how that world developed and how to be effective and responsible citizens of that world. Courses are offered at the Chicago campus and online, providing a rigorous classroom experience. The Department encourages learning outside the classroom through field trips, simulations, foreign travel and internships to enhance experiential learning.

Chair: Matthew J. Costello
Degrees Offered: BA
Academic Year System: Semester
Areas of Specialization: US, Europe, Africa, women, world
Tuition (per academic year): $32800
Enrollment 2018-19:
  Undergraduate Majors: 21
  Degrees in History: 13 BA

Addresses:
  Admissions: http://www.sxu.edu/admissions/
  Financial Aid: http://www.sxu.edu/admissions/financial_aid/

Full-time Faculty

Alaimo, Kathleen (PhD, Wisconsin-Madison 1988; prof.) Europe, social, women; alaimo@sxu.edu

Costello, Matthew J. (PhD, North Carolina, Chapel Hill 1992; prof.) African politics, international relations, comparative politics; costello@sxu.edu

Fojtik, Christine (PhD, Wisconsin, Madison 2013; asst. prof.) modern Germany, Europe, digital; fojtik@sxu.edu

Kirstein, Peter N. (PhD, St. Louis 1973; prof.) modern US, US foreign relations, political ideologies; kirstein@sxu.edu

Lopez, Amanda M. (PhD, Arizona 2010; assoc. prof.) Latin America; alopez@sxu.edu

Taylor, Raymond (PhD, Illinois, Urbana-Champaign 1996; assoc. prof.) Africa and Middle East, world, environmental; taylor@sxu.edu

Salem State University

Dept. of History, 352 Lafayette St., Salem, MA 01970-5353. 978.542.6286. Fax 978.542.7215. Email: dseger@salemstate.edu. Website: https://www.salemstate.edu/academics/college-arts-and-sciences/history.

Salem, Massachusetts is home to the legacies of the China Trade and the 1692 Witch Trials, Nathaniel Hawthorne and Nathaniel Bowditch, spectacular historic buildings, amazing museums, and a university with a history department that is dedicated to teaching as well as utilizing this rich historical legacy.

Chair: Andrew T. Darien
Director of Graduate Studies: Bethany Jay
Degrees Offered: BA, MA, MAT, Cert. (public hist.)
Academic Year System: Semester
Areas of Specialization: world, public, early America, Europe, Asia and Middle East
Undergraduate Tuition (per academic year):
  In-State: $910
  Out-of-State: $7050
Graduate Tuition (per academic year):
  In-State: $2520
  Out-of-State: $4140
Enrollment 2018-19:
  Undergraduate Majors: 200
  New Graduate Students: 32
  Full-time Graduate Students: 9
  Part-time Graduate Students: 105
  Degrees in History: 58 BA, 34 MA
Undergraduate Addresses:
  Admissions: https://www.salemstate.edu/admissions-and-aid/welcome-undergraduate-admissions
  Financial Aid: https://www.salemstate.edu/finaid
Graduate Addresses:
  Admissions: https://www.salemstate.edu/graduate/admissions
  Financial Aid: https://www.salemstate.edu/finaid

Full-time Faculty

Austin, Brad E. (PhD, Ohio State 2001; prof.) modern US, sports, history education; baustin@salemstate.edu

Baker, Emerson W. (PhD, William and Mary 1986; prof.) museum studies, New England; ebaker@salemstate.edu

Chapman-Adisho, Annette R. (PhD, Illinois, Chicago 2006; prof.) modern Europe, French Revolution; achapmanadisho@salemstate.edu

Chomsky, Aviva (PhD, California, Berkeley 1990; prof.) Latin America; achomsky@salemstate.edu

Darien, Andrew T. (PhD, NYU 2000; prof. and chair) 20th-century US, oral, policing, veterans; adarien@salemstate.edu

Fischer, Gayle V. (PhD, Indiana 1995; prof.) gender and women, LGBTQ, 19th-century US; gfischer@salemstate.edu

Jay, Bethany W. (PhD, Boston Coll. 2009; assoc. prof. and dir., grad. studies) America, world; bjay@salemstate.edu

Jensen, Erik S. (PhD, Columbia 2008; assoc. prof.) ancient Greece and Rome; ejensen@salemstate.edu

Kyrou, Alexandros K. (PhD, Indiana 1993; prof.) Byzantium, eastern Europe, Russia; akyrou@salemstate.edu

Li, Li (PhD, North Carolina, Chapel Hill 1997; prof.) East Asia; lli@salemstate.edu

Louro, Michele L. (PhD, Temple 2011; assoc. prof.) modern South Asia, world; mlouro@salemstate.edu

Mauriello, Christopher E. (PhD, Brown 1995; prof.) modern Europe, Holocaust Studies; cmauriello@salemstate.edu

Morrison, Dane A. (PhD, Tufts 1983; prof.) early America, business; dmorrison@salemstate.edu

Okeny, Kenneth (PhD, California, Santa Barbara 1992; assoc. prof.) Africa; kokeny@salemstate.edu

Seger, Donna Amelia (PhD, Brandeis 1991; prof.) medieval, Renaissance, early modern Europe; dseger@salemstate.edu

Shea, Margo (PhD, Massachusetts Amherst 2010; asst. prof.) public, Ireland; mshea@salemstate.edu

Wilson, Jamie J. (PhD, NYU 2005; prof.) African American; jwilson2@salemstate.edu

Retired/Emeritus Faculty

Ames, Charles F., Jr. (PhD, Boston Univ. 1974; prof. emeritus) 19th- and 20th-century US; cames@salemstate.edu

Doyle, James T. (PhD, Ohio State 1967; prof. emeritus) world, recent US; james.doyle@salemstate.edu

Fox, John J. (MA, Lehigh 1964; prof. emeritus) US constitutional, oral, community; john.fox@salemstate.edu

Malloy, Anne E. (EdD, Boston Univ. 1978; prof. emeritus) women, college teaching methods, Europe; anne.malloy@salemstate.edu

Maloney, Joan M. (PhD, Georgetown 1961; prof. emeritus) modern China; joan.maloney@salemstate.edu

Piemonte, Joseph M. (MA, Boston Univ. 1953; prof. emeritus) Latin America

Thomson, William O. (MEd, Northeastern 1963; prof. emeritus) New England

Visiting Faculty

Collins, William Steve (PhD, LaSalle 1997; vis. lect.) world, US; wcollins@salemstate.edu

Martin, Corinne (MA, Providence 2006; vis. instr.) America, world; crichard@salemstate.edu

Martin, Zachary J. (PhD, Hawai'i, Mânoa 2013; vis. lect.) America, world; zmartin@salemstate.edu

McGuire, Michael Edward (PhD, Boston Univ. 2012; vis. lect.) France; mmcguire@salemstate.edu

Miller, Randall H. (MA, Norwich 2007; vis. instr.) world; rmiller2@salemstate.edu

Pano, Gregory (ABD, Tufts; vis. instr.) law, world; gpano@salemstate.edu

Pride, Maria (MA, Salem State 2006; vis. instr.) world; mpride@salemstate.edu

Shaughnessy-Zeena, Colleen (OMS, Worcester State 1994; vis. instr.) world; cshaughnessyzeena@salemstate.edu

Weiss, James R. (PhD, West Virginia 2000; vis. instr.) early modern Europe; jweiss@salemstate.edu

Salisbury University

Dept. of History, 1101 Camden Ave., Salisbury, MD 21801-6860. 410.543.6245. Fax 410.677.5038. Email: efstory@salisbury.edu. Website: https://www.salisbury.edu/academic-offices/liberal-arts/history/.

The Department of History offers an invigorating learning experience that challenges students to ask not just what happened, but why it happened.

Chair: Emily Story
Director of Graduate Studies: Celine Carayon
Degrees Offered: BA,MA
Academic Year System: Semester
Areas of Specialization: Chesapeake studies, Americas, Europe, Africa, Asia
Undergraduate Tuition (per academic year):
In-State: $10044
Out-of-State: $20110
Graduate Tuition (per academic year):
In-State: $7272
Out-of-State: $13032
Enrollment 2018-19:
Undergraduate Majors: 137
New Graduate Students: 4
Full-time Graduate Students: 6
Part-time Graduate Students: 11
Degrees in History: 42 BA, 4 MA
Undergraduate Addresses:
Admissions: http://www.salisbury.edu/admissions/
Financial Aid: http://www.salisbury.edu/admissions/finaid/
Graduate Addresses:
Admissions: http://www.salisbury.edu/gsr/gradstudies/
Financial Aid: http://www.salisbury.edu/admissions/finaid/

Full-time Faculty

Birch, Kevin E. (MA, Maryland, Coll. Park 2009; MA, Washington Coll. 1998; lect.) world civilizations, ancient; kebirch@salisbury.edu

Bowler, Richard Carl (PhD, UCLA 1996; prof.) Germany, Europe, science and technology; rcbowler@salisbury.edu

Carayon, Celine (PhD, William and Mary 2010; assoc. prof. and grad. dir.) colonial America, Native American, Atlantic world; cxcarayon@salisbury.edu

Ference, Gregory C. (PhD, Indiana 1988; prof.) Asia, eastern Europe, Hapsburgs; gxference@salisbury.edu

French, Kara M. (PhD, Michigan 2013; assoc. prof.) US women, gender studies; kmfrench@salisbury.edu

Genvert, Margaret Fisk (MA, Salisbury 1995; lect.) world civilizations, US; mfgenvert@salisbury.edu

Gonzalez, Aston (PhD, Michigan 2014; asst. prof.) African American; aagonzalez@salisbury.edu

Goyens, Tom (PhD, Leuven 2003; assoc. prof.) 19th- and early 20th-century US, urban radicalism; txgoyens@salisbury.edu

Hannon, Claudia A. (MA, Salisbury 1992; lect.) world civilizations, ancient; cahannon@salisbury.edu

Kotlowski, Dean J. (PhD, Indiana 1998; prof.) 20th-century US, US politics, biography; djkotlowski@salisbury.edu

Lelic, Emin (PhD, Chicago 2017; asst. prof.) Ottoman physiognomy, Islam, early modern empires; exlelic@salisbury.edu

Long, Creston S., III (PhD, William and Mary 2002; assoc. prof.) US, Chesapeake studies; cslong@salisbury.edu

McCarty, Michael B. (PhD, Columbia 2013; asst. prof.) Japan, East Asia, war and defeat; mbmccarty@salisbury.edu

Patel, Shruti (PhD, Washington 2017; asst. prof.) Early modern and modern South Asia, colonialism, religious formations; sapatel@salisbury.edu

Ragan, Elizabeth A. (PhD, Pennsylvania 2001; assoc. prof.) anthropology; earagan@salisbury.edu

Story, Emily F. (PhD, Vanderbilt 2006; assoc. prof. and chair) Latin America, urban, environmental; efstory@salisbury.edu

Talbert, Bart R. (PhD, Alabama 1996; assoc. prof.) Civil War, 19th-century America, military; brtalbert@salisbury.edu

Venosa, Joseph (PhD, Ohio 2011; assoc. prof.) Horn of Africa, Islam in African history, modern Middle East; jlvenosa@salisbury.edu

Vicens, Belen (PhD, Notre Dame 2016; asst. prof.) medieval and early modern Spain, medieval Mediterranean world; bxvicenssaiz@salisbury.edu

Walton, Kristen P. (PhD, Wisconsin, Madison 2001; prof.) Britain, early modern Europe, European reformations; kpwalton@salisbury.edu

Whitney, Jeanne E. (PhD, Delaware 1991; assoc. prof.) colonial America, material culture, museum studies; jxwhitney@salisbury.edu

Joint/Cross Appointments

Lewis, Michael L. (PhD, Iowa 2000; prof.; chair, Environmental Studies) environmental; mllewis@salisbury.edu

Pereboom, Maarten L. (PhD, Yale 1991; prof. and dean; Fulton Sch. Liberal Arts) US diplomatic and constitutional, European international; mlpereboom@salisbury.edu

Retired/Emeritus Faculty

Johnson, Norman (PhD, North Carolina, Chapel Hill 1974; prof. emeritus) Germany, 20th-century Europe

Miller, Timothy S. (PhD, Catholic 1975; prof. emeritus) Byzantine, medieval; tsmiller@salisbury.edu

Small, Clara L. (PhD, Delaware 1991; prof. emeritus) African American, civil rights

Whaley, Donald M. (MA, Princeton 1974; assoc. prof. emeritus) 19th-century America, US South, US social and cultural

Sam Houston State University

Dept. of History, SHSU Box 2239, Huntsville, TX 77341-2239. 936.294.1475. Fax 936.294.3938. Email: ham010@shsu.edu; history@shsu.edu. Website: https://www.shsu.edu/academics/history/.

Offering the BA and MA degrees and a certification for teachers, the department is committed to teaching excellence, curriculum innovation, and faculty research.

Chair: Pinar Emiralioglu
Director of Graduate Studies: Brian M. Jordan
Degrees Offered: BA,BS,MA
Academic Year System: Semester
Areas of Specialization: US, Middle East, Europe, Latin America, Africa, military
Undergraduate Tuition (per academic year):
  In-State: $8536
  Out-of-State: $18496

Graduate Tuition (per academic year):
  In-State: $8015
  Out-of-State: $15485
Enrollment 2018-19:
  Undergraduate Majors: 398
  New Graduate Students: 51
  Full-time Graduate Students: 14
  Part-time Graduate Students: 60
  Degrees in History: 91 BA, 33 MA
  Students in Undergraduate Courses: 6607
  Students in Undergraduate Intro Courses: 4542
Undergraduate Addresses:
  Admissions: http://www.shsu.edu/admissions/
  Financial Aid: http://www.shsu.edu/dept/financial-aid/
Graduate Addresses:
  Admissions: http://www.shsu.edu/dept/graduate-admissions/
  Financial Aid: http://www.shsu.edu/dept/financial-aid/

Full-time Faculty

Baker, Nancy E. (PhD, Harvard 2003; assoc. prof.) US, women; neb001@shsu.edu

Barker, Rosanne (PhD, California, Santa Barbara 1994; assoc. prof.) colonial and revolutionary America, women; his_rmb@shsu.edu

Biskupska, Jadwiga (PhD, Yale 2013; asst. prof.) Europe, military, intellectual; jxb074@shsu.edu

Cashion, Ty (PhD, Texas Christian 1993; prof.) American West, Texas; his_rtc@shsu.edu

Cox, Thomas H. (PhD, SUNY, Buffalo 2004; assoc. prof.) US, early national; thc001@shsu.edu

Dean, Amy K. R. (PhD, Purdue 2014; lect.) early modern Europe, European and American women; akd015@shsu.edu

Doleshal, Zachary (PhD, Texas, Austin 2012; lect.) central Europe, public; zad007@shsu.edu

Domitrovic, Brian (PhD, Harvard 2000; prof.) intellectual, economic; bfd001@shsu.edu

Elmore, Maggie J. (PhD, California, Berkeley 2017; asst. prof.) Latino/a, American Catholic studies; mxe053@shsu.edu

Emiralioglu, Pinar (PhD, Chicago 2006; assoc. prof. and chair) Ottoman Empire, historical cartography, Middle East; mpe005@shsu.edu

Heath, Charles V., II (PhD, Tulane 2007; assoc. prof.) Latin America; cvh003@shsu.edu

Hendrickson, Kenneth E., III (PhD, Iowa 1993; prof. and dean; Grad. Studies) British Empire, science; his_keh@shsu.edu

Jordan, Brian Matthew (PhD, Yale 2013; asst. prof. and dir., grad. studies) US Civil War; bmj018@shsu.edu

Littlejohn, Jeffrey Lynn (PhD, Arkansas 2002; prof.) US, civil rights, digital; jll004@shsu.edu

Mass, Sarah Merritt (PhD, Michigan 2018; asst. prof.) Britain, urban; smm154@shsu.edu

Mayes, David C. (PhD, Wisconsin-Madison 2002; assoc. prof.) Europe, Reformation; his_dcm@shsu.edu

Oyugi, Willis (PhD, UCLA 2014; asst. prof.) Africa, environmental; woo002@shsu.edu

Pappas, Nicholas (PhD, Stanford 1983; prof.) Europe, ancient Greece, military; his_ncp@shsu.edu

Park, Benjamin E. (PhD, Cambridge 2014; asst. prof.) US religion, 19th-century US; bep013@shsu.edu

Pruitt, Bernadette (PhD, Houston 2001; assoc. prof.) African American; his_bxp@shsu.edu

Quraishi, Uzma (PhD, Rice 2013; asst. prof.) immigration, US, South Asia; uxq001@shsu.edu

Rapp, Stephen, Jr. (PhD, Michigan 1997; prof.) Caucasus, medieval; shr002@shsu.edu

Retired/Emeritus Faculty

Olson, James S. (PhD, SUNY, Stony Brook 1972; Dist. Prof. emeritus) 20th-century US, medicine; his_jso@shsu.edu

Visiting Faculty

Hyams, Aaron (PhD, Marquette 2016; vis. asst. prof.) Texas, American West; adh061@shsu.edu

University of San Diego

Dept. of History, 5998 Alcala Park, San Diego, CA 92110. 619.260.4756. Fax 619.260.2272. Email: history@sandiego.edu. Website: https://www.sandiego.edu/cas/history/.

The History Department is dedicated to excellent teaching and innovative research. Students learn to work with original sources and to think and write critically about a wide variety of historical problems.

Chair: Colin Fisher
Degrees Offered: BA
Academic Year System: Semester
Areas of Specialization: US, Latin America, Europe, Asia, Africa
Tuition (per academic year): $50450
Enrollment 2018-19:
Undergraduate Majors: 49
Addresses:
Admissions: http://www.sandiego.edu/admissions/undergraduate/
Financial Aid: http://www.sandiego.edu/admissions/tuition-and-fees.php

Adjunct Faculty

Gheissari, Ali (DPhil, Oxford 1990; adj. prof.) modern Middle East, Iran; alig@sandiego.edu

Heisser, Cecily M. (CPhil, California, San Diego 2003; lect.) cheisser@sandiego.edu

Miller, David J. (PhD, California, San Diego 2007; lect.) race and ethnicity; davidmiller@sandiego.edu

Full-time Faculty

Abrecht, Ryan R. (PhD, California, Santa Barbara 2014; asst. prof.) Rome; rabrecht@sandiego.edu

Barton, Thomas William (PhD, Yale 2006; assoc. prof.) medieval and early modern Europe, Spain; barton@sandiego.edu

Fisher, Colin (PhD, California, Irvine 1999; prof. and chair) American environmental, American West and Native American; colinf@sandiego.edu

Gonzalez, Michael J. (PhD, California, Berkeley 1993; prof.) 19th-century US, California, Chicano and borderlands studies; michaelg@sandiego.edu

Gump, James O. (PhD, Nebraska 1980; prof.) modern Europe, Africa, comparative colonialism; gump@sandiego.edu

McClain, Molly Anne (PhD, Yale 1994; prof.) Britain, 18th-century Europe; mmcclain@sandiego.edu

Miller, Channon (PhD, Boston Univ. 2017; asst. prof.) New England, black women; channonmiller@sandiego.edu

Oberle, Clara M. (PhD, Princeton 2006; assoc. prof.) Germany, 20th-century Europe; oberle@sandiego.edu

Serbin, Kenneth P. (PhD, California, San Diego 1993; prof.) modern Latin America, Brazil; kserbin@sandiego.edu

Statler, Kathryn (PhD, California, Santa Barbara 1999; prof.) foreign relations, Vietnam wars; kstatler@sandiego.edu

Sun, Yi (PhD, Washington State 1994; prof.) Asia, China, Japan; ysun@sandiego.edu

Tallie, T.J., Jr. (PhD, Illinois, Urbana-Champaign 2014; asst. prof.) southern Africa, gender and sexuality, 19th-century settler colonialism, Zulu language and culture, British imperialism, global indigenous studies, queer theory

San Diego Mesa College

History Faculty, Social Sciences Dept., 7250 Mesa College Dr., San Diego, CA 92111-4998. 619.388.2417. Fax 619.388.2677. Email: jcrocitt@sdccd.edu. Website: http://www.sdmesa.edu/academics/schools-departments/history/.

The primary objectives of the History program are fulfillment of general education requirements for American Institutions, Humanities, and Social Sciences; completion of the Associate of Arts degree; and preparation for transfer to four-year institutions and completion of general education requirements for students enrolled in four-year institutions.

Chair: John J. Crocitti
Degrees Offered: AA
Academic Year System: Semester
Areas of Specialization: US, Asian American, Native American, US women, Asia, Europe, Latin America, Middle East
Tuition (per academic year):
In-State: $1144
Out-of-State: $7480
Enrollment 2018-19:
Degrees in History: 22 AA
Addresses:
Admissions: http://www.sdmesa.edu/admissions/
Financial Aid: http://www.sdmesa.edu/financial-aid/

Full-time Faculty

Cox, Michael L. (PhD, California, Riverside 2016; assoc. prof.) Native American, colonial/early national US; mcox@sdccd.edu

Crocitti, John J. (PhD, Miami 2001; prof. and chair) Latin America, Brazil, modern US; jcrocitt@sdccd.edu

DebChaudhury, Sudata (PhD, Illinois, Urbana-Champaign 1992; prof.) Asia, modern Europe, decolonialization; sdebchau@sdccd.edu

Holowicki, Alex (PhD, Hawai'i, Mânoa 2017; asst. prof.) world, modern US, First World War; aholowicki@sdccd.edu

Kim, Gloria (PhD, California, San Diego 2013; assoc. prof.) US race/ethnicity/class, 20th-century US social movements, 20th-century US; gkim@sdccd.edu

McLeod, Jonathan W. (PhD, UCLA 1987; prof.) 19th-century US social, race relations, 20th-century education; jmcleod@sdccd.edu

Nondepartmental Historians

Zappia, Charles A. (PhD, California, Berkeley 1994; prof.; dean, Sch. of Social/Behavioral Sciences & Multicultural Studies) US social, labor, ethnic; czappia@sdccd.edu

Part-time Faculty

Cox, Keith W. (PhD, California, Riverside 2007; adj.) Latin America, US, comparative world; kwcox@sdccd.edu

Guthrie, Wayne L. (PhD, California, San Diego 1983; adj.) modern Europe, Anglo-German relations; wguthrie@sdccd.edu

Heisser, Cecily M. (CPhil, California, San Diego 2003; adj.) modern Europe, world, women; cheisserucsd@gmail.com

Hernandez, Jennifer Peoples (PhD, Claremont Grad. 2014; adj.) colonial America, women, 1930s; jehernan@sdccd.edu

Keller, Jean A. (PhD, California, Riverside 2001; adj.) Native American, public, US 1815-77; jkeller@sdccd.edu

Mairot, Mark J. (PhD, UCLA 2013; adj.) Mexico, Latin America, world; mairot@ucla.edu

Miller, Robert David (PhD, California, Riverside 2011; adj.) American West, US since 1920, Native American; rdmiller@sdccd.edu

Nathan, Geoffrey S. (PhD, UCLA 1995; adj.) ancient; genathan47@gmail.com

Nelson, Kristopher A. (PhD, California, San Diego 2016; adj.) science, law, US; knelson001@sdccd.edu

O'Mara, William Edward IV (PhD, California, Irvine 2017; adj.) Middle East, world, Europe; womaraiv@gmail.com

Paligutan, P. James (PhD, California, Irvine 2012; adj.) Asian American, US since 1920, modern Philippines; ppaligut@sdccd.edu

Stout, James Edward (PhD, California, San Diego 2016; adj.) Spain, sport, world; jstout@sdccd.edu

Ulrich-Schlumbohm, Gwen (MA, San Diego State 2006; adj.) women, modern European women, women in colonial North American English colonies; ulrichschlumbohm@gmail.com

San Diego State University

Dept. of History, 5500 Campanile Dr., San Diego, CA 92182-6050. 619.594.5262. Fax 619.594.2210. Email: history@sdsu.edu. Website: https://history.sdsu.edu/.

The history faculty is devoted to teaching excellence and encourages a "community of scholars" atmosphere that includes graduates and undergraduates.

Chair: Edward Beasley
Director of Graduate Studies: Paula DeVos
Degrees Offered: BA,MA
Academic Year System: Semester
Areas of Specialization: Europe, US, Latin America, Asia
Undergraduate Tuition (per academic year):
   In-State: $7488
   Out-of-State: $19368
Graduate Tuition (per academic year):
   In-State: $8922
   Out-of-State: $16050
Enrollment 2018-19:
   Undergraduate Majors: 350
   New Graduate Students: 15
   Full-time Graduate Students: 69
   Degrees in History: 150 BA, 10 MA
Undergraduate Addresses:
   Admissions: http://arweb.sdsu.edu/es/admissions/
   Financial Aid: http://go.sdsu.edu/student_affairs/financialaid/
Graduate Addresses:
   Admissions: http://arweb.sdsu.edu/es/admissions/grad/
   Financial Aid: http://go.sdsu.edu/student_affairs/financialaid/

Full-time Faculty

Asselin, Pierre (PhD, Hawai'i, Manoa 1997; prof. and Dwight E. Stanford Chair) East and Southeast Asian diplomatic

Beasley, Edward J. (PhD, California, San Diego 1993; prof. and chair) 19th-century British Empire; edward.beasley@sdsu.edu

Ben, Pablo Eduardo (PhD, Chicago 2009; assoc. prof.) 19th- and 20th-century South America, Argentina, gender; pben@sdsu.edu

Blum, Edward J. (PhD, Kentucky 2003; prof.) race, religion, Civil War and Reconstruction; eblum@sdsu.edu

Cline, David Phillip (PhD, North Carolina, Chapel Hill 2010; assoc. prof.; Digital Humanities) public and oral, 20th-century social movements

De Vos, Paula S. (PhD, California, Berkeley 2001; prof. and dir., grad. studies) Latin America; pdevos@sdsu.edu

Edgerton-Tarpley, Kathryn (PhD, Indiana 2001; prof.) China, Asia; edgerton@sdsu.edu

Elkind, Sarah (PhD, Michigan 1994; prof.) American environmental, US since 1850, public health; selkind@sdsu.edu

Frieberg, Annika E. (PhD, North Carolina, Chapel Hill 2008; asst. prof.) modern Europe; afrieberg@sdsu.edu

Kazemi, Ranin (PhD, Yale 2012; assoc. prof.) Middle East; rkazemi@sdsu.edu

Kornfeld, Eve (PhD, Harvard 1983; prof.) colonial and revolutionary America, European and American cultural and intellectual; kornfeld@sdsu.edu

Kuefler, Mathew S. (PhD, Yale 1995; prof.) medieval; mkuefler@sdsu.edu

Nieves, Angel David (PhD, Cornell 2001; prof.; Digital Humanities) architecture and urban development, African studies

Passananti, Tom (PhD, Chicago 2001; assoc. prof.) Mexico and Latin America; tpassana@sdsu.edu

Penrose, Walter D., Jr. (PhD, Grad. Center, CUNY 2006; assoc. prof.) ancient; wpenrose@sdsu.edu

Pollard, Elizabeth Ann (PhD, Pennsylvania 2001; prof.) ancient world, Roman and Greek civilizations; epollard@sdsu.edu

Putman, John C. (PhD, California, San Diego 2000; assoc. prof.) 19th- and 20th-century US, American West, California; putman@sdsu.edu

Wiese, Andrew (PhD, Columbia 1993; prof.) 20th-century US urban and social, African American; awiese@sdsu.edu

Yeh, Chiou-ling (PhD, California, Irvine 2001; assoc. prof.) US race and ethnicity, Asian American; cyeh@sdsu.edu

Part-time Faculty

Di Bella, Edward (MA, San Diego State; lect.)

Gastil, George (MA, California, Santa Barbara 1991; lect.)

Harris, Bonnie Mae (PhD, California, Santa Barbara 2009; lect.)

Hillman, Susanne (PhD, California, San Diego 2011; lect.)

Kaffenberger, Schorsch (MA, San Diego State 2014; lect.)

Keller-Lapp, Heidi Marie (PhD, California, San Diego 2005; lect.)

Mahdavi-Izadi, Farid (PhD, Wisconsin, Madison 2000; lect.) Islamic, Middle East; mahdavi@sdsu.edu

Nathan, Geoffrey S. (PhD, UCLA 1995; lect.)

Nobiletti, Frank (ABD, California, San Diego; lect.) US sexuality; fnobilet@sdsu.edu

Parker, Lindsay A. H. (PhD, California, Irvine 2011; lect.)

Sheehan, Kevin J. (PhD, California, Berkeley 2008; lect.)

Stout, Mary Ellen (MA, San Diego State 2016; lect.)

Strom, Yale (lect.)

Tarpley, Van (ABD, Indiana; lect.)

Weeks, William Earl, Jr. (PhD, California, San Diego 1986; lect.)

Yusufjonova-Abman, Zamira (PhD, California, Santa Barbara 2015; lect.)

Retired/Emeritus Faculty

Baron, Lawrence (PhD, Wisconsin, Madison 1974; Nasatir Prof. emeritus) modern Europe, Jewish, modern Germany; lbaron@sdsu.edu

Bartholomew, Francis M., Jr. (PhD, Princeton 1969; assoc. prof. emeritus) Russia and Soviet Union

Cheek, William F., III (PhD, Virginia 1961; prof. emeritus) black American civilization, American biography

Christian, David Gilbert (DPhil, Oxford 1974; prof. emeritus) world, Russia, world environmental; dgchrist@sdsu.edu

Chu, Pao-chin (PhD, Pennsylvania 1970; prof. emeritus) Republican Chinese diplomatic, modern Chinese military, Chinese Communist Party

Cobbs, Elizabeth Anne (PhD, Stanford 1988; prof. emeritus) US, Latin America; ehoffman@sdsu.edu

Colston, Stephen A. (PhD, UCLA 1973; assoc. prof. emeritus) Latin American studies, anthropology, public; colston@sdsu.edu

Cox, Thomas R. (PhD, Oregon 1969; prof. emeritus) forest and conservation, Asian-American economic relations, Gilded Age and Progressive Era

Cunniff, Roger L. (PhD, Texas, Austin 1970; prof. emeritus) Latin America, Brazil; rcunniff@sdsu.edu

Davies, Thomas M., Jr. (PhD, New Mexico 1970; prof. emeritus) 20th-century Peru, Andes, Latin American militarism

DuFault, David V. (PhD, Oregon 1972; assoc. prof. emeritus) Japan, Philippine-US relations, Asian American

Dunn, Ross E. (PhD, Wisconsin, Madison 1968; prof. emeritus) Africa, North Africa, Islamic; dunn@sdsu.edu

Ferraro, Joanne M. (PhD, UCLA 1983; prof. emeritus) Renaissance/early modern Europe, economic and social; ferraro@sdsu.edu

Filner, Robert (PhD, Cornell 1973; assoc. prof. emeritus) science, science and government

Flemion, Philip F. (PhD, Florida 1968; assoc. prof. emeritus) 19th- and 20th-century Central America, independence period Latin America

Hamilton, Charles D. (PhD, Cornell 1968; prof. emeritus) classics, Greek and Roman political, Greek and Roman historiography and numismatics; chamilto@sdsu.edu

Heyman, Neil M. (PhD, Stanford 1972; prof. emeritus) 20th-century Russia, Europe, military; heyman@sdsu.edu

Hoidal, Oddvar K. (PhD, Southern California 1970; prof. emeritus) modern Norway, modern Scandinavia, modern Europe; hoidal@sdsu.edu

Kushner, Howard I. (PhD, Cornell 1970; prof. emeritus) social, medicine

McDean, Harry C. (PhD, UCLA 1969; prof. emeritus) US economic, 20th-century US, US agriculture/business; mcdean@sdsu.edu

O'Brien, Albert C. (PhD, Notre Dame 1968; prof. emeritus) Italy, Catholic church in modern world, Holocaust; obrien1@sdsu.edu

Schatz, Arthur (PhD, Oregon 1965; prof. emeritus and dean, grad. div.) US foreign policy

Smith, Ray T. (PhD, California, Berkeley 1964; prof. emeritus) Asian civilization, India

Starr, Raymond G. (PhD, Texas, Austin 1964; prof. emeritus) local, San Diego, public

Stites, Francis N. (PhD, Indiana 1968; prof. emeritus) American constitutional, early national US

Stoddart, Jess (PhD, California, Berkeley 1966; prof. emeritus) Tudor-Stuart England

Strong, Doug (PhD, Syracuse 1964; prof. emeritus) US environmental, West and frontier

Vartanian, Pershing (PhD, Michigan 1971; prof. emeritus) 19th-century American intellectual, Jacksonian America, American studies; vartania@sdsu.edu

University of San Francisco

Dept. of History, 2130 Fulton St., San Francisco, CA 94117-1080. 415.422.6784. Fax 415.422.5784. Email: history@usfca.edu. Website: https://www.usfca.edu/arts-sciences/undergraduate-programs/history.

Our major and minor curricula are designed by a diverse group of professors and offer a variety of courses in social, cultural, environmental, gender, economic, political, and religious history.

Chair: Heather Hoag
Degrees Offered: BA
Academic Year System: Semester
Areas of Specialization: US, Europe, Asia, Latin America, Africa, Islamic world, global
Tuition (per academic year): $49750
Enrollment 2018-19:
    Undergraduate Majors: 67
    Degrees in History: 20 BA
    Students in Undergraduate Courses: 1464
    Students in Undergraduate Intro Courses: 1243
Addresses:
    Admissions: https://www.usfca.edu/admission/undergraduate
    Financial Aid: https://www.usfca.edu/admission/financial-aid

Adjunct Faculty

Arnold, Chase (PhD, California, Berkeley 2017; instr.) Africa; carnold2@usfca.edu

Banks, Elyse L. (PhD, California, Santa Cruz 2016; instr.) 20th-century US, interracial organizing, social movements, religion, race; bankselyse@gmail.com

O'Sullivan, Chris (PhD, London 1999; instr.) US, foreign policy, California; osullivanc@usfca.edu

von Bothmer, Bernard (PhD, Indiana 2006; instr.) US; bvonbothmer@yahoo.com

Full-time Faculty

Claussen, Martin A. (PhD, Virginia 1991; prof.) medieval Europe; claussenm@usfca.edu

Harrison, Candice L. (PhD, Emory 2008; assoc. prof.) US, African American; clharrison2@usfca.edu

Hoag, Heather Jane (PhD, Boston Univ. 2003; prof. and chair) Africa, environmental; hjhoag@usfca.edu

Kruze, Uldis (PhD, Indiana 1976; prof.) Asia, modern China, modern Japan; kruzeu@usfca.edu

Moreno, Julio E. (PhD, California, Irvine 1998; prof.) Latin America, Mexico, cultural; moreno@usfca.edu

Nasstrom, Kathryn L. (PhD, North Carolina, Chapel Hill 1993; prof.) US, women, oral; nasstromk@usfca.edu

Neaman, Elliot Y. (PhD, California, Berkeley 1992; prof.) 20th-century Europe, Germany; neamane@usfca.edu

Olds, Katrina B. (PhD, Princeton 2009; prof.) early modern Europe, European expansion, European religious; kbolds@usfca.edu

Stanfield, Michael E. (PhD, New Mexico 1992; prof.) Latin America, Amazonia; stanfieldm@usfca.edu

Zaman, Taymiya R. (PhD, Michigan 2007; prof.) Islamic world, South Asia; zamant@umich.edu

Zarsadiaz, James (PhD, Northwestern 2014; asst. prof.) 20th-century US, comparative urban/suburban studies, Asian American; jzarsadiaz@usfca.edu

San José State University

Dept. of History, 1 Washington Sq., San Jose, CA 95192-0117. 408.924.5500. Email: treina.bills@sjsu.edu. Website: http://www.sjsu.edu/history/.

To understand the present and prepare for the future, we must understand the past. The Department of History at San José State University offers both undergraduate and graduate programs that enable students to comprehend the forces that have shaped our world. History majors become teachers, lawyers, journalists, researchers, writers, museum professionals, archivists, administrators, librarians, and they work in all fields of business.

Chair: Glen Gendzel
Director of Graduate Studies: Libra R. Hilde
Director of Undergraduate Studies: Xiaojia Hou
Degrees Offered: BA,MA
Academic Year System: Semester
Areas of Specialization: US political and social, modern Europe, ancient and medieval, Asia, Latin America
Undergraduate Tuition (per academic year):
    In-State: $7852
    Out-of-State: $17356
Graduate Tuition (per academic year):
    In-State: $9286
    Out-of-State: $16414
Enrollment 2018-19:
    Undergraduate Majors: 230
    New Graduate Students: 15
    Full-time Graduate Students: 25
    Part-time Graduate Students: 35
    Degrees in History: 50 BA, 10 MA
Undergraduate Addresses:
    Admissions: http://www.sjsu.edu/admissions/
    Financial Aid: http://www.sjsu.edu/faso/
Graduate Addresses:
    Admissions: http://www.sjsu.edu/gape/
    Financial Aid: http://www.sjsu.edu/faso/

Full-time Faculty

Chopra, Ruma (PhD, California, Davis 2008; prof.) early America, indigenous and African slaveries, environmental; Ruma.Chopra@sjsu.edu

Garcia, Alberto (PhD, California, Berkeley 2016; asst. prof.) Mexico and Latin America, recent US, immigration/political/diplomatic; Alberto.Garcia@sjsu.edu

Gendzel, Glen J. (PhD, Wisconsin, Madison 1998; prof. and chair) California and US West, 19th- and 20th-century US, politics/culture/business/immigration; Glen.Gendzel@sjsu.edu

Hilde, Libra R. (PhD, Harvard 2003; prof. and grad. advisor) 19th-century US, Civil War, gender and race; Libra.Hilde@sjsu.edu

Hill, Patricia Evridge (PhD, Texas, Dallas 1990; prof.) 19th- and 20th-century US, urban, social; Patricia.Hill@sjsu.edu

Hou, Xiaojia (PhD, Cornell 2008; assoc. prof. and undergrad. advisor) modern China, 20th-century Chinese peasants, Mao Zedong; xiaojia.hou@sjsu.edu

Olson, Katharine Kristina (PhD, Harvard 2008; asst. prof.) medieval/early modern Europe, Britain and Ireland, religious/social/cultural/intellectual; katharine.olson@sjsu.edu

Pickering, Mary B. (PhD, Harvard 1988; prof.) 19th- and 20th-century European social and intellectual, modern France, European women; Mary.Pickering@sjsu.edu

Roth, Jonathan P. (PhD, Columbia 1991; prof.) ancient, military, world and Jewish; Jonathan.Roth@sjsu.edu

Vasquez, George L. (PhD, Columbia 1978; prof.) Latin America, modern Europe, Middle East; George.Vasquez@sjsu.edu

Part-time Faculty

Buyco, Ray (MA, San José State 2010; lect.) modern Europe and world, US, politics and ideology; raymand.buyco@sjsu.edu

Chilton, Katherine (PhD, Carnegie Mellon 2009; lect.) African American, US women, slavery and emancipation; katherine.chilton@sjsu.edu

Cirivilleri, Robert (MA, San José State 2000; lect.) US, world; Robert.Cirivilleri@sjsu.edu

Guardino, Laura (MA, San José State 2003; lect.) US, women, education; Laura.Guardino@sjsu.edu

Katsev, Allison Y. (PhD, Stanford 1998; lect.) Russia, historiography, modern Europe; Allison.Katsev@sjsu.edu

McBane, Margo (PhD, UCLA 2001; lect.) California, public and oral, women/race/gender; Margo.McBane@sjsu.edu

Narveson, Eric J. (MA, San José State 1986; lect.) critical thinking, modern military; eric.narveson@evc.edu

Speed, Richard M. (PhD, California, Santa Barbara 1988; lect. emeritus) America, Europe, US; rbspeed@comcast.net

Wilson, Mary Lynn (PhD, UCLA 1999; lect.) world, medieval; Mary.Wilson@sjsu.edu

Retired/Emeritus Faculty

Bernhardt, John W. (PhD, UCLA 1986; prof. emeritus) medieval, ancient; John.Bernhardt@sjsu.edu

Boll, Michael M. (PhD, Wisconsin, Madison 1969; prof. emeritus) Russia, Soviet Union, national defense

Boudreau, Joseph A. (PhD, UCLA 1965; prof. emeritus) Canada, British Empire; josephboudreau@att.net

Conniff, Michael L. (PhD, Stanford 1976; prof. emeritus) Latin America; Michael.Conniff@sjsu.edu

Cornford, Daniel (PhD, California, Santa Barbara 1983; prof. emeritus) 19th- and 20th-century US, California, labor

Cramer, Richard S. (PhD, Stanford 1960; prof. emeritus) US, constitutional, Civil War

Don, Patricia Lopes (PhD, California, Davis 2000; prof. emeritus) colonial Latin America, early modern Europe; Patricia.Don@sjsu.edu

Jensen, Billie (PhD, Colorado, Boulder 1962; prof. emeritus) US, women

Jerke, Iris M. (MA, San José State 2003; lect. emeritus) US, critical thinking; Iris.Jerke@sjsu.edu

Keserich, Charles (PhD, Washington State 1966; prof. emeritus) modern Europe

Kline, Benjamin (PhD, Univ. Coll., Cork, Ireland 1986; lect. emeritus) modern Europe, Africa; bkline555@comcast.net

Kumamoto, Bob (PhD, UCLA 1984; prof. emeritus) 20th-century US, diplomatic

Leonard, Charlene M. (PhD, California, Berkeley 1958; prof. emeritus) France

McNeil, David O. (PhD, Stanford 1972; prof. emeritus) 16th- and 17th-century Europe, France, Renaissance and Reformation; dmcneil@stanfordalumni.org

Moore, George E. (PhD, California, Berkeley 1966; prof. emeritus) Japan, East and South Asia

Propas, Frederic (PhD, UCLA 1982; lect. emeritus) American foreign policy, early American cultural and social; rickpropas@comcast.net

Reynolds, E. Bruce (PhD, Hawai'i, Mânoa 1988; prof. emeritus) Japan, China, Southeast Asia; bruce.reynolds@sjsu.edu

Underdal, Stanley J. (PhD, Columbia 1977; prof. emeritus) US, ethnicity and race, Native Americans

Walsh, James P. (PhD, California, Berkeley 1970; prof. emeritus) US, California, Irish American; James.Walsh@sjsu.edu

Santa Clara University

Dept. of History, 500 El Camino Real, Santa Clara, CA 95053-0285. 408.554.4527. Fax 408.554.2124. Email: historydepartment@scu.edu. Website: https://www.scu.edu/cas/history/.

Santa Clara's History Department strives to be a community of scholars in which students and faculty engage in vigorous inquiry to study and understand the past.

Chair: Nancy C. Unger
Degrees Offered: BA
Academic Year System: Quarter
Areas of Specialization: US, Latin America, Europe, East Asia/South Asia/Indian Ocean, Africa/West Africa/Middle East
Tuition (per academic year): $51081
Enrollment 2018-19:
 Undergraduate Majors: 48
 Degrees in History: 15 BA
Addresses:
 Admissions: http://www.scu.edu/ugrad/
 Financial Aid: http://www.scu.edu/financialaid/

Full-time Faculty

Andrews, Naomi J. (PhD, California, Santa Cruz 1998; assoc. prof.) early modern France, women; nandrews@scu.edu

Liebscher, Arthur F., SJ (PhD, Indiana 1975; assoc. prof.) Latin America, Argentina; aliebscher@scu.edu

Mariani, Paul P. (PhD, Chicago 2007; assoc. prof.) China; pmariani@scu.edu

Molony, Barbara (PhD, Harvard 1982; prof.) Japan, China, women in Asia; bmolony@scu.edu

Newsom Kerr, Matthew Lee (PhD, Southern California 2006; assoc. prof.) science and medicine, modern Europe; mnewsomkerr@scu.edu

Odamtten, Harry Nii Koney (PhD, Michigan State 2010; assoc. prof.) African studies, Atlantic world; hodamtten@scu.edu

Randall, Amy E. (PhD, Princeton 2000; prof.) modern Russia, eastern Europe; arandall@scu.edu

Skinner, David E. (PhD, California, Berkeley 1971; prof.) Africa, Middle East; dskinner@scu.edu

Turley, Thomas (PhD, Cornell 1978; assoc. prof.) ancient and medieval Europe; tturley@scu.edu

Unger, Nancy C. (PhD, Southern California 1985; prof. and chair) US, women, progressivism; nunger@scu.edu

Joint/Cross Appointments

Greenwalt, William S. (PhD, Virginia 1985; prof.; Classics) classical Greece and Macedonia, Rome; wgreenwalt@scu.edu

Hazard, Anthony Q., Jr. (PhD, Temple 2008; asst. prof.; Ethnic Studies) US racism; ahazard@scu.edu

Retired/Emeritus Faculty

French, Dorothea (PhD, California, Berkeley 1986; assoc. prof. emeritus) medieval, late antiquity, church; dfrench@scu.edu

Gelber, Steven (PhD, Wisconsin, Madison 1972; prof. emeritus) 20th-century US, US social and cultural; sgelber@scu.edu

Giacomini, George F., Jr. (MA, California, Berkeley 1957; assoc. prof. emeritus) American and European diplomatic, 19th-century US; ggiacomini@scu.edu

Margadant, Jo Burr (PhD, California, Davis 1987; prof. emeritus) France, modern Europe, European women; jbmargadant@scu.edu

O'Keefe, Timothy J. (PhD, Notre Dame 1968; prof. emeritus) England, Ireland, modern Europe; tokeefe@scu.edu

Pierson, Peter O'Malley (PhD, UCLA 1966; prof. emeritus) Spain, early modern Europe, cultural; pompierson@aol.com

Raman, Sita A. (PhD, UCLA 1992; prof. emeritus) South Asia, India, Southeast Asia; sraman@scu.edu

Senkewicz, Robert M. (PhD, Stanford 1974; prof. emeritus) colonial and revolutionary America, US Southwest; rsenkewicz@scu.edu

The University of Scranton

Dept. of History, St. Thomas Hall 309, Scranton, PA 18510-4699. 570.941.7625. Fax 570.941.5843. Email: david.dzurec@scranton.edu. Website: https://www.scranton.edu/academics/cas/history/.

As a department we stand out because we offer our students a foundation for almost any career they can imagine. Steeped in the tradition of the Jesuit ratio studiorum, we train our students not only as scholars but as citizens.

Chair: David J. Dzurec
Degrees Offered: BA
Academic Year System: Semester
Areas of Specialization: US, Europe, Latin America, women, East Asia
Tuition (per academic year): $42910
Enrollment 2018-19:
 Undergraduate Majors: 78
 Degrees in History: 22 BA
Addresses:
 Admissions: http://www.scranton.edu/admissions/
 Financial Aid: http://www.scranton.edu/financial-aid/

Full-time Faculty

Brennan, Sean Philip (PhD, Notre Dame 2009; assoc. prof.) modern Europe, 20th-century Russia, 20th-century Germany; sean.brennan@scranton.edu

Domenico, Roy (PhD, Rutgers 1987; prof.) 19th- and 20th-century European political and cultural, Italy; roy.domenico@scranton.edu

Dunn, Josephine M. (PhD, Pennsylvania 1991; prof.) medieval to Renaissance art, Pennsylvania oral and local; josephine.dunn@scranton.edu

Dzurec, David J., III (PhD, Ohio State 2008; prof. and chair) American Revolution, early national US, American foreign relations; david.dzurec@scranton.edu

Fan, Shuhua (PhD, North Carolina, Chapel Hill 2007; prof.) world, Asia, modern China and China-US relations; shuhua.fan@scranton.edu

Gillett, Christopher P. (PhD, Brown 2018; asst. prof.) early modern Britain and Ireland, early modern Europe, early modern religious change in global perspective; christopher.gillett@scranton.edu

Kennedy, Lawrence William (PhD, Boston Coll. 1987; prof.) Gilded Age and Progressive Era America, urban and ethnic, modern Ireland; lawrence.kennedy@scranton.edu

Levy, Aiala T. (PhD, Chicago 2016; asst. prof.) Latin America, Atlantic world, digital; aiala.levy@scranton.edu

Poulson, Susan (PhD, Georgetown 1990; prof.) recent America, American women; susan.poulson@scranton.edu

Pratt, Adam J. (PhD, Louisiana State 2012; assoc. prof.) Jacksonian America, borderlands studies, American South; adam.pratt@scranton.edu

Shaffern, Robert (PhD, Notre Dame 1992; prof.) ancient, medieval, early modern Europe; robert.shaffern@scranton.edu

Welsh, W. Jeffrey (PhD, Bowling Green State 1982; prof.) American colonies, US business, public; william.welsh@scranton.edu

Retired/Emeritus Faculty

Conover, Willis M. (EdD, Montana State 1978; prof. emeritus) American West, US, geography; willis.conover@scranton.edu

De Michele, Michael D. (PhD, Penn State 1967; prof. emeritus) modern Europe, England, ethnic; michael.demichele@scranton.edu

Homer, Frank X. J. (PhD, Virginia 1971; prof. emeritus) modern Europe, modern England, European diplomatic; francis.homer@scranton.edu

Williams, Bernard D. (MA, Niagara 1955; prof. emeritus) modern Europe, Latin America, international studies; bernard.williams@scranton.edu

Scripps College

Dept. of History, 1030 Columbia Ave., Claremont, CA 91711-3948. 909.607.2807. Fax 909.621.8323. Email: andrew.aisenberg@scrippscollege.edu. Website: http://www.scrippscollege.edu/departments/history.

The offerings of the Scripps History Department are especially rich in US, European, and Latin American history, and they highlight the importance of race, gender, sexuality, and critical theory for an understanding of human experience in the past.

Chair: Andrew Aisenberg
Degrees Offered: BA
Academic Year System: Semester
Areas of Specialization: early modern and modern Europe, US, African American, Latin America, intellectual/cultural/social/political/economic
Tuition (per academic year): $54806
Enrollment 2018-19:
  Undergraduate Majors: 17
  Degrees in History: 5 BA
Addresses:
  Admissions: http://www.scrippscollege.edu/admission/
  Financial Aid: http://www.scrippscollege.edu/financial-aid/

Full-time Faculty

Aisenberg, Andrew R. (PhD, Yale 1993; prof. and chair) modern Europe, France, medicine; andrew.aisenberg@scrippscollege.edu

Forster, Cindy (PhD, California, Berkeley 1995; prof.) Latin America, labor, women; cindy.forster@scrippscollege.edu

Liss, Julia E. (PhD, California, Berkeley 1990; prof.) US intellectual, cultural, anthropology; julia.liss@scrippscollege.edu

Roberts, Rita (PhD, California, Berkeley 1988; prof.) US, 19th century, African American; rroberts@scrippscollege.edu

Tazzara, Corey S. (PhD, Stanford 2011; assoc. prof.) early modern Italy, economic and political, Ottoman Empire and Mediterranean world; ctazzara@scrippscollege.edu

Retired/Emeritus Faculty

Blaine, Bradford B. (PhD, UCLA 1965; prof. emeritus) medieval Europe, technology

Geerken, John H. (PhD, Yale 1967; prof. emeritus) Renaissance and Reformation Europe, intellectual, legal; jgeerken@scrippscollege.edu

Seattle University

Dept. of History, 901 12th Ave., PO Box 222000, Seattle, WA 98122-1090. 206.296.5450. Fax 206.296.5997. Email: poquizm@seattleu.edu. Website: https://www.seattleu.edu//artsci/departments/history/.

The history program focuses on the values, as well as the ideas, personalities, and institutions that existed in the past and shaped the present. Concerned with perceptions of reality and historic reality itself, the history program attempts to exploit all forms of information concerning the past.

Chair: Hazel Hahn
Degrees Offered: BA
Academic Year System: Quarter
Areas of Specialization: Europe, America, Latin America, Asia, Africa, Middle East
Tuition (per academic year): $40500
Enrollment 2018-19:
  Undergraduate Majors: 80
  Degrees in History: 25 BA
Addresses:
  Admissions: http://www2.seattleu.edu/admissions/
  Financial Aid: http://www2.seattleu.edu/undergraduate-admissions/finances/

Adjunct Faculty

Dean, Michael (PhD, California, Berkeley 2014; adj.) modern central Europe, modern US, social, intellectual, immigration

Ng, Michael K. (PhD, Royal Holloway, London 2008; adj.) ancient Rome

Full-time Faculty

Adejumobi, Saheed Adeyinka (PhD, Texas, Austin 2001; assoc. prof.; Global African Studies) modern Africa, African American, African diaspora intellectual and cultural; s.ade@seattleu.edu

Earenfight, Theresa M. (PhD, Fordham 1997; prof.) medieval and early modern Europe, political, monarchy and gender; theresa@seattleu.edu

Hahn, Hazel (PhD, California, Berkeley 1997; prof. and chair) modern France, Paris, French Empire, French Indochina; hahnh@seattleu.edu

Kamerling, Henry (PhD, Illinois 1998; instr.) 19th- and 20th-century America, world, prisons; kamerlih@seattleu.edu

Kangas, William H. (PhD, Washington 1993; sr. instr.) modern Europe, intellectual and cultural, historical theory/historiography; wkangas@seattleu.edu

Liang, Kan (PhD, Yale 1995; assoc. prof. and assoc. dean) East Asia, China; liang@seattleu.edu

McLeod, Marc C. (PhD, Texas, Austin 2000; assoc. prof.) Latin America, Caribbean; mcleodm@seattleu.edu

Murphy, Thomas R. SJ (PhD, Connecticut 1998; assoc. prof.) US slavery, US Northwest; tmurphy@seattleu.edu

Pepper, Tracey A. (MA, Central Washington 2000; instr.) eastern Europe, Russia, gender; peppert@seattleu.edu

Robinson, Nova (PhD, Rutgers 2015; asst. prof.) Middle East, political, women

Souza, Randall (PhD, California, Berkeley 2014; asst. prof.) ancient Greece, Sicily; souzara@seattleu.edu

Spencer, Heath A. (PhD, Kentucky 1997; sr. instr.) modern Europe, modern Germany, religious and social; spencerh@seattleu.edu

Taylor, Tom W. (PhD, Minnesota 1988; assoc. prof.) World Wars I and II, social, world; twtaylor@seattleu.edu

Retired/Emeritus Faculty

Burnstein, Daniel E. (PhD, Rutgers 1992; assoc. prof. emeritus) US, Progressive Era, social welfare; danielbu@seattleu.edu

Harmon, Robert (MA, Washington 1957; assoc. prof. emeritus) Western civilization

Madsen, David (PhD, Washington 1981; assoc. prof. emeritus) ancient Greece and Rome, humanities, Latin and origins of Christianity; dmadsen@seattleu.edu

Miller, Jacquelyn (PhD, Rutgers 1995; assoc. prof. and assoc. provost emeritus) colonial America, American Revolution, gender and sexuality; jcmiller@seattleu.edu

Seton Hall University

Dept. of History, 400 S. Orange Ave., South Orange, NJ 07079-2687. 973.275.2984. Fax 973.761.7798. Email: thomas.rzeznik@shu.edu; historydept@shu.edu. Website: https://www.shu.edu/history/.

The Department of History offers programs of study leading to the BA and MA degrees. By presenting the story of human achievements, hopes and frustrations, struggles and triumphs, the department helps the inquiring student to understand this complex world and shape its future.

Chair: Thomas F. Rzeznik
Director of Graduate Studies: Dermot A. Quinn
Degrees Offered: BA,BA/MA,MA
Academic Year System: Semester
Areas of Specialization: US, Europe, global, Catholic
Undergraduate Tuition (per academic year): $41460
Graduate Tuition (per academic year): $22662
Enrollment 2018-19:
  Undergraduate Majors: 93
  Full-time Graduate Students: 3
  Part-time Graduate Students: 18
Undergraduate Addresses:
  Admissions: http://admissions.shu.edu
  Financial Aid: https://www.shu.edu/undergraduate-admissions/financial-aid.cfm
Graduate Addresses:
  Admissions: http://www.shu.edu/applying/graduate
  Financial Aid: http://www.shu.edu/graduate-affairs/graduate-financial-aid.cfm

Adjunct Faculty

Koenig, Brigitte A. (PhD, California, Berkeley 2000; adj. assoc. prof.) US social and women; brigitte.koenig@shu.edu
Lucibello, Alan J. (MA, Catholic 1967; adj.) Western civilization; alan.lucibello@shu.edu

Full-time Faculty

Connell, William J. (PhD, California, Berkeley 1989; prof.) Renaissance and Reformation, medieval and early modern Italy, European intellectual; william.connell@shu.edu
Fieldston, Sara (PhD, Yale 2013; asst. prof.) America, US and world, childhood; sara.fieldston@shu.edu
Gedacht, Anne Giblin (PhD, Wisconsin, Madison 2015; asst. prof.) modern Japan, migration and immigration, race and ethnicity; anne.giblin@shu.edu
Greene, Larry A. (PhD, Columbia 1979; prof.) Civil War and Reconstruction, African American, Great Depression and World War II; larry.greene@shu.edu
Harvey, Sean P. (PhD, William and Mary 2009; assoc. prof.) colonial and early Republic, US intellectual and cultural, Native American; sean.harvey@shu.edu
Hoffer, Williamjames Hull (PhD, Johns Hopkins 2003; JD, Harvard 1996; prof.) US legal, economic, military; williamjames.hoffer@shu.edu
Knight, Nathaniel (PhD, Columbia 1995; prof.) Russia, eastern Europe, Central Asia; nathaniel.knight@shu.edu
Matusevich, Maxim (PhD, Illinois, Urbana-Champaign 2001; prof.; dir., Russian & East European Studies Prog.) world, African diaspora, Cold War; maxim.matusevich@shu.edu
May, Vanessa (PhD, Virginia 2007; assoc. prof.) US, women's studies, labor; vanessa.may@shu.edu

Molesky, Mark C. (PhD, Harvard 2000; prof.) Germany, Portugal and France, European intellectual; mark.molesky@shu.edu
Quinn, Dermot A. (PhD, Oxford 1988; prof. and dir., grad. prog.) Great Britain, Ireland, Catholic thought; dermot.quinn@shu.edu
Rekabtalaei, Golbarg (PhD, Toronto 2015; asst. prof.) modern Iran, modern Middle East, Iranian/Middle Eastern cinema; golbarg.rekabtalaei@shu.edu
Rzeznik, Thomas F. (PhD, Notre Dame 2006; assoc. prof. and chair) US Catholic and religious, urban, environmental; thomas.rzeznik@shu.edu
Schultz, Kirsten (PhD, NYU 1998; assoc. prof.) Latin America, Brazil, Iberian empires; kirsten.schultz@shu.edu
Wangerin, Laura (PhD, Wisconsin, Madison 2014; asst. prof.) medieval Europe, politics and society, legal; laura.wangerin@shu.edu

Retired/Emeritus Faculty

Browne, George P. (PhD, Catholic 1972; assoc. prof. emeritus) immigration, Latin America
Driscoll, William (PhD, Fordham 1965; prof. emeritus) legal theory, Jacksonian America
Lurie, Maxine N. (PhD, Wisconsin, Madison 1968; prof. emerita) early America, New Jersey; maxine.lurie@shu.edu
Scholz, Bernhard W. (PhD, Wurzburg, Germany 1964; prof. emeritus) Europe, medieval
Shapiro, Edward S. (PhD, Harvard 1968; prof. emeritus) foreign policy, 20th century, intellectual
Stock-Morton, Phyllis (PhD, Yale 1965; prof. emerita) intellectual, modern France, women
Walz, Ralph C. (PhD, NYU 1970; assoc. prof. emeritus) Germany, French Revolution

Shepherd University

Dept. of History, PO Box 5000, Shepherdstown, WV 25443-5000. 304.876.5277. Fax 304.876.5405. Email: sbrasher@shepherd.edu. Website: https://www.shepherd.edu/history.

Here you'll find faculty and students who share your passion for uncovering and interpreting the past. We offer small class sizes, courses that span from ancient civilization to Renaissance Italy to modern Japan, and the chance to work directly with top faculty in the profession.

Chair: Sally M. Brasher
Degrees Offered: BA
Academic Year System: Semester
Areas of Specialization: Civil War and 19th-century US, historic preservation, public, Europe, non-Western
Tuition (per academic year):
  In-State: $7328
  Out-of-State: $17868
Enrollment 2018-19:
  Undergraduate Majors: 75
  Degrees in History: 32 BA
Addresses:
  Admissions: http://www.shepherd.edu/admissions/
  Financial Aid: http://www.shepherd.edu/faoweb/

Full-time Faculty

Alexander, Keith D. (PhD, Maryland, Coll. Park 2003; asst. prof.) historic preservation, modern Germany, Cuba; kalex@shepherd.edu
Bankhurst, Benjamin (PhD, King's Coll., London 2011; asst. prof.) early America, Atlantic, Appalachia; bbankhur@shepherd.edu

Brasher, Sally Mayall (PhD, Catholic 2001; asst. prof. and chair) medieval and early modern Europe, gender; sbrasher@shepherd.edu

Broomall, James Joseph (PhD, Florida 2011; asst. prof.; dir., GT Moore Civil War Center) 19th-century US, Civil War

Gordon, David B. (PhD, Hawai'i, Manoa 1997; asst. prof.) East Asia, intellectual; dgordon@shepherd.edu

Perego, Elizabeth Marie (PhD, Ohio State 2017; asst. prof.) Africa, Middle East; eperego@shepherd.edu

Sandy, Julia L. (PhD, Massachusetts Amherst 2006; asst. prof.) 20th-century US, public, Latin America; jsandyba@shepherd.edu

Shippensburg University

Dept. of History, 1871 Old Main Dr., DHC 122, Shippensburg, PA 17257-2299. 717.477.1621. Fax 717.477.4062. Email: sbburg@ship.edu. Website: http://www.ship.edu/history/.

Situated in the beautiful Cumberland Valley, a region rich with historic sites and resources, Shippensburg University is the ideal location for studying history. Our student-centered faculty teach a diverse range of fascinating courses, allowing you to immerse yourself in the topics and time periods that you enjoy.

Chair: Steven B. Burg
Director of Graduate Studies: John D. Bloom
Degrees Offered: BA,BSEd,MA
Academic Year System: Semester
Areas of Specialization: world and comparative, Middle East/Europe, Latin America, East and South Asia, US
Undergraduate Tuition (per academic year):
In-State: $9570
Out-of-State: $17362
Graduate Tuition (per academic year):
In-State: $11970
Out-of-State: $16830
Enrollment 2018-19:
Undergraduate Majors: 151
New Graduate Students: 6
Full-time Graduate Students: 20
Part-time Graduate Students: 12
Degrees in History: 35 BA, 11 MA, 15 BSEd
Undergraduate Addresses:
Admissions: http://www.ship.edu/Admissions/Undergraduate/Undergraduate_Home/
Financial Aid: http://www.ship.edu/financial_aid/
Graduate Addresses:
Admissions and Financial Aid: http://www.ship.edu/graduate/

Full-time Faculty

Bloom, John D. (PhD, Minnesota 1991; prof. and dir., grad. studies) US cultural, popular culture, oral; jdbloo@ship.edu

Burg, Steven B. (PhD, Wisconsin-Madison 1999; prof. and chair) public, modern US, public policy; sbburg@ship.edu

Clay, Catherine B. (PhD, Oregon 1989; assoc. prof.) Russian and eastern Europe, comparative women, Central Asia/Inner Asia/Europe; cbclay@ship.edu

Dessants, Betty A. (PhD, California, Berkeley 1995; prof.) US foreign relations, 20th-century US, teaching methods; badess@ship.edu

Dieterich-Ward, Allen J. (PhD, Michigan 2006; assoc. prof.) US, environmental, urban; ajdieterichward@ship.edu

Godshalk, David Fort (PhD, Yale 1992; prof.) African American, US social, American South; dfgods@ship.edu

Klein, Kim M. (PhD, Johns Hopkins 1998; prof.) colonial and revolutionary America, Canada; kmklei@ship.edu

Paul, Chandrika (PhD, Cincinnati 1997; prof.) South and Southeast Asia, British Empire; chpaul@ship.edu

Pierce, Gretchen Kristine (PhD, Arizona 2008; assoc. prof.) Latin America, women's studies; gkpierce@ship.edu

Quist, John W. (PhD, Michigan 1992; prof.) 19th-century US, US Civil War era, US South; jwquis@ship.edu

Senecal, Christine K. (PhD, Boston Coll. 1999; assoc. prof.) early medieval Europe, ancient Rome and Byzantium; cksene@ship.edu

Shaffer, Robert (PhD, Rutgers 2003; prof.) US foreign relations, 20th-century US, teaching methods; roshaf@ship.edu

Skaff, Jonathan K. (PhD, Michigan 1998; prof.) China, Japan, Inner Asia; jkskaf@ship.edu

Spicka, Mark E. (PhD, Ohio State 2000; prof.) Germany, modern Europe, world; mespic@ship.edu

Tulchin, Allan A. (PhD, Chicago 2000; assoc. prof.) early modern France, religion; aatulchin@ship.edu

Ulrich, Brian J. (PhD, Wisconsin, Madison 2008; assoc. prof.) Middle East, Islamic; bjulrich@ship.edu

Skidmore College

Dept. of History, 815 N. Broadway, Saratoga Springs, NY 12866-1632. 518.580.5260. Fax 518.580.5258. Email: tnechtma@skidmore.edu. Website: https://www.skidmore.edu/history/.

History is a way by which men and women come to understand who they are as human beings. It is the mission of the History Department to impart to students a solid knowledge of the past and to develop in them the ways of thinking they will need to make sense of broad patterns of change in different civilizations and cultures.

Chair: Tillman W. Nechtman
Degrees Offered: BA
Academic Year System: Semester
Areas of Specialization: Europe, US, East Asia, Latin America, British Empire
Tuition (per academic year): $54270
Enrollment 2018-19:
Undergraduate Majors: 54
Degrees in History: 28 BA
Addresses:
Admissions: http://www.skidmore.edu/admissions/
Financial Aid: http://www.skidmore.edu/financialaid/

Full-time Faculty

Bastress-Dukehart, Erica (PhD, California, Berkeley 1997; assoc. prof.) medieval and early modern Europe; bastress@skidmore.edu

Delton, Jennifer A. (PhD, Princeton 1997; prof.) 20th-century US, African American; jdelton@skidmore.edu

Dym, Jordana (PhD, NYU 2000; prof.) Latin America; jdym@skidmore.edu

Hockenos, Matthew D. (PhD, NYU 1998; prof.) modern Europe; mhockeno@skidmore.edu

Huangfu Day, Jenny (PhD, California, San Diego 2012; assoc. prof.) Asia; jhuangfu@skidmore.edu

Morser, Eric J. (PhD, Wisconsin, Madison 2002; prof.) early America; emorser@skidmore.edu

Nechtman, Tillman W. (PhD, Southern California 2005; prof. and chair) England, British Empire; tnechtma@skidmore.edu

Yildiz, Murat Cihan (PhD, UCLA 2015; asst. prof.) modern Middle East; myildiz@skidmore.edu

Nondepartmental Historians

Arnush, Michael (PhD, Pennsylvania 1991; assoc. prof.; Classics) Greek and Roman social and political; marnush@skidmore.edu

Retired/Emeritus Faculty

Eyman, David (MA, Ohio 1967; prof. emeritus) US military; deyman@skidmore.edu

Lee, Patricia-Ann (PhD, Columbia 1966; prof. emeritus) England, Tudor-Stuart England; plee@skidmore.edu

Pearson, Margaret J. (PhD, Washington 1983; prof. emeritus) China, Japan; mpearson@skidmore.edu

Van Meter, Robert, Jr. (PhD, Wisconsin, Madison 1971; lect. emeritus) US diplomatic; rvanmeter@skidmore.edu

Slippery Rock University

Dept. of History, 303 Spotts World Culture Bldg., Slippery Rock, PA 16057-1326. 724.738.2053. Fax 724.738.4762. Email: sruhistorydept@sru.edu. Website: https://www.sru.edu/academics/colleges-and-departments/cla/departments/history.

History is made every day, by all of us. We shape our society, our culture, our economy. And in turn, this historical moment makes us who we are. The faculty in the Department of History teaches courses that examine all regions of the world, and countless chapters of the human story. We want our students to understand that everybody's history is interdependent. We offer students the opportunity to be guided by their own interests, while also introducing them to new subjects and new ideas.

Chair: William Bergmann
Director of Graduate Studies: Paula Rieder
Degrees Offered: BA,BS,BSSecEd,MA
Academic Year System: Semester
Areas of Specialization: public, US social/cultural/intellectual, ancient/medieval/modern Europe
Undergraduate Tuition (per academic year):
  In-State: $10477
  Out-of-State: $18443
Graduate Tuition (per academic year):
  In-State: $12659
  Out-of-State: $18215
Enrollment 2018-19:
  Undergraduate Majors: 61
  New Graduate Students: 23
  Full-time Graduate Students: 5
  Part-time Graduate Students: 33
  Degrees in History: 12 BA, 7 MA
Undergraduate Addresses:
  Admissions: http://www.sru.edu/admissions
  Financial Aid: http://www.sru.edu/admissions/financial-aid
Graduate Addresses:
  Admissions: http://www.sru.edu/admissions/graduate-admissions
  Financial Aid: http://www.sru.edu/admissions/financial-aid

Full-time Faculty

Bergmann, William H. (PhD, Cincinnati 2005; assoc. prof. and chair) America; william.bergmann@sru.edu

Cowan, Aaron Bradley (PhD, Cincinnati 2008; assoc. prof.) US public, urban, comparative environmental; aaron.cowan@sru.edu

Denning, Margaret B. (PhD, Zurich, Switzerland 1986; prof.) modern world civilization, China and Japan; mbd@sru.edu

Ford, Melissa (PhD, St. Louis 2016; asst. prof.) American studies; melissa.ford@sru.edu

Levy, Alan H. (PhD, Wisconsin, Madison 1979; prof.) 20th-century US, intellectual, Russia and Soviet Union; alan.levy@sru.edu

Paradis, Lia (PhD, Rutgers 2005; assoc. prof.) 20th-century Britain, empire and decolonization, continental Europe; lia.paradis@sru.edu

Pearcy, Thomas L. (PhD, Miami 1993; prof.) Latin America, 20th-century US, modern world civilization; thomas.pearcy@sru.edu

Rieder, Paula M. (PhD, Illinois, Urbana-Champaign 2000; assoc. prof. and dir., grad. studies) medieval Europe, women, France; paula.rieder@sru.edu

Tuten, Eric E. (PhD, Utah 2000; asst. prof.) contemporary Middle East, Jewish, Islamic; eric.tuten@sru.edu

White, Carlis C. (PhD, Illinois, Urbana-Champaign 2001; assoc. prof.) ancient Rome and Greece; carlis.white@sru.edu

Retired/Emeritus Faculty

Craig, John M. (PhD, William and Mary 1986; prof. emeritus) diplomatic, colonial America, US women; john.craig@sru.edu

Nichols, John A. (PhD, Kent State 1974; prof. emeritus) medieval Europe, women, Renaissance and Reformation; john.nichols@sru.edu

Rotge, Larry R. (PhD, Ball State 1978; assoc. prof. emeritus) Tudor and Stuart England, early modern Europe

Smith College

Dept. of History, 5 Chapin Dr., Wright Hall #227, Northampton, MA 01063. 413.585.3702. Fax 413.585.3389. Email: lminnich@smith.edu. Website: https://www.smith.edu/academics/history.

The Department of History endeavors to cultivate a critical understanding of past and present human societies that will help students to become informed, thoughtful, and engaged participants in the world. By offering our students the opportunity to discover historical inquiry as a meaningful part of their humanistic formation, history contributes directly to the highest intellectual mission of the college.

Chair: Darcy Buerkle
Director of Graduate Studies: Patricia DiBartolo
Director of Undergraduate Studies: Deanna Dixon
Degrees Offered: BA,MA
Academic Year System: Semester
Areas of Specialization: Middle East, East Asia, Europe, US and Latin America, Africa
Tuition (per academic year): $53940
Enrollment 2018-19:
  Undergraduate Majors: 77
  Degrees in History: 30 BA
Undergraduate Addresses:
  Admissions: https://www.smith.edu/admission-aid
  Financial Aid: https://www.smith.edu/admission-aid/tuition-aid
Graduate Addresses:
  Admissions and Financial Aid: https://www.smith.edu/admission-aid/how-apply/graduate

Affiliated Faculty

Sierra Becerra, Diana (PhD, Michigan 2017; postdoc. fellow; Latin American & Latino/a Studies) digital humanities, popular political education; dbecerra@smith.edu

Full-time Faculty

Ahlman, Jeffrey S. (PhD, Illinois, Urbana-Champaign 2011; assoc. prof.) Africa; jahlman@smith.edu

Anderson, Marnie S. (PhD, Michigan 2005; assoc. prof.) Japan; msanders@smith.edu

Benz, Ernest (PhD, Toronto 1988; assoc. prof.) modern Europe; ebenz@smith.edu

Birk, Joshua Colin (PhD, California, Santa Barbara 2006; assoc. prof.) medieval Europe, medieval Islam, borderlands; jcbirk@smith.edu

Buerkle, Darcy C. (PhD, Claremont Grad. 2001; assoc. prof. and chair) modern Europe, women; dbuerkle@smith.edu

Gardner, Daniel K. (PhD, Harvard 1978; prof.) China; dgardner@smith.edu

Guglielmo, Jennifer M. (PhD, Minnesota 2003; assoc. prof.) US, women; jgugliel@smith.edu

Lim, Richard (PhD, Princeton 1991; prof.) ancient, late antiquity; rlim@smith.edu

Pryor, Elizabeth Stordeur (PhD, California, Santa Barbara 2009; assoc. prof.) African American, US women; epryor@smith.edu

Joint/Cross Appointments

Glebov, Sergey (PhD, Rutgers 2004; Five Coll. Assoc. Prof.; Amherst Coll.) Russia, Eurasia; sglebov@smith.edu

Nondepartmental Historians

Kim, Jina Eleanor (PhD, Washington 2006; asst. prof.) Korean Studies, East Asian Studies; jkim@smith.edu

Mathews, Barbara A. (PhD, Brown 1994; lect.; American Studies)

Wilson, Louis E. (PhD, UCLA 1980; prof.; Afro-American Studies) lwilson@smith.edu

Part-time Faculty

Gunn, Peter (MEd, Harvard 1988; lect.) US, education; pgunn@smith.edu

Hall-Witt, Jennifer L. (PhD, Yale 1996; lect.) British Empire; jhallwit@smith.edu

Retired/Emeritus Faculty

Afferica, Joan (PhD, Harvard 1967; prof. emeritus) Russia; jafferic@smith.edu

Haddad, Robert (PhD, Harvard 1965; prof. emeritus) Middle East; rhaddad@smith.edu

Horowitz, Daniel (PhD, Harvard 1967; prof. emeritus) US cultural and intellectual; dhorowit@smith.edu

Horowitz, Helen Lefkowitz (PhD, Harvard 1969; prof. emeritus) US cultural and social, US institutional, women; hhorowit@smith.edu

Little, Lester K., II (PhD, Princeton 1962; prof. emeritus) medieval Latin Christian social and religious; llittle@smith.edu

Nenner, Howard A. (PhD, California, Berkeley 1971; prof. emeritus) England; hnenner@smith.edu

Newbury, David S. (PhD, Wisconsin, Madison 1979; prof. emeritus) sub-Saharan Africa, social, environmental; dnewbury@smith.edu

Salisbury, Neal E. (PhD, UCLA 1972; lect. emeritus) North America to 1820, American Indian; nsalisbu@smith.edu

Stieber, Joachim W. (PhD, Yale 1974; prof. emeritus) late medieval, Renaissance and Reformation Europe; jstieber@smith.edu

Wilson, R. Jackson J. (PhD, Wisconsin, Madison 1964; prof. emeritus) US intellectual; rwilson@wilson.org

Zulawski, Ann (PhD, Columbia 1985; prof. emeritus) Latin America; azulawsk@smith.edu

Sonoma State University

Dept. of History, Stevenson Hall 2070, 1801 E. Cotati Ave., Rohnert Park, CA 94928-3609. 707.664.2313. Fax 707.664.3920. Email: steve.estes@sonoma.edu. Website: http://history.sonoma.edu.

The Department of History at Sonoma State University offers courses in US, European, Asian, and Latin American history in addition to courses with regional and thematic approaches. The department offers a BA and MA in history and a minor in history.

Chair: Steve Estes
Director of Graduate Studies: Stephen Bittner
Degrees Offered: BA, MA
Academic Year System: Semester
Areas of Specialization: US, medieval and early modern Europe, Russia and Soviet Union, Latin America, modern Asia and Pacific Basin
Undergraduate Tuition (per academic year):
  In-State: $7798
  Out-of-State: $17302
Graduate Tuition (per academic year):
  In-State: $9232
  Out-of-State: $18736
Enrollment 2018-19:
  Undergraduate Majors: 191
  New Graduate Students: 5
  Degrees in History: 61 BA, 5 MA
Addresses:
  Admissions: http://admissions.sonoma.edu
  Financial Aid: http://sonoma.edu/finaid

Adjunct Faculty

Chase, Robert G. (PhD, California, Irvine 2013; lect.) 19th- and 20th-century US, California, Australia

Markay, Jesse B. (ABD, New Mexico; lect.) US

Miller, Margaret A. (PhD, Washington 2000; lect.) US, Latin America

Full-time Faculty

Bittner, Stephen V. (PhD, Chicago 2000; prof. and grad. studies coord.) Russia, modern Europe; steve.bittner@sonoma.edu

Cohen, Samuel (PhD, Toronto 2013; asst. prof.) ancient and medieval; samuel.cohen@sonoma.edu

Estes, Steve (PhD, North Carolina, Chapel Hill 2001; prof. and chair) 20th-century US; steve.estes@sonoma.edu

Halavais, Mary Hoyt (PhD, California, San Diego 1997; prof.) early modern Europe, Spain and Latin America, minority; mary.halavais@sonoma.edu

Jolly, Michelle E. (PhD, California, San Diego 1998; prof.) US West, California, women; michelle.jolly@sonoma.edu

Kittelstrom, Amy Marie (PhD, Boston Univ. 2004; assoc. prof.) modern US, transnational intellectual culture; kitt@sonoma.edu

Noonan, Kathleen (PhD, California, Santa Barbara 1989; prof.) British Isles, colonial America, early modern Europe and Atlantic world; noonan@sonoma.edu

Retired/Emeritus Faculty

Abbott, Judith (PhD, Connecticut 1989; prof. emeritus) medieval Europe, Rome; judith.abbott@sbcglobal.net

Alfaro-Velcamp, Theresa (PhD, Georgetown 2001; prof. emeritus) Latin America, Mexico, borderlands

Brown, Robert (PhD, Paris 1963; prof. emeritus)

Dodgen, Randall (PhD, Yale 1989; prof. emeritus) modern Asia and Pacific Basin; dodgen@sonoma.edu

Jefferson, Robert (PhD, Utah 1972; lect. emeritus) late medieval Europe and Islamic, Tudor-Stuart England; rjefferson@sbcglobal.net

Karlsrud, Robert A. (PhD, UCLA 1972; prof. emeritus) American labor and social; bob.karlsrud@sonoma.edu

Markwyn, Daniel W. (PhD, Cornell 1970; prof. emeritus) early America, California and local; daniel.markwyn@sonoma.edu

Mellini, Peter J. D. (PhD, Stanford 1971; prof. emeritus) modern Britain and Europe, journalism and media, Middle East

Poe, William Clay (PhD, Brandeis 1971; prof. emeritus)

Price, Glenn W. (PhD, Southern California 1966; prof. emeritus)

Stasz, Clarice (PhD, Rutgers 1967; prof. emeritus) social, 20th-century US, historical methods; stasz@sonoma.edu

Watrous, Stephen D. (PhD, Washington 1970; prof. emeritus) Russia, modern Europe

White, D. Anthony (PhD, UCLA 1968; prof. emeritus) Latin America

The University of the South

Dept. of History, 735 University Ave., Sewanee, TN 37383-1000. 931.598.1723. Fax 931.598.1145. Email: kjwhitmer@sewanee.edu. Website: https://new.sewanee.edu/programs-of-study/history/.

Sewanee's history professors reflect diverse approaches to the study of the past with emphasis on the history of women and gender, medieval and early modern Europe, Russia, Southern Africa, Latin America and the colonization of the Americas, 19th- and 20th-century popular culture, African American history, and economics and society during and after the Reconstruction, among others.

Chair: Kelly J. Whitmer
Degrees Offered: BA
Academic Year System: Semester
Areas of Specialization: US, Europe, Latin America, Africa and Middle East, Atlantic world
Tuition (per academic year): $44848
Enrollment 2018-19:
Undergraduate Majors: 31
Degrees in History: 31 BA
Addresses:
Admissions and Financial Aid: http://admission.sewanee.edu/

Full-time Faculty

Berebitsky, Julie (PhD, Temple 1997; prof.) US women, family; jberebit@sewanee.edu

Goldberg, Harold J. (PhD, Wisconsin-Madison 1973; Underdown Prof.) Russia, China and East Asia; hgoldber@sewanee.edu

Levine, Roger S. (PhD, Yale 2004; assoc. prof.) Africa, environmental; rlevine@sewanee.edu

Mansker, Andrea N. (PhD, UCLA 2003; assoc. prof.) modern European cultural/intellectual/social, modern France, gender; amansker@sewanee.edu

McEvoy, Carmen E. (PhD, California, San Diego 1995; prof.) Latin America; cmcevoy@sewanee.edu

Mitchell, Matthew David (PhD, Pennsylvania 2012; asst. prof.) Great Britain, Atlantic world, slavery and slave trade; mdmitche@sewanee.edu

Register, Woody (PhD, Brown 1991; Houghteling Prof.) American cultural and intellectual, 20th-century US; wregiste@sewanee.edu

Ridyard, Susan J. (PhD, Cambridge 1983; prof.) medieval England, ancient Rome, medieval Europe; sridyard@sewanee.edu

Roberts, Nicholas Edward (PhD, NYU 2009; asst. prof.) modern Middle East, Islam; nerobert@sewanee.edu

Whitmer, Kelly (PhD, British Columbia 2008; assoc. prof. and chair) early modern Europe, science, social and intellectual; kjwhitme@sewanee.edu

Willis, John C. (PhD, Virginia 1991; duPont Prof.) 19th-century US, US South, environmental; jwillis@sewanee.edu

Retired/Emeritus Faculty

Perry, Charles R. (PhD, Harvard 1976; Kenan Prof. emeritus) modern England

Visiting Faculty

Allen, Jody L. (PhD, William and Mary 2007; vis. asst. prof.) African American; jlallen@sewanee.edu

Bhattacharjee, Dharitri (PhD, Texas, Austin 2015; vis. asst. prof.) India, Indian Ocean; dhbhatta@sewanee.edu

University of South Alabama

Dept. of History, 5991 USA Dr. N., Room 344, Mobile, AL 36688-0002. 251.460.6210. Fax 251.460.6750. Email: history@southalabama.edu. Website: https://www.southalabama.edu/colleges/artsandsci/history/.

Knowledge and awareness of history and society are important ingredients of a liberal education. The Department of History offers general courses for all students, a major and a minor in history, and preparation for students who plan to continue study at the graduate level, to teach history, or to enter related fields.

Chair: David A. Messenger
Director of Graduate Studies: Martha Jane Brazy
Degrees Offered: BA,MA
Academic Year System: Semester
Areas of Specialization: early modern Europe, modern Europe, US, US South, world, Jewish studies, science and medicine
Undergraduate Tuition (per academic year):
In-State: $7896
Out-of-State: $15792
Graduate Tuition (per academic year):
In-State: $7956
Out-of-State: $15912
Enrollment 2018-19:
Undergraduate Majors: 145
New Graduate Students: 5
Full-time Graduate Students: 7
Part-time Graduate Students: 10
Degrees in History: 24 BA, 2 MA
Undergraduate Addresses:
Admissions: http://southalabama.edu/departments/admissions/
Financial Aid: http://southalabama.edu/finaid/
Graduate Addresses:
Admissions and Financial Aid: http://www.southalabama.edu/colleges/artsandsci/history/gradprogram.html

Full-time Faculty

Brazy, Martha Jane L. (PhD, Duke 1998; assoc. prof. and coord., grad. studies) African American, social, southern women; mjbrazy@southalabama.edu

Cage, Claire (PhD, Johns Hopkins 2011; assoc. prof.) France, modern Europe; ccage@southalabama.edu

Faust, Robert E. (PhD, Missouri, Columbia 2003; sr. instr.) Western civilization and US; rfaust@southalabama.edu

Hamilton, Marsha L. (PhD, SUNY, Stony Brook 2001; assoc. prof.) colonial America; mhamilton@southalabama.edu

Kozelsky, Mara V. (PhD, Rochester 2004; prof.) modern Europe, Russia; mkozelsky@southalabama.edu

Lombardo, Timothy J. (PhD, Purdue 2013; asst. prof.) modern US

McKiven, Henry M. (PhD, Vanderbilt 1990; assoc. prof.) US South, Civil War and Reconstruction, American social; hmckiven@southalabama.edu

Meola, David (PhD, British Columbia 2012; asst. prof.) 19th-century Jewish

Messenger, David A. (PhD, Toronto 2000; prof. and chair) 20th-century Europe, modern Spain; davidamessenger@southalabama.edu

Miller, Harrison (PhD, Columbia 2001; prof.) Asia; hsmiller@southalabama.edu

Strong, Michele Marion (PhD, North Carolina, Chapel Hill 2004; assoc. prof.; advisor, Phi Alpha Theta) Great Britain, British Empire; mstrong@southalabama.edu

Urban, Kelly L. (PhD, Pittsburgh 2017; asst. prof.) US, Latin American studies; kurban@southalabama.edu

Williams, Rebecca R. (PhD, McGill 2007; assoc. prof.) Islamic civilization, classical, medieval; rwilliams@southalabama.edu

Part-time Faculty

Donald, William O. (MA, South Alabama 2002; instr.) Western civilization, US; wdonald@southalabama.edu

Green, Elizabeth V. (MA, South Alabama 2011; instr.) US; elizabethgreen@southalabama.edu

McWilliams, Tennant S. (PhD, Georgia 1973; instr.) 20th-century American politics and legal; tmcwilliams@southalabama.edu

Theodore, Philip (PhD, Alabama 1986; instr.) modern Europe, US; ptheodore@southalabama.edu

Tyson, Kara K. (OMS, Springhill 2011; instr.) Western civilization; ktyson@southalabama.edu

Retired/Emeritus Faculty

Brandon, Betty J. (PhD, North Carolina, Chapel Hill 1969; prof. emeritus) modern US, Progressive Era, women; howardbbran@aol.com

DeVore, Donald E. (PhD, Louisiana State 1989; prof. emeritus) US and African American studies; ddevore@southalabama.edu

Holmes, Larry E. (PhD, Kansas 1968; prof. emeritus) Russia, Soviet education, Soviet Union 1917-41

Houston, W. Robert (PhD, Rice 1972; assoc. prof. emeritus) military, military social, modern and contemporary Europe; whouston@jaguar1.usouthal.edu

Monheit, Michael Leonard (PhD, Princeton 1988; assoc. prof. emeritus) Reformation and early modern Europe; mmonheit@southalabama.edu

Rogers, Daniel E. (PhD, North Carolina, Chapel Hill 1990; prof. emeritus) modern Europe, modern Germany, Holocaust; drogers@southalabama.edu

Thomason, Michael V. (PhD, Duke 1968; prof. emeritus) Alabama, archival practice, Africa; jawa1@zebra.net

University of South Carolina Aiken

Dept. of History, Political Science and Philosophy, 471 University Pkwy., Aiken, SC 29801. 803.641.3498. Fax 803.641.3461. Email: georgian@usca.edu. Website: https://www.usca.edu/polisci/.

We are a community of active scholars and researchers, but our greatest source of pride is the quality of teaching we provide. Most of our faculty have either won or have been nominated for teaching awards at the local, state, and national levels. We are especially proud of the individual attention we provide our students, comparable with the kind found at the very best small, exclusive, liberal arts colleges, or at the graduate level.

Chair: D.B. Dillard-Wright
Degrees Offered: BA
Academic Year System: Semester
Areas of Specialization: American religion, immigration and ethnicity, Latin America, modern Europe, Ottoman Empire
Tuition (per academic year):
In-State: $10196
Out-of-State: $20102
Enrollment 2018-19:
Undergraduate Majors: 45
Degrees in History: 15 BA
Addresses:
Admissions: https://www.usca.edu/admissions/
Financial Aid: https://www.usca.edu/financialaid/

Full-time Faculty

Deal, Roger A. (PhD, Utah 2006; assoc. prof.) modern Middle East, Ottoman-Turkey; rogerd@usca.edu

Dwyer-Ryan, Meaghan (PhD, Boston Coll. 2010; asst. prof.) 19th- and 20th-century US, immigration/ethnicity/race, Gilded Age and Progressive Era; mdwyerryan@usca.edu

Georgian, Elizabeth A. (PhD, Delaware 2011; asst. prof.) American religion, early Republic, Methodism; georgian@usca.edu

Helsley, Alexia J. (MA, South Carolina 1974; sr. instr.) South Carolina, US South, public; alexiah@usca.edu

Peterson, Heather Rose (PhD, Texas, Austin 2009; asst. prof.) Mexico, Latin America; heatherp@usca.edu

Pierce, Samuel (PhD, Florida 2007; asst. prof.) Iberia, Europe; samuel.pierce@usca.edu

Retired/Emeritus Faculty

Brockington, William S., Jr. (PhD, South Carolina 1975; dist. prof. emeritus) military, modern Britain, British Empire; billb@usca.edu

Farmer, James O. (PhD, South Carolina 1982; dist. prof. emeritus) America, US South, South Carolina; jimf@usca.edu

Lacy, Elaine (PhD, Arizona State 1991; dist. prof. emeritus) Latin America, Mexico, gender studies; elainel@usca.edu

Lumans, Valdis O. (PhD, North Carolina, Chapel Hill 1979; dist. prof. emeritus) modern Germany, eastern Europe, Russia; vall@usca.edu

Smith, W. Calvin (PhD, North Carolina, Chapel Hill 1971; dist. prof. emeritus) America, US South, colonial

University of South Carolina, Columbia

Dept. of History, Gambrell Hall, Rm. 245, 817 Henderson St., Columbia, SC 29208-0001. 803.777.5165. Fax 803.777.4494. Email: jessicae@mailbox.sc.edu. Website: https://www.sc.edu/study/colleges_schools/artsandsciences/history/.

The Department of History is one of the university's "centers of excellence"—offering a strong and diverse program for both undergraduate and graduate students. The faculty includes outstanding scholars in fields ranging from North America, Latin America, Europe, and the non-Western world. Our Public History program is one of the oldest and storied in the United States.

Chair: Jessica I. Elfenbein
Director of Graduate Studies: Kent Germany

Director of Undergraduate Studies: Kathryn Edwards
Degrees Offered: BA, MA, PhD
Academic Year System: Semester
Areas of Specialization: US, US South, African American, Europe, public, science/technology/environment, medicine
Undergraduate Tuition (per academic year):
  In-State: $12738
  Out-of-State: $33627
Graduate Tuition (per academic year):
  In-State: $13650
  Out-of-State: $29196
Enrollment 2018-19:
  Undergraduate Majors: 350
  New Graduate Students: 11
  Full-time Graduate Students: 65
  Part-time Graduate Students: 3
  Degrees in History: 200 BA, 6 MA, 4 PhD
Undergraduate Addresses:
  Admissions: https://sc.edu/about/offices_and_divisions/undergraduate_admissions/
  Financial Aid: http://sc.edu/financialaid/
Graduate Addresses:
  Admissions and Financial Aid: https://www.sc.edu/study/colleges_schools/artsandsciences/history/study/graduate/

Adjunct Faculty

Risk, James (PhD, South Carolina 2017; adj. prof.) science, technology, transportation, maritime; risk@mailbox.sc.edu

Full-time Faculty

Ames, Christine Caldwell (PhD, Notre Dame 2002; prof.) medieval Europe; amesc@mailbox.sc.edu

Berns, Andrew (PhD, Pennsylvania 2011; assoc. prof.) Jewish, Renaissance Italy; aberns@mailbox.sc.edu

Brown, Thomas J. (PhD, Harvard 1995; prof.) 19th-century America; browntj@mailbox.sc.edu

Childs, Matt D. (PhD, Texas, Austin 2001; assoc. prof.) Cuba, comparative slavery; matchilds@yahoo.com

Coenen-Snyder, Saskia (PhD, Michigan 2008; assoc. prof.) Jewish, modern Europe; snydersc@mailbox.sc.edu

Donaldson, Bobby J. (PhD, Emory 2002; assoc. prof.; Center for Civil Rights History & Research) African American, American South; donaldbj@mailbox.sc.edu

Eatmon, Myisha S. (PhD, Northwestern 2019; instr.)

Edwards, Kathryn A. (PhD, California, Berkeley 1993; prof. and dir., undergrad. studies) Renaissance, Reformation, European sociocultural; edwards@mailbox.sc.edu

Elfenbein, Jessica I. (PhD, Delaware 1996; prof. and chair) American urban, public; jessicae@mailbox.sc.edu

Germany, Kent B. (PhD, Tulane 2000; prof. and dir., grad. studies) oral, modern US; germanyk@mailbox.sc.edu

Grace, Joshua Ryan (PhD, Michigan State 2013; asst. prof.) Africa; gracejr@mailbox.sc.edu

Harrison, Carol E. (DPhil, Oxford 1993; prof.) modern Europe, France, gender and religion; ceharris@mailbox.sc.edu

Holton, Abner L., III (PhD, Duke 1990; McCausland Prof.) early America; aholton@mailbox.sc.edu

Kuenzli, E. Gabrielle (PhD, Wisconsin-Madison 2005; assoc. prof.) Latin America, Andes; kuenzli@mailbox.sc.edu

Lekan, Thomas M. (PhD, Wisconsin-Madison 1999; prof.; Sch. of Earth, Ocean and Environment) modern German cultural, comparative environmental; lekan@sc.edu

Littlefield, Valinda W. (PhD, Illinois, Urbana-Champaign 2003; assoc. prof.; faculty athletic rep.) African American, African American education, African American women; littlevw@mailbox.sc.edu

MacKenzie, S. Paul (DPhil, Oxford 1989; Caroline McKissick Dial Prof.) 20th-century British military, cinema and British society; mackensp@mailbox.sc.edu

Marsh, Allison (PhD, Johns Hopkins 2007; assoc. prof.) public, material culture; marsha@mailbox.sc.edu

Maskiell, Nicole Saffold (PhD, Cornell 2013; asst. prof.) early America; maskiell@mailbox.sc.edu

Melvin-Koushki, Matthew (PhD, Yale 2012; McClausland Faculty Fellow) Islamic world, religion; mmelvink@sc.edu

November, Joseph A. (PhD, Princeton 2006; assoc. prof.) biomedical, computing; november@mailbox.sc.edu

Osokina, Elena A. (PhD, Moscow State 1998; prof.) Russia, modern Europe; osokina@mailbox.sc.edu

Patel, Dinyar (PhD, Harvard 2015; asst. prof.) South Asia; pateldi@mailbox.sc.edu

Schor, Adam M. (PhD, Michigan 2004; assoc. prof.) ancient and medieval Mediterranean; schor@mailbox.sc.edu

Sklaroff, Lauren R. (PhD, Virginia 2003; prof.) modern US; sklaroff@mailbox.sc.edu

Smith, Mark M. (PhD, South Carolina 1995; Carolina Dist. Prof.) slavery, 19th-century US, American South; smithmm@mailbox.sc.edu

Sullivan, Patricia A. (PhD, Emory 1983; prof.) African American, civil rights; psulliv@mailbox.sc.edu

Varlik, Nükhet (PhD, Chicago 2008; prof.) Ottoman Empire, early modern Mediterranean, medicine

Weyeneth, Robert (PhD, California, Berkeley 1984; prof.) public, modern US, environment; weyeneth@mailbox.sc.edu

Wilder, Colin F. (PhD, Chicago 2010; asst. prof.) digital, early modern Germany; wildercf@mailbox.sc.edu

Nondepartmental Historians

Ford, Lacy K., Jr. (PhD, South Carolina 1983; prof.; dean, Coll. of Arts and Sciences) US since 1789, American South; ford@mailbox.sc.edu

Schulz, Constance B. (PhD, Cincinnati 1973; prof. emeritus; editor, Pinckney Papers Project) public, archives, early national; schulz@mailbox.sc.edu

Part-time Faculty

Snyder, David Jonathan (PhD, Southern Illinois, Carbondale 2006; sr. instr.; Maxcy International House) US; snyderd@mailbox.sc.edu

Retired/Emeritus Faculty

Atkinson, Ronald R. (PhD, Northwestern 1978; assoc. prof. emeritus) ethnicity, sub-Saharan Africa; atkinson@mailbox.sc.edu

Augustinos, Gerasimos (PhD, Indiana 1971; prof. emeritus) eastern Europe, eastern Mediterranean, modern Greece; augustg@mailbox.sc.edu

Basil, John D. (PhD, Washington 1966; prof. emeritus) Russia; basil@mailbox.sc.edu

Beardsley, Edward H. (PhD, Wisconsin, Madison 1966; prof. emeritus) US, science, medicine

Carter, Dan T. (PhD, North Carolina, Chapel Hill 1967; prof. emeritus) US South; carterdt@mailbox.sc.edu

Clements, Kendrick A. (PhD, California, Berkeley 1970; prof. emeritus) US diplomatic; clements@mailbox.sc.edu

Doyle, Don H. (PhD, Northwestern 1973; McCausland Prof. emeritus) modern US; doyledh@mailbox.sc.edu

Edgar, Walter B. (PhD, South Carolina 1969; George Washington Dist. Prof. emeritus; dir., Inst. Southern Studies) colonial America, South Carolina; edgar@mailbox.sc.edu

Hendricks, Wanda A. (PhD, Purdue 1990; assoc. prof. emeritus) US, women, African American; hendricw@mailbox.sc.edu

Kinzley, W. Dean (PhD, Washington 1984; assoc. prof. emeritus) Japan, East Asia; kinzley@mailbox.sc.edu

Kross, Jessica (PhD, Michigan 1974; prof. emeritus) colonial America, social/cultural/religion; kross@mailbox.sc.edu

Littlefield, Daniel C. (PhD, Johns Hopkins 1977; Carolina Dist. Prof. emeritus) colonial America, African American; littledc@mailbox.sc.edu

Patterson, Robert B. (PhD, Johns Hopkins 1962; prof. emeritus) medieval Europe, medieval England; pattsn@mailbox.sc.edu

Perkins, Kenneth J. (PhD, Princeton 1973; prof. emeritus) Middle East, North Africa; perkins@mailbox.sc.edu

Peters, Kenneth E. (PhD, Michigan 1972; assoc. prof. emeritus) modern US; kepeters7@att.net

Salomon, Hilel B. (PhD, Columbia 1969; assoc. prof. emeritus) modern China, traditional Chinese political thought, Mongolia; hilele@yahoo.com

Scardaville, Michael C. (PhD, Florida 1977; assoc. prof. emeritus) Latin America, Mexico; scardavm@mailbox.sc.edu

Smith, Michael S. (PhD, Cornell 1972; prof. emeritus) modern France, European economic; smithm@mailbox.sc.edu

Spruill, Marjorie Julian (PhD, Virginia 1989; prof. emeritus) recent US, women; spruillm@mailbox.sc.edu

Synnott, Marcia G. (PhD, Massachusetts 1974; prof. emeritus) recent US, women, desegregation; synnott@mailbox.sc.edu

Terrill, Tom E. (PhD, Wisconsin, Madison 1966; prof. emeritus) US economic, industrial America; terrill@mailbox.sc.edu

Weir, Robert M. (PhD, Case Western Reserve 1966; prof. emeritus) colonial America, American Revolution; ar2weir@gmail.com

Wilson, Clyde N., Jr. (PhD, North Carolina, Chapel Hill 1971; prof. emeritus) US, Middle Period; cwilson@clicksouth.net

Recently Awarded PhDs

Angeloni, Gabriella "Reading Material: Personal Libraries and the Cultivation of Identity in Revolutionary South Carolina"

Cunningham, Candace "'I Hope They Fire Me': Black Teachers in the Fight for Equal Education 1910s"

Foghani, Sadegh "Ayatollahs and Embryos: Science, Politics, and Religion in Post-Revolutionary Iran"

Gunter, Jennifer Holman "Sex and the State: Sexual Politics in South Carolina in the 1970s"

Holmes, Erin Marie "Within the House of Bondage: Constructing and Negotiating the Plantation Landscape in the British Atlantic World, 1670-1820"

Keane-Dawes, Antony Wayne "A Divisive Community: Race, Nation, and Loyalty in Santo Domingo, 1822-1849"

Robinson, Brian "The Popular Education Question in Antebellum South Carolina, 1800-1860"

University of South Dakota

Dept. of History, 414 E. Clark St., East Hall, Vermillion, SD 57069-2390. 605.677.5218. Fax 605.677.5568. Email: history@usd.edu. Website: https://www.usd.edu/arts-and-sciences/history/.

Historians are part sleuth and part research scientist, sharing a curiosity about where we've come from and history's potential to influence where we are going. If you want to know how societies function, why something happened or changed, history will help you find the answers.

Chair: David Burrow
Director of Graduate Studies: Molly Rozum
Degrees Offered: BA,BS,MA

Academic Year System: Semester
Areas of Specialization: American West, South Dakota, 20th-century US, 19th-century US, modern Europe
Undergraduate Tuition (per academic year):
In-State: $7474
Out-of-State: $10248
Graduate Tuition (per academic year):
In-State: $6840
Out-of-State: $12250
Enrollment 2018-19:
Undergraduate Majors: 115
New Graduate Students: 6
Full-time Graduate Students: 12
Part-time Graduate Students: 2
Degrees in History: 15 BA, 20 BS, 4 MA
Undergraduate Addresses:
Admissions: http://www.usd.edu/admissions
Financial Aid: http://www.usd.edu/financial-aid/
Graduate Addresses:
Admissions: http://www.usd.edu/arts-and-sciences/history/graduate.cfm
Financial Aid: http://www.usd.edu/graduate-school/

Full-time Faculty

Boxer, Elise (PhD, Arizona State 2009; asst. prof.) Native American, Mormon, 19th- and 20th-century US; Elise.Boxer@usd.edu

Breuninger, Scott C. (PhD, Wisconsin, Madison 2002; assoc. prof. and dir., Honors Program) modern Britain/Ireland/Atlantic, European intellectual, European social; Scott.Breuninger@usd.edu

Bucklin, Steven J. (PhD, Iowa 1993; prof.) US diplomatic, 20th-century US, South Dakota; Steven.Bucklin@usd.edu

Burrow, David I. (PhD, Wisconsin, Madison 2005; assoc. prof. and chair) Russia, 20th-century Europe; david.burrow@usd.edu

Hackemer, Kurt H. (PhD, Texas A&M 1994; prof. and Univ. provost) 19th-century US, American military and naval, Civil War; Kurt.Hackemer@usd.edu

Lampert, Sara Elisabeth (PhD, Michigan 2012; assoc. prof.) women and gender, colonial and early America, race and ethnicity; Sara.Lampert@usd.edu

Lehmann, Clayton M. (PhD, Chicago 1986; prof.) ancient world, medieval Europe, early modern Europe; clehmann@usd.edu

Rozum, Molly P. (PhD, North Carolina, Chapel Hill 2001; assoc. prof. and dir., grad. studies) 20th-century US, Great Plains and Canadian borderlands, US women; Molly.Rozum@usd.edu

Southeastern Louisiana University

Dept. of History and Political Science, SLU 10895, Hammond, LA 70402. 985.549.2109. Fax 985.549.2012. Email: wrobison@selu.edu. Website: http://www.southeastern.edu/acad_research/depts/hist_ps/.

The Department of History and Political Science is unsurpassed among academic departments at Southeastern Louisiana University in scholarship, teaching, and service.

Chair: William B. Robison
Director of Graduate Studies: William B. Robison
Degrees Offered: BA,MA
Academic Year System: Semester
Areas of Specialization: US South, early US, recent US, Britain, Europe

Undergraduate Tuition (per academic year):
 In-State: $5715
 Out-of-State: $17734
Graduate Tuition (per academic year):
 In-State: $6260
 Out-of-State: $18279
Enrollment 2018-19:
 Undergraduate Majors: 350
 New Graduate Students: 27
 Full-time Graduate Students: 35
 Part-time Graduate Students: 75
 Degrees in History: 77 BA, 13 MA
Undergraduate Addresses:
 Admissions: http://www.southeastern.edu/admin/admissions/
 Financial Aid: http://www.southeastern.edu/admin/fin_aid/
Graduate Addresses:
 Admissions: http://www.southeastern.edu/apply/graduate/
 Financial Aid: http://www.southeastern.edu/admin/fin_aid/

Full-time Faculty

Ambrose, Edith (PhD, Tulane 1999; instr.) Louisiana, labor; Edith. Ambrose@selu.edu

Anderson, Angie (MA, Southeastern Louisiana 1995; instr.) Western civilization, US; aanderson2@selu.edu

Bell, Jeffrey (PhD, Tulane 1992; prof.) intellectual, philosophy; jeffrey.bell@selu.edu

Burns, Barbara (MEd, Southeastern Louisiana 1979; instr.) Western civilization, US; bburns@selu.edu

Cavell, Samantha (PhD, Exeter 2009; asst. prof.) naval, military; Samantha.Cavell@selu.edu

Chauvin, Munson (MA, Southeastern Louisiana; instr.) munson. chauvin@southeastern.edu

Corbello, M. Kurt (PhD, New Orleans 1992; assoc. prof.) southern politics; mcorbello@selu.edu

Doughty, Lauren (PhD, Louisiana State 2017; instr.) Lauren. Doughty@selu.edu

Elliott, Charles (MA, Southeastern Louisiana 1997; instr.) Louisiana; cnelliott@selu.edu

Finley, Keith M. (PhD, Louisiana State 2004; asst. prof.) civil rights, Congress; Keith.Finley@selu.edu

Gonzalez-Perez, Margaret (PhD, Louisiana State 1994; prof.) comparative politics, international relations; mgonzalez@selu. edu

Gratton, Peter (PhD, DePaul 2007; asst. prof.; Philosophy) Peter. Gratton@southeastern.edu

Hester, Bridget (MA, Southern Mississippi; instr.; Political Science) Bridget.Hester@southeastern.edu

Hyde, Samuel C. (PhD, Louisiana State 1992; prof.) Old and New US South, colonial America, East Asia; shyde@selu.edu

Ostarly, Lori (MA, Southeastern Louisiana 1990; instr.) Western civilization, US; lostarly@selu.edu

Perez, Samantha (PhD, Tulane 2018; asst. prof.) late medieval Europe, Renaissance, art; Samantha.Perez@selu.edu

Petrakis, Peter (PhD, Louisiana State 1998; assoc. prof.) political science, civil rights and constitutional, US government; ppetrakis@selu.edu

Price, Benjamin L. (PhD, Louisiana State 1998; instr.) colonial America; Benjamin.Price@selu.edu

Robison, William B., III (PhD, Louisiana State 1983; prof.; chair; and dir., grad. studies) Tudor-Stuart England, Reformation and medieval Europe; wrobison@selu.edu

Saucier, Craig (PhD, Louisiana State 2008; asst. prof.) Western civilization, US; csaucier@selu.edu

Traver, Andrew G. (PhD, Toronto 1996; prof.) medieval Europe, ancient; atraver@selu.edu

Traylor, Ronald (PhD, Houston 2005; instr.) African American, US South; Ronald.Traylor@selu.edu

Part-time Faculty

Fontenot, Michael J. (PhD, Louisiana State 1976; instr.) Russia, Middle East; Michael.Fontenot@southeastern.edu

Retired/Emeritus Faculty

Nichols, C. Howard (MA, Louisiana State 1958; prof. emeritus) Louisiana; hnichols@selu.edu

Visiting Faculty

Isenhower, Zachary C. (PhD, Louisiana State 2018; vis. asst. prof.) zachary.isenhower@selu.edu

University of Southern California

Dept. of History, 3502 Trousdale Pkwy., SOS 153, Los Angeles, CA 90089-0034. 213.740.1657. Fax 213.740.6999. Email: history@ dornsife.usc.edu. Website: https://dornsife.usc.edu/hist.

The History Department is dedicated to core values, which we pursue with a diverse and growing faculty working at the forefront of historical scholarship in a wide range of fields.

Chair: Philip Ethington
Director of Graduate Studies: Paul Lerner
Director of Undergraduate Studies: Lindsay O'Neill
Degrees Offered: BA, PhD
Academic Year System: Semester
Areas of Specialization: Americas, Asia, Europe
Tuition (per academic year): $57256
Enrollment 2018-19:
 Undergraduate Majors: 275
 New Graduate Students: 7
 Full-time Graduate Students: 29
 Degrees in History: 54 BA, 7 MA, 1 PhD
Undergraduate Addresses:
 Admissions: http://www.usc.edu/admission/
 Financial Aid: http://financialaid.usc.edu/
Graduate Addresses:
 Admissions: https://dornsife.usc.edu/hist/graduate/
 Financial Aid: http://financialaid.usc.edu/

Adjunct Faculty

Estrada, William D. (PhD, UCLA 2003; adj. asst. prof.; curator and chair, History; Natural History Museum) California, Los Angeles, public; westrada@nhm.org

Gillerman, Sharon I. (PhD, UCLA 1996; adj. assoc. prof.; Hebrew Union Coll.) German and European Jewish, gender; gillerma@ usc.edu

Holter, Darryl Oliver (PhD, Wisconsin, Madison 1980; assoc. prof.) US and European labor and business, Los Angeles; dholter@usc. edu

Ritchie, Robert C. (PhD, UCLA 1972; prof.; sr. research assoc., Huntington Library) early America, maritime; rritchie@ huntington.org

Westwick, Peter J. (PhD, California, Berkeley 1999; research prof.) modern science and technology, Cold War US, California; westwick@usc.edu

Full-time Faculty

Antaramian, Richard (PhD, Michigan 2014; asst. prof.) Ottoman, Armenia, networks; antarami@usc.edu

Baumgartner, Alice (PhD, Yale 2018; asst. prof.) 19th-century US, US-Mexico borderlands, slavery and emancipation; albaumga@ usc.edu

Becker, Marjorie R. (PhD, Yale 1988; assoc. prof.) Latin America, Latin American and Mexican gender/ethnicity/culture/revolution, creative writing; mbecker@usc.edu

Bleichmar, Daniela (PhD, Princeton 2005; assoc. prof.; Art Hist.) early modern Spanish Empire, science, visual culture; bleichma@usc.edu

Deverell, William (PhD, Princeton 1989; prof.; dir., Huntington-USC Inst. on California and West) US West; deverell@usc.edu

Echols, Alice (PhD, Michigan 1986; prof.) modern US, gender and sexuality, popular music; echols@usc.edu

Ethington, Philip J. (PhD, Stanford 1989; prof. and chair) interdisciplinary urban, 20th-century US, new media; philipje@usc.edu

Fox, Richard Wightman (PhD, Stanford 1975; prof.) American cultural and intellectual; rfox@usc.edu

Glenn, Jason K. (PhD, California, Berkeley 1997; assoc. prof.) medieval Europe; jkglenn@usc.edu

Goldstein, Joshua L. (PhD, California, San Diego 1999; assoc. prof.) East Asia; jlgoldst@usc.edu

Gruner, Wolf (PhD, Tech., Berlin 1994; prof. and Shapell-Guerin Chair in Jewish Studies; dir., USC Shoah Foundation Center fo Advanced Genocide Research) Third Reich and Holocaust in Europe, comparative genocide, 19th- and 20th-century Latin American race relations; gruner@usc.edu

Gualtieri, Sarah M. (PhD, Chicago 2000; assoc. prof.) Arab Americans, modern Middle East, gender and migration; gualtier@usc.edu

Halttunen, Karen (PhD, Yale 1979; prof.) American cultural and intellectual; halttune@usc.edu

Harkness, Deborah E. (PhD, California, Davis 1994; prof.) early modern European science, early modern England, London; deharkne@usc.edu

Hwang, Kyung Moon (PhD, Harvard 1997; prof.) Korea, comparative social and cultural, historical memory; khwang3@gmail.com

Kurashige, Lon Y. (PhD, Wisconsin, Madison 1994; prof.) Asian American, US immigration and ethnicity, cultural; kurashig@usc.edu

Lerner, Paul F. (PhD, Columbia 1996; prof. and dir., grad. studies; dir., Max Kade Inst. for Austrian-German-Swiss Studies) modern central Europe, medicine and psychiatry, German Jewish; plerner@usc.edu

Mancall, Peter C. (PhD, Harvard 1986; Andrew W. Mellon Prof. of Humanities; Linda and Harlan Martens Dir., USC-Huntington Early Modern Studies Inst.) early America, Atlantic world, Native American; mancall@usc.edu

Maskarinec, Maya (PhD, UCLA 2015; asst. prof.) early medieval Europe and Mediterranean, Rome, hagiography and historiography; maskarin@usc.edu

Morgan, Alaina (PhD, NYU 2017; asst. prof.) Islam in North America, African diaspora, African American; alainamo@usc.edu

O'Neill, Lindsay J. (PhD, Yale 2008; teaching asst. prof. and dir., undergrad. studies) early modern England, Atlantic world; ljoneill@usc.edu

Pant, Ketaki (PhD, Duke 2015; asst. prof.) South Asia, Indian Ocean; kpant@usc.edu

Perez Morales, Edgardo (PhD, Michigan 2013; asst. prof.) colonial Latin America, Age of Atlantic Revolutions, slavery and emancipation; perezmor@usc.edu

Perl-Rosenthal, Nathan Raoul (PhD, Columbia 2011; assoc. prof.) colonial America, early modern Europe, Atlantic world; perlrose@usc.edu

Piggott, Joan R. (PhD, Stanford 1987; Gordon L. MacDonald Prof.; dir., Proj. for Premodern Japan Studies/Kambun Workshops)

pre-1600 monarchy/church and state relations, family and gender, city and countryside; joanrp@usc.edu

Ross, Steven J. (PhD, Princeton 1980; prof.; dir., Casden Inst. for the Study of the Jewish Role in American Life) US social, film, political; sjross@usc.edu

Rouighi, Ramzi (PhD, Columbia 2005; assoc. prof.) Mediterranean, medieval, North Africa; rouighi@usc.edu

Rubenstein, Jay C. (PhD, California, Berkeley 1997; prof.) medieval Europe, Crusades, intellectual; jayruben@usc.edu

Sanchez, George J. (PhD, Stanford 1989; prof.) Chicano/a, immigration, American West; georges@usc.edu

Schwartz, Vanessa R. (PhD, California, Berkeley 1993; prof.; Art Hist.) modern Europe, France and US, visual culture; vschwart@usc.edu

Sheehan, Brett G. (PhD, California, Berkeley 1997; prof.) modern China, social, business and economic; bsheehan@usc.edu

Soll, Jacob S. (PhD, Cambridge 1998; Univ. prof.) early modern Europe, politics, economic; soll@usc.edu

Uchiyama, Benjamin (PhD, Southern California 2013; asst. prof.) modern Japan; buchiyam@usc.edu

Velmet, Aro (PhD, NYU 2017; asst. prof.) modern Europe, global, science/technology/medicine; velmet@usc.edu

Joint/Cross Appointments

Birge, Bettine (PhD, Columbia 1992; assoc. prof.; East Asian Languages and Cultures) premodern China and Inner Asia, law, gender and ethnicity; birge@usc.edu

Bitel, Lisa M. (PhD, Harvard 1987; prof.; Religion) early medieval, religion, Celtic; bitel@usc.edu

Braudy, Leo (PhD, Yale 1968; Univ. Prof.; English) 17th- and 18th-century England, post-1945 US, film; braudy@usc.edu

Fischer Bovet, Christelle (PhD, Stanford 2008; assoc. prof.; Classics) Greece, Greco-Roman Egypt, ethnicity; fischerb@usc.edu

Gross, Ariela J. (PhD, Stanford 1996; JD, Stanford 1994; prof.; Law Sch.) legal, slavery and race relations, 19th-century US; agross@law.usc.edu

Klerman, Daniel M. (PhD, Chicago 1998; JD, Chicago 1991; prof.; Law Sch.) legal, economic, England; dklerman@law.usc.edu

Malone, Carolyn M. (PhD, California, Berkeley 1973; prof.; Art Hist.) French Romanesque, English Gothic architecture, medieval liturgy; cmalone@usc.edu

Pollini, John (PhD, California, Berkeley 1978; USC Associates Endowed Prof.; Art History) Roman art and archaeology, Greek art and archaeology, ancient Rome; pollini@usc.edu

Shah, Nayan B. (PhD, Chicago 1995; prof.; American Studies and Ethnicity) US and Canada, gender and sexuality studies, legal and medical; nayansha@dornsife.usc.edu

Sloane, David C. (PhD, Syracuse 1984; prof.; Price Sch. of Public Policy) 20th-century US, cultural and urban, medicine; dsloane@price.usc.edu

Wilson, Francille Rusan (PhD, Pennsylvania 1988; assoc. prof.; American Studies and Ethnicity) African American, labor, women; frwilson@usc.edu

Nondepartmental Historians

Robison, Mark Power (PhD, Colorado, Boulder 2000; assoc. prof.; research assoc. prof., Sch. Education) colonial North America, French and British Canada, New England; mrobison@usc.edu

Retired/Emeritus Faculty

Accampo, Elinor Ann (PhD, California, Berkeley 1984; prof. emerita) French social and cultural, gender/feminism/sexuality, disease and epidemics; accampo@usc.edu

Banner, Lois W. (PhD, Columbia 1970; prof. emerita) gender, social, popular and visual culture; lbanner@usc.edu

Bennett, Judith M. (PhD, Toronto 1981; John R. Hubbard Prof. emerita) late medieval, women and gender, England; judith.bennett@usc.edu

Berger, Gordon M. (PhD, Yale 1972; prof. emeritus) Japan, trans-Pacific relations, psychohistory; gberger@usc.edu

Dingman, Roger V. (PhD, Harvard 1969; prof. emeritus) American diplomatic/naval/military, Pacific and East Asian international; dingmanr@aol.com

Furth, Charlotte D. (PhD, Stanford 1965; prof. emerita) late imperial and modern China, gender, medicine; cdfurth@gmail.com

Herrup, Cynthia B. (PhD, Northwestern 1982; John R. Hubbard Prof. emerita) early modern England, legal, cultural; herrup@usc.edu

Knoll, Paul W. (PhD, Colorado, Boulder 1964; prof. emeritus) late medieval east central Europe, Renaissance, universities; knoll@usc.edu

Mitchell, Franklin D. (PhD, Missouri, Columbia 1964; prof. emeritus) 20th-century US, Truman administration; history@usc.edu

Nagle, D. Brendan (PhD, Southern California 1968; prof. emeritus) Roman Republic, Roman social, ancient Mediterranean; nagle@usc.edu

Rorlich, Azade-Ayse (PhD, Wisconsin, Madison 1976; prof. emeritus) Russia/USSR/Islam in Eurasia, identity, Muslim visual culture; arorlich@usc.edu

Seip, Terry L. (PhD, Louisiana State 1974; assoc. prof. emeritus) American South, Civil War and Reconstruction, quantitative and teaching methods; tseip@usc.edu

Shammas, Carole (PhD, Johns Hopkins 1971; John R. Hubbard Prof. emerita) early America, early modern Britain, socioeconomic; shammas@usc.edu

Recently Awarded PhDs

Stoddard, Angelica "Defining Worthiness: Veteran Mental Health in California, from Uneven Investment to Deinstitutionalization, 1941-67"

Southern Connecticut State University

Dept. of History, Engleman Hall C 205 A, 501 Crescent St., New Haven, CT 06515-1355. 203.392.5600. Fax 203.392.8835. Email: pettoc1@southernct.edu. Website: https://www.southernct.edu/history/.

The History Department offers students a comprehensive curriculum that focuses on a deep understanding of the myriad forces creating our modern world. The department offers a BA or a BS degree, and a BS degree with secondary teaching certification, as well as MA and post baccalaureate degrees.

Chair: Christine M. Petto
Director of Graduate Studies: Byron Nakamura
Degrees Offered: BA,BS,MA
Academic Year System: Semester
Areas of Specialization: US, East and Southeast Asia, Europe, Middle East, Latin America and Africa
Undergraduate Tuition (per academic year):
  In-State: $10954
  Out-of-State: $23463
Graduate Tuition (per academic year):
  In-State: $12143
  Out-of-State: $24345

Enrollment 2018-19:
  Undergraduate Majors: 256
  New Graduate Students: 8
  Full-time Graduate Students: 3
  Part-time Graduate Students: 36
Undergraduate Addresses:
  Admissions: http://www.southernct.edu/admissions/
  Financial Aid: http://www.southernct.edu/admissions/undergraduate/financial-aid/
Graduate Addresses:
  Admissions: http://www.southernct.edu/academics/graduate/
  Financial Aid: http://www.southernct.edu/academics/graduate/financinged.html

Full-time Faculty

Amerman, Stephen K. (PhD, Arizona State 2002; prof.) American West, American Indian, environmental; amermans1@southernct.edu

Beals, Polly A. (PhD, Rutgers 1989; assoc. prof.) modern Britain, European women, socialism and feminism; bealsp1@southernct.edu

Carter-David, Siobhan (PhD, Indiana 2011; assoc. prof.) African American, American culture/fashion/beauty, urban; carterdavis1@southernct.edu

Chrissidis, Nikolaos A. (PhD, Yale 2000; prof.) early modern and modern Russian religious and cultural, Balkans, Eastern Orthodoxy; chrissidisn1@southernct.edu

Coury, Carmen (PhD, Yale 2012; asst. prof.) colonial and modern Latin America, immigration

Judd, Steven C. (PhD, Michigan 1997; prof.) Middle East, Islam; judds1@southernct.edu

Kern, Darcy (PhD, Georgetown 2012; asst. prof.) medieval Spain and Venice political, language and translation, religion; kernd2@southernct.edu

Madison, Julian C. (PhD, Washington 1996; assoc. prof.) African American, 20th-century US sports and culture, racism and American law; madisonj1@southernct.edu

McDaniel, Marie Basile (PhD, California, Davis 2010; assoc. prof.) colonial America, religion, ethnicity; mcdanielm4@southernct.edu

Nakamura, Byron J. (PhD, Washington 1999; assoc. prof. and dir., grad. studies) ancient Greece/Rome, late Roman Empire, ancient religion; nakamurab1@southernct.edu

Paddock, Troy R.E. (PhD, California, Berkeley 1994; prof.) modern Europe and Germany, European intellectual and historiography, environmental; paddockt1@southernct.edu

Petto, Christine M. (PhD, Indiana 1996; prof. and chair) early modern France, science, cartography; pettoc1@southernct.edu

Radice, Thomas A. (PhD, Pennsylvania 2006; assoc. prof.) early China, Chinese intellectual, East Asia; radicet1@southernct.edu

Rondinone, Troy M. (PhD, UCLA 2003; prof.) US, methodology; rondinonet1@southernct.edu

Smith, Jason W. (PhD, Temple 2012; asst. prof.) maritime, military, environmental

Thompson, C. Michele (PhD, Washington 1997; prof.) Southeast Asia, medicine, military intelligence; thompsonc2@southernct.edu

Part-time Faculty

Nakamura, Lisa E. (PhD, Washington 1999; adj.) science, Victorian Britain

Retired/Emeritus Faculty

Davis, Hugh H. (PhD, Ohio State 1969; prof. emeritus) 19th-century US, social/cultural/intellectual; davish1@southernct.edu

Feinberg, Harvey M. (PhD, Boston Univ. 1969; prof. emeritus) West and South Africa, Ghana, European ethnic conflict; feinbergh1@southernct.edu

Friedlander, Alan R. (PhD, California, Berkeley 1982; prof. emeritus) Middle Ages, France, church and inquisition; friedlandea1@southernct.edu

Gerber, Richard A. (PhD, Michigan 1967; prof. emeritus) US and English constitutional, US intellectual, Reconstruction; gerberr1@southernct.edu

House, Lewis (PhD, NYU 1969; prof. emeritus) US, Latin America

Lee, Ta-Ling (PhD, NYU 1967; prof. emeritus) US, East Asia

Metaxas, Virginia A. (PhD, SUNY, Stony Brook 1984; prof. emeritus) US women, medical, Hawaii; metaxasv1@southernct.edu

Purmont, Jon E. (PhD, Columbia 1988; prof. emeritus) US, colonial America, Connecticut; purmontj1@southernct.edu

Wright, William D. (PhD, SUNY, Buffalo 1985; prof. emeritus) Russia, African American, Western civilization

Southern Illinois University Carbondale

Dept. of History, Faner Hall 3374, 1000 Faner Dr., Carbondale, IL 62901-4519. 618.453.4391. Fax 618.453.5440. Email: history@siu.edu. Website: https://cola.siu.edu/history/.

The Department of History is strongly committed to creating an environment that is supportive of students from diverse backgrounds while upholding the most rigorous academic standards. Our courses cover the globe, and students are given ample opportunity to work closely with award-winning teachers and scholars.

Chair: Jonathan Bean
Director of Graduate Studies: Hale Yilmaz
Director of Undergraduate Studies: Joseph Sramek
Degrees Offered: BA,BS,MA,PhD
Academic Year System: Semester
Areas of Specialization: US, Europe, Latin America, Africa, Middle East
Undergraduate Tuition (per academic year): $9638
Graduate Tuition (per academic year):
  In-State: $14085
  Out-of-State: $35213
Enrollment 2018-19:
  Undergraduate Majors: 84
  New Graduate Students: 8
  Full-time Graduate Students: 14
  Part-time Graduate Students: 16
  Degrees in History: 18 BA, 13 BS, 3 MA, 2 PhD
Undergraduate Addresses:
  Admissions: http://siu.edu/admissions/
  Financial Aid: http://fao.siu.edu/
Graduate Addresses:
  Admissions and Financial Aid: https://cola.siu.edu/history/graduate/

Full-time Faculty

Bean, Jonathan J. (PhD, Ohio State 1994; prof. and chair) US economic, business, public policy; jonbean@siu.edu

Benti, Getahun (PhD, Michigan State 2000; assoc. prof.) modern Africa, urbanization and migration; benti@siu.edu

Brown, Ras Michael (PhD, Georgia 2004; assoc. prof.) Atlantic, Africa; rasmlb@siu.edu

Najar, Jose D. (PhD, Indiana 2012; lect.) Latin America, Brazil; jnajar@siu.edu

Player, Tiffany (PhD, Washington, St. Louis 2018; asst. prof.) African American, 19th-century US; tplayer@siu.edu

Smoot, Pamela (PhD, Michigan State 1999; asst. prof.) US, African American, West Africa; olivia@siu.edu

Sramek, Joseph M. (PhD, Grad. Center, CUNY 2007; assoc. prof. and dir., undergrad. studies) British Empire, colonial India; sramek@siu.edu

Weeks, Theodore R. (PhD, California, Berkeley 1992; prof.) Russia, Poland, eastern European nationalities; tadeusz@siu.edu

Whaley, Gray H. (PhD, Oregon 2002; assoc. prof.) American Indian; gwhaley@siu.edu

Yilmaz, Hale (PhD, Utah 2006; assoc. prof. and dir., grad. studies) Islamic, modern Turkey; yilmaz@siu.edu

Retired/Emeritus Faculty

Allen, Howard W. (PhD, Washington 1959; prof. emeritus) recent US; hwallen@siu.edu

Allen, James Smith (PhD, Tufts 1979; prof. and assoc. provost emeritus) modern Europe; jsallen@siu.edu

Argersinger, JoAnn E. (PhD, George Washington 1980; prof. emeritus) American labor; jarger@siu.edu

Argersinger, Peter H. (PhD, Wisconsin, Madison 1970; prof. emeritus) American political and policy, American rural; parger@siu.edu

Batinski, Michael C. (PhD, Northwestern 1969; prof. emeritus) early America, cultural; batinski@siu.edu

Bengtson, Dale R. (PhD, Hartford Seminary Found. 1971; asst. prof. emeritus) religious, Africa; bengtson@siu.edu

Carr, Kay J. (PhD, Chicago 1987; assoc. prof. emeritus) 19th-century US, environmental, American social; kjcarr@siu.edu

Carrott, M. Browning, Jr. (PhD, Northwestern 1966; assoc. prof. emeritus) US constitutional and legal; carrott@siu.edu

Conrad, David E. (PhD, Oklahoma 1962; prof. emeritus) US economic; dconrad@siu.edu

Dotson, John E. (PhD, Johns Hopkins 1969; prof. emeritus) Renaissance, medieval, Italy; jdotson@siu.edu

Fanning, Charles F. (PhD, Pennsylvania 1972; prof. emeritus) Ireland and Irish American, immigration and ethnic studies; celtic42@siu.edu

Gold, Robert L. (PhD, Iowa 1964; prof. emeritus) Latin America

Haller, John S., Jr. (PhD, Maryland, Coll. Park 1968; prof. emeritus) US intellectual, science and medicine; jhaller@notes.siu.edu

Lacey, Vincent A. (, Southern Illinois, Carbondale 1985; assoc. prof. emeritus) US, Southeast Asia, quantitative; vlacey@siu.edu

Lieberman, Robbie (PhD, Michigan 1984; prof. emeritus) recent US, cultural, peace movement; robl@siu.edu

Murphy, James B. (PhD, Louisiana State 1968; assoc. prof. emeritus) US South

O'Day, Edward J., Jr. (MA, Indiana 1956; assoc. prof. emeritus) modern Europe; edoday@siu.edu

Stocking, Rachel L. (PhD, Stanford 1994; assoc. prof. emeritus) Europe, ancient and early medieval; stocking@siu.edu

Werlich, David P. (PhD, Minnesota 1968; prof. emeritus) Latin America, Peru; elmaximo@siu.edu

Wilson, David L. (PhD, Tennessee, Knoxville 1974; prof. emeritus) American foreign relations, 20th-century Sino-American relations; dwilson@siu.edu

Recently Awarded PhDs

Brouwer, Nathan J. "This is Your Nation on Drugs: The War on Drugs and the Making of Contemporary America, 1980-94"

Li, Lu "Find a Way Home: Vietnamese Adoption and the Memory of the Vietnam War"

Podesva, James "Exporting America: The US Information Centers and German Reconstruction"

University of Southern Indiana

Dept. of History, Coll. of Liberal Arts, 8600 University Blvd., Evansville, IN 47712. 812.461.5219. Fax 812.465.7152. Email: jhardgrave@usi.edu. Website: https://www.usi.edu/liberal-arts/history/.

The History Department supports USI's mission of creating an engaged learning community advancing education and knowledge, enhancing civic and cultural awareness and fostering partnerships through comprehensive outreach programs.

Chair: Jason D. Hardgrave
Degrees Offered: BA,BS
Academic Year System: Semester
Areas of Specialization: US, Europe, Middle East, public, secondary education
Tuition (per academic year):
In-State: $6152
Out-of-State: $15085
Enrollment 2018-19:
Undergraduate Majors: 125
Degrees in History: 4 BA, 12 BS
Students in Undergraduate Courses: 1484
Students in Undergraduate Intro Courses: 913
Online-Only Courses: 10%
Addresses:
Admissions: http://www.usi.edu/admission
Financial Aid: http://www.usi.edu/finaid/

Full-time Faculty

Beeby, James M. (PhD, Bowling Green State 1999; prof. and dean) African American, US Gilded Age and Progressive Era; jmbeeby@usi.edu

Dixon, Michael D. (PhD, Ohio State 2000; prof.) Greece, Rome, Greek epigraphy; mdixon@usi.edu

Hardgrave, Jason D. (PhD, Kansas 2004; assoc. prof. and chair) medieval Europe, gender; jhardgrave@usi.edu

Harison, Casey (PhD, Iowa 1993; prof.; dir., Center for Communal Studies) modern Europe, France; charison@usi.edu

Hoyer, Cacee (PhD, Texas, Austin 2016; asst. prof.) history education, modern Africa; choyer@usi.edu

Hughes, Sakina Mariam (PhD, Michigan State 2012; asst. prof.) African American, American Indian, ethnohistory; shughes1@usi.edu

Hunt, Tamara L. (PhD, Illinois, Urbana-Champaign 1989; prof.) early modern Britain, publishing and book, 18th-century caricature; tlhunt@usi.edu

King, Anya (PhD, Indiana 2007; assoc. prof.) medieval Middle East, Silk Road; aking13@usi.edu

Lynn, Denise Marie (PhD, SUNY, Binghamton 2006; assoc. prof.) modern US, women; dmlynn1@usi.edu

Ress, Stella A. (PhD, Loyola, Chicago 2014; asst. prof.) public, modern US, gender; sress@usi.edu

Shefveland, Kristalyn Marie (PhD, Mississippi 2010; assoc. prof.) colonial America, Native American, Atlantic world; kmshefvela@usi.edu

Retired/Emeritus Faculty

Bigham, Darrel E. (PhD, Kansas 1970; prof. emeritus; dir., Hist. Southern Indiana Proj.) Indiana, 20th-century US, religion; dbigham@usi.edu

Pitzer, Donald E. (PhD, Ohio State 1966; prof. emeritus; dir., Center Communal Studies) US social and intellectual, communal utopias, American foreign relations; dpitzer@usi.edu

Reid, Robert Louis (PhD, Northwestern 1968; prof. emeritus) US; rreid@usi.edu

Scavone, Daniel C. (PhD, Loyola, Chicago 1969; prof. emeritus) medieval; dcscavon@usi.edu

University of Southern Maine

Dept. of History, 100 Payson Smith Hall, Portland, ME 04104. 207.780.4283. Fax 207.780.5311. Email: gjohnson@maine.edu; nicole.leclerc@maine.edu. Website: https://usm.maine.edu/history.

Alternate Address: 37 College Ave., Gorham, ME 04038

History majors and minors at USM become familiar with past knowledge, the forces of change and the varieties of historical scholarship that examine cultures and events across all times and places.

Chair: Gary Johnson
Degrees Offered: BA
Academic Year System: Semester
Areas of Specialization: American and African American, Maine and New England, ancient and Near East, East Asia, social studies teaching certification
Tuition (per academic year):
In-State: $7590
Out-of-State: $9120
New England and Canada: $9120
Enrollment 2018-19:
Undergraduate Majors: 165
Degrees in History: 37 BA
Addresses:
Admissions: http://usm.maine.edu/admission
Financial Aid: http://usm.maine.edu/student-financial-services

Full-time Faculty

Bischof, Elizabeth M. (PhD, Boston Coll. 2005; assoc. prof.; dir., Center for Collaboration and Development) US, cultural, photography; Elizabeth.Bischof@maine.edu

Johnson, Gary J. (PhD, Michigan 1984; assoc. prof. and coord.) ancient, religion; gjohnson@maine.edu

Rowe, Leroy Milton (PhD, Missouri, Columbia 2012; asst. prof.) African American, childhood, gender studies; leroy.rowe@maine.edu

Sparks, Lacey A. (PhD, Kentucky 2017; asst. prof.) food, Europe and Africa, women and gender; lacey.sparks@maine.edu

Tuchinsky, Adam Max (PhD, North Carolina, Chapel Hill 2001; assoc. prof.; dean, Coll. of Arts, Humanities, and Social Sciences) 19th-century US, Civil War, intellectual; adam.tuchinsky@maine.edu

Zhao, Jie (PhD, Princeton 1995; assoc. prof.) East Asia, 16th- and 17th-century China, intellectual; zhaoj@maine.edu

Southern Methodist University

William P. Clements Dept. of History, PO Box 750176, Dallas, TX 75275-0176. 214.768.2984. Fax 214.768.2404 Email: hist@smu.edu. Website: https://www.smu.edu/dedman/academics/departments/history.

Alternate Address: For courier delivery: Dept. of History, 3225 University, Suite 71, Dallas, TX 75205

Our faculty members are dedicated teachers and distinguished scholars, specializing in fields ranging from North America, Latin America, Europe, and the non-Western world. We are committed to the pursuit of knowledge and the education of our students.

Chair: Thomas Knock
Director of Graduate Studies: John Chavez
Director of Undergraduate Studies: Sabri Ates
Degrees Offered: BA,MA,PhD
Academic Year System: Semester
Areas of Specialization: America, Europe, US Southwest, Middle East, Asia
Undergraduate Tuition (per academic year): $48190
Graduate Tuition (per academic year): $34776
Enrollment 2018-19:
   Undergraduate Majors: 88
   New Graduate Students: 6
   Full-time Graduate Students: 16
   Part-time Graduate Students: 6
   Degrees in History: 29 BA, 2 MA, 1 PhD
Undergraduate Addresses:
   Admissions: http://www.smu.edu/admission
   Financial Aid: http://www.smu.edu/Admission/FinancialAid
Graduate Addresses:
   Admissions: http://www.smu.edu/Graduate
   Financial Aid: http://www.smu.edu/Admission/FinancialAid

Full-time Faculty

Andrien, Kenneth J. (PhD, Duke 1977; Edmund and Louise Kahn Prof.) colonial Latin America, Atlantic world, Andes; kandrien@smu.edu

Ates, Sabri (PhD, NYU 2005; assoc. prof. and dir., undergrad. studies) modern Middle East, Kurdish, late Ottoman-Iran; sates@smu.edu

Chavez, John R. (PhD, Michigan 1980; prof. and dir., grad. studies) North Atlantic, colonial borderlands, Mexican Americans; jchavez@smu.edu

Countryman, Edward F. (PhD, Cornell 1971; Univ. Dist. Prof.) colonial America, American Revolution, Native Americans; ecountry@smu.edu

DeLuzio, Crista J. (PhD, Brown 1999; assoc. prof.) American women, intellectual, cultural; cdeluzio@smu.edu

Dowling, Melissa Barden (PhD, Columbia 1994; assoc. prof.; dir., Classical Studies) Greece, Rome; mdowling@smu.edu

Engel, Jeffrey A. (PhD, Wisconsin-Madison 2001; assoc. prof.; dir., Center for Presidential History) American political, foreign relations; jaengel@smu.edu

Engel, Katherine Carte (PhD, Wisconsin, Madison 2003; assoc. prof.) early America, Atlantic, religious; kengel@smu.edu

Foley, Neil (PhD, Michigan 1990; Robert and Nancy Dedman Prof.; co-dir., Clements Center for Southwest Studies) US-Mexico borderlands, immigration, race/ethnicity; foleyn@smu.edu

Graybill, Andrew R. (PhD, Princeton 2003; prof.; co-dir., Clements Center for Southwest Studies) US West, borderlands, environmental; agraybill@smu.edu

Guldi, Joanna (PhD, California, Berkeley 2008; asst. prof.) Britain, empire, digital; jguldi@smu.edu

Hamilton, Kenneth M. (PhD, Washington, St. Louis 1978; assoc. prof.; dir., Ethnic Studies) African American, US; kmarvin@smu.edu

Hochman, Erin R. (PhD, Toronto 2010; assoc. prof.) modern Germany; ehochman@smu.edu

Kelly, Jill E. (PhD, Michigan State 2012; asst. prof.) Africa, South Africa; jillk@smu.edu

Knock, Thomas J. (PhD, Princeton 1982; prof. and chair) foreign relations, 20th-century US; tknock@smu.edu

Lopez, Bianca (PhD, Washington, St. Louis 2016; asst. prof.) medieval Europe

McCrossen, Alexis (PhD, Harvard 1995; prof.) US social and cultural; amccross@smu.edu

Orlovsky, Daniel T. (PhD, Harvard 1976; prof.) Russia, Soviet Union; dorlovsk@smu.edu

Ron, Ariel (PhD, California, Berkeley 2012; asst. prof.) Civil War and Reconstruction, early America, scientific agriculture

Shiao, Ling A. (PhD, Brown 2008; asst. prof.) East Asia; lshiao@smu.edu

Wellman, Kathleen (PhD, Chicago 1983; prof.) France, intellectual, early modern Europe; kwellman@smu.edu

Part-time Faculty

Doyle, David D., Jr. (PhD, Grad. Center, CUNY 2003; adj. asst. prof.; dir., Univ. Honors Prog.) US, sexuality; ddoyle@smu.edu

Halperin, Rick (PhD, Auburn 1978; prof. of practice of human rights; dir., Human Rights Education Prog.) antebellum US South, human rights; rhalperi@smu.edu

Miller, Brandon Gray (PhD, Michigan State 2013; adj. asst. prof.) Russia/former Soviet Union, gender; bgmiller@smu.edu

Winnie, Laurence H. (PhD, Michigan 1988; sr. lect.) French church; lwinnie@smu.edu

Retired/Emeritus Faculty

Bakewell, Peter J. (PhD, Cambridge 1969; Edmund and Louise Kahn Prof. emeritus) colonial Latin America; bakewell@smu.edu

Breeden, James O. (PhD, Tulane 1967; prof. emeritus) US South, medicine, science; jbreeden@smu.edu

Davis, Ronald L. (PhD, Texas, Austin 1961; prof. emeritus) US social and cultural

Hargrave, O. T. (PhD, Vanderbilt 1966; prof. emeritus) Tudor-Stuart England

Hopkins, James K. (PhD, Texas, Austin 1972; prof. emeritus) modern Britain; hopkins@smu.edu

Martin, Luis (PhD, Columbia 1966; prof. emeritus) Latin America, Spain

Mears, John A. (PhD, Chicago 1964; assoc. prof. emeritus) early modern Europe; jmears@smu.edu

Niewyk, Donald L. (PhD, Tulane 1968; prof. emeritus) modern Europe, Germany; dniewyk@smu.edu

Smith, Sherry L. (PhD, Washington 1984; prof. emeritus) American West, American Indian, public; sherrys@smu.edu

Recently Awarded PhDs

Zapata, Joel "The Mexican Southern Plains: Creating an Ethnic Mexican Homeland on the Llano"

University of Southern Mississippi

Dept. of History, 118 College Dr. #5047, Hattiesburg, MS 39406-0001. 601.266.4320. Fax 601.266.5757. Email: history@usm.edu. Website: https://www.usm.edu/humanities.

What makes the History Department at Southern Miss unique is our breadth of course offerings, our nationally recognized programs, and our committed faculty. We are big enough to offer quality programs, yet personal enough to give students individual attention. The department's faculty include award-winning authors and teachers--nationally acknowledged experts in their fields. It is a great place to learn.

Chair: Matthew Casey
Director of Graduate Studies: Kyle F. Zelner
Director of Undergraduate Studies: Brian LaPierre
Degrees Offered: BA,MA,MS,PhD,Cert. (public hist.)
Academic Year System: Semester
Areas of Specialization: early America and US, war and society, American South, modern Europe, cultural and gender
Tuition (per academic year):
In-State: $8896
Out-of-State: $10896
Enrollment 2018-19:
Undergraduate Majors: 230
New Graduate Students: 12
Full-time Graduate Students: 46
Part-time Graduate Students: 10
Degrees in History: 61 BA, 6 MA, 1 MS, 3 PhD, 2 Cert.
Undergraduate Addresses:
Admissions: https://www.usm.edu/admissions
Financial Aid: https://www.usm.edu/financial-aid
Graduate Addresses:
Admissions: https://www.usm.edu/graduate-school
Financial Aid: https://www.usm.edu/financial-aid

Full-time Faculty

Abra, Allison J. (PhD, Michigan 2009; assoc. prof.) modern Britain and Europe, popular culture, gender; allison.abra@usm.edu

Bristol, Douglas Walter, Jr. (PhD, Maryland, Coll. Park 2002; assoc. prof.) African American, business, cultural; douglas.bristol@usm.edu

Casey, Matthew (PhD, Pittsburgh 2012; assoc. prof. and dir., Sch. of Humanities) Latin America and Caribbean, race/ethnicity/gender, labor; matthew.casey@usm.edu

Chambers, Douglas Brent (PhD, Virginia 1996; assoc. prof.) sub-Saharan Africa, black Atlantic, comparative slavery; douglas.chambers@usm.edu

Follett, Westley N. (PhD, Toronto 2002; assoc. prof.) medieval, religious, Ireland; westley.follett@usm.edu

Greene, Kevin D. (PhD, North Carolina, Greensboro 2011; asst. prof.) African American, modern US, American music; kevin.greene@usm.edu

Grivno, Max L. (PhD, Maryland, Coll. Park 2007; assoc. prof.) US South, labor, slavery; max.grivno@usm.edu

Haley, Andrew P. (PhD, Pittsburgh 2005; assoc. prof.) US cultural, culinary, class; andrew.haley@usm.edu

Haynes, Joshua S. (PhD, Georgia 2013; asst. prof.) Native American, early America, public; joshua.haynes@usm.edu

LaPierre, Brian (PhD, Chicago 2006; assoc. prof. and dir., undergrad. studies) Soviet Union, 19th-century Russia, social and cultural; brian.lapierre@usm.edu

Luckhardt, Courtney L. (PhD, Notre Dame 2011; asst. prof.) early and high medieval, medieval Mediterranean, hagiography; courtney.luckhardt@usm.edu

Peterson, Joseph W. (PhD, Yale 2017; asst. prof.) modern and revolutionary France, Europe, political, religious; joseph.peterson@usm.edu

Stephens, Deanne (PhD, Southern Mississippi 1996; prof.; assoc. dean, Gulf Coast Campus) pedagogy, Mississippi, social; deanne.nuwer@usm.edu

Stur, Heather Marie (PhD, Wisconsin, Madison 2008; assoc. prof.) 20th-century US, foreign relations, war and gender; heather.stur@usm.edu

Swope, Kenneth M., Jr. (PhD, Michigan 2001; prof.) late imperial China, comparative military, East Asian diplomatic; kenneth.swope@usm.edu

Tuuri, Rebecca A. (PhD, Rutgers 2012; assoc. prof.) African American, civil rights, gender; rebecca.tuuri@usm.edu

Ural, Susannah J. (PhD, Kansas State 2002; prof.) US Civil War era, war and society, Reconstruction South; susannah.ural@usm.edu

Wiest, Andrew A. (PhD, Illinois, Chicago 1990; Univ. Dist. Prof.) war and society, Vietnam War, World War I; andrew.wiest@usm.edu

Zelner, Kyle F. (PhD, William and Mary 2003; assoc. prof. and dir., grad. studies) colonial and revolutionary America, war and society, social; kyle.zelner@usm.edu

Retired/Emeritus Faculty

Ciccarelli, Orazio A. (PhD, Florida 1969; prof. emeritus) Latin America, modern Peru, immigration; ocarelli@msn.com

Farrell, Mary Beth (MA, Southern Mississippi 1986; instr. emeritus) pedagogy, social studies licensure, world; mary.farrell@usm.edu

McMillen, Neil R. (PhD, Vanderbilt 1969; prof. emeritus) 20th-century US, New US South, African American; nmcmillen@aol.com

Morgan, Chester M. (PhD, Memphis 1982; prof. emeritus) US South, politics, Mississippi; b.morgan@usm.edu

Scarborough, William K. (PhD, North Carolina, Chapel Hill 1962; prof. emeritus) Old US South, Civil War; william.scarborough@usm.edu

Smith, James Patterson (PhD, Vanderbilt 1984; prof. emeritus) Britain, colonial, modern Europe; jamespat.smith@usm.edu

Visiting Faculty

Bourdon, Jeffrey Normand (PhD, Mississippi 2010; vis. asst. prof.) 19th-century US, politics, pedagogy

Recently Awarded PhDs

Cantrell, Kelly E. "Consuming Victory: American Women and the Politics of Food Rationing during World War II"

Colbourn, Colin M. "Esprit de Marine Corps: The Making of the Modern Marine Corps through Public Relations, 1911-50"

Wade, Eve J. "Becoming Bronzeville: The Origin of the Black Metropolis in a Southern City"

Southern Oregon University

Dept. of History & Political Science, 1250 Siskiyou Blvd., Ashland, OR 97520-5083. 541.552.6124. Fax 541.552.6439. Email: walcherd@sou.edu. Website: https://sou.edu/academics/history/.

The History Program comprises a community of students, teachers, and scholars who are dedicated to analyzing the past and serving as responsible global citizens. Together we probe the stories and experiences of peoples who have lived throughout the United States and on every corner of the globe, from antiquity to the present. In the process, History students cultivate advanced skills as critical thinkers, researchers, writers, and public speakers.

Chair: Dustin Walcher
Degrees Offered: BA,BS
Academic Year System: Quarter
Areas of Specialization: US, Europe, Latin America, Atlantic world, international
Tuition (per academic year):
In-State: $6600
Out-of-State: $16500
Enrollment 2018-19:
Undergraduate Majors: 80
Degrees in History: 5 BA, 12 BS

Addresses:
Admissions: http://www.sou.edu/enrollment/
Financial Aid: http://www.sou.edu/enrollment/financial-aid/

Full-time Faculty

Hughes, William (PhD, California, Davis 1995; assoc. prof.; Political Science) modern US, comparative political; whughes@sou.edu
McEnroe, Sean F. (PhD, California, Berkeley 2009; assoc. prof.) Latin America, Atlantic world; mcenroes@sou.edu
Pavlich, Paul (JD, California, Berkeley 1982; asst. prof.; Political Science) US constitutional, legal; pavlich@sou.edu
Walcher, Dustin (PhD, Ohio State 2007; prof. and chair) international, US foreign relations, Western Hemisphere; walcherd@sou.edu

Retired/Emeritus Faculty

Carney, Todd F. (PhD, Oregon 1995; assoc. prof. emeritus) American West, environment, family; tcarney@sou.edu
Frey, Richard C., Jr. (PhD, Oregon 1969; prof. emeritus) US, historiography
Gernant, Karen (PhD, Oregon 1980; prof. emeritus) world civilization, China and Japan, women
Harrison, Robert T. (PhD, Southern California 1987; prof. emeritus) world civilization, Britain and England, 20th-century Europe
Kunze, Neil L. (PhD, UCLA 1971; prof. emeritus; dean, Sch. Social Science and Education) modern Britain; kunze@sou.edu
Miller, Gary M. (PhD, Florida 1985; prof. emeritus) world civilization, ancient, early modern Europe; miller@sou.edu
Sundwick, Karen S. (PhD, New Mexico 1986; prof. emeritus) world civilization, Latin America and Mexico, Mexican American

University of South Florida, St. Petersburg

Dept. of History and Politics, 100 Snell House, 501 Second St. S., Saint Petersburg, FL 33701. 729.873.4458. Fax 727.873.4878. Email: jmfrancis1@mail.usf.edu. Website: http://www.usfsp.edu/hp/.

The common thread linking our diverse faculty is a passion for teaching and scholarship. We truly care about the students we teach and want to make a difference by conveying our knowledge in the classroom and through professional outlets in our respective disciplines.

Chair: J. Michael Francis
Director of Graduate Studies: Chris Meindl
Degrees Offered: BA,MLA
Academic Year System: Semester
Areas of Specialization: America, modern Europe, Latin America, Africa, early modern Mediterranean
Undergraduate Tuition (per academic year):
In-State: $5811
Out-of-State: $16726
Graduate Tuition (per academic year):
In-State: $7662
Out-of-State: $15686
Enrollment 2018-19:
Undergraduate Majors: 190
New Graduate Students: 8
Full-time Graduate Students: 6
Part-time Graduate Students: 12
Degrees in History: 26 BA, 7 MLA

Undergraduate Addresses:
Admissions: http://www.usfsp.edu/undergraduate-admissions/
Financial Aid: http://www.usfsp.edu/financial-aid/
Graduate Addresses:
Admissions: http://www.usfsp.edu/graduate-admissions/
Financial Aid: http://www.usfsp.edu/financial-aid/

Adjunct Faculty

Boyer, Patrice (MA, Case Western Reserve 2006; adj.) art
Golenbock, Peter (JD, NYU 1970; adj.) sports
Knudsen, Donna (OMS, South Florida, St. Petersburg 2012; adj.) US
McCreery, Gregory (MA, South Florida 2012; adj.) philosophy
Paris, Christy (MA, Florida State 2013; adj.) art
Shedden, Dawn L. (PhD, Florida 2013; adj.) Europe, Germany, Italy
Slattery, Tim (PhD, South Florida 2014; adj.) modern political thought
Stanfield, Michael (MA, South Florida 2015; MA, Iowa 2010; adj.) philosophy
Vogt, Albert (PhD, Loyola, Chicago 2013; adj.) US, film, music
Walker, David (MA, South Florida, St. Petersburg 2004; JD, Stetson 1965; adj.) US, legal
Weeks, Patricia (PhD, South Florida 2013; adj.) China, politics, cultural

Full-time Faculty

Arsenault, Raymond O. (PhD, Brandeis 1981; John Hope Franklin Prof.) US South, race and civil rights, US political and social; roarsenault@gmail.com
Bundrick, Sheramy (PhD, Emory 1998; assoc. prof.; Art Hist.) classical Greek/Roman/Etruscan art, Van Gogh; bundrick@mail.usf.edu
Francis, J. Michael (PhD, Cambridge 1998; Hough Family Chair and dept. chair) early Florida, colonial Latin America, Spain; jmfrancis1@mail.usf.edu
Jimenez Bacardi, Arturo (PhD, California, Irvine 2015; asst. prof.) international relations, national security
Kopytoff, Larissa (PhD, NYU 2018; instr.) modern Africa, France, French Empire; kopytoff@mail.usf.edu
LaFollette, Hugh (PhD, Vanderbilt 1977; Marie and Leslie E. Cole Chair) ethics, moral philosophy; hhl@mail.usf.edu
Mantilla, Luis-Felipe (PhD, Georgetown 2012; asst. prof.; Politics) comparative politics, Latin America, Middle East; lfm1@mail.usf.edu
Mbatu, Richard (PhD, Oklahoma State 2006; asst. prof.) geography, environmental studies, Africa
McLauchlan, Judithanne Scourfield (PhD, Rutgers 2003; assoc. prof.; Politics) American politics and government, constitutional law, political campaigns; jsm2@usfsp.edu
Meindl, Chris (PhD, Florida 1996; assoc. prof.; dir., Florida Studies Grad. Prog.) Florida, water resources
O'Connor, Adrian D. (PhD, Pennsylvania 2009; asst. prof.) France, French Revolution, modern Europe; oconnora@mail.usf.edu
Smith, Thomas (PhD, Virginia 1997; assoc. prof. and assoc. chair; Politics) political thought, human rights, politics and literature; twsmith2@mail.usf.edu

Nondepartmental Historians

Johns, Rebecca (PhD, Rutgers 1994; Frank Duckwall assoc. prof.; Geography) environmental thought, urban Florida

Retired/Emeritus Faculty

Fernandez, Susan J. (PhD, Florida 1987; assoc. prof. emeritus) Cuba, film

Mormino, Gary R. (PhD, North Carolina, Chapel Hill 1977; prof. emeritus) Florida, foodways
Paulson, Daryl (PhD, Florida State 1975; prof. emeritus) American politics

Visiting Faculty

Heinsen-Roach, Erica (PhD, Miami 2012; vis. asst. prof.) early modern Mediterranean, captivity and slavery, Netherlands; heinsenroach@usf.edu
Jones, Peyton (ABD, Tulane; vis. instr.) US, US South, urban race

University of South Florida, Tampa

Dept. of History, SOC 260, 4202 E. Fowler Ave., Tampa, FL 33620-8100. 813.974.2809. Fax 813.974.6228. Email: lewist@usf.edu. Website: https://www.usf.edu/arts-sciences/departments/history/.

Our faculty seeks to inform and question, to provoke, and to challenge our students to a higher level of understanding of the past. History at USF offers the student an opportunity to explore civilizations from around the globe and from the ancient through contemporary eras.

Chair: Brian Connolly
Director of Graduate Studies: Kees Boterbloem
Director of Undergraduate Studies: Steven Prince
Degrees Offered: BA,MA,PhD
Academic Year System: Semester
Areas of Specialization: US, modern Europe, Latin America, ancient/medieval/early modern world, Russia, digital humanities
Undergraduate Tuition (per academic year):
   In-State: $3927
   Out-of-State: $11895
Graduate Tuition (per academic year):
   In-State: $7829
   Out-of-State: $15471
Enrollment 2018-19:
   Undergraduate Majors: 315
   New Graduate Students: 12
   Full-time Graduate Students: 60
   Part-time Graduate Students: 5
   Degrees in History: 117 BA, 9 MA, 2 PhD
Addresses:
   Admissions: https://www.usf.edu/admissions/
   Financial Aid: https://www.usf.edu/financial-aid/

Full-time Faculty

Belohlavek, John M. (PhD, Nebraska 1970; prof.) 19th-century US, early national, Middle Period; belohlav@usf.edu
Benadusi, Giovanna (PhD, Syracuse 1988; prof.) early modern Europe, gender and social, Italian Renaissance; benadusi@usf.edu
Boterbloem, Kees (Case) (PhD, McGill 1994; prof. and grad. coord.) Soviet Union, Netherlands, European expansion; cboterbl@usf.edu
Cali, Denise (MA, Catania, Italy 2004; instr.) medieval archaeology; denisecali@usf.edu
Connolly, Brian (PhD, Rutgers 2007; assoc. prof. and chair) 19th-century US, family and sexuality; bconnolly@usf.edu
Decker, Michael J. (DPhil, Oxford 2001; prof.) Byzantine, Mediterranean, economy and society; mjdecker@usf.edu
Dosal, Paul J. (PhD, Tulane 1987; prof., on admin. leave) Latin America, Caribbean; pdosal@usf.edu

Dukes-Knight, Jennifer (PhD, Harvard 2011; instr.) Celtic, early medieval, Ireland; jlknight@usf.edu
Fontaine, Darcie S. (PhD, Rutgers 2011; assoc. prof.) modern Europe, French colonial, women and gender; dfontaine@usf.edu
Irwin, Julia F. (PhD, Yale 2009; assoc. prof.) US in world, science; juliai@usf.edu
Johnson, David K. (PhD, Northwestern 2000; prof.) US since 1945, Cold War political culture, gay and lesbian; davidjohnson@usf.edu
King, Matt (PhD, Minnesota 2018; asst. prof.) medieval; matthewking1@usf.edu
Langford, Julie (PhD, Indiana 2005; assoc. prof.) ancient Rome, gender and society; langford@usf.edu
Levy, Philip A. (PhD, William and Mary 2001; prof.) colonial and revolutionary America, historical archaeology; plevy@usf.edu
Murray, William M. (PhD, Pennsylvania 1982; prof.) ancient Greek history and archaeology, ancient naval war and seafaring; murray@usf.edu
Novoa, Adriana I. (PhD, California, San Diego 1998; assoc. prof.) Latin America, science, race and gender; ainovoa@usf.edu
Ottanelli, Fraser M. (PhD, Syracuse 1987; prof.) 20th-century US, US radical movements, labor and ethnicity; ottanelli@usf.edu
Prince, K. Stephen (PhD, Yale 2010; assoc. prof. and undergrad. prog. dir.) 19th- and 20th-century US, modern South, Civil War and Reconstruction; ksp@usf.edu
Ramos, Frances L. (PhD, Texas, Austin 2005; assoc. prof.) colonial Latin America, Mexico; framos@usf.edu
Tanasi, Davide (PhD, Catania, Italy 2012; assoc. prof.) Mediterranean archaeology, digital imaging; dtanasi@usf.edu
Thomas, David Jason (PhD, Brown 2016; instr.) Greece and Rome, medieval, Greek epigraphy; davidjthomas@usf.edu

Part-time Faculty

Murray, Suzanne (PhD, Minnesota 1981; instr.) Bronze Age Greek art and archaeology; spmurray@usf.edu

Retired/Emeritus Faculty

Ingalls, Robert P. (PhD, Columbia 1973; prof. emeritus) 20th-century US, labor
Kleine, Georg H. (PhD, Erlangen-Nurnberg, Germany 1967; assoc. prof. emeritus) modern Europe; kleine@honors.usf.edu

Recently Awarded PhDs

Beeler, David "Persisting in the Negative: the Banishment, Exile, and Execution of Gerard Udinck, 1657-65"
Brown, Jeffrey Neal "A Tall Ship: The Rise of the International Mercantile Marine"
Buchanan, Ashley Lynn "The Politics of Medicine at the Late Medici Court: The Recipe Collection of Anna Maria Luisa de' Medici (1667-1743)"
Hartsfield, Byron J. "Changing Narratives of Martyrdom in the Works of Huguenot Printers during the Wars of Religion"
Laffer, Dennis Ross "Jewish Trail of Tears II: Children Refugee Bills of 1939 and 1940"
Taylor, Joshua S. "'I Think of the Future': The Long 1850s and the Origins of the Americanization of the World"

Southwestern University

Dept. of History, 1001 E. University Ave., Georgetown, TX 78626. 512.863.1414. Fax 512.863.1535. Email: byrnesm@southwestern.edu. Website: https://www.southwestern.edu/history/.

The Southwestern History program provides students with an especially strong global perspective and a solid grounding in the methods and fields of history, while also encouraging interdisciplinary connections.

Chair: Melissa Byrnes
Degrees Offered: BA
Academic Year System: Semester
Areas of Specialization: East Asia, Europe, Latin America, US, science and medicine
Tuition (per academic year): $48430
Enrollment 2018-19:
   Undergraduate Majors: 41
   Degrees in History: 6 BA
   Students in Undergraduate Courses: 341
   Students in Undergraduate Intro Courses: 65
Addresses:
   Admissions: http://www.southwestern.edu/admission/
   Financial Aid: http://www.southwestern.edu/aid/

Full-time Faculty

Byrnes, Melissa K. (PhD, Georgetown 2008; assoc. prof. and chair) modern France, North Africa, immigration and race in Europe; byrnesm@southwestern.edu
Hernandez Berrones, Jethro (PhD, California, San Francisco 2014; asst. prof.) Latin America, medicine, science; hernandj@southwestern.edu
Hower, Jessica S. (PhD, Georgetown 2013; assoc. prof.) early modern Europe, Atlantic world, Britain; howerj@southwestern.edu
Hower, Joseph E. (PhD, Georgetown 2013; asst. prof.) US, labor; howerj2@southwestern.edu

Retired/Emeritus Faculty

Allen, Martha M. (PhD, Texas, Austin 1972; prof. emeritus) colonial America, western and women
Crowley, Weldon S. (PhD, Iowa 1966; prof. emeritus) Europe, historiography, macrohistory
Davidson, Steven C. (PhD, Wisconsin, Madison 1982; prof. emeritus) China, Japan, historiography; davidsos@southwestern.edu
Dawson, Jan C. (PhD, Washington 1976; prof. emeritus) US, women, environmental; dawsonj@southwestern.edu
McClendon, Thomas V. (PhD, Stanford 1995; prof. emeritus) Africa, colonial, legal; mcclendt@southwestern.edu

Spelman College

Dept. of History, Box 823, 350 Spelman Ln. SW, Atlanta, GA 30314-4399. 404.681.3643. Fax 404.270.5508. Email: jmercada@spelman.edu. Website: https://www.spelman.edu/academics/majors-and-programs/history.

The study of history is an important component of a meaningful and comprehensive liberal arts education. As such, our major provides a unique opportunity for students to understand how the past informs our understanding of the present.

Chair: Yan Xu
Degrees Offered: BA
Academic Year System: Semester
Areas of Specialization: US and African American, Europe, Africa, Asia, Latin America and Caribbean

Tuition (per academic year):
   In-State: $27314
   Out-of-State: $40109
Enrollment 2018-19:
   Undergraduate Majors: 25
   Degrees in History: 8 BA
Addresses:
   Admissions: http://www.spelman.edu/admissions
   Financial Aid: http://www.spelman.edu/admissions/financial-aid

Full-time Faculty

Brimmer, Brandi Clay (PhD, UCLA 2005; assoc. prof.) bbrimmer@spelman.edu
De Sousa, Dalila (PhD, Bowling Green State 1987; assoc. prof.) Latin America, Brazil; ddesousa@spelman.edu
Phillips-Lewis, Kathleen (PhD, Manitoba 1994; assoc. prof.) Caribbean, modern Europe; klewis@spelman.edu
Xu, Yan (PhD, Ohio State 2013; asst. prof. and chair) Asia; yxu@spelman.edu

Part-time Faculty

Odari, Catherine (PhD, Georgia State 2017; instr.) Africa; codari@spelman.edu

Retired/Emeritus Faculty

Ganz, Margery A. (PhD, Syracuse 1979; prof. emeritus) Renaissance and Reformation, medieval Europe; mganz@spelman.edu

Stanford University

Dept. of History, 450 Serra Mall, Bldg. 200, Rm. 113, Stanford, CA 94305-2024. 650.723.2651. Fax 650.725.0597 Website: https://history.stanford.edu/.

History is a pragmatic discipline in which the analysis of change over time involves sifting the influences and perspectives that affect the course of events, and evaluating the different forms of evidence historians exploit to make sense of them. Teaching students how to weigh these sources and convert the findings into persuasive analysis lies at the heart of the department's teaching.

Chair: Matthew Sommer
Degrees Offered: BA,MA,MA/JD,JD/PhD,PhD
Academic Year System: Quarter
Areas of Specialization: Africa, Britain, early modern Europe, East Asia, eastern Europe/Russia, science/medicine/technology, Jewish, Latin America, medieval Europe, Middle East and Central Asia, modern Europe, South Asia, transnational/international/global and US
Tuition (per academic year): $50703
Enrollment 2018-19:
   Undergraduate Majors: 120
   New Graduate Students: 16
   Full-time Graduate Students: 80
   Degrees in History: 40 BA, 7 MA, 13 PhD
Undergraduate Addresses:
   Admissions: http://admission.stanford.edu
   Financial Aid: http://financialaid.stanford.edu
Graduate Addresses:
   Admissions: http://gradadmissions.stanford.edu
   Financial Aid: http://financialaid.stanford.edu

Full-time Faculty

Baker, Keith M. (PhD, London 1964; prof.) French Enlightenment, 17th- and 18th-century European social and political theory, social science; kbaker@stanford.edu

Burns, Jennifer L. (PhD, California, Berkeley 2005; assoc. prof.) US, 20th century; jenniferburns@stanford.edu

Cabrita, Joel Marie (PhD, Cambridge 2008; asst. prof.)

Campbell, James T. (PhD, Stanford 1989; prof.) US, African American; jtcampb@stanford.edu

Carson, Clayborne, Jr. (PhD, UCLA 1975; prof.; dir., Martin Luther King Jr. Research and Education Inst.) African American, urban, labor; ccarson@stanford.edu

Chang, Gordon H. (PhD, Stanford 1987; prof.) Asian American, arms control, US foreign relations; gchang@stanford.edu

Como, David R. (PhD, Princeton 1999; prof.) Britain; dcomo@stanford.edu

Crews, Robert D. (PhD, Princeton 1999; prof.) modern Russia, late Ottoman, comparative colonialism; rcrews@stanford.edu

Daughton, J. P. (PhD, California, Berkeley 2002; assoc. prof.) modern France, colonialism; daughton@stanford.edu

Dorin, Rowan (PhD, Harvard 2015; asst. prof.) medieval Europe

Findlen, Paula (PhD, California, Berkeley 1989; prof.) Renaissance through Enlightenment Italy, science and medicine; pfindlen@stanford.edu

Frank, Zephyr L. (PhD, Illinois, Urbana-Champaign 1999; prof.) Latin America; zfrank@stanford.edu

Freedman, Estelle B. (PhD, Columbia 1976; prof.) US social, American women; ebf@stanford.edu

Gienapp, Jonathan Eric (PhD, Johns Hopkins 2013; asst. prof.) early America; jgienapp@stanford.edu

Griffiths, Fiona J. (PhD, Trinity Coll., Cambridge 1999; prof.) medieval Europe; fgriffit@stanford.edu

Hecht, Gabrielle (PhD, Pennsylvania 1992; prof.; Freeman Spogli Inst.) technology; ghecht@stanford.edu

Hobbs, Allyson Vanessa (PhD, Chicago 2009; assoc. prof.) US; ahobbs@stanford.edu

Jolluck, Katherine R. (PhD, Stanford 1995; sr. lect.) eastern Europe; jolluck@stanford.edu

Kollmann, Nancy Shields (PhD, Harvard 1980; prof.) 15th- to 17th-century Russia; kollmann@stanford.edu

Lewis, Mark E. (PhD, Chicago 1985; prof.) China; mel1000@stanford.edu

Lewis, Martin Wayne (PhD, California, Berkeley 1987; sr. lect.) geography; mwlewis@stanford.edu

Minian, Ana Raquel (PhD, Yale 2012; assoc. prof.) modern Latin America, Mexico, 20th-century US; aminian@stanford.edu

Moon, Yumi (PhD, Harvard 2006; assoc. prof.) Korea; ymoon@stanford.edu

Mullaney, Thomas S. (PhD, Columbia 2006; prof.) modern China; tsmullaney@stanford.edu

Naimark, Norman M. (PhD, Stanford 1972; prof.) eastern Europe, Soviet Union; naimark@stanford.edu

Olivarius, Kathryn (DPhil, Oxford 2016; asst. prof.) 19th-century US; koli@stanford.edu

Press, Steven Michael (PhD, Harvard 2014; asst. prof.) modern Europe; smpress@stanford.edu

Proctor, Robert N. (PhD, Harvard 1984; prof.) 20th-century science/technology/medicine; rproctor@stanford.edu

Riskin, Jessica G. (PhD, California, Berkeley 1995; prof.) modern Europe, science; jriskin@stanford.edu

Roberts, Richard (PhD, Toronto 1978; prof.) West Africa, economic and social; rroberts@stanford.edu

Rodrigue, Aron (PhD, Harvard 1985; prof.) Jewish, Ottoman Empire, France; rodrigue@stanford.edu

Satia, Priya (PhD, California, Berkeley 2004; prof.) modern Britain and Empire; psatia@stanford.edu

Schiebinger, Londa L. (PhD, Harvard 1984; prof.) 17th- and 18th-century European intellectual and social, women in science; schieb@stanford.edu

Sommer, Matthew H. (PhD, UCLA 1994; prof. and chair) late imperial and modern China; msommer@stanford.edu

Stokes, Laura P. (PhD, Virginia 2006; assoc. prof.) early modern Europe, social; lpstokes@stanford.edu

Uchida, Jun (PhD, Harvard 2005; assoc. prof.) modern Japan; junu@stanford.edu

Weiner, Amir (PhD, Columbia 1995; assoc. prof.) Soviet Union and Ukraine; weiner@stanford.edu

White, Richard (PhD, Washington 1976; prof.) American West, American Indian, environmental; whiter@stanford.edu

Wigen, Kären E. (PhD, California, Berkeley 1990; prof.) Japan; kwigen@stanford.edu

Winterer, Caroline (PhD, Michigan 1996; prof.) 18th- and 19th-century US, cultural and intellectual; cwinterer@stanford.edu

Wolfe, Mikael D. (PhD, Chicago 2009; asst. prof.) Latin America, Mexico, environmental; mikaelw@stanford.edu

Yaycioglu, Ali (PhD, Harvard 2008; assoc. prof.) Middle East, Ottoman; ayayciog@stanford.edu

Zipperstein, Steven J. (PhD, UCLA 1980; prof.) modern Jewish, Russia, comparative nationalism; szipper@stanford.edu

Joint/Cross Appointments

Haber, Stephen H. (PhD, UCLA 1985; prof.; Political Science) Latin America; haber@stanford.edu

Rakove, Jack N. (PhD, Harvard 1975; prof.; Political Science) American Revolution, early American political; rakove@stanford.edu

Saller, Richard P. (PhD, Cambridge 1978; prof.; Classics) early Roman Empire; rsaller@stanford.edu

Scheidel, Walter (PhD, Vienna 1993; prof.; Classics) Rome, social and economic; scheidel@stanford.edu

Retired/Emeritus Faculty

Beinin, Joel (PhD, Michigan 1982; prof. emeritus) Middle East, economic, labor; beinin@stanford.edu

Bernstein, Barton J. (PhD, Harvard 1963; prof. emeritus) modern US, US foreign policy, recent US social

Camarillo, Albert M. (PhD, UCLA 1975; prof. emeritus) Chicano/a, US urban, American West; camar@stanford.edu

Corn, Joseph J., III (PhD, California, Berkeley 1977; sr. lect. emeritus) US, technology, transport; joecorn@stanford.edu

Duus, Peter (PhD, Harvard 1965; prof. emeritus) modern Japan; pduus@stanford.edu

Emmons, Terence (PhD, California, Berkeley 1966; prof. emeritus) Russian political/social/intellectual, European historiography; ektxe1@gmail.com

Holloway, David (PhD, Cambridge 1984; prof. emeritus; Political Science) Soviet Union and Cold War, nuclear weapons; david.holloway@stanford.edu

Kennedy, David M. (PhD, Yale 1968; prof. emeritus) 20th-century US intellectual; dmk@stanford.edu

Lougee, Carolyn Chappell (PhD, Michigan 1972; prof. emeritus) early modern Europe, women and family; lougee@stanford.edu

Mancall, Mark (PhD, Harvard 1963; prof. emeritus) Zionist and Israel, modern India; mmancall@stanford.edu

Paret, Peter (PhD, London 1960; prof. emeritus) modern Europe

Robinson, Paul A. (PhD, Harvard 1968; prof. emeritus) European intellectual; paulr@stanford.edu

Seaver, Paul S. (PhD, Harvard 1965; prof. emeritus) 16th- and 17th-century England, English Puritan, social; seaver@stanford.edu

Sheehan, James J. (PhD, California, Berkeley 1964; prof. emeritus) modern Germany; sheehan@stanford.edu

Stansky, Peter D. L. (PhD, Harvard 1961; prof. emeritus) 19th- and 20th-century Britain; stansky@stanford.edu

Van Slyke, Lyman P. (PhD, California, Berkeley 1964; prof. emeritus) modern China, Chinese language training, US-East Asian relations; yangtze@stanford.edu

Recently Awarded PhDs

Beacock, Ian P. "Heartbroken: Democratic Emotions, Political Subjectivity, and the Unravelling of the Weimar Republic, 1918-33"

Burge, Russell Patrick "The Promised Republic: Developmental Society and the Making of Modern Seoul, 1961-79"

Carrillo, Mateo J. "Driving Mexican Migration: Constructing Technologies and Mythologies of Mobility, 1940-64"

Hamed-Troyansky, Vladimir "Refugees and Empires: North Caucasus Muslims between the Ottoman and Russian Worlds, 1864-1914"

Hein, Benjamin P. "Emigration and the Industrial Revolution in German Europe, 1820-1900"

Hill, Rachael Anita "Scientists, Healers and Bioprospectors: The Epistemological Politics of Traditional Medicine in Ethiopia, 1930-98"

Hirata, Koji "Steel Metropolis: Industrial Manchuria and the Making of Chinese Socialism, 1916-64"

Huneke, Samuel Clowes "Homosexuality and the State in Cold War Germany"

Kahn, Michelle "Foreign at Home: Turkish-German Migrants and the Boundaries of Europe, 1961-90"

LeBlanc, Hannah "Nutrition for National Defense: American Food Science in World War II and the Cold War"

Martin, Nicole Noelle "In the Name of the Home: The Politics of Gender, Race, and Reconstruction in 19th-Century America"

Meyers, Joshua "To Dance at Two Weddings: Jews, Nationalism, and the Left in Revolutionary Russia"

Ng, Joseph Chong Kong "Entrepreneurial Capitalism, The Making of the Central Pacific Railroad, 1861-99"

Quinn, Stephanie "Labor, Urbanization, and Political Imagination in Namibia, 1943-94"

Seeley, Joseph Andrew "Liquid Geography: The Yalu River and the Boundaries of Empire in East Asia, 1894-1945"

Slobodkin, Yan "Empire of Hunger: Famine and the French Colonial State, 1867-1945"

Suh, Jung Wook "Pacific Crossings: American Encounters with Asians in the Progressive Era of Empire and Exclusion"

College of Staten Island, City University of New York

Dept. of History, 2800 Victory Blvd., 2N-215, Staten Island, NY 10314. 718.982.2870. Fax 718.982.2864. Email: denise.galica@csi.cuny.edu. Website: https://www.csi.cuny.edu/academics-and-research/departments-programs/history

The Department of History at the College of Staten Island is a community of professional historians committed to excellence in teaching and research.

Chair: John Wing
Director of Graduate Studies: Susan Smith-Peter
Degrees Offered: BA, MA
Academic Year System: Semester

Areas of Specialization: US colonial through post-1945, early modern and modern Europe, world, Middle East/Asia/Africa/Latin America and Caribbean, classical antiquity/Western medieval/Byzantine/Islamic

Undergraduate Tuition (per academic year):
In-State: $6930
Out-of-State: $14880

Graduate Tuition (per academic year):
In-State: $11090
Out-of-State: $15390

Enrollment 2018-19:
Undergraduate Majors: 279
New Graduate Students: 10
Full-time Graduate Students: 8
Part-time Graduate Students: 9
Degrees in History: 57 BA, 5 MA

Undergraduate Addresses:
Admissions: http://www.csi.cuny.edu/admissions/
Financial Aid: http://www.csi.cuny.edu/finaid/

Graduate Addresses:
Admissions: http://www.csi.cuny.edu/admissions/grad/
Financial Aid: http://www.csi.cuny.edu/finaid/

Full-time Faculty

Averbuch, Bryan D. (PhD, Harvard 2013; asst. prof.) early modern Asia, Silk Road; bryan.averbuch@csi.cuny.edu

Collins, Jacob (PhD, UCLA 2013; asst. prof.) modern France and Italy, post-1968 French political, autobiography; jacob.collins@csi.cuny.edu

Dixon, John M. (PhD, UCLA 2007; asst. prof.) colonial America, Atlantic world; john.dixon@csi.cuny.edu

Gambetti, Sandra (PhD, California, Berkeley 2003; assoc. prof.) ancient; sandra.gambetti@csi.cuny.edu

Haj, Samira A. (PhD, UCLA 1988; prof.) modern Middle East; samira.haj@csi.cuny.edu

Holder, Calvin B. (PhD, Harvard 1976; prof.) US, Caribbean; calvin.holder@csi.cuny.edu

Ivison, Eric A. (PhD, Birmingham, UK 1993; prof.) medieval Europe/Byzantium, Byzantine/late antiquity studies/archaeology, Byzantine urban/social/cultural/archaeology; eric.ivison@csi.cuny.edu

Kimball, Natalie (PhD, Pittsburgh 2013; asst. prof.) Latin America/Argentina/Bolivia, Caribbean, gender/ethnicity/race/religion; natalie.kimball@csi.cuny.edu

Lavender, Catherine J. (PhD, Colorado, Boulder 1997; assoc. prof.) US women, US West, cultural; catherine.lavender@csi.cuny.edu

Lewis, Mark (PhD, UCLA 2008; assoc. prof.) modern Germany; mark.lewis@csi.cuny.edu

Lufrano, Richard (PhD, Columbia 1987; assoc. prof.) modern China, East Asia; richard.lufrano@csi.cuny.edu

Mbah, Emmanuel (PhD, Texas, Arlington 2006; assoc. prof.) colonial and postcolonial Africa; emmanuel.mbah@csi.cuny.edu

Powers, Richard Gid (PhD, Brown 1969; prof.) US; rgpsi@earthlink.net

Sassi, Jonathan D. (PhD, UCLA 1996; prof.) revolutionary and early Republic US, religion, antislavery and race; jonathan.sassi@csi.cuny.edu

Smith-Peter, Susan J. (PhD, Illinois, Urbana-Champaign 2001; assoc. prof. and dir., grad. studies) Russia and eastern Europe susan.smithpeter@csi.cuny.edu

Wing, John T. (PhD, Minnesota 2009; assoc. prof. and chair) environmental, early modern Europe; john.wing@csi.cuny.edu

Zevin, Alexander (PhD, UCLA 2014; asst. prof.) modern Britain, British economic and political, British imperial; alexander.zevin@csi.cuny.edu

Retired/Emeritus Faculty

Cooper, Sandi E. (PhD, NYU 1967; prof. emeritus) modern
European peace, women; sandi.cooper@csi.cuny.edu

Traboulay, David M. (PhD, Notre Dame 1970; prof. emeritus) Latin
America, South Asia; davidtraboulay@hotmail.com

Weiner, Howard R. (PhD, NYU 1972; assoc. prof. emeritus) US
immigration, Italy, urban; howard.weiner@csi.cuny.edu

Stephen F. Austin State University

*Dept. of History, Box 13013, Nacogdoches, TX 75962.
936.468.3802. Fax 936.468.2478. Email: history@sfasu.edu;
tdavis@sfasu.edu. Website: http://www.sfasu.edu/academics/
colleges/liberal-applied-arts/history.*

*The History Department, a community of scholars and teachers,
serves a diverse undergraduate and graduate student body by
offering a wide variety of courses, seminars, and independent
studies and by pursuing and publishing historical research.*

Chair: Troy Davis
Director of Graduate Studies: Court Carney
Degrees Offered: BA, MA
Academic Year System: Semester
Areas of Specialization: US, Europe and world, Latin America,
Texas
Undergraduate Tuition (per academic year):
In-State: $10947
Out-of-State: $23397
Graduate Tuition (per academic year):
In-State: $7273
Out-of-State: $14743
Enrollment 2018-19:
Undergraduate Majors: 161
New Graduate Students: 12
Full-time Graduate Students: 16
Part-time Graduate Students: 9
Degrees in History: 31 BA, 4 MA
Undergraduate Addresses:
Admissions: http://www.sfasu.edu/admissions/
Financial Aid: http://www.sfasu.edu/faid/
Graduate Addresses:
Admissions: http://www.sfasu.edu/graduate/
Financial Aid: http://www.sfasu.edu/faid/

Adjunct Faculty

Clark, Lea (MA, Stephen F. Austin State 2019; adj.) US; Lea.Clark@
sfasu.edu

Dendy, Charles (MA, Stephen F. Austin State 2012; JD, Texas 1978;
adj.) US; dendyc@sfasu.edu

Devlin, Cynthia M. (MA, Stephen F. Austin State 2005; adj.) US;
devlinc@sfasu.edu

Patterson, Gretchen (MA, Stephen F. Austin State 2018; adj.)
Western civilization; Gretchen.Patterson@sfasu.edu

Weatherly, Megan S. (MA, Nevada, Las Vegas 2010; adj.) US;
msweatherly@sfasu.edu

Full-time Faculty

Allen, Robert B. (PhD, Columbia 1991; assoc. prof.) Old Regime
and French Revolution; rballen@sfasu.edu

Barringer, Mark D. (PhD, Texas Christian 1997; assoc. prof.)
American West, environmental, Texas; mbarringer@sfasu.edu

Beisel, Perky (DA, Middle Tennessee State 2005; assoc. prof.)
public; pbeisel@sfasu.edu

Bentley, Lisa (MA, Stephen F. Austin State 2012; lect.) US, teacher
preparation; bentleylisa@sfasu.edu

Bui, L. Bao (PhD, Illinois, Urbana-Champaign 2016; lect.) US;
builb@sfasu.edu

Carney, Court P. (PhD, Louisiana State 2003; prof. and dir., grad.
studies) African American; carneycp@sfasu.edu

Catton, P. E. (PhD, Ohio 1998; prof.) modern Asia; pcatton@sfasu.
edu

Chakraborty, Suparna (PhD, Purdue 2017; lect.) world;
chakrabos@sfasu.edu

Chakravartty, Aryendra (PhD, Penn State 2013; asst. prof.) South
Asia, world, colonialism/imperialism; chakravaa@sfasu.edu

Cooper, Dana Magill (PhD, Texas Christian 2006; prof.) women,
gender; cooperdc@sfasu.edu

Cox, Randi Barnes (PhD, Indiana 1999; assoc. prof.) modern Russia,
consumer studies, cultural; rcox@sfasu.edu

Davis, Troy D. (PhD, Marquette 1992; prof. and chair) modern
Europe, Ireland, diplomatic; tdavis@sfasu.edu

Hampton, Hunter M. (PhD, Missouri, Columbia 2017; lect.) US;
hamptonh@sfasu.edu

Jackson, Jere L. (PhD, North Carolina, Chapel Hill 1974; regents
prof.) modern Europe, Germany; jjackson@sfasu.edu

Lannen, Andrew C. (PhD, Louisiana State 2002; assoc. prof.)
colonial and revolutionary America; lannenac@sfasu.edu

Moulton, Aaron Coy (PhD, Arkansas 2016; asst. prof.) Latin
America; moultonac@sfasu.edu

Poston, Brook (PhD, Texas Christian 2012; assoc. prof.) early
Republic US, American legal, American constitutional;
postonb@sfasu.edu

Sandul, Paul J. P. (PhD, California, Santa Barbara/California State,
Sacramento 2009; assoc. prof.) public; sandulpj@sfasu.edu

Sosebee, Scott (PhD, Texas Tech 2004; assoc. prof.) Texas, South;
sosebeem@sfasu.edu

Sutherland, Samuel (PhD, Ohio State 2017; asst. prof.) medieval,
ancient; sutherlas@sfasu.edu

Taaffe, Stephen R. (PhD, Ohio 1995; prof.) diplomacy, military;
staaffe@sfasu.edu

Retired/Emeritus Faculty

Dahmus, John (PhD, Cornell 1970; prof. emeritus) ancient,
medieval Europe

Devine, Joseph A., Jr. (PhD, Virginia 1968; prof. emeritus) colonial
America, transportation; jdevine@sfasu.edu

Johnson, Bobby H. (PhD, Oklahoma 1967; regents prof. emeritus)
American West, American social and cultural; bhjohnson@sfasu.
edu

Mathis, Robert N. (PhD, Georgia 1968; prof. emeritus) early
national, Old US South; rmathis@sfasu.edu

Richman, Allen M. (PhD, Minnesota 1973; regents prof. emeritus)
American intellectual, Renaissance and Reformation;
arichman@sfasu.edu

Stockton University

*Historical Studies Program, 101 Vera King Farris Dr., Galloway,
NJ 08205. 609.652.4505. Fax 609.652.4550. Email: history@
stockton.edu. Website: https://stockton.edu/arts-humanities/
historical-studies.html.*

*The Historical Studies curriculum offers courses that teach the
various methods of historical study, provide students with a
broad understanding of the major themes of human history, and
give them the opportunity to propose and implement their own
research projects.*

Chair: Lisa Rosner
Degrees Offered: BA
Academic Year System: Semester
Areas of Specialization: ancient Mediterranean, early modern and modern Europe, US and Atlantic, Indian Ocean
Tuition (per academic year):
  In-State: $8435
  Out-of-State: $15219
Enrollment 2018-19:
  Undergraduate Majors: 113
  Degrees in History: 40 BA
Addresses:
  Admissions: https://stockton.edu/admissions/
  Financial Aid: https://stockton.edu/admissions/financial-aid.html

Full-time Faculty

Gregg, Robert (PhD, Pennsylvania 1989; prof. and dean; General Studies) US 1865-present, African American; robert.gregg@stockton.edu

Hayse, Michael R. (PhD, North Carolina, Chapel Hill 1995; assoc. prof.) modern Germany, eastern Europe, Soviet Union; haysem@stockton.edu

Lubenow, William C. (PhD, Iowa 1968; dist. prof.) modern Europe, modern Britain, methodology and philosophy of history and the history of cognition; william.lubenow@stockton.edu

McDonald, Michelle Craig (PhD, Michigan 2005; assoc. prof. and interim asst. to provost) Atlantic, early America, public and museum studies; michelle.mcdonald@stockton.edu

Murphy, Kameika Samantha (PhD, Clark 2014; asst. prof.) Atlantic

Musher, Sharon Ann (PhD, Columbia 2007; assoc. prof.) modern US, cultural, gender; sharon.musher@stockton.edu

Nichols, Robert H. (PhD, Pennsylvania 1997; prof.) Indian Ocean, South Asia; nicholsr@stockton.edu

Papademetriou, Tom (PhD, Princeton 2001; assoc. prof.; dir., Interdisciplinary Center for Hellenic Studies) Ottoman, Mediterranean, Hellenic; apapadem@stockton.edu

Rosner, Lisa (PhD, Johns Hopkins 1985; prof. and coord.; dir., Stockton Honors Coll.) science and medicine, early modern Europe; rosnerl@stockton.edu

Zucconi, Laura M. (PhD, California, San Diego 2005; assoc. prof.) ancient Mediterranean and Near East, medicine, archaeology; zucconil@stockton.edu

Suffolk University

Dept. of History, 73 Tremont St., Boston, MA 02108. 617.573.8116. Email: preeve@suffolk.edu. Website: https://www.suffolk.edu/cas/degrees-programs/history.

The History Department offers students a major, minor, honors major in History and Literature, and wide-ranging concentrations in the histories of the Americas, regional and global history, and public history. Areas of specialization include the African diaspora, Asian history, black studies, and gender history.

Chair: Patricia A. Reeve
Degrees Offered: BA,BS
Academic Year System: Semester
Areas of Specialization: Americas, regional and global, Asian studies, African diaspora, public, gender
Tuition (per academic year): $40104
Enrollment 2018-19:
  Undergraduate Majors: 70
  Degrees in History: 25 BA, 12 BS

  Students in Undergraduate Courses: 822
  Students in Undergraduate Intro Courses: 307
Undergraduate Addresses:
  Admissions: http://www.suffolk.edu/admission/undergraduate/
  Financial Aid: https://www.suffolk.edu/undergraduate-admission/undergraduate-tuition-aid

Full-time Faculty

Allison, Robert J. (PhD, Harvard 1992; prof.) early/colonial/revolutionary/early Republic America, Native American, Boston; rallison@suffolk.edu

Bellinger, Robert A. (PhD, Boston Coll. 2000; assoc. prof.) African American and African diaspora history and culture, America West African history and culture; rbellinger@suffolk.edu

Greenberg, Kenneth S. (PhD, Wisconsin-Madison 1976; Dist. Prof.) American life to/since Civil War, slavery and anti-slavery, Vietnam War and US South in history/literature/film; kgreenberg@suffolk.edu

Hannigan, Robert E., Jr. (PhD, Princeton 1978; asst. prof.) US foreign relations, modern world, international affairs; rhannigan@suffolk.edu

Lasdow, Kathryn (PhD, Columbia 2018; asst. prof.) colonial and early national America, public, architectural and material culture

Plott, Michele S. (PhD, Yale 1993; assoc. prof.) 19th- and 20th-century France, politics and culture in Europe 1890-1939, Germany in film/visual culture and history since 1945; mplott@suffolk.edu

Reeve, Patricia A. (PhD, Boston Coll. 2007; assoc. prof. and chair) 19th-century US, working-class and labor histories, masculinity and gender studies; preeve@suffolk.edu

Suleski, Ronald (PhD, Michigan 1974; prof.; dir., Rosenberg Inst. for East Asian Studies) modern and pre-modern China/Japan/Korea, 20th-century Manchuria, Chinese and Japanese languages; rsuleski@suffolk.edu

Xue, Yong (PhD, Yale 2004; asst. prof.) modern China, agrarian studies, Japan; yxue@suffolk.edu

Part-time Faculty

Casini, Matteo (PhD, Venice, Italy 1993; lect.) Europe, Mediterranean, Italy; mattcasini@yahoo.com

Lee, Lester P., Jr. (MA, Johns Hopkins 1976; MA, Harvard; lect.) Africa/African American/Atlantic/Britain, comparative slavery, imperialism and world; llee@suffolk.edu

Lenzie, Sharon (MEd, Suffolk; lect. and asst. dean) America; slenzie@suffolk.edu

O'Neill, Stephen (MA, Boston Coll.; lect.) piracy and Atlantic, Plymouth Colony, material culture and public; soneill@suffolk.edu

Shadbash, Shahram (PhD, Boston Univ.; sr. lect.) Middle East, Islam; sshadbash@yahoo.com

Weiss, Camille (PhD, West Virginia 1986; sr. lect.; Humanities) early modern French and Italian courts; cweiss@suffolk.edu

Retired/Emeritus Faculty

McCarthy, Joseph M. (PhD, Boston Coll. 1972; prof. emeritus) ancient and medieval Europe; joemccarthy@suffolk.edu

Sul Ross State University

Dept. of Behavioral and Social Sciences, LH 208, Box C-157, Alpine, TX 79832-9991. 432.837.8157. Fax 432.837.8146. Email: msaka@sulross.edu. Website: https://www.sulross.edu/section/265/behavioral-social-sciences.

The Department of Behavioral and Social Sciences offers bachelor's degrees in History, Psychology, Social Science (General) and Social Science (Political Science focus). Anthropology, Mexican-American Studies and Sociology are offered as minor fields of study only. In addition, limited course work is offered in Geography and Philosophy. Master's degrees are offered in History and Public Administration.

Chair: Mark Saad Saka
Director of Graduate Studies: Mark Saad Saka
Degrees Offered: BA,MA
Academic Year System: Semester
Areas of Specialization: world, Europe, Mexico, Middle East
Tuition (per academic year):
  In-State: $3552
  Out-of-State: $10176
Enrollment 2018-19:
  Undergraduate Majors: 26
  New Graduate Students: 6
  Full-time Graduate Students: 9
  Part-time Graduate Students: 12
  Degrees in History: 10 BA, 4 MA
Addresses:
  Admissions: http://www.sulross.edu/section/234/getting-started
  Financial Aid: http://www.sulross.edu/page/106/financial-aid

Full-time Faculty

Dehart, Kendra (MA, Texas State 2014; asst. prof.) women, Texas, American West; kendra.dehart@sulross.edu
Saka, Mark Saad (PhD, Houston 1995; prof.; chair; and dir., grad. studies) Mexico, modern Middle East and Asia, world religions; msaka@sulross.edu
Williamson, Savannah L. (PhD, Houston 2016; asst. prof.) American slavery, antebellum South, American medical and science; savannah.williamson@sulross.edu

Nondepartmental Historians

Walter, Matthew John (MA, Sul Ross State 2002; lect.; Museum of the Big Bend) Texas, Civil War, American military; mwalter@sulross.edu

Susquehanna University

Dept. of History, 514 University Ave., Selinsgrove, PA 17870-1001. 570.372.4734. Fax 570.372.2870. Email: munozm@susqu.edu. Website: https://www.susqu.edu/academics/majors-and-minors/department-of-history/history.

In the Department of History, you'll know how to think critically, to connect the dots and analyze what you've found, and to convey your ideas in compelling ways.

Chair: Maria Munoz
Degrees Offered: BA
Academic Year System: Semester
Areas of Specialization: US, Europe, Africa, Latin America
Tuition (per academic year): $43160
Enrollment 2018-19:
  Undergraduate Majors: 53
  Degrees in History: 12 BA
Addresses:
  Admissions: https://www.susqu.edu/admission-and-aid
  Financial Aid: https://www.susqu.edu/admission-and-aid/tuition-and-financial-aid

Full-time Faculty

Imhoof, David Michael (PhD, Texas, Austin 2000; prof.) modern Europe and Germany, culture, Holocaust; imhoof@susqu.edu
Munoz, Maria L. O. (PhD, Arizona 2009; assoc. prof. and chair) 20th-century Mexico, indigenous cultures, race and politics; munozm@susqu.edu
Rouphail, Robert (PhD, Illinois, Urbana-Champaign 2019; asst. prof.) East Africa, environmental, science, Mauritius; ropuhail@susqu.edu
Slavishak, Edward S. (PhD, North Carolina, Chapel Hill 2002; assoc. prof.) US, space and landscape, labor and leisure; slavishak@susqu.edu
Weaver, Karol Kimberlee (PhD, Penn State 1999; assoc. prof.) US, science and medicine, women; weaverk@susqu.edu

Nondepartmental Historians

McMillin, Linda A. (PhD, UCLA 1990; prof.; provost; and dean of faculty) medieval, gender, Spain; mcmillin@susqu.edu

Part-time Faculty

Logan, Tim (MA, Villanova 1993; adj. prof.) modern US, diplomatic; logant@susqu.edu
Mulligan, Megan (MA, Arizona 2000; adj. prof.) modern US; mulliganmeg@susqu.edu
Namminga, Darin (MDiv, Western Theological Seminary 2007; adj. prof.) US
Staron, Nicole (MA, Ohio 2006; adj. prof.) modern Europe, Russia; nstaron@pct.edu

Retired/Emeritus Faculty

Housley, Donald D. (PhD, Penn State 1971; prof. emeritus) US, social, higher education; housley@susqu.edu

Swarthmore College

Dept. of History, 500 College Ave., Swarthmore, PA 19081-1397. 610.328.8135. Fax 610.328.8171. Email: history@swarthmore.edu. Website: https://www.swarthmore.edu/history.

The courses and seminars offered by the History Department attempt to give students a sense of the past; an acquaintance with the social, cultural, and institutional developments that have produced the world of today; and an understanding of the nature of history as a discipline.

Chair: Robert Weinberg
Degrees Offered: BA
Academic Year System: Semester
Areas of Specialization: early modern/modern Europe and Ireland, US, Africa, Asia, Latin America, cultural, empire, environmental, sexuality, social, urban, women
Tuition (per academic year): $70744
Enrollment 2018-19:
  Undergraduate Majors: 49
  Degrees in History: 12 BA
  Students in Undergraduate Courses: 411
  Students in Undergraduate Intro Courses: 193
Addresses:
  Admissions: http://www.swarthmore.edu/admissions-aid
  Financial Aid: http://www.swarthmore.edu/admissions-aid/financial-aid-and-cost-information

Full-time Faculty

Armus, Diego C. (PhD, California, Berkeley 1996; prof.) Latin America, urban, social; darmus1@swarthmore.edu

Azfar, Farid M. (PhD, Brown 2009; assoc. prof.) early modern Europe, sexuality, Atlantic; fazfar1@swarthmore.edu

Brown, Megan (PhD, Graduate Center, CUNY 2017; asst. prof.) modern Europe, European integration, empire; megan.brown@swarthmore.edu

Burke, Timothy J. (PhD, Johns Hopkins 1993; prof.) Africa, cultural studies; tburke1@swarthmore.edu

Chen, BuYun (PhD, Columbia 2013; asst. prof.) China, craft and technology, women; bchen5@swarthmore.edu

Dorsey, Allison Gloria (PhD, California, Irvine 1995; prof.) African American, civil rights, food; adorsey1@swarthmore.edu

Dorsey, Bruce A. (PhD, Brown 1993; prof.) US social and cultural, early America, gender; bdorsey1@swarthmore.edu

Murphy, Marjorie (PhD, California, Davis 1981; prof.) American labor, Ireland, women; mmurphy1@swarthmore.edu

Shokr, Ahmad (PhD, NYU 2016; asst. prof.) modern Middle East, decolonization, capitalism; ashokr1@swarthmore.edu

Weinberg, Bob (PhD, California, Berkeley 1985; prof. and chair) Russia, modern Europe, modern Jewish; rweinbe1@swarthmore.edu

Retired/Emeritus Faculty

Bannister, Robert (PhD, Yale 1961; prof. emeritus) US political and intellectual since 1787; rbannis1@swarthmore.edu

Bensch, Stephen P. (PhD, California, Berkeley 1987; prof. emeritus) medieval Europe, Near East; sbensch1@swarthmore.edu

DuPlessis, Robert S. (PhD, Columbia 1974; prof. emeritus) early modern Europe, Atlantic, economic; rduples1@swarthmore.edu

Li, Lillian M. (PhD, Harvard 1975; prof. emerita) China, Japan, cities; lli1@swarthmore.edu

Wright, Harrison M. (PhD, Harvard 1957; prof. emeritus) Africa, European expansion, historiography

Sweet Briar College

Dept. of History, Benedict Hall, Sweet Briar, VA 24595. 434.381.6234. Fax 434.381.6494. Email: llaufenberg@sbc.edu. Website: https://sbc.edu/social-sciences-and-humanities/history/.

Though the liberal arts curriculum traditionally offers knowledge for knowledge's sake, the study of history opens numerous opportunities in a wide range of career fields. History, as one of the cornerstones of a liberal arts education, provides students with a greater ability to think rationally and develop understanding of issues and problems in proper contexts.

Chair: Lynn Marie Laufenberg
Degrees Offered: BA
Academic Year System: Semester
Areas of Specialization: US cultural and social, 20th century; premodern Europe/Mediterranean/British Isles, US and continental legal
Tuition (per academic year): $35800
Enrollment 2018-19:
 Undergraduate Majors: 15
 Degrees in History: 5 BA
Addresses:
 Admissions: http://sbc.edu/admissions
 Financial Aid: http://sbc.edu/financial-aid

Full-time Faculty

Laufenberg, Lynn Marie (PhD, Cornell 2000; assoc. prof. and chair) Renaissance and medieval British Isles, law, gender; llaufenberg@sbc.edu

Waugh, Dwana (PhD, North Carolina, Chapel Hill 2012; asst. prof.) 19th- and 20th-century US, social, African American; dwaugh@sbc.edu

Syracuse University

Dept. of History, 145 Eggers Hall, Syracuse, NY 13244-1020. 315.443.2210. Fax 315.443.5876. Email: history@maxwell.syr.edu. Website: https://www.maxwell.syr.edu/hist/.

Understanding history—the record of what people have thought, said, and done—is essential in understanding the world of today. Undergraduate and graduate students explore not only events of the past, but their meaning and implications for our own lives.

Chair: Norman Kutcher
Director of Graduate Studies: Alan Allport
Degrees Offered: BA, MA, MPhil, PhD
Academic Year System: Semester
Areas of Specialization: Africa, East Asia, Europe, modern Latin America/North America/US, modern and contemporary South Asia
Undergraduate Tuition (per academic year): $50230
Graduate Tuition (per academic year): $28062
Enrollment 2018-19:
 Undergraduate Majors: 138
 New Graduate Students: 12
 Full-time Graduate Students: 44
 Degrees in History: 58 BA, 1 MA, 3 PhD, 3 MPhil
Undergraduate Addresses:
 Admissions: http://admissions.syr.edu/
 Financial Aid: http://financialaid.syr.edu/
Graduate Addresses:
 Admissions: http://graduateschool.syr.edu/
 Financial Aid: http://financialaid.syr.edu/

Full-time Faculty

Allport, Alan (PhD, Pennsylvania 2007; assoc. prof. and dir., grad. studies) modern Britain and Europe; aallport@maxwell.syr.edu

Branson, Susan (PhD, Northern Illinois 1992; prof.) US women, US social, US political; branson@syr.edu

Brege, Brian Anthony (PhD, Stanford 2014; asst. prof.) Renaissance Italy; babrege@maxwell.syr.edu

Champion, Craige B. (PhD, Princeton 1993; prof.) Hellenistic Greece, Greek democracy and republican Rome, classical historiography; cbchamp@maxwell.syr.edu

Cohen, Andrew Wender (PhD, Chicago 1999; prof.) modern US, labor, legal; awcohe01@maxwell.syr.edu

Diem, Albrecht (PhD, Utrecht, Netherlands 2000; assoc. prof.) late antiquity and early medieval; adiem@maxwell.syr.edu

Ebner, Michael R. (PhD, Columbia 2004; assoc. prof.) modern Europe, Italy, fascism; mebner@syr.edu

Faulkner, Carol (PhD, SUNY, Binghamton 1998; prof.) 19th-century America, US women; cfaulkne@maxwell.syr.edu

Gonda, Jeffrey D. (PhD, Yale 2012; assoc. prof.) 20th-century American politics and society, US race and rights, US urban; jdgonda@maxwell.syr.edu

Hagenloh, Paul M. (PhD, Texas, Austin 1999; assoc. prof.) medieval and imperial Russia, Soviet Union; phagenlo@syr.edu

Herrick, Samantha Kahn (PhD, Harvard 2002; assoc. prof.) late medieval 1000-1500; sherrick@maxwell.syr.edu

Kallander, Amy Aisen (PhD, California, Berkeley 2007; assoc. prof.) modern Middle East; akalland@maxwell.syr.edu

Kallander, George (PhD, Columbia 2006; assoc. prof.) Korean and Northeast Asian history and culture; glkallan@maxwell.syr.edu

Khalil, Osamah F. (PhD, California, Berkeley 2010; assoc. prof.) US and Middle East

Kumar, Radha (PhD, Princeton 2014; asst. prof.) modern South Asia, urban, caste in India; rkuma100@maxwell.syr.edu

Kutcher, Norman Alan (PhD, Yale 1991; prof. and chair) late imperial and modern China; nakutcher@maxwell.syr.edu

Kyle, Chris R. (PhD, Auckland 1994; assoc. prof.) British parliaments; chkyle@maxwell.syr.edu

Lasch-Quinn, Elisabeth D. (PhD, Massachusetts 1990; prof.) modern American social, cultural, intellectual; edlasch@maxwell.syr.edu

McCormick, Gladys I. (PhD, Wisconsin-Madison 2009; assoc. prof.) Latin America and Carribean, 19th- and 20th-century Mexico; gmccormi@maxwell.syr.edu

Murphy, Tessa (PhD, Chicago 2016; asst. prof.) early America; temurphy@maxwell.syr.edu

Schmeller, Mark G. (PhD, Chicago 2001; assoc. prof.) 18th- and 19th-century American cultural and intellectual; mschmell@maxwell.syr.edu

Shanguhyia, Martin S. (PhD, West Virginia 2007; assoc. prof.) colonial and postcolonial Africa, African political/economic/cultural, African environment and sustainability; mshanguh@maxwell.syr.edu

Takeda, Junko (PhD, Stanford 2006; assoc. prof.) early modern Europe; jtakeda@maxwell.syr.edu

Terrell, Robert S. (PhD, California, San Diego 2018; asst. prof.) modern Germany

Thompson, Margaret Susan (PhD, Wisconsin, Madison 1979; assoc. prof.) US political, religious, women; msthomps@maxwell.syr.edu

Nondepartmental Historians

Burstyn, Joan N. (PhD, London 1968; prof.; Education) modern; jburstyn@syr.edu

Sernett, Milton C. (PhD, Delaware 1972; prof.; African American Studies) 19th-century American abolitionism, African American religion, American South; mcsernet@syr.edu

Stam, David H. (PhD, Northwestern 1978; Univ. librarian emeritus) dhstam@syr.edu

Wiecek, Willam M. (PhD, Wisconsin, Madison 1968; prof. emeritus; Law) legal and constitutional; wmwiecek@law.syr.edu

Retired/Emeritus Faculty

Bennett, David H. (PhD, Chicago 1963; Meredith Prof. emeritus) 20th-century America, American political extremism, military; dhbennet@maxwell.syr.edu

Marquardt, Frederick D. (PhD, California, Berkeley 1973; Maxwell Prof. emeritus) modern Germany, social and economic, labor; fdmarqua@gmail.com

Marsh, Peter T. (PhD, Cambridge 1962; prof. emeritus) 19th- and 20th-century Britain, international political economy; ptmarsh@powernet.co.uk

Romano, Dennis (PhD, Michigan State 1981; prof. emeritus) Renaissance Italy, early modern social and cultural, Venice; dromano@syr.edu

Sharp, James Roger (PhD, California, Berkeley 1966; prof. emeritus) early national and Middle Period US, political; jrsharp@maxwell.syr.edu

Webb, Stephen S. (PhD, Wisconsin, Madison 1965; Maxwell Prof. emeritus) early America, Anglo-American social and political, Native American; sswebb@maxwell.syr.edu

Recently Awarded PhDs

Avery, Shane P. "To Open the Forests to the Sun-Beam: Place and Landscape in American Geographical Writing, 1783-1860"

Dragoni, Mark "Operating Outside of Empire: Trade and Citizenship in the Atlantic World, 1756-1812"

Gaffney, Mindy Lu "Intimate Collaborations: An Examination of Female Relationships in the Homosocial Environment of Select Women's Colleges during the Early Decades of the 12th Century"

Soljour, Kishauna "Beyond the Banlieue: French Postcolonial Migration and the Politics of a Sub-Saharan Identity"

Stegeman, Henry John III "Indigenismo and Mapuche Politics in 20th-Century Chile"

Webb, Silas "Birmingham Is No Detroit: Migration, Mobilization, and Memory in British Punjabi Politics, 1938-84"

University of Tampa

Dept. of History, Sociology, Geography and Legal Studies, Box Q, 401 W. Kennedy Blvd., Tampa, FL 33606-1490. 813.253.3333. Fax 813.258.7237. Email: ssegalla@ut.edu. Website: http://www.ut.edu/historysociologygeographylegal/.

The Bachelor of Arts in History program is designed to help students see themselves and their society from different times and places, while displaying an informed perspective and a mature view of human nature. The program includes choices of optional interdisciplinary concentrations in Global History & Culture and American History & Law, as well as a standard history program.

Chair: Spencer Segalla
Degrees Offered: BA
Academic Year System: Semester
Areas of Specialization: global, American history and law
Tuition (per academic year): $25202
Enrollment 2018-19:
  Degrees in History: 20 BA
Addresses:
  Admissions: http://www.ut.edu/admissions/
  Financial Aid: http://www.ut.edu/financialaid/

Full-time Faculty

Groh, Charles McGraw (PhD, Connecticut 2005; assoc. prof.) US 1877-1920, public, labor; cmcgraw@ut.edu

Littell-Lamb, Elizabeth (PhD, Carnegie Mellon 2002; assoc. prof.) Asia, women; elittell@ut.edu

Palmer, Kelly D. (PhD, Michigan State 2010; asst. prof. of instruction) modern France, Holocaust; kpalmer@ut.edu

Parssinen, Terry M. (PhD, Brandeis 1968; prof.) European social, World War I, World War II; tparssinen@ut.edu

Pompeian, Edward P. (PhD, William and Mary 2014; asst. prof.) Latin America and Caribbean, Atlantic world

Segalla, Spencer D. (PhD, SUNY, Stony Brook 2003; assoc. prof. and chair) French North Africa, colonialism, disasters; ssegalla@ut.edu

Retired/Emeritus Faculty

Tillson, Albert H., Jr. (PhD, Texas, Austin 1986; prof. emeritus) early America, Latin America, revolutionary and antebellum maritime; atillson@ut.edu

Tarleton State University

Dept. of History, Sociology and Geography, Box T-0660, Tarleton Station, Stephenville, TX 76402. 254.968.9021. Fax 254.968.9798. Email: jvazquez@tarleton.edu. Website: https://www.tarleton.edu/hsgg/.

The mission of the department is to provide quality degree programs to prepare students for a wide range of career options. The department also has a significant role in the College of Liberal and Fine Arts and in accomplishing the mission of the university by guiding all students to become knowledgeable and engaged citizens in their communities through the general education core curriculum.

Chair: Opeyemi Zubair
Director of Graduate Studies: Richard A. Cruz
Degrees Offered: BA,BS,MA,MS
Academic Year System: Semester
Areas of Specialization: 19th- and 20th-century Europe, 19th- and 20th-century US, Texas, US social and cultural, public
Undergraduate Tuition (per academic year):
   In-State: $3695
   Out-of-State: $12119
Graduate Tuition (per academic year):
   In-State: $3311
   Out-of-State: $9089
Enrollment 2018-19:
   Undergraduate Majors: 110
   New Graduate Students: 12
   Full-time Graduate Students: 18
   Part-time Graduate Students: 5
   Degrees in History: 35 BA, 6 MA
Undergraduate Addresses:
   Admissions: http://www.tarleton.edu/admissions/
   Financial Aid: http://www.tarleton.edu/finaid/
Graduate Addresses:
   Admissions: http://www.tarleton.edu/graduate/future/
   Financial Aid: http://www.tarleton.edu/finaid/

Full-time Faculty

Branscombe, Jensen (PhD, Texas Christian 2013; asst. prof.) US-Mexico relations, US immigration policy, recent US; branscombe@tarleton.edu

Cruz, Richard A. (PhD, North Texas 1996; assoc. prof. and grad. studies coord.) early modern Europe, European intellectual and cultural; cruz@tarleton.edu

Funiciello, Patrick (PhD, George Washington 2016; asst. prof.) Latin America, Atlantic world, race smuggling; funiciello@tarleton.edu

George, Aaron (PhD, Ohio State 2017; asst. prof.) ageorge@tarleton.edu

Hickman, Christopher Alan (PhD, George Washington 2010; asst. prof.) US law and politics, US Supreme Court, intellectual; hickman@tarleton.edu

Liles, Deborah (PhD, North Texas 2013; asst. prof. and W.K. Gordon Endowed Chair; coord., W. K. Gordon Center) slavery in northwestern Texas; dliles@tarleton.edu

Peach, Steven Jonathan (PhD, North Carolina, Greensboro 2016; asst. prof.) Creek Indian ethnohistory

Roberts, Ted (MA, Tarleton State 2002; sr. instr.) US, US military, military policy; troberts@tarleton.edu

University of Tennessee at Chattanooga

Dept. of History, 408 Brock Hall, Dept. 2052, 615 McCallie Ave., Chattanooga, TN 37403-2598. 423.425.4561. Fax 423.425.2138. Email: michael-d-thompson@utc.edu. Website: https://www.utc.edu/history/.

The Department of History offers an undergraduate major leading to the BA in history. The department's faculty offer courses in American, European, Asian, African, Middle Eastern, and Latin American history, as well as in numerous thematic fields.

Chair: Michael Thompson
Degrees Offered: BA
Academic Year System: Semester
Areas of Specialization: social, economic, political, legal, religious, labor, public, medical, environmental, race and ethnicity, colonialism and empire, women/gender/sexuality, youth and childhood, slavery
Tuition (per academic year):
   In-State: $8664
   Out-of-State: $24782
Enrollment 2018-19:
   Undergraduate Majors: 99
   Degrees in History: 15 BA
   Students in Undergraduate Courses: 3593
   Students in Undergraduate Intro Courses: 2509
   Online-Only Courses: 24%
Addresses:
   Admissions: http://www.utc.edu/admissions/
   Financial Aid: http://www.utc.edu/financial-aid/

Full-time Faculty

Brudney, Edward (PhD, Indiana 2019; asst. prof.) Latin America, labor, legal, memory studies, oral; edward-brudney@utc.edu

Cummiskey, Julia (PhD, Johns Hopkins 2017; asst. prof.) Africa, public health and medicine; julia-cummiskey@utc.edu

Eckelmann Berghel, Susan (PhD, Indiana 2014; asst. prof.) modern US, childhood/youth, African American, transnationalism; susan-eckelmann@utc.edu

Guilfoyle, James Edward (PhD, Chicago 2009; assoc. lect.) early modern Ireland and Britain, British Empire, political economy, state formation, early modern capitalism, economic thought; james-guilfoyle@utc.edu

Hu, Fang Yu (PhD, California, Santa Cruz 2015; asst. prof.) modern China, Japan, and East Asia, gender, colonialism; fangyu-hu@utc.edu

Johnson, Mark A. (PhD, Alabama 2016; lect.) US, American South, race and politics, African American

Kuby, William (PhD, Pennsylvania 2011; UC Foundation Assoc. Prof.) modern US, women/gender/sexuality, legal, African American; william-kuby@utc.edu

McCormack, Carey Kathleen (PhD, Washington State 2018; lect.) South and Southeast Asia, Indian Ocean world, environment, gender, empire; carey-mccormack@utc.edu

Nelson, Kelli B. (PhD, Mississippi State 2017; lect.) public, environment, death and memorialization; kelli-nelson@utc.edu

Robinson, Kira (PhD, Minnesota 2012; asst. prof.) medieval Europe, medicine, law, religion; kira-robison@utc.edu

Swanson, John C. (PhD, Minnesota 1996; Guerry Prof.) 20th-century Austria and Hungary, politics and ethnicity; john-swanson@utc.edu

Thompson, Michael D. (PhD, Emory 2009; UC Foundation Assoc. Prof. and head) early national and antebellum US, slavery, American South; michael-d-thompson@utc.edu

Tracy Samuel, Annie (PhD, Tel Aviv 2014; asst. prof.) Middle East, Iran; annie-tracysamuel@utc.edu

White, Michelle A. (PhD, York 2001; UC Foundation Prof.) early modern England, women; michelle-white@utc.edu

Retired/Emeritus Faculty

Deierhoi, Tyler (PhD, Duke 1964; prof. emeritus) modern Europe, Germany and Russia, technology; noldane@aol.com

Harbaugh, Jane W. (PhD, Tufts 1957; Guerry Prof. emeritus) Asia, Middle East, Europe, diplomacy

Ingle, H. Larry (PhD, Wisconsin, Madison 1967; prof. emeritus) American intellectual, Quaker, African American; lingle@bellsouth.net

Rice, Richard (PhD, Harvard 1974; prof. emeritus) Asia, contemporary Japanese business and technology; richard-rice@utc.edu

Russell, James Michael (PhD, Princeton 1972; prof. emeritus) American urban, Civil War, US South; james-russell@utc.edu

Ward, James A., III (PhD, Louisiana State 1969; Guerry Prof. emeritus) American economic, transportation, Viking

Wright, William J. (PhD, Ohio State 1969; prof. emeritus) European social, Reformation and early modern Europe, revolutionary change

University of Tennessee at Knoxville

Dept. of History, 915 Volunteer Blvd., Knoxville, TN 37996-4065. 865.974.5421. Fax 865.974.3915. Email: efreeber@utk.edu. Website: https://history.utk.edu/.

The Department of History at the University of Tennessee provides an engaged and exciting place to learn about the past. We have an award-winning faculty that provides a comprehensive undergraduate curriculum. We offer graduate programs in three clusters: modern Europe, American history, and medieval and Renaissance history.

Chair: Ernest Freeberg
Director of Graduate Studies: Alison Vacca
Director of Undergraduate Studies: Charles Sanft
Degrees Offered: BA, MA, PhD
Academic Year System: Semester
Areas of Specialization: US, premodern Europe, modern Europe
Undergraduate Tuition (per academic year):
  In-State: $13006
  Out-of-State: $31426
Graduate Tuition (per academic year):
  In-State: $13120
  Out-of-State: $31538
Enrollment 2018-19:
  Undergraduate Majors: 247
  New Graduate Students: 9
  Full-time Graduate Students: 44
  Degrees in History: 54 BA, 5 MA, 7 PhD
  Students in Undergraduate Courses: 4229
  Students in Undergraduate Intro Courses: 3071
Undergraduate Addresses:
  Admissions: http://www.utk.edu/admissions/
  Financial Aid: http://onestop.utk.edu/
Graduate Addresses:
  Admissions: http://gradschool.utk.edu/
  Financial Aid: http://onestop.utk.edu/

Affiliated Faculty

Black, Winston E., II (PhD, Toronto 2008; postdoc. research assoc.; MARCO Inst.) medieval, medicine, Christianity; wblack3@utk.edu

Friend, John L. (PhD, Texas, Austin 2009; asst. prof.; Classics) Greece, military, Athenian democracy; jlfriend@utk.edu

Hulsether, Mark (PhD, Minnesota 1992; prof.; Religious Studies) American religious; mhulseth@utk.edu

Lafferty, Maura (PhD, Toronto 1993; assoc. prof.; Classics) medieval studies; mlaffert@utk.edu

Magilow, Daniel Howard (PhD, Princeton 2003; assoc. prof.; Modern Foreign Languages and Literatures) German studies, Holocaust studies, visual culture/film and photograph; dmagilow@utk.edu

Shepardson, Christine (PhD, Duke 2003; assoc. prof.; Religious Studies) Near East in late antiquity, Syriac literature and theology; cshepard@utk.edu

Tandy, David (PhD, Yale 1979; prof.; Classics) Greek economic and social; dtandy@utk.edu

Van de Moortel, Aleydis (PhD, Bryn Mawr 1997; asst. prof.; Classics) Bronze Age archaeology, underwater archaeology; advm@utk.edu

Full-time Faculty

Andersen, Margaret Cook (PhD, Iowa 2009; assoc. prof.) France, imperialism; mcookand@utk.edu

Bast, Robert J. (PhD, Arizona 1993; assoc. prof.) early modern Europe; rbast@utk.edu

Black, Chad T. (PhD, New Mexico 2006; asst. prof.) colonial Latin America, gender; cblack6@utk.edu

Black, Monica A. (PhD, Virginia 2006; assoc. prof. and assoc. head) post-1945 Germany; mblack9@utk.edu

Block, Kristen (PhD, Rutgers 2007; assoc. prof.) Atlantic; kblock3@utk.edu

Dessel, J. P. (PhD, Arizona 1991; assoc. prof.) Jewish, ancient; jdessel@utk.edu

Feller, Daniel (PhD, Wisconsin, Madison 1981; prof.; dir. and ed., Andrew Jackson Papers) Jacksonian America, political; dfeller@utk.edu

Freeberg, Ernest (PhD, Emory 1995; prof. and head) 19th-century US, social and cultural, religious; efreeber@utk.edu

Gillis, Matthew Bryan (PhD, Virginia 2009; asst. prof.) early medieval Europe; mgillis1@utk.edu

Harlow, Luke E. (PhD, Rice 2009; asst. prof.) American Civil War and Reconstruction, antebellum US, American religion; lharlow1@utk.edu

Latham, Jacob A. (PhD, California, Santa Barbara 2007; asst. prof.) late antique, early medieval, Rome; jlatham3@utk.edu

Liulevicius, Vejas G. (PhD, Pennsylvania 1994; prof.; dir., Center for Study of War and Soc.) 20th-century Europe, Germany; vliulevi@utk.edu

Magra, Christopher P. (PhD, Pittsburgh 2006; assoc. prof.) colonial America; cmagra@utk.edu

Nenzi, Laura Nenz Detto (PhD, California, Santa Barbara 2004; prof.) modern Japan; lnenzi@utk.edu

Norrell, Robert J. (PhD, Virginia 1983; Schmitt Prof.) New US South, civil rights; rnorrell@utk.edu

Olsson, Tore C. (PhD, Georgia 2013; asst. prof.) 20th-century US and world, food and agriculture; colsson@utk.edu

Phillips, Denise (PhD, Harvard 2004; assoc. prof.) Germany, science; aphill13@utk.edu

Reed, Julie L. (PhD, North Carolina, Chapel Hill 2011; asst. prof.) Cherokee, Native American; jreed56@utk.edu

Rubenstein, Jay C. (PhD, California, Berkeley 1997; prof.) medieval European intellectual, Crusades; jrubens1@utk.edu

Sacco, Lynn (PhD, Southern California 2001; assoc. prof.) women, Progressive era; lsacco@utk.edu

Sanft, Charles (PhD, Muenster 2005; assoc. prof. and dir., undergrad. studies) early Chinese political thought and practice; csanft@utk.edu

Vacca, Alison Marie (PhD, Michigan 2010; asst. prof. and dir., grad. studies) Islamic; avacca@utk.edu

Williams, Shannen Dee (PhD, Rutgers 2013; asst. prof.) US and black Catholic diaspora; swill132@utk.edu

Winford, Brandon Kyron (PhD, North Carolina, Chapel Hill 2014; asst. prof.) US; bwinford@utk.edu

Wu, Shellen Xiao (PhD, Princeton 2010; assoc. prof.) modern China, science, modern Germany; swu5@utk.edu

Nondepartmental Historians

Coens, Thomas M. (PhD, Harvard 2004; assoc. ed.; Papers of Andrew Jackson) formation of Jackson Party 1822-29; tcoens@utk.edu

Cohen, Michael David (PhD, Harvard 2008; asst. ed.; James K. Polk Correspondence Project) mdcohen@utk.edu

Moss, Laura-Eve (PhD, Connecticut 1999; assoc. ed.; Papers of Andrew Jackson) constitutional, New York state; lmoss3@utk.edu

Part-time Faculty

Mariner, Capt Rosemary (MS, National War Coll. 1997; lect.; vis. fellow, Center for Study of War and Soc.) military; rmariner@utk.edu

Retired/Emeritus Faculty

Ash, Stephen V. (PhD, Tennessee, Knoxville 1983; prof. emeritus) Civil War and Reconstruction, Tennessee; sash@utk.edu

Bergeron, Paul H. (PhD, Vanderbilt 1965; prof. emeritus) Tennessee, Jacksonian America, US South; bergeron@utk.edu

Bing, Daniel (PhD, Indiana 1969; assoc. prof. emeritus) ancient Near East, Greece and Rome; dbing@utk.edu

Bohstedt, John (PhD, Harvard 1972; prof. emeritus) modern Britain; bohstedt@utk.edu

Brummett, Palmira (PhD, Chicago 1988; prof. emeritus) Middle East; palmira@utk.edu

Chmielewski, Edward (PhD, Harvard 1957; prof. emeritus) Russia, Poland

Finger, John R. (PhD, Washington 1968; prof. emeritus) westward movement, Indian-white relations; jfinger@utk.edu

Fleming, Cynthia (PhD, Duke 1977; prof. emeritus) African American; cfleming@utk.edu

Haas, Arthur G. (PhD, Chicago 1961; prof. emeritus) Germany, central Europe

Hao, Yen-p'ing (PhD, Harvard 1966; Lindsay Young Prof. emeritus) East Asia, China; yhao@utk.edu

Mayhew, Anne (PhD, Texas, Austin 1966; prof. emeritus) US economic; amayhew@utk.edu

Muldowny, John (PhD, Yale 1959; assoc. prof. emeritus) 19th- and early 20th-century America; jmuldown@utk.edu

Pinckney, Paul J. (PhD, Vanderbilt 1962; assoc. prof. emeritus) Tudor-Stuart England; pinckney@utk.edu

Utley, Jonathan G. (PhD, Illinois, Urbana-Champaign 1970; prof. emeritus) American foreign relations

Wheeler, William Bruce (PhD, Virginia 1967; prof. emeritus) early national America, US urban, regional studies; wwheele1@utk.edu

Recently Awarded PhDs

Eubanks, Elizabeth "Benevolent Patriarchs: Gender and Charity in Colonial South Carolina"

Hodge, Joshua S. "Alabama's Public Wilderness: Reconstruction Politics, Natural Resources, and the End of the Southern Commons, 1866-1905"

Kleinkopf, Kathryn "Encountering the Holy: An Intersectional Study of Early Christian Asceticism"

University of Tennessee at Martin

Dept. of History and Philosophy, 322 Humanities Bldg., 209 Hurt St., Martin, TN 38238-5001. 731.881.7470. Fax 731.881.7584. Email: dcoffey@utm.edu. Website: http://www.utm.edu/departments/history/.

The Department of History and Philosophy's mission is to provide an outstanding undergraduate education by offering an appealing and appropriate array of courses taught by devoted faculty who care deeply about students, individualized, one-on- one academic advising, and opportunities to enhance one's educational experience through internships, faculty-led travel-study, and advanced research and writing.

Chair: David A. Coffey
Degrees Offered: BA,BS
Academic Year System: Semester
Areas of Specialization: US, Europe, military, women, ancient and late antiquity
Tuition (per academic year):
In-State: $8024
Out-of-State: $21968
Enrollment 2018-19:
Undergraduate Majors: 50
Degrees in History: 10 BA, 3 BS
Addresses:
Admissions: http://www.utm.edu/admis.php
Financial Aid: http://www.utm.edu/departments/finaid/

Adjunct Faculty

Camper, Joshua (MA, Murray State 2008; lect.) jcamper@utm.edu

Guyer, Benjamin Michael (PhD, Kansas 2016; lect.) medieval Europe, England; bguyer@utm.edu

Smith, Timothy B. (PhD, Mississippi State 2001; lect.) US, Civil War, military; tims@utm.edu

Full-time Faculty

Barber, David (PhD, California, Davis 2003; prof.) 20th-century US, Africa; dbarber@utm.edu

Carls, Alice-Catherine (PhD, Paris, Sorbonne 1976; prof.) modern Europe, Poland, Russia; accarls@utm.edu

Coffey, David A. (PhD, Texas Christian 1999; prof. and chair) 19th-century US, military, Latin America; dcoffey@utm.edu

Garlitz, Richard P. (PhD, Ohio 2008; assoc. prof.) world, diplomacy, Middle East; rgarlitz@utm.edu

Howard, Nathan Dale (PhD, Arkansas 2005; prof.) ancient and medieval; nhoward@utm.edu

Hur, Hyungju (PhD, Illinois, Urbana-Champaign 2012; asst. prof.) modern China, modern Japan, Korea; hhur1@utm.edu

LaFleur, Renee Anne (PhD, Ohio 2011; assoc. prof.) US, intellectual, Latin America; rlafleur@utm.edu

Lewis, Margaret Brannan (PhD, Virginia 2012; assoc. prof.) Germany, Europe, world civilizations; mlewis47@utm.edu

McDonough, Daniel J. (PhD, Illinois, Urbana-Champaign 1990; prof.) colonial America, England, military; danmc@utm.edu

Retired/Emeritus Faculty

Carroll, Robert L. (OMS, Mississippi 1962; asst. prof. emeritus; asst. vice chancellor, Alumni Affairs) US, US West

Downing, Marvin L. (PhD, Oklahoma 1970; prof. emeritus) 20th-century US, frontier; mdowning@utm.edu

Jones, K Paul (PhD, Wisconsin, Madison 1970; prof. emeritus) Germany, modern Europe, European diplomatic

Maness, Lonnie E. (PhD, Memphis 1980; prof. emeritus) Middle Period US, diplomatic, Tennessee; lmaness@utm.edu

Tennessee State University

Dept. of History, Political Science, Geography, and Africana Studies, 3500 John Merritt Blvd., Nashville, TN 37209-1561. 615.963.5471. Fax 615.963.5497. Email: aoyebade@tnstate.edu. Website: http://www.tnstate.edu/history/.

The majors and minors offered by the Department of HPGA will give you the skills to embark upon a number of different career paths. During your time with our excellent faculty, you will become a much improved writer, a strong analytical thinker, and an informed citizen.

Chair: Adebayo Oyebade
Degrees Offered: BA,BS
Academic Year System: Semester
Areas of Specialization: America, African American, Europe, public, Middle East
Tuition (per academic year):
In-State: $6498
Out-of-State: $19218
Enrollment 2018-19:
Undergraduate Majors: 45
Degrees in History: 8 BA
Addresses:
Admissions: http://students.tnstate.edu/
Financial Aid: http://www.tnstate.edu/financial_aid/

Full-time Faculty

Bertrand, Michael T. (PhD, Memphis 1995; assoc. prof.) 20th-century US, US South; mbertrand@tnstate.edu
Brown, Keisha Alexandria (PhD, Southern California 2015; asst. prof.) East Asia; kbrown110@tnstate.edu
Browne, Sheri B. (PhD, Minnesota 2002; prof.) women and gender, early America; sbrowne@tnstate.edu
Corse, Theron (PhD, Vanderbilt 1995; assoc. prof.) Latin America, science and technology; tcorse@tnstate.edu
Dachowski, Elizabeth H. (PhD, Minnesota 1995; prof.) ancient/medieval/early modern Europe, world; edachowski@tnstate.edu
Dark, Joel H. (PhD, Vanderbilt 1998; prof. and assoc. dean; Liberal Arts) modern Europe; jdark@tnstate.edu
Ewing, K. T. (PhD, Memphis 2014; asst. prof.) African American, women and gender, 20th-century US; kewing6@tnstate.edu
Oyebade, Adebayo O. (PhD, Temple 1995; prof. and chair) Africa; aoyebade@tnstate.edu
Patrick, Andrew J. (PhD, Manchester 2011; asst. prof.) US foreign relations, Middle East, world; apatric2@tnstate.edu
Schmeller, Erik S. (PhD, Southern Illinois, Carbondale 1999; prof.) colonial and early Republic America, British Empire; eschmeller@tnstate.edu
Williams, Learotha, Jr. (PhD, Florida State 2003; assoc. prof.) African American, public, 19th-century US; lwilli22@tnstate.edu

Part-time Faculty

Bobo, Pamela (MEd, Tennessee State 1998; instr.) women, presidential; pbobo@tnstate.edu
Watson, Griff (DA, Middle Tennessee State 1985; instr.) America; gwatson@mytsu.tnstate.edu

Tennessee Technological University

Dept. of History, Box 5064, 5 William Jones Dr., Cookeville, TN 38505. 931.372.3332. Fax 931.372.6142. Email: jjroberts@ tntech.edu. Website: https://www.tntech.edu/cas/history/.

The Department has developed and maintains a comprehensive and successful curriculum for history majors. Majors are expected to think analytically, ascertain facts and make objective judgments, and write clearly, communicating the results of reasoned analysis.

Chair: Jeffery J. Roberts
Degrees Offered: BA,BS
Academic Year System: Semester
Areas of Specialization: US, Europe, regional
Tuition (per academic year):
In-State: $8449
Out-of-State: $16535
Enrollment 2018-19:
Undergraduate Majors: 78
Degrees in History: 6 BA, 12 BS
Addresses:
Admissions: http://www.tntech.edu/admissions/
Financial Aid: http://www.tntech.edu/financialaid/

Adjunct Faculty

Beason, Ed (MA, Tennessee Tech. 2005; adj.) US; ebeason@tntech.edu
Brown, R. Keith (MA, West Georgia; adj.) US; rbrown1@k12tn.net
Schmitzer, Jeanne (MA, Central Florida 1996; adj.) US; jschmitzer@twlakes.net

Full-time Faculty

Akehinmi, Krystal D. F. (PhD, Rutgers 2010; asst. prof.) African American, women; kdfakehinmi@tntech.edu
Banton, Arthur (PhD, Purdue 2016; asst. prof.) sports, urban culture, African American; abanton@tntech.edu
Birdwell, Michael E. (PhD, Tennessee, Knoxville 1996; prof.) cultural, film, World War I; birdie@tntech.edu
Davis, Philip C., Jr. (MA, Wake Forest 1994; instr.) US; pdavis@tntech.edu
Dollar, Kent T. (PhD, Tennessee, Knoxville 2001; prof.) colonial America, early national, Civil War; kdollar@tntech.edu
Driggers, E. Allen, Jr. (PhD, South Carolina 2015; asst. prof.) science, modern England; edriggers@tntech.edu
Hinton, Paula K. (PhD, Miami, Ohio 2001; assoc. prof.) women, gender, crime; phinton@tntech.edu
Laningham, Susan D. (PhD, Arkansas 2001; assoc. prof.) medieval and early modern Europe, Latin America, religion; slaningham@tntech.edu
Propes, C. Elizabeth (PhD, Mississippi 2003; assoc. prof.) modern France, 19th-century Europe, Africa; epropes@tntech.edu
Roberts, Jeffery J. (PhD, Ohio State 1990; prof. and chair) European military, Russia, Middle East; jjroberts@tntech.edu
Smith, Troy Duane (PhD, Illinois, Urbana-Champaign 2011; asst. prof.) western US, Native American, environmental; tdsmith@tntech.edu

Retired/Emeritus Faculty

Brinker, William (PhD, Indiana 1973; prof. emeritus) East Asia, American diplomatic; wbrinker@tntech.edu
Dickinson, W. Calvin (PhD, North Carolina, Chapel Hill 1967; prof. emeritus) Stuart England, Tennessee; cdickinson@tntech.edu

Fernandez, Gilbert G. (PhD, Florida State 1974; prof. emeritus) French Revolution, 19th-century Europe, Spain; gfernandez@tntech.edu

Kharif, Wali R. (PhD, Florida State 1983; prof. emeritus) Afro-American, New and Old South, sports; wrkharif@tntech.edu

Schrader, William C., III (PhD, Catholic 1972; prof. emeritus) early modern Europe, medieval, Germany

Webb, George E. (PhD, Arizona 1978; prof. emeritus) science, American West, modern England; gwebb@tntech.edu

Whiteaker, Larry H. (PhD, Princeton 1977; prof. emeritus) American religious, Civil War; lwhiteaker@tntech.edu

Texas A&M University

Dept. of History, 4236 TAMU, 101 Melbern Glasscock Bldg., College Station, TX 77843-4236. 979.845.7151. Fax 979.862.4314. Email: ckblanton@tamu.edu. Website: https://history.tamu.edu/.

The Department of History at Texas A&M University offers the BA, MA, and PhD. The faculty teach courses on peoples, ideas, and cultures from around the world and across the ages, and are devoted to developing students' critical thinking, reading, and writing skills.

Chair: Carlos K. Blanton
Director of Graduate Studies: Walter Kamphoefner
Director of Undergraduate Studies: Felipe Hinojosa
Degrees Offered: BA,MA,PhD
Academic Year System: Semester
Areas of Specialization: war and society, Caribbean and Atlantic world, Chicano and Latino, Britain and Empire, Southwest and borders
Undergraduate Tuition (per academic year):
In-State: $10764
Out-of-State: $36442
Graduate Tuition (per academic year):
In-State: $7444
Out-of-State: $15958
Enrollment 2018-19:
Undergraduate Majors: 490
New Graduate Students: 10
Full-time Graduate Students: 39
Part-time Graduate Students: 23
Degrees in History: 136 BA, 1 MA, 5 PhD
Addresses:
Admissions: http://www.tamu.edu/admissions/
Financial Aid: https://financialaid.tamu.edu/

Full-time Faculty

Alonzo, Armando Cantu (PhD, Indiana 1991; assoc. prof.) Mexican American, Texas, Spanish borderlands; alonzo@tamu.edu

Anderson, Terry H. (PhD, Indiana 1978; prof.) US since 1930s, 1960s; tha@tamu.edu

Bickham, Troy O. (DPhil, Oxford 2001; prof.) Atlantic world, Britain, US; tbickham@tamu.edu

Blanton, Carlos Kevin (PhD, Rice 1999; prof. and chair) Latino/a, US and Texas; ckblanton@tamu.edu

Bouton, Cynthia A. (PhD, SUNY, Binghamton 1985; prof.) modern France, European women and gender, European social; c-bouton@tamu.edu

Brooks, Charles E. (PhD, SUNY, Buffalo 1988; assoc. prof.) early national US; c-brooks@tamu.edu

Broussard, Albert S. (PhD, Duke 1977; prof.) African American, urban; a-broussard@tamu.edu

Cobbs, Elizabeth Anne (PhD, Stanford 1988; prof.) US, Latin America; cobbs@tamu.edu

Coopersmith, Jonathan C. (DPhil, Oxford 1985; prof.) technology, Soviet Union; j-coopersmith@tamu.edu

Dror, Olga (PhD, Cornell 2003; assoc. prof.) modern East Asia, Vietnam; olgadror@tamu.edu

Emre, Side (PhD, Chicago 2009; assoc. prof.) Islamic; sideemre@tamu.edu

Foote, Lorien L. (PhD, Oklahoma 1999; prof.) war and society; lfoote@tamu.edu

Haefeli, Evan (PhD, Princeton 2000; assoc. prof.) Atlantic world; evanhaefeli@neo.tamu.edu

Hatfield, April Lee (PhD, Johns Hopkins 1997; assoc. prof.) early America, Atlantic world, Caribbean; ahatfield@tamu.edu

Hernandez, Sonia (PhD, Houston 2006; assoc. prof.) Chicano/Latino, Latin America; soniah@tamu.edu

Hinojosa, Felipe (PhD, Houston 2009; assoc. prof. and dir., undergrad. studies) Latino/a, Chicano/a, religion; fhinojosa@tamu.edu

Hudson, Angela Pulley (PhD, Yale 2007; prof.) American Indian and US South; aphudson@tamu.edu

Hudson, David R. C. (PhD, Texas A&M 1998; instructional assoc. prof.) Ireland; david-hudson@tamu.edu

Johnson, Violet Showers (PhD, Boston Coll. 1992; prof.; dir., Africana Studies) US race/ethnicity/immigration, Africa, African diaspora; vmjohnson@tamu.edu

Kamphoefner, Walter D. (PhD, Missouri, Columbia 1978; prof. and dir., grad. studies) 19th-century US, immigration, urban; waltkamp@tamu.edu

Kim, Hoi-eun (PhD, Harvard 2006; assoc. prof.) central Europe and Japan; hekim@tamu.edu

Kirkendall, Andrew J. (PhD, North Carolina, Chapel Hill 1996; prof.) Latin America, Brazil; andykirk@tamu.edu

Lenihan, John H. (PhD, Maryland, Coll. Park 1976; assoc. prof.) recent US, cultural and intellectual; j-lenihan@tamu.edu

Linn, Brian McAllister (PhD, Ohio State 1985; prof.) military, US, Pacific; b-linn@tamu.edu

MacNamara, Trent (PhD, Columbia 2015; asst. prof.) 19th- and early 20th-century US, cultural and intellectual, social

McNamara, Sarah J. (PhD, North Carolina, Chapel Hill 2016; asst. prof.) Latina/o, US, women and gender

Parker, Jason C. (PhD, Florida 2002; prof.) US foreign relations, modern US; jcparker@tamu.edu

Reese, Roger R. (PhD, Texas, Austin 1990; prof.) Soviet Union; rreese@tamu.edu

Resch, Robert P. (PhD, California, Davis 1985; assoc. prof.) modern European intellectual, Marxism, structuralism and poststructuralism; rpresch@tamu.edu

Riegg, Stephen B. (PhD, North Carolina, Chapel Hill 2016; asst. prof.) Russia and eastern Europe, modern Europe

Rouleau, Brian (PhD, Pennsylvania 2010; assoc. prof.) US in world; brianr@tamu.edu

Schloss, Rebecca Hartkopf (PhD, Duke 2003; assoc. prof.) Atlantic world, Caribbean, France; rhschloss@tamu.edu

Schwartz, Daniel Louis (PhD, Princeton 2009; assoc. prof.) late antiquity/early Middle Ages; daniel.schwartz@tamu.edu

Seipp, Adam R. (PhD, North Carolina, Chapel Hill 2005; prof.) European war and society, Germany, transnational; aseipp@tamu.edu

Smith, Philip M. (PhD, Texas A&M 2007; instructional assoc. prof.) pms@tamu.edu

Stranges, Anthony N. (PhD, Wisconsin, Madison 1977; assoc. prof.) science, chemistry; a-stranges@tamu.edu

Unterman, Katherine R. (PhD, Yale 2011; assoc. prof.) 19th-century US

Vaught, David J. (PhD, California, Davis 1997; prof.) US agriculture, labor, Gilded Age and Progressive era; d-vaught@tamu.edu

Wood, Julia Erin (PhD, Yale 2011; asst. prof.) 20th-century US; erin.wood@tamu.edu

Nondepartmental Historians

Konrad, Christoph F. (PhD, North Carolina, Chapel Hill 1985; assoc. prof.; Modern and Classical Languages) Greece and Rome, Roman government and religion, Greek and Latin historiography; konradc@tamu.edu

Retired/Emeritus Faculty

Adams, Ralph J. Q. (PhD, California, Santa Barbara 1972; dist. prof. emeritus) modern Britain; rjqa@tamu.edu

Alpern, Sara (DPhil, Maryland, Coll. Park 1978; assoc. prof. emerita) American social and intellectual, American women; s-alpern@tamu.edu

Bradford, James C. (PhD, Virginia 1976; prof. emeritus) US naval, early national US, maritime; jcbradford@tamu.edu

Dawson, Joseph G. M., III (PhD, Louisiana State 1978; prof. emeritus) American military, Civil War and Reconstruction; jgdawson@tamu.edu

Dunlap, Thomas R. (PhD, Wisconsin, Madison 1975; prof. emeritus) environment, America; t-dunlap@tamu.edu

Dunning, Chester S. L. (PhD, Boston Coll. 1976; prof. emeritus) Russia, early modern Europe; c-dunning@tamu.edu

Rosenheim, James M. (PhD, Princeton 1981; prof. emeritus) early modern and 18th-century Britain, British social; j-rosenheim@tamu.edu

Wang, Di (PhD, Johns Hopkins 1998; prof. emeritus) modern East Asia, China; di-wang@tamu.edu

Yarak, Larry W. (PhD, Northwestern 1983; assoc. prof. emeritus) Africa, comparative slavery; yarak@tamu.edu

Recently Awarded PhDs

Coulthard, Cheryl "The Quest for a Utopian Solution to Social Problems of Race, Gender and Social Inequality: A Comparative Study of Communal Societies in the 19th and 20th Centuries"

Delear, Stephen D. "Death of a Multi-Ethnic Society: Populist and the Bourbon Coup in Texas, 1880-1910"

Harward, Grant Thomas "Holy War: The Romanian Army, Motivation, and the Holocaust, 1941-44"

Linsenbardt, Brooke "Faith In Ourselves: Indigenous Women's Educational (Trans) Creatings in the 1970s and 1980s"

Walters, Katherine Kuehler "The 1920s Texas Ku Klux Klan Revisited: White Supremacy and Structural Power in a Rural County"

Yokell, Marshall "The German Foreign Office and the Developing World, 1871-1914"

Yokell, Matthew A. "Qingdao and the German Experience in China, 1890-1918"

Texas A&M University-Commerce

Dept. of History, PO Box 3011, Commerce, TX 75429. 903.886.5226. Fax 903.468.3230. Email: Sharon.Kowalsky@tamuc.edu. Website: http://www.tamuc.edu/academics/colleges/humanitiesSocialSciencesArts/departments/history/.

The Department of History at Texas A&M University-Commerce cultivates an academic appreciation of diversity and offer opportunities to engage with and serve university, regional, national, and global communities.

Chair: Sharon Kowalsky
Director of Graduate Studies: Andrew Baker

Director of Undergraduate Studies: Derrick McKisick
Degrees Offered: BA,BS,MA,MS
Academic Year System: Semester
Areas of Specialization: US, Europe, Latin America, India, transatlantic, world, public, food, environmental, Russia/Soviet, women and gender; Islamic world, Texas
Undergraduate Tuition (per academic year):
 In-State: $8434
 Out-of-State: $20884
Graduate Tuition (per academic year):
 In-State: $6424
 Out-of-State: $13239
Enrollment 2018-19:
 Undergraduate Majors: 156
 New Graduate Students: 11
 Full-time Graduate Students: 15
 Part-time Graduate Students: 38
 Degrees in History: 2 BA, 20 BS, 4 MA, 9 MS
Undergraduate Addresses:
 Admissions: http://www.tamuc.edu/admissions/
 Financial Aid: http://www.tamuc.edu/admissions/tuitionCosts/
Graduate Addresses:
 Admissions: http://www.tamuc.edu/academics/graduateSchool/graduateAdmissions/
 Financial Aid: http://www.tamuc.edu/admissions/tuitionCosts/

Full-time Faculty

Baker, Andrew C. (PhD, Rice 2014; asst. prof. and dir., grad. studies) US South, Caribbean, environmental/agricultural; Andrew.Baker@tamuc.edu

Brannon-Wranosky, Jessica S. (PhD, North Texas 2010; Dist. Prof.) digital, 19th-century Texas, women; jessica.wranosky@tamuc.edu

Cardona, Mylynka Kilgore (PhD, Texas, Arlington 2015; asst. prof.) transatlantic, public, women's and gender studies; Mylynka.Cardona@tamuc.edu

Ford, Judy Ann (PhD, Fordham 1994; prof.) medieval, Renaissance and Reformation; judy.ford@tamuc.edu

Kowalsky, Sharon A. (PhD, North Carolina, Chapel Hill 2004; assoc. prof. and head; dir., Gender Studies) early Soviet Union, women, criminology; sharon.kowalsky@tamuc.edu

Kuracina, William F. (PhD, Syracuse 2008; prof. and CHSSA dean) modern South Asia, British Empire, modern Britain; william.kuracina@tamuc.edu

McKisick, Derrick Duane (PhD, Arkansas 2007; assoc. prof. and dir., undergrad. studies) African American, Native American, US South; Derrick.McKisick@tamuc.edu

Moreno, E. Mark (PhD, Washington State 2011; assoc. prof.) Latin America, Mexico, Chicano; Mark.Moreno@tamuc.edu

Ross, Cynthia (PhD, Washington State 2011; asst. prof.) world, global environmental, Pacific; Cynthia.Ross@tamuc.edu

Smith, John Howard (PhD, SUNY, Albany 2003; prof.) colonial and revolutionary US, American religious; john.smith@tamuc.edu

Part-time Faculty

Dobbs, Ricky Floyd (PhD, Texas A&M 1996; prof.; assoc. provost, Academic Foundations) Texas, American South; Ricky.Dobbs@tamuc.edu

Retired/Emeritus Faculty

McFarland, Keith D. (PhD, Ohio State 1969; prof. emeritus and Univ. pres. emeritus) American social and intellectual, military, 20th century; keith.mcfarland@tamuc.edu

Wade, Harry (PhD, St. Louis 1967; prof. emeritus) modern Europe, East Asia, world; harry.wade@tamuc.edu

Texas A&M University-Corpus Christi

Dept. of History, 6300 Ocean Dr., Unit 5814, Corpus Christi, TX 78412. 361.825.5783. Fax 361.825.5844. Email: peter.moore@ tamucc.edu. Website: http://cla.tamucc.edu/humanities/ history/.

Our courses provide students the opportunity to deepen their understanding and appreciation of the development of the United States, Latin America, Asia, and Europe; refine their reading, listening, critical thinking, writing, communication, and research skills; and acquire integrated perspectives on political, social, economic, cultural, and military factors, which have shaped the city, the state, the region, the nation, and the world.

Chair: Peter Moore
Director of Graduate Studies: Sandrine Sanos
Degrees Offered: BA,MA
Academic Year System: Semester
Areas of Specialization: US, Texas, Mexican American, Latin America, Europe and Asia
Undergraduate Tuition (per academic year):
  In-State: $6045
  Out-of-State: $17126
Graduate Tuition (per academic year):
  In-State: $6055
  Out-of-State: $14723
Enrollment 2018-19:
  Undergraduate Majors: 133
  New Graduate Students: 7
  Full-time Graduate Students: 8
  Part-time Graduate Students: 4
  Degrees in History: 34 BA, 7 MA
Undergraduate Addresses:
  Admissions: http://admissions.tamucc.edu/
  Financial Aid: http://osfa.tamucc.edu/student_info.html
Graduate Addresses:
  Admissions: http://admissions.tamucc.edu/
  Financial Aid: https://gradschool.tamucc.edu/

Full-time Faculty

Blanke, David (PhD, Loyola, Chicago 1996; prof.) cultural, transportation, Gilded Age and Progressive Era; david.blanke@ tamucc.edu

Brown, Jennifer Corrinne (PhD, Washington State 2012; assoc. prof.) US environmental; jennifer.brown@tamucc.edu

Costanzo, Adam (PhD, California, Davis 2012; professional assoc. prof.) early America, urban; adam.costanzo@tamucc.edu

Moore, Peter N. (PhD, Georgia 2001; prof. and chair) US South, US religion, early national US; peter.moore@tamucc.edu

Quiroz, Anthony (PhD, Iowa 1998; prof.) Mexican American, US labor and social, recent US; anthony.quiroz@tamucc.edu

Robinson, Beth (PhD, Wisconsin, Milwaukee 2013; asst. prof.) US labor, US women; beth.robinson@tamucc.edu

Rueda, Claudia P. (PhD, Texas, Austin 2014; asst. prof.) Latin America; claudia.rueda@tamucc.edu

Sanos, Sandrine (PhD, Rutgers 2004; prof. and grad. prog. coord.) France, modern Europe, European women; sandrine.sanos@ tamucc.edu

Wooster, Robert (PhD, Texas, Austin 1985; Regents Prof.) US West, US military, Texas; robert.wooster@tamucc.edu

Visiting Faculty

Covey, Eric (PhD, Texas, Austin 2014; vis. professional asst. prof.) American studies, cultural geography, feminist and queer theory, Orientalism and imperialism

Johnson, Timothy Scott (PhD, Graduate Center, CUNY 2016; vis. professional asst. prof.) modern France, modern Europe, intellectual; timothy.johnson@tamucc.edu

Jones, Kelly Hacker (PhD, SUNY, Stony Brook 2018; vis. asst. prof.) women and gender, medicine

Texas A&M University-San Antonio

History Program, Dept. of Arts & Humanities, One University Way, San Antonio, TX 78224. 210.784.2200. Fax 210.784.2299. Email: Julie.Hebert@tamusa.edu. Website: http://www.tamusa.edu/ College-of-Arts-and-Sciences/artsandhumanities/history/.

Our program's mission is to provide students with a broad knowledge of the past and an appreciation of the complexities of the contemporary world. The study of History equips students with the necessary skills for success in a wide range of careers in education, public history, social service, law, government, and business. Students receive training in the collection, analysis, and evaluation of information, critical thinking, and oral and written communication.

Chair: Ann Bliss
Degrees Offered: BA
Academic Year System: Semester
Areas of Specialization: US, Latin America, Europe
Tuition (per academic year): $8216
Addresses:
  Admissions: http://www.tamusa.edu/admissions/ undergraduatestudents/
  Financial Aid: http://www.tamusa.edu/financialaid/

Full-time Faculty

Bush, William S. (PhD, Texas, Austin 2004; prof.) US, social and cultural, children and youth, policy, juvenile justice; william. bush@tamusa.edu

Galan, Francis Xavier (PhD, Southern Methodist 2006; asst. prof.) Tejano, slavery/smuggling/revolution/oil in Mexico/Texas/ Louisiana, Sephardic Jewish diaspora in Latin America; francis. galan@tamusa.edu

Porter, Amy M. (PhD, Southern Methodist 2004; assoc. prof.) Spanish colonial borderlands, early US, women, Texas; amy,porter@tamusa.edu

Westermann, Edward B. (PhD, North Carolina, Chapel Hill 2000; prof.) Holocaust and genocide studies, Nazi Germany, World War II, air power; edward.westermann@tamusa.edu

University of Texas at Arlington

Dept. of History, Box 19529, Arlington, TX 76019-0529. 817.272.2861. Fax 817.272.2852. Email: history@uta.edu. Website: http://www.uta.edu/history/.

Our department offers students who major in History a wide range of topical, regional, and chronological courses that broaden their understanding of the field and improve their knowledge of the past. At the graduate level, we offer students a rigorous MA degree as well as a PhD in History that includes innovative offerings in

Public History, Archives Administration, and GIS, as well as North America's only specialized track in the History of Cartography.

Chair: Scott W. Palmer

Director of Graduate Studies: Stephanie Cole (MA) and Kenyon Zimmer (PhD)

Degrees Offered: BA, MA, PhD

Academic Year System: Semester

Areas of Specialization: trans-Atlantic, US Southwest, Europe, Latin America, Africa

Undergraduate Tuition (per academic year):
In-State: $8878
Out-of-State: $17302

Graduate Tuition (per academic year):
In-State: $8000
Out-of-State: $14318

Enrollment 2018-19:
Undergraduate Majors: 312
New Graduate Students: 6
Full-time Graduate Students: 68
Part-time Graduate Students: 39
Degrees in History: 88 BA, 11 MA, 3 PhD

Undergraduate Addresses:
Admissions: https://www.uta.edu/admissions/
Financial Aid: http://www.uta.edu/fao/

Graduate Addresses:
Admissions: https://www.uta.edu/admissions/graduate/
Financial Aid: http://www.uta.edu/fao/

Full-time Faculty

Adam, Thomas (PhD, Leipzig, Germany 1998; prof.) Europe, trans-Atlantic, 19th-century philanthropy; adam@uta.edu

Babiracki, Patryk J. (PhD, Johns Hopkins 2008; assoc. prof.) modern Russia, eastern Europe, transnational; babiracki@uta.edu

Breuer, Kimberly H. (PhD, Vanderbilt 2004; sr. lect.) Latin America; breuer@uta.edu

Cole, Stephanie (PhD, Florida 1994; assoc. prof. and dir., grad. studies) US women, African American, social; scole@uta.edu

Conrad, Paul T. (PhD, Texas, Austin 2011; asst. prof.) Native American, US Southwest, US; conrad@uta.edu

Demhardt, Imre Josef (PhD, Darmstadt, Germany 2003; PhD, Frankfurt Am Main, Germany 1995; endowed prof.) historical geography, cartography, German colonialism; demhardt@uta.edu

Fairbanks, Robert Bruce (PhD, Cincinnati 1981; prof.) US urban; fairbank@uta.edu

Garrigus, John D. (PhD, Johns Hopkins 1988; prof.) Caribbean, colonial Latin America, French Atlantic; garrigus@uta.edu

Goldberg, Joyce S. (PhD, Indiana 1982; assoc. prof.) US diplomatic and military; goldberg@uta.edu

LaFevor, David Clark (PhD, Vanderbilt 2011; asst. prof.) Latin America; dlafevor@uta.edu

Maizlish, Stephen E. (PhD, California, Berkeley 1978; assoc. prof.) antebellum US political, Civil War and Reconstruction; maizlish@uta.edu

Milson, Andrew J. (PhD, Georgia 1999; prof.) social science education/geography; milson@uta.edu

Morris, Christopher (PhD, Florida 1991; prof.) early national, Old US South, US social; morris@uta.edu

Narrett, David E. (PhD, Cornell 1981; prof.) colonial and revolutionary America; narrett@uta.edu

Palmer, Scott W. (PhD, Illinois, Urbana-Champaign 1997; prof. and chair) Russia, technology; scott.palmer@uta.edu

Price, Delaina (PhD, Yale 2017; asst. prof.) African American, transatlantic slave trade, precolonial Africa

Rose, Sarah F. (PhD, Illinois, Chicago 2008; assoc. prof.) disability, US policy, US labor; srose@uta.edu

Salinas, Cristina (PhD, Texas, Austin 2012; asst. prof.) Mexican American, US; csalinas@uta.edu

Sandy, James (PhD, Texas Tech 2016; adj.) American martial culture, special warfare, American culture; james.sandy@uta.edu

Saxon, Gerald D. (PhD, North Texas 1979; assoc. prof.) archival science, Texas and US Southwest, oral and research methods; saxon@uta.edu

Travis, Charles IV (PhD, Trinity Coll., Dublin 2006; asst. prof.) Atlantic, spatial, geographic information systems; charles.travis@uta.edu

Zimmer, Kenyon W. (PhD, Pittsburgh 2010; assoc. prof. and dir., grad. studies) migration, transnational social movements, race/ethnicity/gender; kzimmer@uta.edu

Joint/Cross Appointments

Haynes, Sam W. (PhD, Houston 1988; prof.; dir., Center for Greater Southwestern Studies) 19th-century US, Texas, Anglo-American relations; haynes@uta.edu

Part-time Faculty

Cawthon, Elisabeth A. (PhD, Virginia 1985; assoc. prof. and dean) British constitutional and legal, Tudor-Stuart, legal and medical; cawthon2@uta.edu

Folsom, Bradley Neill (PhD, North Texas 2014; asst. prof.) Texas and Southwest, US; bfolsom@uta.edu

Hunnicutt, Wendell A. (PhD, Texas, Arlington 2010; lect.) trans-Atlantic; hunnicut@uta.edu

Lawrence, Jennifer (PhD, Texas A&M 2004; lect.) US, Texas; jlawrenc@exchange.uta.edu

Retired/Emeritus Faculty

Dulaney, W. Marvin (PhD, Ohio State 1984; prof. emeritus) African American, US; dulaney@uta.edu

Green, George N. (PhD, Florida State 1966; prof. emeritus) US labor, Texas, New US South; ggreen@uta.edu

Jalloh, Alusine (PhD, Howard 1993; assoc. prof. emeritus) Africa; jalloh@uta.edu

Kyle, Donald G. (PhD, McMaster 1981; prof. emeritus) ancient Greece and Rome, ancient sport; kyle@uta.edu

Palmer, Stanley H. (PhD, Harvard 1973; prof. emeritus) modern Britain and Ireland, police, British Empire; spalmer@uta.edu

Philp, Kenneth R. (PhD, Michigan State 1968; prof. emeritus) contemporary US, US historiography, Native American; philp@uta.edu

Reinhardt, Steven G. (PhD, Northern Illinois 1982; assoc. prof. emeritus) early modern Europe, France, colonial Louisiana; reinhard@uta.edu

Richmond, Douglas (PhD, Washington 1976; prof. emeritus) Latin America; richmond@uta.edu

Rodnitzky, Jerome L. (PhD, Illinois, Urbana-Champaign 1967; prof. emeritus) contemporary US social and intellectual; jerry.rodnitzky@uta.edu

Trevino, Roberto R. (PhD, Stanford 1994; assoc. prof. emeritus)

Recently Awarded PhDs

Caldwell, Robert B. "Indians in their Proper Place: Culture Areas, Linguistic Stocks, and the Genealogy of a Map"

Loignon, Austin "Cornflakes, God, and Enemas: John Harvey Kellogg and Global Health Reform in the 19th Century"

Tinkler, Jacqueline Lee "Determinants of Ethnic Formation and Retention as Seen among Belgian Migrants in Northeast Wisconsin"

Towns, Lydia "The Opening of the Atlantic World: England's Transatlantic Interests during the Reign of Henry VIII"

Wells, Cory D "Immigrant Nativists: Irish Protestants' Anti-Catholicism in the Atlantic World, 1830-1930"

University of Texas at Austin

Dept. of History, 128 Inner Campus Dr. B7000, GAR 1.104, Austin, TX 78712-1739. 512.471.3261. Fax 512.475.7222. Email: arturo. flores@austin.utexas.edu. Website: https://liberalarts.utexas. edu/history/.

The history major prepares students not only for diverse workplaces, but also for a life of engaged citizenship, as all of us confront an ever more complicated and interconnected world. As a history student, you will study with some of the finest teachers at UT, graduate with the skills that every job-seeker needs today, and learn about the US and its relations with the rest of the world.

Chair: Jacqueline Jones
Director of Graduate Studies: Alison Frazier
Degrees Offered: BA,MA,PhD
Academic Year System: Semester
Areas of Specialization: US, Europe, Africa, Asia, Latin America
Undergraduate Tuition (per academic year):
In-State: $10112
Out-of-State: $35996
Graduate Tuition (per academic year):
In-State: $8088
Out-of-State: $16032
Enrollment 2018-19:
Undergraduate Majors: 600
New Graduate Students: 10
Full-time Graduate Students: 100
Part-time Graduate Students: 10
Degrees in History: 150 BA, 15 MA, 12 PhD
Undergraduate Addresses:
Admissions: https://admissions.utexas.edu
Financial Aid: http://finaid.utexas.edu/
Graduate Addresses:
Admissions: https://gradschool.utexas.edu/
Financial Aid: http://finaid.utexas.edu/

Affiliated Faculty

Aghaie, Kamran Scot (PhD, UCLA 1999; assoc. prof.; Middle Eastern Studies, Center for Women's and Gender Studies, Center for Middle Eastern Studies) modern Iran, Middle East, Islamic rituals; kamranaghaie@austin.utexas.edu

Ali, Kamran Asdar (PhD, Johns Hopkins 1997; assoc. prof.; Anthropology, Middle Eastern Studies) gender, health, development; asdar@austin.utexas.edu

Alvarez, C.J. (PhD, Chicago 2014; asst. prof.; Mexican American and Latino/a Studies) US-Mexico border; cjalvarez@austin. utexas.edu

Biow, Douglas G. (PhD, Johns Hopkins 1990; prof.; Superior Oil Company-Linward Shivers Cenntenial Prof., Medieval and Renaissance Studies; French and Italian and dir., Center for European Studies) medieval and Renaissance studies, European

Burrowes, Nicole (PhD, Graduate Center, CUNY 2015; asst. prof.; African Studies) comparative histories of racialization and colonialism, black transnationalism, social movements; nburrowes@utexas.edu

Carleton, Don E. (PhD, Houston 1978; sr. lect.; exec. dir., Dolph Briscoe Center for American History) Texas, America; d.carleton@austin.utexas.edu

Chery, Tshepo Masango (PhD, Pennsylvania 2012; asst. prof.; African & African Diaspora Studies) Africa, social movements, religious activism and fundamentalism; tmchery@austin.utexas.edu

Davis, Janet Marie (PhD, Wisconsin-Madison 1998; asst. prof.) American Studies; janetmdavis@austin.utexas.edu

Denbow, James R. (PhD, Indiana; prof.; Anthropology) archaeology, later Stone Age and Iron Age studies, Southern and Centra Africa; jdenbow@austin.utexas.edu

Ebbeler, Jennifer V. (PhD, Pennsylvania 2001; assoc. prof.; Classics) Greco-Roman epistolography, late antique literature and cultural, classical Latin prose; jebbeler@austin.utexas.edu

Forbath, William E. (PhD, Yale 1992; assoc. dean, Research; Lloyd M. Bentsen Chair, Sch. of Law) legal and constitutional; wforbath@law.utexas.edu

Gutterman, Lauren Jae (PhD, NYU 2012; asst. prof.; American Studies) modern US, women/gender/sexuality, LGBT/queer studies; lgutterman@austin.utexas.edu

Inboden, William C. (PhD, Yale 2003; assoc. prof.; exec. dir., Clements Center for History, Strategy & Statecraft) America; inboden@austin.utexas.edu

Jiménez, Mónica Alexandra (PhD, Texas, Austin 2015; asst. prof.; African & African Diaspora Studies) legal history of empire, law and race, 20th-century nationalist movements; majimenez@ utexas.edu

Makalani, Minkah (PhD, Illinois, Urbana-Champaign 2004; assoc. prof.; African & African Diaspora Studies) postcolonial Caribbean, black radicalism; makalani@austin.utexas.edu

Martinich, Aloysius (PhD, California, San Diego 1973; prof.; Philosophy) martinich@mail.utexas.edu

Moin, A. Azfar (PhD, Michigan 2010; assoc. prof.; Middle Eastern Studies) Sufism and sainthood in Islam, sacred kingship, early modern Iran/Central Asia/South Asia; amoin@utexas.edu

Ramos Scharrón, Carlos E. (PhD, Colorado State; prof.; Geography and Environment) hydro-geomorphology, terrestrial carbon and sediment budgets, watershed analyses and land use change; cramos@austin.utexas.edu

Smith, Mark C. (PhD, Texas, Austin 1980; assoc. prof.; American Studies) US; mcsmith@mail.utexas.edu

Thompson, Shirley E. (PhD, Harvard 2001; assoc. prof.; American Studies, African & African Diaspora Studies) African American and African diaspora studies, 19th-century US cultural, slavery and post-emancipation cultures

Woods, Marjorie Curry (PhD, Toronto; prof.; English) medieval literature, medieval and Renaissance rhetoric and pedagogy, composition exercises in premodern classroom; marjoriewoods@austin.utexas.edu

Full-time Faculty

Abzug, Robert H. (PhD, California, Berkeley 1977; prof.) US social; zug@austin.utexas.edu

Berry, Daina Ramey (PhD, UCLA 1998; assoc. prof.) US, African American, slavery; drb@austin.utexas.edu

Bodian, Miriam (PhD, Hebrew 1988; prof.) early modern and medieval Europe, diaspora and migration, race/ethnicity/ nation; bodian@austin.utexas.edu

Brands, H. W. (PhD, Texas, Austin 1985; prof.) US, international relations; hwbrands@austin.utexas.edu

Brower, Benjamin Claude (PhD, Cornell 2005; assoc. prof.) modern France and Mediterranean, colonial Algeria, European imperialism; benbrower@utexas.edu

Brown, Jonathan Charles (PhD, Texas, Austin 1976; prof.) Latin America; j.brown@austin.utexas.edu

Bsumek, Erika (PhD, Rutgers 2000; assoc. prof.) 20th-century US, US West, Native American; embsumek@austin.utexas.edu

Buenger, Walter L., Jr. (PhD, Rice 1979; prof.) Texas, Southwest; w-buenger@austin.utexas.edu

Butler, Matthew (PhD, Bristol, UK 2000; assoc. prof.) postrevolutionary Mexico, local religion, Cristero Rebellion; mbutler@austin.utexas.edu

Cañizares-Esguerra, Jorge (PhD, Wisconsin-Madison 1995; prof.) Latin America; canizares-esguerra@austin.utexas.edu

Chatterjee, Indrani (PhD, London 1996; prof.) South Asia; ichatterjee@austin.utexas.edu

Coffin, Judith G. (PhD, Yale 1985; assoc. prof.) modern France; jcoffin@austin.utexas.edu

Crew, David F. (PhD, Cornell 1975; prof.) modern Germany; dfcrew@uts.cc.utexas.edu

Deans-Smith, Susan (PhD, Cambridge 1984; assoc. prof.) colonial Latin America; sdsmith@austin.utexas.edu

Del Castillo, Lina M. (PhD, Miami 2007; assoc. prof.) Latin America, 19th-century Colombia, US-Latin American relations; delcastillo@austin.utexas.edu

Di-Capua, Yoav (PhD, Princeton 2004; assoc. prof.) Middle East; ydi@austin.utexas.edu

Falola, Toyin O. (PhD, Ife, Nigeria 1981; Jacob & Frances Sanger Mossiker Chair and Univ. Dist. Teaching Prof.) West Africa; toyinfalola@austin.utexas.edu

Farmer, Ashley D. (PhD, Harvard 2013; asst. prof.; African & African Diaspora Studies) African American, African American women, black political thought; adf@austin.utexas.edu

Forgie, George B. (PhD, Stanford 1972; assoc. prof.) US, Jacksonian America; forgie@austin.utexas.edu

Frazier, Alison K. (PhD, Columbia 1998; assoc. prof. and grad. studies advisor) Europe 1300-1500; akfrazier@austin.utexas.edu

Frens-String, Joshua (PhD, NYU 2015; asst. prof.) Latin American and Latino, global food; jfstring@austin.utexas.edu

Garfield, Seth W. (PhD, Yale 1996; prof.) Latin American studies, Brazil; sgarfield@austin.utexas.edu

Garrard, Virginia (PhD, Tulane 1986; prof.) Latin America, race, ethnicity and nation; garrard@austin.utexas.edu

Green, Laurie B. (PhD, Chicago 1999; assoc. prof.) US, 20th century, gender; lbgreen@austin.utexas.edu

Guha, Sumit (PhD, Cambridge 1981; Frances Higginbotham Nalle Centennial Prof.) South Asia; sguha@austin.utexas.edu

Hardwick, Julie (PhD, Johns Hopkins 1991; prof.; dir., Inst. for Hist. Studies) early modern Europe, social and cultural; jhardwick@austin.utexas.edu

Hsu, Madeline Y. (PhD, Yale 1996; prof.; Asian Studies, Center for Asian American Studies) US, East Asia, diaspora and migration; myhsu@austin.utexas.edu

Hunt, Bruce J. (PhD, Johns Hopkins 1984; assoc. prof.) science; bjhunt@austin.utexas.edu

Jones, Jacqueline (PhD, Wisconsin-Madison 1976; prof. and chair) race/ethnicity/nation, diaspora and migration, gender/sexuality/family; jjones@mail.utexas.edu

Joseph, Peniel E. (PhD, Temple 2000; prof.; Lyndon B. Johnson Sch. of Public Affairs) civil rights/Black Power movements, race and public policy, African American

Kamil, Neil (PhD, Johns Hopkins 1989; assoc. prof.) colonial America; kamil@austin.utexas.edu

Lawrence, Mark Atwood (PhD, Yale 1999; assoc. prof.) US; malawrence@austin.utexas.edu

Levine, Philippa J. A. (DPhil, St. Antony's Coll., Oxford 1984; prof.) British studies, Victorian feminism, race and gender; philippa@austin.utexas.edu

Li, Huaiyin (PhD, UCLA 2000; prof.) East Asia, empire and globalization; hli@utexas.edu

Lichtenstein, Tatjana (PhD, Toronto 2009; asst. prof.) 20th-century Jewish history and politics, Israel, Holocaust; lichtens@austin.utexas.edu

Louis, Wm. Roger (LittD, Oxford 1979; DPhil, Oxford 1962; Kerr Chair and Dist. Teaching Prof.) Britain and British Empire, Middle East/India/Africa; britishstudies@austin.utexas.edu

Martinez, Alberto (PhD, Minnesota 2000; prof.) modern Europe, science/technology/medicine; almartinez@austin.utexas.edu

Matysik, Tracie (PhD, Cornell 2001; assoc. prof.) modern European intellectual and cultural; matysik@austin.utexas.edu

Mintz, Steven H. (PhD, Yale 1979; prof.; exec. dir., Inst. for Transformative Learning, UT System) America; smintz@utsystem.edu

Moore, Leonard (PhD, Ohio State 1998; prof.) US, race, ethnicity and nation; leonardmoore@austin.utexas.edu

Neuberger, Joan (PhD, Stanford 1985; prof.) Russia; neuberger@austin.utexas.edu

Neuburger, Mary C. (PhD, Washington 1997; prof.) modern eastern Europe; burgerm@austin.utexas.edu

Newman, Martha G. (PhD, Stanford 1988; assoc. prof.) medieval; newman@austin.utexas.edu

O'Connell, Aaron B. (PhD, Yale 2009; assoc. prof.) 20th-century military, US foreign affairs; aaron.oconnell@austin.utexas.edu

Olwell, Robert A. (PhD, Johns Hopkins 1991; assoc. prof.) colonial America; rolwell@austin.utexas.edu

Osseo-Asare, Abena Dove (PhD, Harvard 2005; assoc. prof.) history and sociology of science/technology/medicine/global health, Ghana/Madagascar/South Africa, nuclear energy/medical isotopes/biotechnology/plants and society; osseo@utexas.edu

Raby, Megan M. (PhD, Wisconsin-Madison 2012; asst. prof.) science, environmental studies; meganraby@austin.utexas.edu

Seaholm, Megan (PhD, Rice 1988; sr. lect.) late 19th- and 20th-century US social and cultural, US women; seaholm@austin.utexas.edu

Spellberg, Denise A. (PhD, Columbia 1989; prof.) Islamic civilization; spellberg@austin.utexas.edu

Stoff, Michael B. (PhD, Yale 1977; assoc. prof.) 20th-century US; planiidirector@austin.utexas.edu

Suri, Jeremi (PhD, Yale 2001; Mack Brown Dist. Chair; modern world, US, policy-making/governance/social movements/cultural (mis)understandings) Lyndon B. Johnson Sch. of Public Affairs; suri@austin.utexas.edu

Talbot, Cynthia (PhD, Wisconsin-Madison 1988; prof.) premodern Indian; ctalbot@austin.utexas.edu

Tully, Alan (PhD, Johns Hopkins 1973; prof.) colonial America; tully@austin.utexas.edu

Twinam, Ann (PhD, Yale 1976; prof.) colonial Latin America; anntwinam@austin.utexas.edu

Vaughn, James Martin (PhD, Chicago 2009; asst. prof.) empire and globalization, business and economic, intellectual; jmvaughn@austin.utexas.edu

Vong, Sam C. (PhD, Yale 2013; asst. prof.) Southeast Asia, Asian American, US

Walker, Juliet E. K. (PhD, Chicago 1976; prof.) African American business; jekwalker@austin.utexas.edu

Wynn, Charters (PhD, Stanford 1987; assoc. prof.) Soviet Russia; wynn@utexas.edu

Zamora, Emilio, Jr. (PhD, Texas, Austin 1983; prof.) Mexican American, American working class; e.zamora@austin.utexas.edu

Retired/Emeritus Faculty

Divine, Robert A. (PhD, Yale 1954; prof. emeritus) American diplomatic; rdivine@austin.rr.com

Gould, Lewis L. (PhD, Yale 1966; prof. emeritus) American political 1880-1920; lgould@austin.rr.com

Graham, Richard (PhD, Texas, Austin 1961; prof. emeritus) Brazil; rgraham@mail.utexas.edu

Hall, Michael G. (PhD, Johns Hopkins 1956; prof. emeritus) colonial America; mghall@mail.utexas.edu

Hopkins, Antony G. (PhD, London 1964; prof. emeritus) British Empire and Commonwealth, Africa, economic, imperialism and globalization; tony.hopkins@austin.utexas.edu

Lamphear, John (PhD, London 1972; prof. emeritus) sub-Saharan Africa; lamphear@mail.utexas.edu

Lasby, Clarence G. (PhD, UCLA 1962; prof. emeritus) US since 1929; clasby@austin.rr.com

Levack, Brian P. (PhD, Yale 1970; prof. emeritus) 16th- and 17th-century Britain; levack@austin.utexas.edu

Marcus, Abraham (PhD, Columbia 1979; prof. emeritus) modern Arabia; amarcus@uts.cc.utexas.edu

Meacham, Standish, Jr. (PhD, Harvard 1961; prof. emeritus) modern England; meachsalz@mail.utexas.edu

Miller, Guy Howard (PhD, Michigan 1970; assoc. prof. emeritus) US, religious thought; hmiller@mail.utexas.edu

Minault, Gail (PhD, Pennsylvania 1972; prof. emeritus) India; gminault@austin.utexas.edu

Monas, Sidney (PhD, Harvard 1955; prof. emeritus) Europe; smonas@mail.utexas.edu

Morgan, M. Gwyn (PhD, Exeter, UK 1962; prof. emeritus) medieval Europe; mgm@mail.utexas.edu

Oshinsky, David M. (PhD, Brandeis 1971; prof. emeritus) 20th-century US; oshinsky@mail.utexas.edu

Pells, Richard H. (PhD, Harvard 1969; prof. emeritus) US, 20th-century intellectual and social; rpells@aol.com

Rhoads, Edward J. M. (PhD, Harvard 1970; prof. emeritus) modern China; erhoads@mail.utexas.edu

Recently Awarded PhDs

Babits, Christopher Michael "To Cure a Sinful Nation: Conversion Therapy and the Making of Modern America, 1940 to Today"

Fisher, Dennis "To Not Sell One Perch: Algonquin Politics and Culture at Kitigan Zibi during the 20th Century"

Flannery, Kristie Patricia "Forging Loyalty to Spain in the 'Catholic Republic' of Manila, 1750-1808"

Minami, Kazushi "From Enemies to Friends: The Rise of US-Chinese Reconciliation, 1964-79"

O'Brien, Elizabeth "Intimate Interventions: The Cultural Politics of Reproductive Surgery in Mexico, 1790-1940"

Rose, Christopher S. "Disease, Depravity, and Revolution: The Breakdown in Public Health in Egypt, 1914-19"

Shore, Edward F. "Avengers of Zumbi: The Rise of the Quilombo Movement and Affirmative Action in Brazil, 1920-2015"

University of Texas at El Paso

Dept. of History, Liberal Arts Bldg., Rm. 320, 500 W. University, El Paso, TX 79968-0532. 915.747.5508. Fax 915.747.5948. Email: history@utep.edu. Website: https://www.utep.edu/liberalarts/history/.

We offer degrees at the undergraduate, master's, and doctoral levels, and our students enjoy many opportunities for research and travel. Our faculty members are committed teachers and scholars, with substantial records of publication and national and international reputations.

Chair: Jeffrey Shepherd

Director of Graduate Studies: Ignacio Martinez (PhD); Joshua Fan (MA)

Degrees Offered: BA,MA,PhD

Academic Year System: Semester

Areas of Specialization: US-Mexico border, Latin America, US, Europe, Africa and Asia

Undergraduate Tuition (per academic year):
In-State: $7050
Out-of-State: $19524

Graduate Tuition (per academic year):
In-State: $6170
Out-of-State: $14878

Enrollment 2018-19:
Undergraduate Majors: 255
New Graduate Students: 9
Full-time Graduate Students: 40
Part-time Graduate Students: 13
Degrees in History: 38 BA, 8 MA, 1 PhD

Undergraduate Addresses:
Admissions: http://www.utep.edu/admit
Financial Aid: http://financialaid.utep.edu

Graduate Addresses:
Admissions: http://graduate.utep.edu
Financial Aid: http://financialaid.utep.edu

Full-time Faculty

Ambler, Charles H. (PhD, Yale 1983; prof.) Africa, Middle East; cambler@utep.edu

Armstrong-Partida, Michelle (PhD, Iowa 2008; assoc. prof.) medieval and early modern Spain, gender, medieval European and Mediterranean Christians/Jews/Muslims; armstrongpartida@gmail.com

Brunk, Samuel F. (PhD, New Mexico 1992; prof.) 20th-century Mexico, Latin America, environmental; sbrunk@utep.edu

Cartwright, Brad J. (PhD, Colorado, Boulder 2006; assoc. prof. of practice; dir., Center for History Teaching and Learning) 19th-century US, Pacific world; bjcartwright@utep.edu

Chavez, Ernesto (PhD, UCLA 1994; prof.) Mexican American; echavez@utep.edu

Chew, Selfa (PhD, Texas, El Paso 2010; asst. prof. of instruction) diaspora, borderlands; sachew@utep.edu

Edison, Paul (PhD, Columbia 1999; assoc. prof.) France, science and empire, world; pedison@utep.edu

Fan, Joshua (PhD, Hawai'i, Manoa 2006; asst. prof. and dir., MA program) modern China, East Asia, world; jfan@utep.edu

Kawashima, Yasuhide (PhD, California, Santa Barbara 1967; prof.) colonial America, American legal, recent Japan; ykawashi@utep.edu

Leyva, Yolanda Chavez (PhD, Arizona 1999; assoc. prof.) public, oral, Mexican American; yleyva@utep.edu

Martinez, Ignacio, Jr. (PhD, Arizona 2013; assoc. prof. and dir., PhD program) colonial Latin America, borderlands; imartinez26@utep.edu

McGee Deutsch, Sandra F. (PhD, Florida 1979; prof.) Latin America, Argentina; sdeutsch@utep.edu

Shepherd, Jeffrey P. (PhD, Arizona State 2002; assoc. prof. and chair) US West, Native American; jpshepherd@utep.edu

Stanfield, Susan Joyce (PhD, Iowa 2013; asst. prof.) 19th-century US, race and gender, food; sjstanfield@utep.edu

Topp, Michael M. (PhD, Brown 1993; assoc. prof.) American immigration and ethnicity, labor; mtopp@utep.edu

Veloz, Larisa (PhD, Georgetown 2015; asst. prof.) borderlands, 20th-century Mexico, migration and gender; llveloz@utep.edu

Waters, Leslie (PhD, UCLA 2012; asst. prof.) eastern Europe, borderlands, migrations; lwaters@utep.edu

Weber, Ronald J. (PhD, Wisconsin, Madison 1983; assoc. prof.) ancient; rweber@utep.edu

Williams, Michael Vinson (PhD, Mississippi 2007; prof.; dir., African American Studies) African American, civil rights movement mvwilliams@utep.edu

Retired/Emeritus Faculty

Hackett, David A. (PhD, Wisconsin, Madison 1971; assoc. prof. emeritus) recent Europe, Germany; davidah@utep.edu

Jackson, Carl T. (PhD, UCLA 1964; prof. emeritus) US social and intellectual; cjackson@utep.edu

Martin, Charles H. (PhD, Tulane 1972; prof. emeritus) recent US, African American, Texas; mcharles@utep.edu

Martin, Cheryl E. (PhD, Tulane 1976; prof. emeritus) Latin America, colonial Mexico; cmartin@utep.edu

Righter, Robert W. (PhD, California, Santa Barbara 1968; prof. emeritus) US West, public, environmental

Recently Awarded PhDs

Orozco, Eva Marie Nohemi "Las Mujeres Sinarquistas (1937-62): Las Manos Ocultas en la Construcción del Sentimiento Nacionalista"

University of Texas-Rio Grande Valley

Dept. of History, 1201 W. University Dr., Edinburg, TX 78539. 956.882.8260. Fax 956.384.5096. Email: thomas.britten@utrgv. edu. Website: https://www.utrgv.edu/history/.

The University of Texas Rio Grande Valley was created by the Texas Legislature in 2013 in a historic move that brings together the resources and assets of UT Brownsville and UT Pan American.

Chair: Thomas Daniel Knight
Director of Graduate Studies: Megan Birk
Degrees Offered: BA,MA
Academic Year System: Semester
Areas of Specialization: US, modern Europe, Latin America, southwestern US borderlands, Chicano studies
Undergraduate Tuition (per academic year):
In-State: $5125
Out-of-State: $13555
Graduate Tuition (per academic year):
In-State: $4163
Out-of-State: $9221
Enrollment 2018-19:
Undergraduate Majors: 392
New Graduate Students: 13
Full-time Graduate Students: 12
Part-time Graduate Students: 27
Degrees in History: 82 BA, 4 MA
Students in Undergraduate Courses: 5000
Students in Undergraduate Intro Courses: 3000
Online-Only Courses: 15%
Addresses:
Admissions: http://www.utrgv.edu/en-us/admissions
Financial Aid: http://www.utrgv.edu/en-us/costs-financial-aid

Full-time Faculty

Avila, Mayra Lizette (PhD, Texas, El Paso 2018; lect.) borderlands, Mexican American; mayra.avila@utrgv.edu

Avila, Rolando (EdD, Texas, Pan American 2013; lect.) US; rolando. avila@utrgv.edu

Balci, Tamer (PhD, Claremont Grad. 2007; assoc. prof.) Middle East and Ottoman Empire, world; tamer.balci@utrgv.edu

Birk, Megan E. (PhD, Purdue 2008; assoc. prof. and dir., grad. studies) Gilded Age, social, women; megan.birk@utrgv.edu

Britten, Thomas A. (PhD, Texas Tech 1994; prof.) Native American, US; thomas.britten@utrgv.edu

Bruehoefener, Friederike (PhD, North Carolina, Chapel Hill 2014; asst. prof.) friederike.bruehoefener@utrgv.edu

Buchberger, Erica (DPhil, Oxford 2013; asst. prof.) ancient and medieval, medieval Spain, world; erica.buchberger@utrgv.edu

Campney, Brent M. S. (PhD, Emory 2007; prof.) African American, regional studies; brentcampney@gmail.com

Diaz, George T. (PhD, Southern Methodist 2010; assoc. prof.) Mexican American, borderlands, US; george.diaz@utrgv.edu

Elkin, Daniel (PhD, Arkansas 2018; lect.) daniel.elkin@utrgv.edu

English, Linda C. (PhD, Oklahoma 2005; assoc. prof.) US West, Texas, women; linda.english@utrgv.edu

Faubion, Michael L (PhD, Texas Tech 1993; assoc. prof.) 20th-century US, diplomatic, military; michael.faubion@utrgv.edu

Fisher, David C. (PhD, Indiana 2003; assoc. prof.) modern Russia, world; david.fisher@utrgv.edu

Goins, John D. (PhD, Houston 2014; instr.) US, gender; john. goins@utrgv.edu

Harp, Jamalin Rae (PhD, Texas Christian 2017; lect.) US, family, women; jamalin.harp@utrgv.edu

Hay, Amy Marie (PhD, Michigan State 2005; assoc. prof.) 20th-century US, women, medicine; amy.hay@utrgv.edu

Hoppens, Robert (PhD, Washington 2009; assoc. prof.) Far East Asia, modern Japan; robert.hoppens@utrgv.edu

Joseph, H. Denise (PhD, North Texas 1976; prof.) colonial Mexico, Texas; harriet.joseph@utrgv.edu

Knight, T. Daniel D. (DPhil, Oxford 2004; assoc. prof.) colonial, US South; thomas.knight@utrgv.edu

Levinson, Irving Walter (PhD, Houston 2003; assoc. prof.) Mexico, Latin America; irving.levinson@utrgv.edu

Miller, Christopher L. (PhD, California, Santa Barbara 1981; prof.) 19th-century US; christopher.miller@utrgv.edu

Mills, James W. (MAIS, Texas, Brownsville 2000; lect.) james.mills@ utrgv.edu

Paul, Nilanjana (PhD, West Virginia 2016; asst. prof.) India, South Asia, world; nilanjana.paul@utrgv.edu

Ridge, Michael Allen, Jr. (PhD, Iowa 2012; lect.) michael.ridge@ utrgv.edu

Samponaro, Philip (PhD, Connecticut 2003; assoc. prof.) 20th-century US social and cultural; philip.samponaro@utrgv.edu

Skowronek, Russell (PhD, Michigan State 1989; prof.; Anthropology) public, historic archaeology, Latin America; russell.skowronek@utrgv.edu

Starling, Jamie Matthew (PhD, Texas, El Paso 2012; assoc. prof.) borderlands, Latin America; jamie.starling@utrgv.edu

Waite, Charles (PhD, Texas Tech 2003; assoc. prof.) Texas; charles. waite@utrgv.edu

Wallace, Ned F. (MA, Texas, Pan American 2008; MBA, Rollins 1999; lect.) ef.wallace@utrgv.edu

Weaver, Michael K. (PhD, North Carolina, Chapel Hill 1990; assoc. prof.) modern Britain, modern Europe, British Empire; michael. weaver@utrgv.edu

Welty, Kyle (PhD, Baylor 2012; instr.) kyle.welty@utrgv.edu

Wirts, Kristine M. (PhD, Auburn 2003; assoc. prof.) early modern Europe, Reformation, France; kristine.wirts@utrgv.edu

University of Texas at San Antonio

Dept. of History, 1 UTSA Cir., San Antonio, TX 78249-0652. 210.458.4333. Fax 210.458.4796. Email: history@utsa.edu. Website: http://history.utsa.edu/.

The mission of the department is to enhance our collective knowledge of the past, train students in how to develop informed and discerning perspectives on the past, and disseminate the benefits of a historical education to the multicultural populations of San Antonio, South Texas, and beyond. The department promotes faculty and student research, teaches a comprehensive curriculum in History and American Studies, and fosters professional contributions to the community by faculty and students.

Chair: Kirsten Gardner
Director of Graduate Studies: Wing Chung Ng
Degrees Offered: BA,MA
Academic Year System: Semester
Areas of Specialization: empires/states/borders, European social and cultural, Latin America, modern East and South Asia, US social and cultural
Undergraduate Tuition (per academic year):
  In-State: $9361
  Out-of-State: $20674
Graduate Tuition (per academic year):
  In-State: $7476
  Out-of-State: $21835
Enrollment 2018-19:
  Undergraduate Majors: 337
  New Graduate Students: 16
  Full-time Graduate Students: 40
  Part-time Graduate Students: 15
  Degrees in History: 100 BA, 25 MA
Undergraduate Addresses:
  Admissions: http://utsa.edu/admissions/undergrad/
  Financial Aid: http://utsa.edu/financialaid/
Graduate Addresses:
  Admissions: http://www.graduateschool.utsa.edu/
  Financial Aid: http://utsa.edu/financialaid/

Adjunct Faculty

Baumgardner, Neel G. (PhD, Texas, Austin 2013; lect.) American studies, parks and wilderness; neel.baumgardner@utsa.edu

Browning, Robert S. (PhD, Wisconsin-Madison 1981; sr. lect.) US, military; robert.browning@utsa.edu

Carr-Shanahan, John Grant (MA, Texas, San Antonio 2009; lect.) US, world civilizations; john.carrshanahan@utsa.edu

Crosson, Andria (MA, Texas, San Antonio 2005; lect.) US, world civilizations; andria.crosson@utsa.edu

Debs, Michele (MA; lect.) US; michele.debs@utsa.edu

Dilley, Jennifer (MA, Texas, San Antonio 2008; lect.) US, world civilizations; jennifer.dilley@utsa.edu

Hansen, David W. (MA, Texas, San Antonio 1995; lect. III) US, computer applications; david.hansen@utsa.edu

Hicks, Lesli Louise (MA, Texas, San Antonio; lect. I) US, Texas; lesli.hicks@utsa.edu

Minten, Rhonda (MA, Texas, San Antonio; lect. I) US, Texas, world civilizations; rhonda.minten@utsa.edu

Peterson, Jodi M. (MA, Texas, San Antonio 2009; lect. I) US; jodi.peterson@utsa.edu

Turney, Elaine C. (PhD, Texas Christian 2007; sr. lect.) US, West, environmental; elaine.turney@utsa.edu

Full-time Faculty

Clinton, Catherine (PhD, Princeton 1980; Denman Endowed Prof.) US, Civil War, gender studies; catherine.clinton@utsa.edu

Davies, Brian L. (PhD, Chicago 1983; prof.) Russia and Soviet Union, European cultural, Islam; brian.davies@utsa.edu

Gardner, Kirsten E. (PhD, Cincinnati 1999; assoc. prof. and chair) US women, social; kirsten.gardner@utsa.edu

Gonzales, Rhonda M. (PhD, UCLA 2002; prof.) Africa, linguistics, diaspora; rhonda.gonzales@utsa.edu

Gonzalez, Gabriela (PhD, Stanford 2005; assoc. prof.) Mexican American, borderlands; gabriela.gonzalez@utsa.edu

Gonzalez, Jerry B. (PhD, Southern California 2009; assoc. prof.) US Latina/o; jerry.gonzalez@utsa.edu

Gray, LaGuana K. (PhD, Houston 2007; assoc. prof.) US, African American; laguana.gray@utsa.edu

Guy, Kolleen M. (PhD, Indiana 1996; assoc. prof.) modern France, Europe, economic and cultural; kolleen.guy@utsa.edu

Hardgrove, Anne (PhD, Michigan 1999; assoc. prof.) South Asia, cultural and social, world; anne.hardgrove@utsa.edu

Kelly, Patrick J. (PhD, NYU 1992; assoc. prof.) modern US, Civil War, social; patrick.kelly@utsa.edu

Komisaruk, Catherine (PhD, UCLA 2000; assoc. prof.) colonial era Mexico and Central America; catherine.komisaruk@utsa.edu

Konove, Andrew Philip (PhD, Yale 2013; asst. prof.) Latin America; andrew.konove@utsa.edu

Michel, Gregg L. (PhD, Virginia 1999; assoc. prof.) US South, political, social; gregg.michel@utsa.edu

Ng, Wing Chung (PhD, British Columbia 1993; prof. and dir., grad. studies) modern China, East Asia, migration; wingchung.ng@utsa.edu

Nolan-Ferrell, Catherine A. (PhD, Texas, Austin 2000; assoc. prof.) modern Mexico, labor; catherine.ferrell@utsa.edu

Reynolds, John F. (PhD, Rutgers 1980; prof.) US political, quantitative, computer applications; john.reynolds@utsa.edu

Valerio-Jimenez, Omar S. (PhD, UCLA 2001; assoc. prof.) Latina/o studies, borderlands; omar.valerio-jimenez@utsa.edu

Retired/Emeritus Faculty

Almaraz, Felix D., Jr. (PhD, New Mexico 1968; prof. emeritus) Texas, American Southwest, borderlands; felix.almaraz@utsa.edu

Boyd, Steven R. (PhD, Wisconsin, Madison 1974; prof. emeritus) colonial America, Constitution and law; steven.boyd@utsa.edu

Daniels, Bruce C. (PhD, Connecticut 1970; prof. emeritus) colonial and revolutionary America, New England, popular culture; bruce.daniels@utsa.edu

Henderson, Dwight F. (PhD, Texas, Austin 1966; prof. emeritus) America, environmental; dwight.henderson@utsa.edu

Johnson, David R. (PhD, Chicago 1972; prof. emeritus) urban, immigration, crime; david.johnson@utsa.edu

Schneider, James C. (PhD, Wisconsin, Madison 1979; prof. emeritus) 20th century, American foreign relations; james.schneider@utsa.edu

University of Texas at Tyler

Dept. of History and Political Science, 3900 University Blvd., Tyler, TX 75799-6699. 903.566.7371. Fax 903.565.5537. Email: mstadelmann@uttyler.edu. Website: https://www.uttyler.edu/history/.

The Department of History and Political Science at The University of Texas at Tyler offers a broad-based liberal arts education to suit each student's individual interests and career goals. UT Tyler undergraduate and graduate programs in history provide excellent preparation for careers in a variety of fields, including elementary, secondary and higher education; library and archival work; law; and government.

Chair: Marcus Stadelmann
Director of Graduate Studies: Colin Snider
Degrees Offered: BA,BS,MA
Academic Year System: Semester
Areas of Specialization: World War I/World War II/Vietnam, diplomatic and military, Civil War and Reconstruction, Africa and Latin America, modern Europe
Undergraduate Tuition (per academic year):
In-State: $6838
Out-of-State: $17518
Graduate Tuition (per academic year):
In-State: $7126
Out-of-State: $15028
Enrollment 2018-19:
Undergraduate Majors: 123
New Graduate Students: 9
Full-time Graduate Students: 21
Degrees in History: 6 BA, 21 BS, 7 MA
Addresses:
Admissions: http://www.uttyler.edu/admissions/apply.php
Financial Aid: http://www.uttyler.edu/financialaid/

Full-time Faculty

Carter, Jill (MA, Texas, Tyler; lect.) jcarter@uttyler.edu
Dotson, M. Rhys (MA, Texas, Tyler 2009; lect.) modern America; mdotson@uttyler.edu
Koster, Mickie (PhD, Rice 2009; assoc. prof.) world, Africa; mkoster@uttyler.edu
Linehan, Mary (PhD, Notre Dame 1991; assoc. prof.) gender, race, sexuality; mlinehan@uttyler.edu
Link, Amanda (PhD, Washington State 2015; asst. prof.) Ireland, World War I and World War II, modern Europe; mlink@uttyler.edu
Newsom, James L. (PhD, Texas Christian 1995; sr. lect.) Texas, diplomatic and military, early America; jnewsom@uttyler.edu
Snider, Colin M. (PhD, New Mexico 2011; assoc. prof. and dir., grad. studies) world, Latin America, Brazil; csnider@uttyler.edu
Stith, Matthew M. (PhD, Arkansas 2010; assoc. prof.) 19th-century US and Civil War, environmental, Vietnam; mstith@uttyler.edu
Tabri, Edward A. (PhD, Virginia 1996; assoc. prof.) ancient, medieval, early modern Europe; etabri@uttyler.edu

Retired/Emeritus Faculty

Falzone, Vincent (PhD, Maryland, Coll. Park 1969; prof. emeritus) vfalzone@uttyler.edu
Gajda, Patricia A. (PhD, Case Western Reserve 1972; prof. emeritus) modern Europe, Russia, central Europe; pgajda@uttyler.edu

Texas Christian University

Dept. of History, TCU Box 297260, Reed Hall 308, 2850 S. University Dr., Fort Worth, TX 76129. 817.257.7288. Fax 817.257.5650. Website: https://addran.tcu.edu/history/.

The department is part of the AddRan College of Liberal Arts. Its mission is to foster an understanding of the past, promote critical inquiry, improve communication skills, and develop an appreciation for cultural diversity in the global community.

Chair: William Meier
Director of Graduate Studies: Rebecca Sharpless
Director of Undergraduate Studies: Alex Hidalgo
Degrees Offered: BA,MA,PhD

Academic Year System: Semester
Areas of Specialization: US, Latin America
Undergraduate Tuition (per academic year): $49160
Graduate Tuition (per academic year): $30780
Enrollment 2018-19:
Undergraduate Majors: 103
New Graduate Students: 8
Full-time Graduate Students: 45
Degrees in History: 32 BA, 2 MA, 3 PhD
Undergraduate Addresses:
Admissions: http://www.admissions.tcu.edu/
Financial Aid: http://www.financialaid.tcu.edu/
Graduate Addresses:
Admissions: http://addran.tcu.edu/history/academics/areas-of-study/graduate-programs/graduate-admissions/
Financial Aid: http://www.financialaid.tcu.edu/

Full-time Faculty

Campbell, Jodi M. (PhD, Minnesota 1999; prof.) early modern Europe, Spain, culture and society, food; j.campbell@tcu.edu
Cantrell, Gregg (PhD, Texas A&M 1988; Lowe Chair) Texas; g.cantrell@tcu.edu
Gallay, Alan (PhD, Georgetown 1986; Lyndon Baines Johnson Chair) early America, Atlantic world, Native American, US South; a.gallay@tcu.edu
Hammad, Hanan (PhD, Texas, Austin 2009; assoc. prof.) Islamic studies; h.hammad@tcu.edu
Hidalgo, Alexander (PhD, Arizona 2013; asst. prof. and dir., undergrad. studies) Latin America, colonial America, Mesoamerican ethnohistory, manuscript and print culture, collecting, sound, Iberian Atlantic, cartography; a.hidalgo@tcu.edu
Hosainy, Hadi (PhD, Texas, Austin 2016; instr.) early modern Middle East, Ottoman Empire, gender, women, slavery, Islamic law, sharia court, pious endowments, family; hadi.hosainy@tcu.edu
Kerstetter, Todd M. (PhD, Nebraska 1997; prof.) American West, US 1877-1920; t.kerstetter@tcu.edu
Krochmal, Max (PhD, Duke 2011; assoc. prof.; Comparative Race and Ethnic Studies) modern America, race, labor; m.krochmal@tcu.edu
Meier, William M. (PhD, Wisconsin-Madison 2009; assoc. prof. and chair) modern Britain and Ireland, British Empire; w.meier@tcu.edu
Menchaca, Celeste Ruiz (PhD, Southern California 2016; asst. prof.) US-Mexico borderlands; c.menchaca@tcu.edu
Navarro, Aaron W. (PhD, Harvard 2004; assoc. prof) Latin America, comparative world, Mexico; aaron.navarro@tcu.edu
Ramirez, Susan E. (PhD, Wisconsin, Madison 1977; Penrose Chair) Latin America; s.ramirez@tcu.edu
Sanders, Claire A. (PhD, North Carolina, Chapel Hill 1996; sr. instr.) modern Europe; c.sanders@tcu.edu
Schoolmaster, F. Andrew (PhD, Kent State 1979; prof. and dean; AddRan Coll.) applied geography; a.schoolmaster@tcu.edu
Sharpless, Rebecca (PhD, Emory 1993; prof. and dir., grad. studies) American studies, women's studies; r.sharpless@tcu.edu
Smith, Gene Allen (PhD, Auburn 1991; prof.) colonial and revolutionary America, early national US, American naval; g.smith@tcu.edu
Szok, Peter Andrew (PhD, Tulane 1998; prof.) Latin America; p.szok@tcu.edu
Vuic, Kara Dixon (PhD, Indiana 2006; assoc. prof.) US, military, women; k.vuic@tcu.edu
Woodworth, Steven E. (PhD, Rice 1987; prof.) Old US South, Civil War and Reconstruction; s.woodworth@tcu.edu

Worthing, Peter M. (PhD, Hawai'i, Manoa 1995; prof.) modern China, Vietnam; p.worthing@tcu.edu

Retired/Emeritus Faculty

Brown, D. Clayton (PhD, UCLA 1970; prof. emeritus) modern US, agricultural

Coerver, Don M. (PhD, Tulane 1973; prof. emeritus) Mexico, business, US Southwest; d.coerver@tcu.edu

McDorman, Kathryne S. (PhD, Vanderbilt 1977; assoc. prof. emeritus) modern Britain, empire; k.mcdorman@tcu.edu

Stevens, Kenneth R. (PhD, Indiana 1982; prof. emeritus) American presidency, US constitutional; k.stevens@tcu.edu

Recently Awarded PhDs

Kosc, Kallie "Daughters of the Nation: Stockbridge Indian Women, Education, and Citizenship in Early America, 1790-1840"

McCutchen, Jennifer Monroe "Gunpowder and the Creek-British Struggle for Power in the Southeast, 1736-76"

Rivas, Brennan Gardner "The Deadly Weapon Laws of Texas: Regulating Guns, Knives, and Knuckles in the Lone Star State, 1836-1930"

Webb, Jessica "Prostitution and Power in Progressive-Era Texas: Entrepreneurship and the Influence of Madams in Fort Worth and San Antonio, 1877-1920"

Wibracht, Brooke "The Texas Fence-Cutting Wars, 1883-90"

Winslow, Brady Glen "Receptivity to Mormonism in the Upper Mississippi River Valley, 1830-60"

Texas Lutheran University

Dept. of History, 1000 W. Court St., Seguin, TX 78155. 830.372.8000. Email: rczuchry@tlu.edu. Website: http://www.tlu.edu/academics/programs/history/.

TLU's history program creates historians who help us understand the present through the study and interpretation of the past.

Chair: Angelika E. Sauer
Degrees Offered: BA
Academic Year System: Semester
Areas of Specialization: continental North America, gender/race/ethnicity, transnational and international, public
Tuition (per academic year): $24860
Enrollment 2018-19:
  Undergraduate Majors: 27
  Degrees in History: 10 BA
Addresses:
  Admissions: http://www.tlu.edu/admissions
  Financial Aid: http://www.tlu.edu/finaid

Full-time Faculty

Czuchry, Rebecca A. Kosary (PhD, Texas A&M 2006; prof.; chair, African American Studies) African American, 19th- and 20th-century North America, racial/gendered violence; rczuchry@tlu.edu

Grace, Philip (PhD, Minnesota 2010; asst. prof.) medieval and early modern Europe, social and cultural, world; pgrace@tlu.edu

Sauer, Angelika E. (PhD, Waterloo 1994; prof. and chair) international migration, 19th- and 20th-century North America, gender, childhood and youth; asauer@tlu.edu

Nondepartmental Historians

Cottrell, Debbie Mauldin (PhD, Texas, Austin 1993; vice pres., Acad. Affairs)

University of Texas of the Permian Basin

Dept. of History, 4901 E. University, Odessa, TX 79762-0001. 432.552.2313. Fax 432.552.3280. Email: martinez_a@utpb.edu. Website: https://www.utpb.edu/cas/academic-departments/history-department/.

The History faculty at UTPB are engaged in a variety of research projects. We offer a range of courses in US, Europe, and world, including new courses in sports history.

Chair: Ana Martinez-Catsam
Director of Graduate Studies: Ana Martinez-Catsam
Degrees Offered: BA, MA
Academic Year System: Semester
Areas of Specialization: America to 1900, 20th-century America, Europe, world
Undergraduate Tuition (per academic year):
  In-State: $6441
  Out-of-State: $16941
Graduate Tuition (per academic year):
  In-State: $5685
  Out-of-State: $13155
Enrollment 2018-19:
  Undergraduate Majors: 49
  New Graduate Students: 3
  Full-time Graduate Students: 2
  Part-time Graduate Students: 10
  Degrees in History: 8 BA, 1 MA
Undergraduate Addresses:
  Admissions: http://www.utpb.edu/admissions
  Financial Aid: http://www.utpb.edu/campus-life/financial-aid
Graduate Addresses:
  Admissions: http://www.utpb.edu/academics/graduate-studies-and-research
  Financial Aid: http://www.utpb.edu/campus-life/financial-aid

Full-time Faculty

Catsam, Derek Charles (PhD, Ohio 2003; Kathlyn Cosper Dunagan Prof.) modern US, South Africa and modern Africa, civil rights and sports; catsam_d@utpb.edu

Frawley, Michael S. (PhD, Louisiana State 2014; asst. prof.) American South, economics; frawley_m@utpb.edu

Martinez-Catsam, Ana Luisa (PhD, Texas Tech 2003; assoc. prof.; chair; and grad. program head) Texas, Mexican American, late 19th- and early 20th-century US; martinez_a@utpb.edu

Paxton, Jennifer (PhD, Texas Tech 2015; sr. lect.) paxton_j@utpb.edu

Spickermann, Roland (PhD, Michigan 1994; assoc. prof.) modern Germany, modern China, world; spickermann_r@utpb.edu

Part-time Faculty

Hinton, Diana Davids (PhD, Yale 1969; J. Conrad Dunagan Chair) oil, Europe; hinton_d@utpb.edu

Texas Southern University

Dept. of History, Geography, and General Studies, 3100 Cleburne Ave., Houston, TX 77004. 713.313.7794. Fax 713.313.7873. Email: cary.wintz@tsu.edu; carywintz@gmail.com. Website: http://www.tsu.edu/academics/colleges-and-schools/colabs/history/.

Through the program of study in History, it is the goal of the department to increase students' awareness of the nature of history, the historical process, and intellectual historical awareness, as well as to expand their knowledge of world history and American history while emphasizing the role of African Americans and other minorities.

Chair: Cary D. Wintz, interim
Director of Graduate Studies: Cary D. Wintz
Degrees Offered: BA,MA
Academic Year System: Semester
Areas of Specialization: African American, US social and political, western Europe, women, Africa, China
Undergraduate Tuition (per academic year):
  In-State: $8552
  Out-of-State: $18512
Graduate Tuition (per academic year):
  In-State: $7569
  Out-of-State: $14139
Enrollment 2018-19:
  Undergraduate Majors: 82
  New Graduate Students: 6
  Full-time Graduate Students: 18
  Degrees in History: 12 BA, 5 MA
Undergraduate Addresses:
  Admissions: http://em.tsu.edu/admissions/
  Financial Aid: http://em.tsu.edu/financialaid/
Graduate Addresses:
  Admissions: http://www.tsu.edu/academics/colleges-and-schools/the-graduate-school/
  Financial Aid: http://em.tsu.edu/financialaid/

Full-time Faculty

Brown Pellum, Kimberly (PhD, Howard 2013; asst. prof.) women, African American, US South; BrownKD@tsu.edu
Chaudhuri, Nupur (PhD, Kansas State 1974; prof.) modern Europe, race and gender, British Empire; nupurc@earthlink.net
Esparza, Jesus Jesse (PhD, Houston 2008; asst. prof.) Mexican American, borderlands, Texas; esparzajj@tsu.edu
Hart, Roger (PhD, UCLA 1997; prof.; dir., Confucius Inst.) China, Asia, science and technology; hartrp@tsu.edu
Kossie-Chernyshev, Karen L. (PhD, Rice 1998; prof.) recent US, US religions, African American; kossie_kl@tsu.edu
Pitre, Merline (PhD, Temple 1976; prof.) African American, US South, women; pitre_mx@tsu.edu

Part-time Faculty

Maddox, Gregory H. (PhD, Northwestern 1988; prof. and dean; Grad. Sch.) Africa, environmental; maddox_gh@tsu.edu
Wintz, Cary D. (PhD, Kansas State 1974; Dist. Prof.; interim chair; and dir., grad. studies) African American, Texas, research methods; wintz_cd@tsu.edu

Visiting Faculty

Hawkins, Gregg (MA, Southern Univ. and A&M 1999; vis. instr.) US, African American
Herbst, James D. (PhD, Yale 2014; vis. asst. prof.) modern France, world; james.herbst@tsu.edu
Meeks, Tomiko Michelle (MA, Houston 2011; vis. instr.) US, African American; Tomiko.Meeks@tsu.edu
Vipond Quesada, Julie (MA, Texas Southern 2011; vis. instr.) US, world; julie.vipond@tsu.edu

Texas State University

Dept. of History, 601 University Dr., San Marcos, TX 78666-4616. 512.245.2142. Fax 512.245.3043. Email: am34@txstate.edu. Website: https://www.txstate.edu/history/.

The Department of History at Texas State offers the BA and MA degrees. Our department has over 30 full-time, PhD- holding faculty who offer a wide variety of courses spanning the globe in coverage while also conducting ground-breaking research.

Chair: Angela F. Murphy
Director of Graduate Studies: Jose Carlos de la Puente
Degrees Offered: BA,MA,MEd
Academic Year System: Semester
Areas of Specialization: US, Europe, Latin America, public, world
Undergraduate Tuition (per academic year):
  In-State: $8496
  Out-of-State: $18288
Graduate Tuition (per academic year):
  In-State: $7398
  Out-of-State: $14742
Enrollment 2018-19:
  Undergraduate Majors: 428
  New Graduate Students: 16
  Full-time Graduate Students: 43
  Part-time Graduate Students: 32
  Degrees in History: 91 BA, 26 MA
Undergraduate Addresses:
  Admissions: http://www.admissions.txstate.edu/
  Financial Aid: http://www.finaid.txstate.edu/
Graduate Addresses:
  Admissions and Financial Aid: http://www.gradcollege.txstate.edu/steps.html

Adjunct Faculty

Alter, Tom (PhD, Illinois, Chicago 2016; lect.) US, Texas, labor; ta1066@txstate.edu
Duffy, Shannon E. (PhD, Maryland, Coll. Park 2008; sr. lect.) US; sd22@txstate.edu
Etienne-Gray, Trace (MA, Texas State, San Marcos 1993; sr. lect.) US, teacher education; te01@txstate.edu
Glass, Bryan S. (PhD, Texas, Austin 2012; sr. lect.) modern Britain, British imperial; bg30@txstate.edu
Hindson, Irene L. (MEd, Texas State, San Marcos 1983; sr. lect.) US; ih01@txstate.edu
Lannon Albrecht, Deirdre (MA, Texas State, San Marcos 2007; sr. lect.) US; dl24@txstate.edu
Law, Debra Anne (PhD, Johns Hopkins 2015; lect.) Brazil; dlaw@txstate.edu
Mann, Bryan (PhD, Leicester 2007; sr. lect.) Europe; bm30@txstate.edu
Mauck, Jeffrey (PhD, Indiana 1991; sr. lect.) US, public; jm81@txstate.edu
Mellard, Jason D. (PhD, Texas, Austin 2009; lect.) music, popular culture; jdm190@txstate.edu
Newcomer, Lara T. (MA, Texas State 2007; lect.) US, teacher education; ln1057@txstate.edu
Paddison, Joshua (PhD, UCLA 2008; lect.) US, American West, religion; j_p532@txstate.edu
Selcraig, James T. (PhD, Illinois, Urbana-Champaign 1981; sr. lect.) modern US; js32@txstate.edu
Siegenthaler, Peter D. (PhD, Texas, Austin 2004; sr. lect.) world, modern Japan; ps30@txstate.edu

Full-time Faculty

Berlage, Nancy Kay (PhD, Johns Hopkins 2000; assoc. prof.) public, 20th-century American social and political; nkb11@txstate.edu

Bishop, Elizabeth A. (PhD, Chicago 1997; assoc. prof.) modern Middle East; eb26@txstate.edu

Bourgeois, Eugene J., II (PhD, Cambridge 1988; prof. and provost) Tudor-Stuart England, English local; eb04@txstate.edu

Brennan, Mary C. (PhD, Miami, Ohio 1988; prof. and dean; Liberal Arts) recent US; mb18@txstate.edu

Brown, Ronald C. (PhD, Illinois, Urbana-Champaign 1975; prof.) mining, American West; rb04@txstate.edu

Cagniart, Pierre F. (PhD, Texas, Austin 1986; assoc. prof.) ancient; pc09@txstate.edu

Damiano, Sara (PhD, Johns Hopkins 2015; asst. prof.) early America, Atlantic world, women; sdamiano@txstate.edu

de la Puente, Jose Carlos (PhD, Texas Christian 2010; assoc. prof. and dir., grad. studies) colonial Latin America; j.c.delapuente@txstate.edu

Dunn, Dennis J. (PhD, Kent State 1970; prof. and Regents' prof.) Russia, eastern Europe; dd05@txstate.edu

Hart, Paul Brian (PhD, California, San Diego 1997; prof.) modern Mexico, Mexican American; ph18@txstate.edu

Hartman, Gary A. (PhD, Texas, Austin 1996; prof.) US, Texas music; gh08@txstate.edu

Helgeson, Jeffrey (PhD, Illinois, Chicago 2008; assoc. prof.) African American, labor, urban; jh221@txstate.edu

Johnson, Ronald Angelo (PhD, Purdue 2010; assoc. prof.) Atlantic world, early US diplomatic, US religious; rj26@txstate.edu

Makowski, Elizabeth M. (PhD, Columbia 1993; prof.) medieval; em13@txstate.edu

Margerison, Kenneth H., Jr. (PhD, Duke 1973; prof.) French Revolution, modern Europe; km04@txstate.edu

McKiernan-Gonzalez, John (PhD, Michigan 2002; assoc. prof.) Mexican American, Latin American studies; jrm259@txstate.edu

McWilliams, James E. (PhD, Johns Hopkins 2001; prof.) US, early America; jm71@txstate.edu

Menninger, Margaret Eleanor (PhD, Harvard 1998; assoc. prof.) modern Germany, Europe; mm48@txstate.edu

Montgomery, Rebecca S. (PhD, Missouri, Columbia 1999; assoc. prof.) Gilded Age and Progressive Era; rm53@txstate.edu

Murphy, Angela (PhD, Houston 2006; prof. and chair) 19th-century US reform, Civil War, Reconstruction; am34@txstate.edu

Pliley, Jessica R. (PhD, Ohio State 2010; assoc. prof.) gender, sexuality; jp74@txstate.edu

Renold, Leah M. (PhD, Texas, Austin 1999; assoc. prof.) South and Southeast Asia; lr22@txstate.edu

Ritter, Caroline (PhD, California, Berkeley 2015; asst. prof.) modern Britain, modern Africa, empire

Rivaya-Martinez, Joaquin (PhD, UCLA 2006; assoc. prof.) ethnohistory; jr59@txstate.edu

Romo, Anadelia A. (PhD, Harvard 2004; assoc. prof.) Latin America, comparative slavery and gender; ar23@txstate.edu

Tillman, Ellen Davies (PhD, Illinois, Urbana-Champaign 2010; assoc. prof.) military, Latin America; et19@txstate.edu

Valencia, Louie Dean (PhD, Fordham 2016; asst. prof.) digital, early and late modern; lv1027@txstate.edu

Watson, Dwight D. (PhD, Houston 1999; assoc. prof.) African American; dw25@txstate.edu

Yick, Joseph K. (PhD, California, Santa Barbara 1988; Ingram prof.) modern China, Chinese communism, world; jy02@txstate.edu

Retired/Emeritus Faculty

Andrews, Gregg (PhD, Northern Illinois 1988; dist. prof. emeritus) US labor; ga05@txstate.edu

Brieger, Alton G. (MA, Texas A&I 1960; prof. emeritus) Europe; ab27@txstate.edu

Bynum, Victoria (PhD, California, San Diego 1987; dist. prof. emeritus) antebellum US South, race and gender; vb03@txstate.edu

de la Teja, Jesus F. (PhD, Texas, Austin 1988; dist. prof. emeritus) Texas, colonial Mexico; delateja@txstate.edu

Jager, Ronald B. (PhD, Texas, Austin 1972; prof. emeritus) US economic, constitutional, Gilded Age; rj18@txstate.edu

Wilson, James A. (PhD, Arizona 1967; prof. emeritus) American West, US; jw04@txstate.edu

Texas Tech University

Dept. of History, Box 41013, Lubbock, TX 79409-1013. 806.742.3744. Fax 806.742.1060. Email: sean.cunningham@ttu. edu. Website: http://www.depts.ttu.edu/history/.

The Department of History at Texas Tech University boasts an outstanding and diverse faculty with expertise in a wide range of specializations.

Chair: Sean P. Cunningham
Director of Graduate Studies: Emily Skidmore
Director of Undergraduate Studies: Julie Willett
Degrees Offered: BA,MA,PhD
Academic Year System: Semester
Areas of Specialization: international politics and political culture, modern US, Southwest/West/borderlands, Vietnam War and military, world
Undergraduate Tuition (per academic year):
  In-State: $4862
  Out-of-State: $13286
Graduate Tuition (per academic year):
  In-State: $4546
  Out-of-State: $10864
Enrollment 2018-19:
  Undergraduate Majors: 375
  New Graduate Students: 18
  Full-time Graduate Students: 85
  Degrees in History: 139 BA, 12 MA, 3 PhD
Undergraduate Addresses:
  Admissions: http://www.admissions.ttu.edu/
  Financial Aid: http://www.financialaid.ttu.edu/
Graduate Addresses:
  Admissions: http://www.depts.ttu.edu/gradschool/admissions/
  Financial Aid: http://www.depts.ttu.edu/history/graduate/programs.php

Full-time Faculty

Adams, Gretchen A. (PhD, New Hampshire 2001; assoc. prof.) US political culture to 1877, history and memory; gretchen.adams@ttu.edu

Barenberg, Alan (PhD, Chicago 2007; asst. prof.) Russia and Soviet Union, gulags; alan.barenberg@ttu.edu

Baum, Jacob M. (PhD, Illinois, Urbana-Champaign 2013; asst. prof.) early modern Germany, Protestant Reformation, cultural; jacob.m.baum@ttu.edu

Bell, Gary (PhD, UCLA 1974; prof.) early modern Britain, Tudor-Stuart England; gary.bell@ttu.edu

Bjerk, Paul K. (PhD, Wisconsin, Madison 2008; asst. prof.) Africa, modern Tanzania; paul.bjerk@ttu.edu

Brittsan, Zachary (PhD, California, San Diego 2010; asst. prof.) modern Mexico, Latin America; zachary.brittsan@ttu.edu

Calkins, Laura M. (PhD, SOAS, London 1990; assoc. prof.) Asia and international relations, intelligence operations; laura.calkins@ttu.edu

Cunningham, Sean P. (PhD, Florida 2007; assoc. prof. and chair) modern US politics, conservatism, Texas and Sunbelt; sean.cunningham@ttu.edu

D'Amico, Stefano (PhD, Studi di Milano, Italy 1993; assoc. prof.) early modern Europe/Italy, urban history and demography; stefano.damico@ttu.edu

Forsythe, Gary (PhD, Pennsylvania 1984; assoc. prof.) ancient Greece and Rome; gary.forsythe@ttu.edu

Franklin, Catharine R. (PhD, Oklahoma 2010; asst. prof.) 19th-century US, military, Native American/American West

Hahn, Barbara M. (PhD, North Carolina, Chapel Hill 2006; asst. prof.) US South, science and technology; barbara.hahn@ttu.edu

Hart, Justin (PhD, Rutgers 2004; assoc. prof.) 20th-century US, US diplomatic and international; justin.hart@ttu.edu

Howe, John M. (PhD, UCLA 1979; prof.) medieval Europe, religion and hagiography; john.howe@ttu.edu

Iber, Jorge (PhD, Utah 1997; prof. and assoc. dean; Coll. Arts and Sciences) Mexican American, Latino/as and US sports; jorge.iber@ttu.edu

Johnson, Matthew (PhD, Temple 2011; asst. prof.) US social movements, civil rights, US since 1945; matthew.j.johnson@ttu.edu

Legacey, Erin-Marie (PhD, Northwestern 2011; asst. prof.) France, French Revolution; erin-marie.legacey@ttu.edu

Levario, Miguel A. (PhD, Texas, Austin 2007; assoc. prof.) US borderlands, Mexican American, US West and Southwest; miguel.levario@ttu.edu

Lutjens, Richard Newton, Jr. (PhD, Northwestern 2012; asst. prof.) modern Germany; richard.lutjens@ttu.edu

McBee, Randy D. (PhD, Missouri, Columbia 1996; assoc. prof. and assoc. dean; Coll. Arts & Sciences) 20th-century US, US labor and social history, masculinity; randy.mcbee@ttu.edu

Milam, Ron (PhD, Houston 2004; assoc. prof.) Vietnam Conflict, US military, US war and society; ron.milam@ttu.edu

Mosher, Jeffrey C. (PhD, Florida 1996; assoc. prof.) modern Latin America, Brazil; jeffrey.mosher@ttu.edu

Pelley, Patricia M. (PhD, Cornell 1993; assoc. prof.) Vietnam, Southeast Asia, world; patricia.pelley@ttu.edu

Skidmore, Emily (PhD, Illinois, Urbana-Champaign 2011; asst. prof. and dir., grad. studies) US gender and sexuality, 19th-century US legal and cultural; emily.skidmore@ttu.edu

Stoll, Mark (PhD, Texas, Austin 1993; assoc. prof.) US environmental, US religious; mark.stoll@ttu.edu

Swingen, Abigail L. (PhD, Chicago 2007; asst. prof.) early modern Britain, early modern British state and empire, Caribbean; abigail.swingen@ttu.edu

Willett, Julie (PhD, Missouri, Columbia 1996; assoc. prof. and dir., undergrad. studies) gender and sexuality, US women and labor, US social and cultural; j.willett@ttu.edu

Wong, Aliza Siu (PhD, Colorado, Boulder 2001; assoc. prof.) modern Europe and Italy, diaspora/race/nation, popular culture and history; aliza.wong@ttu.edu

Recently Awarded PhDs

Batura, Amber "The Effect of Playboy on the Social Awareness of American Soldiers in the Vietnam War"

Headford, Jonathon "The History of Sports and Sports Fandom"

Texas Woman's University

Dept. of History and Political Science, CFO 605, PO Box 425889, Denton, TX 76204-5889. 940.898.2133. Fax 940.898.2130. Email: HistoryGov@twu.edu. Website: https://twu.edu/history-political-science/.

History and Government offers a variety of programs, emphasizing interdisciplinary connections, global perspectives, and multicultural experiences. Programs combine strengths in political and legal analysis with attention to historical evolution in ways that illustrate the complexities of decision-making, the forces producing historical change, and a diversity of intellectual traditions.

Chair: Jonathan Olsen
Degrees Offered: BA,BS,MA
Academic Year System: Semester
Areas of Specialization: women, 20th-century America, Texas
Undergraduate Tuition (per academic year):
  In-State: $4124
  Out-of-State: $12548
Graduate Tuition (per academic year):
  In-State: $3903
  Out-of-State: $10221
Undergraduate Addresses:
  Admissions: http://www.twu.edu/admissions/
  Financial Aid: http://www.twu.edu/finaid/
Graduate Addresses:
  Admissions and Financial Aid: http://www.twu.edu/admissions/graduate/

Full-time Faculty

Blosser, Jacob M. (PhD, South Carolina 2006; prof.) colonial America, Atlantic world; jblosser@twu.edu

Fanning, Sara (PhD, Texas, Austin 2008; prof.) Latin America and Caribbean, African American, transnational; sfanning@twu.edu

Hevron, Parker (PhD, Southern California 2013; asst. prof.) phevron@twu.edu

Hodges, Lybeth (PhD, Texas Tech 1984; prof.) North American frontier, social, Britain; lhodges@twu.edu

Hoye, Timothy K. (PhD, Duke 1977; prof.) political theory, comparative political, American government; thoye@twu.edu

Landdeck, Katherine (PhD, Tennessee, Knoxville 2003; prof.) modern US, women, military; klanddeck@twu.edu

Olsen, Jonathan (PhD, Maryland, Coll. Park 1997; prof. and chair) comparative politics, political theory; jolsen@twu.edu

Travis, Paul D. (PhD, Oklahoma 1975; prof.) US, 20th-century America; ptravis@twu.edu

van Erve, Wouter (PhD, Massachusetts Amherst 2017; asst. prof.) wvanerve@twu.edu

Towson University

Dept. of History, 8000 York Rd., CLA 4210, Baltimore, MD 21252-0001. 410.704.2923. Fax 410.704.5595. Email: ckoot@towson.edu. Website: https://www.towson.edu/cla/departments/history/.

As a history major, you will develop skills that transfer to a diverse range of careers. Learn to become an effective communicator, a critical and creative thinker, and a researcher who can analyze issues, events and data with a high level of competence.

Chair: Christian Koot
Degrees Offered: BA,BS
Academic Year System: Semester
Areas of Specialization: America, Europe, Latin America, Asia, Africa
Tuition (per academic year):
In-State: $10198
Out-of-State: $24334
Enrollment 2018-19:
Undergraduate Majors: 218
Degrees in History: 2 BA, 52 BS
Addresses:
Admissions: http://www.towson.edu/admissions/undergrad
Financial Aid: http://www.towson.edu/admissions/financialaid

Adjunct Faculty

Alduino, Frank W. (PhD, Florida State 1989; adj.) 19th- to 20th-century US, 20th-century Europe, educational leadership; falduino@towson.edu

Anderson, Patricia (PhD, Delaware 2008; adj.) 19th-century social and cultural, public, Maryland; panderson@towson.edu

Full-time Faculty

Chen, Gilbert (PhD, Washington, St. Louis 2019; asst. prof.) late imperial China, Chinese gender and religion; zchen@towson.edu

Costa-Gomes, Rita (PhD, Novade Lisboa 1994; prof.) medieval Europe, Portugal, Spain; rcostagomes@towson.edu

Diemer, Andrew (PhD, Temple 2011; assoc. prof.) 19th-century US, African American, slavery and anti-slavery; adiemer@towson.edu

Dombrowski Risser, Nicole A. (PhD, NYU 1995; prof.) France and Europe, women and family, gender and war; ndombrowski@towson.edu

Fisher, Benjamin Edward (PhD, Pennsylvania 2011; assoc. prof.) early modern Europe, Jewish; bfisher@towson.edu

Gadotti, Alhena (PhD, Johns Hopkins 2005; assoc. prof.) ancient Near East, late 3rd-early 2nd millennium BCE, religion; agadotti@towson.edu

Gray, Elizabeth Kelly (PhD, William and Mary 2002; assoc. prof.) early national and antebellum US, American foreign relations; egray@towson.edu

Katz, Kimberly (PhD, NYU 2001; prof.) 19th- and 20th-century Middle East and North Africa, colonial and postcolonial Tunisian urban history and heritage; kkatz@towson.edu

Koot, Christian J. (PhD, Delaware 2005; prof. and chair) colonial and early US, Atlantic world, economic and commercial; ckoot@towson.edu

Mancini, John (PhD, Catholic 1996; lect.) US; jmancini@towson.edu

Masatsugu, Michael K. (PhD, California, Irvine 2004; assoc. prof.) Asian American, Asian-US relations, 20th-century immigration and race; mmasatsugu@towson.edu

Oduntan, Oluwatoyin (PhD, Dalhousie 2011; assoc. prof.) Africa; ooduntan@towson.edu

Oslund, Karen (PhD, UCLA 2000; prof.) Scandinavia, western Europe and global Artic, environmental; koslund@towson.edu

Pineo, Ronn (PhD, California, Irvine 1987; prof.) late 19th-century to present Latin America, Andes, US-Latin American relations; rpineo@towson.edu

Reinhardt, Akim D. (PhD, Nebraska 2000; prof.) 20th-century American Indian, US West; areinhardt@towson.edu

Rook, Robert (PhD, Kansas State 1996; prof.) US, environmental, military; rrook@towson.edu

Ropers, Erik (PhD, Melbourne 2012; assoc. prof.) modern Japan, East Asia; hropers@towson.edu

Walter, Amanda Lauren (PhD, Wayne State 2019; instr.) US, world; awalter@towson.edu

Zajicek, Benjamin (PhD, Chicago 2009; assoc. prof.) Soviet Union, psychiatry, 20th-century Europe; bzajicek@towson.edu

Part-time Faculty

Siwi, Marcio (PhD, NYU 2017; asst. prof.) Latin America, Caribbean, urbanism

Retired/Emeritus Faculty

Hirschmann, Edwin (PhD, Wisconsin, Madison 1972; prof. emeritus) South and Southeast Asia, Islamic; ehirschmann@verizon.net

Larew, Karl G. (PhD, Yale 1964; prof. emeritus) European intellectual, military; klarew@towson.edu

Phillips, Steve E. (PhD, Georgetown 1998; prof. emeritus) China/Taiwan/East Asia, political and diplomatic, Cold War; sphillips@towson.edu

Piotrowski, Harry (PhD, Syracuse 1971; prof. emeritus) Russia, Soviet Union

Ryon, Roderick N. (PhD, Penn State 1966; prof. emeritus) Jacksonian America, American labor, immigrants

Stallsmith, Allaire (PhD, Pennsylvania 1976; assoc. prof. emeritus) ancient Near East, Rome, Byzantine; astallsmith@towson.edu

Whitman, Mark I. (PhD, Harvard 1973; prof. emeritus) US constitutional; mwhitman@towson.edu

Trinity College

Dept. of History, 300 Summit St., Seabury Hall, Rm. 127, Hartford, CT 06106. 860.297.2397. Fax 860.297.5111. Email: jeffrey.bayliss@trincoll.edu. Website: https://www.trincoll.edu/Academics/MajorsAndMinors/History/.

Historical study at a national liberal arts college like Trinity is an intellectual practice that makes the past come alive, in the US and in the world beyond, in the classroom and outside.

Chair: Jeffrey Bayliss
Degrees Offered: BA
Academic Year System: Semester
Areas of Specialization: Asia, Africa, Europe, Middle East, US and Latin America
Tuition (per academic year): $56380
Enrollment 2018-19:
Undergraduate Majors: 74
Degrees in History: 32 BA
Addresses:
Admissions: http://www.trincoll.edu/Admissions/
Financial Aid: http://www.trincoll.edu/Admissions/finaid/

Full-time Faculty

Alejandrino, Clark Lim (PhD, Georgetown 2019; asst. prof.) China, environmental; clark.alejandrino@trincoll.edu

Bayliss, Jeffrey P. (PhD, Harvard 2003; assoc. prof. and chair) Japan, Korea; jeffrey.bayliss@trincoll.edu

Cocco, Sean F. (PhD, Washington 2004; assoc. prof.) early modern Europe, cultural, Italy; sean.cocco@trincoll.edu

Elukin, Jonathan M. (PhD, Princeton 1993; assoc. prof.) medieval, Christian-Jewish relations, book; jonathan.elukin@trincoll.edu

Figueroa-Martinez, Luis (PhD, Wisconsin, Madison 1991; assoc. prof.) Caribbean, African diaspora in Latin America, Latinos in US; luis.figueroa@trincoll.edu

Greenberg, Cheryl L. (PhD, Columbia 1988; Paul E. Raether Dist. Prof.) African American, 20th-century US, race/ethnicity/social activism; cheryl.greenberg@trincoll.edu

Kassow, Samuel D. (PhD, Princeton 1976; Charles H. Northam Prof.) Russia, eastern Europe, Germany; samuel.kassow@trincoll.edu

Kete, Kathleen J. (PhD, Harvard 1989; Borden W. Painter Jr. '58/H'95 Prof.) modern Europe, France, cultural; kathleen.kete@trincoll.edu

Lestz, Michael E. (PhD, Yale 1980; assoc. prof.) China, Japan; michael.lestz@trincoll.edu

Regan-Lefebvre, Jennifer (PhD, Queen's, Belfast 2007; assoc. prof.) modern Britain and Empire; jennifer.reganlefebvre@trincoll.edu

Reger, Gary L. (PhD, Wisconsin, Madison 1987; Hobart Prof.; Classical Languages) Greece, Rome; gary.reger@trincoll.edu

Joint/Cross Appointments

Antrim, Zayde G. (PhD, Harvard 2005; assoc. prof.; International Studies) Middle East; zayde.antrim@trincoll.edu

Euraque, Dario Aquiles (PhD, Wisconsin, Madison 1990; prof.; International Studies) Central America, race, ethnicity and sexuality; dario.euraque@trincoll.edu

Gac, Scott E. (PhD, Graduate Center, CUNY 2003; assoc. prof.; American Studies) 19th-century US, race and culture, social reform; scott.gac@trincoll.edu

Markle, Seth (PhD, NYU 2010; assoc. prof.; International Studies) Africa; seth.markle@trincoll.edu

Wickman, Thomas Michael (PhD, Harvard 2012; assoc. prof.; American Studies) environment, colonial America, Native American; thomas.wickman@trincoll.edu

Trinity University

Dept. of History, 1 Trinity Pl., San Antonio, TX 78212-7200. 210.999.7621. Fax 210.999.8334. Email: clatimor@trinity.edu. Website: https://new.trinity.edu/academics/departments/history.

The study of history plays a central and formative role at Trinity. Offering new perspectives on the past as well as ongoing influences the past has on the present, history promotes critical thinking, develops analytical skills, nurtures open-minded examination of controversial issues, and encourages writing excellence.

Chair: Carey H. Latimore
Degrees Offered: BA
Academic Year System: Semester
Areas of Specialization: Africa, ancient Greece and Rome, African American and US, East and Southeast Asia, Middle East/Europe/Latin America
Tuition (per academic year): $36214
Enrollment 2018-19:
  Undergraduate Majors: 85
  Degrees in History: 48 BA
Addresses:
  Admissions: http://new.trinity.edu/admissions-aid
  Financial Aid: http://new.trinity.edu/admissions-aid/financial-aid

Full-time Faculty

Ejikeme, Anene (PhD, Columbia 2003; assoc. prof.) Africa, women; aejikeme@trinity.edu

Johnson, Jason Burton (PhD, Northwestern 2011; asst. prof.) modern Europe, 20th-century Germany; jjohnso7@trinity.edu

Kramer, Erin B. (PhD, Wisconsin-Madison 2018; asst. prof.) early America and Native American; ekramer@trinity.edu

Latimore, Carey H. IV (PhD, Emory 2005; assoc. prof. and chair) African American, antebellum US South, Civil War; clatimor@trinity.edu

Lesch, David W. (PhD, Harvard 1991; Halsell Dist. Prof.) Middle East; dlesch@trinity.edu

Loiselle, Kenneth B. (PhD, Yale 2007; asst. prof.) early modern Europe, French Revolution; kloiselle@trinity.edu

Marafioti, Nicole J. (PhD, Cornell 2009; asst. prof.) medieval Europe; nmarafio@trinity.edu

Navarro, Aaron W. (PhD, Harvard 2004; assoc. prof.) Mexico, Latin America; anavarro@trinity.edu

Tam, Gina Anne (PhD, Stanford 2016; asst. prof.) modern China, linguistics, race and ethnicity; gtam@trinity.edu

Turek, Lauren F. (PhD, Virginia 2015; asst. prof.) modern US, diplomatic, public; lturek@trinity.edu

Retired/Emeritus Faculty

Clark, Donald N. (PhD, Harvard 1978; prof. emeritus) East Asia, Korea; dclark@trinity.edu

Kownslar, Allan O. (DA, Carnegie Mellon 1969; prof. emeritus) Texas, teaching methods; akownsla@trinity.edu

McCusker, John J. (PhD, Pittsburgh 1970; prof. emeritus) American economic, colonial, quantitative methods; jmccuske@mac.com

Metcalf, Alida C. (PhD, Texas, Austin 1983; prof. emeritus) Alida.C.Metcalf@rice.edu

Miller, Char (PhD, Johns Hopkins 1980; prof. emeritus) char.miller@pomona.edu

Salvucci, Linda K. (PhD, Princeton 1985; assoc. prof. emeritus) early America, Atlantic empires, colonial Cuba; lsalvucc@trinity.edu

Smart, Terry (PhD, Kansas 1968; prof. emeritus) modern Europe, Russia; tsmart@trinity.edu

Troy University

Dept. of History, University Ave., Troy, AL 36082. 334.670.3412. Email: ajones@troy.edu. Website: http://trojan.troy.edu/artsandsciences/history/.

The History and Philosophy Department at Troy boasts a qualified faculty who offers a wide array of courses spanning the entire historical experience.

Chair: Allen Jones
Degrees Offered: BA,BS
Academic Year System: Semester
Areas of Specialization: colonial/southern/modern US, medieval, French Revolution, Enlightenment, medieval Europe/Africa, science and technology, Cold War
Tuition (per academic year):
  In-State: $7800
  Out-of-State: $15600
Enrollment 2018-19:
  Undergraduate Majors: 130
  Degrees in History: 10 BS
Addresses:
  Admissions: https://www.troy.edu/applications-admissions/
  Financial Aid: https://www.troy.edu/scholarships-costs-aid/

Full-time Faculty

Blum, Elizabeth D. (PhD, Houston 2000; prof. and assoc. chair) US women, US environmental, contemporary America; sblum@troy.edu

Buckner, Timothy R. (PhD, Texas, Austin 2005; assoc. prof.) US South, race and slavery, Atlantic world; tbuckner48602@troy.edu

Carlson, R. David (PhD, Emory 2009; asst. prof.) 19th-century US, Civil War; rdcarlson@troy.edu

Gnoinska, Margaret K. (PhD, George Washington 2010; asst. prof.) modern and eastern Europe, Far East, international Cold War; mgnoinska@troy.edu

Hagler, Aaron M. (PhD, Pennsylvania 2014; asst. prof.) Middle East; hagler@troy.edu

Hoose, Adam L. (PhD, St. Louis 2011; asst. prof.; Dothan) medieval Europe; ahoose@troy.edu

Jones, Allen E., Jr. (PhD, South Carolina 1998; prof. and chair) medieval Europe, ancient, Renaissance Europe; ajones@troy.edu

Kruckeberg, Robert D. (PhD, Michigan 2009; asst. prof.) French Enlightenment, French Revolution; rkruckeberg@troy.edu

McCall, Joseph (ABD, Auburn; sr. lect.) modern US, Alabama; mccalljo@troy.edu

Medeiros, Avington (MEd, Faulkner 2013; lect.) history education; ahmedeiros@troy.edu

Merriman, Scott A., Sr. (PhD, Kentucky 2003; lect.; Montgomery) American constitutional development, African American; smerriman@troy.edu

Mihal, Sandy (EdD, Vanderbilt 1990; lect.; Global) Western civilization, world

O'Sullivan, Robin (PhD, Texas, Austin 2010; lect.; Dothan) US cultural

Olliff, Martin T., III (PhD, Auburn 1998; assoc. prof.; Dothan) public, archives; molliff@tsud.edu

Puckett, Dan J. (PhD, Mississippi State 2005; assoc. prof.; Montgomery) Germany, Holocaust studies; dpuckett45442@troy.edu

Ritter, Luke (PhD, St. Louis 2014; lect.) American West, American religious; ritterl@troy.edu

Robison, Daniel E. (PhD, Auburn 2000; lect.; Global) England, French Revolution

Roper, Mary Wynn (ABD, Auburn; lect.; Global) US

Ross, Karen D. (PhD, Minnesota 2006; assoc. prof.) science, technology, medicine; kdross@troy.edu

Saunders, Robert S., Jr. (PhD, Auburn 1994; assoc. prof.) Civil War, US military

Tucker, Kathryn (PhD, Georgia 2014; lect.) civil rights, US South; ktucker@troy.edu

Retired/Emeritus Faculty

Mitchell, Norma Taylor (PhD, Duke 1967; prof. emeritus) early America, American women, African American

Smith, Earl (PhD, Vanderbilt 1974; assoc. prof. emeritus) Middle Period US, diplomatic, US constitutional

Welch, William M., Jr. (DPhil, Oxford 1978; prof. emeritus) British Commonwealth, Middle East, Africa; wwelch@troy.edu

Truman State University

Dept. of History, Sch. of Social and Cultural Studies, 100 E. Normal, MC 214, Kirksville, MO 63501-4221. 660.785.7102. Fax 660.785.4337. Email: history@truman.edu. Website: https://www.truman.edu/majors-programs/majors-minors/history-major/.

As a history major at Truman, you pursue the wondrous complexities of the past while acquiring the skills and insight necessary to prepare for an exciting and fulfilling future.

Chair: Kathryn Brammall
Degrees Offered: BA, BS
Academic Year System: Semester
Areas of Specialization: US, Europe, Latin America, Asia, Africa
Tuition (per academic year):
  In-State: $7425
  Out-of-State: $14277
Enrollment 2018-19:
  Undergraduate Majors: 188
  Degrees in History: 17 BA, 11 BS
Addresses:
  Admissions: https://www.truman.edu/admission-cost/admission-requirements/
  Financial Aid: http://www.truman.edu/admission-cost/cost-aid/

Full-time Faculty

Becker, Marc (PhD, Kansas 1997; prof.) modern Latin America, revolution; marc@truman.edu

Brammall, Kathryn M. (PhD, Dalhousie 1996; prof. and chair; ed., Sixteenth Century Journal) Tudor and Stuart England, early modern Europe, medieval Europe; brammall@truman.edu

Ling, Huping (PhD, Miami, Ohio 1991; prof.; exec. ed., Journal of Asian American Studies) Asia, Asian American, oral; hling@truman.edu

Mandell, Daniel R. (PhD, Virginia 1992; prof.) early America, Native American; dmandell@truman.edu

Reschly, Steven D. (PhD, Iowa 1994; prof.) US, Amish, frontier and west; sdr@truman.edu

Wandel, Torbjorn V. (PhD, California, Irvine 1998; prof.) modern Europe, France, theory; twandel@truman.edu

West, Sally (PhD, Illinois, Urbana-Champaign 1995; prof.) Russia, modern Europe, theory; swest@truman.edu

Nondepartmental Historians

Orel, Sara (PhD, Toronto 1993; prof.; Art) art, Egypt, Islamic art; orel@truman.edu

Ramberg, Peter (PhD, Indiana 1993; prof.; Chemistry) science, chemistry, Europe; ramberg@truman.edu

Retired/Emeritus Faculty

Gall, Jeffrey (PhD, Missouri, Columbia 1993; prof. emeritus) US, Missouri, history education; jgall@truman.edu

Hanley, Mark Y. (PhD, Purdue 1989; prof. emeritus) 19th-century US; mhanley@truman.edu

Hirsch, Jerrold M. (PhD, North Carolina, Chapel Hill 1984; prof. emeritus) US cultural, African American, oral; jhirsch@truman.edu

Robinson, David K. (PhD, California, Berkeley 1987; prof. emeritus) Europe, Germany, science; drobinso@truman.edu

Rose, M. Lynn (PhD, Minnesota 1995; prof. emerita) ancient world, Greece, disability studies; lynnrose@truman.edu

Zoumaras, Thomas (PhD, Connecticut 1987; prof. emeritus) American diplomatic, 20th-century US, Latin America; zoumaras@truman.edu

Visiting Faculty

McDonald, Jason J. (PhD, Southampton 1993; vis. asst. prof.) US, immigration, public; jasonmcd@truman.edu

Russell, Stephanie L. (MA, Kansas 2009; vis. instr.) medieval Europe, gender; slrussell@truman.edu

Tulane University

Dept. of History, 6823 St. Charles Ave., 115 Hebert Hall, New Orleans, LA 70118-5698. 504.865.5162. Fax 504.862.8739. Email: klane1@tulane.edu. Website: https://liberalarts.tulane. edu/departments/history.

The rich heritage of New Orleans, our award-winning faculty, the outstanding history resources on our campus, and Tulane University's tradition of excellence make history a vital part of "the Tulane experience."

Chair: Thomas Luongo
Director of Graduate Studies: Guadalupe Garcia
Director of Undergraduate Studies: Brian DeMare
Degrees Offered: BA,MA,PhD
Academic Year System: Semester
Areas of Specialization: Africa, Europe, Latin America, Middle East, US
Undergraduate Tuition (per academic year): $59000
Graduate Tuition (per academic year): $45750
Enrollment 2018-19:
　Undergraduate Majors: 120
　New Graduate Students: 4
　Full-time Graduate Students: 42
　Degrees in History: 120 BA, 2 MA, 4 PhD
Undergraduate Addresses:
　Admissions: http://tulane.edu/admission/
　Financial Aid: http://tulane.edu/financialaid/
Graduate Addresses:
　Admissions and Financial Aid: http://tulane.edu/liberal-arts/

Adjunct Faculty

Fitzmorris, Terrence W. (PhD, Louisiana State 1989; adj. instr.; Univ. Coll.) America, modern Louisiana; tfitzmo@tulane.edu

Hill, Lance (PhD, Tulane 1997; exec. dir.; Southern Inst. for Education and Research) civil rights movement, 20th-century radical right-wing movements; lhill@tulane.edu

Raeburn, Bruce Boyd (PhD, Tulane 1991; adj.) New Orleans jazz; raeburn@tulane.edu

Full-time Faculty

Adderley, Laura Rosanne (PhD, Pennsylvania 1996; assoc. prof.) African diaspora, African American, Caribbean; adderley@ tulane.edu

Akin, Yigit (PhD, Ohio State 2011; assoc. prof.) Middle East; yakin@ tulane.edu

Bernstein, Michael A. (PhD, Yale 1982; prof.) economic and political, economic thought, modern public policy; mbernstein@tulane.edu

Boyden, James M. (PhD, Texas, Austin 1988; assoc. prof.) early modern Spain, Renaissance; jboyden@tulane.edu

Clark, Emily (PhD, Tulane 1998; prof.) US, early America; eclark@ tulane.edu

Cruz, Felipe Fernandes (PhD, Texas, Austin 2016; asst. prof.) modern Brazil, technology; fcruz1@tulane.edu

DeMare, Brian James (PhD, UCLA 2007; assoc. prof. and dir., undergrad. studies) modern China, modern Japan, 18th- and 19th-century French cultural; bdemare@tulane.edu

Edwards, Kathryn (PhD, Toronto 2010; asst. prof.) modern France, modern Europe; medward5@tulane.edu

Garcia, Guadalupe (PhD, North Carolina, Chapel Hill 2006; assoc. prof. and dir., grad. studies) Latin America and Caribbean, Cuba, urban studies; ggarcia4@tulane.edu

Gilpin, Robert Blakeslee (PhD, Yale 2009; asst. prof.) US South; rgilpin@tulane.edu

Haber, Carole (PhD, Pennsylvania 1979; prof.) American social and medical; chaber@tulane.edu

Harl, Kenneth W. (PhD, Yale 1978; prof.) classical Greece, Rome, Byzantium; kharl@tulane.edu

Haugeberg, Karissa (PhD, Iowa 2011; asst. prof.) US women, medicine, modern US religion and politics; khaugebe@tulane. edu

Horowitz, Andrew (PhD, Yale 2014; asst. prof.) environmental, modern US political, modern US cultural; ahorowitz@tulane.edu

Isaacson, Walter (BA, Harvard 1974; Univ. Prof.) technology; isaacson@tulane.edu

Lane, Kris E. (PhD, Minnesota 1996; prof.) Latin America; klane1@ tulane.edu

Lipman, Jana K. (PhD, Yale 2006; assoc. prof.) 20th-century US; jlipman@tulane.edu

Luongo, F. Thomas (PhD, Notre Dame 1998; assoc. prof. and chair) medieval Europe, Renaissance, Italy; tluongo@tulane.edu

McMahon, Elisabeth M. (PhD, Indiana 2005; assoc. prof.) Africa, North and West Africa, South and East Africa; emcmahon@ tulane.edu

Otte, Marline Sylta (PhD, Toronto 1999; assoc. prof.) modern Germany, social and cultural, comparative popular culture; motte@tulane.edu

Pollock, Linda A. (PhD, St. Andrews, UK 1982; prof.) Britain, 16th and 17th centuries, European family; pollock@tulane.edu

Ramer, Samuel C. (PhD, Columbia 1971; assoc. prof.) modern Europe, Russia, 19th-century Russian social and intellectual; ramer@tulane.edu

Sparks, Randy J. (PhD, Rice 1988; prof.) US South, US, religion; rsparks1@tulane.edu

Teichgraeber, Richard F. (PhD, Brandeis 1978; prof.) American intellectual, 18th- to 19th-century Britain; rteich@tulane.edu

Wolfe, Justin (PhD, UCLA 1999; assoc. prof.) Central America, Nicaragua; jwolfe@tulane.edu

Retired/Emeritus Faculty

Bernstein, George L. (PhD, Chicago 1978; prof. emeritus) 19th- and 20th-century Britain; gbernst@tulane.edu

Frey, Sylvia R. (PhD, Tulane 1969; prof. emeritus) colonial and revolutionary America, US political traditions and institutions, women; frey@tulane.edu

Latner, Richard (PhD, Wisconsin, Madison 1972; prof. emeritus) Jacksonian America, sectionalism and Civil War, information technology; latner@tulane.edu

MacLachlan, Colin M. (PhD, UCLA 1969; prof. emeritus) Latin American social, Brazil, Mexico; cmaclac@tulane.edu

Malone, Bill C. (PhD, Texas, Austin 1965; prof. emeritus) US social and cultural, American folklore and music

Powell, Lawrence N. (PhD, Yale 1976; prof. emeritus) Civil War and Reconstruction, Louisiana; powell@tulane.edu

Schroeder, Susan (PhD, UCLA 1984; prof. emeritus) colonial Latin America, Native American; sschroe@tulane.edu

Woodward, Ralph Lee, Jr. (PhD, Tulane 1962; prof. emeritus) Latin American economic, Central America; rwoodward@tulane.edu

Yeager, Gertrude M. (PhD, Texas Christian 1972; assoc. prof. emeritus) Latin American social and political, Spanish South America, women and gender; tyeager@tulane.edu

Union College

Dept. of History, 807 Union St., Schenectady, NY 12308-3163. 518.388.6220. Fax 518.388.6422. Email: forougha@union.edu; historychair@union.edu. Website: https://www.union.edu/academic/majors-minors/history.

The History Department is vitally involved in all levels of the College curriculum. The department is large enough to offer a varied and rich selection of offerings to students taking courses as majors or as electives.

Chair: Andrea Foroughi
Degrees Offered: BA
Academic Year System: Trimester
Areas of Specialization: US and public, Europe, Africa and Middle East, East and South Asia, Latin America
Tuition (per academic year): $56853
Enrollment 2018-19:
  Undergraduate Majors: 66
  Degrees in History: 16 BA
Addresses:
  Admissions: http://www.union.edu/admissions/
  Financial Aid: http://www.union.edu/admissions/finaid/

Full-time Faculty

Aslakson, Kenneth Randolph (PhD, Texas, Austin 2007; assoc. prof.) African American, colonial/revolutionary/early Republic America, law/race/Constitution; aslaksok@union.edu

Berk, Stephen M. (PhD, Columbia 1971; Henry & Sally Schaffer Prof.) Judaic studies, Russia and Soviet Union, Holocaust; berks@union.edu

Cramsie, John R., III (PhD, St. Andrews, UK 1997; assoc. prof.) Britain, Ireland, imperial Britain; cramsiej@union.edu

Feffer, Andrew (PhD, Pennsylvania 1987; prof.) 20th century, US cultural and intellectual; feffera@union.edu

Foroughi, Andrea R. (PhD, Minnesota 1999; assoc. prof. and chair) women and gender, 19th century, US social; forougha@union.edu

Madancy, Joyce A. (PhD, Michigan 1995; prof.) East Asia, drugs; madancyj@union.edu

Mazumder, Rajashree (PhD, UCLA 2013; asst. prof.) South and Southeast Asia/Burma, migration, Indian Ocean region; mazumder@union.edu

Meade, Teresa A. (PhD, Rutgers 1984; Florence B. Sherwood Prof.) Latin America, women and gender; meadet@union.edu

Morris, Andrew (PhD, Virginia 2003; assoc. prof.) 20th century, US politics and policy; morrisa@union.edu

Peterson, Brian James (PhD, Yale 2005; assoc. prof.) Africa, Islam, modern France; petersob@union.edu

Sargent, Steven D. (PhD, Pennsylvania 1982; prof.) medieval, Renaissance, science and technology; sargents@union.edu

Walker, Mark (PhD, Princeton 1987; John Bigelow Prof.) modern Europe, science and technology, intellectual; walkerm@union.edu

Part-time Faculty

Brennan, Denis P. (PhD, SUNY, Albany 2003; lect.) 19th-century US, sports, political and social; brennand@union.edu

Lawson, Melinda A. (PhD, Columbia 1998; sr. lect.) 19th century, abolition and Civil War, public; lawsonm@union.edu

Retired/Emeritus Faculty

Hansen, Erik von Stein (PhD, Cornell 1968; prof. emeritus) modern Europe, socialism, imperialism; hansene@union.edu

Thurston, Donald (PhD, Columbia 1970; prof. emeritus) East Asia, Japan; thurstod@union.edu

Wells, Robert V. (PhD, Princeton 1969; prof. emeritus) early America and Revolution, demography, folk music; wellsr@union.edu

Union University

Dept. of History, 1050 Union University Dr., Jackson, TN 38305-3697. 731.661.1818. Fax 731.661.5175. Email: scarls@uu.edu. Website: http://www.uu.edu/dept/history/.

In addition to a two-semester core class in world civilization, the department offers courses in American, European, Latin American, and church history. There are also history internships, a History and Historians course that focuses on historical methodology, and a senior seminar that provides an in-depth research and writing experience.

Chair: Stephen D. Carls
Degrees Offered: BA,BS
Academic Year System: Semester
Areas of Specialization: American foreign policy, 19th-century America, religious, modern Europe
Tuition (per academic year): $32650
Enrollment 2018-19:
  Undergraduate Majors: 28
  Degrees in History: 3 BA
Addresses:
  Admissions: http://www.uu.edu/admissions/
  Financial Aid: http://www.uu.edu/financialaid/

Full-time Faculty

Allen, J. Henry, Jr. (PhD, George Washington 2004; assoc. prof.) US religious, church, 19th-century America; jallen@uu.edu

Bates, David Keith, Jr. (PhD, Kansas State 2006; prof.) 20th-century America, American religious, Reformation Europe; dkbates@uu.edu

Carls, Stephen Douglas (PhD, Minnesota 1982; Univ. Prof. and chair) France, economic, 20th-century Europe; scarls@uu.edu

Lindley, W. Terry (PhD, Texas Christian 1985; Univ. Prof.) American foreign policy, America since 1945, American church; tlindley@uu.edu

Thomas, David C. (PhD, Ohio State 1993; prof.) early America, religious, American Far West; dthomas@uu.edu

Part-time Faculty

Briley, Robert (MEd, Union 1994; adj. instr.) 18th-century America, ancient Rome, Cold War; cp1796@aol.com

Retired/Emeritus Faculty

Baggett, James A. (PhD, North Texas 1972; prof. emeritus and dean emeritus; Arts and Sciences) US South, Civil War and Reconstruction, America; jabaggett3234@att.net

United States Air Force Academy

Dept. of History, 2354 Fairchild Dr., Suite 6F101, Colorado Springs, CO 80840-6246. 719.333.3230. Fax 719.333.2970. Email: mail. DFH@usafa.edu. Website: https://www.usafa.edu/department/history/.

An understanding of history is a critical component to the training of capable, educated officers. The knowledge gained and the perspective developed are important to the education of the professional Air Force officer.

Chair: Col. Meg Martin
Degrees Offered: BS
Academic Year System: Semester
Areas of Specialization: military, America, international
Tuition: Students appointed to the academy become cadets in the US Air Force; they pay no tuition. A nonrefundable deposit of $1,000 is required of each cadet upon entry. Cadets receive a monthly salary approximately half that of a second lieutenant's pay.
Enrollment 2018-19:
Undergraduate Majors: 112
Degrees in History: 27 BS
Addresses:
Admissions: https://www.academyadmissions.com/

Affiliated Faculty

Abbatiello, John J. (PhD, King's Coll., London 2004; chief, Research and Scholarship Div.; Center for Character and Leadership Development) naval and air power, World War I; john.abbatiello@usafa.edu
Randolph, Stephen Patrick (PhD, George Washington 2005; Rokke-Fox Chair; Center for Character and Leadership Development) Air Force, Air Force Academy, profession of arms; stephen.randolph@usafa.edu

Full-time Faculty

Abadi, Jacob (PhD, NYU 1978; prof.) Middle East, British Empire; jacob.abadi@usafa.edu
Clune, Lt Col John (PhD, Kansas 2014; asst. prof.) international, world, Africa; john.clune@usafa.edu
Epper, Michael (MA, Hardin-Simmons 2010; instr.) Michael.Epper@usafa.edu
Fugler, Maj Thomas J. (MA, Colorado, Colorado Springs 2017; instr.) modern Turkey, modern Middle East, leftist groups and radical movements; thomas.fugler@usafa.edu
Hamer, Lt Col Michael D. (MA, Kansas State 2016; instr.) US religion, world, America; michael.hamer@usafa.edu
Honnen, Mark (MA, Georgia State 2013; asst. prof.) world, British imperialism, South Asia; mark.honnen@usafa.edu
Jennings, John M. (PhD, Hawai'i, Manoa 1995; prof.) East Asia; john.jennings@usafa.edu
Johnson, Maj Donald D., III (MA, Purdue 2015; instr.) Europe, decolonization, British Empire; donald.johnson@usafa.edu
Kennedy, Lt Col (Ret.) Doug B. (PhD, Kansas State 2017; temporary asst. prof.) US foreign relations, US airpower; douglas.kennedy@usafa.edu
Leonard, Lt Col Douglas (PhD, Duke 2012; asst. prof.) modern France, Northwest Africa; douglas.leonard@usafa.edu
Lopez, Maj Miguel Angel (MA, Temple 2015; instr.) World War II, German military; miguel.lopez@usafa.edu
Martin, Col Margaret Carol (PhD, North Carolina, Chapel Hill 2014; permanent prof. and dept. head) US, military; margaret.martin@usafa.edu
Menath, Lt Col Ryan (DA, North Dakota 2018; asst. prof.) US military; ryan.menath@usafa.edu
Morris, Lt Col Craig (PhD, Auburn 2015; asst. prof.) technology, aviation, US; craig.morris@usafa.edu
Naaktgeboren, Capt Jason L. (MA, Northern Arizona 2009; instr.) American West, environmental; jason.naaktgeboren@usafa.edu
Patton, Capt Kirsten M. (MA, Central Missouri 2015; instr.) modern America, public, archiving; kirsten.patton@usafa.edu
Roche, Lt Col John David (PhD, North Carolina, Chapel Hill 2015; asst. prof.) America, military, Atlantic; john.roche@usafa.edu
Romans, Maj Timothy (MA, Florida State 2005; asst. prof.) early modern Asia, early modern Europe; timothy.romans@usafa.edu

Rush, Lt Anthony P. (MA, Heidelberg 2013; instr.) anthony.rush@usafa.edu
Scott-Weaver, Meredith L. (PhD, Delaware 2011; instr.) Europe, Jewish, world; meredith.scott-weaver@usafa.edu
Smith, Philip M. (OMS, Harvard 2017; instr.) early modern Britain, Russia; philip.smith@usafa.edu
Steele, Charles (PhD, West Virginia 2000; assoc. prof.) maritime, military, Europe; charles.steele@usafa.edu
Wettemann, Robert Paul (PhD, Texas A&M 2001; assoc. prof.) America, military, Latin America; robert.wettemann@usafa.edu

Nondepartmental Historians

Blyth, Lance R. (PhD, Northern Arizona 2005; instr.) borderlands, American West; lance.blyth@usafa.edu
Carriedo, Lt Col (Ret.) Robert (PhD, New Mexico 2004; assoc. prof.) Latin America; robert.carriedo@usafa.edu
Laslie, Brian D. (PhD, Kansas State 2013; instr.) American military, airpower; brian.laslie@usafa.edu

Visiting Faculty

Etcheson, Nicole (PhD, Indiana 1991; Dist. Vis. Prof.) sectional crisis, Jacksonian era, Civil War and Reconstruction; nicole.etcheson@usafa.edu
Wintz, Cary D. (PhD, Kansas State 1974; Dist. Vis. Prof.) African American, Harlem Renaissance, early 20th-century racial and political ideology; cary.wintz@usafa.edu

United States Army Command and General Staff College

Dept. of Military History, 100 Stimson Ave., Fort Leavenworth, KS 66027. 913.684.2050. Fax 913.684.3869. Email: david.w.mills24.civ@mail.mil. Website: https://usacac.army.mil/organizations/cace/cgsc/cgss.

The academic year does not follow a semester or quarter system. History instruction is provided as part of a year-long program in which field-grade officers in the US Army and sister services, as well as officers from other nations, participate. There are no majors, although students may take electives in history and pursue a master's in military art and science with focus in history during their year at CGSC.

Chair: David G. Cotter
Director of Graduate Studies: Robert F. Baumann
Degrees Offered: MMAS
Academic Year System: Year-long program
Areas of Specialization: military, modern Europe, US
Tuition: None
Addresses:
Admissions: https://usacac.army.mil/

Full-time Faculty

Abel, Jonathan A. (PhD, North Texas 2014; asst. prof.) revolutionary and Napoleonic Europe, Enlightenment, military theory; jonathan.a.abel.civ@mail.mil
Babb, Joseph G. (PhD, Kansas 2012; assoc. prof.) 20th-century China, Chinese military thought; joseph.g.babb.civ@mail.mil
Brown, Gates (PhD, Kansas 2013; asst. prof.) 20th-century US, Cold War; gates.m.brown2.civ@mail.mil
Coss, Edward J. (PhD, Ohio State 2005; prof.; Fort Belvoir) revolutionary and Napoleon Europe, 19th-century Britain; edward.j.coss.civ@mail.mil

Cotter, David G. (MA, Massachusetts 1992; MA, Gratz 2017; asst. prof. and dir.) Napoleonic and Peninsular War, Holocaust and genocide; david.g.cotter.civ@mail.mil

DiMarco, Louis A. (PhD, Kansas State 2010; assoc. prof.) 20th-century US, World War II, cavalry; louis.a.dimarco.civ@mail.mil

Faulkner, Richard S. (PhD, Kansas State 2008; prof. and Stofft Chair) 19th-century US, Spanish-American War, World War I; richard.s.faulkner.civ@mail.mil

Gerges, Mark T. (PhD, Florida State 2005; assoc. prof.) 18th- and 19th-century Europe, French Revolution and Napoleonic eras; mark.t.gerges.civ@mail.mil

Holden, David W. (PhD, Kansas 2015; asst. prof.) diplomatic, 20th-century US; david.w.holden.civ@mail.mil

Hosler, John (PhD, Delaware 2005; assoc. prof.) medieval Europe and Middle East, warfare, Crusades; john.d.hosler.civ@mail.mil

Hospodor, Gregory Scott (PhD, Louisiana State 2000; assoc. prof.) 19th-century US, Jacksonian America; gregory.s.hospodor.civ@mail.mil

Hull, Mark M. (PhD, Univ. Coll., Cork 2000; assoc. prof.) military intelligence, modern Germany, military law; mark.m.hull.civ@mail.mil

Johnson, Christopher (MA, Louisiana State 2009; asst. prof.) international relations, 20th-century US, 20th-century Japan/East Asia; christopher.r.johnson60.civ@mail.mil

Kalic, Sean N. (PhD, Kansas State 2006; prof.) 20th-century US, Cold War, aerospace; sean.n.kalic.civ@mail.mil

Kautt, William H. (PhD, Ulster 2005; prof.) 20th-century Europe, Ireland and Britain, unconventional warfare; william.h.kautt.civ@mail.mil

Kuehn, John T. (PhD, Kansas State 2007; prof. and former Stofft Chair) naval, Asia, World War II; john.t.kuehn.civ@mail.mil

Laver, Harry S. (PhD, Kentucky 1998; prof.) 19th-century US, American Civil War, World War II Europe; harry.s.laver.civ@mail.mil

Mallett, Derek R. (PhD, Texas A&M 2009; asst. prof.; Fort Gordon) 20th-century US, World War II, prisoners of war; derek.r.mallett.civ@mail.mil

Mikolashek, Jon B. (PhD, Florida State 2007; asst. prof.; Fort Belvoir) US, World War II, Afghanistan; jon.b.mikolashek.civ@mail.mil

Mills, David W. (PhD, North Dakota State 2009; asst. prof.) Cold War, Great Plains, Indian wars; david.w.mills24.civ@mail.mil

Mullis, Tony R. (PhD, Kansas 2002; assoc. prof.; Redstone Arsenal) 19th-century US, Jacksonian America, indigenous nations; tony.r.mullis2.civ@mail.mil

Pierce, Marlyn R. (PhD, Kansas State 2013; asst. prof.) 20th century, World War II, aviation; marlyn.r.pierce.civ@mail.mil

Rafuse, Ethan S. (PhD, Missouri-Kansas City 1999; prof.) 19th-century US, early modern Europe; ethan.s.rafuse.civ@mail.mil

Steed, Brian L. (MA, Vermont Coll., Norwich 2006; asst. prof.) brian.l.steed.civ@mail.mil

Stephenson, Donald S. (PhD, Kansas 2007; prof.) 20th-century Germany, World War I; donald.s.stephenson.civ@mail.mil

Valentine, Janet G. (PhD, Alabama 2002; assoc. prof.) Korean War, 20th-century US social and cultural; janet.g.valentine.civ@mail.mil

Vaughn, Mark Kennedy (PhD, Reading, UK 1999; asst. prof.; Fort Lee) medieval Europe, civil-military operations, military governance/peacekeeping operations; mark.k.vaughn.civ@mail.mil

Nondepartmental Historians

Baumann, Robert F. (PhD, Yale 1982; dir., grad. studies) imperial Russia, Central Asia, contemporary peacekeeping operations; robert.f.baumann.civ@mail.mil

Bruscino, Thomas A., Jr. (PhD, Ohio 2005; assoc. prof.; Sch. of Advanced Military Studies) 20th-century US, war and society; thomas.a.bruscino.civ@mail.mil

Butler-Smith, Alice A. (PhD, Kansas 2004; assoc. prof.; Sch. of Advanced Military Studies) Middle East, terrorism; alice.a.butler-smith.civ@mail.mil

Calhoun, Mark T. (PhD, Kansas 2012; assoc. prof.; Sch. of Advanced Military Studies) 20th-century US, World War II; mark.t.calhoun.civ@mail.mil

Carlson, Anthony E. (PhD, Oklahoma 2010; asst. prof.; Sch. of Advanced Military Studies) 20th-century US; anthony.e.carlson9.civ@mail.mil

Davis, Robert T., II (PhD, Ohio 2007; assoc. prof.; Sch. of Advanced Military Studies) Russia, 20th-century Europe; robert.t.davis2.civ@mail.mil

Fullerton, Dan C. (PhD, Kansas 2007; assoc. prof.; Sch. of Advanced Military Studies) Civil War, 20th-century US; dan.c.fullerton.civ@mail.mil

Gorman, G. Scott (PhD, Johns Hopkins 2006; assoc. prof.; deputy dir.; Sch. of Advanced Military Studies) Russia, air power; gerald.s.gorman2.civ@mail.mil

Hanson, Thomas E. (PhD, Ohio State 2006; prof.) 20th-century US, modern Germany, US diplomatic; thomas.e.hanson.civ@mail.mil

Herrera, Ricardo A. (PhD, Marquette 1998; assoc. prof.; Sch. of Advanced Military Studies) colonial America, 19th-century US, Latin America; ricardo.a.herrera.civ@mail.mil

Kennedy, John R. (OMS, US Army Command Coll. 1989; team leader; Fort Lee) 20th-century Europe, Dutch military, military theory; john.r.kennedy16.civ@mail.mil

Lauer, George Stephen (PhD, Florida State 2010; asst. prof.; Sch. of Advanced Military Studies) 20th-century US; george.s.lauer.civ@mail.mil

Martin, James B. (PhD, Texas, Austin 1997; prof.; assoc. dean) 19th-century US, American Civil War, irregular warfare; james.b.martin1.civ@mail.mil

Nowowiejski, Dean A. (PhD, Princeton 2008; assoc. prof.; Ike Skelton Distinguished Chair, Art of War) war and society, 20th-century US, military government; dean.a.nowowiejski.civ@mail.mil

Prigge, Christopher N. (PhD, Harvard 2011; dir.; Advanced Strategic Planning and Policy Prog.) cavalry, education; christopher.n.prigge.mil@mail.mil

Schifferle, Peter J. (PhD, Kansas 2002; prof.; Sch. of Advanced Military Studies) 20th-century US, education; peter.j.schifferele.civ@mail.mil

Stentiford, Barry M. (PhD, Alabama 1998; prof.; Sch. of Advanced Military Studies) 20th-century US, Southeast Asia; barry.m.stentiford.civ@mail.mil

Wright, Donald P. (PhD, Tulane 2002; deputy dir.; Army Press) Russo-Japanese War, World War I, Iraq War/Afghanistan War; donald.p.wright.civ@mail.mil

Retired/Emeritus Faculty

Willbanks, James H. (PhD, Kansas 1998; George C. Marshall Chair emeritus) 20th-century US, Cold War, Vietnam; james.h.willbanks.civ@mail.mil

United States Military Academy

Dept. of History, 600 Thayer Rd., West Point, NY 10996-1793. 845.938.3221. Fax 845.938.3932. Email: krista.hennen@ westpoint.edu. Website: https://westpoint.edu/academics/ academic-departments/history.

Because the core of courses required for graduation emphasizes mathematics, physical sciences, and engineering, the US Military Academy awards all of its graduates the BS. Each cadet, however, may construct a major or a field of study in any of a wide variety of disciplines in mathematics, science, engineering, social sciences, or the humanities.

Chair: Col Gail Yoshitani
Degrees Offered: BS
Academic Year System: Semester
Areas of Specialization: military, strategic, America, Europe, international
Tuition: Students appointed to the academy become cadets in the United States Army; they pay no tuition. A nonrefundable deposit of $1,800 is required of each cadet upon entry. Cadets receive a monthly salary approximately half that of a second lieutenant's pay.
Enrollment 2018-19:
Undergraduate Majors: 262
Degrees in History: 89 BS
Addresses:
Admissions: http://www.westpoint.edu/admissions/

Full-time Faculty

Askew, Maj Mark (MA, Texas A&M 2015; instr.) US Army during Civil War and Reconstruction, US military government in Cuba and Philippines; mark.askew@usma.edu

Bergman, Maj Mark (MA, Pennsylvania 2015; instr.) 19th-century US foreign relations, 19th-century US military/War of 1812/Mexican War, West African colonial; mark.bergman@usma.edu

Black, Lt Col Frederick H., Jr. (PhD, Florida State 2005; asst. prof.) Napoleonic-era military and diplomatic, US military; frederick.black@usma.edu

Browning, Capt Nicholas (MA, Texas Christian 2016; instr.) colonial America and early Republic, American martial development, war and society; nicholas.browning@usma.edu

Bucher, Greta (PhD, Ohio State 1995; prof.) Russia, women and gender, medicine; greta.bucher@usma.edu

Chang, Capt Adam (MA, Western Washington 2016; instr.) late Qing China, military reform; adam.chang@usma.edu

Clason, Capt Nathan (MA, Michigan State 2017; instr.) modern US conservatism, US/Vietnamese diplomatic relations, POW/MIA accounting mission and Vietnam War; Nathan.Clason@usma.edu

Collins, Capt Devon (MA, Ohio State 2017; instr.) 19th- and 20th-century military, prisoners of war, race/ethnicity/nation; devon.collins@usma.edu

Cook, Capt Jessica (MA, Virginia 2017; instr.) colonial American South, cross-cultural encounters and entanglement, frontier and borderland disputes; jessica.cook@usma.edu

Delva, Capt Liliane (MA, Duke 2017; instr.) gender, 19th- and 20th-century Haiti; liliane.delva@usma.edu

Doss, Lt Col John C. (MA, George Washington 2009; asst. prof.) late imperialism and decolonization, World War II, North Africa; john.doss@usma.edu

Fahey, John Edward (PhD, Purdue 2017; instr.) late Habsburg Empire, civil-military relations, Europe; john.fahey@usma.edu

Flores, Maj Benjamin (MA, Arizona 2016; instr.) American foreign policy in Middle East, 20th-century America and Middle East, World War I postwar settlement; benjamin.flores@usma.edu

Frey, David S. (PhD, Columbia 2003; assoc. prof.; dir., Center for Holocaust and Genocide Studies) international/Africa/east central Europe, genocide, Holocaust; david.frey@usma.edu

Garner, Maj Christian (MA, North Texas 2016; instr.) American glider pilot training in World War II, Texas military; christian.garner@usma.edu

Gatzemeyer, Maj Garrett (PhD, Kansas 2018; instr.) war and culture, physicality/sport/body, martial masculinities; garrett.gatzemeyer@usma.edu

Geheran, Michael J. (PhD, Clark 2016; asst. prof.) modern Germany, Holocaust and genocide studies, veterans; michael.geheran@usma.edu

Gibby, Col Bryan (PhD, Ohio State 2004; Academy Prof.) American policy and national strategy in East Asia, military strategy and operations in Korea, war and conflict in Islamic world; bryan.gibby@usma.edu

Gioe, David (PhD, Cambridge 2014; asst. prof.) intelligence and international security studies, Anglo-American intelligence and security services, American foreign relations; david.gioe@usma.edu

Griffin, Benjamin (PhD, Texas, Austin 2018; asst. prof.) American foreign relations, Cold War, grand strategy and policy; ben.griffin@usma.edu

Hatzinger, Maj Kyle (MA, North Texas 2015; instr.) repatriation of American war dead, 20th-century American military; Kyle.Hatzinger@usma.edu

Herman, Maj Thomas (MA, North Texas 2016; instr.) veterans' culture and memory, Vietnam War material culture; thomas.herman@usma.edu

Hinnershitz, Stephanie Dawn (PhD, Maryland, Coll. Park 2013; asst. prof.) immigration, race and ethnicity, civil and human rights; stephanie.hinnershitz@usma.edu

Hoogland, Maj Edward (MA, Hawai'i 2016; instr.) American foreign relations, 20th-century China; edward.hoogland@usma.edu

Hope, Maj Greg (MA, Ohio State 2015; instr.) 20th-century military, US Army; gregory.hope@usma.edu

Hrinko, Lt Col (ret.) Raymond (MA, Illinois 2003; asst. prof.) international, imperial and Soviet Russia; raymond.hrinko@usma.edu

Keating, Maj Christine (MA, Brown 2015; instr.) 20th-century Brazil, US foreign policy, Latin America; christine.keating@usma.edu

Kiesling, Eugenia C. (PhD, Stanford 1988; prof.) military, Europe, ancient; eugenia.kiesling@usma.edu

Kiser, Maj Michael (PhD, Boston Coll. 2016; instr.) American foreign relations, empire and imperialism, grand strategy and leadership; michael.kiser@usma.edu

Krueger, Capt David (MA, Harvard 2017; instr.) 19th-century America, race and gender in military, American foreign policy; david.krueger@usma.edu

Lambert, Maj David (MA, Georgetown 2016; instr.) American political economy, American scientific and industrial, political history of American defense; david.lambert@usma.edu

LeVay, Maj James (MA, Yale 2015; instr.) American civil/military relationships/veterans' affairs, early British Empire, early French Empire; jason.levay@usma.edu

Lovering, Capt Richard (MA, Southern Mississippi 2017; instr.) modern Vietnam, modern Britain, Vietnam War; richard.lovering@usma.edu

Martin, Maj James (MA, Texas 2015; instr.) US-Latin American relations, small wars, religion and foreign policy; James.Martin@usma.edu

McDonald, Robert M. S. (PhD, North Carolina, Chapel Hill 1998; prof.) Revolutionary and early American Republic, Thomas Jefferson, intellectual and political culture; robert.mcdonald@usma.edu

McDonough, Matthew (PhD, Kansas State 2011; asst. prof.) war and memory, 19th-century US, westward expansion; matthew.mcdonough@usma.edu

Mobbs, Maj Michael (MA, Pennsylvania 2017; instr.) US Army and risk, Army doctrine/institutional knowledge/learning, military processes and decision models; michael.mobbs@usma.edu

Moore, Lt Col Tomas (MA, Kansas State 2009; asst. prof.) military manpower/sourcing/recruitment, military and media, topics in military innovation; tomas.moore@usma.edu

Muehlbauer, Matthew S. (PhD, Temple 2008; asst. prof.) colonial America, American military; matthew.muehlbauer@usma.edu

Mukerjee, Anil Kumar (PhD, California, Santa Barbara 2009; asst. prof.) colonial Brazil and Latin America, Portuguese Africa, South Atlantic slaver trade; anil.mukerjee@usma.edu

Musteen, Col Jason R. (PhD, Florida State 2005; Academy Prof.) French Revolutionary and Napoleonic era, military; jason.musteen@usma.edu

Nagel, Amanda (PhD, Mississippi 2014; asst. prof.) US military, US race, Civil Rights Movement; amanda.nagel@usma.edu

Nimick, Thomas G. (PhD, Princeton 1993; assoc. prof.) late imperial China, modern China, East Asian warfare; thomas.nimick@usma.edu

Rogers, Clifford J. (PhD, Ohio State 1994; prof.) military, late medieval Britain and France; clifford.rogers@usma.edu

Salinas, Capt Antonio (MA, Eastern Michigan 2015; instr.) Roman and Greek warfare, counterinsurgency and irregular warfare, Irish Republican Army and conflict in Northern Ireland; antonio.salinas@usma.edu

Sculley, Lt Col Seanegan (MA, Massachusetts 2007; Academy Prof.) America, colonial America, revolutionary America; seanegan.sculley@usma.edu

Seidule, Ty (PhD, Ohio State 1997; prof.) military, West Point, race and gender; ty.seidule@usma.edu

Siry, Lt Col David (MA, Penn State 2003; asst. prof.; dir., Center for Oral History) American Civil War; david.siry@usma.edu

Stapleton, John M., Jr. (PhD, Ohio State 2004; assoc. prof.) military, early modern Europe, Britain and Dutch republic; john.stapleton@usma.edu

Villanueva, Capt James (PhD, Ohio State 2019; instr.) ancient military, American military; james.villanueva@usma.edu

Waddell, Steve (PhD, Texas A&M 1992; prof.) military, World War II; steve.waddell@usma.edu

Watson, Samuel (PhD, Rice 1996; prof.) US state formation and civil-military relations, US military institutions and professionalism, US borderlands and territorial expansion; samuel.watson@usma.edu

Yoshitani, Col Gail E. S. (PhD, Duke 2008; assoc. prof.) military, American foreign relations, 20th century; gail.yoshitani@usma.edu

Ursinus College

Dept. of History, 601 Main St., Collegeville, PA 19426-1000. 610.409.3595. Fax 610.409.3631. Email: history@ursinus.edu. Website: https://www.ursinus.edu/academics/history/.

The mission of the Ursinus College History Department is to cultivate within our community the lifelong habit of actively engaging and critically questioning the relationship between past, present, and future. We affirm that everyone has a history, and that, as global citizens, exploring those histories matters.

Chair: Susanna A. Throop
Degrees Offered: BA
Academic Year System: Semester
Areas of Specialization: America, African American, Native American, world and comparative, Mediterranean and Europe, East Asia, digital humanities, archaeology, oral, gender and sexuality, material culture
Tuition (per academic year): $52050
Enrollment 2018-19:
  Undergraduate Majors: 33
  Degrees in History: 14 BA
  Students in Undergraduate Courses: 264
  Students in Undergraduate Intro Courses: 203
Addresses:
  Admissions: https://www.ursinus.edu/admission/
  Financial Aid: https://www.ursinus.edu/admission/affordability/

Full-time Faculty

Chao, Glenda Ellen (PhD, Columbia 2017; asst. prof.; East Asian Studies) ancient China, East Asia, archaeology; gchao@ursinus.edu

Daggar, Lori J. (PhD, Pennsylvania 2016; asst. prof.) early America, Native American, early Republic race/class/philanthropy; ldaggar@ursinus.edu

Mellis, Johanna (PhD, Florida 2018; asst. prof.) modern European political and social, world, imperialism and colonialism, international relations, sports; jmellis@ursinus.edu

Onaci, Edward (PhD, Illinois, Urbana-Champaign 2012; assoc. prof.) African American, modern US, activism and political movements, culture and music; eonaci@ursinus.edu

Throop, Susanna A. (PhD, Cambridge 2006; assoc. prof. and chair) medieval Europe, medieval Mediterranean, religious and cultural, Christianity; sthroop@ursinus.edu

Retired/Emeritus Faculty

Akin, William E. (PhD, Rochester 1972; prof. emeritus) modern US social and political, baseball; wakin@ursinus.edu

Clark, Hugh R. (PhD, Pennsylvania 1981; prof. emeritus) middle period and modern China, Japan, comparative; hclark@ursinus.edu

University of Utah

Dept. of History, CTIHB 310, 215 S. Central Campus Dr., Salt Lake City, UT 84112-0311. 801.581.6121. Fax 801.585.0580. Email: benjamin.cohen@utah.edu. Website: https://history.utah.edu/.

The University of Utah is a co-educational, non-sectarian, state-supported institution of some 27,000 students and 4,000 faculty. Founded in 1850, it is one of the oldest institutions of higher learning west of the Missouri River. The 1,500 acre campus is located along the foothills of the Wasatch Mountains, the westernmost branch of the Rockies, overlooking Salt Lake City.

Chair: Benjamin Cohen
Director of Graduate Studies: Matt Basso
Director of Undergraduate Studies: Rebecca Horn
Degrees Offered: BA,MA,MS,PhD
Academic Year System: Semester
Areas of Specialization: US, Middle East, Europe, Latin America, Asia
Undergraduate Tuition (per academic year):
  In-State: $5490
  Out-of-State: $17797
Graduate Tuition (per academic year):
  In-State: $5060
  Out-of-State: $16590
Enrollment 2018-19:
  Undergraduate Majors: 268
  New Graduate Students: 12
  Full-time Graduate Students: 29

Part-time Graduate Students: 30
Degrees in History: 61 BA, 12 MA, 1 PhD

Undergraduate Addresses:
Admissions: http://admissions.utah.edu/apply/undergraduate/
Financial Aid: http://financialaid.utah.edu/

Graduate Addresses:
Admissions: http://admissions.utah.edu/apply/graduate/
Financial Aid: http://financialaid.utah.edu/

Adjunct Faculty

Reed, John (PhD, Southern California 1994; assoc. prof./lect.) military; john.reed@history.utah.edu

Thatcher, Mel (PhD, Washington 2004; adj. asst. prof.) China; mel_thatcher@yahoo.com

Thompson, Gregory C. (PhD, Utah 1981; adj. asst. prof.) American Indian, US Southwest; gthompson@library.utah.edu

Full-time Faculty

Arvin, Maile (PhD, California, San Diego 2013; asst. prof.; Gender Studies) Pacific Islands and Pacific Islanders; maile.arvin@utah.edu

Ault, Julia E. (PhD, North Carolina, Chapel Hill 2015; asst. prof.) modern Europe/Germany, Russia and eastern Europe; julia.ault@utah.edu

Basso, Matthew L. (PhD, Minnesota 2001; assoc. prof. and dir., grad. studies) gender, US West; matt.basso@utah.edu

Bresnahan, David (PhD, Wisconsin, Madison 2018; asst. prof.) Africa, world

Cagle, Hugh G. (PhD, Rutgers 2011; assoc. prof.) Latin America and Brazil, science, comparative colonial; hugh.cagle@utah.edu

Clement, Elizabeth (PhD, Pennsylvania 1998; assoc. prof.) US women, sexuality; elizabeth.clement@utah.edu

Cohen, Benjamin B. (PhD, Wisconsin-Madison 2002; prof. and chair) South Asia; benjamin.cohen@utah.edu

Dain, Bruce R. (PhD, Princeton 1996; assoc. prof.) US cultural and intellectual; bruce.dain@utah.edu

Davies, Edward J., II (PhD, Pittsburgh 1977; prof.) world, military; edavies@history.utah.edu

Durbach, Nadja (PhD, Johns Hopkins 2000; prof.) modern Britain; n.durbach@utah.edu

Goldberg, Robert Alan (PhD, Wisconsin, Madison 1977; prof.) American West, social movements, 20th-century US; bob.goldberg@utah.edu

Hinderaker, Eric (PhD, Harvard 1991; prof.) early America; eric.hinderaker@utah.edu

Horn, Rebecca (PhD, UCLA 1989; assoc. prof. and dir., undergrad. studies) Latin America; rebecca.horn@history.utah.edu

Lowey-Ball, Shawnakim (PhD, Yale 2014; asst. prof.) South East Asia; shawnakim.lowey-ball@utah.edu

McDannell, Colleen (PhD, Temple 1984; prof. and McMurrin Chair) American religious; colleen.mcd@utah.edu

Moreira, Isabel A. (PhD, St. Andrews, Scotland 1992; prof.) late ancient, early medieval, Europe; isabel.moreira@utah.edu

Olden, Danielle R. (PhD, Ohio State 2013; asst. prof.) Latina/o, African American, comparative race and ethnicity

Porter, Susie S. (PhD, California, San Diego 1997; prof.) women, Latin America; s.porter@utah.edu

Reeve, W. Paul (PhD, Utah 2002; prof.) Utah, US West; paul.reeve@history.utah.edu

Sasaki-Uemura, Wesley M. (PhD, Cornell 1993; assoc. prof.) Japan; wes.sasaki-uemura@utah.edu

Smoak, Gregory E. (PhD, Utah 1999; assoc. prof.) American Indian; greg.smoak@utah.edu

Theiss, Janet Mary (PhD, California, Berkeley 1998; assoc. prof.) China; janet.theiss@utah.edu

Voltz, Noel Mellick (PhD, Ohio State 2014; asst. prof.) African American, Atlantic world, early America; noel.voltz@utah.edu

Retired/Emeritus Faculty

Adams, Winthrop Lindsay (PhD, Virginia 1974; prof. emeritus) ancient; winthrop.adams@utah.edu

Cannon, Byron (PhD, Columbia 1970; prof. emeritus) modern Middle East, social, legal; byron.cannon@utah.edu

Clayton, James L. (PhD, Cornell 1964; prof. emeritus) economic, legal, recent US; james.clayton@comcast.net

Coleman, Ronald G. (PhD, Utah 1980; assoc. prof. emeritus) African American, Civil War and Reconstruction; rcoleman@utah.edu

Coombs, F. Alan (PhD, Illinois, Urbana-Champaign 1968; assoc. prof. emeritus) 20th-century US, American political; acoombs@history.utah.edu

Gerlach, Larry R. (PhD, Rutgers 1968; prof. emeritus) early America, sports; larry.gerlach@utah.edu

Gunn, Lloyd Ray (PhD, Rutgers 1974; assoc. prof. emeritus) early Republic and Jacksonian America, American political; ray.gunn@utah.edu

Lehning, James (PhD, Northwestern 1977; prof. emeritus) European social, France; jim.lehning@utah.edu

Ojala, Jeanne (PhD, Florida State 1969; prof. emeritus) France

Olsen, Glenn W. (PhD, Wisconsin, Madison 1965; prof. emeritus) medieval, intellectual, religious; glenn.olsen@utah.edu

Parker, Bradley (PhD, UCLA 1998; assoc. prof. emeritus) ancient Near East

Paxton, Roger V. (PhD, Stanford 1968; prof. emeritus) Russia and Soviet Union, Balkans; rpaxton@history.utah.edu

Sluglett, Peter J. (PhD, Oxford 1973; prof. emeritus) 19th- and 20th-century Middle East, political, socioeconomic; sluglett@aol.com

Smelser, Ronald (PhD, Wisconsin, Madison 1970; prof. emeritus) modern Germany, modern European social, modern European cultural; rmsmelse@history.utah.edu

Tompson, Richard (PhD, Michigan 1967; prof. emeritus) modern Britain

Von Sivers, Peter (PhD, Munich, Germany 1967; assoc. prof. emeritus) Middle East, medieval political thought; peter.vonsivers@utah.edu

Utah State University

Dept. of History, 0710 Old Main Hall, Logan, UT 84322-0710. 435.797.1300. Fax 435.797.3899. Email: melissa.maughan@usu.edu. Website: http://history.usu.edu/.

The Department of History's primary mission is to train undergraduates to research, analyze, synthesize, and communicate accurate conclusions about change over time by using the historical method. At the same time we aim to inculcate cultural literacy and provide the knowledge necessary for informed decision making by citizens of Utah, the United States, and the world.

Chair: Tammy Proctor
Director of Graduate Studies: Victoria Grieve
Degrees Offered: BA,BS,MA,MS
Academic Year System: Semester
Areas of Specialization: comparative world, US West, Europe and world wars, religious history and classics, environmental
Undergraduate Tuition (per academic year):
In-State: $6548
Out-of-State: $21087

Graduate Tuition (per academic year):
In-State: $5996
Out-of-State: $20987
Enrollment 2018-19:
Undergraduate Majors: 240
New Graduate Students: 11
Full-time Graduate Students: 18
Part-time Graduate Students: 40
Degrees in History: 28 BA, 12 BS, 4 MA, 4 MS
Undergraduate Addresses:
Admissions: http://www.usu.edu/admissions/
Financial Aid: http://www.usu.edu/finaid/
Graduate Addresses:
Admissions and Financial Aid: http://rgs.usu.edu/
graduateschool/

Full-time Faculty

Andersen, Rebecca (PhD, Arizona State 2015; lect.) public, Utah; rebecca.andersen@usu.edu

Archer, Seth (PhD, California, Riverside 2015; asst. prof.) North American West, health/disease/medicine, Hawai'i; seth.archer@usu.edu

Barton, John D. (MA, Brigham Young 1989; principal lect.) American West and Utah; john.barton@usu.edu

Brown, Clayton D. (PhD, Pittsburgh 2008; assoc. prof.) modern China, East Asia, nationalism; clayton.brown@usu.edu

Bulthuis, Kyle Timothy (PhD, California, Davis 2007; assoc. prof.) early America, social and cultural, race and slavery; kyle.bulthuis@usu.edu

Clendening, Logan (PhD, California, Davis 2018; temp. asst. prof.) race/ethnicity/nationalism, gender and sexuality, religion; logan.clendening@usu.edu

Cogan, Susan M. (PhD, Colorado, Boulder 2012; asst. prof.) early modern social and cultural, religious coexistence, Renaissance and Reformation; susan.cogan@usu.edu

Conte, Christopher A. (PhD, Michigan State 1995; assoc. prof.) Africa, environmental; chris.conte@usu.edu

Culver, Lawrence (PhD, UCLA 2004; assoc. prof.) America, US Southwest borderlands; lawrence.culver@usu.edu

Damen, Mark L. (PhD, Texas, Austin 1985; prof.) Greek and Latin languages, theatre, ancient Near East; mark.damen@usu.edu

Diaz, Angela (PhD, Florida 2013; asst. prof.) US and world, Civil War, borderlands; angela.diaz@usu.edu

Gossard, Julia M. (PhD, Texas, Austin 2015; asst. prof.) early modern France, childhood, gender; julia.gossard@usu.edu

Grayzel, Susan R. (PhD, California, Berkeley 1994; prof.) modern Europe, gender, war; s.grayzel@usu.edu

Grieve, Victoria M. (PhD, George Washington 2004; prof. and dir., grad. studies) America, American cultural, childhood; victoria.grieve@usu.edu

Gupta, Ravi M. (DPhil, Oxford 2004; prof. and Redd Chair) Hinduism, religion; ravi.gupta@usu.edu

Mason, Patrick Q. (PhD, Notre Dame 2005; assoc. prof. and Arrington Chair) Mormonism, American religious, Christianity, violence, peacebuilding; patrick.mason@usu.edu

Mueller, Robert (PhD, California, Santa Barbara 1993; assoc. prof.) early modern Europe, Tudor England; robert.mueller@usu.edu

Neel, Susan Rhoades (PhD, UCLA 1990; assoc. prof.) modern and post-World War II US, environmental, National Park System; susan.neel@usu.edu

O'Neill, Colleen M. (PhD, Rutgers 1997; assoc. prof.) US West, US women, ethnic studies; colleen.oneill@usu.edu

Proctor, Tammy M. (PhD, Rutgers 1995; dist. prof. and head) modern Europe and Britain, gender, imperialism; Tammy.Proctor@usu.edu

Rosenberg, Eliza (PhD, McGill 2015; postdoc. teaching fellow) comparative religious studies, Judaism, Christianity; eliza.rosenberg@usu.edu

Ross, Danielle M. (PhD, Wisconsin-Madison 2011; asst. prof.) Central Asia, Islamic intellectual, Russian imperial and Soviet; danielle.ross@usu.edu

Sanders, James (PhD, Pittsburgh 2000; prof.) Latin America; james.sanders@usu.edu

Shapiro, Susan O. (PhD, Texas, Austin 1992; assoc. prof.) Greece and Rome, classical mythology, Latin and Greek; susan.o.shapiro@usu.edu

Sur, Dominic (PhD, Virginia 2015; asst. prof.) Buddhism, comparative religion; dominic.sur@usu.edu

Titchener, Frances Bonner (PhD, Texas, Austin 1988; dist. prof.; ed., Ploutarchos) Greece, Rome, Greek and Latin languages; frances.titchener@usu.edu

Ward, Joseph P. (PhD, Stanford 1992; prof. and dean) London, social, early modern Britain; joe.ward@usu.edu

Joint/Cross Appointments

Davis, Dan (MA, Wyoming 1997; photograph curator; Special Collections, Merrill-Cazier Library) dandav@usu.edu

Duncan, Jennifer (OMS, Texas, Austin 1997; collection development; Special Collections, Merrill-Cazier Library) Jennifer.Duncan@usu.edu

Parson, Robert (MS, Utah State 1983; Univ. archivist; Special Collections, Merrill-Cazier Library) robert.parson@usu.edu

Pelling, Christopher B. R. (DPhil, Oxford 1975; Regius Prof. of Greek; Christ Church, Oxford) classics

Pumphrey, Clint (MS, Utah State 2009; manuscript curator; Special Collections, Merrill-Cazier Library) American West, environmental; Clint.Pumphrey@usu.edu

Welch, Todd (MA, Western Washington 1995; assoc. dean; Special Collections and Archives, Merrill-Cazier Library) archives administration and records management; todd.welch@usu.edu

Retired/Emeritus Faculty

Barlow, Philip L. (THD, Harvard Divinity Sch. 1988; prof. emeritus) Mormonism and culture; philip.barlow@usu.edu

Glatfelter, R. Edward (PhD, Indiana 1975; assoc. prof. emeritus) Russia, East Asia; edward.glatfelter@usu.edu

Jones, Norman L. (PhD, Cambridge 1978; prof. emeritus) Renaissance and Reformation, medieval, Tudor England; norm.jones@usu.edu

Lewis, David Rich (PhD, Wisconsin, Madison 1988; prof. emeritus) American Indian, environmental, American West; david.r.lewis@usu.edu

McInerney, Daniel J. (PhD, Purdue 1984; prof. emeritus) American intellectual, American studies, antebellum US; daniel.mcinerney@usu.edu

McPherson, Robert S. (PhD, Brigham Young 1987; prof. emeritus) Native American studies; bob.mcpherson@usu.edu

Nicholls, Michael L. (PhD, William and Mary 1972; prof. emeritus) early America; michael.nicholls@usu.edu

Peterson, F. Ross (PhD, Washington State 1968; prof. emeritus) modern US political, African American; ross.peterson@usu.edu

Rosenband, Leonard N. (PhD, Princeton 1981; prof. emeritus) France, social, urban and labor; leonard.rosenband@usu.edu

Utah Valley University

History and Political Science, 800 W. University Pkwy., Mail Stop 185, Orem, UT 84058-5999. 801.863.8487. Fax 801.863.7013. Email: HISTPOLS@uvu.edu. Website: https://www.uvu.edu/hps/.

UVU's History Program is dedicated to developing the 21st-century student. We provide the general student body a broad range of courses that increase global awareness, engagement and informed citizenship, as well as develop critical thinking, writing, and oral expression.

Chair: Jay DeSart
Degrees Offered: AA,AS,BA,BS
Academic Year System: Semester
Areas of Specialization: US, Latin America, Europe and Russia, Africa
Tuition (per academic year):
In-State: $5036
Out-of-State: $15606
Enrollment 2018-19:
Undergraduate Majors: 281
Degrees in History: 5 AA, 20 BA, 21 BS, 25 AS
Students in Undergraduate Courses: 1731
Students in Undergraduate Intro Courses: 1161
Online-Only Courses: 3%
Addresses:
Admissions: https://www.uvu.edu/admissions/
Financial Aid: https://www.uvu.edu/financialaid/

Full-time Faculty

Bennett, Lyn Ellen (PhD, Kansas 1996; prof.) 19th-century US, US West, US women; lbennett@uvu.edu
Goode, Michael J. (PhD, Illinois, Chicago 2012; asst. prof.) early America, Atlantic world, religion and political culture; mgoode@uvu.edu
Hunt, John M. (PhD, Ohio State 2009; asst. prof.) Renaissance Italy, medieval Europe and Mediterranean cultures, ritual and popular culture; john.hunt@uvu.edu
Lentz, Mark W. (PhD, Tulane 2008; asst. prof.) colonial Latin America, early modern Europe; mlentz@uvu.edu
McCarthy, Brendan (PhD, Ohio State 2018; asst. prof.) Roman Republic, ancient Mediterranean, space and communication; Bmccarthy@uvu.edu
Nigro, Jenna C. (PhD, Illinois, Chicago 2014; asst. prof.) modern France, modern European imperialism, colonial West Africa; jenna.nigro@uvu.edu
Snedegar, Keith (DPhil, Oxford 1989; prof.) science and technology, Britain, southern Africa; snedegke@uvu.edu
Winans, Adrienne A. (PhD, Ohio State 2015; asst. prof.) modern US, women/gender/sexuality, Asian American; Adrienne.winans@uvu.edu

Joint/Cross Appointments

Brown, Kathren A. (PhD, Bowling Green State 1997; assoc. prof.; asst. vice pres., Academic Affairs) modern Europe, Russia, eastern Europe; brownkt@uvu.edu
Farnsworth, F. Dennis, Jr. (MA, Brigham Young 1969; prof.; Political Science) international administration, educational leadership and policy, Asian studies; farnswde@uvu.edu

Utica College

Dept. of History, 1600 Burrstone Rd., Utica, NY 13502-4892. 315.792.3147. Fax 315.792.3173. Email: ptdesimo@utica.edu. Website: https://www.utica.edu/academics/programs/history.

Utica College's history program offers remarkable breadth and flexibility. As a history major, students work closely with an accomplished faculty to explore the discipline through scholarship and real-world learning experiences.

Chair: Peter DeSimone
Degrees Offered: BA
Academic Year System: Semester
Areas of Specialization: US, Europe, Asia, African American
Tuition (per academic year): $21560
Enrollment 2018-19:
Undergraduate Majors: 49
Degrees in History: 13 BA
Addresses:
Admissions: http://www.utica.edu/enrollment/admissions/
Financial Aid: http://www.utica.edu/finance/sfs/finaid.cfm

Full-time Faculty

Cash, Sherri G. (PhD, Arizona 2001; assoc. prof.) early America, women and gender, New York; scash@utica.edu
DeSimone, Peter Thomas (PhD, Ohio State 2012; assoc. prof. and chair) Russia and Soviet Union, early modern and modern Europe, Christianity; ptdesimo@utica.edu
Harris, Clemmie L. (PhD, Pennsylvania 2013; asst. prof.) America, Africana studies, urban affairs; clharris@utica.edu
Wittner, David G. (PhD, Ohio State 2000; prof.) modern Japan, technology; dwittner@utica.edu

Valparaiso University

Dept. of History, 1400 Chapel Dr., Valparaiso, IN 46383-6493. 219.464.6962. Fax 219.464.5511. Email: colleen.seguin@valpo.edu. Website: https://www.valpo.edu/history/.

Founded in 1859, Valpo offers a thorough grounding in the liberal arts as well as professional training and graduate study, helping students find their own paths to lifelong personal, spiritual, and professional growth.

Chair: Colleen Seguin
Degrees Offered: BA,MALS
Academic Year System: Semester
Areas of Specialization: US, Europe, East Asia, Africa, Latin America
Undergraduate Tuition (per academic year): $40520
Graduate Tuition (per academic year): $11700
Enrollment 2018-19:
Undergraduate Majors: 54
Part-time Graduate Students: 1
Degrees in History: 4 BA, 2 MA
Undergraduate Addresses:
Admissions: http://www.valpo.edu/admission/
Financial Aid: http://www.valpo.edu/student-financial-services/
Graduate Addresses:
Admissions: http://www.valpo.edu/grad/
Financial Aid: http://www.valpo.edu/student-financial-services/

Full-time Faculty

Ostoyich, Kevin Robert (PhD, Harvard 2006; prof.) modern Europe, Germany; kevin.ostoyich@valpo.edu
Rittgers, Ronald K. (PhD, Harvard 1998; prof. and Erich Markel Chair) Reformation Europe; ron.rittgers@valpo.edu
Schaefer, Charles G. H. (PhD, Chicago 1990; prof.) Africa, Middle East; chuck.schaefer@valpo.edu
Seguin, Colleen M. (PhD, Duke 1997; assoc. prof. and chair) England, early modern Europe; colleen.seguin@valpo.edu
Suarez, Camille A. (PhD, Pennsylvania 2019; asst. prof.) 19th- and 20th-century US, transnational, race, Reconstruction, American Southwest, American empire, borderlands, labor, legal; camille.suarez@valpo.edu

Xia, Yun (PhD, Oregon 2010; assoc. prof.) China, gender, Japan; yun.xia@valpo.edu

Nondepartmental Historians

Rubchak, Marian (PhD, Illinois, Chicago 1987; sr. research prof.) Russia, Soviet Union, western European intellectual; marian.rubchak@valpo.edu

Startt, James Dill (PhD, Maryland, Coll. Park 1965; sr. research prof.) 20th-century Europe, British Empire and Commonwealth; james.startt@valpo.edu

Visiting Faculty

Schwartz Francisco, Diana Lynn (PhD, Chicago 2016; vis. asst. prof.) Latin America, environmental

Vanderbilt University

Dept. of History, PMB 351802, 2301 Vanderbilt Pl., Nashville, TN 37235-1802. 615.322.2575. Fax 615.343.6002. Website: https://as.vanderbilt.edu/history/.

The Department of History's faculty members offer courses that span the globe—from Africa and Asia to Europe, Latin America, and the United States—and that introduce students to a range of historical questions and methodologies.

Chair: Edward Wright-Rios
Director of Graduate Studies: Samira Sheikh
Director of Undergraduate Studies: Lauren Clay
Degrees Offered: BA,BS,PhD
Academic Year System: Semester
Areas of Specialization: America, Asia, Europe, Latin America, Middle East and Africa, global and transnational, science/medicine/technology, law, history and society
Undergraduate Tuition (per academic year): $50800
Graduate Tuition (per academic year): $34380
Enrollment 2018-19:
  Undergraduate Majors: 242
  New Graduate Students: 9
  Full-time Graduate Students: 60
  Degrees in History: 87 BA, 5 MA, 10 PhD
  Students in Undergraduate Courses: 2065
  Students in Undergraduate Intro Courses: 1100
Undergraduate Addresses:
  Admissions: http://admissions.vanderbilt.edu/
  Financial Aid: http://www.vanderbilt.edu/financialaid/
Graduate Addresses:
  Admissions: http://gradschool.vanderbilt.edu/admissions/
  Financial Aid: http://gradschool.vanderbilt.edu/funding/

Full-time Faculty

Applegate, Celia S. (PhD, Stanford 1987; William R. Kenan Endowed Chair) Germany, cultural, music; celia.applegate@vanderbilt.edu

Benton, Lauren A. (PhD, Johns Hopkins 1987; Nelson O. Tyrone Jr. Chair; dean, Coll. of Arts and Science; Law) Atlantic, comparative history of empire, legal; lauren.benton@vanderbilt.edu

Bess, Michael Demaree (PhD, California, Berkeley 1989; Chancellor's Prof. and assoc. chair) 20th-century Europe, environmentalism, social and ethical implications of technology; michael.d.bess@vanderbilt.edu

Blackbourn, David (PhD, Cambridge 1976; Cornelius Vanderbilt Dist. Chair) Germany, environmental, transnational; david.g.blackbourn@vanderbilt.edu

Bryen, Ari Z. (PhD, Chicago 2008; asst. prof.; Classics) Roman history and law, violence/papyrology/rhetoric; ari.z.bryen@vanderbilt.edu

Byrd, Brandon R. (PhD, North Carolina, Chapel Hill 2014; asst. prof.) 19th- and 20th-century US, African American, African diaspora; brandon.r.byrd@vanderbilt.edu

Caferro, William P. (PhD, Yale 1992; Gertrude Conaway Prof.) medieval Europe, economic; william.p.caferro@vanderbilt.edu

Castilho, Celso T. (PhD, California, Berkeley 2008; assoc. prof.) Latin America, Atlantic slavery and abolition, citizenship; celso.t.castilho@vanderbilt.edu

Clay, Lauren R. (PhD, Pennsylvania 2003; assoc. prof. and dir., undergrad. studies) European culture, theatre, French empire; lauren.clay@vanderbilt.edu

Cowie, Jefferson R. (PhD, North Carolina, Chapel Hill 1997; James G. Stahlman Prof.; co-dir., Vanderbilt Hist. Seminar) postwar US politics and culture, labor/class/capitalism, popular culture and transnational; jefferson.cowie@vanderbilt.edu

Crawford, Katherine B. (PhD, Chicago 1997; Cornelius Vanderbilt Prof.; dir., Women's and Gender Studies) gender history/theory, early modern France; katherine.b.crawford@vanderbilt.edu

Dickerson, Dennis C. (PhD, Washington, St. Louis 1978; James M. Lawson Jr. Prof.; Divinity) African American and US religion civil rights movement; dennis.c.dickerson@vanderbilt.edu

Eakin, Marshall C. (PhD, UCLA 1981; prof.) Latin America, 19th- and 20th-century Brazil and Central America; marshall.c.eakin@vanderbilt.edu

Figal, Gerald A. (PhD, Chicago 1992; prof.; dir., Asian Studies) modern Japanese cultural and intellectual, postwar Okinawa, Japanese animation; gerald.figal@vanderbilt.edu

Greble, Emily (PhD, Stanford 2007; assoc. prof.; German, Russian and East European Studies) modern eastern Europe, Balkans and former Yugoslavia; emily.greble@vanderbilt.edu

Halevi, Leor E. (PhD, Harvard 2002; assoc. prof.; Law) Islam, Islamic law; leor.halevi@vanderbilt.edu

Harrington, Joel F. (PhD, Michigan 1989; Centennial Prof.) Reformation, early modern Germany, children and family; joel.harrington@vanderbilt.edu

Igarashi, Yoshikuni (PhD, Chicago 1994; assoc. prof.; Asian Studies) modern Japan; yoshikuni.igarashi@vanderbilt.edu

Igo, Sarah E. (PhD, Princeton 2001; prof.; Law, Political Science, Sociology and dir., American Studies) modern US 1865-present, cultural, human sciences; sarah.igo@vanderbilt.edu

Kramer, Paul Alexander (PhD, Princeton 1998; assoc. prof.) US and world, globalization, immigration; paul.a.kramer@vanderbilt.edu

Lake, Peter G. (PhD, Cambridge 1978; Univ. Dist. Prof.; Martha Rivers Ingram Chair; Divinity Sch.) Tudor-Stuart England, religion; peter.lake@vanderbilt.edu

Landers, Jane G. (PhD, Florida 1988; Gertrude Conaway Prof.) Afro-Latin America, Atlantic world, comparative slave systems; jane.landers@vanderbilt.edu

Lorge, Peter (PhD, Pennsylvania 1996; assoc. prof.; Asian Studies) ancient China, war, Chinese martial arts; peter.lorge@vanderbilt.edu

McGinn, Thomas A. (PhD, Michigan 1986; prof.; Classics) Roman law and social, Latin literature; thomas.a.mcginn@vanderbilt.edu

Molineux, Catherine A. J. (PhD, Johns Hopkins 2005; assoc. prof.) early modern British Atlantic, slavery, race; catherine.a.molineux@vanderbilt.edu

Molvig, Ole R. (PhD, Princeton 2006; asst. prof.; asst. dir., Vanderbilt Inst. for Digital Learning; Physics) physical sciences, technology, modern European intellectual and cultural; ole.molvig@vanderbilt.edu

Ochonu, Moses Ebe (PhD, Michigan 2004; Cornelius Vanderbilt Prof.) Africa, colonialism, political economy; moses.ochonu@vanderbilt.edu

Rijke-Epstein, Tasha (PhD, Michigan 2017; asst. prof.) Africa, urban, science/technology

Robinson, William Francis (PhD, Auburn 1999; asst. prof.) Latin America, Caribbean; william.f.robinson@vanderbilt.edu

Rogaski, Ruth (PhD, Yale 1996; assoc. prof.; co-dir., Vanderbilt Hist. Seminar; interim dir., Asian Studies) 20th-century Chinese cultural, medicine; ruth.rogaski@vanderbilt.edu

Schwartz, Thomas Alan (PhD, Harvard 1985; prof.; Political Science, European Studies) US foreign relations, 20th-century America, international relations; thomas.a.schwartz@vanderbilt.edu

Sheikh, Samira (DPhil, Wolfson Coll., Oxford 2004; assoc. prof. and dir., grad. studies; Asian Studies, Islamic Studies) South Asia; samira.sheikh@vanderbilt.edu

Smith, Helmut W. (PhD, Yale 1991; Martha Rivers Ingram Prof.; European Studies and dir., Digital Humanities) modern Germany; helmut.w.smith@vanderbilt.edu

Tuchman, Arleen M. (PhD, Wisconsin, Madison 1985; prof.) science and medicine, gender and sexuality, disease; arleen.m.tuchman@vanderbilt.edu

Usner, Daniel H., Jr. (PhD, Duke 1981; Holland M. McTyeire Prof.) American Indian, colonial and early national, US South; daniel.h.usner@vanderbilt.edu

Wasserstein, David J. (DPhil, Oxford 1982; Eugene Greener Jr. Prof.; Jewish Studies) medieval Jews, Jews of Islam, medieval Islam; david.wasserstein@vanderbilt.edu

Wcislo, Francis W. (PhD, Columbia 1984; assoc. prof.) reform period Russia, modern Russia; francis.w.wcislo@vanderbilt.edu

Welch, Kim M. (PhD, Maryland, Coll. Park 2012; asst. prof.; Law) North American slavery, US South, women and gender; kimberly.m.welch@vanderbilt.edu

Williams, Rhonda Y. (PhD, Pennsylvania 1998; prof. and John L. Seigenthaler Chair) civil rights and black power, race/class/gender, urban/social movements/social justice; rhonda.williams@vanderbilt.edu

Wright-Rios, Edward N. (PhD, California, San Diego 2004; prof. and chair) modern Latin America and Mexico, religion, ethnohistory; edward.wright-rios@vanderbilt.edu

Joint/Cross Appointments

Ackerman-Lieberman, Phillip (PhD, Princeton 2007; assoc. prof.; Jewish Studies, Law, Religious Studies) medieval Jewish and Islamic, economic/social/legal; phil.lieberman@vanderbilt.edu

Cohen, Julia Phillips (PhD, Stanford 2008; assoc. prof.; Jewish Studies) modern Jewish, Europe, Ottoman; julia.p.cohen@vanderbilt.edu

Collins, William J. (PhD, Harvard 1998; Terrence E. Adderley Jr. Prof.; Economics) economic, labor; william.collins@vanderbilt.edu

Hudnut-Beumler, James (PhD, Princeton 1989; Anne Potter Wilson Dist. Prof.; Divinity Sch.) historiography of religion in American South, 19th- and 20th-century American religious, religion and philanthropy; james.hudnut-beumler@vanderbilt.edu

Joskowicz, Alexander Ari (PhD, Chicago 2008; asst. prof.; Jewish Studies, European Studies) modern Jewish, modern Europe, modern Jewish philosophy and thought; a.joskowicz@vanderbilt.edu

Lim, Paul C-H (PhD, Cambridge 2001; asst. prof.; Religious Studies; Divinity Sch.) early modern English intellectual, Puritanism, Reformation thought; paul.lim@vanderbilt.edu

Loss, Christopher (PhD, Virginia 2007; asst. prof.; Public Policy; Peabody Coll.) US social and political, higher education, public policy; c.loss@vanderbilt.edu

Mayeux, Sara (PhD, Stanford 2016; JD, Stanford Law 2011; asst. prof.; Law) criminal law and procedure, constitutional law, American legal; sara.mayeux@vanderbilt.edu

Metzl, Jonathan (PhD, Michigan 2001; Frederick B. Rentschler II Prof.; Sociology, Psychiatry, and dir., Center for Medicine, Health, and Society) mental illness, medical boundaries, men's health; jonathan.metzl@vanderbilt.edu

Michelson, David A. (PhD, Princeton 2007; asst. prof.; Classics, Religious Studies; Divinity Sch.) Christianity in Middle East/Asia/Africa, Syriac literature and culture; david.a.michelson@vanderbilt.edu

Patterson, Tiffany Ruby (PhD, Minnesota 1995; assoc. prof.; African American and Diaspora Studies) African American, black Atlantic; t.ruby.patterson@vanderbilt.edu

Price, David (PhD, Yale 1985; prof.) neo-Latin poetry, English bible, Renaissance visual art; david.h.price@vanderbilt.edu

Rousseau, Peter L. (PhD, NYU 1995; prof.; Economics) macroeconomics, money and banking, technological change; peter.l.rousseau@vanderbilt.edu

Sharfstein, Daniel (JD, Yale 2000; prof.; Law) American legal, race and law, property law; daniel.sharfstein@vanderbilt.edu

Stark, Laura (PhD, Princeton 2006; assoc. prof.; Center for Medicine, Health and Society) science/medicine/technology, human science; laura.stark@vanderbilt.edu

Wells-Oghoghomeh, Alexis S. (PhD, Emory 2015; asst. prof.; Religious Studies) African American religious, American religious slavery and religion in America; alexis.s.wells@vanderbilt.edu

Part-time Faculty

Downs, Jordan (PhD, California, Riverside 2015; research asst. prof.) early modern London/England/Europe, print and manuscript culture

Jones, Yollette (PhD, Duke 1985; sr. lect. and assoc. dean; Coll. of Arts and Science) African American; yollette.t.jones@vanderbilt.edu

Questier, Michael (PhD, Sussex 1988; research asst. prof.) 16th- and 17th-century English local, ecclesiastical, martyrology; michael.questier@vanderbilt.edu

Retired/Emeritus Faculty

Blackett, Richard J. M. (MA, Manchester, UK 1973; Andrew Jackson Prof. emeritus) African American, antislavery, Caribbean; richard.j.blackett@vanderbilt.edu

Carlton, David L. (PhD, Yale 1977; assoc. prof. emeritus) US South, US business; david.l.carlton@vanderbilt.edu

Conkin, Paul K. (PhD, Vanderbilt 1957; Dist. Prof. emeritus) intellectual, philosophical; paul.k.conkin@vanderbilt.edu

Epstein, James A. (PhD, Birmingham, UK 1977; Dist. Prof. emeritus) modern Britain, imperial; james.a.epstein@vanderbilt.edu

Franklin, Jimmie L. (PhD, Oklahoma 1968; prof. emeritus) US South, African American; jimmiefranklin@comcast.net

Ramsey, Matthew (PhD, Harvard 1978; prof. emeritus) modern Europe, France, medicine; matthew.ramsey@vanderbilt.edu

Voegeli, V. Jacque, III (PhD, Tulane 1965; prof. emeritus) US South; jacque.voegeli@vanderbilt.edu

Winters, Donald L. (PhD, Wisconsin, Madison 1966; prof. emeritus) economic; donald.l.winters@vanderbilt.edu

Recently Awarded PhDs

Bortz, Sean Benjamin "Thinking with Jews: Jews and Judaism and the Struggle for Orthodoxy in Late Medieval and Reformation England"

Bretones Lane, Fernanda "Spanish Religious Sanctuary and Inter-Imperial Marronage in the 18th-Century Caribbean"

Bruno, Dean "This Land Is Our Land: Possession and Remembrance of a Central New York Landscape"

Elrick, Joanna K. "Black Religions with White Faces: The Creolization of Religious Belief and Cultural Practice in Colonial Brazil, Angola, and Cuba, 1600-1889"

Genkins, Daniel "Entangled Empires: England and Spain in the 17th-Century Caribbean"

Lazo, Katherine "'Rigour upon Men's Consciences': National Identity, Religion, and English Catholics during the Interregnum"

Mapes, Christopher David "Germany's Slavery Problem during the Sattelzeit, 1750-1850"

Mosher, Shawn J. "African American Emigrationists and the Building of Liberia from the Top Down, 1847-1900"

Murrell, William S. "Dragomans and Crusaders: The Role of Translators and Translation in the Medieval Eastern Mediterranean, 1098-1291"

Painter, Cassandra Lynn "The Life and Afterlife of Anna Katharina Emmerick: Reimagining Catholicism in Modern Germany"

Picard, Danielle "Analyzing the Human Factor in British Industrial Psychology, 1919-39"

Teague, Aileen T. "Americanizing Mexican Drug Enforcement: The War on Drugs in Mexican Politics and Society, 1964-82"

Williams, J'Nese "The Texture of Empire: British Colonial Botanic Gardens, Science, and Colonial Administration"

Vassar College

Dept. of History, Box 711, 124 Raymond Ave., Poughkeepsie, NY 12604-0711. 845.437.5670. Fax 845.437.7186. Email: lymurdoch@vassar.edu; miwhalen@vassar.edu. Website: https://history.vassar.edu/.

The study of history at Vassar develops a range of skills that can be applied not only to further study but also to a wide variety of careers. Students also enjoy the close mentorship of faculty who help them to become critical thinkers, strong writers and eloquent, incisive speakers. Our graduates aim high, welcome challenges, and stand out on the job market.

Chair: Lydia Murdoch
Degrees Offered: BA
Academic Year System: Semester
Areas of Specialization: US, Europe, Middle East, non-Western, women
Tuition (per academic year): $56130
Enrollment 2018-19:
  Undergraduate Majors: 72
  Degrees in History: 22 BA
Addresses:
  Admissions: http://admissions.vassar.edu/
  Financial Aid: http://admissions.vassar.edu/financial-aid/

Full-time Faculty

Bisaha, Nancy (PhD, Cornell 1997; prof.) Renaissance Italy, medieval; nabisaha@vassar.edu

Brigham, Robert K. (PhD, Kentucky 1994; prof.) US foreign relations, modern America; robrigham@vassar.edu

Choudhury, Mita (PhD, Northwestern 1997; prof.) French Revolution, 18th-century France, early modern Europe; michoudhury@vassar.edu

Cohen, Miriam J. (PhD, Michigan 1978; prof.) modern America, American social, women; cohen@vassar.edu

Edwards, Rebecca B. (PhD, Virginia 1995; prof.) 19th-century America, women, Civil War; reedwards@vassar.edu

Hoehn, Maria (PhD, Pennsylvania 1995; prof.) Germany, 20th-century Europe; mahoehn@vassar.edu

Merrell, James H. (PhD, Johns Hopkins 1982; prof.) colonial and revolutionary America, Native American; merrell@vassar.edu

Mills, Quincy T. (PhD, Chicago 2006; assoc. prof.) African American; qumills@vassar.edu

Murdoch, Lydia (PhD, Indiana 2000; prof. and chair) Victorian Britain, childhood, welfare state; lymurdoch@vassar.edu

Offutt, Leslie S. (PhD, UCLA 1982; assoc. prof.) early Latin America, ethnohistory, Mexico; offutt@vassar.edu

Pohl, Michaela (PhD, Indiana 1999; assoc. prof.) modern Russia, eastern Europe; mipohl@vassar.edu

Rashid, Ismail O. D. (PhD, McGill 1998; prof.) 19th- and 20th-century Africa, West Africa; israshid@vassar.edu

Schreier, Joshua S. (PhD, NYU 2003; prof.) Islamic Middle East/North Africa, modern France; joschreier@vassar.edu

Soon, Wayne (PhD, Princeton 2014; asst. prof.; Asian Studies) East Asia

Retired/Emeritus Faculty

Hodges, Norman E. (PhD, Columbia 1974; assoc. prof. emeritus) 19th- and 20th-century Africa and African diaspora, 20th-century African and Afro-Caribbean liberation movement, 19th-century Afro-American intellectual and social

Schalk, David L. (PhD, Harvard 1964; prof. emeritus) 19th- and 20th-century France, 19th- and 20th-century European intellectual, Spain and Italy since 1815; schalk@vassar.edu

Wohl, Anthony S. (PhD, Brown 1966; prof. emeritus) England, Victorian London, 17th-century Europe; aswohl@aol.com

University of Vermont

Dept. of History, 201 Wheeler House, 133 S. Prospect St., Burlington, VT 05405-0164. 802.656.3180. Fax 802.656.8794. Email: shari.dike@uvm.edu. Website: https://www.uvm.edu/cas/history.

The Department of History faculty are each experts in their unique areas of study as well as talented teacher-mentors. We guide our students in their quest for research and writing skills as well as the development of critical thought.

Chair: Paul Deslandes
Director of Graduate Studies: Dona Brown (hist.); Thomas Visser (hist. preservation)
Director of Undergraduate Studies: Erik Esselstrom
Degrees Offered: BA,MA,MS
Academic Year System: Semester
Areas of Specialization: global, cultural, social, gender, environmental
Undergraduate Tuition (per academic year):
  In-State: $16392
  Out-of-State: $41280
Graduate Tuition (per academic year):
  In-State: $16392
  Out-of-State: $27120
Enrollment 2018-19:
  Undergraduate Majors: 213
  New Graduate Students: 9
  Full-time Graduate Students: 11
  Part-time Graduate Students: 9
  Degrees in History: 50 BA, 6 MA, 4 MS

Undergraduate Addresses:
Admissions: https://www.uvm.edu/admissions/undergraduate
Financial Aid: https://www.uvm.edu/studentfinancialservices
Graduate Addresses:
Admissions: https://www.uvm.edu/graduate/prospective_
student_resources
Financial Aid: https://www.uvm.edu/studentfinancialservices

Full-time Faculty

Briggs, Charles (PhD, North Carolina, Chapel Hill 1993; lect.) late medieval European intellectual and cultural, world, early Europe; charles.briggs@uvm.edu

Brown, Dona L. (PhD, Massachusetts Amherst 1989; prof. and dir., grad. studies) Vermont, US cultural; dona.brown@uvm.edu

Buchanan, Andrew N. (PhD, Rutgers 2011; sr. lect.) US, military; andrew.buchanan@uvm.edu

Carr, Jacqueline Barbara (PhD, California, Berkeley 1998; assoc. prof.) early America, women; jacqueline.carr@uvm.edu

Deslandes, Paul R. (PhD, Toronto 1996; assoc. prof. and chair) Britain, gender, sexualities; paul.deslandes@uvm.edu

Ergene, Bogac A. (PhD, Ohio State 2001; assoc. prof.) Islam and world, social theory and cultural studies; bogac.ergene@uvm.edu

Esselstrom, Erik Warren (PhD, California, Santa Barbara 2004; assoc. prof. and dir., undergrad. studies) modern Japan, comparative East Asia; eesselst@uvm.edu

Field, Sean L. (PhD, Northwestern 2002; prof.) medieval Europe, religious; sean.field@uvm.edu

Gustafson, Melanie S. (PhD, NYU 1993; assoc. prof.) US social, US women, gender politics; melanie.gustafson@uvm.edu

Huener, Jonathan D. (PhD, Illinois, Urbana-Champaign 1998; assoc. prof.) modern Germany, Poland, Holocaust; jonathan.huener@uvm.edu

Kornbluh, Felicia A. (PhD, Princeton 2000; assoc. prof.) US, gender; felicia.kornbluh@uvm.edu

Massell, David P. (PhD, Duke 1997; prof.) Canada, US-Canada relations, environmental; david.massell@uvm.edu

McCullough, Robert (PhD, Cornell 1993; assoc. prof.) historic preservation, architectural, preservation law; robert.mccullough@uvm.edu

McGowan, Abigail (PhD, Pennsylvania 2003; assoc. prof. and assoc. dean) South Asia, India; abigail.mcgowan@uvm.edu

Nicosia, Francis R. (PhD, McGill 1977; prof.) Holocaust; francis.nicosia@uvm.edu

Osten, Sarah E. (PhD, Chicago 2010; asst. prof.) Latin America, Mexico; sarah.osten@uvm.edu

Phelps, Nicole M. (PhD, Minnesota 2008; assoc. prof.) US diplomatic; nicole.phelps@uvm.edu

Schrafstetter, Susanna B. (PhD, Munich, Germany 1998; assoc. prof.) 20th-century Europe; susanna.schrafstetter@uvm.edu

Steinweis, Alan E. (PhD, North Carolina, Chapel Hill 1988; prof.) Holocaust; alan.steinweis@uvm.edu

Stilwell, Sean (PhD, York, Can. 1999; assoc. prof.) Africa, Nigeria; sean.stilwell@uvm.edu

Visser, Thomas D. (MS, Vermont 1986; prof. and dir., hist. preservation) historic preservation, architectural conservation; thomas.visser@uvm.edu

Whitfield, Harvey Amani (PhD, Dalhousie 2003; prof.) African American, Atlantic Canada, Vermont; harvey.whitfield@uvm.edu

Zdatny, Steven (PhD, Pennsylvania 1982; prof.) modern France; steven.zdatny@uvm.edu

Retired/Emeritus Faculty

Andrea, Alfred J. (PhD, Cornell 1969; prof. emeritus) medieval Europe, global; aandrea@uvm.edu

Coleman, Willi (PhD, California, Irvine 1983; assoc. prof. emeritus) African American, US women of color; willi.coleman@uvm.edu

Hutton, Patrick H. (PhD, Wisconsin, Madison 1969; prof. emeritus) European intellectual, historiography, modern France; patrick.hutton@uvm.edu

Liebs, Chester (MS, Columbia 1977; prof. emeritus) historic preservation; cliebs1@aol.com

Metcalfe, William (PhD, Minnesota 1967; prof. emeritus) Tudor-Stuart England; william.metcalfe@uvm.edu

Overfield, James H. (PhD, Princeton 1968; prof. emeritus) global, Renaissance and Reformation, European intellectual; james.overfield@uvm.edu

Spinner, Thomas J., Jr. (PhD, Rochester 1964; prof. emeritus) modern Britain

Steffens, Henry J. (PhD, Cornell 1968; prof. emeritus) science, European cultural, philosophy of history; henry.steffens@uvm.edu

Stoler, Mark A. (PhD, Wisconsin, Madison 1971; prof. emeritus) US diplomatic, US military, World War II; mark.stoler@uvm.edu

Stout, Neil R. (PhD, Wisconsin, Madison 1962; prof. emeritus) colonial and early national America; neil.stout@uvm.edu

True, Marshall (PhD, Virginia 1965; assoc. prof. emeritus) Latin America; cmtrue@verizon.net

Youngblood, Denise J. (PhD, Stanford 1980; prof. emeritus) Russia and eastern Europe, European cultural, film and history; denise.youngblood@uvm.edu

Villanova University

Dept. of History, 800 Lancaster Ave., SAC 403, Villanova, PA 19085-1699. 610.519.4662. Fax 610.519.4450. Email: marc.gallicchio@villanova.edu; vicki.sharpless@villanova.edu. Website: https://www1.villanova.edu/villanova/artsci/history.html.

The History Department is committed to maintaining an intellectual, social, and emotional environment conducive to the development of the necessary components of the human spirit-love, respect, intellect, faith and care-among the undergraduates, graduate students, faculty, and staff who form its community.

Chair: Marc Gallicchio
Director of Graduate Studies: Lynne Hartnett
Degrees Offered: BA,MA
Academic Year System: Semester
Areas of Specialization: modern Europe, US, global, public
Undergraduate Tuition (per academic year): $43840
Graduate Tuition (per academic year): $21600
Enrollment 2018-19:
Undergraduate Majors: 48
New Graduate Students: 18
Full-time Graduate Students: 29
Part-time Graduate Students: 15
Degrees in History: 32 BA, 20 MA
Undergraduate Addresses:
Admissions: http://www1.villanova.edu/villanova/admission.html
Financial Aid: http://www1.villanova.edu/villanova/enroll/finaid.html
Graduate Addresses:
Admissions: http://www1.villanova.edu/main/vuacademics/gradapp.html
Financial Aid: http://www1.villanova.edu/villanova/enroll/finaid.html

Full-time Faculty

Abugideiri, Hibba (PhD, Georgetown 2002; assoc. prof.) Middle East; hibba.abugideiri@villanova.edu

Bailey, Craig (PhD, London 2004; assoc. prof.) Ireland; craig.bailey@villanova.edu

Gallicchio, Marc (PhD, Temple 1986; prof. and chair) American foreign relations, military; marc.gallicchio@villanova.edu

Gettel, Eliza (PhD, Harvard 2019; asst. prof.) ancient

Giesberg, Judith Ann (PhD, Boston Coll. 1999; prof.) US women; judith.giesberg@villanova.edu

Hartnett, Lynne Ann (PhD, Boston Coll. 2000; asst. prof. and dir., grad. hist. prog.) Russia and modern world; lynne.hartnett@villanova.edu

Keita, Maghan (PhD, Howard 1988; prof. and dir., global interdisciplinary studies) Africa; maghan.keita@villanova.edu

Kerrison, Catherine M. (PhD, William and Mary 1999; prof.) North America, pre-1800, US women; catherine.kerrison@villanova.edu

Kolsky, Elizabeth (PhD, Columbia 2002; assoc. prof.) South Asia; elizabeth.kolsky@villanova.edu

Lindenmeyr, Adele (PhD, Princeton 1980; prof. and dean, grad. studies) Russia and Soviet Union; adele.lindenmeyr@villanova.edu

Liu, Andrew (PhD, Columbia 2014; asst. prof.) modern China, East Asia, capitalism; andrew.liu@villanova.edu

Martinko, Whitney A. (PhD, Virginia 2012; asst. prof.) public, early Republic; whitney.martinko@villanova.edu

McCall, Timothy (PhD, Michigan 2005; assoc. prof.) European art; timothy.mccall@villanova.edu

Rosier, Paul C. (PhD, Rochester 1998; prof.) America; paul.rosier@villanova.edu

Ryan, Joseph G. OSA (PhD, American 1997; assoc. prof.) America, American medicine; joseph.ryan@villanova.edu

Soriano, Cristina (PhD, NYU 2011; assoc. prof.) colonial Latin America and Caribbean, social and cultural; cristina.soriano@villanova.edu

Steege, Paul R. (PhD, Chicago 1999; assoc. prof.) Europe; paul.steege@villanova.edu

Sullivan, Mark W. (PhD, Bryn Mawr 1981; asst. prof.) US art; mark.sullivan@villanova.edu

Williams, Shannen Dee (PhD, Rutgers 2013; asst. prof.) African American, women, religious; shannen.williams@villanova.edu

Winer, Rebecca Lynn (PhD, UCLA 1996; assoc. prof.) medieval Europe; rebecca.winer@villanova.edu

Part-time Faculty

Diamond, Kelly-Anne (PhD, Brown 2006; adj. lect.) ancient Egypt; kelly.anne.diamondreed@villanova.edu

Ricci, Emil A. (EdD, Widener 2005; adj. lect.) 18th-century England; emil.ricci@villanova.edu

Varias, Alexander (PhD, NYU 1986; adj. lect.) France; alexander.varias@villanova.edu

Retired/Emeritus Faculty

Johnson, Jeffrey Allan (PhD, Princeton 1980; prof. emeritus) science and technology; jeffrey.johnson@villanova.edu

Little, Lawrence S. (PhD, Ohio State 1993; prof. emeritus) African American; lawrence.little@villanova.edu

Reilly, Bernard Francis (PhD, Bryn Mawr 1966; prof. emeritus) medieval; bernard.reilly@villanova.edu

University of Virginia

Corcoran Dept. of History, Nau Hall, PO Box 400180, Charlottesville, VA 22904-4180. 434.924.7147. Fax 434.924.7891. Email: cnh6g@virginia.edu. Website: http:// history.virginia.edu/.

The University of Virginia's Corcoran Department of History has long been one of the anchors for liberal and humane education in the College of Arts & Sciences. Members of the department are nationally and internationally recognized for their scholarship and teaching.

Chair: Claudrena Harold
Director of Graduate Studies: Jeffrey Rossman
Director of Undergraduate Studies: Cong Ellen Zhang
Degrees Offered: BA,MA,PhD
Academic Year System: Semester
Areas of Specialization: Africa, East Asia, Europe, Latin America/ Middle East/South Asia, US
Undergraduate Tuition (per academic year):
  In-State: $14476
  Out-of-State: $39852
Graduate Tuition (per academic year):
  In-State: $18222
  Out-of-State: $29400
Enrollment 2018-19:
  Undergraduate Majors: 434
  New Graduate Students: 11
  Full-time Graduate Students: 72
  Degrees in History: 187 BA, 4 MA, 12 PhD
Undergraduate Addresses:
  Admissions: http://admission.virginia.edu/
  Financial Aid: http://admission.virginia.edu/financial_aid
Graduate Addresses:
  Admissions: http://gsas.virginia.edu/
  Financial Aid: http://gsas.virginia.edu/funding

Full-time Faculty

Balogh, Brian H. (PhD, Johns Hopkins 1988; prof.) 20th-century America; balogh@virginia.edu

Bishara, Fahad Ahmad (PhD, Duke 2012; asst. prof.) Indian Ocean world, legal and capitalism, maritime; fab7b@virginia.edu

Braun, Herbert (PhD, Wisconsin, Madison 1982; prof.) modern Latin America; hb3r@virginia.edu

Dierksheide, Christa (PhD, Virginia 2009; Brockman Foundation Jefferson Scholars Foundation Prof.) Age of Jefferson; cbd3g@virginia.edu

Edelson, S. Max (PhD, Johns Hopkins 1999; prof.) colonial America; edelson@virginia.edu

Gaines, Kevin K. (PhD, Brown 1991; Julian Bond Prof.; Carter G. Woodson Inst. for African-American and African Studies) African American history and global perspective, civil rights movement, black diaspora, music in cultural production.

Gratien, Christopher (PhD, Georgetown 2015; asst. prof.) Middle East/North Africa, environmental and global; crg8w@virginia.edu

Hale, Grace Elizabeth (PhD, Rutgers 1995; prof. and Commonwealth Chair) US South, cultural; hale@virginia.edu

Halliday, Paul D. (PhD, Chicago 1993; C. Julian Bishko Prof.) legal, early modern Britain; ph4p@virginia.edu

Harold, Claudrena N. (PhD, Notre Dame 2004; prof. and chair) African American, US labor; cnh6g@virginia.edu

Hill Edwards, Justene G. (PhD, Princeton 2015; asst. prof.) African American; jgh7d@virginia.edu

Hitchcock, William I. (PhD, Yale 1994; William W. Corcoran Prof.) 20th-century Europe, international politics and diplomacy; hitch@virginia.edu

Janney, Caroline E. (PhD, Virginia 2005; John L. Nau III Prof.) ladies memorial associations 1865-1900; cej4b@virginia.edu

Kershaw, Paul J. E. (PhD, King's Coll., London 1999; assoc. prof.) medieval; pjk3p@virginia.edu

Klubock, Thomas Miller (PhD, Yale 1993; prof.) modern Latin America; tmk5k@virginia.edu

Kunakhovich, Kyrill (PhD, Princeton 2013; asst. prof.) modern Europe; kmk5ss@virginia.edu

Lambert, Erin (PhD, Wisconsin, Madison 2012; assoc. prof.) early modern Europe; eml7f@virginia.edu

Lendon, Jon E. (PhD, Yale 1991; prof.) ancient; jel4c@virginia.edu

Linstrum, Erik (PhD, Harvard 2012; assoc. prof.) modern Britain; erl2z@virginia.edu

Loeffler, James (PhD, Columbia 2006; Jay Berkowitz Prof.) Jewish; james.loeffler@virginia.edu

Mason, John Edwin, Jr. (PhD, Yale 1992; assoc. prof.) southern Africa, African American cultural and intellectual; jem3a@virginia.edu

McMillen, Christian W. (PhD, Yale 2004; prof.) Native American, US West; cwm6w@virginia.edu

Megill, Allan (PhD, Columbia 1975; prof.) modern Europe; megill@virginia.edu

Meyer, Elizabeth A. (PhD, Yale 1988; T. Cary Johnson Jr. Prof.) ancient; eam2n@virginia.edu

Milov, Sarah E. (PhD, Princeton 2013; asst. prof.) 20th-century America; sem9dw@virginia.edu

Mobley, Christina Frances (PhD, Duke 2015; asst. prof.) Africa; cfm8a@virginia.edu

Nair, Neeti (PhD, Tufts 2005; assoc. prof.) modern South Asia; nn2v@virginia.edu

Owensby, Brian P. (PhD, Princeton 1994; prof.) modern Latin America, Brazil; bpo3a@virginia.edu

Parshall, Karen V. H. (PhD, Chicago 1982; Commonwealth Prof.) science; khp3k@virginia.edu

Reed, Bradly W. (PhD, UCLA 1994; assoc. prof.) late imperial and modern China; bwr4k@virginia.edu

Rossman, Jeffrey J. (PhD, California, Berkeley 1997; assoc. prof. and dir., grad. studies) 20th-century Russia; jrossman@virginia.edu

Seeley, Joseph Andrew (PhD, Stanford 2019; asst. prof.) modern Korea; jas5fz@virginia.edu

Sessions, Jennifer (PhD, Pennsylvania 2005; assoc. prof.) French colonialism in North Africa; jes4fx@virginia.edu

Stagg, J.C.A. (PhD, Princeton 1973; prof.) early national US; js5h@virginia.edu

Stolz, Robert P. (PhD, Chicago 2006; assoc. prof.) modern Japan; rstolz@virginia.edu

Taylor, Alan S. (PhD, Brandeis 1986; Thomas Jefferson Foundation Prof.) colonial America, early US Republic; ast8f@virginia.edu

Thomas, Mark F. (DPhil, Oxford 1984; prof.) American and European economic; mt4w@virginia.edu

Varon, Elizabeth R. (PhD, Yale 1993; Langbourne M. Williams Prof.) American South and Civil War era, women and gender, intellectual and cultural; erv5c@virginia.edu

White, Joshua Michael (PhD, Michigan 2012; assoc. prof.) Middle East and North Africa; jmwhite@virginia.edu

Zelikow, Philip D. (PhD, Fletcher Sch. Diplomacy, Tufts 1993; White Burkett Miller Prof.) Cold War; zelikow@virginia.edu

Zhang, Cong Ellen (PhD, Washington 2003; assoc. prof. and dir., undergrad. studies) early imperial China; cz5h@virginia.edu

Zunz, Olivier (PhD, Paris 1982; James Madison Prof.) American urban, social; oz@virginia.edu

Joint/Cross Appointments

Achilles, Manuela (PhD, Michigan 2005; assoc. prof., general faculty; Germanic Languages and Literatures) modern Germany; ma6cq@virginia.edu

Brown, John K. (PhD, Virginia 1992; assoc. prof.; Science, Tech. and Soc., Engineering and Applied Science) industrial, British and American economic/labor/technological; jkb6d@virginia.edu

Carlson, Bernie (PhD, Pennsylvania 1984; prof.; Science, Tech. and Soc., Engineering and Applied Science) technology; wc4p@virginia.edu

Goluboff, Risa L. (PhD, Princeton 2003; assoc. prof.; Law) American civil rights; rlg3t@virginia.edu

Horne, Janet R. (PhD, NYU 1992; assoc. prof.; French) modern France; jhorne@virginia.edu

Kahrl, Andrew W. (PhD, Indiana 2008; assoc. prof.; Carter G. Woodson Inst. for African American Studies) African American; andrew.kahrl@virginia.edu

Liu, Xiaoyuan (PhD, Iowa 1990; David Dean Prof.; East Asian Studies) East Asia; xyliu@virginia.edu

Olick, Jeffrey K. (PhD, Yale 1993; prof.; Sociology) Germany, memory; jko3k@virginia.edu

Singerman, David (PhD, MIT 2014; asst. prof.; American Studies) US, science and technology; ds2ax@virginia.edu

Von Eschen, Penny M. (PhD, Columbia 1994; William R. Kenan Jr. Prof.; American Studies) US in world and culture, politics of African diaspora; pmv3c@virginia.edu

Weber, Alison (PhD, Illinois, Urbana-Champaign 1975; prof.; Spanish, Italian, and Portuguese) Spain, early modern religion; apw@virginia.edu

White, G. Edward (PhD, Yale 1967; David and Mary Harrison Dist. Prof.; Law) American legal; gew@virginia.edu

Nondepartmental Historians

Coleman, David (PhD, Queensland, Australia 2000; asst. prof.; Presidential Recordings Proj., Miller Center Public Affairs) Cold War foreign policies, Cuban crisis, Berlin crisis; dgcoleman@virginia.edu

Finder, Gabriel N. (PhD, Chicago 1997; lect.; Germanic Languages and Literatures, Jewish Studies Prog.) modern Europe, Jewish; gf6n@virginia.edu

McKee, Guian A. (PhD, California, Berkeley 2002; asst. prof.; Presidential Recordings Proj., Miller Center Public Affairs) 20th-century US, social policy; gam2n@virginia.edu

O'Shaughnessy, Andrew Jackson (DPhil, Oxford 1988; prof.; Saunders Dir., Robert H. Smith Center) 18th-century Atlantic world, British Empire; aoshaughnessy@monticello.org

Selverstone, Marc J. (PhD, Ohio 2000; assoc. prof.; Presidential Recordings Proj., Miller Center Public Affairs) US foreign relations, Cold War, US Cold War culture; selverstone@virginia.edu

Retired/Emeritus Faculty

Aron, Cindy S. (PhD, Maryland, Coll. Park 1981; prof. emeritus) US women; msa5w@virginia.edu

Barnett, Richard B. (PhD, California, Berkeley 1975; assoc. prof. emeritus) medieval and early modern South Asia; rbb@virginia.edu

Crosby, Everett U., II (PhD, Johns Hopkins 1959; prof. emeritus) medieval France and England; euc@virginia.edu

Dimberg, Ronald G. (PhD, Columbia 1970; assoc. prof. emeritus) traditional China, Chinese and Japanese intellectual; rgd@virginia.edu

Edsall, Nicholas C. (PhD, Harvard 1966; prof. emeritus) modern England

Fogarty, Gerald P. (PhD, Yale 1969; prof. emeritus; Religious Studies) American religious; gpf@virginia.edu

Gallagher, Gary W. (PhD, Texas, Austin 1982; John Nau Prof. emeritus) Civil War and Reconstruction; gallagher@virginia.edu

Holt, Michael F. (PhD, Johns Hopkins 1967; Langbourne M. Williams Prof. emeritus) 19th-century American political; mfh6p@virginia.edu

Israel, John W. (PhD, Harvard 1963; prof. emeritus) East Asia, modern China; ji@virginia.edu

Kett, Joseph F. (PhD, Harvard 1964; James Madison Prof. emeritus) American social and intellectual; jfk9v@virginia.edu

Leffler, Melvyn P. (PhD, Ohio State 1972; Edward R. Stettinius Prof. emeritus) American diplomatic; mpl4j@virginia.edu

Leffler, Phyllis K. (PhD, Ohio State 1971; prof. emeritus) public; pkl6h@virginia.edu

McClellan, Woodford (PhD, California, Berkeley 1963; prof. emeritus) Russia, eastern Europe; wdm@virginia.edu

McCurdy, Charles W., Jr. (PhD, California, San Diego 1976; prof. emeritus) American legal; cwm@virginia.edu

Midelfort, H. C. Erik (PhD, Yale 1970; C. Julian Bishko Prof. emeritus) Reformation, early modern Germany; hem7e@virginia.edu

Onuf, Peter S. (PhD, Johns Hopkins 1973; Thomas Jefferson Memorial Found. Prof. emeritus) 18th-century America; dude@virginia.edu

Osheim, Duane J. (PhD, California, Davis 1973; prof. emeritus) Renaissance, early modern Italy; djo@virginia.edu

Schuker, Stephen A. (PhD, Harvard 1969; William W. Corcoran Prof. emeritus) modern Europe; sas4u@virginia.edu

Wilken, Robert L. (PhD, Chicago 1963; Commonwealth Prof. emeritus) early church; rlw2w@virginia.edu

Williams, D. Alan (PhD, Northwestern 1959; assoc. prof. emeritus) colonial America; daw5z@virginia.edu

Recently Awarded PhDs

Butcher, Tom N. "Sexual Spectra: Biology and Sexual Politics in Europe, 1896-1933"

Cohen, Jonathan D. "For a Dollar and a Dream: State Lotteries and American Inequality"

Creer, Tyler "The Iliad and Heike Monogatari and the Historical Ramifications of Comparison"

De Groot, Michael Benjamin "Disruption: Economic Globalization and the End of the Cold War Order in the 1970s"

Erlandson, Erik Moss "Regulator-in-Chief: The Presidency, Red Tape, and the Transformation of the Administrative State, 1975-81"

Evans, Alexandra Tejblum "Reagan's Middle East: Lebanon and the Evolution of US Strategy, 1981-85"

Hursh, Kimberly E. "To Hell or Restitution: Catholic Commercial Justice in New Spain, 1600-1770"

Johnson, Rachael Givens "'Conquered by Words' or 'Taught by Senses': The Body, Affects, and Imagination in Devotional Conflicts of the Spanish Atlantic 18th Century"

Lurie, Shira "Politics at the Poles: Liberty Poles and the Popular Struggle for the New Republic"

Miller, Scott Christopher "A Merchant's Republic: Crisis, Opportunity, and the Development of American Capitalism, 1760-1807"

Thompson, Joseph "Sounding Southern: Music, Militarism, and the Making of the Sunbelt"

Virginia Commonwealth University

Dept. of History, 811 S. Cathedral Pl., Box 842001, Richmond, VA 23284-2001. 804.828.1635. Fax 804.828.7085. Email: jcpowers@vcu.edu. Website: https://history.vcu.edu.

VCU History majors investigate the past across boundaries of time and place and apply their knowledge and skills in capstone courses. The History MA program engages graduate students through analysis of development across time and directs them into independent research and writing.

Chair: John Powers
Director of Graduate Studies: Emilie Raymond
Director of Undergraduate Studies: Leigh Ann Craig
Degrees Offered: BA,MA,Cert. (public hist.)
Academic Year System: Semester
Areas of Specialization: America, US South, African American, Atlantic world, Europe
Undergraduate Tuition (per academic year):
  In-State: $13624
  Out-of-State: $33656
Graduate Tuition (per academic year):
  In-State: $13633
  Out-of-State: $26314
Enrollment 2018-19:
  Undergraduate Majors: 244
  New Graduate Students: 16
  Full-time Graduate Students: 12
  Part-time Graduate Students: 12
  Degrees in History: 90 BA, 5 MA, 2 Cert.
  Students in Undergraduate Courses: 3867
  Students in Undergraduate Intro Courses: 2021
Addresses:
  Admissions: https://vcu.edu/admissions
  Financial Aid: https://finaid.vcu.edu/

Full-time Faculty

Bendersky, Joseph W. (PhD, Michigan State 1975; prof.) Germany, modern Europe; jwbender@vcu.edu

Craig, Leigh Ann (PhD, Ohio State 2001; assoc. prof. and dir., undergrad. studies) medieval, Renaissance, Reformation; lacraig@vcu.edu

Crislip, Andrew T. (PhD, Yale 2002; prof. and Blake Chair) religious studies, ancient Christianity; acrislip@vcu.edu

Daugherity, Brian J. (PhD, William and Mary 2010; assoc. prof.) US South, civil rights, modern America; bjdaugherity@vcu.edu

Dickinson, Michael (PhD, Delaware 2017; asst. prof.) African American; mldickinson@vcu.edu

Eastman, Carolyn (PhD, Johns Hopkins 2001; assoc. prof.) early America, women and gender; ceastman@vcu.edu

Espinoza, G. Antonio (PhD, Columbia 2007; assoc. prof.) Latin America, Peru; gaespinoza@vcu.edu

Ewing, Christopher B. (PhD, Graduate Center, CUNY 2018; asst. prof.) LGBTQ, modern Germany

Gomez, Rocio (PhD, Arizona 2014; asst. prof.) Latin America

Hafez, Melis (PhD, UCLA 2012; assoc. prof.) Middle East, Ottoman Empire; mhafez@vcu.edu

Herman, John (PhD, Washington 1993; assoc. prof.) East Asia; jeherman@vcu.edu

Meacham, Sarah Hand (PhD, Virginia 2003; assoc. prof.) colonial America, women; shmeacham@vcu.edu

Meier, Kathryn Shively (PhD, Virginia 2010; assoc. prof.) Civil War, US military, environmental; ksmeier@vcu.edu

Moitt, Bernard C. (PhD, Toronto 1985; prof.) Africa, Caribbean; bmoitt@vcu.edu

Munro, George E. (PhD, North Carolina, Chapel Hill 1973; prof.) Russia; gemunro@vcu.edu

Newman, Brooke Nicole (PhD, California, Davis 2008; assoc. prof.) early modern Britain, Atlantic world; bnewman@vcu.edu

Powers, John C. (PhD, Indiana 2001; assoc. prof. and chair) science and medicine, early modern Europe; jcpowers@vcu.edu

Rader, Karen A. (PhD, Indiana 1995; prof.) science and medicine, modern America; karader@vcu.edu

Raymond, Emilie (PhD, Missouri, Columbia 2003; prof. and dir., grad. studies) 20th-century America; eeraymond@vcu.edu

Shilaro, Priscilla M. (PhD, West Virginia 2000; collateral asst. prof.) Africa; pmshilaro@vcu.edu

Smith, Ryan K. (PhD, Delaware 2002; prof.) 19th-century America, religious; rksmith3@vcu.edu

Smithers, Gregory D. (PhD, California, Davis 2006; prof.) 19th-century America, Native American; gdsmithers@vcu.edu

Stone, Peter J. (PhD, Cincinnati 2012; collateral asst. prof.) ancient Mediterranean and Near East, Greek archaeology; pjstone@vcu.edu

Thurber, Timothy N. (PhD, North Carolina, Chapel Hill 1996; prof.) 20th-century America; tnthurber@vcu.edu

Turner, Nicole Myers (PhD, Pennsylvania 2013; asst. prof.) African American, religious and political, women and gender; nmturner@vcu.edu

Retired/Emeritus Faculty

Blake, William E. (PhD, Union Theological 1968; prof. emeritus) Renaissance, Reformation; weblake2@verizon.net

Briceland, Alan V. (PhD, Duke 1965; assoc. prof. emeritus) early America, American Revolution; abricela@vcu.edu

Greer, Harold E., Jr. (PhD, Alabama 1965; assoc. prof. emeritus) US, Latin America; hegreer2@comcast.net

Kneebone, John T. (PhD, Virginia 1981; assoc. prof. emeritus) US South, public, oral; jtkneebone@vcu.edu

Messmer, Michael W. (PhD, Yale 1972; prof. emeritus) Europe; mmessmer@vcu.edu

Talbert, Robert M. (PhD, Hebrew Union 1970; assoc. prof. emeritus) ancient Near East; rtalbert@vcu.edu

Trani, Eugene P. (PhD, Indiana 1966; prof. emeritus and pres. emeritus) US, diplomatic; eptrani@vcu.edu

Tunnell, Ted (PhD, California, Berkeley 1978; prof. emeritus) American Civil War and Reconstruction, Virginia; ttunnell@vcu.edu

Urofsky, Melvin I. (PhD, Columbia 1968; prof. emeritus) US, constitutional; murofsky@vcu.edu

Virginia Military Institute

Dept. of History, 536 Scott Shipp Hall, Lexington, VA 24450. 540.464.7338. Fax 540.464.7246. Email: wilkinsonmf@vmi. edu. Website: https://www.vmi.edu/academics/departments/ history/.

The history curriculum is designed to produce men and women educated in the responsibilities of citizenship. It prepares cadets for graduate schools of history or government, and for occupations in which the ability to understand backgrounds, grasp issues, and manage affairs is essential.

Chair: Mark F. Wilkinson
Degrees Offered: BA

Academic Year System: Semester

Areas of Specialization: US, modern Europe, military, ancient, modern East Asia

Tuition (per academic year):
In-State: $29884
Out-of-State: $55928

Enrollment 2018-19:
Undergraduate Majors: 155
Degrees in History: 33 BA

Addresses:
Admissions: http://www.vmi.edu/admissions-and-aid/
Financial Aid: http://www.vmi.edu/admissions-and-aid/ costs-and-aid/

Adjunct Faculty

Minor, Kelly Anne (PhD, Florida 2005; instr.) world; minork@vmi.edu

Full-time Faculty

Andreeva, Elena (PhD, NYU 2001; prof.) Middle East; andreevae@vmi.edu

Arndt, Jochen S. (PhD, Illinois, Chicago 2015; asst. prof.) Africa, world; arndtjs@vmi.edu

Coleman, Bradley Lynn (PhD, Georgia 2001; prof.; John A. Adams '71 Center for Military Hist. and Strategic Analysis) US military, US-Latin American relations; colemanbl@vmi.edu

Dowling, Timothy (PhD, Tulane 1999; prof.) Germany, central Europe; dowlingtc@vmi.edu

Elizondo-Schroepfer, Liz (PhD, Texas, Austin 2016; asst. prof.) Latin American borderlands; elizondol@vmi.edu

Jensen, R. Geoffrey (PhD, Yale 1995; prof. and John C. Biggs Jr. Chair) military, modern Europe; jensenrg@vmi.edu

Johnson, M. Houston V (PhD, Tennessee, Knoxville 2006; assoc. prof.) 20th-century US, aviation; johnsonmh@vmi.edu

Koons, Kenneth E. (DA, Carnegie Mellon 1986; prof.) social; koonske@vmi.edu

Matsui, John H. (PhD, Johns Hopkins 2013; asst. prof.) 19th-century US, American Civil War; matsuijh@vmi.edu

McCleskey, Turk (PhD, William and Mary 1990; prof.) early America; mccleskeynt@vmi.edu

Osborne, Eric W. (PhD, Texas Christian 1999; assoc. prof.) Britain, military, India; osborneew@vmi.edu

Turner, Blair P. (PhD, Florida 1986; prof.) Latin America, military; turnerbp@vmi.edu

Wilkinson, Mark (PhD, Michigan 1982; prof. and head) US diplomatic, modern China; wilkinsonmf@vmi.edu

Yin, Qingfei (PhD, George Washington 2018; asst. prof.) modern China, Chinese foreign relations, Cold War

Part-time Faculty

Clarke, Mariko Asakawa (MA, Fort Hays State 1990; instr.) diplomatic, modern Germany, modern Japan; clarkema@vmi.edu

Retired/Emeritus Faculty

Koeniger, A. Cash (PhD, Vanderbilt 1980; prof. emeritus) American South, Civil War, 20th-century US; koenigerac@vmi.edu

Sheldon, Rose Mary (PhD, Michigan 1987; prof. emeritus) ancient; sheldonrm@vmi.edu

Vandervort, Bruce C. (PhD, Virginia 1989; prof. emeritus; ed., Journal of Military History) modern France, Africa, military; vandervortb@vmi.edu

Virginia Polytechnic Institute and State University

Dept. of History, Major Williams Hall, Rm. 431 (0117), 220 Stanger St., Blacksburg, VA 24061. 540.231.5331. Fax 540.231.8724. Email: lifounta@vt.edu. Website: https://liberalarts.vt.edu/ departments-and-schools/department-of-history.html.

Our history department publishes cutting-edge historical research, trains students to become critical thinkers and strong researchers, and shares our passion for history with the community. Classes are small, and our close-knit History majors and faculty hold regular social events and service activities through our award-winning history honor society.

Chair: Brett L. Shadle
Director of Graduate Studies: Matthew Heaton
Director of Undergraduate Studies: Heather Gumbert
Degrees Offered: BA,MA
Academic Year System: Semester
Areas of Specialization: US, race/gender/ethnicity, science/ technology/medicine/environment, digital/oral/public, war and society
Undergraduate Tuition (per academic year):
  In-State: $11420
  Out-of-State: $29960
Graduate Tuition (per academic year):
  In-State: $13701
  Out-of-State: $27614
Enrollment 2018-19:
  Undergraduate Majors: 220
  New Graduate Students: 4
  Full-time Graduate Students: 14
  Degrees in History: 68 BA, 10 MA
Undergraduate Addresses:
  Admissions: http://www.inventyourfuture.vt.edu/
  Financial Aid: http://www.finaid.vt.edu/
Graduate Addresses:
  Admissions: http://graduateschool.vt.edu/
  Financial Aid: http://www.finaid.vt.edu/

Full-time Faculty

Agmon, Danna (PhD, Michigan 2011; asst. prof.) early modern Europe, India and Indian Ocean, colonialism and imperialism; dagmon@vt.edu

Barrow, Mark V., Jr. (PhD, Harvard 1992; prof.) American environmental, biology; barrow@vt.edu

Bugh, Glenn R. (PhD, Maryland, Coll. Park 1979; assoc. prof.) ancient and Byzantine; gbugh@vt.edu

Demmer, Amanda (PhD, New Hampshire 2017; asst. prof.) military, diplomatic, US

Dufour, Monique (PhD, Virginia Tech 2014; collegiate asst. prof.) medicine; msdufour@vt.edu

Ekirch, A. Roger (PhD, Johns Hopkins 1978; prof.) colonial America; arekirch@vt.edu

Ewing, Tom (PhD, Michigan 1994; assoc. prof. and assoc. dean, grad. studies research) modern Russia, digital; etewing@vt.edu

Gitre, Carmen M. K. (PhD, Rutgers 2011; asst. prof.) Middle East, modern Egypt; cgitre@vt.edu

Gitre, Edward J. K. (PhD, Rutgers 2008; asst. prof.) US, social science, religion; egitre@vt.edu

Gumbert, Heather L. (PhD, Texas, Austin 2006; asst. prof. and assoc. chair) modern Europe; hgumbert@vt.edu

Halpin, Dennis P. (PhD, Rutgers 2013; asst. prof.) US, African American, urban; dphalpin@vt.edu

Harrington Becker, Gertrude (PhD, Florida 2008; sr. instr.) ancient, classical studies reception; thbecker@vt.edu

Heaton, Matthew Michael (PhD, Texas, Austin 2008; asst. prof. and grad. dir.) Africa, world, transnational science and medicine; mheaton@vt.edu

Hirsh, Richard F. (PhD, Wisconsin, Madison 1979; prof.) technology; richards@vt.edu

Holness, Lucien (PhD, Maryland, Coll. Park 2019; M.A., Villanova University 2012; asst. prof.) African American political/urban/ social, early US, slavery and emancipation

Kiechle, Melanie A. (PhD, Rutgers 2012; asst. prof.) US, environmental/science/medicine, urban; mkiechle@vt.edu

Lumba, Allan (PhD, Washington 2013; asst. prof.) colonialism and imperialism, capitalism and labor, Asia/Pacific

Mollin, Marian B. (PhD, Massachusetts 2000; assoc. prof.) US, women and gender, social movements; mmollin@vt.edu

Nelson, Amy K. (PhD, Michigan 1993; assoc. prof.) Russia, animal studies/environmental, cultural; anelson@vt.edu

Polanco, Edward Anthony (PhD, Arizona 2018; asst. prof.) Latin America, indigenous peoples, medicine; polanco@vt.edu

Quigley, Paul D. (PhD, North Carolina, Chapel Hill 2006; assoc. prof.; dir., Virginia Center for Civil War Studies) American Civil War era; pquigley@vt.edu

Schneider, Helen M. (PhD, Washington 2004; asst. prof.) modern China, women and gender; hms@vt.edu

Shadle, Brett L. (PhD, Northwestern 2000; assoc. prof. and chair) Africa, colonialism; shadle@vt.edu

Stephens, Robert P. (PhD, Texas, Austin 2001; assoc. prof.) modern Europe and Germany, popular culture; rosteph2@vt.edu

Taylor, Jessica (PhD, Florida 2017; asst. prof.) oral/public, Native American, early America

Thorp, Daniel B. (PhD, Johns Hopkins 1982; assoc. prof.; assoc. dean, undergrad. academic affairs) colonial America, European colonization of North America; wachau@vt.edu

Wallenstein, Peter (PhD, Johns Hopkins 1973; prof.) US South, Virginia, public policy; pwallens@vt.edu

Winling, LaDale C. (PhD, Michigan 2010; asst. prof.) 20th-century US, digital, urban; lwinling@vt.edu

Joint/Cross Appointments

Schmitthenner, Peter (PhD, Wisconsin, Madison 1991; assoc. prof.; Humanities, Center Interdisciplinary Studies) modern South Asia; pschmitt@vt.edu

Nondepartmental Historians

Gabriele, Matthew (PhD, California, Berkeley 2005; assoc. prof.; Religion and Culture) medieval and early modern studies; mgabriele@vt.edu

Purcell, Aaron D. (PhD, Tennessee 2006; dir.; Special Collections, Univ. Libraries) adp@vt.edu

Reeves, Barbara J. (PhD, Harvard 1980; asst. prof.; Center Study of Science and Society) science; reeves@vt.edu

Retired/Emeritus Faculty

Arnold, Linda (PhD, Texas, Austin 1982; prof. emeritus) Mexico, Latin America; redtape@vt.edu

Baumgartner, Frederic J. (PhD, Wisconsin, Madison 1972; prof. emeritus) France, military, Reformation; treeman@vt.edu

Bunch-Lyons, Beverly A. (PhD, Miami, Ohio 1995; assoc. prof. emeritus) African American, social; blyons@vt.edu

Burr, David D. (PhD, Duke 1967; prof. emeritus) medieval Europe, intellectual; olivi@vt.edu

Howard, Thomas C. (PhD, Florida State 1965; assoc. prof. emeritus) British Empire, Africa; tchoward@vt.edu

Jones, Kathleen W. (PhD, Rutgers 1988; assoc. prof. emeritus) American women, medicine/psychology; kjwj@vt.edu

Nurse, Ronald J. (PhD, Michigan State 1971; assoc. prof. emeritus) American diplomatic

O'Donnell, J. Dean, Jr. (PhD, Rutgers 1970; assoc. prof. emeritus) European diplomatic; odonnell@vt.edu

Ochsenwald, William (PhD, Chicago 1971; prof. emeritus) Middle East; ochsen@vt.edu

Robertson, James I., Jr. (PhD, Emory 1959; prof. emeritus; founding dir., Center for Civil War Studies) Civil War; jircw@vt.edu

Shifflett, Crandall A. (PhD, Virginia 1975; prof. emeritus) US social, US South, Appalachia; shifflet@vt.edu

Shumsky, Neil Larry (PhD, California, Berkeley 1972; assoc. prof. emeritus) American urban; yksmuhs@vt.edu

Wieczynski, Joseph L. (PhD, Georgetown 1966; prof. emeritus) Russia

Williamson, Gustavus G., Jr. (PhD, Johns Hopkins 1954; assoc. prof. emeritus) US economic

Wong, Young-tsu (PhD, Washington 1971; prof. emeritus) China, Japan; ywong@vt.edu

Visiting Faculty

Nichols, Bradley (PhD, Tennessee, Knoxville 2016; vis. asst. prof.) modern Europe, Nazi Germany, military; bradleyn@vt.edu

Wabash College

Dept. of History, PO Box 352, Crawfordsville, IN 47933-0352. 765.361.6028. Fax 765.361.6277. Email: warnerri@wabash.edu. Website: https://www.wabash.edu/academics/history/.

The Wabash History Department is dedicated to promoting the study of history of diverse peoples, with important emphasis on global and cultural historical methods. Students are encouraged not only to study Historians, but to accumulate the skills to BECOME Historians.

Chair: Rick Warner
Degrees Offered: BA
Academic Year System: Semester
Areas of Specialization: world/comparative, Europe, Latin America, US, military/gender/medicine/culture
Tuition (per academic year): $33300
Enrollment 2018-19:
  Undergraduate Majors: 25
  Degrees in History: 25 BA
Addresses:
  Admissions: http://www.wabash.edu/admissions/
  Financial Aid: http://www.wabash.edu/admissions/financialaid

Full-time Faculty

Morillo, Stephen R. (DPhil, Oxford 1985; prof.) military, world, medieval and early modern; morillos@wabash.edu

Rhoades, Michelle K. (PhD, Iowa 2001; assoc. prof.) modern Europe, medicine, gender; rhoadesm@wabash.edu

Royalty, Robert M., Jr. (PhD, Yale 1995; prof.; Religion) Christianity, sociology of religion, critical theory; royaltyr@wabash.edu

Thomas, Sabrina C. (PhD, Arizona State 2015; asst. prof.) US, US foreign policy, mixed populations

Warner, Rick R. (PhD, California, Santa Cruz 1999; assoc. prof. and chair) Latin America, world, Africa; warnerri@wabash.edu

Retired/Emeritus Faculty

Barnes, James J. (PhD, Harvard 1960; prof. emeritus) modern Europe; barnesj@wabash.edu

Visiting Faculty

Kunze, Savitri Maya (PhD, Chicago 2019; vis. asst. prof.) US in world; kunzes@wabash.edu

Wake Forest University

Dept. of History, PO Box 7806, Reynolda Station, Winston Salem, NC 27109-7806. 336.758.5501. Email: gammonlc@wfu.edu. Website: http://history.wfu.edu/.

Our department is committed to deeper conceptualizations of cultural heritages from across the globe. Our faculty members help students develop a critical understanding of the many varied pasts as well as enhance writing, research, analytical, and rhetorical skills.

Chair: Monique O'Connell
Degrees Offered: BA
Academic Year System: Semester
Areas of Specialization: US and US South, medieval and modern Europe, Latin America, Africa and Asia, legal and ancient
Tuition (per academic year): $52348
Enrollment 2018-19:
  Undergraduate Majors: 126
  Degrees in History: 70 BA
Addresses:
  Admissions: http://admissions.wfu.edu/
  Financial Aid: http://admissions.wfu.edu/financial_aid/

Full-time Faculty

Blee, Lisa (PhD, Minnesota 2008; assoc. prof.) US West, Native American; bleelm@wfu.edu

Caron, Simone M. (PhD, Clark 1990; prof.; chair, Women's & Gender Studies) American medical, US since 1877, gender; caron@wfu.edu

Coates, Benjamin Allen (PhD, Columbia 2010; assoc. prof.) US and world, US legal, empire; coatesba@wfu.edu

Frank, Thomas E. (PhD, Emory 1981; prof.; Divinity Sch.) American religion, historic preservation; frankte@wfu.edu

Gillespie, Michele K. (PhD, Princeton 1990; prof. and Coll. dean) US South, labor, US women; gillesmk@wfu.edu

Hellyer, Robert I. (PhD, Stanford 2001; assoc. prof.) early modern and modern Japan, global economic; hellyer@wfu.edu

Hines, Alisha (PhD, Duke 2018; asst. prof.) 19th-century US, slavery, gender/black women/mobility; hinesaj@wfu.edu

Hughes, Michael L. (PhD, California, Berkeley 1981; prof.) modern Germany, late modern Europe; hughes@wfu.edu

Koscak, Stephanie Elaine (PhD, Indiana 2013; asst. prof.) early modern Britain, imperialism and British Empire, long 18th century; koscakse@wfu.edu

Lerner, Jeffrey D. (PhD, Wisconsin-Madison 1993; prof.) ancient world, Hellenistic; lernerjd@wfu.edu

O'Connell, Monique (PhD, Northwestern 2002; prof. and chair) medieval and Renaissance Europe; oconneme@wfu.edu

Parent, Anthony S., Jr. (PhD, UCLA 1982; prof.; dir., MALS & Lifelong Learning Progs.) Afro-American, Atlantic world; parentas@wfu.edu

Plageman, Nathan A. (PhD, Indiana 2008; assoc. prof.) Africa; plagemna@wfu.edu

Rahman, M. Raisur (PhD, Texas, Austin 2008; assoc. prof.) South Asia; rahmanmr@wfu.edu

Ruddiman, John A. (PhD, Yale 2010; assoc. prof.) colonial America; ruddimja@wfu.edu

Rupp, Susan Z. (PhD, Stanford 1992; assoc. prof. and assoc. chair) Russia; rupp@wfu.edu

Sinanoglou, Penny (PhD, Harvard 2008; assoc. prof.) Britain and Middle East; sinanopj@wfu.edu

Trachtenberg, Barry Carl (PhD, UCLA 2004; prof. and Rubin Presidential Chair) European Jewish; trachtbc@wfu.edu

Wilkins, Charles L. (PhD, Harvard 2005; assoc. prof.) Middle East, Ottoman Empire; wilkincl@wfu.edu

Williams, Alan J. (PhD, Yale 1974; prof.) French Revolution, modern France; awill@wfu.edu

Yarfitz, Mir (PhD, UCLA 2012; assoc. prof.) Latin America, gender/sexuality/masculinity; yarfitmh@wfu.edu

Zhang, Qiong (PhD, Harvard 1996; asst. prof.) China, science and medicine; zhangq@wfu.edu

Visiting Faculty

Holmgren, Derek John (PhD, North Carolina, Chapel Hill 2015; vis. asst. prof.) Europe; holmgrdj@wfu.edu

Thomas, Charles S. (PhD, Vanderbilt 1983; vis. prof.) modern German military; thomascs@wfu.edu

Washburn University

Dept. of History, 1700 SW College Ave., Topeka, KS 66621. 785.670.2060. Email: history@washburn.edu. Website: https:// washburn.edu/academics/college-schools/arts-sciences/ departments/history/.

For majors, the department provides a clear map to mastery of the field; a course of study that is diverse in terms of both geographical and temporal ranges; and a capstone experience that calls of students to do history themselves, engaging with primary sources to produce a research paper.

Chair: Thomas Prasch
Degrees Offered: BA
Academic Year System: Semester
Areas of Specialization: US, Europe, Latin America, ancient and medieval, Kansas
Tuition (per academic year):
In-State: $6552
Out-of-State: $14808
Enrollment 2018-19:
Undergraduate Majors: 100
Degrees in History: 25 BA
Addresses:
Admissions: http://www.washburn.edu/admissions/
Financial Aid: http://www.washburn.edu/admissions/paying-for-college/financial-aid/

Adjunct Faculty

Gillaspie, Joel (PhD, Mississippi 2015; adj.) joel.gillaspie@washburn.edu

Wiard, Jennifer (PhD, Missouri, Columbia 2016; adj.) American religion; jennifer.wiard@washburn.edu

Full-time Faculty

Bearman, Alan (PhD, Kansas State 2005; assoc. prof.) colonial America, religious; alan.bearman@washburn.edu

Erby, Kelly K. (PhD, Emory 2010; assoc. prof.) early national; kelly.erby@washburn.edu

Goossen, Rachel W. (PhD, Kansas 1993; prof.) 20th-century US, US women; rachel.goossen@washburn.edu

Mactavish, Bruce (PhD, Mississippi 1993; asst. prof.) 19th-century US, Civil War, African American; bruce.mactavish@washburn.edu

Morse, Kimberly J. (PhD, Texas, Austin 2000; prof.) Latin America, Caribbean; kim.morse@washburn.edu

Prasch, Thomas J. (PhD, Indiana 1995; prof. and chair) Victorian Britain, modern Europe; tom.prasch@washburn.edu

Silvestri, Charles Anthony (PhD, Southern California 1995; lect.) medieval, ancient Rome; tony.silvestri@washburn.edu

Wynn, Kerry (PhD, Illinois, Urbana-Champaign 2005; assoc. prof.) US Gilded Age and Progressive era, Native American; kerry.wynn@washburn.edu

Retired/Emeritus Faculty

Cott, Kennett (PhD, New Mexico 1978; prof. emeritus) Latin America; ken.cott@washburn.edu

Geiger, Marilyn (PhD, Kansas 1979; prof. emeritus) colonial America, US women; zzgeig@washburn.edu

Tucker, Sara W. (PhD, Indiana 1982; prof. emeritus) East Asia, European women; sara.tucker@washburn.edu

Wagnon, William O., Jr. (PhD, Missouri, Columbia 1969; prof. emeritus) 20th-century US; bill.wagnon@washburn.edu

University of Washington

Dept. of History, Smith 318, Box 353560, Seattle, WA 98195-3560. 206.543.5790. Fax 206.543.9451. Email: histmain@uw.edu. Website: https://history.washington.edu/.

The Department of History, which offers degrees both at the undergraduate and graduate levels, as well as opportunities for interested members of the wider community to attend courses as "Access" students, is among the largest at the University of Washington. History Department faculty have received the university's distinguished teaching award more times than those in any other unit on campus.

Chair: Glennys Young
Director of Graduate Studies: Devin Naar
Director of Undergraduate Studies: Robin Stacey
Degrees Offered: BA,MA,PhD
Academic Year System: Quarter
Areas of Specialization: US and Latin America, Asia, ancient to modern Europe, Africa and Middle East, Russia and Central Asia
Undergraduate Tuition (per academic year):
In-State: $11465
Out-of-State: $38166
Graduate Tuition (per academic year):
In-State: $16997
Out-of-State: $29562
Enrollment 2018-19:
Undergraduate Majors: 190
New Graduate Students: 4
Full-time Graduate Students: 42
Part-time Graduate Students: 1
Degrees in History: 87 BA, 4 PhD
Undergraduate Addresses:
Admissions: https://www.washington.edu/admissions/
Financial Aid: https://www.washington.edu/financialaid/
Graduate Addresses:
Admissions: https://history.washington.edu/admissions
Financial Aid: https://history.washington.edu/funding-graduate-students

Affiliated Faculty

Beadie, Nancy (PhD, Syracuse 1989; prof.; Education) education, economics, state formation; nbeadie@uw.edu

Berger, Dan (PhD, Pennsylvania 2010; asst. prof.; Interdisciplinary Arts and Sciences, Washington, Bothell) American studies, critical race theory, social movements; dberger@uwb.edu

Bessner, Daniel M. (PhD, Duke 2013; asst. prof.; International Studies) European intellectual, US foreign affairs, Jewish studies; dbessner@uw.edu

Gowing, Alain M. (PhD, Bryn Mawr 1988; prof.; Classics) ancient Rome, Latin and Greek historiography, Roman Empire literature; alain@uw.edu

Noegel, Scott (PhD, Cornell 1995; prof.; Near Eastern Languages and Civilization) ancient Near East; snoegel@uw.edu

Novetzke, Christian Lee (PhD, Columbia 2003; prof.; International Studies) South Asia; novetzke@uw.edu

Pianko, Noam (PhD, Yale 2004; prof.; International Studies) American Jewish; npianko@uw.edu

Way, Thaisa (PhD, Cornell 2005; prof.; Landscape Architecture) landscape history/theory/design, feminist histories of design; tway@uw.edu

Williams, Michael A. (PhD, Harvard 1977; prof.; International Studies) ancient Christianity and society, religions in Greco-Roman antiquity; maw@uw.edu

Woody, Andrea (PhD, Pittsburgh 1997; prof.; Philosophy) history and philosophy of science; awoody@uw.edu

Yee, Shirley Jo-Ann (PhD, Ohio State 1987; prof.; Gender, Women & Sexuality Studies) women and gender, American women; sjyee@uw.edu

Full-time Faculty

Bailkin, Jordanna (PhD, Stanford 1998; prof.) modern Europe, England and Ireland, colonialism; bailkin@uw.edu

Behlmer, George K. (PhD, Stanford 1977; prof.) modern Britain, family social, medicine; behlmer@uw.edu

Bet-Shlimon, Arbella (PhD, Harvard 2012; asst. prof.) Middle East, comparative colonialisms, urban; shlimon@uw.edu

Campbell, Elena (PhD, Russian Acad. Sciences, St. Petersburg 1999; assoc. prof.) imperial Russia; eicampb@uw.edu

Dhavan, Purnima (PhD, Virginia 2003; assoc. prof.) South Asia; pdhavan@uw.edu

Ebrey, Patricia Buckley (PhD, Columbia 1975; prof.) early imperial China, Song dynasty, social; ebrey@uw.edu

Felak, James R. (PhD, Indiana 1989; prof.) eastern Europe; felak@uw.edu

Findlay, John M. (PhD, California, Berkeley 1982; prof.) American West, Pacific Northwest; jfindlay@uw.edu

Glenn, Susan A. (PhD, California, Berkeley 1983; prof.) 20th-century US, social and cultural, women and gender; glenns@uw.edu

Green, Mira (PhD, Washington 2014; lect.) ancient Rome; mirag@uw.edu

Gregory, James N. (PhD, California, Berkeley 1983; prof. and assoc. chair) 20th-century US, labor/race/politics; gregoryj@uw.edu

Hevly, Bruce (PhD, Johns Hopkins 1987; assoc. prof.) science, technology; bhevly@uw.edu

Jonas, Raymond (PhD, California, Berkeley 1985; prof.) modern France; jonas@uw.edu

Jung, Moon-Ho (PhD, Cornell 2000; assoc. prof.) Asian American, labor; mhjung@u.washington.edu

Marhoefer, Laurie (PhD, Rutgers 2008; assoc. prof.) Germany, sexuality; marl@uw.edu

Metzler, Mark D. (PhD, California, Berkeley 1998; prof.; Jackson Sch. of International Studies) modern Japan, economics; mmetzler@uw.edu

Nash, Linda L. (PhD, Washington 2000; assoc. prof.) environmental, American West, US; lnash@uw.edu

O'Mara, Margaret Pugh (PhD, Pennsylvania 2002; prof.) US politics and policy, urban and environmental, US West; momara@uw.edu

O'Neil, Mary R. (PhD, Stanford 1980; assoc. prof.) Renaissance and Reformation, early modern Europe; oneilmr@uw.edu

Rafael, Vicente L. (PhD, Cornell 1984; prof.) Philippines, colonialism and nationalism, historiography; vrafael@uw.edu

Rodriguez-Silva, Ileana M. (PhD, Wisconsin, Madison 2004; assoc. prof.) postcolonial and modern Latin America; imrodrig@uw.edu

Schmidt, Benjamin (PhD, Harvard 1994; prof.) early modern Europe, Netherlands; schmidtb@uw.edu

Smallwood, Stephanie E. (PhD, Duke 1999; assoc. prof.) Atlantic world, slavery; ses9@uw.edu

Stacey, Robert C. (PhD, Yale 1983; dean and prof.) medieval; bstacey@uw.edu

Stacey, Robin C. (PhD, Yale 1986; prof. and dir., undergrad. studies) medieval, Celtic, women and gender; rcstacey@uw.edu

Thomas, Lynn M. (PhD, Michigan 1997; prof.) Africa, cultural and social, women and gender; lynnmt@uw.edu

Thurtle, Phillip (PhD, Stanford 2002; prof.; Comparative Hist. of Ideas Prog.) history and philosophy of science, technology; thurtle@uw.edu

Urbanski, Charity Leah (PhD, California, Berkeley 2007; sr. lect.) medieval France and England, vernacular historiography; urbanski@uw.edu

Walker, Joel Thomas (PhD, Princeton 1997; assoc. prof.) late antiquity, Byzantium, early Middle Ages; jwalker@uw.edu

Warren, Adam W. V. (PhD, California, San Diego 2004; assoc. prof.) Latin America; awarren2@uw.edu

Joint/Cross Appointments

Dong, Madeleine Y. (PhD, California, San Diego 1996; prof.; International Studies) modern China, cultural/social/urban, women and gender; yuedong@uw.edu

Giebel, Christoph J. F. (PhD, Cornell 1996; assoc. prof.; International Studies) Southeast Asia, Viet Nam; giebel@uw.edu

Mosca, Matthew William (PhD, Harvard 2008; assoc. prof.; International Studies) late imperial China, imperialism and colonialism, borders and borderlands; mosca@uw.edu

Naar, Devin (PhD, Stanford 2011; assoc. prof. and dir., grad. studies; International Studies) Jewish studies, Ottoman Empire, Balkans; denaar@uw.edu

Reid, Joshua L. (PhD, California, Davis 2009; assoc. prof.; American Indian Studies) American Indian, American West, environment; jlreid@uw.edu

Yang, Anand A. (PhD, Virginia 1976; prof.; International Studies) South Asia; aay@uw.edu

Young, Glennys (PhD, California, Berkeley 1989; prof. and chair; International Studies) imperial and Soviet Russia, communism/religion/historiography, emotions/women/gender; glennys@uw.edu

Part-time Faculty

McNally, Deborah (PhD, Washington 2013; lect.) dcm9@uw.edu

Roberts, Nathan E. (PhD, Washington 2014; lect.) ner3@uw.edu

Retired/Emeritus Faculty

Alden, Dauril (PhD, California, Berkeley 1959; prof. emeritus) colonial, Latin America; dauril@earthlink.net

Bacharach, Jere L. (PhD, Michigan 1967; prof. emeritus) early Islamic and modern Middle East, Ottoman Empire, numismatics; jere@uw.edu

Bergquist, Charles W. (PhD, Stanford 1973; prof. emeritus) modern Latin America, labor; caramba@uw.edu

Conlon, Frank F. (PhD, Minnesota 1969; prof. emeritus) South Asia; conlon@uw.edu

Ferrill, Arther (PhD, Illinois, Urbana-Champaign 1964; prof. emeritus) ancient Rome, military; ferrill@uw.edu

Fowler, Wilton (PhD, Yale 1966; prof. emeritus) US diplomatic; willfowl@uw.edu

Gil, Carlos (PhD, UCLA 1974; prof. emeritus) Latin America, Latino/Mexican American; gil@uw.edu

Guy, R. Kent (PhD, Harvard 1981; prof. emeritus; International Studies) China, empire and colonialism; qing@uw.edu

Hankins, Thomas L. (PhD, Cornell 1964; prof. emeritus) science; hankins@uw.edu

Harmon, Alexandra (PhD, Washington 1995; prof. emeritus; American Indian Studies) Native American, race and ethnicity, nationalism; aharmon@uw.edu

Johnson, Richard R. (PhD, California, Berkeley 1972; prof. emeritus) early America, constitutional; rrj@uw.edu

Joshel, Sandra R. (PhD, Rutgers 1977; prof. emeritus) ancient Rome; sjoshel@uw.edu

Kirkendall, Richard S. (PhD, Wisconsin, Madison 1958; prof. emeritus) modern US; rsk@uw.edu

Levy, Fred J. (PhD, Harvard 1960; prof. emeritus) Tudor-Stuart England; flevy@uw.edu

Nam, Hwasook B. (PhD, Washington 2003; assoc. prof. emeritus; International Studies) modern Korea, labor; hsnam@uw.edu

Pyle, Kenneth B. (PhD, Johns Hopkins 1965; prof. emeritus; International Studies) modern Japan, foreign relations, intellectual; kbp@uw.edu

Rorabaugh, W. J. (PhD, California, Berkeley 1976; prof. emeritus) US social, 19th-century US; rorabaug@uw.edu

Sears, Laurie J. (PhD, Wisconsin-Madison 1986; prof. emeritus) Indonesia and Southeast Asia, historiography and comparative colonialisms, psychoanalysis and colonialism; lsears@uw.edu

Taylor, Quintard, Jr. (PhD, Minnesota 1977; prof. emeritus) African American, American West; qtaylor@uw.edu

Thomas, Carol G. (PhD, Northwestern 1965; prof. emeritus) ancient Greece; carolt@uw.edu

Toews, John E. (PhD, Harvard 1973; prof. emeritus) European intellectual and cultural; toews@uw.edu

Ullman, Joan Connelly (PhD, Bryn Mawr 1964; prof. emeritus) modern Spain; ullman@uw.edu

Waugh, Daniel C. (PhD, Harvard 1972; prof. emeritus) medieval Russia, Central Asia and Caucasus, early imperial Russia; dwaugh@uw.edu

Recently Awarded PhDs

Aguirre, Michael Damien "The Wages of Borders: Political Economy, Labor Activism, and Racial Formation in the Imperial-Mexicali Borderlands, 1937-79"

Archibald, Ryan "Traveling Dissent: Activists, Borders, and the US National Security State"

Hall, Emily M. A. "Kim Songhwan's 'Mr. Kobau': Editorial Cartoons as Genre Weapons in the South Korean Search for Democracy, 1945-72"

Lozar, Patrick "The Meaning of this Boundary Line: Indigenous Communities and the Canada-United States Border on the Columbia Plateau, 1850s-1930s"

Mahoney, Eleanor "Beyond Wilderness: Parks, People, and Politics in the Age of Environmentalism"

Meredith, Jesse David "Cities of the Plan: Visions of the Built Environment in Northern England, 1960-85"

Washington and Jefferson College

Dept. of History, 60 S. Lincoln St., Washington, PA 15301. 724.222.4400. Email: tmainwaring@washjeff.edu. Website: https://www.washjeff.edu/history-department.

The Department of History provides a curriculum that develops the knowledge and skills students need to appreciate the past and thrive in the future. The program offers more than 40 courses, ranging from Medieval Civilization and Ancient China to courses focused on colonial America, global Buddhism, and more.

Chair: W. Thomas Mainwaring
Degrees Offered: BA
Academic Year System: Semester
Areas of Specialization: US, Europe, English legal, Europe, China, and Asia
Tuition (per academic year): $47384
Enrollment 2018-19:
   Undergraduate Majors: 39
   Degrees in History: 15 BA
   Students in Undergraduate Courses: 498
   Students in Undergraduate Intro Courses: 187
Addresses:
   Admissions: http://www.washjeff.edu/future-students
   Financial Aid: http://www.washjeff.edu/financial-aid

Full-time Faculty

Caffrey, Patrick J. (PhD, Georgetown 2002; assoc. prof.) Asia, environmental; pcaffrey@washjeff.edu

Kieran, David (PhD, George Washington 2009; asst. prof.) 20th-century US, cultural, American studies; dkieran@washjeff.edu

List, Victoria D. (PhD, Michigan 1991; prof.) England, legal and constitutional; vlist@washjeff.edu

Mainwaring, W. Thomas (PhD, North Carolina, Chapel Hill 1988; prof. and chair) 19th-century America, colonial America; tmainwaring@washjeff.edu

Visiting Faculty

Strittmatter, David (PhD, SUNY, Buffalo 2018; vis. asst. prof.) dstrittmatter@washjeff.edu

Washington and Lee University

Dept. of History, 204 W. Washington St., Newcomb Hall, Lexington, VA 24450. 540.458.8771. Fax 540.458.8498. Email: hemphillk@wlu.edu. Website: https://www.wlu.edu/history-department.

Our department of a dozen faculty members offers a variety of courses and perspectives on the remote and recent histories of the United States, Europe, Latin America, Africa, the Middle East and East Asia. History courses emphasize careful reading and analysis of original sources in order to approach the past on its own terms.

Chair: Molly Michelmore
Degrees Offered: BA
Academic Year System: Semester
Areas of Specialization: Europe, East Asia, Africa, US, Latin America
Tuition (per academic year): $49170
Enrollment 2018-19:
   Undergraduate Majors: 72
   Degrees in History: 21 BA
Addresses:
   Admissions: https://www.wlu.edu/admissions
   Financial Aid: https://www.wlu.edu/financial-aid

Full-time Faculty

Bello, David A. (PhD, Southern California 2001; assoc. prof.) China and Japan; bellod@wlu.edu

Bidlack, Richard (PhD, Indiana 1987; prof.) Europe, Russia and Soviet Union; bidlackr@wlu.edu

Brock, Michelle D. (PhD, Texas, Austin 2012; asst. prof.) Britain, early modern religion and culture, witchcraft and demonology; brockm@wlu.edu

DeLaney, Theodore C. (PhD, William and Mary 1995; assoc. prof.) 19th-century US, African American, slavery; delaneyt@wlu.edu

Gildner, R. Matthew (PhD, Texas, Austin 2012; asst. prof.) gildnerm@wlu.edu

Horowitz, Sarah E. (PhD, California, Berkeley 2008; asst. prof.) France, Europe; horowitzs@wlu.edu

Michelmore, Molly C. (PhD, Michigan 2006; assoc. prof. and chair) 20th-century US; michelmorem@wlu.edu

Myers, Barton A. (PhD, Georgia 2009; assoc. prof.) American Civil War, American South, military; myersb@wlu.edu

Patch, William Lewis, Jr. (PhD, Yale 1981; Wm. R. Kenan Jr. Prof.) modern European cultural, modern German social and political; patchw@wlu.edu

Peterson, David S. (PhD, Cornell 1985; prof.) medieval Europe, Renaissance, Reformation; petersond@wlu.edu

Senechal de la Roche, Roberta (PhD, Virginia 1986; prof.) US social, violence, Gilded Age; senechalr@wlu.edu

Vise, Melissa E. (PhD, Northwestern 2015; asst. prof.) medieval European intellectual/cultural/religious, Italian peninsula; visem@wlu.edu

Retired/Emeritus Faculty

Cecil, Lamar, Jr. (PhD, Johns Hopkins 1962; Wm R. Kenan Jr. Prof. emeritus) Renaissance, Reformation, modern Germany

Jeans, Roger, Jr. (PhD, George Washington 1974; Elizabeth Lewis Otey Prof. emeritus) China and Japan; jeansr@wlu.edu

Machado, Barry (PhD, Northwestern 1975; prof. emeritus) 20th-century US political/military/business/foreign affairs

Merchant, J. Holt, Jr. (PhD, Virginia 1976; prof. emeritus) American South, Civil War and Reconstruction, American Constitution; merchanth@wlu.edu

Porter, Henry P., Jr. (PhD, Duke 1965; prof. emeritus) Canada, Australia and New Zealand, sub-Saharan Africa; porterh@wlu.edu

Sanders, I. Taylor, II (PhD, Virginia 1972; prof. emeritus) ancient Egypt/Greece/Rome/Britain

Washington College

Dept. of History, 300 Washington Ave., Chestertown, MD 21620-1197. 410.778.2800. Fax 410.810.7170. Email: jsorrentino2@washcoll.edu. Website: https://www.washcoll.edu/departments/history/.

History is part of the essence of Washington College-the first college chartered in the new nation, supported by our namesake, George Washington, and located in a quaint colonial town still lined with brick walkways. At the college, history isn't just something to be researched-it's something you can live every day.

Chair: Janet Sorrentino
Degrees Offered: BA
Academic Year System: Semester
Areas of Specialization: colonial and revolutionary era America, 19th- and 20th-century US social, early Islamic civilization, premodern and modern Europe, Asia/Russia/Japan/China
Tuition (per academic year): $45888
Enrollment 2018-19:
  Undergraduate Majors: 45
  Degrees in History: 12 BA

Addresses:
  Admissions: http://www.washcoll.edu/admissions/
  Financial Aid: http://www.washcoll.edu/admissions/tuition-aid/

Full-time Faculty

Black, T. Clayton (PhD, Indiana 1996; assoc. prof.) Russia and Soviet Union, East Asia, 20th-century Russian literature; cblack2@washcoll.edu

Miller, Kenneth J. (PhD, California, Davis 2006; asst. prof.) colonial and revolutionary era America, Latin American culture and literature; kmiller4@washcoll.edu

Sorrentino, Janet T. (PhD, North Carolina, Chapel Hill 1999; assoc. prof. and chair) medieval and early modern intellectual and religious, Islamic civilization; jsorrentino2@washcoll.edu

Striner, Richard (PhD, Maryland, Coll. Park 1982; prof.) American intellectual, political; rstriner2@washcoll.edu

Wilson, Carol E. (PhD, West Virginia 1991; prof.) African American, American women, South Africa; cwilson2@washcoll.edu

Retired/Emeritus Faculty

Smith, Nathan (PhD, Illinois, Urbana-Champaign 1958; prof. emeritus) late imperial Russia, 20th-century Germany, modern Europe; nsmith2@washcoll.edu

Washington State University

Dept. of History, Wilson-Short Hall 301, PO Box 644030, Pullman, WA 99164-4030. 509.335.5139. Fax 509.335.4171. Email: history@wsu.edu. Website: https://history.wsu.edu/.

As both a humanities discipline and a social science, History possesses elements of literary studies, anthropology, economics, and sociology and teaches a variety of skills that are relevant across the entire range of majors offered by the College of Arts and Sciences.

Chair: Matthew Sutton
Director of Graduate Studies: Jeffrey Sanders
Director of Undergraduate Studies: Raymond Sun
Degrees Offered: BA,MA,PhD
Academic Year System: Semester
Areas of Specialization: US, public, early and modern Europe, modern East Asia, world/environmental/war, society/gender
Undergraduate Tuition (per academic year):
  In-State: $10101
  Out-of-State: $24527
Graduate Tuition (per academic year):
  In-State: $11795
  Out-of-State: $25227
Enrollment 2018-19:
  Undergraduate Majors: 295
  New Graduate Students: 12
  Full-time Graduate Students: 36
  Part-time Graduate Students: 2
  Degrees in History: 78 BA, 7 MA, 2 PhD
  Online-Only Courses: 15%
Undergraduate Addresses:
  Admissions: http://admission.wsu.edu/
  Financial Aid: http://finaid.wsu.edu/
Graduate Addresses:
  Admissions: http://gradschool.wsu.edu/
  Financial Aid: http://finaid.wsu.edu/

Adjunct Faculty

Bell, Brett Richard (PhD, Washington State 2015; instr.) US; brett.r.bell@wsu.edu

Chan, Roger Y. (ABD, Washington; instr.) world civilizations, East Asia; rchan@wsu.edu

Dodson, Julian Frank (PhD, New Mexico 2015; postdoc. teaching fellow) Mexico, Latin American-Iberian studies, environment; julian.dodson@wsu.edu

Ellis, Rebecca Ann (PhD, New Mexico 2016; instr.) Latin America; rebecca.ellisdodson@wsu.edu

Franklin, Robert (MA, Washington State 2014; instr.) US, Pacific Northwest; robert.franklin@wsu.edu

Herzog, Shawna (PhD, Washington State 2013; instr.) world; sherzog2@wsu.edu

Hill, Franklin (PhD, Washington State 1996; instr.) world civilizations, 19th-century US, Middle East; fhill002@wsu.edu

Mann, Michelle R. (PhD, Brandeis 2016; postdoc. fellow) Middle East, colonial Africa; michelle.mann@wsu.edu

Miller, Brenna Caroline (PhD, Ohio State 2018; instr.) modern Europe; brenna.miller@wsu.edu

Nobbs-Thiessen, Benjamin James (PhD, Emory 2016; instr.) Latin America

Turner-Rahman, Lipi (PhD, Washington State 2008; instr.) Middle East, Asia; ilipi@wsu.edu

Walsh, Sarah (PhD, Maryland, Coll. Park 2013; instr.) Latin America; sarah.walsh@wsu.edu

Whelchel, Aaron D. (PhD, Washington State 2011; instr.) awhelchel@wsu.edu

Full-time Faculty

Bauman, Robert A. (PhD, California, Santa Barbara 1998; assoc. prof.; Tri-Cities) US, public, African American; rbauman@tricity.wsu.edu

Boag, Peter (PhD, Oregon 1988; prof.) modern US, environment, American West/Pacific Northwest; boag@wsu.edu

Brecher, W. Puck (PhD, Southern California 2005; assoc. prof.) modern Japan; wbrecher@wsu.edu

Farley, Brigit (PhD, Indiana 1991; assoc. prof.; Tri-Cities) eastern Europe, Russia; bfarley@tricity.wsu.edu

Faunce, Ken V. (PhD, Idaho 2000; clinical asst. prof.) world civilizations, 19th- and 20th-century US; kfaunce@uidaho.edu

Fountain, Steven M. (PhD, California, Davis 2007; clinical asst. prof.; Vancouver) US, global environment; sfountain@vancouver.wsu.edu

Gerber, Lydia (PhD, Hamburg, Germany 1998; clinical assoc. prof.) China; lgerber@wsu.edu

Hatter, Lawrence B. A. (PhD, Virginia 2011; asst. prof.) early America, Atlantic world, American West; lawrence.hatter@wsu.edu

Hoch, Steven L. (PhD, Princeton 1983; prof.) modern Russia, European agrarian, historical demography; steven-hoch@wsu.edu

Jordan, Theresa L. (MA, Washington 1991; clinical assoc. prof.) early and modern Europe, medieval; tjordan@wsu.edu

Kale, Steven D. (PhD, Wisconsin, Madison 1987; prof.) modern Europe, modern France; kale@wsu.edu

Kawamura, Noriko (PhD, Washington 1989; assoc. prof.) US foreign relations, Japan; nkawamura@wsu.edu

McCoy, Robert R. (PhD, California, Riverside 2002; assoc. prof.) public, 20th-century US; mccoy@wsu.edu

Mercier, Laurie (PhD, Oregon 1995; prof.; Vancouver) US, public; mercier@vancouver.wsu.edu

Peabody, Sue (PhD, Iowa 1993; prof.; Vancouver) early modern Europe, France; speabody@vancouver.wsu.edu

Phoenix, Karen E. (PhD, Illinois, Urbana-Champaign 2010; clinical asst. prof.) world, women; karen.phoenix@wsu.edu

Sanders, Jeffrey C. (PhD, New Mexico 2005; assoc. prof. and dir., grad. studies) American West, 20th-century US, environmental; jcsanders@wsu.edu

Spohnholz, Jesse A. (PhD, Iowa 2004; assoc. prof.) Renaissance, Reformation, early modern Europe; spohnhoj@wsu.edu

Stratton, Clif (PhD, Georgia State 2010; clinical asst. prof.) world, transnational US; clif.stratton@wsu.edu

Sun, Raymond C. (PhD, Johns Hopkins 1992; assoc. prof. and dir., undergrad. studies) modern Europe, modern Germany; sunray@wsu.edu

Sutton, Matthew Avery (PhD, California, Santa Barbara 2005; prof. and chair) US, modern America; sutton@wsu.edu

Svingen, Orlan J. (PhD, Toledo 1982; prof.) public, Native American; svingen@wsu.edu

Thigpen, Jennifer (PhD, California, Irvine 2007; assoc. prof.) US women; jthigpen@wsu.edu

Wang, Xiuyu (PhD, Carnegie Mellon 2006; assoc. prof.; Vancouver) modern China, Chinese ethnicity/religion/nationalism, modern East Asia; wangx@vancouver.wsu.edu

Weller, Charles (PhD, Al-Farabi Kazakh National 2006; clinical asst. prof.) religious, world, Asian studies; rcw@world-hcrc.com

Whalen, Kathleen N. (PhD, Washington State 2011; clinical asst. prof.) US, women; kfry@wsu.edu

Wright, Ashley (PhD, Cambridge 2008; asst. prof.) British Empire and modern imperialism, world, modern Europe; ashley.wright2@wsu.edu

Part-time Faculty

Berliner, Yvonne G. (PhD, Chile 2006; instr.) Latin America, world civilizations; yberliner@wsu.edu

Ma, Ling (PhD, SUNY, Buffalo 2016; vis. scholar) modern China; ling.ma@wsu.edu

Retired/Emeritus Faculty

Andrews, Margaret W. (PhD, British Columbia 1979; prof. emeritus) Canada, modern Britain, medicine; mwa-jlb@telus.net

Armitage, Susan H. (PhD, London 1968; Meyer Dist. Prof. emeritus) US women, frontier, American studies; armitage@wsu.edu

Ashby, LeRoy (PhD, Maryland, Coll. Park 1966; Regents Prof. emeritus and Johnson Dist. Prof. emeritus) US, recent America; ashby@wsu.edu

Blackwell, Fritz (PhD, Wisconsin, Madison 1973; prof. emeritus) South Asia; blackwell.fw@centurytel.net

Coon, David L. (PhD, Illinois, Urbana-Champaign 1972; assoc. prof. emeritus) early America; coond@wsu.edu

Garretson, E. P., Jr. (PhD, Chicago 1975; assoc. prof. emeritus) early modern Europe, Austria, world; epgjr@wsu.edu

Goucher, Candice (PhD, UCLA 1984; prof. emeritus; Vancouver) Africa, African diaspora; cgoucher@vancouver.wsu.edu

Gough, Jerry B. (PhD, Cornell 1971; assoc. prof. emeritus) science, technology, early Britain; gough@wsu.edu

Hume, Richard L. (PhD, Washington 1969; prof. emeritus) US, Civil War and Reconstruction, Jeffersonian-Jacksonian era; rhume@wsu.edu

Peterson, Jacqueline (PhD, Illinois, Chicago 1981; prof. emeritus) Native American, public, North America; jpeterson1@vancouver.wsu.edu

Schlesinger, Roger (PhD, Illinois, Urbana-Champaign 1970; prof. emeritus) early modern Europe

Stratton, David H. (PhD, Colorado, Boulder 1955; prof. emeritus) US, American frontier, Pacific Northwest; dstratton@wsu.edu

Tolmacheva, Marina A. (PhD, Acad. Science, Leningrad 1970; prof. emeritus) Islamic, Middle East; tolmache@wsu.edu

Williams, Richard S. (PhD, Michigan State 1973; assoc. prof. emeritus) ancient and medieval Europe; sarek@wsu.edu

Recently Awarded PhDs

Atkins, Gregory "Evangelical Mecca: Government, Business, and Christian Organizations in Colorado Springs"

Perry, Katherine Nicole "Mau Mau in the Metropole: The Conservative Party and Kenya's State of Emergency, 1952-60"

Washington University in St. Louis

Dept. of History, One Brookings Dr., Busch Hall, Room 113, Saint Louis, MO 63130-4899. 314.935.5450. Fax 314.935.4399. Email: history@wustl.edu. Website: https://history.wustl.edu/.

The Department of History prides itself on the individual attention faculty mentors provide students. Graduates express great satisfaction with their experience, mentioning in particular faculty's knowledge of the subject matter, dynamic teaching and respect for students.

Chair: Peter J. Kastor
Director of Graduate Studies: Nancy Y. Reynolds
Director of Undergraduate Studies: Cassie Adcock
Degrees Offered: BA, PhD
Academic Year System: Semester
Areas of Specialization: US, Africa and Middle East, Atlantic/Caribbean/Latin America, East and South Asia, Europe
Tuition (per academic year): $50650
Enrollment 2018-19:
  Undergraduate Majors: 88
  New Graduate Students: 4
  Full-time Graduate Students: 27
  Degrees in History: 73 BA, 2 PhD
Undergraduate Addresses:
  Admissions: http://admissions.wustl.edu/
  Financial Aid: https://admissions.wustl.edu/financial-aid
Graduate Addresses:
  Admissions and Financial Aid: http://graduateschool.wustl.edu/

Adjunct Faculty

Bubelis, William S. (PhD, Chicago 2007; assoc. prof.; Classics) ancient Mediterranean world, economics/religion/state, Northern Greece/Cyprus/Cyclades/Achaemenid Empire; wbubelis@wustl.edu

Davis, Adrienne (JD, Yale 1991; William M. Van Cleve Prof.; vice provost, Sch. of Law) law and popular culture, gender and race relations, feminist legal theory; adriennedavis@wustl.edu

Dzuback, Mary Ann (PhD, Columbia 1987; assoc. prof.; Education and dir., Women, Gender and Sexuality Studies) schooling and school policy, feminism intellectual, gender and higher education; madzubac@wustl.edu

Jacobs, Martin (PhD, Free, Berlin 1994; prof.; Jewish, Islamic and Near Eastern Languages and Cultures) medieval and early modern Mediterranean world Jewish, Jews-Muslims religious and cultural encounters, Sephardic diasporas; mjacobs@wustl.edu

Ma, Zhao (PhD, Johns Hopkins 2008; asst. prof.; East Asian Languages and Cultures) modern China, urban culture and women's studies, film and politics; zhaoma@artsci.wustl.edu

Maffly-Kipp, Laurie F. (PhD, Yale 1990; Archer Alexander Dist. Prof.; Danforth Center on Religion and Politics, Religious Studies) Mormonism, African American religions, Pacific borderlands religion; maffly-kipp@wustl.edu

Messbarger, Rebecca (PhD, Chicago 1994; prof.; Romance Languages and dir., Medical Humanities) Italian Enlightenment culture, women in civic/academic/social life, anatomical wax models; rmessbar@wustl.edu

Mumford, Eric (PhD, Princeton 1996; Rebecca and John Voyles Prof.; Architecture; Sam Fox Sch. of Design and Visual Arts) architectural and urban design; epm@wustl.edu

Schmidt, Leigh Eric (PhD, Princeton 1987; Edward C. Mallinckrodt Dist. Univ. Prof.; Danforth Center on Religion and Politics; Religious Studies) American religious culture and holidays, American religion and politics; leigh.e.schmidt@wustl.edu

Valeri, Mark (PhD, Princeton 1985; Reverend Priscilla Wood Neaves Dist. Prof.; Danforth Center on Religion and Politics) American religion/social thought/economics, Reformation theology and Calvinism political, Puritanism and Enlightenment moral philosophy; mvaleri@wustl.edu

Yucesoy, Hayrettin (PhD, Chicago 2002; assoc. prof.; Jewish and Near Eastern Languages and Cultures) medieval Middle East, knowledge production and imperial politics, political messianiam and historiography; yucesoy@wustl.edu

Zwicker, Steven (PhD, Brown 1969; Stanley Elkin Prof.; English) English literature, early modern England, English Civil War and Restoration literature; szwicker@wustl.edu

Full-time Faculty

Allman, Jean M. (PhD, Northwestern 1987; J. H. Hexter Prof.; Humanities; dir., Center for the Humanities) Africa, gender, African colonialism and nationalism; jallman@wustl.edu

Bedasse, Monique (PhD, Miami 2010; asst. prof.) modern Caribbean, African diaspora, modern Africa and transnational; mbedasse@wustl.edu

Bernstein, Iver (PhD, Yale 1985; prof.; dir., American Culture Studies) 19th-century US, slavery, US race and political culture; icbernst@wustl.edu

Bivar, Venus Melissa (PhD, Chicago 2010; asst. prof.) modern Europe, 20th-century French food and farming, environment; vbivar@wustl.edu

Borgwardt, Elizabeth (PhD, Stanford 2002; assoc. prof.) US foreign relations, US role in world affairs, historical perspectives on human rights; eborgwar@wustl.edu

Dube, Alexandre (PhD, McGill 2010; asst. prof.) French empire political culture, natives/planters/thieves political and economic, Atlantic world corruption and patronage of revolutionarie; adube22@wustl.edu

Flowe, Douglas James (PhD, Rochester 2014; asst. prof.) criminality/leisure/masculinity, American cities race/class/space, New York City crime and racial violence; dflowe@wustl.edu

Johnson, Christine R. (PhD, Johns Hopkins 2001; assoc. prof.) Renaissance transformations in knowledge/power/identity, early modern European cultural/religious/economic, central Europe; cjohns@wustl.edu

Kieval, Hillel J. (PhD, Harvard 1981; Gloria M. Goldstein Prof.; Jewish History and Thought) Jewish, east central European Jewish social and cultural, ethnicity/nationalism/anti-Semitism; hkieval@wustl.edu

Knapp, Krister Dylan (PhD, Boston Coll. 2003; sr. lect.; exec. coord., Crisis & Conflict in Historical Perspective) 19th- and 20th-century US cultural and intellectual, international relations, foreign policy; kknapp@wustl.edu

Miles, Steven B. (PhD, Washington 2000; prof.) early modern China, 19th-century China/Eurasia/early modern world; smiles@wustl.edu

Montano, Diana Jeaneth (PhD, Arizona 2014; asst. prof.) construction of modern Latin American societies, technology and nationalism/domesticity, electricity; dmontano@wustl.edu

Pegg, Mark G. (PhD, Princeton 1997; prof.) medieval world, Inquisition, Middle Ages witchcraft and magic; mpegg@wustl.edu

Ramos, Christina (PhD, Harvard 2015; asst. prof.) colonial Latin American medicine, colonial mental hospitals and patients, Latin American medical/religious/indigenous cultures; christina.ramos@wustl.edu

Reynolds, Nancy Y. (PhD, Stanford 2003; assoc. prof. and dir., grad. studies) modern Middle Eastern society and culture, 20th-century Egyptian and decolonization, Middle Eastern political and social; nreynolds@wustl.edu

Treitel, Corinna A. (PhD, Harvard 1999; assoc. prof.) modern Germany and Europe, science, medical humanities; ctreitel@wustl.edu

Watt, Lori (PhD, Columbia 2002; assoc. prof.; dir., East Asian Studies) modern Japanese political and social, imperialism and decolonization, postwar and postcolonial migrations; loriwatt@wustl.edu

Joint/Cross Appointments

Adcock, Cassie (PhD, Chicago 2007; assoc. prof. and dir., undergrad. studies; Religious Studies) modern South Asia, politics of religion and secularism, agriculture; cadcock@wustl.edu

Bornstein, Daniel (PhD, Chicago 1985; Stella K. Darrow Prof.; Religious Studies) medieval and Renaissance Europe, medieval and early modern European religion/culture/society; dbornste@wustl.edu

Chandra, Shefali (PhD, Pennsylvania 2003; assoc. prof.; Women, Gender and Sexuality Studies) South Asian culture and politics, imperialism and sexuality, globalization and postcolonial India; sc23@wustl.edu

Friedman, Andrea S. (PhD, Wisconsin-Madison 1995; prof.; Women, Gender and Sexuality Studies) modern US politics/gender/sexuality; afriedman@wustl.edu

Kastor, Peter J. (PhD, Virginia 1999; prof. and chair; American Culture Studies) digital, federal state-building, North American frontiers and early Republic; pjkastor@wustl.edu

Ludmerer, Ken (PhD, Harvard; Mabel Dorn Reeder Dist. Prof.; Sch. of Medicine) medicine, US medical education reforms; kludmere@wustl.edu

Mustakeem, Sowande' (PhD, Michigan State 2008; assoc. prof.; African and African American Studies) Middle Passage studies, trans-Atlantic slave trade, African diaspora; mustakee@wustl.edu

Parsons, Timothy H. (PhD, Johns Hopkins 1996; prof.; African and African American Studies; International and Area Studies) 20th-century African urban, African social dimensions of military service, African and world Islamic; parsons@wustl.edu

Retired/Emeritus Faculty

Hause, Steven C. (PhD, Washington, St. Louis 1969; sr. scholar; Humanities) French social, women's rights movement and French Protestant minority, modern Europe; shause@wustl.edu

Hirst, Derek M. (PhD, Cambridge 1973; William Eliot Smith Prof. emeritus) Tudor-Stewart Britain, 17th-century English politics and society; dmhirst@wustl.edu

Izenberg, Gerald N. (PhD, Harvard 1969; prof. emeritus) modern Europe, intellectual; gnizenbe@wustl.edu

Konig, David T. (PhD, Harvard 1974; prof. emeritus) early American history and law, American culture studies, Anglo-American legal; konig@wustl.edu

Okenfuss, Max J. (PhD, Harvard 1971; assoc. prof. emeritus) 18th-century Europe, European society and education, 18th-century Russia; okenfuss@wustl.edu

Walter, Richard John (PhD, Stanford 1966; prof. emeritus) Argentina and Chile political and urban, 20th-century US-Latin American relations, Latin American literature and history; rjwalter@wustl.edu

Recently Awarded PhDs

Bin-Kasim, Waseem-Ahmed "Sanitary Segregation: Cleansing Accra and Nairobi, 1908-63"

Chen, Gilbert "Living in this World: An Everyday Life History of Ordinary Monks and Nuns in Late Imperial China"

Duan, Weicong "Ming China as a Gunpowder Empire: Military Technology, Politics, and Fiscal Administration, 1350-1620"

Foti, Luca Roberto "Heretical Communes: The Struggle for Authority in the 14th-Century Papal Territories"

Siegel, Sarah "'By the People Most Affected': Model Cities, Citizen Control, and the Broken Promises of Urban Renewal"

Wayne State University

Dept. of History, 3094 Faculty/Admin. Bldg., 656 W. Kirby, Detroit, MI 48202. 313.577.2525. Fax 313.577.6987. Website: https://clas.wayne.edu/history.

Our department maintains an international reputation for excellence, especially in labor and urban history, gender and women's history, the history of science, technology, and the environment, and the history of politics and the state. We invite you to learn more about how we teach undergraduate students the historian's craft and train graduate students as professional historians in diverse careers in higher education and in public and non-profit cultural and governmental agencies and organizations.

Chair: Elizabeth V. Faue
Director of Graduate Studies: Eric H. Ash
Director of Undergraduate Studies: Elizabeth Dorn Lublin
Degrees Offered: BA, MA, PhD, MAPH, MA/MIS, MAPH/MIS, MA/JD, Cert. (archival and world)
Academic Year System: Semester
Areas of Specialization: US, Europe, gender and women, urban/labor/politics, science/technology/environment, public
Undergraduate Tuition (per academic year):
In-State: $10050
Out-of-State: $21629
Graduate Tuition (per academic year):
In-State: $12724
Out-of-State: $26135
Enrollment 2018-19:
Undergraduate Majors: 135
New Graduate Students: 19
Full-time Graduate Students: 36
Part-time Graduate Students: 19
Degrees in History: 26 BA, 5 MA, 2 PhD, 6 Archival Cert.
Undergraduate Addresses:
Admissions: http://wayne.edu/admissions/undergrad/
Financial Aid: http://finaid.wayne.edu/
Graduate Addresses:
Admissions: http://wayne.edu/admissions/graduate/
Financial Aid: http://wayne.edu/gradschool/funding/

Full-time Faculty

Ash, Eric H. (PhD, Princeton 2000; prof. and dir., grad. studies) early modern England, environmental, science; ao0103@wayne.edu

Bukowczyk, John J. (PhD, Harvard 1980; prof.) American immigration, Polish American; aa2092@wayne.edu

Chinea, Jorge L. (PhD, Minnesota 1994; assoc. prof.; dir., Center for Latino/a and Latin American Studies) Latin America, Caribbean; aa1941@wayne.edu

Cuello, Jose (PhD, California, Berkeley 1981; assoc. prof.) Latin America, Mexico; j.cuello@wayne.edu

Faue, Elizabeth V. (PhD, Minnesota 1987; prof. and chair) modern US, labor, gender and women; ad5247@wayne.edu

Gidlow, Liette Patricia (PhD, Cornell 1997; assoc. prof.) modern US, political, gender and women; gidlow@wayne.edu

Hart, Jennifer Anne (PhD, Indiana 2011; assoc. prof.) modern Africa, world; eu0767@wayne.edu

Hummer, Hans (PhD, UCLA 1997; assoc. prof.) medieval Europe; hummer@wayne.edu

Kershaw, Paul V. (PhD, NYU 2014; asst. prof.) modern US, US and world, capitalism; paul.kershaw@wayne.edu

Kruman, Marc W. (PhD, Yale 1978; prof.; dir., Center for the Study of Citizenship) 19th-century America; m.kruman@wayne.ed

Lanza, Janine M. (PhD, Cornell 1996; assoc. prof.; dir., Gender, Sexuality and Women's Studies Prog.) early modern Europe, gender and women; jmlanza@wayne.edu

Likaka, Osumaka (PhD, Minnesota 1993; assoc. prof.) modern Africa, Central Africa; ad5221@wayne.edu

Lublin, Elizabeth Dorn (PhD, Hawai'i, Manoa 2003; assoc. prof. and dir., undergrad. studies) modern Japan, gender and women; aj8580@wayne.edu

Lupovitch, Howard (PhD, Columbia 1996; assoc. prof.; dir., Cohn-Haddow Center for Judaic Studies) modern Europe, Jewish; hlupovitch@wayne.edu

Lynch, William (PhD, Cornell 1996; assoc. prof.) science, early modern England, environmental; ae8917@wayne.edu

Marrero, Karen (PhD, Yale 2011; asst. prof.) colonial North America, Native American; bx2389@wayne.edu

Neumann, Tracy (PhD, NYU 2010; assoc. prof.) modern US, urban, public; tracyneumann@wayne.edu

Port, Andrew I. (PhD, Harvard 2000; prof.) modern Germany, human rights; ar6647@wayne.edu

Retish, Aaron B. (PhD, Ohio State 2003; assoc. prof.) modern Russia, world; aretish@wayne.edu

Richmond, Marsha (PhD, Indiana 1986; prof.) science, gender and women, environmental; marsha.richmond@wayne.edu

Taschka, Sylvia (PhD, Friedrich Alexander 2003; lect.) modern Germany, foreign relations; sylvia.taschka@wayne.edu

VanBurkleo, Sandra F. (PhD, Minnesota 1988; prof.) American constitutional and legal, gender and women; ad5235@wayne.edu

Williams, Kidada E. (PhD, Michigan 2005; assoc. prof.) African American; kidada.williams@wayne.edu

Nondepartmental Historians

Goldberg, David (PhD, Massachusetts Amherst 2004; assoc. prof.; African American Studies) African American, urban, labor; dgolber@wayne.edu

Seikaly, May (DPhil, Oxford 1983; assoc. prof.; Near East and Asian Studies) modern Middle East; ad6006@wayne.edu

Sheridan Moss, Jennifer (PhD, Columbia 1990; assoc. prof.; Classical and Modern Languages, Literature and Cultures) ancient; aa2191@wayne.edu

Retired/Emeritus Faculty

Aronson, A. Ronald (PhD, Brandeis 1968; dist. prof. emeritus) modern European intellectual; ac7159@wayne.edu

Hyde, Charles K. (PhD, Wisconsin, Madison 1971; prof. emeritus) economic, technology; aa0912@wayne.edu

Johnson, Christopher H. (PhD, Wisconsin, Madison 1968; prof. emeritus) European social and labor; aa4307@wayne.edu

Scott, Samuel F. (PhD, Wisconsin, Madison 1968; prof. emeritus) France, European diplomatic; aa1002@wayne.edu

Shapiro, Stanley (PhD, California, Berkeley 1967; assoc. prof. emeritus) recent America; aa1357@wayne.edu

Shor, Francis (PhD, Minnesota 1976; prof. emeritus) 20th-century US social and cultural; aa2439@wayne.edu

Small, Melvin (PhD, Michigan 1965; dist. prof. emeritus) American diplomatic, peace studies; m.small@wayne.edu

Weinberg, David H. (PhD, Wisconsin, Madison 1971; prof. emeritus) modern Europe, Jewish; davidweinberg@wayne.edu

Recently Awarded PhDs

Hnatow, Andrew "Vestiges of Industry: Deindustrialization and Community in Detroit and Montreal"

Mora, Miriam Eve "From Talking to Carrying a Big Schtick: Jewish Masculinity in 20th-Century America"

Morris, Joshua James "The Many Worlds of American Communism, 1912-2012"

Varlamos, Michael N. "A Quest for Human and Civil Rights: The Legacy of Archbishop Iakovos"

Walter, Amanda Lauren "'I've Always Had A Voice. Now I'm Going to Use It!' The Working Women's Movement and Clerical Unionism in Higher Education"

Weber State University

Dept. of History, 1299 Edvalson St., Dept 1205, Ogden, UT 84408-1205. 801.626.6706. Fax 801.626.7130. Email: history@weber.edu. Website: https://www.weber.edu/history.

The department's chief goal is to transmit both the content of history and the necessary analytical and interpretive skills to its students. More specifically, the department seeks as objectives to prepare students for careers in teaching and history-related fields and to provide courses that contribute to the general education and lifelong learning of all students.

Chair: Sara Dant
Degrees Offered: BA
Academic Year System: Semester
Areas of Specialization: US, Europe, Far East, Latin America
Tuition (per academic year):
 In-State: $3961
 Out-of-State: $12058
Enrollment 2018-19:
 Undergraduate Majors: 263
 Degrees in History: 52 BA
Addresses:
 Admissions: http://weber.edu/admissions
 Financial Aid: http://weber.edu/financialaid

Adjunct Faculty

Kaadan, Abdul Nasser (MD,PhD, Aleppo; vis. international prof.) medicine, Islam; ankaadan@weber.edu

Kronmiller, Brady (MA, Utah State 2004; adj. instr.) US, Europe; bradykronmiller@weber.edu

Nelson, Katie (PhD, Warwick 2011; adj. asst. prof.) England; katienelson2@weber.edu

Rives, Nathan (PhD, Brandeis 2011; adj.) early America, religion; NathanRives@weber.edu

Smith, Tracey D. (MS, Utah State 1996; adj. instr.) US; tsmith@weber.edu

Full-time Faculty

Brower, M. Brady (PhD, Rutgers 2005; prof.) modern Europe, France; mbrower@weber.edu

Dant, Sara (PhD, Washington State 2000; prof. and chair) US, environmental, Far West; sdant@weber.edu

Deakin, Vikki J. (PhD, Missouri, Columbia 2002; prof.) colonial and revolutionary America, African American, religion; vikkivickers@weber.edu

Francis, Stephen S. (PhD, Arizona State 1998; assoc. prof.) Britain, western Europe; sfrancis@weber.edu

Lande, Jonathan (PhD, Brown 2018; asst. prof.) US Civil War, African American; jonlande@gmail.com

Lewis, Gregory Scott (PhD, Arizona State 1999; prof.) East Asia, South Asia, Middle East; glewis@weber.edu

Little, J. Branden (PhD, California, Berkeley 2009; assoc. prof.) US diplomatic, military; jblittle@weber.edu

Mackay, Kathryn Leiani (PhD, Utah 1987; prof.) Native American, women, environmental; kmackay@weber.edu

Matt, Susan J. (PhD, Cornell 1996; prof.) 19th- and early 20th-century US, social and cultural, emotions; smatt@weber.edu

Richey, Jeffrey W. (PhD, North Carolina, Chapel Hill 2012; assoc. prof.) Latin America, Argentina, sports; jeffreyrichey@weber.edu

Romaniello, Matthew P. (PhD, Ohio State 2003; asst. prof.) Russia, early modern Europe, global

Sessions, Gene A. (PhD, Florida State 1974; prof.) Africa, US diplomatic, Far West; gsessions1@weber.edu

Swedin, Eric G. (PhD, Case Western Reserve 1996; prof.) recent US, science/technology/medicine; eswedin@weber.edu

Retired/Emeritus Faculty

Dolph, James A. (PhD, Massachusetts Amherst 1975; prof. emeritus) early America, environmental, Native American; jdolph@weber.edu

Ibarguen, J. Henry (MA, Americas, Mexico 1967; asst. prof. emeritus) Latin America, US Southwest, Chicano; jibarguen@weber.edu

Larkin, LaRae (PhD, Utah 1990; assoc. prof. emeritus) Russia, Soviet Union, eastern Europe; llarkin@weber.edu

Sadler, Richard W. (PhD, Utah 1969; prof. emeritus) Utah, Civil War; rsadler@weber.edu

Sather, Lee (PhD, California, Santa Barbara 1975; prof. emeritus) Scandinavia, early modern Europe, French Revolution; lsather@weber.edu

Ulibarri, Richard (PhD, Utah 1963; prof. emeritus) Far West, military; rulibarri@weber.edu

Wesleyan University

Dept. of History, Public Affairs Center 113, 238 Church St., Middletown, CT 06459-0002. 860.865.2480. Fax 860.685.2078. Email: lflannigan@wesleyan.edu. Website: https://www.wesleyan.edu/history/.

The History Department is home to a distinguished group of scholar-teachers whose work ranges from the medieval to the post-modern, from the Middle East to the Midwest, from gender and sexuality to science and economics, from micro-history to world history.

Chair: Ethan Kleinberg
Degrees Offered: BA
Academic Year System: Semester
Areas of Specialization: North America, modern Europe, Asia/Africa/Latin America, intellectual, religion
Tuition (per academic year): $56704
Enrollment 2018-19:
  Undergraduate Majors: 91
  Degrees in History: 26 BA

Addresses:
  Admissions: http://www.wesleyan.edu/admission/
  Financial Aid: http://www.wesleyan.edu/finaid/

Affiliated Faculty

Hill, Patricia R. (PhD, Harvard 1981; prof.; American Studies) American social, women; phill@wesleyan.edu

Full-time Faculty

Erickson, Paul H. (PhD, Wisconsin, Madison 2006; assoc. prof.) US science; perickson@wesleyan.edu

Eudell, Demetrius L. (PhD, Stanford 1997; prof.) 19th-century US, African American; deudell@wesleyan.edu

Fullilove, Courtney A. (PhD, Columbia 2009; assoc. prof.) 19th century; cfullilove@wesleyan.edu

Greene, Nathanael (PhD, Harvard 1964; prof.) modern Europe, fascism, European socialism; ngreene@wesleyan.edu

Grimmer-Solem, Erik (DPhil, Oxford 1999; assoc. prof.) modern Germany, economic and social thought; egrimmer@wesleyan.edu

Holmes, Oliver W. (PhD, Chicago 1971; prof.) modern European intellectual, comparative political; oholmes@wesleyan.edu

Johnston, William D. (PhD, Harvard 1987; prof.) Japan, East Asia; wjohnston@wesleyan.edu

Kleinberg, Ethan (PhD, UCLA 1998; prof. and chair) European intellectual; ekleinberg@wesleyan.edu

Lennox, Jeffers L. (PhD, Dalhousie 2010; assoc. prof.) colonial/early America; jlennox@wesleyan.edu

Lopez Fadul, Valeria Escauriaza (PhD, Princeton 2015; asst. prof.) Latin America; vlopezfadul@wesleyan.edu

Masters, Bruce (PhD, Chicago 1982; prof.) Ottoman Empire, modern Middle East, Ireland; bmasters@wesleyan.edu

Miller, Cecilia (DPhil, Oxford 1988; prof.) European intellectual; cmiller@wesleyan.edu

Pinch, William R. (PhD, Virginia 1990; prof.) India, South Asia; wpinch@wesleyan.edu

Schatz, Ronald W. (PhD, Pittsburgh 1977; prof.) American labor, social, political; rschatz@wesleyan.edu

Shaw, D. Gary (DPhil, Oxford 1990; prof.) medieval, Britain, social; gshaw@wesleyan.edu

Smolkin-Rothrock, Victoria (PhD, California, Berkeley 2010; assoc. prof.) modern Russia and Soviet Union, religion; vsmolkin@wesleyan.edu

Tan, Ying Jia (PhD, Yale 2015; asst. prof.) China; ytan@wesleyan.edu

Tucker, Jennifer (PhD, Johns Hopkins 1997; assoc. prof.) science, medicine and technology, modern Europe and Britain; jtucker@wesleyan.edu

Twagira, Laura Ann (PhD, Rutgers 2013; asst. prof.) African women and gender; ltwagira@wesleyan.edu

Retired/Emeritus Faculty

Brown, Judith C. (PhD, Johns Hopkins 1977; prof. emeritus) early modern Europe, Italy; jbrown@wesleyan.edu

Buel, Richard V., Jr. (PhD, Harvard 1962; prof. emeritus) pre-Civil War America; rbuel@wesleyan.edu

Elphick, Richard H. (PhD, Yale 1972; prof. emeritus) southern Africa, European imperialism, Canada; relphick@wesleyan.edu

Gillmor, C. Stewart (PhD, Princeton 1968; prof. emeritus) science, quantitative methods; sgillmor@wesleyan.edu

Morgan, David W. (DPhil, Oxford 1969; prof. emeritus) modern Germany; dmorgan@wesleyan.edu

Nussdorfer, Laurie (PhD, Princeton 1985; prof. emeritus) early modern Europe; lnussdorfer@wesleyan.edu

Pomper, Philip (PhD, Chicago 1965; prof. emeritus) Russia, psychohistory, intellectual; ppomper@wesleyan.edu

Schwarcz, Vera (PhD, Stanford 1977; prof. emeritus) China; vschwarcz@wesleyan.edu

Vann, Richard T. (PhD, Harvard 1959; prof. emeritus) European social and intellectual, philosophy of history; rvann@wesleyan.edu

Wightman, Ann M. (PhD, Yale 1983; prof. emeritus) Latin America; awightman@wesleyan.edu

West Chester University

Dept. of History, 404 Wayne Hall, West Chester, PA 19383-2133. 610.436.2201. Fax 610.436.3069. Email: rkodosky@wcupa.edu. Website: https://www.wcupa.edu/arts-humanities/History/.

WCU has one of the most affordable and high-quality undergraduate programs in the nation. Our 18 full-time faculty members, all experts in their fields, value both excellent teaching, active scholarship, and engagement with our community.

Chair: Robert J. Kodosky
Director of Graduate Studies: Brenda Gaydosh
Degrees Offered: BA,MA,MEd
Academic Year System: Semester
Areas of Specialization: US, Europe, world, Holocaust and genocide studies, American studies
Undergraduate Tuition (per academic year):
  In-State: $9026
  Out-of-State: $19616
Graduate Tuition (per academic year):
  In-State: $10322
  Out-of-State: $14522
Enrollment 2018-19:
  Undergraduate Majors: 236
  New Graduate Students: 15
  Full-time Graduate Students: 10
  Part-time Graduate Students: 21
  Degrees in History: 73 BA, 10 MA
Undergraduate Addresses:
  Admissions: http://www.wcupa.edu/_admissions/sch_adm/
  Financial Aid: http://www.wcupa.edu/_services/fin_aid/
Graduate Addresses:
  Admissions: http://www.wcupa.edu/_admissions/sch_dgr/
  Financial Aid: http://www.wcupa.edu/_services/fin_aid/

Adjunct Faculty

Kincade, Vance R., Jr. (PhD, Miami, Ohio 1996; instr.) US; vkincade@wcupa.edu

Repousis, Angelo (PhD, Temple 2002; instr.) US; arepousis@wcupa.edu

Full-time Faculty

Chien, Cecilia L. F. (PhD, Harvard 1994; prof.) East Asia, China, comparative; cchien@wcupa.edu

Donkor, Martha (PhD, Toronto 2000; assoc. prof.; Women's and Gender Studies) Africa, women, transnational; mdonkor@wcupa.edu

Fournier, Eric (PhD, California, Santa Barbara 2008; assoc. prof. and asst. chair) late antiquity, ancient, medieval; efournier@wcupa.edu

Friedman, Jonathan (PhD, Maryland, Coll. Park 1996; prof.) Holocaust, modern Europe, modern Jewish; jfriedman@wcupa.edu

Gaydosh, Brenda L. (PhD, American 2010; assoc. prof. and dir., grad. studies) Germany, modern Europe, early modern Europe; bgaydosh@wcupa.edu

Gedge, Karin E. (PhD, Yale 1994; prof. and dir., social studies) US religion, social studies education, women; kgedge@wcupa.edu

Gimber, Steven G. (PhD, American 2000; assoc. prof.) colonial America, American Revolution, American studies; sgimber@wcupa.edu

Hanley, Wayne M. (PhD, Missouri, Columbia 1998; prof.) modern France, 18th-century Europe, social studies education; whanley@wcupa.edu

Hardy, Charles A., III (PhD, Temple 1989; prof.) popular culture, Pennsylvania, environmental; chardy@wcupa.edu

Kirschenbaum, Lisa A. (PhD, California, Berkeley 1993; prof.) Russia, social studies education, women's studies; lkirschenb@wcupa.edu

Kodosky, Robert J. (PhD, Temple 2006; assoc. prof. and chair) US military, US diplomatic, social studies education; rkodosky@wcupa.edu

Krulikowski, Anne E. (PhD, Delaware 2001; assoc. prof.) Gilded Age, US urban, American studies; akrulikowski@wcupa.edu

Legg, Thomas J. (PhD, William and Mary 1994; assoc. prof.) US technology, maritime, social studies education; tlegg@wcupa.edu

Malkin, Tia E. (PhD, Brown 2003; asst. prof.) Latin America, Brazil, social studies education; tmalkin-fo@wcupa.edu

Ruswick, Brent J. (PhD, Wisconsin, Madison 2006; asst. prof.) social studies education, science, Gilded Age/Progressive Era; bruswick@wcupa.edu

Scythes, James Michael (MA, Villanova 1997; asst. prof.) US, Western civilization; jscythes@wcupa.edu

Smucker, Janneken L. (PhD, Delaware 2010; assoc. prof.) digital, material culture, American studies; jsmucker@wcupa.edu

Thames-Taylor, LaTonya (PhD, Mississippi 2005; assoc. prof.) African American, US South, US social; lthames-taylor@wcupa.edu

Urban, Elizabeth (PhD, Chicago 2012; asst. prof.) Islamic world, women, social; eurban@wcupa.edu

Western Carolina University

Dept. of History, 225 McKee Bldg, Cullowhee, NC 28723. 828.227.7243. Fax 828.227.2419. Email: mengel@email.wcu.edu. Website: https://www.wcu.edu/learn/departments-schools-colleges/cas/humanities/history/.

Whether you're enrolled in our undergraduate program (which includes Social Sciences Education and the Public History Certificate) or the graduate program, our expert faculty will prepare you for your future—inside the classroom and through special opportunities such as internships and community engagement projects.

Chair: Mary Ella Engel
Director of Graduate Studies: Alex Macaulay
Degrees Offered: BA, BS, BSEd, MA, MAEd, MAT, Cert. (public hist.)
Academic Year System: Semester
Areas of Specialization: US, South, Appalachia/Native American, global, public
Undergraduate Tuition (per academic year):
  In-State: $1000
  Out-of-State: $5000
Graduate Tuition (per academic year):
  In-State: $4950
  Out-of-State: $10154

Enrollment 2018-19:
Undergraduate Majors: 165
New Graduate Students: 7
Full-time Graduate Students: 17
Degrees in History: 3 BA, 19 BS, 4 MA
Undergraduate Addresses:
Admissions: http://www.wcu.edu/apply/undergraduate-admissions
Financial Aid: http://www.wcu.edu/apply/financial-aid
Graduate Addresses:
Admissions and Financial Aid: http://www.wcu.edu/apply/graduate-school

Full-time Faculty

Aderinto, Saheed A. (PhD, Texas, Austin 2010; assoc. prof.) Africa, Nigeria; saderinto@email.wcu.edu

Clines, Robert John (PhD, Syracuse 2014; asst. prof.) early modern Europe, Mediterranean world; rjclines@email.wcu.edu

Denson, Andrew (PhD, Indiana 2000; assoc. prof.) Native American, Cherokee; denson@email.wcu.edu

Dorondo, David R. (DPhil, Oxford 1988; Creighton Sossomon assoc. prof.) modern Europe, modern Germany; dorondo@email.wcu.edu

Engel, Mary Ella (PhD, Georgia 2009; assoc. prof. and chair) 19th-century America, American religion, Appalachia; mengel@email.wcu.edu

Ferguson, Robert Hunt (PhD, North Carolina, Chapel Hill 2012; asst. prof.) modern US, US South, North Carolina; rhferguson@email.wcu.edu

Francis-Fallon, Benjamin (PhD, Georgetown 2012; asst. prof. and coord., social sciences education) 20th-century US, immigration and ethnicity, Latin America; bfrancisfallon@email.wcu.edu

Graham, Gael N. (PhD, Michigan 1990; prof.) American social, women, China; graham@email.wcu.edu

Harvey, Kyle Edmund (PhD, Cornell 2019; asst. prof.) Latin America

Macaulay, Alexander S., Jr. (PhD, Georgia 2003; assoc. prof. and dir., grad. studies) modern America, gender, cultural; macaulay@email.wcu.edu

McRae, Elizabeth Gillespie (PhD, Georgia 2003; assoc. prof.) American South, civil rights movement, women; mcrae@email.wcu.edu

Philyaw, L. Scott (PhD, North Carolina, Chapel Hill 1995; assoc. prof.; Coulter Faculty Commons) early America, North Carolina; philyaw@wcu.edu

Starnes, Richard D. (PhD, Auburn 1999; assoc. prof. and dean; Coll. of Arts and Sciences) US South, Civil War and Reconstruction, North Carolina; starnes@wcu.edu

Swigger, Jessica I. (PhD, Texas, Austin 2008; assoc. prof.) public, modern America, urban; jswigger@email.wcu.edu

Szabo, Vicki Ellen (PhD, Cornell 2000; assoc. prof.) medieval Europe, Greece and Rome; szabo@email.wcu.edu

Thomas, Adam James (PhD, California, Irvine 2016; asst. prof.) early America, slavery

Retired/Emeritus Faculty

Anderson, William L. (PhD, Alabama 1974; prof. emeritus) 18th-century Europe, Cherokee Indian

Bell, John L. (PhD, North Carolina, Chapel Hill 1970; prof. emeritus) North Carolina, Reconstruction, military; jbell@wcu.campus.mci.edu

Blethen, H. Tyler, III (PhD, North Carolina, Chapel Hill 1972; prof. emeritus) Appalachia, England, Europe; blethen@email.wcu.edu

Hulbert, Ellerd M. (PhD, Chicago 1970; prof. emeritus) Russia

Lewis, James A. (PhD, Duke 1975; prof. emeritus) Latin America, colonial America; lewis@email.wcu.edu

Schwartz, Gerald (PhD, Washington State 1969; prof. emeritus) modern America

Williams, Max R. (PhD, North Carolina, Chapel Hill 1965; prof. emeritus) US South, Civil War and Reconstruction, public; swilliams@dnet.net

Wood, Curtis W., Jr. (PhD, North Carolina, Chapel Hill 1971; prof. emeritus; sr. research assoc., Mountain Heritage Center) England, southern Appalachia, public; woodcw@email.wcu.edu

Western Connecticut State University

Dept. of History and Non-Western Cultures, 181 White St., Danbury, CT 06810. 203.837.8484. Fax 203.837.8905. Email: maym@wcsu.edu. Website: http://www.wcsu.edu/history/.

Western's history majors receive a first-class history education and learn to think and read critically, write well, and plan and execute complex projects.

Chair: Joshua Rosenthal and Marcy May
Director of Graduate Studies: Wynn Gadkar-Wilcox
Degrees Offered: BA,BS,MA
Academic Year System: Semester
Areas of Specialization: US, Europe, Latin America, Southeast Asia, Middle East
Undergraduate Tuition (per academic year):
In-State, NY, NJ: $10017
Out-of-State: $22878
Graduate Tuition (per academic year):
In-State: $11298
Out-of-State: $24098
Enrollment 2018-19:
Undergraduate Majors: 81
New Graduate Students: 3
Full-time Graduate Students: 3
Part-time Graduate Students: 17
Degrees in History: 29 BA, 3 MA
Undergraduate Addresses:
Admissions: http://www.wcsu.edu/admissions/ugrad.asp
Financial Aid: http://www.wcsu.edu/finaid/
Graduate Addresses:
Admissions: http://www.wcsu.edu/graduate/
Financial Aid: http://www.wcsu.edu/finaid/

Full-time Faculty

Allocco, Katherine Gretchen (PhD, Texas, Austin 2004; prof.) medieval Europe, gender, Britain; alloccok@wcsu.edu

Duffy, Jennifer Nugent (PhD, NYU 2008; prof.) US ethnic, urban, teacher education; duffyj@wcsu.edu

Gadkar-Wilcox, Wynn W. (PhD, Cornell 2002; prof. and dir., grad. studies) Southeast Asia, intellectual, historiography; wilcoxw@wcsu.edu

Gutzman, Kevin R. C. (PhD, Virginia 1999; JD, Texas, Austin 1990; prof.) revolutionary America, US South, constitutional; gutzmank@wcsu.edu

Lindenauer, Leslie J. (PhD, NYU 1997; prof.) colonial America, women, museum studies; lindenauerl@wcsu.edu

May, Martha E. (PhD, SUNY, Binghamton 1984; prof. and co-chair) 20th-century US, women, political; mmay89@gmail.com

Nolan, Michael E. (PhD, Brandeis 2001; prof.) modern France and Germany; nolanm@wcsu.edu

Rosenthal, Joshua M. (PhD, Columbia 2001; prof. and co-chair) Colombia, Brazil, Latin America; rosenthalj@wcsu.edu

Saad, Abubaker M. (PhD, Washington 1987; prof.) Middle East, Islam; saada@wcsu.edu

Part-time Faculty

Campanaro, Amy E (MA, SUNY, Albany 2002; instr.) US; campanaroa@wcsu.edu

Coleman, George A. (MS, Teachers, Columbia 1977) African American; colemang@wcsu.edu

Flanagan, Stephen T. (MA, Western Connecticut State 1984; MA, St. John's, NY 1996) US; flanagans@wcsu.edu

Friedman, Laurence N. (CERT, Southern Connecticut State 1986) US; friedmanl@wcsu.edu

Jackson, Gregory E. (PhD, SUNY, Stony Brook 2013) Brazil, sports; jacksong@wcsu.edu

Rossi, Maryann (PhD, St. Louis 1983; asst. dean; Professional Studies) early US, material culture, historic preservation; rossim@wcsu.edu

Walens, Susann M. (PhD, Union Inst. Grad. Sch. 1994) US; walenss@wcsu.edu

Retired/Emeritus Faculty

Detzer, David W. (PhD, Connecticut 1970; prof. emeritus) US

Linabury, George O. (PhD, Columbia 1970; prof. emeritus) ancient Egypt; linaburyg@wcsu.edu

Western Illinois University

Dept. of History, 438 Morgan Hall, 1 University Cir., Macomb, IL 61455-1390. 309.298.1053. Fax 309.298.2540. Email: KA-Boeckelman@wiu.edu. Website: http://www.wiu.edu/cas/history/.

While the faculty members of WIU's History Department have individual fields of research and teaching specialization, we all incorporate many diverse approaches into our teaching. Our Department offers specialists and courses relating to many kinds of historical analysis, across a wide range of chronological and geographical emphases.

Chair: Keith Boeckelman
Director of Graduate Studies: Timothy Roberts
Degrees Offered: BA,MA
Academic Year System: Semester
Areas of Specialization: US and Europe, 19th and 20th centuries, political and social, comparative labor, women
Undergraduate Tuition (per academic year): $7104
Graduate Tuition (per academic year): $6102
Enrollment 2018-19:
Undergraduate Majors: 100
New Graduate Students: 5
Full-time Graduate Students: 15
Part-time Graduate Students: 3
Degrees in History: 24 BA, 8 MA
Online-Only Courses: 20%
Undergraduate Addresses:
Admissions: http://www.wiu.edu/admissions/
Financial Aid: http://www.wiu.edu/student_services/financial_aid/
Graduate Addresses:
Admissions and Financial Aid: http://www.wiu.edu/graduate_studies/

Full-time Faculty

Boynton, Virginia R. (PhD, Ohio State 1995; prof.) US women, 20th-century US, colonial Latin America; VR-Boynton@wiu.edu

Brice, Lee L. (PhD, North Carolina, Chapel Hill 2003; prof.) ancient Greece and Rome, ancient military, film and history; LL-Brice@wiu.edu

Chamberlin, Ute Elisabeth (PhD, Arizona State 2007; assoc. prof.) modern Europe and Germany, urban, European women; UE-Chamberlin@wiu.edu

Cole, Peter (PhD, Georgetown 1997; prof.) urban and labor, US 1877-1914, South Africa; P-Cole@wiu.edu

Filipink, Richard M., Jr. (PhD, SUNY, Buffalo 2003; prof.) US 1945-present, Vietnam, political and diplomatic; RM-Filipink@wiu.edu

Hall, Gregory D. (PhD, Washington State 1999; prof.) US West, Illinois, environmental; G-Hall@wiu.edu

McNabb, Jennifer Lynn (PhD, Colorado, Boulder 2003; prof.) early modern Europe, England, medieval Europe; JL-McNabb@wiu.edu

Pamonag, Febe D. (PhD, Alberta 2006; assoc. prof.) modern Japan, Japanese women, Asia; F-Pamonag@wiu.edu

Roberts, Timothy M. (DPhil, Oxford 1998; prof. and dir., grad. studies) US to Civil War and Reconstruction, trans-Atlantic, legal; TM-Roberts@wiu.edu

Woell, Edward J. (PhD, Marquette 1997; prof.) Old Regime Europe, Enlightenment, French Revolution and Napoleon; EJ-Woell@wiu.edu

Nondepartmental Historians

Stierman, John (MA, Iowa 1987; MLS, Northern Iowa 1986; prof.; research librarian, Malpass Library) colonial America, antebellum America, American intellectual; JP-Stierman@wiu.edu

Retired/Emeritus Faculty

Balsamo, Larry T. (PhD, Missouri, Columbia 1967; prof. emeritus) Civil War and Reconstruction, US South; LT-Balsamo@wiu.edu

Brown, Spencer H. (PhD, Northwestern 1964; prof. emeritus) Africa, modern Europe, methodology; SH-Brown@wiu.edu

Cady, Darrel (PhD, Kansas 1974; assoc. prof. emeritus) 20th-century US

Combs, William L. (PhD, Purdue 1982; prof. emeritus) Germany, modern Europe; WL-Combs@wiu.edu

Egler, David G. (PhD, Arizona 1977; prof. emeritus) Japan, China, India; DG-Egler@wiu.edu

Hopkins, George E. (PhD, Texas, Austin 1969; prof. emeritus) US 1945-present, presidential assassinations, Asia; GE-Hopkins@wiu.edu

Jelatis, Virginia G. (PhD, Minnesota 1999; assoc. prof. emeritus) colonial and revolutionary America, Native American; VG-Jelatis@wiu.edu

Kernek, Sterling J. (PhD, Cambridge 1971; prof. emeritus) European diplomatic, modern Europe; SJ-Kernek@wiu.edu

Kirk, Gordon W. (PhD, Michigan State 1970; prof. emeritus) urban, US 1877-1914, quantitative methods; cargord@rcn.com

Kretchik, Walter E. (PhD, Kansas 2001; prof. emeritus) US military, US diplomatic, global/transnational warfare

Ledbetter, Rosanna (PhD, Northern Illinois 1967; prof. emeritus) modern Europe, Russia

Leonard, Virginia W. (PhD, Florida 1975; prof. emeritus) Latin America, US Navy in Latin America; V-Leonard@wiu.edu

O'Brien, Charles H. (PhD, Columbia 1967; prof. emeritus) medieval Europe, European intellectual, historiography

Pano, Nicholas C. (MA, Johns Hopkins 1958; prof. emeritus) Russia to 1917, Soviet Union 1917, central and eastern Europe

Watkins, Sharon B. (PhD, North Carolina, Chapel Hill 1971; assoc. prof. emeritus) France, 19th- and 20th-century Europe; stw300@comcast.net

Watkins, Thomas H. (PhD, North Carolina, Chapel Hill 1972; prof. emeritus) ancient Greece, ancient Rome, medieval Europe; stw300@comcast.net

Western Kentucky University

Dept. of History, 1906 College Heights Blvd., #21086, Bowling Green, KY 42101-1086. 270.745.3841. Fax 270.745.2950. Email: eric.reed@wku.edu. Website: https://www.wku.edu/history/.

The History Department offers a variety of programs for students interested in studying, researching or learning how to teach the past.

Chair: Eric Reed
Director of Graduate Studies: Marko Dumancic
Degrees Offered: BA,MA
Academic Year System: Semester
Areas of Specialization: US, Europe, world
Undergraduate Tuition (per academic year):
  In-State: $10602
  Out-of-State: $26496
Graduate Tuition (per academic year):
  In-State: $14568
  Out-of-State: $21576
Undergraduate Addresses:
  Admissions: http://www.wku.edu/atwku/admissions.php
  Financial Aid: http://www.wku.edu/financialaid/
Graduate Addresses:
  Admissions and Financial Aid: http://www.wku.edu/graduate/

Full-time Faculty

Browder, Dorothea (PhD, Wisconsin, Madison 2008; assoc. prof.) American women, gender; dorothea.browder@wku.edu

Brown, Kate E. (PhD, Virginia 2015; asst. prof.) US and British legal, early US; kate.brown@wku.edu

Dietle, Robert L. (PhD, Yale 1991; assoc. prof.) French Revolution, modern intellectual; robert.dietle@wku.edu

Dumancic, Marko (PhD, North Carolina, Chapel Hill 2010; assoc. prof. and dir., grad. studies) Russia/Soviet Union, gender and sexuality, film; marko.dumancic@wku.edu

Eagle, Marc V. (PhD, Tulane 2005; assoc. prof.) Latin America; marc.eagle@wku.edu

Harkins, Anthony A. (PhD, Wisconsin, Madison 1999; prof.) 20th-century US social and cultural, popular culture, American studies; tony.harkins@wku.edu

Jennings, Audra (PhD, Ohio State 2008; assoc. prof.) US, disability; audra.jennings@wku.edu

Kondratieff, Eric John (PhD, Pennsylvania 2003; assoc. prof.) ancient Rome and political culture, epigraphy and numismatics; eric.kondratieff@wku.edu

LaFantasie, Glenn W. (PhD, Brown 2005; prof.) Civil War; glenn.lafantasie@wku.edu

Miner, Jeffrey David (PhD, Stanford 2011; asst. prof.) medieval Europe, early modern Europe, precolonial Africa; jeffrey.miner@wku.edu

Minter, Patricia Hagler (PhD, Virginia 1994; prof.) American legal, 19th- and 20th-century US, American South; patricia.minter@wku.edu

Olson, Alexander I. (PhD, Michigan 2013; assoc. prof.) US, American studies, North American West, indigenous studies, biopolitics; alexander.olson@wku.edu

Reed, Eric S. (PhD, Syracuse 2001; prof. and chair) modern Europe, France; eric.reed@wku.edu

Romero, Juan (PhD, Texas, Austin 2008; assoc. prof.) modern Middle East, Islamic world; juan.romero@wku.edu

Rosa, Andrew J. (PhD, Massachusetts 2006; assoc. prof.) US, African American and African diaspora, African American studies; andrew.rosa@wku.edu

Sanderfer, Selena Ronshaye (PhD, Vanderbilt 2010; assoc. prof.) African American, Africa; selena.sanderfer@wku.edu

Serafini, David (MA, Western Kentucky 1997; instr.) modern US; david.serafini@wku.edu

Van Dyken, Tamara (PhD, Notre Dame 2008; assoc. prof.) modern US, American religious; tamara.vandyken@wku.edu

Walton-Hanley, Jennifer A (PhD, Kentucky 2009; assoc. prof.) 19th-century US; jennifer.walton-hanley@wku.edu

Retired/Emeritus Faculty

Baker, James T. (PhD, Florida State 1968; prof. emeritus) European social and intellectual, Renaissance and Reformation, contemporary American religious; james.baker@wku.edu

Bussey, Charles J. (PhD, Kentucky 1975; prof. emeritus) Middle Period, American studies; charles.bussey@wku.edu

Crowe-Carraco, Carol E. (PhD, Georgia 1970; prof. emeritus) Kentucky, Tudor-Stuart, women; carol.crowecarraco@wku.edu

Hardin, John A. (PhD, Michigan 1989; prof. emeritus) African American, Africa; john.hardin@wku.edu

Haynes, Robert V. (PhD, Rice 1959; prof. emeritus) early national, African American, Jacksonian Era; robert.haynes@wku.edu

Lee, David (PhD, Ohio State 1975; prof. emeritus) 20th-century US South, American political; david.lee@wku.edu

Lucas, Marion B. (PhD, South Carolina 1965; prof. emeritus) Middle Period, Civil War and Reconstruction, US South; marion.lucas@wku.edu

Murphy, Frederick I. (PhD, Florida 1970; prof. emeritus) medieval, Renaissance and Reformation, American diplomatic; frederick.murphy@wku.edu

Stone, Richard G., Jr. (PhD, Tennessee, Knoxville 1973; prof. emeritus) colonial America, 20th-century Europe, New US South; richard.stone@wku.edu

Troutman, Richard L. (PhD, Kentucky 1958; prof. emeritus) colonial America, early national; richard.troutman@wku.edu

Weigel, Richard D. (PhD, Delaware 1973; prof. emeritus) ancient, medieval, genealogy; richard.weigel@wku.edu

Western Michigan University

Dept. of History, 4301 Friedmann Hall, Kalamazoo, MI 49008-5334. 269.387.4650. Fax 269.387.4651. Email: wilson.warren@wmich.edu. Website: https://wmich.edu/history/.

WMU is classified by the Carnegie Foundation as a "research institution with high research activity." The history department offers four undergraduate majors (Liberal Education, Secondary Education: History, Secondary Education: Social Studies, and Public History), as well as master's and doctoral degrees. Our faculty members offer a wide array of courses in North American and European history, with a particular concentration on the history of the pre-1800, and especially medieval, world.

Chair: Wilson Warren
Director of Graduate Studies: Sally Hadden
Degrees Offered: BA,MA,PhD
Academic Year System: Semester
Areas of Specialization: North America, Europe, medieval, public
Undergraduate Tuition (per academic year):
  In-State: $12161
  Out-of-State: $15201

Graduate Tuition (per academic year):
   In-State: $11728
   Out-of-State: $22177
Enrollment 2018-19:
   Undergraduate Majors: 120
   New Graduate Students: 9
   Full-time Graduate Students: 22
   Part-time Graduate Students: 9
   Degrees in History: 25 BA, 6 MA
   Students in Undergraduate Courses: 1848
   Students in Undergraduate Intro Courses: 1700
   Online-Only Courses: 19%
Undergraduate Addresses:
   Admissions: http://www.wmich.edu/admissions/
   Financial Aid: http://www.wmich.edu/finaid/
Graduate Addresses:
   Admissions: http://www.wmich.edu/grad/
   Financial Aid: http://www.wmich.edu/history/

Adjunct Faculty

Cox, Anna-Lisa G. (PhD, Illinois, Urbana-Champaign 2002; adj.) African American, US, Midwest

Norris, L. Patrick (PhD, Minnesota 1976; prof.) public, US intellectual; pnorris@kvcc.edu

Toledo Pereyra, Luis (PhD, Minnesota 1984; prof.) medicine and health care

Wickstrom, John B. (PhD, Yale 1969; prof.) medieval, monasticism, iconography; john.wickstrom@kzoo.edu

Full-time Faculty

Benac, David T. (PhD, Missouri, Columbia 2003; assoc. prof.) public, environmental; david.benac@wmich.edu

Berkhofer, Robert F., III (PhD, Harvard 1997; assoc. prof.) medieval Europe, France, England; robert.berkhofer@wmich.edu

Berto, Luigi Andrea (PhD, Venice 2001; prof.) early Middle Ages, war and violence, Italy; luigi.berto@wmich.edu

Beyan, Amos (PhD, West Virginia 1985; prof.) West Africa, African American, Africana studies; amos.beyan@wmich.edu

Borish, Linda J. (PhD, Maryland, Coll. Park 1990; assoc. prof.) 19th-century US, women, sport; linda.borish@wmich.edu

Brandao, Jose Antonio (PhD, York, Can. 1994; prof.) 17th- and 18th-century American Indian, colonial America, Canada; jose.brandao@wmich.edu

Cousins, James P. (PhD, Kentucky 2010; faculty specialist II) education, US; james.cousins@wmich.edu

Dooley, Howard J. (PhD, Notre Dame 1976; prof.) modern Middle East, global and contemporary; howard.dooley@wmich.edu

Hadden, Sally E. (PhD, Harvard 1993; JD, Harvard 1989; assoc. prof. and dir., grad. studies) colonial America, antebellum US South, US constitutional and legal; sally.hadden@wmich.edu

Kachun, Mitch (PhD, Cornell 1997; prof.) African American, 19th-century US; mitch.kachun@wmich.edu

Martini, Edwin A., III (PhD, Maryland, Coll. Park 2004; prof.) post-World War II US, US-Vietnam relations, diplomacy and culture; edwin.martini@wmich.edu

Murray, James M. (PhD, Northwestern 1983; prof.) medieval and early modern Europe; james.murray@wmich.edu

Nassaney, Michael S. (PhD, Massachusetts Amherst 1992; prof.) ethnohistory, North American fur trade; michael.nassaney@wmich.edu

Palmitessa, James R. (PhD, NYU 1995; assoc. prof.) early modern Europe, urban, material culture; james.palmitessa@wmich.edu

Pyenson, Lewis Robert (PhD, Johns Hopkins 1974; prof.) science; lewis.pyenson@wmich.edu

Rubin, Eli (PhD, Wisconsin, Madison 2004; prof.) Germany, 20th-century eastern Europe, material culture; eli.rubin@wmich.edu

Simon, Larry J. (PhD, California, Los Angeles 1989; assoc. prof.) Crusades, Muslim-Christian-Jewish relations, medieval Spain and Italy; larry.simon@wmich.edu

Strong, Anise K. (PhD, Columbia 2005; assoc. prof.) ancient social and cultural, gender and sexuality, reception studies; anise.strong@wmich.edu

Tabor, Nathan L. M. (PhD, Texas, Austin 2014; asst. prof.) Islamic, Muslim South Asia; nathan.tabor@wmich.edu

Warren, Wilson J. (PhD, Pittsburgh 1992; prof. and chair) social science education, labor, 20th-century US; wilson.warren@wmich.edu

Xiong, Victor (PhD, Australian National 1989; prof.) China, urban, cultural; victor.xiong@wmich.edu

Yoshida, Takashi (PhD, Columbia 2001; prof.) modern Japan, history and memory, Japanese American; takashi.yoshida@wmich.edu

Joint/Cross Appointments

Ogbomo, Onaiwu (PhD, Dalhousie 1993; prof.; Africana Studies) Africa, African American, gender; onaiwu.ogbomo@wmich.edu

Perez-Villa, Angela (PhD, Michigan 2017; asst. prof; Gender and Women's Studies) Afro-Latin American history and culture, women's and gender studies

Saillant, John D. (PhD, Brown 1989; prof.; English) African American, diaspora religious literature; john.saillant@wmich.edu

Nondepartmental Historians

Carlson, Sharon (PhD, Western Michigan 2002; prof.; dir., Archives and Regional Hist. Collection) archives, public, US; sharon.carlson@wmich.edu

Durham, Lofty (PhD, Pittsburgh 2009; assoc. prof.; Theatre) theatre, script analysis, script analysis for production; lofton.durham@wmich.edu

Heasley, Lynne (PhD, Wisconsin, Madison 2000; assoc. prof.; Inst. of the Environment and Sustainability) environmental, cultural geography; lynne.heasley@wmich.edu

Kubiski, Joyce M. (PhD, Washington 1994; assoc. prof.; dir., Sch. Art) medieval and Renaissance art; joyce.kubiski@wmich.edu

Steuer, Susan M. B. (PhD, Minnesota 2001; assoc. prof.; head, Special Collections and Rare Books, Library) medieval Europe, England, women; susan.steuer@wmich.edu

Retired/Emeritus Faculty

Beech, George T. (PhD, Johns Hopkins 1960; prof. emeritus) medieval, social; george.beech@wmich.edu

Carlson, Lewis H. (PhD, Michigan State 1967; prof. emeritus) 20th-century US, popular culture, minorities; lewis.carlson@wmich.edu

Coryell, Janet L. (PhD, William and Mary 1986; prof. emeritus) 19th-century US, women; janet.coryell@wmich.edu

Davis, Ronald W. (PhD, Indiana 1968; prof. emeritus) Islamic, West Africa; ronald.davis@wmich.edu

Elder, E. Rozanne (PhD, Toronto 1968; prof. emeritus) medieval church; e.rozanne.elder@wmich.edu

Ferreira, James M. (PhD, Minnesota 1971; prof. emeritus) 20th-century US cultural and intellectual, Cold War/Vietnam era/anticommunism; james.ferreira@wmich.edu

Gray, Marion W., Jr. (PhD, Wisconsin, Madison 1971; prof. emeritus) 18th- and 19th-century Germany, European gender, environmental; marion.gray@wmich.edu

Haight, Bruce M. (PhD, Northwestern 1981; prof. emeritus) West Africa, Islamic; bruce.haight@wmich.edu

Havira, Barbara S. (PhD, Michigan State 1986; assoc. prof. emeritus) 19th- and 20th-century US, labor, women; barbara.havira@wmich.edu

Lyon-Jenness, Cheryl (PhD, Western Michigan 1998; master faculty specialist; dir., undergrad. studies emeritus) 19th-century US, horticultural and agricultural, gender; cheryl.lyon-jenness@wmich.edu

Maier, Paul L. (PhD, Basel, Switzerland 1957; prof. emeritus) ancient, Christianity, Reformation; paul.maier@wmich.edu

Stone, Judith F. (PhD, SUNY, Stony Brook 1979; Mary Meader Prof. emeritus) modern France, cultural and political, gender; judith.stone@wmich.edu

Western Oregon University

Dept. of History, 345 N. Monmouth Ave., Monmouth, OR 97361-1394. 503.838.8288. Fax 503.838.8635. Email: swedoe@wou.edu. Website: http://www.wou.edu/history/.

Western Oregon University, steadily emerging as a leading comprehensive public liberal arts institution, is committed to changing lives, strengthening communities, and transforming our world.

Chair: Elizabeth M. Swedo
Director of Graduate Studies: Bao Hua Hsieh
Degrees Offered: BA,BS
Academic Year System: Quarter
Areas of Specialization: East and West Asia, Africa/Latin America, North America, Europe/Russia, comparative and transnational
Tuition (per academic year):
  In-State: $8112
  Out-of-State: $23895
Enrollment 2018-19:
  Undergraduate Majors: 60
  Degrees in History: 3 BA, 8 BS
Addresses:
  Admissions: http://www.wou.edu/student/admissions/
  Financial Aid: http://www.wou.edu/finaid

Adjunct Faculty

Cocoltchos, Christopher N. (PhD, UCLA 1979; adj.) US, social and urban; cocoltchosc@wou.edu

Full-time Faculty

Doellinger, David (PhD, Pittsburgh 2002; prof.) modern Russia, east central Europe, Germany; doellind@wou.edu

Goldsworthy-Bishop, Patricia M. (PhD, California, Irvine 2009; assoc. prof.) North Africa, Europe, transnational; goldswop@wou.edu

Hsieh, Bau Hwa (PhD, Illinois, Urbana-Champaign 1992; prof. and dir., grad. studies) modern and premodern China, East Asia, crosscultural comparative women; hsiehb@wou.edu

Jensen, Kimberly S. (PhD, Iowa 1992; prof.) women and gender, World War I, 20th-century US; jenseki@wou.edu

Rector, John L. (PhD, Indiana 1976; prof.) Latin America, Chile, Puerto Rico; rectorj@wou.edu

Swedo, Elizabeth M. (PhD, Minnesota, Twin Cities 2012; asst. prof. and chair) medieval and early modern Europe; swedoe@wou.edu

Retired/Emeritus Faculty

Cotroneo, Ross R. (PhD, Idaho 1966; prof. emeritus) Pacific Northwest, military, constitutional law

Dortmund, Erhard K. (MA, California, Berkeley 1960; assoc. prof. emeritus) US intellectual, modern Germany

Geier, Max G. (PhD, Washington State 1990; prof. emeritus) public, environmental, North American West; geierm@wou.edu

Huxford, Gary L. (PhD, Washington 1963; prof. emeritus) colonial and 20th-century America, historiography

Sil, Narasingha P. (PhD, Oregon 1978; prof. emeritus) Tudor-Stuart England, Europe, Africa; siln@wou.edu

Western Washington University

Dept. of History, 516 High St., MS 9061, Bellingham, WA 98225-9061. 360.650.3429. Fax 360.650.7789. Email: jennie.huber@wwu.edu. Website: https://chss.wwu.edu/history.

We offer several undergraduate and graduate degree programs in history to match your interests and educational goals. The study of history facilitates the development of research, analytical, evaluative, and interpretive skills.

Chair: Johann Neem
Director of Graduate Studies: Christopher C. Friday
Degrees Offered: BA,MA
Academic Year System: Quarter
Areas of Specialization: Europe, US and Western Hemisphere, Africa and Middle East, East Asia, archives and records management
Undergraduate Tuition (per academic year):
  In-State: $8130
  Out-of-State: $23544
Graduate Tuition (per academic year):
  In-State: $11442
  Out-of-State: $22566
Enrollment 2018-19:
  Undergraduate Majors: 251
  New Graduate Students: 9
  Full-time Graduate Students: 8
  Degrees in History: 68 BA, 11 MA
Undergraduate Addresses:
  Admissions: https://admissions.wwu.edu/
  Financial Aid: https://admissions.wwu.edu/financial-aid
Graduate Addresses:
  Admissions: http://www.wwu.edu/gradschool/
  Financial Aid: http://www.wwu.edu/gradschool/financial-aid-work-study.shtml

Adjunct Faculty

Greenberg, Mark I. (PhD, Florida 1997; dean; Western Libraries) American ethnic; Mark.Greenberg@wwu.edu

Joffrion, Elizabeth (MA, New Orleans 1989; MLIS, Maryland, Coll. Park 1997; dir., Heritage Resources; Western Libraries) archives and records management; Elizabeth.Joffrion@wwu.edu

Kurtz, Anthony (MA, Western Washington 1998; records mgr. and Univ. archivist; Western Libraries) archives and records management; Anthony.Kurtz@wwu.edu

Schulze-Oechtering, Michael A. (PhD, California, Berkeley 2016; instr.) ethnic studies, Asian American studies; Michael.Schulze-Oechtering@wwu.edu

Steele, Ruth (MA, Western Washington 2002; archivist; Center for Pacific Northwest Studies) archives and records management; Ruth.Steele@wwu.edu

Takagi, Midori (PhD, Columbia 1995; assoc. prof.; Fairhaven Coll.) slavery, ethnic; midori.takagi@wwu.edu

Full-time Faculty

Anderson, Charles W. (PhD, NYU 2013; asst. prof.) Middle East; Charles.Anderson@wwu.edu

Bushelle, Emi Foulk (PhD, UCLA 2016; asst. prof.) premodern Japan; Emi.Foulk@wwu.edu

Cameselle, Pedro M. (PhD, Fordham 2017; asst. prof.) Latin America, world; pedro.cameselle@wwu.edu

Cerretti, Josh (PhD, SUNY, Buffalo 2014; asst. prof.) women/gender/sexuality studies; josh.cerretti@wwu.edu

Costanzo, Susan E. (PhD, Northwestern 1994; assoc. prof.) Russia and Soviet Union, Europe; Susan.Costanzo@wwu.edu

Diehl, Peter D. (PhD, UCLA 1991; assoc. prof.) medieval, ecclesiastical, social; Peter.Diehl@wwu.edu

Eurich, Susan Amanda (PhD, Emory 1988; prof.) early modern Europe, France; Amanda.Eurich@wwu.edu

Friday, Chris (PhD, UCLA 1991; prof. and dir., grad. studies) American Indian, Asian American, Pacific Northwest; Chris.Friday@wwu.edu

Garfinkle, Steven J. (PhD, Columbia 2000; prof.) ancient Near East and Mediterranean, historical theory and methods; Steven.Garfinkle@wwu.edu

Hardesty, Jared Ross (PhD, Boston Coll. 2014; assoc. prof.) colonial America; Jared.Hardesty@wwu.edu

Jimerson, Randall C. (PhD, Michigan 1977; prof.) archival administration, information and records management, US; Rand.Jimerson@wwu.edu

Lopez, Abel Ricardo (PhD, Maryland, Coll. Park 2008; prof.) Latin America; Ricardo.Lopez@wwu.edu

Neem, Johann N. (PhD, Virginia 2004; prof. and chair) early American Republic; Johann.Neem@wwu.edu

Pihos, Peter Constantine (PhD, Pennsylvania 2015; asst. prof.) African American; peter.pihos@wwu.edu

Price, Matthew Hunter (PhD, Ohio State 2014; asst. prof.) early American Republic; Hunter.Price@wwu.edu

Seltz, Jennifer (PhD, Washington 2005; assoc. prof.) 19th and 20th century, US West; Jennifer.Seltz@wwu.edu

Stewart, Mart A. (PhD, Emory 1988; prof.) 19th-century US social and cultural, environmental, Civil War and Reconstruction; Mart.Stewart@wwu.edu

Thompson, Roger R. (PhD, Yale 1985; prof.) China; Roger.Thompson@wwu.edu

Zarrow, Sarah Ellen (PhD, NYU 2015; asst. prof.) modern Jewish, modern Europe, Holocaust; sarah.zarrow@wwu.edu

Zimmerman, Sarah J. (PhD, California, Berkeley 2011; assoc. prof.) West Africa; Sarah.Zimmerman@wwu.edu

Retired/Emeritus Faculty

Danysk, Cecilia A. (PhD, McGill 1991; assoc. prof. emeritus) Canada

Helfgott, Leonard M. (PhD, Maryland, Coll. Park 1973; prof. emeritus) Middle East, Jewish, modern Europe; Leonard.Helfgott@wwu.edu

Mariz, George (PhD, Missouri, Columbia 1970; prof. emeritus) European intellectual, Britain; George.Mariz@wwu.edu

Ritter, Harry, Jr. (PhD, Virginia 1969; prof. emeritus) 20th-century Germany, 19th-century Habsburg monarchy; Harry.Ritter@wwu.edu

Schwarz, Henry (PhD, Wisconsin, Madison 1962; prof. emeritus) modern China, Mongolia, Chinese Central Asia; Henry.Schwarz@wwu.edu

Truschel, Louis W. (PhD, Northwestern 1970; assoc. prof. emeritus) southern Africa, modern Africa, modern Europe; Louis.Truschel@wwu.edu

Whisenhunt, Donald W. (PhD, Texas Tech 1966; prof. emeritus) US, 1930s; Donald.Whisenhunt@wwu.edu

Visiting Faculty

Johnston, Christine (PhD, UCLA 2016; vis. asst. prof.) ancient Near East, Mediterranean, economic; christine.johnston@wwu.edu

Van Huizen, Philip (PhD, British Columbia 2013; vis. asst. prof.) Canada; Philip.VanHuizen@wwu.edu

University of West Georgia

Dept. of History, TLC Bldg. 3200, 1601 Maple St., Carrollton, GA 30118. 678.839.6508. Fax 678.839.4160. Email: history@westga.edu. Website: https://www.westga.edu/academics/coah/history/.

The History Department's mission is to teach students about the past and about the discipline of history as an integral part of a complete liberal arts education for citizens in our complex, culturally diverse, and increasingly global society.

Chair: Timothy Schroer

Director of Graduate Studies: Stephanie Chalifoux

Degrees Offered: BA,MA

Academic Year System: Semester

Areas of Specialization: US, modern and early modern Europe, East and Southeast Asia, Latin America, public

Undergraduate Tuition (per academic year):
In-State: $4264
Out-of-State: $15048

Graduate Tuition (per academic year):
In-State: $5448
Out-of-State: $21168

Enrollment 2018-19:
Undergraduate Majors: 141
New Graduate Students: 11
Full-time Graduate Students: 27
Part-time Graduate Students: 15
Degrees in History: 24 BA, 12 MA

Undergraduate Addresses:
Admissions: https://www.westga.edu/admissions/
Financial Aid: https://www.westga.edu/student-services/financialaid/

Graduate Addresses:
Admissions: https://www.westga.edu/academics/gradstudies/
Financial Aid: https://www.westga.edu/student-services/financialaid/

Full-time Faculty

Bohannon, Keith S. (PhD, Penn State 2001; prof.) Civil War and Reconstruction, US South, 19th-century US; kbohanno@westga.edu

Chalifoux, Stephanie M. (PhD, Alabama 2013; asst. prof. and dir., grad. studies) women's studies; schalifo@westga.edu

de Nie, Michael W. (PhD, Wisconsin, Madison 2001; prof.) modern Britain and Ireland; mdenie@westga.edu

Genell, Aimee M. (PhD, Columbia 2013; asst. prof.) Middle East/Islamic; agenell@westga.edu

Goodson, Steve (PhD, Emory 1995; prof.) Gilded Age, Progressive Era, US cultural and social; hgoodson@westga.edu

Lipp, Charles T. (PhD, SUNY, Buffalo 2005; prof.) early modern Europe, early modern France; clipp@westga.edu

MacKinnon, Elaine McClarnand (PhD, Emory 1995; prof.) Russia, Soviet Union, modern Europe; emcclarn@westga.edu

McCleary, Ann (PhD, Brown 1996; prof. and dir., Public Hist.) public, US women, material culture; amcclear@westga.edu

McCullers, Molly L. (PhD, Emory 2012; assoc. prof.) Africa; mmcculle@westga.edu

Pacholl, Keith A. (PhD, California, Riverside 2002; prof.) colonial America, American Revolution, social and cultural; kpacholl@westga.edu

Pidhainy, Ihor O. (PhD, Toronto 2007; asst. prof.) Asia; ipidhain@westga.edu

Rivers, Larry O. (PhD, Vanderbilt 2010; assoc. prof.) African American, US religion, 20th-century US; lrivers@westga.edu

Schroer, Timothy Louis (PhD, Virginia 2002; prof. and chair) Germany, 20th-century Europe, race; tschroer@westga.edu

Stoutamire, William F. (PhD, Arizona State 2013; asst. prof.) public; wstoutam@westga.edu

Van Valen, Gary (PhD, New Mexico 2003; assoc. prof.) Latin America, ethnohistory, Bolivia; gvanvale@westga.edu

Vasconcellos, Colleen A. (PhD, Florida International 2004; assoc. prof.) Atlantic world, comparative slavery and emancipation, childhood studies; cvasconc@westga.edu

Williams, Daniel K. (PhD, Brown 2005; prof.) 20th-century US, US religion, US politics; dkw@westga.edu

Williams, Nadejda (PhD, Princeton 2008; assoc. prof.) classics, ancient world; nwilliam@westga.edu

Westminster College

Dept. of History, 319 S. Market St., New Wilmington, PA 16172-0001. 724.946.7248. Fax 724.946.7256. Email: clarkpg@westminster.edu. Website: https://www.westminster.edu/academics/majors-programs/history/.

History students at Westminster College learn to read critically, analyze systematically, communicate effectively, write convincingly, work collaboratively, and think globally about the past.

Chair: Patricia Clark
Degrees Offered: BA
Academic Year System: Semester
Areas of Specialization: US, Russia, Latin America, Africa
Tuition (per academic year): $35360
Enrollment 2018-19:
  Undergraduate Majors: 39
  Degrees in History: 9 BA
Addresses:
  Admissions: http://www.westminster.edu/admissions/
  Financial Aid: http://www.westminster.edu/admissions/financial-aid/index.cfm

Full-time Faculty

Clark, Patricia G. (PhD, Illinois, Urbana-Champaign 2002; assoc. prof. and chair) modern Europe, Latin America, Africa; clarkpg@westminster.edu

Cuff, Timothy (PhD, Pittsburgh 1998; prof.) US economic, 19th-century America, anthropometric; cufft@westminster.edu

Lahr, Angela M. (PhD, Northern Illinois 2005; assoc. prof.) modern America, Cold War, religion in America; lahram@westminster.edu

Martin, Russell Edward (PhD, Harvard 1996; prof.) Russia, medieval and early modern Europe, Eastern Orthodoxy; martinre@westminster.edu

Retired/Emeritus Faculty

Castro, A. Dwight (PhD, Indiana 1972; prof. emeritus) classical languages, early church, ancient Greece and Rome; castroad@westminster.edu

Twining, David C. (PhD, Case Western Reserve 1988; prof. emeritus) 1960s America, revolutionary and early America, African American; twinindc@westminster.edu

Westmont College

Dept. of History, 955 La Paz Rd., Santa Barbara, CA 93108-1099. 805.565.6155. Fax 805.565.6255. Email: pointer@westmont.edu. Website: https://www.westmont.edu/history.

Our faculty are strikingly international, with strong ties to five different countries and PhDs from three. Westmont history majors leave prepared to serve the world.

Chair: Richard W. Pointer
Degrees Offered: BA
Academic Year System: Semester
Areas of Specialization: Europe, US, South Asia, Middle East
Tuition (per academic year): $44130
Enrollment 2018-19:
  Undergraduate Majors: 35
  Degrees in History: 6 BA
Addresses:
  Admissions: http://www.westmont.edu/admissions/
  Financial Aid: http://www.westmont.edu/admissions/financial-aid.html

Adjunct Faculty

Beeman, Randal S. (PhD, Iowa State 1995; adj.) US agricultural and rural, environmental; rbeeman@westmont.edu

Robertson Huffnagle, Holly R. (MA, Georgetown 2013; adj.) 20th-century Europe, Holocaust

Thompson, William Keene (PhD, California, Santa Barbara 2019; adj.) early modern Europe

Full-time Faculty

Chapman, Alister (PhD, Cambridge 2004; prof.) 20th-century Britain, modern Europe; chapman@westmont.edu

Keaney, Heather Nina (PhD, California, Santa Barbara 2003; assoc. prof.) Middle East; hkeaney@westmont.edu

Mallampalli, Chandra S. (PhD, Wisconsin, Madison 2000; prof.) South Asia; mallampa@westmont.edu

Pointer, Richard W. (PhD, Johns Hopkins 1981; prof. and chair) American religious, colonial America, Native American; pointer@westmont.edu

Robins, Marianne A. (PhD, Sorbonne, France 1999; prof.) early modern Europe, France; robins@westmont.edu

Winslow, Rachel (PhD, California, Santa Barbara 2012; asst. prof.) US social policy/family/childhood/race; rwinslow@westmont.edu

Retired/Emeritus Faculty

Wilt, Paul C. (PhD, American 1970; prof. emeritus) US intellectual; wilt@westmont.edu

West Virginia University

Dept. of History, PO Box 6303, Morgantown, WV 26506-6303. 304.293.2421. Fax 304.293.3616. Email: Joseph.Hodge@mail.wvu.edu. Website: https://www.wcupa.edu/arts-humanities/History/.

The Department of History, part of the Eberly College of Arts and Sciences at West Virginia University, offers a variety of courses for the interested undergraduate and graduate student. Our faculty includes professors of West Virginia history, US history, African, Latin American, Asian, and European history.

Chair: Joseph Hodge
Director of Graduate Studies: Brian Luskey
Degrees Offered: BA,MA,PhD
Academic Year System: Semester
Areas of Specialization: US, Appalachia, modern Europe, modern Africa
Undergraduate Tuition (per academic year):
In-State: $8496
Out-of-State: $25344
Graduate Tuition (per academic year):
In-State: $9594
Out-of-State: $26208
Enrollment 2018-19:
Undergraduate Majors: 205
New Graduate Students: 20
Full-time Graduate Students: 55
Part-time Graduate Students: 9
Degrees in History: 55 BA, 7 MA, 5 PhD
Undergraduate Addresses:
Admissions: https://admissions.wvu.edu/
Financial Aid: http://financialaid.wvu.edu
Graduate Addresses:
Admissions: https://graduateadmissions.wvu.edu/
Financial Aid: http://financialaid.wvu.edu

Full-time Faculty

Aaslestad, Katherine B. (PhD, Illinois, Urbana-Champaign 1997; prof.) modern Europe, Germany, cultural; Katherine.Aaslestad@mail.wvu.edu

Arthurs, Joshua W. (PhD, Chicago 2007; assoc. prof.) modern Europe, Italy; joshua.arthurs@mail.wvu.edu

Bingmann, Melissa R. (PhD, Arizona State 2003; assoc. prof.) public, modern US; melissa.bingmann@mail.wvu.edu

Blobaum, Robert E. (PhD, Nebraska 1981; Eberly Prof.) modern central and east Europe; Robert.Blobaum@mail.wvu.edu

Fones-Wolf, Elizabeth A. (PhD, Massachusetts Amherst 1990; prof.) 20th-century US, social, economic; efwolf@wvu.edu

Fones-Wolf, Ken (PhD, Temple 1985; prof.) 19th-century US, labor, Appalachia and West Virginia; kfoneswo@wvu.edu

Gorby, William Hal (PhD, West Virginia 2014; teaching asst. prof.) West Virginia, Appalachia, 20th-century US working class; William.Gorby@mail.wvu.edu

Hodge, Joseph M. (PhD, Queen's, Can. 1999; assoc. prof. and chair) Britain and Empire, decolonization, development and modernization; Joseph.Hodge@mail.wvu.edu

Luskey, Brian Patrick (PhD, Emory 2004; assoc. prof. and dir., grad. studies) early Republic US, urban, gender; brian.luskey@mail.wvu.edu

M'bayo, Tamba E. (PhD, Michigan State 2009; assoc. prof.) Africa, West Africa; Tamba.Mbayo@mail.wvu.edu

Maxon, Robert M. (PhD, Syracuse 1972; prof.) East Africa, colonial Kenya; Robert.Maxon@mail.wvu.edu

McArdle Stephens, Michele (PhD, Oklahoma 2011; asst. prof.) Latin America, Mexico, race and gender; Michele.Stephens@mail.wvu.edu

Phillips, Jason K. (PhD, Rice 2003; Eberly Prof.) Civil War and Reconstruction, US South, 19th-century America; jason.phillips@mail.wvu.edu

Siekmeier, James F. (PhD, Cornell 1993; assoc. prof.) US diplomatic, Latin America; James.Siekmeier@mail.wvu.edu

Smart, Devin (PhD, Illinois, Urbana-Champaign 2017; asst. prof.) Africa, environmental, food and consumption; devin.smart@mail.wvu.edu

Staples, Kate Kelsey (PhD, Minnesota 2006; assoc. prof. and assoc. chair) medieval, women, England; Kate.Staples@mail.wvu.edu

Tauger, Mark B. (PhD, UCLA 1991; assoc. prof.) Russia and Soviet Union, world and comparative, historiography; mtauger@wvu.edu

Thornton, Jennifer (PhD, California, Riverside 2018; teaching asst. prof.) public, cultural resource management; jennifer.thornton@mail.wvu.edu

Vester, Matthew A. (PhD, UCLA 1997; prof.) early modern Europe, Italy, kinship; matt.vester@mail.wvu.edu

Retired/Emeritus Faculty

Arnett, William S. (PhD, Ohio State 1973; assoc. prof. emeritus) ancient; William.Arnett@mail.wvu.edu

Hammersmith, Jack L. (PhD, Virginia 1970; prof. emeritus) East Asia, recent US, American diplomatic; Jack.Hammersmith@mail.wvu.edu

Howe, Barbara J. (PhD, Temple 1976; assoc. prof. emeritus) social, women, women's studies; bhowe@wvu.edu

Lewis, Ronald L. (PhD, Akron 1974; Robbins Prof. emeritus) US social and labor, Appalachia and West Virginia; Ronald.Lewis@mail.wvu.edu

Lustig, Mary Lou (PhD, Syracuse 1982; prof. emeritus) colonial and revolutionary America, political and cultural; MaryLou.Lustig@mail.wvu.edu

McCluskey, Stephen C. (PhD, Wisconsin, Madison 1974; prof. emeritus) medieval, science; scmcc@wvu.edu

McMahon, Michal (PhD, Texas, Austin 1970; assoc. prof. emeritus) 19th-century US, urban, environmental; Michal.McMahon@mail.wvu.edu

Super, John C. (PhD, UCLA 1973; prof. emeritus) Latin America, Americas, comparative religious; John.Super@mail.wvu.edu

Visiting Faculty

Super, Joseph F. (PhD, West Virginia 2014; vis. instr.) US; joseph.super@mail.wvu.edu

Recently Awarded PhDs

Gramith, Luke "Liberation by Emigration: Italian Communists, the Cold War, and West-East Migration in Venezia Guilia in the Early Postwar Period"

Himes, Henry Edward III "Privately Secure? Miners, Steelworkers, and the Post-World War II Public-Private Welfare State"

McGee, Megan "Jacob Schmick and Moravian Missionary Activity among Native Americans"

Morgan-Cutright, Betsy L. "The Margins of Middle: Poverty and Community in a Shropshire Parish, c. 1601-1834"

Sanko, Marc A. "Britishers in Two Worlds: Maltese Immigrants in Detroit and Toronto, 1919-70"

Welsko, Charles R. III "A World Full of Mutations: Loyalty and Allegiance as a Cultural Process in Civil War Era America, 1850-80"

Wheaton College

Dept. of History, 501 College Ave., Blanchard Hall 2 West, Wheaton, IL 60187-5593. 630.752.5130. Fax 630.752.5294. Email: history@wheaton.edu. Website: https://www.wheaton.edu/academics/programs/history/.

The history department at Wheaton College offers a major or minor in history, and also a history/social science major which is a teacher education concentration. You'll graduate with a foundational understanding of past contexts, and the ability to interpret and impact God's world today, and tomorrow.

Chair: R. Tracy McKenzie
Degrees Offered: BA

Academic Year System: Semester

Areas of Specialization: early modern and modern Europe, US, Asia, Africa

Tuition (per academic year): $37700

Enrollment 2018-19:

Undergraduate Majors: 71

Degrees in History: 19 BA

Addresses:

Admissions: http://www.wheaton.edu/Admissions-and-Aid/Undergrad

Financial Aid: http://www.wheaton.edu/Admissions-and-Aid/Financial-Aid

Full-time Faculty

Franklin-Harkrider, Melissa L. (PhD, North Carolina, Chapel Hill 2003; assoc. prof.) medieval and early modern Europe, 16th-century England, women and family; melissa.harkrider@wheaton.edu

Johnson, Karen J. (PhD, Illinois, Chicago 2013; assoc. prof.) US, race; karen.johnson@wheaton.edu

Kim, Hanmee Na (PhD, UCLA 2015; asst. prof.) East Asia; hanmee.kim@wheaton.edu

Lundin, Matthew D. (PhD, Harvard 2006; assoc. prof.) early modern Germany, modern France, medieval intellectual; matthew.lundin@wheaton.edu

McKenzie, R. Tracy (PhD, Vanderbilt 1988; prof. and chair) 19th-century US, Civil War and Reconstruction, American South; tracy.mckenzie@wheaton.edu

Riddle, Jonathan D. (PhD, Notre Dame 2019; asst. prof.) America, religion, medicine; jonathan.riddle@wheaton.edu

Stringham, Noel (PhD, Virginia 2016; asst. prof.) Africa; noel.stringham@wheaton.edu

Nondepartmental Historians

Farney, Kirk (PhD, Notre Dame 2016; asst. prof.; vice pres., Advancement, Vocation, and Alumni Engagement) American religious; kirk.farney@wheaton.edu

Shuster, Robert D. (MA, Wisconsin, Madison 1975; Archives, Billy Graham Center) US religious; robert.shuster@wheaton.edu

Retired/Emeritus Faculty

Blumhofer, Edith L. (PhD, Harvard 1977; prof. emeritus) US religion, Christianity; Edith.L.Blumhofer@wheaton.edu

Kay, Thomas O. (PhD, Chicago 1974; assoc. prof. emeritus) ancient, medieval Europe, 20th-century Russia; thomas.kay@wheaton.edu

Long, Kathryn T. (PhD, Duke 1993; assoc. prof. emeritus) US religious, US women, Latin America; Kathryn.T.Long@wheaton.edu

Maas, David E. (PhD, Wisconsin, Madison 1972; prof. emeritus) American Revolution and Loyalist, Civil War, local; david.maas@wheaton.edu

Noll, Mark A. (PhD, Vanderbilt 1975; prof. emeritus) US and Canadian Christianity; mnoll@nd.edu

Rapp, Dean R. (PhD, Johns Hopkins 1971; prof. emeritus) Victorian and 20th-century England, modern Europe; dean.rapp@wheaton.edu

Weber, Charles W. (PhD, Chicago 1982; prof. emeritus) colonial Africa, European expansion, modern East Asia; charles.w.weber@wheaton.edu

Wheaton College Massachusetts

Dept. of History, Knapton Hall, 26 E. Main St., Norton, MA 02766-2322. 508.286.3639. Fax 508.286.3640. Email: bezis-selfa_john@wheatoncollege.edu. Website: https://wheatoncollege.edu/academics/programs/history/.

Learning takes place both in and out of the classroom. We are committed to fostering a sense of intellectual community among students and faculty. One of the strengths of the history department is our innovative courses.

Chair: John Bezís-Selfa

Degrees Offered: BA

Academic Year System: Semester

Areas of Specialization: US, women, Europe, Asia

Tuition (per academic year): $54118

Enrollment 2018-19:

Undergraduate Majors: 64

Degrees in History: 19 BA

Students in Undergraduate Courses: 530

Students in Undergraduate Intro Courses: 204

Addresses:

Admissions: http://wheatoncollege.edu/admission

Financial Aid: http://wheatoncollege.edu/sfs

Adjunct Faculty

Zangani, Federico (BA, Oxford 2014; Brown-Wheaton Fellow) ancient Near East, Egypt, languages; zangani_federico@wheatoncollege.edu

Full-time Faculty

Bezis-Selfa, John (PhD, Pennsylvania 1995; assoc. prof. and chair) US Latino/a, colonial North America, Latin America; jbeselfa@wheatonma.edu

Bloom, Alexander (PhD, Boston Coll. 1979; prof.) modern US, US intellectual; abloom@wheatoncollege.edu

Cathcart, Dolita (PhD, Boston Coll. 2004; assoc. prof.) US social, race/class/gender identity, African American; dcathcar@wheatoncollege.edu

Cecil, Anni (PhD, Boston Coll. 1997; prof.) modern Europe, military, US-Europe relations; cecil_anni@wheatoncollege.edu

Li, Shenglan (PhD, Binghamton, SUNY 2017; asst. prof.) East Asia, science/technology/medicine, global and gender; li_shenglan@wheatoncollege.edu

Polanichka, Dana M. (PhD, UCLA 2009; assoc. prof.) medieval France and Germany, early medieval cultural, medieval Christian architecture; polanichka_dana@wheatoncollege.edu

Tomasek, Kathryn (PhD, Wisconsin, Madison 1995; prof.) US women, 19th-century US; ktomasek@wheatoncollege.edu

Retired/Emeritus Faculty

Chandra, Vipan (PhD, Harvard 1977; prof. emeritus) East Asia, Korea, India; vchandra@wheatonma.edu

Helmreich, Paul C. (PhD, Harvard 1964; prof. emeritus) modern Europe, Russia; phelmrei@wheatonma.edu

Visiting Faculty

Henry, Wanda Sanville (PhD, Brown 2017; vis. instr.) medieval/early modern Europe, women, medicine; henry_wanda@wheatoncollege.edu

Whitman College

Dept. of History, 345 Boyer Ave., Walla Walla, WA 99362. 509.527.5798. Fax 509.527.5026. Email: dottbr@whitman.edu; heilbrunr@whitman.edu. Website: https://www.whitman.edu/academics/departments-and-programs/history.

We offer a curriculum that is incredibly diverse for a school of our size. In small classes you will be able to explore historical phenomena across the globe and across time.

Chair: Lynn Sharp
Degrees Offered: BA
Academic Year System: Semester
Areas of Specialization: Africa, Europe, US, East Asia, Latin America, Islamic world, environmental, ancient Mediterranean
Tuition (per academic year): $53420
Enrollment 2018-19:
  Undergraduate Majors: 38
  Degrees in History: 9 BA
  Students in Undergraduate Courses: 507
  Students in Undergraduate Intro Courses: 109
Addresses:
  Admissions: http://www.whitman.edu/admission-and-aid/applying-to-whitman
  Financial Aid: http://www.whitman.edu/admission-and-aid/financial-aid-and-costs

Full-time Faculty

Arch, Jakobina (PhD, Harvard 2014; asst. prof.) environmental, early modern Japan; archjk@whitman.edu
Charlip, Julie A. (PhD, UCLA 1995; prof.) Latin America; charlija@whitman.edu
Cotts, John D. (PhD, California, Berkeley 2000; prof.) medieval and early modern Europe; cottsjd@whitman.edu
Davies, Sarah H. (PhD, Texas, Austin 2012; assoc. prof.) ancient Mediterranean; daviessh@whitman.edu
Dott, Brian R. (PhD, Pittsburgh 1998; assoc. prof.) China, East Asia; dottbr@whitman.edu
Lerman, Nina E. (PhD, Pennsylvania 1993; assoc. prof.) 19th-century US, technology social; lermanne@whitman.edu
Semerdjian, Elyse (PhD, Georgetown 2003; prof.) Islamic world; semerdve@whitman.edu
Sharp, Lynn L. (PhD, California, Irvine 1996; assoc. prof. and chair) modern Europe, France, rural; sharpll@whitman.edu
Woodfork, Jacqueline Cassandra (PhD, Texas, Austin 2001; assoc. prof.) Africa; woodfojc@whitman.edu

Retired/Emeritus Faculty

Schmitz, David F. (PhD, Rutgers 1985; Skotheim Chair emeritus) diplomatic, 20th-century US; schmitdf@whitman.edu
Weingart, J. Walter (PhD, Northwestern 1976; prof. emeritus) England, early modern Europe; weingart@whitman.edu

Whittier College

Dept. of History, 13406 Philadelphia St., PO Box 634, Whittier, CA 90608. 562.907.4200. Fax 562.698.4067. Email: lmcenaney@whittier.edu. Website: https://www.whittier.edu/academics/history.

Within the Department of History at Whittier College, you'll find a diverse group of teachers and scholars committed to working with students who want to engage the study of history. Our broad range of courses and teaching styles helps students understand human beings and their societies in a global context. Students who enroll in our classes learn how to do the detective work of the historian and are expected to become historians themselves through close reading and analysis of historical documents, essay writing, and class discussion. This education prepares our graduates with a wide range of critical thinking and writing skills that allow them to pursue a diverse array of meaningful and successful career paths—from law, business, and health, to museum and archival work, to secondary school teaching, and to graduate work in history. We have even had two history majors go to medical school. To the question, "What can I do with a history degree," we answer: "Anything you are interested in and are willing to work hard for."

Chair: Laura McEnaney
Degrees Offered: BA
Academic Year System: Semester
Areas of Specialization: East Asia, Europe, Latin America, US
Tuition (per academic year): $42690
Enrollment 2018-19:
  Undergraduate Majors: 75
  Degrees in History: 14 BA
Addresses:
  Admissions: http://www.whittier.edu/admission
  Financial Aid: http://www.whittier.edu/financialaid

Full-time Faculty

Marks, Robert B. (PhD, Wisconsin, Madison 1978; prof.) modern China, environmental, social and economic; rmarks@whittier.edu
McEnaney, Laura (PhD, Wisconsin, Madison 1996; prof.) modern US, gender, post-1945 US; lmcenaney@whittier.edu
Orozco, Jose (PhD, Harvard 1997; assoc. prof.) modern Mexico, race, comparative immigration; jorozco@whittier.edu
Ortega, Jose Guadalupe (PhD, UCLA 2007; asst. prof.) colonial Latin America, Cuba, slavery; jortega@whittier.edu
Sage, Elizabeth M. (PhD, Chicago 1996; assoc. prof.) modern Europe, modern French social and intellectual; esage@whittier.edu
Zappia, Natale (PhD, California, Santa Cruz 2008; asst. prof. and chair) colonial America, Native American, borderlands; nzappia@whittier.edu

Retired/Emeritus Faculty

Archer, Richard L. (PhD, California, Santa Barbara 1968; prof. emeritus) early America, American social and cultural
Breese, Donald (PhD, UCLA 1964; prof. emeritus) European cultural, Civil War
Fairbanks, Joseph (PhD, Arizona 1971; prof. emeritus) colonial and revolutionary America

Whitworth University

Dept. of History, 300 W. Hawthorne Rd., Spokane, WA 99251. 509.777.3270. Fax 509.777.3711. Email: aclark@whitworth.edu. Website: https://www.whitworth.edu/History/.

The history department strives to embody Whitworth's education of mind and heart through excellent teaching, open and robust debate, scholarship, mentoring, and thorough preparation of students for careers with purpose and potential.

Chair: Anthony E. Clark
Degrees Offered: BA
Academic Year System: 4-1-4

Areas of Specialization: US and African American, Europe, public, East Asia
Tuition (per academic year): $43800
Enrollment 2018-19:
Undergraduate Majors: 53
Degrees in History: 24 BA
Addresses:
Admissions: http://www.whitworth.edu/cms/administration/admissions/
Financial Aid: http://www.whitworth.edu/cms/administration/financial-aid/

Affiliated Faculty

Soden, Dale (PhD, Washington 1980; prof.; dir., Weyerhaeuser Center for Christian Faith and Learning and vice pres., planning) US, Pacific Northwest, American intellectual; dsoden@whitworth.edu

Full-time Faculty

Clark, Anthony E. (PhD, Oregon 2005; assoc. prof. and chair) Asia and China, non-Western, world; aclark@whitworth.edu
Leal, K. Elise (PhD, Baylor 2018; asst. prof.) US to 1877, American religion, gender theory and European women 1300-1750; eleal@whitworth.edu
Slack, Corliss K. (PhD, Oxford 1988; prof.) Europe, Crusades; cslack@whitworth.edu

Retired/Emeritus Faculty

Migliazzo, Arlin Charles (PhD, Washington State 1982; prof. emeritus) antebellum South, recent US, ethnicity and race; amigliazzo@whitworth.edu

Wichita State University

Dept. of History, 1845 Fairmount, Wichita, KS 67260-0045. 316.978.3150. Fax 316.978.3473. Email: jay.price@wichita.edu. Website: https://www.wichita.edu/academics/fairmount_college_of_liberal_arts_and_sciences/history/.

A Bachelor of Arts (BA) in history from Wichita State offers several specialized areas of study. As a history student, you'll improve your ability to think, write, speak, reason and solve problems—skills vital to success in graduate school and in virtually every career. And you'll be able to combine your degree with other disciplines, such as teaching, political science, journalism and others.

Chair: Jay M. Price
Director of Graduate Studies: Robin Henry
Degrees Offered: BA,MA
Academic Year System: Semester
Areas of Specialization: US, local, ancient and medieval world, modern Europe
Undergraduate Tuition (per academic year):
In-State: $4164
Out-of-State: $10591
Graduate Tuition (per academic year):
In-State: $4217
Out-of-State: $11141
Enrollment 2018-19:
Undergraduate Majors: 137
New Graduate Students: 29
Full-time Graduate Students: 7
Part-time Graduate Students: 53
Degrees in History: 24 BA, 8 MA

Undergraduate Addresses:
Admissions: http://www.wichita.edu/thisis/admissions/
Financial Aid: http://www.wichita.edu/thisis/home/?u=finaid_home
Graduate Addresses:
Admissions and Financial Aid: http://www.wichita.edu/thisis/academics/graduate/

Full-time Faculty

Ballout, Laila K. (PhD, Northwestern 2017; asst. prof.) 20th-century US, US and world; laila.ballout@wichita.edu
Dehner, George Joseph (PhD, Northeastern 2005; assoc. prof.) world, environmental; george.dehner@wichita.edu
Dreifort, John E. (PhD, Kent State 1970; prof.) modern France, 19th- and 20th-century Europe; john.dreifort@wichita.edu
Hayton, Jeff Patrick (PhD, Illinois, Urbana-Champaign 2013; asst. prof.) modern Europe, Germany, popular culture; jeff.hayton@wichita.edu
Henry, Robin C. (PhD, Indiana 2006; assoc. prof. and dir., grad. studies) gender, sexuality, legal; robin.henry@wichita.edu
Hundley, Helen S. (PhD, Illinois, Urbana-Champaign 1984; asst. prof.) Russia, Soviet Union, Siberia; helen.hundley@wichita.edu
Owens, Robert M. (PhD, Illinois, Urbana-Champaign 2003; assoc. prof.) colonial and revolutionary America; robert.owens@wichita.edu
Price, Jay M. (PhD, Arizona State 1997; assoc. prof. and chair) public, social; jay.price@wichita.edu
Thelle, Rannfrid (PhD, Oslo, Norway 1999; asst. prof.; Religion) Old Testament, New Testament, Biblical studies topics, Biblical Hebrew; rannfrid.thelle@wichita.edu
Torbenson, Craig L. (PhD, Oklahoma 1992; assoc. prof.) geography, family; craig.torbenson@wichita.edu
Weems, Robert E., Jr. (PhD, Wisconsin-Madison 1987; prof.) African American, African American business, American business; robert.weems@wichita.edu

Retired/Emeritus Faculty

Duram, James C. (PhD, Wayne State 1968; prof. emeritus) American constitutional and legal
Johnson, Judith R. (PhD, New Mexico 1987; assoc. prof. emeritus) 20th-century America, Latin America; judith.johnson@wichita.edu
Loftus, Ariel (PhD, Michigan 1992; assoc. prof. emeritus) ancient, Greece and Rome, women in antiquity; ariel.loftus@wichita.edu
Thomas, Phillip Drennon (PhD, New Mexico 1965; prof. emeritus) medieval, environmental; phillip.thomas@wichita.edu

Wilkes University

Dept. of History, 84 W. South St., Wilkes Barre, PA 18766. 570.408.4530. Fax 570.408.7829. Email: john.hepp@wilkes.edu. Website: https://www.wilkes.edu/history.

Located in the heart of Wilkes-Barre's vibrant historic district, Wilkes University is a great place to study history because the past is all around you.

Chair: Christopher Zarpentine
Degrees Offered: BA
Academic Year System: Semester
Areas of Specialization: urban/business/technology/energy, women and gender/social and cultural, public, digital, Asia, print culture/foodways
Tuition (per academic year): $34454

Enrollment 2018-19:
Undergraduate Majors: 37
Degrees in History: 5 BA
Students in Undergraduate Courses: 752
Students in Undergraduate Intro Courses: 616
Online-Only Courses: 1%

Addresses:
Admissions: http://www.wilkes.edu/admissions/
Financial Aid: http://www.wilkes.edu/admissions/financial-aid/

Full-time Faculty

Hepp, John H. IV (PhD, North Carolina, Chapel Hill 1998; prof.) American cultural, technology and business, urban and diplomatic; john.hepp@wilkes.edu

Kuiken, Jonathan R. (PhD, Boston Coll. 2013; asst. prof.) oil industry and energy, Great Britain, Middle East; jonathan.kuiken@wilkes.edu

Riggs, Paul T. (PhD, Pittsburgh 1997; prof. and dean) modern Britain, Scotland, legal; paul.riggs@wilkes.edu

Shimizu, Akira (PhD, Illinois, Urbana-Champaign 2011; asst. prof.) Japan, Asia and world, food and foodways; akira.shimizu@wilkes.edu

Sopcak-Joseph, Amy (PhD, Connecticut 2019; asst. prof.) print culture, early America, Atlantic world

Retired/Emeritus Faculty

Berlatsky, Joel A. (PhD, Northwestern 1970; prof. emeritus) Britain, early modern Europe, South Asia; joel.berlatsky@wilkes.edu

Cox, Harold E. (PhD, Virginia 1958; prof. emeritus) American social and cultural, technology and business, diplomatic; harold.cox@wilkes.edu

Hupchick, Dennis P. (PhD, Pittsburgh 1983; prof. emeritus) eastern Europe, Russia, Ottoman; dennis.hupchick@wilkes.edu

Rodechko, James P. (PhD, Connecticut 1967; prof. emeritus) American social and intellectual, ethnic, World War II; james.rodechko@wilkes.edu

Wenger, Diane E. (PhD, Delaware 2002; prof. emeritus) women, colonial, early Republic; diane.wenger@wilkes.edu

Willamette University

Dept. of History, 900 State St., Salem, OR 97301-3931. 503.370.6061. Fax 503.370.6944. Email: eeisenbe@willamette.edu. Website: http://www.willamette.edu/cla/history/.

The program in history is designed to provide a firm foundation in the histories of Western civilization, American society and culture, East Asian and Middle Eastern cultures. The department is especially strong in social, cultural and intellectual history and emphasizes an understanding of the nature of historical inquiry.

Chair: Ellen Eisenberg
Degrees Offered: BA
Academic Year System: Semester
Areas of Specialization: ancient and medieval Europe, European intellectual and political, American social and intellectual, modern Middle East and East Asia
Tuition (per academic year): $49750
Enrollment 2018-19:
Undergraduate Majors: 46
Degrees in History: 14 BA
Students in Undergraduate Courses: 450
Addresses:
Admissions: http://www.willamette.edu/admission
Financial Aid: http://www.willamette.edu/admission/tuition-aid

Full-time Faculty

Cotlar, Seth (PhD, Northwestern 2000; prof.) American intellectual/political/cultural, early Republic, revolutionary era; scotlar@willamette.edu

Eisenberg, Ellen M. (PhD, Pennsylvania 1990; Dwight and Margaret Lear Prof. and chair) American social, 20th-century America; eeisenbe@willamette.edu

McCaffrey, Cecily M. (PhD, California, San Diego 2003; assoc. prof.) China, East Asia; cmccaffr@willamette.edu

Petersen Boring, Wendy (PhD, Yale 2004; assoc. prof.) medieval and Renaissance Europe, intellectual and cultural; wpeterse@willamette.edu

Sadeghian, Saghar (PhD, Sorbonne Nouvelle 2014; asst. prof.) Middle East, environmental, minority groups; ssadeghian@willamette.edu

Smaldone, William T. (PhD, SUNY, Binghamton 1989; prof.) modern Europe, 20th-century Germany, Latin America; wsmaldon@willamette.edu

Joint/Cross Appointments

Chenault, Robert R. (PhD, Michigan 2008; assoc. prof.; Classics) ancient Greece, Rome; rchenaul@willamette.edu

Loftus, Ronald P. (PhD, Claremont Grad. 1975; prof.; Foreign Languages and Literatures) Japan; rloftus@willamette.edu

Part-time Faculty

Dunlap, Leslie K. (PhD, Northwestern 2001; asst. prof.) 20th-century American women, American families; ldunlap@willamette.edu

Jopp, Jennifer (PhD, SUNY, Binghamton 1992; asst. prof.) American legal, colonial Latin America; jjopp@willamette.edu

Retired/Emeritus Faculty

Duvall, William E. (PhD, California, Santa Barbara 1973; prof. emeritus) European intellectual, modern France; bduvall@willamette.edu

Lucas, Robert (PhD, Columbia 1966; prof. emeritus) ancient, medieval Europe, Renaissance; rlucas@willamette.edu

McCowen, George S. (PhD, Emory 1966; prof. emeritus) American intellectual, colonial and revolutionary America

College of William and Mary

Lyon Gardiner Tyler Dept. of History, PO Box 8795, Williamsburg, VA 23187-8795. 757.221.3720. Fax 757.221.2111. Email: histo2@wm.edu. Website: https://www.wm.edu/as/history/.

Named for Lyon Gardiner Tyler, the college's 17th president, the Department of History's dedicated faculty and distinctive history give it a unique character among public institutions and create a learning environment that fosters close interaction among students and professors.

Chair: Frederick Corney
Director of Graduate Studies: Paul Mapp
Director of Undergraduate Studies: Tuska Benes
Degrees Offered: BA,MA,PhD
Academic Year System: Semester
Areas of Specialization: early America, US, comparative, Europe, Latin America and Africa
Undergraduate Tuition (per academic year):
In-State: $17434
Out-of-State: $40089
Graduate Tuition (per academic year):
In-State: $16440
Out-of-State: $34800

Enrollment 2018-19:
Undergraduate Majors: 242
New Graduate Students: 11
Full-time Graduate Students: 65
Degrees in History: 101 BA, 6 MA, 4 PhD

Undergraduate Addresses:
Admissions: http://www.wm.edu/admission/
undergraduateadmission/
Financial Aid: http://www.wm.edu/admission/financialaid/

Graduate Addresses:
Admissions and Financial Aid: https://www.wm.edu/as/history/
gradprogram/

Adjunct Faculty

Butler, Michael (PhD, Virginia 1980; adj. asst. prof.) American
foreign policy, 20th-century US, 20th-century Europe;
mabutler01@wm.edu

Limoncelli, Amy (PhD, Boston Coll. 2016; adj. asst. prof.) modern
Britain, modern Europe, British Empire; aelimo@wm.edu

Affiliated Faculty

Brown, Marley R., III (PhD, Brown 1972; research prof.; dir.,
Archaeological Excavation and Conservation, Colonial
Williamsburg Found.) historical archaeology; mrbro1@wm.edu

Carson, Cary (PhD, Harvard 1974; lect.; vice pres., Research Div.,
Colonial Williamsburg Found.) early modern England, America;
carycarson@earthlink.net

Hobson, Charles F. (PhD, Emory 1971; lect.; ed., Papers of John
Marshall) early national America; cfhobs@wm.edu

Horn, James P. P. (PhD, Sussex, UK 1982; lect.; Colonial
Williamsburg Found.) American studies; jhorn@cwf.org

Kelso, William M. (PhD, Emory 1971; adj. assoc. prof.; dir.,
Research & Interpretation, Jamestown Rediscovery) historical
archaeology; wkelso@preservationvirginia.org

Kern, Susan A. (PhD, William and Mary 2005; vis. assoc. prof.; dir.,
Internships, National Inst. American Hist. and Democracy) early
America, Age of Jefferson, American South, material culture,
public; sakern@wm.edu

Lounsbury, Carl (PhD, George Washington 1983; adj. assoc.
prof.; sr. architectural historian, Colonial Williamsburg Found.)
vernacular architecture; crloun@wm.edu

Zimmerli, Nadine (PhD, Wisconsin-Madison 2011; asst. editor;
Omohundro Inst.) modern Germany; nizimmerli@wm.edu

Full-time Faculty

Allen, Jody L. (PhD, William and Mary 2007; asst. prof.; co-dir.,
Lemon Project) African American, US South; jlalle@wm.edu

Benes, Kveta E. (PhD, Washington 2001; Clark G. and Elizabeth
H. Diamond Assoc. Prof. and dir., undergrad. studies) modern
Europe, cultural and intellectual, modern Germany; kebene@
wm.edu

Chouin, Gerard (PhD, Syracuse 2009; asst. prof.) pre-Atlantic, early
modern Atlantic West Africa; glchouin@wm.edu

Corney, Frederick C. (PhD, Columbia 1997; prof. and chair) modern
Europe, Russia; fccorn@wm.edu

Daileader, Philip H. (PhD, Harvard 1996; Harrison assoc. prof.)
medieval Europe; phdail@wm.edu

Ely, Melvin Patrick (PhD, Princeton 1985; William R. Kenan Jr. Prof.)
African American, US South; mpelyx@wm.edu

Fisher, Andrew H. (PhD, Arizona State 2003; assoc. prof.) 20th-
century cultural, environmental, American Indian and West;
ahfis2@wm.edu

Grasso, Christopher D. (PhD, Yale 1992; prof.) early America,
religious and intellectual; cdgras@wm.edu

Han, Eric (PhD, Columbia 2008; assoc. prof.) East Asia, Japan;
echan@wm.edu

Homza, LuAnn (PhD, Chicago 1992; prof.) Spain, Renaissance and
Reformation Europe; lahomz@wm.edu

Hubbard, Joshua (PhD, Michigan 2017; asst. prof.) China;
jahubbard@wm.edu

Karakaya-Stump, Ayfer (PhD, Harvard 2008; asst. prof.) Ottoman,
Islamic and Arabic, medieval Europe; akstump@wm.edu

Kitamura, Hiroshi (PhD, Wisconsin, Madison 2004; assoc. prof.) US
foreign relations, East Asia, cultural and intellectual; hxkita@
wm.edu

Koloski, Laurie S. (PhD, Stanford 1998; assoc. prof.) eastern and
modern Europe; lskolo@wm.edu

Konefal, Betsy O. (PhD, Pittsburgh 2005; assoc. prof.; dir., Latin
American Studies) Latin America, ethnohistory, race and
gender; bokone@wm.edu

Levitan, Kathrin (PhD, Chicago 2006; assoc. prof.) modern Britain,
social thought, British Empire; khlevi@wm.edu

Mapp, Paul W. (PhD, Harvard 2001; William E. Pullen Prof. and dir.,
grad. studies) colonial North America, early modern Europe,
international relations; pwmapp@wm.edu

Middleton, Simon (PhD, Graduate Center, CUNY 1998; assoc. prof.)
colonial New York; smiddleton@wm.edu

Petty, Adrienne Monteith (PhD, Columbia 2004; assoc. prof.)
modern US; ampetty@wm.edu

Piker, Joshua A. (PhD, Cornell 1998; prof.; editor, William and Mary
Quarterly) Atlantic world, early America, US; japiker@wm.edu

Pope, Jeremy (PhD, Johns Hopkins 2010; asst. prof.) Africa;
jwpope@wm.edu

Popper, Nicholas (PhD, Princeton 2007; Kohlhagen Assoc. Prof.)
Tudor-Stuart England, early modern European intellectual;
nspopper@wm.edu

Prado, Fabricio (PhD, Emory 2009; asst. prof.) colonial Latin
America, Rio de la Plata and Portugese America, transimperial
and transnational networks; fpprado@wm.edu

Richter, Julie (PhD, William and Mary 1992; lect.) colonial America,
colonial Virginian race/class/gender; cjrich@wm.edu

Schechter, Ronald B. (PhD, Harvard 1993; assoc. prof.) modern
Europe, French cultural and Jewish; rbsche@wm.edu

Sheriff, Carol (PhD, Yale 1993; Pullen Prof.) early 19th-century US,
social; cxsher@wm.edu

Vinson, Robert Trent (PhD, Howard 2001; Frances L. and Edwin L.
Cummings assoc. prof.) black Atlantic, South Africa, African and
African American studies; rtvins@wm.edu

Whittenburg, James P. (PhD, Georgia 1974; prof.) colonial America,
early national, quantitative methods; jpwhit@wm.edu

Wulf, Karin A. (PhD, Johns Hopkins 1993; prof.; dir., Omohundro
Inst.) US women, colonial America; kawulf@wm.edu

Zutshi, Chitralekha (PhD, Tufts 2000; Plumeri Fellow and prof.)
South Asia; cxzuts@wm.edu

Joint/Cross Appointments

Brown, Chandos Michael (PhD, Harvard 1987; assoc. prof.;
American Studies) American intellectual and cultural, early
national US; cmbrow@wm.edu

McGovern, Charles F. (PhD, Harvard 1993; assoc. prof.; dir.,
American Studies) American cultural, popular culture, consumer
culture; cfmcgo@wm.edu

Meyer, Leisa D. (PhD, Wisconsin-Madison 1993; assoc. prof.; dir.,
American Studies) US women, gender and sexuality, military;
ldmeye@wm.edu

Rosen, Hannah (PhD, Chicago 1999; asst. prof.; American Studies)
US death/race/segregation; hrosen@wm.edu

Thelwell, Chinua Akimaro (PhD, NYU 2011; asst. prof.; Africana
Studies) African diaspora, idea of race in Atlantic world, South
Africa; cathelwell@wm.edu

Turtis, Richard (PhD, Chicago 1997; asst. prof.; Africana Studies and Latin American Studies) Caribbean; rturits@wm.edu

Nondepartmental Historians

Campbell, Bruce B. (PhD, Wisconsin, Madison 1988; assoc. prof.; Modern Languages) modern Germany, paramilitarism, radio; bbcamp@wm.edu

Fitzgerald, Maureen A. (PhD, Wisconsin, Madison 1992; assoc. prof.; Religious Studies) US women, religion/immigration/welfare; mafitz@wm.edu

Retired/Emeritus Faculty

Abdalla, Ismail H. (PhD, Wisconsin, Madison 1981; prof. emeritus) Africa, Middle East; ixabda@wm.edu

Axtell, James L. (PhD, Cambridge 1967; Kenan Prof. emeritus) colonial North America, American Indian-white relations, European exploration; jlaxte@wm.edu

Canning, Craig N. (PhD, Stanford 1975; prof. emeritus) East Asia, China and Japan, US-China relations; cncann@wm.edu

Crapol, Edward P. (PhD, Wisconsin, Madison 1968; Pullen Prof. emeritus) US foreign policy, Cold War; edpcal@wm.edu

Esler, Anthony J. (PhD, Duke 1961; prof. emeritus) modern Europe, global, intellectual

Funigiello, Philip J. (PhD, NYU 1966; prof. emeritus) recent America, urban America; pjfuni@yahoo.com

Hoak, Dale E. (PhD, Cambridge 1971; Chancellor Prof. emeritus) Tudor-Stuart England, early modern Europe; dehoak@wm.edu

Johnson, Ludwell H., III (PhD, Johns Hopkins 1955; prof. emeritus) antebellum and Civil War political and economic

McArthur, Gilbert H. (PhD, Rochester 1968; prof. emeritus) modern Europe, Russia; ghmcar@wm.edu

Price, Richard S. (PhD, Harvard 1970; Dittman Prof. emeritus) sociocultural anthropology and history, Afro-American maroons, Caribbean; rspric@wm.edu

Rafeq, Abdul-Karim (PhD, London 1963; prof. emeritus) Arab Middle Eastern studies; akrafe@wm.edu

Smith, J. Douglas (PhD, Virginia 1960; assoc. prof. emeritus) America

Strong, George V. (PhD, North Carolina, Chapel Hill 1969; prof. emeritus) modern Germany, Austro-Hungarian Empire, social and intellectual; gvstro@wm.edu

Walker, Helen Campbell (MA, Yale 1966; prof. emeritus) new US South, African Americans since 1861, southern women; hcwalk@wm.edu

Recently Awarded PhDs

Butler, Amelia M. "'They Are Instructed in Useful Learning': 'Colored' Orphan Asylums in Progressive-Era Virginia"

Ward, David Lawrence "A School for Leaders: Continental Army Officer Training and Civilian Leadership in the Trans-Appalachian West"

William Paterson University

Dept. of History, 300 Pompton Rd., Atrium 217, Wayne, NJ 07470. 973.720.2319. Fax 973.720.3079. Email: mcmahonlu@wpunj. edu. Website: https://www.wpunj.edu/cohss/departments/history/.

Emphasizing breadth of study and comparative inquiry as well as more specialized research, the Department of History provides strong support and unique opportunities for both undergraduates and graduate students.

Chair: Lucia McMahon
Director of Graduate Studies: Joanne Miyang Cho

Degrees Offered: BA,MA
Academic Year System: Semester
Areas of Specialization: US, Europe and Russia, Latin America and Brazil, East Asia and South Asia, Middle East
Undergraduate Tuition (per academic year):
  In-State: $12574
  Out-of-State: $17868
Graduate Tuition (per academic year):
  In-State: $14958
  Out-of-State: $19764
Enrollment 2018-19:
  Undergraduate Majors: 160
  New Graduate Students: 10
  Full-time Graduate Students: 5
  Part-time Graduate Students: 9
  Degrees in History: 75 BA, 4 MA
Undergraduate Addresses:
  Admissions: http://www.wpunj.edu/admissions/undergraduate
  Financial Aid: http://www.wpunj.edu/financial-aid
Graduate Addresses:
  Admissions: http://www.wpunj.edu/admissions/graduate
  Financial Aid: http://www.wpunj.edu/financial-aid

Full-time Faculty

Ambroise, Jason (PhD, California, Berkeley 2006; assoc. prof.) America since 1607, science, African American studies; ambroisej@wpunj.edu

Bone, Jonathan A. (PhD, Chicago 2003; asst. prof.) Russia, Soviet Union, economic; bonej@wpunj.edu

Cho, Joanne Miyang (PhD, Chicago 1993; prof.) modern Germany, Germany and Asia, theories of civilization; choj@wpunj.edu

Cook, Theodore Failor, Jr. (PhD, Princeton 1987; prof.; dir., Asian Studies) East Asia, international relations, military; cookt@wpunj.edu

Dai, Yingcong (PhD, Washington 1996; prof.) imperial and modern China, Southeast Asia, information technology; daiy@wpunj.edu

Finnegan, Terence R. (PhD, Illinois, Urbana-Champaign 1993; prof.) US social and quantitative, race relations, information technology; finnegant@wpunj.edu

Gill, Navyug (PhD, Emory 2014; asst. prof.; Asian Studies) modern South Asia, labor, caste and religious politics

Gonzalez, Evelyn (PhD, Columbia 1993; prof.) US, urban, minorities; gonzaleze@wpunj.edu

Koistinen, David J. (PhD, Yale 1999; assoc. prof.) US economic; koistinend@wpunj.edu

Livingston, John W. (PhD, Princeton 1968; assoc. prof.) modern Middle East, Islamic civilization, science; livingstonj@wpunj.edu

MacLeod, Dewar (PhD, Grad. Center, CUNY 1998; prof.) America, cultural studies; macleodg@wpunj.edu

McDonough, Scott J. (PhD, UCLA 2005; assoc. prof.) late antiquity; mcdonoughs21@wpunj.edu

McMahon, Lucia (PhD, Rutgers 2004; prof. and chair) colonial to present America, women and gender; mcmahonlu@wpunj.edu

Meaders, Daniel E. (PhD, Yale 1990; assoc. prof.) colonial and revolutionary America, African American; meadersd@wpunj.edu

O'Donnell, Krista Molly (PhD, SUNY, Binghamton 1996; prof.) women, Europe and Africa, imperialism; odonnellk@wpunj.edu

Robb, George (PhD, Northwestern 1990; prof.) modern Britain, social, women; robbg@wpunj.edu

Zeller, Neici M. (PhD, Illinois, Chicago 2010; assoc. prof.) Latin America, women; zellern@wpunj.edu

Retired/Emeritus Faculty

Edelstein, Melvin A. (PhD, Princeton 1965; prof. emeritus) French Revolution, 18th-century Europe

Geissler-Bowles, Suzanne (PhD, Syracuse 1976; prof. emerita) colonial and revolutionary America, early national US, American religion; bowless@wpunj.edu

Gruber, Carol S. (PhD, Columbia 1968; prof. emeritus) 20th-century US, war and society

Nalle, Sara T. (PhD, Johns Hopkins 1983; prof. emeritus) early modern Spain and France, medieval France; nalles@wpunj.edu

Tirado, Isabel A. (PhD, California, Berkeley 1985; prof. emeritus) late modern Europe, imperial Russia and USSR; tiradoi@wpunj.edu

Williams College

Dept. of History, 85 Mission Park Dr., Hollander Hall, Williamstown, MA 01267. 413.597.2394. Fax 413.597.3673. Email: lsaharcz@williams.edu. Website: https://history.williams.edu/.

The History Department seeks to cultivate a critical understanding and awareness of the past and the development of our students' intellectual, analytical, and rhetorical abilities.

Chair: Anne Reinhardt
Degrees Offered: BA
Academic Year System: Semester
Areas of Specialization: Africa, East Asia and South Asia, Europe and Russia, Middle East, North and South America, global
Tuition (per academic year): $56970
Enrollment 2018-19:
  Undergraduate Majors: 87
  Degrees in History: 49 BA
Addresses:
  Admissions: http://admission.williams.edu
  Financial Aid: http://finaid.williams.edu

Full-time Faculty

Bernhardsson, Magnus T. (PhD, Yale 1999; Brown Prof.) modern Middle East, Iraq, nationalism and religion; mbernhar@williams.edu

Bevilacqua, Alexander (PhD, Princeton 2014; asst. prof.) early modern European cultural and intellectual, globalization and cultural exchange, Europe and Islamic world; ab24@williams.edu

Chapman, Jessica M. (PhD, California, Santa Barbara 2006; assoc. prof.) US and world, US foreign relations, Vietnam; jmc1@williams.edu

DeLucia, Christine M. (PhD, Yale 2012; asst. prof.) Native American/indigenous, early America, settler colonialism, environment and place, memory and commemoration, material culture and museums, and decolonizing methodologies

Dew, Charles B. (PhD, Johns Hopkins 1964; Ephraim Williams Prof.) US South, Civil War and Reconstruction; cdew@williams.edu

Dubow, Sara L. (PhD, Rutgers 2003; prof.) US gender, sexuality, law; sld1@williams.edu

Garbarini, Alexandra (PhD, UCLA 2003; prof.) modern Germany, Holocaust, Jews in modern Europe; agarbari@williams.edu

Kapadia, Aparna (PhD, SOAS, London 2010; assoc. prof.) early modern South Asia, modern South Asia; ak16@williams.edu

Kittleson, Roger A. (PhD, Wisconsin, Madison 1997; prof.) modern Latin America, Brazil, sport and nationalism; rkittles@williams.edu

Kohut, Thomas A. (PhD, Minnesota 1983; Sue and Edgar Wachenheim III Prof.) Germany, 20th-century Europe, psychological dimensions of past; tkohut@williams.edu

Long, Gretchen (PhD, Chicago 2003; prof.) African American, 19th-century US, American medicine; glong@williams.edu

Merrill, Karen R. (PhD, Michigan 1994; Frederick Rudolph '42 - C/O 1965 Prof.) US political and international, US West, environmental; kmerrill@williams.edu

Reinhardt, Anne H. (PhD, Princeton 2002; prof. and chair) modern China, imperialism and colonialism; areinhar@williams.edu

Siniawer, Eiko Maruko (PhD, Harvard 2003; prof.) modern Japan, waste and wastefulness, political violence; emaruko@williams.edu

Skorobogatov, Yana (PhD, California, Berkeley 2018; asst. prof.) Russia and Soviet Union; ys3@williams.edu

Waters, Chris (PhD, Harvard 1985; Hans W. Gatzke '38 Prof.) Britain, 20th-century Europe, sexuality; cwaters@williams.edu

Whalen, Carmen T. (PhD, Rutgers 1994; Carl W. Vogt '58 Prof.) US Latino/a, US labor; cwhalen@williams.edu

Wong, K. Scott (PhD, Michigan 1992; Charles R. Keller Prof.) Asian American, immigration, American West; kwong@williams.edu

Part-time Faculty

Mandel, Maud S. (PhD, Michigan 1998; prof. and Coll. pres.) Jewish; msm8@williams.edu

Valk, Anne (PhD, Duke 1996; lect.; assoc. dir., Public Humanities) oral, public, 20th-century US social; av7@williams.edu

Retired/Emeritus Faculty

Dalzell, Robert F., Jr. (PhD, Yale 1966; Fred Rudolph Prof. emeritus) 18th- and 19th-century US, American civilization, business; rdalzell@williams.edu

Frost, Peter Kip (PhD, Harvard 1966; Frederich L. Schuman Prof. emeritus) modern Japan, Vietnam, US-Asian relations; pkf1@williams.edu

Hyde, John M. (PhD, Harvard 1963; Brown Prof. emeritus) modern Europe, modern France, European diplomatic; jhyde@williams.edu

Oakley, Francis C. (PhD, Yale 1960; Edward Dorr Griffin Prof. emeritus) medieval Europe, European intellectual; foakley@williams.edu

Singham, Shanti Marie (PhD, Princeton 1990; prof. emeritus) French Revolution, modern Europe, colonialism and imperialism; ssingham@williams.edu

Wagner, William G. (DPhil, Oxford 1981; Brown Prof. emeritus) Russia, 19th- and 20th-century Europe; wwagner@williams.edu

Wood, James B. (PhD, Emory 1973; Charles R. Keller Prof. emeritus) early modern Europe, military; jwood@williams.edu

Visiting Faculty

Bohlen, Casey (PhD, Harvard 2016; vis. asst. prof.; Religion) American religion, modern politics and social movements, US intellectual; cdb024@williams.edu

Swagler, Matthew (PhD, Columbia 2017; vis. asst. prof.) Francophone West and Central Africa, decolonization and postcolonial African politics, African Marxisms, African gender and sexuality; mps7@williams.edu

Winthrop University

Dept. of History, Oakland Ave., Rock Hill, SC 29733. 803.323.2173. Fax 803.323.4023. Email: criderg@winthrop.edu. Website: https://www.winthrop.edu/cas/history/.

Winthrop's Department of History is home to several faculty members who cover a wide range of fields and who have been honored with numerous awards. The department offers programs of study leading to the BA and MA.

Chair: Gregory S. Crider
Director of Graduate Studies: J. Edward Lee
Degrees Offered: BA,MA
Academic Year System: Semester
Areas of Specialization: US South, Latin America, modern Europe, Asia, Mediterranean
Undergraduate Tuition (per academic year):
   In-State: $14870
   Out-of-State: $28786
Graduate Tuition (per academic year):
   In-State: $14810
   Out-of-State: $28530
Enrollment 2018-19:
   Undergraduate Majors: 90
   New Graduate Students: 7
   Full-time Graduate Students: 13
   Part-time Graduate Students: 9
   Degrees in History: 31 BA, 3 MA
Undergraduate Addresses:
   Admissions: http://www.winthrop.edu/admissions/
   Financial Aid: http://www.winthrop.edu/finaid/
Graduate Addresses:
   Admissions and Financial Aid: http://www.winthrop.edu/graduateschool/

Full-time Faculty

Bell, Gregory Donald (PhD, Duke 2007; asst. prof.) Mediterranean, medieval Europe; bellgd@winthrop.edu

Chang, Chia-Lan (PhD, Southern California 2007; asst. prof.) modern China, Japan, migration; changc@winthrop.edu

Crider, Gregory S. (PhD, Wisconsin-Madison 1996; prof. and chair) Latin America, modern Mexico, labor studies; criderg@winthrop.edu

Dixon-McKnight, Otha Jennifer (PhD, North Carolina, Chapel Hill 2017; asst. prof.) African American studies, gender studies, modern US

Doyle, L. Andrew (PhD, Emory 1998; assoc. prof.) modern US South, sports; doylea@winthrop.edu

Lee, J. Edward (PhD, South Carolina 1987; prof. and dir., grad. studies) US since 1876, US diplomatic, South Carolina; leee@winthrop.edu

Pretty, Dave (PhD, Brown 1997; assoc. prof.) Russia, central Europe; prettyd@winthrop.edu

Williams, Virginia S. (PhD, Florida State 1993; prof.) Latin America, historiography, peace studies; williamsv@winthrop.edu

Part-time Faculty

Doom, Jason W. (MA, North Carolina, Charlotte 2013; adj. instr.) US diplomatic, Latin America, US cultural; doomj@winthrop.edu

Lee, Brian Edward (PhD, North Carolina, Greensboro 2015; adj. instr.) modern US; leeb@winthrop.edu

Silverman, Jason H. (PhD, Kentucky 1981; prof. emeritus) US Old South, Civil War, American ethnic; silvermanj@winthrop.edu

University of Wisconsin-Eau Claire

Dept. of History, Hibbard 701, Eau Claire, WI 54702-4004. 715.836.5501. Fax 715.836.3540. Website: https://www.uwec.edu/academics/college-arts-sciences/departments-programs/history/.

The mission of the UW-Eau Claire history department is to provide a high quality liberal education, based upon rigorous scholarly inquiry, to all of the students it serves. The department also seeks to engage the community through public history.

Chair: Louisa Rice
Director of Graduate Studies: John W.W. Mann
Degrees Offered: BA,BS,MA
Academic Year System: Semester
Areas of Specialization: US, Europe, public, American Indian, global
Undergraduate Tuition (per academic year):
   In-State: $8692
   Out-of-State: $16265
Graduate Tuition (per academic year):
   In-State: $8774
   Out-of-State: $17905
Enrollment 2018-19:
   Undergraduate Majors: 177
   New Graduate Students: 10
   Full-time Graduate Students: 9
   Part-time Graduate Students: 19
   Degrees in History: 30 BA, 5 MA
Undergraduate Addresses:
   Admissions: http://www.uwec.edu/admissions/
   Financial Aid: http://www.uwec.edu/finaid/
Graduate Addresses:
   Admissions: http://www.uwec.edu/Admissions/graduate.htm
   Financial Aid: http://www.uwec.edu/finaid/

Adjunct Faculty

Chamberlain, Oscar B. (PhD, South Carolina 1995; sr. lect. emeritus) 19th-century America; chambeob@uwec.edu

Orser, Joseph Andrew (PhD, Ohio State 2010; sr. lect.) orserja@uwec.edu

Ott, Daniel P. (PhD, Loyola, Chicago 2015; lect.) US, public; ottdp@uwec.edu

Weber, Margaret Baker (PhD, Iowa State 2018; lect.) 20th-century US, rural and agricultural, women; webermb@uwec.edu

Full-time Faculty

Ducksworth-Lawton, Selika Marianne (PhD, Ohio State 1993; prof.) 20th-century US, African American; duckswsm@uwec.edu

Mann, John W. W. (PhD, Washington State 2001; prof. and dir., grad. studies) America, public; mannjw@uwec.edu

Oberly, James W. (PhD, Rochester 1983; prof.) American economic, Civil War; joberly@uwec.edu

Patrick, Sue C. (PhD, Indiana 1988; prof.) US; business and finance; sue.patrick@uwc.edu

Rice, Louisa C. (PhD, Rutgers 2006; assoc. prof. and chair) modern Europe, global and comparative; ricelc@uwec.edu

Sanislo, Teresa (PhD, Michigan 2000; prof.) modern Germany, Europe, gender; sanisltm@uwec.edu

Shinno, Reiko (PhD, Stanford 2002; prof.) East Asia; shinnor@uwec.edu

Sturtevant, Andrew K. (PhD, William and Mary 2011; asst. prof.) Native American, early America; sturteak@uwec.edu

Turner, Patricia Regina (PhD, Michigan 1994; prof.) modern France, Europe; turnerpr@uwec.edu

Nondepartmental Historians

Licon, Gerardo (PhD, Southern California 2009; assoc. prof.; Latin American Studies) US Latino; licong@uwec.edu

Soll, David J. (PhD, Brandeis 2009; assoc. prof.; Watershed Inst. for Environmental Studies) environmental; solld@uwec.edu

Waters, Matthew W. (PhD, Pennsylvania 1997; prof.; chair, Languages) ancient Mediterranean; watersmw@uwec.edu

Retired/Emeritus Faculty

Gosch, Stephen S. (PhD, Rutgers 1972; prof. emeritus) world, social; stephengosch9@gmail.com

Gough, Deborah M. (PhD, Pennsylvania 1978; prof. emeritus) US women; goughdm@uwec.edu

Gough, Robert J. (PhD, Pennsylvania 1977; prof. emeritus) American social, social stratification and mobility, family; goughrj@uwec.edu

Haywood, Carl (PhD, Boston Univ. 1967; prof. emeritus and dean; Coll. of Arts and Sciences) Africa, Middle East; haywoocn@uwec.edu

Lang, Katherine Howe (PhD, Chicago 1997; prof. emeritus) Middle East, world, historiography; langkh@uwec.edu

Lauber, Jack M. (PhD, Iowa 1967; prof. emeritus) Russia, modern Europe, East Asia; lauberjm@uwec.edu

Lazda, Paulis I. (PhD, Wisconsin, Madison 1987; prof. emeritus) central and eastern Europe; lazdapi@uwec.edu

Mickel, Ronald E. (PhD, Wayne State 1961; prof. emeritus) US intellectual and cultural, US 1920-50; mickelre@uwec.edu

Miller, Thomas F. (PhD, Virginia 1981; prof. emeritus) early modern Europe, German Reformation, late medieval Europe; millert@uwec.edu

Pederson, Jane M. (PhD, Columbia 1987; prof. emeritus) Gilded Age, US women; pedersjm@uwec.edu

Pinero, Eugene (PhD, Connecticut 1987; prof. emeritus) Latin America; pineroe@uwec.edu

St. Germaine, Richard D. (PhD, Arizona State 1975; prof. emeritus) American Indian; stgermrd@uwec.edu

Wussow, Walter J. (PhD, Colorado, Boulder 1966; prof. emeritus) France, Germany, Reformation; wussowwj@uwec.edu

---

University of Wisconsin-La Crosse

Dept. of History, Rm. 401 Carl Wimberly Hall, 1725 State St., La Crosse, WI 54601-3742. 608.785.8350. Fax 608.785.8370. Email: jgrider@uwlax.edu. Website: https://www.uwlax.edu/history/.

The History Department offers instruction and opportunities in the history of regions and topics that span the entire world. In fact, the world is the specialty of this department. We are committed to a world history approach that forms the basis of our General Education survey courses, and also allows us to offer upper-division courses covering a vast variety of regions, time periods and themes.

Chair: John T. Grider
Degrees Offered: BA,BS
Academic Year System: Semester
Areas of Specialization: world, public/policy, social/cultural
Tuition (per academic year):
  In-State: $9258
  Out-of-State: $17928
Enrollment 2018-19:
  Undergraduate Majors: 159
  Degrees in History: 1 BA, 8 BS
Addresses:
  Admissions: http://www.uwlax.edu/admissions/
  Financial Aid: http://www.uwlax.edu/finaid/

Full-time Faculty

Beaujot, Ariel F. (PhD, Toronto 2008; assoc. prof.) public, modern Britain; abeaujot@uwlax.edu

Buffton, Deborah (PhD, Wisconsin-Madison 1987; prof.) China, France; dbuffton@uwlax.edu

Chavalas, Mark W. (PhD, UCLA 1988; prof.) Greece, Rome, ancient Near East; chavalas.mark@uwlax.edu

Grider, John T. (PhD, Colorado, Boulder 2006; prof. and chair) modern US; jgrider@uwlax.edu

Hardy, Penelope K. (PhD, Johns Hopkins 2017; asst. prof.) science and technology; phardy@uwlax.edu

Iguchi, Gerald Scott (PhD, California, San Diego 2006; assoc. prof.) modern Japan; iguchi.gera@uwlax.edu

Longhurst, James L. (PhD, Carnegie Mellon 2004; prof.) modern US, environmental; longhurs.jame@uwlax.edu

Macias-Gonzalez, Victor M. (PhD, Texas Christian 1999; prof.) Latin America; macias.vict@uwlax.edu

Morrison, Heidi (PhD, California, Santa Barbara 2009; assoc. prof.) modern Middle East; hmorrison@uwlax.edu

Pai, Gita V. (PhD, California, Berkeley 2010; assoc. prof.) South Asia, India; gpai@uwlax.edu

Shatara, Hanadi (MS, Pennsylvania 2009; asst. prof.) social studies education

Shonk, Kenneth Lee, Jr. (PhD, Marquette 2010; assoc. prof.) modern Ireland, world, history education; kshonk@uwlax.edu

Stovey, Patricia Ann (PhD, Wisconsin-Madison 2010; asst. prof.) education; pstovey@uwlax.edu

Trimmer, Tiffany A. (PhD, Northeastern 2007; assoc. prof.) social, migration and labor; ttrimmer@uwlax.edu

Trost, Jennifer (PhD, Carnegie Mellon 1996; assoc. prof.) American crime, surveillance and identification/identity theft, race relations; jtrost@uwlax.edu

Retired/Emeritus Faculty

Hollenback, Jess B. (PhD, UCLA 1988; assoc. prof. emeritus) world religions; hollenba.jess@uwlax.edu

Lee, Charles R. (PhD, SUNY, Buffalo 1978; prof. emeritus) oral and public; clee@uwlax.edu

Lybeck, Marti M. (PhD, Michigan 2007; retired asst. prof.) gender, modern Europe; lybeck.mart@uwlax.edu

Sinclair, Shelley A. (PhD, New Mexico 1991; assoc. prof. emeritus) Europe, medieval; sinclair.shel@uwlax.edu

Wegner, Gregory (PhD, Wisconsin-Madison 1989; prof. emeritus) Holocaust education; gwegner@uwlax.edu

---

University of Wisconsin-Madison

Dept. of History, 3211 Mosse Humanities Bldg., 455 N. Park St., Madison, WI 53706-1405. 608.263.1800. Fax 608.263.5302. Email: ankennison@wisc.edu. Website: https://history.wisc.edu/.

The History Department at the University of Wisconsin-Madison is consistently ranked among the very best in the nation. Our internationally recognized faculty offer training in a comprehensive array of regional and transnational fields, with strengths in virtually all areas of the world.

Chair: Leonora Neville
Director of Graduate Studies: Joseph R. Dennis
Director of Undergraduate Studies: Sarah Thal
Degrees Offered: BA,BS,MA,PhD
Academic Year System: Semester
Areas of Specialization: Africa, Asia, Europe, Latin America and Caribbean, US/North America, science/medicine/technology, gender and women, Jewish, war in society and culture

Undergraduate Tuition (per academic year):
In-State: $10556
Out-of-State: $37805
Graduate Tuition (per academic year):
In-State: $12010
Out-of-State: $25336
Enrollment 2018-19:
Undergraduate Majors: 400
New Graduate Students: 17
Full-time Graduate Students: 131
Degrees in History: 143 BA, 33 BS, 10 MA, 14 PhD
Undergraduate Addresses:
Admissions: https://www.wisc.edu/admissions/
Financial Aid: https://www.admissions.wisc.edu/prepare/costs.php
Graduate Addresses:
Admissions: https://grad.wisc.edu/apply/
Financial Aid: https://grad.wisc.edu/funding/

Affiliated Faculty

Chopra, Preeti (PhD, California, Berkeley 2003; assoc. prof.; Languages and Cultures of Asia) architecture and urbanism after 1750, spatial landscapes of empire, visual cultures of South Asia; chopra@wisc.edu

Clark-Pujara, Christy (PhD, Iowa 2009; assoc. prof.; Afro-American Studies) African American to 1900, US slavery, slavery and capitalism; clarkpujara@wisc.edu

Ermakoff, Ivan (PhD, Chicago; prof.; Sociology) political contention/regime breakdowns/state violence, Weimar Republic, French Third Republic/Vichy France; ermakoff@ssc.wisc.edu

Greene, Christina R. (PhD, Duke 1996; assoc. prof.; Afro-American Studies) black women, civil rights movement; cgreene2@wisc.edu

McGarr, Kathryn Jane (PhD, Princeton 2017; asst. prof.; School of Journalism & Mass Communication) 20th-century US, political, media; kmcgarr@wisc.edu

Nelson, Adam R. (PhD, Brown 1998; asst. prof.; Educational Policy Studies) America, intellectual and education, American social and political; anelson@education.wisc.edu

Sharafi, Mitra (PhD, Princeton 2006; assoc. prof.; Law Sch.) South Asian legal, colonialism, British Empire; sharafi@wisc.edu

Stern, Walter C (PhD, Tulane 2014; asst. prof.; Educational Policy Studies) US, urban, education, race; wcstern@wisc.edu

Full-time Faculty

Banerjee, Mou (PhD, Harvard 2018; asst. prof.) modern South Asia, religion and politics; mbanerjee4@wisc.edu

Boswell, Laird (PhD, California, Berkeley 1988; prof.) modern France, European social and political; lboswell@wisc.edu

Callaci, Emily J. (PhD, Northwestern 2012; assoc. prof.) Africa, urban, gender and sexuality; ejcallaci@wisc.edu

Chamedes, Giuliana R (PhD, Columbia 2013; asst. prof.) Europe, religious, Catholicism; chamedes@wisc.edu

Chan, Shelly P. (PhD, California, Santa Cruz 2009; assoc. prof.) modern China, diaspora/nation/gender, world; shelly.chan@wisc.edu

Cheng, Cindy I-Fen (PhD, California, Irvine 2004; prof.) US Cold War culture, Asian American history and culture, urban poverty; cicheng@wisc.edu

Ciancia, Kathryn (PhD, Stanford 2011; asst. prof.) modern Poland, 20th-century eastern Europe, nationalism; ciancia@wisc.edu

Cronon, William J. (DPhil, Oxford 1981; PhD, Yale 1990; Vilas Research Prof.) US West, environmental; bill@williamcronon.net

Dennis, Joe (PhD, Minnesota 2004; JD, Minnesota 1991; assoc. prof. and dir., grad. studies) Chinese social, Chinese print culture, Chinese legal; dennis3@wisc.edu

Desan, Suzanne (PhD, California, Berkeley 1985; prof.) early modern Europe, French Revolution; smdesan@wisc.edu

Enstad, Nan C. (PhD, Minnesota 1993; prof.) 20th-century US women, popular culture, race; nenstad@wisc.edu

Glotzer, Paige (PhD, Johns Hopkins 2016; asst. prof.) US, urban, politics and business

Hall, John W. (PhD, North Carolina, Chapel Hill 2007; assoc. prof.) military, American Indian, US; jwhall3@wisc.edu

Hansen, Anne (PhD, Harvard 1999; prof.) religion and Theravada Buddhism, Southeast Asia, religion and colonialism; arhansen@wisc.edu

Haynes, April R. (PhD, California, Santa Barbara 2009; assoc. prof. and assoc. chair) women and gender, sexuality, US 1790-1860; ahaynes4@wisc.edu

Hirsch, Francine (PhD, Princeton 1998; prof.) Russia and Soviet Union; fhirsch@wisc.edu

Hsia, Florence C. (PhD, Chicago 1999; prof.) early modern science, Scientific Revolution, science and print culture; fchsia@wisc.edu

Iber, Patrick J. (PhD, Chicago 2011; asst. prof.) Latin America, US foreign relations, intellectual; piber@wisc.edu

Kantrowitz, Stephen D. (PhD, Princeton 1995; prof.) 19th-century US, race, gender; skantrow@wisc.edu

Kennedy, Devin (PhD, Harvard 2019; asst. prof.) technology, computing, STS, business, US

Kim, Charles R. (PhD, Columbia 2007; assoc. prof.) Korea, cultural, diaspora; charles.kim@wisc.edu

Kinzley, Judd C. (PhD, California, San Diego 2012; assoc. prof.) modern China, environmental, political economy; kinzley@wisc.edu

Kleijwegt, Marc (PhD, Leiden, Netherlands 1991; prof.) community and society in Roman Empire, childhood and youth, slavery; marc.kleijwegt@wisc.edu

Kodesh, Neil R. (PhD, Northwestern 2004; prof.) precolonial Africa, eastern Africa; kodesh@wisc.edu

Lapina, Elizabeth (PhD, Johns Hopkins 2007; assoc. prof.) medieval, Crusades, Chronicles; lapina@wisc.edu

McCoy, Alfred William (PhD, Yale 1977; prof.) Southeast Asia, modern empires, global drug trafficking; awmccoy@wisc.edu

McDonald, David M. (PhD, Columbia 1988; prof.) imperial Russia, modern Europe; dmmcdon1@wisc.edu

Michels, Anthony E. (PhD, Stanford 1998; prof.) American Jewish, labor; aemichels@wisc.edu

Murthy, Viren (PhD, Chicago 2007; assoc. prof.) Asia, modern philosophy; vmurthy2@wisc.edu

Neville, Leonora (PhD, Princeton 1998; prof. and chair) Byzantium, late antiquity, Crusades; leonora.neville@wisc.edu

Nyhart, Lynn K. (PhD, Pennsylvania 1986; Bablitch-Keltch Vilas Prof.) modern biology, museums and informal education, evolutionary theory; lknyhart@wisc.edu

Ratner-Rosenhagen, Jennifer (PhD, Brandeis 2003; prof.) US cultural and intellectual; ratnerrosenh@wisc.edu

Roberts, Mary Louise (PhD, Brown 1990; prof.) modern France, European women, European cultural; maryroberts@wisc.edu

Rock-Singer, Aaron White (PhD, Princeton 2016; asst. prof.) Middle East, Islam, social movements; rocksinger@wisc.edu

Shoemaker, Karl B. (PhD, California, Berkeley 2001; prof.) medieval Europe, legal; kbshoemaker@wisc.edu

Stolz, Daniel (PhD, Princeton 2013; asst. prof.) Middle East, Islamic, science and technology; dastolz@wisc.edu

Sweet, James H. (PhD, Grad. Center, CUNY 1999; prof.) African diaspora, Brazil; jhsweet@wisc.edu

Taylor, Claire (PhD, Cambridge 2006; assoc. prof.) ancient Greece, social, gender; claire.taylor@wisc.edu

Thal, Sarah (PhD, Columbia 1999; prof. and dir., undergrad. studies) modern Japan, political, religion; thal@wisc.edu

Ussishkin, Daniel (PhD, California, Berkeley 2007; assoc. prof.) modern Britain, war and society, social sciences; ussishkin@wisc.edu

Wandel, Lee Palmer (PhD, Michigan 1985; prof.) early modern Europe, Reformation, cultural; lpwandel@wisc.edu

Whiting, Gloria McCahon (PhD, Harvard 2015; asst. prof.) early America, race and slavery in Atlantic world, women/gender/family; gwhiting@wisc.edu

Williford, Daniel J. (ABD, Michigan; asst. prof.) technology, North Africa and Middle East, environment

Young, Louise (PhD, Columbia 1993; prof.) modern Japan, social and cultural, international; louiseyoung@wisc.edu

Joint/Cross Appointments

Bitzan, Amos (PhD, California, Berkeley 2011; asst. prof.; Center for Jewish Studies) modern European Jewish, intellectual; abitzan@wisc.edu

Brown, Ashley (PhD, George Washington 2017; asst. prof.; African American Studies) African American, US, sports; abrown62@wisc.edu

Enke, A. Finn (PhD, Minnesota 1999; prof.; Gender and Women's Studies) gender, sexuality, US social movements; aenke@wisc.edu

Gómez, Pablo F. (PhD, Vanderbilt 2010; assoc. prof.; Medical Hist. and Bioethics) medicine, Latin America, Caribbean; pgomez@wisc.edu

Hennessy, Elizabeth A. (PhD, North Carolina, Chapel Hill 2014; asst. prof.; Nelson Inst.) world environmental, animal studies, geography; ehennessy2@wisc.edu

Houck, Judith A. (PhD, Wisconsin, Madison 1998; assoc. prof.; Medical Hist. and Bioethics) women's health, sexuality, body; jahouck@wisc.edu

Ipsen, Pernille (PhD, Copenhagen 2008; assoc. prof.; Gender and Women's Studies) Atlantic slave trade, gender and women; pipsen@wisc.edu

Keller, Richard C. (PhD, Rutgers 2001; prof.; Medical Hist. and Bioethics) psychiatry, colonial medicine, European medicine; rckeller@wisc.edu

Lederer, Susan E. (PhD, Wisconsin, Madison 1987; Robert Turell Prof.; chair, Medical Hist. and Bioethics) human experimentation, American science and medicine; selederer@wisc.edu

Mitman, Gregg (PhD, Wisconsin-Madison 1988; Vilas Research Prof.; Medical Hist. and Bioethics) environmental, science and medicine, American cultural; gmitman@med.wisc.edu

Nelson, Nicole C. (PhD, Cornell 2011; asst. prof.; Medical Hist. and Bioethics) science, medicine, science and technology studies; nicole.nelson@wisc.edu

Plummer, Brenda G. (PhD, Cornell 1981; prof.; Afro-American Studies) Afro-American, international; bplummer@wisc.edu

Ramirez, Marla Andrea (PhD, California, Santa Barbara 2015; asst. prof.; Chicana/o and Latina/o Studies) US, US-Mexico borderlands, race and ethnicity, gender and sexuality; ramireztahua@wisc.edu

Reese, William John (PhD, Wisconsin, Madison 1980; Vilas Research Prof.; Education Policy Studies) American education, reform movements; wjreese@wisc.edu

Nondepartmental Historians

Carlsson, Eric (PhD, Wisconsin-Madison 2006; assoc. lect.; Religious Studies) early modern Europe, intellectual and philosophical, religion; eric.carlsson@wisc.edu

Cullinane, Michael M. (PhD, Michigan 1989; teaching assoc.; Center for Southeast Asian Studies) 19th- and 20th-century Philippines, modern Southeast Asia, Southeast Asians in US; mmcullin@wisc.edu

Keyser, Richard L. (PhD, Johns Hopkins 2001; teaching assoc.; Center for Law, Society & Justice) medieval and early modern France, Europe, legal and environmental; rkeyser@wisc.edu

Rider, Robin E. (PhD, California, Berkeley 1980; sr. lect.; dir., Special Collections, Memorial Library) mathematics, printing; rrider@library.wisc.edu

Retired/Emeritus Faculty

Archdeacon, Thomas J. (PhD, Columbia 1971; prof. emeritus) immigration, quantitative analysis, ethnicity; tjarchde@wisc.edu

Barker, John W., Jr. (PhD, Rutgers 1961; prof. emeritus) Byzantine, music; jwbarker@wisc.edu

Broman, Thomas H. (PhD, Princeton 1987; prof. emeritus) 18th-century science, early modern medicine, science and public; thbroman@wisc.edu

Chamberlain, Michael M. (PhD, California, Berkeley 1992; prof. emeritus) medieval Middle East, Mediterranean, comparative; mchamber@wisc.edu

Coffman, Edward M. (PhD, Kentucky 1959; prof. emeritus) US military

Cohen, Charles Lloyd (PhD, California, Berkeley 1982; prof. emeritus) colonial North America, American religious, American Indian to 1815; clcohen@wisc.edu

Cooper, John Milton, Jr. (PhD, Columbia 1968; prof. emeritus) late 19th- and early 20th-century US, US South; jmcooper@wisc.edu

Courtenay, William J. (PhD, Harvard 1967; prof. emeritus) medieval social and intellectual, paleography; wjcourte@wisc.edu

Dickey, Laurence W., III (PhD, California, Berkeley 1980; prof. emeritus) European intellectual; laurencedickey@gmail.com

Donnelly, James Stephen, Jr. (PhD, Harvard 1971; prof. emeritus) modern Britain and Ireland; jsdonnel@wisc.edu

Dunlavy, Colleen A. (PhD, MIT 1988; prof. emeritus) capitalism, US business and technology, comparative; cdunlavy@wisc.edu

Frykenberg, Robert E. (PhD, London 1961; prof. emeritus) modern India, South Indian political/religious/social/cultural; frykenberg@wisc.edu

Gordon, Linda (PhD, Yale 1970; prof. emeritus) 20th-century US social/political/social policy, women and gender, family; lgordon@wisc.edu

Hamalainen, Pekka K. (PhD, Indiana 1966; prof. emeritus) Scandinavia; pkhamala@wisc.edu

Hilts, Victor L. (PhD, Harvard 1967; prof. emeritus) social and behavioral sciences; vlhilts@wisc.edu

Hollingsworth, J. Rogers (PhD, Chicago 1960; prof. emeritus) American social and political; hollingsjr@aol.com

Koshar, Rudy J., Jr. (PhD, Michigan 1979; prof. emeritus) European intellectual, religious, Germany; rjkoshar@wisc.edu

Leavitt, Judith W. (PhD, Chicago 1975; prof. emeritus) American medicine and public health, women and medicine; jwleavit@wisc.edu

Lee, Jean Butenhoff (PhD, Virginia 1984; prof. emerita) revolutionary America, US South to 1835, historical memory; jblee@wisc.edu

Lin, Yu-sheng (PhD, Chicago 1970; prof. emeritus) Chinese social and intellectual; yslin@wisc.edu

Mallon, Florencia E. (PhD, Yale 1980; prof. emeritus) Latin America, gender and ethnicity, nationalism; femallon@wisc.edu

Mazzaoui, Maureen F. (PhD, Bryn Mawr 1966; prof. emeritus) medieval economic, Renaissance Italy; mazzaoui@wisc.edu

McCormick, Thomas J. (PhD, Wisconsin, Madison 1960; prof. emeritus) American foreign relations; tmccormi@wisc.edu

Morgan, David O. (PhD, London 1977; prof. emeritus) premodern Middle East and Central Asia; domorgan@wisc.edu

Numbers, Ronald L. (PhD, California, Berkeley 1969; Hilldale and William Coleman Prof. emeritus) medical, American medicine and science, science/medicine/religion; rnumbers@wisc.edu

Payne, Stanley G. (PhD, Columbia 1960; prof. emeritus) Europe, fascism, Spain and Portugal; sgpayne@wisc.edu

Scarano, Francisco A. (PhD, Columbia 1978; prof. emeritus) Caribbean; fscarano@wisc.edu

Schultz, Stanley K. (PhD, Chicago 1969; prof. emeritus) US, urban; skschult@wisc.edu

Sewell, Richard H. (PhD, Harvard 1962; prof. emeritus) Civil War and Reconstruction; rhsewell@wisc.edu

Shank, Michael H. (PhD, Harvard 1983; prof. emeritus) medieval and early modern science; mhshank@wisc.edu

Sharpless, John B., II (PhD, Michigan 1975; prof. emeritus) 19th-century and early American social and cultural, quantitative methods; jbsharpl@wisc.edu

Siegel, Daniel M. (PhD, California, Berkeley 1967; prof. emeritus) modern physics; dmsiegel@wisc.edu

Sommerville, Johann (PhD, Cambridge 1981; prof. emeritus) early modern Britain, European intellectual; jsommerv@wisc.edu

Sorkin, David (PhD, California, Berkeley 1983; prof. emeritus) European Jewish, Enlightenment and religion, comparative toleration and emancipation; djsorkin@gmail.com

Spear, Thomas T. (PhD, Wisconsin, Madison 1974; prof. emeritus) precolonial Africa, eastern and southern Africa; tspear@wisc.edu

Stern, Steve J. (PhD, Yale 1979; prof. emeritus) Latin America, social; sjstern@wisc.edu

Winichakul, Thongchai (PhD, Sydney, Australia 1988; prof. emeritus) Southeast Asia; twinicha@wisc.edu

Wink, Andre (PhD, Leiden, Netherlands 1984; prof. emeritus) India and Indian Ocean area; awink@wisc.edu

Recently Awarded PhDs

Bae, So Yeon "Rewriting Domitian's Tyranny"

Bilotte, Meggan L. "Becoming Native: Family Labor and the Construction of Belonging in Northern Colorado Sugar Beet Communities, 1900-75"

Cedillo, Adela "Intersections between the Dirty War and the War on Drugs in Northwestern Mexcio, 1969-85"

Essame, Jeanne "Diaspora as Detour: Haitian Émigrés during the Duvalier Years, 1950s-80s"

George, Brendon "Mile High Metropole: Denver and the US Empire"

Greeney, Spring "Line Dry: An Environmental History of Laundry Work, 1845-1992"

Park, Eunhee "Bittersweet Home: Navigating the Elusive Middle-Class Aspiration of Homeownership through Women's Financial Strategies in South Korea from the 1960s to the 1970s"

Puchalski, Piotr "Beyond Empire: Interwar Poland and Maritime Colonialism, 1918-39"

Reiter, Matthew "The Rustbelt Right: The Midwestern Origins of Modern Conservatism"

Shannon, Benjamin T. "The Political Evensong: Christian Renewal and the West German New Left"

Stanton, Megan "All in the Family: Ecclesiastical Authority and Family Theology in The Church of Jesus Christ of Latter-day Saints"

Wells, Richard Evan "The Manchurian Bean: How the Soybean Shaped the Modern History of China's Northeast, 1862-1945"

Wersan, Kate "Between the Calendar and the Clock: An Environmental History of American Timekeeping, 1660-1920"

University of Wisconsin-Milwaukee

Dept. of History, PO Box 413, Milwaukee, WI 53201-0413. 414.229.4361. Fax 414.229.2435. Email: history@uwm.edu. Website: https://uwm.edu/history/.

WM Department of History's faculty, staff, and students pursue research and teaching interests that span the globe. We provide undergraduate and graduate students with the opportunity to engage in the process of historical discovery and analysis, giving them skills and knowledge that will be useful in every kind of work and in civic life.

Chair: Joseph A. Rodriguez
Director of Graduate Studies: Joe Austin
Director of Undergraduate Studies: Lex Renda and Lisa Silverman
Degrees Offered: BA,MA,MA/MLIS,PhD
Academic Year System: Semester
Areas of Specialization: public, modern, global, urban
Undergraduate Tuition (per academic year):
  In-State: $9588
  Out-of-State: $20867
Graduate Tuition (per academic year):
  In-State: $11884
  Out-of-State: $24921
Enrollment 2018-19:
  Undergraduate Majors: 85
  New Graduate Students: 16
  Full-time Graduate Students: 57
  Part-time Graduate Students: 9
  Degrees in History: 40 BA, 9 MA, 3 PhD
Undergraduate Addresses:
  Admissions: http://www4.uwm.edu/admission/
  Financial Aid: http://uwm.edu/financialaid
Graduate Addresses:
  Admissions: https://uwm.edu/history/graduate/
  Financial Aid: http://uwm.edu/financialaid

Full-time Faculty

Alinder, Jasmine (PhD, Michigan 1999; assoc. prof.) public, visual culture, museum studies; jalinder@uwm.edu

Austin, Joe (PhD, Minnesota 1996; assoc. prof. and dir., grad. studies) modern US urban, popular, youth culture; jaustin@uwm.edu

Buff, Rachel (PhD, Minnesota 1995; prof.) modern US social and cultural, immigration and ethnicity; rbuff@uwm.edu

Cantwell, Christopher D. (PhD, Cornell 2011; asst. prof.) fundamentalism and lay Bible study practices, gender and lived religion in America

Carlin, Martha (PhD, Toronto 1984; prof.) medieval, Britain, London; carlin@uwm.edu

Carter, Gregory (PhD, Texas, Austin 2007; assoc. prof.) mixed race identity, comparative ethnic studies, popular culture; cartergt@uwm.edu

Chu, Winson W. (PhD, California, Berkeley 2006; assoc. prof.) modern central Europe; wchu@uwm.edu

Divalerio, David (PhD, Virginia 2011; assoc. prof.) religion, Tibetan Buddhism; divaleri@uwm.edu

Evans, Christine Elaine (PhD, California, Berkeley 2010; assoc. prof.) modern Russia/Soviet Union; evansce@uwm.edu

Filippello, Marcus (PhD, California, Davis 2010; assoc. prof.) sub-Saharan Africa, environmental; filippem@uwm.edu

Haigh, Thomas (PhD, Pennsylvania 2003; assoc. prof.) computing; thaigh@uwm.edu

Howland, Douglas R. (PhD, Chicago 1989; prof.) modern China and Japan, cultural interaction, international law and state; dhowland@uwm.edu

Kim, Nan (PhD, California, Berkeley 2007; assoc. prof.) modern Korea, family and gender, cultural and public; ynkp@uwm.edu

McGuinness, Aims C., III (PhD, Michigan 2001; assoc. prof.) Latin America, global; smia@uwm.edu

Pease, Neal H. (PhD, Yale 1982; prof.) Poland, eastern Europe; pease@uwm.edu

Renda, Lex (PhD, Virginia 1991; assoc. prof. and co-dir., undergrad. studies) mid-19th-century US; renlex@uwm.edu

Rodriguez, Joseph A. (PhD, California, Berkeley 1990; prof. and chair) US minorities, urban; joerod@uwm.edu

Rothfels, Nigel T. (PhD, Harvard 1994; assoc. prof.) rothfels@uwm.edu

Seligman, Amanda I. (PhD, Northwestern 1999; prof.) US urban and social, public policy, community organizing; seligman@uwm.edu

Silverman, Lisa (PhD, Yale 2004; assoc. prof. and co-dir., undergrad. studies) modern Jewish, cultural, gender; silverld@uwm.edu

Vang, Chia Youyee (PhD, Minnesota 2006; prof.) modern Hmong/Southeast Asia; vangcy@uwm.edu

Joint/Cross Appointments

Eichner, Carolyn J. (PhD, UCLA 1996; assoc. prof.; Women's and Gender Studies) women's studies, modern Europe, modern France; eichner@uwm.edu

Retired/Emeritus Faculty

Anderson, Margo J. (PhD, Rutgers 1978; prof. emeritus) US urban and social, quantitative methods; margo@uwm.edu

Bartley, Russell H. (PhD, Stanford 1971; prof. emeritus) Latin America, Spain and Portugal, historiography; bartleyr@uwm.edu

Buck, David D. (PhD, Stanford 1972; prof. emeritus) China, urban; davebuck@uwm.edu

Gordon, Michael A. (PhD, Rochester 1977; assoc. prof. emeritus) US labor, public; mgordon@uwm.edu

Hamdani, Abbas (PhD, London 1950; prof. emeritus) Islamic, Middle East and North Africa, medieval; ahamdani@uwm.edu

Hitz, Elizabeth (PhD, NYU 1978; sr. lect. emeritus) US social and technology, women, public; ehitz@uwm.edu

Hoeveler, J. David, Jr. (PhD, Illinois, Urbana-Champaign 1971; prof. emeritus) US intellectual, religious; jdh2@uwm.edu

Horsman, Reginald (PhD, Indiana 1958; prof. emeritus) early national US, US expansion, 19th-century US diplomatic; horsman@uwm.edu

Levine, Marc V. (PhD, Pennsylvania 1982; prof. emeritus) North American urban, public policy, Canada and Québec; veblen@uwm.edu

McBride, Genevieve (PhD, Wisconsin, Madison 1989; prof. emeritus) US women, advertising and popular culture, Wisconsin; gmcbride@uwm.edu

Merrick, Jeffrey W. (PhD, Yale 1979; prof. emeritus) early modern France, intellectual and cultural, gender and sexuality; jmerrick@uwm.edu

Meyer, Stephen, III (PhD, Rutgers 1977; prof. emeritus) 20th-century US social/labor/cultural/gender; stemey@uwm.edu

Miller, Nathan (PhD, Columbia 1960; prof. emeritus) US economic; knmiller@uwm.edu

Pycior, Helena M. (PhD, Cornell 1976; prof. emeritus) science, intellectual, women; helena@uwm.edu

Ross, Ronald J. (PhD, California, Berkeley 1971; prof. emeritus) Germany, modern social and political, military; rjross@uwm.edu

Ruggiero, Kristin (PhD, Indiana 1979; prof. emeritus) Latin America; ruggiero@uwm.edu

Schroeder, John H. (PhD, Virginia 1971; prof. emeritus) 19th-century US, naval and maritime, diplomatic; jhs@uwm.edu

Shashko, Philip (PhD, Michigan 1969; prof. emeritus) modern Russia and Balkans, intellectual; pshashko@uwm.edu

Trattner, Walter I. (PhD, Wisconsin, Madison 1964; prof. emeritus) US social, social welfare and poverty, women; wit@uwm.edu

Weare, Walter B. (PhD, North Carolina, Chapel Hill 1970; assoc. prof. emeritus) Afro-American, US social, US South; bweare@uwm.edu

Wiesner-Hanks, Merry E. (PhD, Wisconsin-Madison 1979; prof. emeritus; Women's and Gender Studies) Renaissance, women, Christianity; merrywh@uwm.edu

Visiting Faculty

Cornell, Akikwe (ABD, Minnesota; vis. asst. prof.) American Indian, military; cornelaj@uwm.edu

Recently Awarded PhDs

Anthony, Steven A. "The Elaine Riot of 1919: Race, Class, and Labor in the Arkansas Delta"

Grensavitch, Krista M. "Reimagining the Object Lesson: A Method for Teaching and Learning in the Contemporary Feminist Classroom"

University of Wisconsin-Oshkosh

Dept. of History, 800 Algoma Blvd., Sage 3612, Oshkosh, WI 54901. 920.424.2456. Fax 920.424.0938. Email: kercher@uwosh. edu. Website: https://uwosh.edu/history/.

The Department of History at University of Wisconsin Oshkosh is dedicated to teaching and researching the history of the world. We believe that obtaining a nuanced and informed historical perspective can help every citizen think critically, clearly, and creatively.

Chair: Stephen Kercher
Degrees Offered: BA,BS
Academic Year System: Semester
Areas of Specialization: US, Europe, Russia, India and Southeast Asia, Latin America
Tuition (per academic year):
  In-State: $7357
  Out-of-State: $14930
Enrollment 2018-19:
  Undergraduate Majors: 145
  Degrees in History: 27 BA, 25 MA
Addresses:
  Admissions: http://admissions.uwosh.edu
  Financial Aid: http://admissions.uwosh.edu/costs-and-aid

Full-time Faculty

Frey, James W. (PhD, Wisconsin, Madison 2000; assoc. prof.) South Asia; freyj@uwosh.edu

Kapelusz-Poppi, Ana Maria (PhD, Illinois, Chicago 2002; assoc. prof.) Latin America; kapelusz@uwosh.edu

Kercher, Stephen E. (PhD, Indiana 2000; prof. and chair) 20th-century US; kercher@uwosh.edu

Kuhl, Michelle M. (PhD, SUNY, Binghamton 2004; assoc. prof.) 19th-century US; kuhlm@uwosh.edu

Loewenstein, Karl E. (PhD, Duke 1999; assoc. prof.) Russia, eastern Europe; loewenst@uwosh.edu

Loiacono, Gabriel J. (PhD, Brandeis 2008; asst. prof.) early America, 19th-century US social/political/legal; loiacong@uwosh.edu

Mouton, Michelle (PhD, Minnesota 1997; assoc. prof.) modern Europe, Germany, women; mouton@uwosh.edu

Rivers, Kimberly A. (PhD, Toronto 1995; prof.) medieval Europe; rivers@uwosh.edu

Rutz, Michael A. (PhD, Washington, St. Louis 2002; prof.) Britain, Africa; rutz@uwosh.edu

Joint/Cross Appointments

Feldman, James W. (PhD, Wisconsin, Madison 2004; assoc. prof.; Environmental Studies) US West, 20th-century US, environmental; feldmanj@uwosh.edu

Rensing, Susan M. (PhD, Minnesota 2006; asst. prof.; Women's Studies) US, women, science; rensings@uwosh.edu

Part-time Faculty

Pickron, Jeffrey W. (PhD, SUNY, Binghamton 2013; lect.) US, Europe; pickronj@uwosh.edu

Rowland, Thomas J. (PhD, George Washington 1992; sr. lect.) US, Europe; rowland@uwosh.edu

University of Wisconsin-Platteville

Dept. of History, 1 University Plaza, Platteville, WI 53818-3099. 608.342.1787. Fax 608.342.6039. Email: stanleya@uwplatt.edu; savoyr@uwplatt.edu. Website: https://campus.uwplatt.edu/history.

UW-Platteville offers a major and minor in history. The strengths developed in the study of history (analysis, synthesis, and communication) make history an excellent liberal arts base for advanced professional training in law or business.

Chair: Adam Stanley
Degrees Offered: BA,BS
Academic Year System: Semester
Areas of Specialization: US, Europe, Asia, Latin America
Tuition (per academic year):
  In-State: $6298
  Out-of-State: $13871
Enrollment 2018-19:
  Undergraduate Majors: 81
  Degrees in History: 16 BA
Addresses:
  Admissions: http://campus.uwplatt.edu/admission
  Financial Aid: http://campus.uwplatt.edu/financial-aid

Adjunct Faculty

Carey, Delbert (PhD, Marquette 2000; adj.) world civilization, modern Europe, France; careyd@uwplatt.edu

Grant, Paul G. (PhD, Wisconsin, Madison 2017; adj.) Africa, world religions, migration; grantp@uwplatt.edu

Gurman, Scott (PhD, Northern Illinois 2012; adj.) US foreign relations, world, Philippines; gurmans@uwplatt.edu

Full-time Faculty

Gormley, Melissa E. (PhD, California, Davis 2006; assoc. prof. and interim dean; Coll. of Liberal Arts & Education) Latin America, medicine/women and gender, Atlantic world and Africa; gormleym@uwplatt.edu

Ivanov, Andrey V. (PhD, Yale 2012; asst. prof.) Russia, early modern Russian church, Central Asia; ivanovan@uwplatt.edu

Krugler, David (PhD, Illinois, Urbana-Champaign 1997; prof.) 20th-century America, African American; kruglerd@uwplatt.edu

Lee, Joong-Jae (PhD, NYU 2000; assoc. prof.) American labor, East Asia, technology; leejo@uwplatt.edu

Stanley, Adam C. (PhD, Purdue 2004; prof. and chair) early modern and 20th-century Europe, France and Germany, gender; stanleya@uwplatt.edu

Tesdahl, Eugene R. H. (PhD, Colorado, Boulder 2012; asst. prof.) Native American, colonial America, American women; tesdahle@uwplatt.edu

Turner, Nancy L. (PhD, Iowa 1996; prof.) medieval/Renaissance/Reformation Europe, Middle East, science; turnern@uwplatt.edu

Retired/Emeritus Faculty

Hellert, Susan (MA, Loras 1986; sr. lect. emeritus) world civilization, US survey, Wisconsin; hellert@uwplatt.edu

Nelson, Paula M. (PhD, Iowa 1984; prof. emeritus) American West, American women, American social; nelsonp@uwplatt.edu

Roberts, Tracey Lee (MA, Illinois, Chicago 1986; sr. lect. emeritus) world civilizations, 19th-century Europe, US immigration; robertstra@uwplatt.edu

Rowley, David G. (PhD, Michigan 1982; prof. emeritus) modern Europe, Russia, Great Britain; rowleyd@uwplatt.edu

University of Wisconsin-Stevens Point

Dept. of History and International Studies, 477 Collins Classroom Center, Stevens Point, WI 54481-1909. 715.346.2334. Fax 715.346.4489. Email: lwillis@uwsp.edu. Website: https://www.uwsp.edu/history/.

The traditional history major and history minor are designed for students preparing to teach and for those interested in such fields as law and library science. The department requires students to take coursework in US, world regional, and global/comparative history. Students may also take a concentration in race and ethnicity.

Chair: Lee L. Willis
Director of Graduate Studies: Edgar Francis
Degrees Offered: BA,BS,MST
Academic Year System: Semester
Areas of Specialization: world/global, US and Native American, Europe, Latin America, Asia, Africa and Middle East
Enrollment 2018-19:
  Undergraduate Majors: 107
  Degrees in History: 15 BA, 14 BS
Undergraduate Tuition (per academic year):
  In-State: $7511
  Out-of-State: $15084
Graduate Tuition (per academic year):
  In-State: $8718
  Out-of-State: $17849
Addresses:
  Admissions: http://www.uwsp.edu/admissions/
  Financial Aid: http://www.uwsp.edu/finaid/

Full-time Faculty

Barker, Brett R. (PhD, Wisconsin, Madison 2001; prof.) US, Native American, African American, Europe; bbarker@uwsp.edu

Barske, Valerie H. (PhD, Illinois, Urbana-Champaign 2008; assoc. prof.) East Asia; vbarske@uwsp.edu

Francis, Edgar Walter IV (PhD, UCLA 2005; assoc. prof. and dir., grad. studies) Islamic studies; efrancis@uwsp.edu

Hale, Brian J. (PhD, Wisconsin, Madison 1992; assoc. prof.) Germany, western Europe; bhale@uwsp.edu

Harper, Rob (PhD, Wisconsin, Madison 2008; assoc. prof.) US, Native American; rharper@uwsp.edu

Jessee, E. Jerry (PhD, Montana State, Bozeman 2012; asst. prof.) science, global environmental; jerry.jessee@uwsp.edu

Kleiman, Jeffrey (PhD, Michigan State 1985; prof.) Holocaust, American religion and politics, American ethnic, Jews and Judaism; jkleiman@uwc.edu

Leigh, Jeffrey T. (PhD, Indiana 1997; prof.) Russia; jleigh@uwsp.edu

LoPatin-Lummis, Nancy (PhD, Washington, St. Louis 1988; prof.) modern Britain; nlopatin@uwsp.edu

Prendergast, Neil D. (PhD, Arizona 2011; assoc. prof.) US environmental; nprender@uwsp.edu

Scripps, Sarah Michel (PhD, South Carolina 2014; asst. prof.) public; sscripps@uwsp.edu

Willis, Lee L., III (PhD, Florida State 2006; prof. and chair) US, African American, American South; lwillis@uwsp.edu

Nondepartmental Historians

Summers, Gregory S. (PhD, Wisconsin, Madison 2001; assoc. prof.; provost and vice chancellor) US, environmental, Wisconsin; gsummers@uwsp.edu

Yonke, Eric J. (PhD, North Carolina, Chapel Hill 1990; prof.; dir., International Progs.) modern Germany; eyonke@uwsp.edu

Retired/Emeritus Faculty

Brewer, Susan A. (PhD, Cornell 1991; prof. emeritus) American foreign relations; sbrewer@uwsp.edu

Kaminski, Theresa (PhD, Illinois, Urbana-Champaign 1992; prof. emeritus) US women; tkaminsk@uwsp.edu

University of Wisconsin-Whitewater

Dept. of History, 5221 Laurentide Hall, 800 W. Main St., Whitewater, WI 53190-1705. 262.472.1103. Fax 262.472.1611. Email: thibodj@uww.edu. Website: https://www.uww.edu/cls/departments/history.

The History Department at UW-Whitewater offers students three 36-unit tracks in history, public history, or secondary education, as well as a two minor programs in history and history education. The department offers BA and BS degrees and also offers a BS in education for students wishing to teach history or social studies at the elementary, middle, or high school level.

Chair: Jennifer Thibodeaux
Degrees Offered: BA,BS,BSE
Academic Year System: Semester
Areas of Specialization: US and Latin America, Africa, East Asia, Europe, public
Tuition (per academic year):
  In-State: $7692
  Out-of-State: $16265
Enrollment 2018-19:
  Undergraduate Majors: 149
Addresses:
  Admissions: http://www.uww.edu/admissions
  Financial Aid: http://www.uww.edu/financialaid/

Full-time Faculty

Brown, Karl William (PhD, Texas, Austin 2007; asst. prof.) Europe; brownk@uww.edu

Coons, James (PhD, Wisconsin, Madison 2014; asst. prof.) modern Europe

Gulig, Anthony G. (PhD, Saskatchewan 1997; assoc. prof.) American and Canadian West, American Indian and Canadian First Nations, environmental; guliga@uww.edu

Hyun, Sinae (PhD, Wisconsin-Madison 2014; asst. prof.) East Asia

Kreitlow, Bert S. (PhD, Iowa 2002; lect.) Latin America; kreitlob@uww.edu

Levy, James Anders (PhD, Rutgers 2006; assoc. prof.) America, race and ethnicity in America, public; levyj@uww.edu

Nath, Kimberly (PhD, Delaware 2016; asst. prof.) colonial America

Paddock, Adam John (PhD, Texas, Austin 2012; assoc. prof.) Africa; paddocka@uww.edu

Patterson, Molly Benjamin (PhD, Wisconsin, Madison 2009; assoc. prof.) Middle East; pattersm@uww.edu

Thibodeaux, Jennifer D. (PhD, Kansas 2004; prof. and chair) ancient, medieval Europe; thibodej@uww.edu

Vang, Nengher N. (PhD, Minnesota 2010; asst. prof.) transnational, foreign policy, America; vangn@uww.edu

Nondepartmental Historians

Hachten, Elizabeth A. (PhD, Wisconsin, Madison 1991; asst. dean; Coll. Letters and Sciences) Russia, medicine and science; hachtene@uww.edu

Wisconsin Lutheran College

Dept. of History, 8800 W. Bluemound Rd., Milwaukee, WI 53226-4699. 414.443.8561. Email: aaron.palmer@wlc.edu. Website: http://www.wlc.edu/History/.

WLC's history faculty have earned graduate degrees from top-level institutions and regularly present at conferences and publish books and articles. Our faculty members are teaching scholars who personally interact with students, get to know them, involve students in scholarship, and use their scholarship to enhance the student's experience in the classroom. All WLC history courses are taught from a Lutheran theological perspective. Instruction is shaped according to Scripture and the Lutheran Confessions—a focus virtually unique in American higher education.

Chair: Aaron J. Palmer
Degrees Offered: BA,BS
Academic Year System: Semester
Areas of Specialization: US, Europe, early America, Atlantic, military, ancient
Enrollment 2018-19:
  Undergraduate Majors: 20
  Degrees in History: 5 BA
Tuition (per academic year): $30850
Addresses:
  Admissions and Financial Aid: http://www.wlc.edu/admissions-and-aid/

Full-time Faculty

Beck, Paul (PhD, Marquette 1996; prof.) US Civil War, Native American, military; paul.beck@wlc.edu

Finnigan, Sheena (ABD, Wisconsin, Madison; asst. prof.) ancient Rome, medieval, Islam, women; sheena.finnigan@wlc.edu

Palmer, Aaron (PhD, Georgetown 2009; prof.) colonial America, American Revolution; aaron.palmer@wlc.edu

Retired/Emeritus Faculty

Kiecker, James (PhD, Marquette 1978; prof. emeritus) Reformation, European intellectual, church

Wittenberg University

Dept. of History, PO Box 720, Springfield, OH 45501-0720. 937.327.7836. Fax 937.327.7893. Email: craffensperger@ wittenberg.edu. Website: https://www5.wittenberg.edu/ academics/history.

As a history major, you will acquire skills in articulating different points of views, analyzing evidence and ideas, enhancing your ability to communicate your ideas in writing, and persuasively presenting your work to an audience. Critical thinking and the ability to understand divergent views is a universal skill you will develop while at Wittenberg.

Chair: Christian Raffensperger
Degrees Offered: BA
Academic Year System: Semester
Areas of Specialization: ancient and medieval, Eurasia, America and diplomacy, Africa, world
Tuition (per academic year): $38030
Enrollment 2018-19:
 Undergraduate Majors: 56
 Degrees in History: 13 BA
Addresses:
 Admissions: http://www.wittenberg.edu/admission
 Financial Aid: http://www.wittenberg.edu/admission/financials

Full-time Faculty

Brooks Hedstrom, Darlene L. (PhD, Miami, Ohio 2001; prof. and Wray Chair, Humanities; Archaeology) late antiquity and archaeology, Byzantium, ancient Mediterranean; dbrookshedstrom@wittenberg.edu

Raffensperger, Christian A. (PhD, Chicago 2006; assoc. prof. and chair) Russia, Byzantium, medieval Europe; craffensperger@ wittenberg.edu

Rosenberg, Scott P. (PhD, Indiana 1998; prof.) Africa, African American; srosenberg@wittenberg.edu

Taylor, Thomas T. (PhD, Illinois, Urbana-Champaign 1988; prof.) early America, American intellectual and religious; ttaylor@ wittenberg.edu

Wood, Molly M. (PhD, South Carolina 1998; prof.) modern US, US diplomatic, Latin America; mwood@wittenberg.edu

Retired/Emeritus Faculty

Behrman, Cynthia F. (PhD, Boston Univ. 1965; prof. emeritus) modern England, women; cbehrman@wittenberg.edu

Cutler, Robert S. (PhD, Michigan State 1970; assoc. prof. emeritus) ancient, medieval and early modern; bob8954@yahoo.com

Hartje, Robert G. (PhD, Vanderbilt 1955; prof. emeritus) colonial America, early 19th-century America, US South

Hayden, Albert A. (PhD, Wisconsin, Madison 1959; prof. emeritus) Britain

Huffman, James L. (PhD, Michigan 1972; prof. emeritus) modern Japan, press; jhuffman@wittenberg.edu

O'Connor, Joseph E. (PhD, Virginia 1968; prof. emeritus) Russia and former Soviet Union; jeoconnor@wittenberg.edu

Ortquist, Richard T. (PhD, Michigan 1968; prof. emeritus) recent US, US diplomatic, legal and constitutional; rortquist@ wittenberg.edu

College of Wooster

Dept. of History, Kauke Hall, 400 E. University St., Wooster, OH 44691. 330.263.2463. Fax 330.263.2614. Email: history@ wooster.edu. Website: https://www.wooster.edu/departments/ history/.

At Wooster, we believe that the best way to understand history is to do history. We encourage students to ask questions about the past (and the present), to bring their own skills of critical thinking and interpretation to the sources of history.

Chair: Shannon King
Degrees Offered: BA
Academic Year System: Semester
Areas of Specialization: US, Europe, Asia, Africa, Latin America
Tuition (per academic year): $50250
Enrollment 2018-19:
 Undergraduate Majors: 108
 Degrees in History: 33 BA
Addresses:
 Admissions: http://www.wooster.edu/admissions/
 Financial Aid: http://www.wooster.edu/admissions/aid/

Full-time Faculty

Hettinger, Madonna J. (PhD, Indiana 1986; prof.) late medieval Europe, social and cultural; mhettinger@wooster.edu

Holt, Katherine (PhD, Princeton 2005; assoc. prof.) Latin America; kholt@wooster.edu

King, Shannon (PhD, SUNY, Binghamton 2006; asst. prof. and chair) African American, intellectual; sking@wooster.edu

Ng, Margaret Wee-Siang (PhD, McGill 2013; asst. prof.) Chinese medicine, gender; mng@wooster.edu

Pozefsky, Peter C. (PhD, UCLA 1993; prof.) Russia, Europe, cultural and intellectual; ppozefsky@wooster.edu

Roche, Jeff (PhD, New Mexico 2001; assoc. prof.) recent US, political, regional; jroche@wooster.edu

Sene, Ibra (PhD, Michigan State 2008; asst. prof.) Africa; isene@ wooster.edu

Shaya, Gregory K. (PhD, Michigan 2000; assoc. prof.) modern France, Europe, North Africa; gshaya@wooster.edu

Walters, Jordan Biro (PhD, New Mexico 2015; asst. prof.) 20th-century US, western America, women/gender/sexuality/LGBTQ; jbiro@wooster.edu

Welsch, Christina C. (PhD, Princeton 2016; asst. prof.) Britain, military; cwelsch@wooster.edu

Joint/Cross Appointments

Friedman, Joan S. (PhD, Columbia 2003; assoc. prof.; Religious Studies) modern Jewish; jfriedman@wooster.edu

Nondepartmental Historians

Hickey, Damon D. (PhD, South Carolina 1989; library dir. emeritus) American religious; dhickey@wooster.edu

Meyer, Jimmy E. Wilkinson (PhD, Case Western Reserve 1993; asst. ed.; Wooster magazine) women; jmeyer@wooster.edu

Miller, David B. (PhD, Yale 1971; financial aid dir. emeritus) church; dmiller@wooster.edu

Retired/Emeritus Faculty

Calhoun, Daniel F. (PhD, Chicago 1959; prof. emeritus) Soviet and imperial Russia; dcalhoun@wooster.edu

Copeland, Henry J. (PhD, Cornell 1966; prof. emeritus) modern France, modern Europe; hcopeland@wooster.edu

Gates, John M. (PhD, Duke 1967; prof. emeritus) war and revolution; jgates@wooster.edu

Gedalecia, David (PhD, Harvard 1971; prof. emeritus) China, Japan; dgedalecia@wooster.edu

Hodges, James A. (PhD, Vanderbilt 1963; prof. emeritus) 20th-century US, US South, labor; jhodges@wooster.edu

Holliday, Vivian L. (PhD, North Carolina, Chapel Hill 1961; prof. emeritus) ancient; vholliday@wooster.edu

Schilling, Hayden (PhD, Vanderbilt 1970; prof. emeritus) early modern Europe, Tudor-Stuart England, Britain since 1714; hschilling@wooster.edu

Taylor, Karen (PhD, Duke 1988; assoc. prof. emeritus) early US, gender and sexuality; ktaylor@wooster.edu

Worcester State University

Dept. of History and Political Science, 486 Chandler St., Worcester, MA 01602-2597. 508.929.8162. Fax 508.929.8155. Email: mflibbert@worcester.edu; challer1@worcester.edu. Website: https://www.worcester.edu/History-and-Political-Science/.

Build a deeper understanding of our contemporary world by studying the past. You will develop a strong foundation in historical thinking, research skills and methods, and expand your capacity to contribute to our increasingly global society as a well-informed citizen. In lively, interactive classroom exchanges, you'll analyze the meaning of past events and acquire an informed perspective on your own heritage and the heritage of people around the world.

Chair: Charlotte Haller
Director of Graduate Studies: Tona Hangen
Degrees Offered: BA,MA
Academic Year System: Semester
Areas of Specialization: political science, pre-law, Middle East studies, public
Undergraduate Tuition (per academic year):
In-State: $10160
Out-of-State: $16240
Graduate Tuition (per academic year): $5800
Enrollment 2018-19:
Undergraduate Majors: 150
New Graduate Students: 6
Part-time Graduate Students: 34
Degrees in History: 40 BA, 8 MA
Students in Undergraduate Courses: 1240
Students in Undergraduate Intro Courses: 870
Online-Only Courses: 15%
Undergraduate Addresses:
Admissions: http://www.worcester.edu/Admissions/
Financial Aid: http://www.worcester.edu/Financial-Aid/
Graduate Addresses:
Admissions: http://worcester.edu/Graduate/
Financial Aid: http://www.worcester.edu/Financial-Aid/

Adjunct Faculty

Baker, Michael (MA, Worcester State 2014; instr.) US, Civil War, political science; mbaker4@worcester.edu

Corvi, Steven J. (PhD, Northeastern 2003; adj.) British military

Killeen, Patrick Ryan (MA, Worcester State 2013; instr.) US, political science; pkilleen@worcester.edu

LaFleche, Paul V. (BA, Assumption; adj.) 19th- and early 20th-century US; plafleche@worcester.edu

Full-time Faculty

Angelo, Nathan J. (PhD, New School 2015; asst. prof.) American politics, racial and ethnic politics, civil liberties and civil rights; nangelo@worcester.edu

Briesacher, Erika L. (PhD, Kent State 2012; assoc. prof.) Europe, Germany, public; ebriesacher@worcester.edu

Dell'Aera, Anthony D. (PhD, Brown 2008; asst. prof.) American government, political theory, methodology; adellaera@worcester.edu

Fromm, Martin (PhD, Columbia 2010; assoc. prof.) Asia; mfromm@worcester.edu

Garcia-Guevara, Aldo Vladimir (PhD, Texas, Austin 2007; prof.) Latin America; agarciaguevara@worcester.edu

Gesin, Michael (PhD, Brandeis 2007; prof.) Jewish, Holocaust, Europe; mgesin@worcester.edu

Haller, Charlotte A. (PhD, Wisconsin-Madison 2000; prof. and chair) America, US women; challer1@worcester.edu

Hangen, Tona J. (PhD, Brandeis 1999; assoc. prof. and dir., grad. studies) US social and cultural, 19th- and 20th-century US, religion and popular culture; thangen@worcester.edu

Holloran, Peter C. (PhD, Boston Univ. 1982; prof.) American social and ethnic, popular culture, US; pholloran@worcester.edu

Mears, Tanya M. (PhD, Massachusetts Amherst 2005; assoc. prof.) African American, early America, New England; tmears@worcester.edu

Okuda, Alison K. (PhD, NYU 2016; asst. prof.) Africa; aokuda@worcester.edu

Saliba, Najib E. (PhD, Michigan 1971; prof.) Middle East studies, Middle East politics, 19th-century Europe; nsaliba@worcester.edu

Smith, Robert W. (PhD, William and Mary 1997; prof.) American foreign relations; rsmith1@worcester.edu

Retired/Emeritus Faculty

Baratta, Joseph P. (PhD, Boston Univ. 1982; assoc. prof. emeritus) diplomatic, Britain, science and technology; jbaratta@worcester.edu

Cohen, Bruce S. (ABD, Rutgers 1964; assoc. prof. emeritus) labor, US, women; bcohen@worcester.edu

Twiss, David (MA, Assumption 1968; assoc. prof. emeritus) political science, American government

Visiting Faculty

Sculos, Bryant W. (PhD, Florida International 2017; vis. asst. prof.) international political theory, global politics, critical theory; bsculos@worcester.edu

University of Wyoming

Dept. of History & American Studies, Dept. 3198, 1000 E. University Ave., Laramie, WY 82071-3198. 307.766.5101. Fax 307.766.5192. Email: uwhistory@uwyo.edu. Website: https://www.uwyo.edu/history/.

Long committed to the history of the American West, the History Department at UW is uniquely positioned to situate this field in a global context. Drawing on expertise ranging from Europe, East and Central Asia, Africa, and the Americas, we strive to explore historical questions with thematic as well as comparative approaches. Our goal is to give students a truly global perspective on history.

Chair: Isadora Helfgott
Director of Graduate Studies: Jeffrey Means
Degrees Offered: BA,MA

Academic Year System: Semester
Areas of Specialization: US/US West/Native American, Africa, Atlantic world, modern Germany, medieval Europe
Undergraduate Tuition (per academic year):
In-State: $4747
Out-of-State: $14803
Graduate Tuition (per academic year):
In-State: $6289
Out-of-State: $16009
Enrollment 2018-19:
Undergraduate Majors: 150
New Graduate Students: 5
Full-time Graduate Students: 9
Degrees in History: 39 BA, 5 MA
Students in Undergraduate Courses: 1367
Students in Undergraduate Intro Courses: 526
Online-Only Courses: 32%
Undergraduate Addresses:
Admissions: http://www.uwyo.edu/admissions/
Financial Aid: http://www.uwyo.edu/sfa/
Graduate Addresses:
Admissions: http://www.uwyo.edu/admissions/graduate/
Financial Aid: http://www.uwyo.edu/history/

Adjunct Faculty

Devine, Michael J. Esq. (PhD, Ohio State 1974; adj. prof.) public, US
Simpson, Peter K. (PhD, Oregon 1973; prof.) US West, Wyoming; psimpson@telegraph.uwyo.edu
Utterback, Kristine T. (PhD, Toronto 1985; assoc. prof.) medieval, ancient; utterbck@uwyo.edu

Full-time Faculty

Helfgott, Isadora A. (PhD, Harvard 2006; assoc. prof. and chair) 20th-century US cultural, museum studies; ihelfgot@uwyo.edu
Kelly, Alexandra (PhD, Stanford 2014; asst. prof.; Anthropology) Africa, Atlantic trade; alexandra.kelly@uwyo.edu
Laegreid, Renee M. (PhD, Nebraska 2002; prof.) 19th-century US, US West and transnational, gender; rlaegrei@uwyo.edu
Logan, Barbara Ellen (PhD, California, Santa Cruz 2002; extended term professional lect.; Gender & Women's Studies) medieval Europe, gender; blogan@uwyo.edu
Means, Jeff D. (PhD, Oklahoma 2007; assoc. prof. and dir., grad. studies) Plains Indians; jmeans4@uwyo.edu
Roberts, Phil (PhD, Washington 1990; prof.) Wyoming, American West, public and legal; philr@uwyo.edu

Retired/Emeritus Faculty

Dieterich, Herbert R. (PhD, New Mexico 1958; prof. emeritus) American studies, US cultural; herbrd@uwyo.edu
Hardy, Deborah W. (PhD, Washington 1968; prof. emeritus) modern Russia, 19th-century Europe
Kohler, Eric D. (PhD, Stanford 1971; assoc. prof. emeritus) modern Germany, 20th-century Europe
Moore, William H. (PhD, Texas, Austin 1971; prof. emeritus) US social, 20th-century US

Xavier University of Louisiana

Dept. of History, 1 Drexel Dr., New Orleans, LA 70125-1098. 504.520.7581. Fax 504.520.7938. Email: history@xula.edu. Website: https://www.xula.edu/department?id=history_e2642ea.

The History Department at Xavier University is made up of a diverse group of professors and dedicated students set within an intimate atmosphere. Our areas of expertise range from the United States to the ancient Mediterranean, from modern Latin America to 19th-century France, and from 20th-century Africa to colonial and postcolonial African diaspora studies.

Chair: Steven J. Salm
Degrees Offered: BA
Academic Year System: Semester
Areas of Specialization: Africa and African diaspora, African American, Latin America, US and Europe, women
Tuition (per academic year): $20594
Enrollment 2018-19:
Undergraduate Majors: 28
Degrees in History: 8 BA
Students in Undergraduate Courses: 425
Students in Undergraduate Intro Courses: 320
Addresses:
Admissions: http://www.xula.edu/admissions/
Financial Aid: http://www.xula.edu/financial-aid/

Full-time Faculty

Gaudin, Wendy A. (PhD, NYU 2005; asst. prof.) oral, immigration, diaspora studies; wgaudin@xula.edu
Huda, Shamsul (PhD, Illinois, Urbana-Champaign 1989; assoc. prof.) 19th-century US, South Asia; shuda@xula.edu
Manley, Elizabeth S. (PhD, Tulane 2008; assoc. prof.) Caribbean, Latin America, women; emanley1@xula.edu
Rotondo-McCord, Jonathan (PhD, Yale 1991; assoc. prof.) medieval Europe, comparative world, Southeast Asia; jrotondo@xula.edu
Salm, Steven J. (PhD, Texas, Austin 2003; prof. and chair) Africa, popular culture, urban; sjsalm@xula.edu
Sinegal-DeCuir, Sharlene Sinegal (PhD, Louisiana State 2009; assoc. prof.) African American, US, New Orleans; ssinegal@xula.edu
St. Julien, Danielle E. (MA, Louisiana, Lafayette 2009; instr.) 20th-century US political, African American, Louisiana

Nondepartmental Historians

Cox, Marcus (PhD, Northwestern 2001; prof.; assoc. dean, Grad. Programs and Summer Sch.) military, African American; mcox1@xula.edu
Lachoff, Irwin (PhD, New Orleans 1993; assoc. archivist) Jews in New Orleans, US southern Jews; ilachoff@xula.edu

Retired/Emeritus Faculty

Donaldson, Gary (PhD, Louisiana State 1983; prof. emeritus) modern US, presidential; gdonalds@xula.edu
Hughes, Barbara, CSJ (PhD, St. Louis 1972; prof. emeritus) modern Europe; bhughes@xula.edu

Xavier University

Dept. of History, 1496 Dana Ave., Cincinnati, OH 45207-5161. 513.745.2888. Fax 513.745.2074. Email: smythe@xavier.edu. Website: https://www.xavier.edu/history/.

Xavier's history department boasts a particularly active set of scholars committed to bringing historical perspective to some of the important questions faced by the world today. Our location in a large city with a rich history gives our students ample opportunities to see many aspects of history in the surrounding landscape, as well as in many of the fine cultural institutions nearby.

Chair: Kathleen Smythe
Degrees Offered: BA
Academic Year System: Semester

Areas of Specialization: US, England and Ireland, Europe, Latin America, Africa

Tuition (per academic year): $40220

Enrollment 2018-19:
Undergraduate Majors: 97
Degrees in History: 19 BA

Addresses:
Admissions: http://www.xavier.edu/admission/
Financial Aid: http://www.xavier.edu/financial-aid/

Full-time Faculty

Anderson, M. Christine (PhD, Ohio State 1986; assoc. prof.) American women, modern US; andersoc@xavier.edu

Browne, Randy M. (PhD, North Carolina, Chapel Hill 2012; asst. prof.) global, Atlantic slavery, African diaspora; browner@xavier.edu

Chrastil, Rachel A. (PhD, Yale 2005; prof. and assoc. dean) modern Europe, France; chrastilr@xavier.edu

Fairfield, John D. (PhD, Rochester 1984; prof.) modern America, recent US; fairfiel@xavier.edu

Grayson, Jennifer (PhD, Johns Hopkins 2017; asst. prof.) graysonj2@xavier.edu

Mengel, David C. (PhD, Notre Dame; prof. and dean) medieval Europe and Bohemia; mengel@xavier.edu

O'Hara, Julia Cummings (PhD, Indiana 2004; assoc. prof.) Latin America, Mexico; ohara@xavier.edu

O'Hara, Paul (PhD, Indiana 2007; assoc. prof.) modern US, American studies; oharas@xavier.edu

Rzeczkowski, Frank Roman (PhD, Northwestern 2003; teaching prof.) Native American; rzeczkowskif@xavier.edu

Smythe, Kathleen R. (PhD, Wisconsin, Madison 1997; prof. and chair) modern Africa; smythe@xavier.edu

Tiro, Karim Michel (PhD, Pennsylvania 1999; prof.) early America, Native American, Canada; tiro@xavier.edu

von Weissenberg, Marita (PhD, Yale 2013; asst. prof.) late medieval religious and social; vonweissenbergm@xavier.edu

Whipple, Amy C. (PhD, Northwestern 2004; assoc. prof.) modern Britain; whipplea@xavier.edu

Retired/Emeritus Faculty

Fortin, Roger A. (PhD, Lehigh 1969; prof. emeritus) US intellectual; fortin@xavier.edu

Korros, Alexandra S. (PhD, Columbia 1974; prof. emerita) Tsarist Russia, Soviet Union, Russian Jewish; korros@xavier.edu

LaRocca, John J. SJ (PhD, Rutgers 1977; prof. emeritus) Tudor-Stuart England, Reformation, popular piety; larocca@xavier.edu

Visiting Faculty

Quinn, James T. (PhD, Kansas 2011; temporary instr.) modern Europe; quinnj9@xavier.edu

Yale University

Dept. of History, PO Box 208324, New Haven, CT 06520-8324. 203.432.1366. Fax 203.432.7587. Email:dana.lee@yale.edu. Website: https://history.yale.edu/.

Alternate Address: 1037 Chapel St., New Haven, CT 06511

Yale's distinguished History faculty, among the most eminent in the world, teach and write the histories of Africa, Asia, Europe, Latin America, the Middle East, and the United States and Canada, from ancient times to the present, seeking to make its study as exciting and rewarding in the 21st century as it was when President Thomas Clap first introduced it at Yale before the American Revolution.

Chair: Alan Mikhail
Director of Graduate Studies: Paul Sabin
Director of Undergraduate Studies: Edward Rugemer
Degrees Offered: BA,MA,MPhil,PhD
Academic Year System: Semester
Areas of Specialization: Africa, early modern Europe, East Asia, global, Jewish, Latin America, medieval, Middle East, modern Europe, Russia and eastern Europe, Southeast Asia, US

Undergraduate Tuition (per academic year): $55500
Graduate Tuition (per academic year): $43300
Enrollment 2018-19:
Undergraduate Majors: 426
New Graduate Students: 24
Full-time Graduate Students: 179
Part-time Graduate Students: 5
Degrees in History: 137 BA, 27 MA, 18 PhD, 20 MPhil

Undergraduate Addresses:
Admissions: https://admissions.yale.edu/
Financial Aid: https://finaid.yale.edu/

Graduate Addresses:
Admissions: https://gsas.yale.edu/admission-graduate-school
Financial Aid: https://gsas.yale.edu/funding

Full-time Faculty

Allen, Jennifer L. (PhD, California, Berkeley 2015; asst. prof.) modern Europe; j.allen@yale.edu

Amanat, Abbas (DPhil, Oxford 1981; prof.) Middle East; abbas.amanat@yale.edu

Antonov, Sergei (PhD, Columbia 2011; asst. prof.) modern Russia; sergei.antonov@yale.edu

Bertucci, Paola (PhD, Oxford 2001; assoc. prof.) early modern science and medicine; paola.bertucci@yale.edu

Blight, David W. (PhD, Wisconsin-Madison 1985; prof.) US, Civil War; david.blight@yale.edu

Botsman, Daniel V. (PhD, Princeton 1999; prof.) Japan; daniel.botsman@yale.edu

Bushkovitch, Paul A. (PhD, Columbia 1975; prof.) pre-Petrine Russia, economic; paul.bushkovitch@yale.edu

Coen, Deborah Rachel (PhD, Harvard 2004; prof.) science and medicine; deborah.coen@yale.edu

De, Rohit (PhD, Princeton 2013; asst. prof.) South Asia; rohit.de@yale.edu

Dean, Carolyn J. (PhD, California, Berkeley 1987; prof.) 20th-century France, intellectual, gender studies; carolyn.dean@yale.edu

Drixler, Fabian F. (PhD, Harvard 2009; prof.) premodern Japan; fabian.drixler@yale.edu

Echeverri, Marcela (PhD, NYU 2008; asst. prof.) Latin America; marcela.echeverri@yale.edu

Eire, Carlos M. N. (PhD, Yale 1979; prof.; Religious Studies) Reformation; carlos.eire@yale.edu

Eller, Anne (PhD, NYU 2011; asst. prof.) Latin America; anne.eller@yale.edu

Freedman, Paul Harris (PhD, California, Berkeley 1978; prof.) medieval Europe, Spain; paul.freedman@yale.edu

Freeman, Joanne B. (PhD, Virginia 1998; prof.) early Republic US, American Revolution, politics; joanne.freeman@yale.edu

Gaddis, John Lewis (PhD, Texas, Austin 1968; prof.) Cold War, historical methodology, biography; john.gaddis@yale.edu

Gage, Beverly (PhD, Columbia 2004; prof.) 20th-century US politics; beverly.gage@yale.edu

Grandin, Greg (PhD, Yale 1999; prof.) Latin America

Hansen, Valerie (PhD, Pennsylvania 1987; prof.) premodern China, Silk Road, Chinese religion; valerie.hansen@yale.edu

Harms, Robert Wayne (PhD, Wisconsin, Madison 1978; prof.) Africa, environmental, slave trade; robert.harms@yale.edu

Ho, Denise Y. (PhD, Harvard 2009; asst. prof.) 20th-century China; denise.ho@yale.edu

Jacobson, Matthew F. (PhD, Brown 1992; prof.; American Studies) 20th-century US cultural, immigration, ethnicity; matthew.jacobson@yale.edu

Joseph, Gilbert M. (PhD, Yale 1978; prof.) Latin America, Mexico; gilbert.joseph@yale.edu

Kennedy, Paul M. (DPhil, Oxford 1970; prof.) Britain, international relations; paul.kennedy@yale.edu

Kiernan, Benedict F. (PhD, Monash, Australia 1983; prof.) early and modern Southeast Asia, Cambodian history and politics, genocide; ben.kiernan@yale.edu

Klein, Jennifer Lisa (PhD, Virginia 1999; prof.) US 1945-present; jennifer.klein@yale.edu

Magaziner, Daniel R. (PhD, Wisconsin, Madison 2007; prof.) modern Africa

Marcus, Ivan G. (PhD, Jewish Theological Sem. 1975; prof.; Religious Studies) medieval Jewish, Judaism; ivan.marcus@yale.edu

Merriman, John M. (PhD, Michigan 1972; prof.) modern France; john.merriman@yale.edu

Meyerowitz, Joanne (PhD, Stanford 1983; prof.) US women; joanne.meyerowitz@yale.edu

Mikhail, Alan (PhD, California, Berkeley 2008; prof. and chair) early modern Middle East; alan.mikhail@yale.edu

Nakhimovsky, Isaac (PhD, Harvard 2008; asst. prof.; Humanities) early modern intellectual; isaac.nakhimovsky@yale.edu

Pitti, Stephen J. (PhD, Stanford 1998; prof.; American Studies) Mexican American; stephen.pitti@yale.edu

Rankin, William J. (PhD, Harvard 2011; asst. prof.) science and medicine; william.rankin@yale.edu

Rugemer, Edward B. (PhD, Boston Coll. 2005; assoc. prof. and dir., undergrad. studies; African American Studies) pre-1863 African American; edward.rugemer@yale.edu

Sabin, Paul E. (PhD, California, Berkeley 2000; prof. and dir., grad. studies) environmental; paul.sabin@yale.edu

Schwartz, Stuart B. (PhD, Columbia 1968; prof.) Latin America, Brazil; stuart.schwartz@yale.edu

Shore, Marci (PhD, Stanford 2001; assoc. prof.) European cultural and intellectual; marci.shore@yale.edu

Snyder, Timothy (DPhil, Oxford 1997; prof.) modern eastern central Europe; timothy.snyder@yale.edu

Sorkin, David (PhD, California, Berkeley 1983; prof.; Judaic Studies) modern Jewish; david.sorkin@yale.edu

Tannenbaum, Rebecca J. (PhD, Yale 1996; sr. lect.) early America; rebecca.tannenbaum@yale.edu

Westad, O. A. (PhD, North Carolina, Chapel Hill 1991; prof.) diplomatic

Winroth, Anders (PhD, Columbia 1996; prof.) medieval, legal, Scandinavia; anders.winroth@yale.edu

Wrightson, Keith (PhD, Cambridge 1974; prof.) Britain 1500-1750, social/economic/cultural; keith.wrightson@yale.edu

Joint/Cross Appointments

Blackhawk, Ned (PhD, Washington 1999; prof.; American Studies) Native American; ned.blackhawk@yale.edu

Lamoreaux, Naomi R. (PhD, Johns Hopkins 1979; prof.; Economics) US economic and business; naomi.lamoreaux@yale.edu

Lui, Mary T. (PhD, Cornell 2000; prof.; American Studies) Asian American; mary.lui@yale.edu

Manning, Joseph G. (PhD, Chicago 1992; prof.; Classics) Hellenistic world; joseph.manning@yale.edu

Moyn, Samuel Aaron (LLD, California, Berkeley 2000; prof.; Law Sch.) law; samuel.moyn@yale.edu

Stout, Harry S. (PhD, Kent State 1974; prof.; Religious Studies, American Studies) American religious, early America, Civil War; harry.stout@yale.edu

Warner, John H. (PhD, Harvard 1984; prof.; Hist. of Medicine) 19th-century US social and cultural, life sciences; john.warner@yale.edu

Nondepartmental Historians

Cohn, Ellen R. (BA, Wesleyan 1977; sr. research scholar; ed., Papers of Benjamin Franklin) ellen.cohn@yale.edu

Part-time Faculty

Gitlin, Jay L. (PhD, Yale 2002; lect.) US social and cultural, Native American; jay.gitlin@yale.edu

Ramalingam, Chitra (PhD, Harvard 2009; lect.) science; chitra.ramalingam@yale.edu

Rogers, Naomi (PhD, Pennsylvania 1986; prof.; Hist. of Medicine) women, medicine; naomi.rogers@yale.edu

Semmel, Stuart (PhD, Harvard 1997; sr. lect.) Britain; stuart.semmel@yale.edu

Retired/Emeritus Faculty

Agnew, Jean-Christophe (PhD, Harvard 1977; prof. emeritus; American Studies) US cultural; jean-christophe.agnew@yale.edu

Banac, Ivo (PhD, Stanford 1975; prof. emeritus) modern Balkans, communist movement; ivo.banac@yale.edu

Bartlett, Beatrice S. (PhD, Yale 1980; prof. emeritus) Chinese archives and documents, Qing and modern political and historiography; beatrice.bartlett@yale.edu

Butler, Jon (PhD, Minnesota 1972; prof. emeritus) American religious, colonial America, American urban religion 1870-1940; jon.butler@yale.edu

Demos, John P. (MA, California, Berkeley 1961; prof. emeritus) colonial America, family; john.demos@yale.edu

Engelstein, Laura (PhD, Stanford 1976; prof. emeritus) Russia; laura.engelstein@yale.edu

Faragher, John Mack (PhD, Yale 1977; prof. emeritus) US West, Native American; john.faragher@yale.edu

Gilmore, Glenda E. (PhD, North Carolina, Chapel Hill 1992; prof. emeritus) US, American South, African American; glenda.gilmore@yale.edu

Howard, Michael E. (MA, Oxford 1948; prof. emeritus) modern Europe, modern military and naval

Kagan, Donald (PhD, Ohio State 1958; prof. emeritus) Greece, political thought; donald.kagan@yale.edu

Kevles, Daniel J. (PhD, Princeton 1964; prof. emeritus) science, US since 1877; daniel.kevles@yale.edu

Lamar, Howard R. (PhD, Yale 1951; prof. emeritus) US West

Layton, Bentley (PhD, Harvard 1971; prof. emeritus) religion; bentley.layton@yale.edu

MacMullen, Ramsay (PhD, Harvard 1957; prof. emeritus) Rome; ramsay.macmullen@yale.edu

Matthews, John F. (DPhil, Oxford 1969; prof. emeritus) late Roman social, economic, legal and political; john.matthews@yale.edu

Smith, Gaddis (PhD, Yale 1961; prof. emeritus) US diplomatic, maritime; gaddis.smith@yale.edu

Snowden, Frank M. (DPhil, Oxford 1975; prof. emeritus) modern Italy, medicine; frank.snowden@yale.edu

Spence, Jonathan D. (PhD, Yale 1965; prof. emeritus) China since 1600; jonathan.spence@yale.edu

Totman, Conrad (PhD, Harvard 1964; prof. emeritus) pre-Meiji Japan, Japanese forestry

Winter, Jay M. (PhD, Cantab. 1970; prof. emeritus) modern Britain, comparative Europe; jay.winter@yale.edu

Recently Awarded PhDs

Abney Salomon, Charlotte "Products of the Mineral Kingdom: Mineral Science in Sweden, 1740-1820"

Barzilay, Aner "Michel Foucault and First Philosophy: A Nietzschean End to Metaphysics in Postwar France, 1952-84"

Brackney, Kathryn Leigh "Phantom Geographies: An Alternative History of Holocaust Consciousness"

Burset, Christian Russo "A Common Law? Legal Pluralism in the 18th-Century British Empire"

Cratty, Flynn Jamison "'The Soul in Paraphrase': Prayer and the Changing Mental Worlds of Early Modern France and England"

Graham, Johns Webb III "Environmental, Social, and Political Change in the Otomi Heartland: A Hydraulic History of the Ixmilquilpan Valley (Hidalgo State, Mexico)"

Healey, Katherrine "Couldn't Believe Their Ears: Hearing, Deafness, and Aural Citizenship in World War II America"

Hogan, Andrew "The Auction of Pharoah: Institutions, Markets, and Culture in the Mediterranean during the First Millennium BC"

Lawrence, Tanya Elal "An Age of Trans-Imperial Vernacularisms: The Iranian Dissident Community of the Late Ottoman Empire"

Lockshin, Lauren Gottlieb "Bernard Lazare: From Antisemitism to Socialist Zionism in Fin-de-Siecle France"

Lord, Kevin L. "Law, Custom, and Honor in the Case of Ludwig IV of Bavaria, 1323-47"

Lorek, Timothy "Developing Paradise: Agricultural Science in the Conflicted Landscape of Colombia's Cauca Valley, 1927-67"

Mas, Catherine "The Culture Brokers: Medicine and Anthropology in Global Miami, 1960-95"

Mazur, Zachary "Financing the Nation: The Polish State and Economic Growth, 1918-39"

Munoz Arbelaez, Santiago "The New Kingdom of Granada: The Making and Unmaking of Spain's Atlantic Empire, 1530-1620"

Waycott, Laurel "The Pattern-Seekers: The Science of Discernment, 1850-1920"

Zdencanovic, Ben "From Cradle to Grave: The United States in a World of Welfare, 1940-53"

Zhang, Huasha "Our Kind of Tibetans: The Political Life and Times of Liu Manqing, 1906-42"

York College of Pennsylvania

Dept. of History and Political Science, Humanities Center, Room 100, 441 Country Club Rd., York, PA 17403. 717.815.1329. Fax 717.849.1681. Email: jaltman@ycp.edu. Website: https://www.ycp.edu/academics/school-of-the-arts-communication-and-global-studies/programs/history/.

Our students are the kind that want to help shape public policy and diplomatic efforts, see the world and make a global impact, or use what's happened before to influence how we approach future decisions. A global perspective comes standard here.

Chair: John A. Altman
Degrees Offered: BA
Academic Year System: Semester
Areas of Specialization: colonial era, 19th- and 20th-century America, western Europe, medieval era, public
Tuition (per academic year): $18910
Enrollment 2018-19:
 Undergraduate Majors: 23
 Degrees in History: 10 BA
 Students in Undergraduate Courses: 1136
 Students in Undergraduate Intro Courses: 700

Addresses:
 Admissions: http://www.ycp.edu/admissions/
 Financial Aid: http://www.ycp.edu/admissions/cost-and-financial-aid/

Full-time Faculty

Altman, John (PhD, Tennessee 1997; prof. and chair; Political Science) comparative state policy analysis; jaltman@ycp.edu

Beatty, Jacqueline (PhD, George Mason 2016; asst. prof.) early America, women and gender, public; jbeatty@ycp.edu

Brooks, Corey (PhD, California, Berkeley 2010; assoc. prof.) 19th-century US; cbrooks4@ycp.edu

Kennedy, Padraic C. (PhD, Washington, St. Louis 1997; assoc. prof.) Britain; pkennedy@ycp.edu

Krug, Ilana C. (PhD, Toronto 2006; assoc. prof.) medieval studies; ikrug@ycp.edu

Levy, Peter B. (PhD, Columbia 1986; prof.) 20th-century US; plevy@ycp.edu

McAdams, Kay L. (PhD, Indiana 1999; assoc. prof.) modern Europe; kmcadams@ycp.edu

Youngstown State University

Dept. of History, 1 University Plaza, DEBH 519, Youngstown, OH 44555-3452. 330.941.3456. Fax 330.941.2304. Email: bbonhomme@ysu.edu. Website: https://ysu.edu/academics/college-liberal-arts-social-sciences/history-major.

The Department of History at Youngstown State University is dedicated to the discovery and dissemination of knowledge about the past. The department promotes and integrates scholarship, teaching, and service to educate its undergraduate and graduate students. It promotes civic engagement with the wider community.

Chair: Brian Bonhomme
Director of Graduate Studies: Daniel Ayana
Degrees Offered: BA,BS,BSEd,MA
Academic Year System: Semester
Areas of Specialization: US, Europe, Middle East, Africa, applied
Undergraduate Tuition (per academic year):
 In-State: $8087
 Out-of-State: $14087
Graduate Tuition (per academic year):
 In-State: $12115
 Out-of-State: $18115
Enrollment 2018-19:
 Undergraduate Majors: 150
 New Graduate Students: 5
 Full-time Graduate Students: 11
 Part-time Graduate Students: 1
 Degrees in History: 15 BA, 7 MA
 Students in Undergraduate Courses: 1500
 Students in Undergraduate Intro Courses: 1000
 Online-Only Courses: 20%
Undergraduate Addresses:
 Admissions: http://web.ysu.edu/admissions
 Financial Aid: http://cfweb.cc.ysu.edu/finaid/
Graduate Addresses:
 Admissions: http://cms.ysu.edu/college-graduate-studies/domestic-admissions
 Financial Aid: http://cms.ysu.edu/college-graduate-studies/financial-aid

Full-time Faculty

Ayana, Daniel (PhD, Illinois, Urbana-Champaign 1995; prof. and dir., grad. studies) Africa, environmental, intellectual; dayana@ysu.edu

Bonhomme, Brian (PhD, Grad. Center, CUNY 2000; prof. and acting chair) Russia, environmental; bbonhomme@ysu.edu

Congdon, Eleanor A. (PhD, Cambridge 1997; assoc. prof.) medieval, Mediterranean trade, Renaissance; eacongdon@ysu.edu

DeBlasio, Donna M. (PhD, Kent State 1980; prof.) applied, 20th-century America; dmdeblasio@ysu.edu

Fluker, Amy L (PhD, Mississippi 2015; asst. prof.) 19th-century US, Civil War

Labendz, Jacob Ari (PhD, Washington, St. Louis 2014; asst. prof.) modern Europe, Jewish, Holocaust

Leary, Thomas (PhD, Brown 1985; assoc. prof.) historic preservation, labor, steel industry; teleary@ysu.edu

Pallante, Martha I. (PhD, Pennsylvania 1988; prof. and assoc. dean) colonial America, revolutionary America, material culture; mipallante@ysu.edu

Simonelli, David (PhD, Tulane 2001; prof.) Europe, Britain, 20th-century world; dsimonelli@ysu.edu

Viehe, Fred W. (PhD, California, Santa Barbara 1983; prof.) urban, crime; fwviehe@ysu.edu

Retired/Emeritus Faculty

Berger, Martin E. (PhD, Pittsburgh 1969; prof. emeritus) modern Europe, Germany, World Ward II; meberger@ysu.edu

York, Anne Marie (PhD, UCLA 1992; prof. emeritus) early modern France, French Revolution, modern and contemporary France; ayork@ysu.edu

Canadian Departments

University of Alberta

Dept. of History and Classics, 2-28 Henry Marshall Tory Bldg., Edmonton, AB T6G 2H4, Canada. 780.492.3270. Fax 780.492.9125. Email: histclass@ualberta.ca. Website: https://www.ualberta.ca/history-classics/.

We take pride in being one of the finest Departments of History and Classics in Canada, with around 40 faculty members in the two divisions. We teach in all areas of these two disciplines, with a large group of Majors and healthy honours programs.

Chair: Ryan Dunch
Director of Graduate Studies: Adam Kemezis
Director of Undergraduate Studies: Jaymie Heilman
Degrees Offered: BA,BS,MA,PhD
Academic Year System: Semester
Areas of Specialization: Europe, Britain, Canada, Asia, US
Tuition:
Canadian undergraduate $6,116, international undergraduate $17,593, Canadian graduate thesis-based $5,537, international graduate thesis-based $8,605 (incl. fees)
Enrollment 2018-19:
Undergraduate Majors: 181
New Graduate Students: 16
Full-time Graduate Students: 63
Part-time Graduate Students: 12
Degrees in History: 35 BA, 5 BS, 10 MA, 4 PhD
Undergraduate Addresses:
Admissions: http://admission.ualberta.ca/
Financial Aid: http://www.registrarsoffice.ualberta.ca/
Graduate Addresses:
Admissions and Financial Aid: http://www.gradstudies.ualberta.ca/

Adjunct Faculty

Couture, Claude (PhD, Montréal 1987; prof.; Faculté Saint-Jean) Canadian studies, intellectual and social; ccouture@ualberta.ca
Freed, Joann Zeiset (PhD, Alberta 1982; adj. prof.) archaeology of Carthage, Punic and Roman transport amphoras, Father Alfred-Louis Delatre; freed@ualberta.ca
Fujiwara, Aya (PhD, Alberta 2007; dir.; Prince Takamado Japan Centre for Teaching and Research) fujiwara@ualberta.ca
Klid, Bohdan W. (PhD, Alberta 1992; faculty service officer; Canadian Inst. of Ukrainian Studies) bohdan.klid@ualberta.ca
Mills, David C. (PhD, Carleton, Can. 1981; assoc. prof.) Canadian social and intellectual, sports, women; david.mills@ualberta.ca
Rowe, Allan A. (PhD, Alberta 2008; adj.) Canada, immigration and ethnicities, social; aarowe@ualberta.ca

Full-time Faculty

Carter, Sarah A. (PhD, Manitoba 1987; Henry Marshall Tory Chair and prof.; Native Studies) Canada, western Canada, social; scarter@ucalgary.ca
Coleman, Heather (PhD, Illinois, Urbana-Champaign 1998; Canada Research Chair and assoc. prof.) imperial Russia; heather.coleman@ualberta.ca
Cormack, Lesley B. (PhD, Toronto 1988; prof. and dean, Arts) science and technology, Britain; Lesley.Cormack@ualberta.ca
Dunch, Ryan (PhD, Yale 1996; assoc. prof. and chair; chair, East Asian Studies) modern China; ryan.dunch@ualberta.ca

Ede, Andrew G. (PhD, Toronto; assoc. prof.; dir., Science, Tech. and Soc.) science and technology; aede@ualberta.ca
Ens, Gerhard J. (PhD, Alberta 1989; prof.) western Canada, native peoples; gens@ualberta.ca
Gouglas, Sean (PhD, McMaster 2001; assoc. prof.; dir., Office of Interdisciplinary Studies) Canadian environment and agriculture; sean.gouglas@ualberta.ca
Gow, Andrew C. (PhD, Arizona 1993; prof.; dir., Religious Studies) late medieval, early modern Europe; andrew.gow@ualberta.ca
Haagsma, Margriet (PhD, Groningen, Netherlands 1989; assoc. prof.) Greek archaeology; margriet.haagsma@ualberta.ca
Harris, John (PhD, Illinois, Urbana-Champaign 1997; assoc. prof.) Greek language and literature, Greek and Roman philosophy; john.harris@ualberta.ca
Heilman, Jaymie Patricia (PhD, Wisconsin, Madison 2006; assoc. prof. and assoc. chair, undergrad. studies) Latin America; jaymie.heilman@ualberta.ca
Hendrickson, Jocelyn N. (PhD, Emory 2009; asst. prof.; Religious Studies) Islamic law and society, medieval and early modern North Africa and Iberia; jnhendri@ualberta.ca
Hijmans, Steven E. (PhD, Groningen, Netherlands 1989; assoc. prof.) Roman art and archaeology; shijmans@ualberta.ca
Himka, John-Paul (PhD, Michigan 1977; prof.) eastern Europe, Ukraine; jhimka@ualberta.ca
Jay, Jennifer (PhD, Australian National 1983; prof.) China; jjay@ualberta.ca
Kemezis, Adam (PhD, Michigan 2006; assoc. prof. and assoc. chair, grad. studies) Latin literature; kemezis@ualberta.ca
Kitchen, John (PhD, Toronto 1989; assoc. prof.; Religious Studies) medieval religion, medieval intellectual; jkitchen@ualberta.ca
Kravchenko, Volodymyr (PhD, National Acad. of Sciences, Ukraine 1997; prof.; dir., Canadian Inst. of Ukrainian Studies) Ukraine, Russian empire, historical writing; vkravche@ualberta.ca
Lemire, Beverly J. (DPhil, Oxford 1985; Henry Marshall Tory Chair and prof.; Material Culture Inst.) industrial era, Britain; lemire@ualberta.ca
MacFarlane, Kelly (PhD, Alberta 2002; faculty lect.) classics, Latin; kelly.macfarlane@ualberta.ca
Mackay, Christopher S. (PhD, Harvard 1994; prof.) Rome, Latin literature; csmackay@ualberta.ca
Marples, David R. (PhD, Sheffield, UK 1985; Dist. Univ. Prof.) Russia and Soviet Union, eastern Europe, Ukraine; david.marples@ualberta.ca
McDougall, E. Ann (PhD, Birmingham, UK 1980; prof.) African social and economic; ann.mcdougall@ualberta.ca
Moure, Kenneth J. (PhD, Toronto 1988; prof.) modern Europe; moure@ualberta.ca
Muir, James (PhD, York, Can. 2004; assoc. prof.; Faculty of Law) Canadian legal; james.muir@ualberta.ca
Nagel, Rebecca (PhD, Harvard 1995; assoc. prof.) Latin literature, Greek prose; rebecca.nagel@ualberta.ca
Patrouch, Joseph F., III (PhD, California, Berkeley 1991; prof.; dir., Wirth Inst. for Austrian and Central European Studies) early modern central Europe; patrouch@ualberta.ca
Piper, Elizabeth (PhD, York, Can. 2005; assoc. prof.) Canadian environmental; epiper@ualberta.ca
Pownall, Frances S. (PhD, Toronto 1993; prof. and assoc. chair, undergrad. prog.) Greece; frances.pownall@ualberta.ca
Rice, Candace M. (DPhil, Oxford 2012; asst. prof.) classical archaeology, Mediterranean archaeology; cmrice@ualberta.ca

Romeo, Sharon Elizabeth (PhD, Iowa 2009; asst. prof.) US; sharon.romeo@ualberta.ca

Rossiter, Jeremy J. (PhD, Alberta 1986; prof.) Roman province archaeology; jeremy.rossiter@ualberta.ca

Samson, Jane D. (PhD, London 1994; prof. and assoc. chair, grad. studies) Britain, exploration; jane.samson@ualberta.ca

Skidmore, Colleen (PhD, Alberta 1999; prof.) Canadian photography and art, Canadian and US women and photography; colleen.skidmore@ualberta.ca

Smith, Robert W. (PhD, Cambridge 1979; prof.) science and technology, US; rwsmith@ualberta.ca

Smith, Susan L. (PhD, Wisconsin, Madison 1991; prof.) women, health and medicine, African American and Asian American; susan.l.smith@ualberta.ca

Stewart, Selina (PhD, Cornell 1989; assoc. prof.; Modern Languages) Greek and Latin literature, classical linguistics; selinas@ualberta.ca

Stunden Bower, Shannon Stunden (PhD, British Columbia 2006; asst. prof.) Canadian prairies, environmental, Canada; stundenbower@ualberta.ca

Sweeney, Dennis J. (PhD, Michigan 1994; assoc. prof.) modern Germany, Europe; dsweeney@ualberta.ca

Sysyn, Frank (PhD, Harvard 1976; prof.; Canadian Inst. of Ukrainian Studies) frank.sysyn@ualberta.ca

Szabo, Franz A.J. (PhD, Alberta 1976; prof.) early modern Europe, Germany, Austria; franz.szabo@ualberta.ca

Wujastyk, Dominik (DPhil, Oxford 1982; prof.) ancient India; wujastyk@gmail.com

Retired/Emeritus Faculty

Ben Zvi, Ehud (PhD, Emory 1990; prof. emeritus) Hebrew scriptures, historical-critical approaches, ancient literature; ehud.ben.zvi@ualberta.ca

Braun, Richard E. (PhD, Texas, Austin 1969; prof. emeritus)

Braun, Willi (PhD, Toronto 1993; prof. emeritus) early Christian literature, theories of religion; willi.braun@ualberta.ca

Fracchia, Helena (PhD, California, Berkeley 1979; prof. emeritus) Greek and Italian art and archaeology; helena.fracchia@ualberta.ca

Gualtieri, Maurizio (PhD, Pennsylvania; prof. emeritus) Italian archaeology, Rome; mgualt@unipg.it

Hall, David J. (PhD, Toronto 1973; prof. emeritus) post-Confederation Canada; david.hall@ualberta.ca

Hett, Robert R. (PhD, Rochester 1969; prof. emeritus) pre-Confederation Canada

Johnson, David C. (PhD, California, Berkeley 1975; prof. emeritus) Latin America; david.johnson@ualberta.ca

Jones, William J. (PhD, London; prof. emeritus) Elizabethan and early Stuart Britain

Landy, Francis (DPhil, Sussex, UK 1983; prof. emeritus) Hebrew Bible, Judaism, religion and psychoanalysis; francis.landy@ualberta.ca

Lightner, David L. (PhD, Cornell 1969; prof. emeritus) American economic and labor; david.lightner@ualberta.ca

MacLaren, Ian S. (PhD, Western Ontario 1985; prof. emeritus) Canadian North, social; ian.maclaren@ualberta.ca

Macleod, Roderick C. (PhD, Duke 1971; prof. emeritus) western Canada, social; rmacleod@ualberta.ca

Moss, David J. (DPhil, Oxford; prof. emeritus) 19th-century Britain, economic and social; d.j.moss@exeter.ac.uk

Munro, Kenneth J. (PhD, Ottawa 1973; prof. emeritus) French Canada; ken.munro@ualberta.ca

Neumaier, Eva K. (PhD, Ludwig-Maximillian, Munich; prof. emeritus) India, Tibetan and Mongolian studies

Nielsen, Rosemary M. (PhD, Washington; prof. emeritus) Greek and Latin poetry, women's studies

Owram, Douglas R. (PhD, Toronto 1976; prof. emeritus) post-Confederation Canadian cultural/intellectual/economic

Prestwich, Patricia E. (PhD, Stanford 1973; prof. emeritus) modern France, women; pat.prestwich@ualberta.ca

Prithipaul, Kchetrepal (PhD, Paris; prof. emeritus)

Small, Allistair M. (DPhil, Oxford; prof. emeritus) Italian archaeology, Rome; asmall@torphichen.demon.co.uk

Small, Carola M. (Other, Oxford; prof. emeritus) medieval France; hiscss@srv0.arts.ed.ac.uk

Smith, Burton M. (PhD, Washington State 1970; prof. emeritus) 19th-century US, social and intellectual; bmsmith@ualberta.ca

Smith, Richard C. (PhD, Illinois, Urbana-Champaign 1961; prof. emeritus) ancient Near East and Hellenistic

Swyripa, Frances A. (PhD, Alberta 1988; prof. emeritus) Canadian ethnic and immigration, women; fswyripa@ualberta.ca

Voisey, Paul L. (PhD, Toronto 1979; prof. emeritus) western Canada, social and economic; pvoisey@ualberta.ca

Waugh, Earle (PhD, Chicago 1972; prof. emeritus) Islam, comparative and religious studies; earle.waugh@ualberta.ca

Wilson, Harold E. (PhD, British Columbia 1975; prof. emeritus) modern Southeast Asia

Wilson, John R. (PhD, California, Berkeley; prof. emeritus) Greek literature and linguistics

Visiting Faculty

Baskerville, Peter A. (PhD, Queen's, Can. 1973; vis. prof.; chair, Modern Western Canadian Hist.) Canada; pab@ualberta.ca

Recently Awarded PhDs

Au Yong, Ke-Xin "The History of Mathematics in China between the Sixth and Twelfth Centuries"

Bilous, Larysa "Jewish Community of Kyiv during World War I: Social and Economical Transformations"

Vynnyk, Oksana "Postwar 'Normalization': The Adaptation of the Handicapped War Veterans and the Civil Life in Interwar Lviv"

Brandon University

Dept. of History, 270 18th St., Brandon, MB R7A 6A9, Canada. 204.727.9664. Fax 204.726.0473. Email: history@brandonu.ca. Website: https://www.brandonu.ca/history/.

Brandon University's History Department offers courses in social history, gender and women's history, cultural history, public history, as well as those in national and world history reflect the increasing diversity of historical studies. Small classes allow students to discuss and debate historical developments and to work closely with professors, all of whom are active researchers and writers.

Chair: David Winter
Degrees Offered: BA, BA Hon
Academic Year System: Semester
Areas of Specialization: world, Canada, Europe, public
Tuition: Canadian $4,706
Enrollment 2018-19:
  Undergraduate Majors: 48
  Degrees in History: 15 BA
Addresses:
  Admissions: http://www.brandonu.ca/future-students/
  Financial Aid: http://www.brandonu.ca/future-students/tuition/

Full-time Faculty

Harms, Patricia F. (PhD, Arizona State 2007; assoc. prof.) Latin American women, gender, indigenous; harmsp@brandonu.ca

Hinther, Rhonda (PhD, McMaster 2005; assoc. prof.) western Canada, public, gender; hintherr@brandonu.ca

MacKay, Lynn (PhD, York, Can. 1991; prof.) Britain and Ireland, Europe, social; mackay@brandonu.ca

Naylor, James (PhD, York, Can. 1988; prof.) 20th-century social, working class; naylor@brandonu.ca

Strang, G. Bruce (PhD, McMaster 2000; prof.) modern Italy, 20th-century Britain, international relations; strangb@brandonu.ca

Winter, David R. (PhD, Toronto 2000; assoc. prof. and chair) medieval Europe, preaching and pastoralia, demons; winterd@brandonu.ca

Retired/Emeritus Faculty

Mott, Morris K. (PhD, Queen's, Can. 1980; prof. emeritus) Canada, Canadian West, sports; mott@brandonu.ca

Pernal, Andrew B. (PhD, Ottawa 1977; prof. emeritus) Poland, Russia, Ukraine; pernal@brandonu.ca

University of British Columbia

Dept. of History, Room 1297, 1873 East Mall, Vancouver, BC V6T 1Z1, Canada. 604.822.2099. Fax 604.822.6658. Email: history. dept@ubc.ca. Website: http://www.history.ubc.ca/.

The History Department at the University of British Columbia is an intellectually vibrant centre of scholarship and teaching. We are one of five original departments in the Faculty of Arts that commenced offering undergraduate classes when the University of British Columbia accepted its first students in the fall of 1915. The Department has special strengths in East Asian history and the history of science.

Chair: Eagle Glassheim
Director of Graduate Studies: John Roosa
Director of Undergraduate Studies: Bradley Miller
Degrees Offered: BA,MA,PhD
Academic Year System: Eight-month term
Areas of Specialization: Canada, East Asia, Europe, US, Latin America, Africa, South and Southeast Asia, science
Undergraduate Tuition (per academic year):
  In-State: $5189
  Out-of-State: $34847
Graduate Tuition (per academic year):
  In-State: $4896
  Out-of-State: $8604
Enrollment 2018-19:
  Undergraduate Majors: 305
  New Graduate Students: 11
  Full-time Graduate Students: 52
  Degrees in History: 81 BA, 9 MA, 1 PhD
  Students in Undergraduate Courses: 5736
  Students in Undergraduate Intro Courses: 1969
Addresses:
  Admissions and Financial Aid: https://www.ubc.ca/admissions/

Full-time Faculty

Booker, Courtney Matthew (PhD, UCLA 2002; assoc. prof.) medieval, Carolingian European intellectual and political; cbooker@mail.ubc.ca

Brain, Robert M. (PhD, UCLA 1995; assoc. prof.) 19th-century French science, instruments cultural, industrial exhibitions; rbrain@mail.ubc.ca

Brook, Timothy J. (PhD, Harvard 1984; prof.) modern China; tim.brook@ubc.ca

Byrne, Jeffrey James (PhD, London Sch. Economics 2011; assoc. prof.) developing world international, modern Africa, revolutionary movements and transfer of revolutionary ideologies/practices; jeffrey.byrne@ubc.ca

Christopoulos, John (PhD, Toronto 2013; asst. prof.) early modern Europe, premodern medicine, early modern Italian social and cultural; john.christopoulos@ubc.ca

Dixon, Joy (PhD, Rutgers 1993; assoc. prof.) 19th- and early 20th-century Britain, gender and cultural; joy.dixon@ubc.ca

Ducharme, Michel (PhD, McGill 2005; assoc. prof.) pre-Confederation Canada; Michel.Ducharme@ubc.ca

French, William E. (PhD, Texas, Austin 1990; assoc. prof.) 20th-century Mexico, labor; wfrench@mail.ubc.ca

Glassheim, Eagle (PhD, Columbia 2000; prof. and head) modern Europe; eagle.g@ubc.ca

Gorsuch, Anne E. (PhD, Michigan 1992; prof.) Soviet Union, popular culture; gorsuch@mail.ubc.ca

Ishiguro, Laura (PhD, Univ. Coll. London 2011; asst. prof.) British Columbia, British Empire, comparative empire and settler colonialism; laura.ishiguro@ubc.ca

Kojevnikov, Alexei (PhD, Inst. Hist. of Science and Tech., Moscow 1989; assoc. prof.) science, Russia and Soviet Union, Cold War nuclear; anikov@mail.ubc.ca

Lee, Steven H. (DPhil, Oxford 1991; assoc. prof.) Canadian foreign relations, 20th-century diplomatic; stevenhl@mail.ubc.ca

Loo, Tina M. (PhD, British Columbia 1990; prof.) law social, 19th-century Canada, British Columbia; tina.loo@ubc.ca

Mayer, Tara (PhD, London 2012; instr. I) colonial South Asia, empire and aesthetic influence, Indo-European commodity exchanges; tara.mayer@ubc.ca

Menkis, Richard (PhD, Brandeis 1988; assoc. prof.) Middle East, Holocaust, Jewish; menkis@mail.ubc.ca

Miller, Bradley J. (PhD, Toronto 2012; assoc. prof. and dir., undergrad. studies) law and legal, state formation, political; brmiller@ubc.ca

Morton, David (PhD, Minnesota 2015; asst. prof.) 20th-century Mozambique urban, slums, Africa from imperialism to independence; david.morton@ubc.ca

Paris, Leslie M. (PhD, Michigan 2000; assoc. prof.) US cultural, social and gender; lparis@mail.ubc.ca

Peterson, Glen D. (PhD, British Columbia 1992; prof.) modern China; glpeters@mail.ubc.ca

Prange, Sebastian R. (PhD, London 2008; asst. prof.) premodern South Asia, trans-oceanic networks; s.prange@ubc.ca

Raibmon, Paige (PhD, Duke 2000; prof.) First Nations; praibmon@mail.ubc.ca

Roosa, John P. (PhD, Wisconsin, Madison 1998; assoc. prof. and dir., grad. studies) Southeast and South Asia, nationalism, colonialism; jroosa@mail.ubc.ca

Sindelar, Arlene (PhD, Mississippi 1997; sr. instr.) medieval legal and social, women and family; arlene.sindelar@ubc.ca

Thrush, Coll (PhD, Washington 2002; prof.) indigenous, environmental studies; cthrush@mail.ubc.ca

Tworek, Heidi J. (PhD, Harvard 2012; asst. prof.) international history of news, business and legal, Germany and Europe; htworek@mail.ubc.ca

Unwalla, Pheroze (PhD, SOAS, London 2014; instr.) modern Middle East, Turkey and Ottoman Empire, memory studies, nations and nationalism; pheroze@mail.ubc.ca

Wang, Jessica (PhD, MIT 1995; assoc. prof.) post-1865 US, political and intellectual, political theory; jessica.wang@ubc.ca

Yu, Henry (PhD, Princeton 1994; assoc. prof.) American intellectual, Asian American, race and immigration; henry.yu@ubc.ca

Joint/Cross Appointments

Cheek, Timothy C. (PhD, Harvard 1986; prof.; Sch. of Public Policy and Global Affairs) Chinese Communist Party, political system in modern China; t.cheek@ubc.ca

Shin, Leo K. (PhD, Princeton 1999; assoc. prof.; Asian Studies) premodern China; lkshin@mail.ubc.ca

Retired/Emeritus Faculty

Friedrichs, Christopher R. (PhD, Princeton 1974; prof. emeritus) early modern European urban and social, Germany 1500-1800, German Jewish; crf@mail.ubc.ca

Krause, Paul L. (PhD, Duke 1987; assoc. prof. emeritus) 19th-century social and labor, US political culture; krause@mail.ubc.ca

Recently Awarded PhDs

Peotto, Thomas "Dark Mimesis: A Cultural History of the Scalping Paradigm"

Brock University

Dept. of History, 1812 Sir Isaac Brock Way, St. Catharines, ON L2S 3A1, Canada. 905.688.5550. Fax 905.984.4849. Email: history@ www.brocku.ca. Website: https://brocku.ca/humanities/ history/.

Brock history students benefit from a rich diversity of course offerings, including first-year surveys to advanced fourth- year and graduate seminars. All lectures are paired with small weekly seminars where students hone their skills in critical thinking, analysis, and presentation in a nurturing setting.

Chair: Maureen Lux
Director of Graduate Studies: Renee Lafferty-Salhany
Degrees Offered: BA,MA
Academic Year System: Semester
Areas of Specialization: Canada, US, Europe, Africa, science and technology
Tuition:
    Canadian $6,466.90
    International $19,938.50
Enrollment 2018-19:
    Undergraduate Majors: 298
    New Graduate Students: 7
    Full-time Graduate Students: 8
    Degrees in History: 83 BA, 9 MA
Undergraduate Addresses:
    Admissions: and Financial Aid: https://brocku.ca/admissions/
Graduate Addresses:
    Admissions and Financial Aid: https://brocku.ca/safa/

Full-time Faculty

Bonnett, John (PhD, Ottawa 2002; assoc. prof.) intellectual, history and computing; jbonnett@brocku.ca

Clark, Jessica P. (PhD, Johns Hopkins 2012; assoc. prof.) health/beauty culture/body; jclark@brocku.ca

Friedman, Tami J. (PhD, Columbia 2001; assoc. prof.) 20th-century US social, economic, foreign policy; tfriedman@brocku.ca

Kranjc, Gregor (PhD, Toronto 2006; asst. prof.) east central Europe; gkranjc@brocku.ca

Lafferty-Salhany, Renee (PhD, Dalhousie 2003; asst. prof. and dir., grad. studies; Canadian Studies) modern Canadian culture, religion and denominationalism; rlaffert@brocku.ca

Lux, Maureen (PhD, Simon Fraser 1996; prof. and chair) Canadian aboriginal, western Canada; mlux@brocku.ca

McDonald, R. Andrew (PhD, Guelph 1993; prof.) medieval Britain and Europe, Celtic, ancient; amcdonal@brocku.ca

McLeod, Jane A (PhD, York, Can. 1987; assoc. prof.) early modern France, social, censorship; jmcleod@brocku.ca

Mirzai, Behnaz (PhD, York, Can. 2004; prof.) Iran, Middle East, slavery; bmirzai@brocku.ca

Neswald, Elizabeth R. (PhD, Humboldt 2004; assoc. prof.) science; eneswald@brocku.ca

Ojo, Olatunji (PhD, York, Can. 2003; assoc. prof.) African social and economic, slavery, African diaspora; oojo@brocku.ca

Patrias, Carmela K. (PhD, Toronto 1985; prof.) post-Confederation Canada, immigration and labor, women; cpatrias@brocku.ca

Samson, Daniel J. (PhD, Queen's, Can. 1997; assoc. prof.) Canadian rural, Atlantic Canada; dsamson@brocku.ca

Schimmelpenninck, David (PhD, Yale 1997; prof.) Russia, Inner Asia; dschimme@brocku.ca

Spencer, Mark G. (PhD, Western Ontario 2001; assoc. prof.) early America, Enlightenment; mspencer@brocku.ca

Suescun Pozas, Maria del Carmen (PhD, McGill 2005; assoc. prof.) modern Latin America, gender, art; msuescunpozas@brocku.ca

Vlossak, Elizabeth (PhD, Cambridge 2004; assoc. prof.) modern Europe; evlossak@brocku.ca

Wang, Ning (PhD, British Columbia 2005; assoc. prof.) modern China; nwang@brocku.ca

Wickett, Murray R. (PhD, Toronto 1996; assoc. prof.) US, race relations; mwickett@brocku.ca

Joint/Cross Appointments

Driedger, Michael D. (PhD, Queen's, Can. 1996; assoc. prof.; Liberal Arts) early modern Germany, comparative religious movements and minorities; mdriedge@brocku.ca

Retired/Emeritus Faculty

Hanyan, Craig R. (PhD, Harvard 1964; assoc. prof. emeritus) early national US, US political, 19th-century US; chanyan@cogeco.ca

Sainsbury, John A. (PhD, McGill 1975; prof. emeritus) early modern Britain, colonial America; jsainsbu@brocku.ca

Taylor, Robert R. (PhD, Stanford 1970; prof. emeritus) modern Germany, Niagara, architecture; rratcliffetaylor@yahoo.com

University of Calgary

Dept. of History, 2500 University Dr. NW, SS656, Calgary, AB T2N 1N4, Canada. 403.220.6401. Fax 403.289.8566. Email: histdept@ucalgary.ca. Website: https://hist.ucalgary.ca/.

We are a community of 25 faculty members, several professors emeriti and adjunct professors, more than 50 graduate students, and about 300 undergraduate majors and honours students. Not only do we all share a passion for the study of the past, we firmly believe that the study of history has contemporary relevance and is an excellent preparation for a wide range of careers.

Chair: Mark Konnert
Director of Graduate Studies: Hendrik Kraay
Director of Undergraduate Studies: Paul Chastko
Degrees Offered: BA,MA,PhD
Academic Year System: Semester

Areas of Specialization: Canada, science and medicine, Latin America, medieval and early modern Europe, military/diplomatic, modern Europe and Britain, US, Africa, world

Undergraduate Tuition (per academic year):
Canadian: $5,385.59
International $7402.55

Graduate Tuition (per academic year):
Canadian: $5,593.50
International graduate $12,695.88

Enrollment 2018-19:
Undergraduate Majors: 273
New Graduate Students: 2
Full-time Graduate Students: 43
Part-time Graduate Students: 2
Degrees in History: 49 BA, 6 MA, 2 PhD

Undergraduate Addresses:
Admissions: http://www.ucalgary.ca/admissions/
Financial Aid: http://www.ucalgary.ca/studentfinance/

Graduate Addresses:
Admissions and Financial Aid: https://hist.ucalgary.ca/graduate

Full-time Faculty

Bercuson, David J. (PhD, Toronto 1971; prof.) post-1914 Canadian political/military/diplomatic, strategic studies; bercuson@ucalgary.ca

Campbell, Lyndsay (PhD, California, Berkeley 2008; assoc. prof.) Canadian and US legal; lcampbe@ucalgary.ca

Chastko, Paul A. (PhD, Ohio 2002; sr. instr. and dir., undergrad. prog.) energy and environment; pchastko@ucalgary.ca

Colpitts, George (PhD, Alberta 2000; prof.) Canada, environmental; colpitts@ucalgary.ca

Devine, Heather (PhD, Alberta 2002; assoc. prof.; Communication and Culture) Canadian native, American Indian policy, Western Canadian ethnic; hdevine@ucalgary.ca

Dolata, Petra (PhD, Ruhr, Bochum, Germany; assoc. prof. and Tier II Canada Research Chair) energy, diplomatic and international; pdolata@ucalgary.ca

Elofson, Warren M. (DPhil, Oxford 1977; prof.) Canadian agriculture, 18th-century Britain, Rockingham Whigs; elofson@ucalgary.ca

Ferris, John R. (PhD, King's Coll., UK 1986; prof.) 20th-century British and European diplomatic/intelligence, 19th- and 20th-century imperial, interwar Europe; ferris@ucalgary.ca

Hill, Alexander A. (PhD, Cambridge 2001; prof.) Soviet military, military, naval; hilla@ucalgary.ca

Janovicek, Nancy E. A. (PhD, Simon Fraser 2002; assoc. prof.) Canadian women's movement, violence against women, social movements and community organizations; njanovic@ucalgary.ca

Kiddle, Amelia M. (PhD, Arizona 2010; assoc. prof.) Latin American international relations, Mexican cultural/political/diplomatic; akiddle@ucalgary.ca

Konnert, Mark W. (PhD, Southern California 1988; prof. and chair) early modern France and Europe, Reformation and religious wars, urban; mkonnert@ucalgary.ca

Konshuh, Courtnay (PhD, Winchester 2014; asst. prof.) state development and cultural exchange in medieval world, classical period to Reformation; courtnay.konshuh@ucalgary.ca

Kraay, Hendrik (PhD, Texas, Austin 1995; prof. and dir., grad. prog.) Brazilian social/political/cultural/military, slavery and race, civic rituals and festivals; kraay@ucalgary.ca

Macmillan, Kenneth R. (PhD, McMaster 2001; prof.) Britain; macmillk@ucalgary.ca

Marshall, David B. (PhD, Toronto 1987; prof.) Canadian social/intellectual/religious, First World War, Canadian popular culture; marshall@ucalgary.ca

Moore, Anne (PhD, Claremont Grad. 2004; assoc. prof.) origins of Christianity, intertestamental literature, religion and place; amoore@ucalgary.ca

Spangler, Jewel L. (PhD, California, San Diego 1996; assoc. prof.) American social and cultural 1750-1850, American South, early American religious; spangler@ucalgary.ca

Stahnisch, Frank W. (PhD, Free, Berlin 2001; MD, Humboldt (Charité), Berlin 1998; prof.) history and philosophy of science, history and philosophy of neurosciences, physiology; fwstahni@ucalgary.ca

Stapleton, Timothy (PhD, Dalhousie 1993; prof.) Africa, military, war and society; timothy.stapleton@ucalgary.ca

Stortz, Paul James (PhD, Toronto; assoc. prof.; Communication and Culture) Canada, diversity/ethnicity/gender/race, social/educational/intellectual; pjstortz@ucalgary.ca

Timm, Annette F. (PhD, Chicago 1999; prof.) modern Europe/modern Germany/Holocaust, 20th-century war and society, gender and sexuality; atimm@ucalgary.ca

Towers, Frank H. (PhD, California, Irvine 1993; assoc. prof.) US Civil War, social, political; ftowers@ucalgary.ca

Wilkinson, Glenn (PhD, Lancaster; sr. instr. and dir., undergrad. studies) film and media, modern Britain, military; grwilkin@ucalgary.ca

Wright, David C. (PhD, Princeton 1993; assoc. prof.) imperial Chinese foreign relations and diplomacy, Mongol world empire, pre-20th-century Taiwan; wrightd@ucalgary.ca

Retired/Emeritus Faculty

Archer, Christon I. (PhD, SUNY, Stony Brook 1971; prof. emeritus) Mexico, military, Pacific exploration; archer@ucalgary.ca

Brennan, Patrick H. (PhD, York, Can. 1989; prof. emeritus) 20th-century Canadian politics and military; brennan@ucalgary.ca

Francis, R. Douglas (PhD, York, Can. 1975; prof. emeritus) 20th-century Canadian intellectual and social, western Canadian intellectual and social; francis@ucalgary.ca

Herwig, Holger H. (PhD, SUNY, Stony Brook 1971; prof. emeritus) German imperial/military/political/diplomatic, strategic studies; herwig@ucalgary.ca

Jameson, Elizabeth A. (PhD, Michigan 1987; prof. emeritus) US social, American West, working class and women; jameson@ucalgary.ca

Knafla, Louis A. (PhD, UCLA 1965; prof. emeritus) English social/intellectual/legal 1485-1760, Canadian legal 1760-1940; knafla@ucalgary.ca

Michaud, Francine (PhD, Laval 1989; assoc. prof. emeritus) medieval Europe, social/religious/family; michaud@ucalgary.ca

Randall, Stephen J. (PhD, Toronto 1972; prof. emeritus) 19th- and 20th-century US political/social/economic, US diplomatic, Latin America and Caribbean; srandall@ucalgary.ca

Rasporich, Anthony W. (PhD, Manitoba 1970; prof. emeritus) Canadian intellectual, ethnic and immigration, western Canadian regional and resource development; awraspor@ucalgary.ca

Smith, Donald B. (PhD, Toronto 1975; prof. emeritus) native peoples, early Canadian West, French Canadians in Canadian West; smithd@ucalgary.ca

Staum, Martin S. (PhD, Cornell 1971; prof. emeritus) Enlightenment, French Revolution, 18th- and 19th-century French social sciences; mstaum@ucalgary.ca

Travers, Timothy H. E. (PhD, Yale 1970; prof. emeritus) 19th- and 20th-century warfare, modern tactical and strategic thought, film and history

Recently Awarded PhDs

Barrios Giraldo, David "Memory and Commemorations in Colombia at the Turn of the 19th Century. The Centennial of Independence in 1910"

Glover, Fred "Dispatches from the Wilderness: A History of the Canadian Missionaries and Korean Protestants in Northern Korea and Manchuria, 1893-1928"

Kurbegovic, Erna "Eugenics in Comparative Perspective: Explaining Manitoba and Alberta's Divergence on Eugenics Policy, 1910-30s"

Wiley, Andrew "'A Steady Opposition to Every Evolution of Radicalism': Western Conservatism in Civil War Era Indiana"

Carleton University

Dept. of History, 400 Paterson Hall, 1125 Colonel By Dr., Ottawa, ON K1S 5B6, Canada. 613.520.2828. Email: chair.history@carleton.ca; grad.history@carleton.ca. Website: https://carleton.ca/history/.

Carleton's Department of History offers an intellectually stimulating culture, encourages students to participate in their communities and provides opportunities unique to the national capital. When students graduate, they are well prepared for employment in a wide range of professions.

Chair: James Miller
Director of Graduate Studies: Paul Nelles
Director of Undergraduate Studies: Michel Hogue
Degrees Offered: BA,MA,PhD
Academic Year System: Semester
Areas of Specialization: Canada, women/gender/sexuality, public, Europe, international
Undergraduate Tuition (per academic year):
  Canadian: $7,847.01
  International $26,490.01
Graduate Tuition (per academic year):
  Canadian MA: $7,135.08
  International MA: $16,415.08
  Canadian PhD: $6,829.08
  International PhD: $15,009.08
Enrollment 2018-19:
  Undergraduate Majors: 368
  New Graduate Students: 18
  Full-time Graduate Students: 38
  Part-time Graduate Students: 16
  Degrees in History: 68 BA, 15 MA, 3 PhD
  Students in Undergraduate Courses: 2748
  Students in Undergraduate Intro Courses: 773
  Online-Only Courses: 6%
Undergraduate Addresses:
  Admissions: http://admissions.carleton.ca/
  Financial Aid: http://carleton.ca/awards/
Graduate Addresses:
  Admissions: http://graduate.carleton.ca/
  Financial Aid: http://graduate.carleton.ca/financial-assistance/

Adjunct Faculty

Abel, Kerry (PhD, Queen's, Can. 1985; adj. prof.) Northern Canada, First Nations; kerry.abel@carleton.ca

Allina-Pisano, Eric (PhD, Yale 2002; adj. research prof.; assoc. prof., Ottawa) Africa, slavery, African diaspora; eric.allinapisano@carleton.ca

Badgley, Ian (MA, Toronto; adj. research prof.; archaeologist, Heritage Program, National Capital Commission) cultural heritage; ian.badgley@carleton.ca

Barber, Marilyn J. (PhD, London 1975; adj. research prof.) Canada, women, immigration; marilyn.barber@carleton.ca

Brandon, Laura E. (PhD, Carleton, Can. 2002; adj. research prof.; research assoc., Canadian War Museum; adj. research prof., School for Studies in Art & Culture, Carleton) contemporary and historical Canadian and international art and artists

Burtch, Andrew P. (PhD, Carleton, Can. 2009; adj. research prof.; post-1945 historian, Canadian War Museum) 20th-century Canadian political/diplomatic/military, 20th-century America, Soviet/Russia; andrew.burtch@carleton.ca

Campbell, Isabel (PhD, Laval 2000; adj. research prof.; historian, National Defence Headquarters) military and naval, Cold War allied intelligence, security state, military families; isabel.campbell@carleton.ca

Cavell, Janice (PhD, Carleton, Can. 2003; adj. research prof.) print culture, exploration, polar regions; janice.cavell@carleton.ca

Cook, Tim (PhD, Australian Defence Force Acad. 2002; adj. prof.) Canadian military; tim.cook@warmuseum.ca

Donaghy, Gregory S. (PhD, Waterloo 1998; adj. research prof.; head, Historical Section, Foreign Affairs and International Trade Canada) Canadian history and diplomacy, Canadian foreign policy; greg.donaghy@carleton.ca

Douglas, W.A.B. (PhD, Queen's, Can. 1973; adj. research prof.) Canadian military; w.douglas@carleton.ca

Erlank, Natasha (PhD, Cambridge 1999; adj. research prof.) natasha.erlank@carleton.ca

Fedorowicz, Jan (PhD, King's Coll., Cambridge; adj. prof.) central Europe and Russia, futurist thought, terrorism in history; jan.fedorowicz@carleton.ca

Florez-Malagon, Alberto (PhD, SUNY, Stony Brook 1994; adj. research prof.; prof., Ottawa) cultural studies, postcolonial and subaltern studies, Latin American studies; alberto.florezmalagon@carleton.ca

Goldman, Hal (PhD, Massachusetts Amherst 2000; adj. prof.) 19th- and 20th-century US social and cultural, US gender/women/sexuality, US legal and constitutional; harold.goldman@carleton.ca

Goodwin, G. Frederick (PhD, Princeton 1978; adj. prof.) 20th-century US, US foreign policy; fred.goodwin@carleton.ca

Graham, Sean (PhD, Ottawa 2014; adj. research prof.; historian, Parks Canada Agency) North American media and broadcasting; Sean.Graham3@carleton.ca

Gray, Charlotte (MA, Oxford 1977; adj. research prof.) Canadian social and cultural; charlotte.gray@carleton.ca

Hinther, Rhonda (PhD, McMaster 2005; adj. research prof.; assoc. prof., Brandon) Canadian public; rhonda.hinther@carleton.ca

Hodge, Shannon (MLIS, McGill 2004; adj. prof.; corporate archivist, Corporate Records and Archives, Carleton); shannon.hodge@carleton.ca

Horrall, Andrew (PhD, Cambridge 1998; adj. prof.; sr. archivist, Library and Archives Canada) andrew.horrall@carleton.ca

Huffer, Damien (PhD, Australian National 2012; adj. research prof.) global and Southeast Asian antiquities trade, human remains trafficking; damien.huffer@carleton.ca

Keane, Lloyd (adj. prof.; coord., Archives and Rare Books, Archives and Research Collections, Carleton) lloyd.keane@carleton.ca

Mackenzie, Hector (DPhil, Oxford 1981; adj. research prof.; sr. historian and academic outreach advisor, Global Affairs Canada)

Canadian political and diplomatic; hector.mackenzie@carleton.ca

McKean, Matthew (PhD, Queen's, Can. 2009; adj. research prof.; assoc. dir., Education, Conference Board of Canada) 19th- and 20th-century Britain; matthew.mckean@carleton.ca

Molloy, Michael (BA, Notre Dame Univ. Coll.; adj. research prof.) immigration policy, refugee policy and resettlement programs and processes, humanitarian immigration, Middle East current affairs; michael.molloy@carleton.ca

Morin, Jean-Pierre (MA, Ottawa; adj. research prof.; staff historian, Aboriginal Affairs and Northern Development Canada) treaties between government and aboriginal people, government policy and administration of AANDC

Oliver, Dean Frederick (PhD, York, Can. 1996; adj. prof.; dir., Research, Canadian Museum of History) Canadian military; dean.oliver@carleton.ca

Petrou, Michael (DPhil, Oxford 2006; adj. research prof.) Canadians in Spanish Civil War, modern Middle East; michael.petrou@carleton.ca

Robertson, Beth A. (PhD, Carleton, Can. 2013; adj. research prof.; project dir. and postdoctoral fellow, International Development Research Centre) body and senses, queer theory, visual and material culture; beth.robertson@carleton.ca

Schwartz, Joan M. (PhD, Queen's, Can. 1998; adj. research prof.) photography, geographical imagination, landscape and travel, Canada, archives management, art/fact/artifact; joan.schwartz@carleton.ca

Terretta, Meredith E. (PhD, Wisconsin, Madison 2004; adj. research prof.; assoc. prof., Ottawa) modern Africa, human rights, women and nationalism; meredith.terretta@carleton.ca

van Rahden, Till (PhD, Bielefeld, Germany 1999; adj. research prof.; Canada Research Chair, Montréal) modern Germany and Europe, gender, Jewish; till.vanrahden@carleton.ca

Willis, John (PhD, Laval; adj. research prof.; historian, Canadian Museum of History) social history of postal communication in Canada; john.willis@carleton.ca

Full-time Faculty

Anderson, Mark C. (PhD, California, Riverside 1995; prof.) Latin American and Caribbean studies, American popular culture/zombies/frontier myth/westerns, imperialism in Americas/American behavior; mark.anderson@carleton.ca

Bellamy, Matthew J. (PhD, Carleton, Can. 2001; assoc. prof.) 19th- and 20th-century Canadian political/economic/business/cultural, consumption, brewing industry; matthew.bellamy@carleton.ca

Dean, David M. (PhD, Cambridge 1984; prof.; co-dir., Carleton Centre for Public History) early modern British political/social/cultural, public, historical representation and performance in museums/film/theatre; david.dean@carleton.ca

Dean, Joanna E. (PhD, Carleton, Can. 1999; assoc. prof.) Canada, women and gender, environmental; joanna.dean@carleton.ca

Diptee, Audra (PhD, Toronto 2005; assoc. prof.) Caribbean, comparative slavery, Atlantic world; audra.diptee@carleton.ca

Evans, Jennifer V. (PhD, SUNY, Binghamton 2001; prof.) modern Europe, Germany, social and cultural, sexuality; jennifer.evans@carleton.ca

Fraser, Erica L. (PhD, Illinois, Urbana-Champaign 2009; asst. prof.) Russia and Soviet Union, sports and leisure in communist states, gender; erica.fraser@carleton.ca

Graham, Shawn (PhD, Reading 2002; assoc. prof.) digital humanities, ancient Rome, public, computational creativity; shawn.graham@carleton.ca

Hillmer, G. Norman (PhD, Cambridge 1974; Chancellor's Prof.; Norman Paterson Sch. of International Affairs) Canada diplomatic, Canada-US relations, peacekeeping; norman.hillmer@carleton.ca

Hogue, Michel (PhD, Wisconsin, Madison 2009; assoc. prof. and dir., undergrad. studies) aboriginal peoples, Great Plains, North American West/borderlands, Metis and First Nations, fur trade; michel.hogue@carleton.ca

Jangam, Chinnaiah (PhD, SOAS, London 2005; assoc. prof.) South Asia, Dalit, India, decolonization/nationalism/politics of identity; chinnaiah.janggam@carleton.ca

Johnston, Andrew M. (PhD, Cambridge 1996; assoc. prof.) 20th-century US foreign relations, international, humanitarian intervention/human rights/power, gender/pragmatism/feminism/social theory; andrew.johnston@carleton.ca

Kinsey, Danielle C (PhD, Illinois, Urbana-Champaign 2010; asst. prof.) 19th-century Europe, Britain and empire, material culture and consumption; danielle.kinsey@carleton.ca

Klausen, Susanne (PhD, Queen's, Can. 1999; prof.) Africa, social and medical; susanne.klausen@carleton.ca

Kovalio, Jacob (PhD, Pittsburgh 1981; assoc. prof.) Japanese diplomatic/foreign policy/political culture/nationalism, Chinese hegemonism/international relations in Indo-Pacific area, Pan-Asianism/Asian international relations

Laird, W. R. (PhD, Toronto 1983; prof.) ancient/medieval/Renaissance science, mechanics and science of motion; WRLaird@carleton.ca

Lipsett-Rivera, Sonya (PhD, Tulane 1988; prof.) Latin America, colonial Mexico, environmental and social, popular culture and violence; sonya.lipsettrivera@carleton.ca

Madokoro, Laura (PhD, British Columbia 2012; assoc. prof.) refugees and humanitarianism, migration, human rights, race, settler colonialism; laura.madokoro@carleton.ca

Marshall, Dominique (PhD, Montreal 1989; prof.) 20th-century Québec, state formation, social policy, welfare, families, children's rights and humanitarian aid in international perspective; dominique.marshall@carleton.ca

McNeil, Daniel (PhD, Toronto 2007; assoc. prof.) migration, Atlantic world, diasporas and intellectuals; daniel.mcneil@carleton.ca

Miller, James D. (PhD, Emory 1996; assoc. prof. and chair) slavery and emancipation in US and Atlantic world, experiences and representations of insanity and asylum life, history of art brut/outsider art; james.miller@carleton.ca

Nelles, Paul (PhD, Johns Hopkins, 1995; assoc. prof. and dir., grad. studies) 16th- to 18th-century France and Italy, early modern European cultural/religious/intellectual, history of the book/libraries/communication/food, early modern Catholicism, Jesuits; paul.nelles@carleton.ca

Opp, James (PhD, Carleton, Can. 2000; prof.; assoc. dean, Faculty of Grad. and Postdoc. Affairs) Canadian social/cultural/religious, history of the body and gender, photography, public memory and national/regional identities

Phillips, Roderick G. (DPhil, Oxford 1975; prof.) French Revolution, family, women, alcohol/wine/food; roderick.phillips@carleton.ca

Saurette, Marc (PhD, Toronto 1998; assoc. prof.) medieval France, monastic reform, intellectual and cultural, digital manuscript studies, Middle Ages in popular culture; marc.saurette@carleton.ca

Walker, Pamela J. (PhD, Rutgers 1992; prof.) modern Britain, comparative women, Christianity and missions, race and racial identity in historical perspective; pamela.walker@carleton.ca

Walsh, John C. (PhD, Guelph 2001; asst. prof.; co-dir., Carleton Centre for Public History) 19th-century Canada, social, environmental, public, space and place, governmentality, epistemology, maps and mapping; john.walsh@carleton.ca

Whitney, Susan (PhD, Rutgers 1994; assoc. prof.) 20th-century social and political, modern France, women and gender, European youth, communism and Catholicism; susan.whitney@carleton.ca

Joint/Cross Appointments

Azzi, Stephen (PhD, Waterloo 1996; assoc. prof.; Political Management) Canadian politics and international relations; stephen.azzi@carleton.ca

Downie, Susan (PhD, Toronto; instr. III; Coll. of the Humanities, Greek and Roman Studies) Greek political and social, classical mythology and religion, ancient art and architecture; susan.downie@carleton.ca

Fisher, Greg (DPhil, Oxford; assoc. prof.; Coll. of the Humanities, Greek and Roman Studies) ancient Rome, Near Eastern archaeology, Iran in late antiquity; greg_fisher@carleton.ca

Gentile, Patrizia (PhD, Queen's, Can. 2006; assoc. prof.; Indigenous & Canadian Studies; Sociology & Anthropology) Canadian women, sexuality, national security; patrizia_gentile@carleton.ca

Hanes, Roy (PhD, McGill; assoc. prof.; Sch. of Social Work) disability in Canada; roy.hanes@carleton.ca

Hassim, Shireen (PhD, York, Can.; prof. and Canada 150 Research Chair in Gender and African Politics; Institute of African Studies) feminist theory, politics, social movements and collective action; Shireen.Hassim@carleton.ca

Litt, Paul (PhD, Toronto 1989; prof.; Indigenous and Canadian Studies) Canada, cultural policy, public, heritage imaginary/tourism/historic sites in postwar Ontario, mass media and politics of image; paul.litt@carleton.ca

Patterson, Monica (PhD, Michigan 2009; asst. prof.; Inst. of Interdisciplinary Studies) modern South Africa, anthropology, childhood; monica.patterson@carleton.ca

Shewell, Hugh (PhD, Toronto 1995; assoc. prof.; Sch. of Social Work) indigenous-state relations in Canada, social welfare, poverty and ideology; hugh.shewell@carleton.ca

Sobers, Candace (PhD, Toronto 2014; asst. prof.; Global and International Studies) international, modern international relations; candace.sobers@carleton.ca

Trainor, Christopher (archivist and dept. head, Archives & Research Collections; MacOdrum Library) chris.trainor@carleton.ca

Trépanier, Anne (PhD, Laval 2005; assoc. prof.; Indigenous & Canadian Studies; French) Quebec political and cultural identity, Quebec and Canadian nationalism, rhetoric and discourse analysis; anne.trepanier@carleton.ca

Wolfart, Johannes C. (PhD, Cambridge 1993; assoc. prof.; Coll. of the Humanities, Religion) modern Christianity, religion and violence, historiography and historical writing; johannes.wolfart@carleton.ca

Wright, J. Barry (PhD, York, Can. 1990; prof.; Law; Institute of Criminology & Criminal Justice) Canadian political trials and national security, criminal and constitutional law, 19th-century British colonial and postcolonial governance

Retired/Emeritus Faculty

Bellamy, John G. (PhD, Nottingham, UK 1966; prof. emeritus) medieval England, legal; john.bellamy@carleton.ca

Bennett, Y. Aleksandra (PhD, McMaster 1984; retired assoc. prof.) 20th-century England, international; Aleksandra.Bennett@carleton.ca

Black, J. Laurence (PhD, McGill 1968; Dist. Research Prof.) modern Russia, Soviet foreign and domestic policy; larry.black@carleton.ca

Curtis, Bruce (PhD, Toronto 1980; prof. emeritus; Sociology and Anthropology) state formation, moral regulation, Canada and British Empire 1780-1900; bruce.curtis@carleton.ca

Elliott, Bruce S. (PhD, Carleton, Can. 1984; prof. emeritus) Canadian social, local, immigration; Bruce.Elliott@carleton.ca

Gorham, Deborah (PhD, Ottawa 1982; Dist. Research Prof.) 19th-century England, women; deborah.gorham@carleton.ca

Griffiths, Naomi E. S. (PhD, London 1969; Dist. Research Prof.) Acadia, France, French Canada; naomi.griffiths@carleton.ca

Jones, Raymond A. (PhD, London Sch. of Economics 1968; prof. emeritus) diplomatic and international, 20th century, British foreign policy; raymond.jones@carleton.ca

Kantowicz, Edward R. (PhD, Chicago 1972; prof. emeritus) 20th-century US, US church; edward.kantowicz@carleton.ca

King, Peter J. (PhD, Illinois, Urbana-Champaign 1961; prof. emeritus) US, American Revolution, American Socialist Labor Party; peter.king2@carleton.ca

McDowall, Duncan L. (PhD, Carleton, Can. 1978; prof. emeritus) 20th-century Canada, business; Duncan.McDowall@Carleton.ca

McKillop, A. Brian (PhD, Queen's, Can. 1976; prof. emeritus) Intellectual and cultural, cultural production and expression, biography of journalist/historian/media celebrity Pierre Berton, historiography/theory and method in history

Merkley, Paul C. (PhD, Toronto 1965; prof. emeritus) US religious; paul.merkley@carleton.ca

Muise, Delphin A. (PhD, Western Ontario 1971; prof. emeritus) Canada, Maritimes, public; Del.Muise@Carleton.ca

Phillips, Mark Saber (PhD, Toronto 1974; prof. emeritus; Inst. for Comparative Studies in Literature, Art, and Culture) European intellectual and cultural, historical theory; mark.phillips@carleton.ca

Taylor, John H. (MA, British Columbia 1976; prof. emeritus) Canadian urban and social; john.taylor@carleton.ca

Recently Awarded PhDs

Lundrigan, Meghan "Holocaust Memory and Visuality in the Age of Social Media"

Murphy, Romalie "Colonizing Space and Producing Territory: John and Elizabeth Simcoe and Water, Power, and Empire in Upper Canada, 1792-96"

Smith, Dorothy-Jane "The Ottawa Valley Journal and the Modern Countryside: A City-Country Newspaper and the New Journalism in Eastern Ontario, 1887-1925"

Concordia University

Dept. of History, 1455 de Maisonneuve Blvd. W., Montreal, QC H3G 1M8, Canada. 514.848.2424. Fax 514.848.4538. Email: history@concordia.ca; Donna.Whittaker@concordia.ca. Website: http://www.concordia.ca/artsci/history.html

The History Department at Concordia University is a dynamic centre of research and teaching that produces innovative scholarship and trains students to use knowledge about the past both within academia and beyond it.

Chair: Matthew Penney
Director of Graduate Studies: Anya Zilberstein
Director of Undergraduate Studies: Gavin Taylor; Alison Rowley (honours programs)
Degrees Offered: BA, MA, PhD
Academic Year System: Semester
Areas of Specialization: cultural/public/oral, new media, gender and sexuality, genocide and human rights, transnational

Tuition:

Québec undergraduate $3,700 to $4,600, Canadian undergraduate $8,900 to $10,000, international undergraduate $20,600 to $27,000; Québec MA $6,000 to $6,300, Canadian MA $14,100 to $14,300, international MA $29,000 to $40,000

Enrollment 2018-19:

Undergraduate Majors: 825

New Graduate Students: 17

Full-time Graduate Students: 48

Part-time Graduate Students: 3

Degrees in History: 150 BA, 8 MA, 1 PhD

Undergraduate Addresses:

Admissions: http://www.concordia.ca/admissions/

Financial Aid: http://www.concordia.ca/offices/faao/

Graduate Addresses:

Admissions and Financial Aid: http://www.concordia.ca/artsci/history/programs/graduate.html

Full-time Faculty

Berger, Rachel (PhD, Cambridge 2007; assoc. prof.; dir., individualized program (MA & PhD), Sch. of Graduate Studies) modern South Asia, medicine, gender and sexuality; Rachel.Berger@concordia.ca

Bergholz, Max A. (PhD, Toronto 2010; assoc. prof.) Balkans and eastern Europe, genocide and mass violence, memory and remembrance; Max.Bergholz@concordia.ca

Carr, Graham (PhD, Maine 1983; prof.; interim Univ. pres.; and vice chancellor) Canadian cultural and intellectual; Graham.Carr@concordia.ca

Chalk, Frank Robert (PhD, Wisconsin, Madison 1970; prof.) US foreign relations, Africa; Frank.Chalk@concordia.ca

Foster, Gavin M. (PhD, Notre Dame 2009; assoc. prof.; Sch. of Irish Studies) modern Ireland and Britain, social and cultural, nationalism; Gavin.Foster@concordia.ca

Ghabrial, Sarah (PhD, McGill 2014; asst. prof.; Political Science) modern Maghreb, law and society, colonialism/gender/family; Sarah.Ghabrial@concordia.ca

Gossage, Peter J. (PhD, Québec, Montréal 1991; prof.) Québec society, family and gender, historical demography; Peter.Gossage@concordia.ca

High, Steven (PhD, Ottawa 1999; prof.) North America, oral, public; Steven.High@concordia.ca

Ingram, Norman (PhD, Edinburgh 1988; prof.) modern France, peace movements, international relations; Norman.Ingram@concordia.ca

Ivaska, Andrew M. (PhD, Michigan 2003; assoc. prof.) modern Africa, popular culture, urban social change in Africa; Andrew.Ivaska@concordia.ca

Jacob, Wilson Chacko (PhD, NYU 2005; assoc. prof.) modern Middle East, cultural, gender and sexuality; Wilson.Jacob@concordia.ca

Jaffary, Nora E. (PhD, Columbia 2000; prof.) colonial Latin America, Mexico, gender; Nora.Jaffary@concordia.ca

Lehrer, Erica (PhD, Michigan 2005; prof.) post-Holocaust Jewry, heritage and museums, post-conflict memory and identity; Erica.Lehrer@concordia.ca

Lorenzkowski, Barbara (PhD, Ottawa 2002; assoc. prof.) Canada and US, ethnicity and gender, cultural and social; Barbara.Lorenzkowski@concordia.ca

McCormick, Ted G. (PhD, Columbia 2005; assoc. prof.) early modern Europe, intellectual, colonialism; Ted.McCormick@concordia.ca

McGaughey, Jane G. V. (PhD, London 2008; prof.; Sch. of Irish Studies) colonial Canada, diasporas and empire, sexuality; Jane.McGaughey@concordia.ca

McSheffrey, Shannon (PhD, Toronto 1992; prof.) late medieval England, gender and social, law; Shannon.McSheffrey@concordia.ca

Penney, Matthew (PhD, Auckland 2007; assoc. prof. and chair) modern Japan, war memory, popular culture and film; Matthew.Penney@concordia.ca

Razlogova, Elena (PhD, George Mason 2004; assoc. prof.) 20th-century US cultural, US in global context, digital; Elena.Razlogova@concordia.ca

Reiter, Eric H. (PhD, Toronto 1994; LLM, McGill 2004; assoc. prof.) Canadian legal, law and society; Eric.Reiter@concordia.ca

Rowley, Alison (PhD, Duke 2000; prof. and dir., honours programs) Russian and Soviet social, cultural, women; Alison.Rowley@concordia.ca

Rudin, Ronald (PhD, York, Can. 1977; prof.) French Canada and Ireland, cultural and social, public; Ronald.Rudin@concordia.ca

Taylor, Gavin J. (PhD, William and Mary 2000; asst. prof.; assoc. chair; and dir., undergrad. programs) colonial North America, Native America, Atlantic world; Gavin.Taylor@concordia.ca

Ventura, Theresa M. (PhD, Columbia 2009; asst. prof.) US, environment, international relations; Theresa.Ventura@concordia.ca

Zilberstein, Anya (PhD, MIT 2008; assoc. prof. and dir., grad. studies) environmental, early modern Atlantic and British Empire, science/medicine/technology; anya.zilberstein@concordia.ca

Nondepartmental Historians

Krantz, Frederick (PhD, Cornell 1970; prof.; Liberal Arts Coll.) Renaissance Europe; fkrantz@videotron.ca

Retired/Emeritus Faculty

Bertrand, Charles L. (PhD, Wisconsin, Madison 1969; prof. emeritus) modern Italy; charlesbertrand_2@sympatico.ca

Bode, Frederick A. (PhD, Yale 1969; prof. emeritus) 19th-century US, 19th-century US South, US film; Frederick.Bode@concordia.ca

Decarie, M. Graeme (PhD, Queen's, Can. 1972; assoc. prof. emeritus) modern Canada, Canadian social; graemedecarie1@gmail.com

Fick, Carolyn E. (PhD, Concordia, Can. 1980; assoc. prof. emeritus) Haitian and French revolutions, 16th- to 19th-century Atlantic, European colonialism; Carolyn.Fick@concordia.ca

Hill, John L. (PhD, Duke 1967; assoc. prof. emeritus) modern India

Schade, Rosemarie (PhD, York, UK 1985; assoc. prof. emeritus) 20th-century Germany, German youth and women's movements; Rosemarie.Schade@concordia.ca

Scheinberg, Stephen J. (PhD, Wisconsin, Madison 1966; prof. emeritus) American working class, Canadian-American relations; Stephen.Scheinberg@concordia.ca

Shlosser, F. E. (PhD, McGill 1981; assoc. prof. emeritus) ancient, Byzantine and medieval

Tittler, Robert B. (PhD, NYU 1971; dist. prof. emeritus) Tudor-Stuart England; Robert.Tittler@concordia.ca

van Nus, Walter (PhD, Toronto 1976; assoc. prof. emeritus) Canadian social and urban

Vipond, Mary (PhD, Toronto 1974; dist. prof. emeritus) Canadian cultural and intellectual; Mary.Vipond@concordia.ca

Recently Awarded PhDs

Fillion, Eric "Experiments in Cultural Diplomacy: Music as Mediation in Canadian-Brazilian Relations, 1940s-60s"

Dalhousie University

*Dept. of History, Marion McCain Bldg., Rm. 1158, 6135
University Ave., PO Box 15000, Halifax, NS B3H 4R2, Canada.
902.494.2011. Fax 902.494.3349. Email: history@dal.ca.
Website: https://www.dal.ca/faculty/arts/history.html.*

*As historians must be able to communicate analyses and
arguments clearly and convincingly, Dalhousie's history faculty
are especially committed to teaching our students the necessary
skills, in both written and oral expression, to make their research
results accessible, clear, and persuasive.*

Chair: Krista Kesselring
Director of Graduate Studies: Colin Mitchell
Director of Undergraduate Studies: Christopher Bell
Degrees Offered: BA,MA,PhD
Academic Year System: Semester
Areas of Specialization: Canada, America, Africa, Britain, Europe
Undergraduate Tuition (per academic year):
    Canadian: $8,939
    International: $19,345
Graduate Tuition (per academic year):
    Canadian: $10,179
    International: $20.393
Enrollment 2018-19:
    Undergraduate Majors: 96
    New Graduate Students: 9
    Full-time Graduate Students: 20
    Part-time Graduate Students: 1
    Degrees in History: 49 BA, 3 MA
Undergraduate Addresses:
    Admissions: http://www.dal.ca/admissions.html
    Financial Aid: http://www.dal.ca/admissions/
        money_matters.html
Graduate Addresses:
    Admissions: http://www.dal.ca/admissions/graduate.html
    Financial Aid: http://www.dal.ca/admissions/
        money_matters.html

Adjunct Faculty

Cross, Michael (PhD, Toronto 1968; adj. prof.) Canadian social;
    michael.cross@dal.ca
Sutherland, David (PhD, Toronto 1975; adj. prof.) Canadian social
    and economic, Atlantic Canada; david.sutherland@dal.ca

Affiliated Faculty

Benzaquen, Adriana S. (PhD, York, Can. 1999; assoc. prof.; Mount
    St. Vincent) Europe, childhood, science; adriana.benzaquen@
    msvu.ca
Clow, Barbara (PhD, Toronto 1994; exec. dir.; Atlantic Centre of
    Excellence for Women's Health) medicine; barbara.clow@dal.ca
Cottreau-Robins, Catherine (PhD, Dalhousie 2012; curator; Nova
    Scotia Museum) slavery in Loyalist era, archaeology of Atlantic
    Canada, cultural geography; catherine.cottreau-robins@
    novascotia.ca
Forestell, Nancy M. (PhD, Toronto 1993; prof.; St. Francis Xavier)
    Canada; nforeste@stfx.ca
Frost, Karolyn Smardz (PhD, Waterloo 2003; adj. prof.; Acadia)
    Canada, Atlantic, cultural; ksmardz@acadiau.ca
Gechtman, Roni (PhD, NYU 2005; assoc. prof.; Mount St. Vincent)
    Europe, Jewish, labor; roni.gechtman@msvu.ca
Haigh, Elizabeth (PhD, Wisconsin, Madison 1973; prof.; St. Mary's,
    Can.) Russia; elizabeth.haigh@smu.ca

Hubley, Martin (PhD, Ottawa 2009; curator; Nova Scotia Museum)
    museum studies, naval; hubleym@gov.ns.ca
Kehoe, S. Karly (PhD, Glasgow 2005; Canada Research Chair;
    Saint Mary's Univ., Can.) British Atlantic, Catholicism, rural
    development; karly.kehoe@smu.ca
MacDonald, Monica (PhD, York, Can. 2007; mgr., research; acting
    chief curator, Canadian Museum of Immigration at Pier 21)
    Canada, cultural, environmental; mmmacdonald@eastllink.ca
MacKinnon, Lachlan (PhD, Concordia, Can. 2016; asst. prof.; Cape
    Breton) Canada, Atlantic, social; lachlan_mackinnon@cbu.ca
Marsters, Roger (PhD, Dalhousie 2013; curator; Nova Scotia
    Museum) maritime, cultural landscapes, Canadian cultural;
    roger.marsters@novascotia.ca
McOuat, Gordon (PhD, Toronto 1992; prof.; King's, Can.) science;
    gmcouat@dal.ca
Neatby, Nicole (PhD, Montréal 1993; prof.; St. Mary's, Can.)
    Canada; nicole.neatby@smu.ca
Reid, John G. (PhD, New Brunswick 1976; prof.; St. Mary's, Can.)
    Canada; john.reid@smu.ca
Roberts, Jonathan (PhD, Dalhousie 2015; asst. prof.; Mount St.
    Vincent) Africa, medical, social; jonathan.roberts@msvu.ca
Sewell, William S. (PhD, British Columbia 2000; assoc. prof.; St.
    Mary's, Can.) Japan, China; bill.sewell@smu.ca
Slumkoski, Corey (PhD, New Brunswick 2009; asst. prof.; Mount St.
    Vincent) Atlantic Canada; corey.slumkoski@msvu.ca
Snobelen, Stephen (PhD, Cambridge 2000; assoc. prof.; King's,
    Can.) Britain; snobelen@dal.ca
Stretton, Tim (PhD, Cambridge 1993; prof.; St. Mary's, Can.) legal;
    tim.stretton@smu.ca
Summerby-Murray, Robert (PhD, Toronto 1992; prof.; St. Mary's,
    Can.) Canada, environmental, heritage; robsummerbymurray@
    gmail.com
Twohig, Peter L. (PhD, Dalhousie 1999; prof.; St. Mary's, Can.)
    medicine; peter.twohig@smu.ca
Walls, Martha (PhD, New Brunswick 2006; asst. prof.; Mount St.
    Vincent) Atlantic Canada indigenous; martha.walls@msvu.ca
Whidden, James (PhD, London 1998; prof.; Acadia) Middle East,
    Egypt, Africa; jamie.whidden@acadiau.ca

Full-time Faculty

Bannister, Jerry (PhD, Toronto 1999; assoc. prof.) Canada, Atlantic,
    legal; jerry.bannister@dal.ca
Bell, Christopher M. (PhD, Calgary 1998; prof. and dir., undergrad.
    studies) modern Britain, international, military; bellcm@dal.ca
Bingham, John P. (PhD, York, Can. 1997; asst. prof.) modern
    Europe, Germany, urban; john.bingham@dal.ca
Binkley, Lisa (PhD, Queen's, Can. 2016; asst. prof.) material culture,
    textiles, indigenous/settler relations; lbinkley@mta.ca
Bleasdale, Ruth (PhD, Western Ontario 1984; asst. prof.) Canadian
    cultural, legal, labor; ruth.bleasdale@dal.ca
Cooper, Afua (PhD, Toronto 2000; assoc. prof.) Africa, Canada;
    afua.cooper@dal.ca
Hanlon, Gregory (OPhD, Bordeaux, France 1983; prof.) early
    modern Italy and France, behavioural history from Darwin;
    gregory.hanlon@dal.ca
Kesselring, Krista J. (PhD, Queen's, Can. 2000; prof. and chair) early
    modern England, social and legal; krista.kesselring@dal.ca
Kozlov, Denis (PhD, Toronto 2005; assoc. prof.) modern Russia,
    intellectual, cultural; denis.kozlov@dal.ca
Kynoch, Gary (PhD, Dalhousie 2000; assoc. prof.) Africa, southern
    Africa, crime and conflict; gary.kynoch@dal.ca
McCallum, Todd (PhD, Queen's, Can. 2004; asst. prof.) Canada,
    social, Marxism; todd.mccallum@dal.ca

Mitchell, Colin P. (PhD, Toronto 2002; assoc. prof. and dir., grad. studies) medieval and early modern Islamic world, political, religious; c.mitchell@dal.ca

Pekacz, Jolanta T. (PhD, Alberta 1998; PhD, Warsaw 1987; assoc. prof.) 18th- and 19th-century Europe, social history of music; jpekacz@dal.ca

Roberts, Justin L. (PhD, Johns Hopkins 2008; assoc. prof.) slavery, early America, Atlantic world; justin.roberts@dal.ca

Zachernuk, Philip (PhD, Toronto 1991; assoc. prof.) global, Africa, social and intellectual; pzachern@dal.ca

Joint/Cross Appointments

Holmlund, Mona (PhD, Cambridge 2006; asst. prof.; Fountain School of Performing Arts) art, visual culture, 19th-century England

Kirk, John (PhD, British Columbia 1977; prof.; Spanish) Latin America; john.kirk@dal.ca

Parasram, Ajay (PhD, Carleton, Can. 2017; asst. prof.; International Development Studies) modern/colonial South Asia, decolonial, international relations; parasram@dal.ca

Treiger, Alexander (PhD, Yale 2008; assoc. prof.; Classics) Islam, Eastern Christianity, comparative religion; atreiger@dal.ca

Ulicki, Theresa (PhD, Sussex, UK 2006; asst. prof.; International Development Studies) gender and development, southern Africa; ulickit@dal.ca

Warwick, Jacqueline (PhD, UCLA 2002; assoc. prof.; Music) musicology; jwarwick@dal.ca

Retired/Emeritus Faculty

Crowley, John E. (PhD, Johns Hopkins 1970; Munro Prof. emeritus) early Anglo-America, material culture, landscape; jack.crowley@dal.ca

Flint, John E. (PhD, London 1957; prof. emeritus) Africa, British Empire, Third World

Neville, Cynthia J. (PhD, Aberdeen, UK 1983; prof. emeritus) medieval Scotland and England, legal, social; cynthia.neville@dal.ca

Pereira, Norman (PhD, California, Berkeley 1970; prof. emeritus) Russia; norman.pereira@dal.ca

Tillotson, Shirley M. (PhD, Queen's, Can. 1992; prof. emeritus) Canada, politics, gender; shirley.tillotson@dal.ca

Traves, Thomas (PhD, York, Can. 1976; prof. emeritus and pres. emeritus) Canadian economic and labor, Canadian public policy; tom.traves@dal.ca

Waite, Peter B. (PhD, Toronto 1954; prof. emeritus) 19th- and 20th-century Canada

University of Guelph

Dept. of History, MacKinnon Extension, Guelph, ON N1G 2W1, Canada. 519.824.4120. Email: histsec@uoguelph.ca. Website: https://www.uoguelph.ca/history.

The Tri-University Graduate Program in History combines the faculty and resources at the University of Guelph, Wilfrid Laurier University, and the University of Waterloo. Students register at the university where their advisor is located and receive their degree from that university but do their coursework jointly at all three universities.

Chair: Sofie Lachapelle
Director of Graduate Studies: Susan Nance
Director of Undergraduate Studies: Susannah Ferreira
Degrees Offered: BA, MA, PhD

Academic Year System: Trimester
Areas of Specialization: Scotland, Canada, medieval and modern Europe, gender/family/women, global
Undergraduate Tuition (per academic year):
In-State: $7319
Out-of-State: $21173
Graduate Tuition (per academic year):
In-State: $9114
Out-of-State: $20870
Enrollment 2018-19:
Undergraduate Majors: 276
New Graduate Students: 17
Full-time Graduate Students: 37
Part-time Graduate Students: 2
Degrees in History: 91 BA, 15 MA, 4 PhD
Students in Undergraduate Courses: 5189
Students in Undergraduate Intro Courses: 1486
Online-Only Courses: 8%
Undergraduate Addresses:
Admissions: http://admission.uoguelph.ca
Financial Aid: http://www.uoguelph.ca/registrar/studentfinance/
Graduate Addresses:
Admissions and Financial Aid: http://www.triuhistory.ca

Full-time Faculty

Abraham, Tara H. (PhD, Toronto 2000; assoc. prof.) science and medicine, 20th-century America; taabraha@uoguelph.ca

Carstairs, Catherine (PhD, Toronto 2000; prof.) Canadian and US social and cultural; ccarstai@uoguelph.ca

Cormack, William S. (PhD, Queen's, Can. 1992; assoc. prof.) modern Europe, French Revolution; wcormack@uoguelph.ca

Ewan, Elizabeth L. (PhD, Edinburgh, Scotland 1985; prof. and Univ. Research Chair) medieval and early modern Scotland, early modern Europe; eewan@uoguelph.ca

Ferreira, Susannah Humble (PhD, Johns Hopkins 2003; assoc. prof. and dir., undergrad. studies) medieval, premodern Europe; shumble@uoguelph.ca

Fraser, James (PhD, Edinburgh 2003; assoc. prof. and Scottish Studies Found. Chair) early medieval northern Britain and Ireland, transition from Roman Iron Age; jfrase08@uoguelph.ca

Goddard, Peter A. (DPhil, Oxford 1990; assoc. prof.) early modern Europe, 16th- to 18th-century France; pgoddard@uoguelph.ca

Gordon, Alan (PhD, Queen's, Can. 1997; prof.) Canada, political, heritage; alan.gordon@uoguelph.ca

Hayday, Matthew C. (PhD, Ottawa 2003; prof.) Canada, French Canada, bilingualism; mhayday@uoguelph.ca

James, Kevin J. (PhD, Edinburgh, Scotland 2000; prof.) 19th-century Britain, migration, tourism; kjames@uoguelph.ca

Kolapo, Femi J. (PhD, York, Can. 1998; assoc. prof.) Africa; kolapof@uoguelph.ca

Lachapelle, Sofie (PhD, Notre Dame 2002; prof. and chair) science, European women; slachap@uoguelph.ca

Luby, Brittany (PhD, York, Can. 2016; asst. prof.) North American indigenous; brittany.luby@uoguelph.ca

Mahood, Linda L. (PhD, Glasgow, Scotland 1992; prof.) social control, 19th- and 20th-century Scotland, gender; lmahood@uoguelph.ca

McCook, Stuart (PhD, Princeton 1996; prof.) Latin America, Caribbean, environment; sgmccook@uoguelph.ca

Murray, Jacqueline (PhD, Toronto 1987; prof.) medieval Europe, sexuality; jacqueline.murray@uoguelph.ca

Nance, Susan (PhD, California, Berkeley 2003; prof. and dir., grad. studies) US; snance@uoguelph.ca

Palsetia, Jesse S. (PhD, Toronto 1996; assoc. prof.) South Asia, 19th-century colonialism; palsetia@uoguelph.ca

Racine, Karen (PhD, Tulane 1996; assoc. prof.) Latin America, 19th-century republicanism, omen; kracine@uoguelph.ca

Smith, Norman D. (PhD, British Columbia 2003; prof.) Asian studies, women's studies; nsmith06@uoguelph.ca

Wilson, Catharine A. (PhD, Queen's, Can. 1989; prof.) Canadian social and rural, migration studies; cawilson@uoguelph.ca

Worringer, Renee E. (PhD, Chicago 2001; asst. prof.) Middle East, Far East, Turkey; rworring@uoguelph.ca

Joint/Cross Appointments

Inwood, Kris E. (PhD, Toronto 1984; prof.; Economics) economic, Canada, quantitative methods; kinwood@uoguelph.ca

McDougall, Alan (DPhil, Oxford 2001; assoc. prof.; Sch. of Languages and Literatures) Germany, European studies; amcdouga@uoguelph.ca

Retired/Emeritus Faculty

Andrew, Donna T. (PhD, Toronto 1977; Univ. prof. emerita) 18th- and 19th-century British social, women; dandrew@uoguelph.ca

Boehnert, Gunnar C. (PhD, London 1977; prof. emeritus) Cold War, post-1945 Germany, European defense issues; gboehner@uoguelph.ca

Cassidy, Keith M. (PhD, Toronto 1974; prof. emeritus) 20th century, US social and intellectual; kcassidy@uoguelph.ca

Crowley, Terence A. (PhD, Duke 1975; Univ. prof. emeritus) French Canada, women, Canadian social and rural; tcrowley@uoguelph.ca

Farrell, David R. (PhD, Western Ontario 1968; prof. emeritus) American West, revolutionary to Civil War America, US military; dfarrell@uoguelph.ca

McCalla, Douglas W. (DPhil, Oxford 1972; Univ. prof. emeritus) Canada, rural, economic; dmccalla@uoguelph.ca

Munford, Clarence J. (DPhil, Leipzig, Germany 1962; prof. emeritus) black studies, 17th-century Caribbean slavery, Third World national liberation movements

Murray, David R. (PhD, Cambridge 1968; prof. emeritus) Canadian foreign policy, Latin America and Caribbean; dmurray@uoguelph.ca

Reiche, Eric G. (PhD, Delaware 1972; prof. emeritus) 20th-century German social and political; egreiche@uoguelph.ca

Reid, Richard M. (PhD, Toronto 1976; prof. emeritus) Civil War social, early 19th-century Upper Canada; rreid@uoguelph.ca

Stelter, Gilbert A. (PhD, Alberta 1968; prof. emeritus) Canadian and European urban and town planning, colonial towns; gstelter@uoguelph.ca

Recently Awarded PhDs

Cogan, Theodore "'Sharing the Nation's Heart Globally': Foreign Aid and the Canadian Public, 1950-80"

Devlin, Shayna "'Whatever the World Admires in a Prince': Robert Stewart Duke of Albany, Power, Politics, and Family in Late Medieval Scotland"

Sholdice, Mark McIntosh "The Ontario Experiment: Hydroelectricity, Public Ownership, and Transnational Progressivism, 1906-39"

Yuan, Jianda "Utilizing the Intruders: Re-Examining Chinese-Speaking Elite Experiences in Manchukuo, 1931-37"

University of Manitoba

Dept. of History, 403 Fletcher Argue Bldg., Winnipeg, MB R3T 2N2, Canada. 204.474.8401. Fax 204.474.7579. Email: history@umanitoba.ca. Website: http://umanitoba.ca/faculties/arts/departments/history/.

The department includes faculty members with advanced degrees from leading universities in Canada, Great Britain, the United States, and Europe. They teach an average of fifty undergraduate courses each year, as well as offering seminars at the graduate level and supervising thesis research. The faculty includes specialists in virtually every type of historical study: intellectual, cultural, political, economic and business, Aboriginal, women's, diplomatic, global, comparative, and World history, as well as archival studies and computer applications. The Master's Programme is offered jointly by the History Departments of the University of Manitoba and the University of Winnipeg.

Chair: Tina Mai Chen
Director of Graduate Studies: Len Kuffert
Degrees Offered: BA, BA Hon, BA Adv, MA, PhD
Academic Year System: Full year
Areas of Specialization: Canada and Americas, Europe, modern world, medieval, Asia
Undergraduate Tuition (per academic year):
 Canadian: $3,526.80 Can.
 International: $12,344.10 Can.
Graduate Tuition (per academic year):
 Canadian: $3,928.48 Can.
 International: $7,856.96 Can.
Enrollment 2018-19:
 Undergraduate Majors: 152
 New Graduate Students: 23
 Full-time Graduate Students: 60
 Part-time Graduate Students: 1
 Degrees in History: 10 MA
Undergraduate Addresses:
 Admissions: http://umanitoba.ca/admissions/
 Financial Aid: http://umanitoba.ca/student/fin_awards/
Graduate Addresses:
 Admissions and Financial Aid: http://umanitoba.ca/faculties/arts/departments/history/graduate/

Full-time Faculty

Baader, Benjamin Maria (PhD, Columbia 2002; assoc. prof.) Europe and modern Germany, Jewish, gender; benjamin.baader@umanitoba.ca

Bak, Greg (PhD, Dalhousie 2001; assoc. prof.) archival theory, digital archives, digital information theory; greg.bak@umanitoba.ca

Brownlie, Robin Jarvis (PhD, Toronto 1996; prof.) Canada, aboriginal, colonialism; robin.brownlie@umanitoba.ca

Chadya, Joyce M. (PhD, Minnesota 2005; assoc. prof.) African women, Africa social, southern Africa; joyce.chadya@umanitoba.ca

Chen, Tina Mai (PhD, Wisconsin, Madison 1999; prof. and chair) modern China, political culture, gender; tina.chen@umanitoba.ca

Churchill, David S. (PhD, Chicago 2000; prof.) 20th-century US, gender and sexuality, postwar intellectual; david.churchill@umanitoba.ca

Cossar, Roisin A. (PhD, Toronto 1999; prof.) later Middle Ages, religion and society, medieval Italy; roisin.cossar@umanitoba.ca

Dueck, Jennifer M. (DPhil, Merton Coll., Oxford 2005; asst. prof.) Middle East, youth and politics, cultural; jennifer.dueck@umanitoba.ca

Elvins, Sarah Lynn (PhD, York, Can. 2001; assoc. prof.) America, social and cultural; sarah.elvins@umanitoba.ca

Ferguson, Barry G. (PhD, York, Can. 1982; prof.) Canada, intellectual, political; barry.ferguson@umanitoba.ca

Finlay, John L. (PhD, Manitoba 1968; prof.) Canada, modern Europe, modern intellectual

Frank, Christopher (PhD, York, Can. 2003; assoc. prof.) Britain, labor, legal; chris.frank@umanitoba.ca

Gabbert, Mark A. (PhD, California, Santa Barbara 1973; assoc. prof.) modern Europe, labor, socialism; mark.gabbert@umanitoba.ca

Gibbings, Julie A. (PhD, Wisconsin-Madison 2012; asst. prof.) Central America, ethnohistory, diaspora studies; julie.gibbings@umanitoba.ca

Guard, Julie (PhD, Toronto/OISE 1994; prof.; Labour Studies) Canadian labour studies, gender and women, social movements; julie.guard@umanitoba.ca

Heller, Henry (PhD, Cornell 1969; prof.) early modern Europe, political and social, culture; henry.heller@umanitoba.ca

Jones, Esyllt (PhD, Manitoba 2003; prof.) Canada; esyllt.jones@umanitoba.ca

Kuffert, Leonard B. (PhD, McMaster 2000; prof. and grad. chair) 20th-century Canada, cultural, broadcasting; len.kuffert@umanitoba.ca

Nallim, Jorge A. (PhD, Pittsburgh 2002; prof.) Latin America, Argentina; jorge.nallim@umanitoba.ca

Perry, Adele (PhD, York, Can. 1997; prof.) colonialism, Canada, gender; adele.perry@umanitoba.ca

Smith, Greg T. (PhD, Toronto 1999; assoc. prof.) early modern Britain, cultural, crime and legal; greg.smith@umanitoba.ca

Thomson, Erik M. (PhD, Johns Hopkins 2005; assoc. prof.) early modern Europe, comparative, cultural; erik.thomson@umanitoba.ca

Thorpe, Jocelyn (PhD, York, Can. 2008; assoc. prof.; Women's Studies) environmental, colonialism, Canada; jocelyn.thorpe@umanitoba.ca

Part-time Faculty

Friesen, Jean Usher (PhD, British Columbia 1969; assoc. prof.) Canada, northern Canada, preconfederation Canada; jean.friesen@umanitoba.ca

Gerus, Oleh W. (PhD, Toronto 1970; sr. scholar) Russia, modern Ukraine, Ukrainians in Canada; oleh.gerus@umanitoba.ca

Kendle, John E. (PhD, London 1965; sr. scholar) Canada, British Commonwealth and Ireland

Kerr, Ian J. (PhD, Minnesota 1975; sr. scholar) colonial India, railways, labor and technology; ian.kerr@umanitoba.ca

Kinnear, E. Mary (PhD, Oregon 1973; sr. scholar) women; e.kinnear@umanitoba.ca

Kinnear, Michael S. R. (DPhil, Oxford 1965; sr. scholar) British and western European voting patterns, American congressional elections, modern European minority nationalities; michael.kinnear@umanitoba.ca

Moulton, Edward C. (PhD, London 1964; sr. scholar) Asian studies, modern South Asia, colonialism and nationalism

Nesmith, Thomas C. (PhD, Carleton, Can. 1988; prof.) archival studies; thomas.nesmith@umanitoba.ca

Steiman, Lionel B. (PhD, Pennsylvania 1970; sr. scholar) modern Europe, anti-Semitism, Holocaust; lionel.steiman@umanitoba.ca

Vaitheespara, Ravindiran (PhD, Toronto 1999; sr. scholar) colonial and postcolonial South Asia, nationalism; ravi.vaithees@umanitoba.ca

Retired/Emeritus Faculty

Anna, Timothy E. (PhD, Duke 1969; Dist. Prof. emeritus) Latin America, Mexico; timothy.anna@umanitoba.ca

Bailey, Peter C. (PhD, British Columbia 1974; sr. scholar emeritus) British social, 19th-century leisure and popular culture; baileypc@cc.umanitoba.ca

Carroll, Francis M. (PhD, Dublin 1970; prof. emeritus) US diplomatic, Anglo-American relations, Ireland; francis.carroll@umanitoba.ca

Friesen, Gerald A. (PhD, Toronto 1974; Dist. Prof. emeritus) Canada, prairies, communication; gerald.friesen@umanitoba.ca

Lebrun, Richard A. (PhD, Minnesota 1963; prof. emeritus) modern Europe, 18th- and 19th-century French intellectual

Sandiford, Keith A. P. (PhD, Toronto 1966; prof. emeritus) 19th-century British political, diplomatic, social

Wortley, John T. (PhD, London 1969; prof. emeritus) medieval, Byzantine

Recently Awarded PhDs

Coutts, Robert James "The Language of Place: Heritage, Memory, and Historic Sites in Western Canada"

McGill University

Dept. of History and Classical Studies, 845 Sherbrooke St. W., Leacock Bldg., 7th Fl., Montreal, QC H3A 2T7, Canada. 514.398.3975. Fax 514.398.8365. Email: undergraduate.history@mcgill.ca; graduate.history@mcgill.ca. Website: https://www.mcgill.ca/history/.

This is one of the largest History departments in Canada, with an active and dynamic research culture. The department is home to an extensive undergraduate program, with classes taught by nearly 50 full-time faculty. The graduate program in History offers training towards the MA and PhD degrees in a variety of areas and fields of specialization in historical research. The department sponsors events, talks, and workshops, along with our affiliated research groups in History, across the Faculty of Arts, and in the wider Montreal community.

Chair: Jason Opal
Director of Graduate Studies: Griet Vankeerberghen
Director of Undergraduate Studies: Jarrett Rudy
Degrees Offered: BA,MA,PhD
Academic Year System: Semester
Areas of Specialization: Africa/Asia/Middle East, Americas, Europe, global, thematic
Tuition:
BA: Québec $4,038, non-Québec Canadian $7,728, international $17,125; MA: Québec $4,018, non-Québec Canadian $7,708, international $16,991; PhD: Québec $4,018, non-Québec Canadian $4,017, international $15,505
Enrollment 2018-19:
Undergraduate Majors: 529
New Graduate Students: 39
Full-time Graduate Students: 88
Degrees in History: 252 BA, 26 MA, 6 PhD
Undergraduate Addresses:
Admissions: http://www.mcgill.ca/admissions/
Financial Aid: http://www.mcgill.ca/studentaid/
Graduate Addresses:
Admissions and Financial Aid: http://www.mcgill.ca/gps/

Full-time Faculty

Anastassiadis, Tassos (PhD, Sciences-Po, Paris 2006; asst. prof.) 19th- and 20th-century Greek religion/state formation/nationalism, European missionaries in eastern Mediterranean, activism and institutional change

Basu, Subho (PhD, Cambridge 1994; assoc. prof.) South Asia; subho.basu@mcgill.ca

Beck, Hans (DPhil, Erlangen, Germany; prof.; dir., Classical Studies) archaic and classical Greece, Roman Republic; hans.beck@mcgill.ca

Bruce, Travis (PhD, Western Michigan 2010; PhD, Toulouse 2009; asst. prof.) medieval Mediterranean world; travis.bruce@mcgill.ca

Campbell, Gwyn (PhD, Wales, Swansea 1985; prof.) East Africa, Indian Ocean, world; gwyn.campbell@mcgill.ca

Clarke, Paula C. (PhD, London 1982; assoc. prof.) Italian Renaissance; paula.clarke@mcgill.ca

Cowan, Brian W. (PhD, Princeton 2000; assoc. prof.) early modern Britain; brian.cowan2@mcgill.ca

Desbarats, Catherine (PhD, McGill 1993; assoc. prof.) Canada, New France social and economic; catherine.desbarats@mcgill.ca

Dew, Nicholas (DPhil, Oxford 2000; assoc. prof.) early modern Europe, France; nicholas.dew@mcgill.ca

Downey, D. Allan (PhD, Wilfrid Laurier 2014; asst. prof.) Canadian indigenous; allan.downey@mcgill.ca

Elbourne, Elizabeth (DPhil, Oxford 1992; assoc. prof.) modern Britain; elizabeth.elbourne@mcgill.ca

Fitzpatrick, Shanon (PhD, California, Irvine 2013; lect.) US; shanon.fitzpatrick@mcgill.ca

Fronda, Michael P. (PhD, Ohio State 2003; assoc. prof.) early Roman empire, Latin literature of Republic, late antiquity and classical Greece; michael.fronda@mcgill.ca

Greer, Allan (PhD, York, Can. 1980; prof.) pre-Confederation Canada and Quebec, early modern colonialism; allan.greer@mcgill.ca

Heaman, Elsbeth (PhD, Toronto 1996; assoc. prof.) Canada; elsbeth.heaman@mcgill.ca

Hellman, John W. (PhD, Harvard 1969; prof.) European intellectual, modern France; john.hellman@mcgill.ca

Hoffmann, Peter C. (PhD, Munich, Germany 1961; prof.) early modern and modern Germany; peter.hoffmann@mcgill.ca

Krapfl, James (PhD, California, Berkeley 2007; asst. prof.) eastern and central Europe; james.krapfl@mcgill.ca

LeGrand, Catherine (PhD, Stanford 1980; assoc. prof.) Latin America, Iberia; catherine.legrand@mcgill.ca

Lewis, Brian D. (PhD, Harvard 1994; prof.) modern Britain; brian.lewis@mcgill.ca

Luethi, Lorenz Martin (PhD, Yale 2003; assoc. prof.) international relations; lorenz.luthi@mcgill.ca

Madokoro, Laura (PhD, British Columbia 2012; asst. prof.) modern Canada; laura.madokoro@alumni.ubc.ca

Moore, Leonard J. (PhD, UCLA 1985; assoc. prof.) 19th- and 20th-century US, social; leonard.moore@mcgill.ca

Morton, Suzanne (PhD, Dalhousie 1990; prof.) Canadian social; suzanne.morton@mcgill.ca

Opal, Jason M. (PhD, Brandeis 2003; assoc. prof. and chair) early America; jason.opal@mcgill.ca

Partner, Nancy F. (PhD, California, Berkeley 1975; prof.) medieval, historiography, critical theory; nancy.partner@mcgill.ca

Rudy, Jarrett (PhD, McGill 2001; assoc. prof. and dir., undergrad. studies) modern Québec; jarrett.rudy@mcgill.ca

Soske, Jon Dylan (PhD, Toronto 2009; asst. prof.) 20th-century African intellectual, Indian Ocean genealogies of race, South Asian diaspora; jon.soske@mcgill.ca

Studnicki-Gizbert, Daviken F. (PhD, Yale 2001; assoc. prof.) Latin America and early modern Iberia, world; daviken.studnicki@mcgill.ca

Szapor, Judith (PhD, York, Can. 2001; lect.) eastern Europe; judith.szapor@mcgill.ca

Tai, Jeremy (PhD, California, Santa Cruz 2015; asst. prof.) late imperial and modern China; jeremy.tai@mcgill.ca

Vankeerberghen, Griet (PhD, Princeton 1996; assoc. prof. and dir., grad. studies) early China; griet.vankeerberghen@mcgill.ca

Walker, Gavin (ABD, Cornell; special category asst. prof.; East Asian Studies) Japan; gavin.walker@mcgill.ca

Zucchi, John E. (PhD, Toronto 1983; prof.) modern Canada, immigration; john.zucchi@mcgill.ca

Joint/Cross Appointments

Abisaab, Malek (PhD, SUNY, Binghamton 2001; assoc. prof.; Islamic Studies) modern Middle East, women; malek.abisaab@mcgill.ca

Hundert, Gershon David (PhD, Columbia 1978; prof.; Jewish Studies) Jewish, early modern Poland; gershon.hundert@mcgill.ca

Parsons, Laila (DPhil, Oxford 1995; assoc. prof.; Islamic Studies) modern Middle East; laila.parsons@mcgill.ca

Tone, Andrea E. (PhD, Emory 1992; prof.; Social Studies of Medicine) US social/gender/industry; andrea.tone@mcgill.ca

Wallis, Faith (PhD, Toronto 1985; assoc. prof.; Social Studies of Medicine) medieval; faith.wallis@mcgill.ca

Wright, David (DPhil, Oxford 1993; prof.; McGill Inst. for Health and Social Policy) health and medicine; david.wright@mcgill.ca

Yates, Robin D. S. (PhD, Harvard 1980; prof.; East Asian Studies) traditional China, Chinese science/technology/philosophy, historical theory; robin.yates@mcgill.ca

Retired/Emeritus Faculty

Boss, Valentin J. (PhD, Harvard 1962; prof. emeritus) modern Russia, Slavic, 17th- and 18th-century science; valentin.boss@mcgill.ca

Echenberg, Myron (PhD, Wisconsin-Madison 1971; prof. emeritus) Africa, French empire in Africa, social history of medicine in Africa; myron.echenberg@mcgill.ca

Levesque, Andree (PhD, Duke 1973; prof. emeritus) Quebec, social and economic, gender; andree.levesque@mcgill.ca

Maxwell, Michael P. (PhD, McGill 1966; prof. emeritus) Tudor-Stuart Britain, Ireland; michael.maxwell@mcgill.ca

Miller, Carman I. (PhD, London 1970; prof. emeritus) Canadian social and political, maritime; carman.miller@mcgill.ca

Morton, Desmond (PhD, London 1968; prof. emeritus) Canadian military, political, industrial relations; desmond.morton@mcgill.ca

Ota, Yuzo (PhD, Tokyo 1976; prof. emeritus) Japan, Japanese intellectual; yuzo.ota@mcgill.ca

Schachter, Albert (DPhil, Oxford 1968; prof. emeritus) ancient Greece; jaschachter@compuserve.com

Young, Brian J. (PhD, Queen's, Can. 1973; prof. emeritus) Canada, 19th-century Quebec; brian.young@mcgill.ca

Recently Awarded PhDs

Dial, Andrew "The 'Lavalette Affair': Jesuits and Money in the French Atlantic"

Gilmour, C. Brett "Heldenpolitik: Ritterkreuz, Ideologies and the Complexities of Hero Culture under National Socialism"

Greven, Jeannette F. "Palestine and America's 'Global War on Terror': A History, 2000-2008"

McMaster University

Dept. of History, Chester New Hall, Rm. 619, 1280 Main St. W., Hamilton, ON L8S 4L9, Canada. 905.525.9140. Fax 905.777.8316. Email: histdept@mcmaster.ca. Website: https://history.humanities.mcmaster.ca/.

We offer a broad range of courses at the undergraduate and graduate levels to challenge your perception of the past and the present. Whether you are interested in the medieval or the modern world, national or global history, our diverse and flexible programs will suit you. Our courses are designed to foster key skill sets: how to ask probing questions and seek thoughtful answers, how to read critically, write effectively and speak persuasively.

Chair: Stephen Heathorn
Director of Graduate Studies: Martin Horn
Director of Undergraduate Studies: Megan Armstrong
Degrees Offered: BA, MA, PhD
Academic Year System: Semester
Areas of Specialization: Britain and Europe, Canada, war and society, gender, health and medicine
Undergraduate Tuition (per academic year):
  In-State: $7765
  Out-of-State: $27151
Graduate Tuition (per academic year):
  In-State: $6400
  Out-of-State: $17096
Enrollment 2018-19:
  Undergraduate Majors: 152
  New Graduate Students: 22
  Full-time Graduate Students: 45
  Part-time Graduate Students: 1
  Degrees in History: 53 BA, 17 MA, 6 PhD
  Students in Undergraduate Courses: 2857
  Students in Undergraduate Intro Courses: 518
  Online-Only Courses: 11%
Undergraduate Addresses:
  Admissions: http://registrar.mcmaster.ca/
  Financial Aid: http://sfas.mcmaster.ca/
Graduate Addresses:
  Admissions and Financial Aid: http://graduate.mcmaster.ca/

Adjunct Faculty

Dagenais, Maxime (PhD, Ottawa 2011; adj.) British North America, French North America; dagenam@mcmaster.ca

Harris, Richard (PhD, Queen's, Can.; prof.; Geography) urban; harrisr@mcmaster.ca

Full-time Faculty

Armstrong, Megan Cathleen (PhD, Toronto 1998; assoc. prof. and dir., undergrad. studies) early modern Europe, social and cultural, religious; marmstr@mcmaster.ca

Balcom, Karen A. (PhD, Rutgers 2001; assoc. prof.) modern America, social, women; balcomk@mcmaster.ca

Bouchier, Nancy (PhD, Western Ontario 1990; prof.) sports, Canadian local; bouchier@mcmaster.ca

Cruikshank, Ken (PhD, York, Can. 1988; prof.; dean, Faculty of Humanities) Canada, business, administrative; cruiksha@mcmaster.ca

De Barros, Juanita L. (PhD, York, Can. 1998; prof.) Atlantic world, slavery, British Guyana; debarr@mcmaster.ca

Downey, Allan (PhD, Wilfrid Laurier 2014; assoc. prof.; Indigenous Studies) indigenous nationhood/sovereignty/self-determination; downea2@mcmaster.ca

Egan, Michael (PhD, Washington State 2004; assoc. prof.) science and technology, environmental; egan@mcmaster.ca

Frager, Ruth (PhD, York, Can. 1986; assoc. prof.) Canada, labor, women; frager@mcmaster.ca

Gauvreau, Michael (PhD, Toronto 1985; prof.) Canada, intellectual, social; mgauvrea@mcmaster.ca

Heathorn, Stephen J. (PhD, Toronto 1996; prof. and chair) modern Britain; heaths@mcmaster.ca

Horn, Martin (PhD, Toronto 1994; assoc. prof. and dir., grad. studies) 20th-century Europe, finance; mhorn@mcmaster.ca

Ibhawoh, Bonny (PhD, Dalhousie 2002; prof.) Africa, slavery; ibhawoh@mcmaster.ca

McDonald, Tracy A. (PhD, Toronto 2002; assoc. prof.) Soviet Union, Russia; tmcdon@mcmaster.ca

McKay, Ian G. (PhD, Dalhousie 1983; L. R. Wilson Prof.; Wilson Inst. for Canadian Hist.) Canada, political, social; mckayi@mcmaster.ca

McQueen, Alison (PhD, Pittsburgh 1998; prof.; dir., Sch. of the Arts) cultural and art, 19th-century France; ajmcq@mcmaster.ca

Song, Jaeyoon Harr (PhD, Harvard 2007; assoc. prof.) China; songjae@mcmaster.ca

Streeter, Stephen M. (PhD, Connecticut 1994; assoc. prof.) modern US foreign relations, Latin America; streete@mcmaster.ca

Swett, Pamela E. (PhD, Brown 1999; prof.) 20th-century Europe, Germany; swettp@mcmaster.ca

Weaver, John C. (PhD, Duke 1974; Dist. Univ. Prof.) Canada, social, urban; jweaver@mcmaster.ca

Nondepartmental Historians

Bone, Andrew (PhD, McMaster 1994; ed.; Russell Centre) bone@mcmaster.ca

Retired/Emeritus Faculty

Aksan, Virginia H. (PhD, Toronto 1991; prof. emeritus) Islam, Ottoman Empire; vaksan@mcmaster.ca

Alsop, James Douglas (PhD, Cambridge 1978; prof. emeritus) Tudor-Stuart England, government and economic, military; alsopj@mcmaster.ca

Barrett, David Peter (PhD, SOAS, London 1978; prof. emeritus) China, Asian studies; dpbarrett@sympatico.ca

Cassels, Alan (PhD, Michigan 1961; prof. emeritus) Italy, fascism; cassels@sympatico.ca

Fritz, Paul (PhD, Cambridge 1966; prof. emeritus) 18th-century Britain

Haley, Evan W. (PhD, Columbia 1986; assoc. prof. emeritus) Rome; haleyev@mcmaster.ca

Johnston, Charles (PhD, Pennsylvania 1954; prof. emeritus) British Empire, Canada, native

Kaczynski, Bernice M. (PhD, Yale 1975; prof. emeritus) early Middle Ages; kaczynb@mcmaster.ca

Levenstein, Harvey (PhD, Wisconsin, Madison 1966; prof. emeritus) US, labor radicalism, food social; levenst@mcmaster.ca

Nelles, Henry Vivian (PhD, Toronto 1970; L. R. Wilson Prof. emeritus; Wilson Inst. for Canadian Hist.) Canada, economic; nellesh@mcmaster.ca

Rempel, Richard A. (DPhil, Oxford 1967; prof. emeritus) modern Britain, pacifism, liberalism; rempelr@mcmaster.ca

Russo, David J. (PhD, Yale 1966; prof. emeritus) US, American towns

Thorpe, Wayne L. (PhD, British Columbia 1979; prof. emeritus) modern European labor and radical, political culture in 20th-century Europe, ideologies in 20th-century Europe; thorpew@mcmaster.ca

Recently Awarded PhDs

Clemens, Michael "Framing Nature and Nation: The Environmental Cinema of the National Film Board, 1939-74"

Coschi, Mario Nathan "From Wilhelm to Hans: Ethnicity, Citizenship, and the German Community of Berlin/Kitchener, Ontario, 1871-1970s"

Gataveckas, Brittany "'The Kindness of Uncle Sam'? American Aid to France and the Politics of Postwar Relief, 1944-48"

Johnston, Scott A. "The Construction of Modern Timekeeping in the Anglo-American World, 1876-1913"

Jorgenson, Mica A. R. "'Treasure House to the World': A Global Environmental History of the Porcupine Gold Rush, 1909-29"

Manning, Richard P. "Firebugs, Rustlers, Vandals and Vigilantes: Crime and Criminal Justice in Late 19th- and Early 20th-Century Rural Ontario"

Rowan, Michael "Crash Landing: Citizens, the State, and Protest against Federal Airport Planning, 1968-75"

Shoalts, Adam "Tracking the Sasquatch: Accounts of Monsters in North American Explorers' Journals, 1492-1900"

Memorial University of Newfoundland

Dept. of History, Arts & Admin. Bldg., Rm. A4019, St. John's, NL A1C 5S7, Canada. 709.864.8420. Fax 709.737.2164 Email: stephanc@mun.ca; agushue@mun.ca. Website: https://www. mun.ca/history/.

Our teaching and research focuses on a broad range of geographical areas ranging from Newfoundland to the entire globe. The core of our mission is to promote excellence in teaching and research, fostering a spirit of curiosity and inquiry about all facets of the human past.

Chair: Stephan Curtis
Director of Graduate Studies: Neil Kennedy
Director of Undergraduate Studies: Stephan Curtis
Degrees Offered: BA,BA Hon,MA,PhD
Academic Year System: Semester
Areas of Specialization: Canada, Maritime, Newfoundland and Labrador
Undergraduate Tuition (per academic year):
  Canadian: $3,825
  International: $13,200
Graduate Tuition (per academic year):
  Canadian: $3,939 (MA), $10,156 (PhD)
  International: $5,118 (MA), $13,836 (PhD)
Enrollment 2018-19:
  Undergraduate Majors: 158
  New Graduate Students: 14
  Full-time Graduate Students: 21
  Part-time Graduate Students: 2
  Degrees in History: 24 BA, 6 MA, 2 PhD, 8 BA Hon
Undergraduate Addresses:
  Admissions: http://www.mun.ca/undergrad/apply/
  Financial Aid: http://www.mun.ca/scholarships/home/ index.php
Graduate Addresses:
  Admissions: http://www.mun.ca/become/graduate/
  Financial Aid: http://www.mun.ca/scholarships/financialaid/

Full-time Faculty

Bezzina, Edwin (PhD, Toronto 2004; asst. prof.; Grenfell) early modern Europe, 17th-century French Protestant-Catholic relations; ebezzina@grenfell.mun.ca

Bishop Stirling, Terry L. (MA, Queen's, Can. 1985; asst. prof.) Newfoundland; tstirlin@mun.ca

Bosak, Edita (PhD, London 1982; assoc. prof.) central and eastern Europe, Britain; ebosak@mun.ca

Bregent-Heald, Dominique (PhD, Duke 2004; assoc. prof.) US, Canada, film; dbheald@mun.ca

Burton, Valerie C. (PhD, London 1988; prof.) Maritime, Britain, masculinity; vburton@mun.ca

Cadigan, Sean (PhD, Memorial, Newfoundland 1991; prof.) Canada, Newfoundland, environment; scadigan@mun.ca

Cassis, Marica C. (PhD, Toronto 2007; assoc. prof.) ancient, religion, archaeology; mcassis@mun.ca

Curtis, Stephan M. (PhD, Carnegie Mellon 2000; assoc. prof.; chair; and dir., undergrad. studies) Germany, medicine, family; stephanc@mun.ca

Fantauzzo, Justin S.J. (PhD, Cambridge 2014; asst. prof.) military and World War I, British Empire and Middle East, soldier heroism/masculinity; jfantauzzo@mun.ca

Janzen, Olaf U. (PhD, Queen's, Can. 1983; prof.; Grenfell) Canada, naval, 18th-century Newfoundland; olaf@grenfell.mun.ca

Kennedy, Neil (PhD, Western Ontario 2002; assoc. prof. and dir., grad. studies) Atlantic, colonial, maritime; nkennedy@mun.ca

Kirkpatrick, Michael D. (PhD, Saskatchewan 2013; asst. prof.) global, Guatemala, cultural change; michael.kirkpatrick@mun. ca

Korneski, Kurt (PhD, Memorial, Newfoundland 2004; assoc. prof.) Canada, US, labor; kkornesk@mun.ca

Panjabi, Ranee K. L. (PhD, Peradeniya, India 1980; prof.) Asia, 20th century; rpanjabi@mun.ca

Rossignol, Sebastien (PhD, Lille 3/Göttingen 2008; asst. prof.) medieval Central Europe, urbanization, uses of writing; srossignol@mun.ca

Sandlos, John (PhD, York, Can. 2005; prof.) environment, Canada; jsandlos@mun.ca

Sweeny, Robert (PhD, McGill 1985; Honourary Research Prof.) Canada, US, Industrial Revolution; rsweeny@mun.ca

Webb, Jeff A. (PhD, New Brunswick 1994; prof.) communications, Newfoundland, Maritime; jeff.webb@mun.ca

White, Bonnie (PhD, McMaster 2008; asst. prof.; Grenfell) World War I, Europe, 20th-century Britain; bjwhite@grenfell.mun.ca

Joint/Cross Appointments

Baehre, Rainer (PhD, York, Can. 1985; assoc. prof.; head, Grenfell, Social/Cultural Studies) Canada; rbaehre@grenfell.mun.ca

Connor, James T. H. (PhD, Waterloo 1989; John Clinch Prof.; Medical Humanities, Hist. of Medicine) jconnor@mun.ca

Connor, Jennifer J. (PhD, Western Ontario 1992; prof.) Medical Humanties, Hist of Medicine; jennifer.connor@med.mun.ca

Retired/Emeritus Faculty

Bassler, Gerhard P. (PhD, Kansas 1966; prof. emeritus) modern Europe, migration; gbassler@mun.ca

Hiller, James K. (PhD, Cambridge 1972; prof. emeritus) British Empire, Newfoundland; jhiller@mun.ca

Recently Awarded PhDs

Robinson, Curtis "Ethnic Elites, Propaganda, Recruiting and Intelligence in German-Canadian Ontario, 1914-18"

Université de Montréal

Dept. d'histoire, CP 6128, succursale Centre-ville, Montreal, QC H3C 3J7, Canada. 514.343.6238. Fax 514.343.2483. Email: hst@umontreal.ca. Website: https://histoire.umontreal.ca/.

Alternate Address: Adresse civique: Dépt. d'histoire, C-6128, Pavillon Lionel-Groulx, 3150 Jean-Brillant, Montreal, QC H3T 1N8

Le Département d'histoire de l'Université de Montréal s'impose comme un acteur clé de la recherche historique au Québec et au Canada. Il se distingue par l'ouverture de ses programmes, le caractère cosmopolite de son corps professoral et une perspective interdisciplinaire marquée.

Chair: Jacques Perreault
Director of Graduate Studies: Ollivier Hubert
Degrees Offered: BA,MA,PhD
Academic Year System: Trimester
Areas of Specialization: ancient and Middle Ages, modern and contemporary Europe, Canada/Québec/Americas, East Asia, sciences
Tuition:
Québec resident $1,768.20; Canadian $5,140.80; international undergraduate $11,886, international graduate MA $11,886, PhD $10,673.40
Enrollment 2018-19:
Undergraduate Majors: 305
New Graduate Students: 43
Full-time Graduate Students: 127
Part-time Graduate Students: 11
Degrees in History: 49 BA, 19 MA, 3 PhD
Addresses:
Admissions and Financial Aid: http://admission.umontreal.ca/admission/

Adjunct Faculty

Poulin, Joseph-Claude (PhD, Aix-Marseille, France 1969; research assoc.) medieval Europe; joseph-claude.poulin@umontreal.ca
Ruelland, Jacques G. (PhD, Montréal 1994; research assoc.) science; jgruelland@progression.net

Full-time Faculty

Baillargeon, Denyse (PhD, Montréal 1990; prof.) women and family, Canada; denyse.baillargeon@umontreal.ca
Blennemann, Gordon (PhD, Mainz 2007; prof.) gordon.blennemann@umontreal.ca
Bonnechere, Pierre (OPhD, Louvain-la-Neuve, Belgium 1992; prof.) ancient Greece; pierre.bonnechere@umontreal.ca
Bouchard, Carl (PhD, Montréal 2004; asst. prof.) 20th-century international relations; carl.bouchard@umontreal.ca
Carley, Michael Jabara (PhD, Queen's, Can. 1976; prof. titulaire) 20th-century France and USSR/Russia, international relations; michael.j.carley@umontreal.ca
Dagenais, Michele (PhD, Québec, Montréal 1992; prof.) political, Canada; michele.dagenais@umontreal.ca
Dalton, Susan (PhD, Montréal 1999; assoc. prof.) 18th-century Europe, gender and cultural; susan.dalton@umontreal.ca
Deslandres, Dominique (PhD, Montréal 1990; prof.) early modern Europe, France; dominique.deslandres@umontreal.ca
Dessureault, Christian (PhD, Montréal 1986; assoc. prof.) Canadian economic and social 1760-1850; christian.dessureault@umontreal.ca

Dewar, Helen (PhD, Toronto 2012; asst. prof.) New France; Helen.Dewar@umontreal.ca
Genequand, Philippe (PhD, Genève 2004; asst. prof.) Middle Ages
Hamzah, Dyala (OPhD, Freie, Berlin/EHESS, Paris 2008; asst. prof.) Middle East, Islamic studies; dyala.hamzah@umontreal.ca
Huberman, Michael (PhD, Toronto 1985; prof.) 19th- and 20th-century Britain; michael.huberman@umontreal.ca
Hubert, Ollivier (PhD, Laval 1997; assoc. prof. and dir., grad. studies) Canadian social and cultural 1760-1850; ollivier.hubert@umontreal.ca
Meren, David J. (PhD, McGill 2008; asst. prof.) Canadian international relations, Québec, Canada; david.meren@umontreal.ca
Milton, Cynthia E. (PhD, Wisconsin, Madison 2002; assoc. prof.) Latin America, Andes; cynthia.milton@umontreal.ca
Monnais, Laurence (PhD, Paris 1997; assoc. prof.) East Asia since 1800; laurence.monnais-rousselot@umontreal.ca
Ownby, David (PhD, Harvard 1990; prof.) China; david.ownby@umontreal.ca
Perreault, Jacques (PhD, EHESS, France 1984; prof. and dir.) Greek archaeology; jacques.y.perreault@umontreal.ca
Rabkin, Yakov (PhD, Moscow 1972; prof.) science; yakov.rabkin@umontreal.ca
Ramirez, Bruno (PhD, Toronto 1975; prof.) 19th- and 20th-century US, labor and immigration; bruno.ramirez@umontreal.ca
Raschle, Christian (PhD, Fribourg, Switzerland 1999; asst. prof.) Rome; christian.raschle@umontreal.ca
Saul, Samir (OPhD, Paris, Vincennes 1991; assoc. prof.) contemporary France, international relations; samir.saul@umontreal.ca
Wien, Thomas (PhD, McGill 1988; assoc. prof.) New France, social and economic; thomas.wien@umontreal.ca

University of New Brunswick

Dept. of History, PO Box 4400, Fredericton, NB E3B 5A3, Canada. 506.453.4621. Fax 506.453.5068. Email: history@unb.ca. Website: https://www.unb.ca/fredericton/arts/departments/history/.

The Department of History at UNB offers students a range of courses and areas of study normally found only at much larger universities. We have award-winning teachers, and scholars whose work is at the cutting edge of research in their fields. But History at UNB is, above all, a community of individuals passionate about teaching and learning. The classes are small, the professors friendly and accessible, the students smart and motivated, and the atmosphere warm and welcoming.

Chair: Jeffrey S. Brown
Director of Graduate Studies: Lisa Todd
Degrees Offered: BA,MA,PhD
Academic Year System: Semester
Areas of Specialization: Atlantic Canada, Atlantic world, 20th-century international and military, early modern, women and gender, health and medicine
Undergraduate Tuition (per academic year):
In-State: $7700
Out-of-State: $17357
Graduate Tuition (per academic year):
In-State: $6843
Out-of-State: $14100

Enrollment 2018-19:
Undergraduate Majors: 54
New Graduate Students: 12
Full-time Graduate Students: 29
Part-time Graduate Students: 10
Degrees in History: 18 BA, 7 MA, 1 PhD
Undergraduate Addresses:
Admissions: http://www.unb.ca/admissions/
Financial Aid: http://www.unb.ca/moneymatters/financial/
Graduate Addresses:
Admissions and Financial Aid: http://www.unb.ca/gradstudies/

Adjunct Faculty

Dutcher, Stephen (PhD, New Brunswick 2001; adj. prof.) co-operatives, indigenous-settler society relations, nature of power; sdutcher@unb.ca

Huskins, Bonnie L. (PhD, Dalhousie 1991; adj. prof.) loyalists and freemasons in American Revolution, Atlantic Canada, Atlantic world; bhuskins@unb.ca

Mullin, Janet (PhD, New Brunswick 2008; adj. prof.) 18th-century England, middle classes, leisure culture; mullinj@unb.ca

Full-time Faculty

Brown, Jeffrey Scott (PhD, Rochester 2001; assoc. prof. and chair) post-1865 US, modernity and modernism, American therapeutics; jsbrown@unb.ca

Churchill, Wendy (PhD, McMaster 2005; assoc. prof.) early modern Britain and Atlantic world, medicine social; wchurchi@unb.ca

Corke, Sarah-Jane (PhD, New Brunswick 2000; assoc. prof.) American foreign relations, 20th-century US, US Intelligence; s-j.corke@unb.ca

Fury, Cheryl A. (PhD, McMaster 1998; assoc. prof.) early modern Europe, Elizabethan England, social/maritime/religious; cfury@unb.ca

Hunt-Kennedy, Stefanie Dawn (PhD, Toronto 2015; asst. prof.) early modern Atlantic world, Caribbean and African diaspora, slavery; hunt.kennedy@unb.ca

Kennedy, Sean (PhD, York, Can. 1998; prof.) contemporary Europe, 20th-century France, fascism; skennedy@unb.ca

Lindsay, Debra (PhD, Manitoba 1989; assoc. prof.) 19th-century US, women, science; dlindsay@unbsj.ca

MacDonald, Heidi E. (PhD, New Brunswick 2000; prof.) post-Confederation Canada, Atlantic Canada women, youth, oral; heidimacdonald@unb.ca

Mancke, Elizabeth (PhD, Johns Hopkins 1990; prof.) Atlantic Canada, Atlantic world, British imperial; emancke@unb.ca

Marquis, Gregory (PhD, Queen's, Can. 1987; prof.) Canadian legal, law enforcement, crime; gmarquis@unbsj.ca

Milner, J. Marc (PhD, New Brunswick 1983; prof.; dir., Gregg Centre) military and naval; milner@unb.ca

Morton, Erin (PhD, Queen's, Can. 2009; asst. prof.) visual and material culture, Atlantic Canada; emorton@unb.ca

Mullally, Sasha (PhD, Toronto 2005; assoc. prof.) Canada, post-Civil War US, health and medicine; sasham@unb.ca

Parenteau, William M. (PhD, New Brunswick 1994; prof.) post-Confederation Canada, Atlantic Canadian environmental; wparent@unb.ca

Todd, Lisa M. (PhD, Toronto 2005; assoc. prof. and dir., grad. studies) modern Germany, gender and sexuality, war and society; ltodd@unb.ca

Waite, Gary K. (PhD, Waterloo 1986; prof.) early modern Europe; waite@unb.ca

Whitney, Robert (PhD, Queen's, Can. 1996; assoc. prof.) Latin America; whitney@unbsj.ca

Windsor, Lee (PhD, New Brunswick 2006; research assoc.; deputy dir., Gregg Centre) war, modern warfare, Canadian military; lwindsor@unb.ca

Retired/Emeritus Faculty

Campbell, Gail G. (PhD, Clark 1983; prof. emeritus) 19th-century Canadian social and political culture, quantitative, New Brunswick; campbell@unb.ca

Charters, David (PhD, London 1980; retired prof.) war studies, insurgency and counter-insurgency; charters@unb.ca

Conrad, Margaret (PhD, Toronto 1979; prof. emeritus) Canada, women's studies; mconrad@unb.ca

Frank, David A. (PhD, Dalhousie 1979; retired prof.) Canadian social and labour; dfrank@unb.ca

Kealey, Gregory S. (PhD, Rochester 1977; prof. emeritus) Canadian social, Canadian security and intelligence, North American working class; gkealey@unb.ca

Kealey, Linda (PhD, Toronto 1982; prof. emeritus) America, Canadian women and gender; lkealey@unb.ca

Kent, Peter C. (PhD, London/London Sch. Econ. 1978; prof. emeritus) Italian foreign policy, Holy See foreign policy; kent@unb.ca

Turner, R. Steven (PhD, Princeton 1973; prof. emeritus) science; turner@unb.ca

Recently Awarded PhDs

Devor, Teresa "'Living Weather' for Survival: Cultivating Local Climatic Knowledge in New Brunswick, c. 1790-1870"

University of Northern British Columbia

Dept. of History, 3333 University Way, Prince George, BC V2N 4Z9, Canada. 250.960.5594. Fax 250.960.5545. Email: history@unbc.ca. Website: https://www.unbc.ca/history.

The study of history contributes to critical thinking, helps to develop intellectual maturity, and assists students to present ideas clearly and accurately. Courses in our department blend thematic and geographic approaches to the study of history.

Chair: Ted Binnema
Director of Graduate Studies: Dana Wessell Lightfoot
Degrees Offered: BA, BA Hon, MA
Academic Year System: Semester
Areas of Specialization: British Columbia, women and gender, legal, Iberian world and Latin America, environmental and indigenous peoples
Undergraduate Tuition (per academic year):
In-State: $4171
Out-of-State: $14598
Graduate Tuition (per academic year): $3232
Enrollment 2018-19:
Undergraduate Majors: 48
New Graduate Students: 2
Full-time Graduate Students: 5
Degrees in History: 32 BA, 3 MA
Undergraduate Addresses:
Admissions: http://www.unbc.ca/apply
Financial Aid: http://www.unbc.ca/financial-aid
Graduate Addresses:
Admissions: https://www.unbc.ca/history/graduate-program
Financial Aid: http://www.unbc.ca/financial-aid

Full-time Faculty

Binnema, Theodore (PhD, Alberta 1998; prof. and chair) indigenous, environmental, science; Ted.Binnema@unbc.ca

Bryce, Benjamin (PhD, York, Can. 2013; asst. prof.) Latin America and Canada, transnationalism and migration, health; benjamin.bryce@unbc.ca

Holler, Jacqueline S. (PhD, Emory 1998; assoc. prof.) colonial Latin America, gender, religion; holler@unbc.ca

Lightfoot, Dana Wessell (PhD, Toronto 2005; assoc. prof. and dir., grad. studies) medieval Spain, women and gender, medieva Europe; lightfoot@unbc.ca

Swainger, Jonathan (PhD, Western Ontario 1991; prof.) Canadian legal, western Canada; swainger@unbc.ca

Retired/Emeritus Faculty

Jago, Charles (PhD, Cambridge 1969; prof. emeritus) early modern Spain; charles.jago@unbc.ca

Martel, Gordon (PhD, Toronto 1977; prof. emeritus) international, historiography; martel@unbc.ca

Morrison, William (PhD, Western Ontario 1973; prof. emeritus) northern Canada; morrison@unbc.ca

Université du Québec à Montréal

Département d'histoire, CP 8888, succursale Centre-Ville, Montreal, QC H3C 3P8, Canada. 514.987.4154. Fax 514.987.7813. Email: dept.histoire@uqam.ca. Website: https://histoire.uqam.ca/.

Le Département d'histoire se situe dans une tradition de couverture large de l'histoire du monde occidental, mais il a ouvert ses champs de spécialisation bien au-delà, en engageant de nouveaux professeurs en histoire des relations internationales, du Moyen-Orient, de l'Asie du Sud-Est et de la Chine, en passant par l'Egypte ancienne et l'Amérique latine. Les domaines d'enseignement et de recherche touchent un large éventail de champs spatio-temporels et thématiques.

Chair: Lyse Roy
Director of Graduate Studies: Alain Beaulieu
Director of Undergraduate Studies: Isabelle Lehuu
Degrees Offered: BA, MA, PhD
Academic Year System: Trimester
Areas of Specialization: Québec and Canada, US, Latin America, modern and contemporary Europe, antiquity, Middle Ages, Asia
Undergraduate Tuition (per academic year):
  Québec $3,095 Can.
  Canadian $8,270 Can.
  International $17,450 Can.
Graduate Tuition (per academic year):
  MA First Year Québec: $3,565 Can.
  MA First Year Canadian: $9,390 Can.
  MA First Year International: $19,720 Can.
  PhD First Year: $3,565 Can.
Enrollment 2018-19:
  Undergraduate Majors: 300
  New Graduate Students: 40
  Full-time Graduate Students: 100
  Part-time Graduate Students: 50
Addresses:
  Admissions: http://www.etudier.uqam.ca/
  Financial Aid: http://vie-etudiante.uqam.ca/aide-financiere/

Full-time Faculty

Alexeeva, Olga (PhD, Paris Diderot-Paris VII 2010; prof.) 19th- and 20th-century East Asia and China; alexeeva.olga@uqam.ca

Barros, Andrew (PhD, Cambridge 2000; prof.) 20th-century international relations; barros.andrew@uqam.ca

Bastien, Pascal (PhD, Laval 2002; PhD, Paris XIII; prof.) 18th-century France, political and cultural; bastien.pascal@uqam.ca

Beaulieu, Alain (PhD, Laval 1993; prof. and dir., grad. studies) 17th to 19th centuries, New France, indigenous; beaulieu.alain@uqam.ca

Burgess, Joanne (PhD, Québec, Montréal 1987; prof.) 19th-century Canada, 19th-century Québec; burgess.joanne@uqam.ca

Cohen, Yolande J. (PhD, Paris 1978; prof.) 20th-century Europe, France, 20th-century women; cohen.yolande@uqam.ca

Colantonio, Laurent (PhD, Paris 8-Saint-Denis 2001; prof.) 19th- and 20th-century United Kingdom; colantonio.laurent@uqam.ca

Depatie, Sylvie (PhD, McGill 1988; prof.) 18th- and 19th-century Canada; depatie.sylvie@uqam.ca

Deruelle, Benjamin (PhD, Paris I-Panthéon-Sorbonne 2011; prof.) modern Europe, military, digital humanities; deruelle.benjamin@uqam.ca

Dorais, Geneviève (PhD, Wisconsin, Madison 2014; prof.) Latin America, 19th to 20th century; dorais.genevieve@uqam.ca

Drendel, John (PhD, Toronto 1990; prof.) Middle Ages; drendel.john_v@uqam.ca

Fahrni, Magda (PhD, York, Can. 2001; prof.) 20th-century Québec and Canada, women and gender, health and welfare; fahrni.magda@uqam.ca

Fougeres, Dany (PhD, INRS Urbanisation 2002; prof.) 19th- to 20th-century Canada/Québec; fougeres.dany@uqam.ca

Gagnon, Robert (PhD, Montréal 1990; prof.) technology and education; gagnon.robert@uqam.ca

Garneau, Jean-Philippe (PhD, Québec, Montréal 2003; prof.) 18th- and 19th-century Canada; garneau.jean-philippe@uqam.ca

Gingras, Yves (PhD, Montréal 1984; prof.) science and technology; gingras.yves@uqam.ca

Goscha, Christopher E. (PhD, Sorbonne 2001; prof.) 20th-century international relations; goscha.christopher@uqam.ca

Lehuu, Isabelle (PhD, Cornell 1992; prof. and dir., undergrad. studies) antebellum US, social and cultural; lehuu.isabelle@uqam.ca

Levesque, Jean (PhD, Toronto 2003; prof.) modern Russia and eastern Europe; levesque.jean@uqam.ca

Marquis, Dominique (PhD, Québec, Montréal 1999; prof.) 20th-century Québec and Canada; marquis.dominique@uqam.ca

Nagy, Piroska (PhD, EHSS, Paris; prof.) Middle Ages; nagy.piroska@uqam.ca

Petitclerc, Martin (PhD, Québec, Montréal 2004; prof.) 19th- and 20th-century Québec and Canada; petitclerc.martin@uqam.ca

Pollard, Richard (PhD, Cambridge 2009; prof.) Middle Ages, medieval Italy, intellectual culture; pollard.richard@uqam.ca

Poyet, Julia (PhD, Montréal 2009; prof.) poyet.julia@uqam.ca

Revez, Jean (PhD, Paris-Sorbonne (Paris IV) 1999; prof.) Egyptology; revez.jean@uqam.ca

Robinson, Greg J. (PhD, NYU 2000; prof.) 20th-century US, social; robinson.greg@uqam.ca

Ross, Daniel (PhD, York, Can. 2017; prof.) 20th-century Canada and Québec, urban, political

Roy, Lyse (PhD, Montréal 1994; prof. and chair) modern Europe; roy.lyse@uqam.ca

Savard, Stéphane (PhD, Laval 2010; prof.) 20th-century Canada and Québec political; savard.stephane@uqam.ca

Steinhoff, Anthony J. (PhD, Chicago 1996; prof.) 19th- and 20th-century Europe and Germany; steinhoff.anthony@uqam.ca

Theriault, Gaetan (PhD, Laval 1994; prof.) ancient Greece and Rome; theriault.gaetan@uqam.ca

Winter, Stefan (PhD, Chicago 2002; prof.) Middle East and Maghreb; winter.stefan@uqam.ca

Zwarich, Natasha (MA, Québec, Montréal 2004; prof. and archivist) records and archives management; zwarich.natasha@uqam.ca

Queen's University

Dept. of History, 49 Bader Ln., Watson Hall, 212, Kingston, ON K7L 3N6, Canada. 613.533.2150. Fax 613.533.6298. Email: collinsj@queensu.ca. Website: https://www.queensu.ca/history/.

When you study History at Queen's University you'll follow in the footsteps of thousands of alumni who have occupied and currently hold positions in the commanding heights of government, law, business, education, management consulting, public relations, advertising, journalism, publishing, and the heritage sector.

Chair: Jeffrey Collins, acting
Director of Graduate Studies: Adnan Husain
Director of Undergraduate Studies: Amitava Chowdhury
Degrees Offered: BA, BA Hon, MA, PhD
Academic Year System: Semester
Areas of Specialization: Europe, North America, Africa, Atlantic world, labor/religious/rural/women
Undergraduate Tuition (per academic year):
In-State: $7943
Out-of-State: $41173
Graduate Tuition (per academic year):
In-State: $7610
Out-of-State: $14747
Enrollment 2018-19:
Undergraduate Majors: 379
New Graduate Students: 33
Full-time Graduate Students: 92
Degrees in History: 128 BA, 21 MA, 7 PhD
Undergraduate Addresses:
Admissions: http://www.queensu.ca/admission/
Financial Aid: http://www.queensu.ca/studentawards/financial-aid
Graduate Addresses:
Admissions: http://www.queensu.ca/sgs/applications-admissions
Financial Aid: https://www.queensu.ca/sgs/prospective-students/applying-scholarships

Full-time Faculty

Akenson, Donald H. (PhD, Harvard 1967; prof.) England and Ireland, rural; 8da8@queensu.ca

Brison, Jeffrey (PhD, Queen's, Can. 1998; asst. prof.) modern Canada; brisonj@queensu.ca

Caron, Caroline-Isabelle (PhD, McGill 2001; assoc. prof.) French Canada; caronc@queensu.ca

Carson, James T. (PhD, Kentucky 1996; prof.) antebellum US, Native American ethnohistory; jc35@queensu.ca

Chowdhury, Amitava (PhD, Washington State 2008; asst. prof. and undergrad. chair) Caribbean; a.chowdhury@queensu.ca

Collins, Jeffrey R. (PhD, Harvard 1999; assoc. prof. and acting chair) early modern England; collinsj@queensu.ca

Currarino, Rosanne (PhD, Rutgers 1999; assoc. prof.) late 19th- and early 20th-century US, labor; rc16@queensu.ca

den Otter, Sandra (DPhil, Oxford 1990; assoc. prof.) modern Britain, political thought; denotter@queensu.ca

Dueck, Gordon B. (PhD, Queen's, Can. 1999; asst. prof.) modern Jewish; dueckg@queensu.ca

English, Allan Douglas (PhD, Queen's, Can. 1993; assoc. prof.) Canadian military; english_a@rmc.ca

Errington, E. Jane (PhD, Queen's, Can. 1981; prof.) 18th- and 19th-century North America, women, intellectual; errington_j@rmc.ca

Greenfield, Richard (PhD, London 1985; prof.) middle and late Byzantine history and religion; greenfie@queensu.ca

Haidarali, Laila S. (PhD, York, Can. 2007; assoc. prof.) modern US; laila.haidarali@queensu.ca

Hardwick, Martina L. (PhD, Queen's, Can. 1998; asst. prof.) colonial Upper Canada; hardwick@queensu.ca

Hill, Emily Miriam (PhD, Cornell 1996; assoc. prof.) modern China; hillem@queensu.ca

Husain, Adnan A. (PhD, California, Berkeley 1998; assoc. prof. and grad. chair) medieval Western, Middle East; ah28@queensu.ca

Jainchill, Andrew J. S. (PhD, California, Berkeley 2004; assoc. prof.) early modern Europe; andrew.jainchill@queensu.ca

Manley, Rebecca (PhD, California, Berkeley 2004; assoc. prof.) Soviet Russia; manleyr@queensu.ca

Maynard, Steven (MA, Queen's, Can. 1987; lect.) Canadian social; maynards@queensu.ca

McNairn, Jeffrey L. (PhD, Toronto 1997; assoc. prof. and assoc. chair) colonial and early national Canada; mcnairnj@queensu.ca

Pande, Ishita (PhD, Princeton 2005; assoc. prof.) South Asia; pande@queensu.ca

Parker, David S. (PhD, Stanford 1991; assoc. prof.) modern Latin America; parkerd@queensu.ca

Pasolli, Lisa (PhD, Victoria 2012; assoc. prof.) 20th-century Canada; lisa.pasolli@queensu.ca

Salzmann, Ariel C. (PhD, Columbia 1995; assoc. prof.) Ottoman Empire; as45@queensu.ca

Sen, Aditi (PhD, Deccan Coll. Post-Graduate and Research Inst., India 2007; asst. prof.) ancient India, gender and food; senadit@gmail.com

Siljak, Ana (PhD, Harvard 1997; prof.) Russia; siljaka@queensu.ca

Smith, Timothy B. (PhD, Columbia 1994; prof.) modern France, European social, welfare state; tbs@queensu.ca

van Deusen, Nancy E. (PhD, Illinois, Urbana-Champaign 1995; prof.) colonial Latin America; nancy.vandeusen@queensu.ca

Walker, Barrington (PhD, Toronto 2003; assoc. prof.) black and immigrant experience in Canada; walkerb@queensu.ca

Weldemichael, Awet Tewelde (PhD, UCLA 2008; asst. prof.) Africa, world; awet.weldemichael@queensu.ca

Woolf, Daniel Robert (DPhil, Oxford 1983; prof.) Tudor and Stuart Britain; woolfd@queensu.ca

Joint/Cross Appointments

Adelman, Howard (PhD, Brandeis 1985; assoc. prof.) early modern Italy; adelman@queensu.ca

Bruno-Jofre, Rosa (PhD, Calgary 1983; prof.; Education) education; brunojor@queensu.ca

Christou, Theodore (PhD, Queen's, Can.; assoc. prof.; Education) social studies, education and curriculum; theodore.christou@queensu.ca

D'Elia, Anthony Francis (PhD, Harvard 2000; prof.; Classics) Renaissance Italy; deliaa@queensu.ca

Dubinsky, Karen (PhD, Queen's, Can. 1991; prof.; Global Development Studies) women, modern Canada; dubinsky@queensu.ca

Epprecht, Marc A. (PhD, Dalhousie 1992; prof.; Global Development Studies) southern Africa, gender; epprecht@queensu.ca

Healey, Jenna (PhD, Yale 2016; asst. prof.) medicine; jenna.healey@queensu.ca

Retired/Emeritus Faculty

Christianson, Paul K. (PhD, Minnesota 1971; prof. emeritus) Tudor-Stuart England; christia@queensu.ca

Duffin, Jacalyn M. (OPhD, Sorbonne, France 1985; prof. emerita) medicine; duffinj@queensu.ca

Jeeves, Alan H. (PhD, Queen's, Can. 1971; prof. emeritus) southern Africa; alanjeeves@cs.com

Mah, Harold (PhD, Stanford 1982; prof. emeritus) modern European cultural and intellectual; hem@queensu.ca

Malcolmson, Robert W. (PhD, Warwick, UK 1970; prof. emeritus) rural England, 1940s; malcolms@queensu.ca

McCready, William D. (PhD, Toronto 1971; prof. emeritus) medieval intellectual; mccready@queensu.ca

Shenton, Robert (PhD, Toronto 1982; prof. emeritus) sub-Saharan African development; shentonr@queensu.ca

Smith, Geoffrey S. (PhD, California, Santa Barbara 1969; prof. emeritus) US diplomatic, US social; smithgs@queensu.ca

Stayer, James M. (PhD, Cornell 1964; prof. emeritus) Reformation Europe; jms2@queensu.ca

Van Die, Marguerite (PhD, Western Ontario 1987; prof. emerita) religious, Canadian church; vandiem@queensu.ca

Recently Awarded PhDs

Couchman, Michael "Apologists, Prohibitionists, and Systemic Inertia: The Origins of Global Drug Control, 1900-45"

Duffett, Angela "Making Home: Performance, Sociability, and Identity in St John's, Newfoundland, 1810-60"

Liu, Yun "Launching Environmental Protection Policies in Hubei, China, 1970-90"

Mackechnie, Johan "Migration and Its Impact on the Household: Medieval Valencia after the Black Death Plague, 1348-1453"

Martin, Valerie "Loyalty, Racializing Power, and the Gendering of the Press: The Newspapers and the Making of an Authoritative Voice for Canadien and Anglo Gentlemen in the Province of Quebec, 1764-1791"

Nesbitt, Douglas "Days of Action: Ontario's Extra-Parliamentary Opposition to the Common Sense Revolution, 1995-98"

Tait, Jackson "The English State Lottery-Loan and the Origins of Modern Public Finance in the Atlantic World, 1694-1826"

Royal Military College of Canada

Dept. of History, PO Box 17000 STN Forces, Kingston, ON K7K 7B4, Canada. 613.541.6000. Fax 613.541.6056. Email: kevin.brushett@rmc.ca. Website: https://www.rmc-cmr.ca/en/history/History-department.

The Department of History shares in the primary mission of the college's academic wing, to provide university-level education to officer cadets as one of the essential elements of their professional development. To this end, the programme in history is designed to meet the specific needs of two types of students: those who major in history and those taking degrees in other departments who have an interest in the discipline.

Chair: Kevin Brushett
Degrees Offered: BA,MA,PhD
Academic Year System: Semester
Areas of Specialization: Canada, military, diplomatic

Tuition: Domestic undergraduate $5,720 Can.; domestic graduate $5,790 Can., international graduate $13,560 Can.

Enrollment 2018-19: Undergraduate Majors: 44
Degrees in History: 15 BA

Undergraduate Addresses: Admissions: https://www.rmc-cmr.ca/en/registrars-office/welcome-admissions

Graduate Addresses: Admissions: https://www.rmc-cmr.ca/en/registrars-office/admission-graduate-studies

Full-time Faculty

Brushett, Kevin (PhD, Queen's, Can. 2001; asst. prof. and chair) Canada, social, urban; brushett-k@rmc.ca

Carrier, Richard (PhD, Laval 2002; asst. prof.) Italy, military; richard.carrier@rmc.ca

Coombs, Howard (PhD, Queen's, Can. 2009; asst. prof.) military education, Canadian military history in modern era; howard.coombs@rmc.ca

Delaney, Douglas E. (PhD, Royal Military, Can. 2003; prof.) Canadian and British Commonwealth military; delaney-d@rmc.ca

Deleuze, Magali (PhD, Montréal 1999; assoc. prof.) Canada, France, peacekeeping; deleuze-m@rmc.ca

Doucet, Marie-Michèle (PhD, Montréal 2015; asst. prof.) France, gender, international relations; Marie-Michele.Doucet@rmc.ca

Grodzinski, Tanya J. (PhD, Royal Military, Can. 2010; assoc. prof.) Canadian military, colonial North American military; Tanya.Grodzinski@rmc.ca

Gullachsen, Arthur W. (PhD, Western Ontario 2016; asst. prof.) Canadian and German military, Britain; Arthur.Gullachsen@rmc.ca

Hennessy, Michael A. (PhD, New Brunswick 1995; prof.) military, naval and maritime, 20th-century Canada; hennessy-m@rmc.ca

Kenny, James (PhD, Carleton, Can. 1994; assoc. prof.) modern Canada, political economy, environmental; kenny-j@rmc.ca

Lamarre, Jean (PhD, Montréal 1996; prof.) immigration, US; jean.lamarre@rmc.ca

Legault, Roch (PhD, Montréal 1996; prof.) Canadian military, preindustrial Canada; legault-r@rmc.ca

Maloney, Sean M. (PhD, Temple 1998; prof.) Canadian military, Cold War; sean.maloney@rmc.ca

Oliveira, Vanessa Dos Santos (PhD, York, Can. 2016; asst. prof.) Africa, slavery and gender; Vanessa.Dos-Santos-Oliveira@rmc.ca

Varey, David (PhD, Royal Military, Can. 2005; asst. prof.) international relations, British foreign policy; varey-d@rmc.ca

Wakelam, Randall (PhD, Wilfrid Laurier 2006; assoc. prof.) air power, Canadian military, military education; randall.wakelam@rmc.ca

Retired/Emeritus Faculty

Dreisziger, N.A.F. (PhD, Toronto 1974; prof. emeritus) modern Canada, eastern Europe, World War II; dreisziger-n@rmc.ca

Errington, E. Jane (PhD, Queen's, Can. 1981; prof. emeritus) 19th-century North America, women; errington_j@rmc.ca

Haycock, Ronald G. (PhD, Western Ontario 1976; prof. emeritus) war and technology, Canadian military, theories of war; haycock-r@rmc.ca

Ion, A. Hamish (PhD, Sheffield, UK 1978; prof. emeritus) modern Japan, Canadian-Japanese relations, Japanese Christianity; ion-h@rmc.ca

Klepak, Hal P. (PhD, London 1985; prof. emeritus) Canada, Latin America, strategy; klepak-h@rmc.ca

McKercher, Brian J. C. (PhD, London Sch. Economics 1979; prof. emeritus) 19th- to 20th-century British foreign policy, Great Powers in modern era, Anglo-American relations since 1900; mckercher-b@rmc.ca

Prete, Roy A. (PhD, Alberta 1979; assoc. prof. emeritus) modern western Europe, French Revolution and Napoleon, World Wars I and II; prete-r@rmc.ca

Saint Mary's University

Dept. of History, McNally North 214, 923 Robie St., Halifax, NS B3H 3C3, Canada. 902.420.5756. Fax 902.420.5141. Email: history@smu.ca. Website: https://smu.ca/academics/departments/history.html.

The department's faculty members have expertise in American, East Asian, Canadian, European, and Latin American History, the quality of which has been recognized through an array of fellowships, grants, prizes, and awards.

Chair: Michael Vance
Director of Graduate Studies: Kirrily Freeman
Degrees Offered: BA,MA
Academic Year System: Semester
Areas of Specialization: Atlantic Canada, Canada, early modern and modern Europe, Americas and Brazil, modern East Asia
Undergraduate Tuition (per academic year):
In-Province: $6,288.50 Can.
Out-of-Country: $12,304.50 Can.
Graduate Tuition (per academic year):
In-Province: $6,776.50 Can.
Out-of-Country: $11,204 Can.
Enrollment 2018-19:
Undergraduate Majors: 74
New Graduate Students: 2
Full-time Graduate Students: 4
Degrees in History: 60 BA, 2 MA
Undergraduate Addresses:
Admissions: http://www.smu.ca/future-students/welcome.html
Financial Aid: http://www.smu.ca/academics/money-matters.html
Graduate Addresses:
Admissions: http://www.smu.ca/academics/fgsr-future-students.html
Financial Aid: http://www.smu.ca/academics/fgsr-future-scholarships-and-awards.html

Adjunct Faculty

Codignola, Luca (LittD, St. Mary's, Can. 2003; LittD, Rome 1970; adj.) luca.codignola@smu.ca

McGowan, Mark G. (PhD, Toronto 1988; adj. prof.) mark.mcgowan@utoronto.ca

Perrins, Robert John (PhD, York, Can. 1996; prof.; Acadia) China, Japan, medicine; robert.perrins@acadiau.ca

Saney, Isaac (PhD, London 2014; adj.) isaac.saney@dal.ca

Full-time Faculty

Barbosa, Rosana (PhD, Toronto 1998; assoc. prof.) Latin America, Brazil, immigration; rosana.barbosa@smu.ca

Brown, Blake (PhD, Dalhousie 2005; asst. prof.) 19th- and 20th-century Canada, legal, Nova Scotia; blake.brown@smu.ca

Freeman, Kirrily (PhD, Waterloo 2005; asst. prof. and dir., grad. studies) modern Europe, France, social and cultural; kirrily.freeman@smu.ca

Morrison, James H. (PhD, Ibadan, Nigeria 1976; prof.) global, Canadian ethnicity, Atlantic migration; james.morrison@smu.ca

Munro, John J. (PhD, California, Santa Barbara 2009; asst. prof.) modern US, race, Cold War and anticolonialism; John.Munro@smu.ca

Neatby, Nicole (PhD, Montréal 1993; assoc. prof.) modern Canada, Québec, public; nicole.neatby@smu.ca

Reid, John G. (PhD, New Brunswick 1976; prof.) colonial northeastern North America, Maritime provinces, Canadian higher education; john.reid@smu.ca

Sewell, William S. (PhD, British Columbia 2000; assoc. prof.) China, Japan, imperialism; bill.sewell@smu.ca

Stretton, Tim (PhD, Cambridge 1993; assoc. prof.) Tudor and Stuart Britain, social and legal, women's legal rights; tim.stretton@smu.ca

Sun, Xiaoping (PhD, California, Santa Cruz 2008; asst. prof.) China, gender; xiaoping.sun@smu.ca

Vance, Michael (PhD, Guelph 1990; prof. and chair) British emigration, Scotland, Ireland; michael.vance@smu.ca

Warner, Lyndan (PhD, Cambridge 1996; assoc. prof.) early modern Europe, family, print culture; lyndan.warner@smu.ca

Joint/Cross Appointments

Kehoe, S. Karly (PhD, Glasgow 2005; research chair; Atlantic Canada Studies) Atlantic Canada communities; karly.kehoe@smu.ca

Murphy, Terry (PhD, Newcastle-Upon-Tyne; prof. emeritus; Religious Studies) religions in Canada and Atlantic Canada; Terry.Murphy@smu.ca

Twohig, Peter L. (PhD, Dalhousie 1999; assoc. prof.; Atlantic Canada Studies) Atlantic Canada, health and medicine; peter.twohig@smu.ca

Retired/Emeritus Faculty

Carrigan, D. Owen (PhD, Maine 1966; prof. emeritus) Canadian crime and punishment, 20th-century US

Howell, Colin D. (PhD, Cincinnati 1976; prof. emeritus) sport, Canada, Atlantic Canada studies; colin.howell@smu.ca

Maccormack, John R. (PhD, Toronto 1960; prof. emeritus) Long Parliament, human values

Young, George F.W. (PhD, Chicago 1969; prof. emeritus) modern Europe, 19th- and 20th-century Germany, 19th- and 20th-century Latin America; geofw.young@smu.ca

University of Saskatchewan

Dept. of History, 9 Campus Dr., Saskatoon, SK S7N 5A5, Canada. 306.966.8712. Fax 306.966.5852. Email: history.department@usask.ca. Website: https://artsandscience.usask.ca/history/.

The Department of History at the University of Saskatchewan is one of the strongest history departments in Canada. We are recognized for our innovative methods and excellence in teaching. Our groundbreaking research has secured millions of dollars in research funding in national and international competitions.

Chair: Jim Handy
Director of Graduate Studies: Angela Kalinowski
Director of Undergraduate Studies: Simonne Horwitz
Degrees Offered: BA,MA,PhD
Academic Year System: Semester
Areas of Specialization: colonial/postcolonial/indigenous, environmental/prairies/US West, science/medicine/health, gender and sexuality, history and politics of memory
Undergraduate Tuition (per academic year):
In-State: $6347
Out-of-State: $17327

Graduate Tuition (per academic year):
In-State: $4137
Out-of-State: $6536
Enrollment 2018-19:
Undergraduate Majors: 98
New Graduate Students: 9
Full-time Graduate Students: 46
Degrees in History: 24 BA, 8 MA, 4 PhD
Undergraduate Addresses:
Admissions: http://explore.usask.ca/admissions/
Financial Aid: http://students.usask.ca/money/scholarships.php
Graduate Addresses:
Admissions: http://www.usask.ca/cgsr/applying/index.php
Financial Aid: http://www.usask.ca/cgsr/funding/

Adjunct Faculty

Barnhart, Gordon (PhD, Saskatchewan 1998; adj. prof.) Canadian prairie, post-Confederation Canada, formation of Germany before World War I; gordon.barnhart@usask.ca

Fairbairn, Brett T. (DPhil, Oxford 1987; adj. prof.) modern Germany, modern European economic, cooperative movements; brett.fairbairn@usask.ca

Jensen, Gordon (PhD, Univ. of St. Michael's Coll. 1992; adj. prof.) Luther, Reformation; gordon.jensen@usask.ca

Klaassen, Walter (DPhil, Oxford 1963; prof.) radical reformation; wrkl@sasktel.net

Sider, Robert (DPhil, Oxford 1965; adj.) ancient, late antiquity; sider@sask.usask.ca

Affiliated Faculty

MacKinnon, Janice C. (PhD, Queen's, Can. 1977; assoc. member; Sch. of Public Policy) Canadian public policy, Canadian fiscal and health policy, federal-provincial relations; janice.mackinnon@usask.ca

Full-time Faculty

Androsoff, Ashleigh (PhD, Toronto 2011; asst. prof.) Western Canada, ethnic diversity, gender; ashleigh.androsoff@usask.ca

Clifford, Jim (PhD, York, Can. 2011; asst. prof.) Britain, environmental, digital; jim.clifford@usask.ca

Cunfer, Geoff (PhD, Texas 1999; prof.) Great Plains, environmental; geoff.cunfer@usask.ca

David, Mirela Violeta (PhD, NYU 2014; asst. prof.) eugenics/birth control, gender; mirela.david@usask.ca

Desbrisay, Gordon R. (PhD, St. Andrews, UK 1989; assoc. prof.; vice dean, Academic) early modern Britain, Scotland, urban/social/intellectual; gordon.desbrisay@usask.ca

Dyck, Erika (PhD, McMaster 2005; prof. and Canada Research Chair) medicine, psychiatry, eugenics; erika.dyck@usask.ca

Englebert, Robert A. (PhD, Ottawa 2010; assoc. prof.) colonial North America, French colonial; r.englebert@usask.ca

Handy, Jim (PhD, Toronto 1986; prof. and head) Central America, 19th century capitalism, peasant; jim.handy@usask.ca

Horwitz, Simonne (DPhil, Oxford 2006; assoc. prof. and dir., undergrad. studies) medicine, colonialism, South Africa; simonne.horwitz@usask.ca

Hoy, Benjamin T. K. (PhD, Stanford 2015; asst. prof.) First Nations, borderlands, North America; benjamin.hoy@usask.ca

Kalinowski, Angela (PhD, Toronto 1996; assoc. prof. and dir., grad. studies) ancient Rome, urban and cultural; angela.kalinowski@usask.ca

Keyworth, George (PhD, UCLA 2001; asst. prof.) medieval Chinese and Japanese religious; george.keyworth@usask.ca

Klaassen, Frank (PhD, Toronto 1999; assoc. prof.; dir., Classical, Medieval, and Renaissance Studies) Renaissance, later Middle Ages 1000-1500, science/technology; frank.klaassen@usask.ca

Korinek, Valerie J. (PhD, Toronto 1996; prof.) 20th-century Canadian cultural/gender/social; valerie.korinek@usask.ca

Labelle, Kathryn Magee (PhD, Ohio State 2011; assoc. prof.) Huron/Wendat/Wyandot diaspora, indigenous North America, settler colonialism; kathryn.labelle@usask.ca

Labelle, Maurice Jr. M., Jr. (PhD, Akron 2012; asst. prof.) Arab decolonization, US-Middle East relations, Arab-Israeli conflict; maurice.jr.labelle@usask.ca

McLeister, Kyle (PhD, McMaster 2011; instr.) medical terminology, ancient medicine and classics; kyle.mcleister@usask.ca

Meyers, Mark F. (PhD, Brown 2000; assoc. prof.) modern European intellectual and cultural, gender and sexuality, modern France; mark.meyers@usask.ca

Neufeld, Matthew (PhD, Alberta 2008; assoc. prof.) early modern Britain, health care systems, cultural memory; matthew.neufeld@usask.ca

Porter, John R. (PhD, Toronto 1990; assoc. prof.) ancient Greek and Latin literature, Attic orators and social; john.porter@usask.ca

Smith, Martha (PhD, Toronto 1997; prof.) 20th-century US foreign relations, Cold War, Asia Pacific; martha.smith@usask.ca

Stiles, Lewis (MA, British Columbia; instr.) medical and scientific terminology, etymology, Greek and Latin poetry; stilesl@shaw.ca

Troupe, Cheryl (PhD, Saskatchewan 2019; asst. prof.) Metis, indigenous, environment and food, gender, indigenous research methodologies, community-engaged research, historical GIS; cheryl.troupe@usask.ca

Watson, Andrew (PhD, York, Can. 2014; asst. prof.) environment, energy, Canada, sustainability, agroecosystems, commodities; a.watson@usask.ca

Joint/Cross Appointments

Khanenko-Friesen, Natalia (PhD, Alberta; assoc. prof.; head, Religion and Culture, St. Thomas More Coll.) oral, ethnic studies, diaspora studies; khanenko-friesen@stmcollege.ca

Wright, Sharon Hubbs (PhD, Toronto 2006; asst. prof.; St. Thomas More Coll.) medieval Britain, medieval women; sharon.wright@stmcollege.ca

Retired/Emeritus Faculty

Bietenholz, Peter G. (DPhil, Basel, Switzerland 1958; prof. emeritus) Renaissance and Reformation, Reformation Italy, Erasmus of Rotterdam; bietenholz@sask.usask.ca

Biggs, Lesley (PhD, Toronto 1990; assoc. prof. emeritus) health care, body, gender; lesley.biggs@usask.ca

Deutscher, Thomas B. (PhD, Toronto 1978; prof. emeritus; St. Thomas More Coll.) Renaissance and Reformation, 16th-century Italian clerical education, Erasmus of Rotterdam; tdeutscher@stmcollege.ca

Grogin, Robert C. (PhD, NYU 1969; prof. emeritus) 20th-century Europe, interwar France

Hayden, J. Michael (PhD, Loyola, Chicago 1963; prof. emeritus) 17th-century Europe, 16th- and 17th-century French social and religious; michael.hayden@usask.ca

Kent, Christopher A. (DPhil, Sussex, UK 1969; prof. emeritus; ed., Canadian Journal of History) 19th-century English social and intellectual, women, arts and society; chris.kent@usask.ca

Kitzan, Laurence (PhD, Toronto 1965; prof. emeritus) British Empire; kitzan@sask.usask.ca

Miller, James R. (PhD, Toronto 1972; prof. and Canada Research Chair emeritus) native-newcomer relations, post-Confederation Canada; jim.miller@usask.ca

Miquelon, Dale B. (PhD, Toronto 1974; prof. emeritus) Canada to 1867, French Canada to 1800, French-Canadian nationalism; dale.miquelon@usask.ca

Regehr, Theodore D. (PhD, Alberta 1967; prof. emeritus) western Canada, business; tregehr@ucalgary.ca

Stewart, Larry (PhD, Toronto 1978; prof. emeritus) early modern science and technology; stewartl@sask.usask.ca

Swan, P. Michael (PhD, Harvard 1965; prof. emeritus) ancient Rome, ancient Greece, dynasty of Caesars; swan@sask.usask.ca

Waiser, William A. (PhD, Saskatchewan 1983; prof. emeritus) western and northern Canada; bill.waiser@usask.ca

Recently Awarded PhDs

Beninger, Carling "Does the Church Really Care: The Indigenous Policies of the Anglican, Presbyterian, and United Churches of Canada, 1946-90"

DeWitt, Jessica Marie "Middle Parks: Development of State and Provincial Parks in the United States and Canada, 1890-1990"

Iceton, Glenn "Defining Space: How History Has Shaped and Informed Notions of Kaska Land Use and Occupancy"

Razumenko, Fedir "Clinical Trials, Cancer, and the Emergence of Human Subject Research Ethics in Canada, 1921-80"

Spinney, Erin Elizabeth "Naval and Military Nursing in the British Empire, c. 1763-1830"

Troupe, Cheryl "Mapping Métis Stories: Land Use, Gender and Kinship in the Qu'Appelle Valley, 1850-1950"

Simon Fraser University

Dept. of History, 8888 University Dr., Burnaby, BC V5A 1S6, Canada. 778.782.3521. Email: histgo@sfu.ca; histgrad@sfu.ca. Website: http://www.sfu.ca/history.html.

The Department of History provides courses that introduce students to major world regions and cultures, to historical periods, and to social, political, cultural and economic themes. Our offerings reflect our local context while also providing a global perspective.

Chair: Jennifer Spear
Director of Graduate Studies: Mary-Ellen Kelm
Director of Undergraduate Studies: Nicolas Kenny
Degrees Offered: BA,MA,PhD
Academic Year System: Trimester
Areas of Specialization: Europe, Americas, Middle East, Asia
Undergraduate Tuition (per academic year):
　In-State: $5647
　Out-of-State: $25220
Graduate Tuition (per academic year): $5726
Enrollment 2018-19:
　Undergraduate Majors: 238
　New Graduate Students: 14
　Full-time Graduate Students: 32
　Degrees in History: 132 BA, 4 MA, 2 PhD
　Students in Undergraduate Courses: 3149
　Students in Undergraduate Intro Courses: 1127
Undergraduate Addresses:
　Admissions: http://www.sfu.ca/admission/undergraduate.html
　Financial Aid: http://www.sfu.ca/students/financialaid/
Graduate Addresses:
　Admissions and Financial Aid: http://www.sfu.ca/history/graduate.html

Full-time Faculty

Adcock, Christina (PhD, Cambridge 2010; asst. prof.) modern Canada, northern and circumpolar, cultural; tina.adcock@sfu.ca

Brown, Jeremy (PhD, California, San Diego 2008; assoc. prof.) modern China; jeremy_brown@sfu.ca

Chenier, Elise R. (PhD, Queen's, Can. 2001; prof.) Canada, women and gender, sexuality; echenier@sfu.ca

Clossey, Luke (PhD, California, Berkeley 2004; assoc. prof.) early modern world; lclossey@sfu.ca

Craig, John (PhD, Cambridge 1992; prof.) early modern England; johnc@sfu.ca

Garfinkel, Paul A. (PhD, Brandeis 2004; assoc. prof.) modern Italy, legal and social, criminal law; pgarfink@sfu.ca

Geiger, Andrea (PhD, Washington 2006; assoc. prof.) trans-Pacific and borderlands, race/contact relations/migration, legal; aageiger@sfu.ca

Ghazal, Amal (PhD, Alberta 2005; assoc. prof.; dir., Centre for the Comparative Study of Muslim Societies and Cultures) modern Arab world, Islamic intellectual, Islam in Africa; amal_ghazal@sfu.ca

Kelm, Mary-Ellen (PhD, Toronto 1995; prof. and grad. chair) modern Canada, indigenous peoples, health and gender; kelm@sfu.ca

Kenny, Nicolas (PhD, Montréal and Libre de Bruxelles 2008; assoc. prof. and undergrad. chair) Canada/Quebec, cultural and urban, Europe; nicolas_kenny@sfu.ca

Keough, Willeen (PhD, Memorial, Newfoundland 2002; prof.) Atlantic Canada and Ireland, gender and ethnicity, cultural memory; wkeough@sfu.ca

Kuehn, Thomas (PhD, NYU 2005; assoc. prof.) modern Middle East, Ottoman Empire; thomas_kuehn@sfu.ca

Leier, Mark (PhD, Memorial, Newfoundland 1991; prof.) Labor and the left, anarchism, post-Confederation Canada; leier@sfu.ca

Matsumura, Janice (PhD, York, Can. 1994; assoc. prof.) modern Japan; jmatsumu@sfu.ca

Pabel, Hilmar M. (PhD, Yale 1992; prof.) early modern Europe, Reformation; pabel@sfu.ca

Panchasi, Roxanne (PhD, Rutgers 2002; assoc. prof.) modern France; panchasi@sfu.ca

Ray, Bidisha (PhD, Manchester 2008; sr. lect.) modern South Asia; bray@sfu.ca

Sedra, Paul (PhD, NYU 2006; assoc. prof.) modern Arab Middle East; pdsedra@sfu.ca

Spear, Jennifer M. (PhD, Minnesota 1999; assoc. prof. and chair) early North America, race, gender and sexuality; jennifer_spear@sfu.ca

Taylor, Joseph E., III (PhD, Washington 1996; prof.) western North America, environmental; taylorj@sfu.ca

Vinkovetsky, Ilya (PhD, California, Berkeley 2002; assoc. prof.) modern Russia and Soviet Union; ivink@sfu.ca

Walshaw, Sarah (PhD, Washington, St. Louis 2005; sr. lect.) Africa; sarah_walshaw@sfu.ca

Windel, Aaron M. (PhD, Minnesota 2010; asst. prof.) modern Britain and British Empire, media and technology, rural economics and colonial development; awindel@sfu.ca

Joint/Cross Appointments

Doxiadis, Evdoxios (PhD, California, Berkeley 2007; assoc. prof.; Stavros Niarchos Found. Centre for Hellenic Studies) Greek women's roles 1750-1900, Romaniote Jews; edoxiadi@sfu.ca

Ferguson, Karen (PhD, Duke 1996; prof.; Urban Studies) 20th-century US; kjfergus@sfu.ca

O'Brien, Emily D. (PhD, Brown 2005; assoc. prof.; Humanities) Italian Renaissance; eobrien@sfu.ca

Nondepartmental Historians

Campbell, Lara (PhD, Queen's, Can. 2003; prof.; chair, Gender, Sexuality, Women's Studies) Confederation women and gender, political protest in North America, gender and welfare state; lcampbel@sfu.ca

Krallis, Dimitris (PhD, Michigan 2006; assoc. prof.; Stavros Niarchos Found. Centre for Hellenic Studies) Byzantium; dkrallis@sfu.ca

Retired/Emeritus Faculty

Boyer, Richard E. (PhD, Connecticut 1973; prof. emeritus) colonial Latin America, Mexico, urbanization; boyer@sfu.ca

Day, Charles R. (PhD, Harvard 1964; prof. emeritus) Europe, France, social; charles_day@sfu.ca

Debo, Richard K. (PhD, Nebraska 1964; prof. emeritus) Russia, modern Europe, international relations

Ingram, Edward (PhD, London Sch. Economics 1968; prof. emeritus) Britain as Great Power, British India, Middle Eastern international

Johnston, Hugh J. M. (PhD, London 1970; prof. emeritus) Canada, immigration; hjohnsto@sfu.ca

Kitchen, J. Martin (PhD, London 1966; prof. emeritus) modern Germany, Austria, socialism; kitchen@sfu.ca

Little, John I. (PhD, Ottawa 1976; prof. emeritus) French Canada, 19th-century Canada; jlittle@sfu.ca

Maclean, Derryl N. (PhD, McGill 1985; assoc. prof. emeritus) Islamic studies, Middle East; maclean@sfu.ca

Stubbs, John D. (DPhil, Oxford 1973; prof. emeritus) Britain, imperial, Canada; jstubbs@sfu.ca

Recently Awarded PhDs

Golbasi, Edip "The Anti-Armenian Riots of 1895-97: The 'Climate of Violence' and Intercommunal Conflict in Istanbul and the Eastern Anatolian Provinces of the Ottoman Empire"

Grueter, Mark "Anarchism and the Working Class: The Union of Russian Workers in the North American Labor Movement, 1910s"

Knickerbocker, Madeline "A Sovereign Culture: The Politics of Stó:lo Heritage in the 20th Century"

University of Toronto

Dept. of History, Sidney Smith Hall, Room 2074, 100 St. George St., Toronto, ON M5S 3G3, Canada. 416.978.3363. Fax 416.978.4810. Email: history.frontdesk@utoronto.ca. Website: https://history.utoronto.ca/.

The department offers exciting opportunities to interpret the past and probe its significance through research, education, and lifelong learning. Each year, our internationally renowned faculty guide more than 7,000 talented students through the fascinating realm of historical study. One of the largest history departments in North America, we are home to a critical mass of expertise and are ranked 6th among public universities worldwide and 4th in North America.

Chair: Alison Smith
Director of Graduate Studies: Steve Penfold; Sean Mills (MA)
Director of Undergraduate Studies: Nhung Tran
Degrees Offered: BA, MA, PhD
Academic Year System: Semester
Areas of Specialization: Canada, Britain, US, Asia, Latin America
Tuition:
  MA Program: http://history.utoronto.ca/graduate/ma/tuition-funding
  PhD Program: http://history.utoronto.ca/graduate/phd/tuition-funding
Enrollment 2018-19:
  Undergraduate Majors: 862
  New Graduate Students: 40
  Full-time Graduate Students: 162

Part-time Graduate Students: 7
Degrees in History: 372 BA, 15 MA, 10 PhD
Undergraduate Addresses:
  Admissions: https://www.utoronto.ca/future-students
  Financial Aid: http://www.future.utoronto.ca/finances
Graduate Addresses:
  Admissions and Financial Aid: http://www.history.utoronto.ca/graduate

Full-time Faculty

Anastakis, Dimitry (PhD, York, Can. 2001; prof. and L.R. Wilson/R.J. Currie Chair; Rotman Sch. of Business) Canada, US, economy, technology and society, state/politics/law; dimitry.anastakis@utoronto.ca

Bartlett, Kenneth (PhD, Toronto 1978; prof.) Renaissance Europe; kenneth.bartlett@utoronto.ca

Bender, Daniel E. (PhD, NYU 2001; prof.; Scarborough) urban, food; debender@utsc.utoronto.ca

Bergen, Doris L. (PhD, North Carolina, Chapel Hill 1991; prof.) Holocaust studies; doris.bergen@utoronto.ca

Bertram, Laurie (PhD, Toronto 2010; asst. prof.) modern Canada, gender, material culture; l.bertram@utoronto.ca

Birla, Ritu (PhD, Columbia 1999; assoc. prof.; dir., Asian Inst.) modern South Asia, colonial and postcolonial cultural studies, feminist and social; r.birla@utoronto.ca

Bohaker, Heidi (PhD, Toronto 2006; assoc. prof.) aboriginal; heidi.bohaker@utoronto.ca

Bothwell, Robert (PhD, Harvard 1972; prof.) modern Canadian political, diplomatic, military; bothwell@chass.utoronto.ca

Brown, Elspeth H. (PhD, Yale 2000; assoc. prof.; Mississauga) American social and cultural; elspeth.brown@utoronto.ca

Chen, Li (PhD, Columbia 2009; assoc. prof.; chair, Scarborough) late imperial and modern China; lchen@utsc.utoronto.ca

Chin, Carol C. (PhD, Ohio State 2001; assoc. prof.) international relations, Asian American relations; carol.chin@utoronto.ca

Cochelin, Isabelle (PhD, Montréal 1996; assoc. prof.) medieval; isabelle.cochelin@utoronto.ca

Cohen, Paul E. (PhD, Princeton 2001; assoc. prof.) early modern France; p.cohen@utoronto.ca

Coleman, Kevin P. (PhD, Indiana 2012; asst. prof.; Mississauga) modern Latin America, US-Latin American relations, visual culture; kevin.coleman@utoronto.ca

Emon, Anver M. (PhD, UCLA 2005; OPhD, Yale Law Sch. 2009; prof. and Canada Research Chair; Faculty of Law) Islamic law, legal, legal philosophy; anver.emon@utoronto.ca

Everett, Nicholas C. (PhD, Cambridge 1997; prof.) medieval Europe; n.everett@utoronto.ca

Ewing, Cindy (PhD, Yale 2018; asst. prof.; Trinity Coll.) international relations, contemporary international, Asia-Middle Eastern transnational

Fujitani, Takashi (PhD, California, Berkeley 1986; prof.) modern and contemporary Japan, East Asia, Asian American and transnational; t.fujitani@utoronto.ca

Gabaccia, Donna R. (PhD, Michigan 1979; prof.; Scarborough) gender, immigration, diaspora; donna.gabaccia@utoronto.ca

Gervers, Michael (PhD, Toronto 1972; prof.; Scarborough) medieval, social, archaeology; m.gervers@utoronto.ca

Gettler, Brian (PhD, Québec, Montréal 2011; asst. prof.; Mississauga) aboriginal, Québec, capitalism; brian.gettler@utoronto.ca

Ghosh, Shami (PhD, Toronto 2009; asst. prof.) Centre for Medieval Studies; shami.ghosh@utoronto.ca

Grewal, Anup (PhD, Chicago 2012; asst. prof.; Scarborough) modern China, cultural studies, gender studies; anup.grewal@utoronto.ca

Halpern, Rick (PhD, Pennsylvania 1989; prof.) US; rick.halpern@utoronto.ca

Hanssen, Jens (DPhil, Oxford 2001; assoc. prof.; Mississauga) Mediterranean urban, Ottoman and Arab, intellectual/cultural/political; jens.hanssen@utoronto.ca

Hastings, Paula Pears (PhD, Duke 2010; asst. prof.; Scarborough) Canada, British Empire, Caribbean; paula.hastings@utsc.utoronto.ca

Hawkins, Sean (PhD, Cambridge 1989; assoc. prof.) Africa, animals; sean.hawkins@utoronto.ca

Hill, Susan (PhD, Trent 2006; assoc. prof.; dir., Centre for Indigenous Studies) indigenous histories, culture and linguistics; susan.hill@utoronto.ca

Hood, Adrienne D. (PhD, California, San Diego 1988; assoc. prof.) America, material culture; a.hood@utoronto.ca

Iacovetta, Franca (PhD, York, Can. 1988; prof.; Scarborough) Canada, immigration, women and social; f.iacovetta@utoronto.ca

Jacobson, Brian (PhD, Southern California 2011; asst. prof.; Cinema Studies Inst.) history and theory of moving image media, history and philosophy of technology, environmental; brian.jacobson@utoronto.ca

Jenkins, Jennifer Louise (PhD, Michigan 1997; assoc. prof.) modern Europe; jl.jenkins@utoronto.ca

Jennings, Eric T. (PhD, California, Berkeley 1998; prof.) modern western Europe, 20th-century France, colonialism; eric.jennings@utoronto.ca

Johnson, W. Christopher (PhD, Yale 2014; asst. prof.; Women and Gender Studies Inst.) African American, gender, transnational studies; wchris.johnson@utoronto.ca

Kasekamp, Andres (PhD, London 1996; prof.; chair, Estonian Studies) Estonian studies, international relations; andres.kasekamp@utoronto.ca

Kasturi, Malavika (PhD, Cambridge 1998; assoc. prof.; Mississauga) 19th- and 20th-century colonial South Asia and British Empire; malavika.katsuri@utoronto.ca

Kazal, Russell A. (PhD, Pennsylvania 1998; assoc. prof.; Scarborough) modern America, social and urban, immigration and ethnicity; rkazal@utsc.utoronto.ca

Keil, Charles (PhD, Wisconsin, Madison 1995; prof.; principal, Innis Coll.) modern America, cinema; charlie.keil@utoronto.ca

Lahusen, Thomas (OPhD, Lausanne, Switzerland 1982; prof.) Russia, cinema; thomas.lahusen@utoronto.ca

Lam, Tong (PhD, Chicago 2003; assoc. prof.; Mississauga) modern China, East Asia; tong.lam@utoronto.ca

Loeb, Lori (PhD, Toronto 1992; assoc. prof.) Britain; lori.loeb@utoronto.ca

MacArthur, Julie (PhD, Cambridge 2010; asst. prof.) African studies, film, cartography; julie.macarthur@utoronto.ca

Macmillan, Margaret (DPhil, Oxford 1974; prof., on leave) late 19th- and early 20th-century British Empire, international relations; margaret.macmillan@utoronto.ca

Magocsi, Paul R. (PhD, Princeton 1972; prof.) Ukrainian economic, social, political

Mar, Lisa R. (PhD, Toronto 2002; assoc. prof. and Richard Charles Lee Chair) Chinese Canadian studies; lisa.mar@utoronto.ca

McGowan, Mark G. (PhD, Toronto 1988; prof.) modern Canada, religious, social and immigration; mark.mcgowan@utoronto.ca

Meyerson, Mark D. (PhD, Toronto 1987; prof.) medieval; meyerson@chass.utoronto.ca

Mills, Sean (PhD, Queen's, Can. 2008; assoc. prof. and MA coord.) Canada, Quebec, empire; sean.mills@utoronto.ca

Mishler, Max (PhD, NYU 2016; asst. prof.) African diaspora, Atlantic world, America

Mori, Jennifer (PhD, Worcester Coll., Oxford 1992; prof.) arly modern Britain; jennifer.mori@utoronto.ca

Murphy, Michelle (PhD, Harvard 1998; prof.) modern America, gender, race; michelle.murphy@utoronto.ca

Musisi, Nakanyike (PhD, Toronto 1991; assoc. prof.) Africa, women's studies; nakanyike.musisi@utoronto.ca

Nelson, William Max (PhD, UCLA 2006; asst. prof.; Scarborough) Europe, France, intellectual; wnelson@utsc.utoronto.ca

Newton, Melanie J. (PhD, Oxford 2001; assoc. prof.) Caribbean, gender; melanie.newton@utoronto.ca

Penfold, Steve (PhD, York, Can. 2002; assoc. prof. and assoc. chair, grad. studies) modern Canada, social, economic and cultural; steve.penfold@utoronto.ca

Pilcher, Jeffrey M. (PhD, Texas Christian 1993; prof.) food history and studies; jeffrey.pilcher@utoronto.ca

Pruessen, Ronald W. (PhD, Pennsylvania 1968; prof.) 20th-century American political and diplomatic; pruessen@chass.utoronto.ca

Raman, Bhavani (PhD, Michigan 2007; assoc. prof.; Scarborough) colonial law, scribal culture; bhavani.raman@utoronto.ca

Retallack, James (PhD, Oxford 1983; prof.) modern western Europe, political, social; james.retallack@utoronto.ca

Rockel, Stephen J. (PhD, Toronto 1997; assoc. prof.; Scarborough) Africa; stephen.rockel@utoronto.ca

Rothman, E. Natalie (PhD, Michigan 2006; assoc. prof.; Scarborough) early modern Europe; rothman@utsc.utoronto.ca

Sayle, Timothy Andrews (PhD, Temple 2014; asst. prof.) international relations; tim.sayle@utoronto.ca

Sharma, Jayeeta (PhD, Cambridge 2003; assoc. prof.; Scarborough) South Asia and British Empire, labor, environment and food; sharma@utsc.utoronto.ca

Shorter, Edward L. (PhD, Harvard 1968; prof.) modern western Europe, social, medicine; history.medicine@utoronto.ca

Silano, Giulio (PhD, Toronto 1982; prof.) medieval, ecclesiastical, institutional and legal; gsilano@chass.utoronto.ca

Smith, Alison K. (PhD, Chicago 2000; prof. and chair) imperial Russia; alison.smith@utoronto.ca

Sweeney, Shauna J. (PhD, NYU 2015; asst. prof.; Women and Gender Studies Inst.) African diaspora, Atlantic world, women's and gender studies; shauna.sweeney@nyu.edu

Tavakoli-Targhi, Mohamad (PhD, Chicago 1988; prof.; Mississauga) Iran and Middle East, modernity, gender studies; m.tavakoli@utoronto.ca

Terpstra, Nicholas (PhD, Toronto 1989; prof.) early modern Europe, Italian Renaissance; nicholas.terpstra@utoronto.ca

Tran, Nhung T. (PhD, UCLA 2004; assoc. prof. and assoc. chair, undergrad. studies) Southeast Asia, gender; nhungtuyet.tran@utoronto.ca

van Isschot, Luis (PhD, McGill 2010; asst. prof.) modern Latin America, human rights, law and society; luis.vanisschot@utoronto.ca

Viola, Lynne (PhD, Princeton 1984; prof.) 20th-century Russia; lynne.viola@utoronto.ca

Virani, Shafique (PhD, Harvard 2001; prof.; Mississauga) Islam studies; shafique.virani@utoronto.ca

Walker, Tamara J. (PhD, Michigan 2007; asst. prof.) Latin America, slavery, gender

Wang, Yiwen Yvon (PhD, Stanford 2014; asst. prof.) modern China, gender; yyvon.wang@utoronto.ca

Wilson, David Alexander (PhD, Queen's, Can. 1983; prof.) Ireland, Celtic; david.wilson@utoronto.ca

Wittmann, Rebecca E. (PhD, Toronto 2001; assoc. prof.; chair, Mississauga) modern Germany; wittmann@chass.utoronto.ca

Woods, Rebecca (PhD, Massachusetts Inst. of Tech. 2013; asst. prof.; Inst. for the Hist. and Philosophy of Sci. and Tech.) rebecca.woods@utoronto.ca

Wrobel, Piotr (PhD, Warsaw 1984; assoc. prof.) Poland; piotr.wrobel@utoronto.ca

Retired/Emeritus Faculty

Abray, Jane (PhD, Yale 1978; prof. emeritus) early modern Europe, Reformation; jane.abray@utoronto.ca

Aster, Sidney (PhD, London Sch. Econ. 1969; prof. emeritus; Mississauga) modern Britain, international relations; sidney.aster@utoronto.ca

Berger, Carl C. (PhD, Toronto 1967; prof. emeritus) modern Canada, cultural and social, historiography

Berman, William C. (PhD, Ohio State 1963; prof. emeritus) 20th-century America, political/social/diplomatic

Blanchard, Peter H. (PhD, London 1975; prof. emeritus) modern Latin America, social, political; blanchar@chass.utoronto.ca

Cairns, John C. (PhD, Cornell 1951; prof. emeritus) modern western Europe, French intellectual/political/diplomatic, historiography

Callahan, William J., Jr. (PhD, Harvard 1964; prof. emeritus) early modern western Europe, Spanish social/economic/political; wj.callahan@utoronto.ca

Dent, Julian (PhD, London 1965; prof. emeritus) early modern Western Europe, French social and political, historiography

Dowler, Wayne (PhD, London Sch. Econ. 1973; prof. emeritus; Scarborough) modern Russia, intellectual, political; dowler@utsc.utoronto.ca

Dyck, Harvey L. (PhD, Columbia 1963; prof. emeritus) modern eastern Europe, Russian social/economic/political/diplomatic; hldyck@chass.utoronto.ca

Eksteins, Modris (DPhil, Oxford 1970; prof. emeritus; Scarborough) modern western Europe, political, intellectual; eksteins@utsc.utoronto.ca

Estes, James M. (PhD, Ohio State 1964; prof. emeritus) early modern western Europe, German religious and political; james.estes@utoronto.ca

Finlyason, Michael (PhD, Toronto 1968; prof. emeritus) early modern Britain, social/religious/political

Goering, Joseph W. (PhD, Toronto 1977; prof. emeritus) medieval; goering@chass.utoronto.ca

Goffart, Walter A. (PhD, Harvard 1961; prof. emeritus) early medieval Europe, Rome and institutional, historiography; walter.goffart@yale.edu

Grendler, Paul F. (PhD, Wisconsin, Madison 1964; prof. emeritus) early modern western Europe, Italian intellectual/social/religious

Ingham, John N. (PhD, Pittsburgh 1973; prof. emeritus) modern America, business/social/cultural, 19th- and 20th-century America

Israel, Milton (PhD, Michigan 1965; prof. emeritus) modern Asia, British Empire, Indian social and political

Johnson, Robert E. (PhD, Cornell 1974; prof. emeritus; Mississauga) modern eastern Europe, Russia, social; johnson@chass.utoronto.ca

Keep, J.L.H. (PhD, London 1954; prof. emeritus) modern eastern Europe

Kivimae, Juri (PhD, Estonian Acad. Science 1981; prof. emeritus) early modern Estonia and Baltic, economic; jkivimae@chass.utoronto.ca

Klein, Martin A. (PhD, Chicago 1964; prof. emeritus) modern Africa, social and political; martin.klein@utoronto.ca

Kornberg, Jacques (PhD, Harvard 1964; prof. emeritus) modern Europe, Jewish, Holocaust; kornberg@chass.utoronto.ca

MacDowell, Laurel S. (PhD, Toronto 1979; prof. emeritus) modern Canada, labour and social, environmental; laurel.macdowell@utoronto.ca

Marrus, Michael R. (PhD, California, Berkeley 1968; prof. emeritus) modern Europe, fascism, Holocaust; michael.marrus@utoronto.ca

Morton, Desmond (PhD, London 1968; prof. emeritus) modern Canada, social, economic/political/military

Murray, Alexander C. (PhD, Toronto 1976; prof. emeritus; Mississauga) medieval, late Rome, early modern Europe; alexander.murray@utoronto.ca

Nelson, William H. (PhD, Columbia 1958; prof. emeritus) colonial America, intellectual/social/political

Noel, Jan (PhD, Toronto 1987; assoc. prof. emeritus; Mississauga) pre-Confederation Canada, French Canada, gender; jnoel@utm.utoronto.ca

Penslar, Derek Jonathan (PhD, California, Berkeley 1987; prof. emeritus) modern Jewish, Europe and Israel

Raby, David L. (PhD, Warwick 1971; prof. emeritus) Latin America, Mexico, 20th-century Portuguese social/economic/political

Radforth, Ian W. (PhD, York, Can. 1985; prof. emeritus) Canada, 19th- and 20th-century Ontario, social and economic; i.radforth@utoronto.ca

Robertson, Ian (PhD, Toronto 1974; prof. emeritus; Scarborough) post-Confederation Canada, political, intellectual; robertson@utsc.utoronto.ca

Rossos, Andrew (PhD, Stanford 1971; prof. emeritus) modern eastern Europe, Czech political and diplomatic

Rutherford, Paul F. W. (PhD, Toronto 1973; prof. emeritus) modern Canada, cultural/social, political; prutherf@chass.utoronto.ca

Silver, Arthur I. (PhD, Toronto 1973; prof. emeritus) modern Canada, French Canadian, social and intellectual; asilver@chass.utoronto.ca

Smyth, Denis (PhD, Cambridge 1978; prof. emeritus) international

Spencer, Robert A. (PhD, Oxford 1959; prof. emeritus) modern western Europe, German political/diplomatic/military

Todd, Barbara J. (PhD, Oxford 1985; prof. emeritus) early modern Britain, women; b.todd@utoronto.ca

Van Kirk, Sylvia (PhD, London 1975; prof. emeritus) early Canadian West, women

Wagle, Narendra K. (PhD, London 1963; prof. emeritus) South Asia, medieval India

Wark, Wesley K. (PhD, London Sch. Econ. 1984; prof. emeritus) 20th-century Britain, foreign and defense policy, international relations and intelligence

Wayne, Michael (PhD, Yale 1979; prof. emeritus) 19th-century America; michael.wayne@utoronto.ca

Recently Awarded PhDs

Barbour, Dale "Undressed Toronto: A Social of Toronto's Waterfront, 1870-1930"

Carpenter, Sandy Kealani "Moving Relics, Moving Power: Sacred Space and the Peace of God in Southern France at the Turn of the 11th Century"

Colbourn, Susan "Defining Détente: NATO's Struggle for Identity, 1975-83"

Cousins, Karen Shears "The Virgin of Chiquinquira: Imagining Christianity and the Mother of God in the New Kingdom of Granada"

Douglas, Justin "History of the Credit Card"

Fisk, Bethan "'The Wilderness Within': African Diasporic Religion in New Granada and the Atlantic World"

Harris, Dustin "Muslims in Marseille: North Africa Immigration and French Social Welfare in the Late Colonial and Early Post-Colonial Eras"

Lin, Nimrod "People Who Count: Zionism, Democracy, and Demography in Mandate Palestine"

Logue, Alexandra "The 'Metes and Bounds' of Manhood: Gender, Property, and Violence in Early Modern England"

Lukas, Benjamin "Hommes de guerre: Nobility, Masculinity, and Mental Violence in the 16th-Century France"

McVicker, Ben A. "Afgantsy: The Social, Political, and Cultural Legacy of a Forgotten Generation"

Nash, Shannon "Through the Shadows: The Myth and Reality of Sleeper Cells"

Pourtavaf, Leila "The Representation of Qajar Women in 19th-Century Travelogues"

Savage, Michael Gray "The Metropolitan Moment: Municipal Boundaries, Segregation, and Civil Rights Possibilities in the American North"

Sproule, Joseph "Merchants of War: Mercenaries, Economy, and Society in the Late 16th-Century Baltic"

Webb, Michael "Interwoven Texts: Connections among Monasteries in Charente during the Central Middle Ages"

Wellum, Caleb "Energizing the Right: Economy, Ecology, and Culture in the 1970s"

Wiens, Gavin J. "In the Service of Kaiser and King: State Sovereignty, Nation-Building, and the German Army, 1866-1918"

Yoshinari, Mary Ann Hiloko "Economic Sovereignty in Iran, 1928-53"

Trent University

Dept. of History, Lady Eaton College South S101, 1600 West Bank Dr., Peterborough, ON K9L 0G2, Canada. 705.748.1011. Fax 705.748.1821. Email: history@trentu.ca. Website: https://www.trentu.ca/history/.

The History Department at Trent University remains committed to small group learning and close faculty-student interaction. Our courses emphasize the development of diverse research and communications skills.

Chair: Antonio Cazorla-Sanchez
Director of Graduate Studies: David Sheinin
Degrees Offered: BA, BA Hon, MA
Academic Year System: Semester
Areas of Specialization: medieval/early modern/modern Britain and Europe, Canada and US, Asia/Africa/Middle East, Latin America and Russia, Iberian studies
Undergraduate Tuition (per academic year):
 Canadian: $6,820 Can.
 International: $17,522 Can.
Graduate Tuition (per academic year):
 Canadian: $8,017 Can.
 International: $10,740 Can.
Enrollment 2018-19:
 Undergraduate Majors: 290
 New Graduate Students: 5
 Full-time Graduate Students: 12
 Part-time Graduate Students: 2
 Degrees in History: 125 BA, 1 MA
Undergraduate Addresses:
 Admissions: http://www.trentu.ca/applying/
 Financial Aid: http://www.trentu.ca/financialaid/
Graduate Addresses:
 Admissions: http://www.trentu.ca/graduatestudies/
 Financial Aid: http://www.trentu.ca/graduatestudies/financialsupport.php

Full-time Faculty

Andriewsky, Olga (PhD, Harvard 1991; assoc. prof.) imperial Russia; oandriewsky@trentu.ca

Bialuschewski, Arne (PhD, Kiel 1999; asst. prof.) early modern Atlantic, piracy, cross-cultural relations; abialu@trentu.ca

Boulby, Marion (PhD, Toronto 1996; assoc. prof.) Near and Middle East, Islamic; marionboulby@trentu.ca

Cazorla-Sanchez, Antonio (PhD, Granada 1994; prof. and chair) modern Europe, fascism and dictatorships, Spain; acazorla@trentu.ca

Dunaway, Finis (PhD, Rutgers 2001; prof.) America, cultural, environmental; finisdunaway@trentu.ca

Durand, Caroline (PhD, McGill 2011; asst. prof.) Québec, social/cultural/political; carolinedurand@trentu.ca

Elbl, Ivana (PhD, Toronto 1986; prof.) late medieval, Portugal, European expansion; ielbl@trentu.ca

Harris-Stoertz, Fiona (PhD, California, Santa Barbara 1999; assoc. prof.) high medieval England, social and cultural, women; fharris@trentu.ca

Hurl-Eamon, Jennine (PhD, York, Can. 2001; prof.) early modern Britain, western social and crime, women/plebeian marriage/war and society/childhood; jenninehurleamon@trentu.ca

Kay, Carolyn H. (PhD, Yale 1994; prof.) modern Germany, cultural and social; ckay@trentu.ca

Miron, Janet (PhD, York, Can. 2004; assoc. prof.) 19th-century Canada, prisons and asylums, crime and mental illness; janetmiron@trentu.ca

Nguyen-Marshall, Van (PhD, British Columbia 2002; assoc. prof.) Vietnam; vannguyenmarshall@trentu.ca

Sheinin, David M. K. (PhD, Connecticut 1989; prof. and dir., grad. studies) Latin America, modern US; dsheinin@trentu.ca

Siena, Kevin (PhD, Toronto 2001; assoc. prof.) early modern Britain, medicine and sexuality, urban poverty and welfare; ksiena@trentu.ca

Wright, Robert A. (PhD, Queen's, Can. 1989; prof.) Canadian cultural and diplomatic; rawright@trentu.ca

Retired/Emeritus Faculty

Barker, John C. (PhD, Toronto 1967; prof. emeritus) intellectual, historiography

Hodgins, Bruce W. (PhD, Duke 1965; prof. emeritus) Canadian North, Australia, aboriginal

Jennings, John N. (PhD, Toronto 1979; assoc. prof. emeritus) Canadian West and US; jjennings@trentu.ca

Jones, Elwood H. (PhD, Queen's, Can. 1971; prof. emeritus) Canada, colonial America; ejones@trentu.ca

McCalla, Douglas W. (DPhil, Oxford 1972; prof. emeritus) Canadian social and economic; dmccalla@uoguelph.ca

Morton, Patricia M. (PhD, Toronto 1976; prof. emeritus) modern Britain, slavery, US South

Robson, Stuart T. (DPhil, Oxford 1966; prof. emeritus) World Wars I and II, modern Germany

Standen, S. Dale (PhD, Toronto 1975; prof. emeritus) Canada, Québec; dstanden@trentu.ca

Taylor, Graham D. (PhD, Pennsylvania 1972; prof. emeritus) 20th-century US, business; gtaylor@trentu.ca

Walden, Keith (PhD, Queen's, Can. 1980; prof. emeritus) Canadian cultural and intellectual; kwalden@trentu.ca

Wilson, G. Alan (PhD, Toronto 1959; prof. emeritus) Canada, maritime provinces

University of Waterloo

Dept. of History, 200 University Ave. W., Hagey Hall, Waterloo, ON N2L 3G1, Canada. 519.888.4567. Fax 519.746.2658. Email: history@uwaterloo.ca. Website: https://uwaterloo.ca/history/.

The Tri-University Graduate Program in History combines the faculty and resources at the University of Guelph, Wilfrid Laurier University, and the University of Waterloo. Students register at the university where their advisor is located and receive their degree from that university but do their coursework jointly at all three universities.

Chair: Julia Roberts
Director of Graduate Studies: Susan Roy
Director of Undergraduate Studies: Geoffrey Hayes
Degrees Offered: BA,MA,PhD
Academic Year System: Semester
Areas of Specialization: Canada, early modern/Reformation/modern Europe, Britain and British Empire, war and society, US
Undergraduate Tuition (per academic year):
   Canadian: $7,306
Graduate Tuition (per academic year):
   Canadian: $8,681
Enrollment 2018-19:
   Undergraduate Majors: 86
   New Graduate Students: 16
   Full-time Graduate Students: 26
   Part-time Graduate Students: 1
   Degrees in History: 44 BA, 10 MA, 1 PhD
Undergraduate Addresses:
   Admissions: http://uwaterloo.ca/registrar/
   Financial Aid: http://uwaterloo.ca/student-awards-financial-aid/
Graduate Addresses:
   Admissions: https://uwaterloo.ca/history/graduate
   Financial Aid: http://uwaterloo.ca/graduate-studies/awards-funding

Affiliated Faculty

Bednarski, Steven (PhD, Québec, Montréal 2002; assoc. prof.; St. Jerome's) late medieval and early modern French social/cultural/criminal/gender; stevenb@uwaterloo.ca

Epp, Marlene (PhD, Toronto 1996; prof.; Conrad Grebel Univ. Coll.) Canada, immigration, women and family; mgepp@uwaterloo.ca

Lackenbauer, Whitney (PhD, Calgary 2004; assoc. prof.; St. Jerome's) modern Canada, international relations, native-newcomer relations; pwlacken@uwaterloo.ca

Osborne, Troy D. (PhD, Minnesota 2007; asst. prof.; Conrad Grebel Univ. Coll.) early modern European religious and cultural, Dutch republic, Mennonite; t3osborne@uwaterloo.ca

Touhey, Ryan (PhD, Waterloo 2006; assoc. prof.; St. Jerome's) Canadian foreign relations, Canadian political relations, Cold War; rmtouhey@uwaterloo.ca

Full-time Faculty

Bruce, Gary S. (PhD, McGill 1998; assoc. prof.) 20th-century Germany; gsbruce@uwaterloo.ca

Gorman, Daniel P. (PhD, McMaster 2003; assoc. prof.) modern Britain and British Empire, global governance, intellectual property; dpgorman@uwaterloo.ca

Hayes, Geoffrey (PhD, Western Ontario 1992; assoc. prof. and assoc. chair, undergrad. studies) Canadian military, modern Canada; ghayes@uwaterloo.ca

Hunt, Andrew E. (PhD, Utah 1997; prof.) US since 1877, Vietnam War; aehunt@uwaterloo.ca

Kroeker, Greta G. (PhD, California, Berkeley 2004; assoc. prof.) early modern Europe; gkroeker@uwaterloo.ca

MacDougall, Heather (PhD, Toronto 1982; assoc. prof.) Canada, medicine, public; hmacdoug@uwaterloo.ca

Milligan, Ian (PhD, York, Can. 2011; assoc. prof.) Canadian youth, digital; i2milligan@uwaterloo.ca

Muirhead, Bruce W. (PhD, York, Can. 1986; prof.) Canada-US trade relations, Canada-India trade relations; muirhead@uwaterloo.ca

Nicholas, Jane (PhD, Waterloo 2007; assoc. prof.; Sexuality, Marriage, and Family Studies) history of body in Canada, women and gender, feminist pedagogy; jane.nicholas@uwaterloo.ca

Peers, Douglas M. (PhD, London 1988; prof. and dean, Arts) British imperialism 1750-1900, India 1700-1947, historiography; dpeers@uwaterloo.ca

Roberts, Julia (PhD, Toronto 1999; assoc. prof. and chair) Canadian social; robertsj@uwaterloo.ca

Roy, Susan (PhD, British Columbia; asst. prof. and assoc. chair, grad. studies) aboriginal; susan.roy@uwaterloo.ca

Sbardellati, John (PhD, California, Santa Barbara 2006; assoc. prof.) US diplomatic; jsbardel@uwaterloo.ca

Statiev, Alex (PhD, Calgary 2004; assoc. prof.) Soviet Union and eastern Europe, totalitarianism, popular resistance and counterinsurgency; astatiev@uwaterloo.ca

Taylor, Lynne (PhD, Michigan 1992; assoc. prof.) 20th-century Europe, international, France; ltaylor@uwaterloo.ca

Walker, James (PhD, Dalhousie 1973; prof.) Canadian black, race relations, Africa; jwwalker@uwaterloo.ca

Retired/Emeritus Faculty

Cuthbert-Brandt, Gail (PhD, York, Can. 1977; prof. emeritus) Canada and Québec, women, labour; gcbrandt@uwaterloo.ca

English, John R. (PhD, Harvard 1973; prof. emeritus) 20th-century Canada, political and international; jenglish@uwaterloo.ca

Harrigan, Patrick J. (PhD, Michigan 1967; Dist. Prof. emeritus) modern Europe and France, social, sport; harrigan@uwaterloo.ca

McLaughlin, Kenneth (PhD, Toronto 1974; Dist. Prof. emeritus) 19th- and 20th-century Canada, public, historic sites and museums; kmclaughlin@uwaterloo.ca

Mitchinson, Wendy (PhD, York, Can. 1977; prof. emeritus) Canada, social, women; wlmitchi@uwaterloo.ca

Snyder, Arnold (PhD, McMaster 1981; prof. emeritus) 16th-century Europe, radical Reformation, church; casnyder@uwaterloo.ca

University of Western Ontario (Western University)

Dept. of History, Lawson Hall, Rm. 2201, London, ON N6A 5B8, Canada. 519.661.3645. Fax 519.661.3010. Email: history-inquiries@uwo.ca. Website: https://www.history.uwo.ca/.

The Department provides a diverse and dynamic environment for undergraduates, graduate students, and faculty. For undergraduates and graduate students alike, the Department of History at Western University offers a wide array of educational opportunities.

Chair: Francine McKenzie
Director of Graduate Studies: Nancy Rhoden
Director of Undergraduate Studies: Jonathan Vance
Degrees Offered: BA,BA Hon,MA,PhD
Academic Year System: Trimester
Areas of Specialization: Canada, US, digital, international and transnational, public history and memory

Undergraduate Tuition (per academic year):
Canadian: $8,262.45
International: $30,906.45
Graduate Tuition (per academic year):
Canadian: $4,711.34
International: $11,926
Enrollment 2018-19:
Undergraduate Majors: 278
New Graduate Students: 33
Full-time Graduate Students: 63
Part-time Graduate Students: 3
Degrees in History: 91 BA, 27 MA, 6 PhD
Undergraduate Addresses:
Admissions: https://welcome.uwo.ca/admissions/
Financial Aid: https://registrar.uwo.ca/student_finances/
Graduate Addresses:
Admissions: https://www.grad.uwo.ca/admissions/
Financial Aid: https://www.grad.uwo.ca/finances/

Adjunct Faculty

Berest, Julia P. (PhD, Western Ontario 2009; adj. prof.) modern Russian thought and political culture; jberest2@uwo.ca

Christie, Nancy (PhD, Sydney 1987; adj. prof.) nchrist8@uwo.ca

Devine, Shauna (PhD, Western Ontario 2010; adj. prof.) sdevine7@uwo.ca

Murison, Barbara C. (PhD, Western Ontario 1981; adj. prof.) British Empire, early modern Europe, Scottish diaspora; bmurison@uwo.ca

Stewart, Geoffrey Charles (PhD, Western Ontario 2009; adj. asst. prof.) US, global engagement at intersection of decolonization, Cold War; gstewa4@uwo.ca

Tovey, Mark (PhD, Carleton, Can. 2011; adj. asst. prof.) public, architectural heritage, technologies, theatre; mark@uwo.ca

Full-time Faculty

Dove, Michael F. (PhD, Western Ontario 2008; asst. prof.) public; mdove2@uwo.ca

Flath, James A. (PhD, British Columbia 2000; assoc. prof.) modern China, culture, public; jflath@uwo.ca

Fleming, Keith R. (PhD, Western Ontario 1988; prof.) Canada, business; kfleming@uwo.ca

Halpern, Monda M. (PhD, Queen's, Can. 1997; assoc. prof.) Canada, gender; halpern@uwo.ca

Hamilton, Michelle (PhD, Western Ontario 2004; assoc. prof.) public; mhamilt3@uwo.ca

Hernandez-Saenz, Luz Maria (PhD, Arizona 1993; prof.) Latin America, Atlantic studies, medicine; lmhs@uwo.ca

Krats, Peter V. (PhD, Western Ontario 1988; asst. prof.) Canada, northern development, immigration; pkrats@uwo.ca

MacDougall, Robert (PhD, Harvard 2004; assoc. prof.) 20th-century US, business, technology, cultural and political history of information, communication, science; rmacdou@uwo.ca

MacEachern, Alan (PhD, Queen's, Can. 1997; prof.) Canada, public, environment, climate; amaceach@uwo.ca

May, Allyson N. (PhD, Toronto 1997; assoc. prof.) 18th- to 19th-century Britain, legal, cultural; amay6@uwo.ca

McGlynn, Margaret (PhD, Toronto 1998; prof. and assoc. dean) late medieval and early Tudor England, church and law; mmcglyn@uwo.ca

McKenzie, Francine (PhD, Cambridge 1995; prof. and chair) international, Canada, British Empire; fmckenzi@uwo.ca

Nathans, Eli A. (PhD, Johns Hopkins 2001; assoc. prof.) 20th-century Germany, modern Western culture; enathans@uwo.ca

Rhoden, Nancy L. (PhD, Princeton 1994; assoc. prof. and grad. chair) Atlantic studies, colonial Britain, early America, American

Revolution, religious and social, political change, British Empire; nrhoden@uwo.ca

Schumacher, Frank (PhD, Cologne 1997; assoc. prof.) American foreign policy, colonialism, global history of genocide and mass violence; fschuma@uwo.ca

Sendzikas, Aldona (PhD, Hawai'i 2002; assoc. prof.) warfare, 20th-century US, American studies; asendzi2@uwo.ca

Shatzmiller, Maya (PhD, Aix-en-Provence, France 1974; prof.) medieval, Islamic, women; maya@uwo.ca

Shire, Laurel (PhD, George Washington 2008; assoc. prof.) US, race and culture, American studies; lshire@uwo.ca

Turkel, William J. (PhD, MIT 2004; prof. and research chair) environment, Canada; wturkel@uwo.ca

Vance, Jonathan F. W. (PhD, York, Can. 1993; prof. and chair, undergrad. studies) Canada, culture and conflict, warfare; jvance@uwo.ca

Wardhaugh, Robert (PhD, Manitoba 1995; prof.) Canada, politics; rwardhau@uwo.ca

Young, Carl (PhD, London 2004; assoc. prof.) Korea, Japan, international relations; cyoung73@uwo.ca

Joint/Cross Appointments

Dyczok, Marta (PhD, Oxford 1996; assoc. prof.; Political Science) international politics, east central Europe and Eurasia, Ukraine, mass media, migration, post-communism and World War II; mdyczok@uwo.ca

McKellar, Shelley (PhD, Toronto 1999; assoc. prof.; Surgery) Canada, US, medicine; smckell@uwo.ca

McKenna, Katherine (PhD, Queen's, Can. 1987; assoc. prof.; Women's Studies) Canada, women, public, gender; kmckenna@uwo.ca

Part-time Faculty

Acres, William (PhD, Cambridge 1992; asst. prof.) Britain, Tudor-Stuart, politics; wacres@uwo.ca

Compeau, Timothy (PhD, Western Ontario 2015; part-time faculty) colonial North America and Atlantic world, revolutionary cultural; tcompeau@uwo.ca

Drachewych, Oleska (PhD, McMaster 2017; asst. prof.) Russian foreign policy, international communism, transitional anti-imperialism; odrachew@uwo.ca

Dyck, Jason Chad (PhD, Toronto 2012; asst. prof.) colonial religion, missionary work, sacred history in early modern Spanish world; jdyck3@uwo.ca

Iarocci, Andrew (PhD, Wilfrid Laurier 2005; asst. prof.) World War I, military transportation, material culture of modern conflict; aiarocc@uwo.ca

Lloydlangston, Amber (PhD, Ottawa 2002; asst. prof.) alloydla@uwo.ca

Spanner, Donald (PhD, Western Ontario 1994; asst. prof.; Faculty of Information and Media Studies) archival studies, reference services and outreach development, conservation and preservation management, Ontario; dspanner@uwo.ca

Takagaki, Cary (PhD, Toronto 1999; asst. prof.) East Asian studies, Japanese studies; ctakagak@uwo.ca

Vacante, Jeff (PhD, Western Ontario 2005; asst. prof.) Canada, intellectual, Quebec political and gender; jvacant2@uwo.ca

Retired/Emeritus Faculty

Avery, Donald H. (PhD, Western Ontario 1973; prof. emeritus) Canada, science, international relations; avery@uwo.ca

Emerson, Roger L. (PhD, Brandeis 1962; prof. emeritus) Scotland, European intellectual; emerson@uwo.ca

Emery, George N. (PhD, British Columbia 1970; prof. emeritus) methodology, demography, Canada; emery@uwo.ca

Flaherty, David H. (PhD, Columbia 1967; prof. emeritus) colonial America, legal; david@flaherty.com

Forster, J. J. Benjamin (PhD, Toronto 1982; assoc. prof. emeritus) Canada, business, economic history; bforster@uwo.ca

Guinsburg, Thomas N. (PhD, Columbia 1969; prof. emeritus) American foreign policy; pcetng@uwo.ca

Hahn, Erich J. C. (PhD, Yale 1971; assoc. prof. emeritus) Germany, international relations, Modern Europe; ejhahn@uwo.ca

Hall, Roger D. (PhD, Cambridge 1974; assoc. prof. emeritus) Canada, culture, Ontario; hallmartin@sympatico.ca

Hyatt, A. M. Jack (PhD, Duke 1964; prof. emeritus) Canada, military, oral; hyatt@uwo.ca

Kellow, Margaret M. R. (PhD, Yale 1992; assoc. prof. emeritus) 19th-century US, women, slavery and abolition; mmkellow@uwo.ca

Matthews, Jean V. (PhD, Harvard 1977; prof. emeritus) 19th century American intellectual, women; jmatthews@california.net

Millard, J. Rodney (PhD, Toronto 1982; asst. prof. emeritus) Canada, technology; rmillar2@uwo.ca

Neary, Peter F. (PhD, London 1965; prof. emeritus) Canada, politics, warfare, Newfoundland; neary@uwo.ca

Ogelsby, John C. M. (PhD, Washington 1963; prof. emeritus) Latin America, Canada

Reynard, Pierre Claude (PhD, York, Can. 1994; assoc. prof. emeritus) France, technology, environment, Early-modern Europe; preynard@uwo.ca

Ruud, Charles A. (PhD, California, Berkeley 1965; prof. emeritus) Russia; ruud@uwo.ca

Sea, Thomas F. (PhD, California, Berkeley 1974; assoc. prof. emeritus) Reformation, Germany; tsea@uwo.ca

Simpson, Craig M. (PhD, Stanford 1972; assoc. prof. emeritus) 19th-century US, Old US South; csimpso1@uwo.ca

Soranaka, Isao (PhD, Wisconsin, Madison 1974; assoc. prof. emeritus) Japan, business; isoranak@uwo.ca

Steele, Ian K. (PhD, London 1964; prof. emeritus) British Empire, early America, Atlantic studies; isteele@uwo.ca

Thompson, J. Neville (PhD, Princeton 1967; prof. emeritus) modern Britain, politics; jnthomps@uwo.ca

Visiting Faculty

Beaujot, Ariel F. (PhD, Toronto 2008; vis. asst. prof.) public, everyday life; abeaujot@uwo.ca

Recently Awarded PhDs

Baxter, Megan "Would You Sell Yourself for a Drink, Boy? Masculinity and Fraternalism in the Ontario Temperance Movement, 1850-1914"

Chase, Jordan "'For Weariness Cannot but Fill Our Men after So Long a Period of Hardship and Endurance': War Weariness in the Canadian Corps in the First World War"

Desroches, Samantha "Tanks and Tinsel: The American Celebration of Christmas during World War II"

Garrett, Jeremy "Tribute to the Fallen: The Evolution of Canadian Battlefield Burials during the First World War"

Habkirk, Evan "Co-opting Militarism: Changes in Six Nations Militarism, 1814-1914"

Malek, Jonathan "The Pearl of the Prairies: The History of the Winnipeg Filipino Community"

Phillips, Graeme "'An Articulate Minority': Studies in the Ideas of Canadian Peace, 1945-63"

Worsfold, Elliot "Welcoming Strangers: Race, Religion, and Ethnicity in German Lutheran Ontario and Missouri, 1939-70"

Wilfrid Laurier University

Dept. of History, 75 University Ave. W., DAWB 4-135, Waterloo, ON N2L 3C5, Canada. 519.884.1970. Fax 519.746.3655. Email: hvogel@wlu.ca. Website: https://students.wlu.ca/programs/arts/history/.

The Tri-University Graduate Program in History combines the faculty and resources at the University of Guelph, Wilfrid Laurier University, and the University of Waterloo. Students register at the university where their advisor is located and receive their degree from that university but do their coursework jointly at all three universities.

Chair: Darren Mulloy
Director of Graduate Studies: Blaine Chiasson
Director of Undergraduate Studies: Amy Milne-Smith
Degrees Offered: BA,MA,PhD
Academic Year System: Semester
Areas of Specialization: Canada, US, Europe, Africa, Asia
Tuition:
  Canadian undergraduate $754.84 per 0.50 credit; Canadian graduate $2,914.35 per term; international undergraduate $2,410.37 per 0.50 credit, international graduate $6,682.92 per term
Enrollment 2018-19:
  Undergraduate Majors: 293
  New Graduate Students: 18
  Full-time Graduate Students: 29
  Part-time Graduate Students: 1
  Degrees in History: 51 BA, 10 MA, 3 PhD
Undergraduate Addresses:
  Admissions: https://www.wlu.ca/future-students/
  Financial Aid: https://students.wlu.ca/registration-and-finances/financial-aid/
Graduate Addresses:
  Admissions and Financial Aid: http://www.wlu.ca/graduatestudies

Full-time Faculty

Bogaert, Kandace (PhD, McMaster 2015; asst. prof.) health and disease, military medicine, 20th-century Canada; kbogaert@wlu.ca

Brockett, Gavin (PhD, Chicago 2003; assoc. prof.) Middle East, Turkey; gbrockett@wlu.ca

Chiasson, Blaine (PhD, Toronto 2002; assoc. prof. and grad. officer) Asia, China and Manchuria, Russia; bchiasson@wlu.ca

Comacchio, Cynthia (PhD, Guelph 1987; prof.) Canadian gender, family and class; ccomacch@wlu.ca

Crerar, Adam (PhD, Toronto 1999; assoc. prof.) modern Canada, social, cultural; acrerar@wlu.ca

Dee, Darryl (PhD, Emory 2004; assoc. prof.) early modern Europe, early modern France, social and cultural; ddee@wlu.ca

Friesen, Leonard G. (PhD, Toronto 1988; prof.) imperial Russia, Soviet Union, international relations; lfriesen@wlu.ca

Grischow, Jeff D. (PhD, Queen's, Can. 1999; assoc. prof.) Africa, Ghana, comparative development studies; jgrischow@wlu.ca

Milne-Smith, Amy G. (PhD, Toronto 2006; assoc. prof. and undergrad. officer) Victorian Britain, masculinity and class, mental illness; amilnesmith@wlu.ca

Monod, David (PhD, Toronto 1988; prof.) 20th-century US, cultural; dmonod@wlu.ca

Mulloy, Darren (PhD, East Anglia, UK 2001; prof. and chair) 20th-century US, political extremism, American Right; dmulloy@wlu.ca

Neylan, Susan L. (PhD, British Columbia 1999; assoc. prof.) Canadian aboriginal, Canadian social and cultural; sneylan@wlu.ca

Nighman, Chris (PhD, Toronto 1996; assoc. prof.) late medieval and early Renaissance Europe, intellectual and ecclesiastical, humanities computing; cnighman@wlu.ca

Plach, Eva Anna (PhD, Toronto 2001; assoc. prof.) eastern Europe, Poland, gender; eplach@wlu.ca

Sarty, Roger (PhD, Toronto 1982; prof.) Canada, war and society, naval; rsarty@wlu.ca

Smith, David A. (PhD, Harvard 2007; assoc. prof.) early modern Britain, English in Carribean, law and society; dasmith@wlu.ca

Weiner, Dana E. (PhD, Northwestern 2007; assoc. prof.) 19th-century US, abolition/slavery/race, gender; dweiner@wlu.ca

Zeller, Suzanne (PhD, Toronto 1986; prof.) 19th-century Canada, science and environment, culture and ideas; szeller@wlu.ca

Retired/Emeritus Faculty

Copp, Terry (MA, McGill 1962; prof. emeritus; Laurier Centre for Military Strategic and Disarmament Studies) military; tcopp@wlu.ca

Gough, Barry (PhD, London 1969; prof. emeritus) naval and imperial affairs, native peoples, constitutional and external affairs; bgough@wlu.ca

Haberer, Erich E. (PhD, Toronto 1987; assoc. prof. emeritus) modern Germany, Third Reich, Holocaust; ehaberer@wlu.ca

Laband, John (PhD, Natal 1991; prof. emeritus) war and society, South Africa, Zulu Kingdom; jlaband@wlu.ca

Lorimer, Doug A. (PhD, British Columbia 1972; prof. emeritus) Victorian Britain, racism and empire; dlorimer@wlu.ca

Lorimer, Joyce (PhD, Liverpool 1973; prof. emeritus) early modern Britain, English in South America and Caribbean; jlorimer@wlu.ca

Recently Awarded PhDs

Cross, Gwenith "Modernizing Midwifery: Managing Childbirth in Ontario and the British Isles, 1900-50"

Falcon, Kyle "The Ghost Story of the Great War: Spiritualism, Psychical Research, and the British War Experience, 1914-39"

Muller, Ian "The Complexity of Canadian Anti-Communism, 1945-67"

Rosenthal, Lyndsay "Venus in the Trenches: The Treatment of Venereal Disease in the Canadian Expeditionary Force, 1914-19"

University of Windsor

Dept. of History, Chrysler Hall North 1184, 401 Sunset Ave., Windsor, ON N9B 3P4, Canada. 519.253.3000. Fax 519.971.3610. Email: history@uwindsor.ca. Website: http://www.uwindsor.ca/history/.

The History program at the University of Windsor provides outstanding teaching from a variety of professors who are engaged in fascinating and wide-ranging research. The program encourages students to develop sharpened critical thinking and writing skills, all the while being engaged in a challenging discipline.

Chair: Robert Nelson
Degrees Offered: BA, BA Hon, MA
Academic Year System: Semester
Areas of Specialization: Americas, Europe, Middle East, Africa, social
Undergraduate Tuition (per academic year):
In-State: $8032
Out-of-State: $26716

Graduate Tuition (per academic year):
In-State: $8345
Out-of-State: $27028
Enrollment 2018-19:
Undergraduate Majors: 61
New Graduate Students: 6
Full-time Graduate Students: 16
Degrees in History: 39 BA, 8 MA
Addresses:
Admissions: http://www.uwindsor.ca/registrar/admissions
Financial Aid: http://www.uwindsor.ca/studentawards/

Adjunct Faculty

Dienesch, Robert M. (PhD, New Brunswick 2006; sessional instr.) America, military; rdienesc@uwindsor.ca

Kulisek, Larry L. (PhD, Wayne State 1973; assoc. prof.) Canada, local, urban; kulisek@uwindsor.ca

Pole, Adam (PhD, Trinity Coll., Dublin 2006; adj. prof.) Ireland, crime; adampole@uwindsor.ca

Full-time Faculty

Atkin, Natalie (PhD, Wayne State 1999; ancillary academic learning specialist) America, women; natalie9@mnsi.net

Burr, Christina (PhD, Memorial, Newfoundland 1991; assoc. prof.) Canada; burrc@uwindsor.ca

Huffaker, Shauna (PhD, California, Santa Barbara 2008; asst. prof.) Middle East, early modern, social; huffaker@uwindsor.ca

Lazure, Guy (PhD, Johns Hopkins 2003; assoc. prof.) modern Europe; glazure@uwindsor.ca

Mohamed, H. Mohamed (PhD, Alberta 2004; assoc. prof.) Africa, diaspora; mmohamed@uwindsor.ca

Nelson, Robert L. (PhD, Cambridge 2003; assoc. prof. and chair) modern Europe, international relations; rnelson@uwindsor.ca

Palmer, Steven P. (PhD, Columbia 1990; assoc. prof.) Latin America, postcolonial; spalmer@uwindsor.ca

Phipps, Pauline A. (PhD, Carleton, Can. 2004; sessional lect.) Britain, women; pphipps@uwindsor.ca

Takai, Yukari (PhD, Montréal 1998; asst. prof.) America, gender, migration; ytakai@uwindsor.ca

Teasdale, Guillaume (PhD, York, Can. 2010; asst. prof.) French of Detroit River region; gteasdal@uwindsor.ca

Way, Peter (PhD, Maryland, Coll. Park 1991; prof.) labor, Atlantic world, military; peterway@uwindsor.ca

Wright, Miriam (PhD, Memorial, Newfoundland 1997; assoc. prof.) Canada, state and society, fisheries; mwright@uwindsor.ca

Retired/Emeritus Faculty

Howsam, Leslie (PhD, York, Can. 1989; prof. emeritus) British cultural, book; lhowsam@uwindsor.ca

Klinck, David M. (PhD, Wisconsin, Madison 1973; prof. emeritus) French intellectual, French Revolution; klinck@uwindsor.ca

McCrone, Kathleen E. (PhD, NYU 1971; prof. emeritus) Victorian British social, women; kem@uwindsor.ca

Pryke, Kenneth G. (PhD, Duke 1963; prof. emeritus) Canada; p49@uwindsor.ca

Sautter, Udo (PhD, Tübingen 1969; prof. emeritus) Germany; gzsst01@uni-tuebingen.de

Simmons, Christina (PhD, Brown 1982; assoc. prof. emeritus) American social, women; simmonc@uwindsor.ca

Tucker, E. Bruce (PhD, Brown 1979; prof. emeritus) American social and cultural; tucker1@uwindsor.ca

University of Winnipeg

Dept. of History, 515 Portage Ave., Winnipeg, MB R3B 2E9, Canada. 204.786.9382. Fax 204.774.4134. Email: history@ uwinnipeg.ca; s.tolman@uwinnipeg.ca. Website: https://www. uwinnipeg.ca/history/.

The Department of History offers courses designed to lead students, in stages, to an understanding of the historian's craft and of the historical process. As a student of History, you will improve your ability to evaluate evidence and learn how to present your interpretations in clear and logical written and oral arguments. The Master's Programme is offered jointly by the History Departments of the University of Manitoba and the University of Winnipeg.

Chair: James Hanley
Director of Graduate Studies: Janis Thiessen
Degrees Offered: BA,BA Hon,MA
Academic Year System: Terms
Areas of Specialization: Canada and US, social and labour, indigenous, immigration and ethnicity, science and medicine
Undergraduate Tuition (per academic year):
  Canadian: $3,883 Can.
  International: $12,658
Graduate Tuition (per academic year):
  Canadian: $3,928 Can.
  International: $7,857
Enrollment 2018-19:
  Undergraduate Majors: 345
  New Graduate Students: 15
  Degrees in History: 190 BA, 10 MA
Undergraduate Addresses:
  Admissions: https://www.uwinnipeg.ca/future-student/
  Financial Aid: https://www.uwinnipeg.ca/awards/
Graduate Addresses:
  Admissions and Financial Aid: https://www.uwinnipeg.ca/graduate-studies/

Adjunct Faculty

Borys, Stephen (PhD, McGill 1994; adj. prof.; Winnipeg Art Gallery) European landscape painting 1600-1900, Canadian art, architectural and 20th-century design; s.borys@uwinnipeg.ca
Bovey, Patricia FRSA (MA, Toronto 1970; adj. prof.) curatorial, Canadian art; p.bovey@uwinnipeg.ca

Full-time Faculty

Abreu-Ferreira, Darlene (PhD, Memorial, Newfoundland 1996; prof.) early modern Europe, Portuguese women and crime, sexuality/gender/race; d.abreu@uwinnipeg.ca
Alexander, Emma C. (PhD, Cambridge 2002; assoc. prof.) South Asia, childhood, labor; e.alexander@uwinnipeg.ca
Bohr, Roland (PhD, Manitoba 2006; assoc. prof.) Canada, indigenous; r.bohr@uwinnipeg.ca
Caudano, Anne-Laurence (PhD, Cambridge 2004; assoc. prof.) medieval, Byzantium and eastern Slavic culture, medieval sciences; a.caudano@uwinnipeg.ca
Eyford, Ryan C. (PhD, Manitoba 2011; assoc. prof.) indigenous and settler interaction, Canadian West, Canada and Empire; r.eyford@uwinnipeg.ca
Freund, Alexander (PhD, Bremen, Germany 2000; prof.; chair, German-Canadian Studies) German Canadian, oral, 20th century; a.freund@uwinnipeg.ca

Gavrus, Delia (PhD, Toronto 2011; assoc. prof.) science/medicine/technology, 19th and 20th century, Canada and US social and cultural; d.gavrus@uwinnipeg.ca
Hanley, James G. (PhD, Yale 1998; prof. and chair) Britain, science, medicine; j.hanley@uwinnipeg.ca
Keshavjee, Serena (PhD, Toronto 2002; prof.) art, architecture, modernism; s.keshavjee@uwinnipeg.ca
Labrecque, Claire (PhD, Laval 2008; asst. prof.; Art History) medieval and northern Renaissance art and architecture, pilgrimage art and architecture; c.labrecque@uwinnipeg.ca
Lawrie, Paul R. D. (PhD, Toronto 2011; assoc. prof.) America, African American, labour; p.lawrie@uwinnipeg.ca
Loewen, Royden K. (PhD, Manitoba 1990; prof.; chair, Mennonite Studies) Canadian social, immigration; r.loewen@uwinnipeg.ca
McCallum, Mary Jane L. (PhD, Manitoba 2008; assoc. prof.) indigenous, gender and women, labor; m.mccallum@uwinnipeg.ca
McCormack, Ross (PhD, Western Ontario 1973; prof.) Canada, immigration, Latin America; r.mccormack@uwinnipeg.ca
Meuwese, Mark (PhD, Notre Dame 2004; prof.) indigenous America, colonial Americas, Atlantic world; m.meuwese@uwinnipeg.ca
Nagam, Julie (PhD, York, Can. 2011; asst. prof.; Art History) indigenous art; j.nagam@uwinnipeg.ca
Seyhun, Ahmet (PhD, McGill 2002; assoc. prof.) Islamic, Ottoman, Islamic legal developments; a.seyhun@uwinnipeg.ca
Sibanda, Eliakim R. (PhD, Colorado, Boulder 2001; prof.) African liberation movements, agrarian policies, biographical; e.sibanda@uwinnipeg.ca
Thiessen, Janis L. (PhD, New Brunswick 2006; assoc. prof. and dir., grad. studies) labor, religious, oral; ja.thiessen@uwinnipeg.ca
Wall, Sharon (PhD, York, Can. 2003; assoc. prof.) social and cultural, childhood and youth, gender and sexuality; s.wall@uwinnipeg.ca
Yaremko, Jason M. (PhD, Manitoba 1997; assoc. prof.) Latin America, indigenous, culture and imperialism; j.yaremko@uwinnipeg.ca
Zayarnyuk, Andriy (PhD, Alberta 2003; assoc. prof.) modern eastern Europe, nationalism and peasants, urban; a.zayarnyuk@uwinnipeg.ca

Retired/Emeritus Faculty

Daniels, Bruce C. (PhD, Connecticut 1970; sr. scholar) Puritanism, New England
Reilly, J. Nolan (PhD, Dalhousie 1983; prof. emeritus) Canadian labor, social
Stevens, Wesley M. (PhD, Emory 1968; sr. scholar)
Stone, Daniel Z. (PhD, Indiana 1972; sr. scholar) Poland, ethnic, Winnipeg; stone@uwinnipeg.ca
Werner, Hans (PhD, Manitoba 2002; sr. scholar) Mennonite studies, settlement of western Canada, Canadian immigration; h.werner@uwinnipeg.ca
Young, Robert J. (PhD, London 1969; sr. scholar) Third French Republic 1870-1940, interwar international politics, biography; r.young@uwinnipeg.ca

York University

Dept. of History, Faculty of Liberal Arts & Prof. Studies, 4700 Keele St., Toronto, ON M3J 1P3, Canada. 416.736.5123. Fax 416.736.5836. Email: lapshist@yorku.ca. Website: https:// history.laps.yorku.ca/.

The Department consistently ranks among the best in the world. It enjoys an international reputation for scholarship, while retaining a commitment to excellence and innovation in teaching. The History Department has a strong record of research accomplishment, as measured in its members' publications and in internal and external grant competitions.

Chair: Thabit Abdullah
Director of Graduate Studies: Jeremy Trevett
Degrees Offered: BA,MA,PhD,International BA
Academic Year System: Eight-month term (undergraduate); trimester (graduate)
Areas of Specialization: Canada and US, modern Europe and Britain, ancient, Africa/Latin America/East Asia, social/cultural/gender/race relations/political
Undergraduate Tuition (per academic year):
   In-State: $7258
   Out-of-State: $21306
Graduate Tuition (per academic year):
   In-State: $5547
   Out-of-State: $19587
Enrollment 2018-19:
   Undergraduate Majors: 648
   New Graduate Students: 36
   Full-time Graduate Students: 85
   Part-time Graduate Students: 29
   Degrees in History: 232 BA, 26 MA, 16 PhD
Undergraduate Addresses:
   Admissions: http://futurestudents.yorku.ca/
   Financial Aid: http://sfs.yorku.ca/aid/
Graduate Addresses:
   Admissions: http://futurestudents.yorku.ca/graduate
   Financial Aid: http://www.yorku.ca/grads/

Full-time Faculty

Abdullah, Thabit A. J. (PhD, Georgetown 1992; prof. and chair) Islamic, modern Middle East; athabit@yorku.ca

Bonnell, Jennifer (PhD, Toronto 2010; asst. prof.) Canada, environment, public; bonnellj@yorku.ca

Brooke, Stephen J. (DPhil, Oxford 1988; prof.) 20th-century Britain, cultural; sjbrooke@yorku.ca

Cohen, Elizabeth S. (PhD, Toronto 1978; prof.) early modern Europe, women; ecohen@yorku.ca

Cohen, Thomas V. (PhD, Harvard 1974; prof.; Humanities) early modern Europe; tcohen@yorku.ca

Cothran, Boyd, III (PhD, Minnesota 2012; assoc. prof.) 19th-century US, cultural, indigenous studies; cothran@yorku.ca

Curto, Jose C. (PhD, UCLA 1996; assoc. prof.) Africa, slavery; jcurto@yorku.ca

Durston, Alan (PhD, Chicago 2004; assoc. prof.) colonial Latin America, Andes; durston@yorku.ca

Edmondson, Jonathan C. (PhD, Cambridge 1985; prof.) ancient Rome, Roman empire, Roman social; jedmond@yorku.ca

Fogel, Joshua (PhD, Columbia 1980; prof. and Canada Research Chair) China, Japan; fogel@yorku.ca

Gekas, Athanasios (PhD, Essex, UK 2004; assoc. prof.) modern Greece; agekas@yorku.ca

Johnson, Michele A. (PhD, Johns Hopkins 1995; assoc. prof.) blacks in the Americas, American social, Caribbean social; johnsonm@yorku.ca

Jones-Imhotep, Edward (PhD, Harvard 2001; assoc. prof.) technology, science; imhotep@yorku.ca

Judge, Joan (PhD, Columbia 1993; prof.) China, 19th and 20th century, women; judge@yorku.ca

Jurdjevic, Mark (PhD, Northwestern 2002; assoc. prof.; Glendon) Italian Renaissance, early modern European political culture; mjurdjevic@glendon.yorku.ca

Kelly, Benjamin (DPhil, Oxford 2003; assoc. prof.) ancient, Rome, Roman Egypt; benkelly@yorku.ca

Kheraj, Sean (PhD, York, Can. 2007; assoc. prof.) Canada, environmental, social; kherajs@yorku.ca

Kim, Janice C. H. (PhD, London 2001; assoc. prof.) 20th-century East Asia, Korea, labor; jkim@yorku.ca

Koffman, David S. (PhD, NYU 2011; asst. prof.) Canadian and US Jewish, empire and religion, inter-ethnicity; koffman@yorku.ca

Koopmans, Rachel M. (PhD, Notre Dame 2001; assoc. prof.) medieval Europe; koopmans@yorku.ca

Ladd-Taylor, Molly (PhD, Yale 1986; assoc. prof.) US social, women; mltaylor@yorku.ca

Langlois, Suzanne (PhD, McGill 1997; assoc. prof.; Glendon) modern Europe, 20th century; slanglois@glendon.yorku.ca

Lovejoy, Paul E. (PhD, Wisconsin, Madison 1973; dist. research prof.) Africa, African diaspora, slavery; plovejoy@yorku.ca

Martel, Marcel (PhD, York, Can. 1994; prof.) Canada, political, social; mmartel@yorku.ca

McGillivray, Gillian A. (PhD, Georgetown 2001; assoc. prof.; Glendon) modern Latin America, Cuba; gmcgilli@glendon.yorku.ca

McPherson, Kathryn M. (PhD, Simon Fraser 1990; prof.) western Canada, women; kathryn@yorku.ca

Neill, Deborah J. (PhD, Toronto 2005; assoc. prof.) modern Germany, imperialism; dneill@yorku.ca

Perin, Roberto (PhD, Ottawa 1975; prof.; Glendon) French Canada, immigration; rperin@yorku.ca

Podruchny, Carolyn (PhD, Toronto 1999; assoc. prof.) early Canada, aboriginal; carolynp@yorku.ca

Price, Betsey B. (PhD, Toronto 1983; prof.; Glendon) medieval, intellectual; bprice@glendon.yorku.ca

Pyee, Audrey (PhD, York, Can. 2005; asst. prof.; Glendon) Canada, French Canada, public; apyee@yorku.ca

Rubenstein, Anne (PhD, Rutgers 1994; assoc. prof.) Latin America, US; arubenst@yorku.ca

Schotte, Margaret (PhD, Princeton 2014; asst. prof.) early modern Europe, cultural, social; mschotte@yorku.ca

Shore, Marlene (PhD, Toronto 1984; prof.) North American studies, cultural; mshore@yorku.ca

Shubert, Adrian (PhD, London 1982; Univ. prof.) modern Spain, European social and cultural; adriansh@yorku.ca

Stephen, Jennifer (PhD, Toronto 2000; assoc. prof.) Canada, political, social; stephenj@yorku.ca

Sturino, Franc (PhD, Toronto 1974; assoc. prof.; Humanities) modern Europe, Canadian immigration; fsturino@yorku.ca

Trevett, Jeremy (DPhil, Oxford 1990; assoc. prof. and dir., grad. studies) ancient Greece; jtrevett@yorku.ca

Trotman, David V. (PhD, Johns Hopkins 1980; prof.) Atlantic, Caribbean, cultural; dtrotman@yorku.ca

Weiser, Keith Ian (PhD, Columbia 2001; assoc. prof.; Humanities) Holocaust and eastern Europe, Jewish, Poland; kweiser@yorku.ca

Wicken, William C. (PhD, McGill 1994; prof.) colonial North America, European-native contact; wwicken@yorku.ca

Nondepartmental Historians

Agnew, Vijay (PhD, Toronto 1976; prof.; Social Science) women, India, immigrants in Canada; vagnew@yorku.ca

Anderson, Katharine Mary (PhD, Northwestern 1994; assoc. prof.; Humanities) modern science and technology, Britain, environment; kateya@yorku.ca

Burke, Tony (PhD, Toronto 2001; assoc. prof.; Humanities) early Christianity, Roman social; tburke@yorku.ca

Coates, Colin M. (PhD, York, Can. 1992; assoc. prof.; Glendon; Canadian Studies) Canada, New France, sociocultural; ccoates@gl.yorku.ca

Davies, Megan J. (PhD, McGill 1994; assoc. prof.; Social Science) health, rural health/women and health/old age, British Columbia; daviesmj@yorku.ca

Ehrlich, Carl S. (PhD, Harvard 1991; prof.; Humanities) biblical, ancient Near East, ancient Israel; ehrlich@yorku.ca

Ewen, Geoffrey (PhD, York, Can. 1998; asst. prof.; Glendon; Canadian Studies) 20th-century Canada, labor; gewen@glendon.yorku.ca

Girard, Philip (PhD, Dalhousie 1999; prof.; Osgoode Hall Law Sch.) Canada, legal; pgirard@osgoode.yorku.ca

Harland, Philip A. (PhD, Toronto 1999; prof.; Humanities) early Christianity, Roman Empire religious life; pharland@yorku.ca

Jenkins, William (PhD, Toronto 2001; assoc. prof.; Geography) Canadian immigration, Irish migration; wjenkins@yorku.ca

Kipping, Mathias (PhD, Munich 1993; prof.; Schulich Sch. of Business) business; mkipping@schulich.yorku.ca

Kroker, Kenton (PhD, Toronto 2000; assoc. prof.; Science & Technology Studies) medicine; kkroker@yorku.ca

Lightman, Bernard V. (PhD, Brandeis 1979; prof.; Humanities) Britain, Victorian era, intellectual; lightman@yorku.ca

McNab, David (PhD, Lancaster 1978; assoc. prof.; Equity Studies) native studies, equity studies; dtmcnab@yorku.ca

Naddaf, Gerard (OPhD, Paris IV, Sorbonne; prof.; Philosophy) ancient Greek philosophy; naddaf@yorku.ca

Reaume, Geoffrey Francis (PhD, Toronto 1997; assoc. prof.; Critical Disability Studies Graduate Prog.) madness, people with disabilities, medical; greaume@yorku.ca

Scardellato, Gabriele P. (PhD, British Columbia 1983; assoc. prof.; Languages, Literatures, Linguistics) 20th-century Canada, Canadian multiculturalism, immigration; gpscar@yorku.ca

Schweitzer, Marlis (PhD, Toronto 2005; assoc. prof.; Theatre, Fine Arts) transnational commodity culture, fashion and beauty, US theatre; schweit@yorku.ca

Wood, Patricia (PhD, Duke 1995; prof.; Geography) Canada, political/immigration/identity/aboriginal; pwood@yorku.ca

Retired/Emeritus Faculty

Bradbury, Bettina (PhD, Concordia, Can. 1984; prof. emerita) Canada, social, women; bettina@yorku.ca

Egnal, Marc M. (PhD, Wisconsin, Madison 1974; prof. emeritus) colonial and 19th-century America; megnal@yorku.ca

Gentles, Ian (PhD, London 1969; prof. emeritus; Glendon) 17th-century Britain, Ireland, military; igentles@glendon.yorku.ca

Hay, C. Douglas (PhD, Warwick, UK 1975; prof. emeritus) Canada, British legal; dhay@yorku.ca

Heron, Craig (PhD, Dalhousie 1981; prof. emeritus) Canadian labor; cheron@yorku.ca

Maidman, Maynard P. (PhD, Pennsylvania 1976; prof. emeritus) ancient, Mesopotamia; mmaidman@yorku.ca

Neeson, Jeanette M. (PhD, Warwick, UK 1978; assoc. prof. emerita) early modern England; jmneeson@yorku.ca

Rogers, Nicholas C. (PhD, Toronto 1975; Dist. Research Prof. emeritus) modern Britain; nickrog@yorku.ca

Singer, Martin (PhD, Michigan 1977; prof. emeritus) modern China, traditional China, Japan; singerm@yorku.ca

Steinisch, Irmgard (PhD, Munich 1982; assoc. prof. emerita) modern Germany; imgards@yorku.ca

Recently Awarded PhDs

Aikenhead, Paul "Maple Music: A Gender History of Canadian Rock, 1983-94"

Chrisman, Kevin "Selling Modernity in Mexico: A Cultural History of the Sanborns Dept Store, 1903-2003"

Gravelle, Mario "Politics and Franco-Ontarian Public Opinion from the Repeal of Regulation 17 to the 1960s"

Hay, Travis "The Science of Settler Colonialism: A Canadian History of the Thrifty Gene Hypothesis"

Leoni, Tommaso "Natura Benivolentissimus! Imperial Ideology and Propaganda under Titus"

Wytenbroek, Lydia "Contested Health Care: Gender, Faith, Professionalism, Nationalism and American Mission Medicine in Iran, 1920-60"

Yaari, Noa "Visual Literacy in History: An Analytical Approach to Using Visual Evidence in Histography of Early Modern Italy in the 19th-21st Century"

Historical Organizations

American Catholic Historical Association

Mount St. Mary's Univ., 16300 Old Emmitsburg Rd., Emmitsburg, MD 21727. 301.447.5799. Email: cstrauss@achahistory.org. Website: https://achahistory.org/.

The American Catholic Historical Association is a conference of scholars, archivists, and teachers of Catholic studies. Founded by the distinguished church historian Peter Guilday who, in 1919, assembled a group of scholars in Cleveland, Ohio, it was intended to be a national society that would bring together scholars scattered across the country and their nonprofessional supporters, all of whom were interested in the history of the Catholic Church or Catholic aspects of secular history.

A. Collections and Libraries

Not applicable.

B. Programs

From its earliest years the Association has pursued two main objectives. One is to promote a deeper and more widespread knowledge of the history of the Catholic Church broadly considered, which encompasses its internal life—its growth and expansion from the apostolic age to the present and in all quarters of the Earth; its evolving doctrine, discipline, polity, liturgy, spirituality, and piety; and its missionary, charitable, and educational activities—as well as its external life—its relations with the civil government; its members' individual and collective influence on the intellectual, cultural, political, and social progress of mankind; and its members' attitudes toward their contemporary circumstances and problems.

The other important aim is the advancement of historical scholarship in all fields among its members by rendering them various services, offering them opportunities for utilizing their talents, and according them public recognition for their demonstrated merits. The Association has always enjoyed the support of Catholic universities, colleges, and seminaries and has endeavored, in turn, to make itself especially helpful to their teachers, scholars, and students. In more recent times, the Association has invited diocesan and religious archivists and historians to become a part of the ACHA family.

The ACHA meets annually in conjunction with the American Historical Association's annual meeting in early January. The association also sponsors a spring conference in March/April of each year at a local college or university. For conference information, see the website at www.achahistory.org.

C. Publications

The Catholic Historical Review is the official organ of the ACHA, published quarterly by Catholic University of America Press.

D. Fellowships and Awards

The American Catholic Historical Association awards the following prizes annually:

The *John Gilmary Shea Prize* for a published book on the history of the Catholic Church broadly considered. The prize is given annually to the author of a book, published during a preceding 12-month period, which is judged by a committee of experts to have made the most original and distinguished contribution to knowledge of the history of the Catholic Church. Any author who is a citizen or permanent resident of the United States or Canada is eligible.

The *Howard R. Marraro Prize* for a work on Italian history or Italo-American history or relations. The prize is given annually to the author of a book that is judged by a committee of experts to be the most distinguished work dealing with Italian history or Italo-American history or relations that has been published in a preceding twelve-month period. It is named in memory of Howard A. Marraro (1879–1972), who was a professor in Columbia University and the author of more than a dozen books on Italian literature, history, and culture. Entries must first have been published in English by a historian whose usual residence is North America.

The *Peter Guilday Prize* is awarded for a manuscript, accepted by the editor of the *Catholic Historical Review*, that is the author's first scholarly publication. Entries must be submitted as articles; those received in the editorial office by September 1 of any year will be considered for that year's prize. The winning article will be published in the following year. Any author who is a citizen or permanent resident of the United States or Canada is eligible.

The *John Tracy Ellis Dissertation Award*, memorializes the scholarship and teaching of Monsignor Ellis (1905–92). Its purpose is to assist a graduate student working on some aspect of the history of the Catholic Church. Those wishing to enter the competition for the award must be citizens or authorized residents (i.e., permanent residents or on student visas) of the United States or Canada, and must be enrolled in a doctoral program at a recognized institution of higher education.

The *ACHA President's Award* provides partial funding to two graduate students whose papers have been accepted by the program chair. The award provides partial assistance to attend either the January or Spring conference where the student is presenting his/her work.

The *ACHA Distinguished Service Awards* are presented in three categories: for teaching, scholarship, and contribution to Catholic studies. The association's *Distinguished Achievement Award for Scholarship* is bestowed on that scholar who, in the opinion of the committee making the selection, has during a long career made a significant impact on the understanding of Catholic history. The award is not for one book or any single piece of scholarship, but for a sustained series of contributions which have fundamentally animated the research of others besides being significant in their own right. The association's *Award for Service to Catholic Studies* acknowledges the exceptional contributions of those who "promote study and research of the history of Catholicism broadly conceived" apart from teaching and publication. The term "service" may include any and all of the following, but are not restricted to them: service to the Association, archival management, museum displays that advance public knowledge of Catholic history, media and other activities that promote the role and place of Catholic studies to a wide audience. The association presents a *Distinguished Teaching Award* annually to a college or university professor who has demonstrated a high commitment to teaching beyond the expected requirements of their position and through their influence and skill have promoted Catholic studies from one generation of scholars to another. Through this award the ACHA recognizes the importance of creative and effective teaching in the growth of Catholic studies.

The *Graduate Student Summer Research Grants* will be awarded to four ACHA graduate student members who are ABD and attending an accredited institution of higher learning. The deadline for applying for funding is April 10, 2019; notification will be no later than April 30, 2019.

For further information on all prizes and grants, visit the Association website at www.achahistory.org.

Officers

Barber, Marian J. (PhD, Texas, Austin 2010; member, Executive Council; dir., Catholic Archives of Texas) immigration, race and ethnicity; marianj.barber@gmail.com

Burns, Jeffrey M. (PhD, Notre Dame 1982; member, Executive Council; Franciscan Sch. of Theology) immigrant church; burnsjm@burnsjm.cnc.net

Carroll, James T. (PhD, Notre Dame 1997; vice pres.; Iona) Native American, education and pedagogy, transnational studies; JCarroll@iona.edu

Dugan, Katherine A. (PhD, Northwestern 2015; member, Executive Council; Springfield Coll.) US religion, American Catholicism, religion and gender, interfaith studies; kdugan@springfield.edu

Endres, David J. (PhD, Catholic; member, Executive Council; assoc. prof. and dean, Athenaeum of Ohio and Mount St. Mary's Seminary) US Catholicism; dendres@athenaeum.edu

Gribble, Richard E. CSC (PhD, Catholic 1995; past pres.; prof., Stonehill) 20th-century American Catholicism; rgribble@stonehill.edu

Hayes, Patrick J. (PhD, Catholic 2003; member, Executive Council; Archives of the Redemptorist Fathers, Baltimore Province) American Catholicism, immigration, social ethics; pjhayesphd@gmail.com

Holscher, Kathleen (PhD, Princeton 2008; pres.; assoc. prof., New Mexico) religion, social theory; holscher@unm.edu

Koeth, Stephen Mark (MPhil, Columbia 2015; MA, Columbia 2014; member, Executive Council) smkoeth@gmail.com

Menke, Martin R. (PhD, Boston Coll. 1996; member, Executive Council; prof., Rivier) 20th-century German political Catholicism; mmenke@rivier.edu

Twomey, Carolyn (PhD, Boston Coll. 2017; member, Executive Council) ctwomey@stlawu.edu

Staff

Minnich, Nelson H. (PhD, Harvard 1977; ed., Catholic Historical Review; prof., Catholic) Renaissance, Reformation; minnich@cua.edu

Strauss, Charles Thomas (PhD, Notre Dame 2012; exec. secretary-treasurer) US in world, US religious; strauss@msmary.edu

American Historical Association

Headquarters Office, 400 A St. SE, Washington, DC 20003. 202.544.2422. Fax 202.544.8307. Email: info@historians.org. Website: https://www.historians.org.

The American Historical Association (AHA) is a nonprofit membership organization founded in 1884 and incorporated by Congress in 1889 for the promotion of historical studies. The AHA provides leadership for the discipline, protects academic freedom, develops professional standards, aids in the pursuit and dissemination of scholarship, and supplies various services to sustain and enhance the work of its members.

A. Collections and Libraries

The AHA headquarters office holds complete sets of the *American Historical Review*; the AHA's *Annual Reports*; *Writings on American History*; and *Perspectives on History* (including its predecessors, the *AHA Newsletter* and *Perspectives*). The papers of the American Historical Association are available through the Manuscripts Division of the Library of Congress. The Association has digitized many of these materials, which are available online at www.historians.org/about-aha-and-membership/aha-history-and-archives.

In addition to its website at www.historians.org, the AHA can be found on Facebook, Twitter, LinkedIn, and YouTube.

B. Programs

The Association's principal functions fall within five realms: research/publication, teaching, advocacy, professional development, and networking. As the largest association of professional historians in the world, the AHA serves historians representing every historical period and geographical area. The approximately 12,000 members include academics at universities, two- and four-year colleges, museums, historical organizations, libraries and archives, independent historians, students, K-12 teachers, government and business professionals, and many people who, whatever their profession, possess an abiding interest in history.

Much of the work of the Association is conducted through its governing Council and committees of historians. The Professional Division of the Council articulates ethical standards and best practices in the historical profession and works to ensure fair treatment of all historians. These principles are expressed in the *Statement on Standards of Professional Conduct*, which addresses dilemmas and concerns about the practice of history that historians have regularly brought to the Association seeking guidance and counsel. The Research Division promotes historical scholarship, encourages the collection and preservation of historical documents and artifacts, ensures equal access to information, and fosters the dissemination of information about historical records and research. The Teaching Division focuses on history education at all levels, in addition to the preparation and professional development of history teachers.

Permanent committees include the Annual Meeting Program and Local Arrangements Committees; the *AHR* Board of Editors; the Committee on Affiliated Societies; the Council Committee on the Annual Meeting; the Finance Committee; and the Investment Committee. Standing committees include the Committee on Gender Equity; the Committee on International Historical Activities; the Committee on LGBTQ Status in the Profession; the Committee on Minority Historians; and the Graduate and Early Career Committee.

The AHA promotes historical thinking and practice in a wide variety of venues, including educational and research institutions, government, and the private and nonprofit sectors. Through its membership in the National Coalition for History, the National Humanities Alliance, Consortium of Social Science Associations, Social Science Research Council, and American Council of Learned Societies, the Association collaborates with other organizations to vigorously support the rights of individuals and institutions involved in historical work. The AHA also serves as a liaison with foreign scholars and historical organizations, advocating for the rights of historians abroad.

The AHA holds an annual meeting each January. The AHA Program Committee schedules about 300 sessions addressing a wide range of topics, including scholarly research, teaching methodology, and professional concerns. Throughout the four-day meeting, the AHA operates a Career Fair and an Exhibit Hall. Approximately four dozen affiliated societies meet jointly with the AHA, scheduling sessions, annual and business meetings, luncheons, receptions, and other events. Attendance at the annual meeting averages 4,000 to 5,000.

C. Publications

The AHA publishes a wide variety of periodical, annual, and other publications of service and interest to professional historians and the general public. The *American Historical Review* is published five times per year. It has been the journal of record for the historical discipline in the United States since 1895. One of the few journals in the world that brings together scholarship from every major field of historical study, the *AHR* publishes articles that make a significant contribution to historical knowledge, as well as approximately 1,000 reviews of books and other historical materials per year, surveying and assessing the most important contemporary historical scholarship.

Perspectives on History, the newsmagazine of the AHA, appears nine times a year. For the past 50 years, *Perspectives* has been the principal source for news and information about the historical discipline. The core of the publication includes articles on topics concerning historical work in the United States and around the world. The Association covers current news and information about history and the work of historians through online-only articles on Perspectives Daily, at historians.org/perspectives.

The AHA's website also offers a rich array of resources and teaching materials for history professionals, aspiring historians, and the general public. The site includes the AHA Directory Online (historians.org/directorysearch), which provides for detailed searching of faculty/staff and their field specializations, as well as the ability to do benchmarking comparisons between departments. The most comprehensive information available on the state of doctoral education in history can now be found as part of the main AHA Directory Online. The listings for departments offering PhD degrees include specific descriptions of the programs and statistics. The AHA also maintains the Directory of Dissertations, which contains a list of over 55,000 dissertations that were completed or are currently in progress at history departments in the United States and Canada. The website also offers a calendar of historical activities (including award deadlines, conferences, and interpretive program and museum exhibitions). In addition, the site offers a robust collection of primary source materials.

The Association also publishes a wide range of pamphlets on teaching, research, and professional issues. These include series that provide synthetic overviews of important fields in the discipline, such as New Essays on Constitutional History (published in association with the Institute for Constitutional Studies), Regions and Regionalisms in the Modern World, and Historical Perspectives on Technology, Society, and Culture (with the Society for the History of Technology). The Association's pamphlets aid members of the discipline at every stage in their careers, from *Historical Research in Archives: A Practical Guide* by Samuel J. Redman to *A Historian's Guide to Copyright* by Michael Les Benedict. Descriptions, prices, and ordering instructions can be found on the AHA's website.

D. Fellowships and Awards

The Association currently administers two major fellowships, 32 prizes for publications (books, articles, films, and other formats), four research grants, three travel grants, and several other awards for professional and scholarly achievement.

Prizes for Publications:

Herbert Baxter Adams Prize, which rotates between European history from ancient history through 1815 and from 1815 through the 20th century; *George Louis Beer Prize* for the best book on European international history since 1895; *Jerry Bentley Prize* for any book published in English dealing with global or world-scale history, with connections or comparisons across continents, in any period; *Albert J. Beveridge Award* for the best book in English on the history of the United States, Latin America, or Canada since 1492; *Paul Birdsall Prize* for a major work on European military and strategic history since 1870; *James Henry Breasted Prize* for an outstanding book in any field of history prior to CE 1000; *Albert B. Corey Prize* for the best book on the history of Canadian-American relations or the history of both countries (administered jointly with the Canadian Historical Association); *Raymond J. Cunningham Prize* for the best article by an undergraduate; *John H. Dunning Prize* for the best book in US history by a first- or second-time author; *John K. Fairbank Prize* for the best book on East Asian history since 1800; *Morris D. Forkosch Prize* for the best book in British, British imperial, or British Commonwealth history since 1485; *Leo Gershoy Award* for the best book in English on 17th- and 18th-century western European history; *William and Edwyna Gilbert Award* for the best journal or serial article on teaching history; *Clarence H. Haring Prize* for an outstanding book in Latin American history by a Latin American, published in any language; *J. Franklin Jameson Award* for an outstanding achievement in editing historical sources; *Friedrich Katz Prize* for the best book in Latin American and Caribbean history; *Joan Kelly Memorial Prize* for the best book in women's history or feminist theory that incorporates a historical perspective; *Martin A. Klein Prize* to recognize the most distinguished book on African history published in English; *Waldo G. Leland Prize* for an outstanding reference tool in the field of history; *Littleton-Griswold Prize* for the best book in US law and society, broadly defined; *J. Russell Major Prize* for the best book in English on French history; *Helen and Howard R. Marraro Prize* for the best book on Italian history or Italian-American relations; *George L. Mosse Prize* for the best book in European intellectual and cultural history since the Renaissance; *John E. O'Connor Film Award* for outstanding interpretations of history through the medium of film or video; *Eugenia M. Palmegiano Prize* for the most outstanding book published in English on any aspect of the history of journalism; *James Rawley Prize* for writing that explores aspects of integration of Atlantic worlds before the 20th century; *Premio del Rey* for the best book in English in the field of early Spanish history and culture prior to 1516; *John F. Richards Prize* for the most distinguished work of scholarship on South Asian history published in English; *James Harvey Robinson Prize* for the best history teaching aid; *Dorothy Rosenberg Prize* for the most distinguished work of scholarship on the history of the Jewish Diaspora published in English; *Roy Rosenzweig Prize* for work on an innovative and freely available new media project that reflects thoughtful, critical, and rigorous engagement with technology and the practice of history; and *Wesley-Logan Prize* for an outstanding book on some aspect of the history of the dispersion, settlement, and the return of people originally from Africa (sponsored jointly with the Association for the Study of African American Life and History).

Prizes for Professional and Scholarly Achievement:

Troyer Steele Anderson Prize for contributions to the advancement of the purposes of the Association; *Eugene Asher Award* for distinguished postsecondary history teaching; *Beveridge Family Teaching Prize* for K–12 teachers, either as individuals or a group; *Equity Award* that recognizes and publicizes individuals and institutions that have achieved excellence in recruiting and retaining underrepresented racial and ethnic groups into the historic profession; *Herbert Feis Award* for distinguished contributions to public history; *Honorary Foreign Member Award* for foreign scholars who are distinguished for their work in the field of history and who have markedly assisted the work of American historians in the scholar's country; *Nancy Lyman Roelker Mentorship Award* for outstanding mentorship to students; *Theodore Roosevelt-Woodrow Wilson Award*, given occasionally to honor a public official or other civil servant who has made extraordinary contributions to the study, teaching, and public understanding of history; and *Awards for Scholarly Distinction* for lifetime achievement of quality work in the historical profession.

Grants and Fellowships:

J. Franklin Jameson Fellowship in American History, jointly sponsored by the AHA and the Library of Congress, supports significant scholarly research by young historians and *Fellowship in Aerospace History*, supported by the National Aeronautics and Space Administration, funds one research project for six to nine months in aerospace science, technology, management, law, or policy.

Research Grants. Only AHA members are eligible to apply for these grants. All grants are offered annually and are intended to further research in progress. They may be used for travel to a library or archive; microfilming, photography, or photocopying; borrowing or access fees; or similar research expenses. *Beveridge Research Grants* are available to support research in the history of the Western hemisphere. *Michael Kraus Research Grants* are offered in colonial American history, with particular reference to the intercultural aspects of American and European relations. *Littleton-Griswold Grants* award research in US legal history and the field of law and society, broadly defined. *Bernadotte Schmitt Grants* support research in the history of Europe, Asia, and Africa.

Travel Grants. Only AHA members are eligible to apply for these grants. The AHA offers the AHA Council Annual Meeting Travel Grants, the Dorothy Rosenberg Phi Beta Kappa Annual Meeting Travel Grants, and the Jerry Bentley World History Travel Grants to help graduate students and early career historians attend the annual meeting.

See the AHA's website for details and application requirements.

Staff

Brookins, Julia Akinyi (PhD, Chicago 2013; special projects coord.) US immigration, citizenship, 19th-century US; jbrookins@historians.org

Connor, Megan (BA, Mary Washington 2017; program assoc.) mconnor@historians.org

Denbo, Seth (PhD, Warwick 2002; dir., scholarly communication and digital initiatives) digital, 18th-century Britain, social and cultural; sdenbo@historians.org

Doyle, Debbie Ann (PhD, American 2003; meetings mgr.) US cultural, urban, public; ddoyle@historians.org

Flanagan, Christopher (PhD, Notre Dame 2019; vis. fellow) American Revolution and early Republic, early expansion and state-building; cflanagan@historians.org

Grossman, James R. (PhD, California, Berkeley 1982; exec. dir.) US social and urban, African American, history and public culture; jgrossman@historians.org

Hewitt, Michelle (BA, Maryland Univ. Coll. 2013; membership asst. mgr.) mhewitt@historians.org

Kaefer, Katie (MA, Houston 2012; marketing mgr.) America, public; kkaefer@historians.org

Keough, Matthew Thomas (MA, George Mason 2014; archives and office asst.) mkeough@historians.org

Lou, Karen (BA, Emory 2019; editorial asst.) klou@historians.org

Martin, Elyse (BA, Smith 2011; assoc. ed., web content and social media) emartin@historians.org

Medina Del Toro, Victor, Jr. (BA, Haverford 2017; meetings and executive asst.) science, antiquities trafficking and art crime; vmedina@historians.org

Miller, Allison (PhD, Rutgers 2012; ed., Perspectives on History) modern US cultural, women, sexuality; amiller@historians.org

Orgodol, Betsy (MPA, Strayer 2008; accounting mgr.) borgodol@historians.org

Reich, Devon (BA, Ohio State 2018; operations and marketing asst.) world politics and anthropoology; dreich@historians.org

Ruediger, Dylan (PhD, Georgia State 2017; coord., Career Diversity for Historians and institutional research) Native American, settler colonialism, English Atlantic world; druediger@historians.org

Schaffer, Dana Lanier (MA, American 2004; deputy dir.) public, African American; dschaffer@historians.org

Scott-Pinkney, Pamela M. (membership mgr.) ppinkney@historians.org

Swafford, Emily L. (PhD, Chicago 2014; dir., academic and professional affairs) war and society, women and gender, modern US; eswafford@historians.org

Townsend, Liz (BA, Catholic 1989; mgr., data admin. and integrity) database administration; ltownsend@historians.org

American Jewish Historical Society

15 W. 16th St., New York, NY 10011. 212.294.6160. Fax 212.294.6161. E-mail: ajhs@ajhs.org. Web page: http://www.ajhs.org.

Alternate Address: 101 Newbury St., Boston, MA 02116-3062. 617.226.1245.

The American Jewish Historical Society was founded in 1892 to collect, preserve, catalog, exhibit, publish, and otherwise disseminate information relating to the American Jewish experience. It does so through the society's publications, research collections, conferences, and exhibits.

A. Collections and Libraries

AJHS holds over 1,500 collections related to the American Jewish experience, from the colonial period to the present. The society serves as a major archival resource for a number of national American Jewish organizations of the past and present.

B. Programs

The society sponsors a variety of conferences, lectures and exhibitions.

C. Publications

AJHS publishes the scholarly quarterly journal *American Jewish History*.

D. Fellowships and Awards

AJHS offers the Ruth B. Fein Prize, a graduate student travel stipend; the Sid and Ruth Lapidus Fellowship for use of AJHS's colonial collections; and the Saul Veiner Book Prize.

Staff

Elder, Tanya (MA, NYU; sr. archivist) telder@ajhs.cjh.org

Malbin, Susan L. (PhD, Brandeis, 1980; dir., Library & Archives) smalbin@ajhs.org

Polland, Annie (PhD, Columbia, 2005; exec. dir.) Jewish, US, apolland@ajhs.org

American Society of Church History

PO Box 141553, Minneapolis, MN 55414. 215.821.8107. Email: asch@churchhistory.org. Website: http://www.churchhistory.org/.

The American Society of Church History is a community of scholars, dedicated to studying the history of Christianity in relation to broader culture, across all time periods, locations, and cultural contexts.

A. Collections and Libraries

The papers of the society are housed at the Presbyterian Historical Society, the National Archives of the PC(USA), in Philadelphia. In addition, Cambridge University Press maintains an electronic archive of all issues of the society's journal, *Church History: Studies in Christianity and Culture*, at Cambridge Journals Online (CJO).

B. Programs

The society holds its annual conference as part of the annual meeting of the American Historical Association in January. Spring conferences are typically held every other year.

C. Publications

The society publishes *Church History: Studies in Christianity and Culture* on a quarterly basis. The journal is devoted to publishing articles and book reviews that treat the entire history of Christianity and related subjects, as well as the historical interaction between religious expressions and culture. Issues of the journal can be accessed through Cambridge Journals Online (CJO), JSTOR, and ATLA/ATLAS (through EBSCO).

D. Fellowships and Awards

The Society offers annually a series of book and article awards. All nominations and entries must be submitted to the Executive Secretary at the American Society of Church History office.

The Frank S. and Elizabeth D. Brewer Prize, offered annually and limited to authors publishing their first scholarly work, is an award of $2,500. (The book may be in print or the author may have a contract for the book to be published.) Entries in their final form must be received by March 1.

The Albert C. Outler Prize is an annual award in the amount of $2,500 to the author of the best book published in the published in the prior calendar year, that illumines the diversity of global Christianity, issues of Christian unity and disunity (doctrinal, cultural, institutional), and/or the interactions between Christianity and other religions, in any period and area of the history of Christianity. Nominations must be received by March 1.

The Philip Schaff Prize is an award in the amount of $5,000 to the author of the best book in the history of Christianity by a North American scholar published in the prior calendar year. Nominations must be received by March 1.

The Jane Dempsey Douglass Prize is an annual award in the amount of $500 for the author of the best essay published during the previous calendar year on any aspect of the role of women in the history of Christianity. Nominations, accompanied by a copy of the article, must be received by March 1.

The Sidney E. Mead Prize, offered annually, is an award in the amount of $500 for the author of the best unpublished essay in any field of church history written by a doctoral candidate or recent graduate whose manuscript stems directly from doctoral research. The manuscript will be published in *Church History*. Entries must be submitted by July 1.

Officers

Keen, Ralph (PhD, Chicago 1990; past pres.) 16th-century religious, medieval and modern political thought; ralph.keen@churchhistory.org

Lim, Paul C-H (PhD, Cambridge 2001; pres.) Reformation Europe, evangelicalism, world Christianities; paul.lim@vanderbilt.edu

Ramírez, Daniel (PhD, Duke 2005; pres.-elect) migration, religious culture; dramire@umich.edu

Staff

Maskell, Caleb J. D. (PhD, Princeton 2019; exec. secretary) American Christianities, American religion, race and religion in America; caleb.maskell@churchhistory.org

Sterk, Andrea L. (PhD, Princeton Theological Seminary 1994; editor, *Church History*) mission and conversion 300-1000; sterk@umn.edu

Arthur and Elizabeth Schlesinger Library on the History of Women in America

Radcliffe Inst. for Advanced Study, 3 James St., Cambridge, MA 02138-3630. 617.495.8647. Fax 617.496.8340. Email: slref@radcliffe.harvard.edu. Website: https://www.radcliffe.harvard.edu/schlesinger-library.

The Arthur and Elizabeth Schlesinger Library was established at Radcliffe College (now the Radcliffe Institute for Advanced Study, Harvard University) in 1943, when alumna Maud Wood Park gave papers, books, and memorabilia documenting the 72-year suffrage movement (1848-1920) and women's political and reform work after 1920.

A. Collections and Libraries

The Schlesinger Library is in the vanguard of collecting on the history of women in America. Its holdings of books, manuscripts, periodicals, photographs, ephemera, oral histories, and audiovisual materials document the social, cultural, and political history of women in the United States, with an emphasis on women's rights movements, social reform, women's health issues, and family lives. The library is open to the public, but materials do not circulate.

The library houses nearly 4,000 manuscript collections, including the personal papers of notable women such as Susan B. Anthony, Lydia Maria Child, Charlotte Perkins Gilman, Dorothy West, Julia Child, Betty Friedan, Judy Chicago, and Pauli Murray. Family papers, as well as the papers of lesser-known women, are also abundant and equally important for a full understanding of women's place in history. The library houses the records of women's organizations and of groups and agencies concerned with women's issues, among them the Boston and Cambridge YWCAs, the National Organization for Women, the Boston Women's Health Book Collective, National Abortion Rights Action League, and several Boston-area settlement houses.

The approximately 130,000-volume book collection covers all aspects of the social and intellectual history of women and includes scholarly works, bibliographies, fiction, and more than 20,000 volumes on cookery and household management. The library subscribes to over 225 periodicals on a wide range of women's issues and interests. Approximately 100,000 photographs, hundreds of oral history transcripts, videotapes, and other materials are also available to scholars.

All of the library's manuscript collections, as well as most books and periodicals, are cataloged on HOLLIS, Harvard University's OnLine Library Information System. Finding aids for all of the library's manuscript collections are available on OASIS, Harvard's Online Archival Search Information System, and nearly half of the library's photographs are available through VIA, the university's Visual Information Access database. The library has an active digitization program that numbers more than half a million images from the collection and hundreds of digitized books. All digital images are linked to finding aids and some may be viewed through an on-line digital delivery platform http://schlesinger.radcliffe.harvard.edu/onlinecollections.

B. Programs

The Library hosts a series of lectures, symposia, and workshops on a broad range of topics concerning gender and women's history. During the academic year, the library sponsors a monthly film series featuring films and documentaries by and about women.

C. Publications

Library publications include the *Schlesinger Library Newsletter*. Other library-related publications include *The Black Women Oral History Project: From the Arthur and Elizabeth Schlesinger Library on the History of Women in America, Radcliffe College* (Westport, Conn.: Meckler, 1991); Eva Steiner Moseley, ed., *Women, Information, and the Future: Collecting and Sharing Resources Worldwide*(Fort Atkinson, Wis.: Highsmith Press, 1995); Susan von Salis, compiler, *Revealing Documents: A Guide to African American Manuscript Sources in the Schlesinger Library and the Radcliffe College Archives* (Boston: G. K. Hall, 1993); and Susan Ware, ed., *New Viewpoints in Women's History: Working Papers from the Schlesinger Library 50th Anniversary Conference, March 4–5, 1994*(Cambridge, Mass.: Arthur and Elizabeth Schlesinger Library on the History of Women in America, Radcliffe College, 1994).

D. Fellowships and Awards

The Schlesinger Library offers short-term research grants for those using the library's holdings. The Carol K. Pforzheimer Student Fellowships are open to Harvard undergraduates. Dissertation grants for doctoral research, the Alice Stone Blackwell grant for work on women's rights in the United States and abroad, and Research Support grants for postdoctoral and independent research are open to graduate students or faculty from any college or university and to independent scholars. Additionally, the library participates in the New England Regional Fellowship Consortium. For further information about Schlesinger Library grants, please consult the library's web page.

Staff

Aloisio, Paula (MA, Simmons 2001; manuscript cataloger) pkaczor@radcliffe.harvard.edu

Altieri, Marylene (MA, Harvard 1975; MSLS, Simmons 1984; curator; rare books and printed materials) maltieri@radcliffe.harvard.edu

Benson, Amy (OMS, Simmons 1991; librarian/archivist; digital initiatives) amy_benson@radcliffe.harvard.edu

Brown, Emilyn Laura (MLIS, Pratt Inst. 2007; MA, Columbia 2002; manuscripts cataloger) Emilyn_Brown@radcliffe.edu

Carey, Diana (MLS, Pratt Inst. 2004; reference librarian; visual resources) dcarey@radcliffe.harvard.edu

Carll, Johanna A. (MLS, Simmons 2000; manuscript cataloger) jcarll@radcliffe.harvard.edu

Donovan, Joanne (MA, Harvard Extension Sch. 2004; audiovisual and photograph cataloger) jdonovan@radcliffe.harvard.edu

Dunn, Marilyn (MA, Massachusetts 1990; MSLS, Simmons 1978; exec. dir.) mdunn@radcliffe.harvard.edu

Earle, Susan (MSLS, Simmons 1992; manuscripts cataloger) searle@radcliffe.harvard.edu

Engelhart, Anne (MS, Simmons 1984; MLA, Harvard Extension Sch. 1992; head; collection services) annee@radcliffe.harvard.edu

Fauxsmith, Jennifer (MLIS, Simmons 2002; research librarian) jennifer_fauxsmith@radcliffe.harvard.edu

Gotwals, Jennifer (MA, NYU 2001; manuscripts cataloger) jgotwals@radcliffe.harvard.edu

Hill, Ruth Edmonds (BS, Simmons 1948; audiovisual coord.) ruth_hill@radcliffe.harvard.edu

Holbrook, Catherine (MLIS, Simmons 2001; manuscripts cataloger) cholbroo@radcliffe.harvard.edu

Hutcheon, Sarah (MS, Simmons 2000; reference librarian) hutcheon@radcliffe.harvard.edu

Jacob, Kathryn Allamong (PhD, Johns Hopkins 1986; curator; manuscripts) kjacob@radcliffe.harvard.edu

Kamensky, Jane (PhD, Yale 1993; Pforzheimer Family Foundation Dir.; prof., Harvard) colonial America, American social and cultural; kamensky@g.harvard.edu

Moody, Honor (MLIS, Simmons 2005; rare book cataloger) hmoody@radcliffe.harvard.edu

Moore, Amber (archivist) amber_moore@radcliffe.harvard.edu

Morales Henry, Pablo (MSLIS, Simmons 2013; programmer and born-digital archivist) pablo_moraleshenry@radcliffe.harvard.edu

Peimer, Laura (MA, NYU 1996; manuscript processor) laura_peimer@radcliffe.harvard.edu

Shea, Ellen (MLIS, Simmons 1995; head; Research Services) eshea@radcliffe.harvard.edu

Strauss, Amanda Elizabeth (MS, Simmons 2013; research librarian) amanda_strauss@radcliffe.harvard.edu

Tuck, Sherrie (PhD, Harvard 1985; published materials cataloger) stuck@radcliffe.harvard.edu

Unsinn, Summer (MLIS, Simmons 2004; backlog cataloger) sunsinn@radcliffe.harvard.edu

Vassar, Mark (MLIS, Simmons 2002; manuscripts cataloger) mark_vassar@radcliffe.harvard.edu

Weintraub, Jennifer (MLIS, Michigan 1996; digital librarian/archivist) jennifer_weintraub@radcliffe.harvard.edu

Canadian Historical Association/ La Société Historique du Canada

1912-130, Albert St., Ottawa, ON K1P 5G4, Canada. 613.233.7885. Fax 613.565.5445. Email: cha-shc@cha-shc.ca; mduquet@cha-shc.ca. Website: https://cha-shc.ca/.

Founded in 1922, the Canadian Historical Association | La Société historique du Canada is a bilingual not-for-profit and charitable association devoted to fostering the scholarly study and communication of history in Canada. It is the largest of its kind in the country.

A. Collections and Libraries

The CHA does not maintain a research collection but relies on the proximity of Library and Archives Canada.

B. Programs

The CHA's many committees are responsible for much of the association's work and much of its influence. Among the society's committees and portfolios are the Advocacy (External Relations, Copyright adviser, Census); Communications (*Bulletin*, Electronic Committee, Webmaster); Outreach (Membership, Chairs Liaison; Affiliated Committees); CHA/AHA Joint Committee (Corey Prize); Graduate Students; Regional History Committee (Clio Awards); Prizes; and Publications (*Journal* liaison; books and booklets). Regional and subject interest organizations have been granted affiliated status within the CHA: Canadian Committee on Women's History; Canadian Committee on History and Computing; Graduate Students Committee; Canadian Committee on the History of Sexuality; the Canadian Committee on Labour History; History of Children and Youth Group; Canadian Committee on the Second World War; Economic Historians in Canada;

Canadian Committee on Military History; Canadian Urban History Association; Business History Group; Native History Group; the Northern History Group; the Public History Group; the Oral History Group; and the Environmental History Group.

The CHA holds an annual meeting each spring in conjunction with the Congress of the Humanities and Social Sciences at various cities across Canada, bringing together interested members for conference and discussion on wide-ranging themes and diversity of topics. Each annual meeting combines business sessions with the largest annual historical conference in Canada.

C. Publications

The CHA has a broadly based program of publications. The *Bulletin* (published three times a year) is a forum of importance to all historians, containing news on historians and their activities, information on forthcoming conferences, prizes, fellowships, research grants, and opinion pieces on issues in academic and public history. The *Journal of the Canadian Historical Association/ Revue de la Société historique du Canada* (two issues per year, one online) is a refereed journal of the best papers presented to the Editorial Board for consideration, in any field of history and in either official language. The CHA publishes Historical Booklets (now online) on pertinent historical topics and in collaboration with the federal Multiculturalism Program, an ongoing series in ethnic history and a new series of short books on specialized themes designed for undergraduate students. The CHA publishes an online *Register of Post-Graduate Dissertations in Progress in History and Related Subjects* and *Becoming a Historian*, a guide for students (online edition in preparation). In addition, members who wish to subscribe to a number of Canadian journals may do so through the association.

D. Fellowships and Awards

The CHA offers the *François-Xavier Garneau Medal Prize* for an outstanding work in the field of history over a five-year period. The *Sir John A. Macdonald Prize* is awarded annually for the best nonfiction work of Canadian history judged to have the most significant contribution to an understanding of the Canadian past. The *Wallace K. Ferguson Prize* is awarded annually to the author of an outstanding scholarly book in the field of history other than Canadian history. The *Albert B. Corey Prize* is given every two years jointly with the American Historical Association for the best book dealing with the history of Canadian-American relations or with the history of both countries. The *John Bullen Prize* is awarded annually for the best doctoral dissertations in history. The *CLIO Awards* are given annually for meritorious publications or for exceptional contributions by individuals or organizations to regional history. The *CHA Journal Prize* is awarded every year for the best essay published each year in the Journal of the Canadian Historical Association. The *Jean-Marie Fecteau Prize* is awarded for the best article published in a peer-reviewed journal (including peer-reviewed student journals) by a PhD of MA-level member, in French or in English.

Officers

Bryden, Penny E. (PhD, York, Can. 1994; pres.) pbryden@uvic.ca
Duquet, Michel (PhD, Ottawa 2006; exec. dir.) mduquet@cha-shc. ca
McCutcheon, Jo-Anne (PhD, Ottawa 2002; treasurer) jomac@ history2knowledge.ca
Perry, Adele (PhD, York, Can. 1997; past pres.) colonialism, Canada; adele.perry@umanitoba.ca

Center for History of Physics

American Inst. of Physics, 1 Physics Ellipse, College Park, MD 20740-3843. 301.209.3165. Fax 301.209.0882. Email: chp@aip. org; photos@aip.org. Website: https://www.aip.org/history-programs/physics-history.

A division of the American Institute of Physics, the Center for History of Physics is the oldest and best-known institution dedicated to the history of a scientific discipline. Established in 1961, the center's mission is to preserve and make known the history of the physical sciences.

A. Collections and Libraries

The Center's library is the Niels Bohr Library & Archives. Holdings include the Emilio Segrè Visual Archives, comprising some 30,000 portraits and other historical photographs, drawings, and film and video clips; an extensive collection of books related to physics; more than 2,000 archival and manuscript collections; tape-recorded materials, including some 1,400 recordings of reminiscences and a large collection of oral history interviews; hundreds of manuscript autobiographies and unpublished histories of physics institutions, and much else.

The International Catalog of Sources (ICOS) is also maintained in the Niels Bohr Library & Archives. ICOS contains records for unpublished source materials in the archives and over 700 other repositories worldwide. The period of interest is chiefly from about 1890 to the present, but ICOS also contains information on 19th-century collections of interest, and even earlier ones of major importance. In addition to collections that are in libraries and archives, ICOS has information on papers in private hands (especially if they are available for research use) and information on papers of significant scientists that have been destroyed. The library also maintains the Physics History Finding Aids web site, which provides access to finding aids for more than 100 collections at 12 major science archives.

B. Programs

Working to document the history of modern science is the Center's best-known activity. Through research, the staff builds a sound base for advising scientists and institutions on how they may safeguard the record of their achievements. Meanwhile, the Center maintains its own strategy for documenting physics history worldwide. One part of this strategy is a program of oral history interviewing to save for posterity the recollections of eminent physical scientists. The Center has conducted some 3,000 hours of interviews with over 1,500 individuals, while assisting many outside scholars in further interviewing. Most of the tapes are transcribed, indexed, and available for use.

Still more important has been saving correspondence, notebooks, and other unpublished materials. By aiding scientists, their families, and archivists at many institutions around the world, the Center helps assure the survival of collections that might otherwise have been lost forever. The Center normally does not try to acquire such collections for itself but seeks to preserve them at the most appropriate repository. The Center also microfilms collections of letters, notebooks, and the like. On a broader scale, the Center promotes the preservation of endangered historical records created by large nonacademic research laboratories, multi-institutional collaborations, and corporations.

The Center plays an active role in explaining the heritage of physics and allied sciences to the scientific community and to society at large. Besides providing help to educators and the media, the staff write their own historical articles and books, both scholarly and popular. From time to time they also undertake projects such as exhibits and posters for the benefit of science museums, teachers, and the public. Exhibits on the web at http://www.aip.org/history/exhibit.htm attract students and teachers.

C. Publications

The Center publishes a semiannual newsletter, the *Center for History of Physics Newsletter*. This newsletter includes reports on work in the history of the physical, carried out at the American Institute of Physics and elsewhere. It also includes reports on archival materials, bibliographies, photos, and more. Other publications include *AIP Studies of Multi-Institutional Collaborations*, which presents findings of the AIP Center's studies of the organizational structures and functions of large research collaborations; *Documentation of Postwar Physics*, developed during the AIP Center's study of recordkeeping and records appraisal at US Department of Energy Laboratories; *Guide to the Archival Collections in the Niels Bohr Library at the American Institute of Physics*; and online exhibits explaining aspects of physics history. For access to publications visit the Center's web site.

D. Fellowships and Awards

The Center has a program of grants-in-aid for research in the history of the physical sciences and their social interactions. Grants can be up to $2,500 each. They can be used only to reimburse direct expenses connected with the work. Preference will be given to those who need part of the funds for travel and subsistence to use the resources of AIP's Niels Bohr Library & Archives in College Park, Maryland (easily accessible from Washington, DC), or to microfilm papers or to record oral history interviews with a copy deposited in the library. Applicants should either be working toward a graduate degree in the history of science (in which case they should include a letter of reference from their thesis adviser), or show a record of publication in the field. Deadlines for receipt of applications are April 15 and November 15 of each year.

Grants to archives are intended to make accessible records and papers that document the history of modern physics and allied fields. Grants can be up to $10,000 each and can be used only to cover direct expenses connected with preserving, inventorying, arranging, describing, or cataloging appropriate collections. Expenses may include acid-free storage materials and staff salary/benefits, but not overhead. For grant guidelines or for more information on the Center and its programs, check the web site at www.aip.org/history-programs/physics-history/grants, or call the Center.

Staff

Burch, Lance (MA, Florida State 2016; assoc. historian) science, environmental science and policy, marine science; lburch@aip.org

Calhoun, Chip (MLS, Maryland, Coll. Park 2005; digital archivist) processing, digital tools; ccalhoun@aip.org

Good, Gregory A. (PhD, Toronto 1982; dir.) 19th- and 20th-century physical and earth science; ggood@aip.org

Hearty, Ryan (MA, Johns Hopkins 2019; oral history fellow) 20th-century engineering, environmental science; rhearty@aip.org

Henderson, Gabriel David (PhD, Michigan State 2014; assoc. historian) environmental politics and science, science and public policy, 20th-century America; ghenders@aip.org

Holland, Samantha (MLS, Maryland 2019; archives asst.) processing, biographical research, digital/web; sholland@aip.org

Jankowski, Stephanie (BS, Maryland 1984; sr. administrative support) oral histories, meetings and conferences, database; sjankows@aip.org

Lengel, Audrey (MLS, Maryland, Coll. Park 2015; photo archivist) image collections, copyright; alengel@aip.org

Mona, Corinne (MA, Bergen, Norway 2012; asst. librarian) cataloging, preservation; cmona@aip.org

Mueller, Melanie J. (MLS, Maryland, Coll. Park 2005; dir.) documentary strategy, administration, collection development; mmueller@aip.org

Rein, Allison (MLS, Maryland, Coll. Park 2011; asst. dir.; Special Collections) cataloging, collection development, preservation; arein@aip.org

Weirich, Sarah (MLIS, Southern Mississippi 2018; metadata specialist) cataloging, preservation; sweirich@aip.org

Colonial Society of Massachusetts

87 Mount Vernon St., Boston, MA 02108. 617.227.2782. Fax 617.227.0521. Email: jtyler1776@gmail.com. Website: https://www.colonialsociety.org/.

Founded in 1892, the Colonial Society of Massachusetts is a non-profit educational foundation designed to promote the study of Massachusetts history from earliest settlement through the first decades of the nineteenth century.

A. Collections and Libraries

Not applicable.

B. Programs

The Colonial Society of Massachusetts publishes documents related to early Massachusetts history and holds occasional scholarly conferences on related topics, often printing the proceedings. The society also conducts workshops and provides other support for K–12 history teachers in Massachusetts and holds periodic forums for graduate students to share work in progress.

C. Publications

The society has published 89 volumes of documents related to early Massachusetts history.

D. Fellowships and Awards

The society provides a subvention to the *New England Quarterly* and awards annually the Walter Muir Whitehill Prize ($2,500 and publication in the *New England Quarterly*) for a distinguished essay in colonial history, previously unpublished. Preference is given to New England topics. Submissions should be received by the society by December 31 of each calendar year.

Staff

Tyler, John (PhD, Princeton 1980; ed., publications) colonial America, 17th- and 18th-century Britain, American architecture and decorative arts; jtyler1776@gmail.com

The Committee on Lesbian, Gay, Bisexual, and Transgender History

c/o Emily Hobson, Univ. of Nevada, Reno, 1664 N. Virginia St., MS 0046, Reno, NV 89557-0046. 775.682.6482. Email: ehobson@unr.edu. Website: http://clgbthistory.org/.

The Committee on Lesbian and Gay History was founded in 1979, and its name was changed to the Committee on Lesbian, Gay, Bisexual, Transgender History in January 2009. Since 1982, the Committee has been officially recognized as an affiliate of the American Historical Association and meets annually in conjunction with the AHA conference, where we sponsor sessions on lesbian, gay, bisexual, transgender, and queer history. One need not be a member of the AHA to join the Committee.

A. Collections and Libraries

Not applicable.

B. Programs

Since 1982, the Committee on LGBT History has been officially recognized as an affiliate of the American Historical Association. The Committee on LGBT History encourages the development of specialized courses in LGBTQ studies as well as the inclusion of LGBTQ topics in general history courses. It promotes local history archives and projects and coordinates activities with other professional caucuses. The Committee on LGBT History also seeks to prevent discrimination against lesbian, gay, bisexual, transgender, and queer historians, in keeping with AHA policies.

The Committee on LGBT History meets annually in conjunction with the AHA, where it sponsors sessions on lesbian, gay, bisexual, transgender, and queer history. One need not be a member of the AHA to join the Committee on LGBT History.

C. Publications

The Committee on LGBT History publishes a newsletter two times a year and maintains an e-mail announcements list, a Facebook page, and a web page.

D. Fellowships and Awards

The Committee on LGBT History awards six scholarly prizes in alternating years. The John Boswell, Joan Nestle, and Don Romesburg Prizes are awarded in odd-numbered years. The *John Boswell Prize* is awarded for an outstanding book on lesbian, gay, bisexual, transgender, and/or queer history published in English. The *Joan Nestle Prize* is awarded for an outstanding paper on lesbian, gay, bisexual, transgender, and/or queer history completed in English by an undergraduate student. The Nestle Prize is funded by the generous contributions of the Committee on LGBT History lifetime members. The *Don Romesburg Prize* is awarded for outstanding K-12 curriculum in LGBT history.

The Gregory Sprague, Audre Lorde, and Allan Bérubé Prizes are awarded in even-numbered years. The *Gregory Sprague Prize* is awarded for an outstanding published or unpublished paper, article, book chapter, or dissertation chapter on lesbian, gay, bisexual, transgender, and/or queer history completed in English by a graduate student. The *Audre Lorde Prize* is awarded for an outstanding article on lesbian, gay, bisexual, transgender, and/or queer history written in English by a North American. The *Allan Bérubé Prize* is awarded for an outstanding public history project on lesbian, gay, bisexual, transgender, and/or queer history. For details on submissions (including deadlines) see http://clgbthistory.org/prizes/.

Officers

Capo, Julio C., Jr. (PhD, Florida International 2011; co-chair) capo@history.umass.edu

Haynes, April R. (PhD, California, Santa Barbara 2009; book review ed.) april.haynes@wisc.edu

Hobson, Emily K. (PhD, Southern California 2009; co-chair) ehobson@unr.edu

Royles, Dan (PhD, Temple 2014; newsletter ed.) droyles@gmail.com

Skidmore, Emily (PhD, Illinois, Urbana-Champaign 2011; treasurer-secretary) emily.skidmore@ttu.edu

Cushwa Center for the Study of American Catholicism

Univ. of Notre Dame, 407 Geddes Hall, Notre Dame, IN 46556-5611. 574.631.5441. Fax 574.631.8471. Email: cushwa@nd.edu. Website: https://cushwa.nd.edu/.

The Charles and Margaret Hall Cushwa Center for the Study of American Catholicism is located at the University of Notre Dame. Begun in 1975, the center promotes and encourages the scholarly study of the American Catholic tradition.

A. Collections and Libraries

The Cushwa Center's activities embrace four areas: instruction, research, publication, and collection of materials. In each of these areas, the center pursues a multidisciplinary approach and does not limit its activities or programs to any one particular methodology or discipline.

The library and archives of the University of Notre Dame house an extensive collection of Catholic Americana. This collection includes Catholic newspapers, literature, records of 20th-century Catholic organizations, histories of midwestern and American Catholics, reports of European missionary societies, and other material related to the American Catholic community.

B. Programs

The Cushwa Center sponsors the American Catholic Studies Seminars. Scholars from across the country are invited to present papers at these seminars, which are held at the university several times a year. These papers are available to the public for the cost of mailing. The center also sponsors the Notre Dame Seminar in American Religion, a gathering of selected historians of American religion. The Cushwa Center also sponsors occasional conferences on topics related to American Catholicism and research on topics such as the American Catholic parish, the history of American Catholic seminary education, and Hispanic Catholics in America, among others. The center also presents an annual Hibernian lecture. For more information on any of these programs, contact the director.

The Lived History of Vatican II project, which began in 2011, broke new ground in the study of religion and modernity, the relationship between local and global realities, and the international impact of the Second Vatican Council. The project's ultimate goal is to spark further works on this topic and incite a body of scholarly work on the international impact of the Council. A volume encompassing the project's findings is forthcoming.

C. Publications

The Cushwa Center posts a semiannual newsletter on its web site at cushwa.nd.edu/newsletter, *American Catholic Studies*. This newsletter reports on the latest scholarship in American Catholic studies, features personal news items, provides information on major archival holdings in the United States, and publishes essays on recent research.

D. Fellowships and Awards

Research Travel Grants are awarded by the center to scholars wishing to use the university's library and archival collections of Catholic Americana. The Hibernian Research Award for Irish American Studies is funded by an endowment from the Ancient Order of Hibernians. This award is granted annually to scholars researching the Irish experience in America. In conjunction with

Italian Studies at the University of Notre Dame (italianstudies. nd.edu), the center offers an annual funding opportunity, the Peter R. D'Agostino Research Travel Grant. Designed to facilitate the study of the American past from an international perspective, this competitive award of $5,000 will support research in Roman archives for a significant publication project on US Catholic history. Theodore M. Hesburgh Research Travel Grants support research projects in any academic discipline that consider and incorporate the work of the Rev. Theodore M. Hesburgh, C.S.C., former president of the University of Notre Dame. Grants are made twice yearly. Contact the center's director for information on any of these grants or fellowships.

Staff

Cummings, Kathleen Sprows (PhD, Notre Dame 1999; dir.) American women, Catholicism and ethnicity; cummings.23@ nd.edu

Folger Institute

Folger Shakespeare Library, 201 E. Capitol St. SE, Washington, DC 20003-1094. 202.675.0312. Fax 202.675.0378. Email: institute@ folger.edu. Website: https://www.folger.edu/folger-institute.

A. Collections and Libraries

The Folger Institute is a dedicated center for advanced study and collections-focused research in the humanities at the Folger Shakespeare Library, home to the world's largest Shakespeare collection as well as major collections of rare books, manuscripts, prints, and works of art, from the early modern period through to the present day. The Institute fosters targeted investigations of these world-class collections through multi-disciplinary, formal programs and residential research fellowships. The Institute gathers knowledge communities and establishes fresh research and teaching agendas for the humanities. Its advanced undergraduate and early-stage graduate student initiatives introduce students to rare materials and the research questions that can be explored with those materials. Plans are also underway to organize multi-year, collaborative research initiatives.

The work of the Institute in all its many parts has been generously supported by endowments from the Andrew W. Mellon Foundation, program and fellowship grants from the National Endowment for the Humanities, the sustaining memberships of the universities of the Institute's consortium, and support from a variety of other sources, including private donors and scholarly societies. The Folger Institute helps set the intellectual agenda for early modern humanities. Through their interpretations of primary source materials, its associated scholars bring to light important issues from early modernity that still resonate today.

B. Programs

A collaborative enterprise sponsored by the Folger Shakespeare Library and over forty universities offers a multi-disciplinary program of seminars, workshops, conferences, colloquia, and lectures. For the most up-to-date information on Folger Institute consortium programs, please visit the Institute's Scholarly Programs website.

Grants-in-aid in support of program participation are available to affiliates of the consortium universities listed below. Unless otherwise specified, registration fees are automatically waived for affiliates of the Folger and Newberry Library consortia. Applicants may use the online application portal.

The consortium universities include: University of Alabama; American University; Amherst College; Boston University; Brown University; University at Buffalo, SUNY; University of Chicago; The City University of New York; Columbia University; University of Connecticut; University of Delaware; Duke University; Emory University; Fordham University; George Mason University; The George Washington University; Georgetown University; Harvard University; Howard University; The Johns Hopkins University; University of Maryland, Baltimore County; University of Maryland, College Park; University of Massachusetts, Amherst; New York University; University of North Carolina at Chapel Hill; University of North Carolina at Greensboro; North Carolina State University; University of Notre Dame; The Ohio State University; University of Pennsylvania; Pennsylvania State University; Princeton University; Queen's University Belfast; University of Rochester; Rutgers University; University of St. Andrews; University of South Carolina; Syracuse University; Texas A&M University; University of Toronto; Tulane University; Vanderbilt University; University of Virginia; Washington University in St. Louis; West Virginia University; and Yale University.

C. Publications

A list of long-term fellows' publications can be found on the Folgerpedia website at Publications by Folger Institute Fellows.

A list of publications that have grown out of the seminars, conferences, and symposia sponsored by the Institute and its two centers—the Center for Shakespeare Studies and the Center for the History of British Political Thought—can be found on the Folgerpedia website at Selected publications resulting from Folger Institute seminars.

D. Fellowships and Awards

The Folger Institute offers research fellowships to cultivate ongoing, lively multi-disciplinary dialogue and collaboration among scholars and artists and to encourage use of the exceptional collections of the Folger Shakespeare Library. Fellowships are supported by the funds from the Andrew W. Mellon Foundation, The National Endowment for the Humanities, and the Folger Shakespeare Library, and a variety of private endowments and public partnerships. For more information about Folger Institute Fellowships, please visit the Institute's Fellowships Programs website.

Staff

Herbert, Amanda E. (PhD, Johns Hopkins 2010; assoc. dir., fellowships) early modern Britain, gender and sexuality, body, food; aherbert@folger.edu

Lynch, Kathleen (PhD, Pittsburgh 1982; exec. dir.) 17th-century English literature, regulation of religion and book trade; klynch@folger.edu

Williams, Owen (PhD, Pennsylvania 2003; assoc. dir., scholarly programs) Elizabethan prose, religion, law; owilliams@folger. edu

Gerald R. Ford Presidential Library

1000 Beal Ave., Ann Arbor, MI 48109-2114. 734.205.0555. Fax 734.205.0571. Email: ford.library@nara.gov. Website: https:// www.fordlibrarymuseum.gov/.

The Library in Ann Arbor, Michigan, and the Ford Presidential Museum in Grand Rapids, Michigan, form one institution that is part of the National Archives and Records Administration's system of presidential libraries.

A. Collections and Libraries

The Library collects, preserves, and makes accessible to the public a rich body of archival materials on US domestic issues, foreign relations, and political affairs during the Cold War era. Current holdings include over 25 million pages of memos, letters, meeting notes, reports, and other historical documents. There are also 500,000 audiovisual items, including photographs, videotapes of network news broadcasts, audiotapes of speeches and press briefings, film, and campaign commercials.

The presidential papers of Gerald Ford and his White House staff form the core collection. These are supplemented by the pre- and post-presidential papers of Gerald Ford, the papers of Betty Ford, the papers of many former government officials and political associates, the records of the National Security Council, oral histories, and much more.

PRESNET, a powerful internal collection description database, gives quick subject access to most of the open materials at the Library. Upon request, archivists can generate detailed lists of folders (with estimates of the number of pages in each) in response to queries for materials on almost any topic.

B. Programs

The library presents speakers, lobby exhibits, educational programs, and other events. It collaborates on additional programs with its partner institution, the Gerald R. Ford Presidential Museum in Grand Rapids, Michigan. The Gerald R. Ford Presidential Foundation provides major support for many of these programs.

C. Publications

A comprehensive guide to all research collections, with detailed inventories to all of the "open" collections, is available at the library's web site. Cabinet and National Security Council meeting minutes, and selected other documents and photos are available on the web site.

D. Fellowships and Awards

The Gerald R. Ford Presidential Foundation awards grants of up to $2,200 each in support of research in the holdings of the Ford Presidential Library. A grant defrays North American travel, living, and photocopy expenses of a research trip to the Ford Library. Please contact the library for information about application procedures as well as holdings related to your project. Each year's application deadlines are March 15 and September 15.

The Gerald R. Ford Scholar Award in Honor of Robert Teeter, in the amount of $5,000, has been established by the library and the University of Michigan with gifts from the Teeter family, the UPS Foundation, and others. The award is given annually to support dissertation research on an aspect of the US political process during the latter part of the 20th century. Award recipients may wish to conduct a portion of their research in the Robert Teeter Papers, 1972–2004. Mr. Teeter, who worked in several Republican presidential campaigns, was one of the nation's foremost public opinion analysts. The application deadline is May 1.

Staff

Davis, Stacy (MLS, Maryland, Coll. Park; archivist) modern US; stacy.davis@nara.gov

Didier, Elaine (PhD, Michigan; dir., Library and Museum) library/museum management, modern US; elaine.didier@nara.gov

Druga, Elizabeth (MLIS, Pittsburgh; audiovisual archivist) modern US; elizabeth.druga@nara.gov

Gundersen, Geir (MA, North Dakota State; supervisory archivist) library management, modern US, 1970s US foreign relations; geir.gundersen@nara.gov

Holtz, Tim (MLIS, Wayne State; archives specialist) modern US, 1970s US foreign relations; tim.holtz@nara.gov

O'Connell, John (MA, Wayne State; archives technician) modern US; john.o'connell@nara.gov

Senger, Jeffrey (MA, Western Michigan; archives technician) modern US; jeffrey.senger@nara.gov

German Historical Institute

1607 New Hampshire Ave. NW, Washington, DC 20009. 202.387.3355. Fax 202.387.6437. Email: info@ghi-dc.org. Website: https://www.ghi-dc.org/.

The German Historical Institute (GHI) was established in April 1987 as an independent nonprofit foundation dedicated to the promotion of historical research and to the dissemination of historical knowledge. Since 2002 it has been part of the Max Weber Foundation. In 2017, the GHI opened a Pacific Regional Office, GHI West, in Berkeley, CA. The institute receives funding from the government of the Federal Republic of Germany but also seeks grants and accepts support from other sources.

A. Collections and Libraries

The GHI has established a research library that includes a reference section; finding aids of German and American archives; a collection of periodicals, focusing especially on German Americana, German regional and local history, and recent publications on German and American history, with emphasis on German-American relations.

B. Programs

The GHI provides a permanent basis for historical research in the fields of German history, North American history, global and transregional history and digital history. It lends support and advice to German and North American historians and scholars in related fields and advances scholarly cooperation by organizing conferences, lecture series and other academic formats.

C. Publications

The GHI maintains an active publication program in English and German as part of its effort to foster international scholarly dialogue. It publishes important contributions to the fields of German, North American, and transatlantic history. The GHI has several ongoing peer-reviewed book series, as well as its own journal: *Publications of the German Historical Institute* (with Cambridge University Press), *Transatlantische Historische Studien* (with Steiner Verlag), *Studies in German History* (with Berghahn Books), the bi-annual bulletin, and a bulletin supplement on special themes. In addition, the GHI manages the History of Knowledge blog, a venue for the exchange of ideas and information on the history of knowledge.

D. Fellowships and Awards

Each year, the institute awards the Steiner Prize for Transatlantic History, the Friends of the GHI annually award the Fritz Stern Dissertation Prize for the best North American dissertation in German History. The GHI also offers fellowships to fund the research of German and North American doctoral students and postdocs. Since 2015 the GHI has also been granting two German-American binational tandem fellowships for scholars at various academic levels. In 2017 it added another binational Tandem fellowship at its Pacific Regional Office, GHI West. In addition, the GHI is part of the Max Weber Foundation's travel grants network. To further promote scholars in the early stages of their career, the GHI organizes an annual Transatlantic Doctoral Seminar, an Archival Seminar, the Seminar in Jewish History, a

Medieval History Seminar (with the GHI in London) and a Young Scholars Forum (at GHI West).

Staff

Augustin, Anna-Carolin (PhD, Potsdam 2016; research fellow) modern German-Jewish history and culture, women and gender, Jewish material culture, Nazi art looting and postwar restitution; augustin@ghi-dc.org

Engel, Elisabeth (PhD, Free, Berlin 2014; research fellow) early and modern North America, postcolonial studies, Atlantic and transnational; engel@ghi-dc.org

Hughes, Thomas L. (JD, Yale Law Sch. 1952; sr. vis. fellow) Brandenburg/Magdeburg/Poland 1555-66; thoshughes@aol.com

Jansen, Axel (PhD, Goethe 2001; deputy dir.) US, science; a.jansen@ghi-dc.org

Jansen, Jan C. (PhD, Konstanz 2011; research fellow) colonial and imperial, modern Europe, freemasonry; jansen@ghi-dc.org

Laessig, Simone (PhD, Dresden 1990; dir.) 19th- and 20th-century cultural and social, Jewish; prolaessig@ghi-dc.org

Lazar, David (MA, Stanford 1986; sr. editor) lazar@ghi-dc.org

Livingston, R. Gerald (PhD, Harvard 1959; sr. vis. fellow) post-World War II Germany, American foreign policy in Europe; jliving844@aol.com

McCullough, Kelly A. (PhD, Bryn Mawr 2003; project mgr., GHDI) expressionism, garden city movement, architecture and politics; mccullough@ghi-dc.org

Pertilla, Atiba K. (PhD, NYU 2016; research assoc.) economic, digital; pertilla@ghi-dc.org

Roesch, Claudia (PhD, Muenster 2014; research fellow) family, migration, reproductive rights, transatlantic; roesch@ghi-dc.org

Stoneman, Mark R. (PhD, Georgetown 2007; editor) military, Germany, social; stoneman@ghi-dc.org

Sutcliffe, Patricia (PhD, Texas, Austin 2000; editor) sutcliffe@ghi-dc.org

Urbansky, Sören (PhD, Konstanz 2014; research fellow) Russia, 18th-to 20th-century Soviet Union and China, Chinese diaspora in Pacific, borders; urbansky@ghi-dc.org

von der Krone, Kerstin (PhD, Erfurt 2010; research fellow) modern Jewish/Jewish education, intellectual/ book/knowledge production; krone@ghi-dc.org

Westermann, Andrea (PhD, Bielefeld 2006; fellow, GHI West) science; westermann@ghi-dc.org

Wetzell, Richard (PhD, Stanford 1991; research fellow) 19th- and 20th-century Germany, modern German legal/intellectual/cultural, science; wetzell@ghi-dc.org

Hagley Museum and Library

PO Box 3630, 298 Buck Rd. E., Wilmington, DE 19807. 302.658.2400. Fax 302.658.3690. Email: mmoeller@hagley.org. Website: https://www.hagley.org/.

A. Collections and Libraries

The Hagley Museum and Library is a nonprofit educational institution dedicated to America's economic and technological heritage. It houses an important collection of manuscripts, photographs, books, digital assets, oral histories, and artifacts documenting the history of America's business and technology. Hagley initially focused its collecting on the Middle Atlantic region, but in recent years the scope of collecting has broadened to include records of and works about business organizations and companies of national importance.

The Published Collections Department manages approximately 300,000 volumes and 12,500 microforms, including books, serials, pamphlets, maps and atlases, city directories, trade catalogs and journals, theses, and government documents. Business history and biography comprise more than one-third of the imprints collections. Included are works on economics and economic history, labor, energy, transportation and communication, commerce, consumerism, industrial design, commercial architecture, consumer electronics, advertising, finance, and corporate history. Company annual reports, stockholder and employee magazines, advertising literature, and public relations pieces complement archival collections.

Hagley possesses a distinguished collection for the study of the history of technology. The 66,000 trade catalogs, most of which were published between 1880 and 2010, are important resources for the study of America's commercial, technological, and industrial development. The catalogs are also useful for historic restorations, artifact identification, and race and gender studies. The trade catalog collection has been described in a separate collections guide. Hagley's collection of guidebooks and catalogs for the great international expositions trace international technology transfer and the introduction of manufactured goods to the public. The American fairs at Philadelphia (1876), Chicago (1893), and St. Louis (1904) are especially well represented in Hagley's collection, as is the London Crystal Palace Exhibition of 1851.

The European roots of American business and technological development are documented in the rare book and pamphlet collections, which include works on 18th-century French history and economic theory, with a particular emphasis on physiocracy. It is the most significant collection of French Enlightenment documents describing these subjects outside France.

The Guttman Collection of pyrotechnics consists of some 800 books and many pamphlets on explosives and military subjects; it is particularly strong in books about fireworks published between 1500 and 1900.

Hagley's 38,000 linear feet of manuscripts collections, managed by the Manuscripts and Archives Department, contain the records of several thousand firms as well as the personal papers of the entrepreneurs who helped build them. The library is also the repository for the records of national business and trade organizations, including the US Chamber of Commerce, the National Association of Manufacturers, the American Iron and Steel Institute, and the National Foreign Trade Council.

The companies represented range from the mercantile houses of the late 18th century through the artisan workshops of the 19th, to the multinational corporations of the 20th century through the dot-com businesses of the 21st. The collections illustrate the impact of the enterprise system on American society—its economic, social, technological, political, cultural, and labor history.

The business and personal papers of the DuPont Company and family were the core collections around which the library developed. The papers of Pierre Samuel du Pont de Nemours (1739–1817) are an important resource for students of 18th-century French history. Those of his son, E. I. du Pont, and other family members document the 1802 founding and subsequent operation of the DuPont Company's powder mills. Twentieth-century records describe the transformation of the company into a modern corporation. The papers of the three cousins most responsible for this transformation (T. Coleman, Alfred I., and Pierre S. du Pont) are also in the collections, and are among the critical collections (along with the papers of members of Pew family of Pennsylvania, also at Hagley) informing scholarship in the history of modern philanthropy and the resurgence of modern conservatism in the United States.

The history of the northeastern railways is well represented in Hagley's collections, which include the records of the Philadelphia and Reading Railroad and significant parts of the Pennsylvania Railroad archives. Records and photographs documenting the history of energy development and use can be found in the archives of the Sun Company, the Westmoreland Coal Company, the Penn Virginia Corporation, and St. Clair Coal Company. The archives of the Pennsylvania Power and Light Company trace the development of the electric industry in eastern Pennsylvania. Similarly, the history of the iron and steel industry can be traced through the records of Bethlehem Steel Corporation, Lukens Steel Company, Alan Wood Steel Company, and Phoenix Steel Corporation.

Many collections chronicle the progress of high technology in the 20th century. The Elmer Sperry papers and the papers and photographs of the Sperry Gyroscope Company (1909–65) document the history of pioneering scientific and technical firms that became important military contractors. Records and photographs of Sperry-UNIVAC, the Eckert-Mauchly Company, Engineering Research Associates, and the IBM antitrust suit trace the early history of the computer and aeronautics industries. Hagley owns the largest collection of documents describing the development and operations of the Radio Corporation of America (RCA) and its iconic leader of nearly four decades, David Sarnoff. Hagley also has major collections on the history of atomic energy from the Manhattan Project onward. Records of the MCI Communications Corporation detail many aspects of the computer and communications revolution, the development of electronic mail, and the evolution of national telecommunications policies. Hagley has acquired collections describing the dot-com phenomenon stradling the 20th and 21st centuries, and the development of electronic voluntary consensus standards vital for our modern networked environment.

In recent years, Hagley has begun to document the history of advertising and America's consumer culture. It holds the papers of Ernest Dichter, founder of the Institute for Motivational Research. Dichter advised hundreds of American and European firms on applying psychological techniques to advertising. Focus groups are one of his innovations. The records of Joseph E. Seagram & Sons Company and Avon Products provide invaluable information on mass marketing, advertising, and market research. Product and package design are well represented in the papers of industrial designers Raymond Loewy, Thomas Lamb, and Marc Harrison, William Pahlmann, Irv Koons, Richard Hollerith, Ken White, Marshall Johnson, and others.

The Department of Audiovisual Collections and Digital Initiatives provides visual and aural documentation within the scope of Hagley's research areas. Many of the collections, which vary in size from one image to more than 100,000, are directly related to holdings in the Manuscripts and Archives Department. The collections include a multitude of 20th-century black-and-white still photography. Other formats found throughout the holdings range from daguerreotypes to Polaroid prints, lithographs and engravings, motion pictures, negatives in a variety of formats, videotapes, and sound recordings, including oral histories collected and developed by Hagley's Oral History Office. Hagley's pictorial archives are organized by individual collections; finding aids to specific collections contain entries for the major subjects covered.

The artifact collections of the Hagley Museum number approximately 250,000 objects. They range from historic architecture and landscape to decorative and fine arts to scientific instruments, hand tools, and industrial machinery. Second in size only to the Smithsonian Institution's own is Hagley's collection of US patent models, small-scale versions of inventions submitted along with patent applications to the Commissioner of Patents. Also noteworthy is the decorative arts collection assembled by Louise duPont Crowninshield, which is particularly strong in hooked rugs, English ceramics, and American and English textiles. During the past 40 years, Hagley's collections have formed the basis of many classic studies in economic, business, and technological history. In recent years, younger scholars working on broad interdisciplinary projects that transcend the boundaries between business, technological, labor, social, and cultural history, have begun to make use of the library. Environmental history, the history of capitalism, marketing, commercial art and industrial design, market segmentation and its impact on women and minorities, the rise of the digital marketplace and multinational corporations are just some of the recent topics pursued by researchers using Hagley's collections.

B. Programs

The Center for the History of Business, Technology, and Society is Hagley's office of advanced studies. It sponsors a number of programs. Its research seminar series circulates work-in-progress essays to interested individuals, and holds discussions of these papers six times during each academic year. The center sponsors periodic conferences that highlight Hagley's collections, scholarly issues documented in Hagley's holdings, or important historical topics and anniversaries. It also organizes occasional lunchtime discussions, where staff and visiting scholars discuss their research and use of Hagley collections. The seminars, conferences, and discussions are directed to the scholarly community broadly conceived, including students, faculty, the staff of historical societies and museums, and unaffiliated individuals. The center also sponsors periodic public lectures, oriented toward the general public, and serves as the principal administrative office for the Business History Conference.

C. Publications

The Hagley Museum and Library publishes materials that pertain to its collections, exhibits, and resources. It maintains two book series with academic presses, the Hagley Perspectives on Business and Culture, collected papers from its conferences published with the University of Pennsylvania Press; and the Hagley Library Studies on Business, Technology, and Politics, a monograph series on topics related to collections at Hagley published with the Johns Hopkins University Press. A series of brochures on Hagley's research collections include overviews of holdings relevant to a variety of historical topics, including commercial architecture, business and politics, consumer culture, advertising, design, public relations, women's history, computers and automation, and iron and steel. Hagley also has published a biography of architect John McShain, responsible for a number of buildings in the nation's capital, as well as an analytical treatment of the influential work of industrial designer Raymond Loewy that accompanied a major exhibition at Hagley. Hagley also maintains a Collections & Research News blog, whose posts are summarized and sent to followers at the end of every month.

D. Fellowships and Awards

Hagley's Center for the History of Business, Technology, and Society awards numerous grants and fellowships every year. Grants-in-aid support exploratory and short-term research visits to the collections. Ph.D. candidates working on appropriate dissertations can apply for four-months' funding through the Henry Belin du Pont Dissertation Fellowship Program, or twelve-months' funding through the Jefferson Scholars-Hagley Library Dissertation Fellowships in Business and Politics, supported jointly by Hagley and the University of Virginia. Postgraduate scholars may apply for four- or eight-months' support through the

NEH-Hagley Postdoctoral Fellowships on Business, Culture, and Society. Hagley also supports the Hagley Prize in Business History, awarded by the Business History Conference annually to the best book in business history published in the previous two years.

Staff

Bockrath, Diane (MLS, Maryland 2010; processing archivist; Manuscripts and Archives) bookbinding; dbockrath@hagley.org

Clawson, Lucas R. (MA, Delaware 2008; MA, Appalachian State 2006; reference archivist; Manuscripts and Archives) lclawson@hagley.org

DiMeo, Michelle (PhD, Warwick 2010; assoc. dir.; Manuscripts and Archives) women, science, medicine; mdimeo@hagley.org

Gross, Linda (MS, North Carolina 1987; MA, Pennsylvania 1983; reference librarian; Published Collections) lgross@hagley.org

Hanes, Alice (MLS, North Carolina Central; technical services librarian; Published Collections) ahanes@hagley.org

Horowitz, Roger (PhD, Wisconsin, Madison 1990; assoc. dir.; Center for the Hist. of Business, Tech., and Soc.) 20th-century America, labor; rhorowitz@hagley.org

Hughes, Debra (MA, Texas Tech 1981; curator; Collections and Exhibits) material culture; dhughes@hagley.org

Martin, Kevin (MA, Delaware 2003; curator; Audiovisual and Digital Initiatives) kmartin@hagley.org

Moeller, Max (MA, Villanova 1997; MSLS, Clarion 2008; curator; Published Collections) automotive history; mmoeller@hagley.org

Rau, Erik P. (PhD, Pennsylvania 1999; dir.; Library Services) US political culture, postcolonial development; erau@hagley.org

Ruminski, Clayton (MLIS, Kent State 2015; MA, Youngstown State 2013; managing archivist; Manuscripts and Archives) cruminski@hagley.org

Sather, Laurie (MSLS, Drexel 2010; MA, Penn State 2007; audiovisual archivist; Audiovisual and Digital Initiatives) lsather@hagley.org

Schad, Angela (MA, Delaware 2014; reference archivist; Audiovisual and Digital Initiatives) aschad@hagley.org

Herbert Hoover Presidential Library-Museum

210 Parkside Dr., PO Box 488, West Branch, IA 52358. 319.643.5301. Fax 319.643.6045. Email: hoover.library@nara. gov. Website: https://hoover.archives.gov/.

A. Collections and Libraries

The Herbert Hoover Presidential Library contains approximately 2,200 cubic feet of the papers of Herbert Hoover. Included are papers documenting his career as a mining engineer, his activities as director of relief agencies during and following World War I, his tenure as Secretary of Commerce (1921–28), his Presidency (1929–33), and his post-presidential activities. Along with Hoover's personal papers are copies of selected records from the National Archives that document the activities of federal agencies associated with Hoover, such as the US Food Administration, or conferences that he convened, such as the White House Conference on Child Health. Also included are the papers of his wife, Lou Henry Hoover.

In addition to the Hoover Papers, the Library contains 300 other collections of papers from individuals who either worked with Herbert Hoover, or were associated with him through shared areas of interest or activity. Some of the more prominent collections include the papers of Hoover associate and chairman of the Atomic Energy Commission Lewis Strauss, US Senators

Gerald Nye of North Dakota and Bourke Hickenlooper of Iowa, chairman of Sears, Roebuck & Company Robert E. Wood, conservative newspaper columnists Westbrook Pegler, Walter Trohan, and Clark Mollenhoff, as well as writer and journalist Rose Wilder Lane, whose papers include correspondence with and manuscripts from her mother, Laura Ingalls Wilder. Along with Hoover's life and presidency, other areas of research interest covered by the manuscript collections include atomic energy, aviation, international relief work, agricultural economics, the isolationist movement prior to World War II, and conservative political thought in the mid-20th century.

Audiovisual holdings include 39,500 still photographs, 153,000 feet of 16mm movies, 420 hours of audiotape, 19 hours of videotape, and 78 audio discs. Transcripts of 443 oral history interviews are also available for use. A book collection of over 20,000 volumes—most relating to the period of Herbert Hoover's public life—is available in the Reading Room, as are periodicals related to Hoover, and microfilmed newspapers, theses, and dissertations.

B. Programs

The Library and the Hoover Presidential Foundation, a non-profit organization that supports the work of the Library-Museum and the Herbert Hoover National Historic Site, periodically host featured speakers and conferences pertaining to issues related to Hoover, and more broadly, 20th-century US political and diplomatic history. Topics of recent conferences have included the history of international food relief, First Ladies of Iowa, Laura Ingalls Wilder, and newly-published biographies of Herbert Hoover.

C. Publications

Comprehensive guides to all research collections are available on the Library's website. The Library publishes a monthly electronic newsletter.

D. Fellowships and Awards

The Hoover Presidential Foundation annually awards grants to researchers to enable them to visit West Branch and use the Library's holdings. The guidelines for this program and application forms can be found at the Foundation's web site at http://hooverpresidentialfoundation.org/travel-grant.php. Recent books that have resulted from research funded by the Hoover Presidential Foundation include *Making the World Safe: The American Red Cross and a Nation's Humanitarian Awakening* by Julia F. Irwin (Oxford, 2013), *Herbert Hoover in the White House: The Ordeal of the Presidency* by Charles Rappleye (Simon and Schuster, 2016), *Libertarians on the Prairie: Laura Ingalls Wilder, Rose Wilder Lane, and the Making of the Little House Books* by Christine Woodside (Arcade Publishing, 2016), *Hoover: An Extraordinary Life in Extraordinary Times* by Kenneth Whyte (Knopf, 2017), *World War I: A Short History* by Tammy Proctor (Wiley-Blackwell, 2017), and *Prairie Fires: The American Dreams of Laura Ingalls Wilder* by Caroline Fraser (Metropolitan Books, 2017).

The Foundation also hosts the annual Uncommon Student Award, a scholarship granted to three or more outstanding high school juniors for projects that improve the quality of life in their communities.

Staff

Dinschel, Elizabeth (MA, North Florida 2007; education specialist) elizabeth.dinschel@nara.gov

Eckhardt, Marcus (BA, Northern Iowa 1997; curator) marcus. eckhardt@nara.gov

Schaefer, Matthew T. (MA, Michigan 1990; archivist) matthew. schaefer@nara.gov

Schwartz, Thomas F. (PhD, Illinois, Urbana-Champaign 2000; dir.) thomas.schwartz@nara.gov

Smith, Lynn A. (MLIS, Denver 1999; MA, Colorado State 1991; archivist) lynn.smith@nara.gov

Wier, Melanie (MA, Western Illinois 2010; exhibit specialist) melanie.wier@nara.gov

Wright, Craig G. (MLIS, Michigan 1990; supervisory archivist) craig. wright@nara.gov

The Historical Society of Pennsylvania

Library, 1300 Locust St., Philadelphia, PA 19107-5699. 215.732.6200. Fax 215.732.2680. Email: library@hsp.org; webmaster@hsp.org. Website: https://hsp.org/.

The Historical Society of Pennsylvania (HSP), a special collections research library, is dedicated to making the rich variety of America's past accessible to all. The HSP is a private, nonprofit institution. The governing board of councilors currently consists of 24 members who serve three-year terms and 6 emeritus members. The society has a staff of 21 professional and support personnel and a membership of 1,650.

A. Collections and Libraries

Founded in 1824, and significantly augmented by the Balch Institute for Ethnic Studies in 2002, the Historical Society of Pennsylvania has been one of the nation's most important resources for scholars of American history and the social sciences. The society's collections of 21 million manuscripts, books, and graphics provide essential primary documentation for numerous scholarly works.

The collections document the social, political, commercial, ethnic, and cultural history of Pennsylvania and the Middle Atlantic region, with an emphasis on Philadelphia, from the 17th century to the present and its importance in US history, particularly during the colonial, revolutionary, and early national periods.

The HSP's manuscript and archive holdings of more than 20 million items include the papers of William Penn and the Penn family, Benjamin Franklin, the third largest collection of George Washington papers, Matthew Carey, Nicholas Biddle, the James Buchanan Presidential Library, Jay Cooke, Gen. George Gordon Meade, the Pennsylvania Abolition Society, the Bank of North America, the Baldwin Locomotive Works, and other personal, business, and organization records; 7,500 Pennsylvania maps and atlases dating from 1683 to the present; and 312,000 photographs, prints, watercolors, sketches, and architectural drawings. The library houses 560,000 books and pamphlets, published and unpublished genealogical material (including the collections of the Genealogical Society of Pennsylvania), newspapers, and periodicals. The library is open Tuesday and Thursday 12:30–5:30 p.m., Wednesday 12:30–8:30 p.m., and Friday from 10 a.m. to 5:30 p.m. Off-site researchers can access the society's collections through the fee-based Research-by-Mail service.

B. Programs

The society sponsors exhibits, lectures, workshops, and a range of programs that introduce its collections to members and the public.

C. Publications

The society's principal scholarly publication, the *Pennsylvania Magazine of History and Biography*, is the oldest continuously published journal of its kind in the United States. It is circulated to HSP members, libraries, and individuals throughout the world. Included in the journal are articles of original scholarship on the mid-Atlantic region and Pennsylvania-related subjects and book reviews. *Pennsylvania Legacies*, a newsmagazine geared to educators and the curious public, is currently on hiatus. Both publications are available online through JSTOR. *Sidelights* is HSP's newsletter for members and keeps them apprised of the society's activities and acquisitions. The *Guide to the Manuscript Collections of the Historical Society of Pennsylvania*, published in 1991, summarizes 2,100 collections of over 12 million documents covering more than 300 years of American history. *Serving History in a Changing World: The Historical Society of Pennsylvania in the 20th Century* by Sally F. Griffith was published in 2001.

D. Fellowships and Awards

The Historical Society of Pennsylvania and the Library Company of Philadelphia jointly offer approximately 25 one-month fellowships for research in residence. Independently, the Historical Society awards 2 Balch fellowships in ethnic and immigrant and/or 20th-century history and 1 Greenfield fellowship in 20th-century history.

Staff

Arnold, Lee (DPhil, South Africa, Pretoria 2016; sr. dir. & COO, library and collections) Philadelphia, genealogy, travel and tourism; larnold@hsp.org

Cullen, Charles T. (PhD, Virginia 1970; pres. & CEO) Thomas Jefferson, revolutionary period, early national period; ccullen@hsp.org

DiGiovanni, Anthony (BA, Rutgers, Camden 2015; cataloguer, copy) Pennsylvania, African American, early Republic America, American Reconstruction; adigiovanni@hsp.org

Haugaard, David G. (MA, Pennsylvania 1986; dir., research services) colonial Pennsylvania politics and society; dhaugaard@hsp.org

Hayden, Caroline E. (MLIS, Maryland 2016; dir., digital services) digitization, metadata; chayden@hsp.org

Heim, Sarah (MLS, Maryland 2004; MA, Maryland 2004; librarian, research services) Americana, gender studies; sheim@hsp.org

Hutto, Cary (MA, John F. Kennedy 2004; dir., archives) Pennsylvania region, costume and theatre, archival processing; chutto@hsp.org

Larocco, Christina G. (PhD, Maryland, Coll. Park 2012; editor, PMHB) culture, women; clarocco@hsp.org

O'Brien, Tara (MFA, Univ. of the Arts 2005; dir., preservation and conservation) book arts, book binding and printmaking, education; tobrien@hsp.org

Rolph, Daniel N. (PhD, Pennsylvania 1992; historian & head, reference) frontier, military, genealogy; drolph@hsp.org

Smith, Steve (MA, Rutgers, Camden 2001; librarian, public services) America, Native American, animal rights and conservation; ssmith@hsp.org

Twiss-Houting, Beth (MA, Delaware 1983; sr. dir., programs) American vernacular architecture, early national period, museum interpretation; btwisshouting@hsp.org

Historic New Orleans Collection

533 Royal St., New Orleans, LA 70130-2179. 504.523.4662. Fax 504.598.7108. Email: wrc@hnoc.org. Website: https://www.hnoc.org/.

A. Collections and Libraries

The Historic New Orleans Collection is a museum, research center, and publisher dedicated to the study and preservation of the history and culture of New Orleans and the Gulf South region. In a complex of historic French Quarter buildings at 520 and 533 Royal Street, the collection operates a museum, which includes the Louisiana History Galleries, French Quarter Galleries, and Education Galleries, tracing the history of the city from its founding to the present day; the Williams Residence, a house museum; a museum shop; and a cafe. The Williams Research Center at 410 Chartres Street makes available to researchers the collection's holdings, which comprise some 35,000 library items, more than two miles of documents and manuscripts, and approximately 400,000 photographs, prints, drawings, paintings, and other artifacts.

Notable collections include the Butler Family papers, the William C. Cook War of 1812 in the South Collection, the Pierre Clément Laussat papers, the Frederic Ramsey Jr. papers on American music, the William Russell Jazz Collection, the Fred W. Todd Tennessee Williams Collection, and the Vieux Carré Survey, as well as land tenure, architectural, and cemetery records. Examples of outstanding pictorial materials include maps from the 16th through the 20th centuries; photographs by J. D. Edwards, Charles L. Franck, Richard Koch, Clarence John Laughlin, Daniel S. Leyrer, Stuart M. Lynn, Michael P. Smith, Sam R. Sutton, and Doris Ulmann; drawings and paintings by Josephine Crawford, Boyd Cruise, Charles Reinike, Alfred R. Waud, Ellsworth Woodward, and William Woodward; architectural drawings by James Gallier Sr. and Jr.; and prints by Morris Henry Hobbs and Jules Lion. Each year the collection acquires and catalogs thousands of additional items by donation or purchase. Published guides to the photographic collections and the Vieux Carré Survey are available, and new acquisitions are regularly described in *The Historic New Orleans Collection Quarterly*. A general *Guide to Research at the Williams Research Center* is available upon request, as are back issues of the *Quarterly*.

B. Programs

The Historic New Orleans Collection encourages research into the history and culture of Louisiana and the Gulf South at the Williams Research Center. The collection also offers a variety of programs for visitors of all ages and backgrounds: guided tours, gallery talks, seminars, lectures, changing exhibitions, photographic services, a speakers' bureau, and educational outreach. The Williams Research Center Symposium is held annually in January/February and the New Orleans Antiques Forum in August.

C. Publications

Exhibition catalogues, historical monographs, biographies and memoirs, and reference works are among THNOC's major publications. Recent titles include *Enigmatic Stream: Industrial Landscapes of the Lower Mississippi River*, by Richard Sexton (2019); *New Orleans, the Founding Era / La Nouvelle-Orleans, les années fondatrices*, edited by Erin M. Greenwald (2018); *Guidebooks to Sin: The Blue Books of Storyville, New Orleans*, by Pamela D. Arceneaux (2017); *Garden Legacy*, by Mary Louise Mossy Christovich and Roulhac Bunkley Toledano (2016); *A Life in Jazz*, by Danny Barker, edited by Alyn Shipton, with a new introduction by Gwen Thompkins (2016); *The Katrina Decade: Images of an Altered City*, by David G. Spielman (exh. cat. 2015); *Henry Howard: Louisiana's Architect*, by Robert S. Brantley with Victor McGee, photographs by Robert S. Brantley and Jan White Brantley (2015; copublished by Princeton Architectural Press); *French Baroque Music of New Orleans: Spiritual Songs from the Ursuline Convent (1736) [Musique française baroque à la Nouvelle-Orléans: Recueil d'airs spirituels des Ursulines (1736)]* (2014); *A Fine Body of Men: The Orleans Light Horse, Louisiana Cavalry, 1861–1865*, by Donald Peter Moriarty II (2014); *Creole World: Photographs of New Orleans and the Latin Caribbean Sphere*, by Richard Sexton (exh. cat. 2014); *A Company Man: The Remarkable French-Atlantic Voyage of a Clerk for the Company of the Indies*, by Marc-Antoine Caillot, edited and with an introduction by Erin Greenwald (2013); *Perique: Photographs by Charles Martin* (exh. cat. 2012); *Ernie K-Doe: The R&B Emperor of New Orleans*, by Ben Sandmel (2012); *Furnishing Louisiana: Creole and Acadian Furniture, 1735–1835*, edited by Jessica Dorman and Sarah R. Doerries (2010); *Unfinished Blues: Memories of a New Orleans Music Man*, by Harold Battiste Jr. with Karen Celestan (2010); *Drawn to Life: Al Hirschfeld and the Theater of Tennessee Williams* (exh. cat. 2010); *In Search of Julien Hudson: Free Artist of Color in Pre-Civil War New Orleans*, by William Keyse Rudolph and Patricia Brady, with an introduction by Erin Greenwald (exh. cat. 2010); *In the Spirit: The Photography of Michael P. Smith from The Historic New Orleans Collection* (exh. cat. 2009); *Josephine Crawford: An Artist's Vision*, by Louise C. Hoffman (2009); *A Closer Look: The Antebellum Photographs of Jay Dearborn Edwards, 1858-1861* (exh. cat. 2008); *Birds of a Feather: Wildfowl Carving in Southeast Louisiana* (exh. cat. 2007); *Vaudechamp in New Orleans*, by William Keyse Rudolph (2007); *Crescent City Silver* (repr. 2007; exh. cat. 1980); *Printmaking in New Orleans*, edited by Jessie J. Poesch (2006; copublished by University Press of Mississippi); *Common Routes: St. Domingue–Louisiana* (exh. cat. 2006); *A British Eyewitness at the Battle of New Orleans: The Memoirs of Royal Navy Admiral Robert Aitchison, 1808–1827*, edited by Gene Smith (2004); *From Louis XIV to Louis Armstrong: A Cultural Tapestry* (exh. cat. 2004); *George L. Viavant: Artist of the Hunt*, by George E. Jordan (2003); *Charting Louisiana: Five Hundred Years of Maps*, edited by Alfred E. Lemmon, John T. Magill, and Jason R. Wiese, consulting editor John R. Hebert (2003); *Queen of the South: New Orleans, 1853–1862, The Journal of Thomas K. Wharton* (1999); *Jazz Scrapbook: Bill Russell and Some Highly Musical Friends* (1998); *Haunter of Ruins: The Photography of Clarence John Laughlin* (1997; copublished by Bullfinch Press) *Complementary Visions of Louisiana Art: The Laura Simon Nelson Collection at the Historic New Orleans Collection* (1996); and *Bibliography of New Orleans Imprints, 1764–1864*, by Florence M. Jumonville (1989).

The collection's two periodical publications are *The Historic New Orleans Collection Quarterly*, with articles on the history and culture of Louisiana as well as news of exhibitions, acquisitions, staff, donors, and publications, and the *Tennessee Williams Annual Review*. Back issues of the *Manuscripts Division Update*, published annually from 1982 to 1994 and organized thematically by research field, are available upon request.

D. Fellowships and Awards

The Historic New Orleans Collection invites applications for the Dianne Woest Fellowship in the Arts and Humanities. The fellowship carries a stipend of $4,000 to support research in the history and culture of Louisiana and the Gulf South. Additionally, in cooperation with the Louisiana Historical Association, THNOC awards the annual General L. Kemper Williams Prize in Louisiana History to the best published work about Louisiana history. Additional information about both programs is available at www. hnoc.org/research/prizes-and-fellowships.

Staff

Arceneaux, Pamela D. (MLS, Louisiana State 1977; sr. librarian/rare books curator; Williams Research Center) Louisiana, popular culture; pamela@hnoc.org

Ball, Dorothy (BA, North Carolina, Chapel Hill 2004; sr. editor; Publications) dorothyb@hnoc.org

Bartels, Carol O. (MA, New Orleans 1993; dir.; Technology) archives and records administration; carol@hnoc.org

Berman, Viola (MLIS, Louisiana State 1992; assoc. registrar; Collections) vberman@hnoc.org

Blackmore, Lydia (MA, Delaware, Winterthur Prog. 2013; decorative arts curator; Museum Programs) decorative arts, material culture; lydiab@hnoc.org

Bonner, Judith (MA, Tulane 1983; sr. curator; Museum Programs) southern art, 19th-century culture; jbonner@hnoc.org

Boyer, Lori (MS, New Orleans 2007; head; Visitor Services) urban, historic preservation; lorib@hnoc.org

Cave, Mark (MLIS, Kentucky 1991; sr. curator and oral historian; Williams Research Center) personal narrative, literary arts, 20th-century New Orleans; markc@hnoc.org

Dorman, Jessica A. (PhD, Harvard 1996; dir.; Publications) journalism, 19th- and 20th-century literature; jessicad@hnoc.org

Duggan, Sarah (MA, Delaware/Winterthur 2011; coord. and research curator, Classical Institute of the South; Museum Programs) American decorative arts and material culture, religious history and culture; sduggan@hnoc.org

Dunn, Katherine Jolliff (BA, Tulane; collections processor; Williams Research Center) art, architecture; katherined@hnoc.org

Eberle, Susan (BA, St. Edward's 2001; asst. registrar; Collections) art, collections care; susane@hnoc.org

Eichhorn, Mary Lou (BA, Loyola, New Orleans 1983; sr. reference assoc.; Williams Research Center) New Orleans religious, genealogy; marylou@hnoc.org

Everrett, Aimee (MLIS, Louisiana State 2007; assoc. curator; Williams Research Center) aimee@hnoc.org

Farah, W. Mattison (MA, Tulane 2010; assoc. curator, traveling exhibitions; Museum Programs) US political, early modern Spain; mattf@hnoc.org

Garsaud, Mary M. (MA, New Orleans 2009; sr. editor; Publications) maryg@hnoc.org

Gaudry, Rachel (MA, Washington 2011; education coord.; Education) rachelg@hnoc.org

Ghabrial, Jennifer Rebuck (BA, Tulane 2006; head registrar; Collections) collections care/management; jghabrial@hnoc.org

Hammer, Daniel (OMS, Tulane 2008; vice pres. and deputy dir.; Administration) German language and culture, historic preservation; danielh@hnoc.org

Harrell, Kevin T. (PhD, Mississippi 2013; collections cataloger; Williams Research Center) colonial America, native South, Atlantic world; kevinh@hnoc.org

Hébert Veit, Kristin (MA, Louisiana State 2013; curatorial cataloger; Williams Research Center) kristinhv@hnoc.org

Hickey, Maclyn Le Bourgeois (MA, Tulane 2015; curatorial conservation coord.; Museum Programs) maclynh@hnoc.org

Hines, Kelley (MA, Chicago 2016; asst. registrar; Collections) archaeology and cultural anthropology of race/gender/sexuality; kelleyh@hnoc.org

Howorth, Vasser B. (MLIS, Louisiana State 2012; manuscripts cataloger; Williams Research Center) vasserh@hnoc.org

Lavigne, Brian (records manager; Williams Research Center) brianl@hnoc.org

Lawrence, John H. (BA, Vassar 1975; dir.; Museum Programs) American photography, conservation; johnl@hnoc.org

Lawrence, Priscilla O'Reilly (BFA, Mississippi, Women 1971; pres. and CEO; Administration) New Orleans lithography, collections management; priscill@hnoc.org

Lemmon, Alfred E. (PhD, Tulane 1981; dir.; Williams Research Center) performing arts, archival management; alfredl@hnoc.org

Lemoine, Leidy (MLS, Drexel 2013; manuscripts cataloger; Williams Research Center) oral, vernacular culture; leidyc@hnoc.org

Longbrake, Margit (MA, NYU 1996; sr. editor; Publications) English literature, American literature; margitl@hnoc.org

Margot, Howard (MA, Tulane 1989; curator; Williams Research Center) howardm@hnoc.org

McFillen, Amanda (MMS, Toronto 2007; assoc. dir.; Museum Programs) amandam@hnoc.org

McKiernan, Siobhan (MLIS, Louisiana State 2007; assoc. editor; Publications) siobhanm@hnoc.org

Mizell-Nelson, Cathe (MA, Tulane 1995; editor; Publications) 18th-century Caribbean, 19th-century Louisiana; cathemn@hnoc.org

Neidenbach, Libby C. (PhD, William and Mary 2015; visitor services asst.; Visitor Services) New Orleans history and culture, Atlantic world freedom and slavery, material culture, African American history and culture; Libby.Neidenbach@hnoc.org

Ogden, Elizabeth (MA, Sotheby's Inst. 2007; special projects coord.; Administration) elizabetho@hnoc.org

Redmann, Michael (MLS, Emporia State 2009; manuscripts cataloger; Williams Research Center) michaelr@hnoc.org

Schwartzberg, Jenny (MA, Georgia 2010; curator; Education) modern Europe; jennifers@hnoc.org

Seiferth, Eric A. (MA, Tulane 2008; curator; Museum Programs) 20th-century New Orleans, American music; erics@hnoc.org

Smith, Rebecca (MLIS, Louisiana State 2005; head, reader services; Williams Research Center) disaster preparedness, rights and repros; rebeccas@hnoc.org

Solomon, Jude (curator; Museum Programs) photographic collections; jude@hnoc.org

Szafran, Heather (MS, Simmons 2014; reference assoc.; Williams Research Center) heathers@hnoc.org

Taylor, Mallory (MA, Ryerson 2010; assoc. curator; Museum Programs) photo preservation, collections management; malloryt@hnoc.org

Ticknor, Robert (MA, Tulane 2007; reference assoc.; Williams Research Center) Europe; robertt@hnoc.org

Weldon, Nick (BS, Northwestern 2010; assoc. editor; Publications) journalism; nickw@hnoc.org

Wiese, Jason (MLIS, Louisiana State 1999; assoc. dir.; Williams Research Center) archival, early America, cartography; jasonw@hnoc.org

Woods, Warren J. (BA, Syracuse 1976; exhibitions coord.; Museum Programs) popular culture; warrenw@hnoc.org

Woynowski, Kent (MS, Simmons 2001; digital assets manager; Technology) digital archives; kentw@hnoc.org

History Associates Incorporated

300 N. Stonestreet Ave., Rockville, MD 20850-1655. 301.279.9697. Fax 301.279.9224. Email: hai@historyassociates.com. Website: https://www.historyassociates.com/.

History Associates Incorporated, founded in 1981, provides professional historical research and writing, archival and records management, collections management, exhibits, and interpretive planning services to federal, state, and local governments and to private industry and the professions throughout the United States and abroad.

A. Collections and Libraries

History Associates maintains a collection of reference works for internal use.

B. Programs

History Associates' services include research and writing of historical monographs and policy-related studies; oral histories; historical exhibits; interpretive planning; litigation research and expert testimony (historical studies and document research); archives management (needs assessments, design and operation of archives, and development of schedules for electronic and paper records); museum collections management; and archival storage. History Associates staff are especially knowledgeable about government records in the federal records centers and the National Archives.

C. Publications

History Associates produces a variety of books, reports, finding aids, and other publications for its clients. Among those publicly available are Kenneth D. Durr, *From Sea to Soup: The Evolution of Blount Fine Foods, 1946-2011* (2012); Kenneth D. Durr, *The First 40: A History of DAI* (2010); Halley L. Fehner and James P. Rife, *40 Years of Self Determination: A Commemorative History of the California Rural Indian Health Board, Inc.* (2009); William Lanouette, *Richards, Layton & Finger: An Illustrated History* (2009); James P. Rife and Capt. Alan J. Dellapenna, Jr., *Caring and Curing: A History of the Indian Health Service* (2009); Kenneth D. Durr, *Life of the Party: Kenneth F. Simpson and the Survival of the Republicans in 1930s New York* (2009); James P. Rife and Rodney P. Carlisle, *The Sound of Freedom: Naval Weapons Technology at Dahlgren, Virginia, 1918–2006* (2007); Kenneth D. Durr, *A Company With a Mission: Rodman Rockefeller and the International Basic Economy Corporation, 1947–85* (2006); Adrian Kinnane, *Durable Legacy: A History of Morris, Nichols, Arsht & Tunnell* (2005); Adrian Kinnane, *DuPont: From the Banks of the Brandywine to the Miracles of Science* (2002); Rodney P. Carlisle, *Powder and Propellants: Energetic Materials at Indian Head, Maryland, 1890–2001,* 2nd ed. (2002); Dian O. Belanger and Adrian Kinnane, *Managing American Wildlife: A History of the International Association of Fish and Wildlife Agencies,* centennial ed. (2002); Kenneth D. Durr and Philip L. Cantelon, *Never Stand Still: The History of Consolidated Freightways, Inc. and CNF Transportation Inc., 1929–2000* (1999); Rodney P. Carlisle, *Where the Fleet Begins: A History of the David Taylor Research Center* (1998); Rodney P. Carlisle with Joan M. Zenzen, *Supplying the Nuclear Arsenal: American Production Reactors, 1942–1992* (1996); Philip L. Cantelon and Kenneth D. Durr, *The Roadway Story* (1996); Philip L. Cantelon, *The History of MCI: The Early Years, 1968–88* (1993); and Richard G. Hewlett, *Jessie Ball duPont* (1992); Kenneth D. Durr, *The Best Made Plans: Robert R. Nathan and 20th Century Liberalism* (2013); James P. Rife, *Changes, Challenges, Champions: A History of the Fort Worth District US Army Corps of Engineers 2000-2011* (2013); Halley L. Fehner, *Celebrating the Past, Creating the Future, Improving Health Every Day, 125th Anniversary, Sentara* (2013); Jason H. Gart, *He Shall Direct Thy Paths: The Early Life of George W. Carver* (2014); James P. Rife, *Moving Metal, 75 Years of Reliance Steel & Aluminum Co.* (2014); Kimberly L. Silvi, *More Than Meets the Eye, The CooperVision Story* (2015); Adrian Kinnane, *Arnold & Porter: The Early Years 1946-1980* (2016); Kenneth D. Durr with Jerome S. Noll, *The Evolution of a Profession: The First 75 Years of the American College of Foot and Ankle Surgeons 1942-2017* (2016); Philip L. Cantelon, *Nuclear Safety Has No Borders: A History of the World Association of Nuclear Operators* (2016); report entitled *Predecessors of ABM AMRO Bank N.V. and Connections to African Slavery in the United States and the Americas* (April 2006) for ABN AMRO; report to JPMorgan Chase on connections to slavery (spring 2005); major contributor to report for Ford Motor Company entitled *Research Findings about Ford-Werke under the Nazi Regime* (2001); Department of Homeland Security fifth anniversary historical documents entitled *Senior Leadership: The First Five Years: 2003–08* and *Brief Documentary History of the Department of Homeland Security*; *Moving Inactive Records Out of the Office*, procedures manual for National Institutes of Health Office of Management Assessment; online finding aids for the Smithsonian Institution Archives of American Art to the Richard York Gallery Records, Doll & Richards Gallery Records, Galerie Chalette Records, Lillian and Frederick Kiesler Papers, Research Material on Amedeo Modigliani, Helen DeMott Papers, Roko Gallery Records, and Leo Castelli Gallery Records; online finding aids to a number of collections at the National Library of Medicine, including Joshua Lederberg Papers, Marshall W. Nirenberg Papers, Sol Spiegelman Papers, Telford H. Work Papers, Adrian Kantrowitz Papers, Clarence Dennis Papers, and American Association for the Surgery of Trauma Archives; an online finding aid for the Library of Congress to the Maxine Singer Collection; and online finding aids to a number of collections for the Online Archive of California, including Scripps (Ellen B.) Collection 1840–2000, Empire Mine State Historic Park Collection 1866–1985, California Institute of the Arts Photographic Materials Collection, Ruth Chandler Williamson Gallery Archival Collection 1870–2005, Scripps College Fine Arts Foundation Collection, Southern California Edison Records 1848–1989, Phelan (James D.) Papers 1855–1941, and Guide to the California Institute of the Arts Collection 1925–1988. Complete design and production services are available in-house through the Montrose Press.

D. Fellowships and Awards

History Associates offers occasional internship opportunities for students in archival and/or historical studies.

Staff

Anderson, Megan L. (BA, St. Mary's 2011; historian) Europe; manderson@historyassociates.com

Bergen, Hilary (BA, American 2013; historian) Europe; hbergen@historyassociates.com

Cantelon, Philip L. (PhD, Indiana 1971; sr. historian; CEO; and founder) contemporary America; pcantelon@historyassociates.com

Carlisle, Rodney P. (PhD, California, Berkeley 1965; founder) technology, energy, military and naval; carlisle@rutgers.edu

Conn, Christina F. (MA, Cooperstown Grad. Prog. 2010; sr. collections mgr.) museum studies; cconn@historyassociates.com

Delosier, Nikole Ember (MA, Drexel 2013; archivist) library and information science, archives; ndelosier@historyassociates.com

Eisen, Mimi (MA, Brown 2018; research historian) history, law, society; meisen@historyassociates.com

Fehner, Halley L. (BA, St. Mary's 2008; sr. historian, CIP) US; hfehner@historyassociates.com

Gage, Marielle (MLIS, Catholic 2016; MA, Catholic 2015; archivist) medieval; mgage@historyassociates.com

Gart, Jason H. (PhD, Arizona State 2006; sr. historian) 20th-century US, American West, technology; jgart@historyassociates.com

Giambrone, Jennifer A. (BA, Gettysburg 2010; historian) US, sociology, museum studies; jgiambrone@historyassociates.com

Goguen, Matthew (MS, Vermont 2015; historian) historic preservation; mgoguen@historyassociates.com

Hallgren, Kate N. (PhD, Graduate Center, CUNY 2012; sr. historian) public, modern US, women; khallgren@historyassociates.com

Hill, Jenna (MA, American 2018; research historian) public; jhill@historyassociates.com

Holsinger, Janet L. (MA, North Carolina 2000; sr. historian) Europe; jholsinger@historyassociates.com

Jae, Kendra (MSLIS, Simmons 2015; archivist) archives management; kjae@historyassociates.com

Kim, Colleen (MA, Georgetown 2018; research historian) English and speech language hearing science, history; ckim@historyassociates.com

Lathrop, Kelly (MLS, Maryland 2015; certified archivist) art photography; klathrop@historyassociates.com

Livesey, Elizabeth (MA, George Washington 2016; archivist) Jewish cultural arts, museum studies; elivesey@historyassociates.com

Maser, Beth G. (MLIS, Wisconsin-Milwaukee; pres.) Federal Records Management, CSM, ECMp, PMP; bmaser@historyassociates.com

McDougal, Phoebe (BA, Goucher 2008; historian) history and political science; pmcdougal@historyassociates.com

McIntyre, James K. (MLIS, Kent State 2005; certified archivist) archives; jmcintyre@historyassociates.com

Nardi, Eric (MA, Salisbury 2015; historian) colonial America, colonial Chesapeake; enardi@historyassociates.com

O'Hern-Crook, Megan (MA,MLS, Maryland 2016; certified archivist) art history, library science; mohern@historyassociates.com

Orme, Jennifer (MLIS, Wayne State 2015; archivist) history, archival administration; jorme@historyassociates.com

Phillips, Mary Claire (BA, Texas 2018; research historian) government and history; mphillips@historyassociates.com

Rebadow, Allison (MA, American 2013; historian) public; arebadow@historyassociates.com

Reis, Michael C. (MA, George Washington 1981; sr. historian) US, political, environmental; mreis@historyassociates.com

Rife, James P. (MA, Virginia Tech 1999; sr. historian) early America, military; jrife@historyassociates.com

Silvi, Kimberly L. (BA, St. Mary's 2007; historian) US, Latin America; ksilvi@historyassociates.com

Simpson, Andrew T. (MA, George Washington 2009; sr. historian) US; asimpson@historyassociates.com

Starr, Laura Kopp (MLS, Maryland, Coll. Park 2009; certified archivist) archives, US South; lstarr@historyassociates.com

Sullivan, Emily (MA, American 2018; research historian) public; esullivan@historyassociates.com

Swaim, Carlyn M. (MA, Maryland 2016; sr. historian) US; cswaim@historyassociates.com

Vierick, Robert Scott (BA, William and Mary 2015; historian) history and government; svierick@historyassociates.com

Williams, Erica C. (MLS, Simmons 2006; certified archivist) archives; ewilliams@historyassociates.com

Williams, Robert C. (PhD, Harvard 1966; founder) Russia, cryptography, nuclear; bob03harmony@yahoo.com

Howard Thurman Papers Project

Boston Univ., Sch. of Theology, 745 Commonwealth Ave., Ste. 111A, Boston, MA 02215. 617.358.4221. Email: wfluker@bu.edu. Website: https://www.bu.edu/htpp/.

The Howard Thurman Papers Project was founded in 1992. Through the publication of The Papers of Howard Washington Thurman, the Project makes the documentary record of Thurman's long and productive career accessible to the widest possible audience-scholars, non-academics, religious practitioners, students, and the broader public. The edition is published by the University of South Carolina Press.

A. Collections and Libraries

The Howard Thurman Papers Project has reviewed over 50,000 documents produced by or relating to pastor, author, educator, and civil rights leader Howard Thurman (1899–1981). The documents include correspondence, sermons, unpublished writings, and speeches from the principal collection of Howard Thurman's papers held by the Howard Gotlieb Archival Research Center at Boston University, collections of Thurman papers held by Howard University and Emory University, and the Thurman family's personal collection. The Project also has reviewed documents from a variety of related collections, including the papers of Sue Bailey Thurman, Mordecai Wyatt Johnson, Benjamin Mays, Mary McLeod Bethune, Eleanor Roosevelt, Martin Luther King, Jr., John Hope, Rufus Jones, the National YMCA and YWCA, the Fellowship of Reconciliation, the Church for the Fellowship of All Peoples, and the Congress of Racial Equality.

B. Programs

The Project is publishing the five-volume edition of *The Papers of Howard Washington Thurman*. It also maintains a website that provides free access to selected Thurman-related materials, including a chronology of events in Thurman's life with links to sites providing further information on selected topics. The Project is planning to publish a digital edition of its work.

C. Publications

Published in 2009, *Volume 1: My People Need Me, June 1918–March 1936* begins with Thurman's early years in his native Daytona, Florida; moves through his formal education, his leadership in the student movement, and his years at Howard University as a professor of philosophy and religion; and ends with Thurman's historic trip to India and his meeting with Mahatma Gandhi in 1936. The second volume of the edition, *Christian, Who Calls Me Christian? April 1936–August 1943*, published in 2012, documents the second half of Thurman's career at Howard University as Dean of Rankin Chapel following his return from India; and his role as a leading figure in the nascent civil rights movement, including his involvement with pacifism during the period of World War II. Published in 2015, *Volume 3: The Bold Adventure, September 1943–May 1949* documents Thurman's founding, and leadership, of the Church for the Fellowship of All Peoples in San Francisco, California—the nation's first major interracial, interfaith church. Published in 2017, *Volume 4: The Soundless Passion of a Single Mind, June 1949–December 1962* covers Thurman's tenure as the Dean of Marsh Chapel at Boston University, where he became the first African American Dean of Chapel at a majority-white college or university in the United States. Forthcoming in 2019, *Volume 5: The Wider Ministry, January 1963–April 1981* documents Thurman's activities as Director of the Howard Thurman Educational Trust to the months shortly before his death.

D. Fellowships and Awards

The Howard Thurman Papers Project is funded through generous grants from the Lilly Endowment, Inc.; the National Endowment for the Humanities (NEH); the Henry Luce Foundation; the Pew Charitable Trusts, Inc.; and the National Historical Publications and Records Commission (NHPRC).

Staff

Fluker, Walter Earl (PhD, Boston Univ.; editor and dir.) social ethics, theory and practice of ethical leadership, African American theological/religious/moral traditions; wfluker@bu.edu

Huntington Library, Art Collections, and Botanical Gardens

1151 Oxford Rd., San Marino, CA 91108-1218. 626.405.2194. Fax 626.449.5703. Website: http://www.huntington.org/.

A. Collections and Libraries

The Huntington Library is a research institution devoted primarily to the study of British and American history, literature, art history, and history of science and medicine. The library has exceptional collections of manuscripts and rare books in the fields in which it specializes. In American history its holdings of the printed accounts of early explorers are virtually complete; its collections in the period to 1800 number more than 7,000 American imprints as well as extensive manuscript archives; its holdings on the Civil War and the West are among the most extensive in the nation. The library's holdings in British medieval history are unparalleled in the United States; in the postmedieval period its collections include more than seventy percent of all books printed in England before 1641 as well as more than seventy collections of manuscripts. The total number of collections for postmedieval British and American history is more than 800.

These historical collections are supplemented by equally extensive holdings of literary books and manuscripts. For American literature there is a remarkable collection of American fiction before 1900 and manuscript collections containing the papers of such notable writers as Jack London and Wallace Stevens. In British literature the collections on the English Renaissance are quite extensive and the later periods are equally well represented with notable collections in theater history.

The Huntington and Virginia Steele Scott Galleries contain many remarkable paintings, and the collections have nearly 50,000 drawings, watercolors, and prints. There are also approximately 800,000 photographs with especially rich holdings in the American West.

The Burndy Library is now available to scholars and adds enormously to The Huntington's already fine history of science holdings. Accompanying the library is the Dibner History of Science Program at The Huntington. This program funds long- and short-term fellowships, an annual conference, and a lecture series.

B. Programs

The Huntington co-sponsors a number of seminars that meet regularly, including early modern British history, Renaissance English literature, and early American history. "Brown Bag" lunch seminars are held on a regular basis. The Huntington also organizes conferences and hosts meetings of scholarly societies, in addition to sponsoring a lecture series.

C. Publications

There are published guides to the manuscript collections. The Huntington Library Press publishes the *Huntington Library Quarterly*.

D. Fellowships and Awards

The Huntington awards approximately 150 short-term fellowships each year to doctoral and postdoctoral scholars. There are several long-term fellowships, including three sponsored by the National Endowment for the Humanities. For information regarding any of these grants, please contact the office of the Director of Research.

Staff

Blodgett, Peter J. (PhD, Yale 2007; curator; Western American Hist.) American West; pblodgett@huntington.org

Brooke, Sandra Ludig (MLS, SUNY 1999; MA, Williams 1982; dir.; Library) art; sbrooke@huntington.org

Chase, Erin (BA, California, Santa Cruz 1994; asst. curator; Architecture and Photography) architecture and historical photographs; echase@huntington.org

Funke, Claudia (MA, Columbia 1998; chief curator and assoc. dir.; Library Collections) cfunke@huntington.org

Glisson, James (PhD, Northwestern 2012; asst. curator; American Art) American art; jglisson@huntington.org

Hess, Catherine (MA, UCLA 1984; chief curator; European Art) 15th- through 19th-century European art, Continental sculpture and decorative arts; chess@huntington.org

Hindle, Steve (PhD, Cambridge 1993; dir.; Research) early modern England; shindle@huntington.org

Klein, Joel A. (PhD, Indiana 2014; curator; Medicine and Allied Sciences) early science and medicine, chymistry; jklein@huntington.org

Lewis, Daniel (PhD, California, Riverside 1997; sr. curator; Hist. of Science and Technology) science, technology; dlewis@huntington.org

McCurdy, Melinda (PhD, California, Santa Barbara 2005; assoc. curator; British Art) 18th- and 19th-century British art; mmccurdy@huntington.org

Mihaly, David (MA, Cooperstown Grad. Prog. 1983; curator; Graphic Arts and Social Hist.) dmihaly@huntington.org

Ritchie, Robert C. (PhD, UCLA 1972; sr. research assoc.) early America; rritchie@huntington.org

Russell, Natalie (MLIS, San José State 2009; asst. curator; Literary Collections) American literary manuscripts; nrussell@huntington.org

Satrum, Krystle (MLS, Simmons 2008; asst. curator; Jay T. Last Collection) 19th-century America; ksatrum@huntington.org

Stalls, Clay (PhD, UCLA 1991; curator; California Collections) California; cstalls@huntington.org

Tabor, Stephen (MLS, UCLA 1977; curator; Rare Books) early printed books; stabor@huntington.org

Tsapina, Olga (PhD, Lomonosov Moscow State 1998; curator; American Hist.) America, trans-Atlantic Enlightenment; otsapina@huntington.org

Watts, Jennifer (MA, Fuller Theological Sem. 1990; curator; Photography and Visual Culture) historical photographs; jwatts@huntington.org

Wilkie, Vanessa Jean (PhD, California, Riverside 2009; curator; Medieval Manuscripts and British Hist.) medieval Britain; vwilkie@huntington.org

Yang, Li Wei (MLIS, San Jose State 2008; curator; Pacific Rim Collections) American West; lwyang@huntington.org

Kentucky Historical Society

Thomas D. Clark Center for Kentucky History, 100 W. Broadway, Frankfort, KY 40601-1931. 502.564.1792. Website: https://history.ky.gov/.

Staff and volunteers of the Kentucky Historical Society (KHS) operate the Kentucky History Center & Museums (KHC&M), in historic downtown Frankfort, Kentucky. KHC&M comprises the Thomas D. Clark Center for Kentucky History, housing KHS's headquarters, signature museum and exhibits, a research facility, museum store, classrooms, collections and archival storage, and public events spaces; the Old State Capitol; and the State Arsenal, home of the Kentucky Military History Museum.

Through the years, students, history enthusiasts, genealogists, scholars and tourists from all over the state, nation and world have come to KHC&M to experience and learn about the commonwealth's robust past, conduct scholarly research or explore their family's roots. As such a destination, KHC&M serves as an important educational resource that also contributes to regional tourism development.

KHS is a nonprofit membership organization founded in 1836 and in continuous operation since 1896. Its mission is to educate and engage people through Kentucky's history in order confront the challenges of the future.

A. Collections and Libraries

KHS has extensive archival, library and museum collections that document the people, organizations and businesses of the commonwealth. It maintains online catalogs for offsite research, provides fee-based research services for people who need more information and cannot visit KHC&M, and has a full research library for onsite visitors. Collections include, but are not limited to, manuscripts, photographs, oral histories, artifacts, periodicals and publications. KHS collections attract scholars from around the world, and around the state. Kentucky family history is a special area of emphasis.

B. Programs

KHS serves a broad audience and gears its programming to its different segments.

Public Programs: KHS presents several types of programs for adults and children at KHC&M, including, but not limited to, exhibits (both permanent and temporary), film screenings, talks, workshops and camps.

Student Programs: Field trips to KHC&M are the primary means through which KHS engages K-12 students. However, KHS also works with students and teachers through the Kentucky Junior Historical Society, a club-based program; and National History Day in Kentucky, an individual or group contest-based program where students conduct original research on a specific theme and present their findings for judging and potential advancement to a national contest. KHS in-school programs include Traveling Trunks, topic-based lessons and activities; Museums to Go, mobile panel displays; and HistorySmarts, combining history with a related hands-on arts activity. Teacher Programs: KHS museum educators provide such teacher professional development opportunities as the annual Kentucky History Education Conference and specific-topic workshops throughout the school year.

Community Engagement: KHS has several community engagement programs. One of the most popular is the Kentucky Historical Marker program, which allows communities to identify and commemorate their own histories. KHS also administers the Local History Trust Fund, a tax check-off where Kentucky state taxpayers contribute to a grant pool for history-minded organizations in the commonwealth; operates the HistoryMobile, an exhibit within a tractor-trailer that is available for community organizations and schools; and administers the Kentucky Oral History Commission (KOHC). KOHC provides several types of grants to encourage the collection and preservation of historically valuable interviews.

C. Publications

The Register of the Kentucky Historical Society: KHS has published the state's scholarly quarterly continually since 1903. It features articles that focus primarily on Kentucky history and includes an extensive book review section. *Kentucky Ancestors*: KHS started this publication in 1965 to provide articles for and resources to people researching family history in Kentucky. Originally a quarterly print publication, *Kentucky Ancestors* transitioned to an online publication in 2013. *Civil War Governors of Kentucky Digital Documentary Edition*: This online "publication" contains thousands of documents that the Kentucky Governor's Office generated or received between 1860 and 1865. They show what life was like for public officials and everyday civilians during wartime. KHS staff and graduate assistants are annotating each one with biographical information and adding metadata to help create a research platform that will allow people to access, understand and analyze the information in new ways.

D. Fellowships and Awards

Research Fellowships: KHS offers short-term fellowships (one to four weeks) to promote scholarship on any facet of Kentucky's history. They are available to independent scholars, college and university teachers, graduate students and scholars working in disciplines related to an aspect of Kentucky history. *Kentucky History Awards*: KHS sponsors annual awards to recognize outstanding achievements by historians, public history professionals, volunteers, business and civic leaders, communities and historical organizations throughout the commonwealth. *Internships*: KHS internships offer hands-on experience in a variety of areas to help undergraduate and graduate students aspiring to a career in museums or history attain their goals. KHS designs internships to help meet specific organizational needs, but often can tailor individual projects to an intern's skills, interests and academic requirements.

Staff

Alvey, Scott (BA, Western Kentucky 1990; exec. dir.) scott.alvey@ ky.gov

Higgins, Amanda Leigh (PhD, Kentucky 2013; community engagement admin.) 20th-century Kentucky, America; amanda. higgins@ky.gov

Lang, Stephanie (PhD, Kentucky 2009; assoc. editor; Register of the Kentucky Hist. Soc.) Appalachia; stephanie.lang@ky.gov

Sanders, Stuart (BA, Centre 1995; history advocate) Civil War; stuart.sanders@ky.gov

Schmitt, Sarah (MA, Western Kentucky; oral hist. admin.; Kentucky Oral Hist. Commission) sarahm.schmitt@ky.gov

La Guardia and Wagner Archives

La Guardia Comm. Coll., CUNY, 31-10 Thomson Ave., Rm. E-238, Long Island City, NY 11101-3007. 718.482.6068. Fax 718.482.5069. Email: richardli@lagcc.cuny.edu. Website: http:// www.laguardiawagnerarchive.lagcc.cuny.edu/.

The La Guardia and Wagner Archives was established in 1982 to collect, preserve, and make available primary materials documenting the social and political history of New York City, with an emphasis on the mayoralty and the borough of Queens. The Archives serves researchers, journalists, students, scholars, exhibit planners, and policy makers. Its website provides a webdatabase to the collections, which include almost 100,000 digitized photos, and nearly 2.5 million digitized documents. The Archives is located a five-minute walk from the 33rd Street/ Rawson St. stop on the #7 line, which can be boarded at the Times Square and Grand Central Stations in Manhattan. Hours for researchers are Monday to Friday, 9:30AM to 4:30PM. Please call or e-mail for a research appointment.

A. Collections and Libraries

This growing repository contains several major collections. View samples on YouTube, Flickr, Facebook, Blog, and PodBean.

Fiorello H. La Guardia Collection: As mayor during the turbulent period from 1934–45, La Guardia initiated major reforms during the Depression and World War II. In 1982, the mayor's widow, Marie La Guardia, donated her husband's personal papers to La Guardia Community College. These documents, photographs, and personal artifacts chronicle Mayor La Guardia's life and times.

The collection contains transcripts of La Guardia's speeches, the texts of his 1942-45 Sunday Radio Broadcasts, personal correspondence, and more than 3,000 photographs. The Archives holds a microfilm copy of selected series of La Guardia's mayoral papers housed at the New York City Municipal Archive, and a microfilm copy of La Guardia's Congressional papers housed at the New York Public Library. The collection contains more than 100 hours of audio and videotapes.

Robert F. Wagner Collection: Mayor Wagner was the second generation of the Wagner family to devote himself to public service. His father was US Senator Robert F. Wagner, a major figure on the national scene in the New Deal era who sponsored landmark labor, civil rights, health, social security, and social welfare legislation. The mayor's son, Robert F. Wagner Jr., served as a member of the New York City Council, Chair of the New York City Planning Commission, deputy mayor for policy, and president of the New York City Board of Education.

Mayor Wagner served as chief executive of New York City for three terms. From 1954–65, he oversaw the construction of housing, parks, roadways, and schools. He championed the growth and empowerment of municipal labor unions, sponsored the creation of the City University of New York, and mobilized resources for the War on Poverty. The Collection consists of correspondence, transcripts of 3,000 speeches, over 7,000 photographs, personal artifacts, and a 100-interview oral history collection. Also available are the papers of Wagner's executive assistant Julius Edelstein, a major figure in the redevelopment of the Upper West Side and a driving force in urban housing throughout the city. Portions of Sen. Wagner's papers, held by Georgetown University, are available on microfilm. In 1994, the archives received the personal papers of Robert F. Wagner Jr., documenting the third and final generation of the Wagner family to serve in a public role.

Abraham D. Beame Collection: Beame enjoyed a long and distinguished career in public service, including a term as mayor, 1974–77. The Beame Collection consists of 1,800 photographs, more than 100 artifacts, and an assortment of papers. These include the fiscal crisis of the 1970s and the bicentennial celebration. The Beame oral history project has gathered unique recollections of more than 30 associates and contemporaries of the mayor.

Edward I. Koch Collection: New York's dynamic 105th mayor served three terms, 1978–89. This collection of post-mayoral materials includes more than 3,700 photographs, videos, and a variety of documents. Included in the collection are materials donated by contemporaries and associates of the mayor, on such issues as charter revision and economic development. A portion of Mayor Koch's mayoral speeches, which deal with some of the defining issues of the 1980s, is now available online. Dozens of oral history transcripts offer insights into the Koch years.

New York City Council: This collection represents an unparalleled snapshot of the legislative history of America's biggest city from the 1930s into the 21st century. It includes copies of the thousands of enacted laws and official publications, and also the records of public hearings and committee files on legislation under consideration and ad hoc investigations, numerous photographs and negatives, maps, artifacts, scrapbooks, audio and videotapes, as well as the papers of dozens of individual council members. Legislative documents from 1955–2007 are searchable on the website. Nearly 1.5 million of these are now available in full-text online, along with more than 67,000 searchable photographs.

New York City Housing Authority (NYCHA): Founded in 1934, NYCHA was the first US housing authority. The collection covers the period from the 1920s to the 1990s. It documents the construction of New York's public housing projects and provides information about the lives of the residents. The collection contains correspondence, reports, news-clippings, testimony, and surveys of neighborhoods and tenant populations. It also has more than 100,000 images, including photos of city neighborhoods before the projects were built. About 5,000 can be viewed online.

Steinway & Sons: Henry Z. Steinway donated the papers of the Steinway & Sons piano company to the archives in 1985. Steinway figures prominently in American immigration, business, cultural, urban, and labor history. The family founded a piano company in Manhattan in 1853, and in 1870 built a factory in Queens and constructed street railways and housing. The collection consists of family, business, and workers' records from 1853–2007. The collection also contains more than 4,800 photographs, and more than 50 hours of audio and videotapes.

Queens History Collection: The Archives houses a collection on the social history of Queens from the 19th to the 20th century. This includes a 3,000-image plus photo collection. It contains views of transportation, leisure, work, and family life in New York's largest borough, especially Astoria, Long Island City, and Woodside. The images show the transformation from a rural county in the late 19th century to an urban borough by 1950. The collection also has more than 90 oral histories. An additional aspect is the papers of two settlement houses, Forest Hills Community House and Sunnyside Community Services. The Archives also contains a small collection of documents, framed photographs and artifacts from former New York State Senator, Serphin R. Maltese and State Assemblyman Mark Weprin,

Real Estate Board of New York (REBNY) Collection: The Papers of REBNY, donated to the Archives by the Board in 2017, document the history of private real estate in New York City from the Board's founding, in 1896, to 2018. The largest portion of the Collection consists of the "Property Cards" (~200,000), produced by REBNY, which chronicle the real estate history of Manhattan properties. The other documents (~ 24 cf) are divided between those published by REBNY (i.e., Manual and Diaries, REBNY Minutes, Annual Journals and Reports, and an Annual Banquet publication), and Non-REBNY publications (i.e., Newsclippings, and Brooklyn Street Maps). There is also a Subject Files Series, which includes office occupancy surveys, and there are several folders of REBNY President Steven Spinola's correspondence. The Collection also contains 38 Videos, 24 audiocassettes, about 3 cf of photos, 25 artifacts, and 20 real estate handbooks/guides.

The LGBTQ Collection: is presently being processed, and will be added to the online database for researchers as they become available. Presently, the bulk of this collection comes from the Papers of Daniel Dromm and Senator/Assemblyman Tom Duane. The Daniel Dromm Papers, expected to be available to researchers in the summer of 2019, consists of 24 cubic ft of documents and artifacts, illuminating Queens LGBT history and activism from the 1990s to the early 2010s. Dromm, a Queens public school teacher from 1984 to 2009, was a founder of the Queens Lesbian and Gay Pride Committee and an organizer of the Queens Pride Parade and Festival, inaugurated in Jackson Heights in 1993. The Senator Thomas Duane LGBTQ Papers consist of two Series: the Gay Literature Series (the Christopher Magazine from 1976 to 1993) and the Personal Gay Files Series (documents collected by Senator Duane, before, during and after his time in political office).

In addition, the Archives has acquired microfilm copies of the papers of all the NYC mayors since La Guardia (O'Dwyer, Impellitteri, Wagner, Lindsay, Beame, Koch, Dinkins, and the Digital Collection of Giuliani. The Archives has begun to develop its collection of Lindsay Photographs, having received a donation from the Mayor's son John Lindsay Jr. and daughter, Kathleen Lake.

B. Programs

The La Guardia and Wagner Archives produces a variety of public programs, including history calendars; k-12 curricula; tours; and exhibits.

New York State mandates that 4th and 5th graders study local history, but does not provide instructors with materials to teach this subject. Helping to fill this void, the Archives has published curriculum for students in New York City's public schools.

The Archives maintains multiple exhibits throughout the hallways of the college and at other cultural institutions. Tours of the Archives facility are offered to the college community, which include an introduction to archival procedures, a visit to the storage room, and group sessions during which Archives' staff assist students in interpreting a historical document.

Each year the Archives works with LAGCC faculty members to work with a cohort of students on a year-long research and fieldwork project utilizing different collections. The students are trained in different historical methodologies, and do a variety of fieldwork assignments that bring their work into the public eye through photography, interviewing, podcasting, conference panels and writing.

C. Publications

Besides the yearly curricula, Archives has published an annual history calendar since 1979.

D. Fellowships and Awards

Not applicable.

Staff

Ciego, Soraya (MLS, Queens, CUNY 2009; deputy dir.) sciego@lagcc.cuny.edu

DiCarlo, Douglas (MA, Long Island 1994; MLS, Queens, CUNY 2002; archivist) 19th-century US social; ddicarlo@lagcc.cuny.edu

Garfunkel, Amanda (MLIS, San José State 2017; asst. archivist) amellinger@lagcc.cuny.edu

Kleban, Oleg (AS, Kiev Industrial, Ukraine 1993; info. systems assoc. II) okleban@lagcc.cuny.edu

Lieberman, Richard K. (PhD, NYU 1976; dir.) US, urban, New York City; richardli@lagcc.cuny.edu

Mezick, David (MLIS, Long Island, CW Post 2019; library coord.) dmezick@lagcc.cuny.edu

Petrus, Stephen (PhD, Grad. Center, CUNY 2010; historian) American public; spetrus@lagcc.cuny.edu

Rodriguez, Miguelina (PhD, Rutgers, Camden 2017; deputy coord.) migrodriguez@lagcc.cuny.edu

Rosner, Molly (ABD, Rutgers, Newark; asst. dir.; Education Progs.) American social and cultural; mrosner@lagcc.cuny.edu

Weinstein, Stephen (PhD, Columbia 1984; asst. to dir.) urban, sports, US and New York City; sweinstein@lagcc.cuny.edu

Leo Baeck Institute, Inc.

15 W. 16th St., New York, NY 10011-6301. 212.744.6400. Fax 212.988.1305. Email: lbaeck@lbi.cjh.org. Website: https://www.lbi.org/.

A. Collections and Libraries

The 80,000-volume library of the Leo Baeck Institute (LBI) is recognized as the foremost reference source in the field of German-speaking Jewish history. Rich in rarities ranging from early 16th-century writings to Moses Mendelssohn first editions and dedication copies of works by prominent writers of recent generations, many of the library's volumes were salvaged from famous Jewish libraries destroyed by the Nazis. The library includes a comprehensive collection of belles lettres written by Jews, extensive material on the "Jewish Problem" and anti-Semitism, and more than 750 periodicals published by Jews from the 18th to the 20th centuries.

The Leo Baeck Institute Archives is the outstanding documentation center of its kind in the world. Thousands of family, business, institutional, and community records touch upon virtually every phase of German Jewish life during the past 200 years. Material in the archives relates not only to famous names of the past; a unique collection of over 2,000 memoirs and more than 30,000 photographs mirrors the life of the average Jew.

One hundred twenty paintings as well as several thousand drawings and prints further enhance the significance of the institute as an impressive repository of the cultural legacy of German-speaking Jewry.

The catalog to the holdings of the library and archives is available online. The archival collections are converted for digital access and made available via the LBI website (DigiBaeck at www.lbi.org/DigiBaeck) as well as through InternetArchive (www.archive.org).

B. Programs

At monthly lectures and the annual Leo Baeck Memorial Lecture, prominent speakers share their knowledge on a broad range of subjects.

Every year the institute presents two or three exhibits of material from its collection. Major exhibits utilizing LBI holdings have attracted broad attention nationwide.

The institute is a vibrant research center; its facilities are used by students, scholars, and private individuals from throughout the world. An ongoing public program of lectures, symposia, and international conferences encourages a lively exchange of ideas.

LBI is a partner organization in the Center for Jewish History with YIVO Institute for Jewish Research, American Jewish Historical Society, American Sephardic Federation, and Yeshiva University Museum. The web site for the center is www.cjh.org.

C. Publications

The LBI has published well over 100 books in English, German, and Hebrew. The LBI's London center issues the highly acclaimed *Year Book*. A variety of scholarly essays in German appear in the *Almanach*, edited by the Jerusalem Institute. The New York institute publishes the *LBI News* for its members.

D. Fellowships and Awards

The LBI assists doctoral candidates and younger academics with projects leading to doctoral dissertations or scholarly works. The application deadline for the joint Leo Baeck Institute/German Academic Exchange Service (DAAD) Fellowship, the Fritz Halbers Fellowship, and the David Baumgardt Memorial Fellowship is

November 1, the deadline for the Career Development Fellowship is March 1. Application forms are available on the LBI's website.

Officers

Bamberger, Michael A. (vice pres.) michael.bamberger@dentons.com

Baum, Dennis (secretary)

Detjen, David W. (vice pres.) david.detjen@alston.com

Gundersheimer, Werner L. (PhD, Harvard 1963; vice pres.) gundershei@folger.edu

Houston, Amy (treasurer)

Sobel, Ronald B. (pres.)

Staff

Evers, Renate (OMS, Rutgers; MLS, Frankfurt, Germany; dir., collections) revers@lbi.cjh.org

Mecklenburg, Frank (PhD, Tech., Berlin 1981; chief archivist and dir., research) German and German-Jewish, 19th and 20th century; fmecklenburg@lbi.cjh.org

Simonson, Michael (MLS, Pratt Inst.; archivist and registrar) msimonson@lbi.cjh.org

Teifer, Hermann (MLS, Queens, CUNY; MA, Vienna, Austria; head archivist) hteifer@lbi.cjh.org

Weitzer, William H. (PhD, Massachusetts Amherst 1981; exec. dir.) wweitzer@lbi.cjh.org

Library Company of Philadelphia

1314 Locust St., Philadelphia, PA 19107-5698. 215.546.3181. Fax 215.546.5167. Email: refdept@librarycompany.org. Website: https://librarycompany.org/.

A. Collections and Libraries

The Library Company of Philadelphia is an independent research library with collections documenting every aspect of the history and background of American culture from the colonial period to the end of the 19th century. A rare book collection of national importance, its holdings number about 750,000 rare books, pamphlets, newspapers, broadsides, and items of ephemera, 100,000 graphics, and 160,000 manuscripts. These collections are available to all researchers without charge.

From its founding in 1731 through the 19th century, the Library Company actively collected books, newspapers, pamphlets, and prints, British and continental as well as American, reflecting all the varied interests of its learned and cosmopolitan clientele. These materials now form an unparalleled collection of primary research materials, constantly augmented by gift and purchase, which provides a comprehensive representation of American print culture in the 18th and 19th centuries. The following areas receive particular attention: African American history; American science, technology, architecture, agriculture, natural history, education, philanthropy, and popular medicine; business and economic history; German-Americana; American Judaica; Philadelphia area history; the history of printing, book collecting, and reading; women's history; household and family life; popular literature; historic visual culture, and printmaking, mapmaking, and photography in Philadelphia.

The Library Company maintains a reciprocal housing agreement with the Historical Society of Pennsylvania in which the Historical Society's rare book collection is housed in the Library Company and the Library Company's manuscript collection is housed in the Historical Society. Included in the Library Company's manuscripts are the papers of John Dickinson; Dr. Benjamin Rush; Pierre Eugène Du Simitière, an 18th-century ephemera collector and artist; Ann Hampton Brewster, 19th

century novelist and journalist; John A. McAllister, Philadelphia antiquarian and ephemera collector; and the Smith family.

There is a significant art and artifact collection that includes paintings, sculpture, furniture, and decorative arts dating from the 18th century (when the library maintained a "cabinet of curiosities") through the end of the 19th century. A separate Print and Photograph Department manages the institution's graphics collections, which extend up to the mid-20th century.

Readers are assisted in their research by a knowledgeable staff. The Library Company provides a web site for further information about the library and its collections, with links to an online catalog of records for books, graphics, serials, broadsides, and collections (WolfPAC) and to a separate catalog for digital image collections (ImPAC).

Fully searchable digital images of many of the Library Company's early American books, pamphlets, and broadsides are accessible through the Readex/Newsbank digital Archive of Americana, including Afro-Americana Imprints from the Library Company of Philadelphia, 1535-1922 (which will eventually contain over 12,000 titles); and Early American Imprints, Series I (1639-1800) and II (1801-1819), including new Supplements from the Library Company of Philadelphia for both Series. In addition, Adam Matthew Digital has published a digital archive called Popular Medicine in America, 1800-1900, drawn from the Library Company's collections.

B. Programs

The Library Company offers a changing exhibition program, and sponsors a variety of public programs including lectures and symposia. Exhibitions are open free of charge during regular library hours.

The Library Company has established formal programs in four subject areas, each of which sponsor conferences, public programs, publications, exhibitions, and residential fellowships. The Program in African American History (PAAH) brings together scholars and interested members of the public to explore and discuss every aspect of the experience of people of African descent in the Americas from the beginnings of European colonization through 1900. In 2013, PAAH made an ambitious commitment to promoting scholarship in early African American History and increasing the diversity of scholars in the field with the help of a generous grant from the Andrew W. Mellon Foundation. The Program in Early American Economy and Society (PEAES) is dedicated to promoting scholarship and public understanding about the origins and development of the early North American and Atlantic economy, including such topics as the cultures of business, local and international commerce, manufacturing, labor, political economy, households, gender, and technology. The Visual Culture Program (VCP@LCP) promotes the use of historical images as primary sources for studying the past and fosters research, collection, and interpretation of historic visual material. Finally, the Davida T. Deutsch Program in Women's History is committed to the ongoing work of "recovering" women's history from the resources in the collections. Its goal is to recognize and honor women for who they were in their historical moment.

C. Publications

The Library Company's Annual Report provides a lively account of new acquisitions, discoveries, programs and activities. It is sent to all members and to libraries throughout the world. Its newsletter, the *Occasional Miscellany*, is published twice a year. The Library Company also publishes exhibition catalogs, bibliographies, and monographs. Among recent publications are *Philadelphia on Stone: Commercial Lithography in Philadelphia,*

1828-1878, edited by Erika Piola (co-published with Penn State University Press); *Early African American Print Culture*, edited by Lara Langer Cohen and Jordan Alexander Stein (co-published with the University of Pennsylvania Press); and two books marking the Franklin Tercentenary and the 275th anniversary of the Library Company's founding: *Benjamin Franklin, Writer and Printer*, by James N. Green and Peter Stallybrass (co-published with Oak Knoll Press and the British Library, 2006) and *The Library of Benjamin Franklin*, by Edwin Wolf 2nd and Kevin Hayes (co-published with the American Philosophical Society, 2006). The PEAES book series, "Studies in Early American Economy and Society from the Library Company of Philadelphia," is co-published with the Johns Hopkins University Press. Fourteen titles have appeared in this series, most recently Joseph Adelman's *Revolutionary Networks: The Business and Politics of Printing the News*. See also *Economic History in the Philadelphia Region: Guide to Manuscripts and Print Resources for Research* by Cathy Matson and Wendy Woloson.

D. Fellowships and Awards

Each year the Library Company offers about 45 fellowships for research in residence in its collections. Many of them are one-month fellowships jointly sponsored with the Historical Society of Pennsylvania, supporting research in both libraries; among these are Barra International Fellowships for non-US citizens living abroad. The PEAES and the PAAH both offer short- and long-term post-doctoral and dissertation fellowships in their respective subject areas. PAAH fellowships are funded by the Andrew W. Mellon Foundation as part of the Mellon Scholars Program, which also includes summer internships for recent college graduates and summer workshops for recent college graduates or students in their first year of graduate study. The National Endowment for the Humanities Post-doctoral Fellowships and the Albert M. Greenfield Foundation Dissertation Fellowships support research in any subject area appropriate to the Library Company's collections. The stipends range from $2,000 to $5,500 per month. The application deadline for the long-term post-doctoral fellowships is November 1. For all other awards the deadline is March 1. The project proposal should demonstrate that the collection contains primary sources central to the research topic; applicants are encouraged to inquire about the appropriateness of the proposed topic. A renovated historic house next door to the library serves as a fellows' residence. For more information visit the library's web site or e-mail James Green at jgreen@librarycompany.org.

Staff

August, Linda (MA, Arts 2004; reference and artifacts curator) museum studies; laugust@librarycompany.org

Barsanti, Michael J. (PhD, Pennsylvania 2002; dir.) mbarsanti@librarycompany.org

Cooper Owens, Deirdre B. (PhD, UCLA 2008; dir.; Prog. in African American Hist.) African American, gender, medicine; Deirdre.CooperOwens@qc.cuny.edu

D'Agostino, Rachel (MSLS, Clarion, Pa. 2007; OMS, Harvard 2000; curator; Printed Books) early American imprints; rdagostino@librarycompany.org

Fenton, William D. (PhD, Fordham 2018; dir., scholarly innovation) digital humanities, American literature; wfenton@librarycompany.org

Green, James (MLS, Columbia 1976; MPhil, Yale 1972; librarian) printing and publishing; jgreen@librarycompany.org

King, Cornelia S. (MA, Temple 1989; MS, Drexel 1980; chief; Reference) women's studies; cking@librarycompany.org

Matson, Cathy (PhD, Columbia 1985; dir.; Prog. in Early American Econ. and Soc.) early America, economic; cmatson@librarycompany.org

Piola, Erika (MA, Pennsylvania 1996; asst. curator; Prints and Photographs) graphics; epiola@librarycompany.org

Rosner, Jennifer (BFA, Arts 1978; head; Bindery/Conservation) bookbinding; bindery@librarycompany.org

Smith, Jasmine R. (MLIS, Kent State 2016; reference librarian) African American; jsmith@librarycompany.org

Weatherwax, Sarah (MA, William and Mary 1984; curator; Prints and Photographs) Philadelphia, early photography; printroom@librarycompany.org

Massachusetts Historical Society

1154 Boylston St., Boston, MA 02215-3695. 617.646.0512. Fax 617.859.0074. Email: fellowships@masshist.org; library@masshist.org. Website: http://www.masshist.org/.

A. Collections and Libraries

The Massachusetts Historical Society was founded in 1791 for the threefold purpose of collecting, preserving, and disseminating resources for the study of American history. It was not only the first North American historical society, but also the first institution of any kind to devote its attention primarily to collecting and publishing in American history.

The society's collections cannot be matched either in scope or in depth by those of any similar American institution. The area of primary interest is the manuscript collection of more than 12 million pieces in 3,600 separate collections of personal papers and institutional records. These holdings, exceeded in importance only by those of the Library of Congress, cover such diverse subjects as the history of religion, law, education, and medicine; diplomacy and international commerce; the American Revolution and the Civil War; and environmental and women's history. Although the holdings in the history of New England and in the period from colonization through the late 19th century are especially strong, the society also has significant materials for the study of the West Indies, Latin America, the China trade, and the 20th century.

The society holds 200,000 published items including large collections of early Massachusetts printing and New England local history. More than a dozen special libraries of rare books and manuscripts, several of them given by 19th-century collectors, augment these holdings. Published materials include more than 20,000 broadsides, 30,000 18th- and 19th-century pamphlets, 5,000 maps, and more than 150,000 microforms. The society also houses more than 100,000 historic photographs.

B. Programs

The society sponsors research projects and scholarly conferences and hosts five monthly colloquia on early American history, modern American society & culture, environmental history, African American history, and on the history of women, gender, and sexuality. A sixth seminar series—on biography—meets several times each year. A seventh series focusing on digital history is under development. The society also organizes annual series of public lectures, symposia, and brown bag lunches. In September 2017, the society hosted a workshop on "The Future of History." The MHS's Center for the Teaching of History promotes history and civics education through programs, web-based resources, fellowships, and support for National History Day.

C. Publications

The society issued the first volume of its *Collections* series in 1792. Over the course of more than two centuries it has published hundreds of items, most of them in continuing series, including the *Collections* (edited documents), the *Massachusetts Historical Review* (a scholarly periodical), and *Sibley's Harvard Graduates* (biographical sketches of 17th- and 18th-century Harvard students). The society is also home to the *Adams Papers* documentary editing project.

In recent years, the society has also made important materials available through its web site, including maps of the French and Indian War; *The Adams Papers Digital Edition*; the *Thomas Jefferson Digital Edition*; and curricular materials for K–12 teachers.

D. Fellowships and Awards

Each year the society offers at least two long-term fellowships, several summer teaching fellowships, a two-month award (in collaboration with the Boston Athenaeum) on the Civil War, and more than 20 short-term fellowships. The application deadline for long-term fellowships, funded in large part by the National Endowment for the Humanities, is January 15; the final submission date for proposals for the Civil War grant is February 15; the deadline for proposals for short-term awards is March 1. The society is also a member of the New England Regional Fellowship Consortium, a collaboration of 30 research institutions. In 2019, the NERFC will offer at least 25 awards, each for a minimum of 40 working days, portable among the participating organizations. The deadline for NERFC applications is February 1. For information on research fellowships at the MHS, see the society's web site or contact the Research Department. For information on K-12 teacher fellowships, contact the Center for Teaching History.

Staff

Allgor, Catherine A. (PhD, Yale 1998; pres.) women's lives and gender, early Republic, politics; callgor@masshist.org

Barlow, Rhonda (PhD, Virginia 2016; asst. editor; Adams Papers) American foreign policy; rbarlow@masshist.org

Barzilay, Karen N. (PhD, William and Mary 2009; JQ Adams diary digital project; Adams Papers) 18th century; kbarzilay@masshist.org

Beardsley, Deborah (BS, Rochester Inst. Tech. 1986; public engagement coord.; Education and Community Engagement) American folk art, mourning jewelry; dbeardsley@masshist.org

Beauchard, Oona (BFA, Massachusetts Coll. Art 1996; paper conservator and registrar; Collections) film; obeauchard@masshist.org

Beauchard, Sabina (reproductions coord.; Library) sbeauchard@masshist.org

Beck, William (OMS, Boston Univ. 1999; web developer; Collections) bbeck@masshist.org

Bentley, Anne E. (BA, Syracuse 1973; curator, art & artifacts; Collections) early American numismatics, material culture; abentley@masshist.org

Bertulli, Sarah (BA, Maine 2010; CERT, Tufts 2018; public programs coord.; Education and Community Engagement) sbertulli@masshist.org

Bush, Alexandra (MSLS, Simmons 2018; digital production asst.; Adams Papers) abush@masshist.org

Chand, Rakashi (BS, Northeastern 2002; sr. library asst.; Library) rchand@masshist.org

Clutterbuck-Cook, Anna J. (MA,MLIS, Simmons 2011; reference librarian; Library) education, feminism; acook@masshist.org

Coveney, Chris (BA, Ithaca 1987; chief tech. and media officer; Finance and Administration) technology, travel, community activism; ccoveney@masshist.org

Drummey, Peter (MLS, Columbia 1977; Stephen T. Riley Librarian; Library) historical archaeology, travel and discovery, World War I; pdrummey@masshist.org

Elder, Hannah (MLIS, Simmons 2019; library asst.; Library) helder@masshist.org

Finn, Katie (BA, Massachisetts Amherst 1999; executive asst. to pres. and secretary to the board) kfinn@masshist.org

Fries, Gwen (BA, Elizabethtown 2016; asst. production editor; Adams Papers) book production; gfries@masshist.org

Georgini, Sara E. (PhD, Boston Univ. 2016; series editor; Adams Papers) American religion; sgeorgini@masshist.org

Grant, Amanda (MA, Salem State 2011; donor engagement manager; Development) agrant@masshist.org

Griffin, Katherine H. (MA, Northeastern 1984; Nora Saltonstall Preservation Librarian; Collections) kgriffin@masshist.org

Gutierrez, Florentina (BA, Wellesley 2015; library asst.) classical civilizations; fgutierrez@masshist.org

Hamond, Tammy (BA, St. Anselm 1991; controller; Finance and Administration) thamond@masshist.org

Hayes, Annie (MA, Boston Architectural 2014; sr. development assoc.; Development) ahayes@masshist.org

Heavey, Elaine (MLIS, Simmons 2008; dir.; Library) late 19th century; eheavey@masshist.org

Heywood, Nancy (MLS, Simmons 1996; sr. archivist, digital initiatives; Collections) archives; nheywood@masshist.org

Hinchen, Dan (MLS, Simmons 2010; reference librarian; Library) dhinchen@masshist.org

Kleespies, Gavin (MA, Chicago 1999; dir., programs, exhibitions, and community partnerships; Education and Community Engagement) American economic; gkleespies@masshist.org

Knauff, Carol (BA,BFA, Cornell 1999; vice pres.; Communications & Marketing) Communications; cknauff@masshist.org

Kolbet, Kelsey (BA, Smith 2017; library asst.; Library) kkolbet@masshist.org

Lane, Jonathan (BA, Harvard Extension School; coord., Revolution 250; Education and Community Engagement) jlane@masshist.org

Lawson, Brenda M. (MSLS, Simmons 1988; vice pres.; Collections) diaries, medicine, social welfare; blawson@masshist.org

LeBlanc, Ondine (PhD, Michigan 1994; Worthington C. Ford Editor; Publications) women's diaries, humanities text encoding; oleblanc@masshist.org

Lowell, Laura Scott (MSLS, Simmons 2009; processing archivist and internship coord.; Collections) Massachusetts towns; llowell@masshist.org

Mahmoud, Shakira (MEd, Lesley, 2015; gifts and database manager) women's rights movement. Civil Rights Movement; smahmoud@masshist.org

Major, George (operations asst.; Finance and Administration) gmajor@masshist.org

Martin, Sara (PhD, Melbourne 2008; editor in chief; Adams Papers) women and family; saram@masshist.org

Martin, Susan (MSLS, Simmons 2005; processing archivist and EAD coord.; Collections) smartin@masshist.org

Melchior, Kate (MA, Bristol 2015; asst. dir., education; Education and Community Engagement) public, historical memory, Holocaust commemoration; kmelchior@masshist.org

Millikan, Neal Elizabeth (PhD, South Carolina 2008; digital projects editor; Adams Papers) 19th-century American social, digitization; nmillikan@masshist.org

Minty, Christopher F. (PhD, Stirling 2015; asst. editor; Adams Papers) 18th-century America, loyalists; cminty@masshist.org

Mitchell, Theresa (BA, Wellesley 2016; library asst.) tmitchell@masshist.org

Morris, Katy (MA, Columbia 2013; research coord. and book review editor; Research) women/gender/sexuality, American West, oral; kmorris@masshist.org

Nguyen, Maureen (MBA, Babson Coll. 2008; vice pres.; Development) mnguyen@masshist.org

Norton, Amanda (BA, Boston Coll. 2008; digital production editor; Adams Papers) digitization, John Adams; anorton@masshist.org

Rec, Agnieszka (PhD, Yale 2016; assoc. editor; Publications) Middle Ages, alchemy; arec@masshist.org

Renault, Tess (MA, Emerson 2018; editorial asst.; Adams Papers and Publications) transcription; trenault@masshist.org

Smith, Jennifer (operations asst.; Finance and Administration) jensmith@masshist.org

Snyder, Clara (MA, Simmons 2019; library asst.; Library) csnyder@masshist.org

Sweeney, Dan (facility manager; Finance and Administration) dsweeney@masshist.org

Tardif, Elyssa (PhD, Purdue 2013; dir., education; Education and Community Engagement) early New England women, museum studies; etardif@masshist.org

Tsoules, Will (MBA,MS, Northeastern 2003; vice pres. and CFO; Finance and Administration) wtsoules@masshist.org

Williams, Ashley (MSLS, Simmons 2019; library asst./processing asst.; Library) awilliams@masshist.org

Wongsrichanalai, Kanisorn (PhD, Virginia 2010; dir.; Research) 19th-century US, Civil War era, gender, oral, food, human and animal interactions; kwongsrichanalai@masshist.org

Woodward, Hobson (MSLS, Simmons 2004; series editor, Adams family correspondence; Adams Papers) Adams family; hwoodward@masshist.org

Wright, Conrad E. (PhD, Brown 1980; Sibley Editor; Research) colonial and early national America; cwright@masshist.org

Wulf, Laura (BFA, Sch. Museum of Fine Arts, Boston 1996; photographic and digital imaging specialist; Collections) lwulf@masshist.org

Yacovone, Mary E. (MSLS, Simmons 1991; sr. cataloger; Collections) American printing, genealogy; myacovone@masshist.org

The McNeil Center for Early American Studies

Univ. of Pennsylvania, 3355 Woodland Walk, Philadelphia, PA 19104-4531. 215.898.9251. Fax 215.573.3391. Email: mceas@ccat.sas.upenn.edu. Website: http://www.mceas.org/.

The McNeil Center for Early American Studies (MCEAS) facilitates research and scholarly inquiry into the histories and cultures of North America in the Atlantic world before 1850, with a particular but by no means exclusive emphasis on the mid-Atlantic region.

A. Collections and Libraries

Established in 1978 as the Philadelphia Center for Early American Studies, the MCEAS is endowed by gifts from the Robert L. McNeil Jr. Charitable Trust, the Andrew W. Mellon Foundation, the Barra Foundation, the University of Pennsylvania, and other generous donors. It operates as a consortium of mid-Atlantic research and educational institutions. The MCEAS conducts a fellowship program designed to capitalize upon Philadelphia's magnificent manuscript, book, and museum collections; a seminar program intended to promote intellectual community among local and visiting faculty and graduate students; and a publication program intended to disseminate the best new research in early American studies.

The MCEAS holds a small reference library for the use of its fellows but does not itself maintain a research collection. Fellows have access to the University of Pennsylvania library system and to other major Philadelphia-area archives and research libraries.

B. Programs

The MCEAS sponsors a seminar that meets approximately three times a month between September and May, with the paper for each session circulated in advance. Over 200 people attend at least once a year, with an average attendance of 40 to 50 at meetings held at half a dozen different sites in the Delaware Valley. While most of the regular attendees are graduate students and faculty from institutions in the Philadelphia area, participants come from as far afield as Long Island, New York City, Princeton, Baltimore, Annapolis, and Washington. In addition to its seminar, the MCEAS organizes informal works-in-progress discussions, evening colloquia, and other venues for sharing research. It also sponsors or co-sponsors occasional major national conferences, including a biennial graduate student conference held in the fall of odd-numbered years. Recent national conferences include Human Trafficking in Early America, Port Cities in the Early Modern World, 1500-1800, and Situation Critical: Critique, Theory, and Early American Studies.

C. Publications

The scholarly journal *Early American Studies* is published quarterly, edited by Roderick McDonald. An MCEAS *Early American Studies* monograph series is published by the University of Pennsylvania Press; inquiries should be addressed to the MCEAS director. Recent titles include Cornelia Dayton and Sharon Salinger, *Robert Love's Warnings: Searching for Strangers in Colonial Boston*; Juliana Barr and Edward Countryman, eds., *Contested Spaces of Early America*; Brian Connolly, *Domestic Intimacies: Incest and the Liberal Subject in Nineteenth-Century America*; Jean R. Soderlund, *Lenape Country: Delaware Valley Society Before William Penn*; Bethel Saler, *The Settlers' Empire: Colonialism and State Formation in America's Old Northwest*; Brian P. Luskey and Wendy A. Woloson, eds., Capitalism By Gaslight: Illuminating the Economy of Nineteenth-Century America; Michael Leroy Oberg, *Professional Indian: The American Odyssey of Eleazer Williams*; Robert Michael Morrissey, *Empire by Collaboration: Indians, Colonists, and Governments in Colonial Illinois Country*; William Huntting Howell, *Against Self-Reliance: The Arts of Dependence in the Early United States*; Ignacio Gallup-Diaz, Andrew Shankman, and David J. Silverman, eds., *Anglicizing America: Empire, Revolution, Republic*; Jen Manion, *Liberty's Prisoners: Carceral Culture in Early America*; and Padraig Riley, *Slavery and the Democratic Conscience: Political Life in Jeffersonian America*.

D. Fellowships and Awards

The MCEAS offers approximately ten predoctoral dissertation fellowships each year most with a stipend of $21,000 for a term of nine months, beginning September 1. Dissertation fellows are provided with office and computer facilities in the MCEAS building on Penn's campus. Advanced graduate students from any PhD-granting institution who are in the dissertation research or writing stage are eligible to compete for these fellowships. So far, in annual competitions, grants have been awarded to more than 200 graduate students from many US, Canadian, and European universities. Most fellows have been historians and literary scholars, but dissertators in half a dozen other fields have also won awards. The application deadline for all 2016–17 dissertation fellowships is March 1, 2016.

The MCEAS also offers at least one annual postdoctoral fellowship and a sabbatical fellowship. For additional information on fellowship programs and for application deadlines, contact the director or visit the MCEAS web site.

The MCEAS also annually appoints a number of research associates. This service is offered to qualified scholars visiting Philadelphia for two months or longer who wish to participate in MCEAS activities and are capable of providing their own financial support. Research associates are provided with University of Pennsylvania library and computer privileges and—if space permits—with office space in the MCEAS building. For additional information, consult the director.

Staff

Baxter-Bellamy, Amy L. (MA, Catholic 1998; assoc. dir.) Tudor-Stuart England; abaxter@sas.upenn.edu

Dunn, Richard S. (PhD, Princeton 1955; dir. emeritus and Nichols Prof. emeritus) early America, Caribbean; rdunn@amphilsoc.org

Richter, Daniel K. (PhD, Columbia 1984; Richard S. Dunn Dir.) early America, Native American; drichter@history.upenn.edu

National Aeronautics and Space Administration

History Division & Office of Communications, Attn: Nadine Andreassen/ 5S14, MS C072, 300 E St. SW, Washington, DC 20546-0001. 202.358.0384. Fax 202.358.2866. Email: hq-histinfo@nasa.gov. Website: https://history.nasa.gov/.

A. Collections and Libraries

Materials for research in the history of aeronautics, astronautics, and space science are available at National Aeronautics and Space Administration (NASA) Headquarters (in Washington, DC) and at NASA centers across the country. The NASA Headquarters Historical Reference Collection has approximately 2,000 cubic feet of published and unpublished materials and has access to the retired records of the agency at the Washington National Records Center in Suitland, Maryland. A complete, though somewhat dated, description of the program, entitled *Research in NASA History* (SP-2009-4543), is available on request and is online at history.nasa.gov/sp4543.pdf. The Headquarters Historical Reference Collection space has been renovated. There are now 6 large researcher work stations available for use. To make arrangements for research at NASA Headquarters please email hq-histinfo@nasa.gov or call 202-358-0384.

The NASA History Program also has an active and extensive presence on the Web. Basic reference materials on most major NASA programs, bibliographies, links to information about NASA history at its field centers, and free electronic copies of all NASA History publications are available on the website at http://history.nasa.gov.

B. Programs

The NASA History Program includes the preparation of published histories and reference works; the preparation or sponsorship of occasional studies for internal use or limited distribution; the preservation of NASA records of historical value; and the stimulation, encouragement, and support of historical study of NASA-related activities by researchers from outside the government. The History Program also communicates information about NASA History and History Program activities through our web site (www.nasa.gov/topics/history), Twitter (@NASAHistory), and Facebook (NASA History).

C. Publications

Most publications are prepared by scholars working under contract with NASA. Principal investigators on contract proposals should hold a PhD or demonstrate similar competence. Most of NASA's history is in, or closely related to, the field of recent technology and science. Contract proposals are normally sought for specific projects and will be advertised via government procurement channels - primarily at www.fbo.gov.

NASA History publications are available free in electronic versions online at: http://history.nasa.gov/series95.html. Hard copies of new publications are available from the NASA Headquarters Information Center. Some older titles are also available from the Information Center. Availability and ordering information for the Information Center are at www.hq.nasa.gov/office/hqlibrary/ic/ic2.htm.

The NASA History Program also publishes a quarterly newsletter. The current issue, and archives of earlier issues, are available free at http://history.nasa.gov/histnews.htm">http://history.nasa.gov/histnews.htm.

D. Fellowships and Awards

NASA supports an annual Fellowship in Aerospace History, administered by the American Historical Association. This fellowship is open to US citizens who hold a doctoral degree in history or a closely related field, or who are enrolled in and have completed all course work for a doctoral degree-granting program. The fellowship term is for six months to one year and carries a maximum stipend of $20,000. Current details can be found at: www.historians.org/nasafellowship.

NASA also supports two similar fellowships, one through the History of Science Society (HSS) and the other through the Society for the History of Technology (SHOT). For information on the HSS Fellowship in the History of Space Science see www.hssonline.org/about/society_NASAFellowship.html. For information on the SHOT NASA Fellowship, see www.historyoftechnology.org/awards/nasa.html.

The NASA History Program seeks interns for fall, spring and summer terms. Interns must be currently enrolled in a degree-granting program at the undergraduate or graduate level, and must be US citizens or legal residents. Typical intern duties include social media work, handling complex and detailed queries on aerospace history; editing and proofreading of manuscripts; and writing short articles for the web site or newsletter. Please see www.nasa.gov/content/nasa-history-division-student-internships for more information.

Staff

Andreassen, Nadine (NASA History Program specialist) nadine.j.andreassen@nasa.gov

Barry, William P. (DPhil, Oxford 1996; chief historian) aerospace, Soviet Union/Russia; bill.barry@nasa.gov

Garber, Stephen J. (MS, Virginia Tech 2002; OMS, Pittsburgh 1993; historian) aeronautics, astronautics, technology; steve.garber@hq.nasa.gov

Rodgers, Robyn K. (MLIS, San Jose State 2012; chief archivist) women, Army, archival; robyn.k.rodgers@nasa.gov

National Coalition for History

400 A St. SE, Washington, DC 20003. 202.544.2422. Fax 202.544.8307. Email: lwhite@historycoalition.org. Website: http://historycoalition.org/.

Since 1982, the National Coalition for History (formerly known as the National Coordinating Committee for the Promotion of

History) has served as a national advocacy office for the historical and archival professions.

A. Collections and Libraries

Not applicable.

B. Programs

A consortium of over 50 organizations, the NCH represents the historical and archival professions on issues involving federal funding and policy issues that have an impact on historical research and teaching, the employment of historians, public policy issues relating to history, historic preservation, and the dissemination of historical information. The NCH operates from an office in the American Historical Association headquarters building on Capitol Hill in Washington.

The NCH works on a wide range of federal issues from information policy to historic preservation, providing testimony at congressional hearings, presenting briefings to NCH member organizations, participating in advocacy strategy sessions, and writing legislative updates. The major issues for the NCH during recent years include funding for the National Endowment for the Humanities, funding and policies of the National Archives, funding for the grants program of the National Historical Publications and Records Commission as well as the Department of Education ("Teaching American History" grants), declassification policy, access to presidential and other federal records, historic preservation, the historical program of the National Park Service, and telecommunications policy.

C. Publications

In January 1995, the organization began publishing regular "Washington Updates" on H-Net. In 2007, the National Coalition for History launched a new web site and RSS feed providing real-time access to history-related news from Washington. NCH's weekly reports provide current information on legislation, hearings, markups, and federal policy issues of concern to historians and archivists. The web site also provides in-depth issue briefs on major legislation. For a free subscription, visit the web page.

D. Fellowships and Awards

Not applicable.

Staff

White, Leland J. (JD, Catholic 1981; MA, George Mason 2000; exec. dir.) lwhite@historycoalition.org

National Defence Headquarters

Directorate of History and Heritage, NDHQ / CMP | QGDN / CPM, 101 Colonel By Dr., Ottawa, ON K1A 0K2, Canada. 613.998.7058. Fax 613.990.8579. Email: stephen.harris@forces. gc.ca; warren.sinclair@forces.gc.ca. Website: http://www.cmp-cpm.forces.gc.ca/dhh-dhp/.

The Directorate of History and Heritage (DHH) includes historians, archivists, experts in current Canadian Forces regulations pertaining to heritage and tradition, and Canadian Forces museums administrators. DHH is under the chief of military personnel. Its offices are located in South-East Ottawa, near the Heron and Walkley road junction.

A. Collections and Libraries

In cooperation with the National Archives of Canada, the Directorate of History and Heritage is, in essence, the archives of the Canadian Armed Forces. During the Second World War,

the Royal Canadian Navy, Canadian Army, and Royal Canadian Air Force appointed historical officers to produce reports for the future record and to form the basis of official histories. All of these reports are available for research at DHH. The reading room is open to the general public for archival and library research on Tuesdays and Wednesdays, from 8:30 a.m. to 4:30 p.m.

The most formal and comprehensive collection of reports was created by historical officers at the Canadian Military Headquarters (CMHQ) in London. The *CMHQ Reports* are being made available electronically over time. These reports are available only in English. Other collections include:

Book Collection: Official histories of allied and enemy forces, general histories, campaign histories, and some technical works, as well as numerous Canadian and British regimental histories. Some bound runs of periodicals are held. There is an extensive collection of officers' lists and printed regulations and administrative orders, mostly Canadian.

Kardex Collection: Papers from the Canadian Army and the Royal Canadian Air Force, mainly 1939–64, filed according to the directorate Kardex classification system. The files includes the papers of Lieutenant-Colonel H. M. Jackson, who compiled information on a number of military topics—in particular his heavily used notes on the careers of First World War Canadian officers. The Kardex Collection was closed to acquisitions in 1971.

Document Collection: Begun in 1971, the Document Collection is catalogued on cards, and includes all documents, reports, and narratives received between 1971 and December 1994. This collection is now closed to acquisitions.

InMagic Databases: As of June 1995, an archival database contains descriptions of archival collections. These collections include new materials on peacekeeping.

Archeion: The online database of descriptions of records located in archives across Ontario is held in the Archeion database. About 730 fonds level and 550 series level descriptions held in the Directorate of History and Heritage archives are uploaded to Archeion and searchable at the following link: https://www.archeion.ca/

Permanent Reference Files: Working files of booklets, newspaper clippings, photographs, and similar ephemeral materials. Files have been created for Canadian bases in Canada and abroad, Canadian units, Canadian ships, squadrons of the Royal Canadian Air Force and Canadian Forces, and aircraft types, both Canadian and foreign.

Biographical Files: Open working files for many Canadian servicemen and civilians, of all ranks and professions, and for some selected foreigners. The biographical files are supplemented by card files of Second World War honors and awards, casualties, prisoners of war, etc., for Canadian personnel. There is also a card file of Canadians who served in the British flying services in the First World War.

Steiger Materials: The late Mr. Steiger's collection of documents in the German language which originated in Germany during the Second World War. Many are translated into English. They also include documents relating to research on specific aspects of the First World War, lists of documents held in other archives, and some secondary published material about German military history in general.

Public Record Office and Related Materials: Large quantities of Public Record Office documents photocopied in London for research on the Royal Canadian Air Force and Royal Canadian Navy histories.

Naval Historian's Collection: Large collection of naval materials arranged by the old Royal Canadian Navy file number and catalogued in a separate Kardex.

Photographs Collection: The Directorate does not hold photographs. A bank of recent images is available at Combat Camera: www.combatcamera.forces.gc.ca, you may also contact Canada's National Defence Public Inquiries office at www.forces.gc.ca/en/contact.page. Images more than 7 years old are in the Documentary Art and Photography Division, National Archives of Canada.

B. Programs

Not applicable.

C. Publications

DHH publishes a broad range of books to meet the varying needs of the Canadian Forces. Popular and social histories provide background and overview to build a sense of historical evolution and identity. Critical histories dispassionately note lessons learned and a professional requirement to prepare, organize, and train for future operations.

DHH maintains and publishes a variety of documents for research purposes. Recent publications include *French Canadians and Bilingualism in the Canadian Armed Forces, Vol. 1: 1969–87; Official Languages: National Defence's Response to the Federal Policy; Canadian Military Heritage, Vol. I: 1000–1754* and *Vol. II: 1755–1871; The Canadian Military Experience, 1867–1995: A Bibliography; Canada and the Battle of Vimy Ridge, 9–12 April 1917; A Rattle of Pebbles: The First World War Diaries of Two Canadian Airmen; The Crucible of War, 1939–45; Liberation: The Canadians in Europe; Normandy 1944: The Canadian Summer; Canadians and the Italian Campaign; To Serve Canada: A History of the Royal Military College of Canada since the Second World War; Canadian Forces Dress Instructions; Honours, Flags, and Heritage Structure of the Canadian Forces and Lineages and Insignia of the Canadian Forces, Vol. I: Miscellaneous Units, Vol. II: Ships, Vol. III: Combat Arms Regiments,* and *Vol. IV: Flying Squadrons; Canadian Forces Museums: Operations and Administration; A History of Women in the Canadian Military; Canada and the Korean War; No Higher Purpose (The Official History of the Royal Canadian Navy 1939–43); A Blue Water Navy (The Official History of the Royal Canadian Navy 1943–45);* and *The Seabound Coast (The Official History of the Royal Canadian Navy, 1867-1939); Aboriginal People in the Canadian Military (A Commemorative History of).*

Our more recent in print publications may be available commercially.

D. Fellowships and Awards

Not applicable.

Staff

Campbell, Isabel (PhD, Laval 2000; historian) postwar Canadian foreign and defense policy, NATO, Royal Canadian Navy; isabel.campbell@forces.gc.ca

Delaney, Jason (MA, Waterloo 1999; historian) Canadian naval and maritime, Arctic; jason.delaney@forces.gc.ca

Harris, Stephen John (PhD, Duke 1979; dir.) 20th-century military, Canada, British imperial; stephen.harris@forces.gc.ca

Johnston, William C. (MA, Waterloo 1982; historian) Royal Canadian Air Force, Korea, Royal Canadian Navy; william.johnston@forces.gc.ca

Kletke, Carl (MA, Royal Military College, Can. 2006; historian) heritage, customs and traditions of Canadian military; carl.kletke@forces.gc.ca

Litalien, Michel (MA, Ottawa 2003; historian) French Canadian military, 20th-century Canadian military; michel.litalien@forces.gc.ca

MacFarlane, John D. W. (PhD, Laval 1995; historian) heritage, 20th-century Canadian foreign policy, Southeast Asia; john.macfarlane@forces.gc.ca

McKillip, James Duncan (PhD, Ottawa 2012; historian) military, comparative colonial, indigenous Canada; james.mckillip@forces.gc.ca

Reynolds, Kenneth W. (PhD, McGill 1997; historian) 20th-century and Canadian military, Germany, heritage; ken.reynolds@forces.gc.ca

Sinclair, Warren (MLS, Western Ontario 1989; chief archivist) archives, native, military; warren.sinclair@forces.gc.ca

Tremblay, Yves (PhD, Laval 1993; historian) Canadian peacekeeping, technology, Canadian Army; yves.tremblay@forces.gc.ca

Whitby, Michael (MA, Carleton, Can. 1987; historian) Royal Canadian Navy, 20th-century naval; michael.whitby@forces.gc.ca

---

National History Center of the American Historical Association

400 A St. SE, Washington, DC 20003. 202.450.3209. Fax 202.544.8307. Website: https://nationalhistorycenter.org/.

A. Collections and Libraries

The center does not maintain a research collection.

B. Programs

The National History Center was established to provide opportunities for historians from all over the world to exchange ideas and to help them reach out to broader audiences by providing the historical context necessary to understand today's events.

The center's programs reinforce the critical role that history and historical knowledge play in public decision making and civic life. Capitalizing on its Washington, DC, location, the center offers briefings, lectures, seminars, and workshops for scholars, journalists, government officials and staff, as well as students and the public. Its programs include Congressional Briefings in which historians help Congressional staff understand the background of topics of current legislative concern; a mock policy briefing program that helps educators teach their students about the relevance of studying the past to understanding the present; and in partnership with the Woodrow Wilson International Center for Scholars, seminars open to the public in which historians place current events in historical perspective.

C. Publications

The center, in cooperation with Oxford University Press, publishes a monograph series called Reinterpreting History. The series addresses a key element in the historian's craft: how the interpretation of specific historical events evolves over time. Volumes analyze how historical issues change when viewed from diverse perspectives and from one generation to the next. The first, *Making Sense of the Vietnam Wars*, was edited by Mark Philip Bradley and Marilyn B. Young. Jack Greene and Philip Morgan edited the second, *Atlantic History: A Critical Appraisal*. The most recent volume, *The Human Rights Revolution: An International History*, was published in January 2012, edited by Akira Iriye, Petra Goedde, and William I. Hitchcock. Volumes in development examine the Cold War in the developing world, the role of exploration in history, the Jacksonian era, the French Revolution, the intersection of military and environmental history, rethinking the "Progressive Era," and the dawning of a post-Cold War world. For further information, contact the center.

The center maintains a website at www.nationalhistorycenter. org, a Facebook page at National History Center, and a Twitter presence at @historyctr.

D. Fellowships and Awards

Not applicable.

Officers

Bundles, A'Lelia P. (MA, Harvard Coll. 1974; member, Board of Trustees)

Grossman, James R. (PhD, California, Berkeley 1982; chair, Board of Trustees) jgrossman@historians.org

Kohn, Richard H. (PhD, Wisconsin-Madison 1968; member, Board of Trustees)

Kraut, Alan (PhD, Cornell 1975; member, Board of Trustees)

Lawrence, John Alan (PhD, California, Berkeley 1979; member, Board of Trustees)

Marcum, Deanna B. (PhD, Maryland, Coll. Park 1991; treasurer)

McNeill, John R. (PhD, Duke 1981; member, Board of Trustees)

Mueller, Gordon 'Nick' Herbert (PhD, North Carolina, Chapel Hill 1970; member, Board of Trustees)

Norton, Mary Beth (PhD, Harvard 1969; member, Board of Trustees)

Roberts, Cokie (BA, Wellesley 1964; member, Board of Trustees)

Stovall, Tyler E. (PhD, Wisconsin-Madison 1984; member, Board of Trustees)

Staff

Kennedy, Dane K. (PhD, California, Berkeley 1981; dir.) modern Britain, colonialism, world; dkennedy@historians.org

National Library of Medicine

History of Medicine Division, 8600 Rockville Pike, MSC 3819, Bethesda, MD 20894-3819. 301.496.5405. Fax 301.402.0872. Email: hmdref@nlm.nih.gov. Website: https://www.nlm.nih. gov/hmd/.

The National Library of Medicine houses one of the world's largest history of medicine collections. We collect, preserve, and make available to researchers and the public, print and non-print materials that document the history of medicine, health, and disease in all time periods and cultures. We invite scholars, researchers, and the general public to explore our catalogs, finding aids, online exhibitions, and other resources on our website.

A. Collections and Libraries

The National Library of Medicine's (NLM) resources for historical studies in medicine and in related sciences and specialties are among the richest in the world. Its holdings cover every age from antiquity to the present and represent the medical thought and institutions of virtually every country. The collections include printed monographs and serials, institutional reports, theses, manuscripts, archives, films, prints, photographs and other visual materials, and other works in all major languages. The library's online public catalog, LocatorPlus, is accessible on the World Wide Web at https://locatorplus.gov. Finding aids for NLM's manuscript collections are available at https://oculus.nlm.nih. gov/cgi/f/findaid/findaid-idx. NLM Digital Collections, a growing resource encompassing a variety of formats, is available at https:// collections.nlm.nih.gov.

The History of Medicine Division (HMD) administers the older segments of the library's monographs, serials, and audiovisuals collections (at present, monographs published before 1914, serials published before 1871, and audiovisuals produced before 1970), while more recent works are available through the adjoining divisions of the library. HMD is also responsible for manuscripts collections, both early and modern; an extensive prints and photographs collection; and the library's exhibitions program.

HMD has created a History of Medicine Subset of PubMed at www.pubmed.gov. The History of Medicine Subset includes citations to more than 30,000 journal articles in the history of medicine and related fields published since 1964. To use the History of Medicine Subset, select "Topic-Specific Queries" under PubMed Tools on the PubMed homepage, then select "History of Medicine" as the subject.

B. Programs

HMD organizes programs for the scholarly community and the general public. Visit www.nlm.nih.gov/hmd to learn more.

Additionally, HMD celebrates its historical collections through its Exhibition Program. The program develops and presents exhibitions and multidisciplinary educational tools that make the National Library of Medicine's historical collections available to audiences around the world. Through special displays onsite, traveling banner shows that tour the world, and online K–12 and higher education resources, the Exhibition Program advances public awareness about medicine, science, and history. Exhibitions and special displays focus on a variety of topics including medicine and the arts, science and society, patients and practitioners, and the technology of medicine. Visit the Exhibition Program online to learn more: www.nlm.nih.gov/exhibition.

C. Publications

HMD has published separate catalogs of its 16th-, 17th-, and 18th-century monograph collections. HMD also maintains an online catalog of its prints and photographs collection, "Images from the History of Medicine," at www.nlm.nih.gov/hmd/ihm. HMD, with other branches of NLM, produces an online digital publication of selected manuscripts collections with commentary, "Profiles in Science," at https://profiles.nlm.nih.gov. HMD maintains the *Directory of History of Medicine Collections* online at https://hmddirectory.nlm.nih.gov. HMD provides reference support for IndexCat, the digitized *Index-Catalogue of the Library of the Surgeon General's Office, 1880–1961.* IndexCat includes over 3.5 million citations to books, dissertations, and journal articles dated from antiquity through the 1950s at https://indexcat.nlm. nih.gov. Additionally, HMD maintains a blog, *Circulating Now,* which highlights the Library's historical collections, programs, collaborations, and activities. You can read it and subscribe at https://circulatingnow.nlm.nih.gov.

D. Fellowships and Awards

In February 2016, the National Library of Medicine announced its receipt of a generous gift from The DeBakey Medical Foundation to support enhanced access to the Michael E. DeBakey Archives at the NLM and to establish the Michael E. DeBakey Fellowship in the History of Medicine. Learn more about this fellowship program here: www.nlm.nih.gov/hmd/ informationfor/debakeyfellowship.html.

The National Library of Medicine also offers financial assistance to scholars for the preparation of book-length manuscripts and other scholarly works of value to US health professionals, public health officials, biomedical researchers and historians of the health sciences. For further information about the NLM Grants for Scholarly Works in Biomedicine and Health (G13) see www.nlm. nih.gov/ep/GrantPubs.html.

Staff

Eilers, Sarah (MLS, Maryland 2005; archivist, Historical Audiovisuals) mental health in film, film as primary source in history of medicine, medical knowledge and practice in life of Alexander Hamilton; sarah.eilers@nih.gov

Greenberg, Stephen J. (PhD, Fordham 1983; head; Rare Books and Early Manuscripts Section) medicine, book, Tudor-Stuart England; stephen.greenberg@nih.gov

Koyle, Kenneth M. (MEd, Penn State 2009; MA, Uniformed Services Univ., Health Sciences 2009; deputy chief) military medical, US Civil War, medical innovation; ken.koyle@nih.gov

Moffatt, Christie (MSLS, North Carolina, Chapel Hill 2000; archivist; Digital Manuscripts) digitization and manuscripts, 20th-century science/medicine/public health; moffattc@mail.nih.gov

Newmark, Jill L. (BA, Denver 1982; exhibition specialist/curator) African Americans in Civil War medicine; newmarj@mail.nlm.nih.gov

Rees, John (MLIS, Texas, Austin 1997; archivist and digital resources mgr.; Images and Archives) 18th- to 20th-century American South, American cultural and intellectual, libraries and archives; reesj@mail.nlm.nih.gov

Reznick, Jeffrey Stephen (PhD, Emory 1999; chief) 20th-century social and cultural, medicine and medical material culture, military/veterans/wartime voluntary aid; jeffrey.reznick@nih.gov

Roth, Ginny A. (MSLS, Catholic 2007; curator, Prints & Photographs) color theory, identification and preservation of photographic and photomechanical print processes, visual materials cataloging; ginny.roth@nih.gov

Rothfeld, Anne (PhD, American 2016; historian; Public Services) 19th- and 20th-century Europe, economics and culture, art provenance and restitution; rothfea@mail.nih.gov

Speaker, Susan L. (PhD, Pennsylvania 1992; curator-historian) medicine, 19th- and 20th-century cultural, drug and alcohol use and abuse; speakes1@mail.nih.gov

Warlow, Rebecca (MA, Northeastern 1993; head; Images and Archives) archives management, digitization and metadata, online access and engagement to archives; rebecca.warlow@nih.gov

Naval War College

John B. Hattendorf Center, 686 Cushing Rd., Newport, RI 02841-1207. 401.841.3719. Fax 401.841.3579. Email: david.kohnen@usnwc.edu. Website: https://usnwc.edu/Research-and-Wargaming/Research-Centers/Hattendorf-Center.

The US Naval War College is the oldest naval war college in the world and the highest professional educational institution in the United States Navy. Established in 1884 by Navy Department General Order No. 325, the Naval War College today consists of six resident schools and several research centers. The John B. Hattendorf Center for Maritime Historical Research serves as a central resource for naval history matters, from exploration and theory to strategy and operations. In addition to contributing to the curriculum and publishing original research, our faculty helps preserve our institutional history.

A. Collections and Libraries

The John B. Hattendorf Center for Maritime Historical Research (HHC): The Hattendorf Historical Center resides under the Naval War College's College of Leadership and Ethics. The Center was established in 2017 and is named for AHA member John B. Hattendorf (Kenyon, AB, 1964; Brown, AM, 1971; Oxford, DPhil, 1979, DLitt, 2016), who served as the College's Ernest J.

King Professor of Maritime History for 32 years, 1984-2016. The Hattendorf Historical Center manages the College's maritime history and sea service heritage programs. This Center serves as a resource and contact point for the Naval War College in all matters relating to research in maritime history and heritage and has particular responsibility for the College's collections of art and historical materials, and for the use and display of such materials.

The department has three complementary and interrelated functional divisions: (1) an Historical Section, which conducts research and writing in naval and maritime history; (2) a Museum Section, which maintains in cooperation with the Naval History and Heritage Command a museum of naval warfare that collects, preserves, and interprets historical properties that illustrate (a) key concepts in the evolution of maritime strategy and naval operations from antiquity to the present, (b) the history of naval activity in the Narragansett Bay region from the colonial period to the present, and (c) the institutional history of the NWC since 1884; (3) an Archives, Manuscripts, and Rare Books Section, the Naval Historical Collection, that manages the College's collection of historical materials.

Naval Historical Collection: The College's archives and manuscript collection, the Naval Historical Collection, is part of the Hattendorf Historical Center located in Mahan Hall. The Naval Historical Collection (NHC), the Naval War College's archives and manuscript repository, comprises more than 6000 linear feet of records documenting the history of the US Naval War College, the history of naval warfare in general, and the history of the Navy in Narragansett Bay. The College Archives within the collection detail the administrative and curricular history of the institution from its founding in 1884 to the present. Included in these holdings are administrative correspondence and memorandums, staff studies, reports and surveys, student theses, papers, faculty and guest lectures, college publications, intelligence and technical research source collections, conference records, and photographs. In addition to the College Archives, the manuscript holdings of the NHC consist of more than 400 collections of personal papers and corporate records, and over 900 individual manuscript items. Significant naval warfare collections include papers of Fleet Admiral Ernest J. King and former college presidents Stephen B. Luce, Alfred Thayer Mahan, Charles H. Stockton, William Veazie Pratt, William S. Sims, Raymond A. Spruance, James B. Stockdale, and Richard G. Colbert. Additional collections include the records of the Newport Naval Training Station, the Newport Naval Base, the Quonset Naval Air Station, and the Naval Torpedo Station. An extensive oral history collection, newspapers, pamphlets, and naval history subject files are also available for research. In addition, the NHC manages the College's 4000+ volume Rare Book collection focused on naval, military and maritime history.

More information about the collections and an increasing number of digital collections are available online through the NHC's website: https://www.usnwcarchives.org.

Naval War College Museum: The NWC Museum is one of the US Navy's 10 official historical museums and is part of the system of museums that is managed under the Director, Naval History and Heritage Command, Washington, DC. The Naval War College Museum is located in Founders Hall, a National Historic Landmark. The building, built originally as a poor house in 1819-20, was where the college began in 1884 and where the second president and lecturer on naval strategy, Captain Alfred Thayer Mahan, delivered the first of his famous lecture series on The Influence of Sea Power Upon History, 1660–1783, first published in 1890. In addition, the museum maintains a loan exhibit to nearby Fort Adams State Park.

The Naval War College Museum collects and preserves materials relating to the history of the art and science of naval warfare, and the naval heritage of the Narragansett Bay, and makes use of these materials for educational exhibitions and associated programs. Generally speaking, museum exhibitions seek to identify the milestones in the evolutionary development of war at sea; explain the importance of the sea as a factor in the formulation and achievement of national policy objectives and as the arena wherein decisions are made through diplomacy and arms; and describe the eventful relationship of the US Navy with Narragansett Bay and with the people of Rhode Island from the birth of the nation to recent times.

Further information is available on the museum's website: https://usnwc.edu/NWC-Museum.

Under the Hattendorf Historical Center, the NWC Museum and Naval Historical Collection serve as the corporate memory of the navy in the region and of the college, as well as a clearinghouse for information on US naval history for the interested public and scholars in the southern New England area. The museum collection is open to study by graduate students and specialists. The museum director, a maritime historian, counsels researchers, delivers talks, and publishes books as well as articles in newspapers, magazines, and scholarly journals.

Library: The Henry E. Eccles Library of the Naval War College in Hewirr Hall, houses a collection of about 500,000. The collection is particularly strong in subjects of interest to the naval profession: naval and military science, history and strategy, defense management, economics, international law, international relations, and contemporary world issues.

B. Programs

The graduate course curriculum comprises elements of strategy, management, and naval operations, and is taught during a ten-month academic year. Although courses taught at the college are open only to selected officers of the armed forces and officials in other government agencies, the college's collections and archives are open to the public; interested parties should write to the president of the college. The college is accredited to award a Master of Arts degree in National Security and Strategic Studies to its senior-level students and the Master of Arts Degree in Defense and Strategic Studies to its intermediate-level students. In addition, the Hattendorf Historical Center faculty offer a Graduate Certificate in Maritime History.

The College sponsors a series of occasional public lectures, which include the Admiral Raymond Spruance Memorial lecture series. Various conferences and lectures afford opportunities to exchange ideas among academic, political, military, and cultural leaders. The programs are open to the public by invitation.

C. Publications

The Naval War College Press publishes the *Naval War College Review*, *The Newport Papers*, the Hattendorf Historical Monograph series, a series of registers and guides to its naval historical collections, and a variety of other special studies on naval warfare, international law, and related subjects that are available to the interested public. A catalog of publications may be found on the college's web site (click on "NWC Press"). Two publications of general interest for historians are *Ubi Sumus? The State of Naval and Maritime History* (1994), *Doing Naval History: Essays toward Improvement* (1995). Recent historical books published by the Naval War College Press by faculty members include *The Evolution of the US Navy's Maritime Strategy, 1977–1986* (2004); *US Naval Strategy in the 1990s: Selected Documents* (2006); *Waves of Hope: the US Navy's Response to the Tsunami in Northern Indonesia* (2007); *US Naval Strategy in the 1980s: Selected Documents* (2008);

Somalia ... From the Sea (2009); *Nineteen-Gun Salute: Case Studies of Operational, Strategic, and Diplomatic Leadership during the 20th and Early 21st Centuries* (2010); *Talking about Naval History* (2012); and *The Hattendorf Prize Lectures* (2019).

D. Fellowships and Awards

The Naval War College Foundation awards annually the $1,500 Edward S. Miller Research Fellowship in Naval History to the researcher who has the greatest need and can make the optimum use of research materials for naval history located in the Naval War College's Archives, Naval Historical Collection, and Henry E. Eccles Library. The recipient is a research fellow in the Hattendorf Historical Center, which provides administrative support. Application deadline October 1.

Since 2011, the Naval War College has awarded at approximately two-year intervals the Hattendorf Prize for Distinguished Original Research in Maritime History. Given to a senior scholar on an international basis, the Prize consists of a $10,000 award, a bronze medal, and a citation along with the awardee's presentation of the Hattendorf Prize Lecture. The Hattendorf Prize Laureates are N.A.M. Rodger, All Souls College, Oxford University (2011); Paul M. Kennedy, Yale University (2014); Captain Dr. Werner Rahn, German Navy (ret.) (2016); Geoffrey Till, King's College, London (2018).

Full-time Faculty

Carpenter, Stanley D. M. (PhD, Florida State 1998; prof.; Strategy and Policy, Coll. Distance Education, Newport) British military/naval, American Revolution, Tudor-Stuart Britain; carpents@usnwc.edu

Carter, Bradley (PhD, Kansas 2004; faculty; Strategy and Policy, Coll. Distance Education, Newport) war and religion, military chaplains, US cultural; bradley.carter@usnwc.edu

Chadbourn, Charles C., III (PhD, Washington 1976; prof.; Strategy and Policy, Coll. Distance Education, Washington, DC) American diplomatic, US naval, US Civil War; chadbouc@usnwc.edu

Chisholm, Donald W. (PhD, California, Berkeley 1984; Stephen B. Luce Prof.; Joint Military Operations) Korean War, World War II naval operations, naval administration; chisholm@usnwc.edu

Creely, Thomas E. (PhD, Salve Regina 2006; prof.; dir., Ethics & Emerging Military Technology Grad. Prog., Leadership & Ethics) ethics of technology, applied ethics; tomcreely@icloud.com

Dancy, Jeremiah Ross (DPhil, Oxford 2012; asst. prof.; Hattendorf Hist. Center) naval and maritime 1700 to present; jeremiah.dancy@usnwc.edu

Demy, Timothy James (PhD, Salve Regina 2003; prof.; Operational and Strategic Leadership) religion and security, US naval, 19th-century American naval; timothy.demy@usnwc.edu

Dennis, Michael A. (PhD, Johns Hopkins 1991; prof.) American science and technology, military, strategy; michael.dennis@usnwc.edu

Elleman, Bruce A. (PhD, Columbia 1993; W.V. Pratt Prof.) China, Japan, Russia; ellemanb@usnwc.edu

Fiorey, Mark E. (MA, Naval War Coll. 2017; asst. prof. and deputy dir.; Hattendorf Hist. Center) US naval, Asia-Pacific, Vietnam; mark.fiorey@usnwc.edu

Getchell, Michelle D. (PhD, Texas, Austin 2014; asst. prof.; Strategy & Policy) Cold War international, Latin America, Soviet Union; michelle.getchell@usnwc.edu

Gvosdev, Nikolas K. (DPhil, Oxford 1996; prof.; National Security Affairs) Russian political, imperial expansion, international affairs; nikolas.gvosdev@usnwc.edu

Helfont, Samuel (PhD, Princeton 2015; asst. prof.; Strategy and Policy, Monterey) modern Middle East, international; samuel.helfont@nps.edu

Hime, Douglas N. (PhD, Salve Regina 2002; prof.; Joint Military Operations) technology, military planning; himed@usnwc.edu

Holmes, James (PhD, Tufts 2003; prof.; Strategy and Policy) maritime strategy in Asia; james.holmes@usnwc.edu

Hoyt, Timothy D. (PhD, Johns Hopkins 1997; prof.; Strategy and Policy) Irish Republicanism, strategic thought, South Asia; hoytt@usnwc.edu

Jones, Michael W. (PhD, Florida State 2004; S&W Prof.; Strategy and Policy, Coll. Distance Education, Monterey) Europe 1715-1815, Napoleon, French Revolution; michael.jones@usnwc.edu

Kelly, Jason M. (PhD, Cornell 2017; asst. prof.; Strategy & Policy) modern China, modern East Asia, US foreign relations; jason.kelly@usnwc.edu

Kohnen, David (PhD, King's Coll., London 2013; dir.; Hattendorf Hist. Center) maritime, civil-military relations, museums and popular culture; david.kohnen@usnwc.edu

Lane, Heidi E. Rutz (PhD, UCLA 2003; assoc. prof.; Strategy and Policy and dir., Middle East Regional Group) terrorism, ethno-religious nationalism, Middle East political development; heidi.lane@usnwc.edu

Luke, Ivan T. (PhD, Salve Regina 2012; assoc. prof.; Joint Military Operations) maritime, maritime security, homeland security; ivan.luke@usnwc.edu

Maurer, John H. (PhD, Tufts 1988; A.T. Mahan Prof.; Strategy and Policy) modern military and naval, world wars, international relations; john.maurer@usnwc.edu

McCranie, Kevin D. (PhD, Florida State 2001; assoc. prof.; Strategy and Policy) naval and maritime, 18th- and 19th-century Europe; kevin.mccranie@usnwc.edu

Mulready-Stone, Kristin K. (PhD, Yale 2009; assoc. prof.; Writing and Teaching Excellence Center) modern China, Vietnam War, Asia-Pacific; kristin.mulreadystone@usnwc.edu

Murray, Nicholas A. (DPhil, Oxford 2007; faculty; Strategy and Policy) modern Britain and Europe, evolution of warfare, military education; nicholas.murray@usnwc.edu

Norton, Richard J. (PhD, Fletcher Sch., Tufts 2003; prof.; National Security Affairs) international relations, colonial wars 1847-1939, South America; nortonr@usnwc.edu

Paine, Sarah C. M. (PhD, Columbia 1993; W.S. Sims Prof.; Strategy and Policy) China, Japan, Russia; sally.paine@usnwc.edu

Pavkovic, Michael F. (PhD, Hawai'i, Manoa 1991; William L. Rodgers Prof. and chair; Strategy and Policy) ancient Greece and Rome, early modern Europe, comparative military; michael.pavkovic@usnwc.edu

Ross, Angus (MA, Providence 2005; prof.) Victorian and Edwardian Royal Navy, 20th-century US Navy, naval innovation/transformation; rossak@usnwc.edu

Sampson, Joyce E. (PhD, Florida State 2000; S&W Prof.; Strategy and Policy, Coll. Distance Education, Monterey) Tudor-Stuart Britain, modern Europe, military and naval; jesampso@nps.navy.mil

Sarantakes, Nicholas E. (PhD, Southern California 1997; assoc. prof.; Strategy and Policy) modern diplomatic and military, US foreign policy; nick.sarantakes@usnwc.edu

Satterfield, George David (PhD, Illinois, Urbana-Champaign 2002; assoc. prof.; Strategy and Policy) early modern military, modern military, strategy; george.satterfield@usnwc.edu

Schultz, Timothy (PhD, Duke 2007; assoc. dean; Electives) science and technology, military, medicine; timothy.schultz@usnwc.edu

Sheehan, John M. (PhD, Naval Postgrad. Sch. 2013; assoc. prof.; Strategy and Policy) American imperialism, US foreign policy, US political; john.sheehan@usnwc.edu

Shuster, Richard J. (PhD, George Washington 2000; faculty; Joint Military Operations) modern Europe, modern military, diplomatic; richard.shuster@usnwc.edu

Stone, David R. (PhD, Yale 1997; prof.; chair, Strategy & Policy) Soviet military and diplomatic, contemporary Russia, South Asia; david.stone@usnwc.edu

Sweeney, Patrick C. (PhD, Salve Regina 2002; prof.; Joint Military Operations) military planning; sweeneyp@usnwc.edu

Toprani, Anand (PhD, Georgetown 2012; asst. prof.; Strategy and Policy) modern diplomatic and military, intelligence, energy geopolitics; anand.topriani@usnwc.edu

Vego, Milan Nikola (PhD, George Washington 1981; R.K. Turner Prof.; Joint Military Operations) naval and military theory, German/Austrian military and naval, Pacific naval war 1941-45; vegom@usnwc.edu

Walling, Karl F. (PhD, Chicago 1992; prof.; Strategy and Policy, Monterey) ancient and modern political philosophy, American political thought, strategy and grand strategy; kfwallin@nps.edu

Wilson, Andrew R. (PhD, Harvard 1998; prof.; Strategy and Policy) China; wilsona@usnwc.edu

Wilson, Evan (DPhil, Oxford 2015; asst. prof.; Hattendorf Hist. Center) naval and maritime 1700 to present; evan.wilson@usnwc.edu

Retired/Emeritus Faculty

Baer, George W. (PhD, Harvard 1965; A.T. Mahan Prof. and chair emeritus; Strategy and Policy) modern naval, military, international relations; gwbaer6@comcast.net

Blanton, Harold D. (PhD, Florida State 1999; S&W Prof. emeritus; Strategy and Policy, Coll. Distance Education, Monterey) Napoleon, French Revolution, modern Europe; hdblanto@gmail.com

Cook, Martin L. (PhD, Chicago 1985; James Bond Stockdale Prof. emeritus) military ethics, ancient, airpower; martin.cook@usafa.edu

Fuller, William C., Jr. (PhD, Harvard 1980; prof. emeritus; Strategy and Policy) Russia, terrorism; fullerw@comcast.net

Gatchel, Theodore L. (MS, Naval Postgrad. Sch. 1971; prof. emeritus; Joint Military Operations) 20th-century amphibious warfare, fortifications, infantry weapons and tactics; gatchelt@gmail.com

Hagan, Kenneth J. (PhD, Claremont Grad. 1970; prof. emeritus; Strategy and Policy, Coll. Distance Education, Monterey) US naval, US military, 19th-century US; kenhagan@comcast.net

Hattendorf, John Brewster (LITTD, Oxford 2016; Ernest J. King prof. emeritus and sr. mentor) maritime, naval, early modern Europe 1689-1815; john.hattendorf@usnwc.edu

Kaiser, David E. (PhD, Harvard 1976; prof. emeritus; Strategy and Policy) modern diplomatic, US foreign policy

Lee, Bradford A. (PhD, Cambridge 1974; prof. emeritus; Strategy and Policy) 20th-century military, diplomatic, economic; balee22@verizon.net

Masakowski, Yvonne R. (PhD, CUNY 1996; assoc. prof. emeritus; Leadership & Ethics) foreign policy, artificial intelligence, leadership, EEMT; dym46@yahoo.com

Ohls, Gary J. (PhD, Texas Christian 2008; JMO Prof. emeritus; Joint Military Operations, Coll. Distance Education, Monterey) military, naval, amphibious; garyohls@aol.com

Owens, MacKubin Thomas (PhD, Dallas 1982; prof. emeritus; National Security Affairs and assoc. dean, Academics and Electives) American military, US civil-military relations, American Civil War; owensm@usnwc.edu

Smith, Douglas V. (PhD, Florida State 2005; prof. emeritus; Coll. Distance Education, Newport) US and European military, naval, 19th-century Russia; smithdv@usnwc.edu

Waghelstein, John D. (PhD, Temple 1990; prof. emeritus; Joint Military Operations) Latin America, world military thought, American military; john.waghelstein@usnwc.edu

Staff

Cembrola, Robert (BA, Rhode Island 1977; exhibits mgr.; Naval War Coll. Museum) US naval, maritime, underwater archaeology; robert.cembrola@usnwc.edu

Delmage, Elizabeth (MLIS, Rhode Island; asst. archivist) archives, 20th-century US, US naval; elizabeth.delmage@usnwc.edu

DeLucia, Elizabeth (MA, Marist 2014; dir., education and public outreach) museum education, social studies education, volunteer coordination; elizabeth.delucia@usnwc.edu

Doane, Rob (MA, Loyola, Chicago 2003; curator; Naval War Coll. Museum) US naval, maritime; robert.doane@usnwc.edu

Parillo, Stacie (MS, Simmons 2011; MA, Suffolk 2003; dir.; Naval Hist. Collection Archives) stacie.parillo@usnwc.edu

New York State Archives

New York State Education Dept., 11A42 Cultural Education Center, Empire State Plaza, 222 Madison Ave., Albany, NY 12230. 518.474.8955. Fax 518.408.1940. Email: archref@nysed.gov. Website: http://www.archives.nysed.gov/.

The New York State Archives is responsible for ensuring the preservation of, and access to, all records of New York state government that have enduring legal and historical value. The archives is a unit of the Office of Cultural Education in the State Education Department.

A. Collections and Libraries

The New York State Archives regulates the disposition and archival preservation of state and local government records, provides guidance and services to help governments better manage their records, and supports statewide activities to strengthen historical records programs in both the public and private sectors.

The archives contains over 150,000 cubic feet of records that document many aspects of New York state's history and heritage. The archives' holdings date from the 17th-century Dutch colonial period to the present and exist on parchment, paper, and microfilm, and in computer-readable formats. These government records document the organization, functions, policies, and programs of the agencies and offices that created them. They also document the interaction of the state and its citizens—people from diverse social and economic backgrounds whose lives are affected by the activities of their government.

The holdings of the archives are particularly strong in the following areas: Dutch and British colonial periods, Erie Canal, War of 1812, Civil War, World Wars I and II, social welfare, correctional and mental health services, state lands, banking and insurance industry, colonial and state courts, environmental issues, motion picture scripts and censorship, and radical political activities.

B. Programs

The archives has extensive microfilm holdings. Copies of unrestricted microfilms can be purchased or borrowed by libraries. Digital Collections is available providing access to thousands of images of archival records, particularly photographs and maps. Selected records of genealogical and historical interest have been digitized and indexed by Ancestry.com.

C. Publications

The state archives has an online catalog and finding aids with current information on holdings. Numerous topical guides and several special indexes/databases are available on its web site. It published a *Guide* (1995) to its holdings as well as guides available both online and/or in print on specific subject areas: *The Union Preserved: A Guide to Civil War Records in the New York State Archives*; *Duely and Constantly Kept: A History of the New York Supreme Court*; *The Mighty Chain: A Guide to Canal Records*; *Enduring Images: A Guide to Photographic Records*; *The Lusk Committee: A Guide to the Records of the Joint Legislative Committee to Investigate Seditious Activities*; *Guide to Records Relating to the Revolutionary War*; *A Spirit of Sacrifice: New York's Response to the Great War*; and *They Also Served: New Yorkers on the Home Front (World War II)*. A complete list of publications is available from the state archives. Information about archives holdings and services is available through the archives' web site.

D. Fellowships and Awards

The Larry J. Hackman Research Residency Program offers travel grants for research in the state archives. The program is supported by the New York State Archives Partnership Trust. Information and applications can be obtained from New York Archives, 11A42 Cultural Education Center, Albany, NY 12230. 518.474.8955 or online at www.nysarchivestrust.org. E-mail: hackmanres@nysed.gov.

Staff

Allen, Emily (MS, SUNY, Albany 2005; sr. archivist) accessioning, archival outreach; emily.allen@nysed.gov

Arpey, Andrew W. (PhD, SUNY, Albany 2000; assoc. archivist) electronic access, legal and corrections records; andrew.arpey@nysed.gov

Backman, Prudence (MLIS, Simmons 1980; principal archivist) collections management, electronic access; prudence.backman@nysed.gov

Brinkman, Jamie (sr. archivist) digitization; jamie.brinkman@nysed.gov

Bumpers, Jasmine (MS, SUNY, Albany 2012; sr. archivist) cataloging; jasmine.bumpers@nysed.gov

Carroll, Heather (BA, Bard 2005; sr. archivist) statewide archival advisory services

Diefenderfer, John (MA,MLS, SUNY, Albany 2002; sr. archivist) statewide archival advisory services; john.diefenderfer@nysed.gov

Folts, James D., Jr. (PhD, Rochester 1976; principal archivist and head; Researcher Services) records access, outreach, court records, special projects; jim.folts@nysed.gov

Gonsalves, Maggi (sr. archivist) electronic records; maggi.gonsalves@nysed.gov

Gorman, William P. (MA, SUNY, Albany 1979; sr. archivist) reference; bill.gorman@nysed.gov

Gray, Monica (MA, Univ. Coll., London 1993; assoc. archivist and asst. head) reference, digitization; monica.gray@nysed.gov

Hess, AnnMarie (BA, SUNY, Buffalo 2005; sr. archivist) collections management; annmarie.hess@nysed.gov

Maloney, Michael (MSIS, SUNY, Albany 2012; sr. archivist) collections management; michael.maloney@nysed.gov

McPeters, Jackson (MLS, SUNY, Albany 1992; sr. archivist) accessioning; jackson.mcpeters@nysed.gov

Swaney, Keith (MA,MLS, Maryland, Coll. Park 2007; sr. archivist) digitization, electronic access, cataloging; keith.swaney@nysed.gov

Weddle, Bonita (MA, Kent State 1998; assoc. archivist) electronic records; bonita.weddle@nysed.gov

North Carolina Office of Archives and History

109 E. Jones St., Raleigh, NC 27601-2807. 919.814.6640. Email: ahweb@ncdcr.gov. Website: https://www.ncdcr.gov/about/ office-archives-and-history.

Alternate Address: 4610 Mail Service Center, Raleigh, NC 27699

A. Collections and Libraries

The *Division of State History Museums* is comprised of the main North Carolina Museum of History in Raleigh, and six regional museums: the Museum of the Albemarle in Elizabeth City; the Museum of the Cape Fear Historical Complex in Fayetteville; the Mountain Gateway Museum and Heritage Center in Old Fort; the North Carolina Maritime Museum in Beaufort; the North Carolina Maritime Museum at Southport; and the Graveyard of the Atlantic Museum in Hatteras. The division collects and preserves artifacts and other historical materials relating to the history and heritage of North Carolina. Its collections feature more than 150,000 items representing six centuries of North Carolina history. These artifacts are classified as: decorative arts, furnishings, costumes, uniforms, tools and equipment, industry, folklife, numismatics, currency, weapons, textiles, anthropology, paintings, graphics, maritime, military, medicine, transportation, toys, tobacco, and North Carolina history and culture. Museum patrons can access information about artifacts in the collection via the Internet. Select images and artifact records can be located on the museum's website at www.ncdcr.gov/places-to-go/museums.

The *North Carolina State Archives* contains over 50,000 cubic feet of material dating from 1663, consisting of official records of the colony and state of North Carolina. It includes legislative, executive, and judicial records of state agencies; original and microfilmed records of the North Carolina counties; and special collections materials that supplement and complement the public records of North Carolina. These consist of private manuscript collections of individuals and families active in state and national life, or which document the history and culture of the state, including hundreds of account books from the 18th through the 20th centuries. There are records of statewide civic, professional, fraternal, and social organizations, and student academic and financial aid files from defunct post-secondary schools and colleges in the state. Other special collections materials include pre-1913 records of birth, marriage, and death from family Bibles; a significant collection of maps portraying all or parts of North Carolina; and papers and records documenting North Carolina's military heritage and its participation in wars in which the United States has been involved. Significant audiovisual materials include a reference file containing over two million negatives from the 1890s to the present day, photograph collections, motion picture film, and audio recordings. The Outer Banks History Center collects coastal and maritime history. The Western Regional Archives in Asheville collects private manuscripts, organizational records, and photographic collections related to the western region of the state, with an emphasis on Black Mountain College. The State Archives provides online access to many of these materials through digital collections, social media, websites, and an online catalog. The Historic Sites Collection includes artifacts that fall under the classifications of decorative arts and furnishings, costumes and uniforms, photography, industry, archaeology, folklore, currency, weapons, textiles, anthropology, paintings, graphics, medicine, agriculture, literature, and transportation. The Historic Property Inventory Files contain information and photographs of significant historic and architectural properties in North Carolina and include over 9,000 individual files on such properties.

The *Office of State Archaeology* holds over a million artifacts from prehistoric Native American, colonial, Civil War, and historic shipwreck sites throughout the state, including the internationally famous *Queen Anne's Revenge* pirate shipwreck.

B. Programs

The *Office of Archives and History* cooperates with other historical agencies, colleges, and universities to offer seminars, workshops, and lectures on many aspects of the state's history. Through the Federation of North Carolina Historical Societies, the office assists local historical societies and museums by providing information and professional training in such areas as preservation, museum collections and exhibits, and records management. Student internships are developed in conjunction with colleges and universities. The office also sponsors History Day in North Carolina.

The office operates 27 state-owned historic sites associated with various aspects of North Carolina's political, social, and economic history, including Native American and African American sites. These sites, located throughout the state, regularly offer guided tours and special programs. A number of them have visitor centers with permanent and temporary exhibits. Some charge admission fees.

The office operates seven museums across the state, which interpret North Carolina history, including regional and maritime history and other topics through short- and long-time exhibitions. A variety of educational programming and publications are available to the visitor on-site or through distance-learning technologies. All museums offer admittance free-of-charge, with the exception of some special exhibitions that may charge a fee.

The *Archaeology* and *Historic Preservation* sections are responsible for identifying and protecting the state's archaeological and architectural resources. Included among their responsibilities are issuing permits for exploration of sites on state lands and shipwrecks in state waters, operating the National Register program, reviewing projects for effects on historic resources, and advising constituents on matters of archaeology, preservation, and restoration.

The *State Archives* manages the state's large record collection and provides services to researchers doing historical and genealogical work, including offering annual workshops, online tutorials, and blog posts on North Carolina history and records management. Staff members also advise local governments and private agencies on imaging and records management, as well as providing best practices documents on the creation, management, and preservation of electronic records.

C. Publications

The office publishes a softcover series of books covering a wide range of North Carolina historical topics; the popular *North Carolina Troops, 1861–1865: A Roster* series; and the quarterly journal *North Carolina Historical Review*.

D. Fellowships and Awards

Not applicable.

Staff

Bartos, Ramona (JD,OMS, Georgia 2002; dir., Division of Historical Resources; admin., Hist. Preservation Section and deputy state hist. preservation officer) historic preservation, environmental review, local historic preservation programs

Cherry, Kevin (PhD, North Carolina, Chapel Hill 2010; dir., Office of Archives and History; state hist. preservation officer) North Carolina, higher education; kevin.cherry@ncdcr.gov

Futch, Jeff (MA, North Carolina State 1994; admin., Western Office of Dept. of Cultural Resources) public; jeff.futch@ncdcr.gov

Howard, Kenneth (JD, Wake Forest Law Sch. 1982; dir., Division of State History Museums) ken.howard@ncdcr.gov

Koonts, Sarah E. (MA, North Carolina State 1993; dir., Division of Archives and Records) archival materials, records management; sarah.koonts@ncdcr.gov

Lanier, Michelle (MA, North Carolina, Chapel Hill; dir., Division of State Historic Sites and Properties) inclusion/equity/accessibility/diversity, museum and site management, emergency response, African American history and culture

Mintz, John (MA, Arkansas 1989; state archaeologist) economic anthropology, ethnohistory, public archaeology; john.mintz@ncdcr.gov

Ohio History Connection

800 E. 17th Ave., Columbus, OH 43211-2474. 800.686.6124. Fax 614.297.2411. Website: https://www.ohiohistory.org/.

Alternate Address: 1-71 and 17th Ave., Columbus, OH

Founded in 1885, the nonprofit Ohio History Connection provides a wide array of statewide services and programs related to collecting, preserving, and interpreting Ohio's rich archaeological and natural history.

A. Collections and Libraries

Since 1885, the Ohio History Connection has collected more than two million items related to the state's heritage. With a network of more than 50 historical sites across the state and over 7,000 members, the Ohio History Connection is one of the largest state historical organizations in the country. Its mission is to spark discovery of Ohio's stories, embrace the present, share the past, and transform the future.

A private, nonprofit organization, the Ohio History Connection serves as the state's agent in historical matters in return for an appropriation that constitutes, typically, about 40% of its total budget. Other financial resources include gifts, grants, contract services, admissions, sales revenues and state capital funds. As a service to the state of Ohio, Ohio History Connection offers varied educational services for teachers and students; manages the state museum archives, and historic preservation office; provides support and services to regional and local historical organizations across the state; and oversees a network of historical sites and museums, which attracts nearly half a million visitors annually. The Ohio History Connection has a 21-member board of trustees. Nine trustees appointed by the governor. Nine are elected by the membership. And, three are elected by the Board itself.

The Ohio History Connection maintains an extensive historical research library that reflects the diverse cultural, historical, political, and industrial achievements of the state of Ohio. The collections are comprised of 142,000 volumes of books; more than 15,000 maps; 85,000 rolls of microfilm; 12,000 sheets of microfiche; 10,700 cubic feet of manuscript material; and 8,500 cubic feet of audiovisual material, including 1 million photographic images. Included in the library holdings are documents from the settlement of the Northwest Territory, and extensive Civil War papers, and correspondence. The society houses the largest collection of early and modern Ohio newspapers in existence. The collection is comprised of 4,500 titles, 20,000 volumes, and 49,979 rolls of microfilm. As the State Archives of Ohio, the Ohio History Connection collects, maintains, and provides access to 13,500 cubic feet of local government records and 20,000 cubic feet of state archives. Digital exhibits and online databases such as the *African American Experience in*

Ohio, Beyond the Call of Duty, Fight for the Colors, Ohio Memory Online Scrapbook, OhioPix, and the *Online Death Index* allow collection access to more than 1,000,000 visitors a year.

The archives/library presents a variety of workshops throughout the year to historical and genealogical organizations. Individual researchers have the opportunity to attend workshops designed to introduce family history researchers to the extensive amount of records and resources available. The state archives participates in the state's records management program, assists local governments with records management issues, and provides leadership and guidance in developing solutions for preservation of government records in electronic formats.

The Ohio History Connection's museum collections represent a broad range of natural, cultural, social, political, and industrial materials from prehistoric times to the present. In total, its three-dimensional objects number just under 2,000,000 items. The collections consist of over 1,000,000 archeological items, primarily prehistoric American Indian cultures in Ohio. Of these, the collections relating to the Hopewell, Adena, and Fort Ancient cultures are particularly strong. The history collections contain approximately 250,000 items, featuring a broad range of objects that document life in Ohio from the first settlement of the Northwest Territories to the present. These collections are strong in ceramics, glass, textiles, firearms, and Ohio aviation history. The natural history collections consist of over 350,000 specimens and are outstanding in Ohio fossils, skeletal collections, insects, and minerals.

B. Programs

Each year, the Ohio History Connection offers an array of exhibits, tours, field trip opportunities, seminars, lectures, educational workshops, audiovisual presentations, and special events. It coordinates distance learning programs, a traveling case program for schools, the National History Day in Ohio program for students in grades 6–12, and manages an online encyclopedia, *Ohio History Central,* designed for students and teachers. The organization's educational programs also provide extensive teacher professional development programs for history teachers through the Teaching American History program. In addition, this unit partners with and provides administrative support for the Ohio Academy of History, a 300-member association of history professors across Ohio, and for the Ohio Council for Social Studies, the state's 1300-member association for K–12 social studies teachers.

The Ohio History Connection maintains 50+ historic, archaeological, and natural history sites and museums throughout the state. Nine are accredited by the American Association of Museums—the Ohio Historical Center, Ohio Village, Adena Mansion & Gardens, Armstrong Air & Space Museum, Campus Martius Museum, Fort Ancient, Fort Meigs, Hayes Presidential Center, and Johnston Farm & Indian Agency. Four archaeological sites are on the United States' World Heritage Tentative List—Fort Ancient, Newark Earthworks, and Serpent Mound. Thirteen are designated National Historic Landmarks (such as Dunbar House, Grant Boyhood Home, Harding Home and Tomb, and Rankin House), three are National Natural Landmarks (including Cedar Bog and Fort Hill), and two are listed on the National Register of Historic Places for their national significance (including Zoar Village). Thirty six more are listed on the National Register for state or local significance such as Flint Ridge and Schoenbrunn Village. Three are dedicated state nature preserves including Wahkeena. Major museums include the Museum of Ceramics, the National Afro-American Museum and Cultural Center, National Road/Zane Grey Museum, the Ohio River Museum, and Youngstown Historical Center of Industry & Labor.

Today, 49 of these historic sites and museums are managed by a total of 42 local organizations and agencies on behalf of the Ohio History Connection.

The Ohio Historic Preservation Office is the official historic preservation agency of the state of Ohio. A division of the Ohio History Connection, it has developed since 1967 when the Ohio History Connection was designated to manage responsibilities delegated to the state by Congress in the National Historic Preservation Act of 1966. It is funded in part by an annual grant from the US Department of the Interior's Historic Preservation Fund, matched by the Ohio History Connection, the state of Ohio, and other public and private sources. A staff of preservation professionals identifies historic places and archaeological sites in Ohio through the Ohio Historic Inventory and Ohio Archaeological Inventory; nominates eligible Ohio properties to the National Register of Historic Places; reviews proposed rehabilitation work on historic buildings for state and federal tax credits; consults on more than 7,500 federally funded or licensed undertakings a year in Ohio, to ensure that alternatives are considered in any action that would damage or destroy properties listed on, or eligible for, the National Register, qualifies communities in Ohio whose programs meet federal standards for Certified Local Government status and oversees grants to them; and consults on conservation of buildings and sites, offering free technical advice. The Ohio Historic Preservation Office also offers a preservation library, Building Doctor Clinics, and publications like the *Old-Building Owner's Manual*. Outstanding contributions to preservation of Ohio's historic, architectural, and archaeological resources are honored annually with Ohio Historic Preservation Office Awards.

Through a partnership with the Ohio Local History Alliance, the Ohio History Connection Local History Office works with more than 600 historical organizations in the state. The office provides technical assistance through workshops, on site consultation, historical organization assessments, and strategic planning. It also organizes and administers 10 regional meetings, an awards program, and a statewide Annual Meeting. The office also publishes the association's newsletter, *The Local Historian*. The Local History Office also provides administrative support to the Society of Ohio Archivists, a statewide organization of over 650 archivists.

C. Publications

The Ohio History Connection publishes Echoes Magazine, a bi-monthly history magazine and newsletter, and *Ohio Histor-e-news*, an online newsletter.

D. Fellowships and Awards

Not applicable.

Omohundro Institute of Early American History and Culture

PO Box 8781, Williamsburg, VA 23187-8781. 757.221.1114. Fax 757.221.1047. Email: oieahc@wm.edu. Website: https://oieahc.wm.edu/.

Alternate Address: 400 Landrum Dr., Ground Fl., Swem Library, Williamsburg, VA 23185

A. Collections and Libraries

The Omohundro Institute supports early American scholarship broadly understood to include the Atlantic World roughly during the years 1450 to 1820. Except for a limited microfilm collection, chiefly of early American newspapers, the OI does not maintain a research collection. The staff will assist visiting scholars in using materials in the libraries of William & Mary (W&M).

B. Programs

The OI is the publisher of the leading journal for historians of early America, the *William and Mary Quarterly*, as well as an award-winning series of monographs. Additional support for scholars of Vast Early America is provided in the form of pre and postdoctoral fellowships, conferences, seminars, colloquia and online finding aids—the List, the Map, and Works-in-Progress—for scholars interested in learning more about events and fellowships around the world of particular interest to historians of Vast Early America. A blog (*Uncommon Sense*) and a podcast (*Ben Franklin's World* with host Liz Covart) provide additional vehicles for the Early Americanist community to reach colleagues in the field as well as the broader public. The OI also is a primary partner with W&M, King's College London and the Royal Archives on the Georgian Papers Programme. You can read about all of these programs and more on their website, https://oieahc.wm.edu.

In partnership with the Department of History at William & Mary, the OI provides apprenticeships in scholarly editing to students pursuing the M.A. and Ph.D. degrees in history at W&M. Participants work directly with the OI's publications staff. Address admissions inquiries to the Director of Graduate Studies, Dept. of History, William & Mary, PO Box 8795, Williamsburg, VA 23187.

C. Publications

The *William and Mary Quarterly* is the leading journal of early American history, an interdisciplinary academic publication that has featured history, political science, art history, literature, architecture and material culture, and digital humanities. Nearly half a million user sessions accessed the *WMQ* last year, making it among the top 3% of the now 17,000 journals housed in JSTOR. One of the ten founding journals in JSTOR, the *WMQ* has a subscription list of over 3,500 people and institutions, including nearly 400 located outside the United States. The OI's book program has published more than 200 volumes; many are regarded as classics and are regularly adopted for classroom use at both the undergraduate and graduate levels. OI books, released at an average rate of five per year, have received over 150 major commendations, including a Pulitzer Prize, a National Book Award, two Frederick Douglass Book Prizes, and seven Bancroft Prizes—mostly recently for the 2017 publication of Douglas Winiarski's *Darkness Falls on the Land of Light: Experiencing Religious Awakenings in Eighteenth-Century New England*. Significant scholarly editions published by the OI include *The Papers of John Marshall* and *The Law Papers of St. George Tucker*.

D. Fellowships and Awards

The OI annually awards approximately thirty fellowships to scholars at many levels, including advanced graduate students and senior scholars. The majority of fellowship applications are due *November 1* each year. Applications for an additional round of the OI–Jamestown Rediscovery Foundation short-term fellowships and the Georgian Papers Programme fellowships are due March 1 each year.

The *OI-NEH Postdoctoral Fellowship* is a two-year postdoctoral fellowship awarded to an entry-level scholar in any field of early American studies. Applications are due November 1 for the term beginning the following July. Foreign nationals are eligible to apply. Fellows must have completed all requirements for the doctorate, *including defense*, by the close of the application period and may not have previously published a book or have a book under contract. The OI holds first claim on publishing the appointed fellow's completed manuscript. The fellowship includes concurrent appointment in the appropriate department as visiting professor in the appropriate department at William & Mary and teaching a total of six semester hours during the two-year term.

The OI also offers short-term fellowship opportunities. These include opportunities offered in conjunction with the Jamestown Rediscovery Foundation, the Folger Shakespeare Library, and the Georgian Papers Programme. Scholars at the pre and postdoctoral levels are invited to apply.

Jamestown Rediscovery–Omohundro Institute (JR-OI) fellowships support the study of topics that relate directly to the holdings at the JRF. Up to four month-long fellowships may be offered in a year over the course of two application periods, one of which closes November 1 and the other of which closes March 1.

Folger Shakespeare Library fellowships support scholars with strong interests in Atlantic history, colonial history, literary studies, performance history, and material culture so that they may make use of the collections at the Folger Shakespeare Library for one month as well as participate in the Folger Institute's intellectual community. Applications are due November 1 each year.

The *Georgian Papers Programme* is a collaborative project with W&M, King's College London and the Royal Archives to study and digitize the papers housed at Windsor Castle pertaining to the Georgian period. Up to eight awards are offered each year by the OI. Applications are due November 1 and March 1. Fellows must be US or UK citizens. Successful applicants must undergo a security clearance before beginning work at Windsor Castle.

Untenured faculty may apply for the *Scholars' Workshop*, an opportunity to work with the editorial staff and colleagues in the early American field during a ten day period in July on either a book manuscript or journal article already in progress. Books under contract to a publisher will not be considered. Up to eight participants are chosen each year. Applications are due November 1.

The *Lapidus-OIEAHC Predoctoral Fellowships* offer up to eight $1000 fellowships annually to support advanced graduate student research related to Early American and transatlantic print culture, including authorship, production, circulation, and reception. Applications are due November 1.

Scholars in conjunction with archivists and librarians at historical collections are invited to apply jointly for the *Lapidus Initiative for Digital Collections Fellowships*. Awards of up to $5,000 are given to promote creative use of digital tools and materials, and bring scholars and collections specialists together to make collections available for digital scholarship. Applications are due November 1.

New in 2019! Scholars of the American revolution and early republic, in conjunction with collections specialists, are invited to apply jointly for the *OI–Mount Vernon Fellowships for Digital Collections in the American Founding Era*. Up to two awards of up to $5,000 each are given to promote creative use of digital tools and materials, and bring scholars and collections specialists together to make collections related to the American Founding era, broadly defined to span from 1763 to 1800, with preference for projects connected to George Washington and his world, available for digital scholarship. Applications are due November 1.

Additional information regarding all application requirements and deadlines is available at oieahc.wm.edu/fellowships/.

Staff

Adelman, Joseph M. (PhD, Johns Hopkins 2010; asst. editor, Digital Initiatives) US printing and news circulation, US post office, new media and blogging; adelman.joseph@gmail.com

Amundsen, Karin Alana (PhD, Southern California, 2017; postdoc. fellow) early America, metallurgy, mining, English colonization; kamundsen@wm.edu

Arena, Carolyn Marie (PhD, Columbia 2017; postdoctoral fellow) early modern colonization, slavery and trade, colonial Caribbean; cmarena@wm.edu

Arnette, Carol (BA, Richmond 1988; asst. editor, William and Mary Quarterly) cgarnette@wm.edu

Bassi, Daniella F. (MA, William and Mary; editorial asst.; Publications)

Burdette, M. Kathryn (BA, Connecticut Coll. 1994; sr. project editor, Books; Publications) editing, early America, science fiction; mkburd@wm.edu

Chew, Virginia Montijo (MA, William and Mary 2001; managing editor, Books; Publications) editing, early America; vlmont@wm.edu

Covart, Elizabeth M. (PhD, California, Davis 2011; editor, Digital Projects) podcasts and new media, American Revolution; liz@benfranklinsworld.com

Daen, Laurel R. (PhD, William and Mary 2016; postdoctoral fellow) disability and sickness in early America, 18th century, 19th century; lrdaen@wm.edu

Holl, Shawn A. (BA, Notre Dame 1992; dir., Development) saholl@wm.edu

Howard, Martha (MA, Chicago 1991; dir., Conferences & Communications) mxhowa@wm.edu

Kelly, Catherine E. (PhD, Rochester 1992; editor, Books; Publications) women, 18th century, 19th century; cekelly01@wm.edu

Musselwhite, Margaret T. (MA, William and Mary 2006; managing editor, William and Mary Quarterly) editing, early America; mstill@wm.edu

Piker, Joshua A. (PhD, Cornell 1998; editor, William and Mary Quarterly) Native Americans, Creek peoples, early America; japiker@wm.edu

Popper, Nicholas (PhD, Princeton 2007; book review editor, William and Mary Quarterly) early modern Britain; nspopper@wm.edu

Singh, Vineeta (PhD, California, San Diego 2018; postdoctoral fellow) institutions, slavery; vsingh@email.wm.edu

Stevenson, Kaylan M. (MA, William and Mary 2013; manuscript editor, Books; Publications) early America, women; kmstevenson@wm.edu

White, Holly N. Stevens (PhD, William and Mary 2017; asst. editor, Digital Projects; Publications) children in early America; hnstevens@wm.edu

Wulf, Karin A. (PhD, Johns Hopkins 1993; exec. dir.) colonial America, women, gender; kawulf@wm.edu

Zimmerli, Nadine (PhD, Wisconsin-Madison 2011; assoc. editor, Books; Publications) American Indian, early America, modern Europe; nizimmerli@wm.edu

Organization of American Historians

112 N. Bryan Ave., Bloomington, IN 47408-4141. 812.855.7311. Fax 812.855.0696. Email: oah@oah.org. Website: https://www.oah.org/.

From its beginning as a small regional group, the Organization of American Historians (OAH) has grown into a large international association of more than 7,500 individual members and institutional subscribers interested in the full scope of US history.

A. Collections and Libraries

The Archives of the OAH is located at the Ruth Lilly Library at Indiana University-Purdue University Indianapolis (IUPUI).

B. Programs

The organization was founded in 1907 as the Mississippi Valley Historical Association (MVHA) and was headquartered in Lincoln, Nebraska, for nearly half a century. Originally focusing on the history of the Mississippi Valley, the association evolved into the primary organization of specialists in US history. Membership is open to anyone interested in the organization's mission: promoting excellence in the scholarship, teaching, and presentation of American history, and encouraging the wide discussion of historical questions and the equitable treatment of all practitioners of history.

Each spring the OAH holds a four-day annual meeting, which is attended by approximately 2,000 people, along with nearly 75 exhibiting companies that display and sell their recent publications in American history. The program committee organizes approximately 250 sessions and workshops concerned with scholarly and professional matters of interest to specialists in US history at all levels and in all settings. In addition, many smaller historical groups use the OAH conference to schedule speakers and discussions at breakfasts, luncheons, and special sessions.

The OAH Distinguished Lectureship Program, established by OAH President Gerda Lerner in 1981, coordinates and arranges lectures by prominent scholars on a variety of historical topics. More than 500 speakers who have made major contributions to the many fields of US history participate in the program. Lectureship fees, beginning at $1,000 and paid directly as donations to the OAH, enable the organization to function more effectively on behalf of the historical profession. Host institutions also pay the lecturer's travel and lodging expenses. A list of lecturers and their specific topics is available at the OAH web site.

The OAH is governed by an executive board of 15 voting members and has a number of committees that work to promote history and focus on topics of particular interest to the organization. The OAH also has representatives on committees that function jointly with other organizations. The OAH's service committees are: Annual Meeting Local Resource Committee; Annual Meeting Program Committee; Committee on Committees; Committee on Academic Freedom; Committee on Community Colleges; Committee on Disability and Disability History; OAH-Japanese Association for American Studies Japan Historians Collaborative Committee; Committee on Marketing and Communications; International Committee; OAH Committee on National Park Service Collaboration; Committee on Part-Time, Adjunct, and Contingent Employment; Committee on Public History; Committee on Research and Government; Committee on the Status of African American, Latino/a, Asian American, and Native American (ALANA) Historians and ALANA Histories; Committee on the Status of Lesbian, Gay, Bisexual, Transgender, and Queer (LGBTQ) Historians and Histories; Committee on the Status of Women in the Historical Profession; Committee on Teaching; International Committee; Journal of American History Editorial Board; Leadership Advisory Council; and Membership Committee.

The OAH's joint committees and groups to which it sends representatives are: the Advisory Committee on Historical Diplomatic Documentation; American Council of Learned Societies; National Historical Publications and Records Commission; National Museum of Afro-American History and Culture Planning Council; National Council for History Education; and the National Humanities Alliance.

C. Publications

The OAH publishes the *Journal of American History,* the leading scholarly publication in the field of US history and well known as the major resource for the study, investigation, and teaching of the nation's past. Appearing quarterly since 1914—first as the *Mississippi Valley Historical Review* (1914–64) and then as the *Journal of American History* (1964–)—the *Journal* has a distinguished history, publishing many prize-winning and widely reprinted scholarly articles. The *Journal* also features historiographic essays and reviews of books, films, exhibitions, and web sites. Its ongoing initiative in internationalization places American history in a global context, and the "Teaching the JAH" web project brings the latest scholarly research into the US history classroom. The *Journal's* recent scholarship bibliography is now available to OAH members as an online searchable database. See the website at www.journalofamericanhistory.org.

The American Historian is the OAH's newest publication and debuted in August 2014. The quarterly magazine covers the broad variety of needs and interests of OAH members, including primary and secondary teaching, professional development, research, recent scholarship, public history, digital history, and contemporary debates about the past.

Published from July 1973 to November 2009, the *OAH Newsletter* included historical essays, regular columns, articles on current developments in the historical profession, and professional opportunity announcements. The *OAH Newsletter* ceased its print edition in November 2009 and its content has been moved to the organization's website.

Beginning in the fall of 2011, the organization started publishing *OAH Update,* a semi-monthly electronic newsletter for all members. Each issue contains news of the profession, advocacy updates, and timely information about OAH programs and services.

The quarterly *OAH Magazine of History,* published from 1985 to 2013, was a valuable teaching resource and addressed the interests, needs, and concerns facing teachers of US history from middle school through the university level. Each issue of the *OAH Magazine* featured historical scholarship on a specific period or area where contemporary research has yielded new information and insights. While no longer published, OAH members receive access to the entire archive of the *OAH Magazine* online.

D. Fellowships and Awards

The OAH sponsors or cosponsors awards and prizes in recognition of scholarly and professional achievement in the fields of US history. The *Roy Rosenzweig Distinguished Service Award* is presented each year to an individual or individuals whose contributions have significantly enriched the understanding of and appreciation for American history. The *Ray Allen Billington Prize* is given for the best book on American frontier history, while the *Lawrence W. Levine Award* recognizes the best book in American cultural history. The *Merle Curti Award* recognizes books in the fields of American social and intellectual history. The Binkley-Stephenson Award is for the best scholarly article published in the *Journal of American History* during the preceding calendar year. The *Frederick Jackson Turner Award* is given to the author of a book on American history who has not previously published a book-length work. The *OAH Tachau Teacher of the Year Award* is given annually to a precollegiate teacher who has enhanced the intellectual development of other history teachers and/or students. The *Louis Pelzer Memorial Award* is given for the best essay in American history by a graduate student. The *OAH Friend of History Award* recognizes an individual who is not a professional historian, or an institution or organization, for outstanding support for the pursuit of historical research, for the public presentation of history, or for the work of the organization. The *Erik Barnouw Award* is given in recognition of an outstanding television program or documentary film concerned with American history.

The *Lerner-Scott Prize* is awarded annually for the best doctoral dissertation in US women's history. The *Mary Jurich Nickliss Prize* is given for "the most original" book in US Women's and/or Gender History. The *Darlene Clark Hine Award* is an annual award for the best book in African American women's and gender history. The *Avery O. Craven Award* is awarded to the most original book on the coming of the Civil War, the Civil War years, or the Era of Reconstruction, with the exception of works of purely military history. The *Liberty Legacy Foundation Award* is given for the best book on any historical aspect of the struggle for civil rights. The *James A. Rawley Prize* is given for a book dealing with race relations in the United States. *David Montgomery Award* is given annually by the OAH with co-sponsorship by the Labor and Working-Class History Association (LAWCHA) for the best book on a topic in American labor and working-class history. The *Richard W. Leopold Prize* recognizes a book written by a historian connected with federal, state, or municipal government in the areas of foreign policy, military affairs broadly construed, the historical activities of the federal government, or biography in one of the these areas. The *Ellis W. Hawley Prize* is awarded annually for the best book on the political economy, politics, or institutions of the United States, concerning its domestic or international affairs, from the Civil War to the present.

The *Willi Paul Adams Award* for the best foreign language book on the American past and the *David Thelen Award* for best foreign language article on the American past are awarded biennially. The OAH also cosponsors, with the Japanese Association for American Studies, an exchange program for Japanese and US scholars, as well as a residency program in Germany, through collaboration with the Fritz Thyssen Foundation, as well as an exchange program with China, through its relationship with the American History Research Association of China. The *Huggins-Quarles Award* is given annually to one or two graduate students of color to assist them with expenses related to travel to research collections for the completion of the PhD dissertation. In 2017, the OAH awarded its first *John D'Emilio LGBTQ History Dissertation Award* for the best PhD dissertation in US LGBTQ history. The OAH offers the *John Higham Research Fellowship* to provide research funds for a graduate student writing his or her doctoral dissertation in American history. The *Merrill Graduate Student Travel Grants* are supported by a bequest from the Merrill Trust and are given annually to help sponsor the travel-related costs of graduate students who are confirmed as participants on the OAH conference program and who incur expenses traveling to the annual meeting. Grants from the *President's Travel Fund for Emerging Scholars* are made each year to enable graduate students and young scholars to attend the OAH Annual Meeting. For more information on OAH awards and prizes, visit the OAH website.

Officers

Goodgold, Jay S. (treasurer)
Lewis, Earl (PhD, Minnesota 1984; past pres.)
Meyerowitz, Joanne (PhD, Stanford 1983; pres.)
Sanchez, George J. (PhD, Stanford 1989; vice pres.)

Staff

Andrews, Stephen Douglas (PhD, Stanford 2005; managing editor; Journal of American History) US antebellum, religion, reform; standrew@indiana.edu

Apgar, Jonathan (BA,Other, Southwestern 2007; accounting and financial support specialist) jmapgar@oah.org
Barker, Karen (BA, Indiana 1983; accounting specialist) kbarker@oah.org
Black, James M. (BS, Indiana 2012; systems analyst and developer) jmblack@oah.org
Clark-Huckstep, Andrew E. (PhD, Indiana 2017; production editor) aclark@oah.org
Finley, Katherine Mandusic (PhD, Union Inst. 2007; exec. dir.) nonprofit management, public and museums, medicine; kmfinley@oah.org
Hamm, Kara (committee coord.) khamm@oah.org
Hanchett, Sally R. (MLS, East Carolina 2011; distinguished lectureship coord.) shanchett@oah.org
Irvin, Benjamin H. (PhD, Brandeis 2004; exec. editor) American Revolution and eaarly American studies, national identity, disability
King, Chris (BA, Purdue 2013; web specialist) kingchan@oah.org
Marsh, Elisabeth M. (PhD, Indiana 2012; membership dir.) immigration, ethnicity, post-1865 US; emarsh@oah.org
Selby, Hajnalka Gajdacs (MA, Liverpool 2005; meetings dir.) hselby@oah.org
Warner, Jonathan (PhD, Indiana 2016; editor, The American Historian) Latin America; jonwarne@oah.org
Zwirecki, Paul Jason (PhD, SUNY, Buffalo 2014; public history manager) pzwirecki@oah.org

Phi Alpha Theta History Honor Society, Inc.

Univ. of South Florida, 4202 E. Fowler Ave., SOC107, Tampa, FL 33620-8100. 813.974.6235. Fax 813.974.8215. Email: info@phialphatheta.org. Website: http://www.phialphatheta.org/.

Phi Alpha Theta History Honor Society, Inc., was founded at the University of Arkansas on March 17, 1921. Since then, the society has grown to over 950 chapters in 50 states. Initiates total more than 270,000.

A. Collections and Libraries

Not applicable.

B. Programs

Phi Alpha Theta is composed of chapters in properly accredited colleges and universities. All students in those institutions who have completed the required number of history courses and are maintaining high standards in their college or university studies are eligible for membership.

Phi Alpha Theta is a professional society with the objective of promoting the study of history through the encouragement of research, good teaching, publication, and the exchange of learning and ideas among historians. Its mission is to bring students, teachers, and writers of history together intellectually and socially, and it encourages and assists historical research and publication by its members.

At its Biennial Convention, undergraduate and graduate students are provided an opportunity to meet with distinguished historians and to present papers. Phi Alpha Theta is one of the few honor and professional historical societies to encourage student paper presentations in its programs. A number of outstanding historians also appear on the program of every Biennial Convention, so that members have the opportunity to hear their contributions to historical scholarship. Through these meetings, students and professors have the opportunity to get acquainted with colleagues and to enjoy social and intellectual dialogue. The cost of transportation of a delegate from each attending chapter is partially underwritten. Each Biennial Convention is also the occasion for an active social program that generally includes a reception and tours.

The society also sponsors special programs at the annual meetings of the Organization of American Historians, the Southern Historical Association, the Western History Association, the Pacific Coast Branch of the American Historical Association, the Southwest Social Science Association, and many state historical associations. Phi Alpha Theta is expanding its participation in other annual meetings as well.

On the local level, each of its chapters conducts many activities for the benefit and enjoyment of its members. The local chapter sponsors speakers, debates and seminars of a scholarly nature, book forums, and many other programs in cooperation with local and area historical societies. It serves in many ways as an adjunct to the department of history in its college or university and often is a helpful outlet for the expression of the opinions and wishes of the students of history in their relations with the department, the library, and the college. Through the local chapter's promotion of social activities, students and faculty become better acquainted in an informal setting.

Another beneficial aspect of the society's work is the regional activity of chapters located in close proximity. Some 35 regional meetings are held each year, and more than 700 student papers are presented and the members of numerous chapters are brought together. These activities are the lifeblood of the society.

Initiation into a chapter of Phi Alpha Theta confers lifetime membership. The initiation fee is the only financial expense for membership. However, there are three voluntary means of continuing to actively support the projects of the society. For $50 an individual receives both *The Historian* and *The News Letter* for one year, with the balance going to the endowment fund. For $30 a one-year subscription to *The Historian* is offered. A member may also elect to subscribe individually to *The News Letter*.

C. Publications

The society, as part of its mission to encourage historical study, publishes *The Historian*, a distinguished quarterly, whose pages are open to its members for the publication of the results of their studies in all fields of history. It also contains reviews of the most important current books. *The Historian* has the second-largest circulation among scholarly historical journals in the world. Each initiate receives a year's subscription as part of the initiation fee.

A second publication, *The News Letter*, reaches subscribing members three times a year and carries news items covering all activities (such as regional meetings and Biennial Conventions) and awards and grants of the society. It focuses on chapters and individual members.

Further information can be found on Phi Alpha Theta's web site.

D. Fellowships and Awards

To promote the study of history, Phi Alpha Theta has established a number of prizes and awards for its members.

Six annual Paper Prize Awards are granted for papers written by society members. The George P. Hammond Award of $500 is presented for the best paper by a graduate student member; the Lynn W. Turner Award of $500 is awarded for the best paper by an undergraduate student member. Four additional $350 awards are available to student members of the society.

The papers in this competition may be devoted to any field of history. Each must be of high scholarly quality and recommended by the faculty advisor of the Phi Alpha Theta chapter to which the submitting student belongs or by the history department chair.

The prizewinning papers are reviewed by the editor of *The Historian* and, if of publishable quality, will be printed in *The Historian* at the author's request. Interested members should consult the announcements of these awards for instructions as to format, deadlines, etc., on the web site at www.phialphatheta.org.

Phi Alpha Theta also offers its members graduate scholarship awards. The A. F. Zimmerman Scholarship in the amount of $1,250, the Thomas S. Morgan Memorial Scholarship of $1,000, and the William E. Parrish Scholarship of $1,000 are presented to student members entering graduate school for the first time for work leading to the MA degree in history. The Phi Alpha Theta Scholarship Award and the John Pine Memorial Award, each in the amount of $1,000, are awarded to graduate student members for final work leading to the PhD in history. The $1,000 Graydon A. Tunstall Jr. Award is for juniors majoring in European history.

The Gordon Morris Bakken Scholarship in Western History awards $500 to a graduate student in history researching the Trans-Mississippi West. Applications must detail the research questions, the agenda including travel to archives, and probable date of completion.

The Phi Alpha Theta Faculty Advisor Award offers a $1,000 award for research, writing, or travel to an outstanding faculty member who has served as faculty advisor for five or more years.

To encourage greater chapter activity, the society offers annual Best Chapter Awards, each in the amount of $250, for activities and projects carried on by the local chapter. The chapters are divided into six groups predicated upon the enrollment of the college/university where the chapter is established. A separate category has been created for multi-year winners.

To encourage publication in history, Phi Alpha Theta offers two annual $1,000 awards for books written by its members: one for the best first book in history and a second for the best second or subsequent one.

Another Phi Alpha Theta program is student internships. *The Historian* editorial office receives editorial internships, as does the book review editor's office at Ohio Wesleyan University.

All applications or requests for further information should be directed to the executive director.

Officers

Blosser, Jacob M. (PhD, South Carolina 2006; vice pres.) colonial America, Atlantic world; jblosser@twu.edu

Burgtorf, Jochen (PhD, Heinrich-Heine, Duesseldorf, Germany 2001; chair, Advisory Board) Crusades and Latin East, medieval papacy

Drees, Clayton J. (PhD, Claremont Grad. 1993; pres.) medieval and early modern Europe, Africa and Islamic; cdrees@vwc.edu

Staff

Decker, Michael J. (DPhil, Oxford 2001; exec. dir.) Byzantine archaeology, agricultural economy and society; info@ phialphatheta.org

O'Connor, Adrian D. (PhD, Pennsylvania 2009; editor, The Historian) 18th-century European cultural and political, French Revolution; oconnora@mail.usf.edu

Spall, Richard F., Jr. (PhD, Illinois, Urbana-Champaign 1985; book review editor, The Historian) Great Britain, Empire and Commonwealth, modern Europe; rfspall@owu.edu

Robert H. Smith International Center for Jefferson Studies

Thomas Jefferson Found., PO Box 316, Charlottesville, VA 22902. 434.984.7500. Fax 434.296.1992. Email: ICJSfellowships@ monticello.org; wpippin@monticello.org. Website: http://www. monticello.org/icjs/.

The Robert H. Smith International Center for Jefferson Studies at Monticello was established by the Thomas Jefferson Foundation in 1994 in cooperation with the University of Virginia, and incorporates the Departments of Archaeology, Adult Programs, and Research, as well as The Papers of Thomas Jefferson: Retirement Series and the Jefferson Library.

A. Collections and Libraries

The dual purpose of the center is research and education, to promote Jefferson scholarship nationally and internationally. Located at Kenwood, a residential estate near Monticello, the center carries on an active program of conferences, international events, research, publications, seminars, lectures, residential fellowships, internships, and short courses.

The Jefferson Library provides bibliographic access to all known writings by and about Thomas Jefferson, inventories of unpublished materials and audiovisual resources, plus voluminous files and reports containing the results of research conducted over the years at Monticello. See the web page at www.monticello.org/library.

B. Programs

The center sponsors conferences, lectures, seminars, international events, fellowships, research, publications, field schools, and short courses (credit and noncredit) related to the life, times, and legacy of Thomas Jefferson.

C. Publications

In addition to co-publishing and underwriting reprints of standard titles in the Jefferson field, the center sponsors two series of Jefferson-related publications.

The Robert H. Smith International Center for Jefferson Studies sponsors *The Papers of Thomas Jefferson: Retirement Series*, the definitive edition of Jefferson's correspondence and papers for the period between his retirement from the presidency in 1809 and his death in 1826. A resident staff of professional editors will prepare a letterpress edition of at least 20 volumes, published by Princeton University Press, and related electronic research tools.

D. Fellowships and Awards

The fellowship and grants program is supported by the First Union Corporation, the Batten Foundation and the Peter Nicolaisen fund and is open to all scholars working on Jefferson or Jefferson-related projects, but gives preference to three classes of candidates: doctoral students working on dissertations, scholars preparing manuscripts for publication, and international scholars.

Short-term fellowships are awarded for one or more months of residency at the Robert H. Smith International Center for Jefferson Studies and may include lodging, which is available on a very limited basis. The award for US and Canadian fellows is $2,000 plus pre-approved travel expenses; the Peter Nicolaisen award for international fellows is $3,000 plus pre-approved travel expenses. Fellows will have access to the research resources of Monticello, as well as the extensive collections of the Alderman Library, University of Virginia. Applications must be received by April 1 or November 1 and should include a 500-word description of the project, a one-paragraph summary of the project, a current résumé, and arrange to have two letters of reference sent electronically to the center. Send applications to the Fellowship Committee at the Robert H. Smith International Center for Jefferson Studies Fellowship Committee (ICJSfellowships@ monticello.org).

Staff

Bates, Lynsey (PhD, Pennsylvania 2015; DAACS sr. archaeological analyst) lbates@monticello.org

Berkes, Anna (MLS, Illinois 2004; research librarian; Jefferson Library) aberkes@monticello.org

Bollwerk, Elizabeth (PhD, Virginia 2012; DAACS archaeological analyst) ebollwerk@monticello.org

Cooper, Leslie (BA, South Carolina 1998; DAACS sr. archaeological analyst) lcooper@monticello.org

Coughlan, Katelyn (MA, Massachusetts Boston 2014; DAACS sr. archaeological analyst) kcoughlan@monticello.org

Dahm, Kerry Anne (MA, Virginia 2013; editorial asst.; Jefferson Papers) kdahm@monticello.org

Devine, Christine Styrna (PhD, William and Mary 1990; archaeological analyst) cdevine@monticello.org

Francavilla, Lisa A. (PhD, George Mason 2018; managing editor; Jefferson Papers) lfrancavilla@monticello.org

Galle, Jillian (PhD, Virginia 2006; project dir.; Digital Archaeological Archive of Comparative Slavery) jgalle@monticello.org

Gray, Andrea R. (MA, North Carolina State 2008; asst. editor; Jefferson Papers) agray@monticello.org

Haggard, Robert F. (PhD, Virginia 1997; sr. assoc. editor; Jefferson Papers) social reform in Victorian Britain, late Victorian diplomacy; rhaggard@monticello.org

Hickman, Ellen C. (MA, Wisconsin, Madison 2005; assoc. editor; Jefferson Papers) ehickman@monticello.org

Lautenschlager, Julie L. (PhD, William and Mary 2003; assoc. editor; Jefferson Papers) jlautenschlager@monticello.org

Looney, J. Jefferson (PhD, Princeton 1983; Daniel P. Jordan editor in chief; Jefferson Papers) jlooney@monticello.org

Mueller, Alison (BA, Virginia 2017; archaeological analyst) amueller@monticello.org

Neiman, Fraser (PhD, Yale 1990; dir., archaeology) fneiman@ monticello.org

O'Shaughnessy, Andrew Jackson (DPhil, Oxford 1988; Saunders Dir.) aoshaughnessy@monticello.org

Perdue, Martin C. (MA, Virginia 1993; processing tech.; Jefferson Library) mperdue@monticello.org

Pippin, Whitney (BA, Mary Baldwin; program and fellowship coord.) wpippin@monticello.org

Ptacek, Crystal (MA, Tennessee 2013; archaeological field research mgr.) cptacek@monticello.org

Ragosta, John A. (PhD, Virginia 2008; historian) jragosta@ monticello.org

Robertson, Jack (MA, Michigan 1977; Fiske and Marie Kimball Librarian) jrobertson@monticello.org

Sawyer, Elizabeth (BA, William and Mary 2005; archaeological analyst) esawyer@monticello.org

Scott-Fleming, Mary (BA, London Coll.; dir., adult education) mscottfleming@monticello.org

Sellick, Gary D. (MA, South Carolina 2016; editorial asst.; Jefferson Papers) gsellick@monticello.org

Spengler, Susan (MS, West Virginia 2017; tech. specialist; Jefferson Papers) sspengler@monticello.org

Tay, Endrina (MLS, North Carolina, Chapel Hill; assoc. found. librarian for tech. services; Jefferson Library); etay@monticello. org

Viterbo, Paula (PhD, SUNY, Stony Brook 2000; editorial asst.; Jefferson Papers) pviterbo@monticello.org
Wheeler, Derek (MA, Virginia 1996; research archaeologist) dwheeler@monticello.org
Wilson, Gaye (PhD, Edinburgh 2012; sr. historian) gwilson@monticello.org

Science History Institute

315 Chestnut St, Philadelphia, PA 19106. 215.925.2222. Fax 215.925.1954. Email: info@sciencehistory.org. Website: https://www.sciencehistory.org/.

A. Collections and Libraries

The Othmer Library of Chemical History contains significant holdings of primary resources for the history of chemistry and related sciences, technologies, and industries, dating from the 15th century through the 21st century. Items of particular interest include 1,800 journal titles and approximately 7,000 rare books and manuscripts dating from 1425 onward; over 6,000 linear feet of archival materials from leading scientists and innovative individuals, corporations, industries, and professional organizations; over 100,000 volumes of monographs and journals that are primary and secondary historical sources covering a broad subject range in the sciences; over 50,000 historical images in a variety of formats illustrating notable chemists, laboratories, instrumentation, and artifacts; and hundreds of oral history interviews with leading figures in chemistry, chemical engineering, bio-medicine, and related fields. The Science History Institute Museum holds over 700 scientific instruments with a particular strength in 20th-century analytical instruments; fine art representing a wide variety of chemical and alchemical subjects with more than 90 paintings and 200 works on paper; over 600 pieces of glass apparatus; and a collection of some 100 chemistry sets.

The printed book, oral history, and archival collections can be searched through the online catalog at http://othmerlib.sciencehistory.org. The digital collection can be searched at http://digital.sciencehistory.org. The oral histories can also be searched or browsed at https://oh.sciencehistory.org. Research Guides to Othmer Library collections are available at http://guides.othmerlibrary.sciencehistory.org.

B. Programs

The Science History Institute (formerly the Chemical Heritage Foundation) is a Library, Museum, and Center for Scholars that fosters dialogue on science and technology in society. We focus on historical issues surrounding matter and materials and their effects on our modern world in territory ranging from the physical sciences and industries, through the chemical sciences and engineering, to the life sciences and technologies. We collect, preserve, and exhibit historical artifacts; engage communities of scientists and engineers; and tell the stories of the people behind breakthroughs and innovations.

The Center for Historical Research is Science History Institute's independent scholarly research center. Its Beckman Center for the History of Chemistry supports around 20 fellows (long- and short-term) in residence to foster a community of scholarship in the history of science, technology, and medicine, with a focus on chemical and material topics, and to take greater advantage of the collections held by the Institute. The Center holds weekly lunchtime lectures during the academic year by its staff, fellows, and special guests. The biweekly writing seminar series allows staff and fellows to present works-in-progress for discussion and comment. The Rohm and Haas Fellow in Focus lecture series presents semiannual public talks by Institute fellows on their work. The Synthesis lecture series presents regular public talks by authors of books in the *Synthesis* series of monographs, a joint venture of the Institute and the University of Chicago Press. The Center also sponsors the annual Gordon Cain Conference on an historical topic related to contemporary issues in chemistry, chemical engineering, and/or chemical industries, organized by a leading scholar from outside the Institute, as well as occasional conferences on topics relating to the history of chemistry, construed broadly.

The Institute for Research identifies key issues at the intersections of science, technology, and medicine that can benefit from careful research, analysis, and new perspectives. The Institute for Research develops projects that mobilize history using archives, interviews, case studies, and oral histories in order to bring original perspectives on contemporary science and technology-based societal challenges. Its work and findings are packaged in multiple forms to meet the needs of diverse constituencies, including individuals in the private, public, and non-profit sectors, as well as current and future researchers. The Institute for Research is a hybrid institution, uniting academe's strong foundation in original research with the passion of a non-profit think tank capable of taking the results of that research to those who need it most. The Institute for Research's staff utilizes tools developed in the fields of science and technology studies; the history of science, technology, and medicine; public history; and the arts to offer unique insights into contemporary science and technology issues, from the development of new materials to the role of federal policies in the development of pharmaceuticals. The Center for Oral History provides a unifying structure of method—the use of in-depth interviews—which under-girds the Institute for Research's programmatic initiatives and connects them to the Science History Institute's core collection and preservation mission.

The Roy Eddleman Institute for Interpretation and Education, the outreach arm of the Science History Institute, brings the history of chemistry, chemical engineering, and the life sciences to a broad audience through public programs, print and Web-based publications, and educational materials. The Eddleman Institute also operates the Science History Institute Museum.

The Science History Institute Museum features a permanent exhibition and changing exhibits that explore the history of chemistry, chemical engineering, and the life sciences and the role science plays in the modern world. *Making Modernity*, the Museum's permanent exhibition, shows how chemistry has impacted our lives—frequently in unexpected ways. Visitors can trace scientific progress in the laboratory, the factory, and their homes and learn how chemistry created and continues to shape the modern world. Drawn from the Institute's collections, *Making Modernity* includes scientific instruments and apparatus, rare books, fine art, and the personal papers of prominent scientists. Topics range from alchemy, synthetics, and the chemical-instrument revolution to chemistry education, electrochemistry, chemistry sets, and the science of color. The museum is free of charge and open to the public Tuesday through Saturday, 10 a.m. to 5 p.m., and to 8 p.m. on the first Friday of every month (March-June and August-December). Closed on major holidays.

C. Publications

The Science History Institute publishes *Distillations*, an accessibly written online magazine that explores stories at the intersections of materials science, history, and culture. For information on submissions or subscriptions, write to the editor at editor@sciencehistory.org or visit the magazine's web site at www.sciencehistory.org/distillations. In association with the magazine, the Institute also produces a *Distillations* blog, podcast, and occasional videos.

In addition, the Institute is a partner with the University of Chicago Press in publishing *Synthesis*, a scholarly, peer-reviewed book series on the history of chemistry, broadly defined. Series titles can be browsed at the *Synthesis* website, www.press. uchicago.edu/ucp/books/series/SYN.html.

D. Fellowships and Awards

The Science History Institute hosts scholars from all parts of the world through its Fellowship and Travel Grant Program. Through the Beckman Center for the History of Chemistry, the Institute offers peer-reviewed long-term (2-year 80/20 postdoctoral and 9-month dissertation) and short-term research (1-4 months) fellowships in residence as well as travel grants for research in the collections. Fellowship applications are welcome from scholars from a broad spectrum of disciplines whose research touches on some aspect of the history of science, technology, and medicine. All fellows have the opportunity to give informal talks at the weekly brown-bag lecture series and present works-in-progress at biweekly seminars. All scholars have access to the Othmer Library of Chemical History, as well as a wealth of area resources. Applications for all fellowships must be received by January 2 for the term beginning the following September. Fellowships can be taken up by doctoral candidates, postdoctoral scholars, academic faculty, and independent scholars. For details on all fellowships please visit the web site at www.sciencehistory.org/fellowships.

The Institute for Research periodically seeks postdoctoral fellows working in fields related to the history and social study of science for subject-specific or directed long-term (1–3 years) projects. Fellows form research groups around particular topics of interest, pilot new areas of research, and connect research with the collections and outreach. Research topics draw upon the department's strengths in oral history, public history, digital humanities, science studies, and history of science. Research fellows collaborate to coordinate workshops, reading groups, and research reports that provide critical perspectives on emerging areas of study.

Staff

Abney Salomon, Charlotte (PhD, Yale 2019; Price postdoc. fellow) science, technology, material culture; cabney@sciencehistory. org

Anderson, Robert G. W. (DPhil, Oxford 1970; pres. and CEO) chemistry, museums, scientific instrumentation; randerson@ sciencehistory.org

Augustyniak, Ashley (MLIS, Florida State 2006; reference librarian and fellowship coord.) library science; aaugustyniak@ sciencehistory.org

Berry, Lee Sullivan (MMS, Notre Dame 1998; curator, oral hist.) oral, science, digital humanities; lberry@sciencehistory.org

Biro, Zackary Joseph (MA, Lehigh 2014; program asst.; Center for Applied Hist.) public, digital humanities, America; zbiro@ sciencehistory.org

Bowden, Mary Ellen (PhD, Yale 1974; sr. research fellow) chemistry, astrology; mebowden@sciencehistory.org

Bowen, Ashley (PhD, Brown 2016; digital engagement mgr.) medical, museum studies, digital humanities; abowen@ sciencehistory.org

Boytim, Jacqueline (BA, Pennsylvania 2010; program assoc.; Center for Oral Hist.) science, oral; jboytim@sciencehistory.org

Brashear, Ronald (MS, Louisville 1984; dir.; Othmer Library) book, science, astrophysics; rbrashear@sciencehistory.org

Cansler, Clay (BA, North Carolina, Chapel Hill 1998; managing editor; Distillations) visual culture, science in popular culture, politics and ethics in science; ccansler@sciencehistory.org

Carr, Mariel (OMS, California, Berkeley 2013; multimedia producer) medicine, public health, gender studies; mcarr@sciencehistory. org

Caruso, David J. (PhD, Cornell 2008; dir.; Center for Oral Hist.) military medicine, biomedical science, technology; dcaruso@ sciencehistory.org

Dahlberg, Britt (PhD, Pennsylvania 2015; dir.; Center for Applied Hist.) science/technology/medicine, environmental, digital humanities; bdahlberg@sciencehistory.org

Geehr, Shelley Wilks (BA, Muhlenberg 1983; dir.; Eddleman Inst. for Interpretation and Education) educational gaming, informal education; sgeehr@sciencehistory.org

Jaehnig, Kenton (MA, Wright State 1996; processing archivist) America, archives; kjaehnig@sciencehistory.org

Joniec, Nicole (MSLIS, Drexel 2016; digital coll. and metadata librarian) digital asset management, library and information science, digital humanities; njoniec@sciencehistory.org

Kaplan, Rebecca (PhD, California, San Francisco 2013; Cain postdoctoral fellow) medicine, environmental, American; rkaplan@sciencehistory.org

Kativa, Hillary S. (MA, Villanova 2008; MA, Rutgers 2010; chief curator, audiovisual and digital coll.) digital humanities, American political, public; hkativa@sciencehistory.org

Klett, Joseph (PhD, Yale 2015; research fellow; Inst. for Research) cultural sociology, sound studies, social theory; jklett@ sciencehistory.org

Martucci, Jessica (PhD, Pennsylvania 2011; research fellow) science, gender studies, disability studies; jmartucci@ sciencehistory.org

Meyer, Michal (PhD, Florida 2009; editor-in-chief and mgr.; public hist. initiatives) science popularization, 19th-century intellectual and cultural; mmeyer@sciencehistory.org

Mitchell, Daniel Jon (DPhil, Oxford 2010; dir., Center of Historical Research) science; dmitchell@sciencehistory.org

Ockerbloom, Mary Mark (MS, Saskatchewan 1991; wikipedian-in-residence) digital humanities, information science, science; mockerbloom@sciencehistory.org

Ockert, Ingrid (PhD, Princeton 2018; Haas postdoctoral fellow) science, visual culture, digital humanities; iockert@ sciencehistory.org

Ortenberg, Rebecca (MA, SUNY, Oneonta 2013; social media editor) museum studies, intersections of gender and labor history, popular culture; rortenberg@sciencehistory.org

Orzechowski, Victoria (MLIS, Drexel 2013; librarian) library science; vorzechowski@sciencehistory.org

Pedrick, Alexis (MA, Arcadia 2012; mgr., public progs.) America, death and mourning culture, museum studies; apedrick@ sciencehistory.org

Rochkind, Jonathan (MLIS, Washington 2006; software developer/tech. lead) digital asset management, library and information science, software engineering; jrochkind@sciencehistory.org

Rubeiz, Edward (MSLIS, Drexel 2016; library applications developer) digital asset management, library and information science, science, records management; erubeiz@sciencehistory. org

Sampson, Molly (MA, Christie's Education 2009; collections mgr. and registrar) museum studies, visual culture, public art; msampson@sciencehistory.org

Schneider, Christy (MA, Univ. of the Arts 2002; exhibitions project mgr.) exhibit development, museum education, intersections of science/art/history; cschneider@sciencehistory.org

Shea, Patrick (MA, Delaware 2004; chief curator; Archives and Manuscripts) technology, archives; pshea@sciencehistory.org

Tomlinson, Andrea (MLIS,OMS, Drexel 2008; tech. services librarian) library and information science; atomlinson@sciencehistory.org

Tritton, Thomas R. (PhD, Boston Univ. 1973; sr. research fellow) biophysical chemistry, pharmacology, cancer chemotherapy; ttritton@sciencehistory.org

Turner, Roger (PhD, Pennsylvania 2010; research fellow; Inst. for Research) science, public, digital humanities; rturner@sciencehistory.org

Van Tiggelen, Brigitte (PhD, Catholique de Louvain 1998; dir.; Office of the President, Europe) science; bvantiggelen@sciencehistory.org

Voelkel, James R. (PhD, Indiana 1994; curator; Rare Books and resident scholar, Beckman Center for Hist. of Chemistry) early modern science, book; jvoelkel@sciencehistory.org

Wiener, Ann Elizabeth (BFA, Minneapolis Coll. of Art and Design 1990; museum operations mgr.) medicine, science, material culture; awiener@sciencehistory.org

Shelby Cullom Davis Center for Historical Studies

Dept. of History, Princeton Univ., 136 Dickinson Hall, Princeton, NJ 08544-1017. 609.258.4997. Fax 609.258.5326. Email: davisctr@princeton.edu. Website: https://history.princeton.edu/centers-programs/shelby-cullom-davis-center.

The Davis Center was established in 1968 as a center for historical research at Princeton University and to stimulate intellectual exchange both within the Department of History and between the department and visiting scholars. The center is supported by the George Henry Davis 1886 and Shelby Cullom Davis 1930 funds.

A. Collections and Libraries

Not applicable.

B. Programs

The center supports the Davis Research Seminar, which gathers together a group of research scholars from America and abroad around a core of members of the department, all of whom are working on a common problem. The focus of interest in the seminar changes every two years. The seminar meets most Friday mornings during the academic year. Scholars wanting to offer a paper to the seminar should write to the director.

During the academic years 2020–21 and 2021–22, the Shelby Cullom Davis Center for Historical Studies will focus on the topic of "Revolutionary Change." Historians have always considered moments of revolutionary change to be central objects of study. These moments do not necessarily involve politics, and are not limited to the modern world. The word "revolutionary" itself may be a relatively recent coinage (dating from the early modern period), but the sorts of change that it denotes have taken place in every area of human activity, and in every time and place. Revolutionary change is rapid and destabilizing. It is also dynamic, in the sense that it does not simply reflect or extend the forces which originally generated it, but builds on itself in original and often wholly-unpredictable ways. It can be both destructive and creative. It can entail a frightful human cost, but it can also open up new human possibilities and freedoms. It can take place on many different spatial and temporal scales—and at the same time, it can radically transform human understandings of the scales themselves.

Under the directorship of David A. Bell beginning in 2020, the Davis Center seeks applications from historians working on revolutionary change in any period of human history, and in any area, including (but not limited to) the histories of politics, culture, ideas, social structure, gender relations, sexuality, race relations, religion and the environment. We also welcome applications from historians working on the concept of revolutionary change itself, on how moments of such change are retrospectively identified, and on failed, incomplete or ineffective examples. We are particularly interested in developing conversations among historians working on revolutionary change in different areas and periods.

C. Publications

Initiatives of The Davis Center result in the publication of many books. *Shelby Cullom Davis Center Volumes*: The Center's theme has formed the basis for many multi-author volumes. Most recently, these collections of essays have been published in partnership with Princeton University Press. *The Lawrence Stone Lectures*: The Davis Center and Princeton University Press have also partnered to bring important and innovative historical scholarship to a broad audience through the Lawrence Stone Lectures. Each year, the Davis Center brings a major historian to campus for a week of informal meetings and three thematically linked lectures. These lectures serve as the foundation for the Lawrence Stone Lectures volumes. For a list of titles, see the center's website.

D. Fellowships and Awards

The Center will offer a limited number of research fellowships for one or two semesters, running from September to January and from February to June. Early career scholars must have their doctoral degrees in hand at the time of the application. Fellows are expected to live in Princeton in order to take an active part in the intellectual interchange with other members of the Seminar. Funds are limited, and candidates are, therefore, strongly urged to apply to other grant-giving institutions as well as the Center if they wish to come for a full year.

To apply, please link to http://history.princeton.edu/fellowship-information. The deadline for receipt of applications and letters of recommendation for fellowships for 2020–21 is December 1, 2019. Please note that we will not accept faxed applications. Applicants must apply online and submit a CV, cover letter, research proposal, abstract of proposal, and contact information for three references. For further information about the Davis Center, please go to www.princeton.edu/dav. Princeton University is an equal opportunity employer and complies with applicable EEO and affirmative action regulations.

Staff

Creager, Angela N. H. (PhD, California, Berkeley 1991; dir. and Thomas M. Siebel Prof.) 20th-century biology; creager@princeton.edu

Society for Historians of American Foreign Relations

Middle Tennessee State Univ., Dept. of History, 1301 E. Main St., Box 23, Murfreesboro, TN 37132. 617.458.6156. Fax 615.898.5881. Email: amy.sayward@shafr.org. Website: https://shafr.org/.

A. Collections and Libraries

The SHAFR Archives include correspondence relating to the founding of the society, records of its business office, and materials relating to the publication of *Diplomatic History*. The Archives is housed in the Ohio State University Library & Archives in Columbus, OH.

B. Programs

SHAFR holds an annual meeting, usually in June, featuring some 75-80 sessions on all aspects of American foreign relations history, broadly defined, as well as various plenary sessions, roundtable panels, and keynote lectures on a variety of topics.

SHAFR is a member of the National Coalition for History and underwrites its efforts to represent academic historians in Washington, DC. SHAFR is an affiliate of the American Historical Association, sponsoring panels at its annual meeting and sponsoring an annual luncheon and reception.

The SHAFR website posts valuable information about the society, its governance, programs, prizes, and publications. It also contains links to other web sites of interest to researchers in the field. The Syllabus Initiative involves posting online the syllabi of undergraduate and graduate courses in US diplomatic history, for the benefit of teachers and professors who are conceptualizing or reforming courses in the field. More information on these programs is provided on the website.

C. Publications

The society publishes *Diplomatic History*, the journal of record in the field of US foreign relations history, five times per year. It also publishes *Passport: The Society for Historians of American Foreign Relations Review*, three times per year. These two periodicals are provided to all members of the society and are available through subscriptions by libraries and individuals.

New in 2018 is the third, on-line edition of the *SHAFR Guide*, which provides an updated annotated guide to the literature on US foreign relations and international history since 1600. Its some 2.1 million words makes it the premier source for those beginning research in this area. Starting in 2019, access is provided free of charge to SHAFR members; information on purchasing this publication is posted at www.shafr.org/publications/guide.

D. Fellowships and Awards

SHAFR offers members and others a variety of research fellowships and achievement prizes; full information is available at shafr.org/members.

SHAFR offers a Marilyn B. Young Dissertation Completion Fellowship of $25,000 for advanced doctoral candidates nearing completion of their dissertations.

Among SHAFR's fellowships are the following: The Michael J. Hogan Fellowship of up to $4,000 is awarded annually to a graduate student member of SHAFR to defray the costs of studying foreign languages needed for research. The W. Stull Holt Dissertation Fellowship of up to $4,000 is awarded annually to a doctoral candidate writing a dissertation in the field of the history of American foreign relations, to defray costs of travel. The Lawrence Gelfand-Armin Rappaport-Walter LaFeber Fellowship of $4,000 is awarded annually to defray the costs of dissertation research travel by a doctoral candidate in the field. Stuart L. Bernath Dissertation Grants of up to $4,000 are awarded annually to help doctoral students who are members of SHAFR defray expenses encountered in the writing of their dissertations. The Myrna F. Bernath Fellowship of up to $2,500 is awarded

biannually (in odd years) to a woman doctoral candidate or recent PhD conducting research in the field. The Robert A. and Barbara Divine Graduate Student Travel Grant program subsidizes travel to the SHAFR annual meeting by selected graduate students who are presenting papers. Several Samuel Flagg Bemis Dissertation Research Grants and William Appleman Williams Junior Faculty Research Grants of up to $4,000 and $2,000, respectively, are also awarded annually.

SHAFR also offers the following achievement prizes: The Norman and Laura Graebner Award of $2,000, issued biannually (in even years), is a lifetime achievement award intended to recognize a senior historian of US foreign relations who has significantly contributed to the development of the field, through scholarship, teaching, and/or service, over his or her career. The Peter L. Hahn Distinguished Service Award recognizes career-long contributions to the growth and development of SHAFR. The Robert H. Ferrell Book Prize of $2,500 is awarded annually to the best book in the field (beyond the author's first book). The Stuart L. Bernath Book Prize of $2,500 is awarded annually to the best first book on any aspect of the history of American foreign relations. The Michael H. Hunt Prize in International History is awarded to the best first book in international history utilizing records in more than one language. The Myrna F. Bernath Book Award of $2,500 is awarded biannually (in even years) to the author of the best book written by a woman in the field and published during the preceding two calendar years. The Arthur S. Link-Warren F. Kuehl Prize for Documentary Editing of $1,000 is presented biannually (in odd years) to the best book featuring analytical scholarly editing of documents relevant to the history of American foreign relations and published during the preceding two calendar years. The Stuart L. Bernath Lecture Prize of $1,000 is awarded annually to recognize excellence in teaching and research in the field of foreign relations by younger scholars. The Stuart L. Bernath Scholarly Article Prize of $1,000 is awarded annually to the author of a distinguished article appearing in a scholarly journal or edited book on any topic in US foreign relations. The Betty M. Unterberger Dissertation Prize of $1,000 is awarded biannually (in odd years) to the best dissertation, completed during the previous two calendar years, on any topic in United States foreign relations history. The Oxford University Press USA Dissertation Prize in International History of $1,000 is awarded biannually (in even years) to recognize the best dissertation writing by a rising historian who has completed a research project defined as international history.

Officers

Hoganson, Kristin L. (PhD, Yale 1995; vice pres.) US cultural, foreign relations; hoganson@illinois.edu
Keys, Barbara J. (PhD, Harvard 2001; pres.) emotions, human rights; bkeys@unimelb.edu.au

Staff

Foster, Anne L. (PhD, Cornell 1995; editor; Diplomatic History) US foreign relations; anne.foster@indstate.edu
Goedde, Petra (PhD, Northwestern 1995; editor; Diplomatic History) pgoedde@temple.edu
Johns, Andrew L. (PhD, California, Santa Barbara 2000; editor; Passport) US foreign relations; andrew_johns@byu.edu
McPherson, Alan L. (PhD, North Carolina, Chapel Hill 2001; assoc. editor; Diplomatic History) alan.mcpherson@temple.edu
Sayward, Amy L. (PhD, Ohio State 1998; exec. dir.) Tennessee death penalty, United Nations; amy.sayward@mtsu.edu

Society for History Education, Inc.

,Dept. of History, California State Univ., 1250 N. Bellflower Blvd., Long Beach, CA 90840-1601. 562.985.2573. Fax 562.985.5431. Email: info@thehistoryteacher.org; info@ societyforhistoryeducation.org. Website: http://www. societyforhistoryeducation.org/.

The Society for History Education is an educational and historical non-profit organization affiliated with the American Historical Association, and was founded for the purpose of improving the teaching of history in the university, community college, and precollegiate school classroom. Its peer-reviewed quarterly journal, The History Teacher, has been published since 1967.

A. Collections and Libraries

The Society maintains a complete collection of *The History Teacher* in both physical and electronic archives. Additionally, full-text, open-access to recent issues and archives of *The History Teacher* is available at www.thehistoryteacher.org.

B. Programs

AHA Member Discounts are available to individual and institutional members of the American Historical Association, offering 15% savings on subscriptions to *The History Teacher*. This option may be added when starting or renewing AHA membership.

C. Publications

Society members receive *The History Teacher*, published quarterly in November, February, May, and August, the most widely recognized professional publication in the United States devoted to the teaching of history in the university, community college, and precollegiate school. The society maintains a library of back issues of *The History Teacher*, which are available for purchase.

D. Fellowships and Awards

The Eugene Asher Distinguished Teaching Award, established in 1986, recognizes outstanding teaching and advocacy for history teaching at two-year, four-year, and graduate colleges and universities. The award is named for the late Eugene Asher, for many years a leading advocate for history teaching. The Society for History Education (SHE) shares with the AHA sponsorship of the award. It recognizes inspiring teachers whose techniques and mastery of subject matter made a lasting impression and substantial difference to students of history. Members of the AHA and SHE submit nominations to the Committee on Teaching Prizes. Visit www.historians.org/awards-and-grants/awards-and-prizes/eugene-asher-award for more information and deadlines.

The Richard and Louise Wilde Award, offered in conjunction with the Department of History at California State University, Long Beach invites applications from CSULB students in master's, credential, and advanced undergraduate programs. The award is named for the late Richard Wilde and his wife Louise Wilde, a duo who helped shape the history of California State University, Long Beach as well as the *The History Teacher*. Applicants must demonstrate strong interest in pedagogy, specifically in teaching history. The recipient also receives a year-long student internship with the editorial board of the *The History Teacher*. Visit www. cla.csulb.edu/departments/history/awards-and-scholarships for more information and deadlines.

Staff

Alkana, Linda Kelly (PhD, California, Irvine 1985; Editorial Board member) modern Europe, women, critical thought; linda.alkana@csulb.edu

Binkiewicz, Donna M. (PhD, UCLA 1997; Editorial Board member) social, cultural; donna.binkiewicz@csulb.edu

Dabel, Jane E. (PhD, UCLA 2000; secretary and editor; The History Teacher) late 19th-century US, Afro-American, gender; jane.dabel@csulb.edu

Hamilton, Gail (MA, California State, Long Beach 2010; Editorial Board member) history education, middle school, world; ghamilton@csulb.edu

Herrera, Elisa (MA, California State, Long Beach 2007; dir. and managing editor; The History Teacher) history education, US, Middle East; herrera@thehistoryteacher.org

Igmen, Ali F. (PhD, Washington 2004; Editorial Board member) Central Asia, Soviet Union, Turkic diaspora; ali.igmen@csulb.edu

Keirn, Tim W. (OMS, London Sch. Econ. 1982; pres.) history education, Britain; tim.keirn@csulb.edu

Kuo, Margaret (PhD, UCLA 2003; Editorial Board member) modern China; margaret.kuo@csulb.edu

Luhr, Eileen S. (PhD, California, Irvine 2004; Editorial Board member) US, cultural, religious; eileen.luhr@csulb.edu

Neumann, Dave (PhD, Southern California 2016; Editorial Board member) history education, US; dave.neumann@csulb.edu

Shafer, David (PhD, London 1994; treasurer) French social and cultural; david.shafer@csulb.edu

Weber, William A. (PhD, Chicago 1970; Editorial Board member) modern Europe, music social; william.weber@csulb.edu

Society for Military History

George C. Marshall Library, Lexington, VA 24450-1600. 540.464.7468. Fax 540.464.7330. Email: jmhsmh@vmi.edu. Website: http://www.smh-hq.org/.

Established in 1933 as the American Military History Foundation, renamed in 1939 the American Military Institute, and renamed again in 1990 the Society for Military History, the society is devoted to stimulating and advancing the study of military history. Its membership (today more than 2,600) has included many of the nation's most prominent scholars, soldiers, and citizens interested in military history.

A. Collections and Libraries

The Society for Military History Archives is held by the Richard L. D. Morse Department of Special Collections, Hale Library, Kansas State University, Manhattan, Kansas.

B. Programs

The society, in coordination with local hosts, sponsors an annual spring meeting and conference with panels representing the diversity of military history.

Past meetings include the society's 2018 annual meeting April 5-8 at the Galt House Hotel Louisville, KY, and the 2017 annual meeting March 30–April 2 at the Hyatt Regency Jacksonville-Riverfront Jacksonville, Florida, hosted by the Institute on World War II and the Human Experience and the Department of History, Florida State University; 2016 annual meeting April 14–17 in Ottawa, Ontario, Canada, at the Ottawa Marriott Hotel, hosted by the Canadian Museum of History and the Canadian War Museum; 2015 annual meeting April 9–12 in Montgomery, Alabama, at the Renaissance Montgomery Hotel & Spa, hosted by The Air University Foundation, Maxwell Air Force Base; 2014, at the Westin Crown Center Hotel in Kansas City, Missouri, hosted by Command

and General Staff College Foundation, Liberty Memorial–National World War I Museum, Harry S. Truman Library Institute, and Department of History, University of Kansas with the theme "Transformational Conflicts: War and Its Legacy through History"; 2013, in New Orleans, Louisiana, at the Sheraton New Orleans Hotel, hosted by University of Southern Mississippi, the National World War II Museum, and Southeastern Louisiana University with the theme "War, Society, and Remembrance"; 2012, in Arlington, Virginia, hosted by the Army Historical Foundation with the theme "The Politics of War"; 2011, in Lisle, Illinois, hosted by the Cantigny First Division Foundation with the theme "Ways of War"; 2010, in Lexington, Virginia, jointly hosted by the Virginia Military Institute and the George C. Marshall Foundation with the theme "Causes Lost and Won"; 2009, in Murfreesboro, Tennessee, hosted by Middle Tennessee State University with the theme "Warfare and Culture"; 2008, in Ogden, Utah, sponsored by Weber State University with the theme "The Military and Frontiers"; 2007, in Frederick, Maryland, sponsored by the Catoctin Center for Regional Studies at Frederick Community College with the theme "Crossroads of War"; and 2006, in Manhattan, Kansas, sponsored by Kansas State University.

Future Meetings: The 2018 annual meeting will be April 5–8 in Louisville, Kentucky, hosted by the College of Arts & Sciences and the Department of History, University of Louisville.

C. Publications

The *Journal of Military History*, the quarterly journal of the Society for Military History, has published scholarly articles on the military history of all eras and geographical areas since 1937. The *Journal* is fully refereed. It publishes articles, book reviews, a list of recent articles dealing with military history published by other journals, an annual list of doctoral dissertations in military history, and an annual index. The *Journal of Military History* is published by the society with assistance from the George C. Marshall Foundation and the Virginia Military Institute. The *Journal of Military History* is available online from EBSCOhost. *Headquarters Gazette* is the society's quarterly newsletter. The society maintains a Guide to Graduate Programs in Military History on its web site.

D. Fellowships and Awards

The society confers several awards and prizes. The *Samuel Eliot Morison Prize* recognizes not any one specific achievement, but a body of contributions in the field of military history, extending over time and reflecting a spectrum of scholarly activity contributing significantly to the field. The *Edward H. Simmons Memorial Service Award* is presented for long, distinguished, or particularly outstanding service to the Society for Military History. *Distinguished Book Awards* recognize the best book-length publications in English on military history, whether monograph, bibliography, guide, or other project copyrighted in the previous three calendar years. An award has been established for the best military history web site. The *Moncado Prizes* are awarded annually to the authors of the four best articles published in the *Journal of Military History* during the previous calendar year. These awards include a plaque and monetary prize. The *Russell F. Weigley Graduate Student Travel Grant Awards* honor one of the great American military historians of the 20th century and support participation by promising graduate students in the society's annual meeting. The *SMH/ABC-CLIO Research Grants* are designated specifically to support the work of advanced graduate students and those scholars who do not hold a doctoral degree but are employed full-time as historians. These funds may be used for travel, purchase of microfilm or other research materials, photocopying, and similar expenses. The *Edward M. Coffman Prize* honors a devoted member of the society and professor by

granting an award to the best first manuscript in military history and brings publication consideration by the University of North Carolina Press. The Society for Military History, in partnership with The George C. Marshall Foundation, offers the *SMH-GCMF Prize for the Use of Digital Technology in Teaching Military History* for an individual, group or institution that creates, designs and implements material for use in teaching military history utilizing evolving digital technology. The *Allan R. Millett Dissertation Research Fellowship* honors an eminent scholar and professor by awarding funds for doctoral dissertation research on a topic in any field of military history.

Officers

Felker, C.C. (PhD, Duke 2004; exec. dir.) naval, military; ccfelker@msn.com

Hall, John W. (PhD, North Carolina, Chapel Hill 2007; pres.) US military, Native American; jwhall3@wisc.edu

Kumbier, Ashley (OMS, Wisconsin, Madison 2008; treasurer)

Mansoor, Peter R. (PhD, Ohio State 1995; vice pres.) military, national security and policy studies; mansoor.1@osu.edu

Staff

Arnold, James R. (BA, Colby 1974; asst. editor; Journal of Military History) burrostn@cfw.com

Barnett, Tracy L. (MA, Southern Mississippi 2017; Mark Grimsley Fellow in Social Media)

Dowling, Timothy (PhD, Tulane 1999; assoc. editor; Journal of Military History) military, Germany; dowlingtc@vmi.edu

Friedman, Hal M. (PhD, Michigan State 1995; recording secretary) US national security affairs; friedman@hfcc.edu

Hackemer, Kurt H. (PhD, Texas A&M 1994; newsletter editor and webmaster) 19th-century US naval and military; kurt.hackemer@usd.edu

Turner, Blair P. (PhD, Florida 1986; asst. editor; Journal of Military History) Latin American military, US-Latin American relations turnerbp@vmi.edu

Turner, Vicki (business mgr.) vturner@vmi.edu

Vandervort, Bruce C. (PhD, Virginia 1989; editor; Journal of Military History) imperialism, colonial warfare; vandervortb@vmi.edu

Wells, Anne S. (MA, Mississippi State 1975; MLS, Alabama 1981; asst. editor; Journal of Military History) military, World War II, 20th-century US; awells@rockbridge.net

Wiener, Roberta (managing editor; Journal of Military History) wienerr@vmi.edu

Society for the History of Technology

c/o Foundation for History of Tech., Eindhoven U., Atlas Building 8.401, PO Box 513, Eindhoven, 5600 MB, Netherlands. +31.402.4746. Email: SHOT.secretariaat@tue.nl. Website: https://www.historyoftechnology.org/.

A. Collections and Libraries

Not applicable.

B. Programs

The Society for the History of Technology (SHOT) holds an annual meeting, usually in October, featuring papers, panels, and other programs representing ongoing research in the field of history of technology, broadly defined. The annual meeting is also the location for meetings of SHOT's Special Interest Groups, which bring together researchers from specific fields; SIGs include groups focusing on the history of engineering, history of aviation and aerospace, electricity and communications, history of computers, history of the environment, military tech, technology museums, and women in the history of technology.

In 1991, SHOT launched its International Scholars Program to encourage greater participation in the society by scholars outside North America, to improve communication among historians of technology around the world, and to foster an international community of scholars in the field. The program also offers encouragement to those just beginning their careers, hoping that recognition by SHOT will enable them to find the means to attend SHOT's annual meetings. Nominees must reside outside the United States and may be junior or more advanced scholars, but emphasis is given to more junior historians. Those selected for two-year terms will receive a subscription to *Technology and Culture* and be encouraged to attend SHOT's meetings. They also will be asked to prepare a short description of the history of technology in their country for possible publication in the newsletter. A new class of International Scholars is selected each year, with appointments made by a selection committee and by the president and announced at the annual meeting. Self-nomination is permitted. All nominations must include a brief personal statement, list of publications and activities, and c.v. For more information, please see the SHOT web site.

SHOT also has programs to provide annual meeting participants (particularly graduate students and international scholars) with travel grants to support travel to SHOT's annual meeting. For details, see SHOT's web site.

C. Publications

The society publishes a quarterly journal, *Technology and Culture,* devoted to scholarship on all aspects of technology and its interaction with society. The society also publishes a periodic newsletter, usually in the summer to provide information about the annual meeting and elections. SHOT also has partnered with the American Historical Association to publish a joint booklet series on the history of technology. For more information, please visit www.historyoftechnology.org/booklets.html.

D. Fellowships and Awards

The Society for the History of Technology sponsors or administers 12 prizes designed to encourage and recognize distinguished contributions to scholarship or museum exhibits in the history of technology. Application for all prizes may be made to the appropriate prize committee. Deadlines vary, but most fall between 15 January and 1 April each year. For up-to-date deadlines and details, please see the SHOT web site at www.historyoftechnology.org/awards.html.

The Leonardo de Vinci Medal is the highest recognition of the society; it is presented annually to an individual who has made an outstanding contribution to the history of technology, through research, teaching, publication, and other activities. A certificate accompanies the medal.

The Edelstein Prize is awarded for an outstanding book in the history of technology published during any of the three years preceding the award. Authors should arrange for three copies of their work to be sent to the committee by the publisher. The prize consists of $3,500 and a plaque.

The Abbott Payson Usher Prize was established to honor the scholarly contributions of the late Dr. Usher and to encourage the publication of original research of the highest standard. It is awarded annually to the author of the best scholarly work published during the preceding three years under the auspices of the Society for the History of Technology. The prize consists of $400 and a certificate.

The Joan Cahalin Robinson Prize is awarded annually for the best presentation at the society's annual meeting. Those presenters who are giving their first paper at a SHOT annual meeting will be eligible for the prize. Candidates for the award are judged not only on the quality of the historical research and scholarship demonstrated in the written papers submitted to the Prize Committee before the meeting but also on the effectiveness of their oral presentations. The Robinson Prize consists of a cash prize and certificate.

The Samuel Eleazar and Rose Tartakow Levinson Prize is awarded annually for an original essay in the history of technology that is the author's first work intended for publication. The essay must explicitly examine in some detail a technology or technological device within the framework of social or intellectual history. The prize consists of a certificate and cash prize.

The IEEE Life Members' Prize in Electrical History recognizes the best paper in electrical history published in the previous year. Established by the History Committee of the Institute of Electrical and Electronics Engineers (IEEE), supported by the IEEE Life Members' Fund, and administered by the society, the prize consists of $500 and a certificate. Any historical paper published in a learned journal or magazine is eligible if it treats the art or engineering aspects of electrotechnology and its practitioners. Electrotechnology encompasses power, electronics, telecommunications, and computer science. The cash portion of the prize is shared among all joint authors; individual certificates are presented to each joint author.

The Dibner Prize, made possible by grants from Bern Dibner and the Charles Edison Fund, recognizes excellence in museum exhibits that interpret the history of technology, industry, and engineering to the general public. The winning exhibit, in addition to being well designed and produced, should raise pertinent historical issues. It should be based on scholarship that is solid and current, correct, and complete in its factual content and implication. Artifacts and images should be used in a manner that interests, teaches, and stimulates both the general public and historians. Nomination procedures can be found on the SHOT web site.

The Melvin Kranzberg Award is a dissertation fellowship in honor of the memory of the co-founder of the society. The award of $1,000 will be granted to a doctoral student engaged in the preparation of a dissertation on the history of technology, broadly defined.

The Sally Hacker Prize recognizes the best popular book written in the three years preceding the award. The prize, consisting of a cash prize and certificate, recognizes books in the history of technology that are directed to a broad audience of readers, including students and the interested public. The books should assume that the reader has no prior knowledge of the subject or its method of treatment, and should provide an elucidating explanation of technological change in history, with a minimum of technical or academic prose. The book may be nominated by anyone, including the author or the book's publisher.

The Brooke Hindle Postdoctoral Fellowship provides $10,000 in support of any purpose connected with research and writing in the history of technology for a period of not less than four months. Applicants must hold a doctorate in the history of technology or a related field. The fellowship can be held concurrently with another fellowship and is awarded every other year.

The Eugene S. Ferguson Prize is awarded every other year for outstanding and original reference work that will support future scholarship in the history of technology. Eligible materials include bibliographies, biographical dictionaries, critical editions of primary sources, exhibition catalogues, guides to the field, historical dictionaries and encyclopedias, CDs, web sites, electronic databases, and more. The prize consists of a plaque and cash prize. Material can be nominated by authors, publishers, or others.

The NASA Fellowship in the History of Space Technology, offered by SHOT, will fund one predoctoral or postdoctoral fellow for up to one academic year, for $17,000, to undertake a research project related to the history of space technology.

Officers

Bix, Amy S. (PhD, Johns Hopkins 1994; treasurer) women in engineering, technological unemployment; abix@iastate.edu

Korsten, Jan (PhD, Nijmegen 1996; secretary) technology; j.w.a.korsten@tue.nl

Krige, John (PhD, Sussex, UK 1979; past pres.) science/technology/ US foreign policy; john.krige@hts.gatech.edu

Misa, Thomas J. (PhD, Pennsylvania 1987; pres.) interactions of technology and modern culture; tmisa@umn.edu

Mohun, Arwen Palmer (PhD, Case Western Reserve 1992; vice pres.) technology, risk; mohun@udel.edu

Moon, Suzanne Marie (PhD, Cornell 2000; editor; Technology and Culture) technological change in colonial Indonesia; suzannemoon@ou.edu

The Society of the Cincinnati

2118 Massachusetts Ave. NW, Washington, DC 20008-2810. 202.785.2040. Fax 202.785.0729. Email: library@ societyofthecincinnati.org. Website: https://www. societyofthecincinnati.org/.

The Society of the Cincinnati was founded in 1783 by American military officers and their French counterparts who served during the War for American Independence. Perpetuated by descendants of the original members and other qualified officers, the society is a nonprofit educational institution that supports the American Revolution Institute at its national headquarters at Anderson House in Washington, D.C. The Institute promotes advanced scholarship, conducts public programs, advocates preservation and makes resources available to teachers and students to enrich knowledge and understanding of the achievements of the American Revolution.

A. Collections and Libraries

The Society of the Cincinnati library houses a growing research collection of more than 50,000 items focusing on the people and events of the American Revolution, with a particular concentration on the military and naval history of the period. At the core of the rare book collection are approximately 8,000 works on the art of war, including treatises on fortification, naval architecture, medical texts, artillery and drill manuals, and officers' guides. Other highlights include a nearly complete collection of British army lists for the years between 1755 and 1783, *Ordonnances du Roi* relating to the French army and navy, memoirs of American and British officers, Loyalists tracts, and Indian captivity narratives. Complementing the early printed books are historical manuscripts, maps, broadsides, graphic arts, and the archives of the founding of the society. In addition, a modern reference collection supports research on the Revolutionary War period and the history of the Society of the Cincinnati and its members. The library is open to researchers by appointment, weekdays from 10 a.m. to 4 p.m.

B. Programs

The library and museum mount two exhibitions annually at the society headquarters at Anderson House, and organize lectures, book signings, concerts, and other public programs.

C. Publications

The society publishes exhibition catalogs and brochures, as well as an *Annual Report and Cincinnati Fourteen*, a semi-annual newsletter available to members of the society.

D. Fellowships and Awards

Several annual research fellowships are available to students and faculty at the thesis level and beyond on a competitive basis. The Society of the Cincinnati Prize is awarded to the author of a distinguished work on the era of the American Revolution. Deadline for submissions for the 2020 prize (for a work published in 2019) is December 31, 2019.

Staff

Clark, Ellen McCallister (MLS, Catholic 1997; library dir.) emclark@ societyofthecincinnati.org

Hong, E. K. (MLS, Maryland 1988; cataloger and systems librarian) ekhong@societyofthecincinnati.org

Nellis, Rachel (MSIS, Texas 2016; research services librarian) rnellis@societyofthecincinnati.org

State Historical Society of Missouri

1020 Lowry St., Columbia, MO 65201-7298. 573.882.7083. Fax 573.884.4950. Email: contact@shsmo.org. Website: https:// shsmo.org/.

The State Historical Society of Missouri was founded in 1898 as a research facility for the study of the Show Me State's heritage. As charged by state statute, the society collects, preserves, makes accessible, and publishes material relating to the history of Missouri and the Midwest. Headquartered in Columbia, the society maintains research centers throughout Missouri. The current center locations are in Cape Girardeau, Columbia, Kansas City, Rolla, St. Louis, and Springfield.

A. Collections and Libraries

The State Historical Society of Missouri research centers collect and maintain materials that include but are not limited to manuscripts, newspaper archives, photo archives, maps, oral histories, reference works, and an art collection for public and scholarly use.

A constantly growing collection of primary sources has been assembled to document all aspects of life in Missouri and the Midwest. In addition to the more traditional political, military, and diplomatic records, users will find information on religion, the arts, education, the professions, ethnic and social groupings and movements, all aspects of the economy, and data on the lives of both famous and obscure individuals that in totality illustrate the experience and culture of the region. Finding aids to the manuscript collections are available online at http://shsmo.org/ manuscripts.

The society has the largest and most complete collection of Missouri newspapers in the nation. State newspapers from 1808 to the present are preserved on more than 56,000 reels of microfilm. In addition, more than 200 current newspapers from every Missouri county arrive weekly. A guide to the newspaper collection on microfilm and a searchable index to selected papers are available on the society's web site. The society also maintains a growing collection of digitized historic newspapers that is searchable by keyword and may be accessed at http://shsmo.org/ newspaper/mdnp.

The photograph archives contain more than 100,000 photographs, postcards, and other graphic materials. The collection is an outstanding research source for students, scholars, writers, local historians, genealogists, and others interested in images of the people and the events that shaped the development of Missouri, the Midwest, and the West. A growing collection of digitized images is available online and may be accessed at http://shsmo.org/photograph.

More than 4,400 maps, ranging from early river routes, trails, and roads to modern railroad and highway routes, are owned by the society. Atlases, gazetteers, early guidebooks, and statistical maps are on file, as is a complete assemblage of the state's official topographic maps. The earliest map in the collection, published in 1684, charts the Louisiana Territory claimed for France by LaSalle. Digital collections available online include aerial photographs and plat maps of Missouri.

The oral history program actively produces and collects oral history interviews that preserve the history and culture of Missouri and Missourians. Ongoing projects include Missouri veterans, politics in Missouri, Missouri environmental history, desegregation and civil rights, and other topics.

The society's reference collections contain books, pamphlets, journals, and official publications that document the history of the state and the Midwest. The holdings range from monographs and biographies to city directories and county histories to family and organizational histories.

The society's art collection contains the major national collection of paintings and portraits by 19th-century artist George Caleb Bingham. The Thomas Hart Benton Collection includes signed lithographs, drawings, watercolors, and the World War II Year of Peril series. Ninety colored engravings by Karl Bodmer depicting Western Plains Indians greatly enhance the collection. Contemporary Missouri artists are represented by the works of Frank B. Nuderscher, Frederick Oakes Sylvester, William Knox, Carl Gentry, Fred Geary, Fred Shane, Charles Schwartz, Frank Stack, Siegfried Reinhardt, Larry Young, and Roscoe Misselhorn. The editorial cartoon collection, national in scope, includes original works by Daniel Fitzpatrick, S. J. Ray, Bill Mauldin, Don Hesse, Tom Engelhardt, and others.

The collections at the Columbia headquarters are open to the public Tuesday–Friday, 8 a.m.–4:45 p.m., and Saturday, 8 a.m.–3:30 p.m., except legal holidays and the Saturdays preceding Monday-observed holidays. The art galleries, located in Columbia, are open Tuesday–Friday, 9 a.m.–4:30 p.m., and Saturday, 9 a.m.–3:15 p.m. The Cape Girardeau center is open to the public Monday–Friday, 9 a.m.–1 p.m. and by appointment. The Kansas City, Rolla, and St. Louis centers are open Tuesday–Friday, 8 a.m.–4:45 p.m. The Springfield center is open Monday–Friday, 8 a.m.–5 p.m.

B. Programs

The society, in conjunction with the Missouri Humanities Council, sponsors the Missouri component of the National History Day competition for junior and senior high school students. Permanent and changing exhibitions featuring works from the society's art collection appear in the art galleries. Public programming includes workshops, lecture series, a statewide speakers' bureau for not-for-profit organizations, and administration of the annual Missouri Conference on History.

C. Publications

The *Missouri Historical Review*, the society's quarterly journal, contains the nation's most extensive collection of articles and edited documents on the history of Missouri. The society also publishes scholarly books; a quarterly newsletter; online publications such as the Historic Missourians biographical series for young readers; and occasional directories, guides, and indexes related to the holdings. Descriptions and ordering information can be obtained from the society's web site.

D. Fellowships and Awards

The society's Center for Missouri Studies offers annual competitive fellowships to support ongoing scholarship on selected Missouri topics. Sponsored by the Richard S. Brownlee Fund, each fellowship awards a $5,000 stipend and presents opportunities to publish work in the *Missouri Historical Review* and to deliver a public lecture. Interested scholars should check the society's web site or contact the society for further information.

A $1,500 cash award is presented annually for the best book written on the history of Missouri or Missourians; submission deadline is June 30 for books published during the previous calendar year. The $1,000 biennial Eagleton-Waters Award recognizes the best book published on the political history of Missouri during the two preceding years. The submission deadline is June 30 of odd-numbered years.

The *Missouri Historical Review* Award of $750 is given annually for the best article appearing in the journal. The biennial Mary Neth Prize of $500 is awarded to the author of the best article on women's or gender history to appear in the journal in the preceding two volumes.

The Lewis E. Atherton Prizes annually recognize an outstanding master's thesis and doctoral dissertation on Missouri history or biography. The winning thesis receives a $500 cash award; $1,000 is awarded to the winning dissertation. Nominations are made by the department granting the degrees; submission deadline is June 30.

Staff

Adams, Lucinda (asst. dir., Kansas City) adamslu@shsmo.org
Bradbury, John F., Jr. (BA, Missouri-Rolla 1974; Center for Missouri Studies fellow) JFB@shsmo.org
Brenner, John (managing editor) brennerj@shsmo.org
Cox, Anne (photo archivist) coxan@shsmo.org
Eddleman, William R. (assoc. dir., Cape Girardeau) EddlemanW@shsmo.org
Engel, Elizabeth (sr. archivist) engelel@shsmo.org
Forester, Rachel (archivist, Kansas City) foresterrl@shsmo.org
George, Christina (sr. strategic comm. assoc.) georgecr@shsmo.org
George, Kevin (librarian) georgeke@shsmo.org
Goggin, Carole (library info. asst., Rolla) goggincj@shsmo.org
Hargett, Dean (acquisitions specialist) hargettd@shsmo.org
Harper, Kimberly (assoc. editor) harperk@shsmo.org
Heinzmann, Whitney (archivist, Kansas City) heinzmannw@shsmo.org
Hirsch, Gerald (sr. assoc. dir.) hirschg@shsmo.org
Jolley, Laura (asst. dir., Manuscripts) jolleyl@shsmo.org
Konzal, John C. (archivist) konzalj@shsmo.org
Kraus, Erin (conservator) krause@shsmo.org
Kremer, Gary R. (PhD, American 1978; exec. dir.) kremerg@shsmo.org
Kremer-Wright, Garret (archivist, Cape Girardeau) KremerWrightG@shsmo.org
Leeman, Lauren (librarian) leemanl@shsmo.org
Lewis, Jami A (BA, Drury 2008; archivist, Springfield) LewisJami@shsmo.org
Lohmann, Mary Ellen (strategic comm.) lohmannm@shsmo.org
Loran, Michele (archivist, Kansas City) LoranM@shsmo.org
Luebbert, Patsy (grant mgr.) LuebbertP@shsmo.org
Marks, Claire P. (archivist, St. Louis) MarksCP@shsmo.org
Mayhan, Maggie (coord., National Hist. Day in Missouri) mayhanm@shsmo.org
McCarthy, Peter (library info. asst.) mccarthyp@shsmo.org
Medlock, A. J. (archivist, St. Louis) MedlockA@shsmo.org

Pace, Jeneva (advancement officer and board liaison) pacejp@shsmo.org
Richmond, Heather (archivist) richmondh@shsmo.org
Rost, Sean (PhD, Missouri, Columbia 2018; oral historian) RostS@shsmo.org
Rowden, Aubrey (admin. coord.) RowdenAu@shsmo.org
Schneider, John (asst. preparator)
Seale, Kathleen (sr. archivist, Rolla) sealek@shsmo.org
Shinn, Tatyana N. (asst. dir., Reference) ShinnTn@shsmo.org
Smither, Erin (sr. archivist, Springfield) smithere@shsmo.org
Sporleder, Josephine (media specialist, St. Louis) sporlederj@shsmo.org
Stack, Joan (art curator) stackj@shsmo.org
Sweeney, Michael (Bicentennial coord.) SweeneyMic@shsmo.org
Thomas, Kenn (sr. archivist, St. Louis) thomask@shsmo.org
Thompson, Greig (chief museum preparator) thompsong@shsmo.org
Van Vranken, Erika (librarian) vanvrankene@shsmo.org
Wagner, Wende (membership prog. coord.) wagnerwl@shsmo.org
Walsh, Kevin (security) walshkr@shsmo.org
Waters, Amy L. (librarian) watersa@shsmo.org
Wilkinson, Melissa (mgr. II business admin.) wilkinsonme@shsmo.org

United States Capitol Historical Society

200 Maryland Ave. NE, Washington, DC 20002-5796. 202.543.0629. Fax 202.544.8244. Email: uschs@uschs.org. Website: https://uschs.org/.

A. Collections and Libraries

Not applicable.

B. Programs

The US Capitol Historical Society, a privately funded nonprofit educational organization chartered by the US Congress, conducts and sponsors several programs promoting the history and art of the Capitol and the Congress, including fellowship programs, annual symposia, lunchtime lectures, publications, traveling exhibits, and research for publication.

Foremost among the society's programs is its symposia series, alternating annually between congressional history, and the art and architectural history of the Capitol and Capitol campus. In recognition of the centennial of the ratification of the 19th Amendment, the upcoming (2020) congressional history symposium will focus on the evolution of voting rights in American history. Prior congressional history symposia have examined the American Revolution, the Confederation Period, the Constitution, and the history of Congress in the Federalist, Antebellum, Civil War, and the Reconstruction periods. Prior art/architectural history symposia have examined the role of Montgomery Meigs, and the "politics of ethnicity" in the Capitol's design. For more information, consult the society's web site.

The Society's educational outreach department furnishes many educational resources through its every-expanding website features. The Society also provides many "live" educational programs for students, teachers, and the general public. The Society's lunchtime lecture series presents book talks or other hour-long presentations monthly throughout the year, and weekly every August. "Where Freedom Speaks" is an interdisciplinary program distributed nationwide, designed to teach elementary-level students about the history of the Capitol and their constitutional rights and responsibilities. "We the People" is a day-long program held throughout the public school academic year, exposing eighth-graders in the DC area to sites and related themes associated with the functioning of the US Constitution and federal government. An annual series of youth forums creates a dialogue about public service between past and present members of Congress, congressional staff, and high school students.

C. Publications

The history department of the society conducts and publishes research into the history of the Capitol and of the Congress. Publications include *The Capitol Dome* magazine of history, published twice yearly; *Creating Capitol Hill*; *The United States Capitol: An Annotated Bibliography* (Univ. of Oklahoma Press); *The Speakers of the US House of Representatives: A Bibliography* (Johns Hopkins Univ. Press); *Foreign Visitors to Congress: Speeches and History* (Kraus International); *The Committee on Ways and Means: A Bicentennial History* (GPO); and *Accidental Architect: William Thornton and the Cultural Life of Early Washington* (Ohio Univ. Press). Books based on the annual symposia have been published for the society by the University Press of Virginia and Ohio University Press. Works by fellows of the society have been published by the Yale University Press, the University of Delaware Press, and by the society itself, which has also originated *We, the People*; *Washington Past and Present*; *Where the People Speak*; and several other books, pamphlets, and videos on the Capitol; Washington, DC; and related historical subjects.

D. Fellowships and Awards

The US Capitol Historical Society's fellowship program is designed to encourage and assist research and publication on the art and architectural history of the US Capitol complex. The program, jointly administered with the Office of the Architect of the Capitol, currently offers monthly stipends of $2,500, available for up to a maximum of one year. The fellowship is open to graduate students enrolled in a degree program in art or architectural history, American history, or American studies; professors; and independent scholars with a proven record of research and publication. Application deadline is March 15 for the fellowship year beginning the following September. Interested parties should contact Dr. Michele Cohen, Curator, Architect of the Capitol, Washington, DC 20515.

The Society also administers summer- or semester-long internships for undergraduate and graduate students interested in researching for any of the History Department's various publications, and assisting with any aspect of its public history programs.

Every year the Society's Freedom Award ceremony recognizes and honors individuals and organizations that have advanced greater public understanding and appreciation for freedom as represented by the US Capitol and Congress.

Staff

Borchard, Lauren E. (MA, George Washington 2004; dir., Historical Progs.) women, cultural, 20th-century US; lauren@uschs.org
diGiacomantonio, William C. (MA, Chicago 1988; chief historian) early Congress, congressional biography, early Native American relations; cdigiacomo@uschs.org

United States Department of State

Office of the Historian, FSI/OH, 2300 E St. NW, SA-4D, Washington, DC 20372. 202.955.0200. Fax 202.955.0268. Email: history@state.gov. Website: https://history.state.gov/.

A. Collections and Libraries

Documents and collections maintained in the office are for internal use only.

B. Programs

The Office of the Historian at the Department of State publishes the official record of US foreign policy in the Foreign Relations of the United States series in accordance with 22 USC 4351 et seq. The Office also counsels scholars on documentary resources, conducts oral history interviews, and provides historical reference services to government officials, scholars, and the general public. Historians also frequently teach at the Foreign Service Institute. Ongoing offerings taught by office staff include modules on diplomatic history and related subjects for the Foreign Service Institute's A–100 training (the basic education received by all new Foreign Service Officers) and a number of area studies courses.

C. Publications

The Foreign Relations of the United States series presents the official documentary record of major US foreign policy decisions and significant diplomatic activity. The series began in 1861 and now comprises more than 500 individual volumes. The volumes published over the last two decades contain declassified records from all of the US foreign policy agencies. Historians conduct research in the Presidential Libraries, Departments of State and Defense, National Security Council, Central Intelligence Agency, Agency for International Development, and other relevant agencies. Volumes in the series since 1952 are organized chronologically according to Presidential administrations, and geographically and topically within each series. A total of 32 volumes cover the Kennedy administration; 36 cover the Johnson administration; 65 of 67 volumes scheduled have been published for the Nixon and Ford administrations; 24 of 33 volumes scheduled have been published for the Carter administration; and 4 of 52 scheduled have been published for the Reagan administration. All new volumes and the entirety of the back catalog volumes are available on the Office's website, history.state.gov.

The Office also produces both classified and unclassified research studies, with some of the latter available on its website. The website also features extensive, publicly accessible digital archives devoted to various aspects of the Department's history and US foreign policy. Contents include Recognition and Relations, an encyclopedia of US diplomatic relations with every country; Principal Officers of the Department and US Chiefs of Mission, a thorough record of key Department staff; and a World-Wide Diplomatic Archives Index, which directs readers to diplomatic archives and record services across the world. The website also offers searchable chronologies of Foreign Travels of the Secretary of State and Presidential Visits Abroad.

D. Fellowships and Awards

The Department of State periodically offers internships through the Virtual Student Federal Service program (unpaid), the Department of State's Internship program (unpaid), and the Pathways Internship program (paid).

Staff

Ahlberg, Kristin L. (PhD, Nebraska 2003; asst. to the general editor) US diplomatic, US presidency, foreign assistance policy

Ashley, Carl Edward (PhD, Catholic 2003; div. chief, Declassification) European intellectual, US-European relations, NATO politics

Ball, Margaret Sewall (PhD, Colorado, Boulder 2013; historian)

Barnum, Forrest S. L. (MA, British Columbia 2012; historian) modern Europe, US diplomatic, comparative politics

Berndt, Sara E. (PhD, George Washington 2011; historian) Latin America, religion and culture, imperialism/politics/international relations

Botts, Joshua D. (PhD, Virginia 2009; historian) US diplomatic, Cold War

Burton, Myra Frances (MA, San Diego 1995; div. chief, Africa and Americas) Africa, African American, US diplomatic

Cabrera, Tiffany H. (PhD, Howard 2014; historian) 20th-century US, Vietnam War, civil rights

Chalou, Mandy (MA, New Hampshire 2004; div. chief, Editing & Publishing) modern Europe, British imperialism and Commonwealth, Atlantic

Charles, Elizabeth C. (PhD, George Washington 2010; historian) modern Russia and Soviet Union, US diplomatic, Cold War

Eckroth, Stephanie L. (PhD, Texas Tech 2011; historian) bibliography, textual studies, scholarly editing

Faith, Thomas I. (PhD, George Washington 2008; historian) modern US, military, technology

Garrett, Amy C. (PhD, Pennsylvania 2004; div. chief, Policy Studies) propaganda and diplomacy

Geyer, David C. (MA, Maryland, Coll. Park 1993; div. chief, Europe) modern Germany, Cold War, US diplomatic

Goings, Renee A. (MA, Texas 2000; deputy historian) Middle East, Anglo-American diplomacy

Hawley, Charles V. (PhD, Iowa 1999; historian) US international relations, US culture, Asian American

Hite, Kerry E. (BS, Radford 1990; historian) politics, international relations

Holly, Susan K. (PhD, Essex, UK 1987; historian) Anglo-American diplomacy, Middle East, oil diplomacy

Howard, Adam M. (PhD, Florida 2003; dir.) US diplomatic, transnational, modern Middle East

Husain, Aiyaz (PhD, Tufts 2011; historian) US diplomatic, modern Middle East, South Asia

Kolar, Laura R. (PhD, Virginia 2011; historian) modern US, political culture, environment

Marrs, Aaron W. (PhD, South Carolina 2006; historian) US to 1877, US diplomacy with sub-Saharan Africa

McAllister, William Brian (PhD, Virginia 1996; div. chief, Special Projects) international and transnational, diplomatic, modern Europe

McCoyer, Michael T. M. (PhD, Northwestern 2007; joint historian) US since 1865, social and cultural, immigration and ethnicity

Morrison, Christopher A. (PhD, Georgetown 2009; historian) 19th- and 20th-century imperialism, US relations with Iran, Philippines and East Asia

Munteanu, Mircea A. (MPhil, George Washington 2008; historian) US diplomatic, Cold War, eastern Europe

Nickles, David P. (PhD, Harvard 2000; div. chief, Middle East and Asia) culture and history of US diplomacy, technology, US relations with East Asia

Pitman, Paul M. (PhD, Columbia 1997; historian) international economic relations, strategy and policy, modern and contemporary Europe

Poster, Alexander O. (PhD, Ohio State 2010; historian) US diplomatic, disaster relief, Latin America

Rasmussen, Kathleen Britt (PhD, Toronto 2001; div. chief, Global Issues and General) US diplomatic, international economy, Canadian diplomatic

Regan, Matthew R. G. (MA, Catholic 2004; historian) Southeast Asia, US foreign relations, international development

Ross, Amanda (MSLS, North Carolina, Chapel Hill 2008; program analyst) library science, archives

Rotramel, Seth Amiel (PhD, Georgetown 2010; historian) modern Europe, international relations, medicine

Rubin, Daniel A. (PhD, Maryland, Coll. Park 2010; historian) US diplomatic, Cold War, Sino-American relations

Smith, Nathaniel Lee (PhD, North Carolina, Chapel Hill 2007; historian) diplomatic and international, 20th-century world, US

Taylor, Melissa Jane (PhD, South Carolina 2006; historian) US immigration policy, modern Europe, Jewish

Tudda, Chris (PhD, American 2002; historian) US diplomatic, Cold War, revolutionary America

Weatherhead, Dean (MA, George Washington 1993; historian) military policy, intelligence operations

Wicentowski, Joseph C. (PhD, Harvard 2007; digital history advisor) modern East Asia, social, public health

Wieland, Alexander R. (PhD, London 2006; historian) Anglo-American diplomacy, Middle East

Wilson, James Graham (PhD, Virginia 2011; historian) US diplomatic, Cold War, Soviet Union

Woodroofe, Louise Prentis (PhD, London 2007; historian) US diplomatic, US-African relations, Cold War

Zierler, David (PhD, Temple 2008; historian) US diplomatic, environment, national security policy

United States Senate Historical Office

201 Hart Senate Office Bldg., Washington, DC 20510-7108. 202.224.6900. Email: historian@sec.senate.gov. Website: https://www.senate.gov/history.

A. Collections and Libraries

The US Senate Historical Office serves as institutional memory for the US Senate. It collects and provides information on significant events, dates, precedents, and historical comparisons of current and past Senate activities for use by senators and staff, the media, scholars, and the general public. The office maintains files of biographical information and Senate-related subjects, scholarly articles, newsclippings, and photographs and other images.

B. Programs

The office advises senators and Senate committees on preservation of noncurrent office files, assists scholars in researching topics of Senate history, provides historical information to the public and the media, and maintains a register of biographical information and locations of former senators' research collections. Staff provides assistance in the use of congressional source materials and in the understanding of the history of current Senate procedures and precedents. Office historians and archivists provide regular talks and presentations on Senate history as well as specially-designed historical tours for senators and staff. Historians identify and conduct oral history interviews with retired senators, Senate officers, and staff.

C. Publications

The office publishes printed and online narrative histories of the Senate and reference works designed to provide concise information about various aspects of the Senate's institutional history, including contested elections, impeachment trials, notable investigations, and committee proceedings. It edits for publication historically significant transcripts and minutes of selected Senate committees and party organizations. It publishes brochures, booklets, reference works, and scholarly books and monographs. It creates and maintains the Senate portion of the printed and online *Biographical Directory of the United States Congress*. The office produces and maintains all historical information on the US Senate website at www.senate.gov.

D. Fellowships and Awards

The office participates in the summer internship program of the Secretary of the US Senate.

Staff

Baker, Richard A. (PhD, Maryland, Coll. Park 1982; historian emeritus) US political; senateshistorian@gmail.com

Baumann, Mary T. (MA, George Mason 2001; historical writer and online content mgr.) US political; mary_baumann@sec.senate.gov

Butler, Elisabeth F. (MA, William and Mary 2005; deputy archivist for accessioning and processing) US political, archival; elisabeth_butler@sec.senate.gov

Camilleri, Amy (BA, Detroit Mercy 2001; executive asst.) amy_camilleri@sec.senate.gov

Hahn, Beth (MA, George Mason 1998; historical editor) US political; beth_hahn@sec.senate.gov

Holt, Daniel (PhD, Virginia 2008; asst. historian) US political, legal, political economy; daniel_holt@sec.senate.gov

Koed, Betty K. (PhD, California, Santa Barbara 1999; historian/dir.) US political, public, oral; betty_koed@sec.senate.gov

Moore, Heather (MA,MLS, Maryland, Coll. Park 1997; photo historian) US political, archival; heather_moore@sec.senate.gov

Paul, Karen D. (MA, Virginia 1973; archivist) US political, archival; karen_paul@sec.senate.gov

Ritchie, Donald A. (PhD, Maryland, Coll. Park 1975; historian emeritus) US political, oral; donritchie.historian@gmail.com

Scott, Katherine A. (PhD, Temple 2009; assoc. historian/deputy dir.) US political, oral; kate_scott@sec.senate.gov

White, M. Alison (MS, Tennessee 2002; deputy archivist for digital archives) US judicial, political, archival; alison_white@sec.senate.gov

Virginia Museum of History and Culture

PO Box 7311, Richmond, VA 23221-0311. 804.358.4901. Fax 804.355.2399. Email: reference@VirginiaHistory.org. Website: https://www.virginiahistory.org/.

The Virginia Museum of History & Culture is owned and operated by the Virginia Historical Society—a private, non-profit organization established in 1831. For use in its state history museum and its renowned research library, the historical society cares for a collection of nearly nine million items representing the ever-evolving story of Virginia. It has a staff of about 75 professional and support personnel and a membership of about 7,200 across all 50 states.

A. Collections and Libraries

The research library, museum, and offices are located at 428 North Boulevard in Richmond. Virginia House, a house museum owned and operated by the society, is located at 4301 Sulgrave Road in Richmond.

The society began collecting manuscripts and objects shortly after its founding, and its library is one of the largest repositories of nonofficial documents in the Southeast. Because the society was established as an independent, privately supported scholarly institution, its jurisdiction has never extended to the official records of the state.

The manuscript collections, holding more than 8,000,000 processed items, embrace personal, family, and corporate papers dating from the seventeenth century to the present. Included are the correspondence of colonial families, royal governors, Revolutionary patriots, Virginia-born presidents, the Confederate hierarchy, and twentieth-century Virginians; diaries, commonplace books, and plantation records; and the papers of businesses, churches, and educational and charitable organizations. Finding aids on the African American, Civil War, and women's manuscript collections provide an overview of the most important groupings of documents.

Although manuscripts constitute the largest single segment of the society's holdings, they are only a part of the total collection. Holdings in books and serials number nearly 150,000 volumes. Rare books include early tracts on the settlement of Virginia, travel narratives, Virginia and Confederate imprints, and an extensive collection of seventeenth- and eighteenth-century architectural books and volumes once owned by celebrated Virginians. The map collection includes some 6,500 items dating from 1590 to the present. Virginia newspapers, from the first surviving copy of the *Virginia Gazette* (1736) to papers published in the mid-twentieth century, are available both in the original form and on microfilm. The museum collections embrace original portraiture (more than 900 pieces), prints, photographs, and outstanding examples of southern furniture, silverware, and decorative arts, as well as bookplates, sheet music, paper currency, paper ephemera, and the largest collection of Confederate-made weaponry in existence. In the society's library and on its web site, an online catalog gives researchers access to all of these collections.

B. Programs

In its effort to advance the interpretation of Virginia history, the Virginia Museum of History & Culture sponsors public lectures, symposia, and exhibitions. The annual Stuart G. Christian, Jr. Lecture, the Hazel and Fulton Chauncey Lecture, and the J. Harvie Wilkinson, Jr. Lecture bring to the society speakers of national prominence. Lunchtime Banner Lectures in the Robins Family Forum mark events, such as Black History Month and Women's History Month, and present other topics related to Virginia and American history.

The museum's education staff serves teachers, students, out-of-school adults, and local historical societies. Programs offered include teacher recertification workshops, symposia and conferences, innovative teacher institutes, and such classroom kits as "Teaching with Documents" and "Teaching with Photographs." Since 2012, staff have reached a national audience through HistoryConnects, the society's interactive video conferencing program. In 2017, the museum became the permanent site for the annual Virginia History Day competition.

Museum exhibitions interpret Virginia history in its broadest context. Past exhibitions have examined the lives of such historical figures as Pocahontas and George Washington, Virginia's ratification of the Constitution, medical history, the escape from slavery and the colonization of Liberia, World War II's effect on the Old Dominion, the Civil War on home front and battlefield, Virginia's role in westward expansion, and the history of African Americans in Virginia from the first arrival in Jamestown to the twenty-first century. Additionally, the museum organizes traveling exhibitions, smaller versions of exhibitions that have appeared at the institution.

C. Publications

The society has published the *Virginia Magazine of History and Biography* quarterly since 1893. The journal features articles of original scholarship and book reviews on Virginia and Virginia-related subjects. A newsletter keeps members informed about the museum's activities. The website is a continuously updated publication of activities and provides access to the online catalog of its holdings. The museum has published monograph-length catalogs to accompany a number of its major exhibitions. These books include *The Virginia Landscape: A Cultural History*; *Lost Virginia: Vanished Architecture of the Old Dominion*; *Bound Away: Virginia and the Westward Movement*; *Old Virginia: The Pursuit of a Pastoral Ideal*; *Treasures Revealed from the Paul Mellon Library of Americana*; *Jamestown, Québec, Santa Fe: Three North American Beginnings*; *Lee and Grant*; and *Photography in Virginia*. In addition, the museum has highlighted its major collections with such books as *Eye of the Storm: A Civil War Odyssey Written and Illustrated by Private Robert Knox Sneden* and *Images from the Storm*. In 2006 the society published its own history in Melvin I. Urofsky's *The Virginia Historical Society: The First 175 Years, 1831–2006*. In 2018, the museum published *The Story of Virginia: Highlights from the Virginia Museum of History & Culture*. In 2019, the museum published *A Time for Moderation: J. Sargeant Reynolds and Virginia's New Democrats, 1960–1971* by C. Matthew West.

D. Fellowships and Awards

Each year the research library administers a program of short-term research fellowships to help defray the travel and living expenses of scholars visiting the society's library. Grants include the Andrew W. Mellon Research Fellowship in Virginia and American history; the Guy Kinman Award, which support work on such topics as lesbian and gay studies, civil rights, and First Amendment issues; the Betty Sams Christian Fellowship in business history; and the Frances Lewis Fellowship in Gender and Women's History. The deadline for applying each year is February 1.

The museum confers annual cash awards for the best overall article in the *Virginia Magazine of History & Biography*, the best article by a graduate student in the *Virginia Magazine*, the outstanding history teacher of the year, the outstanding secondary school student of the year, and the Richard Slatten Award for excellence in Virginia biography.

Staff

Beattie, Heather Dawn (MA, Virginia Commonwealth 2002; collections mgr.) photography, digital imaging, museum studies; hbeattie@VirginiaHistory.org

Bosket, Jamie O. (MA, George Washington 2008; pres. and CEO) museum studies, public administration; jbosket@VirginiaHistory.org

Bryan, Tracy L. (MA, Phoenix 2004; dir., facilities) human resources, historic site management; tbryan@VirginiaHistory.org

Dozier, Graham (MA, Virginia Tech 1992; editor) Civil War, military, editing; gdozier@VirginiaHistory.org

Jones, Amber Elizabeth (MLIS, Alabama 2014; proj. cataloging/digital librarian) women; ajones@VirginiaHistory.org

Mason, Mary Ann (MA, James Madison 2015; proj. archivist) 19th century, women, Civil War; mmason@VirginiaHistory.org

McClure, John M. (MA, Virginia Commonwealth 2003; reference dept. mgr.) Reconstruction, New South, Jim Crow; jmcclure@VirginiaHistory.org

Nesossis, Jennifer R. (MA, Virginia Commonwealth 2007; visual communications officer) pre-Colombian art, digital media; jennifer@VirginiaHistory.org

Newman, L. Paige (MLS, Catholic 2004; asst. archivist) Virginia; pnewman@VirginiaHistory.org

Oglesby, Elizabeth H. (MFA, Savannah Coll. Art and Design 2006; mgr., public relations and marketing) photography, public relations, marketing; loglesby@VirginiaHistory.org

Parris, L. Eileen (MLS, North Carolina 1992; archivist) colonial Virginia, Old US South, women; eparris@VirginiaHistory.org

Plumb, Michael B. (MA, George Mason 2011; vice pres., guest engagement) colonial America, revolutionary America, public; mplumb@VirginiaHistory.org

Rasmussen, William M. S. (PhD, Delaware 1979; sr. curator) Virginia art, Virginia architecture; wrasmussen@VirginiaHistory.org

Rusch, Stacy J. (MLS, UCLA 1988; chief, conservation) book and paper conservation; srusch@VirginiaHistory.org

Scher, Adam E. (MA, George Washington 1985; vice pres., collections) material culture, interpretation, collections management; ascher@VirginiaHistory.org

Schneider, Tracy D. (MA, George Washington 1997; vice pres., marketing & communications) art, marketing; tschneider@VirginiaHistory.org

Schwarting, Paulette S. (MSLS, Catholic 1982; dir., tech. services) conservation and preservation, automation; pschwarting@VirginiaHistory.org

Sherry, Karen A. (PhD, Delaware 2011; curator, exhibitions) American art, material culture; ksherry@VirginiaHistory.org

Stoner, Laura E. G. (MA, Virginia Commonwealth 2004; asst. archivist) Virginia business; lstoner@VirginiaHistory.org

Talkov, Andrew H. (MA, Virginia Commonwealth 2013; vice pres., exhibitions & publications) mid-19th-century America, Civil War; atalkov@VirginiaHistory.org

Western History Association

Univ. of Nebraska at Omaha, 6001 Dodge St., Omaha, NE 68182. 402.554.5999. Email: westernhistoryassociation@gmail.com. Website: https://www.westernhistory.org/.

The Western History Association was founded in 1961 by a group of professional and avocational historians bound by their belief in the American West as a place rich in history and deserving of further study. The Western History Association strives to be a congenial home for the study and teaching of all aspects of North American Wests, frontiers, homelands, and borderlands. Our mission is to cultivate the broadest appreciation of this diverse history.

A. Collections and Libraries

Not applicable.

B. Programs

The first meeting of what was to become the Western History Association was held in Santa Fe, New Mexico in October 1961. The WHA continues to hold an annual conference in October. Conference programs are mailed in July.

The WHA is governed by its members who elect a president, president-elect, council, and nominating committee. The WHA offers membership to anyone interested in the study of the North American West. An annual membership includes a one year subscription to *Western Historical Quarterly*, the premier scholarly journal in the field, with articles and book reviews by leading

western historians; discounted rates for the annual conference; and eligibility for awards and prizes in recognition of scholarly achievements in Western history.

C. Publications

The *Western Historical Quarterly* is the official, peer-reviewed journal of the Western History Association. Reflecting the association's mission to cultivate diverse scholarship, the *Western Historical Quarterly* publishes original articles dealing with the North American West, undefined expansion and colonization, indigenous histories, regional studies (including western Canada, northern Mexico, Alaska, and Hawaii), and transnational, comparative, and borderland histories. Articles undergo rigorous peer review and appear online as part of JSTOR's Current Scholarship Program.

D. Fellowships and Awards

The association sponsors a number of annual and biennial awards for books and articles, and an editorial fellowship is offered by the *Western Historical Quarterly*.

Officers

Sandweiss, Martha A. (PhD, Yale 1985; pres.; prof., Princeton) masand@princeton.edu

Wrobel, David M. (PhD, Ohio 1991; pres.-elect; prof., Oklahoma) david.wrobel@ou.edu

Staff

Hyde, Anne (PhD, California, Berkeley 1988; editor, Western Historical Quarterly; prof., Oklahoma) anne.hyde@ou.edu

Nelson, Elaine Marie (PhD, New Mexico 2011; exec. dir.) American West, race and gender, tourism; emnelson@unomaha.edu

World History Association

Northeastern Univ., Dept. of History, 245 Meserve Hall, 360 Huntington Ave., Boston, MA 02115. 617.373.6818. Fax 617.373.2661. Email: info@thewha.org. Website: https://www.thewha.org/.

A. Collections and Libraries

The collection of papers and documents since the founding of the World History Association (WHA) in 1987 is maintained at the World History Association headquarters at Northeastern University.

B. Programs

The WHA holds an annual conference, usually in the last week of June or occasionally in July. Every three years the annual conference is held outside of the United States. Conference information is included in mailings to members, in the *World History Bulletin*, and on the WHA website. The WHA also holds tightly focused symposia at various times and locations throughout the year. Regional affiliates have their own meeting schedules and conferences; see the WHA website for links and complete details. The WHA sponsors or co-sponsors annual institutes and workshops for teachers of world history across the nation, including sessions concerning the AP world history program.

C. Publications

The WHA's official journal is the quarterly *Journal of World History* and WHA also publishes the semi-annual (Spring and Fall) *World History Bulletin*. As the premier source for the dissemination of recent scholarship in world history, the *Journal of World History* serves as a forum for historical scholarship undertaken from a trans-national, trans-cultural, and trans-regional point of view. Its articles and reviews feature comparative and cross-cultural themes. The *Journal of World History* (E-ISSN: 1527-8050) is now available (from Vol. 7) in the Project MUSE electronic database of journals in the humanities and social sciences. Access is restricted to subscribing institutions. For more details, e-mail or visit http://muse.jhu.edu/journals/jwh.

Full-text articles are available through JSTOR. In addition, abstracts dating to Volume I (1990) can be accessed through the University of Hawai`i Press web site at www.uhpress.hawaii.edu/journals/jwh. All early volumes of *Journal of World History* (from three years before the current volume) are now available in the JSTOR electronic journal archive. For details, visit www.jstor.org/journals/10456007.html. *Journal of World History* vols. 14–19 (2003–08) are also available at the History Cooperative collection of online history scholarship at www.historycooperative.org.

The *World History Bulletin* functions as a WHA newsletter and as a source of articles, textbook reviews, and practical ideas for teaching world history at the secondary and college levels. Both are included with membership.

The WHA Teaching Committee supports publications concerning the teaching of world history, including the online journal *World History Connected*, at worldhistoryconnected.press.uiuc.edu, which particularly addresses the needs of class-room teachers.

The WHA also encourages the discussion of scholarly and pedagogical issues through H-World and through the AP World History listserv.

D. Fellowships and Awards

The WHA is committed to fostering excellence in teaching and scholarship at all levels of education. In cooperation with the Phi Alpha Theta History Honor Society, the WHA awards an annual World History Student Paper Prize ($500 each) for the best undergraduate and graduate papers in world history. The World Historian Student Essay Competition Prize ($500) is awarded to a student at the K–12 level. An annual WHA Book Prize ($500) to recognize new scholarly studies that make a significant contribution to the growing field of world history is offered annually. Two awards for the WHA conferences area also available, as well as conference registration fee waivers. The World Scholar Travel Fund is to fund scholars to attend the annual conference and is primarily for those residing outside of North America. The William H. McNeill Teacher Scholarship is also awarded to fund travel and expenses for K–12 and community college instructors (two awards). The WHA Dissertation Prize awards the best dissertation submitted within the prior year. Finally, the WHA Bentley Book Prize awards $500 to the best new book on world history published in the prior year. Complete details on all prizes and scholarships can be found at www.thewha.org.

Officers

Louro, Michele L. (PhD, Temple 2011; treasurer) modern South Asia, world; mlouro@salemstate.edu

Mitchell, Laura J. (PhD, UCLA 2001; vice pres.) Africa, environment, world; mitchell@uci.edu

Rhett, Maryanne A. (PhD, Washington State 2008; secretary) world history during WWI; mrhett@monmouth.edu

Vieira, Kerry (MA, Providence 2009; exec. dir.) Europe; info@thewha.org

Warner, Rick R. (PhD, California, Santa Cruz 1999; immediate past pres.) Latin America; warnerri@wabash.edu

Wiesner-Hanks, Merry E. (PhD, Wisconsin-Madison 1979; pres.) Renaissance, women; merrywh@uwm.edu

Guide to Historians

The Guide to Historians performs two functions: it is an index to all the historians and history specialists listed in this *Directory* as institutional faculty and staff, and a list of the members of the AHA as of August 9, 2019. If a historian was found on both lists, his or her entries were combined.

The listings include both AHA members (whose names are in ***bold italic***) and nonmembers. *Italicized* institutional names indicate that the historian is included in that specific *Directory* entry. The basic index entry for a historian listed in the *Directory* includes the individual's name, department or organization, and current e-mail address. AHA members have more detailed entries depending on how much information they supplied. Their listings include city and state; one or more institutional affiliations; e-mail address; and their current research topics.

A small proportion of members requested that their information not be made public; some of these members who are listed as faculty or staff in an institutional *Directory* entry are included in the Guide. We regret any errors that remain. AHA members can access and search our online membership directory by logging in at http://www.historians.org/myaha. Members can also update and correct any erroneous information in their listings.

A a

***Aaslestad*, *Katherine B*.**, *West Virginia*. Morgantown, WV. Email: Katherine. Aaslestad@mail.wvu.edu. Research: wars of liberation/war memories/gender, 1815 as postwar era.

Abadi, Jacob, *US Air Force Acad*. Email: jacob. abadi@usafa.edu.

Abadie, H. Dale, *Mississippi*.

Abajian*, *Christine. Woodmere, NY. Affil: G.W. Hewlett-Woodmere High Sch. Email: cabajian@hewlett-woodmere.net. Research: world.

Abaka, Edmund, *Miami*. Email: e.abaka@miami. edu.

Abbas*, *Amber Heather, *St. Joseph's*. Philadelphia, PA. Email: aabbas@sju.edu. Research: India's partition, Aligarh Muslim university.

Abbatiello, John J., *US Air Force Acad*. Email: john.abbatiello@usafa.edu.

Abbay, Alemseged, *Frostburg State*. Email: aabbay@frostburg.edu.

Abbey*, *Jefferson William. Fort Collins, CO. Affil: Colorado State. Email: jeffabbe@gmail.com.

Abbott*, *Carl, *Portland State*. Portland, OR. Email: abbottc@pdx.edu. Research: western US city planning and politics, science fiction and social theory.

Abbott*, *Charles. Cheverly, MD. Affil: Maryland, Coll. Park. Email: charlesabbott@tanzanica. com.

Abbott, John, *Illinois, Chicago*. Email: jabbot1@ uic.edu.

Abbott, Judith, *Sonoma State*. Email: judith. abbott@sbcglobal.net.

Abbott*, *Marie Estelle. Columbus, IN. Email: marie.garrison101@comcast.net.

Abbott*, *Nicholas J., *Old Dominion*.

Abbott, William M., *Fairfield*. Email: wmabbott@ fairfield.edu.

Abdalla, Ismail H., *William and Mary*. Email: ixabda@wm.edu.

Abdella*, *Charles. Boylston, MA. Affil: St. John's High Sch. Email: chuckabdella@gmail.com.

Abdul-Korah, Gariba B., *St. Rose*. Email: abdulkog@strose.edu.

Abdullah, Thabit A. J., *York, Can*. Email: athabit@yorku.ca.

Abdul-Tawwab*, *Qasim. Daytona Beach, FL. Affil: Building The Right Foundation. Email: qasimat@yahoo.com. Research: African American Islam.

Abeel*, *Scott F.. Middleburg, VA. Email: sfabeel@ gmail.com.

Abel, Jonathan A., *US Army Command Coll*. Email: jonathan.a.abel.civ@mail.mil.

Abel, Kerry, *Carleton, Can*. Email: kerry.abel@ carleton.ca.

Abele*, *Michael Thomas. Greensboro, NC. Affil: North Carolina, Chapel Hill. Email: mabele@ email.unc.edu. Research: property.

Abelson*, *Elaine S., *New School*. New York, NY. Email: abelson@newschool.edu. Research: 1930s gender and urban homelessness, 1930s US Great Depression.

Abercrombie*, *Thomas A., *NYU*. New York, NY. Email: thomas.abercrombie@nyu.edu. Research: sexuality/gender/honor/violence, festivals/urban culture/social memory.

Abi*, *Ceren. Los Angeles, CA. Affil: UCLA. Email: cerenabi@ucla.edu.

Abidogun*, *Jamaine M., *Missouri State*. Email: jamaineabidogun@missouristate.edu.

Abi-Hamad, Saad G., *Florida International*. Email: sabihama@fiu.edu.

Abi-Mershed*, *Osama W., *Georgetown*. Email: Osama.AbiMershed@georgetown.edu.

Abiola*, *Ofosuwa Mutashat. Temple Hills, MD. Affil: Howard. Email: ofosuwa.abiola@howard. edu. Research: African/African diaspora dance, cultural/performance and identity.

Abisaab*, *Malek, *McGill*. Email: malek.abisaab@ mcgill.ca.

Ablard*, *Jonathan D., *Ithaca*. Ithaca, NY. Email: jablard@ithaca.edu. Research: conscription and suffrage in Argentina, nutrition.

Ablavsky*, *Gregory. Stanford, CA. Affil: Stanford Law Sch. Email: ablavsky@law.stanford.edu.

Ables*, *Gisela Renate. Houston, TX. Affil: Houston Comm. Coll. Northwest. Email: gisela.ables@hccs.edu. Research: US-Middle East relations, Americans and Middle East societies.

Ablovatski*, *Eliza, *Kenyon*. Email: ablovatskie@ kenyon.edu.

Abney Salomon, Charlotte, *Science History Inst*. Email: cabney@sciencehistory.org.

Abou-El-Haj, Rifaat Ali, *Binghamton, SUNY*. Email: rasultani@aol.com.

Abra*, *Allison J., *Southern Mississippi*. Hattiesburg, MS. Email: allison.abra@usm.edu. Research: modern Britain and Europe, popular culture.

Abraham*, *Blake M.. Newark, DE. Affil: Delaware. Email: bma@udel.edu.

Abraham*, *David. Miami, FL. Affil: Miami. Email: dabraham@law.miami.edu. Research: comparative citizenship in neoliberal era, historical political economy.

Abraham*, *Lee B. New York, NY. Affil: Columbia. Email: lba2133@columbia.edu.

Abraham, Tara H., *Guelph*. Email: taabraha@ uoguelph.ca.

Abrahamian, Ervand, *Graduate Center, CUNY*. Email: ervand.abrahamian@baruch.cuny.edu.

Abrahamse*, *Dorothy de F., *California State, Long Beach*. Email: dabraham@csulb.edu.

Abrahamson*, *Hannah R.. Atlanta, GA. Affil: Emory. Email: hannah.rose.abrahamson@ emory.edu. Research: women in early colonial Yucatán, social.

Abrams*, *Daniel J.. Bronx, NY. Email: djabronx@ yahoo.com.

Abray, Jane, *Toronto*. Email: jane.abray@ utoronto.ca.

Abrecht*, *Ryan R., *San Diego*. Email: rabrecht@ sandiego.edu.

Abreu*, *Christina Denise, *Northern Illinois*. DeKalb, IL. Email: cabreu@niu.edu. Research: US Latino/a social and cultural, Afro-Latin American and Caribbean.

Abreu-Ferreira*, *Darlene, *Winnipeg*. Winnipeg, MB, Canada. Email: d.abreu@uwinnipeg.ca. Research: early modern Europe, Portuguese women and crime.

Abromeit, John, *SUNY, Buffalo State*. Email: abromejd@buffalostate.edu.

Abruzzi*, *Raymond J.. Brooklyn, NY. Affil: Columbia. Email: rja2150@columbia.edu.

Abruzzo, Margaret N., *Alabama, Tuscaloosa*. Email: mabruzzo@ua.edu.

Abugideiri, Hibba, *Villanova*. Email: hibba. abugideiri@villanova.edu.

Abul-Magd, Zeinab A, *Oberlin*. Email: zeinab. abul-magd@oberlin.edu.

Abu-Rish, Ziad M., *Ohio*. Email: abuz@ohio.edu.

Abu-Shumays*, *Mary D. Oceanside, CA. Affil: Pittsburgh. Email: ika001@hotmail.com.

Abzug*, *Robert H., *Texas, Austin*. Austin, TX. Email: zug@austin.utexas.edu. Research: psychology and religion in American life, America and Holocaust.

Accampo*, *Elinor Ann, *Southern California*. Los Angeles, CA. Email: accampo@usc.edu. Research: 1918 flu pandemic in France/ Britain/US, WWI.

Accardi, Dean, *Connecticut Coll.* Email: daccardi@conncoll.edu.

Acevedo, John Felipe. Tuscaloosa, AL. Affil: Alabama, Tuscaloosa. Email: jacevedo@law. ua.edu. Research: criminal law in colonial New England, police brutality in contemporary America.

Acevedo-Field, Rafaela. Dillon, MT. Affil: Montana Western. Email: rafrsrch@gmail.com. Research: Iberian Atlantic, Inquisition.

Achebe, Nwando, *Michigan State.* East Lansing, MI. Email: achebe@msu.edu. Research: Africa and West Africa, women/gender/sexuality studies.

Achee, Henri A. Houston, TX. Affil: Houston Comm. Coll. Email: henri.achee@hccs.edu.

Achenbaum, Andrew, *Houston.* Email: achenbaum@uh.edu.

Achilles, Manuela, *Virginia.* Charlottesville, VA. Email: ma6cq@virginia.edu. Research: Weimar Germany.

Acker, Caroline J., *Carnegie Mellon.* Berkeley, CA. Email: acker@andrew.cmu.edu. Research: medicine and drugs, policy.

Ackerberg-Hastings, Amy K. Rockville, MD. Affil: Maryland Univ. Coll. Email: aackerbe@verizon. net. Research: Scottish mathematics/science, mathematics education.

Ackerman, Evelyn B., *Graduate Center, CUNY; Lehman, CUNY.* Email: eackerman7@att.net.

Ackerman-Lieberman, Phillip, *Vanderbilt.* Email: phil.lieberman@vanderbilt.edu.

Ackert, Lloyd Thomas, Jr., *Drexel.* Email: lta24@ drexel.edu.

Acosta, Sal, *Fordham.* Email: sacosta3@fordham. edu.

Acree, Jill O. Las Vegas, NV. Affil: Southern Nevada. Email: jllacree@gmail.com.

Acres, William, *Western Ontario.* Email: wacres@ uwo.ca.

Acsay, Peter, *Missouri–St. Louis.* Saint Louis, MO. Email: acsayp@umsl.edu. Research: US monetary policy, Cold War economic.

Adair, Jennifer, *Fairfield.* Fairfield, CT. Email: jadair@fairfield.edu; jenniferadair@gmail. com. Research: Latin American transitions to democracy, welfare.

Adal, Raja, *Pittsburgh.* Pittsburgh, PA. Email: raja.adal@pitt.edu; raja.adal@gmail.com. Research: modern Egyptian cultural, modern Japanese cultural.

Adalet, Begum. Ithaca, NY. Affil: Cornell. Email: ba375@cornell.edu.

Adalian, Rouben P. Washington, DC. Affil: Armenian National Inst. Email: rouben. adalian@ani-dc.org. Research: Armenia, Turkey.

Adam, Thomas, *Texas, Arlington.* Arlington, TX. Email: adam@uta.edu. Research: philanthropy, transnational.

Adamiak, Patrick John. San Diego, CA. Affil: California, San Diego. Email: padamiak@ucsd. edu.

Adamiak, Stanley, *Central Oklahoma.* Email: sadamiak@uco.edu.

Adamo, Edwarda. San Marcos, CA. Affil: California State, San Marcos. Email: adamo009@cougars.csusm.edu.

Adamo, Phillip C., *Augsburg.* Email: adamo@ augsburg.edu.

Adams, Catherine J., *SUNY, Coll. Geneseo.* Email: adamsc@geneseo.edu.

Adams, Christa. Brunswick, OH. Affil: Cuyahoga Comm. Coll. Email: christaadams@gmail.com.

Adams, Christine M., *St. Mary's, Md.* Email: cmadams@smcm.edu.

Adams, David B., *Missouri State.* Email: dba995f-sgf@missouristate.edu.

Adams, David Wallace, *Cleveland State.* Email: d.adams@csuohio.edu.

Adams, Elizabeth C., *Frostburg State.*

Adams, Gretchen A., *Texas Tech.* Email: gretchen.adams@ttu.edu.

Adams, Julia Potter. New Haven, CT. Affil: Yale. Email: Julia.adams@yale.edu. Research: early modern European states and empires, theory and history.

Adams, Kara. Brighton, MA. Email: kmadams258@gmail.com.

Adams, Kevin John, *Kent State.* Email: kadams9@kent.edu.

Adams, Larry Donell. Hillside, NJ. Email: poindextera8@aol.com. Research: pre-WWI Europe, pre-WWI US.

Adams, Lucinda, *State Hist. Soc. of Missouri.* Email: adamslu@shsmo.org.

Adams, Matthew Stephen. Loughborough, United Kingdom. Affil: Loughborough. Email: m.s.adams@lboro.ac.uk. Research: anarchism, modern British intellectual and cultural.

Adams, Matthew. Peekskill, NY. Affil: American. Email: ma3832a@american.edu.

Adams, Meredith L., *Missouri State.* Email: meredithadams@missouristate.edu.

Adams, Michael C. C., *Northern Kentucky.* Email: adamsm@nku.edu.

Adams, Michelle, *Central Florida.* Email: Michelle.Adams@ucf.edu.

Adams, Mikaela M., *Mississippi.* Email: mmadams@olemiss.edu.

Adams, Paul V. Shippensburg, PA. Affil: Shippensburg. Email: pvg6724@aol.com. Research: southeast Asian environmental, comparative historical demography.

Adams, Ralph J. Q., *Texas A&M.* Email: rjqa@ tamu.edu.

Adams, Sean Patrick, *Florida.* Gainesville, FL. Email: spadams@ufl.edu. Research: 19th-c coal industry, American political economy.

Adams, Thomas M. Washington, DC. Email: adamspt@earthlink.net. Research: comparative social welfare, work and assistance in Europe.

Adams, Thomas P. Davis, CA. Affil: California Dept. of Education. Email: tadams@cde. ca.gov.

Adams, William Drea. Falmouth, ME. Affil: Mellon Foundation. Email: wda@mellon.org.

Adams, Winthrop Lindsay, *Utah.* Email: winthrop.adams@utah.edu.

Adamson, Carol A. Stockholm, Sweden. Email: caradamson@gmail.com.

Adamson, Walter Luiz, *Emory.* Email: wadamso@emory.edu.

Adas, Michael P., *Rutgers.* New Brunswick, NJ. Email: madas@rci.rutgers.edu. Research: wars of attrition and hegemon's decline, WWI as global conflict.

Adcock, Cassie, *Washington, St. Louis.* Email: cadcock@wustl.edu.

Adcock, Christina, *Simon Fraser.* Email: tina. adcock@sfu.ca.

Adderley, Laura Rosanne, *Tulane.* New Orleans, LA. Email: adderley@tulane.edu. Research: African diaspora, Caribbean basin.

Addington, Larry H., *Citadel.* Email: larrya103@ aol.com.

Addis, Cameron Clark, *Austin Comm. Coll.* Email: caddis@austincc.edu.

Addy, George M., *Brigham Young.*

Adebayo, A. G., *Kennesaw State.* Email: aadebayo@kennesaw.edu.

Adedze, Agbenyega Tony, *Illinois State.* Email: adedze@ilstu.edu.

Adejumobi, Saheed Adeyinka, *Seattle.* Email: s.ade@seattleu.edu.

Adekunle, Julius, *Monmouth.* Email: jadekunl@ monmouth.edu.

Adeleke, R. Tunde, *Iowa State.* Email: tadeleke@ iastate.edu.

Adelman, Howard, *Queen's, Can.* Email: adelman@queensu.ca.

Adelman, Jeremy I., *Princeton.* Princeton, NJ. Email: adelman@princeton.edu. Research: Latin America.

Adelman, Joseph M., *Framingham State; Omohundro Inst.* Framingham, MA. Email: jadelman@framingham.edu; adelman. joseph@gmail.com. Research: American Revolution circulation of political news, rise and fall of post office in America.

Adelman, Melvin L., *Ohio State.* Email: adelman.1@osu.edu.

Adelman, Sarah Mulhall, *Framingham State.* Email: sadelman1@framingham.edu.

Adelson, Roger, *Arizona State.* Email: adelsonr@ asu.edu.

Adelusi-Adeluyi, Ademide, *California, Riverside.* Email: ademide.adelusi-adeluyi@ucr.edu.

Aderinto, Saheed A., *Western Carolina.* Email: saderinto@email.wcu.edu.

Adkins, Tracy. Mesquite, TX. Email: tracy@ tracyadkinscpa.com. Research: US Native American governmental policy, European international trade 800-1500 CE.

Adkisson, Michael Colton. Ames, IA. Affil: Iowa State. Email: Cadksn@iastate.edu.

Adler, Ayden, *DePauw.* Email: aydenadler@ depauw.edu.

Adler, Eliyana R., *Penn State.* Email: era12@psu. edu.

Adler, Jeffrey S., *Florida.* Gainesville, FL. Email: jadler@ufl.edu. Research: US urban, crime.

Adler, Jessica L., *Florida International.* Miami, FL. Email: jadler@fiu.edu. Research: modern America, health care.

Adler, Paul K., *Colorado Coll.* Colorado Springs, CO. Email: padler@coloradocollege.edu. Research: US.

Adrian, Christine. Champaign, IL. Affil: Jefferson Middle Sch.; American Hist. Teachers Collaborative. Email: mschris6@comcast.net.

Adyanga, Onek C., *Millersville, Pa.* Email: onek. adyanga@millersville.edu.

Afary, Janet, *California, Santa Barbara.* Email: afary@religion.ucsb.edu.

Afferica, Joan, *Smith.* Email: jafferic@smith.edu.

Afinogenov, Gregory, *Georgetown.* Cambridge, MA. Email: gda8@georgetown.edu; gafinogenov@gmail.com. Research: Russia.

Afolayan, Funso S., *New Hampshire, Durham.* Email: funso.afolayan@unh.edu.

Afshari, Reza, *Pace.* Email: rafshari@pace.edu.

Aftonomos, Anthony, *Nebraska, Omaha.*

Agan, John A. Minden, LA. Affil: Bossier Parish Comm. Coll. Email: jagan58@mac.com. Research: 20th-c US South, political.

Agarwal, *Kritika*. Arlington, VA. Email: Kritika.agarwal@gmail.com. Research: US immigration, Asian American studies.

Agee, **Christopher L.**, *Colorado Denver*. Email: chris.agee@ucdenver.edu.

Aghaie, **Kamran Scot**, *Texas, Austin*. Austin, TX. Email: kamranaghaie@austin.utexas.edu; kamransaghaie@gmail.com. Research: Shi'ism and modern political Islam, Iranian nationalism and historiography.

Agmon, **Danna**, *Virginia Tech*. Blacksburg, VA. Email: dagmon@vt.edu. Research: French imperialism in India, colonial intermediaries.

Agnani, **Sunil**, *Illinois, Chicago*. Email: sagnani1@uic.edu.

Agnew, **Christopher M.** King George, VA. Email: drcma2@yahoo.com.

Agnew, **Christopher Stephen**, *Dayton*. Dayton, OH. Email: cagnew1@udayton.edu. Research: Asia.

Agnew, **Hugh L.**, *George Washington*. Washington, DC. Email: agnew@gwu.edu. Research: nationalism in eastern Europe/Czech, political symbol and ritual.

Agnew, **Jean-Christophe**, *Yale*. New Haven, CT. Email: jean-christophe.agnew@yale.edu. Research: US cultural.

Agnew, **Vijay**, *York, Can*. Email: vagnew@yorku.ca.

Agnitti, **Allen**, *American International*. Email: allen.agnitti@aic.edu.

Agocs, **Andreas**. Stockton, CA. Affil: Pacific. Email: aagocs@pacific.edu. Research: 20th-c Central Europe, German Democratic Republic.

Agoston, **Gabor J.**, *Georgetown*. Email: agostong@georgetown.edu.

Agrait, **Nicolas**, *Long Island, Brooklyn*. Brooklyn, NY. Email: Nicolas.Agrait@liu.edu. Research: 14th-c Spain, Alfonso XI 1312-50.

Agresta, **Abigail Newton**. Washington, DC. Affil: George Washington. Email: abigailagresta@gwu.edu.

Aguilar, **Emiliano, II**. Whiting, IN. Affil: Northwestern. Email: aguilare1992@gmail.com. Research: Northwest Indiana/Latinx politics.

Aguilar, **Kevan Antonio**. Cherry Valley, CA. Affil: California, San Diego. Email: aguilar.kevan@gmail.com. Research: space and radical movements, Spanish exiles in Mexico.

Aguirre, **Carlos**, *Oregon*. Email: caguirre@uoregon.edu.

Aguirre, **Dennis**. Greeley, CO. Affil: Northern Colorado. Email: Dennis.Aguirre@unco.edu. Research: US, Chicana/o.

Aguirre, **Nancy**, *Citadel*. Email: naguirre@citadel.edu.

Aguirre-Mandujano, **Oscar**, *Pennsylvania*.

Agyepong, **Tera**, *DePaul*. Email: tagyepon@depaul.edu.

Ahlberg, **Kristin L.**, *US Dept. of State*. Alexandria, VA. Email: ahlbergkl@state.gov. Research: Lyndon Johnson administration, food aid policies.

Ahlman, **Jeffrey S.**, *Smith*. Northampton, MA. Email: jahlman@smith.edu. Research: African intellectual and political, African nationalism and nation-building.

Ahluwalia, **Sanjam**, *Northern Arizona*. Email: sanjam.ahluwalia@nau.edu.

Ahmad, **Diana L.**, *Missouri Science and Tech*. Email: ahmadd@mst.edu.

Ahmad, **Feroz**, *Massachusetts, Boston*.

Ahmadi, **Shaherzad R.**, *St. Thomas, Minn*. Email: srahmadi@stthomas.edu.

Ahmed, **Faiz**, *Brown*. Providence, RI. Email: faiz_ahmed@brown.edu. Research: Ottoman Empire and Islamicate world, Islamic legal and constitutional.

Ahmed, **Manan**, *Columbia (Hist.)*. New York, NY. Email: ma3179@columbia.edu. Research: philosophy of history/Islam/Pakistan, space/memory/hermeneutics/intellectual.

Ahn, **Byungil**, *Saginaw Valley State*. Email: bahn@svsu.edu.

Ahn, **Chong Eun**, *Central Washington*. Email: ahnc@cwu.edu.

Ahr, **Johan**, *Hofstra*. Email: johan.ahr@hofstra.edu.

Aibel, **Mina A**. Great Neck, NY. Email: loudan@aol.com. Research: New York City, Chicago.

Aidinoff, **Marc**. Cambridge, MA. Affil: MIT. Email: marc.aidinoff@gmail.com.

Aidt-Guy, **Anita L**. Derwood, MD. Affil: Notre Dame, Md.

Aieta, **Joseph, III**. Framingham, MA. Affil: Lasell. Email: jaieta@lasell.edu.

Aiken, **Katherine G.**, *Idaho*. Email: kaiken@uidaho.edu.

Aikin, **Elizabeth Jane**. Alexandria, VA. Email: jaikin@verizon.net. Research: institutional, cultural institutions.

Ailes, **Mary E.**, *Nebraska, Kearney*. Email: ailesm@unk.edu.

Aisenberg, **Andrew R.**, *Scripps*. Claremont, CA. Email: andrew.aisenberg@scrippscollege.edu. Research: modern Europe and France, medicine.

Aiyar, **Sana**, *MIT*. Cambridge, MA. Email: aiyar@mit.edu. Research: South Asian diaspora in colonial Kenya, British Empire.

Akanda, **Albab**. Ashburn, VA. Email: albabakanda@gmail.com.

Akarli, **Engin D.**, *Brown*. Email: Engin_Akarli@Brown.edu.

Akasoy, **Anna**, *Graduate Center, CUNY*. Email: aa739@hunter.cuny.edu.

Akcam, **Taner**, *Clark*. Email: takcam@clarku.edu.

Akehinmi, **Krystal D. F.**, *Tennessee Tech*. Email: kdfakehinmi@tntech.edu.

Akenson, **Donald H.**, *Queen's, Can*. Email: 8da8@queensu.ca.

Akiboh, **Alvita**. Evanston, IL. Affil: Northwestern. Email: AlvitaAkiboh@u.northwestern.edu. Research: US colonial empire, national material culture.

Akin, **William E.**, *Ursinus*. Email: wakin@ursinus.edu.

Akin, **Yigit**, *Tulane*. New Orleans, LA. Email: yakin@tulane.edu. Research: modern Middle East, WWI.

Akita, **George**, *Hawai'i, Manoa*.

Aksakal, **Mustafa**, *Georgetown*. Email: Mustafa.Aksakal@georgetown.edu.

Aksamit, **Nerissa Kalee**. Pittsburgh, PA. Affil: West Virginia. Email: nkaksamit@mix.wvu.edu.

Aksan, **Virginia H.**, *McMaster*. Email: vaksan@mcmaster.ca.

Akturk, **Ahmet Serdar**, *Georgia Southern*. Email: aakturk@georgiasouthern.edu.

Akyeampong, **Emmanuel K.**, *Harvard (Hist.)*. Cambridge, MA. Email: akyeamp@fas.harvard.edu. Research: sub-Saharan West Africa.

Al Huneidi, **Said S**. Amman, Jordan. Email: saidhuneidi@gmail.com. Research: war horses

in ancient world, Egyptian and Hittite Bronze Age chariots.

Alagirisamy, **Darinee**. Hong Kong. Email: darinee.alagirisamy@cantab.net.

Alagona, **Peter S.**, *California, Santa Barbara*. Email: alagona@history.ucsb.edu.

Alaichamy, **Martin**. Zion, IL. Email: martinalaichamy@gmail.com.

Alaimo, **Kathleen**, *St. Xavier*. Email: alaimo@sxu.edu.

Alam, **Asiya**, *Louisiana State*. Email: aalam@lsu.edu.

Alam, **Eram**, *Harvard (Hist. of Science)*. Email: ealam@fas.harvard.edu.

Alamri, **Neama**. Merced, CA. Affil: California, Merced. Email: nalamri@ucmerced.edu.

Alarid, **Michael Joseph**, *Nevada, Las Vegas*. Email: michael.alarid@unlv.edu.

Albanese, **David**, *Bentley*. Email: dalbanese@bentley.edu.

Albani, **Michael**. East Lansing, MI. Affil: Michigan State. Email: malbani@luc.edu. Research: Native and Euro-American relations, Great Lakes fur trade.

Albarran, **Elena Jackson**, *Miami, Ohio*. Email: albarrej@miamioh.edu.

Alberi, **Mary L.**, *Pace*. Email: malberi@pace.edu.

Alberto, **Paulina Laura**, *Michigan, Ann Arbor*. Ann Arbor, MI. Email: palberto@umich.edu. Research: Brazilian black politics/intellectuals, race in contemporary Argentina.

Albi, **Christopher**, *SUNY, New Paltz*. New Paltz, NY. Email: albic@newpaltz.edu. Research: Latin American economic/legal/political, rule of law in Mexico.

Albin, **Roger L**. Ann Arbor, MI. Affil: Michigan, Ann Arbor. Email: ralbin@umich.edu. Research: Parkinson disease, dementias.

Albisetti, **James C.**, *Kentucky*. Email: jcalbi01@uky.edu.

Alborn, **Timothy L.**, *Graduate Center, CUNY; Lehman, CUNY*. Bronx, NY. Email: timothy.alborn@lehman.cuny.edu. Research: British financial services, science.

Albright, **Laura Merrifield**, *Indianapolis*. Email: albrightlm@uindy.edu.

Albritton Jonsson, **Fredrik L.**, *Chicago*. Email: fljonsso@uchicago.edu.

Alcalde, **Angel**. Melbourne, Australia. Affil: Melbourne. Email: angel.alcalde@unimelb.edu.au.

Alcenat, **Westenley**, *Fordham*. Email: walcenat@fordham.edu.

Alchon, **Guy**, *Delaware*. Email: galchon@udel.edu.

Aldana, **Gerardo V.**, *California, Santa Barbara*. Email: gvaldana@chicst.ucsb.edu.

Aldana, **Jessica**. Stafford, TX. Affil: St. Thomas, Tex. Email: jessicaaldana91@gmail.com.

Alden, **Dauril**, *Washington, Seattle*. Email: dauril@earthlink.net.

Alder, **Ken L.**, *Northwestern*. Evanston, IL. Email: k-alder@northwestern.edu. Research: science and technology, France and US.

Alderman, **Myles H.**, **Sr**. North Haven, CT. Email: maldermansr@gmail.com.

Aldous, **Richard**, *Bard*. Email: raldous@bard.edu.

Aldridge, **Daniel W.**, **III**, *Davidson*. Email: daaldridge@davidson.edu.

Alduino, **Frank W.**, *Towson*. Email: falduino@towson.edu.

Alegi, **Peter C.**, *Michigan State*. Email: alegi@ msu.edu.

Alejandrino, **Clark Lim**, *Trinity Coll., Conn.* Washington, DC. Email: clark.alejandrino@ trincoll.edu; cla50@georgetown.edu.

Alekna, **John**. Princeton, MA. Affil: Princeton. Email: jalekna@princeton.edu.

Alessi-Friedlander, **R. Z.** Fayetteville, NC. Affil: US Army. Email: zachaf17@gmail.com.

Alexander, **Amber**, *Nebraska, Kearney*. Email: alexanderaj@unk.edu.

Alexander, **Amir**, *UCLA*. Email: amiralex@ucla. edu.

Alexander, **Ann Field**, *Mary Baldwin*. Email: aalexand@mbc.edu.

Alexander, **Anna Rose**, *California State, East Bay*. Email: anna.alexander@csueastbay.edu.

Alexander, **Benjamin F.** Bloomfield, NJ. Affil: Bloomfield. Email: benalexandernyc@ yahoo.com. Research: Armenian-American immigrant, modern US ethnic and cultural politics.

Alexander, **Charles C.**, **Jr.**, *Ohio*. Email: calexa35@peoplepc.com.

Alexander, **Emma C.**, *Winnipeg*. Email: e.alexander@uwinnipeg.ca.

Alexander, **Jennifer K.**, *Minnesota (Hist. of Science)*. Email: alexa056@umn.edu.

Alexander, **John K.**, *Cincinnati*. Email: john.k.alexander@uc.edu.

Alexander, **June G.** Cincinnati, OH. Email: june. alexander67@gmail.com. Research: US ethnic groups in Cold War era, slavic immigration and ethnic groups.

Alexander, **Keith D.**, *Shepherd*. Email: kalex@ shepherd.edu.

Alexander, **Kimberly S.**, *New Hampshire, Durham*. Email: kimberly.alexander@unh.edu.

Alexander, **Kristine**. Lethbridge, AB, Canada. Affil: Lethbridge. Email: kristine.alexander@ gmail.com. Research: Girl Guides, children and childhood during WWI.

Alexander, **Leslie M.**, *Oregon*. Email: lalexand@ uoregon.edu.

Alexander, **Michael C.**, *Illinois, Chicago*. Pittsburgh, PA. Email: micalexa@uic.edu. Research: Roman politics.

Alexander, **Roberta S.**, *Dayton*.

Alexander, **Ruth M.**, *Colorado State*. Email: ruth. alexander@colostate.edu.

Alexander, **Ryan M.**, *SUNY, Plattsburgh*. Email: ralex006@plattsburgh.edu.

Alexander, **Shawn Leigh**, *Kansas*. Email: slalexan@ku.edu.

Alexander, **Thomas G.**, *Brigham Young*. Provo, UT. Email: thomas_alexander@byu.edu. Research: Mormonism 1847-present, western US environmental.

Alexander, **William H.** Chesapeake, VA. Affil: Norfolk State. Email: whalexander@nsu.edu. Research: modern Europe, world.

Alexander-Davey, **Ethan**, *Campbell*. Email: alexander-davey@campbell.edu.

Alexanderson, **Kris**. Stockton, CA. Affil: Pacific. Email: kalexanderson@pacific.edu. Research: global maritime networks and Dutch empire.

Alexeeva, **Olga**, *Québec, Montréal*. Email: alexeeva.olga@uqam.ca.

Alexis, **Yveline**, *Oberlin*. Email: yalexis@oberin. edu.

Aley, **Ginette**, *Kansas State*. Email: galey@ksu. edu.

Alfaro-Velcamp, **Theresa**, *Sonoma State*.

Alfonso, **Alyssa**. Miami, FL. Affil: Westwood Christian Sch. Email: aalfonso@ westwoodchristian.org.

Al-Ghadeed, **Hamad Beraik**. Mc Lean, VA. Affil: Morgan State. Email: haalg1@morgan.edu. Research: Middle Eastern oil, US.

Ali, **Kamran Asdar**, *Texas, Austin*. Email: asdar@ austin.utexas.edu.

Ali, **Mohammed Hassen**, *Georgia State*. Email: mali@gsu.edu.

Ali, **Omar H.** Greensboro, NC. Affil: North Carolina, Greensboro. Email: ohali@uncg.edu. Research: African diaspora in Indian Ocean world, Afro-Peru.

Aliano, **David**, *Mount St. Vincent*. Email: david. aliano@mountsaintvincent.edu.

Alie, **Remi**. Berkeley, CA. Affil: California, Berkeley. Email: remi_alie@berkeley.edu.

Al-Imad, **Leila S.**, *East Tennessee State*. Email: alimad@etsu.edu.

Alimagham, **Pouya**, *MIT*. Email: ipouya@mit. edu.

Alinder, **Jasmine**, *Wisconsin-Milwaukee*. Milwaukee, WI. Email: jalinder@uwm.edu. Research: public, visual culture.

Alitto, **Guy S.**, *Chicago*. Email: galitto@uchicago. edu.

Alkana, **Linda Kelly**, *California State, Long Beach; Soc. for Hist. Education*. Email: linda. alkana@csulb.edu.

Allain, **Michael L.**, *James Madison*. Email: allainml@jmu.edu.

Allee, **Mark A.**, *Loyola, Chicago*. Email: mallee@ luc.edu.

Allemand, **Kevin**, **Jr**. Perkinston, MS. Affil: Hancock High Sch. Email: kevin. allemand1848@gmail.com.

Allen, **Aaron C.**, *Roger Williams*. Email: aallen@ rwu.edu.

Allen, **Ann T.**, *Louisville*. Louisville, KY. Email: ann.allen@louisville.edu; atalle1201@gmail. com. Research: modern Germany, European intellectual.

Allen, **Austin L.**, *Houston-Downtown*. Email: allena@uhd.edu.

Allen, **Barbara C.**, *La Salle*. Email: allenb@lasalle. edu.

Allen, **Chadrick John**. Ankeny, IA. Affil: Des Moines Area Comm. Coll. Email: chad. allen07@gmail.com.

Allen, **Conrad**. Madison, WI. Affil: Wisconsin, Madison. Email: callen25@wisc.edu.

Allen, **David B.**, *SUNY, Maritime Coll.* Email: dallen@sunymaritime.edu.

Allen, **E. John**, *Plymouth State*.

Allen, **Emily**, *New York State Archives*. Email: emily.allen@nysed.gov.

Allen, **Howard W.**, *Southern Illinois, Carbondale*. Email: hwallen@siu.edu.

Allen, **J. Henry**, **Jr**., *Union*. Jackson, TN. Email: jallen@uu.edu. Research: American religious, church.

Allen, **James B.**, *Brigham Young*.

Allen, **James Smith**, *Southern Illinois, Carbondale*. Carbondale, IL. Email: jsallen@siu. edu. Research: women in French freemasonry, personal and historical memory.

Allen, **Jennifer L.**, *Yale*. Email: j.allen@yale.edu.

Allen, **Jody L.**, *South; William and Mary*. Email: jlallen@sewanee.edu; jlalle@wm.edu.

Allen, **Joel W.**, *Graduate Center, CUNY; Queens, CUNY*. Email: jallen@gc.cuny.edu; joel.allen@ qc.cuny.edu.

Allen, **Judith A.**, *Indiana*. Email: juallen@ indiana.edu.

Allen, **Lee N.** Mountain Brook, AL. Affil: Samford. Email: lnallen@samford.edu. Research: modern US, church.

Allen, **Marcus Anthony**, *North Carolina A&T State*. Email: maallen5@ncat.edu.

Allen, **Martha M.**, *Southwestern*.

Allen, **Michael J.**, *Northwestern*. Email: m-allen1@northwestern.edu.

Allen, **Richard B.**, *Framingham State*. Framingham, MA. Email: rallen1@ framingham.edu. Research: Mascarene/ Indian Ocean social/economic, slave trade/ comparative slave societies.

Allen, **Robert B.**, *Stephen F. Austin State*. Email: rballen@sfasu.edu.

Allen, **Stephen D.**, *California State, Bakersfield*. Email: sallen13@csub.edu.

Allgor, **Catherine A.**, *Massachusetts Hist. Soc.* Email: callgor@masshist.org.

Allgor, **Kenneth Robert**. Virginia Beach, VA. Affil: Salem Middle Sch. Email: rammad1@aol.com.

Allina-Pisano, **Eric**, *Carleton, Can.* Ottawa, ON, Canada. Affil: Ottawa. Email: eric. allinapisano@carleton.ca; eric.allina@uottawa. ca. Research: slavery and colonial rule in Africa, Africans in post/socialist Europe.

Allinson, **Rayne**, *Pacific Lutheran*. Email: allinsra@plu.edu.

Allison, **Benjamin V**. Kent, OH. Affil: Kent State. Email: balliso7@kent.edu.

Allison, **Christopher Mark Brady**. Watertown, MA. Affil: Harvard. Email: christopher.m.b.allison@gmail.com. Research: early American encounters with the body, material culture in Protestantism.

Allison, **James Robert, III**, *Christopher Newport*. Email: james.allison@cnu.edu.

Allison, **Jessica L.** Springfield, MO. Email: jalli003@fiu.edu. Research: 20th-c Cuban public health, Rockefeller Foundation/science discourse.

Allison, **Robert J.**, *Suffolk*. Boston, MA. Email: ballison@suffolk.edu. Research: colonial/ revolutionary/early Republic America, Native American.

Allison, **William Thomas**, *Georgia Southern*. Email: billallison@georgiasouthern.edu.

Allitt, **Patrick N.**, *Emory*. Email: pallitt@emory. edu.

Allman, **Jean M.**, *Washington, St. Louis*. Saint Louis, MO. Email: jallman@wustl.edu. Research: African environment and health, global and imperial.

Allmendinger, **David F.**, **Jr.**, *Delaware*. Email: dfa@udel.edu.

Allocco, **Katherine Gretchen**, *Western Connecticut State*. Email: alloccok@wcsu.edu.

Allosso, **Dan**, *Bemidji State*. Email: daniel. allosso@bemidjistate.edu.

Allport, **Alan**, *Syracuse*. Email: aallport@ maxwell.syr.edu.

Allswang, **John M.**, *California State, Los Angeles*. Email: allswang@adelphia.net.

Allyn, **William Noah**. Denver, CO. Affil: Colorado, Denver. Email: noahallyn@me.com.

Al-Marashi, **Ibrahim**, *California State, San Marcos*. Email: ialmarashi@csusm.edu.

Almaraz, **Felix D.**, **Jr.**, *Texas, San Antonio*. Email: felix.almaraz@utsa.edu.

Almeida, **James**. Boston, MA. Affil: Harvard. Email: jamesalmeida2015@gmail.com. Research: social conflict, self/other identification.

Al-Nakib, **Farah**, *California Polytechnic State*.

Aloisio, **Paula**, *Arthur and Elizabeth Schlesinger Library*. Email: pkaczor@radcliffe.harvard.edu.

Alonso, **Francesca**. El Paso, TX. Affil: Northwest Early College High Sch. Email: falonso@canutillo-isd.org.

Alonso, **Paula**, *George Washington*. Washington, DC. Email: palonso@gwu.edu. Research: Latin American politics/culture/ideas.

Alonzo, **Armando Cantu**, *Texas A&M*. College Station, TX. Email: alonzo@tamu.edu. Research: US-Mexico border 1848-1942, 17th-/19th-c New Spain.

Alpaugh, **Micah**, *Central Missouri*. Email: alpaugh@ucmo.edu.

Alpe, **Alyssa**. Berthoud, CO. Affil: Northern Water. Email: aalpe@northernwater.org.

Alpern, **Sara**, *Texas A&M*. Email: s-alpern@tamu.edu.

Alpers, **Benjamin L**. Norman, OK. Affil: Oklahoma. Email: balpers@ou.edu. Research: uses of the past in 1970s America.

Alpers, **Edward A**., *UCLA*. Gualala, CA. Email: alpers@history.ucla.edu. Research: Indian Ocean, slave trade and abolition.

Alpert, **Alan M**. Denver, CO. Email: alpert5532@gmail.com. Research: paleovirology.

Alpert, **Jennifer S**., *Bentley*. Email: jalpert@bentley.edu.

Al-Qattan, **Najwa**, *Loyola Marymount*. Email: nalqatta@lmu.edu.

Al-Rustom, **Hakem**, *Michigan, Ann Arbor*. Email: hakemaa@umich.edu.

Alsop, **James Douglas**, *McMaster*. Email: alsopj@mcmaster.ca.

Al-Sowayel, **Dina**, *Houston*. Email: dina@chasecom.net.

Altan, **Selda**, *Randolph*. Gainesville, FL. Email: saltan@randolphcollege.edu; selda.altan@ufl.edu. Research: China, labor.

Alter, **George C**., *Michigan, Ann Arbor*. Email: altergc@umich.edu.

Alter, **Stephen G**. Wenham, MA. Affil: Gordon, Mass. Email: steve.alter@gordon.edu. Research: human sciences in 18th-c America, linguistic Darwinism.

Alter, **Tom**, *Texas State*. Email: ta1066@txstate.edu.

Alteras, **Isaac**, *Queens, CUNY*. Email: ialteras@aol.com.

Altieri, **Marylene**, *Arthur and Elizabeth Schlesinger Library*. Email: maltieri@radcliffe.harvard.edu.

Al-Tikriti, **Nabil Sirri**, *Mary Washington*. Fredericksburg, VA. Email: naltikri@umw.edu. Research: Ottoman Islamic religious identity, Ottoman historiography.

Altman, **Ida**, *Florida; New Orleans*. Gainesville, FL. Email: ialtman@ufl.edu; ialtman@uno.edu. Research: conquest of western Mexico, early Spanish Caribbean.

Altman, **John**, *York, Pa*. Email: jaltman@ycp.edu.

Altrichter, **Doug**. Alexandria, VA. Email: dmaltrichter@aol.com.

Altschiller, **Donald**. Cambridge, MA. Affil: Boston Univ. Email: donaltsc@bu.edu.

Altschuler, **Glenn**, *Cornell*. Email: gca1@cornell.edu.

Altstadt, **Audrey**, *Massachusetts, Amherst*. Email: altstadt@history.umass.edu.

Alvah, **Donna**, *St. Lawrence*. Canton, NY. Email: dalvah@stlawu.edu. Research: children and youth in Cold War/Vietnam War, children/youth/nuclear weapons/war.

Alvarado, **Christian David**. Santa Cruz, CA. Affil: California, Santa Clara. Email: chdalvar@ucsc.edu.

Alvarez, **C.J.**, *Texas, Austin*. Email: cjalvarez@austin.utexas.edu.

Alvarez, **Jose E**., *Houston-Downtown*. Email: alvarezj@uhd.edu.

Alvarez, **Luis A**., *California, San Diego*. Email: luisalvarez@ucsd.edu.

Alvarez, **Thomas A**., *California State, Dominguez Hills; California State, Los Angeles*. Email: talvarez@csudh.edu; talavar10@calstatela.edu.

Alvarez-Rivera, **Ferdinand**, **Jr**. Hatillo, PR, Puerto Rico. Affil: Puerto Rico, Utuado. Email: Ferdialvarez@gmail.com. Research: cultural, microhistory.

Alveal, **Carmen Margarida Oliveira**. Natal, Brazil. Affil: Federal do Rio Grande do Norte. Email: carmenalveal@uol.com.br. Research: land property/legal history.

Alves, **Abel A**., *Ball State*. Email: aalves@bsu.edu.

Alvey, **Scott**, *Kentucky Hist. Soc*. Email: scott.alvey@ky.gov.

Alwine, **Andrew**, *Charleston*. Email: alwineat@cofc.edu.

Amador, **Emma Balbina**, *Connecticut, Storrs*. Email: emma.amador@uconn.edu.

Amador, **Jose**, *Miami, Ohio*. Email: amadorj@miamioh.edu.

Amanat, **Abbas**, *Yale*. Email: abbas.amanat@yale.edu.

Amar, **Tarik Cyril**, *Columbia (Hist.)*. Email: tca2109@columbia.edu.

Amatori, **Franco**. Milano, Italy. Affil: Bocconi. Email: franco.amatori@unibocconi.it. Research: 20th-c comparative business, 20th-c Italian firms.

Ambaras, **David Richard**, *North Carolina State*. Email: david_ambaras@ncsu.edu.

Ambler, **Charles H**., *Texas, El Paso*. El Paso, TX. Email: cambler@utep.edu. Research: Africa, Middle East.

Ambroise, **Jason**, *William Paterson*. Email: ambroisej@wpunj.edu.

Ambrose, **Douglas**, *Hamilton*. Email: dambrose@hamilton.edu.

Ambrose, **Edith**, *Southeastern Louisiana*. Email: Edith.Ambrose@selu.edu.

Ambrosius, **Lloyd E**., *Nebraska, Lincoln*. Lincoln, NE. Email: lambrosius1@unl.edu. Research: US foreign relations, presidency.

Amdur, **Kathryn E**., *Emory*. Email: kamdur@emory.edu.

Amelang, **James S**. Madrid, Spain. Affil: Autonoma de Madrid. Email: james.amelang@uam.es. Research: autobiography, urban discourse.

Ament, **Suzanne E**., *Radford*. Email: seament@radford.edu.

Americo, **Maria**, *St. Peter's*. Email: mamerico@saintpeters.edu.

Amerman, **Stephen K**., *Southern Connecticut State*. Email: amermans1@southernct.edu.

Ames, **Charles F**., **Jr**., *Salem State*. Email: cames@salemstate.edu.

Ames, **Christine Caldwell**, *South Carolina, Columbia*. Columbia, SC. Email: amesc@sc.edu. Research: wine.

Ames, **Scott C**. Ipswich, MA. Affil: Ipswich High Sch. Email: sames477@gmail.com. Research: France under Napoleon and settlements, US Revolution.

Amin, **Julius A**., *Dayton*. Email: jamin1@udayton.edu.

Amin, **Neel**, *James Madison*. Email: aminnn@jmu.edu.

Ammon, **Francesca Russello**. Philadelphia, PA. Affil: Pennsylvania. Email: francesca.ammon@gmail.com. Research: urban and suburban, built environment.

Ammons, **Jacynda**, *Missouri State*. Email: JacyndaAmmons@MissouriState.edu.

Amos, **Janice**. Elgin, IL. Affil: Southern New Hampshire. Email: j.amos@snhu.edu.

Amos, **N. Scott**, *Lynchburg*. Email: amos.n@lynchburg.edu.

Amponsah, **Nana Akua**, *North Carolina, Wilmington*. Email: amponsahn@uncw.edu.

Amrith, **Sunil**, *Harvard (Hist.)*. Email: amrith@fas.harvard.edu.

Amsterdam, **Daniel**, *Georgia Inst. of Tech*. Email: daniel.amsterdam@hts.gatech.edu.

Amundson, **Michael A**., *Northern Arizona*. Email: michael.amundson@nau.edu.

Amussen, **Susan D**. Merced, CA. Affil: California, Merced. Email: samussen@ucmerced.edu. Research: 17th-c English cultural and social, language/festivity/violence.

Amzi-Erdogdular, **Leyla**, *Rutgers, Newark/New Jersey Inst. of Tech*. Email: leyla.amzi@rutgers.edu.

Anastakis, **Dimitry**, *Toronto*. Email: dimitry.anastakis@utoronto.ca.

Anastassiadis, **Tassos**, *McGill*. Email: tassos.anastassiadis@mcgill.ca.

Anastazievsky, **Walter**. Saint Paul, MN. Email: vlodko62@gmail.com.

Anbinder, **Jacob**. Cambridge, MA. Affil: Harvard. Email: anbinder@g.harvard.edu. Research: urban, business.

Anbinder, **Tyler G**., *George Washington*. Arlington, VA. Email: anbinder@gwu.edu. Research: 19th-c American immigration, nativism.

Ancekewicz, **Elaine M**. Port Jefferson Station, NY. Email: emafr@aol.com. Research: early modern philosophy of history, continental historiography.

Andaya, **Leonard Y**., *Hawai'i, Manoa*. Email: andaya@hawaii.edu.

Andersen, **Margaret Cook**, *Tennessee, Knoxville*. Knoxville, TN. Email: mcookand@utk.edu. Research: France and demographic debate, French gender.

Andersen, **Rebecca**, *Utah State*. Email: rebecca.andersen@usu.edu.

Andersen, **Thomas B**., *St. Michael's*.

Anderson, **Alan Marshall**. Shoreview, MN. Affil: King's Coll., London. Email: amanderson5987@comcast.net. Research: laws of war and military/naval/strategy, international arbitration.

Anderson, **Angie**, *Southeastern Louisiana*. Email: aanderson2@selu.edu.

Anderson, **Betty S**., *Boston Univ*. Boston, MA. Email: banderso@bu.edu. Research: education in Lebanon, urban studies in Amman.

Anderson, Bonnie S. Brooklyn, NY. Affil: CUNY. Email: bonniea100@gmail.com. Research: biography of Ernestine Rose, feminism.

Anderson, Bryan. West Islip, NY. Email: lulu.callie.griffy@gmail.com.

Anderson, Carol Susan. Reseda, CA. Email: philosophula@gmail.com.

Anderson, Carol, *Emory*. Atlanta, GA. Email: carol.anderson@emory.edu. Research: African American anti-colonialism, African American human rights.

Anderson, Chad L., *Hartwick*. Email: andersonc2@hartwick.edu.

Anderson, Charles W., *Western Washington*. Email: Charles.Anderson@wwu.edu.

Anderson, Charles, Jr. Fayetteville, NC. Affil: Fayetteville State. Email: cander30@uncfsu.edu.

Anderson, Daniele. New York, NY. Affil: Columbia. Email: danieleanderson13@gmail.com.

Anderson, David L. Monterey, CA. Affil: California State, Monterey Bay. Email: danderson@csumb.edu. Research: Vietnam War, Cold War.

Anderson, David M., *Louisiana Tech*. Shreveport, LA. Email: davida@latech.edu. Research: US Gilded Age, 20th century.

Anderson, Douglas F., *Northwestern Coll*. Email: firth@nwciowa.edu.

Anderson, Elaine. Washington, DC. Affil: US Dept. of State. Email: AndersonElaine.

Anderson, Electa E. Oceanside, CA. Affil: El Toro High Sch. Email: electab@gmail.com. Research: print culture, Progressive era US West.

Anderson, Fred, *Colorado, Boulder*. Boulder, CO. Email: fred.anderson@colorado.edu. Research: American Revolution, early national.

Anderson, Gary C., *Oklahoma (Hist.)*. Email: gcanderson@ou.edu.

Anderson, Greg, *Ohio State*. Email: anderson.1381@osu.edu.

Anderson, Hillary, *Central Arkansas*. Email: handerson7@uca.edu.

Anderson, Iain. Tulsa, OK. Affil: Northeastern State. Email: ianderson182@gmail.com. Research: jazz/American culture/1960s, immigration and ethnic institutions.

Anderson, James A., *North Carolina, Greensboro*. Email: jamie_anderson@uncg.edu.

Anderson, James D., *Illinois, Urbana-Champaign*. Email: janders@illinois.edu.

Anderson, James R., *Michigan State*. Email: anders90@msu.edu.

Anderson, Jennifer L., *SUNY, Stony Brook*. Huntington, NY. Email: Jennifer.L.Anderson@stonybrook.edu. Research: mahogany trade/environmental, Atlantic material culture.

Anderson, Joel, *Maine, Orono*. Email: joel.anderson@maine.edu.

Anderson, John B. Galena, OH.

Anderson, John B., *Holy Cross*. Email: jbanders@holycross.edu.

Anderson, Karen S., *Arizona*. Email: karena@u.arizona.edu.

Anderson, Katharine Mary, *York, Can*. Email: kateya@yorku.ca.

Anderson, M. Christine, *Xavier, Ohio*. Email: andersoc@xavier.edu.

Anderson, Margaret Lavinia. Berkeley, CA. Affil: California, Berkeley. Email: mlavinia@berkeley.

edu. Research: Germany and Ottoman Empire, Armenian massacres 1890s-1933.

Anderson, Margo J., *Wisconsin-Milwaukee*. Milwaukee, WI. Email: margo@uwm.edu. Research: statistics/surveys/federal government, women.

Anderson, Mark C., *Carleton, Can*. Email: mark.anderson@carleton.ca.

Anderson, Mark, *Loyola Marymount*.

Anderson, Marnie S., *Smith*. Email: msanders@smith.edu.

Anderson, Megan L., *Hist. Assoc*. Email: manderson@historyassociates.com.

Anderson, Nancy Fix, *Loyola, New Orleans*.

Anderson, Patricia, *Towson*. Email: panderson@towson.edu.

Anderson, Perry, *UCLA*. Email: fanderso@ucla.edu.

Anderson, R. Bentley, SJ, *Fordham*.

Anderson, Robert G. W., *Science History Inst*. Email: randerson@sciencehistory.org.

Anderson, Robin L., *Arkansas State*.

Anderson, Rodney D. Havana, FL. Affil: Florida State. Email: rdanderson@fsu.edu. Research: rural to urban migration.

Anderson, Scott M. Waco, TX. Affil: Baylor. Email: smacw@live.com. Research: contemporary religion and politics, Civil War religion and politics.

Anderson, Sheldon R., *Miami, Ohio*. Email: anderss@miamioh.edu.

Anderson, Stewart Hurst, *Brigham Young*. Email: stewart_anderson@byu.edu.

Anderson, Terry H., *Texas A&M*. Email: tha@tamu.edu.

Anderson, Thomas L., Jr., *Henry Ford Coll*. Email: tomlanderson@sbcglobal.net.

Anderson, Tonnia L. Chickasha, OK. Affil: Univ. of Science and Arts, Okla. Email: tonnia.anderson@yahoo.com. Research: material culture in American South, photography and racial identity.

Anderson, Virginia D., *Colorado, Boulder*. Boulder, CO. Email: virginia.anderson@colorado.edu. Research: American Revolution, colonial America.

Anderson, Warwick H. Sydney, Australia. Affil: Sydney. Email: warwick.anderson@sydney.edu.au. Research: science/medicine/public health, racial thought.

Anderson, William L., *Western Carolina*.

Anderson-Bricker, Kristin M. Dubuque, IA. Affil: Loras. Email: Kristin.AndersonBricker@loras.edu. Research: black civil rights, influenza 1918.

Andes, Stephen J. C., *Louisiana State*. Email: sandes@lsu.edu.

Ando, Clifford, *Chicago*. Email: cando@uchicago.edu.

Andrade, Nathanael J., *Binghamton, SUNY*. Binghamton, NY. Email: nandrade@binghamton.edu. Research: Hellenistic and Roman Near East, Greek colonialism and Roman imperialism.

Andrade, Tonio A., *Emory*. Email: tandrad@emory.edu.

Andrade Diniz de Araujo, Maria Paula. Nashville, TN. Affil: Vanderbilt. Email: mp.andrade@vanderbilt.edu. Research: epidemics, religion.

Andrea, Alfred J., *Vermont*. Burlington, VT. Email: aandrea@uvm.edu. Research: crusades, Afro-Eurasian travel before 1450.

Andreasen, Bethany, *Minot State*. Minot, ND. Email: bethany.andreasen@minotstateu.edu. Research: education philosophy and curriculum, frontier women.

Andreassen, Nadine, *NASA*. Email: nadine.j.andreassen@nasa.gov.

Andreeva, Elena, *Virginia Military Inst*. Email: andreevae@vmi.edu.

Andrei, George. Bloomington, IN. Affil: Indiana. Email: ga6895@outlook.com.

Andres, Benny J., Jr., *North Carolina, Charlotte*. Email: bandres@uncc.edu.

Andrew, Donna T., *Guelph*. Email: dandrew@uoguelph.ca.

Andrews, Bridie, *Bentley*. Email: bandrews@bentley.edu.

Andrews, Dee E., *California State, East Bay*. Hayward, CA. Email: dee.andrews@csueastbay.edu. Research: American Revolution and religion, early American antislavery.

Andrews, Edward E., *Providence*. Email: eandrews@providence.edu.

Andrews, George Reid, *Pittsburgh*. Pittsburgh, PA. Email: reid1@pitt.edu. Research: Afro-Latin America, Latin American black.

Andrews, Gordon, *Grand Valley State*. Email: andrewgo@gvsu.edu.

Andrews, Gregg, *Texas State*. Email: ga05@txstate.edu.

Andrews, James T., *Iowa State*. Email: andrewsj@iastate.edu.

Andrews, John. Rockville, MD. Affil: Maryland, Coll. Park. Email: jandre81@umd.edu.

Andrews, Margaret W., *Washington State, Pullman*. Email: mwa-jlb@telus.net.

Andrews, Margaret, *Chicago*. Email: margaretandrews@uchicago.edu.

Andrews, Matthew P., *North Carolina, Chapel Hill*. Email: andrewsm@email.unc.edu.

Andrews, Naomi J., *Santa Clara*. Portola Valley, CA. Email: nandrews@scu.edu; nja@andlev.com. Research: Romantic socialism, colonialism.

Andrews, Rebecca. Arlington, VA. Affil: Georgetown. Email: andrews.becky@gmail.com.

Andrews, Stephen Douglas, *Indiana; OAH*. Email: standrew@indiana.edu.

Andrews, Thomas G., *Colorado, Boulder*. Email: thomas.andrews@colorado.edu.

Andrien, Kenneth J., *Ohio State; Southern Methodist*. Dallas, TX. Email: andrien.1@osu.edu; kandrien@smu.edu. Research: Spanish Atlantic world 1700-96, colonial Andes.

Andriewsky, Olga, *Trent*. Email: oandriewsky@trentu.ca.

Androsoff, Ashleigh, *Saskatchewan*. Email: ashleigh.androsoff@usask.ca.

Angel, Edward. Washington, DC. Affil: Morgan, Angel & Assoc. Email: Ed@Morganangel.com. Research: Native American, natural resource policy.

Angel, Lauren. Huntington, WV. Affil: George Washington. Email: lacangel@gwmail.gwu.edu.

Angell, James E. West Springfield, MA. Email: mrangell@hotmail.com. Research: Cold War, racism in America.

Angelo, Nathan J., *Worcester State*. Email: nangelo@worcester.edu.

Angelov, Dimiter, *Harvard (Hist.)*. Email: dangelov@fas.harvard.edu.

Angelova, **Diliana**, *California, Berkeley*. Email: angelova@berkeley.edu.

Anishanslin, **Zara**, *Delaware*. Email: zma@udel. edu.

Anna, **Timothy E.**, *Manitoba*. Email: timothy. anna@umanitoba.ca.

Annis, *Lee*. Silver Spring, MD. Affil: Montgomery. Email: jleeannis@gmail.com. Research: South, US political.

Anooshahr, **Ali**, *California, Davis*. Email: aanooshahr@ucdavis.edu.

Ansiaux, **Robert R.**, *Dallas*. Email: ransiaux@ udallas.edu.

Ansley, *John*. Poughkeepsie, NY. Affil: Marist. Email: john.ansley@marist.edu. Research: Cold War era, Tibet's relations with US.

Anslover, **Nicole L.**, *Indiana, Northwest*. Email: nanslove@iun.edu.

Anson, **Edward M.**, **IV**, *Arkansas, Little Rock*. Email: emanson@ualr.edu.

Antaramian, **Richard**, *Southern California*. Email: antarami@usc.edu.

Anthony, **David H.**, **III**, *California, Santa Cruz*. Email: danthony@ucsc.edu.

Anthony, **Douglas A.**, *Franklin & Marshall*. Email: douglas.anthony@fandm.edu.

Antkiewicz, **Henry J.**, *East Tennessee State*. Email: antkiewh@etsu.edu.

Antler, **Joyce**, *Brandeis*. Email: antler@brandeis. edu.

Antoninis, *Jacob A.* Bethpage, NY. Affil: US Immigration and Customs Enforcement. Email: jacob.antoninis@dhs.gov.

Antonov, **Sergei**, *Yale*. Email: sergei.antonov@ yale.edu.

Antonova, **Katherine Pickering**, *Queens, CUNY*. Email: katherine.antonova@qc.cuny.edu.

Antonovich, **Jacqueline**, *Muhlenberg*. Email: jacquelineanotovich@muhlenberg.edu.

Antonucci, *Nicholas*. Riverhead, NY. Affil: Suffolk County Comm. Coll., SUNY. Email: nab8@ columbia.edu. Research: US foreign policy/ Near East 1915-41, Arab nationalism 1900-50.

Antos, *Bethany J.* Sleepy Hollow, NY. Affil: Rockefeller Archive Center. Email: bantos@ rockarch.org. Research: Rockefeller Univ.

Antov, **Nikolay**, *Arkansas, Fayetteville*. Email: antov@uark.edu.

Antrim, **Zayde G.**, *Trinity Coll., Conn*. Email: zayde.antrim@trincoll.edu.

Anuik, *Jonathan David*. Edmonton, AB, Canada. Affil: Alberta. Email: anuik@ualberta.ca.

Anyanwu, **Ogechi**, *Eastern Kentucky*. Email: ogechi.anyanwu@eku.edu.

Anzilotti, **Cara**, *Loyola Marymount*. Email: cara. anzilotti@lmu.edu.

Apaliski, *Sierra*. Wildwood, NJ. Affil: American. Email: sa6461a@american.edu.

Apgar, **Jonathan**, *OAH*. Email: jmapgar@oah. org.

Appelbaum, **Nancy P.**, *Binghamton, SUNY*. Email: nappel@binghamton.edu.

Appelbaum, *Patricia*. Amherst, MA. Affil: Ronin Inst. Email: Patricia.Appelbaum@ RoninInstitute.org. Research: Protestant culture, St. Francis of Assisi.

Appelbaum, *Yoni*. Washington, DC. Affil: The Atlantic. Email: yoni.appelbaum@gmail.com. Research: Gilded Age, capitalism.

Appelhans, *Jeffery R.* Newark, DE. Affil: Delaware. Email: appeljr@udel.edu. Research: politics and culture of early America, early American Catholicism.

Apple, *Kaelyn Grace*. Cupertino, CA. Affil: Oxford. Email: kaelynapple@gmail.com.

Appleby, *R. Scott*, *Notre Dame*. Email: Appleby.3@nd.edu.

Appleford, *Simon*, *Creighton*. Omaha, NE. Email: simonappleford@creighton.edu. Research: digital humanities, US.

Applegate, **Celia S.**, *Vanderbilt*. Nashville, TN. Email: celia.applegate@vanderbilt.edu. Research: German music and society, German nationalism and regionalism.

Applegate, **Howard L.** Honey Brook, PA. Affil: Lebanon Valley. Email: applegat@lvc.edu. Research: modern US, business.

Appleton, **Thomas H.**, **Jr.**, *Eastern Kentucky*. Email: tom.appleton@eku.edu.

Appuhn, *Karl R.*, *NYU*. New York, NY. Email: appuhn@nyu.edu. Research: European epizootics 1600-1800, early modern concepts of nature.

Appy, **Christian G.**, *Massachusetts, Amherst*. Email: appy@history.umass.edu.

Apter, *Andrew*, *UCLA*. Los Angeles, CA. Email: aapter@history.ucla.edu. Research: black Atlantic studies, historical memory.

Aquino, **Hilary C.**, *Albright*. Email: haquino@ albright.edu.

Arah, **Benjamin**, *Bowie State*. Email: barah@ bowiestate.edu.

Araiza, *Lauren*, *Denison*. Granville, OH. Email: araizal@denison.edu. Research: civil rights movement.

Aranda, *Jose Luis*. Las Cruces, NM. Affil: New Mexico State, Dona Ana. Email: jaranda2@ nmsu.edu. Research: Library of Congress, web archives.

Arata, *Laura J.*, *Oklahoma State*. Stillwater, OK. Email: larata@okstate.edu. Research: American West, race.

Araujo, *Ana Lucia*. Washington, DC. Affil: Howard. Email: aaraujo@howard.edu. Research: memory of slavery, visual culture of slavery.

Arbelaez, **Maria S.**, *Nebraska, Omaha*. Email: marbelaez@unomaha.edu.

Arcenas, *Claire Rydell*, *Montana*. Email: claire. arcenas@mso.umt.edu.

Arceneaux, **Pamela D.**, *Hist. New Orleans*. Email: pamela@hnoc.org.

Arceneaux, *William*. Baton Rouge, LA. Affil: Louisiana State. Email: warcenea@lsu.edu. Research: Acadia.

Arch, *Jakobina*, *Whitman*. Email: archjk@ whitman.edu.

Archambeau, **Nicole A.**, *Colorado State*. Email: nicole.archambeau@colostate.edu.

Archdeacon, **Thomas J.**, *Wisconsin-Madison*. Email: tjarchde@wisc.edu.

Archer, **Christon I.**, *Calgary*. Email: archer@ ucalgary.ca.

Archer, **Richard L.**, *Whittier*.

Archer, **Robert D.**, *California State, Chico*. Email: rarcher@csuchico.edu.

Archer, *Seth*, *Utah State*. Logan, UT. Email: seth. archer@usu.edu. Research: Native North America, Hawai'i.

Archibald, **Robert**, *Northern Michigan*. Email: roarchib@nmu.edu.

Archibald, **Ryan**, *California State, Dominguez Hills*.

Ardrey, *Becky*. Fairhope, AL. Affil: South Alabama. Email: beckyardrey@gmail.com.

Arena, *Carolyn Marie*, *Omohundro Inst*. Email: cmarena@wm.edu.

Arens, **Olavi**, *Georgia Southern*. Email: oarens@ georgiasouthern.edu.

Arenson, *Adam*, *Manhattan*. Riverdale, NY. Email: adam.arenson@manhattan.edu. Research: Civil War and American West, African Americans back from Canada.

Argersinger, **JoAnn E.**, *Southern Illinois, Carbondale*. Email: jarger@siu.edu.

Argersinger, *Peter H.*, *Southern Illinois, Carbondale*. Williamsburg, VA. Email: parger@ siu.edu. Research: American political and policy, American rural.

Argote-Freyre, *Frank*, *Kean*. Email: fargotef@ kean.edu.

Ariail, *Cat*. Clarksville, GA. Affil: Miami. Email: cat.m.ariail@gmail.com. Research: postwar track and field, black athletes.

Aricanli, *Sare*. Durham, United Kingdom. Affil: Durham. Email: sare.aricanli@durham.ac.uk. Research: medicine.

Ari-Chachaki, *Waskar T.*, *Nebraska, Lincoln*. Lincoln, NE. Email: wari2@unl.edu. Research: nationalism in Andes, race in Latin America.

Ariel, *Ari*, *Iowa*. New York, IA. Email: ari-ariel@ uiowa.edu. Research: Middle East, Jews in Arab countries.

Arista, *Noelani M.*, *Hawai'i, Manoa*. Email: arista@hawaii.edu.

Arkush, *Alan*, *Binghamton, SUNY*. Email: arkjustbb@aol.com.

Armanios, *Febe Y.*, *Middlebury*. Email: farmanio@middlebury.edu.

Armantrout, *George L.*, *Portland State*. Email: d1ga@pdx.edu.

Armbruster-Sandoval, *Ralph*, *California, Santa Barbara*. Email: armbrust@chicst.ucsb.edu.

Armitage, *David*, *Harvard (Hist.)*. Cambridge, MA. Email: armitage@fas.harvard.edu. Research: British Civil War, international political thought.

Armitage, *Susan H.*, *Washington State, Pullman*. Email: armitage@wsu.edu.

Armon, *Adi*. Madison, WI. Affil: Wisconsin, Madison. Email: aarmon@wisc.edu. Research: intellectual, Europe.

Armstead, *Myra B. Young*, *Bard*. Annandale On Hudson, NY. Email: armstead@bard.edu. Research: antebellum African American, antebellum US social/cultural.

Armstrong, *Anne E.* Sylmar, CA. Email: KennewickSkull@hotmail.com. Research: American cultural, rituals/beliefs and festivals.

Armstrong, *Ayanna*, *North Carolina A&T State*. Email: ararmst3@ncat.edu.

Armstrong, *Charles K.*, *Columbia (Hist.)*. New York, NY. Email: cra10@columbia.edu. Research: US-East Asian relations, Korea since 1945.

Armstrong, *Megan Cathleen*, *McMaster*. Email: marmstr@mcmaster.ca.

Armstrong, *Stephen A.*, *Central Connecticut State*. Email: armstrong@ccsu.edu.

Armstrong, *Tenisha Hart*. Stanford, CA. Affil: Martin Luther King Jr. Papers Project. Email: tenisha@stanford.edu.

Armstrong, *Thom M*. Claremont, CA. Affil: Barstow. Email: thomarm@gmail.com. Research: early republic diplomacy and politics, Peter Paul & Mary.

Armstrong-Partida, Michelle, *Texas, El Paso*. El Paso, TX. Email: armstrongpartida@gmail.com; marmstrongpartida@utep.edu. Research: Iberia, church and clerical masculinity.

Armstrong-Price, Amanda, *Fordham*. Email: aarmstrongprice@fordham.edu.

Armstrong-Roche, Michael. Middletown, CT. Affil: Wesleyan. Email: marmstrong@wesleyan.edu. Research: Cervantes, early modern Spanish and European theater.

Armus, Diego C., *Swarthmore*. Email: darmus1@swarthmore.edu.

Arnau, Ariel, *St. Joseph's*.

Arndt, J. Chris, *James Madison*. Email: arndtjc@jmu.edu.

Arndt, Jochen S., *Virginia Military Inst*. Lexington, VA. Email: arndtjs@vmi.edu. Research: African ethno-linguistic identities, production of knowledge.

Arnesen, Eric, *George Washington*. Washington, MD. Email: arnesen@gwu.edu. Research: A. Philip Randoph, civil rights and the left.

Arnett, William S., *West Virginia*. Email: William.Arnett@mail.wvu.edu.

Arnette, Carol, *Omohundro Inst*. Email: cgarnette@wm.edu.

Arnn, Larry P., *Hillsdale*. Email: larnn@hillsdale.edu.

Arno, Joan E. Zephyrhills, FL. Email: joan2mike@verizon.net.

Arnold, Andrew B., *Kutztown*. Email: arnold@kutztown.edu.

Arnold, Brie Swenson, *Coe*. Email: barnold@coe.edu.

Arnold, Bruce Makoto, *Ohio State*. Email: arnold.1041@osu.edu.

Arnold, Catherine, *Memphis*. Email: crnold13@memphis.edu.

Arnold, Chase, *San Francisco*. Email: carnold2@usfca.edu.

Arnold, Douglas M. Washington, DC. Email: arndoum@earthlink.net. Research: historical documents, early Republic Connecticut.

Arnold, Ellen F., *Ohio Wesleyan*. Email: efarnold@owu.edu.

Arnold, James R., *Soc. for Military Hist*. Email: burrostn@cfw.com.

Arnold, Katherine. London, CA. Affil: London Sch. of Economics. Email: K.E.Arnold@lse.ac.uk.

Arnold, Lauren. Mountain View, CA. Affil: Ricci Inst., San Francisco. Email: laurenarnold@cs.com. Research: East-West cultural interaction 1250-1528, post-1250 Europeans in Central Asia/China.

Arnold, Laurie, *Gonzaga*. Email: arnoldl@gonzaga.edu.

Arnold, Lee, *Hist. Soc. of Pennsylvania*. Email: larnold@hsp.org.

Arnold, Linda, *Virginia Tech*. Email: redtape@vt.edu.

Arnold, Stanley, *Northern Illinois*. Email: sarnold@niu.edu.

Arnold, Thomas J. Rancho Santa Fe, CA. Affil: San Diego Mesa. Email: thjarn@yahoo.com. Research: environment and cities, WWII.

Arnold, Trina. Oklahoma City, OK. Affil: Mid-America Christian. Email: trina.arnold@macu.edu.

Arnold, W. Vincent, *Concordia Coll*. Email: arnold@cord.edu.

Arnstein, Walter L. Urbana, IL. Affil: Illinois, Urbana-Champaign. Email: warnstei@illinois.edu. Research: Queen Victoria, Victorian religion.

Arnush, Michael, *Skidmore*. Email: marnush@skidmore.edu.

Aron, Cindy S., *Virginia*. Email: msa5w@virginia.edu.

Aron, Stephen, *UCLA*. Los Angeles, CA. Email: saron@ucla.edu. Research: Concord in American West, frontiers and borderlands.

Aronowsky, Leah. Urbana, IL. Affil: Illinois, Urbana-Champaign. Email: aronowsk@illinois.edu.

Aronson, A. Ronald, *Wayne State*. Email: ac7159@wayne.edu.

Aronson, Jay David, *Carnegie Mellon*. Email: aronson@andrew.cmu.edu.

Arpaia, Paul-Marie T., *Indiana, Pa.* Indiana, PA. Email: paul.arpaia@iup.edu. Research: Italian liberalism/nationalism/fascism, 19th-/20th-c Italian culture and politics.

Arpey, Andrew W., *New York State Archives*. Email: andrew.arpey@nysed.gov.

Arrington, Andrea Lynn, *Indiana State*. Email: Andrea.Arrington@indstate.edu.

Arrom, Silvia M., *Brandeis*. Email: arrom@brandeis.edu.

Arsenault, Raymond O., *South Florida, St. Petersburg*. Saint Petersburg, FL. Email: roarsenault@gmail.com. Research: civil rights movement.

Arthurs, Joshua W., *West Virginia*. Morgantown, WV. Email: joshua.arthurs@mail.wvu.edu. Research: fall of Mussolini/society and memory, everyday life in Fascist Italy.

Artun, Tuna, *Rutgers*. Email: tuna.artun@rutgers.edu.

Aruga, Natsuki. Tokyo, Japan. Affil: Saitma. Email: natsukia@nifty.com. Research: post-WWII US occupation and gender, comparative transnational/global.

Arvanigian, Mark E., *California State, Fresno*. Email: marvanig@csufresno.edu.

Arvin, Maile, *Utah*. Email: maile.arvin@utah.edu.

Asaka, Ikuko, *Illinois, Urbana-Champaign*. Email: iasaka@illinois.edu.

Asaka, Megan, *California, Riverside*. Email: megan.asaka@ucr.edu.

Aschenbrenner, Nathanael. San Diego, CA. Affil: Harvard. Email: aschenbrenner@fas.harvard.edu.

Aschenbrenner, Peter J. Columbia, MD. Email: aschenbrenner.historian@gmail.com. Research: 1787 Constitutional Convention, constitutional law.

Ascher, Abraham, *Graduate Center, CUNY*. New York, NY. Email: a.ascher@att.net. Research: Russia.

Aselmeyer, Norman. Berlin, Germany. Affil: European Univ. Inst. Email: norman.aselmeyer@eui.eu.

Asen, Daniel, *Rutgers, Newark/New Jersey Inst. of Tech*. Email: da467@rutgers.edu.

Ash, Eric H., *Wayne State*. Email: ao0103@wayne.edu.

Ash, Mitchell G. Vienna, Austria. Affil: Vienna. Email: mitchell.ash@univie.ac.at. Research: modern science, modern Germany.

Ash, Stephen V., *Tennessee, Knoxville*. Email: sash@utk.edu.

Ashbaugh, William B., *SUNY, Oneonta*. Email: william.ashbaugh@oneonta.edu.

Ashby, LeRoy, *Washington State, Pullman*. Email: ashby@wsu.edu.

Ashcom, Susan R. Arlington, VA. Email: susanrashcom@gmail.com.

Ashcraft-Eason, Lillian, *Bowling Green State*. Email: lashcra@bgsu.edu.

Ashenmiller, Joshua. Los Angeles, CA. Affil: Fullerton Coll. Email: jashenmiller@fullcoll.edu. Research: 1969 national environmental policy act, environmental policy and conservatism.

Asher, Florence, *Hunter, CUNY*. Email: fasher@hunter.cuny.edu.

Asher, Robert, *Connecticut, Storrs*.

Ashford, Evan Howard, *SUNY, Oneonta*. Oneonta, NY. Email: evan.ashford@oneonta.edu. Research: African American.

Ashley, Carl Edward, *US Dept. of State*. Washington, DC. Email: carl@cashley.org. Research: European intellectual, US-European relations.

Ashley, Susan A., *Colorado Coll*. Colorado Springs, CO. Email: sashley@coloradocollege.edu. Research: modern Europe, France.

Ashman, Patricia Shaw, *Central Missouri*.

Ashmore, Faith. Troy, MI. Affil: American. Email: fa1516a@american.edu.

Ashmore, Susan Youngblood, *Emory*. Decatur, GA. Email: sashmor@emory.edu. Research: War on Poverty and civil rights in Alabama, religion and grassroots change in Alabama.

Ashurov, Barakatullo. Affil: Harvard. Email: barakatulloashurov@gmail.com.

Ashworth, William B., *Missouri–Kansas City*. Email: ashworthw@umkc.edu.

Asim, Ina, *Oregon*. Email: inaasim@uoregon.edu.

Askew, Maj Mark, *US Military Acad*. Email: mark.askew@usma.edu.

Askman, Douglas Victor, *Hawai'i Pacific*. Email: daskman@hpu.edu.

Aslakson, Kenneth Randolph, *Union Coll*. Email: aslaksok@union.edu.

Aslanian, Sebouh David, *UCLA*. Email: saslanian@history.ucla.edu.

Aso, Michitake, *SUNY, Albany*. Email: maso@albany.edu.

Aso, Noriko, *California, Santa Cruz*. Email: naso@ucsc.edu.

Asselin, Pierre, *San Diego State*.

Astarita, Tommaso, *Georgetown*. Washington, DC. Email: astaritt@georgetown.edu. Research: early modern Europe, Mediterranean.

Aster, Sidney, *Toronto*. Email: sidney.aster@utoronto.ca.

Astor, Aaron, *Maryville*. Maryville, TN. Email: aaron.astor@maryvillecollege.edu. Research: grassroots politics, US Civil War and Reconstruction.

Astourian, Stephan, *California, Berkeley*. Email: astour@berkeley.edu.

Astren, Fred. San Francisco, CA. Affil: San Francisco State. Email: fastren@sfsu.edu.

Atamaz-Topcu, Serpil, *California State, Sacramento*. Email: atamaztopcu@csus.edu.

Atassi, Ahmad Nazir, *Louisiana Tech*. Email: aatassi@latech.edu.

Atchison, Devon H., *Bellevue*. Email: devon.atchison@bellevuecollege.edu.

Atencio, August. Stowe, VT. Affil: American. Email: aa4681a@american.edu.

Ates, Sabri, *Southern Methodist*. Email: sates@smu.edu.

Atkin, *Muriel A.*, *George Washington.* Washington, DC. Email: matkin@gwu.edu. Research: Russia, Tajikistan.

Atkin, *Natalie*, *Windsor.* Email: natalie9@mnsi. net.

Atkins, *E. Taylor*, *Northern Illinois.* Dekalb, IL. Email: etatkins@niu.edu. Research: Japanese colonialism, Baha`i faith.

Atkins, *Gregory.* Hays, KS. Affil: Fort Hays State. Email: gjatkins@fhsu.edu. Research: religion, American West.

Atkins, *Jonathan M.*, *Berry.* Email: jatkins@berry. edu.

Atkinson, *Clarissa W.* Cambridge, MA. Email: clarissa.w.atkinson@gmail.com.

Atkinson, *Connie Zeanah*, *New Orleans.* Email: c.atkinson@uno.edu.

Atkinson, *David Christopher*, *Purdue.* West Lafayette, IN. Email: atkinsod@purdue.edu. Research: culture and American foreign relations, immigration and American foreign relations.

Atkinson, *Evelyn H.* Madison, WI. Affil: Chicago. Email: ematkinson@uchicago.edu.

Atkinson, *Kenneth R.*, *Northern Iowa.* Email: kenneth.atkinson@uni.edu.

Atkinson, *Roark*, *Ramapo.* Email: atkinson@ ramapo.edu.

Atkinson, *Ronald R.*, *South Carolina, Columbia.* Email: atkinson@mailbox.sc.edu.

Atto, *William J.*, *Dallas.* Email: atto@udallas.edu.

Attreed, *Lorraine C.*, *Holy Cross.* Worcester, MA. Email: lattreed@holycross.edu. Research: medieval Anglo-Iberian diplomacy, use of film in teaching history.

Atwill, *David G.*, *Penn State.* University Park, PA. Email: dga11@psu.edu; dgatwill@me.com. Research: 19th-c Chinese borderlands, Tibetan Muslims.

Atwood, *Christopher P.* Philadelphia, PA. Affil: Pennsylvania. Email: catwood@sas.upenn. edu. Research: Mongol empire, post-imperial Mongol historiography.

Audain, *Mekala S.*, *New Jersey.*

Auerbach, *Jeffrey A.*, *California State, Northridge.* Email: jeffrey.auerbach@csun.edu.

Auerbach, *Karen*, *North Carolina, Chapel Hill.* Email: kauerbach@unc.edu.

Auerbach, *Stephen D.*, *Georgia Coll. and State.* Email: stephen.auerbach@gcsu.edu.

August, *Andrew*, *Penn State.* Email: axa24@psu. edu.

August, *Linda*, *Library Co. of Philadelphia.* Email: laugust@librarycompany.org.

Augustin, *Anna-Carolin*, *German Hist. Inst.* Email: augustin@ghi-dc.org.

Augustine, *Dolores L.*, *St. John's, NY.* Email: augustid@stjohns.edu.

Augustinos, *Gerasimos*, *South Carolina, Columbia.* Email: augustg@mailbox.sc.edu.

Augustyn, *Frederick J., Jr.* Greenbelt, MD. Affil: Library of Congress. Email: augustynfrederick5@gmail.com. Research: adult literacy, 20th-c popular culture.

Augustyniak, *Ashley*, *Science History Inst.* Email: aaugustyniak@sciencehistory.org.

Ault, *Julia E.*, *Utah.* Email: julia.ault@utah.edu.

Auman, *Karen E.*, *Brigham Young.* Email: kauman@byu.edu.

Aumoithe, *George, Jr.* Princeton, NJ. Affil: Princeton. Email: george.aumoithe@gmail. com. Research: comparative welfare states, health planning.

Aune, *Stefan*, *NYU.*

Auricchio, *Laura*, *New School.* Email: auricchl@ newschool.edu.

Auslander, *Diane P.*, *Lehman, CUNY.* Email: diane.auslander@lehman.cuny.edu.

Auslander, *Leora*, *Chicago.* Chicago, IL. Email: lausland@uchicago.edu. Research: cultural revolutions, interwar European Jewish.

Aust, *Martin E.* Bonn, Germany. Affil: Rheinische Friedrich-Wilhelms, Bonn. Email: martin.aust@ uni-bonn.de. Research: Russia/empire/global, Russia/autobiography.

Austen, *Ralph A.*, *Chicago.* Email: wwb3@ uchicago.edu.

Austin, *Allan W.* Dallas, PA. Affil: Misericordia. Email: aaustin@misericordia.edu. Research: race and ethnicity in 20th-c US, American identity.

Austin, *Brad E.*, *Salem State.* Email: baustin@ salemstate.edu.

Austin, *Bradley.* Marion, IL. Email: bvb813@ hotmail.com.

Austin, *Curtis J.*, *Oregon.* Email: caustin@ uoregon.edu.

Austin, *Gareth.* Cambridge, United Kingdom. Affil: Cambridge. Email: gma31@cam.ac.uk. Research: West African markets/slaves/ states, economic development and the Anthropocen.

Austin, *Joe*, *Wisconsin-Milwaukee.* Email: jaustin@uwm.edu.

Austin, *Lyudmila.* Ann Arbor, MI. Email: austinly@msu.edu.

Austin, *Paula*, *Boston Univ.; California State, Sacramento.* Email: paula.austin@csus.edu.

Austin, *Shawn Michael*, *Arkansas, Fayetteville.* Email: saustin1@uark.edu.

Avella, *Steven M.*, *Marquette.* Milwaukee, WI. Email: steven.avella@marquette.edu. Research: religion and urban life, California.

Avent, *Glenn J.*, *Hastings.* Email: gavent@ hastings.edu.

Averbeck, *Robin Marie*, *California State, Chico.* Email: rmaverbeck@csuchico.edu.

Averbuch, *Bryan D.*, *Staten Island, CUNY.* Email: bryan.averbuch@csi.cuny.edu.

Averill, *Stephanie Trombley.* Hudson, NH. Affil: Southern New Hampshire. Email: s.averill@snhu.edu. Research: rhetoric and foreign policy formulation, status of forces agreements.

Avery, *Donald H.*, *Western Ontario.* Email: avery@uwo.ca.

Avetissian, *Karine A.* St. Petersburg, Russia. Affil: St. Petersburg. Email: stepkars@icsps.ru. Research: ancient Greece, Russian emigrant historians in US.

Avila, *Alfredo.* Mexico. Affil: Nacional Autónoma de México. Email: alfredo.avila@unam.mx. Research: 19th-c Latin American politics, independence of Latin America.

Avila, *Edward David.* Santa Ana, CA. Affil: Trinity Law Sch. Email: avilaedward1972@gmail.com. Research: labor law, border studies.

Avila, *Eric R.*, *UCLA.* Email: eavila@ucla.edu.

Avila, *Mayra Lizette*, *Texas-Rio Grande Valley.* McAllen, TX. Email: mayra.avila@utrgv. edu; mayra_avila49@yahoo.com. Research: immigration, gender.

Avila, *Rolando*, *Texas-Rio Grande Valley.* Email: rolando.avila@utrgv.edu.

Avina, *Joshua.* Fresno, CA. Affil: Illinois, Springfield. Email: josh.avina78@gmail.com.

Aviña, *Alexander*, *Arizona State.* Tempe, AZ. Email: alexander.avina@asu.edu. Research: Mexican guerrilla movements, drugs and state violence.

Avitabile, *Matthew*, *SUNY, Oneonta.* Email: matthew.avitabile@oneonta.edu.

Avraamides, *Achilles*, *Iowa State.*

Avrutin, *Eugene M.*, *Illinois, Urbana-Champaign.* Email: eavrutin@illinois.edu.

Awad, *Habeeb*, *Hope.* Email: hawad@hope.edu.

Awn, *Peter J.*, *Columbia (Hist.).* Email: pja3@ columbia.edu.

Axel, *Paul Joseph.* Chicago, IL. Affil: Air Force Academy High Sch. Email: paxel@cps.edu.

Axelrod, *Jeremiah Borenstein*, *Occidental.* Pasadena, CA. Email: axelrod@oxy.edu; jem@ inventingautopia.com. Research: Los Angeles gender/race/mobility, Southern California urbanism and planning.

Axtell, *James L.*, *William and Mary.* Email: jlaxte@ wm.edu.

Ayana, *Daniel*, *Youngstown State.* Email: dayana@ysu.edu.

Aydin, *Cemil*, *North Carolina, Chapel Hill.*

Ayers, *Edward L.*, *Richmond.* Charlottesville, VA. Email: eayers@richmond.edu. Research: US South.

Azfar, *Farid M.*, *Swarthmore.* Email: fazfar1@ swarthmore.edu.

Azimi, *Fakhreddin*, *Connecticut, Storrs.* Email: fakhreddin.azimi@uconn.edu.

Azuma, *Eiichiro*, *Pennsylvania.* Email: eazuma@ sas.upenn.edu.

Azzi, *Stephen*, *Carleton, Can.* Email: stephen. azzi@carleton.ca.

B b

Baack, *Lawrence J.* Berkeley, CA. Email: larry@ thebaacks.com. Research: Carsten Niebuhr and Arabian journey, Antarctic in history.

Baader, *Benjamin Maria*, *Manitoba.* Email: benjamin.baader@umanitoba.ca.

Babayan, *Kathryn*, *Michigan, Ann Arbor.* Email: babayan@umich.edu.

Babb, *Joseph G.*, *US Army Command Coll.* Email: joseph.g.babb.civ@mail.mil.

Babcock, *Robert S.*, *Hastings.* Email: rbabcock@ hastings.edu.

Baber, *R. Jovita*, *Illinois, Chicago.* Email: jbabe@ comcast.net.

Babiracki, *Patryk J.*, *Texas, Arlington.* Email: babiracki@uta.edu.

Babits, *Christopher Michael.* Austin, TX. Affil: Texas, Austin. Email: chris.babits@utexas.edu.

Babits, *Lawrence E.*, *East Carolina.* Email: babitsl@ecu.edu.

Babou, *Cheikh A. M.*, *Pennsylvania.* Email: cheikh@sas.upenn.edu.

Babovic, *Jovana*, *SUNY, Coll. Geneseo.* Email: babovic@geneseo.edu.

Baca-Winters, *Keenan.* Albuquerque, NM. Affil: Gilbert L. Sena Charter High Sch. Email: kbacawint@gmail.com.

Bach, *Damon R.* Navasota, TX. Affil: Texas A&M. Email: bachdr@hotmail.com. Research: American counterculture, international counterculture.

Bach, *Jose Alfredo.* San Marcos, TX. Affil: Portentious Buffoon. Email: jabach1228@cox. net.

Bach, *Morten*, *Ohio.* Email: bach@ohio.edu.

Bacharach, Jere L., *Washington, Seattle*. Email: jere@uw.edu.

Bachin, Robin F., *Miami*. Miami, FL. Email: rbachin@miami.edu. Research: urban planning, sustainability.

Bachman, Jessica Leigh. Edmonds, WA. Affil: Washington. Email: jlb49@uw.edu. Research: global Cold War, postcolonial South Asia.

Bachrach, Bernard S., *Minnesota (Hist.)*. Email: bachr001@umn.edu.

Bachrach, David Stewart, *New Hampshire, Durham*. Email: david.bachrach@unh.edu.

Bacino, Leo J., *Northeastern Illinois*. Email: L-Bacino@neiu.edu.

Backfish, Charles G., *SUNY, Stony Brook*. Email: charles.backfish@stonybrook.edu.

Backman, Clifford R., *Boston Univ*. Boston, MA. Email: cbackman@bu.edu. Research: Crown of Aragon, medieval intellectual.

Backman, Prudence, *New York State Archives*. Email: prudence.backman@nysed.gov.

Bacon, Ewa K., *Lewis*. Wheaton, IL. Email: baconew@lewisu.edu. Research: science, global.

Bacon, Reginald W. Newburyport, MA. Affil: Historic New England. Email: rwbacon@comcast.net. Research: American vaudeville, American circus.

Bacopoulos-Viau, Alexandra, *NYU*.

Badgley, Ian, *Carleton, Can*. Email: ian.badgley@carleton.ca.

Badran, Margot. Washington, DC. Email: m-badran@northwestern.edu.

Bae, Kyoungjin, *Kenyon*. Email: baek@kenyon.edu.

Baehler, Joel Edward. Cleveland Heights, OH. Affil: Kent State. Email: jbaehler@kent.edu. Research: citizenship and LGBT communities, post-WWII cultural and intellectual.

Baehre, Rainer, *Memorial, Newfoundland*. Email: rbaehre@grenfell.mun.ca.

Baer, Andrew Scott, *Alabama, Birmingham*. Birmingham, AL. Email: abaer@uab.edu; asbaer81@gmail.com. Research: race and criminal justice, social movements.

Baer, George W., *Naval War Coll*. Email: gwbaer6@comcast.net.

Baer, Marc B., *Hope*. Email: baer@hope.edu.

Baernstein, P. Renee, *Miami, Ohio*. Oxford, OH. Email: baernspr@miamioh.edu. Research: early modern Europe, Renaissance.

Baesler, John, *Saginaw Valley State*. Email: jbaesler@svsu.edu.

Bagby, Ross F. Columbus, OH. Email: rfbagby@aol.com.

Baggett, Ashley, *North Dakota State*. Email: ashley.baggett@ndsu.edu.

Baggett, Holly, *Missouri State*. Email: hollybaggett@missouristate.edu.

Baggett, James A., *Union*. Email: jabaggett3234@att.net.

Baghoolizadeh, Beeta, *Bucknell*. Email: bb038@bucknell.edu.

Bahar, Matthew Robert, *Oberlin*. Email: mbahar@oberlin.edu.

Bahler, Gary M. Stockbridge, MA. Email: gary.bahler@gmail.com.

Bahr, Katrin. Amherst, MA. Affil: Massachusetts Amherst. Email: katrin.bahr@gmail.com.

Baics, Gergely, *Barnard, Columbia*. New York, NY. Email: gbaics@barnard.edu. Research: urban history / historical GIS, economic history.

Baig, *Hamzah Mirza*. New Haven, CT. Affil: Yale. Email: hamzah.baig@yale.edu.

Bailey, Anne C., *Binghamton, SUNY*. Email: abailey@binghamton.edu.

Bailey, Beth L., *Kansas*. Lawrence, KS. Email: blbailey@ku.edu. Research: US gender and sexuality, 20th-c US cultural and social.

Bailey, Craig, *Villanova*. Email: craig.bailey@villanova.edu.

Bailey, Heather, *Illinois, Springfield*. Email: hbail2@uis.edu.

Bailey, John Christian. Purchase, NY. Affil: Purchase, SUNY. Email: johnchristianbailey@gmail.com. Research: German-Jewish love, emotions.

Bailey, John W., Jr., *Centenary, La.* Email: jbailey2@centenary.edu.

Bailey, John Wendell, Jr. Kenosha, WI. Affil: Carthage. Research: US military and Indians, American West.

Bailey, Johnny. Trenton, NJ. Email: dr.jonbailey@gmail.com.

Bailey, Michael D., *Iowa State*. Ames, IA. Email: mdbailey@iastate.edu. Research: late medieval religion, magic and superstition.

Bailey, Michael T. Brookline, MA. Affil: Boston Coll. Email: baileymp@bc.edu.

Bailey, Peter C., *Manitoba*. Email: baileypc@cc.umanitoba.ca.

Bailey, Rebecca J., *Northern Kentucky*. Email: baileyr4@nku.edu.

Bailey, Richard A., *Canisius*. Email: bailey22@canisius.edu.

Bailey, Roger Alan. Herndon, VA. Affil: Maryland, Coll. Park. Email: rabailey@terpmail.umd.edu.

Bailey, Stuart C. Tewksbury, MA. Affil: Purdue; Massachusetts Lowell. Email: stucbailey@gmail.com.

Bailey, Telisha Dionne. Charlottesville, VA. Affil: Virginia. Email: tdb6d@virginia.edu. Research: African American women/carceral state, gender/mass incarceration/race.

Bailey, Trent. Urbandale, IA. Affil: Colorado, Colorado Springs. Email: trent.j.bailey@gmail.com.

Bailey, W. Richard, Esq. Reedley, CA. Email: rich020950@aol.com.

Bailey Fischer, Valerie. Williamstown, MA. Affil: Williams. Email: valerie_bailey@brontes.org. Research: US Episcopal Church, women in Holy Orders.

Bailey Glasco, Sharon, *Linfield*. Email: sglasco@linfield.edu.

Bailkin, Jordanna, *Washington, Seattle*. Seattle, WA. Email: bailkin@u.washington.edu. Research: decolonization and migration, social science.

Baillargeon, Denyse, *Montréal*. Email: denyse.baillargeon@umontreal.ca.

Bailley, Jean-Louis David. Cincinnati, OH. Affil: Kenyon. Email: jlbaillely2@gmail.com.

Bailony, Reem, *Agnes Scott*. Email: rbailony@agnesscott.edu.

Baily, Samuel L., III, *Rutgers*. Email: bailysj@comcast.net.

Bailyn, Bernard, *Harvard (Hist.)*. Belmont, MA. Email: bailyn@fas.harvard.edu. Research: America.

Bain, Bob, *Michigan, Ann Arbor*. Ann Arbor, MI. Email: bbain@umich.edu. Research: teaching and learning history, history education.

Bain, Donald E., Jr., *St. John Fisher*. Email: dbain@sjfc.edu.

Baird, Andrew T., *Columbus State*. Email: baird_andrew@columbustate.edu.

Baird, Deborah F. Los Altos, CA.

Baird, Jay W., *Miami, Ohio*. Oxford, OH. Email: bairdjw@muohio.edu. Research: literature in Third Reich, Germany in WWII.

Baird, Melissa F., *Michigan Tech*. Email: mfbaird@mtu.edu.

Baird, W. David, *Pepperdine*. Email: david.baird@pepperdine.edu.

Bajalan, Djene Rhys, *Missouri State*. Email: DRBajalan@MissouriState.edu.

Bak, Greg, *Manitoba*. Email: greg.bak@umanitoba.ca.

Bak, Joan Lamaysou, *Richmond*. Email: jbak@richmond.edu.

Bakari, Adonijah L., *Middle Tennessee State*. Email: adonijah.bakari@mtsu.edu.

Baker, Andrew C., *Texas A&M, Commerce*. Email: Andrew.Baker@tamuc.edu.

Baker, Andrew David, *Bates*. Email: abaker2@bates.edu.

Baker, Bruce E. Newcastle Upon Tyne, United Kingdom. Affil: Newcastle. Email: bruce.baker@ncl.ac.uk. Research: US South, Reconstruction.

Baker, Christine D., *Indiana, Pa.* Email: cbaker@iup.edu.

Baker, Elizabeth Anne, *Grove City*. Grove City, PA. Email: bakerea@gcc.edu.

Baker, Emerson W., *Salem State*. Email: ebaker@salemstate.edu.

Baker, Erik. Cambridge, MA. Affil: Harvard. Email: ebaker@g.harvard.edu. Research: US political conservatism, US social science.

Baker, Florence M. Glendale, CA. Affil: El Camino. Email: fmbaker2@earthlink.net. Research: modern world planted landscapes, Asian religious culture and traditions.

Baker, H. Robert, *Georgia State*. Atlanta, GA. Email: robertbaker@gsu.edu. Research: fugitive slaves in antebellum US, constitutional.

Baker, James F., *Central Oklahoma*. Email: jbaker@uco.edu.

Baker, James T., *Western Kentucky*. Email: james.baker@wku.edu.

Baker, Jeffrey, *Duke*. Email: jeffrey.baker@duke.edu.

Baker, Keith M., *Stanford*. Stanford, CA. Email: kbaker@stanford.edu. Research: French Revolution, political culture.

Baker, Michael, *Worcester State*. Email: mbaker4@worcester.edu.

Baker, Nancy E., *Sam Houston State*. Email: neb001@shsu.edu.

Baker, Norman, *SUNY, Buffalo*. Email: nbaker@buffalo.edu.

Baker, Patricia Anne. Whitstable, United Kingdom. Affil: Kent. Email: pattyanne_baker@hotmail.com. Research: garden, health and scences.

Baker, Paul, *NYU*. Email: prbaker2@aol.com.

Baker, Paula, *Ohio State*. Email: baker.973@osu.edu.

Baker, Richard A., *US Senate Hist. Office*. Kensington, MD. Email: senatehistorian@gmail.com; senatehistorian@comcast.net. Research: parliamentary rules of procedure, senator-constituency communications.

Baker, **Thomas L**. Rio Vista, TX. Affil: W.K. Gordon Center. Email: tbaker@tarleton.edu. Research: wind power, social and cultural studies.

Baker, **Thomas N**., *SUNY, Coll. Potsdam*. Email: bakertn@potsdam.edu.

Baker, **Vaughan B**., *Louisiana, Lafayette*.

Baker, **William J**., *Maine, Orono*. Email: william. baker@maine.edu.

Bakewell, **Peter J**., *Southern Methodist*. Email: bakewell@smu.edu.

Bakhash, **Shaul**, *George Mason*. Email: sbakhash@gmu.edu.

Bakhle, **Janaki**, *California, Berkeley*. Email: jbakhle@berkeley.edu.

Bakhmetyeva, **Tatyana V**., *Rochester*. Email: tatyana.bakhmetyeva@rochester.edu.

Balabanlilar, **Lisa Ann**, *Rice*. Houston, TX. Email: balabanlilar@rice.edu. Research: Mughal imperial identity, comparative islamic empire.

Balachandran, **Jyoti Gulati**, *Penn State*. University Park, PA. Email: jzb461@psu. edu; jyotigul@gmail.com. Research: Islam in medieval/early modern Gujarat, scholarly networks in Indian Ocean world.

Balasubramanian, **Aditya**. Acton, Australia. Affil: Australian National. Email: aditya. balasubramanian@gmail.com.

Balberg, **Mira**, *California, San Diego*. Email: mbalberg@ucsd.edu.

Balcerski, **Thomas J**., *Eastern Connecticut State*. Willimantic, CT. Email: balcerskit@easternct. edu. Research: antebellum US, political.

Balci, **Tamer**, *Texas-Rio Grande Valley*. Email: tamer.balci@utrgv.edu.

Balcom, **Karen A**., *McMaster*. Email: balcomk@ mcmaster.ca.

Baldacci, **Alexis**. Gainesville, FL. Affil: Bates. Email: anbalda@ufl.edu. Research: material culture, citizen response to authoritarian states.

Baldanza, **Kathlene T**., *Penn State*. State College, PA. Email: ktb3@psu.edu; katybaldanza@ gmail.com. Research: Sino-Viet relations in Ming, early modern world.

Balderrama, **Francisco**, *California State, Los Angeles*. Email: fbalder@calstatela.edu.

Baldwin, **Deborah J**., *Arkansas, Little Rock*. Email: djbaldwin@ualr.edu.

Baldwin, **Peter C**., *Connecticut, Storrs*. Storrs Mansfield, CT. Email: pbaldwin@uconn.edu. Research: public space, urban children.

Baldwin, **Peter**, *UCLA*. New York, NY. Email: pbaldwin@ucla.edu. Research: modern Europe, comparative Europe-US.

Baldwin, **Roger**, *California State, East Bay*. Email: roger.baldwin@csueastbay.edu.

Baldwin-Glenn, **JoAnn**. Chicago, IL. Email: jbaldwinglenn@gmail.com.

Balfour, **David B**. Rutland, VT. Affil: St. Joseph. Email: dbalfour@csj.edu.

Balik, **Shelby M**. Centennial, CO. Affil: Metropolitan State, Denver. Email: smbalik@ gmail.com. Research: colonial religious culture, family and religious life.

Balkenende, **Teresa**. Seattle, WA. Affil: Highline Comm. Coll. Email: teri_balkenende@yahoo. com. Research: modern central European public health and economic.

Ball, **Alan M**., *Marquette*. Email: alan.ball@ marquette.edu.

Ball, **Dorothy**, *Hist. New Orleans*.

Ball, **Erica L**., *Occidental*. Email: balle@oxy.edu.

Ball, **Jeremy R**., *Dickinson*. Email: ballj@ dickinson.edu.

Ball, **L. Durwood**, **Jr**., *New Mexico*. Email: lball@ unm.edu.

Ball, **Larry D**., **Sr**., *Arkansas State*.

Ball, **Margaret Sewall**, *US Dept. of State*.

Ball, **Molly C**., *Rochester*. Rochester, NY. Email: mollycball@rochester.edu. Research: labor market inequality in Brazil, early 20th-c working women.

Ballah, **Henryatta**, *Connecticut Coll*. Email: hballah@conncoll.edu.

Ballan, **Mohamad**, *SUNY, Stony Brook*.

Ballard, **Allen B**., *SUNY, Albany*. Email: aballard@ albany.edu.

Balleisen, **Edward J**., *Duke*. Durham, NC. Email: eballeis@duke.edu. Research: US commercial fraud, economic regulation.

Ballinger, **Pamela L**., *Michigan, Ann Arbor*. Email: pballing@umich.edu.

Ballone, **Angela**. Sassari, Italy. Affil: Nacional Autónoma de México. Email: angela.ballone@ gmail.com. Research: early modern, legal.

Ballout, **Laila K**., *Wichita State*. Wichita, KS. Email: laila.ballout@wichita.edu; LailaBallout2013@u.northwestern.edu. Research: US foreign relations, immigration.

Balogh, **Brian H**., *Virginia*. Email: balogh@ virginia.edu.

Balsamo, **Larry T**., *Western Illinois*. Email: LT-Balsamo@wiu.edu.

Balserak, **Jon**, *Illinois, Chicago*. Email: J.Balserak@bristol.ac.uk.

Baltacioglu-Brammer, **Ayse**, *Binghamton, SUNY; NYU*. Email: abaltaci@binghamton.edu; abb12@nyu.edu.

Baltimore, **Lester B**., *Adelphi*. Email: baltimor@ adelphi.edu.

Balto, **Simon Ezra**, *Iowa*. Iowa City, IA. Email: simon-balto@uiowa.edu. Research: early-/mid-20th-c US race/policing, organic community roots of Black Power.

Baltovski, **Alexander Edward**. Staten Island, NY. Affil: Graduate Center, CUNY. Email: siralex5@ gmail.com.

Balzarini, **Stephen E**., *Gonzaga*. Email: balzarini@gonzaga.edu.

Balzer, **Harley D**., *Georgetown*. Cabin John, MD. Email: balzerh@georgetown.edu. Research: middle classes, education/science/ technology.

Bamba, **Abou**, *Gettysburg*. Email: abamba@ gettysburg.edu.

Bamberger, **Michael A**., *Leo Baeck Inst*. Email: michael.bamberger@dentons.com.

Bamford, **Tyler**. Souderton, PA. Affil: Temple. Email: bamford.tyler@gmail.com.

Banac, **Ivo**, *Yale*. Email: ivo.banac@yale.edu.

Banerjee, **Mou**, *Wisconsin-Madison*. Clemson, SC. Affil: Clemson. Email: mbanerjee4@ wisc.edu; moubanerjee082007@gmail.com. Research: modern South Asia, politics of religion in colonial India.

Banerjee, **Somaditya**, *Austin Peay State*. Email: banerjees@apsu.edu.

Banerjee, **Swapna M**., *Brooklyn, CUNY*. Brooklyn, NY. Email: banerjee@brooklyn.cuny.edu. Research: children and fathers in colonial India, gender/family/domesticity.

Bangura, **Joseph J**, *Kalamazoo*. Email: bangura@kzoo.edu.

Banke, **Rachel**. Mishawaka, IN. Affil: Missouri, Columbia. Email: rbanke@alumni.nd.edu.

Banker, **James R**., *North Carolina State*. Email: james_banker@ncsu.edu.

Bankhurst, **Benjamin**, *Shepherd*. Email: bbankhur@shepherd.edu.

Banks, **Bryan Andrew**, *Columbus State*. Email: banks_bryan@columbusstate.edu.

Banks, **Elizabeth**. New York, NY. Affil: NYU. Email: elizabethbanks@gmail.com. Research: Soviet-Mozambican relations, chronology of international socialism.

Banks, **Elyse L**., *San Francisco*. Email: bankselyse@gmail.com.

Banner, **James M**., **Jr**. Washington, DC. Email: jbanner@aya.yale.edu. Research: American national state, historians' professional practices.

Banner, **Lois W**., *Southern California*. Email: lbanner@usc.edu.

Banner-Haley, **Charles Pete**, *Colgate*. Cortland, NY. Email: cbannerhaley@mail.colgate.edu. Research: African American intellectual, Afro-Americans in Upstate New York.

Bannister, **Jerry**, *Dalhousie*. Email: jerry. bannister@dal.ca.

Bannister, **Robert**, *Swarthmore*. Email: rbannis1@swarthmore.edu.

Bannon, **Cynthia J**., *Indiana*. Email: cbannon@ indiana.edu.

Banta, **Brady**, *Arkansas State*. Email: bbanta@ astate.edu.

Banton, **Arthur**, *Tennessee Tech*. Email: abanton@tntech.edu.

Banton, **Caree Ann Marie**, *Arkansas, Fayetteville*. Email: cabanton@uark.edu.

Banulescu, **Sultana**. New York, NY. Affil: Graduate Center, CUNY. Email: sbanules@ gmail.com. Research: medicine and science, cultural and intellectual.

Baptist, **Edward E**., *Cornell*. Email: eeb36@ cornell.edu.

Baracco, **Tony S**. Farmington Hills, MI. Affil: Oakland Comm. Coll. Email: tbaracco@yahoo. com.

Barahona, **Renato**, *Illinois, Chicago*. Chicago, IL. Email: barahona@uic.edu. Research: sexual criminality/honor/law, popular culture/ women/social control.

Barajas, **Frank P**., *California State, Channel Islands*. Email: frank.barajas@csuci.edu.

Barakat, **Abdul A**. Van Nuys, CA. Email: abdulbarakat@gmail.com.

Baran, **Emily B**., *Middle Tennessee State*. Murfreesboro, TN. Email: Emily.Baran@mtsu. edu; emily.b.baran@gmail.com. Research: Jehovah's Witnesses in Soviet Union, Pentecostals in Soviet Union.

Baranov, **Alexander**. Berlin, Germany. Affil: Free, Berlin. Email: ordoteutonicus@gmail.com. Research: medieval Livonia, Teutonic Order.

Baranowski, **Shelley O**. West Palm Beach, FL. Affil: Akron. Email: sbarano@comcast.net. Research: German imperialism, tourism and consumer culture.

Baratta, **Joseph P**., *Worcester State*. Email: jbaratta@worcester.edu.

Barba, **Paul**, *Bucknell*.

Barbee, **David**. Arlington, OH. Affil: Pennsylvania. Email: dmbarbee@hotmail.com.

Barber, **Cary Michael**, *California State, San Bernardino*. Email: barberc@wfu.edu.

Barber, **David**, *Tennessee, Martin*. Email: dbarber@utm.edu.

Barber, Harry. Bartlett, TN. Affil: Memphis. Email: Harrybarber@bellsouth.net. Research: American culture wars, evolution/creationism.

Barber, Katrine, *Portland State*. Email: barberk@pdx.edu.

Barber, Marian J., *American Catholic Hist. Assoc.* Austin, TX. Email: marianj.barber@gmail.com. Research: race in Texas-Mexico borderlands, post-1820 European emigration.

Barber, Marilyn J., *Carleton, Can.* Email: marilyn.barber@carleton.ca.

Barber, Marlin Christopher, *Missouri State*. Email: mcbarber@missouristate.edu.

Barber, Stephen P., *Columbus State*. Email: barber_stephen@columbusstate.edu.

Barber, Tom Ewing. Baton Rouge, LA. Affil: Louisiana State, Baton Rouge. Email: tbarbe6@lsu.edu. Research: American philanthropy, poverty.

Barberis, Daniela S. Naperville, IL. Affil: North Central. Email: dsbarberis@noctrl.edu. Research: science, French intellectual 1789-1914.

Barbezat, Michael David. East Melbourne, Australia. Affil: Australian Catholic. Email: michael.barbezat@acu.edu.au. Research: Hell/Purgatory/eschatology, identity/minorities/persecution.

Barbier, Mary Kathryn, *Mississippi State*. Mississippi State, MS. Email: kathryn.barbier@msstate.edu. Research: George C. Marshall/Bernard L. Montgomery, Lily Sergueiew.

Barbieri-Low, Anthony J., *California, Santa Barbara*. Email: barbieri-low@history.ucsb.edu.

Barbosa, Rosana, *St. Mary's, Can.* Email: rosana.barbosa@smu.ca.

Barbosa Ribeiro, Braulia Ines. New Haven, CT. Affil: Yale Divinity Sch. Email: braulia@gmail.com.

Barbour, Barton, *Boise State*. Email: bbarbour@boisestate.edu.

Barchiesi, Franco. Columbus, OH. Affil: Ohio State. Email: barchiesi.1@osu.edu. Research: states and labor regimes/Atlantic, racialization/liberalism/antiblackness.

Barclay, David E., *Kalamazoo*. Largo, FL. Affil: German Studies Assoc. Email: david.barclay@kzoo.edu; director@thegsa.org. Research: modern Germany, modern France and Britain.

Barclay, Jenifer L. Pullman, WA. Affil: Washington State, Pullman. Email: jenifer.barclay@wsu.edu. Research: US slavery/antebellum America, disability.

Barclay, Michael Emil. Pittsburgh, PA. Affil: Southern New Hampshire. Email: m.barclay1@snhu.edu.

Barclay, Paul David, *Lafayette*. Easton, PA. Email: barclayp@lafayette.edu. Research: comparative colonialism, colonial Taiwan.

Bardes, John. New Orleans, LA. Affil: Tulane. Email: bardesj@gmail.com.

Bare, Daniel Robert. College Station, TX. Affil: Texas A&M, Coll. Station. Email: DanielBare@gmail.com.

Barefoot, Danielle Blalock. Tucson, AZ. Affil: Arizona. Email: dblalock@email.arizona.edu. Research: Chilean university student activism.

Barefoot, James Collin. Tucson, AZ. Affil: Arizona. Email: jamesbarefoot@email.arizona.edu.

Barenberg, Alan, *Texas Tech*. Email: alan.barenberg@ttu.edu.

Barger, Lilian Calles. El Prado, NM. Email: lilian@lilianbarger.com. Research: feminist thought, American thought.

Baring, Edward G. Madison, NJ. Affil: Drew. Email: ebaring@drew.edu. Research: postwar French philosophy, transnational intellectual.

Barish, Daniel, *Baylor*. Waco, TX. Email: daniel_barish@baylor.edu; dan.barish@gmail.com.

Barkacs, Michael. Cleveland, OH. Email: mebarkacs@yahoo.com. Research: Angevin England, Reformation art.

Barkan, Elazar, *Columbia (Hist.)*. Email: eb2302@columbia.edu.

Barkawi, Tarak. London, United Kingdom. Affil: London Sch. of Economics. Email: tarak.barkawi@gmail.com.

Barker, Brett R., *Wisconsin-Stevens Point*. Email: bbarker@uwsp.edu.

Barker, Caitlin Ayrault. Lansing, MI. Affil: Michigan State. Email: caitlinbarker@gmail.com.

Barker, Gordon S. Ste. Agathe des Monts, QC, Canada. Affil: Bishop's. Email: gbarker@ubishops.ca. Research: African American, early Republic.

Barker, Hannah, *Arizona State*. Email: hannah.barker@asu.edu.

Barker, John C., *Trent*.

Barker, John W., **Jr.**, *Wisconsin-Madison*. Email: jwbarker@wisc.edu.

Barker, Karen, *OAH*. Email: kbarker@oah.org.

Barker, Peter, *Oklahoma (Hist. of Science)*. Email: barkerp@ou.edu.

Barker, Ray C., *Canisius*. Buffalo, NY. Affil: Erie Comm. Coll., South. Email: barker@canisius.edu; barker@ecc.edu. Research: contemporary British politics, role of leader of opposition.

Barker, Rosanne, *Sam Houston State*. Email: his_rmb@shsu.edu.

Barker-Benfield, Graham John, *SUNY, Albany*. Email: benfield@albany.edu.

Barkin, Kenneth David, *California, Riverside*. Email: kenneth.barkin@ucr.edu.

Barkley Brown, Elsa, *Maryland, Coll. Park*. College Park, MD. Email: barkleyb@umd.edu. Research: Afro-American and women.

Barksdale, Kevin T., *Marshall*. Email: barksdale@marshall.edu.

Barlow, Philip L., *Utah State*. Email: philip.barlow@usu.edu.

Barlow, Rhonda, *Massachusetts Hist. Soc.* Email: rbarlow@masshist.org.

Barlow, Richard, *Arizona State*.

Barlow, Tani E., *Rice*. Houston, TX. Email: tb5@rice.edu; barlow.tani@gmail.com. Research: Chinese social science in 1920s-30s, gender and history of sociology.

Barlow Robles, Whitney. Cambridge, MA. Affil: Harvard. Email: whitney.a.robles@gmail.com.

Barman, Roderick J. Vancouver, BC, Canada. Affil: British Columbia. Email: roderick.j.barman@ubc.ca. Research: Brazil 1852-1910.

Barnes, Andrew E., *Arizona State*. Email: andrew.barnes@asu.edu.

Barnes, Aneilya K., *Coastal Carolina*. Email: abarnes@coastal.edu.

Barnes, Gordon Randolph, **Jr.** Brooklyn, NY. Affil: Graduate Center, CUNY. Email: grbarnesjr@gmail.com. Research: Mauritius/Jamaica/British Empire, slavery/post-emancipation/violence.

Barnes, Iris Leigh. Havre de Grace, MD. Affil: Hosanna Sch. Museum. Email: iris.barnes@hosannaschoolmuseum.org.

Barnes, James J., *Wabash*. Crawfordsville, IN. Email: barnesj@wabash.edu. Research: International copyright, German intelligence organization.

Barnes, Kenneth C., *Central Arkansas*. Email: kennethb@uca.edu.

Barnes, Mark, *Morgan State*. Email: mark.barnes@morgan.edu.

Barnes, Melvin Laneer, Jr. Columbus, OH. Affil: Ohio State. Email: Barnes.724@osu.edu. Research: Sino-African American interaction.

Barnes, Nicole E., *Duke*. Durham, NC. Email: nicole.barnes@duke.edu. Research: 20th-c Chinese medicine, early 20th-c Chinese ethnic identity.

Barnes, Rhae Lynn, *Princeton*. Email: rlbarnes@princeton.edu.

Barnes, Robin Bruce, *Davidson*. Davidson, NC. Email: robarnes@davidson.edu. Research: Reformation, early modern Europe.

Barnes, Steven A., *George Mason*. Email: sbarnes3@gmu.edu.

Barnes, Teresa A., *Illinois, Urbana-Champaign*. Email: tbarnes2@illinois.edu.

Barnes, Timothy M., *California Polytechnic State*. Email: tbarnes@calpoly.edu.

Barnet, Edward Halley. New York, NY. Affil: Stanford. Email: ehbarnet@stanford.edu.

Barnett, Carlton Carter, III. Austin, TX. Affil: Texas, Austin. Email: c.barnett@utexas.edu. Research: religion, Christianity.

Barnett, Lydia, *Northwestern*. Evanston, IL. Email: lydia.barnett@northwestern.edu. Research: natural disasters, labor and science.

Barnett, Redmond J. Tacoma, WA. Email: redmondbarnett@nventure.com. Research: US West since 1850, social.

Barnett, Richard B., *Virginia*. Email: rbb@virginia.edu.

Barnett, Suzanne Wilson. Tacoma, WA. Affil: Puget Sound. Email: sbarnett@pugetsound.edu. Research: Chinese geographical writings, US-China relations.

Barnett, Tracy L., *Soc. for Military Hist.*

Barnett, William C., *North Central*. Email: wcbarnett@noctrl.edu.

Barney, William L., *North Carolina, Chapel Hill*. Chapel Hill, NC. Email: wbarney@email.unc.edu. Research: 19th-c US political and social.

Barnhart, Adam D. Whittier, CA. Affil: UCLA. Email: adbarnhart@gmail.com. Research: urban ports, deindustrialization.

Barnhart, Gordon, *Saskatchewan*. Email: gordon.barnhart@usask.ca.

Barnhart, Michael A., *SUNY, Stony Brook*. Email: michael.barnhart@stonybrook.edu.

Barnhart, Rodney R., *Henry Ford Coll.*

Barnhart, Terry A., *Eastern Illinois*. Email: tabarnhart@eiu.edu.

Barnhouse, Lucy Christine. Waverly, IA. Affil: Wartburg. Email: lucy.barnhouse@wartburg.edu. Research: late medieval hospitals, medieval medical manuscripts.

Barnum, Forrest S. L., *US Dept. of State*.

Barnwell, Kristi N., *Illinois, Springfield*. Email: kbarn2@uis.edu.

Baron, Beth, *Graduate Center, CUNY*. Email: bbaron@gc.cuny.edu.

Baron, **Christopher**. Notre Dame, IN. Affil: Notre Dame. Email: cbaron1@nd.edu. Research: Greek and Roman historical writing, memory and identity in ancient world.

Baron, **Lawrence**, *San Diego State*. Email: lbaron@sdsu.edu.

Baron, **Sabrina Alcorn**, *Maryland, Coll. Park*. Email: sbaron@umd.edu.

Barr, **Beth Allison**, *Baylor*. Email: beth_barr@baylor.edu.

Barr, **John M**. Kingwood, TX. Affil: Lone Star, Kingwood. Email: john.m.barr@lonestar.edu. Research: Abraham Lincoln and colonization, Reconstruction violence in Texas.

Barr, **Juliana**, *Duke*. Durham, NC. Email: juliana.barr@duke.edu. Research: 16th-/17th-c Spanish borderlands, Indian enslavement.

Barr, **Kara E.**, *Bowling Green State*. Email: kebarr@bgsu.edu.

Barr, **Nicolaas P**. Seattle, WA. Affil: Washington, Seattle. Email: nickbarr@uw.edu. Research: critical theory in the Netherlands.

Barragan, **Yesenia**, *Rutgers*. Email: yesenia.barragan@rutgers.edu.

Barraza Mendoza, **Elsa**. Washington, DC. Affil: Georgetown. Email: eb939@georgetown.edu. Research: universities and slavery, early US politics and religion.

Barrera, **Antonio**, *Colgate*. Email: abarrera@colgate.edu.

Barrett, **David Peter**, *McMaster*. Email: dpbarrett@sympatico.ca.

Barrett, **Marsha E.**, *Illinois, Urbana-Champaign*. Urbana, IL. Email: meb@illinois.edu; marsha.barrett@gmail.com. Research: US political, African American.

Barrett, **Michael B.**, *Citadel*.

Barrett, **Tracy C.**, *North Dakota State*. Email: tracy.barrett@ndsu.edu.

Barrie, **Amanda**. Surrey, United Kingdom. Affil: Greenwich. Email: mandybarrie@hotmail.com. Research: votes for women, suffragettes.

Barringer, **Mark D.**, *Stephen F. Austin State*. Email: mbarringer@sfasu.edu.

Barringer, **Whitney**. Little Rock, AR. Affil: Central Arkansas. Email: wbarringer1@uca.edu. Research: state institutions and mental health, community organizing in rural areas.

Barrington, **John P. T.**, *Furman*. Email: john.barrington@furman.edu.

Barrios Giraldo, **David**. Calgary, AB, Canada. Affil: Calgary. Email: david.barriosgiraldo@ucalgary.ca. Research: commemorations, historical memory.

Barr-Melej, **Patrick**, *Ohio*. Athens, OH. Email: barr-mel@ohio.edu. Research: 20th-c Chilean political/cultural, youth 1960s-70s.

Barron, **Charrise**. Providence, RI. Affil: Brown. Email: Charrise_Barron@brown.edu.

Barron, **Gloria J.**, *Framingham State*.

Barros, **Andrew**, *Québec, Montréal*. Email: barros.andrew@uqam.ca.

Barrow, **Ian J.**, *Middlebury*. Email: ibarrow@middlebury.edu.

Barrow, **Mark V.**, **Jr.**, *Virginia Tech*. Email: barrow@vt.edu.

Barrow, **Robert M.**, *Georgia Southern*.

Barrows, **Leland C**. Blackville, SC. Affil: Voorhees. Email: lbarrows@voorhees.edu. Research: French colonial empire, Romania.

Barrows, **Robert G.**, *Indiana–Purdue, Indianapolis*. Email: rbarrows@iupui.edu.

Barry, **Boubakar**. Dakar-Fann, Senegal. Email: bbarry@orange.sn.

Barry, **Erin**. Saint Louis, MO. Affil: Washington, St. Louis. Email: erinbarry@wustl.edu.

Barry, **William D.**, *Puget Sound*. Email: bbarry@pugetsound.edu.

Barry, **William P.**, *NASA*. Email: bill.barry@nasa.gov.

Barsanti, **Michael J.**, *Library Co. of Philadelphia*. Email: mbarsanti@librarycompany.org.

Barshay, **Andrew E.**, *California, Berkeley*. Email: abars@berkeley.edu.

Barske, **Valerie H.**, *Wisconsin-Stevens Point*. Email: vbarske@uwsp.edu.

Barsotti, **Edoardo Marcello**. Brooklyn, NY. Affil: Fordham. Email: edoardo.barsotti@gmail.com.

Bartchy, **S. Scott**, *UCLA*. Email: bartchy@history.ucla.edu.

Bartee, **Wayne C.**, *Missouri State*. Email: waynebartee@missouristate.edu.

Bartel, **Michael Fritz**. New Haven, CT. Affil: Yale. Email: fritz.bartel@yale.edu. Research: Atlantic Charter, 1940s international.

Bartels, **Carol O.**, *Hist. New Orleans*. Email: carol@hnoc.org.

Barth, **Jonathan E.**, *Arizona State*. Email: jonathan.barth@asu.edu.

Barthelemy, **Melissa Jane**. Goleta, CA. Affil: California, Santa Barbara. Email: barthelemy@ucsb.edu.

Bartholomew, **Francis M.**, **Jr.**, *San Diego State*.

Bartholomew, **James R.**, *Ohio State*. Washington, DC. Email: bartholomew.5@osu.edu. Research: Nobel science and medicine prizes, modern Japanese scientists and science.

Bartlett, **Beatrice S.**, *Yale*. Email: beatrice.bartlett@yale.edu.

Bartlett, **Kenneth**, *Toronto*. Email: kenneth.bartlett@utoronto.ca.

Bartlett, **Stephen M.**, *Kennesaw State*. Email: sbartlet@kennesaw.edu.

Bartley, **Karen**, *Dayton*. Email: kbartley1@udayton.edu.

Bartley, **Russell H.**, *Wisconsin-Milwaukee*. Email: bartleyr@uwm.edu.

Bartoloni-Tuazon, **Kathleen**. Vienna, VA. Affil: First Federal Congress Project. Email: kbartoloni.tuazon@gmail.com. Research: executive power/popular sovereignty, presidential title controversy of 1789.

Barton, **Carlin Adele**, *Massachusetts, Amherst*. Email: cbarton@history.umass.edu.

Barton, **Christopher**, *Francis Marion*. Email: cbarton@fmarion.edu.

Barton, **John D.**, *Utah State*. Email: john.barton@usu.edu.

Barton, **Josef**, *Northwestern*. Email: j-barton@northwestern.edu.

Barton, **Keith C.**, *Indiana*. Email: kcbarton@indiana.edu.

Barton, **Richard E.**, *North Carolina, Greensboro*. Email: rebarton@uncg.edu.

Barton, **Thomas William**, *San Diego*. San Diego, CA. Email: barton@sandiego.edu. Research: Muslim-Christian frontiers in Iberia, Crown of Aragon.

Bartos, **Ramona**, *North Carolina Office of Archives*. Email: ramona.bartos@ncdcr.gov.

Bartov, **Omer**, *Brown*. Providence, RI. Email: Omer_Bartov@Brown.edu. Research: Holocaust and comparative genocide, eastern Europe and interethnic relations.

Bartram, **Faye Lin**, *Iowa*. Email: faye-bartram@uiowa.edu.

Bartrop, **Paul**, *Florida Gulf Coast*. Email: pbartrop@fgcu.edu.

Barty, **Peter F.**, *North Alabama*.

Barua, **Pradeep**, *Nebraska, Kearney*. Email: baruap@unk.edu.

Barzilay, **Karen N.**, *Massachusetts Hist. Soc.* Email: kbarzilay@masshist.org.

Basalla, **George**, *Delaware*. Email: basalla@udel.edu.

Baseler, **Marilyn C**. Ledyard, CT. Affil: Connecticut. Email: m.baseler@sbcglobal.net.

Basham, **Greg W**. Visalia, CA. Email: gregba@cos.edu. Research: Progressive Era, Gilded Age.

Bashara, **Charles G. N**. Washington, DC. Affil: US Dept. of Justice. Email: cgnbashara@gmail.com. Research: early modern European church/state/spirituality, Near Eastern education and nationalism.

Bashaw, **Carolyn**, *Le Moyne*. Email: bashawct@lemoyne.edu.

Bashir, **Shahzad**, *Brown*. Barrington, RI. Email: shahzad_bashir@brown.edu. Research: Islamic humanities.

Bashiri, **Iraj**, *Minnesota (Hist.)*. Email: bashi001@umn.edu.

Basil, **John D.**, *South Carolina, Columbia*. Email: basil@mailbox.sc.edu.

Baskerville, **Peter A.**, *Alberta*. Email: pab@ualberta.ca.

Baskes, **Jeremy A.**, *Ohio Wesleyan*. Email: jabaskes@owu.edu.

Baskind, **Stephen**. Ben Wheeler, TX. Affil: Tyler Jr. Coll. Email: sbas@tjc.edu. Research: Old Bailey, violence in Europe.

Bass, **Jeffrey D**. Winchester, VA. Affil: Arizona State. Email: jdbass33@yahoo.com.

Bassett, **Ross Knox**, *North Carolina State*. Raleigh, NC. Email: ross_bassett@ncsu.edu; rkbassett@gmail.com. Research: semiconductor technology, computing.

Bassi, **Daniella F.**, *Omohundro Inst.*

Bassi Arevalo, **Ernesto**, *Cornell*. Email: eb577@cornell.edu.

Bassler, **Gerhard P.**, *Memorial, Newfoundland*. Email: gbassler@mun.ca.

Basso, **Matthew L.**, *Utah*. Salt Lake City, UT. Email: matt.basso@utah.edu. Research: masculinity, aging.

Bast, **Robert J.**, *Tennessee, Knoxville*. Email: rbast@utk.edu.

Bastedo, **Spencer C**. Astoria, NY. Affil: Graduate Center, CUNY. Email: sbastedo@gradcenter.cuny.edu. Research: 20th-c Iraq, Islamist movements.

Bastian, **Audrey**. Silver Spring, MD. Email: audrey.bastian@gmail.com.

Bastien, **Pascal**, *Québec, Montréal*. Email: bastien.pascal@uqam.ca.

Bastress-Dukehart, **Erica**, *Skidmore*. Email: bastress@skidmore.edu.

Basu, **Subho**, *McGill*. Email: subho.basu@mcgill.ca.

Batalden, **Stephen K.**, *Arizona State*. Email: stephen.batalden@asu.edu.

Batchelor, **Robert Kinnaird, Jr.**, *Georgia Southern*. Statesboro, GA. Email: batchelo@georgiasouthern.edu. Research: London 1660-1740, contact between Britain and China 1600-1793.

Bates, David Keith, Jr., *Union*. Email: dkbates@uu.edu.

Bates, Edward, *Elmhurst*. Email: edward.bates@elmhurst.edu.

Bates, Lynsey, *Robert H. Smith Center*. Email: lbates@monticello.org.

Bates, Rebecca J., *Berea*. Berea, KY. Email: rebecca_bates@berea.edu. Research: philanthropy in Great Britain, labor and national identity.

Bates, Robert William, Esq. Weaverville, CA. Affil: Prepa Tec High Sch. Email: greenbaby1212@gmail.com. Research: German American, northeastern Africa.

Bates, Robin Duffin. Chicago, IL. Affil: Northwestern. Email: rdbates@uchicago.edu. Research: education in postrevolutionary France, political theory 1750-1850.

Bates, Toby Glenn, *Mississippi State*. Email: tgb52@msstate.edu.

Bathory Vidaver, Mary Martha. Oxford, MS. Affil: Mississippi. Email: mbathory@go.olemiss.edu. Research: Social Gospel and 20th-c southern reform, 20th-c religion and labor movement.

Batinski, Michael C., *Southern Illinois, Carbondale*. Carbondale, IL. Email: batinski@siu.edu. Research: historical consciousness in Midwest, US war and peace.

Batruni, Catherine. Danville, CA. Affil: American, Beirut. Email: cbatruni@gmail.com.

Battick, John F., *Maine, Orono*. Email: jbattick@adelphia.net.

Battisti, Danielle, *Nebraska, Omaha*. Email: dbattisti@unomaha.edu.

Batza, Katie P. Lawrence, KS. Affil: Kansas. Email: batza@ku.edu. Research: 1970s gay and lesbian health activism, HIV/AIDS epidemic.

Batzell, Rudi E., *Lake Forest*. Chicago, IL. Email: batzell@mx.lakeforest.edu; rbatzell@gmail.com. Research: welfare state formation, class/gender/racial inequality.

Bauer, Brian, *Illinois, Chicago*. Email: bsb@uic.edu.

Bauer, Deborah, *Purdue, Fort Wayne*. Email: bauerd@pfw.edu.

Bauer, Jeremiah, *Nebraska, Omaha*.

Bauer, William J., Jr., *Nevada, Las Vegas*. Las Vegas, NV. Email: wbauer@unlv.edu. Research: Native Americans and labor, Native Americans and sports.

Bauerle, Ellen A. Ann Arbor, MI. Affil: Univ. of Michigan Press. Email: bauerle@umich.edu.

Baugh, Daniel A., *Cornell*. Williamsburg, VA. Email: dab3@cornell.edu. Research: modern English political/social/economic 1688-1918, European maritime 1600-1800.

Baughan, Elizabeth, *Richmond*. Email: ebaughan@richmond.edu.

Baughman, John J., *DePauw*. Greencastle, IN. Email: jbaughm@comcast.net. Research: modern France, modern Mediterranean.

Baukol, Bard, *North Dakota*. Email: bard.baukol@und.edu.

Baum, Dennis, *Leo Baeck Inst.*

Baum, Emily L., *California, Irvine*. Irvine, CA. Email: emily.baum@uci.edu. Research: modern China, psychology and medicine.

Baum, Jacob M., *Texas Tech*. Lubbock, TX. Email: jacob.m.baum@ttu.edu. Research: senses, temporality and millenarianism.

Baum, Robert M. Hanover, NH. Affil: Dartmouth. Email: robert.m.baum@dartmouth.edu. Research: African religions, West Africa.

Bauman, John F., *California, Pa.*

Bauman, Melissa. Apo, AP. Affil: Maryland Univ. Coll. Email: missmelbau@gmail.com.

Bauman, Robert A., *Washington State, Pullman*. Richland, WA. Email: rbauman@tricity.wsu.edu. Research: race and social policy, race in American West.

Baumann, Mary T., *US Senate Hist. Office*. Email: mary_baumann@sec.senate.gov.

Baumann, Robert F., *US Army Command Coll*. Email: robert.f.baumann.civ@mail.mil.

Baumann, Roland M., *Oberlin*. Email: roland.m.baumann@oberlin.edu.

Baumgardner, Neel G., *Texas, San Antonio*. Email: neel.baumgardner@utsa.edu.

Baumgartner, Alice, *Southern California*. Email: albaumga@usc.edu.

Baumgartner, Frederic J., *Virginia Tech*. Email: treeman@vt.edu.

Baumler, Alan, *Indiana, Pa.* Email: baumler@iup.edu.

Baun, Dylan, *Alabama, Huntsville*. Nashville, TN. Email: dylan.baun@uah.edu. Research: modern Middle East youth/young people, mid-20th-c street politics in Lebanon.

Bauschatz, John, *Arizona*. Email: jbausch1@email.arizona.edu.

Bauss, Rudy. Austin, TX. Affil: Austin Comm. Coll. Email: xmasrudy@yahoo.com. Research: Indian and Chinese opium trade 1770-1840, Portuguese Empire trade and commerce.

Bavaria, Melanie. Brooklyn, NY. Affil: NYU. Email: mb5476@nyu.edu.

Bavery, Ashley Johnson, *Eastern Michigan*. Email: abavery@emich.edu.

Baxendale, Susannah F. Culver City, CA. Affil: UCLA. Email: susannahbaxendale@gmail.com. Research: business partnerships and patrimony.

Baxter, Colin F., *East Tennessee State*. Email: baxterc@etsu.edu.

Baxter, Douglas C., *Ohio*. Email: baxter@ohio.edu.

Baxter, Randolph W. Fullerton, CA. Affil: California State, Fullerton. Email: rbaxter@fullerton.edu. Research: McCarthyism, homophobia and politics.

Baxter, Stephen, *North Carolina, Chapel Hill*.

Baxter-Bellamy, Amy L., *McNeil Center*. Email: abaxter@sas.upenn.edu.

Bay, Alexander R., *Chapman*. Email: bay@chapman.edu.

Bay, Mia E., *Pennsylvania*. Philadelphia, PA. Email: mbay@sas.upenn.edu. Research: Jim Crow travel, black thought.

Bayandor, Darioush. Nyon, Switzerland. Email: dbayandor@gmail.com.

Baydoun, Shatha, *Henry Ford Coll.* Email: sbaydoun@hfcc.edu.

Bayer, Ronald, *Columbia (Hist. Public Health)*. Email: rb8@columbia.edu.

Bayliss, Jeffrey P., *Trinity Coll., Conn.* Email: jeffrey.bayliss@trincoll.edu.

Baylor, Michael, *Lehigh*. Email: mgb2@lehigh.edu.

Baynton, Douglas C., *Iowa*. Email: douglas-baynton@uiowa.edu.

Bayor, Ronald H., *Georgia Inst. of Tech.* Email: ronald.bayor@hts.gatech.edu.

Bazemore, Georgia B., *Eastern Washington*. Email: gbazemore@ewu.edu.

Bazzaz, Sahar, *Holy Cross*. Email: sbazzaz@holycross.edu.

Beach, Alison Isdale, *Ohio State*. New York, NY. Email: beach.174@osu.edu. Research: European medieval, religious.

Beach, Robert L. Utica, NY. Affil: SUNY, Albany. Email: blbeach@albany.edu. Research: US-French relations since 1945, Horatio Seymour and Election of 1868.

Beach, Todd. Minneapolis, MN. Affil: Eastview High Sch. Email: todd.beach@district196.org.

Beachy, Robert M. Incheon, South Korea. Affil: UIC Yonsei. Email: rmbeachy@yonsei.ac.kr.

Beacock, Ian P. Vancouver, BC, Canada. Affil: British Columbia. Email: beacock@mail.ubc.ca.

Beadie, Nancy, *Washington, Seattle*. Email: nbeadie@uw.edu.

Beail, Linda, *Point Loma Nazarene*. Email: lindabeail@pointloma.edu.

Beal, Thomas D., *SUNY, Oneonta*. Email: thomas.beal@oneonta.edu.

Beale, Sarah, *North Carolina A&T State*. Email: sjbeale@ncat.edu.

Beales, Ross W., Jr., *Holy Cross*. Reading, MA. Email: rbeales@holycross.edu; r.beales@yahoo.com. Research: 18th-c Westborough MA.

Beall, Jonathan, *North Georgia*. Email: jonathan.beall@ung.edu.

Beals, Polly A., *Southern Connecticut State*. Email: bealsp1@southernct.edu.

Beaman, Greg A. Alexandria, VA. Affil: Georgetown. Email: gregabeaman@gmail.com. Research: New Orleans.

Bean, Jonathan J., *Southern Illinois, Carbondale*. Email: jonbean@siu.edu.

Beard, Rebecca E. Columbus, OH. Affil: Ohio State. Email: rebecca.e.beard29@gmail.com.

Beardsley, Deborah, *Massachusetts Hist. Soc.* Email: dbeardsley@masshist.org.

Beardsley, Edward H., *South Carolina, Columbia*.

Beardsley, Thomas R., *Bentley*. Email: tbeardsley@bentley.edu.

Bearman, Alan, *Washburn*. Email: alan.bearman@washburn.edu.

Beasley, Edward J., *San Diego State*. San Diego, CA. Email: edward.beasley@sdsu.edu. Research: Victorian communication web, Victorian social investigation.

Beasley, Shannon. Paragould, AR. Affil: Crowley's Ridge. Email: sbeasley@crc.edu.

Beason, Ed, *Tennessee Tech*. Email: ebeason@tntech.edu.

Beaton, Brian W., *California Polytechnic State*. Email: brbeaton@calpoly.edu.

Beattie, Blake R., *Louisville*. Email: blake.beattie@louisville.edu.

Beattie, Heather Dawn, *Virginia Museum of Hist.* Email: hbeattie@VirginiaHistory.org.

Beattie, Mary E., *Maine, Orono*. Email: beattie@maine.edu.

Beattie, Peter M., *Michigan State*. Email: beattiep@msu.edu.

Beatty, Edward N., *Notre Dame*. Notre Dame, IN. Email: ebeatty@nd.edu. Research: Latin America, modern Mexico.

Beatty, Jacqueline, *York, Pa.* Email: jbeatty@ycp.edu.

Beatty, **Richard K**. San Francisco, CA. Affil: California, San Francisco. Email: wolf_fritsche@yahoo.com. Research: power and politics in Europe 1918-45, youth and idealism in Europe 1918-50.

Beauchard, **Oona**, *Massachusetts Hist. Soc.* Email: obeauchard@masshist.org.

Beauchard, **Sabina**, *Massachusetts Hist. Soc.* Email: sbeauchard@masshist.org.

Beaudreau, **Sylvie**, *SUNY, Plattsburgh.* Email: beaudrsm@plattsburgh.edu.

Beaujot, **Ariel F.**, *Wisconsin-La Crosse; Western Ontario.* Email: abeaujot@uwlax.edu; abeaujot@uwo.ca.

Beaulieu, **Alain**, *Québec, Montréal.* Email: beaulieu.alain@uqam.ca.

Beaver, **Daniel C.**, *Penn State.* Email: dxb28@psu.edu.

Bebber, **Brett M.**, *Old Dominion.* Email: bbebber@odu.edu.

Beben, **Daniel Joseph**. Houston, TX. Affil: Nazarbayev. Email: djbeben@gmail.com.

Becerra, **Juana**. Cambridge, MA. Affil: Harvard. Email: juanabecerra@g.harvard.edu.

Becher, **Harvey**, *Northern Arizona.* Email: harvey.becher@nau.edu.

Bechtol, **Jonathan**, *California State, San Marcos.* Email: jbechtol@csusm.edu.

Beck, **David R. M.**, *Montana.* Email: david.beck@mso.umt.edu.

Beck, **Hans**, *McGill.* Email: hans.beck@mcgill.ca.

Beck, **Hermann**, *Miami.* Miami, FL. Email: hbeck@miami.edu. Research: Weimar and Nazi Germany, anti-Semitism in modern Germany.

Beck, **Jason**. Blairstown, NJ. Affil: Blair Academy. Email: beckj@blair.edu.

Beck, **Paul**, *Wisconsin Lutheran.* Email: paul.beck@wlc.edu.

Beck, **Roger B.**, *Eastern Illinois.* Email: rbbeck@eiu.edu.

Beck, **William**, *Massachusetts Hist. Soc.* Email: bbeck@masshist.org.

Becker, **Ann M**. Mount Sinai, NY. Affil: Empire State Coll., SUNY. Email: ann.becker@esc.edu. Research: smallpox in American Revolution, Revolutionary War pensions.

Becker, **Jane S.**, *Massachusetts, Boston.* Email: jane.becker@umb.edu.

Becker, **Marc**, *Truman State.* Kirksville, MO. Email: marc@truman.edu; marc@yachana.org. Research: Ecuadorian Indian and peasant movements, Latin American revolutionary theory.

Becker, **Marjorie R.**, *Southern California.* Email: mbecker@usc.edu.

Becker, **Michael John**. Durham, NC. Affil: Duke. Email: mjb87@duke.edu.

Becker, **Robert K**. Binghamton, NY. Affil: Broome Comm. Coll., SUNY. Email: beckerrk@sunybroome.edu.

Becker, **Seymour**, *Rutgers.* New York, NY. Email: seymourb@nyc.rr.com; sbeck915@gmail.com. Research: Russian national consciousness, Russian borderlands policy.

Becker, **William H.**, *George Washington.* Email: whbecker@gwu.edu.

Beckert, **Sven**, *Harvard (Hist.).* Cambridge, MA. Email: beckert@fas.harvard.edu. Research: capitalism, transnational.

Beckett, **Thomas L**. Pinellas Park, FL. Email: tb10432@aol.com. Research: historiography, Western civilization.

Beck-King, **Natasha R**. San Antonio, TX. Email: natashapuryear@gmail.com.

Beckman, **Eric**. Saint Paul, MN. Affil: Anoka High Sch. Email: eric@ebeckman.org.

Beckmann Tessel, **Nicole Cecilia**. Chicago, IL. Affil: Chicago. Email: nicobeen@uchicago.edu. Research: diplomatic.

Beckwith, **Guy**, *Auburn.* Email: beckwgv@auburn.edu.

Beda, **Steven**, *Oregon.* Email: sbeda@uoregon.edu.

Bedal, **Leigh-Ann**, *Penn State, Erie.* Email: lxb41@psu.edu.

Bedasse, **Monique**, *Washington, St. Louis.* Email: mbedasse@wustl.edu.

Bederman, **Gail**, *Notre Dame.* Email: Bederman.1@nd.edu.

Bednarski, **Steven**, *Waterloo.* Email: stevenb@uwaterloo.ca.

Bedos-Rezak, **Brigitte Miriam**, *NYU.* New York, NY. Email: bbr2@nyu.edu. Research: 10th- to 12th-c signs of identity, prescholastic semiotics.

Beebe, **Kathryne Elizabeth**, *North Texas.* Email: kathryne.beebe@unt.edu.

Beebe, **Ralph**, *George Fox.* Email: rbeebe@georgefox.edu.

Beebe, **Rose Marie**. San Jose, CA. Affil: Santa Clara. Email: rosemariebeebe@gmail.com.

Beebe, **William**. Gold Canyon, AZ. Email: bbau79@yahoo.com. Research: colonial US, US Constitution.

Beeby, **James M.**, *Southern Indiana.* Email: jmbeeby@usi.edu.

Beech, **George T.**, *Western Michigan.* Email: george.beech@wmich.edu.

Beecher, **Jonathan F.**, *California, Santa Cruz.* Santa Cruz, CA. Email: jbeecher@ucsc.edu. Research: intellectuals and 1848, utopia and dystopia.

Beede, **Benjamin R**. North Brunswick, NJ. Affil: Rutgers. Email: brbeede@scarletmail.rutgers.edu. Research: 19th-/20th-c US counterinsurgency, US Progressivism 1900-20.

Beekman, **Scott M**. Athens, OH. Affil: Rio Grande. Email: sbeekman@columbus.rr.com. Research: American sports and popular culture, American ethnic.

Beeler, **John F.**, *Alabama, Tuscaloosa.* Tuscaloosa, AL. Email: jbeeler@ua.edu. Research: naval and military, modern Britain and Empire/Commonwealth.

Beeman, **Randal S.**, *Westmont.* Email: rbeeman@westmont.edu.

Beer, **Barrett L.**, *Kent State.* Email: bbeer@kent.edu.

Beer, **John J.**, *Delaware.* Email: johnbeer@udel.edu.

Beers, **Laura D.**, *American.* Email: beers@american.edu.

Beezley, **William H.**, *Arizona.* Email: beezley@u.arizona.edu.

Begay, **Michael E**. South Deerfield, MA. Affil: Massachusetts Amherst. Email: begay@schoolph.umass.edu. Research: National Health Insurance, politics of health care.

Begemann, **Rosemary E.**, *Georgia Coll. and State.*

Beggs, **Alvin Dwayne**, *Lourdes.* Findlay, OH. Email: abeggs@lourdes.edu. Research: abdication of war powers by Congress, rise of nationalism in Vietnam.

Behlmer, **George K.**, *Washington, Seattle.* Email: behlmer@uw.edu.

Behnken, **Brian D.**, *Iowa State.* Email: bbehnken@iastate.edu.

Behr, **Haley Patricia**. Dearborn, MI. Affil: Detroit Mercy. Email: haleypbehr@gmail.com.

Behr, **Thomas Chauncey**, *Houston.* Email: thomasbehr@earthlink.net.

Behre, **Patricia E.**, *Fairfield.* Email: pbehre@fairfield.edu.

Behrend, **Justin J.**, *SUNY, Coll. Geneseo.* Geneseo, NY. Email: behrend@geneseo.edu. Research: postemancipation black politics, fugitive slaves.

Behrend-Martinez, **Edward J.**, *Appalachian State.* Email: behrendmarte@appstate.edu.

Behrends, **Frederick**, *North Carolina, Chapel Hill.*

Behrendt, **Andrew E.**, *Missouri Science and Tech.* Email: behrendta@mst.edu.

Behrent, **Michael C.**, *Appalachian State.* Email: behrentmc@appstate.edu.

Behrman, **Cynthia F.**, *Wittenberg.* Email: cbehrman@wittenberg.edu.

Beihammer, **Alexander**, *Notre Dame.* Email: Alexander.D.Beihammer.1@nd.edu.

Beil, **Richard**. Copperas Cove, TX. Affil: Parlor Songs Academy. Email: iwojimajoe1775@gmail.com.

Beilein, **Joseph, Jr.**, *Penn State, Erie.* Email: jmb79@psu.edu.

Beiler, **Rosalind J.**, *Central Florida.* Email: rosalind.beiler@ucf.edu.

Beineke, **John A.**, *Arkansas State.* Email: jbeineke@astate.edu.

Beinin, **Joel**, *Stanford.* Stanford, CA. Email: beinin@stanford.edu. Research: Egyptian labor movements, political economy of Islamic movements.

Beirich, **Gregory S.**, *California State, Los Angeles.* Email: gbeiric@calstatela.edu.

Beiriger, **Alexandra M**. Libertyville, IL. Affil: DePaul. Email: revelwithacause@gmail.com. Research: anti-violence activism, feminism.

Beiriger, **Eugene E.**, *DePaul.* Gurnee, IL. Email: ebeirige@depaul.edu. Research: Anglo-German relations 1900-45, British politics 1886-1964.

Beisel, **Perky**, *Stephen F. Austin State.* Email: pbeisel@sfasu.edu.

Beisswenger, **Martin**. Suessen, Germany. Affil: Higher Sch. of Economics, Moscow. Email: martin.beisswenger@gmail.com. Research: Eurasianism/Russian intellectual, Russian postrevolutionary emigration.

Beito, **David T.**, *Alabama, Tuscaloosa.* Email: dbeito@bama.ua.edu.

Bejan, **Cristina Adriana**. Raleigh, NC. Affil: Duke. Email: bejan.cristina@gmail.com. Research: interwar Romanian cultural and intellectual, Romanian secret police/dissidence under Ceausescu.

Bekele, **Getnet**, *Oakland.* Email: bekele@oakland.edu.

Beland, **Matthew R**. Madison, NJ. Affil: Drew. Email: mbeland@drew.edu. Research: Crane Brinton's Anatomy of Revolution, book.

Belcik, **Nathaniel Todd**. Lake Oswego, OR. Affil: Portland State. Email: nbelcik@gmail.com.

Belco, **Michelle Helene**. Houston, TX. Affil: Houston. Email: mbelco@uh.edu. Research: Congress shaping presidential power, meaning of citizenship.

Belco, **Victoria C.**, *Portland State*.

Belew, **Kathleen K.**, *Chicago*. Email: belew@uchicago.edu.

Bell, **Albert A.**, **Jr.**, *Hope*. Email: bell@hope.edu.

Bell, **Andrew William**. Farley, IA. Affil: Boston Univ. Email: andrew.william.bell@gmail.com.

Bell, **Brett Richard**, *Washington State, Pullman*. Email: brett.r.bell@wsu.edu.

Bell, **Caryn Cosse'**. Lafitte, LA. Affil: Massachusetts, Lowell. Email: Caryn_Bell@uml.edu. Research: 19th-c Creole New Orleans, Louisiana/Caribbean/France.

Bell, **Christopher M.**, *Dalhousie*. Email: bellcm@dal.ca.

Bell, **David A.**, *Princeton*. New York, NY. Email: dabell@princeton.edu; david.avrom.bell@gmail.com. Research: early modern Europe/France, political culture in age of Revolutions.

Bell, **David Jonathan**. Taipei City, Taiwan, Province Of China. Affil: National Taiwan. Email: davidbell98@gmail.com. Research: legal thought in Qin and Han China, ceremonial/burial art in Qin and Han China.

Bell, **David**, *North Greenville*. Email: david.bell@ngu.edu.

Bell, **Gary**, *Texas Tech*. Email: gary.bell@ttu.edu.

Bell, **Gregory Donald**, *Winthrop*. Waxhaw, NC. Email: bellgd@winthrop.edu. Research: logistics during First Crusade, medieval looting and ravaging.

Bell, **Harris E.**, *Austin Comm. Coll*. Email: hbell@austincc.edu.

Bell, **Jacob**. Urbana, IL. Affil: Illinois, Urbana-Champaign. Email: jsbell3@illinois.edu.

Bell, **Jeffrey**, *Southeastern Louisiana*. Email: jeffrey.bell@selu.edu.

Bell, **Jessica L.** Post Falls, ID. Email: jlbell@eagles.ewu.edu.

Bell, **John Frederick**. Worcester, MA. Affil: Assumption. Email: j.frederick.bell@gmail.com. Research: social reform, race.

Bell, **John L.**, *Western Carolina*. Email: jbell@wcu.campus.mci.edu.

Bell, **John P.**, *Purdue, Fort Wayne*. Email: bellj@ipfw.edu.

Bell, **Julia Hopson**. Palmer, TX. Affil: Southern New Hampshire. Email: julia.bell@snhu.edu.

Bell, **Karen Cook**, *Bowie State*. Email: kcookbell@bowiestate.edu.

Bell, **Matthew**. San Francisco, CA. Affil: Lowell High Sch. Email: mattbell510@gmail.com.

Bell, **Richard J.**, *Maryland, Coll. Park*. Email: rjbell@umd.edu.

Bell, **Robert Joseph**. Brooklyn, NY. Affil: NYU. Email: rjb487@nyu.edu.

Bell, **Rudolph M.**, *Rutgers*. Email: rbell@history.rutgers.edu.

Bell, **Sarah**. Lawrence, KS. Affil: Kansas. Email: sarahkaybell@gmail.com.

Bell, **Stephen**, *UCLA*. Email: sbell@geog.ucla.edu.

Bellamy, **John G.**, *Carleton, Can*. Email: john.bellamy@carleton.ca.

Bellamy, **Matthew J.**, *Carleton, Can*. Email: matthew.bellamy@carleton.ca.

Bellamy, **Micah Paul**. Longwood, FL. Affil: Master's Academy. Email: micahbellamy57@gmail.com.

Bellany, **Alastair J.**, *Rutgers*. New Brunswick, NJ. Email: bellany@rci.rutgers.edu. Research: early modern Britain.

Bellavia, **Steven**. Bowling Green, OH. Affil: Bowling Green State. Email: srbella@bgsu.

edu. Research: Cold War/popular culture, 20th-c US.

Belli, **Mériam**, *Iowa*. Email: meriam-belli@uiowa.edu.

Bellinger, **Robert A.**, *Suffolk*. Email: rbellinger@suffolk.edu.

Bellitto, **Christopher M.**, *Kean*. Email: cbellitt@kean.edu.

Bello, **David A.**, *Washington and Lee*. Lexington, VA. Email: bellod@wlu.edu. Research: Qing China frontier, Qing China ethnic and environmental.

Bellon, **Richard**, *Michigan State*. Email: bellonr@msu.edu.

Bellot, **Leland J.**, *California State, Fullerton*. Email: lbellot@fullerton.edu.

Bellows, **Amanda Brickell**. New York, NY. Affil: North Carolina, Chapel Hill. Email: amanda.b.bellows@gmail.com. Research: comparative US and Russia, cultural.

Belmonte, **Laura A.**, *Oklahoma State*. Stillwater, OK. Email: laura.belmonte@okstate.edu. Research: AIDS and US foreign relations, international LGBT rights movement.

Belohlavek, **John M.**, *South Florida, Tampa*. Email: belohlav@usf.edu.

Belonick, **Paul**. San Francisco, CA. Affil: UC Hastings Coll. of Law. Email: pb8p@virginia.edu.

Belozerova, **Olga A.** Altadena, CA. Email: oab1991@yahoo.com.

Belsky, **Natalie**, *Minnesota Duluth*. Email: nbelsky@d.umn.edu.

Belsky, **Richard D.**, *Hunter, CUNY*. Email: rbelsky@hunter.cuny.edu.

Belue, **Ted Franklin**, *Murray State*. Email: tbelue@murraystate.edu.

Belz, **Herman**, *Maryland, Coll. Park*. Email: redbelz@comcast.net.

Belzer, **Allison S.**, *Georgia Southern*. Savannah, GA. Email: abelzer@georgiasouthern.edu.

Bemel, **Kevin**. Beverly Hills, CA. Affil: Center for the Study of Everyday Life. Email: kbemel@gmail.com.

Bemporad, **Elissa**, *Graduate Center, CUNY; Queens, CUNY*. Email: elissa.bemporad@qc.cuny.edu.

Ben, **Pablo Eduardo**, *San Diego State*. Email: pben@sdsu.edu.

Ben Atar, **Doron**, *Fordham*. Email: benatar@fordham.edu.

Ben Taleb, **Baligh B. A.**, **Jr.** Lincoln, NE. Affil: Nebraska, Lincoln. Email: beligh.taleb@huskers.unl.edu.

Ben Zeev, **Nimrod**. Philadelphia, PA. Affil: Pennsylvania. Email: nimrodb@sas.upenn.edu.

Ben Zvi, **Ehud**, *Alberta*. Email: ehud.ben.zvi@ualberta.ca.

Benac, **David T.**, *Western Michigan*. Email: david.benac@wmich.edu.

Benadusi, **Giovanna**, *South Florida, Tampa*. Tampa, FL. Email: benadusi@usf.edu. Research: early modern state building, law/culture/gender.

Ben-Amos, **Avner**. Tel Aviv, Israel. Affil: Tel Aviv. Email: benamos@post.tau.ac.il. Research: modern French political culture, Israeli collective memory.

Bender, **Daniel E.**, *Toronto*. Toronto, ON, Canada. Email: debender@utsc.utoronto.ca. Research: sweatshops, industrialization cultural.

Bender, **Jill C.**, *North Carolina, Greensboro*. Email: jcbender@uncg.edu.

Bender, **John Elijah**, *Concordia Coll*. Email: bender@cord.edu.

Bender, **Matthew V.**, *New Jersey*. Email: bender@tcnj.edu.

Bender, **Noah Daniel**. Berkeley, CA. Affil: California, Berkeley. Email: noah.bender@berkeley.edu. Research: German migration, European nationalism and empire.

Bender, **Norman J.**, *Colorado Colorado Springs*.

Bender, **Thomas**, *NYU*. Brooklyn, NY. Email: thomas.bender@nyu.edu. Research: US in global perspective, metropolitan culture.

Bender, **Tovah L.**, *Florida International*. Email: tbender@fiu.edu.

Bendersky, **Joseph W.**, *Virginia Commonwealth*. Email: jwbender@vcu.edu.

Benedict, **Carol A.**, *Georgetown*. Washington, DC. Email: benedicc@georgetown.edu. Research: Republic of China 1912-49, Ch'ing Dynasty 1644-1911.

Benedict, **Hope Ann**, *Idaho State*. Salmon, ID. Affil: Lemhi County Hist. Museum. Email: benehope@isu.edu; hbenedict78@gmail.com. Research: development of community in Lemhi County ID, historical change/New West in Idaho.

Benedict, **Jerrad**, *California State, Chico*. Email: jbenedict4@csuchico.edu.

Benedict, **Michael Les**, *Ohio State*. Columbus, OH. Email: benedict.3@osu.edu. Research: Reconstruction politics and law.

Benedict, **Philip J.** Philadelphia, PA. Affil: Geneva. Email: philip.benedict@unige.ch. Research: French wars of religion, Calvinism.

Beneke, **Chris**, *Bentley*. Email: cbeneke@bentley.edu.

Benes, **Kveta E.**, *William and Mary*. Email: kebene@wm.edu.

Ben-Ghiat, **Ruth**, *NYU*. New York, NY. Email: rb68@nyu.edu. Research: empire.

Bengtson, **Dale R.**, *Southern Illinois, Carbondale*. Email: bengtson@siu.edu.

Benish, **Dawn Colleen**. Ogden, UT. Affil: Weber Innovation High Sch. Email: dcbenish@gmail.com. Research: gender/polygamy/suffrage, Chinese ethnic enclaves and criminality.

Benite, **Zvi Ben-Dor**, *NYU*. Email: zvi@nyu.edu.

Benjamin, **Jody**, *California, Riverside*. Email: jody.benjamin@ucr.edu.

Benjamin, **Karen A.**, *Elmhurst*. Email: karen.benjamin@elmhurst.edu.

Benjamin, **Michael**, *Georgia Southern*. Email: mbenjamin@georgiasouthern.edu.

Benjamin, **Thomas L.**, *Central Michigan*. Email: benja1t@cmich.edu.

Benjamins, **Ira Lee**. Houston, TX. Affil: San Jacinto Coll. North. Email: lee.benjamins@yahoo.com. Research: slavery and abolition, masculinity studies.

Benkert, **Volker**, *Arizona State*. Email: volker.benkert@asu.edu.

Bennet, **Cynthia D**. Rosemount, MN. Affil: Iowa State. Email: cyndb@netins.net. Research: popularization of science/technology in US, social/cultural response to technology.

Bennett, **Anna**. Miami, FL. Affil: Miami. Email: anb121@miami.edu.

Bennett, **Bruce S**. Gaborone, Botswana. Affil: Botswana. Email: bennett@mopipi.ub.bw. Research: British religion and politics, British Empire and Botswana.

Bennett, **David H.**, *Syracuse*. Email: dhbennet@maxwell.syr.edu.

Bennett, **Evan P.**, *Florida Atlantic*. Email: ebennett@fau.edu.

Bennett, *Herman L.*, *Graduate Center, CUNY*. New York, NY. Email: hbennett@gc.cuny.edu. Research: freedom in 17th century, African diaspora.

Bennett, *Jean H*. Westport, CT. Affil: Weston High Sch. Email: jeaniebennett@gmail.com.

Bennett, *Joshua Maxwell Redford*. Oxford, United Kingdom. Affil: Oxford. Email: joshua.bennett@chch.ox.ac.uk. Research: Intellectual, Religious.

Bennett, *Judith M.*, *North Carolina, Chapel Hill; Southern California*. Portland, OR. Email: judithb@usc.edu. Research: medieval women, singlewomen in England 1300-1550.

Bennett, *Lyn Ellen*, *Utah Valley*. Orem, UT. Email: lbennett@uvu.edu. Research: 19th-c US, US West.

Bennett, *Norman Robert*. Duxbury, MA. Email: normanbennett@earthlink.net. Research: port wine 1750-1910, wine.

Bennett, *Todd*, *East Carolina*. Greenville, NC. Email: bennettm@ecu.edu. Research: intelligence, historical memory.

Bennett, *Tomas Ricardo*. Orlando, FL. Affil: Freedom High Sch. Email: Bennett2@ocps.net. Research: dictatorship of Jose Antonio Paez, Jacksonian democracy.

Bennett, **Y. Aleksandra**, *Carleton, Can*. Email: Aleksandra.Bennett@carleton.ca.

Bennette, **Rebecca Ayako**, *Middlebury*. Email: rbennett@middlebury.edu.

Benowitz, **Elliot**, *Portland State*.

Benowitz, *June Melby*. Sarasota, FL. Affil: South Florida, Sarasota. Email: benowitz@sar.usf.edu. Research: right-wing women/baby boom generation, 20th-c US women and religion.

Bensch, **Stephen P.**, *Swarthmore*. Email: sbensch1@swarthmore.edu.

Bensel, *Richard F.*, *Cornell*. Ithaca, NY. Email: rfb2@cornell.edu. Research: American political development, political economy.

Benson, **Amy**, *Arthur and Elizabeth Schlesinger Library*. Email: amy_benson@radcliffe.harvard.edu.

Benson, *Dalton Michael*. Iowa City, IA. Affil: Iowa. Email: dalton.michael.benson@gmail.com. Research: German immigration, German culture outside of Germany.

Benson, *Darcy*. Columbus, OH. Affil: Ohio State. Email: benson.436@buckeyemail.osu.edu.

Benson, *Devyn Spence*. Davidson, NC. Affil: Davidson. Email: debenson@davidson.edu. Research: Cuba, African diaspora studies.

Benson, *Maxine F.* Boulder, CO. Email: bensoncook@msn.com. Research: Edwin James 1797-1861.

Benson, *Neal W*. Manchester, CT. Affil: Connecticut River Academy. Email: nbenson@ctriveracademy.org.

Benson, **Ronald M.**, *Millersville, Pa*.

Benson, *Sharon*. Arlington, VA. Affil: Northern Virginia Comm. Coll. Email: sharonea124@gmail.com.

Benson, *T. Lloyd*, *Furman*. Greenville, SC. Email: lloyd.benson@furman.edu. Research: US before 1860, Civil War.

Benti, **Getahun**, *Southern Illinois, Carbondale*. Email: benti@siu.edu.

Benting, *Scott*. Beaverton, OR. Email: scott.benting@gmail.com. Research: US-Nordic relations at start of Cold War, Armor of God.

Bentley, **Anne E.**, *Massachusetts Hist. Soc*. Email: abentley@masshist.org.

Bentley, **Lisa**, *Stephen F. Austin State*. Email: bentleylisa@sfasu.edu.

Benton, **Bradley T.**, *North Dakota State*. Email: bradley.benton@ndsu.edu.

Benton, *Lauren A.*, *Vanderbilt*. Nashville, TN. Email: lauren.benton@vanderbilt.edu. Research: comparative colonial, legal.

Benton-Cohen, *Katherine A.*, *Georgetown*. Washington, DC. Email: kab237@georgetown.edu. Research: immigration, race.

Ben-Ur, *Aviva*, *Massachusetts, Amherst*. Amherst, MA. Email: aben-ur@judnea.umass.edu. Research: Eurafricans in Suriname, US ethnohistory.

Benz, **Ernest**, *Smith*. Email: ebenz@smith.edu.

Benzaquen, **Adriana S.**, *Dalhousie*. Email: adriana.benzaquen@msvu.ca.

Beranek, *Karen*. Unalakleet, AK. Affil: Bering Strait Sch. District. Email: kel381@hotmail.com.

Berberian, **Houri**, *California, Irvine*. Email: houri.berberian@uci.edu.

Bercuson, **David J.**, *Calgary*. Email: bercuson@ucalgary.ca.

Berduc, *Manuel*. Ithaca, NY. Affil: Cornell. Email: mb2582@cornell.edu. Research: pre-1917 anarchist/early socialism, radical visual culture.

Berebitsky, **Julie**, *South*. Email: jberebit@sewanee.edu.

Bereiter, *Gregory*. Alexandria, VA. Affil: Naval Hist. Command. Email: gregory.bereiter@navy.mil; greg.bereiter@gmail.com. Research: military history, religious violence.

Berend, **Ivan**, *UCLA*. Email: iberend@history.ucla.edu.

Berenson, *Edward G.*, *NYU*. Tarrytown, NY. Email: edward.berenson@nyu.edu. Research: exploration and colonialism, journalism.

Berest, **Julia P.**, *Western Ontario*. Email: jberest2@uwo.ca.

Beretz, *Elaine M*. Bryn Mawr, PA. Affil: Bryn Mawr. Email: eberetz@brynmawr.edu. Research: social history of art, Christian iconography.

Berg, *Anne Kristina*, *Pennsylvania*. Ann Arbor, MI. Affil: Michigan, Ann Arbor. Email: akberg@umich.edu. Research: film and cinematic culture in Hamburg.

Berg, *Catherine Diane*. Marshall, MN. Email: Cberg@iw.net.

Berg, **Matthew P.**, *John Carroll*. Email: mberg@jcu.edu.

Berg, *Scott*. Midlothian, TX. Email: scottm.berg@gmail.com. Research: toleration and pluralism in Austria.

Berg, *Walter L*. Bainbridge Island, WA.

Berg Burin, **Nikki**, *North Dakota*. Email: nikki.berg@und.edu.

Bergad, **Laird W.**, *Graduate Center, CUNY; Lehman, CUNY*. Email: lbergad@gc.cuny.edu.

Bergen, **Doris L.**, *Toronto*. Email: doris.bergen@utoronto.ca.

Bergen, **Hilary**, *Hist. Assoc*. Email: hbergen@historyassociates.com.

Bergen, *Jessica DeJohn*. Lake Charles, LA. Affil: Texas, El Paso. Email: jdbergen@miners.utep.edu. Research: borderlands.

Berger, **Albert I.**, *North Dakota*. Email: albert.berger@und.edu.

Berger, **Carl C.**, *Toronto*.

Berger, **Dan**, *Washington, Seattle*. Email: dberger@uwb.edu.

Berger, *David*. New York, NY. Affil: Yeshiva. Email: dberger@yu.edu. Research: Jewish-Christian relations, Jewish Messianism.

Berger, **Gordon M.**, *Southern California*. Email: gberger@usc.edu.

Berger, *Iris*, *SUNY, Albany*. Albany, NY. Email: iberger@albany.edu. Research: 20th-c South African women, African Americans and South Africa.

Berger, *Martin E.*, *Youngstown State*. Youngstown, OH. Email: meberger@ysu.edu.

Berger, *Michael L*. Maple Glen, PA. Affil: Arcadia. Email: berger@arcadia.edu. Research: sociocultural impact of automobile.

Berger, **Molly W.**, *Case Western Reserve*. Email: molly.berger@case.edu.

Berger, **Patrice**, *Nebraska, Lincoln*. Email: pberger1@unl.edu.

Berger, **Rachel**, *Concordia, Can*. Email: Rachel.Berger@concordia.ca.

Berger, **Ronald M.**, *SUNY, Albany*. Email: rberger@albany.edu.

Bergeron, **Paul H.**, *Tennessee, Knoxville*. Email: bergeron@utk.edu.

Bergerson, **Andrew Stuart**, *Missouri–Kansas City*. Email: bergersona@umkc.edu.

Berghahn, *Volker R.*, *Columbia (Hist.)*. New York, NY. Email: vrb7@columbia.edu. Research: modern western Europe, Germany.

Bergholz, **Max A.**, *Concordia, Can*. Email: Max.Bergholz@concordia.ca.

Bergman, *James Henry*. Springfield, PA. Affil: Temple. Email: jamesbergman@gmail.com. Research: atmospheric sciences, concepts of stability.

Bergman, *Jay A.*, *Central Connecticut State*. New Britain, CT. Email: bergmanj@ccsu.edu. Research: Andrei Sakharov.

Bergman, **Maj Mark**, *US Military Acad*. Email: mark.bergman@usma.edu.

Bergmann, **Peter E.**, *Florida*. Email: bergmann@ufl.edu.

Bergmann, **William H.**, *Slippery Rock*. Email: william.bergmann@sru.edu.

Bergquist, **Charles W.**, *Washington, Seattle*. Email: caramba@uw.edu.

Bergstrom, **Randolph E.**, *California, Santa Barbara*. Email: bergstro@history.ucsb.edu.

Beringer, **Richard E.**, *North Dakota*.

Berk, **Stephen E.**, *California State, Long Beach*. Email: sberk@csulb.edu.

Berk, **Stephen M.**, *Union Coll*. Email: berks@union.edu.

Berkeley, **Kathleen Christine**, *North Carolina, Wilmington*. Email: berkeleyk@uncw.edu.

Berkes, **Anna**, *Robert H. Smith Center*. Email: aberkes@monticello.org.

Berkey, *Jonathan M.*, *Concord*. Athens, WV. Email: berkeyj@concord.edu. Research: Civil War in Shenandoah Valley.

Berkey, **Jonathan P.**, *Davidson*. Email: joberkey@davidson.edu.

Berkhofer, **Robert F.**, **III**, *Western Michigan*. Email: robert.berkhofer@wmich.edu.

Berkman, **Joyce A.**, *Massachusetts, Amherst*. Email: jberkman@history.umass.edu.

Berkovitz, **Jay**, *Massachusetts, Amherst*. Email: jrb@judnea.umass.edu.

Berkowitz, **Aaron Max**. Springfield, IL. Affil: Lincoln Land Comm. Coll. Email: Aaron.Berkowitz@llcc.edu. Research: Cold War, US anticommunism.

Berkowitz, **Carin**. Swarthmore, PA. Affil: New Jersey Council for the Humanities. Email: carin.berkowitz@gmail.com. Research: medicine and art, science and pedagogy.

Berkowitz, Edward D., *George Washington*. Email: ber@gwu.edu.

Berktay, **Asligul**. Istanbul, Turkey. Affil: Sabanci. Email: asligul.berktay@gmail.com.

Berlage, Nancy Kay, *Texas State*. Email: nkb11@txstate.edu.

Berlatsky, **Joel A.**, *Wilkes*. Email: joel.berlatsky@wilkes.edu.

Berler, **Anne**, *Coastal Carolina*. Email: aberler@coastal.edu.

Berliner, **Brett**, *Morgan State*. Email: brett.berliner@morgan.edu.

Berliner, **Yvonne G.**, *Washington State, Pullman*. Email: yberliner@wsu.edu.

Berman, **Cassandra Nicole**. Waltham, MA. Affil: Brandeis. Email: cnberman@brandeis.edu.

Berman, **Constance H.**, *Iowa*. Iowa City, IA. Email: constance-berman@uiowa.edu. Research: Middle Ages religious women, economic and women.

Berman, Viola, *Hist. New Orleans*. Email: vberman@hnoc.org.

Berman, William C., *Toronto*.

Bernard, **Lance V.** Cloverdale, CA. Affil: Nevada State. Email: lvbernard@gmail.com.

Bernard, Sheila Curran, *SUNY, Albany*. Albany, NY. Email: sbernard@albany.edu.

Bernardi, **Claudia**. Roma, Italy. Affil: Roma Tre. Email: clod.zeta@gmail.com.

Bernardino, **Erik**. Capitola, CA. Affil: California, Santa Cruz. Email: ebernar1@ucsc.edu.

Bernath, **Michael T.**, *Miami*. Miami, FL. Email: mbernath@miami.edu.

Berndt, Sara E., *US Dept. of State*.

Bernhard, **Winfred E.**, *Massachusetts, Amherst*. Norfolk, MA. Email: winbern@comcast.net. Research: colonial New England.

Bernhardsson, Magnus T., *Williams*. Email: mbernhar@williams.edu.

Bernhardt, John W., *San José State*. Email: John.Bernhardt@sjsu.edu.

Bernhardt, Kathryn, *UCLA*. Email: bernhard@history.ucla.edu.

Bernhardt, **Mark A.** Clinton, MS. Affil: Jackson State. Email: mabhardt@gmail.com. Research: media/gender/war, journalism.

Bernier, Julia Wallace, *North Alabama*. Email: jbernier@una.edu.

Berns, Andrew, *South Carolina, Columbia*. Email: aberns@mailbox.sc.edu.

Bernstein, **Alan Edgar**, *Arizona*. Oakland, CA. Email: aebern@email.arizona.edu. Research: belief in hell, religion and cultural.

Bernstein, Andrew W., *Lewis & Clark*. Email: awb@lclark.edu.

Bernstein, **Aryeh**. Modiin, Israel. Email: abbernstein@gmail.com. Research: religious zionism.

Bernstein, Barton J., *Stanford*.

Bernstein, David A., *California State, Long Beach*. Email: dbernste@csulb.edu.

Bernstein, Gail Lee, *Arizona*. Email: glbernst@u.arizona.edu.

Bernstein, George L., *Tulane*. Email: gbernst@tulane.edu.

Bernstein, **Hilary J.**, *California, Santa Barbara*. Email: bernstein@history.ucsb.edu.

Bernstein, **Iver**, *Washington, St. Louis*. Email: icbernst@wustl.edu.

Bernstein, **John Andrew**, *Delaware*. Email: johnbern@udel.edu.

Bernstein, **Joseph M.** West Bloomfield, MI. Email: jmbernstein@yahoo.com.

Bernstein, Laurie, *Rutgers, Camden*. Email: lbernste@camden.rutgers.edu.

Bernstein, Lee, *SUNY, New Paltz*. Email: bernstel@newpaltz.edu.

Bernstein, Michael A., *Tulane*. Email: mbernstein@tulane.edu.

Bernstein, **Shana B.** Evanston, IL. Affil: Northwestern. Email: sbbsparkle@yahoo.com. Research: 20th-c Los Angeles race relations, race relations.

Berolzheimer, **Alan R**. Norwich, VT. Affil: Vermont Hist. Soc. Email: bercress@sover.net.

Berquist Soule, **Emily K.**, *California State, Long Beach*. Long Beach, CA. Email: emily.berquist@csulb.edu. Research: slavery and abolition in the Atlantic, Spanish Empire.

Berrey, **Stephen A.**, *Michigan, Ann Arbor*. Ann Arbor, MI. Email: sberrey@umich.edu. Research: African American, African diaspora.

Berrin, **Kathleen Joyce**. Laguna Woods, CA. Affil: California, Irvine. Email: kberrin@uci.edu. Research: Cold War, arts and culture.

Berry, **Chad T.**, *Berea*. Berea, KY. Email: chad_berry@berea.edu. Research: country music, Appalachian studies.

Berry, **Chelsea L.**, *Randolph*. Washington, DC. Email: cberry@randolphcollege.edu; cb1098@georgetown.edu. Research: Caribbean, comparative slavery.

Berry, **Daina Ramey**, *Texas, Austin*. Austin, TX. Email: drb@austin.utexas.edu. Research: enslaved prices in US, African American.

Berry, **David A**. Palm City, FL. Affil: Essex County Coll. Email: berry@essex.edu.

Berry, **Dawn Alexandrea**. Kaneohe, HI. Affil: Defense POW/MIA Accounting Agency. Email: dawn.berry@gmail.com. Research: polar regions, Monroe Doctrine.

Berry, **James**. Boulder, CO. Email: jabe0086@colorado.edu.

Berry, Lee Sullivan, *Science History Inst*. Email: lberry@sciencehistory.org.

Berry, **Mary Elizabeth**. Berkeley, CA. Affil: California, Berkeley. Email: meberry@berkeley.edu. Research: print culture, work and rules of consumption.

Berry, **Mary F.**, *Pennsylvania*. Email: mfberry@sas.upenn.edu.

Berry, **Michelle K.**, *Arizona*. Tucson, AZ. Email: mkberry@email.arizona.edu.

Berry, Sara S., *Johns Hopkins (Hist.)*. Email: sberry@jhu.edu.

Berry, **Stephen Joseph**. Archdale, NC. Affil: Iowa. Email: stephen-berry@uiowa.edu. Research: 20th-c American journalism, American civil rights and press.

Berry, Stephen William, II, *Georgia*. Email: berry@uga.edu.

Berry, **Walter**. Autun, France. Affil: Dijon. Email: berryweb01@aol.com.

Berryman, Thomas G., *Henry Ford Coll*. Email: berryman@hfcc.edu.

Bertaina, David, *Illinois, Springfield*. Email: dbert3@uis.edu.

Bertellini, **Giorgio**. Ann Arbor, MI. Affil: Michigan. Email: giorgiob@umich.edu. Research: Hollywood and US political leadership, US fascism.

Berthold, Richard M., *New Mexico*. Email: qqduckus@unm.edu.

Berto, Luigi Andrea, *Western Michigan*. Email: luigi.berto@wmich.edu.

Bertolette, **William F**. Baton Rouge, LA. Affil: Baton Rouge Comm. Coll. Email: wbertolette@cox.net. Research: national image and identity, 19th-c imperial rivalries.

Bertoloni Meli, **Domenico**, *Indiana*. Email: dbmeli@indiana.edu.

Bertolotti, **David John**. Joliet, IL. Affil: Gratz. Email: david.bertolotti72@gmail.com. Research: Holocaust.

Bertram, Laurie, *Toronto*. Email: l.bertram@utoronto.ca.

Bertrand, Charles L., *Concordia, Can*. Email: charlesbertrand_2@sympatico.ca.

Bertrand, **Daniel Alan**. Taylorsville, UT. Affil: Utah State. Email: dbertrand21@gmail.com.

Bertrand, **Michael T.**, *Tennessee State*. Nashville, TN. Email: mbertrand@tnstate.edu. Research: post-WWII popular music and culture, southern race relations.

Bertucci, Paola, *Yale*. Email: paola.bertucci@yale.edu.

Bertulli, Sarah, *Massachusetts Hist. Soc*. Email: sbertulli@masshist.org.

Bertz, Ned O., *Hawai'i, Manoa*. Email: bertz@hawaii.edu.

Beshimov, **Bakyt**. Affil: Northeastern. Email: bakytbj@yahoo.com.

Beshwate, **Benjamin James**. Ridgecrest, CA. Affil: Cerro Coso Comm. Coll. Email: ben@beshwate.com. Research: 20th-c American social, modern Europe.

Bess, **Michael Demaree**, *Vanderbilt*. Nashville, TN. Email: m.bess@vanderbilt.edu. Research: human enhancement technologies, political centrism.

Besse, Susan K., *Graduate Center, CUNY*. Email: skbesse@earthlink.net.

Bessner, **Daniel M.**, *Washington, Seattle*. Email: dbessner@uw.edu.

Best, Jeremy, *Iowa State*. Email: bestja@iastate.edu.

Best, **Wallace D.**, *Princeton*. Princeton, NJ. Email: wbest@princeton.edu. Research: religion and literature, Pentecostal women preachers.

Beswick, **Spencer**. Ithaca, NY. Affil: Cornell. Email: spencerbeswick@gmail.com.

Betik, **Jessica Bilhartz**. Irving, TX. Affil: Aberdeen. Email: jessica@betik.com. Research: early modern England/Scotland/Ireland, women's education.

Bet-Shlimon, **Arbella**, *Washington, Seattle*. Seattle, WA. Email: shlimon@uw.edu. Research: modern Iraq, modern Persian Gulf.

Bettendorf, **Nicole M**. McHenry, IL. Affil: Western Kentucky. Email: nbett2@gmail.com. Research: 20th-c US social movements, US race/women/gender.

Bettine, **Aiden Michael**. Iowa City, IA. Affil: Iowa. Email: aiden-bettine@uiowa.edu. Research: public memory/Native Americans/Chicago, public history/digital history/teaching.

Bettinger, **Rikki**. Katy, TX. Affil: Houston. Email: rikkidiane@gmail.com.

Beugoms, **Jean-Pierre**. Philadelphia, PA. Email: jpbeugoms@gmail.com.

Beuttler, *Fred W*. Chicago, IL. Affil: Chicago, Graham Sch. Email: fredbeuttler@gmail.com. Research: 20th-c US, political.

Bevel, **Felicia**, *North Florida*. Email: felicia_bevel@brown.edu.

Beveridge, *Albert J*., *III*. Washington, DC. Affil: Beveridge & Diamond P.C. Email: beveridgeiii@gmail.com. Research: business and federal government.

Beverley, **Eric L**., *SUNY, Stony Brook*. Email: eric.beverley@stonybrook.edu.

Bevilacqua, **Alexander**, *Williams*. Email: ab24@williams.edu.

Beyan, **Amos**, *Western Michigan*. Email: amos.beyan@wmich.edu.

Beyerchen, **Alan D**., *Ohio State*. Portland, OR. Email: beyerchen.1@osu.edu; beyerchen.1@gmail.com. Research: modern Germany.

Beyler, **Richard H**., *Portland State*. Email: beylerr@pdx.edu.

Bezark, **Michelle**. Wilmette, IL. Affil: Northwestern. Email: michellebezark2020@u.northwestern.edu.

Bezerra, **Nielson**. Rio de Janeiro, Brazil. Affil: Estado do Rio de Janeiro. Email: bezerranielson@hotmail.com.

Bezilla, **Michael**, *Penn State*. Email: mxb13@psu.edu.

Bezis-Selfa, *John*, *Wheaton, Mass*. Norton, MA. Email: jbeselfa@wheatonma.edu. Research: colonial America, US Latino/a.

Bezucha, **Robert J**., *Amherst*. Email: rjbezucha@amherst.edu.

Bezzina, **Edwin**, *Memorial, Newfoundland*. Email: ebezzina@grenfell.mun.ca.

Bhagavan, **Manu B**., *Graduate Center, CUNY; Hunter, CUNY*. Email: mbhagava@hunter.cuny.edu.

Bhagirat-Rivera, *Ramaesh Joseph*. Central Falls, RI. Affil: Boston Coll. Email: rjbhagirat@gmail.com. Research: race/nation/performative culture, Caribbean/Guyana/Trinidad.

Bhattacharjee, **Dharitri**, *South*. Email: dhbhatta@sewanee.edu.

Bhattacharya, **Tithi**, *Purdue*. Email: tbhattac@purdue.edu.

Bhattacharyya, **Debjani**, *Drexel*. Email: db893@drexel.edu.

Biale, **David**, *California, Davis*. Email: dbiale@ucdavis.edu.

Bialuschewski, **Arne**, *Trent*. Email: abialu@trentu.ca.

Bian, *He*, *Princeton*. Princeton, NJ. Email: hbian@princeton.edu. Research: early modern China, medicine.

Bian, **Morris L**., *Auburn*. Email: bianmor@auburn.edu.

Bianchi, *Lorrey J*. Boston, MA. Affil: Boston Univ. Email: ljbianchi@msn.com.

Bianchini, **Janna C**., *Maryland, Coll. Park*. Email: jcwb@umd.edu.

Bias, *Brett D*. Lawrence, KS. Affil: Kansas. Email: bdbias@ku.edu.

Biba, **Catherine**, *Hastings*. Email: cbiba@hastings.edu.

Bibbee, **Jeffrey R**., *North Alabama*. Email: jrbibbee@una.edu.

Bibler, *Jared S*. Fremont, OH. Affil: Global Pathways Inst. Email: jaredbibler@yahoo.com. Research: social movements in Latin America.

Bicha, **Karel D**., *Marquette*.

Bickford, **Charlene Bangs**, *George Washington*. Email: bickford@gwu.edu.

Bickham, **Troy O**., *Texas A&M*. Email: tbickham@tamu.edu.

Biddick, *Kathleen A*. Philadelphia, PA. Affil: Temple. Email: kathleen.biddick@temple.edu. Research: sovereignty and archives, temporality and periodization.

Bidegain, **Ana Maria**, *Florida International*. Email: bidegain@fiu.edu.

Bidelman, *Patrick K*. Nokomis, FL. Email: Bidelman@comcast.net.

Bidlack, **Richard**, *Washington and Lee*. Email: bidlackr@wlu.edu.

Bieber, **Jason Parker**, *Dayton*. Email: jbieber1@udayton.edu.

Bieber, *Judy*, *New Mexico*. Albuquerque, NM. Email: jbieber@unm.edu. Research: 19th-c Brazilian politics/frontiers, Brazilian indigenous peoples.

Biel, *Justin*, *Minnesota State, Mankato*. Mankato, MN. Email: justin.biel@mnsu.edu. Research: Indian secularism, Enlightenment.

Biel, *Pamela*. Berlin, Germany. Email: pamelas.pug@googlemail.com.

Bieler, *Jan Stacey*. East Lansing, MI.

Bielski, *Mark Francis*. New Orleans, LA. Affil: Stephen Ambrose Hist. Tours. Email: mfbielski@yahoo.com. Research: American Civil War, WWII.

Bienstock, *Barry W*. Bronx, NY. Affil: Horace Mann Sch. Email: barrybienstock@yahoo.com. Research: late 19th-c American West, 19th-c Native American.

Bienvenu, **Richard T**., *Missouri, Columbia*. Email: bienvenur@missouri.edu.

Bier, **Laura**, *Georgia Inst. of Tech*. Email: laura.bier@hts.gatech.edu.

Bierma, *David L*. Wildomar, CA. Email: david@7hlcattle.com.

Biess, **Frank P**., *California, San Diego*. Email: fbiess@ucsd.edu.

Bietenholz, **Peter G**., *Saskatchewan*. Email: bietenholz@sask.usask.ca.

Bieter, **John**, *Boise State*. Email: johnbieter@boisestate.edu.

Bigelow, **Bruce L**., *Butler*. Email: bbigelow@butler.edu.

Bigelow, **Gerald F**., *Bates*. Email: gbigelow@bates.edu.

Biggs, *David A*., *California, Riverside*. Riverside, CA. Email: dbiggs@ucr.edu. Research: Southeast Asia, environmental.

Biggs, **Douglas L**., *Nebraska, Kearney*. Email: biggsdl@unk.edu.

Biggs, *James*. La Habra, CA. Affil: Whittier Christian High Sch. Email: jbiggs@wchs.com.

Biggs, **Lesley**, *Saskatchewan*. Email: lesley.biggs@usask.ca.

Biggs, **Lindy B**., *Auburn*. Email: biggslb@auburn.edu.

Bigham, **Darrel E**., *Southern Indiana*. Evansville, IN. Email: dbigham@usi.edu; bighamd8@gmail.com. Research: African Americans on Lower Ohio 1850-90, reform movements in IN/IL/KY 1830-90.

Bigott, *Joseph C*. Naperville, IL. Affil: Purdue Northwest, Hammond. Email: bigott@pnw.edu.

Bihler, **Lori G**., *Framingham State*. Email: lbihler@framingham.edu.

Biles, **Amanda B**., *Minot State*. Email: amanda.biles@minotstateu.edu.

Biletz, **Frank A**., *Loyola, Chicago*. Evanston, IL. Email: fbiletz@luc.edu; fbiletz@att.net. Research: Western civilization.

Bilinkoff, **Jodi E**., *North Carolina, Greensboro*. Greensboro, NC. Email: jodi_bilinkoff@uncg.edu. Research: early modern Catholic Europe, gender/religion/life writing.

Bilka, **Monika**. Chandler, AZ. Affil: Chandler-Gilbert Comm. Coll. Email: monika.bilka@cgc.edu.

Billheimer, **Jonathan D**., *Appalachian State*. Email: billheimerjd@appstate.edu.

Billinger, **Robert D**., *Jr*. Indian Trail, NC. Affil: Wingate. Email: billingr@wingate.edu. Research: German confederation of Metternich era, German POWs in America 1942-46.

Billings, **Mathieu W**., *Indianapolis*. Email: billingsm@uindy.edu.

Billings, **Warren M**., *New Orleans*. Email: wbilling@uno.edu.

Billows, **Richard A**., *Columbia (Hist.)*. Email: rab4@columbia.edu.

Bilodeau, **Christopher J**., *Dickinson*. Carlisle, PA. Email: bilodeac@dickinson.edu. Research: colonial northern New England, colonial Quebec and Wabanaki Indians.

Bilof, *Edwin G*. New Milford, NJ. Email: fre99nj@aol.com. Research: Russian military historiography, battlefield memorials.

Bilsky, **Lester J**., *Arkansas, Little Rock*.

Bindas, *Kenneth J*., *Kent State*. Kent, OH. Email: kbindas@kent.edu. Research: Depression-era US and modernity, music and Depression era.

Binford, **Henry C**., *Northwestern*. Email: hcbin@northwestern.edu.

Bing, **Daniel**, *Tennessee, Knoxville*. Email: dbing@utk.edu.

Bingham, *Emily S*. Louisville, KY. Email: emily@emilybingham.net.

Bingham, **John P**., *Dalhousie*. Email: john.bingham@dal.ca.

Bingmann, **Melissa R**., *West Virginia*. Morgantown, WV. Email: melissa.bingmann@mail.wvu.edu. Research: myth of West, 20th-c masculinity.

Bin-Kasim, **Waseem-Ahmed**, *Elon*. Email: wbinkasim@gmail.com.

Binkiewicz, **Donna M**., *Soc. for Hist. Education*. Email: donna.binkiewicz@csulb.edu.

Binkley, **Lisa**, *Dalhousie*. Email: lbinkley@mta.ca.

Binnema, **Theodore**, *Northern British Columbia*. Email: Ted.Binnema@unbc.ca.

Binnenkade, *Alexandra*. Basel, Switzerland. Affil: Basel. Email: alexandra.binnenkade@unibas.ch. Research: pedagogy/learning about historical violence, cultural studies/memory and identity.

Binnington, **Ian**, *Allegheny*. Email: ibinning@allegheny.edu.

Biondi, **Martha**, *Northwestern*. Email: m-biondi@northwestern.edu.

Biondo, *Michael*. Des Plaines, IL. Affil: Maine South High Sch. Email: History.mrb@gmail.com.

Biow, **Douglas G**., *Texas, Austin*. Email: biow@austin.utexas.edu.

Birch, **Kevin E**., *Salisbury*. Email: kebirch@salisbury.edu.

Birchok, *Daniel Andrew*. Flint, MI. Affil: Michigan, Flint. Email: dbirchok@umflint. edu. Research: Islamic narrative and ritual, genealogical narratives and the nation.

Bird, *Danielle*. Logan, UT. Affil: Stevens-Henager. Email: danielle.bird@stevenshenager.edu.

Birdwell, **Michael E.**, *Tennessee Tech*. Email: birdie@tntech.edu.

Birge, *Bettine*, *Southern California*. Los Angeles, CA. Email: birge@usc.edu. Research: Chinese Yuan dynasty law, Mongol ethnicity/gender/law.

Birk, *Joshua Colin*, *Smith*. Northampton, MA. Email: jcbirk@smith.edu. Research: medieval Mediterranean.

Birk, **Megan E.**, *Texas-Rio Grande Valley*. Email: megan.birk@utrgv.edu.

Birkenmeier, **John W.**, *Maryland, Baltimore County*. Email: jwbirk@umbc.edu.

Birkner, **Michael J.**, *Gettysburg*. Email: mbirkner@gettysburg.edu.

Birla, *Ritu*, *Toronto*. Toronto, ON, Canada. Email: r.birla@utoronto.ca. Research: capitalism and governance, ethics/culture/modern subject.

Birn, **Donald S.**, *SUNY, Albany*. Email: dbirn@albany.edu.

Biro, **Zackary Joseph**, *Science History Inst*. Email: zbiro@sciencehistory.org.

Birt, **Robert**, *Bowie State*. Email: rbirt@bowiestate.edu.

Birzer, **Bradley J.**, *Hillsdale*. Email: bbirzer@hillsdale.edu.

Bisaha, **Nancy**, *Vassar*. Email: nabisaha@vassar.edu.

Bischof, **Christopher R.**, *Richmond*.

Bischof, **Elizabeth M.**, *Southern Maine*. Email: Elizabeth.Bischof@maine.edu.

Bischof, *Guenter J.*, *New Orleans*. New Orleans, LA. Email: gjbischo@uno.edu. Research: 20th-c US-Austrian relations, WWII POWs/postwar historical memory.

Bishara, *Fahad Ahmad*, *Virginia*. Charlottesville, VA. Email: fab7b@virginia.edu; fabishara@gmail.com. Research: Indian Ocean economic and legal, Islamic law and capitalism.

Bishku, **Michael B.**, *Augusta*. Email: mbishku@augusta.edu.

Bishop, **Elizabeth A.**, *Texas State*. Email: eb26@txstate.edu.

Bishop, **Jane C.**, *Citadel*. Email: bishopj@citadel.edu.

Bishop, *Russell K*. Ipswich, MA. Affil: Gordon, Mass. Email: rusbish@yahoo.com. Research: medieval, Renaissance and Reformation.

Bishop Stirling, **Terry L.**, *Memorial, Newfoundland*. Email: tstirlin@mun.ca.

Biskupska, **Jadwiga**, *Sam Houston State*. Email: jxb074@shsu.edu.

Biskupski, **M. B. B.**, *Central Connecticut State*. Email: biskupskim@ccsu.edu.

Bissett, **James**, *Elon*. Email: bissett@elon.edu.

Bisson, **Cynthia S.**, *Belmont*. Email: cynthia.bisson@belmont.edu.

Bisson, **Douglas R.**, *Belmont*. Email: douglas.bisson@belmont.edu.

Bisson, *Thomas N.*, *Harvard (Hist.)*. Cambridge, MA. Email: tnbisson@fas.harvard.edu. Research: experience of power in Latin Europe.

Bissonnette, *Richard Joseph*. Norwalk, CT. Email: win4870@yahoo.com.

Bistis, *Margo*. Los Angeles, CA. Affil: Art Center Coll. of Design. Email: Margo.Bistis@artcenter.edu. Research: modern Europe, cultural.

Bitel, *Lisa M.*, *Southern California*. Los Angeles, CA. Email: bitel@usc.edu. Research: religious visions and apparitions, contemporary religion and visual culture.

Bittel, **Carla J.**, *Loyola Marymount*. Email: cbittel@lmu.edu.

Bitter, **Michael J.**, *Hawai'i, Hilo*. Email: bitter@hawaii.edu.

Bittle, **William G.**, *Kent State*. Email: wbittle@kent.edu.

Bittner, *Stephen V.*, *Sonoma State*. Rohnert Park, CA. Email: steve.bittner@sonoma.edu. Research: Black Sea winemaking, Soviet cultural politics 1953-91.

Bitzan, **Amos**, *Wisconsin-Madison*. Email: abitzan@wisc.edu.

Bivar, **Venus Melissa**, *Washington, St. Louis*. Email: vbivar@wustl.edu.

Bivins, **Joshua**. Lincoln, NE. Affil: Southeast Comm. Coll. Email: jbivins2@huskers.unl.edu.

Bix, **Amy S.**, *Iowa State; Soc. for Hist. of Tech*. Email: abix@iastate.edu.

Bix, **Herbert P.**, *Binghamton, SUNY*. Email: hbix@binghamton.edu.

Bjerk, **Paul K.**, *Texas Tech*. Email: paul.bjerk@ttu.edu.

Bjerke, *Jillian M.* Boulder, CO. Affil: Colorado, Boulder. Email: jillian.bjerke@colorado.edu.

Bjornlie, **Shane**, *Claremont McKenna*. Email: shane.bjornlie@cmc.edu.

Blaakman, *Michael Albert*, *Princeton*. Princeton, NJ. Email: blaakman@princeton.edu. Research: early America.

Black, *Ashley L*. Turlock, CA. Affil: California State, Stanislaus. Email: ablack5@csustan.edu. Research: modern Mexican political, Cold War Latin America-US relations.

Black, **Brian**, *Penn State*. Email: bcb4@psu.edu.

Black, **Chad T.**, *Tennessee, Knoxville*. Email: cblack6@utk.edu.

Black, *Edson*. Malverne, NY. Email: edson111@hotmail.com.

Black, **J. Laurence**, *Carleton, Can*. Email: larry.black@carleton.ca.

Black, **James M.**, *OAH*. Email: jmblack@oah.org.

Black, *Jennifer M.* Dallas, PA. Affil: Misericordia. Email: jenblack1@gmail.com. Research: advertising, visual culture.

Black, **Kayla**, *North Greenville*. Email: kayla.black@ngu.edu.

Black, **Liza**, *Indiana*. Email: blackli@indiana.edu.

Black, **Lt Col Frederick H.**, **Jr.**, *US Military Acad*. Email: frederick.black@usma.edu.

Black, *Maclin Taylor*. Chattanooga, TN. Email: mblack14@vols.utk.edu.

Black, *Megan Ann*. London, United Kingdom. Affil: London Sch. of Economics. Email: megan.ann.black@gmail.com. Research: US in global context, Native American studies.

Black, *Monica A.*, *Tennessee, Knoxville*. Knoxville, TN. Email: mblack9@utk.edu. Research: folk medicine, popular religion.

Black, **Paul V.**, *California State, Long Beach*. Email: pvblack@csulb.edu.

Black, **Sara**, *Christopher Newport*. Email: sara.black@cnu.edu.

Black, **Scott M.**, *SUNY, Buffalo State*.

Black, **T. Clayton**, *Washington Coll*. Email: cblack2@washcoll.edu.

Black, **Winston E.**, **II**, *Tennessee, Knoxville*. Email: wblack3@utk.edu.

Blackbourn, *David*, *Harvard (Hist.); Vanderbilt*. Nashville, TN. Email: dgblackb@fas.harvard.edu; david.blackbourn@vanderbilt.edu. Research: German environmental, German transnational.

Blackett, *Richard J. M.*, *Vanderbilt*. Nashville, TN. Email: richard.j.blackett@vanderbilt.edu. Research: African American, antislavery.

Blackey, *Robert A.*, *California State, San Bernardino*. Claremont, CA. Email: rblackey@csusb.edu. Research: Dutch art and social life.

Blackford, *Mansel G.*, *Ohio State*. Columbus, OH. Email: blackford.1@osu.edu. Research: American business and economic.

Blackhawk, *Ned*, *Yale*. New Haven, CT. Email: ned.blackhawk@yale.edu. Research: Great Basin Indian, southwestern Indian slavery.

Blackman, **Dexter Lee**, *Morgan State*. Email: dexter.blackman@morgan.edu.

Blackman, *Robert*. Hampden Sydney, VA. Affil: Hampden-Sydney. Email: rblackman@hsc.edu. Research: French Revolution, cultural.

Blackmar, *Elizabeth*, *Columbia (Hist.); Columbia (Hist. Public Health)*. New York, NY. Email: eb16@columbia.edu. Research: social, urban.

Blackmore, **Lydia**, *Hist. New Orleans*. Email: lydiab@hnoc.org.

Blackwell, **Fritz**, *Washington State, Pullman*. Email: blackwell.fw@centurytel.net.

Blackwell, *John C.* Collinsville, MS. Email: John.blackwell1293@gmail.com.

Blade, *Melinda K.* Coronado, CA. Affil: Academy of Our Lady of Peace. Email: cortemplar@aol.com. Research: Shroud of Turin, Knights Templar.

Blaich, **Kristian B.**, *Agnes Scott*. Email: kblaich@agnesscott.edu.

Blain, *Keisha N.*, *Pittsburgh*. Princeton, NJ. Email: Keisha.Blain@gmail.com. Research: 20th-c US, African American.

Blaine, **Bradford B.**, *Scripps*. Claremont, CA. Email: Blaine1066@aol.com. Research: medieval Europe, technology.

Blaine, **Marcia Schmidt**, *Plymouth State*. Email: mblaine@plymouth.edu.

Blair, *Ann*, *Harvard (Hist.)*. Cambridge, MA. Email: amblair@fas.harvard.edu. Research: book history and methods of scholarship, science and religion.

Blair, **Carl**, *Michigan Tech*. Email: cblair@mtu.edu.

Blair, **Cynthia M.**, *Illinois, Chicago*. Email: cmblair@uic.edu.

Blair, **George Alexander**, *SUNY, Buffalo State*. Email: blairga@buffalostate.edu.

Blair, **Karen J.**, *Central Washington*. Email: blairk@cwu.edu.

Blair, **Melissa Estes**, *Auburn*. Email: mab0122@auburn.edu.

Blair, *Melissa F.*, *Maryland, Baltimore County*. Baltimore, MD. Email: mfblair@umbc.edu. Research: cultural landscapes, central Maryland.

Blair, **William Alan**, *Penn State*. Email: wab120@psu.edu.

Blaisdell, **Muriel L.**, *Miami, Ohio*. Email: blaisdml@miamioh.edu.

Blake, *Casey N.*, *Columbia (Hist.)*. New York, NY. Email: cb460@columbia.edu. Research: US intellectual and cultural, American studies.

Blake, Corinne, *Rowan*. Email: blake@rowan. edu.

Blake, Rachel. Brooklyn, NY. Affil: Uncommon Preparatory Charter High Sch. Email: rblake@ uncommonprepcharter.org.

Blake, Stanley E., *Ohio State*. Email: blake.166@ osu.edu.

Blake, Timothy R. South Burlington, VT. Affil: Penn State, Erie, Behrend. Email: blake.timr@ gmail.com.

Blake, William E., *Virginia Commonwealth*. Email: weblake2@verizon.net.

Blakelock, Emily. Toronto, ON, Canada. Affil: Toronto. Email: emily.blakelock@gmail.com.

Blakely, Allison. Silver Spring, MD. Affil: Howard. Email: ablakely@bu.edu. Research: Europe and African diaspora, Russian democracy.

Blakely, David. Lindon, UT. Affil: Nebraska, Kearney. Email: dgblakely@comcast.net.

Blakemore, Porter R., *Mary Washington*. Email: pblakemo@umw.edu.

Blakney, Sharece. Philadelphia, PA. Affil: Rutgers. Email: shasilly@scarletmail.rutgers. edu.

Blan, Noah, *Lake Forest*. Email: blan@lakeforest. edu.

Blanchard, Corey David. Los Angeles, CA. Email: cdi5@wildcats.unh.edu. Research: British Atlantic, Native American.

Blanchard, Peter H., *Toronto*. Email: blanchar@ chass.utoronto.ca.

Blanchfield, Lyn A., *SUNY, Oswego*. Email: lyn. blanchfield@oswego.edu.

Blanck, Dag, *Augustana*. Email: dagblanck@ augustana.edu.

Blanck, Emily V., *Rowan*. Email: blancke@rowan. edu.

Bland, Sidney R., *James Madison*. Email: blandsr@jmu.edu.

Blane, Andrew. New York, NY.

Blang, Eugenie M. Norfolk, VA. Affil: Hampton. Email: eblang1@cox.net. Research: US relations with postwar Germany, Erhard/ Brandt relations with US.

Blank, Hanne. Newark, OH. Affil: Denison. Email: hanne.blank@gmail.com. Research: feminist health, lesbian feminism.

Blanke, David, *Texas A&M, Corpus Christi*. Email: david.blanke@tamucc.edu.

Blanke, Richard D., *Maine, Orono*. Email: blanke@maine.edu.

Blankenship, Anne Michele, *North Dakota State*. Email: anne.blankenship@ndsu.edu.

Blankholm, Joseph, *California, Santa Barbara*. Email: blankholm@religion.ucsb.edu.

Blanks, David R., *Arkansas Tech*. Email: dblanks@atu.edu.

Blansett, Kent, *Nebraska, Omaha*. Email: kblansett@unomaha.edu.

Blanton, Carlos Kevin, *Texas A&M*. College Station, TX. Email: ckblanton@tamu.edu. Research: bilingual instruction, Mexican Americans in Texas.

Blanton, Harold D., *Naval War Coll*. Email: hdblanto@gmail.com.

Blanton, S. Walker, Jr., *Jacksonville*. Email: sblanto@ju.edu.

Blanton, Timothy. Gainesville, FL. Affil: Florida. Email: tblanton@ufl.edu. Research: cultural history of consumer capitalism, timekeeping/ leisure & recreation.

Blantz, Thomas E., *CSC*, *Notre Dame*. Notre Dame, IN. Email: tblantz@nd.edu. Research:

US political since 1920, Gilded Age political and religious.

Blaschke, Anne. Cambridge, MA. Affil: Holy Cross. Email: blaschke@bu.edu. Research: post-WWII cultural politics and athletics, African American feminists in sports.

Blasenheim, Peter L., *Colorado Coll*. Email: pblasenheim@coloradocollege.edu.

Blasi, Joseph R. New Brunswick, NJ. Affil: Rutgers. Email: blasi@smlr.rutgers.edu.

Blaszak, Barbara J., *Le Moyne*. Syracuse, NY. Email: blaszabj@lemoyne.edu. Research: empire/UK&US special relationship, women/ memory.

Blaszczyk, Agata. Watford, United Kingdom. Affil: Polish Univ. Abroad in London. Email: caucor@hotmail.com.

Blatchford, Barrie. The Bronx, NY. Affil: Columbia. Email: barrieblatchford@gmail. com. Research: hunting in the American West, introduction of new plants/animals to US.

Blatt, Joel R., *Connecticut, Storrs*. Email: joel. blatt@uconn.edu.

Blatt, Martin Henry, *Northeastern*. Email: m.blatt@northeastern.edu.

Blaufarb, Rafe, *Florida State*. Tallahassee, FL. Email: rblaufarb@fsu.edu. Research: early modern/revolutionary/Napoleonic France, military.

Blaylock, David W., *Eastern Kentucky*. Email: david.blaylock@eku.edu.

Blazich, Frank Arthur, Jr. Alexandria, VA. Affil: National Museum of American Hist. Email: frank.blazich@gmail.com. Research: disaster policy, military and society.

Bleasdale, Ruth, *Dalhousie*. Email: ruth. bleasdale@dal.ca.

Blecher, Joel. Washington, DC. Affil: George Washington. Email: jblecher@gwu.edu. Research: commentary traditions on Qur'an and Hadith, revival and reform in Islam.

Bledsoe, Wayne M., *Missouri Science and Tech*. Email: wbledsoe@mst.edu.

Bledstein, Burton J., *Illinois, Chicago*. Chicago, IL. Email: bjb@uic.edu. Research: US intellectual and social thought.

Blee, Lisa, *Wake Forest*. Email: bleelm@wfu.edu.

Bleichmar, Daniela, *Southern California*. Email: bleichma@usc.edu.

Blennemann, Gordon, *Montréal*. Email: gordon. blennemann@umontreal.ca.

Blethen, H. Tyler, III, *Western Carolina*. Email: blethen@email.wcu.edu.

Blevins, Brooks, *Missouri State*. Email: brblevins@missouristate.edu.

Blevins, Cameron, *Northeastern*. Email: c.blevins@northeastern.edu.

Blibo, Frank Kofi. Cambridge, MA. Affil: Harvard. Email: blibo@g.harvard.edu. Research: cardiology, neurosciences.

Blight, David W., *Yale*. New Haven, CT. Email: david.blight@yale.edu. Research: Civil War memory, Frederick Douglass.

Blinka, Daniel D. Greendale, WI. Affil: Marquette. Email: Daniel.Blinka@mu.edu. Research: jury trials in revolutionary America, trials in Progressive era.

Bliss, Brenden, *Hawai'i Pacific*. Email: bbliss@ hpu.edu.

Bliss, Robert M., Jr., *Missouri–St. Louis*. Email: rmbliss@umsl.edu.

Blitstein, Peter A. Appleton, WI. Affil: Lawrence. Email: peter.a.blitstein@lawrence.edu.

Research: Soviet nationalities policy, comparative colonialism.

Blobaum, Robert E., *West Virginia*. Morgantown, WV. Email: Robert.Blobaum@mail.wvu.edu. Research: 20th-c Poland, state and society.

Bloch, Brandon. Cambridge, MA. Affil: Harvard. Email: bloch@fas.harvard.edu.

Bloch, Ruth, *UCLA*. Email: bloch@history.ucla. edu.

Block, Kristen, *Tennessee, Knoxville*. Email: kblock3@utk.edu.

Block, Michael D. San Francisco, CA. Affil: Southern California. Email: michael.d.block@ gmail.com. Research: US trade with China, US conquest of California.

Block, Nelson R. Houston, TX. Affil: Winstead PC. Email: nblock@winstead.com. Research: Western intellectual, youth movements.

Block, Sharon, *California, Irvine*. Email: sblock@ uci.edu.

Blodgett, Peter J., *Huntington Library*. San Marino, CA. Email: pblodgett@huntington. org. Research: tourism in Rocky Mountain West, American national parks.

Bloodworth, William, *Augusta*. Email: wbloodwo@augusta.edu.

Bloom, Alexander, *Wheaton, Mass*. Email: abloom@wheatoncollege.edu.

Bloom, John D., *Shippensburg*. Email: jdbloo@ ship.edu.

Bloom, Matthew David. Austin, TX. Affil: Concordia, Tex. Email: mbloom9@gmail.com. Research: 19th-c US economic development, urban-rural interactions.

Bloom, Peter, *California, Santa Barbara*. Email: pblom@filmandmedia.ucsb.edu.

Blosenhauer-Leaton, Aubrie R. Rochester, NY. Email: aubrieleaton@gmail.com.

Blosser, Jacob M., *Texas Woman's; Phi Alpha Theta*. Email: jblosser@twu.edu.

Blouin, Francis X., Jr., *Michigan, Ann Arbor*. Ann Arbor, MI. Email: fblouin@umich.edu. Research: archival administration.

Blower, Brooke L., *Boston Univ*. Boston, MA. Email: bblower@bu.edu. Research: Americans in world at war 1914-45.

Blum, Dan, *SUNY, Buffalo State*. Email: blumdm@ buffalostate.edu.

Blum, Edward J., *San Diego State*. Email: eblum@sdsu.edu.

Blum, Elizabeth D., *Troy*. Email: sblum@troy. edu.

Blum, Hilary. Knoxville, TN. Affil: Claremont Graduate. Email: hilary.blum@cgu.edu.

Blum, Mark E., *Louisville*. Email: mark.blum@ louisville.edu.

Blum, Michael A. Greenville, SC. Email: blum9725@yahoo.com.

Blume, Kenneth John. Altamont, NY. Affil: Albany Coll. of Pharmacy. Email: Kenneth. blume@acphs.edu. Research: African Americans in US diplomacy 1865-1914, US maritime industry.

Blumengarten, Louis H. New York, NY. Email: lhb070@gmail.com.

Blumenthal, Debra G., *California, Santa Barbara*. Email: blumenthal@history.ucsb.edu.

Blumenthal, Edward. Paris, France. Affil: Sorbonne Nouvelle (Paris 3). Email: edoblum@ gmail.com. Research: exile in 19th-c Latin America, codification of international law.

Blumenthal, Susanna, *Minnesota (Hist.)*. Email: blume047@umn.edu.

AHA members in **bold italic**; Directory-listed affiliations in *italic*

574 Blumhofer, Edith L. • Bonner, Robert E. Guide to Historians

Blumhofer, Edith L., *Wheaton, Ill.* Email: Edith.L.Blumhofer@wheaton.edu.

Blumin, Stuart M., *Cornell.* New York, NY. Email: smb5@cornell.edu. Research: American social/cultural/demographic, American urban.

Blunt, John. Jamaica, NY. Affil: Kingsborough Comm. Coll., CUNY. Email: jblunt@kbcc.cuny.edu.

Blutinger, Jeffrey C., *California State, Long Beach.* Email: jeffrey.blutinger@csulb.edu.

Blyden, Nemata, *George Washington.* Email: nemata@gwu.edu.

Blyth, Lance R., *US Air Force Acad.* Colorado Springs, CO. Affil: NORAD and US Northern Command. Email: lance.blyth@usafa.edu; lance.r.blyth.civ@mail.mil. Research: Navajo-New Mexico war 1800-68, global pastoral borderlands wars.

Blythe, James M., *Memphis.* Email: jmblythe@memphis.edu.

Boaden, Richard. Melbourne, Australia. Email: Rboaden@vicbar.com.au.

Boag, Peter, *Washington State, Pullman.* Email: boag@wsu.edu.

Boanes, Phyllis, *Earlham.* Email: phyllisb@earlham.edu.

Boantza, Victor, *Minnesota (Hist. of Science).* Email: vboantza@umn.edu.

Boatwright, Mary T., *Duke.* Email: tboat@duke.edu.

Boaz, Rachael E., *Baldwin Wallace.* Email: rboaz@bw.edu.

Bobadilla, Eladio B., *Kentucky.* Durham, NC. Affil: Duke. Email: eladio.bobadilla@uky.edu; eladio.bobadilla@duke.edu.

Bobo, Pamela, *Tennessee State.* Email: pbobo@tnstate.edu.

Bobroff, Ronald P., *Bryant.* Jamestown, NC. Affil: Oglethorpe. Email: ronbobroff@hotmail.com; rbobroff@oglethorpe.edu. Research: imperial Russian diplomatic, origins of WWI.

Bobrycki, Shane. Cambridge, MA. Affil: Harvard. Email: sbobryck@fas.harvard.edu. Research: crowds in Middle Ages, early medieval politics and written word.

Bocchine, Kristin. Blythewood, SC. Affil: North Texas. Email: kristinbocchine@my.unt.edu.

Bock, Nils. Trier, Germany. Affil: Westfälische Wilhelms, Münster. Email: nils.bock@uni-muenster.de. Research: money/debt/credit, heralds/court culture/political culture.

Bockelman, Brian. Ripon, WI. Affil: Ripon. Email: bockelmanb@ripon.edu. Research: Argentine cultural 1880-1930, 1970s Bertrand Russell tribunal.

Bockrath, Diane, *Hagley Museum and Library.* Email: dbockrath@hagley.org.

Bode, Frederick A., *Concordia, Can.* Email: Frederick.Bode@concordia.ca.

Bodek, Richard H., *Charleston.* Email: bodekr@cofc.edu.

Bodel, John P., *Brown.* Email: John_Bodel@Brown.edu.

Bodemer, Margaret, *California Polytechnic State.* Email: mbodemer@calpoly.edu.

Boden, Michael. Poughkeepsie, NY. Affil: Dutchess Comm. Coll., SUNY. Email: bodenma@yahoo.com. Research: Friedrich Engels, Socialist military thought.

Bodenhamer, David J., *Indiana–Purdue, Indianapolis.* Email: intu100@iupui.edu.

Bodet, Gerald P., *New Orleans.* Email: gbodet@uno.edu.

Bodian, Miriam, *Texas, Austin.* Austin, TX. Email: bodian@austin.utexas.edu. Research: Inquisition, early modern European thought.

Bodnar, John E., *Indiana.* Email: bodnar@indiana.edu.

Boeck, Brian J., *DePaul.* Email: bboeck@depaul.edu.

Boehling, Rebecca, *Maryland, Baltimore County.* Baltimore, MD. Email: boehling@umbc.edu. Research: postwar transitional justice.

Boehlke, Frederick J., Jr. Paoli, PA. Affil: Eastern. Email: fboehlke@eastern.edu.

Boehm, Lisa Krissoff. Grafton, MA. Affil: Bridgewater State. Email: lkrissoffboehm@bridgew.edu. Research: women and work, images of cities.

Boehnert, Gunnar C., *Guelph.* Email: gboehner@uoguelph.ca.

Boeke, Kristine E., *Austin Comm. Coll.* Email: kboeke@austincc.edu.

Boenker, Dirk, *Duke.* Durham, NC. Email: db48@duke.edu. Research: German and US militarism 1870-1918.

Boerner, Curt. Greenville, MI. Email: curtboerner@hotmail.com. Research: American popular culture, historiography.

Boero, Dina, *New Jersey.* Trenton, NJ. Email: boerod@tcnj.edu. Research: late antiquity, ancient and medieval.

Boerrigter, Carly. Fort Collins, CO. Affil: Colorado State, Fort Collins. Email: carly.boerrigter@colostate.edu.

Bogaert, Kandace, *Wilfrid Laurier.* Email: kbogaert@wlu.ca.

Boggs, Robert, *North Greenville.* Email: robert.boggs@ngu.edu.

Bogue, Sarah. Atlanta, GA. Affil: Emory. Email: sbogue@emory.edu.

Bohac, Rodney D., *Brigham Young.* Email: rodney_bohac@byu.edu.

Bohaker, Heidi, *Toronto.* Email: heidi.bohaker@utoronto.ca.

Bohan, Nancy Ellen. Baltimore, MD. Email: nbohan@gmail.com.

Bohanan, Donna J., *Auburn.* Email: bohandj@auburn.edu.

Bohannon, Keith S., *West Georgia.* Email: kbohanno@westga.edu.

Bohlen, Casey, *Williams.* Email: cdb024@williams.edu.

Bohlen, Michael William. Fayetteville, AR. Affil: Arkansas, Fayetteville. Email: mwbohlen@uark.edu. Research: education in antebellum South.

Bohling, Joseph, *Portland State.* Email: jbohling@pdx.edu.

Bohr, Roland, *Winnipeg.* Email: r.bohr@uwinnipeg.ca.

Bohstedt, John, *Tennessee, Knoxville.* Email: bohstedt@utk.edu.

Boin, Douglas, *St. Louis.* Email: boindr@slu.edu.

Boittin, Jennifer Anne, *Penn State.* Email: jab808@psu.edu.

Bokina, John. Chicago, IL. Affil: Texas Rio Grande Valley. Email: castus8@aol.com. Research: political thought of Herbert Marcuse, Spartacus revolt.

Bokovoy, Melissa K., *New Mexico.* Albuquerque, NM. Email: mbokovoy@unm.edu; jugo333@msn.com. Research: Yugoslavia and memory, collectivization and eastern Europe.

Bolaños, Isacar, *Loyola, Md.*

Boles, John B., *Rice.* Email: boles@rice.edu.

Boles, Richard J., *Oklahoma State.*

Bolin, James Duane, *Murray State.* Email: jbolin@murraystate.edu.

Boll, Michael M., *San José State.*

Bolle, Kees W., *UCLA.* Email: kbolle@gwi.net.

Bollettino, Maria Alessandra, *Framingham State.* Framingham, MA. Email: mbollettino@framingham.edu; bollettino@gmail.com. Research: Atlantic world, race.

Bollwerk, Elizabeth, *Robert H. Smith Center.* Email: ebollwerk@monticello.org.

Bolman, Brad. Cambridge, MA. Affil: Harvard. Email: bolman@g.harvard.edu.

Bolt, Robert, *Calvin.*

Bolt, William, *Francis Marion.* Email: wbolt@fmarion.edu.

Bolton, Charles C., *North Carolina, Greensboro.* Email: ccbolton@uncg.edu.

Bolton, S. Charles, *Arkansas, Little Rock.* Email: scbolton@ualr.edu.

Bomboy, Scott. Perkasie, PA. Affil: National Constitution Center. Email: sbomboy@yahoo.com.

Bon Tempo, Carl, *SUNY, Albany.* Email: cbontempo@albany.edu.

Bonafide, John, *SUNY, Albany.* Email: john.bonafide@oprhp.state.ny.us.

Bonafont, Melissa N., *Austin Comm. Coll.* Email: mbonafon@austincc.edu.

Bonanca, Jasmine Sue. Taunton, MA. Email: jasmine.bonanca@gmail.com.

Bond, Beverly Greene, *Memphis.* Email: bgbond@memphis.edu.

Bond, Elizabeth Andrews, *Ohio State.* Columbus, OH. Email: bond.282@osu.edu. Research: early modern Europe, modern Europe.

Bond, Mona G. Boxford, MA. Affil: Arizona State. Email: Mgmbond4653@gmail.com. Research: New Mexico, American Southwest.

Bond, Sarah E., *Iowa.* Email: sarah-bond@uiowa.edu.

Bone, Andrew, *McMaster.* Email: bone@mcmaster.ca.

Bone, Jonathan A., *William Paterson.* Email: bonej@wpunj.edu.

Bongers, Robert Martin, II. Stanardsville, VA. Affil: Nebraska, Kearney. Email: robert.bongers.07@gmail.com.

Bongiorno, Joseph, *St. John's, NY.* Email: bongiorj@stjohns.edu.

Bonhomme, Brian, *Youngstown State.* Email: bbonhomme@ysu.edu.

Boniece, Sally A., *Frostburg State.* Email: sboniece@frostburg.edu.

Bonnechere, Pierre, *Montréal.* Email: pierre.bonnechere@umontreal.ca.

Bonnell, Jennifer, *York, Can.* Email: bonnellj@yorku.ca.

Bonnell-Freidin, Anna, *Michigan, Ann Arbor.* Email: freidin@umich.edu.

Bonner, Christopher James, *Maryland, Coll. Park.* College Park, MD. Email: cjbonner@umd.edu. Research: 19th-c black intellectuals.

Bonner, Judith, *Hist. New Orleans.* Email: jbonner@hnoc.org.

Bonner, Michael, *Michigan, Ann Arbor.* Email: mbonner@umich.edu.

Bonner, Robert E., *Carleton Coll.* Email: rbonner@carleton.edu.

Bonner, Robert E., *Dartmouth.* Email: robert.bonner@dartmouth.edu.

AHA members in **bold italic**; Directory-listed affiliations in *italic*

Bonnett, **John**, *Brock*. Email: jbonnett@brocku. ca.

Bono, **James J.**, *SUNY, Buffalo*. Buffalo, NY. Email: hischaos@buffalo.edu. Research: early modern science/medicine/religion, metaphor/narrative/science.

Bonomi, **Patricia U.**, *NYU*. Email: pub1@nyu. edu.

Bontrager, **Shannon T**. Cartersville, GA. Affil: Georgia Highlands, Cartersville. Email: Shannon.bontrager@gmail.com. Research: commemorations and public memory, death and burial of military dead.

Booker, **Anna Fay**. Bellingham, WA. Affil: Whatcom Comm. Coll. Email: anna.booker@ gmail.com. Research: local, digital humanities.

Booker, **Courtney Matthew**, *British Columbia*. Vancouver, BC, Canada. Email: cbooker@ interchange.ubc.ca. Research: Carolingian Europe, representations of political crisis.

Booker, **Matthew Morse**, *North Carolina State*. Email: matthew_booker@ncsu.edu.

Booker, **Vaughn A**. Hanover, NH. Affil: Dartmouth. Email: vaughn.a.booker@ dartmouth.edu.

Boone, **Daniel H**. Gilbert, AZ. Affil: Social Security Administration. Email: dbhist1775@ gmail.com. Research: American Revolutionary period, Seven Years War.

Boone, **Paul Thaddeus**. Bottineau, ND. Affil: Dakota, Bottineau. Email: drpaulboone@ gmail.com. Research: teachers, popular culture.

Boone, **Rebecca Ard**, *Lamar*. Beaumont, TX. Email: raboone@my.lamar.edu. Research: Renaissance political culture, Spanish Empire.

Boonshoft, **Mark**, *Norwich*. Northfield, VT. Email: mboonsho@norwich.edu; mark.boonshoft@ gmail.com. Research: colonial America.

Boonstra, **John**. Falmouth, MA. Affil: European Univ. Inst. Email: john.boonstra@eui.eu.

Boorn, **Alida Scott**. Kent, WA. Email: alidaboorn@gmail.com. Research: tourism, material culture.

Boos, **Lance**. Islip Terrace, NY. Affil: SUNY, Stony Brook. Email: lance.boos@stonybrook.edu.

Boosel, **Brian D.**, *OSB*. Latrobe, PA. Affil: St. Vincent. Email: 00boosel@cua.edu.

Booth, **Alan R.**, *Ohio*. Email: boothar@gmail. com.

Booth, **Jonathon**. Somerville, MA. Affil: Harvard. Email: jonathon.booth@gmail.com.

Booth, **Ryan W.** Pullman, WA. Affil: Washington State, Pullman. Email: ryan.booth@wsu.edu. Research: US West, US Indian Scouts.

Booth, **Stephane Elise**, *Kent State*. Email: sbooth@kent.edu.

Booth, **Teddy W.**, **II**, *Lincoln Memorial*. Email: teddy.booth@lmunet.edu.

Boothe, **Leon E.**, *Northern Kentucky*. Email: boothel@nku.edu.

Borah, **Abikal**. Austin, TX. Affil: Texas, Austin. Email: aborah@utexas.edu.

Borbonus, **Dorian**, *Dayton*. Email: borbondo@ notes.udayton.edu.

Borchard, **Lauren E.**, *US Capitol Hist. Soc.* Email: lauren@uschs.org.

Borchert, **James A.**, *Cleveland State*. Email: jamesborchert@netscape.net.

Borders, **Hillary**. Smyrna, TN. Affil: Middle Tennessee State. Email: hillaryelizabethborders@gmail.com.

Bordewich, **Chloe**. Cambridge, MA. Affil: Harvard. Email: cbordewich@g.harvard.edu.

Bordewich, **Fergus M**. San Francisco, CA. Email: fergus.bordewich@yahoo.com. Research: antebellum US politics, US Civil War.

Borg, **Daniel R.**, *Clark*.

Borg, **Kevin L.**, *James Madison*. Email: borgkl@ jmu.edu.

Borgen, **Robert**, *California, Davis*. Email: rborgen@ucdavis.edu.

Borges, **Charles J.**, **SJ**, *Loyola, Md.* Email: cborges@loyola.edu.

Borges, **Dain E.**, *Chicago*. Chicago, IL. Email: dborges@uchicago.edu. Research: Latin America, Brazil.

Borges, **Marcelo J.**, *Dickinson*. Carlisle, PA. Email: borges@dickinson.edu. Research: Latin America, comparative migrations.

Borgwardt, **Elizabeth**, *Washington, St. Louis*. Saint Louis, MO. Email: eborgwar@wustl.edu. Research: Nuremberg trials, human rights.

Boris, **Eileen**, *California, Santa Barbara*. Santa Barbara, CA. Email: boris@femst.ucsb.edu. Research: gender/race/social policy, home as workplace/domestic labor.

Borish, **Linda J.**, *Western Michigan*. Kalamazoo, MI. Email: linda.borish@wmich.edu. Research: American women/sport/gender, American Jewish women and sport.

Borja, **Melissa May**. New York, NY. Affil: Michigan, Ann Arbor. Email: mborja@umich. edu. Research: refugee studies, oral.

Borland, **Luke**. Iowa City, IA. Affil: Iowa. Email: Luke-borland@uiowa.edu.

Bornstein, **Daniel**, *Washington, St. Louis*. Saint Louis, MO. Email: dbornste@wustl.edu. Research: late medieval Italian religious culture, medieval/Renaissance Italian women.

Borrello, **Mark E.**, *Minnesota (Hist. of Science)*. Email: borrello@umn.edu.

Borrero, **Mauricio**, *St. John's, NY*. Jamaica, NY. Email: borrerom@stjohns.edu. Research: Russia.

Borriello, **Giovanni**. Naples, Italy. Affil: Tuscia. Email: giovanni.borriello77@gmail.com. Research: Japanese modernization/Oyatoi gaikokuj, medical officer in Japanese history.

Borrut, **Antoine**, *Maryland, Coll. Park*. Email: aborrut@umd.edu.

Borsch, **Stuart James**, *Assumption*. Email: sborsch@assumption.edu.

Borstelmann, **Tim**, *Nebraska, Lincoln*. Lincoln, NE. Email: tborstelmann2@unl.edu; tborstelmann@neb.rr.com. Research: race and foreign relations, 1970s.

Bortner, **Michael A**. Belvedere, CA. Email: japanesehistorytoday@gmail.com.

Bortz, **Jeffrey L.**, *Appalachian State*. Email: bortzjl@appstate.edu.

Borucki, **Alex F.**, *California, Irvine*. Irvine, CA. Email: aborucki@uci.edu. Research: African diaspora, early modern Atlantic world.

Borus, **Daniel H.**, *Rochester*. Email: daniel. borus@rochester.edu.

Boruta-Sadkowski, **Alicja**, *Northern Iowa*. Email: alicja.boruta-sadkowski@uni.edu.

Borys, **Stephen**, *Winnipeg*. Email: s.borys@ uwinnipeg.ca.

Borza, **Eugene N.**, *Penn State*. Email: borza@ comcast.net.

Bos, **Linda Marie**. Elm Grove, WI. Affil: Mount Mary. Email: boslm@mtmary.edu. Research:

education changed by industrialization, online teaching methods in history.

Bosak, **Edita**, *Memorial, Newfoundland*. Email: ebosak@mun.ca.

Bosak-Schroeder, **Clara**, *Illinois, Urbana-Champaign*. Email: cbosak@illinois.edu.

Bosch, **William J.**, **SJ**, *Le Moyne*. Email: BoschWJ@lemoyne.edu.

Boschert, **Sherry**. San Francisco, CA. Email: sherry.boschert@gmail.com. Research: Title IX, women.

Bose, **Purnima**, *Indiana*. Email: pbose@indiana. edu.

Bose, **Sarmila**. Oxford, United Kingdom. Affil: Oxford. Email: sarmila.bose@post.harvard. edu. Research: genetic analysis/Bengal kayastha origins, roots of conflicts NE India/ Baluchistan.

Bose, **Sugata**, *Harvard (Hist.)*. Email: sbose@fas. harvard.edu.

Bosket, **Jamie O.**, *Virginia Museum of Hist*. Email: jbosket@VirginiaHistory.org.

Bosley, **Blaire Tracy**. Stone Mountain, GA. Affil: Wooster. Email: bbosley18@wooster.edu.

Boss, **Valentin J.**, *McGill*. Email: valentin.boss@ mcgill.ca.

Bossler, **Beverly**, *California, Davis*. Email: bjbossler@ucdavis.edu.

Bossy, **Denise Ileana**, *North Florida*. Email: denise.bossy@unf.edu.

Bost, **Darius**. Salt Lake City, UT. Email: bostdr4@ gmail.com.

Boster, **Tania**. Oberlin, OH. Affil: Oberlin. Email: tboster@oberlin.edu. Research: community-based learning and research, intellectual biography.

Bostick, **Theodore P.**, *Christopher Newport*. Email: tbostick@cnu.edu.

Boston, **Amanda**. Brooklyn, NY. Affil: NYU. Email: amanda.boston@nyu.edu. Research: gentrification, critical geography.

Boswell, **Laird**, *Wisconsin-Madison*. Madison, WI. Email: lboswell@wisc.edu. Research: European borderlands, 20th-c France.

Bosworth, **Amanda Leigh**. Vicksburg, MI. Affil: Cornell. Email: alb399@cornell.edu. Research: American maritime, Russian maritime.

Bosworth, **Amy K.**, *Ball State*. Email: akbosworth@bsu.edu.

Bosworth, **Stephen D**. Austin, TX. Affil: Austin Comm. Coll. Email: sbosworth2011@hotmail. com. Research: early 20th-c Chilean labor.

Botelho, **Lynn**, *Indiana, Pa.* Email: botelho@iup. edu.

Boterbloem, **Kees (Case)**, *South Florida, Tampa*. Email: cboterbl@usf.edu.

Bothwell, **Robert**, *Toronto*. Email: bothwell@ chass.utoronto.ca.

Botjer, **George F**. Belleair, FL. Affil: Tampa. Email: geoghist@aol.com. Research: western European economic geography, US economic.

Botsman, **Daniel V.**, *Yale*. New Haven, CT. Email: daniel.botsman@yale.edu. Research: Tokugawa Japan 1600-1868, Meiji Restoration 1868-1912.

Botstein, **Leon**, *Bard*. Email: botstein@bard.edu.

Bottiger, **Patrick Gary**, *Kenyon*. Email: bottigerp@kenyon.edu.

Bottigheimer, **Karl S.**, *SUNY, Stony Brook*. Email: Karl.Bottigheimer@stonybrook.edu.

Botts, **Joshua D.**, *US Dept. of State*.

Bouchard, **Carl**, *Montréal*. Email: carl. bouchard@umontreal.ca.

Bouchard, Gerard. Chicoutini, QC, Canada. Email: gerard_bouchard@uqac.ca.

Boucher, Christophe, *Charleston*. Email: boucherc@cofc.edu.

Boucher, Diane M. Gardner, MA. Affil: Clark. Email: dianem.boucher@gmail.com. Research: East Florida frontier borderlands, African American migration/Reconstruction.

Boucher, Ellen R., *Amherst*. Email: eboucher@amherst.edu.

Boucher, Philip P., *Alabama, Huntsville*. Huntsville, AL. Email: boucherp@uah.edu; philippboucher@gmail.com. Research: early modern Europe, colonial expansion.

Bouchier, Nancy, *McMaster*. Email: bouchier@mcmaster.ca.

Boudreau, Joseph A., *San José State*. Email: josephboudreau@att.net.

Boughan, Kurt M., *Citadel*. Mount Pleasant, SC. Email: kurt.boughan@citadel.edu. Research: Italian scholastic medicine, medieval psychology.

Bouk, Dan, *Colgate*. Email: dbouk@colgate.edu.

Boulby, Marion, *Trent*. Email: marionboulby@trentu.ca.

Bouldin, Elizabeth, *Florida Gulf Coast*. Fort Myers, FL. Email: ebouldin@fgcu.edu; bouldin.elizabeth@gmail.com. Research: early modern British Atlantic, gender and religion.

Bouley, Bradford Albert, *California, Santa Barbara*. Email: bouley@history.ucsb.edu.

Boulton, Alexander O. Baltimore, MD. Affil: Stevenson. Email: aoboulton@hotmail.com. Research: Jefferson and race, Peloponnesian War.

Boulton, D'Arcy Jonathan D., *Notre Dame*. Email: Boulton.2@nd.edu.

Bouquet, Dorothee M., *Purdue*. Email: dbouquet@purdue.edu.

Bourboun, Jake. Manvel, ND. Affil: North Dakota. Email: Jacob.bourboun@und.edu. Research: maritime Philadelphia 1740-75, 18th-c American sailors.

Bourdon, Jeffrey Normand, *Southern Mississippi*.

Bourdon, Roger J., *Mary Washington*. Email: rbourdon@umw.edu.

Bourg, Julian Edward, *Boston Coll.* Email: julian.bourg.1@bc.edu.

Bourgeois, Eugene J., II, *Texas State*. Email: eb04@txstate.edu.

Bouril, Thomas. Syracuse, NY. Affil: Syracuse. Email: tbouril@syr.edu.

Bourque, Stephen A. Kansas City, MO. Affil: US Army Command Coll. Email: profbourque@mac.com. Research: France in WWII, US WWII.

Boutelle, Alyssa. Oakland, CA. Email: arboutelle@gmail.com.

Bouton, Cynthia A., *Texas A&M*. College Station, TX. Email: c-bouton@tamu.edu. Research: modern France, European women and gender.

Bouton, R. Terry, *Maryland, Baltimore County*. Email: bouton@umbc.edu.

Bovee, David S. Thiensville, WI. Affil: Fort Hays State. Email: dsbovee@fhsu.edu. Research: American Catholic rural life, religion of US presidents.

Bovey, Patricia, FRSA, *Winnipeg*. Email: p.bovey@uwinnipeg.ca.

Bowden, Mary Ellen, *Science History Inst.* Email: mebowden@sciencehistory.org.

Bowen, Ashley, *Science History Inst.* Email: abowen@sciencehistory.org.

Bowen, Cecilia. Lake Elsinore, CA. Email: cbowe002@ucr.edu. Research: Reconstruction Era Mississippi, colonial Virginia.

Bowen, Daniel A. Berkeley, CA. Affil: California, Berkeley. Email: dabowen01@gmail.com.

Bowen, Michael D., *John Carroll*. Email: mbowen@jcu.edu.

Bowen, Paula Lynn. Lawton, OK. Affil: Lawton Public Sch. Email: paula4134@sbcglobal.net.

Bowen, Wayne H., *Central Florida*. Email: Wayne.Bowen@ucf.edu.

Bower, Kevin P., *Nebraska Wesleyan*. Email: kbower@nebrwesleyan.edu.

Bower, Stephanie B., *Indiana, Southeast*. Email: sbower@ius.edu.

Bowers, Douglas E. Vienna, VA. Affil: US Dept. of Agriculture. Email: dougbowers@aol.com.

Bowers, Kristy Wilson, *Missouri, Columbia*. Columbia, MO. Email: bowersks@missouri.edu; kswbowers@gmail.com. Research: epidemics and public health, medical and scientific networks.

Bowes, John P., *Eastern Kentucky*. Richmond, KY. Email: john.bowes@eku.edu. Research: Native American, American West.

Bowie, Nikolas. Cambridge, MA. Affil: Harvard. Email: nbowie@law.harvard.edu.

Bowler, Richard Carl, *Salisbury*. Email: rcbowler@salisbury.edu.

Bowles, Brett C., *Indiana*. Email: bowlesb@indiana.edu.

Bowling, Kenneth R., *George Washington*. Email: kbowling@gwu.edu.

Bowling, Lawson H., III, *Manhattanville*. Purchase, NY. Email: Lawson.Bowling@mville.edu. Research: American sports.

Bowlus, Charles R., *Arkansas, Little Rock*. Email: crbowlus@ualr.edu.

Bowman, Brad, *Louisville*. Email: brad.bowman@lousville.edu.

Bowman, Denvy A., *Capital*. Email: dbowman@capital.edu.

Bowman, Jeffrey A., *Kenyon*. Gambier, OH. Email: bowmanj@kenyon.edu. Research: Iberian hagiography, law/conflict/disputes.

Bowman, Joye L., *Massachusetts, Amherst*. Email: jbowman@history.umass.edu.

Bowman, Matthew. Claremont, CA. Affil: Claremont Graduate. Email: matthew.bowman@cgu.edu. Research: evangelicalism, Mormonism.

Bowman, Nancy Lynn. Seattle, WA. Affil: Bush Sch. Email: nlbowman89@hotmail.com. Research: American identity between 1880 and 1930.

Bowman, Sarah K., *Columbus State*. Email: bowman_sarah@columbusstate.edu.

Bowman, Steven B., *Cincinnati*. Email: steven.bowman@uc.edu.

Bowman, William D., *Gettysburg*. Email: wbowman@gettysburg.edu.

Bowser, Matthew J. Boston, MA. Affil: Northeastern. Email: mattbowser129@gmail.com. Research: British imperial and world, social and economic history of Myanmar.

Box, Benjamin Matthew. Carrollton, TX. Email: benbox2112@gmail.com.

Boxer, Elise, *South Dakota*. Email: Elise.Boxer@usd.edu.

Boxer, Marilyn J. Berkeley, CA. Affil: San Francisco State. Email: mboxer@sfsu.edu.

Research: 18th- to 20th-c European women, 19th- to early 20th-c socialism.

Boyd, Catherine Elaine, *James Madison*.

Boyd, Charles O'Halloran. Atlanta, GA. Affil: Georgia State. Email: charlesboyd135@gmail.com. Research: slavery and abolitionism, Jim Crow and civil rights.

Boyd, Edward L. Hillsboro, IL. Email: edboyde@hotmail.com.

Boyd, Kelly King. London, United Kingdom. Affil: Inst. of Hist. Research. Email: k.boyd@blueyonder.co.uk. Research: 1950s television and national culture, national identity in postwar Britain.

Boyd, Steven R., *Texas, San Antonio*. Email: steven.boyd@utsa.edu.

Boyd-Bragg, Dorothy, *James Madison*.

Boyden, James M., *Tulane*. Baton Rouge, LA. Email: jboyden@tulane.edu. Research: Spanish honor/piety/elite ethos, Spanish historiography of French wars.

Boyer, Christopher R., *Illinois, Chicago*. Chicago, IL. Email: crboyer@uic.edu. Research: peasant movements, Mexican environment and culture.

Boyer, John W., *Chicago*. Email: jwboyer@uchicago.edu.

Boyer, Lori, *Hist. New Orleans*. Email: lorib@hnoc.org.

Boyer, Patrice, *South Florida, St. Petersburg*.

Boyer, Richard E., *Simon Fraser*. Email: boyer@sfu.ca.

Boyer Lewis, Charlene, *Kalamazoo*. Email: clewis@kzoo.edu.

Boylan, Anne M., *Delaware*. Newark, DE. Email: aboylan@udel.edu. Research: early 19th-c women's organizations, historical memory.

Boyle, Kevin, *Northwestern*. Evanston, IL. Email: kevin.boyle@northwestern.edu. Research: 20th-c US.

Boyle, Sarah. Overland Park, KS. Affil: Johnson County Comm. Coll. Email: sboyle4@jccc.edu.

Boynton, Virginia R., *Western Illinois*. Email: VR-Boynton@wiu.edu.

Boytim, Jacqueline, *Science History Inst.* Email: jboytim@sciencehistory.org.

Bozeman, T. Dwight, *Iowa*. Email: d-bozeman@uiowa.edu.

Bozian, Ashley Mariam. Larchmont, NY. Affil: St. John's, NY. Email: Boziana@stjohns.edu.

Bozyk, Dennis P. Westland, MI. Affil: Madonna. Email: dbozyk@gmail.com. Research: modern world, teaching/learning.

Brackett, John K., *Cincinnati*.

Brackett, Shawn. Calgary, AB, Canada. Affil: Calgary. Email: shawn.brackett@ucalgary.ca. Research: normal schools, student life/student affairs.

Bracy, Alexander Charles. College Park, MD. Affil: Maryland, Coll. Park. Email: alexcbracy@gmail.com.

Bradburn, Douglas M. Mount Vernon, VA. Affil: Binghamton, SUNY. Email: dbradburn@mountvernon.org. Research: early US citizenship and nationhood, British Empire policy and ideology.

Bradbury, Bettina, *York, Can.* Email: bettina@yorku.ca.

Bradbury, John F., Jr., *Missouri Science and Tech.; State Hist. Soc. of Missouri*. Email: jfb@mst.edu; JFB@shsmo.org.

Bradbury, Miles L., *Maryland, Coll. Park*. Email: bradbuml@umd.edu.

Brade, *Laura Elizabeth*, *Albion*. Albion, MI. Email: lbrade@albion.edu. Research: migration/refugees/Holocaust, 20th-c Germany and Czechoslovakia.

Braden, *James Allen*. Washington, DC. Affil: US Dept. of Justice. Email: napoleon101041@gmail.com. Research: Chinese military thought 1900-47, Islamic military thought 1900-2000.

Bradford, *Alfred S.*, *Oklahoma (Hist.)*. Email: abradford@ou.edu.

Bradford, *James C.*, *Texas A&M*. Email: jcbradford@tamu.edu.

Bradley, *Cheryl*. Henderson, NV. Affil: Nevada, Las Vegas. Email: cherylbradley2020@gmail.com.

Bradley, *Christopher Michael*. Tempe, AZ. Email: cmbradley@cox.net.

Bradley, *Evelyn*. Logan, UT. Email: eib3015@gmail.com.

Bradley, *Jonathan Gerald*. Rouses Point, NY. Affil: McGill. Email: jon.bradley@mcgill.ca.

Bradley, *Joseph C.*, *Jr*. Alexandria, VA. Affil: Tulsa. Email: joseph-bradley@utulsa.edu. Research: 19th-c Russia, voluntary associations and civil society.

Bradley, *Keith R.*, *Notre Dame*. Email: Bradley.45@nd.edu.

Bradley, *Mark Philip*, *Chicago*. Chicago, IL. Email: mbradley@uchicago.edu. Research: human rights, Vietnam and postcolonialism.

Bradley, *Michelle Anne*. Fayetteville, GA. Affil: National Archives. Email: mbradley92@yahoo.com. Research: pre-WWI battleships, Korean War.

Bradley-Perrin, *Ian*. New York, NY. Affil: Columbia. Email: ifb2105@columbia.edu.

Brady, *Benjamin*. Saint Louis, MO. Email: bkb7fy@virginia.edu.

Brady, *Lisa M.*, *Boise State*. Email: lisabrady@boisestate.edu.

Brady, *Robert Louis*. Reno, NV. Email: robertbrady535@yahoo.com.

Braff, *Paul Alexander*. Boston, MA. Affil: Temple. Email: paul.braff@temple.edu.

Bragg, *Beverly Lynn*. Portland, TN. Email: footnotes312@gmail.com. Research: post-Civil War black educational institutions, Reformation/theater/hybrid spaces.

Bragg, *John Kenneth*, *New Jersey City*. Email: JBragg@njcu.edu.

Brain, *Robert M.*, *British Columbia*. Email: rbrain@mail.ubc.ca.

Brain, *Stephen*, *Mississippi State*. Email: scbrain@history.msstate.edu.

Brakke, *David*, *Ohio State*. Columbus, OH. Email: brakke.2@osu.edu. Research: ancient Christian monasticism, gnosticism.

Bramhall, *David D.*. Farmington, NM. Affil: San Juan. Email: bramhalld@sanjuancollege.edu. Research: Jeffersonian philosophy, social change in modern America.

Brammall, *Kathryn M.*, *Truman State*. Kirksville, MO. Email: brammall@truman.edu. Research: early modern England, science and culture.

Bramson, *Loni*. Portland, OR. Affil: American Public Univ. System. Email: bramsonloni@gmail.com.

Bramwell, *Lincoln L.*. Fort Collins, CO. Affil: USDA Forest Service. Email: lincoln.bramwell@gmail.com. Research: USDA Forest Service, Fire.

Brand, *Peter J.*, *Memphis*. Email: pbrand@memphis.edu.

Brandao, *Jose Antonio*, *Western Michigan*. Email: jose.brandao@wmich.edu.

Brandenberger, *David*, *Richmond*. Email: dbranden@richmond.edu.

Brandenburgh, *Crystal Dawn*. Council Bluffs, IA. Affil: Iowa State. Email: cdbrandenburgh@gmail.com.

Brandfon, *Robert L.*, *Holy Cross*.

Brandom, *Eric W.*, *Kansas State*. Email: brandom@ksu.edu.

Brandon, *Betty J.*, *South Alabama*. Chapel Hill, NC. Email: howardbbran@aol.com. Research: modern US, Progressive Era.

Brandon, *Jacqueline*. New York, NY. Affil: Princeton. Email: jvbrandon@princeton.edu.

Brandon, *Laura E.*, *Carleton, Can*. Email: laura.brandon@carleton.ca.

Brandon, *Tyler Blake*. Pennsville, NJ. Email: tylerblake.brandon@gmail.com. Research: American Civil War guerrilla warfare, Western martial arts in modern age.

Brands, *H. W.*, *Texas, Austin*. Email: hwbrands@austin.utexas.edu.

Brandt, *Allan M.*, *Harvard (Hist. of Science)*. Newton, MA. Email: brandt@fas.harvard.edu. Research: American medicine and science, health and public policy.

Brannan, *Emora Thomas*. Baltimore, MD. Affil: Lovely Lane Museum; St. Mary's Seminary & Univ. Email: emorabrannan@verizon.net. Research: 18th-c English Wesleyan, historical theology/justification.

Brannon, *Rebecca*, *James Madison*. Harrisonburg, VA. Email: brannorn@jmu.edu. Research: reconciliation and American Revolution, violence and its effects on politics.

Brannon-Wranosky, *Jessica S.*, *Texas A&M, Commerce*. Commerce, TX. Email: jessica.wranosky@tamuc.edu. Research: gender/racial/ethnic enfranchisement, digital humanities.

Branscombe, *Jensen*, *Tarleton State*. Email: branscombe@tarleton.edu.

Branson, *Margaret S.*. Casper, WY.

Branson, *Susan*, *Syracuse*. Email: branson@syr.edu.

Brashear, *Ronald*, *Science History Inst*. Email: rbrashear@sciencehistory.org.

Brasher, *Sally Mayall*, *Shepherd*. Email: sbrasher@shepherd.edu.

Brasil, *Paul D.*. Coeur D Alene, ID. Affil: North Idaho. Email: paul_brasil@nic.edu. Research: Portugal.

Braslow, *Joel*, *UCLA*. Email: jbraslow@ucla.edu.

Brasseaux, *Carl A.*, *Louisiana, Lafayette*.

Brathwaite, *Kamau*, *NYU*. Email: kb5@nyu.edu.

Bratt, *James D.*, *Calvin*. Email: jbratt@calvin.edu.

Bratt, *Jordan Frazier*. Maricopa, AZ. Affil: George Mason. Email: jfbratt@gmail.com. Research: Mormonism.

Brattain, *Michelle*, *Georgia State*. Atlanta, GA. Email: mbrattain@gsu.edu. Research: cultural and intellectual, labor.

Bratton, *Lisa M*. Tuskegee Institute, AL. Affil: Tuskegee. Email: drbratt@hotmail.com.

Braude, *Ann D.*. Cambridge, MA. Affil: Harvard Divinity Sch. Email: ann_braude@harvard.edu. Research: women in religion, feminism.

Braude, *Benjamin*, *Boston Coll*. Email: braude@bc.edu.

Braudy, *Leo*, *Southern California*. Email: braudy@usc.edu.

Braun, *Herbert*, *Virginia*. Charlottesville, VA. Email: hb3r@virginia.edu. Research: modern Latin America.

Braun, *John R*. McMinnville, OR. Affil: Willamette. Email: braunjr@comcast.net. Research: interwar French politics, Bertrand de Jouvenel.

Braun, *Lindsay Frederick*, *Oregon*. Eugene, OR. Email: lfbraun@uoregon.edu. Research: colonialism, cartography and surveying.

Braun, *Mark E*. Cobleskill, NY. Affil: SUNY, Coll. of A&T. Email: braunme@cobleskill.edu.

Braun, *Richard E.*, *Alberta*.

Braun, *Willi*, *Alberta*. Email: willi.braun@ualberta.ca.

Braund, *Kathryn H.*, *Auburn*. Email: braunkh@auburn.edu.

Braun-Strumfels, *Lauren H*. Somerville, NJ. Affil: Raritan Valley Comm. Coll. Email: lbraun@raritanval.edu. Research: Italian migration, immigration restriction.

Braunum, *Jake*. Miami, FL. Affil: Miami. Email: jdb251@miami.edu.

Brautigam, *Jeffrey C*. Hanover, IN. Affil: Hanover. Email: brautgm@hanover.edu. Research: Victorian cultural, Victorian science.

Bray, *Mark*. Lebanon, NH. Affil: Dartmouth. Email: mark.bray@dartmouth.edu.

Braziel, *Bradley*. Malvern, AR. Affil: Ouachitas. Email: braziellessonplans@yahoo.com.

Brazinsky, *Gregg A.*, *George Washington*. Email: brazinsk@gwu.edu.

Brazy, *Martha Jane L.*, *South Alabama*. Buffalo, NY. Email: mjbrazy@southalabama.edu. Research: African American, social.

Brecher, *W. Puck*, *Washington State, Pullman*. Pullman, WA. Email: wbrecher@wsu.edu. Research: modern Japan.

Breckman, *Warren Glen*, *Pennsylvania*. Philadelphia, PA. Email: breckman@sas.upenn.edu. Research: 19th-/20th-c intellectual, political thought.

Bredbenner, *Candice*, *North Carolina, Wilmington*. Portland, ME. Email: bredbennerc@uncw.edu. Research: citizenship, interwar culture and politics.

Bredovskis, *Eriks Eduards*. Burlington, ON, Canada. Affil: Toronto. Email: bredovsk@gmail.com. Research: modern Germany, urban cultural.

Breeden, *James O.*, *Southern Methodist*. Email: jbreeden@smu.edu.

Breen, *Ben*, *California, Santa Cruz*. Email: bebreen@ucsc.edu.

Breen, *Louise A.*, *Kansas State*. Email: breen@ksu.edu.

Breen, *Michael P.*, *Reed*. Portland, OR. Email: michael.breen@reed.edu. Research: lawyers and social/cultural change, state-building and royal absolutism.

Breen, *Patrick H.*, *Providence*. Email: pbreen@providence.edu.

Breen, *Timothy H.*, *Northwestern*. Email: t-breen@northwestern.edu.

Breese, *Donald*, *Whittier*.

Brege, *Brian Anthony*, *Syracuse*. Syracuse, NY. Email: babrege@maxwell.syr.edu; babrege@gmail.com. Research: Renaissance Italy.

Bregent-Heald, *Dominique*, *Memorial, Newfoundland*. Email: dbheald@mun.ca.

Bregman, *Jay A.*, *Maine, Orono*. Email: jay.bregman@umit.maine.edu.

Bregoli, *Francesca*, Graduate Center, CUNY; Queens, CUNY. Flushing, NY. Email: francesca. bregoli@qc.cuny.edu. Research: 18th-c Mediterranean, early modern Jewish-Christian relations.

Breihan, **John R.**, Loyola, Md. Email: breihan@ loyola.edu.

Breiseth, *Christopher N*. Ticonderoga, NY. Affil: Franklin & Eleanor Roosevelt Inst. Email: cnbreiseth@aol.com.

Breitman, *Richard*, American. Bethesda, MD. Email: rbreit@american.edu. Research: modern Germany, European social and political.

Brekus, *Catherine A*. Auburndale, MA. Affil: Harvard. Email: cbrekus@hds.harvard.edu.

Brembt, *Kristopher*. Hewitt, NJ. Email: kristbrembt@yahoo.com.

Bremer, **Francis J.**, Millersville, Pa. Email: francis. bremer@millersville.edu.

Bremer, **Jeff R.**, Iowa State. Email: jrbremer@ iastate.edu.

Brenes, *Michael A*. Hamden, CT. Affil: Yale. Email: michael.brenes@yale.edu. Research: American diplomacy, American conservatism.

Brennan, **Denis P.**, Union Coll. Email: brennand@union.edu.

Brennan, **James P.**, California, Riverside. Email: james.brennan@ucr.edu.

Brennan, *James R.*, Illinois, Urbana-Champaign. Urbana, IL. Email: jbrennan@illinois.edu. Research: East African nationalism and race, varieties of Islam in East Africa.

Brennan, *Katherine Stern*, Loyola, Md. Annapolis, MD. Email: kbrennan@loyola. edu. Research: academies provincial France, women and translation.

Brennan, *Kristine B*. Stamford, CT. Affil: Brunswick Sch. Email: KBrennan@ brunswickschool.org.

Brennan, *Margaret*. Champaign, IL. Affil: Illinois, Urbana-Champaign. Email: mlbrennan10@ gmail.com.

Brennan, **Mary C.**, Texas State. Email: mb18@ txstate.edu.

Brennan, **Patrick H.**, Calgary. Email: brennan@ ucalgary.ca.

Brennan, *Sean Philip*, Scranton. Scranton, PA. Email: sean.brennan@scranton.edu. Research: Catholic Relief Services in Europe, United Nations in 1950s.

Brenner, *Arthur D*. Albany, NY. Affil: SUNY, Albany. Email: abrenner@albany.edu. Research: Jews in Europe in WWI, German political culture/civic values.

Brenner, **John**, State Hist. Soc. of Missouri. Email: brennerj@shsmo.org.

Brenner, **Michael**, American. Email: mbrenner@ american.edu.

Brenner, *Rebecca B*. Arlington, VA. Affil: American. Email: Rb5078a@student.american. edu.

Brenner, **Robert P.**, UCLA. Email: brenner@ history.ucla.edu.

Brescia, **Michael M.**, Arizona. Email: brescia@ email.arizona.edu.

Breslin, *Thomas Aloysius*, Florida International. Miami, FL. Email: breslint@fiu.edu. Research: China Sea disputes, China's borderlands during GPCR.

Breslow, *Boyd*, Florida Atlantic. Boca Raton, FL. Email: breslow@fau.edu. Research: England, London.

Breslow, **Marvin A.**, Maryland, Coll. Park. Email: mab@umd.edu.

Bresnahan, **David**, Utah.

Bresson, *Alain*, Chicago. Chicago, IL. Email: abresson@uchicago.edu. Research: ancient world.

Breting-Garcia, *Victoria M*. Houston, TX. Email: vickimarga2@aol.com. Research: North American environmental.

Breuer, **Karin H.**, Ithaca. Email: kbreuer@ithaca. edu.

Breuer, **Kimberly H.**, Texas, Arlington. Email: breuer@uta.edu.

Breuninger, **Scott C.**, South Dakota. Email: Scott.Breuninger@usd.edu.

Brevda, *Scott*. Jackson Heights, NY. Email: sbrevda@fordham.edu.

Brew, *Gregory Ralph*. Dallas, TX. Affil: Southern Methodist. Email: gbrew@smu.edu. Research: US-Iran relationship, political economy of energy.

Brewer, *Helen Louise*. Williamsburg, VA. Email: h.brewer333@gmail.com.

Brewer, **Herbert**, Morgan State. Email: herbert. brewer@morgan.edu.

Brewer, *Holly*, Maryland, Coll. Park. College Park, MD. Email: hbrewer@umd.edu. Research: early debates about slavery in British Empire, family and dependency.

Brewer, **John**, California Inst. of Tech. Email: jbrewer@caltech.edu.

Brewer, *Susan A.*, Wisconsin-Stevens Point. Piseco, NY. Email: sbrewer@uwsp.edu. Research: American foreign relations.

Breyfogle, *Nicholas*, Ohio State. Columbus, OH. Email: breyfogle.1@osu.edu. Research: 19th-c Russian colonization/religion, Eurasian environmental/Lake Baikal.

Brian, **Amanda M.**, Coastal Carolina. Email: abrian@coastal.edu.

Brian, *Kathleen M*. Mountlake Terrace, WA. Affil: Western Washington. Email: kathleen.brian@ wwu.edu. Research: suicide, eugenics.

Brice, **Lee L.**, Western Illinois. Email: LL-Brice@ wiu.edu.

Briceland, **Alan V.**, Virginia Commonwealth. Email: abricela@vcu.edu.

Brick, *Aaron*. San Francisco, CA. Affil: City Coll., San Francisco. Email: abrick@ccsf.edu.

Brick, *Christopher E.*, George Washington. Washington, DC. Email: cbrick@gwu.edu. Research: US populism and gender, marriage as universal human right.

Brick, *Howard*, Michigan, Ann Arbor. Ann Arbor, MI. Email: hbrick@umich.edu. Research: modern social theory, social movements.

Bricker, **Renee Pilette**, North Georgia. Email: renee.bricker@ung.edu.

Bridenthal, *Renate*. New York, NY. Affil: Brooklyn, CUNY. Email: RBriden440@gmail. com. Research: Economic crime and state formation.

Bridger, *Sarah*, California Polytechnic State. Brooklyn, NY. Email: sbridger@calpoly.edu. Research: science and ethics, Cold War.

Bridges, **Amy**, California, San Diego. Email: abridges@weber.ucsd.edu.

Bridges, *Mary*. Nashville, TN. Affil: Vanderbilt. Email: mbridges@gmail.com.

Bridges, *Roger D*. Bloomington, IL. Affil: Rutherford B. Hayes Presidential Center. Email: rdbridges@comcast.net. Research:

19th-c African American/Illinois, end of Reconstruction.

Briegel, *Kaye*. Long Beach, CA. Affil: California State, Long Beach. Email: kbriegel@csulb.edu.

Brieger, **Alton G.**, Texas State. Email: ab27@ txstate.edu.

Brier, *Jennifer*, Illinois, Chicago. Chicago, IL. Email: jbrier@uic.edu. Research: gay and lesbian, women.

Briesacher, **Erika L.**, Worcester State. Email: ebriesacher@worcester.edu.

Briggs, **Charles**, Vermont. Email: charles. briggs@uvm.edu.

Briggs, *Jonathyne W.*, Indiana, Northwest. Gary, IN. Email: jwbriggs@iun.edu. Research: postwar France, globalization.

Briggs, **Laura J.**, Massachusetts, Amherst. Email: ljbriggs@wost.umass.edu.

Briggs, **Pamela R.**, Austin Peay State. Email: briggsp@apsu.edu.

Brigham, *Robert K.*, Vassar. Poughkeepsie, NY. Email: robrigham@vassar.edu. Research: US foreign relations, modern America.

Bright, **Charles C.**, Michigan, Ann Arbor. Email: cbright@umich.edu.

Brignac, *Kelly*. Cambridge, MA. Affil: Harvard. Email: brignac@g.harvard.edu.

Briley, **Robert**, Union. Email: cp1796@aol.com.

Briley, *Ron F.* Albuquerque, NM. Affil: Sandia Prep Sch. Email: rbriley@sandiaprep.org. Research: Woody Guthrie and American left, cinematic depiction of baseball in 1950s.

Brilliant, *Mark R.*, California, Berkeley. Email: mbrill@berkeley.edu.

Brimmer, **Brandi Clay**, Spelman. Email: bbrimmer@spelman.edu.

Brinegar, *Sara*. Washington, DC. Email: sgbrinegar@gmail.com.

Bringas-Nostti, *Raul*. San Pedro Cholula, Mexico. Email: raul.bringas@udlap.mx. Research: US-Mexico relations, Mexican business.

Brink, **Maryann E.**, Massachusetts, Boston. Email: maryann.brink@umb.edu.

Brinker, **William**, Tennessee Tech. Email: wbrinker@tntech.edu.

Brinkley, **Douglas G.**, Rice. Email: douglas. brinkley@rice.edu.

Brinkman, **Jamie**, New York State Archives. Email: jamie.brinkman@nysed.gov.

Brinkmann, *Tobias*, Penn State. University Park, PA. Email: thb10@psu.edu. Research: modern Jewish, migration and immigration.

Brinley, *Michael A*. Newbury Park, CA. Affil: Pennsylvania. Email: mical@sas.upenn.edu. Research: city planning, Soviet social.

Brinster, *Kyle*. Jersey City, NJ. Affil: St. John's, NY. Email: kyle.brinster@gmail.com.

Briones, **Matthew Manuel**, Chicago. Email: brio@uchicago.edu.

Briscoe, *Dolph*, *IV*. San Antonio, TX. Affil: Texas A&M, San Antonio. Email: dbriscoe@utexas. edu. Research: Texas politics since 1945, 20th-c US political and social.

Brison, **Jeffrey**, Queen's, Can. Email: brisonj@ queensu.ca.

Bristol, **Douglas Walter**, **Jr.**, Southern Mississippi. Email: douglas.bristol@usm.edu.

Bristol, **Joan**, George Mason. Email: jbristol@ gmu.edu.

Bristow, *Edward*, Fordham. Email: ebristow@ fordham.edu.

Bristow, Nancy K., *Puget Sound*. Email: nbristow@pugetsound.edu.

Brito de Freitas, Iohana. Chicago, IL. Email: iohanamail@gmail.com.

Britsch, R. Lanier, *Brigham Young*. Email: lanny@byu.edu.

Britt, Andrew Graham. Winston Salem, NC. Affil: North Carolina Sch. of the Arts. Email: andrewgbritt@gmail.com.

Brittain, James E., *Georgia Inst. of Tech.*

Britten, Thomas A., *Texas-Rio Grande Valley*. Email: thomas.britten@utrgv.edu.

Britto, Lina M., *Northwestern*. Evanston, IL. Email: lina.britto@northwestern.edu. Research: marijuana/narcotrafficking/war on drugs, state formation/popular culture/identity.

Britton, Jason. Calhan, CO. Affil: Bureau of Reclamation. Email: jcbritton@protonmail.com.

Britton, John A., *Francis Marion*. Email: jbritton@fmarion.edu.

Brittsan, Zachary, *Texas Tech*. Lubbock, TX. Email: zachary.brittsan@ttu.edu. Research: 19th-c Mexico, social and cultural.

Brizuela-Garcia, Esperanza, *Montclair State*. Email: brizuelagare@mail.montclair.edu.

Broadbridge, Anne F., *Massachusetts, Amherst*. Email: broadbridge@history.umass.edu.

Broadhead, Will, *MIT*. Email: williamb@mit.edu.

Brobst, Peter John, *Ohio*. Email: brobst@ohio.edu.

Broc, Loren A. Schenectady, NY. Email: labroc@capital.net. Research: revivalism in antebellum US, religious enthusiasm and insanity.

Brock, Julia, *Alabama, Tuscaloosa*. Email: jbrock2@ua.edu.

Brock, Lisa A., *Kalamazoo*. Email: lbrock@kzoo.edu.

Brock, Michelle D., *Washington and Lee*. Lexington, VA. Email: brockm@wlu.edu. Research: religion and culture in early modern Scotland, religion in Atlantic world.

Brockett, Gavin, *Wilfrid Laurier*. Email: gbrockett@wlu.ca.

Brockey, Liam Matthew, *Michigan State*. East Lansing, MI. Email: brockey@msu.edu. Research: early modern southern Europe, Portuguese Empire.

Brockington, William S., Jr., *South Carolina Aiken*. Email: billb@usca.edu.

Brockopp, Jonathan, *Penn State*. Email: jeb38@psu.edu.

Brockwell, Charles W., *Louisville*.

Brodbeck, David, *California, Irvine*. Email: david.brodbeck@uci.edu.

Brodie, Janet Farrell, *Claremont Grad*. Pacific Palisades, CA. Email: janet.brodie@cgu.edu. Research: Cold War social, post-WWII US.

Brodrecht, Grant R. Winter Park, FL. Affil: Geneva Sch. Email: grantb@alumni.nd.edu. Research: Civil War and Reconstruction, religion and politics.

Brodsky, Adriana Mariel, *St. Mary's, Md*. Email: ambrodsky@smcm.edu.

Brody, David, *California, Davis*. Kensington, CA. Email: brodyiir@berkeley.edu. Research: labor and New Deal, American labor law.

Broedel, Hans Peter, *North Dakota*. Email: hans.broedel@und.edu.

Broesamle, John J., *California State, Northridge*.

Brogdon, Frederick W., *Georgia Southern*.

Broggie, Matthew D., *Austin Peay State*. Email: broggiem@apsu.edu.

Brogi, Alessandro, *Arkansas, Fayetteville*. Email: abrogi@uark.edu.

Broich, John E., *Case Western Reserve*. Email: john.broich@case.edu.

Brokaw, Cynthia J., *Brown*. Email: Cynthia_Brokaw@Brown.edu.

Broman, Thomas H., *Wisconsin-Madison*. Email: thbroman@wisc.edu.

Brondarbit, Alex. Santa Cruz, CA. Affil: California, Santa Cruz. Email: arbrondarbit@gmail.com. Research: medieval high politics and government, gender and sexuality.

Bronson, Adam P. Durham, United Kingdom. Affil: Durham. Email: adam.p.bronson@durham.ac.uk. Research: democracy and political culture, rumors.

Bronstein, Jamie L., *New Mexico State*. Email: jbronste@nmsu.edu.

Brook, Eva Paulette. Moscow, ID. Affil: Idaho. Email: broo7518@vandals.uidaho.edu.

Brook, Timothy J., *British Columbia*. Vancouver, BC, Canada. Email: tim.brook@ubc.ca. Research: modern China.

Brooke, John L., *Ohio State*. Columbus, OH. Email: brooke.10@osu.edu. Research: 1860 US civil society/public sphere, global environmental.

Brooke, Sandra Ludig, *Huntington Library*. Email: sbrooke@huntington.org.

Brooke, Stephen J., *York, Can*. Email: sjbrooke@yorku.ca.

Brookins, Julia Akinyi, *AHA*. Austin, TX. Email: jbrookins@historians.org. Research: German immigration to US Southwest, reproduction of nationalism and race.

Brooks, A. Taeko. Northampton, MA. Affil: Massachusetts Amherst. Email: atbrooks@research.umass.edu. Research: early Chinese historiography, early Chinese philosophy.

Brooks, Cecelia R. Langston, OK. Affil: Oklahoma State. Email: revcrbrooks@aol.com. Research: American black progressives/New Deal, public.

Brooks, Charles E., *Texas A&M*. Email: c-brooks@tamu.edu.

Brooks, Clayton M., *Mary Baldwin*. Email: cbrooks@mbc.edu.

Brooks, Corey, *York, Pa*. Email: cbrooks4@ycp.edu.

Brooks, Danielle DiMauro. Brentwood, NY. Affil: Suffolk County Comm. Coll., SUNY. Email: dimaurd@sunysuffolk.edu. Research: sexuality in ancient Roman Empire, Walt Disney and WWII propaganda.

Brooks, E. Willis, *North Carolina, Chapel Hill*. Email: ewbrooks@live.unc.edu.

Brooks, Emily. Brooklyn, NY. Affil: Graduate Center, CUNY. Email: ebrooks@gradcenter.cuny.edu. Research: 20th-c US crime.

Brooks, George E., Jr., *Indiana*.

Brooks, James F., *California, Santa Barbara*. Email: jbrooks@history.ucsb.edu.

Brooks, Jeffrey P., *Johns Hopkins (Hist.)*. Baltimore, MD. Email: brooksjp@jhu.edu; brooksjef@gmail.com. Research: Russian high and low culture, Russian literature/art/popular culture.

Brooks, Jennifer E., *Auburn*. Email: jebrooks@auburn.edu.

Brooks, Michael E., *Bowling Green State*. Email: mebrook@bgsu.edu.

Brooks, Nathan M., *New Mexico State*. Arlington, VA. Email: nbrooks@nmsu.edu. Research: Russian chemistry, D.I. Mendeleev.

Brooks, Pam E., *Oberlin*. Email: pam.brooks@oberlin.edu.

Brooks, Susannah J. Freiburg, Germany. Affil: Albert-Ludwigs. Email: sus.j.brooks@gmail.com. Research: American disaster relief in 1920s China, humanitarianism/philanthropy.

Brooks Hedstrom, Darlene L., *Wittenberg*. Email: dbrookshedstrom@wittenberg.edu.

Broomall, James Joseph, *Shepherd*.

Brophy, Christina S. Chicago, IL. Affil: Triton. Email: christinabrophy@triton.edu. Research: folklore, death customs.

Brophy, James M., *Delaware*. Newark, DE. Email: jbrophy@udel.edu. Research: popular political culture 1789-1848, political literacy in Europe 1850-1941.

Brose, Eric Dorn, *Drexel*. Email: broseed@drexel.edu.

Brosnan, Kathleen Anne, *Oklahoma (Hist.)*. Norman, OK. Email: kbrosnan@ou.edu. Research: California wine, transnational wine.

Brosseder, Claudia R., *Illinois, Urbana-Champaign*. Email: cbrossed@illinois.edu.

Brostowski, Allen A. Mullica Hill, NJ.

Brough, Kerry. Phoenix, AZ. Email: kbrough@cox.net.

Broussard, Albert S., *Texas A&M*. Email: a-broussard@tamu.edu.

Broussard, Joyce L., *California State, Northridge*. Email: joyce.broussard@csun.edu.

Browder, Dewey A., *Austin Peay State*. Email: browderd@apsu.edu.

Browder, Dorothea, *Western Kentucky*. Email: dorothea.browder@wku.edu.

Browder, Tom. Seeley Lake, MT. Affil: BL Solutions LLC. Email: tbrowder@yahoo.com.

Brower, Benjamin Claude, *Texas, Austin*. Email: benbrower@utexas.edu.

Brower, M. Brady, *Weber State*. Email: mbrower@weber.edu.

Brown, Alex R. Alexandria, VA. Affil: Work4U?. Email: alexb.42@yahoo.com.

Brown, Ashley, *Wisconsin-Madison*. Email: abrown62@wisc.edu.

Brown, Blake, *St. Mary's, Can*. Email: blake.brown@smu.ca.

Brown, Carolyn A., *Rutgers*. Email: cbrown@panix.com.

Brown, Chandos Michael, *William and Mary*. Email: cmbrow@wm.edu.

Brown, Christopher L., *Columbia (Hist.)*. New York, NY. Email: clb2140@columbia.edu. Research: early British Empire, slavery.

Brown, Clayton D., *Utah State*. Email: clayton.brown@usu.edu.

Brown, Courtney. Pensacola, FL. Email: cbrown052010@gmail.com.

Brown, D. Clayton, *Texas Christian*.

Brown, Dona L., *Vermont*. Burlington, VT. Email: dona.brown@uvm.edu. Research: agriculture, regional.

Brown, Dorothy M., *Georgetown*. Email: brownd@georgetown.edu.

Brown, Elizabeth A. R. New York, NY. Affil: Brooklyn, CUNY; Graduate Center, CUNY. Email: earbrown160@aol.com. Research: feudalism, medieval and early modern France.

Brown, *Elspeth H.*, *Toronto*. Toronto, ON, Canada. Email: elspeth.brown@utoronto.ca. Research: visual culture, American social and cultural.

Brown, *Emilyn Laura*, *Arthur and Elizabeth Schlesinger Library*. Email: Emilyn_Brown@radcliffe.edu.

Brown, *Frederick L.* Seattle, WA. Email: fbrown1455@gmail.com.

Brown, Gates, *US Army Command Coll.* Email: gates.m.brown2.civ@mail.mil.

Brown, Gregory Stephen, *Nevada, Las Vegas.* Email: gbrown@unlv.nevada.edu.

Brown, H. Haines, *Central Connecticut State.* Email: BrownH@mail.ccsu.edu.

Brown, Howard G., *Binghamton, SUNY.* Email: hgbrown@binghamton.edu.

Brown, Jeffrey P., *New Mexico State.* Email: jbrown@nmsu.edu.

Brown, *Jeffrey Scott*, *New Brunswick.* Email: jsbrown@unb.ca.

Brown, Jennifer Corrinne, *Texas A&M, Corpus Christi.* Email: jennifer.brown@tamucc.edu.

Brown, *Jeremy*, *Simon Fraser.* Email: jeremy_brown@sfu.ca.

Brown, Jerome F., *New Mexico State.*

Brown, John K., *Virginia.* Email: jkb6d@virginia.edu.

Brown, *Jonathan Charles*, *Texas, Austin.* Austin, TX. Email: j.brown@austin.utexas.edu. Research: Cold War, Cuban Revolution.

Brown, *Joshua*, *Graduate Center, CUNY.* New York, NY. Email: jbrown@gc.cuny.edu. Research: visual culture of US Civil War, 19th-c visual culture.

Brown, *Judith C.*, *Wesleyan.* Berkeley, CA. Email: jbrown@wesleyan.edu. Research: higher education, grand ducal Tuscany.

Brown, Karl William, *Wisconsin-Whitewater.* Email: brownk@uww.edu.

Brown, Kate E., *Western Kentucky.* Email: kate.brown@wku.edu.

Brown, Kate Pride, *Georgia Inst. of Tech.* Email: k.p.brown@gatech.edu.

Brown, *Kathleen M.*, *Pennsylvania.* Merion Station, PA. Email: kabrown@sas.upenn.edu. Research: colonial America, popular culture.

Brown, Kathren A., *Utah Valley.* Email: brownkt@uvu.edu.

Brown, *Keisha Alexandria*, *Tennessee State.* Lithonia, GA. Email: kbrown110@tnstate.edu; keishab241@gmail.com. Research: modern China, transnational/race and ethnic studies.

Brown, Kendall Walker, *Brigham Young.* Email: kwb3@byu.edu.

Brown, Kenny L., *Central Oklahoma.* Email: kebrown@uco.edu.

Brown, *LaKisha Lasha.* Fresno, TX. Affil: Texas Southern. Email: lklbrown16@gmail.com.

Brown, Marie, *Kansas.* Email: mgbrown@ku.edu.

Brown, Marley R., III, *William and Mary.* Email: mrbro1@wm.edu.

Brown, *Mary Elizabeth.* Staten Island, NY. Affil: Marymount Manhattan. Email: mbrown1@mmm.edu. Research: post-WWII DPs traveling through NYC.

Brown, *Megan*, *Swarthmore.* Swarthmore, PA. Email: megan.brown@swarthmore.edu. Research: modern Europe, European integration.

Brown, *Melissa J.* Cambridge, MA. Affil: Harvard-Yenching Inst. Email: melbrown@fas.harvard.

edu. Research: rural Chinese female labor/footbinding 1880-1950, gender/kinship/economy in China 1600-2010.

Brown, Nikki Lynn Marie, *New Orleans.* Email: nlbrown2@uno.edu.

Brown, *Peter B.* West Hartford, CT. Affil: Rhode Island Coll. Email: cany@snet.net. Research: Muscovite administrative, East Slavic/Finno-Ugric associations 800-1500.

Brown, Philip C., *Ohio State.* Email: brown.113@osu.edu.

Brown, R. Keith, *Tennessee Tech.* Email: rbrown1@k12tn.net.

Brown, Ras Michael, *Southern Illinois, Carbondale.* Email: rasmlb@siu.edu.

Brown, Richard D., *Connecticut, Storrs.* Email: richard.d.brown@uconn.edu.

Brown, Robert, *Sonoma State.*

Brown, Roger H., *American.* Email: rbrown9@aol.com.

Brown, Ronald C., *Texas State.* Email: rb04@txstate.edu.

Brown, Scot D., *UCLA.* Email: sbrown@history.ucla.edu.

Brown, *Shana J.*, *Hawai'i, Manoa.* Honolulu, HI. Email: shanab@hawaii.edu. Research: Qing-republican Chinese cultural, republican economic.

Brown, *Simon.* Berkeley, CA. Affil: California, Berkeley. Email: simon.brown@berkeley.edu.

Brown, Spencer H., *Western Illinois.* Email: SH-Brown@wiu.edu.

Brown, *Stanford Maxwell.* Macon, GA. Affil: Auburn. Email: stanbrown32@aol.com. Research: southern US religious, southern US educational.

Brown, Tamara L., *Bowie State.* Email: tlbrown@bowiestate.edu.

Brown, Tammy L., *Miami, Ohio.* Email: browntl3@miamioh.edu.

Brown, Theodore M., *Rochester.* Email: theodore_brown@urmc.rochester.edu.

Brown, Thomas A., *Augustana.* Email: tombrown@augustana.edu.

Brown, Thomas J., *South Carolina, Columbia.* Email: browntj@mailbox.sc.edu.

Brown, Timothy Scott, *Northeastern.* Email: ti.brown@neu.edu.

Brown, Tristan, *MIT.* Email: tristanb@mit.edu.

Brown, Victoria Bissell, *Grinnell.* Email: brownv@grinnell.edu.

Brown, Vincent Aaron, *Harvard (Hist.).* Email: brown8@fas.harvard.edu.

Brown, Walter R., *Memphis.* Email: wrbrown@memphis.edu.

Brown, Warren C., *California Inst. of Tech.* Email: wcb@hss.caltech.edu.

Brown, *Willa H.* Cambridge, MA. Affil: Harvard. Email: willabrown@fas.harvard.edu.

Brown, William Allan Sazie, *Miami, Ohio.* Email: brownwa3@miamioh.edu.

Brown Pellum, Kimberly, *Texas Southern.* Email: BrownKD@tsu.edu.

Brown-Coronel, *Margie*, *California State, Fullerton.* Fullerton, CA. Email: mbrown-coronel@fullerton.edu. Research: US.

Browne, *Alice.* Brooklyn, NY. Affil: New-York Hist. Soc. Email: Alicebrowne@mindspring.com.

Browne, George P., *Seton Hall.*

Browne, Janet, *Harvard (Hist. of Science).* Email: jbrowne@fas.harvard.edu.

Browne, *Randy M.*, *Xavier, Ohio.* Cincinnati, OH. Email: browner@xavier.edu; randybrowne@

gmail.com. Research: Atlantic slavery, British Caribbean.

Browne, *Sheri B.*, *Tennessee State.* Email: sbrowne@tnstate.edu.

Brownell, *Blaine A.* Evanston, IL. Email: babrownell@gmail.com. Research: universities.

Brownell, *Kathryn Cramer*, *Purdue.* West Lafayette, IN. Email: brownell@purdue.edu. Research: Hollywood and politics, media/politics/popular culture.

Browning, Capt Nicholas, *US Military Acad.* Email: nicholas.browning@usma.edu.

Browning, Christopher R., *North Carolina, Chapel Hill.* Email: cbrownin@email.unc.edu.

Browning, *Elizabeth Grennan.* Bloomington, IN. Affil: Indiana. Email: eabrowni@indiana.edu. Research: environmental, intellectual.

Browning, Judkin, *Appalachian State.* Email: browningjj@appstate.edu.

Browning, Reed S., *Kenyon.* Email: browninr@kenyon.edu.

Browning, Robert S., *Texas, San Antonio.* Email: robert.browning@utsa.edu.

Browning, *Robert.* China Township, MI. Email: robertbrowning421@yahoo.com.

Brownlee, *W. Elliot*, *California, Santa Barbara.* Santa Barbara, CA. Email: brownlee@history.ucsb.edu. Research: American economic.

Brownlie, Robin Jarvis, *Manitoba.* Email: robin.brownlie@umanitoba.ca.

Brown-Nagin, *Tomiko*, *Harvard (Hist.).* Cambridge, MA. Email: tbrownnagin@law.harvard.edu. Research: US legal, US social.

Broxmeyer, *Jeffrey.* Ferndale, MI. Email: jeffrey.broxmeyer@utoledo.edu.

Broyld, Daniel J., *Central Connecticut State.* Email: d.broyld@ccsu.edu.

Brubaker, *Jared.* San Francisco, CA. Email: jbrubaker@gmail.com.

Brubaker, Jeffrey, *SUNY, Coll. Geneseo.* Email: brubaker@geneseo.edu.

Brubaker, *Robert Paul.* Fayetteville, AR. Affil: Arkansas, Fayetteville. Email: robertb@umich.edu.

Bruce, *Emily Claire.* Morris, MN. Affil: Minnesota, Morris. Email: bruce088@umn.edu.

Bruce, Gary S., *Waterloo.* Email: gsbruce@uwaterloo.ca.

Bruce, *Judith Ball.* Sandston, VA. Affil: Virginia Commonwealth. Email: jbbruce45@comcast.net.

Bruce, Scott G., *Fordham.* Email: sbruce3@fordham.edu.

Bruce, *Shaun.* Chicago, IL. Affil: Pritzker Coll. Prep. Email: shaun.p.bruce@gmail.com.

Bruce, Travis, *McGill.* Email: travis.bruce@mcgill.ca.

Brucken, Rowland M., *Norwich.* Email: rbrucken@norwich.edu.

Bruckner, *Daniel R.* Jefferson, PA. Email: brucknerdan05@comcast.net.

Brudney, Edward, *Tennessee, Chattanooga.* Email: edward-brudney@utc.edu.

Brueck, Gregory J., *California State, East Bay.* Email: gregory.brueck@csueastbay.edu.

Brueckenhaus, Daniel, *Beloit.* Email: brueckenhausd@beloit.edu.

Bruegel, *Martin.* Paris, France. Affil: Institut National de la Recherche Agronomique. Email: Martin.Bruegel@inra.fr.

Bruehoefener, **Friederike**, *Texas-Rio Grande Valley*. Email: friederike.bruehoefener@utrgv. edu.

Bruening, **Michael W.**, *Missouri Science and Tech*. Email: bruening@mst.edu.

Bruess, **Gregory L.**, *Northern Iowa*. Email: gregory.bruess@uni.edu.

Bruey, **Alison Jane**, *North Florida*. Jacksonville, FL. Email: alison.bruey@unf.edu. Research: social movements, Chile.

Bruggemann, **Julia C.**, *DePauw*. Email: jbruggemann@depauw.edu.

Brummett, **Palmira**, *Tennessee, Knoxville*. Email: palmira@utk.edu.

Brundage, **Anthony**. Claremont, CA. Affil: California State Polytechnic, Pomona. Email: albrundage@cpp.edu. Research: English poor laws 1750-1930, British and US historians 1870-1930.

Brundage, **David**, *California, Santa Cruz*. Santa Cruz, CA. Email: brundage@ucsc.edu. Research: Irish nationalism in US, civil rights in US and Northern Ireland.

Brundage, **James A.**, *Kansas*. Email: jabrun@ukans.edu.

Brundage, **W. Fitzhugh**, *North Carolina, Chapel Hill*. Chapel Hill, NC. Email: brundage@email. unc.edu. Research: torture in US, African Americans and mass culture.

Brune, **Jeffrey A.** Washington, DC. Affil: Gallaudet. Email: jeff.brune@gallaudet.edu. Research: modern US disability.

Brunelle, **Gayle K.**, *California State, Fullerton*. Fullerton, CA. Email: gbrunelle@fullerton.edu. Research: 17th-c French colonization, France 1930-45.

Brunelli, **Giampiero**. Roma, Italy. Email: giampiero.brunelli@gmail.com.

Brungardt, **Maurice P.**, *Loyola, New Orleans*. Email: brungard@loyno.edu.

Brunk, **Samuel F.**, *Texas, El Paso*. El Paso, TX. Email: sbrunk@utep.edu. Research: Mexican political culture, Chihuahuan Desert environmental.

Bruno, **Andy R.**, *Northern Illinois*. Email: abruno2@niu.edu.

Bruno, **Michael JS**. Yonkers, NY. Affil: St. Joseph's Seminary. Email: mbruno@dunwoodie.edu.

Bruno-Jofre, **Rosa**, *Queen's, Can.* Kingston, ON, Canada. Email: brunojor@queensu. ca. Research: education, women religious/ teaching congregations.

Brunsman, **Denver A.**, *George Washington*. Email: brunsman@gwu.edu.

Bruscino, **Thomas A.**, **Jr.**, *US Army Command Coll.* Email: thomas.a.bruscino.civ@mail.mil.

Brushett, **Kevin**, *Royal Military*. Email: brushett-k@rmc.ca.

Bruther, **Betty J.** Indianapolis, IN. Email: bjmilhist@aol.com. Research: medieval institutional, medieval and modern serial murder.

Bryan, **Jimmy L.**, **Jr.**, *Lamar*. Email: jlbryan@lamar.edu.

Bryan, **Mark Evans**. Granville, OH. Affil: Denison. Email: bryanm@denison.edu. Research: 18th-c US popular culture, long 19th-c US theatre.

Bryan, **Peter Cullen**. Middletown, PA. Affil: Penn State, Capital Campus. Email: pcb144@psu. edu.

Bryan, **Tracy L.**, *Virginia Museum of Hist.* Email: tbryan@VirginiaHistory.org.

Bryans, **William S.**, *Oklahoma State*. Email: bill. bryans@okstate.edu.

Bryant, **Chad**, *North Carolina, Chapel Hill*. Email: bryantc@email.unc.edu.

Bryant, **Elizabeth Ann**. Houston, TX. Affil: Houston Comm. Coll. Email: drelizabethbryant@gmail.com. Research: homosexuality in Holocaust, US during Holocaust.

Bryant, **Jonathan M.**, *Georgia Southern*. Email: jbryant@georgiasouthern.edu.

Bryant, **Lawrence M**. Chico, CA. Affil: California State, Chico. Email: lbryant@csuchico.edu.

Bryant, **Michael Scott**, *Bryant*. Email: mbryant@bryant.edu.

Bryant, **Sherwin K.**, *Northwestern*. Email: s-bryant@northwestern.edu.

Bryant, **William Andrew**. Tulare, CA. Email: bryant@cvc.org.

Bryce, **Benjamin**, *Northern British Columbia*. Prince George, BC, Canada. Email: benjamin. bryce@unbc.ca; benbryce@gmail.com. Research: migration/immigration, education/ health.

Brychta, **Savannah MacLeod**. Atlantic Beach, FL. Email: n00712756@unf.edu.

Bryden, **Penny E.**, *Canadian Hist. Assoc.* Email: pbryden@uvic.ca.

Bryen, **Ari Z.**, *Vanderbilt*. Email: ari.z.bryen@vanderbilt.edu.

Brzycki, **Melissa A.**, *Monmouth*. West Long Branch, NJ. Email: mbrzycki@monmouth.edu.

Bsheer, **Rosie**, *Harvard (Hist.)*. Email: rbsheer@fas.harvard.edu.

Bsumek, **Erika**, *Texas, Austin*. Email: embsumek@austin.utexas.edu.

Bu, **Liping**, *Alma*. Alma, MI. Email: bulipi@alma. edu. Research: China's modernization and public health, Western influence in Asia.

Bubelis, **William S.**, *Washington, St. Louis*. Email: wbubelis@wustl.edu.

Bucca, **Robert D.**, **III**. Russellville, TN. Email: rbucca@vols.utk.edu. Research: Civil War, Reconstruction.

Buccellati, **Giorgio**, *UCLA*. Email: buccella@ucla. edu.

Bucco, **Jack A.**, *Austin Comm. Coll.* Email: jbucco@austincc.edu.

Buchanan, **Andrew N.**, *Vermont*. Email: andrew. buchanan@uvm.edu.

Buchanan, **Elizabeth**. Tryon, NC. Affil: Findlay. Email: elizabeth.f.buchanan@gmail.com. Research: premodern economies, early Christian rhetoric and law.

Buchanan, **Shirley E**. Mililani, HI. Affil: Hawaii, Manoa. Email: sbuchana@hawaii.edu.

Buchberger, **Erica**, *Texas-Rio Grande Valley*. Email: erica.buchberger@utrgv.edu.

Buchberger, **Kyle**. Tacoma, WA. Email: buchberg12@gmail.com.

Buchbinder, **Lorraine**, *North Georgia*. Email: lorraine.buchbinder@ung.edu.

Buchenau, **Jurgen**, *North Carolina, Charlotte*. Charlotte, NC. Email: jbuchenau@uncc.edu. Research: Mexican Revolution, Mexico in world affairs.

Bucher, **Greta**, *US Military Acad.* Email: greta. bucher@usma.edu.

Bucher, **Henry Hale**, **Jr.**, *Austin Coll.* Email: hbucher@austincollege.edu.

Bucher, **Jesse W.**, *Roanoke*. Email: bucher@roanoke.edu.

Bucholz, **Arden K.**, **Jr.** Brockport, NY. Affil: SUNY, Coll. Brockport. Email: abucholz@brockport. edu.

Bucholz, **Robert**, *Loyola, Chicago*. Email: rbuchol@luc.edu.

Buchwald, **Jed Z.**, *California Inst. of Tech.* Email: buchwald@hss.caltech.edu.

Buck, **David D.**, *Wisconsin-Milwaukee*. Milwaukee, WI. Email: davebuck@uwm.edu. Research: 19th-c tea trade, 20th-c Chinese urban.

Buck, **Xavier**. Richmond, CA. Affil: California, Berkeley. Email: xavierbuck12@gmail.com.

Buckaloo, **Derek N.**, *Coe*. Cedar Rapids, IA. Email: dbuckalo@coe.edu. Research: Vietnam syndrome.

Buckelew, **Richard**. Port Orange, FL. Affil: Bethune-Cookman. Email: buckelewr@cookman.edu.

Buckey, **Christopher McNally**. Coronado, CA. Email: ChrisBuckey@msn.com. Research: late 19th-early 20th-c navies, UK Royal Navy 1889-1921.

Buckheit, **Elizabeth**. New Haven, CT. Affil: Yale. Email: elizabeth.buckheit@yale.edu.

Bucki, **Cecelia**, *Fairfield*. Fairfield, CT. Email: cbucki@fairfield.edu. Research: New Deal social policy and taxation, urban labor politics in 1930s.

Bucking, **Scott J.**, *DePaul*. Email: sbucking@depaul.edu.

Buckingham, **Peter H.**, *Linfield*. Email: pbucking@linfield.edu.

Buckley, **Constance R.**, *Loyola, Chicago*. Email: cbuckl@luc.edu.

Buckley, **Eve E.**, *Delaware*. Email: ebuckley@udel.edu.

Buckley, **Jay H.**, *Brigham Young*. Email: jay_buckley@byu.edu.

Buckley, **Roger Norman**, *Connecticut, Storrs*. Email: roger.buckley@uconn.edu.

Bucklin, **Steven J.**, *South Dakota*. Email: Steven. Bucklin@usd.edu.

Buckner, **Timothy R.**, *Troy*. Email: tbuckner48602@troy.edu.

Buckridge, **Steeve O.**, *Grand Valley State*. Email: buckrids@gvsu.edu.

Bucur, **Maria**, *Indiana*. Email: mbucur@indiana. edu.

Buehler-Rappold, **Teresa Leigh**. Austin, TX. Affil: American Public Univ. System. Email: LeighB82@hotmail.com.

Buehner, **Henry**, *Chestnut Hill*. Email: buehnerh@chc.edu.

Buel, **Richard V.**, **Jr.**, *Wesleyan*. Essex, CT. Email: rbuel@wesleyan.edu. Research: pre-Civil War America.

Buenger, **Walter L.**, **Jr.**, *Texas, Austin*. Austin, TX. Email: w-buenger@austin.utexas.edu. Research: Texas and South 1887-1930, 1920s Ku Klux Klan.

Bueno, **Christina M.**, *Northeastern Illinois*. Email: C-Bueno@neiu.edu.

Buerglener, **Robert F.** Durham, NC. Email: rpbuergl@gmail.com. Research: consumer culture, transportation.

Buerkle, **Darcy C.**, *Smith*. Email: dbuerkle@smith.edu.

Buettinger, **Craig**, *Jacksonville*. Email: cbuetti@ju.edu.

Buettner, **Elizabeth A**. Amsterdam, Netherlands. Affil: Amsterdam. Email: E.A.Buettner@uva.nl. Research: Europe after empire, South Asian culture in postwar Britain.

Buff, *Rachel*, *Wisconsin-Milwaukee*. Email: rbuff@uwm.edu.

Buffett, *Neil Philip*. Selden, NY. Affil: Suffolk County Comm. Coll., SUNY. Email: buffetn@sunysuffolk.edu. Research: high school student activism, suburban US.

Buffton, *Deborah*, *Wisconsin-La Crosse*. Email: dbuffton@uwlax.edu.

Buford, *Kellie Wilson*, *Arkansas State*. Email: kbuford@astate.edu.

Bugh, *Glenn R.*, *Virginia Tech*. Email: gbugh@vt.edu.

Buhle, *Mari Jo*, *Brown*. Email: Mari_Buhle@Brown.edu.

Buhle, *Paul M.*, *Brown*. Email: Paul_Buhle@Brown.edu.

Buhler, *Peter*, *Boise State*. Email: pbuhler@boisestate.edu.

Bui, *L. Bao*, *Stephen F. Austin State*. Email: builb@sfasu.edu.

Bukey, *Evan B.*, *Arkansas, Fayetteville*. Fayetteville, AR. Email: ebukey@uark.edu. Research: Nazi Austria, WWII.

Bukowczyk, *John J.*, *Wayne State*. Detroit, MI. Email: aa2092@wayne.edu. Research: American immigration, Polish American.

Bulkley, *Robert D.*, *Jr.* Beaverton, OR. Email: robert.bulkley@frontier.com.

Bull, *Jonathan*. Sapporo, Japan. Affil: Hokkaido. Email: j_e_bull@slav.hokudai.ac.jp.

Bull, *Marcus G.*, *North Carolina, Chapel Hill*. Email: mgbull@email.unc.edu.

Bullard, *Melissa M.*, *North Carolina, Chapel Hill*. Email: mbullard@email.unc.edu.

Bullard, *Wanda Lee*. Lynchburg, VA. Affil: Liberty. Email: bullard1@liberty.edu.

Bulliet, *Richard W.*, *Columbia (Hist.)*. Email: rwb3@columbia.edu.

Bullion, *John L.*, *Missouri, Columbia*. Email: bullionj@missouri.edu.

Bullock, *Michaella*. Sacramento, CA. Email: michaellabullock@gmail.com.

Bulman, *William J.*, *Lehigh*. Email: wib311@lehigh.edu.

Bult, *Conrad J.*, *Calvin*. Email: cbult@calvin.edu.

Bulthuis, *Kyle Timothy*, *Utah State*. Email: kyle.bulthuis@usu.edu.

Bultman, *C. Baars*, *Hope*. Email: bultmanb@hope.edu.

Bumpers, *Jasmine*, *New York State Archives*. Email: jasmine.bumpers@nysed.gov.

Bunch, *Jeffrey*. Santa Clara, CA. Affil: Mission. Email: jbunch14@gmail.com.

Bunch, *Lonnie*. Washington, DC. Affil: Smithsonian Inst. Email: bunchl@si.edu.

Bunch, *Michael C.* Colorado Springs, CO. Affil: Colorado, Colorado Springs. Email: michael.c.bunch@gmail.com. Research: Kosovar-Albanian diaspora/Germany, East Prussian refugees.

Bunch-Lyons, *Beverly A.*, *Virginia Tech*. Alexandria, VA. Email: blyons@vt.edu. Research: juke joints, middle-class African Americans.

Bundles, *A'Lelia P.*, *National Hist. Center*. Washington, DC. Affil: National Archives Found. Email: abundles@gmail.com. Research: Harlem Renaissance and A'Lelia Walker, American business women/African American.

Bundrick, *Sheramy*, *South Florida, St. Petersburg*. Email: bundrick@mail.usf.edu.

Bunk, *Brian D.*, *Massachusetts, Amherst*. Email: bunk@history.umass.edu.

Bunker, *Rachel*. Jersey City, NJ. Affil: Rutgers. Email: rbunker@history.rutgers.edu.

Bunker, *Steven B.*, *Alabama, Tuscaloosa*. Email: sbunker@bama.ua.edu.

Buonincontro, *William E.* Tower Lakes, IL. Affil: Roosevelt. Email: buonincontro@aol.com. Research: Vietnam era.

Burbank, *Jane R.*, *NYU*. New York, NY. Email: jane.burbank@nyu.edu. Research: law, empire.

Burch, *Jessica*. Salt Lake City, UT. Affil: Utah. Email: jessicakburch@gmail.com.

Burch, *Lance*, *Center for Hist. of Physics*. Email: lburch@aip.org.

Burch, *Susan*. Middlebury, VT. Affil: Middlebury. Email: sburch@middlebury.edu. Research: disability/race/ethnicity/nation.

Burchett, *Julie*. Saint Louis, MO. Affil: Webster Groves High Sch. Email: burchett.julie@wgmail.org. Research: US civil rights movement, women's issues.

Burchfield, *Joe D.*, *Northern Illinois*. Email: burchfield@niu.edu.

Burckel, *Nicholas C.* Milwaukee, WI. Affil: Marquette. Email: nicholas.burckel@marquette.edu.

Burdette, *M. Kathryn*, *Omohundro Inst.* Email: mkburd@wm.edu.

Burds, *Jeffrey*, *Northeastern*. Email: j.burds@neu.edu.

Burford, *Dave*. Starkville, MS. Affil: Mississippi State. Email: db2400@msstate.edu.

Burg, *B. Richard*, *Arizona State*.

Burg, *Steven B.*, *Shippensburg*. Shippensburg, PA. Email: sbburg@ship.edu. Research: public, modern US.

Burgess, *Ashley*. Austell, GA. Email: apb4291@students.kennesaw.edu.

Burgess, *Debra*. Terrace Park, OH. Affil: Cincinnati. Email: dburgess202@yahoo.com. Research: early 20th-c immigration, Progressive Era.

Burgess, *Joanne*, *Québec, Montréal*. Email: burgess.joanne@uqam.ca.

Burgess, *Larry E.*, *California, Riverside*. Email: admin@aksmiley.org.

Burgess, *William D.*, *East Tennessee State*. Email: burgessw@etsu.edu.

Burggraaff, *Winfield J.*, *Missouri, Columbia*. Email: burggraaffw@missouri.edu.

Burghart, *William Devon*. Tacoma, WA. Affil: Washington, Tacoma. Email: burghw@uw.edu.

Burgin, *Angus Robinson*, *Johns Hopkins (Hist.)*. Baltimore, MD. Email: burgin@jhu.edu. Research: 20th-c US political/economic/capitalism.

Burgin, *Say*, *Dickinson*. Email: burgins@dickinson.edu.

Burgos, *Adrian*, *Jr.*, *Illinois, Urbana-Champaign*. Email: burgosjr@illinois.edu.

Burgos, *Robert Gilbert*. Chicago, IL. Affil: Chicago. Email: rburgos@uchicago.edu. Research: community formation in 20th-c urban Japan, material culture in minority communities.

Burgtorf, *Jochen*, *California State, Fullerton; Phi Alpha Theta*. Fullerton, CA. Email: jburgtorf@fullerton.edu. Research: Crusades and Latin East, medieval papacy.

Burgwyn, *H. James*, *Jr.* Philadelphia, PA. Affil: West Chester. Email: jburgwyn2@verizon.net.

Burin, *Eric*, *North Dakota*. Email: eric.burin@und.edu.

Burk, *Kathleen*. Harwell, United Kingdom. Affil: Univ. Coll., London. Email: k.burk@ucl.ac.uk. Research: Anglo-American relations since 1497, British and American empires.

Burke, *Chloe S.*, *California State, Sacramento*. Email: cburke@csus.edu.

Burke, *Colin B.*, *Maryland, Baltimore County*. Email: burke@umbc.edu.

Burke, *Edmund M.*, *Coe*.

Burke, *Edmund*, *III*, *California, Santa Cruz*. Email: eburke@ucsc.edu.

Burke, *Flannery*, *St. Louis*. Saint Louis, MO. Email: flannery.burke@slu.edu. Research: early 20th-c art colonies in West.

Burke, *James*, *Capital*.

Burke, *Keelin*. Oak Park, IL. Affil: Newberry Library. Email: burkek@newberry.org.

Burke, *Kyle Bradford*, *Hartwick*. Email: burkek@hartwick.edu.

Burke, *Laurence Mitchell*, *II*. Sterling, VA. Affil: US Naval Acad. Email: BurkeL@si.edu. Research: US Naval Aviation, military innovation.

Burke, *Martin Joseph*, *Graduate Center, CUNY; Lehman, CUNY*. Bronx, NY. Email: mburke1@gc.cuny.edu; martin.burke@lehman.cuny.edu. Research: American cultural, intellectual.

Burke, *Timothy J.*, *Swarthmore*. Email: tburke1@swarthmore.edu.

Burke, *Tony*, *York, Can.* Email: tburke@yorku.ca.

Burkett, *Melanie Lynne*. North Epping, Australia. Affil: Macquarie. Email: melb2001@gmail.com. Research: British Empire, colonial Australia.

Burkholder, *Jared S.*, *Grace*. Email: burkhojs@grace.edu.

Burkholder, *Mark A.*, *Missouri–St. Louis*. Saint Louis, MO. Email: burkholder@umsl.edu; burkm@swbell.net. Research: 18th-c Spanish imperial administration.

Burkholder, *Peter J.* Morristown, NJ. Affil: Fairleigh Dickinson, Florham. Email: burk0032@fdu.edu.

Burkle, *Aaron Scott*, *John Carroll*. Email: aburkle@jcu.edu.

Burks, *John L.*, *Henry Ford Coll.* Email: jburks@hfcc.edu.

Burlingame, *Michael A.*, *Illinois, Springfield*. Email: mburl2@uis.edu.

Burlingham, *Kate*, *California State, Fullerton*. Fullerton, CA. Email: kburlingham@fullerton.edu. Research: US foreign relations, Africa and development.

Burman, *Thomas E.*, *Notre Dame*. Email: tburman@nd.edu.

Burnett, *Amy Nelson*, *Nebraska, Lincoln*. Email: aburnett1@unl.edu.

Burnett, *D. Graham*, *Princeton*. Email: dburnett@princeton.edu.

Burnette, *Rand*. Jacksonville, IL. Affil: MacMurry. Research: Thomas Hutchins, cartography.

Burnham, *Louisa A.*, *Middlebury*. Email: lburnham@middlebury.edu.

Burno, *Philip M.* Chicago, IL.

Burns, *Andrea A.*, *Appalachian State*. Email: burnsaa@appstate.edu.

Burns, *Barbara*, *Southeastern Louisiana*. Email: bburns@selu.edu.

Burns, *Ian*. Columbus, OH. Affil: Northern Illinois. Email: Ian.Burns13@gmail.com. Research: Irish Volunteers (IV), 20th-c Irish nationalism.

Burns, *Jeffrey M.*, *American Catholic Hist. Assoc.* Oceanside, CA. Affil: Academy of American Franciscan Hist. Email: burnsjm@burnsjm.cnc. net; acadafh@fst.edu.

Burns, *Jennifer L.*, *Stanford.* Stanford, CA. Email: jenniferburns@stanford.edu. Research: US right wing thought, political culture.

Burns, *Kathryn J.*, *North Carolina, Chapel Hill.* Chapel Hill, NC. Email: kjburns@email.unc. edu. Research: colonial Andes, gender/power.

Burns, *Linda Green.* Oak Park, IL. Affil: Oak Park River Forest High Sch. Email: lburns@oprfhs. org. Research: teaching of history.

Burns, *Michael*, *Mount Holyoke.* Email: mburns@ mtholyoke.edu.

Burns, *Paul E.*, *Nevada, Las Vegas.*

Burns, *Richard Dean*, *California State, Los Angeles.* Email: rdburns@earthlink.net.

Burns, *Richard.* Maryland Heights, MO. Email: richardburns@mac.com.

Burns, *Susan L.*, *Chicago.* Chicago, IL. Email: slburns@uchicago.edu. Research: 19th-c Japanese medicine and body.

Burns, *Thomas S.*, *Emory.* Email: histsb@emory. edu.

Burnside, *Ron*, *Presbyterian.*

Burnstein, *Daniel E.*, *Seattle.* Email: danielbu@ seattleu.edu.

Burr, *Christina*, *Windsor.* Email: burrc@ uwindsor.ca.

Burr, *David D.*, *Virginia Tech.* Email: olivi@vt.edu.

Burrell, *Kristopher Bryan.* New York, NY. Affil: Hostos Comm. Coll., CUNY. Email: kbryanburrell@yahoo.com. Research: civil rights movement, black intellectuals.

Burrill, *Emily Susan*, *North Carolina, Chapel Hill.* Email: eburrill@email.unc.edu.

Burrow, *David I.*, *South Dakota.* Vermillion, SD. Email: david.burrow@usd.edu. Research: public opinion in early 19th-c Russia, social history of intelligentsia.

Burrowes, *Nicole*, *Texas, Austin.* Email: nburrowes@utexas.edu.

Burson, *Jeffrey D.*, *Georgia Southern.* Statesboro, GA. Email: jburson@georgiasouthern. edu. Research: radical and theological enlightenments, comparative European enlightenments.

Burson, *Phyllis J.* Bethesda, MD. Email: pburson@verizon.net.

Burstein, *Andrew*, *Louisiana State.* Email: aburstein@lsu.edu.

Burstein, *Stanley M.*, *California State, Los Angeles.* Email: sburste@calstatela.edu.

Burstyn, *Joan N.*, *Syracuse.* Email: jburstyn@ syr.edu.

Burt, *Sean*, *North Dakota State.* Email: sean. burt@ndsu.edu.

Burtch, *Andrew P.*, *Carleton, Can.* Email: andrew.burtch@carleton.ca.

Burton, *Antoinette M.*, *Illinois, Urbana-Champaign.* Urbana, IL. Email: aburton@ illinois.edu. Research: British Empire, world.

Burton, *Chris.* Lethbridge, AB, Canada. Affil: Lethbridge. Email: christopher.burton@uleth. ca. Research: postwar Russia, environment.

Burton, *Danny E.*, *North Alabama.* Email: deburton@una.edu.

Burton, *John*, *DePaul.* Email: jburton@depaul. edu.

Burton, *Myra Frances*, *US Dept. of State.*

Burton, *Orville Vernon.* Ninety Six, SC. Affil: Clemson. Email: vburton@clemson.edu.

Research: sectional conflict/Civil War/ Reconstruction, civil rights movement.

Burton, *Valerie C.*, *Memorial, Newfoundland.* Email: vburton@mun.ca.

Burton-Rose, *Daniel J.*, *Northern Arizona.* Email: Daniel.Burton-Rose@nau.edu.

Burwell, *Fred*, *Beloit.* Email: burwellf@beloit. edu.

Burzlaff, *Jan.* Sundern, Germany. Affil: Harvard. Email: burzlaff@g.harvard.edu.

Busch, *Allan*, *Jr.*, *Fort Hays State.*

Busch, *David.* Ann Arbor, MI. Affil: Carnegie Mellon. Email: dbusch@andrew.cmu.edu.

Buschmann, *Rainer F.*, *California State, Channel Islands.* Email: rainer.buschmann@csuci.edu.

Buseman, *Michael*, *North Georgia.* Email: michael.buseman@ung.edu.

Bush, *Alexandra*, *Massachusetts Hist. Soc.* Email: abush@masshist.org.

Bush, *Erin N.*, *North Georgia.* Centreville, VA. Email: erin.bush@ung.edu; ebush3@gmu. edu. Research: violent women in the South, gender and capital crimes in America.

Bush, *Gregory W.*, *Miami.* Email: publicbush@ gmail.com.

Bush, *Kelly A.* New York, NY. Email: kbush99@ yahoo.com. Research: modern art, 19th-c art.

Bush, *Paul Westley.* Washington, DC. Affil: Catholic. Email: 68bush@cardinalmail.cua. edu. Research: Carolingian diplomatics.

Bush, *Scott.* Austin, TX. Affil: Texas ESC Region 13. Email: knowthepast@gmail.com.

Bush, *William S.*, *Texas A&M, San Antonio.* Email: william.bush@tamusa.edu.

Bushelle, *Emi Foulk*, *Western Washington.* Email: Emi.Foulk@wwu.edu.

Bushkovitch, *Paul A.*, *Yale.* Email: paul. bushkovitch@yale.edu.

Bushman, *Richard L.*, *Columbia (Hist.).* Email: rlb7@columbia.edu.

Bushnell, *Amy Turner*, *Brown.* East Greenwich, RI. Email: Amy_Bushnell@Brown.edu. Research: indigenous Americans to 1900, frontiers and borderlands to 1900.

Bushnell, *John S.*, *Northwestern.* Evanston, IL. Email: j-bushnell@northwestern.edu. Research: Russia.

Bushnell, *Paul E.*, *Illinois Wesleyan.* Email: bushnell@iwu.edu.

Busquets, *Lizette.* Athens, GA. Affil: Georgia. Email: lbusquet@uga.edu.

Bussan, *Samuel*, *Lehman, CUNY.* Email: sbussan@gradcenter.cuny.edu.

Bussel, *Bob*, *Oregon.* Email: bussel@uoregon. edu.

Bussey, *Charles J.*, *Western Kentucky.* Email: charles.bussey@wku.edu.

Bussiere, *David W.*, *Jr.* Easton, PA. Email: dbussiere@trhistorical.com.

Bustamante, *Michael*, *Florida International.* Miami, FL. Email: mbustama@fiu.edu. Research: historical memory, Cuban Revolution.

Busto, *Rudy*, *California, Santa Barbara.* Email: rude@religion.ucsb.edu.

Butcher, *Tom N.* Charlottesville, VA. Affil: Virginia. Email: tmbutcher@virginia.edu. Research: Europe/Germany/Austria, sex/ gender/sexuality.

Butkis, *John F.* Beaumont, CA. Email: jbutkis@ hotmail.com.

Butko, *Brian*, *Duquesne.* Email: butkob@duq. edu.

Butler, *Elisabeth F.*, *US Senate Hist. Office.* Email: elisabeth_butler@sec.senate.gov.

Butler, *James Michael*, *Jr.* St. Augustine, FL. Affil: Flagler. Email: mbutler1@flagler.edu. Research: Civil Rights Movement, African American since 1969.

Butler, *Jon*, *Yale.* Minneapolis, MN. Email: jon. butler@yale.edu. Research: New York City religion 1870-1960.

Butler, *Kim D.*, *Rutgers.* Piscataway, NJ. Email: kbutler@africana.rutgers.edu. Research: Brazil, African diaspora in Americas.

Butler, *Larry*, *George Mason.*

Butler, *Leslie A.*, *Dartmouth.* Email: leslie. butler@dartmouth.edu.

Butler, *Lisa L.* Port Orange, FL. Email: historygal65@gmail.com. Research: southern Maryland mulatto family.

Butler, *Matthew*, *Texas, Austin.* Email: mbutler@ austin.utexas.edu.

Butler, *Michael*, *William and Mary.* Email: mabutler01@wm.edu.

Butler, *Robert W.*, *Elmhurst.* Email: robb@ elmhurst.edu.

Butler, *Ryan.* Woodway, TX. Affil: Baylor. Email: Ryan_Butler@baylor.edu. Research: religion, abolition.

Butler, *Sara M.*, *Ohio State.* Email: butler.960@ osu.edu.

Butler-Smith, *Alice A.*, *US Army Command Coll.* Email: alice.a.butler-smith.civ@mail.mil.

Butrica, *Andrew J.* Bethesda, MD. Email: abutrica@earthlink.net. Research: electronics and communication technology, space.

Butt, *John J.*, *James Madison.* Email: buttjj@jmu. edu.

Butterfield, *Jo E.*, *Iowa.* Email: jo-butterfield@ uiowa.edu.

Butterfield, *Kevin C.* Mount Vernon, VA. Affil: Fred W. Smith National Library. Email: kbutterfield@mountvernon.org. Research: law and American voluntary associations.

Butts, *Michele T.*, *Austin Peay State.* Email: buttsmt@apsu.edu.

Buxton, *Bridget A.*, *Rhode Island.* Email: babuxton@uri.edu.

Buyco, *Ray*, *San José State.* Email: raymand. buyco@sjsu.edu.

Buzanski, *Peter M.* Monte Sereno, CA. Affil: San Jose State. Email: buzanski@earthlink.net.

Buzard Boyett, *Patricia M.*, *Loyola, New Orleans.* Email: pbboyett@loyno.edu.

Buzzanco, *Robert*, *Houston.* Email: buzz@ uh.edu.

Buzzell, *Rolfe G.* Anchorage, AK. Affil: Alaska State Office of Hist. and Archaeology. Email: rolfe.buzzell@gmail.com. Research: Alaskan gold rush, Alaskan mining.

Byczkiewicz, *Romuald K.*, *Central Connecticut State.* Email: byczkiewiczr@ccsu.edu.

Byers, *Richard*, *North Georgia.* Email: richard. byers@ung.edu.

Byfield, *Judith A.*, *Cornell.* Email: jab632@ cornell.edu.

Byington, *Richard B.* Winter Park, FL. Affil: Central Florida. Email: rchbying@aol. com. Research: officer advancement in Napoleonic Navy, 16th-c French persecution of Huegonots.

Byler, *Charles A.*, *Carroll.* Email: cbyler@carrollu. edu.

Bynum, **Caroline W.**, *Columbia (Hist.)*. New York, NY. Affil: Inst. for Advanced Study. Email: cwb4@columbia.edu; cwbynum@ias.edu. Research: medieval Christian theology and practice, history of the body.

Bynum, **Cornelius Lyn**, *Purdue*. Email: clbynum@purdue.edu.

Bynum, **Victoria**, *Texas State*. Email: vb03@txstate.edu.

Byrd, **Alexander X.**, *Rice*. Houston, TX. Email: axb@rice.edu. Research: urban South since Brown v. Board, black migration.

Byrd, **Brandon R.**, *Vanderbilt*. Nashville, TN. Email: brandon.r.byrd@vanderbilt.edu. Research: African Americans and Haiti.

Byrne, **Daniel**, *Evansville*. Evansville, IN. Email: db89@evansville.edu. Research: US policy on decolonization, Cold War diplomacy in North Africa.

Byrne, **Frank J.**, *SUNY, Oswego*. Email: frank.byrne@oswego.edu.

Byrne, **James Steven**. Squamish, BC, Canada. Affil: Quest. Email: james.s.byrne@gmail.com. Research: 15th-c astronomy, medieval natural philosophy.

Byrne, **Jeffrey James**, *British Columbia*. Vancouver, BC, Canada. Email: jeffrey.byrne@ubc.ca. Research: 20th-c Third World, Cold War and decolonization.

Byrne, **Patricia**. West Hartford, CT. Affil: Trinity Coll., Conn. Email: patricia.byrne@trincoll.edu.

Byrnes, **Joseph F.**, *Oklahoma State*. Email: joseph.byrnes@okstate.edu.

Byrnes, **Mark Stephen**. Spartanburg, SC. Affil: Wofford. Email: byrnesms@wofford.edu. Research: 20th-c US, US diplomatic.

Byrnes, **Melissa K.**, *Southwestern*. Email: byrnesm@southwestern.edu.

C c

Cabage, **Daniel**. Davenport, IA. Affil: German American Heritage Center and Museum. Email: daniel.cabage@snhu.edu. Research: Columbian Exchange, constitutional intent.

Cabanes, **Bruno**, *Ohio State*. Bexley, OH. Email: cabanes.2@osu.edu. Research: war and society, transnational.

Cable, **John Henry**. Thomasville, GA. Affil: Florida State. Email: jhc15b@my.fsu.edu. Research: African American, race and class.

Cabrera, **Tiffany H.**, *US Dept. of State*.

Cabrera Geserick, **Marco A.**, *Gustavus Adolphus*. Email: cabrerageserick@gustavus.edu.

Cabrita, **Joel Marie**, *Stanford*.

Caccipuoti, **Christine**. Farmingdale, NY. Affil: Footnoting Hist. Email: CJCaccipuoti@gmail.com.

Caciola, **Nancy A.**, *California, San Diego*. Email: ncaciola@ucsd.edu.

Cadava, **Geraldo Lujan**, *Northwestern*. Evanston, IL. Email: g-cadava@northwestern.edu. Research: US-Mexico borderlands, Latina/o.

Caddell, **Joseph W.**, *North Carolina, Chapel Hill; North Carolina State*. Email: caddellj@email.unc.edu; jcaddell@ncsu.edu.

Cadden, **Joan**, *California, Davis*. Email: jcadden@ucdavis.edu.

Caddoo, **Cara**, *Indiana*. Bloomington, IN. Email: ccaddoo@indiana.edu. Research: film and media, religion.

Cade, **Nancy**. Pikeville, KY. Affil: Pikeville. Email: nancycade@upike.edu.

Cadegan, **Una M.**, *Dayton*. Dayton, OH. Email: cadegan@udayton.edu. Research: US Catholic literary culture, US Catholicism and popular culture.

Caden, **Mara**. Chicago, IL. Affil: Massachusetts Hist. Soc. Email: mara.caden@gmail.com.

Cadigan, **Sean**, *Memorial, Newfoundland*. Email: scadigan@mun.ca.

Cady, **Benjamin**. Minneapolis, MN. Affil: Blake Sch. Email: bcady@blakeschool.org.

Cady, **Daniel J.**, *California State, Fresno*. Email: dcady@csufresno.edu.

Cady, **Darrel**, *Western Illinois*.

Cady, **William P.**. Malibu, CA. Affil: Santa Monica High Sch. Email: Patcady@verizon.net.

Caferro, **William P.**, *Vanderbilt*. Email: william.p.caferro@vanderbilt.edu.

Caffee, **Cheryl Ann**, *Central Oklahoma*. Email: ccaffee@uco.edu.

Caffrey, **Margaret M.**, *Memphis*. Email: mcaffrey@memphis.edu.

Caffrey, **Patrick J.**, *Washington and Jefferson*. Email: pcaffrey@washjeff.edu.

Cage, **Claire**, *South Alabama*. Email: ccage@southalabama.edu.

Cagle, **Hugh G.**, *Utah*. Email: hugh.cagle@utah.edu.

Caglioti, **Angelo Matteo**. New York, NY. Affil: Barnard, Columbia. Email: am.caglioti@gmail.com. Research: science and environment, empire.

Cagniart, **Pierre F.**, *Texas State*. Email: pc09@txstate.edu.

Cahan, **David**, *Nebraska, Lincoln*. Email: dcahan2@unl.edu.

Cahill, **Cathleen D.**, *Penn State*. University Park, PA. Email: czc335@psu.edu. Research: federal government in US West, Native American.

Cahill, **Justin**. New York, NY. Affil: WW Norton & Co. Email: jcahill@wwnorton.com.

Cahill, **Richard Andrew**, *Berea*. Email: richard_cahill@berea.edu.

Cahill, **Suzanne E.**, *California, San Diego*.

Cahn, **Susan K.**, *SUNY, Buffalo*. Email: cahn@buffalo.edu.

Cai, **Liang**, *Notre Dame*. Notre Dame, IN. Email: lcai@nd.edu; irisliangcai@gmail.com. Research: Han Confucianism.

Cain, **Courtney**, *Lake Forest*. Email: cain@mx.lakeforest.edu.

Cain, **Mary Cathryn**, *Agnes Scott*. Email: mcain@agnesscott.edu.

Cain, **Victoria**, *Northeastern*. Email: v.cain@neu.edu.

Caires, **Michael T**. Charlottesville, VA. Email: mtc2p@virginia.edu.

Cairney, **Christian Charles**. London, United Kingdom. Affil: Roehampton. Email: cairneycc@gmail.com.

Cairns, **John C.**, *Toronto*. Toronto, ON, Canada. Email: johncairns@sympatico.ca.

Calabrese, **Victoria**, *Lehman, CUNY*. Larchmont, NY. Email: victoria.calabrese@lehman.cuny.edu; vcalabrese@hotmail.com. Research: Italian emigration, Italian Southern Question.

Calder, **Bruce J.**, *Illinois, Chicago*. Email: bcalder@uic.edu.

Calder, **Lendol G.**, *Augustana*. Rock Island, IL. Email: lendolcalder@augustana.edu. Research: history teaching and learning, consumer culture.

Calderon, **Roberto R.**, *North Texas*. Email: beto@unt.edu.

Calderón, **Fernando H.**, *Northern Iowa*. Email: fernando.calderon@uni.edu.

Caldwell, **Craig H., III**, *Appalachian State*. Email: caldwellch@appstate.edu.

Caldwell, **Holly**, *Chestnut Hill*. Gladwyne, PA. Email: caldwellh@chc.edu; hollyc@udel.edu. Research: medicine, deaf history.

Caldwell, **John Walter, Jr**. San Angelo, TX. Email: jcaldwel@wcc.net.

Caldwell, **Lee Ann**, *Augusta*. Email: lcaldwel@augusta.edu.

Caldwell, **Peter C.**, *Rice*. Email: caldwell@rice.edu.

Caldwell, **Robert B**. Many, LA. Affil: Texas, Arlington. Email: Robert.Caldwell@mavs.uta.edu.

Calhoun, **Charles W.**, *East Carolina*. Washington, DC. Email: calhounc@ecu.edu. Research: Gilded Age politics, presidency of Ulysses S. Grant.

Calhoun, **Chip**, *Center for Hist. of Physics*. Email: ccalhoun@aip.org.

Calhoun, **Daniel F.**, *Wooster*. Email: dcalhoun@wooster.edu.

Calhoun, **Daniel H**. Santa Rosa, CA. Affil: California, Davis. Email: dhcalhoun@ucdavis.edu. Research: Jacksonian period, 19th-c cultural.

Calhoun, **Mark T.**, *US Army Command Coll.* Email: mark.t.calhoun.civ@mail.mil.

Cali, **Denise**, *South Florida, Tampa*. Email: denisecali@usf.edu.

Calkins, **Kenneth R.**, *Kent State*. Email: kcalk@aol.com.

Calkins, **Laura M.**, *Texas Tech*. Email: laura.calkins@ttu.edu.

Call, **Lewis**, *California Polytechnic State*. Email: lcall@calpoly.edu.

Callaci, **Emily J.**, *Wisconsin-Madison*. Email: ejcallaci@wisc.edu.

Callaghan, **Jennifer A**. Chicago, IL. Affil: Northwestern. Email: Jennifera.callaghan@gmail.com.

Callahan, **Daniel F.**, *Delaware*. Newark, DE. Email: dfcao@udel.edu. Research: Jerusalem pilgrims 950-1050, Western heresy 950-1050.

Callahan, **Kathy J.**, *Murray State*. Email: kcallahan@murraystate.edu.

Callahan, **Raymond A., Jr.**, *Delaware*. Email: rac@udel.edu.

Callahan, **William J., Jr.**, *Toronto*. Email: wj.callahan@utoronto.ca.

Callan, **John F**. Elgin, SC. Affil: Brentwood Senior High Sch. Email: jcallan@att.net.

Callaway, **Shelby**. Cheverly, MD. Affil: US Dept. of Agriculture. Email: slcallaw@gmail.com. Research: Soil Conservation, USDA.

Callcott, **George H.**, *Maryland, Coll. Park*. College Park, MD. Email: gcallcott@aol.com. Research: US South, Maryland.

Callejas, **Karla**, *California State, Los Angeles*. Email: Karla.Callejas4@calstatela.edu.

Calloway, **Colin G.**, *Dartmouth*. Hanover, NH. Email: colin.calloway@dartmouth.edu. Research: Native American.

Calvert, **Jane E.**, *Kentucky*. Email: jane.calvert@uky.edu.

Calvert, **John**, *Creighton*. Email: johncalvert@creighton.edu.

Calvert, **Kenneth**, *Hillsdale*. Email: kcalvert@hillsdale.edu.

Camarillo, **Albert M.**, *Stanford*. Stanford, CA. Email: camar@stanford.edu. Research: comparative race and ethnicity.

Cameron, **Brian**. Dumont, NJ. Affil: Garfield Sch. District. Email: bcameron@gboe.org.

Cameron, **Calla**. Claremont, CA. Affil: Claremont McKenna. Email: cjcsunflower16@gmail.com. Research: US war crimes, Trujillo Dictatorship.

Cameron, **Christopher Alain**, *North Carolina, Charlotte*. Durham, NC. Email: ccamer17@uncc.edu. Research: slavery/religion/black abolitionists, freethought/secularism/humanism.

Cameron, **Euan K.**, *Columbia (Hist.)*. New York, NY. Affil: Union Theological Seminary. Email: ecameron@uts.columbia.edu. Research: scholasticism and superstition, theology of church history.

Cameron, **Jessica May**. Roanoke, VA. Email: mrsjessyc@gmail.com.

Cameron, **Justin Ross**. Roanoke, VA. Email: jcameron1683@gmail.com. Research: indigeonous America/colonial America.

Cameron, **Ross J.** Springfield, VA. Email: rcameron49@earthlink.net.

Cameron, **Sarah I.**, *Maryland, Coll. Park*. Email: scameron@umd.edu.

Cameselle, **Pedro M.**, *Western Washington*. Email: pedro.cameselle@wwu.edu.

Camilleri, **Amy**, *US Senate Hist. Office*. Email: amy_camilleri@sec.senate.gov.

Camiscioli, **Elisa**, *Binghamton, SUNY*. Email: ecamis@binghamton.edu.

Camp, **Richard L.**, *California State, Northridge*. Santa Monica, CA. Email: richard.camp@csun.edu. Research: Italian futurism, 20th-c modernist culture.

Campanaro, **Amy E**, *Western Connecticut State*. Email: campanaroa@wcsu.edu.

Campbell, **Brian**. Champaign, IL. Affil: Illinois, Urbana-Champaign. Email: bcmpbll2@illinois.edu.

Campbell, **Bruce B.**, *William and Mary*. Williamsburg, VA. Email: bbcamp@wm.edu. Research: state violence/paramilitarism, radio.

Campbell, **Caroline Jane**, *North Dakota*. Grand Forks, ND. Email: caroline.campbell@und.edu. Research: French interwar years gender, nationalism/fascism/empire.

Campbell, **Claire**, *Bucknell*. Email: cec036@bucknell.edu.

Campbell, **Daniel**, *Austin Peay State*. Email: campbelld@apsu.edu.

Campbell, **D'Ann M**. Billings, MT. Affil: Culver-Stockton. Email: dcampbell@culver.edu. Research: teaching American history.

Campbell, **Debra**. Waterville, ME. Affil: Colby. Email: dcampbe@colby.edu. Research: American women/religion/autobiography, religion and WWII.

Campbell, **Elena**, *Washington, Seattle*. Email: eicampb@uw.edu.

Campbell, **Elizabeth**, *Denver*. Denver, CO. Email: ecampbell@du.edu. Research: post-WWII recovery of Nazi looted art, post-WWII cultural policy Western Europe.

Campbell, **Gail G.**, *New Brunswick*. Email: campbell@unb.ca.

Campbell, **George**, *Eastern Kentucky*.

Campbell, **Gwyn**, *McGill*. Email: gwyn.campbell@mcgill.ca.

Campbell, **Ian Wylie**, *California, Davis*. Woodland, CA. Email: iwcampbell@ucdavis.

edu; iwcampbell@gmail.com. Research: Russian Empire and 19th-c Europe, comparative colonialism and imperialism.

Campbell, **Isabel**, *Carleton, Can.; National Defence Headquarters*. Email: isabel.campbell@carleton.ca; isabel.campbell@forces.gc.ca.

Campbell, **Jacqueline Glass**, *Francis Marion*. Email: jcampbell@fmarion.edu.

Campbell, **James P.** Rockford, IL. Email: jpcampbell67@gmail.com. Research: early modern Europe, early Christianity.

Campbell, **James T.**, *Stanford*. Email: jtcampb@stanford.edu.

Campbell, **Jodi M.**, *Texas Christian*. Fort Worth, TX. Email: j.campbell@tcu.edu. Research: representations of faces, early modern Spanish politics and culture.

Campbell, **Karl E.**, *Appalachian State*. Email: campbllke@appstate.edu.

Campbell, **Kathleen**. Atlanta, GA. Affil: Westminster Sch. Email: katiecampbell@westminster.net.

Campbell, **Kenneth L.**, *Monmouth*. Perryville, MD. Email: campbell@monmouth.edu. Research: comparative Western civilization, English religious nonconformity.

Campbell, **Lara**, *Simon Fraser*. Email: lcampbel@sfu.ca.

Campbell, **Lyndsay**, *Calgary*. Email: lcampbe@ucalgary.ca.

Campbell, **Mark T.** Burlingame, CA. Email: MarkT.Campbell@yahoo.com.

Campbell, **Mavis C.**, *Amherst*.

Campbell, **Michael T**. San German, PR. Affil: Puerto Rico, Ponce. Email: mcampbell1957@gmail.com.

Campbell, **Monica**. Jonesboro, AR. Affil: Mississippi. Email: mcampbe6@go.olemiss.edu. Research: postwar urbanization/urban renewal, neoliberalism.

Campbell, **Randolph B. 'Mike'**, *North Texas*. Email: mike@unt.edu.

Campbell, **Robert Dean**. Williamsport, IN. Email: robertdeancampbell2010@gmail.com.

Campbell, **Robin**, *SUNY, Albany*.

Campbell, **Roy B.**, *Presbyterian*. Email: rbcamp@presby.edu.

Campbell, **Stanley L.**, *Purdue, Fort Wayne*.

Campbell, **Stephen**. La Verne, CA. Affil: California Polytechnic State. Email: swcampbell83@gmail.com. Research: political, economic.

Campbell, **Tracy**, *Kentucky*. Email: tracamp@uky.edu.

Camper, **Joshua**, *Tennessee, Martin*. Email: jcamper@utm.edu.

Campion, **David A.**, *Lewis & Clark*. Portland, OR. Email: campion@lclark.edu. Research: colonial policing in British India, Irish and Indian nationalism.

Campney, **Brent M. S.**, *Texas-Rio Grande Valley*. Email: brentcampney@gmail.com.

Campos, **Amie**. Downey, CA. Affil: California, San Diego. Email: amcampos@ucsd.edu.

Campos, **Isaac P.**, *Cincinnati*. Email: camposip@ucmail.uc.edu.

Campos, **Luis**, *New Mexico*. Email: luiscampos@unm.edu.

Campos, **Michelle U.**, *Florida*. Gainesville, FL. Email: mcampos@ufl.edu. Research: Ottoman citizenship, Islamic modernism.

Canaday, **Margot**, *Princeton*. Email: mcanaday@princeton.edu.

Canale, **Joshua P.** Syracuse, NY. Affil: Jefferson Comm. Coll. Email: jcanale1@binghamton.edu. Research: early America, American Revolution.

Candeloro, **Dominic**, *Loyola, Chicago*. Email: dcandeloro@luc.edu.

Candiani, **Vera Silvina**, *Princeton*. Email: candiani@princeton.edu.

Candida Smith, **Richard**. Evanston, IL. Affil: California, Berkeley. Email: candidas@berkeley.edu. Research: US and Latin America, art and culture.

Candido, **Mariana P.**, *Notre Dame*. Email: mcandido@nd.edu.

Cane-Carrasco, **James A.**, *Oklahoma (Hist.)*. Email: cane@ou.edu.

Canedo, **Oscar R.** El Cajon, CA. Affil: Grossmont. Email: oscar.canedo@gcccd.edu.

Canedo, **Oscar**. San Marcos, CA. Affil: California State, San Marcos. Email: caned006@cougars.csusm.edu.

Cañeque, **Alejandro**, *Maryland, Coll. Park*. College Park, MD. Email: acaneque@umd.edu. Research: politics of martyrdom in Spanish empire, 16th-17th-c New Spain.

Caner, **Daniel F.**, *Indiana*. Email: dcaner@indiana.edu.

Cangemi, **Michael Joseph**. Syracuse, NY. Affil: Connecticut Coll. Email: mcangemi@conncoll.edu. Research: diplomatic, Cold War.

Cañizares-Esguerra, **Jorge**, *Texas, Austin*. Email: canizares-esguerra@austin.utexas.edu.

Cannadine, **David N.**, *Princeton*. Princeton, NJ. Email: dcannadi@princeton.edu. Research: modern Britain.

Cannato, **Vincent J.**, *Massachusetts, Boston*. Email: vincent.cannato@umb.edu.

Canning, **Craig N.**, *William and Mary*. Email: cncann@wm.edu.

Canning, **Kathleen M.**, *Michigan, Ann Arbor; Rice*. Houston, TX. Email: kcanning@umich.edu; kcanning@rice.edu. Research: German gender and citizenship, WWI/postwar revolutions.

Canning, **Paul M.**, *Connecticut, Storrs*. Email: paul.canning@uconn.edu.

Cannon, **Brian Q.**, *Brigham Young*. Email: brian_cannon@byu.edu.

Cannon, **Brian**. Malvern, PA. Email: bcannon@sas.upenn.edu.

Cannon, **Byron**, *Utah*. Email: byron.cannon@utah.edu.

Cannon, **Jessica A.**, *Central Missouri*. Email: jacannon@ucmo.edu.

Cansler, **Clay**, *Science History Inst*. Email: ccansler@sciencehistory.org.

Cantelon, **Philip L.**, *Hist. Assoc*. Email: pcantelon@historyassociates.com.

Cantisano, **Pedro**, *Kenyon*. Email: cantisanop@kenyon.edu.

Canton, **David A.**, *Connecticut Coll*. Email: dacan@conncoll.edu.

Cantor, **Louis**, *Purdue, Fort Wayne*. Email: louiscantor@earthlink.net.

Cantor, **Milton**, *Massachusetts, Amherst*. Email: mcantor@history.umass.edu.

Cantrell, **Gregg**, *Texas Christian*. Email: g.cantrell@tcu.edu.

Cantrell, **Phillip Allen, II**, *Longwood*. Email: cantrellpa@longwood.edu.

Cantres, **James, Jr**. Brooklyn, NY. Affil: Hunter, CUNY. Email: james.cantres@hunter.cuny.edu. Research: African diaspora, Caribbean diaspora in Britain.

Cantwell, Christopher D., *Wisconsin-Milwaukee*.

Capeci, Dominic J., Jr., *Missouri State*. Email: dominiccapeci@missouristate.edu.

Capello, Ernesto B., *Macalester*. Saint Paul, MN. Email: ecapello@macalester.edu. Research: Quito space/history/modernity, popular response to 1969 Rockefeller Mission.

Caplan, Karen D., *Rutgers, Newark/New Jersey Inst. of Tech*. Email: kcaplan@rutgers.edu.

Caplinger, Christopher, *Georgia Southern*. Email: caplinca@georgiasouthern.edu.

Capo, Julio C., Jr., *Florida International; Massachusetts, Amherst; Committee on LGBT Hist.* Amherst, MA. Email: Julio.capo@fiu.edu; capo@history.umass.edu. Research: 20th-c queer Miami, transnational Caribbean-US sexuality.

Capozzola, Christopher, *MIT*. Cambridge, MA. Email: capozzol@mit.edu. Research: WWI homefront, Philippines.

Cappello, Lawrence, *Alabama, Tuscaloosa*. Northport, NY. Email: lcappello@ua.edu; lawrencecappello@gmail.com. Research: 20th-c US.

Capper, Charles H., *Boston Univ*. Boston, MA. Email: capper@bu.edu. Research: American transcendentalist movement, romanticism and American reform.

Capps, Alan P. Alexandria, VA. Affil: George Mason. Email: acapps1@masonlive.gmu.edu. Research: biographies of WWII fighter A/C design, domestic scandals/foreign policy.

Capps, Christopher Edwin. Chicago, IL. Affil: Elgin High Sch. Email: chriscapps@u-46.org.

Capps, Hubert Donald. Fuquay-Varina, NC. Email: cappshd@gmail.com. Research: US automotive competition prior to 1920.

Caprice, Kevin R. Charlottesville, VA. Email: krc5p@virginia.edu.

Capron, Dennis. Columbia, MD. Email: cornellis01@verizon.net. Research: colonial/early Republic imminent domain, Georgia and road to revolution.

Capshew, James H., *Indiana*. Email: jcapshew@indiana.edu.

Caputo, Nina, *Florida*. Gainesville, FL. Email: ncaputo@ufl.edu. Research: late medieval Jewish-Christian relations, conversion-religion and culture.

Caraher, William R., *North Dakota*. Email: william.caraher@und.edu.

Caraway, David Todd. San Antonio, TX. Affil: Keystone Sch. Email: dcaraway@grandecom.net. Research: Netherlands and Belgium 1813-39, Netherlands 1914-18.

Carayon, Celine, *Salisbury*. Salisbury, MD. Email: cxcarayon@salisbury.edu. Research: French-Indian nonverbal communication, 16th/17th-c French Atlantic.

Carbonneau, Ara. Iowa City, IA. Affil: Iowa. Email: Ara-carbonneau@uiowa.edu.

Carbonneau, Robert E. Scranton, PA. Affil: Ricci Inst. Email: robcarb@cpprov.org. Research: Catholic missions in China, US Catholicism.

Carden, Allen. Fresno, CA. Affil: Fresno Pacific. Email: ACarden@aol.com. Research: Lincoln, American slavery.

Cardon, Nathan. Edgbaston, Birmingham, United Kingdom. Affil: Birmingham. Email: nathan.cardon@mail.utoronto.ca. Research: modernity and empire in New South, trans-imperial technology.

Cardona, Cynthia, *California State, Los Angeles*. Email: ccardon7@calstatela.edu.

Cardona, Mylynka Kilgore, *Texas A&M, Commerce*. Email: Mylynka.Cardona@tamuc.edu.

Cardoza, Anthony L., *Loyola, Chicago*. Email: acardoz@luc.edu.

Carenen, Caitlin Elisabeth, *Eastern Connecticut State*. Email: carenenc@easternct.edu.

Caretti, Erin J. Mercersburg, PA. Affil: Mercersburg Academy. Email: eringate@hotmail.com.

Carey, Anthony Gene, *Appalachian State*. Email: careyag@appstate.edu.

Carey, David, Jr., *Loyola, Md.* Email: drcarey@loyola.edu.

Carey, Delbert, *Wisconsin-Platteville*. Email: careyd@uwplatt.edu.

Carey, Diana, *Arthur and Elizabeth Schlesinger Library*. Email: dcarey@radcliffe.harvard.edu.

Carey, Elaine K. Hammond, IN. Affil: Purdue Northwest. Email: elaine.carey@pnw.edu. Research: crime, narcotics.

Carey, Mark, *Oregon*. Email: carey@uoregon.edu.

Carey, Miya. Trenton, NJ. Affil: Rutgers. Email: miyacarey@gmail.com.

Carey, Vincent, *SUNY, Plattsburgh*. Email: careyvp@plattsburgh.edu.

Cargill, Jack, *Rutgers*. Email: jcargill@scarletmail.rutgers.edu.

Carhart, Michael C., *Old Dominion*. Email: mcarhart@odu.edu.

Carignan, Michael Ian, *Elon*. Email: mcarignan@elon.edu.

Carlat, Louis E., *Rutgers*. Email: carlat@taep.rutgers.edu.

Carlebach, Elisheva, *Columbia (Hist.)*. Email: ec607@columbia.edu.

Carleton, Don E., *Texas, Austin*. Email: d.carleton@austin.utexas.edu.

Carlevale, John, *Berea*. Email: john_carlevale@berea.edu.

Carley, Michael Jabara, *Montréal*. Email: michael.j.carley@umontreal.ca.

Carlin, Martha, *Wisconsin-Milwaukee*. Email: carlin@uwm.edu.

Carlisle, Rodney P., *Rutgers, Camden; Hist. Assoc.* Email: carlisle@rutgers.edu.

Carll, Johanna A., *Arthur and Elizabeth Schlesinger Library*. Email: jcarll@radcliffe.harvard.edu.

Carlock, Robert. Bowling Green, OH. Affil: Bowling Green State. Email: robcarlock@gmail.com.

Carls, Alice-Catherine, *Tennessee, Martin*. Email: accarls@utm.edu.

Carls, Stephen Douglas, *Union*. Jackson, TN. Email: scarls@uu.edu. Research: 20th-c Europe, economic.

Carlson, Andrew J., *Capital*. Email: acarlson@capital.edu.

Carlson, Anthony E., *US Army Command Coll.* Email: anthony.e.carlson9.civ@mail.mil.

Carlson, Bernie, *Virginia*. Email: wc4p@virginia.edu.

Carlson, Christi, *Northern Arizona*. Email: christi.carlson@nau.edu.

Carlson, Eric Josef. Saint Peter, MN. Affil: Gustavus Adolphus. Email: ecarlson@gustavus.edu. Research: English Reformation effects, anger/sin/emotion.

Carlson, Erik D., *Florida Gulf Coast*. Email: ecarlson@fgcu.edu.

Carlson, Leonard A., *Emory*. Email: econlac@emory.edu.

Carlson, Lewis H., *Western Michigan*. Email: lewis.carlson@wmich.edu.

Carlson, Lynne Ann. Largo, MD. Affil: Prince George's Comm. Coll. Email: carlsola@pgcc.edu.

Carlson, Marifran. Chicago, IL. Research: Argentine women, human rights in Latin America.

Carlson, Marybeth, *Dayton*. Dayton, OH. Email: mcarlson1@udayton.edu. Research: poor relief, Atlantic world.

Carlson, R. David, *Troy*. Email: rdcarlson@troy.edu.

Carlson, Sharon, *Western Michigan*. Email: sharon.carlson@wmich.edu.

Carlson, Thomas A., *Oklahoma State*.

Carlsson, Eric, *Wisconsin-Madison*. Madison, WI. Email: eric.carlsson@wisc.edu. Research: German Enlightenment, Protestant theology.

Carlton, Dana. Fairfield, CA. Affil: Southern New Hampshire. Email: dana.carlton@snhu.edu.

Carlton, David L., *Vanderbilt*. Email: david.l.carlton@vanderbilt.edu.

Carmical, Oline, Jr., *Cumberlands*. Email: oline.carmical@ucumberlands.edu.

Carmichael, Ann G., *Indiana*. Email: carmicha@indiana.edu.

Carmichael, Peter S., *Gettysburg*. Email: pcarmich@gettysburg.edu.

Carmona, Juan Pablo. Donna, TX. Affil: Donna High Sch. Email: jpc9965@yahoo.com. Research: US/Mexican border studies, America.

Carnaghi, Benedetta. Ithaca, NY. Affil: Cornell. Email: bc552@cornell.edu. Research: Fascist and Nazi secret police, Resistance and Holocaust.

Carnes, Mark C., *Barnard, Columbia*. New York, NY. Email: mc422@columbia.edu. Research: American social, gender.

Carnes, Todi S. Alexandria, VA. Affil: George Mason. Email: todicarnes@verizon.net.

Carnevale, Nancy C., *Montclair State*. Email: carnevalen@mail.montclair.edu.

Carney, Amy, *Penn State, Erie*. Erie, PA. Email: abc13@psu.edu. Research: modern Europe, Germany and fascism.

Carney, Court P., *Stephen F. Austin State*. Nacogdoches, TX. Email: carneycp@sfasu.edu. Research: politics of black art, jazz and modern American culture.

Carney, Todd F., *Southern Oregon*. Email: tcarney@sou.edu.

Carnie, Henry Joseph. Irvine, CA. Affil: Irvine Valley. Email: hcarnie@ivc.edu.

Caron, Caroline-Isabelle, *Queen's, Can.* Email: caronc@queensu.ca.

Caron, Simone M., *Wake Forest*. Email: caron@wfu.edu.

Caron, Vicki, *Cornell*. Ithaca, NY. Email: vc21@cornell.edu. Research: Jewish refugee crisis in France 1933-42, post-1870 French Jewish-Catholic relations.

Carotenuto, Matthew P., *St. Lawrence*. Email: mcarotenuto@stlawu.edu.

Carothers, Ryan M. San Jose, CA. Email: academyoftheeons@gmail.com. Research: Second Temple Judaism, Christian origins.

Carp, *Benjamin L.*, *Brooklyn, CUNY*. Brooklyn, NY. Email: BCarp@brooklyn.cuny.edu. Research: Revolutionary War, cosmopolitanism.

Carp, **E. Wayne**, *Pacific Lutheran*. Email: carpw@plu.edu.

Carpenter, **Gerald G.**, *Niagara*. Email: cgc@niagara.edu.

Carpenter, *Jason Robert*. Salt Lake City, UT. Affil: Utah. Email: carpenterteacher@gmail.com.

Carpenter, *Joel A.*, *Calvin*. Grand Rapids, MI. Email: jcarpent@calvin.edu. Research: new universities in Africa/Asia/Latin America, non-Western Christianity.

Carpenter, *Joseph H.* Arlington, TX. Affil: Texas, Arlington. Email: jcinrockwall@yahoo.com. Research: Europe/Russia/America 1900-17, Panama Revolution 1903.

Carpenter, *Kyle Burton*. Fort Worth, TX. Affil: Southern Methodist. Email: kbcarpenter@smu.edu.

Carpenter, *Roger M*. Monroe, LA. Affil: Louisiana, Monroe. Email: carpenter@ulm.edu. Research: native and European contacts, natives/Europeans/liberty.

Carpenter, **Stanley D**. **M.**, *Naval War Coll*. Email: carpents@usnwc.edu.

Carpenter, *Stephanie A.*, *Andrews*. Berrien Springs, MI. Email: carpenter@andrews.edu. Research: 20th-c US, agricultural.

Carpenter, *William C*. Falls Church, VA. Affil: National Archives. Email: wcarpent@gmu.edu. Research: Orangeism in Ireland.

Carr, **Graham**, *Concordia, Can*. Email: Graham.Carr@concordia.ca.

Carr, *Jacien George*. Blacklick, OH. Affil: Sch. of Oriental and African Studies. Email: 634262@soas.ac.uk. Research: Poro Society/Liberia and Sierra, African military.

Carr, **Jacqueline Barbara**, *Vermont*. Email: jacqueline.carr@uvm.edu.

Carr, **Karen E.**, *Portland State*.

Carr, **Kay J.**, *Southern Illinois, Carbondale*. Email: kjcarr@siu.edu.

Carr, **Mariel**, *Science History Inst.* Email: mcarr@sciencehistory.org.

Carr Childers, **Leisl Ann**, *Colorado State*. Email: leisl.carr_childers@colostate.edu.

Carrafiello, *Michael L.*, *Miami, Ohio*. Email: carrafml@miamioh.edu.

Carrasquillo, **Rosa E.**, *Holy Cross*. Email: rcarrasq@holycross.edu.

Carreras, **Charles E.**, *Ramapo*. Email: ccarrera@ramapo.edu.

Carretta, *Vincent*. Springfield, VA. Affil: Maryland, Coll. Park. Email: vac@umd.edu. Research: 18th-c Anglophone-African writers, 18th-c British writers.

Carrick, *Christina R.*, *Princeton*. Newtown, PA. Email: ccarrick@princeton.edu; carrickc@bu.edu. Research: revolutionary America.

Carriedo, **Lt Col (Ret.) Robert**, *US Air Force Acad*. Email: robert.carriedo@usafa.edu.

Carrier, **Richard**, *Royal Military*. Email: richard.carrier@rmc.ca.

Carrigan, **D**. **Owen**, *St. Mary's, Can*.

Carrigan, *Michelle D.* Fort Pierce, FL. Affil: Indian River State. Email: chelle2122@yahoo.com. Research: divorce in 18th-c New York, law/culture/gender relationships.

Carrigan, **William D.**, *Rowan*. Email: carrigan@rowan.edu.

Carriker, *Jay*. Marshall, TX. Affil: Wiley. Email: jcarriker@wileyc.edu.

Carriker, **Robert Charles**, *Gonzaga*. Email: carriker@gonzaga.edu.

Carriker, **Robert M.**, *Louisiana, Lafayette*. Email: carriker@louisiana.edu.

Carrillo, *Charles C*. Whittier, CA. Affil: Azusa Pacific. Email: chascarrillo@aol.com. Research: late medieval and early modern Spain, historical geography.

Carrillo, *Mateo J*. Santa Barbara, CA. Affil: California, Santa Barbara. Email: mateoc.history@gmail.com.

Carrington, **Laurel**, *St. Olaf*. Email: carringt@stolaf.edu.

Carrington-Farmer, **Charlotte Victoria**, *Roger Williams*. Email: ccarrington@rwu.edu.

Carroll, **Bret Evan**, *California State, Stanislaus*. Email: bcarroll@csustan.edu.

Carroll, *Charles F*. Harvard, MA.

Carroll, *Charles*. Providence, RI. Affil: Brown. Email: charles_carroll@brown.edu. Research: universities, masculinities.

Carroll, *Christina B.*, *Kalamazoo*. Kalamazoo, MI. Email: christina.carroll@kzoo.edu; christinabcarroll@gmail.com. Research: French empire and nationalism 1870-1914, literary and political culture 1870-1914.

Carroll, *Francis M.*, *Manitoba*. Winnipeg, MB, Canada. Email: fcarrol@cc.umanitoba.ca. Research: US diplomatic, Anglo-American relations.

Carroll, *Fred*, *Kennesaw State*. Acworth, GA. Email: fred.carroll@kennesaw.edu. Research: African American, journalism.

Carroll, **Heather**, *New York State Archives*.

Carroll, *James T.*, *American Catholic Hist. Assoc.* New Rochelle, NY. Affil: Iona. Email: JCarroll@iona.edu. Research: American religion, education.

Carroll, **John M.**, *Lamar*. Email: jmcarroll1@my.lamar.edu.

Carroll, **Mark M.**, *Missouri, Columbia*. Email: carrollmm@missouri.edu.

Carroll, *Peter J.*, *Northwestern*. Evanston, IL. Email: p-carroll@northwestern.edu. Research: modernity and urbanism, gender and sexuality.

Carroll, **Robert L.**, *Tennessee, Martin*.

Carroll, *Rosemary F.*, *Coe*.

Carroll, *Tamar W*. Rochester, NY. Affil: Rochester Inst. of Tech. Email: tamar.carroll@rit.edu. Research: Rochester NY and Eastman Kodak Co., social movements in post-1945 US.

Carrott, **M. Browning**, **Jr.**, *Southern Illinois, Carbondale*. Email: carrott@siu.edu.

Carr-Shanahan, **John Grant**, *Texas, San Antonio*. Email: john.carrshanahan@utsa.edu.

Carson, **Carolyn**, *Pittsburgh*. Email: cjlc@pitt.edu.

Carson, **Cary**, *William and Mary*. Email: carycarson@earthlink.net.

Carson, **Cathryn L.**, *California, Berkeley*. Email: clcarson@berkeley.edu.

Carson, *Clayborne*, **Jr.**, *Stanford*. Stanford, CA. Email: ccarson@stanford.edu. Research: Martin Luther King Jr., global liberation movements.

Carson, **David A.**, *SUNY, Buffalo State*. Email: carsonda@buffalostate.edu.

Carson, **James T.**, *Queen's, Can*. Email: jc35@queensu.ca.

Carson, *John*, *Michigan, Ann Arbor*. Ann Arbor, MI. Email: jscarson@umich.edu. Research: medical jurisprudence, human sciences.

Carson, *Sarah*. Cornwall-on-Hudson, NY. Affil: Princeton. Email: scarson@princeton.edu.

Carson, **Thomas Edward**, *Henry Ford Coll.* Email: tecarson@hfcc.edu.

Carson-Bird, *Elizabeth Ann*. Bonne Terre, MO. Affil: Clayton High Sch. Email: fumcat@msn.com. Research: 15th-c Latin poetry, 15th-c papacy/cultural.

Carstairs, **Catherine**, *Guelph*. Email: ccarstai@uoguelph.ca.

Carter, **Bradley**, *Naval War Coll.* Email: bradley.carter@usnwc.edu.

Carter, *Brian Charles*. Ukiah, CA. Affil: Carter Momsen PC. Email: bcarter@cartermomsen.com.

Carter, **Dan T.**, *South Carolina, Columbia*. Email: carterdt@mailbox.sc.edu.

Carter, **Daryl Anthony**, *East Tennessee State; North Carolina A&T State*. Email: carterda@etsu.edu; dacarter1@ncat.edu.

Carter, **David**, *Auburn*. Email: cartedc@auburn.edu.

Carter, **Derrais**, *Portland State*. Email: derrais@pdx.edu.

Carter, *Gregory Matthew*. Carbondale, IL. Affil: Southern Illinois, Carbondale. Email: Greg1832@siu.edu. Research: Progressive Era, Caribbean interventions.

Carter, *Gregory*, *Wisconsin-Milwaukee*. Email: cartergt@uwm.edu.

Carter, *Heath W*. Valparaiso, IN. Affil: Valparaiso. Email: heath.carter@ptsem.edu. Research: religion and industrial order, religion and Chicago race riot.

Carter, **James H.**, *St. Joseph's*. Email: jcarter@sju.edu.

Carter, **Jill**, *Texas, Tyler*. Email: jcarter@uttyler.edu.

Carter, *Jim*. Ann Arbor, MI. Affil: Michigan. Email: jimrc@umich.edu. Research: Italian literature, European intellectual history.

Carter, *John*. Kennett, MO. Affil: Southern Mississippi. Email: john.c.carter@usm.edu.

Carter, *Karen E.*, *Brigham Young*. Provo, UT. Email: karen_carter@byu.edu. Research: religious education in early modern France, religions practice in 18th-c. France.

Carter, *Katlyn*. Ann Arbor, MI. Affil: Michigan, Ann Arbor. Email: katlync@umich.edu. Research: political culture, Age of Revolutions.

Carter, **Lucia**, *Mars Hill*. Email: lcarter@mhu.edu.

Carter, **Michael S.**, *Dayton*. Email: carterms@notes.udayton.edu.

Carter, *Mitchell*. Plano, IL. Affil: Plano Community Unit Sch. District No. 88. Email: CartersCornerPR@gmail.com.

Carter, **Sarah A.**, *Alberta*. Email: scarter@ucalgary.ca.

Carter, *Todd*. Oxford, United Kingdom. Affil: Oxford. Email: todd.carter@univ.ox.ac.uk. Research: Cold War, Anglo-American relations.

Carter, *W. Burlette*. Washington, DC. Affil: George Washington University Law Sch. Email: bcarter@law.gwu.edu.

Carter-David, **Siobhan**, *Southern Connecticut State*. Email: carterdavis1@southernct.edu.

Cartney, *Susan*. Annapolis, MD. Email: susan.cartney@gmail.com.

Carton, **Benedict**, *George Mason*. Email: bcarton1@gmu.edu.

Cartwright, **Brad J.**, *Texas, El Paso*. Email: bjcartwright@utep.edu.

Cartwright, Charlotte, *Christopher Newport*. Email: charlotte.cartwright@cnu.edu.

Cartwright, Katherine. Williamsburg, VA. Affil: William and Mary. Email: kscartwright@email.wm.edu.

Caruso, David J., *Science History Inst*. Email: dcaruso@sciencehistory.org.

Caruso, Virginia P., *Henry Ford Coll*. Email: tuffey10@aol.com.

Carver, Michael M., *Bowling Green State*. Email: mcarver@bgsu.edu.

Cary, Noel D., *Holy Cross*. Email: ncary@holycross.edu.

Casale, Giancarlo L., *Minnesota (Hist.)*. Email: casale@umn.edu.

Casanova-Fuentes, Clarissa. Westbury, NY. Affil: W. T. Clarke High Sch. Email: ccasanova@emufsd.us.

Casas, Maria Raquel, *Nevada, Las Vegas*. Email: maria.casas@unlv.edu.

Casavantes Bradford, Anita, *California, Irvine*. San Diego, CA. Email: acasavan@uci.edu; anitacasavantesbradford@gmail.com. Research: Cuban diaspora/exile, immigration/race/ethnicity.

Case, Holly A., *Brown*. Providence, RI. Email: holly_case@brown.edu. Research: international history of 19th-/20th-c Europe, contested territory and minority rights.

Case, Jay. Canton, OH. Affil: Malone. Email: jcase@malone.edu. Research: world Christianity, evangelicalism.

Case, Theresa A., *Houston-Downtown*. Houston, TX. Email: caset@uhd.edu. Research: labor, social.

Casey, Christopher A. Washington, DC. Affil: Library of Congress. Email: caseyc@mac.com.

Casey, Leo E. Washington, DC. Email: leoecasey@gmail.com.

Casey, Marion T. Notre Dame, IN. Affil: Maryland. Email: caseyemery@aol.com. Research: Vietnam-American War, Cold War.

Casey, Mary. Los Angeles, CA. Affil: California State, Northridge. Email: mcplywrt@aol.com.

Casey, Matthew, *Southern Mississippi*. Email: matthew.casey@usm.edu.

Casey-Leininger, Charles F., *Cincinnati*. Email: caseylcf@ucmail.uc.edu.

Cash, Sherri G., *Utica*. Email: scash@utica.edu.

Cashdollar, Charles D. Indiana, PA. Affil: Indiana, Pa. Email: cashdolr@auxmail.iup.edu.

Cashin, Joan E., *Ohio State*. Email: cashin.2@osu.edu.

Cashion, Ty, *Sam Houston State*. Email: his_rtc@shsu.edu.

Cashwell, Meggan Farish. Raleigh, NC. Affil: Duke. Email: maf48@duke.edu. Research: US race and gender formation, law in early national period.

Casiano, Michael Ray. Baltimore, MD. Affil: Maryland, Coll. Park. Email: mc3267@gmail.com.

Casini, Matteo, *Suffolk*. Email: mattcasini@yahoo.com.

Casini, Tommaso. Firenze, Italy. Email: casini.tommaso@gmail.com. Research: 13th-c rural aristocracy in Tuscany, early 14th-c rural society in Tuscany.

Cason, Kevin. Nashville, TN. Email: kevin.h.cason@gmail.com. Research: advertising and material culture, Tennessee agriculture.

Casper, Scott E., *Nevada, Reno*. Email: casper@unr.edu.

Casper, Stephen T. Potsdam, NY. Affil: Clarkson. Email: scasper@clarkson.edu. Research: neurology and neuroscience, Anglo-American biomedicine.

Cassanelli, Lee, *Pennsylvania*. Email: lcassane@sas.upenn.edu.

Cassanello, Robert V., *Central Florida*. Orlando, FL. Affil: H-Net. Email: Robert.Cassanello@ucf.edu. Research: segregation, transportation.

Cassel, Par K., *Michigan, Ann Arbor*. Email: cassel@umich.edu.

Cassella-Blackburn, Michael. Port Angeles, WA. Affil: Peninsula. Email: mblackburn@pencol.edu. Research: 1970s US society and culture, Russian-American relations.

Cassels, Alan, *McMaster*. Email: cassels@sympatico.ca.

Casserly, Brian G., *Bellevue*. Bellevue, WA. Email: brian.casserly@bellevuecollege.edu. Research: civilian-military relations in US West, environmental politics.

Cassidy, Keith M., *Guelph*. Email: kcassidy@uoguelph.ca.

Cassidy, Michelle, *Central Michigan*. Oxford, OH. Affil: Miami, Ohio. Email: cassi2m@cmich.edu; mckrysia@umich.edu. Research: American Indian, Civil War.

Cassiere, Katrina Louise. Spokane, WA. Affil: Washington State, Pullman. Email: klcassiere@gmail.com.

Cassimere, Raphael, Jr., *New Orleans*. New Orleans, LA. Email: rcassime@uno.edu. Research: African Americans in New Orleans since Civil War.

Cassis, Marica C., *Memorial, Newfoundland*. Email: mcassis@mun.ca.

Castaneda, Chris J., *California State, Sacramento*. Email: cjc@csus.edu.

Casteel, William. North Las Vegas, NV. Affil: Norwich. Email: casteel.william1307@gmail.com. Research: mid-20th-c popular culture, gender and sexuality.

Casteen, Elizabeth Ingeborg, *Binghamton, SUNY*. Binghamton, NY. Email: ecasteen@binghamton.edu. Research: raptus in medieval Europe, gender/sexuality.

Castiglione, Caroline F., *Brown*. Providence, RI. Email: Caroline_Castiglione@Brown.edu. Research: early modern Europe, politics and society.

Castilho, Celso T., *Vanderbilt*. Brentwood, TN. Email: celso.t.castilho@vanderbilt.edu; ccastilho@hotmail.com. Research: Atlantic slavery and emancipation, citizenship and state formation.

Castillo, David M. El Paso, TX. Email: dmcastillo5@miners.utep.edu.

Castillo, Dennis. East Aurora, NY. Affil: Christ the King Seminary. Email: dcastillo@cks.edu. Research: Catholicism, Malta.

Castillo, Erin M. Tehachapi, CA. Affil: Southern New Hampshire. Email: erin.castillo11@gmail.com.

Castillo, Joshua Mark. Chicopee, MA. Affil: Boston Univ. Email: jcafhist@bu.edu.

Castillo, Pedro, *California, Santa Cruz*. Email: pcastle@ucsc.edu.

Castillo, Thomas A., *Coastal Carolina*. Conway, SC. Email: tcastillo@coastal.edu; tcasti02@gmail.com. Research: 20th-c US, class and political economy.

Castillo Reyna, Angélica. Silver Spring, MD. Affil: North Carolina, Chapel Hill. Email: luzangel2787@gmail.com. Research: Mexican masculinities and horsemanship, Mexican post-revolutionary nationalism.

Castillo-Munoz, Veronica, *California, Santa Barbara*. Arcadia, CA. Email: castillomunoz@history.ucsb.edu. Research: gender and land reform in Mexico, transnational migration.

Castle, David B., *Ohio*. Email: castle@ohio.edu.

Castonguay, Andrea Lee. Chicago, IL. Affil: Notre Dame. Email: andrea.castonguay@gmail.com. Research: Almoravid and Almohad Dynasties, Iberia and North Africa.

Castora, Joseph Charles. New Hyde Park, NY. Affil: City Coll., NY. Email: jcastora@ccny.cuny.edu. Research: 12th-c Renaissance, Cistercian Order.

Castro, A. Dwight, *Westminster*. Email: castroad@westminster.edu.

Castro, J. Justin, *Arkansas State*. Jonesboro, AR. Email: jcastro@astate.edu. Research: technology and engineering in Mexico, technology in Latin America.

Castro, Mauricio Fernando. Atlanta, GA. Affil: Georgia State. Email: mauricio.castro@duke.edu. Research: US, urban.

Castro, Myrtle. Des Plaines, IL. Affil: Eastern Illinois. Email: castro.myrtle42@gmail.com.

Castro, Sara Bush. Chapel Hill, NC. Affil: North Carolina, Chapel Hill. Email: sara.castro@unc.edu. Research: US-China relations, intelligence/national security.

Castronova, Edward. Bloomington, IN. Affil: Indiana. Email: castro@indiana.edu. Research: games/Prussian military training.

Casu, Igor. Chisinau, Moldova. Affil: State Univ., Moldova. Email: igorcasu@gmail.com.

Cater, Benjamin Michael, *Point Loma Nazarene*. Email: bencater@pointloma.edu.

Cates, Joseph E. Northfield, VT. Affil: Norwich. Email: jcates@norwich.edu. Research: US military, 19th-c Americans in Italy.

Cathcart, Dolita, *Wheaton, Mass.* Email: dcathcar@wheatoncollege.edu.

Catlin, Jonathon James. Princeton, NJ. Affil: Princeton. Email: jcatlin@princeton.edu.

Catlos, Brian A. Boulder, CO. Affil: Colorado, Boulder. Email: brian.catlos@colorado.edu. Research: Muslim-Christian-Jewish relations, Mudejares of Crown of Aragon.

Caton, Brian P., *Luther*. Decorah, IA. Email: catobr01@luther.edu. Research: colonial South Asia/Punjab, animal husbandry/breeding/vet medicine.

Catris, Sandrine Emmanuelle, *Augusta*. Augusta, GA. Email: scatris@augusta.edu. Research: post-1949 Xinjiang identity, cultural revolution and memory.

Catsam, Derek Charles, *Texas, Permian Basin*. Email: catsam_d@utpb.edu.

Catterall, W. Douglas, *Cameron*. Oklahoma City, OK. Email: dougc@cameron.edu. Research: cultural impact of migration, early modern Atlantic world.

Catton, P. E., *Stephen F. Austin State*. Nacogdoches, TX. Email: pcatton@sfasu.edu. Research: modern Asia.

Caudano, Anne-Laurence, *Winnipeg*. Email: a.caudano@uwinnipeg.ca.

Caulfield, Norman E., *Fort Hays State*. Email: ncaulfie@fhsu.edu.

Caulfield, **Sueann**, *Michigan, Ann Arbor*. Ann Arbor, MI. Email: scaul@umich.edu. Research: Latin America, women.

Caulkins, **Tamara**. Ellensburg, WA. Affil: Oregon State. Email: tamaracaulkins@hotmail.com. Research: diagrammatic movement notations, early modern body and gesture.

Causey, **Virginia E.**, *Columbus State*. Email: causey_virginia@columbusstate.edu.

Cauvin, **Thomas**, *Colorado State*. Email: thomas.cauvin@colostate.edu.

Cavallo, **Bradley**. Westville, IN. Affil: Marian. Email: bradleycavallo@yahoo.com.

Cavanaugh, **Robert L**. Frederick, MD. Email: mamlukman@aol.com.

Cave, **Mark**, *Hist. New Orleans*. Email: markc@hnoc.org.

Cave, **Scott**. Abingdon, VA. Affil: Penn State. Email: scottcuevas87@gmail.com. Research: conquest, communication after conquest.

Cavell, **Janice**, *Carleton, Can*. Email: janice.cavell@carleton.ca.

Cavell, **Samantha**, *Southeastern Louisiana*. Email: Samantha.Cavell@selu.edu.

Cavender, **Mary Wells**, *Ohio State*. Email: cavender.13@osu.edu.

Caverly, **Matthew Mark**. Cochran, GA. Affil: Middle Georgia State. Email: matthewcvrl@gmail.com. Research: presidential-congressional relations, foreign and domestic policy analysis.

Cavert, **William M.**, *St. Thomas, Minn*. Email: william.cavert@stthomas.edu.

Cawthon, **Elisabeth A.**, *Texas, Arlington*. Email: cawthon2@uta.edu.

Cawthra, **Benjamin**, *California State, Fullerton*. Fullerton, CA. Email: bcawthra@fullerton.edu. Research: African American culture, visual studies and history.

Cayton, **Mary Kupiec**, *Miami, Ohio*. Columbus, OH. Affil: Ohio State. Email: caytonmk@miamioh.edu. Research: American Evangelicalism, 19th-c US religious and cultural.

Cazorla-Sanchez, **Antonio**, *Trent*. Email: acazorla@trentu.ca.

Cebul, **Brent**, *Pennsylvania*.

Cebula, **Larry**, *Eastern Washington*. Email: lcebula@ewu.edu.

Cecil, **Anni**, *Wheaton, Mass*. Email: cecil_anni@wheatoncollege.edu.

Cecil, **Lamar**, **Jr.**, *Washington and Lee*.

Cecil, **Patrick William**, *Chapman*. Email: pcecil@chapman.edu.

Cedillo, **Adela**. Cedar Falls, IA. Affil: Wisconsin, Madison. Email: acedillo@wisc.edu. Research: revolutionary movements, drug wars.

Celani, **Lawrence**. Columbia, MO. Affil: Missouri, Columbia. Email: lcytb@mail.missouri.edu.

Celello, **Kristin M.**, *Queens, CUNY*. Email: kristin.celello@qc.cuny.edu.

Celenza, **Christopher S**. Washington, DC. Affil: Georgetown. Email: ccelenza@georgetown.edu. Research: Renaissance views of history of philosophy, social world of Renaissance intellectuals.

Çelik, **Zeynep**, *Rutgers, Newark/New Jersey Inst. of Tech*. Email: zeynep.celik@njit.edu.

Celinscak, **Mark**, *Nebraska, Omaha*. Email: mcelinscak@unomaha.edu.

Cembrola, **Robert**, *Naval War Coll*. Email: robert.cembrola@usnwc.edu.

Cenci, **Luther Cox**. Stanford, CA. Affil: Stanford. Email: lcenci1@stanford.edu.

Censer, **Jack R.**, *George Mason*. Fairfax, VA. Email: jcenser@gmu.edu. Research: France and Europe, social and intellectual.

Censer, **Jane T.**, *George Mason*. Fairfax, VA. Email: jcense1@gmu.edu. Research: 19th-c southern women, 19th-/early 20th-c women novelists.

Cerasano, **Susan P**. Hamilton, NY. Affil: Colgate. Email: scerasano@colgate.edu.

Ceric, **Meliha**, *St. Thomas, Minn*. Email: mceric@stthomas.edu.

Cerillo, **Augustus**, **Jr.**, *California State, Long Beach*. Email: acerillo@vanguard.edu.

Cerretti, **Josh**, *Western Washington*. Email: josh.cerretti@wwu.edu.

Cesario, **Brad**. College Station, TX. Affil: Texas A&M, Coll. Station. Email: cesario2@tamu.edu. Research: relationship between military & press, Royal Navy 1815-1916.

Cevasco, **Carla**. Somerset, NJ. Affil: Rutgers. Email: carla.cevasco@rutgers.edu.

Chabot, **Philip Vernon**. Hudson, WI. Email: pvchabotsr@comcast.net.

Chadbourn, **Charles C.**, **III**, *Naval War Coll*. Email: chadbouc@usnwc.edu.

Chadwick, **Bruce**, *New Jersey City*. Email: bchadwick@njcu.edu.

Chadwick, **Tara**. Fort Lauderdale, FL. Affil: Fort Lauderdale Hist. Soc. Email: wabigun@yahoo.com. Research: pleuri-perspective interpretive design, contemporary art as historical record.

Chadya, **Joyce M.**, *Manitoba*. Email: joyce.chadya@umanitoba.ca.

Chafe, **William H.**, *Duke*. Chapel Hill, NC. Email: william.chafe@duke.edu; william.chafe@gmail.com. Research: 20th-c US, oral.

Chaffee, **John W.**, *Binghamton, SUNY*. Email: chaffee@binghamton.edu.

Chaiklin, **Martha**. Columbia, MD. Email: chaiklin@pitt.edu. Research: ivory carving and trade, shoes.

Cha-Jua, **Sundiata K.**, *Illinois, Urbana-Champaign*. Email: schajua@illinois.edu.

Chakars, **Melissa**, *St. Joseph's*. Email: mchakars@sju.edu.

Chakrabarty, **Dipesh**, *Chicago*. Chicago, IL. Email: dipesh@uchicago.edu. Research: modern Indian cultural and social, Bengal.

Chakraborty, **Suparna**, *Stephen F. Austin State*. Email: chakrabos@sfasu.edu.

Chakravarti, **Ananya**, *Georgetown*. New Cairo, Egypt. Affil: American, Cairo. Email: ac1646@georgetown.edu; chakravarti_ananya@yahoo.com. Research: colonial Brazil, early modern South Asia.

Chakravartty, **Aryendra**, *Stephen F. Austin State*. Email: chakravaa@sfasu.edu.

Chalhoub, **Sidney**, *Harvard (Hist.)*. Email: chalhoub@fas.harvard.edu.

Chalifoux, **Stephanie M.**, *West Georgia*. Email: schalifo@westga.edu.

Chalk, **Frank Robert**, *Concordia, Can*. Email: Frank.Chalk@concordia.ca.

Challu, **Amilcar E.**, *Bowling Green State*. Bowling Green, OH. Email: achallu@bgsu.edu. Research: famine/hunger and living standards, economic.

Chalmers, **David**, *Florida*. Email: chi@ufl.edu.

Chalou, **Mandy**, *US Dept. of State*.

Chamberlain, **David Moylan**. East Burke, VT. Affil: Burke Mountain Academy. Email: cribgochridge@yahoo.com. Research:

environmental citizenship, political economy of Edward Abbey.

Chamberlain, **Douglas**. Jamestown, RI. Affil: Naval War Coll. Email: douglas.chamberlain@usnwc.edu.

Chamberlain, **Mary Ava**. Dayton, OH. Affil: Wright State. Email: ava.chamberlain@wright.edu. Research: early American religious, gender.

Chamberlain, **Michael M.**, *Wisconsin-Madison*. Email: mchamber@wisc.edu.

Chamberlain, **Oscar B.**, *Wisconsin-Eau Claire*. Email: chambeob@uwec.edu.

Chamberland, **Celeste C.**, *Roosevelt*. Email: cchamberland@roosevelt.edu.

Chamberlin, **Foster Pease**. San Diego, CA. Affil: San Diego Miramar. Email: fosterpchambers@gmail.com. Research: interwar democratic collapse, police.

Chamberlin, **Paul T.**, *Columbia (Hist.)*. Email: ptc2121@columbia.edu.

Chamberlin, **Ute Elisabeth**, *Western Illinois*. Macomb, IL. Email: UE-Chamberlin@wiu.edu. Research: German urban and women, German women in post-WWI politics.

Chambers, **Douglas Brent**, *Southern Mississippi*. Email: douglas.chambers@usm.edu.

Chambers, **Glenn Anthony**, *Michigan State*. East Lansing, MI. Email: chamb311@msu.edu. Research: Latinos and Afro-Latinos/US South, African diaspora/migration.

Chambers, **Henry E.**, *California State, Sacramento*. Email: hchamber@csus.edu.

Chambers, **John W.**, **II**, *Rutgers*. Email: chamber@history.rutgers.edu.

Chambers, **Kevin C.**, *Gonzaga*. Email: chambersk@gonzaga.edu.

Chambers, **Lee**, *Colorado, Boulder*. Email: chambers@colorado.edu.

Chambers, **Mark Milton**. Central Islip, NY. Affil: SUNY, Stony Brook. Email: markc1717@gmail.com. Research: Native American/Euro-American convergence, early mining practices/technology.

Chambers, **Mortimer**, *UCLA*. Email: chambers@history.ucla.edu.

Chambers, **Sarah C.**, *Minnesota (Hist.)*. Minneapolis, MN. Email: chambers@umn.edu. Research: Spanish American independence, 19th-c Chilean family and politics.

Chambliss, **Julian Carlos**. East Lansing, MI. Affil: Michigan State. Email: chambl91@msu.edu. Research: urban planning, urbanization.

Chambliss, **Melanie**. Chicago, IL. Affil: Columbia Coll., Chicago. Email: mchambliss@colum.edu.

Chambres, **William F**. La Mott, PA. Affil: Westbrook-Rock Hill Foundation. Email: contactus@historic-lamott-pa.com. Research: Cheltenham Township PA, Camp William Penn.

Chamedes, **Giuliana R**, *Wisconsin-Madison*. Madison, WI. Email: chamedes@wisc.edu; giuliana.chamedes@gmail.com. Research: international, modern Europe.

Chamosa, **Oscar**, *Georgia*. Athens, GA. Email: chamo01@uga.edu. Research: folklore and politics of cultural nationalism, Civic associations and development.

Champa, **David A**. Crawfordsville, IN. Email: dachampa@att.net. Research: Civil War governors, Holocaust in Italy.

Champion, **Claire**. Sewickley, PA. Email: championclaire@yahoo.com.

Champion, Craige B., *Syracuse*. Email: cbchamp@maxwell.syr.edu.

Champion, Matthew S. London, United Kingdom. Affil: Birkbeck, London. Email: m.champion@bbk.ac.uk. Research: late medieval Northern Europe, temporalities.

Chan, Man Ning. Hong Kong. Email: chanmanning413@gmail.com.

Chan, Roger Y., *Washington State, Pullman*. Email: rchan@wsu.edu.

Chan, Shelly P., *Wisconsin-Madison*. Madison, WI. Email: shelly.chan@wisc.edu. Research: modern and global China, migration and diaspora.

Chan, Wellington, *Occidental*. Email: wkchan@oxy.edu.

Chand, Rakashi, *Massachusetts Hist. Soc.* Email: rchand@masshist.org.

Chande, Abdin, *Adelphi*. Email: chande@adelphi.edu.

Chandler, Abby B. Lowell, MA. Affil: Massachusetts, Lowell. Email: abigail_chandler@uml.edu. Research: colonial American legal, political uprisings.

Chandler, **D. S.**, *Miami, Ohio*. Email: chandlds@miamioh.edu.

Chandler, *Kegan A.* Kingwood, TX. Affil: Atlanta Bible. Email: keganchandler@yahoo.com.

Chandler, *Tom*. Melbourne, Australia. Affil: Monash. Email: tom.chandler@monash.edu.

Chandra, Shefali, *Washington, St. Louis*. Email: sc23@wustl.edu.

Chandra, Vipan, *Wheaton, Mass.* Email: vchandra@wheatonma.edu.

Chaney, Wesley B., *Bates*. Email: wchaney@bates.edu.

Chang, Amanda. Washington, DC. Affil: Woodrow Wilson High Sch. Email: amanda.chang@dc.gov.

Chang, Capt Adam, *US Military Acad.* Email: adam.chang@usma.edu.

Chang, Chia-Lan, *Winthrop*. Email: changc@winthrop.edu.

Chang, Chun-Shu, *Michigan, Ann Arbor*. Ann Arbor, MI. Email: cschang@umich.edu. Research: ancient and Ch'in-Han China, Sung-Ming-Ch'ing China.

Chang, David A., *Minnesota (Hist.)*. Email: dchang@umn.edu.

Chang, Derek S., *Cornell*. Email: dsc37@cornell.edu.

Chang, Gordon H., *Stanford*. Stanford, CA. Email: gchang@stanford.edu. Research: US-Pacific relations, Asian American.

Chang, Hao, *Ohio State*.

Chang, Hui-hua, *Elon*. Email: hchang@elon.edu.

Chang, Jason Oliver, *Connecticut, Storrs*. Email: jason.o.chang@uconn.edu.

Chang, Kornel, *Rutgers, Newark/New Jersey Inst. of Tech.* Email: kchang4@rutgers.edu.

Chang, Lung-chih. Nankang, Taipei, Taiwan. Affil: Academia Sinica. Email: lchang@gate.sinica.edu.tw. Research: Japanese colonial discourse in Taiwan, contemporary Taiwanese historiography.

Chang, Michael G., *George Mason*. Email: mchang5@gmu.edu.

Chang, Vivien. London, United Kingdom. Affil: Virginia. Email: vlc5ds@virginia.edu.

Chanis, Shery. Austin, TX. Affil: Texas, Austin. Email: schanis@utexas.edu. Research: early modern China.

Chao, Anne Shen, *Rice*. Email: annechao@rice.edu.

Chao, Glenda Ellen, *Ursinus*. Email: gchao@ursinus.edu.

Chao, Yuan-ling, *Middle Tennessee State*. Email: YuanLing.Chao@mtsu.edu.

Chaparro Silva, Alexander. Austin, TX. Affil: Texas, Austin. Email: alexander.chaparro@utexas.edu. Research: Spanish-American political culture 1700-1851, Spanish-American intellectual 1700-1851.

Chapdelaine, Robin P., *Duquesne*. Email: chapdelainer@duq.edu.

Chapel, Lesley Lynne. Auburn Hills, MI. Affil: Nevada State. Email: Lesley.Chapel@nsc.edu.

Chapin, Christy Ford, *Maryland, Baltimore County*. Email: cchapin@umbc.edu.

Chaplin, Joyce, *Harvard (Hist.)*. Cambridge, MA. Email: chaplin@fas.harvard.edu. Research: around-the-world travel, colonial America.

Chaplin, Tamara, *Illinois, Urbana-Champaign*. Email: tchaplin@illinois.edu.

Chapman, Alice L., *Grand Valley State*. Email: chapmali@gvsu.edu.

Chapman, Alister, *Westmont*. Email: chapman@westmont.edu.

Chapman, Erin D., *George Washington*. Washington, DC. Email: echapman@gwu.edu. Research: black feminism/African American gender, race/gender/film/popular culture.

Chapman, Herrick E., *NYU*. Brookline, MA. Email: hc3@nyu.edu. Research: France/French empire, social/economic/political.

Chapman, Jessica M., *Williams*. Email: jmc1@williams.edu.

Chapman, Richard M., *Concordia Coll.* Moorhead, MN. Email: chapman@cord.edu. Research: solidarity work in Central America, Lutherans and slavery.

Chapman, Richard N., *Francis Marion*. Email: rchapman@fmarion.edu.

Chapman, Ryan, *North Carolina, Wilmington*. Email: chapmanrj@uncw.edu.

Chapman Williams, Sara E., *Oakland*. Email: chapman@oakland.edu.

Chapman-Adisho, Annette R., *Salem State*. Email: achapmanadisho@salemstate.edu.

Chapnick, Adam. Toronto, ON, Canada. Affil: Canadian Forces Coll. Email: a.chapnick@gmail.com. Research: UN Security Council, Canadian foreign policy.

Chappel, James G., *Duke*. Email: jgc@duke.edu.

Chappell, David A., *Hawai'i, Manoa*. Email: dchappel@hawaii.edu.

Chappell, David L., *Oklahoma (Hist.)*. Norman, OK. Email: dchappell@ou.edu. Research: US social and intellectual, cultural.

Chappell, L. Stephen, *James Madison*. Email: chappesx@jmu.edu.

Chard, Daniel S. Amherst, MA. Affil: Massachusetts Amherst. Email: dchard@history.umass.edu. Research: terrorism and political violence, surveillance and policing.

Chardell, Daniel. Deerfield, IL. Affil: Harvard. Email: dchardell@g.harvard.edu. Research: end of Cold War in Middle East, US military intervention.

Charenko, Melissa, *Michigan State*. Email: charenko@msu.edu.

Chariton, Jesse David. Columbus, GA. Affil: Iowa State. Email: chariton@iastate.edu. Research: Irish famine immigration to US, race/ethnicity and religion in America.

Charles, Douglas M. Mckeesport, PA. Affil: Penn State, Greater Allegheny. Email: dmc166@psu.edu. Research: FBI surveillance of gays/obscenity, FBI.

Charles, Elizabeth C., *US Dept. of State*.

Charles, Jeffrey, *California State, San Marcos*. Email: jcharles@csusm.edu.

Charlip, Julie A., *Whitman*. Walla Walla, WA. Email: charlija@whitman.edu. Research: domestic security forces of Costa Rica.

Charney, Lena London. Bronx, NY.

Charney, Paul J., *Frostburg State*. Email: pcharney@frostburg.edu.

Charnoff, Deborah B. New York, NY. Affil: Graduate Center, CUNY. Email: dcharnoff@gradcenter.cuny.edu. Research: colonial American intellectual, early modern English intellectual.

Charnow, Sally, *Hofstra*. Brooklyn, NY. Email: sally.charnow@hofstra.edu. Research: turn-of-the-century Paris, cultural politics and modernism.

Charters, David, *New Brunswick*. Email: charters@unb.ca.

Chartier, Roger A., *Pennsylvania*. Paris, France. Affil: Ecole des Hautes Etudes en Sci. Sociales. Email: chartier@history.upenn.edu. Research: written culture, culture and sociology of texts.

Charumbira, Ruramisai A. Bern, Switzerland. Affil: Bern. Email: r-c@aya.yale.edu. Research: historical memory, empire and immigration.

Chary, Frederick B., *Indiana, Northwest*.

Chase, Erin, *Huntington Library*. Email: echase@huntington.org.

Chase, Joseph. Coralville, IA. Email: jchase11@gmail.com. Research: Indigenous studies, Religious studies.

Chase, Lawrence J., *Eastern Kentucky*. Email: larry.chase@eku.edu.

Chase, Michelle Chi, *Pace*. New York, NY. Email: chase.michelle@gmail.com. Research: Cuban Revolution.

Chase, Philander D. Charlottesville, VA. Affil: Virginia. Email: pdc1732@gmail.com. Research: George Washington Papers, Revolutionary War.

Chase, Robert G., *Sonoma State*. San Mateo, CA. Email: chaserobert@yahoo.com. Research: Great White Fleet, Pacific world's fairs.

Chase, Robert T., *SUNY, Stony Brook*. Email: robert.chase@stonybrook.edu.

Chase, William J., *Pittsburgh*. Email: wchase@pitt.edu.

Chase-Levenson, Alexander, *Pennsylvania*. Email: alchase@sas.upenn.edu.

Chassen-Lopez, Francie R., *Kentucky*. Lexington, KY. Email: frclopz@uky.edu. Research: Latin American gender and state formation, women and power.

Chastain, Andra Brosy. Vancouver, WA. Affil: Washington State, Vancouver. Email: andra.chastain@wsu.edu. Research: urban development in Latin America, technology and expertise.

Chastain, James G., *Ohio*. Email: jameschastain5@yahoo.com.

Chasteen, John C., *North Carolina, Chapel Hill*. Email: chasteen@email.unc.edu.

Chastko, Paul A., *Calgary*. Email: pchastko@ucalgary.ca.

Chatani, Sayaka. Singapore. Affil: National, Singapore. Email: sc2049@columbia.edu.

Chatelain, **Marcia**, *Georgetown*. Washington, DC. Email: mc899@georgetown.edu. Research: childhood and youth, women.

Chatfield, **Andrew**. Washington, DC. Affil: American. Email: ac5668a@student.american.edu. Research: American diplomatic, Progressive era.

Chatterjee, **Choi**, *California State, Los Angeles*. Email: cchatte@calstatela.edu.

Chatterjee, **Indrani**, *Texas, Austin*. Email: ichatterjee@austin.utexas.edu.

Chatterjee, **Rohan**. Chicago, IL. Affil: Chicago. Email: rchatterjee@uchicago.edu.

Chatterjee, **Sumita**, *Miami*. Email: s.chatterjee@miami.edu.

Chattopadhyaya, **Utathya**, *California, Santa Barbara*. Santa Barbara, CA. Email: utathya@ucsb.edu. Research: modern South Asia.

Chaturvedi, **Vinayak**, *California, Irvine*. Irvine, CA. Email: vinayak@uci.edu. Research: Hindu nationalism intellectual, 20th-c Gujarat history and politics.

Chaudhry, **Faisal Iqbal**. Dayton, OH. Affil: Dayton. Email: fchaudhry1@udayton.edu. Research: early modern/modern South Asia, globalization of classical legal thought.

Chaudhuri, **Meghna**. New York, NY. Affil: NYU. Email: mc4426@nyu.edu.

Chaudhuri, **Nupur**, *Texas Southern*. Houston, TX. Email: nupurc@earthlink.net. Research: national identity and Alsace, nationalism in Egypt/India/Nigeria.

Chauncey, **George**, *Columbia (Hist.)*. Email: george.chauncey@columbia.edu.

Chauvin, **Kenneth**, *Appalachian State*. Email: chauvinkm@appstate.edu.

Chauvin, **Munson**, *Southeastern Louisiana*. Email: munson.chauvin@southeastern.edu.

Chauvin, **Thomas N.**, *Central Connecticut State*. Email: chauvinthn@mail.ccsu.edu.

Chavalas, **Mark W.**, *Wisconsin-La Crosse*. Email: chavalas.mark@uwlax.edu.

Chavez, **Eric**. El Paso, TX. Affil: Texas, El Paso; El Paso Comm. Coll. Email: echavez24@miners.utep.edu.

Chavez, **Ernesto**, *Texas, El Paso*. El Paso, TX. Email: echavez@utep.edu. Research: film/sexuality, Latino.

Chavez, **Joaquin M.**, *Illinois, Chicago*. Chicago, IL. Email: chavezj1@uic.edu. Research: Cold War in Latin America, intellectuals/peace and conflict.

Chavez, **John R.**, *Southern Methodist*. Dallas, TX. Email: jchavez@smu.edu. Research: Zacatecas and US Southwest, North Atlantic world.

Chavez, **Meghann**. Miami Beach, FL. Affil: Florida International. Email: mchav097@fiu.edu.

Chavez, **Miguel M.**, *Lamar*. Email: miguel.chavez@lamar.edu.

Chávez, **David**. Pasadena, CA. Affil: California, Riverside. Email: dchav014@ucr.edu.

Chavez-Garcia, **Miroslava**, *California, Santa Barbara*. Email: mchavezgarcia@history.ucsb.edu.

Chavis, **Charles Lester, Jr**. Columbia, MD. Affil: George Mason. Email: charles.chavis18@alumni.morgan.edu.

Chazan, **Robert**, *NYU*. Email: rc2@nyu.edu.

Chazelle, **Celia**, *New Jersey*. Email: chazelle@tcnj.edu.

Chazkel, **Amy**. Brooklyn, NY. Affil: Columbia. Email: amychazkel@gmail.com. Research:

criminality and justice in modern Brazil, urban slavery in Brazil.

Cheape, **Charles W.**, **III**, *Loyola, Md*. Email: ccheape@loyola.edu.

Checkovich, **Alex**, *Richmond*. Email: acheckov@richmond.edu.

Cheek, **Timothy C.**, *British Columbia*. Email: t.cheek@ubc.ca.

Cheek, **William F.**, **III**, *San Diego State*.

Chehabi, **Houchang E.**, *Boston Univ*. Email: chehabi@bu.edu.

Chen, **Anne Hunnell**, *Hofstra*. Email: anne.h.chen@hofstra.edu.

Chen, **BuYun**, *Swarthmore*. Swarthmore, PA. Email: bchen5@swarthmore.edu. Research: fashion/silk production, women's work.

Chen, **Candace S**. Richmond, CA. Email: candaceschen@gmail.com.

Chen, **Chi-yun**, *California, Santa Barbara*.

Chen, **Constance J. S.**, *Loyola Marymount*. Email: cchen@lmu.edu.

Chen, **Gilbert**, *Towson*.

Chen, **Janet Y.**, *Princeton*. Email: jychen@princeton.edu.

Chen, **Jeffery Chun-Jung**. Stanford, CA. Affil: Stanford. Email: jefferyc@stanford.edu.

Chen, **Jian**, *Cornell*. Ithaca, NY. Email: jc585@cornell.edu. Research: Sino-American relations, China.

Chen, **John C**. San Gabriel, CA. Affil: Claremont Graduate. Email: jcchendrew@aol.com. Research: American religion, Sinicizing Christianity in China.

Chen, **John Tseh-han**. Brooklyn, NY. Affil: Columbia. Email: jtc2148@columbia.edu. Research: Islam and Muslims in China, science and medicine.

Chen, **Joseph T.**, *California State, Northridge*.

Chen, **Li**, *Toronto*. Email: lchen@utsc.utoronto.ca.

Chen, **Min-sun**. Thunder Bay, ON, Canada. Affil: Lakehead. Email: mchen1@lakeheadu.ca.

Chen, **Shiau-Yun**, *Ball State*. Email: schen5@bsu.edu.

Chen, **Shiwei**, *Lake Forest*. Email: chen@lakeforest.edu.

Chen, **Shuang**, *Iowa*. Email: shuang-chen@uiowa.edu.

Chen, **Tina Mai**, *Manitoba*. Email: tina.chen@umanitoba.ca.

Chen, **Wei-ti**. Somerville, MA. Affil: Harvard. Email: weitichen1631@gmail.com. Research: East Asia, China and Japan.

Chen, **Xiaoming**, *Ohio Wesleyan*. Email: xmchen@owu.edu.

Chen, **Yixin**, *North Carolina, Wilmington*. Email: cheny@uncw.edu.

Chen, **Yong**, *California, Irvine*. Email: y3chen@uci.edu.

Chenault, **Robert R.**, *Willamette*. Email: rchenaul@willamette.edu.

Cheney, **Charise**, *Oregon*. Email: ccheney@uoregon.edu.

Cheney, **David M**. Overland Park, KS. Email: dmcheney@gmail.com. Research: Catholic hierarchy.

Cheney, **Paul B.**, *Chicago*. Chicago, IL. Email: cheney@uchicago.edu. Research: intellectual, European economic expansion.

Cheng, **Cindy I-Fen**, *Wisconsin-Madison*. Email: cicheng@wisc.edu.

Cheng, **Kimberly**. Arlington, VA. Affil: NYU. Email: kac780@nyu.edu.

Cheng, **Rachel K**. Fremont, CA. Affil: Dominican Sisters of Mission San Jose. Email: rachel.k.cheng@gmail.com. Research: gender, race and ethnicity.

Chenier, **Elise R.**, *Simon Fraser*. Email: echenier@sfu.ca.

Chen-Lin, **Diana**, *Indiana, Northwest*. Email: dchenlin@iun.edu.

Chenut, **Helen Harden**, *California, Irvine*. Email: hchenut@uci.edu.

Cheong, **Caroline**, *Central Florida*. Email: Caroline.Cheong@ucf.edu.

Cherian, **Divya**, *Princeton*. Email: dcherian@princeton.edu.

Cherian, **Reema**. Sacramento, CA. Affil: California, Davis. Email: rcherian@ucdavis.edu.

Chernock, **Arianne J.**, *Boston Univ*. Boston, MA. Email: chernock@bu.edu. Research: male feminism, comparative ethnography.

Cherny, **Robert W**. San Francisco, CA. Affil: San Francisco State. Email: robt.cherny@gmail.com.

Cherry, **David**, *Montana State, Bozeman*. Email: dcherry@montana.edu.

Cherry, **Haydon L.**, *Northwestern*. Evanston, IL. Email: haydon.cherry@northwestern.edu. Research: Vietnamese social, Vietnamese intellectual.

Cherry, **Kevin**, *North Carolina Office of Archives*. Email: kevin.cherry@ncdcr.gov.

Cherry, **Megan Lindsay**, *North Carolina State*. Email: megan_cherry@ncsu.edu.

Chervin, **Reed**. Hong Kong. Affil: Hong Kong. Email: chervin@hku.hk.

Chervinsky, **Lindsay Mitchell**. Los Angeles, CA. Affil: California, Davis. Email: lindsay.chervinsky@gmail.com. Research: origins of the president's cabinet.

Chery, **Tshepo Masango**, *Houston; Texas, Austin*. Email: tmchery@central.uh.edu; tmchery@austin.utexas.edu.

Chesley, **Emily Ruth**. Princeton, NJ. Affil: Princeton Theological Seminary. Email: emily.chesley@ptsem.edu.

Chesney, **Peter**. Los Angeles, CA. Affil: UCLA. Email: mrpchesney@gmail.com.

Chesnut, **Glenn F.**, *Indiana, South Bend*. Email: gchesnut@iusb.edu.

Chester, **Lucy**, *Colorado, Boulder*. Boulder, CO. Email: chester@colorado.edu. Research: connections between India and Palestine, maps in Indian nationalism.

Chesterton, **Bridget M.**, *SUNY, Buffalo State*. Email: chesterbm@buffalostate.edu.

Chet, **Guy**, *North Texas*. Email: guychet@unt.edu.

Cheta, **Omar**, *Bard*. Annandale On Hudson, NY. Email: ocheta@bard.edu. Research: Middle East and Ottoman, economic and legal.

Chettiar, **Teri Anne**, *Illinois, Urbana-Champaign*. Email: chettiar@illinois.edu.

Cheung-Miaw, **Calvin**. Daly City, CA. Affil: Stanford. Email: calvin.miaw@gmail.com.

Chevalier, **Cheryl**. Arlington, VA. Email: cherylmchevalier@verizon.net.

Chevalier, **Genevieve**. Tecumseh, ON, Canada. Affil: Windsor. Email: chevalig@uwindsor.ca.

Chew, **Richard S.**, **III**. Williamsburg, VA. Affil: Virginia State. Email: rchew@vsu.edu. Research: American Revolution and Atlantic economy, colonial Chesapeake and Atlantic world.

Chew, Selfa, *Texas, El Paso*. Email: sachew@utep.edu.

Chew, Virginia Montijo, *Omohundro Inst*. Email: vlmont@wm.edu.

Chhabria, Sheetal, *Connecticut Coll*. New London, CT. Email: schhabri@conncoll.edu. Research: South Asia, urbanization.

Chhun, Maura Elizabeth, *Metropolitan State*. Minneapolis, MN. Email: maura.chhun@metrostate.edu; maura.chhun@gmail.com. Research: Britain and empire, gender.

Chi, Xiang. Los Angeles, CA. Affil: UCLA. Email: thuchix@gmail.com.

Chia, Jack Meng-Tat. Singapore. Affil: National, Singapore. Email: mc2286@cornell.edu. Research: Buddhism, overseas Chinese.

Chia, Lucille, *California, Riverside*. Riverside, CA. Email: lucille.chia@ucr.edu. Research: traditional China, social and cultural.

Chiang, Connie Y., *Bowdoin*. Email: cchiang@bowdoin.edu.

Chiang, Howard Hsueh-Hao, *California, Davis*. Davis, CA. Email: hhchiang@ucdavis.edu. Research: medicine, transsexuality.

Chiang, Yung-chen, *DePauw*. Email: ychiang@depauw.edu.

Chiasson, Blaine, *Wilfrid Laurier*. Email: bchiasson@wlu.ca.

Chickering, Roger P., *Georgetown*. South Beach, OR. Email: chickerr@georgetown.edu. Research: German agriculture/political.

Chien, Cecilia L. F., *West Chester*. Email: cchien@wcupa.edu.

Chiero, Heather J., *Augusta*. Email: hchiero@augusta.edu.

Chikowero, Moses, *California, Santa Barbara*. Email: chikowero@history.ucsb.edu.

Childers, Christopher, *Pittsburg State*. Email: rchilders@pittstate.edu.

Childers, Jason. Macclenny, FL. Email: childerssage@gmail.com.

Childers, Michael Wayne, *Colorado State*. Email: michael.childers@colostate.edu.

Childers, Thomas, Jr., *Pennsylvania*. Email: childers@sas.upenn.edu.

Childress, Faith J., *Rockhurst*. Email: faith.childress@rockhurst.edu.

Childrose, Nicole C. Hudson, NY. Affil: Columbia-Greene Comm. Coll. Email: nicole.childrose@sunycgcc.edu.

Childs, Greg L., *Brandeis*. Email: gchilds@brandeis.edu.

Childs, Lisa C. Fayetteville, AR. Affil: Arkansas, Fayetteville. Email: lcchilds@uark.edu.

Childs, Matt D., *South Carolina, Columbia*. Columbia, SC. Email: matchilds@yahoo.com; childsmd@mailbox.sc.edu. Research: Havana and African diaspora, black militia soldiers in Latin America.

Childs, Travis Madison, *Cameron*. Email: tchilds@cameron.edu.

Childs, William R., *Ohio State*. Austin, TX. Email: childs.1@osu.edu; billchildstex@gmail.com. Research: energy policy and environment, 20th-c consumer culture.

Chiles, Robert, *Maryland, Coll. Park*. Email: rchiles@umd.edu.

Chilton, Katherine, *San José State*. Email: katherine.chilton@sjsu.edu.

Chilton, Madeleine. Saint Louis, MO. Affil: American. Email: mm7357a@american.edu.

Chilukuri, Shaan. Chevy Chase, MD. Affil: American. Email: sc2672a@american.edu.

Chin, Angelina, *Pomona*. Email: angelina.chin@pomona.edu.

Chin, Carol C., *Toronto*. Toronto, ON, Canada. Email: carol.chin@utoronto.ca. Research: US-East Asia relations 1890-1920, culture and US foreign relations.

Chin, Hue-ping. Springfield, MO. Affil: Drury. Email: hchin@drury.edu. Research: modern China, women.

Chin, Rita C-K, *Michigan, Ann Arbor*. Ann Arbor, MI. Email: rchin@umich.edu. Research: European Left, immigration in New Europe.

Chinea, Jorge L., *Wayne State*. Email: aa1941@wayne.edu.

Ching, Erik K., *Furman*. Greenville, SC. Email: erik.ching@furman.edu. Research: 19th-c El Salvador, 20th-c Central American communism.

Chinnici, Joseph P. Oceanside, CA. Affil: Franciscan Sch. of Theology. Email: jchinnici@fst.edu. Research: American religious, medieval Franciscan.

Chira, Adriana, *Emory*. Email: adriana.chira@emory.edu.

Chirhart, Ann S., *Indiana State*. Email: Ann.Chirhart@indstate.edu.

Chisholm, Donald W., *Naval War Coll*. Email: chisholm@usnwc.edu.

Chisick, Harvey. Haifa, Israel. Affil: Haifa. Email: hchisick@gmail.com.

Chism, Jonathan, *Houston-Downtown*. Email: chismj@uhd.edu.

Chittur, Debra. Huntsville, AL. Email: dchittur@gmail.com.

Chiu, Cheng-Chang. Sacramento, CA. Email: ccchiu50@gmail.com.

Chmielewski, Edward, *Tennessee, Knoxville*.

Cho, Heesoo. University City, MO. Affil: Washington, St. Louis. Email: heesoocho@wustl.edu.

Cho, Hwisang. Atlanta, GA. Affil: Emory. Email: hwisang.cho@emory.edu. Research: Korean storytelling and charisma, Eurasian Nexus in Korean textual culture.

Cho, Joanne Miyang, *William Paterson*. Email: choj@wpunj.edu.

Cho, Jun Hee, *Amherst*. Email: jcho@amherst.edu.

Cho, Sue Jean. Arlington, VA. Affil: Northern Virginia Comm. Coll. Email: suejeancho@gmail.com. Research: Korean immigration to US, citizenship and transnationalism.

Choate, Mark I., *Brigham Young*. Email: mark_choate@byu.edu.

Chodorow, Stanley, *California, San Diego*. La Jolla, CA. Email: schodorow@ucsd.edu. Research: medieval legal, libraries.

Choe, Yong-ho, *Hawai'i, Manoa*. Email: choeyh@hawaii.edu.

Choi, Hye Eun. New York, NY. Affil: Columbia. Email: choi.hyeeun@gmail.com.

Choi, Sung-Eun, *Bentley*. Email: schoi@bentley.edu.

Chojnacki, Stanley J., *North Carolina, Chapel Hill*. Email: venetian@live.unc.edu.

Chomsky, Aviva, *Salem State*. Email: achomsky@salemstate.edu.

Chopas, Mary Elizabeth Basile. Concord, MA. Affil: Harvard Law Sch. Email: marychopas@gmail.com.

Chopra, Preeti, *Wisconsin-Madison*. Email: chopra@wisc.edu.

Chopra, Ruma, *San José State*. Mountain View, CA. Email: Ruma.Chopra@sjsu.edu. Research: colonial America, Latin America.

Choquette, Leslie P., *Assumption*. Email: lchoquet@assumption.edu.

Chou, Catherine, *Grinnell*. Email: choucath@grinnell.edu.

Choudhury, Mita, *Vassar*. Email: michoudhury@vassar.edu.

Choudhury, Rishad, *Oberlin*. Oberlin, OH. Email: rchoudhu@oberlin.edu. Research: South Asia.

Chouin, Gerard, *William and Mary*. Email: glchouin@wm.edu.

Chow, Kai-wing, *Illinois, Urbana-Champaign*. Email: kchow1@illinois.edu.

Chowdhury, Amitava, *Queen's, Can*. Email: a.chowdhury@queensu.ca.

Chowkwanyun, Merlin, *Columbia (Hist. Public Health)*. Email: mc2028@cumc.columbia.edu.

Chowning, Margaret, *California, Berkeley*. Berkeley, CA. Email: chowning@berkeley.edu. Research: colonial and 19th-c Mexican women/church.

Chrastil, Rachel A., *Xavier, Ohio*. Cincinnati, OH. Email: chrastilr@xavier.edu. Research: childlessness.

Chretien, Lisa. Hermiston, OR. Affil: Hermiston High Sch. Email: lisa.chretien@hermistonsd.org. Research: American Revolution/missed history, Oregon/Pacific Northwest/West.

Chrislock, C. Winston, *St. Thomas, Minn*. Email: cwchrislock@stthomas.edu.

Chrissanthos, Stefan G., *California State, Fullerton; California, Riverside*. Email: schrissanthos@fullerton.edu; stefan.chrissanthos@ucr.edu.

Chrissidis, Nikolaos A., *Southern Connecticut State*. Email: chrissidisn1@southernct.edu.

Christ, Matthew, *Indiana*. Email: mrchrist@indiana.edu.

Christelow, Allan, Jr., *Idaho State*.

Christelow, Stephanie Mooers, *Idaho State*.

Christensen, Carl C., *Colorado, Boulder*.

Christensen, Daniel Eric, *Biola; California State, Fullerton*. Email: daniel.christensen@biola.edu; dchristensen@fullerton.edu.

Christensen, Kurt L. Leawood, KS. Affil: Missouri, Kansas City. Email: klckb4@mail.umkc.edu. Research: unemployment, retirement benefits.

Christensen, Robert. Santa Fe, NM. Affil: Georgetown. Email: rc1317@georgetown.edu.

Christian, David Gilbert, *San Diego State*. Email: dgchrist@sdsu.edu.

Christiansen, Samantha M. R., *Colorado Colorado Springs*. Email: schrist3@uccs.edu.

Christianson, Eric H., *Kentucky*. Email: ehchri01@uky.edu.

Christianson, J. R., *Luther*. Minneapolis, MN. Email: christianson@luther.edu. Research: royal courts, Scandinavian cultural.

Christianson, Paul K., *Queen's, Can*. Email: christia@queensu.ca.

Christie, Nancy, *Western Ontario*. Email: nchrist8@uwo.ca.

Christman, Robert J., *Luther*. Email: chriro05@luther.edu.

Christman, Victoria, *Luther*. Email: chrivi02@luther.edu.

Christmas, Farah. Hazlehurst, MS. Affil: Jackson State. Email: farah.l.christmas@jsums.edu. Research: global, women.

Christmas, *Sakura*, *Bowdoin*. Brunswick, ME. Email: schristm@bowdoin.edu. Research: environment, science and technology studies.

Christofferson, **Michael**, *Adelphi*. Email: mchristofferson@adelphi.edu.

Christopher, **Chad A.**, *Northern Iowa*. Email: chad.christopher@uni.edu.

Christopoulos, **John**, *British Columbia*. Email: john.christopoulos@ubc.ca.

Christou, **Theodore**, *Queen's, Can*. Email: theodore.christou@queensu.ca.

Christy, **Alan S.**, *California, Santa Cruz*. Email: achristy@ucsc.edu.

Chu, **Jonathan M.**, *Massachusetts, Boston*. Email: jonathan.chu@umb.edu.

Chu, **Pao-chin**, *San Diego State*.

Chu, *Pey-Yi*, *Pomona*. Claremont, CA. Email: peyyichu@gmail.com. Research: earth sciences, transnational scientific exchanges.

Chu, **Richard T.**, *Massachusetts, Amherst*. Email: rtchu@history.umass.edu.

Chu, *Winson W.*, *Wisconsin-Milwaukee*. Milwaukee, WI. Email: wchu@uwm.edu; winson.w.chu@gmail.com. Research: German minorities, cities in east central Europe.

Chuchiak, **John F.**, **IV**, *Missouri State*. Email: johnchuchiak@missouristate.edu.

Chudacoff, **Howard P.**, *Brown*. Email: Howard_Chudacoff@Brown.edu.

Chudzinski, *Adrienne Elyse*. Fremont, OH. Affil: Stanford Online High Sch. Email: adriennechudzinski@stanford.edu. Research: modern US, memory and public history.

Chulos, *Chris John*, *Roosevelt*. Oak Park, IL. Email: cchulos@roosevelt.edu. Research: collective memory, modern Russia.

Chumney, **James R.**, **Jr.**, *Memphis*. Email: jchumney@memphis.edu.

Chung, **Patrick**. College Park, MD. Affil: Maryland, Coll. Park. Email: pchung10@umd.edu. Research: US military, modern South Korea.

Chung, *Sue Fawn*, *Nevada, Las Vegas*. Email: suefawn.chung@unlv.edu.

Church, *Christopher M.*, *Nevada, Reno*. Reno, NV. Email: christopherchurch@unr.edu. Research: digital, late modern Europe.

Church, *Rebecca Ellen*, *Metropolitan State*. Saint Paul, MN. Email: rebecca.church@metrostate.edu. Research: Iberian peninsula and southern France, monastic women.

Churchill, *Bernardita Reyes*. Washington, DC. Affil: Philippines. Email: nitachurchill@hotmail.com. Research: local/regional, colonial Philippines/Spain/Japan/US.

Churchill, *David S.*, *Manitoba*. Winnipeg, MB, Canada. Email: david.churchill@umanitoba.ca. Research: 20th-c US, gender and sexuality.

Churchill, **Lindsey Blake**, *Central Oklahoma*. Email: lchurchill@uco.edu.

Churchill, **Robert H.**, *Hartford*. Email: churchill@hartford.edu.

Churchill, **Wendy**, *New Brunswick*. Email: wchurchi@unb.ca.

Churchman, **John H.** Arlington, VA. Email: churchm3@comcast.net.

Churella, **Albert J.**, *Kennesaw State*. Email: achurell@kennesaw.edu.

Chused, *Richard H.* New York, NY. Affil: New York Law Sch. Email: rhchused@gmail.com. Research: American gender and law, history and property.

Ciancia, *Kathryn*, *Wisconsin-Madison*. Madison, WI. Email: ciancia@wisc.edu. Research: Poland 1918-39.

Ciani, **Kyle E.**, *Illinois State*. Email: keciani@ilstu.edu.

Ciarlo, *David M.*, *Colorado, Boulder*. Boulder, CO. Email: david.ciarlo@colorado.edu. Research: visual, German colonialism.

Ciccarelli, **Orazio A.**, *Southern Mississippi*. Email: ocarelli@msn.com.

Cichopek-Gajraj, **Anna**, *Arizona State*. Email: anna.cichopek-gajraj@asu.edu.

Ciego, **Soraya**, *La Guardia and Wagner Archives*. Email: sciego@lagcc.cuny.edu.

Cieslak, **Marta**, *Arkansas, Little Rock*. Email: mxcieslak@ualr.edu.

Cikota, **Javier**, *Bowdoin*. Email: jcikota@bowdoin.edu.

Cimbala, **Paul A.**, *Fordham*. Email: cimbala@fordham.edu.

Cimino, *Eric C.* Jackson Heights, NY. Affil: Molloy. Email: ecimino@molloy.edu. Research: 20th-c travelers' aid movement, Progressive Era social reform.

Cinq-Mars, *Tom Jay*. Warwick, RI. Affil: Duke. Email: tjc30@duke.edu. Research: Soviet oil industry 1948-91.

Cintron Hause, *Omayra*. Stoystown, PA. Affil: Central Connecticut State. Email: omayracintronhause@gmail.com. Research: Puerto Rico, immigration.

Cioc-Ortega, **Mark**, *New Mexico State*. Email: mcioc@nmsu.edu.

Cipa, **Hakki Erdem**, *Michigan, Ann Arbor*. Email: ecipa@umich.edu.

Cipriano, *Salvatore*, *Jr*. Cambridge, MA. Affil: Boston Coll. Email: cipriansjr@gmail.com. Research: 17th-c universities in Scotland/Ireland.

Ciriacono, **Salvatore**. Padova, Italy. Affil: Padova. Email: salvatore.ciriacono@unipd.it.

Cirivilleri, **Robert**, *San José State*. Email: Robert.Cirivilleri@sjsu.edu.

Citino, *Nathan J.*, *Rice*. Houston, TX. Email: citino@rice.edu. Research: US diplomatic, economic development.

Citino, *Robert M.* New Orleans, LA. Affil: National WWII Museum. Email: rob.citino@nationalww2museum.org. Research: WWII, postwar world.

Claflin, *Kyri Watson*. Concord, NH. Affil: Boston Univ. Email: kyriclaflin@comcast.net. Research: French world war/food and culture, food in world history.

Claggett, *Nicola*. Bowie, MD. Email: ms.claggett@outlook.com.

Clancy-Smith, *Julia A.*, *Arizona*. Tucson, AZ. Email: juliac@u.arizona.edu. Research: 19th-c North African trans-med settlement, colonial North African women/gender/education.

Clansy, **Benjamin**, *St. Rose*. Email: bclansy@mail.strose.edu.

Clardy, **Brian Keith**, *Murray State*. Email: bclardy@murraystate.edu.

Clare, **Rod**, *Elon*. Email: rclare@elon.edu.

Clark, **Anna K.**, *Minnesota (Hist.)*. Email: clark106@umn.edu.

Clark, **Anthony E.**, *Whitworth*. Email: aclark@whitworth.edu.

Clark, *Cassandra L.* Bountiful, UT. Affil: Utah. Email: cassandra.clark@utah.edu. Research: race/whiteness/gender/sexuality, 19th-/20th-c science.

Clark, **Charles W.**, **III**, *Augusta*.

Clark, **Christopher F.**, *Connecticut, Storrs*. Email: c.clark@uconn.edu.

Clark, **Claire Ducharme**, *Kentucky*. Email: claire.clark@uky.edu.

Clark, *Clifford E.*, *Carleton Coll*. Northfield, MN. Email: cclark@carleton.edu. Research: material culture, community studies.

Clark, *Constance Areson*. Worcester, MA. Affil: Worcester Polytechnic Inst. Email: cclark@wpi.edu. Research: science/technology/culture, environmental history and science.

Clark, *Cullen Thomas*. Eunice, LA. Email: cullentclark@hotmail.com. Research: nonconformity and free church, evangelicalism.

Clark, **Daniel A.**, *Indiana State*. Email: Dan.Clark@indstate.edu.

Clark, *Daniel J.*, *Oakland*. Ann Arbor, MI. Email: djclark@oakland.edu. Research: Detroit labor/oral.

Clark, *Denis*. Calgary, AB, Canada. Affil: Calgary. Email: jdenis.clark@ucalgary.ca. Research: eastern/western European relations, influence of attitudes/perceptions in diplomacy.

Clark, *Donald N.*, *Trinity, Tex*. Email: dclark@trinity.edu.

Clark, *Douglas H.* Thompsons Station, TN. Affil: Vanderbilt. Email: douglas.brown.clark@gmail.com. Research: American religious, race and civil rights movement.

Clark, **Ellen McCallister**, *Soc. of Cincinnati*. Email: emclark@societyofthecincinnati.org.

Clark, *Emily*, *Tulane*. New Orleans, LA. Email: eclark@tulane.edu. Research: free people of color in Haiti and Louisiana, internal colonialism.

Clark, *Frederic Nolan*. New York, CA. Affil: Southern California. Email: fredernc@usc.edu.

Clark, **Geoffrey W.**, *SUNY, Coll. Potsdam*. Email: clarkgw@potsdam.edu.

Clark, **Hugh R.**, *Ursinus*. Email: hclark@ursinus.edu.

Clark, **J.C.D.**, *Kansas*. Email: jcdclark@ku.edu.

Clark, *J.M.H.*, *Kentucky*. Email: jmhclark@uky.edu.

Clark, **James C.**, *Central Florida*. Email: James.Clark@ucf.edu.

Clark, **Jessica P.**, *Brock*. Email: jclark@brocku.ca.

Clark, *Joshua Tyler*. Chicopee, MA. Affil: Chicopee Comprehensive High Sch. Email: jclark1092@gmail.com. Research: travel writers and lecturers in 1800s US, Americans' view on Middle East in 1800s.

Clark, *Justin Tyler*. Singapore. Affil: Nanyang Tech. Email: justintylerclark@gmail.com. Research: visual culture, time.

Clark, **Katherine Ann**, *SUNY, Coll. Brockport*. Email: kaclark@brockport.edu.

Clark, **Katherine R. P.**, *Kansas*. Email: krpclark@ku.edu.

Clark, **Lea**, *Stephen F. Austin State*. Email: Lea.Clark@sfasu.edu.

Clark, *Linda L.*, *Millersville, Pa*. Long Beach, CA. Email: linda.l.clark@millersville.edu. Research: women in French civil service, French women's education.

Clark, *Malcolm C.*, *Charleston*. Charleston, SC. Research: US diplomatic.

Clark, *Meri L.* Springfield, MA. Affil: Western New England. Email: meri.clark@wne.edu. Research: Colombia/independence/nation/state, literacy/handwriting/gender.

Clark, Michael D., *New Orleans.* Email: mdclark1@uno.edu.

Clark, Nancy, *Louisiana State.* Email: nclark@lsu.edu.

Clark, Patricia G., *Westminster.* Email: clarkpg@westminster.edu.

Clark, Richard Dennis Harold. Falls Church, VA. Affil: US Dept. of Defense. Email: rdhclark@gmail.com.

Clark, Shannan Wayne, *Montclair State.* Brooklyn, NY. Email: clarksh@montclair.edu.

Clark, Thomas R. Sacramento, CA. Affil: California State, Sacramento. Email: tomclark@saclink.csus.edu. Research: California water rights, Max Radin and legal realism.

Clark, Tim J. Philadelphia, PA. Affil: Nazareth Academy High Sch. Email: clark@nazarethacademyhs.org.

Clark, Vincent A. Overland Park, KS. Affil: Johnson County Comm. Coll. Email: vclark@jccc.edu. Research: German middle classes, intellectuals in Germany.

Clarke, Brian P. Toronto, ON, Canada. Affil: Emmanuel, Toronto. Email: b.clarke@utoronto.ca. Research: 19th-/early 20th-c Canada, public religion and popular piety.

Clarke, Christopher. Rochester, NY. Email: clarkecsc@gmail.com.

Clarke, Frances M. Sydney, Australia. Affil: Sydney. Email: frances.clarke@sydney.edu.au. Research: American Civil War, gender.

Clarke, J. Calvitt, III, *Jacksonville.* Email: jclarke@ju.edu.

Clarke, Mariko Asakawa, *Virginia Military Inst.* Email: clarkema@vmi.edu.

Clarke, Paula C., *McGill.* Email: paula.clarke@mcgill.ca.

Clarke, Robert. Orlando, FL. Affil: Central Florida. Email: robert.clarke@ucf.edu.

Clark-Huckstep, Andrew E., *OAH.* Email: aclark@oah.org.

Clark-Pujara, Christy, *Wisconsin-Madison.* Madison, WI. Email: clarkpujara@wisc.edu. Research: slavery and emancipation in Rhode Island, northern US slavery.

Clark-Wiltz, Meredith. Franklin, IN. Affil: Franklin. Email: mclark-wiltz@franklincollege.edu.

Clary, Mary Kate Stringer, *Coastal Carolina.* Email: mclary@coastal.edu.

Clason, Capt Nathan, *US Military Acad.* Email: Nathan.Clason@usma.edu.

Claudiu Ramon, Butculescu D. Bucuresti, Romania. Affil: Acad. Andrei Radulescu. Email: butculescu@yahoo.com. Research: heraldry, medieval.

Clauss, Errol M. Clemmons, NC. Affil: Salem. Email: emclauss37@aol.com. Research: America/East Asia, Holocaust.

Claussen, Martin A., *San Francisco.* San Francisco, CA. Email: claussenm@usfca.edu.

Clavey, Charles H. Cambridge, MA. Affil: Harvard. Email: cclavey@g.harvard.edu.

Clavin, Matthew J., *Houston.* Houston, TX. Email: mjclavin@uh.edu. Research: Haitian Revolution, Civil War.

Clawson, Lucas R., *Hagley Museum and Library.* Email: lclawson@hagley.org.

Clay, Catherine B., *Shippensburg.* Email: cbclay@ship.edu.

Clay, Eugene. Tempe, AZ. Affil: Arizona State. Email: clay@asu.edu. Research: old believers and sectarians, Orthodox church.

Clay, Lauren R., *Vanderbilt.* Nashville, TN. Email: lauren.clay@vanderbilt.edu. Research: commercialization, theater.

Claypool, James C., *Northern Kentucky.* Email: claypoolj@nku.edu.

Clayson, S. Hollis, *Northwestern.* Email: shc@northwestern.edu.

Clayton, Bruce L., *Allegheny.* Email: bclayton39@yahoo.com.

Clayton, James L., *Utah.* Email: james.clayton@comcast.net.

Clayton, Lawrence A., *Alabama, Tuscaloosa.* Email: lclayton@simplecom.net.

Cleary, Patricia A., *California State, Long Beach.* Email: patricia.cleary@csulb.edu.

Cleaveland, Timothy, *Georgia.* Email: tcleave@uga.edu.

Clegg, Amelia. London, United Kingdom. Affil: Birkbeck, London. Email: aclegg01@mail.bbk.ac.uk. Research: military/colonialism/empire.

Clegg, Claude A., III, *North Carolina, Chapel Hill.* Email: cclegg@email.unc.edu.

Clegg, Mindy Lea. Conyers, GA. Affil: Georgia State. Email: mindy.clegg@gmail.com. Research: Popular music/recording industry, cold war/consumer capitalism.

Cleland, Joel S., *Lander.*

Clemens, Paul G.E., *Rutgers.* Metuchen, NJ. Email: clemens@history.rutgers.edu. Research: early American labor, early American material culture/consumerism.

Clemens, Raymond. Woodbridge, CT. Affil: Beinecke Rare Book and Manuscript Library. Email: raymond.clemens@yale.edu. Research: cult of Mary Magdalen, maps in Gregorio Dati's Sfera.

Clemens-Bruder, Susan W., *Muhlenberg.* Email: clemens@muhlenberg.edu.

Clement, Elizabeth, *Utah.* Email: elizabeth.clement@utah.edu.

Clemente, Deirdre, *Nevada, Las Vegas.* Email: deirdre.clemente@unlv.edu.

Clements, Kendrick A., *South Carolina, Columbia.* Email: clements@mailbox.sc.edu.

Clemmons, Linda M., *Illinois State.* Email: lmclemm@ilstu.edu.

Clendening, Logan, *Utah State.* Sacramento, CA. Email: logan.clendening@usu.edu; lwclendening@ucdavis.edu.

Cleveland, Jordan. Oxford, MS. Affil: Mississippi. Email: Jclevela@go.olemiss.edu. Research: neutrality, small states and liberalism.

Cleveland, Todd C., *Arkansas, Fayetteville.* Email: tcclevel@uark.edu.

Clever, Iris. Los Angeles, CA. Affil: UCLA. Email: irisclever@ucla.edu. Research: science and medicine/anthropometry, colonial interactions.

Clifford, Dale Lothrop, *North Florida.* Email: clifford@unf.edu.

Clifford, Jim, *Saskatchewan.* Email: jim.clifford@usask.ca.

Clifford, Nicholas R., *Middlebury.* Middlebury, VT. Email: clifford@middlebury.edu. Research: travel writing on China.

Clifford, Roderick A., *DePauw.* Email: clifford@depauw.edu.

Clifton, Alice. Atlanta, GA. Affil: Georgia Inst. of Tech. Email: alice.clifton@gmail.com.

Cline, David Phillip, *San Diego State.* San Diego, CA. Email: dpcline@sdsu.edu. Research: public and oral, 20th-c social movements.

Cline, Diane Harris, *George Washington.* Email: drcline@gwu.edu.

Cline, Douglas H. Williamsport, MD. Email: DLPooh@verizon.net.

Cline, Eric H., *George Washington.* Email: ehcline@gwu.edu.

Cline, Sarah, *California, Santa Barbara.* Goleta, CA. Email: cline@history.ucsb.edu. Research: colonial Mexico, religion in Latin America.

Clines, Robert John, *Western Carolina.* Cullowhee, NC. Email: rjclines@wcu.edu. Research: early modern Europe, Mediterranean world.

Clingan, Edmund. Woodside, NY. Affil: Queensborough Comm. Coll., CUNY. Email: EClingan@qcc.cuny.edu. Research: money and power in world history, Western economy of 1920s-30s.

Clinton, Catherine, *Texas, San Antonio.* San Antonio, TX. Email: catherine.clinton@utsa.edu; Catherineclinton@mac.com. Research: US Civil War, gender studies.

Clinton, Maggie, *Middlebury.* Email: mclinton@middlebury.edu.

Clinton, Michael G. Gwynedd Valley, PA. Affil: Gwynedd Mercy. Email: Clinton.Michael@gmercyu.edu. Research: peace movements, trans- and international organizations.

Cliver, Robert K. Arcata, CA. Affil: Humboldt State. Email: rc61@humboldt.edu. Research: Shanghai silk industry 1945-65, labor and gender in the PRC.

Clokey, Richard M., *Indiana State.* Email: Richard.Clokey@indstate.edu.

Close, Christopher W., *St. Joseph's.* Philadelphia, PA. Email: cclose@sju.edu. Research: urban reformation in Swabia, rural reform in Swabia.

Closmann, Charles, *North Florida.* Email: cclosman@unf.edu.

Clossey, Luke, *Simon Fraser.* Email: lclossey@sfu.ca.

Cloud, Samantha. Saint Louis, MO. Affil: St. Louis. Email: scloud@slu.edu.

Clouse, Michele L., *Ohio.* Email: clousem@ohio.edu.

Clow, Barbara, *Dalhousie.* Email: barbara.clow@dal.ca.

Clow, Richmond, *Montana.* Email: clowrl@mso.umt.edu.

Clubb, Jerome M. Port Angeles, WA. Email: jerryc@olypen.com.

Clulee, Nicholas H., *Frostburg State.* Email: nclulee@frostburg.edu.

Clune, Lori A., *California State, Fresno.* Email: lclune@csufresno.edu.

Clune, Lt Col John, *US Air Force Acad.* Email: john.clune@usafa.edu.

Clutterbuck-Cook, Anna J., *Massachusetts Hist. Soc.* Email: acook@masshist.org.

Clymer, Kenton J., *Northern Illinois.* Wayzata, MN. Email: kclymer@niu.edu. Research: US relations with Burma.

Coady, Joseph W., *Mount St. Vincent.*

Coate, Charles. Portland, OR. Affil: Eastern Oregon. Email: ccoate@gmail.com. Research: 1960s politics.

Coates, Benjamin Allen, *Wake Forest.* Email: coatesba@wfu.edu.

Coates, Colin M., *York, Can.* Email: ccoates@gl.yorku.ca.

Coates, **Timothy J.**, *Charleston*. Email: coatest@cofc.edu.

Coatsworth, *John H.*, *Columbia (Hist.); Harvard (Hist.)*. New York, NY. Email: jhc2125@columbia.edu. Research: Mexican economic 1700-1910, 20th-c Latin American international.

Cobb, **Daniel M.**, *North Carolina, Chapel Hill*. Email: dcobb@unc.edu.

Cobb, **James C.**, *Georgia*. Email: cobby@uga.edu.

Cobble, *Dorothy Sue*, *Rutgers*. Princeton, NJ. Email: cobble@rutgers.edu. Research: labor and women's internationalism, US social democracy.

Cobbs, *Elizabeth Anne*, *San Diego State; Texas A&M*. La Mesa, CA. Email: ehoffman@sdsu.edu; cobbs@tamu.edu. Research: post-WWII US reform, foreign relations.

Coble, *Parks M.*, *Jr.*, *Nebraska, Lincoln*. Lincoln, NE. Email: pcoble1@unl.edu. Research: Sino-Japanese War 1937-45.

Cobo Betancourt, *Juan Fernando*, *California, Santa Barbara*. Santa Barbara, CA. Email: jcobo@history.ucsb.edu. Research: religion in colonial Latin America, race in colonial Latin America.

Cocco, **Sean F.**, *Trinity Coll., Conn.* Email: sean.cocco@trincoll.edu.

Cocenza, *Nathalia*. Columbia, SC. Affil: South Carolina, Columbia. Email: nathalia.cocenza@gmail.com.

Cochelin, **Isabelle**, *Toronto*. Email: isabelle.cochelin@utoronto.ca.

Cochran, *Joseph*. North Riverside, IL. Affil: Trinity Evangelical Divinity Sch. Email: jtcochran82@gmail.com.

Cochran, *Philip Michael*. Austin, TX. Affil: Austin Comm. Coll. Email: cochranpm@gmail.com. Research: British educational reform.

Cochran, **Sherman Gilbert**, *Cornell*. Email: sgc11@cornell.edu.

Cockfield, **Jamie H.**, *Mercer*.

Cocks, *Geoffrey C.*, *Albion*. Carmel, CA. Email: gcocks@albion.edu. Research: illness in Nazi Germany, Stanley Kubrick and Germany.

Coclanis, *Peter A.*, *North Carolina, Chapel Hill*. Chapel Hill, NC. Email: coclanis@unc.edu. Research: world rice trade, US South.

Cocoltchos, *Christopher N.*, *Western Oregon*. Portland, OR. Email: cocoltchosc@wou.edu; chubbacat1@msn.com.

Codignola, **Luca**, *St. Mary's, Can.* Email: luca.codignola@smu.ca.

Cody, *Christopher*. Brooklyn, NY. Email: codyc@stjohns.edu.

Cody, *Lisa Forman*, *Claremont McKenna*. South Pasadena, CA. Email: lisa.cody@cmc.edu. Research: obstetrics and midwifery, visual culture.

Coe, **Stephen H.**, *Eastern Kentucky*.

Coe, *Steven*. Washington, DC. Affil: US Dept. of Justice. Email: Steve.Coe@usdoj.gov.

Coelho, *John J.* Acton, MA. Affil: Scottish Rite Masonic Museum & Library. Email: johnjcoelho@gmail.com. Research: Abraham Lincoln, antebellum/Civil War/Reconstruction.

Coen, *Deborah Rachel*, *Yale*. New Haven, CT. Email: deborah.coen@yale.edu. Research: Europe, science.

Coen, *Ross Allen*. Fairbanks, AK. Affil: Alaska Fairbanks. Email: racoen@alaska.edu. Research: fisheries/salmon, race.

Coenen-Snyder, **Saskia**, *South Carolina, Columbia*. Email: snydersc@mailbox.sc.edu.

Coens, **Thomas M.**, *Tennessee, Knoxville*. Email: tcoens@utk.edu.

Coerver, **Don M.**, *Texas Christian*. Email: d.coerver@tcu.edu.

Coffey, **David A.**, *Tennessee, Martin*. Email: dcoffey@utm.edu.

Coffey, **Michele L.**, *Memphis*. Email: mlcoffey@memphis.edu.

Coffin, *Judith G.*, *Texas, Austin*. Austin, TX. Email: jcoffin@austin.utexas.edu. Research: postwar Europe, gender and sexuality.

Coffman, **Edward M.**, *Wisconsin-Madison*.

Coffman, *Elesha*, *Baylor*. Waco, TX. Email: elesha_coffman@baylor.edu. Research: church, US intellectual and religious.

Cogan, *Jacob Katz*. Cincinnati, OH. Affil: Cincinnati. Email: jacob.cogan@uc.edu.

Cogan, *Susan M.*, *Utah State*. Logan, UT. Email: susan.cogan@usu.edu. Research: early modern social and cultural, religious coexistence.

Coghill, *Jeff*. Atlanta, GA. Affil: Georgia State. Email: coghill758@gmail.com.

Cogswell, **Thomas**, *California, Riverside*. Email: thomas.cogswell@ucr.edu.

Cohen, **Aaron J.**, *California State, Sacramento*. Email: cohenaj@csus.edu.

Cohen, **Andrew Wender**, *Syracuse*. Email: awcohe01@maxwell.syr.edu.

Cohen, *Benjamin B.*, *Utah*. Salt Lake City, UT. Email: benjamin.cohen@utah.edu. Research: South Asia.

Cohen, **Brian M**. Putney, VT. Affil: Landmark. Email: bcohen@landmark.edu.

Cohen, *Bruce S.*, *Worcester State*. Worcester, MA. Email: bcohen@worcester.edu. Research: Massachusetts labor 1865-1920, New England labor 1865-1920.

Cohen, **Charles Lloyd**, *Wisconsin-Madison*. Email: clcohen@wisc.edu.

Cohen, **Daniel A.**, *Case Western Reserve*. Email: daniel.a.cohen@case.edu.

Cohen, **David A.**, *Assumption*.

Cohen, **David Wm.**, *Michigan, Ann Arbor*. Email: dwcohen@umich.edu.

Cohen, *Deborah A.*, *Northwestern*. Evanston, IL. Email: deborah-cohen@northwestern.edu. Research: modern Britain and Europe.

Cohen, *Deborah*, *Missouri–St. Louis*. Saint Louis, MO. Email: deborah.cohen@umsl.edu. Research: gender and sexuality, migration.

Cohen, *Debra*. West Windsor, NJ. Affil: Thomas Grover Middle Sch. Email: debra.cohen@ww-p.org.

Cohen, *Elizabeth S.*, *York, Can.* Email: ecohen@yorku.ca.

Cohen, **G. Daniel**, *Rice*. Email: gdcohen@rice.edu.

Cohen, *Gary B.*, *Minnesota (Hist.)*. Minnetonka, MN. Email: gcohen@umn.edu. Research: modern European social, Habsburg Monarchy.

Cohen, *Harvey G*. Strand, London, United Kingdom. Affil: King's Coll., London. Email: harvey.cohen@kcl.ac.uk. Research: historical significance of Duke Ellington, 18th-20th-c American music.

Cohen, *Ira*. New York, NY. Email: icohen3@nyc.rr.com. Research: urban growth.

Cohen, *Julia Phillips*, *Vanderbilt*. Nashville, TN. Email: julia.p.cohen@vanderbilt.edu.

Research: modern Jewish, Europe and Ottoman.

Cohen, **Julie T.**, *California State, Los Angeles*. Email: Julie.Cohen6@calstatela.edu.

Cohen, *Lizabeth*, *Harvard (Hist.)*. Cambridge, MA. Email: cohen3@fas.harvard.edu. Research: urban built environment after WWII, 20th-c US social.

Cohen, *Michael David*, *Tennessee, Knoxville*. Oakdale, MN. Email: mdcohen@utk.edu. Research: James K. Polk, documentary editing.

Cohen, **Miriam J.**, *Vassar*. Email: cohen@vassar.edu.

Cohen, **Norman S.**, *Occidental*. Email: cohen@oxy.edu.

Cohen, **Patricia Cline**, *California, Santa Barbara*. Email: pcohen@history.ucsb.edu.

Cohen, *Paul A*. Cambridge, MA. Affil: Harvard. Email: pcohen@fas.harvard.edu. Research: interaction between story and history, historiography.

Cohen, **Paul E.**, *Toronto*. Email: p.cohen@utoronto.ca.

Cohen, **Ronald D.**, *Indiana, Northwest*.

Cohen, **Samuel**, *Sonoma State*. Email: samuel.cohen@sonoma.edu.

Cohen, *Sharon*. Silver Spring, MD. Affil: Springbrook High Sch. Email: sharon_c_cohen@mcpsmd.org. Research: Americas, China.

Cohen, **Sheldon S.**, *Loyola, Chicago*. Email: scohen@luc.edu.

Cohen, *Stephen F*. New York, NY. Affil: NYU. Email: sfc1@nyu.edu. Research: interpreting Soviet history, interpreting post-Soviet history.

Cohen, **Susan**, *Montana State, Bozeman*. Email: scohen@montana.edu.

Cohen, *Theodore*. Kirkwood, MO. Affil: Lindenwood. Email: tcohen4@gmail.com. Research: Mexico, African diaspora.

Cohen, *Thomas M*. Washington, DC. Affil: Catholic. Email: cohent@cua.edu; thomasmcohen@gmail.com. Research: Texas history and politics 1920-2010, early modern European religious.

Cohen, *Thomas V.*, *York, Can.* Toronto, ON, Canada. Email: tcohen@yorku.ca. Research: Renaissance Italy anthropology/rural life, narrative invention for historians.

Cohen, **Warren I.**, *Maryland, Baltimore County*. Email: wcohen@umbc.edu.

Cohen, *William*, *Hope*. Holland, MI. Email: cohen@hope.edu. Research: James Miller McKim, antislavery.

Cohen, **Yolande J.**, *Québec, Montréal*. Email: cohen.yolande@uqam.ca.

Cohn, *Edward D.*, *Grinnell*. Grinnell, IA. Email: cohned@grinnell.edu. Research: expulsion in Soviet Communist Party, KGB in Lithuania.

Cohn, **Ellen R.**, *Yale*. Email: ellen.cohn@yale.edu.

Coifman, **Victoria Bomba**, *Minnesota (Hist.)*. Email: coifm@umn.edu.

Coker, *Amanda*. Croton On Hudson, NY. Affil: Humane Soc. Legislative Fund. Email: ac8474a@american.edu.

Coker, **Charlie**, *Presbyterian*.

Colantonio, **Laurent**, *Québec, Montréal*. Email: colantonio.laurent@uqam.ca.

Colbert, **John**. Statesboro, GA. Email: john.m.colbert@gmail.com.

Colburn, David R., *Florida*. Email: colburn@ufl.edu.

Cole, Angel. Boydton, VA. Affil: Norwich. Email: angel@bannerfieldfarm.com.

Cole, Edward A., *Grand Valley State*. Email: colee@gvsu.edu.

Cole, Festus, *Bowie State*. Email: fcole@bowiestate.edu.

Cole, Gibril R., *Louisiana State*. Email: gcole@lsu.edu.

Cole, Joshua H., *Michigan, Ann Arbor*. Email: joshcole@umich.edu.

Cole, Juan R. I., *Michigan, Ann Arbor*. Ann Arbor, MI. Email: jrcole@umich.edu. Research: Iraq/Afghanistan/War on Terror, French in Egypt.

Cole, Lauren Elizabeth, *Loyola Marymount*. Email: lcole14@lmu.edu.

Cole, Mark B., *Cleveland State*. Email: m.b.cole@csuohio.edu.

Cole, Mary Hill, *Mary Baldwin*. Staunton, VA. Email: mhcole@marybaldwin.edu. Research: Tudor women.

Cole, Michael S., *Florida Gulf Coast*. Email: mcole@fgcu.edu.

Cole, Olen, Jr., *North Carolina A&T State*. Email: colen@ncat.edu.

Cole, Peter, *Western Illinois*. Email: P-Cole@wiu.edu.

Cole, Richard G., *Luther*. Email: coler@luther.edu.

Cole, Simon, *California, Irvine*. Email: scole@uci.edu.

Cole, Stephanie, *Texas, Arlington*. Email: scole@uta.edu.

Cole, Thomas R. Houston, TX. Affil: UTHealth Houston. Email: thomas.cole@uth.tmc.edu.

Coleman, Aaron Nathan, *Cumberlands*. Email: nathan.coleman@ucumberlands.edu.

Coleman, Alexander Taylor. Stillwater, MN. Email: alexcoleman@outlook.com.

Coleman, Anne Gilbert. Notre Dame, IN. Affil: Notre Dame. Email: acolema3@nd.edu. Research: 20th-c US West, society/culture/landscape/environment/gender.

Coleman, Billy. Vancouver, BC, Canada. Affil: British Columbia. Email: billycoleman84@hotmail.com. Research: political culture, music.

Coleman, Bradley Lynn, *Virginia Military Inst.* Lexington, VA. Email: colemanbl@vmi.edu; colemanbl@appliedhistorycenter.com. Research: US-Latin American relations, forensic anthropology.

Coleman, Charly, *Columbia (Hist.)*. New York, NY. Email: cc3472@columbia.edu. Research: economic theology, selfhood.

Coleman, David, *Virginia*. Email: dgcoleman@virginia.edu.

Coleman, Dwain Conrad. Iowa City, IA. Affil: Iowa. Email: dwain-coleman@uiowa.edu. Research: African American Civil War veterans, Midwest African American communities.

Coleman, George A., *Western Connecticut State*. Email: colemang@wcsu.edu.

Coleman, Heather, *Alberta*. Edmonton, AB, Canada. Email: hcoleman@ualberta.ca. Research: Russian Empire religion and nationality, Ukraine religion.

Coleman, Jon T., *Notre Dame*. Email: jcolema2@nd.edu.

Coleman, Kevin P., *Toronto*. Email: kevin.coleman@utoronto.ca.

Coleman, Michael. Jyvaskyla, Finland. Affil: Jyvaskyla. Email: michael.coleman@jyu.fi. Research: comparative American Indian/Irish education, postmodernist critiques of history.

Coleman, Ronald G., *Utah*. Email: rcoleman@utah.edu.

Coleman, Sterling J., Jr. Springfield, OH. Affil: Clark State Comm. Coll. Email: augustdewinter1@yahoo.com. Research: library history of British Empire, Ethiopia during WWII.

Coleman, Willi, *Vermont*. Email: willi.coleman@uvm.edu.

Colen, Arthur Leonard. Raleigh, NC. Email: alcolen@yahoo.com. Research: slavery, Reconstruction.

Coles, Amanda Jo, *Illinois Wesleyan*. Email: acoles@iwu.edu.

Coles, David J., *Longwood*. Farmville, VA. Email: colesdj@longwood.edu. Research: American Civil War, military.

Coles, David, *Purdue, Fort Wayne*. Email: colesd@ctsfw.edu.

Coles, Melissa. Notre Dame, IN. Affil: Notre Dame. Email: mcoles@nd.edu.

Colgrove, James, *Columbia (Hist. Public Health)*. Email: jc988@columbia.edu.

Colish, Marcia L., *Oberlin*. Guilford, CT. Affil: Yale. Email: marcia.colish@yale.edu. Research: stoicism in Middle Ages, Renaissance humanism.

Coller, Ian, *California, Irvine*. Email: i.coller@uci.edu.

Colley, Linda Jane, *Princeton*. Princeton, NJ. Email: lcolley@princeton.edu. Research: British constitution-making and world, Sir Philip Francis and gender.

Collier, Christopher, *Connecticut, Storrs*. Email: ccollier@mindspring.com.

Collier, T. Nelson. Alexandria, VA. Email: tc755@georgetown.edu.

Collier-Thomas, Bettye. Cherry Hill, NJ. Affil: Temple. Email: collierthomas@att.net. Research: African American women and religion, civil rights/Black Power Movement.

Collini, Sara. Fairfax, VA. Affil: George Mason. Email: scolli16@gmu.edu.

Collins, Capt Devon, *US Military Acad.* Email: devon.collins@usma.edu.

Collins, Cary C. Maple Valley, WA. Affil: Tahoma Senior High Sch. Email: CCollins@tahomasd.us.

Collins, David J., *Georgetown*. Email: djc44@georgetown.edu.

Collins, Deborah J. Elkton, FL. Affil: Florida State. Email: wordweavers@aol.com. Research: Mughal India, early modern Europe.

Collins, Donald, *East Carolina*. Email: collinsd@ecu.edu.

Collins, Jacob, *Staten Island, CUNY*. Email: jacob.collins@csi.cuny.edu.

Collins, James B., *Georgetown*. Email: collinja@georgetown.edu.

Collins, Jeffrey R., *Queen's, Can.* Kingston, ON, Canada. Email: collinsj@queensu.ca. Research: Thomas Hobbes, English Revolution.

Collins, John Michael, *Eastern Washington*. Email: jcollins2@ewu.edu.

Collins, Keith E., *California State, Long Beach*. Email: keith.collins@csulb.edu.

Collins, Michael. Juneau, AK. Affil: Alaska Southeast. Email: mdcollin190@gmail.com.

Collins, Nathan E. Birmingham, MI. Affil: Roeper Sch. Email: max.collins@roeper.org.

Collins, Robert M., *Missouri, Columbia*. Email: collinsr@missouri.edu.

Collins, Samuel W., *George Mason*. Email: scolline@gmu.edu.

Collins, Stephen L. Jamaica Plain, MA. Affil: Babson. Email: Collins@Babson.edu. Research: late medieval England, self/identity.

Collins, Steven Morris. Aubrey, TX. Affil: North Texas. Email: steven.collins@unt.edu. Research: East Germany, US foreign policy.

Collins, Sue L. Pittsburgh, PA. Affil: Carnegie Mellon. Email: sc24@andrew.cmu.edu.

Collins, Theresa M., *Rutgers*. Email: theresac@taep.rutgers.edu.

Collins, William J., *Vanderbilt*. Email: william.collins@vanderbilt.edu.

Collins, William Steve, *Salem State*. Email: wcollins@salemstate.edu.

Colman, David M., *Ramapo*. Email: dlewisc@ramapo.edu.

Colman, Kevin. Princeton, NJ.

Colman, Patty. Moorpark, CA. Affil: Moorpark. Email: pcolman@vcccd.edu. Research: African Americans in early Los Angeles, women homesteaders.

Colpitts, George, *Calgary*. Email: colpitts@ucalgary.ca.

Colston, Stephen A., *San Diego State*. Email: colston@sdsu.edu.

Colton, Robert G. Arlington, VA. Affil: Library of Congress. Email: rcolton4@verizon.net. Research: Union Army, American Revolution.

Coltrain, James, *Nebraska, Lincoln*. Email: jcoltrain2@unl.edu.

Comacchio, Cynthia, *Wilfrid Laurier*. Email: ccomacch@wlu.ca.

Combs, William L., *Western Illinois*. Email: WL-Combs@wiu.edu.

Comerford, Kathleen M., *Georgia Southern*. Statesboro, GA. Email: kcomerfo@georgiasouthern.edu. Research: Renaissance, Reformation.

Comerford, Richard Vincent. County Kildare, Ireland. Affil: National, Ireland, Maynooth. Email: rvcomerford@gmail.com. Research: bases of mobilization in modern Ireland, comparative nationality and culture.

Comfort, Nathaniel C., *Johns Hopkins (Hist. of Science)*. Email: nccomfort@gmail.com.

Comiskey, Gregory Donald. Waverly Hall, GA. Affil: Jordan Vocational High Sch. Email: comiskeysmail@yahoo.com. Research: Christianity in the new millennium., cultural and societal decline.

Commager, Mary Powlesland. Amherst, MA. Email: mcommager@yahoo.com. Research: pre-revolutionary Mexico, Yucatan Peninsula.

Commins, David, *Dickinson*. Email: commins@dickinson.edu.

Como, David R., *Stanford*. Stanford, CA. Email: dcomo@stanford.edu. Research: early modern Britain.

Compeau, Timothy, *Western Ontario*. Email: tcompeau@uwo.ca.

Compton, Aaron, *Austin Peay State*. Email: comptona@apsu.edu.

Compton, Amy Elizabeth. Austin, TX. Affil: Texas A&M, Central Texas. Email: blaidddrwg.ac@gmail.com.

Comshaw, *Benjamin Wesley*. Massillon, OH. Affil: Akron. Email: bcomsha1@yahoo.com. Research: Anglo-Norman, medieval writing/manuscript production.

Con Diaz, *Gerardo*. Davis, CA. Affil: California, Davis. Email: condiaz@ucdavis.edu. Research: software, intellectual property law.

Conant, **Jonathan P.**, *Brown*. Email: Jonathan_Conant@Brown.edu.

Conard, **Rebecca A.**, *Middle Tennessee State*. Iowa City, IA. Email: Rebecca.Conard@mtsu.edu. Research: post-emancipation African American communities, public history/history and philosophy.

Conerly, **Gregory**, *Cleveland State*. Cleveland, OH. Email: g.conerly@csuohio.edu. Research: LGBTQ, African American.

Confer, **Clarissa W.**, *California, Pa.* Email: confer_c@calu.edu.

Confino, *Alon*, *Massachusetts, Amherst*. Amherst, MA. Email: confino@umass.edu. Research: Holocaust/Jewish, Israel/Palestine.

Cong, *Xiaoping*, *Houston*. Houston, TX. Email: mikecon@optonline.net; xcong@central.uh.edu. Research: modern China, women.

Congdon, *Eleanor A.*, *Youngstown State*. Youngstown, OH. Email: eacongdon@ysu.edu. Research: late medieval Mediterranean trade, cultural contacts between East and West.

Congdon, **Lee W.**, *James Madison*. Email: congdolw@jmu.edu.

Conger, **Vivian Bruce**, *Ithaca*. Email: vconger@ithaca.edu.

Conides, **Cynthia**, *SUNY, Buffalo State*. Email: conideca@buffalostate.edu.

Conis, *Elena*. Berkeley, CA. Affil: California, Berkeley. Email: econis@berkeley.edu. Research: 20th-c US medicine, public health.

Conkin, **Paul K.**, *Vanderbilt*. Email: paul.k.conkin@vanderbilt.edu.

Conklin, *Alice L.*, *Ohio State*.

Conklin, **Carli N.**, *Missouri, Columbia*. Email: conklinc@missouri.edu.

Conlan, *Thomas D.*, *Princeton*. Princeton, NJ. Email: tconlan@princeton.edu. Research: premodern Japan.

Conley, **Carolyn A.**, *Alabama, Birmingham*. Email: cconley@uab.edu.

Conley, *Mary A.*, *Holy Cross*. Worcester, MA. Email: mconley@holycross.edu. Research: gender/sexuality/maritime, childhood and empire.

Conley, *Maximilian*. Chapel Hill, NC. Email: maximilian.p.conley@gmail.com.

Conlin, **Erin L.**, *Indiana, Pa.* Email: erin.conlin@iup.edu.

Conlin, **Michael F.**, *Eastern Washington*. Email: mconlin@ewu.edu.

Conlon, *Frank F.*, *Washington, Seattle*. Seattle, WA. Email: conlon@u.washington.edu. Research: Bombay/Saraswat Brahmans, Modern India.

Conn, **Christina F.**, *Hist. Assoc.* Email: cconn@historyassociates.com.

Conn, *Phyllis*. Queens, NY. Affil: St. John's, NY. Email: connp@stjohns.edu. Research: Brighton Beach NY.

Conn, *Steven*, *Miami, Ohio*. Yellow Springs, OH. Email: conns@miamioh.edu; steven.conn1@gmail.com. Research: American cultural, urban.

Conn, *Zachary Isaac*. Owings Mills, MD. Affil: Yale. Email: zachary.conn@yale.edu. Research: early US Indian agents.

Connell, **Charles W.**, *Northern Arizona*. Email: charles.connell@nau.edu.

Connell, *Timothy C.* Cleveland Heights, OH. Affil: Laurel Sch. Email: tconnell@laurelschool.org.

Connell, *Tula A.* Washington, DC. Affil: National Coalition of Independent Scholars. Email: tulaconnell@gmail.com. Research: roots of conservatism in 1950s, philosophies of urbanism.

Connell, *William F.*, *Christopher Newport*. Newport News, VA. Email: wconnell@cnu.edu. Research: Latin America, world civilizations.

Connell, *William J.*, *Seton Hall*. South Orange, NJ. Email: william.connell@shu.edu. Research: Renaissance Italy, early modern European intellectual.

Connell Szasz, **Margaret**, *New Mexico*. Email: conszasz@unm.edu.

Connelly, **James T.**, *CSC*, *Portland*.

Connelly, **John**, *California, Berkeley*. Email: jfconnel@berkeley.edu.

Connelly, *Matthew J.*, *Columbia (Hist.); Columbia (Hist. Public Health)*. New York, NY. Email: mjc96@columbia.edu. Research: Algerian war for independence, population control.

Conner, **Caroline J.**, *Kennesaw State*. Email: conne33@kennesaw.edu.

Conner, **Robin**, *Georgia State*. Email: rconner@gsu.edu.

Conner, **Thomas H.**, *Hillsdale*. Email: tconner@hillsdale.edu.

Conniff, **Michael L.**, *San José State*. Email: Michael.Conniff@sjsu.edu.

Connolly, **Brian**, *South Florida, Tampa*. Email: bconnolly@usf.edu.

Connolly, *James J.*, *Ball State*. Muncie, IN. Email: jconnoll@bsu.edu. Research: US party politics 1840-1920, print culture 1880-1920.

Connolly, *Jonathan S.* Princeton, NJ. Affil: Shelby Cullom Davis Center. Email: jsc5@princeton.edu.

Connolly, *Michael J.* Westville, IN. Affil: Purdue Northwest, Westville. Email: mconnoll@pnw.edu. Research: antebellum America, railroads.

Connolly, **Nathan D.**, *Johns Hopkins (Hist.)*. Email: nconnol2@jhu.edu.

Connor, **James T. H.**, *Memorial, Newfoundland*. Email: jconnor@mun.ca.

Connor, **Jennifer J.**, *Memorial, Newfoundland*. Email: jennifer.connor@med.mun.ca.

Connor, *John Peter*. Charlottesville, VA. Affil: Virginia. Email: jpc7cq@virginia.edu.

Connor, *Megan*, *AHA*. Washington, DC. Email: mconnor@historians.org.

Connors, **Thomas G.**, *Northern Iowa*. Email: thomas.connors@uni.edu.

Conolly-Smith, **Peter**, *Queens, CUNY*. Email: peter.conollysmith@qc.cuny.edu.

Conover, *Cornelius B.*, *V.* Sioux Falls, SD. Affil: Augustana, SD. Email: Cconover@augie.edu. Research: religion and imperialism in Spanish Empire, early modern saints and liturgy.

Conover, **Willis M.**, *Scranton*. Email: willis.conover@scranton.edu.

Conrad, *Celeste M.* Las Cruces, NM. Affil: New Mexico State. Email: cmconrad@zianet.com. Research: religious orders in New Spain, church/state relations in New Spain.

Conrad, **David E.**, *Southern Illinois, Carbondale*. Email: dconrad@siu.edu.

Conrad, **David**, *SUNY, Oswego*. Email: bastigi@earthlink.net.

Conrad, **Margaret**, *New Brunswick*. Email: mconrad@unb.ca.

Conrad, *Nick*. Houston, TX. Affil: Awty International Sch. Email: nconrad@awty.org.

Conrad, *Paul T.*, *Texas, Arlington*. Email: conrad@uta.edu.

Conrad, *Sharron Wilkins*. Irving, TX. Affil: Texas, Dallas. Email: sharronconrad@gmail.com.

Conroy, *Mary E. Schaeffer*, *Colorado Denver*. Englewood, CO. Email: mary.conroy@ucdenver.edu; maryesconroy@gmail.com. Research: Russia.

Conroy-Krutz, *Emily*, *Michigan State*. East Lansing, MI. Email: conroyk5@msu.edu. Research: 18th-/19th-c America, American reform and religion.

Conser, *Walter H., Jr.*, *North Carolina, Wilmington*. Wilmington, NC. Email: conserw@uncw.edu. Research: American religious.

Constable, *Giles*. Princeton, NJ. Affil: Inst. for Advanced Studies.

Constant, *Eric*, *Grand Valley State*. Email: constane@gvsu.edu.

Constuble, *Melanie*. Crofton, MD. Email: melanieconstuble@yahoo.com.

Conte, **Christopher A.**, *Utah State*. Email: chris.conte@usu.edu.

Conte, *Stephanie*. Washingtonville, NY. Email: sconte327@gmail.com.

Contosta, **David R.**, *Chestnut Hill*. Email: contostad@yahoo.com.

Contreni, **John J., Jr.**, *Purdue*. Email: contreni@purdue.edu.

Contreras, *Carlos Alberto*. San Diego, CA. Affil: Grossmont. Email: carloscontreras611@gmail.com. Research: Mexico/ US-Mexico, US-Latin America relations.

Contreras, **Eduardo A.**, *Hunter, CUNY*. Email: econtre@hunter.cuny.edu.

Contreras, **Raoul**, *Indiana, Northwest*. Email: rcontrer@iun.edu.

Conway, *Brian*. Stony Brook, NY. Affil: SUNY, Stony Brook. Email: brian.conway.1@stonybrook.edu.

Conway, *Dennis H.* Whitewater, WI. Email: dconway@netwurx.net.

Conway, *Hannah Caroline*. Cambridge, MA. Affil: Harvard. Email: hannah.caroline.c@gmail.com. Research: science and technology.

Conway, *James David*. Fort Worth, TX. Affil: Tarrant County Coll. Email: drjdconway@gmail.com. Research: Civil Rights Movement, Black Power.

Conway, *Richard*, *Montclair State*. Email: conwayr@mail.montclair.edu.

Conyne, *George*. Canterbury, United Kingdom. Email: grconyne@gmail.com.

Conzen, *Kathleen Neils*, *Chicago*. Chicago, IL. Email: k-conzen@uchicago.edu. Research: 19th-c immigration and ethnicity, American urban.

Coogan, *Peter F.*, *Hollins*. Roanoke, VA. Email: pcoogan@hollins.edu. Research: 20th-c US, international relations.

Cook, **Bernard A.**, *Loyola, New Orleans*. Email: cook@loyno.edu.

Cook, **Blanche Wiesen**, *Graduate Center, CUNY*. Email: Blanchewcook@gmail.com.

Cook, **Capt Jessica**, *US Military Acad*. Email: jessica.cook@usma.edu.

Cook, Christine. Ann Arbor, MI. Affil: Wayne State. Email: christine.cook2@wayne.edu. Research: women in military, world.

Cook, Edward M., Jr., *Chicago.* Email: ecook@uchicago.edu.

Cook, Elizabeth. Richmond, VA. Affil: Virginia Dept. of Historic Resources. Email: libbycook@gmail.com.

Cook, Harold J., *Brown.* Providence, RI. Email: Harold_Cook@Brown.edu. Research: medicine and global, transcultural movements.

Cook, James W., Jr., *Michigan, Ann Arbor.* Ann Arbor, MI. Email: jwcook@umich.edu. Research: popular and mass culture, race and ethnicity.

Cook, Jeffery B., *North Greenville.* Email: jeff.cook@ngu.edu.

Cook, Laurence L., Jr. Dallas, PA. Email: contact@larrycookhistorian.com.

Cook, Martin L., *Naval War Coll.* Email: martin.cook@usafa.edu.

Cook, Michael A., *Princeton.* Email: mcook@princeton.edu.

Cook, Michael D. Phoenix, AZ. Affil: West Coast. Email: michaelcook1@cox.net.

Cook, Noble David, *Florida International.* Coral Gables, FL. Email: cookn@fiu.edu; ndcook@yahoo.com. Research: Franciscan Luis Geronimo de Ore, material culture in Seville 1570-1620.

Cook, Philip C., *Louisiana Tech.*

Cook, Theodore Failor, Jr., *William Paterson.* Wayne, NJ. Email: cookt@wpunj.edu. Research: Asian and Pacific War 1931-45, total war and cultural consequences.

Cook, Tim, *Carleton, Can.* Email: tim.cook@warmuseum.ca.

Cook, William R., *SUNY, Coll. Geneseo.* Email: cookb@geneseo.edu.

Cooley, Angela Jill, *Minnesota State, Mankato.* Mankato, MN. Email: angela.cooley@mnsu.edu. Research: foodways, constitutional.

Cooley, Mackenzie Anne, *Hamilton.* Email: mcooley@hamilton.edu.

Cooley, Richard, *Grand Valley State.* Email: cooleyri@gvsu.edu.

Coolidge, Grace E., *Grand Valley State.* Email: coolidgg@gvsu.edu.

Coolidge, Robert T. Westmount, QC, Canada.

Cools, Amy Marie. Edinburgh, United Kingdom. Affil: Edinburgh. Email: amymcools@gmail.com.

Coombs, F. Alan, *Utah.* Salt Lake City, UT. Email: acoombs@history.utah.edu; alan.margie2@q.com. Research: Sen. Joseph C. O'Mahoney.

Coombs, Howard, *Royal Military.* Email: howard.coombs@rmc.ca.

Coon, David L., *Washington State, Pullman.* Email: coond@wsu.edu.

Coon, Lynda L., *Arkansas, Fayetteville.* Email: llcoon@uark.edu.

Coons, James, *Wisconsin-Whitewater.*

Coons, Lorraine, *Chestnut Hill.* Norristown, PA. Email: lcoons@chc.edu. Research: modern Europe, social and cultural.

Coons, Ronald E., *Connecticut, Storrs.* West Hartford, CT. Email: ronald.coons@uconn.edu; recoons@hotmail.com. Research: Austria 1815-48, Viennese urban.

Coope, Jessica A., *Nebraska, Lincoln.* Email: jcoope1@unl.edu.

Cooper, Abigail J., *Brandeis.* Email: abcooper@brandeis.edu.

Cooper, Afua, *Dalhousie.* Email: afua.cooper@dal.ca.

Cooper, Alan Ralph, *Colgate.* Email: acooper@colgate.edu.

Cooper, Alix, *SUNY, Stony Brook.* Stony Brook, NY. Email: alix.cooper@stonybrook.edu. Research: early modern gender and household, European environmental/occupational health.

Cooper, Barbara M., *Rutgers.* New Brunswick, NJ. Email: bacooper@rci.rutgers.edu. Research: childbirth, illicit trade.

Cooper, Brittney. New Brunswick, NJ. Affil: Rutgers. Email: brittneyccooper@gmail.com.

Cooper, Dana Magill, *Stephen F. Austin State.* Email: cooperdc@sfasu.edu.

Cooper, Frederick, *NYU.* New York, NY. Email: fred.cooper@nyu.edu. Research: colonialism and decolonization, labor.

Cooper, Gail, *Lehigh.* Email: gail.cooper@lehigh.edu.

Cooper, Glen M. Springville, UT. Affil: Independent Scholar. Email: glenmcooper@gmail.com. Research: medicine and astrology and birth of science, Byzantium and Islam intellectual exchanges.

Cooper, Heather L. Iowa City, IA. Affil: Iowa. Email: heather-cooper@uiowa.edu. Research: African American performance culture, memory of Civil War and slavery.

Cooper, James Ferguson. New York, NY. Affil: New Sch. for Social Reearch. Email: coopj399@newschool.edu.

Cooper, Jeffrey Scott. APO, AE. Affil: US Air Force. Email: jcooper0351@yahoo.com.

Cooper, Jerry M., *Missouri–St. Louis.* Email: cooperj@msx.umsl.edu.

Cooper, John Milton, Jr., *Wisconsin-Madison.* Email: jmcooper@wisc.edu.

Cooper, Leslie, *Robert H. Smith Center.* Email: lcooper@monticello.org.

Cooper, Mandy L. Morrisville, NC. Email: mandy.cooper.phd@gmail.com.

Cooper, Melissa L., *Rutgers, Newark/New Jersey Inst. of Tech.* Email: melissa.cooper@rutgers.edu.

Cooper, Neal. Claremont, CA. Email: neal.m.cooper@gmail.com.

Cooper, Sandi E., *Graduate Center, CUNY; Staten Island, CUNY.* New York, NY. Email: sandi.cooper@csi.cuny.edu; coopercsi@gmail.com. Research: women in war and peace 1914-45.

Cooper, Sheila M., *Indiana–Purdue, Indianapolis.*

Cooper, Tracey-Anne, *St. John's, NY.* Email: coopert@stjohns.edu.

Cooper, William J., Jr., *Louisiana State.* Atlanta, GA. Email: wcooper@lsu.edu. Research: US South, 19th-c US.

Cooper Owens, Deirdre B., *Nebraska, Lincoln; Library Co. of Philadelphia.* Brooklyn, NY. Email: Deirdre.CooperOwens@qc.cuny.edu. Research: slavery, women.

Cooperman, Bernard D., *Maryland, Coll. Park.* College Park, MD. Email: cooperma@umd.edu. Research: early modern Jewry, autobiography and memory.

Coopersmith, Jonathan C., *Texas A&M.* College Station, TX. Email: j-coopersmith@tamu.edu. Research: fax machine 1843-present, communications technologies/pornography.

Cope, Don, *Columbus State.* Email: cope_don@columbusstate.edu.

Cope, Jenel Carpenter. Aberdeen, WA. Affil: Grays Harbor. Email: jenelcc@gmail.com.

Cope, Joseph A., *SUNY, Coll. Geneseo.* Email: cope@geneseo.edu.

Cope, R. Douglas, *Brown.* Email: Robert_Cope@Brown.edu.

Copeland, Henry J., *Wooster.* Email: hcopeland@wooster.edu.

Copelman, Dina M., *George Mason.* Email: dcopelma@gmu.edu.

Copenhaver, Amie Brooke. Huntington, WV. Affil: Marshall. Email: copenhaver6@marshall.edu.

Copenhaver, Brian P., *UCLA.* Email: brianc@college.ucla.edu.

Coplin, James R. Minneapolis, MN. Email: james@ticalun.net.

Copp, Terry, *Wilfrid Laurier.* Email: tcopp@wlu.ca.

Coppa, Frank J. Brooklyn, NY. Affil: St. John's, NY. Email: coppaf@stjohns.edu. Research: papacy and Holocaust, fascist Italy.

Coray, Michael, *Nevada, Reno.* Email: mcoray@unr.edu.

Corbello, M. Kurt, *Southeastern Louisiana.* Email: mcorbello@selu.edu.

Corbesero, Susan. Pittsburgh, PA. Affil: Ellis Sch. Email: corbeseros@theellisschool.org. Research: Soviet and Russian visual culture, Sochi Olympics and New Russia.

Corbitt, Jennifer. Dickson, TN. Email: jenniferdcorbitt@hotmail.com.

Corbman, Rachel. Brooklyn, NY. Affil: SUNY, Stony Brook. Email: rachel.corbman@stonybrook.edu.

Corcoran, James R., *Hawai'i Pacific.* Email: jcorcoran@hpu.edu.

Cordero, Alberto, *Queens, CUNY.* Email: alberto.cordero@qc.cuny.edu.

Cordery, Simon C. E., *Iowa State.* Ames, IA. Email: scordery@iastate.edu. Research: modern Britain, comparative railroads.

Cordery, Stacy A., *Iowa State.* Ames, IA. Email: cordery@iastate.edu. Research: Juliette Gordon Low, first ladies.

Cordia, Madelina Marie. Lincoln, NE. Affil: Nebraska, Lincoln. Email: mmcordia@gmail.com. Research: Bracero Program/ethnicity/race/class, local/labor/agriculture/20th century/PNW.

Cordileone, Diana Reynolds, *Point Loma Nazarene.* Email: dianacordileone@pointloma.edu.

Cordova, Cary. Austin, TX. Affil: Texas, Austin. Email: cordova@austin.utexas.edu.

Corey, Mary F., *UCLA.* Email: mcorey@ucla.edu.

Corey, Michael N. Palm Bay, FL. Affil: Brevard Comm. Coll. Email: mikenc2421@aol.com.

Corey, Steven Hunt. Chicago, IL. Affil: Columbia Coll., Chicago. Email: shcorey@gmail.com. Research: New York City environmental, urban environmental.

Corinealdi, Kaysha L. Boston, MA. Affil: Emerson. Email: kcorinealdi@gmail.com. Research: Latin American/Caribbean immigration to US, black diaspora studies.

Corke, Sarah-Jane, *New Brunswick.* Email: s-j.corke@unb.ca.

Corlett, David Michael. Fountain Hills, AZ. Affil: Arizona State. Email: dmcorlett01@gmail.com. Research: Indian wars and early American culture, Indian/white relations in early America.

Corley, *Christopher R.*, *Minnesota State, Mankato*. Mankato, MN. Email: christopher. corley@mnsu.edu. Research: law and family in early modern Burgundy, legal culture in early modern Europe.

Cormack, *Lesley B.*, *Alberta*. Email: Lesley. Cormack@ualberta.ca.

Cormack, *William S.*, *Guelph*. Email: wcormack@ uoguelph.ca.

Corn, *Joseph J.*, *III*, *Stanford*. Email: joecorn@ stanford.edu.

Cornelius, *Alexandra*, *Florida International*. Email: acdiallo@fiu.edu.

Cornelius, *Mary*. Glasgow, United Kingdom. Affil: Glasgow. Email: M.cornelius.1@research. gla.ac.uk. Research: early colonial Grenada, history of religion.

Cornell, *Akikwe*, *Wisconsin-Milwaukee*. Email: cornelaj@uwm.edu.

Cornell, *Cecilia Stiles*, *Illinois, Springfield*. Email: cornell.cecilia@uis.edu.

Cornell, *Chester Warren*, *Jr*. North Little Rock, AR. Affil: Arkansas State, Beebe. Email: cwcornell@asub.edu. Research: African American Islam, black nationalism.

Cornell, *John J.*, *III*. Woburn, MA. Affil: Burlington High Sch. Email: jacktennis87@ yahoo.com.

Cornell, *John S.* Warszawa, Poland. Affil: Pilecki Inst. Email: j.cornell@instytutpileckiego.pl.

Cornell, *John S.*, *Butler*. Email: jcornell@butler. edu.

Cornell, *Sarah E.*, *Massachusetts, Amherst*.

Cornell, *Saul A.*, *Fordham*. Email: scornell1@ fordham.edu.

Cornell, *Travis Brian*. Knoxville, TN. Email: travisbcornell3584@gmail.com. Research: American South/American West, ancient through modern Europe.

Corney, *Frederick C.*, *William and Mary*. Williamsburg, VA. Email: fccorn@wm.edu. Research: modern Europe, Russia.

Cornford, *Daniel*, *San José State*.

Corning, *Caitlin*, *George Fox*. Email: ccorning@ georgefox.edu.

Corona, *Michael John*. Riverside, CA. Email: coronamichael60@gmail.com.

Coronado, *Juan*, *Central Connecticut State*. Email: jdcoronado@ccsu.edu.

Coronado Guel, *Luis Edgardo*, *Sr.*, *Arizona*. Email: luisguel@email.arizona.edu.

Corrado, *Sharyl*, *Pepperdine*. Email: sharyl. corrado@pepperdine.edu.

Correa-Kuyumjian, *Marilia*. Urbana, IL. Affil: Illinois, Urbana-Champaign. Email: kuyumjn2@illinois.edu. Research: Latin America, Brazil.

Corse, *Theron*, *Tennessee State*. Email: tcorse@ tnstate.edu.

Cortada, *James W.* Madison, WI. Affil: Minnesota. Email: jcortada@umn.edu. Research: business, information technology.

Corteguera, *Luis*, *Kansas*. Email: lcortegu@ ku.edu.

Cortes, *Angel de Jesus*. Notre Dame, IN. Affil: Holy Cross Coll. Email: acortes@hcc-nd.edu. Research: higher education.

Cortes, *Carlos E.*, *California, Riverside*. Email: carlos.cortes@ucr.edu.

Cortes, *Enrique*, *California State, Dominguez Hills*.

Corvi, *Steven J.*, *Worcester State*.

Cory, *Stephen Charles*, *Cleveland State*. Email: s.cory@csuohio.edu.

Coryell, *Janet L.*, *Western Michigan*. Email: janet. coryell@wmich.edu.

Cosby, *Patrick H.*, *Penn State, Erie*. Email: phc14@psu.edu.

Cosgrove, *Richard A.*, *Arizona*. Email: rcosgrov@u.arizona.edu.

Cosgrove, *Sean*. Ithaca, NY. Email: scos4577@ uni.sydney.edu.au. Research: culture, urban and gender.

Coss, *Edward J.*, *US Army Command Coll*. Email: edward.j.coss.civ@mail.mil.

Cossar, *Roisin A.*, *Manitoba*. Winnipeg, MB, Canada. Email: roisin.cossar@umanitoba.ca. Research: popular religion in medieval Italy, clerical culture.

Cosson, *Jayne G*. Reston, VA. Affil: Fairfax County Public Sch. Email: jc2013a@student. american.edu. Research: 20th-c US foreign policy, 20th-c Europe.

Costa-Gomes, *Rita*, *Towson*. Baltimore, MD. Email: rcostagomes@towson.edu. Research: medieval societies in Iberia, Iberian landscapes.

Costanzo, *Adam*, *Texas A&M, Corpus Christi*. Corpus Christi, TX. Email: adam.costanzo@ tamucc.edu; adam.costanzo@gmail.com. Research: Washington DC in early Republic.

Costanzo, *Susan E.*, *Western Washington*. Bellingham, WA. Email: Susan.Costanzo@ wwu.edu. Research: Soviet culture 1957-91.

Costello, *Angela Lee*. Atlantic Beach, FL. Affil: USS Midway Museum. Email: angela.l.costello@gmail.com. Research: Byzantium, material culture.

Costello, *David R.*, *Canisius*. Email: costello@ canisius.edu.

Costello, *Matthew J.*, *St. Xavier*. Email: costello@ sxu.edu.

Costenoble, *Charlotte Lila*. Myrtle Beach, SC. Affil: thyssenkrupp Elevator. Email: ch.costenoble@gmail.com.

Costigliola, *Frank C.*, *Connecticut, Storrs*. Email: frank.costigliola@uconn.edu.

Cotelo, *Enrique R*. University, MS. Affil: Mississippi. Email: ecotelo@olemiss.edu. Research: 19th-c Brazil/Uruguay/Argentina borderland, nation services/rural life/ education.

Cothran, *Boyd*, *III*, *York, Can*. Email: cothran@ yorku.ca.

Cotkin, *George B.*, *California Polytechnic State*. San Luis Obispo, CA. Email: gcotkin@calpoly. edu. Research: American moral moments, conceptual revolutions of 1960s.

Cotlar, *Seth*, *Willamette*. Salem, OR. Email: scotlar@willamette.edu. Research: trans-Atlantic radicalism, nostalgia in antebellum America.

Cotroneo, *Ross R.*, *Western Oregon*.

Cott, *Kennett*, *Washburn*. Email: ken.cott@ washburn.edu.

Cott, *Nancy F.*, *Harvard (Hist.)*. Cambridge, MA. Email: ncott@fas.harvard.edu. Research: US social and women.

Cotter, *David G.*, *US Army Command Coll*. Email: david.g.cotter.civ@mail.mil.

Cottreau-Robins, *Catherine*, *Dalhousie*. Email: catherine.cottreau-robins@novascotia.ca.

Cottrell, *Debbie Mauldin*, *Texas Lutheran*.

Cottrell, *Robert Charles*, *California State, Chico*. Email: bcottrell@csuchico.edu.

Cottrol, *Robert J.*, *George Washington*. Washington, DC. Email: bcottrol@law.gwu. edu. Research: legal, comparative race relations.

Cotts, *John D.*, *Whitman*. Walla Walla, WA. Email: cottsjd@whitman.edu. Research: 12th-c ecclesiastical culture, spirituality and clergy.

Coughlan, *Katelyn*, *Robert H. Smith Center*. Email: kcoughlan@monticello.org.

Coughlin, *Michelle Marchetti*. Hingham, MA. Email: mmcoughlin@comcast.net. Research: early American women's writings, colonial New England slavery.

Coughtry, *Jay*, *Nevada, Las Vegas*. Email: jay. coughtry@unlv.edu.

Coulibaly, *Sylvie*, *Kenyon*. Email: coulibalys@ kenyon.edu.

Coulson, *Hilary Louise*. Harrisburg, PA. Affil: Penn State. Email: hlc11@psu.edu.

Coulthard, *Cheryl*. Woodstock, VA. Email: cheryllcoulthard@gmail.com. Research: Utopian communities, social movements.

Coulton, *Juliana Elise*. North Bethesda, MD. Affil: Bradley Hills Presbyterian Church Nursery Sch. Email: juliecoulton@gmail.com.

Countryman, *Edward F.*, *Southern Methodist*. Email: ecountry@smu.edu.

Countryman, *Matthew Jon*, *Michigan, Ann Arbor*. Email: mcountry@umich.edu.

Courey, *Renee*. Sausalito, CA. Affil: Columbia Southern. Email: rcourey@gmail.com.

Courtenay, *William J.*, *Wisconsin-Madison*. Email: wjcourte@wisc.edu.

Courtney-Batson, *Deirdre*, *Pace*. Email: dcourtneybatson@pace.edu.

Courtwright, *David T.*, *North Florida*. Jacksonville, FL. Email: dcourtwr@unf.edu. Research: opioid use and policy, addiction.

Courtwright, *Julie R.*, *Iowa State*. Email: jcourtw@iastate.edu.

Coury, *Carmen*, *Southern Connecticut State*. New York, NY. Email: carmenkordick@gmail.com. Research: Costa Rican emigration to New Jersey, nation building in Costa Rica.

Couser, *Jonathan B.*, *Plymouth State*. Email: jbcouser@mail.plymouth.edu.

Cousins, *James P.*, *Western Michigan*. Email: james.cousins@wmich.edu.

Cousins, *Karen Shears*. Jacksonville, FL. Affil: North Florida. Email: karen.s.cousins@ comcast.net. Research: colonial Spanish American religious change, miracles and developing Marian devotions.

Couture, *Claude*, *Alberta*. Email: ccouture@ ualberta.ca.

Couturier, *Edith B*. Washington, DC. Affil: National Coalition of Independent Scholars. Email: ecouturier@aol.com. Research: 18th-c social, Mexican biography.

Couvares, *Francis G.*, *Amherst*. Amherst, MA. Email: fgcouvares@amherst.edu. Research: free speech/censorship/urban/labor, historiography.

Covart, *Elizabeth M.*, *Omohundro Inst*. Boston, MA. Email: liz@benfranklinsworld.com; emcovart@wm.edu. Research: identity creation and adaptation in early America, New England migration into New York.

Coven, *Robert*. Apex, NC. Affil: Cary Academy. Email: robert_coven@caryacademy.org. Research: threshold concepts in history, (post) secondary innovative pedagogy.

Coveney, Chris, *Massachusetts Hist. Soc.* Email: ccoveney@masshist.org.

Covert, Lisa Pinley, *Charleston.* Email: covertl@cofc.edu.

Covey, Eric, *Texas A&M, Corpus Christi.*

Covington, Sarah Amy, *Graduate Center, CUNY; Queens, CUNY.* Email: sarah.covington@qc.cuny.edu.

*Covo, **Manuel**, California, Santa Barbara.* Email: mcovo@history.ucsb.edu.

Cowan, Aaron Bradley, *Slippery Rock.* Email: aaron.cowan@sru.edu.

*Cowan, **Benjamin Arthur**, California, San Diego.* San Diego, CA. Email: bacowan@ucsd.edu; bacon1980@gmail.com. Research: Cold War sexuality in Americas, right-wing politics and military.

Cowan, Brian W., *McGill.* Email: brian.cowan2@mcgill.ca.

Cowan, Ruth S., *SUNY, Stony Brook.* Email: Ruth.Cowan@stonybrook.edu.

*Cowan, **William Joseph**.* Chino, CA. Affil: Southern California. Email: wcowan@usc.edu. Research: American West/Pacific Rim, environmental.

Cowans, Jon, *Rutgers, Newark/New Jersey Inst. of Tech.* Email: jonco58@aol.com.

*Cowart, **Kimberly B**.* Hewitt, TX. Affil: Robinson High Sch. Email: braycowart@gmail.com.

Cowie, Jefferson R., *Vanderbilt.* Email: jefferson.cowie@vanderbilt.edu.

Cowles, Henry M., *Michigan, Ann Arbor.* Email: cowles@umich.edu.

Cox, Anna-Lisa G., *Western Michigan.*

Cox, Anne, *State Hist. Soc. of Missouri.* Email: coxan@shsmo.org.

*Cox, **David George**.* Southampton, United Kingdom. Affil: Southampton. Email: d.g.cox@soton.ac.uk. Research: modern America.

Cox, Donald, *Appalachian State.* Email: coxda@appstate.edu.

Cox, Edward L., *Rice.* Email: ecox@rice.edu.

*Cox, **Graham**, North Texas.* Denton, TX. Email: graham.cox@unt.edu. Research: Holocaust/Nuremberg war crimes trials, African American.

Cox, Harold E., *Wilkes.* Email: harold.cox@wilkes.edu.

*Cox, **J. Wendel**.* Hanover, NH. Affil: Dartmouth. Email: j.wendel.cox@dartmouth.edu. Research: urban animals.

*Cox, **Jeffrey L.**, Iowa.* Iowa City, IA. Email: jeffrey-cox@uiowa.edu. Research: modern European religion, missionaries.

Cox, John K., *North Dakota State.* Email: john.cox.1@ndsu.edu.

*Cox, **Karen L.**, North Carolina, Charlotte.* Email: kcox@uncc.edu.

Cox, Keith W., *San Diego Mesa.* Email: kwcox@sdccd.edu.

Cox, Marcus, *Xavier, La.* Email: mcox1@xula.edu.

Cox, Marvin R., *Connecticut, Storrs.* Email: marvin.cox@uconn.edu.

*Cox, **Michael K**.* Davenport, IA. Affil: Wilson Middle Sch. Email: geocox304@aol.com.

Cox, Michael L., *San Diego Mesa.* Email: mcox@sdccd.edu.

*Cox, **Nicholas Patrick**.* Sugar Land, TX. Affil: Houston Comm. Coll. Email: npcox@uh.edu. Research: interracial families, Kentucky Jacksonian party formation.

*Cox, **Randi Barnes**, Stephen F. Austin State.* Nacogdoches, TX. Email: rcox@sfasu.edu. Research: Cold War culture.

Cox, Robert S., *Massachusetts, Amherst.* Email: rscox@library.umass.edu.

*Cox, **Shae Vaughn**.* Las Vegas, NV. Affil: Nevada, Las Vegas. Email: coxs6@unlv.nevada.edu. Research: Civil War uniforms, identity and memory.

Cox, Thomas H., *Sam Houston State.* Email: thc001@shsu.edu.

Cox, Thomas R., *San Diego State.*

*Coy, **Andrew William**.* North Fort Myers, FL. Affil: Riverdale High Sch. Email: andycoy22@comcast.net.

*Coy, **Jason Philip**, Charleston.* Email: coyj@cofc.edu.

*Coyle, **Alexander**.* Madaba, Jordan. Affil: King's Academy. Email: alexander.coyle@gmail.com.

Crabbs, Jack A., Jr., *California State, Fullerton.* Email: jcrabbs@fullerton.edu.

Crabtree, Mari N., *Charleston.* Email: crabtreemn@cofc.edu.

Cracraft, James E., *Illinois, Chicago.* Email: cracraft@uic.edu.

Craft, George S., Jr., *California State, Sacramento.* Email: gcraft@csus.edu.

Crafts, Lydia, *Manhattan.* Email: lcrafts01@manhattan.edu.

Cragin, Thomas J., *Muhlenberg.* Email: cragin@muhlenberg.edu.

*Craib, **Raymond B**., Cornell.* Ithaca, NY. Email: rbc23@cornell.edu. Research: geography/cartography, anarchism/the Left.

Craig, Albert M., *Harvard (Hist.).* Email: acraig@fas.harvard.edu.

*Craig, **Bruce**.* Charlottetown, PE, Canada. Affil: Prince Edward Island. Email: rbcraig84@hotmail.com. Research: Cold War espionage.

*Craig, **Douglas B**.* Canberra, Australia. Affil: Australian National. Email: Douglas.Craig@anu.edu.au. Research: 20th-c US political, media.

Craig, John M., *Slippery Rock.* Email: john.craig@sru.edu.

Craig, John Paul, *Chestnut Hill.* Email: craigj@chc.edu.

Craig, John, *Simon Fraser.* Email: johnc@sfu.ca.

*Craig, **Kalani**, Indiana.* Bloomington, IN. Email: craigkl@indiana.edu. Research: divine agency, conflict resolution.

Craig, Kate Melissa, *Auburn.* Email: kmc0088@auburn.edu.

Craig, Leigh Ann, *Virginia Commonwealth.* Email: lacraig@vcu.edu.

*Craig, **Susan J**.* Richmond Hill, NY. Email: scraig14@yahoo.com. Research: theology and culture, film and culture.

*Crais, **Clifton C**., Emory.* Atlanta, GA. Email: ccrais@emory.edu. Research: Africa, cross-cultural.

*Cramer, **Kevin Charles**, Indiana–Purdue, Indianapolis.* Indianapolis, IN. Email: kcramer@iupui.edu. Research: philanthropy/religion/humanitarianism, diasporas/nationalism.

Cramer, Richard S., *San José State.*

*Cramer van den Bogaart, **Annette M**.* Stony Brook, NY. Email: amcvdb@gmail.com. Research: 17th-/18th-c women in Dutch Atlantic.

Cramsie, John R., III, *Union Coll.* Email: cramsiej@union.edu.

Crandell, Jill N., *Brigham Young.* Email: jill_crandell@byu.edu.

*Crane, **Elaine Forman**, Fordham.* New York, NY. Email: ecrane@fordham.edu. Research: early American legal, early American gender.

*Crane, **Susan A**., Arizona.* Tucson, AZ. Email: scrane@u.arizona.edu. Research: modern Europe, cultural and intellectual.

*Crannell-Ash, **Marissa**.* Rochester, NY. Affil: Rochester. Email: mcrannel@ur.rochester.edu.

Crapol, Edward P., *William and Mary.* Email: edpcal@wm.edu.

*Cratty, **Flynn Jamison**.* New Haven, CT. Affil: Yale. Email: flynn.cratty@yale.edu.

Craun, Christopher Carl, *Central Arkansas.* Email: craunc@uca.edu.

*Craver, **Earlene**.* Pismo Beach, CA. Affil: California Polytechnic State. Email: earlenecl@charter.net. Research: immigration and nationalization, intellectual migration from Europe.

Crawford, Charles W., *Memphis.* Email: cwcrwfrd@memphis.edu.

*Crawford, **Elva**.* Fairfax, VA. Email: ebcrawford@aol.com.

*Crawford, **Jonathan A**.* Navarre, FL. Email: jonc-2748@mchsi.com. Research: use of militia in southern frontier, Albigensian crusade and Cathars.

*Crawford, **Katherine B**., Vanderbilt.* Nashville, TN. Email: katherine.b.crawford@vanderbilt.edu. Research: women and desire in French Renaissance, French Wars of Religion.

Crawford, Matthew J., *Kent State.* Email: mcrawf11@kent.edu.

*Crawford, **Michael J**.* Fairfax, VA. Affil: Naval Hist. Command. Email: michael.crawford@navy.mil; crawford.michael.john@gmail.com. Research: American Revolution naval, 19th-c US Navy petty officers.

Crawford, Paul F., *California, Pa.* Email: crawford_p@calu.edu.

Crawley, William B., Jr., *Mary Washington.* Email: wcrawley@umw.edu.

Cray, Robert E., *Montclair State.* Email: crayr@mail.montclair.edu.

Creager, Angela N. H., *Princeton; Shelby Cullom Davis Center.* Email: creager@princeton.edu.

Creagh, C. Dianne, *Penn State.* Email: cdc16@psu.edu.

*Crean, **Jeffrey Peter**.* College Station, TX. Affil: Texas A&M, Coll. Station. Email: jeff.crean@gmail.com. Research: US-China relations, US military public affairs.

Creasman, Allyson F., *Carnegie Mellon.* Email: allysonc@andrew.cmu.edu.

*Creason, **Carl C**.* Prospect, KY. Affil: Northwestern. Email: carlcreason2022@u.northwestern.edu.

Crecelius, Daniel, *California State, Los Angeles.* Email: dcrecel@calstatela.edu.

*Creciun Graff, **Ala**.* College Park, MD. Affil: Maryland, Coll. Park. Email: acreciun@umd.edu. Research: monarchic legitimacy/19th-c Russia, press/nationalism.

*Creech, **Joseph W., Jr**.* Valparaiso, IN. Affil: Valparaiso. Email: joseph.creech@valpo.edu.

Creekmore, Marion, Jr., *Emory.* Email: mcreekm@emory.edu.

Creely, Thomas E., *Naval War Coll.* Email: tomcreely@icloud.com.

Creighton, Margaret S., *Bates.* Email: mcreight@bates.edu.

Cremer, *Douglas J*. Burbank, CA. Affil: Woodbury. Email: douglas.cremer@woodbury.edu. Research: postmodernism and theology, terrorism and religion.

Cremin, **Dennis H.**, *Lewis*. Email: creminde@lewisu.edu.

Crerar, **Adam**, *Wilfrid Laurier*. Email: acrerar@wlu.ca.

Crespino, *Joseph H.*, *Emory*. Decatur, GA. Email: jcrespi@emory.edu. Research: civil rights, race and religion.

Cressler, *Matthew J*. Charleston, SC. Affil: Charleston. Email: mjcressler@gmail.com. Research: African American Catholics in Chicago, Black Power Movement.

Cressman, *Dale L*. Spanish Fork, UT. Affil: Brigham Young. Email: cressman@byu.edu. Research: television news, media coverage/US Civil Rights Movement.

Cressy, **David**, *Ohio State*. Email: cressy.3@osu.edu.

Creswell, **Michael H.**, *Florida State*. Email: mcreswell@fsu.edu.

Crew, **David F.**, *Texas, Austin*. Email: dfcrew@uts.cc.utexas.edu.

Crewe, **Ryan D.**, *Colorado Denver*. Email: ryan.crewe@ucdenver.edu.

Crews, **Daniel A.**, *Central Missouri*. Email: crews@ucmo.edu.

Crews, **Robert D.**, *Stanford*. Email: rcrews@stanford.edu.

Cribelli, **C. Teresa**, *Alabama, Tuscaloosa*. Email: ctcribelli@bama.ua.edu.

Crider, **Destiny**, *Luther*. Email: cridde01@luther.edu.

Crider, *Ernest A*. Centreville, VA. Affil: General Dynamics Information Tech. Email: eacrider1968@verizon.net.

Crider, **Gregory S.**, *Winthrop*. Email: criderg@winthrop.edu.

Crider, *Jonathan B*. Lubbock, TX. Affil: Temple. Email: flywitheagles@gmail.com.

Crider, *Louis Michael*. Millersburg, OH. Email: Mrcrider240@gmail.com.

Crilly, *Mark W*. Niles, IL. Affil: Maryland Univ. Coll. Email: tuppers1@gmail.com.

Crim, **Brian E.**, *Lynchburg*. Email: crim@lynchburg.edu.

Crimmins, **Timothy J.**, *Georgia State*. Email: tcrimmin@gsu.edu.

Crimmins, **Timothy**. South Barrington, IL. Affil: Chicago. Email: crimmins@uchicago.edu.

Crisa, **Antonino**. Milano, Italy. Affil: Warwick. Email: crisa.antonino@gmail.com. Research: archaeology/Sicily, antiquarianism/numismatics.

Crisanti, *Giulia*. Bronx, NY. Affil: Fordham. Email: gcrisanti@fordham.edu.

Crislip, **Andrew T.**, *Virginia Commonwealth*. Email: acrislip@vcu.edu.

Crisp, **James E.**, *North Carolina State*. Email: james_crisp@ncsu.edu.

Critchlow, **Donald Thomas**, *Arizona State*. Email: donald.critchlow@asu.edu.

Croak, **Thomas M.**, **CM**, *DePaul*. Email: tcroak@depaul.edu.

Crocitti, **John J.**, *San Diego Mesa*. Email: jcrocitt@sdccd.edu.

Crocker, **Matthew H.**, *Keene State*. Email: mcrocker@keene.edu.

Crocker, **Ruth C.**, *Auburn*. Email: crockrc@auburn.edu.

Crockett, **Beverly A**. Wilmette, IL. Affil: Oakton Comm. Coll. Email: beverlyac@gmail.com. Research: 19th-c fiction, 19th-c US and Europe.

Crofts, **Daniel W.**, *New Jersey*. Southampton, PA. Email: crofts@tcnj.edu. Research: 19th-c American South, North-South sectional conflict.

Croll, **Sophia D**. Chicago, IL. Affil: Loyola, Chicago. Email: scroll1@luc.edu.

Cromwell, **Alisha Marie**, *Coastal Carolina*. Email: scromwell@coastal.edu.

Cromwell, *Jesse Levis*, *Mississippi*. University, MS. Email: cromwell@olemiss.edu; jesse_Cromwell@hotmail.com. Research: contraband in Venezuela and Colombia, South American trade social.

Cronenberg, **Allen T.**, *Auburn*.

Cronin, **James E.**, *Boston Coll*. Email: croninj@bc.edu.

Cronon, *William J.*, *Wisconsin-Madison*. Madison, WI. Email: bill@williamcronon.net. Research: Portage Wisconsin, recent US environmental politics.

Crooks, **James B.**, *North Florida*. Email: jamesbcrooks@comcast.net.

Croom, *Dan*. Tifton, GA. Email: dbcroom@ncsu.edu.

Cropper, **John S.**, *Charleston*. Email: cropperjs@cofc.edu.

Crosby, *Emilye J.*, *SUNY, Coll. Geneseo*. Geneseo, NY. Email: crosby@geneseo.edu. Research: civil rights movement, Mississippi African American.

Crosby, **Everett U.**, **II**, *Virginia*. Email: euc@virginia.edu.

Crosby, **Heather**, *Charleston*. Email: crosbyhe@cofc.edu.

Cross, **C. Wallace**, *Austin Peay State*. Email: crossw@apsu.edu.

Cross, *Gary S.*, *Penn State*. University Park, PA. Email: gsc2@psu.edu. Research: late industrial society, western Europe/England/US.

Cross, **Michael**, *Dalhousie*. Email: michael.cross@dal.ca.

Crossley, **Pamela Kyle**, *Dartmouth*. Email: pamela.crossley@dartmouth.edu.

Crosson, **Andria**, *Texas, San Antonio*. Email: andria.crosson@utsa.edu.

Crosswell, **Daniel K. R.**, *Columbus State*. Email: crosswell_daniel@columbusstate.edu.

Crothers, *A. Glenn*, *Louisville*. Louisville, KY. Email: glenn.crothers@louisville.edu. Research: economy/society in early national South, antebellum upper South.

Crouch, *Christian Ayne*, *Bard*. Email: crouch@bard.edu.

Crouse, *Maurice A.*, *Memphis*. Memphis, TN. Email: mcrouse@memphis.edu. Research: colonial and revolutionary America.

Crout, *Robert Rhodes*, *Charleston*. Email: croutr@cofc.edu.

Crouthamel, *Jason P.*, *Grand Valley State*. Email: crouthaj@gvsu.edu.

Crow, *John L*. Tallahassee, FL. Affil: Florida State. Email: jlcrow@fsu.edu. Research: American religion, Western esotericism.

Crow, *Matthew*. Geneva, NY. Affil: Hobart and William Smith. Email: mecrow@gmail.com. Research: early American legal, legal and political thought.

Crowe, **David M.**, **Jr.**, *Elon*. Email: crowed@elon.edu.

Crowe, **Michael**, *Notre Dame*. Email: Crowe.13@nd.edu.

Crowe, **Nathan P.**, *North Carolina, Wilmington*. Email: crowen@uncw.edu.

Crowe-Carraco, **Carol E.**, *Western Kentucky*. Email: carol.crowecarraco@wku.edu.

Crowley, *James P*. Riverside, RI. Affil: Brown. Email: jcrowley9802@gmail.com. Research: development of blood grouping concepts, early theories of antibody formation.

Crowley, *John E.*, *Dalhousie*. Halifax, NS, Canada. Email: crowley@dal.ca. Research: 18th-c British imperialism/visual culture.

Crowley, *Mark James*. Cambridge, MA. Affil: Wuhan. Email: mjcrowley@fas.harvard.edu.

Crowley, **Terence A.**, *Guelph*. Email: tcrowley@uoguelph.ca.

Crowley, **Weldon S.**, *Southwestern*.

Crowston, *Clare*, *Illinois, Urbana-Champaign*. Urbana, IL. Email: crowston@illinois.edu. Research: 18th-c French women/credit/fashion, apprenticeship in early modern France.

Crowther, *Kathleen M.*, *Oklahoma (Hist. of Science)*. Email: kcrowther@ou.edu.

Crubaugh, *Anthony*, *Illinois State*. Normal, IL. Email: acrubau@ilstu.edu. Research: 18th-c France.

Crudele, *Kristin Marie*. Islip, NY. Email: kristincrudele@gmail.com.

Cruikshank, **Ken**, *McMaster*. Email: cruiksha@mcmaster.ca.

Crummey, **Robert O.**, *California, Davis*. Email: rocrummey@ucdavis.edu.

Crutchfield, **Lisa L.**, *Lynchburg*. Email: crutchfield_l@lynchburg.edu.

Cruz, **Felipe Fernandes**, *Tulane*. Email: fcruz1@tulane.edu.

Cruz, *Jesus*, *Delaware*. Newark, DE. Email: jesus@udel.edu. Research: material culture and consumption, modern Spain.

Cruz, **Richard A.**, *Tarleton State*. Email: cruz@tarleton.edu.

Csete, **Anne A.**, *St. Lawrence*. Email: acsete@stlawu.edu.

Csirkes, *Ferenc Peter*. Istanbul, Turkey. Affil: Sabanci. Email: fcsirkes@sabanciuniv.edu. Research: vernacularization in Islamic world, Turkish literature and literacy in Iran.

Csiszar, *Alex*, *Harvard (Hist. of Science)*. Cambridge, MA. Email: acsiszar@fas.harvard.edu. Research: scientific communication, physical sciences.

Csorba, *Mrea*, *Duquesne*. Email: csorba@duq.edu.

Cuddihy, *William J*. Pomona, CA. Affil: Golden West; Long Beach City. Email: wcuddihyphd@yahoo.com.

Cuddy, *Brian*. North Ryde, Australia. Affil: Macquarie. Email: bjc249@cornell.edu. Research: international law in world politics, America's Vietnam War.

Cuddy, *Zachary*. Chula Vista, CA. Affil: Southwestern. Email: zcuddy@swccd.edu.

Cuello, **Jose**, *Wayne State*. Email: j.cuello@wayne.edu.

Cuff, *Timothy*, *Westminster*. New Wilmington, PA. Email: cufft@westminster.edu. Research: 19th-c US economic development, 19th-c US health and welfare.

Cugini, *Cesidio Joseph*. Roxbury, MA. Email: cc2manj@verizon.net. Research: 20th-c labor, 20th-c popular culture.

Culclasure, Scott P. Greensboro, NC. Email: sculclasure@aha-net.org. Research: early Republic and American Revolution, French assignats.

Culibrk, Jelena. Santa Monica, CA. Email: culibrk@usc.edu.

Cullather, Nick B., *Indiana*. Bloomington, IN. Email: ncullath@indiana.edu. Research: US foreign relations, intelligence and modernization.

Cullen, Charles T., *Hist. Soc. of Pennsylvania*. Email: ccullen@hsp.org.

Cullen, David, *Arkansas Tech*. Email: dcullen@atu.edu.

Cullinan, William Harvey. Refugio, TX. Affil: Dialogue Inst. Email: wcullina2002@yahoo.com. Research: Confucian philosophy and economics, inter-religious dialogue.

Cullinane, Michael M., *Wisconsin-Madison*. Email: mmcullin@wisc.edu.

Cullison, Jennifer L. Provo, UT. Affil: Colorado, Boulder. Email: cullison@colorado.edu.

Culp, Alyssa. Knoxville, TN. Affil: Tennessee, Knoxville. Email: aculp1@vols.utk.edu.

Culp, Robert J., *Bard*. Email: culp@bard.edu.

Culpepper, Kenneth Scott. Sioux Center, IA. Affil: Dordt. Email: scott.culpepper@dordt.edu. Research: English separatism, Enlightenment historiography.

Culver, Annika A., *Florida State*. Tallahassee, FL. Email: aculver@fsu.edu. Research: advertising/Japan's empire in East Asia, visual cultures US occupation of Japan.

Culver, Gregory, *Austin Peay State*. Email: culverg@apsu.edu.

Culver, Lawrence, *Utah State*. Logan, UT. Email: lawrence.culver@usu.edu. Research: climate and climate change, North American West/borderlands.

Culver, William W. Mooers Forks, NY. Affil: SUNY, Plattsburgh. Email: william.culver@plattsburgh.edu. Research: politics and history of copper metallurgy, historical chemistry.

Cumbler, John T., **Jr.**, *Louisville*. Email: cumbler@louisville.edu.

Cumiford, William, *Chapman*. Email: cumiford@chapman.edu.

Cumings, Bruce, *Chicago*. Chicago, IL. Email: rufus88@uchicago.edu. Research: international, East Asian political economy.

Cumming, John B. Carlsbad, CA. Email: jbcumming@aol.com. Research: emergence of Anglo California, Walther Rathenau and Jewish identity.

Cummings, Alex Sayf, *Georgia State*. Atlanta, GA. Email: alexcummings@gsu.edu. Research: piracy and intellectual property, landscape and information technology.

Cummings, Kathleen Sprows, *Notre Dame*; *Cushwa Center*. Notre Dame, IN. Email: cummings.23@nd.edu. Research: Catholic saints, women religious.

Cummins, Brendan. Lethbridge, AB, Canada. Affil: Lethbridge. Email: brendan.cummins@uleth.ca. Research: new religious movements, Mormon studies.

Cummins, Light T., *Austin Coll*. Email: lcummins@austincollege.edu.

Cummins, Victoria H., *Austin Coll*. Email: vcummins@austincollege.edu.

Cummiskey, Julia, *Tennessee, Chattanooga*. Email: julia-cummiskey@utc.edu.

Cunfer, Geoff, *Saskatchewan*. Email: geoff.cunfer@usask.ca.

Cunigan, Nicholas, *Calvin*. Email: njcunigan@calvin.edu.

Cunniff, Roger L., *San Diego State*. Email: rcunniff@sdsu.edu.

Cunningham, Eric P., *Gonzaga*. Email: cunningham@gonzaga.edu.

Cunningham, Floyd T. Taytay Rizal, Philippines. Affil: Asia Pacific Nazarene Theological Seminary. Email: fcunningham@apnts.org. Research: Philippine Protestantism, Nazarene Church.

Cunningham, Geoffrey. Olympia, WA. Email: cunningg@evergreen.edu.

Cunningham, Sean P., *Texas Tech*. Email: sean.cunningham@ttu.edu.

Cunningham, Shannon. Milwaukee, WI. Affil: Medieval Inst. Publications. Email: s.cunningham@aup.nl.

Cuno, Kenneth M., *Illinois, Urbana-Champaign*. Urbana, IL. Email: kmcuno@illinois.edu. Research: family in modern Egypt, Islamic law in Ottoman Empire and Egypt.

Cupchoy, Lani, *California State, Los Angeles*. Montebello, CA. Email: lcupcho@calstatela.edu; lcupchoy@gmail.com. Research: US, Chicana/o and Latina/o studies.

Cupples, Cynthia J. Laurel, MD. Email: cyncupples@verizon.net.

Curcio-Nagy, Linda A., *Nevada, Reno*. Email: lindacurcio@unr.edu.

Curley, Augustine James. Newark, NJ. Affil: St. Benedict's Abbey, Newark. Email: acurley@sbp.org. Research: Catholic Church in New Jersey.

Curley, George. Santa Ana, CA. Affil: California, Riverside. Email: gcurley@pacbell.net.

Curley, Robert E. Guadalajara, Jalisco, Mexico. Affil: Guadalajara. Email: recurley@gmail.com. Research: Mexican Revolution, Catholicism.

Curp, T. David, *Ohio*. Email: curp@ohio.edu.

Curran, R. Emmett, *Georgetown*. Email: currane@georgetown.edu.

Currarino, Rosanne, *Queen's, Can*. Email: rc16@queensu.ca.

Curras, Ricardo. Lodi, NJ. Affil: Univision New York - Channel 41. Email: ricardo_curras@hotmail.com. Research: 20th-c international relations.

Curren, Jennifer, *California State, Los Angeles*. Email: jcurren@calstatela.edu.

Currier, Vic. Sierra Vista, AZ. Email: rvcurrier@gmail.com.

Curry, Dawne Yvette, *Nebraska, Lincoln*. Email: dcurry2@unl.edu.

Curry, Earl R., *Hope*. Email: curry@hope.edu.

Curry, John J., **IV**, *Nevada, Las Vegas*. Email: john.curry@unlv.edu.

Curry, Lawrence H., **Jr.**, *Houston*. Email: lcurry@uh.edu.

Curry, Lynne, *Eastern Illinois*. Email: lecurry@eiu.edu.

Curta, Florin, *Florida*. Email: fcurta@ufl.edu.

Curtin, Mary Ellen, *American*. Email: curtin@american.edu.

Curtis, Bruce, *Carleton, Can*. Email: bruce.curtis@carleton.ca.

Curtis, Christopher M., *Georgia Southern*. Email: ccurtis@georgiasouthern.edu.

Curtis, Heather D. Needham, MA. Affil: Tufts. Email: heather.curtis@tufts.edu. Research: Christianity, American religion.

Curtis, James C., *Delaware*. Email: jcurtis@udel.edu.

Curtis, Jesse Nathaniel. Philadelphia, PA. Affil: Temple. Email: tuf72715@temple.edu.

Curtis, Kenneth R., *California State, Long Beach*. Email: kenneth.curtis@csulb.edu.

Curtis, Kip, *Ohio State*. Email: curtis.457@osu.edu.

Curtis, Sarah A. San Francisco, CA. Affil: San Francisco State. Email: scurtis@sfsu.edu. Research: French colonialism, women missionaries.

Curtis, Stephan M., *Memorial, Newfoundland*. Email: stephanc@mun.ca.

Curtis, Susan, *Purdue*. Email: curtis@purdue.edu.

Curto, Jose C., *York, Can*. Email: jcurto@yorku.ca.

Curwood, Anastasia C., *Kentucky*. Email: anastasia.curwood@uky.edu.

Cusack, Gregory Daniel. Portland, OR. Email: gregcusack43@gmail.com.

Cushman, Gregory T., *Kansas*. Email: gcushman@ku.edu.

Cushman, Sarah M. Evanston, IL. Affil: Northwestern. Email: sarah.cushman@northwestern.edu. Research: war crimes trials, women in Holocaust.

Cusick, James, *Florida*. Email: jgcusick@ufl.edu.

Cusimano, Richard C., *Louisiana, Lafayette*.

Cutcliffe, Stephen H., *Lehigh*. Email: shc0@lehigh.edu.

Cuthbert-Brandt, Gail, *Waterloo*. Email: gcbrandt@uwaterloo.ca.

Cuthbertson, Susan E. Las Vegas, NV. Affil: Virginia. Email: sec5e@virginia.edu. Research: politics/empire/Italian society.

Cutler, Brock, *Radford*. Email: bcutler2@radford.edu.

Cutler, Kenneth E., *Indiana-Purdue, Indianapolis*. Email: kcutler@iupui.edu.

Cutler, Robert S., *Wittenberg*. Email: bob8954@yahoo.com.

Cutler, William W., **III**. Jenkintown, PA. Affil: Temple. Email: wcutler@temple.edu. Research: 19th-/20th-c school politics, scholarship of teaching and learning.

Cutter, Barbara A., *Northern Iowa*. Email: barbara.cutter@uni.edu.

Cutter, Charles R., *Purdue*. Email: cutter@purdue.edu.

Cutter, Doug, *Illinois State*. Email: dacutte@ilstu.edu.

CuUnjieng Aboitiz, Nicole. New York, NY. Affil: Clare Hall, Cambridge. Email: nec34@cam.ac.uk. Research: Global intellectual history, Southeast Asian history.

Cuyler, Zachary Davis. Brooklyn, NY. Affil: NYU. Email: zack.cuyler@gmail.com.

Cvijetic, Silvije. Nacka, Sweden. Email: silvije@hotmail.com.

Cwiek, Brian E., *Bates*. Email: bcwiek@bates.edu.

Cygan, Mary E., *Connecticut, Storrs*. Email: mary.cygan@uconn.edu.

Cymbala, Amy, *Duquesne*. Email: cymbalaa@duq.edu.

Cypkin, Diane. Brooklyn, NY. Affil: Pace. Email: dcypkin@pace.edu.

Czap, Peter, Jr., *Amherst*. Email: pczap@amherst.edu.

Czitrom, **Daniel J.**, *Mount Holyoke*. South Hadley, MA. Email: dczitrom@mtholyoke.edu. Research: US intellectual and cultural, 20th century.

Czuchry, **Rebecca A. Kosary**, *Texas Lutheran*. Email: rczuchry@tlu.edu.

D d

Dabel, **Jane E.**, *California State, Long Beach; Soc. for Hist. Education*. Email: jane.dabel@csulb.edu.

Dabrowski, **Patrice M**. Natick, MA. Affil: Vienna. Email: pmd@post.harvard.edu. Research: nation-building and commemorations, Carpathian Mountain region.

Dabrowski, **Tomash**. Chicago, IL. Email: tomcdabrowski@gmail.com.

Dachowski, **Elizabeth H.**, *Tennessee State*. Email: edachowski@tnstate.edu.

Dack, **Mikkel**, *Rowan*. Email: dack@rowan.edu.

Daddis, **Gregory A.**, *Chapman*. Email: daddis@chapman.edu.

Daddow, **Kirk Glenn**. Ames, IA. Affil: Des Moines Area Comm. Coll. Email: k.daddow@mchsi.com. Research: Cathar culture in France, Chemin de St Jacques.

Daen, **Laurel R.**, *Omohundro Inst.* Williamsburg, VA. Email: lrdaen@wm.edu; laureldaen@gmail.com. Research: disability, early America.

Dagbovie, **Pero G.**, *Michigan State*. Email: dagbovie@msu.edu.

Dagenais, **Maxime**, *McMaster*. Email: dagenam@mcmaster.ca.

Dagenais, **Michele**, *Montréal*. Email: michele.dagenais@umontreal.ca.

Daggar, **Lori J.**, *Ursinus*. Email: ldaggar@ursinus.edu.

D'Agostino, **Rachel**, *Library Co. of Philadelphia*. Email: rdagostino@librarycompany.org.

Dahl, **Jessa Kennedy**, *Chicago*. Chicago, IL. Affil: Chicago. Email: jdahl@uchicago.edu.

Dahl, **Roger M**. Des Plaines, IL. Affil: National Bahai Archives. Email: rmdahl46@gmail.com.

Dahl, **Victor C.**, *Portland State*.

Dahlberg, **Britt**, *Science History Inst.* Email: bdahlberg@sciencehistory.org.

Dahlstrand, **Frederick C.**, *Ohio State*. Email: dahlstrand.1@osu.edu.

Dahlstrand, **Kate**. Athens, GA. Affil: Georgia. Email: ksd60480@uga.edu.

Dahm, **Kerry Anne**, *Robert H. Smith Center*. Email: kdahm@monticello.org.

Dahmus, **John**, *Stephen F. Austin State*.

Dai, **Yingcong**, *William Paterson*. Wayne, NJ. Email: daiy@wpunj.edu. Research: frontier politics of Qing/Ch'ing, military system of Qing/Ch'ing.

Dail, **Chrystyna Marta**. Ithaca, NY. Affil: Ithaca. Email: cdail@ithaca.edu. Research: political theatre and performance, Ukrainian diasporic communities.

Daileader, **Philip H.**, *William and Mary*. Williamsburg, VA. Email: phdail@wm.edu. Research: medieval Europe.

Dailey, **Barbara R**. Watertown, MA. Email: bdailey45@verizon.net.

Dailey, **Jane**, *Chicago*. Chicago, IL. Email: dailey@uchicago.edu. Research: race and politics 1865-1970, human rights/law/religion.

Daily, **Andrew M.**, *Memphis*. Email: amdaily@memphis.edu.

Daily, **Gary W.**, *Indiana State*. Email: gdaily@isugw.indstate.edu.

Dain, **Bruce R.**, *Utah*. Email: bruce.dain@utah.edu.

Daitoku, **Takaaki**. Yokohama, Japan. Affil: MIT. Email: t-daitoku@u.northwestern.edu. Research: nuclear proliferation, international organizations.

Dal Lago, **Enrico**. Galway, Ireland. Affil: National, Ireland, Galway. Email: enrico.dallago@nuigalway.ie. Research: antebellum America, comparative slavery in New and Old World.

Dale, **Elizabeth**, *Florida*. Email: edale@ufl.edu.

Dale, **Melissa Suzanne**. San Francisco, CA. Affil: San Francisco. Email: mdale3@usfca.edu. Research: Qing social, eunuchs/gender/medical.

Dale, **Stephen F.**, *Ohio State*. Email: dale.1@osu.edu.

Daley, **John L. S.**, *Pittsburg State*. Email: jdaley@pittstate.edu.

Daley, **Matthew Lawrence**, *Grand Valley State*. Email: daleym@gvsu.edu.

Dalin, **Miriam R.**, *Florida Atlantic*. Email: msanua@fau.edu.

Dallasheh, **Leena**. Arcata, CA. Affil: Humboldt State. Email: leena.dallasheh@gmail.com. Research: modern Palestine, citizenship/colonialism/decolonization.

Dallek, **Matthew**. Washington, DC. Affil: George Washington. Email: mdallek@gwu.edu. Research: political management.

Dallek, **Robert**, *UCLA*. Email: rdallek@ucla.edu.

Dalstrom, **Harl A.**, *Nebraska, Omaha*. Email: kdalstrom@msn.com.

Dalton, **Chris**, *St. Bonaventure*. Email: cdalton@sbu.edu.

Dalton, **Christopher B**. Elmore, Australia. Affil: Golburn Murray Water Board. Email: chris.dalton@gmwater.com.au.

Dalton, **Susan**, *Montréal*. Email: susan.dalton@umontreal.ca.

Daly, **Arik Nicholas**. Enid, OK. Email: arikdaly@gmail.com.

Daly, **Jennifer P**. Chicago, IL. Affil: Chicago. Email: jpd@uchicago.edu.

Daly, **John P.**, *SUNY, Coll. Brockport*. Email: jdaly@brockport.edu.

Daly, **Jonathan W.**, *Illinois, Chicago*. Email: daly@uic.edu.

Daly, **Kathleen**, *Bryant*. Email: kdaly1@bryant.edu.

Daly, **Lawrence J.**, *Bowling Green State*. Email: ldaly@bgsu.edu.

Daly, **Patrick E.**, **Esq**. West Hartford, CT. Email: vmfa334ped@sbcglobal.net. Research: US Middle East relations, Spanish Civil War.

Daly Bednarek, **Janet R.**, *Dayton*. Centerville, OH. Email: jbednarek1@udayton.edu. Research: municipal airports, city planning.

Daly-Jones, **Benjamin**. London, United Kingdom. Affil: Oxford. Email: benjamin.daly-jones@lincoln.ox.ac.uk.

Dalzell, **Robert F.**, **Jr.**, *Williams*. Email: rdalzell@williams.edu.

D'Amboise, **Paul**. St. Hubert, QC, Canada. Affil: Comm. Coll. of Vermont. Email: paul.damboise@gmail.com. Research: 20th-c policing in rural Quebec, historical thinking and consciousness.

Damen, **Mark L.**, *Utah State*. Email: mark.damen@usu.edu.

Dameron, **George W.**, *St. Michael's*. Colchester, VT. Email: gdameron@smcvt.edu. Research: medieval Florentine church, medieval Tuscany.

Dames, **Tom J**. Cornwall On Hudson, NY. Affil: Mount St. Mary. Email: tdames@my.msmc.edu. Research: baseball in US history, 1600s Dutch Golden Age.

Damiano, **Sara**, *Texas State*. Email: sdamiano@txstate.edu.

D'Amico, **Stefano**, *Texas Tech*. Lubbock, TX. Email: stefano.damico@ttu.edu. Research: Spanish Milan.

Damms, **Richard V.**, *Mississippi State*. Email: rdamms@history.msstate.edu.

D'Amore, **Laura**, *Roger Williams*. Email: ldamore@rwu.edu.

Dancy, **Jeremiah Ross**, *Naval War Coll.* Email: jeremiah.dancy@usnwc.edu.

Dandelet, **Thomas**, *California, Berkeley*. Berkeley, CA. Email: tdandelet@berkeley.edu. Research: Mediterranean.

D'Andrea, **David M.**, *Oklahoma State*. Email: david.dandrea@okstate.edu.

Dandrow, **Edward M.**, *Central Florida*. Email: edward.dandrow@ucf.edu.

Dane, **Jennifer**. Belmont, CA. Affil: Ohio State. Email: jenniferldane@gmail.com. Research: postrevolution French Catholic convents, dynamics of French nuns' education.

Daniel, **E. Randolph**. Lexington, KY. Affil: Kentucky. Email: erdani01@email.uky.edu. Research: Middle Ages apocalypticism, Middle Ages religious orders.

Daniel, **Evan Matthew**, *Queens, CUNY*. Email: evan.daniel@qc.cuny.edu.

Daniel, **G. Reginald**, *California, Santa Barbara*. Email: rdaniel@soc.ucsb.edu.

Daniel, **Jason**. Miami, FL. Affil: Florida International. Email: jasonmdaniel@gmail.com. Research: early modern Atlantic maritime, colonial Caribbean.

Daniel, **Josiah M.**, **III**. Dallas, TX. Affil: Vinson & Elkins LLP. Email: josiahmdaniel3@gmail.com. Research: Chapter 9 municipal bankruptcy, bankruptcy law.

Daniel, **Marcus L.**, *Hawai'i, Manoa*. Email: marcusd@hawaii.edu.

Daniel, **Pete**. Washington, DC. Email: petedanielr@gmail.com. Research: African American farmers and civil rights, 1950s southern popular culture.

Daniel, **Tracy**. Houston, TX. Affil: Texas Southern. Email: danieltracy6@gmail.com.

Daniel, **Vicki**, *Case Western Reserve*. Email: vicki.daniel@case.edu.

Daniel, **Wallace L.**, **Jr.**, *Baylor; Mercer*. Email: wallace_daniel@baylor.edu; daniel_wl@mercer.edu.

Daniell, **Jere R.**, **II**, *Dartmouth*. Email: jere.daniell@dartmouth.edu.

Daniels, **Bruce C.**, *Texas, San Antonio; Winnipeg*. Email: bruce.daniels@utsa.edu.

Daniels, **Douglas**, *California, Santa Barbara*. Email: daniels@blackstudies.ucsb.edu.

Daniels, **Mario**, *Georgetown*. Email: md1367@georgetown.edu.

Daniels, **Nathan**. Baltimore, MD. Affil: Johns Hopkins. Email: nathan.daniels@jhu.edu. Research: medieval social, medieval cultural.

Daniels, Roger, *Cincinnati*. Bellevue, WA. Email: roger.daniels@uc.edu; roger.daniels@att.net. Research: immigration and immigration policy, era of FDR.

Danielson, Leilah Claire, *Northern Arizona*. Email: leilah.danielson@nau.edu.

Danielsson, Sarah K. Bronx, NY. Affil: Queensborough Comm. Coll., CUNY. Email: sdanielsson@qcc.cuny.edu. Research: Germanic world/European intellectual, genocide.

Dankenbring, Danielle. Bradenton, FL. Affil: Florida Maritime Museum. Email: dmdankenbring@gmail.com.

Dannies, Kate. Oxford, OH. Affil: Miami, Ohio. Email: kd576@georgetown.edu. Research: WWI in Ottoman Empire, women and gender.

Danon, Dina, *Binghamton, SUNY*. Email: ddanon@binghamton.edu.

Danos, Despina O. Neshanic Station, NJ. Email: ddanos@comcast.net.

Danquah, Rochelle E. Farmington Hills, MI. Affil: Wayne State. Email: redanquah@yahoo.com. Research: antislavery movement/Underground Railroad, 19th-c African American.

Dant, Sara, *Weber State*. Ogden, UT. Email: sdant@weber.edu. Research: environment and American West, Land and Water Conservation Fund Act.

Dantas, Mariana L., *Ohio*. Email: dantas@ohio.edu.

Danysk, Cecilia A., *Western Washington*.

Danzer, Gerald A., *Illinois, Chicago*. Itasca, IL. Email: gdanzer@uic.edu; oldwalnutstreet@aol.com. Research: mapping in US, Chicago.

Danziger Halperin, Anna Klein. New York, NY. Affil: Columbia. Email: ad2117@columbia.edu.

Darby, Darron Ray. Tallahassee, FL. Affil: Wallace Comm. Coll. Email: ddarby@wallace.edu.

Darby, Melissa. Portland, OR. Affil: Lower Columbia Research & Archaeology LLC. Email: lowercolumbia@gmail.com. Research: Francis Drake on the NW Coast, Native American architecture.

Darcy, Cornelius P. Westminster, MD. Affil: McDaniel.

Darden, Lindley, *Maryland, Coll. Park*. Email: darden@umd.edu.

Dardess, John, *Kansas*. Email: jdardess@ku.edu.

Darien, Andrew T., *Salem State*. Salem, MA. Email: adarien@salemstate.edu. Research: identity in history, criminal justice/police.

Dark, Joel H., *Tennessee State*. Nashville, TN. Email: jdark@tnstate.edu. Research: Germany and US civil rights.

Darling, Linda T., *Arizona*. Email: ldarling@u.arizona.edu.

Darling, Marsha J., *Adelphi*. Email: darling@adelphi.edu.

Darnton, Robert C., *Harvard (Hist.)*. Cambridge, MA. Email: robert_darnton@harvard.edu. Research: 18th-c book trade, comparative censorship.

D'Arpa, Christine. Detroit, MI. Affil: Wayne State. Email: CL0091@wayne.edu.

Darrow, David W., *Dayton*. Email: david.darrow@notes.udayton.edu.

Darrow, Margaret, *Dartmouth*. Email: margaret.darrow@dartmouth.edu.

Darty, Amy, *Central Florida*. Email: Amy.Darty@ucf.edu.

Daryaee, Touraj, *California, Irvine*. Email: tdaryaee@uci.edu.

Das, Joanna Dee. Saint Louis, MO. Affil: Washington, St. Louis. Email: joanna.d.das@wustl.edu. Research: African diaspora, dance.

Das, Ronin Alec. Eden Prairie, MN. Email: ronind13@gmail.com.

Dasgupta, Ananya, *Case Western Reserve*. Email: ananya.dasgupta@case.edu.

Dash Moore, Deborah, *Michigan, Ann Arbor*. Ann Arbor, MI. Email: ddmoore@umich.edu. Research: American Jewish, New York City.

Daston, Lorraine J. Berlin, Germany. Affil: MPI fur Wissenschaftsgeschichte. Email: ldaston@mpiwg-berlin.mpg.de.

Datiles, J. Michelle. Washington, DC. Affil: Catholic. Email: datilesj@cua.edu.

Datoo, Sabrina. Chicago, IL. Affil: Chicago. Email: sdatoo@uchicago.edu. Research: Avicennian medicine, colonial India.

Dator, James F. Towson, MD. Affil: Goucher. Email: James.Dator@goucher.edu. Research: Leeward Islands, slave resistance.

Datta, Arunima, *Idaho State*. Email: dattarun@isu.edu.

Dauben, Joseph W., *Graduate Center, CUNY; Lehman, CUNY*. Email: jdauben@att.net.

Dauer, Quinn P., *Indiana, Southeast*. Louisville, KY. Email: qdauer@ius.edu; quinndauer@gmail.com. Research: environmental, nation-state building and formation.

Daugherity, Brian J., *Virginia Commonwealth*. Email: bjdaugherity@vcu.edu.

Daughton, J. P., *Stanford*. Email: daughton@stanford.edu.

Daum, Andreas W., *SUNY, Buffalo*. Washington, DC. Email: adaum@buffalo.edu. Research: 19th-/20th-c German transnational, 18th-/20th-c science and culture.

Dausch, Andrew Richard. Florence, MA. Affil: Massachusetts Amherst. Email: ard@history.umass.edu.

Daut, Marlene L. Charlottesville, VA. Affil: Virginia. Email: mdaut@virginia.edu.

Dauverd, Celine, *Colorado, Boulder*. Email: celine.dauverd@colorado.edu.

Davenport, R. Dean. Mckinney, TX. Affil: Kaplan. Email: rddavenport@gmail.com.

Davenport, Sadie Jane. Elk Grove, CA. Email: sadiedavenport05@gmail.com.

Davenport, Stewart A., *Pepperdine*. Email: stewart.davenport@pepperdine.edu.

Davey, Frances E., *Florida Gulf Coast*. Fort Myers, FL. Email: fdavey@fgcu.edu. Research: women's clothing 1873-1914, medicalization of female body.

Davey, Joseph, *Houston-Downtown*. Email: daveyj@uhd.edu.

David, Andrew Nicholas, *Boston Univ*. Email: andavid@bu.edu.

David, Kyle Ellison. Irvine, CA. Affil: California, Irvine. Email: kedavid@uci.edu. Research: modern East Asia, children and childhood.

David, Mirela Violeta, *Saskatchewan*. Email: mirela.david@usask.ca.

David, Sheri I. Reston, VA. Affil: Northern Virginia Comm. Coll. Email: sheridk@gmail.com.

Davidann, Jon Thares, *Hawai'i Pacific*. Email: jdavidann@hpu.edu.

David-Fox, Michael, *Georgetown*. Washington, DC. Email: md672@georgetown.edu.

Research: Smolensk province 1930s-1940s, WWII on the Eastern front.

Davidova, Evguenia N., *Portland State*. Email: evguenia@pdx.edu.

Davidson, Ben. Rye, NY. Affil: NYU. Email: ben.davidson@nyu.edu. Research: Civil War and Reconstruction, childhood.

Davidson, Christina Cecelia. Somerville, MA. Affil: Harvard. Email: christinacecelia.davidson@gmail.com. Research: 20th-c Caribbean/Dominican Republic, religion/Protestantism.

Davidson, David Anthony. New York, NY. Affil: Dalton Sch. Email: dadavidson@gmail.com. Research: early US entrepreneurship, early US ideas about economic progress.

Davidson, Denise Z., *Georgia State*. Atlanta, GA. Email: ddavidson2@gsu.edu. Research: urban life in France 1800-30, gender and class in France 1750-1850.

Davidson, Jessica B., *James Madison*. Email: davidsjb@jmu.edu.

Davidson, Matt. Whitby, ON, Canada. Affil: Miami. Email: mad320@miami.edu.

Davidson, Roger A., **Jr**, *Bowie State*. Email: rdavidson@bowiestate.edu.

Davidson, Steven C., *Southwestern*. Email: davidsos@southwestern.edu.

Davie, Grace, *Queens, CUNY*. Email: grace.davie@qc.cuny.edu.

Davies, Brian L., *Texas, San Antonio*. Email: brian.davies@utsa.edu.

Davies, Edward J., **II**, *Utah*. Email: edavies@history.utah.edu.

Davies, Gwyn, *Florida International*. Email: daviesg@fiu.edu.

Davies, John. Newark, DE. Affil: Delaware. Email: davies2110@gmail.com. Research: Saint Domingun refugees in US, Catholicism in early Republic.

Davies, Megan J., *York, Can*. Email: daviesmj@yorku.ca.

Davies, Richard O., *Nevada, Reno*. Reno, NV. Email: ridavies@unr.edu. Research: American sports, Nevada and American gambling.

Davies, Sarah H., *Whitman*. Email: daviessh@whitman.edu.

Davies, Surekha. Utrecht, Netherlands. Affil: Utrecht. Email: surekha.davies@gmail.com. Research: cultural encounters/empire, science/knowledge/mentalities.

Davies, Thomas M., **Jr.**, *San Diego State*.

Davies, Wade, *Montana*. Email: wade.davies@mso.umt.edu.

d'Avignon, Robyn, *NYU*. New York, NY. Email: robyn.davignon@nyu.edu. Research: West Africa, extraction.

Davila, Carl, *SUNY, Coll. Brockport*. Email: cdavila@brockport.edu.

Davila, Jerry, *Illinois, Urbana-Champaign*. Urbana, IL. Email: jdavila@illinois.edu. Research: Brazil.

Davin, Eric Leif. Pittsburgh, PA. Affil: Pittsburgh. Email: ericdavin@hotmail.com. Research: Labor, Political.

Davis, Adam J., *Denison*. Email: davisaj@denison.edu.

Davis, Adam W., *Duquesne*. Email: davisa1@duq.edu.

Davis, Adrienne, *Washington, St. Louis*. Email: adriennedavis@wustl.edu.

Davis, Amira Rose, *Penn State*. Email: ard51@psu.edu.

Davis, **Andrea Rebecca**, *Arkansas State*. State University, AR. Email: andavis@astate.edu; andrea.r.davis@gmail.com. Research: digital humanities/oral history archive, urban politics and memory in Spain.

Davis, **Belinda J.**, *Rutgers*. Philadelphia, PA. Email: bedavis@rci.rutgers.edu. Research: modern Europe, Germany.

Davis, **Bradley Camp**, *Eastern Connecticut State; Hartford*. Willimantic, CT. Email: davisbrad@easternct.edu; bcampdavis@gmail.com. Research: Sino-Vietnamese borderlands, ethnography in China and Southeast Asia.

Davis, **C. Earl, Jr.**, *Charleston*. Email: davisce@cofc.edu.

Davis, **Christian S.**, *James Madison*. Email: davis2cs@jmu.edu.

Davis, **Christopher Anderson**, *Florida Atlantic*. Email: christopherdavis@fau.edu.

Davis, **Colin J.**, *Alabama, Birmingham*. Pelham, AL. Affil: Indian Springs Sch. Email: cjdavis@uab.edu; colin.davis@indiansprings.org. Research: comparative US/UK labor.

Davis, **Cory**, *Illinois, Chicago*. Email: cdavis26@uic.edu.

Davis, **Cullom**, *Illinois, Springfield*.

Davis, **Dan**, *Utah State*. Email: dandav@usu.edu.

Davis, **Darién J.**, *Middlebury*. Middlebury, VT. Email: davis@middlebury.edu. Research: popular culture, human rights.

Davis, **Darnella**. Washington, DC. Affil: National Coalition of Independent Scholars. Email: drdarnella@msn.com. Research: triracial lens on Allotment Era impacts, revisioning Five Tribes' racial legacy.

Davis, **Diana**, *California, Davis*. Email: geovet@ucdavis.edu.

Davis, **Donald G., Jr.** Austin, TX. Affil: Texas, Austin. Email: dgdavis@ischool.utexas.edu.

Davis, **Edward L.**, *Hawai'i, Manoa*. Email: edavis@hawaii.edu.

Davis, **Frederick R.**, *Purdue*. Email: frdavis@purdue.edu.

Davis, **Gerald H.**, *Georgia State*. Email: ghdavis3@aol.com.

Davis, **Hugh H.**, *Southern Connecticut State*. Email: davish1@southernct.edu.

Davis, **Jack E.**, *Florida*. Email: davisjac@ufl.edu.

Davis, **Janet Marie**, *Texas, Austin*. Email: janetmdavis@austin.utexas.edu.

Davis, **Jeffrey A.**, *Bloomsburg*. Email: jdavis@bloomu.edu.

Davis, **Jennifer Rebecca**. Washington, DC. Affil: Catholic. Email: davisj@cua.edu. Research: early medieval political culture, post-Roman social change.

Davis, **John A.**, *Connecticut, Storrs*. Email: john.davis@uconn.edu.

Davis, **Justin Allen**. Lees Summit, MO. Affil: Missouri, Kansas City. Email: justindavisphd@gmail.com. Research: Pietists, post-Reformation theology.

Davis, **Kimberly**. Milford, WA. Email: lankfordlk@yahoo.com.

Davis, **Lane**. Fort Worth, TX. Affil: Southern Methodist. Email: davisle@smu.edu.

Davis, **Laura June**. Cedar City, UT. Affil: Southern Utah. Email: laurajunedavis@suu.edu. Research: Civil War Navy, gender.

Davis, **Leroy**, *Emory*. Email: ldavi04@emory.edu.

Davis, **Marni**, *Georgia State*. Email: marnidavis@gsu.edu.

Davis, **Michael**, *Liberty*. Email: madavis6@liberty.edu.

Davis, **Mike**. Hampton, VA. Affil: Hampton. Email: michael.davis@hamptonu.edu. Research: anti-secretism, fundamentalist turn.

Davis, **Natalie Z.** Toronto, ON, Canada. Affil: Toronto. Email: nz.davis@utoronto.ca.

Davis, **Philip C., Jr.**, *Tennessee Tech*. Email: pdavis@tntech.edu.

Davis, **R. Hunt, Jr.**, *Florida*. Email: hdavis@ufl.edu.

Davis, **Rebecca L.**, *Delaware*. Newark, DE. Email: rldavis@udel.edu. Research: marriage and American culture, sexuality.

Davis, **Rebecca Miller**, *Missouri–Kansas City*. Email: davisrebe@umkc.edu.

Davis, **Robert C.**, *Ohio State*. Email: davis.711@osu.edu.

Davis, **Robert T., II**, *US Army Command Coll*. Email: robert.t.davis2.civ@mail.mil.

Davis, **Robyn Lily**, *Millersville, Pa*. Millersville, PA. Email: robyn.davis@millersville.edu. Research: science in early America.

Davis, **Roger**, *Nebraska, Kearney*. Email: davisr@unk.edu.

Davis, **Ronald L.**, *Southern Methodist*.

Davis, **Ronald L. F.**, *California State, Northridge*. Email: ronald.davis@csun.edu.

Davis, **Ronald W.**, *Western Michigan*. Email: ronald.davis@wmich.edu.

Davis, **Samantha**. University Park, PA. Affil: Penn State. Email: samidavis5@gmail.com.

Davis, **Simon**, *Graduate Center, CUNY*. Email: simon.davis@bcc.cuny.edu.

Davis, **Stacy**, *Gerald Ford Presidential Library*. Email: stacy.davis@nara.gov.

Davis, **Stephen R.**, *Kentucky*. Email: srda227@g.uky.edu.

Davis, **Steve**. Porter, TX. Affil: Lone Star, Kingswood. Email: steve.davis@lonestar.edu.

Davis, **Thomas H., III**. North Hollywood, CA. Email: thd3noho@sbcglobal.net.

Davis, **Thomas J.**, *Arizona State*. Tempe, AZ. Email: tjdavis@asu.edu. Research: race and US law, identity and law.

Davis, **Troy D.**, *Stephen F. Austin State*. Email: tdavis@sfasu.edu.

Davis-Cline, **Jennifer J.**, *Oklahoma (Hist.)*. Email: jennifer.j.davis@ou.edu.

Davis-Doyle, **Jennifer M.**, *Campbell*. Email: davisj@campbell.edu.

Davis-Secord, **Sarah C.**, *New Mexico*. Email: scds@unm.edu.

Davis-Witherow, **Leah**, *Colorado Colorado Springs*. Email: ldavis2@uccs.edu.

Davulis, **Laura Beth**. Baltimore, MD. Affil: Johns Hopkins Univ. Press. Email: lbd@press.jhu.edu.

Dawidoff, **Robert**, *Claremont Grad*. Email: robert.dawidoff@cgu.edu.

Dawley, **Evan N.** Towson, MD. Affil: Goucher. Email: evan.dawley@goucher.edu. Research: Taiwanese ethnic identity formation.

Dawson, **Alexander S**. Albany, NY. Affil: SUNY, Albany. Email: asdawson@albany.edu. Research: peyote, indigenous self-determination.

Dawson, **Jan C.**, *Southwestern*. Email: dawsonj@southwestern.edu.

Dawson, **Joseph G. M., III**, *Texas A&M*. Email: jgdawson@tamu.edu.

Dawson, **Mark Stanley**. Canberra, Australia. Affil: Australian National. Email: mark.dawson@anu.edu.au. Research: European

body 1550-1750, Anglo-Atlantic race 1550-1750.

Dawson, **Michael C**. Chicago, IL. Affil: Chicago. Email: mc-dawson@uchicago.edu.

Dawson, **Sandra**. Columbia, MD. Affil: Maryland, Baltimore County. Email: execadmin@berksconference.org. Research: medicine and midwifery, women and war.

Dawson, **Virginia**, *Case Western Reserve*. Email: vpd@historyenterprises.com.

Day, **Alexander F.**, *Occidental*. Email: aday@oxy.edu.

Day, **Anastasia**. Newark, DE. Affil: Delaware. Email: anastasiaday@me.com. Research: victory gardens in WWII, food waste in America.

Day, **Anne L.**, *Clarion, Pa*. Email: aday@clarion.edu.

Day, **Carolyn Anne**, *Furman*. Email: carolyn.day@furman.edu.

Day, **Charles R.**, *Simon Fraser*. Email: charles_day@sfu.ca.

Day, **Thomas R**. Urbana, IL. Affil: Illinois, Urbana-Champaign. Email: trday3@illinois.edu.

Day Moore, **Celeste**, *Hamilton*. Email: cdmoore@hamilton.edu.

Dayal, **Subah**, *Tulane*. New Orleans, LA. Email: sdayal@tulane.edu. Research: early modern South Asia, Persian/Dakhni Urdu/Deccan sultanates.

Daynes, **Kathryn M.**, *Brigham Young*. Email: kathryn_daynes@byu.edu.

Dayton, **Cornelia H.**, *Connecticut, Storrs*. Ashford, CT. Email: cornelia.dayton@uconn.edu. Research: health and disease, social.

De, **Rohit**, *Yale*. Email: rohit.de@yale.edu.

de Almeida, **Leitao**. Evanston, IL. Affil: Northwestern. Email: marcosrrs21@hotmail.com.

De Aragon, **RaGena**, *Gonzaga*. Email: dearagon@gonzaga.edu.

De Barros, **Juanita L.**, *McMaster*. Email: debarr@mcmaster.ca.

de Boer, **Wietse T.**, *Miami, Ohio*. Oxford, OH. Email: deboerwt@miamioh.edu. Research: education of senses, Castiglione's courtier.

de Caprariis, **Luca**. Roma, Italy. Affil: John Cabot. Email: ldecaprariis@johncabot.edu.

de Chadarevian, **Soraya**, *UCLA*. Email: chadarevian@history.ucla.edu.

de Chantal, **Julie**, *Georgia Southern*. Email: jdechantal@georgiasouthern.edu.

De Graaf, **Lawrence B.**, *California State, Fullerton*. Email: ldegraaf@fullerton.edu.

De Grand, **Alexander Joseph**, *North Carolina State*. Email: alex_degrand@ncsu.edu.

de Grazia, **Victoria**, *Columbia (Hist.)*. New York, NY. Email: vd19@columbia.edu; victoriadegrazia@gmail.com. Research: modern western Europe, gender and politics.

De Hart, **Jane S.**, *California, Santa Barbara*. Santa Barbara, CA. Email: dehart@history.ucsb.edu. Research: biography and feminist jurisprudence, women and public policy.

de Jong, **Greta E.**, *Nevada, Reno*. Reno, NV. Email: gdejong@unr.edu. Research: African Americans after 1965.

De Krey, **Gary S.**, *St. Olaf*. Email: dekrey@stolaf.edu.

de la Cruz, **Deirdre**, *Michigan, Ann Arbor*. Email: ddelac@umich.edu.

de la Fuente, **Alejandro**, *Harvard (Hist.)*. Email: delafuente@fas.harvard.edu.

de la Fuente, Ariel, *Purdue*. West Lafayette, IN. Email: delafuen@purdue.edu. Research: Latin America.

de la Garza, Andrew, *Louisiana, Lafayette*. Email: adelagarza@louisiana.edu.

De La Pedraja Toman, Rene A., *Canisius*. Buffalo, NY. Email: delapedr@canisius.edu. Research: Latin American military.

de la Puente, Jose Carlos, *Texas State*. San Marcos, TX. Email: jd65@txstate.edu. Research: Andean natives and Atlantic world, Indigenous Legal and Political Cultures.

de la Teja, Jesus F., *Texas State*. Email: delateja@txstate.edu.

De la Torre, Oscar. Charlotte, NC. Affil: North Carolina, Charlotte. Email: odelator@uncc.edu. Research: black peasants in Latin America, Atlantic environmental.

de Leon, Cynthia Aminta. Little Elm, TX. Affil: Prestonwood Christian Academy. Email: missd250@icloud.com.

De Lorenzi, James. New York, NY. Affil: John Jay, CUNY. Email: jdelorenzi@jjay.cuny.edu. Research: Red Sea region, colonial experts.

de Luna, Kathryn M., *Georgetown*. Email: deLuna@georgetown.edu.

De Michele, Michael D., *Scranton*. Email: michael.demichele@scranton.edu.

de Montluzin, E. Lorraine, *Francis Marion*. Florence, SC. Email: edemontluzin@fmarion.edu. Research: 18th-c English press.

de Nie, Michael W., *West Georgia*. Carrollton, GA. Email: mdenie@westga.edu. Research: Irish and British identity, 19th-c British press.

de Pee, Christian, *Michigan, Ann Arbor*. Email: cdepee@umich.edu.

de Schweinitz, Rebecca L., *Brigham Young*. Email: rld@byu.edu.

De Sousa, Dalila, *Spelman*. Email: ddesousa@spelman.edu.

de Syon, Guillaume P., *Albright*. Reading, PA. Email: gdesyon@albright.edu. Research: tourism and travel in post-WWII Germany, air transport advertising.

de Vera, Samantha. La Jolla, CA. Affil: California, San Diego. Email: samdevera@gmail.com. Research: African American Women, California.

De Vos, Paula S., *San Diego State*. Email: pdevos@sdsu.edu.

De Vries, Bert, *Calvin*. Email: dvrb@calvin.edu.

Deacon, David W., *SUNY, Oswego*. Email: david.deacon@oswego.edu.

Deak, Istvan, *Columbia (Hist.)*. New York, NY. Email: id1@columbia.edu. Research: WWII resistance/collaboration, WWII retribution.

Deak, John D., *Notre Dame*. Notre Dame, IN. Email: jdeak@nd.edu. Research: Austria-Hungary in WWI, Interwar Europe.

Deakin, Vikki J., *Weber State*. Email: vikkivickers@weber.edu.

Deal, Robert C., *Marshall*. Email: dealr@marshall.edu.

Deal, Roger A., *South Carolina Aiken*. Email: rogerd@usca.edu.

Dealing, James R., *Central Michigan*. Email: j.dealing@cmich.edu.

Dean, Adam W., *Lynchburg*. Email: dean.aw@lynchburg.edu.

Dean, Amy K. R., *Sam Houston State*. Huntsville, TX. Email: amydean13@shsu.edu. Research: early modern Europe, European and American women.

Dean, Ashleigh, *Georgia Coll. and State*. Email: ashleigh.dean@gcsu.edu.

Dean, Austin L., *Nevada, Las Vegas*. Email: austin.dean@unlv.edu.

Dean, Carolyn J., *Yale*. New Haven, CT. Email: carolyn.dean@yale.edu. Research: Holocaust representation in Europe, gender and sexuality.

Dean, David M., *Carleton, Can*. Email: david.dean@carleton.ca.

Dean, David M., *Frostburg State*. Email: ddean@frostburg.edu.

Dean, Joanna E., *Carleton, Can*. Email: joanna.dean@carleton.ca.

Dean, Michael, *Seattle*. Seattle, WA. Email: michaelwdean@posteo.net. Research: Effective teaching.

Dean, Robert, *Eastern Washington*. Email: rdean@ewu.edu.

Deane, Jennifer Kolpacoff. Morris, MN. Affil: Minnesota, Morris. Email: deanej@morris.umn.edu. Research: medieval heresy and inquisition, gender/lay religiosity/monasticism.

DeAngelo, Angela D., *Kennesaw State*. Email: adeangel@kennesaw.edu.

Deans-Smith, Susan, *Texas, Austin*. Austin, TX. Email: sdsmith@austin.utexas.edu. Research: social and cultural, visual and material culture.

Dear, Peter R., *Cornell*. Email: prd3@cornell.edu.

Deardorff, Max. Frankfurt am Main, Germany. Affil: Max Planck Inst. for European Legal Hist. Email: deardorff.max@gmail.com. Research: race/ethnicity/Iberian world, law.

Deathridge, Kristen Baldwin, *Appalachian State*. Email: baldwindeathridgekd@appstate.edu.

Deb Roy, Rohan. Reading, United Kingdom. Affil: Reading. Email: rohan.debroy@gmail.com. Research: South Asia.

DebChaudhury, Sudata, *San Diego Mesa*. Email: sdebchau@sdccd.edu.

DeBlasi, Anthony, *SUNY, Albany*. Email: deblasi@albany.edu.

DeBlasio, Donna M., *Youngstown State*. Email: dmdeblasio@ysu.edu.

Debnam, Jewell, *Morgan State*. Email: jewell.debnam@morgan.edu.

Debo, Richard K., *Simon Fraser*.

DeBrakeleer, Betsy. Biddeford, ME. Email: bdebrake@gmail.com.

Debs, Michele, *Texas, San Antonio*. Email: michele.debs@utsa.edu.

Decarie, M. Graeme, *Concordia, Can*. Email: graemedecarie1@gmail.com.

DeCaroli, Robert, *George Mason*. Email: rdecarol@gmu.edu.

DeCesare, Catherine Osborne, *Rhode Island*. Email: cdecesare@uri.edu.

Decker, Corrie R., *California, Davis*. Email: crdecker@ucdavis.edu.

Decker, Hannah S., *Houston*. Email: hsdecker@uh.edu.

Decker, Jefferson A. Brooklyn, NY. Affil: Rutgers. Email: jeffersondecker@hotmail.com. Research: political, legal.

Decker, Joseph. Fairbanks, AK. Affil: Wayland Baptist. Email: joseph.m.decker@gmail.com.

Decker, Michael J., *South Florida, Tampa; Phi Alpha Theta*. Email: info@phialphatheta.org; mjdecker@usf.edu.

Decker, Philip Krasovsky. Upper Arlington, OH. Affil: Oxford. Email: pdeck2@gmail.com.

Decker, Rhonda. Hendersonville, NC. Email: rldmlt@yahoo.com.

Deckrow, Andre Kobayashi. Ann Arbor, MI. Affil: Columbia. Email: akd2120@columbia.edu. Research: Japanese-Brazilian migration.

DeCoster, Jonathan. Westerville, OH. Affil: Otterbein. Email: jdecoster@otterbein.edu. Research: 16th-c Florida and Virginia, colonial strategy regarding natives.

Decter, Avi Y. Philadelphia, PA. Affil: Hist. Now.

DeDe-Panken, Madeline, *Lehman, CUNY*. Email: mdedepanken@gradcenter.cuny.edu.

Dee, Darryl, *Wilfrid Laurier*. Email: ddee@wlu.ca.

Deeds, Susan M., *Northern Arizona*. Email: susan.deeds@nau.edu.

Deem, Ken. Rogers, OH. Email: kennydeem@gmail.com.

Deets, Mark W. Ithaca, NY. Affil: Cornell. Email: mwd45@cornell.edu. Research: Senegambian social and cultural, space/geography/cartography.

DeFonso, Chet R., *Northern Michigan*. Marquette, MI. Email: cdefonso@nmu.edu. Research: Britain, gender.

DeForest, Dallas, *California State, Chico*. Email: ddeforest@csuchico.edu.

DeFrank, Joseph Thompson. Young Harris, GA. Affil: Young Harris. Email: jtdefrank@yhc.edu.

Defries, David J., *Kansas State*. Manhattan, KS. Email: ddefries@ksu.edu. Research: hagiography, Flanders.

Deglmann, Ludwig A. Bonn, Germany. Email: InternationalEliteStudent809812@yahoo.com.

deGraffenried, Julie K., *Baylor*. Email: julie_degraffenried@baylor.edu.

DeGroat, Judith A., *St. Lawrence*. Canton, NY. Email: jdegroat@stlawu.edu. Research: socialist feminist Pauline Roland, gender and political exiles.

Degroot, Dagomar, *Georgetown*. Washington, DC. Email: dd865@georgetown.edu; dagomard@gmail.com. Research: environmental, climate and historical climatology.

DeGruccio, Michael E., *St. Peter's*. Email: mdegruccio@saintpeters.edu.

DeHaan, Heather D., *Binghamton, SUNY*. Binghamton, NY. Email: hdehaan@binghamton.edu. Research: Russian city planning/urban space, modernization of Nizhnii Novgorod.

DeHaan, Jeffrey T. Texarkana, TX.

Dehart, Kendra, *Sul Ross State*. Email: kendra.dehart@sulross.edu.

Dehne, Phillip A. Brooklyn, NY. Affil: St. Joseph, Brooklyn. Email: pdehne@sjcny.edu. Research: Britain and South America during WWI.

Dehner, George Joseph, *Wichita State*. Wichita, KS. Email: george.dehner@wichita.edu. Research: diseases, world.

DeHoff, Kenneth H. Honolulu, HI. Affil: Pacific Aviation Museum Pearl Harbor. Email: ken.dehoff@pacificaviationmuseum.org.

Deierhoi, Tyler, *Tennessee, Chattanooga*. Email: noldane@aol.com.

DeKosky, Robert K., *Kansas*. Email: rdekosky@ku.edu.

Del Castillo, Lina M., *Texas, Austin*. Austin, TX. Email: delcastillo@austin.utexas.edu. Research: cartography and Colombia, Latin American race/class/gender/place.

Del Corso, Robert Engel, *Old Dominion*. Newport News, VA. Email: rdelcors@odu.edu; delcorso@earthlink.net. Research: Western civilization, world.

Del Mar, David P., *Portland State*. Email: delmard@pdx.edu.

Del Rio, Chelsea N. Sunnyside, NY. Affil: LaGuardia Comm. Coll., CUNY. Email: cheldel@umich.edu.

Del Soldato, Eva. Philadelphia, PA. Affil: Pennsylvania. Email: evadel@sas.upenn.edu.

Del Testa, David W., *Bucknell*. Lewisburg, PA. Email: ddeltest@bucknell.edu. Research: French Indochina, education and society.

DeLacy, Margaret E. Portland, OR. Affil: Northwest Independent Scholars Assoc. Email: margaretdelacy@comcast.net. Research: medicine, 18th-c British contagionism/reform.

DeLaMater, Paul Matthew. Glens Falls, NY. Affil: SUNY, Albany. Email: mdelamater@albany.edu.

Delaney, Douglas E., *Royal Military*. Email: delaney-d@rmc.ca.

Delaney, Jason, *National Defence Headquarters*. Email: jason.delaney@forces.gc.ca.

DeLaney, Jeane, *St. Olaf*. Email: delaney@stolaf.edu.

Delaney, John J., *Kutztown*. Email: delaney@kutztown.edu.

DeLaney, Theodore C., *Washington and Lee*. Email: delaneyt@wlu.edu.

Delano, David Ivan. West Hartford, CT. Affil: California, Berkeley. Email: david.delano@berkeley.edu.

DeLay, Brian, *California, Berkeley*. Berkeley, CA. Email: delay@berkeley.edu. Research: Indians and US-Mexico relations, arms trade in 19th-c Americas.

Delay, Cara, *Charleston*. Email: delayc@cofc.edu.

Delbanco, Andrew, *Columbia (Hist.)*. New York, NY. Email: andrew.delbanco@columbia.edu. Research: colonial America.

Delbourgo, James, *Rutgers*. New Brunswick, NJ. Email: jdelbourgo@history.rutgers.edu. Research: 17th-/18th-c early modern science, colonial British America/Atlantic world.

Delear, Stephen D. College Station, TX. Affil: Texas A&M. Email: sdelear77840@gmail.com. Research: Depression-era US, legal.

Delegard, Kirsten. Minneapolis, MN. Email: kdelegard@gmail.com.

Delehanty, William, *St. Thomas, Minn*. Email: wmdelehanty@stthomas.edu.

DeLeon, David. Washington, DC. Affil: Howard. Email: profwire@aol.com. Research: African American historiography, contemporary US radical movements.

Deleuze, Magali, *Royal Military*. Email: deleuze-m@rmc.ca.

Delgado, Grace Peña, *California, Santa Cruz*. Email: gpdelgad@ucsc.edu.

Delgado, Jessica L. Princeton, NJ. Affil: Princeton. Email: jessicad@princeton.edu. Research: lay women and church in colonial Mexico, colonial Mexican popular religion.

D'Elia, Anthony Francis, *Queen's, Can*. Email: deliaa@queensu.ca.

Deliyannis, Deborah Mauskopf, *Indiana*. Email: ddeliyan@indiana.edu.

Della Cava, Ralph, *Queens, CUNY*. Email: rd79@columbia.edu.

Dell'Aera, Anthony D., *Worcester State*. Email: adellaera@worcester.edu.

Dellheim, Charles, *Arizona State; Boston Univ.* Email: dellheim@bu.edu.

deLlobet, Ruth. Barcelona, Spain. Affil: Pompeu Fabra. Email: ruthdellobet@gmail.com.

Dell'Omo, Augusta Lynn. Austin, TX. Affil: Texas, Austin. Email: augusta.dellomo@gmail.com.

Delmage, Elizabeth, *Naval War Coll.* Email: elizabeth.delmage@usnwc.edu.

Delmont, Matthew, *Dartmouth*. Email: matthew.delmont@dartmouth.edu.

DeLong, Mary E. Newton, MA. Affil: Museum of Fine Arts, Boston. Email: med62956@gmail.com. Research: women's studies, WWII.

DeLorenzo, Christopher Scott. Arlington, VA. Affil: Georgetown. Email: cdelorenzo2@gmail.com. Research: 20th-c Bolivia, coca leaf substitution.

Deloria, Philip, *Harvard (Hist.)*. Email: deloria@fas.harvard.edu.

Delorso, Robert, Jr. Bluefield, WV. Affil: Bluefield State. Email: rdelorso9@gmail.com.

Delosier, Nikole Ember, *Hist. Assoc.* Email: ndelosier@historyassociates.com.

DeLossa, Robert. Lowell, MA. Affil: Lowell High Sch. Email: rdelossa@lowell.k12.ma.us.

Delph, Ronald K., *Eastern Michigan*. Email: rdelph@emich.edu.

Delton, Jennifer A., *Skidmore*. Email: jdelton@skidmore.edu.

DeLucia, Christine M., *Williams*. Email: cd10@williams.edu.

DeLucia, Elizabeth, *Naval War Coll.* Email: elizabeth.delucia@usnwc.edu.

DeLuna, D. N. Baltimore, MD. Affil: Madison Area Tech. Email: rich8d@aol.com. Research: 18th-c British politics, 18th-c British journalism.

DeLuzio, Crista J., *Southern Methodist*. Email: cdeluzio@smu.edu.

Delva, Capt Liliane, *US Military Acad.* Email: liliane.delva@usma.edu.

DeMaio, Alicia. Allston, MA. Affil: Harvard. Email: demaio@g.harvard.edu. Research: US botanical gardens 1800-60.

Demand, Nancy, *Indiana*.

DeMandel, Sherry Long. Belvedere Tiburon, CA.

DeMarco, Elizabeth Ann. Wenatchee, WA. Affil: American Military. Email: lizdemarco@nwi.net. Research: women rulers throughout history, historiography of environmental history.

DeMare, Brian James, *Tulane*. New Orleans, LA. Email: bdemare@tulane.edu. Research: land reform and political culture.

Demarest, William J. New York, NY. Affil: SUNY, Stony Brook. Email: william.demarest@stonybrook.edu. Research: urban space/shopping/consumerism, Latin American middle class 1950s-70s.

Demas, Lane, *Central Michigan*. Mount Pleasant, MI. Email: demas1lt@cmich.edu. Research: sport, African American.

Dembiczak, Angela, *Coastal Carolina*. Email: ajdembic@coastal.edu.

Demetrides, Sara, *Austin Peay State*. Email: demetridess@apsu.edu.

Demetriou, Denise, *California, San Diego*. Email: dedemetriou@ucsd.edu.

Demhardt, Imre Josef, *Texas, Arlington*. Email: demhardt@uta.edu.

D'Emilio, James P. Flagstaff, AZ. Affil: South Florida. Email: demilio@mail.usf.edu.

Research: Compostela cult/cathedral/pilgrimage, Romanesque art.

D'Emilio, John A., *Illinois, Chicago*. Chicago, IL. Email: demilioj@uic.edu; demilioj@aol.com. Research: sexuality, social movements.

Deming, James C. Princeton, NJ. Affil: Princeton Theological Seminary. Email: james.deming@ptsem.edu. Research: religion and identity, religion and sports.

Demmer, Amanda, *Virginia Tech*. Blacksburg, VA. Email: amandademmer@gmail.com. Research: US-Vietnam normalization, human rights.

DeMoro, Don. Napa, CA. Email: rddemoro@gmail.com.

Demos, John P., *Yale*. Email: john.demos@yale.edu.

Dempsey, Brian, *North Alabama*. Email: bdempsey@una.edu.

Dempsey, Sean Thomas, *Loyola Marymount*. Los Angeles, CA. Email: sean.dempsey@lmu.edu; dempsean@sas.upenn.edu. Research: 20th-c US, religion.

Demshuk, Andrew T., *American*. Email: demshuk@american.edu.

Demuth, Bathsheba, *Brown*. Providence, RI. Email: bathsheba_demuth@brown.edu. Research: environmental, comparative Russia and US.

Demy, Timothy James, *Naval War Coll.* Email: timothy.demy@usnwc.edu.

Den Hartog, Jonathan J. Saint Paul, MN. Affil: Northwestern, St. Paul. Email: jdenhartog@unwsp.edu. Research: Federalist Party in early Republic, religion and politics.

den Otter, Sandra, *Queen's, Can*. Email: denotter@queensu.ca.

Denault, Chelsea. Chicago, IL. Affil: Loyola, Chicago. Email: cdenault@luc.edu.

Denault, Leigh T. Cambridge, United Kingdom. Affil: Cambridge. Email: ltd22@cam.ac.uk. Research: family in colonial North India, 20th-c mutual aid associations.

DenBeste, Michelle D., *California State, Fresno*. Email: mdenbest@csufresno.edu.

Denbo, Seth, *AHA*. Washington, DC. Email: sdenbo@historians.org. Research: digital scholarship, scholarly communication.

Denbow, James R., *Texas, Austin*. Email: jdenbow@austin.utexas.edu.

Dench, Emma, *Harvard (Hist.)*. Email: dench@fas.harvard.edu.

Dendy, Charles, *Stephen F. Austin State*. Email: dendyc@sfasu.edu.

Deneen, Terrence M. Chicago, IL. Email: Trance1147@aol.com. Research: 12th-c Normandy, Cistercian Order.

Denery, Dallas G., II, *Bowdoin*. Email: ddenery@bowdoin.edu.

Denial, Catherine J. Galesburg, IL. Affil: Knox. Email: cdenial@knox.edu. Research: family/gender/race/nation-building, meaning of nation in 19th-c West.

Denis, Watson R. Plantation, FL. Affil: State Univ., Haiti. Email: watsondenis@yahoo.com. Research: US, Caribbean.

Denman, Michael. Las Vegas, NV. Affil: Southern Nevada. Email: michael.denman@csn.edu. Research: martial arts, martial arts and religion.

Denmark, Lisa L., *Georgia Southern*. Email: ldenmark@georgiasouthern.edu.

Dennar, Obinna. Sugar Land, TX. Affil: Rice. Email: obi.dennar@rice.edu.

Dennard, David C., *East Carolina*. Email: dennardd@ecu.edu.

Dennehy, Kristine, *California State, Fullerton*. Email: kdennehy@fullerton.edu.

Dennerline, Jerry P., *Amherst*. Northampton, MA. Email: jpdennerline@amherst.edu. Research: families and shrines of Wuxi China, 19-20c religion/education/reform.

Dennie, Garrey M, *St. Mary's, Md.* Leonardtown, MD. Email: gmdennie@smcm.edu; mannkeba@aol.com. Research: Africa, Caribbean.

Dennie, Nneka. Davidson, NC. Affil: Davidson. Email: nndennie@davidson.edu.

Denning, Andrew, *Kansas*. Lawrence, KS. Email: asdenning@ku.edu. Research: modern Europe, environmental.

Denning, Margaret B., *Slippery Rock*. Email: mbd@sru.edu.

Denning, Robert V. Westerville, OH. Affil: Southern New Hampshire. Email: rdenning13@gmail.com. Research: California environmental policy, Ohio urban.

Dennis, Ashley. Evanston, IL. Affil: Northwestern. Email: Ashley.Dennis@u.northwestern.edu.

Dennis, David B., *Loyola, Chicago*. Email: dennis@luc.edu.

Dennis, Dawn Amber, *California State, Los Angeles*. Email: ddennis3@calstatela.edu.

Dennis, Joe, *Wisconsin-Madison*. Email: dennis3@wisc.edu.

Dennis, Matthew J., *Oregon*. New York, NY. Email: mjdennis@uoregon.edu. Research: American commemoration/memory/identity, relics/material culture.

Dennis, Michael A., *Naval War Coll.* Newport, RI. Email: michael.dennis@usnwc.edu; madennis@comcast.net. Research: Cold War science and technology.

Dennis, Michael G. Houston, TX. Affil: Austin Comm. Coll. Email: mgdennis@comcast.net.

Dennison, Tracy, *California Inst. of Tech.* Email: tkd@hss.caltech.edu.

Dennison, William D., *Covenant*. Email: dennison@covenant.edu.

Deno, Vivian E., *Butler*. Email: vdeno@butler.edu.

deNoyelles, Adrienne. Gainesville, FL. Affil: Florida. Email: addenoyelles@ufl.edu. Research: public health, immigration.

Densford, Kathryn Elizabeth. Elizabethtown, PA. Affil: Elizabethtown. Email: densfordk@etown.edu.

Denson, Andrew, *Western Carolina*. Email: denson@email.wcu.edu.

Dent, Gary L., *Roanoke*. Roanoke, VA. Affil: Virginia Western Comm. Coll. Email: dent@roanoke.edu; gdcubs@verizon.net. Research: sports in America, architecture in America.

Dent, Julian, *Toronto*.

Dent, Rosanna, *Rutgers, Newark/New Jersey Inst. of Tech.* Email: rdent@njit.edu.

Dentler, Jonathan Lowell. Gig Harbor, WA. Affil: Southern California. Email: dentler@usc.edu.

Denton, John William, III. Nashville, NC. Email: dentonjw@gmail.com. Research: ancient Near East, Assyriology.

Denton-Spalding, Grace E. Chicago, IL. Email: gdentonspalding@gmail.com.

d'Entremont, John P., *Randolph*. Email: jdentremont@randolphcollege.edu.

DePalma Digeser, Elizabeth, *California, Santa Barbara*. Email: edepalma@history.ucsb.edu.

DePasquale, Jhestarri. Willow Grove, PA. Affil: Norwich. Email: Jhestarri_p@aol.com.

Depatie, Sylvie, *Québec, Montréal*. Email: depatie.sylvie@uqam.ca.

DePauw, Linda Grant, *George Washington*. Email: minervacen@aol.com.

DePillis, Mario S., *Massachusetts, Amherst*. Email: depillis@history.umass.edu.

DePinto, Jenise R., *St. Rose*. Albany, NY. Email: depintoj@mail.strose.edu; albionia64@hotmail.com. Research: sexuality and political economy, gender/empire/class.

DePriest, Jon P. Santee, CA. Email: jdepriest50@gmail.com. Research: religion and foreign policy.

Der Matossian, Bedross, *Nebraska, Lincoln*. Email: bdermatossian2@unl.edu.

Derby, Robin, *UCLA*. Santa Monica, CA. Email: derby@history.ucla.edu. Research: Latin American studies.

Derfler, Leslie, *Florida Atlantic*. Email: derflerl@fau.edu.

Deringer, William Peter, *MIT*. Cambridge, MA. Email: deringer@mit.edu. Research: science and technology, economic and financial.

Derks, Tracy L. Kingwood, TX. Affil: American Public. Email: tlderks@usa.com. Research: Amer military involvement in Vietnam, WWII Luzon '45.

Dermon, Dave, IV. Franklin, TN. Affil: St. Andrews. Email: dave.dermon4@comcast.net.

Derner, Aaron Timothy. Waterford, WI. Email: atderner@gmail.com.

DeRosa, Christopher S., *Monmouth*. Oakhurst, NJ. Email: cderosa@monmouth.edu. Research: US military, political.

Derousie, Anne M. Lodi, NY. Email: advent@empacc.net.

Derr, Eric Allen. Carlow, Co. Carlow, Ireland. Affil: Carlow. Email: ederr@carlowcollege.ie. Research: prosopography/Irish Catholicism, Jacobite studies/networks.

Derr, Jennifer L., *California, Santa Cruz*. Email: jderr@ucsc.edu.

Derr, Patricia Norred, *Kutztown*. Email: derr@kutztown.edu.

Derrick, Stephanie L. Los Angeles, CA. Affil: Independent. Email: stephanielderrick@gmail.com. Research: Christian reading and print culture, religion and technology.

Deruelle, Benjamin, *Québec, Montréal*. Email: deruelle.benjamin@uqam.ca.

Des Forges, Roger V., *SUNY, Buffalo*. Email: rvd@buffalo.edu.

Desai, Sukumar P. Boston, MA. Affil: Brigham and Women's Hospital. Email: sdesai@partners.org. Research: anesthesia, medicine.

Desai, Tripta, *Northern Kentucky*. Email: desai@nku.edu.

Desan, Suzanne, *Wisconsin-Madison*. Email: smdesan@wisc.edu.

Desbarats, Catherine, *McGill*. Montreal, QC, Canada. Email: catherine.desbarats@mcgill.ca. Research: Canada, New France social and economic.

Desbrisay, Gordon R., *Saskatchewan*. Email: gordon.desbrisay@usask.ca.

DeSchaepdrijver, Sophie C. M., *Penn State*. Email: scd10@psu.edu.

DeSilva, Jennifer Mara, *Ball State*. Muncie, IN. Email: jmdesilva@bsu.edu. Research: late medieval and early modern Europe, Renaissance and Reformation.

DeSimone, Peter Thomas, *Utica*. Email: ptdesimo@utica.edu.

Deslandes, Paul R., *Vermont*. Burlington, VT. Email: paul.deslandes@uvm.edu. Research: British male beauty cultural, imperial travel to Canada.

Deslandres, Dominique, *Montréal*. Email: dominique.deslandres@umontreal.ca.

Deslippe, Dennis A., *Franklin & Marshall*. Lancaster, PA. Email: dennis.deslippe@fandm.edu. Research: equal employment, contemporary social protest.

Desloge, Taylor Hadley. Saint Louis, MO. Affil: Washington, St. Louis. Email: tdesloge@wustl.edu.

Desnoyers, Charles A., *La Salle*. Harleysville, PA. Email: desnoyer@lasalle.edu. Research: Chinese self-strengthening, 19th-c Chinese accounts of America.

Desrochers, Michael, *California State, Dominguez Hills*. Pacific Palisades, CA. Email: mdesrochers@csudh.edu; mjdesrochers@earthlink.net. Research: world.

Dessants, Betty A., *Shippensburg*. Shippensburg, PA. Email: badess@ship.edu; badessants@pa.net. Research: US Cold War, intellectual foundations of US Cold War.

Dessel, J. P., *Tennessee, Knoxville*. Email: jdessel@utk.edu.

Dessureault, Christian, *Montréal*. Email: christian.dessureault@umontreal.ca.

Detch, Andrew Ross. Denver, CO. Affil: Colorado, Boulder. Email: andrew.detch@colorado.edu. Research: circum-Atlantic revolutionary discourses, revolutionary symbolism.

Detjen, David W., *Leo Baeck Inst.* Email: david.detjen@alston.com.

Detzer, David W., *Western Connecticut State*.

Deutsch, Christopher Robert. Columbia, MO. Affil: Missouri, Columbia. Email: crdkf9@mail.missouri.edu. Research: food policy/food ecology, 20th-c US political/capitalism.

Deutsch, Nathaniel, *California, Santa Cruz*. Email: ndeutsch@ucsc.edu.

Deutsch, Sarah J., *Duke*. Durham, NC. Email: sdeutsch@duke.edu. Research: American social, American women.

Deutsch, Tracey Ann, *Minnesota (Hist.)*. Email: tdeutsch@umn.edu.

Deutscher, Thomas B., *Saskatchewan*. Email: tdeutscher@stmcollege.ca.

Devaney, Shawn. Fort Worth, TX. Affil: Texas Christian. Email: s.devaney@tcu.edu. Research: American Civil War.

Devaney, Thomas C., *Rochester*. Pittsford, NY. Email: thomas.devaney@rochester.edu. Research: public spectacle/interfaith relations, emotions/pilgrimage/community.

DeVaro, Lawrence J., Jr. Stratford, NJ. Affil: Camden County Coll. Email: ldevaro@faculty.camdencc.edu. Research: slavery/abolition/resistance, constitutional.

DeVaughn, Booker T. West Hartford, CT. Affil: Three Rivers Comm. Coll. Email: btdevaughn@msn.com.

DeVault, Ileen A., *Cornell*. Email: iad1@cornell.edu.

Deverell, Richard Donald. Macedon, NY. Affil: SUNY, Buffalo. Email: rddeverell87@gmail.com. Research: Cold War culture, media censorship.

Deverell, William, *Southern California*. Email: deverell@usc.edu.

Devereux, **Andrew**, *California, San Diego.* La Jolla, CA. Email: adevereux@ucsd.edu; awdevereux@gmail.com. Research: 15th-c Spanish political thought, Mediterranean world.

Devereux, **David R.**, *Canisius.* Amherst, NY. Email: devereud@canisius.edu. Research: Cold War and decolonization in Asia.

Devine, **Christine Styrna**, *Robert H. Smith Center.* Email: cdevine@monticello.org.

Devine, **Heather**, *Calgary.* Email: hdevine@ucalgary.ca.

Devine, **Joseph A.**, **Jr.**, *Stephen F. Austin State.* Houston, TX. Email: jdevine@sfasu.edu; jomar@suddenlink.net.

Devine, **Michael J.**, **Esq.**, *Wyoming.* Seattle, WA. Email: Mikej_devine@hotmail.com. Research: public, US.

Devine, **Shauna**, *Western Ontario.* Email: sdevine7@uwo.ca.

Devine, **Thomas W.**, *California State, Northridge.* Email: tom.devine@csun.edu.

DeVita, **George A.**, **Jr.**, *Central Connecticut State.* Email: devitag@ccsu.edu.

Devlin, **Cynthia M.**, *Stephen F. Austin State.* Email: devlinc@sfasu.edu.

Devlin, **Dennis S.**, *Grand Valley State.* Email: devlind@gvsu.edu.

Devlin, **Erin K.**, *Mary Washington.* Fredericksburg, VA. Email: edevlin@umw.edu. Research: public, America.

Devlin, **Rachel Jennifer**, *Rutgers.* New Brunswick, NJ. Email: rachel.devlin@rutgers.edu. Research: girls and civil rights, feminism and humor.

Devlin, **Rebecca A.**, *Louisville.* Email: rebecca.devlin@louisville.edu.

Devlin, **Shayna**. North Tonawanda, NY. Affil: Guelph. Email: sdevli01@uoguelph.ca. Research: Albany Stewarts/medieval Scottish nobles, medieval British Isles.

DeVore, **Donald E.**, *South Alabama.* Email: ddevore@southalabama.edu.

Devoti, **John**. Roebling, NJ. Affil: Philadelphia. Email: jdevoti@comcast.net. Research: 20th-c popular culture.

DeVries, **Annalise Kinkel**. Birmingham, AL. Affil: Samford. Email: adevries@samford.edu.

deVries, **Jacqueline R.**, *Augsburg.* Minneapolis, MN. Email: devries@augsburg.edu. Research: religion and British feminism, British suffrage movement.

Devries, **Kelly**, *Loyola, Md.* Email: kdevries@loyola.edu.

DeVries, **Kirsten Marie**. Roanoke, VA. Affil: Virginia Western Comm. Coll. Email: kdevrie1970@gmail.com. Research: Merovingian Francia, episcopal identity.

DeVun, **Leah**, *Rutgers.* New Brunswick, NJ. Email: leah.devun@rutgers.edu. Research: sex and gender, medicine and surgery.

Dew, **Charles B.**, *Williams.* Williamstown, MA. Email: charles.b.dew@williams.edu. Research: US South, Civil War and Reconstruction.

Dew, **Nicholas**, *McGill.* Email: nicholas.dew@mcgill.ca.

Dewald, **Jonathan**, *SUNY, Buffalo.* Buffalo, NY. Email: jdewald@buffalo.edu. Research: European nobility, European historiography.

Dewar, **Helen**, *Montréal.* Montreal, QC, Canada. Email: Helen.Dewar@umontreal.ca. Research: sovereignty and state formation, French Atlantic legal regimes.

DeWeese, **Devin A.**, *Indiana.* Email: deweese@indiana.edu.

Dewey, **Alicia M.**, *Biola.* La Mirada, CA. Email: alicia.dewey@biola.edu. Research: US-Mexico border, business.

Dewey, **Robert F.**, **Jr.**, *DePauw.* Email: rdewey@depauw.edu.

Dewhurst, **Ruth**. Marietta, GA. Affil: Georgia State. Email: ruthdewhurst@gmail.com. Research: early 19th-c German nationalism, 19th-/20th-c capitalism.

Dewindt, **Anne R.** Vienna, VA. Affil: Detroit Mercy. Email: aande@att.net. Research: peasant prosopography, late medieval England.

DeWitt, **Petra**, *Missouri Science and Tech.* Email: dewittp@mst.edu.

DeWolf, **Rebecca L.** Rockville, MD. Affil: American. Email: rdewolf416@gmail.com. Research: gender/politics, citizenship theory.

Dey, **Arnab**, *Binghamton, SUNY.* Ithaca, NY. Email: adey@binghamton.edu. Research: environment/labor/law, south asia.

Deyle, **Steven H.**, *Houston.* Houston, TX. Email: shdeyle@uh.edu. Research: 19th-c US social, slavery.

Dhada, **Mustafah**, *California State, Bakersfield.* San Diego, CA. Email: mdhada@csub.edu; dhada@mindspring.com. Research: Islamic world/Middle East/North Africa, Luso-Africa/liberation wars.

D'Haeseleer, **Tineke**, *Muhlenberg.* Email: tinekedhaeseleer@muhlenberg.edu.

Dhavan, **Purnima**, *Washington, Seattle.* Seattle, WA. Email: pdhavan@uw.edu. Research: Mughal literary cultures, early modern information networks.

Dhillon, **Hardeep Kaur**. Sacramento, CA. Affil: Harvard. Email: hdhillon@g.harvard.edu.

Dhulipala, **Venkat**, *North Carolina, Wilmington.* Email: dhulipalav@uncw.edu.

Di Bella, **Edward**, *San Diego State.*

Di Gioacchino, **Massimo**. Roma, Italy. Affil: Scuola Normale Superiore. Email: massimo.digioacchino@sns.it.

Di Iorio, **Anthony**. Arlington, VA. Email: anthony.diiorio@apsva.us.

Di Nunzio, **Mario R.**, *Providence.* Email: dinunzio@providence.edu.

Di Palma, **Vittoria**. Los Angeles, CA. Affil: Southern California. Email: dipalma@usc.edu.

Di Pasqua, **Federico**, *Hofstra.*

Di Ponio, **Mario**, *Henry Ford Coll.* Email: mariodiponio19@gmail.com.

Di Scala, **Spencer**, *Massachusetts, Boston.* Email: spencer.discala@umb.edu.

Diambri, **Michael**. Burlington, VT. Affil: Vermont. Email: Michael.Diambri@uvm.edu. Research: queer, urban.

Diamond, **Jeffrey M.**, *Clarion, Pa.* Email: jdiamond@clarion.edu.

Diamond, **Kelly-Anne**, *Villanova.* Email: kelly.anne.diamondreed@villanova.edu.

Dias, **Eurico José Gomes**. Torres Novas, Portugal. Affil: Instituto Superior de Ciências Policiais e Segurança Interna. Email: eurico_dias@sapo.pt.

Diaz, **Angela**, *Utah State.* Email: angela.diaz@usu.edu.

Diaz, **Arlene J.**, *Indiana.* Email: ardiaz@indiana.edu.

Diaz, **George T.**, *Texas-Rio Grande Valley.* Email: george.diaz@utrgv.edu.

Diaz, **Maria Elena**, *California, Santa Cruz.* Email: mediaz@ucsc.edu.

Diaz, **Monica**, *Kentucky.* Email: monica.diaz@uky.edu.

Diaz, **Robert Jesus**. El Paso, TX. Affil: Texas, El Paso. Email: rjdiaz.ofa@gmail.com. Research: science, transnational interactions.

Diaz Montejo, **Maria**, *Central Oklahoma.* Email: mdiazmontejo@uco.edu.

Diaz-Arias, **David Gustavo**. San Pedro de Montes, Costa Rica. Affil: Costa Rica. Email: david.diaz@ucr.ac.cr.

Diaz-Miranda, **Mariano**, *Austin Comm. Coll.* Email: marianod@austincc.edu.

Dibbern, **John**. Bethesda, MD. Email: dibbern@stanfordalumni.org. Research: US Indian policy.

DiBiase, **Benjamin**. Rockledge, FL. Affil: Florida Hist. Soc. Email: bdibiase@gmail.com.

Dibua, **Jeremiah**, *Morgan State.* Email: jeremiah.dibua@morgan.edu.

Di-Capua, **Yoav**, *Texas, Austin.* Austin, TX. Email: ydi@austin.utexas.edu. Research: Arab intellectual.

DiCarlo, **Douglas**, *La Guardia and Wagner Archives.* Email: ddicarlo@lagcc.cuny.edu.

Dick, **Wesley A.**, *Albion.* Email: wdick@albion.edu.

Dicke, **Thomas S.**, *Missouri State.* Email: tomdicke@missouristate.edu.

Dickens, **Mark**. Edmonton, AB, Canada. Affil: Alberta. Email: dickens@ualberta.ca. Research: Christianity in Central Asia, Central Asia in Syriac literature.

Dickerman, **Edmund**, *Connecticut, Storrs.*

Dickerson, **Dennis C.**, *Vanderbilt.* Email: dennis.c.dickerson@vanderbilt.edu.

Dickey, **Jennifer**, *Kennesaw State.* Email: jdickey2@kennesaw.edu.

Dickey, **Laurence W.**, **III**, *Wisconsin-Madison.* Email: laurencedickey@gmail.com.

Dickinson, **Edward R.**, *California, Davis.* Davis, CA. Email: erdickinson@ucdavis.edu. Research: 20th-c European cultural and political, welfare state.

Dickinson, **Frederick R.**, *Pennsylvania.* Swarthmore, PA. Email: frdickin@sas.upenn.edu. Research: interwar Japanese politics/society.

Dickinson, **Michael**, *Virginia Commonwealth.* Email: mldickinson@vcu.edu.

Dickinson, **W. Calvin**, *Tennessee Tech.* Email: cdickinson@tntech.edu.

Dickmeyer, **Laurie Jean**. San Angelo, TX. Affil: California, Irvine. Email: ldickmey@uci.edu. Research: 19th-c US-China relations/trade.

Dicks, **Samuel E.**, *Emporia State.* Emporia, KS. Email: dickssam@emporia.edu; samdicks@yahoo.com. Research: Emporia State Univ.

Dickson, **Edward M**. Charlotte, NC. Affil: Providence Day Sch. Email: ted.dickson@providenceday.org. Research: globalizing the survey, creating materials for AP US.

Dickson, **Samantha**. Milwaukee, WI. Affil: American. Email: samantha.dickson432@gmail.com.

Didier, **Elaine**, *Gerald Ford Presidential Library.* Email: elaine.didier@nara.gov.

DiDomenico, **Joseph**. Fort Riley, KS. Affil: Norwich. Email: Joseph.j.didomenico@gmail.com. Research: Marine Corps tank doctrine in the PTO, innovation in interwar years.

Diefenderfer, John, *New York State Archives*. Email: john.diefenderfer@nysed.gov.

Diefendorf, Barbara B. Kittery, ME. Affil: Boston Univ. Email: bdiefend@bu.edu. Research: French Wars of Religion, Catholic Reformation.

Diefendorf, Jeffry M. Kittery, ME. Affil: New Hampshire, Durham. Email: jeffryd@unh.edu. Research: Holocaust, urban culture and urban identity.

Diehl, Chad R., *Loyola, Md.* Charlottesville, VA. Email: crdiehl@loyola.edu; crd2109@caa. columbia.edu. Research: Japan, East Asia.

Diehl, James M., *Indiana*. Email: diehl@indiana. edu.

Diehl, Peter D., *Western Washington*. Email: Peter.Diehl@wwu.edu.

Diem, Albrecht, *Syracuse*. Email: adiem@ maxwell.syr.edu.

Diemer, Andrew, *Towson*. Baltimore, MD. Email: adiemer@towson.edu. Research: African American, US.

Diener, Laura Michele, *Marshall*. Email: diener@ marshall.edu.

Dienesch, Robert M., *Windsor*. Windsor, ON, Canada. Email: rdienesc@uwindsor.ca; sethkephra202@hotmail.com. Research: WWII American naval, American intelligence.

Diephouse, David J., *Calvin*. Grand Rapids, MI. Email: ddiephou@calvin.edu.

Dierenfield, Bruce J., *Canisius*. Email: dierenfb@ canisius.edu.

Dierenfield, Kate M., *Canisius*. Email: dierenfk@ wehle.canisius.edu.

Dierks, Konstantin, *Indiana*. Email: kdierks@ indiana.edu.

Dierksheide, Christa, *Virginia*. Email: cbd3g@ virginia.edu.

Dierksmeier, Laura Virginia. Tübingen, Germany. Affil: Eberhard Karls, Tübingen. Email: laura.dierksmeier@gmail.com. Research: Atlantic studies, confraternities.

Diestelow, Kevin. Williamsburg, VA. Affil: William and Mary. Email: kjdiestelow@email.wm.edu.

Dieterich, Herbert R., *Wyoming*. Email: herbrd@ uwyo.edu.

Dieterich-Ward, Allen J., *Shippensburg*. Email: ajdieterichward@ship.edu.

Dietle, Robert L., *Western Kentucky*. Email: robert.dietle@wku.edu.

Dietrich, Christopher R. W., *Fordham*. Email: cdietrich2@fordham.edu.

Dietz, Maribel, *Louisiana State*. Email: maribel@ lsu.edu.

Dietz, Vivien E., *Davidson*. Email: vidietz@ davidson.edu.

DiFilippo, Steven. San Diego, CA. Email: steven_ difilippo@yahoo.com.

diGiacomantonio, William C., *US Capitol Hist. Soc.* Washington, DC. Email: cdigiacomo@ uschs.org; chuck.digi@gmail.com. Research: early America, Quaker.

DiGiacomo, Mark A. Lawrenceville, NJ. Affil: Pennington Sch. Email: markdigiacomo@ yahoo.com.

DiGiovanni, Anthony, *Hist. Soc. of Pennsylvania*. Glendora, NJ. Email: adigiovanni@hsp.org; adigiovanni84@gmail.com. Research: African Americans in military, Philadelphia public school system.

DiGirolamo, Vincent Richard. Setauket, NY. Affil: Baruch, CUNY. Email: vincent. digirolamo@baruch.cuny.edu. Research: labor, journalism.

D'Ignazio, Catherine M. Swarthmore, PA. Affil: Rutgers, Camden. Email: dignazio@camden. rutgers.edu. Research: schoolgirl sport, urban education.

Digre, Brian, *Elon*. Email: digreb@elon.edu.

Dilday, Aaron. Caldwell, TX. Affil: Texas A&M, Coll. Station. Email: adilday@tamu.edu.

Dilgard, Carla Terase. Glen Cove, NY. Email: carla.jaszczerski@gmail.com. Research: information-seeking behavior, technology.

Dillard, P. David, *James Madison*. Email: dillardp@jmu.edu.

Dillenburg, Elizabeth. Milwaukee, WI. Affil: Minnesota, Twin Cities. Email: eadillenburg@ gmail.com. Research: British imperial culture and identity, women and children in British Empire.

Dilley, Jennifer, *Texas, San Antonio*. Email: jennifer.dilley@utsa.edu.

Dillman, Troy A. Tarpon Springs, FL. Affil: South Florida. Email: tdillm@tampabay.rr.com.

Dillon, Micah. Saint Paul, MN. Affil: Concordia Coll., Minn. Email: micahdillon@gmail.com.

Dillon, Nara. Cambridge, MA. Affil: Harvard. Email: ndillon@fas.harvard.edu.

DiMarco, Louis A., *US Army Command Coll.* Email: louis.a.dimarco.civ@mail.mil.

Dimas, Carlos S., *Nevada, Las Vegas*. Email: carlos.dimas@unlv.edu.

Dimberg, Ronald G., *Virginia*. Email: rgd@ virginia.edu.

DiMeo, Michelle, *Hagley Museum and Library*. Email: mdimeo@hagley.org.

Dimmock, Ethan. Cambridge, MA. Email: ethan. dimmock@gmail.com.

Dineen, Tim. Cumming, GA. Affil: Gwinnett Tech. Email: timothy.dineen@gmail.com. Research: wine, Byzantium.

Diner, Hasia R., *NYU*. New York, NY. Email: hrd1@ nyu.edu. Research: American immigrant, modern Jewish.

Diner, Steven J., *Rutgers, Newark/New Jersey Inst. of Tech.* New York, NY. Email: sdiner@ andromeda.rutgers.edu. Research: higher education, urban and suburban studies.

Dingman, Jacob Smigrod. Washington, DC. Affil: Georgetown. Email: jsd75@georgetown. edu. Research: Westerners in Tibet.

Dingman, Roger V., *Southern California*. Email: dingmanr@aol.com.

Dinius, Oliver J., *Mississippi*. University, MS. Email: dinius@olemiss.edu. Research: economic development in Vargas era, inequality and development policy.

Dinkin, Robert J. Anna Maria, FL. Email: robertjdinkin@gmail.com. Research: Election Day, American voting.

D'Innocenzo, Michael, *Hofstra*. Mineola, NY. Email: michael.dinnocenzo@hofstra.edu. Research: revolutionary America, New York state.

Dinschel, Elizabeth, *Herbert Hoover Presidential Library*. Email: elizabeth.dinschel@nara.gov.

Dintenfass, Michael, *Connecticut, Storrs*. Email: michael.dintenfass@uconn.edu.

Diouf, Mamadou, *Columbia (Hist.)*. Email: md2573@columbia.edu.

DiProfio, Matthew Michael. Union, NJ. Affil: Passaic Public Sch. Email: diprofim@kean.edu.

Diptee, Audra, *Carleton, Can.* Email: audra. diptee@carleton.ca.

Dirks, Jacqueline K., *Reed*. Email: jacqueline. dirks@reed.edu.

Dirks, Nicholas B., *California, Berkeley; Columbia (Hist.)*. Email: ndirks@berkeley.edu.

Dirks, Whitney, *Gustavus Adolphus*. Email: dirksw@gustavus.edu.

Dirrim, Allen W., *California State, Northridge*.

Dise, Robert L., Jr., *Northern Iowa*. Email: robert. dise@uni.edu.

Diskin, Harrison Mitchell. New York, NY. Affil: Southern California. Email: hdiskin@usc.edu.

Dittmar, Katherine K. Houston, TX. Affil: Rice. Email: kdittmar548@gmail.com. Research: revolutionary and early Republic America, American South and American West.

Dittmer, John, *DePauw*. Email: rip@depauw. edu.

Ditz, Toby L., *Johns Hopkins (Hist.)*. Baltimore, MD. Email: toby.ditz@jhu.edu. Research: 18th-c Philadelphia merchant cultural, 18th-c masculinity/gender.

Divalerio, David, *Wisconsin-Milwaukee*. Email: divaleri@uwm.edu.

Divine, Donna Robinson. West Hartford, CT. Affil: Smith. Email: drdivine@smith.edu.

Divine, Robert A., *Texas, Austin*. Email: rdivine@ austin.rr.com.

Divita, James J. Indianapolis, IN. Affil: Marian. Email: jdivita@marian.edu. Research: Indiana, Italian immigration.

Diwan, Pietra. Doral, FL. Affil: PUC-SP / Brazil. Email: pietrasd@gmail.com. Research: eugenics in Americas, 19th-/20th-c body as object.

Dixie, Quinton, *Purdue, Fort Wayne*. Email: dixieq@pfw.edu.

Dixon, Doug. Austin, TX. Email: dad.daddyo@ aol.com.

Dixon, Ina Cornelia. Chapel Hill, NC. Affil: Virginia Foundation for the Humanities. Email: inaelsabe@gmail.com.

Dixon, John M., *Staten Island, CUNY*. Email: john. dixon@csi.cuny.edu.

Dixon, Joy, *British Columbia*. Vancouver, BC, Canada. Email: joydixon@interchange.ubc. ca. Research: modern British religion and sexuality, desire/body/religious modernism.

Dixon, Michael D., *Southern Indiana*. Email: mdixon@usi.edu.

Dixon-Fyle, M. Samuel, *DePauw*. Email: macdixon@depauw.edu.

Dixon-McKnight, Otha Jennifer, *Winthrop*.

Dize, Nathan Hobson. Nashville, TN. Affil: Vanderbilt. Email: nathan.dize@gmail.com.

Djata, Sundiata, *Northern Illinois*. Email: sdjata@ niu.edu.

Dlamini, Jacob S. T., *Princeton*. Email: jdlamini@ princeton.edu.

Dluger, Marc. Burke, VA. Affil: Northern Virginia Comm. Coll. Email: mdluger@yahoo.com.

Dmitriev, Sviatoslav, *Ball State*. Email: dmitriev@bsu.edu.

Dmytryshyn, Basil, *Portland State*.

Do Paco, David. Paris, France. Affil: Sciences Po. Email: david.dopaco@sciencespo.fr. Research: Austria and Ottoman Empire, cross-cultural regional integration.

do Val, PJ. Nashua, NH. Affil: Endicott. Email: pjdoval@gmail.com. Research: Greek humanism and American Revolution, Athena and art & design.

Doaiji, Nora. Wakefield, MA. Affil: Harvard. Email: noradoaiji@g.harvard.edu.

Doan, Natalia. Oxford, United Kingdom. Affil: Oxford. Email: natalia.doan@sant.ox.ac.uk.

Doan, **Robert A.**, *Bellevue*. Email: rdoan@bellevuecollege.edu.

Doane, **Rob**, *Naval War Coll.* Email: robert.doane@usnwc.edu.

Dobbins, *Kerry Evalyn*. McPherson, KS. Affil: McPherson. Email: dobbinsk@mcpherson.edu. Research: infanticide.

Dobbs, **Charles M.**, *Iowa State*.

Dobbs, *Matthew Glen*. Houston, TX. Affil: Sterling High Sch. Email: dobbs.m4@gmail.com.

Dobbs, *Richard*. Gadsden, AL. Affil: Gadsden State Comm. Coll. Email: rdobbs@gadsdenstate.edu.

Dobbs, **Ricky Floyd**, *Texas A&M, Commerce*. Email: Ricky.Dobbs@tamuc.edu.

Dobies, **Eric**, *SUNY, Buffalo State*. Email: dobiesem@buffalostate.edu.

Dobson, **John M.**, *Iowa State*. Santa Fe, NM. Affil: Oklahoma State. Email: jmdobson9@gmail.com. Research: diplomatic historical concepts.

Dochuk, **Darren T.**, *Notre Dame*. Notre Dame, IN. Email: ddochuk@nd.edu. Research: post-1920s US religion and politics.

Dodd, **Douglas W.**, *California State, Bakersfield*. Email: ddodd@csub.edu.

Dodds, **Ben**, *Florida State*. Email: bdodds@fsu.edu.

Dodge, **Meredith D.** Santa Fe, NM. Email: mdodge@zianet.com.

Dodgen, **Randall**, *Sonoma State*. Email: dodgen@sonoma.edu.

Dodman, **Thomas William**. New York, NY. Affil: Columbia. Email: td2551@columbia.edu. Research: modern France, Emotions.

Dodson, **Heidi Lorraine**. Buffalo, NY. Affil: SUNY, Buffalo. Email: heidildodson@gmail.com. Research: African American landownership, African American environmental.

Dodson, **Julian Frank**, *Washington State, Pullman*. Email: julian.dodson@wsu.edu.

Dodson, **Michael S.**, *Indiana*. Email: msdodson@indiana.edu.

Dodt, *Kimberly*. Miami, FL. Affil: Miami. Email: Kxd353@miami.edu.

Doe, *James Ernest*. Visalia, CA. Email: jedoe2@sbcglobal.net. Research: American imperialism, Anglo-Norman administration.

Doebler, **Scott W.** State College, PA. Affil: Penn State. Email: swd6@psu.edu.

Doel, **Ronald E.**, *Florida State*. Tallahassee, FL. Email: rdoel@fsu.edu. Research: rise of environmental sciences, 20th-c international relations of science.

Doellinger, **David**, *Western Oregon*. Email: doellind@wou.edu.

Doenecke, **Justus D.** Sarasota, FL. Affil: New Coll., Fla. Email: doenecke@ncf.edu. Research: US and WWI 1914-20, US 1931-41.

Doenmez, *Sarah*. Dublin, NH. Affil: Dublin Sch. Email: sdoenmez@dublinschool.org.

Doherty, *Charles Edward*. Madison, WI. Affil: Viking Cruises. Email: Cedoherty@hotmail.com.

Doherty, *Sarah E.* Oak Park, IL. Affil: North Park. Email: sedoherty@northpark.edu. Research: women of the Ku Klux Klan, museum studies.

Dohrn, *Michael Robert*. Zephyrhills, FL. Affil: South Florida. Email: mrdohrn@yahoo.com.

Dolan, **Jay P.**, *Notre Dame*. Email: Dolan.1@nd.edu.

Dolata, **Petra**, *Calgary*. Email: pdolata@ucalgary.ca.

Dolbilov, **Mikhail**, *Maryland, Coll. Park*. Email: dolbilov@umd.edu.

Doleshal, *Zachary*, *Sam Houston State*. Huntsville, TX. Email: zad007@shsu.edu. Research: central Europe, business.

Dolkart, **Ron**, *California State, Bakersfield*.

Doll, **Kristin L.** Seattle, WA. Affil: Northwestern. Email: kristindoll2008@u.northwestern.edu. Research: medieval church fires, medieval disasters.

Dollar, **Kent T.**, *Tennessee Tech*. Email: kdollar@tntech.edu.

Dollard, **Catherine L.**, *Denison*. Email: dollard@denison.edu.

Dolph, **James A.**, *Weber State*. Email: jdolph@weber.edu.

Domber, **Gregory F.**, *California Polytechnic State*. Email: gdomber@calpoly.edu.

Dombrowski Risser, **Nicole A.**, *Towson*. Baltimore, MD. Email: ndombrowski@towson.edu. Research: 20th-c refugees, women and military conflict.

Dombrowsky, **Thomas**, *Gettysburg*. Email: tdombrowsky@gettysburg.edu.

Domby, *Adam H*, *Charleston*. Charleston, SC. Email: dombyah@cofc.edu. Research: Civil War memory fraud and lies, Divided communities and legacies of war.

Domenico, **Roy**, *Scranton*. Email: roy.domenico@scranton.edu.

Domingo Gygax, *Marc*. Princeton, NJ. Affil: Princeton. Email: mdomingo@princeton.edu. Research: ancient Greece, modern historiography.

Domingues da Silva, *Daniel B.*, *Rice*. Houston, TX. Email: domingues@rice.edu. Research: transatlantic slave trade, comparative slavery.

Dominguez, **Freddy C.**, *Arkansas, Fayetteville*. Email: fcdoming@uark.edu.

Dominick, **Raymond H.**, **III**, *Ohio State*. Email: dominick.1@osu.edu.

Domitrovic, **Brian**, *Sam Houston State*. Email: bfd001@shsu.edu.

Domurad, *Frank*. Portland, OR. Email: frankdomurad@comcast.net.

Don, **Patricia Lopes**, *San José State*. Email: Patricia.Don@sjsu.edu.

Donabed, **Sargon**, *Roger Williams*. Email: sdonabed@rwu.edu.

Donaghay, *Marie M.* Upper Darby, PA. Affil: East Stroudsburg. Email: mdonaghay@po-box.esu.edu.

Donagher, **Richard J.**, *Rosemont*. Email: rdonagher@rosemont.edu.

Donaghue, *Matthew Thomas*. San Antonio, TX. Affil: Norwich. Email: matthew.donaghue@gmail.com.

Donaghy, **Gregory S.**, *Carleton, Can.* Email: greg.donaghy@carleton.ca.

Donahue, **Brian**, *Brandeis*. Email: bdonahue@brandeis.edu.

Donahue, *Connie Meale*. Boyds, MD. Email: conniemeale@hotmail.com. Research: 19th-c southern black political expectations, Reconstruction Louisiana.

Donahue, **Kelly Lynn**, *St. Thomas, Minn.* Email: dona9875@stthomas.edu.

Donald, **Donna Davis**, *Liberty*. Email: ddonald@liberty.edu.

Donald, **William O.**, *South Alabama*. Email: wdonald@southalabama.edu.

Donaldson, **Bobby J.**, *South Carolina, Columbia*. Email: donaldbj@mailbox.sc.edu.

Donaldson, **Gary**, *Xavier, La.* Email: gdonalds@xula.edu.

Donaldson, **Le'Trice D.** University, MS. Affil: Mississippi. Email: lddonald@olemiss.edu. Research: African American military/gender, African American citizenship/identity.

Donaldson, **Rachel Clare**, *Charleston*. Email: donaldsonrc@cofc.edu.

Donaldson, *Robert C.*, *California State, Sacramento*. Carmichael, CA. Research: modern Europe.

Dong, **Madeleine Y.**, *Washington, Seattle*. Email: yuedong@uw.edu.

Donkor, **Martha**, *West Chester*. Email: mdonkor@wcupa.edu.

Donley, **Richard**, *Eastern Washington*.

Donnelly, **James Stephen**, **Jr.**, *Wisconsin-Madison*. Oregon, WI. Email: jsdonnel@wisc.edu. Research: modern Britain, modern Ireland.

Donnelly, **John Patrick**, **SJ**, *Marquette*. Milwaukee, WI. Email: john.p.donnelly@marquette.edu; jdonnelly@jesuits.org. Research: early Jesuits, Peter Martyr Vermigli.

Donnelly, **Mary Beth**. Falls Church, VA. Affil: Swanson Middle Sch. Email: mbdonnelly524@gmail.com.

Donnelly, **Robert C.**, *Gonzaga*. Email: donnelly@gonzaga.edu.

Donnelly-Rutledge, *Jeremey*. Austin, NY. Affil: Texas, Austin. Email: jdonnellyrutledge@gmail.com.

Donoghue, **John L.**, *Loyola, Chicago*. Email: jdonoghue@luc.edu.

Donoghue, **Michael E.**, *Marquette*. Email: michael.donoghue@marquette.edu.

Donohue, **Kathleen G.**, *Central Michigan*. Email: donoh1k@cmich.edu.

Donovan, *Bill Michael*, *Loyola, Md.* Louisville, KY. Affil: Bellarmine. Email: donovan@loyola.edu; bdonovan@bellarmine.edu. Research: 18th-c Atlantic social/economic, European expansion.

Donovan, **Brian E.**, *Iowa*. Email: brian-donovan@uiowa.edu.

Donovan, *James M.*, *Penn State*. Gettysburg, PA. Email: jmd9@psu.edu. Research: Europe, French social.

Donovan, **Joanne**, *Arthur and Elizabeth Schlesinger Library*. Email: jdonovan@radcliffe.harvard.edu.

Donovan, **John T.**, *California State, Los Angeles*. Hacienda Heights, CA. Email: jdonova@calstatela.edu. Research: 20th-c American Catholicism, Los Angeles Police Dept.

Donson, **Andrew C.**, *Massachusetts, Amherst*. Email: adonson@german.umass.edu.

Doody, **Colleen P.**, *DePaul*. Email: cdoody@depaul.edu.

Dooley, **Brendan**. Cork, Ireland. Affil: Univ. Coll., Cork. Email: b.dooley@ucc.ie. Research: cultural, science.

Dooley, **Howard J.**, *Western Michigan*. Email: howard.dooley@wmich.edu.

Doom, **Jason W.**, *Winthrop*. Email: doomj@winthrop.edu.

Doppelt, *Arthur*. Winter Park, FL. Email: adoppelt@caa.columbia.edu. Research: Charles Andler 1866-1933, Lucien Herr 1864-1926.

Dorais, **Geneviève**, *Québec, Montréal*. Email: dorais.genevieve@uqam.ca.

Doran, Connemara. Potomac, MD. Affil: Harvard. Email: cdoran@fas.harvard.edu. Research: mathematics/physics/cosmology/astronomy, peak oil/energy resources/economics.

Doran, Luke. Mahopac, NY. Email: thelukedoran@gmail.com.

Doran, Timothy, *California State, Los Angeles*. Email: tdoran@calstatela.edu.

Dorin, Rowan, *Stanford*.

Dorinson, Joseph, *Long Island, Brooklyn*. Email: joseph.dorinson@liu.edu.

Dormady, Jason H., *Central Washington*. Email: dormadyj@cwu.edu.

Dorman, Daniel M. Bailey Island, ME. Email: d.v.dorman@comcast.net. Research: clinical pathologist Frank Whittier, 19th-c Maine historic house.

Dorman, Jacob S., *Nevada, Reno*. Reno, NV. Email: jdorman@unr.edu. Research: African American alternative religions, US cultural.

Dorman, Jessica A., *Hist. New Orleans*. New Orleans, LA. Email: jessicad@hnoc.org. Research: journalism, 19th-/20th-c literature.

Dorment, Maureen, *Monmouth*. Email: mdorment@monmouth.edu.

Dormon, James H., Jr., *Louisiana, Lafayette*.

Dorn, Ashley H. Iowa City, IA. Affil: Iowa. Email: ashley-dorn@uiowa.edu. Research: Immigration/Migration, Labor.

Dorn, Sherman J. Tempe, AZ. Affil: Arizona State West. Email: Sherman.dorn@asu.edu.

Dorner, Jennifer. Berkeley, CA. Affil: California, Berkeley. Email: dorner@berkeley.edu.

Doron, Roy. Winston Salem, NC. Affil: Winston-Salem State. Email: doronrs@wssu.edu.

Dorondo, David R., *Western Carolina*. Email: dorondo@email.wcu.edu.

Dorsey, Allison Gloria, *Swarthmore*. Email: adorsey1@swarthmore.edu.

Dorsey, Bruce A., *Swarthmore*. Email: bdorsey1@swarthmore.edu.

Dorsey, Kurk, *New Hampshire, Durham*. Email: kurk.dorsey@unh.edu.

Dorsey, Leathen, *Nebraska, Lincoln*. Email: ldorsey1@unl.edu.

Dorsey, Marion Girard, *New Hampshire, Durham*. Durham, NH. Email: mlgirard@unh.edu. Research: Europe, diplomatic and military.

Dortmund, Erhard K., *Western Oregon*.

Dorwart, Jeffery M., *Rutgers, Camden*. Email: dorwart@camden.rutgers.edu.

dos Santos, George M. New Bedford, MA. Affil: Bishop Connolly High Sch. Email: g.dossantos@att.net. Research: modern Portuguese colonial theory, Sebastianism and nationalism.

Dosal, Paul J., *South Florida, Tampa*. Email: pdosal@usf.edu.

Dosemeci, Mehmet, *Bucknell*. Email: md053@bucknell.edu.

Doss, Harriet E. Amos, *Alabama, Birmingham*. Email: hadoss@uab.edu.

Doss, Jacob Westbrook. Austin, TX. Affil: Texas, Austin. Email: jacobwdoss@utexas.edu.

Doss, Lt Col John C., *US Military Acad.* Email: john.doss@usma.edu.

Dossey, Leslie D., *Loyola, Chicago*. Email: ldossey@luc.edu.

Dostourian, Ara. Harmony, RI. Affil: West Georgia.

Doti, Robert Anthony. Indianapolis, IN. Affil: Ivy Tech. Email: dotirobert@gmail.com.

Dotolo, Frederick Henry, III, *St. John Fisher*. Email: fdotolo@sjfc.edu.

Dotson, David W. Poultney, VT. Email: dotson@together.net.

Dotson, Jerome Kern, Jr. Tucson, AZ. Affil: Arizona. Email: jkdotson@wisc.edu. Research: race and medicine/food studies, popular culture.

Dotson, John E., *Southern Illinois, Carbondale*. Email: jdotson@siu.edu.

Dotson, M. Rhys, *Texas, Tyler*. Email: mdotson@uttyler.edu.

Dott, Brian R., *Whitman*. Walla Walla, WA. Email: dottbr@whitman.edu. Research: Chinese cultural, religion and gender.

Dou, Yu. West Lafayette, IN. Affil: Purdue. Email: dou5@purdue.edu. Research: Chinese exclusion era 1882-1943, Chinese migrants in US Midwest.

Doubleday, Simon R., *Hofstra*. Astoria, NY. Email: simon.r.doubleday@hofstra.edu. Research: medieval Spain, Alfonso X.

Doucet, Marie-Michèle, *Royal Military*. Email: Marie-Michele.Doucet@rmc.ca.

Doucette, Courtney. Philadelphia, PA. Affil: Franklin & Marshall. Email: courtneydoucette@yahoo.com. Research: modern Europe, women and gender.

Doucette, Siobhan. Cincinnati, OH. Affil: Xavier. Email: Siobhandoucette@hotmail.com.

Dougan, Michael B., *Arkansas State*.

Dougherty, Dave. Evening Shade, AR. Affil: Lakeside Ranch. Email: D2@nwlog.com.

Doughty, Lauren, *Southeastern Louisiana*. Email: Lauren.Doughty@selu.edu.

Doughty, Marla Denise. Portland, OR. Affil: Portland. Email: doughtym@up.edu.

Douglas, Lawrence H., *Plymouth State*.

Douglas, R.M. M., *Colgate*. Email: rdouglas@colgate.edu.

Douglas, W.A.B., *Carleton, Can.* Email: w.douglas@carleton.ca.

Douglass, John E., *Cincinnati*. Email: john.douglass@uc.edu.

Douglass, Larissa C. Dalkeith, ON, Canada. Affil: St. Antony's, Oxford. Email: larissa.douglass@googlemail.com. Research: Habsburg Empire legal and constitutional, British Empire legal and constitutional.

Doumani, Beshara B., *Brown*. Email: bdoumani@brown.edu.

Dove, Michael F., *Western Ontario*. Email: mdove2@uwo.ca.

Dover, Paul Marcus, *Kennesaw State*. Email: pdover@kennesaw.edu.

Dovern, Lukas. Stanford, CA. Affil: Stanford. Email: ldovern@stanford.edu. Research: globalization, finance.

Dowd, Gregory, *Michigan, Ann Arbor*. Ann Arbor, MI. Email: dowdg@umich.edu. Research: American Indian, early America.

Dowden-White, Priscilla A., *Missouri–St. Louis*. Email: padhist@umsl.edu.

Dower, John W., *MIT*.

Dowler, Wayne, *Toronto*. Email: dowler@utsc.utoronto.ca.

Dowling, Abigail P., *Mercer*. Email: dowling_ap@mercer.edu.

Dowling, Matthew J., *Providence*. Email: mdowling@providence.edu.

Dowling, Melissa Barden, *Southern Methodist*. Email: mdowling@smu.edu.

Dowling, Timothy, *Virginia Military Inst.; Soc. for Military Hist.* Email: dowlingtc@vmi.edu.

Downey, Allan, *McMaster*. Email: downea2@mcmaster.ca.

Downey, D. Allan, *McGill*. Email: allan.downey@mcgill.ca.

Downey, Dennis B., *Millersville, Pa.* Email: dennis.downey@millersville.edu.

Downey, Elizabeth A., *Gonzaga*. Email: downey@gonzaga.edu.

Downey, Thomas M., *Princeton*. Email: tdowney@princeton.edu.

Downie, Susan, *Carleton, Can.* Email: susan.downie@carleton.ca.

Downing, Marvin L., *Tennessee, Martin*. Email: mdowning@utm.edu.

Downs, Alan Craig, *Georgia Southern*. Email: acdowns@georgiasouthern.edu.

Downs, Gregory P., *California, Davis*. Davis, CA. Email: gdowns@ucdavis.edu; gregorypdowns@gmail.com. Research: Civil War and Reconstruction, comparative occupation.

Downs, James T., Jr., *Connecticut Coll.* Email: james.downs@conncoll.edu.

Downs, Jordan, *Vanderbilt*.

Downs, Murray, *North Carolina State*. Email: downs@unity.ncsu.edu.

Doxiadis, Evdoxios, *Simon Fraser*. Burnaby, BC, Canada. Email: edoxiadi@sfu.ca; evdoxios.doxiadis@gmail.com. Research: Greek women's roles 1750-1900, Romaniote Jews.

Doyle, Christopher L. Simsbury, CT. Affil: Avon Old Farms Sch. Email: chrisdoyle_384@hotmail.com. Research: secondary history education, training history educators.

Doyle, David D., Jr., *Southern Methodist*. Email: ddoyle@smu.edu.

Doyle, Debbie Ann, *AHA*. Washington, DC. Email: ddoyle@historians.org. Research: tourism and resorts, mass culture.

Doyle, Don H., *South Carolina, Columbia*. Folly Beach, SC. Email: don.doyle@sc.edu. Research: US Civil War/Reconstruction/world, nationalism/separatism/international.

Doyle, James T., *Salem State*. Email: james.doyle@salemstate.edu.

Doyle, L. Andrew, *Winthrop*. Email: doylea@winthrop.edu.

Doyle, Mark E., *Middle Tennessee State*. Email: Mark.Doyle@mtsu.edu.

Doyle, Michael Wm. Muncie, IN. Affil: Ball State. Email: mwdoyle@bsu.edu. Research: cultural radicalism, 1960s counterculture.

Doyle, Nora. Winston Salem, NC. Affil: Salem. Email: doylenor@gmail.com. Research: early America, women/gender/sexuality.

Doyle-Raso, John. East Lansing, MI. Affil: Michigan State. Email: doyleras@msu.edu.

Doyno, Mary Harvey. San Francisco, CA. Affil: California State, Sacramento. Email: marydoyno@gmail.com. Research: medieval Italy, saints' cults.

Dozier, Graham, *Virginia Museum of Hist.* Email: gdozier@VirginiaHistory.org.

Drache, Hiram, *Concordia Coll.* Email: drache@cord.edu.

Drachewych, Oleska, *Western Ontario*. Email: odrachew@uwo.ca.

Dracobly, Alexander, *Oregon*. Email: dracobly@uoregon.edu.

Dragnich, **George S**. Arlington, VA. Email: dragnich3@gmail.com.

Drago, **Edmund L.**, *Charleston*. Email: dragoe@cofc.edu.

Dragostinova, **Theodora**, *Ohio State*. Email: dragostinova.1@osu.edu.

Drahan, **Casimir Matthew**. Maumee, OH. Affil: Toledo. Email: casimir.drahan@utoledo.edu.

Drake, **Brian**, *Georgia*. Email: bdrake@uga.edu.

Drake, **Frederic**, *Massachusetts, Amherst*. Email: fwdrake@gmail.com.

Drake, **George A**., *Grinnell*. Grinnell, IA. Email: drake@grinnell.edu. Research: 17th-c England, southern Africa/Lesotho.

Drake, **Harold A.**, *California, Santa Barbara*. Email: drake@history.ucsb.edu.

Drake, **James D**. Denver, CO. Affil: Metropolitan State, Denver. Email: drakeja@msudenver.edu. Research: Rocky Mountain West, historical geography.

Drake, **Janine Giordano**, *Indiana*. Email: jgdrake@iu.edu.

Drake, **Paul W.**, *California, San Diego*. Email: pdrake@ucsd.edu.

Drake, **Richard B.**, *Berea*.

Drake, **Richard R.**, *Montana*. Missoula, MT. Email: richard.drake@umontana.edu. Research: modern Italy, modern European social and intellectual.

Drake, **Tim**. Wabash, IN. Email: tsdrake@hotmail.com.

Drake Brown, **Sarah**, *Ball State*. Muncie, IN. Email: sedrakebrown@bsu.edu. Research: teaching and learning, education.

Drakeman, **Donald Lee**. Hilton Head Island, SC. Affil: Notre Dame. Email: ddrakema@nd.edu. Research: law, religion.

Drakman, **Annelie Elisabeth**. Hägersten, Sweden. Affil: Uppsala. Email: anneliedrakman@hotmail.com.

Drane, **Lindsay Nicole**. Collingswood, NJ. Affil: Houston. Email: lindsay.drane@gmail.com. Research: modern US, food stamps/food politics.

Draney, **Hollie**. Syracuse, UT. Affil: North Davis Preparatory Academy. Email: hollie.draney@gmail.com.

Drapeau, **Blanca**. San Marcos, CA. Affil: California State, San Marcos. Email: drape008@cougars.csusm.edu.

Draper, **Jesse James**. East Lansing, MI. Affil: H-Net. Email: draperje@mail.h-net.org. Research: post-WWII urban development, sports.

Draper, **Timothy Dean**. Sugar Grove, IL. Affil: Waubonsee Comm. Coll. Email: tdraper@waubonsee.edu. Research: 1970s US urban culture, transnational historical pedagogy.

Drees, **Clayton J.**, *Phi Alpha Theta*. Email: cdrees@vwc.edu.

Dreifort, **John E.**, *Wichita State*. Email: john.dreifort@wichita.edu.

Dreisziger, **N.A.F.**, *Royal Military*. Email: dreisziger-n@rmc.ca.

Dreizen, **Alison M.**, *Esq*. New York, NY. Affil: Carter Ledyard & Milburn LLP. Email: dreizen@clm.com.

Drell, **Joanna H.**, *Richmond*. Richmond, VA. Email: jdrell@richmond.edu. Research: medieval Europe, Italy.

Drendel, **John**, *Québec, Montréal*. Email: drendel.john_v@uqam.ca.

Drescher, **Nuala M.**, *SUNY, Buffalo State*.

Drescher, **Seymour**, *Pittsburgh*. Pittsburgh, PA. Email: syd@pitt.edu. Research: slavery and abolition, transatlantic slave trade.

Dresner, **Jonathan F.**, *Pittsburg State*. Pittsburg, KS. Email: jdresner@pittstate.edu. Research: Japanese local, emigration impact on sending communities.

Dressler, **Nicole**. Williamsburg, VA. Affil: William and Mary. Email: nkdress@gmail.com.

Drew, **Katherine Fischer**, *Rice*. Houston, TX. Email: kdrew@rice.edu. Research: early medieval, medieval.

Driedger, **Michael D.**, *Brock*. Email: mdriedge@brocku.ca.

Dries, **Angelyn**, *OSF*. Milwaukee, WI. Affil: St. Louis. Email: driesa@slu.edu. Research: US Catholic missions overseas, women/culture/missions.

Dries, **Mark Pierre**, *Eastern Illinois*. Charleston, IL. Email: mpdries@eiu.edu. Research: Latin America, Peru.

Driggers, **E. Allen**, **Jr.**, *Tennessee Tech*. Email: edriggers@tntech.edu.

Drinkard-Hawkshawe, **Dorothy Lee**, *East Tennessee State*. Email: drinkard@etsu.edu.

Driscoll, **Timothy**. Cambridge, MA. Affil: Harvard Univ. Archives. Email: timothy_driscoll@harvard.edu.

Driscoll, **William**, *Seton Hall*.

Driskell, **Jay Winston**, **Jr.** Takoma Park, MD. Affil: Jay Winston Driskell Research and Consulting. Email: drjaywdriskell@gmail.com. Research: Progressive Atlanta community organizing, race and labor politics in Jacksonville FL.

Drivas, **Eleni**. Whitestone, NY. Affil: St. John's, NY. Email: eleni.history@gmail.com. Research: Gender in southeastern Europe, Civil War.

Driver, **Beau**. McMinnville, TN. Affil: Colorado, Boulder. Email: beaudriver@gmail.com. Research: working-class identity, academia.

Driver, **Richard D.** San Antonio, TX. Affil: McLennan Comm. Coll. Email: rdriver@mclennan.edu. Research: US rock 'n' roll/popular music, US work culture.

Drixler, **Fabian F.**, *Yale*. Email: fabian.drixler@yale.edu.

Droessler, **Holger**. Cambridge, MA. Affil: Harvard. Email: hdroessl@fas.harvard.edu. Research: Euro-American imperialism in Pacific, global hip hop.

Drogan, **Mara**. Troy, NY. Affil: City of Troy. Email: maradrogan@gmail.com. Research: nuclear technology, Cold War foreign policy.

Drohan, **Brian**. Colorado Springs, CO. Email: brian.drohan@gmail.com. Research: human rights and warfare, Cold War and decolonization.

Drompp, **Michael R.**, *Rhodes*. Email: drompp@rhodes.edu.

Dror, **Olga**, *Texas A&M*. Email: olgadror@tamu.edu.

Droubie, **Paul**, *Manhattan*. Email: paul.droubie@manhattan.edu.

Druga, **Elizabeth**, *Gerald Ford Presidential Library*. Email: elizabeth.druga@nara.gov.

Drummey, **Peter**, *Massachusetts Hist. Soc.* Email: pdrummey@masshist.org.

Drummond, **Benjamin**, *Austin Peay State*. Email: drummondb@apsu.edu.

Drummond, **Elizabeth A.**, *Loyola Marymount*. Los Angeles, CA. Email: edrummon@lmu.edu. Research: German-Polish national conflict, gender and nationalism.

Drummond, **Laura**. Atlanta, GA. Affil: Georgia State. Email: Laura@atlantapreservation.com.

Du, **Dan**, *North Carolina, Charlotte*. Email: ddu2@uncc.edu.

Du, **Yongtao**, *Oklahoma State*. Email: yongtao.du@okstate.edu.

Du, **Yue**, *Cornell*. Ithaca, NY. Email: yd514@nyu.edu. Research: Law, State-building.

Du Laney, **Claire**. Chapel Hill, NC. Email: cdulane@ncsu.edu.

Du Mez, **Kristin Kobes**, *Calvin*. Grand Rapids, MI. Email: dumez@calvin.edu. Research: Hillary Clinton's religious history, evangelical masculinity and politics.

Duah, **Manna**, *Miami, Ohio*. Email: duahm@miamioh.edu.

Duan, **Lei**. Ann Arbor, MI. Affil: Michigan. Email: duanl@umich.edu.

Duan, **Ruodi**. Brooklyn, NY. Email: rduan44@gmail.com.

Duan, **Xiaolin**, *North Carolina State*. Email: xduan4@ncsu.edu.

Duara, **Prasenjit**, *Chicago; Duke*. Email: prasenjit.duara@duke.edu.

Dubcovsky, **Alejandra**, *California, Riverside*. Riverside, CA. Email: alejandra.dubcovsky@ucr.edu. Research: colonial Southeast SC/GA/FL, communication networks.

Dube, **Alexandre**, *Washington, St. Louis*. Email: adube22@wustl.edu.

Dube, **Francis**, *Morgan State*. Email: francis.dube@morgan.edu.

Duberman, **Martin**, *Lehman, CUNY*. Email: martinduberman@aol.com.

Dubin, **Lois**. Northampton, MA. Affil: Smith. Email: ldubin@smith.edu. Research: 18th-c Habsburg Jews, civil marriage and divorce.

Dubinsky, **Karen**, *Queen's, Can.* Email: dubinsky@queensu.ca.

Dublin, **Thomas**, *Binghamton, SUNY*. Berkeley, CA. Email: tdublin@binghamton.edu. Research: gender and working class, US immigration.

Dubnov, **Arie M.** Washington, DC. Affil: George Washington. Email: dubnov@gwu.edu. Research: Israel studies/Jewish/intellectual, British colonial and imperial/Mideast.

Dubofsky, **Melvyn**, *Binghamton, SUNY*. Binghamton, NY. Email: dubof@binghamton.edu. Research: comparative labor, workers/state/public policy.

DuBois, **Daniel M.** Wesley Chapel, FL. Affil: St. Leo. Email: daniel.dubois@saintleo.edu. Research: US-East Asian relations, US sports.

DuBois, **Ellen C.**, *UCLA*. Email: edubois@ucla.edu.

Dubois, **Katharine Brophy**, *Duke*. Email: kbd6@duke.edu.

Dubois, **Laurent M.**, *Duke*. Email: laurent.dubois@duke.edu.

DuBose-Simons, **Carla J.** Yonkers, NY. Affil: Westchester Comm. Coll., SUNY. Email: carla.dubose@sunywcc.edu. Research: 20th-c New York City, African American.

Dubow, **Sara L.**, *Williams*. Email: sld1@williams.edu.

Dubrulle, **Hugh F.**, *St. Anselm*. Manchester, NH. Email: hdubrull@anselm.edu. Research: Anglo-American relations.

Ducey, **Michael T.** Centennial, CO. Affil: Veracruzana. Email: olartismo@gmail.com. Research: 19th-c Mexico, colonial Mexican indigenous communities.

Ducharme, Michel, *British Columbia*. Email: Michel.Ducharme@ubc.ca.

Ducksworth-Lawton, Selika Marianne, *Wisconsin-Eau Claire*. Email: duckswsm@uwec. edu.

Dudden, Alexis, *Connecticut, Storrs*. Email: alexis.dudden@uconn.edu.

Dudden, Faye E., *Colgate*. Email: fdudden@ colgate.edu.

Dudley, Chris. East Stroudsburg, PA. Affil: East Stroudsburg. Email: cdudley@esu. edu. Research: origins of political parties as institutions, political economy and economic modernization.

Dudley, Leigh, *Central Oklahoma*. Email: ldudley2@uco.edu.

Dudley, Wade G., *East Carolina*. Email: dudleyw@ecu.edu.

Dudziak, Mary L., *Emory*. Atlanta, GA. Email: mary.dudziak@emory.edu. Research: war and American politics, global reach of US military.

Dueck, Gordon B., *Queen's, Can*. Email: dueckg@queensu.ca.

Dueck, Jennifer M., *Manitoba*. Email: jennifer. dueck@umanitoba.ca.

Duenas, Alcira, *Ohio State*. Email: duenas.2@ osu.edu.

Duenas-Vargas, Guiomar, *Memphis*. Email: gduenas@memphis.edu.

Duerden, Tim, *SUNY, Oneonta*. Email: timothy. duerden@oneonta.edu.

Duerkes, Wayne Nelson. Ames, IA. Affil: Iowa State. Email: wduerkes@yahoo.com. Research: Civil War Western Theater, Civil War Eastern Theater.

DuFault, David V., *San Diego State*.

Duff, Sarah Emily, *Colby*. Email: seduff@colby. edu.

Duffaut, Chad, Jr. Slidell, LA. Email: chad. duffaut-2@selu.edu. Research: Nativist rhetoric in Early Modern Japan, Recreational facilities and civil rights.

Duffin, Jacalyn M., *Queen's, Can*. Email: duffinj@ queensu.ca.

Duffy, Alicia, *Central Florida*. Email: alicia.duffy@ ucf.edu.

Duffy, Edward G., *Clarion, Pa*.

Duffy, Eve M., *Duke*. Email: eve.duffy@duke.edu.

Duffy, Jennifer Nugent, *Western Connecticut State*. Email: duffyj@wcsu.edu.

Duffy, Kevin Barry. Newtown, PA. Affil: Drew. Email: kduffyusa@hotmail.com.

Duffy, Shannon E., *Texas State*. Email: sd22@ txstate.edu.

Dufour, Monique, *Virginia Tech*. Email: msdufour@vt.edu.

Dufour, Ronald P. Providence, RI. Affil: Rhode Island Coll. Email: rdufour@ric.edu. Research: colonial and revolutionary America, historiography.

Dugan, Eileen T., *Creighton*. Email: etdugan@ creighton.edu.

Dugan, Katherine A., *American Catholic Hist. Assoc*. Email: kdugan@springfield.edu.

Duggan, Chris R. Saint Paul, MN. Email: crdduggan@comcast.net.

Duggan, Lawrence G. J., *Delaware*. Email: lgjd@ udel.edu.

Duggan, Sarah, *Hist. New Orleans*. Email: sduggan@hnoc.org.

Dugre, Neal T., *Houston-Clear Lake*. Houston, TX. Email: dugre@uhcl.edu; ndugre@gmail.com.

Research: 17th-c New England, intercolonial relations.

Duiker, William J., III, *Penn State*. Email: wjd2@ psu.edu.

Duis, Perry R., *Illinois, Chicago*. Email: prduis@ uic.edu.

Dukas, Neil B. Kingston, ON, Canada. Affil: National Coalition of Independent Scholars. Email: neil@dukas.org. Research: pre-annexation Hawaiian military, biography of Colonel Volney V. Ashford.

Duke Bryant, Kelly M., *Rowan*. Email: duke-bryant@rowan.edu.

Duker, Adam Asher, *Mount Holyoke*. New Cairo, Egypt. Affil: American, Cairo. Email: aduker@ mtholyoke.edu; adam.duker@aucegypt.edu. Research: early modern Europe/Reformation, France/Switzerland/religious wars.

Dukes, Jack R. Sturgeon Bay, WI. Affil: Carroll. Email: jackjoannedukes@gmail.com. Research: pre-WWI military expansion, armaments/alliances/war planning.

Dukes-Knight, Jennifer, *South Florida, Tampa*. Email: jlknight@usf.edu.

Dulaney, W. Marvin, *Texas, Arlington*. Email: dulaney@uta.edu.

Dull, Laura D. University Center, MI. Affil: Delta. Email: lauradull@delta.edu. Research: gender and conduct, Book of the Knight.

Dumaine, Danielle. Storrs Mansfield, CT. Affil: Connecticut, Storrs. Email: danielle.dumaine@ uconn.edu. Research: utopias and communes, race and gender.

Dumancic, Marko, *Western Kentucky*. Email: marko.dumancic@wku.edu.

Dumas, Genevieve. Sherbrooke, QC, Canada. Affil: Sherbrooke. Email: genevieve.dumas@ usherbrooke.ca. Research: science and medicine, health and health care.

Dumenil, Lynn, *Occidental*. Email: dumenil@ oxy.edu.

Dumett, Raymond E., *Purdue*. Email: rdumett@ purdue.edu.

DuMontier, Benjamin, *Arizona*. Email: bjohnd@ email.arizona.edu.

Dunagin, Amy M., *Kennesaw State*. Email: adunagin@kennesaw.edu.

Dunai, Suzanne. La Jolla, CA. Affil: California, San Diego. Email: SDunai@ucsd.edu. Research: food policy, Franco dictatorship.

Dunak, Karen M. New Concord, OH. Affil: Muskingum. Email: kdunak@muskingum.edu. Research: media and celebrity, gender and citizenship.

Dunar, Andrew J., *Alabama, Huntsville*. Email: dunara@uah.edu.

Dunaway, Finis, *Trent*. Email: finisdunaway@ trentu.ca.

Dunbar, Erica R. Armstrong, *Rutgers*. Email: erica.dunbar@rutgers.edu.

Duncan, Jennifer, *Utah State*. Logan, UT. Email: Jennifer.Duncan@usu.edu. Research: Special Collections.

Duncan, John, *UCLA*. Email: duncan@humnet. ucla.edu.

Duncan, Leanna. Urbana, IL. Affil: Illinois, Urbana-Champaign. Email: lddunca2@illinois. edu.

Duncan, Natanya, *Lehigh*. Bethlehem, PA. Email: nad415@lehigh.edu. Research: Pan-Africanism, diasporic women and nation building.

Duncan, Richard, *Georgetown*. Email: duncanr@ georgetown.edu.

Duncan, Robert H., *California, Irvine*.

Duncan, Stephen Riley. New York, NY. Affil: Bronx Comm. Coll., CUNY. Email: Stephen. Duncan@bcc.cuny.edu. Research: US culture/ Cold War/urban, transnational.

Dunch, Ryan, *Alberta*. Email: ryan.dunch@ ualberta.ca.

Dungy, Kathryn, *St. Michael's*. Email: kdungy@ smcvt.edu.

Dunk, Charles Joseph. Chicago, IL. Affil: Nebraska, Kearney. Email: Cjdunk1@gmail. com.

Dunkelgruen, Theodor William. Cambridge, United Kingdom. Affil: Cambridge. Email: theodor.dunkelgrun@gmail.com. Research: Basel edition of Talmud, editorial history of Hebrew Bible.

Dunkley, Daive Anthony, *Missouri, Columbia*. Email: dunkleyd@missouri.edu.

Dunkley, Peter, *Georgetown*. Email: dunkleyp@ georgetown.edu.

Dunlap, Christopher. Centreville, VA. Affil: Naval Postgraduate Sch. Email: ctdunlap.phd@ gmail.com. Research: nuclear technology and energy, 20th-c Southern Cone political.

Dunlap, Leslie K., *Willamette*. Email: ldunlap@ willamette.edu.

Dunlap, Thomas R., *Texas A&M*. Email: t-dunlap@tamu.edu.

Dunlavey, Reid, *SUNY, Buffalo State*. Email: dunlavrv@buffalostate.edu.

Dunlavy, Colleen A., *Wisconsin-Madison*. Madison, WI. Email: cdunlavy@wisc.edu. Research: comparative corporate governance, standardization of commodities.

Dunlea, Claudia, *Florida Atlantic*. Email: cdunlea@fau.edu.

Dunlop, Catherine T., *Montana State, Bozeman*. Email: catherine.dunlop@montana.edu.

Dunn, Brian R., *Clarion, Pa*. Email: bdunn@ clarion.edu.

Dunn, Caroline C. Clemson, SC. Affil: Clemson. Email: cdunn@clemson.edu. Research: medieval English women/law/society, abduction of women.

Dunn, Dennis J., *Texas State*. San Marcos, TX. Email: dd05@txstate.edu. Research: Catholic Church in Soviet Russia, Orthodox/Islamic/ Western worlds.

Dunn, Josephine M., *Scranton*. Email: josephine.dunn@scranton.edu.

Dunn, Katherine Jolliff, *Hist. New Orleans*. Email: katherined@hnoc.org.

Dunn, Marilyn, *Arthur and Elizabeth Schlesinger Library*. Email: mdunn@radcliffe.harvard.edu.

Dunn, Mary Corley. Saint Louis, MO. Affil: St. Louis. Email: mdunn12@slu.edu.

Dunn, Richard S., *McNeil Center*. Email: rdunn@ amphilsoc.org.

Dunn, Ross E., *San Diego State*. Email: dunn@ sdsu.edu.

Dunne, Brian Thomas, *Florida Atlantic*. Email: bdunne1@fau.edu.

Dunne, Matthew W. Bridgeport, CT. Affil: Housatonic Comm. Coll. Email: mdunne@hcc. commnet.edu. Research: Cold War, post-WWII US cultural.

Dunnell, Ruth, *Kenyon*. Email: dunnell@kenyon. edu.

Dunning, Chester S. L., *Texas A&M*. Email: c-dunning@tamu.edu.

Dunstan, **Helen**. Sydney, Australia. Affil: Sydney. Email: helen.dunstan@sydney.edu.au. Research: corpses and burial in 18th-c China, provincial finance in 18th-c China.

Dunstan, **Sarah Claire**. Stanmore, Australia. Affil: Sydney. Email: sdun9166@uni. sydney.edu.au. Research: African American intellectual, transnational.

Dunston-Coleman, **Aingred G.**, *Eastern Kentucky*. Email: a.dunston@eku.edu.

Dunwoody, **Sean F.**, *Binghamton, SUNY*. Binghamton, NY. Email: sdunwood@ binghamton.edu; sean.f.dunwoody@gmail. com. Research: early modern Europe, premodern Europe.

DuPlessis, **Robert S.**, *Swarthmore*. Email: rduples1@swarthmore.edu.

Dupont, **Carolyn R.**, *Eastern Kentucky*. Email: carolyn.dupont@eku.edu.

Dupont, **Robert L.**, *New Orleans*. Email: rldupont@uno.edu.

Dupras, **Nickolas**, *Northern Michigan*. Email: ndupras@nmu.edu.

Dupre, **Daniel**, *North Carolina, Charlotte*. Charlotte, NC. Email: ddupre@uncc.edu. Research: American Revolution to Civil War.

Dupree, **A. Hunter**. Cambridge, MA. Affil: Brown.

Dupree, **James E.**, **Jr.** Norman, OK. Affil: Oklahoma. Email: james.e.dupree-1@ou.edu.

Dupuis, **Dana**. Moorpark, CA. Affil: American. Email: dupuis.dana@gmail.com.

Duquet, **Michel**, *Canadian Hist. Assoc.* Email: mduquet@cha-shc.ca.

Duram, **David**, *Grand Valley State*. Email: dduram@hpseagles.net.

Duram, **James C.**, *Wichita State*.

Durand, **Caroline**, *Trent*. Email: carolinedurand@trentu.ca.

Durant, **Kendra Lynn**. Chazy, NY. Email: kldurant@asu.edu. Research: prostitution and gender marginalization, gender and migration.

Duranti, **Marco Leonard Ochs**. Sydney, Australia. Affil: Sydney. Email: mloduranti@ gmail.com. Research: international human rights law, European integration.

Durbach, **Nadja**, *Utah*. Email: n.durbach@utah. edu.

Durfee, **Michael Jordan**, *Niagara*. Email: mdurfee@niagara.edu.

Durham, **Brian**. Independence, LA. Affil: Southeastern Louisiana. Email: brn.durham@ gmail.com. Research: Anglican/British ecclesiastical, classic Maya.

Durham, **Lofty**, *Western Michigan*. Email: lofton. durham@wmich.edu.

Durika, **Nathan**. Norfolk, VA. Email: durika1@ yahoo.com.

Durrill, **Wayne K.**, *Cincinnati*. Email: wayne. durrill@uc.edu.

Dursteler, **Eric R**, *Brigham Young*. Provo, UT. Email: ericd@byu.edu. Research: Mediterranean foodways, Mediterranean language and communication.

Durston, **Alan**, *York, Can.* Email: durston@yorku. ca.

Dusch, **Charles Donald**, **Jr.** USAF Academy, CO. Affil: US Air Force Acad. Email: charles.dusch@ usafa.edu. Research: Great War, gender roles in commemoration.

Duskin, **J. Eric**, *Christopher Newport*. Email: eduskin@cnu.edu.

Dutcher, **Stephen**, *New Brunswick*. Email: sdutcher@unb.ca.

Dutra, **Francis A.**, *California, Santa Barbara*. Email: dutra@history.ucsb.edu.

Dutt, **Rajeshwari**. Mandi, India. Affil: Indian Inst. of Tech., Mandi. Email: rdutt@iitmandi.ac.in. Research: 19th-c Yucatan, indigenous studies.

Dutton, **Paul V.**, *Northern Arizona*. Email: paul. dutton@nau.edu.

Duus, **Peter**, *Stanford*. Email: pduus@stanford. edu.

DuVal, **Kathleen**, *North Carolina, Chapel Hill*. Chapel Hill, NC. Email: duval@unc.edu.

Duvall, **William E.**, *Willamette*. Email: bduvall@ willamette.edu.

Duvick, **Brian**, *Colorado Colorado Springs*. Email: bduvick@uccs.edu.

Dweck, **Yaacob H.**, *Princeton*. Email: jdweck@ princeton.edu.

Dworkin, **Dennis L.**, *Nevada, Reno*. Reno, NV. Email: dworkin@unr.edu. Research: cultural theory, modern Britain.

Dwyer, **Ellen**, *Indiana*. Email: dwyer@indiana. edu.

Dwyer, **Erin Austin**, *Oakland*. Email: dwyer@ oakland.edu.

Dwyer, **John Joseph**, *Duquesne*. Email: dwyer@ duq.edu.

Dwyer-McNulty, **Sally**. Poughkeepsie, NY. Affil: Marist. Email: sally.dwyer-mcnulty@marist. edu.

Dwyer-Ryan, **Meaghan**, *South Carolina Aiken*. Email: mdwyerryan@usca.edu.

Dyck, **Erika**, *Saskatchewan*. Email: erika.dyck@ usask.ca.

Dyck, **Harvey L.**, *Toronto*. Email: hldyck@chass. utoronto.ca.

Dyck, **Jason Chad**, *Western Ontario*. St. Catharines, ON, Canada. Email: jdyck3@ uwo.ca; dyckjc@hotmail.com. Research: Spanish colonial historiography, Francisco de Florencia.

Dyczok, **Marta**, *Western Ontario*. Email: mdyczok@uwo.ca.

Dye, **Alan**, *Columbia (Hist.)*. Email: ad245@ columbia.edu.

Dye, **Keith Anthony**. Detroit, MI. Affil: Michigan, Dearborn. Email: keithdye@hotmail.com. Research: African American, US foreign policy/empire.

Dyke, **Bradley F.** Lees Summit, MO. Affil: Hawkeye Comm. Coll. Email: bfdyke@msn. com.

Dykema, **Peter**, *Arkansas Tech*. Email: pdykema@atu.edu.

Dykes, **De Witt S.**, **Jr.**, *Oakland*. Rochester, MI. Email: dykes@oakland.edu. Research: African Americans in Michigan, biography and family.

Dykstra, **Maura D.**, *California Inst. of Tech.* Email: maura@caltech.edu.

Dykstra, **Robert**, *SUNY, Albany*. Email: dykstra39@aol.com.

Dym, **Jeffrey A.**, *California State, Sacramento*. Email: dym@csus.edu.

Dym, **Jordana**, *Skidmore*. Email: jdym@ skidmore.edu.

Dymond, **Russell Floyd**, **Jr.** Aurora, CO. Affil: Denver Police Department. Email: dymondr@ netzero.net.

Dyreson, **Mark**, *Penn State*. Email: mxd52@psu. edu.

Dyson, **Stephen Lee**. Buffalo, NY. Affil: SUNY, Buffalo. Email: cldyson@buffalo.edu.

Dzamba, **Anne O.** Westtown, PA. Email: aodz@ aol.com.

Dzanic, **Dzavid**, *Austin Peay State*. Email: dzanicd@apsu.edu.

Dziedziak, **Caryll Batt**, *Nevada, Las Vegas*. Las Vegas, NV. Email: caryll.dziedziak@unlv. edu. Research: US women, women's political cultures.

Dzuback, **Mary Ann**, *Washington, St. Louis*. Email: madzubac@wustl.edu.

Dzurec, **David J.**, **III**, *Scranton*. Scranton, PA. Email: david.dzurec@scranton.edu. Research: foreign relations in early Republic, American Jesuits.

E e

Eacott, **Jonathan P.**, *California, Riverside*. Riverside, CA. Email: jeacott@ucr.edu. Research: British Empire/India trade, 18th-c Britain and America.

Eads, **Kathy A.** Pasadena, TX. Affil: J. Frank Dobie High Sch. Email: kaeads@sbcglobal.net.

Eagan, **Curtis John**. Herriman, UT. Email: curtis. eagan@gmail.com.

Eagan, **Eileen M**. Portland, ME. Affil: Southern Maine. Email: eileen.eagan@maine.edu. Research: Irish and Irish-American women, women and public art.

Eagle, **Marc V.**, *Western Kentucky*. Email: marc. eagle@wku.edu.

Eagles, **Charles W.**, *Mississippi*. Email: eagles@ olemiss.edu.

Eaglin, **Jennifer**, *Ohio State*. Email: eaglin.5@ osu.edu.

Eakin, **Marshall C.**, *Vanderbilt*. Nashville, TN. Email: marshall.c.eakin@vanderbilt.edu. Research: nationalism and nation-building, Brazil.

Eamon, **William**, *New Mexico State*. Email: weamon@nmsu.edu.

Earenfight, **Theresa M.**, *Seattle*. Seattle, WA. Email: theresa@seattleu.edu. Research: queenship/kingship/monarchy, political.

Earle, **Susan**, *Arthur and Elizabeth Schlesinger Library*. Email: searle@radcliffe.harvard.edu.

Earles, **Rebecca**. Houston, TX. Affil: Rice. Email: rearles93@gmail.com.

Earley-Spadoni, **Tiffany**, *Central Florida*. Email: Tiffany.Earley-Spadoni@ucf.edu.

Earls, **Averill E**. North Tonawanda, NY. Affil: Mercyhurst. Email: averille@buffalo.edu. Research: queer Dublin, gay tourism in Ireland.

Easley, **Roxanne I.**, *Central Washington*. Email: easleyr@cwu.edu.

Eastman, **Carolyn**, *Virginia Commonwealth*. Richmond, VA. Email: ceastman@vcu.edu; carolyn.eastman@gmail.com. Research: gender, media.

Eastman, **Scott B.**, *Creighton*. Email: seastman@ creighton.edu.

Easton, **Laird M.**, *California State, Chico*. Email: leaston@csuchico.edu.

Easum, **Taylor Matthew**. Stevens Point, WI. Affil: Wisconsin, Stevens Point. Email: teasum@ uwsp.edu. Research: modern Thailand, Southeast Asian cities.

Eatmon, **Myisha S.**, *South Carolina, Columbia*.

Eaton, **Brynnlee Blair**. Fort Washington, MD. Email: btervet@gmail.com.

Eaton, **David**, *Grand Valley State*. Allendale, MI. Email: eatond@gvsu.edu. Research: Africa.

Eaton, Joe. Pryor, OK. Affil: National Chengchi. Email: wjeaton@hotmail.com. Research: American nationalism, Anglo-American literary relations.

Eaton, Nicole M., *Boston Coll.* Email: nicole. eaton.2@bc.edu.

Eaton, Richard M., *Arizona.* Email: reaton@u. arizona.edu.

Eaves, Shannon Camille, *Charleston.* Email: eavessc@cofc.edu.

Ebbeler, Jennifer V., *Texas, Austin.* Email: jebbeler@austin.utexas.edu.

Eberle, Jared L. Stillwater, OK. Affil: Oklahoma State. Email: jared.eberle@okstate.edu. Research: native rights movements, Native American identity.

Eberle, Susan, *Hist. New Orleans.* Email: susane@hnoc.org.

Ebersole, Gary L., *Missouri–Kansas City.* Email: ebersoleg@umkc.edu.

Ebert, Christopher C., *Brooklyn, CUNY.* Brooklyn, NY. Email: cebert@brooklyn.cuny.edu; christophercebert@gmail.com. Research: Salvador da Bahia, colonial Brazil.

Ebner, Michael H., *Lake Forest.* Lake Forest, IL. Email: ebner@lakeforest.edu. Research: rapid suburban growth 1945-90, metropolitan Chicago Illinois.

Ebner, Michael R., *Syracuse.* Email: mebner@ syr.edu.

Ebrey, Patricia Buckley, *Washington, Seattle.* Seattle, WA. Email: ebrey@uw.edu. Research: early imperial China, social.

Echenberg, Myron, *McGill.* Email: myron. echenberg@mcgill.ca.

Echeverri, Marcela, *Yale.* Email: marcela. echeverri@yale.edu.

Echols, Alice, *Southern California.* Email: echols@usc.edu.

Eckelmann Berghel, Susan, *Tennessee, Chattanooga.* Email: susan-eckelmann@utc. edu.

Eckert, Astrid M., *Emory.* Atlanta, GA. Email: aeckert@emory.edu. Research: Federal Republic of Germany, German borderlands.

Eckert, Carter J. Cambridge, MA. Affil: Harvard. Email: eckert@fas.harvard.edu. Research: modern Korea, Korean militarism.

Eckert, Ryan. Brick, NJ. Affil: Monmouth. Email: ryanjeckert@icloud.com.

Eckes, Alfred E., **Jr.**, *Ohio.* Email: eckes777@ gmail.com.

Eckhardt, David. Saint Johnsbury, VT. Affil: St. Johnsbury Academy. Email: deckhardt@ stjacademy.org.

Eckhardt, Marcus, *Herbert Hoover Presidential Library.* Email: marcus.eckhardt@nara.gov.

Eckroth, Stephanie L., *US Dept. of State.*

Eckstein, Arthur M., *Maryland, Coll. Park.* Email: ameckst1@umd.edu.

Ector, Richard Haley. Sterling, VA. Affil: Envisioning Hist., Inc. Email: rick.ector@ envisioninghistory.org. Research: Battle of the Atlantic.

Eddleman, William R., *State Hist. Soc. of Missouri.* Email: EddlemanW@shsmo.org.

Eddy, Matthew Daniel. Durham, United Kingdom. Affil: Durham. Email: m.d.eddy@ durham.ac.uk. Research: modern science/ medicine/technology, modern print/ manuscript/visual culture.

Ede, Andrew G., *Alberta.* Email: aede@ualberta. ca.

Edelman, Robert, *California, San Diego.* Email: redelman@ucsd.edu.

Edelson, S. Max, *Virginia.* Charlottesville, VA. Email: edelson@virginia.edu. Research: British American geography and cartography, Martimes/Floridas/Windward Islands.

Edelstein, Dan. Stanford, CA. Affil: Stanford. Email: danedels@stanford.edu. Research: Enlightenment rights, revolutionary authority.

Edelstein, Melvin A., *William Paterson.*

Eden, Jason E., *St. Cloud State.* Email: jeeden@ stcloudstate.edu.

Eden, Jeffrey, *St. Mary's, Md.* Email: jeeden@ smcm.edu.

Edenfield, Nate. Washington, DC. Affil: American. Email: ne6111a@american.edu.

Eder, Sandra, *California, Berkeley.* Email: s.eder@ berkeley.edu.

Ederer, Martin, *SUNY, Buffalo State.* Email: ederermf@buffalostate.edu.

Edgar, Adrienne, *California, Santa Barbara.* Email: edgar@history.ucsb.edu.

Edgar, Walter B., *South Carolina, Columbia.* Email: edgar@mailbox.sc.edu.

Edgerton-Tarpley, Kathryn, *San Diego State.* Email: edgerton@sdsu.edu.

Edgren, Allison, *Loyola, New Orleans.*

Edington, Claire, *California, San Diego.* Email: cedington@ucsd.edu.

Edison, Paul, *Texas, El Paso.* El Paso, TX. Email: pedison@utep.edu. Research: France, science and empire.

Edmonds, Kelton R., *California, Pa.* Email: edmonds_k@calu.edu.

Edmondson, C. Earl, *Davidson.* Email: eaedmondson@davidson.edu.

Edmondson, Jonathan C., *York, Can.* Email: jedmond@yorku.ca.

Edsall, Nicholas C., *Virginia.*

Edson, Evelyn. Scottsville, VA. Affil: Piedmont Virginia Comm. Coll. Email: eedson@pvcc.edu. Research: medieval cartography.

Edwards, Carl N., **Esq.** Temple, TX. Affil: Baylor. Email: cedwards@socialaw.com. Research: behavioral theory, American communism.

Edwards, David Wayne, *Arkansas, Fayetteville.* Email: dedwards@uark.edu.

Edwards, Erika Denise, *North Carolina, Charlotte.* Charlotte, NC. Email: eedwar27@ uncc.edu. Research: African diaspora in Argentina, childhood and motherhood.

Edwards, Frank T., *California, Pa.*

Edwards, Gary T., *Arkansas State.* Email: gedwards@astate.edu.

Edwards, Jane, *Loyola, Md.* Email: jedwards@ loyola.edu.

Edwards, Jason Lee. Carrboro, NC. Affil: North Carolina, Chapel Hill. Email: jason.l.edwards82@gmail.com.

Edwards, Jason R., *Grove City.* Email: jredwards@gcc.edu.

Edwards, Jennifer C., *Manhattan.* Email: jennifer.edwards@manhattan.edu.

Edwards, Jerome E., *Nevada, Reno.* Email: jedwards@unr.nevada.edu.

Edwards, Kathryn A., *South Carolina, Columbia.* Columbia, SC. Email: kathrynedwards@sc.edu. Research: natural and supernatural, social discipline.

Edwards, Kathryn, *Tulane.* New Orleans, LA. Email: medward5@tulane.edu. Research: colonial reform, Guernut Commission.

Edwards, Laura F., *Duke.* Durham, NC. Email: ledwards@duke.edu. Research: legal, US women.

Edwards, Lillie J. Montclair, NJ. Affil: Drew. Email: ledwards@drew.edu. Research: African American missionaries, African American women and education.

Edwards, Lisa M. Lowell, MA. Affil: Massachusetts, Lowell. Email: Lisa_Edwards@ uml.edu. Research: political parties, Catholic Church.

Edwards, Owen Dudley. Edinburgh, United Kingdom. Affil: Edinburgh.

Edwards, Rebecca A. R. Rochester, NY. Affil: Rochester Inst. of Tech. Email: edwards.rar@ gmail.com. Research: Deaf culture.

Edwards, Rebecca B., *Vassar.* Email: reedwards@vassar.edu.

Edwards, Tai. Overland Park, KS. Affil: Johnson County Comm. Coll. Email: taied@jccc.edu.

Edwards, William Pearson. Mattituck, NY. Affil: SUNY, Stony Brook. Email: peconic@gmail. com. Research: pilgrimage, Crusades.

Eeckhout, Stephanie. Severn, MD. Affil: American Military. Email: xenafatboylo@ gmail.com. Research: ancient and classical, ancient Celts.

Effland, Anne B. Myersville, MD. Affil: US Dept. of Agriculture. Email: anne.effland@usda.gov. Research: US agricultural policy, agricultural trade and development.

Efford, Alison Clark, *Marquette.* Email: alison. efford@marquette.edu.

Effros, Bonnie, *Florida.* Email: beffros@ufl.edu.

Efron, John, *California, Berkeley.* Email: efron@ berkeley.edu.

Egan, Michael, *McMaster.* Email: egan@ mcmaster.ca.

Egas, Oswaldo Leigh. Orange Beach, AL. Affil: West Georgia. Email: jenniferwh@yahoo. com. Research: backcountry before American Revolution, American women to 1877.

Eger, A. Asa, *North Carolina, Greensboro.* Email: aaeger@uncg.edu.

Egerton, Douglas R., *Le Moyne.* Email: egertodr@lemoyne.edu.

Egge, James, *Eastern Michigan.* Email: jegge@ emich.edu.

Egger, Vernon O., *Georgia Southern.* Email: voegger@georgiasouthern.edu.

Eghigian, Greg, *Penn State.* University Park, PA. Email: gae2@psu.edu. Research: psychiatry/psychotherapy/psychology, UFOs/ paranormal.

Egler, David G., *Western Illinois.* Email: DG-Egler@wiu.edu.

Eglin, John A., *Montana.* Email: john.eglin@ umontana.edu.

Egnal, Marc M., *York, Can.* Email: megnal@ yorku.ca.

Ehlers, Benjamin, *Georgia.* Email: behlers@uga. edu.

Ehlers, Carol Jean. Port Ludlow, WA.

Ehlers, Maren Annika, *North Carolina, Charlotte.* Charlotte, NC. Email: mehlers@uncc.edu. Research: poor relief in early modern Japan, early modern Japanese social.

Ehret, Christopher, *UCLA.* Email: ehret@history. ucla.edu.

Ehrhardt, George R. Durham, NC. Email: gre120@aol.com. Research: popularization of science, science in American culture.

Ehrick, *Christine T.*, *Louisville*. Louisville, KY. Email: ehrick@louisville.edu. Research: Latin American gender and state, Latin American women and radio.

Ehrlich, **Carl S.**, *York, Can.* Email: ehrlich@yorku.ca.

Ehrstine, **Glenn**, *Iowa*. Email: glenn-ehrstine@uiowa.edu.

Eichbauer, **Melodie Harris**, *Florida Gulf Coast*. Email: meichbauer@fgcu.edu.

Eichhorn, **Mary Lou**, *Hist. New Orleans*. Email: marylou@hnoc.org.

Eichler, *Jeremy*. Newton, MA. Affil: NEH. Email: jeremy.eichler@gmail.com.

Eichner, **Carolyn J.**, *Wisconsin-Milwaukee*. Email: eichner@uwm.edu.

Eid, **Leroy V.**, *Dayton*. Email: leroy.eid@notes.udayton.edu.

Eidahl, *Kyle*. Tallahassee, FL. Affil: Florida A&M. Email: kyle.eidahl@famu.edu.

Eifler, *Mark A.*, *Portland*. Portland, OR. Email: eiflerm@up.edu. Research: geopolitics of world exploration, US colonial western frontier.

Eilers, **Sarah**, *National Library of Medicine*. Email: sarah.eilers@nih.gov.

Einbinder, *Susan L.* Storrs Mansfield, CT. Affil: Connecticut, Storrs. Email: susan.einbinder@uconn.edu. Research: expulsion poetry/Jews from France 1306.

Eire, **Carlos M. N.**, *Yale*. Email: carlos.eire@yale.edu.

Eisel, *Christine L.*, *Memphis*. Berkey, OH. Email: cleisel@memphis.edu. Research: women and law in colonial Virginia.

Eisen, **Jordan Koerth**. Seattle, WA. Affil: Seattle. Email: eisenj1@seattleu.edu.

Eisen, **Mimi**, *Hist. Assoc.* Email: meisen@historyassociates.com.

Eisen, **Sydney**. Willowdale, ON, Canada. Affil: York, Can. Email: seisen@yorku.ca.

Eisenberg, **Andrew**, *Northeastern Illinois*. Email: a-eisenberg@neiu.edu.

Eisenberg, **Ariel**, *Rhodes*. Email: eisenberga@rhodes.edu.

Eisenberg, *Carolyn*, *Hofstra*. Brooklyn, NY. Email: carolyn.eisenberg@hofstra.edu; hiscze@aol.com. Research: 20th-c foreign relations, Nixon-Kissinger era.

Eisenberg, *Ellen M.*, *Willamette*. Salem, OR. Email: eeisenbe@willamette.edu. Research: Jewish community in American West, ethnic relations in American West.

Eisenberg, **Laurie Zittrain**, *Carnegie Mellon*. Email: le3a@andrew.cmu.edu.

Eisenberg, **Merle**. Annapolis, MD. Affil: National Socio-Environmental Synthesis Center. Email: merlee@princeton.edu.

Eisenman, **Harry J.**, *Missouri Science and Tech.* Email: hje@mst.edu.

Eisenstadt, **Marvin**. Syosset, NY. Research: bereavement, parental loss.

Eisenstadt, **Peter C.** Clemson, SC. Affil: Howard Thurman Papers Project. Email: peisenst@gmail.com. Research: African American culture and history, New York state.

Eiss, **Paul**, *Carnegie Mellon*. Email: pke@andrew.cmu.edu.

Eissenstat, **Howard L.**, *St. Lawrence*. Email: heissenstat@stlawu.edu.

Ejikeme, **Anene**, *Trinity, Tex.* Email: aejikeme@trinity.edu.

Ekbladh, *David K.* Medford, MA. Affil: Tufts. Email: david.ekbladh@tufts.edu. Research: US and world, modern US.

Ekechi, **Felix K.**, *Kent State*. Email: fekechi@kent.edu.

Eken, *Mattias*. Wokingham, United Kingdom. Affil: St Andrews. Email: mjee@st-andrews.ac.uk. Research: culture wars, weapons of mass destruction.

Ekinci, *Arianne Marie*. Chapel Hill, NC. Affil: North Carolina, Chapel Hill. Email: ariannem@live.unc.edu.

Ekirch, *A. Roger*, *Virginia Tech.* Email: arekirch@vt.edu.

Eklof, *A. Ben*, *Indiana*. Email: eklof@indiana.edu.

Eklund, *Christopher R.* Winston-Salem, NC. Affil: West Forsyth High Sch. Email: creklund@gmail.com.

Ekmekcioglu, **Lerna**, *MIT*. Email: lerna@mit.edu.

Eksteins, **Modris**, *Toronto*. Email: eksteins@utsc.utoronto.ca.

El Hamel, **Chouki**, *Arizona State*. Email: chouki.elhamel@asu.edu.

El Shakry, *Omnia*, *California, Davis*. Oakland, CA. Email: oselshakry@ucdavis.edu. Research: modern Arab and European intellectual, gender and sexuality/Middle East.

Elbl, *Ivana*, *Trent*. Email: ielbl@trentu.ca.

Elbourne, **Elizabeth**, *McGill*. Email: elizabeth.elbourne@mcgill.ca.

Elder, **E. Rozanne**, *Western Michigan*. Email: e.rozanne.elder@wmich.edu.

Elder, **Hannah**, *Massachusetts Hist. Soc.* Email: helder@masshist.org.

Elder, **Robert**, *Baylor*. Email: robert_elder@baylor.edu.

Elder, *Sace E.*, *Eastern Illinois*. Charleston, IL. Email: seelder@eiu.edu. Research: criminal violence in Weimar Germany.

Elder, **Tanya**, *American Jewish Hist. Soc.* Email: telder@ajhs.cjh.org.

Eldevik, **John T.**, *Hamilton*. Email: jeldevik@hamilton.edu.

Elena, **Eduardo D.**, *Miami*. Email: edelena@miami.edu.

Eley, *Geoff*, *Michigan, Ann Arbor*. Ann Arbor, MI. Email: ghe@umich.edu. Research: European left 1800-2000, British and German history and nation.

Elfenbein, **Caleb**, *Grinnell*. Email: elfenbei@grinnell.edu.

Elfenbein, **Jessica I.**, *South Carolina, Columbia*. Email: jessicae@mailbox.sc.edu.

Elfenbein, *Madeleine*. Goettingen, Germany. Affil: Goettingen. Email: elfenbein@uchicago.edu.

El-Hibri, *Tayeb*. Amherst, MA. Affil: Massachusetts Amherst. Email: telhibri@judnea.umass.edu.

Elias, *Christopher Michael*, *St. Olaf*. Minneapolis, MN. Email: christophermelias@gmail.com. Research: modern US.

Elias, *Megan Joanna*. Boston, MA. Affil: Boston Univ. Email: mjelias@bu.edu. Research: food, gender.

Eliason, *William T.* Washington, DC. Affil: National Defense. Email: william.t.eliason.civ@msc.ndu.edu.

Eliot, *Lewis Bartholomew Heneke*. Columbia, SC. Affil: South Carolina, Columbia. Email: leliot@email.sc.edu. Research: kidnapping in British Caribbean, emotions of US emancipation.

Elison, *William*, *California, Santa Barbara*. Email: welison@religion.ucsb.edu.

Elizondo-Schroepfer, *Liz*, *Virginia Military Inst.* Email: elizondol@vmi.edu.

El-Kati, **Mahmoud**, *Macalester*.

Elkin, *Daniel*, *Texas-Rio Grande Valley*. Email: daniel.elkin@utrgv.edu.

Elkind, *Jessica B.* Orinda, CA. Affil: San Francisco State. Email: jelkind@sfsu.edu. Research: American diplomatic, 20th-c US.

Elkind, **Sarah**, *San Diego State*. Email: selkind@sdsu.edu.

Elkins, **Carole Diane**. Studio City, CA. Affil: UCLA. Email: cael.512@ucla.edu. Research: visual culture, cultural memory.

Elkins, **Caroline M.**, *Harvard (Hist.)*. Email: elkins@fas.harvard.edu.

el-Leithy, **Tamer M.**, *Johns Hopkins (Hist.); NYU*. Email: tamer.elleithy@jhu.edu; tel3@nyu.edu.

Elleman, *Bruce A.*, *Naval War Coll.* Portsmouth, RI. Email: bruce.elleman@usnwc.edu. Research: China and Japan, Russia.

Eller, *Anne*, *Yale*. Email: anne.eller@yale.edu.

Eller, *Saword Broyles*. Liberty, NC. Email: histoirededame@gmail.com. Research: women soldiers of American Civil War, slavery/manumission/abolition.

Ellington, *Jason*. Fredericksburg, VA. Affil: King George High Sch. Email: jellington1971@gmail.com.

Elliot-Meisel, *Elizabeth B.*, *Creighton*. Email: elmeis@creighton.edu.

Elliott, *Bruce S.*, *Carleton, Can.* Email: Bruce.Elliott@carleton.ca.

Elliott, *Charles*, *Southeastern Louisiana*. Email: cnelliott@selu.edu.

Elliott, *Colin*, *Indiana*. Email: cpe@indiana.edu.

Elliott, *Dyan H.*, *Northwestern*. Email: d-elliott@northwestern.edu.

Elliott, *Emily J.*, *Kalamazoo*. Lansing, MI. Email: elliottemilyj@gmail.com. Research: labor migration, Soviet.

Elliott, **Jessica Marin**, *Missouri State*. Email: JessicaElliott@MissouriState.edu.

Elliott, **Mark C.**, *Harvard (Hist.)*. Email: elliott3@fas.harvard.edu.

Elliott, **Mark E.**, *North Carolina, Greensboro*. Email: meelliot@uncg.edu.

Elliott, *Mary, Esq.* Silver Spring, MD. Affil: Smithsonian Inst. Email: Marynelliott@aol.com. Research: African American, migration and community development.

Elliott, *Richard Paul*. Shaker Heights, OH. Affil: Kent State. Email: rpe01@aol.com. Research: Miguel Primo de Rivera.

Ellis, *Alexander Hampton*. Burlington, VT. Affil: Vermont. Email: ahellis22@gmail.com.

Ellis, *Clyde*, *Elon*. Email: ellisrc@elon.edu.

Ellis, **David L.**, *Augustana*. Email: davidellis@augustana.edu.

Ellis, **Donald W.**, *Memphis*.

Ellis, **Elizabeth N.**, *NYU*. Email: ene1@nyu.edu.

Ellis, **Jack D.**, *Alabama, Huntsville*. Email: jellis1789@comcast.net.

Ellis, *John P.*, *Bemidji State*. Bemidji, MN. Email: jellis@bemidjistate.edu. Research: religion in early Republic, young men in early Republic.

Ellis, **Joseph J.**, *III*, *Mount Holyoke*. Email: jellis@mtholyoke.edu.

Ellis, **Mark Robert**, *Nebraska, Kearney*. Email: ellismr@unk.edu.

Ellis, *Rebecca Ann*, *Washington State, Pullman*. Email: rebecca.ellisdodson@wsu.edu.

Ellis, Reginald K. Tallahassee, FL. Affil: Florida A&M. Email: reginald.ellis@famu.edu. Research: US since 1865, African American.

Ellis, Richard A. Mill Valley, CA. Email: a.r.ellis@att.net.

Ellis, Tomas Javier. Jacksonville, FL. Affil: North Florida. Email: tjellis1225@gmail.com. Research: political/Early Republic, sectionalism/politics/race.

Ellis, William E., *Eastern Kentucky*. Email: william.ellis@eku.edu.

Ellison, Christopher Alan. Houston, TX. Affil: Rice. Email: christopher.ellison@gmail.com. Research: comparative modernization, political and economic development.

Ellison, Curtis W., *Miami, Ohio*. Email: ellisocw@miamioh.edu.

Ellison, Karin D. Tempe, AZ. Affil: Arizona State. Email: karin.ellison@asu.edu. Research: American engineering, water resources.

Ellisor, John, *Columbus State*. Email: ellisor_john@columbusstate.edu.

Ellithorpe, Corey James, *North Carolina, Wilmington*.

Ellstrand, Nathan. Chicago, IL. Affil: Loyola, Chicago. Email: nellstrand@luc.edu. Research: sanctuary movement, Mexico-US borderlands.

Elm, Susanna K., *California, Berkeley*. Berkeley, CA. Email: elm@berkeley.edu. Research: slavery and Christianity in late antiquity, ancient medicine.

Elman, Benjamin A., *UCLA*. Email: elman@history.ucla.edu.

Elmer, Hannah. New York, NY. Affil: Columbia. Email: hannah.m.elmer@gmail.com.

Elmore, Bartow Jerome, *Ohio State*.

Elmore, Kathleen C. Marysville, PA. Affil: Wilson. Email: vajgs@aol.com.

Elmore, Maggie J., *Sam Houston State*. Huntsville, TX. Email: mxe053@shsu.edu; m.elmore@berkeley.edu. Research: migration/immigration, religion.

Elofson, Warren M., *Calgary*. Email: elofson@ucalgary.ca.

Elovitz, Paul, *Ramapo*. Email: pelovitz@ramapo.edu.

Elphick, Richard H., *Wesleyan*. Email: relphick@wesleyan.edu.

Els, Brian, *Portland*. Email: els@up.edu.

Elsey, Brenda, *Hofstra*. Hempstead, NY. Email: brenda.elsey@hofstra.edu. Research: 20th-c Chile local politics/popular culture, urban history and civic associations.

Elshakry, Marwa S., *Columbia (Hist.)*. Email: me2335@columbia.edu.

Eltabib, Sarah. Garden City, NY. Affil: Adelphi. Email: seltabib@adelphi.edu.

Eltis, David, *Emory*. Email: deltis@emory.edu.

Elukin, Jonathan M., *Trinity Coll., Conn.* Email: jonathan.elukin@trincoll.edu.

Eluwawalage, Damayanthie. Reading, PA. Affil: Delaware State. Email: deluwawalage@desu.edu. Research: theories/philosophies of fashion/costume, aviation.

Elvins, Sarah Lynn, *Manitoba*. Email: sarah.elvins@umanitoba.ca.

Elwood, Ann, *California State, San Marcos*. Email: aelwood@csusm.edu.

Ely, Christopher David, *Florida Atlantic*. Jupiter, FL. Email: cely@fau.edu. Research: urban, political undergrounds.

Ely, Melvin Patrick, *William and Mary*. Email: mpelyx@wm.edu.

Elzey, Christopher, *George Mason*. Email: celzey@gmu.edu.

Emberton, Carole T., *SUNY, Buffalo*. Buffalo, NY. Email: emberton@buffalo.edu. Research: Civil War, Reconstruction.

Emch-Deriaz, Antoinette. Vancouver, WA. Affil: Florida. Email: aedz1959@gmail.com. Research: 18th-c European medicine, 18th-c Switzerland and Geneva.

Emeagwali, Gloria, *Central Connecticut State*. Email: emeagwali@ccsu.edu.

Emerson, Roger L., *Western Ontario*. Email: emerson@uwo.ca.

Emery, George N., *Western Ontario*. Email: emery@uwo.ca.

Emery, Jacqueline. New York, NY. Affil: SUNY, Old Westbury. Email: emeryj@oldwestbury.edu.

Emiralioglu, Pinar, *Sam Houston State*. Email: mpe005@shsu.edu.

Emmerich, Lisa E., *California State, Chico*. Email: lemmerich@csuchico.edu.

Emmons, David M., *Montana*. Email: david.emmons@umontana.edu.

Emmons, Terence, *Stanford*. Email: ektxe1@gmail.com.

Emon, Anver M., *Toronto*. Email: anver.emon@utoronto.ca.

Emre, Side, *Texas A&M*. Email: sideemre@tamu.edu.

Emrich, John S. Rockville, MD. Affil: American Assoc. of Immunologists. Email: jemrich@aai.org. Research: immunology, professional societies/organizations.

Enacar, Ekin. Chicago, IL. Affil: Chicago. Email: ekin@uchicago.edu.

Enax, Peggy. San Antonio, TX. Affil: ACCD Northeast Lakeview. Email: penax@alamo.edu.

Enck, Henry S., *Central Connecticut State*.

Endelman, Todd, *Michigan, Ann Arbor*. Email: endelman@umich.edu.

Enderle, Kimberly A. Northampton, MA. Email: enderleka@gmail.com.

Endicott, Elizabeth, *Middlebury*. Email: endicott@middlebury.edu.

Endo, Yasuo T. Tokyo, Japan. Email: endou@ask.c.u-tokyo.ac.jp.

Endres, David J., *American Catholic Hist. Assoc.* Email: dendres@athenaeum.edu.

Endy, Christopher, *California State, Los Angeles*. Email: cendy@calstatela.edu.

Engel, Barbara A., *Colorado, Boulder*. Email: barbara.engel@colorado.edu.

Engel, David, *NYU*. New York, NY. Email: de2@nyu.edu. Research: international diplomatic Jewish question, eastern European interethnic relations.

Engel, Elisabeth, *German Hist. Inst.* Washington, DC. Email: engel@ghi-dc.org. Research: early and modern North America, postcolonial studies.

Engel, Elizabeth, *State Hist. Soc. of Missouri*. Email: engelel@shsmo.org.

Engel, Jeffrey A., *Southern Methodist*. Dallas, TX. Email: jaengel@smu.edu. Research: American political.

Engel, Katherine Carte, *Southern Methodist*. Dallas, TX. Email: kengel@smu.edu. Research: religion in American Revolution, international Protestantism.

Engel, Mary Ella, *Western Carolina*. Email: mengel@email.wcu.edu.

Engelbourg, Saul. Newton, MA. Affil: Boston Univ.

Engelhardt, Carroll L., *Concordia Coll.* Moorhead, MN. Email: cengelha@cord.edu. Research: American thought and culture, modern England.

Engelhart, Anne, *Arthur and Elizabeth Schlesinger Library*. Email: annee@radcliffe.harvard.edu.

Engels, Donald, *Arkansas, Fayetteville*.

Engelstein, Gil. Chicago, IL. Affil: Northwestern. Email: GilEngelstein2020@u.northwestern.edu.

Engelstein, Laura, *Yale*. Chicago, IL. Email: laura.engelstein@yale.edu. Research: Russia.

Engen, Darel Tai, *California State, San Marcos*. Email: dengen@csusm.edu.

Engerman, David C. New Haven, CT. Affil: Yale. Email: david.engerman@yale.edu. Research: American foreign policy, international and cultural.

Engl, Rachel A. Bethlehem, PA. Affil: Lehigh. Email: rae210@lehigh.edu. Research: American Revolution, manhood and gender.

Engle, Stephen D., *Florida Atlantic*. Email: engle@fau.edu.

Englebert, Robert A., *Saskatchewan*. Email: r.englebert@usask.ca.

Englehart, Stephen F. Los Angeles, CA. Affil: California State Polytechnic. Email: sfenglehart@cpp.edu. Research: ideologies, world history theory.

Englemann, Stephen, *Illinois, Chicago*. Email: sengelma@uic.edu.

Engler, Mark. Beatrice, NE. Affil: Homestead National Monument of America. Email: home_information@nps.gov.

English, Allan Douglas, *Queen's, Can.* Email: english_a@rmc.ca.

English, Beth Anne. Pennington, NJ. Email: baengl@verizon.net.

English, Charles J., IV. Sierra Vista, AZ. Email: charlie.j.english@outlook.com.

English, Edward Donald. Santa Barbara, CA. Affil: California, Santa Barbara. Email: english@history.ucsb.edu. Research: medieval, world.

English, John R., *Waterloo*. Email: jenglish@uwaterloo.ca.

English, John (Jack) A. Kingston, ON, Canada. Email: jaenglish@cogeco.ca. Research: WWII Western Front, Canadian Army.

English, Linda C., *Texas-Rio Grande Valley*. Email: linda.english@utrgv.edu.

English, Paul G. Newmarket, NH. Affil: Southern New Hampshire. Email: paul.english@snhu.edu.

English, Peter, *Duke*. Email: penglish@duke.edu.

English, Sara. Marshall, IL. Affil: Eastern Illinois. Email: senglish@eiu.edu. Research: Tudor/Reformation/Stuarts/Jacobite, gender transportation/witchcraft.

English, Thomas R. Langhorne, PA. Affil: George Sch. Email: trenglish78@gmail.com. Research: army organization and education, Tasker H. Bliss.

Englund, Steven L. Vestal, NY. Affil: American, Paris. Email: amdgsle@aol.com.

Engstrom, Eric J. Berlin, Germany. Affil: Humboldt, Berlin. Email: eje@online.de. Research: forensic cultures in imperial Berlin.

Engwenyu, **Joseph**, *Eastern Michigan*. Email: jengwenyu@emich.edu.

Enke, **A. Finn**, *Wisconsin-Madison*. Email: aenke@wisc.edu.

Enlil, *Rhiannon*. New Orleans, LA. Affil: New Orleans. Email: renlil@uno.edu. Research: beverage/alcohol/liquor/cocktails.

Ennis, *William Thomas*, *III*. Catonsville, MD. Affil: Gallaudet. Email: william.ennis@gallaudet. edu. Research: European Deaf community 1700-1900, 1911 Nebraska oral law.

Enright, *Kelly*. Saint Augustine, FL. Affil: Flagler. Email: kenright@flagler.edu. Research: museums, nature.

Enríquez, *Sandra Ivette*, *Missouri–Kansas City*. Kansas City, MO. Email: enriquezs@umkc.edu. Research: urban, Chicana/o.

Ens, **Gerhard J.**, *Alberta*. Email: gens@ualberta. ca.

Enssle, **Manfred J.**, *Colorado State*. Email: manfred.enssle@colostate.edu.

Enstad, **Nan C.**, *Wisconsin-Madison*. Email: nenstad@wisc.edu.

Enstam, *Elizabeth York*. Dallas, TX. Email: enstam@sbcglobal.net. Research: woman suffrage, community.

Enszer, *Julie R*. Dover, FL. Email: JulieREnszer@ gmail.com.

Enteen, **George M.**, *Penn State*. Email: gxe1@ psu.edu.

Entenmann, **Robert E.**, *St. Olaf*. Email: entenman@stolaf.edu.

Enyeart, **John P.**, *Bucknell*. Email: jenyeart@ bucknell.edu.

Eow, *Gregory T*. Boston, MA. Affil: MIT. Email: gteddyeow@gmail.com.

Epp, **Marlene**, *Waterloo*. Email: mgepp@ uwaterloo.ca.

Epper, **Michael**, *US Air Force Acad*. Email: Michael.Epper@usafa.edu.

Epple, **Michael J.**, *Florida Gulf Coast*. Email: mepple@fgcu.edu.

Epprecht, **Marc A.**, *Queen's, Can*. Email: epprecht@queensu.ca.

Epps, **Kristen K.**, *Central Arkansas*. Email: kkepps@uca.edu.

Epstein, *Catherine A.*, *Amherst*. Amherst, MA. Email: caepstein@amherst.edu. Research: Nazi Germany.

Epstein, *Donald B*. Wilsonville, OR. Affil: Clackamas Comm. Coll. Email: epsteindone@ aol.com.

Epstein, *James A.*, *Vanderbilt*. Nashville, TN. Email: james.a.epstein@vanderbilt.edu. Research: modern Britain.

Epstein, **Katherine C.**, *Rutgers, Camden*. Email: kce17@camden.rutgers.edu.

Epstein, **Steven A.**, *Kansas*. Email: sae@ku.edu.

Erb, *Claude C*. Pottstown, PA. Email: curterb@ aol.com.

Erbelding, *Rebecca*. Hyattsville, MD. Affil: US Holocaust Memorial Museum. Email: rerbelding@gmail.com. Research: American response to Holocaust.

Erbig, *Jeffrey Alan*, *Jr*. Santa Cruz, CA. Affil: California, Santa Cruz. Email: erbig@ucsc.edu. Research: cartography and native peoples, Bourbon/Pombaline reforms.

Erby, **Kelly K.**, *Washburn*. Email: kelly.erby@ washburn.edu.

Ereline, *Ann*. Portland, OR. Email: aereline@ gmail.com. Research: Muller v. Oregon, US legal.

Erenberg, *Lewis A.*, *Loyola, Chicago*. Email: lerenbe@luc.edu.

Erenrich, *Susan J*. Arlington, VA. Email: ccscsusie@aol.com. Research: social movements, artists in movements of protest/ resistance.

Erfurth, *Nathaniel*. Soldotna, AK. Email: nathan@erfurth.co.

Ergene, **Bogac A.**, *Vermont*. Email: bogac. ergene@uvm.edu.

Erginbas, **Vefa**, *Providence*. Email: erginbas@ providence.edu.

Ericksen, **Robert P.**, *Pacific Lutheran*. Email: ericksrp@plu.edu.

Erickson, **Ansley T.**, *Columbia (Hist.)*. Email: erickson@tc.columbia.edu.

Erickson, **Brice**, *California, Santa Barbara*. Email: berickson@classics.ucsb.edu.

Erickson, **Bruce A.**, *Le Moyne*. Email: ericksba@ lemoyne.edu.

Erickson, **Christine K.**, *Purdue, Fort Wayne*. Email: ericksoc@pfw.edu.

Erickson, *Kirsten*. Sammamish, WA. Affil: King County Library System. Email: krerickson16@ gmail.com. Research: Ulster Women's Unionist Council, Gender and political participation.

Erickson, *Paul H.*, *Wesleyan*. Middletown, CT. Email: perickson@wesleyan.edu. Research: game theory and Cold War culture, scientific conceptions of history.

Ericson, *Steven J.*, *Dartmouth*. Hanover, NH. Email: steven.ericson@dartmouth.edu. Research: Japan, East Asia.

Erlacher, *Trevor F.* Pittsburgh, PA. Affil: Pittsburgh. Email: erlacher@email.unc.edu.

Erlank, **Natasha**, *Carleton, Can*. Email: natasha. erlank@carleton.ca.

Erlebacher, **Albert**, *DePaul*. Email: aerlebac@ depaul.edu.

Erling, *Maria E*. Gettysburg, PA. Affil: United Lutheran Seminary. Email: merling@uls.edu. Research: religious life of 19th-c immigrants, missionary movements and translation.

Ermakoff, *Ivan*, *Wisconsin-Madison*. Madison, WI. Email: ermakoff@ssc.wisc.edu. Research: interwar period in Europe, regime breakdown.

Ermarth, **H. Michael**, *Dartmouth*. Email: michael.ermarth@dartmouth.edu.

Ermer, *John T.*, *Jr*. El Portal, FL. Affil: Florida International. Email: jerme001@fiu.edu. Research: masculinity in 19th-c US, US intervention in Mexican Revolution.

Ermus, *Cindy*. Lethbridge, AB. Affil: Lethbridge. Email: cindy.ermus@uleth.ca. Research: Marseille plague in global context, 18th-c disasters.

Ernst, *Daniel R.*, *Georgetown*. Washington, DC. Email: ernst@georgetown.edu. Research: New Deal lawyers.

Errazzouki, *Samia*. Davis, CA. Affil: California, Davis. Email: serrazzouki@ucdavis.edu. Research: state formation, nationalism.

Errington, **E. Jane**, *Queen's, Can.; Royal Military*. Email: errington_j@rmc.ca.

Ertz, *Simon*. Stanford, CA. Affil: Stanford. Email: ertz@stanford.edu. Research: Soviet political.

Ervin, **Keona Katrice**, *Missouri, Columbia*. Email: ervink@missouri.edu.

Erwin, *Brittany*. Austin, TX. Affil: Texas, Austin. Email: brittany.erwin@utexas.edu.

Eschelbach, *Karl*, *III*. Port Washington, NY. Email: keschelbach@gmail.com.

Escobar, **Edward J.**, *Arizona State*. Email: edward.escobar@asu.edu.

Escobar, **Gayle Gullett**, *Arizona State*. Email: gayle.gullett@asu.edu.

Escobedo, **Elizabeth R.**, *Denver*. Email: elizabeth.escobedo@du.edu.

Esenbel, *Selcuk*. Istanbul, Turkey. Affil: Bogazici. Email: esenbel@boun.edu.tr. Research: Japanese Asianism and world of Islam, Western culture in Japan and Turkey.

Esenwein, *George R.*, *Florida*. Gainesville, FL. Email: gesenwei@ufl.edu. Research: propaganda and war, case of Spain 1936-39.

Eshelman-Lee, *Julie A*. New Roads, LA. Affil: Creole West Productions. Email: director@ creolewest.com. Research: Louisiana.

Esherick, *Joseph W.*, *California, San Diego*. Berkeley, CA. Email: jesherick@ucsd.edu. Research: Chinese Revolution, wartime China.

Esing, **Christopher**, *Austin Peay State*. Email: esingc@apsu.edu.

Eskew, **Glenn T.**, *Georgia State*. Email: gteskew@ gsu.edu.

Eskridge-Kosmach, **Elena**, *Francis Marion*. Email: aeskridgekosmach@fmarion.edu.

Esler, **Anthony J.**, *William and Mary*.

Esparza, **Jesus Jesse**, *Texas Southern*. Email: esparzajj@tsu.edu.

Espinosa, *Mariola*, *Iowa*. Iowa City, IA. Email: mariola-espinosa@uiowa.edu. Research: disease/public health/empire.

Espinoza, **G. Antonio**, *Virginia Commonwealth*. Email: gaespinoza@vcu.edu.

Espiritu, *Augusto F.*, *Illinois, Urbana-Champaign*. Email: aespirit@illinois.edu.

Esposito, **Chiarella**, *Mississippi*. Email: esposito@olemiss.edu.

Esposito, **Frank J.**, *Kean*. Email: fesposit@kean. edu.

Esquilin, **Marta**, *Rutgers, Newark/New Jersey Inst. of Tech*. Email: marta.esquilin@rutgers. edu.

Ess, *John*. San Marcos, CA. Affil: California State, San Marcos. Email: ess001@cougars.csusm. edu.

Essah, **Patience**, *Auburn*. Email: essahpa@ auburn.edu.

Essame, **Jeanne**, *Bates*. Email: jessame@bates. edu.

Esselstrom, *Erik Warren*, *Vermont*. Burlington, VT. Email: eesselst@uvm.edu. Research: Japanese antiwar movement in China, Japanese leftists during occupation.

Essien, **Kwame**, *Lehigh*. Email: kwe212@lehigh. edu.

Essin, **Emmett M.**, **III**, *East Tennessee State*. Email: essine@etsu.edu.

Essington, *Amy*, *California State, Fullerton*. Email: aessington@fullerton.edu.

Esson, *Dylan J*. Salt Lake City, UT. Affil: Waterford Sch. Email: dylanesson@waterfordschool. org. Research: US tourism and sports, German tourism and sports.

Esswein, *Benjamin Thomas*, *Liberty*. Email: btesswein@liberty.edu.

Estabrook, **Carl B.**, *Dartmouth*. Email: carl. estabrook@dartmouth.edu.

Estes, *James M.*, *Toronto*. Email: james.estes@ utoronto.ca.

Estes, *Steve*, *Sonoma State*. Rohnert Park, CA. Email: steve.estes@sonoma.edu. Research: American civil rights movement, masculinity.

Estes, Todd A., *Oakland*. Rochester, MI. Email: estes@oakland.edu. Research: early national US, colonial and revolutionary America.

Estrada, William D., *Southern California*. Email: westrada@nhm.org.

Estruth, Jeannette Alden, *Bard*. New York, NY. Affil: NYU. Email: jae292@nyu.edu.

Etcheson, Nicole, *Ball State; US Air Force Acad.* Muncie, IN. Email: netcheson@bsu.edu; nicole.etcheson@usafa.edu. Research: sectional crisis, Civil War and Reconstruction.

Etefa, Tsega, *Colgate*. Hamilton, NY. Email: tetefa@colgate.edu. Research: Africa.

Etheridge, Bryant. North Conway, NH. Affil: Southern Methodist. Email: bletheridge1@gmail.com.

Etheridge, Elizabeth W., *Longwood*.

Etherington, Norman Alan. North Adelaide, Australia. Affil: West Australia. Email: norman.etherington@uwa.edu.au. Research: 19th-c South Africa, British and European imperialism.

Ethington, Philip J., *Southern California*. Email: philipje@usc.edu.

Etienne-Gray, Trace, *Texas State*. Email: te01@txstate.edu.

Ettinger, Patrick W., *California State, Sacramento*. Email: ettinger@csus.edu.

Ettouney, Osama, *Miami, Ohio*. Email: ettounom@miamioh.edu.

Etulain, Richard W., *New Mexico*. Email: baldbasq@unm.edu.

Eudell, Demetrius L., *Wesleyan*. Middletown, CT. Email: deudell@wesleyan.edu. Research: 19th-c US, African American.

Euler, Carrie E., *Central Michigan*. Mount Pleasant, MI. Email: euler1ce@cmich.edu. Research: Renaissance and Reformation, early modern schools and universities.

Euraque, Dario Aquiles, *Trinity Coll., Conn.* Email: dario.euraque@trincoll.edu.

Eurich, Susan Amanda, *Western Washington*. Email: Amanda.Eurich@wwu.edu.

Eustace, Nicole E., *NYU*. New York, NY. Email: nicole.eustace@nyu.edu. Research: emotion.

Evans, Andrew D., *SUNY, New Paltz*. Email: evansa@newpaltz.edu.

Evans, Catherine L. Toronto, ON, Canada. Affil: Toronto. Email: evans.catherine@gmail.com.

Evans, Charles T. Reston, VA. Affil: Northern Virginia Comm. Coll. Email: cevans@nvcc.edu.

Evans, Christine Elaine, *Wisconsin-Milwaukee*. Email: evansce@uwm.edu.

Evans, Christopher Wayne. Tarboro, NC. Affil: Chowan. Email: christopher.wayne.evans@gmail.com.

Evans, David. Tolland, CT. Affil: Connecticut, Storrs. Email: dave1230evans@yahoo.com.

Evans, Ellen L., *Georgia State*. Email: ele1730@mindspring.com.

Evans, Jennifer V., *Carleton, Can.* Ottawa, ON, Canada. Email: jennifer_evans@carleton.ca. Research: memory/social media/sexuality, homosexuality/subculture/deviance.

Evans, John K., *Minnesota (Hist.)*. Email: evans002@umn.edu.

Evans, Kelly L. Loveland, CO. Affil: Thompson Sch. District. Email: kellye1224@gmail.com. Research: gender and sexuality, middle ground in Midwest.

Evans, Sara M., *Minnesota (Hist.)*. Saint Paul, MN. Email: s-evan@umn.edu. Research: 20th-c US social, American women.

Evans-Grubbs, Judith A., *Emory*. Decatur, GA. Email: jevansg@emory.edu. Research: Roman law and family, imperial and late antique Rome.

Everdell, William R. Brooklyn, NY. Affil: St. Ann's Sch. Email: weverdell@earthlink.net. Research: evangelicalism in abrahamic religions, modernism in sciences and arts 1872-1913.

Evered, Emine Onhan, *Michigan State*. Email: evered@msu.edu.

Everett, Nicholas C., *Toronto*. Email: n.everett@utoronto.ca.

Everman, Henry E., *Eastern Kentucky*. Email: hank.everman@eku.edu.

Everrett, Aimee, *Hist. New Orleans*. Email: aimee@hnoc.org.

Evers, Renate, *Leo Baeck Inst.* Email: revers@lbi.cjh.org.

Eversman, Paul K. Huntington Station, NY. Affil: SUNY, Old Westbury. Email: MrVaudeville@outlook.com.

Eves, Jamie, *Eastern Connecticut State*. Email: evesj@easternct.edu.

Evtuhov, Catherine, *Columbia (Hist.); Georgetown*. New York, NY. Email: ce2308@columbia.edu; evtuhovc@georgetown.edu. Research: imperial Russia, ideas/culture/religion.

Ewald, Carl. Mount Prospect, IL. Affil: Illinois, Chicago. Email: cewald3@uic.edu. Research: local Chicago women in politics, postwar right/conservative consensus.

Ewald, Janet J., *Duke*. Email: jewald@duke.edu.

Ewan, Elizabeth L., *Guelph*. Email: eewan@uoguelph.ca.

Ewen, Geoffrey, *York, Can.* Email: gewen@glendon.yorku.ca.

Ewen, Jeff. Terre Haute, IN. Affil: Ivy Tech. Email: jewen@drew.edu. Research: public health, medicine.

Ewer, Daniel. South Saint Paul, MN. Affil: Minnesota National Guard. Email: JustCallMeSarge@gmail.com. Research: Camp Cody NM, US Army 34th Infantry Division.

Ewing, Christopher B., *Virginia Commonwealth*. Richmond, VA. Email: cewing@gradcenter.cuny.edu. Research: migration and Islam in Germany, postcolonial sex tourism.

Ewing, Cindy, *Toronto*. Toronto, ON, Canada. Email: cindy.ewing@utoronto.ca. Research: Cold War, Human Rights.

Ewing, K. T., *Tennessee State*. Email: kewing6@tnstate.edu.

Ewing, Tabetha, *Bard*. Email: ewing@bard.edu.

Ewing, Tom, *Virginia Tech*. Blacksburg, VA. Email: etewing@vt.edu. Research: Russian gender and education.

Eyal, Yonatan. Montgomery, OH. Affil: Cincinnati. Email: yeyal@post.harvard.edu. Research: Young America movement in antebellum US, 19th-c Romantic politics.

Eyferth, Jacob, *Chicago*. Email: eyferth@uchicago.edu.

Eyford, Ryan C., *Winnipeg*. Email: r.eyford@uwinnipeg.ca.

Eyler, John M., *Minnesota (Hist. of Science)*. Email: eyler001@umn.edu.

Eyman, David, *Skidmore*. Email: deyman@skidmore.edu.

F f

Fabella, Yvonne E. Philadelphia, PA. Affil: Pennsylvania. Email: fabella@sas.upenn.edu. Research: Cultural history of race and slavery, Politics of fashion.

Fabian, Ann V., *Rutgers*. New York, NY. Email: afabian@scarletmail.rutgers.edu; ann.v.fabian@gmail.com. Research: US, cultural.

Fagal, Andrew J. B., *Princeton*. Yardley, PA. Email: afagal@princeton.edu; andrewfagal@gmail.com. Research: early American Republic political economy of war.

Fagan, Elizabeth G. A. Chicago, IL. Affil: Chicago. Email: egafagan@uchicago.edu. Research: Caucasus, identity and authority.

Faggioli, Massimo. Villanova, PA. Affil: Villanova. Email: massimo.faggioli@gmail.com. Research: church, religion/politics/religious movements.

Fahey, David M., *Miami, Ohio*. Email: faheydm@miamioh.edu.

Fahey, John Edward, *US Military Acad.* Email: john.fahey@usma.edu.

Fahmy, Ziad A., *Cornell*. Email: zaf3@cornell.edu.

Fahoum, Basma. Stanford, CA. Affil: Stanford. Email: basma@stanford.edu.

Fahrenthold, Stacy D., *California, Davis*. Email: sfahrenthold@ucdavis.edu.

Fahrer, Charles, *Georgia Coll. and State*. Email: chuck.fahrer@gcsu.edu.

Fahrmeir, Andreas. Oberursel, Germany. Affil: Frankfurt. Email: afahrmeir@yahoo.co.uk. Research: 19th-c London, 19th-c Germany.

Fahrni, Magda, *Québec, Montréal*. Email: fahrni.magda@uqam.ca.

Fahs, Alice, *California, Irvine*. Email: afahs@uci.edu.

Fahy, Barbara M., *Albright*. Email: bfahy@albright.edu.

Fain, W. Taylor, III, *North Carolina, Wilmington*. Wilmington, NC. Email: fainwt@uncw.edu. Research: post-1945 American foreign relations, US-British diplomacy and end of empire.

Fair, Laura J., *Michigan State*. Email: fairl@msu.edu.

Fairbairn, Brett T., *Saskatchewan*. Email: brett.fairbairn@usask.ca.

Fairbanks, Joseph, *Whittier*.

Fairbanks, Robert Bruce, *Texas, Arlington*. Email: fairbank@uta.edu.

Fairfield, John D., *Xavier, Ohio*. Email: fairfiel@xavier.edu.

Fair-Schulz, Axel, *SUNY, Coll. Potsdam*. Email: fairsca@potsdam.edu.

Faison, Elyssa, *Oklahoma (Hist.)*. Norman, OK. Email: efaison@ou.edu. Research: prewar Japanese labor and gender, Japanese race/ethnicity/national identity.

Faith, Thomas I., *US Dept. of State*.

Falato, Betty K. Norman, OK. Email: bkfalato@aol.com.

Falcone, Kelly. Stamford, CT. Email: klyoung9@gmail.com.

Falcone, Marc. New York, NY. Affil: Teachers, Columbia. Email: marc.at.nyc@gmail.com.

Falk, Andrew J., *Christopher Newport*. Newport News, VA. Email: falk@cnu.edu. Research: Cold War cultural export, human rights and NGOs.

Falk, **Francesca**. Ostermundigen, Switzerland. Affil: Fribourg. Email: francesca_falk@yahoo.com.

Falk, **Joyce Duncan**. Santa Barbara, CA. Affil: California. Email: joycedfalk@cox.net. Research: online database searching, bibliography.

Falk, **Oren**, *Cornell*. Email: of24@cornell.edu.

Falk, **Stanley L**. Alexandria, VA. Email: stanfalk@verizon.net. Research: WWII.

Fallavollita, **Paul**. Travelers Rest, SC. Affil: Liberty. Email: pfallavollita@liberty.edu. Research: US foreign policy and sovereignty, American conservative ideology.

Fallaw, **Ben W.**, *Colby*. Email: ben.fallaw@colby.edu.

Fallon, **Cara Kiernan**. New York, NY. Affil: Harvard. Email: cara.kiernan.fallon@gmail.com.

Fallon, **John**, **III**. Lacey, WA. Affil: American Public Univ. System. Email: johnmarjiefallon@hotmail.com.

Falls, **James S.**, *Missouri–Kansas City*. Email: fallsj@umkc.edu.

Falola, **Toyin O.**, *Texas, Austin*. Round Rock, TX. Email: toyinfalola@austin.utexas.edu. Research: Africa, diaspora and migration.

Fals Henderson, **Audrey**. Atlanta, GA. Affil: Emory. Email: audrey.henderson2@emory.edu. Research: agrarian transformation, urban development and change.

Falzone, **Vincent**, *Texas, Tyler*. Email: vfalzone@uttyler.edu.

Fan, **Fa-Ti**, *Binghamton, SUNY*. Email: ffan@binghamton.edu.

Fan, **Joshua**, *Texas, El Paso*. Email: jfan@utep.edu.

Fan, **Shuhua**, *Scranton*. Email: shuhua.fan@scranton.edu.

Fancy, **Hussein**, *Michigan, Ann Arbor*. Ann Arbor, MI. Email: fancy@umich.edu. Research: Muslim soldiers in Christian armies, criminal trade networks.

Fancy, **Nahyan**, *DePauw*. Email: nahyanfancy@depauw.edu.

Fang, **Qiang**, *Minnesota Duluth*. Email: qfang@d.umn.edu.

Fanning, **Charles F.**, *Southern Illinois, Carbondale*. Email: celtic42@siu.edu.

Fanning, **Eugene Charles**. Baltimore, MD. Affil: Maryland, Coll. Park. Email: Ecfanning@gmail.com. Research: immigration and labor, Latin America and US.

Fanning, **Sara**, *Texas Woman's*. Email: sfanning@twu.edu.

Fansher, **Bradley**. Nashville, TN. Email: bradfansher4@hotmail.com.

Fansler, **Jordan A.P.** Dover, NH. Affil: New Hampshire. Email: japfansler@gmail.com. Research: federal system, veterans.

Fantauzzo, **Justin S.J.**, *Memorial, Newfoundland*. Email: jfantauzzo@mun.ca.

Faragher, **John Mack**, *Yale*. Email: john.faragher@yale.edu.

Farah, **W. Mattison**, *Hist. New Orleans*. Email: mattf@hnoc.org.

Farber, **Barry**. Amherst, MA. Email: farber@uhs.umass.edu.

Farber, **David**, *Kansas*. Email: dfarber@ku.edu.

Farber, **Hannah A.**, *Columbia (Hist.)*. Email: hannah.farber@columbia.edu.

Farhani Monfared, **Mahdi**. Affil: Northeastern. Email: m.f.monfared@gmail.com.

Farinas Borrego, **Maikel**. Chapel Hill, NC. Affil: North Carolina, Chapel Hill. Email: maikelfb@outlook.com. Research: Latin America since 1900, Chicano(a)/Latino(a).

Farless, **Patricia L.**, *Central Florida*. Email: Patricia.Farless@ucf.edu.

Farley, **Brigit**, *Washington State, Pullman*. Email: bfarley@tricity.wsu.edu.

Farley, **Ena L.** Brockport, NY. Affil: SUNY, Coll. Brockport. Email: efarley@brockport.edu.

Farmer, **Ashley D.**, *Texas, Austin*. Email: adf@austin.utexas.edu.

Farmer, **Edward L.**, *Minnesota (Hist.)*. Minneapolis, MN. Email: efarmer@umn.edu. Research: Ming gazetteer illustrations.

Farmer, **James O.**, *South Carolina Aiken*. Email: jimf@usca.edu.

Farmer, **Jared**, *SUNY, Stony Brook*. Email: jared.farmer@stonybrook.edu.

Farmer, **Sarah B.**, *California, Irvine*. Irvine, CA. Email: sfarmer@uci.edu. Research: 20th-c European cultural, modern France.

Farmer, **Sharon A.**, *California, Santa Barbara*. Email: farmer@history.ucsb.edu.

Farmer, **Thomas R.** Gastonia, NC. Email: tfarmer1398@gmail.com. Research: early medieval Cologne.

Farmer-Kaiser, **Mary**, *Louisiana, Lafayette*. Email: kaiser@louisiana.edu.

Farnbach Pearson, **Amy W.** Albuquerque, NM. Affil: Oh the Humanities, LLC. Email: amy@ohthehumanitiesllc.com. Research: tuberculosis in 19th-c Scotland.

Farney, **Gary D.**, *Rutgers, Newark/New Jersey Inst. of Tech.* Email: gfarney@rutgers.edu.

Farney, **Kirk**, *Wheaton, Ill.* Hinsdale, IL. Email: kirk.farney@wheaton.edu. Research: American religious.

Farnham Pope, **Christie A.**, *Iowa State*. Email: cfpope@iastate.edu.

Farnia, **Navid**, *Eastern Illinois*.

Farnsworth, **F. Dennis**, **Jr.**, *Utah Valley*. Email: farnswde@uvu.edu.

Farnsworth, **Susan H.** Arlington, VA. Affil: Trinity Washington. Email: SHFarn1@aol.com. Research: Victorian Britain science and politics, Victorian imperial policy.

Farnsworth-Alvear, **Ann C.**, *Pennsylvania*. Email: farnswor@sas.upenn.edu.

Farr, **James R.**, *Purdue*. Email: jrfarr@purdue.edu.

Farr, **William E.**, *Montana*. Email: farr@crmw.org.

Farrell, **Amy Erdman**. Carlisle, PA. Affil: Dickinson. Email: farrell@dickinson.edu.

Farrell, **David R.**, *Guelph*. Email: dfarrell@uoguelph.ca.

Farrell, **Jay**. Erie, CO. Affil: Colorado, Boulder. Email: jay.farrell@colorado.edu.

Farrell, **Mary Beth**, *Southern Mississippi*. Email: mary.farrell@usm.edu.

Farrell, **Sean M.**, *Northern Illinois*. Dekalb, IL. Email: sfarrel1@niu.edu. Research: 19th-c Irish religion and violence, nation and empire.

Farrelly, **Maura Jane**. Waltham, MA. Affil: Brandeis. Email: farrelly@brandeis.edu. Research: 18th-/19th-c American Catholicism, journalism.

Farrington, **Brenda**, *Chapman*. Email: farringt@chapman.edu.

Farrington, **Elliot**, *North Carolina A&T State*. Email: cefarrin@aggies.ncat.edu.

Farris, **John**. Dunwoody, GA. Affil: Georgia State. Email: jfarris@gsu.edu.

Farris, **William Wayne**, *Hawai'i, Manoa*. Email: wfarris@hawaii.edu.

Farriss, **Nancy M.**, *Pennsylvania*.

Farsolas, **James J.**, *Coastal Carolina*. Email: farsolas@coastal.edu.

Farzaneh, **Mateo Mohammad**, *Northeastern Illinois*. Email: m-farzaneh@neiu.edu.

Fasolt, **Constantin**, *Chicago*. Email: icon@uchicago.edu.

Fass, **Paula S**. Berkeley, CA. Affil: California, Berkeley. Email: psfass@berkeley.edu. Research: US children and childhood, society/culture/family.

Faubion, **Michael L**, *Texas-Rio Grande Valley*. Email: michael.faubion@utrgv.edu.

Faue, **Elizabeth V.**, *Wayne State*. Ann Arbor, MI. Email: ad5247@wayne.edu. Research: occupational risk and endangerment, gender/labor/memory.

Faulkenbury, **Evan**. Cortland, NY. Affil: SUNY, Coll. Cortland. Email: evan.faulkenbury@cortland.edu.

Faulkner, **Carol**, *Syracuse*. Syracuse, NY. Email: cfaulkne@maxwell.syr.edu. Research: women's rights, anti-slavery.

Faulkner, **Lisa**. Oak Park, IL. Affil: Oak Park and River Forest High Sch. Email: lmfaulkner@hotmail.com.

Faulkner, **Richard S.**, *US Army Command Coll.* Email: richard.s.faulkner.civ@mail.mil.

Faull, **Matthew Scott**. Carthage, NC. Affil: American Public Univ. System. Email: matthew.faull07@gmail.com. Research: Michael Servetus, Condorcet.

Faunce, **Ken V.**, *Washington State, Pullman*. Email: kfaunce@uidaho.edu.

Faundez, **Gaby**. Miami, FL. Affil: Miami. Email: gaf70@miami.edu.

Faurt, **Anaïs**. Highland Park, NJ. Affil: Rutgers. Email: anais.faurt@rutgers.edu.

Faussette, **Risa**, *St. Rose*. Email: faussetr@strose.edu.

Faust, **Drew G.**, *Harvard (Hist.)*. Email: drew_faust@harvard.edu.

Faust, **Robert E.**, *South Alabama*. Email: rfaust@southalabama.edu.

Fausto, **Boris**. São Paulo, Brazil.

Fausz, **J. Frederick**, *Missouri–St. Louis*. Email: jff@umsl.edu.

Fauxsmith, **Jennifer**, *Arthur and Elizabeth Schlesinger Library*. Email: jennifer_fauxsmith@radcliffe.harvard.edu.

Fawaz, **Leila T**. Cambridge, MA. Affil: Tufts. Email: leila.fawaz@tufts.edu. Research: WWI in Middle East social, modern Levant Ottoman social.

Fawver, **Kate M.**, *California State, Dominguez Hills*. Email: kfawver@csudh.edu.

Fay, **Matthew Martin**. Cincinnati, OH. Email: matthewmfay@gmail.com.

Fea, **John**, *Messiah*. Email: jfea@messiah.edu.

Fear, **Sean**. Leeds, United Kingdom. Affil: Leeds. Email: S.Fear@leeds.ac.uk. Research: US foreign policy, modern Southeast Asia.

Fears-Heinzel, **Gloria Cassandra**. Frankfurt am Main, Germany. Affil: Goethe, Frankfurt. Email: Fears-Heinzel@em.uni-frankfurt.de.

Featherling, **Jacob**. Hattiesburg, MS. Affil: Southern Mississippi. Email: jacob.featherling@usm.edu.

Fechner, **Roger J**. Adrian, MI. Affil: Adrian. Email: RogerFechner@tc3net.com. Research: American Enlightenment, Scottish Enlightenment.

Fede, **Andrew T**. Bogota, NJ. Email: andyfede@ aol.com. Research: slavery law in US and British colonies, comparative slavery law approaches.

Federspiel, **Michael**, *Central Michigan*. Email: feder1mr@cmich.edu.

Fedman, **David**, *California, Irvine*. Email: dfedman@uci.edu.

Fedorowicz, **Jan**, *Carleton, Can*. Email: jan. fedorowicz@carleton.ca.

Fedyashin, **Anton**, *American*. Email: fedyashi@ american.edu.

Feeley, **Kathleen A**. Redlands, CA. Affil: Redlands. Email: kathleen_feeley@redlands. edu. Research: 20th-c US cultural and political, gender/popular culture/media.

Feffer, **Andrew**, *Union Coll*. Email: feffera@ union.edu.

Fegley, **Randall Arlin**, *Penn State*. Email: raf8@ psu.edu.

Fehler, **Timothy G**., *Furman*. Email: timothy. fehler@furman.edu.

Fehner, **Halley L**., *Hist. Assoc*. Email: hfehner@ historyassociates.com.

Fehr, **Russell MacKenzie**. Sacramento, CA. Affil: California, Riverside. Email: rfehr001@ucr.edu. Research: urban political, pre-1927 sound film.

Fehrenbach, **Heide**, *Northern Illinois*. Dekalb, IL. Email: hfehrenbach@niu.edu. Research: visual history of humanitarianism, childhood/war/internationalism.

Fei, **Si-yen**, *Pennsylvania*. Email: siyen@sas. upenn.edu.

Feierman, **Steven M**., *Pennsylvania*. Email: feierman@sas.upenn.edu.

Fein, **Gene**. White Plains, NY. Affil: Fordham. Email: fein@fordham.edu. Research: Christian Front in NYC, Father Charles Coughlin.

Feinberg, **Harvey M**., *Southern Connecticut State*. Email: feinbergh1@southernct.edu.

Feinberg, **Melissa**, *Rutgers*. New Brunswick, NJ. Email: mfeinberg@history.rutgers.edu. Research: Cold War Europe.

Feingold, **Merrick Brent**. Oxford, MS. Email: littleroundtop@hotmail.com. Research: Spanish-American-Cuban War, memory.

Feingold, **Mordechai**, *California Inst. of Tech*. Email: feingold@hss.caltech.edu.

Feinman, **Ronald L**. Boca Raton, FL. Affil: Florida Atlantic, Boca Raton. Email: ron@polithist. com. Research: America in 1930s, America in 1960s.

Feinmark, **Rachel**. Glen Rock, NJ. Affil: Lower East Side Tenement Museum. Email: rfeinmark@uchicago.edu.

Feinstein, **Margarete Myers**. Los Angeles, CA. Affil: Loyola Marymount. Email: mfeinste@ lmu.edu. Research: postwar German political culture, Jewish displaced persons.

Feinstein, **Tamara D. N**., *St. Lawrence*. Canton, NY. Email: tfeinstein@stlawu.edu; tashafeinstein@hotmail.com. Research: political violence and human rights, Latin American Left.

Felak, **James R**., *Washington, Seattle*. Email: felak@uw.edu.

Felber, **Garrett**, *Mississippi*.

Feld, **Marjorie N**. Babson Park, MA. Affil: Babson. Email: mfeld@babson.edu. Research: Lillian D Wald.

Feld, **Mark Ryan**. Hauppauge, NY. Affil: Suffolk County Comm. Coll., SUNY. Email: MarkRyanFeld@gmail.com.

Feldman, **Benjamin**. Washington, DC. Affil: Georgetown. Email: bjf43@georgetown.edu.

Feldman, **James W**., *Wisconsin-Oshkosh*. Email: feldmanj@uwosh.edu.

Feldman, **Lauren Brooke**. Washington, DC. Affil: Johns Hopkins. Email: lauren.feldman@jhu. edu.

Feldman, **Robert S**., *California State, Fullerton*. Email: rfeldman@fullerton.edu.

Feldstein, **Ruth S**., *Rutgers, Newark/New Jersey Inst. of Tech*. Email: feldst@rutgers.edu.

Felix, **David**. New York, NY. Affil: CUNY. Email: dflixx@msn.com. Research: 20th-c political economy, biography.

Felker, **C.C**., *Soc. for Military Hist*. Email: ccfelker@msn.com.

Felker-Kantor, **Max**, *Ball State*. Muncie, IN. Email: mfelkerkanto@bsu.edu; mfkantor@gmail. com. Research: modern US, urban.

Fell, **James E**., **Jr**., *Colorado Denver*. Email: james. fell@ucdenver.edu.

Feller, **Daniel**, *Tennessee, Knoxville*. Knoxville, TN. Email: dfeller@utk.edu. Research: Jacksonian America, political.

Feller, **Laura J**. Washington, DC. Email: fellerl47@verizon.net.

Fellman, **Anita Clair**. Norfolk, VA. Affil: Old Dominion. Email: afellman@odu.edu. Research: mother-in-law/daughter-in-law relations.

Fels, **Anthony D**. Philadelphia, PA. Affil: San Francisco. Email: felsa@usfca.edu. Research: US, religion.

Felt, **Matthieu**. Gainesville, FL. Affil: Florida. Email: mfelt@ufl.edu.

Felten, **Peter G**., *Elon*. Email: pfelten@elon.edu.

Feltman, **Brian K**., *Georgia Southern*. Email: bfeltman@georgiasouthern.edu.

Felton, **Ann**, *Boise State*. Email: annfelton@ boisestate.edu.

Fenech, **Louis E**., *Northern Iowa*. Email: lou. fenech@uni.edu.

Feng, **Cho-Chien**. Saint Louis, MO. Affil: St. Louis. Email: cfeng3@slu.edu. Research: American Revolution, New York Loyalists.

Fenn, **Elizabeth**, *Colorado, Boulder*. Email: elizabeth.fenn@colorado.edu.

Fenrich, **Eric Brett**. Santa Barbara, CA. Affil: California, Santa Barbara. Email: eric@ fenrich.net. Research: space race, Cold War propaganda and ideology.

Fenton, **Edwin**, *Carnegie Mellon*. Email: ef19@ andrew.cmu.edu.

Fenton, **William D**., *Library Co. of Philadelphia*. Email: wfenton@librarycompany.org.

Fenyo, **Mario D**., *Bowie State*. Email: mfenyo@ bowiestate.edu.

Ferber, **Susan**. New York, NY. Affil: Oxford Univ. Press. Email: susan.ferber@oup.com.

Ferdinando, **Peter**, *North Carolina, Charlotte*. Email: pferdina@uncc.edu.

Ference, **Gregory C**., *Salisbury*. Salisbury, MD. Email: gxference@salisbury.edu. Research: eastern Europe, Hapsburgs.

Ferentinos, **Susan**. Bloomington, IN. Affil: Public History Consultant. Email: susan@ susanferentinos.com. Research: public, LGBTQ.

Feres, **Angela**. El Cajon, CA. Affil: Grossmont. Email: aferes@mail.sdsu.edu. Research: early modern Catholics, early modern identity.

Fergeson, **Larissa Smith**, *Longwood*. Email: fergesonls@longwood.edu.

Fergus, **Devin**, *Missouri, Columbia*. Email: fergusd@missouri.edu.

Ferguson, **Barry G**., *Manitoba*. Email: barry. ferguson@umanitoba.ca.

Ferguson, **Christopher John**, *Auburn*. Auburn, AL. Email: cjf0006@auburn.edu. Research: city in Britain, 19th-c material culture.

Ferguson, **Clyde R**., *Kansas State*.

Ferguson, **Earline Rae**, *Rhode Island*. Email: erferguson@uri.edu.

Ferguson, **Heather Lynn**, *Claremont McKenna*. Upland, CA. Email: heather.ferguson@ claremontmckenna.edu; heathfergus@gmail. com. Research: imperial strategies of rule/ideology, moral economies of Ottoman Empire/Greater Syria.

Ferguson, **Karen**, *Simon Fraser*. Email: kjfergus@ sfu.ca.

Ferguson, **Michael**. Danbury, CT. Email: mferguson91@comcast.net.

Ferguson, **Neal**, *Nevada, Reno*. Email: nealf@ unr.edu.

Ferguson, **Robert Hunt**, *Western Carolina*. Email: rhferguson@email.wcu.edu.

Ferguson, **Susanna**. New York, NY. Affil: Columbia. Email: susanna.ferguson@gmail. com.

Ferland, **Jacques**, *Maine, Orono*. Email: jferland@maine.edu.

Ferleger, **Louis A**., *Boston Univ*. Email: ferleger@ bu.edu.

Fermaglich, **Kirsten L**., *Michigan State*. Email: fermagli@msu.edu.

Fernandez, **Damian**, *Northern Illinois*. Dekalb, IL. Email: dfernandez@niu.edu. Research: ancient, late antiquity.

Fernandez, **Delia**, *Michigan State*. Email: dmf@ msu.edu.

Fernandez, **Gilbert G**., *Tennessee Tech*. Email: gfernandez@tntech.edu.

Fernandez, **Jose B**., *Central Florida*. Email: Jose. Fernandez@ucf.edu.

Fernandez, **Leonel**. Santo Domingo, Dominican Republic. Affil: Fundacion Global Democracia y Desarrollo. Email: suscripcionesbjb@gmail. com.

Fernandez, **Lilia**, *Rutgers*. Piscataway, NJ. Email: lilia.fernandez@rutgers.edu. Research: Mexican and Puerto Rican history in US.

Fernandez, **Mark F**., *Loyola, New Orleans*. Email: mffernan@loyno.edu.

Fernandez, **Susan J**., *South Florida, St. Petersburg*.

Fernandez Galeano, **Javier**. Providence, RI. Affil: Brown. Email: javier_fernandez_galeano@ brown.edu.

Fernandez-Armesto, **Felipe**, *Notre Dame*. Notre Dame, IN. Email: Felipe.Fernandez-Armesto@ nd.edu. Research: modern Europe.

Fernandez-Guevara, **Daniel Jesus**. Gainesville, FL. Affil: Florida. Email: djfernandez17@ufl. edu.

Fernlund, **Kevin Jon**, *Missouri–St. Louis*. Email: fernlund@umsl.edu.

Fernsebner, **Susan R**., *Mary Washington*. Email: sfernseb@umw.edu.

Feros, Antonio, *Pennsylvania*. Email: aferos@sas.upenn.edu.

Ferrara degli Uberti, *Carlotta*. Pisa, Italy. Affil: Univ. Coll. London. Email: c.ferrara@ucl.ac.uk. Research: Italy.

Ferrari, Mary C., *Radford*. Email: mferrari@radford.edu.

Ferraro, Joanne M., *San Diego State*. Email: ferraro@sdsu.edu.

Ferraro, *William M*. Charlottesville, VA. Affil: Virginia. Email: wmf4f@virginia.edu. Research: Sherman-Ewing family, 19th-c US male-female relationships.

Ferreira, James M., *Western Michigan*. Email: james.ferreira@wmich.edu.

Ferreira, *Joseph J*., *Jr*. Wrentham, MA. Affil: King Philip Regional High Sch. Email: ferreiraj@kingphilip.org. Research: teaching world history with technology, 19th-/20th-c British imperialism.

Ferreira, Roquinaldo, *Pennsylvania*.

Ferreira, Susannah Humble, *Guelph*. Email: shumble@uoguelph.ca.

Ferrell, Claudine, *Mary Washington*. Email: cferrell@umw.edu.

Ferrell, Henry C., *Jr.*, *East Carolina*. Email: ferrellh@ecu.edu.

Ferrell, Lacy Spotswood, *Central Washington*. Email: ferrelll@cwu.edu.

Ferrell, Lori Anne, *Claremont Grad*. Email: lori.ferrell@cgu.edu.

Ferrer, *Ada*, *NYU*. New York, NY. Email: af6@nyu.edu. Research: Latin American race/nationalism/citizenship, Haitian Revolution in Atlantic world.

Ferrill, Arther, *Washington, Seattle*. Email: ferrill@uw.edu.

Ferrin, *Ciuin*. Iowa City, IA. Affil: Iowa. Email: Wendy-millis@uiowa.edu.

Ferris, John R., *Calgary*. Email: ferris@ucalgary.ca.

Ferris, *Michele*. Winthrop Harbor, IL. Affil: Chicago. Email: mmferris@uchicago.edu.

Ferris, *Norman B*. Murfreesboro, TN. Email: n.b.ferris@comcast.net. Research: William Lewis Dayton, William Henry Seward.

Ferris, William R., *North Carolina, Chapel Hill*. Email: wferris@email.unc.edu.

Ferry, *Peter*. Philadelphia, PA. Affil: Pennsylvania. Email: pcpferry@gmail.com.

Ferry, Robert J., *Colorado, Boulder*. Email: robert.ferry@colorado.edu.

Festle, *Mary Jo*. *Elon*. Elon, NC. Email: festle@elon.edu. Research: 20th-c US, gender and sexuality.

Fett, *Anna*. Chicago, IL. Affil: Notre Dame. Email: afett@nd.edu. Research: people-to-people exchange programs, US youth peacebuilding programs.

Fett, *Sharla M*., *Occidental*. Los Angeles, CA. Email: sfett@oxy.edu. Research: slavery and antebellum medicine, 19th-c slave trade and US suppression.

Fetter, *Henry D*. Los Angeles, CA. Email: hdfetter@aol.com. Research: US relations with Israel, sports.

Feurer, Rosemary, *Northern Illinois*. Email: rfeurer@niu.edu.

Few, *Martha*, *Penn State*. University Park, PA. Email: mzf52@psu.edu. Research: Latin America, medicine and animals.

Fialka, Andrew, *Middle Tennessee State*. Email: Andrew.Fialka@mtsu.edu.

Fichter, *James R*. Pokfulam, Hong Kong. Affil: Hong Kong. Email: fichter@post.harvard.edu. Research: British Empire, French colonialism.

Fichter, *Madigan A*. New York, NY. Affil: Holy Family. Email: madigan.fichter@gmail.com. Research: eastern Europe/Balkans, nationalism.

Fichtner, *Paula S*. Brooklyn, NY. Email: psfichtner@aol.com. Research: Habsburg empire 1450-1848.

Fick, Carolyn E., *Concordia, Can*. Email: Carolyn.Fick@concordia.ca.

Fickes, *Brett Robert*. South Holland, IL. Email: fickes.brett@district205.net.

Fickle, James E., *Memphis*. Email: jfickle@memphis.edu.

Fidelis, *Malgorzata*, *Illinois, Chicago*. Chicago, IL. Email: gosia01@uic.edu. Research: women/labor/communism, eastern European gender.

Fiege, *Mark*, *Montana State, Bozeman*. Bozeman, MT. Email: mark.fiege@montana.edu. Research: American environmental, western America.

Field, *Arthur*, *Indiana*. Bloomington, IN. Email: afield@indiana.edu. Research: Italian Renaissance, early modern intellectual.

Field, *Corinne T*. Charlottesville, VA. Affil: Virginia. Email: cf6d@virginia.edu. Research: women's rights, aging.

Field, Lester L., *Jr.*, *Mississippi*. Email: hsfield@olemiss.edu.

Field, Phyllis F., *Ohio*. Email: field@ohio.edu.

Field, Sean L., *Vermont*. Email: sean.field@uvm.edu.

Field, *Thomas C*. Prescott, AZ. Affil: Embry-Riddle. Email: Thomas.Field@erau.edu. Research: global Cold War, Latin America and world.

Fields, Barbara J., *Columbia (Hist.)*.

Fields, Jill S., *California State, Fresno*. Email: jfields@csufresno.edu.

Fields, *Kollin*. Fate, TX. Affil: Texas, Dallas. Email: kollin.fields@gmail.com.

Fields, Lanny B., *California State, San Bernardino*.

Fields-Black, Edda L., *Carnegie Mellon*. Pittsburgh, PA. Email: fieldsblack@cmu.edu. Research: pre-colonial West Africa, African diaspora.

Fieldston, *Sara*, *Seton Hall*. South Orange, NJ. Email: sara.fieldston@shu.edu; sara.fieldston@gmail.com. Research: America, US and world.

Fiero, Gloria K., *Louisiana, Lafayette*.

Fierstien, *Robert E*. Lakewood, NJ.

Figal, *Gerald A*., *Vanderbilt*. Email: gerald.figal@vanderbilt.edu.

Figliulo-Rosswurm, *Joseph*. Tigard, OR. Affil: California, Santa Barbara. Email: jfigliulorosswurm@gmail.com. Research: gendered violence in medieval Italy, medieval lordship and peasantry.

Figueira, *Robert C*., *Lander*. Greenwood, SC. Email: figueira@lander.edu. Research: medieval papacy, medieval canon law.

Figueira, *Thomas J*. New Brunswick, NJ. Affil: Rutgers. Email: figueira@rci.rutgers.edu. Research: 5th-c Athenian hegemony, Greek social and economic structures.

Figueroa-Martinez, Luis, *Trinity Coll., Conn*. Email: luis.figueroa@trincoll.edu.

Filene, Peter G., *North Carolina, Chapel Hill*. Email: filene@live.unc.edu.

Fileri, *Philip D*. Washington, DC. Affil: Harvard. Email: pfileri@post.harvard.edu. Research: European integration, international political thought.

Filipink, *Richard M*., *Jr.*, *Western Illinois*. Email: RM-Filipink@wiu.edu.

Filippello, *Marcus*, *Wisconsin-Milwaukee*. Northbrook, IL. Email: filippem@uwm.edu; mbfilippello@gmail.com. Research: sub-Saharan Africa, environmental.

Filippini, *Orietta*. Toscanella d Dozza, Italy. Affil: Erfurt. Email: o.filippini@mail.com. Research: archival sciences, early modern Europe.

Filner, *Robert*, *San Diego State*.

Finan, *Barbara*. Concord, MA. Affil: New Hampshire. Email: bfinanp@aol.com. Research: immigration, industrial.

Finan, Thomas J., *St. Louis*. Email: finantj@slu.edu.

Finch, Aisha K., *UCLA*. Email: akfinch@ucla.edu.

Finchelstein, Federico, *New School*. Email: finchelf@newschool.edu.

Finder, *Gabriel N*., *Virginia*. Earlysville, VA. Email: gf6n@virginia.edu. Research: Jews in postwar Poland, Jewish survivors' memory of Holocaust.

Findlay, *Eileen J*., *American*. Washington, DC. Email: efindla@american.edu. Research: Latin America and Caribbean, race and gender.

Findlay, John M., *Washington, Seattle*. Email: jfindlay@uw.edu.

Findlen, Paula, *Stanford*. Email: pfindlen@stanford.edu.

Findley, *Carter V*., *Ohio State*. Columbus, OH. Email: findley.1@osu.edu. Research: Ottoman Empire, Ignatius Mouradgea d'Ohsson.

Findling, John E., *Indiana, Southeast*. Email: jfindlin@ius.edu.

Fine, John V. A., *Jr.*, *Michigan, Ann Arbor*. Email: jvafine@umich.edu.

Fine, *Julia*. Chevy Chase, MD. Email: jfine@college.harvard.edu.

Fine, *Lisa Michelle*, *Michigan State*. East Lansing, MI. Email: fine@msu.edu. Research: US working class relationship to land.

Finegan, Caleb P.S., *Indiana, Pa*. Email: cfinegan@iup.edu.

Finger, John R., *Tennessee, Knoxville*. Email: jfinger@utk.edu.

Finger, *Tara Kristin*. Franklin, NY. Email: TaraKristin610@gmail.com. Research: Mongol Empire/Ill Khanate/Golden Horde, imperial Russia/Soviet Union.

Finger, Thomas David, *Northern Arizona*. Email: thomas.finger@nau.edu.

Fink, *Carole K*., *North Carolina, Wilmington; Ohio State*. Wilmington, NC. Email: fink.24@osu.edu. Research: West Germany and Israel 1966-74, human rights in Europe since 1945.

Fink, *Jeff*. New Braunfels, TX. Affil: Cross Lutheran Sch. Email: jfink@crosslcmsschool.org.

Fink, *Leon*, *Illinois, Chicago*. Washington, DC. Email: leonfink@uic.edu. Research: US labor and immigration, Gilded Age and Progressive Era.

Finkel, Stuart D., *Florida*. Email: sfinkel@ufl.edu.

Finkelstein, *Alexander*. Norman, OK. Affil: Oklahoma. Email: alex.finkelstein@ou.edu.

Finkelstein, Gabriel W., *Colorado Denver*. Email: gabriel.finkelstein@ucdenver.edu.

Finkenbine, Roy E., *Detroit Mercy*. Email: finkenre@udmercy.edu.

Finlay, John L., *Manitoba.*

Finlay, Robert, *Arkansas, Fayetteville.* Email: rfinlay@uark.edu.

Finley, Katherine Mandusic, *OAH.* Bloomington, IN. Email: kmfinley@oah.org. Research: public and museums, 1850-1870 US.

Finley, Keith M., *Southeastern Louisiana.* Email: Keith.Finley@selu.edu.

Finley-Croswhite, S. Annette, *Old Dominion.* Email: acroswhi@odu.edu.

Finlyason, Michael, *Toronto.*

Finn, Jennifer, *Marquette.* Milwaukee, WI. Email: jennifer.finn@marquette.edu. Research: ancient Greece and Rome, Assyria.

Finn, Katie, *Massachusetts Hist. Soc.* Email: kfinn@masshist.org.

Finnegan, Terence R., *William Paterson.* Email: finnegant@wpunj.edu.

Finney, Nathan. Honolulu, HI. Affil: Kansas. Email: finneynk@gmail.com.

Finney, P. Corby, *Missouri–St. Louis.* Email: finneyp@msx.umsl.edu.

Finnigan, Sheena, *Wisconsin Lutheran.* Milwaukee, WI. Email: sheena.finnigan@wlc.edu. Research: pregnancy and childbirth in Rome, women and power in Rome.

Finucane, Adrian, *Florida Atlantic.* Email: afinucane@fau.edu.

Finzsch, Norbert. Koeln, Germany. Affil: Koeln. Email: norbert.finzsch@uni-koeln.de. Research: African American, masculinity.

Fiorey, Mark E., *Naval War Coll.* Email: mark.fiorey@usnwc.edu.

Fireman, Janet. Tucson, AZ. Affil: Natural Hist. Museum of Los Angeles County. Email: jfireman@nhm.org. Research: California, American West.

Firey, Abigail A., *Kentucky.* Email: afire2@uky.edu.

Firkatian, Mari A., *Hartford.* Email: firkatian@hartford.edu.

Firpo, Christina E., *California Polytechnic State.* Email: cfirpo@calpoly.edu.

Firsching, Lorenz J. Vestal, NY. Affil: Broome Comm. Coll. Email: Firsching_L@sunybroome.edu.

First, Joshua J., *Mississippi.* Email: jfirst@olemiss.edu.

Firtko, Stefan F. Bethlehem, PA.

Fischel, Jack R., *Millersville, Pa.* Email: jack.fischel@millersville.edu.

Fischer, Bernd J., *Purdue, Fort Wayne.* Email: fischer@ipfw.edu.

Fischer, Brodwyn M., *Chicago.* Chicago, IL. Email: bmf@uchicago.edu. Research: abolition/migration/urbanization, Josué de Castro.

Fischer, Christopher J., *Indiana State.* Email: Christopher.Fischer@indstate.edu.

Fischer, David Hackett, *Brandeis.* Email: fischer@brandeis.edu.

Fischer, Fritz. Longmont, CO. Affil: Northern Colorado. Email: fritz.fischer@unco.edu. Research: history education, US.

Fischer, Gayle V., *Salem State.* Salem, MA. Email: gfischer@salemstate.edu; gayle.fischer@salemstate.edu. Research: rules regarding clothing, local.

Fischer, John Ryan. River Falls, WI. Affil: Wisconsin, River Falls. Email: john.ryan.fischer@uwrf.edu. Research: biological invasions and native peoples, early connections between CA and HI.

Fischer, Kathleen G., *Pittsburg State.*

Fischer, Kirsten, *Minnesota (Hist.).* Minneapolis, MN. Email: kfischer@umn.edu. Research: early Republic rational religion, early American race/class/gender.

Fischer, Sibylle Maria, *NYU.* New York, NY. Email: smf287@nyu.edu. Research: Caribbean literature and culture, Spanish American independence.

Fischer Bovet, Christelle, *Southern California.* Los Angeles, CA. Email: fischerb@usc.edu; christelle_fischer@mac.com. Research: army and society in Ptolemaic Egypt, ancient Mediterranean ethnicity and status.

Fisette, Jonathan. Jacksonville, FL. Affil: Liberty. Email: valhallaready@gmail.com.

Fisher, Amy A., *Puget Sound.* Email: afisher@pugetsound.edu.

Fisher, Andrew B., *Carleton Coll.* Email: afisher@carleton.edu.

Fisher, Andrew H., *William and Mary.* Email: ahfis2@wm.edu.

Fisher, Benjamin Edward, *Towson.* Email: bfisher@towson.edu.

Fisher, Christopher T., *New Jersey.* Ewing, NJ. Email: fisherc@tcnj.edu. Research: 20th-c American diplomacy, Cold War.

Fisher, Christopher. New Milford, CT. Affil: Trinity Coll., Conn. Email: Fisher057@gmail.com. Research: business as a public resource, New England home as an ideal.

Fisher, Colin, *San Diego.* Email: colinf@sandiego.edu.

Fisher, David C., *Texas-Rio Grande Valley.* Email: david.fisher@utrgv.edu.

Fisher, Geoffrey M. Bolivia, NC. Affil: American Public Univ. System. Email: gmf51179@temple.edu. Research: public, military.

Fisher, Greg, *Carleton, Can.* Email: greg_fisher@carleton.ca.

Fisher, Jeremiah J. Tallahassee, FL. Affil: Florida State. Email: jeremiah.fisher@fsu.edu. Research: Acadian settlement and diaspora, Irish political development.

Fisher, Jerry K., *Macalester.* Email: fisher@macalester.edu.

Fisher, Linford D., *Brown.* Providence, RI. Email: Linford_Fisher@Brown.edu. Research: 18th-c American Indian Christianity, comparative North American colonialism.

Fisher, Michael H., *Oberlin.* Email: michael.fisher@oberlin.edu.

Fisher, Riley. Bethesda, MD. Email: ref0731@cs.com.

Fishman, Laura Schrager. Brooklyn, NY. Affil: York, CUNY. Email: fishman@york.cuny.edu. Research: French colonialism in Americas.

Fishman, Louis, *Brooklyn, CUNY.* Email: lfishman@brooklyn.cuny.edu.

Fishman, Sarah, *Houston.* Houston, TX. Email: sfishman@uh.edu. Research: postwar France, gender and family.

Fissel, Mark Charles, *Augusta.* Email: mfissel@augusta.edu.

Fissell, Mary E., *Johns Hopkins (Hist. of Science).* Baltimore, MD. Email: mfissell@jhmi.edu; mfissell@jhu.edu. Research: popular medicine 1700-1920, gender and sexuality 1700-1850.

Fitch, Nancy E., *California State, Fullerton.* Email: nfitch@fullerton.edu.

Fitchett Climenhaga, Alison. Fitzroy, Australia. Affil: Australian Catholic. Email: alison.fitchettclimenhaga@acu.edu.au.

Fitts, Leon, *Dickinson.* Email: fitts@dickinson.edu.

Fitz, Caitlin A., *Northwestern.* Email: c-fitz@northwestern.edu.

Fitzgerald, David. Cork, Ireland. Affil: Univ. Coll. Cork. Email: davidfitzger@gmail.com. Research: counterinsurgency, military culture.

Fitzgerald, Deborah K., *MIT.* Email: dkfitz@mit.edu.

Fitzgerald, Joseph R., *Cabrini.* Radnor, PA. Email: joseph.r.fitzgerald@cabrini.edu. Research: gender in civil rights and black power, critical race theory.

Fitzgerald, Maureen A., *William and Mary.* Email: mafitz@wm.edu.

Fitzgerald, Michael W., *St. Olaf.* Northfield, MN. Email: fitz@stolaf.edu. Research: Reconstruction in Alabama, Emancipation.

Fitzgerald, Timothy J., *James Madison.* Harrisonburg, VA. Email: fitzgetj@jmu.edu. Research: Mamluk-Ottoman transition in Arab world, legal culture and institutions.

Fitzgibbon, Edward M., Jr., *Ohio.* Email: fitzgibb@ohio.edu.

Fitz-Gibbon, Desmond, *Mount Holyoke.* Email: dfitzgib@mtholyoke.edu.

Fitzharris, Joseph, *St. Thomas, Minn.* Email: jcfitzharris@stthomas.edu.

Fitzmorris, Terrence W., *Tulane.* Email: tfitzmo@tulane.edu.

Fitzpatrick, Ellen F., *New Hampshire, Durham.* Email: ellen.fitzpatrick@unh.edu.

Fitzpatrick, Shanon, *McGill.* Email: shanon.fitzpatrick@mcgill.ca.

Fitzpatrick, Sheila, *Chicago.* Email: sf13@uchicago.edu.

Fitzpatrick Behrens, Susan R., *California State, Northridge.* Email: susan.fitzpatrick@csun.edu.

Fix, Douglas L., *Reed.* Email: dfix@reed.edu.

Fixico, Donald L., *Arizona State.* Mesa, AZ. Email: donald.fixico@asu.edu. Research: American Indian identity, Osceola.

Flack, J. Kirkpatrick, *Maryland, Coll. Park.* Email: jflack@umd.edu.

Flader, Susan L., *Missouri, Columbia.* Email: fladers@missouri.edu.

Flaherty, Darryl, *Delaware.* Email: flaherty@udel.edu.

Flaherty, David H., *Western Ontario.* Email: david@flaherty.com.

Flaherty, Randall Lewis. Charlottesville, VA. Affil: Virginia. Email: rflaherty@law.virginia.edu.

Flamm, Michael W., *Ohio Wesleyan.* Delaware, OH. Email: mwflamm@owu.edu. Research: conservatism and liberalism, politics of crime and law enforcement.

Flamming, Douglas, *Georgia Inst. of Tech.* Email: doug.flamming@hts.gatech.edu.

Flanagan, Christopher, *AHA.* Washington, DC. Email: cflanagan@historians.org.

Flanagan, Drew Edward. Waltham, MA. Affil: Brandeis. Email: dflanaga@brandeis.edu. Research: post-WWII French far right, western European comparative right wing movements.

Flanagan, Jeffrey Michael. Blacksburg, VA. Affil: Virginia Tech. Email: jmflanagan@vt.edu.

Flanagan, Stephen T., *Western Connecticut State.* Danbury, CT. Email: flanagans@wcsu.edu. Research: US.

Flanders, Robert, *Missouri State.*

Flandreau, Marc, *Pennsylvania.*

Flannery, Christopher, *Azusa Pacific*. Email: cflannery@apu.edu.

Flaten, David D. Dryden, NY. Affil: Tompkins Cortland Comm. Coll. Email: flatend@ tompkinscortland.edu. Research: King George II, early modern Britain.

Flath, James A., *Western Ontario*. Email: jflath@uwo.ca.

Flatt, Emma J., *North Carolina, Chapel Hill*.

Fleagle, Alexandra L. Stony Brook, NY. Affil: Wisconsin, Madison. Email: fleagle@wisc. edu. Research: health and sexuality, children's health and institutions.

Fleche, Andre M. Castleton, VT. Affil: Castleton. Email: Andre.Fleche@castleton.edu.

Fleegler, Robert L., *Mississippi*. Memphis, TN. Email: fleegler@olemiss.edu. Research: US immigration and ethnicity, 1988 US presidential election.

Fleetham, Deborah L., *Purdue*. Email: dfleetham@purdue.edu.

Fleischer, Cornell H., *Chicago*. Email: c-fleischer@uchicago.edu.

Fleischer, Mitchell. Ann Arbor, MI. Affil: Wayne State. Email: mfleischer@comcast.net. Research: Detroit, urban renewal.

Fleischer, Sam. Pullman, WA. Affil: Washington State, Pullman. Email: sxfleischer@gmail. com. Research: sports in America, US space program.

Fleischman, Thomas, *Rochester*. Email: tfleisch@ur.rochester.edu.

Fleischmann, Ellen L., *Dayton*. Email: efleischmann1@udayton.edu.

Flemer, Paul A., *St. Mary's, Calif.* Email: pflemer@stmarys-ca.edu.

Fleming, Cynthia, *Tennessee, Knoxville*. Email: cfleming@utk.edu.

Fleming, J. Andrew. Allentown, PA. Affil: Slippery Rock. Email: jxf1070@sru.edu.

Fleming, James Rodger, *Colby*. Email: james. fleming@colby.edu.

Fleming, Katherine E., *NYU*. New York, NY. Email: katherine.fleming@nyu.edu. Research: Jews in Greece/Mediterranean, early 20th-c Greece.

Fleming, Keith R., *Western Ontario*. Email: kfleming@uwo.ca.

Fleming, Robin, *Boston Coll*. Email: robin. fleming@bc.edu.

Fleming, Tessa. Mission Viejo, CA. Affil: Santa Margarita Catholic High Sch. Email: tessafleming@gmail.com.

Fleming, Tyler D., *Louisville*. Louisville, KY. Email: tyler.fleming@louisville.edu. Research: popular cultures, 20th-c South Africa.

Flemion, Philip F., *San Diego State*.

Fletcher, Alison. Huntingdon, PA. Affil: Juniata. Email: fletcher@juniata.edu. Research: British Empire.

Fletcher, Allan W., *Boise State*. Email: afletch@boisestate.edu.

Fletcher, Angharad. Leicester, United Kingdom. Affil: King's Coll., London; Hong Kong. Email: angharad.fletcher@kcl.ac.uk.

Fletcher, Brian. Poulsbo, WA. Affil: Washington. Email: fletch42@uw.edu.

Fletcher, Carol. Longs, SC. Affil: Coastal Carolina. Email: carolannmfletcher@hotmail.com.

Fletcher, Christopher. Chicago, IL. Affil: Newberry Library Center for Renaissance Studies. Email: fletcherc@newberry.org. Research: medieval intellectual life, medieval religious thought.

Fletcher, Ian C., *Georgia State*. Email: icfletcher@gsu.edu.

Fletcher, Kami L., *Albright*.

Fletcher, Marvin E., *Ohio*. Email: fletcher@ohio. edu.

Fletcher, W. Miles, III, *North Carolina, Chapel Hill*. Email: wmfletch@email.unc.edu.

Flickinger, Joseph J. Cincinnati, OH. Email: jflickinger275@gmail.com. Research: Cincinnati suburbs, local.

Fliegelman, Mark Steven. Valrico, FL. Affil: American Military. Email: msfliegelman@msn. com. Research: war and diplomacy in West, Atlantic world.

Flint, John E., *Dalhousie*.

Flint, Karen Elizabeth, *North Carolina, Charlotte*. Email: kflint@uncc.edu.

Flippen, John Brooks. McKinney, TX. Affil: Southeastern Oklahoma State. Email: bflippen@se.edu. Research: modern America, environmental.

Flockerzie, Lawrence J., *Dayton*. Email: lflockerzie1@udayton.edu.

Florea, Cristina, *Cornell*.

Flores, Christina. Bakersfield, CA. Affil: Chicago. Email: christinaflores@uchicago.edu.

Flores, Dan L., *Montana*. Email: dlfnewmexico@aol.com.

Flores, John H., *Case Western Reserve*. Email: john.flores@case.edu.

Flores, Lori A., *SUNY, Stony Brook*. Email: lori. flores@stonybrook.edu.

Flores, Maj Benjamin, *US Military Acad*. Email: benjamin.flores@usma.edu.

Flores, Norma Lisa. Las Vegas, NV. Affil: Nevada, Las Vegas. Email: norma.flores@unlv.edu. Research: Nazi Germany, 20th-c US.

Flores, Ruben, *Kansas; Rochester*. Email: flores@ku.edu; ruben.flores@rochester.edu.

Flores-Villalobos, Joan Victoria, *Ohio State*. Email: flores-villalobos.1@osu.edu.

Florez-Malagon, Alberto, *Carleton, Can*. Ottawa, ON, Canada. Affil: Ottawa. Email: alberto. florezmalagon@carleton.ca; aflorezm@ uottawa.ca. Research: cultural studies, environmental studies.

Florio, Christopher Michael, *Hollins*. Arnold, MD. Email: cflorio@hollins.edu; chrisflorio12@ gmail.com.

Florvil, Tiffany Nicole, *New Mexico*. Email: tflorvil@unm.edu.

Flory, Lynsay, *Minot State*. Email: lynsay.flory@ndsu.edu.

Flowe, Douglas James, *Washington, St. Louis*. Email: dflowe@wustl.edu.

Flowers, Deidre B. New York, NY. Affil: Teachers, Columbia. Email: dbennettfl@me.com. Research: HBCUs, women's education.

Flowers, James. Baltimore, MD. Affil: Johns Hopkins. Email: jflower6@jhmi.edu. Research: patients and healers in Korea 1910-45, patients and healers in Manchuria.

Floyd, Brendon Gray. Columbia, MO. Affil: Missouri, Columbia. Email: bgfloyd@mail. missouri.edu. Research: Irish America, United Irishmen.

Floyd, Michael Ryan, *Lander*. Email: mrfloyd@lander.edu.

Fluhman, J. Spencer, *Brigham Young*. Provo, UT. Email: fluhman@byu.edu. Research: Christianity, Mormonism.

Fluker, Amy L, *Youngstown State*.

Fluker, Walter Earl, *Howard Thurman Papers Proj*. Email: wfluker@bu.edu.

Flynn, James T., *Holy Cross*. Email: jflynn@holycross.edu.

Flynn, Robert J. Portland, OR. Affil: Portland Comm. Coll. Email: robert.flynn@pcc.edu. Research: Western civilization, US and Middle East.

Flynn, Roger J. Anderson, SC. Affil: Anderson, SC. Email: rflynn@andersonuniversity.edu. Research: political science, US transportation.

Flynt, Wayne, *Auburn*. Email: henkewi@duc. auburn.edu.

Fobare, Christopher J. Amherst, MA. Affil: Massachusetts Amherst. Email: cfobare@umass.edu. Research: Reconstruction, race.

Foda, Omar. Ellicott City, MD. Affil: Pennsylvania. Email: ofoda@sas.upenn.edu. Research: economic, social.

Fogarty, Gerald P., *Virginia*. Charlottesville, VA. Email: gpf@virginia.edu. Research: Catholic Church in Virginia, Vatican and US in WWII.

Fogarty, Richard S., *SUNY, Albany*. Albany, NY. Email: rfogarty@albany.edu. Research: France and WWI, military race relations/policy.

Fogel, Joshua, *York, Can*. Email: fogel@yorku.ca.

Fogelson, Robert M., *MIT*. Email: foge@mit.edu.

Fogg, Harry M. New Hampton, NY. Affil: Rockland Comm. Coll. Email: mnefogg@twc. com.

Fogg, Kevin W. Richmond, VA. Affil: Oxford. Email: kevinwfogg@gmail.com. Research: Muslim nationalism in independent Indonesia, traditionalist Islam in Indonesia.

Fogg, Raymond. Marshall, TX. Affil: Wiley. Email: rkfogg@wileyc.edu.

Fogg, Shannon, *Missouri Science and Tech*. Rolla, MO. Email: sfogg@mst.edu. Research: modern France, French Revolution.

Fogle, Kate. Washington, DC. Affil: Ryerson. Email: kfogle@ryerson.ca.

Fogleman, Aaron Spencer, *Northern Illinois*. Email: aaronfogleman@niu.edu.

Fogleman, Andrew M., *California State, Fullerton*. Email: afogleman@fullerton.edu.

Foglesong, David S., *Rutgers*. Email: dsfoglesong@gmail.com.

Fogu, Claudio, *California, Santa Barbara*. Email: cfogu@french-ital.ucsb.edu.

Fojtik, Christine, *St. Xavier*. Email: fojtik@sxu. edu.

Foley, Malcolm Brian. Waco, TX. Affil: Baylor. Email: Malcolm_Foley@baylor.edu.

Foley, Neil, *Southern Methodist*. Dallas, TX. Email: foleyn@smu.edu. Research: immigration, comparative ethnic relations.

Foley, Sean E., *Middle Tennessee State*. Email: Sean.Foley@mtsu.edu.

Foley, Tom. Silver Spring, MD. Affil: Georgetown. Email: tfoley2@gmail.com.

Foley, Vernard L., *Purdue*. Email: foleyv@purdue.edu.

Foley, William E., *Central Missouri*. Email: foleyw@charter.net.

Follett, Richard R., *Covenant*. Lookout Mountain, GA. Email: follett@covenant.edu. Research: 19th-c British culture and politics, contemporary Europe/European integration.

Follett, Westley N., *Southern Mississippi*. Email: westley.follett@usm.edu.

Folmar, J. K., *California, Pa.*

Folsom, Bradley Neill, *Texas, Arlington*. Email: bfolsom@uta.edu.

Folsom, Gabriella Virginia. Lancaster, NY. Affil: American. Email: gf1549a@american.edu.

Folsom, Raphael B., *Oklahoma (Hist.)*. Norman, OK. Email: raphael.folsom@ou.edu. Research: Yaqui people under Spanish rule, war and ethnicity in early Mexico.

Folts, James D., Jr., *New York State Archives*. Email: jim.folts@nysed.gov.

Foner, Eric, *Columbia (Hist.)*. New York, NY. Email: ef17@columbia.edu. Research: Civil War and Reconstruction, slavery.

Fones-Wolf, Elizabeth A., *West Virginia*. Email: efwolf@wvu.edu.

Fones-Wolf, Ken, *West Virginia*. Email: kfoneswo@wvu.edu.

Fonge, Fuabeh P., *North Carolina A&T State*. Email: fpfonge@ncat.edu.

Fontaine, Darcie S., *South Florida, Tampa*. Email: dfontaine@usf.edu.

Fontana, Jason Gregory. Miami, FL. Affil: Florida International. Email: jasonfontana.salon@gmail.com.

Fontenot, Erica Nicole. Bastrop, LA. Affil: Arizona. Email: eri.nic@hotmail.com. Research: battlefield preservation, dark and tourist.

Fontenot, Garrett Andrew. New Orleans, LA. Affil: Tulane. Email: gafonten@gmail.com.

Fontenot, Michael J., *Southeastern Louisiana*. Email: Michael.Fontenot@southeastern.edu.

Fonvielle, Chris E., Jr., *North Carolina, Wilmington*. Email: fonviellec@uncw.edu.

Foote, Lorien L., *Texas A&M*. Email: lfoote@tamu.edu.

Foote, Nicola Claire. Tempe, AZ. Affil: Arizona State. Email: Nicola.Foote@asu.edu. Research: 20th-c Ecuador, race and gender in Caribbean.

Foote, Stephanie. Brevard, NC. Affil: John N. Gardner Inst. for Excellence. Email: foote@jngi.org.

Foppiani, Oreste. Bellevue, Switzerland. Affil: Webster, Geneva. Email: foppiani@webster.ch. Research: Italian-German-Japanese relations in WWII, Fascist Italian Red Cross 1943-45.

Foray, Jennifer L., *Purdue*. West Lafayette, IN. Email: jforay@purdue.edu. Research: imperialism and decolonization, Holocaust.

Forbath, William E., *Texas, Austin*. Email: wforbath@law.utexas.edu.

Forbes, Geraldine M., *SUNY, Oswego*. Syracuse, NY. Email: geraldine.forbes@oswego.edu. Research: South Asian colonial and women, South Asian photography.

Forbes, Michael. White Bear Lake, MN. Email: michaeljayforbes@gmail.com.

Forbes, Robert P. New Haven, CT. Affil: Southern Connecticut State. Email: robert.forbes@aya.yale.edu. Research: pre-1860 African American culture, construction of race.

Force, Pierre, *Columbia (Hist.)*. Email: pf3@columbia.edu.

Ford, Bridget, *California State, East Bay*. Hayward, CA. Email: bridget.ford@csueastbay.edu. Research: antebellum religious, cultural.

Ford, Caroline C., *UCLA*. Email: cford@history.ucla.edu.

Ford, Charles H. Norfolk, VA. Affil: Norfolk State. Email: chfor888@gmail.com. Research: Afro-Caribbean religions, religion and politics in Atlantic world.

Ford, Coleman M. Argyle, TX. Email: coleman.ford@gmail.com.

Ford, Eileen Mary, *California State, Los Angeles*. Los Angeles, CA. Email: eford@calstatela.edu. Research: childhood, visual culture.

Ford, Jennifer Putnam. King of Prussia, PA. Affil: Villanova. Email: jenniferlputnam@gmail.com. Research: archaeology, early America.

Ford, Judy Ann, *Texas A&M, Commerce*. Email: judy.ford@tamuc.edu.

Ford, Lacy K., Jr., *South Carolina, Columbia*. Email: ford@mailbox.sc.edu.

Ford, Lisa Lynn. New Haven, CT. Affil: Yale Center for British Art. Email: drllford@yahoo.com. Research: early modern political, visual culture and propaganda.

Ford, Melissa, *Slippery Rock*. Email: melissa.ford@sru.edu.

Ford, Nancy Gentile, *Bloomsburg*. Email: nford@bloomu.edu.

Ford, Tanisha C., *Delaware*. Email: tcford@udel.edu.

Forderhase, Nancy K. K., *Eastern Kentucky*.

Forderhase, R. E., *Eastern Kentucky*.

Foreman, Matthew. Evanston, IL. Affil: Northwestern. Email: matthewforeman2021@u.northwestern.edu.

Foreman, P. Gabrielle, *Delaware*. Email: gforeman@udel.edu.

Foreman, Tony. Lincoln, NE. Email: tonyforeman@rocketmail.com.

Forest, Timothy Steven, *Cincinnati*.

Forestell, Nancy M., *Dalhousie*. Email: nforeste@stfx.ca.

Forester, Rachel, *State Hist. Soc. of Missouri*. Email: foresterrl@shsmo.org.

Forgie, George B., *Texas, Austin*. Austin, TX. Email: forgie@mail.utexas.edu. Research: US, Jacksonian America.

Forland, Tor Egil. Blindern, Oslo, Norway. Affil: Oslo. Email: t.e.forland@iakh.uio.no. Research: student revolt and radicalization 1960s-70s, explanation in historiography.

Forman, Brian D. Evanston, IL. Affil: Northwestern. Email: brianforman2021@u.northwestern.edu.

Forman, Paul. Lincoln, MA. Email: formanp@gmail.com. Research: modernity and postmodernity, physics.

Forman-Brunell, Miriam, *Missouri–Kansas City*. Kansas City, MO. Email: forman-brunellm@umkc.edu. Research: girlhood, children and youth.

Formichi, Chiara, *Cornell*. Email: cf398@cornell.edu.

Formwalt, Lee W. Bloomington, IN. Email: lee.formwalt@gmail.com. Research: Southwest Georgia, civil rights.

Forner, Sean A., *Michigan State*. East Lansing, MI. Email: saforner@msu.edu. Research: post-1945 political culture and democracy, post-1950s European First New Left.

Foroohar, Manzar, *California Polytechnic State*. Email: mforooha@calpoly.edu.

Foroughi, Andrea R., *Union Coll.* Schenectady, NY. Email: forougha@union.edu. Research: women and gender, 19th century.

Forrest, Bernice E., *Colorado Colorado Springs*. Email: bguillau@uccs.edu.

Forrest, Kaitlyn. Fallbrook, CA. Email: kforrest1222@gmail.com.

Forrester, Max, *St. Thomas, Minn*. Email: mforrester@stthomas.edu.

Forret, Jeffrey Paul, *Lamar*. Email: forretjp@lamar.edu.

Forsberg, Carl. Kansas City, MO. Affil: Texas, Austin. Email: carl.w.forsberg@gmail.com.

Forsdyke, Sara L., *Michigan, Ann Arbor*. Email: forsdyke@umich.edu.

Forse, James H., *Bowling Green State*. Email: jforse@bgsu.edu.

Forsman, Deanna Dawn. San Jose, CA. Affil: North Hennepin Comm. Coll. Email: deanna.forsman@nhcc.edu. Research: Anglo-Saxon England, Merovingian Frankia.

Forss, Amy Helene. Omaha, NE. Affil: Metropolitan Comm. Coll. Email: aforss@mccneb.edu. Research: African American/Mildred Brown, women/Equal Rights Amendment process.

Forster, Cindy, *Scripps*. Email: cindy.forster@scrippscollege.edu.

Forster, J. J. Benjamin, *Western Ontario*. Email: bforster@uwo.ca.

Forster, Marc R., *Connecticut Coll.* New London, CT. Email: mrfor@conncoll.edu. Research: taverns and inns in German villages, Catholic Germany 1500-1800.

Forster, Robert, *Johns Hopkins (Hist.)*. Cockeysville, MD. Email: elbobf@aol.com. Research: 18th-/19th-c French social and economic.

Forsyth, Adam B. Washington, DC. Email: adambforsyth@gmail.com.

Forsyth, Douglas J., *Bowling Green State*. Bowling Green, OH. Email: dougfor@bgsu.edu. Research: comparative economic policy, comparative national financial systems.

Forsythe, Gary, *Texas Tech*. Email: gary.forsythe@ttu.edu.

Forsythe, James L., *Fort Hays State*. Email: jforsyth@fhsu.edu.

Fortenberry, Nelson. Kalispell, MT. Affil: Montana State, Bozeman. Email: nelson.fortenberry@gmail.com.

Forth, Aidan, *Loyola, Chicago*. Email: aforth@luc.edu.

Forth, Christopher E., *Kansas*. Email: ce.forth@anu.edu.au.

Fortin, David W. Philadelphia, PA. Affil: St. Joseph's Preparatory Sch. Email: dfortin@sjprep.org. Research: British social 1300-1600, Welsh social 1300-1600.

Fortin, Roger A., *Xavier, Ohio*. Email: fortin@xavier.edu.

Fortner, Laura Kate. Marks, MS. Email: laurakatefortner@gmail.com.

Fortney, Jeffrey, *Florida Gulf Coast*. Email: jfortney@fgcu.edu.

Fortuna, James J. Winsted, CT. Affil: St Andrews. Email: jf253@st-andrews.ac.uk. Research: architecture and imagery of New Deal, architectural diplomacy.

Fosl, Catherine A., *Louisville*. Email: cfosl@louisville.edu.

Foss, Christopher. Portland, OR. Affil: Portland. Email: foss2007@gmail.com. Research: Pacific Northwest, sports.

Foss, Clive F., *Massachusetts, Boston*.

Foss, Sarah, *Oklahoma State*.

Fossella, Jason Curtis. Saint Louis, MO. Affil: St. Louis. Email: jcfossella@gmail.com.

Foster, A. Kristen, *Marquette*. Email: kristen.foster@marquette.edu.

Foster, Amy E., *Central Florida*. Email: Amy.Foster@ucf.edu.

Foster, **Anne L.**, *Indiana State; Soc. for Hist. of American Foreign Relations*. Terre Haute, IN. Email: Anne.Foster@indstate.edu. Research: opium in Southeast Asia, US imperialism.

Foster, **Buckley T.**, *Central Arkansas*. Email: bfoster@uca.edu.

Foster, **Carrie A.**, *Miami, Ohio*. Email: fosterca@miamioh.edu.

Foster, **Christopher G.** Gales Ferry, CT. Affil: Soc. of Automotive Hist. Email: kit@kitfoster.com. Research: steam automobiles, Anglo-American automobile ventures.

Foster, **Cody James**. Lexington, KY. Affil: Kentucky. Email: cjfoster@indiana.edu. Research: Vietnam War, anti-war movement.

Foster, **Elizabeth A.** Medford, MA. Affil: Tufts. Email: elizabeth.foster@tufts.edu. Research: church and state in colonial Senegal, religion and politics in Third Republic France.

Foster, **Gaines M.**, *Louisiana State*. Baton Rouge, LA. Email: hyfost@lsu.edu. Research: New South.

Foster, **Gavin M.**, *Concordia, Can.* Email: Gavin.Foster@concordia.ca.

Foster, **Jonathan L.** Elko, NV. Affil: Great Basin. Email: jonathan.foster@gbcnv.edu. Research: Civilian Conservation Corps.

Foster, **Lawrence**, *Georgia Inst. of Tech.* Email: lawrence.foster@hts.gatech.edu.

Foster, **Letoshia**. Memphis, TN. Affil: Memphis. Email: mstosh62@yahoo.com. Research: African American, medical.

Foster, **Martha Harroun**, *Middle Tennessee State*. Email: Martha.Foster@mtsu.edu.

Foster, **Robert W.**, *Berea*. Berea, KY. Email: robert_foster@berea.edu. Research: East Asia, Asian philosophies and religions.

Foster, **Stephen**, *Northern Illinois*. Chicago, IL. Email: sfoster@niu.edu. Research: British North America within empire, 18th-c New England religion and politics.

Foster, **Teresa Bass**. Sneads Ferry, NC. Affil: Howard Comm. Coll. Email: fostert1@umbc.edu. Research: 18th-c British convict transportation, colonial Maryland women/labor.

Foster, **Theodore**, *Louisiana, Lafayette*. Email: theodore.foster@louisiana.edu.

Foster, **Thomas A.** Washington, DC. Affil: Howard. Email: taf_2@hotmail.com. Research: gender, sexuality.

Foti, **Luca Roberto**. Saint Louis, MO. Affil: Washington, St. Louis. Email: l.r.foti@wustl.edu. Research: late medieval communal Italy, Inquisition and heresy.

Fouad, **Geoffrey**, *Monmouth*. Email: gfouad@monmouth.edu.

Fougeres, **Dany**, *Québec, Montréal*. Email: fougeres.dany@uqam.ca.

Fought, **Leigh**, *Le Moyne*. Email: foughtlk@lemoyne.edu.

Foulkes, **Julia**, *New School*. New York, NY. Email: foulkesj@newschool.edu. Research: 20th-c US arts, arts/politics/urbanization.

Fountain, **Aaron Gregory**, *Jr.* Bloomington, IN. Affil: Indiana. Email: aafounta@iu.edu.

Fountain, **Steven M.**, *Washington State, Pullman*. Vancouver, WA. Email: sfountain@wsu.edu. Research: European-Native American contact, environment and culture.

Fouraker, **Lawrence**, *St. John Fisher*. Email: lfouraker@sjfc.edu.

Fourmy, **Signe Peterson**. Austin, TX. Affil: Texas, Austin. Email: signepfourmy@utexas.edu.

Fournier, **Eric**, *West Chester*. Email: efournier@wcupa.edu.

Fourshey, **C. Cymone**, *Bucknell*. Lewisburg, PA. Email: ccf014@bucknell.edu. Research: Tanzanian agricultural, hospitality.

Fousek, **John H.** New York, NY. Affil: NYU. Email: john.fousek@nyu.edu. Research: origins of Cold War, ideology and US foreign policy in 1990s.

Fousekis, **Natalie M.**, *California State, Fullerton*. Email: nfousekis@fullerton.edu.

Fouser, **David C.**, *Chapman*. Email: fouser@chapman.edu.

Foust, **Clifford M.**, *Jr.*, *Maryland, Coll. Park*. Email: cfoust@wam.umd.edu.

Fowler, **Charles Collin**. Atlantic Beach, FL. Affil: US Navy. Email: charlescfowler@icloud.com.

Fowler, **Mayhill C.** DeLand, FL. Affil: Stetson. Email: mfowler@stetson.edu. Research: theatre in Soviet Ukraine, military entertainment.

Fowler, **William M.**, *Jr.*, *Northeastern*. Email: w.fowler@neu.edu.

Fowler, **Wilton**, *Washington, Seattle*. Email: willfowl@uw.edu.

Fox, **Carrie**, *Central Oklahoma*. Email: cfox@uco.edu.

Fox, **Daniel M.** New York, NY. Affil: Milbank Memorial Fund. Email: dmfox@milbank.org. Research: US health politics and policy, comparative health politics and policy.

Fox, **Frank W.**, *Brigham Young*. Email: frank_fox@byu.edu.

Fox, **John J.**, *Salem State*. Email: john.fox@salemstate.edu.

Fox, **John W.** Brewster, NY. Email: npsguide@gmail.com.

Fox, **Levi**. Somers Point, NJ. Affil: Temple. Email: levi.fox@temple.edu.

Fox, **Richard Wightman**, *Southern California*. Email: rfox@usc.edu.

Fox, **Ronald Charles**. Waco, TX. Affil: American Public. Email: foxrapp@aol.com. Research: role of Navy in Civil War, General James B. McPherson.

Fox Keller, **Evelyn**, *MIT*. Email: efkeller@mit.edu.

Fox-Amato, **Matthew**, *Idaho*. Email: mamato@uidaho.edu.

Foxley, **Curtis**. Norman, OK. Affil: Oklahoma. Email: curtfoxley@ou.edu.

Foy, **Charles R.**, *Eastern Illinois*. Email: crfoy@eiu.edu.

Fozdar, **Vahid J.**, *California State, East Bay*. Hayward, CA. Email: vahid.fozdar@csueastbay.edu. Research: Indian Freemasonry and nationalism, British Freemasonry and imperialism.

Fracchia, **Helena**, *Alberta*. Email: helena.fracchia@ualberta.ca.

Fracchia, **Joseph**, *Oregon*. Email: fracchia@uoregon.edu.

Frader, **Laura Levine**, *Northeastern*. Boston, MA. Email: l.frader@neu.edu. Research: 20th-c French gender and society, 20th-c French race and empire.

Fraga, **Mike**, *Chapman*. Email: fraga@chapman.edu.

Fraga, **Sean**. Princeton, NJ. Affil: Princeton. Email: seanfraga@gmail.com.

Frager, **Ruth**, *McMaster*. Email: frager@mcmaster.ca.

Frake, **Amy**. Houston, TX. Affil: Holocaust Museum Houston. Email: amyfrake@gmail.com.

Frakes, **Robert M.**, *Clarion, Pa.* Bakersfield, CA. Affil: California State, Bakersfield. Email: rfrakes@clarion.edu; rfrakes1@csub.edu. Research: Roman law, Roman historiography.

Fraley, **J. David**, *Jr.*, *Birmingham-Southern*.

Francavilla, **Lisa A.**, *Robert H. Smith Center*. Email: lfrancavilla@monticello.org.

Francesconi, **Federica**, *SUNY, Albany*. Email: ffrancesconi@albany.edu.

Francis, **Charles**. Washington, DC. Email: ccfrancis@aol.com.

Francis, **Edgar Walter, IV**, *Wisconsin-Stevens Point*. Email: efrancis@uwsp.edu.

Francis, **J. Michael**, *South Florida, St. Petersburg*. Email: jmfrancis1@mail.usf.edu.

Francis, **Joan A.** Takoma Park, MD. Affil: Washington Adventist. Email: jfrancis@wau.edu. Research: social and women, African American urban.

Francis, **R. Douglas**, *Calgary*. Email: francis@ucalgary.ca.

Francis, **Stephen S.**, *Weber State*. Email: sfrancis@weber.edu.

Francis, **Walter**, *Jr.* Capron, VA. Affil: American. Email: wf0295a@american.edu.

Francis-Fallon, **Benjamin**, *Western Carolina*. Cullowhee, NC. Email: bfrancisfallon@email.wcu.edu; francisfallon@gmail.com. Research: US Latino politics, nativism.

Franco, **Bradley**, *Portland*. Email: franco@up.edu.

Franco, **Robert**. Philadelphia, PA. Affil: Duke. Email: robert.franco@duke.edu. Research: Communism, homophobia.

Francois, **Marie E.**, *California State, Channel Islands*. Camarillo, CA. Email: marie.francois@csuci.edu. Research: housekeeping as cultural production, domestic service.

Francois, **Samantha Yates**, *California State, East Bay*. Email: samantha.francois@csueastbay.edu.

Franczak, **Michael Edward**. Chestnut Hill, MA. Affil: Boston Coll. Email: franczam@bc.edu.

Franczyk, **David**, *SUNY, Buffalo State*. Email: franczda@buffalostate.edu.

Frangakis-Syrett, **Elena**, *Graduate Center, CUNY; Queens, CUNY*. Email: elenafs@aol.com; elena_frangakis-syrett@qc.cuny.edu.

Frangos, **John E.**, *Lehman, CUNY*. Manhasset, NY. Email: jefny60@verizon.net. Research: health care and disease, modern Europe.

Frank, **Andrew K.**, *Florida State*. Email: afrank@fsu.edu.

Frank, **Christopher**, *Manitoba*. Email: chris.frank@umanitoba.ca.

Frank, **Dana**, *California, Santa Cruz*. Email: dlfrank@ucsc.edu.

Frank, **Daniel**, *Ohio State*. Email: frank.152@osu.edu.

Frank, **David A.**, *New Brunswick*. Email: dfrank@unb.ca.

Frank, **Jerritt J.**, *Missouri, Columbia*. Email: frankje@missouri.edu.

Frank, **Joshua**. Santa Ana, CA. Affil: New Mexico. Email: jstjoshn@unm.edu.

Frank, **Richard I.**, *California, Irvine*. Email: rifrank@uci.edu.

Frank, **Robert G.**, *Jr.*, *UCLA*. Email: rfrankj@ucla.edu.

Frank, **Ronald**, *Pace*. Email: rfrank2@pace.edu.

Frank, **Ross H**. La Jolla, CA. Affil: California, San Diego. Email: rfrank@ucsd.edu. Research: American Indian/indigenous studies, colonial North America.

Frank, **Stephen**, *UCLA*. Email: frank@history.ucla.edu.

Frank, **Thomas E.**, *Wake Forest*. Email: frankte@wfu.edu.

Frank, **Zephyr L.**, *Stanford*. Email: zfrank@stanford.edu.

Frank Johnson, **Alison**, *Harvard (Hist.)*. Cambridge, MA. Email: afrank@fas.harvard.edu. Research: Habsburg maritime empire, abolition of death penalty in Austria.

Frankel, **Oz**, *New School*. Email: frankelo@newschool.edu.

Frankel, **Richard E.**, *Louisiana, Lafayette*. Email: frankel@louisiana.edu.

Frankforter, **A. Daniel, III**, *Penn State*. Email: adf1@psu.edu.

Frankle, **Robert J.**, *Memphis*. Email: rfrankle@memphis.edu.

Franklin, **Arnold**, *Queens, CUNY*. Email: arnold.franklin@qc.cuny.edu.

Franklin, **Brian Russell**. Dallas, TX. Affil: Southern Methodist. Email: brfranklin@smu.edu. Research: missions/denominationalism, religion/region/nationalism.

Franklin, **Catharine R.**, *Texas Tech*.

Franklin, **J. S.** Cambridge City, IN. Affil: Indiana East. Email: jsfrankl@iu.edu.

Franklin, **Jimmie L.**, *Vanderbilt*. Email: jimmiefranklin@comcast.net.

Franklin, **John K.** Lamoni, IA. Affil: Graceland. Email: jkfrankl@graceland.edu.

Franklin, **Robert**, *Washington State, Pullman*. Email: robert.franklin@wsu.edu.

Franklin, **Sarah L.**, *North Alabama*. Email: sfranklin@una.edu.

Franklin, **V. P.**, *California, Riverside*. New Orleans, LA. Email: vp.franklin@ucr.edu; vpf1019@aol.com. Research: African American, American education.

Franklin-Harkrider, **Melissa L.**, *Wheaton, Ill.* Email: melissa.harkrider@wheaton.edu.

Franklin-Rahkonen, **Sharon**, *Indiana, Pa.* Email: franklin@iup.edu.

Franks, **Joel S.** San Jose, CA. Affil: San Jose State. Email: joel.franks@sjsu.edu. Research: Asian American sport, race/ethnicity/sport.

Franks, **Luke A.**, *North Central*. Email: lafranks@noctrl.edu.

Frankum, **Ronald B, Jr.**, *Millersville, Pa.* Email: ronald.frankum@millersville.edu.

Frantz, **Edward O.**, *Indianapolis*. Indianapolis, IN. Email: efrantz@uindy.edu. Research: US 1877-1920, Midwest.

Frantz, **John B.**, *Penn State*. Email: jbf2@psu.edu.

Frantz (Parsons), **Elaine**, *Kent State*. Email: eparso12@kent.edu.

Franz, **John D.** Pensacola, FL. Email: jdf3638@gmail.com.

Franzen, **Katharine G.**, *Mary Baldwin*. Email: kfranzen@mbc.edu.

Franzen, **Trisha**, *Albion*. Email: tfranzen@albion.edu.

Fraser, **Erica L.**, *Carleton, Can.* Ottawa, ON, Canada. Email: erica.fraser@carleton.ca. Research: gender and Cold War, masculinities and political cultures.

Fraser, **James W.** New York, NY. Affil: NYU. Email: jwf3@nyu.edu. Research: teaching US history in high school, teacher education.

Fraser, **James**, *Guelph*. Email: jfrase08@uoguelph.ca.

Fraser, **Max**, *Miami*. Email: history@miami.edu.

Fraser, **Steven**. New York, NY.

Fraser Connolly, **Mary Beth**. Porter, IN. Affil: Purdue Northwest, Westville. Email: mbfconnolly@outlook.com. Research: American Catholic women religious, American Catholic Church.

Frassetto, **Michael**, *La Salle*. Email: frassetto83@lasalle.edu.

Fratantuono, **Ella**, *North Carolina, Charlotte*. Charlotte, NC. Email: efratant@uncc.edu. Research: Islamic world.

Fraterrigo, **Elizabeth S.**, *Loyola, Chicago*. Email: efrater@luc.edu.

Frawley, **Michael S.**, *Texas, Permian Basin*. Odessa, TX. Email: frawley_m@utpb.edu. Research: antebellum southern industry.

Frazee, **Charles A.**, *California State, Fullerton*. Email: cfrazee@sbcglobal.net.

Frazier, **Alison K.**, *Texas, Austin*. Email: akfrazier@austin.utexas.edu.

Frazier, **Lessie Jo**, *Indiana*. Email: frazierl@indiana.edu.

Frazier, **Nishani**, *Miami, Ohio*. Email: frazien@miamioh.edu.

Frazier, **Tony A.** Durham, NC. Affil: North Carolina Central. Email: tfrazie5@nccu.edu. Research: slavery in 18th-c London, African American.

Frede, **Victoria**, *California, Berkeley*. Email: vfrede@berkeley.edu.

Frederick, **Jake**. Appleton, WI. Affil: Lawrence. Email: jake.frederick@lawrence.edu. Research: colonial Mexico, Fire.

Frederick, **John Henry**. Lafayette, LA. Affil: South Louisiana Comm. Coll. Email: augustknight251989@gmail.com.

Frederick, **Julia**, *Louisiana, Lafayette*. Email: julia@louisiana.edu.

Frederick, **William H.**, *Ohio*. Email: frederic@ohio.edu.

Frederickson, **Kari**, *Alabama, Tuscaloosa*. Email: kfrederi@as.ua.edu.

Frederickson, **Mary E.**, *Miami, Ohio*. Email: frederme@miamioh.edu.

Fredette, **Allison Dorothy**, *Appalachian State*. Email: fredettead@appstate.edu.

Freeberg, **Ernest**, *Tennessee, Knoxville*. Email: efreeber@utk.edu.

Freed, **Joann Zeiset**, *Alberta*. Email: freed@ualberta.ca.

Freed, **John B**. Bloomington, IL. Affil: Illinois State. Email: jbfreed@ilstu.edu. Research: Illinois State U., Frederick Barbarossa.

Freed, **Libbie J.**, *SUNY, Coll. Potsdam*. Email: freedlj@potsdam.edu.

Freedman, **Estelle B.**, *Stanford*. Stanford, CA. Email: ebf@stanford.edu. Research: rape in US, feminism.

Freedman, **Joseph S**. Montgomery, AL. Affil: Alabama State. Email: joseph-freedman@usa.net. Research: schools and universities 1400-1800, intellectual 1400-1800.

Freedman, **Katherine**. Northampton, MA. Affil: Massachusetts Amherst. Email: kfreedman@library.umass.edu. Research: Quakerism, Slavery.

Freedman, **Paul Harris**, *Yale*. New Haven, CT. Email: paul.freedman@yale.edu. Research: food and cuisine, medieval Catalonia.

Freehling, **William W**. Fredericksburg, VA. Affil: Kentucky. Email: wwf4n@virginia.edu.

Freeland, **Richard M.**, *Northeastern*. Email: r.freeland@neu.edu.

Freeman, **David Fors**, *Missouri–Kansas City*. Email: freemandf@umkc.edu.

Freeman, **David**, *California State, Fullerton*. Email: dafreeman@fullerton.edu.

Freeman, **Erik John**. Wallingford, CT. Affil: Choate Rosemary Hall. Email: efreeman@choate.edu.

Freeman, **Joanne B.**, *Yale*. Email: joanne.freeman@yale.edu.

Freeman, **John Rich**, *Duke*. Email: jrf15@duke.edu.

Freeman, **Joshua B.**, *Graduate Center, CUNY; Queens, CUNY*. Email: jfreeman@gc.cuny.edu.

Freeman, **Joshua**. Cambridge, MA. Affil: Harvard. Email: freeman01@g.harvard.edu. Research: modern China, 20th-c socialism.

Freeman, **Julie D.**, *SUNY, Oneonta*. Email: julie.freeman@oneonta.edu.

Freeman, **Kirrily**, *St. Mary's, Can*. Email: kirrily.freeman@smu.ca.

Freeman, **Mary T.**, *Maine, Orono*. Email: mary.t.freeman@maine.edu.

Freeman, **Stephanie**, *Mississippi State*.

Freeman, **Susan K**. Kalamazoo, MI. Affil: Western Michigan. Email: susan.freeman@wmich.edu. Research: LGBT studies.

Freeze, **ChaeRan**, *Brandeis*. Email: cfreeze@brandeis.edu.

Freeze, **Gregory L.**, *Brandeis*. Email: freeze@brandeis.edu.

Frehner, **Brian W.**, *Missouri–Kansas City*.

Freifeld, **Alice**, *Florida*. Email: freifeld@ufl.edu.

Freije, **Vanessa**. Seattle, WA. Affil: Washington, Seattle. Email: vfreije@uw.edu. Research: modern Mexico, politics/scandal/press.

Freire, **Carl**. Suginami-ku, Tokyo, Japan. Affil: Kokugakuin. Email: carl@carlfreire.com. Research: religion and civil society, religious cooperation.

Freitag, **Jason P.**, *Ithaca*. Email: jfreitag@ithaca.edu.

Freitas, **Frederico Santos Soares**, *North Carolina State*. Raleigh, NC. Email: f_freitas@ncsu.edu. Research: Brazil, digital.

Fremion, **Brittany Bayless**, *Central Michigan*. Mount Pleasant, MI. Email: fremi1b@cmich.edu. Research: environmental activism, gender and environment.

French, **Amy Holtman**. University Center, MI. Affil: Delta. Email: amyfrench@delta.edu. Research: Gilded Age labor/gender/law, Michigan workers and crisis of masculinity.

French, **Dorothea**, *Santa Clara*. Email: dfrench@scu.edu.

French, **Gregg Michael**. Amherstburg, ON, Canada. Affil: Western Ontario. Email: gfrench4@uwo.ca. Research: US-Spanish relations/American empire, inter-imperial transfers/world history.

French, **John D.**, *Duke*. Email: jdfrench@duke.edu.

French, **Kara M.**, *Salisbury*. Email: kmfrench@salisbury.edu.

French, **Katherine L.**, *Michigan, Ann Arbor*. Ann Arbor, MI. Email: frenchk@umich.edu. Research: medieval women, medieval material culture.

French, **Scot A**., *Central Florida*. Orlando, FL. Email: scot.french@ucf.edu. Research: geographic mobility and social networks, digital methods andl historiography.

French, **William E**., *British Columbia*. Email: wfrench@mail.ubc.ca.

Frens-String, **Joshua**, *Texas, Austin*. Email: jfstring@austin.utexas.edu.

Frentzos, **Christos G**., *Austin Peay State*. Email: frentzosc@apsu.edu.

Frenzer, **Meagan Therese**. Gainesville, FL. Affil: Florida. Email: mfrenzer@ufl.edu.

Fretwell, **Elizabeth**. Portland, OR. Affil: Reed. Email: Efretwell@uchicago.edu. Research: African urban and global, colonialism and empire.

Freund, **Alexander**, *Winnipeg*. Email: a.freund@uwinnipeg.ca.

Freund, **David M. P**., *Maryland, Coll. Park*. Email: dmfreund@umd.edu.

Freund, **Richard**, *Hartford*. Email: freund@hartford.edu.

Freundschuh, **Aaron C**., *Queens, CUNY*. Email: aaron.freundschuh@qc.cuny.edu.

Frey, **David S**., *US Military Acad*. Email: david.frey@usma.edu.

Frey, **James W**., *Wisconsin-Oshkosh*. Email: freyj@uwosh.edu.

Frey, **Linda S**., *Montana*. Email: linda.frey@umontana.edu.

Frey, **Marsha L**., *Kansas State*. Email: mfrey@ksu.edu.

Frey, **Richard C**., **Jr**., *Southern Oregon*. Ashland, OR. Research: US, historiography.

Frey, **Sylvia R**., *Tulane*. Email: frey@tulane.edu.

Freyer, **Tony**, *Alabama, Tuscaloosa*. Email: tfreyer@law.ua.edu.

Freyhofer, **Horst H**., *Plymouth State*.

Frick, **David**, *California, Berkeley*. Email: frick@berkeley.edu.

Friday, **Chris**, *Western Washington*. Email: Chris.Friday@wwu.edu.

Fridenson, **Patrick**. Paris, France. Affil: Centre de Recherches Historiques. Email: fridenso@ehess.fr.

Frieberg, **Annika E**., *San Diego State*. Email: afrieberg@sdsu.edu.

Fried, **John W**. Ossining, NY. Email: johnwfried@mac.com.

Fried, **Richard M**., *Illinois, Chicago*. Glen Ellyn, IL. Email: rmfried@uic.edu. Research: 20th-c US political, foreign policy.

Friedel, **Robert D**., *Maryland, Coll. Park*. Email: friedel@umd.edu.

Friedland, **Paul**, *Cornell*. Email: paf67@cornell.edu.

Friedlander, **Alan R**., *Southern Connecticut State*. Email: friedlandea1@southernct.edu.

Friedlander, **Saul**, *UCLA*. Email: friedlan@history.ucla.edu.

Friedman, **Andrea S**., *Washington, St. Louis*. Saint Louis, MO. Email: afriedman@wustl.edu. Research: sex and politics in 1950s, obscenity regulation.

Friedman, **Bernard**, *Indiana–Purdue, Indianapolis*.

Friedman, **Frank A**. Robesonia, PA.

Friedman, **Gail**. Yardley, PA. Email: gbfriedman21@gmail.com.

Friedman, **Hal M**., *Henry Ford Coll.; Soc. for Military Hist*. Email: friedman@hfcc.edu.

Friedman, **Jason**. Winchendon, MA. Affil: Winchendon Sch. Email: drjasonfriedman@

gmail.com. Research: late 1970s politics, presidential image and power.

Friedman, **Jerome**, *Kent State*.

Friedman, **Joan S**., *Wooster*. Wooster, OH. Email: jfriedman@wooster.edu. Research: American Judaism, debutante culture.

Friedman, **Jonathan**, *West Chester*. Email: jfriedman@wcupa.edu.

Friedman, **Laurence N**., *Western Connecticut State*. Email: friedmanl@wcsu.edu.

Friedman, **Lawrence J**., **Jr**., *Indiana*. Email: ljfriedm@indiana.edu.

Friedman, **Max Paul**, *American*. Washington, DC. Email: friedman@american.edu. Research: 20th-c US foreign relations.

Friedman, **Rebecca**, *Florida International*. Email: friedmar@fiu.edu.

Friedman, **Tami J**., *Brock*. Email: tfriedman@brocku.ca.

Friedrichs, **Christopher R**., *British Columbia*. Vancouver, BC, Canada. Email: crf@interchange.ubc.ca. Research: early modern German cities, German Jewish communities.

Friefeld, **Jacob Kane**. Lincoln, NE. Affil: Nebraska, Lincoln. Email: jfriefeld@huskers.unl.edu. Research: 19th century, administrative state.

Friend, **Craig Thompson**, *North Carolina State*. Email: craig_friend@ncsu.edu.

Friend, **John L**., *Tennessee, Knoxville*. Email: jlfriend@utk.edu.

Frierson, **Cathy A**., *New Hampshire, Durham*. Email: cathy.frierson@unh.edu.

Frierson, **Elizabeth B**., *Cincinnati*. Email: elizabeth.frierson@uc.edu.

Friery, **James**, *SUNY, Oneonta*. Email: james.friery@oneonta.edu.

Fries, **Gwen**, *Massachusetts Hist. Soc*. Email: gfries@masshist.org.

Friesen, **Abraham**, *California, Santa Barbara*.

Friesen, **Gerald A**., *Manitoba*. Email: gerald.friesen@umanitoba.ca.

Friesen, **Jean Usher**, *Manitoba*. Email: jean.friesen@umanitoba.ca.

Friesen, **Leonard G**., *Wilfrid Laurier*. Email: lfriesen@wlu.ca.

Friesen, **Oris D**. Scottsdale, AZ. Email: oris@orisfriesen.com.

Friguglietti, **James**. Billings, MT. Affil: Montana State, Billings. Email: jfriguglietti@msubillings.edu.

Frink, **Brenda D**., *Portland State*. Email: brenda.frink@pdx.edu.

Frink, **Sandra M**., *Roosevelt*. Email: sfrink@roosevelt.edu.

Friot, **Elena**. Tampa, FL. Affil: New Mexico. Email: efriot@unm.edu. Research: WWII memory and commemoration, New Mexico and the Pacific Theater.

Frisch, **Michael H**., *SUNY, Buffalo*. Email: mfrisch@buffalo.edu.

Friss, **Evan Jay**, *James Madison*. Harrisonburg, VA. Email: frissej@jmu.edu; ejfriss@gmail.com. Research: public.

Fritz, **Harry W**., *Montana*. Email: harry.fritz@umontana.edu.

Fritz, **Paul**, *McMaster*.

Fritz, **Stephen G**., *East Tennessee State*. Email: fritzs@etsu.edu.

Fritz, **Timothy David**, *Mount St. Mary's*. Email: fritz@msmary.edu.

Fritz, **Torie**. Syracuse, NY. Affil: Syracuse. Email: vrfritz@syr.edu. Research: Roma and Sinti, Nazi Germany.

Fritzsche, **Peter**, *Illinois, Urbana-Champaign*. Urbana, IL. Email: pfritzsc@illinois.edu. Research: modern Europe, 20th-c Germany.

Froehlich, **Judith**. Zurich, Switzerland. Affil: Zurich. Email: jmf@khist.uzh.ch. Research: transnational, 19th-c Japan.

Frohman, **Lawrence S**., *SUNY, Stony Brook*. Email: lawrence.frohman@stonybrook.edu.

Froide, **Amy M**., *Maryland, Baltimore County*. Baltimore, MD. Email: froide@umbc.edu. Research: female investors and single women, Britain 1500-1800.

Froiland, **Samuel David**. Eagan, MN. Affil: Illinois, Urbana-Champaign. Email: sdf3@illinois.edu. Research: extinction, Minnehaha Creek.

Frometa, **Maria Isabel**. Downey, CA. Email: maria.frometa@gmail.com.

Fromherz, **Allen**, *Georgia State*. Email: afromherz@gsu.edu.

Fromke, **Kara**. Kannapolis, NC. Email: karlynfro@mac.com. Research: empire and religion.

Fromm, **Martin**, *Worcester State*. Email: mfromm@worcester.edu.

Frommer, **Benjamin R**., *Northwestern*. Email: b-frommer@northwestern.edu.

Fronc, **Jennifer**, *Massachusetts, Amherst*. Email: jfronc@history.umass.edu.

Fronda, **Michael P**., *McGill*. Email: michael.fronda@mcgill.ca.

Frost, **Amanda Clark**. Santa Barbara, CA. Affil: California, Santa Barbara. Email: acfsb@aol.com. Research: medieval England and Normandy, Reign of Henry I 1100-35.

Frost, **Dennis J**., *Kalamazoo*. Email: dennis.frost@kzoo.edu.

Frost, **Frank**, *California, Santa Barbara*.

Frost, **Karolyn Smardz**, *Dalhousie*. Email: ksmardz@acadiau.ca.

Frost, **Peter Kip**, *Williams*. Email: pkf1@williams.edu.

Froysland, **Hayley**, *Indiana, South Bend*. Email: hfroysla@iusb.edu.

Fruhstuck, **Sabine**, *California, Santa Barbara*. Santa Barbara, CA. Email: fruhstuck@eastasian.ucsb.edu. Research: modern/contemp Japan/history/ethnography, sexuality/war/childhood.

Frumer, **Yulia**, *Johns Hopkins (Hist. of Science)*. Email: yfrumer@jhu.edu.

Fry, **Joseph A**., *Nevada, Las Vegas*. Email: joseph.fry@unlv.edu.

Fry, **Poppy**, *Puget Sound*. Email: pfry@pugetsound.edu.

Frydman, **Hannah Clare**. Somerville, MA. Affil: Rutgers. Email: hannah.frydman@rutgers.edu.

Frye, **David**, *Eastern Connecticut State*. Email: fryed@easternct.edu.

Fryer, **Darcy R**. New York, NY. Affil: Brearley Sch. Email: drfryer@aya.yale.edu. Research: economic and family life, youth in early America.

Fryer, **Heather E**., *Creighton*. Omaha, NE. Email: heatherfryer@creighton.edu. Research: American West during WWII, visual culture in American West.

Frykenberg, **Robert E**., *Wisconsin-Madison*. Email: frykenberg@wisc.edu.

Frykman, Niklas, *Pittsburgh*. Pittsburgh, PA. Email: nfrykman@gmail.com. Research: maritime radicalism, Atlantic age of revolution.

Frymire, John M., *Missouri, Columbia*. Email: frymirej@missouri.edu.

Fthenakis, Lisa. Washington, DC. Affil: Smithsonian Inst. Email: lisa.fthenakis@gmail.com.

Fu, Jia-Chen Wendy. Atlanta, GA. Affil: Emory. Email: jia-chen.fu@emory.edu. Research: health and nutrition in republican China.

Fu, Poshek, *Illinois, Urbana-Champaign*. Email: poshekfu@illinois.edu.

Fuentes, Marisa J., *Rutgers*. New Brunswick, NJ. Email: fuentesm@rci.rutgers.edu. Research: 18th-c Caribbean, slavery and women.

Fuentes, Pamela. New York, NY. Affil: Pace. Email: pfuentesperalta@pace.edu.

Fugler, Maj Thomas J., *US Air Force Acad*. Email: thomas.fugler@usafa.edu.

Fuhrer, Mary Babson. Littleton, MA. Email: mfuhrer@verizon.net. Research: New England 1800-1850, revolutionary/early Republic New England.

Fuhrmann, Christopher Joseph, *North Texas*. Email: cfuhrmann@unt.edu.

Fujita, James Hiroshi. Pearl City, HI. Affil: Leeward Comm. Coll., Hawaii System. Email: fujitaja@hawaii.edu. Research: US diplomatic, US military.

Fujitani, Takashi, *California, San Diego; Toronto*. Toronto, ON, Canada. Email: tfujitani@ucsd.edu; t.fujitani@utoronto.ca. Research: modern Japan, modern and contemporary Japanese cultural.

Fujita-Rony, Dorothy P., *California, Irvine*. Email: dfr@uci.edu.

Fujiwara, Aya, *Alberta*. Email: fujiwara@ualberta.ca.

Fulgham, Melissa Ellen. Mount Pleasant, TX. Affil: Northeast Texas Comm. Coll. Email: mwrockymountains@gmail.com.

Fulks, Barry A. Pittsburgh, PA. Affil: St. Vincent. Email: baf426@comcast.net.

Fullagar, Kate. Erskineville, Australia. Affil: Macquarie. Email: kate.fullagar@mq.edu.au.

Fuller, A. James, *Indianapolis*. Email: afuller@uindy.edu.

Fuller, Harcourt T., *Georgia State*. Email: hfuller@gsu.edu.

Fuller, Mary C. Cambridge, MA. Affil: MIT. Email: mcfuller@mit.edu.

Fuller, Mia. Berkeley, CA. Affil: California, Berkeley. Email: miafuller@gmail.com. Research: Italian colonial architecture, Italian Fascist-era New Towns.

Fuller, William C., Jr., *Naval War Coll*. Email: fullerw@comcast.net.

Fullerton, Dan C., *US Army Command Coll*. Email: dan.c.fullerton.civ@mail.mil.

Fullerton, Samuel Curtis. Riverside, CA. Affil: California, Riverside. Email: sfull005@ucr.edu.

Fullilove, Courtney A., *Wesleyan*. Email: cfullilove@wesleyan.edu.

Fulton, Robert Jay, Jr. Franklin Springs, GA. Affil: Emmanuel. Email: rfulton@ec.edu. Research: Louis XIV and France, Atlantic World networks.

Fulton Brown, Rachel L., *Chicago*. Email: rfulton@uchicago.edu.

Fulwider, Chad R., *Centenary, La.* Email: cfulwider@centenary.edu.

Fulwiler, Danielle. Algoma, WI. Email: dfulwilerrhs@gmail.com.

Funiciello, Patrick, *Tarleton State*. Email: funiciello@tarleton.edu.

Funigiello, Philip J., *William and Mary*. Email: pjfuni@yahoo.com.

Funk, Krista Marie. Sand Springs, OK. Email: Funkkrista@yahoo.com.

Funke, Claudia, *Huntington Library*. Email: cfunke@huntington.org.

Furdell, Elizabeth Lane, *North Florida*. Email: efurdell@unf.edu.

Fure-Slocum, Eric J., *St. Olaf*. Northfield, MN. Email: furesloc@stolaf.edu. Research: recent working-class political culture, mid-20th-c urban.

Furey, Constance, *Indiana*. Email: cfurey@indiana.edu.

Furgol, Mary T. Delhi, NY. Affil: Montgomery. Email: mary.furgol@montgomerycollege.edu.

Furlong, Jennifer Elizabeth. Cupertino, CA. Affil: Cupertino Hist. Soc. and Museum. Email: jennifer@cupertinohistoricalsociety.org.

Furlong, Patrick J., *Alma*. Alma, MI. Email: furlong@alma.edu. Research: comparative fascism, South African politics 1930s-40s.

Furlong, Patrick J., *Indiana, South Bend*. South Bend, IN. Email: pfurlong@iusb.edu. Research: Indiana, Arthur St. Clair and Northwest Territory.

Furner, Mary O., *California, Santa Barbara*. Email: furner@history.ucsb.edu.

Furstenberg, Francois, *Johns Hopkins (Hist.)*. Baltimore, MD. Email: f.furstenberg@jhu.edu. Research: US nationalism/early Republic, France in North America c. 1750-1820.

Furth, Charlotte D., *Southern California*. Email: cdfurth@gmail.com.

Fury, Cheryl A., *New Brunswick*. Email: cfury@unb.ca.

Futch, Jeff, *North Carolina Office of Archives*. Email: jeff.futch@ncdcr.gov.

Futrell, Alison, *Arizona*. Email: afutrell@u.arizona.edu.

Fysh, William. Toronto, ON, Canada. Affil: Toronto. Email: williamfysh@gmail.com.

G g

Gaab, Jeffrey S. Farmingdale, NY. Affil: Farmingdale State, SUNY. Email: gaabjs@farmingdale.edu. Research: 20th-c Europe, German political and cultural.

Gabaccia, Donna R., *Toronto*. Email: donna.gabaccia@utoronto.ca.

Gabbert, Mark A., *Manitoba*. Email: mark.gabbert@umanitoba.ca.

Gabel, Isabel. Philadelphia, PA. Affil: Pennsylvania. Email: gabel@sas.upenn.edu. Research: 20th-c biology, philosophy of history.

Gabin, Nancy F., *Purdue*. West Lafayette, IN. Email: ngabin@purdue.edu. Research: US social, women and labor.

Gabriel, Dexter J., *Connecticut, Storrs*. Storrs Mansfield, CT. Email: dexter.gabriel@uconn.edu.

Gabriel, Elun T., *St. Lawrence*. Canton, NY. Email: egabriel@stlawu.edu. Research: German anarchism and socialism, utopian socialism in Europe.

Gabriel, Michael P., *Kutztown*. Email: gabriel@kutztown.edu.

Gabriele, Matthew, *Virginia Tech*. Blacksburg, VA. Email: mgabriele@vt.edu. Research: apocalyptic expectation, Crusades.

Gac, Scott E., *Trinity Coll., Conn*. Hartford, CT. Email: scott.gac@trincoll.edu. Research: culture and antebellum reform, violence in American imagination.

Gaca, Kathy Lynn. Nashville, TN. Affil: Vanderbilt. Email: kathy.L.gaca@vanderbilt.edu. Research: ancient Greek to Byzantine, Rome.

Gaddis, John Lewis, *Yale*. Email: john.gaddis@yale.edu.

Gadkar-Wilcox, Wynn W., *Western Connecticut State*. Email: wilcoxw@wcsu.edu.

Gadotti, Alhena, *Towson*. Email: agadotti@towson.edu.

Gadsden, Brett V., *Northwestern*. Email: brett.gadsden@northwestern.edu.

Gaetano, Matthew, *Hillsdale*. Email: mgaetano@hillsdale.edu.

Gaffey, James P. Little River, CA. Email: JPGaffey@aol.com.

Gaffield, Chad. Ottawa, ON, Canada. Affil: Ottawa. Email: gaffield@uottawa.ca. Research: digital scholarship, official language identities.

Gaffield, Julia, *Georgia State*. Email: jgaffield@gsu.edu.

Gaffin, Virgilette Nzkngha. Cheyney, PA. Affil: Cheyney, Pa. Email: vgaffin@cheyney.edu.

Gage, Beverly, *Yale*. Email: beverly.gage@yale.edu.

Gage, Marielle, *Hist. Assoc*. Email: mgage@historyassociates.com.

Gaggio, Dario, *Michigan, Ann Arbor*. Ann Arbor, MI. Email: dariog@umich.edu. Research: technology and society, economic behavior and social values.

Gagliardi, Jess R. Alamosa, CO. Affil: Adams State. Email: jgagliardi@adams.edu. Research: US First Ladies, African Americans/civil rights movement.

Gagnon, Robert, *Québec, Montréal*. Email: gagnon.robert@uqam.ca.

Gahan, Daniel, *Evansville*. Email: dg23@evansville.edu.

Gahan, Jairan. Toronto, ON, Canada. Affil: Toronto. Email: jairan.gahan@mail.utoronto.ca.

Gaida, Margaret. Norman, OK. Affil: Oklahoma. Email: margaret.gaida@ou.edu.

Gaines, Kevin K., *Virginia*. Email: kkg2u@virginia.edu.

Gaitors, Beau D.J. Winston Salem, NC. Affil: Winston-Salem State. Email: gaitorsbd@wssu.edu. Research: African diaspora, public health.

Gajda, Patricia A., *Texas, Tyler*. Email: pgajda@uttyler.edu.

Galambos, Louis P., *Johns Hopkins (Hist.)*. Baltimore, MD. Email: galambos@jhu.edu. Research: US economic and political, institutional change since 1880.

Galan, Francis Xavier, *Texas A&M, San Antonio*. Email: francis.galan@tamusa.edu.

Galan-Guerrero, Luis Gabriel. Oxford, United Kingdom. Affil: Oxford. Email: luis.galan-guerrero@st-annes.ox.ac.uk.

Galanter, Lea. Kirkland, WA. Affil: Gallant Editorial Services. Email: lea@gallanteditorial.com. Research: early Celtic studies, Roman Britain.

Galbraith, **Gretchen**, *Grand Valley State.* Allendale, MI. Email: galbraig@gvsu.edu. Research: modern Britain, gender.

Galderisi, **Michael D.** Suffolk, VA. Email: mike@mdgalderisi.com.

Galgano, **Michael J.**, *James Madison.* Harrisonburg, VA. Email: galganmj@jmu.edu. Research: 17th-c gender conversations, 17th-c Catholic/Quaker women.

Galgano, **Michael**, *Hofstra.*

Galgano, **Robert C.**, *Richmond.* Email: rgalgano@richmond.edu.

Galili, **Ziva**, *Rutgers.* Email: galili@scarletmail.rutgers.edu.

Galishoff, **Stuart E.**, *Georgia State.*

Galison, **Peter L.**, *Harvard (Hist. of Science).* Email: galison@fas.harvard.edu.

Gall, **Jeffrey**, *Truman State.* Email: jgall@truman.edu.

Gallagher, **Charles R.**, **SJ**, *Boston Coll.* Email: gallagch@bc.edu.

Gallagher, **Gary W.**, *Virginia.* Email: gallagher@virginia.edu.

Gallagher, **Jennifer Ann.** Blacksburg, VA. Affil: Virginia Tech. Email: jennigal@vt.edu.

Gallagher, **Joseph Patrick.** Bayonne, NJ. Email: Ez4u2bee@gmail.com.

Gallagher, **Julie A.**, *Penn State.* Bethlehem, PA. Email: jag63@psu.edu. Research: women and politics, African Americans and politics.

Gallagher, **Michael Paul.** Chicago, IL. Email: mwgallagher@rcn.com.

Gallagher, **Nancy**, *California, Santa Barbara.* Email: gallagher@history.ucsb.edu.

Gallagher, **Ned.** Wallingford, CT. Affil: Choate Rosemary Hall. Email: ngallagher@choate.edu.

Gallagher, **Patrick**, *St. Joseph's.*

Gallagher, **Philip F.**, *Brooklyn, CUNY.* Email: philipg@brooklyn.cuny.edu.

Gallanis, **Thomas P.**, *Iowa.* Email: thomas-gallanis@uiowa.edu.

Gallant, **Thomas W.**, *California, San Diego.* La Jolla, CA. Email: tgallant@ucsd.edu. Research: modern Greece, violence and crime.

Gallay, **Alan**, *Ohio State; Texas Christian.* Fort Worth, TX. Email: gallay.1@osu.edu; a.gallay@tcu.edu. Research: Sir Walter Raleigh and English overseas, Indian slave trade.

Galle, **Jillian**, *Robert H. Smith Center.* Email: jgalle@monticello.org.

Galler, **Robert W.**, **Jr.**, *St. Cloud State.* Email: rwgaller@stcloudstate.edu.

Gallia, **Andrew B.**, *Minnesota (Hist.).* Email: abgallia@umn.edu.

Gallicchio, **Marc**, *Villanova.* Email: marc.gallicchio@villanova.edu.

Gallimore, **Mark K.**, *Canisius.* Email: gallimom@canisius.edu.

Gallman, **J. Matthew**, *Florida.* Email: gallmanm@ufl.edu.

Gallman, **Nancy O.**, *Lewis & Clark.* Portland, OR. Email: ngallman@lclark.edu. Research: Florida borderlands, law.

Gallo, **David M.**, *Mount St. Vincent.* Email: david.gallo@mountsaintvincent.edu.

Gallo, **Marcia M.**, *Nevada, Las Vegas.* Email: marcia.gallo@unlv.edu.

Gallo, **Marcus T.**, *John Carroll.* Broadview Heights, OH. Email: mgallo@jcu.edu. Research: backcountry surveying, land speculation.

Gallon, **Kim Teresa**, *Purdue.* Email: kgallon@purdue.edu.

Gallup-Diaz, **Ignacio J.**, *Bryn Mawr.* Email: igallupd@brynmawr.edu.

Galpern, **Allan N.**, *Pittsburgh.* Email: riocoa@pitt.edu.

Galpern, **Steven G.** Arlington, VA. Affil: US Dept. of State. Email: stevengalpern@comcast.net. Research: modern Palestinian politics, Middle East peace process in Oslo and after.

Galush, **William J.**, *Loyola, Chicago.* Email: wgalush@aol.com.

Galvan Mora, **Jojo.** Cicero, IL. Email: JC.Galvan@outlook.com.

Galvin, **Melissa.** Medford, NJ. Affil: American. Email: mg5556a@american.edu.

Gamache, **Emily.** Redmond, WA. Email: emgamache@gmail.com.

Gamal-Eldin, **Mohamed A.** Jersey City, NJ. Affil: New Jersey Inst. of Tech. Email: arabmny84@gmail.com.

Gamber, **Wendy E.**, *Indiana.* Bloomington, IN. Email: wgamber@indiana.edu. Research: 19th-c boarding houses, women business and labor.

Gambetti, **Sandra**, *Staten Island, CUNY.* Email: sandra.gambetti@csi.cuny.edu.

Gamble, **Richard M.**, *Hillsdale.* Email: rgamble@hillsdale.edu.

Gamble, **Vanessa Northington**. Washington, DC. Affil: George Washington. Email: vngamble@gwu.edu. Research: black women physicians, race.

Gambone, **Michael David**, *Kutztown.* Kutztown, PA. Email: gambone@kutztown.edu; montella.michaeld@gmail.com. Research: Latin America, recent US.

Games, **Alison F.**, *Georgetown.* Washington, DC. Email: gamesa@georgetown.edu. Research: early modern world, Atlantic.

Gamm, **Gerald H.**, *Rochester.* Email: gerald.gamm@rochester.edu.

Gampel, **Benjamin R.** New York, NY. Affil: Jewish Theological Seminary. Email: begampel@jtsa.edu. Research: late 14th-c Iberian Jewries.

Gamsjager, **Bryan David**. Yukon, OK. Affil: Yukon Public Sch. Email: bryangamsjager@yahoo.com.

Gan, **Cheong Soon**. Superior, WI. Affil: Wisconsin, Superior. Email: cheongsoon@gmail.com.

Ganaway, **Bryan F.**, *Charleston.* Email: ganawayb@cofc.edu.

Gandila, **Andrei**, *Alabama, Huntsville.* Email: andrei.gandila@uah.edu.

Gandle, **David L.** New London, NH. Affil: Mainz. Email: dlgandle3@gmail.com. Research: American expatriates in Weimar Germany, Lost Generation in 1920s Europe.

Gannon, **Barbara A.**, *Central Florida.* Email: Barbara.Gannon@ucf.edu.

Gannon, **Grael Brian**. Bismarck, ND. Email: grael.gannon@ndsu.edu.

Gannon, **Kevin M.** Des Moines, IA. Affil: Grand View. Email: kgannon@grandview.edu. Research: teaching and learning, race/racisms in history and higher education.

Ganor, **Sheer**. Berkeley, CA. Affil: California, Berkeley. Email: sheerganor@berkeley.edu. Research: German-Jewish migration and diaspora.

Ganson, **Barbara A.**, *Florida Atlantic.* Boca Raton, FL. Email: bganson@fau.edu. Research: Guarani encounters with Jesuits, aviation.

Gant, **Jesse John**. Saint Louis, MO. Affil: Wisconsin, Madison. Email: gant2@wisc.edu. Research: Republican Party, Old Northwest.

Gant, **Philip Alexander**. Palos Verdes Peninsula, CA. Affil: Harvard. Email: philipgant@fas.harvard.edu.

Ganyard, **Clifton**. Green Bay, WI. Affil: Wisconsin, Green Bay. Email: ganyardc@uwgb.edu. Research: nationalism and Weimar political culture, comparative Germany and Japan.

Ganz, **A. Harding**, *Ohio State.* Email: ganz.1@osu.edu.

Ganz, **Cheryl R**. Winfield, IL. Affil: Smithsonian National Postal Museum. Email: cherylganz@yahoo.com. Research: world's fairs, Great Depression.

Ganz, **Margery A.**, *Spelman.* Avondale Estates, GA. Email: mganz@spelman.edu. Research: 15th-c Florentine social and political, conspiracies against Medici.

Gao, **James Z.**, *Maryland, Coll. Park.* Email: jzgao@umd.edu.

Gao, **Jie**, *Murray State.* Email: selinahistory@gmail.com.

Gao, **Ruchen**. Minneapolis, MN. Affil: Minnesota, Twin Cities. Email: gaoxx444@umn.edu. Research: family dynamics, social and political movements of women.

Gao, **Xiaofei**, *Mount Holyoke.* Cambridge, MA. Email: xgao@mtholyoke.edu; gao.xiaofei09@gmail.com. Research: Manchuria, maritime.

Gaposchkin, **Cecilia**, *Dartmouth.* Email: m.c.gaposchkin@dartmouth.edu.

Garbarini, **Alexandra**, *Williams.* Williamstown, MA. Email: agarbari@williams.edu. Research: pogroms and human rights, self-writing/ego documents.

Garber, **Elizabeth**, *SUNY, Stony Brook.* Email: Elizabeth.Garber@stonybrook.edu.

Garber, **Marilyn**, *California State, Dominguez Hills.*

Garber, **Stephen J.**, *NASA.* Email: steve.garber@hq.nasa.gov.

Garbutt, **Tara**. Gretna, LA. Email: tlynellj@hotmail.com.

Garceau, **Dee**, *Rhodes.* Email: garceau@rhodes.edu.

Garcia, **Alberto**, *San José State.* Email: Alberto.Garcia@sjsu.edu.

Garcia, **Ashley Nicole**. Austin, TX. Affil: Texas, Austin. Email: ashleyngarcia@utexas.edu. Research: early American political radicals, American political development.

Garcia, **Guadalupe**, *Tulane.* Email: ggarcia4@tulane.edu.

Garcia, **Ignacio M.**, *Brigham Young.* Email: ignacio_garcia@byu.edu.

Garcia, **Joseph**. Oceanside, CA. Email: josepmg2@uci.edu.

Garcia, **Juan Ramon**, *Arizona.* Email: jugarcia@u.arizona.edu.

Garcia, **Maria Cristina**, *Cornell.* Ithaca, NY. Email: mcg20@cornell.edu. Research: US Latino/a, refugees.

Garcia, **Mario T.**, *California, Santa Barbara.* Email: garcia@history.ucsb.edu.

Garcia, **Matthew John**, *Dartmouth.* Email: matthew.garcia@dartmouth.edu.

Garcia, **Octavio Delgadillo**, *California State, San Marcos.* La Mesaa, CA. Affil: San Diego State. Email: ogarcia@csusm.edu; odgarcia@sdsu.edu. Research: African population in Central America, African population in Mexico.

AHA members in **bold italic**; Directory-listed affiliations in *italic*

Garcia, Ricardo M. Los Angeles, CA. Affil: Santa Monica. Email: rmedinagarcia@g.ucla.edu. Research: prehistory/history Mesoamerican ballgame, pictographic/alphabetic literacy.

Garcia, Richard A., *California State, East Bay*. Email: richard.garcia@csueastbay.edu.

Garcia, William. Lawrence, KS. Affil: Kansas. Email: williamgarcia8267@gmail.com. Research: Historical literacy in urban communities, media literacy and historical thinking.

Garcia de la Torre, Armando. Miami, FL. Affil: West Indies. Email: agt928@gmail.com. Research: 19th-c Cuba, 18th-19th-c Atlantic world.

Garcia Solares, Israel. Notre Dame, IN. Affil: Notre Dame. Email: isgarcia@colmex.mx.

Garcia y Griego, L. Manuel, *New Mexico*. Email: mgarciay@unm.edu.

Garcia-Bryce, Inigo L., *New Mexico State*. Email: igarciab@nmsu.edu.

Garcia-Guevara, Aldo Vladimir, *Worcester State*. Worcester, MA. Email: aguevara@worcester. edu. Research: Latin America.

Gardinier, David E., *Marquette*.

Gardner, Daniel K., *Smith*. Email: dgardner@ smith.edu.

Gardner, James B. Washington, DC. Email: gardnerjb@gmail.com. Research: museums and public.

Gardner, Kirsten E., *Texas, San Antonio*. San Antonio, TX. Email: kirsten.gardner@utsa.edu. Research: diabetes, women's health.

Gardner, Leigh A. London, United Kingdom. Affil: London Sch. of Economics and Political Sci. Email: l.a.gardner@lse.ac.uk. Research: British Empire, political economy.

Gardner, Lloyd C., *Rutgers*. Email: lgardner79@ gmail.com.

Gardner, Sarah E., *Mercer*. Macon, GA. Email: gardner_se@mercer.edu. Research: Civil War era America, print culture/history of the book.

Garfield, Robert, *DePaul*. Email: rgarfiel@depaul. edu.

Garfield, Seth W., *Texas, Austin*. Austin, TX. Email: sgarfield@mail.utexas.edu. Research: Latin American studies, Brazil.

Garfinkel, Paul A., *Simon Fraser*. Email: pgarfink@sfu.ca.

Garfinkle, Steven J., *Western Washington*. Email: Steven.Garfinkle@wwu.edu.

Garfunkel, Amanda, *La Guardia and Wa_ner Archives*. Email: amellinger@lagcc.cuny.edu.

Gargola, Daniel J., *Kentucky*. Email: djgarg01@ uky.edu.

Garhart, Margaret Anne. Millersville, MD. Affil: Case Western Reserve. Email: magarhart20@ gmail.com.

Garikes, George. Washington, DC. Affil: St. Stephens and St. Agnes Sch. Email: bgarikes@ sssas.org.

Garland, Amber Maree. Dobbin, TX. Affil: Lone Star; Blinn. Email: agarland@consolidated.net.

Garland, Martha MacMackin, *Ohio State*. Email: garland.1@osu.edu.

Garlitz, Richard P., *Tennessee, Martin*. Email: rgarlitz@utm.edu.

Garmon, Frank Warren, Jr. Newport News, VA. Affil: Christopher Newport. Email: fwg3gc@ virginia.edu. Research: American taxation and fiscal policy, wealth inequality and social mobility.

Garneau, Jean-Philippe, *Québec, Montréal*. Email: garneau.jean-philippe@uqam.ca.

Garner, Maj Christian, *US Military Acad*. Email: christian.garner@usma.edu.

Garnhart-Bushakra, Alexandra. Knoxville, TN. Affil: Tennessee, Knoxville. Email: agarnhar@ vols.utk.edu.

Garofalo, Leo J., *Connecticut Coll*. Email: lgar@ conncoll.edu.

Garon, Sheldon M., *Princeton*. Email: garon@ princeton.edu.

Garone, Philip F., *California State, Stanislaus*. Turlock, CA. Email: pgarone@csustan.edu. Research: wetlands/reclamation/restoration, climate change/public lands/Great Basin.

Garosi, Frank J., *California State, Sacramento*. Email: garosi@saclink.csus.edu.

Garrard, Virginia, *Texas, Austin*. Email: garrard@ austin.utexas.edu.

Garretson, E. P., Jr., *Washington State, Pullman*. Email: epgjr@wsu.edu.

Garrett, Alexandra. Charlottesville, VA. Affil: Virginia. Email: asg4c@virginia.edu. Research: early American Republic, women and gender/ slavery/entrepreneurs.

Garrett, Amy C., *US Dept. of State*.

Garrett, Clarke W., *Dickinson*.

Garrett, David T., *Reed*. Portland, OR. Email: david.garrett@reed.edu. Research: late colonial Cusco indigenous elites, Toledan reforms.

Garrett, Phillip. Florence, AL. Affil: Brooks High Sch. Email: phillip.garrett@lcschools.org.

Garrett-Goodyear, R. H., *Mount Holyoke*. South Hadley, MA. Email: hgarrett@mtholyoke.edu.

Garrett-Scott, Shennette, *Mississippi*. Email: mgscott@olemiss.edu.

Garrigus, John D., *Texas, Arlington*. Arlington, TX. Email: garrigus@uta.edu. Research: race and nation in Haiti, free people of color in slave societies.

Garriott, Caroline. San Marcos, TX. Affil: Duke. Email: carolinegarriott@gmail.com. Research: colonial Brazil, visual culture.

Garris, Renee. Fredericksburg, VA. Affil: Germanna Comm. Coll. Email: reneegarris@ hotmail.com. Research: women in Viet Nam Conflict, Jewish women WWII worldwide.

Garrison, J. Ritchie, *Delaware*. Email: jrg@udel. edu.

Garrison, Tim Alan, *Portland State*. Email: timgarrison@pdx.edu.

Garrity, Timothy Francis. Mount Desert, ME. Affil: Mount Desert Island Hist. Soc. Email: tim.garrity@mdihistory.org. Research: Borderlands Acadia National Park, Maine.

Garsaud, Mary M., *Hist. New Orleans*. Email: maryg@hnoc.org.

Gart, Jason H., *Hist. Assoc*. Email: jgart@ historyassociates.com.

Garthwaite, Gene R., *Dartmouth*. Email: gene. garthwaite@dartmouth.edu.

Garver, Bruce M., *Nebraska, Omaha*. Omaha, NE. Email: bgarver@unomaha.edu. Research: modern Europe, military.

Garver, Karen K., *Nebraska, Omaha*. Email: kgarver@unomaha.edu.

Garver, Valerie L., *Northern Illinois*. Email: vgarver@niu.edu.

Garza, Alejandra Christiana. Austin, TX. Affil: Texas, Austin. Email: alejandracgarza@ yahoo.com. Research: South Texas ranching, vaqueros and celebration.

Garza, James Alex, *Nebraska, Lincoln*. Email: jgarza2@unl.edu.

Garza, Melita Marie. Fort Worth, TX. Affil: Texas Christian. Email: melita.garza@tcu.edu.

Gasaway, Jared Matthew. Kernersville, NC. Email: jaredgasaway@gmail.com.

Gasdia, Russell Anthony. New York, NY. Affil: Yale. Email: russell.gasdia@yale.edu.

Gaskin, Thomas M. Everett, WA. Email: depat123@comcast.net. Research: Lyndon B. Johnson, Henry M. Jackson.

Gaspar, David Barry, *Duke*. Durham, NC. Email: dgaspar@duke.edu. Research: slavery and law in colonial British America, war and slave society in Americas.

Gasper, Michael E., *Occidental*. Los Angeles, CA. Email: gasper@oxy.edu. Research: history and memory in Arab world, secularism and nationalism in Middle East.

Gasser, Erika, *Cincinnati*.

Gastil, George, *San Diego State*.

Gaston, Jessie, *California State, Sacramento*. Email: gaston@csus.edu.

Gatchel, Theodore L., *Naval War Coll*. Email: gatchelt@gmail.com.

Gates, Allyson. Tallahassee, FL. Affil: Florida State. Email: astanton@fsu.edu. Research: WWII Pacific Theater, interservice relations.

Gates, Benton E., *Purdue, Fort Wayne*. Email: gatesb@pfw.edu.

Gates, John M., *Wooster*. Email: jgates@wooster. edu.

Gates, Rustin B. Coralville, IA. Affil: Bradley. Email: rustin.gates@gmail.com. Research: Japanese foreign policy 1868-1945, foreign minister Uchida Yasuya.

Gates-Coon, Rebecca A. North Potomac, MD. Affil: Library of Congress. Email: rgatcn@ gmail.com.

Gatson, Torren L., *North Carolina, Greensboro*. Greensboro, NC. Email: tlgatson@uncg.edu. Research: housing, material culture.

Gatti, Evan, *Elon*. Email: egatti@elon.edu.

Gatto, Chris. Deerfield, IL. Affil: Chicago. Email: gatto6189@gmail.com.

Gatzemeyer, Maj Garrett, *US Military Acad*. Email: garrett.gatzemeyer@usma.edu.

Gatzke, Andrea F., *SUNY, New Paltz*. Email: gatzkea@newpaltz.edu.

Gauderman, Kimberly A., *New Mexico*. Email: kgaud@unm.edu.

Gaudin, Wendy A., *Xavier, La.* Email: wgaudin@ xula.edu.

Gaudry, Rachel, *Hist. New Orleans*. Email: rachelg@hnoc.org.

Gaughan, Judy E., *Colorado State, Pueblo*. Email: judy.gaughan@csupueblo.edu.

Gauss, Susan M. Boston, MA. Affil: Massachusetts, Boston. Email: susan.gauss@ umb.edu. Research: Latin America, Mexico.

Gaustad, Blaine C. Arlington, MA. Email: blaine. gaustad@rcn.com. Research: late imperial Chinese popular religion, religion and state in China.

Gaut, Gregory A. Minneapolis, MN. Email: greggaut@gmail.com. Research: historic preservation, Minnesota.

Gautam, Sanjay, *Colorado, Boulder*. Email: sanjay.gautam@colorado.edu.

Gauthier, Ethan. Monrovia, CA. Email: epg25@ ymail.com.

Gautreau, Abigail, *Grand Valley State*. Email: gautreaa@gvsu.edu.

Gauvreau, Michael, *McMaster*. Email: mgauvrea@mcmaster.ca.

Gavac, Donna Broderick. Langley, WA. Affil: Alaska.

Gavitt, Philip R., *St. Louis*. Email: gavitt@slu.edu.

Gavorsky, Scott A. Elko, NV. Affil: Great Basin. Email: scott.gavorsky@gmail.com. Research: civil society and private associations, local government and education.

Gavrus, Delia, *Winnipeg*. Email: d.gavrus@uwinnipeg.ca.

Gawrych, George W., *Baylor*. Email: george_gawrych@baylor.edu.

Gawthrop, Richard L. Franklin, IN. Affil: Franklin. Email: rgawthrop@franklincollege.edu. Research: German Protestant reform movements, origins of German nationalism.

Gayan, Melissa Faris, *Georgia Southern*. Email: mfgayan@georgiasouthern.edu.

Gaydosh, Brenda L., *West Chester*. Email: bgaydosh@wcupa.edu.

Gayle, Carol, *Lake Forest*. Email: gayle@lakeforest.edu.

Gayle, Janette Elice. Geneva, NY. Affil: Hobart and William Smith. Email: gayle@hws.edu. Research: black women and 1940s civil rights movement, black women in New York garment industry.

Gayne, Mary K., *James Madison*. Email: gaynemk@jmu.edu.

Geary, Patrick J., *UCLA*. Princeton, NJ. Affil: Inst. for Advanced Study. Email: geary@ucla.edu; geary@ias.edu. Research: ethnicity, memory.

Gechtman, Roni, *Dalhousie*. Email: roni.gechtman@msvu.ca.

Gedacht, Anne Giblin, *Seton Hall*. South Orange, NJ. Email: anne.gedacht@shu.edu. Research: immigration/diaspora, identity formation/regionalism.

Gedalecia, David, *Wooster*. Email: dgedalecia@wooster.edu.

Gedge, Karin E., *West Chester*. Email: kgedge@wcupa.edu.

Gee, Teri. Sugar City, ID. Affil: Brigham Young, Idaho. Email: terigee43@gmail.com.

Geehr, Shelley Wilks, *Science History Inst*. Email: sgeehr@sciencehistory.org.

Geelhoed, E. Bruce, *Ball State*. Email: bgeelhoed@bsu.edu.

Geerken, John H., *Scripps*. Email: jgeerken@scrippscollege.edu.

Geggus, David P., *Florida*. Email: dgeggus@ufl.edu.

Geheran, Michael J., *US Military Acad*. Email: michael.geheran@usma.edu.

Gehlert, Zachariah. Bourbon, MO. Affil: Missouri, St. Louis. Email: zcgrbm@mail.umsl.edu.

Gehrke, Jules Philip, *Saginaw Valley State*. University Center, MI. Email: jgehrke@svsu.edu. Research: modern England, Europe.

Geier, Max G., *Western Oregon*. Email: geierm@wou.edu.

Geiger, Andrea, *Simon Fraser*. Burnaby, BC, Canada. Email: aageiger@sfu.ca. Research: US-Canadian borderlands, Meiji-era Japanese immigration.

Geiger, Marilyn, *Washburn*. Email: zzgeig@washburn.edu.

Geismer, Lily, *Claremont McKenna*. Email: lgeismer@cmc.edu.

Geissler-Bowles, Suzanne, *William Paterson*. Florham Park, NJ. Email: bowless@wpunj.edu.

Research: 19th-c Episcopal church, Bishop John Croes.

Gekas, Athanasios, *York, Can*. Email: agekas@yorku.ca.

Gelbart, Nina R., *Occidental*. Email: gelbart@oxy.edu.

Gelber, Steven, *Santa Clara*. Email: sgelber@scu.edu.

Gelfand, H. Michael, *James Madison*. Harrisonburg, VA. Email: gelfanhm@jmu.edu. Research: US, research methods.

Gelfand, Mark I., *Boston Coll*. Email: mark.gelfand@bc.edu.

Gelfand, Rachel. Chapel Hill, NC. Affil: Salem State. Email: gelfand@email.unc.edu.

Gellately, Robert J., *Florida State*. Email: rgellately@fsu.edu.

Geller, Jay Howard, *Case Western Reserve*. Cleveland, OH. Email: jhg72@case.edu. Research: Gershom Scholem and his family, Jewish modernism in Weimar Germany.

Gellman, David N., *DePauw*. Greencastle, IN. Email: dgellman@depauw.edu. Research: US antislavery and abolition, US politics and reform 1760-1860.

Gellman, Erik S., *North Carolina, Chapel Hill*. Email: egellman@email.unc.edu.

Geltmaker, Ty E. Los Angeles, CA. Email: echobamboo@tygeltmaker.com. Research: disease and public health, postwar Italian literature.

Gelvin, James L., *UCLA*. Email: gelvin@history.ucla.edu.

Gemorah, Solomon. Great Neck, NY.

Gencturk, Ahmet. Thesalloniki, Greece. Affil: Rome 2 Tor Vergata. Email: ahmetgencturk@gmail.com. Research: Protestant Missionaries in Near East.

Gendzel, Glen J., *San José State*. Email: Glen.Gendzel@sjsu.edu.

Genell, Aimee M., *West Georgia*. Decatur, GA. Email: agenell@westga.edu. Research: international law and imperial expansion, British occupation of Egypt.

Genequand, Philippe, *Montréal*.

Genetin-Pilawa, C. Joseph, *George Mason*. Fairfax, VA. Email: cgenetin@gmu.edu. Research: federal Indian policy, state formation.

Gengenbach, Heidi, *Massachusetts, Boston*. Email: heidi.gengenbach@umb.edu.

Genkins, Daniel. Providence, RI. Affil: Brown. Email: daniel.genkins@gmail.com.

Genova, James E., *Ohio State*. Email: genova.2@osu.edu.

Gent, Malcolm. Nashua, NH. Affil: New Hampshire, Durham. Email: malcgent@yahoo.com. Research: Cold War, espionage.

Genter, Robert B. Jackson Heights, NY. Affil: Nassau Comm. Coll. Email: Robert.Genter@ncc.edu. Research: American modernism, American left.

Gentile, Patrizia, *Carleton, Can*. Email: patrizia_gentile@carleton.ca.

Gentles, Ian, *York, Can*. Email: igentles@glendon.yorku.ca.

Gentry, Jonathan, *Kennesaw State*. Atlanta, GA. Email: jgentr30@kennesaw.edu. Research: German musical culture, Nationalism.

Gentry, Judith F., *Louisiana, Lafayette*. Email: jfgentry@louisiana.edu.

Genvert, Margaret Fisk, *Salisbury*. Email: mfgenvert@salisbury.edu.

Geoghegan, Jeffrey C. La Jolla, CA. Affil: Bishop's Sch. Email: geogheganj@bishops.com. Research: ancient Near East, comparison of ancient historiography.

George, Aaron, *Tarleton State*. Email: ageorge@tarleton.edu.

George, Abosede A., *Barnard, Columbia*. New York, NY. Email: ageorge@barnard.edu; abosedeg@gmail.com. Research: West Africa and Atlantic world, 19th-c African migrations.

George, Alice L. Philadelphia, PA. Email: letter1962@aol.com. Research: John F. Kennedy and Lyndon B. Johnson, Cuban Missile Crisis.

George, Christina, *State Hist. Soc. of Missouri*. Email: georgecr@shsmo.org.

George, Eva, *Capital*. Email: egeorge@capital.edu.

George, James H., **Jr.**, *California State, Bakersfield*. Email: jgeorge@csub.edu.

George, Jessica A. Jersey Shore, PA. Affil: Jersey Shore Area Sr. High Sch. Email: jessica.george@jsasd.org.

George, Kevin, *State Hist. Soc. of Missouri*. Email: georgeke@shsmo.org.

George, Nate. Houston, TX. Affil: Rice. Email: ngeorge@rice.edu.

George, Teresa M. Atascadero, CA. Affil: California Polytechnic State. Email: tgeorge@calpoly.edu.

George, Timothy S., *Rhode Island*. Email: tgeorge@uri.edu.

Georges, Pericles B., *Lake Forest*. Email: georges@lakeforest.edu.

Georgian, Elizabeth A., *South Carolina Aiken*. Aiken, SC. Email: georgian@usca.edu. Research: early American Methodism.

Georgini, Sara E., *Massachusetts Hist. Soc.* Boston, MA. Email: sgeorgini@masshist.org. Research: providentialism in American culture, revolutionary Anglicanism.

Georgy, Joshua T. Williamsport, PA. Affil: Massachusetts Amherst. Email: jtg2102@columbia.edu. Research: Coptic and Ethiopian Orthodox relations, Coptic Church's African missions.

Geppert, Alexander C.T. New York, NY. Affil: NYU. Email: alexander.geppert@nyu.edu. Research: outer space and astroculture, time and temporality.

Geraghty, David Alan, *Longwood*. Email: geraghtyda@longwood.edu.

Gerard, Ezra. Madison, WI. Affil: Wisconsin, Madison. Email: egerard2@wisc.edu.

Gerber, David A., *SUNY, Buffalo*. Buffalo, NY. Email: dagerber@buffalo.edu. Research: letters from immigrants to their homelands, personal and social identities.

Gerber, Jane S., *Graduate Center, CUNY*. Email: gerberjs@aol.com.

Gerber, Larry G., *Auburn*. Email: gerbelg@auburn.edu.

Gerber, Lydia, *Washington State, Pullman*. Email: lgerber@wsu.edu.

Gerber, Matthew Dean, *Colorado, Boulder*. Longmont, CO. Email: matthew.gerber@colorado.edu. Research: French Atlantic colonization and law, early modern European politics of terror.

Gerber, Richard A., *Southern Connecticut State*. Glastonbury, CT. Email: gerberr1@southernct.edu; clioii@cox.net. Research: liberal Republicans of 1872, Civil Rights Act of 1875.

AHA members in **bold italic**; Directory-listed affiliations in *italic*

Gerberding, Richard A., *Alabama, Huntsville.* Email: gerberdingr@uah.edu.

Gerbner, Katharine, *Minnesota (Hist.).* Minneapolis, MN. Email: kgerbner@umn.edu. Research: Atlantic world, early America.

Gerbracht, Frederick W. Wantagh, NY. Affil: George Mercer Jr. Memorial Sch. of Theology. Email: ted.gerbracht@gmail.com. Research: early medieval preaching, 19th-c US Anglicanism.

Gerdow, George, *Northeastern Illinois.* Email: G-Gerdow@neiu.edu.

Gere, Catherina, *California, San Diego.* Email: cgere@ucsd.edu.

Gerges, Mark T., *US Army Command Coll.* Email: mark.t.gerges.civ@mail.mil.

Gerlach, David W., *St. Peter's.* Email: dgerlach@saintpeters.edu.

Gerlach, Larry R., *Utah.* Salt Lake City, UT. Email: larry.gerlach@utah.edu. Research: sport.

Gerlich, Robert S., *SJ, Loyola, New Orleans.* Email: gerlich@loyno.edu.

Germana, Nicholas A., *Keene State.* Email: ngermana@keene.edu.

Germany, Kent B., *South Carolina, Columbia.* Email: germanyk@mailbox.sc.edu.

Gernant, Karen, *Southern Oregon.*

Gerona, Carla, *Georgia Inst. of Tech.* Decatur, GA. Email: cgerona@hts.gatech.edu. Research: Atlantic world and borderlands.

Geroulanos, Stefanos N., *NYU.* Email: sg127@nyu.edu.

Gerrish, Jennifer L., *Charleston.*

Gerson, Stephane A. New York, NY. Affil: NYU. Email: stephane.gerson@nyu.edu.

Gerstein, Linda G. Haverford, PA. Affil: Haverford. Email: lgerstei@haverford.edu. Research: 20th-c Russia and Europe, European intellectual.

Gerstle, Gary L. Cambridge, United Kingdom. Affil: Cambridge. Email: glgerstle@gmail.com. Research: 20th-c US, immigration.

Gerteis, Louis S., *Missouri–St. Louis.* Email: gerteis@umsl.edu.

Gerth, Karl, *California, San Diego.* La Jolla, CA. Email: kgerth@ucsd.edu; karlgerth@gmail.com. Research: consumerism, China.

Gerus, Oleh W., *Manitoba.* Email: oleh.gerus@umanitoba.ca.

Gervers, Michael, *Toronto.* Email: m.gervers@utoronto.ca.

Gerwin, David M. New York, NY. Affil: Queens, CUNY. Email: davidlisa@mindspring.com. Research: 1960s community organizing, secondary social studies.

Geselowitz, Michael N. Hoboken, NJ. Affil: Stevens Inst. of Tech. Email: m.geselowitz@ieee.org. Research: science, technology and society.

Gesick, Lorraine, *Nebraska, Omaha.* Email: lgesick@unomaha.edu.

Gesick, Patrick S. Henderson, NV. Email: patrickg389@yahoo.com.

Gesin, Michael, *Worcester State.* Email: mgesin@worcester.edu.

Gesink, Indira Falk, *Baldwin Wallace.* Berea, OH. Email: igesink@bw.edu. Research: intersex in premodern Islamic societies, gender and law.

Gessner, Ann M. Chestnut Hill, MA. Email: agessner@rcn.com.

Gessner, James S. Chestnut Hill, MA. Email: jgessner@rcn.com.

Getahun, Solomon Addis, *Central Michigan.* Email: getah1sa@cmich.edu.

Getchell, Michelle D., *Naval War Coll.* Email: michelle.getchell@usnwc.edu.

Gettel, Eliza, *Villanova.*

Gettig, Eric, *Georgetown.* Washington, DC. Email: etg22@georgetown.edu. Research: US-Latin American relations, energy.

Gettler, Brian, *Toronto.* Email: brian.gettler@utoronto.ca.

Getty, J. Arch, *UCLA.* Email: getty@ucla.edu.

Getz, Lynne M., *Appalachian State.* Email: getzlm@appstate.edu.

Getz, Trevor Russell. Berkeley, CA. Affil: San Francisco State. Email: tgetz@sfsu.edu. Research: slavery/emancipation in Senegal/Ghana, African diaspora and links to new world.

Geva Halperin, Rotem. Tel Aviv, Israel. Affil: Hebrew. Email: rotemgeva@gmail.com.

Gevinson, Alan Cary. Washington, DC. Affil: Library of Congress. Email: agev@loc.gov. Research: civil rights movement, politics and entertainment.

Geyer, David C., *US Dept. of State.*

Geyer, Martin H. Groebenzell, Germany. Affil: Munich. Email: mhgeyer@lrz.uni-muenchen.de.

Geyer, Michael E., *Chicago.* Chicago, IL. Email: mgeyer@uchicago.edu. Research: 19th-/20th-c Germany, globalization.

Ghabrial, Jennifer Rebuck, *Hist. New Orleans.* Email: jghabrial@hnoc.org.

Ghabrial, Sarah, *Concordia, Can.* Email: Sarah.Ghabrial@concordia.ca.

Ghachem, Malick Walid, *MIT.* Newton Center, MA. Email: mghachem@mit.edu. Research: Atlantic revolutions, French Indies Company.

Ghanoui, Saniya Lee. Urbana, IL. Affil: Illinois, Urbana-Champaign. Email: ghanoui2@illinois.edu.

Gharala, Norah Linda Andrews, *Houston.* Lakewood, NJ. Affil: Georgian Court. Email: nlgharal@central.uh.edu; ngharala@georgian.edu. Research: colonial Afromexico.

Ghazal, Amal, *Simon Fraser.* Email: amal_ghazal@sfu.ca.

Ghazzal, Zouhair A., *Loyola, Chicago.* Email: zghazza@luc.edu.

Ghebre-Ab, Habtu, *Cincinnati.* Email: habtu.ghebre-ab@uc.edu.

Gheissari, Ali, *San Diego.* Email: alig@sandiego.edu.

Gherini, Claire E., *Fordham.* Bronx, NY. Email: cgherini@gmail.com. Research: West Indian medicine, British Atlantic world.

Ghosh, Arunabh, *Harvard (Hist.).* Cambridge, MA. Email: aghosh@fas.harvard.edu. Research: modern China, science and statecraft.

Ghosh, Durba, *Cornell.* Ithaca, NY. Email: dg256@cornell.edu. Research: colonialism, sexuality.

Ghosh, Shami, *Toronto.* Email: shami.ghosh@utoronto.ca.

Giacomini, George F., Jr., *Santa Clara.* Email: ggiacomini@scu.edu.

Giacumakis, George, *California State, Fullerton.* Email: ggiacumakis@fullerton.edu.

Giambrone, Jennifer A., *Hist. Assoc.* Email: jgiambrone@historyassociates.com.

Giandrea, Mary Frances, *American.* Email: giandrea@american.edu.

Giannakopoulos, Georgios. London, United Kingdom. Affil: Durham. Email: giannakopoulos.george@gmail.com.

Gianotti, Mark. Silverdale, WA. Email: jpcj574@yahoo.com.

Gianoutsos, Jamie, *Mount St. Mary's.* Email: gianoutsos@msmary.edu.

Giardina, Carol A., *Queens, CUNY.* Email: cgia@juno.com.

Gibbings, Julie A., *Manitoba.* Email: julie.gibbings@umanitoba.ca.

Gibbon, Peter. New Haven, CT. Affil: Boston Univ. Email: peterhgibbon@comcast.net.

Gibbons, John. Mc Lean, VA. Email: pgibbons@msn.com.

Gibbs, Chad Steven Andrew. Madison, WI. Affil: Wisconsin, Madison. Email: cgibbs4@wisc.edu. Research: Holocaust and genocide studies, Holocaust resistance.

Gibbs, David N., *Arizona.* Email: dgibbs@u.arizona.edu.

Gibbs, Fred, *New Mexico.* Albuquerque, NM. Email: fwgibbs@unm.edu; fwgibbs@gmail.com. Research: science, medieval medicine.

Gibbs, Gary G., *Roanoke.* Salem, VA. Email: gibbs@roanoke.edu. Research: Tudor-Stuart England, early modern Europe.

Gibbs, Janis M., *Hope.* Holland, MI. Email: gibbs@hope.edu. Research: Germany, Reformation.

Gibbs, Jenna M., *Florida International.* Miami, FL. Email: jgibbs@fiu.edu. Research: global imperial-indigenous relations, transatlantic performative culture.

Gibbs, Michael H., *Denver.* Denver, CO. Email: mgibbs@du.edu. Research: Japan, social and cultural.

Gibby, Col Bryan, *US Military Acad.* Email: bryan.gibby@usma.edu.

Gibert, Julie S., *Canisius.* Email: gibert@canisius.edu.

Giblin, Daniel F., *Auburn; Citadel.*

Giblin, James L., *Iowa.* Iowa City, IA. Email: james-giblin@uiowa.edu. Research: Africa.

Giblin, Molly. Oak Park, IL. Affil: Dominican, Ill. Email: mgiblin@dom.edu. Research: French Empire, Pacific world.

Gibson, Amanda W. Richmond, VA. Affil: William and Mary. Email: amandawgibson@gmail.com.

Gibson, Bryan R., *Hawai'i Pacific.* Ewa Beach, HI. Email: brgibson@hpu.edu. Research: Iraq/Iran/Kurds/US, American foreign policy.

Gibson, Fred L., III. Clinton Township, MI. Affil: Oakland. Email: FredLGibsonIII@Yahoo.com.

Gibson, John W., *Henry Ford Coll.* Email: jwgibson@hfcc.edu.

Gibson, Kelly, *Dallas.* Email: kgibson@udallas.edu.

Gibson, Khemani. Orange, NJ. Affil: NYU. Email: khemanig2@gmail.com. Research: citizenship and nationalism, migration.

Gibson, Mary S., *Graduate Center, CUNY.* New York, NY. Affil: John Jay, CUNY. Email: mgibson@jjay.cuny.edu. Research: law/crime/punishment, gender and deviance.

Gibson, Shimon, *North Carolina, Charlotte.* Email: S.Gibson@uncc.edu.

Gidlow, Liette Patricia, *Wayne State.* Email: gidlow@wayne.edu.

Giebel, Christoph J. F., *Washington, Seattle.* Email: giebel@uw.edu.

Giebelhaus, *August W., Jr.*, *Georgia Inst. of Tech.* Email: gus.giebelhaus@hts.gatech.edu.

Gienapp, *Jonathan Eric*, *Stanford.* Stanford, CA. Email: jgienapp@stanford.edu. Research: America in revolutionary era, American constitutionalism.

Giere-Frye, *Wendy L.* Atlanta, GA. Affil: Livingston Collegiate Acad. Email: wgierefrye@gmail.com. Research: efficacy of language on social change, efficacy of language on peace.

Giesberg, **Judith Ann**, *Villanova.* Email: judith.giesberg@villanova.edu.

Giesen, *James C.*, *Mississippi State.* Mississippi State, MS. Email: jgiesen@history.msstate.edu. Research: boll weevil.

Giffin, **Frederick**, *Arizona State.*

Giffin, **William W.**, *Indiana State.* Email: william.giffin@indstate.edu.

Gifford, *Daniel.* Louisville, KY. Affil: Louisville. Email: historiangifford@gmail.com. Research: American holidays, whaling and museums.

Gifford, **Ronald M.**, *Illinois State.* Email: rmgiffo@ilstu.edu.

Gigantino, *James John, II*, *Arkansas, Fayetteville.* Email: jgiganti@uark.edu.

Giggie, **John Michael**, *Alabama, Tuscaloosa.* Email: jmgiggie@bama.ua.edu.

Giglio, **James N.**, *Missouri State.* Email: jamesgiglio@missouristate.edu.

Gigova, **Irina**, *Charleston.* Email: gigovai@cofc.edu.

Giguere, *Joy M.* Dallastown, PA. Affil: Penn State, York. Email: jmg66@psu.edu. Research: commemorative culture, Civil War memory.

Gil, **Carlos**, *Washington, Seattle.* Email: gil@uw.edu.

Gilbert, *Claire*, *St. Louis.* Email: gilbertcm@slu.edu.

Gilbert, **Daniel**, *Illinois, Urbana-Champaign.* Email: gilbertd@illinois.edu.

Gilbert, **David Walker**, *Mars Hill.*

Gilbert, **Erik O.**, *Arkansas State.* Email: egilbert@astate.edu.

Gilbert, **James B.**, *Maryland, Coll. Park.* Email: gilbertj@umd.edu.

Gilbert, **Marc Jason**, *Hawai'i Pacific.* Email: mgilbert@hpu.edu.

Gilbertson-Thompson, *Nicole*, *California, Irvine.* Irvine, CA. Email: gilbertn@uci.edu. Research: US social, gender.

Gilburd, *Eleonory*, *Chicago.* Buffalo Grove, IL. Email: egilburd@uchicago.edu; gilburd@yahoo.com. Research: Russia, late Soviet Russia.

Gildner, **R. Matthew**, *Washington and Lee.* Email: gildnerm@wlu.edu.

Gildrie, **Richard P.**, *Austin Peay State.* Email: gildrier@apsu.edu.

Giles, *Geoffrey J.*, *Florida.* Gainesville, FL. Email: ggiles@ufl.edu. Research: alcohol social, Holocaust.

Gilfoyle, *Timothy J.*, *Loyola, Chicago.* Chicago, IL. Email: tgilfoy@luc.edu. Research: 19th-c US social, urban.

Gilhooley, *Simon Joseph.* Annandale On Hudson, NY. Affil: Bard. Email: sgilhool@bard.edu. Research: constitutional interpretation, American political theory.

Gilje, *Paul A.*, *Oklahoma (Hist.).* Philadelphia, PA. Email: pgilje@ou.edu. Research: US 1492-1865, colonial America.

Gill, **Jill K.**, *Boise State.* Email: jgill@boisestate.edu.

Gill, *Navyug*, *William Paterson.*

Gill, *Tiffany M.*, *Delaware.* Email: tgill@udel.edu.

Gillaspie, *Joel*, *Washburn.* Email: joel.gillaspie@washburn.edu.

Gillen, *Amanda*, *Duquesne.* Email: gillena@duq.edu.

Gillen, **Jerome J.**, *St. Peter's.* Email: jgillen2@saintpeters.edu.

Gillerman, *Sharon I.*, *Southern California.* Los Angeles, CA. Affil: Hebrew Union. Email: gillerma@usc.edu; sgillerman@huc.edu. Research: popular culture and entertainment.

Gillespie, *Deanna M.*, *North Georgia.* Email: dee.gillespie@ung.edu.

Gillespie, **Michele K.**, *Wake Forest.* Email: gillesmk@wfu.edu.

Gillett, **Christopher P.**, *Scranton.* Email: christopher.gillett@scranton.edu.

Gillette, *Aaron K.*, *Houston-Downtown.* Email: gillettea@uhd.edu.

Gillette, *Howard F.*, *Rutgers, Camden.* Haddonfield, NJ. Email: hfg@camden.rutgers.edu. Research: urban, urban policy.

Gillette, *William*, *Rutgers.* Email: begillet@infionline.net.

Gilley, **B. H.**, *Louisiana Tech.*

Gillingham, **John R., III**, *Missouri–St. Louis.* Email: gillingham@umsl.edu.

Gillingham, **Paul**, *Northwestern.* Email: paul.gillingham@northwestern.edu.

Gillis, **Brendan J.**, *Lamar.* Email: bgillis@lamar.edu.

Gillis, **Delia**, *Central Missouri.* Email: dgillis@ucmo.edu.

Gillis, **Gregory R.**, *Austin Peay State.* Email: gillisg@apsu.edu.

Gillis, *John R.*, *Rutgers.* Berkeley, CA. Email: gottgillis@cs.com. Research: comparative islands, worldwide coastal cultures.

Gillis, **Matthew Bryan**, *Tennessee, Knoxville.* Email: mgillis1@utk.edu.

Gillman, **Howard**, *California, Irvine.* Email: chancellor@uci.edu.

Gillmor, **C. Stewart**, *Wesleyan.* Email: sgillmor@wesleyan.edu.

Gillon, *Steven M.* Miami Beach, FL. Affil: Oklahoma. Email: smgillon@aol.com.

Gilman, *Richard.* Broken Arrow, OK. Affil: Tulsa Comm. Coll. Email: rickgilman@yahoo.com.

Gilmartin, **David P.**, *North Carolina State.* Email: david_gilmartin@ncsu.edu.

Gilmore, **Allison B.**, *Ohio State.* Email: gilmore.24@osu.edu.

Gilmore, **Glenda E.**, *Yale.* Email: glenda.gilmore@yale.edu.

Gilmore, *Kimberly.* New York, NY. Affil: HISTORY. Email: kimberly.gilmore@aetn.com.

Giloi, *Eva D.*, *Rutgers, Newark/New Jersey Inst. of Tech.* Newark, NJ. Email: evagiloi@rutgers.edu. Research: material culture of monarchy, fame and charisma.

Gilpin, **Robert Blakeslee**, *Tulane.* Email: rgilpin@tulane.edu.

Gilpin, *W. Clark.* Stevensville, MI. Affil: Chicago. Email: wgilpin@uchicago.edu. Research: comparative religion, letters from prison.

Gilyard, *Vanessa H.* Tampa, FL. Affil: Strayer. Email: vanessa.gilyard@strayer.edu. Research: 18th-c Western civilization.

Gimber, **Steven G.**, *West Chester.* Email: sgimber@wcupa.edu.

Gingerich, **Mark P.**, *Ohio Wesleyan.* Email: mpginger@owu.edu.

Gingerich, *Owen J.*, *Harvard (Hist. of Science).* Email: ogingerich@cfa.harvard.edu.

Gingras, *Yves*, *Québec, Montréal.* Email: gingras.yves@uqam.ca.

Gingrich, *Kurt A.*, *Radford.* Email: kgingric@radford.edu.

Ginsberg, *Stuart.* Arlington, VA. Affil: George Washington. Email: sginsberg@law.gwu.edu. Research: presidential cabinets, congressional behavior.

Ginzberg, *Lori*, *Penn State.* Philadelphia, PA. Email: ldg1@psu.edu. Research: Elizabeth Cady Stanton, 19th-c women's political identities.

Ginzburg, *Carlo*, *UCLA.* Bologna, Italy. Affil: Scuola Normale Superiore, Pisa. Email: ginzburg@history.ucla.edu. Research: Italian Renaissance, early modern Europe.

Gioe, *David*, *US Military Acad.* Email: david.gioe@usma.edu.

Gioielli, *Emily Rebecca.* Saint Joseph, MO. Affil: Missouri Western State. Email: emily.gioielli@gmail.com. Research: violence and nonviolence, revolution.

Gioielli, **Robert R.**, *Cincinnati.*

Giordani, *Angela Marie.* San Marcos, TX. Affil: Columbia. Email: amg2287@columbia.edu. Research: modern Arab intellectual, modern Arabic literature.

Giordano, *Mariella Maria.* Peachtree City, GA. Email: Mmgio0403@gmail.com.

Giovacchini, *Saverio*, *Maryland, Coll. Park.* Email: saverio@umd.edu.

Gipson, *Maurice.* State University, AR. Affil: Mississippi. Email: mdgipson@go.olemiss.edu.

Gipson, *Nicole.* Manchester, United Kingdom. Affil: Manchester. Email: nicole.gipson@postgrad.manchester.ac.uk. Research: urban marginality, housing exclusion/homelessness.

Girard, *Jolyon P.*, *Cabrini.* Email: jgirard@cabrini.edu.

Girard, *Philip*, *York, Can.* Email: pgirard@osgoode.yorku.ca.

Giselbrecht, *Rebecca.* Bern, Switzerland. Affil: Bern. Email: rebecca.giselbrecht@theol.unibe.ch. Research: 16th-c Reformed spirituality, Alsatian noblewoman.

Gisolfi, **Monica Richmond**, *North Carolina, Wilmington.* Email: gisolfim@uncw.edu.

Gispen, **Kees**, *Mississippi.* Email: hsgispen@olemiss.edu.

Gitlin, **Jay L.**, *Yale.* Email: jay.gitlin@yale.edu.

Gitre, *Carmen M. K.*, *Virginia Tech.* Blacksburg, VA. Email: cgitre@vt.edu; carmenkhair@hotmail.com. Research: modern Middle East.

Gitre, **Edward J. K.**, *Virginia Tech.* Email: egitre@vt.edu.

Giustino, *Cathleen M.*, *Auburn.* Auburn, AL. Email: giustcm@auburn.edu. Research: modern central Europe.

Given, *James B.*, *California, Irvine.* Camas, WA. Email: jbgiven@uci.edu. Research: core-periphery relations in medieval Europe, 13th-c Eurasia.

Givens, *Bryan Alan*, *Pepperdine.* Malibu, CA. Email: bryan.givens@pepperdine.edu; bryaninlisbon@yahoo.com. Research: European millenarianism, Inquisition.

Givens, *Cameron James.* Hopkinton, NH. Email: givenscam@comcast.net.

Givens, Robert D., *Cornell Coll.* Email: rgivens@
cornellcollege.edu.

Glade, Mary E., *St. Cloud State.* Email: beglade@
stcloudstate.edu.

Glanz, Lenore M. Chicago, IL. Email:
lenoreglanz@yahoo.com. Research: medieval
trading companies, English legal.

Glasco, Jeffrey D., *Linfield.* Email: jglasco@
linfield.edu.

Glasco, Laurence, *Pittsburgh.* Email: lag1@pitt.
edu.

Glaser, Leah Suzanne, *Central Connecticut
State.* Email: glaserles@ccsu.edu.

Glasker, Wayne, *Rutgers, Camden.* Email:
glasker@camden.rutgers.edu.

Glass, Bryan S., *Texas State.* Email: bg30@
txstate.edu.

Glassberg, David, *Massachusetts, Amherst.*
Email: glassberg@history.umass.edu.

Glassheim, Eagle, *British Columbia.* Email:
eagle.g@ubc.ca.

Glassman, Jonathon, *Northwestern.* Email:
j-glassman@northwestern.edu.

Glatfelter, R. Edward, *Utah State.* Email:
edward.glatfelter@usu.edu.

Glatthaar, Joseph T., *North Carolina, Chapel Hill.*
Email: jtg@unc.edu.

Glaze, Florence Eliza, *Coastal Carolina.* Email:
fglaze@coastal.edu.

Glazer, Steven A. Lamoni, IA. Affil: Graceland.
Email: glazer@graceland.edu.

Gleason, Bruce Philip. Lauderdale, MN. Affil: St.
Thomas, Minn. Email: brucegleason@comcast.
net. Research: world horse-mounted military
bands.

Gleason, J. Philip, *Notre Dame.* Evanston,
IL. Email: jgleason@nd.edu. Research: US
immigration, US religious.

Glebe, Ellen Yutzy. Kassel, Germany. Affil:
self-employed. Email: eyg@writinghistory.de.
Research: Anabaptism and Reformation in
Hesse, Christian resistance in Nazi Germany.

Glebov, Sergey, *Amherst; Smith.* Email:
sglebov@amherst.edu; sglebov@smith.edu.

Glen, Robert A. New Haven, CT. Affil: New
Haven. Email: RGlen@newhaven.edu.
Research: English methodism, Caribbean
methodism.

Glenn, Jason K., *Southern California.* Email:
jkglenn@usc.edu.

Glenn, Susan A., *Washington, Seattle.* Seattle,
WA. Email: glenns@uw.edu. Research: 20th-c
US cultural and social, women and Jewish
identities.

Glennon, Travis James. Exeter, NH. Affil: Tabor
Academy. Email: travisjglennon@gmail.com.

Glickman, Lawrence B., *Cornell.* Ithaca, NY.
Email: lbg49@cornell.edu. Research: meaning
of free enterprise, post-Civil War US.

Glickstein, Jonathan A., *California, Santa
Barbara.*

Gliserman, Nicholas. Salt Lake City, UT.
Affil: Southern California. Email: nicholas.
gliserman@gmail.com. Research: cartography,
political culture.

Glisson, James, *Huntington Library.* Email:
jglisson@huntington.org.

Gloege, Timothy E. W. Grand Rapids, MI. Email:
gloege@gmail.com. Research: Protestant
liberals, business/class/culture.

Glosser, Susan, *Lewis & Clark.* Email: sglosser@
lclark.edu.

Gloster Coates, Patricia, *Pace.* New York, NY.
Email: pglostercoates@pace.edu. Research:
Islamic and West Africa, Afro-American.

Glotzer, Paige, *Wisconsin-Madison.* Madison, WI.
Email: pglotzer@wisc.edu. Research: housing,
development.

Glover, Jimmy. North Las Vegas, NV. Email:
jimlingv4@yahoo.com.

Glover, Lorri M., *St. Louis.* Email: lglover1@slu.
edu.

Glover, William J., *Michigan, Ann Arbor.* Email:
wglover@umich.edu.

Glovsky, David Newman. East Lansing, MI. Affil:
Michigan State. Email: glovskyd@msu.edu.

Gluck, Carol N., *Columbia (Hist.).* New York, NY.
Email: cg9@columbia.edu. Research: war and
memory, modern Japan.

Gluck, Mary, *Brown.* Email: Mary_Gluck@Brown.
edu.

Gluck, Sherna, *California State, Long Beach.*
Email: sbgluck@csulb.edu.

Glueckert, Leo G. Chicago, IL. Email: twitmeistr@
hotmail.com.

Glymph, Thavolia, *Duke.* Email: thavolia@duke.
edu.

Gnoinska, Margaret K., *Troy.* Email:
mgnoinska@troy.edu.

Goan, Melanie Beals, *Kentucky.* Email: melanie.
goan@uky.edu.

Gobat, Michel, *Pittsburgh.* Pittsburgh, PA. Email:
mgobat@pitt.edu. Research: modern Latin
America.

Goble, Andrew E., *Oregon.* Email: platypus@
uoregon.edu.

Goble, Luke J. Portland, OR. Affil: Warner Pacific.
Email: lgoble@warnerpacific.edu. Research:
national formation and indigenous people,
comparative US-South America studies.

Goda, Norman J. W., *Florida.* Email: goda@ufl.
edu.

Godbeer, Richard. Chesterfield, VA. Affil: Virginia
Commonwealth. Email: rgodbeer@vcu.
edu. Research: early America, religious and
cultural.

Godbille, Lara. Malibu, CA. Affil: Naval Hist.
Command. Email: lara.godbille@navy.
mil; laragodbille@gmail.com. Research: US
naval construction in Vietnam War, cultural
property and local identity.

Godbold, E. Stanly, Jr., *Mississippi State.* Email:
stjean@joimail.com.

Goddard, Peter A., *Guelph.* Email: pgoddard@
uoguelph.ca.

Godfrey, Katherine Alexandra. University Park,
PA. Affil: Penn State. Email: kategodfr3y@
gmail.com. Research: New Kingdom of
Granada, 16th-c Mesoamerica.

Godfried, Nathan, *Maine, Orono.* Orono, ME.
Email: godfried@maine.edu. Research:
organized labor and mass media, broadcast
journalists and Cold War.

Godinez, Adelaido, III. Alexandria, VA. Affil:
Kansas. Email: adgodinez@ku.edu. Research:
American first encounters, Mexican-American
War.

Godshalk, David Fort, *Shippensburg.* Email:
dfgods@ship.edu.

Goduti, Philip A. Cromwell, CT. Affil: Quinnipiac.
Email: philip.goduti@quinnipiac.edu.
Research: US Civil Rights Movement, WWII.

Goedde, Petra, *Soc. for Hist. of American Foreign
Relations.* Email: pgoedde@temple.edu.

Goering, Joseph W., *Toronto.* Email: goering@
chass.utoronto.ca.

Goetting, Brittany Patricia. Orono, ME. Affil:
Maine, Orono. Email: brittany.cathey@maine.
edu. Research: early US Republic, colonial
Canada.

Goetz, Rebecca A., *NYU.* Email: rag11@nyu.edu.

Goff, Alice M., *Chicago.* Chicago, IL. Email:
agoff@uchicago.edu. Research: 19th-c
German cultural/intellectual, museums/
collections/material culture.

Goff, Brendan M. Sarasota, FL. Affil: New Coll.,
Fla. Email: bgoff@ncf.edu. Research: US
international, Progressive Era.

Goff, James R., Jr., *Appalachian State.* Email:
goffjr@appstate.edu.

Goff, Krista, *Miami.* Email: kgoff@miami.edu.

Goff, Phiip, *Indiana–Purdue, Indianapolis.* Email:
pgoff@iupui.edu.

Goffart, Walter A., *Toronto.* Email: walter.
goffart@yale.edu.

Goffman, Daniel, *DePaul.* Email: dgoffman@
depaul.edu.

Goforth, Sean, *North Carolina, Wilmington.*
Email: goforths@uncw.edu.

Goggin, Carole, *State Hist. Soc. of Missouri.*
Email: gogginc@shsmo.org.

Gogliettino, John C. Danbury, CT. Email:
jcgogliettino@aol.com.

Goguen, Matthew, *Hist. Assoc.* Email:
mgoguen@historyassociates.com.

Goines, L. Patrick, *Austin Comm. Coll.* Email:
pgoines@austincc.edu.

Goings, Kenneth W., *Ohio State.* Email:
goings.14@osu.edu.

Goings, Renee A., *US Dept. of State.*

Goins, John D., *Texas-Rio Grande Valley.* Email:
john.goins@utrgv.edu.

Gokcek, Mustafa, *Niagara.* Email: gokcek@
niagara.edu.

Golan, Tal, *California, San Diego.* Email: tgolan@
ucsd.edu.

Golas, Peter J., *Denver.* Email: pgolas@du.edu.

Gold, Carol. Bloomington, MN. Affil: Alaska
Fairbanks. Email: cgold@alaska.edu. Research:
preindustrial urban working women, women
in Denmark.

Gold, Robert L., *Southern Illinois, Carbondale.*

Gold, Stuart. Maplewood, NJ. Affil: Rutgers.
Email: stuart.gold@gmail.com. Research:
slavery in New Jersey, rule of law.

Gold McBride, Sarah. Berkeley, CA.
Affil: California, Berkeley. Email:
sarahgoldmcbride@berkeley.edu.

Goldberg, Ann E., *California, Riverside.* Email:
ann.goldberg@ucr.edu.

Goldberg, Barry, *Fordham.* Email: bgoldberg@
fordham.edu.

Goldberg, David J., *Cleveland State.* Email:
d.goldberg@csuohio.edu.

Goldberg, David P. Bronx, NY. Affil: Michigan,
Ann Arbor. Research: progressive politics after
WWII, 1968 effects in German society/culture.

Goldberg, David, *Wayne State.* Email: dgolber@
wayne.edu.

Goldberg, Eric J., *MIT.* Email: egoldber@mit.edu.

Goldberg, Harold J., *South.* Sewanee, TN. Email:
hgoldber@sewanee.edu. Research: Battle of
Saipan, WWII in Europe.

Goldberg, Hillel. Denver, CO. Affil:
Intermountain Jewish News. Email: hillel@ijn.
com.

Goldberg, *Jan*. Essen, Germany. Affil: St. Antony's, Oxford. Email: jgoldberg@hotmail.de. Research: modern Egyptian legal, legal reception.

Goldberg, *Jessica L.*, *UCLA*. Los Angeles, CA. Email: goldberg@history.ucla.edu. Research: medieval Mediterranean trading networks.

Goldberg, *Joyce S.*, *Texas, Arlington*. Arlington, TX. Email: goldberg@uta.edu. Research: US diplomatic and military.

Goldberg, **Mark Allan**, *Houston*. Email: magoldberg@uh.edu.

Goldberg, *Robert Alan*, *Utah*. Salt Lake City, UT. Email: bob.goldberg@utah.edu. Research: 20th-c US politics, 20th-c US social.

Goldberg, *Sasha T*. Chicago, IL. Email: stg@iu.edu.

Golden, **Janet**, *Rutgers, Camden*. Email: jgolden@camden.rutgers.edu.

Golden, *Peter B.*, *Rutgers, Newark/New Jersey Inst. of Tech*. Princeton Junction, NJ. Email: pgolden@rutgers.edu. Research: Turkic nomads, medieval Eurasia.

Golden, *Richard M.*, *North Texas*. Highland Village, TX. Email: Richard.Golden@unt.edu. Research: early modern European witchcraft, early modern French Noailles family.

Goldenberg, *Lila Rice*. Philadelphia, PA. Affil: Pennsylvania. Email: lilagold@sas.upenn.edu.

Goldenberg, **Robert**, *SUNY, Stony Brook*. Email: Robert.Goldenberg@stonybrook.edu.

Golder, *Lauren*. Lancaster, CA. Affil: Penn State. Email: ljgolder@gmail.com. Research: immigration and radicalism, US/Europe.

Goldfield, *David R.*, *North Carolina, Charlotte*. Charlotte, NC. Email: drgoldfi@uncc.edu. Research: US South, urban.

Goldfrank, **David M.**, *Georgetown*. Email: goldfrad@georgetown.edu.

Goldgar, *Anne*. London, United Kingdom. Affil: King's Coll. London. Email: anne.goldgar@kcl.ac.uk. Research: collecting/scholarship/science, European cultural interchange.

Goldich, *Robert L*. Fairfax, VA. Affil: Library of Congress. Email: rgoldich@cox.net. Research: conscription/voluntary military service, military manpower/personnel policies.

Goldish, **Matt**, *Ohio State*. Email: goldish.1@osu.edu.

Goldkamp, *Francis Joseph Michael*. Saint Louis, MO. Affil: Washington, St. Louis. Email: f.joseph.m.goldkamp@wustl.edu. Research: US/UK/Canada Charity/Philanthropy, Contemporary US/Commonwealth Culture.

Goldman, *Andrea S.*, *UCLA*. Los Angeles, CA. Email: goldman@history.ucla.edu. Research: urban culture in 18th-/19th-c China, performance and politics of aesthetics.

Goldman, **Andrew**, *Gonzaga*. Email: goldman@gonzaga.edu.

Goldman, **Hal**, *Carleton, Can*. Email: harold.goldman@carleton.ca.

Goldman, **Joanne A.**, *Northern Iowa*. Email: joanne.goldman@uni.edu.

Goldman, *Leah*. Portland, OR. Affil: Lewis & Clark. Email: lgoldman@lclark.edu. Research: modern Europe, Russia/Soviet Union.

Goldman, *Rachael B*. Bayonne, NJ. Affil: Rutgers. Email: rbg21@scarletmail.rutgers.edu. Research: ancient, global.

Goldman, **Steven**, *Lehigh*. Email: slg2@lehigh.edu.

Goldman, *Wendy Z.*, *Carnegie Mellon*. Pittsburgh, PA. Email: goldman@andrew.cmu.edu. Research: Stalinism, WWII.

Goldmon, *Camille*. Atlanta, GA. Affil: Emory. Email: cgoldmo@emory.edu.

Goldner, *Erik*, *California State, Northridge*. Northridge, CA. Email: erik.goldner@csun.edu. Research: corruption in 17th-/18th-c France.

Goldschmidt, *Arthur E.*, *Penn State*. State College, PA. Email: axg2@psu.edu. Research: Middle East, International Assoc. of Torch Clubs.

Goldsmith, *Julie A*. Indianapolis, IN. Affil: Indiana-Purdue, Indianapolis. Email: jgoldsm@iupui.edu. Research: media, media innovation.

Goldsmith, *William Dixon*. Durham, NC. Affil: North Carolina, Chapel Hill. Email: william.goldsmith@unc.edu. Research: economic development policy, inequality.

Goldstein, **Eric L.**, *Emory*. Email: egoldst@emory.edu.

Goldstein, **Erik**, *Boston Univ*. Email: goldstee@bu.edu.

Goldstein, *Jan E.*, *Chicago*. Chicago, IL. Email: jegoldst@uchicago.edu. Research: 19th-c. racial theory/France, moral thinking/historiography.

Goldstein, *Jonathan*. Chestnut Hill, MA. Affil: West Georgia. Research: China, American-East Asian relations.

Goldstein, **Joshua L.**, *Southern California*. Email: jlgoldst@usc.edu.

Goldstein, *Robert J*. Ann Arbor, MI. Affil: Oakland. Email: goldstei@oakland.edu.

Goldstein, **Thomas William**, *Central Missouri*.

Goldstein, **Warren J.**, *Hartford*. Email: wgoldstei@hartford.edu.

Goldstein-Kane, *Marta Rosa*. Austin, TX. Affil: Paul Valery. Email: martarosakane@gmail.com. Research: student exchanges between France and US, French contributions to US encyclopedias.

Goldsworthy-Bishop, **Patricia M.**, *Western Oregon*. Email: goldswop@wou.edu.

Goldthree, *Reena N*. Princeton, NJ. Affil: Princeton. Email: RGoldthree@princeton.edu. Research: Caribbean, Latin America.

Goldthwaite, **Richard**, *Johns Hopkins (Hist.)*.

Goldwyn, *John P*. Ann Arbor, MI. Affil: King Coll. Prep. High Sch. Email: jpgoldwyn@gmail.com. Research: Great Britain c. 300-1065.

Goldy, **Charlotte Newman**, *Miami, Ohio*. Email: goldycn@miamioh.edu.

Goldy, **Robert**, *Miami, Ohio*.

Golenbock, **Peter**, *South Florida, St. Petersburg*.

Golia, *Julie A*. Brooklyn, NY. Affil: Brooklyn Hist. Soc. Email: julie.golia@gmail.com. Research: advice columns in American newspapers.

Golinski, *Jan V.*, *New Hampshire, Durham*. Email: jan.golinski@unh.edu.

Golland, *David Hamilton*. University Park, IL. Affil: Governors State University. Email: dgolland@gmail.com. Research: civil rights, biography.

Golob, *Stephanie R*. New York, NY. Affil: Baruch, CUNY. Email: Stephanie.Golob@baruch.cuny.edu.

Golombek, **Joseph**, *SUNY, Buffalo State*. Email: golombj@buffalostate.edu.

Goluboff, *Risa L.*, *Virginia*. Washington, DC. Email: goluboff@law.virginia.edu. Research: 1940s modern civil rights development.

Gomez, *Andrew*, *Puget Sound*. Email: andrewgomez@pugetsound.edu.

Gomez, *Michael A.*, *NYU*. New York, NY. Email: michael.gomez@nyu.edu. Research: West Africa, African diaspora.

Gomez, *Rocio*, *Virginia Commonwealth*.

Gomez, *Sonia C*. Chicago, IL. Affil: Chicago. Email: scgomez@uchicago.edu. Research: Japanese immigration, gender and immigration.

Gómez, *Pablo F.*, *Wisconsin-Madison*. Madison, WI. Email: pgomez@wisc.edu. Research: early modern Caribbean body knowledge, Iberian Atlantic medicine.

Gomez-del-Moral, *Alejandro Jose*. Helsinki, Finland. Affil: Helsinki. Email: alejandro.gomezdelmoral@helsinki.fi. Research: consumer culture in Francoist Spain, popular culture in contemporary Spain.

Gomez-Quinones, *Juan*, *UCLA*. Los Angeles, CA. Email: quinones@history.ucla.edu. Research: Latin American intellectual, social change and nationalism.

Gonda, *Jeffrey D.*, *Syracuse*. Email: jdgonda@maxwell.syr.edu.

Gondola, **Ch. Didier**, *Indiana–Purdue, Indianapolis*. Email: gondola@iupui.edu.

Gonsalves, **Maggi**, *New York State Archives*. Email: maggi.gonsalves@nysed.gov.

Gonser, *Kelly D*. Manteca, CA. Affil: California State, Stanislaus. Email: kgonser@yahoo.com. Research: modern Europe/modern Germany, early postwar Germany.

Gonzaba, *Eric N*. Washington, DC. Affil: George Mason. Email: egonzaba@gmu.edu.

Gonzales, *Christian M.*, *Rhode Island*. Durham, CT. Email: cgonzal@uri.edu; cgonzales1998@gmail.com. Research: early US cultural, early US intellectual.

Gonzales, *Ethan Leonard*. Waterford, MI. Affil: Oakland. Email: ethangonzales52@yahoo.com.

Gonzales, **Michael**, *Northern Illinois*. Email: gonzales@niu.edu.

Gonzales, *Phillip B*. Albuquerque, NM. Affil: New Mexico. Email: gonzales@unm.edu. Research: New Mexico Hispanics, ethnic nationalism.

Gonzales, **Rhonda M.**, *Texas, San Antonio*. Email: rhonda.gonzales@utsa.edu.

Gonzales, *Trinidad*. Edinburg, TX. Affil: South Texas. Email: trinidadgonzales99@gmail.com. Research: Latino intellectual, Mexican American civil rights.

Gonzalez, **Aston**, *Salisbury*. Email: aagonzalez@salisbury.edu.

Gonzalez, *Evelyn*, *William Paterson*. Staten Island, NY. Email: gonzaleze@wpunj.edu. Research: US urban, minorities.

Gonzalez, *Fabiola Andrea*. Trujillo Alto, PR. Affil: Univ. Gardens High Sch. Email: fgonzaherna@gmail.com.

Gonzalez, *Gabriela*, *Texas, San Antonio*. San Antonio, TX. Email: gabriela.gonzalez@utsa.edu. Research: Mexican American, transnational.

Gonzalez, *German W*. Woodbridge, VA. Email: germangonzalez@verizon.net.

Gonzalez, *Jennifer*, *Grand Valley State*. Email: gonzalje@gvsu.edu.

Gonzalez, **Jerry B.**, *Texas, San Antonio*. Email: jerry.gonzalez@utsa.edu.

Gonzalez, **Luis A.**, *Indiana.* Email: luisgonz@ indiana.edu.

Gonzalez, **Michael J.**, *San Diego.* San Diego, CA. Email: michaelg@sandiego.edu. Research: 19th-c US, Chicano and borderlands studies.

Gonzalez, **Rafael.** La Crescenta, CA. Affil: High Desert Medical Grooup. Email: rafgonzalezrubio@aol.com.

Gonzalez, **Sergio M.**, *Marquette.* Milwaukee, WI. Email: sergio.gonzalez@marquette.edu. Research: 20th-c US, Latinx studies.

Gonzalez, **Tiffany Jasmin.** Bryan, TX. Affil: Texas A&M, Coll. Station. Email: tiffanygonzalez@ ymail.com.

Gonzalez, **Victoria.** Hackensack, NJ. Email: vicsgon@gmail.com.

González de Bustamante, **Celeste**, *Arizona.* Email: celesteg@email.arizona.edu.

Gonzalez Jimenez, **Elizabeth.** Miami Beach, FL. Affil: Miami. Email: e.gonzalezjimenez@ umiami.edu.

Gonzalez Quintero, **Nicolas Alejandro.** Austin, TX. Affil: Texas, Austin. Email: nagonzalezq@ utexas.edu. Research: transnational, Age of Revolution.

Gonzalez-Perez, **Margaret**, *Southeastern Louisiana.* Email: mgonzalez@selu.edu.

Gonzalez-Vales, **Luis E.** San Juan, PR.

Good, **Cassandra A.** Arlington, VA. Affil: Marymount. Email: cgood@umw.edu; cgood@marymount.edu. Research: early America, gender.

Good, **David F.**, *Minnesota (Hist.).* Email: goodx001@umn.edu.

Good, **Gregory A.**, *Center for Hist. of Physics.* Email: ggood@aip.org.

Good, **McBarrett Steven.** Hickory, NC. Affil: Appalachian State. Email: mcbarrettsgood@ gmail.com.

Good, **Robert**, *Mercer.* Email: good_rm@mercer. edu.

Goodale, **James A.**, *Bucknell.* Email: jgoodale@ bucknell.edu.

Goodall, **Jamie LeAnne Hager.** Owings Mills, MD. Affil: Stevenson. Email: jhagergoodall@ stevenson.edu. Research: Atlantic, piracy.

Goodart, **Margaret M.**, *California State, Sacramento.* Email: goodartm@saclink.csus. edu.

Goodblatt, **David M.**, *California, San Diego.* Email: dgoodblatt@ucsd.edu.

Goode, **James F.**, *Grand Valley State.* Email: goodej@gvsu.edu.

Goode, **Joshua S.**, *Claremont Grad.* Claremont, CA. Email: joshua.goode@cgu.edu. Research: comparative racial theories.

Goode, **Michael J.**, *Utah Valley.* Orem, UT. Email: mgoode@uvu.edu. Research: religion and political culture, peace and violence.

Goode, **Sophia.** Camas, WA. Email: swimgirl310@gmail.com.

Goodfriend, **Joyce D.**, *Denver.* Denver, CO. Email: jgoodfri@du.edu. Research: colonial America, immigration.

Goodgold, **Jay S.**, *OAH.*

Goodheart, **Adam.** Chestertown, MD. Affil: Starr Center. Email: agoodheart2@washcoll.edu. Research: 19th-c America, cultural and social.

Goodheart, **Lawrence B.**, *Connecticut, Storrs.* Email: lawrence.goodheart@uconn.edu.

Goodier, **Susan**, *SUNY, Oneonta.* Oneonta, NY. Email: susan.goodier@oneonta.edu. Research:

women and politics, political and social movements.

Goodlett, **David E.**, *Fort Hays State.* Email: dgoodlet@fhsu.edu.

Goodman, **Adam**, *Illinois, Chicago.* Email: asig@ uic.edu.

Goodman, **Bryna**, *Oregon.* Eugene, OR. Email: bgoodman@uoregon.edu. Research: urban and gender, public culture and press.

Goodman, **Dena**, *Michigan, Ann Arbor.* Ann Arbor, MI. Email: goodmand@umich.edu. Research: consumption and material culture, women and writing.

Goodman, **James**, *Rutgers, Newark/New Jersey Inst. of Tech.* Email: goodmanj@rutgers.edu.

Goodman, **Joshua Ross.** Canton, NY. Affil: St. Lawrence. Email: jgoodman@stlawu.edu. Research: British Mandate for Palestine, policy and counterinsurgency.

Goodrich, **Robert W.**, *Northern Michigan.* Email: rgoodric@nmu.edu.

Goodson, **Steve**, *West Georgia.* Email: hgoodson@westga.edu.

Goodstein, **Elizabeth S.**, *Emory.* Email: egoodst@emory.edu.

Goodwin, **G. Frederick**, *Carleton, Can.* Email: fred.goodwin@carleton.ca.

Goodwin, **Janet R.** Los Angeles, CA. Email: jan@ cs.csustan.edu.

Goodwin, **Joanne L.**, *Nevada, Las Vegas.* Email: joanne.goodwin@unlv.edu.

Goodwin, **John A.** Phoenix, AZ. Affil: Arizona State. Email: jagoodwi@mainex1.asu.edu. Research: Native American education, 20th-c Native American activism.

Goodwin, **Paul B., Jr.**, *Connecticut, Storrs.* Email: paul.goodwin@uconn.edu.

Goodwin, **Sage Meredith.** Oxford, United Kingdom. Affil: Rothermere American Inst. Email: sage.goodwin@hotmail.co.uk.

Goossen, **Benjamin.** Topeka, KS. Affil: Harvard. Email: bengoossen@g.harvard.edu.

Goossen, **Rachel W.**, *Washburn.* Email: rachel. goossen@washburn.edu.

Gootenberg, **Paul E.**, *SUNY, Stony Brook.* Email: paul.gootenberg@stonybrook.edu.

Gorby, **William Hal**, *West Virginia.* Email: William.Gorby@mail.wvu.edu.

Gordanier, **Amy**, *Charleston.* Email: gordanieraw@cofc.edu.

Gordier, **Eric.** Superior, CO. Affil: Colorado, Boulder. Email: eric.gordier@colorado.edu.

Gordin, **Michael D.**, *Princeton.* Email: mgordin@ princeton.edu.

Gordon, **Adi**, *Amherst.* Amherst, MA. Email: agordon@amherst.edu. Research: modern Jewish, European intellectual.

Gordon, **Alan**, *Guelph.* Email: alan.gordon@ uoguelph.ca.

Gordon, **Andrew**, *Harvard (Hist.).* Cambridge, MA. Email: agordon@fas.harvard.edu. Research: modern Japan.

Gordon, **Ann D.**, *Rutgers.* Email: agordon@ scarletmail.rutgers.edu.

Gordon, **Bertram M.** Oakland, CA. Affil: Mills. Email: bmgordon@mills.edu. Research: 1968 Revolt, WWII collaboration.

Gordon, **Colin H.**, *Iowa.* Iowa City, IA. Email: colin-gordon@uiowa.edu. Research: 20th-c US.

Gordon, **Courtney.** West Haven, CT. Email: cgordon9@asu.edu.

Gordon, **Daniel L.**, *Massachusetts, Amherst.* Email: dgordon@history.umass.edu.

Gordon, **David B.**, *Shepherd.* Email: dgordon@ shepherd.edu.

Gordon, **David M.**, *Graduate Center, CUNY.* Email: dmgordon@mindspring.net.

Gordon, **David Malcolm**, *Bowdoin.* Email: dgordon@bowdoin.edu.

Gordon, **Edward E.** Chicago, IL. Affil: Imperial Consulting. Email: imperialcorp@juno.com.

Gordon, **Fon L.**, *Central Florida.* Email: Fon. Gordon@ucf.edu.

Gordon, **Hilary E.** Topanga, CA. Affil: Claremont Graduate. Email: hgordon@tulane.edu. Research: colonial Louisiana, Spanish Civil War print culture.

Gordon, **Joel**, *Arkansas, Fayetteville.* Email: joelg@uark.edu.

Gordon, **John L., Jr.**, *Richmond.* Email: jgordon@ richmond.edu.

Gordon, **John W., Jr.**, *Citadel.* Email: gordonjw@ tecom.usmc.mil.

Gordon, **Leonard A.** New York, NY. Affil: Brooklyn, CUNY. Email: lg17@columbia. edu. Research: 19th-/20th-c US-South Asia relations, impact of Mahatma Gandhi worldwide.

Gordon, **Lesley J.**, *Alabama, Tuscaloosa.* Tuscaloosa, AL. Email: ljgordon1@ua.edu. Research: antebellum US South, Civil War and Reconstruction Era.

Gordon, **Linda**, *NYU; Wisconsin-Madison.* New York, NY. Email: linda.gordon@nyu.edu; lgordon@wisc.edu. Research: gender and imperialism, photography.

Gordon, **Matthew S.**, *Miami, Ohio.* Email: gordonms@miamioh.edu.

Gordon, **Michael A.**, *Wisconsin-Milwaukee.* Email: mgordon@uwm.edu.

Gordon, **Peter E.**, *Harvard (Hist.).* Email: pgordon@fas.harvard.edu.

Gordon, **Rhianna Marie.** Rochester, NY. Affil: Rochester. Email: rgord15@ur.rochester.edu.

Gordon, **Sarah Barringer**, *Pennsylvania.* Philadelphia, PA. Email: sbgordon@law.upenn. edu. Research: same-sex marriage, legal definition of religion.

Gordon, **Tammy**, *North Carolina State.* Email: tammy_gordon@ncsu.edu.

Gordon, **Wendy**, *SUNY, Plattsburgh.* Plattsburgh, NY. Email: gordonwm@plattsburgh.edu. Research: migration, Scotland.

Gordon Baty, **Christy.** Albany, CA. Email: cgbaty@gmail.com.

Gordon-Reed, **Annette**, *Harvard (Hist.).* Cambridge, NY. Email: agordonreed@law. harvard.edu. Research: Jefferson, slavery.

Gorecki, **Piotr S.**, *California, Riverside.* Email: piotr.gorecki@ucr.edu.

Goren, **Arthur**, *Columbia (Hist.).* Email: aag3@ columbia.edu.

Gorentz, **John B.** Battle Creek, MI. Email: john. gorentz@spokesrider.com.

Gorham, **Deborah**, *Carleton, Can.* Email: deborah.gorham@carleton.ca.

Gorman, **Daniel P.**, *Waterloo.* Email: dpgorman@uwaterloo.ca.

Gorman, **Daniel, Jr.** Rochester, NY. Affil: Rochester. Email: dgormanj@u.rochester.edu. Research: religion in American culture and society.

Gorman, **G. Scott**, *US Army Command Coll.* Email: gerald.s.gorman2.civ@mail.mil.

Gorman, **Hugh S.**, *Michigan Tech*. Email: hsgorman@mtu.edu.

Gorman, *James L*. Knoxville, TN. Affil: Johnson. Email: jgorman@johnsonu.edu. Research: Christianity, Stone-Campbell Movement.

Gorman, **Kathleen L.**, *Minnesota State, Mankato*. Email: kathleen.gorman@mnsu.edu.

Gorman, *Vanessa B.*, *Nebraska, Lincoln*. Email: vgorman1@unl.edu.

Gorman, **William P.**, *Monmouth*. Email: wgorman@monmouth.edu.

Gorman, **William P.**, *New York State Archives*. Email: bill.gorman@nysed.gov.

Gormley, **Melissa E.**, *Wisconsin-Platteville*. Email: gormleym@uwplatt.edu.

Gorn, *Cathy*. College Park, MD. Affil: National Hist. Day. Email: cathy@nhd.org.

Gorn, **Elliott J.**, *Loyola, Chicago*. Email: egorn@luc.edu.

Gorsuch, **Anne E.**, *British Columbia*. Email: gorsuch@mail.ubc.ca.

Gorsuch, **Edwin N.**, *Georgia State*. Email: egorsuch@gsu.edu.

Gosch, *Stephen S.*, *Wisconsin-Eau Claire*. Madison, WI. Email: stephengosch9@gmail.com. Research: modern Germany.

Goscha, *Christopher E.*, *Québec, Montréal*. Montreal, QC, Canada. Email: goscha.christopher@uqam.ca. Research: 20th-c international relations.

Gose, *Allison H.* Chapel Hill, NC. Affil: North Carolina, Chapel Hill. Email: agose@live.unc.edu.

Gosfield, *Margaret W*. Santa Barbara, CA.

Goshgarian, **Rachel**, *Lafayette*. Email: goshgarr@lafayette.edu.

Gosner, *Kevin M.*, *Arizona*. Tucson, AZ. Email: kgosner@u.arizona.edu. Research: 19th-c Maya studies, colonial cotton economy in New Spain.

Goss, *Andrew*, *Augusta*. Augusta, GA. Email: angoss@augusta.edu. Research: Indonesian science.

Goss, *Ben*. Claremont, CA. Email: ben@jdgossinc.com.

Goss, *K. David*. Wenham, MA. Affil: Gordon, Mass. Email: david.goss@gordon.edu. Research: public, museum studies.

Gossage, **Peter J.**, *Concordia, Can*. Email: Peter.Gossage@concordia.ca.

Gossard, *Julia M.*, *Utah State*. Logan, UT. Email: julia.gossard@usu.edu. Research: childhood, education.

Gosse, *Johanna*, *Idaho*. Email: johannagosse@gmail.com.

Gosse, *Van E.*, *Franklin & Marshall*. Lancaster, PA. Email: van.gosse@fandm.edu. Research: African American politics, Cold War.

Gosselin, **Edward A.**, *California State, Long Beach*. Email: egosseli@csulb.edu.

Gostisha, *Zackery*. Tacoma, WA. Affil: Pacific Lutheran. Email: gostiszk@plu.edu. Research: early European nationalism.

Goswami, *Manu*, *NYU*. New York, NY. Email: manu.goswami@nyu.edu. Research: nationalism and internationalism, political economy/economic thought.

Gotkowitz, *Laura E. S.*, *Pittsburgh*. Pittsburgh, PA. Email: lgotkowi@pitt.edu. Research: modern Latin America, Andes.

Gotte, *Amanda*. Oak Park, IL. Affil: Loyola, Chicago. Email: agotte83@gmail.com.

Gottlieb, *Beatrice*. New York, NY. Email: beagott@gmail.com.

Gottlieb, **Gabriele**, *Grand Valley State*. Email: gottlieg@gvsu.edu.

Gottreich, **Emily R.**, *California, Berkeley*. Email: emilyrg@berkeley.edu.

Gotwals, **Jennifer**, *Arthur and Elizabeth Schlesinger Library*. Email: jgotwals@radcliffe.harvard.edu.

Goucher, *Candice*, *Washington State, Pullman*. Email: cgoucher@vancouver.wsu.edu.

Goudsouzian, *Aram G.*, *Memphis*. Memphis, TN. Email: agoudszn@memphis.edu. Research: race and American popular culture, civil rights movement.

Goudsouzian, *Chrystal Elaine*, *Memphis*. Email: cdykes@memphis.edu.

Gough, **Allison J.**, *Hawai'i Pacific*. Email: agough@hpu.edu.

Gough, **Barry**, *Wilfrid Laurier*. Email: bgough@wlu.ca.

Gough, **Deborah M.**, *Wisconsin-Eau Claire*. Email: goughdm@uwec.edu.

Gough, **Jerry B.**, *Washington State, Pullman*. Email: gough@wsu.edu.

Gough, *Robert J.*, *Wisconsin-Eau Claire*. Eau Claire, WI. Email: goughrj@uwec.edu. Research: career patterns of Wisconsin teachers 1900-50.

Gough, *Terrence J.* Arlington, VA. Email: tjgough@verizon.net. Research: military-business relations, industrial/economic mobilization for war.

Gouglas, **Sean**, *Alberta*. Email: sean.gouglas@ualberta.ca.

Gould, **Eliga H.**, *New Hampshire, Durham*. Email: eliga.gould@unh.edu.

Gould, **Jeffrey L.**, *Indiana*. Email: gouldj@indiana.edu.

Gould, **Lewis L.**, *Texas, Austin*. Email: lgould@austin.rr.com.

Goulding, **Marc C.**, *Central Oklahoma*. Email: mgoulding@uco.edu.

Goulding, **Robert D.**, *Notre Dame*. Email: Goulding.2@nd.edu.

Gourley, *Bruce T*. Manhattan, MT. Affil: Montana State. Email: mail@brucegourley.com. Research: American religion, Montana and US West.

Gourley, *Gregory*. Berkeley, CA. Email: Gregorykgourley@gmail.com.

Gourrier, **Francis, Jr.**, *Kenyon*. Email: gourrier@kenyon.edu.

Gouverneur, **Joseph**, *North Carolina, Wilmington*. Email: gouverneurj@uncw.edu.

Gouwens, **Kenneth**, *Connecticut, Storrs*. Email: kenneth.gouwens@uconn.edu.

Govens, *Gordon Allen*. Clarkston, GA. Affil: Center for the Study of the Law and Religion. Email: gordongovens@yahoo.com.

Gow, **Andrew C.**, *Alberta*. Email: andrew.gow@ualberta.ca.

Gowans, **Frederick R.**, *Brigham Young*.

Gower, *Kylie Marie*. Laramie, WY. Affil: Wyoming. Email: kgower@uwyo.edu.

Gowing, *Alain M.*, *Washington, Seattle*. Email: alain@uw.edu.

Goyens, **Tom**, *Salisbury*. Email: txgoyens@salisbury.edu.

Grab, **Alexander Israel**, *Maine, Orono*. Email: agrab@maine.edu.

Graber, **Anna**, *Minnesota (Hist. of Science)*. Email: agraber@umn.edu.

Graber, *Jennifer*. Austin, TX. Affil: Texas, Austin. Email: jgraber@austin.utexas.edu.

Grabowski, *John J.*, *Case Western Reserve*. Cleveland, OH. Email: john.grabowski@case.edu. Research: Turkish immigration to US, museum collecting policies.

Grace, **Joshua Ryan**, *South Carolina, Columbia*. Email: gracejr@mailbox.sc.edu.

Grace, *Philip*, *Texas Lutheran*. Seguin, TX. Email: pgrace@tlu.edu; philip.grace1@gmail.com. Research: fatherhood in theory and practice, cultural and intellectual.

Grace, **Richard J.**, *Providence*. Email: rjgrace@providence.edu.

Graden, *Dale T.*, *Idaho*. Moscow, ID. Email: graden@uidaho.edu. Research: comparative slavery, race.

Gradwell, *Jill M.*, *SUNY, Buffalo State*. Email: gradwejm@buffalostate.edu.

Gradwohl, *Alexandra*. Chicago, IL. Affil: Loyola, Chicago. Email: amgradwohl@gmail.com.

Graefser, *Benjamin Myles*. Saint Peters, MO. Email: bgraefser23@gmail.com. Research: importance of alcohol in nation-states, economic benefits of colonialization.

Graeser, *Marcus*. Bad Vilbel, Germany. Affil: Linz, Austria. Email: Marcus.Graeser@jku.at. Research: welfare state, urban.

Graff, *Daniel A.*, *Notre Dame*. Notre Dame, IN. Email: dgraff@nd.edu. Research: race/labor/citizenship in 19th-c US, post-WWII employment policies in US.

Graff, *David A.*, *Kansas State*. Manhattan, KS. Email: dgraff@ksu.edu. Research: medieval Chinese warfare, founding of T'ang dynasty.

Graff, *Henry F.*, *Columbia (Hist.)*. Rye, NY. Email: hfg1@columbia.edu; preshist@aol.com. Research: presidency.

Grafflin, **Dennis**, *Bates*. Email: dgraffli@bates.edu.

Grafton, *Anthony T.*, *Princeton*. Princeton, NJ. Email: grafton@princeton.edu. Research: Renaissance, Reformation.

Gragg, **Larry D.**, *Missouri Science and Tech*. Email: lgragg@mst.edu.

Graham, **Benjamin Jon**, *Memphis*. Email: bjgraham@memphis.edu.

Graham, *Daniel*. Columbia, MD. Affil: Catholic. Email: eildan@gmail.com. Research: British commodity networks, tropical medicine and empire technology.

Graham, **Emily E.**, *Oklahoma State*.

Graham, *Gael N.*, *Western Carolina*. Cullowhee, NC. Email: graham@email.wcu.edu. Research: small-town South, 1960s.

Graham, **Jessica L.**, *California, San Diego*. Email: jlgraham@ucsd.edu.

Graham, *Kenneth A*. Stratford, CT. Affil: Sacred Heart. Email: kengraham@sbcglobal.net.

Graham, *Lisa Jane*. Haverford, PA. Affil: Haverford. Email: lgraham@haverford.edu. Research: early modern Europe, France.

Graham, **Loren R.**, *Harvard (Hist. of Science); MIT*. Email: lrg@mit.edu.

Graham, **Mark W.**, *Grove City*. Email: mwgraham@gcc.edu.

Graham, *Patricia Albjerg*. Cambridge, MA. Affil: Harvard. Email: Patricia_Graham@harvard.edu. Research: American education.

Graham, *Richard*, *Texas, Austin*. Santa Fe, NM. Email: rgraham@mail.utexas.edu; rgraham@newmexico.com. Research: slavery and race, city of Salvador Bahia.

Graham, **Sean**, *Carleton, Can.* Email: Sean. Graham3@carleton.ca.

Graham, **Shawn**, *Carleton, Can.* Email: shawn. graham@carleton.ca.

Graham, **Stacey R.**, *Middle Tennessee State.* Email: Stacey.Graham@mtsu.edu.

Graham, *Teri*. Jackson Heights, NY. Affil: Hofstra. Email: tgraham1@pride.hofstra.edu.

Graham, **Timothy C.**, *New Mexico.* Email: tgraham@unm.edu.

Graizbord, **David I.**, *Arizona.* Email: dlgraizb@ email.arizona.edu.

Gram, **John R.**, *Missouri State.* Email: JohnRGram@MissouriState.edu.

Grama, **Emanuela**, *Carnegie Mellon.* Email: egrama@andrew.cmu.edu.

Gramer, *Jennifer A.* Madison, WI. Affil: Wisconsin, Madison. Email: gramer@wisc.edu. Research: art and culture under Third Reich, postwar Germany.

Gramer, *Regina Ursula*. New York, NY. Affil: NYU. Email: gramer@nyu.edu.

Gramith, *Luke*. Morgantown, WV. Affil: West Virginia. Email: lwgramith@mix.wvu.edu. Research: West-East migration in early Cold War, resistance and long liberation in Italy.

Gramlich-Oka, *Bettina*. Tokyo, NY. Affil: Sophia. Email: gramlich-oka@sophia.ac.jp. Research: women in Tokugawa Period Japan, gender studies within intellectual history.

Gran, *Peter*. Philadelphia, PA. Affil: Temple. Email: pgran@temple.edu. Research: Middle East, comparative and political economy.

Granata, **Cora**, *California State, Fullerton.* Email: cgranata@fullerton.edu.

Grandin, **Greg**, *NYU; Yale.* Email: grandin@nyu. edu.

Grandstaff, **Mark R.**, *Brigham Young.* Email: mark_grandstaff@byu.edu.

Granieri, *Ronald J.* West Chester, PA. Affil: Pennsylvania. Email: rongranieri@me.com. Research: Christian Democracy and European integration, European-American relations.

Graninger, *C. Denver*, *California, Riverside.* Riverside, CA. Email: denver.graninger@ucr. edu. Research: ancient Greece and Rome, material culture.

Granquist, **Carl R.**, **Jr.**, *Keene State.* Email: cgranqui@keene.edu.

Grant, **Amanda**, *Massachusetts Hist. Soc.* Email: agrant@masshist.org.

Grant, *Barbara H.* Belmont, MA. Affil: Commonwealth Sch. Email: avicenna@qotw. net.

Grant, **Curtis R.**, *California State, Stanislaus.*

Grant, *Daniel Aaron*. Madison, WI. Affil: Wisconsin, Madison. Email: dagrant2@wisc. edu.

Grant, *Jacqueline C.* Miami, FL. Affil: Palmer Trinity Sch. Email: jacqueline60@mac.com. Research: 19th-c Cuba, Caribbean and Latin American identity.

Grant, *Jeanne E.*, *Metropolitan State.* Saint Paul, MN. Email: jeanne.grant@metrostate.edu. Research: pre- and Hussite Bohemia, medieval and early modern Holy Roman Empire.

Grant, *Jonathan A.*, *Florida State.* Email: jgrant@ fsu.edu.

Grant, *Jordan Daniel*. Washington, DC. Affil: American. Email: jordandgrant@gmail.com.

Grant, *Keith*. Moncton, NB, Canada. Affil: Crandall. Email: keith.grant@crandallu.ca. Research: loyalism, evangelicalism.

Grant, **Ken A.**, *Detroit Mercy.* Email: grantka@ udmercy.edu.

Grant, *Kevin P.*, *Hamilton.* Clinton, NY. Email: kgrant@hamilton.edu. Research: hunger strikes.

Grant, **Paul G.**, *Wisconsin-Platteville.* Email: grantp@uwplatt.edu.

Grasberger, *Brooke*. Providence, RI. Email: brooke.grasberger@gmail.com.

Grasso, *Christopher D.*, *William and Mary.* Williamsburg, VA. Email: cdgras@wm.edu. Research: early America, religious and intellectual.

Gratien, **Christopher**, *Virginia.* Email: crg8w@ virginia.edu.

Gratton, **Brian**, *Arizona State.* Email: brian@asu. edu.

Gratton, **Peter**, *Southeastern Louisiana.* Email: Peter.Gratton@southeastern.edu.

Grau, *Nathan*. Cambridge, MA. Affil: Harvard. Email: mgrau@g.harvard.edu. Research: imperial, military and cultural.

Graubard, *Stephen R.*, *Brown.* Email: stephengraubard@aol.com.

Graubart, *Karen B.*, *Notre Dame.* Notre Dame, IN. Email: kgraubar@nd.edu. Research: colonial Latin America and late medieval Iberia.

Grauvogel, *Kate*. Philadelphia, PA. Affil: Science Hist. Inst. Email: kgrauvog@indiana.edu.

Graves, **Kori A.**, *SUNY, Albany.* Email: kgraves@ albany.edu.

Gray, **Andrea R.**, *Robert H. Smith Center.* Email: agray@monticello.org.

Gray, **Charlotte**, *Carleton, Can.* Email: charlotte. gray@carleton.ca.

Gray, *Edward G.*, *Florida State.* Tallahassee, FL. Email: egray@fsu.edu. Research: 18th-c radicalism, life insurance.

Gray, **Elizabeth Kelly**, *Towson.* Email: egray@ towson.edu.

Gray, **Emily Fisher**, *Norwich.* Email: egray1@ norwich.edu.

Gray, **Hanna H.**, *Chicago.* Email: h-gray@ uchicago.edu.

Gray, **LaGuana K.**, *Texas, San Antonio.* Email: laguana.gray@utsa.edu.

Gray, *Marion W.*, *Jr.*, *Western Michigan.* Kalamazoo, MI. Email: marion.gray@wmich. edu. Research: gender transitions in Germany 1750-1830, German environmental/agrarian.

Gray, **Monica**, *New York State Archives.* Email: monica.gray@nysed.gov.

Gray, **Ralph D.**, *Indiana–Purdue, Indianapolis.* Email: rgray@iupui.edu.

Gray, *Stephanie*, *Duquesne.* Columbia, SC. Affil: South Carolina, Columbia. Email: segray@ email.sc.edu.

Gray, *Susan E.*, *Arizona State.* Tempe, AZ. Email: segray@asu.edu. Research: 19th-c ethnohistory, Canada-US borderlands.

Gray, *Susan*. Aiken, SC. Affil: Severn Sch. Email: susanwalsky@gmail.com.

Gray, *Taylor*. San Diego, CA. Affil: California, San Diego. Email: t1gray@ucsd.edu.

Gray, *William G.*, *Purdue.* West Lafayette, IN. Email: wggray@purdue.edu. Research: Europe and wider world since 1945, capitalism in international politics.

Graybill, *Andrew R.*, *Southern Methodist.* Dallas, TX. Email: agraybill@smu.edu. Research: waning racial inclusiveness in US West, comparative US and Canadian frontiers.

Grayson, **Jennifer**, *Xavier, Ohio.* Email: graysonj2@xavier.edu.

Grayzel, *Susan R.*, *Utah State.* Logan, UT. Email: s.grayzel@usu.edu. Research: 20th-c Europe, war/gender/material culture.

Greble, *Emily*, *Vanderbilt.* Nashville, TN. Email: emily.greble@vanderbilt.edu. Research: Bosnia, Islam in Europe.

Gredel-Manuele, **Zdenka**, *Niagara.* Email: zgm@niagara.edu.

Greeley, *Horace*. Gig Harbor, WA. Email: hgreeley@sonic.net.

Greeley, *June-Ann T.* Fairfield, CT. Affil: Sacred Heart. Email: juneanng@gmail.com. Research: medieval religious, medieval women.

Green, *Adam Paul*, *Chicago.* Chicago, IL. Email: apgreen@uchicago.edu. Research: African American cultural production, African American friendship.

Green, *Arnold H.*, *Brigham Young.* Email: arnold_green@byu.edu.

Green, *Damita Drayton*. Buckeystown, MD. Affil: Yesteryear Perspectives LLC. Email: DGreen@YesteryearPerspectives.com.

Green, *Elizabeth V.*, *South Alabama.* Email: elizabethgreen@southalabama.edu.

Green, **Elna C.**, *Augusta.* Email: elngreen@ augusta.edu.

Green, **George D.**, *Minnesota (Hist.).* Email: green007@umn.edu.

Green, **George N.**, *Texas, Arlington.* Email: ggreen@uta.edu.

Green, *Hilary Nicole*. Tuscaloosa, AL. Affil: Alabama, Tuscaloosa. Email: hn_green@ hotmail.com. Research: black education in Reconstruction.

Green, *Jack Michael-Freer*. Utica, NY. Affil: Central Connecticut State. Email: mikegreen@ civilizationinthewest.com. Research: American political, 20th-c American labor.

Green, *Jacob*. Los Angeles, CA. Affil: UCLA. Email: Jacobogreen@gmail.com.

Green, *James N.*, *Brown.* New York, NY. Email: James_Green@Brown.edu. Research: 20th-c US-Brazilian relations, 19th-c Brazilian urban.

Green, *James*, *Library Co. of Philadelphia.* Philadelphia, PA. Email: jgreen@ librarycompany.org. Research: printing and publishing.

Green, *Jane Fiegen*. Arlington, VA. Affil: Greater Greater Washington. Email: jane.f.green@ gmail.com. Research: youth and adulthood, capitalism.

Green, *Jay D.*, *Covenant.* Email: jdgreen@ covenant.edu.

Green, *Kerry Jo*. Waltham, MA. Affil: Brandeis. Email: kerryjogreen@gmail.com. Research: women of Pittsburgh in Civil War, women of Easter Rising 1916.

Green, **Laurie B.**, *Texas, Austin.* Email: lbgreen@ austin.utexas.edu.

Green, *Matthew Jason*. Annapolis, MD. Affil: George Washington. Email: mjg.ten@gmail. com.

Green, **Michael K.**, *Eastern Washington.*

Green, *Michael S.*, *Nevada, Las Vegas.* Las Vegas, NV. Email: michael.green@unlv.edu; michael.green@pcb-aha.org. Research: 19th-c America, American West.

Green, *Michael*. Fort Worth, TX. Affil: Texas Christian. Email: michael.e.green@tcu.edu.

Green, **Mira**, *Washington, Seattle.* Email: mirag@ uw.edu.

Green, *Monica H.*, *Arizona State*. Email: monica.green@asu.edu.

Green, *Nathan Allen*. Holden, WV. Affil: Southern West Virginia Comm. and Tech. Coll. Email: nathan.green02@icloud.com.

Green, *Nathaniel C*. Arlington, VA. Affil: Northern Virginia Comm. Coll. Email: ncgreen@nvcc.edu. Research: early US presidency.

Green, *Nile*, *UCLA*. Email: green@history.ucla.edu.

Green, *Patrice*. Athens, GA. Affil: Georgia. Email: patrice.green25@uga.edu.

Green, *Sharony A.*, *Alabama, Tuscaloosa*. Tuscaloosa, AL. Email: sagreen1@ua.edu; sharonyagreen@gmail.com. Research: urban/Miami/sports/migration, urban/Miami/borderlands.

Green, *Shiloh C*. Merced, CA. Affil: California, Merced. Email: sgreen8@ucmerced.edu.

Green, *Shirley L.*, *Bowling Green State*. Email: shirllg@bgsu.edu.

Green, *Susan M.*, *California State, Chico*. Email: sgreen@csuchico.edu.

Green, *Thomas A.*, *Michigan, Ann Arbor*. Ann Arbor, MI. Email: tagreen@umich.edu. Research: English and American criminal justice, British Isles c. 1000-1800.

Green, **William A.**, **Jr.**, *Holy Cross*.

Green, **William D.**, *Augsburg*. Email: greenb@augsburg.edu.

Green Rioja, *Romina A*. Los Angeles, CA. Affil: California, Irvine. Email: rominaakemi@gmail.com. Research: race and nation building in Chile, transnational colonization politics.

Greenberg, *Amy S.*, *Penn State*. University Park, PA. Email: amygreenberg@psu.edu. Research: 19th-c expansionism, politics and culture.

Greenberg, *Berkeley*. Van Nuys, CA. Email: berkeleygreenberg@outlook.com.

Greenberg, *Brian*. Shrewsbury, NJ. Affil: Monmouth. Email: bgreenbe@monmouth.edu. Research: political economy of industrialization, labor.

Greenberg, *Cheryl L.*, *Trinity Coll., Conn.* Hartford, CT. Email: cheryl.greenberg@trincoll.edu. Research: civil rights and civil liberties, African Americans and LGBTQ issues.

Greenberg, **Daniel J.**, *Pace*. Email: dgreenberg2@pace.edu.

Greenberg, *David*, *Rutgers*. New York, NY. Email: davidgr@rutgers.edu. Research: US since 1920, political.

Greenberg, *Douglas S.*, *Rutgers*. Baltimore, MD. Email: doug.greenberg@rutgers.edu. Research: genocide and survivor testimony, technology/libraries/scholarship.

Greenberg, *Janelle*, *Pittsburgh*. Email: janelleg@pitt.edu.

Greenberg, *Kenneth S.*, *Suffolk*. Newton Center, MA. Email: kgreenbe@suffolk.edu. Research: Nat Turner slave rebellion, southern honor.

Greenberg, **Mark I.**, *Western Washington*. Email: Mark.Greenberg@wwu.edu.

Greenberg, **Stephen J.**, *National Library of Medicine*. Email: stephen.greenberg@nih.gov.

Greenberg, *Udi*, *Dartmouth*. Hanover, NH. Email: udi.greenberg@dartmouth.edu. Research: Weimar intellectual, German emigre intellectuals and Cold War.

Greenblatt, *Joel*. Clawson, MI. Affil: International Academy. Email: jgreenblatt@gmail.com.

Greene, *Alison Collis*. Atlanta, GA. Affil: Emory. Email: acgree4@emory.edu. Research: religion and rural life/rural activism, race/religion/labor in South.

Greene, **Ann N**. Philadelphia, PA. Affil: Pennsylvania. Email: angreene@sas.upenn.edu.

Greene, *Benjamin P.*, *Bowling Green State*. Bowling Green, OH. Email: greeneb@bgsu.edu. Research: Cold War international, cultural diplomacy.

Greene, *Caleb*. Big Stone Gap, VA. Affil: Mountain Empire Comm. Coll. Email: cgreene@mecc.edu.

Greene, **Christina R.**, *Wisconsin-Madison*. Email: cgreene2@wisc.edu.

Greene, *Daniel A.*, *Illinois, Chicago*. Evanston, IL. Affil: Northwestern/US Holocaust Memorial Museum. Email: daniel.greene@northwestern.edu; dannygreene73@gmail.com. Research: public history/museums, Holocaust/American response.

Greene, *Douglas G.*, *Old Dominion*. Email: dgreene@odu.edu.

Greene, **J**. **Megan**, *Kansas*. Email: mgreene@ku.edu.

Greene, *Jack P.*, *Brown; Johns Hopkins (Hist.)*. East Greenwich, RI. Affil: John Carter Brown Library. Email: jack_greene@brown.edu. Research: Jamaica settlers 1750s, identity in British plantation colonies.

Greene, **Jeremy Alan**, *Johns Hopkins (Hist. of Science)*. Email: jgree115@jhmi.edu.

Greene, *Jodi*. Birdsboro, PA. Affil: Reading Area Comm. Coll. Email: jgreene@racc.edu. Research: infanticide in early America, women in popular culture.

Greene, *Julie M.*, *Maryland, Coll. Park*. College Park, MD. Email: jmg@umd.edu. Research: labor, migration and immigration.

Greene, **Kevin D.**, *Southern Mississippi*. Email: kevin.greene@usm.edu.

Greene, *Larry A.*, *Seton Hall*. South Orange, NJ. Email: larry.greene@shu.edu.

Greene, **Maggie**, *Montana State, Bozeman*. Email: margaret.greene1@montana.edu.

Greene, *Molly*, *Princeton*. Princeton, NJ. Email: greene@princeton.edu. Research: modern Greece and Ottoman.

Greene, **Nathanael**, *Wesleyan*. Email: ngreene@wesleyan.edu.

Greene, **Rebecca S**. South Orange, NJ. Email: rsg1114@aol.com.

Greene, **Robert H.**, *Montana*. Email: robert.greene@umontana.edu.

Greene, **Robin J.**, *Providence*. Email: rgreene2@providence.edu.

Greene, *Sandra E.*, *Cornell*. Ithaca, NY. Email: seg6@cornell.edu. Research: colonialism, Ghana.

Greene, *Thomas A.*, *North Georgia*. Oakwood, GA. Email: thomas.greene@ung.edu. Research: emotions/senses, Carolingian religion/monsticism/exegesis.

Greene, **Timothy J**. Jersey Shore, PA. Affil: Jersey Shore Area Sch. District. Email: timothyjgreene@verizon.net.

Greeney, *Spring*. Philadelphia, PA. Affil: Baldwin Sch. Email: sgreeney@gmail.com.

Greenfield, *Richard*, *Queen's, Can.* Email: greenfie@queensu.ca.

Greenidge, *Kerri K*. Medford, MA. Affil: Tufts. Email: kerri.greenidge@tufts.edu. Research:

African American political, late 19th-c race and citizenship.

Greenlee, *John Wyatt*. Ithaca, NY. Affil: Cornell. Email: jwg239@cornell.edu. Research: spatial and cartographic, cultural history of eels in England.

Greenly, *Eric M*. Elyria, OH. Email: EGreenl11@yahoo.com.

Green-Mercado, *Marya T.*, *Rutgers, Newark/New Jersey Inst. of Tech.* Email: mayte.green@rutgers.edu.

Greenough, *Paul R.*, *Iowa*. Iowa City, IA. Email: paul-greenough@uiowa.edu. Research: Indian public health, Indian environmental.

Greenspan, **Ian G.**, *Oakland*. Email: greenspa@oakland.edu.

Greenstein, **Elijah J**. New Brunswick, NJ. Affil: Princeton. Email: ejgreenstein@gmail.com.

Greenwald, *Emily*. Missoula, MT. Affil: Hist. Research Assoc. Email: egreenwald@hrassoc.com. Research: 1887 Dawes Act, national parks.

Greenwald, *Lisa*. New York, NY. Affil: Stuyvesant High Sch. Email: Lgreenwald2@schools.nyc.gov.

Greenwald, **Maurine W.**, *Pittsburgh*. Email: greenwal@pitt.edu.

Greenwald, *Richard A.*, *Fairfield*. Fairfield, CT. Email: rgreenwald@fairfield.edu. Research: rise of freelancers, garment workers.

Greenwald, **W**. **James**, **Jr.**, *Arkansas State*.

Greenwalt, **William S.**, *Santa Clara*. Email: wgreenwalt@scu.edu.

Greenwood, **Janette Thomas**, *Clark*. Email: jgreenwood@clarku.edu.

Greenwood, **Jonathan Edward**, *Rochester*. Email: jonathan.greenwood@rochester.edu.

Greenwood, *Neil V*. Delano, TN. Affil: Cleveland State Comm. Coll. Email: ngreenwood@clevelandstatecc.edu.

Greer, *Allan*, *McGill*. Email: allan.greer@mcgill.ca.

Greer, *Edward*. Brookline, MA. Email: greer1996@rcn.com.

Greer, **Harold E.**, **Jr.**, *Virginia Commonwealth*. Email: hegreer2@comcast.net.

Greer, **William H.**, **Jr**. Chevy Chase, MD.

Greer Golda, *Nicole Renee*. Roanoke, VA. Affil: Ferrum. Email: ngreergolda@ferrum.edu. Research: migration, Americanization, gender.

Greet, **Michele**, *George Mason*. Email: mgreet@gmu.edu.

Gregg, **Christopher**, *George Mason*. Email: cgregg@gmu.edu.

Gregg, **Robert**, *Stockton*. Email: robert.gregg@stockton.edu.

Gregg, **Sara M.**, *Kansas*. Email: sgregg@ku.edu.

Gregory, *Aaron J*. Norfolk, VA. Affil: Norfolk Collegiate. Email: ajgreg@email.wm.edu.

Gregory, *Anthony Lee*. Albany, CA. Affil: California, Berkeley. Email: anthony.gregory@berkeley.edu.

Gregory, *Brad S.*, *Notre Dame*. South Bend, IN. Email: bgregor3@nd.edu. Research: early modern Christianity, Reformation.

Gregory, **Candace**, *California State, Sacramento*. Email: cgregory@csus.edu.

Gregory, **Frederick**, *Florida*. Email: fgregory@ufl.edu.

Gregory, *James N.*, *Washington, Seattle*. Seattle, WA. Email: gregoryj@uw.edu. Research: 20th-c migration/race/regions, socialism and radicalism.

Gregory, Timothy E., *Ohio State*. Email: gregory.4@osu.edu.

Grehan, James P., *Portland State*. Portland, OR. Email: grehanjp@pdx.edu. Research: popular religion, popular culture.

Grem, Darren E., *Mississippi*.

Grendler, Paul F., *Toronto*.

Grenier, Judson, *California State, Dominguez Hills*. Email: jgrenier@csudh.edu.

Grenier, Katherine H., *Citadel*. Email: grenierk@citadel.edu.

Grennell, Katherine, *SUNY, Buffalo State*. Email: grenneke@buffalostate.edu.

Gresehover, Lloyd. Topinabee, MI. Email: kbam4591@charter.net.

Gressang, Corinne. Lexington, KY. Affil: Kentucky. Email: corinne.gressang@uky.edu.

Greven, Philip J., Jr., *Rutgers*. Email: pgreven@aol.com.

Grever, John H., *Loyola Marymount*. Email: john.grever@lmu.edu.

Grew, Raymond, *Michigan, Ann Arbor*. Ann Arbor, MI. Email: rgrew@umich.edu. Research: Italian political culture, French church and social change.

Grewal, Anup, *Toronto*. Email: anup.grewal@utoronto.ca.

Gribble, Richard E., CSC, *American Catholic Hist. Assoc.* Email: rgribble@stonehill.edu.

Grider, John T., *Wisconsin-La Crosse*. Email: jgrider@uwlax.edu.

Griech-Polelle, Beth Ann, *Pacific Lutheran*. Graham, WA. Email: griechba@plu.edu. Research: Catholic Church in Nazi Germany, antisemitism and Nazi Germany.

Grieco, Patrick. Suffolk, VA. Affil: US Navy. Email: griecopd@hotmail.com. Research: Declaration of Arbroath, Late Byzantium.

Grieco, Viviana L., *Missouri–Kansas City*. Email: griecov@umkc.edu.

Grieder, Jerome B., *Brown*. Email: Jerome_Grieder@Brown.edu.

Grier, Katherine C., *Delaware*. Email: kcgrier@udel.edu.

Griesmer, Daniel R. Stow, OH. Affil: Akron. Email: dgriesmer@hotmail.com. Research: 19th-c Native Americans and Ohio, 18th-c Native Americans and Ohio.

Grieve, Victoria M., *Utah State*. Logan, UT. Email: victoria.grieve@usu.edu. Research: America, American cultural.

Griffey, Trevor, *California State, Dominguez Hills*.

Griffin, Benjamin, *US Military Acad.* Leavenworth, KS. Email: ben.griffin@usma.edu; ben.griffin@utexas.edu. Research: American foreign relations, Cold War.

Griffin, Carl L. Imperial, CA. Affil: American Military. Email: carl.l.griffin@outlook.com.

Griffin, Christopher. Owensboro, KY. Affil: Brescia. Email: christopher.griffin@brescia.edu.

Griffin, Eric. Miami, FL. Affil: Miami. Email: emg164@miami.edu.

Griffin, Katherine H., *Massachusetts Hist. Soc.* Email: kgriffin@masshist.org.

Griffin, Oliver, *St. John Fisher*. Rochester, NY. Email: ogriffin@sjfc.edu. Research: 19th-/20th-c Europe, modern Germany.

Griffin, Patrick, *Notre Dame*. Notre Dame, IN. Email: pgriffi4@nd.edu. Research: Irish American, early America.

Griffin, Roger A., *Austin Comm. Coll.* Email: rgriffin1@austin.rr.com.

Griffin, Sean G. Brooklyn, NY. Affil: Brooklyn, CUNY. Email: sgriffin@gradcenter.cuny.edu. Research: US antislavery and labor.

Griffith, Brian J. Goleta, CA. Affil: California, Santa Barbara. Email: brianjgriffith@gmail.com. Research: fascist Italy, Roma diaspora in modern Europe.

Griffith, Jeffrey. Broadway, NC. Email: griffjef@gmail.com. Research: Muslim communities in western Europe.

Griffith, Luke. Athens, OH. Affil: Ohio. Email: lgriffith@rio.edu.

Griffith, Michael Dennis. Oakland, CA. Email: griffith.mje@sbcglobal.net.

Griffith, Zoe Ann. New York, NY. Affil: Baruch, CUNY. Email: zoe.griffith@baruch.cuny.edu.

Griffiths, Fiona J., *Stanford*. Stanford, CA. Email: fgriffit@stanford.edu. Research: women, literacy and education.

Griffiths, Naomi E. S., *Carleton, Can.* Email: naomi.griffiths@carleton.ca.

Griffiths, Paul D., *Iowa State*. Email: pgriff@iastate.edu.

Grigg, John A., *Nebraska, Omaha*. Email: jgrigg@unomaha.edu.

Grill, Johnpeter H., *Mississippi State*. Email: grillb1@bellsouth.net.

Grimes, Richard, *Duquesne*. Email: grimesr1@duq.edu.

Grimmer-Solem, Erik, *Wesleyan*. Middletown, CT. Email: egrimmer@wesleyan.edu. Research: German social reform 1848-1918, German imperialism.

Grimsley, Mark, *Ohio State*. Email: grimsley.1@osu.edu.

Grimsted, David A., *Maryland, Coll. Park*. Email: grimsted@umd.edu.

Grimsted, Patricia K. Cambridge, MA. Affil: Harvard Ukrainian Research Inst. Email: grimsted@fas.harvard.edu. Research: trophy and displaced archives, NIS archival heritage.

Grinberg, Claire C. Sarasota, FL. Affil: Binghamton Univ. Art Museum. Email: cresearchart@aol.com. Research: Austrian and German political caricatures, WW I and WW II.

Grinberg, Ronnie Avital, *Oklahoma (Hist.)*. Oklahoma City, OK. Email: grinberg@ou.edu; ronnie.grinberg@gmail.com. Research: New York intellectuals, masculinity.

Gripentrog, John G., *Mars Hill*. Email: jgripentrog@mhu.edu.

Grischkan, Jamie. Boston, MA. Affil: Boston Univ. Email: jgrisch@bu.edu.

Grischow, Jeff D., *Wilfrid Laurier*. Email: jgrischow@wlu.ca.

Griswold, Robert L., *Oklahoma (Hist.)*. Email: rgriswold@ou.edu.

Griswold, Sarah Kephart, *Oklahoma State*. Tulsa, OK. Email: skgriswold@gmail.com. Research: France, museum studies/public.

Griswold, Stephanie Valeska. Temecula, CA. Affil: San Diego State. Email: griswold.stephanie@gmail.com. Research: new religious movements, digital public history.

Griswold, William J., *Colorado State*. Email: william.griswold@colostate.edu.

Gritter, Elizabeth, *Indiana, Southeast*. New Albany, IN. Email: egritter@ius.edu. Research: US, civil rights.

Grivno, Max L., *Southern Mississippi*. Email: max.grivno@usm.edu.

Grjebine, Liv. Cambridge, MA. Affil: Harvard. Email: liv1@hotmail.fr.

Grober, Max C., *Austin Coll.* Denison, TX. Email: mgrober@austincollege.edu. Research: early modern Europe, intellectual.

Grodzins, Dean D. Cambridge, MA. Affil: Harvard Business Sch. Email: grodzins@gmail.com. Research: fugitive slaves, American democracy.

Grodzinski, Tanya J., *Royal Military*. Email: Tanya.Grodzinski@rmc.ca.

Groeger, Cristina V., *Lake Forest*. Chicago, IL. Email: groeger@lakeforest.edu. Research: education, labor markets.

Groetsch, Ulrich, *North Alabama*. Email: ugroetsch@una.edu.

Groft, Tammis, *SUNY, Albany*. Email: grofttk@albanyinstitute.org.

Grogin, Robert C., *Saskatchewan*.

Groh, Charles McGraw, *Tampa*. Email: cmcgraw@ut.edu.

Grohman, Gregory. Iowa City, IA. Affil: Iowa. Email: Gregory-grohman@uiowa.edu.

Gronau, Jack Anthony. Cambridge, MA. Affil: Northeastern. Email: jagronau@gmail.com. Research: French Empire and Feminism.

Gronbeck-Tedesco, John, *Ramapo*. Email: jgronbec@ramapo.edu.

Gronewold, Sue, *Kean*. Email: sgronewo@kean.edu.

Gronningsater, Sarah L. H., *Pennsylvania*. Email: gronning@sas.upenn.edu.

Gronowicz, Anthony. New York, NY. Affil: Borough of Manhattan Comm. Coll., CUNY. Email: abgronowicz@gmail.com. Research: US, New York City.

Groppo, Martha Johanna, *Berea*. Email: groppom@berea.edu.

Gross, Ariela J., *Southern California*. Email: agross@law.usc.edu.

Gross, Benjamin H., *Missouri–Kansas City*. Email: grossb@lindahall.org.

Gross, David L., *Colorado, Boulder*. Email: david.l.gross@colorado.edu.

Gross, Dean. Bronxville, NY. Affil: PS 68. Email: dgrosskitman@yahoo.com.

Gross, Jo-Ann, *New Jersey*. Email: gross@tcnj.edu.

Gross, Kali Nicole, *Rutgers*. Email: kali.gross@rutgers.edu.

Gross, Linda, *Hagley Museum and Library*. Email: lgross@hagley.org.

Gross, Michael B., *East Carolina*. Email: grossm@ecu.edu.

Gross, Miriam D., *Oklahoma (Hist.); Oklahoma (Hist. of Science)*. Norman, OK. Email: mdgross@ou.edu. Research: Maoist PRC rural public health, PRC introduction of popular science.

Gross, Robert A., *Connecticut, Storrs*. Concord, MA. Email: robert.gross@uconn.edu. Research: transcendentalism and society, history of the book.

Gross, Stephen Gerard, *NYU*. Email: sg152@nyu.edu.

Grossberg, Michael C., *Indiana*. Bloomington, IN. Email: grossber@indiana.edu. Research: 19th-/20th-c children and law, law and social policy.

Gross-Diaz, Theresa J., *Loyola, Chicago*. Email: tgross@luc.edu.

Grossman, *David Michael*. Coconut Grove, FL. Email: davidmichaelgrossman@gmail.com.

Grossman, *James F.*, *AHA; National Hist. Center*. Washington, DC. Email: jgrossman@historians.org. Research: African American, history and public culture.

Grossman, *Luke*. Holland, MI. Affil: North Carolina, Chapel Hill. Email: LG64Biz@gmail.com. Research: German Army Officer Corps 1900-55, German Society/Army relations 1900-55.

Grossman, *Martin R*. Boston, MA. Affil: State of Massachusetts.

Grossman, *Richard*, *Northeastern Illinois*. Email: R-Grossman@neiu.edu.

Grossmann, *Atina*. New York, NY. Affil: Cooper Union. Email: ag93@nyu.edu. Research: post-WWII Germany/gender, WWII and Holocaust/refugees.

Grout, **Holly L.**, *Alabama, Tuscaloosa*. Email: hlgrout@bama.ua.edu.

Grove, *Jama McMurtery*. Fayetteville, AR. Affil: Arkansas, Fayetteville. Email: jamagrove@gmail.com.

Grover, *Warren*. Short Hills, NJ. Email: minuteman1996@msn.com.

Groves, *Amber Justine*. Oak Harbor, WA. Email: amberjgroves@gmail.com.

Groves, *Philip V.* Bronx, NY. Affil: Monroe. Email: wonderphil666@gmail.com.

Grow, **Michael R.**, *Ohio*. Email: grow@ohio.edu.

Grubb, **Farley**, *Delaware*. Email: grubbf@lerner.udel.edu.

Grubb, **James S.**, *Maryland, Baltimore County*. Email: grubb@umbc.edu.

Grubbs, **Larry**, *Georgia State*. Email: lgrubbs@gsu.edu.

Gruber, **Carol S.**, *William Paterson*.

Gruber, *Ira D.*, *Rice*. Bellaire, TX. Email: gruber@rice.edu. Research: 18th-c warfare theory and practice, British army officers in American Revolution.

Grucza, *Emily*. Riverside, CA. Email: egruc001@ucr.edu.

Gruder, *Vivian R.*, *Queens, CUNY*. Email: vrgruder@att.net.

Gruenwald, **Kim M.**, *Kent State*. Email: kgruenwa@kent.edu.

Grunden, **Walter Eugene**, *Bowling Green State*. Email: wgrund@bgsu.edu.

Grunder, *Sarah L.* Baldwin, NY. Affil: Suffolk County Comm. Coll., SUNY. Email: slgrun@email.wm.edu. Research: national identity and print culture, US 1877-1945.

Grundmeier, *Timothy D.* New Ulm, MN. Affil: Martin Luther. Email: grundmtd@mlc-wels.edu. Research: religion and Civil War Era, American Lutheranism.

Grundset, *Eric G.* Burke, VA. Email: eggrundset@aol.com. Research: Virginia, New England.

Grundy, *Harry*. Washington, DC. Affil: American. Email: hgrundy@american.edu.

Gruner, *Wolf*, *Southern California*. Email: gruner@usc.edu.

Grzebien, **Thomas W.**, **III**, *Providence*. Email: grzebien@providence.edu.

Gualtieri, **Maurizio**, *Alberta*. Email: mgualt@unipg.it.

Gualtieri, **Sarah M.**, *Southern California*. Email: gualtier@usc.edu.

Guard, **Julie**, *Manitoba*. Email: julie.guard@umanitoba.ca.

Guardino, **Laura**, *San José State*. Email: Laura.Guardino@sjsu.edu.

Guardino, *Peter F.*, *Indiana*. Bloomington, IN. Email: pguardin@indiana.edu. Research: Mexican peasantry, political culture and poor.

Guarneri, *Carl J.*, *St. Mary's, Calif.* Moraga, CA. Email: cguarner@stmarys-ca.edu. Research: US social and intellectual 1830-1930, comparative/transnational.

Guasco, *Michael J.*, *Davidson*. Davidson, NC. Email: miguasco@davidson.edu. Research: Anglo-Atlantic world, racial slavery.

Gubbels, *Thomas*. Jefferson City, MO. Affil: Lincoln, Mo. Email: tjgubbels@gmail.com.

Guberman, *Rachel M.* Philadelphia, PA. Affil: American Academy of Arts & Sciences. Email: guberman@gmail.com. Research: metropolitan/urban studies, post-1960s politics and political culture.

Gubler, *Greg*. Limerick, PA. Email: greggubler@clear.net. Research: diplomacy of imperial Japan, Japanese family/genealogical sources.

Gubser, *Michael D.*, *James Madison*. Harrisonburg, VA. Email: gubsermd@jmu.edu. Research: ethics in phenomenological tradition, historiography and international development.

Gude, *Susana*. Anaheim, CA. Affil: American. Email: sg3305a@american.edu.

Gudgeirsson, *Meg*. Alameda, CA. Affil: Santa Clara. Email: meppel@ucsc.edu. Research: late 19th-c US Mormon.

Gudis, **Catherine**, *California, Riverside*. Email: catherine.gudis@ucr.edu.

Gudmestad, **Robert**, *Colorado State*. Email: robert.gudmestad@colostate.edu.

Gudmundson, **Lowell**, *Mount Holyoke*. Email: lgudmund@mtholyoke.edu.

Guelzo, *Allen C.* Gettysburg, PA. Affil: Gettysburg. Email: aguelzo@gettysburg.edu. Research: Abraham Lincoln.

Guenther, *Katja*, *Princeton*. Princeton, NJ. Email: kguenthe@princeton.edu. Research: US and European psychiatry, transfer of scientific knowledge.

Guenther, **Michael B.**, *Grinnell*. Email: guenthmb@grinnell.edu.

Guerra, *Lillian*, *Florida*. Gainesville, FL. Email: lillian.guerra@ufl.edu. Research: Cuban Revolution, 20th-c Cuba.

Guerrier, **Steve**, *James Madison*. Email: guerrisw@jmu.edu.

Guerrini, *Anita*. Corvallis, OR. Affil: Oregon State. Email: anita.guerrini@oregonstate.edu. Research: early modern anatomy and experimentation, history and ecological restoration.

Guerry, *Ethan Joel*. Hockessin, DE. Affil: Nemours Estate. Email: ethan.j.guerry@gmail.com.

Guerty, **Phillip Michael**, *North Georgia*. Email: phillip.guerty@ung.edu.

Guettel, **Jens-Uwe**, *Penn State*. Email: jug17@psu.edu.

Guevarra, *Rudy P.*, *Jr.* Tempe, AZ. Affil: Arizona State. Email: rpguevarra@asu.edu. Research: Chicanos and Filipinos in San Diego, race relations and biracial identity.

Guglielmo, **Jennifer M.**, *Smith*. Email: jgugliel@smith.edu.

Guglielmo, *Thomas A*. Washington, DC. Affil: George Washington. Email: tguglielmoGW@gmail.com.

Guha, *Ramachandra*. Bangalore, India. Email: ramguha@gmail.com. Research: India, environmental.

Guha, *Sumit*, *Texas, Austin*. Austin, TX. Email: sguha@austin.utexas.edu. Research: Indian socio-cultural, premodern Indian environment.

Guia-Conca, **Aitana**, *California State, Fullerton*. Email: aguia@fullerton.edu.

Guilbault, *Alexis Helen*. Bloomington, IN. Affil: Indiana. Email: memorycentral8@gmail.com. Research: colonial and early American borderlands.

Guild, **Joshua Bruce**, *Princeton*. Email: jguild@princeton.edu.

Guiler, *Thomas A.*, *IV*. Wilmington, DE. Affil: Winterthur Museum, Gardens, and Library. Email: tguiler@winterthur.org.

Guilfoyle, **James Edward**, *Tennessee, Chattanooga*. Email: james-guilfoyle@utc.edu.

Guiliano, *Jennifer E.*, *Indiana–Purdue, Indianapolis*. Indianapolis, IN. Email: guiliano@iupui.edu; jenguiliano@gmail.com. Research: digital humanities, popular culture.

Guillen, *Nalleli M.* Brooklyn, NY. Affil: Brooklyn Hist. Soc. Email: nallelig@gmail.com. Research: visual culture, race.

Guillerm, *Gabrielle*. Chicago, IL. Affil: Northwestern. Email: gabrielleguillerm2019@u.northwestern.edu.

Guillow, **Lawrence**, *California State, Los Angeles*. Email: lguillo@calstatela.edu.

Guimont, *Edward*. Storrs Mansfield, CT. Affil: Connecticut, Storrs. Email: edward.guimont@uconn.edu.

Guingona, *Phillip B*. Pullman, WA. Affil: Washington State, Pullman. Email: phillipg@buffalo.edu. Research: Asia.

Guinsburg, **Thomas N.**, *Western Ontario*. Email: pcetng@uwo.ca.

Guldi, **Joanna**, *Southern Methodist*. Email: jguldi@smu.edu.

Gulema, *Shimelis B*. Stony Brook, NY. Affil: SUNY, Stony Brook. Email: shimelis.gulema@stonybrook.edu.

Gulig, **Anthony G.**, *Wisconsin-Whitewater*. Email: guliga@uww.edu.

Gullace, **Nicoletta F.**, *New Hampshire, Durham*. Email: nfg@unh.edu.

Gullachsen, **Arthur W.**, *Royal Military*. Email: Arthur.Gullachsen@rmc.ca.

Gullickson, **Gay L.**, *Maryland, Coll. Park*. Email: glg@umd.edu.

Gullotta, *Daniel Nicholas*. Hillsborough, CA. Affil: Stanford. Email: gullotta@stanford.edu.

Gumbert, *Heather L.*, *Virginia Tech*. Blacksburg, VA. Email: hgumbert@vt.edu. Research: television and visual culture, postwar Europe/West.

Gump, *James O.*, *San Diego*. San Diego, CA. Email: gump@sandiego.edu. Research: André Tchelistcheff, post-Prohibition Napa Valley.

Gundersen, **Geir**, *Gerald Ford Presidential Library*. Email: geir.gundersen@nara.gov.

Gundersen, **Joan R.**, *California State, San Marcos*.

Gundersheimer, **Werner L.**, *Leo Baeck Inst.* Email: gundershei@folger.edu.

Gundlach, *Bradley J.* Lindenhurst, IL. Affil: Trinity International. Email: bgundlac@tiu.edu. Research: evolution and religion, B.B. Warfield.

Gunn, Christopher, *Coastal Carolina*. Email: cgunn@coastal.edu.

Gunn, Jennifer L., *Minnesota (Hist. of Science)*. Email: gunnx005@umn.edu.

Gunn, Lloyd Ray, *Utah*. Email: ray.gunn@utah.edu.

Gunn, Peter, *Smith*. Email: pgunn@smith.edu.

Gunns, Albert F., *California State, Long Beach*. Email: agunns@csulb.edu.

Gunther, Karl A., *Miami*. Email: k.gunther@miami.edu.

Gunther, Michael G. Suwanee, GA. Affil: Georgia Gwinnett. Email: mgunther@ggc.edu. Research: environment/American Revolution, women's nature writings/postwar America.

Gunther, Vanessa Ann, *Chapman*. Email: vagunthe@chapman.edu.

Guo, Qitao, *California, Irvine*. Email: guoq@uci.edu.

Guo, Weiting. Coquitlam, BC, Canada. Affil: Simon Fraser. Email: weitingguo@gmail.com. Research: late imperial and republican China, Chinese legal.

Gupta, Ravi M., *Utah State*. Email: ravi.gupta@usu.edu.

Gupta, Surendra K., *Pittsburg State*. Bettendorf, IA. Email: surengupta68@gmail.com. Research: Russian foreign policy since 1991, Indo-Russian and Indo-US relations.

Guridy, Frank A., *Columbia (Hist.)*. Email: fg2368@columbia.edu.

Gurkas, Hakki, *Kennesaw State*. Email: hgurkas@kennesaw.edu.

Gurman, Scott, *Wisconsin-Platteville*. Email: gurmans@uwplatt.edu.

Gurner, John J. Pell City, AL. Email: jgurner1745@gmail.com. Research: Scottish Loyalistist in Am Revolution.

Gurowsky, David. Silver Spring, MD. Email: davidgurowsky@gmail.com.

Gurwitz, Beatrice. Chevy Chase, MD. Affil: National Humanities Alliance. Email: bdgurwitz@gmail.com.

Gusella, Christina Elizabeth. Cypress, TX. Affil: Emory. Email: christina.elizabeth.gusella@emory.edu. Research: Soviet cultural diplomacy 1960s-90s, US foreign relations with USSR.

Gust, Sandra J. Bethesda, MD. Email: sjgust@msn.com.

Gustafson, James M., *Indiana State*. Email: james.gustafson@indstate.edu.

Gustafson, Kaaryn. Irvine, CA. Affil: California, Irvine. Email: kgustafson@law.uci.edu.

Gustafson, Melanie S., *Vermont*. Burlington, VT. Email: melanie.gustafson@uvm.edu. Research: US social, US women.

Gustafson, Sarah Helene. Cambridge, MA. Email: sarahgustafson@g.harvard.edu.

Gutarra Cordero, Dannelle. San Juan, PR. Affil: Princeton. Email: dgutarra@princeton.edu. Research: Caribbean, Atlantic world.

Gutek, Gerald L. La Grange, IL. Email: glgutek@yahoo.com.

Gutfeld, David Lawrence. Rochmond, CA. Affil: Sir Francis Drake High Sch. Email: davidlawrencegutfeld@gmail.com. Research: global, California.

Gutfreund, Zevi, *Louisiana State*. Email: zgutfreund@lsu.edu.

Guthman, Joshua, *Berea*. Email: joshua_guthman@berea.edu.

Guthrie, Charles C., *Indianapolis*.

Guthrie, Wayne L., *San Diego Mesa*. Email: wguthrie@sdccd.edu.

Gutierrez, David G., *California, San Diego*. Email: dggutierrez@ucsd.edu.

Gutierrez, Florentina, *Massachusetts Hist. Soc.* Email: fgutierrez@masshist.org.

Gutierrez, Laura D. Stockton, CA. Affil: Pacific. Email: lgutierrez2@pacific.edu. Research: US-Mexico migration, Mexican deportation and return migration.

Gutierrez, Ramon A., *Chicago*. Chicago, IL. Email: rgutierrez@uchicago.edu. Research: Chicano/a, Spanish borderlands.

Gutierrez, Samuel. San Antonio, TX. Email: sgutie517@gmail.com.

Gutierrez, Veronica A., *Azusa Pacific*. Azusa, CA. Email: vgutierrez@apu.edu. Research: Nahua Christianity in colonial Mexico, Franciscans in colonial Mexico.

Gutierrez-Romine, Alicia Mariel. Riverside, CA. Affil: La Sierra. Email: agutierr@lasierra.edu. Research: abortion in California/gender/sex, 20th-c California.

Gutman, David Edward, *Manhattanville*. Purchase, NY. Email: David.Gutman@mville.edu; degutman@gmail.com. Research: late Ottoman, migration.

Gutman, Sanford J., Esq. Ithaca, NY. Affil: SUNY, Cortland. Email: gutmans@cortland.edu.

Gutmann, Myron P., *Colorado, Boulder*. Boulder, CO. Email: myron.gutmann@colorado.edu. Research: population/land use/environment, demography of western US.

Gutterman, Lauren Jae, *Texas, Austin*. Austin, TX. Email: lgutterman@utexas.edu. Research: 20th-c US, women/gender/sexuality.

Gutzke, David W., *Missouri State*. Email: davidgutzke@missouristate.edu.

Gutzman, Kevin R. C., *Western Connecticut State*. Email: gutzmank@wcsu.edu.

Guy, Donna J., *Arizona; Ohio State*. Tucson, AZ. Email: dguy@earthlink.net; guy.60@osu.edu. Research: Juan and Eva Peron, sexuality.

Guy, Kolleen M., *Texas, San Antonio*. Email: kolleen.guy@utsa.edu.

Guy, R. Kent, *Washington, Seattle*. Email: qing@uw.edu.

Guyer, Benjamin Michael, *Tennessee, Martin*. Email: bguyer@utm.edu.

Guyette, Elise A. South Burlington, VT. Email: eguy949@gmail.com.

Guzik, Michael A., SJ, *Le Moyne*. Email: guzikma@lemoyne.edu.

Guzman, Romeo, *California State, Fresno*. Email: romeog@csufresno.edu.

Guzzetta, Melissa. Irvine, CA. Email: Info@PrivateLucky.com.

Gvosdev, Nikolas K., *Naval War Coll.* Email: nikolas.gvosdev@usnwc.edu.

Gyug, Richard F., *Fordham*. Email: gyug@fordham.edu.

H h

Ha, Arang. Houston, TX. Affil: Rice. Email: arang.ha@rice.edu. Research: 19th-c US, Civil War and Reconstruction.

Ha, Songho. Anchorage, AK. Affil: Alaska Anchorage. Email: songhoha@hotmail.com. Research: American system 1801-29, Albert Gallatin.

Haagsma, Margriet, *Alberta*. Email: margriet.haagsma@ualberta.ca.

Haak, Candis L., *SUNY, Oswego*. Email: candis.haak@oswego.edu.

Haas, Amanda Christine. Amarillo, TX. Affil: Wayland Baptist. Email: ahaas878@gmail.com.

Haas, Arthur G., *Tennessee, Knoxville*.

Haas, Grant Timothy. Greeley, CO. Affil: Arizona State. Email: gthaas@asu.edu.

Haas, Lisbeth, *California, Santa Cruz*. Email: lhaas@ucsc.edu.

Haas, Louis B., *Middle Tennessee State*. Murfreesboro, TN. Email: lhaas@mtsu.edu. Research: medieval and early modern family, medieval and early modern saints.

Haas, Martin R., *Adelphi*. Email: haas@adelphi.edu.

Haber, Carole, *Tulane*. Email: chaber@tulane.edu.

Haber, Samuel. Berkeley, CA. Affil: California, Berkeley. Email: zanvil@socrates.berkeley.edu.

Haber, Stephen H., *Stanford*. Email: haber@stanford.edu.

Haberer, Erich E., *Wilfrid Laurier*. Email: ehaberer@wlu.ca.

Haberkern, Phillip Nelson, *Boston Univ.* Email: phaberke@bu.edu.

Haberland, Michelle, *Georgia Southern*. Email: mah@georgiasouthern.edu.

Haberman, Aaron L. Greeley, CO. Affil: Northern Colorado. Email: aaron.haberman@unco.edu. Research: conservative Christianity and politics.

Haberman, Arthur. Toronto, ON, Canada. Affil: York, Can. Email: arthurh@yorku.ca.

Haberski, Raymond J., *Indiana–Purdue, Indianapolis*. Email: haberski@iupui.edu.

Hachten, Elizabeth A., *Wisconsin-Whitewater*. Email: hachtene@uww.edu.

Hackel, Steven W., *California, Riverside*. Pasadena, CA. Email: shackel@ucr.edu. Research: American West, colonial America.

Hackemer, Kurt H., *South Dakota; Soc. for Military Hist.* Email: kurt.hackemer@usd.edu.

Hacker, Barton C. Annapolis, MD. Affil: National Museum of American Hist. Email: hackerb@si.edu. Research: comparative military technology, women and military institutions.

Hacker, J. David, *Minnesota (Hist.)*. Email: hacke010@umn.edu.

Hackett, Brian, *Northern Kentucky*. Email: hackettb1@nku.edu.

Hackett, David A., *Texas, El Paso*. Email: davidah@utep.edu.

Hackett, David G., *Florida*. Email: dhackett@ufl.edu.

Hackett, William H., *Henry Ford Coll.* Email: pwhackett@wowway.com.

Hackmann, Wm. Kent, *Idaho*. Andover, NH. Email: hackmann@uidaho.edu. Research: West India interest in House of Commons.

Hacnik, Christopher. Washington, DC. Affil: American. Email: chacnik@renocavanaugh.com.

Hacohen, Malachi Haim, *Duke*. Durham, NC. Email: mhacohen@duke.edu. Research: modern Europe, intellectual.

Hacsi, Tim A., *Massachusetts, Boston*. Newton, MA. Email: tim.hacsi@umb.edu; tahacsi@yahoo.com. Research: higher education and access, social mobility and poverty.

Haddad, Robert, *Smith*. Email: rhaddad@smith.edu.

Haddad, **William W.**, *California State, Fullerton.* Email: whaddad@fullerton.edu.

Haddad, **Yvonne**, *Georgetown.* Email: haddady@georgetown.edu.

Hadden, *Sally E.*, *Western Michigan.* Kalamazoo, MI. Email: sally.hadden@wmich.edu. Research: 18th-c American law, legal cultures/cities/slavery.

Hadfield, **Leslie**, *Brigham Young.* Email: leslie_hadfield@byu.edu.

Hadi, *Erum*. Briarcliff Manor, NY. Affil: St. John's. Email: erum.hadi17@stjohns.edu. Research: Indo-Islamic material culture, Northwest India material culture.

Hadley, **Erik J.**, *Boise State.* Email: erikhadley@boisestate.edu.

Haeberlein, *Mark C*. Bamberg, Germany. Affil: Bamberg. Email: Mark.Haeberlein@uni-bamberg.de. Research: merchant communities, religious pluralism.

Haefeli, *Evan*, *Texas A&M.* College Station, TX. Email: evanhaefeli@tamu.edu. Research: colonial America, early American religious.

Haeger, **John D.**, *Northern Arizona.* Email: john.haeger@nau.edu.

Hafez, **Melis**, *Virginia Commonwealth.* Email: mhafez@vcu.edu.

Hafter, *Daryl M*. Ann Arbor, MI. Affil: Eastern Michigan. Email: dhafter@emich.edu. Research: 18th-c French women's work, guilds and pre-industrial technology.

Hagan, *Carrie Settle*. Pittsburgh, PA. Affil: Carnegie Mellon. Email: csh@andrew.cmu. edu. Research: youth culture, juvenile court.

Hagan, **Kenneth J.**, *Naval War Coll.* Email: kenhagan@comcast.net.

Hagedorn, *Olivia*. Champaign, IL. Affil: Illinois, Urbana-Champaign. Email: ohagedo2@illinois.edu.

Hagel, **Jonathan C.**, *Kansas.* Email: jhagel@ku.edu.

Hagemann, *Karen*, *North Carolina, Chapel Hill.* Chapel Hill, NC. Email: hagemann@unc.edu. Research: nation/culture/gender, military/war/gender/masculinity.

Hagen, *William W.*, *California, Davis.* Davis, CA. Email: wwhagen@ucdavis.edu. Research: central and eastern European nationality relations, German social and political.

Hagenloh, **Paul M.**, *Syracuse.* Email: phagenlo@syr.edu.

Hager, *Christopher*. Canton, CT. Affil: Trinity Coll., Conn. Email: Christopher.Hager@trincoll.edu.

Hagerty, **Bernard**, *Pittsburgh.* Email: kazuo@pitt.edu.

Haggard, **Robert F.**, *Robert H. Smith Center.* Email: rhaggard@monticello.org.

Hagler, **Aaron M.**, *Troy.* Email: hagler@troy.edu.

Hagler, *Anderson*. Durham, NC. Affil: Duke. Email: anderson.hagler@duke.edu.

Hagood, **Jonathan D.**, *Hope.* Email: hagood@hope.edu.

Hagopian, *Patrick*. Lancaster, United Kingdom. Affil: Lancaster. Email: p.hagopian@lancaster.ac.uk. Research: Vietnam War commemoration, public/race and slavery.

Hagstrom, *Jacob*. Bloomington, IN. Affil: Indiana. Email: jnhagstr@indiana.edu. Research: Second Seminole War.

Hague, *Stephen G.*, *Rowan.* Philadelphia, PA. Email: hague@rowan.edu; sghague@hotmail.com. Research: social status/architecture/

material culture, 18th-c British empire/Atlantic world.

Hahamian, *Laura V.* Irvine, CA. Email: lhahamia@stu.norwich.edu.

Hahamovitch, *Cindy*, *Georgia.* Athens, GA. Email: cxhaha@uga.edu. Research: guestworkers around the globe, international labor migration.

Hahamovitch, *Reynolds Nelson*. Athens, GA. Email: rnhahamovitch@gmail.com.

Hahn, *Barbara M.*, *Texas Tech.* Lubbock, TX. Email: barbara.hahn@ttu.edu. Research: industrialization, technology and economics.

Hahn, **Beth**, *US Senate Hist. Office.* Email: beth_hahn@sec.senate.gov.

Hahn, **Erich J. C.**, *Western Ontario.* Email: ejhahn@uwo.ca.

Hahn, **Hazel**, *Seattle.* Email: hahnh@seattleu.edu.

Hahn, *Peter L.*, *Ohio State.* Columbus, OH. Email: hahn.29@osu.edu. Research: US diplomacy in Middle East, US-Israel relations.

Hahn, **Steven C.**, *St. Olaf.* Email: hahn@stolaf.edu.

Hahn, *Steven H.*, *NYU.* New York, NY. Email: shh5@nyu.edu. Research: US 1830-1900.

Hahner, *June E.*, *SUNY, Albany.* Delmar, NY. Email: jhahner@albany.edu. Research: 19th-c Brazilian women and education, women.

Haidarali, *Laila S.*, *Queen's, Can.* Email: laila.haidarali@queensu.ca.

Haider, *Najam*. New York, NY. Affil: Barnard, Columbia. Email: nih2104@columbia.edu.

Haigh, **Elizabeth**, *Dalhousie.* Email: elizabeth.haigh@smu.ca.

Haigh, **Thomas**, *Wisconsin-Milwaukee.* Email: thaigh@uwm.edu.

Haight, **Bruce M.**, *Western Michigan.* Email: bruce.haight@wmich.edu.

Haight, *Christopher*. Houston, TX. Affil: Houston Comm. Coll. Email: cphaight@gmail.com. Research: LGBTQ, hate crime and violence.

Hailstork, **Qiu Jin**, *Old Dominion.* Email: qjin@odu.edu.

Haine, *W. Scott*. Passaic, NJ. Affil: Alcohol and Drugs Hist. Soc. Email: shaine@aol.com. Research: cafes of France, culture of France.

Haines, *Amy Renee*. Colorado Springs, CO. Affil: Colorado, Colorado Springs. Email: amelarenee@gmail.com. Research: labor in Reconstruction South, 19th-c spiritualism.

Haire, *Melissa*. San Marcos, CA. Affil: California State, San Marcos. Email: haire003@cougars.csusm.edu.

Haith, **Evonda**, *North Carolina A&T State.* Email: erhaith@ncat.edu.

Haj, **Samira A.**, *Graduate Center, CUNY; Staten Island, CUNY.* Email: samirahaj@nyc.rr.com; samira.haj@csi.cuny.edu.

Hajdarpasic, **Edin**, *Loyola, Chicago.* Email: ehajdarpasic@luc.edu.

Hajduk, *John C*. Dillon, MT. Affil: Montana Western. Email: john.hajduk@umwestern.edu. Research: American popular music industry, 20th-c political humor.

Hajkowski, *Thomas*. Dallas, PA. Affil: Misericordia. Email: thajkowski@misericordia.edu. Research: national identity, imperialism.

Hajo, *Cathy Moran*, *NYU; Ramapo.* Mahwah, NJ. Email: cathy.hajo@nyu.edu; chajo@ramapo.edu. Research: documentary editing, US birth control clinics.

Hakim, **Carol D.**, *Minnesota (Hist.).* Email: hakimc@umn.edu.

Hakim, *Joy Frisch*. Chevy Chase, MD. Affil: Oxford Univ. Press. Email: joyhakim@gmail.com. Research: evolutionary biology, science.

Hakkenberg, **Michael A.**, *Roanoke.* Email: hakkenbe@roanoke.edu.

Halavais, *Mary Hoyt*, *Sonoma State.* Rohnert Park, CA. Email: halavais@sonoma.edu. Research: early modern Europe/Mediterranean, Spain and Spanish Empire.

Hale, *Bradley R.*, *Azusa Pacific.* Azusa, CA. Email: bhale@apu.edu. Research: world, modern Europe.

Hale, **Brian J.**, *Wisconsin-Stevens Point.* Email: bhale@uwsp.edu.

Hale, *Dana S*. APO, AE. Email: danahale@hotmail.com. Research: French colonial propaganda, representations of colonial peoples.

Hale, **Grace Elizabeth**, *Virginia.* Email: hale@virginia.edu.

Hale, *Jon*. Columbia, SC. Affil: South Carolina. Email: jnhale@mailbox.sc.edu. Research: US civil rights.

Hale, *Korcaighe P.*, *Ohio.* Zanesville, OH. Email: halek@ohio.edu. Research: postwar European neutrality, German assets in neutral countries.

Hale, *Matthew Rainbow*. Silver Spring, MD. Affil: Goucher. Email: mhale@goucher.edu. Research: colonial America, early Republic.

Hale, **Piers J.**, *Oklahoma (Hist. of Science).* Email: phale@ou.edu.

Hale, *Wesley Ryan*. Narragansett, RI. Affil: Rhode Island. Email: wrhale2006@gmail.com.

Hales, **Barbara**, *Houston-Clear Lake.* Email: hales@uhcl.edu.

Halevi, *Leor E.*, *Vanderbilt.* Nashville, TN. Email: leor.halevi@vanderbilt.edu. Research: trade between Muslims and non-Muslims, social and religious rituals.

Haley, **Andrew P.**, *Southern Mississippi.* Email: andrew.haley@usm.edu.

Haley, *Evan W.*, *McMaster.* Email: haleyev@mcmaster.ca.

Haley, *Heather Marie*. Auburn, AL. Affil: Auburn. Email: hmh0050@auburn.edu. Research: US Navy, race/gender/LGBTQ.

Haley, **John Hamilton**, *North Carolina, Wilmington.* Email: haleyj@uncw.edu.

Halfin, *Jonothan*. Rio Vista, CA. Affil: American Public. Email: jonothan.halfin@mycampus.apus.edu.

Halfond, *Gregory Isaac*, *Framingham State.* Framingham, MA. Email: ghalfond@framingham.edu. Research: Frankish kingdoms/Merovingians/church, canon law.

Halfond, *Irwin*. Edwardsville, IL. Affil: McKendree. Email: irhalf@aol.com. Research: French diplomacy and WWI, late 19th-c Russian liberalism.

Haliczer, **Stephen H.**, *Northern Illinois.* Email: shaliczer@niu.edu.

Hall, **Bruce S.**, *California, Berkeley.* Email: bruce.hall@berkeley.edu.

Hall, *Clarence Jefferson*, *Jr.* Oakland Gardens, NY. Affil: Queensborough Comm. Coll., CUNY. Email: chall@qcc.cuny.edu. Research: environmental, carceral state.

Hall, **David J.**, *Alberta.* Email: david.hall@ualberta.ca.

Hall, **David R.**, *California State, Fullerton.* Email: dhall@fullerton.edu.

Hall, *Diana Komo*. Clarkston, GA. Affil: Credent. Email: dhall@kh2inc.com.

Hall, *Donald*. Silver Spring, MD. Affil: Uniformed Services Univ., Health Sci. Email: don4hall@aol.com. Research: Vietnam War medical, WWII US military medical.

Hall, *Edwin C*. Grosse Pointe, MI. Email: ae8747@wayne.edu.

Hall, **Eric A.**, *Northern Illinois*. Email: ehall4@niu.edu.

Hall, **Gregory D.**, *Western Illinois*. Email: G-Hall@wiu.edu.

Hall, *Gwendolyn Midlo*, *Rutgers*. Laredo, TX. Affil: Michigan State. Email: ghall1929@gmail.com. Research: Atlantic world slave database.

Hall, **Hines H.**, *Auburn*. Email: hallhin@auburn.edu.

Hall, *Jacquelyn Dowd*, *North Carolina, Chapel Hill*. Chapel Hill, NC. Affil: Center for the Study of the American South. Email: jhall@email.unc.edu. Research: 19th-/20th-c southern women workers, 20th-c women writers/intellectuals.

Hall, *John W.*, *Wisconsin-Madison; Soc. for Military Hist.* Madison, WI. Email: jwhall3@wisc.edu. Research: Indian removal, race and war.

Hall, **Jonathan M.**, *Chicago*. Email: jhall@uchicago.edu.

Hall, **Joseph M.**, *Jr.*, *Bates*. Email: jhall2@bates.edu.

Hall, *Kari M*. Arroyo Grande, CA. Affil: Cuesta. Email: karihallag@gmail.com.

Hall, **Kenneth R.**, *Ball State*. Email: khall2@bsu.edu.

Hall, **Linda B.**, *New Mexico*. Email: lbhall@unm.edu.

Hall, **Linda Jones**, *St. Mary's, Md.* Email: ljhall@smcm.edu.

Hall, **Mark**, *George Fox*. Email: mhall@georgefox.edu.

Hall, **Michael G.**, *Texas, Austin*. Email: mghall@mail.utexas.edu.

Hall, **Michael R.**, *Georgia Southern*. Email: mrhall@georgiasouthern.edu.

Hall, *Mitchell K.*, *Central Michigan*. Mount Pleasant, MI. Email: hall1mk@cmich.edu. Research: Vietnam War era, US popular culture.

Hall, **Randal Lee**, *Rice*. Email: rh@rice.edu.

Hall, *Richard Charles*. Swansea, United Kingdom. Affil: Swansea. Email: r.c.hall@swansea.ac.uk. Research: Braddock Plan of 1755, American colonies and the British Empire.

Hall, **Robert G.**, *Ball State*. Email: rghall@bsu.edu.

Hall, **Robert L.**, *Northeastern*. Email: r.hall@neu.edu.

Hall, **Roger D.**, *Western Ontario*. Email: hallmartin@sympatico.ca.

Hall, **Roger**, *California Polytechnic State*. Email: rhall05@calpoly.edu.

Hall, **Ryan C.**, *Colgate*. Email: rhall@colgate.edu.

Hall, *Van Beck*, *Pittsburgh*. Pittsburgh, PA. Email: vanbeck@pitt.edu. Research: 19th-c Virginia, 19th-c political.

Hallam, *Nathan*. Sacramento, CA. Affil: California State, Sacramento. Email: nathan.hallam@csus.edu. Research: American West urban/regional, collective memory and local.

Haller, **Charlotte A.**, *Worcester State*. Email: challer1@worcester.edu.

Haller, **John S.**, **Jr.**, *Southern Illinois, Carbondale*. Email: jhaller@notes.siu.edu.

Haller, *Stephen F*. Glendale, NY. Affil: St. John's, NY. Email: sfhaller@gmail.com. Research: early Republic American education, Scottish Enlightenment.

Hallett, *Hilary*, *Columbia (Hist.)*. Email: hah2117@columbia.edu.

Hallgren, *Kate N.*, *Hist. Assoc.* Email: khallgren@historyassociates.com.

Halliday, *Paul D.*, *Virginia*. Charlottesville, VA. Email: ph4p@virginia.edu. Research: material culture of law, imperial law.

Hallion, *Richard P*. Shalimar, FL. Affil: Florida Polytechnic. Email: DrHypersonic1@hotmail.com.

Hallman, *Clive R.*, *James Madison*. Email: hallmacr@jmu.edu.

Hall-Witt, **Jennifer L.**, *Smith*. Email: jhallwit@smith.edu.

Halperin, *Charles J*. Bloomington, IN. Email: chalperi@iu.edu. Research: Russo-Tatar relations, Ivan the Terrible.

Halperin, *Paula*. Purchase, NY. Affil: Purchase, SUNY. Email: paula.halperin@purchase.edu. Research: film studies, public sphere and media.

Halperin, **Rick**, *Southern Methodist*. Email: rhalperi@smu.edu.

Halpern, *Martin*. Madison, WI. Affil: Henderson State. Email: halpern@hsu.edu. Research: unionization of Ford Motor Co., 20th-c radical politics.

Halpern, **Monda M.**, *Western Ontario*. Email: halpern@uwo.ca.

Halpern, *Paul G*. Tallahassee, FL. Affil: Florida State. Email: phalpern@fsu.edu. Research: Mediterranean naval situation 1900-39, Austro-Hungarian Navy.

Halpern, **Rick**, *Toronto*. Toronto, ON, Canada. Email: rick.halpern@utoronto.ca. Research: photography, labor.

Halpin, **Dennis P.**, *Virginia Tech*. Email: dphalpin@vt.edu.

Halsey, **Stephen Robert**, *Miami*. Email: s.halsey@miami.edu.

Halsey Leckerling, *Christian*. Vershire, VT. Affil: Mountain Sch. of Milton Academy. Email: kit.leckerling@mountainschool.org. Research: forestry in mid-20th-c California, copper mining in late 19th-c Vermont.

Halttunen, **Karen**, *Southern California*. Email: halttune@usc.edu.

Halty, *Nina Isabel*. Cambridge, MA. Affil: Harvard. Email: ninahalty@g.harvard.edu.

Halverson, *Sean C*. Normal, AL. Affil: Alabama A&M. Email: sean.halverson@aamu.edu. Research: colonial and revolutionary America.

Halvorsen, *Jesse Ronald*. Los Angeles, CA. Affil: California, Santa Barbara. Email: halvorsen@uwalumni.com.

Halvorson, **Kristin D.**, *Charleston*. Email: halvorsonkd@cofc.edu.

Halvorson, **Michael J.**, *Pacific Lutheran*. Email: halvormj@plu.edu.

Ham, **Herbert**, *Central Oklahoma*. Email: hham@uco.edu.

Hamalainen, **Pekka K.**, *Wisconsin-Madison*. Email: pkhamala@wisc.edu.

Hamashita, *Takeshi*. Tokyo, Japan. Affil: Sun Yat-sen. Email: thasiapacific@gmail.com.

Hamblin, *Terry*, *Jr*. Unadilla, NY. Affil: SUNY, Delhi. Email: thamblin@yahoo.com. Research: US political, US Cold War.

Hamblin, **William**, *Brigham Young*. Email: william_hamblin@byu.edu.

Hamburg, *Gary M.*, *Claremont McKenna*. Email: gary.hamburg@cmc.edu.

Hamby, *Alonzo L.*, *Ohio*. Athens, OH. Email: hambya@ohio.edu. Research: Franklin D. Roosevelt.

Hamdani, **Abbas**, *Wisconsin-Milwaukee*. Email: ahamdani@uwm.edu.

Hamdani, **Sumaiya A.**, *George Mason*. Email: shamdani@gmu.edu.

Hamed-Troyansky, *Vladimir*, *Furman*. Greenville, SC. Email: vladimir.hamed-troyansky@furman.edu. Research: refugee migration, refugee resettlement.

Hameed, *Chaudhry*. Dallas, TX. Affil: Southern Methodist. Email: chameed@mail.smu.edu.

Hameeteman, *Elizabeth*. Boston, MA. Affil: Boston Univ. Email: ehameete@bu.edu.

Hamel, **Gildas**, *California, Santa Cruz*. Email: gweltaz@ucsc.edu.

Hamel, *Paul A*. San Rafael, CA. Affil: Marin Catholic High Sch. Email: phamel@marincatholic.org.

Hamer, *Lt Col Michael D.*, *US Air Force Acad*. Colorado Springs, CO. Email: michael.hamer@usafa.edu; o4selhamer@yahoo.com. Research: US religion, world.

Hamerla, **Ralph R.**, *Oklahoma (Hist. of Science)*. Email: rhamerla@ou.edu.

Hames, **Gina L.**, *Pacific Lutheran*. Email: hamesgl@plu.edu.

Hametz, *Maura E.*, *James Madison*. Harrisonburg, VA. Email: hametzme@jmu.edu. Research: modern Italy, Habsburg/Adriatic.

Hamilton, *Andrew John*. La Crosse, WI. Affil: Viterbo. Email: ajhamilton@viterbo.edu. Research: trade and empire in Atlantic world, slavery and capitalism.

Hamilton, **Charles D.**, *San Diego State*. Email: chamilto@sdsu.edu.

Hamilton, **David E.**, *Kentucky*. Email: dehami01@uky.edu.

Hamilton, *Gail*, *Soc. for Hist. Education*. Email: ghamilton@csulb.edu.

Hamilton, **Jeffrey S.**, *Baylor*. Email: jeffrey_hamilton@baylor.edu.

Hamilton, **Kenneth M.**, *Southern Methodist*. Email: kmarvin@smu.edu.

Hamilton, *Louis I.*, *Rutgers, Newark/New Jersey Inst. of Tech*. Email: louis.i.hamilton@njit.edu.

Hamilton, *Marsha L.*, *South Alabama*. Mobile, AL. Email: mhamilton@southalabama.edu. Research: 17th-c New England, early modern Atlantic world.

Hamilton, *Mary Jane*. Carmichael, CA. Email: mj.hamilton@pacbell.net.

Hamilton, *Michael S*. Bremerton, WA. Affil: Seattle Pacific. Email: mhamilton@spu.edu.

Hamilton, **Michelle**, *Western Ontario*. Email: mhamilt3@uwo.ca.

Hamilton, *Phillip F.*, *Christopher Newport*. Email: phamilt@cnu.edu.

Hamilton, **Sarah R.**, *Auburn*. Email: srhamilton@auburn.edu.

Hamilton, **Shane L.**, *Georgia*. Email: shamilto@uga.edu.

Hamilton, *Tracy Chapman*. Henrico, VA. Affil: Virginia Commonwealth. Email: tracychamilton21@gmail.com.

Hamlin, Christopher S., *Notre Dame*. Email: chamlin@nd.edu.

Hamlin, David, *Fordham*. Email: hamlin@fordham.edu.

Hamlin, Francoise N., *Brown*. Email: Francoise_Hamlin@Brown.edu.

Hamlin, Kelly Fisk. Pulaski, TN. Email: kelly.fisk.hamlin@gmail.com. Research: contraband camps in Alabama & Tennessee, postwar communities in rural South.

Hamlin, Kimberly A., *Miami, Ohio*. Email: hamlinka@miamioh.edu.

Hamm, Kara, *OAH*. Email: khamm@oah.org.

Hamm, Richard F., *SUNY, Albany*. Albany, NY. Email: rhamm@albany.edu. Research: Arthur Garfield Hays, Women's Party and jury service.

Hamm, Thomas D., *Earlham*. Richmond, IN. Email: tomh@earlham.edu. Research: Quakerism, antislavery.

Hammack, David C., *Case Western Reserve*. Cleveland, OH. Email: David.Hammack@cwru.edu. Research: nonprofit organizations/civil society, charitable foundations/endowments.

Hammack, Maria Esther. Austin, TX. Affil: Texas, Austin. Email: mariaesther@utexas.edu. Research: slavery, borderlands.

Hammad, Hanan, *Texas Christian*. Email: h.hammad@tcu.edu.

Hammel, Sabrinna Elizardo. Universal City, TX. Affil: Northeast Lakeview. Email: sabrinahammel@aol.com.

Hammer, Daniel, *Hist. New Orleans*. Email: danielh@hnoc.org.

Hammer, Paul E. J., *Colorado, Boulder*. Email: paul.hammer@colorado.edu.

Hammersmith, Jack L., *West Virginia*. Email: Jack.Hammersmith@mail.wvu.edu.

Hammond, Gregory S., *Austin Peay State*. Nashville, TN. Email: hammondg@apsu.edu; krakesone@hotmail.com. Research: women's suffrage, 20th-c Peru.

Hammond, Kelly, *Arkansas, Fayetteville*. Email: kah018@uark.edu.

Hammond, Kenneth, *New Mexico State*. Email: khammond@nmsu.edu.

Hammond, Lauren, *Augustana*. Email: laurenhammond@augustana.edu.

Hammond, Leslie, *Pittsburgh*. Email: lhammond@pitt.edu.

Hammond, William E., *Missouri State*.

Hammonds, Evelynn M., *Harvard (Hist. of Science)*. Cambridge, MA. Email: evelynn_hammonds@harvard.edu. Research: race and gender in science.

Hamner, Christopher Heald, *George Mason*. Email: chamner@gmu.edu.

Hamond, Tammy, *Massachusetts Hist. Soc.* Email: thamond@masshist.org.

Hampton, Hunter M., *Stephen F. Austin State*. Email: hamptonh@sfasu.edu.

Hampton, Valerie Dawn. Newberry, FL. Affil: Western Michigan. Email: valerie.d.hampton@wmich.edu.

Hamroun, Mahel. Berkeley, CA. Affil: California, Berkeley. Email: mhamroun@berkeley.edu.

Hamscher, Albert N., *Kansas State*. Email: aham@ksu.edu.

Hamza, Ibrahim, *Franklin & Marshall*. Email: ihamza@fandm.edu.

Hamza, Shireen. Cambridge, MA. Affil: Harvard. Email: shireenhamza@g.harvard.edu. Research: medicine in Islamic world, Indian Ocean.

Hamzah, Dyala, *Montréal*. Email: dyala.hamzah@umontreal.ca.

Han, Eric, *William and Mary*. Email: echan@wm.edu.

Han, Song Yeol. Tinton Falls, NJ. Affil: Seton Hall. Email: syhan0512@gmail.com. Research: book circulation in modern East Asia, transnational nationalism in East Asia.

Han, Weibin. Warsaw, Poland. Affil: Coll. of Europe Natolin Campus. Email: weibinhan@icloud.com. Research: German minority in Central Europe, Ideological influence on migration.

Hanawalt, Barbara A., *Ohio State*. Email: hanawalt.4@osu.edu.

Hanchett, Sally R., *OAH*. Email: shanchett@oah.org.

Hancock, Alton O., *Centenary, La.* Email: aohancock@charter.net.

Hancock, Christin Lee, *Portland*. Email: hancock@up.edu.

Hancock, David John, *Michigan, Ann Arbor*. Email: hancockd@umich.edu.

Hancock, Eleanor. Canberra, Australia. Affil: Australian Defence Force Academy. Email: e.hancock@adfa.edu.au. Research: Ernst Roehm and the SA, Prussia.

Hancock, Jonathan Todd. Conway, AR. Affil: Hendrix. Email: hancockj@hendrix.edu. Research: New Madrid earthquakes 1811-12, American Indians in Early Republic.

Hancock, Mary E., *California, Santa Barbara*. Email: hancock@anth.ucsb.edu.

Hancock, Michael John. Voorhees, NJ. Email: mhancock@stu.norwich.edu.

Hancock, Scott, *Gettysburg*. Email: shancock@gettysburg.edu.

Hand, Robert S. Las Vegas, NV. Email: robhand@arhatmedia.com. Research: medieval astronomy.

Handel, John Martin. Northlake, TX. Affil: California, Berkeley. Email: jmhandel@berkeley.edu.

Handke, Margaretta S., *Minnesota State, Mankato*. Email: margaretta.handke@mnsu.edu.

Handy, Jim, *Saskatchewan*. Email: jim.handy@usask.ca.

Handy-Marchello, Barbara, *North Dakota*. Email: barbara.handy.marchello@und.edu.

Handyside, Philip David. Deland, FL. Affil: Stetson. Email: phandysi@stetson.edu. Research: French translation of William of Tyre, military orders in Wales.

Hanebrink, Paul A., *Rutgers*. Email: hanebrin@history.rutgers.edu.

Hanes, Alice, *Hagley Museum and Library*. Email: ahanes@hagley.org.

Hanes, Jeffrey, *Oregon*. Eugene, OR. Email: hanes@uoregon.edu. Research: modern Japan.

Hanes, Roy, *Carleton, Can.* Email: roy.hanes@carleton.ca.

Haney, David Paul, *Austin Comm. Coll.* Email: dhaney@austincc.edu.

Hang, Xing, *Brandeis*. Email: xinghang@brandeis.edu.

Hangen, Tona J., *Worcester State*. Stow, MA. Email: thangen@worcester.edu; professortona@gmail.com. Research: UN, nongovernmental organizations.

Hanifi, Shah Mahmoud, *James Madison*. Email: hanifism@jmu.edu.

Hanioglu, M. Sukru, *Princeton*. Email: hanioglu@princeton.edu.

Hankins, Barry G., *Baylor*. Email: barry_hankins@baylor.edu.

Hankins, James, *Harvard (Hist.)*. Email: jhankins@fas.harvard.edu.

Hankins, Jeffrey R., *Louisiana Tech*. Email: jhankins@latech.edu.

Hankins, Michael. Washington, DC. Affil: Smithsonian Air and Space Museum. Email: mwhankins82@gmail.com. Research: military technology/culture, air power/aviation.

Hankins, Thomas L., *Washington, Seattle*. Email: hankins@uw.edu.

Hanley, Anne G., *Northern Illinois*. DeKalb, IL. Email: ahanley@niu.edu. Research: municipal finance/public services, standardization/domestic economy.

Hanley, James G., *Winnipeg*. Email: j.hanley@uwinnipeg.ca.

Hanley, Mark Y., *Truman State*. Email: mhanley@truman.edu.

Hanley, Sarah, *Iowa*. Scituate, MA. Affil: Huntington Library. Email: sarah-hanley@uiowa.edu. Research: legal and political theory, family formation and state building.

Hanley, Wayne M., *West Chester*. Cochranville, PA. Email: whanley@wcupa.edu. Research: French Revolution and Napoleon, 18th-c Europe.

Hanley, Will, *Florida State*. Tallahassee, FL. Email: whanley@fsu.edu; willpdfs@gmail.com. Research: Nationality in Egypt, International law.

Hanlon, David, *Hawai'i, Manoa*. Email: hanlon@hawaii.edu.

Hanlon, Gregory, *Dalhousie*. Email: gregory.hanlon@dal.ca.

Hanna, David Montgomery. New York, NY. Affil: Stuyvesant High Sch. Email: dhanna@stuy.edu. Research: Italo Balbo, 1933 Chicago World's Fair.

Hanna, Jonathan Anthony. Claremont, CA. Affil: Claremont Graduate. Email: jonathan.hanna@cgu.edu. Research: gay and lesbian history/literature.

Hanna, Mark G., *California, San Diego*. La Jolla, CA. Email: m1hanna@ucsd.edu. Research: early Anglophone literature, law.

Hanna, Martha T., *Colorado, Boulder*. Email: martha.hanna@colorado.edu.

Hannaway, Caroline C. Baltimore, MD. Email: channaway@aol.com.

Hanne, Eric J., *Florida Atlantic*. Email: ehanne@fau.edu.

Hannigan, Robert E., Jr., *Suffolk*. Email: rhannigan@suffolk.edu.

Hannon, Brian P. D. Phoenix, AZ. Email: bpdhannon@yahoo.com. Research: war correspondents, WWII.

Hannon, Claudia A., *Salisbury*. Email: cahannon@salisbury.edu.

Hannon, Peter J., FSC, *Lewis*. Email: hannonpe@lewisu.edu.

Hanretta, Sean A., *Northwestern*. Evanston, IL. Email: sean.hanretta@northwestern.edu. Research: Islam in West Africa, religious and social change in West Africa.

Hansen, Alexa Noelle. Naperville, IL. Affil: Illinois State. Email: abeeman94@aol.com.

Hansen, Anne, *Wisconsin-Madison*. Email: arhansen@wisc.edu.

Hansen, Arthur A., *California State, Fullerton*. Email: ahansen@fullerton.edu.

Hansen, Bert W. New York, NY. Affil: Baruch, CUNY. Email: bert.hansen@baruch.cuny.edu. Research: science and medicine.

Hansen, David W., *Texas, San Antonio*. Email: david.hansen@utsa.edu.

Hansen, Erik von Stein, *Union Coll*. Email: hansene@union.edu.

Hansen, James E., **II**, *Colorado State*. Email: james.hansen@colostate.edu.

Hansen, James Roger, *Auburn*. Email: hansejr@auburn.edu.

Hansen, Jan E. Berlin, Germany. Affil: Humboldt, Berlin. Email: jan-eric.hansen@geschichte.hu-berlin.de.

Hansen, Jason D., *Furman*. Email: jason.hansen@furman.edu.

Hansen, Karen V., *Brandeis*. Email: khansen@brandeis.edu.

Hansen, Peo. Norrköping, Sweden. Affil: Linkoping. Email: peo.hansen@liu.se.

Hansen, Peter H. Worcester, MA. Affil: Worcester Polytechnic Inst. Email: phansen@wpi.edu.

Hansen, Valerie, *Yale*. New Haven, CT. Email: valerie.hansen@yale.edu. Research: premodern China, Silk Road.

Hanser, Jessica. Singapore. Affil: Yale-NUS Coll. Email: jessicahanserync@gmail.com.

Hanshew, Karrin M., *Michigan State*. Email: hanshew@msu.edu.

Hanson, Danielle. Grand Forks, ND. Email: daniellehanson727@gmail.com.

Hanson, Holly E., *Mount Holyoke*. Email: hhanson@mtholyoke.edu.

Hanson, John, *Indiana*. Email: jhhanson@indiana.edu.

Hanson, Joyce A., *California State, San Bernardino*. Email: jahanson@csusb.edu.

Hanson, Kenneth, *Central Florida*. Email: Kenneth.Hanson@ucf.edu.

Hanson, Marta E., *Johns Hopkins (Hist. of Science)*. Email: mhanson4@jhmi.edu.

Hanson, Matthew M., *St. Joseph's*.

Hanson, Paul R., *Butler*. Indianapolis, IN. Email: phanson@butler.edu. Research: comparing revolutionary terrors.

Hanson, Richard Simon, *Luther*. Email: hansri01@luther.edu.

Hanson, Shawn R. Corpus Christi, TX. Affil: Texas A&M, Corpus Christi. Email: shanson4@islander.tamucc.edu.

Hanson, Thomas E., *US Army Command Coll*. Email: thomas.e.hanson.civ@mail.mil.

Hanson, Victor Davis, *Hillsdale*. Email: vhanson@hillsdale.edu.

Hanson, Woodward S. Fort Myers, FL. Affil: South Florida. Email: wshanson@gmail.com.

Hanssen, Jens, *Toronto*. Email: jens.hanssen@utoronto.ca.

Hanssen, Susan E., *Dallas*. Email: shanssen@udallas.edu.

Hantula, James N. Murphy, NC. Email: hdjne98@cabletvonline.net. Research: cartography and world maps, early US iron works.

Hantzmon, Richard C. Charlottesville, VA. Affil: Brandeis. Email: hantzmon@brandeis.edu. Research: wildlife conservation law, hunting and fishing regulation.

Hanyan, Craig R., *Brock*. Lewiston, NY. Email: chanyan@cogeco.ca. Research: New York state law and politics 1790-1830.

Hao, Yen-p'ing, *Tennessee, Knoxville*. Email: yhao@utk.edu.

Happy, Raymond. Bethlehem, CT. Email: Rphappy13@gmail.com.

Haque, Jameel, *Minnesota State, Mankato*. Email: jameel.haque@mnsu.edu.

Har, Katherine. New York, NY. Affil: Oxford. Email: katherine.j.har@gmail.com. Research: medieval England, legal.

Harbaugh, Jane W., *Tennessee, Chattanooga*.

Harcourt, Felix A., *Austin Coll*. Sherman, TX. Email: fharcourt@austincollege.edu; farharcourt@googlemail.com. Research: Ku Klux Klan in 1920s America.

Hardeman, Martin J., *Eastern Illinois*. Charleston, IL. Email: mjhardeman@eiu.edu. Research: 19th-c US, African American.

Harden, Michael Wayne, *Lincoln Memorial*. Email: michael.harden@lmunet.edu.

Harden, Victoria A. Silver Spring, MD. Affil: National Inst. of Health. Email: vharden@outlook.com. Research: AIDS epidemic, US federal government health activities.

Harder, Mette, *SUNY, Oneonta*. Email: mette.harder@oneonta.edu.

Hardesty, Jared Ross, *Western Washington*. Bellingham, WA. Email: Jared.Hardesty@wwu.edu. Research: slavery in colonial Americas, early modern British Empire.

Hardgrave, Jason D., *Southern Indiana*. Email: jhardgrave@usi.edu.

Hardgrove, Anne, *Texas, San Antonio*. Email: anne.hardgrove@utsa.edu.

Hardin, John A., *Western Kentucky*. Email: john.hardin@wku.edu.

Hardin, Sarah F., *St. Anselm*. Email: shardin@anselm.edu.

Harding, Jeannie C., *James Madison*. Email: hardinjc@jmu.edu.

Harding, Timothy F., *California State, Los Angeles*.

Hardman, Elizabeth L. Hartsdale, NY. Affil: Bronx Comm. Coll., CUNY. Email: Elizabeth.Hardman@bcc.cuny.edu. Research: socio-economic roles of medieval women, medieval notarial records & courts.

Hardmond, Robert L. Brooklyn, NY. Affil: Brooklyn Tech. High Sch. Email: aminn101@juno.com.

Hardwick, Julie, *Texas, Austin*. Email: jhardwick@austin.utexas.edu.

Hardwick, Kevin R., *James Madison*. Email: hardwikr@jmu.edu.

Hardwick, Martina L., *Queen's, Can*. Email: hardwick@queensu.ca.

Hardy, Charles A., **III**, *West Chester*. West Chester, PA. Email: chardy@wcupa.edu. Research: Pennsylvania.

Hardy, Deborah W., *Wyoming*.

Hardy, Duncan, *Central Florida*. Email: Duncan.Hardy@ucf.edu.

Hardy, Eric M., *Loyola, New Orleans*. Email: emhardy@loyno.edu.

Hardy, James D., **Jr.**, *Louisiana State*.

Hardy, Jeffrey S., *Brigham Young*. Provo, UT. Email: jeff_hardy@byu.edu. Research: Soviet penal system 1953-64.

Hardy, Penelope K., *Wisconsin-La Crosse*. La Crosse, WI. Email: phardy@uwlax.edu. Research: oceanography, technology.

Hardy, Robin Aspasia, *Montana State, Bozeman*. Email: rahardy25@gmail.com.

Hare, J. Laurence, *Arkansas, Fayetteville*. Email: lhare@uark.edu.

Hargett, Dean, *State Hist. Soc. of Missouri*. Email: hargettd@shsmo.org.

Hargrave, O. T., *Southern Methodist*.

Hargrett, Elizabeth. Oakland, CA. Affil: California, Berkeley. Email: elizabeth.hargrett@berkeley.edu.

Harison, Casey, *Southern Indiana*. Evansville, IN. Email: charison@usi.edu. Research: cholera epidemic of 1832, modern Paris.

Harkavy, Ira, *Pennsylvania*. Email: harkavy@pobox.upenn.edu.

Harkins, Anthony A., *Western Kentucky*. Email: tony.harkins@wku.edu.

Harkness, Deborah E., *Southern California*. Email: deharkne@usc.edu.

Harl, Kenneth W., *Tulane*. Email: kharl@tulane.edu.

Harlan, David Craig, *California Polytechnic State*. Email: charlan@calpoly.edu.

Harlan, Stephen G. North Plainfield, NJ. Affil: US Army. Email: stephen_harlan@verizon.net. Research: 99th RRC in GWOT, Continental Army.

Harland, Philip A., *York, Can*. Email: pharland@yorku.ca.

Harland-Jacobs, Jessica L., *Florida*. Email: harlandj@ufl.edu.

Harless, Richard. Lorton, VA. Affil: Northern Virginia Comm. Coll. Email: rgh4@cox.net. Research: George Washington and Native Americans.

Harley, David E. Cockeysville, MD.

Harley, Sharon. College Park, MD. Affil: Maryland, Coll. Park. Email: sharley@umd.edu. Research: African American women and labor, Du Bois and gender.

Harline, Craig, *Brigham Young*. Email: craig_harline@byu.edu.

Harling, Philip, *Kentucky*. Email: harling@uky.edu.

Harlow, Luke E., *Tennessee, Knoxville*. Email: lharlow1@utk.edu.

Harlow, Thomas James. Grand Forks, ND. Affil: North Dakota. Email: tomharlow@msn.com. Research: US/gender/women's associations, 19th-/20th-c US social.

Harmon, Alexandra, *Washington, Seattle*. Email: aharmon@uw.edu.

Harmon, David Leroy. Apo, AE. Affil: Maryland Univ. Coll. Email: drharmon.harmon@gmail.com. Research: recreational vehicles and camping, engineering program curriculum changes.

Harmon, Elizabeth. Washington, DC. Affil: Michigan, Ann Arbor. Email: liz.harmon@gmail.com. Research: American political economy, philanthropy.

Harmon, Robert, *Seattle*.

Harmon, Sandra D. Normal, IL. Affil: Illinois State. Email: sdharmo@ilstu.edu. Research: US women's education.

Harmon, Stephen A., *Pittsburg State*. Email: sharmon@pittstate.edu.

Harms, Patricia F., *Brandon*. Email: harmsp@brandonu.ca.

Harms, Robert Wayne, *Yale*. Email: robert.harms@yale.edu.

Harold, Claudrena N., *Virginia*. Email: cnh6g@virginia.edu.

Haroon, **Sana**, *Massachusetts, Boston*. Boston, MA. Email: sana.haroon@umb.edu. Research: Institutions, public sphere.

Harootunian, **Harry D.**, *Chicago; NYU*. Email: hh3@nyu.edu.

Harp, **Gillis J.**, *Grove City*. Email: gjharp@gcc.edu.

Harp, **Jamalin Rae**, *Texas-Rio Grande Valley*. Email: jamalin.harp@utrgv.edu.

Harper, **April**, *SUNY, Oneonta*. Email: april.harper@oneonta.edu.

Harper, *John L*. Bologna, Italy. Affil: Johns Hopkins Univ. Center. Email: jharper@jhubc.it. Research: Alexander Hamilton, contemporary US foreign policy.

Harper, **Kimberly**, *State Hist. Soc. of Missouri*. Email: harperk@shsmo.org.

Harper, **Kristine C.**, *Florida State*. Email: kcharper@fsu.edu.

Harper, **Kyle**, *Oklahoma (Hist.)*. Email: kyleharper@ou.edu.

Harper, **Matt J. Z.**, *Mercer*. Email: harper_mjz@mercer.edu.

Harper, **Mattie Marie**. Saint Paul, MN. Affil: Minnesota Hist. Soc. Email: mattiemharper@gmail.com. Research: 18th-c African Americans in Indian country, Great Lakes region.

Harper, *Misti Nicole*, *Gustavus Adolphus*. Fayetteville, AR. Affil: Arkansas, Fayetteville. Email: mnharper@gustavus.edu; mxh040@uark.edu. Research: intersectionality, civil rights.

Harper, *Rob*, *Wisconsin-Stevens Point*. Stevens Point, WI. Email: rharper@uwsp.edu. Research: upper Ohio Valley politics and violence.

Harper, *Tobias Joel*, *Arizona State*. Tempe, AZ. Email: tobias.harper@asu.edu; tobias.harper@gmail.com. Research: modern Britain, British Empire.

Harran, **Marilyn J.**, *Chapman*. Email: harran@chapman.edu.

Harreld, **Donald J.**, *Brigham Young*. Email: donald_harreld@byu.edu.

Harrell, *David E.*, *Auburn*. Ponte Vedra Beach, FL. Email: harrede@auburn.edu. Research: 20th-c American religion.

Harrell, **Kevin T.**, *Hist. New Orleans*. Email: kevinh@hnoc.org.

Harrie, **Jeanne E.**, *California State, Bakersfield*. Email: jharrie@csub.edu.

Harrigan, **Patrick J.**, *Waterloo*. Email: harrigan@uwaterloo.ca.

Harrill, **J. Albert**, *Ohio State*. Email: harrill.5@osu.edu.

Harrington, **Ann M.**, **BVM**, *Loyola, Chicago*. Email: aharri1@luc.edu.

Harrington, **Anne**, *Harvard (Hist. of Science)*. Email: aharring@fas.harvard.edu.

Harrington, *Joel F.*, *Vanderbilt*. Nashville, TN. Email: joel.f.harrington@vanderbilt.edu. Research: early modern Germany, law/religion/society.

Harrington, **Joseph F.**, **Jr.**, *Framingham State*. Email: jharrington@framingham.edu.

Harrington, *Matthew Craig*. Tallahassee, FL. Affil: James S. Rickards High Sch. Email: harringtonma@leonschools.net.

Harrington, **Wade**, *Azusa Pacific*. Email: jharrington@apu.edu.

Harrington, *William D*. Orchard Park, NY. Affil: SUNY, Buffalo. Email: wharrington@brownkelly.com.

Harrington Becker, **Gertrude**, *Virginia Tech*. Email: thbecker@vt.edu.

Harris, *Amy B.*, *Brigham Young*. Provo, UT. Email: amy.harris@byu.edu. Research: English families, poverty and singleness.

Harris, **Barbara J.**, *North Carolina, Chapel Hill*. Email: bharris@live.unc.edu.

Harris, **Benjamin**, *New Hampshire, Durham*. Email: bh5@unh.edu.

Harris, **Bonnie Mae**, *San Diego State*.

Harris, **Brice**, **Jr.**, *Occidental*. Email: bharris@oxy.edu.

Harris, *Carmen V*. Simpsonville, SC. Affil: South Carolina Upstate. Email: charris@uscupstate.edu. Research: black extension workers, slavery in South Carolina.

Harris, **Charles H.**, **III**, *New Mexico State*.

Harris, *Clemmie L.*, *Utica*. Utica, NY. Email: clharris@utica.edu; harriscl@sas.upenn.edu. Research: northern race and partisan politics, Pan-Africanism.

Harris, *Curtis*. Washington, DC. Affil: American. Email: curtismharris@gmail.com. Research: labor rights in professional sports.

Harris, **David**, *North Carolina A&T State*. Email: harrisda@ncat.edu.

Harris, *Frank W*. New Hyde Park, NY. Affil: Farmingdale State, SUNY. Email: frankwjh@juno.com. Research: Irish Tudor-Stuart, English and Irish legal.

Harris, **Glen Anthony**, *North Carolina, Wilmington*. Email: harrisg@uncw.edu.

Harris, *J. William*, *Jr.* Boston, MA. Affil: New Hampshire, Durham. Email: jw.harris@unh.edu. Research: New South social, quantitative methods.

Harris, **James F.**, *Maryland, Coll. Park*. Email: jharris@umd.edu.

Harris, *James*. San Juan Capistrano, CA. Affil: St. Margaret's Episcopal Sch. Email: jharris@smes.org. Research: late imperial China, world.

Harris, *Jay M*. Cambridge, MA. Affil: Harvard. Email: jharris@g.harvard.edu. Research: Jewish studies.

Harris, **John**, *Alberta*. Email: john.harris@ualberta.ca.

Harris, **Kristine M.**, *SUNY, New Paltz*. Email: harrisk@newpaltz.edu.

Harris, **Lane J.**, *Furman*. Email: lane.harris@furman.edu.

Harris, *LaShawn D.*, *Michigan State*. East Lansing, MI. Email: harri859@msu.edu. Research: 20th-c cultural/social/urban, women and gender.

Harris, **Lauren McArthur**, *Arizona State*. Email: lauren.harris.1@asu.edu.

Harris, *Leslie M.*, *Northwestern*. Evanston, IL. Email: leslie.harris@northwestern.edu. Research: southern slavery and masculinity, 20th-c New Orleans.

Harris, **Lynn B.**, *East Carolina*. Email: harrisly@ecu.edu.

Harris, **Marc L.**, *Penn State*. Email: mlh6@psu.edu.

Harris, **Matthew L.**, *Colorado State, Pueblo*. Email: matt.harris@csupueblo.edu.

Harris, *Moira Claire*. Richmond, VA. Affil: George Mason. Email: moiraharris518@gmail.com.

Harris, **Neil**, *Chicago*. Email: nh16@uchicago.edu.

Harris, *Patrick William*. Warren, MI. Affil: Oakland Comm. Coll. Email: patrick.harris@

fulbrightmail.org. Research: assimilation in 12th-c Toledo, medieval Leonese/Castilian identity.

Harris, **Richard**, *McMaster*. Email: harrisr@mcmaster.ca.

Harris, *Robert L.*, *Jr.* Fulton, MD. Affil: Cornell. Email: rlh10@cornell.edu. Research: African American since 1940, MLK in history and memory.

Harris, **Stephen John**, *National Defence Headquarters*. Email: stephen.harris@forces.gc.ca.

Harris, *Steven E.*, *Mary Washington*. Fredericksburg, VA. Email: sharris@umw.edu. Research: Soviet mass housing, Aeroflot.

Harris, *Steven*. San Francisco, CA. Affil: San Francisco State. Email: sharris@steveharris.net.

Harris, **Tim J.**, *Brown*. Email: Tim_Harris@Brown.edu.

Harris, **William C.**, *North Carolina State*. Email: william_harris@ncsu.edu.

Harris, **William James**, **Sr.**, *Presbyterian*. Email: wjharris@presby.edu.

Harris, **William L.**, *Citadel*.

Harrison, **Benjamin T.**, *Louisville*. Email: ben.harrison@louisville.edu.

Harrison, **Candice L.**, *San Francisco*. Email: clharrison2@usfca.edu.

Harrison, *Carol E.*, *South Carolina, Columbia*. Columbia, SC. Email: ceharris@mailbox.sc.edu. Research: French religion 1750-1914, gender.

Harrison, **Cynthia E.**, *George Washington*. Email: harrison@gwu.edu.

Harrison, **Daniel F.**, *Henry Ford Coll.* Email: dharrisn@hfcc.edu.

Harrison, *David Wayne*. Edmond, OK. Affil: Southern New Hampshire. Email: dhloveshistory@gmail.com.

Harrison, *Emily A*. Cambridge, MA. Affil: Harvard. Email: harrison@post.harvard.edu.

Harrison, **Hope M.**, *George Washington*. Email: hopeharr@gwu.edu.

Harrison, *Patricia Greenwood*. Mobile, AL. Affil: Spring Hill. Email: harrison@shc.edu. Research: British and American suffrage movements.

Harrison, **Robert T.**, *Southern Oregon*.

Harrison, *Victoria Lee*. Edwardsville, IL. Affil: Southern Illinois, Edwardsville. Email: harri5716@gmail.com. Research: 19th-c US, African American.

Harris-Stoertz, **Fiona**, *Trent*. Email: fharris@trentu.ca.

Harrod, *Richard Frederick*. St. Louis, IL. Affil: Washington, St. Louis. Email: rharrod@wustl.edu.

Harrold, **Frances L.**, *Georgia State*.

Harry, **Elizabeth A.**, *St. Thomas, Minn*. Email: eaharry@stthomas.edu.

Harsanyi, **Doina P.**, *Central Michigan*. Email: harsa1dp@cmich.edu.

Harsch, *Donna T.*, *Carnegie Mellon*. Pittsburgh, PA. Email: dh44@andrew.cmu.edu. Research: post-1945 comparative health policies, post-1945 German health cultures.

Harsch, *Lloyd A*. New Orleans, LA. Affil: New Orleans Baptist Theological Sem. Email: lharsch@nobts.edu. Research: religious liberty and law, ethnic expressions of Baptist tenets.

Harshman, **Deirdre Ruscitti**, *Christopher Newport*. Email: deirdre.harshman@cnu.edu.

Harshman, **Matthew James**, *Christopher Newport*. Email: matthew.harshman@cnu.edu.

Harsin, Jill, *Colgate*. Email: jharsin@colgate.edu.

Hart, Daniel Rielly. Boston, MA. Email: drh375@g.harvard.edu.

Hart, Darryl G., *Hillsdale*. Hillsdale, MI. Email: dhart@hillsdale.edu; dgh1530@comcast.net. Research: secularization in 20th-c US, church and state in 19th-c US.

Hart, James S., Jr., *Oklahoma (Hist.)*. Email: jshart@ou.edu.

Hart, Jennifer Anne, *Wayne State*. Detroit, MI. Email: jennifer.hart4@wayne.edu. Research: transportation in postcolonial Ghana, public culture of religion in Ghana.

Hart, John Mason, *Houston*. Email: jhart@uh.edu.

Hart, Justin, *Texas Tech*. Email: justin.hart@ttu.edu.

Hart, Mitchell, *Florida*. Gainesville, FL. Email: hartm@ufl.edu. Research: European and American Jewish.

Hart, Paul Brian, *Texas State*. Email: ph18@txstate.edu.

Hart, Richard. Winthrop, WA. Affil: Hart West & Assoc. Email: e.richard.hart@gmail.com.

Hart, Roger, *Texas Southern*. Email: hartrp@tsu.edu.

Hart, Russell A., *Hawai'i Pacific*. Email: rhart@hpu.edu.

Hart, T. Robert, *North Carolina, Wilmington*. Email: hartt@uncw.edu.

Hart, Tanya, *Pepperdine*. Email: tanya.hart@pepperdine.edu.

Hart, William B., *Middlebury*. Email: hart@middlebury.edu.

Hartch, Todd F., *Eastern Kentucky*. Richmond, KY. Email: todd.hartch@eku.edu. Research: Ivan Illich and Cuernavaca, Charismatic Catholics in Mexico.

Hartenian, Larry R. Plymouth, MA. Affil: Curry. Email: lharteni@curry.edu. Research: propaganda of George W. Bush administration.

Harter, Kevin L., *James Madison*. Email: harterkl@jmu.edu.

Harth, A. C. Ridgeland, MS. Affil: St. Andrew's Episcopal Sch. Email: harthc@gosaints.org. Research: global studies education, geopolitical change and IR.

Harth, Amy E. Overland Park, KS. Affil: Union Inst. and Univ. Email: amy.harth@email.myunion.edu. Research: representations of Africa in western media, narratives of economic development.

Hartigan, Francis X., *Nevada, Reno*. Email: hartigan@unr.edu.

Hartigan-O'Connor, Ellen, *California, Davis*. Davis, CA. Email: eoconnor@ucdavis.edu. Research: colonial Newport RI and Charleston SC, gender/consumption/credit.

Hartje, Robert G., *Wittenberg*.

Hartlerode, Holly A., *Bowling Green State*. Email: curator@woodcountyhistory.org.

Hartman, Andrew G., *Illinois State*. Email: ahartma@ilstu.edu.

Hartman, Gary A., *Texas State*. Email: gh08@txstate.edu.

Hartman, Janine C., *Cincinnati*. Email: janine.hartman@uc.edu.

Hartmann, Susan M., *Ohio State*. Columbus, OH. Email: hartmann.1@osu.edu. Research: US policy and politics since 1945, US second wave feminism.

Hartnett, Jeremy. Crawfordsville, IN. Affil: Wabash. Email: Hartnetj@wabash.edu.

Hartnett, Lynne Ann, *Villanova*. Email: lynne.hartnett@villanova.edu.

Hartog, Hendrik A. Princeton, NJ. Affil: Princeton. Email: hartog@princeton.edu. Research: legal history global/local, property relations.

Hartog, Joanne D., *James Madison*. Email: hartogjd@jmu.edu.

Hartshorne, Thomas L., *Cleveland State*. Email: t.hartshorne@csuohio.edu.

Hartston, Barnet P. Saint Petersburg, FL. Affil: Eckerd. Email: hartstbp@eckerd.edu. Research: anti-Semitism in imperial Germany, German legal.

Hartung, Felicitas. La Jolla, CA. Affil: California, San Diego. Email: fhartung@ucsd.edu. Research: US-GER relations, peace movement and emotions.

Hartzok, Justus G., *Gettysburg*. Email: jhartzok@gettysburg.edu.

Harvell, Elle Evelyn. Los Angeles, CA. Affil: UCLA. Email: eharvell@ucla.edu. Research: American Civil War, 19th-c America.

Harvey, David Allen. Sarasota, FL. Affil: New Coll., Fla. Email: dharvey@ncf.edu. Research: occultism and politics in 19th-c France, religion/science/popular culture.

Harvey, David, *Graduate Center, CUNY*. Email: dharvey@gc.cuny.edu.

Harvey, John Layton, *St. Cloud State*. Email: jlharvey@stcloudstate.edu.

Harvey, Kyle Edmund, *Western Carolina*. Ithaca, NY. Affil: Cornell. Email: keh236@cornell.edu.

Harvey, Marcus G. Peterborough, ON, Canada. Affil: Trent Univ. Faculty Assoc. Email: marcusgharvey@gmail.com.

Harvey, Mark, *North Dakota State*. Email: mark.harvey@ndsu.edu.

Harvey, Morgan Rhea. Arcata, CA. Affil: Humboldt County Hist. Soc. Email: mrh426@humboldt.edu.

Harvey, Paul William, *Colorado Colorado Springs*. Colorado Springs, CO. Email: pharvey@uccs.edu. Research: religion and race in South 1860-2000, music and culture.

Harvey, Richard L., *Ohio*. Email: harvey@ohio.edu.

Harvey, Sean P., *Seton Hall*. Email: sean.harvey@shu.edu.

Harwell, Debbie Z., *Houston*. Email: dzharwel@central.uh.edu.

Hasegawa, Masato, *NYU*. Email: masato.hasegawa@nyu.edu.

Hasegawa, Tsuyoshi, *California, Santa Barbara*. Email: hasegawa@history.ucsb.edu.

Haskell, Alexander B., *California, Riverside*. Email: alexander.haskell@ucr.edu.

Haskett, Robert Stephen, *Oregon*. Email: rhaskett@uoregon.edu.

Haskins, Victoria Katharine. Callahagan, Australia. Affil: Newcastle. Email: Victoria.Haskins@newcastle.edu.au.

Haslam, Gerald M., *Brigham Young*. Email: gerald_haslam@byu.edu.

Hassan, Amina. Washington, DC. Affil: Ohio. Email: aminahassanphd@gmail.com. Research: Loren Miller, African American business/California.

Hassan, Mona, *Duke*. Email: mona.hassan@duke.edu.

Hassani, Hannah. Bethesda, MD. Email: hjhannah@gwu.edu.

Hassett, Matthew J., *Coastal Carolina; North Carolina, Wilmington*. Email: mhassett@coastal.edu; hassetm@uncw.edu.

Hassim, Shireen, *Carleton, Can*. Email: Shireen.Hassim@carleton.ca.

Hasso, Frances, *Duke*. Email: frances.hasso@duke.edu.

Hassoun, Rosina. Saginaw, MI. Email: rhassoun@svsu.edu.

Hastings, Derek K., *Oakland*. Email: hastings@oakland.edu.

Hastings, Paula Pears, *Toronto*. Email: paula.hastings@utsc.utoronto.ca.

Hastings, Sally Ann, *Purdue*. West Lafayette, IN. Email: sahnolte@purdue.edu. Research: Japanese women, missionary.

Hata, Donald Teruo, Jr., *California State, Dominguez Hills*. Redondo Beach, CA. Email: dhata@csudh.edu. Research: Japanese American historiography.

Hatala, Josh. Troy, NY. Affil: Emma Willard Sch. Email: jhatala@emmawillard.org.

Hatch, David A. Columbia, MD.

Hatch, John. Salt Lake City, UT. Affil: Signature Books. Email: john@signaturebooks.com.

Hatch, Robert A., *Florida*. Email: ufhatch@ufl.edu.

Hatfield, April Lee, *Texas A&M*. College Station, TX. Email: ahatfield@tamu.edu. Research: 17th-/18th-c Atlantic world, Anglo-Spanish relations.

Hatfield, Douglas W., *Rhodes*. Email: hatfield@rhodes.edu.

Hatfield, Edward Adair. Atlanta, GA. Affil: Emory. Email: edwardhat@gmail.com. Research: urban, political.

Hatfield, Jason Travis. Durham, NC. Affil: Lucas Middle Sch. Email: stagewalker@hotmail.com. Research: Japan, America.

Hatfield, Kevin D., *Oregon*. Email: kevhat@uoregon.edu.

Hathaway, Jane, *Ohio State*. Email: hathaway.24@osu.edu.

Hathaway, Sonja Natalie. Grand Forks, ND. Email: snhathaway215@gmail.com.

Hattam, Victoria C., *New School*. Email: hattamv@newschool.edu.

Hattem, Michael D. New Haven, CT. Affil: New-York Hist. Soc. Email: mdhattem@gmail.com. Research: 18th-c US history culture, 18th-c US memory and politics.

Hattendorf, John Brewster, *Naval War Coll*. Newport, RI. Affil: Naval Hist. Command. Email: john.hattendorf@usnwc.edu. Research: Stephen B. Luce 1827-1917, Anglo-French naval wars 1689-1815.

Hatter, Lawrence B. A., *Washington State, Pullman*. Email: lawrence.hatter@wsu.edu.

Hattingh, Alistair V. New Concord, OH. Affil: Muskingum. Email: hattingh@muskingum.edu. Research: 20th-c Argentina.

Hattori, Akira. Fukuoka, Japan. Affil: Fukuoka. Email: hattori@fukuoka-u.ac.jp.

Hatzenbuehler, Ronald, *Idaho State*. Email: hatzrona@isu.edu.

Hatzinger, Maj Kyle, *US Military Acad*. Email: Kyle.Hatzinger@usma.edu.

Hau, Michael G. Clayton, Australia. Affil: Monash. Email: michael.hau@monash.edu. Research: Weimar and Nazi period sports science, hygiene.

Hauck, *Gregory Lee*. Stafford, VA. Email: gregory.hauck@gmail.com.

Haude, *Sigrun*, *Cincinnati*. Cincinnati, OH. Email: sigrun.haude@uc.edu. Research: continental Europe, Reformation.

Haug, **C. James**, *Mississippi State*. Email: ncentralmiss@yahoo.com.

Haug, **Robert J.**, *Cincinnati*. Email: haugrt@ucmail.uc.edu.

Haugaard, *David G.*, *Hist. Soc. of Pennsylvania*. Philadelphia, PA. Email: dhaugaard@hsp.org. Research: colonial Pennsylvania politics and society.

Haugeberg, *Karissa*, *Tulane*. New Orleans, LA. Email: khaugebe@tulane.edu. Research: anti-abortion movement, gender.

Haugh Holtan, *Alexandra M.* Naperville, IL. Email: amholtan@gmail.com. Research: indigenous Siberia, Russian empire in Siberia.

Haulman, **Kate**, *American*. Email: haulman@american.edu.

Haumann, *Sebastian*. Darmstadt, Germany. Affil: Technische, Darmstadt. Email: haumann@pg.tu-darmstadt.de. Research: natural resources, urban.

Haun, *Faye*. New York, NY. Affil: Graduate Center, CUNY. Email: fhaun@gradcenter.cuny.edu.

Hauptman, *Laurence M.*, *SUNY, New Paltz*. New Paltz, NY. Email: hauptmal@newpaltz.edu; Rlhauptman@aol.com. Research: Iroquois, Seneca and Oneida.

Haurand, *F. Robert*, *Jr.* Henrico, VA. Affil: Sanborn Regional Middle Sch. Email: frhjr@yahoo.com.

Haus, **Jeffrey**, *Kalamazoo*. Email: jhaus@kzoo.edu.

Hause, *Steven C.*, *Missouri–St. Louis; Washington, St. Louis*. Saint Louis, MO. Email: shause@wustl.edu. Research: Protestantism in France 1860-1914.

Hauselmann, *Hans*. Modesto, CA. Affil: Modesto Jr. Coll. Email: hauselmannh@yosemite.edu.

Hauser, **Reine**, *SUNY, Buffalo State*. Email: hauserr@buffalostate.edu.

Hauser, **Robert**, *Penn State*. Email: reh6@psu.edu.

Hauser, **William**, *Rochester*. Email: william.hauser@rochester.edu.

Haushofer, *Lisa*. Cambridge, MA. Affil: Harvard. Email: lisa.haushofer@utoronto.ca. Research: medicine/science, food.

Hausmann, *Stephen R.*, *St. Thomas, Minn.* St. Paul, MN. Email: srhausmann@stthomas.edu. Research: Rapid City SD/Black Hills, 1972 flood/indigenous segregation.

Hausse, *Heidi*. Auburn, AL. Affil: Auburn. Email: heidi.hausse@gmail.com.

Havens, *T.R.H.*, *Northeastern*. Lexington, MA. Email: thavens@bhavens.com. Research: postwar Japan, Meiji Restoration 1868-1912.

Haverty-Stacke, *Donna Truglio*, *Hunter, CUNY*. Bronxville, NY. Email: dhaverty@hunter.cuny.edu. Research: 1941 Smith Act trial SWP/Teamsters 544, US working-class/radical political culture.

Havira, **Barbara S.**, *Western Michigan*. Email: barbara.havira@wmich.edu.

Hawes, **Clement**, *Michigan, Ann Arbor*. Email: cchawes@umich.edu.

Hawes, **Joseph M.**, *Memphis*. Email: jhawes@memphis.edu.

Hawk, **Angela S.**, *California State, Long Beach*. Email: angela.hawk@csulb.edu.

Hawk, *Emily Ann*. New York, NY. Affil: Columbia. Email: EmilyAnnHawk@gmail.com. Research: dance.

Hawke, *Jason G.*, *Roanoke*. Email: hawke@roanoke.edu.

Hawkins, *Cynthia*. Rochester, NY. Affil: SUNY, Buffalo. Email: hawkins.cynthia@gmail.com. Research: African American agency and art object, agency/art/identity/citizenship.

Hawkins, **Gregg**, *Texas Southern*.

Hawkins, *Gregory J.* East Sandwich, MA.

Hawkins, *J. Russell*. Marion, IN. Affil: Indiana Wesleyan. Email: rusty.hawkins@indwes.edu. Research: race and religion, US civil rights.

Hawkins, **Michael**, *Creighton*. Email: michaelhawkins@creighton.edu.

Hawkins, **Sean**, *Toronto*. Email: sean.hawkins@utoronto.ca.

Hawkins, *Timothy Paul*, *Indiana State*. Terre Haute, IN. Email: Timothy.Hawkins@indstate.edu. Research: Napoleonic intervention in Latin America, independence in Spanish Empire.

Hawkinson, *Charles*. Madison, AL. Affil: Athens State. Email: clhawkinson@gmail.com.

Hawley, **Charles V.**, *US Dept. of State*.

Hawley, *Ellis W.*, *Iowa*. Iowa City, IA. Email: ellis.hawley@mchsi.com. Research: Herbert Hoover, US economic policy.

Haworth, **Daniel S.**, *Houston-Clear Lake*. Email: haworth@uhcl.edu.

Haws, **Robert J.**, *Mississippi*.

Hawthorne, **Walter W.**, *III*, *Michigan State*. Email: walterh@msu.edu.

Hay, **Amy Marie**, *Texas-Rio Grande Valley*. Email: amy.hay@utrgv.edu.

Hay, **C. Douglas**, *York, Can.* Email: dhay@yorku.ca.

Hay, *Carla H.*, *Marquette*. Milwaukee, WI. Email: carla.hay@marquette.edu. Research: popular politics, Catharine Macaulay.

Hay, *Chelsey*. Columbus, OH. Email: chelseyellen@gmail.com.

Hay, *Robert P.*, *Marquette*. Milwaukee, WI. Research: US social/cultural/intellectual 1783-1861.

Hay, *Sebastian*. Boone, NC. Email: hays@appstate.edu.

Hay, **William Anthony**, *Mississippi State*. Email: wilhay6248@aol.com.

Hayashi, **Brian M.**, *Kent State*. Email: bhayashi@kent.edu.

Hayashida-Knight, *Christopher H.* Chico, CA. Affil: California State, Chico. Email: chayashida-knight@csuchico.edu. Research: patriotism and nationalism, African American women.

Haycock, **Ronald G.**, *Royal Military*. Email: haycock-r@rmc.ca.

Hayda, *Chad Alan*. Monticello, MN. Email: chadhayda@gmail.com.

Hayday, *Matthew C.*, *Guelph*. Email: mhayday@uoguelph.ca.

Hayden, *Albert A.*, *Wittenberg*. Springfield, OH. Research: Britain.

Hayden, **Caroline E.**, *Hist. Soc. of Pennsylvania*. Email: chayden@hsp.org.

Hayden, *Erica Rhodes*. Nashville, TN. Affil: Trevecca Nazarene. Email: erica.r.hayden@gmail.com. Research: criminal punishments and women, antebellum US society.

Hayden, **J. Michael**, *Saskatchewan*. Email: michael.hayden@usask.ca.

Hayden-Roy, **Patrick M.**, *Nebraska Wesleyan*. Email: phr@nebrwesleyan.edu.

Hayes, **Annie**, *Massachusetts Hist. Soc.* Email: ahayes@masshist.org.

Hayes, *Dawn Marie*, *Montclair State*. Montclair, NJ. Email: hayesd@mail.montclair.edu. Research: perceptions of body 1100-1400, perceptions of sacred space 1100-1400.

Hayes, **Geoffrey**, *Waterloo*. Email: ghayes@uwaterloo.ca.

Hayes, **John**, *Augusta*. Email: jhayes22@augusta.edu.

Hayes, *Patrick J.*, *American Catholic Hist. Assoc.* Philadelphia, PA. Affil: Archives of the Redemptorist Fathers, Baltimore Province. Email: pjhayesphd@gmail.com.

Hayes, **Peter F.**, *Northwestern*. Email: p-hayes@northwestern.edu.

Hayes, **Roland C.**, *Austin Comm. Coll*. Email: rhayes@austincc.edu.

Hayford, *Charles W.* Evanston, IL. Email: Chayford@aol.com. Research: US-China relations, film and food.

Haykel, *Bernard*, *Princeton*. Princeton, NJ. Email: haykel@princeton.edu. Research: Islamic intellectual and legal, marginals and legal norms in Islam.

Haynes, *April R.*, *Wisconsin-Madison; Committee on LGBT Hist.* Email: april.haynes@wisc.edu.

Haynes, *Christine S.*, *North Carolina, Charlotte*. Charlotte, NC. Email: chaynes@uncc.edu. Research: book trade, work.

Haynes, **Douglas E.**, *Dartmouth*. Email: douglas.haynes@dartmouth.edu.

Haynes, **Douglas M.**, *California, Irvine*. Email: dhaynes@uci.edu.

Haynes, **Joshua S.**, *Southern Mississippi*. Email: joshua.haynes@usm.edu.

Haynes, **Robert V.**, *Western Kentucky*. Email: robert.haynes@wku.edu.

Haynes, **Sam W.**, *Texas, Arlington*. Email: haynes@uta.edu.

Haynold, *Oliver M.* Evanston, IL. Affil: Northwestern. Email: omhpublic@haynold.com. Research: constitutional thought in Württemberg.

Hays, *Jo N.*, *Loyola, Chicago*. Oak Park, IL. Email: jhays@luc.edu; jnhays111@comcast.net. Research: disease and 19th-c imperialism.

Hayse, *Michael R.*, *Stockton*. Swarthmore, PA. Email: haysem@stockton.edu. Research: German Federal Republic/Allied occupation 1945-59, Holocaust.

Hayter, *Julian Maxwell*, *Richmond*. University of Richmond, VA. Email: jhayter@richmond.edu. Research: modern US, modern African American.

Hayton, **Jeff Patrick**, *Wichita State*. Email: jeff.hayton@wichita.edu.

Haywood, **Carl**, *Wisconsin-Eau Claire*. Email: haywoocn@uwec.edu.

Haywood, **D'Weston L.**, *Hunter, CUNY*. Email: dh2036@hunter.cuny.edu.

Haywood, **Elisabeth Kalé**, *Allegheny*. Email: khaywood@allegheny.edu.

Hazard, **Anthony Q.**, *Jr.*, *Santa Clara*. Email: ahazard@scu.edu.

Hazinski, *Ryan Walter*. Lake Elsinore, CA. Affil: Canyon Springs High Sch. Email: ryan.hazinski@gmail.com.

Hazkani, Shay, *Maryland, Coll. Park*. Email: hazkani@umd.edu.

Hazlett, David L. Fountain, CO. Affil: Fountain-Ft. Carson High Sch. Email: dhazlett@ffc8.org.

He, Belinda. Seattle, WA. Affil: Washington, Seattle. Email: chailude@gmail.com.

He, Qiliang, *Illinois State*. Email: qhe@ilstu.edu.

He, Rowena Xiaoqing, *St. Michael's*. Email: rhe@smcvt.edu.

He, Sophia Wenli. Horseheads, NY. Affil: Cornell. Email: sh787@cornell.edu.

Head, David, *Central Florida*. Email: David.Head@ucf.edu.

Head, Randolph C., *California, Riverside*. Riverside, CA. Email: randolph.head@ucr.edu. Research: European institutional cultures, archives.

Headle, Barbara A., *Colorado Colorado Springs*. Email: bheadle@uccs.edu.

Headrick, Daniel R., *Roosevelt*. Email: dheadric@roosevelt.edu.

Healey, Jenna, *Queen's, Can*. Email: jenna.healey@queensu.ca.

Healey, Mark Alan, *Connecticut, Storrs*. Storrs Mansfield, CT. Email: mark.healey@uconn.edu. Research: modern Argentina/Brazil, disasters/environment/populism/cities.

Healy, Catherine. Dublin, Ireland. Affil: Trinity Coll. Dublin. Email: healyc7@tcd.ie.

Healy, Gavin. Jackson Heights, NY. Affil: Columbia. Email: gh148@columbia.edu.

Healy, Maureen, *Lewis & Clark*. Email: healy@lclark.edu.

Healy-Clancy, Meghan Elisabeth. Canton, MA. Affil: Bridgewater State. Email: healy.meghan@gmail.com. Research: politics of culture in anti-apartheid, Nadine Gordimer.

Heaman, Elsbeth, *McGill*. Email: elsbeth.heaman@mcgill.ca.

Heaney, Christopher H., *Penn State*. State College, PA. Email: cuh282@psu.edu. Research: grave-opening in Peru and Americas, race and science in Andes.

Heaphy, Leslie A., *Kent State*. North Canton, OH. Email: lheaphy@kent.edu. Research: US, sports.

Hearden, Patrick J., *Purdue*. Email: phearden@purdue.edu.

Hearst, Kathryn P. New Rochelle, NY. Affil: Sarah Lawrence. Email: katehearst1@gmail.com. Research: Film & Media Studies, US Gender Studies.

Hearty, Ryan, *Center for Hist. of Physics*. Columbia, MD. Email: rhearty@aip.org; rhearty1@jhu.edu.

Heasley, Lynne, *Western Michigan*. Email: lynne.heasley@wmich.edu.

Heath, Charles V., II, *Sam Houston State*. Email: cvh003@shsu.edu.

Heath, Orland G. Silver Spring, MD. Email: orlandheath@verizon.net.

Heath, Vicki Marie. Austin, TX. Affil: Texas A&M, Coll. Station. Email: vicki_heath_78@tamu.edu. Research: 18th-c prostitution in London, Harris's List.

Heathcott, Joseph E., *New School*. Email: heathcoj@newschool.edu.

Heathorn, Stephen J., *McMaster*. Email: heaths@mcmaster.ca.

Heaton, Matthew Michael, *Virginia Tech*. Email: mheaton@vt.edu.

Heavey, Elaine, *Massachusetts Hist. Soc*. Email: eheavey@masshist.org.

Heavner, Elizabeth Anne. Norman, OK. Email: elizabeth.heavner@snhu.edu.

Hebert, Keith S., *Auburn*. Email: heberks@auburn.edu.

Hébert Veit, Kristin, *Hist. New Orleans*. Email: kristinhv@hnoc.org.

Hebrard, Jean M., *Johns Hopkins (Hist.)*. Baltimore, MD. Email: jhebrard@jhu.edu. Research: social and cultural history of slavery, post-slavery societies of Atlantic world.

Hecht, David K., *Bowdoin*. Email: dhecht@bowdoin.edu.

Hecht, Gabrielle, *Stanford*. Stanford, CA. Email: ghecht@stanford.edu. Research: Anthropocene, scale/materiality/waste/slow violence.

Hecht, Richard D., *California, Santa Barbara*. Email: ariel@religion.ucsb.edu.

Heckart, Beverly A., *Central Washington*. Ellensburg, WA. Email: heckartb@cwu.edu. Research: urban Germany.

Heckman, Alma, *California, Santa Cruz*. Email: aheckman@ucsc.edu.

Hedrick, Charles W., Jr., *California, Santa Cruz*. Email: hedrick@ucsc.edu.

Hedstrom, Matthew S. Charlottesville, VA. Affil: Virginia. Email: hedstrom@virginia.edu. Research: liberal religion and print culture, popular religion 1921-50.

Hedtke, James R., *Cabrini*. Email: james.r.hedtke@cabrini.edu.

Heed, Thomas, *Ramapo*. Email: theed@ramapo.edu.

Heefner, Gretchen A., *Northeastern*. Boston, MA. Email: g.heefner@neu.edu. Research: domestic impact of Cold War, Cold War memory.

Heerman, Scott, *Miami*. Email: s.heerman@miami.edu.

Heern, Zackery M., *Idaho State*. Email: heerzack@isu.edu.

Heffelfinger, T. Jane. Austin, TX. Affil: Texas State. Email: tjaneheffelfinger@gmail.com. Research: African American Cemeteries, Medical.

Hegi, Jeremy Paul. Lubbock, TX. Affil: Boston Univ. Email: jphegi@bu.edu.

Heidbrink, Ingo, *Old Dominion*. Email: iheidbri@odu.edu.

Heiden, William. Bloomfield, CT. Affil: Trinity Coll., Conn. Email: billheiden@gmail.com.

Heidenreich, Donald E., Jr. Saint Charles, MO. Affil: Lindenwood. Email: dheidenreich@lindenwood.edu. Research: national security and early Republic, origins of US Constitution and politics.

Heil, Michael W., *Arkansas, Little Rock*. Email: mwheil@ualr.edu.

Heilman, Jaymie Patricia, *Alberta*. Email: jaymie.heilman@ualberta.ca.

Heim, Sarah, *Hist. Soc. of Pennsylvania*. Email: sheim@hsp.org.

Hein, Benjamin P., *Brown*. Email: benjamin_hein@brown.edu.

Hein, Christine M. Fruita, CO. Affil: Colorado Mesa. Email: chein@coloradomesa.edu.

Hein, Laura E., *Northwestern*. Evanston, IL. Email: l-hein@northwestern.edu. Research: Japanese economic/cultural/intellectual, remembrance of WWII/comparative.

Heine, Steven, *Florida International*. Email: heines@fiu.edu.

Heineman, Elizabeth D., *Iowa*. Iowa City, IA. Email: elizabeth-heineman@uiowa.edu. Research: sexuality, consumer culture.

Heinrichs, Erik Anton. Winona, MN. Affil: Winona State. Email: eheinrichs@winona.edu. Research: early modern religion and medicine, Protestant and Catholic Reformations.

Heinsen-Roach, Erica, *South Florida, St. Petersburg*. Email: heinsenroach@usf.edu.

Heintzman, Kathryn. Cambridge, MA. Affil: Harvard. Email: kheintzman@fas.harvard.edu.

Heinz, Annelise, *Oregon*. Eugene, OR. Email: heinzam@gmail.com. Research: women and gender.

Heinzen, James W., *Rowan*. Email: heinzen@rowan.edu.

Heinzmann, Whitney, *State Hist. Soc. of Missouri*. Email: heinzmannw@shsmo.org.

Heise, Steven K. F. Marlborough, MA. Affil: Holyoke Comm. Coll. Email: sheise@hcc.edu. Research: Atlantic world, slavery and abolition.

Heiser, Richard R., *Presbyterian*. Email: rrheiser@presby.edu.

Heisey, M. J., *SUNY, Coll. Potsdam*. Email: heiseymj@potsdam.edu.

Heiss, Mary Ann, *Kent State*. Kent, OH. Email: mheiss@kent.edu. Research: Anglo-American visions of empire, British decolonization.

Heisser, Cecily M., *San Diego; San Diego Mesa*. Email: cheisser@sandiego.edu; cheisserucsd@gmail.com.

Heitmann, John A., *Dayton*. Email: john.heitmann@notes.udayton.edu.

Held, Joseph, *Rutgers, Camden*.

Helfand, William A. West Berlin, NJ. Email: whelfand@comcast.net.

Helfferich, Tryntje, *Ohio State*. Email: helfferich.1@osu.edu.

Helfgott, Isadora A., *Wyoming*. Email: ihelfgot@uwyo.edu.

Helfgott, Leonard M., *Western Washington*. Email: Leonard.Helfgott@wwu.edu.

Helfont, Samuel, *Naval War Coll*. Email: samuel.helfont@nps.edu.

Helfrich, William. Washington, DC. Affil: American. Email: wh4891a@american.edu.

Helg, Aline. Geneva, Switzerland. Affil: Genève. Email: Aline.Helg@unige.ch. Research: race and nation-making, blacks after slavery.

Helgeson, Jeffrey, *Texas State*. Email: jh221@txstate.edu.

Helgren, Jennifer Hillman. San Ramon, CA. Affil: Pacific. Email: jhelgren@pacific.edu. Research: Camp Fire Girls, US girlhood.

Hellbeck, Jochen, *Rutgers*. Email: hellbeck@history.rutgers.edu.

Heller, Darryl. Iowa City, IA. Affil: Indiana, South Bend. Email: daheller@iusb.edu. Research: construction of race, Black/Jewish relations.

Heller, Henry, *Manitoba*. Email: henry.heller@umanitoba.ca.

Hellert, Susan, *Wisconsin-Platteville*. Email: hellert@uwplatt.edu.

Hellman, John W., *McGill*. Email: john.hellman@mcgill.ca.

Hellrigel, MaryAnn C. Woodland Park, NJ. Affil: IEEE. Email: mahellrigel@gmail.com. Research: Thomas Edison/utilities/consumption, industrial revolutions and world.

Helly, **Dorothy O**. New York, NY. Affil: CUNY. Email: dohelly@aol.com. Research: women and journalism, journalism and empire.

Hellyer, **Robert I.**, *Wake Forest*. Email: hellyer@wfu.edu.

Helmreich, **Jonathan E.**, *Allegheny*. Email: jhelmrei@allegheny.edu.

Helmreich, **Paul C.**, *Wheaton, Mass*. Norton, MA. Email: phelmrei@wheatonma.edu. Research: modern Europe, Russia.

Helms, **Michael Jon**. Baton Rouge, LA. Affil: North Carolina State. Email: mike@mikehelms.org. Research: Ku Klux Klan/Reconstruction, firearms/military weapons.

Helps, **David**. Ypsilanti, MI. Affil: Michigan, Ann Arbor. Email: davidrhhelps@gmail.com.

Helsley, **Alexia J**. *South Carolina Aiken*. Email: alexiah@usca.edu.

Helstosky, **Carol F.**, *Denver*. Denver, CO. Email: chelstos@du.edu. Research: modern Europe, Italy.

Helton, **Laura E**. Philadelphia, PA. Affil: Delaware. Email: laura.helton@nyu.edu. Research: African American archives 1900-60, print culture and book.

Helton, **William L**. Fredericksburg, VA. Affil: Commonwealth of Virginia. Email: wlhelton@netscape.net.

Helyar, **Joseph P**. Atlanta, GA. Email: joehelyar@comcast.net.

Hemenway, **Betsy Jones**, *Loyola, Chicago*. Email: ehemenway@luc.edu.

Heming, **Carol P.**, *Central Missouri*. Email: heming@ucmo.edu.

Hemphill, **Katie**, *Arizona*. Email: khemphill@email.arizona.edu.

Hempson, **Leslie**, *Denison*. Email: hempsonl@denison.edu.

Hench, **John B**. Shrewsbury, MA. Affil: American Antiquarian Soc. (retired). Email: minnechusetts@gmail.com. Research: US WWII magazines.

Hendershot, **Gillian**, *Grand Valley State*. Email: hendersg@gvsu.edu.

Hendershot, **Robert M**. Grand Rapids, MI. Affil: Grand Rapids Comm. Coll. Email: rhenders@grcc.edu. Research: Anglo-American special relationship, influence of culture upon diplomacy.

Henderson, **Dwight F.**, *Texas, San Antonio*. Email: dwight.henderson@utsa.edu.

Henderson, **Gabriel David**, *Center for Hist. of Physics*. Oberlin, OH. Email: ghenders@aip.org; Hende270@gmail.com. Research: climate politics and policy, environmental studies.

Henderson, **James D.**, *Coastal Carolina*. Conway, SC. Email: henderj@coastal.edu. Research: modern Latin America, international studies.

Henderson, **Jarett**. Santa Barbara, CA. Affil: California, Santa Barbara. Email: jhenderson@history.ucsb.edu.

Henderson, **John E**. Auburn, ME. Email: stairiuil@gmail.com.

Henderson, **Jonathan**. Cumming, GA. Affil: Forsyth Central High Sch. Email: henderson678@gmail.com.

Henderson, **Marc Robert**. Annandale, VA. Affil: Vietnam War Commemoration. Email: flynavynu98@hotmail.com. Research: 19th-c US naval, 19th-c diplomatic.

Henderson, **Michael**, *California State, San Marcos*. Email: mhenderson@csusm.edu.

Henderson, **Peter V. N**. Cape Coral, FL. Affil: Winona State. Email: phenderson@winona.edu. Research: Latin America.

Henderson, **Rodger C.**, *Penn State*. Email: rch5@psu.edu.

Hendley, **Matthew C.**, *SUNY, Oneonta*. Email: matthew.hendley@oneonta.edu.

Hendon, **David W.**, *Baylor*. Email: david_hendon@baylor.edu.

Hendricks, **Charles D**. Laytonsville, MD. Email: anncharley@comcast.net. Research: James Maccubbin Lingan 1752-1812.

Hendricks, **Christopher E.**, *Georgia Southern*. Email: chendricks@georgiasouthern.edu.

Hendricks, **Derick Antony**, *Morgan State*. Email: derick.hendricks@morgan.edu.

Hendricks, **Wanda A.**, *South Carolina, Columbia*. Email: hendricw@mailbox.sc.edu.

Hendrickson, **Jocelyn N.**, *Alberta*. Edmonton, AB, Canada. Email: jnhendri@ualberta.ca. Research: medieval to early modern Islamic law, Muslims in Spain post-Reconquest.

Hendrickson, **Kenneth E.**, **III**, *Sam Houston State*. Email: his_keh@shsu.edu.

Hendrickson, **Mark G.**, *California, San Diego*. San Diego, CA. Email: ghendrickson@ucsd.edu. Research: US labor, capitalism.

Hendrix, **Melanie L**. Cantonment, FL. Affil: Tate High Sch. Email: melhendrix2@yahoo.com.

Hendrix, **Scott**, *Carroll*. Email: shendrix@carrollu.edu.

Hendrix-Komoto, **Amanda L.**, *Montana State, Bozeman*. Email: amanda.hendrixkomoto@montana.edu.

Hendryx, **Benjamin**. Concord, NH. Email: bdhendryx@gmail.com.

Heng, **Derek**, *Northern Arizona*. Email: derek.heng@nau.edu.

Hengerer, **Mark Sven**. Muenchen, Germany. Affil: Ludwig-Maximilians, Munich. Email: hengerer@lmu.de. Research: French maritime, Holy Roman Empire and Habsburg monarchy.

Henkin, **David**, *California, Berkeley*. Email: marhevka@berkeley.edu.

Henley, **Lauren Nicole**. Austin, TX. Affil: Texas, Austin. Email: lhenley@utexas.edu.

Hennessy, **Elizabeth A.**, *Wisconsin-Madison*. Email: ehennessy2@wisc.edu.

Hennessy, **Michael A.**, *Royal Military*. Email: hennessy-m@rmc.ca.

Henning, **Joseph M**. Rochester, NY. Affil: Rochester Inst. of Tech. Email: joseph.henning@rit.edu.

Henning, **Lori**, *Auburn; St. Bonaventure*.

Henning, **Stefan**. Evanston, IL. Affil: Northwestern. Email: stefan-henning@northwestern.edu. Research: anthropology and history, modern Chinese Muslim activists.

Henold, **Mary J.**, *Roanoke*. Email: henold@roanoke.edu.

Henretta, **James A.**, *Maryland, Coll. Park*. Email: henretta@umd.edu.

Henriksen, **Margot A.**, *Hawai'i, Manoa*. Email: henrikm@hawaii.edu.

Henriksson, **Anders H**. Harpers Ferry, WV. Affil: Shepherd. Email: ahenriks@shepherd.edu. Research: Russia, modern Europe.

Henriques, **Peter R.**, *George Mason*.

Henry, **James Daryn**. Charlottesville, VA. Affil: Virginia. Email: james.daryn.henry@gmail.com. Research: American religion, revivals.

Henry, **Maura A**. Waltham, MA. Affil: Holyoke Comm. Coll. Email: mhenry@post.harvard.edu. Research: 18th-c British aristocracy, 18th-c European travel.

Henry, **Robin C.**, *Wichita State*. Email: robin.henry@wichita.edu.

Henry, **Terrence**, *SUNY, Buffalo State*. Email: henrytj@buffalostate.edu.

Henry, **Todd A.**, *California, San Diego*. Email: tahenry@ucsd.edu.

Henry, **Wanda Sanville**, *Wheaton, Mass.* Providence, RI. Email: henry_wanda@wheatoncollege.edu; Wanda_Henry@alumni.brown.edu. Research: death industry.

Hentschke, **Jens R**. Newcastle-upon-Tyne, United Kingdom. Affil: Newcastle. Email: j.r.hentschke@ncl.ac.uk. Research: Latin American positivism, Brazilian education.

Hepler, **Reed Carson**. Logan, UT. Email: whosyourmaestro@gmail.com.

Hepler-Smith, **Evan**. Brighton, MA. Affil: Boston Coll. Email: heplers@bc.edu. Research: chemical industry and environment, information technology.

Hepp, **John H.**, **IV**, *Wilkes*. Email: john.hepp@wilkes.edu.

Heppler, **Jason A**. Omaha, NE. Affil: Nebraska, Omaha. Email: jason.heppler@gmail.com. Research: urban environmental politics, North American West.

Hepworth, **Jonathan David**. Athens, GA. Affil: Georgia. Email: jhepwor@uga.edu.

Herb, **Patricia Ann**. Mansfield, OH. Affil: North Central State. Email: paherb52@gmail.com.

Herber, **Charles J.**, *George Washington*. Arlington, VA. Email: cherber@gwu.edu. Research: Germany, Reformation.

Herber, **Tyler**. West Lafayette, IN. Affil: Purdue. Email: herber0@purdue.edu.

Herbert, **Amanda E.**, *Folger Inst*. Email: aherbert@folger.edu.

Herbert, **Eugenia W.**, *Mount Holyoke*. Email: eherbert@mtholyoke.edu.

Herbert, **Jason W**. Lake Placid, FL. Affil: Minnesota, Twin Cities. Email: herbe195@umn.edu.

Herbert, **Sandra**, *Maryland, Baltimore County*. Chester, MD. Email: herbert@umbc.edu. Research: science, intellectual.

Herbert, **Tim**. Chicago, IL. Affil: Illinois, Chicago. Email: therbe2@uic.edu.

Herbon, **Lorraine Dias**. Knoxville, TN. Affil: Tennessee, Knoxville. Email: lherbon@vols.utk.edu.

Herbst, **James D.**, *Texas Southern*. Email: james.herbst@tsu.edu.

Herbst, **Matthew T**. La Jolla, CA. Affil: California, San Diego. Email: mtherbst@ucsd.edu. Research: Byzantine and world, experiential learning and study abroad.

Herder, **Michelle M.**, *Cornell Coll*. Email: mherder@cornellcollege.edu.

Herf, **Jeffrey C.**, *Maryland, Coll. Park*. College Park, MD. Email: jherf@umd.edu. Research: Nazi propaganda in Middle East.

Herff, **Emily**. Portland, OR. Affil: American Public Univ. System. Email: emily.herff@gmail.com.

Herlan, **Ronald W.**, *SUNY, Coll. Brockport*.

Herman, **Benjamin**. West Chester, PA. Affil: Penn State. Email: bjh5316@psu.edu.

Herman, **Charles W**. Stewartville, MN. Affil: Sioux Falls. Email: charles.herman@usiouxfalls.edu. Research: early modern French government and religion, early modern French social and political.

Herman, Daniel J., *Central Washington*. Email: hermand@cwu.edu.

Herman, Ellen P., *Oregon*. Eugene, OR. Email: eherman@uoregon.edu. Research: child adoption, social science and engineering.

Herman, James. Farmers Branch, TX. Affil: Parish Episcopal Sch. Email: jamesherman15@gmail.com.

Herman, John, *Virginia Commonwealth*. Email: jeherman@vcu.edu.

Herman, Maj Thomas, *US Military Acad*. Email: thomas.herman@usma.edu.

Herman, Mark C. Fort Myers, FL. Affil: Florida SouthWestern State. Email: mherman@fsw.edu. Research: 17th-/18th-c diplomacy, 17th-/18th-c nonconformists/dissenters.

Herman, Rebecca, *California, Berkeley*. Email: rebeccaherman@berkeley.edu.

Hermann, Robin, *Louisiana, Lafayette*. Email: rhermann@louisiana.edu.

Hermanson, John, *Bentley*. Email: jhermanson@bentley.edu.

Hermeling, Andrew Dyrli. Lancaster, PA. Affil: Lehigh. Email: adh411@lehigh.edu.

Hermes, Katherine A., *Central Connecticut State*. Email: hermesk@ccsu.edu.

Hermosilla, Matias N. Stony Brook, NY. Affil: SUNY, Stony Brook. Email: matias.hermosilla@stonybrook.edu. Research: humor, popular music.

Hernandez, Bonar L., *Iowa State*. Email: bhernand@iastate.edu.

Hernandez, Carlos Ricardo, III. New Haven, CT. Affil: Yale. Email: carlos.hernandez@yale.edu. Research: memory of Mexican independence, Mexican tourism.

Hernandez, Idolina. Kirkwood, MO. Affil: St. Louis. Email: idolina.hernandez@slu.edu. Research: refugees, empire.

Hernandez, Jennifer Peoples, *San Diego Mesa*. Email: jehernan@sdccd.edu.

Hernandez, Jose Angel, *Houston*.

Hernandez, Leonardo F., *SUNY, Oswego*. Email: leonardo.hernandez@oswego.edu.

Hernandez, Richard L., *East Carolina*. Email: hernandezr@ecu.edu.

Hernandez, Sonia, *Texas A&M*. Email: soniah@tamu.edu.

Hernandez Berrones, Jethro, *Southwestern*. Georgetown, TX. Email: hernandj@southwestern.edu. Research: Mexico, health sciences and public health.

Hernandez-Matos, Antonio. Harrington, DE. Affil: Puerto Rico, Rio Piedras. Email: antonio.hernandezmatos@upr.edu. Research: fashion and modernity, Latinos in US.

Hernandez-Saenz, Luz Maria, *Western Ontario*. Email: lmhs@uwo.ca.

Herndon, Ruth Wallis, *Bowling Green State*. Bowling Green, OH. Email: rwhernd@bgsu.edu. Research: Children in early America, New England Indians.

Herod, Brittany Anne. Wichita, KS. Affil: Wichita State. Email: bherod1@usd259.net.

Heron, Craig, *York, Can*. Email: cheron@yorku.ca.

Herr, Joshua. St Louis, MO. Email: herrjoshua2017@gmail.com. Research: early modern China-Vietnam border, frontier southwest China.

Herr, Pilar M. Greensburg, PA. Affil: Pittsburgh, Greensburg. Email: pmh3@pitt.edu. Research:

Southern Cone state formation/frontiers, Southern Cone ethnic.

Herran Avila, Luis Alberto, *New Mexico*. Email: lherranavila@unm.edu.

Herren, Jeremy E. Savannah, GA. Email: herren1906@gmail.com.

Herrera, Elisa, *Soc. for Hist. Education*. Westminster, CA. Email: herrera@thehistoryteacher.org. Research: history education, US.

Herrera, Ricardo A., *US Army Command Coll*. Kansas City, MO. Email: ricardo.a.herrera.civ@mail.mil; r.herrera0@icloud.com. Research: Valley Forge, Mexican War.

Herrera, Robinson A., *Florida State*. Email: rherrera@fsu.edu.

Herrick, Samantha Kahn, *Syracuse*. Email: sherrick@maxwell.syr.edu.

Herringer, Carol Englehardt, *Georgia Southern*. Email: cherringer@georgiasouthern.edu.

Herrington, Philip, *James Madison*. Email: herrinpm@jmu.edu.

Herrlinger, Page, *Bowdoin*. Portland, ME. Email: pherrlin@bowdoin.edu. Research: late imperial Russia 1881-1917, Russia 1917-91.

Herrman, Judson, *Allegheny*. Email: jherrman@allegheny.edu.

Herron, John, *Missouri–Kansas City*. Email: herronj@umkc.edu.

Herron, Laura Bender. Oberlin, OH. Affil: Oberlin. Email: laura.herron@oberlin.edu.

Herrup, Cynthia B., *Duke; Southern California*. Portland, OR. Email: cherrup@acpub.duke.edu; herrup@usc.edu. Research: early modern England, legal.

Hersch, Matthew, *Harvard (Hist. of Science)*. Cambridge, MA. Email: hersch@fas.harvard.edu. Research: Cold War Era aerospace/computer/military.

Hersey, Mark D., *Mississippi State*. Mississippi State, MS. Email: mhersey@history.msstate.edu. Research: US South, environmental and agricultural.

Hershatter, Gail, *California, Santa Cruz*. Santa Cruz, CA. Email: gbhers@ucsc.edu. Research: rural women in 1950s China, gender and memory.

Hershberg, James G., *George Washington*. Email: jhershb@gwu.edu.

Hershenzon, Daniel Bernardo. New York, NY. Affil: Connecticut. Email: daniel.hershenzon@uconn.edu. Research: Mediterranean, historical anthropology.

Hertz, Deborah, *California, San Diego*. Email: dhertz@ucsd.edu.

Hertzberg, Suzanne. Pacific Palisades, CA. Affil: National Coalition of Independent Scholars. Email: shertzberg@gmail.com. Research: WWII era US-Mexico relations, Roosevelt-era labor and politics.

Hertzman, Marc Adam, *Illinois, Urbana-Champaign*. Urbana, IL. Email: hertzman@illinois.edu; mahertzman@gmail.com. Research: Brazilian race/sexuality/music, intellectual property after slavery.

Hervey, Norma J., *Luther*. Email: herveynj@luther.edu.

Herwig, Holger H., *Calgary*. Email: herwig@ucalgary.ca.

Herzberg, David L., *SUNY, Buffalo*. Buffalo, NY. Email: herzberg@buffalo.edu. Research: prescription drug abuse, drug control regimes.

Herzog, Barbara. Washington, DC. Affil: Herzog Career Consulting. Email: Herzog1@rcn.com.

Herzog, Dagmar, *Graduate Center, CUNY*. Email: dherzog@gc.cuny.edu.

Herzog, Shawna, *Washington State, Pullman*. Pullman, WA. Email: sherzog2@wsu.edu; shawnaherzog@gmail.com. Research: colonial prostitution, British Empire.

Herzog, Tamar, *Harvard (Hist.)*. Email: therzog@fas.harvard.edu.

Heschel, Susannah. Newton, MA. Affil: Dartmouth. Email: susannah.heschel@dartmouth.edu. Research: Jewish scholarship on Islam, Jewish historiography.

Hess, Andrew C. Medford, MA. Affil: Tufts. Email: andrew.hess@tufts.edu.

Hess, AnnMarie, *New York State Archives*. Email: annmarie.hess@nysed.gov. Research:, Y.

Hess, Catherine, *Huntington Library*. Email: chess@huntington.org.

Hess, Christian A. Tokyo, Japan. Affil: Sophia. Email: cahess@sophia.ac.jp. Research: Chinese urban, Sino-Japanese relations.

Hess, Daniel. San Mateo, CA. Affil: Junior State of America. Email: dhessindc@gmail.com.

Hess, Earl J., *Lincoln Memorial*. Email: earl.hess@lmunet.edu.

Hess, Gary R., *Bowling Green State*. Email: ghess@bgsu.edu.

Hesse, Carla A., *California, Berkeley*. Berkeley, CA. Email: chesse@berkeley.edu. Research: Old Regime and revolutionary France.

Hessel, Beth Shalom. Elkins Park, PA. Affil: Presbyterian Hist. Soc. Email: bhessel@history.pcusa.org. Research: WWII religion and Japanese American internment, US West ethnicity/gender/religion.

Hesselink, Reinier H., *Northern Iowa*. Email: reinier.hesselink@uni.edu.

Hessinger, Rodney J., *John Carroll*. Email: rhessinger@jcu.edu.

Hessler, Julie M., *Oregon*. Email: hessler@uoregon.edu.

Hest, John Edward. Moorhead, MN. Affil: North Dakota State. Email: john.e.hest@gmail.com.

Hester, Bridget, *Southeastern Louisiana*. Email: Bridget.Hester@southeastern.edu.

Hester, Torrie R., *St. Louis*. Email: thester4@slu.edu.

Hetnal, Adam A. Kornik, Poland.

Hett, Benjamin C., *Graduate Center, CUNY; Hunter, CUNY*. New York, NY. Email: bhett@hunter.cuny.edu. Research: intellectual history and jurisprudence, popular culture.

Hett, Robert R., *Alberta*.

Hettinger, Madonna J., *Wooster*. Email: mhettinger@wooster.edu.

Hettle, Wallace A., *Northern Iowa*. Email: wallace.hettle@uni.edu.

Hetzner, Donald R., *SUNY, Buffalo State*.

Heuer, Jennifer N., *Massachusetts, Amherst*. Email: heuer@history.umass.edu.

Heuman, Gad J. London, United Kingdom. Affil: Warwick. Email: g.j.heuman@warwick.ac.uk.

Heuman, Susan Eva. New York, NY. Email: susanheuman@gmail.com. Research: Cold War film.

Hevert, Joshua Paul. El Paso, TX. Affil: El Paso Comm. Coll. Email: jhevert@epcc.edu. Research: medieval heresy, medieval cultural.

Hevia, James L., *Chicago*. Chicago, IL. Email: jhevia@uchicago.edu. Research: military intelligence, technology and imperialism.

Hevly, Bruce, *Washington, Seattle*. Email: bhevly@uw.edu.

Hevron, Parker, *Texas Woman's*. Email: phevron@twu.edu.

Hewitt, Michelle, *AHA*. Email: mhewitt@historians.org.

Hewitt, Nancy A., *Rutgers*. Email: nhewitt@scarletmail.rutgers.edu.

Heyck, Hunter, *Oklahoma (Hist. of Science)*. Email: hheyck@ou.edu.

Heydari, Keanu. Ann Arbor, MI. Affil: Michigan, Ann Arbor. Email: keanuheydari@ucla.edu. Research: 19th-c French popular culture, 19th-c American Protestantism.

Heye, Brittany L. Laramie, WY. Affil: Wyoming. Email: bheye@uwyo.edu.

Heyman, Neil M., *San Diego State*. Email: heyman@sdsu.edu.

Heyn, Udo, *California State, Los Angeles*. Email: uheyn@calstatela.edu.

Heyrman, Christine Leigh, *Delaware*. Email: cheyrman@udel.edu.

Heywood, Linda M., *Boston Univ*. Email: heywood@bu.edu.

Heywood, Nancy, *Massachusetts Hist. Soc.* Email: nheywood@masshist.org.

Hibbard, John Douglass. Little Rock, AR. Affil: B.H. Carroll Theological Inst. Email: jhibbard@bhcarroll.edu.

Hickey, Damon D., *Wooster*. Email: dhickey@wooster.edu.

Hickey, Donald Thomas. Capitola, CA. Affil: California, Santa Cruz. Email: donaldthomashickey@gmail.com. Research: 19th-c US, American Civil War era culture/politics.

Hickey, Maclyn Le Bourgeois, *Hist. New Orleans*. Email: maclynh@hnoc.org.

Hickey, Michael C., *Bloomsburg*. Email: mhickey@bloomu.edu.

Hickman, Christopher Alan, *Tarleton State*. Email: hickman@tarleton.edu.

Hickman, Ellen C., *Robert H. Smith Center*. Email: ehickman@monticello.org.

Hicks, Anasa Samantha, *Florida State*. Email: ahicks@fsu.edu.

Hicks, Cheryl D., *Delaware*. Email: cdhicks@udel.edu.

Hicks, D. Bruce, *Cumberlands*. Email: bruce.hicks@ucumberlands.edu.

Hicks, Hannah Katherine. Nashville, TN. Affil: Vanderbilt. Email: hannah.k.hicks@vanderbilt.edu.

Hicks, Hilarie M. Orange, VA. Affil: James Madison's Montpelier. Email: hhicks@montpelier.org. Research: plantation life, James and Dolley Madison.

Hicks, Lesli Louise, *Texas, San Antonio*. Email: lesli.hicks@utsa.edu.

Hicks, Philip S. Notre Dame, IN. Affil: St. Mary's, Ind. Email: phicks@saintmarys.edu. Research: Catharine Macaulay, Anglo-American political thought.

Hicks Few, Maria L., *North Carolina A&T State*. Email: mlhicks@ncat.edu.

Hidalgo, Alexander, *Texas Christian*. Email: a.hidalgo@tcu.edu.

Hier, Charles B., *Duquesne*. Email: hierc@duq.edu.

Higbee, Mark D., *Eastern Michigan*. Ypsilanti, MI. Email: mhigbee@emich.edu. Research: scholarship of teaching and learning, civil rights movement.

Higbie, Frank Tobias, *UCLA*. Email: higbie@history.ucla.edu.

Higginbotham, Ann R., *Eastern Connecticut State*. Email: higginbotham@easternct.edu.

Higginbotham, Evelyn Brooks, *Harvard (Hist.)*. Auburndale, MA. Email: ebhiggin@fas.harvard.edu. Research: memoirs of A. Leon Higginbotham Jr., race and citizenship.

Higgins, Amanda Leigh, *Kentucky Hist. Soc.* Email: amanda.higgins@ky.gov.

Higgins, Claire. Sydney, Australia. Affil: New South Wales. Email: c.higgins@unsw.edu.au.

Higgins, Padhraig. Philadelphia, PA. Affil: Mercer County Comm. Coll. Email: higginsp@mccc.edu. Research: 18th-c Irish political culture, urban poor in Dublin.

Higginson, John Edward, *Massachusetts, Amherst*. Email: jeh@history.umass.edu.

High, Douglas. Frankfort, KY. Affil: Kentucky Hist. Soc. Email: doug.high@ky.gov.

High, Steven, *Concordia, Can*. Email: Steven.High@concordia.ca.

Higham, Carol Alexander, *North Carolina, Charlotte*. Email: ahigham@uncc.edu.

Highsmith, Andrew Robert, *California, Irvine*.

Hightower, Victoria P., *North Georgia*. Email: victoria.hightower@ung.edu.

Hightower, W. Patrick, *North Georgia*. Email: patrick.hightower@ung.edu.

Higonnet, Patrice Louis-Rene, *Harvard (Hist.)*. Email: higonnet@fas.harvard.edu.

Higuchi, Toshihiro, *Georgetown*. Email: th233@georgetown.edu.

Hijar, Katherine, *California State, San Marcos*. Email: khijar@csusm.edu.

Hijiya, James. South Dartmouth, MA. Email: jhijiya@comcast.net. Research: US in 1960s, American Liberal tradition.

Hijmans, Steven E., *Alberta*. Email: shijmans@ualberta.ca.

Hild, Matthew. Atlanta, GA. Affil: Georgia Inst. of Tech. Email: matt77b@gmail.com.

Hilde, Libra R., *San José State*. Email: Libra.Hilde@sjsu.edu.

Hildebrand, Reginald F. Durham, NC. Affil: Durham Tech. Comm. Coll. Email: hildebrandr@durhamtech.edu. Research: American South.

Hildner, Jacob. Chicago, IL. Email: jhildner@oprfhs.org.

Hildreth, Martha L., *Nevada, Reno*. Email: hildreth@unr.edu.

Hilgendorff, Sally. Reading, MA. Email: smhilgendorff27@juno.com. Research: 13th New Jersey Volunteer Infantry, veterans' experiences upon war's return.

Hilken, Charles A., *St. Mary's, Calif.* Moraga, CA. Email: chilken@stmarys-ca.edu. Research: south Italian necrologies, medieval Benedictine chapter room.

Hill, Alexander A., *Calgary*. Email: hilla@ucalgary.ca.

Hill, Ben. Vancouver, BC, Canada. Email: ben_hill@hotmail.com.

Hill, Bracy V., II, *Baylor*. Email: bracy_hill@baylor.edu.

Hill, Christopher L. New York, NY. Affil: Michigan. Email: clhill.mail@gmail.com. Research: nationalism and nationality, social thought.

Hill, Christopher V., *Colorado Colorado Springs*. Email: chill@uccs.edu.

Hill, Corinna Sara. Rochester, NY. Affil: Rochester. Email: corinnasara@gmail.com. Research: gender, disability.

Hill, Emily Miriam, *Queen's, Can*. Email: hillem@queensu.ca.

Hill, Franklin, *Washington State, Pullman*. Email: fhill002@wsu.edu.

Hill, James L. Starkville, MS. Affil: Pittsburgh. Email: james.hill@pitt.edu.

Hill, Jenna, *Hist. Assoc.* Email: jhill@historyassociates.com.

Hill, John L., *Concordia, Can*.

Hill, Joshua Benjamin, *Ohio*. Athens, OH. Email: hillj6@ohio.edu; joshuabhill@aya.yale.edu.

Hill, Kevin D., *Iowa State*. Email: kdhill@iastate.edu.

Hill, Kimberly D. Richardson, TX. Affil: Texas, Dallas. Email: hill.kim@gmail.com. Research: US Protestant foreign missions, US race relations.

Hill, Lamar M., *California, Irvine*. Email: lmhill@uci.edu.

Hill, Lance, *Tulane*. Email: lhill@tulane.edu.

Hill, Marvin S., *Brigham Young*.

Hill, Patricia Evridge, *San José State*. Email: Patricia.Hill@sjsu.edu.

Hill, Patricia R., *Wesleyan*. Email: phill@wesleyan.edu.

Hill, Peter P., *George Washington*. Email: pphill@gwu.edu.

Hill, Robert A., *UCLA*. Email: rhill@history.ucla.edu.

Hill, Ruth Edmonds, *Arthur and Elizabeth Schlesinger Library*. Email: ruth_hill@radcliffe.harvard.edu.

Hill, Susan, *Toronto*. Email: susan.hill@utoronto.ca.

Hill, Zach. San Diego, CA. Affil: California, San Diego. Email: wzhill@ucsd.edu.

Hill Edwards, Justene G., *Virginia*. Email: jgh7d@virginia.edu.

Hiller, James K., *Memorial, Newfoundland*. Email: jhiller@mun.ca.

Hilliard, Constance Bernette, *North Texas*. Email: connie@unt.edu.

Hilliard, Kathleen M., *Iowa State*. Ames, IA. Email: khilliar@iastate.edu. Research: slavery, antebellum US South.

Hilliard, Paul C. Mundelein, IL. Affil: St. Mary of the Lake. Email: philliard@cantab.net. Research: early medieval biblical exegesis, Bede.

Hillis, Faith C., *Chicago*. Chicago, IL. Email: hillis@uchicago.edu; faith.hillis@gmail.com. Research: late imperial Russia/19th-c eastern Europe.

Hillje, John. New Braunfels, TX. Affil: Rider. Email: hillje@rider.edu.

Hillman, Susanne, *San Diego State*.

Hillmer, G. Norman, *Carleton, Can*. Email: norman.hillmer@carleton.ca.

Hillyer, Reiko, *Lewis & Clark*. Email: rhillyer@lclark.edu.

Hiltebeitel, Alf, *George Washington*. Email: beitel@gwu.edu.

Hilton, Laura J. New Concord, OH. Affil: Muskingum. Email: lhilton@muskingum.edu. Research: displaced persons and refugees, identity and nationality.

Hilton, Marjorie L., *Murray State*. Email: mhilton@murraystate.edu.

Hilton, Stanley, *Louisiana State*.

Hiltpold, Paul J., *California Polytechnic State.* Email: philtpol@calpoly.edu.

Hilts, Victor L., *Wisconsin-Madison.* Email: vlhilts@wisc.edu.

Hime, Douglas N., *Naval War Coll.* Email: himed@usnwc.edu.

Himebaugh, Brian A. Lima, OH. Affil: Ohio State, Lima. Email: himebaugh.3@osu.edu.

Himka, John-Paul, *Alberta.* Email: jhimka@ualberta.ca.

Himmelberg, Robert F., *Fordham.* Email: himmelberg@fordham.edu.

Himmelfarb, Gertrude, *Graduate Center, CUNY.* Washington, DC. Email: Ghimn@aol.com. Research: intellectual, Europe.

Himmerich y Valencia, Robert, *New Mexico.*

Hinchen, Dan, *Massachusetts Hist. Soc.* Email: dhinchen@masshist.org.

Hinderaker, Eric, *Utah.* Salt Lake City, UT. Email: eric.hinderaker@utah.edu. Research: politics of memory, comparative colonization.

Hinderliter, Jillian Michele. Columbia, SC. Affil: South Carolina, Columbia. Email: hinderlj@email.sc.edu. Research: Jewish women, Health activism.

Hindle, Steve, *Huntington Library.* San Marino, CA. Email: shindle@huntington.org. Research: labour markets, estate management.

Hindmarch-Watson, Katie A., *Johns Hopkins (Hist.).* Email: katie.hw@jhu.edu.

Hinds, Wayne L. Turlock, CA. Email: whinds43@hotmail.com.

Hindson, Irene L., *Texas State.* Email: ih01@txstate.edu.

Hine, Darlene Clark, *Northwestern.* Email: d-hine@northwestern.edu.

Hinely, Susan D., *SUNY, Stony Brook.* Setauket, NY. Email: susan.hinely@stonybrook.edu. Research: modern Europe, political theory.

Hines, Alisha, *Wake Forest.* Durham, NC. Email: hinesaj@wfu.edu; alisha.hines@gmail.com. Research: 19th-c US, slavery.

Hines, Kelley, *Hist. New Orleans.* Email: kelleyh@hnoc.org.

Hines, Robert R. San Antonio, TX. Affil: Palo Alto. Email: rhines@alamo.edu.

Hines, Sarah Thompson, *Oklahoma (Hist.).* Norman, OK. Email: sarahthines@ou.edu. Research: Bolivia, environmental.

Hines, Thomas S., *Jr.*, *UCLA.* Email: hines@history.ucla.edu.

Hingson, Jesse, *Jacksonville.* Jacksonville, FL. Email: jhingso@ju.edu. Research: family and gender, political culture.

Hinnershitz, Stephanie Dawn, *Cleveland State; US Military Acad.* Email: s.hinnershitz@csuohio.edu; stephanie.hinnershitz@usma.edu.

Hinojosa, Felipe, *Texas A&M.* College Station, TX. Email: fhinojosa@tamu.edu. Research: Latino/Chicano race/ethnicity/gender, religion/evangelicals.

Hinrichs, TJ, *Cornell.* Ithaca, NY. Email: th289@cornell.edu; hinrichs@post.harvard.edu. Research: Sung Dynasty responses to epidemics, Sung Dynasty uses of medical knowledge.

Hinther, Rhonda, *Brandon; Carleton, Can.* Email: hintherr@brandonu.ca; rhonda.hinther@carleton.ca.

Hinton, Diana Davids, *Texas, Permian Basin.* Email: hinton_d@utpb.edu.

Hinton, Elizabeth Kai, *Harvard (Hist.).* Email: ehinton@fas.harvard.edu.

Hinton, Paula K., *Tennessee Tech.* Cookeville, TN. Email: phinton@tntech.edu. Research: crime in America, nursing.

Hirano, Katsuya, *UCLA.* Los Angeles, CA. Email: hirano@history.ucla.edu. Research: power and popular culture, capitalism and subject formation.

Hirota, Hidetaka. Tokyo, Japan. Affil: Waseda. Email: hidetakahirota@aoni.waseda.jp. Research: 19th-c US, American immigration.

Hirsch, Francine, *Wisconsin-Madison.* Madison, WI. Email: fhirsch@wisc.edu. Research: Soviet international law, Soviet nationality policy.

Hirsch, Gerald, *State Hist. Soc. of Missouri.* Email: hirschg@shsmo.org.

Hirsch, Jerrold M., *Truman State.* Email: jhirsch@truman.edu.

Hirsch, Steven J. Saint Louis, MO. Affil: Washington, St. Louis. Email: sjhirsch@wustl.edu. Research: Latin American/Peru anarchism, Latin American populism/Peru's APRA.

Hirsch, Susan E., *Loyola, Chicago.* Email: shirsch@luc.edu.

Hirschfield, John M., *St. Mary's, Md.*

Hirschmann, Edwin, *Towson.* Cockeysville, MD. Email: ehirschmann@verizon.net; eahirschmann@yahoo.com. Research: British press in India, Viceroy Robert Lytton.

Hirsh, Richard F., *Virginia Tech.* Email: richards@vt.edu.

Hirst, Derek M., *Washington, St. Louis.* Email: dmhirst@wustl.edu.

Hirt, Paul W., *Arizona State.* Email: paul.hirt@asu.edu.

Hise, Greg, *Nevada, Las Vegas.* Email: hise@unlv.edu.

Hitchcock, James F., *St. Louis.* Email: hitchcpj@slu.edu.

Hitchcock, William I., *Virginia.* Email: hitch@virginia.edu.

Hitchins, Keith A., *Illinois, Urbana-Champaign.* Email: khitchin@illinois.edu.

Hite, Kerry E., *US Dept. of State.*

Hitz, Elizabeth, *Wisconsin-Milwaukee.* Email: ehitz@uwm.edu.

Hitz, John R. New York, NY. Email: evhitz@gmail.com.

Ho, Angela, *George Mason.* Email: aho5@gmu.edu.

Ho, Chi Fung. Iowa City, IA. Affil: Iowa. Email: Chifung-ho@uiowa.edu.

Ho, Colleen C., *Maryland, Coll. Park.* Email: coho@umd.edu.

Ho, Dahpon D., *Rochester.* Email: dho2@mail.rochester.edu.

Ho, Denise Y., *Yale.* New Haven, CT. Email: denise.ho@yale.edu. Research: cultural relics, museums and monuments.

Ho, Hon-Wai. Nankang, Taipei, Taiwan. Affil: Inst. of Hist. & Philosophy. Email: a525.b423@msa.hinet.net.

Ho, Joseph W., *Albion.* Albion, MI. Email: jwho@umich.edu. Research: photography/visual culture, transnational/global.

Hoag, Heather Jane, *San Francisco.* Email: hjhoag@usfca.edu.

Hoak, Dale E., *William and Mary.* Email: dehoak@wm.edu.

Hoang, Linh. Loudonville, NY. Affil: Siena. Email: lhoang@siena.edu. Research: Asian American Catholics, race and religion.

Hobbins, Daniel, *Notre Dame.* Email: dhobbins@nd.edu.

Hobbs, Allyson Vanessa, *Stanford.* Email: ahobbs@stanford.edu.

Hobbs, Robert Michael. Hawthorne, CA. Email: robohobbs@gmail.com.

Hobbs, Troy. Midland, TX. Affil: Texas, Permian Basin. Email: Troy79705@gmail.com.

Hoberman, Louisa S. Austin, TX. Email: lshoberman@att.net.

Hobson, Aimee Suzanne. Soquel, CA. Affil: Adams State. Email: aimeesue@sbcglobal.net. Research: Annales School impact in US.

Hobson, Charles F., *William and Mary.* Email: cfhobs@wm.edu.

Hobson, Emily K., *Nevada, Reno; Committee on LGBT Hist.* Reno, NV. Email: ehobson@unr.edu. Research: LGBTQ and HIV/AIDS activism 1970s-90s, US prison activism 1970s-90s.

Hobson, Julius W., *Jr.* Washington, DC. Affil: George Washington. Email: julius.hobson@verizon.net. Research: US Congress.

Hoch, Steven L., *Washington State, Pullman.* Richland, WA. Email: steven-hoch@wsu.edu. Research: modern Russia, European agrarian.

Hochfelder, David, *SUNY, Albany.* Albany, NY. Email: dhochfelder@albany.edu. Research: US technology, public and business.

Hochman, Erin R., *Southern Methodist.* Email: ehochman@smu.edu.

Hochman, Steven H., *Emory.* Atlanta, GA. Affil: Carter Center. Email: shochma@emory.edu. Research: American presidents, American presidency.

Hochschild, Jennifer L. Cambridge, MA. Affil: Harvard. Email: hochschild@gov.harvard.edu. Research: American race and ethnic relations, education policy and politics.

Hockenos, Matthew D., *Skidmore.* Email: mhockeno@skidmore.edu.

Hocter, Keith. South Orange, NJ. Affil: Bellwether Consulting. Email: keith.hocter@bellwetherconsulting.net.

Hodapp, Christopher. Indianapolis, IN. Affil: Journal of the Masonic Soc. Email: hodapp@aol.com.

Hodas, Mike. Sun City West, AZ. Email: mikelaurieh2@gmail.com. Research: William D. Kelley, Robert M. La Follette Sr.

Hodes, Martha, *NYU.* New York, NY. Email: martha.hodes@nyu.edu. Research: 19th-c US, race/Civil War/Reconstruction.

Hodge, Adam R., *Lourdes.* Sylvania, OH. Email: ahodge@lourdes.edu. Research: US to 1865, environmental.

Hodge, Bob, *Beloit.* Email: hodgeb@beloit.edu.

Hodge, Joseph M., *West Virginia.* Email: Joseph.Hodge@mail.wvu.edu.

Hodge, Shannon, *Carleton, Can.* Email: shannon.hodge@carleton.ca.

Hodges, Adam J., *Houston-Clear Lake.* Email: hodgesaj@uhcl.edu.

Hodges, Graham R., *Colgate.* Email: ghodges@colgate.edu.

Hodges, James A., *Wooster.* Email: jhodges@wooster.edu.

Hodges, Lybeth, *Texas Woman's.* Email: lhodges@twu.edu.

Hodges, Norman E., *Vassar.*

Hodgins, Bruce W., *Trent.*

Hodgkinson, Rebekah Naomi. York, United Kingdom. Affil: Warwick. Email: rnhodgkinson@gmail.com.

Hodgman, Laura S., *Eastern Washington*. Email: lhodgman@ewu.edu.

Hodgson, Jessica R. Arlington, VA. Affil: Fairfax High Sch. Email: jrhodgson@fcps.edu.

Hodson, Christopher G., *Brigham Young*. Provo, UT. Email: chris_hodson@byu.edu. Research: French Atlantic.

Hoeflich, Michael H., *Kansas*. Email: hoeflich@ku.edu.

Hoefte, Rosemarijn. Leiden, Netherlands. Affil: KITLV. Email: hofte@kitlv.nl. Research: 20th-c Suriname social/cultural, Suriname sports.

Hoehn, Maria, *Vassar*. Email: mahoehn@vassar.edu.

Hoel, Nikolas, *Northeastern Illinois*. Email: N-Hoel@neiu.edu.

Hoenicke Moore, Michaela M., *Iowa*. Iowa City, IA. Email: michaela-hoenicke-moore@uiowa.edu. Research: American nationalism, 20th-c US foreign policy.

Hoenig, John M. Denton, TX. Affil: Texas Woman's. Email: jhoenig@gmail.com. Research: consumerism and environment, railroads/West/consumer goods.

Hoeveler, J. David, Jr., *Wisconsin-Milwaukee*. Milwaukee, WI. Email: jdh2@uwm.edu. Research: John Bascom, Darwin in America.

Hoffecker, Carol E., *Delaware*.

Hoffenberg, Peter H., *Hawai'i, Manoa*. Email: peterh@hawaii.edu.

Hoffer, Peter C., *Georgia*. Athens, GA. Email: pchoffer@uga.edu. Research: early America, legal.

Hoffer, Williamjames Hull, *Seton Hall*. South Orange, NJ. Email: williamjames.hoffer@shu.edu. Research: development of US national state, bureaucracy in public and private life.

Hoffert, Brian, *North Central*. Email: bhoffert@noctrl.edu.

Hoffman, Beatrix R., *Northern Illinois*. Dekalb, IL. Email: beatrix@niu.edu. Research: human right to health care.

Hoffman, Colin Spencer. Rancho Cordova, CA. Email: colinshoffman@gmail.com. Research: German-American Bund in California, California vs. Robert Noble et al.

Hoffman, Matthew, *Franklin & Marshall*. Email: matthew.hoffman@fandm.edu.

Hoffman, Paul E., *Louisiana State*. Baton Rouge, LA. Email: hyhoff@lsu.edu. Research: Spanish Florida and Louisiana, Louisiana State Univ.

Hoffman, Philip T., *California Inst. of Tech*. Email: pth@hss.caltech.edu.

Hoffman, Steven J. Cape Girardeau, MO. Affil: Southeast Missouri State. Email: shoffman@semo.edu. Research: African American community building, urban.

Hoffman, Zachary Adam. Charlottesville, VA. Affil: Virginia. Email: zah3pn@virginia.edu. Research: imperial Russia, popular culture.

Hoffmann, David L., *Ohio State*. Email: hoffmann.218@osu.edu.

Hoffmann, Peter C., *McGill*. Email: peter.hoffmann@mcgill.ca.

Hoffmann, Richard C. King City, ON, Canada. Affil: York, Can. Email: medfish@yorku.ca. Research: preindustrial environments and economies, fisheries in medieval Europe.

Hoffmann, Stefan-Ludwig, *California, Berkeley*. Email: slhoffmann@berkeley.edu.

Hoffnung-Garskof, Jesse, *Michigan, Ann Arbor*. Email: jessehg@umich.edu.

Hoffschwelle, Mary S., *Middle Tennessee State*. Email: Mary.Hoffschwelle@mtsu.edu.

Hofmann, Julie A. Winchester, VA. Affil: Shenandoah. Email: jhofmann@su.edu. Research: eastern Carolingian social groups, women and property in Eastern Francia.

Hofmann, Reto. Tokyo, Japan. Affil: Waseda. Email: retohofmann01@gmail.com.

Hofsommer, Don L., *St. Cloud State*. Saint Cloud, MN. Email: dlhofsommer@stcloudstate.edu. Research: public, Minnesota.

Hogan, Andrew J., *Creighton*. Email: andrewhogan@creighton.edu.

Hogan, Heather, *Oberlin*. Email: heather.hogan@oberlin.edu.

Hogan, Michael J., *Illinois, Springfield; Ohio State*. Columbus, OH. Email: hogan.5@osu.edu; michaeljhogan12@gmail.com. Research: American diplomatic, recent US.

Hogan, Michael Robert. Morgantown, WV. Affil: West Virginia. Email: mrh0024@mix.wvu.edu.

Hogan, Michael. Laredo, TX. Email: michael.hogan@asfg.edu.mx.

Hoganson, Kristin L., *Illinois, Urbana-Champaign; Soc. for Hist. of American Foreign Relations*. Urbana, IL. Email: hoganson@illinois.edu. Research: globalization/transnational/world/empire, agriculture/trade/migration/postcolonial.

Hogarth, Rana, *Illinois, Urbana-Champaign*. Champaign, IL. Email: rhogarth@illinois.edu; rana.hogarth@gmail.com. Research: African American, medicine.

Hogg, Kevin. Cranbrook, BC, Canada. Affil: Mount Baker Secondary Sch. Email: kdohogg@gmail.com.

Hoglund, Sarah L. Garden City, ID. Affil: SUNY, Stony Brook. Email: Slhoglund@gmail.com.

Hogue, Gina, *Arkansas State*. Email: ghogue@astate.edu.

Hogue, James Keith, *North Carolina, Charlotte*. Email: jhogue@uncc.edu.

Hogue, Michel, *Carleton, Can*. Email: michel.hogue@carleton.ca.

Hogue, William Curtis, III. New York, NY. Affil: Fordham. Email: whogue@fordham.edu.

Hohenstein, Kurt A. Homer, NE. Email: khohey@yahoo.com.

Hohl, Elizabeth, *Fairfield*. Riverside, CT. Email: ehohl@fairfield.edu; lizhohl@hotmail.com. Research: new Negro woman 1890-1930, social justice movements.

Hohlfelder, Bob, *Colorado, Boulder*. Email: robert.hohlfelder@colorado.edu.

Hoidal, Oddvar K., *San Diego State*. San Diego, CA. Email: hoidal@mail.sdsu.edu. Research: Scandinavia and the two world wars, Post-1945 Scandinavia.

Hoisington, William A., Jr., *Illinois, Chicago*. Email: williamh@uic.edu.

Holbo, Paul S., *Oregon*. Eugene, OR. Email: pholbo@oregon.uoregon.edu. Research: scandal and foreign policy, Truman and Cold War.

Holbrook, Catherine, *Arthur and Elizabeth Schlesinger Library*. Email: cholbroo@radcliffe.harvard.edu.

Holbrook, Daniel U., *Marshall*. Email: holbrook@marshall.edu.

Holbrook, Joseph W., *Florida International*. Email: jholbroo@fiu.edu.

Holc, Janine P. Baltimore, MD. Affil: Loyola, Md. Email: jholc@loyola.edu. Research: gender and culture, political institutions.

Holcombe, Alec, *Ohio*. Email: holcombe@ohio.edu.

Holcombe, Charles W., *Northern Iowa*. Email: charles.holcombe@uni.edu.

Holden, Charles J., *St. Mary's, Md*. Email: cjholden@smcm.edu.

Holden, Christine. Lewiston, ME. Affil: Southern Maine. Email: holden@maine.edu. Research: Ravensbrueck Mahn-und Gedenkstaette, American Intervention in Russian North.

Holden, David W., *US Army Command Coll*. Email: david.w.holden.civ@mail.mil.

Holden, Robert H., *Old Dominion*. Email: rholden@odu.edu.

Holden, Stacy E., *Purdue*. West Lafayette, IN. Email: sholden@purdue.edu. Research: colonial urbanism, historic preservation.

Holden, Vanessa M., *Kentucky*. Email: vanessa.holden@uky.edu.

Holder, Calvin B., *Staten Island, CUNY*. Email: calvin.holder@csi.cuny.edu.

Holdzkom, Marianne, *Kennesaw State*. Email: mholdzko@kennesaw.edu.

Holguin, Sandie E., *Oklahoma (Hist.)*. Norman, OK. Email: sholguin@ou.edu. Research: nationalism and Spain, flamenco.

Holian, Anna, *Arizona State*. Email: anna.holian@asu.edu.

Holl, Jack M., *Kansas State*. Email: jackholl@ksu.edu.

Holl, Shawn A., *Omohundro Inst*. Email: saholl@wm.edu.

Holland, Jennifer Louise, *Oklahoma (Hist.)*. Email: jennifer.holland@ou.edu.

Holland, Karen A., *Providence*. Email: kholland@providence.edu.

Holland, Robert M., *Henry Ford Coll*.

Holland, Samantha, *Center for Hist. of Physics*. Email: sholland@aip.org.

Hollander, Craig Benjamin, *New Jersey*.

Hollander, David B., *Iowa State*. Email: dbh8@iastate.edu.

Hollander, Katherine. Somerville, MA. Affil: Simmons. Email: katherine.hollander@simmons.edu; kah@marlboro.edu. Research: European women and gender, modern Germany.

Hollander, Nancy Caro, *California State, Dominguez Hills*.

Holle, Bruce F., *Kentucky*. Email: bholl2@uky.edu.

Hollenback, Jess B., *Wisconsin-La Crosse*. La Crosse, WI. Email: hollenba.jess@uwlax.edu; jesshollenback@gmail.com. Research: world religions, mysticism.

Holler, Jacqueline S., *Northern British Columbia*. Email: holler@unbc.ca.

Holliday, Vivian L., *Wooster*. Email: vholliday@wooster.edu.

Holliday, William C., Jr., *Longwood*. Email: hollidaywc@longwood.edu.

Holliman Way, Irene, *Kennesaw State*. Email: iway@kennesaw.edu.

Hollinger, David A. Berkeley, CA. Affil: California, Berkeley. Email: davidhol@berkeley.edu. Research: Protestant missionaries, census categories.

Hollingsworth, J. Rogers, *Wisconsin-Madison*. Email: hollingsjr@aol.com.

AHA members in **bold italic**; Directory-listed affiliations in *italic*

Hollins, Nathan. Arlington, TX. Email: nhollins96@gmail.com.

Hollis, Sylvea. Arlington, VA. Affil: National Park Service. Email: sylvea.hollis@gmail.com.

Hollon, Cory S. Prattville, AL. Affil: Air War. Email: cshollon@gmail.com.

Holloran, Peter C., *Worcester State*. Email: pholloran@worcester.edu.

Holloway, Anna Gibson. Alexandria, VA. Affil: SEARCH, Inc. Email: anna.holloway@searchinc.com. Research: Civil War ironclads/USS Monitor, 19th-c maritime salvage.

Holloway, David, *Stanford*. Email: david.holloway@stanford.edu.

Holloway, Jonathan Scott. Evanston, IL. Affil: Northwestern. Email: jonathan.holloway@northwestern.edu. Research: black politics after WWII, cultural studies.

Holloway, Kenneth William, *Florida Atlantic*. Email: khollow4@fau.edu.

Holloway, Pippa E., *Middle Tennessee State; Richmond*. Email: Pippa.Holloway@mtsu.edu.

Holloway, Thomas H., *California, Davis*. Email: thholloway@ucdavis.edu.

Holly, Nathaniel. Chesnee, SC. Affil: William and Mary. Email: nfholly@email.wm.edu. Research: urban places in colonial America, Southeastern American Indians.

Holly, Susan K., *US Dept. of State*.

Holly, William C. Tempe, AZ. Affil: Arizona State. Email: william.holly@asu.edu. Research: cultural, US since 1970.

Hollywood, Mary, *Illinois State*. Email: meholly@ilstu.edu.

Holm, April E., *Mississippi*. University, MS. Email: aholm@olemiss.edu. Research: sectionalism and evangelicalism, border states in 19th-c US.

Holmes, Blair R., *Brigham Young*. Email: blair_holmes@byu.edu.

Holmes, Chad. Morgantown, WV. Affil: West Virginia. Email: crholmes@mix.wvu.edu.

Holmes, Erin Marie. Philadelphia, PA. Affil: American Philosophical Soc. Email: holmese6@email.sc.edu. Research: comparative studies of plantation culture, colonial Virginia and Carolinas/Atlantic.

Holmes, James, *Naval War Coll*. Email: james.holmes@usnwc.edu.

Holmes, John Dewey. Oakland, CA. Affil: Merritt. Email: jdholmes@igc.org. Research: Russian Revolution and American Communism, Soviet Union and Stalinism.

Holmes, Larry E., *South Alabama*.

Holmes, Oliver W., *Wesleyan*. Email: oholmes@wesleyan.edu.

Holmgren, Derek John, *Wake Forest*. Email: holmgrdj@wfu.edu.

Holmlund, Mona, *Dalhousie*.

Holness, Lucien, *Virginia Tech*.

Holo, Joshua David, *California, Berkeley*. Email: jholo@huc.edu.

Holowicki, Alex, *San Diego Mesa*. Email: aholowicki@sdccd.edu.

Holquist, Peter I., *Pennsylvania*. Philadelphia, PA. Email: holquist@sas.upenn.edu. Research: 19th-c international law of war, Russian politics and society 1860-1929.

Holscher, Kathleen, *American Catholic Hist. Assoc*. Corrales, NM. Affil: New Mexico. Email: kholscher@unm.edu.

Holsinger, Janet L., *Hist. Assoc*. Email: jholsinger@historyassociates.com.

Holstein, Diego, *Pittsburgh*. Email: holstein@pitt.edu.

Holt, Daniel, *US Senate Hist. Office*. Email: daniel_holt@sec.senate.gov.

Holt, Edward. Ruston, LA. Affil: Grambling State. Email: holte@gram.edu. Research: kingship, political theology and liturgy.

Holt, Frank Lee, *Houston*. Houston, TX. Email: fholt@uh.edu. Research: ancient, Greece and Rome.

Holt, Katherine, *Wooster*. Wooster, OH. Email: kholt@wooster.edu. Research: Latin America.

Holt, Mack P., *George Mason*. Woodbridge, VA. Email: mholt@gmu.edu. Research: popular religion and politics, Reformation and wars of religion.

Holt, Michael F., *Virginia*. Email: mfh6p@virginia.edu.

Holt, Thomas C., *Chicago*. Chicago, IL. Email: tholt@uchicago.edu. Research: 19th-c US southern political, Reconstruction.

Holter, Darryl Oliver, *Southern California*. Los Angeles, CA. Affil: Shammas Group. Email: dholter@usc.edu; dholter@shammasgroup.com. Research: business and labor relations, Woody Guthrie.

Holter, Howard R., *California State, Dominguez Hills*. Email: hholter@csudh.edu.

Holton, Abner L., III, *South Carolina, Columbia*. Columbia, SC. Email: holton@sc.edu. Research: origins of US Constitution, blacks in Revolutionary War.

Holton, Gerald, *Harvard (Hist. of Science)*. Email: holton@physics.harvard.edu.

Holtz, Tim, *Gerald Ford Presidential Library*. Email: tim.holtz@nara.gov.

Holyfield, Stephanie L. Dover, DE. Affil: Wesley. Email: shfield@udel.edu.

Holzhausen, Lucas. Almere, Netherlands. Email: lucaz.h@hotmail.com.

Holzman, MayaLisa. Bend, OR. Affil: Oregon State, Cascades. Email: holzmama@oregonstate.edu. Research: Soviet partisan movement/Komsomol, WWII German-occupied eastern Europe.

Homans, Jennifer, *NYU*. Email: jah20@nyu.edu.

Homberger, Torsten, *Nebraska, Kearney*. Email: hombergert@unk.edu.

Homer, Frank X. J., *Scranton*. Scranton, PA. Email: frankx.homer@scranton.edu. Research: modern Europe/England, European diplomatic.

Hommerding, Christopher. Minneapolis, MN. Email: Cjhommerding@gmail.com.

Hommon, William S., *Central Connecticut State*. Email: hommonbill@comcast.net.

Homsey, James Douglas. Silver Spring, MD. Email: jameshomsey@gmail.com.

Homza, LuAnn, *William and Mary*. Email: lahomz@wm.edu.

Hon, Tze-Ki, *SUNY, Coll. Geneseo*. Hong Kong. Affil: City, Hong Kong. Email: hon@geneseo.edu; t.k.hon@cityu.edu.hk. Research: modern Chinese historiography, Yijing/Book of Changes.

Hong, E. K., *Soc. of Cincinnati*. Email: ekhong@societyofthecincinnati.org.

Hong, Jane H., *Occidental*. Email: janehong@oxy.edu.

Hong, Young-Sun, *SUNY, Stony Brook*. Email: young-sun.hong@stonybrook.edu.

Honhart, Michael W., *Rhode Island*. Email: honhart@uri.edu.

Honig, Emily, *California, Santa Cruz*. Email: ehonig@ucsc.edu.

Honnen, Mark, *US Air Force Acad*. Email: mark.honnen@usafa.edu.

Hoock, Holger, *Pittsburgh*. Pittsburgh, PA. Email: hoock@pitt.edu. Research: 18th-/19th-c British Empire, violence.

Hood, Adrienne D., *Toronto*. Email: a.hood@utoronto.ca.

Hood, Clifton. Geneva, NY. Affil: Hobart and William Smith. Email: hood@hws.edu. Research: urban, New York City.

Hood, Jonathan D. Murfreesboro, TN. Email: johood1862@gmail.com. Research: military medicine.

Hoogland, Maj Edward, *US Military Acad*. Email: edward.hoogland@usma.edu.

Hooker, Ernest, *North Carolina A&T State*. Email: edhooker@ncat.edu.

Hooper, Cynthia V., *Holy Cross*. Email: chooper@holycross.edu.

Hooper, Jane, *George Mason*. Email: jhooper3@gmu.edu.

Hoose, Adam L., *Troy*. Email: ahoose@troy.edu.

Hoover, John, *Missouri–St. Louis*. Email: hooverj@umsl.edu.

Hoover, Roy, *Minnesota Duluth*.

Hope, Maj Greg, *US Military Acad*. Email: gregory.hope@usma.edu.

Hopkins, Antony G., *Texas, Austin*. Email: tony.hopkins@austin.utexas.edu.

Hopkins, Benjamin D., *George Washington*. Email: bhopkins@gwu.edu.

Hopkins, David P., Jr. Midland, TX. Affil: Midland. Email: dhopkins@midland.edu. Research: Civil War refugees/displacement, trans-Mississippi West.

Hopkins, George E., *Western Illinois*. Email: GE-Hopkins@wiu.edu.

Hopkins, George W., *Charleston*. Email: hopkinsg@cofc.edu.

Hopkins, James K., *Southern Methodist*. Email: hopkins@smu.edu.

Hopkins, Kelly Yvonne, *Houston*. Email: kyhopkins@uh.edu.

Hopkins, Matthew P. Westmoreland, TN. Affil: Sumner County Sch. Email: mphopkins12@gmail.com.

Hopkins, Richard J., *Ohio State*. Email: richard_hopkins@hotmail.com.

Hoppe, Kirk A., *Illinois, Chicago*. Email: kahoppe1@uic.edu.

Hoppens, Robert, *Texas-Rio Grande Valley*. Email: robert.hoppens@utrgv.edu.

Hopper, Matthew S., *California Polytechnic State*. San Luis Obispo, CA. Email: mshopper@calpoly.edu. Research: pearl diving, slavery in Middle East.

Hoppes, Karen E. Lake Oswego, OR. Affil: Lakeridge High Sch. Email: hoppesk@loswego.k12.or.us. Research: US fascism 1930-45.

Horan, Caley D., *MIT*. Email: cdhoran@mit.edu.

Horbinski, Andrea. Berkeley, CA. Affil: California, Berkeley. Email: horbinski@berkeley.edu. Research: modern empire and East Asia, comparative ancient East Asia/Europe.

Hore, Jarrod Ray. Sydney, Australia. Affil: Macquarie. Email: jarrod.hore@mq.edu.au. Research: California environmental, comparative settler colonialism.

Horgan, *John C.* Mequon, WI. Affil: Concordia, Wisc. Email: jhorgan@cuw.edu. Research: food, global epidemics and plagues.

Horlick, *Alan Stuart*. Sandy Springs, GA. Affil: American Public. Email: ahorlick@gmail.com.

Horn, James P. P., *William and Mary*. Email: jhorn@cwf.org.

Horn, Jeff, *Manhattan*. Email: jeff.horn@manhattan.edu.

Horn, Martin, *McMaster*. Email: mhorn@mcmaster.ca.

Horn, Rebecca, *Utah*. Email: rebecca.horn@history.utah.edu.

Hornbuckle, *Adam R.* Spring Hill, TN. Email: adamhornbuckle@bellsouth.net. Research: Olympic Games/track and field, athletes of African heritage.

Horne, Cale, *Covenant*. Email: cale.horne@covenant.edu.

Horne, *Gerald C.*, *Houston*. Email: ghorne@uh.edu.

Horne, Janet R., *Virginia*. Email: jhorne@virginia.edu.

Horner, John Benjamin, *Indianapolis*.

Hornibrook, Jeff, *SUNY, Plattsburgh*. Email: hornibjh@plattsburgh.edu.

Hornsby-Gutting, Angela Mandee, *Missouri State*. Email: ahornsbygutting@missouristate.edu.

Horodowich, Liz, *New Mexico State*. Email: lizh@nmsu.edu.

Horowitz, Andrew, *Tulane*. Email: ahorowitz@tulane.edu.

Horowitz, *Daniel*, *Smith*. Cambridge, MA. Email: dhorowit@smith.edu. Research: US cultural and intellectual.

Horowitz, David A., *Portland State*.

Horowitz, *Helen Lefkowitz*, *Smith*. Cambridge, MA. Email: hhorowit@smith.edu. Research: tourism, culinary.

Horowitz, *Joel*, *St. Bonaventure*. Watertown, MA. Email: jhorowit@sbu.edu. Research: Latin America, Europe.

Horowitz, Maryanne Cline, *Occidental*. Email: horowitz@oxy.edu.

Horowitz, *Richard S.*, *California State, Northridge*. Email: richard.s.horowitz@csun.edu.

Horowitz, *Robert F.* Troy, MI. Email: bobh2@comcast.net. Research: American Jewish, film and history.

Horowitz, *Roger*, *Hagley Museum and Library*. Wilmington, DE. Email: rhorowitz@hagley.org; rh@udel.edu. Research: 20th-c America.

Horowitz, *Sarah E.*, *Washington and Lee*. Email: horowitzs@wlu.edu.

Horrall, Andrew, *Carleton, Can*. Email: andrew.horrall@carleton.ca.

Horrocks, *Thomas A.* Cambridge, MA. Email: thomasahorrocks@gmail.com. Research: 19th-c American print and politics, book in American culture.

Horsman, Reginald, *Wisconsin-Milwaukee*. Email: horsman@uwm.edu.

Horsnell, Margaret E., *American International*.

Horst, Rene D. Harder, *Appalachian State*. Email: horstrh@appstate.edu.

Horstmann-Gatti, Stacey M., *Long Island, Brooklyn*. Email: stacey.horstmann@liu.edu.

Horton, *Aaron Dennis*. Deatsville, AL. Affil: Alabama State. Email: greatsasuke88@hotmail.com. Research: post-1945 Germany, Korean War.

Horton, *Lois*, *George Mason*. Reston, VA. Email: lhorton@gmu.edu. Research: race, civil rights.

Horton, Scott, *SUNY, Buffalo State*. Email: hortons@buffalostate.edu.

Hortua, *Giovanni*, *California State, Los Angeles*. Downey, CA. Affil: Golden West. Email: ghortua@calstatela.edu; giovanni.hortua.vargas@gmail.com. Research: Latin America, US.

Horvath-Peterson, *Sandra*, *Georgetown*. Email: horvaths@georgetown.edu.

Horwitz, Gordon J., *Illinois Wesleyan*. Email: ghorwitz@iwu.edu.

Horwitz, Simonne, *Saskatchewan*. Email: simonne.horwitz@usask.ca.

Hosainy, Hadi, *Texas Christian*. Email: hadi.hosainy@tcu.edu.

Hosansky, *David J.* Louisville, CO. Affil: Nebraska, Kearney. Email: dhosansky@gmail.com.

Hosford, David H., *Rutgers, Newark/New Jersey Inst. of Tech*. Email: dhosford@andromeda.rutgers.edu.

Hoskins, *Danielle*. Iowa City, IA. Affil: Iowa. Email: danielle-hoskins@uiowa.edu.

Hosler, John, *US Army Command Coll*. Email: john.d.hosler.civ@mail.mil.

Hospodor, Gregory Scott, *US Army Command Coll*. Email: gregory.s.hospodor.civ@mail.mil.

Hostetler, *Laura E.*, *Illinois, Chicago*. Chicago, IL. Email: hostetle@uic.edu. Research: China and France 1662-1715, early modern world.

Hostetter, *David*. La Crescenta, CA. Affil: Shepherd. Email: dlhostetter@yahoo.com. Research: peace, African American.

Hotle, *Charles Patrick*. Canton, MO. Affil: Culver-Stockton. Email: photle@culver.edu. Research: Tudor and Stuart Britain, Crusades.

Hou, Xiaojia, *San José State*. Email: xiaojia.hou@sjsu.edu.

Houck, *Andrew*. Poitiers, France. Email: akhouck_fr@yahoo.fr.

Houck, Judith A., *Wisconsin-Madison*. Email: jahouck@wisc.edu.

Hough, Mazie Louise, *Maine, Orono*. Email: hough@maine.edu.

Houlihan, Lynn, *California State, East Bay*.

Houlihan, *Timothy*. Brooklyn, NY. Affil: St. Francis, NY. Email: thoulihan@sfc.edu.

Houpt, David W., *North Carolina, Wilmington*. Email: houptd@uncw.edu.

Hourigan, Richard R., III, *Coastal Carolina*. Email: rhouriga@coastal.edu.

House, *Jonathan M.* Leavenworth, KS. Affil: US Army Command and General Staff Coll. Email: j_house245@hotmail.com. Research: Cold War military operations, Soviet-German conflict.

House, Lewis, *Southern Connecticut State*.

Houser, *Myra Ann*. Arkadelphia, AR. Affil: Ouachita Baptist. Email: myra.ann.houser@gmail.com. Research: southern Africa, legal.

Houser, *Teresa*. Fremont, NE. Affil: Midland. Email: houser@midlandu.edu. Research: Great Plains, WWI era food programs.

Housley, Donald D., *Susquehanna*. Email: housley@susqu.edu.

Housman, *Talya*. Cambridge, MA. Affil: Brown. Email: talya_housman@brown.edu. Research: military, gender.

Houston, Amy, *Leo Baeck Inst*.

Houston, W. Robert, *South Alabama*. Email: whouston@jaguar1.usouthal.edu.

Hovannisian, Richard G., *UCLA*. Email: hovannis@history.ucla.edu.

Hovland, *Ingie*. Athens, GA. Affil: Georgia. Email: ingiehovland@uga.edu.

Hovsepian, Melissa, *Houston-Downtown*. Email: hovsepianm@uhd.edu.

Howard, Adam M., *US Dept. of State*.

Howard, *Allen M.*, *Rutgers*. Piscataway, NJ. Email: ahoward@scarletmail.rutgers.edu. Research: Africa, urban.

Howard, Amy L., *Richmond*. Email: ahoward3@richmond.edu.

Howard, Angela Marie, *Houston-Clear Lake*. Email: howarda@uhcl.edu.

Howard, Ashley M., *Iowa; Loyola, New Orleans*. Email: ashley-howard@uiowa.edu; ahoward2@loyno.edu.

Howard, Clayton Charles, *Ohio State*. Email: howard.1141@osu.edu.

Howard, *David*. Fate, TX. Affil: Texas, Dallas. Email: david.howard01@gmail.com. Research: antebellum abolitionism, religious material culture in South.

Howard, Douglas A., *Calvin*. Email: dhoward@calvin.edu.

Howard, *Hanna M.* Raleigh, NC. Affil: North Carolina State. Email: hmhowar2@ncsu.edu.

Howard, *James Carson*. Henderson, NV. Affil: Nevada, Las Vegas. Email: howarj1@unlv.nevada.edu.

Howard, *Jasmin Chantel*. East Lansing, MI. Affil: Michigan State. Email: howar260@msu.edu. Research: student activism at North Carolina HBCUs, civil rights movements in Texas.

Howard, Joshua H., *Mississippi*. Email: jhhoward@olemiss.edu.

Howard, *Judith J.* Arlington, VA. Affil: NEH. Email: judyjeffreyhoward@gmail.com.

Howard, Kenneth, *North Carolina Office of Archives*. Email: ken.howard@ncdcr.gov.

Howard, *Kristen Coan*. Chapel Hill, NC. Affil: Arizona. Email: krcoan@email.arizona.edu. Research: Reformation Geneva, early modern hospitals and healthcare.

Howard, Martha, *Omohundro Inst*. Email: mxhowa@wm.edu.

Howard, Michael E., *Yale*.

Howard, Nathan Dale, *Tennessee, Martin*. Email: nhoward@utm.edu.

Howard, Philip Anthony, *Houston*. Email: pahoward@uh.edu.

Howard, Thomas C., *Virginia Tech*. Email: tchoward@vt.edu.

Howarth, Whitney E., *Plymouth State*. Email: wbhowarth@plymouth.edu.

Howe, Barbara J., *West Virginia*. Email: bhowe@wvu.edu.

Howe, *Daniel Walker*, *UCLA*. Sherman Oaks, CA. Email: howe@history.ucla.edu. Research: US 1815-48, US religion.

Howe, *John M.*, *Texas Tech*. Lubbock, TX. Email: john.howe@ttu.edu. Research: hagiography, medieval ecclesiastical.

Howe, *John R., Jr.*, *Minnesota (Hist.)*. Saint Paul, MN. Email: howex002@umn.edu. Research: American Revolution/oral discourse, revolutionary American language/politics.

Howe, Joshua, *Reed*. Email: jhowe@reed.edu.

Howe, *Lisa Ann*. Miami, FL. Affil: Florida International. Email: lisa.howe@fiu.edu. Research: 19th-c Spiritualism, Emma Hardinge Britten.

Howe, **Mark Lee**. El Paso, TX. Affil: International Boundary and Water Commission. Email: mlhowe1@hotmail.com. Research: military, International Boundary and Water Comm.

Howe, **Stanley R**. Bethel, ME. Affil: Bethel Hist. Soc. Email: chestan@megalink.net. Research: 19th-c northern New England agriculture, same-sex dynamics in northern New England.

Howe, **Timothy R**., *St. Olaf*. Email: howe@stolaf. edu.

Howell, **Colin D**., *St. Mary's, Can*. Email: colin. howell@smu.ca.

Howell, **David L**. Cambridge, MA. Affil: Harvard. Email: dhowell@fas.harvard.edu. Research: violence and social order in Japan, 17th-19th-c Japan.

Howell, **Jesse**. Somerville, MA. Affil: Harvard. Email: jhowell@fas.harvard.edu.

Howell, **Joel D**., *Michigan, Ann Arbor*. Ann Arbor, MI. Email: jhowell@umich.edu. Research: medical technology, health policy and medical.

Howell, **Jordan**. Cambridge, MA. Affil: Harvard. Email: j_howell@g.harvard.edu.

Howell, **Martha C**., *Columbia (Hist.)*. New York, NY. Email: mch4@columbia.edu. Research: northern European urban 1300-1600, economy/society/law/gender.

Howell, **Ocean**, *Oregon*. Email: ohowell@ uoregon.edu.

Howell, **Sally**. Ann Arbor, MI. Affil: Michigan-Dearborn. Email: sfhowell@umich.edu. Research: Arab American, Muslim American.

Howell, **Stephen H**. Hampden, ME. Email: stephenhowell1@twc.com. Research: US economic, US political party evolution.

Hower, **Jessica S**., *Southwestern*. Email: howerj@ southwestern.edu.

Hower, **Joseph E**., *Southwestern*. Georgetown, TX. Email: howerj2@southwestern.edu. Research: US.

Howerton, **James**, *North Carolina A&T State*. Email: howerton@ncat.edu.

Howes, **Rachel T**., *California State, Northridge*. Northridge, CA. Email: rachel.howes@csun. edu. Research: Fatimid Egypt, Buyid Iran.

Howland, **Douglas R**., *Wisconsin-Milwaukee*. Email: dhowland@uwm.edu.

Howlett, **Charles F**. West Islip, NY. Affil: Molloy. Email: chowlett@molloy.edu. Research: philosophy and history, American education.

Howlett, **Daniel**. North Andover, MA. Affil: George Mason. Email: dhowlett@masonlive. gmu.edu.

Howorth, **Vasser B**., *Hist. New Orleans*. Email: vasserh@hnoc.org.

Howsam, **Leslie**, *Windsor*. Email: lhowsam@ uwindsor.ca.

Hoxha, **Artan**. Pittsburgh, PA. Affil: Pittsburgh. Email: arh99@pitt.edu.

Hoxie, **Frederick E**. Evanston, IL. Affil: Illinois, Urbana-Champaign. Email: FHOXIE@ COMCAST.NET. Research: 20th-c American Indian, race in American culture.

Hoxworth, **Richard Duane**, *Sr*. Waco, TX. Affil: McLennan Comm. Coll. Email: rhoxworth@ mclennan.edu.

Hoy, **Benjamin T. K**., *Saskatchewan*. Email: benjamin.hoy@usask.ca.

Hoye, **Timothy K**., *Texas Woman's*. Email: thoye@ twu.edu.

Hoyer, **Cacee**, *Southern Indiana*. Evansville, IN. Email: choyer@usi.edu; cacee.hoyer@gmail.

com. Research: history education, modern world.

Hoyer, **Randal L**. Livonia, MI. Affil: Madonna. Email: RHoyer@madonna.edu.

Hoyt, **Andrew Douglas**. Upland, CA. Affil: Minnesota, Twin Cities. Email: hoytx059@ umn.edu. Research: transatlantic radical print culture 1871-1940, anarchism and long 19th century.

Hoyt, **Jennifer Tamara**, *Berry*. Email: jhoyt@ berry.edu.

Hoyt, **Timothy D**., *Naval War Coll*. Newport, RI. Email: hoytt@usnwc.edu. Research: Irish Republicanism, strategic thought.

Hrdlicka, **James**. Boston, MA. Affil: Pennsylvania. Email: jfh8ys@virginia.edu.

Hrinko, **Lt Col (ret.) Raymond**, *US Military Acad*. Email: raymond.hrinko@usma.edu.

Hronek, **Pamela**, *Arkansas State*. Email: phronek@astate.edu.

Hruska, **Benjamin J**. Mesa, AZ. Affil: Basis Mesa. Email: bhruska@asu.edu. Research: memory studies, veterans' organizations.

Hsia, **Florence C**., *Wisconsin-Madison*. Email: fchsia@wisc.edu.

Hsia, **Ke-chin**, *Indiana*. Email: khsia@indiana. edu.

Hsia, **Ronnie Po-chia**, *Penn State*. Email: rxh46@ psu.edu.

Hsieh, **Andrew**, *Grinnell*. Email: hsieh@grinnell. edu.

Hsieh, **Bau Hwa**, *Western Oregon*. Email: hsiehb@wou.edu.

Hsieh, **Meiyu**, *Ohio State*. Email: hsieh.230@ osu.edu.

Hsieh, **Winston**, *Missouri–St. Louis*. Email: hsiehw@umsl.edu.

Hsu, **Chia Yin**, *Portland State*. Portland, OR. Email: hsuc@pdx.edu. Research: Money in Russian Manchuria, 1900s race and ethnicity in Russia.

Hsu, **Cho-yun**, *Pittsburgh*. Email: hsusun@ yahoo.com.

Hsu, **Funie**. San Jose, CA. Affil: San Jose State. Email: funie.hsu@sjsu.edu.

Hsu, **Madeline Y**., *Texas, Austin*. Austin, TX. Email: myhsu@mail.utexas.edu. Research: migration and transnationalism, foreign policy and immigration law.

Hu, **Aiqun**, *Arkansas State*. Email: aiqunhu@ astate.edu.

Hu, **Fang Yu**, *Tennessee, Chattanooga*. Chattanooga, TN. Email: fangyu-hu@utc. edu; drfangyuhu@gmail.com. Research: colonialism, gender.

Hu, **Minghui**, *California, Santa Cruz*. Santa Cruz, CA. Email: mhu@ucsc.edu. Research: intellectual and political, early modern China.

Hu, **Ping C**., *California, San Diego*.

Hu, **Yongguang**, *James Madison*. Email: hu2yx@ jmu.edu.

Hua, **Rui**. Cambridge, MA. Affil: Harvard. Email: ruihua@fas.harvard.edu.

Huacuja Alonso, **Isabel**, *California State, San Bernardino*. San Bernardino, CA. Email: iha@ csusb.edu. Research: media studies, empire.

Huang, **Junliang**. Northridge, CA. Affil: California State, Northridge. Email: junliang. huang@csun.edu.

Huang, **Philip C**., *UCLA*. Email: huang@history. ucla.edu.

Huang, **Yanjie**. New York, NY. Affil: Columbia. Email: yh2798@columbia.edu.

Huang, **Yiyun**. Knoxville, TN. Affil: Tennessee, Knoxville. Email: yhuang54@vols.utk.edu.

Huangfu Day, **Jenny**, *Skidmore*. Email: jhuangfu@skidmore.edu.

Hubbard, **Charles M**., *Lincoln Memorial*. Email: charles.hubbard@lmunet.edu.

Hubbard, **Charles**. Portland, OR. Affil: Portland State. Email: charlesrhubbard@msn.com. Research: historical perspectives around 1836, American and Prussian cities.

Hubbard, **Eleanor K**., *Princeton*. Princeton, NJ. Email: ehubbard@princeton.edu. Research: women in early modern London 1570-1640, consumption cultural.

Hubbard, **James Patrick**. Columbia, MD. Email: jphubbard65@gmail.com. Research: post-WWII US/UK policy towards Africa.

Hubbard, **Joshua**, *William and Mary*. Email: jahubbard@wm.edu.

Hubbard, **Paul G**., *Arizona State*.

Hubbell, **John T**., *Kent State*.

Hubbs, **Guy W**., *Birmingham-Southern*. Email: ghubbs@bsc.edu.

Hubby, **Clif**. New York, NY. Affil: NYU. Email: jch3@nyu.edu. Research: Europe 1100-1500, rural society in medieval Germany.

Huber, **Melissa**, *Providence*.

Huber, **Patrick J**., *Missouri Science and Tech*. Email: huberp@mst.edu.

Huber, **Thomas Michael**. Lawrence, KS. Affil: US Army Command and General Staff Coll. Email: lexington1.com@gmail.com. Research: modern strategic organization, French Revolution 1789-1791.

Huberman, **Michael**, *Montréal*. Email: michael. huberman@umontreal.ca.

Hubert, **Ollivier**, *Montréal*. Email: ollivier. hubert@umontreal.ca.

Hubley, **Martin**, *Dalhousie*. Email: hubleym@ gov.ns.ca.

Huch, **Ronald K**., *Eastern Kentucky*. Email: ron. huch@eku.edu.

Huda, **Shamsul**, *Xavier, La.* Email: shuda@xula. edu.

Huddle, **Mark A**., *Georgia Coll. and State*. Email: mark.huddle@gcsu.edu.

Hu-DeHart, **Evelyn**, *Brown*. Email: Evelyn_Hu-Dehart@Brown.edu.

Hudnall, **Amy C**., *Appalachian State*. Email: hudnallac@appstate.edu.

Hudnut-Beumler, **James**, *Vanderbilt*. Email: james.hudnut-beumler@vanderbilt.edu.

Hudon, **William V**., *Bloomsburg*. Bloomsburg, PA. Email: whudon@bloomu.edu. Research: Italian devotional literature, Counter-Reformation.

Hudson, **Angela Pulley**, *Texas A&M*. Email: aphudson@tamu.edu.

Hudson, **Benjamin T**., *Penn State*. Email: bth1@ psu.edu.

Hudson, **David R. C**., *Texas A&M*. Email: david-hudson@tamu.edu.

Hudson, **Hugh D**., *Georgia State*. Email: hhudson@gsu.edu.

Hudson, **Larry E**., *Rochester*. Email: larry. hudson@rochester.edu.

Hudson, **Leonne M**., *Kent State*. Email: lhudson@kent.edu.

Hudson, **Lynn M**., *Illinois, Chicago*. Email: hudsonlm@uic.edu.

Hudson, **Peter James**, *UCLA*. Email: pjhudson@ ucla.edu.

Hudson-Richards, *Julia Anne*, *Duquesne*. Wexford, PA. Email: hudsonrichardsj@duq. edu; juliahudsonrichards@gmail.com. Research: Spanish labor and social relations, food and globalization.

Huebner, *Andrew B*. Denton, TX. Affil: North Texas. Email: andrew.huebner88@gmail.com.

Huebner, *Andrew J*., *Alabama, Tuscaloosa*. Email: ahuebner@bama.ua.edu.

Huebner, *Tim*, *Rhodes*. Memphis, TN. Email: huebner@rhodes.edu. Research: US South, 19th century.

Huener, Jonathan D., *Vermont*. Email: jonathan. huener@uvm.edu.

Huerta, *Sheri A*. Dumfries, VA. Affil: George Mason. Email: shuerta@masonlive.gmu.edu. Research: Virginia slave laws and trials, family and social networks.

Huettl, *Margaret*, *Nebraska, Lincoln*. Email: mhuettl2@unl.edu.

Huezo, Stephanie, *Mount Holyoke*. Email: shuezo@mtholyoke.edu.

Hufbauer, Karl, *California, Irvine*. Email: hufbauer@uci.edu.

Huff, Brad, *Columbus State*. Email: huff_brad@ columbusstate.edu.

Huffaker, Shauna, *Windsor*. Email: huffaker@ uwindsor.ca.

Huffer, Damien, *Carleton, Can*. Email: damien. huffer@carleton.ca.

Huffine, Kristin L., *Northern Illinois*. Email: khuffine@niu.edu.

Huffman, James L., *Wittenberg*. Email: jhuffman@wittenberg.edu.

Huffman, *Joseph P*., *Messiah*. Mechanicsburg, PA. Email: jhuffman@messiah.edu. Research: medieval Germany, medieval England.

Hughes, Barbara, CSJ, *Xavier, La*. Email: bhughes@xula.edu.

Hughes, C. Alvin, *Austin Peay State*. Email: hughesc@apsu.edu.

Hughes, Charles L., *Rhodes*. Email: hughesc@ rhodes.edu.

Hughes, Debra, *Hagley Museum and Library*. Email: dhughes@hagley.org.

Hughes, Diane Owen, *Michigan, Ann Arbor*. Email: dohughes@umich.edu.

Hughes, Jennifer S., *California, Riverside*. Email: jennifer.hughes@ucr.edu.

Hughes, Judith M., *California, San Diego*. Email: jhughes@ucsd.edu.

Hughes, L. Patrick, *Austin Comm. Coll*. Email: lpatrick@austincc.edu.

Hughes, *Marianne*. San Marcos, CA. Affil: California State, San Marcos. Email: hughe049@cougars.csusm.edu.

Hughes, *Michael D*. Denver, CO. Affil: Front Range Comm. Coll. Email: corona0278@gmail. com.

Hughes, *Michael L*., *Wake Forest*. Winston Salem, NC. Email: hughes@wfu.edu. Research: German political demonstrations.

Hughes, *Patricia Louise*. Uckfield, United Kingdom. Affil: Warwick. Email: Petrarch555@ gmail.com. Research: William Butler Yeats, Honor Bright.

Hughes, *Rebecca C*. Seattle, WA. Affil: Seattle Pacific. Email: rebecca.becky.hughes@gmail. com. Research: British missionaries in Africa.

Hughes, *Richard Lowry*, *Illinois State*. Normal, IL. Email: rhughes@ilstu.edu. Research: history education, 20th-c America.

Hughes, Sakina Mariam, *Southern Indiana*. Email: shughes1@usi.edu.

Hughes, *Steven C*., *Loyola, Md*. Golden, CO. Email: schughes@loyola.edu. Research: European social, police.

Hughes, Thomas L., *German Hist. Inst*. Email: thoshughes@aol.com.

Hughes, William, *Southern Oregon*. Email: whughes@sou.edu.

Huhn, *Erich M*. Morris Plains, NJ. Email: erichmhuhn@gmail.com.

Hui, *Alexandra*, *Mississippi State*. Mississippi State, MS. Email: ahui@history.msstate. edu; alixhui@gmail.com. Research: modern Germany, European science and intellectual.

Huibregtse, *Jon R*., *Framingham State*. Email: jhuibregtse@framingham.edu.

Hulbert, Ellerd M., *Western Carolina*.

Hulbert, *Roy Joseph*. Seattle, WA. Affil: Washington, Seattle. Email: royh@ washington.edu.

Hulden, *Vilja*, *Colorado, Boulder*. Boulder, CO. Email: vilja.hulden@colorado.edu. Research: workplace governance in US, digital.

Hull, *Charlotte Sanger*. Redwood City, CA. Affil: Stanford. Email: charlotteshull@stanford.edu.

Hull, *Gary W*., *Baylor*. Email: gary_hull@baylor. edu.

Hull, *Isabel V*., *Cornell*. Ithaca, NY. Email: ivh1@ cornell.edu. Research: Germany.

Hull, Mark M., *US Army Command Coll*. Email: mark.m.hull.civ@mail.mil.

Hull, *Richard W*., *NYU*. Email: richard.hull@nyu. edu.

Hulliung, Mark, *Brandeis*. Email: hulliung@ brandeis.edu.

Hulse, James W., *Nevada, Reno*. Email: jhulse@ unr.edu.

Hulsebosch, Daniel, *NYU*. Email: daniel. hulsebosch@nyu.edu.

Hulsether, Mark, *Tennessee, Knoxville*. Email: mhulseth@utk.edu.

Hume, Doug, *Azusa Pacific*. Email: dhume@apu. edu.

Hume, Laura Hunt, *Dayton*. Email: lhume1@ udayton.edu.

Hume, Richard L., *Washington State, Pullman*. Email: rhume@wsu.edu.

Hummel, *Dan*. Madison, WI. Affil: Wisconsin, Madison. Email: dhummel@wisc.edu.

Hummer, Hans, *Wayne State*. Email: hummer@ wayne.edu.

Humphrey, Thomas J., *Cleveland State*. Email: tom.humphrey@csuohio.edu.

Humphreys, *Debra*. Indianapolis, IN. Affil: Lumina Foundation. Email: dhumphreys@ luminafoundation.org.

Humphreys, *James Scott*, *Murray State*. Email: jhumphreys@murraystate.edu.

Humphreys, *James*. Oakdale, TN. Affil: Roane State Comm. Coll. Email: humphreysjr@ roanestate.edu. Research: native Southeast North America, US independence and early Republic.

Humphreys, *Margaret*, *Duke*. Email: meh@duke. edu.

Humphreys, *R. Stephen*, *California, Santa Barbara*. Santa Barbara, CA. Email: humphreys@history.ucsb.edu. Research: non-Muslims in early Islamic Syria, 8th-10th-c Arabic historiography.

Hunczak, Taras, *Rutgers, Newark/New Jersey Inst. of Tech*. Email: thunczak@andromeda.rutgers. edu.

Hundert, *Gershon David*, *McGill*. Montreal, QC, Canada. Email: gershon.hundert@mcgill.ca. Research: Jews in 18th-c Poland, European Jewish communal records.

Hundley, Helen S., *Wichita State*. Email: helen. hundley@wichita.edu.

Hunefeldt, *Christine*, *California, San Diego*. Email: chunefeldt@ucsd.edu.

Huneke, *Erik Georg*, *Central Oklahoma*. Email: ehuneke@uco.edu.

Huneke, *Samuel Clowes*. Stanford, CA. Affil: Stanford. Email: shuneke@gmu.edu.

Huner, *Michael Kenneth*, *Grand Valley State*. Allendale, MI. Email: hunerm@gvsu.edu. Research: Paraguay religion/state formation, Guarani language.

Huneycutt, Lois L., *Missouri, Columbia*. Email: huneycuttl@missouri.edu.

Hunner, Jon, *New Mexico State*. Email: jhunner@ nmsu.edu.

Hunnicutt, *Loretta Long*, *Pepperdine*. Malibu, CA. Email: loretta.hunnicutt@pepperdine.edu. Research: women's missionary societies.

Hunnicutt, Wendell A., *Texas, Arlington*. Email: hunnicut@uta.edu.

Hunt, Andrew E., *Waterloo*. Email: aehunt@ uwaterloo.ca.

Hunt, Bruce J., *Texas, Austin*. Email: bjhunt@ austin.utexas.edu.

Hunt, *Catalina*, *Kenyon*. Columbus, OH. Email: hunt2@kenyon.edu; hunt.351@buckeyemail. osu.edu. Research: Ottoman Empire, Balkans and southeastern Europe.

Hunt, *D. Bradford*. Chicago, IL. Affil: Newberry Library. Email: huntb@newberry.org. Research: public housing, Chicago.

Hunt, *David*, *Massachusetts, Boston*. Email: david.hunt@umb.edu.

Hunt, *Emily*. Carrollton, GA. Affil: Georgia State. Email: ehunt7@student.gsu.edu.

Hunt, *Harry Haywood*. Kissimmee, FL. Email: hhaywoodhunt@hotmail.com. Research: Edouard Daladier and fall of France, post-WWII America/France/Japan.

Hunt, *John M*., *Utah Valley*. Orem, UT. Email: john.hunt@uvu.edu. Research: early modern Italy, popular culture/gambling/sociability.

Hunt, *Jonathan Reid*. London, United Kingdom. Affil: Southampton. Email: jonreidhunt@gmail.com. Research: global nuclear governance, global environmental governance.

Hunt, *Lynn A*., *UCLA*. Los Angeles, CA. Email: lhunt@history.ucla.edu. Research: French Revolution, notions of time.

Hunt, *Margaret R*. Uppsala, Sweden. Affil: Uppsala. Email: margaret.hunt@hist.uu.se. Research: military, women and law courts.

Hunt, *Marta Espejo-Ponce*. San Diego, CA. Email: wgood222@aol.com. Research: 17th-c Meso-America, native acculturation/ resistance.

Hunt, Rebecca A., *Colorado Denver*. Email: rebecca.hunt@ucdenver.edu.

Hunt, *Richard M*. Lincoln, MA. Affil: Harvard. Email: rickmhunt@comcast.net.

Hunt, Robert E., *Middle Tennessee State*. Email: Robert.Hunt@mtsu.edu.

Hunt, *Spencer Thomas Buika*. Mishawaka, IN. Affil: Notre Dame. Email: shunt2@nd.edu.

Hunt, Tamara L., *Southern Indiana*. Evansville, IN. Email: tlhunt@usi.edu. Research: 18th-c publishing, caricatures.

Hunt, William A., Jr., *St. Lawrence*. Email: whunt@stlawu.edu.

Hunt Watkinson, Margery Grace. Sandy Springs, GA. Affil: Arizona State. Email: m.grace.hunt@gmail.com.

Hunter, Antwain Kenton, *Butler*. Indianapolis, IN. Email: ahunter1@butler.edu. Research: firearms, North Carolina.

Hunter, Beth. Warrior, AL. Affil: Alabama, Birmingham; Bevill State Comm. Coll. Email: beth@bethhunter.com.

Hunter, Devin, *Illinois, Springfield*.

Hunter, F. Robert, *Indiana State*. Email: Robert. Hunter@indstate.edu.

Hunter, Tera W., *Princeton*. Email: thunter@princeton.edu.

Hunt-Kennedy, Stefanie Dawn, *New Brunswick*. Fredericton, NB, Canada. Email: hunt. kennedy@unb.ca. Research: Caribbean/Atlantic world/disability, slavery/gender/legal.

Huntley, Katherine V., *Boise State*. Email: kvhuntley@boisestate.edu.

Hupchick, Dennis P., *Wilkes*. Email: dennis. hupchick@wilkes.edu.

Huppert, George, *Illinois, Chicago*. Email: huppert@uic.edu.

Hur, Hyungju, *Tennessee, Martin*. Email: hhur1@utm.edu.

Hurewitz, Daniel, *Hunter, CUNY*. Email: dhurewit@hunter.cuny.edu.

Hurgobin, Yoshina, *Kennesaw State*. Kennesaw, GA. Email: yhurgobi@kennesaw.edu; yoshina. hurgobin@gmail.com. Research: Indian labor diaspora, Indian Ocean.

Hurl-Eamon, Jennine, *Trent*. Email: jenninehurleamon@trentu.ca.

Hurley, Andrew, *Missouri–St. Louis*. Email: ahurley@umsl.edu.

Hurley, F. Jack, *Memphis*. Email: hurleyj1@bellsouth.net.

Hurt, John J., *Delaware*. Email: hurt@udel.edu.

Hurt, R. Douglas, *Purdue*. West Lafayette, IN. Email: doughurt@purdue.edu. Research: 20th-c Great Plains, Civil War-era southern agriculture.

Hurtado, Albert L. Roseville, CA. Affil: Oklahoma. Email: ahurtado@ou.edu. Research: historical profession, equine.

Hurtado, Diego. College Park, MD. Affil: Maryland, Coll. Park. Email: dhurtad1@umd. edu.

Hurwich, Judith J. Stamford, CT. Email: jhurwi@aol.com. Research: early modern German family, Zimmerische Chronik.

Husain, Adnan A., *Queen's, Can*. Email: ah28@queensu.ca.

Husain, Aiyaz, *US Dept. of State*.

Husain, Faisal. University Park, PA. Affil: Penn State. Email: fhh102@psu.edu.

Huskins, Bonnie L., *New Brunswick*. Email: bhuskins@unb.ca.

Hussain, Shahla, *St. John's, NY*. Email: hussains@stjohns.edu.

Huston, James L., *Oklahoma State*. Email: james. huston@okstate.edu.

Huston, Reeve, *Duke*. Email: reeve.huston@duke.edu.

Hustwit, William P., *Birmingham-Southern*. Email: whustwit@bsc.edu.

Hutcheon, Sarah, *Arthur and Elizabeth Schlesinger Library*. Email: hutcheon@radcliffe. harvard.edu.

Hutcheson, John A., Jr. Dalton, GA. Affil: Dalton State. Email: jhutcheson@daltonstate.edu. Research: British Conservative Party since 1880, maritime/naval.

Hutchinson, David Lawrence. Ann Arbor, MI. Affil: Michigan, Ann Arbor. Email: d.law. hutchinson@gmail.com. Research: 19th-/20th-c US race and sexuality.

Hutchison, Deirdre. Andover, MA. Email: deehutch@yahoo.com.

Hutchison, Elizabeth Q., *New Mexico*. Email: ehutch@unm.edu.

Huttenmaier, Kathleen, *Eastern Washington*. Email: khuttenmaier@ewu.edu.

Hutter, Roman. Ann Arbor, MI. Affil: Vienna; Michigan. Email: romanhutter@gmx.at.

Hutto, Cary, *Hist. Soc. of Pennsylvania*. Email: chutto@hsp.org.

Hutto, Gary W. Birmingham, AL. Email: ghuttocpa@bellsouth.net. Research: early WWII/France 1940/Britain, King Philip's War.

Hutton, Patrick H., *Vermont*. Email: patrick. hutton@uvm.edu.

Hutton, Paul, *New Mexico*. Email: hutton@unm. edu.

Hutton, Shennan L. Napa, CA. Affil: California, Davis. Email: slhutton@ucdavis.edu. Research: women and economic activities, late medieval Flemish cities.

Hutvagner, Zsofia. Fort Worth, TX. Affil: Texas Christian. Email: z.hutvagner@tcu.edu.

Huxen, Keith William. New Orleans, LA. Affil: National World War II Museum. Email: keith. huxen@nationalww2museum.org. Research: 20th-c America, modern European political/diplomatic.

Huxford, Gary L., *Western Oregon*.

Huyck, Heather A. Mitchellville, MD. Affil: National Collaborative for Women's Hist. Sites. Email: huyckclapper@earthlink.net. Research: Maggie Walker/black resistance/Jim Crow, public.

Huyette, Frank C., Jr. Auburn, CA. Affil: Auburn Unified Sch. District. Email: fchesq@aol.com. Research: history didactics, media in history.

Huyssen, David Nicholas. Yorkshire, United Kingdom. Affil: York. Email: huyssendn@yahoo.com. Research: capitalism, Alfred Winslow Jones.

Hwang, Kyung Moon, *Southern California*. Email: khwang3@gmail.com.

Hyams, Aaron, *Sam Houston State*. Email: adh061@shsu.edu.

Hyams, Paul R., *Cornell*. Email: prh3@cornell. edu.

Hyatt, A. M. Jack, *Western Ontario*. Email: hyatt@uwo.ca.

Hyatt, Irwin T., Jr., *Emory*.

Hyde, Allen, *Georgia Inst. of Tech.* Email: allen. hyde@hsoc.gatech.edu.

Hyde, Anne, *Oklahoma (Hist.); Western Hist. Assoc.* Norman, OK. Email: anne.hyde@ou.edu. Research: 19th-/20th-c America, US West.

Hyde, Charles K., *Wayne State*. Email: aa0912@wayne.edu.

Hyde, Elizabeth, *Kean*. Somerville, NJ. Email: ehyde@kean.edu. Research: early modern how-to manuals, botanical exchange/garden.

Hyde, John M., *Williams*. Email: jhyde@williams. edu.

Hyde, Samuel C., *Southeastern Louisiana*. Email: shyde@selu.edu.

Hyer, Paul V., *Brigham Young*.

Hyland, John O., *Christopher Newport*. Email: john.hyland@cnu.edu.

Hyland, Steven L., Jr. Wingate, NC. Affil: Wingate. Email: s.hyland@wingate.edu. Research: immigration to Americas, transnational processes/flows of people/commodity.

Hylton, Raymond Pierre. Chester, VA. Affil: Virginia Union. Email: vuuprof@aol.com. Research: Huguenots, African American.

Hylton, Veronica. New York, NY. Affil: Chicago. Email: veronicahylton@gmail.com.

Hyman, Harold M., *Rice*. Email: hyman@rice. edu.

Hyman, Louis R., *Cornell*. Email: lrh62@cornell. edu.

Hymes, Robert P., *Columbia (Hist.)*. Email: hymes@columbia.edu.

Hynson, Rachel M. Middlebury, VT. Email: rachel. hynson@gmail.com. Research: Cuba, sexuality studies.

Hyser, Raymond M., *James Madison*. Email: hyserrm@jmu.edu.

Hyson, Jeffrey N., *St. Joseph's*. Email: jhyson@sju.edu.

Hyun, Sinae, *Wisconsin-Whitewater*.

I i

Iacovetta, Franca, *Toronto*. Email: f.iacovetta@utoronto.ca.

Iacullo-Bird, Maria T. New York, NY. Affil: Pace, New York. Email: miacullobird@pace.edu. Research: New York City, museums and visual culture.

Ialongo, Ernest. New York, NY. Affil: Hostos Comm. Coll., CUNY. Email: eialongo@yahoo. com. Research: antisemitism, fascism.

Iarocci, Andrew, *Western Ontario*. Email: aiarocc@uwo.ca.

Ibarguen, Irvin, *NYU*. Brooklyn, NY. Email: ibarguen@nyu.edu; iibarguen@fas.harvard. edu.

Ibarguen, J. Henry, *Weber State*. Email: jibarguen@weber.edu.

Iber, Jorge, *Texas Tech*. Email: jorge.iber@ttu. edu.

Iber, Patrick J., *Wisconsin-Madison*. Madison, WI. Email: piber@wisc.edu; patrick.iber@gmail. com. Research: Cold War cultural, poverty.

Ibhawoh, Bonny, *McMaster*. Email: ibhawoh@mcmaster.ca.

Ibrahim, Abdullahi, *Missouri, Columbia*. Email: ibrahima@missouri.edu.

Ibrahim, Ahmed H. Greenwich, CT. Affil: Qatar. Email: Ahmed812@qu.edu.qa. Research: Arab-Israeli conflict, American-Arab relations.

Ibrahim, Bilal, *Brooklyn, CUNY*. Email: bibrahim@brooklyn.cuny.edu.

Ibrahim, Vivian, *Mississippi*. University, MS. Email: vibrahim@olemiss.edu. Research: modern Middle East.

Ibson, John D. Fullerton, CA. Affil: California State, Fullerton. Email: jibson@fullerton.edu. Research: American manhood in 1950s, male relationships in visual culture.

Icenhauer-Ramirez, Robert. Austin, TX. Affil: Texas, Austin. Email: rirlawyer@gmail.com.

Iddrisu, Abdulai, *St. Olaf*. Email: iddrisu@stolaf. edu.

Iden, *Michelle C.* Randolph, NJ. Affil: County Coll. of Morris. Email: miden@ccm.edu. Research: memory studies, Irish famine.

Idris, **Amir**, *Fordham*. Email: idris@fordham.edu.

Igarashi, **Yoshikuni**, *Vanderbilt*. Email: yoshikuni.igarashi@vanderbilt.edu.

Igler, **David B.**, *California, Irvine*. Email: digler@uci.edu.

Igmen, **Ali F.**, *California State, Long Beach; Soc. for Hist. Education*. Email: ali.igmen@csulb.edu.

Igo, *Sarah E.*, *Vanderbilt*. Nashville, TN. Email: sarah.igo@vanderbilt.edu. Research: social sciences, popular culture.

Igra, *Annette R.*, *Carleton Coll.* Saint Paul, MN. Email: aigra@carleton.edu.

Iguchi, **Gerald Scott**, *Wisconsin-La Crosse*. Email: iguchi.gera@uwlax.edu.

Ihara, *Randal Homma*. South Riding, VA. Email: bonsai126@hotmail.com.

Ikegami, **Eiko**, *New School*. Email: ikegame1@newschool.edu.

Ikeya, **Chie**, *Rutgers*. Email: chie.ikeya@rutgers.edu.

Ikker, *Norris*. San Marcos, CA. Affil: California State, San Marcos. Email: ikker001@cougars.csusm.edu.

Ilahi, *Shereen F.*, *North Central*. Chicago, IL. Email: silahi@noctrl.edu. Research: British Empire/Ireland/India.

Iles Johnston, **Sarah**, *Ohio State*. Email: johnston.2@osu.edu.

Illuzzi, *Jennifer Grana*, *Providence*. Sharon, MA. Email: jilluzz1@providence.edu; jilluzzi@gmail.com. Research: state-Romany relations in Europe.

Imada, **Adria L.**, *California, Irvine*. Email: aimada@uci.edu.

Imai, **Shiho**, *SUNY, Coll. Potsdam*. Email: imais@potsdam.edu.

Imani, *Jocelyn*. Washington, DC. Affil: National Museum of African American Hist. & Culture. Email: jocelynimani@gmail.com. Research: African Diaspora, Black Power.

Imber, **Elizabeth E.**, *Clark*. Email: eimber@clarku.edu.

Imhoff, **Sarah**, *Indiana*. Email: seimhoff@indiana.edu.

Imholt, **Robert J.** North Haven, CT. Affil: Albertus Magnus. Email: rjimholt@yahoo.com.

Imhoof, **David Michael**, *Susquehanna*. Email: imhoof@susqu.edu.

Immerman, *Richard H.* Philadelphia, PA. Affil: Temple. Email: rimmerma@temple.edu. Research: intelligence and US foreign policy.

Immerwahr, *Daniel*, *Northwestern*. Email: daniel.immerwahr@northwestern.edu.

Imy, *Kate Alison*, *North Texas*. Denton, TX. Email: kate.imy@unt.edu; kate.alison.imy@gmail.com. Research: modern Britain, colonial India.

Inaba, *Yumi*. New York, NY. Email: Tsuiteru.hito@gmail.com.

Inboden, **William C.**, *Texas, Austin*. Email: inboden@austin.utexas.edu.

Inden, **Ronald B.**, *Chicago*. Email: rbinden@uchicago.edu.

Infante De La Cruz, **Bianca Estefania**. Jackson, WY. Email: binfante@uwyo.edu.

Ingalls, **Robert P.**, *South Florida, Tampa*.

Ingerick, **Ryan Eric**, *Appalachian State*. Email: ingerickre@appstate.edu.

Ingersoll, *Thomas Neil*, *Ohio State*. Lima, OH. Email: ingersoll.11@osu.edu. Research: racial mixture in early America, racial thought in early America.

Ingham, **John N.**, *Toronto*.

Ingle, **H. Larry**, *Tennessee, Chattanooga*. Email: lingle@bellsouth.net.

Ingleson, *Elizabeth*. Dallas, TX. Affil: Southern Methodist. Email: eing9204@uni.sydney.edu.au. Research: Sino-American relations, globalization and labor.

Inglis, **Kerri A.**, *Hawai'i, Hilo*. Email: inglis@hawaii.edu.

Ingraham, *Kevin Robert*. North Bennington, VT. Affil: SUNY, Albany. Email: kingraham@albany.edu. Research: American Revolution, Nazi Germany.

Ingram, *Daniel P.*, *Ball State*. Muncie, IN. Email: dpingram@bsu.edu. Research: American Indians and British forts, colonial America and historical memory.

Ingram, **Edward**, *Simon Fraser*.

Ingram, **Norman**, *Concordia, Can*. Email: Norman.Ingram@concordia.ca.

Ingram, **Robert G.**, *Ohio*. Email: ingramr@ohio.edu.

Ingram, *Tammy*, *Charleston*. Charleston, SC. Email: ingramt@cofc.edu. Research: modern South, film.

Ingrao, **Charles W.**, *Purdue*. Email: ingrao@purdue.edu.

Ingrassia, **Joseph**, *SUNY, Oneonta*. Email: joseph.ingrassia@oneonta.edu.

Ingwersen, *Lance R.* Anniston, AL. Affil: Denison. Email: lanceingwersen@gmail.com. Research: theater/politics 19th-c Mexico.

Inikori, **Joseph Eyitemi**, *Rochester*. Email: inik@mail.rochester.edu.

Inkpen, *Dani Hallet*. Cambridge, MA. Affil: Harvard. Email: dani.hallet@gmail.com. Research: science, environmental.

Innes, **John S.**, *Eastern Washington*.

Innis-Jimenez, *Michael D*. Tuscaloosa, AL. Affil: Alabama. Email: ij@ua.edu. Research: Latinos/Latinas in Midwest.

Innocenti, *Gerard G*. Dallas, PA. Affil: Kutztown.

Inoue, *Fumi*. Brighton, MA. Affil: Boston Coll. Email: inouef@bc.edu. Research: American military justice, Status of Forces Agreement.

Inscoe, **John C.**, *Georgia*. Email: jinscoe@uga.edu.

Inwood, **Kris E.**, *Guelph*. Email: kinwood@uoguelph.ca.

Ion, **A. Hamish**, *Royal Military*. Email: ion-h@rmc.ca.

Ioris, **Rafael Rossotto**, *Denver*. Email: rafael.ioris@du.edu.

Ipsen, **Carl D.**, *Indiana*. Email: cipsen@indiana.edu.

Ipsen, **Pernille**, *Wisconsin-Madison*. Email: pipsen@wisc.edu.

Ireland, **Owen S.**, *SUNY, Coll. Brockport*. Email: oireland@brockport.edu.

Irigoin, **Alejandra**, *New Jersey*. Email: irigoin@tcnj.edu.

Irish, **Kerry Eugene**, *George Fox*. Email: kirish@georgefox.edu.

Irish, **Maya Soifer**, *Rice*. Email: maya.s.irish@rice.edu.

Iriye, *Akira*, *Harvard (Hist.)*. Cambridge, MA. Email: airiye@fas.harvard.edu. Research: American diplomatic, American-Asian relations.

Irons, **Charles F.**, *Elon*. Email: cirons@elon.edu.

Irvin, *Aaron William*, *Murray State*. Murray, KY. Email: airvin1@murraystate.edu; awirvin82@gmail.com. Research: imperialism and empire in antiquity, ancient religion and community.

Irvin, *Benjamin H.*, *Indiana; OAH*. Bloomington, IN. Email: bhirvin@indiana.edu. Research: disabled Revolutionary War veterans.

Irvin, *Dakota*. Carrboro, NC. Affil: North Carolina, Chapel Hill. Email: dirvin1@live.unc.edu. Research: Russian Revolution and Civil War, Russian provincial.

Irwin, **Julia F.**, *South Florida, Tampa*. Email: juliai@usf.edu.

Irwin, **Mary Ann**, *California State, East Bay*. Email: maryann.irwin@csueastbay.edu.

Irwin, *Ryan M.*, *SUNY, Albany*. Albany, NY. Email: Irwin.126@gmail.com. Research: decolonization, Cold War.

Isaac, **Steven**, *Longwood*. Email: isaacsw@longwood.edu.

Isaac, **Tseggai**, *Missouri Science and Tech*. Email: tseggai@mst.edu.

Isaacman, **Allen F.**, *Minnesota (Hist.)*. Email: isaac001@umn.edu.

Isaacson, **Walter**, *Tulane*. Email: isaacson@tulane.edu.

Isaenko, **Anatoly**, *Appalachian State*. Email: isaenkoa@appstate.edu.

Isbell, **Joshua**. Salt Lake City, UT. Email: joshua.a.isbell@gmail.com.

Iseminger, **Gordon L.**, *North Dakota*. Email: gordon.iseminger@und.edu.

Isenberg, *Alison E.*, *Princeton*. Princeton, NJ. Email: isenber@princeton.edu. Research: American urban, business culture.

Isenberg, *Andrew C.*, *Kansas*. Lawrence, KS. Email: isenberg@ku.edu. Research: American environmental, American West.

Isenberg, **Nancy G.**, *Louisiana State*. Email: nisenberg@lsu.edu.

Isenhower, **Zachary C.**, *Southeastern Louisiana*. Email: zachary.isenhower@selu.edu.

Isern, **Tom D.**, *North Dakota State*. Email: isern@plainsfolk.com.

Isett, **Christopher M.**, *Minnesota (Hist.)*. Email: isett003@umn.edu.

Isetti, **Ronald**, *St. Mary's, Calif.*

Isherwood, **Ian**, *Gettysburg*. Email: iisherwo@gettysburg.edu.

Ishiguro, **Laura**, *British Columbia*. Email: laura.ishiguro@ubc.ca.

Ishii, **Lomayumtewa C.**, *Northern Arizona*. Email: lomayumtew.ishii@nau.edu.

Ishikawa, *Hanako*. New York, NY. Affil: Consulate General of Japan in New York. Email: hanako_ishikawa@outlook.jp.

Ishikawa, *Tadashi*. Orlando, FL. Affil: Central Florida. Email: ishikawt@oregonstate.edu.

Islam, *Pierre*. Buffalo, NY. Email: pislam1@gmail.com.

Ismail, *Zohra*. Summit, NJ. Affil: Oak Knoll Sch. Email: zohra.ismail@oakknoll.org.

Ismay, *Penelope Gwynn*, *Boston Coll*. Chestnut Hill, MA. Email: ismay@bc.edu. Research: 18th-c British Empire credit/debt/trust, friendly societies 1780-1870.

Isom-Verhaaren, *Christine*, *Brigham Young*. Provo, UT. Email: cisom-verhaaren@byu.edu. Research: Ottoman navy, Ottoman identity.

Ison, *Payton*. Star, ID. Email: paytonison@icloud.com.

Israel, *Charles Alan*, *Auburn*. Email: israeca@auburn.edu.

Israel, Jerry, *Indianapolis*.

Israel, John W., *Virginia*. Email: ji@virginia.edu.

Israel, Jonathan. Princeton, NJ. Affil: Inst. for Advanced Study. Email: jisrael@ias.edu. Research: early modern intellectual, early modern Netherlands.

Israel, Kali, *Michigan, Ann Arbor*. Email: kisrael@umich.edu.

Israel, Milton, *Toronto*.

Israel, Paul B., *Rutgers*. Piscataway, NJ. Email: pisrael@rutgers.edu. Research: invention and innovation, media and communications.

Issel, William. Berkeley, CA. Affil: San Francisco State. Email: bi@sfsu.edu. Research: US urban politics, 20th-c urban US West.

Isser, Natalie K., *Penn State*. Email: nxi1@psu.edu.

Isserman, Maurice, *Hamilton*. Email: misserma@hamilton.edu.

Ito, Koji. Urbana, IL. Affil: Illinois, Urbana-Champaign. Email: kojiito2@illinois.edu. Research: US imperialism, US-Japan relations.

Ittmann, Karl E., *Houston*. Email: kittmann@uh.edu.

Itzkowitz, David C., *Macalester*. Email: itzkowitz@macalester.edu.

Ivanov, Andrey V., *Wisconsin-Platteville*. Email: ivanovan@uwplatt.edu.

Ivaska, Andrew M., *Concordia, Can.* Email: Andrew.Ivaska@concordia.ca.

Iverson, Peter J., *Arizona State*. Email: peter.iverson@asu.edu.

Ivey, Jacob. Melbourne, FL. Affil: Florida Inst. of Tech. Email: jacobivey@gmail.com. Research: Natal/South Africa defensive institution, development of Natal as colonial state.

Ivey, Linda, *California State, East Bay*. Email: linda.ivey@csueastbay.edu.

Ivison, Eric A., *Graduate Center, CUNY; Staten Island, CUNY*. Email: eric.ivison@csi.cuny.edu.

Iyer, Samantha Gayathri, *Fordham*. Email: siyer1@fordham.edu.

Izenberg, Gerald N., *Washington, St. Louis*. Email: gnizenbe@wustl.edu.

Izmirlioglu, Ahmet. Salt Lake City, UT. Affil: Utah State. Email: izmirli73@hotmail.com. Research: world, Ottoman Empire from 1800.

Izzo, Jesse Wolf. Miami, FL. Affil: Minnesota, Twin Cities. Email: jesse.izzo@gmail.com.

J j

Jablonsky, Thomas J., *Marquette*. Email: thomas.jablonsky@marquette.edu.

Jabour, Anya, *Montana*. Email: anya.jabour@umontana.edu.

Jach, Theresa R. Richmond, TX. Affil: Houston Comm. Coll., Northwest. Email: theresa.jach@hccs.edu. Research: prison farms/convict leasing.

Jackle, Robert C. Westminster, MD. Affil: York, Pa. Email: rcjackle@aol.com.

Jacklin, Jillian Marie. Oshkosh, WI. Affil: Wisconsin, Madison. Email: jmjacklin@wisc.edu. Research: labor and capitalism, race and gender.

Jackson, Aaron James. Pollock Pines, CA. Affil: California State, Sacramento. Email: jackson3793@gmail.com.

Jackson, Alicia K., *Covenant*. Email: ajackson@covenant.edu.

Jackson, Briana. Bronx, NY. Affil: NYU. Email: jacksonbc3@gmail.com.

Jackson, Carl T., *Texas, El Paso*. Email: cjackson@utep.edu.

Jackson, Christopher R. Berkeley, CA. Affil: De Anza. Email: crjackson81@gmail.com.

Jackson, Daryl P. Greenbelt, MD. Affil: Catholic. Email: jacksondp@cua.edu.

Jackson, David H., Jr. Tallahassee, FL. Affil: Florida A&M. Email: djackso1906@comcast.net. Research: age of Booker T. Washington, African Americans in Jim Crow America.

Jackson, Donald C, *Lafayette*. Email: jacksond@lafayette.edu.

Jackson, Edward M. Dover, DE. Email: emjackso@comcast.net. Research: American/American studies, African American.

Jackson, Eric R., *Northern Kentucky*. Email: jacksoner@nku.edu.

Jackson, Gabriel, *California, San Diego*.

Jackson, Gregory E., *Western Connecticut State*. Email: jacksong@wcsu.edu.

Jackson, Jeffrey H., *Rhodes*. Email: jacksonj@rhodes.edu.

Jackson, Jere L., *Stephen F. Austin State*. Email: jjackson@sfasu.edu.

Jackson, Jerma A., *North Carolina, Chapel Hill*. Email: jaj@email.unc.edu.

Jackson, Jessica Barbata, *Colorado State*. Email: jessica.jackson@colostate.edu.

Jackson, Justin F. Great Barrington, MA. Affil: Bard Coll., Simon's Rock. Email: jjackson@simons-rock.edu.

Jackson, Kenneth T., *Columbia (Hist.)*. Mount Kisco, NY. Email: ktj1@columbia.edu. Research: suburban development, New York City.

Jackson, Lawrence, *Emory*. Email: lpjacks@emory.edu.

Jackson, Leon. Columbia, SC. Affil: South Carolina, Columbia. Email: JacksoL@mailbox.sc.edu. Research: embarassment and shame in 19th-c America.

Jackson, Lisa M. San Francisco, CA. Affil: California, Santa Cruz. Email: limjacks@ucsc.edu.

Jackson, Maurice, *Georgetown*. Email: jacksonz@georgetown.edu.

Jackson, Myles W., *NYU*. Email: myles.jackson@nyu.edu.

Jackson, Nicole Maelyn, *Bowling Green State*. Email: nmjacks@bgsu.edu.

Jackson, Patrick D., *Allegheny*. Email: pjackson@allegheny.edu.

Jackson, Robyn. Stafford, VA. Affil: Northern Virginia Comm. Coll. Email: genealogylover@msn.com.

Jackson, Stephen James. Sioux Falls, SD. Affil: Sioux Falls. Email: Stephen.Jackson@usiouxfalls.edu. Research: British imperialism, dominions of British Empire.

Jackson, Thomas F., *North Carolina, Greensboro*. Email: tjackson@uncg.edu.

Jackson, Tiffany M. Killeen, TX. Affil: Haynes Elementary Sch. Email: tiffyumhb19@aol.com.

Jackson, Trevor. Washington, DC. Affil: George Washington. Email: twjackson@gwu.edu.

Jackson, W. Sherman, *Miami, Ohio*. Email: jacksows@miamioh.edu.

Jackson, Weldon, *Bowie State*. Email: wjackson@bowiestate.edu.

Jackson, Zoe Marguerite. Silver Spring, MD. Email: zo.mar.jackson@gmail.com.

Jackson-Abernathy, Brenda K., *Belmont*. Email: brenda.jackson@belmont.edu.

Jackson-Ybarra, Shawon M. Clovis, CA. Email: shawonybarra1@yahoo.com.

Jacob, Devin. Alameda, CA. Email: devinjacob@gmail.com.

Jacob, Elizabeth. Stanford, CA. Affil: Stanford. Email: ejacob@stanford.edu. Research: decolonization of French West Africa.

Jacob, Kathryn Allamong, *Arthur and Elizabeth Schlesinger Library*. Email: kjacob@radcliffe.harvard.edu.

Jacob, Margaret C., *UCLA*. Los Angeles, CA. Email: mjacob@history.ucla.edu. Research: scientific culture and industrialization, Bernard Picart and origins of Enlightenment.

Jacob, Wilson Chacko, *Concordia, Can.* Email: Wilson.Jacob@concordia.ca.

Jacobe, Stephanie A. Silver Spring, MD. Affil: Maryland Univ. Coll. Email: aureus@usa.net. Research: 19th-c US social/cultural.

Jacobs, Anton K. Kansas City, MO. Email: antonkjacobs@gmail.com. Research: intellectual history, cultural studies.

Jacobs, Justin Matthew, *American*. Email: jjacobs@american.edu.

Jacobs, Margaret D., *Nebraska, Lincoln*. Email: mjacobs3@unl.edu.

Jacobs, Martin, *Washington, St. Louis*. Email: mjacobs@wustl.edu.

Jacobs, Matthew F., *Florida*. Email: mjacobs@ufl.edu.

Jacobs, Nancy J., *Brown*. Providence, RI. Email: nancy_jacobs@brown.edu. Research: postcolonial science and environment, postcolonial Africa.

Jacobs, Seth S., *Boston Coll.* Email: jacobssd@bc.edu.

Jacobs, Travis Beal, *Middlebury*. Bridport, VT. Email: tjacobs@middlebury.edu. Research: Vermont Sen. Robert Stafford.

Jacobsen, Kristin. Skokie, IL. Affil: Loyola, Chicago. Email: kejcat@gmail.com.

Jacobsen, Nils P. Urbana, IL. Affil: Illinois, Urbana-Champaign. Email: njacobse@illinois.edu. Research: Latin America, Andes.

Jacobsen, Trude, *Northern Illinois*. Email: tjacobsen1@niu.edu.

Jacobson, Brian, *Toronto*. Email: brian.jacobson@utoronto.ca.

Jacobson, Carl W., *Oberlin*. Email: carl.jacobson@oberlin.edu.

Jacobson, Danae Ann, *Colby*.

Jacobson, Jon S., *California, Irvine*. Email: jsjacobs@uci.edu.

Jacobson, Justin. Grayslake, IL. Email: JU.Jacobson87@gmail.com.

Jacobson, Keith, *Henry Ford Coll.* Email: keith2169@hotmail.com.

Jacobson, Lisa S., *California, Santa Barbara*. Goleta, CA. Email: jacobson@history.ucsb.edu. Research: alcohol and food studies, consumer culture.

Jacobson, Matthew F., *Yale*. Email: matthew.jacobson@yale.edu.

Jacobson, Stephen H. Barcelona, Spain. Affil: Pompeu Fabra. Email: stephen.jacobson@upf.edu. Research: lawyers in 19th-c Europe and Spain, Catalan nationalism.

Jacobs-Pollez, Rebecca J. Tishomingo, OK. Affil: Murray State Coll. Email: rjacobspollez@mscok.edu. Research: medieval European women, education of medieval women.

Jacoby, Alex, *Loyola Marymount*.

Jacoby, *Karl H.*, *Columbia (Hist.)*. New York, NY. Email: kj2305@columbia.edu. Research: Great Plains and borderlands, US.

Jacoby, **Russell**, *UCLA*. Email: rjacoby@history.ucla.edu.

Jacoby, **Sanford**, *UCLA*. Email: sanford.jacoby@anderson.ucla.edu.

Jacquet, *Catherine O.*, *Louisiana State*. Email: cjacquet@lsu.edu.

Jae, **Kendra**, *Hist. Assoc.* Email: kjae@historyassociates.com.

Jaede, **Mark G.**, *St. Cloud State*. Email: mgjaede@stcloudstate.edu.

Jaeger, **Sheila**, *Oberlin*. Email: sjaeger@oberlin.edu.

Jaehnig, **Kenton**, *Science History Inst.* Email: kjaehnig@sciencehistory.org.

Jaffary, *Nora E.*, *Concordia, Can.* Montreal, QC, Canada. Email: Nora.Jaffary@concordia.ca. Research: birth monstrosities, Mexican women medical.

Jaffe, *Matthew Lee*. Lancaster, CA. Affil: Antelope Valley. Email: mjaffe@avc.edu. Research: world civilizations, American West and California.

Jaffe, **Tracey Lynn**, *Dayton*. Email: tjaffe1@udayton.edu.

Jagel, *Matthew R.* Malta, IL. Affil: St. Xavier. Email: matthewjagel@gmail.com.

Jager, **Ronald B.**, *Texas State*. Email: rj18@txstate.edu.

Jago, *Charles*, *Northern British Columbia*. Email: charles.jago@unbc.ca.

Jagodinsky, *Katrina L.*, *Nebraska, Lincoln*. Email: kjagodinsky@unl.edu.

Jahanbani, **Sheyda F. A.**, *Kansas*. Email: sfaj@ku.edu.

Jahn, *Hubertus F.* Cambridge, United Kingdom. Affil: Cambridge. Email: hfj21@cam.ac.uk. Research: Caucasus region, Russian imperial.

Jahnke Wegner, *Joanne Marie*. Durand, WI. Affil: Minnesota, Twin Cities. Email: jahnk049@umn.edu. Research: Indian captivity and Native American enslavement, women and gender.

Jainchill, **Andrew J. S.**, *Queen's, Can.* Email: andrew.jainchill@queensu.ca.

Jakeman, **Robert J.**, *Auburn*. Email: jakemrj@auburn.edu.

Jakes, *Aaron George*, *New School*. Brooklyn, NY. Email: jakesa@newschool.edu; aaron.jakes@gmail.com. Research: modern Egyptian social, global environmental history of finance.

Jakle, *John A.* Urbana, IL. Affil: Illinois, Urbana-Champaign.

Jaksic, *Ivan A.* Santiago, Chile. Affil: Stanford.

Jakubs, **Deborah**, *Duke*. Email: jakubs@duke.edu.

Jalal, **Ayesha**. Medford, MA. Affil: Tufts. Email: ayesha.jalal@tufts.edu.

Jalloh, **Alusine**, *Texas, Arlington*. Email: jalloh@uta.edu.

Jallow, **Baba Galleh**, *La Salle*.

James, *Anthony*. Chambersburg, PA. Affil: Shippensburg. Email: jamesanthonyl@gmail.com.

James, **Daniel M.**, *Indiana*. Email: dajames@indiana.edu.

James, **Harold**, *Princeton*. Email: hjames@princeton.edu.

James, *Heyward Parker*. Boston, MA. Affil: Brandeis. Email: hpjames423@gmail.com.

Research: Shanghai Jewish communities 1842-1949, tropical stilt house global.

James, *Keith Marlin*. Dallas, TX. Affil: James Trucking. Email: mammongodofmoney888@gmail.com.

James, *Kevin J.*, *Guelph*. Email: kjames@uoguelph.ca.

James, *Timothy MacDowell*. Beaufort, SC. Affil: South Carolina, Beaufort. Email: tjames@uscb.edu. Research: Mexican legal.

James, *Virginia*. Port Orchard, WA. Email: virginialjames@gmail.com. Research: heretics and spirituality, folklore.

James, **Winston**, *California, Irvine*. Email: wjames@uci.edu.

Jameson, *Elizabeth A.*, *Calgary*. Calgary, AB, Canada. Email: jameson@ucalgary.ca. Research: US-Canada borderlands, women in the North American Wests.

Jameson, *Erica J.* Ashland, OR. Affil: Siskiyous. Email: erica.jameson@me.com.

Jameson, **John R.**, *Kent State*. Email: jjameson@kent.edu.

Jamieson, *J.T.* Berkeley, CA. Affil: California, Berkeley. Email: jtjamieson@berkeley.edu.

Jamison, **Felicia**, *Loyola, Md.*

Jamjoum, *Hazem*. New York, NY. Affil: NYU. Email: hj539@nyu.edu. Research: culture and politics, music and capitalism.

Jampee, *Pheeraphong*. Fargo, ND. Affil: North Dakota State. Email: Pheeraphong.jampee@ndus.edu. Research: colonial and postcolonial mainland Southeast Asia.

Janacek, **Bruce**, *North Central*. Email: bnjanacek@noctrl.edu.

Janak, *Blake Christopher Charles*. Oklahoma City, OK. Affil: Central Oklahoma. Email: bjanak@uco.edu. Research: colonialism in Niger River Delta, early modern English Catholic.

Janda, **Lance**, *Cameron*. Email: lancej@cameron.edu.

Janda, **Sarah Eppler**, *Cameron*. Email: sjanda@cameron.edu.

Janes, *Lauren R. H.*, *Hope*. Holland, MI. Email: janes@hope.edu; laurenhinklejanes@gmail.com. Research: French colonialism, food.

Janet, *Richard J.*, *Rockhurst*. Email: rick.janet@rockhurst.edu.

Jangam, **Chinnaiah**, *Carleton, Can.* Email: chinnaiah.janggam@carleton.ca.

Jani, *Disha Karnad*. Princeton, NJ. Affil: Princeton. Email: djani@princeton.edu.

Janken, *Kenneth R.*, *North Carolina, Chapel Hill*. Chapel Hill, NC. Email: krjanken@email.unc.edu. Research: Wilmington Ten, 20th-c African American.

Jankowski, **James P.**, *Colorado, Boulder*. Email: jankowsk@colorado.edu.

Jankowski, **Paul**, *Brandeis*. Email: jankowski@brandeis.edu.

Jankowski, **Stephanie**, *Center for Hist. of Physics*. Email: sjankows@aip.org.

Jannen, *William*, *Jr*. Boston, MA.

Jannenga, *Stephanie Christine*. Norton Shores, MI. Affil: Kent State. Email: sjanneng@kent.edu.

Jannetta, **Ann B.**, *Pittsburgh*. Email: annj@pitt.edu.

Janney, **Caroline E.**, *Virginia*. Email: cej4b@virginia.edu.

Janovicek, **Nancy E. A.**, *Calgary*. Email: njanovic@ucalgary.ca.

Jansen, *Axel*, *German Hist. Inst.* Washington, DC. Email: a.jansen@ghi-dc.org. Research: 20th-c science and public.

Jansen, **Jan C.**, *German Hist. Inst.* Email: jansen@ghi-dc.org.

Jansen, *Katherine L.* Washington, DC. Affil: Catholic. Email: jansen@cua.edu. Research: peacemaking in late medieval Italy.

Janssen, *Michel*, *Minnesota (Hist. of Science)*. Email: janss011@umn.edu.

Janssen, *Volker*, *California State, Fullerton*. Murrieta, CA. Email: vjanssen@fullerton.edu. Research: post-WWII California prisons, technology in California.

Jantzen, *Mark A.* North Newton, KS. Affil: Bethel, Kans. Email: mjantzen@bethelks.edu. Research: German nationalism, Anabaptists and Mennonites.

Janulis, *Megan E.* Aurora, IL. Email: megan_janulis@yahoo.com. Research: Queen Victoria, feminist in Victorian period.

Janus, **Glenn A.**, *Coe*. Email: gjanus@coe.edu.

Janzen, **Mark Ryan**, *Central Oklahoma*. Email: mjanzen@uco.edu.

Janzen, **Olaf U.**, *Memorial, Newfoundland*. Email: olaf@grenfell.mun.ca.

Janzen, *Philip*. Madison, WI. Affil: Wisconsin, Madison. Email: phil.janzen@gmail.com.

Janzen Loewen, *Patricia*. Winnipeg, MB, Canada. Affil: Providence Univ. Coll. Email: patricia.janzenloewen@prov.ca. Research: Christian biography in late antiquity, historiography and Christianity.

Jara, *Javier*. San Marcos, CA. Affil: California State, San Marcos. Email: jara013@cougars.csusm.edu.

Jarausch, *Konrad H.*, *North Carolina, Chapel Hill*. Email: jarausch@email.unc.edu.

Jarin, *Alexander Wiessmann*. Newtown, PA. Email: jarinalexander@gmail.com. Research: British Jewish life, Atlantic slave trade.

Jaroszynska-Kirchmann, *Anna D.*, *Eastern Connecticut State*. Willimantic, CT. Email: kirchmanna@easternct.edu. Research: recent US, immigration and ethnic.

Jarvinen, **Lisa**, *La Salle*. Email: jarvinen@lasalle.edu.

Jarvis, **Brad D.**, *Saginaw Valley State*. Email: bjarvis@svsu.edu.

Jarvis, **Charles A.**, *Dickinson*. Email: jarvisc@dickinson.edu.

Jarvis, *Eric J.* London, ON, Canada. Affil: King's Univ. Coll., Western Ontario. Research: Canada, warfare.

Jarvis, **Katie L.**, *Notre Dame*. Email: kjarvis@nd.edu.

Jarvis, **Lauren V.**, *North Carolina, Chapel Hill*. Email: ljarvis@email.unc.edu.

Jarvis, **Michael J.**, *Rochester*. Email: michael.jarvis@rochester.edu.

Jasanoff, *Maya*, *Harvard (Hist.)*. Cambridge, MA. Email: mjasanof@fas.harvard.edu. Research: modern Britain, imperial.

Jasper, **Kathryn Lee**, *Illinois State*. Email: kljaspe@ilstu.edu.

Jastrzembski, *Joseph C.*, *Minot State*. Minot, ND. Email: joseph.jastrzembski@minotstateu.edu. Research: American Indian languages, folklore.

Jaundrill, *David Colin*, *Providence*. Providence, RI. Email: djaundri@providence.edu. Research: early modern and modern Japan, social/cultural/military.

Javers, **Quinn Doyle**, *California, Davis*. Email: qdjavers@ucdavis.edu.

Jay, **Bethany W.**, *Salem State*. Salem, MA. Email: bjay@salemstate.edu. Research: memory of American slavery.

Jay, **Jacqueline**, *Eastern Kentucky*. Email: jackie. jay@eku.edu.

Jay, **Jennifer**, *Alberta*. Email: jjay@ualberta.ca.

Jay, **Martin E.** Berkeley, CA. Affil: California, Berkeley. Email: martjay@berkeley.edu. Research: late modern Europe since 1789, intellectual.

Jayasanker, **Laresh Krishna**. Denver, CO. Affil: Metropolitan State, Denver. Email: lareshj@ aol.com.

Jayes, **Janice L.**, *Illinois State*. Normal, IL. Email: jjayes@ilstu.edu.

Jean-Baptiste, **Rachel**, *California, Davis*. Davis, CA. Email: rjeanbaptiste@ucdavis.edu. Research: Gabon gender/sexuality/cities, West African miscegenation and race.

Jeanneney, **John R.**, *Hofstra*.

Jeans, **Roger**, **Jr.**, *Washington and Lee*. Email: jeansr@wlu.edu.

Jebari, **Idriss**, *Bowdoin*. Email: ijebari@bowdoin. edu.

Jebsen, **Henry**, **Jr.**, *Capital*. Email: hjebsen@ capital.edu.

Jeeves, **Alan H.**, *Queen's, Can*. Email: alanjeeves@cs.com.

Jeffers, **James S.**, *California State, Dominguez Hills*. Email: jjeffers@csudh.edu.

Jeffers, **Joshua Jack**, *California State, Dominguez Hills*. La Mirada, CA. Email: jojeffers@csudh. edu; jjeffers58@yahoo.com. Research: Ohio valley/frontier/borderlands, settler colonialism/indigenizing discour.

Jefferson, **Alison Rose**. Los Angeles, CA. Affil: Historian and More. Email: alisonrosejefferson@gmail.com. Research: California, African Americans.

Jefferson, **Robert F.**, **Jr**, *New Mexico*. Email: jeffersonr@unm.edu.

Jefferson, **Robert**, *Sonoma State*. Email: rjefferson@sbcglobal.net.

Jeffery, **Hannah**. Nottingham, United Kingdom. Affil: Nottingham. Email: han.jeffery90@gmail. com.

Jeffrey, **Kirk**, **Jr.**, *Carleton Coll*. Email: kirkjeffrey@icloud.com.

Jeffrey, **Thomas E.**, *Rutgers*. Email: tomjeffrey2001@yahoo.com.

Jeffries, **Hasan Kwame**, *Ohio State*. Email: jeffries.57@osu.edu.

Jeffries, **John W.**, *Maryland, Baltimore County*. Email: jeffries@umbc.edu.

Jelatis, **Virginia G.**, *Western Illinois*. Email: VG-Jelatis@wiu.edu.

Jelavich, **Peter**, *Johns Hopkins (Hist.)*. Baltimore, MD. Email: jelavich@jhu.edu. Research: censorship in modern Germany, modern European cultural and intellectual.

Jelks, **Randal Maurice**, *Kansas*. Email: rmjelks@ ku.edu.

Jellison, **Katherine K.**, *Ohio*. Email: jellison@ ohio.edu.

Jenkins, **Benjamin T.** La Verne, CA. Affil: La Verne. Email: Bjenkins@laverne.edu. Research: agriculture, transportation.

Jenkins, **Destin K.**, *Chicago*. Chicago, IL. Email: destin@uchicago.edu.

Jenkins, **Ellen J.**, *Arkansas Tech*. Email: ejenkins@atu.edu.

Jenkins, **Ernest E**. Lancaster, SC. Affil: South Carolina, Lancaster. Email: ejenkins@mailbox. sc.edu.

Jenkins, **Gareth**. Albuquerque, NM. Email: garethjenkins6@gmail.com.

Jenkins, **Jennifer Louise**, *Toronto*. Toronto, ON, Canada. Email: jl.jenkins@utoronto.ca. Research: transnational, German-Middle Eastern relations.

Jenkins, **Philip**, *Baylor; Penn State*. Email: philip_ jenkins@baylor.edu; jpj1@psu.edu.

Jenkins, **Reese V.**, *Rutgers*. Email: reese638@ aol.com.

Jenkins, **Robert L.**, *Mississippi State*. Email: rjenkins3874@bellsouth.net.

Jenkins, **William**, *York, Can*. Email: wjenkins@ yorku.ca.

Jenks, **Andrew Leslie**, *California State, Long Beach*. Fullerton, CA. Email: andrew.jenks@ csulb.edu. Research: Soviet political iconography, Russian Orthodoxy.

Jenks, **Timothy D.**, *East Carolina*. Greenville, NC. Email: jenkst@ecu.edu. Research: popular loyalism in Georgian Britain.

Jennings, **Audra**, *Western Kentucky*. Email: audra.jennings@wku.edu.

Jennings, **Eric T.**, *Toronto*. Email: eric.jennings@ utoronto.ca.

Jennings, **Evelyn Powell**, *St. Lawrence*. Email: ejennings@stlawu.edu.

Jennings, **John M.**, *US Air Force Acad*. Email: john.jennings@usafa.edu.

Jennings, **John N.**, *Trent*. Email: jjennings@ trentu.ca.

Jennings, **Kailtyn**. Tuttle, OK. Affil: Wheaton. Email: katejay09@gmail.com.

Jennison, **Watson W.**, **III**, *North Carolina, Greensboro*. Email: wwjennis@uncg.edu.

Jenrich, **Marissa**. Tujunga, CA. Affil: UCLA. Email: majenrich@gmail.com.

Jensen, **Billie**, *San José State*.

Jensen, **Cara**. St Louis, MO. Email: cjjens314@ gmail.com.

Jensen, **De Lamar**, *Brigham Young*.

Jensen, **Erik Norman**, *Miami, Ohio*. Oxford, OH. Email: jensenen@miamioh.edu. Research: gender and sport in Weimar Republic, collective memory of Nazi persecution.

Jensen, **Erik S.**, *Salem State*. Georgetown, MA. Email: erik.jensen@salemstate.edu. Research: Roman contacts with northern Europe.

Jensen, **Geoffrey W.** Dewey, AZ. Affil: Embry-Riddle Aeronautical, Ariz. Email: JensenG2@ erau.edu. Research: military/race/society 1945-68, military/gender/sexuality.

Jensen, **Gordon**, *Saskatchewan*. Email: gordon. jensen@usask.ca.

Jensen, **Hilmar L.**, *Bates*. Email: hjensen@bates. edu.

Jensen, **Joan M.**, *New Mexico State*. Email: jjensen@nmsu.edu.

Jensen, **Kimberly S.**, *Western Oregon*. Email: jenseki@wou.edu.

Jensen, **Lionel M.**, *Notre Dame*. Email: ljensen@ nd.edu.

Jensen, **R. Geoffrey**, *Virginia Military Inst*. Email: jensenrg@vmi.edu.

Jensen, **Richard Bach**. Natchitoches, LA. Affil: Northwestern State. Email: jensenr@nsula. edu. Research: diplomacy/police/anarchist terrorism, anarchist terrorism 1870s-1930s.

Jenson, **Carol E**. Minneapolis, MN. Email: celizjenson@comcast.net.

Jeon, **Jaewoong**. Boulder, CO. Affil: Chicago. Email: jwoong@uchicago.edu. Research: Korea and Taiwan, capitalism.

Jepsen, **John**. Iowa City, IA. Affil: Iowa. Email: jwjepsen@uiowa.edu. Research: US energy policy/foreign policy, Native American energy/North Dakota.

Jerke, **Iris M.**, *San José State*. Email: Iris.Jerke@ sjsu.edu.

Jernigan, **Scarlet**. Fort Worth, TX. Affil: Texas Christian. Email: s.jernigan@tcu.edu.

Jersild, **Austin**, *Old Dominion*. Email: ajersild@ odu.edu.

Jesch, **Aaron Douglas**. Pullman, WA. Affil: Washington State, Pullman. Email: aaron. jesch@wsu.edu.

Jespersen, **T. Christopher**, *North Georgia*. Email: christopher.jespersen@ung.edu.

Jessee, **E. Jerry**, *Wisconsin-Stevens Point*. Email: jerry.jessee@uwsp.edu.

Jessen, **Sorn Arthur**. Seattle, WA. Email: sorn. jessen@gmail.com.

Jessner, **Sabine**, *Indiana–Purdue, Indianapolis*.

Jessup, **David**, *St. Olaf*. Email: jessdave@uw.edu.

Jessup, **Kesa**, *North Carolina A&T State*. Email: kcjessup@ncat.edu.

Jestice, **Phyllis G.**, *Charleston*. Email: jesticepg@ cofc.edu.

Jett, **Brandon**. LaBelle, FL. Affil: Florida SouthWestern State. Email: bjett@fsw.edu. Research: crime/violence/criminal justice, race relations.

Jette, **Melinda Marie**. Rindge, NH. Affil: Franklin Pierce. Email: jettem@franklinpierce.edu. Research: French North Americans in US West, Native Americans.

Jewell, **Evan**. New York, NY. Affil: Columbia. Email: evan.jewell@columbia.edu.

Jewell, **Katherine Rye**. Belmont, MA. Affil: Fitchburg State. Email: katejewell@gmail.com. Research: early civil rights movement 1890-1940, resistance/music/social change.

Jewett, **Andrew**. Cambridge, MA. Affil: Harvard. Email: ajewett@fas.harvard.edu. Research: science and religion, US political culture.

Jhala, **Angma D.**, *Bentley*. Email: ajhala@bentley. edu.

Ji, **Fangchao**. Washington, DC. Affil: Georgetown. Email: fj121@georgetown.edu.

Ji, **Yeonjung**. Cambridge, MA. Affil: Harvard. Email: mooae1@gmail.com.

Jiang, **Yue**. Palo Alto, CA. Affil: Stanford. Email: jiangyue@stanford.edu.

Jim, **Bernard L.**, *Case Western Reserve*. Email: bernard.jim@case.edu.

Jimenez, **Christina M.**, *Colorado Colorado Springs*. Colorado Springs, CO. Email: cjimenez@uccs.edu. Research: urban popular movements/popular culture, urban public space and citizenship.

Jimenez, **Mike**, *Biola*. Email: mike.jimenez@ biola.edu.

Jiménez, **Mónica Alexandra**, *Texas, Austin*. Email: majimenez@utexas.edu.

Jimenez Bacardi, **Arturo**, *South Florida, St. Petersburg*.

Jiménez Botta, **Felix A**. Brighton, MA. Affil: Boston Coll. Email: jimenefa@bc.edu.

Jimerson, **Randall C.**, *Western Washington*. Email: Rand.Jimerson@wwu.edu.

Jin, **Michael**, *Illinois, Chicago*. Email: mrjin@uic. edu.

Jin, **Xiaoxing**. Chicago, IL. Affil: Notre Dame. Email: xjin1@nd.edu. Research: science/Darwinian studies, China.

Jirau, **Aura Sofia**. Pittsburgh, PA. Affil: Pittsburgh. Email: asj42@pitt.edu.

Jirik, **Katrina Nancy**. Saint Paul, MN. Affil: Minnesota. Email: jiri0006@umn.edu. Research: institutions and asylums 1875-1920, women's roles in work of institutions.

Jobin, **Nicole V.** Boulder, CO. Affil: Colorado, Boulder. Email: jobin@colorado.edu.

Jobs, **Richard I.** Forest Grove, OR. Affil: Pacific. Email: jobs4049@pacificu.edu. Research: youth and national identity in France, youth/travel/European integration.

Jockusch, **Laura**, *Brandeis*. Email: jockusch@brandeis.edu.

Jodziewicz, **Thomas W.**, *Dallas*. Email: tjodz@udallas.edu.

Joesten, **Daniel McKenna**. Watsonville, CA. Affil: California, Santa Cruz. Email: dmjoeste@ucsc.edu.

Joffe, **Edward**. Asheville, NC. Email: ejoffe@asu.edu.

Joffrion, **Elizabeth**, *Western Washington*. Email: Elizabeth.Joffrion@wwu.edu.

John, **James J.**, *Cornell*. Email: jjj2@cornell.edu.

John, **Maria K.**, *Massachusetts, Boston*. Email: mkj2111@columbia.edu.

John, **Richard R.**, *Columbia (Hist.)*. New York, NY. Email: rrj2115@columbia.edu. Research: business and technology, post-1700 communications.

John, **S. Sandor**, *Hunter, CUNY*. Email: s_an@msn.com.

Johns, **Adrian D. S.**, *Chicago*. Chicago, IL. Email: johns@uchicago.edu. Research: book, early modern science.

Johns, **Andrew L.**, *Brigham Young; Soc. for Hist. of American Foreign Relations*. Provo, UT. Email: andrew_johns@byu.edu. Research: John Sherman Cooper and Cold War 1946-76, Hubert Humphrey and Vietnam.

Johns, **Michael J.**, *Henry Ford Coll.* Email: mjohns@schoolcraft.edu.

Johns, **Rebecca**, *South Florida, St. Petersburg*.

Johnsen, **Erik**. Portland, OR. Affil: Portland Comm. Coll. Email: erik.johnsen@pcc.edu.

Johnson, **Adam Fulton**. Santa Fe, NM. Affil: Michigan, Ann Arbor. Email: adamfjohnson@gmail.com. Research: anthropology, documentation/inscription.

Johnson, **Alan Edward**. Pittsburgh, PA. Affil: Philosophia Publications. Email: alanjohnson10@comcast.net. Research: America 1607-present, England 1509-1815.

Johnson, **Amanda J.** Stillwater, OK. Affil: Oklahoma State. Email: amanda72285@gmail.com. Research: 20th-c Native American Women, 20th-c activism.

Johnson, **Amy M.**, *Elon*. Email: ajohnson60@elon.edu.

Johnson, **Andrea S.**, *California State, Dominguez Hills*. Email: anjohnson@csudh.edu.

Johnson, **Andrew**, *Elmhurst*. Email: andrew.johnson@elmhurst.edu.

Johnson, **Benjamin Daniel**, *Massachusetts, Boston*. Cambridge, MA. Email: benjamin.johnson@umb.edu. Research: colonial Mexico, imperial and republican Brazil.

Johnson, **Benjamin H.**, *Loyola, Chicago*. Chicago, IL. Email: bjohnson25@luc.edu. Research:

conservation social, North American borderlands.

Johnson, **Bethany L.**, *Rice*. Email: bethanyj@rice.edu.

Johnson, **Bobby H.**, *Stephen F. Austin State*. Email: bhjohnson@sfasu.edu.

Johnson, **Carina L.**, *Pitzer*. Claremont, CA. Email: carina_johnson@pitzer.edu.

Johnson, **Charles Lane**. Fort Worth, TX. Affil: Dallas Baptist. Email: charcarjohn@att.net. Research: Anglo-Saxon church, medieval intellectual.

Johnson, **Christine R.**, *Washington, St. Louis*. Email: cjohns@wustl.edu.

Johnson, **Christopher H.**, *Wayne State*. Pleasant Ridge, MI. Email: aa4307@wayne.edu. Research: kinship and bourgeois class formation, 18th-c Paris family conflict.

Johnson, **Christopher**, *US Army Command Coll.* Email: christopher.r.johnson60.civ@mail.mil.

Johnson, **Colin R.**, *Indiana*. Email: crj2@indiana.edu.

Johnson, **Craig**. Oakland, CA. Affil: California, Berkeley. Email: craigjohnson@berkeley.edu. Research: modern Southern Cone, reception of Vatican II in Latin America.

Johnson, **Curtis D.**, *Mount St. Mary's*. Email: johnson@msmary.edu.

Johnson, **Cynthia Nicole**. Oklahoma City, OK. Email: cynthianicolejohnson@gmail.com.

Johnson, **Dana A.** Lexington, KY. Affil: Kentucky. Email: drdajohnson@gmail.com. Research: Appalachian women's health.

Johnson, **Daniel**. Ankara, Turkey. Affil: Bilkent. Email: daniel.johnson@bilkent.edu.tr. Research: Atlantic world, labor.

Johnson, **David A.**, *North Carolina, Charlotte*. Email: dajohns1@uncc.edu.

Johnson, **David Alan**, *Portland State*. Portland, OR. Email: johnsonda@pdx.edu. Research: violence and vigilantism, Charles and Mary Beard.

Johnson, **David B.**, *Illinois State*. Email: dbjohns@ilstu.edu.

Johnson, **David C.**, *Alberta*. Email: david.johnson@ualberta.ca.

Johnson, **David K.**, *South Florida, Tampa*. Tampa, FL. Email: davidjohnson@usf.edu. Research: Cold War race and sexuality, gay consumer culture before Stonewall.

Johnson, **David R.**, *Texas, San Antonio*. Email: david.johnson@utsa.edu.

Johnson, **Diana**, *California State, San Bernardino*. Email: dekjohnson@ucdavis.edu.

Johnson, **Donald F.**, *North Dakota State*. Fargo, ND. Email: donald.f.johnson@ndsu.edu. Research: American Revolution, colonial America.

Johnson, **Donald G.**, *North Carolina, Wilmington*. Email: johnsondg@uncw.edu.

Johnson, **Emily Suzanne**, *Ball State*. Muncie, IN. Email: esjohnson2@bsu.edu; esj312@gmail.com. Research: American evangelicalism, women and conservatism.

Johnson, **Eric A.**, *Central Michigan*. Email: johns1ea@cmich.edu.

Johnson, **Eric F.**, *Kutztown*. Kutztown, PA. Email: ejohnson@kutztown.edu. Research: religious ritual and French Revolution, secularization and modernity.

Johnson, **Eric W.** Redmond, WA. Affil: Washington, Seattle. Email: ejred@u.

washington.edu. Research: trading relations between Russia and Central Asia, pre-1850 multicultural Volga society.

Johnson, **Erica R.**, *Francis Marion*. Florence, SC. Email: ejohnson@fmarion.edu. Research: Europe, Latin America.

Johnson, **Fred L., III**, *Hope*. Email: johnson@hope.edu.

Johnson, **Gary J.**, *Southern Maine*. Email: gjohnson@maine.edu.

Johnson, **Gaye**, *California, Santa Barbara*. Email: gtjohnson@blackstudies.ucsb.edu.

Johnson, **Herbert A**. Black Mountain, NC. Affil: South Carolina. Email: janeherb@charter.net. Research: John Marshall and Supreme Court, 17th-c English constitutional law.

Johnson, **Howard B.**, *Delaware*. Email: howardj@udel.edu.

Johnson, **Ian Ona**, *Notre Dame*. Email: ijohnso2@nd.edu.

Johnson, **Jacquelyn**. Chicago, IL. Affil: City Coll., Chicago. Email: jacquelyn918@yahoo.com.

Johnson, **James E**. Arden Hills, MN. Affil: Bethel, Minn.

Johnson, **James E**. Clayton, NJ. Affil: Rowan. Email: weusi7@aol.com. Research: black Mid-Atlantic in Civil War, inequality and education.

Johnson, **James H., Jr.**, *Boston Univ.* Freeport, ME. Email: jhj@bu.edu. Research: modern France, early modern Italy.

Johnson, **Jason Burton**, *Trinity, Tex.* Email: jjohnso7@trinity.edu.

Johnson, **Jeffrey Alan**, *Providence*. Providence, RI. Email: j.johnson@providence.edu. Research: labor/radicalism/politics, Gilded Age/Progressive era US West.

Johnson, **Jeffrey Allan**, *Villanova*. Villanova, PA. Email: jeffrey.johnson@villanova.edu. Research: German chemistry social-institutional, WWI chemical technologies.

Johnson, **Jennifer**, *Brown*. Email: Jennifer_Johnson1@Brown.edu.

Johnson, **Jeremy**. Helena, MT. Affil: Carroll. Email: jeremypennsylvania@gmail.com.

Johnson, **Jessica Marie**, *Johns Hopkins (Hist.)*. Baltimore, MD. Email: jmjohnso@gmail.com; jmj@jhu.edu. Research: African diaspora, slavery.

Johnson, **Joan Marie**. Evanston, IL. Affil: Northwestern. Email: joanmjohnson@northwestern.edu. Research: women, African American.

Johnson, **Joana Galarza**. Temecula, CA. Affil: La Sierra. Email: joana.g.johnson@gmail.com. Research: Latin America, transatlantic colonial.

Johnson, **John W., Jr**, *St. Peter's*. Plainfield, NJ. Email: jjohnson5@saintpeters.edu. Research: American Civil War, African American.

Johnson, **John W.**, *Northern Iowa*. Email: john.johnson@uni.edu.

Johnson, **Judith R.**, *Wichita State*. Email: judith.johnson@wichita.edu.

Johnson, **Karen J.**, *Wheaton, Ill.* Wheaton, IL. Email: karen.johnson@wheaton.edu. Research: Catholic interracialism, race.

Johnson, **Karl Ellis**, *Ramapo*. Email: kjohnson@ramapo.edu.

Johnson, **Kathryn R.**, *Northern Michigan*. Email: kathryjo@nmu.edu.

Johnson, **Kristin R.**, *Puget Sound*. Email: kristinjohnson@pugetsound.edu.

Johnson, *Laura E*. Marlborough, MA. Affil: Historic New England. Email: ljohnson@historicnewengland.org. Research: New England material culture, comparative Native American-European relations.

Johnson, *Linda L*. Minneapolis, MN. Affil: Concordia Coll., Minn. Email: ljohnson@cord.edu. Research: East Asia, women.

Johnson, *Lloyd*, *Campbell*. Email: johnson@campbell.edu.

Johnson, **Ludwell H.**, **III**, *William and Mary*.

Johnson, **Lyman L.**, *North Carolina, Charlotte*. Email: ljohnson@uncc.edu.

Johnson, **M. Houston**, **V**, *Virginia Military Inst*. Email: johnsonmh@vmi.edu.

Johnson, **Maire N.**, *Emporia State*.

Johnson, **Maj Donald D.**, **III**, *US Air Force Acad*. Email: donald.johnson@usafa.edu.

Johnson, **Marilynn S.**, *Boston Coll*. Email: johnsohi@bc.edu.

Johnson, **Mark A.**, *Tennessee, Chattanooga*.

Johnson, **Martin P.**, *Miami, Ohio*. Email: johnsomp@miamioh.edu.

Johnson, **Matthew**, *Texas Tech*. Email: matthew.j.johnson@ttu.edu.

Johnson, *Michael P*., *Johns Hopkins (Hist.)*. Email: vze1vntz@verizon.net.

Johnson, **Michele A.**, *York, Can*. Email: johnsonm@yorku.ca.

Johnson, *Michelle Kimberly*. New Haven, CT. Affil: Yale. Email: michelle.johnson.mkj25@yale.edu.

Johnson, *Miranda*. Sydney, Australia. Affil: Sydney. Email: miranda.johnson@sydney.edu.au. Research: indigenous, political.

Johnson, **Molly Wilkinson**, *Alabama, Huntsville*. Email: johnsomw@uah.edu.

Johnson, *Nicholas*. Fort Collins, CO. Email: njohnson4189@gmail.com. Research: cannabis.

Johnson, **Norman**, *Salisbury*.

Johnson, *Owen V*. Bloomington, IN. Affil: Indiana. Email: owenvjohnson@gmail.com. Research: 20th-c Slovak news media, Ernie Pyle.

Johnson, **Paul C.**, *Michigan, Ann Arbor*. Email: paulcjoh@umich.edu.

Johnson, *Paula*. Port Republic, MD. Affil: National Museum of American Hist. Email: johnsonpa@si.edu. Research: maritime folklore and folklife, US maritime.

Johnson, **Penelope D.**, *NYU*. Email: pdj1@nyu.edu.

Johnson, *Philip M*. Portland, OR. Affil: Multnomah. Email: pjohnson@multnomah.edu. Research: 19th-c US evangelical masculinity, American revivalism.

Johnson, *Rashauna*, *Dartmouth*. Email: rashauna.r.johnson@dartmouth.edu.

Johnson, *Richard R*., *Washington, Seattle*. Email: rrj@uw.edu.

Johnson, *Robert D*., *Brooklyn, CUNY; Graduate Center, CUNY*. Email: kcjohnson9@gmail.com.

Johnson, *Robert E*., *Toronto*. Toronto, ON, Canada. Email: johnson@chass.utoronto.ca. Research: quantitative research methods, post-1919 USSR urbanization and demography.

Johnson, *Ronald Angelo*, *Texas State*. San Marcos, TX. Email: rj26@txstate.edu. Research: US in Atlantic world, Haitian immigration in early America.

Johnson, *Ronald M*., *Georgetown*. Email: johnsorm@georgetown.edu.

Johnson, *Russell L*. Porterfield, WI. Email: rlj003@yahoo.com. Research: military and American society, disability/poverty/aging.

Johnson, **Sherri Franks**, *Louisiana State*. Email: sfj@lsu.edu.

Johnson, **Sherry**, *Florida International*. Email: johnsons@fiu.edu.

Johnson, *Susan Lee*, *Nevada, Las Vegas*. Madison, WI. Email: sljohnson5@wisc.edu. Research: US West, gender and sexuality.

Johnson, **Tai E.**, *Longwood*.

Johnson, **Thomas P.**, *Massachusetts, Boston*. Email: thomas.johnson@umb.edu.

Johnson, **Timothy Scott**, *Texas A&M, Corpus Christi*. Email: timothy.johnson@tamucc.edu.

Johnson, *Tyler V*. Moss Bluff, LA. Affil: Sowela Tech. Comm. Coll. Email: tylervjohnson@hotmail.com. Research: US-Mexican War 1846-48, immigration and religion.

Johnson, **Violet Showers**, *Texas A&M*. Email: vmjohnson@tamu.edu.

Johnson, **W. Christopher**, *Toronto*. Email: wchris.johnson@utoronto.ca.

Johnson, **Walter**, *Harvard (Hist.)*. Email: johnson2@fas.harvard.edu.

Johnson, **Whittington B.**, *Miami*. Email: whittjo@bellsouth.net.

Johnson, *Winifred*. Daytona Beach, FL. Affil: Bethune-Cookman. Email: johnsonw@cookman.edu.

Johnson, **Yvonne J.**, *Central Missouri*.

Johnston, **Andrew M.**, *Carleton, Can*. Email: andrew.johnston@carleton.ca.

Johnston, **Charles**, *McMaster*.

Johnston, **Christine**, *Western Washington*. Email: christine.johnston@wwu.edu.

Johnston, *Gerald Richard*. Tampa, FL. Affil: South Florida, Tampa. Email: grjohnston@verizon.net.

Johnston, **Hugh J. M.**, *Simon Fraser*. Email: hjohnsto@sfu.ca.

Johnston, *Katherine*, *Beloit*. Beloit, WI. Email: johnstonkm@beloit.edu; kj2248@columbia.edu. Research: Caribbean.

Johnston, *Robert D*., *Illinois, Chicago*. Chicago, IL. Email: johnsto1@uic.edu. Research: vaccination, teaching of history.

Johnston, *Sky Michael*. La Jolla, CA. Affil: California, San Diego. Email: smjohnston@ucsd.edu.

Johnston, *Tamra Banks*. Oklahoma City, OK. Affil: Oklahoma State, Oklahoma City. Email: tamrarb@okstate.edu. Research: political/popular culture.

Johnston, *Wade Robert*. Milwaukee, WI. Affil: Wisconsin Lutheran. Email: wade.johnston@wlc.edu.

Johnston, *Warner W*., *Sr*. Pomona, NY. Email: warner@wwjohnston.com.

Johnston, *Warren James*. Sault Ste. Marie, ON, Canada. Affil: Algoma. Email: warren.johnston@algomau.ca. Research: 17th-c culture/political ideas, 17th-/18th-c sermons.

Johnston, **William C.**, *National Defence Headquarters*. Email: william.johnston@forces.gc.ca.

Johnston, *William D*., *Wesleyan*. Higganum, CT. Email: wjohnston@wesleyan.edu. Research: Japanese public health, cholera in Japan.

Johnston, **William M.**, *Massachusetts, Amherst*. Email: william@etterlink.com.au.

Johnstone, **Steven**, *Arizona*. Email: sjohnsto@u.arizona.edu.

Johnston-White, *Rachel M*. Vienna, Austria. Affil: Vienna Sch. of International Studies. Email: rachel.johnston.white@gmail.com. Research: Christianity and politics, Human rights.

Johstono, **Paul**, *Citadel*. Email: pjohston@citadel.edu.

Joiner, **G. Hewett**, **Jr.**, *Georgia Southern*.

Joinson, *Carla*. Church Hill, TN. Email: joinson@earthlink.net. Research: American Indians and insanity, civilian insurrection.

Jolley, **Harley E.**, *Mars Hill*.

Jolley, **Laura**, *State Hist. Soc. of Missouri*. Email: jolleyl@shsmo.org.

Jolluck, **Katherine R.**, *Stanford*. Email: jolluck@stanford.edu.

Jolly, **James A.**, *Millersville, Pa*.

Jolly, *Karen Louise*, *Hawai'i, Manoa*. Honolulu, HI. Email: kjolly@hawaii.edu. Research: manuscript culture, 10th-c Northumbria.

Jolly, **Kenneth S.**, *Saginaw Valley State*. Email: kjolly@svsu.edu.

Jolly, **Michelle E.**, *Sonoma State*. Email: michelle.jolly@sonoma.edu.

Jonas, *Raymond*, *Washington, Seattle*. Seattle, WA. Email: jonas@uw.edu. Research: Africa/Europe/Americas, Mexican Second Empire.

Jones, *Alexandra*. Johns Island, SC. Affil: Houselore. Email: alexandra@houselore.com.

Jones, **Allen E.**, **Jr.**, *Troy*. Email: ajones@troy.edu.

Jones, **Amber Elizabeth**, *Virginia Museum of Hist*. Email: ajones@VirginiaHistory.org.

Jones, *Anna Trumbore*, *Lake Forest*. Lake Forest, IL. Email: jones@lakeforest.edu. Research: 10th-c French bishops, 10th-c French religious life.

Jones, *Arnita A*. Washington, DC. Email: arnitajones@gmail.com. Research: public, policy.

Jones, *Arun W*. Atlanta, GA. Affil: Emory. Email: arun.w.jones@emory.edu. Research: Asian church, Christian mission.

Jones, **Ashley**, *Austin Peay State*. Email: jonesa@apsu.edu.

Jones, *B. J*. San Antonio, TX. Affil: Wayland Baptist. Email: benjamin.jones.44@us.af.mil.

Jones, **Brad A.**, *California State, Fresno*. Email: brajones@csufresno.edu.

Jones, **Cameron David**, *California Polytechnic State*. Email: cjones81@calpoly.edu.

Jones, *Carolyn Christine*. Iowa City, IA. Affil: Iowa. Email: carolyn-jones@uiowa.edu.

Jones, **Catherine A.**, *California, Santa Cruz*. Santa Cruz, CA. Email: catjones@ucsc.edu. Research: Reconstruction, children.

Jones, *Charles*. Saint Augustine, FL. Email: dr.camj87@gmail.com.

Jones, *Christopher F*., *Arizona State*. Tempe, AZ. Email: cjones36@asu.edu; christopherfjones@gmail.com. Research: environmental, business.

Jones, **Christopher P.**, *Harvard (Hist.)*. Email: cjones@fas.harvard.edu.

Jones, **Christopher**, *Liberty*. Email: cljones5@liberty.edu.

Jones, **Daniel A.**, *Florida Atlantic*. Email: djones89@fau.edu.

Jones, *David S*., *Harvard (Hist. of Science)*. Cambridge, MA. Email: dsjones@harvard.edu. Research: heart disease/cardiology/cardiac surgery, epidemics and health disparities.

Jones, *Donald G.*, *Central Arkansas*. Email: donj@uca.edu.

Jones, *Dorothy V.* Evanston, IL. Research: 20th-c search for international justice, war crimes trials.

Jones, *Dylan*. Liberty, MO. Email: dylancjones1789@gmail.com.

Jones, *Ebony Pearl*, *North Carolina State*.

Jones, *Elizabeth Bright*, *Colorado State*. Email: elizabeth.jones@colostate.edu.

Jones, *Elwood H.*, *Trent*. Email: ejones@trentu.ca.

Jones, *Eric Alan*, *Northern Illinois*. Email: iloveroti@gmail.com.

Jones, *Esyllt*, *Manitoba*. Email: esyllt.jones@umanitoba.ca.

Jones, *Gary*, *American International*. Email: gary.jones@aic.edu.

Jones, *Henry W, III*. Longmont, CO. Affil: Destinations Career Academy of Colorado. Email: hjones@k12.com.

Jones, *Howard*, *Alabama, Tuscaloosa*. Email: hjones@tenhoor.as.ua.edu.

Jones, *Jacqueline*, *Texas, Austin*. Austin, TX. Email: jjones@mail.utexas.edu; Jacqueline.jones999@gmail.com. Research: race/ethnicity/nation, diaspora and migration.

Jones, *Jeannette Eileen*, *Nebraska, Lincoln*. Lincoln, NE. Email: jjones11@unl.edu. Research: US cultural and intellectual, African American studies.

Jones, *Jeffrey W.*, *North Carolina, Greensboro*. Email: jwjones@uncg.edu.

Jones, *Jennifer M.*, *Rutgers*. Email: jemjones@sas.rutgers.edu.

Jones, *Jonathan*. Ithaca, NY. Affil: Binghamton, SUNY. Email: jonesj4927@gmail.com.

Jones, *K Paul*, *Tennessee, Martin*. Santa Fe, NM. Email: kennethpauljones@q.com.

Jones, *Kathleen W.*, *Virginia Tech*. Email: kjwj@vt.edu.

Jones, *Kelly E.*, *Arkansas Tech*.

Jones, *Kelly Hacker*, *Texas A&M, Corpus Christi*.

Jones, *Kenneth R.*, *Baylor*. Email: k_r_jones@baylor.edu.

Jones, *Kevin Michael*, *Georgia*. Email: kevjones@uga.edu.

Jones, *Kimberly F*, *Long Island, Brooklyn*. Email: Kimberly.Jones@liu.edu.

Jones, *Kimberly*. Houston, TX. Affil: Rice. Email: kvj2@rice.edu.

Jones, *Kristin*. Tampa, FL. Email: kristin.jones47@gmail.com.

Jones, *Larry Eugene*, *Canisius*. Email: jones@canisius.edu.

Jones, *Linda*, *Dayton*. Email: linda.jones@notes.udayton.edu.

Jones, *Marian Moser*, *Maryland, Coll. Park*. Email: moserj@umd.edu.

Jones, *Mark A.*, *Central Connecticut State*. Email: jonesm@ccsu.edu.

Jones, *Martha S.*, *Johns Hopkins (Hist.)*. Baltimore, MD. Email: msjonz@jhu.edu. Research: Atlantic world slavery and law, critical race theory.

Jones, *Matthew L.*, *Columbia (Hist.); Columbia (Hist. Public Health)*. Email: mj340@columbia.edu.

Jones, *Maxine D.*, *Florida State*. Email: mjones@fsu.edu.

Jones, *Michael E.*, *Bates*. Email: mjones@bates.edu.

Jones, *Michael W.*, *Naval War Coll.* Email: michael.jones@usnwc.edu.

Jones, *Michelle C.* New York, NY. Affil: NYU. Email: mcj320@nyu.edu.

Jones, *Norman L.*, *Utah State*. Logan, UT. Email: norm.jones@usu.edu. Research: Renaissance and Reformation, medieval.

Jones, *Patrick D.*, *Nebraska, Lincoln*. Email: pjones2@unl.edu.

Jones, *Peyton*, *South Florida, St. Petersburg*.

Jones, *Raymond A.*, *Carleton, Can*. Email: raymond.jones@carleton.ca.

Jones, *Robert E.*, *Massachusetts, Amherst*. Email: rejones@history.umass.edu.

Jones, *Robert F.*, *Fordham*. Email: rfjones51@verizon.net.

Jones, *Robert L.* Las Vegas, NV. Affil: Nevada, Las Vegas. Email: sigung@ikks.net.

Jones, *Ryan M.*, *SUNY, Coll. Geneseo*. Geneseo, NY. Email: jonesr@geneseo.edu. Research: Mexican social movements and sexuality, 20th-c world sexuality.

Jones, *Ryan T.*, *Oregon*. Email: rtj@uoregon.edu.

Jones, *Scott E.* Mira Loma, CA. Affil: La Sierra Academy. Email: sjones@lsak12.com. Research: unskilled railroad laborers in West, social impact of railroads on Native Americans.

Jones, *Susan D.*, *Minnesota (Hist. of Science)*. Email: jone0996@umn.edu.

Jones, *Tiffany F.*, *California State, San Bernardino*. Email: tjones@csusb.edu.

Jones, *Toby C.*, *Rutgers*. Email: tobycjones@yahoo.com.

Jones, *Trenton Cole*, *Purdue*. West Lafayette, IN. Email: colejones@purdue.edu; cole.jones@gmail.com. Research: prisoners of war, American Revolution.

Jones, *William D.*, *Claremont Grad*. Claremont, CA. Affil: Mount San Antonio. Email: joneswmd@gmail.com. Research: political and cultural, 20th-c Germany.

Jones, *William D.* Houston, TX. Affil: Rice. Email: wdj1@rice.edu. Research: identity formation in antebellum Louisiana, internal slave trades/second slavery.

Jones, *William J.*, *Alberta*.

Jones, *William P.*, *Minnesota (Hist.)*. Email: wpjones@umn.edu.

Jones, *Yollette*, *Vanderbilt*. Email: yollette.t.jones@vanderbilt.edu.

Jones-Branch, *Cherisse Renee*, *Arkansas State*. State University, AR. Email: crjones@astate.edu; jcherisse2001@yahoo.com. Research: black and white women, South Carolina civil rights.

Jones-Imhotep, *Edward*, *York, Can*. Email: imhotep@yorku.ca.

Jones-Rogers, *Stephanie E.*, *California, Berkeley*. El Cerrito, CA. Email: sejr@berkeley.edu. Research: gender and slavery, African American.

Joniec, *Nicole*, *Science History Inst*. Email: njoniec@sciencehistory.org.

Jopp, *Jennifer*, *Willamette*. Email: jjopp@willamette.edu.

Joravsky, *David*, *Northwestern*.

Jordan, *Brian Matthew*, *Sam Houston State*. Huntsville, TX. Email: bmj018@shsu.edu. Research: veterans returning home from war, cultural.

Jordan, *David Paul*, *Illinois, Chicago*. Email: dpj@uic.edu.

Jordan, *Donald A.*, *Ohio*. Email: jordand@ohio.edu.

Jordan, *Erin Lynn*, *Old Dominion*. Email: ejordan@odu.edu.

Jordan, *Lisa Vaughan*. South Hill, VA. Affil: Southside Virginia Comm. Coll. Email: lisa.jordan@southside.edu.

Jordan, *Matthew Ryan*. Baton Rouge, LA. Affil: Louisiana State Univ. Libraries. Email: mjord42@lsu.edu.

Jordan, *Nicole T.*, *Illinois, Chicago*. Email: njordan@uic.edu.

Jordan, *Philip D.* Radford, VA. Affil: Hastings. Email: pjordan@hastings.edu. Research: John William Draper and 19th-c science, US Civil War.

Jordan, *Theresa L.*, *Washington State, Pullman*. Email: tjordan@wsu.edu.

Jordan, *William Chester*, *Princeton*. Princeton, NJ. Email: wchester@princeton.edu. Research: church-state relations, Jewish-Christian relations.

Jordine, *Melissa R.*, *California State, Fresno*. Email: mjordine@csufresno.edu.

Jordon, *Cora-Jane*. Bromley, United Kingdom. Email: corajanejordonn@gmail.com.

Jorsch, *Thomas F.* Tulsa, OK. Affil: Oklahoma State. Email: tjorsch@hotmail.com. Research: socialism, progressivism.

Jortner, *Adam*, *Auburn*. Email: ajj0008@auburn.edu.

Joselit, *Jenna Weissman*, *George Washington*. Email: joselit@gwu.edu.

Joseph, *Antoine*, *Bryant*. Email: ajoseph@bryant.edu.

Joseph, *Frances Ann*. Houston, TX. Affil: Houston. Email: francesann26@gmail.com. Research: numismatics, nomads.

Joseph, *Gilbert M.*, *Yale*. Woodbridge, CT. Email: gilbert.joseph@yale.edu. Research: 20th-c Latin America, social and revolutionary movements.

Joseph, *H. Denise*, *Texas-Rio Grande Valley*. Email: harriet.joseph@utrgv.edu.

Joseph, *John*, *Franklin & Marshall*. Email: john.joseph@fandm.edu.

Joseph, *Peniel E.*, *Texas, Austin*.

Josephson, *Paul*, *Colby*. Email: paul.josephson@colby.edu.

Joshel, *Sandra R.*, *Washington, Seattle*. Email: sjoshel@uw.edu.

Joshi, *Sanjay*, *Northern Arizona*. Email: sanjay.joshi@nau.edu.

Joskowicz, *Alexander Ari*, *Vanderbilt*. Email: a.joskowicz@vanderbilt.edu.

Joslyn, *Daniel*. New York, NY. Affil: NYU. Email: daj334@nyu.edu.

Joy, *Natalie Irene*, *Northern Illinois*. Email: njoy@niu.edu.

Joyce, *Barry Alan*, *Delaware*. Email: bjoyce@udel.edu.

Joyce, *Charles F.* Springfield, MO. Email: chafrajoy@yahoo.com. Research: West Africa, European impact on West African history.

Joyce, *Ellen E.*, *Beloit*. Email: joycee@beloit.edu.

Joyce, *Justin A*. Grosse Pointe Park, MI. Affil: Emory. Email: justin.a.joyce@emory.edu.

Joyce, *William L.*, *Penn State*. Princeton Junction, NJ. Email: wlj2@psu.edu; wljoyce42@gmail.com. Research: 19th-c publishing, American newspapers.

Joyner, *Edward Thomas*, *Sr*. New Haven, CT. Affil: Yale; Sacred Heart. Email: joyneredward57@yahoo.com.

Juarez-Dappe, **Patricia I.**, *California State, Northridge*. Email: patricia.juarezdappe@csun. edu.

Jucovy, *Jon*. Great Neck, NY. Affil: Ramaz Sch. Email: jjucovy@gmail.com.

Judaken, **Jonathan**, *Rhodes*. Email: judakenj@ rhodes.edu.

Judd, *Jacob*, *Lehman, CUNY*. Ossining, NY. Email: jjudd18@optonline.net. Research: American Jewish, ancient Jewish.

Judd, *Richard W*., *Maine, Orono*. Email: rjudd@ maine.edu.

Judd, *Robert*. New York, NY. Affil: American Musicological Soc. Email: rjudd@ams-net.org. Research: notation, keyboard music.

Judd, *Robin E*., *Ohio State*. Email: judd.18@osu. edu.

Judd, *Steven C*., *Southern Connecticut State*. Email: judds1@southernct.edu.

Judge, *Edward H*., *Le Moyne*. Email: judge@ lemoyne.edu.

Judge, *Joan*, *York, Can*. Email: judge@yorku.ca.

Judson, *Pieter M*. Philadelphia, PA. Affil: European Univ. Inst. Email: pieter.judson@ eui.eu. Research: borderlands, Habsburg monarchy.

Juen, *Joel Thomas*. White Bear Lake, MN. Affil: Century. Email: joel.juen@century.edu.

Jug, *Steven George*. Waco, TX. Affil: Baylor. Email: steven.jug@gmail.com. Research: masculinity and Red Army, Soviet youth.

Julian, *Kathryn Campbell*. Maryville, TN. Affil: Maryville. Email: kcjulian@gmail.com.

Julius, *Jesse*. Sammamish, WA. Affil: Issaquah Sch. District. Email: jesse_julius@hotmail.com.

Jun, *Hajin*. South San Francisco, CA. Affil: Stanford. Email: hajin.jun@gmail.com.

June, *Matthew R*. Chicago, IL. Affil: Latin Sch. of Chicago. Email: mattjune7@gmail.com. Research: 20th-c US political and social, US drugs and alcohol/crime and punishment.

Jung, *Gyungeil*. Seoul, South Korea. Email: jgee2012@naver.com.

Jung, *Moon-Ho*, *Washington, Seattle*. Seattle, WA. Email: mhjung@u.washington.edu. Research: Asian American, labor.

Jurdjevic, *Mark*, *York, Can*. Email: mjurdjevic@ glendon.yorku.ca.

Jurgens, *Jennifer*. Atlanta, GA. Affil: Emory. Email: jjurge2@emory.edu.

Juricek, *John T*., *Emory*. Email: jjurice@emory. edu.

Jurss, *Jacob*, *Metropolitan State*. Saint Paul, MN. Email: jacob.jurss@metrostate.edu; jurssjac@ msu.edu.

Juster, *Susan*, *Michigan, Ann Arbor*. Email: sjuster@umich.edu.

Justice, *George W*., *North Georgia*. Email: george.justice@ung.edu.

Justiniano, *Maureen*. Washington, DC. Affil: SNA International / Defense POW/MIA Accounting Agency (DPAA). Email: mcs. justiniano@gmail.com. Research: WWII in the Pacific Theater, 19th-/20th-c empires and revolutions.

Jütte, *Daniel*, *NYU*. Email: daniel.juette@nyu. edu.

K k

Kaadan, **Abdul Nasser**, *Weber State*. Email: ankaadan@weber.edu.

Kaatz, **Kevin Warren**, *California State, East Bay*. Email: kevin.kaatz@csueastbay.edu.

Kaba, **Lansine**, *Illinois, Chicago*. Email: lkaba@ uic.edu.

Kabala, **Jakub J.**, *Davidson*. Email: kukabala@ davidson.edu.

Kabat, **Ric**, *North Georgia*. Email: ric.kabat@ung. edu.

Kacerguis, *Edward S*. Troy, NY. Affil: Rensselaer Polytech. Inst. Email: fred@rpi.edu.

Kachun, *Mitch*, *Western Michigan*. Kalamazoo, MI. Email: mitch.kachun@wmich.edu. Research: memory, public commemorations.

Kaczynski, *Bernice M*., *McMaster*. Hamilton, ON, Canada. Email: kaczynb@mcmaster. ca. Research: Christian monasticism, early medieval intellectual.

Kadar Lynn, *Katalin*. St. Helena, CA. Affil: Eotvos Lorand. Email: editor@helenahistorypress. com. Research: post-WWII US emigre political movements, National Committee for Free Europe.

Kadia, **Miriam Kingsberg**, *Colorado, Boulder*. Email: miriam.kingsberg@colorado.edu.

Kadish, **Gerald E.**, *Binghamton, SUNY*. Email: kadishg@binghamton.edu.

Kadric, *Sanja*. Columbus, OH. Affil: Ohio State. Email: kadricsa@gmail.com.

Kaefer, *Katie*, *AHA*. Washington, DC. Email: kkaefer@historians.org. Research: America, women.

Kaegi, *Walter E*., *Chicago*. Chicago, IL. Email: kwal@uchicago.edu. Research: Muslim conquest of Byzantine Africa, Byzantine military.

Kaestle, *Carl F*., *Brown*. Email: Carl_Kaestle@ Brown.edu.

Kaeuper, *Richard W*., *Rochester*. Rochester, NY. Email: richard.kaeuper@rochester.edu. Research: chivalry and lived religion, law and justice.

Kafadar, *Cemal*, *Harvard (Hist.)*. Cambridge, MA. Email: kafadar@fas.harvard.edu. Research: Ottoman, paleography.

Kaffenberger, **Schorsch**, *San Diego State*.

Kafka, *Ben*, *NYU*. Email: kafka@nyu.edu.

Kafker, *Frank A*., *Cincinnati*. Dedham, MA. Email: fkafker@msn.com. Research: encyclopedias, French Revolution and Napoleon.

Kagan, *Donald*, *Yale*. Email: donald.kagan@ yale.edu.

Kagan, *Marc*, *Lehman, CUNY*. Email: marc. kagan@lehman.cuny.edu.

Kagan, *Richard L*., *Johns Hopkins (Hist.)*. Philadelphia, PA. Email: kagan@jhu.edu. Research: early modern Europe, Spanish and Iberian expansion.

Kagan Guthrie, **Zachary**, *Mississippi*.

Kahan, *Alan*, *Florida International*. Email: kahana@fiu.edu.

Kahan, *Michael B*. Stanford, CA. Affil: Stanford. Email: mkahan@stanford.edu. Research: Philadelphia, street life.

Kahle, *Mary*. Austin, TX. Affil: Texas State. Email: maryckahle@kahle.org.

Kahle, *Trish*. Chicago, IL. Affil: Chicago. Email: kahle@uchicago.edu.

Kahm, *Howard H*. Seoul, South Korea. Affil: Yonsei. Email: hkahm@yonsei.ac.kr. Research: modern Korean economic, modern Japanese economic.

Kahn, *Michelle*, *Richmond*. Email: mkahn@ richmond.edu.

Kahrl, *Andrew W*., *Virginia*. Charlottesville, VA. Email: andrew.kahrl@virginia.edu. Research: modern US, African American.

Kaicker, *Abhishek*, *California, Berkeley*. Berkeley, CA. Email: kaicker@berkeley.edu; abhishek3@ gmail.com. Research: late Mughal empire, early colonial rule.

Kaiser, *Alan*, *Evansville*. Email: ak58@evansville. edu.

Kaiser, *Daniel H*., *Grinnell*. Email: kaiser@ grinnell.edu.

Kaiser, *David E*., *Naval War Coll*.

Kaiser, *David*, *MIT*. Email: dikaiser@mit.edu.

Kaiser, *Thomas E*., *Arkansas, Little Rock*. Email: tekaiser@ualr.edu.

Kaiwar, *Vasant*, *Duke*. Email: vkaiwar@duke. edu.

Kaja, *Jeffrey D*., *California State, Northridge*. Email: jeffrey.kaja@csun.edu.

Kaldellis, *Anthony*, *Ohio State*. Email: Kaldellis.1@osu.edu.

Kaldis, *William Peter*, *Ohio*. Hilliard, OH. Email: kaldis@ohio.edu. Research: Balkans, Byzantine Empire.

Kale, *Madhavi*, *Bryn Mawr*. Merion Station, PA. Email: mkale@brynmawr.edu. Research: Indian diaspora and British empire, race and gender.

Kale, **Steven D.**, *Washington State, Pullman*. Email: kale@wsu.edu.

Kalhan, *Anil*. Philadelphia, PA. Affil: Drexel. Email: anil.kalhan@aya.yale.edu.

Kalic, **Sean N.**, *US Army Command Coll*. Email: sean.n.kalic.civ@mail.mil.

Kalin, *Anthony S*. Valparaiso, IN. Email: anthony. kalin@valpo.edu. Research: philosophy of history, postwar Polish poetry.

Kalin, **Berkley**, *Memphis*.

Kalinga, *Owen J*., *North Carolina State*. Email: owen_kalinga@ncsu.edu.

Kalinowski, *Angela*, *Saskatchewan*. Email: angela.kalinowski@usask.ca.

Kalisman, *Hilary Falb*, *Colorado, Boulder*. Email: Hilary.Kalisman@colorado.edu.

Kaliss, *Gregory*, *Franklin & Marshall*. Email: gkaliss@fandm.edu.

Kallander, **Amy Aisen**, *Syracuse*. Email: akalland@maxwell.syr.edu.

Kallander, **George**, *Syracuse*. Email: glkallan@ maxwell.syr.edu.

Kalman, *Laura*, *California, Santa Barbara*. Goleta, CA. Email: kalman@history.ucsb.edu. Research: 20th-c US.

Kalthoff, **Mark A.**, *Hillsdale*. Email: mkalthoff@ hillsdale.edu.

Kamali, *Elizabeth Papp*. Cambridge, MA. Affil: Harvard Law Sch. Email: ekamali@law.harvard. edu.

Kamata, *Saaya*. Houston, TX. Affil: Rice. Email: saaya.kamata@rice.edu.

Kamenov, *Nikolay*. Zurich, Switzerland. Affil: Graduate Inst., geneva. Email: nkamenov@ gmail.com.

Kamensky, *Jane*, *Harvard (Hist.)*; *Arthur and Elizabeth Schlesinger Library*. Email: kamensky@g.harvard.edu.

Kamerick, Kathleen C., *Iowa*. Email: kathleen-kamerick@uiowa.edu.

Kamerling, Henry, *Seattle*. Email: kamerlih@seattleu.edu.

Kamil, Neil, *Texas, Austin*. Email: kamil@austin.utexas.edu.

Kaminski, Andrzej, *Georgetown*. Email: kaminska@georgetown.edu.

Kaminski, Theresa, *Wisconsin-Stevens Point*. Email: tkaminsk@uwsp.edu.

Kaminsky, Arnold P., *California State, Long Beach*. Email: arnold.kaminsky@csulb.edu.

Kaminsky, Howard M., *Florida International*. Email: kaminsky@fiu.edu.

Kammerling, Joy, *Eastern Illinois*. Email: jmkammerling@eiu.edu.

Kamola, Stefan, *Eastern Connecticut State*. Willimantic, CT. Email: kamolas@easternct.edu. Research: Persian historiography under the Mongols, Sasanian legacy reception.

Kamp, Marianne R., *Indiana*. Email: mkamp@indiana.edu.

Kamper, Kathleen G., *La Salle*. Email: kamper@lasalle.edu.

Kamphoefner, Walter D., *Texas A&M*. Bryan, TX. Email: waltkamp@tamu.edu. Research: German immigration and ethnicity.

Kanagawa, Nadia, *Furman*. Email: nadia.kanagawa@furman.edu.

Kane, Adrian. Seattle, WA. Affil: Washington, Seattle. Email: akane14@uw.edu.

Kane, Brendan M., *Connecticut, Storrs*. Email: brendan.kane@uconn.edu.

Kane, Eileen Mary, *Connecticut Coll.* Email: ekane2@conncoll.edu.

Kane, Maeve E., *SUNY, Albany*.

Kane, Paula M. Pittsburgh, PA. Affil: Pittsburgh. Email: pmk@pitt.edu. Research: modern Catholic, American religious.

Kane, Robert G., Jr., *Niagara*. Niagara University, NY. Email: rkane@niagara.edu. Research: modern Japan, US diplomatic.

Kane, Sean Thomas. Kansas City, MO. Affil: Missouri, Kansas City. Email: sthosdkane@gmail.com. Research: national identity, early Tudor England.

Kaneko, Toshiya. Sapporo-Shi Hokkaido, Japan. Email: kane1048@lapis.plala.or.jp. Research: Japanese intellectual, Japanese politics.

Kang, Hugh H. W., *Hawai'i, Manoa*. Email: hwkang@hawaii.edu.

Kang, Hyeok Hweon 'H.H.' Cambridge, MA. Affil: Harvard. Email: hyeokhweonkang@g.harvard.edu. Research: early modern Korea, military.

Kang, Minsoo, *Missouri–St. Louis*. St. Louis, MO. Email: kangmi@umsl.edu. Research: modern European intellectual, early modern Europan intellectual.

Kang, S. Deborah, *California State, San Marcos*. Email: dkang@csusm.edu.

Kang, Sung Pil, *Hawai'i Pacific*. Email: skang@hpu.edu.

Kang, Wenqing, *Cleveland State*. Email: w.kang@csuohio.edu.

Kang, Woong Joe. Potomac, MD. Affil: Virginia Christian. Email: wkang2000@gmail.com.

Kangas, William H., *Seattle*. Seattle, WA. Email: wkangas@seattleu.edu. Research: modern Europe, intellectual and cultural.

Kanipe, Esther S., *Hamilton*. Email: ekanipe@hamilton.edu.

Kanjwal, Hafsa, *Lafayette*. Email: kanjwalh@lafayette.edu.

Kannenberg, Corinne E. Denver, CO. Affil: Princeton. Email: corinnek@princeton.edu.

Kannenberg, Lisa A., *St. Rose*. Email: kannenbl@strose.edu.

Kanogo, Tabitha, *California, Berkeley*. Email: kanogo@berkeley.edu.

Kanter, Deborah, *Albion*. Ann Arbor, MI. Email: dkanter@albion.edu. Research: immigration/religion, Chicano.

Kanter, Douglas, *Florida Atlantic*. Boca Raton, FL. Email: dkanter1@fau.edu. Research: British-Irish relations, 19th-c British politics.

Kantowicz, Edward R., *Carleton, Can.* Email: edward.kantowicz@carleton.ca.

Kantrowitz, Stephen D., *Wisconsin-Madison*. Madison, WI. Email: skantrow@wisc.edu. Research: 19th-c US, race and gender.

Kapadia, Aparna, *Williams*. Email: ak16@williams.edu.

Kapelle, William E., *Brandeis*. Email: wkapelle@brandeis.edu.

Kapelusz-Poppi, Ana Maria, *Wisconsin-Oshkosh*. Email: kapelusz@uwosh.edu.

Kapetanopoulos, Elias, *Central Connecticut State*. Email: kapetanopoulos@mail.ccsu.edu.

Kaplan, Anna F. Washington, DC. Affil: American. Email: Anna.F.Kaplan@gmail.com. Research: memory/legacy of U of MS desegregation, black women's labor.

Kaplan, Cynthia, *California, Santa Barbara*. Email: kaplan@polsci.ucsb.edu.

Kaplan, Debra L. Ramat Gan, Israel. Affil: Bar Ilan. Email: debra.kaplan@biu.ac.il. Research: early modern Europe, Jewish.

Kaplan, Edward. Carlisle, PA. Affil: US Army War. Email: eakaplan@gmail.com. Research: 1950s-60s nuclear strategy, discourses on victory.

Kaplan, Elle. Fayetteville, NY. Affil: California, Davis. Email: ellemk222@gmail.com.

Kaplan, Isabelle. Washington, DC. Affil: Georgetown. Email: kaplanindc@yahoo.com. Research: Russia, Azerbaijan.

Kaplan, Lawrence S., *Kent State*. Rockville, MD. Affil: Georgetown. Email: lkaplan24@aol.com. Research: Jeffersonian era, NATO.

Kaplan, Marion, *NYU*. Email: marion.kaplan@nyu.edu.

Kaplan, Mark, *Pace*.

Kaplan, Michael. Oceanside, NY. Affil: SUNY, Farmingdale; Yeshiva. Email: KaplanMC@aol.com.

Kaplan, Philip G., *North Florida*. Email: pkaplan@unf.edu.

Kaplan, Rebecca, *Science History Inst.* Email: rkaplan@sciencehistory.org.

Kaplan, Steven, *Cornell*. Email: slk8@cornell.edu.

Kaplan, Temma, *Rutgers*. Email: temma555@aol.com.

Kapur, Nick, *Rutgers, Camden*. Email: nick.kapur@rutgers.edu.

Karafantis, Layne. Los Angeles, CA. Email: layne.karafantis@gmail.com.

Karakaya-Stump, Ayfer, *William and Mary*. Email: akstump@wm.edu.

Karamanski, Theodore J., *Loyola, Chicago*. Email: tkarama@luc.edu.

Karamustafa, Ahmet, *Maryland, Coll. Park*. Email: akaramus@umd.edu.

Karant-Nunn, Susan C., *Arizona; Portland State*. Portland, OR. Email: karantnu@email.arizona.edu. Research: medieval, Renaissance and Reformation.

Karathanos, Michael. Tulsa, OK. Email: mkarathanos@cox.net.

Karatzas, Konstantinos. Aigaleo, Athens, Greece. Email: dr.karatzas@yahoo.com.

Karch, Brendan J., *Louisiana State*. Email: bkarch@lsu.edu.

Kargon, Robert A., *Johns Hopkins (Hist. of Science)*. Email: kargon@jhu.edu.

Karibo, Holly M., *Oklahoma State*. Stillwater, OK. Email: hkaribo@okstate.edu. Research: US.

Karl, Erin, *Central Oklahoma*. Email: ekarl@uco.edu.

Karl, Rebecca E., *NYU*. New York, NY. Email: rebecca.karl@nyu.edu. Research: Chinese nationalism, Chinese gender and citizenship.

Karlsen, Carol F., *Michigan, Ann Arbor*.

Karlsrud, Robert A., *Sonoma State*. Email: bob.karlsrud@sonoma.edu.

Karn, Alexander M., *Colgate*. Email: akarn@colgate.edu.

Karnes, Kevin C., *Emory*. Email: kkarnes@emory.edu.

Karp, Jonathan, *Binghamton, SUNY*. Email: jkarp@binghamton.edu.

Karp, Matthew J., *Princeton*. Princeton, NJ. Email: mjkarp@princeton.edu; matthewjkarp@gmail.com. Research: US Civil War, southern slaveholders.

Karp, Michael T. Temecula, CA. Affil: Coll. of the Desert; Temecula Valley Unified Sch. District. Email: karpmichaelt@gmail.com. Research: northwest CA labor/violence/environment, utopian communities/water use/the West.

Karpat, Kemal H. Madison, WI. Affil: Wisconsin, Madison. Email: khkarpat@wisc.edu. Research: Ottoman Empire, modern Turkey.

Karr, David S. Columbia, MO. Affil: Columbia Coll., Mo. Email: dskarr@ccis.edu. Research: political culture, English theater and urban space.

Karr, Ronald Dale. Pepperell, MA. Affil: Massachusetts, Lowell. Email: ronald_karr@uml.edu. Research: John Winthrop, 19th-c suburbs.

Karr, Susan Longfield, *Cincinnati*. Email: karrsn@ucmail.uc.edu.

Karras, Alan L. San Francisco, CA. Affil: California, Berkeley. Email: karras@berkeley.edu. Research: political economy, Corruption.

Karras, Ruth Mazo. Dublin, Ireland. Affil: Trinity Coll., Dublin. Email: profkarras@gmail.com. Research: medieval European women/gender, sexuality.

Kars, Marjoleine, *Maryland, Baltimore County*. Washington, DC. Email: kars@umbc.edu. Research: 1763 Berbice slave rebellion, Native Americans and Amazonia.

Karsner, Douglas G., *Bloomsburg*. Email: dkarsner@bloomu.edu.

Karson, Larry. Houston, TX. Affil: Houston, Downtown. Email: karsonl@uhd.edu. Research: American smuggling.

Karsten, Peter D., *Pittsburgh*. Email: pjk2@pitt.edu.

Karthas, Ilyana, *Missouri, Columbia*. Email: karthasi@missouri.edu.

Karush, Matthew B., *George Mason*. Fairfax, VA. Email: mkarush@gmu.edu. Research: mass culture in Argentina 1920-45.

Kasarda, Adam. Hackettstown, NJ. Email: ajkasarda@live.com.

Kaschak, **Brian J**. Kingston, PA. Affil: Wyoming Seminary Coll. Prep. Sch. Email: bkaschak@wyomingseminary.org. Research: religious politics in France 1500-1700, urban politics in France 1500-1700.

Kasekamp, **Andres**, *Toronto*. Email: andres.kasekamp@utoronto.ca.

Kashanipour, **Ryan Amir**, *Arizona; Northern Arizona*. Email: ryan.kashanipour@nau.edu.

Kashani-Sabet, **Firoozeh**, *Pennsylvania*. Email: fks@history.upenn.edu.

Kasper-Marienberg, **Verena**, *North Carolina State*. Email: vikasper@ncsu.edu.

Kasperski, **Kenneth F**. Homosassa, FL. Email: kkasperski@tampabay.rr.com. Research: American colonials in Philippines, American/Filipino cultural exchange.

Kasson, **John F**., *North Carolina, Chapel Hill*. Email: jfkasson@email.unc.edu.

Kassow, **Samuel D**., *Trinity Coll., Conn*. Email: samuel.kassow@trincoll.edu.

Kaster, **Gregory L**., *Gustavus Adolphus*. Saint Peter, MN. Email: gkaster@gac.edu. Research: slavery and abolition, visual culture.

Kastor, **Peter J**., *Washington, St. Louis*. Email: pjkastor@wustl.edu.

Kasturi, **Malavika**, *Toronto*. Email: malavika.katsuri@utoronto.ca.

Katerberg, **William H**., *Calvin*. Email: wkaterbe@calvin.edu.

Kates, **Gary**, *Pomona*. Claremont, CA. Email: gary_kates@pomona.edu; GK004747@pomona.edu. Research: modern Europe.

Kativa, **Hillary S**., *Science History Inst*. Email: hkativa@sciencehistory.org.

Katsev, **Allison Y**., *San José State*. San Jose, CA. Email: Allison.Katsev@sjsu.edu; akatsev@sonic.net. Research: Russia, historiography.

Katsky, **Clay Silver**. Austin, TX. Affil: George Washington. Email: ckatsky@gmail.com. Research: intelligence studies, Cold War.

Katz, **Elizabeth**. St. Louis, MO. Affil: Washington, St. Louis. Email: elizabethdkatz@gmail.com.

Katz, **Esther**, *NYU*. Email: esther.katz@nyu.edu.

Katz, **Ethan B**., *California, Berkeley*. Berkeley, CA. Email: ebkatz@berkeley.edu; ethan.katz79@gmail.com. Research: Jewish-Muslim relations in France, cultural history of Francophone Bible.

Katz, **Kimberly**, *Towson*. Email: kkatz@towson.edu.

Katz, **Paul R**. Nankang, Taipei, Taiwan. Affil: Inst. of Modern Hist. Email: mhprkatz@gate.sinica.edu.tw. Research: urban religion in modern China, Daoism and temple cults.

Katz, **Paul Ryan**. Brooklyn, NY. Affil: Columbia. Email: paul.ryan.katz@gmail.com. Research: violence and its denunciation, the Left and human rights.

Katz, **Philip M**. Washington, DC. Affil: Council of Independent Colleges. Email: pmkatz@post.harvard.edu. Research: American colony in 19th-c Paris, Civil War in global perspective.

Katz, **Sara**, *Loyola, New Orleans*. Ann Arbor, MI. Email: sarakatz@umich.edu.

Katz, **Sherry J**. Berkeley, CA. Affil: San Francisco State. Email: sjkatz@sfsu.edu.

Katz, **Stanley N**. Princeton, NJ. Affil: Princeton. Email: snkatz@princeton.edu. Research: philanthropy, comparative constitutionalism.

Katz-Hyman, **Martha B**. Newport News, VA. Affil: Jamestown-Yorktown Foundation. Email: martha.katzhyman@gmail.com. Research:

material culture of American slavery, abolition and anti-slavery.

Katznelson, **Ira**, *Columbia (Hist.)*. New York, NY. Email: iik1@columbia.edu.

Kauffeldt, **Jonas**, *North Georgia*. Email: jonas.kauffeldt@ung.edu.

Kauffman, **Jesse C**., *Eastern Michigan*. Email: jesse.kauffman@emich.edu.

Kauffman, **Kelsey**. Greencastle, IN. Affil: Indiana Women's Prison. Email: kelsey.kauffman@gmail.com.

Kaufman, **Asher**, *Notre Dame*. Email: Kaufman.15@nd.edu.

Kaufman, **Burton I**., *Miami, Ohio*. New York, NY. Email: kaufmabi@miamioh.edu. Research: US diplomatic, US presidency.

Kaufman, **Lucy M**., *Alabama, Tuscaloosa*. Email: lmkaufman@ua.edu.

Kaufman, **Suzanne K**., *Loyola, Chicago*. Chicago, IL. Email: skaufma@luc.edu. Research: modern Europe, France.

Kaufman, **V. Scott**, *Francis Marion*. Email: vkaufman@fmarion.edu.

Kaufman-McKivigan, **John R**., *Indiana–Purdue, Indianapolis*. Email: jmckivig@iupui.edu.

Kautt, **William H**., *US Army Command Coll*. Email: william.h.kautt.civ@mail.mil.

Kautz, **Matt**. New York, NY. Email: mk3891@tc.columbia.edu.

Kavey, **Allison**, *Graduate Center, CUNY*. Email: akavey@jjay.cuny.edu.

Kawaguchi, **Lesley A**. Santa Monica, CA. Affil: Santa Monica. Email: kawaguchi_lesley@smc.edu. Research: 19th-c German immigration to US, immigrants in California mining region.

Kawamura, **Noriko**, *Washington State, Pullman*. Pullman, WA. Email: nkawamura@wsu.edu. Research: Emperor Hirohito and Pacific war.

Kawashima, **Kohei**. Tokyo, Japan. Affil: Musashi. Email: kokoharu@cc.musashi.ac.jp. Research: sport and culture, race and athletic performance.

Kawashima, **Yasuhide**, *Texas, El Paso*. Email: ykawashi@utep.edu.

Kay, **Carolyn H**., *Trent*. Email: ckay@trentu.ca.

Kay, **Gwen E**., *SUNY, Oswego*. Syracuse, NY. Email: gwen.kay@oswego.edu. Research: home economics, 19th-c bioethics.

Kay, **Thomas O**., *Wheaton, Ill*. Email: thomas.kay@wheaton.edu.

Kaya, **Murat**. Bamberg, Germany. Affil: Bamberg. Email: murrkayaa@gmail.com.

Kayaalp, **Pinar**, *Ramapo*. Email: pkayaalp@ramapo.edu.

Kayali, **Hasan**, *California, San Diego*. Email: hkayali@ucsd.edu.

Kaye, **Cynthia**. Cedar City, UT. Affil: Arizona State. Email: cynthia.kaye.1960@gmail.com.

Kaye, **Joel B**., *Barnard, Columbia*. New York, NY. Email: jkaye@barnard.edu. Research: medieval, European intellectual/economic/science.

Kaye, **Noah**, *Michigan State*. East Lansing, MI. Email: kayenoah@msu.edu; noahkaye@gmail.com. Research: economic, Greece.

Kazal, **Russell A**., *Toronto*. Toronto, ON, Canada. Email: rkazal@utsc.utoronto.ca. Research: urban ethnicity, regional origins of multiculturalism.

Kazanjian, **David**. Philadelphia, PA. Affil: Pennsylvania. Email: kazanjia@english.upenn.edu.

Kazemi, **Ranin**, *San Diego State*. Email: rkazemi@sdsu.edu.

Kazin, **Michael**, *Georgetown*. Washington, DC. Email: mk8@georgetown.edu. Research: US social movements and politics, Reconstruction to present.

Kazmier, **Lisa A**. Manville, NJ. Email: lisakazmier@yahoo.com. Research: death/funeral practices/cremation, print/cultural constructions of gender.

Kazyulina, **Regina**, *Bates*. Email: rkazyuli@bates.edu.

Kea, **Ray A**., *California, Riverside*. Email: ray.kea@ucr.edu.

Kealey, **Edward J**. Amityville, NY.

Kealey, **Gregory S**., *New Brunswick*. Email: gkealey@unb.ca.

Kealey, **Linda**, *New Brunswick*. Email: lkealey@unb.ca.

Kean, **Melissa Fitzsimons**, *Rice*. Email: kean@rice.edu.

Kean, **Thomas H**. Far Hills, NJ.

Keane, **Katarina**, *Maryland, Coll. Park*. Email: kkeane@umd.edu.

Keane, **Kevan Dale**. Petersburg, VA. Affil: Regent. Email: kevakea@mail.regent.edu.

Keane, **Lloyd**, *Carleton, Can*. Email: lloyd.keane@carleton.ca.

Keane-Dawes, **Antony Wayne**. Columbia, SC. Affil: South Carolina, Columbia. Email: antony@email.sc.edu. Research: nationalism and nation building, Afro-diaspora.

Keaney, **Heather Nina**, *Westmont*. Email: hkeaney@westmont.edu.

Kearney, **Patrick**. Burke, VA. Affil: Virginia Commonwealth. Email: pckearney01@gmail.com.

Keating, **Ann Durkin**, *North Central*. Chicago, IL. Email: adkeating@noctrl.edu. Research: urban, 19th-c US.

Keating, **Maj Christine**, *US Military Acad*. Email: christine.keating@usma.edu.

Keating, **Ryan W**., *California State, San Bernardino*. Email: rkeating@csusb.edu.

Keaton, **Michael Palmer**. Seneca, SC. Affil: Southern Wesleyan. Email: mkeaton@swu.edu. Research: John Locke and Algernon Sidney, US government.

Keber, **Martha L**., *Georgia Coll. and State*.

Keddie, **Nikki R**., *UCLA*. Email: keddie@history.ucla.edu.

Keefe, **Thomas M**., *St. Joseph's*. Philadelphia, PA. Research: France, Germany.

Keefer, **Bradley S**., *Kent State*. Email: bkeefer@kent.edu.

Keegan, **Matthew L**. New York, NY. Affil: Barnard, Columbia. Email: mlk.keegan@gmail.com.

Keegan, **Tara Aine**. Eugene, OR. Affil: Oregon. Email: tkeegan@uoregon.edu.

Keel, **Terence**, *California, Santa Barbara*. Email: tkeel@blackstudies.ucsb.edu.

Keeley, **Theresa**, *Louisville*. Email: theresa.keeley@louisville.edu.

Keeling, **Drew A**. Kuesnacht, Switzerland. Email: drewkeeling@yahoo.com. Research: comparative migration, business and economic.

Keen, **Ralph**, *Illinois, Chicago; American Soc. of Church Hist*. Email: rkeen01@uic.edu; ralph.keen@churchhistory.org.

Keenan, **Barry Campbell**. Worthington, OH. Affil: Denison. Email: keenan@denison.edu.

Keenan, Bethany S., *Coe*. Email: bkeenan@coe. edu.

Keene, Jennifer D., *Chapman*. Orange, CA. Email: keene@chapman.edu. Research: 20th-c US, WWI.

Keene, Thomas H., *Kennesaw State*.

Keep, J.L.H., *Toronto*.

Keesler, Maranda. Alexandria, VA. Affil: George Mason. Email: mkeesler@gmu.edu.

Kefalas, Kalliopi. La Jolla, CA. Affil: California, San Diego. Email: kkefalas@ucsd.edu.

Keffer, Ronald Lee. Homer, AK. Email: annronkeffer@gmail.com.

Kegerreis, Christopher M. Goleta, CA. Affil: California, Santa Barbara. Email: cmkegerreis@ gmail.com. Research: Hellenic geography and exploration, Hellenic political philosophy.

Keghida, Mounira. Brooklyn, NY. Affil: Graduate Center, CUNY. Email: mkeghida@gradcenter. cuny.edu. Research: modern Europe, 19th-c world.

Kehl, James, *Pittsburgh*. Email: jak18@pitt.edu.

Kehoe, Karen A. Latrobe, PA. Affil: St. Vincent. Email: karen.kehoe@stvincent.edu. Research: daughters of regiment/Civil War, Civil War bands.

Kehoe, S. Karly, *Dalhousie; St. Mary's, Can.* Email: karly.kehoe@smu.ca.

Kehrberg, Richard, *Iowa State*. Email: kehrberg@iastate.edu.

Keil, Charles, *Toronto*. Email: charlie.keil@ utoronto.ca.

Keilson, Ana Isabel. Somerville, MA. Affil: Harvard. Email: keilson@fas.harvard.edu. Research: dance, intellectual history and political theory.

Keim, Ben, *Pomona*. Email: benjamin.keim@ pomona.edu.

Keiner, Christine. Rochester, NY. Affil: Rochester Inst. of Tech. Email: keinerc@hotmail.com. Research: environmental, maritime.

Keirn, Tim W., *Soc. for Hist. Education*. Email: tim. keirn@csulb.edu.

Keisman, Philip, *Lehman, CUNY*. Email: pkeisman@gradcenter.cuny.edu.

Keita, Maghan, *Villanova*. Email: maghan. keita@villanova.edu.

Keiter, Lindsay Mitchell. Williamsburg, VA. Affil: Penn State, Altoona. Email: lmk227@psu.edu. Research: economic functions of marriage 1750-1865.

Keith, Charles P., *Michigan State*. Email: ckeith@ msu.edu.

Keitt, Andrew W., *Alabama, Birmingham*. Email: akeitt@uab.edu.

Keliher, Macabe. Dallas, TX. Affil: Southern Methodist. Email: keliher@gmail.com. Research: Qing empire, early modern studies.

Kelikian, Alice A., *Brandeis*. Email: kelikian@ brandeis.edu.

Kellam, James Patrick, *Appalachian State*.

Kellam, Lynda. Brooktondale, NY. Affil: Cornell. Email: lkellam@cornell.edu. Research: human rights, humanitarianism.

Kelland, Lara L., *Louisville; Missouri–St. Louis*. Louisville, KY. Email: lara.kelland@louisville. edu. Research: collective memory and public history.

Kellar, Brenda. Corvallis, OR. Affil: Oregon State. Email: kllrbren@gmail.com. Research: pollination knowledge, beekeeping.

Kelleher, Marie A., *California State, Long Beach*. Email: m.kelleher@csulb.edu.

Kelleher, Patricia, *Kutztown*. Kutztown, PA. Email: kelleher@kutztown.edu. Research: US social, immigration.

Keller, Jean A., *San Diego Mesa*. Email: jkeller@ sdccd.edu.

Keller, Jeffery Wayne. Capon Bridge, WV. Affil: John Handley High Sch. Email: keller@wps. k12.va.us.

Keller, Kathleen A., *Gustavus Adolphus*. Email: kkeller2@gustavus.edu.

Keller, Kenneth W., *Mary Baldwin*. Staunton, VA. Email: kkeller@mbc.edu; tessonf@verizon. net. Research: Virginia frontier, Germans and Scots-Irish.

Keller, Lisa. Purchase, NY. Affil: Purchase, SUNY. Email: lisa.keller@purchase.edu. Research: Europe, women.

Keller, Ralph A., *California State, Northridge*.

Keller, Renata N., *Nevada, Reno*.

Keller, Richard C., *Wisconsin-Madison*. Madison, WI. Email: rckeller@wisc.edu. Research: colonial psychiatry in French North Africa, microbe.

Keller, Shoshana, *Hamilton*. Email: skeller@ hamilton.edu.

Keller, Tait S., *Rhodes*. Email: kellert@rhodes. edu.

Keller, Vera A., *Oregon*. Email: keller@uoregon. edu.

Keller-Lapp, Heidi Marie, *San Diego State*.

Kelley, Allison M. Charlottesville, VA. Affil: Virginia. Email: akc8py@virginia.edu.

Kelley, Avery. Bayonne, NJ. Email: Avery_ Kelley@yahoo.com.

Kelley, Blair, *North Carolina State*. Email: blmkelley@ncsu.edu.

Kelley, David E., *Oberlin*. Email: david.e.kelley@ oberlin.edu.

Kelley, Donald R., *Rutgers*. New Brunswick, NJ. Email: dkelley@scarletmail.rutgers. edu. Research: European intellectual, historiography.

Kelley, Hannah R., *James Madison*. Email: kelleyhr@jmu.edu.

Kelley, Kevin M. Azores, Portugal. Email: kevinmkelley@portugalmail.pt.

Kelley, Lucas. Raleigh, NC. Affil: North Carolina, Chapel Hill. Email: lucaspk@live.unc.edu.

Kelley, Mary C., *Michigan, Ann Arbor*. Lyme Center, NH. Email: mckelley@umich.edu. Research: 19th-/20th-c American intellectual, women.

Kelley, Michelle. Saint Louis, MO. Affil: Washington, St. Louis. Email: mrk241@gmail. com.

Kelley, Robin D. G., *UCLA*. Email: rdkelley@ history.ucla.edu.

Kelley, Samuel J. Waco, TX. Affil: Baylor. Email: sam_kelley@baylor.edu.

Kellison, Kimberly R., *Baylor*. Waco, TX. Email: kimberly_kellison@baylor.edu. Research: US South, Civil War and Reconstruction.

Kellman, Jordan, *Louisiana, Lafayette*. Email: kellman@louisiana.edu.

Kellner, Joseph. Berkeley, CA. Affil: California, Berkeley. Email: joseph.kellner@berkeley.edu. Research: Soviet borders/Finland.

Kellogg, Riley Blanchard. Flushing, NY. Affil: Queens, CUNY. Email: rileybk@gmail.com.

Kellogg, Susan, *Houston*. Email: skellogg@ uh.edu.

Kellow, Margaret M. R., *Western Ontario*. Email: mmkellow@uwo.ca.

Kelly, Alexandra, *Wyoming*. Email: alexandra. kelly@uwyo.edu.

Kelly, Alfred H., *Hamilton*. Clinton, NY. Email: akelly@hamilton.edu. Research: legacy of Franco-Prussian War.

Kelly, Benjamin, *York, Can.* Email: benkelly@ yorku.ca.

Kelly, Catherine E., *Omohundro Inst.* Norman, OK. Email: cekelly01@wm.edu. Research: culture, early America.

Kelly, Chau J., *North Florida*. Email: chau.kelly@ unf.edu.

Kelly, David H. Lake View, NY. Affil: D'Youville. Email: kellyd@dyc.edu. Research: higher education, American Catholic education.

Kelly, Di. Keiraville, Australia. Affil: Wollongong. Email: di@uow.edu.au.

Kelly, Jason M., *Indiana–Purdue, Indianapolis*. Indianapolis, IN. Email: jaskelly@iupui.edu. Research: transatlantic radicalism & Fanny Wright, Anthropocene.

Kelly, Jason M., *Naval War Coll.* Email: jason. kelly@usnwc.edu.

Kelly, Jill E., *Southern Methodist*. Dallas, TX. Email: jillk@smu.edu. Research: Zulu, South Africa.

Kelly, Joanna Louise. Medford, MA. Affil: Boston Coll. Email: joanna.l.kelly@gmail.com. Research: US religion, US politics.

Kelly, M. Ruth Reilly. Lake View, NY. Affil: D'Youville. Email: kellyru@dyc.edu. Research: 19th-c American Catholicism.

Kelly, Mary C. Rindge, NH. Affil: Franklin Pierce. Email: kellymc@franklinpierce.edu. Research: Irish American/Irish New York, Great Famine memory.

Kelly, Mills, *George Mason*. Fairfax, VA. Email: tkelly7@gmu.edu. Research: Appalachian Trail, environmental policy.

Kelly, Patrick J., *Texas, San Antonio*. Email: patrick.kelly@utsa.edu.

Kelly, Samantha L., *Rutgers*. New Brunswick, NJ. Email: slkelly@history.rutgers.edu; samantha. lee.kelly@gmail.com. Research: medieval Europe, Horn of Africa.

Kelly, Sean Q. Camarillo, CA. Affil: California State, Channel Islands. Email: sean.kelly@ csuci.edu.

Kelly, Thomas, *Minnesota (Hist.)*.

Kelly, Timothy I. Latrobe, PA. Affil: St. Vincent. Email: tim.kelly@stvincent.edu. Research: US social, US environmental.

Kelm, Mary-Ellen, *Simon Fraser*. Email: kelm@ sfu.ca.

Kelman, Ari, *California, Davis*. Davis, CA. Email: akelman@ucdavis.edu; kelmanari@gmail.com. Research: US, Civil War.

Kelsch, Anne V., *North Dakota*. Email: anne. kelsch@und.edu.

Kelso, William M., *William and Mary*. Email: wkelso@preservationvirginia.org.

Kemezis, Adam, *Alberta*. Email: kemezis@ ualberta.ca.

Kemmis, Gabrielle Claire. Hazelbrook, Australia. Email: gckemmis@gmail.com. Research: Cold War foreign relations, psychology.

Kemnitz, Thomas M. Unionville, NY. Affil: Royal Fireworks Publishing. Email: rfpress@ frontiernet.net.

Kempf, Elena. Berkeley, CA. Affil: California, Berkeley. Email: elenakempf@berkeley.edu.

Kempker, *Erin M*. Columbus, MS. Affil: Mississippi, Women. Email: emkempker@ muw.edu. Research: conservative and right-wing women, second wave feminism.

Kendall, *Keith H.*, *Northern Michigan*. Marquette, MI. Email: kkendall@nmu.edu. Research: Pope Innocent III, 12th-/13th-c sermons.

Kendall, *Philip W*. Brownsville, TX. Affil: Texas, Brownsville. Email: pwkendall@juno.com.

Kendall, **Richard H.**, *SUNY, Albany*.

Kendi, *Ibram X.*, *American*. Washington, DC. Email: ibramxkendi@aol.com. Research: African American, black social movements.

Kendle, **John E.**, *Manitoba*.

Kenez, **Peter**, *California, Santa Cruz*. Email: kenez@ucsc.edu.

Kenlon, *Philip*. Fort Myers, FL. Affil: Florida International. Email: pkenl001@fiu.edu.

Kennedy, **Christopher M.**, *Francis Marion*. Email: ckennedy@fmarion.edu.

Kennedy, **Cynthia M.**, *Clarion, Pa.* Email: ckennedy@clarion.edu.

Kennedy, *Dane K.*, *George Washington; National Hist. Center*. Washington, DC. Email: dkennedy@gwu.edu. Research: exploration and empire, Sir Richard F. Burton.

Kennedy, *David M.*, *Stanford*. Stanford, CA. Email: dmk@stanford.edu. Research: 20th-c US, post-1945 US and international.

Kennedy, *Devin*, *Wisconsin-Madison*. Madison, WI. Email: devinbkennedy@gmail.com.

Kennedy, **John R.**, *US Army Command Coll.* Email: john.r.kennedy16.civ@mail.mil.

Kennedy, *Katharine D.*, *Agnes Scott*. Atlanta, GA. Email: kkennedy@agnesscott.edu. Research: modern Europe, European women.

Kennedy, **Kathleen A.**, *Missouri State*. Email: kathleenkennedy@missouristate.edu.

Kennedy, *Kevin T*. Bradenton, FL. Affil: State Coll., Fla. Email: kennedk1@scf.edu.

Kennedy, **Larissa**, *Illinois State*. Email: lkenned@ilstu.edu.

Kennedy, *Laura*. Detroit, MI. Affil: Wayne State. Email: fz4835@wayne.edu.

Kennedy, **Lawrence William**, *Scranton*. Email: lawrence.kennedy@scranton.edu.

Kennedy, **Lt Col (Ret.) Doug B.**, *US Air Force Acad.* Email: douglas.kennedy@usafa.edu.

Kennedy, **Neil**, *Memorial, Newfoundland*. Email: nkennedy@mun.ca.

Kennedy, **Padraic C.**, *York, Pa.* Email: pkennedy@ycp.edu.

Kennedy, **Paul M.**, *Yale*. Email: paul.kennedy@yale.edu.

Kennedy, **R. Emmet**, *George Washington*. Email: ekennedy@gwu.edu.

Kennedy, *Rebekah R*. Foley, AL. Affil: Toccoa Falls. Email: rebekah.r.kennedy@gmail.com.

Kennedy, *Rick A.*, *Point Loma Nazarene*. San Diego, CA. Email: rickkennedy@pointloma.edu. Research: Cotton Mather, Aristotelian historiography.

Kennedy, **Ross A.**, *Illinois State*. Email: rkenned@ilstu.edu.

Kennedy, **Sean**, *New Brunswick*. Email: skennedy@unb.ca.

Kennedy, *Wright*. New York, NY. Affil: Columbia. Email: w.kennedy@columbia.edu. Research: spatial history/historical GIS, urban mortality in Gilded Age.

Kennelly, *Laura B*. Berea, OH. Email: lkennelly@gmail.com. Research: 18th-c New England, memoir.

Kenner, *Martin*. Hudson, NY. Affil: Bard Prison Initiative. Email: martinkenner@gmail.com. Research: Anglo-American financial relations, Anglo-American imperial.

Kenney, **Padraic J.**, *Indiana*. Email: pjkenney@indiana.edu.

Kenney, **William H.**, *Kent State*. Email: wkenney@kent.edu.

Kennington, *Kelly Marie*, *Auburn*. Auburn, AL. Email: kennington@auburn.edu. Research: 19th-c America, American South.

Kenny, *Gale L*. New York, NY. Affil: Barnard, Columbia. Email: gkenny@barnard.edu. Research: antislavery movement/religion/gender, transnationalism.

Kenny, **James**, *Royal Military*. Email: kenny-j@rmc.ca.

Kenny, *Kevin*, *Boston Coll.; NYU*. New York, NY. Email: kevin.kenny@bc.edu; kevin.kenny@nyu.edu. Research: migration, 19th century.

Kenny, **Nicolas**, *Simon Fraser*. Email: nicolas_kenny@sfu.ca.

Kent, **Christopher A.**, *Saskatchewan*. Email: chris.kent@usask.ca.

Kent, **Dale V.**, *California, Riverside*. Email: dale.kent@ucr.edu.

Kent, **H. Ren Jr.**, *Austin Comm. Coll.* Email: renk@austincc.edu.

Kent, **Holly M.**, *Illinois, Springfield*. Email: hkent3@uis.edu.

Kent, **Larry J.**, *Coastal Carolina*. Email: lkent@coastal.edu.

Kent, **Peter C.**, *New Brunswick*. Email: kent@unb.ca.

Kent, *Stacie A.*, *Boston Coll.* Email: stacie.kent@bc.edu.

Kent, *Susan Kingsley*, *Colorado, Boulder*. Lyons, CO. Email: susan.kent@colorado.edu. Research: 19th-/20th-c Britain, Europe.

Kenworthy, **Scott M.**, *Miami, Ohio*. Email: kenwors@miamioh.edu.

Kenzer, *Robert C.*, *Richmond*. Richmond, VA. Email: rkenzer@richmond.edu; rkenzer@gmail.com. Research: Virginia's Civil War widows.

Keough, *Matthew Thomas*, *AHA*. Bristow, VA. Email: mkeough@historians.org.

Keough, *Willeen*, *Simon Fraser*. Email: wkeough@sfu.ca.

Keppel, *Ben*, *Oklahoma (Hist.)*. Norman, OK. Email: bkeppel@ou.edu. Research: childhood, US social policy.

Kerber, *Linda K.*, *Iowa*. Iowa City, IA. Email: linda-kerber@uiowa.edu. Research: US women, citizenship.

Kerbow, *Stephen M*. Uvalde, TX. Affil: Southwest Texas Jr. Coll. Email: smkerbow@gmail.com.

Kerby, **Robert L.**, *Notre Dame*. Email: Kerby.1@nd.edu.

Kercher, **Stephen E.**, *Wisconsin-Oshkosh*. Email: kercher@uwosh.edu.

Kerenji, *Emil*. Washington, DC. Affil: Mandel Center for Advanced Holocaust Studies. Email: ekerenji@ushmm.org. Research: Holocaust/genocide, WWII in Yugoslavia.

Kerguelen, *Ricardo Jose*. Bogota, Colombia. Affil: Andes. Email: rkerguel@uniandes.edu.co. Research: 19th-c Colombian economics and politics, conflict and economic performance in Antioquia.

Kerkhof, *Jacqueline*. Chevy Chase, MD. Affil: American. Email: Jk3221a@american.edu.

Kern, **Darcy**, *Southern Connecticut State*. Email: kernd2@southernct.edu.

Kern, *Karen M.*, *Hunter, CUNY*. New York, NY. Email: kkern@hunter.cuny.edu. Research: 19th-/20th-c Ottoman.

Kern, **Kathi**, *Kentucky*. Email: kern@uky.edu.

Kern, *Kevin F*. Akron, OH. Affil: Akron. Email: kkern@uakron.edu. Research: social sciences, eugenics and physical anthropology.

Kern, *Louis J.*, *Hofstra*. Brattleboro, VT. Email: louis.j.kern@hofstra.edu. Research: 19th-c American cultural and intellectual, eugenics and reproductive.

Kern, **Paul B.**, *Indiana, Northwest*.

Kern, **Stephen**, *Ohio State*. Email: kern.193@osu.edu.

Kern, **Susan A.**, *William and Mary*. Email: sakern@wm.edu.

Kernahan, *Peter J*. Saint Paul, MN. Affil: Minnesota. Email: kerna001@umn.edu. Research: surgery as profession.

Kernek, **Sterling J.**, *Western Illinois*. Email: SJ-Kernek@wiu.edu.

Kerns-Robison, **Jennifer**, *Portland State*. Email: jkk@pdx.edu.

Kerr, *Daniel R.*, *American*. Washington, DC. Email: kerr@american.edu. Research: public, oral.

Kerr, **Ian J.**, *Manitoba*. Email: ian.kerr@umanitoba.ca.

Kerr, **K. Austin**, *Ohio State*. Email: kerr.6@osu.edu.

Kerr, *Kelsey*. Pelham, NH. Email: kelsey.kerr1@snhu.edu.

Kerrison, *Catherine M.*, *Villanova*. Villanova, PA. Email: catherine.kerrison@villanova.edu. Research: Jefferson's daughters.

Kerr-Ritchie, *Jeffrey R*. Durham, NC. Affil: Howard. Email: jkerr-ritchie@howard.edu; jrkerrritchie@gmail.com. Research: US coastal slave trade, West Indies Emancipation in US.

Kerry, *Paul E.*, *Brigham Young*. Provo, UT. Email: paul_kerry@byu.edu. Research: European intellectual, 18th-/19th-c historiography.

Kersch, *Ken I*. Chestnut Hill, MA. Affil: Boston Coll. Email: kersch@bc.edu.

Kersey, **Harry A.**, **Jr.**, *Florida Atlantic*. Email: kersey@fau.edu.

Kershaw, **Gordon E.**, *Frostburg State*.

Kershaw, **Paul J. E.**, *Virginia*. Email: pjk3p@virginia.edu.

Kershaw, **Paul V.**, *Wayne State*. Email: paul.kershaw@wayne.edu.

Kersten, *Andrew E*. Bridgeton, MO. Affil: Missouri, St. Louis. Email: kerstena206@gmail.com. Research: American Federation of Labor, Clarence Darrow.

Kerstetter, *Todd M.*, *Texas Christian*. Fort Worth, TX. Email: t.kerstetter@tcu.edu. Research: water in the American West and Plains, religion in American West.

Kertesz, **Judy**, *North Carolina State*. Email: jkertes@ncsu.edu.

Keserich, **Charles**, *San José State*.

Keshavjee, **Serena**, *Winnipeg*. Email: s.keshavjee@uwinnipeg.ca.

Kesler Lund, **Alisa**, *Brigham Young*. Email: alisa.keslerlund@byu.edu.

Kessel, *Martina*. Bielefeld, Germany. Affil: Bielefeld. Email: martina.kessel@uni-bielefeld.de.

Kessell, **John L.**, *New Mexico*. Email: kessell@unm.edu.

Kesselring, **Krista J.**, *Dalhousie*. Email: krista. kesselring@dal.ca.

Kessler, *Amalia Deborah*. Palo Alto, CA. Affil: Stanford. Email: akessler@law.stanford.edu.

Kessler, **Lawrence D.**, *North Carolina, Chapel Hill*. Email: ldk@live.unc.edu.

Kessler-Harris, *Alice*, *Columbia (Hist.)*. Email: ak571@columbia.edu.

Kessner, **Thomas**, *Graduate Center, CUNY*. Email: tkessner@gc.cuny.edu.

Ketchum, *Monica*. Yuma, AZ. Affil: Arizona Western. Email: monica.ketchum@azwestern. edu.

Kete, **Kathleen J.**, *Trinity Coll., Conn.* Email: kathleen.kete@trincoll.edu.

Ketelaar, **James E.**, *Chicago*. Email: jketelaa@ uchicago.edu.

Kett, **Joseph F.**, *Virginia*. Email: jfk9v@virginia. edu.

Kettler, *Mark Thomas*. Notre Dame, IN. Affil: Notre Dame. Email: mkettler@alumni.nd.edu. Research: German occupation of Poland in WWI, empire/nation/Europe.

Keune, *Jon*. East Lansing, MI. Affil: Michigan State. Email: keunejon@msu.edu. Research: South Asian social hierarchy/equality, institutionalization of popular mvmts.

Kevles, **Daniel J.**, *California Inst. of Tech.; Yale*. Email: kevles@hss.caltech.edu; daniel.kevles@ yale.edu.

Kevorkian, *Tanya E.*, *Millersville, Pa.* Millersville, PA. Email: tanya.kevorkian@millersville.edu. Research: early modern Germany, colonial Pennsylvania German.

Key, **Barclay**, *Arkansas, Little Rock*. Email: btkey@ualr.edu.

Key, **Joseph P.**, *Arkansas State*. Email: jkey@ astate.edu.

Key, **Newton E.**, *Eastern Illinois*. Email: nekey@ eiu.edu.

Keyes, *Carl Robert*, *Assumption*. Worcester, MA. Email: ckeyes@assumption.edu. Research: colonial newspaper advertisements, commerce and print culture.

Keyes, *Sarah*, *Nevada, Reno*. Reno, NV. Email: sarah.e.keyes@gmail.com. Research: US West, Overland Trail.

Keylor, **William R.**, *Boston Univ.* Email: wrkeylor@bu.edu.

Keys, *Barbara J.*, *Soc. for Hist. of American Foreign Relations*. Parkville, Australia. Affil: Melbourne. Email: bkeys@unimelb.edu.au; barkeys@gmail.com. Research: emotions, human rights.

Keyser, **Richard L.**, *Wisconsin-Madison*. Email: rkeyser@wisc.edu.

Keyser, *Thomas William*. Flourtown, PA. Affil: Adtalem. Email: tomwkeyser@yahoo.com.

Keysor, *Angela Miller*, *Allegheny*. Willard, OH. Email: akeysor@allegheny.edu. Research: early America, healthcare.

Keyworth, **George**, *Saskatchewan*. Email: george.keyworth@usask.ca.

Khalid, *Adeeb*, *Carleton Coll.* Northfield, MN. Email: akhalid@carleton.edu. Research: Central Asia 1750-present, Islam in USSR.

Khalid, **Amna**, *Carleton Coll.* Email: amkhalid@ carleton.edu.

Khalidi, *Rashid I.*, *Columbia (Hist.)*. New York, NY. Email: rik2101@columbia.edu. Research: Middle East.

Khalil, **Osamah F.**, *Syracuse*.

Khamutaev, *Vladimir*. Email: khandrusai.va55@ gmail.com.

Khan, *Abdul Karim*. Pearl City, HI. Affil: Leeward Comm. Coll., Hawaii. Email: khana@hawaii. edu. Research: modern South Asia, Islamic world and Middle East.

Khan, *Almas*. West Covina, CA. Affil: Georgetown Univ. Law Center. Email: abkhan@stanfordalumni.org.

Khan, **Noor-aiman Iftikhar**, *Colgate*. Email: nikhan@colgate.edu.

Khan, **Suraya**. Houston, TX. Affil: Rice. Email: surayakhan01@gmail.com.

Khanenko-Friesen, **Natalia**, *Saskatchewan*. Email: khanenko-friesen@stmcollege.ca.

Khanmalek, *Tala*. Princeton, NJ. Affil: Princeton. Email: talak@princeton.edu.

Kharif, **Wali R.**, *Tennessee Tech.* Email: wrkharif@ tntech.edu.

Khater, **Akram F.**, *North Carolina State*. Email: akram_khater@ncsu.edu.

Khazeni, **Arash**, *Pomona*. Email: arash_ khazeni@pomona.edu.

Kheraj, **Sean**, *York, Can.* Email: kherajs@yorku. ca.

Khiterer, *Victoria M.*, *Millersville, Pa.* Millersville, PA. Email: victoria.khiterer@millersville.edu. Research: Jews in Kiev, Jewish pogroms.

Khodarkovsky, **Michael**, *Loyola, Chicago*. Email: mkhodar@luc.edu.

Khoury, **Dina R.**, *George Washington*. McLean, VA. Email: dikhy@gwu.edu. Research: Middle East.

Khoury, *Philip S.*, *MIT*. Email: khoury@mit.edu.

Khuri-Makdisi, **Ilham**, *Northeastern*. Email: i.khuri-makdisi@neu.edu.

Kia, **Ardeshir**, *Montana*. Email: ardi.kia@mso. umt.edu.

Kia, **Mehrdad**, *Montana*. Email: mehrdad.kia@ umontana.edu.

Kibbe, **Tina M.**, *Lamar*. Email: tkibbe@lamar.edu.

Kibler, *Ray F.*, *III*. Claremont, CA. Email: ray. kibler.iii@ecunet.org. Research: ecumenical theology and history, religion in North America/California.

Kicklighter, **Joseph A.**, *Auburn*. Email: kicklja@ auburn.edu.

Kidd, **Thomas S.**, *Baylor*. Email: thomas_kidd@ baylor.edu.

Kiddle, *Amelia M.*, *Calgary*. Calgary, AB, Canada. Email: akiddle@ucalgary.ca. Research: 20th-c Mexico, inter-American relations.

Kiechle, *Melanie A.*, *Virginia Tech*. Blacksburg, VA. Email: mkiechle@vt.edu. Research: 19th-c urban industrial odors, 19th-c science popularization.

Kiecker, **James**, *Wisconsin Lutheran*.

Kieckhefer, **Richard**, *Northwestern*. Email: kieckhefer@northwestern.edu.

Kieft, **David O.**, *Minnesota (Hist.)*.

Kiel, *Doug*, *Northwestern*. Evanston, IL. Email: doug.kiel@northwestern.edu. Research: Oneida Nation / Indigenous resistance, settler colonialism/Great Lakes Indians.

Kieran, **David**, *Washington and Jefferson*. Email: dkieran@washjeff.edu.

Kierdorf, **Doug C.**, *Bentley*. Email: dkierdorf@ bentley.edu.

Kiernan, **Benedict F.**, *Yale*. Email: ben.kiernan@ yale.edu.

Kierner, **Cynthia A.**, *George Mason*. Email: ckierner@gmu.edu.

Kierstead, **Raymond F.**, **Jr.**, *Reed*. Email: raymond.kierstead@reed.edu.

Kiesling, **Eugenia C.**, *US Military Acad.* Email: eugenia.kiesling@usma.edu.

Kieswetter, **James K.**, *Eastern Washington*. Email: jkieswetter@ewu.edu.

Kietlinski, *Robin*. New Rochelle, NY. Affil: LaGuardia Comm. Coll., CUNY. Email: robin. kietlinski@gmail.com. Research: Japanese women and sports, Olympics in East Asia.

Kieval, *Hillel J.*, *Washington, St. Louis*. Email: hkieval@wustl.edu.

Kightlinger, *Benjamin N.* New York, NY.

Kilbride, **Daniel**, *John Carroll*. Email: dkilbride@ jcu.edu.

Kilgore, *Trevor J.* Ann Arbor, MI. Affil: Michigan, Ann Arbor. Email: tkilgore@umich.edu.

Kilic-Schubel, **Nurten**, *Kenyon*. Email: kilicn@ kenyon.edu.

Killeen, **Patrick Ryan**, *Worcester State*. Email: pkilleen@worcester.edu.

Killen, **Andreas**, *Graduate Center, CUNY*. Email: akillen@ccny.cuny.edu.

Killenbeck, *Mark R.* Fayetteville, AR. Affil: Arkansas. Email: mkillenb@uark.edu.

Killigrew, **John W.**, *SUNY, Coll. Brockport*.

Kim, *Allen*. Los Angeles, CA. Email: AllenKimAK@ gmail.com.

Kim, **Charles R.**, *Wisconsin-Madison*. Email: charles.kim@wisc.edu.

Kim, *Chong (Sean) Bum*, *Central Missouri*. Email: ckim@ucmo.edu.

Kim, *Chonggil*. Daegu, South Korea. Affil: Kyungpook National. Email: kimkil@knu.ac.kr.

Kim, **Christine**, *Georgetown*. Email: cjk25@ georgetown.edu.

Kim, *Clare*. Cambridge, MA. Affil: MIT. Email: clarek@mit.edu.

Kim, **Colleen**, *Hist. Assoc.* Email: ckim@ historyassociates.com.

Kim, **Gloria**, *San Diego Mesa*. Email: gkim@ sdccd.edu.

Kim, *Hanmee Na*, *Wheaton, Ill.* Email: hanmee. kim@wheaton.edu.

Kim, *Hannah*, *Delaware*. Email: hkim@udel.edu.

Kim, *Harrison*, *Hawai'i, Manoa*. Honolulu, HI. Email: chk7@hawaii.edu; cheehyungkim@ gmail.com. Research: North Korea/East Asia/ socialism, everyday life/labor/ideology/city.

Kim, **Hoi-eun**, *Texas A&M*. Email: hekim@tamu. edu.

Kim, *Hyung-Wook*. Los Angeles, CA. Affil: UCLA. Email: mycello14@yahoo.com. Research: collective memory, nationalism.

Kim, **Jaeyoon**, *Point Loma Nazarene*. Email: jaeyoonkim@pointloma.edu.

Kim, **Janice C. H.**, *York, Can.* Email: jkim@yorku. ca.

Kim, *Jaymin*, *St. Thomas, Minn.* Saint Paul, MN. Email: kim07259@stthomas.edu; jaykim1986@gmail.com. Research: early modern China, Chinese borderlands.

Kim, *Jessica Michelle*, *California State, Northridge*. Los Angeles, CA. Email: jessica. kim@csun.edu. Research: Los Angeles, US-Mexico borderlands.

Kim, **Jina Eleanor**, *Smith*. Email: jkim@smith. edu.

Kim, **Jisoo Monica**, *George Washington*. Email: jsk10@gwu.edu.

Kim, *Jiyul*. Oberlin, OH. Email: jiyulkim@gmail. com. Research: culture and security policy, Oberlin local.

Kim, Kwangmin, *Colorado, Boulder*. Email: kwangmin.kim@colorado.edu.

Kim, Kyu Hyun, *California, Davis*. Email: kyukim@ucdavis.edu.

Kim, Loretta E. Hong Kong. Affil: Hong Kong. Email: lekim@hku.hk. Research: China's frontiers and ethnic minorities, comparative empires.

Kim, Marie Seong-Hak, *St. Cloud State*. Email: mskim@stcloudstate.edu.

Kim, Mi Gyung, *North Carolina State*. Email: migkim@ncsu.edu.

Kim, Miri, *Norwich*. Email: mkim1@norwich.edu.

Kim, Monica, *NYU*. New York, NY. Email: monica.kim@nyu.edu; mstarkim@gmail.com. Research: 20th-c US and world, decolonization and postcolonial Korea.

Kim, Nan, *Wisconsin-Milwaukee*. Milwaukee, WI. Email: ynkp@uwm.edu. Research: contemporary Korea, global Cold War in Northeast Asia.

Kim, Richard J., *California State, East Bay*. Email: richard.kim@csueastbay.edu.

Kim, Sonja, *Binghamton, SUNY*. Email: skim@binghamton.edu.

Kim, Sung Bok, *SUNY, Albany*. Email: sbkim@albany.edu.

Kim, Sung Shin, *North Georgia*. Email: sungshin.kim@ung.edu.

Kim, Young Richard. Fort Lee, NJ. Affil: Onassis Foundation USA. Email: youngrichardkim@gmail.com. Research: Epiphanius of Cyprus, Cyprus.

Kim, Yumi, *Johns Hopkins (Hist.)*. Baltimore, MD. Email: h.yumikim@jhu.edu. Research: modern Japan.

Kimball, Jeffrey, *Miami, Ohio*. Email: jpkimball@miamioh.edu.

Kimball, Natalie, *Staten Island, CUNY*. Staten Island, NY. Email: natalie.kimball@csi.cuny.edu; nlkimball@gmail.com. Research: sex and reproduction, women and gender.

Kimball, R. Alan, *Oregon*. Email: kimball@uoregon.edu.

Kimball, Richard Ian, *Brigham Young*. Email: richard_kimball@byu.edu.

Kimball, Warren F., *Rutgers, Newark/New Jersey Inst. of Tech*. Johns Island, SC. Email: wkimball@rutgers.edu. Research: US Tennis Assoc./business, FDR's foreign policy.

Kimble, Sara L. Chicago, IL. Affil: DePaul. Email: skimble2@depaul.edu. Research: European law and feminism, gender analysis.

Kimler, William, *North Carolina State*. Email: kimler@ncsu.edu.

Kimmich, Christoph, *Graduate Center, CUNY*. Email: ckimmich@gc.cuny.edu.

Kimson, George, *III*. New York, NY. Affil: Columbia. Email: gk2498@columbia.edu.

Kincade, Vance R., Jr., *West Chester*. Pottstown, PA. Affil: Philadelphia. Email: vkincade@wcupa.edu; kincadev@philau.edu. Research: US.

Kincaid, Kenneth Ralph. Hammond, IN. Affil: Purdue Northwest, Hammond. Email: kkincaid@pnw.edu. Research: introduced species in Ecuador and Peru, indigenous identity in Ecuador and Peru.

Kindell, Christopher Steven. Chicago, IL. Affil: Chicago. Email: kindell@uchicago.edu. Research: urbanization and public health in Hawaii, print culture in the Pacific.

Kinder, Douglas C. McArthur, OH. Email: douglas.kinder@ymail.com. Research: US/world narcotics control, Harry J. Anslinger.

Kinder, John M., *Oklahoma State*. Email: john.kinder@okstate.edu.

King, Andrew Joseph. Providence, RI. Email: andrewjking95@gmail.com.

King, Anya, *Southern Indiana*. Email: aking13@usi.edu.

King, Charles E. Washington, DC. Affil: Georgetown. Email: kingch@georgetown.edu.

King, Charles W., *Nebraska, Omaha*. Email: cwking@mail.unomaha.edu.

King, Chris, *OAH*. Email: kingchan@oah.org.

King, Cornelia S., *Library Co. of Philadelphia*. Email: cking@librarycompany.org.

King, David W., *SUNY, Oswego*. Email: david.king@oswego.edu.

King, David. Hood River, OR. Affil: Denver. Email: daviddmking@gmail.com.

King, Farina. Tahlequah, OK. Affil: Northeastern State, Tahlequah. Email: farinasmith@gmail.com. Research: Indian education, Indian identity.

King, Ian M. Lake Forest, IL. Affil: Cambridge. Email: ik361@cam.ac.uk.

King, James. Green Bay, WI. Affil: Providence Academy. Email: jameseking@me.com.

King, Jeremy R., *Mount Holyoke*. Email: jking@mtholyoke.edu.

King, John A., Jr. Miami, FL. Affil: Ransom Everglades Sch. Email: jking@ransomeverglades.org.

King, Joshua, *Azusa Pacific*.

King, Kathleen Marie. El Cajon, CA. Email: kking7370@gmail.com.

King, Kelley Marie. Frisco, TX. Affil: North Texas. Email: king.kelley@gmail.com.

King, Kimberly, *Nebraska, Omaha*.

King, Lamont D, *James Madison*. Email: kingld@jmu.edu.

King, Margaret L., *Brooklyn, CUNY*. Douglaston, NY. Email: marglking@gmail.com. Research: mothers and sons, song and cultural continuity.

King, Martha J., *Princeton*. Email: mjking@princeton.edu.

King, Matt, *South Florida, Tampa*. Temple Terrace, FL. Email: matthewking1@usf.edu. Research: Norman Sicily and southern Italy, medieval North Africa.

King, Michael J. Oak Lawn, IL.

King, Michael. Seattle, WA. Affil: Drew. Email: mking2@drew.edu. Research: European colonialism of Africa.

King, Michelle T., *North Carolina, Chapel Hill*. Email: mtking@email.unc.edu.

King, Pamela Sterne, *Alabama, Birmingham*. Email: pamking@uab.edu.

King, Pauline N., *Hawai'i, Manoa*. Email: paulinek@hawaii.edu.

King, Peter J., *Carleton, Can*. Email: peter.king2@carleton.ca.

King, Shannon, *Fairfield; Wooster*. Wooster, OH. Email: sking@wooster.edu. Research: African American migrations, Caribbean migrations.

King, William M. Lafayette, CO. Affil: Colorado, Boulder. Email: william.king@colorado.edu. Research: Afroamerican studies, citizenship and public affairs.

King, Wilma, *Missouri, Columbia*. Chantilly, VA. Email: kingw@missouri.edu. Research: 19th-c US slavery, US women.

Kingman, Emily. Cottage Grove, WI. Email: emilyekingman@icloud.com.

King-O'Brien, Kelly L. Ithaca, NY. Affil: Cornell. Email: kkobrien@uchicago.edu. Research: US labor, American political.

Kingsland, Sharon E., *Johns Hopkins (Hist. of Science)*. Email: sharon@jhu.edu.

Kingston, Ralph, *Auburn*. Email: rfk0001@auburn.edu.

Kinkley, Jeffrey C. Beaverton, OR. Affil: St. John's, NY. Email: jeffreykinkley@gmail.com. Research: modern China, modern Chinese literature and film.

Kinnear, E. Mary, *Manitoba*. Email: e.kinnear@umanitoba.ca.

Kinnear, Michael S. R., *Manitoba*. Email: michael.kinnear@umanitoba.ca.

Kinney, Jayne. Lincoln, NE. Affil: Minnesota. Email: kinne307@umn.edu. Research: indigenous, women and religion.

Kinney, Martha E. Shirley, NY. Affil: Suffolk County Comm. Coll., SUNY. Email: murph@kinney.net.

Kinoshita, Sharon. Santa Cruz, CA. Affil: California, Santa Cruz. Email: sakinosh@ucsc.edu. Research: medieval Mediterranean literature, Marco Polo and congeners.

Kinra, Rajeev Kumar, *Northwestern*. Evanston, IL. Email: r-kinra@northwestern.edu. Research: Mughal literary and political culture, Indo-Persian world.

Kinsel, Amy J. Shoreline, WA. Affil: Shoreline Comm. Coll. Email: akinsel@shoreline.edu. Research: Gettysburg historic preservation, Civil War cultural memory.

Kinsella, William E., Jr. Vienna, VA. Email: wkinsella@nvcc.edu.

Kinser, Jonathan A. Williamsfield, OH. Email: jak238@case.edu. Research: immigrant resistance to 1920s KKK, Prohibition enforcement and immigrants.

Kinser, Samuel C., *Northern Illinois*. Email: sakinser@aol.com.

Kinsey, Danielle C, *Carleton, Can*. Email: danielle.kinsey@carleton.ca.

Kinzer, Bruce L., *Kenyon*. Email: kinzerb@kenyon.edu.

Kinzley, Judd C., *Wisconsin-Madison*. Email: kinzley@wisc.edu.

Kinzley, W. Dean, *South Carolina, Columbia*. Email: kinzley@mailbox.sc.edu.

Kipping, Mathias, *York, Can*. Email: mkipping@schulich.yorku.ca.

Kirasirova, Masha. New York, NY. Affil: NYU, Abu Dhabi. Email: masha.kirasirova@nyu.edu.

Kirby, Jason, *Francis Marion*. Email: jason.kirby@fmarion.edu.

Kirby, Jeni L. Harrison, AR. Email: jenikirby84@gmail.com.

Kirby, William C., *Harvard (Hist.)*. Email: wkirby@hbs.edu.

Kirk, Andy, *Nevada, Las Vegas*. Las Vegas, NV. Email: andy.kirk@unlv.edu. Research: public, US West.

Kirk, Gordon W., *Western Illinois*. Email: cargord@rcn.com.

Kirk, John A., *Arkansas, Little Rock*. Little Rock, AR. Email: jakirk@ualr.edu. Research: southern politics, civil rights.

Kirk, John, *Dalhousie*. Email: john.kirk@dal.ca.

Kirk, Ryan, *Elon*. Email: rkirk2@elon.edu.

Kirkendall, *Andrew J.*, *Texas A&M*. College Station, TX. Email: andykirk@tamu.edu. Research: Paulo Freire, US and democracy in Latin America.

Kirkendall, *Richard S.*, *Washington, Seattle*. Seattle, WA. Email: rsk@u.washington.edu. Research: Harry S. Truman.

Kirkland, *Andrew*. Davenport, OH. Email: andrew11kirkland@gmail.com.

Kirkland, **John D.**, **Jr.**, *Bucknell*. Email: kirkland@bucknell.edu.

Kirkland, *Justin*. Lubbock, TX. Affil: Iowa. Email: justin-kirkland@uiowa.edu.

Kirkman, *A.* *Larkin*. Raleigh, NC.

Kirkpatrick, **Michael D.**, *Memorial, Newfoundland*. Email: michael.kirkpatrick@mun.ca.

Kirkwood, *Patrick Michael*. Oak Grove, MO. Affil: Metropolitan Comm. Coll., Blue River. Email: patrick.kirkwood@mcckc.edu. Research: American and British Imperialism, Anglo-Saxonism and Progressivism.

Kiron, **Arthur**, *Pennsylvania*.

Kirschenbaum, *Lisa A.*, *West Chester*. West Chester, PA. Email: lkirschenb@wcupa.edu. Research: international communism, Spanish exiles in Soviet Union.

Kirschke, *Amy*, *North Carolina, Wilmington*. Email: kirschkea@uncw.edu.

Kirschke, *Hartmut*. Wesseling, Germany. Email: hartmut.kirschke@gmx.de.

Kirshner, *Julius*, *Chicago*. Email: jkir@uchicago.edu.

Kirstein, *Peter N.*, *St. Xavier*. Chicago, IL. Email: kirstein@sxu.edu. Research: modern US, US foreign relations.

Kisatsky, *Deborah L.*, *Assumption*. Milford, MA. Email: dkisatsk@assumption.edu. Research: US policy toward European right, US policy toward European integration.

Kiser, **Maj Michael**, *US Military Acad*. Email: michael.kiser@usma.edu.

Kissir, *Jessica*. Fenton, MO. Affil: Southern New Hampshire. Email: j.kissir@snhu.edu. Research: ancient Egypt Akhenaten 18th Dynasty, Cold War.

Kist, *Glenn J.* Scottsville, NY. Affil: Rochester Inst. of Tech. Email: gjkgsh@rit.edu.

Kitamura, **Hiroshi**, *William and Mary*. Email: hxkita@wm.edu.

Kitchen, **J. Martin**, *Simon Fraser*. Email: kitchen@sfu.ca.

Kitchen, **John**, *Alberta*. Email: jkitchen@ualberta.ca.

Kithinji, **Michael Mwenda**, *Central Arkansas*. Email: mkithinji@uca.edu.

Kittell, **Ellen E.**, *Idaho*. Email: kittell@uidaho.edu.

Kittelstrom, *Amy Marie*, *Sonoma State*. Rohnert Park, CA. Email: kitt@sonoma.edu. Research: liberalism, religion.

Kitterman, **David H.**, *Northern Arizona*. Email: david.kitterman@nau.edu.

Kittleson, *Roger A.*, *Williams*. West Hartford, CT. Email: rkittles@williams.edu. Research: masculinity and sports, Brazil.

Kitunda, **Jeremiah Mutio**, *Appalachian State*. Email: kitundajm@appstate.edu.

Kitzan, **Laurence**, *Saskatchewan*. Email: kitzan@sask.usask.ca.

Kivelson, *Valerie A.*, *Michigan, Ann Arbor*. Ann Arbor, MI. Email: vkivelso@umich.edu. Research: Russian witchcraft.

Kivimae, **Juri**, *Toronto*. Email: jkivimae@chass.utoronto.ca.

Kizenko, **Nadieszda**, *SUNY, Albany*. Email: kizenko@albany.edu.

Kjeldsen, **Michael**. Charlottenlund, Denmark. Affil: Roskilde Univ. Center. Email: mkj@ruc.dk.

Klaassen, *Frank*, *Saskatchewan*. Email: frank.klaassen@usask.ca.

Klaassen, *Walter*, *Saskatchewan*. Email: wrkl@sasktel.net.

Klapper, **Melissa R.**, *Rowan*. Email: klapper@rowan.edu.

Klaren, *Peter F.*, *George Washington*. Email: klaren@gwu.edu.

Klatte, **Mary Ellen**, *Eastern Kentucky*. Email: maryellen.klatte@eku.edu.

Klausen, **Susanne**, *Carleton, Can*. Email: susanne.klausen@carleton.ca.

Klausner, *Carla L.*, *Missouri–Kansas City*. Shawnee Mission, KS. Email: klausnerc@umkc.edu. Research: Arab-Israeli conflict, medieval/Seljuk period Islamic.

Kleban, **Oleg**, *La Guardia and Wagner Archives*. Email: okleban@lagcc.cuny.edu.

Kledzik, *Philip Andrew*. New Lenox, IL. Affil: Joliet Jr. Coll. Email: philank@hotmail.com.

Kleespies, *Gavin*, *Massachusetts Hist. Soc.* Email: gkleespies@masshist.org.

Klehr, *Harvey*, *Emory*. Email: hklehr@ps.emory.edu.

Kleijwegt, *Marc*, *Wisconsin-Madison*. Email: marc.kleijwegt@wisc.edu.

Kleiman, *Jeffrey*, *Wisconsin-Stevens Point*. Email: jkleiman@uwc.edu.

Kleiman, **Jordan B.**, *SUNY, Coll. Geneseo*. Email: kleiman@geneseo.edu.

Kleimola, **Ann**, *Nebraska, Lincoln*. Email: akleimola1@unl.edu.

Klein, **Benjamin F.**, *California State, East Bay*. Email: bkklein@lmi.net.

Klein, **Dennis B.**, *Kean*. Email: dklein@kean.edu.

Klein, *Gary A.* Bronx, NY. Affil: Westchester Comm. Coll., SUNY. Email: gkhistory@aol.com.

Klein, **Herbert S.**, *Columbia (Hist.)*. Email: hsk1@columbia.edu.

Klein, *Ira*, *American*. Email: iklein@american.edu.

Klein, *Jennifer Lisa*, *Yale*. New Haven, CT. Email: jennifer.klein@yale.edu. Research: US labor and social welfare, 20th-c US political economy.

Klein, **Joanne M.**, *Boise State*. Email: jklein@boisestate.edu.

Klein, **Joel A.**, *Huntington Library*. Email: jklein@huntington.org.

Klein, **Kim M.**, *Shippensburg*. Email: kmklei@ship.edu.

Klein, *Marti*. Laguna Niguel, CA. Affil: MiraCosta. Email: mlklein@miracosta.edu. Research: 19th-c US/British maritime literature, Alta CA colonial/maritime/humanities.

Klein, *Martin A.*, *Toronto*. Toronto, ON, Canada. Email: martin.klein@utoronto.ca. Research: African slavery, 19th-/20th-c Senegal and Mali.

Klein, *Norman Mark*, *Esq*. Los Angeles, CA. Affil: California Inst. of the Arts. Email: nmklein@msn.com. Research: American cultural since 1973, media and social memory.

Klein, **Rachel N.**, *California, San Diego*. Email: rklein@ucsd.edu.

Klein, **Shira**, *Chapman*. Email: sklein@chapman.edu.

Klein, *Thoralf*. Loughborough, Leicestershire, United Kingdom. Affil: Loughborough. Email: T.E.Klein@lboro.ac.uk. Research: internationalization of China, political religion in 20th-c China.

Kleinberg, *Ethan*, *Wesleyan*. Middletown, CT. Email: ekleinberg@wesleyan.edu. Research: modern European intellectual, theory and philosophy of history.

Kleine, **Georg H.**, *South Florida, Tampa*. Email: kleine@honors.usf.edu.

Kleinfeld, **Gerald R.**, *Arizona State*.

Klein-Pejsova, *Rebekah*, *Purdue*. West Lafayette, IN. Email: rkleinpe@purdue.edu. Research: east central European Jewish since 1945.

Kleiser, *Randal Grant*. New York, NY. Affil: Columbia. Email: rk2952@columbia.edu. Research: Greenville/Bourbon/Pombalian reforms, Atlantic world smuggling.

Klejment, **Anne**, *St. Thomas, Minn*. Email: amklejment@stthomas.edu.

Klemek, *Christopher*, *George Washington*. Email: klemek@gwu.edu.

Klemm, **Matthew E.**, *Ithaca*. Email: mklemm@ithaca.edu.

Klepak, **Hal P.**, *Royal Military*. Email: klepak-h@rmc.ca.

Klepper, **Deeana C.**, *Boston Univ.* West Roxbury, MA. Email: dklepper@bu.edu. Research: late medieval Christians and Jews, Bible exegesis and polemic.

Klerman, **Daniel M.**, *Southern California*. Email: dklerman@law.usc.edu.

Kless, **Andrew Hoyt**, *Alfred*.

Kletke, **Carl**, *National Defence Headquarters*. Email: carl.kletke@forces.gc.ca.

Klett, **Joseph**, *Science History Inst*. Email: jklett@sciencehistory.org.

Klid, **Bohdan W.**, *Alberta*. Email: bohdan.klid@ualberta.ca.

Klieman, **Kairn A.**, *Houston*. Email: kklieman@uh.edu.

Klimke, *Martin A.*, *NYU*. New York, NY. Affil: NYU, Abu Dhabi. Email: klimke@nyu.edu. Research: Cold War of 1980s/Reagan America, global dimensions of African American civil rights.

Klinck, **David M.**, *Windsor*. Email: klinck@uwindsor.ca.

Kline, **Benjamin**, *San José State*. Email: bkline555@comcast.net.

Kline, **Ronald R.**, *Cornell*. Email: rkline@ee.cornell.edu.

Kline, **Wendy**, *Purdue*. Email: wkline@purdue.edu.

Klinetobe, **Charles John**, *Nebraska, Omaha*.

Kling, *Samuel*. Evanston, IL. Affil: Chicago Council on Global Affairs. Email: samkling@u.northwestern.edu.

Klingelhofer, *Eric*, *Mercer*. Email: klingelhof_e@mercer.edu.

Klingensmith, *Daniel E.*, *Maryville*. Maryville, TN. Email: dan.klingensmith@maryvillecollege.edu. Research: environmental and colonialism, development.

Klingle, *Matthew W.*, *Bowdoin*. Email: mklingle@bowdoin.edu.

Klitzman, *Zach*. Washington, DC. Affil: President Lincoln's Cottage. Email: zklitzman@gmail.com. Research: Abraham Lincoln, Civil War.

Klooster, *Willem*, *Clark*. Worcester, MA. Email: wklooster@clarku.edu. Research: Atlantic world, Dutch America.

Klopotek, Brian R., *Oregon*. Email: klopotek@uoregon.edu.

Kloppenberg, James T., *Harvard (Hist.)*. Wellesley, MA. Email: jkloppen@fas.harvard.edu. Research: post-1650 American/European democracy, pragmatism in American thought.

Klose, Fabian. Mainz, Germany. Email: klose@ieg-mainz.de. Research: human rights, humanitarianism.

Klosko, Christopher. Philadelphia, PA. Affil: Lehigh Carbon Comm. Coll. Email: cklosko@gmail.com.

Klotz, Audie. Syracuse, NY. Affil: Syracuse. Email: aklotz@maxwell.syr.edu.

Klotz, John M. Dubuque, IA. Affil: Mennonite Hist. Soc. Email: klotzjm120@yahoo.com.

Klubock, Thomas Miller, *Virginia*. Charlottesville, VA. Email: tmk5k@virginia.edu. Research: Chile environmental/labor/gender.

Kluchin, Rebecca M., *California State, Sacramento*. Email: rkluchin@csus.edu.

Klug, Sam. Cambridge, MA. Affil: Harvard. Email: klug@fas.harvard.edu.

Klug, Thomas, *Detroit Mercy*. Email: klugta@udmercy.edu.

K'Meyer, Tracy E., *Louisville*. Email: tracyk@louisville.edu.

Knafla, Louis A., *Calgary*. Email: knafla@ucalgary.ca.

Knafla, Sandra. Snohomish, WA. Email: slknafla@stcloudstate.edu.

Knapp, Carolyn S. Oakland, CA. Affil: California, Berkeley. Email: csknapp@earthlink.net. Research: 18th-c British Empire, nationalism.

Knapp, Keith N., *Citadel*. Email: keith.knapp@citadel.edu.

Knapp, Krister Dylan, *Washington, St. Louis*. Email: kknapp@wustl.edu.

Knapp, Thomas A., *Loyola, Chicago*. Email: tknapp@luc.edu.

Knauff, Carol, *Massachusetts Hist. Soc.* Email: cknauff@masshist.org.

Knechtmann, Jennifer Ann. Carlisle, PA. Affil: Delone Catholic High Sch. Email: jknechtmann@gmail.com.

Knee, Stuart E. Charleston, SC. Affil: Charleston. Email: knees@cofc.edu. Research: American social/cultural/ethnic/diplomatic, ancient/medieval/modern Jewish.

Kneebone, John T., *Virginia Commonwealth*. Email: jtkneebone@vcu.edu.

KnicKrehm, Glenn A. Cambridge, MA. Affil: Constellation Production. Email: gknickrehm@constellationcenter.org. Research: music performance context and space.

Knight, Franklin W., *Johns Hopkins (Hist.)*. Email: fknight@jhu.edu.

Knight, Isabel F., *Penn State*. Email: ifk@psu.edu.

Knight, Kathryn Hall. Clermont, FL. Email: kknight100303@aol.com.

Knight, Louise W. Evanston, IL. Affil: Northwestern. Email: lwk@louisewknight.com. Research: Grimke sisters, early women's rights.

Knight, Nathaniel, *Seton Hall*. Email: nathaniel.knight@shu.edu.

Knight, Stephen M. Dumfries, VA. Affil: World Wildlife Fund. Email: stevekflorida@gmail.com.

Knight, T. Daniel D., *Texas-Rio Grande Valley*. Email: thomas.knight@utrgv.edu.

Knight, **Thomas J.**, *Colorado State*. Email: thomas.knight@colostate.edu.

Knirck, Jason K., *Central Washington*. Ellensburg, WA. Email: jason.knirck@cwu.edu. Research: Irish Free State, politics and revolution.

Knobel, Dale T. Georgetown, TX. Affil: Denison. Email: knobel@denison.edu. Research: US nativism, US immigration.

Knoblauch, Kaleb Jarand. Davis, CA. Affil: California, Davis. Email: knoblauch.kaleb@gmail.com.

Knobler, Adam, *New Jersey*. Email: knobler@tcnj.edu.

Knock, Thomas J., *Southern Methodist*. Email: tknock@smu.edu.

Knoerl, T. Kurt, *Georgia Southern*. Email: kknoerl@georgiasouthern.edu.

Knoespel, Kenneth, *Georgia Inst. of Tech.* Email: kenneth.knoespel@iac.gatech.edu.

Knol, Patricia. Winfield, IL. Email: patriciaknol@triton.edu.

Knoll, Paul W., *Southern California*. Portland, OR. Email: knoll@usc.edu. Research: 15th-c Poland, conciliarism and conciliar theory.

Knoop, Phillip J. Cicero, NY. Email: pjknoop1@gmail.com.

Knopf, Richard C., *Kent State*.

Knopp, Larissa Marie. New York, NY. Affil: St. John's, NY. Email: knoppl@stjohns.edu.

Knorr, Daniel. Chicago, IL. Affil: Chicago. Email: dknorr@uchicago.edu. Research: imperial state-locality relationship, early modern/modern cultural exchange.

Knott, Christopher. Las Vegas, NV. Affil: Nevada, Las Vegas. Email: knott@unlv.nevada.edu.

Knott, Sarah, *Indiana*. Bloomington, IN. Email: saknott@indiana.edu. Research: age of democratic revolutions, selfhood.

Knotts, Kenneth, *Nebraska, Omaha*.

Knouff, Gregory T., *Keene State*. Email: gknouff@keene.edu.

Knowles, Anne Kelly, *Maine, Orono*. Orono, ME. Email: anne.knowles@umit.maine.edu. Research: geographies of Holocaust, historical GIS and spatial history.

Knowles, Scott Gabriel, *Drexel*. Email: sgk23@drexel.edu.

Knowlton, B. C., *Assumption*.

Knox, Lezlie S., *Marquette*. Email: lezlie.knox@marquette.edu.

Knox, Steve. Glenside, PA. Affil: help4resesearchers. Email: skskknox@gmail.com.

Knox, Thomas R., *Bowling Green State*. Email: tknox@bgsu.edu.

Knudsen, Donna, *South Florida, St. Petersburg*.

Knuesel, Ariane. Schinznach-Bad, Switzerland. Affil: Fribourg. Email: ariane.knuesel@yahoo.com. Research: China and Switzerland 1945-1990, Cold War actors and networks.

Knupfer, Peter B., *Michigan State*. Email: knupfer@msu.edu.

Ko, Dorothy, *Barnard, Columbia*. Email: dko@barnard.edu.

Kobo, Ousman M., *Ohio State*. Email: kobo.1@osu.edu.

Kobrin, David R. Eastsound, WA. Email: david70@centurytel.net. Research: teaching history using technology, teaching history using primary sources.

Kobrin, Rebecca, *Columbia (Hist.)*. New York, NY. Email: rk2351@columbia.edu.

Research: American philanthropy, American immigration.

Koch, Alexander M. Troy, ME. Email: akoch05@unity.edu.

Koch, Andrew Karl. Brevard, NC. Affil: John N. Gardner Inst. for Excellence. Email: koch@jngi.org.

Koch, Timothy R., *Esq.* Atlanta, GA. Email: koch.jd.phd@gmail.com. Research: American prophetic movements.

Koch, William Matthew. Jamestown, NY. Email: wk8347@gmail.com. Research: WWI, 19th-c American military.

Kochan, Benjamin John. Chestnut Hill, MA. Affil: Boston Univ. Email: bkochan@bu.edu. Research: northwest Atlantic fishing, piracy.

Kocho-Williams, Alastair. Potsdam, NY. Affil: Clarkson. Email: akochowi@clarkson.edu. Research: Soviet challenge to British India.

Koda, Naoko. Higashi Osaka, Japan. Affil: Kindai. Email: nkoda@nyu.edu.

Kodesh, Neil R., *Wisconsin-Madison*. Email: kodesh@wisc.edu.

Koditschek, Theodore, *Missouri, Columbia*. Columbia, MO. Email: koditschekt@missouri.edu. Research: modern British social.

Kodosky, Robert J., *West Chester*. Email: rkodosky@wcupa.edu.

Koed, Betty K., *US Senate Hist. Office*. Email: betty_koed@sec.senate.gov.

Koeneke, Rodney B., *Portland State*. Email: rodneyk@pdx.edu.

Koenig, Brigitte A., *Seton Hall*. Orinda, CA. Email: brigitte.koenig@shu.edu. Research: US anarchism cultural, biography.

Koenig, Sarah, *Ramapo*. Waldwick, NJ. Email: skoenig1@ramapo.edu. Research: religion in American West, development of academic study of history.

Koeniger, A. Cash, *Virginia Military Inst.* Email: koenigerac@vmi.edu.

Koenker, Diane P. London, United Kingdom. Affil: Univ. Coll., London. Email: dkoenker@illinois.edu. Research: consumption in 1960s USSR, Soviet foodways.

Koepp, Cynthia J. Aurora, NY. Affil: Wells. Email: cjkoepp@wells.edu. Research: 18th-c encyclopedias/Abbé Pluche, 18th-c pedagogy and publishing.

Koerber, Bennett. Pittsburgh, PA. Affil: Carnegie Mellon. Email: bkoerber@andrew.cmu.edu.

Koerber, Jeffrey P., *Chapman*. Email: koerber@chapman.edu.

Koerselman, Rebecca A., *Northwestern Coll.* Orange City, IA. Email: rebecca.koerselman@nwciowa.edu. Research: evangelical youth culture, summer camps 1940s-50s.

Koester, Kendra. Friendswood, TX. Affil: Houston, Clear Lake. Email: koester.k.224@gmail.com. Research: WWII, labor movement.

Koeth, Stephen Mark, *American Catholic Hist. Assoc.* New York, NY. Affil: Columbia. Email: smkoeth@gmail.com. Research: postwar suburbanization and Catholicism, Catholic masculinity.

Koffman, David S., *York, Can.* Toronto, ON, Canada. Email: koffman@yorku.ca. Research: Canadian and US Jewish, empire and religion.

Kogan, Nathaniel. Salt Lake City, UT. Affil: Rowland Hall-St. Mark's Sch. Email: nkogan@gmail.com. Research: transatlantic, disability.

Kogman-Appel, **Katrin**. Münster, Germany. Affil: Westfaelische Wilhelms. Email: kogman@ uni-muenster.de.

Kohl, **Lawrence F.**, *Alabama, Tuscaloosa*. Email: lfkohl@bama.ua.edu.

Kohler, **Eric D.**, *Wyoming*.

Kohler-Hausmann, *Julilly*, *Cornell*. Ithaca, NY. Email: jkh224@cornell.edu. Research: postwar US, political and social.

Kohlstedt, **Sally Gregory**, *Minnesota (Hist.); Minnesota (Hist. of Science)*. Minneapolis, MN. Email: sgk@umn.edu. Research: science in American culture, gender and science.

Kohn, **Richard H.**, *North Carolina, Chapel Hill; National Hist. Center*. Durham, NC. Email: rhkohn@unc.edu. Research: US presidential war leadership, American warmaking.

Kohn, **Shira Miriam**. New York, NY. Affil: Dalton Sch. Email: Shiram19@aol.com. Research: Jewish sororities, American Jews.

Kohnen, **David**, *Naval War Coll.* Email: david. kohnen@usnwc.edu.

Kohout, **Amy**, *Colorado Coll.* Email: akohout@ coloradocollege.edu.

Kohut, **Thomas A.**, *Williams*. Williamstown, MA. Email: Thomas.A.Kohut@williams.edu. Research: 20th-c Germany, cultural.

Koistinen, **David J.**, *William Paterson*. Email: koistinend@wpunj.edu.

Koistinen, **Paul A.**, *California State, Northridge*. North Hills, CA. Research: US economic, sociological.

Kojevnikov, **Alexei**, *British Columbia*. Email: anikov@mail.ubc.ca.

Kokomoor, **Kevin**, *Coastal Carolina*. Email: kkokomoor@coastal.edu.

Kola, *Azeta*. Scarsdale, NY. Affil: Northwestern. Email: ak3279@nyu.edu. Research: Mediterranean world, western Balkans.

Kola, *Ijeoma*. Jersey City, NJ. Affil: Columbia. Email: ie2150@cumc.columbia.edu.

Kolakowski, **Morgan Elizabeth**. Syracuse, NY. Affil: Syracuse. Email: morgan.kolakowski@ gmail.com. Research: capital punishment, gender.

Kolapo, **Femi J.**, *Guelph*. Email: kolapof@ uoguelph.ca.

Kolar, **Kelly A.**, *Middle Tennessee State*. Email: Kelly.Kolar@mtsu.edu.

Kolar, **Laura R.**, *US Dept. of State*.

Kolbas, **Judith**, *Miami, Ohio*. Email: kolbasjg@ miamioh.edu.

Kolbet, **Kelsey**, *Massachusetts Hist. Soc.* Email: kkolbet@masshist.org.

Kolchin, **Peter**, *Delaware*. Newark, DE. Email: pkolchin@udel.edu. Research: comparative US-Russian emancipation, slavery/ emancipation/Reconstruction.

Kole de Peralta, **Kathleen M.**, *Idaho State*. Email: kolekath@isu.edu.

Koll, *Elisabeth*, *Notre Dame*. Notre Dame, IN. Email: ekoll@nd.edu. Research: Chinese business/economic/social, Informal Finance/ Infrastructure.

Kolla, *Edward James*. Washington, DC. Affil: Georgetown, Qatar. Email: ejk55@ georgetown.edu. Research: revolutionary and Napoleonic France, international law.

Kollander, **Patricia A.**, *Florida Atlantic*. Email: kollande@fau.edu.

Kollar, *Rene M.* Latrobe, PA. Affil: St. Vincent. Email: rkollar@stvincent.edu.

Kollegger, *Jacob Ludvig*. Luino, Italy. Email: jacob.kollegger@hotmail.com.

Kollmann, **Nancy Shields**, *Stanford*. Stanford, CA. Email: kollmann@stanford.edu. Research: Russian concepts of justice 1500-1740, visual world of early modern Russia.

Kollmer, **Charles**. New York, NY. Affil: Princeton. Email: ckollmer@princeton.edu.

Kollros, **James C**. Oak Lawn, IL. Affil: St. Xavier. Email: bigjimk@mindspring.com. Research: steel business, steel unionism.

Kolmer, **Elizabeth**, **ASC**, *St. Louis*. Email: kolmere@slu.edu.

Koloski, **Laurie S.**, *William and Mary*. Email: lskolo@wm.edu.

Kolp, **John**, *Augustana*. Email: johnkolp@ augustana.edu.

Kolsky, **Elizabeth**, *Villanova*. Email: elizabeth. kolsky@villanova.edu.

Kolz, *Arno W. F.* South Hamilton, MA. Affil: Gordon, Mass. Email: awfkolz@verizon.net. Research: social policies of Nazi Germany, education in Nazi Germany.

Komisaruk, **Catherine**, *Texas, San Antonio*. San Antonio, TX. Email: catherine.komisaruk@ utsa.edu. Research: colonial Mexico and Guatemala, native peoples.

Konate, *Dior*. Orangeburg, SC. Affil: South Carolina State. Email: dkonate@scsu.edu. Research: prisons and punishments in colonial Africa.

Kondratieff, **Eric John**, *Western Kentucky*. Email: eric.kondratieff@wku.edu.

Konefal, **Betsy O.**, *William and Mary*. Email: bokone@wm.edu.

Kong, **Xurong**, *Kean*. Email: xkong@kean.edu.

Konig, **David T.**, *Washington, St. Louis*. Email: konig@wustl.edu.

Konnersman, **Elizabeth**. Oldenburg, IN. Affil: Christendom. Email: elizabeth.konnersman@ christendom.edu. Research: French Revolution, English monarchy.

Konnert, **Mark W.**, *Calgary*. Email: mkonnert@ ucalgary.ca.

Konove, **Andrew Philip**, *Texas, San Antonio*. San Antonio, TX. Email: andrew.konove@utsa.edu; drew.konove@gmail.com. Research: 17th- /19th-c Mexico, Spanish Empire.

Konrad, **Christoph F.**, *Texas A&M*. Email: konradc@tamu.edu.

Konshuh, **Courtnay**, *Calgary*. Email: courtnay. konshuh@ucalgary.ca.

Konvitz, *Josef W*. Saint-Mandé, France. Email: josef@konvitz.com.

Konzal, **John C.**, *State Hist. Soc. of Missouri*. Email: konzalj@shsmo.org.

Kooi, **Christine**, *Louisiana State*. Email: ckooi1@ lsu.edu.

Koons, **Kenneth E.**, *Virginia Military Inst.* Email: koonske@vmi.edu.

Koonts, **Sarah E.**, *North Carolina Office of Archives*. Email: sarah.koonts@ncdcr.gov.

Koonz, *Claudia Ann*, *Duke*. Chapel Hill, NC. Email: ckoonz@duke.edu. Research: European responses to Muslim immigrants, ethics/ public memory/perpetrators.

Koop, **Allen V.**, *Dartmouth*. Email: allen.koop@ dartmouth.edu.

Koopman, **Nicole**, *Charleston*. Email: koopmannm@cofc.edu.

Koopmans, **Rachel M.**, *York, Can.* Email: koopmans@yorku.ca.

Koos, **Cheryl A.**, *California State, Los Angeles*. Email: ckoos@calstatela.edu.

Koot, **Christian J.**, *Towson*. Baltimore, MD. Email: ckoot@towson.edu. Research: colonial British America, colonial Dutch America.

Koot, **Gerard M.** South Dartmouth, MA. Affil: Massachusetts, Dartmouth. Email: gkoot@ umassd.edu. Research: British and Dutch economic 1500-2000, British economic historiography.

Kopelson, *Heather Miyano*, *Alabama, Tuscaloosa*. Tuscaloosa, AL. Email: heather.m.kopelson@ua.edu. Research: 17th-c religious practice/race/gender, English Atlantic world.

Kopf, **David**, *Minnesota (Hist.)*. Email: kopfx001@ umn.edu.

Kopp, **Frederic M.**, *Lewis*. Email: koppfr@lewisu. edu.

Koppel, **Reynold S.**, *Millersville, Pa.*

Koppes, **Clayton R.**, *Oberlin*. Email: clayton. koppes@oberlin.edu.

Kopytoff, *Larissa*, *South Florida, St. Petersburg*. Saint Petersburg, FL. Email: kopytoff@mail. usf.edu; larissa.kopytoff@nyu.edu. Research: modern Africa, France.

Kordas, *Ann*. Pawtucket, RI. Affil: Johnson & Wales. Email: akordas@jwu.edu. Research: women and food, fortune telling in the US.

Korfhage, *David*. Montclair, NJ. Affil: Montclair Kimberley Academy. Email: dkorfhage@ montclairkimberley.org.

Korieh, **Chima**, *Marquette*. Email: chima.korieh@ marquette.edu.

Korinek, *Allison*. New York, NY. Affil: NYU. Email: arkorinek@nyu.edu.

Korinek, **Valerie J.**, *Saskatchewan*. Email: valerie.korinek@usask.ca.

Kormos-Buchwald, **Diana**, *California Inst. of Tech.* Email: diana_buchwald@caltech.edu.

Kornberg, **Jacques**, *Toronto*. Email: kornberg@ chass.utoronto.ca.

Kornblith, *Gary J.*, *Oberlin*. Oberlin, OH. Email: gary.kornblith@oberlin.edu. Research: race relations in Oberlin OH, coming of Civil War.

Kornbluh, **Andrea T.**, *Cincinnati*. Email: andrea. kornbluh@uc.edu.

Kornbluh, *Felicia A.*, *Vermont*. Burlington, VT. Email: fkornblu@uvm.edu. Research: 20th-c constitutional law, New York City.

Körner, *Axel*. London, United Kingdom. Affil: Univ. Coll. London. Email: a.korner@ucl.ac.uk. Research: modern.

Korneski, **Kurt**, *Memorial, Newfoundland*. Email: kkornesk@mun.ca.

Kornfeld, **Eve**, *San Diego State*. Email: kornfeld@ sdsu.edu.

Kornfuehrer, *Axel*. Hopkins, MN. Email: akornfuehrer@msn.com. Research: village life in Pomerania 1850-1945, family.

Kornhauser, **Anne M.**, *Graduate Center, CUNY*. New York, NY. Affil: City Coll., NY. Email: AKornhauser@ccny.cuny.edu. Research: US in world since 1914, 20thc political/legal thought.

Kornweibel, **Richard**, *California State, Sacramento*. Email: kornweibelr@saclink.csus. edu.

Korobeinikov, **Dimitri**, *SUNY, Albany*. Email: dkorobeynikov@albany.edu.

Korr, **Charles P.**, *Missouri–St. Louis*. Email: cpkorr@umsl.edu.

Korros, Alexandra S., *Xavier, Ohio*. Email: korros@xavier.edu.

Kors, Alan C., *Pennsylvania*. Email: akors@sas.upenn.edu.

Korstad, Robert R., *Duke*. Chapel Hill, NC. Email: rkorstad@duke.edu. Research: War on Poverty, comparative white supremacy.

Korsten, Jan, *Soc. for Hist. of Tech.* Email: j.w.a.korsten@tue.nl.

Kosc, Kallie. Fort Worth, TX. Affil: Texas Christian. Email: kallie.kosc@tcu.edu.

Koscak, Stephanie Elaine, *Wake Forest*. Email: koscakse@wfu.edu.

Koschmann, J. Victor, *Cornell*. Email: jvk1@cornell.edu.

Koshar, Rudy J., Jr., *Wisconsin-Madison*. Email: rjkoshar@wisc.edu.

Koshiro, Yukiko. Mishima, Shizuoka, Japan. Affil: Nihon. Email: koshiro.yukiko@nihon-u.ac.jp. Research: WWII, race/culture/ideology.

Kosicki, Piotr H., *Maryland, Coll. Park*. College Park, MD. Email: kosicki@umd.edu. Research: late modern transnational Europe, Catholic political and intellectual life.

Koslofsky, Craig M., *Illinois, Urbana-Champaign*. Urbana, IL. Email: koslof@illinois.edu. Research: skin in early modern world, cultural origins of European Reformation.

Koslovsky, Mary C. Toledo, OH. Email: mary.koslovsky@gmail.com.

Koslow, Jennifer L., *Florida State*. Email: jkoslow@fsu.edu.

Kosmetatou, Elizabeth, *Illinois, Springfield*. Email: ekosm2@uis.edu.

Kosmin, Jennifer Frances, *Bucknell*. Email: jennifer.kosmin@bucknell.edu.

Kossie-Chernyshev, Karen L., *Texas Southern*. Email: kossie_kl@tsu.edu.

Kosso, Cynthia, *Northern Arizona*.

Koster, Mickie, *Texas, Tyler*. Email: mkoster@uttyler.edu.

Kostlevy, William C. Elgin, IL. Affil: Brethren Hist. Library and Archives. Email: bkostlevy@brethren.org. Research: American religious, Progressive Era.

Kosto, Adam J., *Columbia (Hist.)*. New York, NY. Email: ajkosto@columbia.edu. Research: medieval.

Kostroun, Daniella J., *Indiana–Purdue, Indianapolis*. Indianapolis, IN. Email: dkostrou@iupui.edu. Research: political culture of absolutism, women in Catholic Church.

Kotkin, Stephen M., *Princeton*. Email: kotkin@princeton.edu.

Kotlik, Ronald H., *SUNY, Buffalo State*. Email: kotlikrh@buffalostate.edu.

Kotlowski, Dean J., *Salisbury*. Email: djkotlowski@salisbury.edu.

Kotsonis, Yanni, *NYU*. Email: yanni.kotsonis@nyu.edu.

Kottman, Richard N., *Iowa State*.

Koul, Ashish, *Northwestern*. Email: ashish.koul@northwestern.edu.

Kouri, Emilio, *Chicago*. Chicago, IL. Email: kouri@uchicago.edu. Research: modern Mexico, Latin American social and economic.

Kousser, J. Morgan, *California Inst. of Tech.* Email: kousser@hss.caltech.edu.

Kovach, Jeffrey D. Cheshire, CT. Affil: Charter Oak State. Email: jd_kovach75@yahoo.com. Research: Quaker marital regulations on Nantucket, 18th-c New England religious communities.

Kovalesky, Brian Robert. Glendora, CA. Affil: UCLA. Email: briankov@gmail.com.

Kovalev, Roman K., *New Jersey*. Email: kovalev@tcnj.edu.

Kovalio, Jacob, *Carleton, Can.* Email: jacob.kovalio@carleton.ca.

Kovelsky, Damon. Brooklyn, NY. Affil: Brooklyn, CUNY. Email: dkovelsky@yahoo.com.

Koven, Seth D., *Rutgers*. Email: skoven@history.rutgers.edu.

Kowaleski, Maryanne, *Fordham*. Bronx, NY. Email: kowaleski@fordham.edu. Research: port towns in medieval Britain, medieval women and family.

Kowalski, Michael Dale. Jenison, MI. Email: Kowalskimike@comcast.net. Research: Leon Trotsky, Russian Revolution.

Kowalsky, Sharon A., *Texas A&M, Commerce*. Commerce, TX. Email: sharon.kowalsky@tamuc.edu. Research: crime and gender in Revolutionary Russia.

Kowalzig, Barbara, *NYU*. Email: barbara.kowalzig@nyu.edu.

Kownslar, Allan O., *Trinity, Tex.* Email: akownsla@trinity.edu.

Koya, Riyad S. Santa Rosa, CA. Affil: California, Berkeley. Email: skoya2@berkeley.edu. Research: Indian indentured labor, Family law.

Koyle, Kenneth M., *National Library of Medicine*. Email: ken.koyle@nih.gov.

Kozakiewicz, Laurie, *SUNY, Albany*. Email: lk0550@albany.edu.

Kozakowski, Michael, *Colorado Denver*. Email: michael.kozakowski@ucdenver.edu.

Kozel, Susan J. Cream Ridge, NJ. Email: skozel@kean.edu. Research: slavery in western Monmouth County NJ, Gandhi and US civil rights/King/Hamer 1964.

Kozelsky, Mara V., *South Alabama*. Email: mkozelsky@southalabama.edu.

Koziol, Geoffrey, *California, Berkeley*. Email: gkoz@berkeley.edu.

Kozlov, Denis, *Dalhousie*. Email: denis.kozlov@dal.ca.

Kozlowski, Wojciech. Warsaw, Poland. Affil: Pilecki Inst. Email: w.kozlowski@instytutpileckiego.pl. Research: medieval inter-lordly politics, Polish experience of two totalitarianism.

Kozuh, Michael, *Auburn*. Email: mgk0001@auburn.edu.

Kraay, Hendrik, *Calgary*. Calgary, AB, Canada. Email: kraay@ucalgary.ca. Research: social history of independence, civic rituals.

Kraemer, Joshua. Fairfax, VA. Email: bestie88888@protonmail.com.

Kraft, James P., *Hawai'i, Manoa*. Email: jkraft@hawaii.edu.

Kraig, Beth M., *Pacific Lutheran*. Email: kraigbm@plu.edu.

Kraig, Bruce Z., *Roosevelt*. Email: bkraig@roosevelt.edu.

Krainz, Thomas A., *DePaul*. Email: tkrainz@depaul.edu.

Krais, Jakob. Berlin, Germany. Affil: Gerda Henkel Stiftung. Email: jakob.krais@fu-berlin.de.

Krajewski, Heidi Marie, *Charleston*. Email: krajewskih@cofc.edu.

Krallis, Dimitris, *Simon Fraser*. Email: dkrallis@sfu.ca.

Kramer, Alan. New York, NY. Email: akramer62@aol.com.

Kramer, Alisa. Washington, DC. Affil: American. Email: alisask49@gmail.com. Research: law enforcement.

Kramer, Emil A., *Augustana*. Email: emilkramer@augustana.edu.

Kramer, Erin B., *Trinity, Tex.* Email: ekramer@trinity.edu.

Kramer, Jacob. New York, NY. Affil: Borough of Manhattan Comm. Coll., CUNY. Email: jak163@gmail.com. Research: Progressive reform, radicalism.

Kramer, Lloyd S., *North Carolina, Chapel Hill*. Chapel Hill, NC. Email: lkramer@email.unc.edu. Research: modern European intellectual.

Kramer, Michael J., *SUNY, Coll. Brockport*. Email: mkramer@brockport.edu.

Kramer, Paul Alexander, *Vanderbilt*. Nashville, TN. Email: paul.a.kramer@vanderbilt.edu; paul.kramer49@gmail.com. Research: US and world.

Kramer, Robert S., *St. Norbert*. Email: robert.kramer@snc.edu.

Kramer, William. Austin, TX. Email: williamkramer@utexas.edu.

Kranjc, Gregor, *Brock*. Email: gkranjc@brocku.ca.

Kranking, Glenn Eric, *Gustavus Adolphus*. Email: kranking@gustavus.edu.

Krantz, Frederick, *Concordia, Can.* Email: fkrantz@videotron.ca.

Krapfl, James, *McGill*. Email: james.krapfl@mcgill.ca.

Krasner, Barbara D. Somerset, NJ. Affil: William Paterson. Email: barbarakrasner@att.net. Research: immigration, Holocaust.

Krasovic, Mark, *Rutgers, Newark/New Jersey Inst. of Tech.* Email: krasovic@rutgers.edu.

Krats, Peter V., *Western Ontario*. Email: pkrats@uwo.ca.

Kratz, Jessie. Washington, DC. Affil: National Archives. Email: jessie.kratz@nara.gov.

Kraus, Erin, *State Hist. Soc. of Missouri*. Email: krause@shsmo.org.

Krause, Paul L., *British Columbia*. Email: krause@mail.ubc.ca.

Kraut, Alan, *American; National Hist. Center*. Washington, DC. Email: akraut@american.edu. Research: Americanization of immigrants, US coercion and public health.

Krauthamer, Barbara, *Massachusetts, Amherst*. Email: barbarak@history.umass.edu.

Kravchenko, Volodymyr, *Alberta*. Email: vkravche@ualberta.ca.

Kravetz, Melissa Lynn, *Longwood*. Email: kravetzml@longwood.edu.

Krch, Pamela. Grand Junction, CO. Affil: Texas, El Paso. Email: pkk@montrose.net. Research: 20th-c US, Native American.

Kreader, J. Lee. Los Angeles, CA. Email: lee.kreader@gmail.com. Research: Social Security, Zionism.

Krebs, Daniel, *Louisville*. Email: daniel.krebs@louisville.edu.

Krebsbach, Suzanne. Charleston, SC. Affil: Independent Scholar. Email: 01salish@gmail.com. Research: slavery/race/Catholicism.

Kreider, Jodie A., *Denver*. Email: jkreide2@du.edu.

Kreike, Emmanuel, *Princeton*. Email: kreike@princeton.edu.

Kreiner, Jamie, *Georgia*. Athens, GA. Email: jkreiner@uga.edu; jamie.kreiner@gmail.com. Research: Merovingian culture, premodern pigs.

Kreiner, Jared. Williamsburg, VA. Affil: Chicago. Email: jkreiner@uchicago.edu.

Kreiser, B. Robert. Chevy Chase, MD. Affil: George Mason. Email: brkreiser@gmail.com. Research: French veterinary medical profession, academic freedom.

Kreitlow, Bert S., *Wisconsin-Whitewater*. Email: kreitlob@uww.edu.

Krejci, Adam Joseph, Esq. Edmond, OK. Email: adamjkrejci@gmail.com.

Krekic, Barisa, *UCLA*. Email: bkrekic4@hotmail.com.

Kremer, Gary R., *Missouri, Columbia; State Hist. Soc. of Missouri*. Email: kremerg@umsystem.edu; kremerg@shsmo.org.

Kremer, Richard, *Dartmouth*. Email: richard.kremer@dartmouth.edu.

Kremer-Wright, Garret, *State Hist. Soc. of Missouri*. Email: KremerWrightG@shsmo.org.

Krenn, Michael L., *Appalachian State*. Email: krennml@appstate.edu.

Krentz, Peter M., *Davidson*. Email: pekrentz@davidson.edu.

Kress, Lee B., *Rowan*. Cherry Hill, NJ. Email: lbkress@rowan.edu. Research: US and Latin America, military.

Kretchik, Walter E., *Western Illinois*.

Kretz, Dale. Lubbock, TX. Affil: Texas Tech. Email: dale.kretz@ttu.edu.

Kriegel, Lara H., *Indiana*. Email: lkriegel@indiana.edu.

Krieger, Daniel E., *California Polytechnic State*. Email: dkrieger@calpoly.edu.

Krige, John, *Georgia Inst. of Tech.; Soc. for Hist. of Tech*. Email: john.krige@hts.gatech.edu.

Kriger, Colleen E., *North Carolina, Greensboro*. Greensboro, NC. Email: c_kriger@uncg.edu. Research: Africa.

Krikun, David, *SUNY, New Paltz*. Email: krikund@newpaltz.edu.

Krippner, James M. Haverford, PA. Affil: Haverford. Email: jkrippne@haverford.edu. Research: photography and history, Mexico in 1930s.

Krischer, Elana. Albany, NY. Affil: SUNY, Albany. Email: ekrischer@albany.edu.

Krisciunas, Raymond G. New London, CT. Affil: SUNY, Canton. Email: krisr@canton.edu.

Krivulskaya, Suzanna. South Bend, IN. Affil: Notre Dame. Email: suzanna.krivulskaya@gmail.com.

Krochmal, Max, *Texas Christian*. Fort Worth, TX. Email: m.krochmal@tcu.edu. Research: multiracial left in Texas 1935-75, labor/civil rights/gender/oral.

Kroeber, Clifton B., *Occidental*.

Kroeker, Greta G., *Waterloo*. Email: gkroeker@uwaterloo.ca.

Kroemer, James G. Brown Deer, WI. Email: jameskroemer@gmail.com. Research: Second Crusade, Jews/Christians/Muslims.

Kroen, Sheryl T., *Florida*. Gainesville, FL. Email: stkroen@ufl.edu. Research: European cultural and intellectual, capitalism cultural.

Krohn, Raymond James, *Boise State*. Email: raymondkrohn@boisestate.edu.

Krokar, James P., *DePaul*. Evanston, IL. Email: jkrokar@depaul.edu. Research: 19th-c Croatia, cartography in Southeast Europe.

Kroker, Kenton, *York, Can*. Email: kkroker@yorku.ca.

Krolikowski, Alanna, *Missouri Science and Tech*.

Kroll, Gary M., *SUNY, Plattsburgh*. Email: krollgm@plattsburgh.edu.

Krome, Frederic. Batavia, OH. Affil: Cincinnati. Email: kromefj@ucmail.uc.edu. Research: Anglo-American popular culture, science fiction.

Krome-Lukens, Anna L. Chapel Hill, NC. Affil: North Carolina, Chapel Hill. Email: annakl@email.unc.edu. Research: women/NC eugenics and welfare programs.

Kronmiller, Brady, *Weber State*. Email: bradykronmiller@weber.edu.

Krosby, H. Peter, *SUNY, Albany*. Email: krosby@albany.edu.

Kross, Jessica, *South Carolina, Columbia*. Email: kross@mailbox.sc.edu.

Kroupa, Daniel, *Detroit Mercy*. Email: kroupadr@udmercy.edu.

Krozewski, Gerold. Osaka, Japan. Affil: Osaka. Email: g.krozewski@iai.osaka-u.ac.jp.

Kruckeberg, Robert D., *Troy*. Troy, AL. Email: rkruckeberg@troy.edu. Research: French Enlightenment, French Revolution.

Krueckeberg, John, *Plymouth State*. Plymouth, NH. Email: jkrueckeberg@plymouth.edu. Research: Great Depression, WWII Home Front.

Krueger, Capt David, *US Military Acad*. West Point, NY. Email: david.krueger@usma.edu; davidkrueger@g.harvard.edu. Research: US race/gender/ethnicity, citizenship/nationalism/Army.

Krueger, David W. Fort Collins, CO. Email: krueger5691@att.net.

Kruer, Matthew, *Chicago*. Chicago, IL. Email: kruer@uchicago.edu. Research: Susquehannock Indians, Anglo-Indian violence.

Krug, Ilana C., *York, Pa*. Email: ikrug@ycp.edu.

Krug, Jessica A., *George Washington*. Email: jkrug@gwu.edu.

Kruger, Cole, *Nebraska, Kearney*.

Krugler, David, *Wisconsin-Platteville*. Email: kruglerd@uwplatt.edu.

Krugler, John D., *Marquette*. Email: john.krugler@marquette.edu.

Kruk, William K., *Austin Peay State*. Email: krukw@apsu.edu.

Krukofsky, Howard C., *Fordham*. Email: c.howardkrukofsky@hunter.edu.

Krukones, James H., *John Carroll*. Email: jkrukones@jcu.edu.

Krulder, Joseph J. Chico, CA. Affil: California State, Chico. Email: joekrulder@yahoo.com. Research: 18th-c Britain, Seven Years War.

Krulikowski, Anne E., *West Chester*. Email: akrulikowski@wcupa.edu.

Kruman, Marc W., *Wayne State*. Email: m.kruman@wayne.edu.

Krupar, Jason N., *Cincinnati*. Cincinnati, OH. Email: kruparjn@ucmail.uc.edu. Research: Cold War technology and science, race during Cold War.

Kruse, Kevin M., *Princeton*. Princeton, NJ. Email: kkruse@princeton.edu. Research: origins of religious right, WWII and civil rights.

Kruze, Uldis, *San Francisco*. El Cerrito, CA. Email: kruzeu@usfca.edu. Research: modern China, modern Japan.

Kryder, Daniel, *Brandeis*. Email: kryder@brandeis.edu.

Kryder-Reid, Elizabeth, *Indiana–Purdue, Indianapolis*. Email: ekryderr@iupui.edu.

Krylova, Anna, *Duke*. Durham, NC. Email: krylova@duke.edu. Research: historical theory and method, modern Russia and socialism.

Krysiek, James S., *Gettysburg*. Email: jkrysiek@gettysburg.edu.

Krysko, Michael A., *Kansas State*. Email: mkrysko@ksu.edu.

Krzemienski, Edward, *Ball State*. Email: krzemienski@bsu.edu.

Krzeminski, Stephen, *Florida Atlantic*. Email: skrzeminski2013@fau.edu.

Kselman, Thomas A., *Notre Dame*. Notre Dame, IN. Email: Kselman.1@nd.edu. Research: Catholic-Jewish relations in modern France.

Kubacki, Derek W. Stockdale, TX. Email: derek.kubacki@yahoo.com.

Kube, Sven. Miami, FL. Affil: Florida International. Email: svenkube@gmail.com. Research: popular culture/music/film/literature, North American/Euuropean transatlantic exchange.

Kubiski, Joyce M., *Western Michigan*. Email: joyce.kubiski@wmich.edu.

Kubo, Fumiaki. Tokyo, Japan. Affil: Tokyo. Email: kubo@j.u-tokyo.ac.jp.

Kuby, Emma, *Northern Illinois*. Dekalb, IL. Email: ekuby@niu.edu. Research: modern France.

Kuby, William, *Tennessee, Chattanooga*. Chattanooga, TN. Email: william-kuby@utc.edu. Research: US marriage law, nonmarital practice and cohabitation.

Kudlick, Catherine J. San Francisco, CA. Affil: San Francisco State. Email: kudlick@sfsu.edu. Research: disability/attitudes/blindness, blind people in modern France and US.

Kuech, Andrew. Brooklyn, NY. Affil: New Sch. Email: kueca293@newschool.edu.

Kuefler, Mathew S., *San Diego State*. Email: mkuefler@sdsu.edu.

Kuehn, John T., *US Army Command Coll*. Email: john.t.kuehn.civ@mail.mil.

Kuehn, Thomas J. Clemson, SC. Affil: Clemson. Email: tjkuehn@clemson.edu. Research: Renaissance families, women and gender.

Kuehn, Thomas, *Simon Fraser*. Email: thomas_kuehn@sfu.ca.

Kuehne, Thomas, *Clark*. Worcester, MA. Email: tkuehne@clarku.edu. Research: Holocaust, Germany.

Kuehner, Karl. Berkeley, IL. Affil: Illinois, Chicago. Email: karljkuehner@gmail.com. Research: US religion, interaction between religion/capital.

Kuenker, Paul. Durango, CO. Affil: BASIS Tucson Primary. Email: pfkuenker@gmail.com.

Kuenzli, E. Gabrielle, *South Carolina, Columbia*. Email: kuenzli@mailbox.sc.edu.

Kuersteiner, Sarina Corinne. Cambridge, MA. Affil: Columbia. Email: sck2159@columbia.edu. Research: Italy 1000-1500, emotions and senses.

Kuffert, Leonard B., *Manitoba*. Email: len.kuffert@umanitoba.ca.

Kugel, Rebecca, *California, Riverside*. Riverside, CA. Email: rebecca.kugel@ucr.edu. Research: contested definitions of race, Native American concepts of work/gender.

Kugler, Anne, *John Carroll*. Email: akugler@jcu. edu.

Kugler, Michael James, *Northwestern Coll.* Email: kugler@nwciowa.edu.

Kuhl, Dan H. Sun City West, AZ. Email: dkuhl1950@gmail.com.

Kuhl, Michelle M., *Wisconsin-Oshkosh*. Email: kuhlm@uwosh.edu.

Kuhlman, Erika Ann, *Idaho State*. Email: kuhlerik@isu.edu.

Kuiken, Jonathan R., *Wilkes*. Email: jonathan. kuiken@wilkes.edu.

Kuisel, Richard F., *SUNY, Stony Brook*. Email: Richard.Kuisel@stonybrook.edu.

Kuklick, Bruce, *Pennsylvania*. Email: bkuklick@ sas.upenn.edu.

Kulczycki, John J., *Illinois, Chicago*. Chicago, IL. Email: kul@uic.edu. Research: nationalism in Poland, nationalism under communism.

Kulikoff, Allan, *Georgia*. Email: kulikoff@uga. edu.

Kulikowski, Michael, *Penn State*. University Park, PA. Email: mek31@psu.edu. Research: ancient Rome.

Kulisek, Larry L., *Windsor*. Email: kulisek@ uwindsor.ca.

Kumamoto, Bob, *San José State*.

Kumar, Nita, *Claremont McKenna*. Email: nkumar@cmc.edu.

Kumar, Prakash, *Penn State*. Email: puk15@psu. edu.

Kumar, Radha, *Syracuse*. Email: rkuma100@ maxwell.syr.edu.

Kumarasingham, Harshan. Edinburgh, Scotland, United Kingdom. Affil: Edinburgh. Email: harshan.kumarasingham@ed.ac.uk. Research: decolonization/British Empire, commonwealth/monarchy.

Kumbhar, Kiran. Cambridge, MA. Affil: Harvard. Email: kumbhar@g.harvard.edu.

Kumbier, Ashley, *Soc. for Military Hist.*

Kumekawa, Ian. Cambridge, MA. Affil: Harvard. Email: kumekawa@fas.harvard.edu.

Kumhera, Glenn J., *Penn State, Erie*. Email: gjk19@psu.edu.

Kumolalo, Frederick, *Morgan State*. Email: Frederick.Kumolalo@morgan.edu.

Kumor, Georgia Ann. Seattle, WA.

Kunakhovich, Kyrill, *Virginia*. Email: kmk5ss@ virginia.edu.

Kunath, Robert C. Jacksonville, IL. Affil: Illinois Coll. Email: kunath@ic.edu. Research: cultural nationalism and WWI, interpretations of Holocaust perpetrators.

Kuniholm, Bruce R. Durham, NC. Affil: Duke. Email: bruce.kuniholm@duke.edu. Research: US-Turkish relations, US Middle Eastern policy.

Kunze, Neil L., *Southern Oregon*. Email: kunze@ sou.edu.

Kunze, Savitri Maya, *Wabash*. Chicago, IL. Email: kunzes@wabash.edu; smsedlacek@uchicago. edu.

Kunzel, Regina G., *Princeton*. Princeton, NJ. Email: rkunzel@princeton.edu. Research: modern US, gender and sexuality.

Kuo, Margaret, *California State, Long Beach; Soc. for Hist. Education*. Email: margaret.kuo@ csulb.edu.

Kupel, Douglas E. Phoenix, AZ.

Kupin-Lisbin, Marianne E. Penfield, NY. Affil: Rochester. Email: mkupin@ur.rochester.edu.

Kupper, Samuel Y., *California State, Fullerton*. Email: skupper@fullerton.edu.

Kupperman, Karen Ordahl, *Connecticut, Storrs; NYU*. New York, NY. Email: karen.kupperman@ uconn.edu; karen.kupperman@nyu.edu. Research: Atlantic world connections, early modern environment.

Kuracina, William F., *Texas A&M, Commerce*. Commerce, TX. Email: william.kuracina@ tamuc.edu. Research: Indian nationalist movement.

Kurashige, Lon Y., *Southern California*. Email: kurashig@usc.edu.

Kurhajec, Anna L., *Metropolitan State*. Minneapolis, MN. Affil: St. Thomas, Minn. Email: anna.kurhajec@metrostate.edu; kurh3064@stthomas.edu. Research: radicalism and heteronormativity, 1960s/New Left/student movements.

Kurimay, Anita A., *Bryn Mawr*. Email: akurimay@ brynmawr.edu.

Kuriyama, Shigehisa, *Harvard (Hist. of Science)*. Email: hkuriyam@fas.harvard.edu.

Kuromiya, Hiroaki, *Indiana*. Email: hkuromiy@ indiana.edu.

Kurtz, Anthony, *Western Washington*. Email: Anthony.Kurtz@wwu.edu.

Kuryla, Peter A., *Belmont*. Email: peter.kuryla@ belmont.edu.

Kurz, Johannes L. Brunei Darussalam. Affil: Brunei Darussalam. Email: jolukurz@gmail. com. Research: early Song intellectual, 10th-c China.

Kushner, Howard I., *Emory; San Diego State*. Email: hkushne@emory.edu.

Kushner, Nina J., *Clark*. Worcester, MA. Email: nkushner@clarku.edu. Research: elite prostitution in early modern Paris, women and work in early modern France.

Kuskowski, Ada-Maria, *Pennsylvania*.

Kutcher, Gerald J., *Binghamton, SUNY*. Email: gkutcher@binghamton.edu.

Kutcher, Norman Alan, *Syracuse*. Email: nakutcher@maxwell.syr.edu.

Kutolowski, John F., *SUNY, Coll. Brockport*.

Kutolowski, Kathleen S., *SUNY, Coll. Brockport*. Email: kkutolow@brockport.edu.

Kutulas, Judy A., *St. Olaf*. Northfield, MN. Email: kutulas@stolaf.edu. Research: 1970s popular culture, gender and television.

Kuxhausen, Anna K., *St. Olaf*. Email: kux@stolaf. edu.

Kuykendall, John E., *Charleston Southern*. Email: jkuykendall@csuniv.edu.

Kuykendall, Michael. Big Spring, TX. Email: michaelkuykendall@yahoo.com.

Kuzbida, Gregory. The Villages, FL. Email: gkuzbida@gmail.com.

Kuzdale, Ann E. Chicago, IL. Affil: Chicago State. Email: akuzdale@csu.edu. Research: medieval Europe, women.

Kuznesof, Elizabeth A., *Kansas*. Email: kuznesof@ku.edu.

Kuznick, Peter J., *American*. Email: kuznick@ american.edu.

Kuznitz, Cecile E., *Bard*. New York, NY. Email: kuznitz@bard.edu. Research: modern Jewish, Yiddish culture.

Kwak, Nancy H., *California, San Diego*. Email: nhkwak@ucsd.edu.

Kwak, Tae Yang, *Ramapo*. Email: tkwak@ ramapo.edu.

Kwan, Man Bun, *Cincinnati*. Email: kwanmb@ uc.edu.

Kwass, Michael, *Johns Hopkins (Hist.)*. Baltimore, MD. Email: kwass@jhu.edu. Research: early modern France, political and economic culture.

Kwoba, Brian, *Memphis*. Email: bwkwoba@ memphis.edu.

Kwok, Daniel W. Y., *Hawai'i, Manoa*. Email: dkwok@hawaii.edu.

Kwolek-Folland, Angel, *Florida*. Email: akf@ aa.ufl.edu.

Kwosek, Susan L. DeKalb, IL. Affil: Northern Illinois. Email: Susan.kwosek@gmail.com. Research: Black Atlantic, comparative religion.

Kyle, Chris R., *Syracuse*. Email: chkyle@maxwell. syr.edu.

Kyle, Donald G., *Texas, Arlington*. Email: kyle@ uta.edu.

Kynoch, Gary, *Dalhousie*. Email: gary.kynoch@ dal.ca.

Kyong-McClain, Jeff, *Idaho*. Email: jeffkm@ uidaho.edu.

Kyriakoudes, Louis M., *Middle Tennessee State*. Email: Louis.Kyriakoudes@mtsu.edu.

Kyrou, Alexandros K., *Salem State*. Email: akyrou@salemstate.edu.

Kytle, Ethan J., *California State, Fresno*. Email: ekytle@csufresno.edu.

L l

La Fleur, Melissa. Douglasville, GA. Affil: Mercer. Email: simlafleur@gmail.com.

La Serna, Miguel A., *North Carolina, Chapel Hill*. Chapel Hill, NC. Email: laserna@email.unc.edu. Research: Peru and indigenous peasantry, power/cuture/violence.

La Vere, David L, *North Carolina, Wilmington*. Email: lavered@uncw.edu.

Laaman, John Henry, *Kennesaw State*. Email: jlaaman@kennesaw.edu.

Laas, Nataliia. Waltham, MA. Affil: Brandeis. Email: natalialaas@brandeis.edu. Research: Soviet Union, Cold War.

Laats, Adam, *Binghamton, SUNY*. Email: alaats@ binghamton.edu.

Laband, John, *Wilfrid Laurier*. Email: jlaband@ wlu.ca.

Labaree, Benjamin W., *Jr.* Washington, DC. Affil: St. Albans Sch. Email: blabaree@ stalbansschool.org.

Labelle, Kathryn Magee, *Saskatchewan*. Email: kathryn.labelle@usask.ca.

Labelle, Maurice Jr. M., *Jr.*, *Saskatchewan*. Email: maurice.jr.labelle@usask.ca.

Labendz, Jacob Ari, *Youngstown State*.

Labode, Modupe, *Indiana–Purdue, Indianapolis*. Email: mlabode@iupui.edu.

LaBrecque, Annabel G. Washington, DC. Affil: National Hist. Center. Email: annabel_ labrecque@berkeley.edu.

Labrecque, Claire, *Winnipeg*. Email: c.labrecque@uwinnipeg.ca.

LaBuff, Jeremy, *Northern Arizona*. Email: jeremy. labuff@nau.edu.

LaCapra, Dominick C., *Cornell*. Email: dcl3@ cornell.edu.

Lacey, Vincent A., *Southern Illinois, Carbondale*. Email: vlacey@siu.edu.

LaChance, Daniel, *Emory*. Email: dlachance@ emory.edu.

Lachapelle, Sofie, *Guelph*. Email: slachap@ uoguelph.ca.

Lacher, **Katrina**, *Central Oklahoma*. Email: klacher@uco.edu.

Lachoff, **Irwin**, *Xavier, La.* Email: ilachoff@xula.edu.

Lackenbauer, **Whitney**, *Waterloo*. Email: pwlacken@uwaterloo.ca.

LaCombe, **Michael A**., *Adelphi*. Brooklyn, NY. Email: lacombe@adelphi.edu. Research: food, expertise/law of property.

Lacopo, **Frank**. South Bend, IN. Affil: Ball State. Email: fplacopo@bsu.edu. Research: High Medieval social persecution, deep historical methodology.

LaCortiglia, **Jeffrey M**. Clarksville, TN. Affil: US Army. Email: j_lacortiglia@hotmail.com.

LaCroix, **Alison L**. Chicago, IL. Affil: Chicago. Email: lacroix@uchicago.edu. Research: American federalism, 18th-/19th-c US intellectual.

Lacson, **P. Albert**, *Grinnell*. Email: lacson@grinnell.edu.

Lacy, **Cherilyn M**., *Hartwick*. Email: lacyc@hartwick.edu.

Lacy, **Elaine**, *South Carolina Aiken*. Email: elainel@usca.edu.

Lacy, **Lisa M**. Waco, TX. Affil: Texas Tech, Waco. Email: llacy1989@gmail.com. Research: 19th-c Egyptian political movement, British Empire.

Lacy, **Tim N**. Chicago, IL. Affil: Loyola, Chicago; Illinois. Email: timothy.n.lacy@gmail.com. Research: intellectual/cultural/education, anti-intellectualism/medicine.

Ladd, **Brian K**., *SUNY, Albany*. Altamont, NY. Email: ladd@albany.edu.

Ladd-Taylor, **Molly**, *York, Can.* Toronto, ON, Canada. Email: mltaylor@yorku.ca. Research: US social, women.

Laderman, **Scott**, *Minnesota Duluth*. Duluth, MN. Email: laderman@d.umn.edu. Research: history/tourism/memory in Vietnam, modern US.

Laegreid, **Renee M**., *Wyoming*. Email: rlaegrei@uwyo.edu.

Laemmli, **Whitney**, *Carnegie Mellon*.

Laessig, **Simone**, *German Hist. Inst.* Washington, DC. Email: prolaessig@ghi-dc.org.

LaFantasie, **Glenn W**., *Western Kentucky*. Email: glenn.lafantasie@wku.edu.

LaFauci, **Joseph P**., *Roger Williams*.

LaFeber, **Walter F**., *Cornell*. Ithaca, NY. Email: wfl3@cornell.edu. Research: America, US foreign policy 1750-present.

LaFevor, **David Clark**, *Texas, Arlington*. Fort Worth, TX. Email: dlafevor@uta.edu. Research: modernity/gender/nationalism, circum-Caribbean.

Laffan, **Michael F**., *Princeton*. Email: mlaffan@princeton.edu.

Lafferty, **Maura**, *Tennessee, Knoxville*. Email: mlaffert@utk.edu.

Lafferty-Salhany, **Renee**, *Brock*. Email: rlaffert@brocku.ca.

LaFleche, **Paul V**., *Worcester State*. Email: plafleche@worcester.edu.

LaFleur, **Renee Anne**, *Tennessee, Martin*. Email: rlafleur@utm.edu.

LaFleur, **Robert Andre**, *Beloit*. Email: lafleur@beloit.edu.

LaFollette, **Hugh**, *South Florida, St. Petersburg*. Email: hhl@mail.usf.edu.

LaFreniere, **Donald J**., *Michigan Tech*. Email: djlafren@mtu.edu.

Lafuse, **Madeline**. New York, NY. Affil: Graduate Center, CUNY. Email: mlafuse@gradcenter.cuny.edu.

Lagemann, **Ellen Condliffe**, *Bard*. Email: lagemann@bard.edu.

Lagomarsino, **P. David**, *Dartmouth*. Email: david.lagomarsino@dartmouth.edu.

Lagos, **Katerina G**., *California State, Sacramento*. Email: klagos@csus.edu.

LaGrand, **James B**., *Messiah*. Email: jlagrand@messiah.edu.

Lahlum, **Lori Ann**, *Minnesota State, Mankato*. Mankato, MN. Email: lori.lahlum@mnsu.edu. Research: gender and Great Plains agrarian politics, gender and Norwegian American communities.

Lahr, **Angela M**., *Westminster*. Email: lahram@westminster.edu.

Lahti, **Janne J**. Espoo, Finland. Affil: Helsinki. Email: lahtijjj@hotmail.com. Research: colonialism and postcolonialism, whiteness and class.

Lahusen, **Thomas**, *Toronto*. Email: thomas.lahusen@utoronto.ca.

Lai, **Tracy**. Seattle, WA. Affil: Seattle Central Comm. Coll. Email: tracy.lai@seattlecolleges.edu. Research: kibei women, Hanford nuclear reservation.

Laichas, **Thomas M**. Venice, CA. Affil: Crossroads Sch. Email: tlaichas@gmail.com. Research: world and Los Angeles, curriculum development.

Lain, **Bobby D**., *Austin Comm. Coll.* Email: bdlain@cvtv.net.

Lair, **Meredith H**., *George Mason*. Email: mlair@gmu.edu.

Laird, **Pamela W**., *Colorado Denver*. Denver, CO. Email: pamela.laird@ucdenver.edu. Research: US business culture.

Laird, **W. R**., *Carleton, Can.* Email: WRLaird@carleton.ca.

Lake, **Peter G**., *Vanderbilt*. Email: peter.lake@vanderbilt.edu.

Lakemacher, **Matt J**. Gurnee, IL. Affil: Woodland Middle Sch. Email: mlakemacher@dist50.net.

Lakhani, **Zain**. Philadelphia, PA. Affil: Pennsylvania. Email: zlakhani@sas.upenn.edu. Research: human rights, refugees and migration.

Lakwete, **Angela**, *Auburn*. Email: lakwean@auburn.edu.

Lal, **Priya**, *Boston Coll.* Email: priya.lal@bc.edu.

Lal, **Ruby**, *Emory*. Email: rlal2@emory.edu.

Lal, **Vinay**, *UCLA*. Email: vlal@history.ucla.edu.

Lalaki, **Despina**. Astoria, NY. Affil: Baruch, CUNY. Email: despina.lalaki@baruch.cuny.edu.

Lam, **Tong**, *Toronto*. Email: tong.lam@utoronto.ca.

Lamar, **Howard R**., *Yale*. Orange, CT. Research: US West.

Lamarre, **Jean**, *Royal Military*. Email: jean.lamarre@rmc.ca.

Lamarre, **Lynda**. Augusta, GA. Affil: Georgia Military. Email: llamarre@gmc.edu.

Lambe, **Ariel Mae**, *Connecticut, Storrs*. Email: ariel.lambe@uconn.edu.

Lambe, **Jennifer Lynn**, *Brown*. Email: Jennifer_Lambe@Brown.edu.

Lamberson, **Christine M**. San Angelo, TX. Affil: Angelo State. Email: clamberson@angelo.edu. Research: US violence, domestic Cold War US.

Lambert, **Cornelia C**., *North Georgia*. Email: cornelia.lambert@ung.edu.

Lambert, **David E**., *Azusa Pacific*. Email: dlambert@apu.edu.

Lambert, **Elizabeth Harrington**. Elloree, SC. Affil: Grand Valley State. Email: ehlamber@indiana.edu. Research: space and place, war and society.

Lambert, **Erin**, *Virginia*. Email: eml7f@virginia.edu.

Lambert, **Franklin T**., *Purdue*. Email: flambert@purdue.edu.

Lambert, **Maj David**, *US Military Acad.* Email: david.lambert@usma.edu.

Lambert, **Margo M**., *Cincinnati*.

Lamberti, **Marjorie E**., *Middlebury*. Email: lamberti@middlebury.edu.

Lamberton, **Christine**, *North Carolina, Wilmington*. Email: lambertonc@uncw.edu.

Lamkin, **Bryan J**., *Azusa Pacific*. Email: blamkin@apu.edu.

Lamon, **Lester C**., *Indiana, South Bend*. Email: llamon@iusb.edu.

Lamont, **Thomas**. Groton, MA. Affil: Groton Sch. Email: tlamont@groton.org.

Lamoreaux, **Naomi R**., *Yale*. New Haven, CT. Email: naomi.lamoreaux@yale.edu. Research: patenting and technological change, business and other organizations.

Lampe, **John R**., *Maryland, Coll. Park*. Email: jrlampe@umd.edu.

Lamperd, **Brooke**. Providence, RI. Affil: Brown. Email: brooke_lamperd@brown.edu.

Lampert, **Sara Elisabeth**, *South Dakota*. Email: Sara.Lampert@usd.edu.

Lamphear, **John**, *Texas, Austin*. Email: lamphear@mail.utexas.edu.

Lamphere, **Stephanie**. Rocklin, CA. Affil: Sierra. Email: stephclogs@gmail.com.

Lampson, **Howard Frank**. El Dorado Hills, CA. Affil: California State, Sacramento. Email: redheadhl@aol.com.

Lamson, **Lisa Rose**. Milwaukee, WI. Affil: Marquette. Email: lisa.lamson@marquette.edu. Research: sexuality in colonial America, early modern world legal.

Land, **Isaac E**., *Indiana State*. Terre Haute, IN. Email: Isaac.Land@indstate.edu. Research: methods and pedagogy, cosmopolitan port towns.

Land, **Jeremy**. Rockmart, GA. Affil: Georgia State. Email: land25.jeremy@gmail.com. Research: Atlantic world, economic.

Landau, **Emily Epstein**. Washington, DC. Affil: Maryland, Coll. Park. Email: eelandau@verizon.net. Research: 19th-/20th-c US South, country music.

Landau, **Norma B**., *California, Davis*. Email: nblandau@ucdavis.edu.

Landau, **Paul S**., *Maryland, Coll. Park*. Email: plandau@umd.edu.

Landdeck, **Katherine**, *Texas Woman's*. Email: klanddeck@twu.edu.

Landdeck, **Kevin P**. Yonkers, NY. Affil: Sarah Lawrence. Email: bamboozld@gmail.com. Research: Sino-Japanese War 1937-45.

Lande, **Jonathan**, *Weber State*. New York, NY. Affil: New Sch. Email: jonlande@gmail.com; landej@newschool.edu. Research: US Civil War, US slavery.

Lander, **Brian George**, *Brown*. Providence, RI. Email: bgl2114@columbia.edu. Research: Chinese history and archaeology, environmental.

Landers, Jane G., *Vanderbilt*. Nashville, FL. Email: jane.landers@vanderbilt.edu. Research: Africans in Atlantic world, maroons in Latin America.

Landes, Joan B., *Penn State*. Email: jb15@psu.edu.

Landis, Dennis C. Brooklyn, CT. Affil: Brown. Email: dclandis@gmail.com. Research: German book in early Pennsylvania, dissident views of colonial Ame conquest.

Landis, Michael Todd. Ballston Spa, NY. Affil: SUNY, Ulster. Email: mlandis141@gmail.com. Research: US Civil War, 19th-c US.

Landon, Christopher Thomas. Toronto, ON, Canada. Affil: Toronto. Email: christopher.landon@utoronto.ca.

Landon, Michael de L., *Mississippi*.

Landon, William J., *Northern Kentucky*. Email: landonw1@nku.edu.

Landry, Jeffrey P. Portland, CT. Email: Jefflandry77@gmail.com.

Landry, Marc D., II, *New Orleans*. New Orleans, LA. Email: mdlandr1@uno.edu. Research: Germany, Europe.

Lands, LeeAnn Bishop, *Kennesaw State*. Kennesaw, GA. Email: llands@kennesaw.edu.

Landsberg, Alison, *George Mason*. Email: alandsb1@gmu.edu.

Landsea, Kathryn. Miami, FL. Affil: Miami-Dade County Public Sch. Email: klandsea@dadeschools.net.

Landsman, Ned C., *SUNY, Stony Brook*. Email: ned.landsman@stonybrook.edu.

Landweber, Julia A., *Montclair State*. Email: landweberj@mail.montclair.edu.

Landy, Francis, *Alberta*. Email: francis.landy@ualberta.ca.

Lane, Barbara Miller. Wayne, PA. Affil: Bryn Mawr. Email: blane@brynmawr.edu. Research: American and European housing, suburbs.

Lane, Carl A. Montclair, NJ. Affil: Felician. Email: lanec@felician.edu. Research: surplus and debt freedom in 1835.

Lane, Hannah M. Sackville, NB, Canada. Affil: Mount Allison. Email: hlane@mta.ca. Research: Maine-New Brunswick borderlands, religion and fraternalism.

Lane, Heidi E. Rutz, *Naval War Coll.* Email: heidi.lane@usnwc.edu.

Lane, James B., *Indiana, Northwest*.

Lane, John M. Cincinnati, OH. Affil: Covington Latin Sch. Email: 52jrtak@gmail.com. Research: economics, WWII.

Lane, Jonathan, *Massachusetts Hist. Soc.* Email: jlane@masshist.org.

Lane, Kris E., *Tulane*. New Orleans, LA. Email: klane1@tulane.edu. Research: mining, piracy.

Lane, Lance. Shonto, AZ. Affil: Shonto Prep Sch. Email: lance.lane@gmail.com.

Lane, Roger. Haverford, PA. Affil: Haverford. Email: rlane@haverford.edu.

Laney, Monique, *Auburn*. Auburn University, AL. Email: laney@auburn.edu. Research: immigration, technology.

Lang, Andrew F., *Mississippi State*. Email: alang@history.msstate.edu.

Lang, Henry J., *SUNY, Buffalo State*.

Lang, Katherine Howe, *Wisconsin-Eau Claire*. Email: langkh@uwec.edu.

Lang, Michael, *Maine, Orono*. Email: lang@maine.edu.

Lang, Savannah. Sugar Hill, GA. Affil: Georgia. Email: savannahclang@gmail.com.

Lang, Stephanie, *Kentucky Hist. Soc.* Email: stephanie.lang@ky.gov.

Lang, William L., *Portland State*.

Langbein, John H. New Haven, CT. Affil: Yale Law Sch. Email: john.langbein@yale.edu.

Langdon, John S., *UCLA*. Los Angeles, CA. Email: jlangdon@ucla.edu. Research: John III Ducas Vatatzes, Byzantium and Chinggisids.

Langdon, John W., *Le Moyne*. Email: langdon@lemoyne.edu.

Lange, Allison Kelly. Somerville, MA. Affil: Wentworth Inst. of Tech. Email: allisonklange@gmail.com. Research: visual culture, gender.

Lange, Kevin. Friday Harbor, WA. Email: klange@tkoptions.com.

Lange, Shannon Marie. Schaumburg, IL. Affil: Blocks To Bricks, Inc. Email: ghanaslennon@gmail.com.

Langer, Erick Detlef, *Georgetown*. Washington, DC. Email: langere@georgetown.edu. Research: 19th-/20th-c Franciscan missions, 19th-c South American trade/economic.

Langer, Francesca. Carrboro, NC. Affil: North Carolina, Chapel Hill. Email: francescalanger@unc.edu.

Langer, Lawrence N., *Connecticut, Storrs*. Email: lawrence.langer@uconn.edu.

Langford, Julie, *South Florida, Tampa*. Email: langford@usf.edu.

Langfur, Hal, *SUNY, Buffalo*. Buffalo, NY. Email: hlangfur@buffalo.edu. Research: colonial Brazil, Atlantic world.

Langland, Victoria, *Michigan, Ann Arbor*. Ann Arbor, MI. Email: langland@umich.edu. Research: breastfeeding in Brazil.

Langley, Lester D. San Angelo, TX. Affil: Georgia. Email: lesterd.langley@suddenlink.net. Research: making of two Americas, teaching the Age of Revolution.

Langlois, Matthieu. Laval, QC, Canada. Affil: Québec, Montréal. Email: matthieu_langlois@hotmail.com.

Langlois, Suzanne, *York, Can.* Email: slanglois@glendon.yorku.ca.

Langsam, Miriam Z., *Indiana–Purdue, Indianapolis*. Email: mlangsam@iupui.edu.

Langston, Nancy, *Michigan Tech*. Email: nelangs3@mtu.edu.

Lanier, Gabrielle M., *James Madison*. Email: laniergm@jmu.edu.

Lanier, James C., *Rhodes*. Email: lanier@rhodes.edu.

Lanier, Michelle, *North Carolina Office of Archives*. Email: michelle.lanier@ncdcr.gov.

Lanier Christensen, Colleen. Cambridge, MA. Affil: Harvard. Email: colleenlanier@fas.harvard.edu.

Laningham, Susan D., *Tennessee Tech*. Email: slaningham@tntech.edu.

Lankford, John, *Missouri, Columbia*.

Lankiewicz, Donald P. Needham, MA. Affil: Emerson. Email: lankiewicz@gmail.com. Research: baseball's Deadball Era, early commercial aviation.

Lannen, Andrew C., *Stephen F. Austin State*. Email: lannenac@sfasu.edu.

Lannon Albrecht, Deirdre, *Texas State*. Email: dl24@txstate.edu.

Lansen, Oscar, *North Carolina, Charlotte*. Email: oelansen@uncc.edu.

Lansing, Carol L., *California, Santa Barbara*. Email: lansing@history.ucsb.edu.

Lansing, Charles B., IV, *Connecticut, Storrs*. Email: charles.lansing@uconn.edu.

Lansing, Michael J., *Augsburg*. Minneapolis, MN. Email: lansing@augsburg.edu. Research: urban, environmental.

Lansverk, Ronald Lee. White Bear Township, MN. Email: ronlansverk@gmail.com. Research: silver mining in Neihart MT 1880s-1911.

Lanza, Fabio, *Arizona*. Tucson, AZ. Email: flanza@email.arizona.edu. Research: urban space and politics, communism.

Lanza, Janine M., *Wayne State*. Email: jmlanza@wayne.edu.

Lanzillo, Amanda Marie. Washington, DC. Affil: Indiana. Email: amlanzil@indiana.edu.

Lanzona, Vina, *Hawai'i, Manoa*. Email: vlanzona@hawaii.edu.

LaPierre, Brian, *Southern Mississippi*. Email: brian.lapierre@usm.edu.

LaPierre, Patrick. Canton, NY. Affil: SUNY, Canton. Email: patlapierre@hotmail.com.

Lapin, Hayim, *Maryland, Coll. Park*. Email: hlapin@umd.edu.

Lapina, Elizabeth, *Wisconsin-Madison*. Email: lapina@wisc.edu.

LaPlant, Katie Desireé. Toledo, OH. Affil: Michigan. Email: klaplant@umich.edu. Research: Enlightenment and women, English Civil War and women.

Lapoint, Alice. Riverside, CA. Email: alapo001@ucr.edu.

Lapomarda, Vincent A., *Holy Cross*. Worcester, MA. Email: vlapomar@holycross.edu. Research: Italian Americans, Pope Pius XII.

LaPorta, Alphonse F. Washington, DC. Affil: Trans Pacific Partners, LLC. Email: a_laporta@yahoo.com. Research: East Asia regionalism, Indonesia.

Lapp, Benjamin, *Montclair State*. Email: lappb@mail.montclair.edu.

Lapsley, Joseph W., *Loyola, Chicago*. Email: jlapsle@luc.edu.

Laqueur, Thomas W. Berkeley, CA. Affil: California, Berkeley. Email: tlaqueur@berkeley.edu. Research: Britain since 1509, social.

Lara, Sandra Elizabeth. San Antonio, TX. Affil: Texas A&M, San Antonio. Email: sandraelara@hotmail.com. Research: gender, sexuality.

Laracey, Melvin C. San Antonio, TX. Affil: Texas, San Antonio. Email: mlaracey@utsa.edu.

Larew, Karl G., *Towson*. Email: klarew@towson.edu.

Lark, Kimberly Ann. Livonia, MI. Affil: Schoolcraft. Email: klark@schoolcraft.edu.

Larkin, John A., *SUNY, Buffalo*.

Larkin, Kraig. New London, NH. Affil: Colby-Sawyer. Email: kraig.larkin@colby-sawyer.edu.

Larkin, LaRae, *Weber State*. Email: llarkin@weber.edu.

LaRocca, John J., SJ, *Xavier, Ohio*. Email: larocca@xavier.edu.

Larocco, Christina G., *Hist. Soc. of Pennsylvania*. Email: clarocco@hsp.org.

LaRosa, Michael J., *Rhodes*. Email: larosa@rhodes.edu.

Larres, Klaus W., *North Carolina, Chapel Hill*.

Larsen, Andrew E., *Carroll*. Email: alarsen@carrollu.edu.

Larsen, Clark Spencer, *Ohio State*. Email: larsen.53@osu.edu.

Larsen, Kirk W., *Brigham Young*. Provo, UT. Email: kwlarsen67@gmail.com. Research: modern East Asia, Korea.

Larson, *Atria A*. Saint Louis, MO. Affil: St. Louis. Email: atria.larson@gmail.com. Research: medieval canon law, Gratian.

Larson, *Brooke*, *SUNY, Stony Brook*. Huntington, NY. Email: brooke.larson@stonybrook.edu. Research: Latin America, mining and agrarian change.

Larson, *Carolyne Ryan*, *St. Norbert*. Email: carrie.larson@snc.edu.

Larson, *Edward J.*, *Georgia; Pepperdine*. Email: edlarson@uga.edu; elarson@pepperdine.edu.

Larson, *Ethan*. Urbana, IL. Email: eelarso2@illinois.edu.

Larson, *John L.*, *Purdue*. Email: larsonjl@purdue.edu.

Larson, *Mitchell J*. Madison, WI. Affil: Central Lancashire. Email: larsonmitch@yahoo.com. Research: higher education, European business.

Larson, *Peter L.*, *Central Florida*. Email: Peter.Larson@ucf.edu.

Larson, *Pier M.*, *Johns Hopkins (Hist.)*. Email: larson@jhu.edu.

Larson, *Rachel*, *North Greenville*. Email: rachel.larson@ngu.edu.

Larson, *Thomas*. Yorkville, IL. Email: tlar_00@yahoo.com. Research: depth of understanding of history, WWI.

Larson, *Zeb*. Columbus, OH. Affil: Ohio State. Email: zeb.larson@gmail.com.

Larue, *George M.*, *Clarion, Pa*. Email: larue@clarion.edu.

Larue, *L. E*. Saint Paul, MN. Affil: Iowa. Email: lyla_rue@hotmail.com. Research: French Huguenots, 1930s Great Depression.

Lary, *John Draughon*, *Charleston*. Email: laryjd@cofc.edu.

Lasar, *Matthew*, *California, Santa Cruz*. Email: mlasar@ucsc.edu.

Lasby, *Clarence G.*, *Texas, Austin*. Email: clasby@austin.rr.com.

Lasch-Quinn, *Elisabeth D.*, *Syracuse*. Email: edlasch@maxwell.syr.edu.

Lasdow, *Kathryn*, *Suffolk*.

Laslett, *John H. M.*, *UCLA*. Email: laslett@history.ucla.edu.

Laslie, *Brian D.*, *US Air Force Acad*. Email: brian.laslie@usafa.edu.

Lasser, *Carol S.*, *Oberlin*. Oberlin, OH. Email: carol.lasser@oberlin.edu. Research: 19th-c American women and gender.

Lassiter, *Matthew D.*, *Michigan, Ann Arbor*. Email: mlassite@umich.edu.

Lassner, *Jacob*, *Northwestern*. Evanston, IL. Email: j-lassner@northwestern.edu. Research: medieval Near East, Jews of Islamic lands.

Lasso, *Marixa A*. Bogota, Colombia. Affil: Nacional de Colombia. Email: mlasso@unal.edu.co. Research: Atlantic race, age of revolution.

Latham, *Ernest H*. Washington, DC. Affil: Foreign Service Inst. Email: ernest.lathamjr@gmail.com. Research: 20th-c Romania, origins of Cold War.

Latham, *Jacob A.*, *Tennessee, Knoxville*. Email: jlatham3@utk.edu.

Lathrop, *Kelly*, *Hist. Assoc*. Email: klathrop@historyassociates.com.

Latimore, *Carey H.*, *IV*, *Trinity, Tex*. Email: clatimor@trinity.edu.

Latner, *Richard*, *Tulane*. Email: latner@tulane.edu.

Laub, *Richard*, *Georgia State*. Email: rlaub@gsu.edu.

Laub, *Thomas*. Cleveland, MS. Affil: Delta State. Email: forestfive@mac.com. Research: occupied France 1940-44, 20th-c international law.

Laubacher, *Matthew Dominick*. Surprise, AZ. Affil: Ashford. Email: matthew.laubacher@ashford.edu. Research: modern biology, science and society.

Lauber, *Jack M.*, *Wisconsin-Eau Claire*. Email: lauberjm@uwec.edu.

Lauderback, *David Marcus*, *Austin Comm. Coll*. Email: dlauderb@austincc.edu.

Lauer, *George Stephen*, *US Army Command Coll*. Email: george.s.lauer.civ@mail.mil.

Lauerhass, *Ludwig*, *Jr.*, *UCLA*. Email: lauerhas@ucla.edu.

Lauersdorf, *Aubrey*. Chapel Hill, NC. Affil: North Carolina, Chapel Hill. Email: alauersdorf@unc.edu.

Laufenberg, *Lynn Marie*, *Sweet Briar*. Email: llaufenberg@sbc.edu.

Laughead, *Amanda*. Washington, DC. Affil: American. Email: al5790a@american.edu.

Laughlin, *Kathleen A.*, *Metropolitan State*. Email: kathleen.laughlin@metrostate.edu.

Laughlin-Schultz, *Bonnie Ellen*, *Eastern Illinois*. Email: blaughlinschul@eiu.edu.

Laumann, *Dennis*, *Memphis*. Email: dlaumann@memphis.edu.

Launius, *Roger D*. Auburn, AL. Affil: Launius Hist. Services. Email: launiusr@gmail.com. Research: aerospace, Cold War politics.

Lauren, *Paul Gordon*, *Montana*. Email: paul.lauren@mso.umt.edu.

Laurent-Perrault, *Evelyne*, *California, Santa Barbara*. Santa Barbara, CA. Email: elaurentperrault@history.ucsb.edu; afrolat@gmail.com. Research: Afrodescendants' political activism, 19th-c gender dynamics.

Laurenzo, *Frederick E.*, *Mississippi*.

Lauria-Santiago, *Aldo A.*, *Rutgers*. Email: alauria@lcs.rutgers.edu.

Laurie, *Bruce G.*, *Massachusetts, Amherst*. Email: laurie@history.umass.edu.

Lauritsen, *Catherine Grollman*. Cheney, WA. Email: Lauritsen@CenturyTel.net.

Lauritsen, *Frederick M.*, *Eastern Washington*. Email: flauritsen@mail.ewu.edu.

Laursen, *Christopher*, *North Carolina, Wilmington*. Email: laursenc@uncw.edu.

Lause, *Mark A.*, *Cincinnati*. Email: mark.lause@uc.edu.

Lautenschlager, *Julie L.*, *Robert H. Smith Center*. Email: jlautenschlager@monticello.org.

Laux, *James M.*, *Cincinnati*. Email: jlaux@mpinet.net.

Lauziere, *Henri*, *Northwestern*. Email: h-lauziere@northwestern.edu.

Lauzon, *Matt J.*, *Hawaiʻi, Manoa*. Email: mlauzon@hawaii.edu.

Lavelle, *James*. Brooklyn, NY. Email: james.lavelle193@gmail.com.

Lavender, *Catherine J.*, *Staten Island, CUNY*. Email: catherine.lavender@csi.cuny.edu.

Lavender, *Richard Jordan*. New Haven, CT. Affil: Notre Dame. Email: rlavende@nd.edu.

Laver, *Harry S.*, *US Army Command Coll*. Email: harry.s.laver.civ@mail.mil.

LaVere, *Suzanne Michelle*, *Purdue, Fort Wayne*. Email: laveres@pfw.edu.

Lavery, *Jason E.*, *Oklahoma State*. Stillwater, OK. Email: jason.lavery@okstate.edu. Research: early modern Europe, Germany.

Lavigne, *Brian*, *Hist. New Orleans*. Email: brianl@hnoc.org.

Lavin, *Thomas S*. Riverton, IL. Email: lavin@shg.org.

Lavine, *Matthew B.*, *Mississippi State*. Email: mlavine@history.msstate.edu.

LaVopa, *Anthony J.*, *North Carolina State*. Raleigh, NC. Email: anthony_lavopa@ncsu.edu. Research: Enlightenment gender.

Lavrin, *Asuncion A.*, *Arizona State*. Columbia, MD. Email: lavrind@aol.com; lavrin64@gmail.com. Research: masculinity in Mexico 1550-1750, religious women in Mexico 1550-1800.

Law, *Debra Anne*, *Texas State*. Email: dlaw@txstate.edu.

Law, *Randall D.*, *Birmingham-Southern*. Email: rlaw@bsc.edu.

Law, *Ricky W.*, *Carnegie Mellon*. Pittsburgh, PA. Email: rlaw@andrew.cmu.edu; ricky.w.law@gmail.com. Research: interwar German-Japanese relations, extra-diplomatic international relations.

Lawes, *Carolyn J.*, *Old Dominion*. Email: clawes@odu.edu.

Lawler, *Jeff*, *California State, Long Beach*. Email: jeffrey.lawler@csulb.edu.

Lawless, *John M.*, *Providence*. Email: jlawless@providence.edu.

Lawlor, *Ruth Grace*. Cambridge, United Kingdom. Affil: Cambridge. Email: rgl34@cam.ac.uk.

Lawlor, *William*. Evanston, IL. Email: william.j.lawlor@ms.com.

Lawrance, *Benjamin N*. Rochester, NY. Affil: Arizona. Email: benlaw@email.arizona.edu. Research: asylum/refugees, trafficking/slavery.

Lawrence, *Anna M.*, *Fairfield*. Fairfield, CT. Email: alawrence3@fairfield.edu. Research: colonial and revolutionary America, religious.

Lawrence, *Elizabeth*, *Augustana*. Email: elizabethlawrence@augustana.edu.

Lawrence, *Jennifer*, *Texas, Arlington*. Email: jlawrenc@exchange.uta.edu.

Lawrence, *John Alan*, *National Hist. Center*. Washington, DC. Affil: Univ. of California Washington Center. Email: JAL221B@gmail.com. Research: Congress.

Lawrence, *John H.*, *Hist. New Orleans*. Email: johnl@hnoc.org.

Lawrence, *John K*. Ann Arbor, MI. Email: jlawrence@dickinsonwright.com.

Lawrence, *Mark Atwood*, *Texas, Austin*. Austin, TX. Email: malawrence@austin.utexas.edu. Research: US 1877-1920, 20th-c world.

Lawrence, *Priscilla O'Reilly*, *Hist. New Orleans*. Email: priscill@hnoc.org.

Lawrie, *Paul R. D.*, *Winnipeg*. Email: p.lawrie@uwinnipeg.ca.

Lawson, *Brenda M.*, *Massachusetts Hist. Soc*. Email: blawson@masshist.org.

Lawson, *David Anthony*. Apo, AE. Affil: Columbia Coll., Mo. Email: dalawson86@gmail.com.

Lawson, *J. Kime*, *Chestnut Hill*. Email: lawsonk@chc.edu.

Lawson, *Kirstin L.*, *Pittsburg State*. Pittsburg, KS. Email: klawson@pittstate.edu. Research: Gilded Age and Progressive Era US, women.

Lawson, Melinda A., *Union Coll.* Email: lawsonm@union.edu.

Lawson, Michael Lee. Annandale, VA. Affil: MLL Consulting, LLC. Email: mll_consulting@ yahoo.com.

Lawson, Steven F., *Rutgers.* Email: slawson@ scarletmail.rutgers.edu.

Lawton, Stephanie. Charlottesville, VA. Affil: Virginia. Email: sk.lawton@verizon.net. Research: classics in US political culture, commemoration of American presidents.

Layer, William. Arlington, VA. Email: wlayer@ aol.com.

Layton, Bentley, *Yale.* Email: bentley.layton@ yale.edu.

Layton, Brandon. Davis, CA. Affil: California, Davis. Email: bklayton@ucdavis.edu.

Layton, Donald L., *Indiana State.* Email: dlayton@isugw.indstate.edu.

Lazar, David, *German Hist. Inst.* Email: lazar@ ghi-dc.org.

Lazar, Lance, *Assumption.* Email: llazar@ assumption.edu.

Lazar, Max Harrison. Chapel Hill, NC. Affil: North Carolina, Chapel Hill. Email: maxlazar@ live.unc.edu.

Lazaridis, Nikolaos, *California State, Sacramento.* Email: lazaridi@saclink.csus.edu.

Lazda, Paulis I., *Wisconsin-Eau Claire.* Email: lazdapi@uwec.edu.

Lazich, Michael C., *SUNY, Buffalo State.* Email: lazichmc@buffalostate.edu.

Lazier, Benjamin, *Reed.* Email: lazierb@reed. edu.

Lazo, Ariel R. Jersey City, NJ. Email: ariel.lazo@ hotmail.com.

Lazo, Dimitri D. Greenfield, WI. Affil: Alverno. Email: dimitri.lazo@alverno.edu. Research: US foreign relations, imperialism.

Lazure, Guy, *Windsor.* Email: glazure@uwindsor. ca.

Le Bar, Ann C., *Eastern Washington.* Cheney, WA. Email: alebar@ewu.edu. Research: early modern Europe, cultural and intellectual.

Le Guin, Charles A., *Portland State.*

Le Sueur, James Dean, *Nebraska, Lincoln.* Email: jlesueur@unl.edu.

Le Zotte, Jennifer K., *North Carolina, Wilmington.* Wilmington, NC. Email: lezottej@uncw. edu. Research: new capitalism, gender and sexuality/material culture.

Leach, William R., *Columbia (Hist.).* Email: wrl3@ columbia.edu.

Leacock, Kathryn, *SUNY, Buffalo State.* Email: leacockh@buffalostate.edu.

Leahy, Anne. Salt Lake City, UT. Affil: Birmingham. Email: news@interpreterhistory. com. Research: signed language and Deaf, Mormons with disabilities.

Leahy, William P., *SJ*, *Boston Coll.* Email: leahy@ bc.edu.

Leake, Elisabeth. Cambridge, United Kingdom. Affil: Leeds. Email: elisabeth.leake@aya.yale. edu. Research: Cold War South Asia.

Leal, K. Elise, *Whitworth.* Email: eleal@ whitworth.edu.

Leal, Karen Alexandra. Glendale, CA. Email: kleal@mac.com.

Lean, Eugenia Y., *Columbia (Hist.).* New York, NY. Email: eyl2006@columbia.edu. Research: Chinese consumer culture, science.

Lear, John Robert, *Puget Sound.* Tacoma, WA. Email: lear@ups.edu. Research: working class

and social movements, artists and politics in Mexico.

Learned, Jay D. Merlin, OR. Affil: Springboard International Bilingual Sch. Email: jlearned3@ earthlink.net. Research: American Cold War messianism, Soviet Cold War messianism.

Lears, Jackson, *Rutgers.* New Brunswick, NJ. Email: tjlears@history.rutgers.edu. Research: American cultural and intellectual.

Leary, Patrick. Skokie, IL. Email: pleary@gmail. com. Research: social history of authorship and publish, digital scholarship.

Leary, Thomas, *Youngstown State.* Email: teleary@ysu.edu.

Leathem, Karen T. New Orleans, LA. Affil: Louisiana State Museum. Email: kleathem@ crt.la.gov. Research: Louisiana music, Louisiana foodways.

Leatherwood, Jeffrey Michaeldale. Morgantown, WV. Affil: West Virginia. Email: j_leatherwood@yahoo.com. Research: early 20th-c Carolina streetcar strikes, US Army bomb disposal squads of WWII.

Leavell, Ricky. Chicago, IL. Email: leavric2004@ yahoo.com.

Leavelle, Tracy Neal, *Creighton.* Omaha, NE. Email: tracy.leavelle@creighton.edu. Research: colonization and religious encounters, religion and American empire.

Leavitt, Judith W., *Wisconsin-Madison.* Email: jwleavit@wisc.edu.

Leavitt-Alcantara, Brianna N., *Cincinnati.* Email: leavitba@ucmail.uc.edu.

Lebaron, Alan V., *Kennesaw State.* Email: alebaron@kennesaw.edu.

LeBlanc, Hannah. Ithaca, NY. Affil: Cornell. Email: hannah.leblanc@gmail.com.

LeBlanc, Ondine, *Massachusetts Hist. Soc.* Email: oleblanc@masshist.org.

Lebovic, Nitzan, *Lehigh.* Email: nil210@lehigh. edu.

Lebovic, Sam, *George Mason.* Washington, DC. Email: slebovic@gmu.edu; sam.lebovic@ gmail.com. Research: 19th-/20th-c US, global.

Lebovics, Herman, *SUNY, Stony Brook.* Email: herman.lebovics@stonybrook.edu.

Lebra, Joyce C., *Colorado, Boulder.* Email: joycelebra@gmail.com.

LeBrun, John L., *Kent State.* Canfield, OH. Email: lebrun1@aol.com. Research: modern America.

Lebrun, Richard A., *Manitoba.* North Vancouver, BC, Canada. Email: lebrun@cc.umanitoba.ca. Research: translations of Joseph de Maistre, Joseph de Maistre's politics.

Lebsock, Suzanne D., *Rutgers.* Email: lebsock@ history.rutgers.edu.

LeCain, Timothy James, *Montana State, Bozeman.* Bozeman, MT. Email: tlecain@ montana.edu. Research: environment, science and technology.

Lechner, Zachary James, *Centenary, La.* Email: zlechner@centenary.edu.

Ledbetter, Rosanna, *Western Illinois.*

Leder, Harald Thomas. Baton Rouge, LA. Affil: Louisiana State. Email: hleder@lsu.edu. Research: post-WWII American re-education in Germany, WWII air war over Germany.

Lederer, Susan E., *Wisconsin-Madison.* Madison, WI. Email: selederer@wisc.edu. Research: medical readiness in Cold War America, doctors/diets/therapeutic nutrition.

Ledford, Angela, *St. Rose.* Email: ledforda@mail. strose.edu.

Ledford, Kenneth F., *Case Western Reserve.* Cleveland, OH. Email: kenneth.ledford@case. edu. Research: Prussian judiciary 1848-1933, law/Rechtsstaat/middle class.

LeDonne, Gregory B. Boise, ID. Affil: Boise State. Email: gregledonne@u.boisestate.edu.

LeDonne, John P. Cambridge, MA. Email: jledonne@fas.harvard.edu.

Leduc-Grimaldi, Mathilde. Paris, France. Email: mathilde.leduc@gmail.com.

Lee, Andrew H., *NYU.* Westfield, NJ. Email: andrew.lee@nyu.edu. Research: Spain 1917-39, Scottsboro case.

Lee, Andrew K. Novato, CA. Affil: Graduate Theological Union. Email: alee2@ses.gtu.edu. Research: Medieval Christian mysticism.

Lee, Anthony A. Manhattan Beach, CA. Affil: UCLA. Email: Member1700@gmail.com. Research: Baha'i studies, antebellum slavery.

Lee, Bradford A., *Naval War Coll.* Email: balee22@verizon.net.

Lee, Brendan. Oxford, MS. Email: brendan. lee34@gmail.com. Research: French Resistance during WWII, Spanish Civil War.

Lee, Brian Edward, *Winthrop.* Email: leeb@ winthrop.edu.

Lee, Chana Kai, *Georgia.* Email: chanakai@uga. edu.

Lee, Charles R., *Wisconsin-La Crosse.* Email: clee@uwlax.edu.

Lee, Christopher J., *Lafayette.* Email: leechris@ lafayette.edu.

Lee, David Johnson. Philadelphia, PA. Affil: Philadelphia. Email: dedalive@gmail.com.

Lee, David, *Western Kentucky.* Email: david.lee@ wku.edu.

Lee, Erika, *Minnesota (Hist.).* Minneapolis, MN. Email: erikalee@umn.edu. Research: Chinese immigration to US, US immigration law and policy.

Lee, J. Edward, *Winthrop.* Email: leee@winthrop. edu.

Lee, Jacob, *Penn State.* University Park, PA. Email: jacobflee@psu.edu. Research: early America, social and environmental.

Lee, Jean Butenhoff, *Wisconsin-Madison.* Email: jblee@wisc.edu.

Lee, Jinhee, *Eastern Illinois.* Charleston, IL. Email: jlee@eiu.edu. Research: historical agency and knowledge production, East Asian culture and violence.

Lee, John Joseph, *NYU.* Email: joe.lee@nyu.edu.

Lee, John W. I., *California, Santa Barbara.* Email: jwilee@history.ucsb.edu.

Lee, Jonathan A. Austin, TX. Affil: San Antonio. Email: jlee@alamo.edu.

Lee, Jongmin. Daejeon, Republic of Korea. Affil: Univ. of Science and Tech. Email: jongmin.eu@ gmail.com.

Lee, Joong-Jae, *Wisconsin-Platteville.* Email: leejo@uwplatt.edu.

Lee, Joseph Tse-Hei, *Pace.* New York, NY. Email: jlee@pace.edu. Research: Christianity and Activism in China, Church-State Relations.

Lee, Jun Hee. Chicago, IL. Affil: Chicago. Email: junhlee@uchicago.edu.

Lee, Lester P., Jr., *Suffolk.* Email: llee@suffolk. edu.

Lee, M. Kittiya, *California State, Los Angeles.* Pasadena, CA. Email: klee40@exchange. calstatela.edu. Research: language in colonial Brazil, diversity/social formation/colonial Americas.

Lee, **Mai Na M.**, *Minnesota (Hist.)*. Email: mainalee@umn.edu.

Lee, *Maurice D.*, *Jr.*, *Rutgers*. Cranbury, NJ. Research: Tudor-Stuart Britain.

Lee, *Patricia-Ann*, *Skidmore*. Saratoga Springs, NY. Email: plee@skidmore.edu. Research: late Tudor-Stuart England.

Lee, *Robert*. Cambridge, MA. Affil: Harvard. Email: robertlee27@berkeley.edu.

Lee, **Seok Won**, *Rhodes*. Email: lees@rhodes. edu.

Lee, *Seung-joon*. Singapore. Affil: National, Singapore. Email: hisls@nus.edu.sg. Research: food supply and consumption, science and technology in East Asia.

Lee, **Shelley S.**, *Oberlin*. Email: shelley.lee@ oberlin.edu.

Lee, **Sinwoo**, *California State, Chico*. Email: slee143@csuchico.edu.

Lee, *Sophia Zoila*. Philadelphia, PA. Affil: Pennsylvania. Email: slee@law.upenn. edu. Research: labor law and civil rights, constitutional.

Lee, *Sophia*. Davis, CA. Affil: California State, East Bay. Email: sophia.lee@csueastbay.edu. Research: wartime Beijing 1937-45, hospitals in Hebei province.

Lee, *Steven H.*, *British Columbia*. Vancouver, BC, Canada. Email: stevenhl@mail.ubc.ca. Research: Canadian foreign relations, 20th-c diplomatic.

Lee, *Sukhee*, *Rutgers*. Email: sukhlee@history. rutgers.edu.

Lee, **Susanna M.**, **III**, *North Carolina State*. Email: susanna_lee@ncsu.edu.

Lee, *Susanna*. Chester, SC. Email: Susannl@g. clemson.edu. Research: PTSD.

Lee, **Ta-Ling**, *Southern Connecticut State*.

Lee, *Timothy Sanghoon*. Fort Worth, TX. Affil: Brite Divinity Sch. Email: timsanglee@aol.com. Research: Christianity in Korea, Christianity in East Asia.

Lee, *Tommy David*, *II*, *East Tennessee State*. Email: leet@etsu.edu.

Lee, *Trevor Zane*. Lexington, KY. Email: trevorzlee@gmail.com. Research: atheism in US, religion in politics.

Lee, **Victoria**, *Ohio*. Email: leev@ohio.edu.

Lee, **Wayne E.**, *North Carolina, Chapel Hill*. Email: welee@email.unc.edu.

Lee, *Zardas Shuk-man*. Chapel Hill, NC. Affil: North Carolina, Chapel Hill. Email: zardas@ unc.edu. Research: South and Southeast Asia, global history of anticolonialism.

Leech, **Brian J.**, *Augustana*. Email: brianleech@ augustana.edu.

Leech, *Patrick*. Salado, TX. Affil: Mary Hardin-Baylor. Email: patrick.leech@outlook.com. Research: US-Hungarian relations, Cold War.

Leedom, *Joe W.* Roanoke, VA. Affil: Hollins. Email: jwleedom@yahoo.com. Research: early Europe, social.

Leedy, **Todd H.**, *Florida*. Email: tleedy@ufl.edu.

Leeman, **Lauren**, *State Hist. Soc. of Missouri*. Email: leemanl@shsmo.org.

Leeman, *William P.* Middletown, RI. Affil: Salve Regina. Email: bleeman2@verizon.net. Research: American presidency, American military.

Lees, *Andrew*, *Rutgers, Camden*. Philadelphia, PA. Email: alees@camden.rutgers.edu. Research: cities and making of modern Europe, German views of American urbanization.

Lees, *Jay T.*, *Northern Iowa*. Email: jay.lees@uni. edu.

Lees, *Lorraine M.*, *Old Dominion*. Norfolk, VA. Email: llees@odu.edu. Research: Cold War, ethnicity and national security.

Lees, *Lynn Hollen*, *Pennsylvania*. Philadelphia, PA. Email: lhlees@history.upenn.edu. Research: 19th-c British Empire, plantation economics in Malaya.

Lees, *Lynton Elizabeth*. New York, NY. Affil: Columbia. Email: lel2152@columbia.edu.

Leese, *Michael Stevens*, *New Hampshire, Durham*. Email: michael.leese@unh.edu.

Leeson, **Whitney A. M.**, *Roanoke*. Email: wleeson@roanoke.edu.

LeFevre, *Avatar*. Arlington, VA. Email: alefevre78@gmail.com.

Leff, *Lisa Moses*, *American*. Washington, DC. Affil: US Holocaust Memorial Museum. Email: leff@american.edu. Research: Europe 1789-present.

Leffler, *Melvyn P.*, *Virginia*. Charlottesville, VA. Email: mpl4j@virginia.edu. Research: American diplomatic.

Leffler, **Phyllis K.**, *Virginia*. Email: pkl6h@ virginia.edu.

Lefkovitz, **Alison L.**, *Rutgers, Newark/New Jersey Inst. of Tech.* Email: alefkovi@njit.edu.

Lefkovitz, *Jacob Bruce*. Deerfield, IL. Affil: Deerfield High Sch. Email: Jblefkovitz@gmail. com.

Legacey, *Erin-Marie*, *Texas Tech*. Lubbock, TX. Email: erin-marie.legacey@ttu.edu; elegacey@ gmail.com. Research: postrevolutionary France, cultures of death.

LeGall, *Dina*, *Graduate Center, CUNY; Lehman, CUNY*. Email: dinalegall@aol.com.

Legault, **Roch**, *Royal Military*. Email: legault-r@ rmc.ca.

Legg, *Thomas J.*, *West Chester*. Email: tlegg@ wcupa.edu.

Leggett, *Derrick*. Kansas City, MO. Email: derrickleggett@yahoo.com.

Leggiere, **Michael V.**, *North Texas*. Email: michael.leggiere@unt.edu.

Leggour, *Keely R.* Oakland, NJ. Affil: Indian Hills High Sch. Email: kleggour@rih.org.

LeGrand, *Catherine*, *McGill*. Email: catherine. legrand@mcgill.ca.

Lehfeldt, *Elizabeth A.*, *Cleveland State*. Cleveland, OH. Email: e.lehfeldt@csuohio.edu; llehfeldt@gmail.com. Research: early modern convents, queenship.

Lehmann, **Clayton M.**, *South Dakota*. Email: clehmann@usd.edu.

Lehmann, **Matthias B.**, *California, Irvine*. Email: m.lehmann@uci.edu.

Lehmann, *Philipp N.*, *California, Riverside*. Riverside, CA. Email: philipp.lehmann@ucr. edu; pnlehmannbos@gmail.com. Research: desertification, climate change.

Lehmkuhl, *Ursula*. Trier, Germany. Affil: Trier. Email: lehmkuhl@uni-trier.de. Research: 19th-c US-UK cultural transfers, colonial governance in North America.

Lehner, *Monika*. Mattersburg, Austria. Affil: Vienna. Email: monika.lehner@univie.ac.at. Research: Western images of China, political cartoons and satirical periodicals.

Lehning, **James**, *Utah*. Email: jim.lehning@utah. edu.

Lehrer, **Erica**, *Concordia, Can*. Email: Erica. Lehrer@concordia.ca.

Lehuu, *Isabelle*, *Québec, Montréal*. Montreal, QC, Canada. Email: lehuu.isabelle@uqam.ca. Research: books, reading, southern libraries.

Leib, *Charlotte B.* Cambridge, MA. Affil: Harvard. Email: charlotte.leib@gmail.com.

Leibiger, **Stuart**, *La Salle*. Email: leibiger@ lasalle.edu.

Leibo, **Steven Andrew**, *SUNY, Albany*. Email: leibos@sage.edu.

Leiby, **Richard A.**, *Rosemont*. Email: rleiby@ rosemont.edu.

Leier, **Mark**, *Simon Fraser*. Email: leier@sfu.ca.

Leigh, *Jeffrey T.*, *Wisconsin-Stevens Point*. Email: jleigh@uwsp.edu.

Leighton, *Jared*. Sioux Falls, SD. Email: jaredleighton@gmail.com. Research: African American civil rights movement, intersections of US social movements.

Leisure, *John*. Los Angeles, CA. Affil: UCLA. Email: leisure@ucla.edu.

Leith, *Casey M.* Salem, OR. Affil: Oregon. Email: Cmacleith@gmail.com.

Leiva, *Priscilla*. Los Angeles, CA. Affil: Loyola Marymount. Email: Priscilla.Leiva@lmu.edu. Research: space/place/race, comparative racialization.

Leja, *Meg*, *Binghamton, SUNY*.

Lekan, *Thomas M.*, *South Carolina, Columbia*. Email: lekan@sc.edu.

Leland, *John L.* Salem, WV. Affil: Salem International. Email: jleland@salemu.edu. Research: late medieval English law and politics, late medieval English magic.

Lelic, *Emin*, *Salisbury*. Email: exlelic@salisbury. edu.

Leloudis, *James L.*, *North Carolina, Chapel Hill*. Chapel Hill, NC. Email: leloudis@email. unc.edu. Research: War on Poverty, school desegregation.

LeMahieu, *D. L.*, *Lake Forest*. Wilmette, IL. Email: lemahieu@lakeforest.edu. Research: modern Britain, cultural studies.

LeMaster, **Michelle M.**, *Lehigh*. Email: mil206@ lehigh.edu.

Lemay, **Helen R.**, *SUNY, Stony Brook*. Email: Helen.Lemay@stonybrook.edu.

Lemberg, *Diana*. Bernardsville, NJ. Affil: Lingnan. Email: dianalemberg@LN.edu.hk.

Lembright, **Robert L.**, *James Madison*. Email: lembrirl@jmu.edu.

Lemelle, **Sidney J.**, *Pomona*. Email: sidney. lemelle@pomona.edu.

Lemire, *Beverly J.*, *Alberta*. Edmonton, AB, Canada. Email: lemire@ualberta.ca. Research: cultural impact of global trade, material culture and gender practice.

Lemke-Santangelo, *Gretchen J.*, *St. Mary's, Calif.* Email: glemke@stmarys-ca.edu.

Lemmon, **Alfred E.**, *Hist. New Orleans*. Email: alfredl@hnoc.org.

Lemoine, **Bailey**. Denham Springs, LA. Email: brl1934@louisiana.edu.

Lemoine, **Leidy**, *Hist. New Orleans*. Email: leidyc@hnoc.org.

Lemov, **Rebecca**, *Harvard (Hist. of Science)*. Email: rlemov@fas.harvard.edu.

Lemza, *John*. Richmond, VA. Affil: Virginia Commonwealth. Email: lemzajw@vcu.edu. Research: post-1945 American military communities, post-1945 America culture and society.

Lenaghan, John O., *Rutgers*. Email: lenaghan@scarletmail.rutgers.edu.

Lenahan, Kimberly Spencer. Lakewood, OH. Affil: Cuyahoga Comm. Coll. Email: kimberly.lenahan@tri-c.edu. Research: women and health care in Cleveland OH, medical ethics and professionalization.

Lenburg, L. James, *Mars Hill*. Email: jlenburg@mhu.edu.

Lendon, Jon E., *Virginia*. Email: jel4c@virginia.edu.

Lenel, Laetitia. Berlin, Germany. Affil: Humboldt, Berlin. Email: laetitialenel@hu-berlin.de.

Lengel, Audrey, *Center for Hist. of Physics*. Email: alengel@aip.org.

Lenihan, John H., *Texas A&M*. Email: j-lenihan@tamu.edu.

Lennox, Jeffers L., *Wesleyan*. Email: jlennox@wesleyan.edu.

Lenoe, Matthew Edward, *Rochester*. Email: matthew.lenoe@rochester.edu.

Lentacker, Antoine, *California, Riverside*. Email: antoine.lentacker@ucr.edu.

Lenthall, Bruce, *Pennsylvania*. Email: lenthall@sas.upenn.edu.

Lenti, Joseph Umberto, *Eastern Washington*. Email: jlenti@ewu.edu.

Lentz, Mark W., *Utah Valley*. Orem, UT. Email: mlentz@uvu.edu; markolentz@gmail.com. Research: late colonial Yucatan, law and society.

Lentz, Ralph E., *Appalachian State*. Email: lentzre@appstate.edu.

Lentz-Smith, Adriane D., *Duke*. Durham, NC. Email: adl16@duke.edu. Research: African American politics, nationalism and masculinity.

Lenz, Mark. Falls Church, VA. Email: mlenz@gmu.edu.

Lenzie, Sharon, *Suffolk*. Email: slenzie@suffolk.edu.

Leon, Miguel Angel, *SUNY, Oneonta*. Email: miguel.leon@oneonta.edu.

Leon, Sharon M., *Michigan State*. Fairfax, VA. Email: leonshar@msu.edu; sharonmleon@gmail.com. Research: US Catholicism, digital.

Leonard, Amy E., *Georgetown*. Washington, DC. Email: ael3@georgetown.edu. Research: gender and education in Reformation HRE, nuns and Reformation.

Leonard, Angela M., *Loyola, Md.* Email: aleonard@loyola.edu.

Leonard, Charlene M., *San José State*.

Leonard, Elizabeth D., *Colby*. Email: elizabeth.leonard@colby.edu.

Leonard, Julie E. Quincy, MA. Affil: Fontbonne Academy. Email: eireannj@yahoo.com. Research: early modern women, laboring-class women.

Leonard, Kevin A., *Middle Tennessee State*. Murfreesboro, TN. Email: Kevin.Leonard@mtsu.edu. Research: racial politics, Cold War society.

Leonard, Lt Col Douglas, *US Air Force Acad.* Colorado Springs, CO. Email: douglas.leonard@usafa.edu; dougleonard12@yahoo.com.

Leonard, Thomas M., *North Florida*. Email: tleonard@unf.edu.

Leonard, Virginia W., *Western Illinois*. Sun City Center, FL. Email: V-Leonard@wiu.edu. Research: 19th-c US Navy in Latin America, modern Latin America.

Leonard, William. Washington, DC. Affil: American. Email: wl4166a@american.edu.

Leonard, Zachary. Chicago, IL. Affil: Chicago. Email: leonardzt@gmail.com.

Leonas, Gediminas V. Anaheim, CA. Email: gleonas@sbcglobal.net.

Leone, Janice M., *Middle Tennessee State*. Email: Jan.Leone@mtsu.edu.

Leong, Karen J., *Arizona State*. Tempe, AZ. Email: karen.leong@asu.edu. Research: Japanese Americans in Arizona, Japanese American/American Indian.

Leon-Portilla, Miguel. Coyoacan, DF, Mexico. Affil: Nacional Autónoma de México. Email: portilla@servidor.unam.mx.

Lepler, Jessica M., *New Hampshire, Durham*. Exeter, NH. Email: jessica.lepler@unh.edu; jessica.lepler@gmail.com. Research: Panic of 1837, business culture of lawyers.

Lepore, Jill, *Harvard (Hist.)*. Email: jill_lepore@harvard.edu.

Lepore, Judith. Lancaster, PA. Affil: Pennsylvania. Email: jlm762@psu.edu. Research: Progressivism, public relations.

Lerer, David Samuel. New York, NY. Affil: Columbia. Email: dsl2160@columbia.edu. Research: cultural history of capitalism, economic.

Lerma, Ashley Lauren. Houston, TX. Affil: Lone Star. Email: ashley.l.lerma@lonestar.edu.

Lerman, Nina E., *Whitman*. Email: lermanne@whitman.edu.

Lerner, Barron H., *NYU*. Email: barron.lerner@nyumc.org.

Lerner, Jeffrey D., *Wake Forest*. Email: lernerjd@wfu.edu.

Lerner, Marc H., *Mississippi*. University, MS. Email: mlerner@olemiss.edu. Research: Switzerland, competing notions of freedom and liberty.

Lerner, Mitchell B., *Ohio State*. Email: lerner.26@osu.edu.

Lerner, Paul F., *Southern California*. Los Angeles, CA. Email: plerner@usc.edu. Research: consumer culture, cultural.

Lerner, Robert E., *Northwestern*. Email: rlerner@northwestern.edu.

Lerner Patrón, Adrian. New Haven, CT. Affil: Yale. Email: adrian.lernerpatron@yale.edu.

LeRoy, Francois J., *Northern Kentucky*. Email: leroy@nku.edu.

Leroy, Justin, *California, Davis*. Email: jleroy@ucdavis.edu.

LeRoy Ladurie, Emmanuel Bernard. Paris, France. Affil: Coll. de France. Email: EM.Ladurie@wanadoo.fr.

Lescault, Meghan. Walpole, MA. Email: meghan.c.lescault@gmail.com.

Lesch, David W., *Trinity, Tex*. Email: dlesch@trinity.edu.

Leskovar, Fran. Tacoma, WA. Email: Fleskovar@pugetsound.edu.

Leslie, Stuart W., *Johns Hopkins (Hist. of Science)*. Email: swleslie@jhu.edu.

Leslie, W. Bruce, *SUNY, Coll. Brockport*. Brockport, NY. Email: bleslie@brockport.edu. Research: American and British higher education, German and Danish Americans.

Lesnick, Daniel R., *Alabama, Birmingham*.

Lesser, Jeffrey, *Emory*. Atlanta, GA. Email: jlesser@emory.edu. Research: ethnicity, immigration.

Lessoff, Alan H., *Illinois State*. Bloomington, IL. Email: ahlesso@ilstu.edu. Research: urban planning and development, historiography and historical periodization.

Lessy, Anne. Fairfield, CT. Affil: Yale. Email: anne.lessy@yale.edu. Research: Coercive Labor Regimes in 1930s - 1950s.

Lester, Anne E., *Johns Hopkins (Hist.)*. Baltimore, MD. Email: alester5@jhu.edu. Research: monasticism and religion, Crusades.

Lester, Connie L., *Central Florida*. Oviedo, FL. Email: connie.lester@ucf.edu. Research: US South, Gilded Age and Progressive Era.

Lester, Gustave Allen. Cambridge, MA. Affil: Harvard. Email: glester@g.harvard.edu.

Lester, V. Markham, *Birmingham-Southern*. Birmingham, AL. Email: mlester@bsc.edu. Research: Britain, Middle East.

Lestz, Michael E., *Trinity Coll., Conn.* Email: michael.lestz@trincoll.edu.

Letcher, Kenneth. Rock Island, IL. Affil: London Sch. of Economics. Email: k.letcher@lse.ac.uk.

Letwin, Dan, *Penn State*. Email: dll8@psu.edu.

Leucht, Brigitte. Portsmouth, United Kingdom. Affil: Portsmouth. Email: brigitte.leucht@port.ac.uk. Research: origins of the single market program, competition policy of European Union.

Leuchtenburg, William, *North Carolina, Chapel Hill*.

Leung, John, *Northern Arizona*. Email: john.leung@nau.edu.

Leung, Mei-Ling. Brooklyn, NY. Affil: New Sch. Email: ml.l.meiling.leung@gmail.com.

Leung, Vincent S. Pittsburgh, PA. Affil: Pittsburgh. Email: vshleung@gmail.com. Research: state formation in early China, idea of history in early China.

Leung, Yuen-Sang, *California State, Los Angeles*. Email: yuensleung@cuhk.edu.hk.

Leutzsch, Andreas. Bielefeld, Germany. Email: andreas_leutzsch@hotmail.com. Research: global history and reflection of modernity, Europe and Germany.

Levack, Brian P., *Texas, Austin*. Austin, TX. Email: levack@austin.utexas.edu. Research: demonic possession in Reformation Europe, 17th-c political thought.

Levario, Miguel A., *Texas Tech*. Email: miguel.levario@ttu.edu.

LeVay, Maj James, *US Military Acad.* Email: jason.levay@usma.edu.

Levenson, Alan T., *Oklahoma (Hist.)*. Email: alevenson@ou.edu.

Levenson, Deborah T., *Boston Coll.* Email: levensod@bc.edu.

Levenstein, Harvey, *McMaster*. Email: levenst@mcmaster.ca.

Levenstein, Lisa M., *North Carolina, Greensboro*. Chapel Hill, NC. Email: l_levens@uncg.edu; lisa.levenstein@gmail.com. Research: women, feminism.

Levering, Ralph B., *Davidson*. Email: ralevering@davidson.edu.

Levesque, Andree, *McGill*. Email: andree.levesque@mcgill.ca.

Levesque, Jean, *Québec, Montréal*. Email: levesque.jean@uqam.ca.

Levey, Matthew A., *Birmingham-Southern*. Email: mlevey@bsc.edu.

Levi, Luca Martino. Torino, Italy. Email: llevi@sjd.law.harvard.edu.

Levi, **Scott C**., *Ohio State*. Bexley, OH. Email: levi.18@osu.edu. Research: Khanate of Khoqand, early modern Central Asia.

Levi, **Tamara Jo**. Anniston, AL. Affil: Jacksonville State. Email: tjlevi@gmail.com. Research: rationing of indigenous populations, comparative American Indian/aborigine.

Levidis, **Andrew**. Manchester, United Kingdom. Affil: Central Lancashire. Email: levidis. andrew@gmail.com. Research: international history of conservatism, global history of militarism.

Levin, **Carole B**., *Nebraska, Lincoln*. Lincoln, NE. Email: clevin2@unl.edu. Research: early modern England, women.

Levin, **Eve**, *Kansas*. Email: evelevin@ku.edu.

Levin, **Jacob**. Ellicott City, MD. Affil: American. Email: jl2461a@student.american.edu.

Levin, **Miriam R**., *Case Western Reserve*. Email: miriam.levin@case.edu.

Levin, **N. Gordon**, *Amherst*.

Levine, **Ari Daniel**, *Georgia*. Email: adlevine@ uga.edu.

Levine, **Bruce C**., *California, Santa Cruz*. Email: blevine@ucsc.edu.

Levine, **Emily J**. Greensboro, NC. Affil: North Carolina, Greensboro. Email: emilyjlevine@ gmail.com. Research: cultural and intellectual, Weimar Germany.

Levine, **Marc V**., *Wisconsin-Milwaukee*. Email: veblen@uwm.edu.

Levine, **Marilyn A**., *Central Washington*. Ellensburg, WA. Email: levinem@cwu.edu; mlevine1@charter.net. Research: Chinese biography stats/network analysis, Chinese politics in Europe 1920s-30s.

Levine, **Mark A**., *California, Irvine*. Email: mlevine@uci.edu.

Levine, **Philippa J. A**., *Texas, Austin*. Austin, TX. Email: philippa@austin.utexas.edu. Research: British Empire, race and sexuality.

Levine, **Roger S**., *South*. Email: rlevine@ sewanee.edu.

Levine, **Steven I**. Hillsborough, NC. Affil: Montana. Email: chinabox@bellsouth.net. Research: US China relations, American wars in Asia.

Levine, **Susan B**., *Illinois, Chicago*. Washington, DC. Email: slevine@uic.edu. Research: US women and labor, consumer culture.

Levine, **Zachary Paul**. New York, NY. Affil: Columbia. Email: zjl2104@columbia.edu. Research: Jewish identity, modern and 20th-c Hungary.

Levine-Clark, **Marjorie**, *Colorado Denver*. Email: marjorie.levine-clark@ucdenver.edu.

Levin-Rojo, **Danna Alexandra**. México D.F., Mexico. Affil: Autónoma Metropolitana. Email: levinroj@yahoo.com.

Levinson, **Irving Walter**, *Texas-Rio Grande Valley*. Email: irving.levinson@utrgv.edu.

Levin-Stankevich, **Brian L**. Edgewood, NM. Affil: New Mexico. Email: bstankevich@unm.edu. Research: comparative education, cultural borrowing.

Levis, **Nicholas Evangelos**. Brooklyn, NY. Affil: Graduate Center, CUNY. Email: nicholas. evangelos@gmail.com. Research: modern Greece and diaspora, dictatorship and transition.

Levitan, **Kathrin**, *William and Mary*. Email: khlevi@wm.edu.

Levitt, **Theresa Hilary**, *Mississippi*. Email: tlevitt@olemiss.edu.

Levold, **Erwin**. Ossining, NY. Email: elevold@ hotmail.com.

Levy, **Aiala T**., *Scranton*. Scranton, PA. Email: aiala.levy@scranton.edu; aialalevy@gmail. com. Research: spaces of mass sociability 1850-1930, urban mobility in post-emancip. Brazil.

Levy, **Alan H**., *Slippery Rock*. Email: alan.levy@ sru.edu.

Levy, **Barry J**., *Massachusetts, Amherst*. Email: bjl@history.umass.edu.

Levy, **Carolyn Ann**. University Park, PA. Affil: Penn State. Email: cal65@psu.edu. Research: gender/sexuality, incarceration/reform.

Levy, **Darline G**., *NYU*. Email: darline.levy@nyu. edu.

Levy, **Fred J**., *Washington, Seattle*. Email: flevy@ uw.edu.

Levy, **James Anders**, *Wisconsin-Whitewater*. Email: levyj@uww.edu.

Levy, **Jessica Ann**. Princeton, NJ. Affil: Princeton. Email: jessica.levy.a@gmail.com. Research: transnational black politics/business, US international development.

Levy, **Jonathan Ira**, *Chicago*. Email: jlevy@ uchicago.edu.

Levy, **Juliette**, *California, Riverside*. Email: juliette.levy@ucr.edu.

Levy, **Peter B**., *York, Pa.* York, PA. Email: plevy@ ycp.edu. Research: civil rights movement, 1960s.

Levy, **Philip A**., *South Florida, Tampa*. Email: plevy@usf.edu.

Levy, **Richard S**., *Illinois, Chicago*. Email: rslevy@ uic.edu.

Levy, **Sheldon G**. Ann Arbor, MI. Affil: Wayne State. Email: shelly@umich.edu. Research: psychology of political mass killing, perceived/actuarial risk from military and non.

Levy, **Teresita**, *Lehman, CUNY*. Email: teresita. levy@lehman.cuny.edu.

Lewandowski, **Cristopher J**., *Henry Ford Coll*. Email: clewandow@gmail.com.

Lewin, **Alison Williams**, *St. Joseph's*. Brigantine, NJ. Email: lewin@sju.edu. Research: Ren urban culture, medieval law.

Lewin, **Linda**. Berkeley, CA. Affil: California, Berkeley. Email: llewin@berkeley.edu. Research: Brazilian slavery/color/memory, Brazilian banditry and violence.

Lewin, **Thomas J**., *Kansas*. Email: tomlewin@ ku.edu.

Lewis, **Aaron**. Tampa, FL. Affil: South Florida, Tampa. Email: aaronlewis1@mail.usf.edu. Research: changing memories of Lee/ Jackson/Davis, post-Civil War black and women voices.

Lewis, **Abigail**. Washington, DC. Affil: Wisconsin, Madison. Email: aelewis3@wisc.edu. Research: photojournalism in occupied France, photography and memory of WWII.

Lewis, **Adrian R**., *Kansas*. Email: arl0008@ ku.edu.

Lewis, **Brian D**., *McGill*. Email: brian.lewis@ mcgill.ca.

Lewis, **Carolyn Herbst**, *Grinnell*. Email: lewiscar@grinnell.edu.

Lewis, **Catherine**, *Kennesaw State*. Email: clewis1@kennesaw.edu.

Lewis, **Daniel**, *Claremont Grad.; Huntington Library*. San Marino, CA. Email: dlewis@ huntington.org. Research: Pacific, environmental.

Lewis, **David Levering**, *NYU*. New York, NY. Email: dll7@nyu.edu. Research: US presidency.

Lewis, **David Rich**, *Utah State*. Email: david.r.lewis@usu.edu.

Lewis, **Earl**, *Michigan, Ann Arbor; OAH*. Ann Arbor, MI. Email: earlewis@umich.edu. Research: African American, US.

Lewis, **Erik Braeden**. Tallahassee, FL. Affil: Florida State. Email: ebl15@my.fsu.edu.

Lewis, **Gene D**., *Cincinnati*. Email: gene.lewis@ uc.edu.

Lewis, **Gregory Scott**, *Weber State*. Email: glewis@weber.edu.

Lewis, **James A**., *Western Carolina*. Email: lewis@ email.wcu.edu.

Lewis, **James E**., **Jr**., *Kalamazoo*. Kalamazoo, MI. Email: jlewis@kzoo.edu. Research: American Revolution, methodology.

Lewis, **James F**., **II**. Metuchen, NJ. Affil: Western Governors. Email: jl.james.lewis@gmail.com.

Lewis, **James Michael**, **III**. Hunting Valley, OH. Affil: Univ. Sch. Email: jlewis@us.edu.

Lewis, **Jami A**, *State Hist. Soc. of Missouri*. Email: LewisJami@shsmo.org.

Lewis, **Johanna M**., *Arkansas, Little Rock*. Email: jmlewis@ualr.edu.

Lewis, **L. Michael**, *Eastern Kentucky*. Email: m.lewis@eku.edu.

Lewis, **Lance B**. Midland, MI. Email: lewislmh12@ gmail.com.

Lewis, **Margaret Brannan**, *Tennessee, Martin*. Email: mlewis47@utm.edu.

Lewis, **Mark E**., *Stanford*. Email: mel1000@ stanford.edu.

Lewis, **Mark**, *Graduate Center, CUNY; Staten Island, CUNY*. Email: mark.lewis@csi.cuny.edu.

Lewis, **Martin Wayne**, *Stanford*. Email: mwlewis@stanford.edu.

Lewis, **Mary D**., *Harvard (Hist.)*. Cambridge, MA. Email: mdlewis@fas.harvard.edu. Research: Mediterranean colonialism, Tunisia and France law and society.

Lewis, **Michael L**., *Salisbury*. Email: mllewis@ salisbury.edu.

Lewis, **Ronald L**., *West Virginia*. Email: Ronald. Lewis@mail.wvu.edu.

Lewis, **Stephen E**., *California State, Chico*. Email: slewis2@csuchico.edu.

Lewis, **Susan Ingalls**, *SUNY, New Paltz*. Email: lewiss@newpaltz.edu.

Lewis, **Terrance L**. Winston Salem, NC. Affil: Winston-Salem State. Email: lewistl@wssu. edu. Research: British appeasement, British culture 1919-present.

Lewis, **Thomas T**. Saint Cloud, MN. Email: thomastlewis@hotmail.com.

Lewis, **Wallace Leigh**, *Maryville*.

Lewis, **William B**., *Bowie State*. Email: wlewis@ bowiestate.edu.

Lewis Phillips, **Judith Schneid**, *Oklahoma (Hist.)*. Email: judith.s.lewis-1@ou.edu.

Lewis-Nang'ea, **Amanda E**., *SUNY, Coll. Geneseo*. Email: lewisam@geneseo.edu.

Lew-Williams, **Beth**, *Princeton*. Email: bethlw@ princeton.edu.

Ley, **Douglas A**. Jaffrey, NH. Affil: Franklin Pierce. Email: leyda@franklinpierce.edu. Research: colonial and 19th-c America.

Leyva, Yolanda Chavez, *Texas, El Paso*. Email: yleyva@utep.edu.

Lheureux, Teressa. East Freetown, MA. Affil: Maine, Orono. Email: tess.lheureux@gmail.com. Research: Loyalists during Revolution, African settlements in Nova Scotia.

Lhost, Elizabeth. Madison, WI. Affil: Wisconsin, Madison. Email: lhost@uchicago.edu. Research: Islamic law in South Asia, colonial legal circulations.

Li, Chunhua. Binghamton, NY. Affil: Binghamton, SUNY. Email: cli@binghamton.edu.

Li, Danke, *Fairfield*. Email: dli@fairfield.edu.

Li, Feng, *Columbia (Hist.)*. Email: fl123@columbia.edu.

Li, Guotong, *California State, Long Beach*. Email: guotong.li@csulb.edu.

Li, Hongshan, *Kent State*. Email: hli@kent.edu.

Li, Huaiyin, *Texas, Austin*. Email: hli@utexas.edu.

Li, Huijuan. Chapel Hill, NC. Affil: Duke. Email: hl180@duke.edu.

Li, Jing, *Duquesne*. Email: lij@duq.edu.

Li, Lan, *Rice*.

Li, Li, *Salem State*. Email: lli@salemstate.edu.

Li, Lillian M., *Swarthmore*. Email: lli1@swarthmore.edu.

Li, Lin. Madison, WI. Affil: Wisconsin, Madison. Email: lli265@wisc.edu. Research: world, gender and women.

Li, Linfeng. Heath, TX. Email: lifegreenusa@yahoo.com.

Li, Shenglan, *Wheaton, Mass.* Pawtucket, RI. Email: li_shenglan@wheatoncollege.edu. Research: East Asia, science/technology/medicine.

Li, Xiao. Carbondale, IL. Affil: Southern Illinois, Carbondale. Email: lixiao@siu.edu.

Li, Xiao-Bing, *Central Oklahoma*. Edmond, OK. Email: bli@uco.edu. Research: China and Cold War, Chinese military.

Li, Xiaoxiong, *Plymouth State*. Email: xli@plymouth.edu.

Li, Yan, *Oakland*. Email: yanli@oakland.edu.

Li, Yiwen Ivana. Hong Kong. Affil: City, Hong Kong. Email: Liyiwen0725@gmail.com.

Liang, Kan, *Seattle*. Email: liang@seattleu.edu.

Liang, Yong. Tübingen, Germany. Affil: Tübingen. Email: yong.liang@student.uni-tuebingen.de.

Liao, Edgar. Singapore. Affil: British Columbia. Email: edgarliao@hotmail.sg. Research: youth, student movements.

Libby, Joseph E. Fresno, CA. Affil: Clovis Comm. Coll. Email: joseph.libby@scccd.edu.

Libby, Justin H., *Indiana–Purdue, Indianapolis*. Email: jhlibby@iupui.edu.

Liber, George O., *Alabama, Birmingham*. Email: gliber@uab.edu.

Libson, Scott. Bloomington, IN. Affil: Emory. Email: scott.libson@gmail.com. Research: foreign mission movement, nonprofit fundraising.

Licht, Walter M., *Pennsylvania*. Philadelphia, PA. Email: wlicht@sas.upenn.edu. Research: US, labor and economic.

Lichtenstein, Alex, *Indiana*. Bloomington, IN. Affil: American Hist. Review. Email: lichtens@indiana.edu; alichtens@gmail.com. Research: labor/civil rights/anticommunism, comparative South African/US labor.

Lichtenstein, Nelson N., *California, Santa Barbara*. Email: nelson@history.ucsb.edu.

Lichtenstein, Tatjana, *Texas, Austin*. Email: lichtens@austin.utexas.edu.

Lichtman, Allan J., *American*. Bethesda, MD. Email: lichtman@american.edu. Research: quantitative methods, American political.

Licon, Gerardo, *Wisconsin-Eau Claire*. Email: licong@uwec.edu.

Lidtke, Vernon L., *Johns Hopkins (Hist.)*. Towson, MD. Email: lidtke@jhu.edu. Research: German art and politics 1900-45, Conrad Felixmüller.

Lieb, Emily S. Seattle, WA. Affil: Seattle. Email: esl2003@caa.columbia.edu.

Lieberman, Benjamin. Fitchburg, MA. Affil: Fitchburg State. Email: blieberman@fitchburgstate.edu. Research: ethnic cleansing and genocide, Weimar Republic.

Lieberman, David, *California, Berkeley*. Email: dlieb@law.berkeley.edu.

Lieberman, Richard K., *La Guardia and Wagner Archives*. Long Island City, NY. Email: richardli@lagcc.cuny.edu. Research: America, urban.

Lieberman, Robbie, *Southern Illinois, Carbondale*. Email: robl@siu.edu.

Lieberman, Victor B., *Michigan, Ann Arbor*. Email: eurasia@umich.edu.

Liebeskind, Claudia, *Florida State*. Email: cliebeskind@fsu.edu.

Liebowitz, Jonathan J. Littleton, MA. Affil: Massachusetts, Lowell. Email: jonathan_liebowitz@uml.edu. Research: French tenancy and sharecropping 1850-95, draft animals in Europe and US.

Liebrecht, Bradley. Yakima, WA. Affil: West Valley Sch. District #208. Email: bliebrecht@gmail.com.

Liebs, Chester, *Vermont*. Email: cliebs1@aol.com.

Liebscher, Arthur F., *SJ*, *Santa Clara*. Email: aliebscher@scu.edu.

Liechty, Mark, *Illinois, Chicago*. Email: liechty@uic.edu.

Lierheimer, Linda, *Hawai'i Pacific*. Email: llierheimer@hpu.edu.

Lierse, Robert E. Gainesville, FL. Affil: Florida. Email: rlierse54@ufl.edu.

Lieser, Joshua R. Santa Barbara, CA. Affil: Onxard. Email: jlieser44@gmail.com. Research: 20th-c US, modern Russia.

Lieske, Albert C, III. Eagle Mountain, UT. Affil: Norwich. Email: lieskeac@hotmail.com.

Lifset, Robert D., *Oklahoma (Hist.)*. Norman, OK. Email: robertlifset@ou.edu. Research: energy, politics.

Lifshitz, Felice. Edmonton, AB, Canada. Affil: Alberta. Email: felice.lifshitz@ualberta.ca. Research: early medieval gender and manuscript culture, 20th-c cinematic medievalism.

Light, Jennifer, *MIT*. Email: jslight@mit.edu.

Lightfoot, Dana Wessell, *Northern British Columbia*. Email: lightfoot@unbc.ca.

Lightfoot, Natasha J., *Columbia (Hist.)*. New York, NY. Email: nlightfoot@columbia.edu. Research: emancipation in British West Indies, migration from West Indies from 1900.

Lightman, Bernard V., *York, Can.* Email: lightman@yorku.ca.

Lightman, Harriet, *Northwestern*. Email: h-lightman@northwestern.edu.

Lightner, David L., *Alberta*. Edmonton, AB, Canada. Email: david.lightner@ualberta.ca. Research: 1930s film star Winnie Lightner.

Likaka, Osumaka, *Wayne State*. Email: ad5221@wayne.edu.

Liles, Deborah, *Tarleton State*. Weatherford, TX. Email: dliles@tarleton.edu. Research: slavery in northwestern Texas, oral history of black students.

Lilla, Mark, *Columbia (Hist.)*. Email: mlilla@columbia.edu.

Lillie, Lisa M. Webster Groves, MO. Affil: Maryville. Email: llillie@maryville.edu. Research: transnational trade, early modernity and identity.

Lilly, Carol S., *Nebraska, Kearney*. Email: lillyc@unk.edu.

Lilly, David, *Loyola, New Orleans*. Email: dlilly@loyno.edu.

Lilly, R. Keith, *Concord*. Email: rklilly@concord.edu.

Lim, Hannah Saeyoung. Exeter, NH. Affil: UCLA. Email: hslim@ucla.edu.

Lim, Nancy Kate. Boise, ID. Affil: Fort Hays State. Email: nancyruarklim@gmail.com.

Lim, Paul C-H, *Vanderbilt; American Soc. of Church Hist.* Email: paul.lim@vanderbilt.edu.

Lim, Richard, *Smith*. Email: rlim@smith.edu.

Lim, Shirley, *SUNY, Stony Brook*. Email: shirley.lim@stonybrook.edu.

Lim, Sungyun, *Colorado, Boulder*. Boulder, CO. Email: sungyun.lim@colorado.edu. Research: modern Japan, Korea.

Lim, Susan C., *Biola*. Email: susan.lim@biola.edu.

Limary, Christine. Elverta, CA. Email: cdlimary@hotmail.com.

Limerick, Patricia Nelson, *Colorado, Boulder*. Boulder, CO. Email: patricia.limerick@colorado.edu; pnl@centerwest.org. Research: energy production and consumption, US Dept. of Interior.

Limoncelli, Amy, *William and Mary*. Email: aelimo@wm.edu.

Lin, Mao, *Georgia Southern*. Email: mlin@georgiasouthern.edu.

Lin, Mei-Mei Rose. Taipei, Taiwan. Affil: National Dong Hwa. Email: mmlin@mail2000.com.tw. Research: Christianity in China, world women and religion.

Lin, Shing-Ting. Fremont, CA. Affil: Columbia. Email: sl2814@columbia.edu. Research: science/medicine/gender, 19th-/20th-c Sino-Western relations.

Lin, Xiying. Philadelphia, PA. Affil: Pennsylvania. Email: gniyixnil@gmail.com.

Lin, Yu-sheng, *Wisconsin-Madison*. Email: yslin@wisc.edu.

Lin, Zoe Shan, *Ithaca*. Email: zslin@ithaca.edu.

Linabury, George O., *Western Connecticut State*. Email: linaburyg@wcsu.edu.

Lincicome, Mark E., *Holy Cross*. Email: mlincico@holycross.edu.

Lind, Mary Ann, *Biola*. Email: maryann.lind@biola.edu.

Lind, Vera, *Northern Illinois*. Email: vlind@niu.edu.

Lindeman, Katherine Marie. Hamilton, ON, Canada. Affil: Tel Aviv. Email: katie.lindeman@mail.utoronto.ca. Research: medieval Iberia, medieval church.

Lindemann, Albert S., *California, Santa Barbara*. Email: lindeman@history.ucsb.edu.

Lindemann, Mary, *Miami*. Miami, FL. Email: mlindemann@miami.edu; mlindemann1949@gmail.com. Research: early modern Europe, medicine.

Lindenauer, **Leslie J.**, *Western Connecticut State.* Email: lindenauerl@wcsu.edu.

Lindenfeld, *David F.*, *Louisiana State.* Baton Rouge, LA. Email: hylind@lsu.edu. Research: comparative responses to missionaries, theorizing the irrational.

Lindenmeyer, **Kriste**, *Rutgers, Camden.* Email: kriste.lindenmeyer@camden.rutgers.edu.

Lindenmeyr, *Adele*, *Villanova.* Villanova, PA. Email: adele.lindenmeyr@villanova.edu. Research: Russian women, biography and history.

Linder, *Robert D.*, *Kansas State.* Manhattan, KS. Email: rdl@ksu.edu. Research: Australian religious, religion and politics in Europe/US.

Linderman, **Gerald**, *Michigan, Ann Arbor.* Email: gfl@umich.edu.

Lindgren, *Allana C.* Victoria, BC, Canada. Affil: Victoria. Email: aclind@uvic.ca. Research: performing arts, modernism.

Lindgren, *James*, *SUNY, Plattsburgh.* Email: james.lindgren@plattsburgh.edu.

Lindgren-Gibson, *Alexandra S.*, *Mississippi.* University, MS. Email: aslindgr@olemiss.edu. Research: modern Europe.

Lindholm, *Richard T.* Eugene, OR. Affil: Lindholm Research. Email: rtlindholm@msn.com. Research: Renaissance Italy, early modern economic.

Lindley, **W. Terry**, *Union.* Email: tlindley@uu.edu.

Lindman, *Janet M.*, *Rowan.* Royersford, PA. Email: lindman@rowan.edu. Research: US, women.

Lindner, *Christine Beth*, *Murray State.* Murray, KY. Email: christinebethlindner@gmail.com. Research: missions, 19th-c US and Ottoman Syrian women.

Lindner, **Rudi**, *Michigan, Ann Arbor.* Email: rpl@umich.edu.

Lindo-Fuentes, **Hector**, *Fordham.* Email: hlindo@aol.com.

Lindquist, **Malinda Alaine**, *Minnesota (Hist.).* Email: lindqust@umn.edu.

Lindquist-Dorr, **Lisa J.**, *Alabama, Tuscaloosa.* Email: ldorr@bama.ua.edu.

Lindsay, **Anne M.**, *California State, Sacramento.* Email: anne.lindsay@csus.edu.

Lindsay, **Brendan Charles**, *California State, Sacramento.* Email: brendan.lindsay@csus.edu.

Lindsay, **Debra**, *New Brunswick.* Email: dlindsay@unbsj.ca.

Lindsay, *James E.* Dubuque, IA.

Lindsay, **James E.**, *Colorado State.* Email: james.lindsay@colostate.edu.

Lindsay, *Lisa A.*, *North Carolina, Chapel Hill.* Chapel Hill, NC. Email: lalindsa@email.unc.edu. Research: African American repatriation to Nigeria, colonialism and social change in Africa.

Lindseth, **Erik L.**, *Indiana–Purdue, Indianapolis.* Email: elindset@iupui.edu.

Lindsey, **Howard Odell**, *DePaul.* Email: hlindsey@depaul.edu.

Lindsey, *Mark G.* Hales Corners, WI. Email: lindsey@uwalumni.com.

Linehan, **Mary**, *Texas, Tyler.* Email: mlinehan@uttyler.edu.

Linenthal, **Edward T.**, *Indiana.* Email: etl@indiana.edu.

Ling, **Huping**, *Truman State.* Email: hling@truman.edu.

Lingenfelter, **Scott**, *Grand Valley State.* Email: lingenfs@gvsu.edu.

Lingwood, **Chad Gilbert**, *Grand Valley State.* Email: lingwoch@gvsu.edu.

Link, *Alessandra La Rocca*. Louisville, KY. Affil: Indiana, Southeast. Email: l.alessandra87@gmail.com.

Link, **Amanda**, *Texas, Tyler.* Email: mlink@uttyler.edu.

Link, *Betsy Leland*. Los Angeles, CA.

Link, **Stefan J.**, *Dartmouth.* Email: stefan.j.link@dartmouth.edu.

Link, *William A.*, *Florida.* Gainesville, FL. Email: linkwa@ufl.edu; linkwa@gmail.com. Research: US South.

Linker, *Jessica C.* Philadelphia, PA. Affil: Bryn Mawr. Email: jessica.linker@uconn.edu. Research: women and scientific practice, colonial paper money.

Linkhoeva, *Tatiana*, *NYU.* New York, NY. Email: tatiana.linkhoeva@nyu.edu. Research: modern Japan/intellectual/socialism, Soviet Russia/nationality question.

Linn, **Brian McAllister**, *Texas A&M.* Email: b-linn@tamu.edu.

Linn, *Jason*, *California Polytechnic State.* San Luis Obispo, CA. Email: jalinn@calpoly.edu. Research: world, ancient Greece and Rome.

Linstrum, **Erik**, *Virginia.* Email: erl2z@virginia.edu.

Lintelman, **Joy K.**, *Concordia Coll.* Email: lintelma@cord.edu.

Linton, *Derek S.* Geneva, NY. Affil: Hobart and William Smith. Email: linton@hws.edu. Research: early bacteriology and immunology, WWI disease control.

Lintvedt, *Ane J.* Baltimore, MD. Affil: McDonogh Sch. Email: alintvedt@mcdonogh.org. Research: world/maritime/pedagogy, 18th-19th-c Europe.

Lipartito, *Kenneth J.*, *Florida International.* Miami, FL. Email: lipark@fiu.edu. Research: American economic, business.

Lipkowitz, *Elise S.* Arlington, VA. Affil: National Science Foundation. Email: eliselipkowitz2009@u.northwestern.edu. Research: Atlantic world, science and technology.

Lipman, *Andrew C.*, *Barnard, Columbia.* New York, NY. Email: alipman@barnard.edu. Research: colonial North America and US to 1877, Native Americans.

Lipman, *Jana K.*, *Tulane.* New Orleans, LA. Email: jlipman@tulane.edu. Research: 20th-c US.

Lipman, **Jonathan N.**, *Mount Holyoke.* Email: jlipman@mtholyoke.edu.

Lipp, **Charles T.**, *West Georgia.* Email: clipp@westga.edu.

Lippert, *Amy K.*, *Chicago.* Chicago, IL. Email: lippert@uchicago.edu; alippert@gmail.com. Research: 19th-c West / popular culture, visual culture / celebrity.

Lippert, **Werner D.**, *Indiana, Pa.* Email: lippert@iup.edu.

Lipschultz, **Sybil**, *Miami.* Email: slipschultz@miami.edu.

Lipscomb, **Patrick C.**, *Louisiana State.*

Lipsett-Rivera, **Sonya**, *Carleton, Can.* Email: sonya.lipsettrivera@carleton.ca.

Lipsitz, **George**, *California, Santa Barbara.* Email: glipsitz@blackstudies.ucsb.edu.

Lipson, *Steven J.* Nashville, TN. Affil: Vanderbilt. Email: sjlips@yahoo.com. Research: religous schooling in late 20th cent US, late 20th-c Catholic labor/politics.

Lipstadt, *Deborah E.*, *Emory.* Email: dlipsta@emory.edu.

Lipton, *Sara G.*, *SUNY, Stony Brook.* Email: sara.lipton@stonybrook.edu.

Lirley McCune, *Sarah E.* Columbia, MO. Affil: Columbia Coll., Mo. Email: slirleymccune@ccis.edu. Research: women and gender, death.

Lisio, **Donald J.**, *Coe.*

Liss, **Julia E.**, *Scripps.* Email: julia.liss@scrippscollege.edu.

Liss, *Peggy K*. Washington, DC. Email: pkliss@verizon.net. Research: American exceptionalism, autobiography and history.

List, **Victoria D.**, *Washington and Jefferson.* Email: vlist@washjeff.edu.

Liston, **Ann E.**, *Fort Hays State.*

Liszka, **Kate**, *California State, San Bernardino.* Email: kate.liszka@csusb.edu.

Litaker, **Noria**, *Nevada, Las Vegas.*

Litalien, **Michel**, *National Defence Headquarters.* Email: michel.litalien@forces.gc.ca.

Litchfield, *R. Burr*, *Brown.* Westport, MA. Email: robert_litchfield@Brown.edu. Research: 15th-/19th-c Florence.

Litke, *Andrew*. Falls Church, VA. Affil: Catholic. Email: awlitke@gmail.com.

Litoff, *Judy Barrett*, *Bryant.* Smithfield, RI. Email: jlitoff@bryant.edu. Research: US women and WWII, post-Soviet economies in transition.

Litogot, **Lynda M.**, *Henry Ford Coll.* Email: lylitogot@yahoo.com.

Litt, **Paul**, *Carleton, Can.* Email: paul.litt@carleton.ca.

Littauer, **Amanda H.**, *Northern Illinois.* Email: alittauer@niu.edu.

Littell-Lamb, **Elizabeth**, *Tampa.* Email: elittell@ut.edu.

Little, *Ann M.*, *Colorado State.* Fort Collins, CO. Email: ann.little@colostate.edu. Research: colonial America, women and gender.

Little, *Douglas J.*, *Clark.* Worcester, MA. Email: dlittle@clarku.edu. Research: US and Middle East, US and multinational oil companies.

Little, **Dwayne L.**, *Point Loma Nazarene.* Email: dwaynelittle@pointloma.edu.

Little, **J. Branden**, *Weber State.* Email: jblittle@weber.edu.

Little, **John I.**, *Simon Fraser.* Email: jlittle@sfu.ca.

Little, *Kimberly Kaye*. Athens, OH. Affil: Ohio. Email: littlek@ohio.edu. Research: women and civil rights.

Little, **Kimberly S.**, *Central Arkansas.* Email: klittle@uca.edu.

Little, **Lawrence S.**, *Villanova.* Email: lawrence.little@villanova.edu.

Little, *Lester K.*, *II*, *Smith.* Northampton, MA. Email: llittle@smith.edu. Research: medieval Latin Christian social and religious.

Little, **Monroe H.**, **Jr.**, *Indiana–Purdue, Indianapolis.* Email: mlittle@iupui.edu.

Littlefield, *Daniel C.*, *South Carolina, Columbia.* Columbia, SC. Email: littledc@mailbox.sc.edu. Research: early national race relations, African ethnicity in colonial America.

Littlefield, **Valinda W.**, *South Carolina, Columbia.* Email: littlevw@mailbox.sc.edu.

Littlejohn, **Jeffrey Lynn**, *Sam Houston State.* Email: jll004@shsu.edu.

Litvak, **Olga**, *Cornell.*

Litwack, *Leon F*. Berkeley, CA. Affil: California, Berkeley. Email: llitwack@berkeley.edu. Research: Black South in WWII, 20th-c African Americans.

Litzenberger, **Caroline J.**, *Portland State.*

Litzinger, **Charles A.**, *California State, Bakersfield.*

Liu, **Andrew**, *Villanova.* Email: andrew.liu@villanova.edu.

Liu, *Jennifer*, *Central Michigan*. Mount Pleasant, MI. Email: liu3j@cmich.edu. Research: education in China and Taiwan, military training in China and Taiwan.

Liu, **Tessie P.**, *Northwestern.* Email: t-liu@northwestern.edu.

Liu, **Wenxi**, *Miami, Ohio.* Email: liuw@miamioh.edu.

Liu, *Xiaoyuan*, *Virginia*. Charlottesville, VA. Email: xyliu@virginia.edu. Research: Chinese Central Asian ethnopolitics, 20th-c Sino-US relations.

Liu, *Xinru*, *New Jersey*. Philadelphia, PA. Email: liux@tcnj.edu. Research: ancient India, Silk Road.

Liu, **Xun**, *Rutgers.* Email: xunliu@history.rutgers.edu.

Liu, *Yan*, *SUNY, Buffalo*. Buffalo, NY. Email: yliu253@buffalo.edu. Research: premodern China, cultural history of medicine.

Liu, *Zhaokun*. Pittsburgh, PA. Affil: Carnegie Mellon. Email: zhaokun1@andrew.cmu.edu. Research: forensic science, military.

Liu, *Zhigang*. Boston, MA. Affil: Simmons. Email: zhigang.liu@simmons.edu. Research: American diplomatic, modern China and Japan.

Liu, *Zifeng*. Ithaca, NY. Affil: Cornell. Email: zl564@cornell.edu.

Liulevicius, **Vejas G.**, *Tennessee, Knoxville.* Email: vliulevi@utk.edu.

Liverant, *Bettina*. Calgary, AB, Canada. Affil: Calgary. Email: bllivera@ucalgary.ca.

Livesay, *Daniel*, *Claremont McKenna*. Claremont, CA. Email: dlivesay@cmc.edu. Research: 18th-c US slavery, 18th-c Caribbean slavery.

Livesey, **Elizabeth**, *Hist. Assoc.* Email: elivesey@historyassociates.com.

Livesey, **Steven J.**, *Oklahoma (Hist. of Science).* Email: slivesey@ou.edu.

Livezeanu, **Irina**, *Pittsburgh.* Email: irina1@pitt.edu.

Livie, *Ian Michael*. Petaluma, CA. Affil: Santa Rosa Jr. Coll. Email: ianlivie@gmail.com. Research: criminality and childhood in Britain.

Livingston, *James C.*, *Rutgers*. New York, NY. Email: jameslivingston49@hotmail.com. Research: 19th-/20th-c American economic, intellectual.

Livingston, **Jeffery C.**, *California State, Chico.* Email: jlivingston@csuchico.edu.

Livingston, **John W.**, *William Paterson.* Email: livingstonj@wpunj.edu.

Livingston, **Julie**, *NYU.* Email: jl6877@nyu.edu.

Livingston, **R. Gerald**, *German Hist. Inst.* Email: jliving844@aol.com.

Livschiz, **Ann**, *Purdue, Fort Wayne.* Email: livschia@pfw.edu.

Lizondo, *Mary Ann*. Alexandria, VA. Email: maryannlizondo@comcast.net. Research: European revolutions.

Lloyd, **Brian D.**, *California, Riverside.* Email: brian.lloyd@ucr.edu.

Lloyd, **Craig**, *Columbus State.* Email: craiglloyd40@hotmail.com.

Lloyd, **David T.**, *St. Lawrence.* Email: dlloyd@stlawu.edu.

Lloyd, **Jennifer M.**, *SUNY, Coll. Brockport.* Email: jlloyd@brockport.edu.

Lloyd, *Kiegan Elliot*. White City, SK, Canada. Affil: Luther Coll., Regina. Email: kel470@Uregina.ca.

Lloydlangston, **Amber**, *Western Ontario.* Email: alloydla@uwo.ca.

Lo, *Karl C*. San Francisco, CA. Affil: Law Offices of Karl Lo. Email: Karllo475@gmail.com.

Loader, **Colin T.**, *Nevada, Las Vegas.* Email: loaderc@unlv.nevada.edu.

Loats, *Carol L*. Pueblo, CO. Affil: Colorado State, Pueblo. Email: loats10cl@msn.com. Research: notaries/child transfers/artisans, gender and relationships.

Loayza, **Matthew**, *Minnesota State, Mankato.* Email: matt.loayza@mnsu.edu.

Loberg, *Molly J.*, *California Polytechnic State*. San Luis Obispo, CA. Email: mjloberg@calpoly.edu. Research: consumer culture in Berlin 1920s-30s.

Locke, **Robert R.**, *Hawai'i, Manoa.* Email: blocke@hawaii.edu.

Lockenour, *Jay B*. Wynnewood, PA. Affil: Temple. Email: jay.lockenour@temple.edu. Research: German officer corps, Erich Ludendorff.

Lockhart, *Jessica*. Houston, TX. Affil: Rice. Email: jml20@rice.edu.

Locking, *Alexandra*. Chicago, IL. Affil: Chicago. Email: alexandra.locking@gmail.com. Research: lordship/church reform/Chronicles, 11th-c Europe.

Locklin-Sofer, *Nancy Lynne*, *Maryville*. Maryville, TN. Email: nancy.locklin@maryvillecollege.edu. Research: women's work, marriage law.

Lockman, *Zachary*, *NYU*. New York, NY. Email: zachary.lockman@nyu.edu. Research: modern Middle East.

Lockridge, **Kenneth A.**, *Montana.*

Lodwick, **Kathleen L.**, *Penn State.* Email: kll2@psu.edu.

Loe, **Mary Louise**, *James Madison.* Email: loeml@jmu.edu.

Loeb, **Lori**, *Toronto.* Email: lori.loeb@utoronto.ca.

Loeb, **Lynne**, *California State, Dominguez Hills.* Email: lloeb@csudh.edu.

Loeffler, *James*, *Virginia*. Washington, DC. Email: james.loeffler@virginia.edu. Research: antisemitism, genocide.

Loengard, *Janet*. Bernardsville, NJ. Affil: Moravian. Email: loengardj@moravian.edu. Research: English nuisance law, medieval/early modern English women's property law.

Loewen, **Royden K.**, *Winnipeg.* Email: r.loewen@uwinnipeg.ca.

Loewenberg, *Peter J.*, *UCLA*. Los Angeles, CA. Email: peterl@ucla.edu. Research: Austria 1918, time in history and psychoanalysis.

Loewenstein, **Karl E.**, *Wisconsin-Oshkosh.* Email: loewenst@uwosh.edu.

Lofgren, *Charles A*. Claremont, CA. Affil: Claremont McKenna. Email: clofgren@cmc.edu. Research: war-making constitutional.

Loftus, **Ariel**, *Wichita State.* Email: ariel.loftus@wichita.edu.

Loftus, **Ronald P.**, *Willamette.* Email: rloftus@willamette.edu.

Logan, **Barbara Ellen**, *Wyoming.* Email: blogan@uwyo.edu.

Logan, **Gabe**, *Northern Michigan.* Email: glogan@nmu.edu.

Logan, **Michael F.**, *Oklahoma State.* Email: michael.logan@okstate.edu.

Logan, **Tim**, *Susquehanna.* Email: logant@susqu.edu.

Logevall, *Fredrik*, *Harvard (Hist.)*. Cambridge, MA. Email: fredrik_logevall@harvard.edu. Research: Vietnam wars 1945-75, Cold War.

Logue, **William H.**, *Northern Illinois.* Email: wlogue@mindspring.com.

Lohmann, **Mary Ellen**, *State Hist. Soc. of Missouri.* Email: lohmannm@shsmo.org.

Lohr, *Eric J.*, *American*. Bethesda, MD. Email: elohr@american.edu. Research: Russian citizenship 1860-1930, WWI and end of Russian Empire.

Loiacono, **Gabriel J.**, *Wisconsin-Oshkosh.* Email: loiacong@uwosh.edu.

Loiselle, *Aimee*. Springfield, MA. Affil: Connecticut, Storrs. Email: aimee.loiselle@uconn.edu. Research: Norma Rae and women workers/global, Puerto Rican women in labor.

Loiselle, **Kenneth B.**, *Trinity, Tex.* Email: kloisell@trinity.edu.

Lokken, *Paul*, *Bryant*. Smithfield, RI. Email: plokken@bryant.edu. Research: Africans in colonial Central America, identity in colonial Central America.

Lomax, *John Phillip*. Ada, OH. Email: j-lomax@onu.edu. Research: 13th-c law and politics, 12th-/13th-c Italy.

Lombard, *Anne S.*, *California State, San Marcos.* Email: alombard@csusm.edu.

Lombardi, *John V*. Amherst, MA. Email: lombardi@jvlone.com. Research: Venezuela.

Lombardi, **Joseph**, *Northern Kentucky.* Email: lombardij2@nku.edu.

Lombardo, **Timothy J.**, *South Alabama.*

Lomnitz, **Claudio**, *Columbia (Hist.).* Email: cl2510@columbia.edu.

Londo, **William**, *Oakland.* Email: londo@oakland.edu.

Lonetree, **Amy J.**, *California, Santa Cruz.* Email: lonetree@ucsc.edu.

Long, **Alecia P.**, *Louisiana State.* Email: aplong@lsu.edu.

Long, *Bronson W*. Rome, GA. Affil: Georgia Highlands. Email: blong@highlands.edu. Research: post-1945 Franco-German relations, military occupations.

Long, *C. Thomas*, *George Washington*. Great Falls, VA. Email: tomlong@gwu.edu. Research: early American naval forces social, Revolutionary War naval operations.

Long, **Creston S.**, **III**, *Salisbury.* Email: cslong@salisbury.edu.

Long, **Gretchen**, *Williams.* Email: glong@williams.edu.

Long, **Jeff E.**, *Bloomsburg.* Email: jlon2@bloomu.edu.

Long, **John D.**, *Roanoke.* Email: jlong@roanoke.edu.

Long, **Kathryn T.**, *Wheaton, Ill.* Email: Kathryn.T.Long@wheaton.edu.

Long, **Kelly Ann**, *Colorado State.* Email: kelly.long@colostate.edu.

Long, *Ngo Vinh*, *Maine, Orono*. Email: vinhlong.ngo@maine.edu.

Long, *Pamela O*. Washington, DC. Email: pamlong@pamelaolong.com. Research: engineering in 16th-c Rome, visual representation/Renaissance science/tech.

Long, *Patrick Joseph*. Buffalo, NY. Affil: SUNY, Buffalo. Email: pjlong@buffalo.edu.

Long, Robert E., *California State, Sacramento*. Email: relong@csus.edu.

Long, Robert L., *Elmhurst*. Email: robert.long@elmhurst.edu.

Long, Roger D., *Eastern Michigan*. Email: rlong@emich.edu.

Long, *Sara*. Westminster, CA. Affil: California, Irvine. Email: saralong.edu@gmail.com.

Long, Thomas E., *California State, San Bernardino*. Email: tlong@csusb.edu.

Longbrake, Margit, *Hist. New Orleans*. Email: margitl@hnoc.org.

Longfellow, David L., *Baylor*. Email: david_longfellow@baylor.edu.

Longhurst, James L., *Wisconsin-La Crosse*. Email: longhurs.jame@uwlax.edu.

Longley, Kyle, *Arizona State*. Email: kyle.longley@asu.edu.

Longo, *Dominic S*. Brick, NJ. Email: dsl82@hotmail.com. Research: transportation, Cold War political.

Loo, Tina M., *British Columbia*. Email: tina.loo@ubc.ca.

Loo, Tze May, *Richmond*. Email: tloo@richmond.edu.

Lookingbill, Brad. Columbia, MO. Affil: Columbia Coll., Mo. Email: bdlookingbill@ccis.edu. Research: Indian Wars, armed forces and civil society.

Loomis, Erik S., *Rhode Island*. Email: eloomis@uri.edu.

Looney, *J. Jefferson*, *Robert H. Smith Center*. Email: jlooney@monticello.org.

Loos, Tamara L., *Cornell*. Ithaca, NY. Email: tl14@cornell.edu. Research: historiography, modern Thailand.

LoPatin-Lummis, Nancy, *Wisconsin-Stevens Point*. Email: nlopatin@uwsp.edu.

Lopera Mesa, Gloria Patricia. Miami, FL. Affil: Florida International. Email: glope161@fiu.edu. Research: legal, Native American reservation lands.

Lopes, Maria-Aparecida, *California State, Fresno*. Email: mlopes@csufresno.edu.

Lopez, *Abel Ricardo*, *Western Washington*. Bellingham, WA. Email: Ricardo.Lopez@wwu.edu. Research: American middle class, class relations.

Lopez, Adalberto, *Binghamton, SUNY*.

Lopez, Amanda M., *St. Xavier*. Chicago, IL. Email: alopez@sxu.edu. Research: cemetery reform in Mexico, death and body in Mexico.

Lopez, Bianca, *Southern Methodist*.

Lopez, Kathleen, *Rutgers*. Email: kmlopez@lcs.rutgers.edu.

Lopez, Maj Miguel Angel, *US Air Force Acad*. Email: miguel.lopez@usafa.edu.

Lopez, Maritere, *California State, Fresno*. Email: mariterel@csufresno.edu.

Lopez, Nancy, *Houston-Downtown*. Email: lopezn@uhd.edu.

Lopez, Rick A., *Amherst*. Email: ralopez@amherst.edu.

Lopez, *Russ*. Boston, MA. Email: rptlopez@gmail.com. Research: modern Boston.

Lopez-Alonso, *Moramay*, *Rice*. Houston, TX. Email: moramay@rice.edu. Research: living standards in Mexico, Mexico and the world.

Lopez Fadul, **Valeria Escauriaza**, *Wesleyan*. Email: vlopezfadul@wesleyan.edu.

Lopez Fuentes, *Julia*. Atlanta, GA. Affil: Emory. Email: julia.lopez@emory.edu. Research: democratization/Europeanization in Spain, European community of memory since 1945.

Lopez-Jantzen, *Nicole*. New York, NY. Affil: Borough of Manhattan Comm. Coll., CUNY. Email: nlopezjantzen@bmcc.cuny.edu. Research: Lombard Italy, ideology and identity.

Lopez Lazaro, **Fabio T**., *Hawaiʻi, Manoa*. Honolulu, HI. Email: fll@hawaii.edu. Research: world maritime 1300-1800, imperialism and corporate law.

Lopez Velador, **Johanna**. Iowa City, IA. Affil: Iowa. Email: Johanna-lopez@uiowa.edu.

Loran, Michele, *State Hist. Soc. of Missouri*. Email: LoranM@shsmo.org.

Lorcin, *Patricia M. E*., *Minnesota (Hist.)*. Minneapolis, MN. Email: plorcin@umn.edu. Research: Memory/trauma/nostalgia, West. imperialism/colonial/postcolonial.

Lord, Gary T., *Norwich*. Email: glord@norwich.edu.

Lorek, *Timothy*. New Haven, CT. Affil: Yale. Email: timothy.lorek@yale.edu.

Lorenz, Christine, *Duquesne*. Email: lorenzc@duq.edu.

Lorenz, Edward C., *Alma*. Email: lorenz@alma.edu.

Lorenzkowski, Barbara, *Concordia, Can*. Email: Barbara.Lorenzkowski@concordia.ca.

Lorenz-Meyer, Martin, *Augsburg*. Email: lorenz@augsburg.edu.

Lorge, Peter, *Vanderbilt*. Email: peter.lorge@vanderbilt.edu.

Lorimer, Doug A., *Wilfrid Laurier*. Email: dlorimer@wlu.ca.

Lorimer, Joyce, *Wilfrid Laurier*. Email: jlorimer@wlu.ca.

Loring, Joanna. San Diego, CA. Affil: Fort Hays State. Email: joannaloring@yahoo.com.

LoSavio, JoAnn. DeKalb, IL. Affil: Northern Illinois. Email: jlosavio@niu.edu.

Losier, Toussaint Godley. South Hadley, MA. Affil: Massachusetts Amherst. Email: tlosier@umass.edu.

Losos, Joseph O. Saint Louis, MO.

Loss, Christopher, *Vanderbilt*. Email: c.loss@vanderbilt.edu.

Lotchin, Roger W., *North Carolina, Chapel Hill*. Email: rlotchin@email.unc.edu.

Lotz-Heumann, *Ute*, *Arizona*. Tucson, AZ. Email: ulotzh@email.arizona.edu. Research: European Reformation, German Enlightenment.

Lou, *Karen*, *AHA*. Washington, DC. Email: klou@historians.org.

Lougee, Carolyn Chappell, *Stanford*. Email: lougee@stanford.edu.

Loughlin, Patricia, *Central Oklahoma*. Email: ploughlin@uco.edu.

Loughran, Trish, *Illinois, Urbana-Champaign*. Email: loughran@illinois.edu.

Louis, *Wm. Roger*, *Texas, Austin*. Austin, TX. Email: britishstudies@austin.utexas.edu. Research: Britain and British Empire, Middle East/India/Africa.

Louisa, *Angelo J*. Omaha, NE. Email: pamsampler@aol.com. Research: Baseball, England 1485-1603.

Lounsbury, Carl, *William and Mary*. Email: crloun@wm.edu.

Louro, *Michele L*., *Salem State; World Hist. Assoc*. Marblehead, MA. Email: mlouro@salemstate.edu. Research: modern South Asia, world.

Louthan, Howard P., *Minnesota (Hist.)*. Email: hlouthan@umn.edu.

Lovano, Michael, *St. Norbert*. Email: michael.lovano@snc.edu.

Love, Joseph L., *Jr*. Urbana, IL. Affil: Illinois, Urbana-Champaign. Email: j-love2@uiuc.edu. Research: 20th-c economic, economic ideas.

Loveday, *Amos J*., *Jr*. Columbus, OH. Email: ajloveday@aol.com. Research: energy policy, environmental policy.

Lovejoy, Henry B., *Colorado, Boulder*. Lakewood, CO. Email: hlovejoy@colorado.edu; henlovejoy@gmail.com. Research: West Africa, African diaspora.

Lovejoy, Paul E., *York, Can*. Email: plovejoy@yorku.ca.

Lovelace, *H. Timothy*, *Jr*, *Indiana*. Bloomington, IN. Email: lovelace@indiana.edu. Research: legal, civil rights.

Loveland, Anne C., *Louisiana State*.

Loveland, *James M*. Saint Petersburg, FL. Email: jimloveland52@yahoo.com.

Lovely, *Elizabeth*. Tampa, FL. Affil: South Florida, Tampa. Email: elovely@mail.usf.edu.

Lovering, Capt Richard, *US Military Acad*. Email: richard.lovering@usma.edu.

Lovett, *Christopher C*., *Emporia State*. Topeka, KS. Email: clovett@emporia.edu. Research: American internal security policy, Cold War/Vietnam.

Lovett, *Laura L*., *Massachusetts, Amherst*. Pittsburgh, PA. Affil: Pittsburgh. Email: lovett@history.umass.edu. Research: pronatalism and reproduction, non-sexist education and feminism.

Lovins, *Christopher*. Ulsan, South Korea. Affil: Ulsan National Inst. of Science and Tech. Email: christopher_lovins@hotmail.com. Research: King Chongjo, historical film.

Lovoll, Odd S., *St. Olaf*. Email: lovoll@stolaf.edu.

Low, John, *Ohio State*. Email: low.89@osu.edu.

Low, *Michael C*., *Iowa State*. Ames, IA. Email: low@iastate.edu. Research: Hajj/Islamic pilgrimage to Mecca, Environment/water/infrastructure/energy.

Low, *Ryan*. Cambridge, MA. Affil: Harvard. Email: low@g.harvard.edu.

Lowe, *Ben*, *Florida Atlantic*. Boca Raton, FL. Email: bplowe@fau.edu. Research: mid-Tudor religious and social thought, Reformation and society in Gloucester.

Lowe, Benedict James, *North Alabama*. Email: blowe1@una.edu.

Lowe, *Eugene Y*., *Jr*. Evanston, IL. Affil: Northwestern. Email: eyljr@northwestern.edu. Research: Social Gospel and higher US religion.

Lowe, *Hilary Iris*. Philadelphia, PA. Affil: Temple. Email: hilowe@temple.edu. Research: museums, preservation.

Lowe, *Margaret A*. Bridgewater, MA. Affil: Bridgewater State. Email: mlowe@bridgew.edu. Research: female body, social.

Lowe, William C. Clinton, IA. Email: curlow@ mchsi.com. Research: remembrance of war, war memorials.

Lowell, Laura Scott, *Massachusetts Hist. Soc.* Email: llowell@masshist.org.

Lowen, Rebecca S., *Metropolitan State.* Email: rebecca.lowen@metrostate.edu.

Lowenfeld, Daniel. Jericho, NY. Affil: Nassau Comm. Coll.; St. John's. Email: DanielLowenfeld@aol.com.

Lowengard, Sarah. New York, NY. Affil: Cooper Union. Email: sarahl@panix.com. Research: pre-1795 color printing.

Lower, Michael, *Minnesota (Hist.).* Email: mlower@umn.edu.

Lower, Richard C., *California State, Sacramento.* Email: rclower@csus.edu.

Lower, Wendy Morgan, *Claremont McKenna.* Claremont, CA. Email: wlower@cmc.edu. Research: Holocaust studies, east central Europe.

Lowery, Malinda Maynor, *North Carolina, Chapel Hill.* Email: mmaynor@email.unc.edu.

Lowey-Ball, Shawnakim, *Utah.* Salt Lake City, UT. Email: shawnakim.lowey-ball@utah.edu. Research: South East Asia.

Lowgren, Andrea. Portland, OR. Affil: Portland Comm. Coll. Email: andrea.lowgren@pcc.edu.

Lowry, John S., *Eastern Kentucky.* Email: john. lowry@eku.edu.

Lowy, Dina, *Gettysburg.* Email: dlowy@ gettysburg.edu.

Loyd, Thomas. Washington, DC. Affil: Georgetown. Email: trl44@georgetown.edu.

Lozano, Rosina A., *Princeton.* Princeton, NJ. Email: rlozano@princeton.edu. Research: Mexican American, American West.

Lozar, Patrick. Seattle, WA. Affil: Washington, Seattle. Email: plozar@uw.edu.

Lozovsky, Natalia. San Mateo, CA. Email: lozovsky@yahoo.com. Research: medieval historiography and geo-ethnography, medieval education.

Lu, Emily Qiyan. Johnson City, TN. Affil: East Tennessee State. Email: lueq01@etsu.edu.

Lu, Hanchao, *Georgia Inst. of Tech.* Email: hanchao.lu@hts.gatech.edu.

Lu, Lex Jing, *Clark.* Worcester, MA. Email: lexlu@ clarku.edu. Research: beauty and masculinity, Chinese physiognomy.

Lu, Ling-Pei. Taipei, Taiwan. Email: lulingp@ gm.scu.edu.tw. Research: secession movement, Old South.

Lu, Louis Yi. Cambridge, MA. Affil: Harvard. Email: lu02@g.harvard.edu.

Lu, Sidney Xu, *Michigan State.* Email: slu@msu. edu.

Lu, Soo Chun, *Indiana, Pa.* Email: sclu@iup.edu.

Lu, Weijing, *California, San Diego.* Email: w1lu@ ucsd.edu.

Lu, Yan, *New Hampshire, Durham.* Email: yan.lu@ unh.edu.

Lubamersky, Lynn T., *Boise State.* Email: llubame@boisestate.edu.

Lubar, Steven D., *Brown.* Email: Steven_Lubar@ Brown.edu.

Lubenow, William C., *Stockton.* Email: william. lubenow@stockton.edu.

Lubick, George M., *Northern Arizona.* Email: george.lubick@nau.edu.

Lublin, Elizabeth Dorn, *Wayne State.* Email: aj8580@wayne.edu.

Lubotzky, Asher. Bloomington, IN. Affil: Indiana. Email: asijanlu@gmail.com.

Lubrano, David John. Fairfax, VA. Affil: George Mason. Email: Tmansbestbuddy@Yahoo.com. Research: US presidents, Gilded Age.

Luby, Brittany, *Guelph.* Email: brittany.luby@ uoguelph.ca.

Luca, Francis X., *Florida International.* Email: lucaf@fiu.edu.

Lucas, M. Philip, *Cornell Coll.* Email: plucas@ cornellcollege.edu.

Lucas, Marion B., *Western Kentucky.* Email: marion.lucas@wku.edu.

Lucas, Paul, *Clark.*

Lucas, Robert, *Willamette.* Email: rlucas@ willamette.edu.

Lucas, Wendy E., *Central Arkansas.* Email: wendyc@uca.edu.

Lucci, Diego. Blagoevgrad, Bulgaria. Affil: American, Bulgaria. Email: dlucci@aubg.edu.

Luchetti, Patricia J. Pittston, PA. Email: trishl69@ hotmail.com.

Lucibello, Alan J., *Seton Hall.* Morris Plains, NJ. Email: alan.lucibello@shu.edu; alucib2869@ aol.com. Research: Western civilization.

Luck, Patrick F., *Columbus State.* Email: luck_ patrick@columbustate.ed.

Lucker, Amy Ellen. Brooklyn, NY. Affil: Rutgers, Newark. Email: luckeramy@gmail.com.

Luckett, Thomas M., *Portland State.* Email: luckettt@pdx.edu.

Luckhardt, Courtney L., *Southern Mississippi.* Email: courtney.luckhardt@usm.edu.

Lucky, Jared. Stamford, CT. Affil: Yale. Email: jared.lucky@yale.edu.

Lucky, Nathan. Vancouver, BC, Canada. Email: nathanlucky@protonmail.com.

Lucsko, David N., *Auburn.* Email: dnl0006@ auburn.edu.

Ludden, David E., *NYU.* New York, NY. Email: del5@nyu.edu. Research: inter-Asian connections, empire and globalization.

Ludmerer, Ken, *Washington, St. Louis.* Email: kludmere@wustl.edu.

Luebbert, Patsy, *State Hist. Soc. of Missouri.* Email: LuebbertP@shsmo.org.

Luebke, David M., *Oregon.* Email: dluebke@ uoregon.edu.

Luebke, Frederick C., *Nebraska, Lincoln.* Email: fredluebke@comcast.net.

Luecke, Mirelle G. Mystic, CT. Affil: Mystic Seaport Museum. Email: mgluecke@gmail. com. Research: waterfront communities/ precarious labor, sailor art/art and identity.

Luesink, David N. Pittsburgh, PA. Affil: Pittsburgh. Email: luesink@pitt.edu. Research: modern China, medicine.

Luethi, Lorenz Martin, *McGill.* Montreal, QC, Canada. Email: lorenz.luthi@mcgill.ca; lorenz_luthi@yahoo.com. Research: Cold War, Sino-Soviet relations.

Luff, Jennifer D. Durham, United Kingdom. Affil: Durham. Email: jennifer.luff@durham. ac.uk. Research: US and UK radicalism and antiradicalism, US and UK political development.

Lufrano, Richard, *Graduate Center, CUNY; Staten Island, CUNY.* Email: richard.lufrano@csi.cuny. edu.

Luft, David S., *California, San Diego.* Corvallis, OR. Affil: Oregon State. Email: david.luft@ oregonstate.edu. Research: modern Germany and Austria, modern European intellectual.

Luhr, Eileen S., *California State, Long Beach; Soc. for Hist. Education.* Email: eileen.luhr@csulb. edu.

Lui, Mary T., *Yale.* Email: mary.lui@yale.edu.

Lukashevich, Stephen, *Delaware.*

Lukasiewicz, Mariusz. Leipzig, Germany. Affil: Leipzig. Email: mariusz.Lukasiewicz@uni-leipzig.de.

Luke, Ivan T., *Naval War Coll.* Email: ivan.luke@ usnwc.edu.

Lukes, Igor, *Boston Univ.* Email: lukes@bu.edu.

Lukic, Mark. Bronx, NY. Affil: Purchase, SUNY. Email: marklukich95@gmail.com.

Lumans, Valdis O., *South Carolina Aiken.* Email: vall@usca.edu.

Lumba, Allan, *Virginia Tech.* Ann Arbor, MI. Affil: Michigan, Ann Arbor. Email: lumba@umich. edu. Research: money, authority.

Lummus, Wesley, *St. Thomas, Minn.* Email: lumm2160@stthomas.edu.

Lunbeck, Elizabeth, *Harvard (Hist. of Science).* Cambridge, MA. Email: lunbeck@fas.harvard. edu. Research: women and gender, psychiatry and medicine.

Lund, Carl A. Dickinson, ND. Affil: Dickinson State. Email: carllund@gmail.com. Research: education.

Lundberg, Caitlyn. Corning, CA. Email: lundbergc@gmail.com. Research: First Anglo-Afghan War.

Lundberg, James M., *Notre Dame.* Email: jlundbe1@nd.edu.

Lundeen, Erik. Robinson, TX. Affil: Baylor University. Email: lundeen9@gmail.com. Research: Biblical exegesis, Christian Hebraism.

Lundgren, Burden. Norfolk, VA. Email: blundgren1@alumni.jhu.edu. Research: yellow fever epidemics, health profession regulation.

Lundin, Matthew D., *Wheaton, Ill.* Email: matthew.lundin@wheaton.edu.

Lundy, Phoebe, *Boise State.*

Lungerhausen, Matthew R. Winona, MN. Affil: Winona State. Email: mlungerhausen@ winona.edu. Research: photography and society in east central Europe, Antarctica and science.

Luo, Di, *Alabama, Tuscaloosa.* Email: dluo10@ ua.edu.

Luo, Weiwei, *Grinnell.* Email: luoweiwei@ grinnell.edu.

Luo, Yilan. University Park, PA. Affil: Penn State. Email: yul788@psu.edu.

Luongo, F. Thomas, *Tulane.* New Orleans, LA. Email: tluongo@tulane.edu. Research: religion in medieval Italian cities, image and text in medieval manuscripts.

Luongo, Katherine A., *Northeastern.* Email: k.luongo@neu.edu.

Lupo, Ann, *SUNY, Buffalo State.* Email: lupoak@ buffalostate.edu.

Lupo, Lindsey, *Point Loma Nazarene.* Email: lindseylupo@pointloma.edu.

Lupo, Michael Scott, *California State, Sacramento.* Email: sac69485@csus.edu.

Lupold, John S., *Columbus State.* Email: lupold_ john@columbusstate.edu.

Lupovitch, Howard, *Wayne State.* Detroit, MI. Email: hlupovitch@wayne.edu. Research: Jews of Budapest 1686-1868, cholera epidemic of 1831.

Luquer, **Karone**, *Charleston*. Email: luquerk@ cofc.edu.

Luria, Keith P., *North Carolina State*. Raleigh, NC. Email: keithluria@ncsu.edu. Research: religious coexistence and conflict, early modern Europe.

Lurie, **David Barnett**, *Columbia (Hist.)*. Email: dbl11@columbia.edu.

Lurie, Evan. Palo Alto, CA. Affil: Stanford. Email: evlurie@stanfordalumni.org.

Lurie, Jonathan, *Rutgers, Newark/New Jersey Inst. of Tech*. Piscataway, NJ. Email: jlurie@ scarletmail.rutgers.edu. Research: American military, Civil War and Reconstruction.

Lurie, Maxine N., *Seton Hall*. Piscataway, NJ. Email: maxine.lurie@shu.edu. Research: New Jersey, American Revolution.

Lurtz, Casey M., *Johns Hopkins (Hist.)*. Baltimore, MD. Email: clurtz1@jhu.edu. Research: 19th-c rural development, 19th-c economic.

Luse, **Christopher Allen**, *Mississippi*. Email: caluse@olemiss.edu.

Luskey, **Brian Patrick**, *West Virginia*. Email: brian.luskey@mail.wvu.edu.

Lussier, Vincent. San Marcos, CA. Affil: California State, San Marcos. Email: lussi001@cougars. csusm.edu.

Lustig, **Mary Lou**, *West Virginia*. Email: MaryLou. Lustig@mail.wvu.edu.

Luthman, **Johanna A.**, *North Georgia*. Email: johanna.rickman@ung.edu.

Lutjens, **Richard Newton**, **Jr.**, *Texas Tech*. Email: richard.lutjens@ttu.edu.

Lutts, Ralph H. Meadows of Dan, VA. Affil: Virginia Tech. Email: rhlutts@swva.net. Research: racial violence in American environmental history, place in environmental history.

Lutz, Christopher H. Cambridge, MA. Affil: Maya Educational Foundation. Email: chris.lutz@ me.com. Research: Guatemala conquest and indigenous resistance, urban land use in Spanish Guatemala.

Lutze, **Thomas D.**, *Illinois Wesleyan*. Email: tlutze@iwu.edu.

Lux, **Maureen**, *Brock*. Email: mlux@brocku.ca.

Ly, **Aliou**, *Middle Tennessee State*. Email: Aliou. Ly@mtsu.edu.

Lyandres, **Semion**, *Notre Dame*. Email: Lyandres.1@nd.edu.

Lybeck, Marti M., *Wisconsin-La Crosse*. St Paul, MN. Email: lybeck.mart@uwlax.edu; martilybeck@gmail.com. Research: German female homosexuality 1890-1933, romantic love and film/Weimar era.

Lydon, **Ghislaine E.**, *UCLA*. Email: lydon@ history.ucla.edu.

Lyerly, Cynthia Lynn, *Boston Coll*. Chestnut Hill, MA. Email: lyerly@bc.edu. Research: Thomas Dixon, first great awakening.

Lyftogt, **Kenneth L.**, *Northern Iowa*. Email: ken. lyftogt@uni.edu.

Lynch, **Jennifer**, *Central Oklahoma*. Email: jlynch3@uco.edu.

Lynch, Katherine A., *Carnegie Mellon*. Pittsburgh, PA. Email: kl18@andrew.cmu.edu. Research: charity and poor relief, family.

Lynch, **Kathleen**, *Folger Inst.* Email: klynch@ folger.edu.

Lynch, Michael J., *III*. Pine Bluff, AR. Affil: Arkansas, Pine Bluff. Email: lynchm@uapb. edu.

Lynch, **Michael L.**, *Lincoln Memorial*. Email: michael.lynch02@lmunet.edu.

Lynch, **Ryan Joseph**, *Columbus State*. Email: lynch_ryanj@columbusstate.edu.

Lynch, **Shawn M.**, *Assumption*. Email: slynch@ assumption.edu.

Lynch, **William**, *Wayne State*. Email: ae8917@ wayne.edu.

Lynch-Brennan, Margaret E. Latham, NY. Email: mlynchbrennan@gmail.com. Research: Irish domestic servants 1840-1930, Irish immigrants 1840-1930.

Lynd, Hilary Rybeck. Meriden, NH. Affil: California, Berkeley. Email: hilary.lynd@ berkeley.edu.

Lynk, Beth A. Virginia Beach, VA. Email: blynk1@ cox.net. Research: King-Crane Commission, Balfour Declaration.

Lynn, **Denise Marie**, *Southern Indiana*. Email: dmlynn1@usi.edu.

Lynn, Jennifer M. Billings, MT. Affil: Montana State, Billings. Email: jennifer.lynn1@ msubillings.edu. Research: Weimar Germany visual, women and gender.

Lynn, Jennifer, *California, Santa Cruz*. Email: jklynn@ucsc.edu.

Lynn, Joshua A., *Eastern Kentucky*. Richmond, KY. Email: joshua.lynn@eku.edu; josh1854@gmail. com. Research: antebellum/Civil War political culture, political thought.

Lynn, Kimberly. Bellingham, WA. Affil: Western Washington. Email: Kimberly.Lynn@wwu.edu. Research: Spain 1500-1700, Inquisition and religious.

Lynn, Michael R. Westville, IN. Affil: Purdue Northwest, Westville. Email: mlynn@pnw.edu. Research: ballooning in Europe 1783-1820, irrational in Age of Enlightenment.

Lynn-Sherow, Bonnie, *Kansas State*. Email: blynn@ksu.edu.

Lyon, Gregory B. Asheville, NC. Affil: North Carolina, Asheville. Email: greglyon@alumni. princeton.edu. Research: Reformation historical thought and method, early modern utopias.

Lyon, Jonathan Reed, *Chicago*. Chicago, IL. Email: jlyon@uchicago.edu. Research: medieval politics and society, Holy Roman Empire.

Lyon, Vernon F. New Orleans, LA. Email: vfl@ lyonfirm.com.

Lyon-Jenness, Cheryl, *Western Michigan*. Email: cheryl.lyon-jenness@wmich.edu.

Lyons, **Amelia H.**, *Central Florida*. Email: Amelia. Lyons@ucf.edu.

Lyons, **Clare A.**, *Maryland, Coll. Park*. Email: clyons@umd.edu.

Lyons, Laurence A. Foley, AL. Affil: West Florida. Email: Historylal@aol.com. Research: military communications, military medicine.

Lyons, Molly. Vesta, MN. Email: mollymlyons@ gmail.com. Research: Richard III.

Lyons, **Stephen M.**, *Allegheny*. Email: slyons@ allegheny.edu.

Lyons-Barrett, **Mary**, *Nebraska, Omaha*. Email: mlyonsbarrett@msn.com.

Lytle Hernandez, Kelly, *UCLA*. Email: hernandez@history.ucla.edu.

Lytton, **Randolph H.**, *George Mason*. Email:

Lyu, Zheng. Houston, TX. Email: lv.zheng1990@ gmail.com.

M m

Ma, **Chiemi**, *Bellevue*. Email: chiemi.ma@ bellevuecollege.edu.

Ma, **Haiyun**, *Frostburg State*. Email: hma@ frostburg.edu.

Ma, **Ling**, *SUNY, Coll. Geneseo; Washington State, Pullman*. Email: mal@geneseo.edu; ling.ma@ wsu.edu.

Ma, Marcellin Zhang. Oxnard, CA. Affil: Cornell. Email: mzm23@cornell.edu.

Ma, **Yuxin**, *Louisville*. Email: yuxin.ma@louisville. edu.

Ma, **Zhao**, *Washington, St. Louis*. Email: zhaoma@artsci.wustl.edu.

Maag, **Karin Y.**, *Calvin*. Email: kmaag@calvin. edu.

Maar, Henry Richard, *III*. Simi Valley, CA. Affil: California, Santa Barbara. Email: hrmaar@ gmail.com. Research: nuclear freeze campaign, Catholic Church and Cold War.

Maas, **David E.**, *Wheaton, Ill*. Email: david.maas@ wheaton.edu.

Maas, **Korey**, *Hillsdale*. Email: kmaas@hillsdale. edu.

Maas, Michael R., *Rice*. Houston, TX. Email: maas@rice.edu; maas7@juno.com. Research: ancient Greece and Rome, late Roman Empire and Byzantine.

Maayan, Myriam D. New York, NY. Affil: NYU. Email: myriam.maayan@verizon.net. Research: 20th-/21st-c French intellectuals, postwar European intellectual trends.

Mabie, Chris. Grand Rapids, MI. Email: Christopher@Mabie.net.

Mabli, Peter H. Madison, NJ. Affil: American Social Hist. Project. Email: pmabli@me.com.

MacArthur, **Julie**, *Toronto*. Email: julie. macarthur@utoronto.ca.

Macaulay, Alexander S., *Jr.*, *Western Carolina*. Email: macaulay@email.wcu.edu.

Macauley, Melissa, *Northwestern*. Evanston, IL. Email: m-macauley@northwestern.edu; melissamacauley@yahoo.com. Research: social and legal culture 1600-1949, South China Sea transnational.

Maccaferri, **James T.**, *Clarion, Pa.* Email: jmaccaferri@clarion.edu.

Maccormack, **John R.**, *St. Mary's, Can.*

MacDonald, Adam. Issaquah, WA. Affil: Seattle Academy of Arts and Sci. Email: amacdonald@ seattleacademy.org.

MacDonald, **Heidi E.**, *New Brunswick*. Email: heidimacdonald@unb.ca.

MacDonald, Mairi S. Toronto, ON, Canada. Affil: Toronto. Email: mairi.macdonald@utoronto. ca. Research: independence of Guinea, scramble for Africa.

MacDonald, **Michael**, *Michigan, Ann Arbor*. Email: mmacdon@umich.edu.

MacDonald, **Monica**, *Dalhousie*. Email: mmmacdonald@eastlink.ca.

MacDonald, Robert L. Las Vegas, NV. Affil: Southern Nevada. Email: robert.macdonald@ csn.edu.

MacDougall, **Heather**, *Waterloo*. Email: hmacdoug@uwaterloo.ca.

MacDougall, **Robert**, *Western Ontario*. Email: rmacdou@uwo.ca.

MacDowell, **Laurel S.**, *Toronto*. Email: laurel. macdowell@utoronto.ca.

Mace, Darryl C., *Cabrini*. Email: mace@cabrini. edu.

MacEachern, Alan, *Western Ontario*. Email: amaceach@uwo.ca.

Macekura, Stephen, *Indiana*. Bloomington, IN. Email: smacekur@indiana.edu. Research: US and world, global political economy.

MacFarlane, John D. W., *National Defence Headquarters*. Email: john.macfarlane@forces. gc.ca.

MacFarlane, Kelly, *Alberta*. Email: kelly. macfarlane@ualberta.ca.

MacGiollabhui, Muiris. Santa Cruz, CA. Affil: California, Santa Cruz. Email: mmacgiol@ucsc. edu.

MacGonagle, Elizabeth L., *Kansas*. Email: macgonag@ku.edu.

Macgregor, David, *St. John Fisher*. Email: dmacgregor@sjfc.edu.

MacGugan, Joanna Adele Huckins. Worcester, MA. Affil: Connecticut, Storrs. Email: johuckins@gmail.com. Research: late medieval Dublin and colonization, space and landscape.

Macha, Richard S. North Royalton, OH.

Machado, Barry, *Washington and Lee*.

Machado, Pedro A., *Indiana*. Email: pmachado@ indiana.edu.

Machen, Emily A., *Northern Iowa*. Email: emily. machen@uni.edu.

Maciag, Drew. Rochester, NY. Email: drewhist@ frontiernet.net. Research: conservative and liberal traditions, rise and fall of modern American culture.

Maciak, James. Beverly, MA. Affil: Masconomet Regional High Sch. Email: j.maciak@comcast. net.

Macias, Anna, *Ohio Wesleyan*.

Macias, Marco A., *Fort Hays State*. Email: m_ macias2@fhsu.edu.

Macias-Gonzalez, Victor M., *Wisconsin-La Crosse*. Email: macias.vict@uwlax.edu.

Maciejko, Pawel, *Johns Hopkins (Hist.)*. Email: pmaciej1@jhu.edu.

Mack, Adam C. Chicago, IL. Affil: Sch. of the Art Inst. of Chicago. Email: amack1@saic.edu. Research: American consumer culture, post-1945 US.

Mack, Christopher J., *SUNY, Oswego*. Email: christopher.mack@oswego.edu.

Mack, Dwayne Anthony, *Berea*. Email: dwayne_ mack@berea.edu.

Mack, Graeme. La Jolla, CA. Affil: California, San Diego. Email: grmack@ucsd.edu.

Mack, Jessica Robin. Princeton, NJ. Affil: Princeton. Email: jrmack@princeton.edu. Research: Univ. Nacional Autónoma de México (UNAM).

Mack, Kenneth W. Cambridge, MA. Affil: Harvard Law Sch. Email: kmack@law.harvard. edu. Research: African American lawyers, 20th-c US political and cultural.

Mack, Phyllis B., *Rutgers*. Email: pmack@ scarletmail.rutgers.edu.

Mack, Preston, Jr. El Lago, TX. Affil: Texas City High Sch. Email: prestonrmackjr@gmail.com.

Mack, Willie J., Jr. Brooklyn, NY. Affil: SUNY, Stony Brook. Email: willie.mack@stonybrook. edu.

Mackay, Christopher S., *Alberta*. Email: csmackay@ualberta.ca.

Mackay, Kathryn Leani, *Weber State*. Ogden, UT. Email: kmackay@weber.edu. Research: Native American, women.

MacKay, Lynn, *Brandon*. Email: mackay@ brandonu.ca.

Mackenney, Richard S., *Binghamton, SUNY*. Email: rmackenn@binghamton.edu.

Mackenzie, Cameron A., *Purdue, Fort Wayne*. Email: mackenzc@pfw.edu.

Mackenzie, Hector, *Carleton, Can*. Email: hector. mackenzie@carleton.ca.

MacKenzie, S. Paul, *South Carolina, Columbia*. Email: mackensp@mailbox.sc.edu.

Mackey, Thomas C., *Louisville*. Louisville, KY. Email: thomasmackey@louisville.edu. Research: Legal, Lincoln.

Mackie, Brendan. Oakland, CA. Affil: California, Berkeley. Email: bmackie@berkeley.edu.

Mackil, Emily M., *California, Berkeley*. Email: emackil@berkeley.edu.

MacKinnon, Aran, *Georgia Coll. and State*. Email: aran.mackinnon@gcsu.edu.

MacKinnon, Elaine McClarnand, *West Georgia*. Email: emcclarn@westga.edu.

MacKinnon, Janice C., *Saskatchewan*. Email: janice.mackinnon@usask.ca.

MacKinnon, Lachlan, *Dalhousie*. Email: lachlan_ mackinnon@cbu.ca.

Mackinnon, Stephen R., *Arizona State*. Tempe, AZ. Email: stephen.mackinnon@asu.edu. Research: modern China.

Mackintosh, Michael Dean. Cherry Hill, NJ. Affil: Temple. Email: m_d_mackintosh@yahoo.com. Research: US, environmental.

Mackintosh, Will, *Mary Washington*. Email: wmackint@umw.edu.

Mack-Shelton, Kibibi V. Orangeburg, SC. Affil: Massachusetts, Boston. Email: kibibi99@ yahoo.com. Research: comparative/southern/ women/African American, social/oral/slavery/ race/family/cultural.

MacLachlan, Colin M., *Tulane*. Email: cmaclac@ tulane.edu.

MacLaren, Bruce, *Eastern Kentucky*. Email: bruce.maclaren@eku.edu.

MacLaren, Ian S., *Alberta*. Email: ian.maclaren@ ualberta.ca.

Maclean, Derryl N., *Simon Fraser*. Email: maclean@sfu.ca.

MacLean, Nancy, *Duke*. Durham, NC. Email: nm71@duke.edu; democracyinchainsthebook@gmail.com. Research: US, US women.

MacLean, Rose, *California, Santa Barbara*. Email: maclean@classics.ucsb.edu.

MacLennan, Carol A., *Michigan Tech*. Email: camac@mtu.edu.

Macleod, David, *Central Michigan*. Email: macle1d@cmich.edu.

MacLeod, Dewar, *William Paterson*. Email: macleodg@wpunj.edu.

MacLeod, James L., *Evansville*. Email: jm224@ evansville.edu.

MacLeod, Maureen C. Union, NJ. Affil: Mercy. Email: macleod.maureen@gmail.com. Research: Napoleonic France, 19th-c Europe.

Macleod, Murdo J., *Florida*. Email: macleodmurd@hotmail.com.

Macleod, Roderick C., *Alberta*. Email: rmacleod@ualberta.ca.

Macmillan, Kenneth R., *Calgary*. Email: macmillk@ucalgary.ca.

Macmillan, Margaret, *Toronto*. Email: margaret. macmillan@utoronto.ca.

MacMullen, Ramsay, *Yale*. Email: ramsay. macmullen@yale.edu.

MacNamara, Trent, *Texas A&M*. College Station, TX. Email: t.macnamara@tamu.edu. Research: cultural / intellectual / social, birth control / popular morality.

MacNeil, Ronald Colin. Shelburne, VT. Affil: Vermont. Email: rmacneil@uvm.edu.

MacPhee, Donald A., *California State, Dominguez Hills*.

Macpherson, Anne, *SUNY, Coll. Brockport*. Brockport, NY. Email: amacpher@brockport. edu. Research: women's politics, popular and elite nationalisms.

Macrakis, Kristie, *Georgia Inst. of Tech*. Email: kristie.macrakis@hts.gatech.edu.

Mactavish, Bruce, *Washburn*. Email: bruce. mactavish@washburn.edu.

Madancy, Joyce A., *Union Coll*. Email: madancyj@union.edu.

Madar, Allison, *Oregon*. Email: amadar@ uoregon.edu.

Madden, Sean C., *California, Pa*. Email: madden@calu.edu.

Madden, Thomas F., *St. Louis*. Email: maddentf@slu.edu.

Maddex, Jack P., Jr., *Oregon*. Email: jmaddex@ uoregon.edu.

Maddock, Shane J. North Easton, MA. Affil: Stonehill. Email: smaddock@stonehill.edu. Research: US nuclear nonproliferation policy, Cold War ideology and culture.

Maddox, Gregory H., *Texas Southern*. Houston, TX. Email: maddox_gh@tsu.edu. Research: Africa, environmental.

Maddox, Melanie C., *Citadel*. Email: mmaddox@ citadel.edu.

Maddox, Richard, *Carnegie Mellon*. Email: maddox@andrew.cmu.edu.

Maddox, Robert J., *Penn State*. Email: rjm5@ psu.edu.

Maddox, Steven M., *Canisius*. Email: maddoxs@ canisius.edu.

Maddux, Thomas R., *California State, Northridge*. Email: thomas.maddux@csun.edu.

Mader, Jodie N. Crestview Hills, KY. Affil: Thomas More. Email: Jodie.Mader@Thomasmore.edu. Research: Boer War 1899-1902.

Madigan, Marjorie E. New York, NY. Affil: Marymount Manhattan. Email: mmadcam@ mac.com.

Madison, James H., *Indiana*. Email: madison@ indiana.edu.

Madison, Julian C., *Southern Connecticut State*. Email: madisonj1@southernct.edu.

Madley, Benjamin, *UCLA*. Email: madley@ history.ucla.edu.

Madokoro, Laura, *Carleton, Can.; McGill*. Email: laura.madokoro@carleton.ca; laura. madokoro@alumni.ubc.ca.

Madrid, Joshua Thomas. Birmingham, United Kingdom. Affil: Birmingham. Email: jmadrid001@regis.edu.

Madsen, David, *Seattle*. Email: dmadsen@ seattleu.edu.

Madsen, Grant, *Brigham Young*. Provo, UT. Email: gmadsen@byu.edu. Research: economic policy and democratic practice, intellectual and political.

Madsen-Brooks, Leslie, *Boise State*. Email: lesliemadsen-brooks@boisestate.edu.

Maes, *Cari W.* Corvallis, OR. Affil: Oregon State. Email: cari.maes@oregonstate.edu. Research: maternal and child health, national identity.

Maffly-Kipp, **Laurie F.**, *Washington, St. Louis.* Email: maffly-kipp@wustl.edu.

Magaya, *Aldrin Tinashe*, *DePauw.* Iowa City, IA. Affil: Iowa. Email: aldrintinashe-magaya@uiowa.edu. Research: Africa.

Magaziner, **Daniel R.**, *Yale.*

Mageli, **Paul D.** Kenmore, NY.

Magilow, **Daniel Howard**, *Tennessee, Knoxville.* Email: dmagilow@utk.edu.

Maginn, *Andrew Wyatt*. Chapel Hill, NC. Affil: Howard. Email: andrew.maginn@bison.howard.edu. Research: French Caribbean, Haiti.

Maginn, **Christopher Robert**, *Fordham.* Email: maginn@fordham.edu.

Maglen, **Krista**, *Indiana.* Email: kmaglen@indiana.edu.

Magliari, *Michael F.*, *California State, Chico.* Chico, CA. Email: mmagliari@csuchico.edu. Research: Indian slavery in American West, California agriculture and politics.

Magnaghi, **Russell M.**, *Northern Michigan.* Email: rmagnagh@nmu.edu.

Magner, **Lois N.**, *Purdue.* Email: magnerln@aol.com.

Magnus, **Shulamit**, *Oberlin.* Email: shulamit.magnus@oberlin.edu.

Magnuson, *Diana L.* Saint Paul, MN. Affil: Bethel, Minn. Email: d-magnuson@bethel.edu. Research: US census of population.

Magnuson, *Lynnea*. Saint Louis, MO. Affil: Soldiers Memorial Military Museum. Email: magnusonl@stlouis-mo.gov. Research: gender and Manifest Destiny expansion, gender/politics/imperialism.

Magnusson, **Andrew**, *Central Oklahoma.* Email: amagnusson@uco.edu.

Magnusson, **Roberta**, *Oklahoma (Hist.).* Email: rmagnusson@ou.edu.

Magnusson, *Sigurdur Gylfi*. Reykjavik, Iceland. Affil: Reykjavik Academy. Email: sigm@akademia.is.

Magocsi, **Paul R.**, *Toronto.*

Magra, *Christopher P.*, *Tennessee, Knoxville.* Knoxville, TN. Email: cmagra@utk.edu. Research: Manufacturing, Slavery.

Magruder, **Kerry V.**, *Oklahoma (Hist. of Science).* Email: kmagruder@ou.edu.

Maguire, **Matthew W**, *DePaul.* Email: mmaguir3@depaul.edu.

Mah, **Harold**, *Queen's, Can.* Email: hem@queensu.ca.

Mah, *Sara*. Singapore. Email: saraceciliamah@gmail.com.

Mahan, **Terrance L.**, **SJ**, *Loyola Marymount.* Email: tmahan@lmu.edu.

Mahar, *Karen Ward*. Schenectady, NY. Affil: Siena. Email: kmahar@siena.edu. Research: gender and 20th-c corporate culture.

Maharaja, **Gita**, *Duquesne.* Email: maharaja@duq.edu.

Mahdavi-Izadi, **Farid**, *San Diego State.* Email: mahdavi@sdsu.edu.

Maher, **Bernard**, *St. Joseph's.*

Maher, *Neil M.*, *Rutgers, Newark/New Jersey Inst. of Tech.* Newark, NJ. Email: maher@njit.edu. Research: NASA and nature, New Deal conservation.

Maher, *Thomas John*, *Jr*. Bartlett, TN. Affil: Memphis. Email: tmaherjr@aol.com. Research:

American military and diplomatic relations, American involvement in Barbary Wars.

Mahmudlu, *Ceyhun*. Affil: Cornell. Email: ceyhunmahmudlu@gmail.com.

Mahoney, *Barbara*. Wilsonville, OR. Email: tbmahoney@frontier.com.

Mahoney, **Lynn**, *California State, Los Angeles.* Email: Lynn.Mahoney@calstatela.edu.

Mahoney, *Nicole L.* Philadelphia, PA. Affil: Maryland, Coll. Park. Email: nmahoney@umd.edu.

Mahoney, *Olivia*. Chicago, IL. Affil: Chicago Hist. Museum. Email: mahoney@chicagohistory.org. Research: US social/cultural/material culture.

Mahoney, **Timothy R.**, *Nebraska, Lincoln.* Email: tmahoney1@unl.edu.

Mahony, **Mary Ann**, *Central Connecticut State.* Email: mahonym@ccsu.edu.

Mahood, **Linda L.**, *Guelph.* Email: lmahood@uoguelph.ca.

Maidman, **Maynard P.**, *York, Can.* Email: mmaidman@yorku.ca.

Maier, *Arwen Robertson*. Rolling Hills Estates, CA. Email: arwenkrobertson@gmail.com. Research: medieval trade contacts, Sogdian cultural diffusion.

Maier, *Charles S.*, *Harvard (Hist.).* Cambridge, MA. Email: csmaier@fas.harvard.edu. Research: 20th-c Europe, political/economic/social.

Maier, **Clifford F.**, *Northern Michigan.*

Maier, **Donna J. E.**, *Northern Iowa.* Email: donna.maier@uni.edu.

Maier, **Paul L.**, *Western Michigan.* Email: paul.maier@wmich.edu.

Mailer, **Gideon A.**, *Minnesota Duluth.* Email: gamailer@d.umn.edu.

Main, *Gloria L.*, *Colorado, Boulder.* Boulder, CO. Email: gloria.main@colorado.edu. Research: New England 1750-1830, children/childhood/child labor.

Maines, *Rachel Pearl*. Ithaca, NY. Affil: Columbia. Email: rpmaines@gmail.com. Research: safety codes and standards, leisure artisan technologies.

Mainwaring, **W. Thomas**, *Washington and Jefferson.* Email: tmainwaring@washjeff.edu.

Maiorova, **Olga Yevgenyevna**, *Michigan, Ann Arbor.* Email: maiorova@umich.edu.

Mairot, **Mark J.**, *San Diego Mesa.* Email: mairot@ucla.edu.

Maischak, **Lars**. Fresno, CA. Affil: California State, Fresno. Email: lmaischak@csufresno.edu. Research: political economy, world trade.

Maitra Kumar, *Sikandar*. Ann Arbor, MI. Affil: Michigan, Ann Arbor. Email: smkhist@umich.edu.

Maizlish, *Stephen E.*, *Texas, Arlington.* Arlington, TX. Email: maizlish@uta.edu. Research: US antebellum political, US sectional conflict.

Majeska, **George P.**, *Maryland, Coll. Park.* Email: gm5@umail.umd.edu.

Majewski, **John D.**, *California, Santa Barbara.* Email: majewski@history.ucsb.edu.

Major, **George**, *Massachusetts Hist. Soc.* Email: gmajor@masshist.org.

Majstorovic, **Vojin**, *North Texas.* Email: vojin.majstorovic@unt.edu.

Makalani, *Minkah*, *Texas, Austin.* Austin, TX. Email: makalani@austin.utexas.edu. Research: postcolonial Caribbean, black radicalism.

Makdisi, *Ussama S.*, *Rice.* Houston, TX. Email: makdisi@rice.edu. Research: US-Arab relations, sectarianism.

Makela, **Lee A.**, *Cleveland State.* Email: l.makela@csuohio.edu.

Makowski, *Anthony J.* Lansdale, PA. Affil: Delaware County Comm. Coll. Email: amakow1014@aol.com. Research: modern Poland and Germany, Prussian Poland.

Makowski, **Elizabeth M.**, *Texas State.* Email: em13@txstate.edu.

Makowski, **George J.**, *North Alabama.* Email: gjmakowski@una.edu.

Malamud, **Margaret I.**, *New Mexico State.* Email: mmalamud@nmsu.edu.

Malanson, *Jeffrey J.*, *Purdue, Fort Wayne.* Fort Wayne, IN. Email: malansoj@pfw.edu. Research: diplomatic, political/popular culture.

Malbin, **Susan L.**, *American Jewish Hist. Soc.* Email: smalbin@ajhs.org.

Malchow, *Howard L.* Somerville, MA. Affil: Tufts. Email: howard.malchow@tufts.edu. Research: postwar British youth culture, ethnicity/sexuality/identity.

Malcolm, **Allison**, *Carroll.* Email: amalcom@carrollu.edu.

Malcolmson, **Robert W.**, *Queen's, Can.* Email: malcolms@queensu.ca.

Malczewski, *Joan*, *California, Irvine.* Irvine, CA. Email: jmalczew@uci.edu. Research: philanthropy and education, American political development.

Malczycki, **W. Matt**, *Auburn.* Email: malczycki@auburn.edu.

Malebranche, *Mark Roy*, *II*. Whittier, CA. Affil: Palomar. Email: Mark.Malebranche@gmail.com. Research: Hessian mercenaries in America.

Malefakis, **Edward E.**, *Columbia (Hist.).* Email: eem1@columbia.edu.

Malegam, **Jehangir Yezdi**, *Duke.* Email: jehangir.malegam@duke.edu.

Malena, **Sarah L.**, *St. Mary's, Md.*

Maletz, *Matt*. Roslindale, MA. Affil: Northern Illinois. Email: mattmaletz@hotmail.com. Research: public education in Guatemala, Huelga de Dolores.

Malgouri, *Harrouna*. Lincoln, NE. Affil: Nebraska, Lincoln. Email: harrouna.malgouri@fulbrightmail.org.

Malherek, *Joseph*. Blooming Prairie, MN. Email: malherek@gwmail.gwu.edu. Research: US cultural/political/business/social, immigration/capitalism/economy.

Malhotra, **Anshu**, *California, Santa Barbara.* Email: anshumalhotra@ucsb.edu.

Malik, **Salahuddin**, *SUNY, Coll. Brockport.* Email: smalik@brockport.edu.

Malikov, **Yuriy A.**, *SUNY, Oneonta.* Email: yuriy.malikov@oneonta.edu.

Malin, *Gwynneth C.* Brooklyn, NY. Affil: NYU. Email: gwynnethmalin@gmail.com. Research: 19th-c New York, water.

Malino, *Frances*. Brookline, MA. Affil: Wellesley. Email: fmalino@wellesley.edu. Research: 19th-/20th-c Jewish women teachers, Alliance Israelite Universele.

Malka, **Adam C.**, *SUNY, Buffalo; Oklahoma (Hist.).* Email: adammalk@buffalo.edu; acmalka@ou.edu.

Malkin, *Tia E.*, *West Chester.* Email: tmalkin-fo@wcupa.edu.

Malko, Victoria A. Fresno, CA. Affil: California State, Fresno. Email: vmalko@csufresno.edu. Research: social/cultural/military/women, Eastern Europe/Americas/World.

Mallampalli, Chandra S., *Westmont*. Santa Barbara, CA. Email: mallampa@westmont.edu. Research: colonial Indian religion/law/politics, non-Western Christianity.

Mallary, Michael D. Panama City, FL. Affil: American Sch. Hong Kong. Email: mmallary64@gmail.com.

Mallett, Derek R., *US Army Command Coll.* Email: derek.r.mallett.civ@mail.mil.

Mallon, Florencia E., *Wisconsin-Madison*. Email: femallon@wisc.edu.

Mallon, Grace. Oxford, United Kingdom. Affil: Oxford. Email: grace.mallon@univ.ox.ac.uk.

Malloy, Anne E., *Salem State*. Email: anne.malloy@salemstate.edu.

Malloy, Girard J., *SUNY, Maritime Coll.* Email: gmalloy@sunymaritime.edu.

Malloy, James A., Jr., *American*. Email: malloyjimm@aol.com.

Mally, Lynn, *California, Irvine*. Email: lmally@uci.edu.

Maloba, Wunyabari O., *Delaware*. Newark, DE. Email: maloba@udel.edu. Research: modern Africa, Kenya.

Malone, Bill C., *Tulane*.

Malone, Carolyn A., *Ball State*. Email: camalone@bsu.edu.

Malone, Carolyn M., *Southern California*. Email: cmalone@usc.edu.

Malone, Grettel C. San Diego, CA. Email: charmaine@aggienetwork.com. Research: WWII, Civil War.

Malone, Kevan Quinn. San Diego, CA. Affil: California, San Diego. Email: kqmalone@ucsd.edu. Research: suburbanization, immigration.

Malone, Robert J. Notre Dame, IN. Affil: Hist. of Science Soc. Email: jay@hssonline.org. Research: autobiography in science, planter naturalists.

Maloney, Joan M., *Salem State*. Email: joan.maloney@salemstate.edu.

Maloney, Michael, *New York State Archives*. Email: michael.maloney@nysed.gov.

Maloney, Sean M., *Royal Military*. Email: sean.maloney@rmc.ca.

Malsberger, John W., *Muhlenberg*. Email: malsberg@muhlenberg.edu.

Maltby, William S., *Missouri–St. Louis*. Email: maltbyw@msx.umsl.edu.

Maltempi, Anne. Tallmadge, OH. Affil: Akron. Email: am210@zips.uakron.edu.

Malventano, Amy Justine. Florence, KY. Email: amy.j.canon@gmail.com.

Man, Simeon, *California, San Diego*. La Jolla, CA. Email: siman@ucsd.edu. Research: Asian American, transnational US.

Manasek, Jared, *Pace*. Email: manasek@pace.edu.

Mancall, Mark, *Stanford*. Email: mmancall@stanford.edu.

Mancall, Peter C., *Southern California*. Los Angeles, CA. Email: mancall@usc.edu. Research: early America, Atlantic world.

Man-Cheong, Iona D., *SUNY, Stony Brook*. Email: Iona.Man-Cheong@stonybrook.edu.

Manchester, Laurie, *Arizona State*. Email: laurie.manchester@asu.edu.

Manchester, Margaret M., *Providence*. Email: mmanch@providence.edu.

Mancia, Lauren E., *Brooklyn, CUNY*. Brooklyn, NY. Email: laurenmancia@brooklyn.cuny.edu. Research: medieval monasticism, medieval devotion.

Mancilla, Brandon Joel. Cambridge, MA. Affil: Harvard. Email: bmancilla@g.harvard.edu.

Mancini, JoAnne Marie. Maynooth, Co. Kildare, Ireland. Affil: Maynooth. Email: JoAnne.Mancini@nuim.ie. Research: art criticism and American modernism, migration and comparative historiography.

Mancini, John, *Towson*. Email: jmancini@towson.edu.

Mancini, Matthew. Saint Louis, MO. Affil: St. Louis. Email: matthewjmancini@mac.com. Research: Tocqueville, prisons.

Mancke, Elizabeth, *New Brunswick*. Fredericton, NB, Canada. Email: emancke@unb.ca. Research: empire and state formation 1450-1800, early modern British America.

Mancuso, Charles, *SUNY, Buffalo State*. Email: mancusc@buffalostate.edu.

Mancuso, Rebecca, *Bowling Green State*. Email: rmancus@bgsu.edu.

Mandala, Elias C., *Rochester*. Email: elias.c.mandala@rochester.edu.

Mandel, Maud S., *Williams*. Williamstown, MA. Email: msm8@williams.edu. Research: Jews and Muslims in postwar France.

Mandell, Daniel R., *Truman State*. Email: dmandell@truman.edu.

Manela, Erez, *Harvard (Hist.)*. Cambridge, MA. Email: manela@fas.harvard.edu. Research: Wilsonian Moment, 20th-c international relations.

Maner, Brent E., *Kansas State*. Email: maner@ksu.edu.

Manes, Yael, *Agnes Scott*. Email: ymanes@agnesscott.edu.

Maness, Lonnie E., *Tennessee, Martin*. Email: lmaness@utm.edu.

Maney, Patrick J., *Boston Coll.* Email: patrick.maney@bc.edu.

Maney, Paul, *Appalachian State*. Email: maneyp@appstate.edu.

Mangan, Jane E., *Davidson*. Davidson, NC. Email: jamangan@davidson.edu. Research: Iberian world family/law/culture, Africans in Potosi.

Manganaro, Christine. Baltimore, MD. Affil: Maryland Inst. Coll. of Art. Email: christinemanganaro@gmail.com. Research: race and science, Hawai'i.

Mangrum, Robert G. Early, TX. Affil: Howard Payne. Email: rmangrum@hputx.edu. Research: Howard Payne Univ.

Manion, Jen. Cambridge, MA. Affil: Amherst. Email: manionjen@gmail.com. Research: gender and sexuality, early America.

Manke, John Andrew. Saint Paul, MN. Affil: Minnesota, Twin Cities. Email: johnamanke@gmail.com.

Mankins, Sacha. Cambridge, MA. Email: mankins@simmons.edu.

Manley, Elizabeth S., *Xavier, La.* New Orleans, LA. Email: emanley1@xula.edu. Research: Dominican Republic, gender and authoritarian government.

Manley, Rebecca, *Queen's, Can.* Email: manleyr@queensu.ca.

Mann, Brian, *Eastern Illinois*.

Mann, Bruce H. Cambridge, MA. Affil: Harvard Law Sch. Email: mann@law.harvard.edu. Research: credit and debt, law and society.

Mann, Bryan, *Texas State*. Email: bm30@txstate.edu.

Mann, Gregory, *Columbia (Hist.)*. Email: gm522@columbia.edu.

Mann, Holly Marie, *SUNY, Oswego*. Email: holly.mann@oswego.edu.

Mann, Jakob. Johnson City, TN. Email: mannjakob@gmail.com.

Mann, John W. W., *Wisconsin-Eau Claire*. Eau Claire, WI. Email: mannjw@uwec.edu. Research: America, public.

Mann, Kristin Dutcher, *Arkansas, Little Rock*. Little Rock, AR. Email: kdmann@ualr.edu. Research: mission music, northern New Spanish popular culture.

Mann, Kristin, *Emory*. Email: histkm@emory.edu.

Mann, Michelle R., *Washington State, Pullman*. Email: michelle.mann@wsu.edu.

Mann, Susan Louise, *California, Davis*. Email: slmann@ucdavis.edu.

Mann, William, *Central Connecticut State*. Email: williammann@ccsu.edu.

Manna, Monique S. Southbridge, MA. Affil: Worcester State. Email: mmanna@worcester.edu. Research: Massachusetts industrialization.

Mannard, Joseph G., *Indiana, Pa.* Email: jmannard@iup.edu.

Manney-Kalogera, Myrsini. Tucson, AZ. Affil: Arizona. Email: mmanneykalogera@email.arizona.edu.

Manning, Chandra Miller, *Georgetown*. Email: cmm97@georgetown.edu.

Manning, Christopher E., *Loyola, Chicago*. Email: cmannin@luc.edu.

Manning, Jody R., *Rowan*. Email: manningj@rowan.edu.

Manning, Joseph G., *Yale*. Email: joseph.manning@yale.edu.

Manning, Patrick, *Pittsburgh*. Pittsburgh, PA. Email: pmanning@pitt.edu; ahamanning@gmail.com. Research: demography of African slavery, global historiography.

Manning, Roger B., *Cleveland State*. Email: r.manning@csuohio.edu.

Mannion, Patrick. St. John's, NL, Canada. Affil: Memorial, Newfoundland. Email: patrick.mannion@utoronto.ca. Research: Irish diaspora, Irish nationalism.

Mansfield, Julia P. R. New Haven, CT. Affil: Yale. Email: julia.mansfield@yale.edu. Research: yellow fever in the Americas.

Mansker, Andrea N., *South*. Email: amansker@sewanee.edu.

Manson, Douglas. Flushing, NY. Affil: CUNY. Email: dmanson@qc.cuny.edu.

Manson, Janet M. Portland, OR. Affil: Clemson. Email: jmanson1914@gmail.com. Research: US, modern Europe.

Mansoor, Peter R., *Ohio State; Soc. for Military Hist.* Email: mansoor.1@osu.edu.

Mansour, Ibrahim. Belle Mead, NJ. Affil: California, Santa Barbara. Email: ibrahim@ucsb.edu.

Mansur, Abed H., *Indiana State*.

Mantena, Rama S., *Illinois, Chicago*. Chicago, IL. Email: rmantena@uic.edu. Research: public sphere.

Mantilla, **Luis-Felipe**, *South Florida, St. Petersburg*. Email: lfm1@mail.usf.edu.

Manuel-Scott, **Wendi N.**, *George Mason*. Email: wmanuels@gmu.edu.

Manzione, **Joseph A.**, *Concord*. Email: manzionej@concord.edu.

Mao, **Joyce**, *Middlebury*. Email: jmao@middlebury.edu.

Maor, **Naama**. Chicago, IL. Affil: Chicago. Email: naamam@uchicago.edu.

Mapes, **Christopher David**. Nashville, TN. Affil: Vanderbilt. Email: christopher.mapes@fulbrightmail.org.

Mapes, **Kathleen Anne**, *SUNY, Coll. Geneseo*. Email: mapes@geneseo.edu.

Mapes, **Lynn G.**, *Grand Valley State*. Email: mapesl@gvsu.edu.

Mapes, **Mary L.**, *SUNY, Coll. Geneseo*.

Maple, **John T**. Oklahoma City, OK. Affil: Oklahoma Christian. Email: john.maple@oc.edu.

Mapp, **Paul W.**, *William and Mary*. Williamsburg, VA. Email: pwmapp@wm.edu. Research: colonial North America, early modern Europe.

Maqque, **Victor**. West Lafayette, IN. Affil: Purdue. Email: vmaqque@purdue.edu. Research: colonial Latin America, modern Latin America.

Mar, **Lisa R.**, *Toronto*. Email: lisa.mar@utoronto.ca.

Marafioti, **Nicole J.**, *Trinity, Tex*. Email: nmarafio@trinity.edu.

Marak, **Andrae M**. University Park, IL. Affil: Governors State. Email: amarak@govst.edu. Research: borderlands/transnational, crime/smuggling/vice.

Marashi, **Afshin**, *Oklahoma (Hist.)*. Email: amarashi@ou.edu.

Marasigan, **Cynthia**, *Binghamton, SUNY*. Email: cmarasig@binghamton.edu.

Maravel, **Alexandra C.**, **Esq.**, *Central Connecticut State*. Email: maravela@ccsu.edu.

March, **Kevin Alan**. Falmouth, MA. Email: marchk94@gmail.com.

Marchand, **Suzanne Lynn**, *Louisiana State*. Baton Rouge, LA. Email: smarch1@lsu.edu; smarchand61@gmail.com. Research: German theology/philology/history, 19th-c art and archaeology.

Marchiel, **Rebecca K.**, *Mississippi*.

Marcinizyn, **John**, *Duquesne*. Email: marcinizynj@duq.edu.

Marcon, **Federico**, *Princeton*. Email: fmarcon@princeton.edu.

Marcum, **Deanna B.**, *National Hist. Center*. Kensington, MD. Affil: Ithaka S+R. Email: dmarcum@marcum.org.

Marcum, **Joseph S**. Middlesboro, KY. Affil: Southeast Kentucky Comm. and Tech. Coll. Email: joe.marcum@kctcs.edu.

Marcus, **Abraham**, *Texas, Austin*. Email: amarcus@uts.cc.utexas.edu.

Marcus, **Alan I**, *Iowa State; Mississippi State*. Mississippi State, MS. Email: aimarcus@history.msstate.edu. Research: creation/science of American business, cancer research.

Marcus, **Glenn**. Washington, DC. Affil: Johns Hopkins. Email: gmarcusdc@gmail.com. Research: WWI, nuclear war.

Marcus, **Hannah F.**, *Harvard (Hist. of Science)*. Email: hmarcus@fas.harvard.edu.

Marcus, **Ivan G.**, *Yale*. Email: ivan.marcus@yale.edu.

Marcus, **Kenneth H**. La Verne, CA. Affil: La Verne. Email: kmarcus@laverne.edu. Research: Los Angeles cultural, early modern German social.

Marcus, **Maeva**. Bethesda, MD. Affil: New-York Hist. Soc.; George Washington. Email: maevamarcus1@gmail.com. Research: 18th-c legal and constitutional, US Supreme Court.

Marcuse, **Harold**, *California, Santa Barbara*. Santa Barbara, CA. Email: marcuse@history.ucsb.edu. Research: reception history, museums and ethics education.

Marcy, **William L.**, **IV**, *SUNY, Buffalo State*. Email: marcywl@buffalostate.edu.

Maready, **Aaron**. Redding, CA. Affil: Shasta Comm. Coll. Email: aaron.maready@mycampus.apus.edu.

Mareschal, **Patrice**. Camden, NJ. Affil: Rutgers, Camden. Email: marescha@camden.rutgers.edu.

Margadant, **Jo Burr**, *Santa Clara*. Email: jbmargadant@scu.edu.

Margadant, **Ted W**., *California, Davis*. Davis, CA. Email: twmargadant@ucdavis.edu. Research: summary justice in French Revolution.

Margariti, **Roxani Eleni**, *Emory*. Email: rmargar@emory.edu.

Margerison, **Kenneth H.**, **Jr.**, *Texas State*. San Marcos, TX. Email: kmargerison@txstate.edu. Research: French political culture 1760-90, French colonial policy in India.

Margolf, **Diane C.**, *Colorado State*. Email: diane.margolf@colostate.edu.

Margolis, **Aaron**. Kansas City, KS. Affil: Kansas City Kans. Comm. Coll. Email: amargolis@kckcc.edu.

Margot, **Howard**, *Hist. New Orleans*. Email: howardm@hnoc.org.

Marhoefer, **Laurie**, *Washington, Seattle*. Seattle, WA. Email: marl@uw.edu. Research: Weimar Republic, queer.

Marianetti, **Marie**, *Lehman, CUNY*. Email: marie.marianetti@lehman.cuny.edu.

Mariani, **Paul P.**, *Santa Clara*. Santa Clara, CA. Email: pmariani@scu.edu. Research: Christian missions in China, Catholic Church in modern China.

Mariano, **Isabella**. Pleasanton, CA. Affil: California, Berkeley. Email: sblmariano@gmail.com.

Marietta, **Jack**, *Arizona*. Email: jack-marietta@ns.arizona.edu.

Marietti, **John P.**, *Henry Ford Coll.*

Marilley, **Suzanne M**. Columbus, OH. Affil: Capital. Email: smarille@capital.edu.

Marin, **Craig T**. Providence, RI. Affil: Sea Education Association. Email: ctmarin@gmail.com. Research: Atlantic workers, Atlantic ports social.

Marinari, **Maddalena**, *Gustavus Adolphus*. Email: mmarinar@gustavus.edu.

Mariner, **Capt Rosemary**, *Tennessee, Knoxville*. Email: rmariner@utk.edu.

Marine-Street, **Natalie J**. San Francisco, CA. Affil: Stanford. Email: njmarine@stanford.edu.

Marino, **Katherine Marie**, *UCLA*. Los Angeles, CA. Email: kmarino@history.ucla.edu. Research: women, US social movements.

Marino, **Kelly**, *Central Connecticut State*. Email: kmarino@ccsu.edu.

Marino, **Michael P.**, *New Jersey*. Email: marino@tcnj.edu.

Marinski, **Deborah R.**, *Ohio*. Email: marinski@ohio.edu.

Mariz, **George**, *Western Washington*. Email: George.Mariz@wwu.edu.

Markay, **Jesse B.**, *Sonoma State*.

Markel, **Howard**, *Michigan, Ann Arbor*. Email: howard@umich.edu.

Marker, **Emily**, *Rutgers, Camden*. Camden, NJ. Email: emily.marker@rutgers.edu. Research: late colonial/postcolonial France, Francophone Afro-Atlantic world.

Marker, **Gary J.**, *SUNY, Stony Brook*. Email: gary.marker@stonybrook.edu.

Markham, **Elizabeth**, *Arkansas, Fayetteville*. Email: markham@uark.edu.

Markiewicz, **Gordon J**. Brookfield, CT. Email: uhlan53@hotmail.com. Research: Polish-Soviet War 1919-1920.

Markle, **Seth**, *Trinity Coll., Conn.* Email: seth.markle@trincoll.edu.

Markley, **Jonathan Bruce**, *California State, Fullerton*. Email: jmarkley@fullerton.edu.

Markoe, **Karen E.**, *SUNY, Maritime Coll.* Email: kmarkoe@sunymaritime.edu.

Markovic, **John Jovan**, *Andrews*. Email: jjmarko@andrews.edu.

Markowitz, **Gerald E.**, *Columbia (Hist. Public Health); Graduate Center, CUNY*. New York, NY. Affil: John Jay, CUNY. Email: gmarkowitz@jjay.cuny.edu. Research: occupational and environmental health, public health.

Markowitz, **Norman**, *Rutgers*. Email: markowit@history.rutgers.edu.

Marks, **Claire P.**, *State Hist. Soc. of Missouri*. Email: MarksCP@shsmo.org.

Marks, **John**. Nashville, TN. Affil: American Association for State and Local Hist. Email: johngmarks@gmail.com. Research: free people of color in Atlantic world, comparative race relations.

Marks, **Patricia H**. Princeton, NJ. Affil: Princeton. Email: paramonga@comcast.net. Research: Peru 1700-1825.

Marks, **Robert B.**, *Whittier*. Email: rmarks@whittier.edu.

Marks-Mcrath, **Malik**. Indianapolis, IN. Email: malmark@iu.edu.

Markus, **Michael Hughes**. Montgomery, AL. Affil: Alabama State. Email: michaelmarkus09@gmail.com. Research: 19th-c British politics, 19th-c British foreign relations.

Markwyn, **Abigail M.**, *Carroll*. Email: amarkwyn@carrollu.edu.

Markwyn, **Daniel W.**, *Sonoma State*. Email: daniel.markwyn@sonoma.edu.

Marler, **Scott P.**, *Memphis*. Memphis, TN. Email: spmarler@memphis.edu. Research: New Orleans and Louisiana, merchant capital in Atlantic world.

Marme, **Michael**, *Fordham*. Email: marme@fordham.edu.

Marmon, **Shaun Elizabeth**. Princeton, NJ. Affil: Princeton. Email: marmon@princeton.edu.

Marotta, **Gary M.**, *SUNY, Buffalo State*. Email: marottg@buffalostate.edu.

Marotti, **William**, *UCLA*. Email: marotti@history.ucla.edu.

Maroukis, **Thomas C.**, *Capital*. Email: tmarouki@capital.edu.

Marouti, **Andreh**. Burbank, CA. Email: andre.maroutian@gmail.com.

Marples, **David R.**, *Alberta*. Email: david.marples@ualberta.ca.

Marquardt, Frederick D., *Syracuse*. Email: fdmarqua@gmail.com.

Marques, Nelson Mastracci. Miami, FL. Affil: Miami. Email: nem36@miami.edu.

Marquess, Hollie A., *Fort Hays State*. Email: habailey@fhsu.edu.

Marquez, John C. Urbana, IL. Affil: Illinois, Urbana-Champaign. Email: jcmarqu2@illinois.edu.

Marquez-Osuna, Angelica. Cambridge, MA. Affil: Harvard. Email: marquezosuna@g.harvard.edu.

Marquez-Sterling, Manuel, *Plymouth State*.

Marquis, David Mac. Graham, NC. Affil: William and Mary. Email: djmarquis@email.wm.edu.

Marquis, Dominique, *Québec, Montréal*. Email: marquis.dominique@uqam.ca.

Marquis, Gregory, *New Brunswick*. Email: gmarquis@unbsj.ca.

Marrero, Karen, *Wayne State*. Detroit, MI. Email: bx2389@wayne.edu; karenlmarrero@gmail.com. Research: early Native American, early French American.

Marris, Caroline. Plainsboro, NJ. Affil: Columbia. Email: cfm2123@columbia.edu. Research: early modern Europe.

Marrone, Steven P. Medford, MA. Affil: Tufts. Email: steven.marrone@tufts.edu. Research: High Middle Ages intellectual, rationalization of society 1000-1700.

Marrs, Aaron W., *US Dept. of State*. Washington, DC. Email: awmarrs@gmail.com. Research: US antebellum transportation, US diplomacy with sub-Saharan Africa.

Marrus, Michael R., *Toronto*. Email: michael.marrus@utoronto.ca.

Marsans-Sakly, Silvia, *Fairfield*. Email: smarsans-sakly@fairfield.edu.

Marschall, John P., *Nevada, Reno*. Email: johnm@admin.unr.edu.

Marschall, Wythe. Cambridge, MA. Affil: Harvard. Email: wmarschall@fas.harvard.edu.

Marsden, George M., *Notre Dame*. Email: Marsden.1@nd.edu.

Marsh, Allison, *South Carolina, Columbia*. Email: marsha@mailbox.sc.edu.

Marsh, C.C. Los Angeles, CA. Affil: Getty Research Inst. Email: cmarshc@gmail.com.

Marsh, Dawn G., *Purdue*. Lafayette, IN. Email: dmarsh@purdue.edu. Research: indigenous peoples, global systems.

Marsh, Elisabeth M., *OAH*. Bloomington, IN. Email: emarsh@oah.org. Research: immigration, ethnicity.

Marsh, Kevin R., *Idaho State*. Pocatello, ID. Email: marskevi@isu.edu. Research: groundwater management, urban environment.

Marsh, Margaret S., *Rutgers, Camden*. Haddonfield, NJ. Email: mmarsh@rutgers.edu. Research: women and gender, medicine.

Marsh, Peter T., *Syracuse*. Email: ptmarsh@powernet.co.uk.

Marsh, Sean T. Spartanburg, SC. Affil: South Carolina Upstate. Email: stmarsh@ucdavis.edu. Research: ethnicity and southern frontier in Song China, Song Chinese depictions of maritime Asia.

Marshall, Amani N., *Georgia State*. Email: amarshall@gsu.edu.

Marshall, Amy Bliss, *Florida International*. Email: ammarsha@fiu.edu.

Marshall, Amy. Apex, NC. Email: aemarshallrtc@gmail.com.

Marshall, Anne Elizabeth, *Mississippi State*. Email: amarshall@history.msstate.edu.

Marshall, Byron K., *Minnesota (Hist.)*. Email: marsh004@umn.edu.

Marshall, Christopher, *Metropolitan State*. Email: chris.marshall@metrostate.edu.

Marshall, David B., *Calgary*. Email: marshall@ucalgary.ca.

Marshall, David J., *Elon*. Email: dmarshall@elon.edu.

Marshall, Dominique, *Carleton, Can*. Ottawa, ON, Canada. Email: dominique_marshall@carleton.ca. Research: 20th-c Canada/Africa/Europe/US, humanitarianism/children/rights.

Marshall, James P. Brookline, MA. Affil: WEB Dubois Inst. for African and African American Research. Email: jpbdm19@gmail.com. Research: Mississippi civil rights movement in 1960s, southern civil rights movement in 1960s.

Marshall, Jodie Kay. Jericho, VT. Affil: Michigan State. Email: jodie.kay.marshall@gmail.com.

Marshall, John W., *Johns Hopkins (Hist.)*. Email: jmarsha2@jhu.edu.

Marshall, Jon. Wilmette, IL. Affil: Northwestern. Email: j-marshall@northwestern.edu.

Marshall, Kenneth E., *SUNY, Oswego*. Email: kenneth.marshall@oswego.edu.

Marshall, Lindsay. Norman, OK. Affil: Oklahoma. Email: lindsayerinmarshall@ou.edu. Research: public memory and US history education, horsemanship and indigeneity.

Marshall, Manly Ernest. Charlottesville, VA. Email: emarshallmd@comcast.net.

Marshall, Nicholas Frey. Pittsfield, MA. Affil: Marist. Email: nicholas.marshall@marist.edu. Research: health and writing, material culture.

Marshall, Sherrod Brandon. New York, NY. Affil: Lycee Francais de New York. Email: smarsh1661@gmail.com. Research: diplomacy and culture, France and Venice.

Marshall, Wallace W. Charleston, SC. Email: wmarshall@fminet.com. Research: natural theology, science and religion.

Marsili, Filippo, *St. Louis*. Email: fmarsil1@slu.edu.

Marsilli Cardozo, Maria N., *John Carroll*. Email: mmarsilli@jcu.edu.

Marsot, Afaf, *UCLA*. Email: amarsot@ucla.edu.

Marsters, Roger, *Dalhousie*. Email: roger.marsters@novascotia.ca.

Marszalek, John F., *Mississippi State*. Email: johnmarsz@yahoo.com.

Mart, Michelle A., *Penn State*. Reading, PA. Email: mam20@psu.edu. Research: US chemical pesticides.

Martel, Gordon, *Northern British Columbia*. Email: martel@unbc.ca.

Martel, Heather E., *Northern Arizona*. Email: heather.martel@nau.edu.

Martel, Marcel, *York, Can*. Email: mmartel@yorku.ca.

Martell, Christopher C. Boston, MA. Affil: Massachusetts, Boston. Email: christopher.martell@umb.edu. Research: historical inquiry, culturally relevant pedagogy.

Marten, James A., *Marquette*. Email: james.marten@marquette.edu.

Marten, Jessica Marie. Seekonk, MA. Affil: Massachusetts, Dartmouth. Email: Jm_8210@yahoo.com.

Marti, Donald B., *Indiana, South Bend*. Email: dmarti@iusb.edu.

Martin, A. Lynn. Leabrook, Australia. Affil: Adelaide. Email: lynnmartin1@iprimus.com.au.

Martin, Alexander M., *Notre Dame*. Email: a.m.martin@nd.edu.

Martin, Andrew Joseph. Charlotte, NC. Affil: Gordon-Conwell Theological Seminary. Email: drewjmartin@gmail.com.

Martin, Benjamin F., Jr., *Louisiana State*. Greenville, SC. Email: bmarti9@lsu.edu. Research: modern France, 19th-c Europe.

Martin, Benjamin G. Stockholm, Sweden. Affil: Uppsala. Email: bengmartin@gmail.com. Research: Venice in fascist Italy's 'soft power', cultural treaties in 20th-c Europe.

Martin, Bonnie M. Austin, TX. Affil: Southern Methodist. Email: bonniem@imap.cc. Research: slave mortgages, colonial and antebellum America.

Martin, Bradford D., *Bryant*. Email: bmartin@bryant.edu.

Martin, Brian W. Rockville, MD. Email: bw.martin1401@gmail.com. Research: oil and gas development, business of history.

Martin, Chad A., *Indianapolis*. Email: cmartin@uindy.edu.

Martin, Charles H., *Texas, El Paso*. Email: mcharles@utep.edu.

Martin, Cheryl E., *Texas, El Paso*. El Paso, TX. Email: cmartin@utep.edu. Research: US-Mexico borderlands, 18th-/19th-c political culture.

Martin, Christopher Brenden, *Middle Tennessee State*. Email: Brenden.Martin@mtsu.edu.

Martin, Col Margaret Carol, *US Air Force Acad*. Colorado Springs, CO. Email: margaret.martin@usafa.edu; meggym@aol.com.

Martin, Corinne, *Salem State*. Email: crichard@salemstate.edu.

Martin, Dale, *Montana State, Bozeman*. Email: dlmartin@montana.edu.

Martin, Eliza L. Atlanta, GA. Affil: Texas A&M, Corpus Christi. Email: elizalmartin@gmail.com. Research: water development in southern California, 19th-/20th-c California.

Martin, Elyse, *AHA*. Washington, DC. Email: emartin@historians.org.

Martin, James B., *US Army Command Coll*. Email: james.b.martin1.civ@mail.mil.

Martin, James I., Sr., *Campbell*. Email: martinj@campbell.edu.

Martin, James Kirby, *Houston*. Houston, TX. Email: jmartin@uh.edu. Research: Revolutionary War, smoking in America.

Martin, James W., *Montana State, Bozeman*. Email: jameswm@montana.edu.

Martin, Jamie. Cambridge, MA. Affil: Georgetown. Email: jamie.martin@georgetown.edu. Research: international.

Martin, Janet L. B., *Miami*. Miami, FL. Email: j.martin1@miami.edu. Research: Russia.

Martin, Janice Gunther. Notre Dame, IN. Affil: Notre Dame. Email: jgunther@nd.edu.

Martin, Jay, *Central Michigan*. Email: marti6jc@cmich.edu.

Martin, John Jeffries, *Duke*. Durham, NC. Email: john.j.martin@duke.edu. Research: apocalypticism, Europe and Mediterranean.

Martin, Joseph D. Hammond, IN. Affil: Michigan State. Email: jdmartin@gmail.com. Research: 20th-c solid state physics, 20th-c American science.

Martin, Kevin W., *Georgetown.*

Martin, Kevin, *Hagley Museum and Library.* Email: kmartin@hagley.org.

Martin, Kyle. Dublin, Ireland. Affil: Trinity Coll., Dublin. Email: martinky@tcd.ie.

Martin, Lindsey. Chicago, IL. Affil: Northwestern. Email: lindsey.martin@northwestern.edu.

Martin, Luis, *Southern Methodist.*

Martin, Maj James, *US Military Acad.* Email: James.Martin@usma.edu.

Martin, Michael S., *Louisiana, Lafayette.* Email: docmartin@louisiana.edu.

Martin, Morag, *SUNY, Coll. Brockport.* Email: mmartin@brockport.edu.

Martin, Nathan J., *Charleston Southern.* Email: nmartin@csuniv.edu.

Martin, Phyllis, *Indiana.* Email: martinp@indiana.edu.

Martin, Robert F., *Northern Iowa.* Email: robert.martin@uni.edu.

Martin, Russell Edward, *Westminster.* Hermitage, PA. Email: martinre@westminster.edu. Research: dynastic marriage, death and commemoration.

Martin, Russell L., III. Plano, TX. Affil: DeGolyer Library. Email: rlmartin@mail.smu.edu. Research: bibliography, textual criticism.

Martin, Sara, *Massachusetts Hist. Soc.* Email: saram@masshist.org.

Martin, Scott C., *Bowling Green State.* Email: smartin@bgsu.edu.

Martin, Susan, *Massachusetts Hist. Soc.* Email: smartin@masshist.org.

Martin, Terry D., *Harvard (Hist.).* Email: martin11@fas.harvard.edu.

Martin, Virginia. Monona, WI. Affil: Wisconsin, Madison. Email: vmartin2@wisc.edu. Research: 19th-c Kazakhstan, Russian colonialism.

Martin, Waldo Emerson, Jr., *California, Berkeley.* Berkeley, CA. Email: wmartin@berkeley.edu. Research: civil rights and Black Power, American culture.

Martin, Zachary J., *Salem State.* Email: zmartin@salemstate.edu.

Martindale, Michelle. West Lafayette, IN. Affil: Purdue. Email: mmartind@purdue.edu.

Martinek, Jason D., *New Jersey City.* Jersey City, NJ. Email: jmartinek@njcu.edu. Research: Gilded Age and Progressive Era, cultural.

Martines, Lauro R., *UCLA.* Email: martines@history.ucla.edu.

Martinez, Alberto, *Texas, Austin.* Email: almartinez@austin.utexas.edu.

Martinez, Amanda Marie. Nashville, TN. Affil: UCLA. Email: amamartinez@ucla.edu.

Martinez, Ignacio, Jr., *Texas, El Paso.* El Paso, TX. Email: imartinez26@utep.edu. Research: colonial Mexico, Spanish borderlands.

Martinez, Marta V. Warwick, RI. Affil: Rhode Island Latino Arts. Email: marta@nuestrasraicesri.org. Research: Rhode Island Latino, oral.

Martinez, Miguel. El Paso, TX. Affil: Northwest Early College High Sch. Email: mig400058@gmail.com.

Martinez, Nydia A., *Eastern Washington.* Email: nmartinez9@ewu.edu.

Martinez, Oscar, *Arizona.* Email: oscar-martinez@ns.arizona.edu.

Martinez, Roger Louis, *Colorado Colorado Springs.*

Martinez, Valerie, *Our Lady of the Lake.* Email: vamartinez@ollusa.edu.

Martinez Fernandez, Luis, *Central Florida.* Email: Luis.MartinezFernandez@ucf.edu.

Martinez-Catsam, Ana Luisa, *Texas, Permian Basin.* Email: martinez_a@utpb.edu.

Martinez-Matsuda, Veronica, *Cornell.* Ithaca, NY. Email: vm248@cornell.edu. Research: US Farm Security Admin. migrant labor camps, immigration/migration 1930s-40s.

Martini, Edwin A., III, *Western Michigan.* Email: edwin.martini@wmich.edu.

Martini, Elspeth Ann, *Montclair State.* Worcester, MA. Email: martinie@mail.montclair.edu. Research: US/British Empire indigenous removal 1820s-40.

Martinich, Aloysius, *Texas, Austin.* Email: martinich@mail.utexas.edu.

Martinko, Whitney A., *Villanova.* Email: whitney.martinko@villanova.edu.

Martino, Gina M. Akron, OH. Affil: Akron. Email: gmartino@uakron.edu. Research: women and war in early America.

Martore-Lahm, Simona. Livingston, NJ. Email: simona.martore@gmail.com.

Martucci, Jessica, *Science History Inst.* Email: jmartucci@sciencehistory.org.

Marvin, Laurence W., *Berry.* Mount Berry, GA. Email: lmarvin@berry.edu. Research: Crusades, Fifth Crusade.

Marwil, Jonathan L., *Michigan, Ann Arbor.* Email: jmarwil@umich.edu.

Mas, Catherine, *Florida International.* Email: catherine.mas@fiu.edu.

Masakowski, Yvonne R., *Naval War Coll.* Email: dym46@yahoo.com.

Masarik, Elizabeth Garner. Buffalo, NY. Affil: SUNY, Buffalo. Email: egmasari@buffalo.edu.

Masatsugu, Michael K., *Towson.* Email: mmasatsugu@towson.edu.

Maser, Beth G., *Hist. Assoc.* Email: bmaser@historyassociates.com.

Masghati, Emily. Chicago, IL. Affil: Chicago. Email: emily.masghati@gmail.com.

Maskarinec, Maya, *Southern California.* Email: maskarin@usc.edu.

Maskell, Caleb J. D., *American Soc. of Church Hist.* Media, PA. Email: caleb.maskell@churchhistory.org. Research: American religious, religious identity/imagination/politics.

Maskiell, Nicole Saffold, *South Carolina, Columbia.* Columbia, SC. Email: maskiell@mailbox.sc.edu; nmaskiell@gmail.com. Research: 17th-c Dutch Atlantic slavery, British and Dutch Atlantic slavery.

Maslowski, Peter, *Nebraska, Lincoln.* Email: pmaslowski1@unl.edu.

Masoff, Joy. Litchfield, CT. Affil: Arizona State. Email: JMasoff@asu.edu.

Mason, Addis Xyomara. Portland, ME. Affil: Colby. Email: addis.mason@gmail.com. Research: 19th-c Russian intellectual, national identity.

Mason, Austin, *Carleton Coll.* Northfield, MN. Email: amason@carleton.edu. Research: Cult of the Saints, conversion.

Mason, Brooks. Omaha, NE. Affil: Nebraska, Omaha. Email: rbm31415@gmail.com.

Mason, John B. Ann Arbor, MI.

Mason, John Edwin, Jr., *Virginia.* Email: jem3a@virginia.edu.

Mason, John Paul. Fort Collins, CO. Affil: Wyoming. Email: jmason23@uwyo.edu.

Mason, Kevin George. Buford, GA. Affil: US Army. Email: manchu19@aol.com. Research: Confederate Army of Tennessee, Lt. Gen. von Strachwitz.

Mason, Laura, *Johns Hopkins (Hist.).* Email: lmason@jhu.edu.

Mason, Mary Ann, *Virginia Museum of Hist.* Email: mmason@VirginiaHistory.org.

Mason, Matthew E., *Brigham Young.* Email: matthew_mason@byu.edu.

Mason, Patrick Q., *Utah State.* Email: patrick.mason@usu.edu.

Mason, Thomas A. Indianapolis, IN. Affil: Indiana-Purdue, Indianapolis. Email: thomas.a.mason@comcast.net. Research: Lew Wallace 1827-1905, US 1815-77/Civil War.

Mass, Sarah Merritt, *Sam Houston State.* Email: smm154@shsu.edu.

Masschaele, James P., *Rutgers.* East Brunswick, NJ. Email: massch@rci.rutgers.edu. Research: peasants, states and state formation.

Massell, David P., *Vermont.* Burlington, VT. Email: david.massell@uvm.edu. Research: US-Canada relations, environmental.

Massey, John T. Brooklyn, NY. Affil: Graduate Center, CUNY. Email: JTMassey79@gmail.com. Research: Tudor English Catholics, English Catholic continental seminaries.

Massino, Jill Marie, *North Carolina, Charlotte.* Email: jmassino@uncc.edu.

Masson, Elvira, *New Mexico State.* Email: emasson@nmsu.edu.

Massoth, Katherine Sarah, *Louisville.* Louisville, KY. Email: katherine.massoth@louisville.edu. Research: women and gender, US-Mexican borderlands.

Mast, Herman W., III, *Connecticut, Storrs.*

Mastboom, Joyce M., *Cleveland State.* Email: j.mastboom@csuohio.edu.

Mastel, Malena. Saint Paul, MN. Affil: Minnesota, Twin Cities. Email: maste196@umn.edu.

Masten, April F., *SUNY, Stony Brook.* Setauket, NY. Email: april.masten@stonybrook.edu. Research: Irish/African/Native American dance, women/art/labor.

Masters, Bruce, *Wesleyan.* Email: bmasters@wesleyan.edu.

Masterson, Daniel Matthew. Annapolis, MD. Affil: US Naval Academy. Email: masterdanster@gmail.com. Research: Latin America, American naval.

Masuda, Hajimu. Singapore. Affil: National, Singapore. Email: hm14850@gmail.com. Research: social construction of Cold War, student movements in Asia since 1950.

Masud-Piloto, Felix R., *DePaul.* Email: fmasud-p@depaul.edu.

Masur, Kate, *Northwestern.* Evanston, IL. Email: kmasur@northwestern.edu. Research: African American, urban.

Masur, Louis P., *Rutgers.* Email: louis.masur@rutgers.edu.

Masur, Matthew, *St. Anselm.* Manchester, NH. Email: mmasur@anselm.edu. Research: US-Vietnamese relations, culture and foreign relations.

Masuzawa, Tomoko, *Michigan, Ann Arbor.* Email: masuzawa@umich.edu.

Matar, Nabil, *Minnesota (Hist.).* Email: matar010@umn.edu.

Mataya, Nicholas. San Antonio, TX. Affil: Swansea. Email: nmataya@atonementonline.com. Research: late antique Christianity, late Roman Balkans/Danube.

Mateiro, Ashley Marie. Miami, FL. Affil: Doral Academy Just Arts & Management. Email: Amate002@fiu.edu. Research: southern Africa, Lusophone Africa.

Matenaer, James Michael. Steubenville, OH. Affil: Franciscan, Steubenville. Email: jmatenaer@franciscan.edu. Research: medieval scripture commentaries, medieval universities.

Matera, Marc, *California, Santa Cruz*. Santa Cruz, CA. Email: mmatera@ucsc.edu. Research: black European studies, race/gender/imperialism.

Materson, Lisa G., *California, Davis*. Davis, CA. Email: lgmaterson@ucdavis.edu. Research: women and politics.

Mather, I. Roderick, *Rhode Island*. Email: rodmather@uri.edu.

Matherne, Max. Philadelphia, PA. Affil: Tennessee, Knoxville. Email: mcmatherne@gmail.com.

Mathew, Johan, *Rutgers*. New Brunswick, NJ. Email: johan.mathew@rutgers.edu. Research: Indian Ocean, capitalism.

Mathews, Barbara A., *Smith*. Hadley, MA. Affil: Historic Deerfield. Email: mathews.ba@gmail.com. Research: early American labor and servitude, African Americans in rural New England.

Mathews, Donald G., *North Carolina, Chapel Hill*. Email: dgmathew@bellsouth.net.

Mathews, Linda. San Marcos, CA. Affil: California State, San Marcos. Email: mathe026@cougars.csusm.edu.

Mathews-Benham, Sandra K., *Nebraska Wesleyan*. Email: smathews@nebrwesleyan.edu.

Mathewson, Jon. Middletown Springs, VT. Affil: Dorset Hist. Soc. Email: jonm@vermontel.net.

Mathias, Christine. London, United Kingdom. Affil: King's Coll., London. Email: christine.mathias@kcl.ac.uk. Research: conquest of the Gran Chaco 1870-1955, international investments of Samuel Colt.

Mathieu, Edward C. Rockford, IL. Affil: Rockford. Email: eccm62@live.com. Research: political culture in imperial Germany, modernity in imperial Germany.

Mathieu, Sarah-Jane, *Minnesota (Hist.)*. Email: smathieu@umn.edu.

Mathis, Amanda L. Florence, AL. Affil: Muscle Shoals High Sch. Email: amandy324@gmail.com.

Mathis, Robert N., *Stephen F. Austin State*. Nacogdoches, TX. Email: rmathis@sfasu.edu. Research: southern antislavery, white racial attitudes in Old South.

Mathisen, Erik. London, United Kingdom. Affil: Kent. Email: erik_mathisen@me.com. Research: 19th-c slavery and emancipation, Civil War and Reconstruction.

Mathisen, Ralph W., *Illinois, Urbana-Champaign*. Email: ralphwm@illinois.edu.

Mathur, Nameeta, *Saginaw Valley State*. Email: nmathur@svsu.edu.

Matin-asgari, Afshin, *California State, Los Angeles*. Email: amatina@calstatela.edu.

Matis, Hannah W. Alexandria, VA. Affil: Virginia Theological Seminary. Email: hmatis@vts.edu. Research: early medieval church, Carolingian.

Matkin-Rawn, Story L., *Central Arkansas*. Email: slmatkinrawn@uca.edu.

Matos Rodriguez, Felix V., *Queens, CUNY*.

Matray, James I., *California State, Chico; New Mexico State*. Email: jmatray@csuchico.edu.

Matro, Katharina. Bethesda, MD. Affil: Stone Ridge Sch. of the Sacred Heart. Email: katharina.matro@gmail.com.

Matson, Cathy, *Delaware; Library Co. of Philadelphia*. Email: cmatson@udel.edu; cmatson@librarycompany.org.

Matson, Robert W., *Pittsburgh, Johnstown*. Email: rmatson@pitt.edu.

Matsubara, Hiroyuki. Yokohama, Kanagawa, Japan. Affil: Rikkyo. Email: hiro-m@rikkyo.ac.jp. Research: political culture, Progressive era.

Matsuda, Matt K., *Rutgers*. Email: mmatsuda@echo.rutgers.edu.

Matsui, John H., *Virginia Military Inst.* Lexington, VA. Email: matsuijh@vmi.edu; matsuigeneris@gmail.com. Research: interracial friendship, politics and American Civil War.

Matsumoto, Valerie J., *UCLA*. Email: matsumot@history.ucla.edu.

Matsumura, Janice, *Simon Fraser*. Email: jmatsumu@sfu.ca.

Matsumura, Wendy Y., *California, San Diego*. Email: wmatsumura@ucsd.edu.

Matsusaka, Yoshihisa Tak. Wellesley, MA. Affil: Wellesley. Email: ymatsusa@wellesley.edu. Research: nationalism and democracy in Japan, Japanese imperialism and China.

Matsushita, Elizabeth. Urbana, IL. Affil: Illinois, Urbana-Champaign. Email: matssht2@illinois.edu.

Matt, Susan J., *Weber State*. Ogden, UT. Email: smatt@weber.edu. Research: consumerism, emotions.

Mattay, Alan. Austin, TX. Affil: Texas, Austin. Email: alan.mattay@utexas.edu. Research: African American families and labor, 19th-c black citizenship and freedom.

Mattern, Susan P., *Georgia*. Email: smattern@uga.edu.

Matteson, C. Kieko, *Hawai'i, Manoa*. Email: cmatteso@hawaii.edu.

Matthee, Rudi, *Delaware*. Email: matthee@udel.edu.

Mattheisen, Donald J. Arlington, MA. Affil: Massachusetts, Lowell. Email: djmattheisen@yahoo.com.

Matthew, Laura E., *Marquette*. Milwaukee, WI. Email: laura.matthew@marquette.edu. Research: Mexicans in colonial Guatemala.

Matthews, Brenda Taylor. Fort Worth, TX. Affil: Texas Wesleyan. Email: btmatthews@txwes.edu. Research: Texas Wesleyan 125th Anniversary, Texas WPA Guidebook.

Matthews, Glenna. Laguna Beach, CA. Email: glenna11@verizon.net. Research: Thomas Starr King.

Matthews, Jean V., *Western Ontario*. Email: jmatthews@california.net.

Matthews, John F., *Yale*. Email: john.matthews@yale.edu.

Matthews, John M., *Georgia State*.

Matthews, Jolie. Evanston, IL. Affil: Northwestern. Email: jolie.matthews@northwestern.edu.

Matthews, Lisa J. Pomona, CA. Affil: Claremont Graduate. Email: lisa.matthews@cgu.edu.

Matthews, Michael A., *Elon*. Email: mmatthews6@elon.edu.

Matthews, Michael, *SUNY, Maritime Coll.*

Matthews, Steven Paul, *Minnesota Duluth*. Email: smatthew@d.umn.edu.

Matthews, Weldon C., *Oakland*. Email: matthews@oakland.edu.

Mattingly, Paul H., *NYU*. Email: phm2@nyu.edu.

Mattran, Gerald C. Springfield, VA. Affil: US Dept. of State. Email: gcm1@uchicago.edu. Research: state legislatures, Lebanon 1875-1975.

Mattson, Kevin M., *Ohio*. Email: mattson@ohio.edu.

Mattson, Vernon E., *Nevada, Las Vegas*.

Mattusch, Carol, *George Mason*.

Matus, Zachary A., *Boston Coll.* Email: matusz@bc.edu.

Matusevich, Maxim, *Seton Hall*. Email: maxim.matusevich@shu.edu.

Matusow, Allen J., *Rice*. Houston, TX. Email: matusow@rice.edu. Research: recent America.

Matysik, Tracie, *Texas, Austin*. Austin, TX. Email: matysik@austin.utexas.edu. Research: modern European intellectual, materialism.

Matytsin, Anton. Gainesville, FL. Affil: Florda. Email: anton.matytsin@gmail.com. Research: early modern France, early modern intellectual.

Matzke, Rebecca Berens. Ripon, WI. Affil: Ripon. Email: matzker@ripon.edu. Research: 19th-c British foreign/naval policy, British Empire.

Mauch, Christof U. Muenchen, Germany. Affil: Ludwig-Maximilians. Email: mauch@lmu.de.

Mauck, Jeffrey, *Texas State*. Email: jm81@txstate.edu.

Mauder, Christian. Leipzig, Germany. Email: cmauder@gwdg.de.

Maugere, Dennis P. Fort Lauderdale, FL. Affil: Broward Comm. Coll.; Cooper City High Sch. Email: maugered@aol.com. Research: CIA covert operations, Kennedy administration.

Maulden, Kristopher. Jefferson City, MO. Affil: Versailles High Sch. Email: kristopher.maulden@gmail.com. Research: midwestern politics, African American/Indian relationships.

Maulucci, Thomas W., *American International*. Springfield, MA. Email: thomas.maulucci@aic.edu. Research: East German documentary films.

Maurer, Daniel, *Austin Peay State*. Email: maurerd@apsu.edu.

Maurer, John H., *Naval War Coll.* Email: john.maurer@usnwc.edu.

Mauriello, Christopher E., *Salem State*. Email: cmauriello@salemstate.edu.

Mausbach, Wilfried. Heidelberg, Germany. Affil: Heidelberg Center for American Studies. Email: wmausbach@hca.uni-heidelberg.de. Research: Transatlantic Allliance/Community, Social Movements.

Mauskopf, Seymour, *Duke*. Email: shmaus@duke.edu.

Maveety, Nancy. New Orleans, LA. Affil: Tulane. Email: nance@tulane.edu.

Mavroudi, Maria, *California, Berkeley*. Email: mavroudi@berkeley.edu.

Maxey, Trent Elliott, *Amherst*. Email: tmaxey@amherst.edu.

Maxon, Robert M., *West Virginia*. Email: Robert. Maxon@mail.wvu.edu.

Maxson, Brian Jeffrey, *East Tennessee State*. Johnson City, TN. Email: maxson@etsu.edu. Research: Italian humanism 1300-1550, European politics 1200-1550.

Maxson, Stanley. Rockville, MD. Email: smaxson@terpmail.umd.edu.

Maxwell, Clarence V. H., *Millersville, Pa.* Email: clarence.maxwell@millersville.edu.

Maxwell, Jaclyn L., *Ohio*. Email: maxwelj1@ohio.edu.

Maxwell, Kenneth R. Devon, United Kingdom. Affil: Harvard. Email: kmaxwell@fas. harvard.edu. Research: Ibero-American Enlightenment, Cold War peripheries during detente.

Maxwell, Lindsey Brooke. Miami, FL. Affil: Gulliver Preparatory Sch. Email: lindseymaxwellphd@gmail.com. Research: Pentecostalism, homeschooling.

Maxwell, Michael P., *McGill*. Email: michael. maxwell@mcgill.ca.

May, Allyson N., *Western Ontario*. Email: amay6@uwo.ca.

May, Elaine Tyler, *Minnesota (Hist.)*. Minneapolis, MN. Email: mayxx002@umn.edu. Research: legacy of Cold War at home, quest for security since WWII.

May, Gary, *Delaware*. Email: garymay@udel.edu.

May, Glenn A., *Oregon*. Email: gmay@uoregon. edu.

May, Gregory. Rapidan, VA. Email: Gmay214@gmail.com.

May, Lary, *Minnesota (Hist.)*. Minneapolis, MN. Email: mayxx001@umn.edu. Research: US, film and popular culture.

May, Martha E., *Western Connecticut State*. Brookfield, CT. Email: mmay89@gmail.com. Research: Abraham Lincoln in popular culture, masculinity in 20th-century US.

May, Philip Raymond. Chicago, IL. Affil: Soc. of Colonial Wars in the State of Illiniois. Email: pmay@philip-may.com.

May, Robert E., *Purdue*. Email: mayr@purdue. edu.

May, Timothy M., *North Georgia*. Email: timothy. may@ung.edu.

May, Vanessa, *Seton Hall*. South Orange, NJ. Email: vanessa.may@shu.edu. Research: women and work, public health and sexuality.

Mayer, Andrew M. Staten Island, NY. Affil: Staten Island, CUNY. Email: historian6596@gmail. com.

Mayer, David N., *Capital*. Email: dmayer@law. capital.edu.

Mayer, H. A. Cambridge, MA. Email: havhmayer@gmail.com. Research: US intellectual 1776-1876.

Mayer, Heather M. Tigard, OR. Affil: Portland Comm. Coll. Email: heather.mayer1@pcc.edu. Research: women and Industrial Workers of the World.

Mayer, Holly A., *Duquesne*. Pittsburgh, PA. Email: mayer@duq.edu. Research: civil-military relations, cultural identity formation.

Mayer, Michael S., *Montana*. Missoula, MT. Email: michael.mayer@mso.umt.edu. Research: Eisenhower and civil rights policy, postwar American culture.

Mayer, Tara, *British Columbia*. Email: tara. mayer@ubc.ca.

Mayeri, Serena. Philadelphia, PA. Affil: Pennsylvania. Email: smayeri@law.upenn.edu. Research: feminism/civil rights/law, marriage and marital status.

Mayers, David A., *Boston Univ*. Email: dmayers@bu.edu.

Mayes, April J., *Pomona*. Email: april_mayes@pomona.edu.

Mayes, David C., *Sam Houston State*. Email: his_dcm@shsu.edu.

Mayes, Keith A., *Minnesota (Hist.)*. Email: mayes@umn.edu.

Mayeux, Sara, *Vanderbilt*. Nashville, TN. Email: sara.mayeux@vanderbilt.edu.

Mayhall, Laura E. Nym. Silver Spring, MD. Affil: Catholic. Email: mayhall@cua.edu. Research: political culture, media.

Mayhan, Maggie, *State Hist. Soc. of Missouri*. Email: mayhanm@shsmo.org.

Mayhew, Anne, *Tennessee, Knoxville*. Email: amayhew@utk.edu.

Maymi, Javier. Tampa, FL. Affil: South Florida, St. Petersburg. Email: javierm1@mail.usf.edu.

Maynard, Haley J. Washington, DC. Affil: National Archives. Email: maynardhj@gmail. com.

Maynard, John A., *California State, Bakersfield*.

Maynard, Kelly J., *Grinnell*. Email: maynardk@grinnell.edu.

Maynard, Linda. Hebden Bridge, United Kingdom. Email: mayleaves12@yahoo.co.uk.

Maynard, Steven, *Queen's, Can.* Email: maynards@queensu.ca.

Maynard, William, *Arkansas State*. Email: wmaynard@astate.edu.

Maynes, MaryJo, *Minnesota (Hist.)*. Minneapolis, MN. Email: mayne001@umn.edu. Research: girlhood in Europe 1750-1920, personal narratives in social sciences.

Mayo, C.M. Wichita Falls, TX. Email: cmmayo@me.com.

Mayo, Marlene J., *Maryland, Coll. Park*. College Park, MD. Email: mmayo@umd.edu. Research: Eleanor Roosevelt/Japan, gender/race/class in occupied Japan.

Mayo-Bobee, Dinah, *East Tennessee State*. Unicoi, TN. Email: mayobobee@etsu.edu. Research: early Republic-Civil War US politics, political biography.

Mayr, Norbert J., *Penn State*. Email: njm5@psu. edu.

Mays, Devi Elizabeth, *Michigan, Ann Arbor*.

Mays, Michael. West Richland, WA. Affil: Washington State. Email: Michael.Mays@wsu. edu.

Mays, Nicholas S., *Baldwin Wallace*. Email: nmays@bw.edu.

Maza, Sarah C., *Northwestern*. Evanston, IL. Email: scm@northwestern.edu. Research: 18th-/19th-c French cultural, 18th-/19th-c French social.

Mazak-Kahne, Jeanine M., *Indiana, Pa.* Email: jmkahne@iup.edu.

Mazenko, Lisa. Meridianville, AL. Email: lmazenko.

Mazis, John A. Saint Paul, MN. Affil: Hamline. Email: jmazis@hamline.edu. Research: civil society in imperial Russia, early 20th-c Greek politics.

Mazower, Mark, *Columbia (Hist.)*. Email: mm2669@columbia.edu.

Mazumdar, Sucheta, *Duke*. Email: skmmaz@duke.edu.

Mazumder, Rajashree, *Union Coll.* Email: mazumder@union.edu.

Mazumder, Rajit K., *DePaul*. Email: rmazumde@depaul.edu.

Mazurek, Lindsey, *Oregon*.

Mazurek, Malgorzata, *Columbia (Hist.)*. Email: mm4293@columbia.edu.

Mazza, Edmund J., *Azusa Pacific*. Email: emazza@apu.edu.

Mazzaoui, Maureen F., *Wisconsin-Madison*. Email: mazzaoui@wisc.edu.

Mazzarella, Mario D., *Christopher Newport*. Email: mazz@cnu.edu.

Mazzotti, Massimo, *California, Berkeley*. Email: mazzotti@berkeley.edu.

Mbah, Emmanuel, *Staten Island, CUNY*. Email: emmanuel.mbah@csi.cuny.edu.

Mbah, Ndubueze Leonard, *SUNY, Buffalo*. Buffalo, NY. Email: ndubueze@buffalo.edu. Research: West Africa gender and masculinity, Atlantic slavery and imperialism.

Mbajekwe, Patrick U. Norfolk, VA. Affil: Norfolk State. Email: pumbajekwe@nsu.edu. Research: Nigerian land/social change/urban development, eastern Nigerian trade and urban growth.

Mbatu, Richard, *South Florida, St. Petersburg*.

M'bayo, Tamba E., *West Virginia*. Email: Tamba. Mbayo@mail.wvu.edu.

Mbodj, Mohamed, *Manhattanville*. Email: Mohamed.Mbodj@mville.edu.

McAdams, Kay L., *York, Pa.* Email: kmcadams@ycp.edu.

McAfee, Ward M., *California State, San Bernardino*. Email: wmcafee@csusb.edu.

McAlhany, Joseph, *Connecticut, Storrs*. Storrs Mansfield, CT. Email: joseph.mcalhany@uconn.edu. Research: Roman Republic, ancient scholarship.

McAllen, Mary Margaret. San Antonio, TX. Affil: Witte Museum. Email: mmmcallen1@gmail. com. Research: Civil War, Mexico.

McAllister, Ryan. New Lenox, IL. Email: rmcall622@gmail.com.

McAllister, Stuart, *Central Oklahoma*. Email: smcallister2@uco.edu.

McAllister, Ted, *Pepperdine*. Email: ted. mcallister@pepperdine.edu.

McAllister, William Brian, *US Dept. of State*.

McAndrew, J. Malia, *John Carroll*. Email: jmcandrew@jcu.edu.

McArdle Stephens, Michele, *West Virginia*. Morgantown, WV. Email: Michele.Stephens@mail.wvu.edu. Research: indigenous peoples of Mexico, Latin America.

McArthur, Aaron J., *Arkansas Tech*. Email: amcarthur2@atu.edu.

McArthur, Gilbert H., *William and Mary*. Email: ghmcar@wm.edu.

McAuley, Christopher, *California, Santa Barbara*. Email: mcauley@blackstudies.ucsb. edu.

McBane, Margo, *San José State*. Email: Margo. McBane@sjsu.edu.

McBee, Randy D., *Texas Tech*. Email: randy. mcbee@ttu.edu.

McBrady, Jared. Cortland, NY. Affil: SUNY, Coll. Cortland. Email: jmcbrady@umich.edu. Research: history education, sotl.

McBriarty, Patrick T. Chicago, IL. Affil: Windy City Historians. Email: patrick_mcbriarty@yahoo.com.

McBride, David, *Penn State*. Email: djm9@psu. edu.

McBride, Genevieve, *Wisconsin-Milwaukee*. Email: gmcbride@uwm.edu.

McBride, Preston. Topanga, CA. Affil: UCLA. Email: preston.s.mcbride@gmail.com.

McBride, Theresa M., *Holy Cross*. Email: tmcbride@holycross.edu.

McBride Scheurer, Heather, *Ball State*. Email: hrscheurer@bsu.edu.

McCaa, Robert E., Jr., *Minnesota (Hist.)*. Email: rmccaa@umn.edu.

McCaffray, Susan P., *North Carolina, Wilmington*. Email: mccaffrays@uncw.edu.

McCaffrey, Cecily M., *Willamette*. Email: cmccaffr@willamette.edu.

McCaffrey, Kevin Michael. Evanston, IL. Affil: Dwight Sch. Email: mccaffreyk@gmail.com.

McCaffrey, Lawrence J., *Loyola, Chicago*. Email: ljpmcc@aol.com.

McCahill, Elizabeth M., *Massachusetts, Boston*. Winchester, MA. Email: elizabeth.mccahill@ umb.edu. Research: Renaissance Rome.

McCall, Elena. Denver, CO. Email: emm.303@ gmail.com.

McCall, Joseph, *Troy*. Email: mccalljo@troy.edu.

McCall, Keith Dennis. Houston, TX. Email: kdm7@rice.edu. Research: postemancipation black migration.

McCall, Stacey. Utica, NY. Affil: Mohawk Valley Comm. Coll. Email: smccall@mvcc.edu.

McCall, Timothy, *Villanova*. Email: timothy. mccall@villanova.edu.

McCalla, Douglas W., *Guelph; Trent*. Guelph, ON, Canada. Email: dmccalla@uoguelph. ca. Research: settlement of Canada to 1939, consumption in colonial society.

McCallum, Jack E. Fort Worth, TX. Affil: Texas Christian. Email: jemmd@swbell.net. Research: Leonard Wood, military medicine.

McCallum, Mary Jane L., *Winnipeg*. Email: m.mccallum@uwinnipeg.ca.

McCallum, Todd, *Dalhousie*. Email: todd. mccallum@dal.ca.

McCambridge, Mairead. Cork, Ireland. Email: maireadmccambridge@gmail.com.

McCandless, Amy Thompson, *Charleston*. Email: mccandlessa@cofc.edu.

McCandless, Jamie, *Kennesaw State*. Email: jmccandl@kennesaw.edu.

McCandless, Perry G., *Central Missouri*.

McCann, Bryan, *Georgetown*. Email: bm85@ georgetown.edu.

McCann, Christine, *Norwich*. Email: cmccann@ norwich.edu.

McCann, Frank D. Durham, NH. Affil: New Hampshire, Durham. Email: monteagleridge@ msn.com. Research: Brazil-US relations, Brazilian military.

McCann, James C., *Boston Univ*. Email: mccann@bu.edu.

McCants, Anne E. C., *MIT*. Cambridge, MA. Email: amccants@mit.edu. Research: early modern Europe, social and economic.

McCarron, Barry. Millburn, NJ. Affil: Georgetown. Email: bm323@georgetown. edu.

McCarthy, Brendan, *Utah Valley*. Orem, UT. Email: Bmccarthy@uvu.edu; bjmccarthy89@ gmail.com. Research: Roman Republic, ancient Mediterranean.

McCarthy, David S. Petersburg, VA. Affil: Richard Bland, William and Mary. Email: dsmcca@

email.wm.edu. Research: Central Intelligence Agency.

McCarthy, Jennifer. Savannah, GA. Affil: Georgia Southern, Armstrong. Email: jennimcc@ yahoo.com.

McCarthy, John, *Fordham*. Email: jmccarthy@ fordham.edu.

McCarthy, Joseph M., *Suffolk*. Middleboro, MA. Email: joemccarthy@suffolk.edu. Research: late medieval education, 19th-/20th-c military.

McCarthy, Justin A., Jr., *Louisville*. Email: jmc@ louisville.edu.

McCarthy, Kate, *Illinois State*. Email: kmccart@ ilstu.edu.

McCarthy, Kathleen D., *Graduate Center, CUNY*. Email: kmccarthy@gc.cuny.edu.

McCarthy, Mark M. Sioux Center, IA. Affil: Dordt. Email: mark.mccarthy@dordt.edu. Research: Russian sectarians.

McCarthy, Peter, *State Hist. Soc. of Missouri*. Email: mccarthyp@shsmo.org.

McCarthy, Robert E., *Providence*.

McCarthy, Tara M., *Central Michigan*. Email: mccar1tm@cmich.edu.

McCarthy, Tom. Annapolis, MD. Affil: US Naval Acad. Email: mccarthy@usna.edu. Research: psychology, higher education, New England.

McCarthy, Tony. Dublin, Ireland. Email: tony@ drynan.ie.

McCartin, James P. Jersey City, NJ. Affil: Fordham. Email: jmccartin1@fordham.edu. Research: US Catholics and sex 1830-1990.

McCartin, Joseph A., *Georgetown*. Email: jam6@ georgetown.edu.

McCartney, Sarah E. Greensboro, NC. Affil: North Carolina, Greensboro. Email: semcca@ wm.edu.

McCarty, Jessica S. Williamsburg, VA. Affil: Old Dominion. Email: jmcca004@odu.edu.

McCarty, Michael B., *Salisbury*. Salisbury, MD. Email: mbmccarty@salisbury.edu; michaelbmccarty@gmail.com. Research: Jokyu Disturbance of 1221.

McCaslin, Richard B., *North Texas*. Email: mccaslin@unt.edu.

McCaughey, Robert A., *Barnard, Columbia*. Email: ram31@columbia.edu.

McCauley, Samuel A. Royersford, PA. Email: smccauley1991@gmail.com.

McClain, James L., *Brown*. Email: James_ McClain@Brown.edu.

McClain, Lisa R., *Boise State*. Email: lmcclain@ boisestate.edu.

McClain, Molly Anne, *San Diego*. Email: mmcclain@sandiego.edu.

McClain, Sunshine Brooke. Garden Grove, CA. Affil: Golden West. Email: smcclain@gwc.cccd. edu.

McClay, Wilfred M., *Oklahoma (Hist.)*. Email: wmcclay@ou.edu.

McCleary, Ann, *West Georgia*. Email: amcclear@ westga.edu.

McCleary, Kristen L., *James Madison*. Charlottesville, VA. Email: mccleakl@jmu. edu; kristenmccleary@gmail.com. Research: Argentine theater, film.

McClellan, Charles W., *Radford*. Email: cmcclell@radford.edu.

McClellan, Woodford, *Virginia*. Email: wdm@ virginia.edu.

McClelland, Charles, *New Mexico*. Email: cemcc@unm.edu.

McClelland, James C., *Nebraska, Lincoln*. Email: jmcclelland@neb.rr.com.

McClelland-Nugent, Ruth E., *Augusta*. Email: rmcclel1@augusta.edu.

McClendon, Muriel C., *UCLA*. Los Angeles, CA. Email: mcclendo@history.ucla.edu. Research: Britain 1485-present.

McClendon, Thomas V., *Southwestern*. Email: mcclendt@southwestern.edu.

McCleskey, Turk, *Virginia Military Inst.* Lexington, VA. Email: mccleskeynt@vmi. edu; turk.mccleskey@gmail.com. Research: debt litigation in colonial Virginia, free black activism before Revolution.

McClive, Cathy, *Florida State*. Email: cmcclive@ fsu.edu.

McCloskey, Deirdre, *Illinois, Chicago*. Email: deirdre2@uic.edu.

McClure, Daniel R., *Chapman; Fort Hays State*. Hays, KS. Email: dmcclure@chapman.edu; drmcclure2@fhsu.edu. Research: US popular culture and economics, African diaspora popular culture.

McClure, Ellen, *Illinois, Chicago*. Email: ellenmc@uic.edu.

McClure, George William, *Alabama, Tuscaloosa*. Email: gmcclure@ua.edu.

McClure, James P., *Princeton*. Princeton, NJ. Email: mcclur@princeton.edu. Research: American Revolution, early Republic.

McClure, John M., *Virginia Museum of Hist.* Email: jmcclure@VirginiaHistory.org.

McClurken, Jeffrey W., *Mary Washington*. Fredericksburg, VA. Email: jmcclurk@umw. edu. Research: Confederate veteran families, postbellum Virginia mental institutions.

McCluskey, Stephen C., *West Virginia*. Email: scmcc@wvu.edu.

McCole, John J., *Oregon*. Email: mccole@ uoregon.edu.

McCollom, Michael. Ashland, OR. Affil: Eagle Point Middle Sch. Email: mccollomm@sou. edu.

McComb, David G., *Colorado State*. Fort Collins, CO. Email: david.mccomb@colostate.edu. Research: sports, world.

McConnell, Eleanor H., *Frostburg State*. Email: ehmcconnell@frostburg.edu.

McConnell, Jen. Buckley, WA. Affil: Annie Wright Sch. Email: jen.mcconnell@outlook.com.

McConnell, Kent Alan. Exeter, NH. Affil: Phillips Exeter Academy. Email: kmcconnell@exeter. edu. Research: American Civil War and Gilded Age, religion and culture.

McConnell, Michael N., *Alabama, Birmingham*. Email: mcconnel@uab.edu.

McConnell, Sean James. Galveston, TX. Affil: Wayne State. Email: as2283@wayne.edu. Research: US-Iranian relations, 20th-c US political.

McConville, Brendan, *Boston Univ*. Email: bmcconv@bu.edu.

McCoog, Thomas M. New York, NY. Affil: Fordham. Email: tmmccoog@gmail.com. Research: Jesuits in 16th-/17th-c England, Jesuits in 1570s.

McCook, Stuart, *Guelph*. Email: sgmccook@ uoguelph.ca.

McCord, Edward A., *George Washington*. Silver Spring, MD. Email: mccord@gwu.edu. Research: militia organization in modern China.

McCord, Theodore B., *George Mason*. Email: tmccord@gmu.edu.

McCormack, Carey Kathleen, *Tennessee, Chattanooga*. Chattanooga, TN. Email: carey-mccormack@utc.edu. Research: botany, indigenous guides.

McCormack, Dawn, *Middle Tennessee State*. Email: Dawn.Mccormack@mtsu.edu.

McCormack, Ross, *Winnipeg*. Email: r.mccormack@uwinnipeg.ca.

McCormack, Suzanne Kelley. Foxborough, MA. Affil: Comm. Coll. of Rhode Island. Email: suzannekmccormack@gmail.com. Research: 20th-c US social, history of madness/mental illness.

McCormick, Charles H. Gaithersburg, MD. Email: chmccor.grd.hist@aya.yale.edu. Research: detective-left radical nexus 1917-40, OSS and use of leftists 1942-45.

McCormick, Gladys I., *Syracuse*. Syracuse, NY. Email: gmccormi@syr.edu. Research: Latin America and Carribean, 19th-/20th-c Mexico.

McCormick, Kelly Midori. Los Angeles, CA. Affil: UCLA. Email: kelly.midorim@gmail.com. Research: Japanese camera corporations, postwar visual and consumer culture.

McCormick, Michael, *Harvard (Hist.)*.

McCormick, Nicholas J., *Elmhurst*. Chicago, IL. Affil: Columbia Coll., Chicago. Email: nick.mccormick@elmhurst.edu; historynick@gmail.com. Research: museums and expositions, maritime.

McCormick, P. Andrew, *Loyola, Md.*

McCormick, Richard L., *Rutgers*. Email: rlm@rutgers.edu.

McCormick, Ted G., *Concordia, Can.* Email: Ted.McCormick@concordia.ca.

McCormick, Thomas J., *Wisconsin-Madison*. Email: tmccormi@wisc.edu.

McCorquodale, Wilmer H. Houston, TX. Email: wil.mccorquodale@bcm.edu. Research: early modern Europe, France.

McCowen, George S., *Willamette*.

McCoy, Alfred William, *Wisconsin-Madison*. Email: awmccoy@wisc.edu.

McCoy, Cameron D. Provo, UT. Affil: Brigham Young. Email: cameron_mccoy@byu.edu. Research: African American Marines, 19th-/20th-c African American soldiers.

McCoy, Drew R., *Clark*. Email: dmccoy@clarku.edu.

McCoy, Kelli Ann, *Point Loma Nazarene*. San Diego, CA. Email: kmccoy@pointloma.edu. Research: Progressive Era social reform, Law and gender.

McCoy, Meredith Leigh, *Carleton Coll.* Email: mmccoy@carleton.edu.

McCoy, Robert R., *Washington State, Pullman*. Email: mccoy@wsu.edu.

McCoy, W. James, *North Carolina, Chapel Hill*. Email: wjmccoy@unc.edu.

McCoyer, Michael T. M., *US Dept. of State*. Washington, DC. Email: mmccoyer@gmail.com. Research: Mexican immigration and racial formation.

McCracken, Julia Anne. Arlington, VA. Affil: Arlington Public Sch. Email: amccrackenva@gmail.com.

McCranie, Kevin D., *Naval War Coll.* Email: kevin.mccranie@usnwc.edu.

McCray, Austin. Baton Rouge, LA. Affil: Louisiana State, Baton Rouge. Email: amccra7@lsu.edu.

McCray, Patrick, *California, Santa Barbara*. Email: pmccray@history.ucsb.edu.

McCrea, Heather L., *Kansas State*. Email: hmccrea@ksu.edu.

McCready, William D., *Queen's, Can.* Email: mccready@queensu.ca.

McCredy, Beverly. Suffolk, VA. Email: bmccredy@gmail.com.

McCreery, David J., *Georgia State*. Email: dmccreery@gsu.edu.

McCreery, Gregory, *South Florida, St. Petersburg*.

McCrillis, Neal R.. Chicago, IL. Affil: Illinois, Chicago. Email: nealrm@uic.edu. Research: Anglo-American relations during WWI, Conservative Party and conservatism.

McCrone, Kathleen E., *Windsor*. Windsor, ON, Canada. Email: kem@uwindsor.ca. Research: English women and music, English women and sport.

McCrossen, Alexis, *Southern Methodist*. Email: amccross@smu.edu.

McCulla, Theresa. Washington, DC. Affil: National Museum of American Hist. Email: mcculla@gmail.com. Research: 19th-/20th-c consumer/material culture, race/ethnicity/gender.

McCullers, Molly L., *West Georgia*. Email: mmcculle@westga.edu.

McCulley, Richard T.. Washington, DC. Affil: National Archives. Email: richardmcculley@gmail.com. Research: US Senate, US House of Representatives.

McCulloh, John M., *Kansas State*. Email: jmmcc@ksu.edu.

McCullough, Kelly A., *German Hist. Inst.* Email: mccullough@ghi-dc.org.

McCullough, Morgan. Williamsburg, VA. Affil: William and Mary. Email: mtmccullough@email.wm.edu.

McCullough, Robert, *Vermont*. Email: robert.mccullough@uvm.edu.

McCune, Mary E., *SUNY, Oswego*. Email: mary.mccune@oswego.edu.

McCurdy, Charles W., Jr., *Virginia*. Email: cwm@virginia.edu.

McCurdy, John Gilbert, *Eastern Michigan*. Email: jmccurdy@emich.edu.

McCurdy, Melinda, *Huntington Library*. Email: mmccurdy@huntington.org.

McCurry, Stephanie, *Columbia (Hist.)*. Email: sm4041@columbia.edu.

McCusker, John J., *Trinity, Tex.* San Antonio, TX. Email: jmccuske@mac.com. Research: early modern Atlantic world economy, early modern Atlantic sugar industry.

McCusker, Kristine M., *Middle Tennessee State*. Email: Kristine.Mccusker@mtsu.edu.

McCutchen, Chad, *Minnesota State, Mankato*. Email: chad.mccutchen@mnsu.edu.

McCutcheon, Jo-Anne, *Canadian Hist. Assoc.* Email: jomac@history2knowledge.ca.

McDaniel, Cecily Barker, *North Carolina A&T State*. Email: cmcdaniel@ncat.edu.

McDaniel, David, *Marquette*. Email: david.mcdaniel@marquette.edu.

McDaniel, Layne, *Appalachian State*. Email: mcdanielml1@appstate.edu.

McDaniel, Marie Basile, *Southern Connecticut State*. New Haven, CT. Email: mcdanielm4@southernct.edu. Research: religious adherence, ethnic perceptions.

McDaniel, W. Caleb, *Rice*. Email: caleb.mcdaniel@rice.edu.

McDannell, Colleen, *Utah*. Email: colleen.mcd@utah.edu.

McDean, Harry C., *San Diego State*. Email: mcdean@sdsu.edu.

McDermott, Kathleen. Cambridge, MA. Affil: Harvard Univ. Press. Email: kathleen_mcdermott@harvard.edu.

McDevitt, Patrick F., *SUNY, Buffalo*. Email: mcdevitt@buffalo.edu.

McDonagh, Eileen L.. Boston, MA. Affil: Northeastern. Email: e.mcdonagh@neu.edu. Research: woman suffrage/women's rights, political development/welfare state.

McDonald, Bryan, *Penn State*. Email: blm26@psu.edu.

McDonald, Christel G.. Arlington, VA. Affil: Inst. for Multi-Track Diplomacy. Email: chrisjohnmcdon@aol.com.

McDonald, Daniel L.. Providence, RI. Affil: Brown. Email: daniel_l_mcdonald@brown.edu.

McDonald, David M., *Wisconsin-Madison*. Email: dmmcdon1@wisc.edu.

McDonald, Jason J., *Truman State*. Email: jasonmcd@truman.edu.

McDonald, Jason. New York, NY. Affil: Grace Church Sch. Email: jmcdonald@gcschool.org. Research: identifying WWII photos and film, book on Battle of Tarawa.

McDonald, Kate, *California, Santa Barbara*. Santa Barbara, CA. Email: kmcdonald@history.ucsb.edu. Research: placemaking in East Asia 1912-52, travel and tourism.

McDonald, Kevin P., *Loyola Marymount*. Email: kevin.mcdonald@lmu.edu.

McDonald, Mary, *Georgia Inst. of Tech.* Email: mary.mcdonald@hts.gatech.edu.

McDonald, Michael John. Boerne, TX. Affil: Texas, San Antonio. Email: viperswimmer@yahoo.com.

McDonald, Michelle Craig, *Stockton*. Email: michelle.mcdonald@stockton.edu.

McDonald, R. Andrew, *Brock*. Email: amcdonal@brocku.ca.

McDonald, Robert M. S., *US Military Acad.* Email: robert.mcdonald@usma.edu.

McDonald, Russell Ryan. Dallas, TX. Email: rmcdonaldhistorian@gmail.com.

McDonald, Terrence J., *Michigan, Ann Arbor*. Ann Arbor, MI. Email: tmcd@umich.edu.

McDonald, Tracy A., *McMaster*. Email: tmcdon@mcmaster.ca.

McDonald-Miranda, Kathryn Anne. Brunswick, OH. Affil: Akron. Email: kam296@zips.uakron.edu. Research: 16th-c Scottish monasteries, power and patronage of Stewart monarchs.

McDonnell, James R., *SUNY, Buffalo State*.

McDonnell, Lawrence T., *Iowa State*. Email: lmcd@iastate.edu.

McDonnell, Michael A.. Sydney, Australia. Affil: Sydney. Email: michael.mcdonnell@arts.usyd.edu.au. Research: revolutionary Virginia and America, Native Americans and Great Lakes.

McDonough, Daniel J., *Tennessee, Martin*. Martin, TN. Email: danmc@utm.edu. Research: Boston under British occupation 1774-76, William Molineaux.

McDonough, Katherine L.. London, United Kingdom. Affil: Alan Turing Inst. Email: kmcdonough@turing.ac.uk. Research: political culture of road construction, archival inventories.

McDonough, Kelly. Austin, TX. Affil: Texas, Austin. Email: kelly.s.mcdonough@gmail.com.

McDonough, Matthew, *Coastal Carolina; US Military Acad.* Email: mmcdonoug@coastal. edu; matthew.mcdonough@usma.edu.

McDonough, Scott J., *William Paterson*. Email: mcdonoughs21@wpunj.edu.

McDonough, Susan Alice, *Maryland, Baltimore County*. Baltimore, MD. Email: mcdonoug@ umbc.edu. Research: witness testimony in civil court records, medieval Marseilles gender relations.

McDonough, Zachary Charles. Reading, PA. Affil: Alvernia. Email: zach.mcdonough82@ gmail.com.

McDorman, Kathryne S., *Texas Christian*. Email: k.mcdorman@tcu.edu.

McDougal, Phoebe, *Hist. Assoc.* Email: pmcdougal@historyassociates.com.

McDougall, Alan, *Guelph*. Email: amcdouga@ uoguelph.ca.

McDougall, E. Ann, *Alberta*. Email: ann. mcdougall@ualberta.ca.

McDougall, Sara. New York, NY. Affil: John Jay, CUNY. Email: sara_mcdougall@hotmail.com. Research: medieval law, family.

McDougall, Walter A., *Pennsylvania*. Email: wamcd@sas.upenn.edu.

McDow, Thomas F., *Ohio State*. Email: mcdow.4@osu.edu.

McDowall, Duncan L., *Carleton, Can.* Email: Duncan.McDowall@Carleton.ca.

McDowell, Matt P. Chicago, IL. Affil: Morgan Park Academy. Email: matthewpmcdowell@ gmail.com.

McDowell, Peter. Los Angeles, CA. Email: peter@ petermcdowell.com.

McDowell, Robin Bo Eun. Cambridge, MA. Affil: Harvard. Email: rmcdowell@g.harvard. edu. Research: early petrochemical history of Louisiana, racial capitalism.

McDuffie, Adam G. Winston-Salem, NC. Affil: Emory. Email: mcduffiea@gmail.com.

McDuffie, Clint. Liberty, MO. Affil: Baker. Email: cmcduffie@bakeru.edu. Research: US reform movements/industrial 1850-1915, US sports/ leisure 1850-1915.

McDuffie, Erik S., *Illinois, Urbana-Champaign*. Email: emcduffi@illinois.edu.

McEachnie, Robert J., *North Carolina, Charlotte*.

McElderry, Andrea L., *Louisville*.

McElroy, Micah D. New York, NY. Affil: Columbia. Email: mdm2200@columbia.edu.

McElya, Micki, *Connecticut, Storrs*. Email: micki. mcelya@uconn.edu.

McEnaney, Laura, *Whittier*. Whittier, CA. Email: lmcenaney@whittier.edu. Research: WWII and postwar, working class/gender/race.

McEneaney, Sinead. Birmingham, United Kingdom. Affil: Open. Email: sinead. mceneaney@open.ac.uk. Research: autobiographies of 1960s activists, women in postwar protest movements.

McEnroe, Sean F., *Southern Oregon*. Ashland, OR. Email: mcenroes@sou.edu. Research: Indigenous leadership in European Empire, Syncretic devotional art in the Americas.

McEvoy, Carmen E., *South*. Email: cmcevoy@ sewanee.edu.

McEwan, Diane, *North Georgia*. Email: diane. mcewan@ung.edu.

McEwan, John. Saint Louis, MO. Affil: St. Louis. Email: john.a.mcewan@gmail.com. Research: digital humanities, medieval London.

McEwen, Britta Isabelle, *Creighton*. Omaha, NE. Email: brittamcewen@creighton.edu. Research: sex reform in Austria 1900-34, eugenics in interwar Europe.

McFadden, David W., *Fairfield*. Email: dmcfadden@fairfield.edu.

McFadden, Robert J. South Hamilton, MA. Affil: Gordon-Conwell Theological Seminary. Email: rj83librarian@verizon.net. Research: church and Reformation, colonial American religious.

McFarland, Gerald W., *Massachusetts, Amherst*. Email: geraldm@history.umass.edu.

McFarland, Keith D., *Texas A&M, Commerce*. Email: keith.mcfarland@tamuc.edu.

McFarland, Kelly M. Alexandria, VA. Affil: Georgetown. Email: kmm426@georgetown. edu. Research: US and Middle East/Yemen/ Iraq/Syria, US and Afghanistan.

McFarland, Patricia G. Oregon City, OR. Affil: Clackamas Comm. Coll. Email: patmc@ clackamas.edu.

McFarland, Stephen L., *North Carolina, Wilmington*. Email: mcfarlands@uncw.edu.

McFarland, Victor Robert, *Missouri, Columbia*. Email: mcfarlandv@missouri.edu.

McFarlane, Larry A., *Northern Arizona*. Email: larry.mcfarlane@nau.edu.

McFarren, Allen, *SUNY, Buffalo State*.

McFayden, Elizabeth M. Chicago, IL. Affil: Illinois, Chicago. Email: emcfay2@uic.edu.

McFillen, Amanda, *Hist. New Orleans*. Email: amandam@hnoc.org.

McGahan, Elizabeth W. Saint John, NB, Canada. Affil: New Brunswick. Email: emcgahan@ nbnet.nb.ca. Research: women religious, 19th-c urban institutions.

McGalliard, Michael. San Diego, CA. Email: mcmcgalliard@gmail.com.

McGandy, Michael J. Ithaca, NY. Affil: Cornell Univ. Press. Email: mjm475@cornell.edu.

McGarr, Kathryn Jane, *Wisconsin-Madison*. Email: kmcgarr@wisc.edu.

McGarrah, Robert E., Jr. Bethesda, MD. Affil: Maryland Legal Aid. Email: robert.mcgarrah@ gmail.com.

McGarry, Molly K., *California, Riverside*. Email: molly.mcgarry@ucr.edu.

McGaughey, Jane G. V., *Concordia, Can.* Montreal, QC, Canada. Email: Jane. McGaughey@concordia.ca. Research: masculinities, Irish Canada.

McGeary, Stephen, *Florida Atlantic*. Email: smcgeary2018@fau.edu.

McGee, David H. Lynchburg, VA. Affil: Central Virginia Comm. Coll. Email: mcgeed@ centralvirginia.edu. Research: Civil War and impact on family/community.

McGee, Holly Y., *Cincinnati*. Email: holly. mcgee@uc.edu.

McGee, J. Sears, *California, Santa Barbara*. Santa Barbara, CA. Email: jsmcgee@history.ucsb. edu. Research: early modern Britain, religious and political.

McGee Deutsch, Sandra F., *Texas, El Paso*. El Paso, TX. Email: sdeutsch@utep.edu. Research: extreme right in politics, Jewish women.

McGerr, Michael E., *Indiana*. Email: mmcgerr@ indiana.edu.

McGetchin, Douglas T., *Florida Atlantic*. Email: dmcgetch@fau.edu.

McGill, Alicia, *North Carolina State*. Email: aemcgill@ncsu.edu.

McGill, Kathy O. Oakton, VA. Affil: George Mason. Email: mcgills1@juno.com. Research: 18th-c travel literature, early British nationalism.

McGillivray, Gillian A., *York, Can.* Email: gmcgilli@glendon.yorku.ca.

McGinn, Thomas A., *Vanderbilt*. Email: thomas.a.mcginn@vanderbilt.edu.

McGinness, Frederick J., *Mount Holyoke*. Email: mcginnes@mtholyoke.edu.

McGinnis, Katherine Tucker. Winston Salem, NC. Email: ktmcginn@live.unc.edu. Research: 16th-c Italian dancing masters/manuals, professionalism/court life and patronage.

McGirr, Lisa, *Harvard (Hist.)*. Email: lmcgirr@fas. harvard.edu.

McGlade, Jacqueline, *Penn State*. Email: jam838@psu.edu.

McGlocklin, James Nathan. New Hope, AL. Affil: Athens State. Email: lntnathanm@gmail.com.

McGlynn, Margaret, *Western Ontario*. Email: mmcglyn@uwo.ca.

McGough, Patrick, *Queens, CUNY*. Email: mcgoughs@optonline.net.

McGovern, Bryan P., *Kennesaw State*. Email: bmcgover@kennesaw.edu.

McGovern, Charles F., *William and Mary*. Email: cfmcgo@wm.edu.

McGovern, Constance, *Frostburg State*.

McGovern, Jeffrey. APO, AE. Affil: US Air Force. Email: jtmcgove@gmail.com.

McGowan, Abigail, *Vermont*. Burlington, VT. Email: amcgowan@uvm.edu. Research: South Asia, India.

McGowan, Mark G., *St. Mary's, Can.; Toronto*. Email: mark.mcgowan@utoronto.ca.

McGowen, Randall E., *Oregon*. Email: rmcgowen@uoregon.edu.

McGrath, Ann Margaret. Canberra, Australia. Affil: Australian National. Email: ann. mcgrath@anu.edu.au.

McGrath, Elena C., *Carleton Coll.* Northfield, MN. Email: emcgrath@carleton.edu. Research: Latin America, revolutionary movements.

McGrath, Kate E., *Central Connecticut State*. Email: mcgrathkae@ccsu.edu.

McGrath, Patrick. Hong Kong. Affil: Hong Kong. Email: mcgrath85@gmail.com. Research: Catholic/religion, immigration/ethnicity.

McGrath, Stamatina F. Centreville, VA. Affil: George Mason. Email: vasileus@aol.com. Research: hagiography, women and literature.

McGrath, Stephen, *Central Connecticut State*. Email: mcgraths@ccsu.edu.

McGraw, Eva. New York, NY. Affil: Graduate Center, CUNY. Email: mcgraw.eva@gmail.com.

McGraw, Jason Peter, *Indiana*. Bloomington, IN. Email: jpmcgraw@indiana.edu. Research: Colombia popular politics, postemancipation circum-Caribbean.

McGreevey, Robert C., *New Jersey*. Email: mcgreeve@tcnj.edu.

McGreevy, Erin Elizabeth. Middletown, NJ. Affil: PNC Bank, NA. Email: eem426@nyu.edu. Research: The Troubles in Northern Ireland, Irish-American connections with Ireland.

McGreevy, John T., *Notre Dame*. Notre Dame, IN. Email: Mcgreevy.5@nd.edu. Research: US religious and intellectual, urban.

McGregor, Andrew. Texarkana, TX. Affil: Texas A&M, Texarkana. Email: admcgregor3@gmail.com.

McGregor, Deborah, *Illinois, Springfield*.

McGregor, Robert K., *Illinois, Springfield*. Email: mcgregor.robert@uis.edu.

McGrew, Roderick E. Estes Park, CO. Affil: Temple. Research: Europe and French Revolution, Russian economic 1780-1850.

McGuinness, Aims C., III, *Wisconsin-Milwaukee*. Email: smia@uwm.edu.

McGuinness, Margaret M. Philadelphia, PA. Affil: La Salle. Email: mcguinness@lasalle.edu. Research: US women religious, American Catholicism.

McGuire, Elizabeth A., *California State, East Bay*. Email: elizabeth.mcguire@csueastbay.edu.

McGuire, Heather, *George Mason*. Email: hmcguir@gmu.edu.

McGuire, Melissa M., *California State, San Marcos*. Email: mmcguire@csusm.edu.

McGuire, Michael Edward, *Salem State*. Email: mmcguire@salemstate.edu.

McGuire, Michael J. Olympia, WA. Affil: Brandman. Email: mcguire@brandman.edu.

McHale, Shawn F., *George Washington*. Email: mchale@gwu.edu.

McHugh, William F. Chicago, IL.

McInerney, Daniel J., *Utah State*. Logan, UT. Email: daniel.mcinerney@usu.edu. Research: American intellectual, antebellum US.

McInneshin, Michael T., *St. Joseph's*.

McInnis, Edward C., *Louisville*. Email: ecmcin02@louisville.edu.

McIntosh, Marjorie K., *Colorado, Boulder*. Email: marjorie.mcintosh@colorado.edu.

McIntosh, Terence V., *North Carolina, Chapel Hill*. Chapel Hill, NC. Email: terence_mcintosh@unc.edu. Research: Lutheran clergy in Germany 1550-1806, early Enlightenment in Germany.

McIntosh, Whitney A. New York City, NY. Affil: Columbia. Email: wam2134@columbia.edu.

McIntyre, James K., *Hist. Assoc*. Email: jmcintyre@historyassociates.com.

McIntyre, Kathleen M. Providence, RI. Affil: Rhode Island. Email: kamcintyre@uri.edu. Research: indigenous rights and suffrage in Mexico, Protestantism in Latin America.

McIntyre, Lee. Seattle, WA. Email: leemcintyre@clfoto.net.

McIntyre, Sheila M., *SUNY, Coll. Potsdam*. Email: mcintysm@potsdam.edu.

McIntyre, Stephen L., *Missouri State*. Email: stephenmcintyre@missouristate.edu.

McJimsey, George T., *Iowa State*.

McKay, Ian G., *McMaster*. Dundas, ON, Canada. Email: mckayi@mcmaster.ca; imckay2@cogeco.ca. Research: heritage/history-making/tourism, left.

McKay, Joanne. Mount Olive, NC. Affil: Mount Olive. Email: jmckay@umo.edu.

McKay, Richard A. London, United Kingdom. Affil: Cambridge. Email: ram78@cam.ac.uk. Research: North American AIDS epidemic, venereal disease and homosexuality.

McKean, Matthew, *Carleton, Can*. Email: matthew.mckean@carleton.ca.

McKee, Christopher, *Grinnell*. Email: mckee@grinnell.edu.

McKee, Elizabeth, *Coastal Carolina*. Email: elmckee@coastal.edu.

McKee, Francis, *La Salle*. Email: mckeef@lasalle.edu.

McKee, Guian A., *Virginia*. Email: gam2n@virginia.edu.

McKee, James W., Jr., *East Tennessee State*.

McKee, Sally, *California, Davis*. Email: sjmckee@ucdavis.edu.

McKellar, Shelley, *Western Ontario*. Email: smckell@uwo.ca.

McKenna, Joseph, *California, Irvine*. Email: mckenna@uci.edu.

McKenna, Katherine Rose. Nashville, TN. Affil: Vanderbilt. Email: katherine.r.mckenna@vanderbilt.edu. Research: 17th-c Venetian women's writing.

McKenna, Katherine, *Western Ontario*. Email: kmckenna@uwo.ca.

McKenna, Rebecca Tinio, *Notre Dame*. Email: rtmckenna@nd.edu.

McKenna, Thomas J., *Concord*. Email: tjmckenna@concord.edu.

McKenzie, Beatrice L., *Beloit*. Email: mckenzie@beloit.edu.

McKenzie, Francine, *Western Ontario*. Email: fmckenzi@uwo.ca.

McKenzie, Matthew G., *Connecticut, Storrs*. Email: matthew.mckenzie@uconn.edu.

McKenzie, R. Tracy, *Wheaton, Ill*. Email: tracy.mckenzie@wheaton.edu.

McKeown, James S. Wilkes Barre, PA. Affil: Holy Redeemer High Sch.; Penn State, Wilkes Barre. Email: jsm15@psu.edu. Research: American Indians/governmental relations, Col. Return J. Meigs.

McKercher, Brian J. C., *Royal Military*. Email: mckercher-b@rmc.ca.

McKerley, John William, *Iowa*. Email: john-mckerley@uiowa.edu.

McKevitt, Andrew C., *Louisiana Tech*. Email: mckevitt@latech.edu.

McKiernan, Siobhan, *Hist. New Orleans*. Email: siobhanm@hnoc.org.

McKiernan-Gonzalez, John, *Texas State*. Email: jrm259@txstate.edu.

McKillen, Elizabeth A., *Maine, Orono*. Orono, ME. Email: mckillen@maine.edu. Research: labor and foreign relations.

McKillip, James Duncan, *National Defence Headquarters*. Email: james.mckillip@forces.gc.ca.

McKillop, A. Brian, *Carleton, Can*. Email: brian.mckillop@carleton.ca.

McKinley, Michelle. Eugene, OR. Affil: Oregon. Email: michelle@uoregon.edu. Research: public international law, Latin American legal.

McKinley, Shepherd W., *North Carolina, Charlotte*. Email: swmckinl@uncc.edu.

McKinney, Charles W., Jr., *Rhodes*. Email: mckinneyc@rhodes.edu.

McKinney, Gordon B., *Berea*. Email: gordon_mckinney@berea.edu.

McKinnon, Garrett Dale. Durham, NC. Affil: Duke. Email: garrett.mckinnon@duke.edu.

McKinnon, Jennifer F., *East Carolina*. Email: mckinnonje@ecu.edu.

McKinnon, Mike. Janesville, WI. Email: mckinnon0628@aol.com.

McKinstry, Kenji. Pismo Beach, CA. Affil: California Polytechnic State. Email: kenjimckinstry@ucla.edu.

McKisick, Derrick Duane, *Texas A&M, Commerce*. Commerce, TX. Email: Derrick.McKisick@tamuc.edu. Research: 19th-c US, African American.

McKitrick, Frederick L., *Monmouth*. West Long Branch, NJ. Email: fmckitri@monmouth.edu. Research: modern Germany, modern France.

McKittrick, Meredith K., *Georgetown*. Email: McKittrick@georgetown.edu.

McKiven, Henry M., *South Alabama*. Email: hmckiven@southalabama.edu.

McKnight, Marianne Fellows. Salt Lake City, UT. Affil: Salt Lake Comm. Coll. Email: marianne.mcknight@slcc.edu. Research: US cultural, political philosophy.

McKnight, Stephen A., *Florida*. Email: smcknigh@ufl.edu.

McLain, Owen Thomas. Birmingham, AL. Email: Owentmclain@gmail.com.

McLain, Robert, *California State, Fullerton*. Email: rmclain@fullerton.edu.

McLain, Steven. Beaverton, OR. Email: Mclainst@yahoo.com. Research: Monroe Doctrine and regional security, conservative transitions in US.

McLane, John R., *Northwestern*. Email: jockmcl@northwestern.edu.

McLarnon, John Morrison, III, *Millersville, Pa*. Email: john.mclarnon@millersville.edu.

McLauchlan, Judithanne Scourfield, *South Florida, St. Petersburg*. Email: jsm2@usfsp.edu.

McLaughlin, Kenneth, *Waterloo*. Email: kmclaughlin@uwaterloo.ca.

McLaughlin, Leanna. Fort Worth, TX. Affil: California, Riverside. Email: leanna.h.mclaughlin@gmail.com. Research: dissemination of political ideologies, political poetry.

McLaughlin, Mark J., *Maine, Orono*. Email: mark.j.mclaughlin@maine.edu.

McLaughlin, Sean J., *Murray State*.

McLaughlin, Tiggy. Erie, PA. Affil: Gannon. Email: mclaughl040@gannon.edu. Research: late antique Christianity, early medieval popular culture.

McLaurin, Melton A., *North Carolina, Wilmington*. Email: mclaurinm@uncw.edu.

McLean, Eden Knudsen, *Auburn*. Auburn, AL. Email: ekmclean@auburn.edu. Research: relationship between racism and fascism, political uses of elementary education.

McLees, Bozena Nowicka. Chicago, IL. Affil: Loyola, Chicago. Email: bmclees@luc.edu.

McLeister, Kyle, *Saskatchewan*. Email: kyle.mcleister@usask.ca.

McLennan, Rebecca, *California, Berkeley*. Email: mclennan@berkeley.edu.

McLeod, Devon Anotnio. Portsmouth, VA. Email: dmcle757@gmail.com.

McLeod, Jane A, *Brock*. Email: jmcleod@brocku.ca.

McLeod, John E., *Louisville*. Email: john.mcleod@louisville.edu.

McLeod, Jonathan W., *San Diego Mesa*. San Diego, CA. Email: jmcleod@sdccd.edu. Research: politics of public higher education, community colleges.

McLeod, Marc C., *Seattle*. Email: mcleodm@seattleu.edu.

McLeod, Mark W., *Delaware*. Email: mwm@udel.edu.

McLingberg, Lawrence. San Marcos, CA. Affil: California State, San Marcos. Email: mclin003@cougars.csusm.edu.

McLochlin, Dustin, *Bowling Green State*. Email: DMcLochlin@rbhayes.org.

McLoughlin, Nancy A., *California, Irvine*. Email: nmclough@uci.edu.

McMahon, Cian T., *Nevada, Las Vegas*. Las Vegas, NV. Email: cian.mcmahon@unlv.edu. Research: Irish migration, national and racial identities.

McMahon, Darrin M., *Dartmouth*. Hanover, NH. Email: dmcmahon@dartmouth.edu. Research: French Revolution, European Enlightenment.

McMahon, Eileen, *Lewis*. Email: mcmahoei@lewisu.edu.

McMahon, Elisabeth M., *Tulane*. New Orleans, LA. Email: emcmahon@tulane.edu. Research: South and East Africa, North and West Africa.

McMahon, J. Gregory, *New Hampshire, Durham*. Email: gregory.mcmahon@unh.edu.

McMahon, Kate Elizabeth. Baltimore, MD. Affil: Howard. Email: kemcmahon@mac.com. Research: African diaspora in Atlantic world, people of African descent and maritime.

McMahon, Lucia, *William Paterson*. Email: mcmahonlu@wpunj.edu.

McMahon, Michal, *West Virginia*. Email: Michal.McMahon@mail.wvu.edu.

McMahon, Robert J., *Ohio State*. Columbus, OH. Email: mcmahon.121@osu.edu. Research: US diplomatic.

McMahon, Sarah F., *Bowdoin*. Email: smcmahon@bowdoin.edu.

McMahon, Timothy G., *Marquette*. Email: timothy.g.mcmahon@marquette.edu.

McManamon, John M., *SJ, Loyola, Chicago*. Email: jmcmana@luc.edu.

McManus, Brendan J., *Bemidji State*. Email: brendan.mcmanus@bemidjistate.edu.

McManus, Edgar J., *Queens, CUNY*. Email: edgar.mcmanus@qc.cuny.edu.

McManus, John, *Missouri Science and Tech*. Email: mcmanusj@mst.edu.

McManus, Sheila M. Lethbridge, AB, Canada. Affil: Lethbridge. Email: sheila.mcmanus@uleth.ca. Research: North American West borderlands, race/gender/sexuality.

McMath, Robert C., Jr., *Arkansas, Fayetteville*. Email: bmcmath@uark.edu.

McMeeken, Frances. Alpine, CA. Affil: Grossmont. Email: frances.mcmeeken@gcccd.edu.

McMeekin, Sean A., *Bard*. Email: mcmeekin@bard.edu.

McMillen, Christian W., *Virginia*. Email: cwm6w@virginia.edu.

McMillen, Neil R., *Southern Mississippi*. Email: nmcmillen@aol.com.

McMillen, Ryan J. Brooklyn, NY. Affil: New York City Coll. of Tech., CUNY. Email: rmcmillen@citytech.cuny.edu. Research: spaceflight, American religion and technology.

McMillen, Sally G., *Davidson*. Email: samcmillen@davidson.edu.

McMillian, John C., *Georgia State*. Email: jmcmillian@gsu.edu.

McMillin, Linda A., *Susquehanna*. Email: mcmillin@susqu.edu.

McMillin, Sean. Dallas, TX. Affil: El Centro. Email: seandmcmillin@gmail.com.

McMullen, Emerson Thomas, *Georgia Southern*. Email: etmcmullen@georgiasouthern.edu.

McMurry, Linda O., *North Carolina State*.

McMurry, Nan, *Georgia*. Email: nmcmurry@uga.edu.

McMurry, Sally A., *Penn State*. Email: sam9@psu.edu.

McNab, David, *York, Can*. Email: dtmcnab@yorku.ca.

McNabb, Jennifer Lynn, *Northern Iowa; Western Illinois*. Cedar Falls, IA. Email: Jennifer.mcnabb@uni.edu; JL-McNabb@wiu.edu. Research: early modern courtship and marriage, regional social.

McNair, Bruce G., *Campbell*. Email: mcnair@campbell.edu.

McNair, Glenn, *Kenyon*. Email: mcnairg@kenyon.edu.

McNairn, Jeffrey L., *Queen's, Can*. Email: mcnairnj@queensu.ca.

McNally, Deborah, *Washington, Seattle*. Bothell, WA. Email: dcm9@uw.edu; debbiemcnally9@gmail.com.

McNally, Mark Thomas, *Hawai'i, Manoa*. Email: mmcnally@hawaii.edu.

McNamara, Brenda N. Rancho Palos Verdes, CA. Affil: West High Sch.

McNamara, Brian John. Clinton Township, MI. Affil: Temple. Email: tuf93700@temple.edu. Research: US relations with Angola.

McNamara, Celeste Irene. Cortland, NY. Affil: SUNY, Coll. Cortland. Email: celeste.mcnamara@cortland.edu. Research: early modern Italy, Catholicism.

McNamara, Keith. Madison, WI. Affil: Wisconsin, Madison. Email: kmcnamara3@wisc.edu. Research: US education, US immigration.

McNamara, Michael J. Rancho Palos Verdes, CA.

McNamara, Patrick J., *Minnesota (Hist.)*. Email: pjm@umn.edu.

McNamara, Sarah J., *Texas A&M*. College Station, TX. Email: sarahmc@tamu.edu. Research: immigration, assimilation and Americanization.

McNamee, Heather, *Arkansas State*. Email: hmcnamee@astate.edu.

McNaughton, James C. Alexandria, VA. Email: mcnaughton15@yahoo.com. Research: Japanese Americans in WWII, post-1945 US military.

McNay, John T., *Cincinnati*. Cincinnati, OH. Affil: UC Blue Ash Coll. Email: john.mcnay@uc.edu. Research: Truman/Acheson era foreign policy, modern nationalist movements.

McNeely, Ian Farrell, *Oregon*. Email: imcneely@uoregon.edu.

McNeil, Betty Ann. Chicago, IL. Affil: DePaul. Email: bettyann.mcneil@depaul.edu. Research: Elizabeth Ann Bayley Seton, 19th c. Catholic communities of women.

McNeil, Daniel, *Carleton, Can*. Email: daniel.mcneil@carleton.ca.

McNeil, David O., *San José State*. San Francisco, CA. Email: dmcneil@stanfordalumni.org; dmcneil@alumni.stanford.edu. Research: early modern plagues, medical humanism.

McNeil, Genna Rae, *North Carolina, Chapel Hill*. Email: grmcneil@email.unc.edu.

McNeil, Ross Andrew. Shanghai, China. Affil: World Foreign Language Middle Sch. Email: mcneil.ross@gmail.com.

McNeill, John R., *Georgetown; National Hist. Center*. Washington, DC. Email: mcneilljr@georgetown.edu. Research: Caribbean environmental and epidemics, Cold War environmental.

McNeill, Leila. Dallas, TX. Email: leila.a.mcneill@gmail.com.

McNellis, Lindsey. Morgantown, WV. Affil: West Virginia. Email: limcnellis@mix.wvu.edu. Research: sexual violence in Middle Ages, application of law in Middle Ages.

McNeur, Catherine Clare, *Portland State*. Email: catherine.mcneur@pdx.edu.

McNicholas, Mark P. Altoona, PA. Affil: Penn State, Altoona. Email: mpm17@psu.edu. Research: commoners advising the throne, forgery and impersonation.

McNickle, Chris J. Bronx, NY. Email: cjmcnickle@gmail.com. Research: New York City mayors.

McNulty, John W. Chicago, IL.

McOuat, Gordon, *Dalhousie*. Email: gmcouat@dal.ca.

McPeters, Jackson, *New York State Archives*. Email: jackson.mcpeters@nysed.gov.

McPherson, Alan L., *Soc. for Hist. of American Foreign Relations*. Philadelphia, PA. Affil: Temple. Email: alan.mcpherson@temple.edu. Research: US-Caribbean relations, culture/ideology.

McPherson, James M. Princeton, NJ. Affil: Princeton. Email: jmcphers@princeton.edu. Research: battle of Antietam, Army of the Potomac.

McPherson, Kathryn M., *York, Can*. Email: kathryn@yorku.ca.

McPherson, Natasha L., *California, Riverside*. Email: natasha.mcpherson@ucr.edu.

McPherson, Robert S., *Utah State*. Email: bob.mcpherson@usu.edu.

McQuaid, James Robert. Warren, MI. Affil: Wayne State. Email: james.mcquaid@wayne.edu.

McQueen, Alison, *McMaster*. Email: ajmcq@mcmaster.ca.

McQueeney, Kevin G., *Loyola, New Orleans*.

McQuinn, Ilana R., *Davidson*. Email: ilmcquinn@davidson.edu.

McQuirter, Marya A., *Arizona*. Email: mmcquirter@email.arizona.edu.

McRae, Elizabeth Gillespie, *Western Carolina*. Email: mcrae@email.wcu.edu.

McRae, Heather Thornton. Columbia, MO. Affil: Missouri, Columbia. Email: htmf22@mail.missouri.edu. Research: medieval intellectual/religious/medical, comparative/world.

McRavion, Faye, *North Carolina A&T State*. Email: fmcravion@ncat.edu.

McRee, Ben R., *Franklin & Marshall*. Email: ben.mcree@fandm.edu.

McReynolds, Louise, *North Carolina, Chapel Hill*. Chapel Hill, NC. Email: louisem@ad.unc.edu. Research: Imperial Russia.

McShane, Stephen G., *Indiana, Northwest*. Email: smcshane@iun.edu.

McShea, Bronwen C. Princeton, NJ. Affil: Princeton. Email: bronwenmcshea@gmail.com. Research: 17th-c French colonial empire, early modern Catholicism.

McSheffrey, Shannon, *Concordia, Can*. Email: Shannon.McSheffrey@concordia.ca.

McSweeney, Forrest Cale. Champaign, IL. Affil: Illinois, Urbana-Champaign. Email: saxvalhalla@gmail.com.

McTague, John J., Jr. Saint Leo, FL. Affil: St. Leo. Email: jack.mctague@saintleo.edu. Research: Yasir Arafat and American media.

McTygue, Nancy J. Davis, CA. Affil: California, Davis. Email: njmctygue@ucdavis.edu. Research: K-16 history education.

AHA members in **bold italic**; Directory-listed affiliations in *italic*

McVaugh, Michael R., *North Carolina, Chapel Hill.* Email: mcvaugh@live.unc.edu.

McVety, Amanda Kay, *Miami, Ohio.* Email: mcvetyak@miamioh.edu.

McVicar, Douglas S. Wonalancet, NH. Email: peacefield@myfairpoint.net. Research: late 19th-c balloon ascensions, naming of mountains in NH.

McVicker, Ben A. Toronto, ON, Canada. Affil: Toronto. Email: ben.a.mcvicker@gmail.com.

McWatters, D. Lorne, *Middle Tennessee State.* Email: Lorne.McWatters@mtsu.edu.

McWilliams, James E., *Texas State.* Email: jm71@txstate.edu.

McWilliams, John C., *Penn State.* Email: jcm6@psu.edu.

McWilliams, Tennant S., *Alabama, Birmingham; South Alabama.* Email: tsm@uab.edu; tmcwilliams@southalabama.edu.

Meacham, Sarah Hand, *Virginia Commonwealth.* Email: shmeacham@vcu.edu.

Meacham, Standish, Jr., *Texas, Austin.* Email: meachsalz@mail.utexas.edu.

Mead, Jason A. Knoxville, TN. Affil: Johnson. Email: jmead@johnsonu.edu.

Mead, Rebecca J., *Northern Michigan.* Email: rmead@nmu.edu.

Meade, Teresa A., *Union Coll.* Schenectady, NY. Email: meadet@union.edu. Research: Latin America, gender studies.

Meaders, Daniel E., *William Paterson.* Email: meadersd@wpunj.edu.

Meadows, David W., Jr. Hesperia, CA. Email: dwmeadowsjr@gmail.com.

Meadows, R. Darrell. Alexandria, VA. Affil: National Archives. Email: darrell.meadows@nara.gov.

Meagher, Michael, *Missouri Science and Tech.* Email: mmeagher@mst.edu.

Meaney, Neville K. Sydney, Australia. Affil: Sydney. Email: nmea0681@usyd.edu.au.

Meaney, Thomas. Berlin, Germany. Affil: Columbia. Email: tmallorymeaney@gmail.com.

Means, Jeff D., *Wyoming.* Email: jmeans4@uwyo.edu.

Mears, John A., *Southern Methodist.* Dallas, TX. Email: jmears@smu.edu. Research: development of early civilization, 17th-c Austrian army.

Mears, Tanya M., *Worcester State.* Email: tmears@worcester.edu.

Meckel, Richard, *Brown.* Email: Richard_Meckel@Brown.edu.

Mecklenburg, Frank, *Leo Baeck Inst.* New York, NY. Email: fmecklenburg@lbi.cjh.org. Research: German Jewish.

Meckley, Robert, *Miami, Ohio.* Email: mecklerc@miamioh.edu.

Meddles, Erik. Brooklyn, NY. Affil: NYU. Email: erm345@nyu.edu.

Medeiros, Aimee. Walnut Creek, CA. Affil: California, San Francisco. Email: aimee.medeiros@ucsf.edu.

Medeiros, Avington, *Troy.* Email: ahmedeiros@troy.edu.

Medhi, Abhilash, *Mount Holyoke.* Cambridge, MA. Email: amedhi@mtholyoke.edu; abhilash_medhi@brown.edu.

Medici, Catherine. Omaha, NE. Affil: Creighton. Email: cmedici@huskers.unl.edu. Research: early modern women's political agency, women/gender/medicine.

Medina Del Toro, Victor, Jr., *AHA.* Washington, DC. Email: vmedina@historians.org. Research: science, antiquities trafficking and art crime.

Medley, Brian D. Fairfax, VA. Affil: George Mason. Email: bmedley@masonlive.gmu.edu.

Medlock, A. J., *State Hist. Soc. of Missouri.* Email: MedlockA@shsmo.org.

Medoff, Rafael. Silver Spring, MD. Affil: David Wyman Inst. for Holocaust Studies. Email: rafaelmedoff@aol.com.

Meehan, Patrick. Allston, MA. Affil: Harvard. Email: pmeehan@fas.harvard.edu.

Meeker, Susan G. New York, NY. Email: rpm1066@aol.com.

Meeks, Eric V., *Northern Arizona.* Email: eric.meeks@nau.edu.

Meeks, Joshua. Kirkland, WA. Affil: Northwest. Email: joshua.meeks@northwestu.edu. Research: 18th-/19th-c Mediterranean, British Empire.

Meeks, Tomiko Michelle, *Texas Southern.* Houston, TX. Email: Tomiko.Meeks@tsu.edu. Research: Houston local, race relations.

Meftahi, Ida, *Boise State.* Email: idameftahi@boisestate.edu.

Mega, Thomas B., *St. Thomas, Minn.* Email: tbmega@stthomas.edu.

Megill, Allan, *Virginia.* Charlottesville, VA. Email: megill@virginia.edu. Research: modern thought, philosophy of history/historiography.

Megowan, Erina, *Holy Cross.* Email: emegowan@holycross.edu.

Mehas, Shayna Rene, *Elon.* Email: smehas@elon.edu.

Mehilli, Elidor, *Hunter, CUNY.* Email: em705@hunter.cuny.edu.

Mehl, Eva M., *North Carolina, Wilmington.* Email: mehle@uncw.edu.

Mehrotra, Ajay K. Chicago, IL. Affil: American Bar Foundation. Email: akm@abfn.org. Research: US political economy, American legal.

Mehta, Purvi, *Colorado Coll.* Email: pmehta@coloradocollege.edu.

Mehta, Varad. Yardley, PA. Email: varad.mehta@gmail.com.

Mei, Jiahe. Chicago, IL. Affil: Chicago. Email: jiahe@uchicago.com.

Meier, David A. Dickinson, ND. Affil: Dickinson State. Email: david.meier@ndus.edu. Research: modern Europe, Thirty Years War.

Meier, Dustin. Columbus, OH. Affil: Ohio State. Email: meier.87@buckeyemail.osu.edu.

Meier, Kathryn Shively, *Virginia Commonwealth.* Email: ksmeier@vcu.edu.

Meier, Samuel A., *Ohio State.* Email: meier.3@osu.edu.

Meier, William M., *Texas Christian.* Email: w.meier@tcu.edu.

Meigs, Samantha A., *Indianapolis.* Email: smeigs@uindy.edu.

Meindl, Chris, *South Florida, St. Petersburg.*

Meir, Natan M., *Portland State.* Email: meir@pdx.edu.

Meirowitz, Mark John, *SUNY, Maritime Coll.* Email: mmeirowitz@sunymaritime.edu.

Meisel, Joseph S., *Brown.* Providence, RI. Email: joseph_meisel@brown.edu. Research: British politics and public culture.

Meissner, Daniel J., *Marquette.* Email: daniel.meissner@marquette.edu.

Meister, Richard J., *DePaul.* Ogden Dunes, IN. Email: rmeister@depaul.edu.

Meiton, Fredrik, *New Hampshire, Durham.* Email: fredrik.meiton@unh.edu.

Meixsel, Richard B., *James Madison.* Email: meixserb@jmu.edu.

Mekenye, Reuben, *California State, San Marcos.* Email: rmekenye@csusm.edu.

Melancon, Michael S., *Auburn.* Email: melanms@auburn.edu.

Melchior, Kate, *Massachusetts Hist. Soc.* Email: kmelchior@masshist.org.

Melendez-Badillo, Jorell Alexander, *Dartmouth.* Hanover, NH. Email: jorell.a.melendez-badillo@dartmouth.edu; jorell.melendez_badillo@uconn.edu. Research: Puerto Rican workers' print media, non-migrant transnational imaginaries.

Melendy, Brenda. Kingsville, TX. Affil: Texas A&M, Kingsville. Email: brenda.melendy@tamuk.edu. Research: German expellees' victimization rhetoric, comparative genocide.

Melillo, Edward Dallam, *Amherst.* Email: emelillo@amherst.edu.

Melish, Jacob. Washington, DC. Affil: Northern Colorado. Email: jacob.melish@unco.edu. Research: women and gender relations, early modern Paris.

Melish, Joanne Pope. Wakefield, RI. Affil: Kentucky. Email: jmelish@uky.edu. Research: development of US racial ideologies, post-Rev class formation in US North.

Mell, Julie L., *North Carolina State.* Email: jlmell@ncsu.edu.

Mellard, Jason D., *Texas State.* Email: jdm190@txstate.edu.

Mellen, Abigail, *Lehman, CUNY.* Email: amellen@nyc.rr.com.

Mellen Charron, Katherine, *North Carolina State.* Email: kmcharron@ncsu.edu.

Melleno, Daniel F., *Denver.* Denver, CO. Email: daniel.melleno@du.edu. Research: Carolingians, Viking Age Scandinavia.

Mellini, Peter J. D., *Sonoma State.*

Mellis, Johanna, *Ursinus.* Email: jmellis@ursinus.edu.

Mellone, James T. New York, NY. Affil: Queens, CUNY. Email: james.mellone@qc.cuny.edu.

Mellor, Ronald J., *UCLA.* Email: mellor@history.ucla.edu.

Mellors, Sarah, *Missouri State.* Springfield, MO. Email: SarahMellors@missouristate.edu; scmellors@gmail.com. Research: modern China, gender/medicine.

Mellyn, Elizabeth Walker, *New Hampshire, Durham.* Boston, MA. Email: elizabeth.mellyn@unh.edu; ewmellyn@gmail.com. Research: origins of forensic medicine, credit and credit markets in Italy.

Melosi, Martin V., *Houston.* Houston, TX. Email: histn@central.uh.edu. Research: urban environment, atomic energy.

Meloy, Michael J. Oakland, CA. Affil: State of California. Email: meloymj@gmail.com. Research: California society and politics, immigrants in California.

Melton, James V. H., *Emory.* Email: jmelt01@emory.edu.

Melton, Maurice K., *Columbus State.* Email: melton_maurice@columbusstate.edu.

Melton-Villanueva, Miriam, *Nevada, Las Vegas.* Email: miriam.melton-villanueva@unlv.edu.

Meltsner, David. Gainesville, FL. Affil: Florida. Email: dmeltsner@ufl.edu.

Melvin, Karen, *Bates*. Email: kmelvin@bates. edu.

Melvin-Koushki, Matthew, *South Carolina, Columbia*. Email: mmelvink@sc.edu.

Memarzadeh, Maher. Santa Monica, CA. Email: maher@ucla.edu. Research: medical practitioners in colonial Mexico, 16th-/17th-c Spanish/Mexican society.

Memegalos, Florene S., *Hunter, CUNY*. Jamaica, NY. Email: fmemegal@hunter.cuny.edu. Research: early modern Europe, England.

Menard, Russell R., *Minnesota (Hist.)*. Email: menar001@umn.edu.

Menath, Lt Col Ryan, *US Air Force Acad*. Colorado Springs, CO. Email: ryan.menath@usafa. edu; menath@me.com. Research: American Revolution, pedagogy in history.

Menchaca, Celeste Ruiz, *Texas Christian*. Email: c.menchaca@tcu.edu.

Mendelsohn, Everett I., *Harvard (Hist. of Science)*. Email: emendels@fas.harvard.edu.

Mendez, Alina R. Seattle, WA. Affil: Washington, Seattle. Email: armendez@uw.edu.

Mendez, J. Ignacio, *Northeastern Illinois*. Wood Dale, IL. Email: im999@att.net. Research: Spanish American colonialism, origin of Iberian state in Americas.

Mendez, Michael Scott. Saint Louis, MO. Affil: Washington, St. Louis. Email: michael.s.mendez@wustl.edu. Research: violence and warfare in southern France, land devastation and heresy.

Mendez, S. Cecilia, *California, Santa Barbara*. Email: mendez@history.ucsb.edu.

Mendiola Garcia, Sandra Celia, *North Texas*. Email: sandra.mendiolagarcia@unt.edu.

Mendl, Michael. Takoma Park, MD. Affil: Don Bosco Cristo Rey High Sch. Email: salesianstudies@gmail.com. Research: St. John Bosco, Salesian Society.

Mendle, Michael J., *Alabama, Tuscaloosa*. Email: mmendle@bama.ua.edu.

Mendoza, Alex, *North Texas*. Email: amendoza@ unt.edu.

Mendoza, Mary Elizabeth, *Penn State*.

Mendoza Gutierrez, Natalie, *Colorado, Boulder*. Boulder, CO. Email: natalie. mendozagutierrez@colorado.edu; nmendoza21@berkeley.edu. Research: intellectual, Mexican American.

Menegon, Eugenio, *Boston Univ*. Email: emenegon@bu.edu.

Mengel, David C., *Xavier, Ohio*. Cincinnati, OH. Email: mengel@xavier.edu. Research: medieval Europe and Bohemia.

Mengerink, Mark A, *Lamar*. Beaumont, TX. Email: mark.mengerink@lamar.edu. Research: suicide during the Holocaust, heavy metal music.

Menke, Martin R., *American Catholic Hist. Assoc*. Nashua, NH. Email: mmenke@rivier. edu. Research: political Catholicism, Weimar Germany.

Menking, Christopher Neal. Fort Worth, TX. Affil: North Texas. Email: cnmenking@gmail. com. Research: Mexican American War, Southwest borderlands.

Menkis, Richard, *British Columbia*. Email: menkis@mail.ubc.ca.

Mennel, Timothy. Chicago, IL. Affil: Univ. of Chicago Press. Email: tmennel@uchicago.edu.

Menning, Ralph, *Kent State*. Email: rmenning@ kent.edu.

Menninger, Margaret Eleanor, *Texas State*. San Marcos, TX. Email: mm48@txstate.edu. Research: cultural philanthropy, saxony.

Menon Shivram, Nikhil, *Notre Dame*. Notre Dame, IN. Email: nikhilmenon@nd.edu. Research: modern South Asia, economic life.

Mentzer, Raymond A., Jr., *Iowa*. Iowa City, IA. Email: raymond-mentzer@uiowa.edu. Research: French Reformation, French Protestantism.

Meola, David, *South Alabama*.

Meranze, Michael, *UCLA*. Email: meranze@ history.ucla.edu.

Mercado, Juan Pablo. San Jose, CA. Affil: Chabot. Email: jmercado@chabotcollege.edu. Research: Chicana/o, 20th-c US.

Mercado, Monica L., *Colgate*. Hamilton, NY. Email: mmercado@colgate.edu. Research: US women and gender, religion in American culture.

Mercantini, Jonathan, *Kean*. Union, NJ. Email: jmercant@kean.edu. Research: New Jersey, revolutionary America.

Mercelis, Joris, *Johns Hopkins (Hist. of Science)*. Email: jmercelis@jhu.edu.

Mercer, Kevin Mitchell. Winter Park, FL. Affil: Central Florida. Email: kevin.mercer@knights. ucf.edu. Research: counterculture, youth subcultures.

Mercer, William Davenport. Knoxville, TN. Affil: Tennessee, Knoxville. Email: wmercer@utk. edu.

Merchant, Carolyn, *California, Berkeley*. Email: merchant@nature.berkeley.edu.

Merchant, Emily Klancher. Sacramento, CA. Affil: California, Davis. Email: ekmerchant@ ucdavis.edu. Research: 20th-c population science and politics, digital.

Merchant, J. Holt, Jr., *Washington and Lee*. Email: merchanth@wlu.edu.

Mercier, Laurie, *Washington State, Pullman*. Email: mercier@vancouver.wsu.edu.

Mercogliano, Salvatore R., *Campbell*. Email: mercoglianos@campbell.edu.

Meren, David J., *Montréal*. Email: david.meren@ umontreal.ca.

Mergel, Sarah Katherine. Dalton, GA. Affil: Dalton State. Email: smergel@daltonstate.edu.

Mergenthal, Rebekah M. K., *Pacific Lutheran*. Email: mergenrm@plu.edu.

Mericle, Michele J. Lincoln, RI. Affil: Winthrop Group. Email: michele_mericle@brown.edu.

Meringer, Eric Rodrigo. El Paso, TX. Affil: Texas, El Paso. Email: ermeringer@utep.edu. Research: indigenous Miskito of Nicaragua.

Meringolo, Denise D., *Maryland, Baltimore County*. Email: ddm@umbc.edu.

Merinoff, Stephanie Rae. Raleigh, NC. Affil: North Carolina State. Email: merinoff.steph@ gmail.com.

Merithew, Caroline W., *Dayton*. Email: caroline. merithew@notes.udayton.edu.

Meriwether, James H., *California State, Channel Islands*. Thousand Oaks, CA. Email: james. meriwether@csuci.edu. Research: US connections with Africa, race/Cold War/ decolonization.

Meriwether, Jeffrey L., *Roger Williams*. Email: jmeriwether@rwu.edu.

Meriwether, William. Crescent City, CA. Affil: Redwoods. Email: will_meriwether@hotmail. com.

Merkel-Hess, Kate, *Penn State*. University Park, PA. Email: kxm81@psu.edu. Research: Republic of China 1912-49, world.

Merker, Irwin L., *Rutgers, Newark/New Jersey Inst. of Tech*.

Merkley, Paul C., *Carleton, Can*. Email: paul. merkley@carleton.ca.

Merkowitz, David J. Westerville, OH. Affil: Ohio Humanities. Email: dmerkow@yahoo. com. Research: Philadelphia urban crisis and religion, effects of urban crisis.

Mernitz, Kenneth S., *SUNY, Buffalo State*. Email: mernitks@buffalostate.edu.

Mero, John C., *Campbell*. Email: meroj@ campbell.edu.

Merrell, James H., *Vassar*. Email: merrell@vassar. edu.

Merrell, Laura Y. Bloomington, IN. Affil: Indiana. Email: lmerrell@indiana.edu.

Merriam-Castro, Kelley K. Tucson, AZ. Affil: Arizona; Pima Comm. Coll. Email: kmerriam@ email.arizona.edu. Research: music/ gender/performed identity, social/political movements/resistance.

Merrick, Jeffrey W., *Wisconsin-Milwaukee*. Email: jmerrick@uwm.edu.

Merrill, Dennis J., *Missouri–Kansas City*. Email: merrilld@umkc.edu.

Merrill, Karen R., *Williams*. Email: kmerrill@ williams.edu.

Merriman, John M., *Yale*. New Haven, CT. Email: john.merriman@yale.edu. Research: modern France.

Merriman, Scott A., Sr., *Troy*. Email: smerriman@troy.edu.

Merritt, Eli. San Francisco, CA. Affil: Vanderbilt. Email: elimerritt@gmail.com.

Merritt, Jane T., *Old Dominion*. Email: jmerritt@ odu.edu.

Merrow, Kathleen M., *Portland State*. Portland, OR. Email: merrowk@pdx.edu. Research: Nietzsche in contexts, history and theory of rhetoric.

Mersinger, Max. Miramar, FL. Affil: Whiddon-Rogers DJJ. Email: mmers001@fiu.edu.

Mertz, Adam Ralph. Chicago, IL. Affil: Illinois, Chicago. Email: amertz2@uic.edu. Research: modern US, labor.

Meserve, Margaret H., *Notre Dame*. Email: Meserve.1@nd.edu.

Meskill, Johanna Menzel. Brooklyn, NY.

Messbarger, Rebecca, *Washington, St. Louis*. Email: rmessbar@wustl.edu.

Messenger, David A., *South Alabama*. Mobile, AL. Email: davidamessenger@southalabama. edu. Research: memory Spanish civil war, nazis in European periphery.

Messer, Peter Crozier, *Mississippi State*. Mississippi State, MS. Email: pmesser@ history.msstate.edu. Research: colonial and revolutionary America.

Messer, Robert L., *Illinois, Chicago*. Email: messer@uic.edu.

Messersmith, Eric T., *Florida International*. Email: messerse@fiu.edu.

Messersmith, Thomas Martin. Arlington, VA. Affil: Maryland, Coll. Park. Email: tmessers@ umd.edu.

Messinger, **Penny**. Buffalo, NY. Affil: Daemen. Email: pmessing@daemen.edu. Research: 20th-c Appalachia, women.

Messmer, **Michael W.**, *Virginia Commonwealth*. Email: mmessmer@vcu.edu.

Mestaz, **James**, *Claremont McKenna*. Email: jmestaz@cmc.edu.

Mestyan, **Adam**, *Duke*. Durham, NC. Email: adam.mestyan@duke.edu; mestyan@gmail.com. Research: modern Middle East, nationalism.

Metaxas, **Virginia A.**, *Southern Connecticut State*. Email: metaxasv1@southernct.edu.

Metcalf, **Alida C.**, *Rice; Trinity, Tex*. Houston, TX. Email: alida.c.metcalf@rice.edu. Research: colonial Brazil, Luso Atlantic.

Metcalf, **Barbara**, *California, Davis*. Berkeley, CA. Email: bdmetcalf@ucdavis.edu. Research: Muslim institutions and movements, Islam in South Asia.

Metcalf, **Michael F.**, *Mississippi*. Email: mmetcalf@olemiss.edu.

Metcalf, **Thomas R.** Kensington, CA. Affil: California, Berkeley. Email: tmetcalf@berkeley.edu. Research: British raj in India, empire in Indian Ocean.

Metcalf, **Warren**, *Oklahoma (Hist.)*. Email: wmetcalf@ou.edu.

Metcalfe, **William**, *Vermont*. Email: william.metcalfe@uvm.edu.

Metz, **Donald**, *SUNY, Buffalo State*.

Metz, **John H.** Indianapolis, IN. Email: johnhenrymetz@gmail.com.

Metzger, **Thomas A.**, *California, San Diego*.

Metzl, **Jonathan**, *Vanderbilt*. Email: jonathan.metzl@vanderbilt.edu.

Metzler, **Gabriele**. Berlin, Germany. Affil: Humboldt, Berlin. Email: metzlerg@geschichte.hu-berlin.de. Research: political violence and state.

Metzler, **Mark D.**, *Washington, Seattle*. Email: mmetzler@uw.edu.

Meuwese, **Mark**, *Winnipeg*. Winnipeg, MB, Canada. Email: m.meuwese@uwinnipeg.ca. Research: early modern Atlantic world, ethnohistory of colonial America.

Mewett, **Ryan**. Baltimore, MD. Affil: Johns Hopkins. Email: mewett@jhu.edu.

Meyer, **Alan D.**, *Auburn*. Email: adm0027@auburn.edu.

Meyer, **Andrew S.**, *Brooklyn, CUNY*. Email: ameyer@brooklyn.cuny.edu.

Meyer, **Duane G.**, *Missouri State*.

Meyer, **Elizabeth A.**, *Virginia*. Email: eam2n@virginia.edu.

Meyer, **Gregory**. Geneve, Switzerland. Affil: Geneve. Email: gregory.meyer@unige.ch. Research: international organizations, internationalism.

Meyer, **James H.**, *Montana State, Bozeman*. Email: james.meyer7@montana.edu.

Meyer, **Jimmy E. Wilkinson**, *Wooster*. Lancaster, OH. Email: jmeyer@wooster.edu; jimmywmeyer@gmail.com. Research: contraception, women and health care policy.

Meyer, **Judith P.**, *Connecticut, Storrs*. Email: judith.p.meyer@uconn.edu.

Meyer, **Kathryn**. Dayton, OH. Affil: Wright State. Email: kathryn.meyer@wright.edu. Research: Asia, crime and drugs.

Meyer, **Leisa D.**, *William and Mary*. Williamsburg, VA. Email: ldmeye@wm.edu. Research: 20th-c US, sexuality studies.

Meyer, **Manuella**, *Richmond*. Email: mmeyer@richmond.edu.

Meyer, **Michael A.** Cincinnati, OH. Affil: Hebrew Union. Email: mameyer@huc.edu. Research: 19th-/20th-c German Jewry, American Reform synagogue developments.

Meyer, **Michael**, *California State, Northridge*. Email: michael.meyer@csun.edu.

Meyer, **Michal**, *Science History Inst*. Email: mmeyer@sciencehistory.org.

Meyer, **Stephen, III**, *Wisconsin-Milwaukee*. Email: stemey@uwm.edu.

Meyer-Fong, **Tobie S.**, *Johns Hopkins (Hist.)*. Baltimore, MD. Email: tmeyerf@jhu.edu. Research: 19th-c China, 17th-c China.

Meyerhuber, **Carl I., Jr.**, *Penn State*. Email: cim1@psu.edu.

Meyerowitz, **Joanne**, *Yale; OAH*. New Haven, CT. Email: joanne.meyerowitz@yale.edu. Research: world poverty, foreign assistance.

Meyers, **Andrea Riehs**. Detroit, MI. Email: andrea.historical@gmail.com.

Meyers, **Debra A.**, *Northern Kentucky*. Email: meyersde@nku.edu.

Meyers, **Joshua**. San Leandro, CA. Affil: Stanford. Email: joshmeyers87@gmail.com. Research: Jewish politics in Russian Revolution, transnational Jewish radicalism.

Meyers, **Katherine E.** Austin, TX. Affil: Austin Comm. Coll. Email: katherine.meyers@austincc.edu. Research: political theory, gender theory.

Meyers, **Mark F.**, *Saskatchewan*. Email: mark.meyers@usask.ca.

Meyerson, **Joel D.** Annandale, VA. Affil: US Army Center of Military Hist. Email: joelmey@verizon.net. Research: military operations in Vietnam, military logistics.

Meyerson, **Mark D.**, *Toronto*. Toronto, ON, Canada. Email: mark.meyerson@utoronto.ca. Research: Christian-Muslim-Jewish relations, violence in medieval society.

Mezick, **David**, *La Guardia and Wagner Archives*. Email: dmezick@lagcc.cuny.edu.

Meznar, **Joan E.**, *Eastern Connecticut State*. Email: meznarj@easternct.edu.

Mezvinsky, **Norton H.**, *Central Connecticut State*. New York, NY. Email: mezvinskyn@ccsu.edu. Research: Jewish and Israeli fundamentalism, Oslo peace process.

Michael, **Bernardo A.**, *Messiah*. Email: bmichael@messiah.edu.

Michael, **Christopher**. New York, NY. Email: christopher.warren.michael@gmail.com.

Michaels, **Albert L.**, *SUNY, Buffalo State*. Email: michaeal@buffalostate.edu.

Michaels, **Jonathan**. Holyoke, MA. Affil: Connecticut, Greater Hartford. Email: Jonathan.Michaels@uconn.edu.

Michaelsen, **Rebekka**. Frisco, TX. Affil: Texas, Dallas. Email: rebekka.a.michaelsen@gmail.com.

Michals, **Debra A.** Andover, MA. Affil: Merrimack. Email: michalsd@merrimack.edu.

Michaud, **Francine**, *Calgary*. Email: michaud@ucalgary.ca.

Michel, **Gregg L.**, *Texas, San Antonio*. Email: gregg.michel@utsa.edu.

Michel, **Peter**, *Nevada, Las Vegas*. Email: peter.michel@unlv.edu.

Michel, **Sonya Alice**, *Maryland, Coll. Park*. Email: smichel@umd.edu.

Michelmore, **Molly C.**, *Washington and Lee*. Email: michelmorem@wlu.edu.

Michels, **Anthony E.**, *Wisconsin-Madison*. Email: aemichels@wisc.edu.

Michels, **Georg B.**, *California, Riverside*. Email: georg.michels@ucr.edu.

Michelson, **David A.**, *Vanderbilt*. Email: david.a.michelson@vanderbilt.edu.

Michie, **Lindsay**, *Lynchburg*. Email: michie.l@lynchburg.edu.

Michna, **Gregory**, *Arkansas Tech*. Email: gmichna@atu.edu.

Michney, **Todd M.**, *Georgia Inst. of Tech*. Atlanta, GA. Email: todd.michney@hsoc.gatech.edu; tmichney@gmail.com. Research: race and housing/employment, race/ethnicity/immigration.

Mickel, **Ronald E.**, *Wisconsin-Eau Claire*. Eau Claire, WI. Email: mickelre@uwec.edu. Research: US intellectual and cultural, US 1920-50.

Middlekauff, **Robert L.** Pleasanton, CA. Affil: California, Berkeley. Email: rlmiddlek@berkeley.edu. Research: early American democracy, Mark Twain.

Middleton, **Charles R.**, *Roosevelt*. Cathedral City, CA. Email: cmiddleton@roosevelt.edu. Research: Britain and Ireland 1750-1914, education.

Middleton, **Shelly Ann**, *North Carolina A&T State*. Email: samiddle@ncat.edu.

Middleton, **Simon**, *William and Mary*. Email: smiddleton@wm.edu.

Middleton, **Stephen**, *Mississippi State*. Email: smiddleton@history.msstate.edu.

Midelfort, **H. C. Erik**, *Virginia*. Email: hem7e@virginia.edu.

Midgette, **Nancy Smith**, *Elon*. Email: midgette@elon.edu.

Midtrod, **Tom Arne**, *Iowa*. Email: tom-midtrod@uiowa.edu.

Mieczkowski, **Yanek**, *North Florida*. Cocoa Beach, FL. Email: y.mieczkowski@unf.edu; yanektm@yahoo.com. Research: America, political.

Mielnik, **Tara Mitchell**. Lebanon, TN. Affil: Cumberland. Email: tmielnik@cumberland.edu.

Mierzejewski, **Alfred C.**, *North Texas*. Highland Village, TX. Email: acmierzeje@aol.com. Research: German economy, German pension system.

Miescher, **Stephan F.**, *California, Santa Barbara*. Santa Barbara, CA. Email: miescher@history.ucsb.edu. Research: 19th-/20th-c West Africa, masculinities/gender/modernity.

Mieyal, **Timothy J.**, *Baldwin Wallace*. Email: tmieyal@bw.edu.

Migliazzo, **Arlin Charles**, *Whitworth*. Email: amigliazzo@whitworth.edu.

Mignone, **Lisa M.** New York, NY. Email: lmmignone@gmail.com.

Mihal, **Sandy**, *Troy*.

Mihaly, **David**, *Huntington Library*. Email: dmihaly@huntington.org.

Mihm, **Stephen A.**, *Georgia*. Athens, GA. Email: smihm@uga.edu; mihmstep@yahoo.com. Research: 19th-c antebellum, economic banking money.

Mijangos, **Pablo**. Mexico City, Mexico. Affil: Centro de Investigacion y Docencia Economicas. Email: pablomijangos@hotmail.com.

Mikati, Rana, *Charleston*. Email: mikatir@cofc. edu.

Mikecz, Jeremy. Arcadia, CA. Affil: Southern California. Email: jmmikecz@ucdavis.edu. Research: spatial/GIS, geography.

Mikhail, Alan, *Yale*. New Haven, CT. Email: alan. mikhail@yale.edu. Research: Ottoman Empire environmental, Ottoman Empire and World.

Mikhail, Maged S., *California State, Fullerton*. Email: mmikhail@fullerton.edu.

Miki, Yuko, *Fordham*. New York, NY. Email: ymiki1@fordham.edu. Research: Brazil, slavery.

Mikkelson, Douglas Kent, *Hawai'i, Hilo*. Email: dougmikk@hawaii.edu.

Mikolashek, Jon B., *US Army Command Coll.* Email: jon.b.mikolashek.civ@mail.mil.

Milam, Erika Lorraine, *Princeton*. Princeton, NJ. Email: emilam@princeton.edu. Research: modern life sciences, gender and science.

Milam, Ron, *Texas Tech*. Email: ron.milam@ttu. edu.

Milanesio, Natalia, *Houston*.

Milanich, Nara, *Barnard, Columbia*. Email: nmilanich@barnard.edu.

Milano, Anthony John. Richardson, TX. Affil: Texas, Dallas. Email: a.milano2112@gmail. com. Research: early Republic literary/legal, early Republic politics/religion/gender.

Milazzo, Paul C., *Ohio*. Email: milazzo@ohio. edu.

Miles, Gary B., *California, Santa Cruz*. Email: miles@ucsc.edu.

Miles, Mary Jo, *Oakland*. Email: miles@oakland. edu.

Miles, Rogers B. Walla Walla, WA. Affil: Whitman. Email: miles@whitman.edu. Research: religion and higher education.

Miles, Steven B., *Washington, St. Louis*. Email: smiles@wustl.edu.

Miles, Tiya A. Ann Arbor, MI. Affil: Michigan, Ann Arbor. Email: tiyamiles@fas.harvard. edu. Research: African American and Native American, women of color.

Milewski, Melissa L. Palo Alto, CA. Affil: Sussex. Email: melissamilewski@gmail.com. Research: race and law, African American.

Milford, Timothy A., *St. John's, NY*. Brooklyn, NY. Email: milfordt@stjohns.edu. Research: early national political culture, colonial Anglican church.

Milgrim, Michael R. Elgin, IL. Email: michaelmilgrim@aol.com.

Milkes, Elisa R. New York, NY. Affil: Horace Mann Sch. Email: elisa_milkes@horacemann.org. Research: collective memory and warfare, 19th-c Britain.

Millar, Gilbert J., *Longwood*.

Millard, Andre J., *Alabama, Birmingham*. Email: amillard@uab.edu.

Millard, J. Rodney, *Western Ontario*. Email: rmillar2@uwo.ca.

Miller, Allison, *AHA*. Washington, DC. Email: amiller@historians.org. Research: women, sexuality.

Miller, Andrew H. West Hollywood, CA. Affil: Occidental. Email: ahmiller@ucla.edu.

Miller, Andrew Joseph. Media, PA. Affil: Neumann. Email: millera1777@hotmail. com. Research: local Pennsylvania, American military.

Miller, Anthony Joseph, *Miami, Ohio*. Email: mille932@miamioh.edu.

Miller, Aragorn Storm. Pflugerville, TX. Affil: Central Texas. Email: stormmiller@utexas.edu.

Miller, Benjamin Lee. Baltimore, MD. Affil: Calvert Hall College High Sch. Email: blmill04@gmail.com. Research: religion and American Civil War.

Miller, Bradley J., *British Columbia*. Email: brmiller@ubc.ca.

Miller, Brandon Gray, *Southern Methodist*. Email: bgmiller@smu.edu.

Miller, Brenna Caroline, *Washington State, Pullman*. Email: brenna.miller@wsu.edu.

Miller, Brian JK, *Allegheny*. Meadville, PA. Email: bmiller2@allegheny.edu. Research: return migration/Turkey/identity politics, Turkish-German guest workers.

Miller, Brian Richard. Alexandria, VA. Affil: US Dept. of Education. Email: brianrmiller88@ gmail.com. Research: disability/blind, civil rights movements.

Miller, Brian S, *Charleston Southern*. Email: bmiller@csuniv.edu.

Miller, Burke R., *Northern Kentucky*. Email: millerbu@nku.edu.

Miller, Carman I., *McGill*. Email: carman.miller@ mcgill.ca.

Miller, Cecilia, *Wesleyan*. Email: cmiller@ wesleyan.edu.

Miller, Channon, *San Diego*. Email: channonmiller@sandiego.edu.

Miller, Char, *Pomona; Trinity, Tex.* Email: char. miller@pomona.edu.

Miller, Christine. Saint Augustine, FL. Affil: Florida. Email: Millerchristine04@gmail.com.

Miller, Christopher L., *Texas-Rio Grande Valley*. Email: christopher.miller@utrgv.edu.

Miller, Christopher, *Berea*. Email: christopher_ miller@berea.edu.

Miller, Daniel R., *Calvin*. Email: mill@calvin.edu.

Miller, David B., *Roosevelt*. Chicago, IL. Email: dbmjjm@rcn.com; dbmjjm@gmail.com. Research: transformation of Rus' 1200-1450, Trinity-Sergius Monastery 1350-1605.

Miller, David B., *Wooster*. Email: dmiller@ wooster.edu.

Miller, David J., *San Diego*. Email: davidmiller@ sandiego.edu.

Miller, David W., *Carnegie Mellon*. Email: dwmiller@cmu.edu.

Miller, Donald L., *Lafayette*. Email: millerd@ lafayette.edu.

Miller, Douglas K., *Oklahoma State*. Email: douglas.miller@okstate.edu.

Miller, Eben S. South Portland, ME. Affil: Southern Maine Comm. Coll. Email: emiller@ smccme.edu.

Miller, Edward, *Dartmouth*. Email: edward. miller@dartmouth.edu.

Miller, Emelin E. St. Paul, MN. Affil: Minnesota, Twin Cities. Email: mill6266@umn.edu. Research: early modern Arctic, natural.

Miller, Emily G., *Indianapolis*. Email: millereg@ uindy.edu.

Miller, Erin Nichole. Columbus, IN. Affil: Columbus North High Sch. Email: millerer@ bcsc.k12.in.us.

Miller, Eugene W., Jr., *Penn State*. Email: ewm1@psu.edu.

Miller, F. Thornton, *Missouri State*. Email: ftmiller@missouristate.edu.

Miller, Frederick E., Jr. Fairfield, CT. Email: miller. frederick@att.net.

Miller, Gary M., *Massachusetts, Boston*. Email: gary.miller@umb.edu.

Miller, Gary M., *Southern Oregon*. Email: miller@ sou.edu.

Miller, Gerald Adam, Jr., *Chestnut Hill*. Email: millerg@chc.edu.

Miller, Gregory J. Canton, OH. Affil: Malone. Email: gmiller@malone.edu. Research: development of Christian views of Islam, Christian humanism in Reformation.

Miller, Guy Howard, *Texas, Austin*. Austin, TX. Email: hmiller@mail.utexas.edu. Research: US, religious thought.

Miller, Gwenn A., *Holy Cross*. Email: gmiller@ holycross.edu.

Miller, Harrison, *South Alabama*. Email: hsmiller@southalabama.edu.

Miller, Hilary. Canonsburg, PA. Affil: Penn State. Email: hlm212@psu.edu. Research: National Road/early internal improvement, French and Indian War.

Miller, Ian J., *Harvard (Hist.)*. Cambridge, MA. Email: ian_miller@harvard.edu. Research: environment/science/technology, cultural/ visual culture/exhibitions.

Miller, Ian Matthew, *St. John's, NY*. Email: milleri1@stjohns.edu.

Miller, J. Donald. Washington, DC. Email: donmiller0@gmail.com.

Miller, Jaclyn J.S. Edinburg, TX. Affil: South Texas. Email: jaclyn.miller75@gmail.com. Research: Great Plains, bankers and banking.

Miller, Jacquelyn, *Seattle*. Email: jcmiller@ seattleu.edu.

Miller, James D., *Carleton, Can*. Email: james. miller@carleton.ca.

Miller, James R., *Saskatchewan*. Email: jim. miller@usask.ca.

Miller, Janice J. Chandler, AZ. Affil: Scottsdale Comm. Coll. Email: jan.miller714@cox.net.

Miller, Jeffrey Bruce. Denver, CO. Email: jbmwriter@aol.com. Research: WWI's Commission for Relief in Belgium, WWI German-occupied Belgium.

Miller, Jennifer Michelle, *Dartmouth*. Email: jennifer.m.miller@dartmouth.edu.

Miller, Jess A. Mahomet, IL. Affil: Unit Seven Sch.; Eastern Illinois. Email: jmillscots46@ gmail.com.

Miller, John T. Rising Sun, MD. Email: jmiller8@ zoominternet.net.

Miller, Jonson W., *Drexel*. Email: jwm54@drexel. edu.

Miller, Judith A., *Emory*. Email: histjam@emory. edu.

Miller, Karen A. J., *Oakland*. Email: kjmiller@ oakland.edu.

Miller, Karen E. Bellevue, NE. Email: millerke@ rocketmail.com. Research: church/state relations Ireland/Scotland, military air power.

Miller, Karen K., *Boston Coll*. Email: millerkj@ bc.edu.

Miller, Karen Renee. Brooklyn, NY. Affil: La Guardia Comm. Coll., CUNY. Email: kamiller@ lagcc.cuny.edu. Research: 20th-c Philippines, US in world.

Miller, Katya L. Santa Rosa, CA. Affil: US Capitol Hist. Soc. Email: miller.katya@gmail.com. Research: Statue of Freedom, America on atlases and maps.

Miller, Kenneth J., *Washington Coll*. Email: kmiller4@washcoll.edu.

Miller, **Kerby A.**, *Missouri, Columbia*. Email: millerk@missouri.edu.

Miller, *Kristie*. Washington, DC. Email: krste@aol.com. Research: Ellen Axson Wilson and Edith Bolling Wilson, Mark Hanna.

Miller, *Kye Logan*. Franklin, TN. Email: kye.miller@outlook.com.

Miller, **Laura**, *Missouri–St. Louis*. Email: millerlau@umsl.edu.

Miller, **Linda Angle**, *Roanoke*. Email: lmiller@roanoke.edu.

Miller, *Loren Elan*. Washington, DC. Affil: Smithsonian National Museum of African American Hist. & Culture. Email: loren.e.miller@gmail.com. Research: women in military in WWII, visual and material culture.

Miller, *Luke Anson Weatherlow*. Duxbury, MA. Email: matakeeset@gmail.com.

Miller, *Lynneth J.* Waco, TX. Affil: Baylor. Email: lmiller@andersonuniversity.edu. Research: dance/gender/transgression, performing arts and church.

Miller, **M. Sammye**, *Bowie State*. Email: smiller@bowiestate.edu.

Miller, **Margaret A.**, *Sonoma State*.

Miller, **Mark F.**, *Roanoke*. Email: mmiller@roanoke.edu.

Miller, **Marla R.**, *Massachusetts, Amherst*. Email: mmiller@history.umass.edu.

Miller, **Martin A.**, *Duke*. Email: mmiller@duke.edu.

Miller, **Mary Ashburn**, *Reed*. Email: mary.miller@reed.edu.

Miller, *Maureen C.*, *California, Berkeley*. Berkeley, CA. Email: mcmiller@berkeley.edu. Research: ecclesiastical material culture, gender and medieval clergy.

Miller, *Michael B.*, *Miami*. Miami, FL. Email: mbmiller@miami.edu. Research: France and its waterways, modern France.

Miller, **Montserrat M.**, *Marshall*. Email: millerm@marshall.edu.

Miller, **Nathan**, *Wisconsin-Milwaukee*. Email: knmiller@uwm.edu.

Miller, **Nicholas**, *Boise State*. Email: nmiller@boisestate.edu.

Miller, **Patrick B.**, *Northeastern Illinois*. Email: P-Miller1@neiu.edu.

Miller, *Peter N.* New York, NY. Affil: Bard Graduate Center. Email: miller@bgc.bard.edu. Research: historical research, antiquarianism.

Miller, **Randall H.**, *Salem State*. Email: rmiller2@salemstate.edu.

Miller, **Randall M.**, *St. Joseph's*. Email: miller@sju.edu.

Miller, *Randolph A.* Milwaukee, WI. Affil: Carroll. Email: randymiller2112@yahoo.com.

Miller, **Robert David**, *California State, San Marcos; San Diego Mesa*. Email: romiller@csusm.edu; rdmiller@sdccd.edu.

Miller, *Scott Eric.* Tampa, FL. Affil: SUNY, Buffalo State. Email: semiller11@yahoo.com.

Miller, *Shawn W.*, *Brigham Young*. Provo, UT. Email: miller@byu.edu. Research: Latin America, environmental.

Miller, **Stephen J.**, *Alabama, Birmingham*. Email: sjmiller@uab.edu.

Miller, **Stephen M.**, *Maine, Orono*. Email: stephen.miller@maine.edu.

Miller, **Steven F.**, *Maryland, Coll. Park*. Email: sfmiller@umd.edu.

Miller, **Stuart**, *Connecticut, Storrs*. Email: stuart.miller@uconn.edu.

Miller, **Susan Gilson**, *California, Davis*. Email: sgmiller@ucdavis.edu.

Miller, **Suzanne Mariko**, *George Washington*. Email: smmiller@gwu.edu.

Miller, *Tanya Stabler*, *Loyola, Chicago*. Chicago, IL. Email: tstabler@luc.edu. Research: medieval women, lay religious movements.

Miller, **Thomas F.**, *Wisconsin-Eau Claire*. Email: millert@uwec.edu.

Miller, **Timothy S.**, *Salisbury*. Email: tsmiller@salisbury.edu.

Miller, **Wilbur R., Jr.**, *SUNY, Stony Brook*. Email: wilbur.miller@stonybrook.edu.

Miller, **Worth R.**, *Missouri State*. Email: bobmiller@missouristate.edu.

Miller-Davenport, *Sarah*. Sheffield, NY. Affil: Sheffield. Email: millerdavenport@gmail.com. Research: Hawaii statehood.

Miller-Young, **Mireille L.**, *California, Santa Barbara*. Email: mmilleryoung@femst.ucsb.edu.

Millett, **Allan R.**, *Hawai'i Pacific; New Orleans; Ohio State*. Email: amillett@hpu.edu; amillett@uno.edu; millett.2@osu.edu.

Millett, **Nathaniel C.**, *St. Louis*. Email: nmillet1@slu.edu.

Millette, **James**, *Oberlin*. Email: james.millette@oberlin.edu.

Millette, *Rachael*. Denver, CO. Email: rachaelmillette@gmail.com.

Millevoi, *Jerry*. Doylestown, PA. Email: millevoi@comcast.net. Research: interpreting history through cinema, Native Americans and American West.

Millie, *William Jerome*. Seattle, WA. Email: billtothemill@gmail.com.

Milligan, *Ian*, *Waterloo*. Waterloo, ON, Canada. Email: i2milligan@uwaterloo.ca; ianmilligan1@gmail.com. Research: Canadian youth, digital.

Millikan, *Neal Elizabeth*, *Massachusetts Hist. Soc.* Email: nmillikan@masshist.org.

Milliman, *Paul*, *Arizona*. Tucson, AZ. Email: milliman@email.arizona.edu. Research: games and play in the early world, idea of eastern Europe before the 18th c.

Millin, *Ann E.* Silver Spring, MD. Affil: Stockton. Email: aemillin47@gmail.com. Research: Holocaust in Germany and Austria, Jewish immigration to US.

Millinger, **Susan P.**, *Roanoke*. Email: millinger@roanoke.edu.

Million, *Jacob Tucker*. Rochester, NY. Affil: Rochester. Email: jtuckermillion@gmail.com.

Mills, *Andrew Steven*. Chesapeake, VA. Affil: Miller Sch. of Albemarle, Virginia. Email: millsas.jmu@gmail.com. Research: educational pedagogy effects on memory, national identity construction.

Mills, *Brett Andrew*. Owensboro, KY. Affil: Diocese of Owensboro. Email: BMills9590@aol.com. Research: US sectionalism 1820-60, US presidency.

Mills, **David C.**, *Alberta*. Email: david.mills@ualberta.ca.

Mills, **David W.**, *US Army Command Coll.* Email: david.w.mills24.civ@mail.mil.

Mills, **Frederick**, *Bowie State*. Email: fmills@bowiestate.edu.

Mills, *Hayden*. Fullerton, CA. Affil: Downey Unified Sch. District. Email: hayden.mills@biola.edu.

Mills, **James W.**, *Texas-Rio Grande Valley*. Email: james.mills@utrgv.edu.

Mills, **Kenneth R.**, *Michigan, Ann Arbor*. Email: millsken@umich.edu.

Mills, **Quincy T.**, *Vassar*. Email: qumills@vassar.edu.

Mills, **Sean**, *Toronto*. Email: sean.mills@utoronto.ca.

Mills Robbins, **Ruth Ann**, *Biola*. Email: ruth.mill-robbins@biola.edu.

Millsap, *Matt*. Waco, TX. Affil: Baylor. Email: matt_millsap@baylor.edu.

Millstead, *Brenda Ellen*. Dallas, TX. Email: brenda.ellen.millstead@mail.com.

Millward, **James**, *Georgetown*. Email: millwarj@georgetown.edu.

Millward, **Jessica**, *California, Irvine*. Email: millward@uci.edu.

Milmine, *Karen Leslie*. Lubbock, TX. Affil: Texas Tech. Email: thistledoc@gmail.com. Research: Medieval, Female Mystics/Hagiography.

Milne, **Andrea Elizabeth**, *Case Western Reserve*. Email: andrea.milne@case.edu.

Milne, **George Edward**, *Oakland*. Email: milne@oakland.edu.

Milner, *Brian Patrick*. Fort Myers, FL. Affil: Lely High Sch.; Florida Southwestern State. Email: bmilner@fsw.edu.

Milner, **Clyde A., II**, *Arkansas State*.

Milner, **J. Marc**, *New Brunswick*. Email: milner@unb.ca.

Milne-Smith, **Amy G.**, *Wilfrid Laurier*. Email: amilnesmith@wlu.ca.

Milone, *Louise Irene*. Watkinsville, GA. Affil: Georgia. Email: louise.milone@uga.edu.

Milov, **Sarah E.**, *Virginia*. Email: sem9dw@virginia.edu.

Milowitz, *Bernard E.* Rego Park, NY. Email: bmil0641@yahoo.com.

Milowski, *Daniel*. Tempe, AZ. Affil: Arizona State. Email: dmilowsk@asu.edu.

Milson, **Andrew J.**, *Texas, Arlington*. Email: milson@uta.edu.

Milteer, *Warren E., Jr.*, *North Carolina, Greensboro*.

Miltenberger, *Scott A.* Davis, CA. Affil: JRP Hist. Consulting. Email: smiltenberger@jrphistorical.com. Research: water development, environmental pollution.

Milton, **Cynthia E.**, *Montréal*. Email: cynthia.milton@umontreal.ca.

Mims, *Dennis Michael*. Dallas, TX. Affil: Texas, Dallas. Email: mimsm2@yahoo.com. Research: civil rights and social movements, US foreign relations.

Mims, **La Shonda C.**, *Kennesaw State*. Email: lmims4@kennesaw.edu.

Mimura, **Janis A.**, *SUNY, Stony Brook*. Email: janis.mimura@stonybrook.edu.

Min, **Benjamin**, *SUNY, Buffalo State*.

Minardi, *Margot*, *Reed*. Portland, OR. Email: minardi@reed.edu. Research: slavery and abolition, historical memory.

Minault, **Gail**, *Texas, Austin*. Email: gminault@austin.utexas.edu.

Minawi, **Mostafa**, *Cornell*. Email: mm2492@cornell.edu.

Mindell, **David A.**, *MIT*. Email: mindell@mit.edu.

Mindlin, *Morgan J.* Los Angeles, CA. Email: morgjmindlin@gmail.com.

Minear, **Richard H.**, *Massachusetts, Amherst*. Email: rhminear@history.umass.edu.

Miner, **Jeffrey David**, *Western Kentucky*. Email: jeffrey.miner@wku.edu.

Miner, **Jocelyn J.** Granger, IN. Email: jjminer@well.com.

Miner, **Samuel**. Athens, OH. Affil: Maryland, Coll. Park. Email: sminer1@umd.edu.

Miner, **Steven M.**, *Ohio*. Email: miner@ohio.edu.

Mingus, **Matthew D.** Gallup, NM. Affil: New Mexico, Gallup. Email: mmingus@unm.edu. Research: postwar Germany, cartography.

Mingus, **Thomas Michael**. York, PA. Affil: Liberty. Email: tommingus@comcast.net. Research: American Civil War, 20th-c US.

Mini, **James M.** Kennett Square, PA. Email: jamesmmini@earthlink.net.

Minian, **Ana Raquel**, *Stanford*. Stanford, CA. Email: aminian@stanford.edu. Research: modern Latin America, Mexico.

Mink, **Andrew T.** Durham, NC. Affil: National Humanities Center. Email: amink@nationalhumanitiescenter.org.

Minnich, **Nelson H.**, *American Catholic Hist. Assoc.* Email: minnich@cua.edu.

Minnoe, **Emily Rose**. Syracuse, NY. Email: emilyrhenrich@gmail.com. Research: Performance Art, Feminism.

Minor, **Kelly Anne**, *Virginia Military Inst.* Email: minork@vmi.edu.

Minor, **Ryan Harold**. Goleta, CA. Affil: California, Santa Barbara. Email: rminor@umail.ucsb.edu.

Minsky, **Amir**. Wallingford, PA. Affil: NYU, Abu Dhabi. Email: am4117@nyu.edu. Research: Enlightenment political philosophy, Franco-German emotions.

Minten, **Rhonda**, *Texas, San Antonio*. Email: rhonda.minten@utsa.edu.

Minter, **Patricia Hagler**, *Western Kentucky*. Email: patricia.minter@wku.edu.

Minto, **David**. Durham, United Kingdom. Affil: Durham. Email: david.l.minto@durham.ac.uk.

Minton, **Amanda D.**, *Pittsburg State*.

Minty, **Christopher F.**, *Massachusetts Hist. Soc.* Boston, MA. Email: cminty@masshist.org. Research: colonial/revolutionary America, early Republic.

Mintz, **John**, *North Carolina Office of Archives*. Email: john.mintz@ncdcr.gov.

Mintz, **Steven H.**, *Texas, Austin*. Austin, TX. Email: smintz@utsystem.edu; steven.mintz@outlook.com. Research: childhood, slavery and antislavery.

Mintzker, **Yair**, *Princeton*. Princeton, NJ. Email: mintzker@princeton.edu. Research: German urban, historical linguistics.

Miquelon, **Dale B.**, *Saskatchewan*. Email: dale.miquelon@usask.ca.

Mir, **Farina**, *Michigan, Ann Arbor*. Ann Arbor, MI. Email: fmir@umich.edu. Research: Islam/Muslims in colonial India.

Miracle, **Amanda Lea**, *Emporia State*. Email: amiracle@emporia.edu.

Miranda, **Cecilia S.** Fairfax, VA. Email: csmiranda@cox.net.

Mires, **Charlene**, *Rutgers, Camden*. Email: cmires@camden.rutgers.edu.

Miroff, **Neal I.** Sarasota, FL.

Miron, **Janet**, *Trent*. Email: janetmiron@trentu.ca.

Mirow, **M. C.** Miami, FL. Affil: Florida International. Email: mirowm@fiu.edu.

Mirzai, **Behnaz**, *Brock*. Email: bmirzai@brocku.ca.

Misa, **Thomas J.**, *Minnesota (Hist. of Science); Soc. for Hist. of Tech.* Email: tmisa@umn.edu.

Miscamble, **Wilson D.**, **CSC**, *Notre Dame*. Notre Dame, IN. Email: wmiscamb@nd.edu. Research: Truman/a-bombs/defeat of Japan, Catholics and foreign policy 1898-2008.

Misevich, **Philip**, *St. John's, NY*. Email: misevicp@stjohns.edu.

Mishler, **Max**, *Toronto*.

Mishler, **Paul C.**, *Indiana, South Bend*. Email: pmishler@iusb.edu.

Mishra, **Rupali Raj**, *Auburn*. Email: rrm0009@auburn.edu.

Mitcham, **John Calvin**, *Duquesne*. Email: mitchamj@duq.edu.

Mitchell, **Andrew J.**, *Grove City*. Email: ajmitchell@gcc.edu.

Mitchell, **Brian K.**, *Arkansas, Little Rock*. Email: bkmitchell@ualr.edu.

Mitchell, **Christopher Adam**. Brooklyn, NY. Affil: Hunter, CUNY. Email: chmitche@icloud.com. Research: urban and queer subcultures, sexuality and illicit markets.

Mitchell, **Colin P.**, *Dalhousie*. Email: c.mitchell@dal.ca.

Mitchell, **Daniel Jon**, *Science History Inst.* Email: dmitchell@sciencehistory.org.

Mitchell, **Dennis J.**, *Mississippi State*. Email: dmitchell@meridian.msstate.edu.

Mitchell, **Franklin D.**, *Southern California*. Email: history@usc.edu.

Mitchell, **Gary R.**, *Henry Ford Coll.* Email: grmitchell1@hfcc.edu.

Mitchell, **Gregg Edward**. South Hadley, MA. Affil: Massachusetts Amherst. Email: GMitch132@gmail.com.

Mitchell, **Laura J.**, *California, Irvine; World Hist. Assoc.* Irvine, CA. Email: mitchell@uci.edu. Research: colonial South Africa labor/slavery, African environmental.

Mitchell, **Linda E.**, *Missouri–Kansas City*. Email: mitchelll@umkc.edu.

Mitchell, **Lisa**. Philadelphia, PA. Affil: Pennsylvania. Email: lmitch@sas.upenn.edu. Research: public space and political protest, Indian democracy.

Mitchell, **Maria D.**, *Franklin & Marshall*. Email: maria.mitchell@fandm.edu.

Mitchell, **Mary Niall**, *New Orleans*. New Orleans, LA. Email: molly.mitchell@uno.edu. Research: 19th-c slave emancipation and race, black child.

Mitchell, **Mary X.**, *Purdue*. Lafayette, IN. Email: mitch279@purdue.edu. Research: science/technology/medicine, legal.

Mitchell, **Matthew David**, *South*. Email: mdmitche@sewanee.edu.

Mitchell, **Michele**, *NYU*. New York, NY. Email: michele.mitchell@nyu.edu. Research: US and African American, African diaspora.

Mitchell, **Monika**. Somerville, NJ. Affil: Sarah Lawrence. Email: mmitchell@gm.slc.edu. Research: women.

Mitchell, **Nancy**, *North Carolina State*. Email: nancy_mitchell@ncsu.edu.

Mitchell, **Norma Taylor**, *Troy*. Durham, NC. Email: normatmitchell@gmail.com. Research: women in 20th-c medicine, black and white women in antebellum Virginia.

Mitchell, **Pablo R.**, *Oberlin*. Oberlin, OH. Email: pablo.mitchell@oberlin.edu. Research: Latina/o sexuality, sex and modernity in American West.

Mitchell, **Rebecca Anne**, *Middlebury*. Middlebury, VT. Email: rmitchell@middlebury.edu; rebekah.mitchell@gmail.com. Research: late imperial Russia, music.

Mitchell, **Richard H.**, *Missouri–St. Louis*. Saint Louis, MO. Email: richardmitchell@umsl.edu. Research: modern Japan.

Mitchell, **Robin**, *California State, Channel Islands*. Email: robin.mitchell@csuci.edu.

Mitchell, **Silvia Z.**, *Purdue*. West Lafayette, IN. Email: mitch131@purdue.edu. Research: later 17th-c Spain, queenship/court studies/political culture.

Mitchell, **Theresa**, *Massachusetts Hist. Soc.* Email: tmitchell@masshist.org.

Mitchell, **Virginia R.**, *Central Connecticut State*. Email: mitchellv@ccsu.edu.

Mitchell, **William I.**, *SUNY, Buffalo State*. Email: mitchewi@buffalostate.edu.

Mitchener, **D. Keith**, *North Texas*. Email: donald.mitchener@unt.edu.

Mitchinson, **Wendy**, *Waterloo*. Email: wlmitchi@uwaterloo.ca.

Mitman, **Gregg**, *Wisconsin-Madison*. Madison, WI. Email: gmitman@med.wisc.edu. Research: science/medicine/American empire, expedition and industrial film.

Mitrovic, **Milos**. Toronto, ON, Canada. Affil: York, Can. Email: milosmitrovic14@yahoo.com.

Mittelstadt, **Jennifer L.**, *Rutgers*. Email: jmittel@history.rutgers.edu.

Mitter, **Sreemati**, *Brown*.

Mitton, **Steven Heath**, *Florida Atlantic*. Email: smitton@fau.edu.

Mitzman, **Arthur**. Amsterdam, Netherlands. Affil: Amsterdam. Email: abmitzman@planet.nl. Research: globalization and human culture, European unification.

Mixon, **Gregory L.**, *North Carolina, Charlotte*. Email: gmixon@uncc.edu.

Mixson, **James David**, *Alabama, Tuscaloosa*. Email: jmixson@ua.edu.

Mizelle, **Brett**, *California State, Long Beach*. Email: brett.mizelle@csulb.edu.

Mizelle, **Richard**, **Jr.**, *Houston*. Email: rmmizelle@uh.edu.

Mizell-Nelson, **Cathe**, *Hist. New Orleans*. Email: cathemn@hnoc.org.

Mizuno, **Hiromi**, *Minnesota (Hist.)*. Email: mizuno@umn.edu.

Mo, **Yajun**, *Boston Coll.* Chestnut Hill, MA. Email: yajun.mo@bc.edu. Research: Chinese tourism and travel culture 1860-1955, nationalism and region-making in East Asia.

Moazami, **Behrooz**, *Loyola, New Orleans*. Email: bmoazami@loyno.edu.

Mobbs, **Maj Michael**, *US Military Acad.* Email: michael.mobbs@usma.edu.

Mobery, **Jerry C.** Roseville, CA. Affil: Sacramento City. Email: jistory@surewest.net.

Mobley, **Arthur Scott**, **Jr.** Waunakee, WI. Affil: Wisconsin, Madison. Email: asmobley1221@gmail.com. Research: institutional culture and identity, formation of empire.

Mobley, **Christina Frances**, *Virginia*. Email: cfm8a@virginia.edu.

Mochoruk, **J. D.**, *North Dakota*. Email: james.mochoruk@und.edu.

Mock, **Harold**, **III**. Milledgeville, GA. Affil: Georgia Coll. and State. Email: harold.mock@gcsu.edu.

Mockaitis, **Thomas R.**, *DePaul*. Email: tmockait@depaul.edu.

Modaff, Abigail • Moore, David W. **715**

Modaff, Abigail. Cambridge, MA. Affil: Harvard. Email: amodaff@g.harvard.edu.
Modell, John, *Carnegie Mellon*. Providence, RI. Affil: Brown. Email: exigent@andrew.cmu. edu; John_Modell@brown.edu. Research: comparative education, history and sociology of social sciences.
Moehring, Eugene Peter, *Nevada, Las Vegas*. Email: eugene.moehring@unlv.edu.
Moeller, Max, *Hagley Museum and Library*. Email: mmoeller@hagley.org.
Moeller, Robert G., *California, Irvine*. Email: rgmoelle@uci.edu.
Moentmann, Elise M., *Portland*. Email: moentman@up.edu.
Moerer, Andrea K., *Metropolitan State*. Email: andrea.moerer@metrostate.edu.
Moertle, Garron Ryan. Rocklin, CA. Affil: Whitney High Sch. Email: paleo1209@gmail. com.
Moffatt, Christie, *National Library of Medicine*. Email: moffattc@mail.nih.gov.
Moglia-Bratt, Marie, *Pace*. Email: mmogliabratt@pace.edu.
Mogren, Eric William, *Northern Illinois*. Email: mogren@niu.edu.
Mohamed, H. Mohamed, *Windsor*. Email: mmohamed@uwindsor.ca.
Mohandesi, Salar, *Bowdoin*. Email: smohande@ bowdoin.edu.
Mohr, James C., *Oregon*. Eugene, OR. Email: jmohr@uoregon.edu. Research: medical policy/19th c social policy, law/professions.
Mohun, Arwen Palmer, *Delaware; Soc. for Hist. of Tech.* Newark, DE. Email: mohun@udel.edu. Research: technology, risk.
Moin, A. Azfar, *Texas, Austin*. Austin, TX. Email: amoin@utexas.edu. Research: pre-modern Islamic world, Sufism and sainthood.
Moir, Holly Laura. Woodbridge, VA. Affil: George Mason. Email: hmoir@gmu.edu. Research: consumerism, children/youth/teens.
Moitt, Bernard C., *Virginia Commonwealth*. Email: bmoitt@vcu.edu.
Mokhberi, Susan Marie, *Rutgers, Camden*.
Mokhiber, James P., *New Orleans*. Email: jmokhibe@uno.edu.
Mokhtarian, Jason, *Indiana*. Email: jmokhtar@ indiana.edu.
Mokros, Emily, *Kentucky*. Email: emily.mokros@ uky.edu.
Mokyr, Joel, *Northwestern*. Email: j-mokyr@ northwestern.edu.
Mole, Gregory Thomas, *Memphis*. Email: gmole@memphis.edu.
Molesky, Mark C., *Seton Hall*. Email: mark. molesky@shu.edu.
Molho, Anthony, *Brown*. Email: Anthony_ Molho@Brown.edu.
Molineux, Catherine A. J., *Vanderbilt*. Nashville, TN. Email: catherine.a.molineux@vanderbilt. edu. Research: early modern English cultural, popular representations of race.
Mollenauer, Lynn Wood, *North Carolina, Wilmington*. Email: mollenauerl@uncw.edu.
Mollin, Marian B., *Virginia Tech*. Email: mmollin@vt.edu.
Molloy, Michael, *Carleton, Can.* Email: michael. molloy@carleton.ca.
Molony, Barbara, *Santa Clara*. Santa Clara, CA. Email: bmolony@scu.edu. Research: women's rights movement in Japan, gender and sexuality.

Molvarec, Stephen J. Milwaukee, WI. Affil: Marquette. Email: stephenjmolvarec@ gmail.com. Research: medieval Carthusians, medieval religious life.
Molvig, Ole R., *Vanderbilt*. Email: ole.molvig@ vanderbilt.edu.
Mona, Corinne, *Center for Hist. of Physics*. Email: cmona@aip.org.
Monaghan, Shannon. Wellesley, MA. Affil: Harvard. Email: sfmonaghan@gmail.com.
Monaghan, Tyler N. Chicago, IL. Email: Ty.monaghan@gmail.com.
Monahan, Erika, *New Mexico*. Hanover, NH. Email: emonahan@unm.edu; emonahan@ dartmouth.edu. Research: Russia, early modern Europe.
Monas, Sidney, *Texas, Austin*. Email: smonas@ mail.utexas.edu.
Moneyhon, Carl H., *Arkansas, Little Rock*. Email: chmoneyhon@ualr.edu.
Monfasani, John, *SUNY, Albany*. Email: monf@ albany.edu.
Monheit, Michael Leonard, *South Alabama*. Email: mmonheit@southalabama.edu.
Monico, Amanda Lynn. Round Lake, IL. Email: Amonico8@sbcglobal.net.
Moniz, Amanda B. Washington, DC. Affil: National Museum of American Hist. Email: amanda.moniz@gmail.com. Research: early America, humanitarianism.
Monnais, Laurence, *Montréal*. Email: laurence. monnais-rousselot@umontreal.ca.
Monod, David, *Wilfrid Laurier*. Email: dmonod@ wlu.ca.
Monod, Paul Kleber, *Middlebury*. Email: monod@middlebury.edu.
Monroe, Elizabeth Brand, *Indiana–Purdue, Indianapolis*. Email: emonroe@iupui.edu.
Monroe, John Warne, *Iowa State*. Email: jmonroe@iastate.edu.
Monroe, Lisa A. New Haven, CT. Affil: Teachers, Columbia. Email: lam2265@tc.columbia.edu.
Monroe, William S. Providence, RI. Affil: Brown. Email: William_Monroe@brown.edu. Research: 9th-c Italy, manuscript studies.
Monroy, Douglas, *Colorado Coll.* Email: dmonroy@coloradocollege.edu.
Monson, Andrew P., *NYU*. Email: andrew. monson@nyu.edu.
Monson, Jamie, *Michigan State*. Email: monsonj@isp.msu.edu.
Montagna, Douglas S., *Grand Valley State*. Email: montagnd@gvsu.edu.
Montan, Nils Victor, Jr. Orlando, FL. Email: nils. montan@hotmail.com.
Montana, Ismael M., *Northern Illinois*. Email: montana@niu.edu.
Montano, Diana Jeaneth, *Washington, St. Louis*. Email: dmontano@wustl.edu.
Montano, John P., *Delaware*. Email: jpmon@ udel.edu.
Montcher, Fabien, *St. Louis*. Saint Louis, MO. Email: fabien.montcher@slu.edu. Research: early modern Europe, Atlantic world.
Monteiro, Lyra D., *Rutgers, Newark/New Jersey Inst. of Tech.* Email: lyra.monteiro@rutgers.edu.
Monteleone, Andrea Marie. Staatsburg, NY. Affil: Marist. Email: andrea.monteleone8@ gmail.com.
Monteon, Michael P., *California, San Diego*. Email: mmonteon@ucsd.edu.
Monter, William, *Northwestern*. Email: monter@ northwestern.edu.

Montero, Iris. Providence, RI. Affil: Brown. Email: monterini@gmail.com. Research: early modern science and medicine, indigenous Mesoamerica/colonial LA.
Montgomery, David C., *Brigham Young*.
Montgomery, Garth N., Jr., *Radford*. Email: gmontgom@radford.edu.
Montgomery, Georgina Mary, *Michigan State*. Email: montg165@msu.edu.
Montgomery, Rebecca S., *Texas State*. Email: rm53@txstate.edu.
Montgomery, Robert W., *Baldwin Wallace*. Email: rmontgom@bw.edu.
Montgomery, Stephanie. Northfield, MN. Affil: St. Olaf. Email: montgo6@stolaf.edu.
Montgomery, William E., *Austin Comm. Coll.* Austin, TX. Email: bmontgom@austincc.edu. Research: African American churches.
Montgomery, William. Omaha, NE. Affil: Clarkson. Email: wpmontgomery@gmail.com. Research: nursing education prior to 1900.
Montoya, Maria E., *NYU*. New York, NY. Email: maria.montoya@nyu.edu. Research: US labor, borderlands.
Montoya-Mora, Gregory. Albuquerque, NM. Affil: Chicago. Email: gmontoyamora@ uchicago.edu.
Monty, Christopher Sullivan, *California State, Dominguez Hills*. Email: cmonty@csudh.edu.
Moody, Honor, *Arthur and Elizabeth Schlesinger Library*. Email: hmoody@radcliffe.harvard.edu.
Moon, Krystyn R., *Mary Washington*. Fredericksburg, VA. Email: kmoon@umw.edu. Research: 19th-/20th-c US social/cultural.
Moon, S. Joan, *California State, Sacramento*. Email: joanmoon@csus.edu.
Moon, Selena. Edina, MN. Email: selena.m.moon@gmail.com. Research: multi-racial Japanese Americans, Japanese Americans with disabilities.
Moon, Suzanne Marie, *Oklahoma (Hist. of Science); Soc. for Hist. of Tech.* Email: suzannemoon@ou.edu.
Moon, Yumi, *Stanford*. Email: ymoon@stanford. edu.
Mooney, Graham P., *Johns Hopkins (Hist. of Science)*. Email: gmooney3@jhmi.edu.
Mooney, Katherine, *Florida State*. Email: kmooney@fsu.edu.
Mooney, M. Shaun, *James Madison*. Email: mooneyms@jmu.edu.
Mooney-Melvin, Patricia, *Loyola, Chicago*. Chicago, IL. Email: pmooney@luc.edu. Research: monuments/urban memory/ settlement houses.
Moore, Aaron Stephen, *Arizona State*. Email: aaron.s.moore@asu.edu.
Moore, Amber, *Arthur and Elizabeth Schlesinger Library*. Email: amber_moore@radcliffe. harvard.edu.
Moore, Andrew S., *St. Anselm*. Email: amoore@ anselm.edu.
Moore, Anne, *Calgary*. Email: amoore@ucalgary. ca.
Moore, Brian L., *Colgate*. Email: blmoore@ colgate.edu.
Moore, Carole E., *Georgia Inst. of Tech.* Email: moore@gatech.edu.
Moore, Colleen Mary, *James Madison*.
Moore, David T. Philadelphia, PA. Email: davidtmoore@mail.com.
Moore, David W., *Loyola, New Orleans*. Email: dmoore@loyno.edu.

Moore, **Deirdre**. Cambridge, MA. Affil: Harvard. Email: deirdremoore@gmail.com.

Moore, **Diana M.** New York, NY. Affil: Graduate Center, CUNY. Email: dmoore2@gradcenter.cuny.edu.

Moore, **Emily Elizabeth**. Lexington, KY. Affil: Kentucky. Email: eemo239@uky.edu.

Moore, **Erik A.** Norman, OK. Affil: Oklahoma. Email: erikmoorelaw@gmail.com. Research: US-Latin American relations, law.

Moore, George E., *San José State.*

Moore, **Gregory**. South Euclid, OH. Affil: Notre Dame Coll. Email: gmoore@ndc.edu. Research: American-Chinese relations, intelligence analysis/terrorism.

Moore, Heather, *US Senate Hist. Office.* Email: heather_moore@sec.senate.gov.

Moore, Jamie W., *Citadel.* Email: moorej@cchat.com.

Moore, **John A., Jr.** Claremont, CA. Affil: California State Polytechnic. Email: jamoore2@cpp.edu. Research: 20th-c US foreign policy, 18th-c US.

Moore, John C., *Hofstra.*

Moore, John Robert, *Louisiana, Lafayette.*

Moore, Johnny Stuart, *Radford.* Email: jsmoore@radford.edu.

Moore, Jonathan Allen, *Loyola, New Orleans.* Email: jamoore@loyno.edu.

Moore, **Joseph Hunter**. Nashville, TN. Affil: Middle Tennessee State. Email: Hunterrmo@aol.com.

Moore, Leonard J., *McGill.* Email: leonard.moore@mcgill.ca.

Moore, Leonard, *Texas, Austin.* Email: leonardmoore@austin.utexas.edu.

Moore, **Leslie Steltz**. Fort Collins, CO. Affil: Colorado State. Email: moorel1993@gmail.com.

Moore, Lindsay Rae, *Missouri–Kansas City.* Email: mooreiv@umkc.edu.

Moore, Louis Allen, *Grand Valley State.* Email: moorelou@gvsu.edu.

Moore, Lt Col Tomas, *US Military Acad.* Email: tomas.moore@usma.edu.

Moore, Michael E., *Iowa.* Email: michael-e-moore@uiowa.edu.

Moore, Peter N., *Texas A&M, Corpus Christi.* Email: peter.moore@tamucc.edu.

Moore, R. Laurence, *Cornell.* Email: rlm8@cornell.edu.

Moore, R. Scott, *Indiana, Pa.* Indiana, PA. Email: rsmoore@iup.edu. Research: trade in late antiquity, Cyprus.

Moore, Ray A., *Amherst.* Email: ramoore@amherst.edu.

Moore, **Robert J.** Columbia, SC. Affil: Columbia Coll., SC. Email: bobandmeribeth@hotmail.com.

Moore, Rosemary L., *Iowa.* Email: rosemary-moore@uiowa.edu.

Moore, Scott O., *Eastern Connecticut State.* Wethersfield, CT. Email: mooresc@easternct.edu. Research: modern Europe, central Europe.

Moore, Shirley Ann, *California State, Sacramento.* Email: smoore@csus.edu.

Moore, **Stephen I.** Orange, CA. Affil: California, Riverside. Email: stephen.moore@email.ucr.edu.

Moore, Stephen T., *Central Washington.* Email: moorest@cwu.edu.

Moore, William H., *Wyoming.*

Moore-Pewu, Jamila, *California State, Fullerton.* Email: jmoorepewu@fullerton.edu.

Moorhead, **James H.** Princeton, NJ. Affil: Princeton Theological Seminary. Email: james.moorhead@ptsem.edu.

Moorman, Marissa J., *Indiana.* Email: moorman@indiana.edu.

Mora, Anthony P., *Michigan, Ann Arbor.* Email: apmora@umich.edu.

Mora, **Juan Ignacio**. Urbana, IL. Affil: Illinois, Urbana-Champaign. Email: mora6@illinois.edu.

Mora, **Miriam Eve**. New York City, NY. Affil: Wayne State. Email: miriam.eve.mora@gmail.com. Research: American Jewish masculinity, Holocaust and genocide.

Moralee, Jason W, *Massachusetts, Amherst.* Email: jmoralee@history.umass.edu.

Morales, Daniel, *James Madison.* Charlottesville, VA. Email: moral3dx@jmu.edu. Research: US, Latin America.

Morales, **Powell**. Clovis, NM. Email: a.powell.morales@gmail.com.

Morales Castro, **Carmen Alicia**. Bethesda, MD. Affil: Asociación de historia del viejo San Juan. Email: carmenmorales31@gmail.com.

Morales Henry, Pablo, *Arthur and Elizabeth Schlesinger Library.* Email: pablo_moraleshenry@radcliffe.harvard.edu.

Moran, Bruce T., *Nevada, Reno.* Email: moran@unr.edu.

Moran, **Daniel**. East Brunswick, NJ. Affil: East Brunswick Public Sch. Email: dmoran@ebnet.org. Research: Catholic literature and film, authors' reputations.

Moran, Jeffrey P., *Kansas.* Email: jefmoran@ku.edu.

Moran, Megan Catherine, *Montclair State.* Email: moranm@mail.montclair.edu.

Moran, **Michelle T.** Rockville, MD. Affil: Montgomery. Email: michelle.moran@montgomerycollege.edu. Research: diet, public health.

Moran, Rachel Louise, *North Texas.* Email: rachel.moran@unt.edu.

Moran, **Ryan M.** Yokohama, Kanagawa, Japan. Affil: Keio. Email: ryan.moran415@gmail.com. Research: life insurance, science studies.

Moran, Sean Farrell, *Oakland.* Email: moran@oakland.edu.

Moran, **Timothy L**. Grosse Pointe Park, MI. Affil: Wayne State. Email: cy2558@wayne.edu. Research: American Civil War journalism, Tecumseh/Britain/US/borderlands 1812.

Moran Cruz, **Jo Ann Hoeppner**, *Georgetown.* Washington, DC. Email: moranj@georgetown.edu. Research: Christian/Islam religion and state, Dante.

Morantz-Sanchez, **Regina**, *Michigan, Ann Arbor.* Ann Arbor, MI. Email: reginann@umich.edu. Research: 20th-c gender and acculturation, Jewish family/women/medicine.

Morar, **Florin**. Cambridge, MA. Affil: Harvard. Email: morar@post.harvard.edu.

Mora-Torres, Juan T., *DePaul.* Email: jmorator@depaul.edu.

Moravec, Michelle, *Rosemont.* Email: mmoravec@rosemont.edu.

Morcillo, Aurora G., *Florida International.* Email: morcillo@fiu.edu.

More, **Alexander F.** Hull, MA. Affil: Harvard. Email: afmore@post.harvard.edu. Research:

legal and economic origins of welfare, climate change.

More, **Rebecca Sherrill**. Providence, RI. Affil: Brown. Email: Rebecca_More@brown.edu. Research: early modern Britain/17th-/18th-c US, early modern UK/US social/political/economic.

Morehouse, Maggi M., *Coastal Carolina.* Email: morehouse@coastal.edu.

Moreira, Isabel A., *Utah.* Email: isabel.moreira@utah.edu.

Morel, **Joseph Robert**. Barnard, VT. Affil: Brown. Email: jmorel@simpson.com. Research: colonial American travel to Britain, Anglicizing of American colonies.

Morel, **Michael, Jr.** Arlington, TX. Affil: Texas, Arlington. Email: michael.morel@mavs.uta.edu.

Moreno, E. Mark, *Texas A&M, Commerce.* Commerce, TX. Email: Mark.Moreno@tamuc.edu. Research: Mexican independence to revolution, Mexican American/California.

Moreno, Julio E., *San Francisco.* Email: moreno@usfca.edu.

Moreno, Paul, *Hillsdale.* Email: pmoreno@hillsdale.edu.

Moreno Alvarez, **Leonardo Guillermo**. Pittsburgh, PA. Affil: Pittsburgh. Email: lgm17@pitt.edu.

Moreno Vega, **Jose Manuel**. Carrboro, NC. Affil: North Carolina, Chapel Hill. Email: cuate@live.unc.edu.

Morera, Luis X., *Baylor.* Email: luis_morera@baylor.edu.

Moreton, **Bethany E.**, *Dartmouth.* Hanover, NH. Email: bethany.e.moreton@dartmouth.edu. Research: religion/labor/pro-capitalist activism, missionaries and neoliberalism.

Morgan, Alaina, *Southern California.* Email: alainamo@usc.edu.

Morgan, **Alisa Nicole**. La Verne, CA. Affil: California State, Fullerton. Email: amorgan4806@yahoo.com.

Morgan, Anita, *Indiana–Purdue, Indianapolis.* Email: aashende@iupui.edu.

Morgan, **Brandon B**. Rio Rancho, NM. Affil: Central New Mexico Comm. Coll. Email: bmorgan19@cnm.edu. Research: New Mexico-Chihuahua border violence, Pancho Villa and borderlands.

Morgan, Chester M., *Southern Mississippi.* Email: b.morgan@usm.edu.

Morgan, David O., *Wisconsin-Madison.* Email: domorgan@wisc.edu.

Morgan, David W., *Wesleyan.* Email: dmorgan@wesleyan.edu.

Morgan, Francesca C., *Northeastern Illinois.* Evanston, IL. Email: F-Morgan@neiu.edu. Research: US genealogy.

Morgan, Harold D. Hegins, PA. Email: harolddmorgan@excite.com.

Morgan, J. E. Atlanta, GA. Affil: Emory. Email: elizabeth.morgan@emory.edu.

Morgan, Jennifer L., *NYU.* New York, NY. Email: jm3018@nyu.edu. Research: early America, African American diaspora and women.

Morgan, **Joseph G**. New Rochelle, NY. Affil: Iona. Email: jmorgan@iona.edu. Research: 20th-c America, American diplomatic.

Morgan, Lynda J., *Mount Holyoke.* Email: ljmorgan@mtholyoke.edu.

Morgan, M. Gwyn, *Texas, Austin.* Email: mgm@mail.utexas.edu.

AHA members in **bold italic**; *Directory*-listed affiliations in *italic*

Morgan, M. J., *Kansas State*. Email: morganm@ksu.edu.

Morgan, Marjorie, *Central Washington*. Email: mmorgan@cwu.edu.

Morgan, Michael Cotey, *North Carolina, Chapel Hill*. Email: morgan@unc.edu.

Morgan, Michelle M., *Missouri State*. Email: michellemorgan@missouristate.edu.

Morgan, Philip D., *Johns Hopkins (Hist.)*. Baltimore, MD. Email: pmorgan@jhu.edu. Research: early America, African American.

Morgan, Ruth. Elwood, Australia. Affil: Monash. Email: ruth.morgan@monash.edu.

Morgan, Stephen. Nampa, ID. Affil: Northwest Nazarene. Email: stephenmorgan@nnu.edu. Research: early modern Europe, colonial Southeast Asia.

Morgan, Tabitha A. Philadelphia, PA. Affil: Comm. Coll. of Philadelphia. Email: tabitha.a.morgan@gmail.com.

Morgan, Zachary R., *Penn State*. University Park, PA. Email: zzm20@psu.edu. Research: Brazil, abolition.

Morgenson, Eric. Albany, NY. Affil: SUNY, Albany. Email: emorgenson@albany.edu.

Mori, Jennifer, *Toronto*. Email: jennifer.mori@utoronto.ca.

Morillo, Stephen R., *Wabash*. Crawfordsville, IN. Email: morillos@wabash.edu. Research: comparative warrior elites, world.

Morin, Jean-Pierre, *Carleton, Can*. Email: jeanpierre.morin@carleton.ca.

Morisette, Martin Gabrio. Prineville, OR. Email: martin97754@protonmail.com.

Morison, William, *Grand Valley State*. Email: morisonw@gvsu.edu.

Morith, Bradford James. Bryan, TX. Affil: Texas A&M, Coll. Station. Email: bradfordjm1@tamu.edu.

Moriyama, Takahito. Tokyo, Japan. Affil: Tokyo Univ. of Social Welfare. Email: tmoriyama240@gmail.com. Research: modern American conservatism, political media.

Morland, Barbara Robinson. Arlington, VA. Affil: Library of Congress. Email: barbaramorland@aol.com.

Morley, M. Blake. Atlanta, GA. Affil: Georgia State. Email: mmorley2@student.gsu.edu.

Morley, Margaret R., *Northern Arizona*. Email: margaret.morley@nau.edu.

Morman, Paul J., *Dayton*. Email: paul.morman@notes.udayton.edu.

Mormino, Gary R., *South Florida, St. Petersburg*.

Mormul, Michelle M. Saint Clair Shores, MI. Email: mmormul@udel.edu. Research: linen importation/flax seed exportation, port of Philadelphia 1765-1815.

Morone, James A. Providence, RI. Affil: Brown. Email: james_morone@brown.edu. Research: moral politics, race/gender/ethnicity/health care.

Morony, Michael G., *UCLA*. Email: morony@history.ucla.edu.

Morreale, Laura K. Larchmont, NY. Affil: Fordham. Email: morreale156@verizon.net. Research: global French during Middle Ages, early vernacular historiography.

Morrell, Rex D. Tishomingo, OK. Affil: Murray State Coll. Email: rexm@tishomingo.com.

Morrill, Dan L., *North Carolina, Charlotte*. Email: dlmorril@uncc.edu.

Morrill, James R., III, *Louisville*.

Morris, Andrew D., *California Polytechnic State*. Email: admorris@calpoly.edu.

Morris, Andrew, *Union Coll*. Email: morrisa@union.edu.

Morris, Bonnie J. Santa Cruz, CA. Affil: California, Berkeley. Email: drbon@gwu.edu.

Morris, Christopher, *Texas, Arlington*. Email: morris@uta.edu.

Morris, Colin Jeffrey, *Manhattanville*. Email: colin.morris@mville.edu.

Morris, James M., *Christopher Newport*. Email: mjames792@aol.com.

Morris, Jennifer, *Appalachian State*. Email: morrisjf1@appstate.edu.

Morris, John D., *Kent State*.

Morris, Katy, *Massachusetts Hist. Soc*. Email: kmorris@masshist.org.

Morris, Lt Col Craig, *US Air Force Acad*. Email: craig.morris@usafa.edu.

Morris, M. Michelle J., *Missouri, Columbia*. Email: morrismary@missouri.edu.

Morris, Marilyn A., *North Texas*. Email: mmorris@unt.edu.

Morris, Nathan. Saint Louis, MO. Affil: Washington, St. Louis. Email: rnathanmorris@yahoo.com.

Morris, Robin M., *Agnes Scott*. Email: rmorris@agnesscott.edu.

Morris, Ronald V., *Ball State*. Email: rvmorris@bsu.edu.

Morris, Stephanie A. Bensalem, PA. Affil: Sisters of the Blessed Sacrament. Email: samor9820@aol.com.

Morris, Thomas D., *Portland State*.

Morris, Tiyi M. Newark, OH. Affil: Ohio State. Email: morris.730@osu.edu. Research: civil rights movement, black women.

Morrison, Christopher A., *US Dept. of State*.

Morrison, Dane A., *Salem State*. Email: dmorrison@salemstate.edu.

Morrison, Heather Christine, *SUNY, New Paltz*. Email: morrisoh@newpaltz.edu.

Morrison, Heidi, *Wisconsin-La Crosse*. Email: hmorrison@uwlax.edu.

Morrison, James H., *St. Mary's, Can*. Email: james.morrison@smu.ca.

Morrison, Karl F., *Rutgers*. Princeton, NJ. Email: ankamor@verizon.net. Research: semiology in Christian art, medieval hermeneutics.

Morrison, Kevin. Bakersfield, CA. Affil: Kern High Sch. District. Email: Kmorrison13@liberty.edu.

Morrison, William, *Northern British Columbia*. Email: morrison@unbc.ca.

Morrissey, Katherine G., *Arizona*. Tucson, AZ. Email: kmorriss@u.arizona.edu. Research: North American West, cultural.

Morrissey, Robert Michael, *Illinois, Urbana-Champaign*. Urbana, IL. Email: rmorriss@illinois.edu. Research: Illinois and Michigan Canal, frontier Illinois.

Morrissey, Susan K., *California, Irvine*. Irvine, CA. Email: susan.morrissey@uci.edu. Research: political violence, gender and autobiography.

Morrow, Diane Batts, *Georgia*. Athens, GA. Email: dbmorrow@uga.edu. Research: 19th-c African American, US multicultural.

Morrow, John H., Jr., *Georgia*. Athens, GA. Email: jmorrow@uga.edu. Research: modern Europe, war and society.

Morrow, Joshua Aaron. Columbus, OH. Affil: Ohio State. Email: Morrow.289@buckeyemail.osu.edu.

Morrow, Mary Jane, *Duke*. Email: oscar@duke.edu.

Morrow, Robert W. Red Bank, NJ. Affil: Morgan State. Email: rmorrow602@gmail.com.

Morruzzi, Norma, *Illinois, Chicago*. Email: nmorruzzi@uic.edu.

Morschauser, Scott, *Rowan*. Email: morschauser@rowan.edu.

Morse, Darrell P., *California State, Northridge*.

Morse, Kathryn T., *Middlebury*. Middlebury, VT. Email: kmorse@middlebury.edu. Research: environmental, US West.

Morse, Kimberly J., *Washburn*. Email: kim.morse@washburn.edu.

Morse, Victoria M., *Carleton Coll*. Email: vmorse@carleton.edu.

Morser, Eric J., *Skidmore*. Email: emorser@skidmore.edu.

Morsman, Amy F., *Middlebury*. Email: amorsman@middlebury.edu.

Morstein-Marx, Robert, *California, Santa Barbara*. Email: morstein@classics.ucsb.edu.

Mortensen, Dáša Pejchar, *Davidson*. Email: damortensen@davidson.edu.

Mortimer, Loren Michael. Davis, CA. Affil: California, Davis. Email: lmmortimer@ucdavis.edu. Research: Native American environmental, early American borderlands.

Morton, Charles J. Kintnersville, PA.

Morton, David, *British Columbia*. Vancouver, BC, Canada. Email: david.morton@ubc.ca. Research: Maputo Mozambique, shantytowns.

Morton, Desmond, *McGill; Toronto*. Email: desmond.morton@mcgill.ca.

Morton, Erin, *New Brunswick*. Email: emorton@unb.ca.

Morton, John Davis. Chestnut Hill, MA. Affil: Boston Coll. Email: mortonjo@bc.edu.

Morton, Marian J., *John Carroll*. Email: mmorton@jcu.edu.

Morton, Patricia M., *Trent*.

Morton, Paul J., *Covenant*. Email: morton@covenant.edu.

Morton, Richard A. Atlanta, GA. Affil: Clark Atlanta. Email: rmorton@cau.edu.

Morton, Suzanne, *McGill*. Email: suzanne.morton@mcgill.ca.

Mosca, Matthew William, *Washington, Seattle*. Email: mosca@uw.edu.

Moseley, C. Charlton, *Georgia Southern*.

Mosely, Erin, *Chapman*. Email: mosely@chapman.edu.

Mosely Latham, Janet. Elon, NC. Affil: East Carolina. Email: lathamj16@students.ecu.edu. Research: DG Fairchild & Marian Bell Fairchild, Scientific expeditions.

Moser, Claudia, *California, Santa Barbara*. Email: moser@arthistory.ucsb.edu.

Moser, Mark A., *North Carolina, Greensboro*. Email: mamoser@uncg.edu.

Moses, A. Dirk. Princeton, NJ. Affil: Sydney. Email: dirk.moses@sydney.edu.au. Research: genocide in colonial contexts, genocide concept.

Moses, Adrianne. New Rochelle, NY. Affil: Drew. Email: majmasi@aol.com.

Moses, Claire G., *Maryland, Coll. Park*. Email: cmoses@umd.edu.

Moses, Donna. Los Altos, CA. Affil: Arizona State. Email: mosesdo@msjdominicans.org.

Moses, Jacob D. Cambridge, MA. Affil: Harvard. Email: jacobmoses@fas.harvard.edu. Research: medicine, biotechnology.

Moses, James L., *Arkansas Tech.* Email: jmoses@atu.edu.

Moses, Wilson J., *Penn State.* Email: wjm12@psu.edu.

Mosher, Jeffrey C., *Texas Tech.* Lubbock, TX. Email: jeffrey.mosher@ttu.edu. Research: modern Latin America, Brazil.

Moskowitz, Kara, *Missouri–St. Louis.* Saint Louis, MO. Email: moskowitzk@umsl.edu. Research: Kenya, development and decolonization.

Moss, Alfred A., Jr., *Maryland, Coll. Park.* Email: almoss@umd.edu.

Moss, David J., *Alberta.* Email: d.j.moss@exeter.ac.uk.

Moss, Hilary J., *Amherst.* Email: hmoss@amherst.edu.

Moss, Kelsey Christina. Township of Washington, NJ. Affil: Georgetown. Email: kelseym@princeton.edu.

Moss, Kenneth B., *Johns Hopkins (Hist.).* Baltimore, MD. Email: kmoss5@jhu.edu. Research: nationalism and political thought, Jews Eastern Europe Palestine Israel.

Moss, Laura-Eve, *Tennessee, Knoxville.* Email: lmoss3@utk.edu.

Mosshammer, Alden A., *California, San Diego.* Email: amosshammer@ucsd.edu.

Mosterman, Andrea Catharina, *New Orleans.* New Orleans, LA. Email: amosterm@uno.edu. Research: Atlantic, colonial America.

Mostern, Ruth, *Pittsburgh.* Pittsburgh, PA. Email: rmostern@pitt.edu. Research: Yellow River, digital gazetteers.

Mota, Isadora Moura, *Princeton.* Miami, FL. Email: imota@princeton.edu; isadora.mota@miami.edu. Research: slavery, abolition.

Motadel, David. London, United Kingdom. Affil: London Sch. of Economics and Political Sci. Email: David.Motadel@gmail.com.

Motes, Kevin Daniel, *Rockhurst.* Email: kd.motes@rockhurst.edu.

Mott, Morris K., *Brandon.* Email: mott@brandonu.ca.

Mottahedeh, Roy, *Harvard (Hist.).* Email: mottahed@fas.harvard.edu.

Moudry, Roberta M. Ithaca, NY. Affil: Cornell. Email: rmm5@cornell.edu.

Moudy, John Chase. Hopkins, MN. Affil: US Postal Service. Email: john.moudy18@yahoo.com. Research: archival theory and practice, 20th-c US.

Mougoue, Jacqueline-Bethel Tchouta, *Baylor.* Waco, TX. Email: jb_mougoue@baylor.edu. Research: gendering identities.

Moulds, Loren S. Charlottesville, VA. Affil: Virginia. Email: moulds@virginia.edu. Research: gender, suburban.

Moulton, Aaron Coy, *Stephen F. Austin State.* Nacogdoches, TX. Email: moultonac@sfasu.edu; AaronCoyMoulton@gmail.com. Research: US-Latin American relations, US foreign policy ideology.

Moulton, Edward C., *Manitoba.*

Moulton, Gary E., *Nebraska, Lincoln.* Email: gmoulton1@unl.edu.

Mounter, Michael. Cayce, SC. Affil: South Carolina. Email: mountemr@law.sc.edu. Research: 19th-c African American, American women.

Mouralis, Guillaume. Berlin, Germany. Affil: Centre National de la Recherche Scientifique. Email: g.mouralis@gmail.com.

Moure, Frank, *Austin Peay State.* Email: mouref@apsu.edu.

Moure, Kenneth J., *Alberta.* Edmonton, AB, Canada. Email: moure@ualberta.ca. Research: France and economic change since 1940, 20th-c politics and literature.

Mouris, Katya. Hyattsville, MD. Affil: Catholic. Email: 40mouris@cardinalmail.cua.edu.

Moutafis, George. Lesvos, Greece. Email: gmoutaf@otenet.gr. Research: Greek immigration to New York 1895-1930.

Mouton, Michelle, *Wisconsin-Oshkosh.* Email: mouton@uwosh.edu.

Mouw, Dirk Edward. North Little Rock, AR. Affil: Reformed Church Center. Email: dirk.mouw@comcast.net. Research: British New York religion and society, New Netherland.

Moy, Charlotte Elizabeth Cover. Cleveland, TN. Affil: Lee. Email: charlotte.cover@gmail.com. Research: Venetian convent education, University of Padua.

Moy, Rebecca L. York, ME. Affil: Kennebunk High Sch. RSU 21. Email: rmoy@rsu21.net.

Moya, Jose C., *Barnard, Columbia; UCLA.* New York, NY. Email: jmoya@barnard.edu; moya@history.ucla.edu. Research: Buenos Aires anarchism/labor/women, Argentina/Spain immigration/ethnicity.

Moyd, Michelle, *Indiana.* Bloomington, IN. Email: mimoyd@indiana.edu. Research: African soldiers in colonial armies, comparative racisms.

Moye, J. Todd, *North Texas.* Email: moye@unt.edu.

Moye, Lucy E., *Hillsdale.* Email: lmoye@hillsdale.edu.

Moyer, Ann E., *Pennsylvania.* Philadelphia, PA. Email: moyer@sas.upenn.edu. Research: arts and sciences in later Renaissance, intellectual life in 16th-c Florence.

Moyer, Ian S., *Michigan, Ann Arbor.* Ann Arbor, MI. Email: ianmoyer@umich.edu. Research: Ptolemaic Egypt, Greek-Egyptian relations.

Moyer, Paul B., *SUNY, Coll. Brockport.* Email: pmoyer@brockport.edu.

Moylan, Prudence A., *Loyola, Chicago.* Evanston, IL. Email: pmoylan@luc.edu. Research: British gender/peace movements 1890-1940, US women religious 1850-1990.

Moylan, Thomas, *Central Connecticut State.* Email: moylantom@ccsu.edu.

Moyn, Samuel Aaron, *Yale.* Email: samuel.moyn@yale.edu.

Moynahan, Gregory B., *Bard.* Email: moynahan@bard.edu.

Mozie, Dante E. Columbia, SC. Affil: South Carolina. Email: dmozie@email.sc.edu.

Mrazek, Rudolf, *Michigan, Ann Arbor.* Email: rdlf@umich.edu.

Mrozek, Donald J., *Kansas State.* Email: mrozek@ksu.edu.

Mruck, Armin E. Baltimore, MD. Affil: Towson. Email: amruck@towson.edu. Research: German universities under Allied occupation, WWII and post-WWII.

Mseba, Admire, *Missouri, Columbia.*

Mt. Pleasant, Alyssa. Buffalo, NY. Affil: SUNY, Buffalo. Email: alyssamt@buffalo.edu. Research: Native American.

Mtisi, Richard, *Luther.* Email: mtisri01@luther.edu.

Mueggler, Erik. Ann Arbor, MI. Affil: Michigan, Ann Arbor. Email: mueggler@umich.edu.

Muehlbauer, Matthew S., *US Military Acad.* Email: matthew.muehlbauer@usma.edu.

Muehlberger, Ellen, *Michigan, Ann Arbor.* Email: emuehlbe@umich.edu.

Muehlhahn, Klaus. Berlin, Germany. Affil: Freie, Berlin. Email: kmuehl@zedat.fu-berlin.de. Research: secret services in Cold War, governance in China.

Mueller, Alison, *Robert H. Smith Center.* Email: amueller@monticello.org.

Mueller, Christine L., *Reed.* Email: cmueller@reed.edu.

Mueller, Gordon 'Nick' Herbert, *New Orleans; National Hist. Center.* New Orleans, LA. Affil: National WWII Museum. Email: ghmer@uno.edu; nick.mueller@nationalww2museum.org. Research: WWII and public memory, military and diplomatic.

Mueller, John H., *Central Connecticut State; Hartford.* Email: muellerj@mail.ccsu.edu.

Mueller, Ken S. Lafayette, IN. Affil: Ivy Tech Comm. Coll. Email: kmueller@ivytech.edu. Research: Jacksonian politics, American nationalism 1800-50.

Mueller, Lucas Melvin. Philadelphia, PA. Affil: Science Hist. Inst. Email: lmm@mit.edu.

Mueller, Melanie J., *Center for Hist. of Physics.* Email: mmueller@aip.org.

Mueller, Robert, *Utah State.* Email: robert.mueller@usu.edu.

Mueller, Wolfgang P., *Fordham.* Email: wpmueller2@gmail.com.

Muetterties, Carly. Lexington, KY. Affil: Kentucky. Email: carly.muetterties@uky.edu.

Mufuka, N. Kenneth, *Lander.*

Mugge, Miqueias H. Princeton, NJ. Affil: Princeton. Email: mmugge@princeton.edu.

Muhammad, Devissi, *Henry Ford Coll.* Marshall, TX. Affil: Wiley. Email: Devissi.Muhammad@gmail.com; drdevissi@outlook.com. Research: US and Africa, Latin America.

Muhammad, Robin D. Athens, OH. Affil: Ohio. Email: dearmon@ohio.edu. Research: race/gender/state, environmental/sanitation/health issues.

Muhlfeld, Sharon M. Sauder. Collegeville, PA. Affil: Moravian. Email: smsaud@aol.com. Research: colonial and native North America, American Revolution.

Muigai, Wangui. Waltham, MA. Affil: Brandeis. Email: wmuigai@brandeis.edu.

Muir, Edward W., Jr., *Northwestern.* Evanston, IL. Email: e-muir@northwestern.edu. Research: 17th-c libertines and skeptics, culture of Italian opera.

Muir, Fredric J. Annapolis, MD. Affil: Unitarian Universalist Association. Email: FredMuir@gmail.com.

Muir, James, *Alberta.* Email: james.muir@ualberta.ca.

Muir, Malcolm, Jr., *Austin Peay State.*

Muir-Harmony, Teasel Elizabeth. Washington, DC. Affil: Smithsonian Inst. Email: tmuirharmony@gmail.com. Research: technology, diplomacy.

Muirhead, Bruce W., *Waterloo.* Email: muirhead@uwaterloo.ca.

Muise, Delphin A., *Carleton, Can.* Email: Del.Muise@Carleton.ca.

Mujic, Julie A. Westerville, OH. Affil: Denison. Email: mujicj@denison.edu. Research: Midwest home front, education during Civil War.

Mukerjee, **Anil Kumar**, *US Military Acad.* Email: anil.mukerjee@usma.edu.

Mukharji, *Projit Bihari*. Philadelphia, PA. Affil: Pennsylvania. Email: mukharji@sas.upenn.edu. Research: chemistry, anthropology.

Mukherjee, **Erica**, *North Carolina, Chapel Hill.*

Mukherjee, **Mithi**, *Colorado, Boulder.* Email: mukherjm@colorado.edu.

Mukhina, **Irina A.**, *Assumption.* Email: imukhina@assumption.edu.

Mulcahy, *Matthew B.*, *Loyola, Md.* Baltimore, MD. Email: mmulcahy@loyola.edu. Research: colonial and revolutionary America, social.

Mulderry, **Darra D.**, *Providence.* Email: mulderry@providence.edu.

Muldoon, *James M.*, *Rutgers, Camden.* Bristol, RI. Affil: John Carter Brown Library. Email: james_muldoon@brown.edu. Research: medieval, early modern.

Muldowny, **John**, *Tennessee, Knoxville.* Email: jmuldown@utk.edu.

Mulholland, **James A.**, *North Carolina State.*

Mullally, **Sasha**, *New Brunswick.* Email: sasham@unb.ca.

Mullaney, *Thomas S.*, *Stanford.* Stanford, CA. Email: tsmullaney@stanford.edu. Research: technology/language/modernity, ethnicity/social science/governmentality.

Mullen, *Lincoln*, *George Mason.* Fairfax, VA. Email: lmullen@gmu.edu; lincoln@lincolnmullen.com. Research: American religions, digital.

Muller, **Alexander V.**, *California State, Northridge.*

Muller, *Anna*. Dearborn, MI. Affil: Michigan-Dearborn. Email: anmuller@umich.edu. Research: women prisoners in eastern Europe, gender relations in eastern Europe.

Muller, *Dalia A.*, *SUNY, Buffalo.* Buffalo, NY. Email: daliamul@buffalo.edu. Research: Mexico/Cuba transnational, political/cultural and history of ideas.

Muller, **Edward**, *Pittsburgh.* Email: ekmuller@pitt.edu.

Muller, *Jerry Z.* Silver Spring, MD. Affil: Catholic. Email: mullerj@cua.edu. Research: capitalism, biography of Jacob Taubes 1923-87.

Mulligan, *Ami Sumie*. Mililani, HI. Affil: Hawaii, Manoa. Email: amimalie@hawaii.edu.

Mulligan, **Debra**, *Roger Williams.* Email: dmulligan@rwu.edu.

Mulligan, **Megan**, *Susquehanna.* Email: mulliganmeg@susqu.edu.

Mulligan, **William H.**, **Jr.**, *Murray State.* Email: wmulligan@murraystate.edu.

Mullin, **Janet**, *New Brunswick.* Email: mullinj@unb.ca.

Mullin, **Michael**, *California State, Sacramento.*

Mullins, **Jeffrey A.**, *St. Cloud State.* Email: jamullins@stcloudstate.edu.

Mullins, **John Patrick**, *Marquette.* Email: john.mullins@marquette.edu.

Mullis, **Tony R.**, *US Army Command Coll.* Email: tony.r.mullis2.civ@mail.mil.

Mulloy, **Darren**, *Wilfrid Laurier.* Email: dmulloy@wlu.ca.

Mulready-Stone, **Kristin K.**, *Naval War Coll.* Email: kristin.mulreadystone@usnwc.edu.

Mulrooney, **Margaret M.**, *James Madison.* Email: mulroomm@jmu.edu.

Mulry, **Kate Luce**, *California State, Bakersfield.* Email: kmulry@csub.edu.

Mulsow, *Sandra*. Wilson, TX. Affil: Wilson High Sch. Email: smulsow.67@gmail.com.

Mulvehill, *Tim*. Long Beach, CA. Affil: Millikan High Sch. Email: tmulvehill@lbschools.net.

Mumford, **Eric**, *Washington, St. Louis.* Email: epm@wustl.edu.

Mumford, **Jeremy Ravi**, *Brown.* Email: Jeremy_Mumford@Brown.edu.

Mumford, **Kevin J.**, *Illinois, Urbana-Champaign.* Email: kmumford@illinois.edu.

Mumford, *Robert Craig*. Santa Paula, CA. Affil: Southern New Hampshire. Email: Behindtheinkink@gmail.com.

Mummey, **Kevin Dean**, *St. Olaf.* Email: mummey1@stolaf.edu.

Muncy, *Robyn*, *Maryland, Coll. Park.* College Park, MD. Email: rmuncy@umd.edu. Research: US progressive tradition, US women.

Munda, *Brandon Wayne Dylan*. Richmond, VA. Affil: William and Mary. Email: bwmunda@wm.edu.

Munford, **Clarence J.**, *Guelph.*

Mungello, **D. E.**, *Baylor.* Email: d_e_mungello@baylor.edu.

Munholland, **J. Kim**, *Minnesota (Hist.).* Email: munhollandj@aol.com.

Munochiveyi, **Munya B.**, *Holy Cross.* Email: mmunochi@holycross.edu.

Muñoz, **Laura K.**, *Nebraska, Lincoln.* Email: laura.munoz@unl.edu.

Munoz, **Maria L. O.**, *Susquehanna.* Email: munozm@susqu.edu.

Munro, **George E.**, *Virginia Commonwealth.* Email: gemunro@vcu.edu.

Munro, **John J.**, *St. Mary's, Can.* Email: John.Munro@smu.ca.

Munro, **Kenneth J.**, *Alberta.* Email: ken.munro@ualberta.ca.

Munson, *Howard A.*, *IV*. Angwin, CA. Affil: Pacific Union. Email: hmunson@puc.edu. Research: US mission to aid Turkey, US-Turkish relations.

Munson, **James R.**, *Longwood.* Email: munsonjr@longwood.edu.

Munteanu, **Mircea A.**, *US Dept. of State.*

Muntz, **Charles E.**, *Arkansas, Fayetteville.* Email: cmuntz@uark.edu.

Munz, **John**, *Hofstra.* Email: john.f.munz@hofstra.edu.

Munz, *Tania*. Research Triangle Park, NC. Affil: National Humanities Center. Email: taniamunz@gmail.com. Research: science and medicine, technology.

Munzinger, **Mark R.**, *Radford.* Email: mmunzinge@radford.edu.

Murad, *Hasan Sohaib*. Lahore, Pakistan. Affil: Univ. of Management and Tech. Email: hasan.sohaib.murad@umt.edu.pk. Research: Islam/Muslims, Western civilization.

Murch, **Donna**, *Rutgers.* Email: dmurch@history.rutgers.edu.

Murchie, *David N*. Yokohama-shi, Japan. Affil: Tohoku Gakuin. Email: dnmurchie2000@yahoo.com. Research: Christianity and economics, Christianity and socialism.

Murdoch, *Alexander J*. Edinburgh, United Kingdom. Affil: Edinburgh. Email: alex.murdoch@ed.ac.uk. Research: Scotland and America 1603-1815, Scottish politics 1650-1763.

Murdoch, **Lydia**, *Vassar.* Email: lymurdoch@vassar.edu.

Murdock, **Caitlin E.**, *California State, Long Beach.* Email: c.murdock@csulb.edu.

Murdock, *Scott D*. Denver, CO. Email: scott123murdock@yahoo.com.

Murdza, *Peter J.*, *Jr.* Hanover, NH. Email: Peter.Murdza@uwalumni.com. Research: French-Liberian relations, Liberian political.

Murillo, **Bianca**, *California State, Dominguez Hills.* Email: biancaannamurillo@gmail.com.

Murillo, *Dana Velasco*, *California, San Diego.* La Jolla, CA. Email: dvmurillo@ucsd.edu. Research: urban Indians in colonial Zacatecas, indigenous groups in mining towns.

Murillo, *Lina Maria*, *Iowa.* Iowa City, IA. Email: lina-murillo@uiowa.edu. Research: women's reproductive health, race/class/sexuality.

Murison, **Barbara C.**, *Western Ontario.* Email: bmurison@uwo.ca.

Murmello, *Kelly*. Orefield, PA. Affil: Villanova. Email: kelly.murmello@gmail.com.

Murnane, **M. Susan**, *Case Western Reserve.* Email: susan.murnane@case.edu.

Murokh, *Dina*. Los Angeles, CA. Affil: Southern California. Email: murokh@usc.edu.

Murphree, *Daniel S.*, *Central Florida.* Orlando, FL. Email: daniel.murphree@ucf.edu. Research: colonial Floridas, North American borderlands/frontiers.

Murphy, **Angela**, *Texas State.* Email: am34@txstate.edu.

Murphy, *Brian Phillips*, *Rutgers, Newark/New Jersey Inst. of Tech.* Email: brian.phillips.murphy@rutgers.edu.

Murphy, **Cliona**, *California State, Bakersfield.* Email: cmurphy@csub.edu.

Murphy, **Edward L.**, *Michigan State.* Email: murph367@msu.edu.

Murphy, **Frederick I.**, *Western Kentucky.* Email: frederick.murphy@wku.edu.

Murphy, *Hannah Saunders*. London, United Kingdom. Affil: King's Coll. London. Email: hannah.murphy@kcl.ac.uk. Research: early modern, medical.

Murphy, **J. Thomas**, *Indiana, South Bend.* Email: murphyjt@iusb.edu.

Murphy, **James B.**, *Southern Illinois, Carbondale.*

Murphy, *Jane H.*, *Colorado Coll.* Colorado Springs, CO. Email: jmurphy@coloradocollege.edu. Research: Islamic world, science.

Murphy, **Kameika Samantha**, *Stockton.*

Murphy, **Kathleen Susan**, *California Polytechnic State.* Email: ksmurphy@calpoly.edu.

Murphy, *Kevin A.*, *Evansville.* Binghamton, NY. Affil: Binghamton, SUNY. Email: km421@evansville.edu; kmurphy6@binghamton.edu. Research: US, childhood and youth.

Murphy, *Kevin John*. Levittown, NY. Affil: SUNY, Stony Brook. Email: Kevin.Murphy@stonybrook.edu. Research: early America, Atlantic world.

Murphy, *Kevin P.*, *Minnesota (Hist.).* Minneapolis, MN. Email: kpmurphy@umn.edu. Research: US urban/political/intellectual/cultural, sexuality and masculinity.

Murphy, *Laura*. Poughkeepsie, NY. Affil: Dutchess Comm. Coll., SUNY. Email: murphy@sunydutchess.edu. Research: recent academic labor/contingent faculty, women and US labor movement.

Murphy, **Lucy E.**, *Ohio State.* Email: murphy.500@osu.edu.

Murphy, **Marjorie**, *Swarthmore.* Email: mmurphy1@swarthmore.edu.

Murphy, **Mary**, *Montana State, Bozeman.* Email: mmurphy@montana.edu.

Murphy, Mary-Elizabeth B., *Eastern Michigan.* Email: mmurph54@emich.edu.

Murphy, Michael Curtis. Havertown, PA. Affil: West Chester. Email: Murphymichael923@gmail.com.

Murphy, Michelle, *Toronto.* Email: michelle.murphy@utoronto.ca.

Murphy, Paul V., *Grand Valley State.* Allendale, MI. Email: murphyp@gvsu.edu. Research: 20th-c US, intellectual.

Murphy, Paul V., *John Carroll.* Email: pvmurphy@jcu.edu.

Murphy, Ryan Patrick, *Earlham.* Email: murphry@earlham.edu.

Murphy, Sharon Ann, *Providence.* Email: sharon.murphy@providence.edu.

Murphy, Terry, *St. Mary's, Can.* Email: Terry.Murphy@smu.ca.

Murphy, Tessa, *Syracuse.* Syracuse, NY. Email: temurphy@maxwell.syr.edu. Research:, early America.

Murphy, Thomas R., SJ, *Seattle.* Email: tmurphy@seattleu.edu.

Murphy, Timothy James, III. Lovettsville, VA. Affil: Discover America. Email: tjmurphy02@email.wm.edu.

Murphy, William B., *SUNY, Oswego.* Email: william.murphy@oswego.edu.

Murphyao, Amanda. Chicago, CA. Affil: Carleton. Email: murphy.amanda@gmail.com.

Murray, Alexander C., *Toronto.* Email: alexander.murray@utoronto.ca.

Murray, Catherine. Philadelphia, PA. Affil: Temple. Email: tue85831@temple.edu. Research: America.

Murray, Constance P., *James Madison.* Email: murraycp@jmu.edu.

Murray, Courtney. Cypress, TX. Email: courtloughner@gmail.com.

Murray, David R., *Guelph.* Email: dmurray@uoguelph.ca.

Murray, Dian H., *Notre Dame.* Email: Murray.1@nd.edu.

Murray, Gail S., *Rhodes.* Email: murray@rhodes.edu.

Murray, Heather, *North Georgia.* Email: heather.murray@ung.edu.

Murray, Jacqueline, *Guelph.* Guelph, ON, Canada. Email: jacqueline.murray@uoguelph.ca. Research: medieval masculinity, Middle Ages male sexuality.

Murray, James M., *Western Michigan.* Email: james.murray@wmich.edu.

Murray, Jennifer M., *Oklahoma State.*

Murray, Jeremy Andrew, *California State, San Bernardino.* Email: jmurray@csusb.edu.

Murray, Nancy. Washington, VA. Affil: National Park Service. Email: mvumba@yahoo.com. Research: African American, oral.

Murray, Nicholas A., *Naval War Coll.* Email: nicholas.murray@usnwc.edu.

Murray, Pamela S., *Alabama, Birmingham.* Birmingham, AL. Email: pmurray@uab.edu. Research: women in Latin America, women in 19th-c Colombia.

Murray, Peter C. Fayetteville, NC. Affil: Methodist. Email: pcmurray@methodist.edu. Research: civil rights movement, religion and race.

Murray, Richard David. Plymouth, MA. Email: Rmurraytennis@gmail.com.

Murray, Sean Collins, *Austin Comm. Coll.* Email: smurray@austincc.edu.

Murray, Suzanne, *South Florida, Tampa.* Email: spmurray@usf.edu.

Murray, William M., *South Florida, Tampa.* Email: murray@usf.edu.

Murray, Williamson, *Ohio State.*

Murrin, John M. Lawrenceville, NJ. Affil: Princeton. Email: murrin@princeton.edu.

Murry, Gregory W., *Mount St. Mary's.* Email: murry@msmary.edu.

Murthy, Viren, *Wisconsin-Madison.* Email: vmurthy2@wisc.edu.

Murzyn, John S., *Columbus State.*

Musandu, Phoebe. Washington, DC. Affil: Georgetown, Qatar. Email: pam98@georgetown.edu. Research: press, women.

Muscolino, Micah S., *California, San Diego.* Email: mmuscolino@ucsd.edu.

Muse, Clifford L., Jr. Glenn Dale, MD. Affil: Howard. Email: cmuse@howard.edu. Research: New Deal, Howard University.

Musekamp, Jan. Pittsburgh, PA. Affil: Pittsburgh. Email: jan.musekamp@pitt.edu.

Musgrove, Charles D., *St. Mary's, Md.* Email: cdmusgrove@smcm.edu.

Musgrove, George Derek, *Maryland, Baltimore County.* Washington, DC. Email: derek.musgrove@umbc.edu. Research: Washington DC, post-1965 black politics.

Musgrove, Margaret, *Central Oklahoma.* Email: mmusgrove2@uco.edu.

Mushal, Amanda R., *Citadel.* Email: amanda.mushal@citadel.edu.

Musheff, Victoria. Charleston, SC. Affil: Citadel. Email: vcross.mtp@gmail.com. Research: Acadians in British South Carolina.

Musher, Sharon Ann, *Stockton.* Galloway, NJ. Email: mushers@stockton.edu. Research: New Deal art, women travelers.

Musisi, Nakanyike, *Toronto.* Email: nakanyike.musisi@utoronto.ca.

Musoni, Francis, *Kentucky.* Email: francis.musoni@uky.edu.

Musselwhite, Margaret T., *Omohundro Inst.* Email: mstill@wm.edu.

Musselwhite, Paul P., *Dartmouth.* Hanover, NH. Email: paul.musselwhite@dartmouth.edu. Research: civic culture of English Atlantic towns.

Musser, Jimmy Isaac. Fairview Park, OH. Affil: Cleveland Metropolitan Sch. District. Email: jmusser.pro@gmail.com.

Mustafa, Sam A., *Ramapo.* Email: smustafa@ramapo.edu.

Mustakeem, Sowande', *Washington, St. Louis.* Email: mustakee@wustl.edu.

Mustapha, Marda, *St. Rose.* Email: mustaphm@mail.strose.edu.

Musteen, Col Jason R., *US Military Acad.* Email: jason.musteen@usma.edu.

Musto, Ronald G. New York, NY. Affil: Italica Press, Inc. Email: rgmusto@italicapress.com. Research: Trecento Italy, digital humanities.

Muszynski, Emily. Park Ridge, IL. Affil: Loyola, Chicago. Email: emuszynski12@gmail.com.

Mutchler, J. C., *Arizona.* Email: mutchler@email.arizona.edu.

Mutersbaugh, Bert M., *Eastern Kentucky.*

Mutongi, Kenda B., *MIT.* Williamstown, MA. Email: kmutongi@mit.edu. Research: Kenya, transport and commerce in Africa.

Mutschler, Ben. Corvallis, OR. Affil: Oregon State. Email: bmutschler@oregonstate.edu. Research: early America, disability studies.

Mutti Burke, Diane, *Missouri–Kansas City.* Email: muttiburked@umkc.edu.

Muzorewa, Gwinyai P., *Lamar.* Email: gmuzorewa@lamar.edu.

Mwendo, Ukali. New Orleans, LA. Email: ukali700@gmail.com.

Myczek, Pamela A. Sacramento, CA. Affil: State of California. Email: pam.myczek@gmail.com.

Myers, Alfred F. Enola, PA. Email: vse212@breakthru.com.

Myers, Amrita Chakrabarti, *Indiana.* Bloomington, IN. Email: apmyers@indiana.edu. Research: free black women of Charleston 1800-60, interracial sex in Old South.

Myers, Ariana Natalie. Plainsboro, NJ. Affil: Princeton. Email: aamyers@princeton.edu.

Myers, Barton A., *Washington and Lee.* Email: myersb@wlu.edu.

Myers, Brian. Ruby, SC. Affil: Central High Sch. Email: bmyers60@hotmail.com.

Myers, David N., *UCLA.* Email: myers@history.ucla.edu.

Myers, Duane P. Florence, SC. Affil: Francis Marion. Email: dpmyers95@earthlink.net. Research: Austro-German relations 1918-45, German nationalism in Weimar Republic.

Myers, Janet, *Colorado Colorado Springs.* Email: kpmyers@adelphia.net.

Myers, John, *Columbus State.* Email: myers_jack@columbusstate.edu.

Myers, Kathleen A., *Indiana.* Email: myersk@indiana.edu.

Myers, Marcella J., *Andrews.* Email: marcellm@andrews.edu.

Myers, Mark. Selma, IN. Affil: Ball State. Email: msmyers@bsu.edu.

Myers, Nicholas. Ithaca, NY. Affil: Cornell. Email: ngm34@cornell.edu.

Myers, Peter J. San Antonio, TX. Affil: Palo Alto. Email: pmyers@alamo.edu.

Myers, Richard. Doylestown, PA. Email: Redbuddha10@yahoo.com.

Myers, Sarah, *Messiah.* Mechanicsburg, PA. Email: spmyers@messiah.edu; sarahmyers00@gmail.com. Research: US, gender and war.

Myers, W. David, *Fordham.* Email: dmyers@fordham.edu.

Myers, William A., *California State, Fullerton.* Email: wmyers@fullerton.edu.

Myers, William L. Anchorage, AK. Affil: Alaska Anchorage. Email: wlmyers@alaska.edu. Research: Italian fascism, revolution.

Myers-Shirk, Susan E., *Middle Tennessee State.* Email: Susan.Myers-Shirk@mtsu.edu.

Myovich, Samuel Thomas. Placentia, CA. Affil: Placentia Yorba Linda Unified Sch. District. Email: smyovich@pylusd.org. Research: Cold War foreign policy, Cold War in Latin America.

Myrick, Bismarck, *Old Dominion.* Email: bmyrick@odu.edu.

Myrup, Erik Lars, *Kentucky.* Email: erik.myrup@uky.edu.

N n

Naaktgeboren, Capt Jason L., *US Air Force Acad.* Email: jason.naaktgeboren@usafa.edu.

Naar, Devin, *Washington, Seattle.* Email: denaar@uw.edu.

Nabavi, Negin, *Montclair State.* Email: nabavin@mail.montclair.edu.

Nabhan-Warren, **Kristy**, *Iowa*. Iowa City, IA. Email: kristy-nabhan-warren@uiowa.edu. Research: Catholic studies.

Naclerio, **Richard**. Briarcliff Manor, NY. Affil: Graduate Center, CUNY. Email: richn01@aol. com.

Nadasen, **Premilla**, *Barnard, Columbia*. New York, NY. Email: pnadasen@barnard.edu. Research: domestic worker organizing in US, welfare rights/welfare.

Naddaf, **Gerard**, *York, Can.* Email: naddaf@ yorku.ca.

Naddeo, **Barbara Ann**, *Graduate Center, CUNY*. Email: bnaddeo@ccny.cuny.edu.

Nadel, **James**, **Esq**. Pelham, NY. Affil: Michigan, Ann Arbor. Email: jamnadel@umich.edu.

Nadelhaft, **Jerome J.**, *Maine, Orono*. Email: jjnadelhaft@verizon.net.

Nadell, **Pamela S.**, *American*. Email: pnadell@ american.edu.

Nadri, **Ghulam Ahmad**, *Georgia State*. Email: gnadri@gsu.edu.

Naftali, **Timothy James**, *NYU*. Email: timothy. naftali@nyu.edu.

Nagahara, **Hiromu**, *MIT*. Email: nagahara@mit. edu.

Nagam, **Julie**, *Winnipeg*. Email: j.nagam@ uwinnipeg.ca.

Nagata, **Mary Louise**, *Francis Marion*. Email: mnagata@fmarion.edu.

Nagel, **Amanda**, *US Military Acad.* Leavenworth, KS. Affil: Sch. of Advanced Military Studies. Email: amanda.nagel@usma.edu; amanda.m.nagel.civ@mail.mil. Research: African American military service, citizenship/nationalism/empire.

Nagel, **Rebecca**, *Alberta*. Email: rebecca.nagel@ ualberta.ca.

Nagle, **D. Brendan**, *Southern California*. Email: nagle@usc.edu.

Nagy, **Margit**, **CDP**, *Our Lady of the Lake*. Email: mnagy@ollusa.edu.

Nagy, **Piroska**, *Québec, Montréal*. Email: nagy. piroska@uqam.ca.

Nagy, **Zsolt**, *St. Thomas, Minn.* Email: nagy4291@stthomas.edu.

Nai, **Lawrance**. Queen Creek, AZ. Affil: American Leadership Academy. Email: peacefulwarrior23@gmail.com.

Naiden, **Fred**, *North Carolina, Chapel Hill*. Email: naiden@email.unc.edu.

Naimark, **Norman M.**, *Stanford*. Email: naimark@stanford.edu.

Nair, **Aparna**, *Oklahoma (Hist. of Science)*.

Nair, **Neeti**, *Virginia*. Washington, DC. Email: nn2v@virginia.edu. Research: comparative legal, religion in politics.

Nair, **Rahul S.** Dayton, OH. Affil: Antioch. Email: rnair@antiochcollege.org. Research: demography and population policies, development.

Nair, **Savita**, *Furman*. Email: savita.nair@furman. edu.

Naison, **Mark D.**, *Fordham*. Email: naison@ fordham.edu.

Najar, **Jose D.**, *Southern Illinois, Carbondale*. Email: jnajar@siu.edu.

Najar, **Monica E.**, *Lehigh*. Email: mon2@lehigh. edu.

Najemy, **John M.**, *Cornell*. Email: jmn4@cornell. edu.

Najita, **Tetsuo**, *Chicago*. Email: t-najita@ uchicago.edu.

Najmabadi, **Afsaneh**, *Harvard (Hist.)*. Cambridge, MA. Email: najmabad@fas. harvard.edu. Research: trans-sexuality in contemporary Iran, women's lives in Qajar Iran.

Nakamura, **Byron J.**, *Southern Connecticut State*. Email: nakamurab1@southernct.edu.

Nakamura, **Lisa E.**, *Southern Connecticut State*.

Nakashian, **Craig Meran**. Texarkana, TX. Affil: Texas A&M, Texarkana. Email: craig. nakashian@tamut.edu. Research: medieval religious and military culture, medieval literature and culture.

Nakhimovsky, **Isaac**, *Yale*. Email: isaac. nakhimovsky@yale.edu.

Nalefski, **Matthew Hamilton**. Forsyth, IL. Affil: Illinois State. Email: matthew.nalefski@gmail. com.

Nalezyty, **Susan**. Washington, DC. Affil: Georgetown Visitation Preparatory Sch. Email: susan.nalezyty@visi.org.

Nalle, **Sara T.**, *William Paterson*. New York, NY. Email: nalles@wpunj.edu. Research: early modern Spain and France, medieval France.

Nallim, **Jorge A.**, *Manitoba*. Email: jorge.nallim@ umanitoba.ca.

Nalmpantis, **Kyriakos**, *Baldwin Wallace*. Email: knalmpan@bw.edu.

Nam, **Hwasook B.**, *Washington, Seattle*. Email: hsnam@uw.edu.

Namala, **Doris**, *California State, Dominguez Hills*. Email: dnamala@csudh.edu.

Namminga, **Darin**, *Susquehanna*.

Namorato, **Michael V.**, *Mississippi*. Email: hsmvn@olemiss.edu.

Nancarrow, **William J.** Milton, MA. Affil: Curry. Email: wnancarr0904@curry.edu. Research: Gilded Age/Progressive Era law/politics.

Nance, **Brian Kenneth**, *Coastal Carolina*. Email: brian@coastal.edu.

Nance, **Susan**, *Guelph*. Email: snance@ uoguelph.ca.

Napoli, **Philip**, *Brooklyn, CUNY*. Email: pnapoli@ brooklyn.cuny.edu.

Nappi, **Carla S**. Pittsburgh, PA. Affil: Pittsburgh. Email: nappi@pitt.edu. Research: early modern Chinese science, Chinese-Arabic medical exchange.

Naquin, **Susan**. Princeton, NJ. Affil: Princeton. Email: snaquin@princeton.edu. Research: Chinese material culture.

Nardi, **Eric**, *Hist. Assoc.* Email: enardi@ historyassociates.com.

Nardi, **Patricia**. Woodmere, NY. Affil: George W. Hewlett High Sch. Email: pnwoodmere@aol. com.

Narrett, **David E.**, *Texas, Arlington*. Email: narrett@uta.edu.

Narveson, **Eric J.**, *San José State*. Fremont, CA. Affil: Evergreen Valley. Email: eric.narveson@ evc.edu. Research: critical thinking, modern military.

Nasaw, **David**, *Graduate Center, CUNY*. Email: dnasaw@gc.cuny.edu.

Nash, **Alice**, *Massachusetts, Amherst*. Email: anash@history.umass.edu.

Nash, **Gary Baring**, *UCLA*. Email: gnash@ucla. edu.

Nash, **Jere**. Jackson, MS. Email: jerenash@ bellsouth.net. Research: Reconstruction, southern politics.

Nash, **Linda L.**, *Washington, Seattle*. Email: lnash@uw.edu.

Nash, **Patrick Eamon**. Columbus, OH. Affil: Ohio State. Email: nashpe@gmail.com.

Nash, **Philip**, *Penn State*. Email: pxn4@psu.edu.

Nash, **Roderick W.**, *California, Santa Barbara*.

Nash, **Steven E.**, *East Tennessee State*. Email: nashse@etsu.edu.

Nashat, **Guity**, *Illinois, Chicago*. Email: gnashat@ uic.edu.

Nashel, **Jonathan**, *Indiana, South Bend*. South Bend, IN. Email: jnashel@iusb.edu. Research: modern US, US foreign policy.

Nasiali, **Minayo Anne**, *UCLA*. Los Angeles, CA. Email: mnasiali@history.ucla.edu. Research: modernization and decolonization, politics of housing and social welfare.

Nassaney, **Michael S.**, *Western Michigan*. Email: michael.nassaney@wmich.edu.

Nassar, **Issam**, *Illinois State*. Email: irnassa@ilstu. edu.

Nasstrom, **Kathryn L.**, *San Francisco*. Email: nasstromk@usfca.edu.

Natarajan, **Ambika**. Corvallis, OR. Affil: Oregon State. Email: nataraam@onid.oregonstate.edu.

Natarajan, **Radhika**, *Reed*. Portland, OR. Email: e.radhika@gmail.com; radhika.natarajan@ reed.edu. Research: British Empire, social democracy.

Nath, **Kimberly**, *Wisconsin-Whitewater*.

Nathan, **Geoffrey S.**, *San Diego Mesa; San Diego State*. Email: genathan47@gmail.com.

Nathan, **Mark**, *SUNY, Buffalo*. Email: mnathan@ buffalo.edu.

Nathans, **Benjamin**, *Pennsylvania*. Philadelphia, PA. Email: bnathans@history.upenn.edu. Research: Soviet Union law and rights, Simon Dubnov.

Nathans, **Eli A.**, *Western Ontario*. Ann Arbor, MI. Email: enathans@uwo.ca. Research: 20th-c Germany, modern Western culture.

Nathans, **Sydney H.**, *Duke*. Email: snathans@ duke.edu.

Nation, **Richard F.**, *Eastern Michigan*. Ypsilanti, MI. Email: rnation@emich.edu. Research: 19th-c US, environmental.

Natsoulas, **Theodore**. Poughkeepsie, NY. Affil: Toledo. Email: tnatsou@utnet.utoledo.edu. Research: Africa, Cyprus.

Natsuko, **Matsumori**. Shizuoka, Japan. Affil: Shizuoka. Email: nacha_m@yahoo.co.jp. Research: ideas, early modern Iberian and Atlantic.

Nauert, **Paul Gregory**. Redwood City, CA. Affil: Stanford. Email: paulnauert@gmail.com. Research: environmental/climate, diplomatic, America in world.

Naughton, **Patrick**, **Jr**. Washington, DC. Affil: US Army. Email: patrick.naughtonjr@hotmail. com.

Naujoks, **Natasha S**. Norfolk, VA. Affil: Norfolk Academy. Email: nnaujoks@gmail.com.

Naus, **James L.**, *Oakland*. Email: naus@oakland. edu.

Nava, **Carmen**, *California State, San Marcos*. San Marcos, CA. Email: cnava@csusm.edu. Research: nationalism in Latin America, Chicano/Latino.

Nava, **Julian**, *California State, Northridge*.

Navarro, **Aaron W.**, *Texas Christian; Trinity, Tex.* Email: aaron.navarro@tcu.edu; anavarro@ trinity.edu.

Navarro, **Joseph Anthony**. Loomis, CA. Email: mr.joseph.navarro@gmail.com.

Navarro-Aranguren, Marysa, *Dartmouth.* Email: marysa.navarro@dartmouth.edu.

Navin, John J., *Coastal Carolina.* Email: jnavin@coastal.edu.

Nawaz, Asif, *Maine, Orono.* Email: asif.nawaz@maine.edu.

Nayenga, Peter F., *St. Cloud State.*

Naylor, Celia E., Barnard, Columbia. New York, NY. Email: cnaylor@barnard.edu. Research: slavery in Cherokee nation, slave resistance in Jamaica.

Naylor, James, *Brandon.* Email: naylor@brandonu.ca.

Naylor, John F., *SUNY, Buffalo.* Email: jfnaylor@buffalo.edu.

Naylor, Natalie, *Hofstra.*

Naylor, Phillip C., *Marquette.* Email: phillip.naylor@marquette.edu.

Ndanyi, Samson K., *Rhodes.* Email: ndanyis@rhodes.edu.

Ndege, Conchita, *North Carolina A&T State.* Email: ndegec@ncat.edu.

Ndege, George G., *St. Louis.* Email: ndegego@slu.edu.

Neagle, Michael E. Dudley, MA. Affil: Nichols. Email: michael.neagle@nichols.edu. Research: 20th-c US, War on Terror.

Neal, PJ. Waltham, MA. Email: pjneal@gmail.com.

Neaman, Elliot Y., *San Francisco.* Email: neamane@usfca.edu.

Neary, Peter F., *Western Ontario.* Email: neary@uwo.ca.

Neary, Timothy B. Newport, RI. Affil: Salve Regina. Email: timothy.neary@salve.edu. Research: 20th-c social and cultural, urban.

Neatby, Nicole, *Dalhousie; St. Mary's, Can.* Email: nicole.neatby@smu.ca.

Nebiolo, Molly Elisabeth. Brookline, MA. Affil: Northeastern. Email: nebiolo.m@husky.neu.edu.

Nechtman, Tillman W., *Skidmore.* Wilton, NY. Email: tnechtma@skidmore.edu. Research: British Empire and legal, British Empire and art/cultural.

Necochea, Raul, *North Carolina, Chapel Hill.* Email: necochea@email.unc.edu.

Nedervelt, Ross Michael. Mattawan, MI. Affil: Florida International. Email: RNedervelt@msn.com. Research: British Caribbean, American Revolution in Caribbean.

Nedostup, Rebecca, Brown. Providence, RI. Email: rebecca_nedostup@brown.edu. Research: war and displacement, mass violence/death/dying.

Needell, Jeffrey D., *Florida.* Gainesville, FL. Email: jneedell@history.ufl.edu. Research: Afro-Brazilian political mobilization, abolition of slavery in Brazil.

Needham, Andrew, *NYU.* Email: andrew.needham@nyu.edu.

Needham, Dave, *Presbyterian.*

Neel, Carol L., *Colorado Coll.* Colorado Springs, CO. Email: cneel@coloradocollege.edu. Research: Rome, medieval.

Neel, Susan Rhoades, *Utah State.* Email: susan.neel@usu.edu.

Neely, Jeremy, *Missouri State.* Email: jeremyneely@missouristate.edu.

Neely, Mark E., Jr., *Penn State.* Email: mxn10@psu.edu.

Neely, Sylvia E., *Penn State.* Email: sxn13@psu.edu.

Neem, Johann N., *Western Washington.* Bellingham, WA. Email: Johann.Neem@wwu.edu. Research: civil society, citizenship.

Neer, Robert M. Cambridge, MA. Affil: Hult International Sch. of Business. Email: bobneer@gmail.com. Research: global history of US military, weapons technology.

Neeson, Jeanette M., *York, Can.* Email: jmneeson@yorku.ca.

Neff, Christopher Lee. Camperdown, Australia. Affil: Sydney. Email: christopherneff@gmail.com.

Neff, John R., *Mississippi.* Email: jneff@olemiss.edu.

Neher, Kathleen A., *Henry Ford Coll.* Email: neher@millercanfield.com.

Neidenbach, Libby C., *Hist. New Orleans.* Email: Libby.Neidenbach@hnoc.org.

Neiderhiser, Joshua. Dover, PA. Email: jeneiderhiser@gmail.com.

Neiditch, Michael. Washington, DC. Email: hmneiditch@aol.com. Research: Great Britain's embrace of Zionism, US consul-general in Jerusalem 1941-49.

Neighbors, Jennifer M., *Puget Sound.* Email: jneighbors@pugetsound.edu.

Neill, Deborah J., *York, Can.* Email: dneill@yorku.ca.

Neill, Debra R. Chandler, AZ. Affil: Arizona State East. Email: debneill@asu.edu. Research: Bosnian War, origins of religious liberty and James Madison.

Neill, Jeremy H. Princeton, NJ. Affil: Educational Testing Service. Email: jneill@ets.org. Research: gender and imperialism, popular culture.

Neilson, Joanna, *Lincoln Memorial.* Email: joanna.neilson@lmunet.edu.

Neilson, Reid L. Salt Lake City, UT. Affil: LDS Church. Email: reidnelson@ldschurch.org. Research: Asia, Europe.

Neiman, Fraser, *Robert H. Smith Center.* Email: fneiman@monticello.org.

Neirick, Miriam Beth, *California State, Northridge.* Email: miriam.neirick@csun.edu.

Neis, Rachel, *Michigan, Ann Arbor.* Email: rneis@umich.edu.

Neiwert, Rachel Ann. Saint Paul, MN. Affil: St. Catherine. Email: raneiwert@stkate.edu. Research: children in British Empire, education.

Nejad, Kayhan Aryan. Marietta, GA. Affil: Yale. Email: kayhan.nejad@yale.edu.

Neller, Christopher. Arcata, CA. Affil: Humboldt State. Email: cdn4@humboldt.edu.

Nelles, Henry Vivian, McMaster. Kimberley, ON, Canada. Email: nellesh@mcmaster.ca; vivnelles@gmail.com. Research: Canada, economic.

Nelles, Paul, *Carleton, Can.* Email: paul.nelles@carleton.ca.

Nellis, Rachel, *Soc. of Cincinnati.* Email: rnellis@societyofthecincinnati.org.

Nelson, Adam R., *Wisconsin-Madison.* Email: anelson@education.wisc.edu.

Nelson, Alondra. Princeton, NJ. Affil: Inst. for Advanced Study. Email: anelson@ias.edu. Research: science and medicine, race.

Nelson, Amy K., *Virginia Tech.* Email: anelson@vt.edu.

Nelson, Amy. Notre Dame, IN. Affil: Notre Dame. Email: anelson9@nd.edu. Research: female monasticism in central Europe, memorialization/remembrance and identity.

Nelson, Benjamin Ryan. Visalia, CA. Affil: Porterville Unified Sch. District. Email: benrnelson@ucla.edu. Research: British Atlantic/Anglo-American religion, origins/rise of evangelicalism.

Nelson, Cassandra. Minneapolis, MN. Email: nels1967@yahoo.com. Research: archival studies.

Nelson, Clifford M. Berryville, VA. Affil: US Geological Survey. Email: clunydh@gmail.com. Research: USGS 1939-79, origin and early USGS.

Nelson, Elaine Marie, *Nebraska, Omaha; Western Hist. Assoc.* Email: emnelson@unomaha.edu.

Nelson, Elizabeth Angeline. Indianapolis, IN. Affil: Indiana-Purdue, Indianapolis. Email: eanelson@indiana.edu. Research: deinstitutionalization and disability, medicine/science/technology.

Nelson, Elizabeth White, *Nevada, Las Vegas.* Email: elizabeth.nelson@unlv.edu.

Nelson, Eric W., *Missouri State.* Springfield, MO. Email: ericnelson@missouristate.edu. Research: sacred space, world civilization.

Nelson, Hayden. Missoula, MT. Affil: Montana. Email: hayden1.nelson@umontana.edu.

Nelson, J. Bruce, *Dartmouth.* Email: bruce.nelson@dartmouth.edu.

Nelson, Jacqueline, *Plymouth State.* Email: jenelson@plymouth.edu.

Nelson, John K., *North Carolina, Chapel Hill.* Email: jknelson73@bellsouth.net.

Nelson, John T. Kent, OH. Affil: El Paso Comm. Coll. Email: johntnelson@neo.rr.com. Research: Cold War, popular culture.

Nelson, John William. Lafayette, IN. Affil: Notre Dame. Email: jnelso18@nd.edu.

Nelson, Katie, *Weber State.* Email: katienelson2@weber.edu.

Nelson, Keith L., *California, Irvine.* Email: klnelson@uci.edu.

Nelson, Kelli B., *Tennessee, Chattanooga.* Email: kelli-nelson@utc.edu.

Nelson, Kenneth Ross, *Eastern Kentucky.*

Nelson, Kristopher A., *San Diego Mesa.* Email: knelson001@sdccd.edu.

Nelson, Larry E., *Francis Marion.*

Nelson, Lynn A., *Middle Tennessee State.* Email: Lynn.Nelson@mtsu.edu.

Nelson, Marian, *Nebraska, Omaha.*

Nelson, Michael A., *Presbyterian.* Email: mnelson@presby.edu.

Nelson, Nichole Ashley. New Haven, CT. Affil: Yale. Email: nanelson1@optonline.net. Research: urban, America.

Nelson, Nicole C., *Wisconsin-Madison.* Email: nicole.nelson@wisc.edu.

Nelson, Otto M. Owatonna, MN. Affil: Texas Tech. Research: Germany.

Nelson, Paul David, *Berea.* Email: david_nelson@berea.edu.

Nelson, Paula M., *Wisconsin-Platteville.* Email: nelsonp@uwplatt.edu.

Nelson, Richard C., *Augsburg.* Email: nelson@augsburg.edu.

Nelson, Robert K., *Richmond.* Email: rnelson2@richmond.edu.

Nelson, Robert L., *Windsor.* Email: rnelson@uwindsor.ca.

Nelson, **Scott Reynolds**, *Georgia*. Athens, GA. Email: stinkyscott@gmail.com. Research: Panic of 1873-77, shadow of plantation.

Nelson, **William E.**, *NYU*. Email: william.nelson@nyu.edu.

Nelson, **William H.**, *Toronto*.

Nelson, **William Max**, *Toronto*. Email: wnelson@utsc.utoronto.ca.

Nelzén, *John A*. Tallahassee, FL. Affil: Florida State. Email: jan10d@my.fsu.edu. Research: modern Germany, modern Russia/Soviet Union.

Nemes, *Robert*, *Colgate*. Hamilton, NY. Email: rnemes@colgate.edu. Research: modern central Europe, Germany.

Nenner, **Howard A.**, *Smith*. Email: hnenner@smith.edu.

Nenninger, *Timothy K*. Vienna, VA. Affil: National Archives. Email: tim.nenninger@nara.gov.

Nenzi, **Laura Nenz Detto**, *Tennessee, Knoxville*. Email: lnenzi@utk.edu.

Neptune, *Jessica H*. Chicago, IL. Affil: Bard. Email: jneptune@bard.edu. Research: prisons/drug laws/incarceration, college-in-prison/higher education.

Nerdahl, **Michael D.**, *Bowdoin*. Email: mnerdahl@bowdoin.edu.

Nesmith, **Thomas C.**, *Manitoba*. Email: thomas.nesmith@umanitoba.ca.

Nesossis, **Jennifer R.**, *Virginia Museum of Hist.* Email: jennifer@VirginiaHistory.org.

Ness, **John P.**, *St. Cloud State*.

Nesvig, **Martin A.**, *Miami*. Email: mnesvig@miami.edu.

Neswald, **Elizabeth R.**, *Brock*. Email: eneswald@brocku.ca.

Nethery, *Robert L*. Canton, GA. Email: nethery111@yahoo.com.

Nettesheim Hoffmann, *Margaret*. Brookfield, WI. Affil: Marquette. Email: margaret.nettesheim-hoffmann@marquette.edu. Research: philanthropy, urban.

Netting, *Lara*. Larchmont, NY. Affil: Reed. Email: lnetting@yahoo.com. Research: East Asia.

Neu, *Charles E.*, *Brown; Miami*. Miami, FL. Email: Charles_Neu@Brown.edu; cneu@bellsouth.net. Research: American foreign relations, Vietnam War.

Neuberger, *Joan*, *Texas, Austin*. Austin, TX. Email: neuberger@austin.utexas.edu. Research: Soviet film, visual culture as historical evidence.

Neuburger, **Mary C.**, *Texas, Austin*. Email: burgerm@austin.utexas.edu.

Neufeld, *Matthew*, *Saskatchewan*. Saskatoon, SK, Canada. Email: matthew.neufeld@usask.ca. Research: early modern Britain, health care systems.

Neufeld, *Stephen B.*, *California State, Fullerton*. Fullerton, CA. Email: sneufeld@fullerton.edu. Research: military and gender in Mexico, animals and ecology.

Neuhaus, **Jessamyn Anne**, *SUNY, Plattsburgh*. Email: jessamyn.neuhaus@plattsburgh.edu.

Neulander, **Joelle**, *Citadel*. Email: neulanderj@citadel.edu.

Neumaier, **Eva K.**, *Alberta*.

Neuman, *Johanna C*. Delray Beach, FL. Affil: American. Email: johanna.neuman@me.com. Research: women's suffrage, African American experience.

Neuman, **Mark D.**, *Bucknell*. Email: mneuman@bucknell.edu.

Neumann, *Caryn E.*, *Miami, Ohio*. Columbus, OH. Email: neumance@miamioh.edu; carynneu@gmail.com. Research: 1960s women's political, nursing.

Neumann, **Dave**, *Soc. for Hist. Education*. Email: dave.neumann@csulb.edu.

Neumann, **Kristina M.**, *Houston*.

Neumann, *Tracy*, *Wayne State*. Email: tracyneumann@wayne.edu.

Neuschel, **Kristen B.**, *Duke*. Email: kneusche@duke.edu.

Neville, *Cynthia J.*, *Dalhousie*. Email: cynthia.neville@dal.ca.

Neville, *Joseph B.*, **Jr.** Woodbridge, VA. Affil: NEH. Email: mcjbnevill@verizon.net. Research: German American.

Neville, *Leonora*, *Wisconsin-Madison*. Madison, WI. Email: leonora.neville@wisc.edu. Research: Byzantine religion, Byzantine gender.

Neville, *Richard Benjamin*. Savannah, GA. Email: rbenneville@yahoo.com.

Nevin, *Mark David*, *Ohio*. Lancaster, OH. Email: nevinm@ohio.edu. Research: public opinion polling, Nixon presidency.

Nevius, **Marcus P.**, *Rhode Island*. Email: mpnevius@uri.edu.

Newbury, *Catharine*. East Thetford, VT. Affil: Smith. Email: cnewbury@smith.edu. Research: politics and violence in Rwanda, Congo women and rural politics.

Newbury, *David S.*, *Smith*. East Thetford, VT. Email: dnewbury@smith.edu. Research: African environmental, African social.

Newby, *Brenda Marie*. Chula Vista, CA. Affil: Palomar. Email: brendaschaffner@gmail.com. Research: religion in 20th-c US, American West.

Newby, **Gordon D.**, *Emory*. Email: gdnewby@emory.edu.

Newby-Alexander, *Cassandra*. Chesapeake, VA. Affil: Norfolk State. Email: clnewby-alexander@nsu.edu. Research: modern African American, technology.

Newcomer, **Daniel**, *East Tennessee State*. Email: newcomer@etsu.edu.

Newcomer, **Lara T.**, *Texas State*. Email: ln1057@txstate.edu.

Newell, *Margaret E.*, *Ohio State*. Columbus, OH. Email: newell.20@osu.edu. Research: colonial, early US.

Newfield, **Timothy P.**, *Georgetown*.

Newfont, **Kathryn**, *Kentucky*.

Newhall, *Caroline*. Chapel Hill, NC. Affil: North Carolina, Chapel Hill. Email: cwoodn@live.unc.edu.

Newhall, *Samantha*. Tustin, CA. Email: newhallsamantha@gmail.com.

Newhouse, *Paige*. Ann Arbor, MI. Email: panew@umich.edu.

Newkirk, *Anthony B*. North Little Rock, AR. Affil: Philander Smith. Email: newkirk1938@hotmail.com. Research: US diplomacy in Middle East, covert warfare.

Newlin, *Michael*. Fairfax, VA. Affil: George Mason. Email: mnewlin@masonlive.gmu.edu.

Newman, **Brooke Nicole**, *Virginia Commonwealth*. Email: bnewman@vcu.edu.

Newman, **Elizabeth Terese**, *SUNY, Stony Brook*. Email: elizabeth.newman@stonybrook.edu.

Newman, *Geoffrey J*. Overland Park, KS. Affil: Kansas. Email: geof.newman@ku.edu.

Research: US ethnicity/race/immigration, US since 1865.

Newman, **Gerald G.**, *Kent State*.

Newman, **L. Paige**, *Virginia Museum of Hist.* Email: pnewman@VirginiaHistory.org.

Newman, **Louise M.**, *Florida*. Email: lnewman@ufl.edu.

Newman, **Martha G.**, *Texas, Austin*. Email: newman@austin.utexas.edu.

Newman, **Paul Douglas**, *Pittsburgh, Johnstown*. Email: pnewman@pitt.edu.

Newman, *Rachel Grace*. Northampton, MA. Affil: Smith. Email: rnewman@smith.edu.

Newman, **William R.**, *Indiana*. Email: wnewman@indiana.edu.

Newman Ham, **Debra**, *Morgan State*. Email: newman.ham2@verizon.net.

Newmark, **Jill L.**, *National Library of Medicine*. Email: newmarj@mail.nlm.nih.gov.

Newmyer, *R. Kent*, *Connecticut, Storrs*. Email: k.newmyer@uconn.edu.

Newport, *Melanie Diane*, *Connecticut, Storrs*. West Hartford, CT. Email: melanie.newport@uconn.edu. Research: carceral state/jails, recent US.

Newsom, **James L.**, *Texas, Tyler*. Email: jnewsom@uttyler.edu.

Newsom Kerr, **Matthew Lee**, *Santa Clara*. Email: mnewsomkerr@scu.edu.

Newton, *Barbara Hensley*, *Longwood*. chase City, VA. Email: newtonbh@longwood.edu. Research: republicanism in Age of Jefferson, tertium quids.

Newton, *Carolyn*. North Charleston, SC. Affil: Ashley Hall. Email: newtonc@ashleyhall.org. Research: class/race/gender, macroeconomics.

Newton, *Erin*. Chicago, IL. Affil: Chicago. Email: emnewton@uchicago.edu.

Newton, *Jason L*. Ithaca, NY. Affil: Cornell. Email: jn497@cornell.edu.

Newton, **Lowell W.**, *Louisville*.

Newton, *Melanie J.*, *Toronto*. Email: melanie.newton@utoronto.ca.

Newton, *Ross*. Philadelphia, PA. Affil: La Salle. Email: ross.a.newton@gmail.com. Research: early America, Atlantic world.

Neylan, **Susan L.**, *Wilfrid Laurier*. Email: sneylan@wlu.ca.

Neymeyer, **Robert J.**, *Northern Iowa*. Email: robert.neymeyer@uni.edu.

Ng, *Margaret Wee-Siang*, *Wooster*. Wooster, OH. Email: mng@wooster.edu. Research: Chinese medicine and science, gender and body.

Ng, **Michael K.**, *Seattle*.

Ng, **On-cho**, *Penn State*. Email: oxn1@psu.edu.

Ng, **Wing Chung**, *Texas, San Antonio*. Email: wingchung.ng@utsa.edu.

Ngai, *Mae M.*, *Columbia (Hist.)*. New York, NY. Email: mn53@columbia.edu; Maengai@gmail.com. Research: US, law and immigration.

Ngalamulume, **Kalala J.**, *Bryn Mawr*. Email: kngalamu@brynmawr.edu.

Ngo, *Kimmie*. San Marcos, CA. Affil: California State, San Marcos. Email: ngo020@cougars.csusm.edu.

Ngo, *Lan A.*, **SJ**. Los Angeles, CA. Affil: Loyola Marymount. Email: Lan.Ngo@lmu.edu. Research: Vietnam, Catholicism.

Ngovo, **Samuel Benedict**, *Morgan State*. Email: Samuel.Ngovo@morgan.edu.

Nguyen, *Hai Thanh*. Belmont, MA. Affil: Harvard. Email: hai_nguyen@hks.harvard.edu.

Nguyen, Lien-Hang Thi, *Columbia (Hist.)*. New York, NY. Email: ln2358@columbia.edu. Research: Vietnam War.

Nguyen, Maureen, *Massachusetts Hist. Soc.* Email: mnguyen@masshist.org.

Nguyen, Tim. Middlebury, VT. Affil: Case Western Reserve. Email: tcn23@case.edu.

Nguyen, Uyen. Lubbock, TX. Affil: Texas Tech. Email: uyen.nguyen@ttu.edu.

Nguyen-Marshall, Van, *Trent*. Email: vannguyenmarshall@trentu.ca.

Nicassio, Susan Vandiver, *Louisiana, Lafayette*. Email: svn4713@louisiana.edu.

Nice, Jason A., *California State, Chico*. Email: jnice@csuchico.edu.

Nichol, Todd W., *St. Olaf*. Email: nicholt@stolaf.edu.

Nicholas, Jane, *Waterloo*. Waterloo, ON, Canada. Email: jane.nicholas@uwaterloo.ca. Research: freak show, grief.

Nicholas, Karen, *SUNY, Oswego*. Email: karen.nicholas@oswego.edu.

Nicholas, Mary A. South Thomaston, ME. Email: maineart1@yahoo.com.

Nicholas, William E., III, *Birmingham-Southern*.

Nicholls, Andrew D., *SUNY, Buffalo State*. Email: nicholad@buffalostate.edu.

Nicholls, Michael L., *Utah State*. Email: michael.nicholls@usu.edu.

Nichols, Bradley, *Virginia Tech*. Blacksburg, VA. Email: bradleyn@vt.edu.

Nichols, C. Howard, *Southeastern Louisiana*. Email: hnichols@selu.edu.

Nichols, Christopher McKnight. Corvallis, OR. Affil: Oregon State. Email: christopher.nichols@oregonstate.edu. Research: internationalism and isolationism, US role in world in Gilded Age/Progressive Era.

Nichols, Claude W., *Eastern Washington*.

Nichols, David Andrew, *Indiana State*. Email: Dave.Nichols@indstate.edu.

Nichols, James D. Jackson Heights, NY. Affil: Queensborough Comm. Coll., CUNY. Email: jnichols@qcc.cuny.edu. Research: 19th-c US-Mexican borderlands.

Nichols, John A., *Slippery Rock*. Email: john.nichols@sru.edu.

Nichols, Melvin E., Jr., *Indianapolis*. Email: mnichols@uindy.edu.

Nichols, Robert H., *Stockton*. Email: nicholsr@stockton.edu.

Nichols, Robert L., *St. Olaf*. Email: nichols@stolaf.edu.

Nichols, Roger L., *Arizona*. Tucson, AZ. Email: nichols@email.arizona.edu. Research: US and Indians, American West and Europe.

Nichols, Tiffany, Esq. Cambridge, MA. Affil: Harvard. Email: tiffany_nichols@g.harvard.edu. Research: history and philosophy of physics, big science research endeavors.

Nichols, William G., *Citadel*. Charleston, SC. Email: garynichols1@bellsouth.net. Research: Europe and Russia, military.

Nicholson, Brid, *Kean*. Madison, NJ. Email: cnichols@kean.edu. Research: labor and women, Ireland.

Nicholson, Howard Lee, *Northern Michigan*. Email: hnichols@nmu.edu.

Nickell, Amber N. West Lafayette, IN. Affil: Purdue. Email: anickell@purdue.edu. Research: diaspora and migration, modern Europe.

Nickerson, Michelle M., *Loyola, Chicago*. Chicago, IL. Email: mnickerson@luc.edu. Research: gender, politics.

Nickles, David P., *US Dept. of State*.

Nickliss, Alexandra M. San Francisco, CA. Affil: City Coll., San Francisco. Email: amnickliss@gmail.com. Research: US women/gender social/political/intellectual, US West and Progressive era.

Nicolaides, Becky M. Altadena, CA. Affil: USC & UCLA. Email: becky.nicolaides@outlook.com. Research: social history of postwar suburbia.

Nicoll, Leo A., SJ, *Loyola, New Orleans*. Email: nicoll@loyno.edu.

Nicols, John, *Oregon*. Email: jnicols@uoregon.edu.

Nicosia, Francis R., *St. Michael's; Vermont*. Email: francis.nicosia@uvm.edu.

Nielsen, Cameron C. Urbana, PA. Affil: Penn State. Email: cameron.nielsen@psu.edu. Research: apocalpyticism and new religions, conspiracy theories and alt knowledge.

Nielsen, Fredrick H., *Nebraska, Omaha*. Email: fnielsen@unomaha.edu.

Nielsen, Justin M. Oakdale, CA. Affil: Montana. Email: justin.nielsen@umconnect.umt.edu.

Nielsen, Kim E. Toledo, OH. Affil: Toledo. Email: kim.nielsen2@utoledo.edu. Research: disability, biography.

Nielsen, Matthew Ryan. Kalamazoo, MI. Affil: Carnegie Mellon. Email: mnielsen@andrew.cmu.edu.

Nielsen, Rosemary M., *Alberta*.

Niemeyer, Glenn A., *Grand Valley State*.

Nienkamp, Paul, *Fort Hays State*. Email: pknienkamp@fhsu.edu.

Nierman, J. Harris. Flushing, NY. Email: docnierman@att.net.

Nies, Bryan W. Moore, OK. Affil: Oklahoma. Email: bryan.w.nies@ou.edu.

Niessen, James P. New Brunswick, NJ. Affil: Rutgers. Email: niessen@rutgers.edu. Research: Romania, Hungary.

Niestempski, George. Beaverton, OR. Email: niestempski.george@gmail.com.

Nieto-Phillips, John, *Indiana*. Email: jnietoph@indiana.edu.

Nieves, Angel David, *San Diego State*.

Niewyk, Donald L., *Southern Methodist*. Dallas, TX. Email: dniewyk@smu.edu. Research: Holocaust, Jews in Germany.

Nighman, Chris, *Wilfrid Laurier*. Email: cnighman@wlu.ca.

Nightingale, Carl H. Buffalo, NY. Affil: SUNY, Buffalo. Email: cn6@buffalo.edu. Research: global urban history, US urban/political/cultural.

Nigro, Jenna C., *Utah Valley*. Orem, UT. Email: jenna.nigro@uvu.edu. Research: 19th-c French imperialism in Senegal.

Nikolic, Stefan. Lakewood, OH. Affil: Cleveland State. Email: stefan.nikolic9429@gmail.com. Research: Slavic tribes and their migrations, Yugoslavia.

Nikolich, Katheryn. Lawrenceville, GA. Email: knikolich1@student.gsu.edu.

Nikpour, Golnar S., *Dartmouth*. Email: golnar.nikpour@dartmouth.edu.

Niles, Philip, *Carleton Coll.*

Nilsen, Caswell M. Lutherville, MD. Affil: St. Paul's Sch. Email: boocts@gmail.com. Research: Soviet Union, 1920s.

Nimick, Thomas G., *US Military Acad.* Email: thomas.nimick@usma.edu.

Nimmon, Scott Edward. Williamsburg, VA. Email: scottnlindsay.nimmon@gmail.com. Research: Irish Revolution, American Revolution.

Nimz, Timothy G. Littleton, CO. Affil: Littleton Museum. Email: TNimz@aol.com.

Nirenberg, David, *Chicago*. Chicago, IL. Email: nirenberg@uchicago.edu. Research: Jewish-Christian-Muslim relations, late medieval Spain.

Nishida, Mieko, *Hartwick*. Oneonta, NY. Email: nishidam@hartwick.edu. Research: immigration to/from Brazil, diaspora and identity.

Nishioka, Minami. Knoxville, TN. Affil: Tennessee, Knoxville. Email: mnishiok@vols.utk.edu.

Nishiyama, Takashi, *SUNY, Coll. Brockport*. Email: tnishiya@brockport.edu.

Nishizaki, Fumiko. Tokyo, Japan. Affil: Tokyo. Email: nishizak@ask.c.u-tokyo.ac.jp. Research: Wilsonian diplomacy, peace movement.

Nissen, Karen J., *California State, Chico*. Email: knissen@csuchico.edu.

Nissenbaum, Stephen, *Massachusetts, Amherst*. Email: snissenbaum@history.umass.edu.

Nitz, Theodore A., *Gonzaga*. Email: nitz@gonzaga.edu.

Nivison, Kenneth R. Manchester, NH. Affil: Southern New Hampshire. Email: k.nivison@snhu.edu. Research: 19th-c New England political culture, character and society.

Njoku, Raphael Chijioke, *Idaho State*. Email: njokraph@isu.edu.

Njoroge, Njoroge, *Hawai'i, Manoa*. Email: njoroge@hawaii.edu.

Nkululeko, Ekundayo. Houston, TX. Affil: Texas Southern. Email: ohkusu@gmail.com. Research: black freedmen's towns, gender and imperialism.

Nobbs-Thiessen, Benjamin James, *Washington State, Pullman*.

Nobiletti, Frank, *San Diego State*. Email: fnobilet@sdsu.edu.

Nobili, Mauro, *Illinois, Urbana-Champaign*. Email: nobili@illinois.edu.

Noble, Thomas F. X., *Notre Dame*. Charlottesville, VA. Email: tnoble@nd.edu. Research: Carolingian, papal 300-1100.

Nobles, Gregory H., *Georgia Inst. of Tech*. Email: gregory.nobles@gatech.edu.

Nobles, Melissa. Cambridge, MA. Affil: MIT. Email: mnobles@mit.edu.

Noe, Kenneth W., *Auburn*. Email: noekenn@auburn.edu.

Noegel, Scott, *Washington, Seattle*. Email: snoegel@uw.edu.

Noel, Jan, *Toronto*. Email: jnoel@utm.utoronto.ca.

Noel, Linda, *Morgan State*. Email: linda.noel@morgan.edu.

Noel, Lynn Elizabeth. Waltham, MA. Affil: Digital Heritage Consulting. Email: lynnoel@lynnoel.com.

Noel, Matthew E. Hobart, IN. Affil: Purdue Northwest, Hammond. Email: mnoelbat@yahoo.com.

Noel, Rebecca R., *Plymouth State*. Plymouth, NH. Email: rrnoel@plymouth.edu. Research: 19th-c US schooling/health/gender, US intellectual.

Noel, Thomas J., *Colorado Denver*. Email: tom.noel@ucdenver.edu.

Noellert, **Matthew Z.**, *Iowa*. Email: matthew-noellert@uiowa.edu.

Nofil, *Brianna Lane*. New York, NY. Affil: Columbia. Email: bln2109@columbia.edu.

Nogales, *Pamela Christine*. Wyomissing, PA. Affil: NYU. Email: pam.nogales@gmail.com. Research: American radical politics, from slave to free labor in US.

Nokes, *Jeffery D.*, *Brigham Young*. Provo, UT. Email: jeff_nokes@byu.edu. Research: pedagogy, teaching.

Nolan, **Andrew S.**, *Maryland, Baltimore County*. Email: nolan@umbc.edu.

Nolan, **Cathal J.**, *Boston Univ*. Email: cnolan@bu.edu.

Nolan, **Janet A.**, *Loyola, Chicago*. Email: jnolan@luc.edu.

Nolan, **John A.** Morton Grove, IL. Affil: Northwestern. Email: johnnolan2012@u.northwestern.edu.

Nolan, *Mary*, *NYU*. New York, NY. Email: mn4@nyu.edu. Research: 20th-c global economy, human rights.

Nolan, **Michael E.**, *Western Connecticut State*. Email: nolanm@wcsu.edu.

Nolan, *Rachel*. New York, NY. Affil: Columbia. Email: rn826@nyu.edu. Research: adoptions, civil war/genocide.

Nolan-Ferrell, *Catherine A.*, *Texas, San Antonio*. San Antonio, TX. Email: catherine.ferrell@utsa.edu. Research: Chiapas Mexico state formation 1930s-40s, Chiapas labor and rural.

Nold, **Patrick**, *SUNY, Albany*. Email: pnold@albany.edu.

Nolde, **Lance**, *California State, Channel Islands*. Email: lance.nolde741@csuci.edu.

Noll, **Jody**. Doraville, GA. Affil: Georgia State. Email: jnoll3@gsu.edu.

Noll, *Mark A.*, *Notre Dame; Wheaton, Ill*. Wheaton, IL. Email: mnoll@nd.edu. Research: US religious.

Noll, *Steven G.*, *Florida*. Gainesville, FL. Email: nolls@ufl.edu. Research: US social, institutional.

Noll Venables, *Mary C*. Carrigrohane, CO Cork, Ireland. Email: mary.venables@aya.yale.edu.

Nolte, **Claire E.**, *Manhattan*. Email: claire.nolte@manhattan.edu.

Noonan, *Alan*. Washington, DC. Affil: Library of Congress. Email: ajmnoonan@gmail.com. Research: mining migration, Irish diaspora.

Noonan, **Ellen**, *NYU*. Email: men2022@nyu.edu.

Noonan, **Kathleen**, *Sonoma State*. Email: noonan@sonoma.edu.

Noorlander, **Danny L.**, *SUNY, Oneonta*. Email: danny.noorlander@oneonta.edu.

Noraian, **Monica Cousins**, *Illinois State*. Email: mcnora2@ilstu.edu.

Norberg, **Arthur L.**, *Minnesota (Hist. of Science)*. Email: anorberg@umn.edu.

Norberg, **Kathryn**, *UCLA*. Email: knorberg@ucla.edu.

Nord, *Philip G.*, *Princeton*. Princeton, NJ. Email: pgnord@princeton.edu. Research: modern France.

Nordmann, **David A.**, *Coe*. Email: dnordman@coe.edu.

Nordquist, **Philip A.**, *Pacific Lutheran*. Email: nordqupa@plu.edu.

Nordstrom, **Justin Abel**, *Penn State*. Email: jan13@psu.edu.

Noren, *Erik*. Grand Rapids, MI. Affil: Wayne State. Email: erik.noren17@gmail.com.

Noreña, **Carlos F.**, *California, Berkeley*. Email: norena@berkeley.edu.

Norkunas, **Martha**, *Middle Tennessee State*. Email: Martha.Norkunas@mtsu.edu.

Norling, *Lisa A.*, *Minnesota (Hist.)*. Email: norli001@umn.edu.

Norman, **Matthew**, *Cincinnati*. Email: matthew.norman@uc.edu.

Norman, **Sandra L.**, *Florida Atlantic*. Email: norman@fau.edu.

Norman, **York Allen**, *SUNY, Buffalo State*. Email: normanya@buffalostate.edu.

Norr, *Melissa*. Washington, DC. Email: melissanorr@gmail.com.

Norrell, **Robert J.**, *Tennessee, Knoxville*. Email: rnorrell@utk.edu.

Norrgard, *Julia Marie*. Reston, VA. Affil: American, Kosovo. Email: jnorrgard@aukonline.org.

Norris, *Bethany*. Thomaston, GA. Affil: Upson-Lee High Sch. Email: bnorris@upson.k12.ga.us.

Norris, **L. Patrick**, *Western Michigan*. Email: pnorris@kvcc.edu.

Norris, **Mark M.**, *Grace*. Email: norrismm@grace.edu.

Norris, *Nathan C*. Oxnard, CA. Affil: Cornell. Email: natecnorris@gmail.com.

Norris, *Robert Warren*, *II*. Lancaster, SC. Affil: Banyan Capital Management, LLC. Email: RWNII@BanyanCapitalManagementLLC.com.

Norris, **Stephen M.**, *Miami, Ohio*. Email: norriss1@miamioh.edu.

North, *Brian C*. Fort Hood, TX. Affil: Wisconsin, Madison. Email: brian.north74@gmail.com.

North, *Diane M. T*. Hendersonville, NC. Affil: Maryland Univ. Coll. Email: diane.north@faculty.umuc.edu. Research: WWI, civil liberties.

North, *William L.*, *Carleton Coll*. Northfield, MN. Email: wnorth@carleton.edu. Research: clerical reform and biblical exegesis, political rebellion in medieval Germany.

North Hamill, *Anita*. North Aurora, IL. Affil: Oak Park and River Forest High Sch. Email: anorthhamill@gmail.com.

Northrop, *Douglas T.*, *Michigan, Ann Arbor*. Ann Arbor, MI. Email: northrop@umich.edu. Research: transnational tourism, earthquakes in Eurasia 1880-1990.

Northrup, *David A.*, *Boston Coll*. Email: david.northrup@bc.edu.

Norton, **Amanda**, *Massachusetts Hist. Soc*. Email: anorton@masshist.org.

Norton, *D. Jack*. Minneapolis, MN. Affil: Normandale Comm. Coll. Email: jack.norton@normandale.edu. Research: early modern Spanish women, economic.

Norton, *Marcy*, *George Washington; Pennsylvania*. Washington, DC. Email: mnorton@gwu.edu; marcynorton@gmail.com. Research: colonial Latin America, Atlantic world.

Norton, *Mary Beth*, *Cornell; National Hist. Center*. Ithaca, NY. Email: mbn1@cornell.edu. Research: early Anglo-American gender and politics.

Norton, **Phyllis**, *Central Connecticut State*. Email: pnorton@ccsu.edu.

Norton, **Richard J.**, *Naval War Coll*. Email: nortonr@usnwc.edu.

Norwood, *Dael A.*, *Binghamton, SUNY; Delaware*. Newark, DE. Email: dnorwood@binghamton. edu; dnorwood@udel.edu. Research: US politics of commerce, American imperialism.

Norwood, *Stephen H.*, *Oklahoma (Hist.)*. Oklahoma City, OK. Email: shnorwood@ou.edu. Research: US universities' response to Nazism, American Jewish.

Noseworthy, *William*. Lake Charles, LA. Affil: McNeese State. Email: noseworthy@wisc.edu. Research: religion and state.

Notehelfer, **Fred G.**, *UCLA*. Email: notehelf@history.ucla.edu.

Novak, *Michael Helmut*. Colonia, NJ. Affil: George Washington. Email: mnovak4@gwmail.gwu.edu.

Novak, *William J.*, *Michigan, Ann Arbor*. Email: wnovak@umich.edu.

November, **Joseph A.**, *South Carolina, Columbia*. Email: november@mailbox.sc.edu.

Novetzke, *Christian Lee*, *Washington, Seattle*. Email: novetzke@uw.edu.

Novikoff, *Alex J.*, *Kenyon*. Gambier, OH. Email: novikoff1@kenyon.edu; ajnovikoff@gmail.com. Research: medieval intellectual/cultural, Jewish-Christian-Muslim relations.

Novoa, *Adriana I.*, *South Florida, Tampa*. Email: ainovoa@usf.edu.

Novosel, *Anthony*, *Pittsburgh*. Email: pugachev@pitt.edu.

Novotny, **Sharon K.**, *Indiana, South Bend*. Email: snovotny@iusb.edu.

Nowak, *Martin S*. Melbourne, FL. Email: lgmsn@brighthouse.com. Research: Poland and Polish Americans, lives of US presidents.

Nowowiejski, **Dean A.**, *US Army Command Coll*. Email: dean.a.nowowiejski.civ@mail.mil.

Nti, **Kwaku**, *Georgia Southern*. Email: knti@georgiasouthern.edu.

Nudell, *Joshua Paul*. Columbia, MO. Affil: Missouri, Columbia. Email: jpnwwd@mail.missouri.edu. Research: ancient Greece, Greek historiography.

Nugent, *Patrick Dennis*. Chestertown, MD. Affil: Starr Center. Email: pnugent2@washcoll.edu. Research: Urban Planning, Urban Environments.

Nugent, *Walter*, *Notre Dame*. Highland Park, IL. Email: wnugent@nd.edu. Research: political change in the American West.

Numark, *Mitch*, *California State, Sacramento*. Email: mnumark@saclink.csus.edu.

Numbers, *Ronald L.*, *Wisconsin-Madison*. Madison, WI. Email: rnumbers@wisc.edu. Research: science in America, science/medicine/religion.

Numhauser, *Paulina*. Madrid, Spain. Affil: Alcala. Email: paulina.numhauser@gmail.com. Research: Señores de la coca in Spain/Jesuitas, Documentos Miccinelli/ Cronistas.

Nummedal, *Tara E.*, *Brown*. Providence, RI. Email: Tara_Nummedal@Brown.edu. Research: alchemy, gender and Christianity.

Nunez, *Carmen*. Ultimo, Australia. Email: cnunez2@hotmail.com.

Nunez, **Rachel M.**, *Hollins*. Email: rnunez@hollins.edu.

Nunley, **Tamika Yolanda**, *Oberlin*. Email: tamika.nunley@oberlin.edu.

Nunn, **Frederick M.**, *Portland State*.

Nuno, *John Paul A.*, *California State, Northridge*. Email: johnpaul.nuno@csun.edu.

Nuriddin, *Ayah*. Baltimore, MD. Affil: Johns Hopkins. Email: anuridd1@jhmi.edu. Research: medicine, racism.

AHA members in ***bold italic***; *Directory*-listed affiliations in *italic*

Nurse, Ronald J., *Virginia Tech*.

Nussdorfer, Laurie, *Wesleyan*. Email: lnussdorfer@wesleyan.edu.

Nusseck, Marvin. Amsterdam, Netherlands. Affil: Erasmus, Rotterdam. Email: Marvin@nusseck.com.

Nutt, Katharine F., *Northern Arizona*.

Nutting, Maureen Murphy. Seattle, WA. Affil: North Seattle. Email: maureennutting@msn.com. Research: women in higher education, 20th-c US Catholics.

Nutting, P. Bradley, *Framingham State*. Email: pnutting@framingham.edu.

Nutzman, Megan, *Old Dominion*. Email: mnutzman@odu.edu.

Nwauwa, Apollos O., *Bowling Green State*. Email: nwauwa@bgsu.edu.

Nybakken, Elizabeth, *Mississippi State*. Email: enybakken@cox.net.

Nybakken, Richard R. Napa, CA. Affil: Napa Valley. Email: rnybakken@gmail.com. Research: fascism/anti-fascism, history/memory.

Nye, Jennifer L., *Massachusetts, Amherst*. Email: jlnye@history.umass.edu.

Nygren, Joshua, *Central Missouri*. Email: nygren@ucmo.edu.

Nyhart, Lynn K., *Wisconsin-Madison*. Email: lknyhart@wisc.edu.

Nylan, Michael, *California, Berkeley*. Email: mnylan@berkeley.edu.

Nystrom, Elsa A., *Kennesaw State*. Email: enystrom@kennesaw.edu.

Nystrom, Justin A., *Loyola, New Orleans*. Email: jnystrom@loyno.edu.

O o

Oakes, James, *Graduate Center, CUNY*. New York, NY. Email: joakes@gc.cuny.edu. Research: American political thought, emancipation.

Oakes, Julie, *Maryland, Baltimore County*. Email: juloakes@umbc.edu.

Oakes, Karen, *SUNY, Oswego*. Email: karen.oakes@oswego.edu.

Oakley, Christopher Arris, *East Carolina*. Greenville, NC. Email: oakleyc@ecu.edu. Research: American Indians of North Carolina.

Oakley, David Patrick. Ashburn, VA. Affil: National Defense. Email: david@davidpoakley.com. Research: intelligence, US foreign policy.

Oakley, Eric O., *Kennesaw State*. Kennesaw, GA. Email: eoakley1@kennesaw.edu; eric.o.oakley@gmail.com. Research: maritime fur trade, US in Pacific Ocean.

Oakley, Francis C., *Williams*. Williamstown, MA. Email: Francis.C.Oakley@williams.edu. Research: medieval Europe, European intellectual.

Oast, Jennifer B., *Bloomsburg*. Bloomsburg, PA. Email: joast@bloomu.edu. Research: institutional slavery.

Oates, Stephen B., *Massachusetts, Amherst*. Email: sboates@history.umass.edu.

Ober, Douglas F. Vancouver, BC, Canada. Affil: British Columbia. Email: douglas.ober@ubc.ca.

Oberdeck, Kathryn J., *Illinois, Urbana-Champaign*. Urbana, IL. Email: kjo@illinois.edu. Research: working class, urban space.

Oberg, Barbara B. Princeton, NJ. Affil: Princeton. Email: boberg@princeton.edu. Research: American Revolution, early Republic.

Oberg, Michael L., *SUNY, Coll. Geneseo*. Email: oberg@geneseo.edu.

Oberle, Clara M., *San Diego*. Email: oberle@sandiego.edu.

Oberle, Eric W. Paradise Valley, AZ. Affil: Arizona State. Email: eric@ericoberle.com. Research: German and French social sciences, receptions of Enlightenment.

Oberle, George D., III. Stafford, VA. Affil: George Mason. Email: goberle@gmu.edu. Research: information revolution, learned societies.

Oberly, James W., *Wisconsin-Eau Claire*. Eau Claire, WI. Email: joberly@uwec.edu. Research: American economic, Civil War.

Obermiller, David Tobaru, *Gustavus Adolphus*. Email: dobermil@gustavus.edu.

O'Brassill-Kulfan, Kristin, *Rutgers*. Email: kristin.obrassillkulfan@rutgers.edu.

O'Brien, Albert C., *San Diego State*. Email: obrien1@sdsu.edu.

O'Brien, Brenda. Scituate, MA. Affil: Massachusetts, Boston. Email: brendabeckwith@yahoo.com.

O'Brien, Bruce R., *Mary Washington*. Email: bobrien@umw.edu.

O'Brien, Charles H., *Western Illinois*. Williamstown, MA. Email: obrien@bcn.net. Research: medieval Europe, European intellectual.

O'Brien, David J., *Holy Cross*. Email: dobrien@holycross.edu.

O'Brien, Elizabeth, *Johns Hopkins (Hist. of Science)*.

O'Brien, Emily D., *Simon Fraser*. Email: eobrien@sfu.ca.

O'Brien, Gail W, *North Carolina State*. Email: gail_obrien@ncsu.edu.

O'Brien, George Patrick. Columbia, SC. Affil: South Carolina, Columbia. Email: gpobrien@email.sc.edu.

O'Brien, Greg, *North Carolina, Greensboro*. Email: wgobrien@uncg.edu.

O'Brien, Jean M., *Minnesota (Hist.)*. Minneapolis, MN. Email: obrie002@umn.edu. Research: New England Indians.

O'Brien, John J., *Austin Peay State*. Email: obrienj@apsu.edu.

O'Brien, John M., *Queens, CUNY*.

O'Brien, Kenneth P., *SUNY, Coll. Brockport*. Email: kobrien@brockport.edu.

O'Brien, Maureen M., *St. Cloud State*. Email: mmobrien@stcloudstate.edu.

O'Brien, Patricia, *UCLA*. Email: pobrien@college.ucla.edu.

O'Brien, Patrick G., *Emporia State*.

O'Brien, Patrick Karl. Oxford, United Kingdom. Affil: London Sch. of Economics. Email: patrick.obrien@sant.ox.ac.uk. Research: global economic.

O'Brien, Susan Marie, *Florida*. Email: smobrien@ufl.edu.

O'Brien, Tara, *Hist. Soc. of Pennsylvania*. Email: tobrien@hsp.org.

O'Brien, Thomas F., Jr., *Houston*. Email: tobrien@uh.edu.

O'Bryan, Scott P., *Indiana*. Email: spobryan@indiana.edu.

O'Callaghan, Joseph F., *Fordham*. Email: clonmeen@optonline.net.

Ocegueda, Mark Anthony, *California State, Sacramento*. Sacramento, CA. Email: ocegueda@csus.edu. Research: Chicana/o Latina/o studies, 20th-c US.

Ochoa, Alberto. Cathedral City, CA. Email: aochoa2001@me.com. Research: US, world.

Ochoa, Enrique C., *California State, Los Angeles*. Email: eochoa3@calstatela.edu.

Ochoa, Margarita R., *Loyola Marymount*. Los Angeles, CA. Email: margarita.ochoa@lmu.edu. Research: gender/power/law, ethnohistory/Nahuatl.

Ochocki, Jenn. Punta Gorda, FL. Affil: Florida SouthWestern State. Email: jenn.ochocki@outlook.com.

Ochonu, Moses Ebe, *Vanderbilt*. Email: moses.ochonu@vanderbilt.edu.

Ochsenwald, William, *Virginia Tech*. Blacksburg, VA. Email: ochsen@vt.edu. Research: Saudi Arabia and Islam, Arabia and historiography.

Ocker, Christopher M., *California, Berkeley*. Email: ocker@sfts.edu.

Ockerbloom, Mary Mark, *Science History Inst*. Email: mockerbloom@sciencehistory.org.

Ockert, Ingrid, *Science History Inst*. Email: iockert@sciencehistory.org.

Ocobock, Paul Robert, *Notre Dame*. Notre Dame, IN. Email: pocobock@nd.edu. Research: generation in colonial Kenya, African labor/youth/urban.

O'Connell, Aaron B., *Texas, Austin*. Austin, TX. Email: aaron.oconnell@austin.utexas.edu. Research: US military and military culture, 20th-c US and world.

O'Connell, John, *Gerald Ford Presidential Library*. Email: john.o'connell@nara.gov.

O'Connell, Joseph. Homewood, IL. Affil: DePaul. Email: joseph070@comcast.net.

O'Connell, Kaete Mary. Toms River, NJ. Email: kaete.oconnell@gmail.com.

O'Connell, Libby H. Huntington, NY. Affil: US World War I Centennial Commission. Email: libby.oconnell@gmail.com.

O'Connell, Monique, *Wake Forest*. Winston Salem, NC. Email: oconnme@wfu.edu. Research: Venetian maritime empire/Venetian Crete, political culture and identity.

O'Connell Gennari, Elizabeth. Collingswood, NJ. Affil: SUNY, Stony Brook. Email: evoconnell@yahoo.com.

O'Connor, Adrian D., *South Florida, St. Petersburg; Phi Alpha Theta*. Saint Petersburg, FL. Email: oconnora@mail.usf.edu. Research: 18th-c European cultural and political, French Revolution.

O'Connor, Alice M., *California, Santa Barbara*. Santa Barbara, CA. Email: aoconnor@history.ucsb.edu. Research: politics and culture of wealth, philanthropy.

O'Connor, Carol A., *Arkansas State*.

O'Connor, Eric K. Cincinnati, OH. Affil: Seven Hills Sch. Email: ezoconnor@gmail.com. Research: European integration, post-WWII European reconstruction.

O'Connor, Erin E. Bridgewater, MA. Affil: Bridgewater State. Email: eoconnor@bridgew.edu. Research: Ecuadorian Indian-state relations, Ecuadorian gender relations.

O'Connor, John E., *Rutgers, Newark/New Jersey Inst. of Tech*. Bloomfield, NJ. Email: oconnor@njit.edu; joc@slashmail.org. Research: film and television in history.

O'Connor, Joseph E., *Wittenberg*. Email: jeoconnor@wittenberg.edu.

O'Connor, Kate. Plymouth, MI. Affil: Michigan. Email: kateoco@umich.edu. Research: eugenics, adolescence.

O'Connor, **Kelly**, *Loyola, Chicago*. Burr Ridge, IL. Email: kocon6@luc.edu. Research: US, cultural.

O'Connor, **Kevin C.**, *Gonzaga*. Email: oconnork@gonzaga.edu.

O'Connor, **Maura**, *Cincinnati*. Cincinnati, OH. Email: oconnoma@ucmail.uc.edu. Research: risk/speculation/London Stock Exchange, archive/loss/memory/time's passage.

O'Connor, **Patrick**. Ypsilanti, MI. Affil: Montana. Email: patrick.oconnor@umontana.edu.

O'Connor, **Stephen**, *California State, Fullerton*. Fullerton, CA. Email: soconnor@fullerton.edu. Research: Cl Greek military forces and markets, strategy of Cl Greek land warfare.

O'Connor, **Timothy E.**, *Northern Iowa*. Email: tim.oconnor@uni.edu.

O'Connor, **Tricia L**. Lancaster, OH. Email: oconnortl@hotmail.com.

Oda, **Meredith A.**, *Nevada, Reno*. Email: meredtho@unr.edu.

Odahl, **Charles Matson**, *Boise State*. Boise, ID. Email: codahl@boisestate.edu. Research: Constantine and late Roman Empire, Cicero and Catilinarian conspiracy.

Odamtten, **Harry Nii Koney**, *Santa Clara*. Email: hodamtten@scu.edu.

O'Daniel McCallon, **Hannah**. Chicago, IL. Affil: Wayne State. Email: hannahmodaniel1@gmail.com. Research: disability in archival collections.

Odari, **Catherine**, *Spelman*. Email: codari@spelman.edu.

O'Day, **Edward J.**, **Jr.**, *Southern Illinois, Carbondale*. Email: edoday@siu.edu.

O'Dell, **John P.** Chula Vista, CA. Email: odell.jp@gmail.com.

Odem, **Mary E.**, *Emory*. Email: modem@emory.edu.

Odhiambo, **Godriver**, *Le Moyne*. Email: odhiamga@lemoyne.edu.

Odinga, **Agnes A.**, *Minnesota State, Mankato*. Email: agnes.odinga@mnsu.edu.

Odom, **James L.**, *East Tennessee State*. Email: odomj@etsu.edu.

O'Donnell, **Anne**, *NYU*.

O'Donnell, **Catherine**, *Arizona State*. Email: codonnell@asu.edu.

O'Donnell, **Edward T.**, *Holy Cross*. Worcester, MA. Email: eodonnell@holycross.edu. Research: Gilded Age and Progressive Era, Irish American.

O'Donnell, **J. Dean**, **Jr.**, *Virginia Tech*. Email: odonnell@vt.edu.

O'Donnell, **Krista Molly**, *William Paterson*. Wayne, NJ. Email: odonnellk@wpunj.edu. Research: women and imperialism in German Namibia.

O'Donnell, **Paula**. Austin, TX. Affil: Texas, Austin. Email: Podonnell@utexas.edu.

O'Donovan, **Susan E.**, *Memphis*. Memphis, TN. Email: odonovan@memphis.edu. Research: subaltern politics, gender/work/slavery/emancipation.

Oduntan, **Oluwatoyin**, *Towson*. Email: ooduntan@towson.edu.

O'Dwyer, **Emer Sinead**, *Oberlin*. Email: emer.odwyer@oberlin.edu.

Oelze, **Micah J.**, *Franklin & Marshall*. Email: moelze@fandm.edu.

Oestreicher, **Richard J.**, *Pittsburgh*. Taos, NM. Email: dick@pitt.edu. Research: US labor and working class, US popular culture.

Oetter, **Doug R.**, *Georgia Coll. and State*. Email: doug.oetter@gcsu.edu.

Offen, **Karen**. Woodside, CA. Affil: Stanford. Email: kmoffen@stanford.edu. Research: comparative/women, European/French feminism.

Offenburger, **Andrew**, *Miami, Ohio*. Email: offenba@miamioh.edu.

Officer, **Jane Marie**. Hanover, NH. Email: jane.officer@gmail.com.

Offner, **Amy C.**, *Pennsylvania*. Email: offner@sas.upenn.edu.

Offner, **Arnold A.**, *Lafayette*. Newton, MA. Email: offnera@lafayette.edu. Research: US foreign policy 1941-2000, US political 1930s-present.

Offner, **John L**. Chambersburg, PA. Affil: Shippensburg. Email: jloffner@innernet.net. Research: SHAFR 1898-1902, US annexation of Philippine islands.

Offutt, **Leslie S.**, *Vassar*. Poughkeepsie, NY. Email: offutt@vassar.edu. Research: colonial Mexican ethnohistory.

Offutt, **William M.**, *Pace*. Email: billoffutt@aol.com.

Oftedal, **Evan E**. Bridgewater, NJ. Affil: Watchung Hills Regional High Sch. Email: eoftedal@whrhs.org.

Ogawa, **Manako**. Kyoto, Japan. Affil: Ritsumeikan. Email: m-ogawa@fc.ritsumei.ac.jp.

Ogbar, **Jeffrey Ogbonna**, *Connecticut, Storrs*. Hartford, CT. Email: ogbar@uconn.edu. Research: music, urban.

Ogbomo, **Onaiwu**, *Western Michigan*. Email: onaiwu.ogbomo@wmich.edu.

Ogden, **Elizabeth**, *Hist. New Orleans*. Email: elizabetho@hnoc.org.

Ogelsby, **John C. M.**, *Western Ontario*.

Oggins, **Robin S.**, *Binghamton, SUNY*.

Ogilvie, **Brian W.**, *Massachusetts, Amherst*. Hadley, MA. Email: ogilvie@history.umass.edu. Research: antiquarianism/Ezechiel Spanheim, design/providence/entomology.

Ogilvie, **Marilyn B.**, *Oklahoma (Hist. of Science)*. Email: mogilvie@ou.edu.

Ogle, **Vanessa**, *California, Berkeley*.

Oglesby, **Elizabeth H.**, *Virginia Museum of Hist.* Email: loglesby@VirginiaHistory.org.

Oglesby, **Richard E.**, *California, Santa Barbara*.

Ogline Titus, **Jill L.**, *Gettysburg*. Email: jtitus@gettysburg.edu.

O'Gorman, **Maureen Leneker**. Warwick, RI. Email: maureen@maureen.com.

Ogrady, **James F**. Brooklyn, NY. Affil: SUNY, New Paltz. Email: jfog82@gmail.com.

O'Grady, **Robert Michael**. Arlington, MA. Email: ogr917@gmail.com.

Oh, **Arissa**, *Boston Coll.* Email: arissa.oh@bc.edu.

O'Hara, **David A.**, *Central Arkansas*. Email: dohara@uca.edu.

O'Hara, **Julia Cummings**, *Xavier, Ohio*. Cincinnati, OH. Email: ohara@xavier.edu. Research: indigenous peoples of northern Mexico, modern Mexican religious.

O'Hara, **Matt**, *California, Santa Cruz*. Santa Cruz, CA. Email: mdohara@ucsc.edu. Research: modern Latin America and Mexico, late colonial Latin America.

O'Hara, **Paul**, *Xavier, Ohio*. Email: oharas@xavier.edu.

O'Hear, **Ann**. Chester-le-Street, United Kingdom. Email: ohear18@yahoo.com. Research: slavery, material culture.

O'Hearn, **Amy**. Berkeley, CA. Affil: California, Berkeley. Email: aohearn@berkeley.edu.

O'Hern-Crook, **Megan**, *Hist. Assoc.* Email: mohern@historyassociates.com.

Ohlander, **Erik**, *Purdue, Fort Wayne*. Email: ohlandee@pfw.edu.

Ohls, **Gary J.**, *Naval War Coll.* Email: garyohls@aol.com.

Oidtmann, **Max**. Washington, DC. Affil: Georgetown. Email: max.oidtmann@gmail.com. Research: Qing dynasty and Inner Asia, colonial legal culture.

Ojala, **Jeanne**, *Utah*.

Ojo, **Olatunji**. *Brock*. Email: oojo@brocku.ca.

Okamura, **Lawrence**, *Missouri, Columbia*. Email: okamural@missouri.edu.

Okan, **Orcun Can**. Istanbul, Turkey. Affil: Columbia. Email: oco2105@columbia.edu. Research: post-WWI Turkey and Arab East, governance and diplomacy.

O'Keefe, **John McNelis**, *Ohio*. Email: okeefe@ohio.edu.

O'Keefe, **Kieran**. Alexandria, VA. Affil: George Washington. Email: kjokeefe@gwu.edu. Research: Loyalism in revolutionary New York.

O'Keefe, **Timothy J.**, *Santa Clara*. Email: tokeefe@scu.edu.

O'Keeffe, **Brigid M.**, *Brooklyn, CUNY*. Email: bokeeffe@brooklyn.cuny.edu.

Okenfuss, **Max J.**, *Washington, St. Louis*. Email: okenfuss@wustl.edu.

Okeny, **Kenneth**, *Salem State*. Email: kokeny@salemstate.edu.

Okhovat, **Oren**. Gainesville, FL. Affil: Florida. Email: ookho001@ufl.edu.

Okie, **Packard L**. Columbia, MO. Affil: Moherly Area Comm. Coll. Email: oklairdee@aol.com.

Okie, **William Thomas**, *Kennesaw State*. Email: wokie1@kennesaw.edu.

Okin, **Peter Oliver**. Panacea, FL. Email: pokin@alumni.health.usf.edu. Research: public health policy and law, yellow fever.

Okoh, **Oghenetoja H.**, *Loyola, Md*. Akron, OH. Affil: Akron. Email: ohokoh@loyola.edu; tokoh@uakron.edu. Research: Niger Delta, minority citizenship.

Okuda, **Alison K.**, *Worcester State*. Marlborough, MA. Email: aokuda@worcester.edu. Research: African diaspora, West Africa.

Olasz, **Csaba**. La Jolla, CA. Affil: California, San Diego. Email: colasz@ucsd.edu.

Olberding, **Garret P.**, *Oklahoma (Hist.)*. Email: golberding@ou.edu.

Olbertson, **Kristin A.**, *Alma*. Alma, MI. Email: olbertson@alma.edu. Research: speech and language, gentility and deference.

Olcott, **Jocelyn H.**, *Duke*. Durham, NC. Email: olcott@duke.edu. Research: UN International Women's Year 1975, Concha Michel.

Olden, **Danielle R.**, *Utah*.

Oldenburg, **Veena Talwar**, *Graduate Center, CUNY*.

Oldham, **Patricia**. Brooklyn, NY. Affil: Hostos Comm. Coll., CUNY. Email: northstories2@aol.com. Research: antebellum African American communities, US antislavery movement.

Olds, **Katrina B.**, *San Francisco*. Email: kbolds@usfca.edu.

O'Leary, **Brendan**. Philadelphia, PA. Affil: Pennsylvania. Email: boleary@sas.upenn.edu.

O'Leary, **Wayne**, *Maine, Orono*.

Olejniczak, *William*, *Charleston*. Charleston, SC. Email: olejniczakb@cofc.edu. Research: Enlightenment and French Revolution.

Olek, *Christie J*. Bronx, NY. Email: colek@fordham.edu.

Olenik, *J. Kenneth*, *Montclair State*. Email: olenikk@mail.montclair.edu.

O'Leno, *Kenneth*. San Diego, CA. Email: olenoken@gmail.com. Research: Civil War, WWII.

Olesko, *Kathryn M.*, *Georgetown*. Springfield, VA. Email: oleskok@georgetown.edu. Research: science and technoology, Prussia.

Olick, *Jeffrey K.*, *Virginia*. Email: jko3k@virginia.edu.

Olin, *Spencer C.*, *California, Irvine*. Email: scolin@uci.edu.

Olin, *Timothy John*. Lafayette, IN. Affil: Wabash. Email: timothyjolin@gmail.com. Research: Europe, world.

Oliva, *Marilyn*. Brooklyn, NY. Affil: Fordham. Email: marilyn.oliva11201@gmail.com.

Olivarius, *Kathryn*, *Stanford*. Stanford, CA. Email: koli@stanford.edu. Research: slavery and labor in lower Louisiana, African slave trade ban 1808.

Olivas, *Aaron Alejandro*. Laredo, TX. Affil: Texas A&M International. Email: aaolivas@gmail.com. Research: War of Spanish Succession, transatlantic slave trade.

Oliveira, *Vanessa Dos Santos*, *Royal Military*. Email: Vanessa.Dos-Santos-Oliveira@rmc.ca.

Olivencia, *Deborah Joi*. Temple, TX. Affil: Southern New Hampshire. Email: joiolivencia@yahoo.com.

Oliver, *Bette W*. Austin, TX. Affil: Texas, Austin. Email: betteoliver@sbcglobal.net. Research: Late 18th-c artists/museums, social/cultural effects of French Revolution 1789.

Oliver, *Brian*. Fairborn, OH. Affil: Hong Kong International Sch. Email: brianrandalloliver@gmail.com.

Oliver, *Clementine*, *California State, Northridge*. Email: coliver@csun.edu.

Oliver, *Dean Frederick*, *Carleton, Can*. Gatineau, QC, Canada. Affil: Canadian Museum of Hist. Email: dean.oliver@carleton.ca; dean.oliver@historymuseum.ca. Research: Canadian military.

Oliver, *Graham J.*, *Brown*. Email: Graham_Oliver@Brown.edu.

Oliver, *Megan*, *Duquesne*. Email: oliverm2@duq.edu.

Oliver, *Robert*, *Coastal Carolina*. Email: roliver@coastal.edu.

Olkovsky, *Alex*. Waltham, MA. Affil: Boston Univ. Email: aolk@bu.edu.

Oller, *Anthony L.* Bedford, TX. Affil: South Grand Prairie High Sch. Email: anthonyoller@hotmail.com.

Olliff, *Martin T.*, *III*, *Troy*. Email: molliff@tsud.edu.

Olmstead, *Justin Quinn*, *Central Oklahoma*. Edmond, OK. Email: jolmstead@uco.edu. Research: history education, WWI.

Olmsted, *Brett*. Humble, TX. Affil: Houston. Email: brett.olmsted@gmail.com. Research: Mexican American labor/leisure in MI.

Olmsted, *Kathryn S.*, *California, Davis*. Email: ksolmsted@ucdavis.edu.

Olsen, *Christopher J.*, *Indiana State*. Email: Christopher.Olsen@indstate.edu.

Olsen, *Glenn W.*, *Utah*. Salt Lake City, UT. Email: glenn.olsen@utah.edu. Research: medieval humanism, medieval biblical exegesis.

Olsen, *Jon Berndt*, *Massachusetts, Amherst*. Amherst, MA. Email: jon@history.umass.edu. Research: memory culture in East Germany, travel and leisure in East Germany.

Olsen, *Jonathan*, *Texas Woman's*. Email: jolsen@twu.edu.

Olsen, *Kirstin A.* Ben Lomond, CA. Affil: Georgiana Bruce Kirby Preparatory Sch. Email: kolsen@kirby.org. Research: historical context of Charles Dickens.

Olsen, *Patrice Elizabeth*, *Illinois State*. Email: peolsen@ilstu.edu.

Olsen, *Robert James*. Saint Louis, MO. Affil: St. Louis. Email: robert.olsen@slu.edu.

Olson, *Alexander I.*, *Western Kentucky*. Email: alexander.olson@wku.edu.

Olson, *Alison G.*, *Maryland, Coll. Park*. Email: alisongolson@hotmail.com.

Olson, *Benjamin*. Duvall, WA. Email: benjamin.olson@wsu.edu.

Olson, *James S.*, *Sam Houston State*. Email: his_jso@shsu.edu.

Olson, *Jane Elizabeth Bast*. Washington, DC. Email: jane.e.olson@gmail.com.

Olson, *Katharine Kristina*, *San José State*. San Jose, CA. Email: katharine.olson@sjsu.edu. Research: medieval/early modern Europe/Britain/Ireland, religious/social/cultural/intellectual.

Olson, *Keith W.*, *Maryland, Coll. Park*. Shelburne, VT. Email: kwolson@umd.edu. Research: Eisenhower and civil rights, 20th-c presidents.

Olson, *Liesl*. Chicago, IL. Affil: Newberry Library. Email: olsonl@newberry.org. Research: literary modernism, poetry.

Olson, *Madeleine C.* Austin, TX. Affil: Rollins. Email: molson@utexas.edu.

Olson, *Michael D.* Columbia, MO. Affil: Missouri, Columbia. Email: michaelolson@mail.missouri.edu. Research: African American/radicalism/LGBTQ+.

Olson, *Richard A.*, *St. Olaf*. Email: olsonri@stolaf.edu.

Olson, *Sherri*, *Connecticut, Storrs*. Email: sherri.olson@uconn.edu.

Olson Dowis, *Sian Christina*. Chicago, IL. Affil: Northwestern. Email: SianOlsonDowis2014@u.northwestern.edu.

Olsson, *Tore C.*, *Tennessee, Knoxville*. Knoxville, TN. Email: colsson@utk.edu. Research: green revolution in US and Mexico, globalization of rural New Deal.

Olster, *David M.*, *Kentucky*. Email: dmolst01@uky.edu.

Olteanu, *Mihai*. Chicago, IL. Email: mihaiolteanu96@gmail.com.

Olumwullah, *Osaak*, *Miami, Ohio*. Email: olumwuoa@miamioh.edu.

Olwell, *Robert A.*, *Texas, Austin*. Email: rolwell@austin.utexas.edu.

Olyan, *Saul M.* Providence, RI. Affil: Brown. Email: saul_olyan@brown.edu. Research: ancient Israelite religion, biblical exegesis.

O'Malley, *Gregory E.*, *California, Santa Cruz*. Santa Cruz, CA. Email: gomalley@ucsc.edu. Research: intercolony slave trade, race and identity formation.

O'Malley, *Michael H.*, *George Mason*. Email: momalle3@gmu.edu.

O'Malley, *Paul F.*, *Providence*. Email: pomalley@providence.edu.

O'Malley, *Sean*. Edgewater, MD. Email: so6629a@american.edu.

O'Mara, *Kathleen K.*, *SUNY, Oneonta*. Email: kathleen.omara@oneonta.edu.

O'Mara, *Margaret Pugh*, *Washington, Seattle*. Seattle, WA. Email: momara@uw.edu. Research: metropolitan growth, Cold War.

O'Mara, *William Edward*, *IV*, *California State, Dominguez Hills; Chapman; San Diego Mesa*. Email: womaraiv@csudh.edu; womaraiv@chapman.edu.

Omara-Otunnu, *Amii*, *Connecticut, Storrs*. Email: amii.omara-otunnu@uconn.edu.

Onaci, *Edward*, *Ursinus*. Email: eonaci@ursinus.edu.

Onate-Madrazo, *Andrea*, *California Polytechnic State*. Email: aonatema@calpoly.edu.

O'Neil, *Mary R.*, *Washington, Seattle*. Email: oneilmr@uw.edu.

O'Neil, *Timothy M.*, *Central Michigan*. Email: oneil1tm@cmich.edu.

O'Neill, *Carys*. Chicago, IL. Affil: Central Florida. Email: carys.oneill@yahoo.com. Research: gender and nationalism in heritage, heritage tourism and identity.

O'Neill, *Colleen M.*, *Utah State*. Email: colleen.oneill@usu.edu.

O'Neill, *Johnathan G.*, *Georgia Southern*. Email: joneill@georgiasouthern.edu.

O'Neill, *Kelly*, *Harvard (Hist.)*. Email: koneill@fas.harvard.edu.

O'Neill, *Kevin*, *Boston Coll.* Email: kevin.oneill@bc.edu.

O'Neill, *Lindsay J.*, *Southern California*. Pasadena, CA. Email: ljoneill@usc.edu; ljoyoneill@gmail.com. Research: early modern information distribution, Black experience in Britain.

O'Neill, *Sean*, *Grand Valley State*. Email: oneills@gvsu.edu.

O'Neill, *Stephen*, *Furman*. Email: steve.oneill@furman.edu.

O'Neill, *Stephen*, *Suffolk*. Email: soneill@suffolk.edu.

O'Neill, *Ynez V*. Los Angeles, CA. Email: yvonmhi@ucla.edu.

Ong, *Diccon*. Hudson, OH. Affil: Western Reserve Academy. Email: ongd@wra.net.

Onishi, *Sho*. Kyoto, Japan. Affil: MUFG Bank, Ltd. Email: sho19900805@ezweb.ne.jp.

Onkst, *David H*. Rockville, MD. Email: donkst@verizon.net. Research: US space program, engineers and engineering.

Onstine, *Suzanne L.*, *Memphis*. Email: sonstine@memphis.edu.

Onuf, *Peter S.*, *Virginia*. Email: dude@virginia.edu.

Onyon, *David E.* Cedar Hill, TX. Affil: North Texas. Email: david_onyon@yahoo.com. Research: Second Continental Congress.

Ooms, *Herman*, *UCLA*. Email: ooms@history.ucla.edu.

Ooten, *Melissa D.*, *Richmond*. Email: mooten@richmond.edu.

Opal, *Jason M.*, *McGill*. Email: jason.opal@mcgill.ca.

Opitz, *Donald L.* Chicago, IL. Affil: DePaul. Email: dopitz@depaul.edu.

Opler, *Daniel J.*, *Mount St. Vincent*. Email: daniel.opler@mountsaintvincent.edu.

Opp, **James**, *Carleton, Can.* Email: james.opp@carleton.ca.

Oppenheim, **Samuel A.**, *California State, Stanislaus.* Email: soppenheim@csustan.edu.

Oppenheimer, **Gerald**, *Columbia (Hist. Public Health); Graduate Center, CUNY.* Email: geraldo@brooklyn.cuny.edu; go10@columbia.edu.

Oppenhuizen, **Clayton**. East Lansing, MI. Affil: Michigan State. Email: oppenhu4@msu.edu.

Opperman, **Stephanie Baker**, *Georgia Coll. and State.* Email: stephanie.opperman@gcsu.edu.

Orbach, **Dan**. Jerusalem, Israel. Affil: Hebrew, Jerusalem. Email: dannyorbach@gmail.com. Research: military rebellions/assassinations, political legitimacy/illegal orders.

Ordman, **Jilana**, *Lake Forest.* Chicago, IL. Email: ordman@lakeforest.edu; jordman@luc.edu. Research: Crusades, emotions.

Ore, **Janet**, *Montana State, Bozeman.* Email: janet.ore@montana.edu.

Oreck, **Steven Lewis**. Madison, WI. Affil: Wisconsin, Madison. Email: sloreck@wisc.edu. Research: post-1700 military medicine, military/naval/amphibious war.

O'Reilly, **Kenneth**. Milwaukee, WI. Affil: Milwaukee Area Tech. Email: koreilly2@uaa.alaska.edu. Research: Clinton-Bush era, federal surveillance policy.

O'Reilly, **Sean**. Beverly, MA. Affil: Akita International. Email: seanoreilly@aiu.ac.jp.

Orel, **Sara**, *Truman State.* Email: orel@truman.edu.

Orens, **John R.**, *George Mason.* Email: jorens@gmu.edu.

Oreskes, **Naomi**, *Harvard (Hist. of Science).* Email: oreskes@fas.harvard.edu.

Orgodol, **Betsy**, *AHA.* Email: borgodol@historians.org.

Orihuela, **Amanda Marie**. Englewood, CO. Affil: Vanguard Classical Sch. Email: amanda.marie.orihuela@gmail.com.

Oriji, **John N.**, *California Polytechnic State.* Email: joriji@calpoly.edu.

Orintas, **David A.** Waterbury, CT. Email: dorintas@gmail.com.

Orique, **David Thomas**, *OP, Providence.* Providence, RI. Email: dorique@providence.edu. Research: Bartolome de las Casas, colonial missionaries.

Orisich, **Shari M.**, *Coastal Carolina.* Email: sorisich@coastal.edu.

Orkaby, **Asher**. Brighton, MA. Affil: Harvard. Email: orkaby@post.harvard.edu. Research: Yemeni Civil War, internationalization of Yemeni economy.

Orleck, **Annelise**, *Dartmouth.* Thetford Center, VT. Email: annelise.orleck@dartmouth.edu. Research: black mothers and War on Poverty, migration and immigration.

Orlin, **Eric M.**, *Puget Sound.* Email: eorlin@pugetsound.edu.

Orliski, **Constance I.**, *California State, Bakersfield.*

Orlovsky, **Daniel T.**, *Southern Methodist.* Dallas, TX. Email: dorlovsk@smu.edu. Research: Russia, Soviet Union.

Orlow, **Dietrich O.** Bellevue, WA. Affil: Boston Univ. Email: dorlow@bu.edu. Research: comparative fascism, contemporary European Social Democracy.

Orme, **Jennifer**, *Hist. Assoc.* Email: jorme@historyassociates.com.

Ornee, **Laura**. Charlottesville, VA. Affil: Virginia. Email: lho3by@virginia.edu.

Ornelas-Higdon, **Julia**, *California State, Channel Islands.* Email: julia.ornelas-higdon@csuci.edu.

Oropeza, **Lorena**, *California, Davis.* Email: lboropeza@ucdavis.edu.

Orosz, **Kenneth J.**, *SUNY, Buffalo State.* Buffalo, NY. Email: oroszkj@buffalostate.edu. Research: Imperialism in Africa, Flora Shaw/Lady Lugard.

O'Rourke, **Harmony Susan**, *Pitzer.* Email: harmony_orourke@pitzer.edu.

Orozco, **Cynthia E.** Ruidoso, NM. Affil: Eastern New Mexico. Email: Cynthia.Orozco@enmu.edu. Research: Mexican American civil rights, Lincoln County war.

Orozco, **Jose**, *Whittier.* Email: jorozco@whittier.edu.

Orozco, **Rebecca J.** Bisbee, AZ. Affil: Cochise. Email: orozcor@cochise.edu.

Orquiza, **Alex**, **Jr.**, *Providence.* Email: rorquiza@providence.edu.

Orr, **Andrew**, *Kansas State.* Email: aorr1@k-state.edu.

Orr, **James J.**, *Bucknell.* Email: jamesorr@bucknell.edu.

Orr, **Patricia R.** Austin, TX. Affil: Houston Baptist. Email: patorr@i-ocean.com.

Orr, **Suzanne**, *Kansas State.* Email: sorr1@ksu.edu.

Orr, **Timothy**, *Old Dominion.* Email: torr@odu.edu.

Orru, **Giangiacomo**. Cagliari, Italy. Email: giangiaorru@tiscali.it.

Orser, **Joseph Andrew**, *Wisconsin-Eau Claire.* Email: orserja@uwec.edu.

Orsi, **Jared P.**, *Colorado State.* Email: jared.orsi@colostate.edu.

Orsi, **Robert Anthony**, *Northwestern.* Email: r-orsi@northwestern.edu.

Orsini, **Davide**, *Mississippi State.*

Ort, **Thomas W.**, *Queens, CUNY.* Flushing, NY. Email: thomas.ort@qc.cuny.edu. Research: Capek Generation/interwar Czechoslovakia, Prague/Budapest/Vienna cultural life.

Ortega, **Carolina**. Urbana, IL. Affil: Illinois, Urbana-Champaign. Email: cortega5@illinois.edu.

Ortega, **Jose Guadalupe**, *Whittier.* Email: jortega@whittier.edu.

Ortenberg, **Rebecca**, *Science History Inst.* Email: rortenberg@sciencehistory.org.

Orth, **Joel Jason**, *California Polytechnic State.* Email: jorth@calpoly.edu.

Ortiz, **David**, **Jr.**, *Arizona.* Email: davido@u.arizona.edu.

Ortiz, **Eduardo L.** London, United Kingdom. Affil: Imperial. Email: e.ortiz@ic.ac.uk. Research: exact sciences, US-Latin American scientific exchanges.

Ortiz, **Luz A.** Bronx, NY. Affil: Univ. Coll. of the Cayman Islands. Email: lortiz7620@aol.com. Research: Spanish.

Ortiz, **Paul A.**, *Florida.* Gainesville, FL. Email: portiz@ufl.edu. Research: labor, ethnic studies.

Ortiz, **Stephen R.**, *Binghamton, SUNY.* Email: sortiz@binghamton.edu.

Ortiz Diaz, **Alberto**, *Iowa.* Email: alberto-ortizdiaz@uiowa.edu.

Ortmann, **Susan**, *Millersville, Pa.* Email: susan.ortmann@millersville.edu.

Ortolano, **Guy**, *NYU.* New York, NY. Email: ortolano@nyu.edu. Research: urban, cultural.

Ortquist, **Chelsey**. Muskegon, MI. Email: cortqu@gmail.com.

Ortquist, **Richard T.**, *Wittenberg.* Email: rortquist@wittenberg.edu.

Orttung, **Robin**, *Allegheny.* Email: rorttung@allegheny.edu.

Orzechowski, **Victoria**, *Science History Inst.* Email: vorzechowski@sciencehistory.org.

Orzoff, **Andrea**, *New Mexico State.* Email: aorzoff@nmsu.edu.

Osber, **Stephanie**. Framingham, MA. Affil: BEDA Catholic Sch. Spain. Email: so7706a@student.american.edu.

Osborn, **Emily L.**, *Chicago.* Chicago, IL. Email: eosborn1@uchicago.edu. Research: technology, material culture.

Osborn, **Matthew Warner**, *Missouri–Kansas City.* Email: osbornmw@umkc.edu.

Osborn, **Wayne S.**, *Iowa State.*

Osborne, **Eric W.**, *Virginia Military Inst.* Email: osborneew@vmi.edu.

Osborne, **John B.**, **Jr.**, *Millersville, Pa.*

Osborne, **John M.**, *Dickinson.* Email: osborne@dickinson.edu.

Osborne, **Lori**. Evanston, IL. Affil: Frances Willard House Museum. Email: ljosbo1@comcast.net.

Osborne, **Myles Gregory**, *Colorado, Boulder.* Email: myles.osborne@colorado.edu.

Osborne, **Thomas R.**, *North Alabama.* Florence, AL. Email: trosborne@una.edu. Research: refugees in 20th-c Europe.

Osborne, **Troy D.**, *Waterloo.* Email: t3osborne@uwaterloo.ca.

Osburn, **Katherine**, *Arizona State.* Email: katherine.osburn@asu.edu.

Osei, **Cassandra**. Shawnee, KS. Email: cassie.osei@gmail.com.

Osei-Opare, **Nana**. New York City, NY. Affil: UCLA. Email: oseiopare@ucla.edu. Research: Ghana/Nkrumah/post-colonialism/Cold War, USSR/socialism/capitalism.

Osgood, **Aidyn Perry Morris**. Ann Arbor, MI. Affil: Michigan, Ann Arbor. Email: osgooda@umich.edu. Research: women in European military 1450-1815.

Osgood, **Russell K.**, *Grinnell.* Email: osgood@grinnell.edu.

O'Shaughnessy, **Andrew Jackson**, *Virginia; Robert H. Smith Center.* Charlottesville, VA. Email: aoshaughnessy@monticello.org. Research: colonial America, early American Republic.

O'Shea, **Deirdre Patricia**, *Central Florida.* Email: Deirdre.OShea@ucf.edu.

Osheim, **Duane J.**, *Virginia.* Email: djo@virginia.edu.

Oshinsky, **David M.**, *NYU; Texas, Austin.* Email: oshind01@nyu.edu; oshinsky@mail.utexas.edu.

Osler, **Anne**, *St. Thomas, Minn.* Email: osle6883@stthomas.edu.

Oslund, **Karen**, *Towson.* Email: koslund@towson.edu.

Osman, **Julia Anne**, *Mississippi State.* Mississippi State, MS. Email: josman@history.msstate.edu. Research: prerevolutionary France, Europeans in North America.

Osman, **Suleiman**. Washington, DC. Affil: George Washington. Email: sosman@gwu.edu. Research: gentrification in postwar New York City, brownstone revitalization movement.

Osokina, Elena A., *South Carolina, Columbia*. Email: osokina@mailbox.sc.edu.

Osorio, Alejandra B. Wellesley, MA. Affil: Wellesley. Email: aosorio@wellesley.edu. Research: early modern Atlantic urban, colonial Lima Peru cultural.

Osseo-Asare, Abena Dove, *Texas, Austin*. Email: osseo@utexas.edu.

Ostarly, Lori, *Southeastern Louisiana*. Email: lostarly@selu.edu.

Osten, Sarah E., *Vermont*. Email: sarah.osten@uvm.edu.

Ostendorf, Ann, *Gonzaga*. Email: ostendorf@gonzaga.edu.

Oster, Donald B., *Missouri Science and Tech*. Email: donoster@mst.edu.

Osterhout, Vance. San Marcos, CA. Affil: California State, San Marcos. Email: oster005@cougars.csusm.edu.

Osthaus, Wendy B., *Henry Ford Coll*. Email: wosthaus@aol.com.

Ostler, Jeff, *Oregon*. Eugene, OR. Email: jostler@uoregon.edu. Research: American Indian.

Ostoyich, Kevin Robert, *Valparaiso*. Valparaiso, IN. Email: kevin.ostoyich@valpo.edu. Research: Shanghai Jewish refugees, German migration.

Ostrander, Carolyn. Syracuse, NY. Affil: Syracuse. Email: clostran@syr.edu.

Ostrofsky, Kathryn A. Roslindale, MA. Email: kostrofs@gmail.com. Research: popular music and television, children's entertainment and education.

Ostrom, Jessica L. Lake Bluff, IL. Affil: Fusion Academy. Email: jlostrom8@gmail.com. Research: Anglo-Norman England, social attitudes towards leprosy.

Ostrow, Sonja Gammeltoft. Winston Salem, NC. Affil: Minerva Sch. at KGI. Email: sgostrow@gmail.com. Research: modern Germany, science and technology.

Ostrower, Gary B., *Alfred*. Email: ostrower@alfred.edu.

Ostrum, Nick. Columbus, OH. Affil: Clark State Comm. Coll. Email: nicholasostrum@gmail.com. Research: West German petro-policy, German oil companies in Arab world.

Ostwald, Jamel M., *Eastern Connecticut State*. Email: ostwaldj@easternct.edu.

O'Sullivan, Chris, *San Francisco*. Email: osullivanc@usfca.edu.

O'Sullivan, Donal B., *California State, Northridge*. Email: donal.osullivan@csun.edu.

O'Sullivan, John G. Monmouth Junction, NJ. Email: osullivan.john5@gmail.com.

O'Sullivan, Luke. Singapore. Affil: National, Singapore. Email: polldo@nus.edu.sg.

O'Sullivan, Meg Devlin, *SUNY, New Paltz*. Email: osullivm@newpaltz.edu.

O'Sullivan, Robin, *Troy*.

Ota, Yuzo, *McGill*. Email: yuzo.ota@mcgill.ca.

Ota-Wang, Nick. Denver, CO. Affil: Colorado, Denver. Email: Nick.Ota-Wang@alumni.du.edu.

Otero, Josue. Orlando, FL. Affil: Florida International. Email: joter042@fiu.edu.

Otero, Lydia R., *Arizona*. Email: lotero@email.arizona.edu.

Otheguy, Raquel Alicia. Hamden, CT. Affil: Bronx Comm. Coll., CUNY. Email: raquel.otheguy@bcc.cuny.edu.

Othman, Enaya H. Milwaukee, WI. Affil: Marquette. Email: enaya.othman@marquette. edu. Research: Muslim women and identity negotiation, Building communities in Diaspora.

Otim, Patrick William, *Bates*. Email: potim@bates.edu.

Otis, Jessica Marie, *George Mason*. Email: jotis2@gmu.edu.

O'Toole, James M., *Boston Coll*. Chestnut Hill, MA. Email: otoolejb@bc.edu. Research: American Catholicism.

O'Toole, Rachel Sarah, *California, Irvine*. Irvine, CA. Email: rotoole@uci.edu. Research: colonial casta categories, slavery in Americas.

O'Toole, Timothy Michael. Hilton, NY. Affil: SUNY, Buffalo. Email: tim.otoole72@gmail.com. Research: diplomatic, Cold War.

O'Toole, Tomas, *Metropolitan State*. Email: thomas.otoole@metrostate.edu.

Otori, Yukako. Cambridge, MA. Affil: Harvard. Email: yotori@fas.harvard.edu.

Otovo, Okezi T., *Florida International*. Miami, FL. Email: okezi.otovo@fiu.edu. Research: race and gender in modern Brazil, public health.

Otsubo Sitcawich, Sumiko, *Metropolitan State*. Email: sumiko.otsubo@metrostate.edu.

Ott, Cindy, *Delaware*. Email: cott@udel.edu.

Ott, Daniel P., *Wisconsin-Eau Claire*. Email: ottdp@uwec.edu.

Ott, John S., *Portland State*. Portland, OR. Email: ottj@pdx.edu. Research: medieval and Renaissance Europe.

Ott, Julia, *New School*. Email: ottj@newschool.edu.

Ott, Thomas O., III, *North Alabama*.

Ott, Victoria E., *Birmingham-Southern*. Email: vott@bsc.edu.

Ottanelli, Fraser M., *South Florida, Tampa*. Email: ottanelli@usf.edu.

Ottaway, Susannah R., *Carleton Coll*. Northfield, MN. Email: sottaway@carleton.edu. Research: poverty in early modern England, old age in 18th-c England.

Otte, Marline Sylta, *Tulane*. Email: motte@tulane.edu.

Otter, Christopher J., *Ohio State*. Email: otter.4@osu.edu.

Otterby, Jeff. Saint Charles, IL. Affil: Thompson Middle Sch. Email: big2cat@gmail.com.

Otterness, Philip L. Asheville, NC. Affil: Warren Wilson. Email: pottern@warren-wilson.edu. Research: 18th-c German migration to New York.

Otto, Laura Gene. Huntington, NY. Affil: SUNY, Old Westbury. Email: lgo44@aol.com.

Otto, Paul, *George Fox*. Email: potto@georgefox.edu.

Ottoson, Robin Deich. Hillsboro, KS. Affil: Kansas State. Email: rottoson@ksu.edu. Research: Mennonites in Kansas and Plains, religion factor in political resistance.

Otunnu, Ogenga, *DePaul*. Email: ootunnu@depaul.edu.

Oualdi, M'hamed, *Princeton*. Email: moualdi@princeton.edu.

Ouellet, Nelson. Lutes Mountain, NB, Canada. Affil: Moncton. Email: nelson.ouellet@umoncton.ca. Research: African American migration, Reconstruction/Freedmen's Bureau/Tennessee.

Ouellette, Cathy Marie, *Muhlenberg*. Email: couellette@muhlenberg.edu.

Ouellette, Susan, *St. Michael's*. Email: souellette@smcvt.edu.

Outlaw, Alain C., *Christopher Newport*. Email: aoutlaw@cnu.edu.

Outram, Dorinda, *Rochester*. Email: d.outram@rochester.edu.

Ouzts, Clay, *North Georgia*. Email: clay.ouzts@ung.edu.

Overall, C. Sydney. Cleveland, OH. Email: sydneyoverall@hotmail.com. Research: US 1815-77.

Overfield, James H., *Vermont*. Email: james.overfield@uvm.edu.

Overfield, Richard, *Nebraska, Omaha*.

Overmyer-Velazquez, Mark, *Connecticut, Storrs*. Email: mark.velazquez@uconn.edu.

Ovnick, Merry A., *California State, Northridge*. Email: merry.ovnick@csun.edu.

Oweidat, Nadia, *Kansas State*. Email: oweidat@ksu.edu.

Owen, Alex, *Northwestern*. Email: a-owen@northwestern.edu.

Owen, James T., III. Bainbridge Island, WA. Email: jamesoweniii@yahoo.com. Research: 18th-c British Channel Islands, 1607 English Midlands Revolt.

Owen, Kenneth, *Illinois, Springfield*. Email: kowen8@uis.edu.

Owen, Thomas C., *Louisiana State*.

Owens, Alice B. Brooklyn, NY.

Owens, David. Midlothian, TX. Email: david.owens2011@gmail.com.

Owens, Emily A., *Brown*.

Owens, Harry P., *Mississippi*.

Owens, J. B., *Idaho State*. Boise, ID. Email: owenjack@isu.edu. Research: Castilian government 1400-1700, cooperation.

Owens, Larry, *Massachusetts, Amherst*. Email: lowens@history.umass.edu.

Owens, Leslie, *SUNY, Stony Brook*. Email: leslie.owens@stonybrook.edu.

Owens, MacKubin Thomas, *Naval War Coll*. Email: owensm@usnwc.edu.

Owens, Meranda. Chicago, IL. Affil: Field Museum. Email: mowens@fieldmuseum.org.

Owens, Robert M., *Wichita State*. Email: robert.owens@wichita.edu.

Owens, Roger. Newcastle, Australia. Email: roger.owens56@icloud.com. Research: American Revolution, US politics.

Owensby, Brian P., *Virginia*. Email: bpo3a@virginia.edu.

Owino, Meshack, *Cleveland State*. Email: m.owino@csuohio.edu.

Ownby, David, *Montréal*. Email: david.ownby@umontreal.ca.

Ownby, Ted, *Mississippi*. Email: hsownby@olemiss.edu.

Owram, Douglas R., *Alberta*.

Owre, Maximilian Paul, *North Carolina, Chapel Hill*. Email: owre@email.unc.edu.

Owsley, James. Greenville, TX. Affil: Grayson. Email: owsleyj@grayson.edu.

Owusu-Ansah, David, *James Madison*. Email: owusuadx@jmu.edu.

Oxenboell, Morten, *Indiana*. Email: mortoxen@indiana.edu.

Oxford, Mitchell. Covington, KY. Affil: William and Mary. Email: m.oxford.svp@gmail.com.

Oyebade, Adebayo O., *Tennessee State*. Email: aoyebade@tnstate.edu.

Oyen, Meredith L., *Maryland, Baltimore County*. Email: oyen@umbc.edu.

Oyeniyi, Bukola, *Missouri State*. Email: BukolaOyeniyi@missouristate.edu.

Oyos, Matthew M., *Radford*. Email: moyos@radford.edu.

Oyugi, Willis, *Sam Houston State*. Email: woo002@shsu.edu.

Ozment, Steven E., *Harvard (Hist.)*. Email: ozment@fas.harvard.edu.

Ozoglu, Hakan, *Central Florida*. Email: hakan@ucf.edu.

Ozok Gundogan, Nilay, *Florida State*.

Ozturk, Doga. Columbus, OH. Affil: Ohio State. Email: ozturk.15@osu.edu.

P p

Pabel, Hilmar M., *Simon Fraser*. Email: pabel@sfu.ca.

Pace, Daniel. Philadelphia, PA. Affil: Temple. Email: tug82556@temple.edu.

Pace, David, *Indiana*. Bloomington, IN. Email: dpace@indiana.edu. Research: scholarship of teaching and learning.

Pace, Jeneva, *State Hist. Soc. of Missouri*. Email: pacejp@shsmo.org.

Pace, Michael J. Foley, MN. Email: MJPaceMN@outlook.com.

Paces, Cynthia, *New Jersey*. Email: paces@tcnj.edu.

Pach, Chester J., Jr., *Ohio*. Email: pach@ohio.edu.

Pacholl, Keith A., *West Georgia*. Email: kpacholl@westga.edu.

Pacino, Nicole L., *Alabama, Huntsville*. Huntsville, AL. Email: nicole.pacino@uah.edu. Research: public health in Bolivia.

Pack, Jared. Fayetteville, AR. Affil: Arkansas, Fayetteville. Email: bjpack@uark.edu. Research: transatlantic relations 1969-82, US foreign policy during Nixon admin.

Pack, Sasha David, *SUNY, Buffalo*. Buffalo, NY. Email: sdpack@buffalo.edu. Research: travel and tourism, modern Spanish politics.

Packard, Randall M., *Johns Hopkins (Hist. of Science)*. Email: rpackar2@jhmi.edu.

Packer, Tiffany George Butler. Tallahassee, FL. Affil: Florida A&M. Email: tiffany.packer@famu.edu.

Pacyga, Dominic A. Chicago, IL. Affil: Columbia Coll., Chicago. Email: dpacyga@colum.edu. Research: Chicago, race/ethnic/class relations.

Paczkowski, Carolyn. South Hamilton, MA. Affil: Pingree Sch. Email: cpaczkowska@pingree.org. Research: 19th-c African Americans in abolition movement.

Padberg, John W. Saint Louis, MO. Affil: Inst. of Jesuit Sources. Email: jpadberg@jesuits.org. Research: modern European intellectual and cultural, Jesuit.

Paddison, Joshua, *Texas State*. Email: j_p532@txstate.edu.

Paddock, Adam John, *Wisconsin-Whitewater*. Email: paddocka@uww.edu.

Paddock, Troy R.E., *Southern Connecticut State*. New Haven, CT. Email: paddockt1@southernct.edu. Research: 19th-/20th-c culture and environment, historiography.

Padfield Narayan, Abigail. Baltimore, MD. Affil: Central Florida. Email: akpadfield@gmail.com.

Padilla, Tanalis, *MIT*. Email: tanalis@mit.edu.

Padovano, Daniel S. New York, NY. Affil: Metropolitan, CUNY. Email: spqr212@yahoo.com. Research: urban-suburban mass transit, European Union.

Padula, Anthony. Evanston, IL. Email: apadula88@gmail.com.

Paehler, Katrin, *Illinois State*. Email: katpaehler@ilstu.edu.

Pagden, Anthony, *UCLA*. Email: pagden@ucla.edu.

Page, Allison A. Chicago, IL. Affil: Loyola, Chicago. Email: apage3@luc.edu.

Page, Douglas D. Altoona, PA. Affil: Penn State, Altoona. Email: ddp2@psu.edu.

Page, Max, *Massachusetts, Amherst*. Email: mpage@art.umass.edu.

Page, Melvin E., *East Tennessee State*. Email: pagem@etsu.edu.

Page, Oscar C., *Austin Coll.* Email: opage@austincollege.edu.

Pai, Gita V., *Wisconsin-La Crosse*. Email: gpai@uwlax.edu.

Paik, Shailaja D., *Cincinnati*. Email: shailaja.paik@uc.edu.

Paine, Lincoln P. Portland, ME. Email: Lincoln.Paine@gmail.com. Research: maritime Eurasia 600-1200, maritime literature.

Paine, Sarah C. M., *Naval War Coll.* Portsmouth, RI. Email: sally.paine@usnwc.edu. Research: Russo-Japanese rivalry in China 1931-49.

Painter, Borden W., Jr. Hartford, CT. Affil: Trinity Coll., Conn. Email: borden.painter@trincoll.edu. Research: Rome and fascism.

Painter, David S., *Georgetown*. Email: painterd@georgetown.edu.

Painter, Nell Irvin. Newark, NJ. Affil: Princeton. Email: painter@princeton.edu.

Pajakowski, Philip E., *St. Anselm*. Email: ppajakow@anselm.edu.

Pak, Susie J., *St. John's, NY*. Email: paks1@stjohns.edu.

Pakela, Keith Michael. North Brunswick, NJ. Affil: Monmouth. Email: keithpakela@yahoo.com.

Pal, Carol. North Bennington, VT. Affil: Bennington. Email: cpal@bennington.edu. Research: early modern intellectual culture, history of the book.

Palermo, Joseph A., *California State, Sacramento*. Email: jpalermo@csus.edu.

Palermo, Patrick F., *Dayton*.

Paligutan, P. James, *San Diego Mesa*. Email: ppaligut@sdccd.edu.

Pallante, Martha I., *Youngstown State*. Email: mipallante@ysu.edu.

Palm, Daniel, *Azusa Pacific*. Email: dpalm@apu.edu.

Palmegiano, Eugenia M., *St. Peter's*. Email: epalmegiano@saintpeters.edu.

Palmer, Aaron, *Wisconsin Lutheran*. Milwaukee, WI. Email: aaron.palmer@wlc.edu. Research: colonial America, American Revolution.

Palmer, Ada L., *Chicago*. Email: adapalmer@uchicago.edu.

Palmer, Beverly, *Pomona*. Email: bpalmer@pomona.edu.

Palmer, Brandon, *Coastal Carolina*. Email: bpalmer@coastal.edu.

Palmer, James A., *Florida State*. Tallahassee, FL. Email: japalmer@fsu.edu; kearneymarc@gmail.com. Research: medieval Italy, medieval urban society/culture.

Palmer, Jennifer L., *Georgia*. Athens, GA. Email: palmerjl@uga.edu. Research: 18th-c French slavery/race/gender.

Palmer, Kelly D., *Tampa*. Tampa, FL. Email: kpalmer@ut.edu. Research: modern France, Holocaust.

Palmer, Louise Y., *Fairfield*. Email: lpalmer1@fairfield.edu.

Palmer, Michael A., *East Carolina*. Email: palmerm@ecu.edu.

Palmer, Scott W., *Texas, Arlington*. Email: scott.palmer@uta.edu.

Palmer, Stanley H., *Texas, Arlington*. Two Rivers, WI. Email: spalmer@uta.edu. Research: modern Britain and Ireland, police.

Palmer, Steven P., *Windsor*. Email: spalmer@uwindsor.ca.

Palmer, W. Raymond. Lanesboro, MA. Affil: Carleton. Email: wraymondpalmer@gmail.com. Research: Holocaust.

Palmer, William G., *Marshall*. Email: palmer@marshall.edu.

Palmitessa, James R., *Western Michigan*. Email: james.palmitessa@wmich.edu.

Palmquist, David, *SUNY, Albany*. Email: dpalmqui@mail.nysed.gov.

Palo, Christina Vandenbergh. Vienna, VA. Affil: James Madison High Sch. Email: vandencm@gmail.com.

Palo, Michael F. Brussels, Belgium. Affil: Vesalius. Email: mfpalo.palo4@gmail.com. Research: Belgian neutrality 1839-1945, interdisciplinary approaches to international hist.

Palomino, Pablo. Atlanta, GA. Affil: Emory, Oxford Coll. Email: pablo.palomino@emory.edu. Research: modern Latin America, transnational.

Pals, Daniel L., *Miami*. Email: dpals@miami.edu.

Palsetia, Jesse S., *Guelph*. Email: palsetia@uoguelph.ca.

Palshikar, Shreeyash S., *Albright*. Email: spalshikar@albright.edu.

Pamonag, Febe D., *Western Illinois*. Macomb, IL. Email: F-Pamonag@wiu.edu. Research: modern Japan, Japanese women.

Pan, Ming-te, *SUNY, Oswego*. Email: mingte.pan@oswego.edu.

Pan, Yihong, *Miami, Ohio*. Email: pany@miamioh.edu.

Panchasi, Roxanne, *Simon Fraser*. Burnaby, BC, Canada. Email: panchasi@sfu.ca. Research: Esperanto, science fiction.

Pande, Ishita, *Queen's, Can.* Kingston, ON, Canada. Email: pande@queensu.ca. Research: modern South Asia, childhood and age.

Pandey, Gyanendra, *Emory*. Email: gpande2@emory.edu.

Pandit, Ninad. New Delhi, India. Affil: Indian Inst. for Human Settlements. Email: ninad.pandit@gmail.com. Research: Bombay/Mumbai urban/politics, Left/India/Marxism.

Pandora, Katherine A., *Oklahoma (Hist. of Science)*. Email: kpandora@ou.edu.

Panehal, Alexandria Lee. Kelleys Island, OH. Email: alexipanehal53@yahoo.com.

Panjabi, Ranee K. L., *Memorial, Newfoundland*. Email: rpanjabi@mun.ca.

Pankratz, John R., *Albright*. Email: jpankratz@albright.edu.

Pano, Gregory, *Salem State*. Email: gpano@salemstate.edu.

Pano, Nicholas C., *Western Illinois*.

Pant, Ketaki, *Southern California*. Email: kpant@usc.edu.

Panther, Natalie B., *Central Oklahoma*. Email: npanther@uco.edu.

Pantoja, Matthew. Knoxville, TN. Affil: Tennessee, Knoxville. Email: mpantoj88@yahoo.com.

Pantsov, Alexander V., *Capital*. Westerville, OH. Email: apantsov@capital.edu. Research: 20th-c Europe, China.

Panzer, Sarah Jordan, *Missouri State*. Email: SPanzer@MissouriState.edu.

Paolella, Christopher. Columbia, MO. Affil: Missouri, Columbia. Email: cppqf@mail.missouri.edu. Research: medieval human trafficking, medieval slave trade.

Papacosma, S. Victor, *Kent State*. Email: spapacos@kent.edu.

Papadakis, Aristeides, *Maryland, Baltimore County*. Email: papadaki@umbc.edu.

Papademetriou, Tom, *Stockton*. Email: apapadem@stockton.edu.

Papageorge, Linda M., *Kennesaw State*. Email: lpapageo@kennesaw.edu.

Papaioannou, Stefan Sotiris, *Framingham State*. Maynard, MA. Email: spapaioannou@framingham.edu. Research: Balkan wars 1912-13 and WWI in Macedonia, ideas about violence in Southeast Europe.

Papalas, Anthony J., *East Carolina*. Email: papalasa@ecu.edu.

Papamichos Chronakis, Paris. Chicago, IL. Affil: Illinois, Chicago. Email: pchronakis@gmail.com. Research: Sephardic Jewish and Greek diasporas, Ottoman Empire to successor states.

Papandreu, Dimitri, *California State, Fullerton*. Email: dpapandreu@fullerton.edu.

Papczynski, Courteney Leigh. Jacksonville, FL. Affil: North Florida. Email: clpapczynski@gmail.com.

Paperno, Irina, *California, Berkeley*. Email: ipaperno@berkeley.edu.

Pappademos, Melina, *Connecticut, Storrs*. Email: melina.pappademos@uconn.edu.

Pappas, Dale. Miami, FL. Affil: Miami. Email: dsp59@miami.edu.

Pappas, Nicholas, *Sam Houston State*. Email: his_ncp@shsu.edu.

Pappas, Zoe A.. Hastings On Hudson, NY. Affil: Columbia. Email: zap1@caa.columbia.edu. Research: mythological genealogy.

Paquette, Gabriel, *Oregon*. Eugene, OR. Email: paquette@uoregon.edu; gabriel.paquette@trinity.cantab.net. Research: Spain and Portugal and their colonies, comparative imperial.

Paquette, Jean, *Lander*.

Paradis, David H., *Colorado, Boulder*. Email: david.paradis@colorado.edu.

Paradis, Lia, *Slippery Rock*. Slippery Rock, PA. Email: lia.paradis@sru.edu. Research: identity/memory/movement, British empire/culture/decolonization.

Paradis, Michel. New York, NY. Affil: Columbia. Email: mp3373@columbia.edu.

Paradis, Thomas, *Butler*. Email: tparadis@butler.edu.

Parascandola, John Louis. Bethesda, MD. Affil: Independent Scholar. Email: jparascandola@verizon.net. Research: venereal disease in America, pharmacology.

Parasram, Ajay, *Dalhousie*. Email: parasram@dal.ca.

Parcells, Ashley, *Jacksonville*. Jacksonville, FL. Email: aparcel@ju.edu; aparcells22390@gmail.com. Research: South Africa, apartheid.

Pardoe, Harmon Edward. Williamstown, MA. Affil: Williams. Email: hep2@williams.edu.

Pardon, Mireille Juliette. New Haven, CT. Affil: Yale. Email: mireille.pardon@yale.edu.

Pardue, Jeff D., *North Georgia*. Email: jeff.pardue@ung.edu.

Pare, Karen L., *California State, East Bay*.

Parent, Anthony S., Jr., *Wake Forest*. Email: parentas@wfu.edu.

Parenteau, William M., *New Brunswick*. Email: wparent@unb.ca.

Paret, Peter, *Stanford*.

Parillo, Mark P., *Kansas State*. Email: parillo@ksu.edu.

Parillo, Stacie, *Naval War Coll*. Email: stacie.parillo@usnwc.edu.

Paris, Christy, *South Florida, St. Petersburg*.

Paris, Leslie M., *British Columbia*. Email: lparis@mail.ubc.ca.

Park, Albert L., *Claremont McKenna*. Email: albert.park@cmc.edu.

Park, Alyssa, *Iowa*. Email: alyssa-park@uiowa.edu.

Park, Andrew Thomas. Hong Kong. Affil: Hong Kong. Email: parkat@connect.hku.hk. Research: self-determination, international organisations.

Park, Benjamin E., *Sam Houston State*. Huntsville, TX. Email: bep013@shsu.edu; ben25unc@gmail.com. Research: early American intellectual, antebellum US religious boundaries.

Park, Emma F., *New School*. Email: Parke@newschool.edu.

Park, Haeseong, *Charleston Southern*. Montgomery, AL. Email: hpark@csuniv.edu; parkhscap@gmail.com. Research: East Asian women during modern period, immigration/missionaries/imperialism.

Park, Hong-Kyu. Tyler, TX. Affil: Kilgore. Email: hkpark@suddenlink.net. Research: American-Korean relations since 1945.

Park, Hye Ok. Pomona, CA. Affil: Claremont Graduate. Email: hyeok.park@gmail.com.

Park, Hyunhee, *Graduate Center, CUNY*. Email: hpark@jjay.cuny.edu.

Park, Katharine, *Harvard (Hist. of Science)*. Email: park28@fas.harvard.edu.

Park, Nancy, *California State, East Bay*. Email: nancy.park@csueastbay.edu.

Park, Sandra H.. Henrico, VA. Affil: Chicago. Email: shkpark@uchicago.edu.

Park, Shinyoung. Los Angeles, CA. Affil: Seoul National. Email: shinygpark@naver.com. Research: Korean American, oral.

Park, Sun-Young, *George Mason*. Arlington, VA. Email: spark53@gmu.edu. Research: 19th-c Europe, French cultural.

Park, Young Sun. Winona, MN. Affil: St. Mary's, Minn. Email: p.youngsun@gmail.com. Research: children, welfare.

Parker, Alexander R.. East Amherst, NY. Affil: Carnegie Mellon. Email: ap6693a@gmail.com. Research: Env-Hist of 19th-c American canals, ideas of disease causation.

Parker, Alison M., *Delaware*. Newark, DE. Email: aparker@udel.edu. Research: US Constitution and law, US gender and race.

Parker, Amy. Atlanta, GA. Affil: American Academy of Religion. Email: aparker@aarweb.org.

Parker, Bradley, *Utah*.

Parker, Chad Hunter, *Louisiana, Lafayette*. Lafayette, LA. Email: chparker@louisiana.edu; chadhunterparker@gmail.com. Research: US foreign relations, international.

Parker, Charles H., Jr., *St. Louis*. Email: parkerch@slu.edu.

Parker, Cole. San Diego, CA. Affil: San Diego State. Email: coleparker.ca@gmail.com.

Parker, David B., *Kennesaw State*. Email: dparker@kennesaw.edu.

Parker, David S., *Queen's, Can*. Email: parkerd@queensu.ca.

Parker, Geoffrey, *Ohio State*. Email: parker.277@osu.edu.

Parker, Jason C., *Texas A&M*. Email: jcparker@tamu.edu.

Parker, Joseph. Pocono Lake, PA. Email: jjp93@msn.com.

Parker, Kai Perry. Chicago, IL. Affil: Chicago. Email: kaip@uchicago.edu.

Parker, Katherine Ashley. London, United Kingdom. Affil: Queen Mary, London. Email: kaparker18th@gmail.com. Research: Pacific exploration/encounter, book and cartography.

Parker, Kenneth L. Wexford, PA. Affil: Duquesne. Email: parkerk3@duq.edu. Research: John Henry Newman, 19th-c Roman Catholicism.

Parker, Kunal Madhukar. Coral Gables, FL. Affil: Miami. Email: kparker@law.miami.edu. Research: immigration and citizenship, intellectual.

Parker, Lauren, *Colby*. Email: lauren.parker@colby.edu.

Parker, Lindsay A. H., *San Diego State*.

Parker, Nathan. Cutler Bay, FL. Email: nathanparker@yahoo.com.

Parker, S. Thomas, *North Carolina State*. Raleigh, NC. Email: thomas_parker@ncsu.edu. Research: Roman empire, ancient Mediterranean trade.

Parker, Susan R. Saint Augustine, FL. Affil: Florida-Flagler Coll. Email: drsparker@comcast.net. Research: 18th-c property, Native American assimilation.

Parker, Traci Lynnea. Amherst, MA. Affil: Massachusetts Amherst. Email: traciparker@umass.edu.

Parker, William, *Austin Peay State*. Email: parkerw@apsu.edu.

Parkerson, Donald H., *East Carolina*. Greenville, NC. Email: parkersond@ecu.edu; dparkerson@suddenlink.net. Research: education.

Parkes, Chris. Stoke D'Abernon, United Kingdom. Affil: King's Coll., London. Email: posthumous@gmail.com. Research: Sumner Welles.

Parkin, Katherine, *Monmouth*. West Long Branch, NJ. Email: kparkin@monmouth.edu. Research: American women, American cultural.

Parkinson, John Scott, *Ball State*. Email: sparkins@bsu.edu.

Parkinson, Robert, *Binghamton, SUNY*. Email: rparkins@binghamton.edu.

Parks, Annette P., *Evansville*. Email: ap3@evansville.edu.

Parks, Austin Charles. Baltimore, MD. Affil: Loyola, Md. Email: acparks@loyola.edu. Research: postwar Japanese culture, Japanese photography.

Parks, *Jenifer L*. Billings, MT. Affil: Rocky Mountain. Email: jenifer.parks@rocky.edu. Research: Soviet Union Olympic Committee 1952-80.

Parks, *Katie*. Oakland Township, MI. Affil: Wayne State. Email: gh3858@wayne.edu.

Parlopiano, *Brandon T*., *Loyola, Md*. Silver Spring, MD. Email: brandon.parlopiano@ gmail.com. Research: medieval and early modern jurisprudence, madness and disability studies.

Parman, **Donald L**., *Purdue*. Email: parmand@ purdue.edu.

Parmenter, *Jon*, *Cornell*. Ithaca, NY. Email: jwp35@cornell.edu. Research: northeastern Native Americans, settler colonialism.

Parmet, *Robert D*. Great Neck, NY. Affil: York, CUNY. Email: parmet@york.cuny.edu. Research: Jamaica NY and York Coll. CUNY.

Parnell, *David Alan*, *Indiana, Northwest*. Gary, IN. Email: parnelld@iun.edu; d.a.parnell@ gmail.com. Research: Byzantine family and society, Byzantine view of identity.

Parnell, *Matthew B*. New York, NY. Affil: American, Cairo. Email: matthew.parnell@ aucegypt.edu. Research: children and youth in modern Egypt.

Parot, **Joseph J**., *Northern Illinois*.

Parris, **L. Eileen**, *Virginia Museum of Hist*. Email: eparris@VirginiaHistory.org.

Parrish, **Michael E**., *California, San Diego*. Email: mparrish@ucsd.edu.

Parrish, *T. Michael*, *Baylor*. Waco, TX. Email: michael_parrish@baylor.edu. Research: Civil War.

Parrish, **William E**., *Mississippi State*. Email: whsp@ms.metrocast.net.

Parrott, **Christopher**, *Providence*. Email: parrott@providence.edu.

Parrott, *R. Joseph*, *Ohio State*. Columbus, OH. Email: parrott.36@osu.edu. Research: American diplomatic, global race and politics.

Parrow, *Kathleen A*. Spearfish, SD. Affil: Black Hills State. Email: Kathleen.Parrow@bhsu.edu. Research: pre-1700 French customary law, 16th-c law in French literature.

Parry, *Seth A*. Jackson, MS. Affil: Belhaven. Email: sparry@belhaven.edu.

Parshall, **Karen V. H**., *Virginia*. Email: khp3k@ virginia.edu.

Parson, *George Kenneth*. Upper Marlboro, MD. Email: george.parson@verizon.net.

Parson, **Robert**, *Utah State*. Email: robert. parson@usu.edu.

Parsons, **Anne Elizabeth**, *North Carolina, Greensboro*. Email: aeparson@uncg.edu.

Parsons, **Christopher M**., *Northeastern*. Email: c.parsons@neu.edu.

Parsons, **Gregory S**., *SUNY, Oswego*. Email: gregory.parsons@oswego.edu.

Parsons, **Jotham W**., *Duquesne*. Email: parsonsj@duq.edu.

Parsons, **Laila**, *McGill*. Email: laila.parsons@ mcgill.ca.

Parsons, **Lynn H**., *SUNY, Coll. Brockport*. Email: lparsons@brockport.edu.

Parsons, **Timothy H**., *Washington, St. Louis*. Email: parsons@wustl.edu.

Parssinen, **Terry M**., *Tampa*. Email: tparssinen@ ut.edu.

Parthasarathi, **Prasannan**, *Boston Coll*. Email: parthasa@bc.edu.

Partner, *Nancy F*., *McGill*. Montreal West, QC, Canada. Email: nancy.partner@mcgill.ca. Research: historical theory, narrative theory and history.

Partner, **Simon**, *Duke*. Email: spartner@duke. edu.

Partovi, **Pedram**, *American*. Email: partovi@ american.edu.

Partsch, *Jaime R*. Trujillo Alto, PR. Email: jaime. partsch@gmail.com. Research: 20th-c US-Caribbean relations, Caribbean urban.

Pascoe, **Craig S**., *Georgia Coll. and State*. Email: craig.pascoe@gcsu.edu.

Pascu, *Elaine Weber*. Princeton, NJ. Affil: Princeton. Email: pascuelaine12@gmail.com. Research: American Revolution and early Republic.

Pasierowska, *Rachael Lindsay*. Houston, TX. Affil: Rice. Email: rlp2@rice.edu. Research: slavery, animals.

Paskert, *Nicholas*. New Orleans, LA. Affil: Harvard. Email: npaskert@fas.harvard.edu. Research: slavery and urbanization in New Orleans, labor/architecture/memory 1770-1860.

Paskoff, **Paul F**., *Louisiana State*. Email: ppaskoff@lsu.edu.

Pasley, **Jeffrey L**., *Missouri, Columbia*. Email: pasleyj@missouri.edu.

Pasolli, **Lisa**, *Queen's, Can*. Email: lisa.pasolli@ queensu.ca.

Passananti, **Tom**, *San Diego State*. Email: tpassana@sdsu.edu.

Passman, **Elana M**., *Earlham*. Email: passman@ earlham.edu.

Pastor, *Peter*, *Montclair State*. Wayne, NJ. Email: pastorp@mail.montclair.edu. Research: modern Russia, eastern Europe.

Pastore, *Christopher L*., *SUNY, Albany*. Albany, NY. Email: cpastore@albany.edu; pastorec@ gmail.com. Research: colonial America, environmental.

Pasture, *Patrick*. Leuven, Belgium. Affil: KU Leuven. Email: Patrick.Pasture@kuleuven.be. Research: modern religion, European studies.

Patarino, *Vincent V*., *Jr*. Grand Junction, CO. Affil: Colorado Mesa. Email: vpatarin@ coloradomesa.edu. Research: cultural, early modern maritime.

Patch, **Robert W**., *California, Riverside*. Email: robert.patch@ucr.edu.

Patch, **William Lewis**, *Jr*., *Washington and Lee*. Email: patchw@wlu.edu.

Pate, **Alice K**., *Kennesaw State*. Email: apate9@ kennesaw.edu.

Pate, *Carl Edward*, *Jr*., *Esq*. Trenton, MI. Email: cpate@wideopenwest.com.

Patel, **Alka**, *California, Irvine*. Email: alka.patel@ uci.edu.

Patel, **Dinyar**, *South Carolina, Columbia*. Email: pateldi@mailbox.sc.edu.

Patel, *Shruti*, *Salisbury*. Salisbury, MD. Email: sapatel@salisbury.edu; shruti.a.patel@gmail. com. Research: Gujarat/colonialism/princely states, South Asian religion/historiography.

Patenaude, *Marc Allan*. Regina, SK, Canada. Email: mpaten1@gmail.com. Research: post-1945 American internal security.

Patenaude, *Sara*. Decatur, GA. Affil: Tapestry Development Group. Email: sdpatenaude@ gmail.com. Research: Baltimore, Housing.

Paterson, **Thomas G**., *Connecticut, Storrs*.

Paton, *John R*. Pendleton, FL. Affil: Maine. Email: johnrpaton@gmail.com. Research: US occupation of Dominican Republic, US occupation of Puerto Rico.

Patras, **Louis**, *Kent State*.

Patriarca, *Silvana*, *Fordham*. New York, NY. Email: patriarca@fordham.edu. Research: nationalism, gender.

Patrias, **Carmela K**., *Brock*. Email: cpatrias@ brocku.ca.

Patrick, **Andrew J**., *Tennessee State*. Email: apatric2@tnstate.edu.

Patrick, *Andrew P*. Danville, KY. Affil: Centre. Email: andrew.patrick@centre.edu. Research: Kentucky environmental, Kentucky agriculture.

Patrick, **Joshua**. Gilbertown, AL. Email: joshp6389@hotmail.com.

Patrick, *Justin Charles Michael*. Plainfield, ON, Canada. Affil: Toronto. Email: justin.c.m.patrick@gmail.com.

Patrick, **Leslie C**., *Bucknell*. Email: lpatrick@ bucknell.edu.

Patrick, *Sue C*., *Wisconsin-Eau Claire*. Rice Lake, WI. Email: sue.patrick@uwc.edu. Research: Wisconsin, 1930s.

Patrouch, **Joseph F**., **III**, *Alberta*. Email: patrouch@ualberta.ca.

Patt, **Avinoam**, *Hartford*. Email: patt@hartford. edu.

Patterson, **Catherine F**., *Houston*. Email: cpatters@uh.edu.

Patterson, **Cynthia B**., *Emory*. Email: cpatt01@ emory.edu.

Patterson, **Gretchen**, *Stephen F. Austin State*. Email: Gretchen.Patterson@sfasu.edu.

Patterson, **James T**., *Brown*. Email: James_ Patterson@Brown.edu.

Patterson, *James*. Saylorsburg, PA. Affil: Centenary. Email: pattersonj@ centenaryuniversity.edu.

Patterson, *Jeffery R*. Austin, TX. Affil: Texas, Austin. Email: jefferypatterson@utexas.edu. Research: news media of British Empire, social constructions of history/memory.

Patterson, **Lee E**., *Eastern Illinois*. Email: lepatterson2@eiu.edu.

Patterson, **Michelle Wick**, *Mount St. Mary's*. Email: patterson@msmary.edu.

Patterson, **Molly Benjamin**, *Wisconsin-Whitewater*. Email: pattersm@uww.edu.

Patterson, **Monica**, *Carleton, Can*. Email: monica.patterson@carleton.ca.

Patterson, *Patrick Hyder*, *California, San Diego*. Email: patrickpatterson@ucsd.edu.

Patterson, *Raymond A*. Monkton, VT. Affil: St. Michael's. Email: rpatterson@smcvt.edu. Research: 20th-c American Catholic summer schools, Christian reading circles.

Patterson, *Robert B*., *South Carolina, Columbia*. Columbia, SC. Email: pattsn@mailbox.sc.edu. Research: Anglo-Norman, documentary editing.

Patterson, *Sarah Elizabeth*. Bellevue, NE. Affil: SNA International. Email: sarahepatterson1214@gmail.com. Research: 20th-c gender and Marine Corps, gender in military.

Patterson, *Sarah*. Delmar, NY. Affil: SUNY, Albany. Email: sepatterson@fastmail.fm. Research: women/health/reproduction.

Patterson, **Tiffany Ruby**, *Vanderbilt*. Email: t.ruby.patterson@vanderbilt.edu.

Patterson, **Wayne K.**, *St. Norbert*. DePere, WI. Email: wayne.patterson@snc.edu. Research: modern East Asia, Asian-American relations.

Patterson, **William Brown**. Sewanee, TN. Affil: South. Email: bpatters@sewanee.edu. Research: religion in Britain 1500-1700, politics and law in Britain 1500-1700.

Pattison, **Joel S.** Berkeley, CA. Affil: California, Berkeley. Email: Jpatt12@berkeley.edu. Research: medieval Europe 900-1200.

Patton, **Capt Kirsten M.**, *US Air Force Acad.* Email: kirsten.patton@usafa.edu.

Patton, **John P.**, *John Carroll.* Email: jpatton@jcu.edu.

Patton, **June Odessa**. Chicago, IL. Affil: Governors State. Email: pattonjop@aol.com.

Patton, **Randall L.**, *Kennesaw State.* Email: rpatton@kennesaw.edu.

Pattridge, **Blake D.** Covington, LA. Affil: Babson. Email: pattridge@babson.edu. Research: Univ. of San Carlos Guatemala, 19th-c Guatemala.

Patulli Trythall, **Marisa**. Roma, Italy. Affil: Pontifical Oriental Inst. Email: marisa@mptrythall.com.

Paul, **Andrew**. Asheville, NC. Affil: North Carolina, Asheville. Email: andy.paul.phd@gmail.com.

Paul, **Chandrika**, *Shippensburg.* Email: chpaul@ship.edu.

Paul, **Justus F.** Green Lake, WI. Affil: Wisconsin, Stevens Point. Email: jpaul@uwsp.edu. Research: US political since 1920, Wisconsin.

Paul, **Karen D.**, *US Senate Hist. Office.* Email: karen_paul@sec.senate.gov.

Paul, **Nicholas Lithgow**, *Fordham.* Bronx, NY. Email: npaul@fordham.edu. Research: dynastic memory and noble culture, Crusade and western European culture.

Paul, **Nilanjana**, *Texas-Rio Grande Valley.* Brownsville, TX. Email: nilanjana.paul@utrgv.edu. Research: India, South Asia.

Paulet, **Anne**. Arcata, CA. Affil: Humboldt State. Email: ap23@humboldt.edu. Research: comparative imperialism, comparative aboriginal policy.

Paulette, **Tate**, *North Carolina State.*

Paulson, **Daryl**, *South Florida, St. Petersburg.*

Pauly, **Matthew D.**, *Michigan State.* Email: paulym@msu.edu.

Pauly, **Roger A., Jr.**, *Central Arkansas.* Email: rpauly@uca.edu.

Pavilack, **Jody C.**, *Montana.* Email: jody.pavilack@mso.umt.edu.

Pavkovic, **Michael F.**, *Naval War Coll.* Email: michael.pavkovic@usnwc.edu.

Pavlac, **Brian A.** Wilkes Barre, PA. Affil: King's Coll., Pa. Email: bapavlac@kings.edu. Research: prince-bishops, medieval nobility.

Pavlakis, **Dean**. Helena, MT. Affil: Carroll. Email: pavlakis1@verizon.net. Research: British humanitarian movements, colonial forced labor in Africa.

Pavlich, **Paul**, *Southern Oregon.* Email: pavlich@sou.edu.

Pavuk, **Alexander**, *Morgan State.* Email: alexander.pavuk@morgan.edu.

Pawley, **Emily J.**, *Dickinson.* Email: pawleye@dickinson.edu.

Pawlicki, **Sarah Katharine**. Minneapolis, MN. Affil: Minnesota, Twin Cities. Email: pawli059@umn.edu.

Pawling, **Micah Abell**, *Maine, Orono.* Email: micah.pawling@maine.edu.

Pawlisch, **Hans Scott**. Baltimore, MD. Affil: International Commission on Military Hist. Email: hanspawlisch@msn.com. Research: legal, Anglo-Irish.

Paxton, **Frederick S.**, *Connecticut Coll.* New London, CT. Email: fspax@conncoll.edu. Research: sickness and healing, death and dying.

Paxton, **Jennifer A.** Washington, DC. Affil: Catholic. Email: paxton@cua.edu. Research: 12th-c English historiography, 12th-c English monasticism.

Paxton, **Jennifer**, *Texas, Permian Basin.* Email: paxton_j@utpb.edu.

Paxton, **Robert O.**, *Columbia (Hist.).* Email: rop1@columbia.edu.

Paxton, **Roger V.**, *Utah.* Email: rpaxton@history.utah.edu.

Payan, **Matthew Michael**. Corona, CA. Email: matthew.m.payan@gmail.com.

Payaslian, **Simon**, *Boston Univ.* Boston, MA. Email: payas@bu.edu. Research: US foreign policy in Ottoman Empire/Turkey, US foreign economic.

Payk, **Marcus M.** Hamburg, Germany. Affil: Helmut Schmidt, Hamburg. Email: payk@hsu-hh.de.

Payne, **Brendan John**, *North Greenville.* Email: brendan.payne@ngu.edu.

Payne, **David S.**, *Northern Kentucky.* Email: payneda@nku.edu.

Payne, **Elizabeth Anne**, *Mississippi.* Email: epayne@olemiss.edu.

Payne, **Eva Bernice**, *Mississippi.*

Payne, **James F.**, *Mississippi.*

Payne, **Lynda E.**, *Missouri–Kansas City.* Email: paynel@umkc.edu.

Payne, **Matthew John, III**, *Emory.* Email: mpayn01@emory.edu.

Payne, **Phillip Gene**, *St. Bonaventure.* Email: ppayne@sbu.edu.

Payne, **Richard E., III**, *Chicago.* Email: repayne@uchicago.edu.

Payne, **Samantha Leigh**. Fairfax, VA. Affil: Harvard. Email: spayne@g.harvard.edu.

Payne, **Sarah Ruth**, *Colorado State.* Email: sarah.payne@colostate.edu.

Payne, **Stanley G.**, *Wisconsin-Madison.* Email: sgpayne@wisc.edu.

Payne, **Zoraida J.** San Diego, CA. Affil: San Diego State. Email: zoraidapayne@mac.com.

Paynich, **Timothy John**, *California State, Los Angeles.* Email: tpaynic@calstatela.edu.

Payton, **Claire A.** Charlottesville, VA. Affil: Virginia. Email: claire.payton@virginia.edu. Research: urban history, modern Haiti.

Paz, **Gustavo L.** Buenos Aires, Argentina. Affil: Buenos Aires. Email: glpaz2@yahoo.com.

Peabody, **Sue**, *Washington State, Pullman.* Vancouver, WA. Email: speabody@wsu.edu. Research: early modern French Atlantic, race and slavery.

Peace, **Roger**. Tallahassee, FL. Email: rcpeace3@embarqmail.com. Research: US foreign policy and rhetoric, 1980s Central American peace movements.

Peace, **Thomas Gordon Mackenzie**. London, ON, Canada. Affil: Huron Univ. Coll. Email: tpeace@uwo.ca. Research: indigenous education, contested spaces in Northeast.

Peach, **Steven Jonathan**, *Tarleton State.*

Peachin, **Michael**, *NYU.* Email: mp8@nyu.edu.

Peacock, **Margaret E.**, *Alabama, Tuscaloosa.* Email: mepeacock@ua.edu.

Pearce, **Matthew**. Edmond, OK. Affil: Preservation and Design Studio. Email: mpearce.phd@gmail.com.

Pearcy, **Thomas L.**, *Slippery Rock.* Email: thomas.pearcy@sru.edu.

Pearl, **Deborah L.** Berkeley, CA. Email: pearldeb@gmail.com. Research: modern Europe, European social.

Pearlman, **Jill**, *Bowdoin.* Email: jpearlma@bowdoin.edu.

Pearlman, **Lauren**, *Florida.* Gainesville, FL. Email: lpearlman@ufl.edu; lpearlman@gmail.com. Research: African American, Washington DC.

Pearsall, **Sarah**. Cambridge, United Kingdom. Affil: Cambridge. Email: smsp100@cam.ac.uk. Research: early America and Atlantic, gender and family.

Pearson, **Edward A.**, *Franklin & Marshall.* Email: tpearson@fandm.edu.

Pearson, **Ellen Holmes**. Asheville, NC. Affil: North Carolina, Asheville. Email: epearson@unca.edu. Research: colonial/early national legal culture, changing local/national identity/allegiance.

Pearson, **Jeffrey V.**, *Arkansas Tech.* Email: jpearson9@atu.edu.

Pearson, **Jeremy D.**, *Bryant.* Email: jpearson3@bryant.edu.

Pearson, **Jessica L.**, *Macalester.* Saint Paul, MN. Email: jpearso4@macalester.edu. Research: France and United Nations, public health in French Africa 1945-60.

Pearson, **John M.** Sun City, AZ. Email: valleybonding@cox.net. Research: American Civil War.

Pearson, **Joseph**. Deer Park, TX. Email: joepearson1982@gmail.com.

Pearson, **Kathy L.**, *Old Dominion.* Email: kpearson@odu.edu.

Pearson, **Margaret J.**, *Skidmore.* Email: mpearson@skidmore.edu.

Pearson, **Rudy N.** Folsom, CA. Affil: American River. Email: pearsor@arc.losrios.edu.

Pearson, **Samuel C.** Saint Louis, MO. Affil: Southern Illinois, Edwardsville. Email: spearso@siue.edu. Research: American Protestantism, Chinese responses to American culture.

Pearson, **Susan J.**, *Northwestern.* Evanston, IL. Email: sjp@northwestern.edu. Research: birth registration, state building.

Pearson, **Thomas S.**, *Monmouth.* Email: pearson@monmouth.edu.

Pearson, **Willie, Jr.**, *Georgia Inst. of Tech.* Email: willie.pearsonjr@hts.gatech.edu.

Pease, **Neal H.**, *Wisconsin-Milwaukee.* Email: pease@uwm.edu.

Peçe, **Ugur Z.**, *Lehigh.* Email: uzp218@lehigh.edu.

Peck, **Graham A.** Chicago, IL. Affil: St. Xavier. Email: gpeck@sxu.edu. Research: political antislavery, antebellum Illinois.

Peck, **Gunther W.**, *Duke.* Email: peckgw@duke.edu.

Peck, **James**, *NYU.* Email: jlp7923@nyu.edu.

Peck, **Linda Levy**, *George Washington.* Email: llpeck@gwu.edu.

Peckham, **Hannah**. Greenwich, CT. Email: hannahmpeckham@gmail.com.

AHA members in **bold italic**; *Directory*-listed affiliations in *italic*

Peden, Knox. Parkville, Australia. Affil: Melbourne. Email: knox.peden@unimelb. edu.au.

Pedersen, James T. Brooklyn, NY. Affil: Hunter, CUNY. Email: jamestpedersen@gmail.com.

Pedersen, Jean Elisabeth, *Rochester*. Email: jpedersen@esm.rochester.edu.

Pedersen, Susan, *Columbia (Hist.)*. New York, NY. Email: sp2216@columbia.edu. Research: interwar mandated territories, League of Nations.

Pederson, Jane M., *Wisconsin-Eau Claire*. Email: pedersjm@uwec.edu.

Pederson, William D. Shreveport, LA. Affil: Louisiana State, Shreveport. Email: william. pederson@lsus.edu.

Pedeva-Fazlic, Desislava, *California State, Chico*. Email: dpedeva@csuchico.edu.

Pedrick, Alexis, *Science History Inst*. Email: apedrick@sciencehistory.org.

Peebles, Patrick A., *Missouri–Kansas City*. Email: peeblesp@umkc.edu.

Peeler, Todd. Shelby, NC. Affil: Crest High Sch,; Cleveland County Sch. Email: tpeeler@ clevelandcountyschools.org.

Peers, Douglas M., *Waterloo*. Waterloo, ON, Canada. Email: dpeers@uwaterloo.ca. Research: military and colonial knowledge, British and India.

Pegelow Kaplan, Thomas, *Appalachian State*. Boone, NC. Email: thomaspegelowkaplan@ appstate.edu. Research: Nazi Germany and European-Jewish, West Germany and US in 1950s-80s.

Pegg, Mark G., *Washington, St. Louis*. Email: mpegg@wustl.edu.

Pegler-Gordon, Anna. East Lansing, MI. Affil: Michigan State. Email: gordonap@msu. edu. Research: Asians at Ellis Island, Chinese Americans during WWII.

Pegram, Thomas Ray, *Loyola, Md*. Email: tpegram@loyola.edu.

Pehl, Matthew S. Lubbock, TX. Affil: Augustana, SD. Email: mpehl@augie.edu. Research: religion and class, urban.

Peimer, Laura, *Arthur and Elizabeth Schlesinger Library*. Email: laura_peimer@radcliffe.harvard. edu.

Peirce, Leslie, *NYU*. Email: lp50@nyu.edu.

Peiss, Kathy L., *Pennsylvania*. Philadelphia, PA. Email: peiss@sas.upenn.edu. Research: collecting missions in WWII, mass middle class 1930s-50s.

Pekacz, Jolanta T., *Dalhousie*. Email: jpekacz@ dal.ca.

Pekow, Sara A. Brooklyn, NY. Affil: Graduate Center, CUNY. Email: sarapekow@gmail.com. Research: foodways in French Mandate Syria.

Pelegrino, Alexandre. Nashville, TN. Affil: Vanderbilt. Email: alexandrecpelegrino@ gmail.com.

Pelenski, Jaroslaw, *Iowa*.

Pelfrey, Robert. El Paso, TX. Affil: Manchester. Email: robertcpelfrey@gmail.com.

Pelletier, Cynthia. Goffstown, NH. Email: pelletierthree@comcast.net.

Pelley, Patricia M., *Texas Tech*. Email: patricia. pelley@ttu.edu.

Pelli, Moshe, *Central Florida*. Email: Moshe. Pelli@ucf.edu.

Pelling, Christopher B. R., *Utah State*.

Pellissier, Marie A. Williamsburg, VA. Affil: William and Mary. Email: mapellissier@gmail. com.

Pells, Richard H., *Texas, Austin*. Email: rpells@ aol.com.

Pelon, Leslie E. Porterville, CA. Email: lepelon11@gmail.com. Research: women preachers of Second Great Awakening.

Peloso, Vincent C. Lawrenceville, NJ. Affil: Howard. Email: vcpeloso@gmail.com. Research: 19th-c race and national identity, 16th-20th-c race and ethnicity.

Pelz, Stephen E., *Massachusetts, Amherst*.

Pemberton, Stephen G., *Rutgers, Newark/ New Jersey Inst. of Tech*. Email: stephen. pemberton@njit.edu.

Pembleton, Matthew R. Rockville, MD. Affil: American. Email: matt.pembleton@gmail. com.

Penaloza Patzak, C. Brooke. Vienna, Austria. Affil: Vienna. Email: penaloza.patzak@univie. ac.at.

Pencek, Bruce. Blacksburg, VA. Affil: Virginia Tech. Email: bpencek@vt.edu.

Pendas, Devin Owen, *Boston Coll*. Chestnut Hill, MA. Email: pendas@bc.edu. Research: modern Germany.

Penella, Robert, *Fordham*. Email: rpenella@ fordham.edu.

Penfold, Steve, *Toronto*. Email: steve.penfold@ utoronto.ca.

Peng, Juanjuan, *Georgia Southern*. Email: jpeng@georgiasouthern.edu.

Peng, Tao, *Minnesota State, Mankato*. Email: tao. peng@mnsu.edu.

Penick, James L., **Jr.**, *Alabama, Birmingham*.

Penn, Allie. Bay City, MI. Affil: Wayne State. Email: ga0181@wayne.edu. Research: labor, women.

Penna, Anthony N., *Northeastern*. Email: a.penna@neu.edu.

Penney, Matthew, *Concordia, Can*. Email: Matthew.Penney@concordia.ca.

Penningroth, Dylan C., *California, Berkeley*. Kensington, CA. Email: dcap@law.berkeley. edu. Research: legal, African American.

Pennington, Loren E., *Emporia State*. Emporia, KS. Research: colonial America, England.

Pennington, Reina J., *Norwich*. Email: rpenning@norwich.edu.

Penny, H. Glenn, *Iowa*. Iowa City, IA. Email: h-penny@uiowa.edu. Research: anthropology and colonialism, Germans and Native Americans.

Pennybacker, Susan Dabney, *North Carolina, Chapel Hill*. Email: pennybac@email.unc.edu.

Penrose, G. L., *Hope*. Email: penrose@hope.edu.

Penrose, Walter D., **Jr.**, *San Diego State*. Email: wpenrose@sdsu.edu.

Penry, Sarah Elizabeth, *Fordham*. New York, NY. Email: spenry@fordham.edu. Research: Hispanic political philosophy, Spain and Spanish American political practice.

Pensado, Jaime, *Notre Dame*. Email: jpensado@ nd.edu.

Penslar, Derek Jonathan, *Toronto*.

Pepin, Paulette L. Danbury, CT. Affil: New Haven. Email: ppepin@newhaven.edu. Research: Castilian church 1295-1312, K-12 social studies education.

Pepitone, Ren, *Arkansas, Fayetteville*. Fayetteville, AR. Email: pepitone@uark.edu. Research: modern Britain.

Pepper, Tracey A., *Seattle*. Email: peppert@ seattleu.edu.

Peppers, Kieth, *Baldwin Wallace*. Email: kpeppers@bw.edu.

Pequignot, Jennifer Lynn. Greenville, OH. Affil: Auburn. Email: jlp0029@auburn.edu. Research: 20th-c American advertising, De Beers and N.W. Ayer advertisements.

Perales, Monica, *Houston*. Houston, TX. Email: mperales3@uh.edu. Research: Chicana/o labor and gender.

Peralta, Christine Noelle. Urbana, IL. Affil: Illinois, Urbana-Champaign. Email: christine. noelle.peralta@gmail.com.

Peraza, Steve, *SUNY, Buffalo State*. Email: perazas@buffalostate.edu.

Perdue, Martin C., *Robert H. Smith Center*. Email: mperdue@monticello.org.

Perdue, Peter C., *MIT*. Email: peter.c.perdue@ yale.edu.

Perdue, Theda, *North Carolina, Chapel Hill*. Email: tperdue@live.unc.edu.

Pereboom, Maarten L., *Salisbury*. Salisbury, MD. Email: mlpereboom@salisbury.edu. Research: press and international politics 1919-45, history in film.

Perego, Elizabeth Marie, *Shepherd*. Email: eperego@shepherd.edu.

Peregoy, Alexis. Holland, OH. Affil: Arizona. Email: peregoya@ccp.arizona.edu.

Pereira, Norman, *Dalhousie*. Email: norman. pereira@dal.ca.

Perelman, Elisheva A. Saint Joseph, MN. Affil: St. Benedict-St. John's. Email: eperelman@ csbsju.edu.

Perett, Marcela K., *North Dakota State*. Email: marcela.perett@ndsu.edu.

Perez, Arvid H., *Indiana State*. Email: hiperez@ yahoo.com.

Perez, Bernadette J. Princeton, NJ. Affil: Princeton. Email: bjperez@princeton.edu. Research: American empire, environmental.

Perez, Dorie. Merced, CA. Affil: California, Merced. Email: dorie.dakin.perez@gmail.com.

Perez, Erika, *Arizona*. Tucson, AZ. Email: erikaperez@email.arizona.edu; prof. erikaperez@gmail.com. Research: 1769 to late 19th-c California, gender/kinship/family.

Perez, Jonatan. Stanford, CA. Affil: Stanford. Email: Jonatanp10@gmail.com. Research: US immigration quotas, Mexican guestworkers.

Perez, Kim E., *Fort Hays State*. Email: kperez@ fhsu.edu.

Perez, Lorenzo A. Miami, FL. Affil: American. Email: widtlor@aol.com.

Perez, Louis A., **Jr.**, *North Carolina, Chapel Hill*. Chapel Hill, NC. Email: perez@email.unc.edu. Research: Cuba, Caribbean.

Perez, Samantha, *Southeastern Louisiana*. Email: Samantha.Perez@selu.edu.

Perez Melendez, Jose Juan, *California, Davis*. Email: jjperdez@ucdavis.edu.

Perez Morales, Edgardo, *Southern California*. Email: perezmor@usc.edu.

Perez-Montesinos, Fernando, *UCLA*. Los Angeles, CA. Email: fperez@history.ucla.edu; fcpmm2009@gmail.com. Research: modern Mexico, modern Latin American indigenous people.

Perezvargas, BJ, *MBA CEHP*. Indialantic, FL. Affil: Webster. Email: bperezvargas00@ webster.edu. Research: climate change and sea level rising, salt water marshes.

Perez-Villa, **Angela**, *Western Michigan*.

Pergher, **Roberta**, *Indiana*. Bloomington, IN. Email: rpergher@indiana.edu. Research: Italian fascism and colonialism, settlement policies and practices.

Peri, **Alexis Jean**, *Boston Univ*. Email: alexisp4@bu.edu.

Perin, **Raffaella**. Milano, Italy. Affil: Catholic Univ. of Sacred Heart. Email: raffaella.perin@unicatt.it. Research: Catholic Church, Vatican radio.

Perin, **Roberto**, *York, Can*. Email: rperin@yorku.ca.

Perk, **Aaron Taylor**. Austin, TX. Affil: New Mexico. Email: taylorperk@utexas.edu.

Perkins, **Alfred**, *Berea*. Email: alperk@earthlink.net.

Perkins, **Cody S**. Greensboro, NC. Affil: American Hebrew Academy. Email: perkinscody@gmail.com. Research: coloured South Africans, gendered and sexualized stereotypes.

Perkins, **Kenneth J.**, *South Carolina, Columbia*. Email: perkins@mailbox.sc.edu.

Perkins, **Krisha**. Amarillo, TX. Affil: West Texas A&M. Email: krisha.perkins@gmail.com.

Perkins, **Linda**, *Claremont Grad*. Email: linda.perkins@cgu.edu.

Perkins, **Robert C**. Woodlawn, VA. Affil: Methodist. Email: perkybear@comcast.net. Research: pre-railroad North Carolina and Virginia roads, Roanoke-Dan River valley transportation.

Perkiss, **Abigail L.**, *Kean*. Email: aperkiss@kean.edu.

Perlea, **Georgiana**. New York, NY. Email: georgiana.perlea@gmx.us. Research: intellectual/political, postwar France.

Perlman, **Allison J.**, *California, Irvine*. Irvine, CA. Email: aperlman@uci.edu. Research: media policy and reform, social movements.

Perlman, **Susan**. Burke, VA. Email: susanmmperlman@gmail.com. Research: Franco-American relations, Intelligence.

Perlmann, **Joel**, *Bard*. Email: perlmann@bard.edu.

Perl-Rosenthal, **Nathan Raoul**, *Southern California*. Los Angeles, CA. Email: perlrose@usc.edu; npr2103@columbia.edu. Research: colonial America, early modern Europe.

Perlstein, **Daniel**. Berkeley, CA. Affil: California, Berkeley. Email: danperl@berkeley.edu.

Perman, **Michael**, *Illinois, Chicago*. Email: mperman@uic.edu.

Pernal, **Andrew B.**, *Brandon*. Email: pernal@brandonu.ca.

Pernick, **Martin S.**, *Michigan, Ann Arbor*. Ann Arbor, MI. Email: mpernick@umich.edu. Research: concepts of death since 1740, health and medicine in motion pictures.

Perraud, **Louis**, *Idaho*. Email: phantom@uidaho.edu.

Perreault, **Jacques**, *Montréal*. Email: jacques.y.perreault@umontreal.ca.

Perreault, **Melanie L**. Grand Island, NY. Affil: SUNY, Buffalo State. Email: melanieperreault2@gmail.com. Research: violence in Anglo-Indian encounter, comparative colonization.

Perri, **Michael Hartman**. Texarkana, TX. Affil: Texas A&M, Texarkana. Email: mperri@tamut.edu. Research: Colonial Venezuela.

Perrier, **Craig**. Arlington, VA. Affil: Fairfax County Public Sch. Email: craigperrier19@gmail.com.

Research: nationalism and education, US foreign policy with Brazil.

Perrins, **Robert John**, *St. Mary's, Can*. Email: robert.perrins@acadiau.ca.

Perron, **Anthony M.**, *Loyola Marymount*. Email: aperron@lmu.edu.

Perrone, **Fernanda Helen**. Highland Park, NJ. Affil: Rutgers. Email: fhperrone@verizon.net. Research: Catholic women's higher education, missionaries in East Asia.

Perrone, **Giuliana**, *California, Santa Barbara*. Email: gperrone@history.ucsb.edu.

Perrone, **Nickolas Mario**. Petaluma, CA. Affil: California, Davis. Email: nmperrone@ucdavis.edu.

Perrone, **Sean T.**, *St. Anselm*. Email: sperrone@anselm.edu.

Perrot, **Michelle**. Paris, France.

Perrott, **Claire**, *Florida Atlantic*.

Perry, **Adele**, *Manitoba; Canadian Hist. Assoc*. Email: adele.perry@umanitoba.ca.

Perry, **Amanda B**. Washington, DC. Affil: National Hist. Center. Email: acban123@gmail.com.

Perry, **Charles R.**, *South*.

Perry, **David M**. Minneapolis, MN. Affil: Minnesota, Twin Cities. Email: perr0130@umn.edu. Research: Mediterranean culture, Venice.

Perry, **Heather R.**, *North Carolina, Charlotte*. Charlotte, NC. Email: hrperry@uncc.edu. Research: WWI health and medicine, social/cultural/gender.

Perry, **Jay Martin**. Fort Pierre, SD. Affil: South Dakota Board of Regents. Email: jay.perry@sdbor.edu.

Perry, **Jeffrey B**. Westwood, NJ. Email: jeffreybperry@gmail.com. Research: Hubert H. Harrison, Theodore W. Allen.

Perry, **Joe**, *Georgia State*. East Point, GA. Email: jbperry@gsu.edu. Research: modern Germany, consumer society and mass media.

Perry, **Kennetta Hammond**. Leicester, United Kingdom. Affil: De Montfort. Email: kennetta.perry@dmu.ac.uk. Research: race politics in postwar Britain, migration and African diaspora.

Perry, **Lewis C.**, *St. Louis*. Email: perryl@slu.edu.

Perry, **Mark**. Zhuhai, China. Affil: United International. Email: markperry19@gmail.com.

Perry, **Matthew J**. New York, NY. Affil: John Jay, CUNY. Email: mperry@jjay.cuny.edu. Research: gender and slavery, freedwomen in ancient Rome.

Perry, **Nathan W.**, *California Polytechnic State*. Email: naperry@calpoly.edu.

Perry, **Robyn Paige**. Fremont, CA. Affil: California State, East Bay. Email: robynperry510@gmail.com. Research: rock 'n' roll, American popular culture.

Perry, **Thornton A**, *Bellevue*. Email: tperry@bellevuecollege.edu.

Persell, **S. Michael**, *California State, San Bernardino*.

Person, **John D**. Albany, NY. Affil: SUNY, Albany. Email: johndperson@gmail.com. Research: right-wing intellectual, philosophy.

Pertilla, **Atiba K.**, *German Hist. Inst*. Email: pertilla@ghi-dc.org.

Perucci Gonzalez, **Cristian**. Santiago, Chile. Email: cristianperucci@gmail.com.

Peruccio, **Kara A**. Chicago, IL. Affil: Chicago. Email: kaperuccio@uchicago.edu. Research:

interwar Mediterranean dictatorships, women's literature.

Pescador, **Juan Javier**, *Michigan State*. Email: pescador@msu.edu.

Pescatello, **Ann M**. Berkeley, CA.

Pesely, **George E.**, *Austin Peay State*. Email: peselyg@apsu.edu.

Peskin, **Lawrence A.**, *Morgan State*. Baltimore, MD. Email: lawrence.peskin@morgan.edu. Research: early America.

Pestaina, **Khary S**. Miami, FL. Affil: Florida International. Email: Kharypestaina@gmail.com. Research: 20th-c black radicalism, black British soldiers in WWII West Indies.

Pestana, **Carla G.**, *UCLA*. Los Angeles, CA. Email: cgpestana@history.ucla.edu. Research: English conquest of Jamaica.

Peters, **Dolores A.**, *St. Olaf*. Northfield, MN. Email: petersdo@stolaf.edu. Research: Catholic medical establishment 1920-47, professional identity/autobiography.

Peters, **Edward M.**, *Pennsylvania*. Email: empeters@sas.upenn.edu.

Peters, **Erica J**. Mountain View, CA. Email: e-peters-9@alumni.uchicago.edu. Research: European colonialism.

Peters, **Julie**, *Illinois, Chicago*. Email: jlpeters@uic.edu.

Peters, **Kenneth E.**, *South Carolina, Columbia*. Email: kepeters7@att.net.

Petersen, **Mark Jeffrey**, *Dallas*. Irving, TX. Email: mpetersen@udallas.edu. Research: Latin America.

Petersen Boring, **Wendy**, *Willamette*. Email: wpeterse@willamette.edu.

Peterson, **Andrew C.**, *Grand Valley State*. Email: peteran1@gvsu.edu.

Peterson, **Anna Marie**, *Luther*. Email: petean07@luther.edu.

Peterson, **Barbara Bennett**. Tigard, OR. Affil: Hawaii and East-West Center. Email: fandbpeterson@comcast.net. Research: US since 1920, precontact American Indian.

Peterson, **Benjamin**, *Alma*. Email: petersonbl@alma.edu.

Peterson, **Brian James**, *Union Coll*. Email: petersob@union.edu.

Peterson, **Carl H**. El Granada, CA. Affil: California State, Chico. Email: chpeterson@sbcglobal.net. Research: Jefferson and national identity, Jefferson and women.

Peterson, **Charles A.**, *Cornell*. Email: cap4@cornell.edu.

Peterson, **David S.**, *Washington and Lee*. Lexington, VA. Email: petersond@wlu.edu. Research: Renaissance politics and religion, political thought and church.

Peterson, **Dawn**, *Emory*. Email: dawn.peterson@emory.edu.

Peterson, **Derek R.**, *Michigan, Ann Arbor*. Email: drpeters@umich.edu.

Peterson, **Ebony**. Houston, TX. Affil: Texas Southern. Email: petersonlashay90@outlook.com.

Peterson, **Erik L.**, *Alabama, Tuscaloosa*. Email: elpeterson@ua.edu.

Peterson, **F. Ross**, *Utah State*. Email: ross.peterson@usu.edu.

Peterson, **Glen D.**, *British Columbia*. Email: glpeters@mail.ubc.ca.

Peterson, **Heather Rose**, *South Carolina Aiken*. Email: heatherp@usca.edu.

Peterson, **Jacqueline**, *Washington State, Pullman*. Email: jpeterson1@vancouver.wsu. edu.

Peterson, **Jodi M.**, *Texas, San Antonio*. Email: jodi.peterson@utsa.edu.

Peterson, *Jon A.*, *Queens, CUNY*. Essex, CT. Email: japhistqc@aol.com. Research: US city planning, US beautiful city movement.

Peterson, **Joseph W.**, *Southern Mississippi*. Email: joseph.peterson@usm.edu.

Peterson, **Joyce S.**, *Florida International*. Email: petersoj@fiu.edu.

Peterson, **M. Jeanne**, *Indiana*. Email: petersom@indiana.edu.

Peterson, *Maite Elizabeth*. West Hills, CA. Affil: Glendale Comm. Coll. Email: mpeterson@ glendale.edu.

Peterson, *Mark Allen*. New Haven, CT. Affil: Yale. Email: mark.a.peterson@yale.edu. Research: Boston in Atlantic world 1630-1865, early America.

Peterson, **Maya Karin**, *California, Santa Cruz*. Email: mkpeters@ucsc.edu.

Peterson, **Terrence Gordon**, *Florida International*. Email: Terrence.Peterson@fiu. edu.

Peterson, *Trudy H*. Washington, DC. Email: archivesthp@aol.com.

Peterson, **Willard J.**, *Princeton*. Email: easwjp@ princeton.edu.

Pethel, *Mary Ellen*. Nashville, TN. Affil: Harpeth Hall Sch. Email: mepethel@gmail.com. Research: gender and Gilded/Progressive, Reconstruction to WWII southern education.

Petit, *Jeanne D.*, *Hope*. Holland, MI. Email: petit@ hope.edu. Research: gender and immigration law, Catholic women.

Petitclerc, **Martin**, *Québec, Montréal*. Email: petitclerc.martin@uqam.ca.

Petitjean, *Beth*. Saint Louis, MO. Affil: St. Louis. Email: beth.petitjean@slu.edu.

Petraitis, *Jason Mark*. North Brookfield, MA. Email: jmpetraitis@gmail.com.

Petrakis, *Peter*, *Southeastern Louisiana*. Email: ppetrakis@selu.edu.

Petri, *Olga*. Cambridge, United Kingdom. Affil: Cambridge. Email: op257@cam.ac.uk.

Petrick, **Elizabeth R.**, *Rice*.

Petrik, **Paula**, *George Mason*.

Petrinca, *Ruxandra Canache*. Dorval, QC, Canada. Affil: McGill. Email: ruxandra_ canache@yahoo.com. Research: socialism/ culture/dissent, memory/propaganda.

Petrone, **Karen**, *Kentucky*. Email: petrone@uky. edu.

Petropoulos, *Jonathan*, *Claremont McKenna*. Claremont, CA. Email: jpetropoulos@cmc. edu. Research: modern Europe and Germany, cultural.

Petroski, **Henry**, *Duke*. Email: hp@egr.duke.edu.

Petroski, *Jacob R.* Clinton Township, MI. Email: jrp.dartmouth@gmail.com.

Petrou, *Marissa Helene*. Lafayette, LA. Affil: Louisiana, Lafayette. Email: marissa.petrou@ gmail.com. Research: science, collections.

Petrou, **Michael**, *Carleton, Can*. Email: michael. petrou@carleton.ca.

Petrov, *Nikolay*. Landing, NJ. Affil: Drew. Email: npetrov@drew.edu. Research: church, religious studies.

Petrovich, *Lisa L.* Williamsburg, VA. Affil: Colorado, Boulder. Email: petrovich.lisa@ gmail.com.

Petrovsky-Shtern, *Yohanan*, *Northwestern*. Email: yps@northwestern.edu.

Petrow, *Stefan*. Hobart, Australia. Affil: Tasmania. Email: Stefan.petrow@utas.edu. au. Research: London magistrates 1839-1939, Tasmanian policing 1899-1999.

Petrowski, **William**, *Nebraska, Omaha*.

Petruccelli, **David**, *Dartmouth*. Email: david. petruccelli@dartmouth.edu.

Petrus, *Stephen*, *La Guardia and Wagner Archives*. Brooklyn, NY. Email: spetrus@lagcc. cuny.edu; spetrus364@gmail.com. Research: urban, cultural movements.

Petry, **Carl F.**, *Northwestern*. Email: c-petry@ northwestern.edu.

Petrzela, **Natalia**, *New School*. Email: mehlmann@newschool.edu.

Pettegrew, **David K.**, *Messiah*. Email: dpettegrew@messiah.edu.

Pettigrew, *Erin*, *NYU*. New York, NY. Affil: NYU, Abu Dhabi. Email: erin.pettigrew@nyu.edu. Research: religion, race.

Pettit, *Cheyenne Kacey*. Ann Arbor, MI. Affil: Michigan. Email: ckpett@umich.edu.

Petto, **Christine M.**, *Southern Connecticut State*. Email: pettoc1@southernct.edu.

Petty, *Adrienne Monteith*, *William and Mary*. Williamsburg, VA. Email: ampetty@wm.edu. Research: modern US.

Peucker, *Paul M.* Bethlehem, PA. Affil: Moravian Archives. Email: paul@ moravianchurcharchives.org. Research: Moravians in Europe and America, Radical Pietism.

Peychev, *Stefan*. Champaign, IL. Affil: Illinois, Urbana-Champaign. Email: stefanpeychev@ outlook.com. Research: urban environment, space and place.

Peykov, *Deyan Atanasov*. Hallandale, FL. Affil: Florida International. Email: deyanpeykov@ gmail.com.

Pfeffer, **Paula F.**, *Loyola, Chicago*. Email: ppfeffer@luc.edu.

Pfeifer, **Michael James**, *Graduate Center, CUNY*. Email: mpfeifer@jjay.cuny.edu.

Pfleger, **Birte B.**, *California State, Los Angeles*. Email: bpflege@calstatela.edu.

Pflugfelder, **Gregory M.**, *Columbia (Hist.)*. Email: gmp12@columbia.edu.

Pfund, *Niko*. New York, NY. Affil: Oxford Univ. Press. Email: niko.pfund@oup.com.

Phayer, *Michael*, *Marquette*.

Phelan, *Kaidin*. Great Falls, MT. Email: kaidrphelan@gmail.com.

Phelan, *Owen Michael*. Emmitsburg, MD. Affil: Mount St. Mary's. Email: ophelan@msmary. edu. Research: early medieval religion, early medieval culture.

Phelps, *Christopher*. Nottingham, United Kingdom. Affil: Nottingham. Email: historypolitics@aol.com. Research: sexuality and the left, strikes in social thought.

Phelps, *Nicole M.*, *Vermont*. Burlington, VT. Email: nphelps@uvm.edu. Research: US-Habsburg relations, diplomacy and foreign services.

Phelps, *Robert A.*, *California State, East Bay*. Email: robert.phelps@csueastbay.edu.

Phelps, *Wesley G.*, *North Texas*. Huntsville, TX. Affil: Sam Houston State. Email: wesley. phelps@unt.edu; wesley.g.phelps@gmail.com. Research: War on Poverty, Sunbelt politics.

Phifer, **James R.**, *Coe*. Email: jphifer@coe.edu.

Philip, **Kavita Sara**, *California, Irvine*. Email: kphilip@uci.edu.

Philips, *John Edward*. Hirosaki, Japan. Affil: Hirosaki. Email: philips@gol.com. Research: comparative slavery, Nigerian inter-ethnic relations.

Philliou, **Christine May**, *California, Berkeley*. Email: philliou@berkeley.edu.

Phillips, **C. Robert**, **III**, *Lehigh*. Email: crp0@ lehigh.edu.

Phillips, *Carla Rahn*, *Minnesota (Hist.)*. Wimberley, TX. Email: phill002@umn.edu. Research: early modern maritime, exploration.

Phillips, **Christopher J.**, *Carnegie Mellon*. Email: cjp1@cmu.edu.

Phillips, **Christopher**, *Cincinnati*. Email: christopher.phillips@uc.edu.

Phillips, **David D.**, *UCLA*. Email: phillips@history. ucla.edu.

Phillips, **Denise**, *Tennessee, Knoxville*. Email: aphill13@utk.edu.

Phillips, *Dustin*. Forest, MS. Affil: Forest High Sch. Email: dphillips@forest.k12.ms.us.

Phillips, **George H.**, *Colorado, Boulder*.

Phillips, **Glenn O.**, *Morgan State*. Email: gopper. phillips@gmail.com.

Phillips, **Jason K.**, *West Virginia*. Email: jason. phillips@mail.wvu.edu.

Phillips, *Jenna Rebecca*. Baltimore, MD. Affil: Johns Hopkins. Email: jenna.phillips@gmail. com. Research: 13th-c France and Italy, oral tradition/secular music.

Phillips, *Katrina*, *Macalester*. Osseo, MN. Email: kphilli2@macalester.edu. Research: performance, tourism.

Phillips, **Kim T.**, *Connecticut, Storrs*. Email: kim. phillips@uconn.edu.

Phillips, **Lisa A.**, *Indiana State*. Email: Lisa. Phillips@indstate.edu.

Phillips, **Mark Saber**, *Carleton, Can*. Email: mark.phillips@carleton.ca.

Phillips, **Mary Claire**, *Hist. Assoc*. Email: mphillips@historyassociates.com.

Phillips, *P. Michael*. Gettysburg, PA. Affil: US Army War. Email: poledorus@gmail.com.

Phillips, *Roderick G.*, *Carleton, Can*. Email: roderick.phillips@carleton.ca.

Phillips, *Sarah T.*, *Boston Univ*. Boston, MA. Email: sarahphi@bu.edu. Research: New Deal, political conservatism.

Phillips, **Steve E.**, *Towson*. Email: sphillips@ towson.edu.

Phillips, **Susan**, *Charleston*. Email: phillipss@ cofc.edu.

Phillips, *Victoria*. Brooklyn, NY. Affil: Columbia. Email: lvb3@columbia.edu. Research: cultural diplomacy, US Cold War.

Phillips, *William D.*, *Jr.*, *Minnesota (Hist.)*. Wimberley, TX. Email: phill004@umn.edu. Research: medieval slavery, environmental.

Phillips, **William W.**, *Arizona State*.

Phillips Sawyer, *Laura*. Boston, MA. Affil: Harvard Business Sch. Email: lsawyer@hbs. edu.

Phillips-Fein, *Kim*, *NYU*. New York, NY. Email: kpf2@nyu.edu. Research: post-New Deal business/intellectual, rise of 20th-c conservatism.

Phillips-Lewis, **Kathleen**, *Spelman*. Email: klewis@spelman.edu.

Philp, *Kenneth R.*, *Texas, Arlington*. Email: philp@ uta.edu.

Philpott, **William P.**, *Denver*. Centennial, CO. Email: william.philpott@du.edu. Research: environmental history of tourism, suburban.

Philyaw, **L. Scott**, *Western Carolina*. Email: philyaw@wcu.edu.

Phipps, **Catherine L.**, *Memphis*. Email: cphipps1@memphis.edu.

Phipps, **Pauline A.**, *Windsor*. Email: pphipps@uwindsor.ca.

Phipps, **Sheila**, *Appalachian State*. Email: phippssr@appstate.edu.

Phoenix, **Karen E.**, *Washington State, Pullman*. Email: karen.phoenix@wsu.edu.

Pianko, **Noam**, *Washington, Seattle*. Email: npianko@uw.edu.

Piatt, **Alison**. Miami, FL. Affil: Florida International. Email: alison.m.piatt@gmail.com. Research: immigration/sports/US curling, American popular culture.

Piccato, **Pablo A.**, *Columbia (Hist.)*. Email: pp143@columbia.edu.

Piccione, **Peter A.**, *Charleston*. Email: piccionep@cofc.edu.

Piccirilli, **Tomasso**. Washington, DC. Affil: American. Email: tp9092a@american.edu.

Pickering, **Jeanne Marie**. Topsfield, MA. Email: j_pickering@salemstate.edu.

Pickering, **Mary B.**, *San José State*. San Francisco, CA. Email: Mary.Pickering@sjsu.edu. Research: Auguste Comte, mid-19th-c France.

Pickett, **James Robert**, *Pittsburgh*. Email: pickettj@pitt.edu.

Pickett, **William B**. White Bear Lake, MN. Affil: Rose-Hulman Inst. of Tech. Email: william.pickett@rose-hulman.edu. Research: Gen. Andrew Goodpaster, micro-electronics revolution.

Pickowicz, **Paul G.**, *California, San Diego*. Email: bikewei@ucsd.edu.

Pickron, **Jeffrey W.**, *Wisconsin-Oshkosh*. Email: pickronj@uwosh.edu.

Picone, **Louis**. Succasunna, NJ. Affil: William Paterson; Skyhorse Publishing. Email: lpicone@optonline.net. Research: presidential places, monuments.

Picone, **María de los Ángeles**, *Boston Coll*. Chestnut Hill, MA. Email: piconemb@bc.edu. Research: Patagonia.

Pidhainy, **Ihor O.**, *West Georgia*. Email: ipidhain@westga.edu.

Piecuch, **James R.**, *Kennesaw State*. Email: jpiecuch@kennesaw.edu.

Piehler, **G. Kurt**, *Florida State*. Tallahassee, FL. Email: kpiehler@fsu.edu; militarysage@gmail.com. Research: religion and war, history and memory.

Piemonte, **Joseph M.**, *Salem State*.

Pieper Mooney, **Jadwiga E.**, *Arizona*. Tucson, AZ. Email: jadwiga@email.arizona.edu. Research: Cold War, transnational women's activism/feminism.

Pieragastini, **Steven**. Santa Monica, CA. Affil: San Francisco. Email: spieragastini@gmail.com. Research: modern Shanghai, boderlands/frontiers in East Asia.

Pierard, **Richard V.**, *Indiana State*. Asheville, NC. Email: charrichp@aol.com. Research: Germany, Africa.

Pierce, **Gerald J**. Marietta, GA. Affil: Kennesaw State. Email: gjpierce@mindspring.com. Research: Spanish-American War, typhoid fever.

Pierce, **Gretchen Kristine**, *Shippensburg*. Email: gkpierce@ship.edu.

Pierce, **Marlyn R.**, *US Army Command Coll*. Email: marlyn.r.pierce.civ@mail.mil.

Pierce, **Mary**, *Arizona*. Tucson, AZ. Email: piercem@email.arizona.edu. Research: consumer culture in early modern England, sexualities.

Pierce, **Michael Cain**, *Arkansas, Fayetteville*. Email: mpierce@uark.edu.

Pierce, **Morris A.**, *Rochester*. Email: m.pierce@mail.rochester.edu.

Pierce, **Richard B.**, **II**, *Notre Dame*. Email: rpierce@nd.edu.

Pierce, **Samuel Dare**, **Jr**. Fayetteville, NC. Affil: Womack Army Hospital. Email: sdpierce1nov45@outlook.com.

Pierce, **Samuel**, *South Carolina Aiken*. Email: samuel.pierce@usca.edu.

Piercy, **Jeremy**, *Charleston*. Charleston, SC. Email: piercyjl@cofc.edu; jpiercy@alumni.unc.edu. Research: social and cultural, family dynamics and heredity.

Pierre, **Nathalie Frédéric**. Brooklyn, NY. Affil: Spence Sch. Email: np710@nyu.edu.

Pierson, **Peter O'Malley**, *Santa Clara*. Cathedral City, CA. Email: pompierson@aol.com. Research: Don John of Austria 1547-78, Spanish Habsburgs.

Pietruska, **Jamie L.**, *Rutgers*. Email: pietrusk@history.rutgers.edu.

Pigg, **Jimmy J.**, *Austin Peay State*. Email: piggj@apsu.edu.

Piggott, **Joan R.**, *Southern California*. Email: joanrp@usc.edu.

Pihos, **Peter Constantine**, *Western Washington*. Email: peter.pihos@wwu.edu.

Pijning, **Ernst**, *Minot State*. Minot, ND. Email: ernst.pijning@minotstateu.edu. Research: illegal trade in colonial Brazil, diamonds in Brazil.

Piker, **Joshua A.**, *William and Mary; Omohundro Inst*. Williamsburg, VA. Email: japiker@wm.edu. Research: colonial-era American Indian communities, American Indians in colonial history.

Pilant, **Charles A.**, *Cumberlands*. Email: al.pilant@ucumberlands.edu.

Pilcher, **Jeffrey M.**, *Toronto*. Toronto, ON, Canada. Email: jeffrey.pilcher@utoronto.ca.

Pilgrim, **Danya**. New Haven, PA. Affil: Yale. Email: danya.pilgrim@yale.edu.

Pillai, **Sarath**. Chicago, IL. Affil: Chicago. Email: sarathpillai@uchicago.edu. Research: modern South Asia, legal.

Pillar, **James J.**, **OMI**, *Loyola, New Orleans*.

Pimentel, **Jose Ernesto**, **Jr**., *NYU*.

Piña, **Ulices**, *California State, Long Beach*. Email: ulices.pina@csulb.edu.

Pinaud, **Clémence**, *Indiana*. Email: cpinaud@indiana.edu.

Pinch, **William R.**, *Wesleyan*. Middletown, CT. Email: wpinch@wesleyan.edu. Research: Mutiny-Rebellion of 1857, translation of 18th-c war poetry.

Pincince, **John R.**, *Loyola, Chicago*. Chicago, IL. Email: jpincince@luc.edu; john.pincince@gmail.com. Research: Hindu national identity, V. D. Savarkar.

Pinckney, **Paul J.**, *Tennessee, Knoxville*. Email: pinckney@utk.edu.

Pincus, **Arnold**, *California State, Los Angeles*.

Pincus, **Leslie**, *Michigan, Ann Arbor*. Email: lpincus@umich.edu.

Pincus, **Steven C.**, *Chicago*. Email: spincus@uchicago.edu.

Pineda, **Yovanna**, *Central Florida*. Orlando, FL. Email: ypineda@ucf.edu. Research: gender and work, technology.

Pineo, **Ronn**, *Towson*. Email: rpineo@towson.edu.

Pinero, **Eugene**, *Wisconsin-Eau Claire*. Email: pineroe@uwec.edu.

Ping, **Laura**. Purchase, NY. Affil: Queens, CUNY. Email: lping@gradcenter.cuny.edu. Research: women, dress reform.

Pingree, **Elizabeth Anne**. Brighton, MA. Affil: Boston Coll. Email: betsypingree@gmail.com.

Pinheiro, **Holly Anthony**, **Jr.**, *Augusta*.

Pinkard, **Susan K.**, *Georgetown*. Email: pinkards@georgetown.edu.

Pinkins, **Carlyn Nicole**. Albuquerque, NM. Affil: New Mexico. Email: devinsday@gmail.com. Research: Afro American history in Southwest, 20th-c American Indians.

Pinnow, **Kenneth M.**, *Allegheny*. Email: kpinnow@allegheny.edu.

Pino, **Justin Patrick**. Ridgway, PA. Affil: St. Leo Catholic Church. Email: frjustin@comcast.net.

Pinsker, **Matthew**, *Dickinson*. Mechanicsburg, PA. Email: pinskerm@dickinson.edu. Research: US political, Civil War era and Abraham Lincoln.

Pinto, **Karen C**. Boise, ID. Affil: Boise State. Email: karenpinto@boisestate.edu. Research: Islamic cartography, material culture.

Piola, **Erika**, *Library Co. of Philadelphia*. Email: epiola@librarycompany.org.

Piorkowski, **Thomas**, *Elmhurst*. Email: thomas.piorkowski@elmhurst.edu.

Piotrowski, **Harry**, *Towson*.

Piotrowski, **Sara**, *Lewis*. Email: piotrosa@lewisu.edu.

Piott, **Steven L.**, *Clarion, Pa*. Email: piott@clarion.edu.

Piper, **Delaney McMillan**. Pullman, WA. Affil: Washington State. Email: delaneypiper19@gmail.com.

Piper, **Elizabeth**, *Alberta*. Email: epiper@ualberta.ca.

Piper, **John F.**, **Jr**. Williamsport, PA. Affil: Lycoming. Email: piper@lycoming.edu. Research: American religious and missions, church.

Pipkin Anderson, **Amanda Cathryn**, *North Carolina, Charlotte*. Email: apipkin@uncc.edu.

Pippenger, **Randall Todd**. Adamsville, TN. Affil: Princeton. Email: rpippeng@princeton.edu.

Pippin, **Whitney**, *Robert H. Smith Center*. Charlottesville, VA. Email: wpippin@monticello.org.

Pires, **Ana Paula**. Alhos Vedros, Portugal. Affil: Nova de Lisboa. Email: asoarespires@gmail.com.

Pirillo, **Diego**. Berkeley, CA. Affil: California, Berkeley. Email: dpirillo@berkeley.edu. Research: early modern diplomacy, early modern heterodoxy and religious dissent.

Piro-Biko, **George J**. Turlock, CA. Affil: Santa Clara Univ. Law Sch. Email: gpirobiko@gmail.com.

Pirok, **Alena R.**, *Georgia Southern*. Email: apirok@georgiasouthern.edu.

Piston, **William G.**, *Missouri State*. Email: williampiston@missouristate.edu.

Pit, Chrystel. Concord, MA. Affil: Massachusetts, Lowell. Email: canaghan@hotmail.com.

Pitcaithley, Dwight T., *New Mexico State*. Email: dwightp@nmsu.edu.

Pitcavage, Mark. Hilliard, OH. Affil: Anti-Defamation League. Email: pitcavage@sbcglobal.net. Research: right-wing extremism in US, US military-social.

Pite, Rebekah E., *Lafayette*. Easton, PA. Email: piter@lafayette.edu. Research: southern South America/food/consumption, Argentina food/domestic work/community.

Pitelka, Morgan, *North Carolina, Chapel Hill*. Email: mpitelka@email.unc.edu.

Pitman, Paul M., *US Dept. of State*.

Pitre, Merline, *Texas Southern*. Email: pitre_mx@tsu.edu.

Pitt, Steven, *St. Bonaventure*. West Falls, NY. Email: spitt@sbu.edu; sjp55@pitt.edu. Research: 18th-c Atlantic port cities, seafaring community and culture.

Pittenger, Mark A., *Colorado, Boulder*. Boulder, CO. Email: mark.pittenger@colorado.edu. Research: Liberal religion and social activism, Unitarian theology and social movements.

Pitti, Joseph A., *California State, Sacramento*. Email: japitti@saclink.csus.edu.

Pitti, Stephen J., *Yale*. Email: stephen.pitti@yale.edu.

Pitts, Graham A. Washington, DC. Affil: Georgetown. Email: gap32@georgetown.edu. Research: transregional, environmental.

Pitts, Jennifer. Chicago, IL. Affil: Chicago. Email: jpitts@uchicago.edu.

Pitts, Yvonne M., *Purdue*. Lafayette, IN. Email: ypitts@purdue.edu. Research: US legal, US inheritance law.

Pitzer, Donald E., *Southern Indiana*. Email: dpitzer@usi.edu.

Pivar, David J., *California State, Fullerton*. Email: pivar@fullerton.edu.

Pixton, Paul B., *Brigham Young*. Email: paul_pixton@byu.edu.

Pizzigoni, Caterina L., *Columbia (Hist.)*. New York, NY. Email: cp2313@columbia.edu. Research: social and cultural, nahuatl.

Pizzo, David John, *Murray State*. Email: dpizzo@murraystate.edu.

Plaag, Eric W. Boone, NC. Affil: South Carolina. Email: ericplaag@gmail.com. Research: northern travelers in antebellum South, photography 1840-1940.

Plach, Eva Anna, *Wilfrid Laurier*. Email: eplach@wlu.ca.

Placido, Sandy Isabel, *Queens, CUNY*. Email: Sandy.Placido@qc.cuny.edu.

Plageman, Nathan A., *Wake Forest*. Email: plagemna@wfu.edu.

Plakans, Andrejs, *Iowa State*. Email: aplakans@iastate.edu.

Plaks, Jeff, *Central Oklahoma*. Email: jplaks@uco.edu.

Plamper, Jan. London, United Kingdom. Affil: Goldsmiths, London. Email: j.plamper@gold.ac.uk. Research: emotions, Europe and Russia.

Plane, Ann Marie, *California, Santa Barbara*. Email: plane@history.ucsb.edu.

Plant, Alisa. Baton Rouge, LA. Affil: Louisiana State Univ. Press. Email: alisaplant1@lsu.edu.

Plant, Rebecca Jo, *California, San Diego*. La Jolla, CA. Email: rplant@ucsd.edu. Research: 20th-c US, women and gender.

Plastino, Thomas A. Canton, NY. Email: tplastino@slcida.com. Research: Raquette River Valley 1865-1930, US back to land movements.

Plath, Lydia J. Coventry, United Kingdom. Affil: Warwick. Email: l.j.plath@warwick.ac.uk. Research: slavery in US South, slavery in historical film.

Platow, Dena A. Milwaukee, WI. Affil: Milwaukee Public Sch. Email: platowda@milwaukee.k12.wi.us. Research: Civil War draft riots in Port Washington, WWII submarine warfare in Pacific.

Platt, Brian D., *Indianapolis*.

Platt, Brian W., *George Mason*. Fairfax, VA. Email: bplatt1@gmu.edu. Research: early modern historical consciousness.

Platt, Eric W. Brooklyn, NY. Affil: St. Francis, NY. Email: eplatt@sfc.edu.

Platt, Harold L., *Loyola, Chicago*. Email: hplatt@luc.edu.

Platt, Stephen R., *Massachusetts, Amherst*. Email: platt@history.umass.edu.

Platt, Wilfred C., Jr., *Mercer*.

Player, Tiffany, *Southern Illinois, Carbondale*. Email: tplayer@siu.edu.

Plaza, Samuel Joseph, *Henry Ford Coll*. Email: sjplaza@hfcc.edu.

Pleasants, Julian Mciver, *Florida*. Email: jpleasan@history.ufl.edu.

Pletsch, Carl, *Colorado Denver*. Email: carl.pletsch@ucdenver.edu.

Pliley, Jessica R., *Texas State*. San Marcos, TX. Email: jp74@txstate.edu; jpliley@gmail.com. Research: white slavery, FBI and INS.

Plokhii, Serhii, *Harvard (Hist.)*. Email: plokhii@fas.harvard.edu.

Plotke, David, *New School*. Email: plotked@newschool.edu.

Plott, Michele S., *Suffolk*. Email: mplott@suffolk.edu.

Plumb, Michael B., *Virginia Museum of Hist*. Email: mplumb@VirginiaHistory.org.

Plumley, Ryan G. Freiburg, Germany. Affil: Univ. Coll. Freiburg. Email: ryanplumley@gmail.com. Research: self, global intellectual culture.

Plummer, Brenda G., *Wisconsin-Madison*. Email: bplummer@wisc.edu.

Plummer, Brian, *Azusa Pacific*. Email: bplummer@apu.edu.

Plummer, Jillian. Notre Dame, IN. Affil: Notre Dame. Email: jplumme2@nd.edu.

Pluth, Edward J. Delano, MN. Affil: St. Cloud State. Email: ejpluth@frontiernet.net. Research: 19th-20th-c rural, American Indian.

Pluymers, Keith D., *Illinois State*. Los Angeles, CA. Affil: California Inst. of Tech. Email: kdpluym@ilstu.edu; pluymers@caltech.edu. Research: environmental, English expansion.

Poblete, JoAnna U., *Claremont Grad*. Claremont, CA. Email: joanna.poblete@cgu.edu. Research: US colonialism/immigration/labor, APA/Filipino/Puerto Rico/Hawaii/Samoa.

Pobst, Phyllis E., *Arkansas State*. Email: ppobst@astate.edu.

Poche, Justin David, *Holy Cross*. Email: jpoche@holycross.edu.

Pocock, Emil, *Eastern Connecticut State*. Email: pocock@easternct.edu.

Pocock, John G. A., *Johns Hopkins (Hist.)*. Email: jgap@earthlink.net.

Podair, Jerald E. Appleton, WI. Affil: Lawrence. Email: podairj@lawrence.edu. Research: 20th-c American race, New York City.

Podesva, James. Carbondale, IL. Email: jimpodesva@gmail.com. Research: postwar German reconstruction, postwar British political.

Podleski, Genevieve. Saint Louis, MO. Affil: Federal Reserve Bank of St. Louis. Email: genevieve.podleski@gmail.com.

Podruchny, Carolyn, *York, Can*. Email: carolynp@yorku.ca.

Poe, Brittany Elizabeth. Knoxville, TN. Affil: Tennessee, Knoxville. Email: bpoe3@utk.edu.

Poe, William Clay, *Sonoma State*.

Poen, Monte, *Northern Arizona*. Email: monte.poen@nau.edu.

Pogorelskin, Alexis E., *Minnesota Duluth*. Email: apogorel@d.umn.edu.

Pohl, Michaela, *Vassar*. Email: mipohl@vassar.edu.

Pohlmann, John O. Seal Beach, CA. Affil: California State Polytechnic. Email: jpohlcat@roadrunner.com. Research: American West, ancient Greece.

Poiger, Uta G., *Northeastern*. Email: u.poiger@neu.edu.

Pointer, Richard W., *Westmont*. Santa Barbara, CA. Email: pointer@westmont.edu. Research: American religious, colonial America.

Polak, Emil. Sayville, NY. Affil: Queensborough Comm. Coll., CUNY. Email: ejplpolak@gmail.com. Research: medieval and Renaissance letter writing, secular oratory.

Polakoff, Keith I., *California State, Long Beach*. Email: kip@csulb.edu.

Polanco, Edward Anthony, *Virginia Tech*. Blacksburg, VA. Email: polanco@vt.edu. Research: Central Mexico.

Polanichka, Dana M., *Wheaton, Mass*. Norton, MA. Email: polanichka_dana@wheatoncollege.edu. Research: early medieval ritual, religious aesthetics and sacred space.

Polasky, Janet L., *New Hampshire, Durham*. Durham, NH. Email: janet.polasky@unh.edu. Research: Atlantic revolution, comparative labor.

Pole, Adam, *Windsor*. Email: adampole@uwindsor.ca.

Polecritti, Cynthia L., *California, Santa Cruz*. Email: clpolecr@ucsc.edu.

Polenberg, Richard, *Cornell*. Email: rp19@cornell.edu.

Poley, Jared, *Georgia State*. Atlanta, GA. Email: jpoley@gsu.edu. Research: Atlantic world, cultural and intellectual.

Polgar, Paul J., *Mississippi*. Oxford, MS. Email: pjpolgar@olemiss.edu. Research: slavery/antislavery/race/reform, early Republic America.

Poling, Kristin E. Dearborn, MI. Affil: Michigan-Dearborn. Email: kpoling@umich.edu. Research: 19th-c urban culture, German social thought.

Polk, Andrew, *Middle Tennessee State*. Email: Andrew.Polk@mtsu.edu.

Pollack, Eunice G. Oklahoma City, OK. Affil: North Texas. Email: egpollack@aol.com. Research: psychoanalysis.

Pollack, Mark. Springfield, NJ. Email: mark_pollack@verizon.net.

Pollak, Oliver B., *Nebraska, Omaha*. Richmond, CA. Email: obpomni@aol.com. Research: modern Britain and Commonwealth, legal.

Polland, Annie M., *American Jewish Hist. Soc.* Email: apolland@ajhs.org.

Pollard, Elizabeth Ann, *San Diego State*. Email: epollard@sdsu.edu.

Pollard, Lisa, *North Carolina, Wilmington*. Email: pollardl@uncw.edu.

Pollard, Miranda J., *Georgia*. Email: mpollard@uga.edu.

Pollard, Richard, *Québec, Montréal*. Email: pollard.richard@uqam.ca.

Pollard, Sandra. Carrollton, GA. Affil: West Georgia. Email: spollard@westga.edu.

Pollini, John, *Southern California*. Email: pollini@usc.edu.

Pollnitz, Aysha, *Rice*. Email: aysha.pollnitz@rice.edu.

Pollock, Caitlin. Indianapolis, IN. Affil: Indiana-Purdue, Indianapolis. Email: pollock.caitlin@gmail.com.

Pollock, Ethan M., *Brown*. Providence, RI. Email: Ethan_Pollock@Brown.edu. Research: Russian everyday life, USSR and cold war.

Pollock, Fred E. Liberty Corner, NJ. Email: fpollockv@aol.com.

Pollock, Gordon L. Chicago, IL. Affil: International Churchill Soc. Email: pollocklee@rcn.com.

Pollock, Linda A., *Tulane*. Email: pollock@tulane.edu.

Pollock, Sean. Cincinnati, OH. Affil: Wright State. Email: sean.pollock@wright.edu. Research: Russian expansion into Caucasus, scientific exploration of Caucasus.

Polonsky, Antony, *Brandeis*. London, United Kingdom. Email: polonsky@brandeis.edu. Research: eastern European Jewish, Holocaust studies.

Pomata, Gianna, *Johns Hopkins (Hist. of Science)*. Email: gpomata1@jhmi.edu.

Pomerantz, Linda, *California State, Dominguez Hills*. Email: lpomerantz@csudh.edu.

Pomeranz, Kenneth L., *Chicago*. Chicago, IL. Email: kpomeranz1@uchicago.edu; kennethpomeranz@gmail.com. Research: modern Chinese social/environmental, comparative economic.

Pomerleau, Clark A., *North Texas*. Email: clark.pomerleau@unt.edu.

Pomeroy, John. San Luis Obispo, CA. Email: jwilliampomeroy@gmail.com.

Pomeroy, Sarah B., *Graduate Center, CUNY*. Email: sbpom@aol.com.

Pomeroy, Steven A. Colorado Springs, CO. Email: stevena.pomeroy@outlook.com. Research: mobile ICBM technology and deterrence, mobile missile command and control.

Pompeian, Edward P., *Tampa*. Tampa, FL. Email: eppomp@gmail.com. Research: colonial Latin America, Americas in Age of Revolutions.

Pomper, Philip, *Wesleyan*. Email: ppomper@wesleyan.edu.

Ponce, Pearl T., *Ithaca*. Email: pponce@ithaca.edu.

Ponce de Leon, Charles Leonard, *California State, Long Beach*. San Francisco, CA. Email: charles.poncedeleon@csulb.edu. Research: US cultural and intellectual.

Ponce Vazquez, Juan Jose, *Alabama, Tuscaloosa*. Email: jponcevasquez@ua.edu.

Pong, David B., *Delaware*. Email: dpong@udel.edu.

Ponnet, Luke Francis. Portland, OR. Email: aluke.ponnet@gmail.com.

Pontius, Jennifer. Lynnwood, WA. Email: jenniferjpontius@gmail.com.

Poole, Stafford R., *CM*. Perryville, MO. Email: spoole541@aol.com. Research: 16th-c nahvatl, Our Lady of Guadalupe.

Poole, W. Scott, *Charleston*. Email: poolews@cofc.edu.

Poor, Galen Matthew. Madison, WI. Affil: Wisconsin, Madison. Email: gmpoor@wisc.edu. Research: history education in modern China, four great inventions in modern China.

Poor, Lauren Renee Miller, *Baylor*. Email: lauren_poor@baylor.edu.

Poorman, Elizabeth. Los Angeles, CA. Email: eelliott@historians.org.

Poorman, Joshua Wade. Los Angeles, CA. Affil: Southern California. Email: poorman@usc.edu.

Pope, Andrew, *MIT*. Cambridge, MA. Email: andrewpope@fas.harvard.edu.

Pope, Barbara C., *Oregon*. Email: bcpope@uoregon.edu.

Pope, Daniel, *Oregon*. Email: dapope@uoregon.edu.

Pope, Janis. Roseville, CA. Email: jpope@csus.edu.

Pope, Jeremy, *William and Mary*. Email: jwpope@wm.edu.

Pope, Justin James, *Missouri Science and Tech*.

Pope-Obeda, Emily K. Decatur, GA. Affil: Emory. Email: epopeobeda@gmail.com.

Popescu Berk, Adina. New Haven, CT. Affil: Yale Univ. Press. Email: alp31@columbia.edu. Research: global agricultural markets, humanitarian aid.

Popiel, Jennifer J., *St. Louis*. Email: popiel@slu.edu.

Popkin, Jeremy D., *Kentucky*. Lexington, KY. Email: popkin@uky.edu. Research: French and Haitian revolutions, history and autobiography.

Popova, Polina. Chicago, IL. Affil: Illinois, Chicago. Email: ppopov2@uic.edu.

Poppendorf, Alexandria, *Austin Peay State*. Email: poppendorfa@apsu.edu.

Popper, Nicholas, *William and Mary; Omohundro Inst*. Williamsburg, VA. Email: nspopper@wm.edu. Research: Tudor-Stuart England, early modern European intellectual.

Pore, William Franklin. Pusan, South Korea. Affil: Pusan National. Email: willpore@gmail.com. Research: Confucianism, East Asian interaction.

Port, Andrew I., *Wayne State*. Ann Arbor, MI. Email: ar6647@wayne.edu. Research: modern Germany.

Porter, Abigail. Washington, DC. Email: easporter16@gmail.com.

Porter, Amy M., *Texas A&M, San Antonio*. Email: amy.porter@tamusa.edu.

Porter, David L. Oskaloosa, IA.

Porter, David. Providence, RI. Affil: Yale. Email: dcporter88@gmail.com. Research: ethnic and status identity in Qing China, language and ethnicity in Manchu empire.

Porter, Dorothy E., *California, Berkeley*. Email: dporter@itsa.ucsf.edu.

Porter, Eric, *California, Santa Cruz*. Email: ecporter@ucsc.edu.

Porter, Henry P., Jr., *Washington and Lee*. Lexington, VA. Email: porterh@wlu.edu. Research: Canada, Australia and New Zealand.

Porter, Jess, *Arkansas, Little Rock*. Email: jcporter@ualr.edu.

Porter, John R., *Saskatchewan*. Email: john.porter@usask.ca.

Porter, Jonathan, *New Mexico*. Email: jporter@unm.edu.

Porter, Kimberly K., *North Dakota*. Email: kimberly.porter@und.edu.

Porter, Matthew J. Columbus, OH. Affil: JPMorgan Chase & Co. Email: pjmbuckeyes@gmail.com.

Porter, Megan Elizabeth. Lenox, MA. Affil: Lenox Public Sch. Email: mporter@lenoxps.org.

Porter, Shannon. Ambler, PA. Affil: American. Email: sp8863a@american.edu.

Porter, Stephen R., *Cincinnati*. Email: stephen.porter@uc.edu.

Porter, Susan L. Brookline, MA. Affil: Brandeis Women Studies Research Center. Email: sphistorian@comcast.net. Research: orphans/child welfare/adoption, museums/oral history/women.

Porter, Susie S., *Utah*. Email: s.porter@utah.edu.

Porter, Theodore M., *UCLA*. Los Angeles, CA. Email: tporter@history.ucla.edu. Research: state institutions and human heredity, statistics and quantification.

Porter, Thomas E., *North Carolina A&T State*. Email: portert@ncat.edu.

Porter-Szucs, Brian A., *Michigan, Ann Arbor*. Email: baporter@umich.edu.

Portilla, Rafael Angel, Jr. Miami, FL. Affil: Florida International. Email: Rport055@fiu.edu.

Portillo Villeda, Suyapa. Claremont, CA. Affil: Pitzer. Email: suyapa_portillo@pitzer.edu. Research: gender and labor in Banana regions, Central America.

Portuondo, Maria M., *Johns Hopkins (Hist. of Science)*. Baltimore, MD. Email: mportuondo@jhu.edu. Research: early modern cosmography, early modern Spanish/Latin American science.

Porwancher, Andrew, *Oklahoma (Hist.)*. Email: porwancher@ou.edu.

Posadas, Barbara M., *Northern Illinois*. Morris, MN. Email: bposadas@niu.edu; barbaraposadas@comcast.net. Research: Filipino immigration, Filipino American ethnicity.

Posillico, Ailie Margot. Cambridge, MA. Affil: Harvard Divinity Sch. Email: Aposillico@hds.harvard.edu.

Poska, Allyson M., *Mary Washington*. Fredericksburg, VA. Email: aposka@umw.edu. Research: early modern Spain, early modern women.

Posnansky, Merrick, *UCLA*. Email: merrick@history.ucla.edu.

Pospisek, Patrick Allan, *Grand Valley State*. Email: pospisep@gvsu.edu.

Postel, Charles. Oakland, CA. Affil: San Francisco State. Email: postel@sfsu.edu. Research: populism 1886-96, politics/labor/social protest.

Poster, Alexander O., *US Dept. of State*.

Poston, Brook, *Stephen F. Austin State*. Email: postonb@sfasu.edu.

Poston, Ken, *Lamar*. Email: kposton@lamar.edu.

Potamianos, *George*. Arcata, CA. Affil: Redwoods. Email: george-potamianos@ redwoods.edu. Research: film, cultural studies.

Potter, *Claire Bond*, *New School*. New York, NY. Email: potterc@newschool.edu. Research: 20th-c political culture, sex/gender/state.

Potter, *Edmund D*. Waynesboro, VA. Affil: Mary Baldwin. Email: edmunddpotter@gmail.com. Research: WWI and British interwar housing, technology.

Potter, *Pamela M*. Madison, WI. Affil: Wisconsin, Madison. Email: pmpotter@wisc.edu. Research: musical life in 20th-c Berlin, Nazi aesthetics and cultural policy.

Potter, *Sarah E.*, *Memphis*. Email: spotter1@ memphis.edu.

Potthast, *David R*. Hartford, WI. Email: lcdrdave4-5476@charter.net. Research: Great War and modernism, early Christian church.

Potts, **Louis W.**, *Missouri–Kansas City*.

Potts, **Susan**. Stirling, NJ. Email: pandors1@aol. com.

Poulin, **Joseph-Claude**, *Montréal*. Email: joseph-claude.poulin@umontreal.ca.

Poulson, **Susan**, *Scranton*. Email: susan. poulson@scranton.edu.

Powell, *Carolyn*. Monterey, TN. Affil: Volunteer State Comm. Coll. Email: carolyn.powell@ volstate.edu. Research: US.

Powell, **Jeffrey N.**, *Oakland*. Email: powell2@ oakland.edu.

Powell, **Julie M**. Columbus, OH. Affil: Ohio State. Email: jamc8383@gmail.com.

Powell, **Laura**. Albuquerque, NM. Affil: New Mexico. Email: Lpowel5@unm.edu.

Powell, **Lawrence N.**, *Tulane*. Email: powell@ tulane.edu.

Powell, *Peter J*. Chicago, IL. Affil: St. Augustine's House.

Powell, *Sallie*. Lexington, KY. Affil: Kentucky. Email: sallie.powell@eku.edu. Research: race and women, sports.

Powell, *Stephen George*. Somerset, NJ. Affil: Rutgers. Email: spowell86@me.com. Research: transportation, climate change.

Powell, *Stephen*. Greenwich, CT. Affil: Mississippi State. Email: srp343@msstate.edu.

Power, *Margaret M*. Chicago, IL. Affil: Illinois Inst. of Tech. Email: power@iit.edu. Research: Puerto Rican nationalist party, post-WWII right in Latin America.

Power-Greene, **Ousmane K.**, *Clark*. Email: opowergreene@clarku.edu.

Powers, *Amy Godfrey*. DeKalb, IL. Affil: Waubonsee Comm. Coll. Email: apowers@ waubonsee.edu. Research: benevolent societies in New York City, prostitution regulation.

Powers, **Bernard E.**, **Jr.**, *Charleston*. Email: powersb@cofc.edu.

Powers, **Bill**, *Houston-Clear Lake*. Email: powers@uhcl.edu.

Powers, **David S.**, *Cornell*. Email: dsp4@cornell. edu.

Powers, *James F.*, *Holy Cross*. Worcester, MA. Email: jpowers@holycross.edu. Research: Luso-Hispanic municipal law 1000-1300, military art representations 1000-1300.

Powers, **John C.**, *Virginia Commonwealth*. Email: jcpowers@vcu.edu.

Powers, **Richard Gid**, *Graduate Center, CUNY; Staten Island, CUNY*. Email: rgpsi@earthlink. net.

Pownall, **Frances S.**, *Alberta*. Email: frances. pownall@ualberta.ca.

Poyet, **Julia**, *Québec, Montréal*. Email: poyet. julia@uqam.ca.

Pozefsky, **Peter C.**, *Wooster*. Email: ppozefsky@ wooster.edu.

Prado, *Fabricio*, *William and Mary*. Williamsburg, VA. Email: fpprado@wm.edu. Research: colonialism and sovereignty, contraband trade and corruption.

Prados-Torreira, *Teresa*. Chicago, IL. Affil: Columbia Coll., Chicago. Email: tprados-torreira@colum.edu. Research: 19th-c Cuban women.

Prager, *Stan L*. East Longmeadow, MA. Email: stan@gogeeks.com.

Pragoff, *Edward Scott*. Warreton, VA. Affil: Highland Sch. Email: spragoff@ highlandschool.org.

Prakash, *Archana G*. Berkeley, CA. Affil: California, Berkeley. Email: archanaprakash@ berkeley.edu. Research: 19th-c education.

Prakash, *Gyan*, *Princeton*. Princeton, NJ. Email: prakash@princeton.edu. Research: modern India.

Prall, **Stuart E.**, *Queens, CUNY*.

Prange, *Sebastian R.*, *British Columbia*. Vancouver, BC, Canada. Email: s.prange@ ubc.ca; s.prange@gmail.com. Research: trade networks in medieval South India, piracy in premodern Indian Ocean.

Pranger, *Gary K*. Broken Arrow, OK. Affil: Oral Roberts. Email: gpranger@oru.edu. Research: American home missionary in Midwest, evangelicals and Charismatics and society.

Prasad, *Binay*. New Delhi, India. Affil: Jawaharlal Nehru. Email: binay_jnu@outlook.com. Research: Latin American Studies, Diplomatic History.

Prasad, *Ritika*, *North Carolina, Charlotte*. Charlotte, NC. Email: rprasad2@uncc.edu. Research: South Asia, social history of technology.

Prasch, *Thomas J.*, *Washburn*. Topeka, KS. Email: tom.prasch@washburn.edu. Research: Victorian photography, international exhibitions and museums.

Pratcher, *Anthony Charles*, *II*. Philadelphia, PA. Affil: Brown. Email: pant@sas.upenn.edu.

Pratt, **Adam J.**, *Scranton*. Email: adam.pratt@ scranton.edu.

Pratt, *Bea*. Monrovia, CA. Email: bprattle@gmail. com.

Pratt, **David H.**, *Brigham Young*.

Pratt, *Dorothy O*. Carmel, IN. Affil: South Carolina, Columbia. Email: dorothypratt2@ gmail.com. Research: biography, legal changes for women.

Pratt, **Edward E.**, *Florida Atlantic*. Email: epratt2@fau.edu.

Pratt, **Joseph A.**, *Houston*. Email: joepratt@ uh.edu.

Pratt, **Robert A.**, **III**, *Georgia*. Email: rapratt@ uga.edu.

Pratt, **William C.**, *Nebraska, Omaha*. Email: bpratt@unomaha.edu.

Pratzner, *Phillip R*, *Jr*. South Riding, VA. Email: phil.pratzner@gmail.com.

Pravilova, **Ekaterina**, *Princeton*. Email: kprav@ princeton.edu.

Prazniak, **Roxann**, *Oregon*. Email: prazniak@ uoregon.edu.

Prebish, **Charles S.**, *Penn State*. Email: csp1@ psu.edu.

Preble, *Christopher A*. Washington, DC. Affil: Cato Inst. Email: cpreble@cato.org. Research: US foreign policy 1945-present, US political economy.

Premo, **Bianca**, *Florida International*. Email: premob@fiu.edu.

Prendergast, **John A.**, *La Salle*. Email: prendergastj1@lasalle.edu.

Prendergast, *Neil D.*, *Wisconsin-Stevens Point*. Email: nprender@uwsp.edu.

Prendergast, *Thomas R*. Durham, NC. Affil: Duke. Email: trprendergast@gmail.com.

Presbey, **Gail**, *Detroit Mercy*. Email: presbegm@ udmercy.edu.

Prescott, **Cynthia Culver**, *North Dakota*. Email: cynthia.prescott@und.edu.

Prescott, **Heather Munro**, *Central Connecticut State*. Email: prescott@ccsu.edu.

Presnell, *Hattie Marie*. Fayetteville, NC. Affil: Fayetteville Tech. Comm. Coll. Email: hattie.m.presnell@gmail.com. Research: disease, 16th-17th-c English social.

Press, *Steven Michael*, *Stanford*. Email: smpress@stanford.edu.

Presser, **Stephen**, *Northwestern*. Email: s-presser@northwestern.edu.

Prest, *Wilfrid R*. Adelaide, Australia. Affil: Adelaide. Email: wilfrid.prest@adelaide.edu. au. Research: early modern corruption and law, Blackstone and commentaries.

Presta, *Ana M*. Buenos Aires, Argentina. Affil: Buenos Aires. Email: presta@retina.ar. Research: colonial Charcas race/class/gender, colonial Charcas encomienda/family/work.

Prestholdt, **Jeremy G.**, *California, San Diego*. Email: jpresholdt@ucsd.edu.

Preston, *Andrew*. Cambridge, United Kingdom. Affil: Clare Coll., Cambridge. Email: amp33@ cam.ac.uk. Research: US diplomatic, US religion and politics.

Preston, **David L**, *Citadel*. Email: david.preston@ citadel.edu.

Preston, **David**, *Mary Washington*. Email: dpreston@umw.edu.

Preston, **Joseph H.**, *Grand Valley State*.

Prestwich, **Patricia E.**, *Alberta*. Email: pat. prestwich@ualberta.ca.

Prete, **Roy A.**, *Royal Military*. Email: prete-r@ rmc.ca.

Pretty, *Dave*, *Winthrop*. Rock Hill, SC. Email: prettyd@winthrop.edu. Research: city of Rome and Lazio, early medieval Italy.

Preuss, *Gene B.*, *Houston-Downtown*. Houston, TX. Email: preussg@uhd.edu. Research: Confederate monuments in Texas, US education policy 1980-2000.

Previti, *Kate House*. Rye, NH. Affil: William and Mary. Email: kchouse@email.wm.edu.

Prevost, *Elizabeth E.*, *Grinnell*. Grinnell, IA. Email: prevoste@grinnell.edu. Research: empire/ gender/religion.

Pribble, *Scott*. San Carlos, CA. Affil: San Francisco State. Email: pribb1@yahoo.com.

Price, *Anthony Lee*. Milledgeville, GA. Affil: Georgia Military. Email: tonypr42@aol.com.

Price, **Benjamin L.**, *Southeastern Louisiana*. Email: Benjamin.Price@selu.edu.

Price, **Betsey B.**, *York, Can*. Email: bprice@ glendon.yorku.ca.

Price, *Bryan D*. Santa Ana, CA. Affil: Claremont Graduate. Email: Bdaniel.price@gmail.com.

Price, David, *Vanderbilt*. Email: david.h.price@vanderbilt.edu.

Price, Delaina, *Texas, Arlington*.

Price, Don C., *California, Davis*. Email: dcprice@ucdavis.edu.

Price, Edward J., Jr. Cold Spring Harbor, NY. Email: nedprice@optionline.net.

Price, Eric R. Fort Leavenworth, KS. Affil: US Army Command Coll. Email: erprice@ku.edu. Research: US military advisory operations, US-Korean relations.

Price, Erica Anne. Phoenix, AZ. Affil: Arizona State. Email: ericaanneellis@gmail.com. Research: board games in US.

Price, George, *Montana*. Email: george.price@mso.umt.edu.

Price, Glenn W., *Sonoma State*.

Price, Jay M., *Wichita State*. Email: jay.price@wichita.edu.

Price, Lori Lyn. Winchester, MA. Affil: Harvard Extension Sch. Email: medicalrecipecollector@gmail.com. Research: medical receipt books, colonial New England social.

Price, Matthew Hunter, *Western Washington*. Email: Hunter.Price@wwu.edu.

Price, Melynda J. Lexington, KY. Email: melynda.price@uky.edu.

Price, Polly, *Emory*. Email: pprice@emory.edu.

Price, Richard S., *William and Mary*. Email: rspric@wm.edu.

Price, Richard, *Maryland, Coll. Park*. Email: rnp@umd.edu.

Price, Robert W. Spring City, PA. Affil: Eastern. Email: rprice@eastern.edu.

Priddy, Hervey A. Dallas, TX. Affil: Texas, Austin. Email: Hapriddy@aol.com. Research: energy policy.

Pride, Maria, *Salem State*. Email: mpride@salemstate.edu.

Priest, Tyler, *Iowa*. Email: tyler-priest@uiowa.edu.

Prieto, Juile Irene. Washington, DC. Affil: US Army Center of Military Hist. Email: julieprieto@gmail.com. Research: US-Mexican cultural diplomacy, international news reporting.

Prieto, Laura. Pawtucket, RI. Affil: Simmons. Email: laura.prieto@simmons.edu. Research: gender and American imperialism, visual sources.

Prifogle, Emily A. Princeton, NJ. Affil: Princeton. Email: prifogle@princeton.edu. Research: social movements, race/gender/class.

Prigge, Christopher N., *US Army Command Coll*. Email: christopher.n.prigge.mil@mail.mil.

Primmer, Andrew Thomas. Westbury, United Kingdom. Affil: Bristol. Email: andrewprimmer@gmail.com.

Prince, Carl E., *NYU*. Email: cp2@nyu.edu.

Prince, Eldred E. 'Wink', Jr., *Coastal Carolina*. Email: prince@coastal.edu.

Prince, K. Stephen, *South Florida, Tampa*. Tampa, FL. Email: ksp@usf.edu. Research: visions of South in US culture 1865-1915, New Orleans race riot 1900.

Princehouse, Patricia, *Case Western Reserve*. Email: patricia.princehouse@case.edu.

Principe, Lawrence, *Johns Hopkins (Hist. of Science)*. Email: lmafp@jhu.edu.

Printy, Michael O. New Haven, CT. Affil: Yale. Email: michael.printy@yale.edu. Research: Protestant Enlightenment, Germany.

Prior, Daniel G., *Miami, Ohio*. Email: priordg@miamioh.edu.

Prior, David Matthew, *New Mexico*.

Prior, Polly Anne. Massena, NY. Affil: Empire State Coll., SUNY. Email: polly_prior066@esc.edu. Research: Crazy Horse, fight at Little Big Horn.

Pritchard, Sara B., *Cornell*. Ithaca, NY. Email: sbp65@cornell.edu. Research: light pollution, envirotech.

Prithipaul, Kchetrepal, *Alberta*.

Prochnow, Kyle. Allston, MA. Affil: York, Can. Email: prochnow@yorku.ca.

Procter, Michael Patrick, Sr. Phoenix, AZ. Email: mpprocter@gmail.com. Research: Richard Nixon and 1968 election, Richard Nixon foreign policy initiatives.

Proctor, Alan W. Concord, MA. Affil: Middlesex Sch. Email: wallaceaproctor@gmail.com.

Proctor, Frank Trey, III, *Denison*. Granville, OH. Email: proctorf@denison.edu. Research: slave-master legal contests in Spanish America, slavery in America/Mexico as case study.

Proctor, Pat. Leavenworth, KS. Affil: Kansas State. Email: pproctor@prosimco.com. Research: domestic politics of Vietnam War, media and latter Cold War.

Proctor, Robert N., *Stanford*. Email: rproctor@stanford.edu.

Proctor, Tammy M., *Utah State*. Logan, UT. Email: Tammy.Proctor@usu.edu. Research: WWI, gender.

Profit, Elizabeth L. Arlington, VA. Affil: Chicago. Email: bethprofit@mcmaster.ca. Research: Canada, Christianity.

Prokopowicz, Gerald J., *East Carolina*. Email: prokopowiczg@ecu.edu.

Propas, Frederic, *San José State*. Email: rickpropas@comcast.net.

Propes, C. Elizabeth, *Tennessee Tech*. Email: epropes@tntech.edu.

Propp, William H. C., *California, San Diego*. Email: wpropp@ucsd.edu.

Prosser, Richard T. San Mateo, CA. Affil: Junior Statesmen Foundation. Email: richardtprosser@gmail.com. Research: 20th-c newspaper competition.

Proulx, Michael L., *North Georgia*. Email: michael.proulx@ung.edu.

Prousis, Theophilus C., *North Florida*. Email: tprousis@unf.edu.

Prout, Jerry R. Fairfax Station, VA. Affil: Marquette. Email: gerald.prout@marquette.edu. Research: historiography, capitalism.

Provence, Michael, *California, San Diego*. Email: mprovence@ucsd.edu.

Provost, Joseph. Oswego, NY. Email: jprovost@liberty.edu. Research: American Revolution, American founding.

Prude, Jonathan D., *Emory*. Atlanta, GA. Email: histjp@emory.edu. Research: American social and labor.

Pruessen, Ronald W., *Toronto*. Email: pruessen@chass.utoronto.ca.

Pruitt, Bernadette, *Sam Houston State*. Email: his_bxp@shsu.edu.

Pruitt, Keven. Santa Rosa, CA. Affil: San Francisco State. Email: kevenpruitt@gmail.com.

Pruitt, Lisa J., *Middle Tennessee State*. Email: Lisa.Pruitt@mtsu.edu.

Pruitt, Madeline Lawson. Lago Vista, TX. Affil: California, Berkeley. Email: mlpruitt@berkeley.edu.

Pruitt, Nicholas. Quincy, MA. Affil: Eastern Nazarene. Email: Nicholas.Pruitt@enc.edu. Research: 20th-c US religion, 20th-c US culture.

Prushankin, Jeffery S., *Millersville, Pa.* Email: jeffery.prushankin@millersville.edu.

Pruter, Robert, *Lewis*. Email: pruter@comcast.net.

Pryke, Kenneth G., *Windsor*. Email: p49@uwindsor.ca.

Pryor, Elizabeth Stordeur, *Smith*. Email: epryor@smith.edu.

Przybyszewski, Linda C. A., *Notre Dame*. South Bend, IN. Email: Linda.Przybyszewski.1@nd.edu. Research: US legal, 19th-c US.

Przygrodzki, Robert L. Chicago, IL. Email: rob.przy@hotmail.com. Research: Russians in Warsaw 1863-1915, 19th-c Polish masculinities.

Psilakis, Alexander. Washington, DC. Affil: American. Email: ap8701a@american.edu.

Ptacek, Crystal, *Robert H. Smith Center*. Email: cptacek@monticello.org.

Puaca, Brian M., *Christopher Newport*. Email: bpuaca@cnu.edu.

Puaca, Laura Micheletti, *Christopher Newport*. Email: laura.puaca@cnu.edu.

Puc, Krystyna. Winston Salem, NC. Affil: UNC Sch. of the Arts. Email: puck@uncsa.edu.

Pucek, Kaspar Piotr. Princeton, NJ. Affil: Princeton. Email: kpucek@princeton.edu.

Puckett, Dan J., *Troy*. Email: dpuckett45442@troy.edu.

Puckett, Jerryn Faith. Bristol, VA. Email: Jfpuckett@student.king.edu.

Pudelka, Leonard W., *Hartwick*. Email: pudelkal@hartwick.edu.

Puente, Javier. Northampton, MA. Affil: Smith. Email: jpuente@smith.edu. Research: rural/agrarian/environmental.

Puerto, Alexandra Maria, *Occidental*. Email: apuerto@oxy.edu.

Puff, Helmut, *Michigan, Ann Arbor*. Ann Arbor, MI. Email: puffh@umich.edu. Research: visual/representations of ruins, early modern Germany.

Pugach, Noel H., *New Mexico*. Email: npugach@unm.edu.

Pugach, Sara E., *California State, Los Angeles*. Email: spugach@calstatela.edu.

Pugliano, Valentina, *MIT*. Email: pugliano@mit.edu.

Pugliese, Stanislao G., *Hofstra*. Hempstead, NY. Email: stanislao.pugliese@hofstra.edu. Research: Italian anti-fascism, Italian American.

Puhle, Hans-Juergen. Frankfurt am Main, Germany. Affil: Goethe, Frankfurt. Email: Puhle@soz.uni-frankfurt.de. Research: different trajectories into modernity, democracy and democratization.

Pulido, Michael P., *Bellevue*. Bellevue, WA. Email: michael.pulido@bellevuecollege.edu; michaelpalmerpulido@gmail.com. Research: foreign broadcasting and rumor in GDR.

Pullen, Ann W. Ellis, *Kennesaw State*. Email: apullen@kennesaw.edu.

Pulliam, Sara. Annapolis, MD. Affil: George Washington. Email: spulliam@gwu.edu.

Pulliam, **William**, *Delaware*. Email: wpulliam@udel.edu.

Pulman, **Michael**, *Denver*.

Pulsipher, *Jenny Hale*, *Brigham Young*. Provo, UT. Email: jenny_pulsipher@byu.edu. Research: colonial America, indigenous America.

Pumphrey, **Clint**, *Utah State*. Email: Clint.Pumphrey@usu.edu.

Purcell, **Aaron D.**, *Virginia Tech*. Email: adp@vt.edu.

Purcell, *Allan R.*, *Austin Comm. Coll.* Austin, TX. Email: apurcell@austincc.edu. Research: Civil War, military.

Purcell, *Fernando*. Santiago, Chile. Affil: Pontificia Univ. Catolica. Email: Fpurcell@uc.cl. Research: immigration and California transnationalism, US history abroad/cinema/imperialism.

Purcell, **Jennifer J.**, *St. Michael's*. Email: jpurcell@smcvt.edu.

Purcell, *Sarah J.*, *Grinnell*. Grinnell, IA. Email: purcellsj@grinnell.edu. Research: US patriotic relics, political funerals.

Purcell, *Steven James*. Pleasant View, TN. Affil: Tennessee Coll. of Applied Tech. Email: spurc1064@gmail.com.

Purdie, *Tristie*. Merrifield, VA. Email: tristiep@gmail.com.

Purdue, *Simon*. Boston, MA. Affil: Northeastern. Email: purdue.s@husky.neu.edu.

Purdy, *Erin Lynn*. Kingsland, GA. Affil: Broward Public Library. Email: E.purdy@umiami.edu.

Purdy, *Joseph Lawrence*. Cornelius, NC. Affil: North Carolina, Charlotte. Email: Joe_purdy@yahoo.com.

Purdy, *Kristin*. Brooklyn, NY. Affil: Oxford. Email: kmpurdy@gmail.com.

Purdy, *Mike*. Seattle, WA. Email: mike@PresidentialHistory.com. Research: US presidential, presidential campaigning and elections.

Purdy, **Roger W.**, *John Carroll*. Email: rpurdy@jcu.edu.

Purificato, *David Marc*. Jacksonville, FL. Affil: SUNY, Stony Brook. Email: david.purificato@stonybrook.edu. Research: history of the book, antebellum material culture.

Purinton, *William T*. Seoul, South Korea. Affil: Seoul Theological. Email: wpurinton@gmail.com. Research: Korean War, missionaries in East Asia.

Purmont, **Jon E.**, *Southern Connecticut State*. Email: purmontj1@southernct.edu.

Purnell, **Brian**, *Bowdoin*. Email: bpurnell@bowdoin.edu.

Purry, *Valerie*. Brandon, MS. Affil: Jackson State. Email: valerie.a.purry@jsums.edu.

Pursell, **Carroll**, *Case Western Reserve*.

Purushotham, **Sunil**, *Fairfield*. Fairfield, CT. Email: spurushotham@fairfield.edu. Research: South Asia, decolonization.

Purvis, *Larry*. Greenwood, IN. Email: larrydpurvis@hotmail.com. Research: Senator Sheridan Downey of California, WWII Pacific Theater.

Puskar-Pasewicz, *Margaret*. Pittsburgh, PA. Affil: MargaretEdits. Email: margaret@margaretedits.com. Research: 19th-c vegetarianism, food.

Putman, **John C.**, *San Diego State*. Email: putman@sdsu.edu.

Putnam, **Jackson K.**, *California State, Fullerton*. Email: jputnam@fullerton.edu.

Putnam, *Lara E.*, *Pittsburgh*. Pittsburgh, PA. Email: lep12@pitt.edu. Research: Caribbean migration, Gender and mobility.

Putney, *Clifford W.*, *Bentley*. Somerville, MA. Email: cputney@bentley.edu. Research: modern US.

Putney, *Diane T*. Alexandria, VA. Affil: US Dept. of Defense. Email: dtp123@verizon.net. Research: Civil War and memory.

Pycior, **Helena M.**, *Wisconsin-Milwaukee*. Email: helena@uwm.edu.

Pycior, **Julie L.**, *Manhattan*. Email: julie.pycior@manhattan.edu.

Pyee, **Audrey**, *York, Can.* Email: apyee@yorku.ca.

Pyenson, **Lewis Robert**, *Western Michigan*. Email: lewis.pyenson@wmich.edu.

Pyka, *Marcus*. Sorengo-lugano, Switzerland. Affil: Franklin, Switzerland. Email: mpyka@fus.edu. Research: 19th-/20th-c bourgeoisie, modern Jewish identities.

Pyle, *Cynthia M*. New York, NY. Email: c.m.pyle@nyu.edu.

Pyle, **Kenneth B.**, *Washington, Seattle*. Email: kbp@uw.edu.

Pyne, *John M*. Palm Beach Gardens, FL. Email: jpynejip@mac.com. Research: Wilson era, slavery in Age of Revolution.

Pyne, **Stephen J.**, *Arizona State*. Email: stephen.pyne@asu.edu.

Pyron, **Darden A.**, *Florida International*. Email: pyrond@fiu.edu.

Pytell, *Timothy E.*, *California State, San Bernardino*. Email: tpytell@csusb.edu.

Q q

Qian, *Qichen*. New York City, NY. Affil: Columbia. Email: qq2109@columbia.edu.

Qiao, **Zhijian**, *Amherst*. Email: gqiao@amherst.edu.

Qin, **Yucheng**, *Hawai'i, Hilo*. Email: ycqin@hawaii.edu.

Quadri, **Syed Junaid**, *Illinois, Chicago*. Email: jquadri@uic.edu.

Quale-Leach, *G. Robina*. Albion, MI. Affil: Albion. Email: rleach@albion.edu.

Qualls, **Karl D.**, *Dickinson*. Email: quallsk@dickinson.edu.

Quam-Wickham, *Nancy L.*, *California State, Long Beach*. Long Beach, CA. Email: nancy.quam-wickham@csulb.edu. Research: US West and California, labor.

Quataert, *Jean H.*, *Binghamton, SUNY*. Binghamton, NY. Email: profquat@binghamton.edu. Research: human rights, gender and transnational.

Quealy, *Gerit*. New York, NY. Affil: A&E; Huffington Post. Email: MissGQ@aol.com.

Queen, **Sarah A.**, *Connecticut Coll.* Email: saque@conncoll.edu.

Questier, **Michael**, *Vanderbilt*. Email: michael.questier@vanderbilt.edu.

Quezada-Grant, **Autumn Lee**, *Roger Williams*. Email: aquezada-grant@rwu.edu.

Quigley, *David*, *Boston Coll.* Chestnut Hill, MA. Email: david.quigley@bc.edu. Research: US political and cultural.

Quigley, **Paul D.**, *Virginia Tech*. Email: pquigley@vt.edu.

Quijano, **Carolyn Janice**. New York, NY. Affil: Columbia. Email: cjq2101@columbia.edu.

Quinlan, **Paul D.**, *Providence*. Email: pquinlan@providence.edu.

Quinlan, **Sean M.**, *Idaho*. Email: quinlan@uidaho.edu.

Quinn, **Dermot A.**, *Seton Hall*. Email: dermot.quinn@shu.edu.

Quinn, **Edythe Ann**, *Hartwick*. Email: quinne@hartwick.edu.

Quinn, **James T.**, *Xavier, Ohio*. Email: quinnj9@xavier.edu.

Quinn, **Kathleen**, *Northern Kentucky*. Email: quinnka@nku.edu.

Quinn, *Mary Ann*. Tarrytown, NY. Affil: Rockefeller Archive Center. Email: mquinn@rockarch.org. Research: archives.

Quinney, *Kimber M.*, *California State, San Marcos*. San Marcos, CA. Email: kquinney@csusm.edu. Research: US foreign policy/ethnic identity, Italian Americans and anti-fascism.

Quinones, *Julian Dario*. Lakewood, CA. Email: tutormeq@gmail.com.

Quintana, **Alejandro**, *St. John's, NY*. Email: quintana@stjohns.edu.

Quintanilla, *Linda J*. Austin, TX. Email: ljquintanilla@sbcglobal.net. Research: immigration, Mexican American/Texas.

Quirin, *James*. Nashville, TN. Affil: Fisk. Email: jquirin@fisk.edu. Research: Ethiopia, northwest Ethiopian socioethnic.

Quirk, *Charles E.*, *Northern Iowa*.

Quirke, *Carol*. Brooklyn, NY. Affil: SUNY, Coll. Old Westbury. Email: quirkec@oldwestbury.edu. Research: news photography and media, labor.

Quiros, **Ansley**, *North Alabama*. Email: aquiros@una.edu.

Quiroz, **Anthony**, *Texas A&M, Corpus Christi*. Email: anthony.quiroz@tamucc.edu.

Quist, **John W.**, *Shippensburg*. Email: jwquis@ship.edu.

Quitt, **Martin H.**, *Massachusetts, Boston*. Email: martin.quitt@umb.edu.

Quraishi, *Uzma*, *Sam Houston State*. Huntsville, TX. Email: uxq001@shsu.edu; uquraishi13@gmail.com. Research: immigration, US and South Asia.

Qureshi, *Lubna Z*. Stockholm, Sweden. Email: lubnaqureshi1974@gmail.com. Research: US/Europe, Cold War.

R r

Raab, **Nigel A.**, *Loyola Marymount*. Email: nraab@lmu.edu.

Raaflaub, **Kurt**, *Brown*. Email: Kurt_Raaflaub@Brown.edu.

Rabb, **Insitar**, *Harvard (Hist.)*. Email: irabb@law.harvard.edu.

Rabe, *Stephen G*. Salem, OR. Affil: Texas, Dallas. Email: rabe@utdallas.edu.

Rabe, *Susan A*. Chicago, IL. Affil: North Park. Email: srabe@northpark.edu. Research: religion and politics in Middle Ages, comparative Muslim-Jewish-Christian.

Rabidou, *Ronald Ernest*. Bennington, VT. Affil: SUNY, Albany. Email: rrabidou@comcast.net.

Rabig, *Julia A.*, *Dartmouth*. Norwich, VT. Email: julia.rabig@dartmouth.edu; julia.rabig@gmail.com. Research: Newark NJ, community development corporations.

Rabin, **Dana**, *Illinois, Urbana-Champaign.* Urbana, IL. Email: drabin@illinois.edu. Research: Great Britain/nation/race, 18th-c empire.

Rabin, **Shari Lisa**, *Charleston.* Charleston, SC. Email: rabinsl@cofc.edu. Research: 19th-c Judaism, geographic mobility.

Rabin, **Sheila J.**, *St. Peter's.* Email: srabin@saintpeters.edu.

Rabinbach, **Anson G.** Princeton, NJ. Affil: Princeton. Email: rabin@princeton.edu. Research: German intellectual and cultural, fascism and antifascism.

Rabinovitch-Fox, **Einav**. Shaker Heights, OH. Affil: Case Western Reserve. Email: erf256@nyu.edu. Research: 20th-c US popular culture, early 20th-c women's fashions.

Rabinowitch, **Alexander**, *Indiana.* Bloomington, IN. Email: arabinow@indiana.edu.

Rabinowitz, **Richard**. Brooklyn, NY. Affil: American Hist. Workshop. Email: rrahw@earthlink.net. Research: museums and public engagement, slavery.

Rabitoy, **Neil**, *California State, Los Angeles.*

Rabkin, **Yakov**, *Montréal.* Email: yakov.rabkin@umontreal.ca.

Rable, **George C.**, *Alabama, Tuscaloosa.* Email: grable@ua.edu.

Raby, **David L.**, *Toronto.*

Raby, **Megan M.**, *Texas, Austin.* Austin, TX. Email: meganraby@austin.utexas.edu. Research: science, environment.

Racel, **Masako N.**, *Kennesaw State.* Email: mracel@kennesaw.edu.

Racheotes, **Nicholas S.**, *Framingham State.* Brighton, MA. Email: nracheotes@framingham.edu; nsracheotes@comcast.net. Research: disabled in Russia and USSR, Russian thought.

Rachleff, **Peter J.**, *Macalester; Metropolitan State.* Email: rachleff@macalester.edu; peter.rachleff@metrostate.edu.

Racine, **Karen**, *Guelph.* Guelph, ON, Canada. Email: kracine@uoguelph.ca. Research: Latin American independence, patriotic culture/citizenship/liberty.

Rackmales, **Robert**. Belfast, ME. Email: rrackmales@gmail.com. Research: thought of Isaiah Berlin.

Radcliff, **Pamela B.**, *California, San Diego.* La Jolla, CA. Email: pradcliff@ucsd.edu. Research: 19th-/20th-c Spanish politics/culture, post-1800 France and Italy.

Radding, **Charles M.** Chicago, IL. Affil: Michigan State. Email: radding@msu.edu. Research: 11th-/12th-c European culture, origin of universities.

Radding, **Cynthia**, *North Carolina, Chapel Hill.* Chapel Hill, NC. Email: radding@email.unc.edu. Research: northwestern Mexico, eastern lowland Bolivia.

Rademacher, **Christian E.** Chicago, IL. Affil: Museum of Science and Industry Chicago. Email: cerademacher@yahoo.com.

Rademacher, **Nicholas**. Radnor, PA. Affil: Cabrini. Email: nr725@cabrini.edu.

Rader, **Benjamin G.**, *Nebraska, Lincoln.* Email: brader1@unl.edu.

Rader, **Karen A.**, *Virginia Commonwealth.* Richmond, VA. Email: karader@vcu.edu. Research: American science museums, 20th-c biology.

Radesky, **Caroline Elizabeth**, *Iowa.* Iowa City, IA. Email: caroline-radesky@uiowa.edu. Research: queer history, history and memory.

Radford, **Gail E.**, *SUNY, Buffalo.* Buffalo, NY. Email: radford@buffalo.edu. Research: 20th-c US, political.

Radforth, **Ian W.**, *Toronto.* Email: i.radforth@utoronto.ca.

Radice, **Thomas A.**, *Southern Connecticut State.* Email: radicet1@southernct.edu.

Radner, **Robin**. Marlborough, MA. Affil: Boston Coll. Email: rradner@robinradner.com.

Radwanski, **Kyle**. Vista, CA. Email: k.piper99@gmail.com.

Radway, **Robyn Dora**. Budapest, Hungary. Affil: Central European. Email: radwayr@ceu.edu. Research: Habsburg Vienna, Ottoman Hungary.

Raeburn, **Bruce Boyd**, *Tulane.* Email: raeburn@tulane.edu.

Raeburn, **Gabriel**. Philadelphia, PA. Affil: Pennsylvania. Email: raeburn@sas.upenn.edu.

Rael, **Patrick J.**, *Bowdoin.* Email: prael@bowdoin.edu.

Rafael, **Vicente L.**, *Washington, Seattle.* Email: vrafael@uw.edu.

Rafeq, **Abdul-Karim**, *William and Mary.* Email: akrafe@wm.edu.

Raff, **Daniel**, *Pennsylvania.* Philadelphia, PA. Email: raff@wharton.upenn.edu. Research: book trade in America, evolutionary business.

Raffensperger, **Christian A.**, *Wittenberg.* Springfield, OH. Email: craffensperger@wittenberg.edu. Research: royal kinship and feud, medieval Europe.

Rafferty, **Oliver P.**, **SJ**, *Boston Coll.* Email: oliver.rafferty@bc.edu.

Raffety, **Matthew Taylor**. Redlands, CA. Affil: Redlands. Email: matthew_raffety@redlands.edu. Research: US maritime, US legal and labor.

Rafuse, **Ethan S.**, *US Army Command Coll.* Email: ethan.s.rafuse.civ@mail.mil.

Ragab, **Ahmed**, *Harvard (Hist. of Science).* Email: ahmed_ragab@harvard.edu.

Ragan, **Bryant T.**, **Jr.**, *Colorado Coll.* Colorado Springs, CO. Email: bragan@coloradocollege.edu. Research: early modern Europe, gender and sexuality.

Ragan, **Elizabeth A.**, *Salisbury.* Email: earagan@salisbury.edu.

Ragans, **Aaron**. Lawrenceville, GA. Affil: Georgia Gwinnett. Email: aaronragans@gmail.com.

Ragland, **Evan R.**, *Notre Dame.* Notre Dame, IN. Email: eragland@nd.edu. Research: experimentation and learned medicine, emergence of normative experimentation.

Ragosta, **John A.**, *Robert H. Smith Center.* Charlottesville, VA. Email: jragosta@monticello.org; ragostas@comcast.net. Research: American Revolution/religious freedom, early national.

Ragsdale, **Hugh A.**, **Jr.** Charlottesville, VA.

Ragsdale, **Kathryn**, *California, Irvine.* Email: kragsdal@uci.edu.

Rahe, **Paul**, *Hillsdale.* Email: prahe@hillsdale.edu.

Rahman, **M. Raisur**, *Wake Forest.* Email: rahmanmr@wfu.edu.

Rahmeier, **Tyson Dwight**. Austin, TX. Affil: ACE Academy. Email: trahmeier@austingifted.org.

Raianu, **Mircea Constantin**, *Maryland, Coll. Park.* Email: mraianu@umd.edu.

Raibmon, **Paige**, *British Columbia.* Email: praibmon@mail.ubc.ca.

Raider, **Mark A.**, *Cincinnati.* Cincinnati, OH. Email: raiderma@uc.edu. Research: modern Jewish, American culture.

Railton, **Benjamin A.** Waltham, MA. Affil: Fitchburg State. Email: brailton@fitchburgstate.edu.

Raimo, **John Duke**. New York, NY. Affil: NYU. Email: john.raimo@nyu.edu.

Rainer, **Todd Douglas**. Humble, TX. Affil: Lone Star. Email: todddrainer@gmail.com. Research: human trafficking, rise of fascism.

Raines, **Edgar Frank**, **Jr.** Alexandria, VA. Affil: Office of the Chairman, Joint Chiefs of Staff. Email: rainesedandbecky@verizon.net. Research: invasion of Iraq 2003, J. Franklin Bell.

Rakove, **Jack N.**, *Stanford.* Stanford, CA. Email: rakove@stanford.edu. Research: American Revolution, early American political.

Raleigh, **Donald J.**, *North Carolina, Chapel Hill.* Chapel Hill, NC. Email: djr@email.unc.edu. Research: 20th-c Russia, post-1945 oral.

Ralph, **James R.**, **Jr.**, *Middlebury.* Email: ralph@middlebury.edu.

Ramage, **James A.**, *Northern Kentucky.* Email: ramage@nku.edu.

Ramalingam, **Chitra**, *Yale.* Email: chitra.ramalingam@yale.edu.

Ramambason, **Laurent**. Dunedin, FL. Affil: Antananarivo. Email: lwramambason@yahoo.com. Research: Madagascar mission, historical knowledge.

Raman, **Bhavani**, *Toronto.* Email: bhavani.raman@utoronto.ca.

Raman, **Sita A.**, *Santa Clara.* Email: sraman@scu.edu.

Ramaswamy, **Sumathi**, *Duke.* Email: sr76@duke.edu.

Ramberg, **Peter**, *Truman State.* Email: ramberg@truman.edu.

Ramer, **Samuel C.**, *Tulane.* Email: ramer@tulane.edu.

Ramet, **Sabrina Petra**. Trondheim, Norway. Affil: Norwegian Univ. of Sci. and Tech. Email: sabrina.ramet@ntnu.no.

Ramey, **Jessie B.** Pittsburgh, PA. Affil: Chatham. Email: jessie.b.ramey@gmail.com.

Ramey, **Michael Lee**. Fleming Island, FL. Email: rameymichael8@gmail.com. Research: causes of the War of 1812, early American political ideology.

Ramey, **Michael**. Pasadena, TX. Affil: Houston Comm. Coll. Northwest. Email: michael.ramey@hccs.edu.

Ramge, **James L.** Bowling Green, KY. Affil: Southern New Hampshire. Email: jlramge@yahoo.com. Research: Civil War prisons/Andersonville Prison, prisoners of Civil War.

Ramgopal, **Sailakshmi**, *Columbia (Hist.).* Email: sr3658@columbia.edu.

Ramirez, **Antonio**. Elgin, IL. Affil: Elgin Comm. Coll. Email: anramirez@elgin.edu.

Ramirez, **Bruno**, *Montréal.* Email: bruno.ramirez@umontreal.ca.

Ramirez, **Emilee**. San Marcos, CA. Affil: California State, San Marcos. Email: ramir205@cougars.csusm.edu.

Ramirez, **Marla Andrea**, *Wisconsin-Madison.* Email: ramireztahua@wisc.edu.

Ramirez, **Paul F.**, *Northwestern.* Email: pramirez@northwestern.edu.

Ramirez, **Susan E.**, *Texas Christian*. Fort Worth, TX. Email: s.ramirez@tcu.edu. Research: colonial Latin America, Inca civilization.

Ramirez, **Sylvia**. San Marcos, CA. Affil: California State, San Marcos. Email: ramir301@cougars. csusm.edu.

Ramirez, **Yuridia**. Champaign, IL. Affil: Illinois, Urbana-Champaign. Email: yuri.ramirez89@gmail.com.

Ramírez, **Daniel**, *American Soc. of Church Hist.* Email: dramire@umich.edu.

Ramirez-Shkwegnaabi, **Benjamin**, *Central Michigan*. Email: ramir1b@cmich.edu.

Ramold, **Steven J.**, *Eastern Michigan*. Email: sramold@emich.edu.

Ramos, **Christina**, *Washington, St. Louis*. Email: christina.ramos@wustl.edu.

Ramos, **Donald**, *Cleveland State*. Email: d.ramos@csuohio.edu.

Ramos, **Frances L.**, *South Florida, Tampa*. Tampa, FL. Email: framos@usf.edu. Research: Mexican cultural and social, colonial Puebla political culture.

Ramos, **Gabriela P.** Cambridge, United Kingdom. Affil: Cambridge. Email: gr266@cam.ac.uk. Research: Andean colonial, Andean national period.

Ramos, **Nic John**. Pawtucket, RI. Affil: Brown. Email: ramos.nic@gmail.com.

Ramos, **Raúl A.**, *Houston*. Houston, TX. Email: raramos@uh.edu; josiedog@gmail.com. Research: 19th-c US-Mexico border, transnational identity construction.

Ramos Scharrón, **Carlos E.**, *Texas, Austin*. Email: cramos@austin.utexas.edu.

Rampling, **Jennifer M.**, *Princeton*. Email: rampling@princeton.edu.

Ramsdell, **Ted**. Warner Robins, GA. Affil: Georgia Military. Email: tramsdel@gmc.cc.ga.us.

Ramsey, **Kate**, *Miami*. Miami, FL. Email: kramsey@miami.edu.

Ramsey, **Matthew**, *Vanderbilt*. Email: matthew. ramsey@vanderbilt.edu.

Ramsey, **Michael G. L.** Barbourville, KY. Affil: Union Coll. Email: ramseymgl@yahoo.com.

Ramsey, **Ragan**. Columbia, SC. Email: rvramsey92@gmail.com.

Ramsey, **Sonya Y.**, *North Carolina, Charlotte*. Email: sramse17@uncc.edu.

Ramsey, **William Little**, **III**, *Lander*. Email: wramsey@lander.edu.

Ramusack, **Barbara N.**, *Cincinnati*. Cincinnati, OH. Email: ramusabn@ucmail.uc.edu. Research: maternal and infant welfare, princely elites as politicians.

Rana, **Aziz**, *Cornell*. Email: ar643@cornell.edu.

Rand, **Jacki T.**, *Iowa*. Email: jacki-rand@uiowa. edu.

Rand, **Lisa Ruth**. Madison, WI. Affil: Wisconsin, Madison. Email: lrrand@wisc.edu.

Rand, **Tamara S.**, *Baldwin Wallace*. Email: trand@bw.edu.

Randaccio, **Susan Clark**, *SUNY, Buffalo State*. Email: randacsc@buffalostate.edu.

Randall, **Amy E.**, *Santa Clara*. Email: arandall@scu.edu.

Randall, **Stephen J.**, *Calgary*. Email: srandall@ucalgary.ca.

Randolph, **John W.**, **Jr.**, *Illinois, Urbana-Champaign*. Urbana, IL. Email: jwr@illinois. edu. Research: communications, Russian imperial.

Randolph, **Scott E.** Redlands, CA. Affil: Redlands. Email: scott_randolph@redlands.edu. Research: railways and state 1890-1945, 1930s work and unemployment.

Randolph, **Sherie M.**, *Georgia Inst. of Tech.* Email: sherie.randolph@hsoc.gatech.edu.

Randolph, **Stephen Patrick**, *US Air Force Acad.* Colorado Springs, CO. Email: stephen. randolph@usafa.edu; sprandolph52@gmail. com. Research: military, US presidency.

Rands, **David C.**, *Austin Peay State*. Email: randsd@apsu.edu.

Ranew, **James Joseph**. Clearwater, FL. Email: ranewj@hotmail.com.

Raney, **David Alan**, *Hillsdale*. Email: draney@hillsdale.edu.

Ranft, **Patricia**, *Central Michigan*. Email: patricia. ranft@cmich.edu.

Rankin, **Alisha**. Medford, MA. Affil: Tufts. Email: alisha.rankin@tufts.edu. Research: empiricism, early modern German women and pharmacy.

Rankin, **John M.**, *East Tennessee State*. Email: rankinj@etsu.edu.

Rankin, **Monica**. Richardson, TX. Affil: Texas, Dallas. Email: mrankin@utdallas.edu. Research: propaganda in Mexico during WWII, Mexican popular culture in the 1940s.

Rankin, **William J.**, *Yale*. Email: william.rankin@yale.edu.

Ranlet, **Philip**, *Hunter, CUNY*. Middle Village, NY. Email: pranlet@hunter.cuny.edu. Research: early America, American Revolution.

Ransby, **Barbara**, *Illinois, Chicago*. Chicago, IL. Email: bransby@uic.edu. Research: African American feminists, Eslanda Robeson and anti-colonialists.

Ransel, **David L.**, *Indiana*. San Jose, CA. Email: ransel@indiana.edu. Research: early modern Russian merchant families, loyalties of current Moscow-area workers.

Ransford, **Amy R.** Bloomington, IN. Affil: Indiana. Email: amypurvi@indiana.edu.

Ransmeier, **Johanna Sirera**, *Chicago*. Email: jsransmeier@uchicago.edu.

Ransohoff, **Jake Charles**. Tampa, FL. Affil: Harvard. Email: jransohoff@fas.harvard.edu. Research: corporal punishment in Byzantium, medieval Balkans.

Ransom, **Roger L.**, *California, Riverside*. Email: roger.ransom@ucr.edu.

Ranum, **Orest**, *Johns Hopkins (Hist.)*. Email: pranum@compuserve.com.

Rao, **Anupama P.**, *Barnard, Columbia*. New York, NY. Email: arao@barnard.edu. Research: citizenship, violence.

Rao, **Gautham**, *American*. Email: grao@american.edu.

Rao, **John**, *St. John's, NY*. Email: raoj@stjohns. edu.

Raphael, **Renee J.**, *California, Irvine*. Irvine, CA. Email: renee.raphael@uci.edu. Research: early modern science and technology.

Rapone, **Anita**, *SUNY, Plattsburgh*. Email: raponeaj@plattsburgh.edu.

Raposo, **Pedro M. P.** Chicago, IL. Affil: Adler Planetarium. Email: praposo@adlerplanetarium.org.

Rapp, **Dean R.**, *Wheaton, Ill.* Email: dean.rapp@wheaton.edu.

Rapp, **Stephen**, **Jr.**, *Sam Houston State*. Email: shr002@shsu.edu.

Rappaport, **Erika D.**, *California, Santa Barbara*. Santa Barbara, CA. Email: rappaport@history.ucsb.edu. Research: empire/gender/consumer culture.

Rapple, **Rory**, *Notre Dame*. Email: roryrapple220@gmail.com.

Rapson, **Richard L.**, *Hawai'i, Manoa*. Email: rapson@hawaii.edu.

Raschle, **Christian**, *Montréal*. Email: christian. raschle@umontreal.ca.

Rashid, **Ismail O. D.**, *Vassar*. Email: israshid@vassar.edu.

Rashid, **Taufiq**, *Murray State*. Email: trashid@murraystate.edu.

Rashkow, **Ezra**, *Montclair State*. Email: rashkowe@mail.montclair.edu.

Rasico, **Patrick D.** Nashville, TN. Affil: Vanderbilt. Email: prasico@gmail.com. Research: British Empire, colonial India.

Raska, **Francis D.** Prague, Czech Republic. Affil: Charles. Email: francisraska@gmail.com. Research: Czechoslovak Cold War-era exile, 1960s-70s US radicalism.

Raskin, **Stephen L.** Miami, FL. Email: steveraskin9644@gmail.com.

Rasmussen, **Joel David Stormo**. Hollis, NH. Affil: Oxford. Email: joel.rasmussen@mansfield. ox.ac.uk. Research: 19th-c Christian thought.

Rasmussen, **Kathleen Britt**, *US Dept. of State*.

Rasmussen, **William M. S.**, *Virginia Museum of Hist.* Email: wrasmussen@VirginiaHistory.org.

Rasporich, **Anthony W.**, *Calgary*. Email: awraspor@ucalgary.ca.

Rast, **Lawrence R.** Fort Wayne, IN. Affil: Concordia Theological Seminary. Email: lawrence.rast@ctsfw.edu. Research: Lutheranism in post-1970 US, Dispensational premillennialism to 1900.

Ratchford, **Jamal**, *Colorado Coll.* Email: jratchford@coloradocollege.edu.

Rath, **Eric C.**, *Kansas*. Email: erath@ku.edu.

Rath, **Richard C.**, *Hawai'i, Manoa*. Honolulu, HI. Email: rrath@hawaii.edu. Research: sound and media, digital humainties.

Rathbone, **Keith**. Medina, OH. Affil: Macquarie. Email: keithrathbone7@gmail.com. Research: modern France, sport.

Ratliff, **Thomas**, *Central Connecticut State*. Email: ratlifft@ccsu.edu.

Ratner-Rosenhagen, **Jennifer**, *Wisconsin-Madison*. Madison, WI. Email: ratnerrosenh@wisc.edu. Research: US cultural and intellectual.

Rau, **Erik P.**, *Hagley Museum and Library*. Wilmington, DE. Email: erau@hagley.org. Research: US political culture, postcolonial development.

Rauch, **Alan**. Charlotte, NC. Affil: North Carolina, Charlotte. Email: arauch@uncc.edu. Research: private subscription libraries in UK, science/encyclopedias/codification of knowledge.

Rauchway, **Eric**, *California, Davis*. Davis, CA. Email: earauchway@ucdavis.edu. Research: New Deal and WWII.

Raun, **Toivo U.**, *Indiana*. Email: raunt@indiana. edu.

Rausch, **Franklin David**, *Lander*. Email: fdrausch@hotmail.com.

Rausch, **Jane M.**, *Massachusetts, Amherst*. Amherst, MA. Email: jrausch@history.umass. edu. Research: Latin America, Colombia.

Ravel, **Jeffrey S.**, *MIT*. Cambridge, MA. Email: ravel@mit.edu. Research: 17th-19th-c Europe, France.

Ravina, **Mark**, *Emory*. Email: histmr@emory.edu.

Ravitch, Norman, *California, Riverside.*
Rawat, Ramnarayan S., *Delaware.* Email: rawat@udel.edu.
Rawski, Evelyn S., *Pittsburgh.* Email: esrx@pitt. edu.
Rawson, Don C., *Iowa State.*
Rawson, Kathryn. Cape Town, South Africa. Affil: Cape Town. Email: kathrawson@gmail.com.
Rawson, Michael J., *Brooklyn, CUNY; Graduate Center, CUNY.* Harrison, NY. Email: mrawson@ brooklyn.cuny.edu. Research: urban environment, past visions of environmental future.
Ray, Aaron. Kearney, NE. Email: stinger2011@ hotmail.com.
Ray, Amanda. La Valle, WI. Affil: British Columbia. Email: ray.amandae@gmail.com.
Ray, Bidisha, *Simon Fraser.* Email: bray@sfu.ca.
Ray, Carina E., *Brandeis.* Email: cer15@brandeis. edu.
Ray, Daren E., *Auburn.* Email: dzr0033@auburn. edu.
Ray, Donna E., *New Mexico.* Email: donnaray@ unm.edu.
Ray, Donna Thompson. New York, NY. Affil: Graduate Center, CUNY. Email: dthompson@ gc.cuny.edu.
Ray, Gerda W., *Missouri–St. Louis.* Email: rayg@ umsl.edu.
Ray, Jonathan S. Silver Spring, MD. Affil: Georgetown. Email: Jsr46@georgetown.edu. Research: medieval and early modern Jewish, Christian/Muslim/Jewish societies in Iberia.
Ray, Krishnendu. New York, NY. Affil: NYU. Email: krishnendu.ray@nyu.edu. Research: food, South Asia/Bengali.
Ray, Skylar. Waco, TX. Affil: Baylor. Email: Skylar_ Ray@baylor.edu. Research: 20th-c mainline Protestantism.
Raymakers, Elizabeth. Chanhassen, MN. Affil: American. Email: er8017a@american.edu.
Raymond, C. Elizabeth, *Nevada, Reno.* Email: raymond@unr.edu.
Raymond, Emilie, *Virginia Commonwealth.* Email: eeraymond@vcu.edu.
Raymond, Erik. Kamas, UT. Affil: Norwich. Email: thefreedomkids@gmail.com.
Raz, Mical, *Rochester.* Email: mical.raz@ rochester.edu.
Razlogova, Elena, *Concordia, Can.* Email: Elena. Razlogova@concordia.ca.
Rea, Kenneth W., *Louisiana Tech.* Email: rea@ latech.edu.
Read, Michael Hoppin. Rochester, NY. Affil: Rochester. Email: michaelhoppinread@gmail. com.
Reagan, John. Chagrin Falls, OH. Email: j.f.reagan71@vikes.csuohio.edu.
Reagan, Leslie J., *Illinois, Urbana-Champaign.* Email: lreagan@illinois.edu.
Reagan, Paul Brenton John. Philadelphia, PA. Affil: Temple. Email: paul.reagan@temple.edu.
Reagin, Nancy R., *Pace.* Email: nreagin@aol. com.
Reagon, Bernice Johnson, *American.* Email: breagon@aol.com.
Reames, Jeanne, *Nebraska, Omaha.* Email: mreames@unomaha.edu.
Reardon, Carol, *Penn State.* Email: car9@psu. edu.
Reardon, Erik, *Colby.* Email: erik.reardon@colby. edu.

Reardon, John J., *Loyola, Chicago.* Email: jjreardon7@aol.com.
Reardon, Michael F., *Portland State.*
Rearick, Charles, *Massachusetts, Amherst.* Email: rearick@history.umass.edu.
Reason, Akela, *Georgia.* Email: areason@uga. edu.
Reaume, Geoffrey Francis, *York, Can.* Email: greaume@yorku.ca.
Reaves, Michaela Crawford. Thousand Oaks, CA. Affil: California Lutheran. Email: reaves@ callutheran.edu. Research: women in America, immigration.
Rebadow, Allison, *Hist. Assoc.* Email: arebadow@historyassociates.com.
Rebane, P. Peter, *Penn State.* Email: ppr1@psu. edu.
Rebel, Hermann, *Arizona.* Email: hrebel@u. arizona.edu.
Reber, Vera Blinn. Chambersburg, PA. Affil: Shippensburg. Email: vbrebe@innernet.net. Research: medicine social, Latin American economic.
Rebhorn, Marlette, *Austin Comm. Coll.* Email: mrebhorn@austincc.edu.
Rebillard, Eric, *Cornell.* Ithaca, NY. Email: er97@ cornell.edu. Research: Rome.
Rebman, Scarlett N. Bloomfield, NJ. Affil: Syracuse. Email: snrebman@syr.edu. Research: long civil rights era, war on poverty.
Rec, Agnieszka, *Massachusetts Hist. Soc.* Email: arec@masshist.org.
Reckard, Matthew. Ester, AK. Affil: MKR Design. Email: mkreckard@yahoo.com.
Rector, John L., *Western Oregon.* Email: rectorj@ wou.edu.
Rector, Josiah J., *Houston.* Email: jjrector@ central.uh.edu.
Reda, John E., *Illinois State.* Normal, IL. Email: jreda@ilstu.edu. Research: colonial North America, Illinois and Missouri statehood process.
Redding, Kimberly A., *Carroll.* Waukesha, WI. Email: redding@carrollu.edu. Research: German expellees after WWII, memory and identity.
Redding, Sean, *Amherst.* Email: sredding@ amherst.edu.
Reddy, Sumanth, *Bowie State.* Email: sreddy@ bowiestate.edu.
Reddy, William M., *Duke.* Email: wmr@duke. edu.
Redfield, Peter W. Chapel Hill, NC. Affil: North Carolina, Chapel Hill. Email: redfield@unc. edu. Research: medical humanitarianism, nonprofit technologies.
Rediker, Marcus, *Pittsburgh.* Pittsburgh, PA. Email: red1@pitt.edu; marcusrediker@ fastmail.com. Research: Herman Melville and the motley crew.
Redkey, Elizabeth. Latham, NY. Affil: Western Governors. Email: lizzieredkey@gmail. com. Research: thoroughbred racing, horse breeding.
Redman, Emily T., *Massachusetts, Amherst.* Email: eredman@history.umass.edu.
Redman, Samuel James, *Massachusetts, Amherst.* Email: sredman@history.umass.edu.
Redmann, Michael, *Hist. New Orleans.* Email: michaelr@hnoc.org.
Reed, Bradly W., *Virginia.* Email: bwr4k@ virginia.edu.

Reed, Charles V. Chesapeake, VA. Affil: H-Net. Email: cvreed@ecsu.edu; chas.reed@gmail. com.
Reed, Christopher A., *Ohio State.* Email: reed.434@osu.edu.
Reed, Christopher Robert, *Roosevelt.* Email: creed@roosevelt.edu.
Reed, David Leon, *Bowie State.* Email: dreed@ bowiestate.edu.
Reed, Debbie. Knoxville, TN. Email: ladymyste65@me.com.
Reed, Eric S., *Western Kentucky.* Email: eric. reed@wku.edu.
Reed, Germaine M., *Georgia Inst. of Tech.*
Reed, Howard, *Connecticut, Storrs.* Email: howard.reed@uconn.edu.
Reed, James W., *Rutgers.* Email: jwr@scarletmail. rutgers.edu.
Reed, John, *Utah.* Email: john.reed@history. utah.edu.
Reed, Jordan M. Madison, NJ. Affil: Drew. Email: jreed@drew.edu. Research: American history textbooks.
Reed, Julie L., *Tennessee, Knoxville.* Email: jreed56@utk.edu.
Reed, Justin Alan. Murrieta, CA. Affil: California, Riverside. Email: jreed.history@gmail.com. Research: politics/religion/print 1685-91.
Reed, Linda L., *Houston.* Email: lreed@uh.edu.
Reed, Loretta G., *California State, Sacramento.* Email: lreed@csus.edu.
Reed, Merl E., *Georgia State.* Email: fsmer@ panther.gsu.edu.
Reed, Toure F., *Illinois State.* Email: tfreed@ilstu. edu.
Reed, Vivian. Salem, OR. Email: vreed08@wou. edu.
Reed-Anderson, Paulette. Berlin, Germany. Email: pra.forsch.berlin@gmail.com. Research: Treaty of Versailles and Weimar Republic, empire/culture/international law.
Reeder, Linda, *Missouri, Columbia.* Email: reederl@missouri.edu.
Reeder, Matt. Ithaca, NY. Affil: Cornell. Email: mizzenmatt@yahoo.com. Research: 18th- /19th-c ethnicity/social categories, testimony/ knowledge/truth.
Reeder, Tyson. Waynesboro, VA. Affil: Virginia. Email: tfr5y@virginia.edu. Research: Atlantic commerce, race and revolution.
Reemes, Dana, *California State, Fullerton.* Email: dreemes@fullerton.edu.
Rees, Amanda, *Columbus State.* Email: rees_ amanda@columbusstate.edu.
Rees, John, *National Library of Medicine.* Email: reesj@mail.nlm.nih.gov.
Rees, Jonathan, *Colorado State, Pueblo.* Pueblo, CO. Email: jonathan.rees@csupueblo.edu; drjonathanrees@gmail.com. Research: company unions, ice industry.
Reese, De Anna J., *California State, Fresno.* Email: dreese@csufresno.edu.
Reese, Roger R., *Texas A&M.* Email: rreese@ tamu.edu.
Reese, Scott Steven, *Northern Arizona.* Email: scott.reese@nau.edu.
Reese, Ty M., *North Dakota.* Email: ty.reese@ und.edu.
Reese, William John, *Wisconsin-Madison.* Madison, WI. Email: wjreese@wisc.edu. Research: American education, reform movements.

AHA members in ***bold italic***; Directory-listed affiliations in *italic*

Reeve, **Kay A.**, *Kennesaw State*. Email: kreeve@kennesaw.edu.

Reeve, **Patricia A.**, *Suffolk*. Email: preeve@suffolk.edu.

Reeve, **W. Paul**. *Utah*. Salt Lake City, UT. Email: paul.reeve@utah.edu. Research: religion/whiteness, Mormons/race.

Reeves, **A. Compton**, *Ohio*. Prescott, AZ. Email: reevesc@ohio.edu; profcr@kachina.net. Research: 14th-/15th-c England, medieval March of Wales.

Reeves, **Barbara J.**, *Virginia Tech*. Email: reeves@vt.edu.

Reeves, **Brian R.** Farmington, MO. Affil: Farmington High Sch. Email: breeves@farmington.k12.mo.us.

Reeves, **Eileen A.**, *Princeton*. Email: ereeves@princeton.edu.

Reeves, **Mark**. Chapel Hill, NC. Affil: North Carolina, Chapel Hill. Email: mlreeves@live.unc.edu. Research: anticolonial internationalism, comparative decolonization.

Reeves, **Matt**. Prairie Village, KS. Affil: Missouri, Kansas City. Email: marx93@mail.umkc.edu.

Reeves, **Rachel**. Davis, CA. Affil: California, Davis. Email: rlreeves@ucdavis.edu. Research: 18th-c England, religion.

Regal, **Brian**, *Kean*. Email: bregal@kean.edu.

Regalado, **Samuel O.**, *California State, Stanislaus*. Email: sregalado@csustan.edu.

Regan, **Amanda**. Fairfax, VA. Affil: Southern Methodist. Email: aregan2@gmu.edu. Research: US popular culture 1900-50, Sylvia of Hollywood and physical culture.

Regan, **Joe Patrick**. Norwood, MA. Email: jreganhistory@gmail.com. Research: Irish immigrants in antebellum South, Civil War Era.

Regan, **Matthew R. G.**, *US Dept. of State*.

Regan-Lefebvre, **Jennifer**, *Trinity Coll., Conn.* Email: jennifer.reganlefebvre@trincoll.edu.

Regehr, **Theodore D.**, *Saskatchewan*. Email: tregehr@ucalgary.ca.

Reger, **Gary L.**, *Trinity Coll., Conn.* Email: gary.reger@trincoll.edu.

Reger, **Jeffrey Drew**. Email: jreger@historians.org.

Reger, **William M.**, **IV**, *Illinois State*. Email: wmreger@ilstu.edu.

Regev, **Ronny**. Princeton, NJ. Affil: Hebrew, Jerusalem. Email: ronny.regev@mail.huji.ac.il. Research: 20th-c US, Hollywood and popular culture.

Register, **Woody**, *South*. Email: wregiste@sewanee.edu.

Regosin, **Elizabeth**, *St. Lawrence*. Email: eregosin@stlawu.edu.

Regouby, **Lynnette R.** Tulsa, OK. Affil: Tulsa. Email: lregouby@gmail.com. Research: life sciences/botany/plant physiology, science/medicine/technology.

Rehberger, **Dean**, *Michigan State*. Email: rehberge@msu.edu.

Reich, **Devon**, *AHA*. Washington, DC. Email: dreich@historians.org. Research: world politics and anthropoology.

Reich, **Steven A.**, *James Madison*. Email: reichsa@jmu.edu.

Reichard, **David Andrew**. Seaside, CA. Affil: California State, Monterey Bay. Email: dreichard@csumb.edu.

Reichard, **Ruth D.** Indianapolis, IN. Affil: Marian. Email: rreichar@mac.com.

Reichardt, **Eike**. Schnecksville, PA. Affil: Lehigh Carbon Comm. Coll. Email: ereichardt@lccc.edu. Research: local, military.

Reiche, **Eric G.**, *Guelph*. Email: egreiche@uoguelph.ca.

Reichman, **Henry**. Albany, CA. Affil: California State, East Bay. Email: henry.reichman@csueastbay.edu. Research: academic freedom, Communism.

Reid, **Anne M.**, *California Polytechnic State*. Altadena, CA. Email: anreid@calpoly.edu; areid@usc.edu. Research: US borderlands, California.

Reid, **Charles J.**, **Jr.** Minneapolis, MN. Affil: St. Thomas. Email: cjreid@stthomas.edu. Research: marriage and sexuality, western.

Reid, **David A.** Joliet, IL. Affil: Joliet Jr. Coll. Email: dareid64@hotmail.com. Research: science education in Protestant dissent, early Industrial Revolution scientific knowledge.

Reid, **Debra A.** Dearborn, MI. Affil: The Henry Ford. Email: debrar@thehenryford.org. Research: African Americans and rural reform, museums intellectual.

Reid, **Denisse**. Houston, TX. Affil: Harmony Sch. of Discovery. Email: denisse.r.rubio@gmail.com.

Reid, **Donald M.**, *Georgia State*. Seattle, WA. Email: dreid@gsu.edu. Research: museums/archaeology/Egyptian identity, modern Egypt cultural and intellectual.

Reid, **Donald M.**, *North Carolina, Chapel Hill*. Email: dreid1@email.unc.edu.

Reid, **John G.**, *Dalhousie; St. Mary's, Can.* Email: john.reid@smu.ca.

Reid, **John P.** Exeter, NH. Affil: NYU. Email: john.reid@nyu.edu. Research: early Republic law, fur trade law.

Reid, **Jonathan A.**, *East Carolina*. Email: reidj@ecu.edu.

Reid, **Joshua L.**, *Washington, Seattle*. Seattle, WA. Email: jlreid@uw.edu. Research: indigenous marine space, American Indian identity.

Reid, **Phillip F.** Wilmington, NC. Email: phillipfrankreid@gmail.com. Research: early modern merchant ship technology, Atlantic World maritime 1600-1800.

Reid, **Richard M.**, *Guelph*. Email: rreid@uoguelph.ca.

Reid, **Richard William**. Canberra, Australia. Affil: Australian National. Email: richard.reid@anu.edu.au.

Reid, **Robert Louis**, *Southern Indiana*. Evansville, IN. Email: rreid@usi.edu. Research: disasters, New Deal.

Reidy, **Joseph Jude**, *Kennesaw State*. Email: jjr8934@kennesaw.edu.

Reidy, **Joseph P.** Laurel, MD. Affil: Howard. Email: jreidy@howard.edu. Research: US Navy in Civil War, 19th-c southern plantations.

Reidy, **Michael S.**, *Montana State, Bozeman*. Email: mreidy@montana.edu.

Reiff, **Janice L.**, *UCLA*. Los Angeles, CA. Email: jreiff@ucla.edu. Research: 20th-c US, urban.

Reigel, **Corey W.** Wheeling, WV. Affil: West Liberty. Email: cwreigel@yahoo.com. Research: WWI in colonies, naval warfare.

Reiger, **John F.**, *Ohio*. Email: reiger@ohio.edu.

Reill, **Dominique K.**, *Miami*. Miami Beach, FL. Email: d.reill@miami.edu. Research: 19th-c southern Europe, post-WWI Europe.

Reill, **Peter H.**, *UCLA; Miami*. Email: reill@humnet.ucla.edu.

Reilly, **Benjamin James**. Pittsburgh, PA. Affil: Carnegie Mellon. Email: breilly2@qatar.cmu.edu. Research: environmental, Arab peninsula.

Reilly, **Bernard Francis**, *Villanova*. Email: bernard.reilly@villanova.edu.

Reilly, **Brandon Joseph**. Artesia, CA. Affil: UCLA. Email: brandon_reilly@hotmail.com. Research: religious difference and conflict, colonialism and literature.

Reilly, **Elizabeth Hale**. Saunderstown, RI. Email: b.reilly@cox.net.

Reilly, **J. Nolan**, *Winnipeg*.

Reilly, **John T.** Newburgh, NY. Affil: Mount St. Mary. Email: john.reilly@msmc.edu.

Reilly, **Kevin**. New York, NY. Affil: Raritan Valley. Email: kreilly1@rcn.com. Research: global racism.

Reilly, **Kimberley A.** Green Bay, WI. Affil: Wisconsin, Green Bay. Email: reillyk@uwgb.edu.

Reilly, **Michael**. Norwood, MA. Email: mwr@tommasino.com.

Reilly, **Thomas H.**, *Pepperdine*. Malibu, CA. Email: thomas.reilly@pepperdine.edu. Research: industrial reform in republican China.

Reimann, **Melanie**. Pullman, WA. Affil: Washington State, Pullman. Email: melanie.reimann@wsu.edu.

Reimers, **David**, *NYU*. Email: dr5@nyu.edu.

Reimitz, **Helmut**, *Princeton*. Princeton, NJ. Email: hreimitz@princeton.edu. Research: early medieval.

Rein, **Allison**, *Center for Hist. of Physics*. Email: arein@aip.org.

Reinburg, **Virginia**, *Boston Coll.* Chestnut Hill, MA. Email: reinburg@bc.edu. Research: early modern Europe, religious.

Reinert, **Sophus A.** Boston, MA. Affil: Harvard Business Sch. Email: sreinert@hbs.edu. Research: political economy, capitalism.

Reinert, **Stephen W.**, *Rutgers*. Email: sreinert@history.rutgers.edu.

Reinhard, **Rachel B.** Oakland, CA. Affil: California, Berkeley. Email: rreinhard@berkeley.edu. Research: Mississippi Freedom Democratic Party.

Reinhardt, **Akim D.**, *Towson*. Email: areinhardt@towson.edu.

Reinhardt, **Anne H.**, *Williams*. Email: areinhar@williams.edu.

Reinhardt, **Steven G.**, *Texas, Arlington*. Email: reinhard@uta.edu.

Reinhartz, **Dennis P.** Santa Fe, NM. Affil: Texas, Arlington. Research: 17th-/18th-c cartography, WWII Croatia.

Reinharz, **Jehuda**, *Brandeis*. Email: jreinhar@brandeis.edu.

Reininger, **Molly**. West Haven, UT. Affil: Utah State. Email: molly.reininger@aggiemail.usu.edu.

Reins, **Thomas D.**, *Chapman*. Email: reins@fullerton.edu.

Reinstatler, **William**. Saint George, KS. Email: william.reinstatler@gmail.com.

Reis, **Alberto**, **III**. Santa Rosa, CA. Email: albertoreis923@yahoo.com.

Reis, **Joao Jose**. Salvador, Bahia, Brazil. Affil: Federal da Bahia. Email: jjreisufba@gmail.com. Research: Brazil, slavery and African culture.

Reis, **Michael C.**, *Hist. Assoc.* Silver Spring, MD. Email: mreis@historyassociates.com. Research: US political, environmental.

Reisner, Philipp. Maribor, Slovenia. Affil: Heinrich Heine, Duesseldorf. Email: reisner@phil.hhu.de.

Reiss, Suzanna J., *Hawai'i, Manoa*. Email: sreiss@hawaii.edu.

Reist, Katherine K., *Pittsburgh, Johnstown*. Email: kreist@pitt.edu.

Reitan, Richard M., *Franklin & Marshall*. Email: rreitan@fandm.edu.

Reiter, Eric H., *Concordia, Can*. Email: Eric.Reiter@concordia.ca.

Reith, Louis J. Seward, NE. Email: reith.louis@gmail.com. Research: German Reformation, 19th-/20th-c Czech cultural.

Rekabtalaei, Golbarg, *Seton Hall*. Email: golbarg.rekabtalaei@shu.edu.

Relyea, Scott, *Appalachian State*. Email: relyeas@appstate.edu.

Rembis, Michael A., *SUNY, Buffalo*. Buffalo, NY. Email: marembis@buffalo.edu; mrembis@gmail.com. Research: disability, madness.

Remensnyder, Amy G., *Brown*. Email: Amy_Remensnyder@Brown.edu.

Remer, Rosalind, *Drexel*. Philadelphia, PA. Email: rr569@drexel.edu. Research: women's travel narratives, early American economy.

Remollino, Bernard James. Patterson, CA. Affil: UCLA. Email: amosremollino115@gmail.com.

Rempe, Paul L., *Carroll*. Email: prempe@carrollu.edu.

Rempel, Richard A., *McMaster*. Email: rempelr@mcmaster.ca.

Remus, Emily A., *Notre Dame*. Chicago, IL. Email: eremus@nd.edu; eremus@gmail.com. Research: capitalism, consumer society.

Remy, Jana C., *Chapman*. Email: remy@chapman.edu.

Remy, Steven P., *Brooklyn, CUNY; Graduate Center, CUNY*. Email: sremy@brooklyn.cuny.edu.

Ren, Ke, *Holy Cross*. Email: kren@holycross.edu.

Ren, Yi. Philadelphia, PA. Affil: Pennsylvania. Email: yiren@sas.upenn.edu.

Renault, Tess, *Massachusetts Hist. Soc*. Email: trenault@masshist.org.

Renda, Lex, *Wisconsin-Milwaukee*. Email: renlex@uwm.edu.

Renda, Mary A., *Mount Holyoke*. South Hadley, MA. Email: mrenda@mtholyoke.edu. Research: US imperialism in interwar years, US racism and anti-racism.

Rendina, Naomi R. Cleveland Heights, OH. Affil: Case Western Reserve. Email: naomirendina@yahoo.com.

Rendon-Ramos, Erika Rebecca. Brownsville, TX. Affil: Rice. Email: err3@rice.edu.

Rendsburg, Gary, *Rutgers*. Email: grends@jewishstudies.rutgers.edu.

Renique, Jose Luis, *Graduate Center, CUNY; Lehman, CUNY*. Email: jrenique@aol.com.

Renna, Thomas J. Saginaw, MI. Affil: Saginaw Valley State. Email: renna@svsu.edu. Research: German and American national identity, German humanism and Luther.

Renner, Marguerite. Pasadena, CA. Affil: Glendale Comm. Coll., Calif. Email: prenner@glendale.edu. Research: US women, social.

Renner, Timothy. Montclair, NJ. Affil: Montclair State. Email: rennert@mail.montclair.edu. Research: Roman Egypt, Antonine Rome.

Rennie, Robert William, *Indiana, Southeast*. Jacksonville Beach, FL. Email: robert.rennie@unf.edu. Research: modern European technology/aviation.

Reno, Edward Andrew, III, *Adelphi*. Garden City, NY. Email: ereno@adelphi.edu. Research: medieval canon law, medieval administrative practices.

Renold, Leah M., *Texas State*. Email: lr22@txstate.edu.

Rensenbrink, Greta, *Marshall*. Email: rensenbrink@marshall.edu.

Rensing, Susan M., *Wisconsin-Oshkosh*. Email: rensings@uwosh.edu.

Rensink, Brenden W., *Brigham Young*. Email: bwrensink@byu.edu.

Rentfrow, Cmdr James C. Annapolis, MD. Affil: US Naval Acad. Email: rentfrow@usna.edu; ea6jethro@comcast.net. Research: American naval.

Repousis, Angelo, *West Chester*. Email: arepousis@wcupa.edu.

Repucci, Anthony A. Newburyport, MA. Affil: Massachusetts Amherst. Email: anthonyrepucci@gmail.com. Research: Civil War contraband camps, Southern Unionists.

Resch, Robert P., *Texas A&M*. Email: rpresch@tamu.edu.

Rescher, Nicholas. Pittsburgh, PA. Affil: Pittsburgh. Email: RESCHER@PITT.EDU.

Reschly, Steven D., *Truman State*. Kirksville, MO. Email: sdr@truman.edu. Research: Amish and Mennonite, sexuality.

Resendez, Andres, *California, Davis*. Davis, CA. Email: aresendez@ucdavis.edu. Research: Indian slavery, conquest/colonialism/identity.

Reser, Anna N. Albuquerque, NM. Affil: Oklahoma. Email: areser@ou.edu.

Resis, Albert, *Northern Illinois*. Email: resis@niu.edu.

Resnick, Daniel P., *Carnegie Mellon*. Email: dr0q@andrew.cmu.edu.

Resnick, Kirsten, *California State, Dominguez Hills*. Email: kresnick@csudh.edu.

Resnikoff, Jason Zachary. New York, NY. Affil: Columbia. Email: jzr2101@columbia.edu.

Resovich, Thomas, *California State, Northridge*.

Respess, Amanda. Ypsilanti, MI. Affil: Michigan, Ann Arbor. Email: arespess@umich.edu.

Ress, Stella A., *Southern Indiana*. Email: sress@usi.edu.

Restall, Matthew B., *Penn State*. State College, PA. Email: mxr40@psu.edu. Research: colonial Yucatan, Maya religion.

Retallack, James, *Toronto*. Toronto, ON, Canada. Email: james.retallack@utoronto.ca; jamret@rogers.com. Research: elections/August Bebel, Saxony/press/antisemitism.

Retish, Aaron B., *Wayne State*. Detroit, MI. Email: aretish@wayne.edu. Research: peasantry in Russia 1914-22, Viatka Province/Russia/Udmurtiia.

Reumann, Miriam G., *Rhode Island*. Email: mreumann@uri.edu.

Reut, Jennifer. Takoma Park, MD. Affil: American Soc. of Landscape Architects. Email: jenniferreut@gmail.com. Research: American architecture and landscape, digital humanities.

Reuther, Jessica Catherine, *Ball State*. Email: jcreuther@bsu.edu.

Revel, Jacques, *NYU*. Paris, France. Affil: Centre de Recherches Historiques. Email: jr77@nyu.edu. Research: early and modern European social and cultural, historiography.

Revell, Keith D., *Florida International*. Email: revellk@fiu.edu.

Revez, Jean, *Québec, Montréal*. Email: revez.jean@uqam.ca.

Revill, Joel, *Brown*. Email: Joel_Revill@Brown.edu.

Rewers, Mario. Nashville, TN. Affil: Vanderbilt. Email: mario.rewers@vanderbilt.edu.

Reyerson, Kathryn L., *Minnesota (Hist.)*. Saint Paul, MN. Email: reyer001@umn.edu. Research: France, medieval social.

Reyes, Barbara, *New Mexico*. Email: breyes3@unm.edu.

Reyes, Marc Anthony. Kansas City, MO. Affil: Connecticut, Storrs. Email: marc.reyes@uconn.edu.

Reyes-Johnson, Carmen. San Antonio, TX. Affil: Northeast Lakeview. Email: creyesjohnson@gmail.com.

Reynard, Pierre Claude, *Western Ontario*. Email: preynard@uwo.ca.

Reynolds, Amber Thomas, *Elmhurst*. Email: amber.thomas@elmhurst.edu.

Reynolds, David, *Graduate Center, CUNY*. Email: dreynolds@gc.cuny.edu.

Reynolds, Douglas R., *Georgia State*. Email: dreynolds@gsu.edu.

Reynolds, E. Bruce, *San José State*. Email: bruce.reynolds@sjsu.edu.

Reynolds, Edward, *California, San Diego*. Email: ereynolds@ucsd.edu.

Reynolds, Elaine A. Liberty, MO. Affil: William Jewell. Email: reynoldse@william.jewell.edu. Research: policing in early modern London/England.

Reynolds, Elizabeth Joy. New York, NY. Affil: Columbia. Email: er2370@columbia.edu.

Reynolds, John F., *Texas, San Antonio*. Email: john.reynolds@utsa.edu.

Reynolds, Jonathan T., *Northern Kentucky*. Email: reynoljo@nku.edu.

Reynolds, Kenneth W., *National Defence Headquarters*. Email: ken.reynolds@forces.gc.ca.

Reynolds, Luke A. L. Brooklyn, NY. Affil: Graduate Center, CUNY. Email: lureynol@gmail.com. Research: British Officer Corps, military employment post-Waterloo.

Reynolds, Melissa Buckner. Falls Church, VA. Affil: Rutgers. Email: melissabreynolds@yahoo.com. Research: reading/writing practical knowledge, personal books in script and print.

Reynolds, Nancy Y., *Washington, St. Louis*. Clayton, MO. Email: nreynolds@wustl.edu. Research: modern Middle Eastern social and cultural, 20th-c Egyptian commerce and consumption.

Reynolds, Robert, *Kutztown*. Email: reynolds@kutztown.edu.

Reynolds, Ryan T. Killeen, TX. Affil: Baylor. Email: Ryan_Reynolds@Baylor.edu.

Reynoso, Jacqueline, *California State, Channel Islands*. Email: jacqueline.reynoso@csuci.edu.

Rezai, Hamid. Claremont, CA. Affil: Pitzer. Email: hr2106@caa.columbia.edu. Research: popular mobilization/political violence, migration/diaspora/exile.

Rezner, C. Thomas. Augusta, GA. Email: ctrezner@yahoo.com.

Reznick, Jeffrey Stephen, *National Library of Medicine*. Bethesda, MD. Email: jeffrey.reznick@nih.gov; jeffrey.s.reznick@gmail.com. Research: medicine/medical technology/war, medicine and material culture.

Rhett, Maryanne A., *Monmouth; World Hist. Assoc.* Email: mrhett@monmouth.edu.

Rhoades, Michelle K., *Wabash.* Email: rhoadesm@wabash.edu.

Rhoads, Edward J. M., *Texas, Austin.* Email: erhoads@mail.utexas.edu.

Rhode, Joy, *Michigan, Ann Arbor.* Email: joyrohde@umich.edu.

Rhodehamel, Kelyne. Houston, TX. Affil: Rice. Email: kbr2@rice.edu.

Rhoden, Nancy L., *Western Ontario.* London, ON, Canada. Email: nrhoden@uwo.ca. Research: Atlantic studies, colonial America.

Rhodes, Ken. Erie, PA. Email: kenrhodes3291@gmail.com.

Rhodes, Marissa Christman, *Niagara.* Email: mrhodes@niagara.edu.

Rhyne, George N., *Dickinson.* Email: rhyne@dickinson.edu.

Ribak, Gil, *Arizona.* Email: gribak@email.arizona.edu.

Ribeiro, Alyssa, *Allegheny.* Email: aribeiro@allegheny.edu.

Ribeiro, Flavio Diniz. São Paulo, Brazil. Email: flaviodinizribeiro@gmail.com. Research: modernization theory, Walt Whitman Rostow.

Riben, Joshua David. Lancaster, PA. Email: josh15.jr@gmail.com.

Ribovich, Leslie. Princeton, NJ. Affil: Princeton. Email: ribovich@princeton.edu. Research: character education.

Ricar, Sondra L., *Bellevue.* Email: sondra.ricar@bellevuecollege.edu.

Ricci, Emil A., *Villanova.* Email: emil.ricci@villanova.edu.

Rice, C. David, *Central Missouri.* Email: rice@ucmo.edu.

Rice, Candace M., *Alberta.* Email: cmrice@ualberta.ca.

Rice, James Douglas. Medford, MA. Affil: Tufts. Email: james.rice@tufts.edu. Research: colonial and revolutionary era, indigenous peoples in Americas.

Rice, John Steven. McAllen, TX. Affil: South Texas. Email: jsrice@southtexascollege.edu. Research: 19th-c religion in US and Mexico.

Rice, Louisa C., *Wisconsin-Eau Claire.* Eau Claire, WI. Email: ricelc@uwec.edu. Research: modern Europe, global and comparative.

Rice, Mark. New York, NY. Affil: Baruch, CUNY. Email: mark.rice@baruch.cuny.edu. Research: 20th-c Peru, tourism and development.

Rice, Melinda C., *Mississippi.* Email: mcrice1@olemiss.edu.

Rice, Richard, *Tennessee, Chattanooga.* Email: richard-rice@utc.edu.

Rice, Stephen, *Ramapo.* Email: srice@ramapo.edu.

Rich, Myra L., *Colorado Denver.* Email: myra.rich@ucdenver.edu.

Rich, Norman, *Brown.*

Rich, Paul John. Washington, DC. Affil: Policy Studies Organization. Email: pauljrich@gmail.com. Research: Freemasonry, fraternal societies.

Rich, Tracy E. Reston, VA. Email: tracyrich@jhu.edu.

Richard, Carl J., *Louisiana, Lafayette.*

Richard, Gregory L. Winona, MN. Affil: Winona State. Email: grichard@winona.edu. Research: US constitutional and legal, modern US.

Richard, Mark P., *SUNY, Plattsburgh.* Email: richarmp@plattsburgh.edu.

Richards, Holly, *Central Connecticut State.* Email: richardsh@ccsu.edu.

Richards, Joan L., *Brown.* Email: Joan_Richards@Brown.edu.

Richards, Kent D., *Central Washington.* Email: richardsk@cwu.edu.

Richards, Leonard L., *Massachusetts, Amherst.* Email: llr@history.umass.edu.

Richards, Mary Stovall, *Brigham Young.* Email: mary_richards@byu.edu.

Richards, Natalie Anne. Granby, MA. Email: richardsnataliea@gmail.com.

Richards, Nathan T., *East Carolina.* Email: richardsn@ecu.edu.

Richards, Robert J., *Chicago.* Email: r-richards@uchicago.edu.

Richards, Warren J. Salt Lake City, UT.

Richards, Yevette, *George Mason.* Rockville, MD. Email: yjordan@gmu.edu. Research: African American, women.

Richardson, Caleb W., *New Mexico.* Email: cwr@unm.edu.

Richardson, Heather Cox, *Boston Coll.* Email: heather.richardson@bc.edu.

Richardson, Jean, *SUNY, Buffalo State.* Email: richarje@buffalostate.edu.

Richardson, Kristina, *Queens, CUNY.* Email: kristina.richardson@qc.cuny.edu.

Richardson, Malcolm. Washington, DC. Affil: Independent Scholar. Email: mackrich48@gmail.com. Research: US philanthropy, 20th-c Europe.

Richardson, Nicole. Spartanburg, SC. Affil: South Carolina Upstate. Email: nrichardson@uscupstate.edu.

Richardson, Ronald K., *Boston Univ.* Email: hdarodius@aol.com.

Richardson, Roy. Hobart, IN. Email: pastorroyrichardson@gmail.com.

Richardson, Sarah S., *Harvard (Hist. of Science).* Email: srichard@fas.harvard.edu.

Riches, Daniel L., *Alabama, Tuscaloosa.* Tuscaloosa, AL. Email: dlriches@ua.edu. Research: 17th-c Brandenburg-Swedish relations, interaction of religion and diplomacy.

Richey, Jeffrey W., *Weber State.* Email: jeffreyrichey@weber.edu.

Richman, Allen M., *Stephen F. Austin State.* Email: arichman@sfasu.edu.

Richmond, Douglas, *Texas, Arlington.* Email: richmond@uta.edu.

Richmond, Heather, *State Hist. Soc. of Missouri.* Email: richmondh@shsmo.org.

Richmond, Marsha, *Wayne State.* Email: marsha.richmond@wayne.edu.

Richmond, Stephanie J. Norfolk, VA. Affil: Norfolk State. Email: S_j_richmond@hotmail.com. Research: women and reform in Atlantic world, gender and race in the Atlantic world.

Richter, Amy G., *Clark.* Worcester, MA. Email: arichter@clarku.edu. Research: US women, US urban.

Richter, Christopher. Brooklyn, NY. Affil: St. Ann's Sch. Email: chrisdrichter@gmail.com.

Richter, Daniel K., *Pennsylvania; McNeil Center.* Philadelphia, PA. Email: drichter@history.upenn.edu. Research: early America, Native American.

Richter, Daniel. Wilmington, DE. Affil: Maryland, Coll. Park. Email: drichter@umd.edu.

Richter, Donald C., *Ohio.* Email: richter@ohio.edu.

Richter, Julie, *William and Mary.* Williamsburg, VA. Email: cjrich@wm.edu. Research: colonial America, colonial Virginian race/class/gender.

Ricketts, Elizabeth, *Indiana, Pa.* Email: ricketts@iup.edu.

Rickford, Russell John, *Cornell.* Email: rr447@cornell.edu.

Rico, Monica L. Appleton, WI. Affil: Lawrence. Email: monica.rico@lawrence.edu.

Riddle, John M., *North Carolina State.* Email: john_riddle@ncsu.edu.

Riddle, Jonathan D., *Wheaton, Ill.* Email: jonathan.riddle@wheaton.edu.

Riddle, Nathan J. New York, NY. Email: nriddle@akrf.com. Research: historic preservation.

Rider, Jeff. Middletown, CT. Affil: Wesleyan. Email: jrider@wesleyan.edu. Research: 12th-c Flanders, 12th-c Champagne.

Rider, Robin E., *Wisconsin-Madison.* Email: rrider@library.wisc.edu.

Rider, Tara Suzanne. Islip, NY. Affil: SUNY, Stony Brook. Email: tara.rider@stonybrook.edu. Research: Atlantic maritime/whaling/piracy, environmental.

Ridge, Michael Allen, Jr., *Texas-Rio Grande Valley.* Email: michael.ridge@utrgv.edu.

Ridgeway, Kyle Maxwell. Clearwater, FL. Email: kridgeway10@gmail.com.

Ridgway, Whitman, *Maryland, Coll. Park.* Email: ridgway@umd.edu.

Ridley, Jack B., *Missouri Science and Tech.* Email: ridley@mst.edu.

Ridner, Judy A., *Mississippi State.* Email: jridner@history.msstate.edu.

Ridyard, Susan J., *South.* Email: sridyard@sewanee.edu.

Riebeling, Zachary. Ellis Grove, IL. Affil: Illinois, Urbana-Champaign. Email: yellowpocketshirt@gmail.com. Research: philosophy of history after 1945, trauma and historical consciousness.

Rieber, Alfred J. Budapest, Hungary. Affil: Central European. Email: riebera@ceu.hu. Research: Eurasian empires, Soviet foreign policy.

Riedel, Christopher Tolin, *Albion.*

Riedel, Dagmar A. Edgewater, NJ. Affil: Columbia. Email: dar2111@columbia.edu. Research: book in Arabic script, Oriental and Islamic studies.

Rieder, Paula M., *Slippery Rock.* Email: paula.rieder@sru.edu.

Rieff, Lynne A., *North Alabama.* Email: larieff@una.edu.

Riegg, Stephen B., *Texas A&M.*

Rieppel, Lukas, *Brown.* Email: Lukas_Rieppel@Brown.edu.

Riera, Juan L. Miami, FL. Email: juanr377@gmail.com. Research: missions and presidios, archaeology.

Ries, Linda A. New Cumberland, PA. Affil: Pennsylvania State Archives. Email: jaggers1952@verizon.net.

Riess, Steven A., *Northeastern Illinois.* Skokie, IL. Email: s-riess@neiu.edu. Research: horse racing, US sport.

Riess, Warren C., *Maine, Orono.* Email: riess@maine.edu.

Riesterer, Berthold P., *Indiana-Purdue, Indianapolis.* Email: briester@iupui.edu.

Rietveld, Ronald D., *California State, Fullerton.* Email: rrietveld@fullerton.edu.

Rife, James P., *Hist. Assoc.* Email: jrife@historyassociates.com.

Riff, Michael A., *Ramapo.* Email: mriff@ramapo.edu.

Riffle, Kori. Sacramento, CA. Email: koririffle4@gmail.com.

Rigau-Perez, Jose G. San Juan, PR. Email: jos.rigau@gmail.com. Research: Puerto Rico 1820-23, Puerto Rican scientific research.

Riggin, Lisa, *Biola; California State, Fullerton.* Email: lisa.riggin@biola.edu; lriggin@fullerton.edu.

Riggs, Cheryl, *California State, San Bernardino.* Email: criggs@csusb.edu.

Riggs, Paul T., *Wilkes.* Email: paul.riggs@wilkes.edu.

Riggs, Paula. Marietta, OH. Email: p.riggs@suddenlink.net.

Riggsby, Andrew M. Austin, TX. Affil: Texas, Austin. Email: ariggsby@mail.utexas.edu. Research: cognitive, Roman law and society.

Righter, Robert W., *Texas, El Paso.*

Rigo, Mate. Singapore. Affil: Yale-NUS Coll. Email: mate.rigo@yale-nus.edu.sg. Research: border cities in east-central Europe, gender and urban change in east-central Europe.

Rigogne, Thierry, *Fordham.* Email: rigogne@fordham.edu.

Riismandel, John N. Wanaque, NJ. Affil: Bergen Comm. Coll. Email: riisman@optonline.net.

Riismandel, Kyle, *Rutgers, Newark/New Jersey Inst. of Tech.* Email: kyle.riismandel@njit.edu.

Rijke-Epstein, Tasha, *Vanderbilt.* Nashville, TN. Email: tasha.rijke-epstein@vanderbilt.edu. Research: Africa, urban.

Riker, Wesley Leland. Wimauma, FL. Email: wlriker1@hotmail.com.

Riley, James C., *Indiana.* Email: rileyj@indiana.edu.

Riley, Philip F., *James Madison.* Email: rileypf@jmu.edu.

Riley, Stephanie. Columbia, SC. Email: smriley0323@att.net.

Riley Sousa, Mary Ashley, *Middle Tennessee State.* Email: Ashley.Rileysousa@mtsu.edu.

Rilling, Donna J., *SUNY, Stony Brook.* Email: donna.rilling@stonybrook.edu.

Rimmel, Lesley A., *Oklahoma State.* Email: lesley.rimmel@okstate.edu.

Rimner, Steffen. Utrecht, Netherlands. Affil: Utrecht. Email: steffen.rimner@gmail.com.

Rindfleisch, Bryan Christopher, *Marquette.* Email: bryan.c.rindfleisch@marquette.edu.

Rine, Holly A., *Le Moyne.* Email: rineha@lemoyne.edu.

Rinehart, Nicholas T. Cambridge, MA. Affil: Harvard. Email: ntrinehart@gmail.com.

Riney-Kehrberg, Pamela L., *Iowa State.* Ames, IA. Email: prinkeh@iastate.edu. Research: childhood, rural/agricultural.

Ringelberg, Kirstin, *Elon.* Email: kringelberg@elon.edu.

Ringer, Monica M., *Amherst.* Email: mmringer@amherst.edu.

Ringle, Carter Drew, *Purdue, Fort Wayne.* Email: ringcd01@pfw.edu.

Ringle, Dennis J., *Henry Ford Coll.* Email: djringle@charter.net.

Ringrose, Daniel M., *Minot State.* Minot, ND. Email: daniel.ringrose@minotstateu.edu. Research: European social, France and empire.

Ringrose, David R., *California, San Diego.* Email: dringrose@ucsd.edu.

Ringrose, Kathryn M. Del Mar, CA. Affil: California, San Diego. Email: kringrose@ucsd.edu.

Rink, Oliver A., *California State, Bakersfield.*

Riordan, Liam O., *Maine, Orono.* Orono, ME. Email: riordan@maine.edu. Research: multiculturalism in early America, loyalism and revolutionary Atlantic.

Risch, William Jay, *Georgia Coll. and State.* Milledgeville, GA. Email: william.risch@gcsu.edu. Research: Ukrainian national identity, rock music and youth subcultures.

Rischin, Moses. San Francisco, CA. Affil: San Francisco State. Email: mrischin@sfsu.edu.

Rise, Eric W., *Delaware.* Email: erise@udel.edu.

Rishel, Joseph, *Duquesne.* Email: rishelj@duq.edu.

Risk, James, *South Carolina, Columbia.* Email: risk@mailbox.sc.edu.

Risk, Shannon M., *Niagara.* Email: srisk@niagara.edu.

Riskin, Jessica G., *Stanford.* Email: jriskin@stanford.edu.

Risso, Patricia, *New Mexico.* West Lebanon, NH. Email: prisso@unm.edu. Research: 17th-c Arabian Sea trade-related violence.

Ritchey, Sara M. Washington, DC. Affil: Tennessee, Knoxville. Email: sritchey@utk.edu. Research: medieval Christianity, medieval medicine.

Ritchie, Donald A., *US Senate Hist. Office.* Bethesda, MD. Email: donritchie.historian@gmail.com. Research: media and politics.

Ritchie, Robert C., *Southern California; Huntington Library.* San Marino, CA. Email: rritchie@huntington.org. Research: colonial America, Tudor-Stuart England.

Ritchie, Robert, *Liberty.* Email: rfritchie@liberty.edu.

Ritchie Nutt, Rebecca. Delphos, OH. Affil: Northwestern Ohio. Email: rlrnutt@gmail.com. Research: early American Indian boarding schools, colonial and early US race relations.

Ritschel, Daniel, *Maryland, Baltimore County.* Email: ritschel@umbc.edu.

Ritsema, Alex. Edgewood, WA. Email: Alexmritsema@gmail.com.

Ritter, Caroline, *Texas State.*

Ritter, Christopher. Bern, Switzerland. Email: c_ritter@bluewin.ch. Research: hygienic milk and food, design and education.

Ritter, Harry, Jr., *Western Washington.* Email: Harry.Ritter@wwu.edu.

Ritter, Luke, *Troy.* Email: ritterl@troy.edu.

Ritter, Matthew J. Greenport, NY. Email: mattritter5@aol.com.

Ritter, Ted. Moseley, VA. Affil: Virginia Union. Email: tlritter@vuu.edu. Research: religious rhetoric, US presidency.

Ritterhouse, Jennifer L., *George Mason.* Fairfax, VA. Email: jritterh@gmu.edu. Research: 20th-c US, women and gender.

Rittgers, Ronald K., *Valparaiso.* Email: ron.rittgers@valpo.edu.

Ritvo, Harriet, *MIT.* Cambridge, MA. Email: ritvo@mit.edu. Research: 19th-c British environmental, animals.

Ritzema, Maria Magdalen. Milwaukee, WI. Affil: DuPage. Email: maria.ritzema@gmail.com.

Rivas, Brennan Gardner. Fort Worth, TX. Affil: Texas Christian. Email: brennan.gardner@tcu.edu.

Rivas, Darlene S., *Pepperdine.* Email: darlene.rivas@pepperdine.edu.

Rivaya-Martinez, Joaquin, *Texas State.* Email: jr59@txstate.edu.

Rivera, Eleanor, *Murray State.* Email: erivera@murraystate.edu.

Rivers, Daniel Winunwe, *Ohio State.* Email: rivers.91@osu.edu.

Rivers, Kimberly A., *Wisconsin-Oshkosh.* Email: rivers@uwosh.edu.

Rivers, Larry Eugene. Tallahassee, FL. Affil: Florida A&M. Email: larry.rivers@famu.edu. Research: African American.

Rivers, Larry O., *West Georgia.* Carrollton, GA. Email: lrivers@westga.edu. Research: African American, US religion.

Rives, Nathan, *Weber State.* Bountiful, UT. Email: NathanRives@weber.edu; nrives@gmail.com. Research: 19th-c America, religion.

Rizzo, Mary, *Rutgers, Newark/New Jersey Inst. of Tech.* Email: mary.rizzo@rutgers.edu.

Roach, Samuel F., Jr., *Kennesaw State.* Email: froach@kennesaw.edu.

Roark, James L., *Emory.* Email: jlroark@emory.edu.

Robarts, Andrew Richard. Providence, RI. Affil: Rhode Island Sch. of Design. Email: andrewrobarts@yahoo.com. Research: Black Sea region, Ottoman Bulgaria.

Robb, George, *William Paterson.* Wayne, NJ. Email: robbg@wpunj.edu. Research: modern Britain, social.

Robb, Nicola Elizabeth. Hong Kong. Email: aquabbb@gmail.com.

Robbins, Bryan Keith. Winter Haven, FL. Affil: Liberty. Email: bkrobbins_07@yahoo.com. Research: American Revolution and Civil War, WWII.

Robbins, Karen E., *St. Bonaventure.* Email: krobbins@sbu.edu.

Robbins, Kevin C., *Indiana–Purdue, Indianapolis.* Email: krobbin1@iupui.edu.

Robbins, Richard G., Jr., *New Mexico.* San Francisco, CA. Email: rrobbins@unm.edu. Research: V. F. Dzhunkovskii, Russian institutional.

Robbins, Shonna Summer. Tupelo, MS. Affil: Mississippi. Email: ssrobbi2@go.olemiss.edu. Research: sermons in American Civil War, Romanesque/Gothic art and architecture.

Robcis, Camille, *Columbia (Hist.).* Email: car2129@columbia.edu.

Robert, Brett Eugene. Philadelphia, PA. Affil: Pennsylvania. Email: brettr@sas.upenn.edu. Research: hurricanes in 20th-c Caribbean.

Robert, Dana L. Boston, MA. Affil: Boston Univ. Email: drobdan@bu.edu. Research: Christian mission, world Christianity.

Roberts, Alaina Elizabeth. Pittsburgh, PA. Affil: Penn State. Email: aeroberts711@gmail.com. Research: citizenship in Chickasaw Nation, race and geography.

Roberts, Alan Dana. Wellsville, UT. Affil: Utah State. Email: al.roberts@aggiemail.usu.edu.

Roberts, Alasdair Scott. Amherst, MA. Affil: Massachusetts Amherst. Email: alasdair.roberts@gmail.com.

Roberts, Alexandre. Los Angeles, CA. Affil: Southern California. Email: alexandre.roberts@gmail.com. Research: Byzantium, Middle East.

Roberts, Brian E., *Northern Iowa.* Email: brian.roberts@uni.edu.

Roberts, **Carey M**., *Liberty*. Email: croberts@liberty.edu.

Roberts, **Charles E**., *California State, Sacramento*. Email: cerobts@saclink.csus.edu.

Roberts, **Cokie**, *National Hist. Center*.

Roberts, **Daniel M**., **Jr**., *Richmond*. Email: droberts@richmond.edu.

Roberts, **James S**., *Duke*. Email: jroberts@mail01.adm.duke.edu.

Roberts, *Jeff Lynn*. Conroe, TX. Affil: Sam Houston State. Email: jeff.roberts@shsu.edu. Research: American Civil War, international maritime law.

Roberts, **Jeffery J**., *Tennessee Tech*. Email: jjroberts@tntech.edu.

Roberts, **Jennifer T**., *Graduate Center, CUNY*. Email: robertsjt@aol.com.

Roberts, *Jon H*., *Boston Univ*. Boston, MA. Email: roberts1@bu.edu. Research: US intellectual, Anglo-American religion.

Roberts, **Jonathan**, *Dalhousie*. Email: jonathan.roberts@msvu.ca.

Roberts, **Julia**, *Waterloo*. Email: robertsj@uwaterloo.ca.

Roberts, **Justin L**., *Dalhousie*. Email: justin.roberts@dal.ca.

Roberts, **Kathleen Blain**, *California State, Fresno*. Email: broberts@csufresno.edu.

Roberts, **Kodi Alphonse**, *Louisiana State*. Email: kodiroberts@lsu.edu.

Roberts, **Kyle B**., *Loyola, Chicago*. Email: kroberts2@luc.edu.

Roberts, *Luke S*., *California, Santa Barbara*. Santa Barbara, CA. Email: lukerobt@history.ucsb.edu. Research: Tokugawa political culture, samurai.

Roberts, *Mary Louise*, *Wisconsin-Madison*. Madison, WI. Email: maryroberts@wisc.edu. Research: WWII, 19th-/20th-c gender.

Roberts, **Meghan**, *Bowdoin*. Email: mroberts@bowdoin.edu.

Roberts, **Nathan E**., *Washington, Seattle*. Email: ner3@uw.edu.

Roberts, **Nicholas Edward**, *South*. Email: nerobert@sewanee.edu.

Roberts, **Phil**, *Wyoming*. Email: philr@uwyo.edu.

Roberts, *Priscilla M*. Hong Kong. Affil: Hong Kong. Email: proberts@hkucc.hku.hk. Research: 20th-c US diplomacy.

Roberts, **Randy W**., *Purdue*. Email: rroberts@purdue.edu.

Roberts, *Richard*, *Stanford*. Stanford, CA. Email: rroberts@stanford.edu. Research: colonial legal system social, post-slave social.

Roberts, *Rita*, *Scripps*. Claremont, CA. Email: rroberts@scrippscollege.edu. Research: Civil War era, antebellum African Americans.

Roberts, **Roberta A**., *Framingham State*.

Roberts, **Samuel K**., **Jr**., *Columbia (Hist.); Columbia (Hist. Public Health)*. Email: skr2001@columbia.edu.

Roberts, **Strother E**., *Bowdoin*. Email: seroberts@bowdoin.edu.

Roberts, **Ted**, *Tarleton State*. Email: troberts@tarleton.edu.

Roberts, **Timothy M**., *Western Illinois*. Email: TM-Roberts@wiu.edu.

Roberts, *Timothy R*. Newry, ME. Email: ratramnus@mac.com. Research: Attila and Rome, Maori Wars.

Roberts, **Tracey Lee**, *Wisconsin-Platteville*. Email: robertstra@uwplatt.edu.

Roberts, **Walter E**., *North Texas*. Email: walter.roberts@unt.edu.

Robertson, *Andrew W*., *Graduate Center, CUNY; Lehman, CUNY*. New York, NY. Email: arobertson@gc.cuny.edu; andrew.robertson@lehman.cuny.edu. Research: early Republic political, transnational.

Robertson, **Beth A**., *Carleton, Can*. Email: beth.robertson@carleton.ca.

Robertson, *Breanne*. Quantico, VA. Affil: Marine Corps Hist. Division. Email: breanne@brobertson.us. Research: American art, Pan-Americanism.

Robertson, **Claire C**., *Ohio State*. Email: robertson.8@osu.edu.

Robertson, **David**, *Nebraska, Omaha*.

Robertson, **Diarra Osei**, *Bowie State*. Email: dorobertson@bowiestate.edu.

Robertson, **Ian**, *Toronto*. Email: robertson@utsc.utoronto.ca.

Robertson, **Jack**, *Robert H. Smith Center*. Email: jrobertson@monticello.org.

Robertson, **James I**., **Jr**., *Virginia Tech*. Email: jircw@vt.edu.

Robertson, *James M*. Palo Alto, CA. Research: German liberalism, Immanuel Kant.

Robertson, **James MacEwan**, *California, Irvine*. Email: jamesmr1@uci.edu.

Robertson, **John F**., *Central Michigan*. Email: rober1j@cmich.edu.

Robertson, **Lindsay**, *Oklahoma (Hist.)*. Email: lrobertson@ou.edu.

Robertson, *Mary L*. Los Angeles, CA. Affil: Huntington Library. Email: mrobertson@huntington.org. Research: medieval, Britain.

Robertson, *Nancy Marie*, *Indiana–Purdue, Indianapolis*. Indianapolis, IN. Email: nmrobert@iupui.edu. Research: philanthropy, 20th-c US.

Robertson, **Stacey M**., *SUNY, Coll. Geneseo*. Email: robertsons@geneseo.edu.

Robertson, *Stephen M*., *George Mason*. Fairfax, VA. Affil: Roy Rosenzweig Center for Hist. and New Media. Email: srober30@gmu.edu; srob4757@gmail.com. Research: everyday life in 1920s Harlem, culture of surveillance 1865-1940.

Robertson Huffnagle, **Holly R**., *Westmont*.

Robey, *Sarah*, *Idaho State*. Idaho Falls, ID. Email: robesar5@isu.edu. Research: energy, US cultural.

Robichaud, **Andrew**, *Boston Univ*. Email: andrewr1@bu.edu.

Robin, **Ron Theodore**, *NYU*. Email: ron.robin@nyu.edu.

Robins, **Jonathan E**., *Michigan Tech*. Email: jrobins@mtu.edu.

Robins, **Marianne A**., *Westmont*. Email: robins@westmont.edu.

Robins, *Walker Stansberry*. Medford, MA. Affil: Bridgewater State. Email: walkrobins@gmail.com.

Robinson, *Allison Louise Wigfall*. Philadelphia, PA. Affil: Chicago. Email: alwrobinson@uchicago.edu.

Robinson, *Amy Elizabeth*. Santa Rosa, CA. Email: amy@turningplanet.org. Research: empire and militarism, nonviolent social movements.

Robinson, *Ann E*. Cambridge, MA. Affil: Massachusetts Amherst. Email: ann9robinson@gmail.com. Research: chemistry, classification and nomenclature.

Robinson, **Beth**, *Texas A&M, Corpus Christi*. Email: beth.robinson@tamucc.edu.

Robinson, **Brian**, *North Carolina A&T State*. Email: barobinson@ncat.edu.

Robinson, **Charles F**., **II**, *Arkansas, Fayetteville*. Email: cfrobins@uark.edu.

Robinson, *Daniel*. Berkeley, CA. Affil: California, Berkeley. Email: dan.robinson@berkeley.edu.

Robinson, **Daniel**, *California State, East Bay*. Email: daniel.robinson@csueastbay.edu.

Robinson, *David K*., *Truman State*. Columbia, MO. Email: drobinso@truman.edu. Research: psychology and psychiatry, European higher education.

Robinson, **David M**., *Colgate*. Email: drobinson@colgate.edu.

Robinson, *Edward A*. Visalia, CA. Affil: Sequoias. Email: edandkimrobinson@gmail.com. Research: US.

Robinson, *Eric W*., *Indiana*. Bloomington, IN. Email: ewr@indiana.edu. Research: ancient democracy, Sparta.

Robinson, **Genevieve**, **OSB**, *Rockhurst*. Email: robinsong4@mountosb.org.

Robinson, **Geoffrey B**., *UCLA*. Email: robinson@history.ucla.edu.

Robinson, **Greg J**., *Québec, Montréal*. Email: robinson.greg@uqam.ca.

Robinson, **Harlow L**., *Northeastern*. Email: h.robinson@neu.edu.

Robinson, *Jack Clark*. Albuquerque, NM. Affil: Academy of American Franciscan Hist. Email: jcrofm@ymail.com. Research: Franciscan friars in US since 1800, global Franciscanism.

Robinson, *John Eric*. Alton, IL. Affil: St. Louis Coll. of Pharmacy. Email: Eric.Robinson@stlcop.edu. Research: Roman political, American slavery.

Robinson, **Kira**, *Tennessee, Chattanooga*. Email: kira-robison@utc.edu.

Robinson, *Marc Arsell*, *California State, San Bernardino*. San Bernardino, CA. Email: marc.robinson@csusb.edu. Research: African American.

Robinson, **Marsha R**., *Miami, Ohio*. Email: robins78@miamioh.edu.

Robinson, **Martha K**., *Clarion, Pa*. Email: mrobinson@clarion.edu.

Robinson, **Mary Kathryn Cooney**, *Lourdes*. Email: mrobinson@lourdes.edu.

Robinson, *Michael F*., *Hartford*. West Hartford, CT. Email: microbins@hartford.edu. Research: US exploration cultural, 19th-c science and popular culture.

Robinson, *Morgan Jean*, *Mississippi State*. Mississippi State, MS. Email: mrobinson@history.msstate.edu. Research: Africa, science.

Robinson, *Niklas F*. Cambridge, MD. Affil: Delaware State. Email: nirobinson@desu.edu. Research: Mexican political, environmental.

Robinson, **Nova**, *Seattle*.

Robinson, **Paul A**., *Stanford*. Email: paulr@stanford.edu.

Robinson, *Raymond H*., *Northeastern*. Wellesley, MA. Email: ra.robinson@neu.edu. Research: American history painting, families of Boston's Commonwealth Ave.

Robinson, *Shira N*., *George Washington*. Washington, DC. Email: snrobins@gwu.edu. Research: modern Middle East.

Robinson, **Todd E**., *Nevada, Las Vegas*. Email: todd.robinson@unlv.edu.

Robinson, William Francis, *Vanderbilt*. Email: william.f.robinson@vanderbilt.edu.

Robinson-Dunn, Diane, *Detroit Mercy*. Email: robinsod@udmercy.edu.

Robisheaux, Thomas, *Duke*. Email: trobish@duke.edu.

Robison, Daniel E., *Troy*.

Robison, David. Dallas, TX. Affil: Richland. Email: davidrobison@dcccd.edu.

Robison, Mark Power, *Southern California*. Email: mrobison@usc.edu.

Robison, William B., III, *Southeastern Louisiana*. Email: wrobison@selu.edu.

Robson, David W., *John Carroll*. Email: robson@jcu.edu.

Robson, Laura C., *Portland State*. Email: lrobson@pdx.edu.

Robson, Stuart T., *Trent*.

Roby, Bryan K. Ann Arbor, MI. Affil: Michigan, Ann Arbor. Email: robyb@umich.edu. Research: Israel/Palestine, race and ethnicity.

Rocha, Biff. Mason, OH. Affil: Royalmont Academy. Email: BiffRocha1@aol.com. Research: American Catholics, American Evangelicals.

Rocha, Christian. Chicago, IL. Affil: Chicago. Email: christianrocha@uchicago.edu. Research: urban renewal in Tijuana, authoritarian urban politics.

Rocha, Elaine P. Bridgetown, Barbados. Affil: West Indies, Cave Hill. Email: Elaine.Rocha@cavehill.uwi.edu. Research: Brazilian black history, African diaspora.

Rocha, Gabriel de Avilez, *Drexel*. Philadelphia, PA. Email: gar56@drexel.edu.

Roche, Jeff, *Wooster*. Email: jroche@wooster.edu.

Roche, Lt Col John David, *US Air Force Acad*. Colorado Springs, CO. Email: john.roche@usafa.edu; cocockroach@gmail.com. Research: wartime governance of civilians, just war theory and practice.

Rochelo, Mark, *Georgia Coll. and State*. Email: mark.rochelo@gcsu.edu.

Rochkind, Jonathan, *Science History Inst*. Email: jrochkind@sciencehistory.org.

Rock, David P., *California, Santa Barbara*. Email: rock@history.ucsb.edu.

Rock, Howard B., *Florida International*. Email: rockh@fiu.edu.

Rock, Kenneth W., *Colorado State*. Email: kenneth.rock@colostate.edu.

Rock, William R., *Bowling Green State*.

Rockaway, Robert A. Ramat-Aviv, Israel. Affil: Tel Aviv. Email: rockaway@post.tau.ac.il. Research: 20th-c Jewry, Jewish criminality.

Rocke, Alan J., *Case Western Reserve*. Email: alan.rocke@case.edu.

Rockel, Stephen J., *Toronto*. Email: stephen.rockel@utoronto.ca.

Rockenbach, Stephen Ira. Richmond, VA. Affil: Virginia State. Email: srockenbach@vsu.edu. Research: American Civil War in Ohio River Valley, local and regional.

Rockman, Seth E., *Brown*. Providence, RI. Email: seth_rockman@Brown.edu. Research: early Republic US.

Rockoff, Hugh. Princeton Junction, NJ. Affil: Rutgers. Email: rockoff@econ.rutgers.edu. Research: banking panics, wartime economic controls.

Rock-Singer, Aaron White, *Wisconsin-Madison*. Email: rocksinger@wisc.edu.

Rockwell, Nicholas Ryan. Denver, CO. Email: nicholas.r.rockwell@gmail.com. Research: ancient Greek warfare and politics.

Rockwell, Stephen J. Patchogue, NY. Affil: St. Joseph's, NY. Email: srockwell@sjcny.edu.

Rodechko, James P., *Wilkes*. Email: james.rodechko@wilkes.edu.

Rodell, Paul A., *Georgia Southern*. Email: rodell@georgiasouthern.edu.

Roden, Donald T., *Rutgers*. Email: donroden@aol.com.

Rodgers, Bradley A., *East Carolina*. Email: rodgersb@ecu.edu.

Rodgers, Charles Douglas. Rockville, MD. Affil: Berman Hebrew Academy. Email: cdrodgers622@gmail.com.

Rodgers, Hugh I., *Columbus State*. Email: h_slrodgers@knology.net.

Rodgers, Robyn K., *NASA*. Email: robyn.k.rodgers@nasa.gov.

Rodgers, Sharon Y. Princeton, NJ. Email: syr@theworld.com. Research: monetary experiments in provincial Massachusetts, Atlantic.

Rodgers, Sherelle. Suffolk, VA. Affil: Old Dominion. Email: sherellerodgers61@gmail.com.

Rodner, William S., *Old Dominion*. Norfolk, VA. Email: wrodner@odu.edu. Research: Turner and industrialism, Asian art and artists in Britain.

Rodnitzky, Jerome L., *Texas, Arlington*. Email: jerry.rodnitzky@uta.edu.

Rodrigue, Aron, *Stanford*. Email: rodrigue@stanford.edu.

Rodrigues, Robert, *Duquesne*. Email: rodriguesr@duq.edu.

Rodriguez, Alberto D. Hershey, PA. Affil: American Military. Email: albertodrodriguez@yahoo.com.

Rodriguez, Chantel Renee, *Maryland, Coll. Park*. College Park, MD. Email: chanrod@umd.edu. Research: railroad bracero health, transnational Pullman business and labor.

Rodriguez, Daniel Alonzo. Capitola, CA. Affil: California, Santa Cruz. Email: drodri50@ucsc.edu.

Rodriguez, Daniel Arturo, *Brown*. Email: Daniel_Rodriguez@Brown.edu.

Rodriguez, Dimas, Jr. Houston, TX. Email: dimasrodriguez2@gmail.com.

Rodriguez, Elvia. Fresno, CA. Email: elviarodriguez@csufresno.edu. Research: race riots in American West.

Rodriguez, Fernando. New Orleans, LA. Affil: Louisiana State, Baton Rouge. Email: frodri6@tigers.lsu.edu. Research: 20th-c US diplomatic, Middle East/North Africa.

Rodriguez, Gerardo. Fort Worth, TX. Affil: Texas Christian. Email: gerardorodriguez0877@hotmail.com. Research: colonial Mexico.

Rodriguez, Jaime E., *California, Irvine*. Email: jerodrig@uci.edu.

Rodriguez, Jaime Eloy. New York, NY. Affil: St. John's, NY. Email: rodrigj2@stjohns.edu.

Rodriguez, Joseph A., *Wisconsin-Milwaukee*. Email: joerod@uwm.edu.

Rodriguez, Judy Denise. Mission, TX. Affil: South Texas. Email: judydeniseg@msn.com. Research: Catholicism and Hispanic culture.

Rodriguez, Julia E., *New Hampshire, Durham*. Durham, NH. Email: juliar@unh.edu. Research: sciences in Latin America, gender.

Rodriguez, Manuel R. San Juan, PR. Affil: Puerto Rico. Email: mrrv1967@gmail.com. Research: Cold War in Latin America and Caribbean, early 1900s Progressivism in Puerto Rico.

Rodriguez, Marc Simon, *Portland State*. Portland, OR. Email: msr4@pdx.edu. Research: Chicano/Mexican American civil rights, legal.

Rodriguez, Miguelina, *La Guardia and Wagner Archives*. Email: migrodriguez@lagcc.cuny.edu.

Rodriguez, Miles Vincent, *Bard*. Email: rodriguez@bard.edu.

Rodriguez, Sarah B. Chicago, IL. Affil: Northwestern. Email: srodriguez@northwestern.edu. Research: women's sexual health, women's reproductive health.

Rodriguez, Sarah Katherine Manning, *Arkansas, Fayetteville*. Fayetteville, AR. Email: skrodrig@uark.edu; sark@sas.upenn.edu. Research: 19th-c US, US-Mexico borderlands.

Rodriguez, Victor Jose. San Jose, CA. Affil: Sino-US Coll., Beijing Inst. of Tech. Email: analytical.vic@gmail.com. Research: Progressive education, John Dewey and his influence overseas.

Rodriguez, Victor Raymond, II. San Jose, CA. Affil: Foothill. Email: vrrodriguez02@gmail.com.

Rodriguez, Juanita. Bogota, Colombia. Affil: Binghamton, SUNY. Email: crodri35@binghamton.edu.

Rodriguez V, Jorge Juan. New York, NY. Affil: Union Theological Seminary. Email: jjrodriguezv@me.com. Research: History of Religion, Latin American and Caribbean History.

Rodriguez-Silva, Ileana M., *Washington, Seattle*. Email: imrodrig@uw.edu.

Rodriquez, Alicia E., *California State, Bakersfield*. Email: arodriquez@csub.edu.

Rodriquez, Louis, *Kutztown*. Email: rodrique@kutztown.edu.

Roe, Shirley A., *Connecticut, Storrs*. Email: shirley.roe@uconn.edu.

Roeber, Anthony G., *Penn State*. University Park, PA. Email: agr2@psu.edu. Research: colonial America, early modern Germany.

Roeber, Daniel. Tallahassee, FL. Affil: Florida State. Email: danroeber@gmail.com.

Roebuck, Janet, *New Mexico*. Email: jroebuck@unm.edu.

Roebuck, Kristin, *Cornell*. Email: kar79@cornell.edu.

Roediger, David Randall, *Kansas*. Email: droediger@ku.edu.

Roege, Pernille, *Pittsburgh*. Pittsburgh, PA. Email: per20@pitt.edu. Research: 18th-c France and French imperial, 18th-c political economy.

Roell, Craig H., *Georgia Southern*. Email: croell@georgiasouthern.edu.

Roesch, Claudia, *German Hist. Inst*. Email: roesch@ghi-dc.org.

Roesler, Raymond. Tucson, AZ. Affil: American. Email: rr3234a@american.edu.

Roessner, Patricia, *La Salle*. Email: roessner@lasalle.edu.

Rogan, Liz. Omaha, NE. Affil: Clarkson. Email: lizrogan.edd.rn.cne@gmail.com.

Rogaski, Ruth, *Vanderbilt*. Email: ruth.rogaski@vanderbilt.edu.

Rogel, **Carole R.**, *Ohio State*. Columbus, OH. Email: rogel.1@osu.edu. Research: Yugoslavia's breakup, Slovenia and independence.

Roger Hepburn, Sharon A., *Radford*. Email: shepburn@radford.edu.

Rogers, **Alan**, *Boston Coll*. Chestnut Hill, MA. Email: rogersa@bc.edu. Research: religion/medicine/US law.

Rogers, Amelia, *American International*. Email: amelia.rogers@aic.edu.

Rogers, **Chauncey**. Trimble, MO. Email: rogerschauncey@gmail.com.

Rogers, Clifford J., *US Military Acad*. Email: clifford.rogers@usma.edu.

Rogers, Daniel E., *South Alabama*. Email: drogers@southalabama.edu.

Rogers, **Diane**. Charlestown, MA. Affil: Massachusetts, Boston. Email: diane.rogers-ol@umb.edu.

Rogers, **Donald W.**, *Central Connecticut State*. Vernon Rockville, CT. Email: rogersd@ccsu.edu; donrogershistorian@yahoo.com. Research: American civil liberties, Connecticut Progressvie era.

Rogers, George A., *Georgia Southern*.

Rogers, **Janna**. Stillwater, OK. Affil: Oklahoma State. Email: janna.rogers@okstate.edu. Research: Americanize Christianize Indigenous, forced assimilation identity politics.

Rogers, **Jennifer**. West Bloomfield, MI. Email: jrogers5113@email.phoenix.edu.

Rogers, **John D.** Belmont, MA. Affil: American Inst. for Sri Lankan Studies. Email: rogersjohnd@aol.com. Research: Sri Lanka, nationalism/identity/caste.

Rogers, **Justin Isaac**. Oxford, MS. Affil: Mississippi. Email: jirogers@go.olemiss.edu. Research: American South, 19th/20th-c US.

Rogers, **Kenneth, III**. West Bloomfield, MI. Email: rogersk011@gmail.com.

Rogers, **Naomi**, *Yale*. New Haven, CT. Email: naomi.rogers@yale.edu. Research: alternative medicine, 1960s-70s radical health movements.

Rogers, Nicholas C., *York, Can*. Email: nickrog@yorku.ca.

Rogers, Rick M., *Eastern Michigan*. Email: rrogers@emich.edu.

Rogers, **Thomas D.**, *Emory*. Atlanta, GA. Email: tomrogers@emory.edu. Research: labor/agroecological change/race, northeastern Brazil.

Rogers, Warren, Jr., *North Georgia*. Email: warren.rogers@ung.edu.

Rogers-Stokes, **Lori**. Arlington, MA. Email: lori.stokes@comcast.net. Research: Massachusetts Bay Colony 1630-1692.

Rohl, Darrell, *Calvin*. Email: dr33@calvin.edu.

Rohland, **Eleonora Julia**. Bielefeld, Germany. Affil: Bielefeld. Email: eleonora.rohland@uni-bielefeld.de. Research: Caribbean environmental, climate and disaster.

Rohrbough, Malcolm J., *Iowa*. Email: malcolm-rohrbough@uiowa.edu.

Rohrer, James R., *Nebraska, Kearney*. Email: rohrerjr@unk.edu.

Rohrer, Katherine, *North Georgia*. Email: katherine.rohrer@ung.edu.

Rohrer, **S. Scott**. Arlington, VA. Email: scott.rohrer@sagepub.com. Research: religion and revolution in Atlantic world, Presbyterianism during Revolution.

Rohrer, Scott R., *Florida Gulf Coast*. Email: srohrer@fgcu.edu.

Rohrs, Richard C., *Oklahoma State*. Email: richard.rohrs@okstate.edu.

Roider, Karl A., Jr., *Louisiana State*. Email: kroider@lsu.edu.

Roisman, Joseph, *Colby*. Email: joseph.roisman@colby.edu.

Roitman, Joel M., *Eastern Kentucky*. Email: joel.roitman@eku.edu.

Rojanski, Rachel, *Brown*. Email: Rachel_Rojanski@Brown.edu.

Rojas, **Heath**. New York, NY. Affil: Columbia. Email: hmr2138@columbia.edu.

Rojas, **Rochelle**, *Kalamazoo*. Kalamazoo, MI. Email: Rochelle.Rojas@kzoo.edu. Research: witchcraft, Spanish Inquisition.

Rojer, **Aurora**. Ithaca, NY. Affil: Lehman Alternative Community Sch. Email: aurora.rojer@icsd.k12.ny.us.

Roka, **William B.** Elmhurst, NY. Affil: South Street Seaport Museum. Email: wbroka@gmail.com. Research: rise and fall of empires, steamships and globalization before WWI.

Roland, Alex F., *Duke*. Email: aroland@duke.edu.

Roland, Joan G., *Pace*. Email: jroland@pace.edu.

Roldan, **Mary J.**, *Graduate Center, CUNY; Hunter, CUNY*. New York, NY. Email: mrol@hunter.cuny.edu; maryroldan7@gmail.com. Research: radio/culture/politics, violence/drug trafficking/state.

Rolfs, Richard W., SJ, *Loyola Marymount*. Email: rrolfs@lmu.edu.

Rolinson, Mary G., *Georgia State*. Email: mrolinson1@gsu.edu.

Roll, Jarod H., *Mississippi*. Email: jhroll@olemiss.edu.

Rolle, Andrew F., *Occidental*.

Roller, **Heather Flynn**, *Colgate*. Hamilton, NY. Email: hroller@colgate.edu. Research: colonial Brazil, Amazon.

Rollman, **Wilfrid J.** Portland, ME. Affil: Wellesley. Email: wrollman@wellesley.edu.

Rollo, **Lorraine A.** Lebanon, PA. Email: lorraine.historian@gmail.com.

Rollo-Koster, Joelle, *Rhode Island*. Email: joellekoster@uri.edu.

Rolph, Daniel N., *Hist. Soc. of Pennsylvania*. Email: drolph@hsp.org.

Roman, Emilie, *Lake Forest*. Email: roman@lakeforest.edu.

Roman, Meredith, *SUNY, Coll. Brockport*. Email: mroman@brockport.edu.

Roman, **Reinaldo L.**, *Georgia*. Athens, GA. Email: rroman@uga.edu. Research: religions, politics of culture.

Romaniello, Matthew P., *Weber State*.

Romano, Dennis, *Syracuse*. Email: dromano@syr.edu.

Romano, **John F.** Atchison, KS. Affil: Benedictine. Email: johnfromano@gmail.com. Research: early medieval liturgy, power in medieval Europe.

Romano, **Renee C.**, *Oberlin*. Oberlin, OH. Email: rromano@oberlin.edu. Research: historical memory, modern race relations.

Romans, Maj Timothy, *US Air Force Acad*. Email: timothy.romans@usafa.edu.

Romeo, Sharon Elizabeth, *Alberta*. Email: sharon.romeo@ualberta.ca.

Romer, Frank, *East Carolina*. Email: romerf@ecu.edu.

Romero, **Andrea Michelle**. Silver Spring, MD. Email: msromero1992@gmail.com.

Romero, **Eulogio Kyle**. Hermitage, TN. Affil: Vanderbilt. Email: ekyleromero@gmail.com.

Romero, **Gonzalo**. Lima, Peru. Affil: SUNY, Stony Brook. Email: gonzaloemilio.romerosommer@stonybrook.edu.

Romero, Juan, *Western Kentucky*. Email: juan.romero@wku.edu.

Romero, R. Todd, *Houston*. Email: tromero2@uh.edu.

Romesburg, **Don**. Rohnert Park, CA. Affil: Sonoma State. Email: romesbur@sonoma.edu. Research: adolescence and queerness, transgender social/cultural histories.

Romig, Andrew J., *NYU*. Email: romig@nyu.edu.

Rominger, **Christopher James**, *North Florida*. Jacksonville, FL. Email: chris.rominger@unf.edu.

Rommel, John G., Jr., *Central Connecticut State*.

Rommel-Ruiz, **Bryan**, *Colorado Coll*. Colorado Springs, CO. Email: bruiz@coloradocollege.edu. Research: modernity and black Atlantic, film and history.

Romney, **Charles W.**, *Arkansas, Little Rock*. Little Rock, AR. Email: cwromney@ualr.edu. Research: public, modern US.

Romney, **Paul M.** Baltimore, MD. Email: paulromney03@aim.com. Research: contemporary Canadian constitutional thought, post-1982 Canadian national unity.

Romney, Susanah Shaw, *NYU*. Email: ssr8@nyu.edu.

Romo, Anadelia A., *Texas State*. Email: ar23@txstate.edu.

Ron, **Ariel**, *Southern Methodist*. Dallas, TX. Email: aron@smu.edu. Research: antebellum agricultural reform and politics, 19th-c US economic/political development.

Rondinone, Troy M., *Southern Connecticut State*. Email: rondinonet1@southernct.edu.

Roney, **Jessica Choppin**. Philadelphia, PA. Affil: Temple. Email: jessica.roney@temple.edu. Research: early American civil society, frontier Tennessee/State of Franklin.

Roney, **John B.** Fairfield, CT. Affil: Sacred Heart. Email: roneyj@sacredheart.edu. Research: French Huguenots, Ireland and environment.

Ronholm, **Michelle Emick**. Silver Spring, MD. Email: meronholm@gmail.com.

Ronnenberg, Ryan, *Kennesaw State*. Email: pryan4@kennesaw.edu.

Ronzino, **John**. Seaford, NY. Affil: St. John's, NY. Email: jronzin@schools.nyc.gov. Research: nationalism, education.

Rood, Dan B., *Georgia*. Email: danrood@uga.edu.

Rood, Judith M., *Biola*. Email: judith.rood@biola.edu.

Rood, Paul, *Biola*. Email: paul.rood@biola.edu.

Rook, Robert, *Towson*. Email: rrook@towson.edu.

Roos, Julia, *Indiana*. Email: roos@indiana.edu.

Roosa, John P., *British Columbia*. Email: jroosa@mail.ubc.ca.

Roosth, **Sophia**, *Harvard (Hist. of Science)*. Cambridge, MA. Email: roosth@fas.harvard.edu. Research: 20th-/21st-c life sciences.

Root, David, *Indianapolis*. Email: rootd@uindy.edu.

Root, **Elliot**. Chicago, IL. Affil: Johns Hopkins. Email: eroot1@jhu.edu.

Rop, Jeffrey, *Minnesota Duluth*.

Roper, *Danielle M*. Chicago, IL. Affil: Chicago. Email: droper@uchicago.edu.

Roper, **Donald M.**, *SUNY, New Paltz*. Email: drop@hvi.net.

Roper, **John H.**, *Coastal Carolina*. Email: jroper@coastal.edu.

Roper, **Katherine S.**, *St. Mary's, Calif.* Email: kroper@stmarys-ca.edu.

Roper, *Lou*, *SUNY, New Paltz*. Kingston, NY. Email: roperl@newpaltz.edu. Research: English empire 1610-1780, expansion of England to 1730.

Roper, **Mary Wynn**, *Troy*.

Ropers, **Erik**, *Towson*. Email: hropers@towson.edu.

Rorabaugh, *W. J.*, *Washington, Seattle*. Seattle, WA. Email: rorabaug@uw.edu. Research: alcohol and temperance, 1960s social movements.

Rorlich, **Azade-Ayse**, *Southern California*. Email: arorlich@usc.edu.

Rosa, **Andrew J.**, *Western Kentucky*. Email: andrew.rosa@wku.edu.

Rosa, **John**, *Hawai'i, Manoa*. Email: rosajohn@hawaii.edu.

Rosales, **Steven**, *Arkansas, Fayetteville*. Email: rosales@uark.edu.

Rosario, *Jeffrey*. Jasper, OR. Email: jeffreyrosario@gmail.com.

Rosas, **Ana E.**, *California, Irvine*. Email: arosas1@uci.edu.

Rose, **Anne C.**, *Penn State*. Email: acr5@psu.edu.

Rose, **Chanelle Nyree**, *Rowan*. Email: rosec@rowan.edu.

Rose, *Christine*. Elverta, CA. Email: cdanielson1218@yahoo.com.

Rose, *Christopher S*. Austin, TX. Affil: Texas, Austin. Email: csrose@utexas.edu. Research: public health/disease/prostitution, prerevolutionary social.

Rose, *Dennis*. San Francisco, CA. Email: trit0n@sbcglobal.net.

Rose, *E. M*. Princeton, NJ. Affil: Harvard. Email: profemilyrose@hotmail.com. Research: enacted identity/Christian pedagogy, early American investment.

Rose, *Jonathan E*. Madison, NJ. Affil: Drew. Email: jerose@drew.edu. Research: Winston Churchill's literary career, reading.

Rose, *Louis H*. Westerville, OH. Affil: Otterbein. Email: lrose@otterbein.edu. Research: modern Europe, European intellectual.

Rose, **M. Lynn**, *Truman State*. Email: lynnrose@truman.edu.

Rose, *Mark H*., *Florida Atlantic*. Boca Raton, FL. Email: mrose@fau.edu. Research: American city since 1945, politics of American banking.

Rose, *Norman Robert*. Grafton, OH. Affil: Kent State. Email: norman.rose@yahoo.com. Research: banjo, international corrections.

Rose, **Sarah F.**, *Texas, Arlington*. Email: srose@uta.edu.

Rose, *Savannah Glasenapp*. Dalton, NH. Affil: West Virginia. Email: savannah.g.rose@gmail.com.

Rose, **Shelley E.**, *Cleveland State*. Cleveland, OH. Email: shelley.rose@csuohio.edu. Research: Germany, transnational.

Rose, *Sonya O*., *Michigan, Ann Arbor*. Sarasota, FL. Email: sorose@umich.edu. Research: defining the nation/Britain after 1945, aftermath of war.

Rose, *Stanley*. Antioch, TN. Affil: SUNY, Brockport.

Rose, *Taylor Elliott*. New Haven, CT. Affil: Yale. Email: taylor.elliott.rose@gmail.com. Research: roads in Mt. Hood National Forest, Portland heritage trees.

Rosell, *Garth M*. Peabody, MA. Affil: Gordon-Conwell Theological Seminary. Email: grosell@gcts.edu. Research: spiritual renewal, evangelicalism.

Roseman, *Mark*, *Indiana*. Bloomington, IN. Email: marrosem@indiana.edu. Research: Holocaust, world wars and their impact.

Rosemblatt, *Karin A*., *Maryland, Coll. Park*. College Park, MD. Email: karosemb@umd.edu. Research: 20th-c Latin America, gender.

Rosen, *Deborah A*., *Lafayette*. Easton, PA. Email: rosend@lafayette.edu. Research: early America, legal.

Rosen, *Elliot A*., *Rutgers, Newark/New Jersey Inst. of Tech.* Califon, NJ. Research: 20th-c US economic, New Deal.

Rosen, *Hannah*, *William and Mary*. Williamsburg, VA. Email: hrosen@wm.edu. Research: US death/race/segregation, race and 19th-c rape law.

Rosen, **Richard L.**, *Drexel*. Email: rosenrl@drexel.edu.

Rosen, **Ruth E.**, *California, Davis*. Email: rerosen@ucdavis.edu.

Rosenband, *Leonard N*., *Utah State*. Logan, UT. Email: leonard.rosenband@aggiemail.usu.edu. Research: France, labor.

Rosenbaum, **Arthur L.**, *Claremont McKenna*. Email: arthur.rosenbaum@cmc.edu.

Rosenberg, **Charles E.**, *Harvard (Hist. of Science)*. Email: rosenb3@fas.harvard.edu.

Rosenberg, **Clifford D.**, *Graduate Center, CUNY*. Email: CRosenberg@ccny.cuny.edu.

Rosenberg, **Daniel B.**, *Oregon*. Email: dbr@uoregon.edu.

Rosenberg, **Daniel**, *Adelphi*. Email: rosenber@adelphi.edu.

Rosenberg, *David A*. Arlington, VA. Affil: US Naval Acad. Email: ddrhr@msn.com. Research: American naval/military, American naval heritage.

Rosenberg, **Eliza**, *Utah State*. Email: eliza.rosenberg@usu.edu.

Rosenberg, **Emily S.**, *California, Irvine*. Email: e.rosenberg@uci.edu.

Rosenberg, *Gabriel N*., *Duke*. Durham, NC. Email: gnr3@duke.edu; rosenberg.gabriel@gmail.com. Research: industrialization of US agriculture, US state building and modernization.

Rosenberg, *Jonathan*, *Graduate Center, CUNY; Hunter, CUNY*. Email: jrosen8637@aol.com.

Rosenberg, *Ken*. Ardsley, NY. Affil: Edgemont Junior/Senior High Sch. Email: ksrcn@msn.com.

Rosenberg, *Mark*, *Bentley*. Email: mrosenberg@bentley.edu.

Rosenberg, *Rosalind Navin*, *Barnard, Columbia*. Email: rrosenberg@barnard.edu.

Rosenberg, *Scott P*., *Wittenberg*. Email: srosenberg@wittenberg.edu.

Rosenberg, *William G*., *Michigan, Ann Arbor*. Brunswick, ME. Email: wgr@umich.edu. Research: Russia, Soviet Union.

Rosenblatt, *Helena A*., *Graduate Center, CUNY*. New York, NY. Email: hrosenblatt@gc.cuny.

edu. Research: French liberalism, Jean-Jacques Rousseau.

Rosenbloom, **Joshua**, *Kansas*. Email: jrosenbloom@ku.edu.

Rosenbloom, **Nancy J.**, *Canisius*. Email: rosenbln@canisius.edu.

Rosenblum, **Mark**, *Queens, CUNY*. Email: mrapn@earthlink.net.

Rosenblum, *Warren A*. Saint Louis, MO. Affil: Webster. Email: wrosenbl@webster.edu. Research: Magdeburg justice scandal of 1926, European mental disability.

Rosenfeld, *Gavriel D*., *Fairfield*. Cos Cob, CT. Email: grosenfeld@fairfield.edu. Research: modern Germany, collective memory.

Rosenfeld, *Sophia*, *Pennsylvania*. Philadelphia, PA. Email: srosenf@sas.upenn.edu; sophieanner@gmail.com. Research: Age of Revolutions, political theory.

Rosenfeld, *Susan*. Annapolis, MD. Affil: FSR Associates. Email: suerosenfeld2@gmail.com. Research: US law enforcement and national security, US Constitution and terrorism.

Rosenhaft, *Eve*. Liverpool, United Kingdom. Affil: Liverpool. Email: dan85@liv.ac.uk. Research: life insurance in 18th-c Germany, 'other victims' of the Holocaust.

Rosenheim, *James M*., *Texas A&M*. College Station, TX. Email: j-rosenheim@tamu.edu. Research: unmarried men in England 1625-1775.

Rosenkranz, **Susan A.**, *Florida Atlantic*. Email: srosenk@fau.edu.

Rosenmuller, **Christoph**, *Middle Tennessee State*. Email: Christoph.Rosenmuller@mtsu.edu.

Rosenow, **Michael**, *Central Arkansas*. Email: mrosenow@uca.edu.

Rosenstein, **Nathan S.**, *Ohio State*.

Rosenstone, **Robert Allan**, *California Inst. of Tech.* Email: rr@hss.caltech.edu.

Rosenthal, **Anton**, *Kansas*. Email: surreal@ku.edu.

Rosenthal, **Bernice Glatzer**, *Fordham*. Email: rosenthal@fordham.edu.

Rosenthal, *Caitlin*, *California, Berkeley*. Berkeley, CA. Email: crosenthal@berkeley.edu. Research: political economy of slavery, US social and economic.

Rosenthal, *Gregory*, *Roanoke*. Salem, VA. Email: rosenthal.gregory@gmail.com.

Rosenthal, *Jean-Laurent*, *California Inst. of Tech.* Email: jlr@hss.caltech.edu.

Rosenthal, *Jill*, *Hunter, CUNY*. Email: jr3192@hunter.cuny.edu.

Rosenthal, **Joel T.**, *SUNY, Stony Brook*. Email: joel.rosenthal@stonybrook.edu.

Rosenthal, **Joshua M.**, *Western Connecticut State*. Email: rosenthalj@wcsu.edu.

Rosenthal, **Nicolas G.**, *Loyola Marymount*. Email: ngrosen@lmu.edu.

Rosenthal, *Sarah*. Washington, DC. Affil: Georgetown. Email: sar248@georgetown.edu.

Rosenthal, **Steven**, *Hartford*. Email: srosentha@hartford.edu.

Rosenwein, *Barbara H*., *Loyola, Chicago*. Evanston, IL. Email: brosenw@luc.edu; brosenw@gmail.com. Research: social, emotions.

Roshwald, *Aviel I*., *Georgetown*. Washington, DC. Email: roshwaav@georgetown.edu. Research: comparative nationalism, diplomatic/international.

Rosier, Paul C., *Villanova*. Email: paul.rosier@villanova.edu.

Rosinbum, John Theodore. Tucson, AZ. Affil: BASIS Tucson North. Email: john.rosinbum@gmail.com. Research: Central American refugee crisis in US/CA, digital turn and evolution of education.

Rosner, David, *Columbia (Hist.); Columbia (Hist. Public Health)*. New York, NY. Email: dr289@columbia.edu. Research: public health and 9/11, labor and disease.

Rosner, Jennifer, *Library Co. of Philadelphia*. Email: bindery@librarycompany.org.

Rosner, Lisa, *Stockton*. Galloway, NJ. Email: rosnerl@stockton.edu. Research: 18th-c universities/academy of science.

Rosner, Molly, *La Guardia and Wagner Archives*. Email: mrosner@lagcc.cuny.edu.

Rosof, Patricia J. F. New York, NY. Email: pjfrosof@aol.com. Research: Dr. Florence Rena Sabin.

Rosoff, Nancy G. Glenside, PA. Affil: Arcadia. Email: rosoffn@arcadia.edu. Research: women's athletic activity 1880-1920, education.

Ross, Amanda, *US Dept. of State*.

Ross, Andrew Israel, *Loyola, Md*. Baltimore, MD. Email: aross1@loyola.edu. Research: public sexuality in 19th-c Paris, urban modernity.

Ross, Angus, *Naval War Coll*. Email: rossak@usnwc.edu.

Ross, Charles Kenyatta, *Mississippi*. Email: cross@olemiss.edu.

Ross, Cynthia, *Texas A&M, Commerce*. Email: Cynthia.Ross@tamuc.edu.

Ross, Daniel, *Québec, Montréal*.

Ross, Danielle M., *Utah State*. Logan, UT. Email: danielle.ross@usu.edu. Research: Central Asia, Islamic intellectual.

Ross, Dorothy, *Johns Hopkins (Hist.)*. Washington, DC. Email: dottross@comcast.net. Research: social ethics, historical consciousness.

Ross, Ellen. New York, NY. Affil: Ramapo. Email: ellenross@fastmail.com. Research: women and philanthrophy, female journalists.

Ross, Frances M., *Arkansas, Little Rock*. Email: fmross@ualr.edu.

Ross, James D., Jr., *Arkansas, Little Rock*. Email: jdross@ualr.edu.

Ross, Jecoa. El Paso, TX. Affil: Texas, El Paso. Email: jecoa@live.com. Research: Texas sodomy statutes, sexuality/gender/race on borderlands.

Ross, Jenna Katherine. Virginia Beach, VA. Affil: Southern California. Email: jennaros@usc.edu.

Ross, Joseph Andrew. Thomasville, NC. Affil: North Carolina, Greensboro. Email: jaross@uncg.edu. Research: Nuremberg war crimes trial 1945-46, Justice John Jay Parker.

Ross, Karen D., *Troy*. Email: kdross@troy.edu.

Ross, Kerry L., *DePaul*. Email: kross9@depaul.edu.

Ross, Michael A., *Maryland, Coll. Park*. Email: maross@umd.edu.

Ross, Richard J., *Illinois, Urbana-Champaign*. Champaign, IL. Email: rjross@illinois.edu. Research: legal thought, communications.

Ross, Robert, *Austin Peay State*. Email: rossr@apsu.edu.

Ross, Ronald J., *Wisconsin-Milwaukee*. Milwaukee, WI. Email: rjross@uwm.edu.

Research: Bismarck's kulturkampf, 19th-c German prisons/prisoners.

Ross, Rosetta. Atlanta, GA. Affil: Spelman. Email: rross@spelman.edu.

Ross, Sarah Gwyneth, *Boston Coll*. Chestnut Hill, MA. Email: sarah.ross.1@bc.edu. Research: vernacularization of humanism, medical culture in Renaissance Italy.

Ross, Steven J., *Southern California*. Los Angeles, CA. Email: sjross@usc.edu. Research: Hollywood and politics, Hollywood and anti-fascism 1920-50.

Ross, Steven K., *Louisiana State*. Email: skross@lsu.edu.

Ross, Travis Edward. New Haven, CT. Affil: Yale. Email: travis.ross@yale.edu.

Ross, William, *New Hampshire, Durham*. Email: bill.ross@unh.edu.

Rossabi, Morris, *Graduate Center, CUNY; Queens, CUNY*. Email: mr63@columbia.edu; morris.rossabi@qc.cuny.edu.

Rossell, Daves. Savannah, GA. Affil: Savannah Coll. of Art & Design. Email: erossell@scad.edu. Research: Savannah and Lowcountry, illuminating engineering.

Rosser, John, *Boston Coll*. Email: rosserj@bc.edu.

Rossi, John P., *La Salle*. Email: rossi@lasalle.edu.

Rossi, John Paul, *Penn State; Penn State, Erie*. Email: jpr2@psu.edu.

Rossi, Maryann, *Western Connecticut State*. Email: rossim@wcsu.edu.

Rossi, Michael, *Chicago*. Email: michaelrossi@uchicago.edu.

Rossignol, Sebastien, *Memorial, Newfoundland*. Email: srossignol@mun.ca.

Rossin, Genevieve. Miami, FL. Affil: Florida International. Email: ggonz055@fiu.edu.

Rossinow, Doug, *Metropolitan State*. Email: doug.rossinow@metrostate.edu.

Rossiter, Jeremy J., *Alberta*. Email: jeremy.rossiter@ualberta.ca.

Rossman, Jeffrey J., *Virginia*. Charlottesville, VA. Email: jjr2n@virginia.edu. Research: Stalinism, genocide.

Rossos, Andrew, *Toronto*.

Rosswurm, Steven, *Lake Forest*. Waukegan, IL. Email: rosswurm@lakeforest.edu. Research: US gender, Mexico.

Rost, Sean, *Missouri, Columbia; State Hist. Soc. of Missouri*. Email: rosts@shsmo.org.

Rostam-Kolayi, Jasamin, *California State, Fullerton*. Email: jrostam@fullerton.edu.

Roszman, Jay. Cork, Ireland. Affil: Univ. Coll., Cork. Email: jay.roszman@ucc.ie. Research: 19th-c Ireland.

Rota, Emanuel, *Illinois, Urbana-Champaign*. Email: rota@illinois.edu.

Rotge, Larry R., *Slippery Rock*.

Roth, Benita, *Binghamton, SUNY*. Email: broth@binghamton.edu.

Roth, Cassia Paigen, *Georgia*. Athens, GA. Email: cassia.roth@uga.edu. Research: health/reproduction/sexuality, gender studies.

Roth, Ginny A., *National Library of Medicine*. Email: ginny.roth@nih.gov.

Roth, James L. Grafton, WI. Affil: Alverno. Email: james.roth@alverno.edu; jameslroth@att.net. Research: modern Europe, women.

Roth, Jonathan P., *San José State*. Email: Jonathan.Roth@sjsu.edu.

Roth, Michael S. Middletown, CT. Affil: Wesleyan. Email: mroth@wesleyan.edu.

Research: theory of history, memory and history.

Roth, Randolph A., *Ohio State*. Columbus, OH. Email: roth.5@osu.edu. Research: violent crime and death, history and biology.

Roth, Tanya Lee. Saint Louis, MO. Affil: Mary Inst. and St. Louis Country Day Sch. Email: troth@micds.org. Research: women in US military since 1945.

Rothera, Evan Christopher. Huntsville, TX. Affil: Sam Houston State. Email: ecrothera@gmail.com. Research: 19th-c US, 19th-c transnational America.

Rothfeld, Anne, *National Library of Medicine*. Email: rothfea@mail.nih.gov.

Rothfels, Nigel T., *Wisconsin-Milwaukee*. Email: rothfels@uwm.edu.

Rothman, Adam, *Georgetown*. Washington, DC. Email: ar44@georgetown.edu. Research: US slavery and slave trade, early US politics and society.

Rothman, Aviva Tova, *Case Western Reserve*. Email: aviva.rothman@case.edu.

Rothman, David J., *Columbia (Hist.)*. Email: djr5@columbia.edu.

Rothman, E. Natalie, *Toronto*. Email: rothman@utsc.utoronto.ca.

Rothman, Joshua D., *Alabama, Tuscaloosa*. Tuscaloosa, AL. Email: jrothman@bama.ua.edu. Research: Old Southwest society and culture, mob violence and slave insurrection scares.

Rothmund, David Cameron. Lombard, IL. Affil: Illinois, Chicago. Email: zoso1994@yahoo.com. Research: social movements 1865-1945, Southern Negro Youth Congress.

Rothschild, Emma, *Harvard (Hist.)*. Cambridge, MA. Email: rothsch@fas.harvard.edu. Research: 18th-c French empire, economic ideas.

Rothschild, Norman H., *North Florida*. Email: hrothsch@unf.edu.

Rothwell, Rosalind. Durham, NC. Affil: Duke. Email: rozrothwell@gmail.com. Research: Atlantic, South Asia.

Rotondo-McCord, Jonathan, *Xavier, La*. Email: jrotondo@xula.edu.

Rotramel, Seth Amiel, *US Dept. of State*.

Rotter, Andrew Jon, *Colgate*. Hamilton, NY. Email: arotter@colgate.edu. Research: US diplomatic, recent US.

Rouighi, Ramzi, *Southern California*. Email: rouighi@usc.edu.

Rouleau, Brian, *Texas A&M*. Bryan, TX. Email: brianr@tamu.edu. Research: US in world, 19th-c US.

Rouleau, Laura Walikainen, *Michigan Tech*. Email: lwrouleau@mtu.edu.

Rounds, Jay, *Missouri–St. Louis*. Email: roundsj@msx.umsl.edu.

Rouphail, Robert, *Susquehanna*. Champaign, IL. Email: ropuhail@susqu.edu; rouphai2@illinois.edu.

Rouse, Anderson. Greensboro, NC. Affil: North Carolina, Greensboro. Email: arrouse@uncg.edu.

Rouse, Jacqueline A., *Georgia State*. Email: jrouse@gsu.edu.

Rouse, Richard H., *UCLA*. Email: rouse@history.ucla.edu.

Rouse, Wendy. Santa Clara, CA. Email: wendy.rouse@sjsu.edu.

*AHA members in **bold italic**; Directory-listed affiliations in italic*

Rousmaniere, Kate, *Miami, Ohio*. Email: rousmak@miamioh.edu.

Rousseau, Constance M., *Providence*. Email: rousseau@providence.edu.

Rousseau, Peter L., *Vanderbilt*. Email: peter.l.rousseau@vanderbilt.edu.

Rousselow-Winquist, Jessica. Upland, IN. Affil: Taylor. Email: jsroussel@taylor.edu.

Routledge, Karen. Calgary, AB, Canada. Affil: Parks Canada. Email: kirimsa@gmail.com. Research: Inuit/Eastern Arctic, North American environmental.

Roveri, Mattia. New York, NY. Affil: NYU. Email: mattia.roveri1@gmail.com.

Rowan, Jeremy D., *Florida International*. Email: rowanj@fiu.edu.

Rowan, Steven W., *Missouri–St. Louis*. Email: srowan@umsl.edu.

Rowden, Aubrey, *State Hist. Soc. of Missouri*. Email: RowdenAu@shsmo.org.

Rowe, Allan A., *Alberta*. Email: aarowe@ualberta.ca.

Rowe, David L., *Middle Tennessee State*. Email: David.Rowe@mtsu.edu.

Rowe, Erin Kathleen, *Johns Hopkins (Hist.)*. Email: erowe1@jhu.edu.

Rowe, John A., *Northwestern*. Email: ugandarowe@rowezone.com.

Rowe, Leroy Milton, *Southern Maine*. Email: leroy.rowe@maine.edu.

Rowe, Mary Ellen, *Central Missouri*. Email: rowe@ucmo.edu.

Rowe, Robyn Rebecca. Madison, WI. Affil: Wisconsin, Madison. Email: robyn.r.rowe@gmail.com. Research: Irish social and political thought 1880-1920, transatlantic intellectuals and WWI.

Rowe, Stephanie. Indianapolis, IN. Affil: National Council on Public Hist. Email: rowes@iupui.edu.

Rowe, William T., *Johns Hopkins (Hist.)*. Email: wtrowe@jhu.edu.

Rowland, Ingrid D., *Notre Dame*. Roma, Italy. Email: irowland@nd.edu. Research: ancient Athens and Sicily, 16th-c Italy.

Rowland, Leslie S., *Maryland, Coll. Park*. College Park, MD. Email: lrowland@umd.edu. Research: transition from slavery to freedom, Civil War and Reconstruction.

Rowland, Thomas J., *Wisconsin-Oshkosh*. Email: rowland@uwosh.edu.

Rowley, Alison, *Concordia, Can.* Email: Alison.Rowley@concordia.ca.

Rowley, David G., *Wisconsin-Platteville*. Email: rowleyd@uwplatt.edu.

Rowley, John D., *Arkansas Tech*.

Rowley, Sarah B., *DePauw*. Greencastle, IN. Email: rowley.sarah@gmail.com. Research: political, abortion.

Rowley, William Dean, *Nevada, Reno*. Email: rowley@unr.nevada.edu.

Rowney, Don K., *Bowling Green State*. Email: drowney@bgsu.edu.

Roxborough, Ian, *SUNY, Stony Brook*. Email: ian.roxborough@stonybrook.edu.

Roy, Haimanti, *Dayton*. Dayton, OH. Email: hroy1@udayton.edu; haimanti@gmail.com. Research: citizenship and migration, nationalism and state formations.

Roy, Lyse, *Québec, Montréal*. Email: roy.lyse@uqam.ca.

Roy, Susan, *Waterloo*. Email: susan.roy@uwaterloo.ca.

Royalty, Dale M., *East Tennessee State*. Email: royalty@etsu.edu.

Royalty, Robert M., Jr., *Wabash*. Email: royaltyr@wabash.edu.

Royer, Katherine A., *California State, Stanislaus*. Email: kroyer@csustan.edu.

Royles, Dan, *Florida International; Committee on LGBT Hist.* Miami Beach, FL. Email: droyles@fiu.edu; droyles@gmail.com. Research: African American AIDS activism in America.

Royster, Briana. Brooklyn, NY. Affil: NYU. Email: Bar410@nyu.edu. Research: African diaspora, religion/gender/empire.

Royster, Charles W., *Louisiana State*.

Rozbicki, Michal, *St. Louis*. Email: rozbicmj@slu.edu.

Rozek, Jessica. Lanham, MD. Affil: CALIBRE Systems. Email: jess.rozek@calibresys.com.

Rozenblit, Marsha L., *Maryland, Coll. Park*. College Park, MD. Email: mrozenbl@umd.edu. Research: Jews and Germans in Moravia 1848-1938.

Rozett, John M. Albany, NY. Email: rozettj@gmail.com.

Rozsa, George Gregory. Iowa City, IA. Affil: Iowa. Email: George-rozsa@uiowa.edu.

Rozum, Molly P., *South Dakota*. Vermillion, SD. Email: Molly.Rozum@usd.edu. Research: American studies, folklore.

Rozwadowski, Helen M., *Connecticut, Storrs*. Email: helen.rozwadowski@uconn.edu.

Ruane, Christine. Alexandria, VA. Affil: Tulsa. Email: christine-ruane@utulsa.edu. Research: Russia, social and women.

Rubchak, Marian, *Valparaiso*. Email: marian.rubchak@valpo.edu.

Rubeiz, Edward, *Science History Inst.* Email: erubeiz@sciencehistory.org.

Rubenstein, Anne, *York, Can.* Email: arubenst@yorku.ca.

Rubenstein, Jay C., *Southern California; Tennessee, Knoxville*. Email: jayruben@usc.edu; jrubens1@utk.edu.

Rubin, Anne Sarah, *Maryland, Baltimore County*. Baltimore, MD. Email: arubin@umbc.edu. Research: Civil War, memory.

Rubin, Daniel A., *US Dept. of State*.

Rubin, Eli, *Western Michigan*. Email: eli.rubin@wmich.edu.

Rubin, Jeffrey W., *Boston Univ.* Email: jwr@bu.edu.

Rubin, Joan Shelley, *Rochester*. Rochester, NY. Email: joan.rubin@rochester.edu. Research: 19th-/20th-c American intellectual, women.

Rubinfien, Louisa D., *Maryland, Coll. Park*.

Rubinson, Paul H. Bridgewater, MA. Affil: Bridgewater State. Email: paul.rubinson@bridgew.edu. Research: science and Cold War, human rights.

Rubio, Philip F., *North Carolina A&T State*. Durham, NC. Email: pfrubio@ncat.edu; philrubio1950@gmail.com. Research: black postal workers, civil rights and labor.

Ruck, Rob, *Pittsburgh*. Pittsburgh, PA. Email: ruck439019@aol.com. Research: 20th-c American labor, sports.

Rucker, Walter C. Atlanta, GA. Affil: Emory. Email: drwrucker@gmail.com. Research: slave culture and resistance, black Atlantic.

Rudd, Jon D. Bethesda, MD. Affil: Prince Georges Comm. Coll. Email: jrclio@aol.com.

Ruddiman, John A., *Wake Forest*. Email: ruddimja@wfu.edu.

Ruddy, T. Michael, *St. Louis*. Email: ruddytm@slu.edu.

Rudeen, Christopher Michael. Cambridge, MA. Affil: Harvard. Email: cmrudeen@g.harvard.edu.

Ruderman, Anne. London, United Kingdom. Affil: London Sch. of Economics. Email: a.e.ruderman@lse.ac.uk.

Ruderman, David B., *Pennsylvania*. Philadelphia, PA. Email: ruderman@sas.upenn.edu. Research: early modern and modern Jewish, early modern European intellectual.

Rudin, Ronald, *Concordia, Can.* Email: Ronald.Rudin@concordia.ca.

Rudolph, Julia E., *North Carolina State*. Email: jerudolp@ncsu.edu.

Rudolph, Nicole C., *Adelphi*. Email: nrudolph@adelphi.edu.

Rudolph, Richard L., *Minnesota (Hist.)*. Email: rrudolph11@comcast.net.

Rudwick, Martin J. S., *California, San Diego*. Email: mjsr100@cam.ac.uk.

Rudy, Jarrett, *McGill*. Email: jarrett.rudy@mcgill.ca.

Rueber, Micah. Sturgis, MS. Affil: Mississippi Valley State. Email: micah.rueber@mvsu.edu.

Rueda, Claudia P., *Texas A&M, Corpus Christi*. Email: claudia.rueda@tamucc.edu.

Ruediger, Dylan, *AHA*. Washington, DC. Email: druediger@historians.org. Research: Native American, settler colonialism.

Rueger, Jan Martin. London, United Kingdom. Affil: Birkbeck, London. Email: j.rueger@bbk.ac.uk.

Ruelland, Jacques G., *Montréal*. Email: jgruelland@progression.net.

Ruestow, Edward G., *Colorado, Boulder*. Email: edward.ruestow@colorado.edu.

Ruff, Julius R., *Marquette*. Menomonee Falls, WI. Email: julius.ruff@marquette.edu. Research: early modern European violence, early modern French banditry.

Ruff, Mark Edward, *St. Louis*. Email: ruff@slu.edu.

Ruffini, Giovanni R., *Fairfield*. Email: gruffini@fairfield.edu.

Rugemer, Edward B., *Yale*. Email: edward.rugemer@yale.edu.

Rugenstein, Ernest Richard, IV. Troy, NY. Affil: Hudson Valley Comm. Coll. Email: errugenstein@genusinter.com. Research: Native American cultural, 400-1500 CE Europe.

Ruggere, Christine A., *Johns Hopkins (Hist. of Science)*. Email: ruggere@jhmi.edu.

Ruggiero, Guido, Jr., *Miami*. Miami, FL. Email: gruggiero@miami.edu. Research: Renaissance sexual identity, Renaissance treasure hunting.

Ruggiero, Kristin, *Wisconsin-Milwaukee*. Email: ruggiero@uwm.edu.

Ruggles, Steven, *Minnesota (Hist.)*. Email: ruggles@umn.edu.

Rugh, Susan S., *Brigham Young*. Provo, UT. Email: susan_rugh@byu.edu. Research: travel and tourism in US, rural US and Midwest.

Ruiz, Jesus Guillermo. New Orleans, LA. Affil: Tulane. Email: jruiz3@tulane.edu. Research: colonial Latin America, Atlantic world.

Ruiz, Mario M., *Hofstra*. Philadelphia, PA. Email: mario.ruiz@hofstra.edu. Research: gender in modern Middle East, colonial/postcolonial studies.

Ruiz, **Teofilo F.**, *UCLA.* Los Angeles, CA. Email: tfruiz@history.ucla.edu. Research: medieval and early modern Spain and Mediterranean.

Ruiz, **Vicki L.**, *California, Irvine.* Irvine, CA. Email: vruiz@uci.edu. Research: Latina, labor and social movements.

Rumba, **Amanda**. Lafayette, IN. Affil: Purdue; Ivy Tech Comm. Coll. Email: reason@purdue.edu.

Ruminski, **Clayton**, *Hagley Museum and Library.* Email: cruminski@hagley.org.

Rummell, **Nicholas Lee**. Summerville, SC. Affil: Trident Tech. Email: nicholas.rummell@ tridenttech.edu. Research: WWI propaganda, German and Ottoman/Turkish relations.

Rumsey, **Abby S**. San Francisco, CA. Email: abby@asrumsey.com. Research: libraries and collecting institutions, information technologies/analog and digital.

Runcie, **Sarah Cook**, *Louisiana, Lafayette.*

Rung, **Margaret C.**, *Roosevelt.* Evanston, IL. Email: mrung@roosevelt.edu. Research: labor policy in North America, US civil service 1880-1960.

Runstedtler, **Theresa E.**, *American.* Washington, DC. Email: runstedt@american.edu; runstedtler@aol.com. Research: black internationalism, race and popular culture.

Runyon, **William**. Washington, DC. Affil: L. Ron Hubbard Foundation. Email: bill.runyon@ lronhubbard.org.

Ruoff, **Ken J.**, *Portland State.* Portland, OR. Email: ruoffk@pdx.edu. Research: 2600th anniversary celebrations, midcentury modernity.

Rupakheti, **Sanjog**, *Holy Cross.* Worcester, MA. Email: srupakhe@holycross.edu.

Rupert, **Linda M.**, *North Carolina, Greensboro.* Durham, NC. Email: lmrupert@uncg.edu. Research: early modern Caribbean and Atlantic, creolization.

Rupp, **Leila J.**, *California, Santa Barbara.* Santa Barbara, CA. Email: lrupp@femst.ucsb. edu. Research: transnational homophile movement, global history of love between women.

Rupp, **Susan Z.**, *Wake Forest.* Email: rupp@wfu. edu.

Rupp, **Teresa Pugh**, *Mount St. Mary's.* Email: rupp@msmary.edu.

Rupprecht, **Nancy E.**, *Middle Tennessee State.* Email: Nancy.Rupprecht@mtsu.edu.

Rury, **John L.**, *Kansas.* Lawrence, KS. Email: jrury@ku.edu. Research: American education, race and social inequality.

Rusch, **Stacy J.**, *Virginia Museum of Hist.* Email: srusch@VirginiaHistory.org.

Rush, **Anne Spry**, *Maryland, Coll. Park.* Kensington, MD. Email: arush1@umd.edu; annesprush@gmail.com. Research: British Empire/decolonization, immigration/migration/lawlessness.

Rush, **James R.**, *Arizona State.* Email: james. rush@asu.edu.

Rush, **Kimberly**. Bauxite, AR. Affil: American Public Univ. System. Email: kim.r.rush@gmail. com. Research: early Elizabethan England, Renaissance.

Rush, **Lt Anthony P.**, *US Air Force Acad.* Email: anthony.rush@usafa.edu.

Rushforth, **Brett**, *Oregon.* Eugene, OR. Email: bhrush@uoregon.edu. Research: early American slavery, French Atlantic.

Rushing, **Allen**, *East Tennessee State.* Email: rushinga@etsu.edu.

Rushing, **Tracie**, *Central Arkansas.* Email: trushing@uca.edu.

Ruskola, **Teemu**, *Emory.* Email: teemu.ruskola@ emory.edu.

Rusnock, **Andrea A.**, *Rhode Island.* Email: rusnock@uri.edu.

Russ, **Jonathan S.**, *Delaware.* Email: jruss@udel. edu.

Russell, **Alexandria**. Columbia, SC. Affil: South Carolina. Email: russela@email.sc.edu.

Russell, **Andrew L.** Utica, NY. Affil: SUNY Polytechnic Inst. Email: arussell@arussell.org. Research: information and communication technology, standardization.

Russell, **Edmund P., III**, *Boston Univ.; Carnegie Mellon.* Pittsburgh, PA. Email: edruss@bu.edu; edmundr@andrew.cmu.edu. Research: evolution, telegraphy.

Russell, **Frederick H.**, *Rutgers, Newark/New Jersey Inst. of Tech.* Mount Tabor, NJ. Email: frussell@andromeda.rutgers.edu. Research: Augustine, medieval canon law.

Russell, **James Michael**, *Tennessee, Chattanooga.* Email: james-russell@utc.edu.

Russell, **Jeffrey B.**, *California, Santa Barbara.*

Russell, **Mike R.** Salina, KS. Affil: Kansas Wesleyan. Email: dr.mike@kwu.edu. Research: Holocaust, Cold War.

Russell, **Mona L.**, *East Carolina.* Email: russellm@ ecu.edu.

Russell, **Natalie**, *Huntington Library.* Email: nrussell@huntington.org.

Russell, **Nicholas F.** Traverse City, MI. Email: nfrussell@gmail.com. Research: Chinese influence on Spanish Enlightenment, US from Civil War to present.

Russell, **Stephanie L.**, *Truman State.* Email: slrussell@truman.edu.

Russell, **Timothy Dale**. Eastvale, CA. Email: trussell09@gmail.com.

Russo, **Daniel G.**, *Central Connecticut State.* Email: russod@ccsu.edu.

Russo, **David J.**, *McMaster.*

Rust, **Eric C.**, *Baylor.* Email: eric_rust@baylor.edu.

Rustomji, **Nerina**, *St. John's, NY.* Jamaica, NY. Email: rustomjn@stjohns.edu. Research: Middle East, Islamic world.

Rustow, **Marina**, *Princeton.* Email: mrustow@ princeton.edu.

Ruswick, **Brent J.**, *West Chester.* Email: bruswick@wcupa.edu.

Rutenberg, **Amy**, *Iowa State.* Email: arutenbe@ iastate.edu.

Ruth, **David E.**, *Penn State.* Email: dxr35@psu. edu.

Rutherford, **David E.**, *Central Michigan.* Email: ruthe1de@cmich.edu.

Rutherford, **Emily**. Bronx, NY. Affil: Columbia. Email: emr2213@columbia.edu.

Rutherford, **Paul F. W.**, *Toronto.* Email: prutherf@chass.utoronto.ca.

Rutherford, **Phillip**, *Marshall.* Email: rutherfordp@marshall.edu.

Rutkoff, **Peter M.**, *Kenyon.* Email: rutkoff@ kenyon.edu.

Rutkow, **Eric**, *Central Florida.* Email: Eric. Rutkow@ucf.edu.

Rutledge, **Steven H.**, *Linfield.*

Rutter, **Nick**, *Fairfield.* Email: nrutter@fairfield. edu.

Rutz, **Michael A.**, *Wisconsin-Oshkosh.* Email: rutz@uwosh.edu.

Ruud, **Charles A.**, *Western Ontario.* Email: ruud@ uwo.ca.

Ruzicka, **Stephen Q.**, *North Carolina, Greensboro.* Email: sqruzick@uncg.edu.

Ryan, **Francis**, *La Salle.* Email: ryan@lasalle.edu.

Ryan, **James D.** New York, NY. Affil: Bronx Comm. Coll., CUNY. Email: james.d.ryan@ verizon.net. Research: Crusade and mission, cults of missionary martyrs.

Ryan, **James G.** Webster, TX. Affil: Texas A&M, Galveston. Email: ryanj@tamug.edu. Research: American left and right, world communism.

Ryan, **John P.** Shawnee Mission, KS. Affil: Kansas City Kansas Comm. Coll. Email: jpryan2007@ gmail.com.

Ryan, **Joseph G.**, *OSA*, *Villanova.* Email: joseph. ryan@villanova.edu.

Ryan, **Kelly A.**, *Indiana, Southeast.* Email: ryanka@ius.edu.

Ryan, **Luke C.** Stone Mountain, GA. Affil: Georgia Gwinnett. Email: lryan@ggc.edu.

Ryan, **Mary P.**, *Johns Hopkins (Hist.).* Berkeley, CA. Email: mpryan@jhu.edu. Research: urban, gender.

Ryan, **Michael A.**, *New Mexico.* Albuquerque, NM. Email: ryan6@unm.edu. Research: medieval Spanish cultural and intellectual, medieval Mediterranean cultural and intellectual.

Ryan, **Patrick Joseph**. London, ON, Canada. Affil: Kings Univ. Coll. Email: pryan2@uwo.ca. Research: discourse analysis, ideas.

Ryan, **Shawn Daniel**. Worcester, MA. Email: sryan685@yahoo.com. Research: Dominican Republic/Ulises Heureaux era, Caribbean piracy/capitalism/revolution.

Ryan, **W. Michael**, *Northern Kentucky.* Email: ryanw@nku.edu.

Ryang, **Key Sun**, *Mary Washington.*

Ryckman, **Melissa J.** Columbia, TN. Affil: Matin Methodist. Email: mbruninga@ martinmethodist.edu. Research: heresy, FLDS.

Rydell, **Robert W., II**, *Montana State, Bozeman.* Email: rwrydell@montana.edu.

Ryden, **David Beck**, *Houston-Downtown.* Email: rydend@uhd.edu.

Ryder, **John Gregory**, *Radford.*

Rymer, **George Alfred**. Georgetown, TX. Affil: Texas A&M, Central Texas. Email: Grymer8657@aol.com.

Rymph, **Catherine W.**, *Missouri, Columbia.* Email: rymphc@missouri.edu.

Rymsza-Pawlowlska, **Malgorzata Joanna**, *American.* Email: rymszapa@american.edu.

Ryon, **Roderick N.**, *Towson.*

Ryskamp, **George**, *Brigham Young.* Email: george_ryskamp@byu.edu.

Rzadkiewicz, **Chester M.**, *Louisiana, Lafayette.*

Rzeczkowski, **Frank Roman**, *Xavier, Ohio.* Email: rzeczkowskif@xavier.edu.

Rzeznik, **Thomas F.**, *Seton Hall.* South Orange, NJ. Email: thomas.rzeznik@shu.edu. Research: US Catholic and religious, urban.

S s

Saad, **Abubaker M.**, *Western Connecticut State.* Email: saada@wcsu.edu.

Saada, **Emmanuelle M.**, *Columbia (Hist.).* Email: es2593@columbia.edu.

Saak, Eric Leland, *Indiana–Purdue, Indianapolis*. Indianapolis, IN. Email: esaak@iupui. edu. Research: late medieval Augustinian traditions, late medieval political thought.

Saari, Jon L., *Northern Michigan*. Email: jsaari@nmu.edu.

Saavedra, Yvette J. Eugene, OR. Affil: Oregon. Email: yjs@uoregon.edu. Research: Mexican American racial identity and land policies.

Saba, Elias, *Grinnell*. Email: sabaelia@grinnell.edu.

Saba, Roberto N. P. F., *St. Michael's*. Email: rsaba@smcvt.edu.

Sabathne, James. Roscoe, IL. Affil: Hononegah High Sch. Email: jsabat@hononegah.org.

Sabato, Hilda. Buenos Aires, Argentina. Affil: Buenos Aires. Email: hsabato@arnet.com.ar.

Sabean, David Warren, *UCLA*. Los Angeles, CA. Email: dsabean@history.ucla.edu. Research: kinship and family in Europe, European cultural and social.

Sabin, Margaret Alison. New York, NY. Email: masabin@verizon.net. Research: Robert Feke, 18th-c American culture.

Sabin, Paul E., *Yale*. New Haven, CT. Email: paul.sabin@yale.edu. Research: environmental, energy politics.

Sabol, Steven O'Neal, *North Carolina, Charlotte*. Email: sosabol@uncc.edu.

Sabra, Adam A., *California, Santa Barbara*. Santa Barbara, CA. Email: asabra@history.ucsb.edu. Research: poverty and charity in medieval Egypt, Sufism and society in Ottoman Egypt.

Saburova, Tatiana, *Indiana*. Email: tsaburov@indiana.edu.

Sacco, Lynn, *Tennessee, Knoxville*. Knoxville, TN. Email: lsacco@utk.edu. Research: incest in US, medicine and sexuality.

Sach, Michael Andrew. Oyster Bay, NY. Affil: Half Hollow Hills Sch. District. Email: Michael.sach34@gmail.com.

Sacher, John M., *Central Florida*. Email: john.sacher@ucf.edu.

Sachs, Aaron, *Cornell*. Email: as475@cornell.edu.

Sachs, Honor R., *Colorado, Boulder*. Email: Honor.Sachs@colorado.edu.

Sachs, Miranda Rogow, *Denison*. Email: sachsm@denison.edu.

Sachs, Stephen E. Durham, NC. Affil: Duke. Email: sachs@law.duke.edu. Research: early American legal, medieval English legal.

Sachs, William L. Richmond, VA. Email: wls@aol.com. Research: religion and indigenization, religion and compassion.

Sack, Daniel. Washington, DC. Affil: NEH. Email: sack@alumni.princeton.edu. Research: religion and Great Depression, religion and youth movements.

Sack, James J., *Illinois, Chicago*. Chicago, IL. Email: jsack@uic.edu. Research: 18th-/19th-c Britain.

Sack, Ronald H., *North Carolina State*. Email: ronald_sack@ncsu.edu.

Sackett, Robert E., *Colorado Colorado Springs*. Email: rsackett@uccs.edu.

Sackeyfio-Lenoch, Naaborko, *Dartmouth*. Evanston, IL. Email: naaborko.sackeyfio-lenoch@dartmouth.edu. Research: global Ghana in postindependence era, transnational cultural projects.

Sackley, Nicole, *Richmond*. Email: nsackley@richmond.edu.

Sackman, Douglas C., *Puget Sound*. Email: dsackman@pugetsound.edu.

Sacks, David Harris, *Reed*. Portland, OR. Email: dsacks@reed.edu. Research: early modern political/ethical discourse, Britain and Atlantic world.

Sacks, Kenneth, *Brown*. Email: Kenneth_Sacks@Brown.edu.

Sacks, Marcy S., *Albion*. Albion, MI. Email: msacks@albion.edu. Research: African American, post-Emancipation.

Sadeghian, Saghar, *Willamette*. Email: ssadeghian@willamette.edu.

Sadkowski, Konrad, *Northern Iowa*. Email: konrad.sadkowski@uni.edu.

Sadler, Jesse, *Loyola Marymount*. San Diego, CA. Email: jsadler@ucla.edu. Research: early capitalism in merchant families.

Sadler, Louis R., *New Mexico State*. Email: losadler@nmsu.edu.

Sadler, Richard W., *Weber State*. Email: rsadler@weber.edu.

Sadowsky, Jonathan Hal, *Case Western Reserve*. Email: jonathan.sadowsky@case.edu.

Saeger, James S., *Lehigh*. Email: jss0@lehigh.edu.

Saenz, Charles Nicholas. Alamosa, CO. Affil: Adams State. Email: cnsaenz@adams.edu. Research: political culture in Andalusia, localism and modernity.

Saffell, Cameron L. Lubbock, TX. Affil: Museum of Texas Tech Univ. Email: cameron.saffell@ttu.edu. Research: heritage & museum sciences.

Safford, Frank R., *Northwestern*. Email: f-safford@northwestern.edu.

Safier, Neil F., *Brown*. Providence, RI. Affil: John Carter Brown Library. Email: neil_safier@brown.edu. Research: Amazonian expeditions, ecological practices.

Safley, Thomas M., *Pennsylvania*. Email: tsafley@history.upenn.edu.

Safran, Janina, *Penn State*. Email: jxs57@psu.edu.

Sage, Elizabeth M., *Whittier*. Email: esage@whittier.edu.

Sagendorf, Edward. Scotch Plains, NJ. Affil: Union Catholic High Sch. Email: esagendorf@unioncatholic.org.

Sagers, John H., *Linfield*. Email: jsagers@linfield.edu.

Sahin, Kaya, *Indiana*. Email: iksahin@indiana.edu.

Sahlins, Peter. Berkeley, CA. Affil: California, Berkeley. Email: sahlins@berkeley.edu. Research: early modern France.

Saho, Bala S. K., *Oklahoma (Hist.)*. Email: bsaho1@ou.edu.

Sahotsky, Brian. Randolph, NJ. Affil: County Coll. of Morris. Email: bsahotsky@ccm.edu.

Saidi, Christine, *Kutztown*. Email: saidi@kutztown.edu.

Saikia, Yasmin, *Arizona State*. Paradise Valley, AZ. Email: ysaikia@asu.edu. Research: Muslim cosmopolitanism, postcolonial South Asia.

Saillant, John D., *Western Michigan*. Email: john.saillant@wmich.edu.

Sainsbury, John A., *Brock*. Email: jsainsbu@brocku.ca.

Saitua, Iker. Riverside, CA. Affil: California, Riverside. Email: isaitua@ucr.edu.

Sajdi, Dana, *Boston Coll.* Email: sajdi@bc.edu.

Saka, Mark Saad, *Sul Ross State*. Email: msaka@sulross.edu.

Sakai, Naoki, *Cornell*. Email: ns32@cornell.edu.

Sakmyster, Thomas L., *Cincinnati*. Email: tom.sakmyster@uc.edu.

Saksena, Jyotika, *Indianapolis*. Email: jsaksena@uindy.edu.

Saladino, Salvatore. Massapequa Park, NY. Email: user885963@aol.com.

Salamone, Andrew. Burke, VA. Affil: George Mason. Email: asalamon@gmu.edu.

Salamone, Nicholas. Sherrill, NC. Email: njsalamone@gmail.com.

Salas, Nora, *Grand Valley State*. Email: salasn@gvsu.edu.

Salas Landa, Monica. Easton, PA. Email: salaslam@lafayette.edu.

Salata, Debra A., *Lincoln Memorial*. Email: debra.salata@lmunet.edu.

Salau, Mohammed Bashir, *Mississippi*. Email: bashir@olemiss.edu.

Salazar, Victor. Columbus, GA. Affil: Columbus State. Email: salazar_victor@columbusstate.edu. Research: historical empathy, multiculturalism.

Salazar Rey, Ricardo Raul, *Connecticut, Storrs*. Email: ricardo.salazar-rey@uconn.edu.

Saleh, Walid Ahmad. Toronto, ON, Canada. Affil: Toronto. Email: walid.saleh@utoronto.ca.

Saler, Michael T., *California, Davis*. Berkeley, CA. Email: mtsaler@ucdavis.edu. Research: modernity, mass and elite cultures.

Salerno, Beth A., *St. Anselm*. Manchester, NH. Email: bsalerno@anselm.edu. Research: antislavery and abolition, biography.

Salgado, Justin. Lubbock, TX. Email: justin.salgado@ttu.edu.

Salgado, Onix. San Juan, PR. Affil: Interamericana. Email: neiva00@yahoo.com.

Salhi, Ruma Niyogi. Annandale, VA. Affil: Northern Virginia Comm. Coll. Email: rnsalhi@gmail.com. Research: Byzantium, gender.

Saliba, Najib E., *Worcester State*. Email: nsaliba@worcester.edu.

Salinas, Capt Antonio, *US Military Acad*. Email: antonio.salinas@usma.edu.

Salinas, Cristina, *Texas, Arlington*. Email: csalinas@uta.edu.

Salinas, Salvador, *Houston-Downtown*. Houston, TX. Email: salinass@uhd.edu. Research: water in Mexico, rice in Mexico.

Salinger, Sharon V., *California, Irvine*. Irvine, CA. Email: salinger@uci.edu. Research: 18th-c Boston/migration, free blacks/slaves in colonial Boston.

Salisbury, Neal E., *Smith*. Email: nsalisbu@smith.edu.

Salkeld, Helen. Cary, NC. Email: hasalkeld@gmail.com.

Saller, Richard P., *Stanford*. Email: rsaller@stanford.edu.

Salm, Steven J., *Xavier, La*. New Orleans, LA. Email: sjsalm@xula.edu. Research: youth, Ghana.

Salman, Michael A., *UCLA*. Email: salman@history.ucla.edu.

Salmon, Marylynn. Florence, MA. Affil: Smith. Email: msalmon@email.smith.edu.

Salo, Edward, *Arkansas State*. Email: esalo@astate.edu.

Salomon, Frank. Iowa City, IA. Affil: Wisconsin, Madison. Email: fsalomon@wisc.edu.

Salomon, Hilel B., *South Carolina, Columbia*. Email: hilele@yahoo.com.

Saltamacchia, Martina, *Nebraska, Omaha*. Email: msaltamacchia@unomaha.edu.

Salton-Cox, Glyn, *California, Santa Barbara*. Email: saltoncox@english.ucsb.edu.

Saluppo, Alessandro. Brooklyn, NY. Affil: Studi di Padova. Email: alessandro.saluppo@unipd.it.

Salvatore, Nick, *Cornell*. Ithaca, NY. Email: nas4@cornell.edu. Research: American labor and social.

Salvucci, Linda K., *Trinity, Tex*. San Antonio, TX. Email: lsalvucc@trinity.edu. Research: US-Cuba trade 1760-1898, precollegiate textbooks.

Salyer, Lucy, *New Hampshire, Durham*. Email: lucy.salyer@unh.edu.

Salzer, Kathryn E., *Penn State*. Email: kes30@psu.edu.

Salzman, Michele R., *California, Riverside*. Email: michele.salzman@ucr.edu.

Salzmann, Ariel C., *Queen's, Can*. Email: as45@queensu.ca.

Salzmann, Joshua A. T., *Northeastern Illinois*. Email: J-Salzmann@neiu.edu.

Samaniego, Juan. Chula Vista, CA. Email: jfs51@humboldt.edu.

Samarrai, A. I. Reedsburg, WI.

Sameen, Zoya. Chicago, IL. Affil: Chicago. Email: zsameen@uchicago.edu.

Samji, Karim, *Gettysburg*. Email: ksamji@gettysburg.edu.

Sammartino, Annemarie H., *Oberlin*. Email: annemarie.sammartino@oberlin.edu.

Sammons, Jeffrey T., *NYU*. Email: jeffrey.sammons@nyu.edu.

Samols, Steven Weiss. Los Angeles, CA. Affil: Southern California. Email: ssamols@usc.edu.

Samonte, Cecilia Astraquillo, *Rockhurst*. Email: cecilia.samonte@rockhurst.edu.

Samper Vendrell, Javier. Grinnell, IA. Affil: Grinnell. Email: samperja@grinnell.edu. Research: gender and sexuality in interwar Germany, LGBTQ.

Samponaro, Philip, *Texas-Rio Grande Valley*. Email: philip.samponaro@utrgv.edu.

Sampson, Joyce E., *Naval War Coll*. Email: jesampso@nps.navy.mil.

Sampson, Molly, *Science History Inst*. Email: msampson@sciencehistory.org.

Samson, Daniel J., *Brock*. Email: dsamson@brocku.ca.

Samson, Jane D., *Alberta*. Email: jane.samson@ualberta.ca.

Samuels, Peter S, *SUNY, Coll. Geneseo*. Email: samuels@geneseo.edu.

Samuelson, Richard A., *California State, San Bernardino*. Email: rsamuels@csusb.edu.

San Miguel, Guadalupe, Jr., *Houston*. Email: gsanmiguel@uh.edu.

Sanabria, Enrique A., *New Mexico*. Albuquerque, NM. Email: sanabria@unm.edu. Research: Spanish anticlericalism and nationalism, sport and leisure in modern Spain.

Sanabria, José E. Manatí, PR. Email: profesorsanabria@hotmail.com.

Sanborn, Joshua, *Lafayette*. Easton, PA. Email: sanbornj@lafayette.edu. Research: WWI, violence and society.

Sanceri, Jeffrey. Berkeley, CA. Affil: Alameda. Email: sanceri@gmail.com. Research: incarceration, children.

Sanchez, Danielle, *Colorado Coll.; Muhlenberg*. Email: dsanchez@coloradocollege.edu.

Sanchez, Esperanza. Los Angeles, CA. Affil: LA Plaza de Culturas y Arte. Email: Ekssanchez@gmail.com. Research: Los Angeles Public History, Public Art.

Sanchez, George J., *Southern California; OAH*. Email: georges@usc.edu.

Sanchez, Jason C. Bronx, NY. Affil: Bronx Comm. Coll., CUNY. Email: jcsanchez39@hotmail.com.

Sanchez, Jose M., *St. Louis*. Email: sanchejm@slu.edu.

Sanchez, Magdalena S., *Gettysburg*. Email: msanchez@gettysburg.edu.

Sanchez, Sabrina, *Bellevue*. Email: s.sanchez@bellevuecollege.edu.

Sanchez-Albornoz, Nicolas, *NYU*.

Sanchez-Walker, Marjorie, *California State, Stanislaus*. Email: mwalker@csustan.edu.

Sand, Jordan A., *Georgetown*. Email: sandj@georgetown.edu.

Sandage, Scott A., *Carnegie Mellon*. Pittsburgh, PA. Email: sandage@andrew.cmu.edu. Research: mixed-race identity, Native Americans.

Sandberg, Brian, *Northern Illinois*. DeKalb, IL. Email: bsandberg@niu.edu. Research: French Wars of Religion, Violence and civil conflict studies.

Sander, Joshua R. Knoxville, TN. Affil: Tennessee, Knoxville. Email: jsande49@vols.utk.edu.

Sanderfer, Selena Ronshaye, *Western Kentucky*. Email: selena.sanderfer@wku.edu.

Sanderovitch, Sharon. Kadima-Tsoran, Israel. Affil: Hebrew, Jerusalem. Email: ssharon@berkeley.edu.

Sanders, Charles W., Jr., *Kansas State*. Email: chassan@ksu.edu.

Sanders, Claire A., *Texas Christian*. Email: c.sanders@tcu.edu.

Sanders, Crystal R., *Penn State*.

Sanders, Elizabeth. Ithaca, NY. Affil: Cornell. Email: mes14@cornell.edu.

Sanders, Gary B. Denton, TX. Affil: North Texas. Email: garysanders@my.unt.edu.

Sanders, I. Taylor, II, *Washington and Lee*.

Sanders, James, *Utah State*. Logan, UT. Email: james.sanders@usu.edu. Research: popular politics, Atlantic.

Sanders, Jeffrey C., *Washington State, Pullman*. Email: jcsanders@wsu.edu.

Sanders, John T. Annapolis, MD. Affil: US Naval Acad. Email: sanders@usna.edu. Research: Vladimir Shainskii, Soviet Union.

Sanders, Nichole M., *Lynchburg*. Email: sanders.n@lynchburg.edu.

Sanders, Paula A., *Rice*. Houston, TX. Email: sanders@rice.edu. Research: medieval Middle East, Islamic civilization.

Sanders, Sarah. Farmington Hills, MI. Affil: Johns Hopkins. Email: sksanders3@yahoo.com.

Sanders, Stuart, *Kentucky Hist. Soc*. Email: stuart.sanders@ky.gov.

Sanders, Vivienne. Porthcawl, United Kingdom. Email: viv.sanders@btinternet.com.

Sanders Garcia, Ashley. Los Angeles, CA. Affil: UCLA. Email: asandersgarcia@g.ucla.edu. Research: settler colonialism, American Midwest and French Algeria.

Sanderson, Mary, *Dayton*. Email: msanderson1@udayton.edu.

Sanderson, Warren, *SUNY, Stony Brook*. Email: warren.sanderson@stonybrook.edu.

Sandgren, David P., *Concordia Coll*. Email: sandgren@cord.edu.

Sandiford, Keith A. P., *Manitoba*.

Sandler, Willeke, *Loyola, Md*. Email: wsandler@loyola.edu.

Sandlos, John, *Memorial, Newfoundland*. Email: jsandlos@mun.ca.

Sandman, Alison D., *James Madison*. Email: sandmaad@jmu.edu.

Sandoval-Strausz, Andrew K., *Penn State*. University Park, PA. Email: aus1050@psu.edu. Research: US urban landscapes, Latino history and migration.

Sandstrom, Roy E., *Northern Iowa*.

Sandul, Paul J. P., *Stephen F. Austin State*. Email: sandulpj@sfasu.edu.

Sandulescu, Valentin Adrian. Bucharest, Romania. Affil: Bucharest. Email: valentin.sandulescu@gmail.com. Research: Fascism, Jewish studies.

Sandweiss, Eric, *Indiana*. Email: sesandw@indiana.edu.

Sandweiss, Martha A., *Princeton; Western Hist. Assoc*. Princeton, NJ. Email: masand@princeton.edu. Research: American West, visual culture.

Sandy, James, *Texas, Arlington*. Email: james.sandy@uta.edu.

Sandy, Julia L., *Shepherd*. Email: jsandyba@shepherd.edu.

Sanelli, Maria F., *Kutztown*. Email: msanelli@kutztown.edu.

Saney, Isaac, *St. Mary's, Can*. Email: isaac.saney@dal.ca.

Sanfilippo, Stephen Nicholas. Southold, NY. Affil: Maine Maritime Academy. Email: seasonghistory@gmail.com. Research: seamen's songs and poems as gendered texts, constructions of seamen's masculinity.

Sanford, Donald G., *Central Connecticut State*.

Sanft, Charles, *Tennessee, Knoxville*. Email: csanft@utk.edu.

Sangster, Douglas. Berkeley, CA. Affil: California, Berkeley. Email: doug.sangster10@gmail.com.

Sanislo, Teresa, *Wisconsin-Eau Claire*. Email: sanisltm@uwec.edu.

Sankale, Michelle. Centennial, CO. Email: msankale@aol.com.

Sanko, Marc A., *Clarion, Pa*. Clarion, PA. Email: msanko@clarion.edu; masanko2@gmail.com. Research: immigration and ethnic, North America.

Sanmartin, Jose J. Las Heredades, Spain. Affil: Alicante. Email: jose.sanmartin@ua.es. Research: political theory, US and Canadian political system.

Sanos, Sandrine, *Texas A&M, Corpus Christi*. Email: sandrine.sanos@tamucc.edu.

Santamaria Balmaceda, Gema Karina, *Loyola, Chicago*. Chicago, IL. Email: gsantamaria@luc.edu; gemasantamaria@gmail.com. Research: political/social/criminal violence, legality and legitimacy.

Santamarina, Juan C., *Dayton*. Email: santamar@udayton.edu.

Santana, Saul. Chicago, IL. Email: Sonny.santana5@gmail.com.

Santiago, Myrna I., *St. Mary's, Calif*. Email: msantiag@stmarys-ca.edu.

Santner, Kathryn. Studio City, CA. Affil: London. Email: kathryn.santner@gmail.com.

Santoni, Pedro M., *California State, San Bernardino*. Email: psantoni@csusb.edu.

Santoro, **Anthony R.**, *Christopher Newport*. Yorktown, VA. Email: santoro@cnu.edu. Research: ancient Egypt, Byzantine Empire.

Santoro, **Lily A.** Dexter, MO. Affil: Southeast Missouri State. Email: lsantoro@semo.edu. Research: early Republic religion, early Republic popular science.

Santos, **Brenda J.** New Haven, CT. Affil: Achievement First. Email: brendajsantos23@gmail.com. Research: 20th-c US political/social/cultural, US women and gender.

Santos, **Michael Wayne**, *Lynchburg*. Email: santos@lynchburg.edu.

Santos, **Sharon L.** Blackstone, MA. Email: sharonsantos@me.com.

Sanyal, **Usha**. Wingate, NC. Affil: Wingate. Email: ushasanyal3@gmail.com. Research: girls' madrasa (seminary) education, Al-Huda online community.

Saperstein, **Marc E.**, *George Washington*. Email: msaper@gwu.edu.

Saracoglu, **M. Safa**, *Bloomsburg*. Email: msaracog@bloomu.edu.

Saraiva, **Tiago**, *Drexel*. Email: tfs37@drexel.edu.

Sarantakes, **Nicholas E.**, *Naval War Coll.* Email: nick.sarantakes@usnwc.edu.

Saravia, **Gonzalo M. Quintero**. Lima, Peru. Affil: Embassy of Spain to Peru. Email: gquintero141@hotmail.com.

Sarcevic-Tesanovic, **Rachel**. Evanston, IL. Affil: Northwestern. Email: rachelsarcevic-tesanovic2025@u.northwestern.edu.

Sargeant, **Lynn M.**, *California State, Fullerton*. Email: lsargeant@fullerton.edu.

Sargent, **Daniel J.**, *California, Berkeley*. Berkeley, CA. Email: daniel.sargent@berkeley.edu. Research: 1970s US foreign relations, international system.

Sargent, **Natalie Carroll**. Notre Dame, IN. Affil: Notre Dame. Email: nsargent@nd.edu.

Sargent, **Steven D.**, *Union Coll.* Email: sargents@union.edu.

Sargent Wood, **Linda A.**, *Northern Arizona*. Email: linda.sargent.wood@nau.edu.

Sarkar, **Jayita**. Cambridge, MA. Affil: MIT. Email: jayitasarkar@gmail.com.

Sarkisian, **Aram G.** Chicago, IL. Affil: Northwestern. Email: aram.sarkisian@gmail.com. Research: Eastern Orthodox Christianity in US, nativism/citizenship/state power.

Sarna, **Jonathan D.**, *Brandeis*. Waltham, MA. Email: sarna@brandeis.edu. Research: American Jewish.

Sarnoff, **Daniella**. Irvington, NY. Affil: Social Science Research Council. Email: daniellasarnoff@hotmail.com.

Sarr, **Assan**, *Ohio*. Email: sarr@ohio.edu.

Sarreal, **Julia S.** Phoenix, AZ. Affil: Arizona State New Coll. Email: julia.sarreal@asu.edu. Research: mission, 18th-c economy of Rio de la Plata.

Sarrouh, **Mary Kathleen**. Seven Hills, OH. Affil: Notre Dame Coll. Email: mksarrouh@gmail.com. Research: women in Cleveland OH.

Sarti, **Cathleen**. Wiesbaden, Germany. Affil: Mainz. Email: cathleen.sarti@googlemail.com. Research: depositions of Protestant European monarchs, literature and politics in Stuart England.

Sarti, **Roland**, *Massachusetts, Amherst*. Amherst, MA. Email: sarti@history.umass.edu. Research: risorgimento, biography.

Sartin, **Roy Jo**, *Colorado Colorado Springs*. Email: rsartin@uccs.edu.

Sartori, **Andrew S.**, *NYU*. New York, NY. Email: asartori@nyu.edu. Research: modern South Asia, modern intellectual.

Sartorius, **David A.**, *Maryland, Coll. Park*. Email: das@umd.edu.

Sarty, **Roger**, *Wilfrid Laurier*. Email: rsarty@wlu.ca.

Sarzynski, **Sarah R.**, *Claremont McKenna*. Claremont, CA. Email: ssarzynski@cmc.edu; ssarzynski@hotmail.com. Research: Brazil during Cold War, Amazon.

Sasaki, **Motoe**. Kawasaki-shi, Japan. Affil: Hosei. Email: msasaki1@gmail.com. Research: US imperialism and gender, historical consciousness.

Sasaki-Uemura, **Wesley M.**, *Utah*. Salt Lake City, UT. Email: wes.sasaki-uemura@utah.edu. Research: Japan.

Sassi, **Jonathan D.**, *Graduate Center, CUNY; Staten Island, CUNY*. Cranford, NJ. Email: jsassi@gc.cuny.edu; jonathan.sassi@csi.cuny.edu. Research: antislavery movement in 18th-c NJ, American Revolution/early Republic religion.

Sasson, **Tehila**, *Emory*. Email: tehila.sasson@emory.edu.

Sassoon, **Joseph**, *Georgetown*. Washington, DC. Email: js824@georgetown.edu. Research: modern Arab World, Middle East economic.

Satelmajer, **Nikolaus**. Silver Spring, MD. Affil: Seventh-day Adventist Church. Email: NSatelmajer@gmail.com.

Sater, **William F.** Beverly Hills, CA. Email: ChilePrat@aol.com.

Sater Foss, **M. Nichole**, *California State, Los Angeles*. Email: msaterf@calstatela.edu.

Sather, **Laurie**, *Hagley Museum and Library*. Email: lsather@hagley.org.

Sather, **Lee**, *Weber State*. Email: lsather@weber.edu.

Sather, **Michael W.** Pipe Creek, TX. Affil: Texas, San Antonio. Email: michael.w.sather@gmail.com.

Satia, **Priya**, *Stanford*. Email: psatia@stanford.edu.

Satin, **Nicholas R.** New Tripoli, PA. Email: nicholassatin@gmail.com. Research: US Constitution, Christianity.

Sato, **Yasuko**, *Lamar*. Email: ysato@lamar.edu.

Satori, **Heidi**. Saint Nazianz, WI. Affil: Wisconsin, Green Bay. Email: hrsatori@gmail.com.

Satrum, **Krystle**, *Huntington Library*. Email: ksatrum@huntington.org.

Satter, **Beryl E.**, *Rutgers, Newark/New Jersey Inst. of Tech.* Email: satter@rutgers.edu.

Satterfield, **George David**, *Naval War Coll.* Email: george.satterfield@usnwc.edu.

Saucier, **Craig**, *Southeastern Louisiana*. Email: csaucier@selu.edu.

Sauer, **Angelika E.**, *Texas Lutheran*. Email: asauer@tlu.edu.

Saul, **Norman E.**, *Kansas*. Email: normsaul@ku.edu.

Saul, **Samir**, *Montréal*. Email: samir.saul@umontreal.ca.

Saunders, **Janice M.**, *Roanoke*. Email: saunders@roanoke.edu.

Saunders, **Robert M.**, *Christopher Newport*. Email: saunders@cnu.edu.

Saunders, **Robert S.**, **Jr.**, *Troy*.

Saunt, **Claudio**, *Georgia*. Athens, GA. Email: csaunt@uga.edu. Research: Indian removal, population of North America 1500-1790.

Saurette, **Marc**, *Carleton, Can.* Email: marc.saurette@carleton.ca.

Sause, **Karen E.** South Hadley, MA. Affil: Massachusetts Amherst. Email: karen.e.sause@gmail.com.

Sautter, **Udo**, *Windsor*. Email: gzsst01@uni-tuebingen.de.

Savage, **Amanda Lee Keikialoha**, *Memphis*. Email: aksavage@memphis.edu.

Savage, **Barbara D.** Philadelphia, PA. Affil: Pennsylvania. Email: bdsavage@sas.upenn.edu. Research: African American, intellectual/political/religion.

Savage, **Gail L.**, *St. Mary's, Md.* Alexandria, VA. Email: glsavage@smcm.edu. Research: marriage and divorce in modern England.

Savage, **John M.**, *Lehigh*. Email: savage@lehigh.edu.

Savage, **Robert J.**, *Boston Coll.* Email: savager@bc.edu.

Savage, **Robert Mark**. New York, NY. Affil: Columbia. Email: rms55@columbia.edu. Research: American colonial history and law, American Revolution and Constitution.

Savagian, **John C.** Milwaukee, WI. Affil: Alverno. Email: john.savagian@alverno.edu. Research: Mohican and Stockbridge Indians, early American surveyor and inventor.

Savala, **Joshua**. Ithaca, NY. Affil: Cornell. Email: js2754@cornell.edu.

Savard, **Stéphane**, *Québec, Montréal*. Email: savard.stephane@uqam.ca.

Saville, **Julie**, *Chicago*. Chicago, IL. Email: jsaville@uchicago.edu. Research: African American and Caribbean, slavery and emancipation.

Sawatsky, **Walter**. Elkhart, IN. Affil: Associated Mennonite Biblical Seminary. Email: wsawatsky@aol.com. Research: Slavic evangelicals in transition.

Sawula, **Christopher**. Atlanta, GA. Affil: Emory. Email: cswula@emory.edu. Research: early American labor and class formation, early American race/religion/class.

Sawyer, **Elizabeth**, *Robert H. Smith Center*. Email: esawyer@monticello.org.

Sawyer, **Kathryn Rose**. Notre Dame, IN. Affil: Notre Dame. Email: ksawyer2@nd.edu. Research: Church of Ireland, Reformation in Britain and Ireland.

Saxe, **Robert F.**, *Rhodes*. Email: saxer@rhodes.edu.

Saxine, **Ian Thomas**. Bridgewater, MA. Affil: Bridgewater State. Email: Isaxine@gmail.com. Research: cultures of landownership, northern New England frontier.

Saxon, **Gerald D.**, *Texas, Arlington*. Email: saxon@uta.edu.

Saxton, **Martha**, *Amherst*. Email: msaxton@amherst.edu.

Sayegh, **Sharlene**, *California State, Long Beach*. Email: sharlene.sayegh@csulb.edu.

Sayer, **John W.**, *Metropolitan State*. Email: john.sayer@metrostate.edu.

Sayle, **Timothy Andrews**, *Toronto*. Email: tim.sayle@utoronto.ca.

Sayre, **Pamela G.**, *Henry Ford Coll.* Email: psayre@hfcc.edu.

Sayres, **Shaun**. New Windsor, NY. Affil: Clark. Email: shaunsayres@gmail.com.

Saytanov, Sergey Vasilievich. Moscow, Russia. Affil: International Slavonic Inst. Email: ser. saytanov@gmail.com.

Sayward, Amy L., *Middle Tennessee State; Soc. for Hist. of American Foreign Relations*. Murfreesboro, TN. Email: amy.sayward@mtsu. edu. Research: Tennessee death penalty, United Nations.

Sbardellati, John, *Waterloo*. Email: jsbardel@ uwaterloo.ca.

Scaglia, Ilaria. Lichfield, United Kingdom. Affil: Aston. Email: iscaglia@buffalo.edu. Research: international cooperation, emotions.

Scala, James R. Deep River, CT. Email: jrsunnyside369@gmail.com.

Scalenghe, Sara, *Loyola, Md.* Email: sscalenghe@loyola.edu.

Scallet, Daniel, *Georgia Coll. and State*. Email: daniel.scallet@gcsu.edu.

Scally, Robert J., *NYU*. Email: robert.scally@nyu. edu.

Scalone, Luke Sebastian. Boston, MA. Affil: Northeastern. Email: scalone.l@husky.neu. edu.

Scalvedi, Caterina. Chicago, IL. Affil: Illinois, Chicago. Email: cscalv2@uic.edu.

Scanlan, Kyle T. Big Stone Gap, VA. Affil: Mountain Empire Comm. Coll. Email: kscanlan@me.vccs.edu.

Scanlan, Padraic Xavier. London, United Kingdom. Affil: London Sch. of Economics and Political Sci. Email: p.x.scanlan@lse. ac.uk. Research: slavery and emancipation, bureaucratic practices and development.

Scanlon, Jennifer R. Brunswick, ME. Affil: Bowdoin. Email: jscanlon@bowdoin.edu.

Scarano, Francisco A., *Wisconsin-Madison*. Email: fscarano@wisc.edu.

Scarborough, William K., *Southern Mississippi*. Email: william.scarborough@usm.edu.

Scardaville, Michael C., *South Carolina, Columbia*. Email: scardavm@mailbox.sc.edu.

Scardellato, Gabriele P., *York, Can.* Email: gpscar@yorku.ca.

Scarlett, Sarah Fayen, *Michigan Tech.* Houghton, MI. Email: sfscarle@mtu.edu.

Scarlett, Zachary, *Butler*. Email: zscarlet@butler. edu.

Scarnecchia, Timothy L., *Kent State*. Email: tscarnec@kent.edu.

Scaros, Constantinos Emmanuel. Tarpon Springs, FL. Affil: Colorado Tech. Email: deances@gmail.com. Research: US presidents, 20th-c America.

Scarpellini, Emanuela. Milano, Italy. Affil: Milan. Email: emanuela.scarpellini@unimi.it. Research: consumption, material culture.

Scarpino, Philip V., *Indiana–Purdue, Indianapolis*. Email: pscarpin@iupui.edu.

Scavone, Daniel C., *Southern Indiana*. Email: dcscavon@usi.edu.

Schachter, Albert, *McGill*. Email: jaschachter@ compuserve.com.

Schachter, Judith, *Carnegie Mellon*. Email: jm1e@andrew.cmu.edu.

Schackel, Sandra, *Boise State*. Email: sschack@ boisestate.edu.

Schad, Angela, *Hagley Museum and Library*. Email: aschad@hagley.org.

Schade, Rosemarie, *Concordia, Can.* Email: Rosemarie.Schade@concordia.ca.

Schaefer, Charles G. H., *Valparaiso*. Email: chuck.schaefer@valpo.edu.

Schaefer, Jennifer Lee. Rio Grande, NJ. Affil: Washington State, Vancouver. Email: jennifer. schaefer@wsu.edu.

Schaefer, Matthew T., *Herbert Hoover Presidential Library*. Email: matthew.schaefer@ nara.gov.

Schaefer, Meredith Kate. Beaverdam, VA. Email: kate.m.schaefer@gmail.com. Research: American history and sociology.

Schaefer, Paul. Cedarburg, WI. Email: sunkstr3am@gmail.com.

Schaefer, Richard, *SUNY, Plattsburgh*. Email: schaefr@plattsburgh.edu.

Schaefer, Wolf, *SUNY, Stony Brook*. Email: wolf. schafer@stonybrook.edu.

Schaeper, Thomas J., *St. Bonaventure*. Email: tschaepe@sbu.edu.

Schafer, Daniel E., *Belmont*. Nashville, TN. Email: daniel.schafer@belmont.edu. Research: Russian civil war, Tatar and Bashkir.

Schafer, Daniel L., *North Florida*. Email: dschafer@unf.edu.

Schafer, James A., Jr., *Houston*. Email: jschafer@ uh.edu.

Schafer, Sylvia, *Connecticut, Storrs*. Storrs Mansfield, CT. Email: sylvia.schafer@uconn. edu. Research: modern Europe and France, feminist theory.

Schafer, Typhanie. Audubon, MN. Email: typhschafer@gmail.com.

Schaffer, Benjamin, *Charleston*. Email: schafferbc@cofc.edu.

Schaffer, Dana Lanier, *AHA*. Washington, DC. Email: dschaffer@historians.org.

Schaffner, Heather M., *Northern Iowa*. Email: schaffnh@uni.edu.

Schainker, Ellie, *Emory*. Email: ellie.schainker@ emory.edu.

Schake, Kori. London, United Kingdom. Affil: International Inst. for Strategic Studies. Email: kori.schake@iiss.org.

Schakenbach Regele, Lindsay, *Miami, Ohio*. Oxford, OH. Email: regelels@miamioh. edu. Research: early republican diplomacy, capitalism.

Schalk, David L., *Vassar*. Email: schalk@vassar. edu.

Schaller, Michael R., *Arizona*. Email: schaller@u. arizona.edu.

Schama, Simon, *Columbia (Hist.)*. Email: sms53@columbia.edu.

Schantz, Mark S., *Birmingham-Southern*. Birmingham, AL. Email: mschantz@bsc.edu. Research: 19th-c US, Civil War.

Schapiro, Bob. Montclair, NJ. Affil: Drew. Email: bob@newsfilms.org.

Schapiro, Robert A. Atlanta, GA. Affil: Emory Law Sch. Email: robert.schapiro@emory.edu. Research: state/federal constitutional law in US, judicial federalism.

Schapkow, Carsten, *Oklahoma (Hist.)*. Email: cschapkow@ou.edu.

Schaposchnik, Ana E., *DePaul*. Chicago, IL. Email: aschapos@depaul.edu. Research: colonial Lima, Inquisition and Crypto-Jews in Latin America.

Schapsmeier, Edward L. Oconomowoc, WI.

Scharff, Virginia J., *New Mexico*. Albuquerque, NM. Email: vscharff@unm.edu. Research: US social, women.

Scharnau, Ralph W. Dubuque, IA.

Schatz, Arthur, *San Diego State*.

Schatz, Michal. Philadelphia, PA. Affil: Pennsylvania. Email: mschat@sas.upenn.edu.

Schatz, Ronald W., *Wesleyan*. Middletown, CT. Email: rschatz@wesleyan.edu. Research: conflict resolution and George Shultz, industrial relations.

Schatzberg, Eric. Atlanta, GA. Affil: Georgia Inst. of Tech. Email: eschatzberg3@gatech.edu. Research: technology.

Schauer, Jeff, *Nevada, Las Vegas*. Email: jeff. schauer@unlv.edu.

Schauer, Matthew, *Oklahoma State*. Email: matthew.schauer@okstate.edu.

Schechter, Patricia A., *Portland State*. Email: schechp@pdx.edu.

Schechter, Ronald B., *William and Mary*. Williamsburg, VA. Email: rbsche@wm.edu. Research: modern Europe, French cultural and Jewish.

Scheck, Raffael M., *Colby*. Email: raffael.scheck@ colby.edu.

Scheer, Mary L., *Lamar*. Email: mary.scheer@ my.lamar.edu.

Scheffler, Robin Wolfe, *MIT*. Email: rws42@mit. edu.

Scheiber, Harry N., *California, Berkeley*. Berkeley, CA. Email: scheiber@berkeley.edu. Research: American federalism, ocean law history.

Scheidel, Walter, *Stanford*. Email: scheidel@ stanford.edu.

Scheinberg, Stephen J., *Concordia, Can.* Email: Stephen.Scheinberg@concordia.ca.

Scheinfeldt, Tom, *Connecticut, Storrs*. Email: tom.scheinfeldt@uconn.edu.

Schelbert, Leo, *Illinois, Chicago*. Email: lschelbe@uic.edu.

Schell, Patience A. Aberdeen, United Kingdom. Affil: Aberdeen. Email: p.schell@abdn.ac.uk. Research: science and sociability in Chile.

Schelly, Chelsea, *Michigan Tech.* Email: cschelly@mtu.edu.

Schen, Claire S., *SUNY, Buffalo*. Email: cschen@ buffalo.edu.

Schenck, Marcia C. Berlin, Germany. Affil: Free, Berlin. Email: Marcia.schenck@fu-berlin.de.

Scher, Adam E., *Virginia Museum of Hist.* Email: ascher@VirginiaHistory.org.

Scherer, Mark, *Nebraska, Omaha*. Email: mscherer@unomaha.edu.

Scherer, Stephen, *Central Michigan*. Email: scher1s@cmich.edu.

Schermerhorn, Calvin, *Arizona State*. Email: j.schermerhorn@asu.edu.

Scherzer, Kenneth A., *Middle Tennessee State*. Nashville, TN. Email: scherzer@mtsu.edu. Research: US urban, social and quantitative.

Schevtchuk Armstrong, Elizabeth. Cold Spring, NY. Email: scriptor-exemplar@hotmail.com. Research: 14th-/15th-c Britain, politics.

Schiavone, Terry Michael, II. state college, PA. Affil: Penn State. Email: tms362@psu.edu.

Schiavone Camacho, Julia Maria. Fairborn, OH. Affil: Antioch. Email: Schiavone.Camacho@ gmail.com. Research: Latin American Chinese, gender and family.

Schick, James B. M., *Pittsburg State*. Email: jschick@pittstate.edu.

Schiebinger, Londa L., *Stanford*. Stanford, CA. Email: schieb@stanford.edu. Research: colonial gender/race/science, Caribbean medical botany.

Schieder, Chelsea Szendi. Tokyo, Japan. Affil: Aoyama Gakuin. Email: schieder@meiji.ac.jp.

Schieffelin, **Richard R**. Fairfax, VA. Email: rrschieffelin@gmail.com. Research: Henry S. Randall 1811-76, liberal religion in US 1920-41.

Schiefsky, **Mark**, *Harvard (Hist. of Science)*. Email: mjschief@fas.harvard.edu.

Schields, **Chelsea Angela**, *California, Irvine*. Email: cschield@uci.edu.

Schiesl, **Martin J.**, *California State, Los Angeles*. Email: mschies@calstatela.edu.

Schifferle, **Peter J.**, *US Army Command Coll.* Email: peter.j.schifferele.civ@mail.mil.

Schiffman, **Zachary S.**, *Northeastern Illinois*. Email: Z-Schiffman@neiu.edu.

Schild, **Georg M**. Tübingen, Germany. Affil: Tübingen. Email: georg.schild@uni-tuebingen.de.

Schilling, **Donald G**. Williamsburg, VA. Affil: Denison. Email: schilling@denison.edu. Research: politics in northern Bavaria 1880-1933, historiography of WWII and Holocaust.

Schilling, **Hayden**, *Wooster*. Email: hschilling@wooster.edu.

Schilt, **Cornelis Johannes**. Oxford, United Kingdom. Affil: Oxford. Email: keesjanschilt@gmail.com.

Schimmelpenninck, **David**, *Brock*. Email: dschimme@brocku.ca.

Schlabach, **Elizabeth S.**, *Earlham*. Richmond, IN. Email: schlabe@earlham.edu. Research: African American women and gambling, black Chicago.

Schlachet, **Joshua**, *Arizona*. Email: jschlachet@email.arizona.edu.

Schlafly, **Daniel L.**, **Jr.**, *St. Louis*. Saint Louis, MO. Email: daniel.schlafly@slu.edu. Research: Roman Catholic Church in Russia, Western travellers in Russia.

Schlesinger, **Jonathan**, *Indiana*. Bloomington, IN. Email: joschles@indiana.edu. Research: Qing empire and environment, politics of mining.

Schlesinger, **Roger**, *Washington State, Pullman*.

Schlichting, **Kara Murphy**, *Queens, CUNY*. Email: kara.schlichting@qc.cuny.edu.

Schlimgen, **Veta R.**, *Gonzaga*. Spokane, WA. Email: schlimgen@gonzaga.edu; vschlimgen@gmail.com. Research: US citizenship and empire, Pacific world.

Schlitt, **David Morrill**. Bellingham, WA. Affil: Western Washington. Email: dmschlitt@heinzhistorycenter.org.

Schloesser, **Stephen R.**, **SJ**, *Loyola, Chicago*. Chicago, IL. Email: sschloesser@luc.edu. Research: French Catholic revivalism 1880-1940, modernisms/modernities.

Schloss, **Rebecca Hartkopf**, *Texas A&M*. Email: rhschloss@tamu.edu.

Schlossman, **Steven**, *Carnegie Mellon*. Email: sls+@andrew.cmu.edu.

Schlotterbeck, **John T.**, *DePauw*. Email: jschlot@depauw.edu.

Schlotterbeck, **Marian E.**, *California, Davis*. Davis, CA. Email: mschlotterbeck@ucdavis.edu. Research: Popular Unity period in Concepcion 1970-73, New Left politics and student movements in Chile.

Schlotzhauer, **Ruth A**. San Jose, CA. Affil: St. Joseph Sch. Email: ruth@isfeld.net.

Schluessel, **Eric Tanner**, *Montana*. Email: eric.schluessel@mso.umt.edu.

Schlundt, **Ronald A**. Mainz, Germany. Affil: Maryland, Europe. Email: r.schlundt@t-online.de.

Schmacks, **Yanara**, *Lehman, CUNY*. Email: yschmacks@gradcenter.cuny.edu.

Schmalzer, **Sigrid**, *Massachusetts, Amherst*. Email: sigrid@history.umass.edu.

Schmeller, **Erik S.**, *Tennessee State*. Nashville, TN. Email: eschmeller@tnstate.edu. Research: colonial and early Republic America, British Empire.

Schmeller, **Helmut J.**, *Fort Hays State*.

Schmeller, **Mark G.**, *Syracuse*. Email: mschmell@maxwell.syr.edu.

Schmelzkopf, **Karen**, *Monmouth*. Email: kschmelz@monmouth.edu.

Schmid, **Andre**. Toronto, ON, Canada. Affil: Toronto. Email: andre.schmid@utoronto.ca. Research: Cold War cultural, North and South Korea.

Schmidt, **Aaron**. Saint Joseph, MO. Email: arschmidt1824@gmail.com.

Schmidt, **Albert John**. Washington, DC. Affil: George Washington. Email: 601schmidt@comcast.net. Research: Catherinian Russian town planning, 18th-/19th-c English country attorney.

Schmidt, **Benjamin MacDonald**, *NYU*.

Schmidt, **Benjamin**, *Washington, Seattle*. Email: schmidtb@uw.edu.

Schmidt, **Elizabeth S.**, *Loyola, Md.* Email: eschmidt@loyola.edu.

Schmidt, **Hans R.**, **Jr**. Portland, OR. Email: hello2hans@gmail.com. Research: Nanjing incident 1927, US/China/Iran/Turkey 1919-40.

Schmidt, **James**, *Boston Univ*. Email: jschmidt@bu.edu.

Schmidt, **Jim**, *Northern Illinois*. Dekalb, IL. Email: jschmidt@niu.edu. Research: US law and society, childhood.

Schmidt, **Josiah**. Saint Louis, MO. Affil: Washington, St. Louis. Email: josiahschmidt@gmail.com. Research: peasant life in early modern Hesse, deviancy in early modern Europe.

Schmidt, **Kelly**. Saint Louis, MO. Affil: Loyola, Chicago. Email: kschmidt3@luc.edu.

Schmidt, **Leigh Eric**, *Washington, St. Louis*. St. Louis, MO. Email: leigh.e.schmidt@wustl.edu. Research: American religious, religion and American politics.

Schmidt, **Raymond P**. Franklin, TN. Email: raymondschmidt7702@comcast.net. Research: science and technology, military.

Schmidt, **William F**. Wayne, MI. Email: wschmidt47@yahoo.com. Research: medieval Europe, early modern Atlantic.

Schmidt Horning, **Susan**, *St. John's, NY*. Jamaica, NY. Email: schmidts@stjohns.edu. Research: sound studies, women and technology.

Schmiechen, **James A.**, *Central Michigan*. Email: james.schmiechen@cmich.edu.

Schmitt, **Casey Sylvia**. Philadelphia, PA. Affil: McNeil Center for Early American Studies. Email: csschmitt@email.wm.edu.

Schmitt, **Dale J.**, *East Tennessee State*. Email: schmittd@etsu.edu.

Schmitt, **Sarah**, *Kentucky Hist. Soc.* Email: sarahm.schmitt@ky.gov.

Schmitthenner, **Peter**, *Virginia Tech*. Email: pschmitt@vt.edu.

Schmitz, **David F.**, *Whitman*. Walla Walla, WA. Email: schmitdf@whitman.edu. Research: diplomatic, 20th-c US.

Schmitz, **Philip C.**, *Eastern Michigan*. Email: pschmitz@emich.edu.

Schmitz, **Timothy J**. Spartanburg, SC. Affil: Wofford. Email: schmitztj@wofford.edu. Research: 16th-c Catholic reform, church and state in Spain.

Schmitzer, **Jeanne**, *Tennessee Tech*. Email: jschmitzer@twlakes.net.

Schnabel, **Gerald Michael**. Bemidji, MN.

Schneer, **Jonathan**, *Georgia Inst. of Tech*. Email: jonathan.schneer@hts.gatech.edu.

Schneewind, **Sarah**, *California, San Diego*. Email: sschneewind@ucsd.edu.

Schneider, **Ann Imlah**. Washington, DC. Email: aimlahs@aol.com. Research: internationalizing undergraduate curriculum, internationalizing teacher education.

Schneider, **Birgit**. Kowloon, Hong Kong. Affil: Hong Kong. Email: bschneid@hku.hk. Research: demobilization in Germany 1945, demobilization in Japan 1945.

Schneider, **Christy**, *Science History Inst.* Email: cschneider@sciencehistory.org.

Schneider, **Dorothee**, *Illinois, Urbana-Champaign*. Email: schndr@illinois.edu.

Schneider, **Elena Andrea**, *California, Berkeley*. Berkeley, CA. Email: eschneider@berkeley.edu; elena_schneider@yahoo.com. Research: 18th-c Cuba.

Schneider, **Gregory L.**, *Emporia State*. Email: gschneid@emporia.edu.

Schneider, **Helen M.**, *Virginia Tech*. Blacksburg, VA. Email: hms@vt.edu. Research: 20th-c home economics education, domesticity in 20th-c China.

Schneider, **James C.**, *Texas, San Antonio*. Email: james.schneider@utsa.edu.

Schneider, **Joanne F**. Lincoln, RI. Affil: Rhode Island Coll. Email: joanne_schneider@hotmail.com.

Schneider, **John**, *State Hist. Soc. of Missouri*.

Schneider, **Khal R.**, *California State, Sacramento*. Email: schneider@csus.edu.

Schneider, **Lance William**. Sarasota, FL. Email: lance.w.schneider@gmail.com. Research: Hellenistic and Imperial Greek World, Rome and Italy to 31 BCE.

Schneider, **Norah Lynn**. Falmouth, MA. Affil: Salve Regina. Email: norah.schneider@gmail.com. Research: Holocaust and genocide studies, Jewish.

Schneider, **Robert A.**, *Indiana*. Bloomington, IN. Email: raschnei@indiana.edu. Research: Old Regime France, social and cultural.

Schneider, **Tracy D.**, *Virginia Museum of Hist.* Email: tschneider@VirginiaHistory.org.

Schneider, **Wendie E.**, *Iowa State*. Email: wschneid@iastate.edu.

Schneider, **William H.**, *Indiana–Purdue, Indianapolis*. Email: whschnei@iupui.edu.

Schneider-Hector, **Dietmar**, *New Mexico State*. Email: dschneid@nmsu.edu.

Schneiderman, **David**. Seattle, WA. Email: das1983@gmail.com.

Schneirov, **Richard**, *Indiana State*. Email: Richard.Schneirov@indstate.edu.

Schocket, **Andrew M.**, *Bowling Green State*. Email: aschock@bgsu.edu.

Schoen, **Brian**, *Ohio*. Email: schoen@ohio.edu.

Schoen, *Johanna*, *Rutgers*. Lambertville, NJ. Email: johanna.schoen@rutgers.edu.

Schoenbachler, **Matthew G.**, *North Alabama*. Email: mschoenbachler@una.edu.

Schoenbaum, **David**, *Iowa*. Email: dlschoen@aol.com.

Schoenbrun, **David**, *Northwestern*. Email: dls@northwestern.edu.

Schoenfeld, *Abigail*. Durham, NC. Affil: Princeton. Email: abby.schoenfeld@gmail.com.

Schoenhardt, *Rachael M*. Darien, IL. Email: rachaelschoenhardt@gmail.com.

Schoenig, *Steven A.*, *St. Louis*. Saint Louis, MO. Email: sschoeni@slu.edu; sschoenigsj@gmail.com. Research: Medieval Papacy, Medieval Canon Law.

Schoenkopf, *Austin W*. Oklahoma City, OK. Affil: Oklahoma. Email: austin.schoenkopf@ou.edu.

Schoenstein, *Tasha*. Cambridge, MA. Affil: Harvard. Email: tschoenstein@g.harvard.edu.

Schoenwald, *Jonathan M*. Pinecrest, FL. Affil: Gulliver Sch. Email: jschoenwald@gmail.com. Research: post-WWII American radicalism, American politics and culture.

Schoepflin, **Rennie B.**, *California State, Los Angeles*. Email: rschoep@calstatela.edu.

Schoeppner, *Michael Alan*. Farmington, ME. Affil: Maine, Farmington. Email: michael.schoeppner@maine.edu. Research: US legal, international migration.

Schofield, **Kent M.**, *California State, San Bernardino*.

Scholz, **Bernhard W.**, *Seton Hall*.

Scholz, **Maximilian Miguel**, *Florida State*. Email: mscholz@fsu.edu.

Schoof, *Markus*. Hilliard, OH. Affil: Ohio State. Email: schoof.3@buckeyemail.osu.edu. Research: US-Brazilian relations, US missionary.

Schoolmaster, **F. Andrew**, *Texas Christian*. Email: a.schoolmaster@tcu.edu.

Schoone-Jongen, **Robert P.**, *Calvin*. Email: rps2@calvin.edu.

Schoonover, *Thomas D.*, *Louisiana, Lafayette*. Lafayette, LA. Email: tds@louisiana.edu. Research: US-Latin American relations, Gilded Age-Progressive era.

Schoppa, **R. Keith**, *Loyola, Md.* Email: kschoppa@loyola.edu.

Schor, *Adam M.*, *South Carolina, Columbia*. Columbia, SC. Email: schor@mailbox.sc.edu. Research: late antique social networks, late antique Syrian religious conflict.

Schor, **Laura Strumingher**, *Hunter, CUNY*. Email: lschor@hunter.cuny.edu.

Schor, *Paul A*. Paris, France. Affil: Paris Diderot. Email: paul.schor@univ-paris-diderot.fr. Research: US minority consumers, US modernization and everyday life.

Schorman, *Rob R.*, *Miami, Ohio*. Middletown, OH. Email: schormr@miamioh.edu. Research: advertising and consumer culture, popular culture and mass communications.

Schotte, **Margaret**, *York, Can.* Email: mschotte@yorku.ca.

Schottenstein, *Allison Elizabeth*. Cincinnati, OH. Affil: Texas, Austin. Email: allisonschottenstein@gmail.com.

Schrader, **Abby**, *Franklin & Marshall*. Email: abby.schrader@fandm.edu.

Schrader, *Fred E*. Paris, France. Affil: Fudan, Shanghai. Email: schraderfe@gmx.com.

Research: sociability/civil society/taste, political economy.

Schrader, *William C.*, *III*, *Tennessee Tech*. Louisville, KY. Email: WCSchrader3@gmail.com. Research: Westphalia, ecclesiastical principalities.

Schrafstetter, **Susanna B.**, *Vermont*. Email: susanna.schrafstetter@uvm.edu.

Schrag, **Steven D.**, *Bowling Green State*. Email: sschrag@bgsu.edu.

Schrag, *Zachary M.*, *George Mason*. Fairfax, VA. Email: zschrag@gmu.edu. Research: 1844 Philadelphia riot, institutional review boards.

Schramm, **Jeff**, *Missouri Science and Tech*. Email: schrammj@mst.edu.

Schrank, **Sarah**, *California State, Long Beach*. Email: sarah.schrank@csulb.edu.

Schrecker, *John E.*, *Brandeis*. Waltham, MA. Email: schrecker@brandeis.edu. Research: Sino-American relations, Confucian social theory.

Schreiber, *Abby*. Williamsburg, VA. Affil: William and Mary. Email: abschreiber@wm.edu.

Schreiber, **Roy E.**, *Indiana, South Bend*. Email: rschreib@iusb.edu.

Schreier, **Joshua S.**, *Vassar*. Email: joschreier@vassar.edu.

Schrems, **Melissane Parm**, *St. Lawrence*. Email: mschrems@stlawu.edu.

Schriber, **Carolyn P.**, *Rhodes*. Email: schriber@rhodes.edu.

Schroeder, **Carole**, *Boise State*. Email: caroleschroeder@boisestate.edu.

Schroeder, *Caroline*. Stockton, CA. Affil: Pacific. Email: carrie@carrieschroeder.com.

Schroeder, *James Evan*. Bridgeport, WA. Affil: Washington State. Email: jes@ifiber.tv.

Schroeder, **John H.**, *Wisconsin-Milwaukee*. Email: jhs@uwm.edu.

Schroeder, *Michael J*. Annville, PA. Affil: Lebanon Valley. Email: schroede@lvc.edu; msinpa@gmail.com. Research: Nicaragua, Revolution.

Schroeder, *Nicole Lee*. Charlottesville, VA. Affil: Virginia. Email: nls4te@virginia.edu.

Schroeder, *Paul W*. State College, PA. Affil: Illinois, Urbana-Champaign. Email: pschroed@uiuc.edu. Research: European/world international politics, international relations theory.

Schroeder, **Steven P.**, *Indiana, Pa.* Email: schroder@iup.edu.

Schroeder, **Susan**, *Tulane*. Email: sschroe@tulane.edu.

Schroer, *Haley*. Austin, TX. Affil: Texas, Austin. Email: h.m.schroer@utexas.edu.

Schroer, *Timothy Louis*, *West Georgia*. Carrollton, GA. Email: tschroer@westga.edu. Research: race and law of war.

Schroeter, **Daniel J.**, *Minnesota (Hist.)*. Email: schro800@umn.edu.

Schrum, *Ethan*, *Azusa Pacific*. Azusa, CA. Email: eschrum@apu.edu. Research: American intellectual, US foreign affairs.

Schrunk, **Ivancica**, *St. Thomas, Minn.* Email: idschrunk@stthomas.edu.

Schubert, *Kenneth*. Staten Island, NY. Email: kenschubert1@gmail.com. Research: American Revolution, research methods.

Schuele, *Donna C*. Woodland Hills, CA. Affil: California State, Los Angeles. Email: dcsclv@pacbell.net. Research: US Supreme Court, 19th-c women's rights.

Schuering, *Michael*. Gainesville, FL. Affil: Florida. Email: mick4112003@yahoo.de. Research: technology, environmental.

Schuker, **Stephen A.**, *Virginia*. Email: sas4u@virginia.edu.

Schuler, **Friedrich E.**, *Portland State*. Email: schulerf@pdx.edu.

Schull, **Kent F.**, *Binghamton, SUNY*. Email: kschull@binghamton.edu.

Schulman, **Bruce J.**, *Boston Univ*. Email: bjschulm@bu.edu.

Schulman, **Vanessa**, *George Mason*. Email: vschulma@gmu.edu.

Schult, *Anne*. New York, NY. Affil: NYU. Email: as7415@nyu.edu.

Schult, *Frederick, Jr.*, *NYU*. Email: fs3@nyu.edu.

Schulten, **Susan**, *Denver*. Email: sschulte@du.edu.

Schultheiss, *Katrin*, *George Washington*. Washington, DC. Email: kschulth@gwu.edu. Research: modern France, medicine.

Schultz, **April R.**, *Illinois Wesleyan*. Email: aschultz@iwu.edu.

Schultz, **Jane E.**, *Indiana–Purdue, Indianapolis*. Email: jschult@iupui.edu.

Schultz, *Jenna M.*, *St. Thomas, Minn.* Wayzata, MN. Email: schu2971@stthomas.edu; jennaschultz1012@gmail.com. Research: British social and cultural.

Schultz, **Kevin M.**, *Illinois, Chicago*. Email: schultzk@uic.edu.

Schultz, *Kirsten*, *Seton Hall*. South Orange, NJ. Email: schultki@shu.edu. Research: Latin America and Brazil, Iberian empires.

Schultz, **Mark**, *Lewis*. Email: schultma@lewisu.edu.

Schultz, *Rima M*. Oak Park, IL. Email: rimalunin@ameritech.net. Research: political history of Jane Addams, Progresssive women in social movements.

Schultz, **Robert T.**, *Illinois Wesleyan*. Email: rschultz@iwu.edu.

Schultz, **Roger**, *Liberty*. Email: rschultz@liberty.edu.

Schultz, **Stanley K.**, *Wisconsin-Madison*. Email: skschult@wisc.edu.

Schultz, **Timothy**, *Naval War Coll.* Email: timothy.schultz@usnwc.edu.

Schultz, **Warren C.**, *DePaul*. Email: wschultz@depaul.edu.

Schultz, *William*. Princeton, NJ. Affil: Princeton. Email: will.schultz88@gmail.com. Research: religion in urban West, Cold War and US society.

Schulz, *Constance B.*, *South Carolina, Columbia*. Columbia, SC. Email: schulz@mailbox.sc.edu; cb38406@bellsouth.net. Research: Eliza Lucas Pinckney, Adams/Jefferson religious training.

Schulz, *Joy Elizabeth*. Omaha, NE. Affil: Metropolitan Comm. Coll. Email: Jschulz@mccneb.edu. Research: 19th-c Hawaii, US empire.

Schulz, *Zachary W.*, *Columbus State*. Auburn, AL. Affil: Auburn. Email: schulz_zachary@columbusstate.edu; zws0007@auburn.edu. Research: Stuart England, veterinary medicine.

Schulze, **Susan E.**, *George Mason*. Email: sschulze@gmu.edu.

Schulze-Oechtering, **Michael A.**, *Western Washington*. Email: Michael.Schulze-Oechtering@wwu.edu.

Schulzinger, Robert D., *Colorado, Boulder.* Email: schulzin@colorado.edu.

Schumacher, Frank, *Western Ontario.* Email: fschuma@uwo.ca.

Schumaker, Kathryn Anne, *Oklahoma (Hist.).* Email: schumaker@ou.edu.

Schumann, Dirk H. Goettingen, Germany. Affil: Goettingen. Email: dschuma@uni-goettingen. de. Research: youth in transatlantic perspective 1890-, Weimar Republic.

Schuster, David G., *Purdue, Fort Wayne.* Email: schusted@pfw.edu.

Schutts, Jeff R. New Westminster, BC, Canada. Affil: Douglas. Email: schuttsj@ douglascollege.ca. Research: Coca-Cola in Germany/Americanization, dissent in the military.

Schuyler, David, *Franklin & Marshall.* Email: david.schuyler@fandm.edu.

Schuyler, Lorraine Gates, *Richmond.* Email: lschuyle@richmond.edu.

Schuyler, Robert L. Philadelphia, PA. Affil: Pennsylvania. Email: schuyler@sas.upenn. edu. Research: historical archaeology, modern world 1400-present.

Schwab, Richard N., *California, Davis.* Email: rnschwab@ucdavis.edu.

Schwabe, Klaus. Aachen, Germany. Affil: Historisches Institut. Email: schwabe@rwth-aachen.de.

Schwall, Elizabeth. San Jose, CA. Affil: California, Berkeley. Email: elizabeth.schwall@gmail.com.

Schwaller, John F., *SUNY, Albany.* Albany, NY. Email: jschwaller@albany.edu; jfschwaller@ gmail.com. Research: D. Luis de Velasco 1539-1617, Aztec culture.

Schwaller, Robert C., *Kansas.* Email: rschwaller@ku.edu.

Schwaller, Shawn W., *California State, Chico.* Email: sschwaller@csuchico.edu.

Schwalm, Leslie A., *Iowa.* Email: leslie-schwalm@uiowa.edu.

Schwantes, Carlos A., *Idaho; Missouri–St. Louis.* Email: cmschwantes@aol.com.

Schwarcz, Vera, *Wesleyan.* Email: vschwarcz@ wesleyan.edu.

Schwarting, Paulette S., *Virginia Museum of Hist.* Email: pschwarting@VirginiaHistory.org.

Schwartz, Allison. Minneapolis, MN. Affil: Minnesota, Twin Cities. Email: schw1570@ umn.edu.

Schwartz, Daniel B., *George Washington.* Washington, DC. Email: dbs50@gwu.edu. Research: Spinoza reception, Jewish historical consciousness.

Schwartz, Daniel Louis, *Texas A&M.* Email: daniel.schwartz@tamu.edu.

Schwartz, Donald, *California State, Long Beach.* Email: don.schwartz@csulb.edu.

Schwartz, Gerald, *Western Carolina.*

Schwartz, Hillel. Encinitas, CA. Email: hillel2000@cox.net. Research: millenarianism, senses.

Schwartz, Joan M., *Carleton, Can.* Email: joan. schwartz@carleton.ca.

Schwartz, Kathryn A., *Massachusetts, Amherst.* Email: kaschwartz@umass.edu.

Schwartz, Lori. Omaha, NE. Affil: Nebraska, Omaha. Email: lschwartz@unomaha.edu.

Schwartz, Richard D. Morristown, NJ. Affil: Whippany Park High Sch. Email: richschwartz14@gmail.com.

Schwartz, Robert M., *Mount Holyoke.* Email: rschwart@mtholyoke.edu.

Schwartz, Saundra, *Hawai'i, Manoa.* Email: saundras@hawaii.edu.

Schwartz, Seth R., *Columbia (Hist.).* Email: srs166@columbia.edu.

Schwartz, Shuly R. New York, NY. Affil: Jewish Theological Seminary. Email: shschwartz@jtsa. edu. Research: modern Jewish.

Schwartz, Stuart B., *Yale.* New Haven, CT. Email: stuart.schwartz@yale.edu. Research: Iberian Atlantic world, hurricanes.

Schwartz, Thomas Alan, *Vanderbilt.* Nashville, TN. Email: thomas.a.schwartz@vanderbilt.edu. Research: Henry Kissinger and Richard Nixon, Cold War.

Schwartz, Thomas F., *Herbert Hoover Presidential Library.* Email: thomas.schwartz@ nara.gov.

Schwartz, Vanessa R., *Southern California.* Email: vschwart@usc.edu.

Schwartz Francisco, Diana Lynn, *Valparaiso.*

Schwartzbein, Neil. Cote St. Luc, QC, Canada. Email: neil111@sympatico.ca.

Schwartzberg, Jenny, *Hist. New Orleans.* New Orleans, LA. Email: jennifers@hnoc.org. Research: modern Europe.

Schwarz, Henry, *Western Washington.* Email: Henry.Schwarz@wwu.edu.

Schwatka, Kimberly A. Bowie, MD. Email: kaschwatka@comcast.net. Research: Civil War medicine, Civil War civilians.

Schweishelm, Kathryn. Berlin, Germany. Email: schweishelm@gmail.com.

Schweitzer, Marlis, *York, Can.* Email: schweit@ yorku.ca.

Schweizer, Karl W., *Rutgers, Newark/New Jersey Inst. of Tech.* Email: schweizer@njit.edu.

Schweninger, Loren L. Greensboro, NC. Affil: North Carolina, Greensboro. Email: llschwen@ uncg.edu. Research: America, African American.

Schwenk, Cynthia J., *Georgia State.* Email: cschwenk@gsu.edu.

Schwenkbeck, Rahima. Washington, DC. Affil: George Washington. Email: rahima@gwu. edu. Research: US utopian communities, advertising.

Schweppe, Peter, *Montana State, Bozeman.*

Schwoerer, Lois G., *George Washington.* Washington, DC. Email: lgsch@gwu.edu; lgsch101@msn.com. Research: guns and civilian society.

Sciarcon, Jonathan I., *Denver.* Email: jonathan. sciarcon@du.edu.

Sclar, Arieh, *Hunter, CUNY.* Email: asclar@hunter. cuny.edu.

Scofield, Merry Ellen, *Princeton.* Email: mscofield@princeton.edu.

Scofield, Rebecca Elena, *Idaho.* Email: rscofield@uidaho.edu.

Scopino, A. J., Jr., *Central Connecticut State.* Email: scopinoa@ccsu.edu.

Scorsone, Kristyn. Kearny, NJ. Affil: Rutgers, Newark/NJIT. Email: ykristyn@gmail.com.

Scott, Benjamin John. Oakland, CA. Affil: Nebraska, Kearney. Email: scottbj@lopers.unk. edu. Research: childhood in Gilded Age, child labor laws.

Scott, Blake C. Charleston, SC. Affil: Charleston. Email: scottbc@cofc.edu. Research: travel and tourism, American environmental.

Scott, Craig D. Madison, WI.

Scott, Donald M., *Queens, CUNY.* Email: donald. scott@qc.cuny.edu.

Scott, Erik R., *Kansas.* Email: scott@ku.edu.

Scott, Heidi Victoria, *Massachusetts, Amherst.* Email: hvscott@history.umass.edu.

Scott, Jermaine, *Mississippi State.*

Scott, Joan Wallach, *Graduate Center, CUNY.* Princeton, NJ. Affil: Inst. for Advanced Study. Email: jscott@gc.cuny.edu; jws@ias.edu. Research: modern Europe, gender and theory.

Scott, John Thomas, *Mercer.* Email: scott_jt@ mercer.edu.

Scott, Jonathan G., *Austin Peay State.* Email: scottj@apsu.edu.

Scott, Julius, *Michigan, Ann Arbor.* Email: jsscott@umich.edu.

Scott, Karen, *DePaul.* Email: kscott@depaul.edu.

Scott, Katherine A., *US Senate Hist. Office.* Email: kate_scott@sec.senate.gov.

Scott, Michelle R., *Maryland, Baltimore County.* Email: mscott@umbc.edu.

Scott, Rebecca J., *Michigan, Ann Arbor.* Ann Arbor, MI. Email: rjscott@umich.edu. Research: 19th-c Cuba, Atlantic.

Scott, Roy V., *Mississippi State.* Email: royvandjaneb@aol.com.

Scott, Samuel F., *Wayne State.* Email: aa1002@ wayne.edu.

Scott, Thomas A., *Kennesaw State.* Marietta, GA. Email: tscott@kennesaw.edu. Research: state and local, higher education.

Scott, William B., *Kenyon.* Email: scott@kenyon. edu.

Scott, William Randolph, *Lehigh.* Email: wrs4@ lehigh.edu.

Scott, William V. San Antonio, TX. Email: wmvscott@gmail.com.

Scott-Childress, Reynolds J., *SUNY, New Paltz.* Email: scottchr@newpaltz.edu.

Scott-Fleming, Mary, *Robert H. Smith Center.* Email: mscottfleming@monticello.org.

Scott-Pinkney, Pamela M., *AHA.* Washington, DC. Email: ppinkney@historians.org.

Scott-Weaver, Meredith L., *US Air Force Acad.* Email: meredith.scott-weaver@usafa.edu.

Scranton, Philip B., *Rutgers, Camden.* Philadelphia, PA. Email: scranton@rutgers. edu. Research: American economic, business.

Scribner, Vaughn Paul, *Central Arkansas.* Email: vscribner@uca.edu.

Scripps, Sarah Michel, *Wisconsin-Stevens Point.* Email: sscripps@uwsp.edu.

Scrivener, Laurie L. Norman, OK. Affil: Oklahoma. Email: lscrivener@ou.edu.

Scroop, Daniel. Glasgow, United Kingdom. Affil: Glasgow. Email: daniel.scroop@gla.ac.uk. Research: US politics since 1890, New Deal.

Sculley, Lt Col Seanegan, *US Military Acad.* Email: seanegan.sculley@usma.edu.

Scully, Pamela, *Emory.* Atlanta, GA. Email: pamela.scully@emory.edu. Research: human rights, development.

Scully, Randolph F., *George Mason.* Fairfax, VA. Email: rscully@gmu.edu. Research: household and slavery in revolutionary South, religion and slavery in British Atlantic.

Scully, Robert, SJ, Le Moyne. Syracuse, NY. Email: scullyre@lemoyne.edu. Research: Elizabethan religious, early Jesuit.

Sculos, Bryant W., *Worcester State.* Email: bsculos@worcester.edu.

Scurlock, *Jo Ann*. Chicago, IL. Affil: Elmhurst. Email: r-beal@uchicago.edu. Research: Assyro-Babylonian medicine, Assyrian statecraft.

Scythes, **James Michael**, *West Chester*. Email: jscythes@wcupa.edu.

Sea, **Thomas F.**, *Western Ontario*. Email: tsea@uwo.ca.

Seabrook-Rocha, *Leah M.* Sacramento, CA. Affil: Central Texas. Email: leah@seabrook-rocha.com.

Seager, **Michael Allen**, *California State, Fullerton*. Email: mseager@fullerton.edu.

Seah, *Leander*. DeLand, FL. Affil: Stetson. Email: tlseah78@yahoo.com. Research: maritime China and Chinese migration, Jinan University/Guangzhou China.

Seaholm, **Megan**, *Texas, Austin*. Email: seaholm@austin.utexas.edu.

Seale, **Kathleen**, *State Hist. Soc. of Missouri*. Email: sealek@shsmo.org.

Seale, *Yvonne*, *SUNY, Coll. Geneseo*. Email: seale@geneseo.edu.

Searcy, **Kim**, *Loyola, Chicago*. Email: ksearcy@luc.edu.

Searfoss, **Renee C.**, *Coastal Carolina*. Email: rsearfoss@coastal.edu.

Searles, **Michael N.**, *Augusta*. Email: cowboymike@augusta.edu.

Sears, **Christine E.**, *Alabama, Huntsville*. Huntsville, AL. Email: christine.sears@uah.edu. Research: comparative slavery.

Sears, **Laurie J.**, *Washington, Seattle*. Email: lsears@uw.edu.

Seaver, *James B.* Bloomington, IN. Affil: Indiana. Email: jbseaver@indiana.edu. Research: material culture of WWII, museum studies.

Seaver, *Paul S.*, *Stanford*. Palo Alto, CA. Email: seaver@stanford.edu. Research: London guilds, London puritanism.

Seavoy, **Ronald E.**, *Bowling Green State*. Email: rseavoy@bgsu.edu.

Sebesta, *Kailey Ann*. Corunna, MI. Affil: Alma. Email: sebesta1ka@gmail.com.

Sebestyen, *Joseph P.*, *III*. Pittsburgh, PA. Affil: Baldwin-Whitehall Sch. District. Email: joe.sebestyen@gmail.com.

Secrest, **William L.**, *Henry Ford Coll.* Email: willysecrest@gmail.com.

Sedelow, *Walter A., Jr.* Heber Springs, AR. Affil: Arkansas, Little Rock. Research: computer-based natural language analysis, ontological assumption in historiography.

Sedgwick, *James B.* Wolfville, NS, Canada. Affil: Acadia. Email: jamie.sedgwick@gmail.com. Research: international jurisprudence, war crimes.

Sedgwick, *Mark J.* Aarhus, Denmark. Affil: Aarhus. Email: mjrs@cas.au.dk. Research: Islam, terrorism.

Sedney, *Quentin*. Reisterstown, MD. Affil: Comm. Coll. of Baltimore County. Email: sedneys6@verizon.net. Research: early American religious beliefs, secession decisions of border states.

Sedra, *Paul*, *Simon Fraser*. Email: pdsedra@sfu.ca.

See, **Scott W.**, *Maine, Orono*. Email: scott.see@maine.edu.

Seed, **Patricia**, *California, Irvine; Rice*. Email: seed5@uci.edu.

Seedorf, *Martin F.*, *Eastern Washington*. Cheney, WA. Email: mseedorf@mail.ewu.edu; martinseedorf@gmail.com. Research: modern European diplomacy, Britain and Ireland.

Seefeldt, *Douglas*, *Ball State*. Muncie, IN. Email: wdseefeldt@bsu.edu. Research: digital, public memory.

Seeley, **Joseph Andrew**, *Virginia*. Email: jas5fz@virginia.edu.

Seeley, **Samantha M.**, *Richmond*. Email: sseeley@richmond.edu.

Seely, **Bruce E.**, *Michigan Tech*. Email: bseely@mtu.edu.

Seelye, **James Edward**, *Jr.*, *Kent State*. Email: jseelye@kent.edu.

Seeman, *Erik R.*, *SUNY, Buffalo*. Williamsville, NY. Email: seeman@buffalo.edu. Research: colonial America, religion.

Sefton, **David S.**, *Eastern Kentucky*. Email: david.sefton@eku.edu.

Segal, *Daniel A.*, *Pitzer*. Claremont, CA. Email: dsegal@pitzer.edu. Research: modern world, colonialism and postcolonialism.

Segal, **Ethan I.**, *Michigan State*. Email: segale@msu.edu.

Segal, **Howard P.**, *Maine, Orono*. Orono, ME. Email: segal@maine.edu. Research: late 20th-c utopianism, 20th-c technology.

Segal, **Lester A.**, *Massachusetts, Boston*. Email: lester.segal@umb.edu.

Segal, *Raz*. Philadelphia, PA. Affil: Stockton. Email: Raz.Segal@stockton.edu.

Segalla, *Spencer D.*, *Tampa*. Tampa, FL. Email: ssegalla@ut.edu; ssegalla@yahoo.com. Research: colonial/postcolonial French North Africa, 1960 Agadir Earthquake and decolonization.

Segel, **Edward B.**, *Reed*. Email: edward.segel@reed.edu.

Seger, **Donna Amelia**, *Salem State*. Email: dseger@salemstate.edu.

Seguin, **Colleen M.**, *Valparaiso*. Valparaiso, IN. Email: colleen.seguin@valpo.edu. Research: Catholic women in England, recusancy.

Sehat, **David J.**, *Georgia State*. Email: dsehat@gsu.edu.

Sehlinger, **Peter J.**, *Indiana–Purdue, Indianapolis*. Email: psehling@iupui.edu.

Seibert, **William D.**, *Jr.* Twinsburg, OH. Email: seibertd@yahoo.com.

Seidel, **Robert W.**, *Minnesota (Hist. of Science)*. Email: rws@umn.edu.

Seidelman, **Rhona**, *Oklahoma (Hist.); Oklahoma (Hist. of Science)*. Email: rds@ou.edu.

Seidman, **Michael M.**, *North Carolina, Wilmington*. Email: seidmanm@uncw.edu.

Seidman, **Rachel Filene**, *North Carolina, Chapel Hill*. Email: rachel.seidman@unc.edu.

Seidule, *Ty*, *US Military Acad.* West Point, NY. Email: ty.seidule@usma.edu; ty.seidule@gmail.com. Research: Confederate Memory, Digital History.

Seiferth, **Eric A.**, *Hist. New Orleans*. Email: erics@hnoc.org.

Seifman, *Travis*. Los Angeles, CA. Affil: California, Santa Barbara. Email: tseifman@ucsb.edu. Research: Ryukyu Kingdom, diplomatic/political ritual performance.

Seigel, *Jerrold E.*, *NYU*. Email: jes3@nyu.edu.

Seigel, *Micol*, *Indiana*. Email: mseigel@indiana.edu.

Seigler, *Brandon*. Atlanta, GA. Affil: Woodward Academy. Email: brandon.seigler@woodward.edu.

Seijas, *Tatiana*, *Rutgers*. Email: tatiana.seijas@rutgers.edu.

Seikaly, **May**, *Wayne State*. Email: ad6006@wayne.edu.

Seikaly, *Sherene R.*, *California, Santa Barbara*. Santa Barbara, CA. Email: sseikaly@history.ucsb.edu. Research: nationalism, colonialism.

Seip, **Terry L.**, *Southern California*. Email: tseip@usc.edu.

Seipp, **Adam R.**, *Texas A&M*. College Station, TX. Email: aseipp@tamu.edu. Research: post-1945 West Germany, Holocaust.

Seitz, *John Britton*. Charleston, WV. Affil: Iowa State. Email: j.brittonseitz@gmail.com.

Seitz, **Jonathan W.**, *Drexel*. Email: jwseitz@drexel.edu.

Sekulic, *Ana*. Princeton, NJ. Affil: Princeton. Email: ane.sekulic@gmail.com.

Sela, *Ron*, *Indiana*. Bloomington, IN. Email: rsela@indiana.edu. Research: 16th-/19th-c Muslim world, historiography/philology.

Selbitschka, *Armin*. Munich, Germany. Affil: Ludwig Maximilians, Munich. Email: armin@lmu.de. Research: early Chinese notions of afterlife, state formation on Silk Road.

Selby, **Hajnalka Gajdacs**, *OAH*. Email: hselby@oah.edu.

Selby, **John G.**, *Roanoke*. Email: selby@roanoke.edu.

Selcer, *Perrin*, *Michigan, Ann Arbor*. Ann Arbor, MI. Email: pselcer@umich.edu. Research: environmental, global.

Selcraig, **James T.**, *Texas State*. Email: js32@txstate.edu.

Selcuk, *Iklil*. Istanbul, Turkey. Affil: Özyegin. Email: iklilerefe@gmail.com.

Seldon, **Mary Elisabeth**, *Indiana–Purdue, Indianapolis*.

Seleski, *Patricia S.*, *California State, San Marcos*. Escondido, CA. Email: pseleski@csusm.edu. Research: modern Europe, British Isles.

Selesky, **Harold E.**, *Alabama, Tuscaloosa*. Email: hselesky@tenhoor.as.ua.edu.

Self, **Robert O.**, *Brown*. Providence, RI. Email: robert_self@brown.edu. Research: 20th-c US.

Selig, *Diana M.*, *Claremont McKenna*. Claremont, CA. Email: dselig@cmc.edu. Research: ethnoracial identity and immigration, social science and education.

Seligman, *Amanda I.*, *Wisconsin-Milwaukee*. Milwaukee, WI. Email: seligman@uwm.edu. Research: public policy, Milwaukee WI.

Seligmann, *Gustav L., Jr.*, *North Texas*. Denton, TX. Email: gus@unt.edu. Research: 19th-c US presidential campaigns, 19th-c presidential campaign songs.

Sellars, **Nigel Anthony**, *Christopher Newport*. Email: nsellers@cnu.edu.

Sellers, **Abbylin**, *Azusa Pacific*. Email: asellers@apu.edu.

Sellers, **Chris**, *SUNY, Stony Brook*. Email: christopher.sellers@stonybrook.edu.

Sellers, **Jason R.**, *Mary Washington*. Email: jseller4@umw.edu.

Sellers, *Mortimer Newlin Stead*. Radnor, PA. Affil: Baltimore. Email: msellers@ubalt.edu. Research: US Constitution, republican tradition.

Sellers-Garcia, *Sylvia M.*, *Boston Coll.* Chestnut Hill, MA. Email: sylvia.sellers-garcia@bc.edu. Research: colonial Latin America.

Sellick, **Gary D.**, *Robert H. Smith Center*. Email: gsellick@monticello.org.

AHA members in **bold italic**; *Directory*-listed affiliations in *italic*

Selmanovic, Amir, *Eastern Washington*. Email: aselmanovic29@ewu.edu.

Seltz, Jennifer, *Western Washington*. Bellingham, WA. Email: Jennifer.Seltz@wwu.edu. Research: energy and Reconstruction, 19th-c western health and environment.

Seltzer, Michael. Brooklyn, NY. Email: mseltzer6@optonline.net.

Selverstone, Marc J., *Virginia*. Charlottesville, VA. Email: selverstone@virginia.edu. Research: US foreign relations, Cold War.

Selwood, Jacob W., *Georgia State*. Email: jselwood@gsu.edu.

Semán, Ernesto. Bergen, Norway. Affil: Bergen. Email: Ernesto.Seman@uib.no.

Semendeferi, Ioanna, *Houston*.

Semerdjian, Elyse, *Whitman*. Email: semerdve@whitman.edu.

Semioli, Mark. Chatham, NJ. Affil: Kent Place Sch. Email: semi56@aol.com.

Semley, Lorelle D., *Holy Cross*. Email: lsemley@holycross.edu.

Semmel, Stuart, *Yale*. New Haven, CT. Email: stuart.semmel@yale.edu. Research: Britain.

Semo, Enrique, *New Mexico*.

Semonche, John E., *North Carolina, Chapel Hill*. Email: semche@live.unc.edu.

Semsel, Craig R. Lakewood, OH. Affil: Lorain County Comm. Coll. Email: csemsel@lorainccc.edu.

Sen, Aditi, *Queen's, Can*. Email: senadit@gmail.com.

Sen, Ahmet Tunc, *Columbia (Hist.)*. Email: ats2171@columbia.edu.

Sen, Dwaipayan, *Amherst*. Email: dsen@amherst.edu.

Sen, Sudipta, *California, Davis*. Email: ssen@ucdavis.edu.

Sendzikas, Aldona, *Western Ontario*. Email: asendzi2@uwo.ca.

Sene, Ibra, *Wooster*. Email: isene@wooster.edu.

Senecal, Christine K., *Shippensburg*. Email: cksene@ship.edu.

Senechal de la Roche, Roberta, *Washington and Lee*. Lexington, VA. Email: senechalr@wlu.edu. Research: US social, Gilded Age.

Senger, Jeffrey, *Gerald Ford Presidential Library*. Email: jeffrey.senger@nara.gov.

SenGupta, Gunja, *Brooklyn, CUNY; Graduate Center, CUNY*. Email: sengupta@brooklyn.cuny.edu.

Senkewicz, Robert M., *Santa Clara*. San Jose, CA. Email: rsenkewicz@scu.edu. Research: missions in California and Southwest, society in California and Southwest.

Sennett, Richard, *NYU*. Email: richard.sennett@nyu.edu.

Senning, Calvin F. Cape Porpoise, ME. Affil: Maine, Augusta. Email: csenning@roadrunner.com. Research: Jacobean England, Anglo-Spanish relations under James I.

Senocak, Neslihan, *Columbia (Hist.)*. Email: nsenocak@columbia.edu.

Sensbach, Jon F., *Florida*. Email: jsensbach@ufl.edu.

Senseney, John, *Arizona*. Email: jsenseney@email.arizona.edu.

Sentilles, Renee M., *Case Western Reserve*. Email: renee.sentilles@case.edu.

Seo, Sarah. Iowa City, IA. Affil: Iowa. Email: sarah-seo@uiowa.edu.

Seow, Victor, *Harvard (Hist. of Science)*. Email: seow@fas.harvard.edu.

Sepinwall, Alyssa Goldstein, *California State, San Marcos*. San Marcos, CA. Email: sepinwal@csusm.edu. Research: French Revolution/post-Revolution, Haiti.

Sepkoski, David, *Illinois, Urbana-Champaign*. Email: sepkoski@illinois.edu.

Sepulveda, Charles A. Salt Lake City, CA. Affil: Utah. Email: charles.sepulveda@utah.edu.

Sequin, Caroline. Chicago, IL. Affil: Chicago. Email: sequinc@uchicago.edu. Research: prostitution.

Serafini, David, *Western Kentucky*. Email: david.serafini@wku.edu.

Seraphim, Franziska, *Boston Coll*. Chestnut Hill, MA. Email: seraphim@bc.edu. Research: postwar reconstruction, comparative.

Seratt, Jim, *Lamar*. Email: serattjd@my.lamar.edu.

Serbin, Kenneth P., *San Diego*. San Diego, CA. Email: kserbin@sandiego.edu. Research: modern Latin America, Brazil.

Sergent, Tyler, *Berea*. Email: tyler_sergent@berea.edu.

Sermon, Suzanne, *Boise State*. Email: suzannesermon@boisestate.edu.

Serna, Sarah E. Peoria, AZ. Affil: Norwich. Email: sernajs@outlook.com. Research: indentured labor in colonial Chesapeake, child stealing for labor in Chesapeake.

Sernett, Milton C., *Syracuse*. Email: mcsernet@syr.edu.

Serpa, Ashley. Mountain View, CA. Affil: California, Davis. Email: aserpafl@ucdavis.edu. Research: US foreign relations, Portuguese Colonial War.

Service, Timothy. Albany, NY. Affil: Albany Academies. Email: servicet@albanyacademies.org.

Servos, John W., *Amherst*. Email: jwservos@amherst.edu.

Sessa, Kristina, *Ohio State*. Email: sessa.3@osu.edu.

Sessions, Gene A., *Weber State*. Email: gsessions1@weber.edu.

Sessions, Jennifer, *Virginia*. Charlottesville, VA. Email: jes4fx@virginia.edu. Research: French colonialism in Algeria, microhistory.

Sesso, Gloria. Port Jefferson, NY. Affil: Patchogue Medford Sch. Email: gloriasesso@yahoo.com.

Seth, Michael J., *James Madison*. Email: sethmj@jmu.edu.

Seth, Suman, *Cornell*. Email: ss536@cornell.edu.

Settje, David E. River Forest, IL. Affil: Concordia, Chicago. Email: david.settje@cuchicago.edu.

Sevcenko, Liz, *Rutgers, Newark/New Jersey Inst. of Tech*.

Sevea, Iqbal Singh, *North Carolina, Chapel Hill*. Email: isevea@email.unc.edu.

Severn, John K., *Alabama, Huntsville*. Email: severnj@uah.edu.

Severson, Samuel John. New York, NY. Affil: Yale. Email: samuel.severson@yale.edu.

Severtson, Roald Bradley. Seattle, WA. Email: bradsevertson@live.com. Research: statistical analysis, mathematization of induction.

Sevin, Analie. Longmont, CO. Affil: American. Email: as1311a@american.edu.

Sewell, Richard H., *Wisconsin-Madison*. Email: rhsewell@wisc.edu.

Sewell, William H., *Chicago*. Chicago, IL. Email: wsewell@uchicago.edu. Research: 18th-c France.

Sewell, William S., *Dalhousie; St. Mary's, Can*. Email: bill.sewell@smu.ca.

Sexton, Jay, *Missouri, Columbia*.

Sexton, Mary DuBois. Silver Spring, MD. Affil: Montgomery. Email: mary.d.sexton@verizon.net.

Sextro, Laura Elizabeth, *Dayton*. Email: lsextro1@udayton.edu.

Seyhun, Ahmet, *Winnipeg*. Email: a.seyhun@uwinnipeg.ca.

Seymour, Jeffery, *Columbus State*. Email: seymour_jeffery@columbusstate.edu.

Shabazz, Amilcar, *Massachusetts, Amherst*. Email: shabazz@chancellor.umass.edu.

Shackelford, Jole R., *Minnesota (Hist. of Science)*. Email: shack001@umn.edu.

Shackleton, Stefanie. Austin, TX. Affil: Texas, Austin. Email: smshackleton@utexas.edu.

Shadbash, Shahram, *Suffolk*. Email: sshadbash@yahoo.com.

Shadis, Miriam T., *Ohio*. Email: shadis@ohio.edu.

Shadle, Brett L., *Virginia Tech*. Email: shadle@vt.edu.

Shafer, David, *California State, Long Beach; Soc. for Hist. Education*. Email: david.shafer@csulb.edu.

Shafer, Steve C. Champaign, IL. Affil: Illinois, Urbana-Champaign. Email: scs@illinois.edu. Research: American and British film, American musical theater.

Shaffer, Marguerite S., *Miami, Ohio*. Email: shaffems@miamioh.edu.

Shaffer, Robert, *Shippensburg*. Shippensburg, PA. Email: roshaf@ship.edu. Research: US missionary efforts in China and Japan, mid-20th-c US-Asian relations.

Shaffer-Henry, Sara. Bellevue, NE. Affil: Nebraska, Kearney. Email: sarashafferhenry@gmail.com.

Shaffern, Robert, *Scranton*. Email: robert.shaffern@scranton.edu.

Shafir, Nir, *California, San Diego*. Email: nshafir@ucsd.edu.

Shagan, Ethan H., *California, Berkeley*. Berkeley, CA. Email: shagan@berkeley.edu. Research: Britain, Reformation.

Shah, Nayan B., *Southern California*. Email: nayansha@dornsife.usc.edu.

Shahaf, Nataly. New York, NY. Affil: Columbia. Email: ns3050@columbia.edu.

Shaikh, Juned, *California, Santa Cruz*. Santa Cruz, CA. Email: jmshaikh@ucsc.edu. Research: Mumbai urban, South Asian social and cultural.

Shaler, Andrew. Riverside, CA. Affil: California, Riverside. Email: ashal001@ucr.edu. Research: Native Americans of California, global indigenous studies.

Shammas, Carole, *Southern California*. Los Angeles, CA. Email: shammas@usc.edu. Research: built environment, household consumption.

Shan, Patrick Fuliang, *Grand Valley State*. Allendale, MI. Email: shanp@gvsu.edu. Research: Li Dazhao, Republic of China 1912-49.

Shan, Yi. Columbus, OH. Affil: Ohio State. Email: fredshan412@gmail.com.

Shanafelt, Gary W. Abilene, TX. Affil: McMurry. Email: shanafeg@mcm.edu. Research: Austria-Hungary and WWI, Edith Durham and Albania.

Shanahan, **Brendan Anthony**. New Haven, CT. Affil: Yale. Email: brendan.shanahan@yale.edu. Research: US citizenship and citizenship rights, citizens/noncitizens/alienage.

Shanes, **Joshua M.**, *Charleston.* Email: shanesj@cofc.edu.

Shanguhyia, **Martin S.**, *Syracuse.* Email: mshanguh@maxwell.syr.edu.

Shank, **J. B.**, *Minnesota (Hist.).* Email: jbshank@umn.edu.

Shank, **Michael H.**, *Wisconsin-Madison.* Email: mhshank@wisc.edu.

Shankar, **Shobana**, *SUNY, Stony Brook.* Email: shobana.shankar@stonybrook.edu.

Shankman, **Andrew Benjamin**, *Rutgers, Camden.* Camden, NJ. Email: shankman@camden.rutgers.edu. Research: early America, American political and economic.

Shannon, **Anthony Ryan**. Somerville, MA. Affil: Harvard. Email: ashannon@fas.harvard.edu.

Shannon, **Hope**. Chicago, IL. Affil: Loyola, Chicago. Email: hopejshannon@gmail.com.

Shannon, **Kelly J.**, *Florida Atlantic.* Hollywood, FL. Email: shannonk@fau.edu; kelly.j.shannon@gmail.com. Research: 20th-c US-Iran relations, transnational feminist networks.

Shannon, **Kerry Seiji**. Berkeley, CA. Affil: California, Berkeley. Email: kerryshannon@berkeley.edu.

Shannon, **Silvia C.**, *St. Anselm.* Email: sshannon@anselm.edu.

Shannon, **Timothy J.**, *Gettysburg.* Gettysburg, PA. Email: tshannon@gettysburg.edu. Research: North American Indian captivity, Native American-European diplomacy.

Shao, **Qin**, *New Jersey.* Email: shao@tcnj.edu.

Shapard, **Robert Paine**. Chapel Hill, NC. Affil: North Carolina, Chapel Hill. Email: robshapard@yahoo.com. Research: 20th-c US, environmental.

Shapin, **Steven**, *Harvard (Hist. of Science).* Email: shapin@fas.harvard.edu.

Shapinsky, **Peter D.**, *Illinois, Springfield.* Email: pshap2@uis.edu.

Shapiro, **Aaron**, *North Carolina, Charlotte.* Email: ashapi10@uncc.edu.

Shapiro, **Adam R.** Lancaster, PA. Affil: Consortium for the Hist. of Science, Tech. and Medicine. Email: Adam256@gmail.com. Research: US biology pedagogy 1900-30, science-religion dialogue.

Shapiro, **Alan E.**, *Minnesota (Hist. of Science).* Email: ashapiro@physics.umn.edu.

Shapiro, **Barry M.**, *Allegheny.* Email: bshapiro@allegheny.edu.

Shapiro, **Edward S.**, *Seton Hall.* West Orange, NJ. Email: edshapiro07052@yahoo.com. Research: foreign policy, 20th century.

Shapiro, **Hugh L.**, *Nevada, Reno.* Email: shapiro@unr.edu.

Shapiro, **Shelby**. Bethesda, MD. Email: shelshap1949@yahoo.com.

Shapiro, **Stanley**, *Wayne State.* Email: aa1357@wayne.edu.

Shapiro, **Susan H.** Chicago, IL. Affil: Univ. of Chicago Laboratory Sch. Email: sshapir@gmail.com. Research: Holocaust studies.

Shapiro, **Susan O.**, *Utah State.* Email: susan.o.shapiro@usu.edu.

Shapiro-Shapin, **Carolyn G.**, *Grand Valley State.* Email: shapiroc@gvsu.edu.

Sharafi, **Mitra**, *Wisconsin-Madison.* Madison, WI. Email: mitra.sharafi@wisc.edu. Research: South Asian legal, South Asian history of science.

Sharfstein, **Daniel**, *Vanderbilt.* Email: daniel.sharfstein@vanderbilt.edu.

Sharif, **Lama**. Munster, IN. Affil: Purdue. Email: lelshari@purdue.edu.

Sharlach, **Tonia M.**, *Oklahoma State.* Email: tonia.sharlach@okstate.edu.

Sharma, **Jayeeta**, *Toronto.* Email: sharma@utsc.utoronto.ca.

Sharnak, **Debbie Victoria**, *Rowan.* Cambridge, MA. Affil: Harvard. Email: sharnak@rowan.edu; dsharnak@gmail.com. Research: Uruguay, human rights.

Sharon, **Michael**. Harrisburg, PA. Email: mjsharon@comcast.net.

Sharp, **Buchanan**, *California, Santa Cruz.* Email: bsharp@ucsc.edu.

Sharp, **James Roger**, *Syracuse.* Email: jrsharp@maxwell.syr.edu.

Sharp, **Jason Paul**, **Esq.** Spring, TX. Email: Sharplaw@hotmail.com.

Sharp, **Joy L.** Pine Hill, NM. Affil: Ramah Navajo Sch. Board. Email: joytheobscure@gmail.com.

Sharp, **Kelly Kean**, *Luther.*

Sharp, **Lynn L.**, *Whitman.* Walla Walla, WA. Email: sharpll@whitman.edu. Research: Third Republic dairy production/education, 1830s gender/socialism/religion.

Sharp, **Matthew**. Upper Darby, PA. Affil: Pennsylvania. Email: masharp@sas.upenn.edu.

Sharples, **Jason T.**, *Florida Atlantic.* Email: jsharples@fau.edu.

Sharpless, **John B.**, **II**, *Wisconsin-Madison.* Email: jbsharpl@wisc.edu.

Sharpless, **Rebecca**, *Texas Christian.* Fort Worth, TX. Email: r.sharpless@tcu.edu. Research: women and cooking in US South.

Sharpless, **Richard E.**, *Lafayette.*

Sharrow, **Elizabeth A.**, *Massachusetts, Amherst.* Email: sharrow@polsci.umass.edu.

Sharrow, **Walter B.**, *Canisius.* Email: sharrow@canisius.edu.

Shashko, **Philip**, *Wisconsin-Milwaukee.* Milwaukee, WI. Email: pshashko@uwm.edu. Research: modern Russia and Balkans, intellectual.

Shatara, **Hanadi**, *Wisconsin-La Crosse.*

Shattuck, **Gardiner H.**, **Jr.** Warwick, RI. Email: ghshattuck@cox.net. Research: US churches and social issues, Holocaust and genocide.

Shatz, **Julia Rivkind**, *California State, Fresno.* Fresno, CA. Email: jshatz@csufresno.edu. Research: Middle East, empire.

Shatz, **Marshall S.**, *Massachusetts, Boston.* Email: marshall.shatz@umb.edu.

Shatzmiller, **Joseph**, *Duke.* Email: joshatz@duke.edu.

Shatzmiller, **Maya**, *Western Ontario.* Email: maya@uwo.ca.

Shaughnessy, **Kathryn**. Jamaica, NY. Affil: St. John's, NY. Email: shaughnk@stjohns.edu.

Shaughnessy-Zeena, **Colleen**, *Salem State.* Email: cshaughnessyzeena@salemstate.edu.

Shaul, **Hollis**, *Miami, Ohio.* Email: shaulhe@miamioh.edu.

Shaw, **Caroline Emily**, *Bates.* Portland, ME. Email: cshaw@bates.edu. Research: reputation and the law, humanitarianism and human rights.

Shaw, **D. Gary**, *Wesleyan.* Middletown, CT. Email: gshaw@wesleyan.edu. Research: medieval, Britain.

Shaw, **Deborah J.** Saint Augustine, FL. Email: Deb.shaw@gmail.com.

Shaw, **Dennis E.** Tavares, FL. Affil: Miami-Dade. Email: dshaw6987@aol.com.

Shaw, **Ezel Kural**, *California State, Northridge.*

Shaw, **Fred**. Inverness, IL. Email: flshaw@comcast.net.

Shaw, **Jay**. Saint Robert, MO. Email: jayconradshaw@gmail.com.

Shaw, **Jenny**, *Alabama, Tuscaloosa.* Email: jenny.shaw@ua.edu.

Shaw, **Stephanie J.**, *Ohio State.* Columbus, OH. Email: shaw.1@osu.edu. Research: slavery and female slaves, black women during Great Depression.

Shawcross, **Clare Teresa**, *Princeton.* Email: cshawcro@princeton.edu.

Shaya, **Gregory K.**, *Wooster.* Wooster, OH. Email: gshaya@wooster.edu. Research: sensationalism and French press, public execution/anarchist-terrorism.

Shea, **Ellen**, *Arthur and Elizabeth Schlesinger Library.* Email: eshea@radcliffe.harvard.edu.

Shea, **Gary T.** Milwaukee, WI. Email: gshea@att.net.

Shea, **Gary**. Berkley, MI. Email: gmshea@gmail.com.

Shea, **Margo**, *Salem State.* Email: mshea@salemstate.edu.

Shea, **Matthew**, *SUNY, Oneonta.* Email: matthew.shea@oneonta.edu.

Shea, **Patrick**, *Science History Inst.* Email: pshea@sciencehistory.org.

Shealy, **E. Howard**, *Kennesaw State.* Email: hshealy@kennesaw.edu.

Shear, **Adam**. Pittsburgh, PA. Affil: Pittsburgh. Email: ashear@pitt.edu. Research: Jewish culture in Renaissance Italy, Jewish book.

Shearer, **David R.**, *Delaware.* Email: dshearer@udel.edu.

Shearer, **Jeffrey**. La Verne, CA. Affil: Claremont Graduate. Email: jeffrey.shearer@cgu.edu. Research: human rights/Chicago Police Department, genocide studies.

Shearer, **Tobin Miller**, *Montana.* Missoula, MT. Email: tobin.shearer@umontana.edu. Research: innocence and race in 20th-c US, 20th-c purity/race/Mennonites.

Shedden, **Dawn L.**, *South Florida, St. Petersburg.* Saint Petersburg, FL. Email: ds0420@tampabay.rr.com. Research: French Revolution/Germany/borders, French Revolution/comparative religions.

Shedel, **James P.**, *Georgetown.* Washington, DC. Email: shedelj@georgetown.edu. Research: modernization and rule of law, monarchy and modernization.

Sheehan, **Brett G.**, *Southern California.* Email: bsheehan@usc.edu.

Sheehan, **James J.**, *Stanford.* Berkeley, CA. Email: sheehan@stanford.edu. Research: sovereignty and society of states, 20th-c Europe.

Sheehan, **John M.**, *Naval War Coll.* Email: john.sheehan@usnwc.edu.

Sheehan, **Jonathan L.**, *California, Berkeley.* Berkeley, CA. Email: sheehan@berkeley.edu. Research: Bible scholarship in early modern Europe, development of human sciences.

Sheehan, **Kevin J.**, *San Diego State.*

Sheehan-Dean, Aaron C., *Louisiana State*. Baton Rouge, LA. Email: asd@lsu.edu. Research: Civil War and Reconstruction.

Sheehy, Edward J., *La Salle*. Philadelphia, PA. Email: sheehy@lasalle.edu. Research: modern America, US maritime and military.

Sheets, Kevin B. Cortland, NY. Affil: SUNY, Coll. Cortland. Email: kevin.sheets@cortland.edu. Research: classics in American culture, art in American education and culture.

Sheetz-Nguyen, Jessica Ann, *Central Oklahoma*. Edmond, OK. Email: jsheetznguyen@uco.edu. Research: Victorian London as social space, Victorian welfare policy and women.

Sheffer, Debra, *Park*. Email: debra.sheffer@park.edu.

Sheffler, David L., *North Florida*. Email: dsheffle@unf.edu.

Shefsiek, Kenneth P., *North Carolina, Wilmington*. Email: shefsiekk@uncw.edu.

Sheftall, Mark D., *Auburn; Bucknell*. Lewisburg, PA. Email: mds0020@auburn.edu; mds037@bucknell.edu. Research: British Empire, military.

Shefveland, Kristalyn Marie, *Southern Indiana*. Email: kmshefvela@usi.edu.

Sheikh, Samira, *Vanderbilt*. Email: samira.sheikh@vanderbilt.edu.

Sheinin, David M. K., *Trent*. Email: dsheinin@trentu.ca.

Shelden, Rachel A., *Oklahoma (Hist.)*. Norman, OK. Email: rachel.shelden@ou.edu; rachel.shelden@gmail.com. Research: 19th-c judicial culture, federalism in Confederacy.

Sheldon, Geoffrey Paul. Dules, VA. Affil: King's Coll. London. Email: jgsheldon@gmail.com. Research: US/GB diplomacy 1807-67, impact of British abolitionism campaign.

Sheldon, Kathleen E. Santa Monica, CA. Affil: UCLA. Email: ksheldon@ucla.edu. Research: African women, Mozambique.

Sheldon, Marianne B. Oakland, CA. Affil: Mills. Email: mshel@mills.edu. Research: US social, family.

Sheldon, Rose Mary, *Virginia Military Inst.* Email: sheldonrm@vmi.edu.

Sheldon, William F. Nuremberg, Germany. Email: b.sheldon@arcor.de.

Shelford, April G., *American*. Washington, DC. Email: shelfor@american.edu. Research: early modern Europe, religion and culture.

Sheller, Tina H. Baltimore, MD. Affil: Goucher. Email: tina.sheller@goucher.edu. Research: historic preservation, Maryland.

Shellman, Carey Olmstead. Atlanta, GA. Affil: Georgia Gwinnett. Email: cshellma@ggc.edu.

Shell-Weiss, Melanie R. Allendale, MI. Affil: Grand Valley State. Email: shellm@gvsu.edu. Research: migrant labor/oral, Native American urban.

Shelly, Cara L., *Oakland*. Email: shelly@oakland.edu.

Shelor, Erin J., *Millersville, Pa.* Email: erin.shelor@millersville.edu.

Shelton, Anita, *Eastern Illinois*. Email: ashelton@eiu.edu.

Shelton, Brenda, *SUNY, Buffalo State*.

Shelton, Danielle. Chattanooga, TN. Affil: Middle Tennessee State. Email: sds7k@mtmail.mtsu.edu.

Shelton, Laura M., *Franklin & Marshall*. Email: laura.shelton@fandm.edu.

Shelton, Mary. Nashville, TN. Affil: Tennessee State. Email: sheltonmv@hotmail.com.

Shelton, Robert S., *Cleveland State*. Email: r.s.shelton@csuohio.edu.

Shemo, Connie A., *SUNY, Plattsburgh*. Email: connie.shemo@plattsburgh.edu.

Shen, Grace Yen, *Fordham*. Email: gshen1@fordham.edu.

Shen, Yu, *Indiana, Southeast*. Email: yshen@ius.edu.

Sheng, Michael M., *Missouri State*. Email: msheng@uakron.edu.

Shenk, Gerald E. San Diego, CA. Affil: California State, Monterey Bay. Email: gshenk@csumb.edu. Research: US colonialism/public education in Philippines, Filipinos in US armed forces.

Shenk, Tim. Washington, DC. Affil: Washington, St. Louis. Email: teshenk@gmail.com. Research: political economy, intellectual.

Shenkman, Rick B. Seattle, WA. Affil: Hist. News Network. Email: rickshenkman@gmail.com. Research: presidential.

Shenton, Robert, *Queen's, Can.* Email: shentonr@queensu.ca.

Shepard, Alexandra. Glasgow, United Kingdom. Affil: Glasgow. Email: Alex.Shepard@glasgow.ac.uk. Research: early modern Britain, gender relations.

Shepard, Todd, *Johns Hopkins (Hist.)*. Baltimore, MD. Email: tshep75@jhu.edu. Research: Algerian War and French identity and institutions, sexuality and gender in post-WWII Europe.

Shepardson, Christine, *Tennessee, Knoxville*. Email: cshepard@utk.edu.

Shepherd, Jeffrey P., *Texas, El Paso*. Email: jpshepherd@utep.edu.

Shepherd, Kenneth Reynolds, *Henry Ford Coll.* Email: kshepherd@hfcc.edu.

Shepherd, Michael Alan. Youngstown, OH. Affil: Youngstown State. Email: guinfan1@yahoo.com.

Shepherd, Sam C., Jr., *Centenary, La.* Email: sshepher@centenary.edu.

Shepherd, Sarah. Lewisburg, WV. Affil: Goucher. Email: shshepherd0@gmail.com. Research: American slavery.

Shepherd, Stormy M. Highland, UT. Affil: Utah. Email: stormy@leavehomebooking.com. Research: 20th-c US and Vietnam, social/cultural/military.

Shepkaru, Shmuel, *Oklahoma (Hist.)*. Email: shepkaru@ou.edu.

Sheppard, Eugene R., *Brandeis*. Email: sheppard@brandeis.edu.

Sheppard, Kathleen, *Missouri Science and Tech.* Email: sheppardka@mst.edu.

Sher, Doris, *Rutgers, Newark/New Jersey Inst. of Tech.*

Sher, Richard B., *Rutgers, Newark/New Jersey Inst. of Tech.* Maplewood, NJ. Email: sher@njit.edu. Research: transatlantic Enlightenment culture, communication and technology.

Sherayko, Gerard F., *Randolph*. Lynchburg, VA. Email: gsherayko@randolphcollege.edu. Research: 20th-c consumer culture/advertising, Germany.

Sheridan, Bridgette A., *Framingham State*. Cambridge, MA. Email: bsheridan@framingham.edu. Research: modern Europe, gender.

Sheridan, David Allen, *California State, Long Beach*. Email: david.sheridan@csulb.edu.

Sheridan, George J., *Oregon*. Email: gjs@uoregon.edu.

Sheridan Moss, Jennifer, *Wayne State*. Email: aa2191@wayne.edu.

Sheriff, Carol, *William and Mary*. Email: cxsher@wm.edu.

Sherman, Daniel J., *North Carolina, Chapel Hill*. Chapel Hill, NC. Email: dsherman@email.unc.edu. Research: cultural aspects of colonialism, arts and society in post-WWII France.

Sherman, Janann M., *Memphis*. Email: sherman@memphis.edu.

Shermer, Elizabeth Tandy, *Loyola, Chicago*. Email: eshermer@luc.edu.

Sherow, James E., *Kansas State*. Email: jsherow@ksu.edu.

Sherr, Merrill F. Forest Hills, NY.

Sherrill, Peter T., *Arkansas, Little Rock*. Email: ptsherrill@ualr.edu.

Sherry, Karen A., *Virginia Museum of Hist.* Email: ksherry@VirginiaHistory.org.

Sherry, Michael S., *Northwestern*. Evanston, IL. Email: m-sherry@northwestern.edu. Research: punitive turn in American life.

Sherwin, Martin J., *George Mason*. Washington, DC. Email: msherwin@gmu.edu; martysherwin@gmail.com. Research: Cold War, film.

Shesko, Elizabeth M., *Oakland*. Rochester, MI. Email: shesko@oakland.edu. Research: Bolivian indigenous-state relations, military service.

Sheth, Sudev J. Philadelphia, PA. Affil: Harvard Business Sch. Email: sjsheth@gmail.com.

Sheumaker, Helen, *Miami, Ohio*. Oxford, OH. Email: sheumahd@miamioh.edu. Research: secondhand shopping cultural, 19th-c human hair work.

Shevin-Coetzee, Marilyn. Potomac, MD. Email: mscfc@yahoo.com. Research: nationality and citizenship in WWI.

Shewell, Hugh, *Carleton, Can.* Email: hugh.shewell@carleton.ca.

Shi, Xia. Sarasota, FL. Affil: New Coll., Fla. Email: xshi@ncf.edu. Research: women/gender/family, religion and philanthropy.

Shiao, Ling A., *Southern Methodist*. Email: lshiao@smu.edu.

Shiba, Yoshinobu. Saitama-Ken, Japan.

Shibusawa, Naoko, *Brown*. Email: Naoko_Shibusawa@Brown.edu.

Shields, Anna M. Princeton, NJ. Affil: Princeton. Email: ashields@princeton.edu.

Shields, Johanna N., *Alabama, Huntsville*. Email: shieldsj@uah.edu.

Shields, Sarah D., *North Carolina, Chapel Hill*. Chapel Hill, NC. Email: sshields@email.unc.edu. Research: League of Nations and the Middle East, Nationalism in Middle East.

Shiels, Richard D., *Ohio State*. Email: shiels.1@osu.edu.

Shifflett, Crandall A., *Virginia Tech*. Email: shifflet@vt.edu.

Shifrinson, Joshua Itzkowitz. Brookline, MA. Affil: Boston Univ. Email: jris@bu.edu.

Shilaro, Priscilla M., *Virginia Commonwealth*. Email: pmshilaro@vcu.edu.

Shilcutt, Tracy M. Abilene, TX. Affil: Abilene Christian. Email: tracy.shilcutt@acu.edu. Research: infantry combat medics ETO, Pirate Radio 1960s.

Shimada, **Akira**, *SUNY, New Paltz*. Email: shimadaa@newpaltz.edu.

Shimizu, **Akira**, *Wilkes*. Email: akira.shimizu@wilkes.edu.

Shimizu, *Sayuri Guthrie*, *Rice*. Houston, TX. Email: sg45@rice.edu. Research: ocean resource diplomacy, baseball.

Shin, *Dong Jo*. Slingerlands, NY. Affil: Washington State, Vancouver. Email: shind@strose.edu.

Shin, **Ian**, *Michigan, Ann Arbor*. Email: ianshin@umich.edu.

Shin, **Leo K.**, *British Columbia*. Email: lkshin@mail.ubc.ca.

Shindo, **Charles J.**, *Louisiana State*. Email: cshindo@lsu.edu.

Shiner, **Larry**, *Illinois, Springfield*.

Shinn, **Tatyana N.**, *State Hist. Soc. of Missouri*. Email: ShinnTn@shsmo.org.

Shinno, **Reiko**, *Wisconsin-Eau Claire*. Email: shinnor@uwec.edu.

Shipley, **Neal**, *Massachusetts, Amherst*. Email: n.shipley@comcast.net.

Shipps, **Jan**, *Indiana–Purdue, Indianapolis*. Email: shipps@iupui.edu.

Shire, **Laurel**, *Western Ontario*. Email: lshire@uwo.ca.

Shirley, *Annie*. Moreland, GA. Email: ashirle1@my.westga.edu.

Shkuda, *Aaron P*. Princeton, NJ. Affil: Princeton. Email: ashkuda@gmail.com. Research: gentrification, SoHo/New York City.

Shlala, *Elizabeth H*. Wellesley, MA. Affil: Boston Coll. Email: ehs6@georgetown.edu. Research: world, gender and law.

Shlapentokh, **Dmitry V.**, *Indiana, South Bend*. Email: dshlapen@iusb.edu.

Shlosser, **F. E.**, *Concordia, Can.*

Shmagin, **Viktor**, *Colby*. Email: viktor.e.shmagin@gmail.com.

Shmelev, *Anatol*. Stanford, CA. Affil: Stanford. Email: shmelev@stanford.edu. Research: Russian foreign policy, Russian emigration.

Shneer, **David**, *Colorado, Boulder*. Email: david.shneer@colorado.edu.

Shoemaker, *Karl B.*, *Wisconsin-Madison*. Email: kbshoemaker@wisc.edu.

Shoemaker, *Nancy L.*, *Connecticut, Storrs*. Email: nancy.shoemaker@uconn.edu.

Shoemaker, **Rebecca S.**, *Indiana State*. Email: rshoemaker@isugw.indstate.edu.

Shokr, **Ahmad**, *Swarthmore*. Email: ashokr1@swarthmore.edu.

Shonk, *Kenneth Lee*, *Jr.*, *Wisconsin-La Crosse*. La Crosse, WI. Email: kshonk@uwlax.edu. Research: formation of Irish Republic, decolonization/postcolonialism.

Shook, **John R.**, *Bowie State*. Email: jrshook@bowiestate.edu.

Shopes, *Linda*. Carlisle, PA. Email: lshopes@aol.com. Research: oral, popular notions of history.

Shopkow, *Leah*, *Indiana*. Bloomington, IN. Email: shopkowl@indiana.edu; leah.shopkow@gmail.com. Research: Chronicon Andrensis, medieval intellectual and cultural.

Shor, **Francis**, *Wayne State*. Email: aa2439@wayne.edu.

Shore, **Marci**, *Yale*. Email: marci.shore@yale.edu.

Shore, **Marlene**, *York, Can.* Email: mshore@yorku.ca.

Short, *Courtney Aimee*. Wade, NC. Affil: US Air Force Academy. Email: cakjos@yahoo.com.

Research: post-WWII occupation of Okinawa, identity studies.

Short, *John Phillip*, *Georgia*. Athens, GA. Email: jshort@uga.edu; jake.short@gmail.com. Research: German colonialism 1840s-1918, 19th-c visual culture.

Shortall, **Sarah Elizabeth**, *Notre Dame*. Email: sshortal@nd.edu.

Shorten, *David J*. Boston, MA. Affil: Boston Univ. Email: dshorten@bu.edu.

Shorter, **Edward L.**, *Toronto*. Email: history.medicine@utoronto.ca.

Shovelton, *Tamara*. Wendell, NC. Affil: Wake Tech Comm. Coll.; Meredith. Email: tmshovelton@waketech.edu. Research: Reformation in England, relationships of Princess Elizabeth.

Shovlin, *John*, *NYU*. Email: john.shovlin@nyu.edu.

Showalter, *James L*. Stillwater, OK. Affil: Langston. Email: jimshowalter48@hotmail.com.

Showalter, *Meg*. ANN ARBOR, MI. Affil: Michigan, Ann Arbor. Email: meg.a.showalter@gmail.com.

Shreiner, *Tamara Lynn*, *Grand Valley State*. Email: shreinet@gvsu.edu.

Shriver, *Cameron*, *Miami, Ohio*. Oxford, OH. Email: shrivecm@miamioh.edu. Research: Native American, Miami tribe of Oklahoma.

Shriver, **George H.**, *Georgia Southern*.

Shrock, **Alice Almond**, *Earlham*. Email: alices@earlham.edu.

Shrock, **Randall**, *Earlham*. Email: randalls@earlham.edu.

Shrout, *Anelise H*. Fullerton, CA. Affil: California State, Fullerton. Email: shrouta@gmail.com. Research: transnational philanthropy, popular politics.

Shrum, **Rebecca K.**, *Indiana–Purdue, Indianapolis*. Email: rshrum@iupui.edu.

Shryock, *Grant*. San Diego, CA. Email: grantshryock1@gmail.com.

Shubert, **Adrian**, *York, Can.* Email: adriansh@yorku.ca.

Shuck-Hall, **Sheri Marie**, *Christopher Newport*. Email: sheri.shuckhall@cnu.edu.

Shulman, *Aimee*. Detroit, MI. Email: fz1867@wayne.edu.

Shulman, *Holly C*. Charlottesville, VA. Affil: Virginia. Email: hcs8n@virginia.edu. Research: Dolley Madison and widowhood, electronic editing.

Shulman, **Peter Adam**, *Case Western Reserve*. Email: peter.shulman@case.edu.

Shumpert, *Jeremy Eusebius*. Charlotte, NC. Affil: Charlotte Mecklenburg Sch. Email: jeremyeus@gmail.com.

Shumsky, **Neil Larry**, *Virginia Tech*. Email: yksmuhs@vt.edu.

Shumway, **Gary L.**, *California State, Fullerton*. Email: gshumway@fullerton.edu.

Shumway, *Jeffrey M.*, *Brigham Young*. Provo, UT. Email: jshumway@byu.edu. Research: Argentina, Latin America.

Shurbutt, **T. Ray**, *Georgia Southern*.

Shurts, *Sarah Elizabeth*. Kinnelon, NJ. Affil: Bergen Comm. Coll. Email: sshurts@bergen.edu. Research: modern French intellectual identity construction, development of French extreme right.

Shuster, **Richard J.**, *Naval War Coll.* Email: richard.shuster@usnwc.edu.

Shuster, **Robert D.**, *Wheaton, Ill.* Email: robert.shuster@wheaton.edu.

Shutt, *Allison K*. Conway, AR. Affil: Hendrix. Email: shutt@hendrix.edu. Research: biography, colonial Zimbabwe.

Shy, **John W.**, *Michigan, Ann Arbor*. Email: johnshy@umich.edu.

Shyovitz, *David*, *Northwestern*. Evanston, IL. Email: davidshy@northwestern.edu. Research: medieval Jewish conceptions of nature and body, Jewish law and custom.

Sia, *Rosanne*. Vancouver, BC, Canada. Affil: Southern California. Email: rsia@usc.edu.

Sibaja, *Rwany*. Boone, NC. Affil: Appalachian State. Email: sibajaro@appstate.edu. Research: national/masculine/class identity, Argentina soccer.

Sibanda, **Eliakim R.**, *Winnipeg*. Email: e.sibanda@uwinnipeg.ca.

Sibley, **Katherine A. S.**, *St. Joseph's*. Email: sibley@sju.edu.

Sicherman, *Barbara*. West Hartford, CT. Affil: Trinity Coll., Conn. Email: barbara.sicherman@trincoll.edu. Research: US women's reading, women's studies as academic field.

Sicilia, **David B.**, *Maryland, Coll. Park*. Email: dsicilia@umd.edu.

Sickinger, *Raymond L.*, *Providence*. Email: rsicking@providence.edu.

Sidbury, *James*, *Rice*. Houston, TX. Email: js58@rice.edu. Research: US, Atlantic world.

Siddali, **Silvana R.**, *St. Louis*. Email: siddalis@slu.edu.

Siddiqi, **Asif A.**, *Fordham*. Email: siddiqi@fordham.edu.

Siddiqui, **Osama**, *Providence*.

Sidebotham, **Steven**, *Delaware*. Email: ses@udel.edu.

Sider, *E. Morris*, *Messiah*. Grantham, PA. Email: msider@messiah.edu. Research: Anabaptism, Brethren in Christ Church.

Sider, **Robert**, *Saskatchewan*. Email: sider@sask.usask.ca.

Sides, *Josh A.*, *California State, Northridge*. Email: jsides@csun.edu.

Sieber, *Karen*. Dubquue, IA. Affil: Theodore Roosevelt Center. Email: karenlynnsieber@gmail.com.

Siefert, *Thomas*, *Indiana State*. Email: tsiefert@isugw.indstate.edu.

Siegel, *Benjamin*, *Boston Univ.* Somerville, MA. Email: siegelb@bu.edu. Research: modern South Asia.

Siegel, **Daniel M.**, *Wisconsin-Madison*. Email: dmsiegel@wisc.edu.

Siegel, **Jennifer**, *Ohio State*. Email: siegel.83@osu.edu.

Siegel, *Mona L.*, *California State, Sacramento*. Sacramento, CA. Email: msiegel@csus.edu. Research: interwar Europe, feminism/anti-colonialism/pacifism.

Siegel, *Robert A*. Baltimore, MD. Affil: Baltimore City Public Sch. Email: rsiegel401@aol.com. Research: Jewish/diaspora/conversos/Portuguese, early modern religion/science.

Siegel, *Sarah*. Saint Louis, MO. Affil: Washington, St. Louis. Email: sarah.rachel.siegel@gmail.com.

Siegelbaum, *Lewis Henry*, *Michigan State*. East Lansing, MI. Email: siegelba@msu.edu. Research: labor migration, communism.

Siegenthaler, **Peter D.**, *Texas State*. Email: ps30@txstate.edu.

Siegmund, **Stefanie**. New York, NY. Affil: Jewish Theological Seminary. Email: stsiegmund@jtsa.edu. Research: early modern religious conversion, Jewish women and gender studies.

Siekierski, **Maciej**. Stanford, CA. Affil: Hoover Institution. Email: siekierski@stanford.edu. Research: 16th-/17th-c Polish memoirs.

Siekmeier, **James F.**, *West Virginia*. Email: James.Siekmeier@mail.wvu.edu.

Siena, **Kevin**, *Trent*. Email: ksiena@trentu.ca.

Sierra Becerra, **Diana**, *Smith*. Email: dbecerra@smith.edu.

Sierra Silva, **Pablo Miguel**, *Rochester*. Rochester, NY. Email: sierrapm@gmail.com; pablo.sierra@rochester.edu. Research: 1683 buccaneer raid on Veracruz, Urban slavery in colonial Mexico.

Sies, **Mary Corbin**. College Park, MD. Affil: Maryland, Coll. Park. Email: sies@umd.edu. Research: American suburbia, historic preservation.

Siff, **Paul**. Trumbull, CT. Email: siffct@charter.net.

Sifuentez, **Mario, II**. Merced, CA. Affil: California, Merced. Email: msifuentez@ucmerced.edu.

Sigal, **Pete**, *Duke*. Email: psigal@duke.edu.

Sigel, **Lisa Z.**, *DePaul*. Chicago, IL. Email: lsigel@depaul.edu. Research: sexuality, pornography.

Sigler, **Krista L.**, *Cincinnati*. Cincinnati, OH. Affil: UC Blue Ash Coll. Email: krista.sigler@uc.edu. Research: modernity and revolution, popular memory.

Sigurdson, **Hannah**. Somerset, NJ. Affil: Rutgers. Email: hannah.sigurdson@rutgers.edu.

Sikainga, **Ahmad A.**, *Ohio State*. Email: sikainga.1@osu.edu.

Sikes, **Kathryn**, *Middle Tennessee State*. Email: Kathryn.Sikes@mtsu.edu.

Sikes, **Michelle M.** State College, PA. Affil: Penn State. Email: mxs1600@psu.edu.

Sil, **Narasingha P.**, *Western Oregon*. Email: siln@wou.edu.

Silano, **Francesca**, *Miami, Ohio*. Email: silanofg@miamioh.edu.

Silano, **Giulio**, *Toronto*. Email: gsilano@chass.utoronto.ca.

Silber, **Nina**, *Boston Univ*. Email: nsilber@bu.edu.

Silbey, **David J.** Washington, DC. Affil: Cornell. Email: silbey@cornell.edu. Research: Pearl Harbor, 20th-c military.

Siles, **William H.**, *Illinois, Springfield*. Email: siles.william@uis.edu.

Siljak, **Ana**, *Queen's, Can*. Email: siljaka@queensu.ca.

Silkey, **Sarah L.** Williamsport, PA. Affil: Lycoming. Email: silkey@lycoming.edu. Research: transatlantic reform networks, anti-lynching activism.

Silleras-Fernandez, **Nuria**. Boulder, CO. Affil: Colorado, Boulder. Email: silleras@colorado.edu. Research: Iberian cultural and gender, madness/religion/cutlural contact.

Silliman, **Daniel**. Valparaiso, IN. Affil: Valparaiso. Email: daniel.silliman@valpo.edu. Research: religion, book/journalism.

Silliman, **Robert H.**, *Emory*. Email: rsillim@emory.edu.

Silva, **Jose Pablo**, *Grinnell*. Email: silvajp@grinnell.edu.

Silver, **Arthur I.**, *Toronto*. Email: asilver@chass.utoronto.ca.

Silver, **Judith A.** Portsmouth, NH. Email: argentj@yahoo.com. Research: rural societies, French peasants/agriculture/marketing.

Silver, **Paul L.** Johnson, VT. Affil: Johnson State. Email: paul.silver@jsc.edu.

Silver, **Peter R.**, *Rutgers*. Email: peter.silver@rutgers.edu.

Silver, **Timothy H.**, *Appalachian State*. Email: silverth@appstate.edu.

Silverblatt, **Irene**, *Duke*. Email: isilver@duke.edu.

Silverman, **Dan P.**, *Penn State*. Email: dps1@psu.edu.

Silverman, **David J.**, *George Washington*. Washington, DC. Email: djsilver@gwu.edu. Research: American Indians and firearms.

Silverman, **Debora Leah**, *UCLA*. Email: silverma@history.ucla.edu.

Silverman, **Jason H.**, *Winthrop*. Email: silvermanj@winthrop.edu.

Silverman, **Lisa**, *Wisconsin-Milwaukee*. Email: silverld@uwm.edu.

Silverman, **Victor I.**, *Pomona*. Email: vsilverman@pomona.edu.

Silverstein, **Sara**, *Connecticut, Storrs*. Email: sara.silverstein@uconn.edu.

Silverstrim, **Karen F.**, **Esq.**, *SUNY, Buffalo State*. Email: silverkf@buffalostate.edu.

Silvestri, **Charles Anthony**, *Washburn*. Email: tony.silvestri@washburn.edu.

Silvestrini, **Blanca G.**, *Connecticut, Storrs*. Email: blanca.silvestrini@uconn.edu.

Silvi, **Kimberly L.**, *Hist. Assoc*. Email: ksilvi@historyassociates.com.

Simashvili, **Tengiz**. Telavi, Georgia. Email: tengizsimashvili@yahoo.com. Research: Russian Soviet Union's secret police, young Stalin's biography.

Simba, **Malik**, *California State, Fresno*. Email: maliks@csufresno.edu.

Simmerman, **Christopher Ross**. Eugene, OR. Affil: Oregon. Email: csimmerm@uoregon.edu.

Simmons, **Christina**, *Windsor*. Email: simmonc@uwindsor.ca.

Simmons, **Dana J.**, *California, Riverside*. Email: dana.simmons@ucr.edu.

Simmons, **Jerold**, *Nebraska, Omaha*. Email: jsimmons@unomaha.edu.

Simmons, **LaKisha Michelle**, *Michigan, Ann Arbor*. Email: kisha@umich.edu.

Simon, **Amy**. East Lansing, MI. Affil: Michigan State. Email: simonamy@msu.edu. Research: modern western Europe, Holocaust studies.

Simon, **Cori L.** Madison, WI. Affil: Wisconsin, Madison. Email: corilsimon@gmail.com. Research: Indian Territory.

Simon, **Dwight Edwin**. Boston, MA. Affil: Epiphany Sch. Email: dwightesimon@gmail.com. Research: American religion.

Simon, **Larry J.**, *Western Michigan*. Email: larry.simon@wmich.edu.

Simon, **Mark**, *Queens, CUNY*.

Simon, **Rebecca A.** Los Angeles, CA. Email: rasimon85@gmail.com. Research: Atlantic/British imperialism, colonial America/women/children.

Simon, **Roger D.**, *Lehigh*. Email: rds2@lehigh.edu.

Simon, **William J.**, **Jr**. Kunkletown, PA.

Simonelli, **David**, *Youngstown State*. Email: dsimonelli@ysu.edu.

Simons, **Alex C.** Houston, TX. Affil: Houston. Email: acsimons@uh.edu. Research: American state papers, Islam and West.

Simons, **Peter**, *Hamilton*. Email: psimons@hamilton.edu.

Simons, **Walter P.**, *Dartmouth*. Email: walter.p.simons@dartmouth.edu.

Simons, **William M.**, *SUNY, Oneonta*. Email: william.simons@oneonta.edu.

Simonsen, **Jane E**, *Augustana*. Email: janesimonsen@augustana.edu.

Simonson, **Michael**, *Leo Baeck Inst*. Email: msimonson@lbi.cjh.org.

Simpson, **Andrew T.**, *Duquesne*. Email: simpson4@duq.edu.

Simpson, **Andrew T.**, *Hist. Assoc*. Email: asimpson@historyassociates.com.

Simpson, **Bradley R.**, *Connecticut, Storrs*. Email: bradley.simpson@uconn.edu.

Simpson, **Craig M.**, *Western Ontario*. Email: csimpso1@uwo.ca.

Simpson, **David Bruce**. San Marcos, CA. Affil: California State, San Marcos. Email: simps053@cougars.csusm.edu.

Simpson, **Kaitlin**. Knoxville, TN. Affil: Tennessee, Knoxville. Email: ksimps19@vols.utk.edu.

Simpson, **Lee M. A.**, *California State, Sacramento*. Email: lsimpson@csus.edu.

Simpson, **MacKinnon**. Honolulu, HI. Email: MacKinnon96816@gmail.com. Research: postcontact Hawaii, Hawaii maritime.

Simpson, **Patrick Brent**. Dallas, TX. Affil: Cedar Valley. Email: pbsimpson13@gmail.com. Research: educational methodology, WWII strategic bombing.

Simpson, **Peter K.**, *Wyoming*. Email: psimpson@telegraph.uwyo.edu.

Simpson, **Samuel**. College Station, TX. Email: sam64simpson@tamu.edu.

Simpson-Menzies, **Rebecca**. Rancho Cucamonga, CA. Email: bekkileigh@gmail.com.

Sims, **Anastatia**, *Georgia Southern*. Email: asims@georgiasouthern.edu.

Sims, **Harold D.**, *Pittsburgh*. Email: hdsim1@netzero.com.

Sims, **Katrina Rochelle**, *Hofstra*. Email: katrina.sims@hofstra.edu.

Sims, **Taylor Anne**. Ann Arbor, MI. Affil: Michigan, Ann Arbor. Email: simsta@umich.edu.

Sinanoglou, **Penny**, *Wake Forest*. Email: sinanopj@wfu.edu.

Sinclair, **Katrina Ann**. Williamsport, PA. Affil: Pennsylvania Coll. of Tech. Email: kas19@pct.edu.

Sinclair, **Shelley A.**, *Wisconsin-La Crosse*. Email: sinclair.shel@uwlax.edu.

Sinclair, **Warren**, *National Defence Headquarters*. Email: warren.sinclair@forces.gc.ca.

Sindelar, **Arlene**, *British Columbia*. Email: arlene.sindelar@ubc.ca.

Sinegal-DeCuir, **Sharlene Sinegal**, *Xavier, La*. New Orleans, LA. Email: ssinegal@xula.edu. Research: African American, New Orleans.

Sines, **Ryan M**. Manitowoc, WI. Email: rsines21@gmail.com.

Singer, **Amy**. Tel Aviv, Israel. Affil: Tel Aviv. Email: singer.amy@gmail.com. Research: Ottoman capital of Edirne/Adrianople, Ottoman public kitchens and philanthropy.

Singer, **Mark Alan**, *Minot State*. Minot, ND. Email: mark.singer@minotstateu.edu. Research: early medieval pastoral care, early medieval manuscript studies.

Singer, **Martin**, *York, Can.* Email: singerm@yorku.ca.

Singer, **Sandra L.**, *Alfred.* Email: fsinger@alfred.edu.

Singer, **Wendy**, *Kenyon.* Email: singerw@kenyon.edu.

Singerman, **David**, *Virginia.* Email: ds2ax@virginia.edu.

Singh, **Jennifer**, *Georgia Inst. of Tech.* Email: jennifer.singh@hts.gatech.edu.

Singh, **Nikhil Pal**, *NYU.* Email: nikhil.singh@nyu.edu.

Singh, **Vineeta**, *Omohundro Inst.* Williamsburg, VA. Email: vsingh@wm.edu. Research: institutions, slavery.

Singham, **Shanti Marie**, *Williams.* Email: ssingham@williams.edu.

Singleton, **Gregory H.**, *Northeastern Illinois.* Email: roc1940@comcast.net.

Sinha, **Manisha**, *Connecticut, Storrs.* Sturbridge, MA. Email: manisha.sinha@uconn.edu. Research: African Americans and abolition movement.

Sinha, **Mrinalini**, *Michigan, Ann Arbor.* Ann Arbor, MI. Email: sinha@umich.edu. Research: colonial India, gender/imperial/global interactions.

Siniawer, **Eiko Maruko**, *Williams.* Williamstown, MA. Email: emaruko@williams.edu. Research: modern political violence, waste.

Sinisi, **Kyle S.**, *Citadel.* Email: sinisik@citadel.edu.

Sink, **Jessica**. Tipp City, OH. Email: j-sink@onu.edu.

Sinke, **Suzanne M.**, *Florida State.* Tallahassee, FL. Email: ssinke@fsu.edu. Research: international migration and marriage, gender and epistolary practice.

Sinkoff, **Nancy**, *Rutgers.* Email: nsinkoff@jewishstudies.rutgers.edu.

Sinn, **Andrea A.**, *Elon.* Email: asinn@elon.edu.

Sintes, **Nicole**. Miami, FL. Affil: Miami. Email: nxs1035@miami.edu.

Siotto, **Andrea**. Philadelphia, PA. Email: tug27403@temple.edu.

Sippel, **Cornelius, III**, *DePaul.* Email: csippel@depaul.edu.

Sippial, **Tiffany Anise**, *Auburn.* Email: tat0004@auburn.edu.

Sipress, **Joel M.** Superior, WI. Affil: Wisconsin, Superior. Email: jsipress@uwsuper.edu.

Siraisi, **Nancy G.**, *Graduate Center, CUNY.* Email: nsiraisi@verizon.net.

Sirota, **Brent Stuart**, *North Carolina State.* Raleigh, NC. Email: bssirota@ncsu.edu. Research: secularization, separation of church and state.

Siry, **Lt Col David**, *US Military Acad.* Email: david.siry@usma.edu.

Siry, **Steven E.**, *Baldwin Wallace.* Email: ssiry@bw.edu.

Sisco, **Victoria Peterson**. Gastonia, NC. Affil: Belmont Abbey. Email: kidsisco98@icloud.com.

Sishagne, **Shumet**, *Christopher Newport.* Email: sishagne@cnu.edu.

Siskind, **Peter T.** Philadelphia, PA. Affil: Arcadia. Email: siskindp@arcadia.edu. Research: US political economy, urban/suburban studies.

Sisman, **Cengiz**, *Houston-Clear Lake.* Email: sisman@uhcl.edu.

Sistrunk, **Timothy G.**, *California State, Chico.* Email: tsistrunk@csuchico.edu.

Sivan, **Hagith**, *Kansas.* Email: dinah01@ku.edu.

Sivaramakrishnan, **Kavita**, *Columbia (Hist. Public Health).* Email: ks2890@columbia.edu.

Siverson, **Rolf**. Gilroy, CA. Affil: Pennsylvania. Email: siverson@sas.upenn.edu.

Sivitz, **Paul**. Pocatello, ID. Affil: Idaho State. Email: sivipaul@isu.edu. Research: historical GIS, early America.

Siwi, **Marcio**, *Towson.*

Sizer, **Michael Alan**. Baltimore, MD. Affil: Maryland Inst. Coll. of Art. Email: msizer@mica.edu. Research: pre-modern revolt and political culture, urban society/Paris.

Skabelund, **Aaron H.**, *Brigham Young.* Email: aaron_skabelund@byu.edu.

Skabelund, **Donald E.**, *New Mexico.*

Skaff, **Jonathan K.**, *Shippensburg.* Shippensburg, PA. Email: jkskaf@ship.edu. Research: China's relations with Inner Asia, Silk Road trade.

Skaggs, **David C.**, **Jr.**, *Bowling Green State.* Email: dskaggs@bgsu.edu.

Skala, **Doreen**. Bellmawr, NJ. Email: doreenlord@verizon.net. Research: colonial British America, Hanoverian England.

Skaria, **Ajay**, *Minnesota (Hist.).* Email: skari002@umn.edu.

Skau, **George H**. Ridgewood, NJ. Affil: Bergen Comm. Coll. Email: skaujasper59@yahoo.com. Research: 20th-c US presidents, peace process in Northern Ireland.

Skeen, **C. Edward**, *Memphis.* Email: ceskeen@memphis.edu.

Skelly, **Joseph Morrison**, *Mount St. Vincent.* Email: joe.skelly@mountsaintvincent.edu.

Skemp, **Sheila L.**, *Mississippi.* University, MS. Email: sskemp@olemiss.edu. Research: colonial America, American Revolution.

Skenyon, **Stephanie**. Homestead, FL. Affil: Miami. Email: s.skenyon@miami.edu. Research: Chronicles, identity.

Skib, **Bryan**. Ann Arbor, MI. Affil: Michigan. Email: bskib@umich.edu.

Skidmore, **Colleen**, *Alberta.* Email: colleen.skidmore@ualberta.ca.

Skidmore, **Emily**, *Texas Tech; Committee on LGBT Hist.* Lubbock, TX. Email: emily.skidmore@ttu.edu. Research: US gender and sexual formations, normative citizenship.

Skidmore, **William Everett, II**. Houston, TX. Affil: Rice. Email: wes3@rice.edu. Research: abolition and emancipation, world.

Skidmore-Hess, **Cathy J.**, *Georgia Southern.* Email: cskid@georgiasouthern.edu.

Skillin, **Larry Alexander**. Davenport, IA. Affil: St. Ambrose. Email: skillinlarrya@sau.edu. Research: Pennsylvania's Keithian Schism, development of colonial public sphere.

Skilton, **Liz**, *Louisiana, Lafayette.* Email: skilton@louisiana.edu.

Skinner, **Barbara J.**, *Indiana State.* Bloomington, IN. Email: Barbara.Skinner@indstate.edu. Research: Russian and eastern European church, early Russian empire religious policies.

Skinner, **David E.**, *Santa Clara.* Email: dskinner@scu.edu.

Skinner, **Frederick W.**, *Montana.* Email: frederick.skinner@umontana.edu.

Skinner, **Stephen**. Exeter, United Kingdom. Affil: Exeter. Email: S.J.Skinner@exeter.ac.uk. Research: law in interwar Italy and Britain, law/rule of law/fascism and democracy.

Sklansky, **Jeffrey**, *Illinois, Chicago.* Chicago, IL. Email: sklanskj@uic.edu. Research: money and credit in early America, capitalism.

Sklar, **Kathryn Kish**, *Binghamton, SUNY.* Berkeley, CA. Email: kkslar@binghamton.edu. Research: social rights, online resources.

Sklaroff, **Lauren R.**, *South Carolina, Columbia.* Email: sklaroff@mailbox.sc.edu.

Skloot, **Joseph**. Washington, DC. Affil: Columbia. Email: jskloot@mac.com.

Skolnik, **Jonathan**, *Massachusetts, Amherst.* Email: jskolnik@german.umass.edu.

Skopyk, **Bradley**, *Binghamton, SUNY.* Email: bskopyk@binghamton.edu.

Skorobogatov, **Yana**, *Williams.* Email: ys3@williams.edu.

Skowronek, **Russell**, *Texas-Rio Grande Valley.* Email: russell.skowronek@utrgv.edu.

Skowronek, **Stephen**. New Haven, CT. Affil: Yale. Email: stephen.skowronek@yale.edu.

Skuban, **William E.**, *California State, Fresno.* Fresno, CA. Email: weskuban@csufresno.edu. Research: 20th-c Peru and Chile, nationalism and national identity.

Skwiot, **Christine M**. Castine, ME. Affil: Maine Maritime Academy. Email: christine.skwiot@mma.edu. Research: cross-cultural, global revolutionary era.

Skya, **Walter A**. Fairbanks, AK. Affil: Alaska Fairbanks. Email: walterskya@gmail.com. Research: Asian studies, world.

Slack, **Corliss K.**, *Whitworth.* Email: cslack@whitworth.edu.

Slack, **Edward, Jr.**, *Eastern Washington.* Email: eslack@ewu.edu.

Slap, **Andrew L.**, *East Tennessee State.* Email: slap@etsu.edu.

Slate, **Nico**, *Carnegie Mellon.* Email: nslate@andrew.cmu.edu.

Slater, **Sandra D.**, *Charleston.* Email: slaters@cofc.edu.

Slaton, **Amy**, *Drexel.* Email: slatonae@drexel.edu.

Slaton, **Michael**. Hampton, VA. Affil: US Air Force. Email: mikesl8n@yahoo.com.

Slatta, **Richard W.**, *North Carolina State.* Email: slatta@ncsu.edu.

Slattery, **Michael G.**, *Campbell.* Email: sealsrest@earthlink.net.

Slattery, **Samuel Aldred**. Williamsburg, VA. Affil: William and Mary. Email: saslattery@email.wm.edu. Research: early American fortifications, political organization.

Slattery, **Tim**, *South Florida, St. Petersburg.*

Slaughter, **Jane**, *New Mexico.* Albuquerque, NM. Email: mjane@unm.edu. Research: Italian gender and Cold War, women/revolution/terrorism.

Slaughter, **Michael A**. Van Nuys, CA. Affil: California State Polytechnic. Email: maslaughter@cpp.edu. Research: Los Angeles, education.

Slaughter, **Thomas P.**, *Rochester.* Email: thomas.slaughter@rochester.edu.

Slauter, **Will T**. Paris, France. Affil: Paris Diderot. Email: wslauter@univ-paris-diderot.fr. Research: media, copyright and public domain.

Slaven, Michael D., *California, Pa.* Email: slaven@calu.edu.

Slavenas, Julius P., *SUNY, Buffalo State.*

Slavin, Bridgette, *Canisius.* Email: slavinb@canisius.edu.

Slavin, David H. Decatur, GA. Affil: Clayton State. Email: dhslavi@emory.edu. Research: France and Algeria 1870-1962, comparative US South and Algeria 1870-1962.

Slavishak, Edward S., *Susquehanna.* Selinsgrove, PA. Email: slavishak@susqu.edu. Research: bodily spectacles as civic history, American masculinities 1890-1930.

Slaybaugh, Douglas, *St. Michael's.* Email: dslaybaugh@smcvt.edu.

Slayton, Robert A., *Chapman.* Orange, CA. Email: slayton@chapman.edu. Research: 20th-c US, African American.

Sleeper-Smith, Susan, *Michigan State.* East Lansing, MI. Email: sleepers@msu.edu; sleepers@newberry.org. Research: Ohio River Valley Indian women, Indian artefacts in museums.

Slind, Marvin G., *Luther.* Email: slindmar@luther.edu.

Sloan, David A., *Arkansas, Fayetteville.* Email: dsloan@uark.edu.

Sloan, Herbert E., *Barnard, Columbia.* Email: hsloan@barnard.edu.

Sloan, Kathryn A., *Arkansas, Fayetteville.* Fayetteville, AR. Email: ksloan@uark.edu. Research: Latin America.

Sloan, Keith. Swifton, AR. Affil: Tuckerman High Sch. Email: ksloan@bulldogs.k12.ar.us.

Sloan, Stephen M., *Baylor.* Email: stephen_sloan@baylor.edu.

Sloane, David C., *Southern California.* Email: dsloane@price.usc.edu.

Sloane, Jesse D. Seoul, South Korea. Affil: Yonsei. Email: sloanej@runbox.com. Research: religion in northern China 908-1368, Kingdom of Parhae/Bohai 698-926.

Slocum, Kay B., *Capital.* Email: kslocum@capital.edu.

Sloin, Andrew Jay, *SJ.* New York, NY. Affil: Baruch, CUNY. Email: Andrew.Sloin@baruch.cuny.edu. Research: USSR economic/social, modern Jewish.

Slonecker, Blake. Toppenish, WA. Affil: Heritage. Email: slonecker_b@heritage.edu. Research: New Left, pacifism.

Slonim, Shlomo. Jerusalem, Israel. Affil: Hebrew, Jerusalem. Email: shlomo.slonim@mail.huji.ac.il.

Slonimsky, Nora. New York, NY. Affil: Iona. Email: nslonimsky@gmail.com.

Slotkin, Richard S. Baltimore, MD. Affil: Wesleyan. Email: rslotkin@wesleyan.edu. Research: Civil War, nationality and ethnicity.

Slucki, David S., *Charleston.* Email: sluckds@cofc.edu.

Sluga, Glenda A. Sydney, Australia. Affil: Sydney. Email: glenda.sluga@sydney.edu.au. Research: United Nations, racism and nationalism.

Sluga, McKayla Renee. Lansing, MI. Affil: Michigan State. Email: slugamck@msu.edu. Research: 20th-c US political/intellectual/social, visual culture/radical movements.

Sluglett, Peter J., *Utah.* Email: sluglett@aol.com.

Sluis, Ageeth, *Butler.* Email: asluis@butler.edu.

Slumkoski, Corey, *Dalhousie.* Email: corey.slumkoski@msvu.ca.

Slusher, Lee A. Erie, MI. Affil: Bowling Green State. Email: laslusher@yahoo.com. Research: AP Parts Strike 1984, Toledo unionism 1980s.

Smaby, Beverly P., *Clarion, Pa.* Email: bsmaby@clarion.edu.

Smahel, Frantisek. Praha, Czech Republic.

Smail, Daniel L., *Harvard (Hist.).* Cambridge, MA. Email: smail@fas.harvard.edu. Research: material culture, law and society.

Smail, John, *North Carolina, Charlotte.* Email: jsmail@uncc.edu.

Smaldone, William T., *Willamette.* Salem, OR. Email: wsmaldon@willamette.edu. Research: Weimar social democracy, comparative modern socialism.

Smale, Robert L., *Missouri, Columbia.* Columbia, MO. Email: smaler@missouri.edu. Research: 20th-c Bolivian labor movement, contemporary Bolivian politics.

Small, Allistair M., *Alberta.* Email: asmall@torphichen.demon.co.uk.

Small, Carola M., *Alberta.* Email: hiscss@srv0.arts.ed.ac.uk.

Small, Clara L., *Salisbury.*

Small, Melvin, *Wayne State.* Email: m.small@wayne.edu.

Small, Nora Pat, *Eastern Illinois.* Email: npsmall@eiu.edu.

Smalley, Andrea, *Northern Illinois.* Email: asmalley@niu.edu.

Smallman, Shawn C., *Portland State.* Email: smallmans@pdx.edu.

Smallwood, Arwin D., *North Carolina A&T State.* Greensboro, NC. Email: asmallwo@ncat.edu. Research: Native American, mixed race.

Smallwood, Jonathan, *Lincoln Memorial.* Email: jonathan.smallwood@lmunet.edu.

Smallwood, Stephanie E., *Washington, Seattle.* Email: ses9@uw.edu.

Smart, Devin, *West Virginia.* Morgantown, WV. Email: devin.smart@mail.wvu.edu; dsmart5@illinois.edu. Research: working-class food systems, fishing.

Smart, Terry, *Trinity, Tex.* Email: tsmart@trinity.edu.

Smead, E. Howard, *Maryland, Baltimore County; Maryland, Coll. Park.* Email: smead@umbc.edu; hsmead@umd.edu.

Smelser, Ronald, *Utah.* Email: rmsmelse@history.utah.edu.

Smethurst, Richard, *Pittsburgh.* Email: rsmet@pitt.edu.

Smiar, Nicholas P. Eau Claire, WI. Affil: Wisconsin, Eau Claire. Email: smiarnp@uwec.edu. Research: 16th-c poor law and poor relief, Shakers.

Smiley, Will, *Reed.* Email: william.smiley@reed.edu.

Smit, Timothy J., *Eastern Kentucky.* Richmond, KY. Email: tim.smit@eku.edu; timsmit78@gmail.com. Research: Norman Sicily, cross-cultural contact.

Smith, A. Mark, *III, Missouri, Columbia.* smitham@missouri.edu.

Smith, Alexa. Braddock Heights, MD. Email: lexismith6109@gmail.com.

Smith, Alexander. Canal Winchester, OH. Affil: Southern New Hampshire. Email: phpdba@gmail.com.

Smith, Alison K., *Toronto.* Email: alison.smith@utoronto.ca.

Smith, Amanda H. Sandy Springs, GA. Affil: FCS Teaching Museum. Email: smithah06@gmail.com. Research: public.

Smith, Aminda M., *Michigan State.* East Lansing, MI. Email: amsmith@msu.edu. Research: modern China.

Smith, Amy M. Lincolnville, ME. Affil: Southern Maine. Email: amy.m.smith@maine.edu.

Smith, Andrew M., *II, George Washington.* Email: amsii@gwu.edu.

Smith, Angela J., *North Dakota State.* Fargo, ND. Email: angela.smith.1@ndsu.edu; smithangj@gmail.com. Research: poet and radical John Beecher, history and new media.

Smith, Anthony Burke. Dayton, OH. Affil: Dayton. Email: asmith1@udayton.edu. Research: American religion, popular culture.

Smith, Arthur L., *Jr., California State, Los Angeles.* Email: arthursmith@cox.net.

Smith, Benjamin C. Silver Spring, MD. Email: benjamin.clark.smith@gmail.com.

Smith, Benjamin Dallas. Dunmore, AB, Canada. Affil: Waterloo. Email: benji.smith12@gmail.com.

Smith, Bill L., *Idaho.* Email: bills@uidaho.edu.

Smith, Billy G., *Montana State, Bozeman.* Email: bgs@montana.edu.

Smith, Bonnie G., *Rutgers.* New Brunswick, NJ. Email: bosmith@scarletmail.rutgers.edu. Research: modern Europe, women and gender.

Smith, Bryon Thomas. Alexandria, VA. Email: swoll@cjbs.net.

Smith, Burton M., *Alberta.* Email: bmsmith@ualberta.ca.

Smith, Cecil O., *Jr., Drexel.*

Smith, Charles D., *Jr., Arizona.* Tucson, AZ. Email: cdsmith@u.arizona.edu. Research: US diplomacy and Arab-Israeli conflict, Palestine and Arab-Israel.

Smith, Christopher J., *Liberty.* Email: cjsmith19@liberty.edu.

Smith, Colby Ty. Bedford, TX. Affil: Tarrant County Coll. Email: ty.smith521@gmail.com.

Smith, Courtney Michelle, *Cabrini.* Radnor, PA. Email: cms392@cabrini.edu. Research: Negro League Baseball, intercollegiate athletics.

Smith, Craig A., *California, Pa.* Email: smith_c@calu.edu.

Smith, Dale C. Bethesda, MD. Affil: Uniformed Services Univ., Health Sci. Email: dcsmith@netscape.com.

Smith, Damian J., *St. Louis.* Email: dsmith69@slu.edu.

Smith, Daniel Montgomery. USAF Academy, CO. Affil: US Air Force Academy. Email: danmsmith97@gmail.com. Research: world systems, European peace treaties 1648-1815.

Smith, Daniel. Albany, NY. Affil: Albany Coll. of Pharmacy and Health Sciences. Email: daniel.smith@acphs.edu. Research: US Communist Party, public health policy.

Smith, David A., *Baylor.* Email: david_a_smith@baylor.edu.

Smith, David A., *Wilfrid Laurier.* Email: dasmith@wlu.ca.

Smith, David K., *Eastern Illinois.* Email: dksmith@eiu.edu.

Smith, Dennis J., *Nebraska, Omaha.* Email: dennissmith@unomaha.edu.

Smith, Derick, *North Carolina A&T State.* Email: dksmith@ncat.edu.

Smith, **Don A.**, *Grinnell*. Email: smithd@grinnell. edu.

Smith, **Donald B.**, *Calgary*. Email: smithd@ ucalgary.ca.

Smith, **Douglas V.**, *Naval War Coll*. Email: smithdv@usnwc.edu.

Smith, **Earl**, *Troy*.

Smith, **Elizabeth Parish**. Warrensburg, MO. Affil: Central Missouri. Email: epsmith@ucmo.edu. Research: US women.

Smith, **Emily**. South Bend, IN. Email: esmith35@ nd.edu.

Smith, **Erika Cornelius**. Dudley, MA. Affil: Nichols. Email: erika.smith@nichols.edu.

Smith, **F. Todd**, *North Texas*. Email: ftsmith@unt. edu.

Smith, **Frederick H**. Williamsburg, VA. Affil: St. Nicholas Abbey. Email: caribbeanrum2005@ gmail.com. Research: archaeology, alcohol studies.

Smith, **Gaddis**, *Yale*. Email: gaddis.smith@yale. edu.

Smith, **Gene Allen**, *Texas Christian*. Email: g.smith@tcu.edu.

Smith, **Geoffrey S.**, *Queen's, Can*. Email: smithgs@queensu.ca.

Smith, **Gerald L.**, *Kentucky*. Email: glsmit01@ uky.edu.

Smith, **Greg T.**, *Manitoba*. Email: greg.smith@ umanitoba.ca.

Smith, **Gregory A.**, *Central Michigan*. Email: smith5ga@cmich.edu.

Smith, **Gregory J**. Auburn, IL. Affil: Auburn High Sch. Email: Gregs89@hotmail.com.

Smith, **Harold T.**, *Arkansas, Little Rock*.

Smith, **Hayden R.**, *Charleston*. Email: smithhr1@ cofc.edu.

Smith, **Helmut W.**, *Vanderbilt*. Nashville, TN. Email: helmut.w.smith@vanderbilt.edu. Research: German nationalism, German anti-Semitism.

Smith, **Henry B**. Rochester, NY. Affil: Rochester. Email: jemsmith@frontier.com.

Smith, **Hilary A.**, *Denver*. Denver, CO. Email: hilary.smith@du.edu. Research: medicine and health in East Asia, nutrition and diet.

Smith, **Hilda L.**, *Cincinnati*. Cincinnati, OH. Email: smithh@ucmail.uc.edu. Research: 17th-c British women artisans, early modern women's intellectual.

Smith, **J. Douglas**, *William and Mary*.

Smith, **J. Harvey**, *Northern Illinois*. Email: hsmith@niu.edu.

Smith, **Jake Patrick**, *Colorado Coll*. Email: jpsmith@coloradocollege.edu.

Smith, **James Patterson**, *Southern Mississippi*. Gulfport, MS. Email: jamespat.smith@usm. edu; j_pat.smithj@yahoo.com. Research: Britain, colonial.

Smith, **Jasmine R.**, *Library Co. of Philadelphia*. Email: jsmith@librarycompany.org.

Smith, **Jason S.**, *New Mexico*. Email: jssmith@ unm.edu.

Smith, **Jason W.**, *Southern Connecticut State*.

Smith, **Jay M.**, *North Carolina, Chapel Hill*. Email: jaysmith@email.unc.edu.

Smith, **Jeffrey Allen**, *Hawai'i, Hilo*. Email: smith808@hawaii.edu.

Smith, **Jennifer L.**, *North Georgia*. Email: jennifer.smith@ung.edu.

Smith, **Jennifer**, *Massachusetts Hist. Soc*. Email: jensmith@masshist.org.

Smith, **Joanna Handlin**. Cambridge, MA. Affil: Harvard. Email: jfhsmith@fas.harvard.edu. Research: Ming-Qing social, Early Qing trust/ friendship/networks.

Smith, **John Howard**, *Texas A&M, Commerce*. Email: john.smith@tamuc.edu.

Smith, **John K.**, *Lehigh*. Email: jks0@lehigh.edu.

Smith, **John M.**, *Georgia Inst. of Tech*. Email: john.smith@hts.gatech.edu.

Smith, **John David**, *North Carolina, Charlotte*. Charlotte, NC. Email: jdsmith4@uncc.edu. Research: US South slavery and emancipation, American Civil War.

Smith, **Joshua Caleb**. Waco, TX. Affil: Baylor. Email: joshua_smith4@baylor.edu. Research: supernatural and religion, early modern religious.

Smith, **Judith E.**, *Massachusetts, Boston*. Email: judith.smith@umb.edu.

Smith, **Karen Manners**, *Emporia State*. Email: ksmith@emporia.edu.

Smith, **Kathelene McCarty**. Winston-Salem, NC. Affil: North Carolina, Greensboro. Email: kmsmi24@uncg.edu. Research: WWI, American women in college.

Smith, **Katherine Allen**, *Puget Sound*. Tacoma, WA. Email: kasmith2@pugetsound.edu. Research: monastic penance and asceticism, hagiography and devotional practices.

Smith, **Kelly M**. Huntsville, AL. Affil: Alabama, Huntsville. Email: kms0067@uah.edu. Research: Reformation, Scientific Revolution.

Smith, **Kerry**, *Brown*. Providence, RI. Email: kerry_smith@brown.edu. Research: natural disasters and popular science.

Smith, **Kevin D.**, *SUNY, Coll. Potsdam*. Email: smithkd@potsdam.edu.

Smith, **Kevin E.**, *Ball State*. Email: ksmith@bsu. edu.

Smith, **L. Christian**, *Arizona State*.

Smith, **Laverne Young**. Lynchburg, VA. Affil: Liberty. Email: lsmith4@liberty.edu. Research: 18th-c colonial Virginia.

Smith, **Leonard V.**, *Oberlin*. Email: lvsmith@ oberlin.edu.

Smith, **Lyndsay Danielle**. Portland, OR. Affil: Portland State. Email: l_smith07@yahoo.com. Research: public, environmental.

Smith, **Lynn A.**, *Herbert Hoover Presidential Library*. Email: lynn.smith@nara.gov.

Smith, **Mark A**. Ballwin, MO. Affil: John Burroughs Sch. Email: msmith@jburroughs. org. Research: bioethics, Jefferson.

Smith, **Mark C.**, *Texas, Austin*. Email: mcsmith@ mail.utexas.edu.

Smith, **Mark F**. Washington, DC. Affil: National Education Assoc. Email: marksmith@nea.org.

Smith, **Mark J**. Orlando, FL. Affil: Valencia. Email: msmith01@mail.valenciacollege. edu. Research: land tenure in Florida, environmental change in Florida.

Smith, **Mark M.**, *South Carolina, Columbia*. Email: smithmm@mailbox.sc.edu.

Smith, **Martha**, *Saskatchewan*. Email: martha. smith@usask.ca.

Smith, **Mary Jane**, *St. Lawrence*. Email: msm1@ stlawu.edu.

Smith, **Matthew David**, *Miami, Ohio*. Email: smithmd6@miamioh.edu.

Smith, **Matthew James**. Covington Twp., PA. Affil: Elizabethtown. Email: smithm2@etown. edu.

Smith, **Melvin Charles**, *Cumberlands*. Email: chuck.smith@ucumberlands.edu.

Smith, **Merritt Roe**, *MIT*. Email: roesmith@mit. edu.

Smith, **Michael B.**, *Ithaca*. Email: mismith@ ithaca.edu.

Smith, **Michael G.**, *Purdue*. Email: mgsmith@ purdue.edu.

Smith, **Michael M.**, *Oklahoma State*. Email: michael.m.smith@okstate.edu.

Smith, **Michael S.**, *South Carolina, Columbia*. Columbia, SC. Email: smithm@mailbox. sc.edu. Research: French business since 1800, comparative business.

Smith, **Michael S**. Rowland Heights, CA. Email: smithms17@gmail.com. Research: 18th-c credit/debt in Britain, late 18th-c British political culture.

Smith, **Molly**. Lutherville, MD. Email: msmith@ friendsbalt.org.

Smith, **Molly**. Round Lake Beach, IL. Email: mollymsmith97@gmail.com.

Smith, **Natalie Pifat**. Chicago, IL. Affil: Chicago. Email: Npsmith10@gmail.com. Research: Mediterranean port cities, urbanization.

Smith, **Nathan**, *Washington Coll*. Email: nsmith2@washcoll.edu.

Smith, **Nathaniel Lee**, *US Dept. of State*.

Smith, **Nigel**, *Princeton*. Email: nsmith@ princeton.edu.

Smith, **Norman D.**, *Guelph*. Email: nsmith06@ uoguelph.ca.

Smith, **Pamela C**. Akron, OH. Affil: Akron.

Smith, **Pamela H.**, *Columbia (Hist.)*. New York, NY. Email: ps2270@columbia.edu. Research: craft knowledge and metalworking, science.

Smith, **Philip M.**, *Texas A&M*. Email: pms@tamu. edu.

Smith, **Philip M.**, *US Air Force Acad*. Email: philip. smith@usafa.edu.

Smith, **Phillip T.**, *St. Joseph's*. Email: psmith@ sju.edu.

Smith, **Phyllis L.**, *Mars Hill*. Email: psmith@mhu. edu.

Smith, **Randy Scott**, *Pittsburgh*. Email: smitty@ pitt.edu.

Smith, **Ray T.**, *San Diego State*.

Smith, **Rebecca**, *Hist. New Orleans*. Email: rebeccas@hnoc.org.

Smith, **Rich**. Greensboro, NC. Affil: North Carolina, Greensboro. Email: rsmith33@gmu. edu. Research: early US, antebellum US.

Smith, **Richard C.**, *Alberta*.

Smith, **Richard Dean**, *Colorado Denver*. Email: richard.smith@ucdenver.edu.

Smith, **Richard J.**, *Rice*. Email: smithrj@rice.edu.

Smith, **Richard W.**, *Ohio Wesleyan*. Email: rwsmith@owu.edu.

Smith, **Robert A.**, *Emory*.

Smith, **Robert S.**, *Marquette*. Milwaukee, WI. Email: robert.s.smith@marquette.edu. Research: African American legal, legal activism across African diaspora.

Smith, **Robert W.**, *Worcester State*. Marshfield, MA. Email: rsmith1@worcester.edu; proconsul1@juno.com. Research: American foreign relations, early American republic.

Smith, **Robert W.**, *Alberta*. Email: rwsmith@ ualberta.ca.

Smith, **Robert**, *Pittsburg State*.

Smith, **Ronald D.**, *Arizona State*.

Smith, **Ryan K.**, *Virginia Commonwealth*. Email: rksmith3@vcu.edu.

Smith, **Samuel C.**, *Liberty*. Email: scsmith4@ liberty.edu.

Smith, **Sarah Anne**, *Kansas State*. Email: arcana@ksu.edu.

Smith, **Sean D.** Millersville, PA. Email: seandanlsmith@yahoo.com. Research: Bankruptcy Act of 1898.

Smith, **Sean Morey**. Houston, TX. Affil: Rice. Email: smith318@gmail.com.

Smith, **Sean W.**, *California State, Long Beach*. Email: sean.smith@csulb.edu.

Smith, **Sherry L.**, *Southern Methodist*. Moose, WY. Email: sherrys@smu.edu. Research: American West, American Indian.

Smith, **Shirley Diana**. Fishers, IN. Affil: Grace. Email: shunters@purdue.edu. Research: Gilded Age businessmen in Indianapolis, secret societies during WWI.

Smith, **Solomon Kelly**, *Georgia Southern*. Email: sksmith@georgiasouthern.edu.

Smith, **Stacey L.** Corvallis, OR. Affil: Oregon State. Email: smitstac@onid.orst.edu. Research: race and labor in 19th-c California, Civil War and Reconstruction in American West.

Smith, **Stephanie J.**, *Ohio State*. Columbus, OH. Email: smith.4858@osu.edu. Research: 20th-c Mexico, gender/culture.

Smith, **Steve**, *Hist. Soc. of Pennsylvania*. Email: ssmith@hsp.org.

Smith, **Steven C.**, *Providence*. Email: ssmith32@ providence.edu.

Smith, **Steven L.**, *California State, Fullerton*. Email: stevensmith@fullerton.edu.

Smith, **Stuart Tyson**, *California, Santa Barbara*. Email: stsmith@anth.ucsb.edu.

Smith, **Stuart William**. Great Bookham, United Kingdom. Email: Stuart@iba.uk.net.

Smith, **Susan L.**, *Alberta*. Edmonton, AB, Canada. Email: susan.l.smith@ualberta.ca. Research: US military mustard gas experimentation, racial politics and health.

Smith, **Suzanne E.**, *George Mason*. Fairfax, VA. Email: smisuze@gmu.edu. Research: African American studies, 20th-c cultural.

Smith, **Taylor William**. Phoenix, AZ. Affil: Chandler-Gilbert Comm. Coll. Email: taylor. smith715@me.com. Research: Charlatan revivalism in US, self-selected poverty by missionaries.

Smith, **Theodore L.** Reston, VA. Email: smthted@ aol.com. Research: Russia, Baltic states.

Smith, **Theresa Ann**. Claremont, CA. Affil: Webb Sch. Email: tsmith@webb.org. Research: 18th-c women, Enlightenment.

Smith, **Thomas**, *South Florida, St. Petersburg*. Email: twsmith2@mail.usf.edu.

Smith, **Timothy B.**, *Queen's, Can*. Email: tbs@ queensu.ca.

Smith, **Timothy B.**, *Tennessee, Martin*. Email: tims@utm.edu.

Smith, **Tracey D.**, *Weber State*. Email: tsmith@ weber.edu.

Smith, **Troy Duane**, *Tennessee Tech*. Email: tdsmith@tntech.edu.

Smith, **Tyler Ronald**. Arlington, VA. Affil: George Washington's Mount Vernon. Email: tyandjen1999@yahoo.com.

Smith, **Victoria A. O.**, *Nebraska, Lincoln*. Email: vsmith4@unl.edu.

Smith, **W. Calvin**, *South Carolina Aiken*.

Smith, **Wilda M.**, *Fort Hays State*.

Smith, **Woodruff D.**, *Massachusetts, Boston*. Austin, TX. Email: woodruff.smith@umb.edu. Research: Germany, Africa.

Smith, **Zachary Philip**, *Central Arkansas*.

Smither, **Erin**, *State Hist. Soc. of Missouri*. Email: smithere@shsmo.org.

Smither, **James R.**, *Grand Valley State*. Email: smitherj@gvsu.edu.

Smithers, **Gregory D.**, *Virginia Commonwealth*. Richmond, VA. Email: gdsmithers@vcu.edu. Research: miscegenation, slavery.

Smith-Howard, **Kendra D.**, *SUNY, Albany*. Albany, NY. Email: ksmithhoward@albany. edu. Research: service work, regulation of the cleaning trades.

Smith-Peter, **Susan J.**, *Staten Island, CUNY*. Staten Island, NY. Email: susan.smithpeter@ csi.cuny.edu. Research: Russian regional identity and civil society, Creoles in Russian America and Alaska 1800-1912.

Smith-Pryor, **Elizabeth M.**, *Kent State*. Email: esmith1@kent.edu.

Smith-Rosenberg, **Carroll**, *Michigan, Ann Arbor*. Email: csmithro@umich.edu.

Smits, **Gregory J.**, *Penn State*. Email: gjs4@psu. edu.

Smoak, **Gregory E.**, *Utah*. Email: greg.smoak@ utah.edu.

Smocovitis, **Vassiliki B.**, *Florida*. Email: bsmocovi@ufl.edu.

Smolenski, **John J.**, *California, Davis*. Email: jsmolenski@ucdavis.edu.

Smolkin-Rothrock, **Victoria**, *Wesleyan*. Email: vsmolkin@wesleyan.edu.

Smoller, **Laura Ackerman**, *Rochester*. Rochester, NY. Email: laura.smoller@rochester.edu. Research: saints and miracles, prophecy and astrology.

Smoodin, **Eric**. Davis, CA. Affil: California, Davis. Email: esmoodin@ucdavis.edu. Research: US and French film audiences in 1930s, film education in US schools 1920-45.

Smoot, **Pamela**, *Southern Illinois, Carbondale*. Email: olivia@siu.edu.

Smucker, **Janneken L.**, *West Chester*. Email: jsmucker@wcupa.edu.

Smuksta, **Michael J.** La Crosse, WI. Email: mjsmuksta@viterbo.edu. Research: midwestern Civil War gender relations.

Smuts, **R. Malcolm**, *Massachusetts, Boston*. Email: malcolm.smuts@umb.edu.

Smyrlis, **Konstantinos**, *NYU*. Email: ks113@nyu. edu.

Smyser, **Katherine**. Buffalo, NY. Affil: SUNY, Buffalo. Email: kasmyser@buffalo.edu.

Smyth, **Denis**, *Toronto*.

Smythe, **Kathleen R.**, *Xavier, Ohio*. Email: smythe@xavier.edu.

Snay, **Mitchell**, *Denison*. Email: snay@denison. edu.

Snead, **David L.**, *Liberty*. Email: dlsnead@liberty. edu.

Snedegar, **Keith**, *Utah Valley*. Orem, UT. Email: snedegke@uvu.edu. Research: astronomy, medieval Europe.

Sneeringer, **Julia E.**, *Graduate Center, CUNY; Queens, CUNY*. Email: juliasneeringer@verizon. net.

Snell, **Daniel C.**, *Oklahoma (Hist.)*. Norman, OK. Email: dcsnell@ou.edu. Research: ancient Near Eastern religions, anthology of sources of ancient slavery.

Snell, **Timothy Adam**. Fort Worth, TX. Affil: Texas Christian. Email: timasn@comcast.net. Research: Union army military intelligence, information and Civil War.

Sneller, **Maurice P.**, **Jr.**, *Longwood*.

Snetsinger, **John G.**, *California Polytechnic State*. Email: jsnetsin@calpoly.edu.

Snider, **Christy Jo**, *Berry*. Mount Berry, GA. Email: csnider@berry.edu. Research: 20th-c peace movements, transnational NGOs.

Snider, **Colin M.**, *Texas, Tyler*. Tyler, TX. Email: csnider@uttyler.edu. Research: 20th-c Brazil, social.

Snider, **Jill D.** Washington, DC. Affil: Bering Straits Information Technologies. Email: jdsnider27516@yahoo.com. Research: African Americans and aviation, race/technolgy/ American culture.

Snider, **R. Wayne**, *Grace*.

Sniezek, **Christopher J.** Starkville, MS. Affil: Mississippi State. Email: cjs841@msstate.edu. Research: Civil War era, Civil War memory/ public history.

Snobelen, **Stephen**, *Dalhousie*. Email: snobelen@dal.ca.

Snodgrass, **Michael D.**, *Indiana–Purdue, Indianapolis*. Email: misnodgr@iupui.edu.

Snover, **Chelsea**. San Marcos, CA. Affil: California State, San Marcos. Email: snove001@cougars. csusm.edu.

Snow, **Bradley**, *Montana State, Bozeman*. Email: bdsnow@gmail.com.

Snow, **Whitney Adrienne**. Wichita Falls, TX. Affil: Midwestern State. Email: whitneysnow1941@ gmail.com. Research: US, South.

Snowden, **Emma**. Minneapolis, MN. Affil: Minnesota, Twin Cities. Email: snowd030@ umn.edu.

Snowden, **Frank M.**, *Yale*. Email: frank. snowden@yale.edu.

Snyder, **Amanda J.**, *Central Florida*. Email: amanda.snyder@ucf.edu.

Snyder, **Arnold**, *Waterloo*. Email: casnyder@ uwaterloo.ca.

Snyder, **Cathay L.**, *Messiah*. Email: csnyder@ messiah.edu.

Snyder, **Christina N.**, *Penn State*. University Park, PA. Email: snyderc@psu.edu. Research: Native American, US South.

Snyder, **Christopher A.**, *Mississippi State*. Email: cas741@msstate.edu.

Snyder, **Clara**, *Massachusetts Hist. Soc*. Email: csnyder@masshist.org.

Snyder, **David Jonathan**, *South Carolina, Columbia*. Email: snyderd@mailbox.sc.edu.

Snyder, **David R.**, *Austin Peay State*. Email: snyderdr@apsu.edu.

Snyder, **David**. Fresno, CA. Affil: California, Merced. Email: emtdavidsnyder@gmail.com. Research: medieval March of Wales, medieval English Literature.

Snyder, **Jeremiah**. Colorado Springs, CO. Affil: American InterContinental. Email: jsnyder0002@gmail.com.

Snyder, **John W.**, *Kent State*.

Snyder, **Margaret A.** Sleepy Hollow, NY. Affil: Rockefeller Archive Center. Email: msnyder@ rockarch.org. Research: Rockefeller Univ., accessioning.

Snyder, **Robert W.**, *Rutgers, Newark/New Jersey Inst. of Tech*. Email: rwsnyder@rutgers.edu.

Snyder, **Sarah B**. Washington, DC. Affil: American. Email: sarah.b.snyder@gmail.com. Research: Helsinki process, human rights.

Snyder, **Stephen H**., *Linfield*. Email: ssnyder@linfield.edu.

Snyder, **Timothy**, *Yale*. Email: timothy.snyder@yale.edu.

Soares, **John A.**, **Jr.**, *Notre Dame*. Notre Dame, IN. Email: Soares.2@nd.edu.

Soares, **Leigh**, *Mississippi State*.

Sobak, **Robert**, *Bowdoin*.

Sobania, **Neal**, *Pacific Lutheran*. Email: sobania@plu.edu.

Sobel, **Mechal**. Haifa, Israel. Affil: Haifa. Email: msobel@research.haifa.ac.il.

Sobel, **Ronald B**., *Leo Baeck Inst*.

Sobers, **Candace**, *Carleton, Can*. Email: candace.sobers@carleton.ca.

Sochan, **George**, *Bowie State*. Email: gsochan@bowiestate.edu.

Sochen, **June**, *Northeastern Illinois*. Email: J-Sochen@neiu.edu.

Socolow, **Michael J**., *Maine, Orono*. Email: michael.socolow@maine.edu.

Socolow, **Susan M**., *Emory*. Email: socolow@emory.edu.

Sodeman, **Thomas**. Ottawa Hills, OH. Affil: Toledo. Email: thomas.sodeman@utoledo.edu.

Soden, **Dale**, *Whitworth*. Email: dsoden@whitworth.edu.

Sodergren, **Steven E**., *Norwich*. Northfield, VT. Email: ssodergr@norwich.edu. Research: American Civil War.

Soderlund, **Jean**, *Lehigh*. West Deptford, NJ. Email: jrsa@lehigh.edu. Research: colonial America, African American.

Soderlund, **Richard J**., *Illinois State*. Email: rjsoder@ilstu.edu.

Soderstrom, **Mark**. Aurora, IL. Affil: Aurora University. Email: msoderst@aurora.edu. Research: Russia 1700-1917, Siberia.

Sodhy, **Pamela**. McLean, VA. Affil: Georgetown. Email: psodhy@verizon.net. Research: Assoc. of Southeast Asian Nations, US-ASEAN relations.

Soergel, **Philip M**., *Maryland, Coll. Park*. Email: psoergel@umd.edu.

Sofer, **Douglas O**., *Maryville*. Maryville, TN. Email: doug.sofer@maryvillecollege.edu; historiador@mac.com. Research: Colombian political.

Soffer, **Jonathan M**., *NYU*. Brooklyn, NY. Email: jonathan.soffer@nyu.edu. Research: New York City Tammany Hall, urban infrastructure.

Soffer, **Reba N**., *California State, Northridge*. Pacific Palisades, CA. Email: rsoffer@csun.edu. Research: 20th-c British/American conservatism, British/American historiography.

Sohrabi, **Naghmeh**, *Brandeis*. Email: sohrabi@brandeis.edu.

Soine, **Aeleah H**., *St. Mary's, Calif*. Email: ahs3@stmarys-ca.edu.

Soja, **Taylor**. Seattle, WA. Affil: Washington, Seattle. Email: tsoja@uw.edu.

Sokol, **Jason C**., *New Hampshire, Durham*. Portsmouth, NH. Email: jason.sokol@unh.edu. Research: Northeast race and politics, civil rights movement/white southerners.

Sokolik, **Joseph**. Austin, TX. Affil: Headwaters Sch. Email: j.sokolik@headwaters.org.

Sokolsky, **Mark**. Kingston, ON, Canada. Affil: independent scholar. Email: sokolsky.m@gmail.com. Research: Russian environmental, comparative study of empire.

Sola, **Jose O**., *Cleveland State*. Email: j.sola@csuohio.edu.

Soland, **Birgitte**, *Ohio State*. Email: soland.1@osu.edu.

Soliz, **Carmen**, *North Carolina, Charlotte*. Charlotte, NC. Email: msolizur@uncc.edu; carmen.solizu@gmail.com. Research: Latin American social movements, Bolivia.

Soll, **David J**., *Wisconsin-Eau Claire*. Email: solld@uwec.edu.

Soll, **Jacob S**., *Southern California*. Los Angeles, CA. Email: soll@usc.edu. Research: information and knowledge, political culture and economy.

Solnick, **Bruce B**., *SUNY, Albany*. Email: bsol@albany.edu.

Solomon, **Daniel**. Boone, IA. Email: prdsolomon@gmail.com.

Solomon, **Jude**, *Hist. New Orleans*. Email: jude@hnoc.org.

Solomon-Klebba, **Cindy**. Salt Lake City, UT. Affil: Utah. Email: csolomon.history@gmail.com. Research: medieval church and women, women and progressive era.

Solomou, **Emilios A**. Nicosia, Cyprus. Email: solomou.e@unic.ac.cy. Research: teaching history methodology, Cyprus/Graeco-Turkish relations.

Solon, **Paul D**., *Macalester*. Email: solon@macalester.edu.

Solonari, **Vladimir**, *Central Florida*. Orlando, FL. Email: vladimir.solonari@ucf.edu. Research: WWII in Ukraine, Holocaust in Romania.

Soluri, **John**, *Carnegie Mellon*. Pittsburgh, PA. Email: jsoluri@andrew.cmu.edu. Research: Latin America, environmental.

Somerville, **James K**., *SUNY, Coll. Geneseo*.

Somerville, **Robert**, *Columbia (Hist.)*. Email: somervil@columbia.edu.

Sommar, **Mary E**., *Millersville, Pa*. Email: mary.sommar@millersville.edu.

Sommer, **Barbara A**., *Gettysburg*. Santa Fe, NM. Email: bsommer@gettysburg.edu. Research: Amazonia/ethnohistory/culture/slavery.

Sommer, **Matthew H**., *Stanford*. Stanford, CA. Email: msommer@stanford.edu. Research: wife-selling and polyandry, same-sex union and masculinity.

Sommers, **Susan Mitchell**. Latrobe, PA. Affil: St. Vincent. Email: susan.sommers@stvincent.edu. Research: 18th-c British radicalism, 18th-c freemasonry.

Sommerville, **C. John**, *Florida*. Email: jsommerv@ufl.edu.

Sommerville, **Diane Miller**, *Binghamton, SUNY*. Email: sommervi@binghamton.edu.

Sommerville, **Henry**. Durham, NC. Affil: Rochester. Email: henry.sommerville@gmail.com.

Sommerville, **Johann**, *Wisconsin-Madison*. Email: jsommerv@wisc.edu.

Somogyi, **Allison**. Washington, DC. Affil: North Carolina, Chapel Hill. Email: somogyi@live.unc.edu.

Sondhaus, **Lawrence**, *Indianapolis*. Indianapolis, IN. Email: sondhaus@uindy.edu. Research: modern international, strategy and policy.

Song, **Dieyun**. Miami, FL. Affil: Miami. Email: dxs1138@miami.edu.

Song, **Jaeyoon Harr**, *McMaster*. Email: songjae@mcmaster.ca.

Song, **Nianshen**, *Maryland, Baltimore County*. Baltimore, MD. Email: nianshen@umbc.edu; nianshen@gmail.com. Research: China, East Asia.

Song, **Womai Ignatius**, *Earlham*. Email: songwo@earlham.edu.

Songster, **E. Elena**, *St. Mary's, Calif*. Email: ees4@stmarys-ca.edu.

Sonleiter, **Steven**. Orange, CT. Email: ssonleiter@gmail.com.

Sonmez, **Erdem**. Eskisehir, Turkey. Affil: Bilkent. Email: erdemsz@bilkent.edu.tr.

Sonn, **Richard D**., *Arkansas, Fayetteville*. Email: rsonn@uark.edu.

Sonnino, **Paul M**., *California, Santa Barbara*. Email: sonnino@history.ucsb.edu.

Soon, **Wayne**, *Vassar*.

Sopcak-Joseph, **Amy**, *Wilkes*. Storrs Mansfield, CT. Affil: Connecticut, Storrs. Email: amy.sopcak@uconn.edu. Research: Godey's Lady's Book, female consumers.

Soper, **Bonnie**. Stony Brook, NY. Affil: SUNY, Stony Brook. Email: bonnie.soper@stonybrook.edu. Research: Restoration Scotland, colonial backcountry violence.

Soper, **Steven C**., *Georgia*. Email: ssoper@uga.edu.

Soppelsa, **Peter S**., *Oklahoma (Hist. of Science)*. Email: peter.soppelsa@ou.edu.

Soranaka, **Isao**, *Western Ontario*. Email: isoranak@uwo.ca.

Sordo, **Emma M**., *Florida International*. Email: sordoe@fiu.edu.

SoRelle, **James M**., *Baylor*. Email: james_sorelle@baylor.edu.

Sorensen, **Ingrid**. Berwyn, IL. Affil: Concordia, Chicago. Email: sorensen.ingrid@yahoo.com.

Soriano, **Cristina**, *Villanova*. Villanova, PA. Email: cristina.soriano@villanova.edu. Research: revolution and slave rebellions, transmission of knowledge and social movements.

Soriano, **Timothy S**. Grayslake, IL. Affil: Illinois, Chicago. Email: tsoria2@uic.edu. Research: slavery/West Africa/Sierra Leone, Atlantic world.

Sorin, **Gerald**, *SUNY, New Paltz*. Email: soring@newpaltz.edu.

Sorin, **Gretchen Sullivan**, *SUNY, Albany*. Email: sorings@oneonta.edu.

Sorkin, **David**, *Wisconsin-Madison; Yale*. New Haven, CT. Email: david.sorkin@yale.edu; djsorkin@gmail.com. Research: emancipation of European Jewry, German Jewish.

Sorkin, **Jenni**, *California, Santa Barbara*. Email: jsorkin@arthistory.ucsb.edu.

Sorrels, **Katherine**, *Cincinnati*. Email: katherine.sorrels@uc.edu.

Sorrentino, **Janet T**., *Washington Coll*. Email: jsorrentino2@washcoll.edu.

Sosebee, **Scott**, *Stephen F. Austin State*. Nacogdoches, TX. Email: sosebeem@sfasu.edu. Research: entrepreneurship in American West, formation of identity in West.

Sosin, **Joshua**, *Duke*. Email: joshua.sosin@duke.edu.

Soske, **Jon Dylan**, *McGill*. Email: jon.soske@mcgill.ca.

Sosnowski, **Thomas**, *Kent State*. Email: tsosnow1@kent.edu.

Sotenos, Abner Francisco. La Jolla, CA. Affil: California, San Diego. Email: asotenos@ucsd. edu.

Sotiropoulos, Karen, *Cleveland State*. Email: k.sotiropoulos@csuohio.edu.

Soto Laveaga, Gabriela, *Harvard (Hist. of Science)*. Cambridge, MA. Email: gsotolaveaga@fas.harvard.edu. Research: Mexican physician strikes and public health, secret service/social movements/health.

Sotomayor, Antonio. Urbana, IL. Affil: Illinois, Urbana-Champaign. Email: asotomay@illinois. edu. Research: sport and politics in Puerto Rico, colonialism and national identity.

Sottile, Joseph P. Alameda, CA. Email: jpsottile@ hotmail.com. Research: rise of fascism and Axis, Cold War.

Soucy, Robert J., *Oberlin*.

Souders, Kenneth F., *Jr*. Riegelsville, PA. Email: kenfsouders@gmail.com.

Soulodre-La France, Renee. London, ON, Canada. Affil: King's Univ. Coll. Email: rsoulodr@uwo.ca. Research: colonial Latin America/Nueva Granada, enslaved Africans and indigenous.

Soumakis, Fevronia K. Brooklyn, NY. Affil: Teachers, Columbia. Email: fks2102@ tc.columbia.edu.

Sousa, Lisa M., *Occidental*. Los Angeles, CA. Email: lsousa@oxy.edu. Research: Latin America, gender.

South, Marc A. San Antonio, TX. Email: masouth724@hotmail.com.

Souther, J. Mark, *Cleveland State*. Email: m.souther@csuohio.edu.

Southwood, Michael A. Fairfax, VA. Email: msouthwood13@verizon.net. Research: Byzantine, pre-Sports Act (1978) track and field/running.

Souza, Randall, *Seattle*. Email: souzara@ seattleu.edu.

Sovde, Jennifer L. Canton, NY. Affil: SUNY, Canton. Email: sovdej@canton.edu. Research: children and childhood, children's popular culture.

Sowards, Adam M., *Idaho*. Email: asowards@ uidaho.edu.

Sowerby, Scott Andrew, *Northwestern*. Evanston, IL. Email: sowerby@northwestern. edu. Research: cosmopolitanism, religious nonconformity.

Sowerwine, Charles. Moonee Ponds, Australia. Affil: Melbourne. Email: c.sowerwine@gmail. com. Research: 19th-c gender.

Soybel, Phyllis L., *Elmhurst*. Email: soybelp@ elmhurst.edu.

Soyer, Daniel, *Fordham*. Bronx, NY. Email: soyer@fordham.edu. Research: US urban and ethnic, Jewish.

Spadaccini, Bruce Lorenzo, *Jr*. Bear, DE. Affil: Delaware. Email: bspad@udel.edu. Research: Atlantic world commercial networks, Atlantic ship captains.

Spadafora, David, *Lake Forest*.

Spady, Matthew. New York, NY. Email: matthewspady@audubonparkny.com. Research: Audubon Park in New York City, northern Manhattan.

Spagnoli, Paul G., *Boston Coll*. Email: paul. spagnoli@bc.edu.

Spain, Rufus B., *Baylor*. Email: rufus_spain@ baylor.edu.

Spalding, Karen, *Connecticut, Storrs*. Email: karen.spalding@uconn.edu.

Spalding, Sarah Marie. Washington, DC. Email: sarahmspalding@yahoo.com. Research: women and education in medieval Germany, monastic and scholastic collaboration.

Spall, Richard F., *Jr.*, *Ohio Wesleyan; Phi Alpha Theta*. Delaware, OH. Email: rfspall@owu.edu. Research: free trade, Victorianism.

Spanagel, David I. Worcester, MA. Affil: Worcester Polytechnic Inst. Email: spanagel@ wpi.edu. Research: 18th-c global exploration, ideas about Earth's history.

Spang, Rebecca L., *Indiana*. Bloomington, IN. Email: rlspang@indiana.edu. Research: French Revolution, money.

Spangler, Jewel L., *Calgary*. Email: spangler@ ucalgary.ca.

Spanner, Donald, *Western Ontario*. Email: dspanner@uwo.ca.

Spar, Ira, *Ramapo*. Email: ispar@ramapo.edu.

Sparacio, Matthew John. Durant, OK. Affil: Southeastern Oklahoma State. Email: msparacio@se.edu. Research: Choctaw Indians, Colonial South.

Sparks, Lacey A., *Southern Maine*. Gorham, ME. Email: lacey.sparks@maine.edu.

Sparks, Randy J., *Tulane*. Email: rsparks1@ tulane.edu.

Sparrow, James T., *Chicago*. Chicago, IL. Email: jts@uchicago.edu. Research: mass politics of extraterritoriality, intellectual history of political agency.

Spaulding, Jay L. North Fort Myers, FL. Affil: Kean. Email: jspauldi@kean.edu. Research: Funj Kingdom of Sinnar, medieval Nubia.

Spaulding, Robert Mark, *Jr.*, *North Carolina, Wilmington*. Wilmington, NC. Email: spauldingr@uncw.edu. Research: German lands 1650-1848, European trade 1650-present.

Speaker, Susan L., *National Library of Medicine*. Email: speakes1@mail.nih.gov.

Spear, David S., *Furman*. Greenville, SC. Email: david.spear@furman.edu. Research: Norman cathedral clergy 911-1204, Anglo-Norman prosopography 911-1204.

Spear, Jennifer M., *Simon Fraser*. Email: jennifer_ spear@sfu.ca.

Spear, Thomas T., *Wisconsin-Madison*. Email: tspear@wisc.edu.

Speare, Max. Irvine, CA. Affil: California, Irvine. Email: mspeare@uci.edu.

Spears, Ellen G. Atlanta, GA. Affil: Alabama. Email: egspears@as.ua.edu. Research: environmental health social, US South technology and social change.

Specht, Joshua. South Bend, IN. Affil: Monash. Email: joshspecht@gmail.com. Research: US.

Specht, Neva Jean, *Appalachian State*. Email: spechtnj@appstate.edu.

Speckart, Amy. Charlottesville, VA. Affil: Virginia. Email: amy.speckart@virginia.edu. Research: Virginia 1865-present, African American.

Spector, Daniel E. Jacksonville, AL. Email: drspector@cableone.net.

Spector, Ronald H., *George Washington*. Email: spector@gwu.edu.

Spector, Scott, *Michigan, Ann Arbor*. Email: spec@umich.edu.

Speed, Richard M., *San José State*. Email: rbspeed@comcast.net.

Speidel, Michael P., *Hawai'i, Manoa*. Email: speidel@hawaii.edu.

Spellberg, Denise A., *Texas, Austin*. Email: spellberg@austin.utexas.edu.

Spellman, Susan V., *Miami, Ohio*. Email: spellmsv@miamioh.edu.

Spence, Johnny Hampton, II. Chugiak, AK. Affil: Vernon. Email: j.h.spence@tcu.edu. Research: American/Chinese relations during WWII, WWII Pacific military.

Spence, Jonathan D., *Yale*. Email: jonathan. spence@yale.edu.

Spence, Richard B., *Idaho*. Email: rspence@ uidaho.edu.

Spence, Taylor, *New Mexico*. Brooklyn, NY. Email: tspence@unm.edu; taylor.spence@aya.yale. edu. Research: land use policy, social religious land movements.

Spencer, Alexandra. Fresno, CA. Affil: California State, Fresno. Email: alexandra.spencer@ csufresno.edu.

Spencer, Elaine G., *Northern Illinois*. Sycamore, IL. Email: espencer@niu.edu. Research: 19th-c Germany.

Spencer, Eliot P. Chapel Hill, NC. Affil: North Carolina, Chapel Hill. Email: eliotspencer@ alumni.unc.edu. Research: 19th-c Venezuelan cultural, Atlantic world commerce and connections.

Spencer, George W., *Northern Illinois*. Sycamore, IL. Email: gspencer@niu.edu; gspencer39@ yahoo.com. Research: medieval South India, temples.

Spencer, Heath A., *Seattle*. Email: spencerh@ seattleu.edu.

Spencer, Jacob. Cambridge, MA. Affil: Harvard. Email: jacob.m.spencer@gmail.com.

Spencer, John, *Middlebury*.

Spencer, Mark G., *Brock*. Email: mspencer@ brocku.ca.

Spencer, Robert A., *Toronto*.

Spencer, Robyn C., *Graduate Center, CUNY; Lehman, CUNY*. Email: robyn.spencer@lehman. cuny.edu.

Spencer, Steffan A., *Minnesota Duluth*. Email: saspence@d.umn.edu.

Spencer, Stephanie, *North Carolina State*. Email: stephanie_spencer@ncsu.edu.

Spencer, Thomas Tucker, *Indiana, South Bend*. South Bend, IN. Email: thspence@iusb.edu. Research: recent US.

Spencer, Yolanda D. Santa Clarita, CA. Affil: Kings. Email: ydspencer@gmail.com. Research: Pentecostal movement, holiness movement.

Spendelow, Howard, *Georgetown*. Email: spendelh@georgetown.edu.

Spengler, Susan, *Robert H. Smith Center*. Email: sspengler@monticello.org.

Sperber, Jonathan, *Missouri, Columbia*. Columbia, MO. Email: sperberj@missouri.edu. Research: post-1945 global, post-1945 central Europe.

Spero, Patrick K. Philadelphia, PA. Affil: American Philosophical Soc. Email: librarian@ amphilsoc.org. Research: Shawnees.

Spicer, Kevin P. North Easton, MA. Affil: Stonehill. Email: kspicer@stonehill.edu. Research: German Catholic 1933-45, Holocaust.

Spicka, Mark E., *Shippensburg*. Email: mespic@ ship.edu.

Spickard, **Paul**, *California, Santa Barbara*. Santa Barbara, CA. Email: spickard@history.ucsb. edu. Research: US immigration, race and ethnicity.

Spickermann, **Roland**, *Texas, Permian Basin*. Odessa, TX. Email: spickermann_r@utpb.edu. Research: German-Polish relations in German empire, adoption in Germany.

Spidle, **Jake W.**, **Jr.**, *New Mexico*. Email: jspidle@unm.edu.

Spiegel, **Gabrielle M.**, *Johns Hopkins (Hist.)*. Baltimore, MD. Email: spiegel@jhu.edu. Research: medieval historical writing, critical theory of history.

Spiegel, **Nina S.**, *Portland State*. Email: nspiegel@pdx.edu.

Spiekermann, **Uwe**. Hannover, Germany. Affil: German Hist. Inst. Email: uwe.k.spiekermann@gmail.com. Research: consumption, economic and social.

Spielman, **Loren R.**, *Portland State*. Email: spielman@pdx.edu.

Spielvogel, **Jackson J.**, *Penn State*. Email: jxs12@psu.edu.

Spierling, **Karen E.**, *Denison*. Email: spierlingk@denison.edu.

Spiese, **Monica D.**, *Millersville, Pa.*. Email: monica.spiese@millersville.edu.

Spike, **Tamara S.**, *North Georgia*. Email: tamara.spike@ung.edu.

Spiliotes, **Nicholas J.** Bethesda, MD. Email: nspiliotes@comcast.net.

Spillane, **Joseph F.**, *Florida*. Email: spillane@ufl.edu.

Spillemaeker, **Frederic**. Antony, France. Affil: Ecoles des Hautes Études en Sciences Sociales. Email: fspillemaeker@gmail.com.

Spiller, **James A.**, *SUNY, Coll. Brockport*. Email: jspiller@brockport.edu.

Spillman, **Scott**. Morrison, CO. Affil: Colorado, Denver. Email: scottrspillman@gmail.com.

Spina, **Costan**. Saint Louis, MO. Affil: Villa Duchesne Sch. Email: cspina@vdoh.org. Research: Russia in WWI, Napoleonic wars.

Spinelli, **Michelle A.** Stony Brook, NY. Affil: SUNY, Stony Brook. Email: michelle.spinelli@stonybrook.edu. Research: psychiatry, print culture.

Spinner, **Thomas J.**, **Jr.**, *Vermont*. Chevy Chase, MD. Research: 20th-c British Labor Party, 1945-present Guyana.

Spinney, **Russell Alfred**. Ojai, CA. Affil: Thacher Sch. Email: rspinney@thacher.org. Research: emotions in Weimar Republic everyday life, emotions in social movements and political protest.

Spiro, **Liat N**, *Holy Cross*. Worcester, MA. Email: lnspiro@holycross.edu.

Spitz, **Mark**. Denver, CO. Email: markspitz81@gmail.com.

Spitzer, **Alan B.**, *Iowa*. Bryn Mawr, PA. Email: absandmfs@yahoo.com. Research: French restoration, philosophy of history.

Spitzer, **Leo**, *Dartmouth*. Email: leo.spitzer@dartmouth.edu.

Spivey, **Donald**, *Miami*. Miami, FL. Email: dspivey@miami.edu. Research: sport, racism/labor/music/education.

Spock, **Jennifer B.**, *Eastern Kentucky*. Email: jennifer.spock@eku.edu.

Spodek, **Howard**. Philadelphia, PA. Affil: Temple. Email: spodek@temple.edu. Research: Indian and world urban, Indian urban planning.

Spoehr, **Luther W.**, *Brown*. Email: Luther_Spoehr@Brown.edu.

Spohnholz, **Jesse A.**, *Washington State, Pullman*. Pullman, WA. Email: spohnhoj@wsu.edu. Research: religious toleration.

Spooner, **Matthew P.**, *Michigan, Ann Arbor*. Email: spoonerm@umich.edu.

Sporleder, **Josephine**, *State Hist. Soc. of Missouri*. Email: sporlederj@shsmo.org.

Spornick, **Charles D. G.**, *Emory*. Email: libeds@emory.edu.

Spraul-Schmidt, **Judith**. Cincinnati, OH. Affil: Cincinnati. Email: judith.spraul-schmidt@uc.edu. Research: Flagler and urbanization of Florida, Dillon and municipal law.

Sprayberry, **Gary**, *Columbus State*. Email: sprayberry_gary@columbusstate.edu.

Sprenger, **Nicholas**. Highland Park, NJ. Affil: Rutgers. Email: ns1057@history.rutgers.edu.

Sprenkle, **Daniel Ned**, **Jr**. Tucson, AZ. Email: daniel.sprenkle@gmail.com. Research: Violence in the Old West, Decisive Civil War battles.

Spring, **Kelly A**. Gorham, ME. Affil: Southern Maine. Email: kelly.spring@maine.edu. Research: food, gender studies.

Springer, **Arnold R.**, *California State, Long Beach*. Email: ulanbator@venice-ca.com.

Springer, **Jonathan Ricardo**. Brooklyn, NY. Email: Jonathanspri@gmail.com. Research: Caribbean, migration.

Springer, **Michael M.**, *Central Oklahoma*. Email: mspringer@uco.edu.

Spruill, **Marjorie Julian**, *South Carolina, Columbia*. Email: spruillm@mailbox.sc.edu.

Sprunger, **Keith L**. North Newton, KS. Affil: Bethel. Email: sprunger@bethelks.edu. Research: Mennonites and printing, church architecture.

Sprunger, **Mary S**. Harrisonburg, VA. Affil: Eastern Mennonite. Email: mary.sprunger@emu.edu. Research: Golden Age Dutch Mennonites soc and econ, Golden Age Dutch Mennonite ethnography.

Sprunger, **Michael**. Conway, AR. Affil: Hendrix. Email: sprunger@hendrix.edu. Research: crime and punishment in colonial Korea.

Spunaugle, **Adrianne**. Ann Arbor, MI. Affil: Michigan. Email: aspunaug@umich.edu.

Spyridakis, **Stylianos**, *California, Davis*. Email: svspyridakis@ucdavis.edu.

Squatriti, **Paolo**, *Michigan, Ann Arbor*. Email: pasqua@umich.edu.

Squeri, **Lawrence**. East Stroudsburg, PA. Affil: East Stroudsburg. Email: lsqueri@po-box.esu. edu. Research: Italian American, SETI.

Sramek, **Joseph M.**, *Southern Illinois, Carbondale*. Email: sramek@siu.edu.

Srebnick, **Amy Gilman**, *Montclair State*. Email: srebnicka@mail.montclair.edu.

Sreenivas, **Mytheli**, *Ohio State*. Email: sreenivas.2@osu.edu.

Sreenivasan, **Govind**, *Brandeis*. Email: sreenivasan@brandeis.edu.

Sreenivasan, **Ramya**. Philadelphia, PA. Affil: Pennsylvania. Email: rsreenivasan@sas.upenn. edu. Research: communities in early modern South Asia, colonial modernity in princely states.

Srivastava, **Priyanka**, *Massachusetts, Amherst*. Email: priyanka@history.umass.edu.

Srole, **Carole**, *California State, Los Angeles*. Los Angeles, CA. Email: csrole@calstatela.

edu. Research: millionaire and working class marriages, turn of 20th century.

St. Clare, **Dawn**, *Central Oklahoma*. Email: lstclare@uco.edu.

St. George, **Robert Blair**, *Pennsylvania*. Email: stgeorge@sas.upenn.edu.

St. Germaine, **Richard D.**, *Wisconsin-Eau Claire*. Email: stgermrd@uwec.edu.

St. Jean, **Wendy B**. Hammond, IN. Affil: Purdue Northwest, Hammond. Email: stjeanw@pnw. edu. Research: Native America, environment.

St. John, **Rachel C.**, *California, Davis*. Email: rcstjohn@ucdavis.edu.

St. Julien, **Danielle E.**, *Xavier, La.*

Staats, **Daniel D**. Douglasville, GA. Email: ddstaats54@gmail.com. Research: colonial Charleston SC, colonial GA Coast.

Stabler, **Scott L.**, *Grand Valley State*. Email: stablers@gvsu.edu.

Stacey, **Peter**, *UCLA*. Email: pstacey@history.ucla.edu.

Stacey, **Robert C.**, *Washington, Seattle*. Email: bstacey@uw.edu.

Stacey, **Robin C.**, *Washington, Seattle*. Email: rcstacey@uw.edu.

Stack, **Elizabeth Jane**. Bronx, NY. Affil: Fordham. Email: estack@fordham.edu. Research: Irish immigrants in America, German immigrants in America.

Stack, **Joan**, *State Hist. Soc. of Missouri*. Email: stackj@shsmo.org.

Stackelberg, **Roderick**, *Gonzaga*. Email: stackelberg@gonzaga.edu.

Stacy, **Ian Robert**. Bellingham, WA. Affil: Whatcom Comm. Coll. Email: istacy@whatcom.edu.

Stagg, **J.C.A.**, *Virginia*. Charlottesville, VA. Email: js5h@virginia.edu. Research: early national US.

Staggs, **Stephen Thomas**, *Calvin*. Email: sts2@calvin.edu.

Stagner, **Annessa C**. Lamar, CO. Affil: Lamar Comm. Coll. Email: Annessa.stagner@lamarcc. edu. Research: US shell shock in international perspective, military medicine during WWI.

Stahl, **Dale J.**, *Colorado Denver*. Email: dale.stahl@ucdenver.edu.

Stahl, **Ronit Y.**, *California, Berkeley*. Email: rystahl@berkeley.edu.

Stahler, **Kimberly D**. Cuyahoga Falls, OH. Affil: Case Western Reserve. Email: kstahle2@kent. edu.

Stahnisch, **Frank W.**, *Calgary*. Email: fwstahni@ucalgary.ca.

Staley, **David J.**, *Ohio State*. Email: staley.3@osu.edu.

Staley, **Kimberly N**. Dublin, OH. Affil: Southern New Hampshire. Email: knstaley84@gmail. com.

Stalker, **Nancy K.**, *Hawai'i, Manoa*. Email: nancy.stalker@hawaii.edu.

Stallbaumer-Beishline, **Lisa M.**, *Bloomsburg*. Email: lstallba@bloomu.edu.

Stallings, **Courtenay C**. Malibu, CA. Affil: Pepperdine. Email: courtenay.stallings@pepperdine.edu. Research: media, memory and race.

Stalls, **Clay**, *Huntington Library*. Email: cstalls@huntington.org.

Stallsmith, **Allaire**, *Towson*. Email: astallsmith@towson.edu.

Stam, **David H.**, *Syracuse*. Email: dhstam@syr. edu.

Stamm, Michael R., *Michigan State*. East Lansing, MI. Email: stamm@msu.edu. Research: journalism, print culture.

Stanard, Matthew G., *Berry*. Mount Berry, GA. Email: mstanard@berry.edu. Research: modern European imperialism in Africa.

Standaert, Jackie. Sussex, NJ. Affil: Montclair State. Email: jstandaert@outlook.com.

Standen, S. Dale, *Trent*. Email: dstanden@trentu.ca.

Standifer, Mary M. Austin, TX. Email: marymstandifer@gmail.com. Research: Jean Charles Houzeau.

Standish, Sierra. Boulder, CO. Affil: Colorado, Boulder. Email: sierra.standish@colorado.edu. Research: travels of science, public lands.

Standley, Dabney. San Rafael, CA. Affil: Sacred Heart Cathedral Preparatory. Email: dstandley@shcp.edu.

Stanfiel, Heather Lynn. South Bend, IN. Affil: Notre Dame. Email: stanfiel.2@nd.edu. Research: modern Irish memory and conflict, British imperial cultural.

Stanfield, Michael E., *San Francisco*. Email: stanfieldm@usfca.edu.

Stanfield, Michael, *South Florida, St. Petersburg*. Email: sjstanfield@utep.edu.

Stanfield, Susan Joyce, *Texas, El Paso*. Email: sjstanfield@utep.edu.

Stanfield-Johnson, Rosemary, *Minnesota Duluth*. Email: rstanfie@d.umn.edu.

Stangler, Connor. Kansas City, MO. Affil: Indiana. Email: connorstangler@gmail.com. Research: administrative state, capitalism.

Stango, Marie Elizabeth, *Idaho State*. Email: stanmari@isu.edu.

Stanislawski, Michael F., *Columbia (Hist.)*. Email: mfs3@columbia.edu.

Stanke, Jaclyn, *Campbell*. Fuquay-Varina, NC. Email: stanke@campbell.edu. Research: end of Cold War in popular culture, Cold War as article of consumption.

Stanley, Adam C., *Wisconsin-Platteville*. Email: stanleya@uwplatt.edu.

Stanley, Amy B., *Northwestern*. Evanston, IL. Email: a-stanley@northwestern.edu. Research: 19th-c Japanese social, early modern Japanese women and gender.

Stanley, Amy Dru, *Chicago*. Email: adstanle@uchicago.edu.

Stanley, Jerry, *California State, Bakersfield*.

Stanley, John R., *Kutztown*. Email: stanley@kutztown.edu.

Stanley, Kimberly, *Indiana State*. Email: Kimberly.Stanley@indstate.edu.

Stanley, Matthew E. Albany, GA. Affil: Albany State. Email: matthew.stanley@asurams.edu.

Stannish, Steven M., *SUNY, Coll. Potsdam*. Email: stannism@potsdam.edu.

Stansbury, Ronald J. Rochester, NY. Affil: Roberts Wesleyan. Email: stansbury_ronald@roberts.edu.

Stansell, Christine, *Chicago*. Email: stansell@uchicago.edu.

Stansfield, Michael. National Harbor, MD. Email: mikestans1977@yahoo.com.

Stansky, Peter D. L., *Stanford*. Stanford, CA. Email: stansky@stanford.edu. Research: modern British cultural.

Stanton, Andrea L. Denver, CO. Affil: Denver. Email: andrea.stanton@du.edu. Research: mass media technologies and faith communities, technology and national identity.

Stanton, Megan. Madison, WI. Affil: Wisconsin, Madison. Email: mastanton2@wisc.edu.

Stanwood, Owen C., *Boston Coll*. Chestnut Hill, MA. Email: owen.stanwood@bc.edu. Research: Atlantic world.

Stapell, Hamilton Michael, *SUNY, New Paltz*. Email: stapellh@newpaltz.edu.

Stapleford, Thomas A., *Notre Dame*. Email: tstaplef@nd.edu.

Staples, George H. Madison, NJ.

Staples, Kate Kelsey, *West Virginia*. Email: Kate.Staples@mail.wvu.edu.

Stapleton, John M., Jr., *US Military Acad*. Email: john.stapleton@usma.edu.

Stapleton, Kristin, *SUNY, Buffalo*. Buffalo, NY. Email: kstaple@buffalo.edu. Research: modern and republican China.

Stapleton, Timothy, *Calgary*. Email: timothy.stapleton@ucalgary.ca.

Stark, Bennett S. Ann Arbor, MI. Email: sid1732@gmail.com. Research: 21st-c prospects of humanity, non-linearity in past and future.

Stark, Bruce P. Old Lyme, CT.

Stark, Casey M., *Bowling Green State*. Email: starkcm@bgsu.edu.

Stark, David M., *Grand Valley State*. Email: starkd@gvsu.edu.

Stark, Gary D., *Grand Valley State*. Email: starkg@gvsu.edu.

Stark, Laura, *Vanderbilt*. Email: laura.stark@vanderbilt.edu.

Starkey, Armstrong M., III, *Adelphi*. Email: starkey@adelphi.edu.

Starks, Tricia, *Arkansas, Fayetteville*. Email: tstarks@uark.edu.

Starling, Jamie Matthew, *Texas-Rio Grande Valley*. Email: jamie.starling@utrgv.edu.

Starn, Orin, *Duke*. Email: ostarn@duke.edu.

Starn, Randolph R. Berkeley, CA. Affil: California, Berkeley. Email: rstarn@berkeley.edu. Research: early modern Europe, cultural.

Starnes, Richard D., *Western Carolina*. Email: starnes@wcu.edu.

Staron, Nicole, *Susquehanna*. Email: nstaron@pct.edu.

Starr, Clinton R. Frisco, TX. Affil: Collin County Comm. Coll. Email: cstarr@collin.edu. Research: post-WWII US, bohemianism and countercultures.

Starr, Daniel P., *Canisius*. Email: starr@canisius.edu.

Starr, J. Barton. Pensacola, FL. Affil: Palm Beach Atlantic. Email: starrbr@gmail.com. Research: Protestant missions in China, American Revolution loyalists.

Starr, Laura Kopp, *Hist. Assoc*. Email: lstarr@historyassociates.com.

Starr, Raymond G., *San Diego State*.

Startt, James Dill, *Valparaiso*. Email: james.startt@valpo.edu.

Stasevich, James, Jr. Livonia, MI.

Stasz, Clarice, *Sonoma State*. Email: stasz@sonoma.edu.

Stater, Victor L., III, *Louisiana State*. Email: stater@lsu.edu.

Statiev, Alex, *Waterloo*. Email: astatiev@uwaterloo.ca.

Statler, Kathryn, *San Diego*. Email: kstatler@sandiego.edu.

Staudacher, Urmila. Apex, NC. Email: urmistaud2@yahoo.com. Research: women, cultural.

Staudenmaier, Michael. North Manchester, IL. Affil: Manchester. Email: mjstaudenmaier@manchester.edu. Research: US Latina/o/x, comparative race/ethnicity.

Staudenmaier, Peter, *Marquette*. Milwaukee, WI. Email: peter.staudenmaier@marquette.edu; ps283@cornell.edu. Research: occultism in Nazi Germany and Fascist Italy, racial thought.

Staudt, John, *Hofstra*. Email: john.staudt@hofstra.edu.

Staufenbiel, Baylee M. Yakima, WA. Affil: Wyoming. Email: baylee004@gmail.com. Research: medicine, gender and women's studies.

Stauffer, Adam Q. Rochester, NY. Affil: Rochester. Email: astauff2@ur.rochester.edu. Research: California Gold Rush/print culture, intellectual history/science.

Staum, Martin S., *Calgary*. Email: mstaum@ucalgary.ca.

Stauter-Halsted, Keely D., *Illinois, Chicago*. Email: stauterh@uic.edu.

Stavrou, Theofanis G., *Minnesota (Hist.)*. Email: stavr001@umn.edu.

Stayer, Caren Calendine. Columbus, OH. Affil: Strayer. Email: caren.stayer@strayer.edu.

Stayer, James M., *Queen's, Can*. Email: jms2@queensu.ca.

Stayer, Samuel N., *Birmingham-Southern*. Birmingham, AL. Research: 19th-c US.

Stealey, John E., III. Shepherdstown, WV. Affil: Shepherd. Email: jestealey@outlook.com. Research: post-Civil War Appalachia, early Porfirian Mexico.

Stearn, Catherine L., *Eastern Kentucky*. Email: catherine.stearn@eku.edu.

Stearns, Peter N., *George Mason*. Fairfax, VA. Email: pstearns@gmu.edu. Research: recent US culture and society, emotions/consumerism/world.

Stearns, Susan Gaunt, *Mississippi*. University, MS. Email: sgstearn@olemiss.edu. Research: land speculation, early Republic social.

Stebbins, H. Lyman, *La Salle*.

Stebenne, David L., *Ohio State*. Columbus, OH. Email: stebenne.1@osu.edu. Research: US since 1933, modern US political.

Steck, Andrew N., *Iowa*. Iowa City, IA. Email: andrew-steck@uiowa.edu. Research: crowds in medieval Rome, authority and kingship/queenship/papacy.

Steed, Brian L., *US Army Command Coll*. Email: brian.l.steed.civ@mail.mil.

Steege, Paul R., *Villanova*. Villanova, PA. Email: paul.steege@villanova.edu. Research: Berlin in Cold War, material scarcity/limits of politics.

Steele, Brian D., *Alabama, Birmingham*. Email: bdsteele@uab.edu.

Steele, Charles, *US Air Force Acad*. Email: charles.steele@usafa.edu.

Steele, Ian K., *Western Ontario*. Email: isteele@uwo.ca.

Steele, James K. North Las Vegas, NV. Affil: Nevada, Las Vegas. Email: wolfgangnos@gmail.com.

Steele, James, *North Carolina A&T State*. Email: steelej@ncat.edu.

Steele, Joshua. Gainesville, FL. Affil: Arizona. Email: jbsteele@email.arizona.edu.

Steele, Ruth, *Western Washington*. Email: Ruth.Steele@wwu.edu.

Steen, **Charlie R.**, **III**, *New Mexico*. Albuquerque, NM. Email: csteen@unm.edu. Research: early modern culture, European unity.

Steen, **Ivan D.**, *SUNY, Albany*. Email: oralhis@albany.edu.

Steen, **Kathryn**, *Drexel*. Philadelphia, PA. Email: steen@drexel.edu. Research: US synthetic organic chemicals industry, US patent system.

Steeples, **Doug W.**, *Mercer*.

Steere-Williams, **Jacob**, *Charleston*. Email: steerewilliamsj@cofc.edu.

Stefanov, **Tracy**. Willoughby, OH. Email: tstefanov@andrewsosborne.com.

Steffel, **R. Vladimir**, *Ohio State*. Delaware, OH. Email: steffel.1@osu.edu. Research: British social 1815-1939, India.

Steffen, **Charles G.**, *Georgia State*. Email: csteffen@gsu.edu.

Steffens, **Henry J.**, *Vermont*. Email: henry.steffens@uvm.edu.

Steffes, **Tracy L.**, *Brown*. Providence, RI. Email: tracy_steffes@brown.edu. Research: 20th-c US, education.

Stefon, **Frederick J.**, *Penn State*. Email: fjs3@psu.edu.

Steger, **Werner H.** Poughkeepsie, NY. Affil: Dutchess Comm. Coll., SUNY. Email: steger@sunydutchess.edu. Research: antebellum urban South, immigration and labor.

Stegmaier, **Mark J.** Denton, TX. Email: marks@cameron.edu. Research: US politics and sectional crisis 1850-61.

Stehlin, **David**. Fort Myers, FL. Email: dstehlin@gmail.com.

Stehlin, **Stewart A.**, *NYU*. Email: stewart.stehlin@nyu.edu.

Steigerwald, **Alison Rebecca**. North Liberty, IA. Affil: Iowa. Email: alison-steigerwald@uiowa.edu. Research: dissent/WWI/Britain/American, US and the World.

Steigerwald, **David H.**, *Ohio State*. Email: steigerwald.2@osu.edu.

Steigman, **Andrew L.** Chevy Chase, MD. Affil: Georgetown. Email: steigman@georgetown.edu.

Steigmann-Gall, **Richard Albert**, *Kent State*. Email: rsteigma@kent.edu.

Steiman, **Lionel B.**, *Manitoba*. Email: lionel.steiman@umanitoba.ca.

Stein, **David P.** Los Angeles, CA. Email: david.p.stein@gmail.com.

Stein, **Harry H.** Portland, OR. Email: steinharry14@gmail.com. Research: Oregonian newspaper.

Stein, **Harry**. New York, NY. Affil: City Coll., NY. Email: harry.stein@manhattan.edu. Research: US, education.

Stein, **Kalman**. Teaneck, NJ. Affil: Frisch Sch. Email: kalman.stein@frisch.org.

Stein, **Kenneth W.**, *Emory*. Atlanta, GA. Email: kstein@emory.edu. Research: modern Arab world, modern Israel.

Stein, **Leon**, *Roosevelt*. Email: lstein3100@aol.com.

Stein, **Marc R.** San Francisco, CA. Affil: San Francisco State. Email: marcs@sfsu.edu. Research: law, sexuality.

Stein, **Mark L.**, *Muhlenberg*. Email: stein@muhlenberg.edu.

Stein, **Melissa N.**, *Kentucky*. Email: melissa.stein@uky.edu.

Stein, **Sarah A.**, *UCLA*. Los Angeles, CA. Email: sstein@history.ucla.edu. Research: Jews and race/capitalism/colonialism, Jews in Russia and Ottoman empires.

Stein, **Stanley J.** Princeton, NJ. Affil: Princeton.

Stein, **Stephen J.** Bloomington, IN. Affil: Indiana. Email: stein@indiana.edu. Research: religions in America, free exercise of religion.

Stein, **Stephen K.**, *Memphis*. Memphis, TN. Email: sstein@memphis.edu; stvstein@mac.com. Research: Cold War military policy, bdsm community.

Stein, **Steve J.**, *Miami*. Email: srafael@miami.edu.

Stein, **Susan**. Omaha, NE. Email: ssnstn@aol.com.

Steinacher, **Gerald J.**, *Nebraska, Lincoln*. Lincoln, NE. Email: gsteinacher2@unl.edu. Research: International Red Cross, fascist Italy/Nazi Germany/Europe.

Steinbach, **Steven**. Washington, DC. Affil: Sidwell Friends Sch. Email: steinbachs@sidwell.edu.

Steinberg, **Allen**, *Iowa*. Email: allen-steinberg@uiowa.edu.

Steinberg, **John W.**, *Austin Peay State*. Email: steinbergj@apsu.edu.

Steinberg, **Jonathan**, *Pennsylvania*. Email: steinbej@history.upenn.edu.

Steinberg, **Mark D.**, *Illinois, Urbana-Champaign*. Urbana, IL. Email: steinb@illinois.edu. Research: revolution, utopia/dystopia/heterotopia.

Steinberg, **Michael P.**, *Brown*. Email: Michael_Steinberg@Brown.edu.

Steinberg, **Salme H.**, *Northeastern Illinois*. Email: S-Steinberg@neiu.edu.

Steinberg, **Ted L.**, *Case Western Reserve*. Email: theodore.steinberg@case.edu.

Steinbock-Pratt, **Sarah**, *Alabama, Tuscaloosa*. Tuscaloosa, AL. Email: sksteinbockpratt@ua.edu. Research: race and gender in modern US, US in the world.

Steineker, **Rowan**, *Florida Gulf Coast*. Email: rsteineker@fgcu.edu.

Steingart, **Alma**, *Columbia (Hist.)*. Email: as2475@columbia.edu.

Steinhoff, **Anthony J.**, *Québec, Montréal*. Montreal, QC, Canada. Email: steinhoff.anthony@uqam.ca. Research: Wagner and German culture 1860-1960, religion in modern Europe.

Steinisch, **Irmgard**, *York, Can*. Email: imgards@yorku.ca.

Steinke, **Christopher Joseph**, *Nebraska, Kearney*. Email: steinkecj@unk.edu.

Steinmetz, **Charles Edwin**, **Jr.**, *Duquesne*. Email: steinmetzc@duq.edu.

Steinmetz, **George**. Ann Arbor, MI. Affil: Michigan. Email: geostein@umich.edu.

Steinson, **Barbara J.**, *DePauw*. Email: steinson@depauw.edu.

Steinwedel, **Charles R.**, *Northeastern Illinois*. Email: C-Steinwedel@neiu.edu.

Steinweis, **Alan E.**, *Vermont*. Email: alan.steinweis@uvm.edu.

Stejskal, **Sonya**, *Nebraska, Omaha*.

Stelter, **Gilbert A.**, *Guelph*. Email: gstelter@uoguelph.ca.

Stelzel, **Philipp J.**, *Duquesne*. Email: stelzelp@duq.edu.

Stemler, **Mary Lee**. Bryan, TX. Affil: Blinn. Email: ml.stemler@gmail.com.

Steneck, **Nicholas H.**, *Michigan, Ann Arbor*. Email: nsteneck@umich.edu.

Stenger, **Charles C.** Mentor, OH. Email: chass639@yahoo.com.

Stenner, **David**, *Christopher Newport*. Email: david.stenner@cnu.edu.

Stentiford, **Barry M.**, *US Army Command Coll*. Email: barry.m.stentiford.civ@mail.mil.

Stenzel, **Monica J.** Spokane, WA. Affil: Spokane Falls Comm. Coll. Email: monica.stenzel@sfcc.spokane.edu. Research: Reginald Scot and early modern witchcraft, early American witchcraft.

Stepan, **Nancy L.**, *Columbia (Hist.)*. Email: nls1@columbia.edu.

Stephan, **John J.**, *Hawai'i, Manoa*. Honolulu, HI. Email: stephan@hawaii.edu. Research: American Nikkei in imperial Japan.

Stephan, **Rob**, *Arizona*. Email: rstephan@email.arizona.edu.

Stephan, **Scott M.**, *Ball State*. Email: sstephan@bsu.edu.

Stephan, **Tara D.** Midlothian, VA. Affil: Hampden-Sydney. Email: tstephan@hsc.edu. Research: women and gender, Islamic literature.

Stephanson, **Anders**, *Columbia (Hist.)*. Email: ags8@columbia.edu.

Stephen, **Jennifer**, *York, Can*. Email: stephenj@yorku.ca.

Stephen, **Michael L.** Colorado Springs, CO. Email: mstephe2@uccs.edu. Research: Korean women during colonial period, Seoul public spaces.

Stephens, **Bruce**, *Penn State*. Email: bms3@psu.edu.

Stephens, **Deanne**, *Southern Mississippi*. Email: deanne.nuwer@usm.edu.

Stephens, **Isaac Sean**, *Mississippi*.

Stephens, **Julia A.**, *Rutgers*. Email: julia.stephens@rutgers.edu.

Stephens, **Leigh Vella**. Derwood, MD. Affil: Georgetown. Email: Leighvstephens@gmail.com.

Stephens, **Lester D.** Athens, GA. Affil: Georgia. Email: lstephen@uga.edu. Research: naturalists in American south, respnses to theory of evolution.

Stephens, **Rhiannon**, *Columbia (Hist.)*. New York, NY. Email: rs3169@columbia.edu. Research: motherhood in precolonial Uganda, changing concepts of poverty in East Africa.

Stephens, **Robert P.**, *Virginia Tech*. Blacksburg, VA. Email: rosteph2@vt.edu. Research: film and addiction, drug use and misuse.

Stephens, **Ronald Jemal**. West Lafayette, MI. Affil: Purdue. Email: stephe87@purdue.edu.

Stephenson, **Donald S.**, *US Army Command Coll*. Email: donald.s.stephenson.civ@mail.mil.

Stephenson, **John Tyler**. Memphis, TN. Affil: Southwest Tennessee Comm. Coll. Email: jtstephenso1@southwest.tn.edu. Research: American political and legal, American military.

Stepp, **Russell A.** Fulshear, TX. Affil: Aristoi Classical Academy. Email: xan_stepp_12@hotmail.com.

Steptoe, **Tyina**, *Arizona*. Email: tsteptoe@email.arizona.edu.

Sterk, **Andrea L.**, *Minnesota (Hist.); American Soc. of Church Hist*. Saint Paul, MN. Email: sterk@umn.edu. Research: mission and conversion 300-1000, bishops.

Sterling, **Erica**. Cambridge, MA. Affil: Harvard. Email: esterling@g.harvard.edu.

Sterling-Harris, A. Katie, *California, Davis*. Email: akharris@ucdavis.edu.

Stern, Alexandra Minna, *Michigan, Ann Arbor*. Email: amstern@umich.edu.

Stern, Jessica R., *California State, Fullerton*. Email: jessicastern@fullerton.edu.

Stern, Karen B., *Brooklyn, CUNY*. Brooklyn, NY. Email: kstern@brooklyn.cuny.edu. Research: material culture, ancient Jewish populations.

Stern, Marc J., *Bentley*. Waltham, MA. Email: mstern@bentley.edu. Research: American fitness industry 1960-2000.

Stern, Peter, *Massachusetts, Amherst*. Email: pstern@library.umass.edu.

Stern, Philip J., *Duke*. Email: ps91@duke.edu.

Stern, Steve J., *Wisconsin-Madison*. Madison, WI. Email: sjstern@wisc.edu. Research: Latin America, social.

Stern, Walter C, *Wisconsin-Madison*. Madison, WI. Email: wcstern@wisc.edu. Research: education, US urban.

Sternberg, Frances Glazer. Leawood, KS. Affil: Kansas. Email: fgsternberg@kc.rr.com. Research: east European Jewry, Holocaust studies.

Sternberg, Rachel, *Case Western Reserve*. Email: rachel.sternberg@case.edu.

Sternberg, Robert, *American International*. Email: robert.sternberg@aic.edu.

Sterne, Evelyn, *Rhode Island*. Email: sterne@uri.edu.

Sternfeld, Lior Betzalel, *Penn State*. University Park, PA. Email: lbs18@psu.edu. Research: modern Iran, modern Middle East.

Sterphone, Joseph, III. Goleta, CA. Affil: California, Santa Barbara. Email: jsterphone@gmail.com.

Sterr, Glen R. Kent, WA. Affil: Northwest Sch. Email: grsterr@hotmail.com.

Stertzer, Jennifer. Charlottesville, VA. Affil: Virginia. Email: jes7z@virginia.edu.

Steuer, Susan M. B., *Western Michigan*. Email: susan.steuer@wmich.edu.

Stevens, Carol B., *Colgate*. Email: kstevens@colgate.edu.

Stevens, Donald Fithian, *Drexel*. Philadelphia, PA. Email: stevens@drexel.edu. Research: cholera epidemics, marriage.

Stevens, Jennifer A., *Boise State*. Boise, ID. Affil: Stevens Hist. Research Assoc. Email: jenniferstevens@shraboise.com. Research: US environmental/urban, modern US women.

Stevens, Jennifer L., *Roger Williams*. Email: jstevens@rwu.edu.

Stevens, Kenneth R., *Texas Christian*. Email: k.stevens@tcu.edu.

Stevens, Kevin M., *Nevada, Reno*. Email: kstevens@unr.edu.

Stevens, L. Tomlin, *St. Mary's, Md*. Solomons, MD. Email: ltstevens@smcm.edu. Research: colonial America, 18th-/19th-c America.

Stevens, Rosemary A. New York, NY. Affil: Weill Cornell Medical. Email: ras2023@med.cornell.edu. Research: post-WWI US veterans services, mental health policy.

Stevens, Simon M. Sheffield, United Kingdom. Affil: Sheffield. Email: simon.stevens@sheffield.ac.uk. Research: global anti-apartheid movement, boycotts and sanctions.

Stevens, Thomas. Philadelphia, PA. Affil: Pennsylvania. Email: tstevens@sas.upenn.edu.

Stevens, Wesley M., *Winnipeg*.

Stevenson, Brenda E., *UCLA*. Email: stevenso@history.ucla.edu.

Stevenson, Kaylan M., *Omohundro Inst*. Email: kmstevenson@wm.edu.

Stevenson, Louise L., *Franklin & Marshall*. Email: louise.stevenson@fandm.edu.

Stevenson, Walter N., *Richmond*. Email: wstevens@richmond.edu.

Stever, Sarah N., *Detroit Mercy*. Email: steversn@udmercy.edu.

Steward, Journey Lynne, *Elmhurst*. Email: journey.steward@elmhurst.edu.

Steward, Tyran Kai, *Carleton Coll*. Email: tsteward@carleton.edu.

Stewart, Bruce E., *Appalachian State*. Email: stewartbe1@appstate.edu.

Stewart, Catherine Aileen, *Cornell Coll*. Iowa City, IA. Email: cstewart@cornellcollege.edu. Research: Federal Writers' ex-slave project, African American writers and psychology.

Stewart, Cynthia L. Churchville, NY. Affil: SUNY, Coll. Brockport. Email: cyndiestewart1961@gmail.com.

Stewart, David J., *East Carolina*. Email: stewartda@ecu.edu.

Stewart, Dorshell, *Ball State*. Email: dmstewart@bsu.edu.

Stewart, Geoffrey Charles, *Western Ontario*. Email: gstewa4@uwo.ca.

Stewart, George L. Elyria, OH. Affil: Cleveland State. Email: Loganchase@hotmail.com.

Stewart, H. David, *Hillsdale*. Email: hstewart@hillsdale.edu.

Stewart, James B., *Macalester*. Email: stewart@macalester.edu.

Stewart, Jeffrey, *California, Santa Barbara; MIT*. Email: jstewart@blackstudies.ucsb.edu.

Stewart, John Fraser, II. Stevenson, United Kingdom. Affil: Strathclyde. Email: fraserjoh@googlemail.com.

Stewart, Kenneth J., *Covenant*. Email: kstewart@covenant.edu.

Stewart, Larry, *Saskatchewan*. Email: stewartl@sask.usask.ca.

Stewart, Mart A., *Western Washington*. Bellingham, WA. Email: Mart.Stewart@wwu.edu. Research: climate, enviromental, US South.

Stewart, Matthew Dougall. Caldwell, ID. Affil: Syracuse. Email: mstewart@syr.edu.

Stewart, Pamela J. Phoenix, AZ. Affil: Arizona State. Email: pamela.stewart@asu.edu. Research: women-headed households, women and athletics 1865-present.

Stewart, Peter C., *Old Dominion*. Email: pstewart@odu.edu.

Stewart, Selina, *Alberta*. Email: selinas@ualberta.ca.

Stewart, Sierra Mackenzie. Broomfield, CO. Affil: Colorado, Boulder. Email: sierrastewart@msn.com. Research: cultural, modern America.

Stewart-Winter, Timothy David, *Rutgers, Newark/New Jersey Inst. of Tech*. New York, NY. Email: timsw@rutgers.edu.

Stieber, Joachim W., *Smith*. Email: jstieber@smith.edu.

Stiefbold, Angela Shope. Chapel Hill, NC. Affil: Cincinnati. Email: stiefbas@mail.uc.edu. Research: suburbanization/rural character, planning/zoning/environment.

Stiefel, Catherine J. Jacksonville, FL. Affil: Florida. Email: cstiefel@ufl.edu.

Stierman, John, *Western Illinois*. Email: JP-Stierman@wiu.edu.

Stiles, Lewis, *Saskatchewan*. Email: stilesl@shaw.ca.

Stiles, T. J. Berkeley, CA. Email: tjstiles@earthlink.net. Research: George Armstrong Custer.

Stillman, James R. San Anselmo, CA. Affil: International Postal Artifacts Trust. Email: jstillman@seepost.net. Research: reduction of Ottoman influence in Balkans, Proto-Albania.

Stilwell, Sean, *Vermont*. Email: sean.stilwell@uvm.edu.

Stine, Jordan Hunter. Stillwater, OK. Email: jordan.stine@okstate.edu.

Stinger, Charles L., *SUNY, Buffalo*. Email: stinger@buffalo.edu.

Stinson, Jennifer K., *Saginaw Valley State*. Email: jstinson@svsu.edu.

Stisher, Bryan Franklin. Roswell, GA. Affil: Arizona State. Email: Stishbf@auburn.edu.

Stites, Francis N., *San Diego State*.

Stith, Matthew M., *Texas, Tyler*. Email: mstith@uttyler.edu.

Stock, Catherine McNicol, *Connecticut Coll*. Email: cmsto@conncoll.edu.

Stockdale, Melissa K., *Oklahoma (Hist.)*. Norman, OK. Email: mstockdale@ou.edu. Research: Russia and Soviet Union.

Stockdale, Nancy L., *North Texas*. Email: stockdale@unt.edu.

Stockford, Camron. Tuscaloosa, AL. Affil: Alabama, Tuscaloosa. Email: camron.stockford@gmail.com.

Stocking, Rachel L., *Southern Illinois, Carbondale*. Email: stocking@siu.edu.

Stock-Morton, Phyllis, *Seton Hall*. New York, NY. Research: biography, women.

Stockreiter, Elke E., *American*. Email: estockre@american.edu.

Stockton, Robert P., *Charleston*. Email: stocktonr@cofc.edu.

Stoddart, Jess, *San Diego State*.

Stoff, Laurie. Tempe, AZ. Affil: Arizona State. Email: Laurie.Stoff@asu.edu. Research: gender in Russia during WWI, gender in Russia during revolution.

Stoff, Michael B., *Texas, Austin*. Email: planiidirector@austin.utexas.edu.

Stofferahn, Steven A., *Indiana State*. Email: Steven.Stofferahn@indstate.edu.

Stohler, Jason. Pasadena, CA. Affil: California, Santa Barbara. Email: stohler@gmail.com.

Stohner, Marisa Hera. Colorado Springs, CO. Affil: Maryland Univ. Coll. Email: m.hera.stohner@gmail.com.

Stoil, Rebecca. Baltimore, MD. Affil: Johns Hopkins. Email: rstoil1@jhu.edu.

Stokes, Brian, *Christopher Newport*. Email: brian.stokes@cnu.edu.

Stokes, Kimberly, *Columbus State*. Email: stokes_kimberly@columbusstate.edu.

Stokes, Laura P., *Stanford*. Email: lpstokes@stanford.edu.

Stokes, Lauren Kelsey, *Northwestern*. Evanston, IL. Email: lauren.stokes@northwestern.edu. Research: migration.

Stolarik, M. Mark. Ottawa, ON, Canada. Affil: Ottawa. Email: stolarik@uottawa.ca. Research: Slovakia and Slovaks, North American immigration.

Stolberg, Katja F. Hannover, Germany. Affil: Leibniz, Hannover. Email: c.stolberg@yahoo.de. Research: African American relations to Africa, 19th-c Christian missions in Africa.

Stoldt, *Timothy Hilliard*. North Brunswick, NJ. Email: stoldt.timothy@gmail.com. Research: American Civil War historiography, genocide and memory.

Stolee, **Margaret K.**, *SUNY, Coll. Geneseo*. Email: stolee@geneseo.edu.

Stoler, **Ann Laura**, *New School*. Email: stolera@newschool.edu.

Stoler, *Mark A.*, *Vermont*. Burlington, VT. Email: mark.stoler@uvm.edu. Research: WWII grand alliance/joint chiefs of staff, Franklin D. Roosevelt's foreign policies.

Stoll, *Mark*, *Texas Tech*. Lubbock, TX. Email: mark.stoll@ttu.edu. Research: religion and ideas about nature, capitalism and environment.

Stoll, **Steven**, *Fordham*. Email: stoll@fordham.edu.

Stolns, *E. J.* Worland, WY. Email: ejs@nowcap.com.

Stolte, *Carolien*. Leiden, Netherlands. Affil: Leiden. Email: c.m.stolte@hum.leidenuniv.nl.

Stoltzfus, *Nathan A.*, *Florida State*. Washington, DC. Email: nstoltzfus@fsu.edu. Research: modern Germany, political violence and resistance.

Stolz, **Daniel**, *Wisconsin-Madison*. Email: dastolz@wisc.edu.

Stolz, **Robert P.**, *Virginia*. Email: rstolz@virginia.edu.

Stolzenberg, **Daniel**, *California, Davis*. Email: dstolz@ucdavis.edu.

Stone, *Bailey S.*, *Houston*. Northampton, MA. Email: bstone@uh.edu. Research: 18th-c French diplomacy, French revolutionary diplomacy 1789-99.

Stone, **Christopher**, *Appalachian State*.

Stone, **Daniel Z.**, *Winnipeg*. Email: stone@uwinnipeg.ca.

Stone, **David R.**, *Naval War Coll*. Email: david.stone@usnwc.edu.

Stone, *Elliot Christopher*. Riverside, CA. Affil: Moreno Valley High Sch. Email: elliotcstone@yahoo.com.

Stone, **Judith F.**, *Western Michigan*. Email: judith.stone@wmich.edu.

Stone, *Madelyn Marie*. Atlanta, GA. Affil: Emory. Email: mmstone@emory.edu.

Stone, *Marla S.*, *Occidental*. Los Angeles, CA. Email: mstone@oxy.edu. Research: modern Italy 1860-present, 20th-c Europe.

Stone, **Peter J.**, *Virginia Commonwealth*. Email: pjstone@vcu.edu.

Stone, **Richard G.**, **Jr.**, *Western Kentucky*. Email: richard.stone@wku.edu.

Stonehouse, **Frederick**, *Northern Michigan*. Email: stonef@charter.net.

Stoneman, *Mark R.*, *German Hist. Inst.* Washington, DC. Email: stoneman@ghi-dc.org; markstoneman@mac.com. Research: modern Germany, war and society.

Stoner, *John C.*, *Pittsburgh*. Pittsburgh, PA. Email: stonerjc@pitt.edu. Research: foreign policy of AFL-CIO in Africa, cultural policy of US in Africa.

Stoner, **K**. **Lynn**, *Arizona State*. Email: lynn.stoner@asu.edu.

Stoner, **Laura E. G.**, *Virginia Museum of Hist.* Email: lstoner@VirginiaHistory.org.

Stoops, *Jamie*. Houston, TX. Affil: Arizona. Email: jkstoops@email.arizona.edu. Research: transnational pornography trade, British prison system.

Storch, **Neil T.**, *Minnesota Duluth*. Email: nstorch@d.umn.edu.

Storch, *Randi J.* Cortland, NY. Affil: SUNY, Coll. Cortland. Email: randi.storch@cortland.edu. Research: capitalism and democracy, ethnicity and religion.

Storey, **John W.**, *Lamar*. Email: storeyjw@my.lamar.edu.

Storey, **Margaret M.**, *DePaul*. Email: mstorey@depaul.edu.

Storey, *William K.* Jackson, MS. Affil: Millsaps. Email: storewk@millsaps.edu. Research: environment/technology/imperialism, Cecil Rhodes.

Storrs, *Landon R.*, *Iowa*. Iowa City, IA. Email: landon-storrs@uiowa.edu. Research: red scare politics, social movements and public policy.

Stortz, **Paul James**, *Calgary*. Email: pjstortz@ucalgary.ca.

Story, *Daniel Jackson*. Bloomington, IN. Affil: Indiana. Email: djstory@indiana.edu. Research: advertising in 19th-c America, spatial.

Story, **Emily F.**, *Salisbury*. Email: efstory@salisbury.edu.

Story, **Ronald**, *Massachusetts, Amherst*. Email: rstory@history.umass.edu.

Stott, **Richard**, *George Washington*. Email: rstott@gwu.edu.

Stout, **Harry S.**, *Yale*. Email: harry.stout@yale.edu.

Stout, **James Edward**, *San Diego Mesa*. Email: jstout@sdccd.edu.

Stout, **Joseph A.**, **Jr.**, *Arizona State*.

Stout, **Leon J.**, *Penn State*. Email: lys2@psu.edu.

Stout, **Mary Ellen**, *San Diego State*.

Stout, **Neil R.**, *Vermont*. Email: neil.stout@uvm.edu.

Stoutamire, **William F.**, *West Georgia*. Email: wstoutam@westga.edu.

Stovall, *Tyler E.*, *National Hist. Center*. Santa Cruz, CA. Affil: California, Santa Cruz. Email: tstovall@ucsc.edu. Research: modern France, African Americans in Europe.

Stover, **Justin Dolan**, *Idaho State*. Email: stovjust@isu.edu.

Stover, *Philip*. Deming, NM. Affil: National Coalition of Independent Scholars. Email: pstover@rrvmo.com. Research: Mexican religion and revolution, Mexican Mormon Colonies.

Stovey, *Patricia Ann*, *Wisconsin-La Crosse*. Holmen, WI. Email: pstovey@uwlax.edu. Research: secondary education, Middle West.

Stow, **George B.**, **Jr.**, *La Salle*. Email: stow@lasalle.edu.

Stow, *Kenneth R.* Leeds, MA. Affil: Haifa. Email: kstow@research.haifa.ac.il. Research: Jews in 16th-c Rome, Middle Ages church and Jews.

Stowe, *Steven M.*, *Indiana*. East Lansing, MI. Email: sstowe@indiana.edu.

Strackbein, *Davidde E.* Greenwich, CT.

Stradling, *David S.*, *Cincinnati*. Cincinnati, OH. Email: david.stradling@uc.edu. Research: US urban, environment.

Strahorn, *Eric A.*, *Florida Gulf Coast*. Fort Myers, FL. Email: estraho@fgcu.edu. Research: Green Revolution, wildlife conservation.

Strain, **Christopher B.**, *Florida Atlantic*. Email: cstrain@fau.edu.

Strain, *Rebekah*, *Esq.* Laie, HI. Affil: Brigham Young, Hawaii. Email: rebekah.strain@byuh.edu.

Strand, **David**, *Dickinson*. Email: strand@dickinson.edu.

Strand, *Karla Jean*. Waukesha, WI. Affil: Wisconsin, Madison. Email: karlajstrand@gmail.com.

Strang, *Cameron B.*, *Nevada, Reno*. Email: cstrang@unr.edu.

Strang, **G**. **Bruce**, *Brandon*. Email: strangb@brandonu.ca.

Stranges, **Anthony N.**, *Texas A&M*. Email: a-stranges@tamu.edu.

Stranges, **John B.**, *Niagara*. Email: jbs@niagara.edu.

Strasburg, **James D.**, *Hillsdale*. Email: jstrasburg@hillsdale.edu.

Strasma, *Mary Grace*, *Eastern Michigan*. Email: mstrasma@emich.edu.

Strasser, *Susan M.*, *Delaware*. Takoma Park, MD. Email: strasser@udel.edu. Research: commerce and culture of medicinal herbs, cultural/environment/business.

Strasser, *Ulrike*, *California, San Diego*. Email: ustrasser@ucsd.edu.

Strassfeld, *Jonathan*. Charlottesville, VA. Affil: Rochester. Email: jstrassf@ur.rochester.edu. Research: American phenomenology.

Strate, **David K.**, *Northern Arizona*.

Strate, **Shane R.**, *Kent State*. Email: sstrate@kent.edu.

Stratford, **Edward P.**, *Brigham Young*. Email: edward_stratford@byu.edu.

Strathman, **Andy**, *California State, San Marcos*. Email: astrathm@csusm.edu.

Stratton, **Clif**, *Washington State, Pullman*. Email: clif.stratton@wsu.edu.

Stratton, **David H.**, *Washington State, Pullman*. Email: dstratton@wsu.edu.

Straub, *Alexandra*. Philadelphia, PA. Affil: Temple. Email: tue70313@temple.edu.

Straub, *Eleanor F.* Metairie, LA. Email: estraub@aol.com.

Straumann, *Benjamin*. New York, NY. Affil: NYU. Email: bs1115@nyu.edu. Research: European intellectual, reception of Roman law/Roman ethics.

Straus, **Ryane McAuliffe**, *St. Rose*. Email: strausr@mail.strose.edu.

Strauss, **Amanda Elizabeth**, *Arthur and Elizabeth Schlesinger Library*. Email: amanda_strauss@radcliffe.harvard.edu.

Strauss, **Barry S.**, *Cornell*. Email: bss4@cornell.edu.

Strauss, **Charles Thomas**, *Mount St. Mary's; American Catholic Hist. Assoc.* Emmitsburg, MD. Email: strauss@msmary.edu. Research: US religion and politics in global Cold War, human rights and globalization.

Strauss, **Elizabeth**, *Mount St. Mary's*. Email: estrauss@msmary.edu.

Strauss, *Lauren B.* Chevy Chase, MD. Affil: American. Email: strauss@american.edu. Research: leftwing Jewish artists in 1920s-30s NY, 20th-c American Jewish women.

Strauss, **Paul**, *California State, Stanislaus*. Email: pstrauss@csustan.edu.

Straussberger, **John Fredrick**, **III**, *Florida Gulf Coast*. Email: jstraussberger@fgcu.edu.

Straw, *Carole E.*, *Mount Holyoke*. South Hadley, MA. Email: cstraw@mtholyoke.edu. Research: martyrdom death, Christian and classical culture.

Straw, **Richard Alan**, *Radford*. Email: rstraw@radford.edu.

Strayer, Brian E., *Andrews*. Email: bstrayer@andrews.edu.

Strayer, Robert, *SUNY, Coll. Brockport*. Email: rstrayer@brockport.edu.

Streater, Kristen. Richardson, TX. Affil: Collin. Email: kstreater@collin.edu. Research: Kentucky women and Civil War, women's 19th-c politics.

Strecker, Damien. Cincinnati, OH. Affil: Fordham. Email: dstrecker1@fordham.edu.

Streeter, Stephen M., *McMaster*. Email: streete@mcmaster.ca.

Streets-Salter, Heather E., *Northeastern*. Ipswich, MA. Email: h.streetssalter@neu.edu. Research: Southeast Asian empires, world.

Strelau, Renate. Reseda, CA. Email: strelau@renatestrelau.com.

Stremlau, Rose, *Davidson*.

Stretton, Tim, *Dalhousie; St. Mary's, Can.* Email: tim.stretton@smu.ca.

Streusand, Douglas E. Fredericksburg, VA. Affil: Marine Corps Command & Staff Coll. Email: desphd@aol.com. Research: Ottoman/Safavi/Mughal empires, politics in Islamic societies.

Strick, James E., *Franklin & Marshall*. Email: james.strick@fandm.edu.

Stricker, Frank, *California State, Dominguez Hills*. Email: fstricker@csudh.edu.

Strickland, Jeanna. Concord, NC. Affil: Kannapolis City Sch./Sam Houston State. Email: jeanna0815@gmail.com.

Strickland, Jeff, *Montclair State*. Email: stricklandj@mail.montclair.edu.

Strickland, Peter, *Illinois, Chicago*. Email: pstric2@uic.edu.

Stricklin, David, *Arkansas, Little Rock*.

Strieter, Terry W. Murray, KY. Affil: Murray State. Email: tstrieter@murray-ky.net. Research: French police 1789-1914, art and society 1789-1914.

Strikwerda, Carl. Washington, DC. Email: strikwerdac@etown.edu. Research: WWI origins and impact, globalization.

Striner, Richard, *Washington Coll*. Email: rstriner2@washcoll.edu.

Stringham, Noel, *Wheaton, Ill*. Email: noel.stringham@wheaton.edu.

Strittmatter, David, *Washington and Jefferson*. Email: dstrittmatter@washjeff.edu.

Strobach, Peter. Montreal, QC, Canada. Email: p_strobach@sympatico.ca. Research: use of digital maps, lifelong learning.

Strobel, Margaret A., *Illinois, Chicago*. Ventura, CA. Email: pegs@uic.edu; pegs2013@gmail.com. Research: comparative women, Chicago Women's Liberation Union.

Strobel, Marian E., *Furman*. Greenville, SC. Email: marian.strobel@furman.edu. Research: post-WWII women, recent US social/political.

Strocchia, Sharon T., *Emory*. Atlanta, GA. Email: sstrocc@emory.edu. Research: early modern Italian women, early modern Italian medicine.

Stroinski, Anna. Wood Ridge, NJ. Affil: Boston Univ. Email: annastro@bu.edu.

Strom, Janet E. South Hackensack, NJ. Affil: Bergen County Div. of Cultural & Historic Affairs. Email: jjeess213@gmail.com. Research: Bergen County historic sites, pre-1900 science in NJ.

Strom, Jonathan, *Emory*. Email: jstrom@emory.edu.

Strom, Yale, *San Diego State*.

Stromquist, H. Shelton, *Iowa*. Email: shelton-stromquist@uiowa.edu.

Strong, Anise K., *Western Michigan*. Email: anise.strong@wmich.edu.

Strong, Anthony. Boston, MA. Email: anthony.strong001@umb.edu.

Strong, Doug, *San Diego State*.

Strong, George V., *William and Mary*. Email: gvstro@wm.edu.

Strong, Michele Marion, *South Alabama*. Email: mstrong@southalabama.edu.

Strongin, William, *SUNY, New Paltz*. Email: strongis@newpaltz.edu.

Stross, Wendy Anne. Guelph, ON, Canada. Email: eestross@rogers.com. Research: death in 18th-c London, obituaries in 18th-c London.

Strote, Noah Benezra, *North Carolina State*. Email: nbstrote@ncsu.edu.

Stroud, Ellen, *Penn State*. Email: estroud@psu.edu.

Stroud, Irene Elizabeth. Lawrenceville, NJ. Affil: Princeton. Email: istroud@princeton.edu. Research: Progressive-era Protestantism, eugenics.

Stroup, Alice, *Bard*. Email: stroup@bard.edu.

Stroup, James Nicholas. Irvine, CA. Affil: California, Riverside. Email: jnstroup@gmail.com. Research: transportation and urban planning, technology.

Stroup, John. Houston, TX. Affil: Rice. Email: stroup@rice.edu.

Strub, Whitney, *Rutgers, Newark/New Jersey Inst. of Tech*. Email: wstrub@rutgers.edu.

Struever, Nancy, *Johns Hopkins (Hist.)*. Email: n.struever@jhu.edu.

Strum, Harvey Joel. Albany, NY. Affil: Sage. Email: strumh@hotmail.com. Research: Canadian aid to Ireland 1847/63/80, American aid to Ireland 1847/63/80.

Strupek, Joe. Bloomington, IL. Affil: Norwich. Email: jstrupek@comcast.net.

Struve, Lynn A., *Indiana*. Bloomington, IN. Email: struve@indiana.edu. Research: consciousness, dreams and memory in culture.

Stryker, Julia Connell. Austin, TX. Affil: Texas, Austin. Email: julia.stryker@utexas.edu.

Stryker, Susan. San Francisco, CA. Affil: Arizona. Email: susanstryker@email.arizona.edu. Research: philosophy of embodiment and technology, transgender studies.

Strykowski, Derek Robert. Buffalo, NY. Affil: SUNY, Buffalo. Email: dstrykowski@gmail.com. Research: music composition, music publishing.

Stuard, Susan M. Haverford, PA. Affil: Haverford. Email: sstuard@haverford.edu.

Stuart, Joseph. Sandy, UT. Affil: Utah. Email: joseph.stuart@utah.edu.

Stuart, Kathy, *California, Davis*. Email: kestuart@ucdavis.edu.

Stuart, Kimberly A. New Gloucester, ME. Affil: Southern New Hampshire. Email: kimberlystuart4@outlook.com.

Stubbs, John D., *Simon Fraser*. Email: jstubbs@sfu.ca.

Stubenrauch, Joseph, *Baylor*. Email: joseph_stubenrauch@baylor.edu.

Stuckey, Jacalynn. Canton, OH. Affil: Malone. Email: jstuckey@malone.edu.

Stuckey, Jace A. Arlington, VA. Affil: Marymount. Email: jstuckey@marymount.edu. Research: Crusades, Charlemagne.

Stuckey, Melissa Nicole. Elizabeth City, NC. Affil: Elizabeth City State. Email: melissa.stuckey@gmail.com. Research: African American migration to Oklahoma, blacks and Progressive era.

Studnicki-Gizbert, Daviken F., *McGill*. Email: daviken.studnicki@mcgill.ca.

Stuewer, Roger H., *Minnesota (Hist. of Science)*. Email: rstuewer@physics.umn.edu.

Stuhler, Mary Theresa. New Braunfels, TX. Affil: American Military. Email: marystuhler@verizon.net.

Stump, Daniel H., *Illinois State*. Email: dhstump@ilstu.edu.

Stunden Bower, Shannon Stunden, *Alberta*. Email: stundenbower@ualberta.ca.

Stur, Heather Marie, *Southern Mississippi*. Email: heather.stur@usm.edu.

Sturc, John H. Washington, DC. Affil: George Washington Law Sch. Email: jhsturc@gmail.com.

Sturchio, Jeffrey L. Alexandria, VA. Affil: Rabin Martin. Email: jeffreysturchio@optonline.net. Research: global health and development, pharmaceutical industry.

Sturino, Franc, *York, Can*. Email: fsturino@yorku.ca.

Sturkey, William M., *North Carolina, Chapel Hill*. Chapel Hill, NC. Email: wsturkey@live.unc.edu.

Sturman, Rachel L., *Bowdoin*. Brunswick, ME. Email: rsturman@bowdoin.edu. Research: modern South Asian urban infrastructure/industries, labor/skill/technologies/politics.

Sturtevant, Andrew K., *Wisconsin-Eau Claire*. Email: sturteak@uwec.edu.

Sturtz, Linda L., *Macalester*. Saint Paul, MN. Email: lsturtz@macalester.edu. Research: early North America, Caribbean.

Styles, Eric. Windsor, CT. Affil: Loomis-Chaffee Sch. Email: eric_styles@loomis.org. Research: US collective memory, US publishing.

Su, Alastair. Stanford, CA. Affil: Stanford. Email: asu5512@stanford.edu.

Suarez, Camille A., *Valparaiso*. Philadelphia, PA. Email: camille.suarez@valpo.edu; suarezca@sas.upenn.edu.

Suarez, Tracy. Colorado Springs, CO. Affil: Phoenix. Email: trsuarez54@gmail.com. Research: William de Warren.

Suarez-Potts, William J., *Kenyon; Rice*. Email: suarezpottsw@kenyon.edu; william.suarez-potts@rice.edu.

Subrahmanyam, Sanjay, *UCLA*. Email: subrahma@history.ucla.edu.

Suchma, Philip Charles, *Lehman, CUNY*. Email: philip.suchma@lehman.cuny.edu.

Sudhir, Pillarisetti. Centreville, VA. Email: pillarisetti.sudhir@gmail.com. Research: book, colonialism.

Suescun Pozas, Maria del Carmen, *Brock*. Email: msuescunpozas@brocku.ca.

Sufian, Sandy, *Illinois, Chicago*. Email: sufians@uic.edu.

Suganuma, Unryu. Tokyo, Japan. Affil: Obirin. Email: suganumaphd@yahoo.com. Research: Sino-Japanese historical relations, Chinese historical culture.

Sugarman, Michael. Bristol, United Kingdom. Affil: Bristol. Email: mwsugarman@gmail.com.

Sugiyama, Shigeru. Shizuoka, Japan. Affil: Shizuoka. Email: shsugi@inf.shizuoka.ac.jp. Research: US-Mexican relations in 1930s-40s, US-Mexican-Japanese relations.

Sugrue, **Thomas J.**, *NYU*. New York, NY. Email: tjs7@nyu.edu; thomas.sugrue@gmail.com. Research: late 20th-c US race and politics, real estate in America.

Suh, **Soyoung**, *Dartmouth*. Email: soyoung. suh@dartmouth.edu.

Suhr, **James Leonard**. Glen Allen, VA. Affil: Norwich. Email: jameslsuhr@gmail.com.

Suisman, **David**, *Delaware*. Philadelphia, PA. Email: dsuisman@udel.edu. Research: US popular culture, senses.

Sukenic, **Harvey J.** Brookline, MA. Affil: Hebrew. Email: hsukenic@hebrewcollege. edu. Research: 16th-18th-c Jews in Venetian ghetto.

Suleski, **Ronald**, *Suffolk*. Email: rsuleski@suffolk. edu.

Sullivan, **Brian R.** Rockville, MD. Email: lkfbrs@ aol.com. Research: 20th-c Italian military intelligence, William J. Donovan 1883-1959.

Sullivan, **Charles L.** Los Gatos, CA. Research: wine.

Sullivan, **Charles R.**, *Dallas*. Irving, TX. Email: sullivan@udallas.edu. Research: Scottish Enlightenment literature.

Sullivan, **Elaine**, *California, Santa Cruz*. Email: easulliv@ucsc.edu.

Sullivan, **Emily**, *Hist. Assoc.* Email: esullivan@ historyassociates.com.

Sullivan, **Evan P.** Albany, NY. Affil: SUNY, Albany. Email: esullivan@albany.edu. Research: disability and society, war and society.

Sullivan, **James Edward**. San Francisco, CA. Affil: Dominican, Calif. Email: dmresults2@gmail. com.

Sullivan, **Mark W.**, *Villanova*. Email: mark. sullivan@villanova.edu.

Sullivan, **Michael J.**, *Drexel*. Email: sullivmj@ drexel.edu.

Sullivan, **Patricia A.**, *South Carolina, Columbia*. Email: psulliv@mailbox.sc.edu.

Sullivan, **Renae**. Lewis Center, OH. Affil: Ohio State. Email: sullivan.927@buckeyemail.osu. edu. Research: South Asian women, South Asian diaspora.

Sullivan, **Robert E.**, *Notre Dame*. Email: Sullivan.158@nd.edu.

Sullivan, **Robert J.** Worcester, MA.

Sullivan, **Robert**, *Massachusetts, Amherst*. Email: sullivan@german.umass.edu.

Sullivan, **Stephen Jude**. Cedarhurst, NY. Affil: Lawrence High Sch. Email: sully49@gmail. com. Research: urban/Brooklyn, ethnicity/ immigration/Irish America.

Sullivan, **Thomas J.** Conception, MO. Affil: Conception Abbey. Email: thomassull@gmail. com. Research: prosopography of medieval university, medieval Parisian faculty of theology.

Sullivan-Gonzalez, **Douglass C.**, *Mississippi*. University, MS. Email: dsg@olemiss.edu. Research: 19th-/20th-c Guatemala, church/ state/popular religion.

Sumida, **Jon**, *Maryland, Coll. Park*. Email: jtsumida@umd.edu.

Sumlin, **Amalia Lake**. Eureka Springs, AR. Affil: Arkansas. Email: alsumlin@uark.edu.

Summerby-Murray, **Robert**, *Dalhousie*. Email: robsummerbymurray@gmail.com.

Summerhill, **Thomas**, *Michigan State*. Email: summerhi@msu.edu.

Summerhill, **William, III**, *UCLA*. Email: wrs@ history.ucla.edu.

Summers, **Carol**, *Richmond*. Email: lsummers@ richmond.edu.

Summers, **Gregory S.**, *Wisconsin-Stevens Point*. Email: gsummers@uwsp.edu.

Summers, **Mark W.**, *Kentucky*. Email: msumm2@ uky.edu.

Summers, **Martin**, *Boston Coll.* Email: summermb@bc.edu.

Summers, **Samantha**. Burlington, ON, Canada. Affil: Toronto. Email: samantha.summers@ mail.utoronto.ca.

Summers, **Samuel Aubrey**. Vancouver, WA. Affil: Clark. Email: ssumme12@gmail.com.

Summers, **Suzanne L.**, *Austin Comm. Coll.* Email: smcfadde@austincc.edu.

Summers Sandoval, **Tomas F., Jr.**, *Pomona*. Email: tfss@pomona.edu.

Summey, **Virginia L.** Greensboro, NC. Affil: North Carolina, Greensboro. Email: virginia. summey@gmail.com.

Sumner, **Gregory D.**, *Detroit Mercy*. Email: sumnergd@udmercy.edu.

Sumner, **Jaclyn Ann**, *Presbyterian*. Clinton, SC. Email: jasumner@presby.edu. Research: politics and governance in Mexico, Tlaxcala Mexico.

Sumner, **Margaret**, *Ohio State*. Email: sumner.27@osu.edu.

Sumner, **Raymond Vincent**. Timnath, CO. Affil: Colorado State, Fort Collins. Email: vinnie1990@mac.com.

Sumpter, **Amy**, *Georgia Coll. and State*. Email: amy.sumpter@gcsu.edu.

Sun, **E-tu Zen**, *Penn State*.

Sun, **Laichen**, *California State, Fullerton*. Email: ssun@fullerton.edu.

Sun, **Raymond C.**, *Washington State, Pullman*. Email: sunray@wsu.edu.

Sun, **Simon H.** Cambridge, MA. Affil: Harvard. Email: hongzhesun@g.harvard.edu.

Sun, **Xiaoping**, *St. Mary's, Can.* Email: xiaoping. sun@smu.ca.

Sun, **Yi**, *San Diego*. San Diego, CA. Email: ysun@ sandiego.edu. Research: Chinese women social, Chinese foreign policy.

Sundberg, **Adam**, *Creighton*. Email: adamsundberg@creighton.edu.

Sundberg, **Christine**, *Colorado Denver*. Email: christine.sundberg@ucdenver.edu.

Sundberg, **Eric J.** Jericho, NY. Affil: Jericho Union Free Sch. District. Email: esundberg@ jerichoschools.org.

Sundberg, **Sara B.**, *Central Missouri*. Warrensburg, MO. Email: ssundberg@ucmo. edu. Research: women and property under civil law.

Sunderland, **Willard**, *Cincinnati*. Cincinnati, OH. Email: willard.sunderland@uc.edu. Research: Russian imperialism 1700-1920s, technology.

Sundiata, **Ibrahim K.**, *Brandeis*. Email: sundiata@brandeis.edu.

Sundstrom, **Austin James**. Riverside, IL. Affil: Loyola, Chicago. Email: austin.sundstrom@ yahoo.com.

Sundwick, **Karen S.**, *Southern Oregon*.

Sunseri, **Thaddeus**, *Colorado State*. Email: thaddeus.sunseri@colostate.edu.

Sunshine, **Glenn S.**, *Central Connecticut State*. Email: sunshineg@ccsu.edu.

Sunwall, **Christina**, *Minot State*. Email: christina. sunwall@minotstateu.edu.

Suny, **Ronald Grigor**, *Chicago; Michigan, Ann Arbor*. Ann Arbor, MI. Email: rgsuny@uchicago. edu; rgsuny@umich.edu. Research: Stalin and making of USSR, empires and nations.

Super, **John C.**, *West Virginia*. Email: John. Super@mail.wvu.edu.

Super, **Joseph F.**, *West Virginia*. Fairchance, PA. Email: joseph.super@mail.wvu.edu; jsuper@ liberty.edu. Research: Social Gospel, liberation theology.

Super, **Richard R.**, *Creighton*. Email: super@ creighton.edu.

Suppe, **Frederick C.**, *Ball State*. Muncie, IN. Email: fsuppe@bsu.edu. Research: Celtic, medieval British castle guard.

Supplee, **Joan E.**, *Baylor*. Email: joan_supplee@ baylor.edu.

Sur, **Dominic**, *Utah State*. Email: dominic.sur@ usu.edu.

Surbrug, **Robert Surbrug, Jr.** Holyoke, MA. Affil: Bay Path. Email: rsurbrug@yahoo.com. Research: US antinuclear movement, US peace activism.

Surh, **Gerald D.**, *North Carolina State*. Email: surh@ncsu.edu.

Suri, **Jeremi**, *Texas, Austin*. Austin, TX. Email: suri@austin.utexas.edu. Research: diplomacy and politics 1958-72, 1960s social protests.

Surkis, **Judith**, *Rutgers*. New Brunswick, NJ. Email: judith.surkis@rutgers.edu. Research: law/religion/gender in French Algeria, post-decolonization family law.

Surman, **Emily**. New Providence, NJ. Affil: American. Email: es1307b@american.edu.

Suskind, **Cornelia Kennedy**. Cambridge, MA. Affil: Harvard. Email: cksuskind@gmail.com.

Susmann, **Natalie**, *MIT*. Email: nsusmann@mit. edu.

Suszko, **Marek**, *Loyola, Chicago*. Email: msuszko@luc.edu.

Sutcliffe, **Adam D.** London, United Kingdom. Affil: King's Coll., London. Email: adam. sutcliffe@kcl.ac.uk. Research: early modern European intellectual, Jews and Judaism.

Sutcliffe, **John William, IV.** APO, AE. Affil: Leeds. Email: hyjwsi@leeds.ac.uk.

Sutcliffe, **Patricia**, *German Hist. Inst.* Email: sutcliffe@ghi-dc.org.

Sutherland, **Bobbi Sue**, *Dayton*. Email: bsutherland1@udayton.edu.

Sutherland, **Daniel E.**, *Arkansas, Fayetteville*. Email: dsutherl@uark.edu.

Sutherland, **David**, *Dalhousie*. Email: david. sutherland@dal.ca.

Sutherland, **Donald M. G.**, *Maryland, Coll. Park*. Email: dsutherl@umd.edu.

Sutherland, **Jaclyn Louise**. Arlington, VA. Affil: American. Email: jackiesutherland@nnu.edu. Research: Mary Chesnut, American Civil War.

Sutherland, **Samuel**, *Stephen F. Austin State*. Email: sutherlas@sfasu.edu.

Sutherland, **Suzanne**, *Middle Tennessee State*. Email: suzanne.sutherland@mtsu.edu.

Sutrisno, **Arieanto**. Secaucus, NJ. Email: asutrisn@gmail.com.

Sutt, **Cameron M.**, *Austin Peay State*. Email: suttc@apsu.edu.

Suttell, **Brian William**. Radford, VA. Affil: North Carolina, Greensboro. Email: bsutt34@yahoo. com.

Sutter, **Brenann E.** New Brunswick, NJ. Affil: Rutgers. Email: brenannsutter@gmail.com. Research: gender, pornography.

Sutter, *Paul S.*, *Colorado, Boulder*. Boulder, CO. Email: paul.sutter@colorado.edu. Research: environmental, public health.

Sutterlin, *Siegfried H.* Ottumwa, IA. Email: shsutterlin@yahoo.com. Research: post-WWI Munich revolution, Die Wende.

Sutton, *Angela*. Nashville, TN. Affil: Vanderbilt. Email: angela.c.sutton@vanderbilt.edu. Research: piracy, Atlantic slave trade.

Sutton, *Donald S.*, *Carnegie Mellon*. Email: ds27@andrew.cmu.edu.

Sutton, *Matthew Avery*, *Washington State, Pullman*. Pullman, WA. Email: sutton@wsu.edu. Research: evangelicalism, early religious right.

Sutton-Bosley, *Kellianne*. Northfield, VT. Email: ksutton@alu.norwich.edu. Research: smuggling during War of 1812, Vermont in Hartford Convention.

Suttle, *Danael*. Fayetteville, AR. Affil: Arkansas, Fayetteville. Email: dc.suttle@gmail.com.

Suval, *John*. Columbia, MO. Affil: Missouri, Columbia. Email: john.suval@gmail.com.

Suvanasai, *Apasrin*. Alexandria, VA. Email: asuvanasai@yahoo.com.

Suwanto, *Harry Chandra*. Tempe, AZ. Email: hsuwanto@gmail.com. Research: Salem-Sumatra pepper trade.

Suziedelis, *Saulius A.*, *Millersville, Pa.* Email: ssuziedelis@millersville.edu.

Svingen, *Orlan J.*, *Washington State, Pullman*. Pullman, WA. Email: svingen@wsu.edu; osvingen@gmail.com. Research: public, Native American.

Swafford, *Emily L.*, *AHA*. Washington, DC. Email: eswafford@historians.org. Research: military/state/society, gender and foreign relations.

Swagler, *Matthew*, *Williams*. Email: mps7@williams.edu.

Swaim, *Carlyn M.*, *Hist. Assoc.* Email: cswaim@historyassociates.com.

Swain, *Amanda Jeanne*, *California, Irvine*. Email: ajswain@uci.edu.

Swain, *Brian Sidney*, *Kennesaw State*. Email: bswain3@kennesaw.edu.

Swain, *Martha H.*, *Mississippi State*. Email: mes6@ra.msstate.edu.

Swainger, *Jonathan*, *Northern British Columbia*. Email: swainger@unbc.ca.

Swan, *P. Michael*, *Saskatchewan*. Email: swan@sask.usask.ca.

Swaney, *Keith*, *New York State Archives*. Email: keith.swaney@nysed.gov.

Swanger, *Joanna B.*, *Earlham*. Email: swangjo@earlham.edu.

Swanson, *Carl E.*, *East Carolina*. Email: swansonc@ecu.edu.

Swanson, *John C.*, *Tennessee, Chattanooga*. Chattanooga, TN. Email: john-swanson@utc.edu. Research: 20th-c Austria and Hungary, politics and ethnicity.

Swanson, *Michael R.* Danville, VA. Email: wallstreetwindow@gmail.com. Research: Virginia, labor.

Swanson, *Michael*, *Roger Williams*. Email: mswanson@rwu.edu.

Swanson, *Ryan A.* Albuquerque, NM. Affil: New Mexico. Email: swansonr@unm.edu. Research: sports and segregation.

Swanson, *Scott G.*, *Butler*. Email: sswanson@butler.edu.

Swanson, *Wesley*. Stockton, CA. Affil: San Joaquin Delta. Email: wswanson@deltacollege.edu.

Swarts, *James L.* Rochester, NY. Affil: SUNY, Geneseo. Email: jlswarts@frontiernet.net.

Swartsfager, *Scott*. Little Elm, TX. Affil: Collin. Email: sswartsfager@gmail.com.

Swartz, *Marvin*, *Massachusetts, Amherst*. Email: mswartz@history.umass.edu.

Swayamprakash, *Ramya*. East Lansing, MI. Affil: Michigan State. Email: swayampr@msu.edu. Research: borderlands, urban.

Swayze, *Joshua*. Columbia, NJ. Email: joshua.swayze@gmail.com.

Swecker, *Zoe A.*, *Clarion, Pa.* Clarion, PA. Research: Russia, Reformation.

Sweda, *Krystle Farman*. Lexington, KY. Affil: Graduate Center, CUNY. Email: kfarman@gradcenter.cuny.edu. Research: Afro-Mexico/black experience, religion.

Swedberg, *Gregory John*, *Manhattanville*. Email: gregory.swedberg@mville.edu.

Swedin, *Eric G.*, *Weber State*. Email: eswedin@weber.edu.

Swedo, *Elizabeth M.*, *Western Oregon*. Monmouth, OR. Email: swedoe@wou.edu. Research: Icelandic church and society 1300-1550, cultural responses to natural disasters.

Sweeney, *Dan*, *Massachusetts Hist. Soc.* Email: dsweeney@masshist.org.

Sweeney, *Dennis J.*, *Alberta*. Edmonton, AB, Canada. Email: dsweeney@ualberta.ca. Research: German right, racism/imperialism/colonialism.

Sweeney, *James R.*, *Old Dominion*. Email: jsweeney@odu.edu.

Sweeney, *Kevin M.*, *Amherst*. Email: kmsweeney@amherst.edu.

Sweeney, *Lean*. Albuquerque, NM. Affil: New Mexico. Email: leaswee@yahoo.com.

Sweeney, *Mark*. Cave Creek, AZ. Email: flyhalf@cox.net. Research: presidents and press, Cold War.

Sweeney, *Michael*, *State Hist. Soc. of Missouri*. Email: SweeneyMic@shsmo.org.

Sweeney, *Patrick C.*, *Naval War Coll.* Email: sweeneyp@usnwc.edu.

Sweeney, *Regina M.*, *Dickinson*. Email: sweeneyr@dickinson.edu.

Sweeney, *Shauna J.*, *Toronto*. Email: shauna.sweeney@nyu.edu.

Sweeny, *Robert*, *Memorial, Newfoundland*. Email: rsweeny@mun.ca.

Sweet, *David Graham*, *California, Santa Cruz*. Email: dgsweet@ucsc.edu.

Sweet, *James H.*, *Wisconsin-Madison*. Madison, WI. Email: jhsweet@wisc.edu; jhsweetaha@gmail.com. Research: African diaspora, Brazil.

Sweet, *John W.*, *North Carolina, Chapel Hill*. Email: sweet@unc.edu.

Sweet, *Julie Anne*, *Baylor*. Email: julie_sweet@baylor.edu.

Sweet, *Natalie Heather*, *Lincoln Memorial*. Email: natalie.sweet@lmunet.edu.

Sweets, *John F.*, *Kansas*. Email: exprofjfs@ku.edu.

Sweetser, *Michelle*, *Bowling Green State*.

Sweig, *Julia Ellen*. Takoma Park, MD. Affil: Texas, Austin. Email: juliasweig@yahoo.com.

Sweitz, *Samuel R.*, *Michigan Tech*. Email: srsweitz@mtu.edu.

Swerdlow, *Noel*, *Chicago*. Email: nms@oddjob.uchicago.edu.

Swett, *Pamela E.*, *McMaster*. Email: swettp@mcmaster.ca.

Swierenga, *Robert P.*, *Hope; Kent State*. Email: swierenga@hope.edu.

Swietek, *Francis R.*, *Dallas*. Irving, TX. Email: swietek@udallas.edu. Research: 12th-c monastic, 12th-c literary.

Swift, *Mary G.*, *OSU*, *Loyola, New Orleans*.

Swigger, *Jessica I.*, *Western Carolina*. Email: jswigger@email.wcu.edu.

Swingen, *Abigail L.*, *Texas Tech*. Email: abigail.swingen@ttu.edu.

Swinth, *Kirsten N.*, *Fordham*. Email: swinth@fordham.edu.

Swislocki, *Mark S.*, *NYU*. Email: mark.swislocki@nyu.edu.

Switzer, *Wyatt Peter*. Marlborough, NH. Email: w_switzer@dublinschool.org.

Swope, *Kenneth M., Jr.*, *Southern Mississippi*. Email: kenneth.swope@usm.edu.

Swords, *Molly Elizabeth*. Moscow, ID. Affil: Idaho. Email: mswords@uidaho.edu.

Swyripa, *Frances A.*, *Alberta*. Email: fswyripa@ualberta.ca.

Sydorenko, *Alexander*, *Arkansas State*. Email: asydorenko@astate.edu.

Sylla, *Edith D.*, *North Carolina State*. Email: edith_sylla@ncsu.edu.

Sylvester, *Roshanna P.* Evanston, IL. Affil: DePaul. Email: roshanna.sylvester@gmail.com. Research: girls/science/technology, Cold War.

Sylwester, *H. James*, *Central Missouri*.

Symcox, *Geoffrey W.*, *UCLA*. Email: symcox@history.ucla.edu.

Syme, *Samuel A., Jr.* Myrtle Beach, SC.

Symes, *Carol*, *Illinois, Urbana-Champaign*. Urbana, IL. Email: symes@illinois.edu. Research: premodern media and communication, WWI and medieval past.

Symons, *Van J.*, *Augustana*. Email: vansymons@augustana.edu.

Synakowski, *Robert*. Syracuse, NY. Affil: Syracuse Polish Community. Email: rsynakow@twcny.rr.com.

Synnott, *Marcia G.*, *South Carolina, Columbia*. Columbia, SC. Email: synnott@mailbox.sc.edu. Research: white women as civil rights activists, affirmative action and coeducation.

Synofzick, *Marie*. Iowa City, IA. Affil: Iowa. Email: Marie-synofzick@uiowa.edu.

Synycia, *Natasha Nicole*. Anaheim, CA. Email: natashasynycia@gmail.com. Research: geneology of ideal feminine beauty, post-1945 US and world.

Syrett, *Nicholas L.* Lawrence, KS. Affil: Kansas. Email: nsyrett@gmail.com. Research: child marriage in 19th-c America, 20th-c queer.

Syrrakos, *Barbara*. New York, NY. Affil: City Coll., NY. Email: bsyrrakos@ccny.cuny.edu. Research: West Africa independence, agriculture.

Sysyn, *Frank*, *Alberta*. Email: frank.sysyn@ualberta.ca.

Szabla, *Christopher*. Ithaca, NY. Affil: Cornell. Email: cjs392@cornell.edu.

Szabo, *Franz A.J.*, *Alberta*. Email: franz.szabo@ualberta.ca.

Szabo, *Vicki Ellen*, *Western Carolina*. Email: szabo@email.wcu.edu.

Szafran, *Heather*, *Hist. New Orleans*. Email: heathers@hnoc.org.

Szafranski, *Tanya*. Norman, OK. Affil: Oklahoma. Email: persephone@ou.edu. Research: Greek identity in Roman Empire.

Szaluta, *Jacques*. Westbury, NY. Affil: US Merchant Marine Acad. Email: szalutajs@aol.com.

Szapor, **Judith**, *McGill*. Email: judith.szapor@mcgill.ca.

Szczepaniak, *Tracy R*. San Antonio, TX. Email: lady_pilot@hotmail.com. Research: US foreign policy in Middle East, security studies.

Szechi, **Daniel**, *Auburn*. Email: daniel.szechi@manchester.ac.uk.

Szewczyk, *Frank Jacob*. Lisle, IL. Email: frankjacob@live.com.

Szok, **Peter Andrew**, *Texas Christian*. Email: p.szok@tcu.edu.

Szonyi, **Michael**, *Harvard (Hist.)*. Email: szonyi@fas.harvard.edu.

Szporluk, **Roman**, *Harvard (Hist.)*. Email: szporluk@fas.harvard.edu.

Szuchman, **Mark D**., *Florida International*. Email: mark.szuchman@gmail.com.

Szylvian, *Kristin M*., *St. John's, NY*. Jamaica, NY. Email: szylviak@stjohns.edu. Research: US housing policy.

Szymanski, **Mallory**, *Alfred*. Email: szymanski@alfred.edu.

Szymczak, **Robert B**., *Penn State*. Email: rxs16@psu.edu.

T t

Taaffe, **Stephen R**., *Stephen F. Austin State*. Email: staaffe@sfasu.edu.

Taber, *Robert D*. Fayetteville, NC. Affil: Fayetteville State. Email: robtaber@gmail.com. Research: colonial Saint-Domingue, property in early Americas.

Tabili, *Laura E*., *Arizona*. Tucson, AZ. Email: tabili@u.arizona.edu. Research: Britain, modern Europe.

Tabor, *Alex*. Athens, OH. Affil: Cincinnati. Email: taboralexd@gmail.com.

Tabor, *Nathan L. M*., *Western Michigan*. Kalamazoo, MI. Email: nathan.tabor@wmich.edu. Research: Islamic, Muslim South Asia.

Tabor, **Stephen**, *Huntington Library*. Email: stabor@huntington.org.

Tabri, **Edward A**., *Texas, Tyler*. Email: etabri@uttyler.edu.

Tabuteau, **Emily Z**., *Michigan State*. Email: tabuteau@msu.edu.

Tabyshalieva, **Anara**, *Marshall*. Email: tabyshalieva@marshall.edu.

Tachau, **Katherine H**., *Iowa*. Email: katherine-tachau@uiowa.edu.

Tackett, *Nicolas O*., *California, Berkeley*. Berkeley, CA. Email: tackett@berkeley.edu. Research: China.

Tackett, **Timothy N**., *California, Irvine*. Irvine, CA. Email: ttackett@uci.edu. Research: French Revolution/origins/violence, Old Regime/religious culture.

Taddeo, **Julie Anne**, *Maryland, Coll. Park*. Email: taddeo@umd.edu.

Taffet, *Jeffrey F*. Kings Point, NY. Affil: US Merchant Marine Academy. Email: taffetj@usmma.edu. Research: US and Chile in 1960s, foreign aid and natural resources.

Taft, *Alexander E*. Austin, TX. Affil: Texas, Austin. Email: ataft@utexas.edu.

Tagliacozzo, *Eric*, *Cornell*. Email: et54@cornell.edu.

Tague, *Ingrid H*., *Denver*. Denver, CO. Email: itague@du.edu. Research: early modern Europe, Great Britain.

Tague, *Joanna Teresa*, *Denison*. Email: taguej@denison.edu.

Tai, *Emily Sohmer*. Long Island City, NY. Affil: Queensborough Comm. Coll., CUNY. Email: etai@qcc.cuny.edu. Research: medieval piracy, medieval Mediterranean.

Tai, **Hue-Tam Ho**, *Harvard (Hist.)*. Email: hhtai@fas.harvard.edu.

Tai, **Jeremy**, *McGill*. Email: jeremy.tai@mcgill.ca.

Taiz, *Lillian K*., *California State, Los Angeles*. Email: ltaiz@calstatela.edu.

Takacs, *Sarolta A*. Staten Island, NY. Affil: Staten Island, CUNY. Email: sarolta.takacs@csi.cuny.edu. Research: Rome and Byzantium, digital humanities.

Takagaki, **Cary**, *Western Ontario*. Email: ctakagak@uwo.ca.

Takagi, **Midori**, *Western Washington*. Email: midori.takagi@wwu.edu.

Takai, **Yukari**, *Windsor*. Email: ytakai@uwindsor.ca.

Takats, **Sean P**., *George Mason*. Email: stakats@gmu.edu.

Takeda, **Junko**, *Syracuse*. Email: jtakeda@maxwell.syr.edu.

Takenaka, *Akiko*, *Kentucky*. Lexington, KY. Email: a.takenaka@uky.edu. Research: Japanese war responsibility/reconciliation, cultural heritage.

Takeuchi, *Michiko*, *California State, Long Beach*. Long Beach, CA. Email: michiko.takeuchi@csulb.edu. Research: women and feminism(s) in Northeast Asia, sexuality.

Takla, *Nefertiti*, *Manhattan*. Email: ntakla01@manhattan.edu.

Takougang, **Joseph**, *Cincinnati*. Email: joseph.takougang@uc.edu.

Takriti, **Abdel Razzaq**, *Houston*.

Tal, *Yuval*. Baltimore, MD. Affil: Johns Hopkins. Email: ytal2@jhu.edu.

Talamante, **Laura R. E**., *California State, Dominguez Hills*. Email: ltalamante@csudh.edu.

Talbert, **Bart R**., *Salisbury*. Email: brtalbert@salisbury.edu.

Talbert, **Richard J. A**., *North Carolina, Chapel Hill*. Email: talbert@email.unc.edu.

Talbert, **Robert M**., *Virginia Commonwealth*. Email: rtalbert@vcu.edu.

Talbert, **Roy**, **Jr**., *Coastal Carolina*. Email: talbert@coastal.edu.

Talbot, *Christine*. Greeley, CO. Affil: Northern Colorado. Email: christine.talbot@unco.edu. Research: 19th-c US Mormon, feminist theory/gender/citizenship.

Talbot, *Cynthia*, *Texas, Austin*. Austin, TX. Email: ctalbot@austin.utexas.edu. Research: historical traditions of pre-1800 India, early modern courtly culture.

Talbott, **John E**., *California, Santa Barbara*. Email: talbott@history.ucsb.edu.

Talbott, **Robert D**., *Northern Iowa*.

Talkov, *Andrew H*., *Virginia Museum of Hist*. Email: atalkov@VirginiaHistory.org.

Tallackson, *Stephen Ronald*. Ogden Dunes, IN. Affil: Purdue Northwest. Email: stevertallackson1944@gmail.com.

Tallie, **T.J.**, **Jr**., *San Diego*. Email: ttallie@sandiego.edu.

Tallman, **Ronald Duea**, *Roosevelt*. Email: rtallman@roosevelt.edu.

Tallon, *James N*., *Lewis*. Email: tallonja@lewisu.edu.

Tam, *Gina Anne*, *Trinity, Tex*. Email: gtam@trinity.edu.

Tam, *Yue-Him*, *Macalester*. Email: tam@macalester.edu.

Tamaki, *Nobuhiko*. Niiza-shi, Japan. Affil: Kanagawa. Email: tamaki.nobuhiko@gmail.com.

Tamarin, *David*, *SUNY, Coll. Geneseo*. Email: tamarin@geneseo.edu.

Tamayo, *David*. Albany, CA. Affil: California, Berkeley. Email: tamayo.d@gmail.com. Research: American service clubs in Latin America.

Tamboli, *Vikram*. Palos Verdes Estates, CA. Affil: London. Email: vikramtamboli@gmail.com. Research: Guyana/Venezuela/borderlands/rumor, violence/race/spirituality/politics.

Tambor, *Molly*. New York, NY. Affil: Long Island, Post. Email: mrt18@columbia.edu. Research: women/constitutions/citizenship, policing/female officers 20th c Europe.

Tambs, **Lewis**, *Arizona State*.

Tan, *Chun Kiang Isaac Kiang*. New York, NY. Affil: Columbia. Email: ct2810@columbia.edu.

Tan, *Wei Yu Wayne*, *Hope*. Holland, MI. Email: tan@hope.edu. Research: Japan, Disability studies.

Tan, **Ying Jia**, *Wesleyan*. Email: ytan@wesleyan.edu.

Tanaka, *Stefan*. La Jolla, CA. Affil: California, San Diego. Email: stanaka@ucsd.edu. Research: time, Meiji Japan.

Tananbaum, *Duane A*., *Lehman, CUNY*. Bronx, NY. Email: duane.tananbaum@lehman.cuny.edu. Research: Herbert H. Lehman, president-congress relations in foreign affairs.

Tanasi, **Davide**, *South Florida, Tampa*. Email: dtanasi@usf.edu.

Tandy, *Charles*. Ann Arbor, MI. Affil: Center for Interdisciplinary Philosophic Studies. Email: cetandy@gmail.com. Research: philosophy, knowledge evolution/revolution.

Tandy, **David**, *Tennessee, Knoxville*. Email: dtandy@utk.edu.

Tanenhaus, **David S**., *Nevada, Las Vegas*. Email: david.tanenhaus@unlv.edu.

Tang, **Christopher**, *California State, Bakersfield*. Email: ctang3@csub.edu.

Tani, *Karen*. Berkeley, CA. Affil: California, Berkeley. Email: ktani@law.berkeley.edu. Research: US social welfare law and policy.

Tanielian, *Melanie*, *Michigan, Ann Arbor*. Ann Arbor, MI. Email: meltan@umich.edu. Research: WWI as lived and remembered in Beirut, Middle East home front social and cultural.

Taniguchi, **Nancy J**., *California State, Stanislaus*. Email: ntaniguchi@csustan.edu.

Tanis, *Kaitlyn L*. Bear, DE. Affil: Delaware. Email: kltanis@udel.edu.

Tannenbaum, **Rebecca J**., *Yale*. Email: rebecca.tannenbaum@yale.edu.

Tanner, **Harold M**., *North Texas*. Email: htanner@unt.edu.

Tanner, *Heather J*., *Ohio State*. Mansfield, OH. Email: tanner.87@osu.edu. Research: 13th-c northern French countesses, feudalism and inheritance.

Tanner, Kevin, Jr., *Austin Peay State*. Email: tannerk@apsu.edu.

Tannoury-Karam, Sana. New York, NY. Affil: Lebanese American. Email: sanatannoury@gmail.com. Research: Middle East.

Tannous, Jack B., *Princeton*. Email: jtannous@princeton.edu.

Tanny, Jarrod, *North Carolina, Wilmington*. Email: tannyj@uncw.edu.

Tantillo, Astrida Orle. Chicago, IL. Affil: Illinois, Chicago. Email: tantillo@uic.edu. Research: 18th-c science, 18th-c philosophy.

Tanzer, Frances Anne. Brooklyn, NY. Affil: Clark. Email: ftanzer@clarku.edu.

Tao, Bo. New Haven, CT. Affil: Yale. Email: bo.tao@yale.edu.

Tappan, Jennifer N., *Portland State*. Email: jtappan@pdx.edu.

Taranto, Stacie, *Ramapo*. Email: staranto@ramapo.edu.

Taratko, Carolyn D. Nashville, TN. Affil: Vanderbilt. Email: carolyn.taratko@vanderbilt.edu.

Tardif, Elyssa, *Massachusetts Hist. Soc.* Email: etardif@masshist.org.

Tarpley, Van, *San Diego State*.

Tarr, Joel A., *Carnegie Mellon*. Email: jt03@andrew.cmu.edu.

Tartakoff, Paola, *Rutgers*. Email: paola.tartakof@rutgers.edu.

Tarter, Brent. Richmond, VA. Affil: Library of Virginia. Email: brent.tarter@lva.virginia.gov. Research: Virginia, American Revolution.

Tarulevicz, Nicole T. Hobart, Australia. Affil: Tasmania. Email: nicole.tarulevicz@utas.edu.au. Research: food.

Tarver, H. Micheal, *Arkansas Tech*. Email: mtarver@atu.edu.

Tasar, Eren M., *North Carolina, Chapel Hill*. Email: etasar@email.unc.edu.

Taschka, Sylvia, *Wayne State*. Email: sylvia.taschka@wayne.edu.

Tashjian, Victoria B., *St. Norbert*. Email: victoria.tashjian@snc.edu.

Tassin, Kristin Shawn. Metairie, LA. Affil: Episcopal Sch. of Acadiana. Email: kristintassin@hotmail.com. Research: state and society in Nasserist Egypt, governmentality in rural Egypt.

Tassinari, Edward J., *SUNY, Maritime Coll.* Email: etassinari@sunymaritime.edu.

Tatarewicz, Joseph N., *Maryland, Baltimore County*. Woodstock, MD. Email: tatarewicz@umbc.edu. Research: Cold War science and technology, culture of science and technology.

Tate, James B., *Kennesaw State*.

Tate, Michael L., *Nebraska, Omaha*. Email: mtate@unomaha.edu.

Tate, Sarah, *Grand Valley State*. Email: tatesara@gvsu.edu.

Tatlock, Jason Robert, *Georgia Southern*. Email: jtatlock@georgiasouthern.edu.

Tauber, James Franklin. Harrisburg, NC. Email: jtauber@carolina.rr.com.

Tauger, Mark B., *West Virginia*. Morgantown, WV. Email: mtauger@wvu.edu. Research: famine, collectivization.

Tavakoli-Targhi, Mohamad, *Toronto*. Email: m.tavakoli@utoronto.ca.

Taves, Ann, *California, Santa Barbara*. Email: taves@religion.ucsb.edu.

Tavolacci, Laura. Santiago Centro, Chile. Affil: California, Davis. Email: ltavolacci@ucdavis.edu. Research: agricultural 'improvement', transition from early modern to modern.

Tawil, Randa M. New Haven, CT. Affil: Yale. Email: randa.tawil@yale.edu.

Tay, Endrina, *Robert H. Smith Center*. Email: etay@monticello.org.

Taylor, Alan S., *California, Davis; Virginia*. Email: astaylor@ucdavis.edu; ast8f@virginia.edu.

Taylor, Amy Murrell, *Kentucky*. Email: amtaylor1@uky.edu.

Taylor, Anna Lisa, *Massachusetts, Amherst*. Email: annat@history.umass.edu.

Taylor, Camelia. San Marcos, CA. Affil: California State, San Marcos. Email: taylo220@cougars.csusm.edu.

Taylor, Christiane Diehl, *Eastern Kentucky*. Email: chris.taylor@eku.edu.

Taylor, Claire, *Wisconsin-Madison*. Email: claire.taylor@wisc.edu.

Taylor, Clarence W., *Graduate Center, CUNY*. Email: clarence.taylor@baruch.cuny.edu.

Taylor, Darrick N. Kansas City, MO. Email: suntleones@msn.com. Research: early modern public sphere, John Locke's religious beliefs.

Taylor, Durahn A. B., *Pace*. Email: dtaylor@pace.edu.

Taylor, Edgar Curtis, III. Chamberlain, TN. Affil: Johannesburg. Email: edgarjac@umich.edu. Research: urban protest in East Africa, Ugandan Asians.

Taylor, Frank, *Boston Coll.* Email: taylorfa@bc.edu.

Taylor, Gail Marlow. Rancho Santa Margarita, CA. Affil: California, Irvine. Email: gail.marlow.taylor@gmail.com. Research: botany/pharmacy/medicine, science.

Taylor, Gavin J., *Concordia, Can.* Email: Gavin.Taylor@concordia.ca.

Taylor, Graham D., *Trent*. Email: gtaylor@trentu.ca.

Taylor, Gregory S. Murfreesboro, NC. Affil: Chowan. Email: taylog@chowan.edu. Research: International Labor Defense.

Taylor, Jackson, Jr., *Mississippi*. Oxford, MS. Email: happyjack3047@aol.com.

Taylor, Jennifer Whitmer, *Duquesne*. Email: taylorj8@duq.edu.

Taylor, Jessica, *Virginia Tech*. Gainesville, FL. Email: jxtayl@ufl.edu. Research: colonial South, material culture studies.

Taylor, John H., *Carleton, Can.* Email: john.taylor@carleton.ca.

Taylor, Jon E., *Central Missouri*. Email: jtaylor01@ucmo.edu.

Taylor, Joseph E., III, *Simon Fraser*. Email: taylorj@sfu.ca.

Taylor, Karen, *Wooster*. Email: ktaylor@wooster.edu.

Taylor, Kathryn. Philadelphia, PA. Affil: Pennsylvania. Email: kataylor@sas.upenn.edu.

Taylor, Keith W., *Cornell*. Email: kwt3@cornell.edu.

Taylor, Kenneth L., *Oklahoma (Hist. of Science)*. Email: ktaylor@ou.edu.

Taylor, Kerry W., *Citadel*. Email: kerry.taylor@citadel.edu.

Taylor, Larissa Juliet, *Colby*. Email: larissa.taylor@colby.edu.

Taylor, Lynne, *Waterloo*. Email: ltaylor@uwaterloo.ca.

Taylor, Mallory, *Hist. New Orleans*. Email: malloryt@hnoc.org.

Taylor, Martha, *Loyola, Md.* Email: mtaylor@loyola.edu.

Taylor, Matthew D., *Rice*. Email: ptt@rice.edu.

Taylor, Melissa Jane, *US Dept. of State*. Washington, DC. Email: mjt1999@gmail.com. Research: Jewish immigration to US during Holocaust, American diplomats during WWII.

Taylor, Michael H. Kennesaw, GA. Affil: Kennesaw State. Email: mtayl221@kennesaw.edu. Research: James Wilson 1742-1798, presidency of James Madison.

Taylor, Michael. Whispering Pines, NC. Email: mjt67merc@yahoo.com.

Taylor, Nathan. University Of Richmond, VA. Affil: Virginia Baptist Hist. Soc. Email: nathanltaylor365@gmail.com.

Taylor, Nathaniel L. Barrington, RI. Email: ntaylor@post.harvard.edu. Research: historiography of genealogy.

Taylor, Nikki Marie. Washington, DC. Affil: Howard. Email: nikki.taylor@howard.edu. Research: antebellum US, urban.

Taylor, Quintard, Jr., *Washington, Seattle*. Email: qtaylor@uw.edu.

Taylor, Rachel Lanier. Seattle, WA. Affil: Washington, Seattle. Email: rachellt@uw.edu.

Taylor, Raymond, *St. Xavier*. Email: taylor@sxu.edu.

Taylor, Richard S. Springfield, IL. Email: rst2136@comcast.net. Research: Protestantism, social reform/abolitionism.

Taylor, Robert R., *Brock*. Email: rratcliffetaylor@yahoo.com.

Taylor, Romeyn, *Minnesota (Hist.)*. Email: taylo0017@aol.com.

Taylor, Scott K., *Kentucky*. Email: scottktaylor@uky.edu.

Taylor, Terry L. Shoreline, WA. Affil: Shoreline Comm. Coll. Email: ttaylor@shoreline.edu.

Taylor, Thomas F., *Norwich*. Email: ttaylor@norwich.edu.

Taylor, Thomas T., *Wittenberg*. Email: ttaylor@wittenberg.edu.

Taylor, Tom W., *Seattle*. Email: twtaylor@seattleu.edu.

Taylor, William Alan. San Angelo, TX. Affil: Angelo State. Email: william.taylor@angelo.edu. Research: American policy/politics/society, Civil-military relations.

Taylor, William B. Brunswick, ME. Affil: California, Berkeley. Email: wtaylor@berkeley.edu. Research: Mexican spiritual geography, colonial period shrines and pilgrimage.

Taylor-Perry, Maria. Charlotte, NC. Affil: Charlotte Mecklenburg Sch. Email: aperry65@att.net. Research: America's entry into WWI, funeral customs in US South.

Taylor-Poleskey, Molly, *Middle Tennessee State*. Murfreesboro, TN. Email: molly.taylor-poleskey@mtsu.edu. Research: digital, early modern Europe.

Tazzara, Corey S., *Scripps*. Email: ctazzara@scrippscollege.edu.

Tchen, John Kuo Wei, *NYU; Rutgers, Newark/New Jersey Inst. of Tech*. Email: jack.tchen@nyu.edu; jack.tchen@rutgers.edu.

Teaford, Jon C., *Purdue*. Email: teaford@purdue.edu.

Teasdale, Guillaume, *Windsor*. Email: gteasdal@uwindsor.ca.

Teasdale, **Steven**. Toronto, ON, Canada. Affil: Toronto. Email: steven.teasdale@mail. utoronto.ca. Research: Genoa and early modern Mediterranean, medieval and early modern slavery.

Teasley, **Kenneth Chadwick**. Aiea, HI. Affil: US Navy. Email: chad.teasley@yahoo.com. Research: naval, military.

Tebbenhoff, **Edward H.**, *Luther*. Email: tebbened@luther.edu.

Tebeau, **Mark T.**, *Arizona State*. Email: mark. tebeau@asu.edu.

TeBrake, **William H.**, *Maine, Orono*. Okatie, SC. Email: tebrake@maine.edu. Research: hydraulic eng. in late medieval Holland, peasant revolts in 14th-c Europe.

Tedeschi, **John A**. Ferryville, WI. Email: tede@ mwt.net.

Tedesco, **Marie**, *East Tennessee State*. Email: tedescom@etsu.edu.

Teed, **Melissa Ladd**, *Saginaw Valley State*. Email: mteed@svsu.edu.

Teed, **Paul E.**, *Saginaw Valley State*. Email: pteed@svsu.edu.

Teeter, **Timothy M.**, *Georgia Southern*. Email: tmteeter@georgiasouthern.edu.

Teevens, **Joey**. Acton, MA. Affil: Westborough High Sch. Email: teevensj@westboroughk12. org.

Tegeder, **David**, *Florida*. Email: dtegeder@ufl. edu.

Tegegne, **Habtamu M.**, *Rutgers, Newark/New Jersey Inst. of Tech*. Email: habtamu.tegegne@ rutgers.edu.

Teichgraeber, **Richard F.**, *Tulane*. Email: rteich@ tulane.edu.

Teifer, **Hermann**, *Leo Baeck Inst*. Email: hteifer@ lbi.cjh.org.

Teixeira, **Melissa**, *Pennsylvania*.

Tejada, **Cristina**. Charleston, SC. Affil: American. Email: ct2638@american.edu.

Tejani, **James**, *California Polytechnic State*. Email: jtejani@calpoly.edu.

Telesca, **William John**, *Le Moyne*.

Teller, **Adam**, *Brown*. Email: Adam_Teller@ Brown.edu.

Tellez, **Frank R.**, **Sr**. Asheville, NC. Affil: New Mexico. Email: ftellez@unm.edu. Research: Hispanics as tenured/tenure-track profs, critical race theory.

Tellier, **Cassandra L.**, *Capital*. Email: ctellier@ capital.edu.

Telman, **D. A. Jeremy**. Valparaiso, IN. Affil: Valparaiso. Email: jeremy.telman@valpo.edu. Research: legal theory, national security law.

Temin, **Peter**, *MIT*. Email: ptemin@mit.edu.

Temkin, **Moshik**. Cambridge, MA. Affil: Harvard. Email: moshik_temkin@harvard.edu. Research: 20th-c US politics and culture, 20th-c European politics and culture.

Templin, **Thomas E**. Lexington, KY.

Tenbus, **Eric G**. Milledgeville, GA. Affil: Georgia Coll. and State. Email: eric.tenbus@gcsu.edu. Research: 19th-c English Catholicism.

Tenenbaum, **Barbara A**. Washington, DC. Affil: Library of Congress. Email: bten@comcast.net.

Teng, **Emma J.**, *MIT*. Cambridge, MA. Email: eteng@mit.edu. Research: China studies, Asian American.

Tenkotte, **Paul A.**, *Northern Kentucky*. Email: tenkottep@nku.edu.

Tenorio, **Mauricio**, *Chicago*. Email: tenoriom@ uchicago.edu.

Tent, **James F.**, *Alabama, Birmingham*. Email: jtent@uab.edu.

Tentler, **Thomas N.**, *Michigan, Ann Arbor*. Email: ttentler@umich.edu.

Teplitsky, **Joshua**, *SUNY, Stony Brook*. Stony Brook, NY. Email: joshua.teplitsky@ stonybrook.edu. Research: early modern Europe 1500-1750, diaspora studies.

Terazawa, **Yuki**, *Hofstra*. Email: yuki.terazawa@ hofstra.edu.

Terem, **Etty**, *Rhodes*. Email: tereme@rhodes.edu.

Teriba, **Adedoyin**. Brooklyn, NY. Affil: Pratt Inst. Email: ateriba@pratt.edu.

Terpstra, **Martin W**. Chicago, IL. Affil: Plante & Moran, PLLC. Email: martin.terpstra@ plantemoran.com. Research: NAFTA studies, fraud.

Terpstra, **Nicholas**, *Toronto*. Email: nicholas. terpstra@utoronto.ca.

Terraciano, **Kevin**, *UCLA*. Los Angeles, CA. Email: terra@history.ucla.edu. Research: colonial Latin America.

Terrall, **Mary**, *UCLA*. Email: terrall@history.ucla. edu.

Terrazas Williams, **Danielle**, *Oberlin*. Sierra Madre, CA. Email: dterraza@oberlin.edu. Research: African diaspora, women.

Terrell, **Robert S.**, *Syracuse*. Syracuse, NY. Email: rsterrel@maxwell.syr.edu. Research: Germany in world.

Terretta, **Meredith E.**, *Carleton, Can*. Email: meredith.terretta@carleton.ca.

Terrill, **Tom E.**, *South Carolina, Columbia*. Email: terrill@mailbox.sc.edu.

Terry, **Bryan**. Atlanta, GA. Affil: Georgia State. Email: btterry7@gmail.com. Research: postwar global religious dissent, Cold War imperialism.

Terry, **David D.**, *Grand Valley State*. Email: terrydav@gvsu.edu.

Terry, **David Taft**, *Morgan State*. Email: david. terry@morgan.edu.

Terry, **Jennifer Robin**. Fair Oaks, CA. Affil: California, Berkeley. Email: jenterry@ berkeley.edu. Research: children/labor/WWII, nationalism/consumerism.

Terry-Roisin, **Elizabeth Ashcroft**, *Florida International*. Miami, FL. Email: eterryro@fiu. edu. Research: Moriscos/nobility/Spanish Renaissance.

Terzian, **Barbara A.**, *Ohio Wesleyan*. Email: baterzia@owu.edu.

Terzian, **Sevan**, *Florida*. Email: sterzian@coe. ufl.edu.

Tesdahl, **Eugene R. H.**, *Wisconsin-Platteville*. Platteville, WI. Email: tesdahle@uwplatt.edu. Research: smuggling in early New France and New York, French Atlantic world.

Teska, **Wallace Kilpatrick**. Stanford, CA. Affil: Stanford. Email: wteska@stanford.edu.

Teslow, **Tracy L.**, *Cincinnati*. Email: tracy.teslow@ uc.edu.

Testasecca, **Rick**. St. Augustine, FL. Affil: St. Johns Tech. High Sch. Email: rickt100258@ icloud.com.

Teter, **Magda**, *Fordham*. Bronx, NY. Email: mteter@fordham.edu. Research: medieval and early modern Jewish, early modern eastern Europe.

Tetrault, **Lisa M.**, *Carnegie Mellon*. Email: tetrault@andrew.cmu.edu.

Tetzlaff, **Monica Maria**, *Indiana, South Bend*. Email: mtetzlaf@iusb.edu.

Teuscher, **Kevin J**. Santa Rosa, CA. Affil: Sonoma State. Email: kteuscher01@gmail.com.

Tezcan, **Baki**, *California, Davis*. Email: btezcan@ ucdavis.edu.

Thacker, **Molly**. Arlington, VA. Affil: Georgetown. Email: mt1003@georgetown.edu.

Thackeray, **Frank W.**, *Indiana, Southeast*. Email: fthacker@ius.edu.

Thai, **Philip**, *Northeastern*. Email: p.thai@neu. edu.

Thakar, **Milind**, *Indianapolis*. Email: mthakar@ uindy.edu.

Thal, **Sarah**, *Wisconsin-Madison*. Email: thal@ wisc.edu.

Thale, **Christopher P**. Evanston, IL. Affil: Columbia Coll., Chicago. Email: thalechris@ gmail.com.

Thames-Taylor, **LaTonya**, *West Chester*. Email: lthames-taylor@wcupa.edu.

Thane, **James L.**, **Jr**. Scottsdale, AZ. Email: jlthane@hotmail.com.

Thapar, **Romila**. New Delhi, India.

Tharp, **Brent W.**, *Georgia Southern*. Email: btharp@georgiasouthern.edu.

Thatcher, **Mel**, *Utah*. Email: mel_thatcher@ yahoo.com.

Thavenet, **Dennis**, *Central Michigan*. Email: d.thavenet@cmich.edu.

Thayer, **Anne T**. Lancaster, PA. Affil: Lancaster Theological Seminary. Email: athayer@ lancasterseminary.edu. Research: sermons, pastoral care.

Thayer, **John A.**, *Minnesota (Hist.)*. Email: thaye001@umn.edu.

Theibault, **John C**. Voorhees, NJ. Email: jtheibault@comcast.net. Research: digital humanities, early modern Europe.

Theilmann, **John M**. Chesnee, SC. Affil: Converse. Email: john.theilmann@converse. edu. Research: late medieval England, new institutionalism.

Theiss, **Janet Mary**, *Utah*. Email: janet.theiss@ utah.edu.

Theiss, **Raymond W**. Liverpool, NY. Affil: SUNY, Oswego. Email: rtheiss@oswego.edu.

Thelen, **David P.**, *Indiana*.

Thelen, **Elizabeth M**. Berkeley, CA. Affil: California, Berkeley. Email: ethelen@berkeley. edu. Research: pilgrimage towns/Rajasthan.

Thelin, **Alexandra**. Clifton, NJ. Affil: Drew. Email: athelin@drew.edu.

Thelle, **Rannfrid**, *Wichita State*. Email: rannfrid. thelle@wichita.edu.

Thelwell, **Chinua Akimaro**, *William and Mary*. Williamsburg, VA. Email: cathelwell@wm.edu. Research: blackface minstrelsy in South Africa.

Theobald, **Brianna**, *Rochester*.

Theodore, **Philip**, *South Alabama*. Email: ptheodore@southalabama.edu.

Theodorou, **Nicholas**. Haverhill, MA. Affil: Foley Hoag LLP. Email: nct@foleyhoag.com.

Theoharis, **Athan G.**, *Marquette*.

Theriault, **Gaetan**, *Québec, Montréal*. Email: theriault.gaetan@uqam.ca.

Theriault, **Noah**, *Carnegie Mellon*. Email: noaht@andrew.cmu.edu.

Thernstrom, **Stephan**, *Harvard (Hist.)*. Email: thernstr@fas.harvard.edu.

Thiam, **Madina**. Los Angeles, CA. Affil: UCLA. Email: mthiam@ucla.edu.

Thibodeaux, **Jennifer D.**, *Wisconsin-Whitewater*. Email: thibodej@uww.edu.

AHA members in **bold italic**; *Directory*-listed affiliations in *italic*

Thick, Matthew Robert. Flint, MI. Affil: Michigan-Flint. Email: mthick@umflint.edu; matthewrthick@gmail.com. Research: early identity Great Lakes natives.

Thiel, John Robert. Roscommon, MI. Affil: Kirtland Comm. Coll. Email: john.thiel@kirtland.edu. Research: public, Michigan.

Thierer, Joyce M., *Emporia State*. Email: jthierer@emporia.edu.

Thiessen, Janis L., *Winnipeg*. Email: ja.thiessen@uwinnipeg.ca.

Thigpen, Jennifer, *Washington State, Pullman*. Email: jthigpen@wsu.edu.

Thilly, Peter Dewitt, *Mississippi*. Oxford, MS. Email: pdthilly@olemiss.edu; peter.thilly@gmail.com. Research: China/crime/opium/smuggling.

Thinn, Marquett Nasell. Lawrenceville, GA. Affil: Georgia Military. Email: mthinn1@student.gsu.edu. Research: historical materialism, Arabian perspectives.

Thomas, Aaron. Starkville, MS. Affil: Mississippi State. Email: tat233@msstate.edu.

Thomas, Adam James, *Western Carolina*. Columbus, OH. Email: thomasaj@uci.edu.

Thomas, Carol G., *Washington, Seattle*. Email: carolt@uw.edu.

Thomas, Chantz. Seattle, WA. Email: chantzthomas@gmail.com.

Thomas, Charles S., *Georgia Southern; Wake Forest*. Email: cthomas@georgiasouthern.edu; thomascs@wfu.edu.

Thomas, Christine, *California, Santa Barbara*. Email: thomas@religion.ucsb.edu.

Thomas, David C., *Union*. Email: dthomas@uu.edu.

Thomas, David Jason, *South Florida, Tampa*. Email: davidjthomas@usf.edu.

Thomas, David. Seattle, WA. Affil: Temple. Email: dwthomas1782@temple.edu.

Thomas, Denise. Elk Grove, CA. Email: Dthomas.t@comcast.net.

Thomas, Felicia Y., *Morgan State*. Email: felicia.thomas@morgan.edu.

Thomas, Glen R., *Mary Washington*.

Thomas, Hugh M., *Miami*. Miami, FL. Email: h.thomas@miami.edu. Research: secular clergy of England, medieval English ethnic identity.

Thomas, I. Job, *Davidson*. Email: jothomas@davidson.edu.

Thomas, Jack Ray, *Bowling Green State*. Email: tomjack@bgsu.edu.

Thomas, Joan Maria. Torredembarra (Tarragona), Spain. Affil: Rovira-Virgili. Email: joanmaria.thomas@urv.cat. Research: fascism and francoism, Roosevelt era US.

Thomas, John Joseph. Sun City West, AZ. Email: johnthomas1342@gmail.com.

Thomas, Julia Adeney, *Notre Dame*. Chicago, IL. Email: Thomas.165@nd.edu; thomasjna@aol.com. Research: Japan, modern political and intellectual.

Thomas, Kenn, *State Hist. Soc. of Missouri*. Email: thomask@shsmo.org.

Thomas, Lorrin Reed, *Rutgers, Camden*. Camden, NJ. Email: lthomas2@camden.rutgers.edu. Research: Puerto Rican migrants in US, citizenship.

Thomas, Lynn M., *Washington, Seattle*. Email: lynnmt@uw.edu.

Thomas, Mark F., *Virginia*. Email: mt4w@virginia.edu.

Thomas, Patrick Ewan. London, United Kingdom. Affil: House of Commons. Email: patrick.e.thomas@gmail.com.

Thomas, Patrick M., *Evansville*. Email: pt4@evansville.edu.

Thomas, Phillip Drennon, *Wichita State*. Email: phillip.thomas@wichita.edu.

Thomas, Rachel C., *George Fox*. Email: rthomas@georgefox.edu.

Thomas, Sabrina C., *Wabash*.

Thomas, Steven R. Windcrest, TX. Email: srthomas72@yahoo.com.

Thomas, Teresa Fava. Fitchburg, MA. Affil: Fitchburg State. Email: tthomas@fitchburgstate.edu. Research: 20th-c immigration/Italy/Venice, Italy in world wars.

Thomas, Teresa M., *Austin Comm. Coll*. Email: tmthomas@austincc.edu.

Thomas, William G., III, *Nebraska, Lincoln*. Lincoln, NE. Email: wgt@unl.edu. Research: American railroad development, digital scholarship.

Thomason, Michael V., *South Alabama*. Email: jawa1@zebra.net.

Thompkins, Bennel. Los Angeles, CA. Affil: Waverly Sch. Email: bennelthompkins@gmail.com.

Thompsell, Angela, *SUNY, Coll. Brockport*. Brockport, NY. Email: athompse@brockport.edu. Research: peacekeeping/security, exploration/travel.

Thompson, Angela T., *East Carolina*. Email: thompsona@ecu.edu.

Thompson, Antonio Scott, *Austin Peay State*. Email: thompsonas@apsu.edu.

Thompson, Aubrey, *Morgan State*. Email: aubrey.thompson@morgan.edu.

Thompson, Augustine Craig, OP. Oakland, CA. Affil: St. Albert the Great Priory. Email: athompson@dspt.edu. Research: medieval church and Italy, medieval philosophy/theology/lay piety.

Thompson, Bruce A., *California, Santa Cruz*. Santa Cruz, CA. Email: brucet@ucsc.edu. Research: European and Jewish intellectual and cultural, France.

Thompson, C. Michele, *Southern Connecticut State*. Email: thompsonc2@southernct.edu.

Thompson, Catherine L., *Holy Cross*. Email: catherine.thompson@uconn.edu.

Thompson, Christopher S., *Ball State*. Muncie, IN. Email: cthompso@bsu.edu. Research: identities in modern France, immigration/citizenship in modern France.

Thompson, Courtney, *Mississippi State*.

Thompson, Douglas E., *Mercer*. Email: thompson_d@mercer.edu.

Thompson, Drew Anthony, *Bard*.

Thompson, Elizabeth F., *American*. Washington, DC. Email: eft@american.edu. Research: constitutionalism/liberalism/Islam, cinema/public sphere/gender/empire.

Thompson, Emily, *Princeton*. Princeton, NJ. Email: emilyt@princeton.edu. Research: early sound motion pictures, phonograph.

Thompson, Gregory C., *Utah*. Email: gthompson@library.utah.edu.

Thompson, Greig, *State Hist. Soc. of Missouri*. Email: thompsong@shsmo.org.

Thompson, H. Paul, Jr., *North Greenville*. Greenville, SC. Email: pthompson@ngu.edu. Research: postemancipation Atlanta urban reform.

Thompson, Heather Ann, *Michigan, Ann Arbor*. Birmingham, MI. Email: hthompsn@umich.edu. Research: urban, justice and crime.

Thompson, J. Neville, *Western Ontario*. Email: jnthomps@uwo.ca.

Thompson, Janet M. Albuquerque, NM. Email: JThomp3789@aol.com. Research: US labor law, US welfare reform.

Thompson, Jennifer, *California State, Fullerton*. Email: jethompson@fullerton.edu.

Thompson, Jerry Lee, *Lamar*. Email: jlthompson1@my.lamar.edu.

Thompson, John B. New York, NY. Affil: Columbia. Email: jbt2112@columbia.edu. Research: war and China, technology/politics/statecraft.

Thompson, John Herd, *Duke*. Email: jthompso@duke.edu.

Thompson, Joseph, *Mississippi State*.

Thompson, Katrina Dyonne, *St. Louis*. Email: kthomp35@slu.edu.

Thompson, Kelly C., Esq. Romulus, MI. Affil: Wayne County Comm. Coll. Email: kcthompson734@gmail.com. Research: religious beginnings and connections, Renaissance and Reformation.

Thompson, Lauren MacIvor. Marietta, GA. Affil: Georgia State. Email: lmacivor1@gsu.edu. Research: medicine, law.

Thompson, Mack E., *California, Riverside*.

Thompson, Margaret Susan, *Syracuse*. Email: msthomps@maxwell.syr.edu.

Thompson, Mark L. Groningen, Netherlands. Affil: Groningen. Email: m.l.thompson@rug.nl. Research: 17th-c Delaware Valley, colonial surveyors.

Thompson, Maureen Sherrard. Hollywood, FL. Affil: Florida International. Email: mthom232@fiu.edu.

Thompson, Melissa Marie. Lubbock, TX. Email: melissa.m.thompson@ttu.edu.

Thompson, Michael D., *Tennessee, Chattanooga*. Email: michael-d-thompson@utc.edu.

Thompson, Michael Kyle, *Pittsburg State*. Email: mkthompson@pittstate.edu.

Thompson, Nancy M., *California State, East Bay*. Challenge, CA. Email: nancy.thompson@csueastbay.edu. Research: medieval Europe, world civilizations.

Thompson, Phyllis E. P. Newton, MA. Affil: Harvard. Email: pepthompsonphd@gmail.com.

Thompson, Roger R., *Western Washington*. Email: Roger.Thompson@wwu.edu.

Thompson, Shirley E., *Texas, Austin*. Email: s.thompson@austin.utexas.edu.

Thompson, Stephen P. Woodbridge, VA. Affil: US Army. Email: stephen.p.thompson3@gmail.com.

Thompson, Tommy R., *Nebraska, Omaha*. Email: tthompson@unomaha.edu.

Thompson, V. Elaine, *Louisiana Tech*. Email: elainet@latech.edu.

Thompson, Victoria E., *Arizona State*. Email: victoria.thompson@asu.edu.

Thompson, Wayne W. Washington, DC. Affil: Air Force Hist. Studies Office. Email: waynewthompson@msn.com.

Thompson, William Keene, *Westmont*. Santa Barbara, CA. Email: wkthompson@ucsb.edu. Research: religious identity formation, iconoclasm and iconophilia.

AHA members in **bold italic**; Directory-listed affiliations in *italic*

Thomson, *Alexander*. Livonia, MI. Affil: Schoolcraft. Email: athomson@schoolcraft. edu.

Thomson, *Erik M.*, *Manitoba*. Winnipeg, MB, Canada. Email: erik.thomson@umanitoba.ca. Research: statecraft and commerce, networks.

Thomson, *Jennifer*, *Bucknell*. Email: j.thomson@ bucknell.edu.

Thomson, *Rodney*, *California State, Chico*. Chico, CA. Email: rthomson2@csuchico.edu; rodney.l.thomson@gmail.com. Research: early sectarianism in Islam, religion's role in culture and politics.

Thomson, *Sinclair S.*, *NYU*. New York, NY. Email: st19@nyu.edu. Research: colonial Andes.

Thomson, **William O.**, *Salem State*.

Thorn, **Samuel A.**, *Purdue, Fort Wayne*.

Thornberry, *Elizabeth*, *Johns Hopkins (Hist.)*. Email: liz.thornberry@gmail.com.

Thorne, *Susan E.*, *Duke*. Durham, NC. Email: sthorne@duke.edu. Research: Dickens/urban/ crime/race, US South/Saint Domingue/Haiti/ SC.

Thorne, **Tanis C.**, *California, Irvine*. Email: tcthorne@uci.edu.

Thornton, **David W.**, *Campbell*. Email: thornton@campbell.edu.

Thornton, *J. Mills, III*, *Michigan, Ann Arbor*. Montgomery, AL. Email: jmthrntn@umich. edu. Research: US civil rights movement, US Civil War origins.

Thornton, *Jennifer*, *West Virginia*. Morgantown, WV. Email: jennifer.thornton@mail.wvu.edu.

Thornton, **John K.**, *Boston Univ*. Email: jkthorn@ bu.edu.

Thornton, *Michael Alan*. New Haven, CT. Affil: Yale. Email: michael.a.thornton@yale.edu. Research: Meiji Japan, urban.

Thornton, **Richard C.**, *George Washington*. Email: rthornto@gwu.edu.

Thornton, *Sybil*, *Arizona State*. Email: sybil. thornton@asu.edu.

Thornton, **Tamara Plakins**, *SUNY, Buffalo*. Email: thornton@buffalo.edu.

Thorp, *Daniel B.*, *Virginia Tech*. Email: wachau@ vt.edu.

Thorp, *Malcolm R.*, *Brigham Young*. Email: malcolm_thorp@byu.edu.

Thorpe, *Jocelyn*, *Manitoba*. Email: jocelyn. thorpe@umanitoba.ca.

Thorpe, **Wayne L.**, *McMaster*. Email: thorpew@ mcmaster.ca.

Thorsheim, *Peter*, *North Carolina, Charlotte*. Charlotte, NC. Email: peter.thorsheim@uncc. edu. Research: recycling in Britain during WWII, environmental consequences of militarism.

Thrasher, *Rosemary*, *North Greenville*. Email: rosemary.thrasher@ngu.edu.

Threat, *Charissa J.*, *Chapman*. Atlanta, GA. Affil: Spelman. Email: threat@chapman.edu; cthreat@spelman.edu. Research: US civil rights and gender, military and civic society relationships.

Threlkeld, *Megan S.*, *Denison*. Granville, OH. Email: threlkeldm@denison.edu. Research: US women's internationalism, world organization 1890-1950.

Throntveit, *Trygve Van Regenmorter*. Minneapolis, MN. Affil: Minnesota, Twin Cities. Email: throntv@gmail.com. Research: American intellectual, international.

Throop, *Susanna A.*, *Ursinus*. Collegeville, PA. Email: sthroop@ursinus.edu. Research: ideas of crusading, emotions.

Thrush, **Coll**, *British Columbia*. Email: cthrush@ mail.ubc.ca.

Thuesen, *Peter J.* Indianapolis, IN. Affil: Indiana-Purdue, Indianapolis. Email: pthuesen@iupui. edu. Research: American religious, 18th-c book trade.

Thum, *Gregor*, *Pittsburgh*. Pittsburgh, PA. Email: thum@pitt.edu. Research: German-East European relations, modern Central Europe.

Thum, *Michael*. Hildesheim, Germany. Email: dr.mthum@gmx.de.

Thum, *Rian*, *Loyola, New Orleans*. New Orleans, LA. Email: thum@loyno.edu. Research: Uyghur historiography.

Thuma, *Emily*, *California, Irvine*. Email: ethuma@ uci.edu.

Thurber, *Timothy N.*, *Virginia Commonwealth*. Email: tnthurber@vcu.edu.

Thurman, *Kira L.*, *Michigan, Ann Arbor*. Email: thurmank@umich.edu.

Thurner, *Lance C.* Bronx, NY. Affil: Rutgers. Email: lancethurner@gmail.com.

Thurner, *Mark W.*, *Florida*. Email: mthurner@ ufl.edu.

Thurston, *Donald*, *Union Coll*. Email: thurstod@ union.edu.

Thurston, *Robert William*, *Miami, Ohio*. Oxford, OH. Email: thurstrw@miamioh.edu. Research: lynching, coffee.

Thurston, *Rosemary Fox*, *New Jersey City*. Email: rthurston2@njcu.edu.

Thurtle, *Phillip*, *Washington, Seattle*. Email: thurtle@uw.edu.

Thyret, *Isolde R.*, *Kent State*. Email: ithyret@ kent.edu.

Tickner, *Karen Elizabeth*. Silver Spring, MD. Email: KarenTickner127@gmail.com.

Ticknor, *Robert*, *Hist. New Orleans*. Email: robertt@hnoc.org.

Tiedemann, *Joseph S.*, *Loyola Marymount*. Email: jtiedema@lmu.edu.

Tiegreen, *Christopher*. Atlanta, GA. Affil: Georgia State. Email: ctiegreen1@student. gsu.edu.

Tieleman, *Matthijs T.* Los Angeles, CA. Affil: UCLA. Email: matthijs.tieleman@gmail.com.

Tiemeyer, *Phil*, *Kansas State*. Email: tiemeyerp@ ksu.edu.

Tierney, *Brian*, *Cornell*. Ithaca, NY. Email: bt20@ cornell.edu. Research: medieval church law, medieval political theory.

Tiersten, *Lisa S.*, *Barnard, Columbia*. New York, NY. Email: ltiersten@barnard.edu. Research: capitalism and culture, colonialism.

Tiffany, *David M.* Fredonia, NY. Affil: SUNY, Fredonia.

Tighe, *William J.*, *Muhlenberg*. Email: tighe@ muhlenberg.edu.

Tijerina, *Andres*, *Austin Comm. Coll.* Austin, TX. Email: andrest@austincc.edu. Research: Great Plains and borderlands, Chicano/Latino.

Tikoff, *Valentina K.*, *DePaul*. Email: vtikoff@ depaul.edu.

Tilburg, *Patricia A.*, *Davidson*. Email: patilburg@ davidson.edu.

Tilchin, *William*. Pawtucket, RI. Affil: Boston Univ. Email: wnt@bu.edu. Research: American foreign relations since 1800, modern US political and social.

Tilford, *Matthew B.* Varysburg, NY. Affil: Bucknell. Email: matt.tilford@gmail.com. Research: long civil rights movement, memory studies and public.

Tilitz, *Thomas*, *Queens, CUNY*.

Tillerson-Brown, *Amy J.*, *Mary Baldwin*. Email: atillers@mbc.edu.

Tillery, *Tyrone*, *Houston*. Email: ttillery@mail. uh.edu.

Tilley, *Helen L.*, *Northwestern*. Email: helen. tilley@northwestern.edu.

Tillman, *Ellen Davies*, *Texas State*. Email: et19@ txstate.edu.

Tillman, *Margaret Mih*, *Purdue*. West Lafayette, IN. Email: mmtillman@purdue.edu. Research: modern China, childhood and family.

Tillotson, *Shirley M.*, *Dalhousie*. Email: shirley. tillotson@dal.ca.

Tillson, *Albert H., Jr.*, *Tampa*. Email: atillson@ ut.edu.

Tils, *Rachel*. Newton, MA. Affil: Kings Academy. Email: rtils@kingsacademy.edu.jo.

Tilton, *Lauren*. Richmond, VA. Affil: Richmond. Email: lauren.tilton@gmail.com. Research: participatory media, digital humanities.

Timm, *Annette F.*, *Calgary*. Email: atimm@ ucalgary.ca.

Timmerman, *Jay M.* Middleton, WI. Email: wict106@mac.com.

Timmons-Hill, *Deborah L.*, *Georgia Southern*. Email: deborahhill@georgiasouthern.edu.

Timonin, *Michael*. Elmira, NY. Affil: Broome Comm. Coll. Email: mike.timonin@gmail.com. Research: post-WWII US demobilization, WWII gender identity.

Tindle, *Emilie*. Collinsville, OK. Affil: Oklahoma State. Email: etindle@okstate.edu.

Tinker, *Greg J.* San Francisco, CA. Affil: Manchester. Email: greg.j.tinker@gmail.com. Research: modern British/European culture/ politics, cultural memory of WWII in Europe.

Tinker Salas, *Miguel Roberto*, *Pomona*. Email: mtinkersalas@pomona.edu.

Tinkler, *Robert S.*, *California State, Chico*. Email: rtinkler@csuchico.edu.

Tinley, *Lynn C.* Atlanta, GA. Email: lynntinley@ comcast.net.

Tinsman, *Heidi E.*, *California, Irvine*. San Pedro, CA. Email: hetinsma@uci.edu. Research: Chile and Americas consumer culture, gender/ sexuality/labor.

Tippeconnic, *Eric*, *California State, Fullerton*. Email: etippeconnic@fullerton.edu.

Tirado, *Isabel A.*, *William Paterson*. New York, NY. Email: tiradoi@wpunj.edu. Research: 1920s Soviet youth, party and komsomol in NEP countryside.

Tirado, **Thomas C.**, *Millersville, Pa.* Email: tctirado@millersville.edu.

Tiro, **Karim Michel**, *Xavier, Ohio*. Email: tiro@ xavier.edu.

Tirosh-Samuelson, *Hava*, *Arizona State*. Email: hava.samuelson@asu.edu.

Tiryakian, *Josefina C.* Durham, NC. Email: jctiryak@duke.edu. Research: national identity in late colonial Peru, Franciscan missiology and enlightened thought.

Tisby, *Jemar*. Helena-West Helena, AR. Affil: Mississippi. Email: jtisby@go.olemiss.edu.

Tischler, *Barbara L.* New York, NY. Affil: Speyer Legacy Sch. Email: Tischlerb@gmail.com. Research: civil rights movement, American culture.

Tise, *Larry E*. Philadelphia, PA. Affil: East Carolina. Email: ltise@attglobal.net. Research: early aviation in US and Europe, founding fathers and fascism.

Titchener, Frances Bonner, *Utah State*. Email: frances.titchener@usu.edu.

Tittler, Robert B., *Concordia, Can*. Email: Robert.Tittler@concordia.ca.

Tlusty, B. Ann, *Bucknell*. Email: tlusty@bucknell.edu.

Tobbell, Dominique A., *Minnesota (Hist. of Science)*. Email: dtobbell@umn.edu.

Tobey, Jerry L., *California State, Sacramento*. Email: wuff@saclink.csus.edu.

Tobey, Ronald C., *California, Riverside*. Email: ronald.tobey@ucr.edu.

Tobias, Norman, *Rutgers, Newark/New Jersey Inst. of Tech*. Email: tobias@njit.edu.

Tobin, Catherine, *Central Michigan*. Email: tobin1c@cmich.edu.

Tobin, *Eugene M*. New York, NY. Affil: Andrew W. Mellon Foundation. Email: emt@mellon.org.

Tobin, *Kathleen Ann*. Hammond, IN. Affil: Purdue Northwest, Hammond. Email: tobink@pnw.edu. Research: population policy, birth control.

Tobler, Douglas F., *Brigham Young*.

Tocci, *Charles*. Chicago, IL. Affil: Loyola, Chicago. Email: ctocci@luc.edu.

Todd, *Andrew D*. Morgantown, WV. Email: a_d_todd@rowboats-sd-ca.com.

Todd, Barbara J., *Toronto*. Email: b.todd@utoronto.ca.

Todd, Elizabeth K., *Case Western Reserve*. Email: elizabeth.todd@case.edu.

Todd, Ellen Wiley, *George Mason*.

Todd, *Kathryn Gwyn*. Napa, CA. Email: kgtodd@gmail.com. Research: AIDS epidemic in San Francisco.

Todd, Lisa M., *New Brunswick*. Email: ltodd@unb.ca.

Todd, Margo, *Pennsylvania*. Email: mtodd@sas.upenn.edu.

Todd, *Molly*, *Montana State, Bozeman*. Bozeman, MT. Email: molly.todd@montana.edu; mollynmntodd@gmail.com. Research: Central America/El Salvador, trans-American solidarity/human rights.

Todd-Breland, *Elizabeth S.*, *Illinois, Chicago*. Chicago, IL. Email: etoddbre@uic.edu. Research: urban education and politics, race and inequality.

Todes, Daniel P., *Johns Hopkins (Hist. of Science)*. Email: dtodes@jhmi.edu.

Todesca, James C., *Georgia Southern*. Email: jtodesca@georgiasouthern.edu.

Todorova, *Maria N.*, *Illinois, Urbana-Champaign*. Urbana, IL. Email: mtodorov@illinois.edu. Research: Balkan identity and nationalism, hero worship.

Todt, *Michael A*. Durango, CO. Affil: Center of Southwest Studies. Email: miketodt@gmail.com. Research: Canada/US national health insurance, health care in western states.

Toews, *John E.*, *Washington, Seattle*. Seattle, WA. Email: toews@uw.edu. Research: psychoanalysis, modernism and masculinity.

Toff, *Nancy E*. New York, NY. Affil: Oxford Univ. Press. Email: nancy.toff@oup.com.

Toffoli, *Erica*. Maple, ON, Canada. Affil: Toronto. Email: erica.toffoli@mail.utoronto.ca.

Toffolo-Cresce, *Mary E.*, *Esq*. Davidsonville, MD. Affil: Our Lady of Perpetual Help Sch. Email: toffolocresce@gmail.com.

Toft, *Amir A*. Chicago, IL. Email: atoft@uchicago.edu.

Tolan, *John V*. Nantes, France. Affil: Nantes. Email: john.tolan@univ-nantes.fr. Research: Muslim and Christian mission and polemic, Mediterranean world culture and exchange.

Tolbert, Lisa C., *North Carolina, Greensboro*. Email: lctolber@uncg.edu.

Toledo Pereyra, Luis, *Western Michigan*.

Toler, *Pamela D*. Chicago, IL. Email: pdtoler@sbcglobal.net. Research: women war correspondents in WWII, women warriors.

Tolin-Schultz, *Alexandra*. Oneonta, NY. Affil: SUNY, Oneonta. Email: alexandratolinschultz@yahoo.com. Research: Enlightenment, 18th-c racial discourse.

Tollefson, Harold, *New Mexico State*. Email: hatollef@nmsu.edu.

Tolles, Bryant, *Delaware*. Email: bftolles@udel.edu.

Tollison, Courtney L., *Furman*. Email: courtney.tollison@furman.edu.

Tolmacheva, Marina A., *Washington State, Pullman*. Email: tolmache@wsu.edu.

Tolpin, Martha, *Bentley*. Email: mtolpin@bentley.edu.

Tomasek, Kathryn, *Wheaton, Mass*. Providence, RI. Email: ktomasek@wheatoncollege.edu. Research: TEI for account books, business and economy 1840-65.

Tomes, Nancy J., *SUNY, Stony Brook*. East Northport, NY. Email: nancy.tomes@stonybrook.edu. Research: US social, women.

Tomich, Dale W., *Binghamton, SUNY*. Email: dtomich@binghamton.edu.

Tomita, *Yoka*. New York, NY. Affil: Columbia. Email: yokatomita@gmail.com.

Tomlin, *J. L.*, *North Texas*. Denton, TX. Email: J.Tomlin@unt.edu. Research: early America, Atlantic world.

Tomlins, *Christopher Lawrence*. Berkeley, CA. Affil: California, Berkeley. Email: ctomlins@law.berkeley.edu. Research: Turner Rebellion, philosophy of history.

Tomlinson, Andrea, *Science History Inst*. Email: atomlinson@sciencehistory.org.

Tomlinson, Tristan, *Colgate*. Email: ttomlinson@colgate.edu.

Tomoff, *Kiril*, *California, Riverside*. Riverside, CA. Email: kiril.tomoff@ucr.edu. Research: USSR cultural exchange, Soviet music.

Tompkins, David G., *Carleton Coll*. Email: dtompkin@carleton.edu.

Tompson, Doug, *Columbus State*. Email: tompson_doug@columbusstate.edu.

Tompson, Richard, *Utah*.

Tonat, *Ian Edward*. Reston, VA. Affil: William and Mary. Email: ietonat@email.wm.edu. Research: Native American, early American West.

Tone, Andrea E., *McGill*. Email: andrea.tone@mcgill.ca.

Tone, John Lawrence, *Georgia Inst. of Tech*. Email: john.tone@hts.gatech.edu.

Tonks, *Henry Miles James*. Allston, MA. Email: henrymjtonks@aol.com.

Tonomura, Hitomi, *Michigan, Ann Arbor*. Email: tomitono@umich.edu.

Tooch, *Eric Richard*. New Brighton, PA. Email: erictooch@yahoo.com.

Tooley, T. Hunt, *Austin Coll*. Email: htooley@austincollege.edu.

Toomey, *Michael*, *Lincoln Memorial*. Harrogate, TN. Email: michael.toomey@lmunet.edu. Research: southern Appalachia, Tennessee.

Tooze, *J. Adam*, *Columbia (Hist.)*. New York, NY. Email: adam.tooze@columbia.edu. Research: modern Germany.

Topdar, *Sudipa*, *Illinois State*. Normal, IL. Email: stopdar@ilstu.edu; sudipa.topdar@gmail.com. Research: colonial schooling, colonial childhoods.

Topik, *Steven C.*, *California, Irvine*. Irvine, CA. Email: sctopik@uci.edu. Research: commodity.

Toplin, Robert Brent, *North Carolina, Wilmington*. Email: toplinrb@uncw.edu.

Topp, Michael M., *Texas, El Paso*. Email: mtopp@utep.edu.

Toprani, Anand, *Naval War Coll*. Email: anand.topriani@usnwc.edu.

Tor, Deborah G., *Notre Dame*. Email: dtor@nd.edu.

Torain, Corey, *North Carolina A&T State*. Email: cltorain@ncat.edu.

Torbenson, Craig L., *Wichita State*. Email: craig.torbenson@wichita.edu.

Torbett, *Skyler Michael*. Austin, TX. Email: skyler.torbett@g.austincc.edu.

Torget, *Andrew J.*, *North Texas*. Email: torget@unt.edu.

Toro-Sepulveda, *Kalia*. Mayaguez, PR, Puerto Rico. Email: k_toro@yahoo.com.

Torpey, John, *Graduate Center, CUNY*. Email: jtorpey@gc.cuny.edu.

Torre, Jose R., *SUNY, Coll. Brockport*. Email: jrtorre@brockport.edu.

Torres, *Marco*. Chicago, IL. Affil: Chicago. Email: mtorres3@uchicago.edu.

Torres, *Ricardo*. Cayey, PR. Affil: Centro de Estudios Avanzados de Puerto Rico y el Caribe. Email: rigelto@yahoo.com.

Torrey, Glenn E., *Emporia State*.

Tortorici, *Zeb*. New York, NY. Affil: NYU. Email: zebbie@gmail.com. Research: sexuality in colonial Latin America, suicide/abortion/infanticide.

Tosko Bello, *Brian K*. Washington, DC. Affil: Arizona State. Email: btosko@asu.edu.

Totani, *Yuma*, *Hawai'i, Manoa*. Email: yuma.totani@hawaii.edu.

Toth, *Wesley Brooks*. Kent, OH. Email: wtoth21@gmail.com. Research: Cold War, Sports.

Totman, Conrad, *Yale*.

Totten, *Marie Cathryn*. Russellville, AR. Affil: Arkansas. Email: mcf003@uark.edu.

Toudji, Sonia, *Central Arkansas*. Email: stoudji@uca.edu.

Touhey, Ryan, *Waterloo*. Email: rmtouhey@uwaterloo.ca.

Touhill, Blanche M., *Missouri–St. Louis*. Email: touhillb@msx.umsl.edu.

Toulin, *Alana*. Chicago, IL. Affil: Northwestern. Email: alanatoulin2019@u.northwestern.edu.

Tounsel, *Christopher*, *Penn State*. Email: cut70@psu.edu.

Touwaide, *Alain*. San Marino, CA. Affil: Inst. for the Preservation of Medical Traditions. Email: atouwaide@hotmail.com. Research: biomedical sciences, transmission of knowledge.

Tovey, Mark, *Western Ontario*. Email: mark@uwo.ca.

Towers, Frank H., *Calgary*. Email: ftowers@ucalgary.ca.

Towey, Alexander. San Marcos, CA. Affil: California State, San Marcos. Email: towey001@cougars.csusm.edu. Research: esotericism/secret societies/occult.

Towles, David Wayne. Elizabeth City, NC. Email: dtowles1969@gmail.com.

Towne, Stephen E., *Indiana–Purdue, Indianapolis*. Email: setowne@iupui.edu.

Townend, Paul A., *North Carolina, Wilmington*. Email: townendp@uncw.edu.

Townsend, Camilla D., *Rutgers*. Highland Park, NJ. Email: ctownsend@history.rutgers.edu. Research: Latin America, comparative.

Townsend, Colby. Centerville, UT. Affil: Utah State. Email: colby.townsend@aggiemail.usu.edu.

Townsend, Kenneth W., *Coastal Carolina*. Email: ken@coastal.edu.

Townsend, Liz, *AHA*. Washington, DC. Email: ltownsend@historians.org.

Townsend, Robert B. Alexandria, VA. Affil: American Academy of Arts and Sciences. Email: rbthisted@gmail.com. Research: history profession(s), quantitative.

Townsend, Sarah. Indianapolis, IN. Affil: American Military. Email: kellardt@comcast.net.

Toxqui, Aurea. Peoria, IL. Affil: Bradley. Email: atoxqui@fsmail.bradley.edu. Research: popular places of social interaction, popular culture.

Toy, Chase Douglas. Northridge, CA. Affil: California State, Northridge. Email: chasetoy@gmail.com. Research: colonial/Southwest US, Europe 1815-1914.

Toy, Ernest W., *California State, Fullerton*. Email: etoy@fullerton.edu.

Traboulay, David M., *Staten Island, CUNY*. Email: davidtraboulay@hotmail.com.

Tracey, Ainsworth, *North Carolina A&T State*. Email: altracey@ncat.edu.

Trachtenberg, Barry Carl, *Wake Forest*. Winston Salem, NC. Email: trachtbc@wfu.edu. Research: modern Jewish, Nazi Holocaust.

Tracy, Arthur L., *Mary Washington*. Email: atracy@umw.edu.

Tracy, James D., *Minnesota (Hist.)*. Email: tracy001@umn.edu.

Tracy, Sarah, *Oklahoma (Hist.); Oklahoma (Hist. of Science)*. Email: swtracy@ou.edu.

Tracy Samuel, Annie, *Tennessee, Chattanooga*. Email: annie-tracysamuel@utc.edu.

Traflet, Janice M. Lewisburg, PA. Affil: Bucknell. Email: jtraflet@bucknell.edu. Research: stock market, marketing.

Trafzer, Clifford E., *California, Riverside*. Email: clifford.trafzer@ucr.edu.

Traille, E. Kay, *Kennesaw State*. Email: etraille@kennesaw.edu.

Trainor, Christopher, *Carleton, Can*. Email: chris.trainor@carleton.ca.

Trainor, Richard H. Oxford, United Kingdom. Affil: Oxford. Email: richard.trainor@exeter.ox.ac.uk. Research: British middle class elites 1850-1950, British universities 1850-2000.

Traitor, Ann, *SUNY, Oneonta*. Email: ann.traitor@oneonta.edu.

Tran, Lisa, *California State, Fullerton*. Email: lisatran@fullerton.edu.

Tran, Nhung T., *Toronto*. Email: nhungtuyet.tran@utoronto.ca.

Tran, Nu-Anh, *Connecticut, Storrs*. Email: nu-anh.tran@uconn.edu.

Tran, Tommy. Merced, CA. Affil: California, Merced. Email: ttran299@ucmerced.edu.

Trani, Eugene P., *Virginia Commonwealth*. Email: eptrani@vcu.edu.

Transchel, Kate, *California State, Chico*. Email: ktranschel@csuchico.edu.

Traore, M. Ousmane, *Pomona*. Email: makhroufi.traore@pomona.edu.

Trask, David S. Fort Collins, CO. Email: traskds@earthlink.net. Research: missionary-Sioux relations 1860-1940, American ideas of national identity.

Trask, Jeffrey Lee. New York, NY. Affil: Georgia State. Email: trask.jeffrey@gmail.com. Research: cultural democracy, urban landscape studies.

Trattner, Walter I., *Wisconsin-Milwaukee*. Email: wit@uwm.edu.

Traugh, Geoffrey, *Georgetown*. Richmond, VA. Email: geoffrey.traugh@nyu.edu. Research: Africa.

Traugott, Mark, *California, Santa Cruz*. Email: traugott@ucsc.edu.

Trauschweizer, Ingo, *Ohio*. Email: trauschw@ohio.edu.

Trautmann, Thomas R., *Michigan, Ann Arbor*. Email: ttraut@umich.edu.

Traver, Andrew G., *Southeastern Louisiana*. Email: atraver@selu.edu.

Travers, Thomas Robert, *Cornell*. Email: trt5@cornell.edu.

Travers, Timothy H. E., *Calgary*.

Traverso, Enzo, *Cornell*. Email: vt225@cornell.edu.

Traves, Thomas, *Dalhousie*. Email: tom.traves@dal.ca.

Travis, Anthony R., *Grand Valley State*. Email: travisa@gvsu.edu.

Travis, Charles, IV, *Texas, Arlington*. Email: charles.travis@uta.edu.

Travis, Frederick F. Rhinebeck, NY. Affil: John Carroll. Email: fftravis10@yahoo.com. Research: international relations, US since World War II.

Travis, Paul D., *Texas Woman's*. Denton, TX. Email: ptravis@twu.edu. Research: 20th-c America.

Travis, Tara Elisabeth. Cortez, CO. Affil: National Park Service. Email: 610travis@gmail.com. Research: Public History, US West.

Travis, Trysh, *Florida*. Email: ttravis@ufl.edu.

Traweek, Sharon, *UCLA*. Email: traweek@history.ucla.edu.

Traylor, Jack. Dayton, TN. Affil: Bryan. Email: trayloja@aol.com. Research: WWII, Franklin Roosevelt.

Traylor, Ronald, *Southeastern Louisiana*. Email: Ronald.Traylor@selu.edu.

Traylor-Heard, Nancy Jane. Mississippi State, MS. Affil: Mississippi State. Email: njt50@msstate.edu.

Treadgold, Warren T., *St. Louis*. Saint Louis, MO. Email: warren.treadgold@slu.edu. Research: Byzantine historians, American universities.

Treadway, John D., *Richmond*. Email: jtreadwa@richmond.edu.

Treadway, Sarah. McKees Rocks, PA. Affil: Pittsburgh. Email: streadway24@ymail.com. Research: Nazi Germany, Holocaust.

Treadwell, Aaron, *Middle Tennessee State*. Email: Aaron.Treadwell@mtsu.edu.

Treanor, Patrick Joseph. Wheaton, MD. Email: patrickjtreanor@cs.com. Research: Albanians and WWII, Britain and Bulgaria 1918-23.

Treckel, Paula A., *Allegheny*. Email: ptreckel@allegheny.edu.

Tree, Robert L. Fairfield, IA. Email: rtree@lisco.com.

Treiger, Alexander, *Dalhousie*. Email: atreiger@dal.ca.

Treitel, Corinna A., *Washington, St. Louis*. Saint Louis, MO. Email: ctreitel@wustl.edu. Research: food and diet reform in modern Germany.

Tremblay, Yves, *National Defence Headquarters*. Email: yves.tremblay@forces.gc.ca.

Trepanier, Nicolas, *Mississippi*. Email: ntrepani@olemiss.edu.

Trepanier, Trent. Bemidji, MN. Email: trenttrepanier@gmail.com. Research: ultranationalists in Showa Japan, Communism in Germany.

Trépanier, Anne, *Carleton, Can*. Email: anne.trepanier@carleton.ca.

Trevett, Jeremy, *York, Can*. Email: jtrevett@yorku.ca.

Trevino, Roberto R., *Texas, Arlington*.

Trice, Tom R., *California Polytechnic State*. Email: ttrice@calpoly.edu.

Trier, Mike. Fort Wayne, IN. Affil: East Allen County Sch. Email: mjtbmr@hotmail.com.

Trigg, Scott. Notre Dame, IN. Affil: Notre Dame. Email: strigg@nd.edu. Research: medieval Islamic astronomy/philosophy, commentaries and knowledge transmission.

Trimarchi, Carolyn, *Duquesne*. Email: trimarchic@duq.edu.

Trimble, William F., *Auburn*. Email: trimbwf@auburn.edu.

Trimmer, Tiffany A., *Wisconsin-La Crosse*. Email: ttrimmer@uwlax.edu.

Triner, Gail D., *Rutgers*. Email: gtriner@gmail.com.

Trinidad, Michael E., *Jr*. El Paso, TX. Affil: Texas, El Paso. Email: metrinidad@miners.utep.edu.

Tripp, Bernell E. Gainesville, FL. Affil: Florida. Email: btripp@jou.ufl.edu. Research: abolitionist press, 19th-c black press.

Tripp, Steven E., *Grand Valley State*. Email: tripps@gvsu.edu.

Trisco, Robert F. Washington, DC. Affil: Catholic. Email: trisco@cua.edu. Research: post-16th-c US and UK Catholic Church, 19th-/20th-c papacy.

Tristano, Richard. Winona, MN. Affil: St. Mary's, Minn. Email: rtristan@smumn.edu. Research: 15th-/16th-c Ferrara, Borso d'Este.

Tritle, Lawrence A., *Loyola Marymount*. Email: ltritle@lmu.edu.

Tritton, Thomas R., *Science History Inst*. Email: ttritton@sciencehistory.org.

Trivedi, Lisa, *Hamilton*. Email: ltrivedi@hamilton.edu.

Trivellato, Francesca. New Haven, CT. Affil: Yale. Email: ft@ias.edu. Research: continental Europe.

Troche, Julia D., *Missouri State*. Email: JuliaTroche@missouristate.edu.

Troester, Patrick Thomas. Dallas, TX. Affil: Southern Methodist. Email: ptroester1@gmail.com. Research: 19th-c US-Mexico borderlands, early America.

Trofimov, Leonid T., *Bentley*. Email: ltrofimov@bentley.edu.

Trolander, Judith Ann, *Minnesota Duluth*. Email: jtroland@d.umn.edu.

Trollinger, Abigail P., *St. Norbert*. DePere, WI. Email: abby.trollinger@snc.edu. Research: New Deal social movements and welfare.

Trollinger, William V., Jr., *Dayton*. Dayton, OH. Email: wtrollinger1@udayton.edu. Research: creationism, politics and Christian right.

Tromly, Benjamin K., *Puget Sound*. Email: btromly@pugetsound.edu.

Troost, Kristina, *Duke*. Email: kristina.troost@duke.edu.

Tropp, Jacob A., *Middlebury*. Email: jtropp@middlebury.edu.

Trost, Jennifer, *Wisconsin-La Crosse*. Email: jtrost@uwlax.edu.

Trotman, David V., *York, Can.* Email: dtrotman@yorku.ca.

Trotter, Joe William, Jr., *Carnegie Mellon*. Pittsburgh, PA. Email: trotter@andrew.cmu.edu. Research: 20th-c African American urban, 20th-c African American labor.

Trotti, Michael Ayers, *Ithaca*. Email: mtrotti@ithaca.edu.

Troupe, Cheryl, *Saskatchewan*. Email: cheryl.troupe@usask.ca.

Trout, Dennis, *Missouri, Columbia*. Email: trout@missouri.edu.

Troutman, Richard L., *Western Kentucky*. Email: richard.troutman@wku.edu.

Troutt Powell, Eve M., *Pennsylvania*. Philadelphia, PA. Email: troutt@sas.upenn.edu. Research: African slavery in Middle East, religion and slavery.

Trowbridge, David J., *Marshall*. Email: david.trowbridge@marshall.edu.

Troxler, Carole Watterson, *Elon*. Email: troxlerc@elon.edu.

Troxler, George, *Elon*. Email: troxlerg@elon.edu.

Troy, Gil. Jerusalem, Israel. Affil: McGill. Email: gil.troy@mcgill.ca. Research: moderation in America, modern American presidency.

Troyan, Brett. Cortland, NY. Affil: SUNY, Coll. Cortland. Email: BrTroyan@gmail.com.

Troyansky, David G., *Brooklyn, CUNY; Graduate Center, CUNY*. Brooklyn, NY. Email: troyansky@brooklyn.cuny.edu. Research: early modern and modern Europe, France.

Truant, Cynthia M., *California, San Diego*. La Jolla, CA. Email: ctruant@ucsd.edu. Research: Old Regime Paris guildswomen, popular theater and working class.

True, Marshall, *Vermont*. Email: cmtrue@verizon.net.

Truelove, Joshua M. Brighton, MA. Affil: Boston Coll. Email: truelove@bc.edu.

Truett, Samuel, *New Mexico*. Email: truett@unm.edu.

Truitt, Elly, *Bryn Mawr*. Email: etruitt@brynmawr.edu.

Truitt, Jonathan G., *Central Michigan*. Mount Pleasant, MI. Email: truit1jg@cmich.edu. Research: Latin America.

Trumbach, Randolph, *Graduate Center, CUNY*. New York, NY. Affil: Baruch, CUNY. Email: randolph.trumbach@baruch.cuny.edu. Research: 18th-c sexuality, 18th-c religion.

Trumper, Camilo, *SUNY, Buffalo*. Email: ctrumper@buffalo.edu.

Truschel, Louis W., *Western Washington*. Email: Louis.Truschel@wwu.edu.

Truschke, Audrey, *Rutgers, Newark/New Jersey Inst. of Tech.* Newark, NJ. Email: audrey.

truschke@gmail.com. Research: India, South Asia.

Truxes, Thomas M., *NYU*. Email: thomas.truxes@nyu.edu.

Trybus, Karl J. Spartanburg, SC. Affil: Limestone. Email: karl.trybus@gmail.com. Research: Vatican actions in Spanish Civil War, 20th-c European film and identity.

Tryon, Kevin. Haverford, PA. Affil: Haverford Sch. Email: KTryon@Haverford.org.

Tsacoyianis, Beverly A., *Memphis*. Email: btscynis@memphis.edu.

Tsai, Shih-Shan Henry, *Arkansas, Fayetteville*. Email: htsai@uark.edu.

Tsai, Wei-chieh. New Taipei, Taiwan. Affil: National Chengchi. Email: weictsai@gmail.com. Research: Mongols and Manchus under Ch'ing rule, cultural.

Tsal, Yotam. Tel Aviv, Israel. Affil: California, Berkeley. Email: ytsal@berkeley.edu.

Tsapina, Olga, *Huntington Library*. San Marino, CA. Email: otsapina@huntington.org. Research: Seven Years' War and British America, transatlantic religious Enlightenment.

Tscherne, Joel W. Ashland, KY. Affil: Southern New Hampshire. Email: me@joelt.org. Research: presidential recordings, film.

Tschetter, Ann. Lincoln, NE. Affil: Nebraska, Lincoln. Email: atschetter2@unl.edu.

Tseng, Gloria S., *Hope*. Email: tseng@hope.edu.

Tshimanga-Kashama, Charles, *Nevada, Reno*. Email: ckashama@unr.edu.

Tsikitas, Arianna M. Niantic, CT. Affil: Connecticut. Email: arianna.tsikitas@uconn.edu.

Tsin, Michael T., *North Carolina, Chapel Hill*. Email: tsin@email.unc.edu.

Tsitlanadze, Tea. Tbilisi, Georgia. Email: tea.tsitlanadze@tsu.ge.

Tsoukas, Liann E., *Pittsburgh*. Email: lit2@pitt.edu.

Tsoules, Will, *Massachusetts Hist. Soc.* Email: wtsoules@masshist.org.

Tsouna, Voula, *California, Santa Barbara*. Email: vtsouna@philosophy.ucsb.edu.

Tsouvala, Georgia, *Illinois State*. Email: gtsouva@ilstu.edu.

Tsu, Cecilia M., *California, Davis*. Email: cmtsu@ucdavis.edu.

Tubb, Douglas. Danville, KY. Email: ucrhistory@hotmail.com.

Tubbs, David L. New York, NY. Affil: King's Coll. Email: dtubbs@tkc.edu.

Tubbs, Melanie, *Arkansas Tech*.

Tuchinsky, Adam Max, *Southern Maine*. Email: adam.tuchinsky@maine.edu.

Tuchman, Arleen M., *Vanderbilt*. Email: arleen.m.tuchman@vanderbilt.edu.

Tuchscherer, Konrad T., Jr., *St. John's, NY*. Email: tuchschk@stjohns.edu.

Tuck, Michael W., *Northeastern Illinois*. Email: M-Tuck@neiu.edu.

Tuck, Sherrie, *Arthur and Elizabeth Schlesinger Library*. Email: stuck@radcliffe.harvard.edu.

Tucker, Alicia Liberty. Manassas, VA. Affil: Northern Virginia Comm. Coll., Manassas. Email: atucker@nvcc.edu.

Tucker, Ann L., *North Georgia*. Email: ann.tucker@ung.edu.

Tucker, Barbara M., *Eastern Connecticut State*. Email: tuckerb@easternct.edu.

Tucker, David M., *Memphis*.

Tucker, David V., *Iowa*. Email: david-tucker@uiowa.edu.

Tucker, E. Bruce, *Windsor*. Email: tucker1@uwindsor.ca.

Tucker, Jennifer, *Wesleyan*. Email: jtucker@wesleyan.edu.

Tucker, John A., *East Carolina*. Email: tuckerjo@ecu.edu.

Tucker, Judith E., *Georgetown*. Email: Judith.Tucker@georgetown.edu.

Tucker, Kathryn, *Troy*. Email: ktucker@troy.edu.

Tucker, Sara W., *Washburn*. Email: sara.tucker@washburn.edu.

Tucker, William F., *Arkansas, Fayetteville*. Email: wtucker@uark.edu.

Tudda, Chris, *US Dept. of State*.

Tuell, Yvette. Pocatello, ID. Affil: Utah. Email: y.tuell@utah.edu.

Tueller, James B. Laie, HI. Affil: Brigham Young, Hawaii. Email: tuellerj@byuh.edu. Research: Spanish Empire in Pacific Ocean, Christianization of Chamorros.

Tuennerman, Laura A., *California, Pa.* Email: tuennerman@calu.edu.

Tulchin, Allan A., *Shippensburg*. Email: aatulchin@ship.edu.

Tulchin, Joseph S. Brookline, MA. Affil: Harvard. Email: joe.tulchin@gmail.com. Research: US foreign policy, Argentina-US relations.

Tull, Charles J., *Indiana, South Bend*.

Tullos, Allen E., *Emory*. Email: allen.tullos@emory.edu.

Tully, Alan, *Texas, Austin*. Austin, TX. Email: tully@austin.utexas.edu. Research: colonial America.

Tully, John D., *Central Connecticut State*. New Britain, CT. Email: tullyj@ccsu.edu. Research: social studies education, American foreign relations.

Tumblin, Jesse Cole. Newton Center, MA. Affil: Boston Coll. Email: tumblin@bc.edu. Research: British Empire, 20th-c international relations.

Tumpek-Kjellmark, Katharina C. Des Moines, IA. Affil: Grand View. Email: ktumpek@grandview.edu. Research: women in 20th-c world, post-WWII German women.

Tuna, Mustafa O., *Duke*. Email: mustafa.tuna@duke.edu.

Tune, Michael. Springfield, VA. Affil: George Washington. Email: tune.michael@gmail.com. Research: African American.

Tunnell, Ted, *Virginia Commonwealth*. Email: ttunnell@vcu.edu.

Tunstall, Graydon A., Jr. Tampa, FL. Affil: South Florida, Tampa. Email: tunstall@usf.edu. Research: WWI Eastern Front.

Turan, Ebru, *Fordham*. Email: turan@fordham.edu.

Turek, Lauren F., *Trinity, Tex.* San Antonio, TX. Email: lturek@trinity.edu. Research: evangelicals and US foreign policy, Pentecostalism and global capitalism.

Turiano, Evan. New York, NY. Affil: Graduate Center, CUNY. Email: evan.turiano@gmail.com.

Turk, Katherine Lee, *North Carolina, Chapel Hill*. Email: kturk@email.unc.edu.

Turk, Richard W., *Allegheny*. Email: rturk@allegheny.edu.

Turkel, William J., *Western Ontario*. Email: wturkel@uwo.ca.

Turley, **Richard E.**, **Jr**. Salt Lake City, UT. Affil: Church of Jesus Christ of Latter-day Saints. Email: turleyre@ldschurch.org.

Turley, **Thomas**, *Santa Clara*. Santa Clara, CA. Email: tturley@scu.edu. Research: ancient and medieval Europe.

Turnage, **Anne-Marie**. Petersburg, VA. Affil: Virginia State. Email: aturnage@vsu.edu.

Turner, **Alexis**. Cambridge, MA. Affil: Harvard. Email: txturner@g.harvard.edu.

Turner, **Andrew A.**, *Columbus State*. Email: turner_andrew@columbusstate.edu.

Turner, **Blair P.**, *Virginia Military Inst.; Soc. for Military Hist*. Email: turnerbp@vmi.edu.

Turner, **Brian David**, *Portland State*. Email: brian.turner@pdx.edu.

Turner, **Catherine**, *Appalachian State*. Email: turnerce@appstate.edu.

Turner, **Dennise Mickelle**. Atlanta, GA. Affil: Georgia State, Perimeter Coll. Email: dmt6700@aol.com. Research: race/identity/culture, immigration.

Turner, **Eldon R.**, *Florida*. Email: eturner@ufl.edu.

Turner, **Felicity M.**, *Georgia Southern*. Savannah, GA. Email: fturner@georgiasouthern.edu. Research: intersection of medicine and law.

Turner, **James**, *Notre Dame*. El Prado, NM. Email: jturner2@nd.edu. Research: formation of academic disciplines, William Robertson Smith.

Turner, **John P.**, *Colby*. Email: john.turner@colby.edu.

Turner, **John**, *Nebraska, Lincoln*. Email: jturner2@unl.edu.

Turner, **Julie**. Cincinnati, OH. Affil: UC Blue Ash Coll. Email: jtz_email@yahoo.com. Research: Greenbelt communities of New Deal, post-WWII US society/culture.

Turner, **Karen Gottschang**, *Holy Cross*. Email: kturner@holycross.edu.

Turner, **Kate**. Madison, WI. Affil: Wisconsin, Madison. Email: keturner2@wisc.edu. Research: 20th-c Britain, gender.

Turner, **Michael**, *Appalachian State*. Email: turnermj@appstate.edu.

Turner, **Nancy L.**, *Wisconsin-Platteville*. Platteville, WI. Email: turnern@uwplatt.edu. Research: Christians and Jews in late Middle Ages, science c. 1200-1750.

Turner, **Nicole Myers**, *Virginia Commonwealth*. Email: nmturner@vcu.edu.

Turner, **Patricia Regina**, *Wisconsin-Eau Claire*. Eau Claire, WI. Email: turnerpr@uwec.edu. Research: civil society and sociability, comparative revolutions.

Turner, **R. Steven**, *New Brunswick*. Email: turner@unb.ca.

Turner, **Roger**, *Science History Inst*. Email: rturner@sciencehistory.org.

Turner, **Sasha**. Hamden, CT. Affil: Quinnipiac. Email: sturner@quinnipiac.edu. Research: women and slavery, Atlantic world.

Turner, **Vicki**, *Soc. for Military Hist*. Email: vturner@vmi.edu.

Turner, **Wendy J.**, *Augusta*. Email: wturner1@augusta.edu.

Turner-Rahman, **Lipi**, *Washington State, Pullman*. Email: ilipi@wsu.edu.

Turney, **Elaine C.**, *Texas, San Antonio*. Email: elaine.turney@utsa.edu.

Turning, **Patricia**, *Albright*. Email: pturning@albright.edu.

Turnmire, **Rebekah**. Mouth of Wilson, VA. Affil: South Carolina. Email: turnmire@email.sc.edu.

Turpin, **Andrea L.**, *Baylor*. Waco, TX. Email: andrea_turpin@baylor.edu. Research: gender and religion in US higher education, YWCA.

Turtis, **Richard**, *William and Mary*. Email: rturits@wm.edu.

Tusan, **Michelle E.**, *Nevada, Las Vegas*. Las Vegas, NV. Email: michelle.tusan@unlv.edu. Research: refugees and genocide, Middle East and Europe interwar years.

Tusay, **Michael Andrew**, **III**. North Huntingdon, PA. Affil: Duquesne. Email: tusaymichael@gmail.com. Research: formation of Mamluk Sultanate, medieval manuscript studies.

Tuten, **Eric E.**, *Slippery Rock*. Email: eric.tuten@sru.edu.

Tutino, **John**, *Georgetown*. Washington, DC. Email: tutinoj@georgetown.edu. Research: Latin America and Mexico, social/cultural/political.

Tutino, **Stefania**, *UCLA*. Email: tutino@history.ucla.edu.

Tuttle, **Gray**, *Columbia (Hist.)*. Email: gwt2102@columbia.edu.

Tuttle, **Lilly**. Brooklyn, NY. Affil: Museum of the City of New York. Email: lillytuttle@gmail.com. Research: New York City 1970s and 1980s, public space/visual culture/public art.

Tuttle, **Mary**. Vestal, NY. Affil: Binghamton, SUNY. Email: mtuttle@binghamton.edu.

Tuttle, **Meredith**. West Lafayette, IN. Affil: Purdue. Email: tuttle13@purdue.edu. Research: imperial Russia, European social/cultural/diplomatic.

Tuuri, **Rebecca A.**, *Southern Mississippi*. Hattiesburg, MS. Email: rebecca.tuuri@usm.edu. Research: National Council of Negro Women, international development in 1970s.

Twagira, **Benjamin E.**, *Agnes Scott*. Email: btwagira@agnesscott.edu.

Twagira, **Laura Ann**, *Wesleyan*. Email: ltwagira@wesleyan.edu.

Tweed, **Thomas**, *Notre Dame*. Notre Dame, IN. Email: ttweed@nd.edu. Research: religion in Americas, migration.

Tweton, **D. Jerome**, *North Dakota*.

Twinam, **Ann**, *Cincinnati; Texas, Austin*. Lakeway, TX. Email: ann.twinam@uc.edu; anntwinam@austin.utexas.edu. Research: illegitimacy in Spanish Atlantic world, lost women of the HAHR.

Twing, **Christina**. Leander, TX. Affil: Arizona State. Email: christinatwing@gmail.com.

Twining, **David C.**, *Westminster*. Email: twinindc@westminster.edu.

Twiss, **David**, *Worcester State*.

Twiss-Houting, **Beth**, *Hist. Soc. of Pennsylvania*. Email: btwisshouting@hsp.org.

Twitty, **Anne S.**, *Mississippi*. Email: atwitty@olemiss.edu.

Twohig, **Peter L.**, *Dalhousie; St. Mary's, Can*. Email: peter.twohig@smu.ca.

Twomey, **Alfred E.**, *Central Missouri*.

Twomey, **Carolyn**, *American Catholic Hist. Assoc*. Chestnut Hill, MA. Affil: Boston Coll. Email: ctwomey@stlawu.edu; carolyn.twomey@bc.edu.

Tworek, **Heidi J.**, *British Columbia*. Vancouver, BC, Canada. Email: htworek@mail.ubc.ca; heidievans@gmail.com. Research: 19th-/20th-c news agencies, modern Germany.

Tyce, **Spencer**. Fairmont, WV. Affil: Fairmont State. Email: spencertyce@gmail.com. Research: early colonial Venezuela, Caribbean economic.

Tye, **Nathan Thomas**, *Nebraska, Kearney*. Email: tyen@unk.edu.

Tyler, **Daniel**, *Colorado State*. Email: rockydan@aol.com.

Tyler, **Jacki Hedlund**, *Eastern Washington*. Email: jtyler5@ewu.edu.

Tyler, **John**, *Colonial Soc. of Massachusetts*. Boston, MA. Email: jtyler1776@gmail.com.

Tyler, **Lyon Gardiner**, **Jr.**, *Citadel*.

Tyrrell, **Brian Patrick**, *Reed*.

Tyrrell, **Ian R**. Marrickville, Australia. Affil: New South Wales. Email: i.tyrrell@unsw.edu.au. Research: idea of American exceptionalism, Theodore Roosevelt and US conservation policy.

Tyson, **Amy Marie**, *DePaul*. Email: atyson2@depaul.edu.

Tyson, **Kara K.**, *South Alabama*. Email: ktyson@southalabama.edu.

Tyvela, **Kirk A**. West Bend, WI. Affil: Wisconsin, Washington County. Email: kirk.tyvela@uwc.edu. Research: US-Latin American relations, Cold War.

Tzortzopoulou-Gregory, **Lita**, *Ohio State*. Email: gregory.257@osu.edu.

U u

Uchida, **Jun**, *Stanford*. Stanford, CA. Email: junu@stanford.edu. Research: Japanese colonialism in Korea.

Uchiyama, **Benjamin**, *Southern California*. Email: buchiyam@usc.edu.

Udeze, **Clement Okafor**, *California State, Dominguez Hills*. Email: cudeze@csudh.edu.

Udovic, **Edward R.**, *CM*, *DePaul*. Chicago, IL. Email: eudovic@depaul.edu. Research: modern French religious.

Uffelman, **Minoa D.**, *Austin Peay State*. Email: uffelmanm@apsu.edu.

Uhalde, **Kevin**, *Ohio*. Email: uhalde@ohio.edu.

Uhlman, **James Todd**, *Dayton*. Email: juhlman1@udayton.edu.

Ulate, **Christopher**. Montclair, CA. Affil: Bishop Amat High Sch. Email: chris.ulate@gmail.com.

Uldricks, **Teddy J**. Las Vegas, NV. Affil: Nevada, Las Vegas. Email: uldrickst@yahoo.com. Research: WWII-era appeasement/global, Soviet foreign policy.

Ulibarri, **Richard**, *Weber State*. Email: rulibarri@weber.edu.

Ulicki, **Theresa**, *Dalhousie*. Email: ulickit@dal.ca.

Ullman, **Joan Connelly**, *Washington, Seattle*. Email: ullman@uw.edu.

Ullman, **Sharon R.**, *Bryn Mawr*. Email: sullman@brynmawr.edu.

Ullrich, **Rebecca A**. Albuquerque, NM. Affil: Sandia National Laboratories. Email: raullri@sandia.gov. Research: US Cold War science and technology, 19th-c British voyages of exploration.

Ulrich, **Brian J.**, *Shippensburg*. Shippensburg, PA. Email: bjulrich@ship.edu. Research: empires and kinship societies, Persian Gulf.

Ulrich, **David**, *SUNY, Buffalo State*. Email: ulrichdl@buffalostate.edu.

Ulrich, **Laurel T.**, *Harvard (Hist.)*. Email: ulrich@fas.harvard.edu.

Ulrich-Schlumbohm, Gwen, *San Diego Mesa*. Email: ulrichschlumbohm@gmail.com.

Ulrickson, Maria Cecilia. Hyattsville, MD. Affil: Morgan State. Email: mariaceciliapluta@gmail.com. Research: African diaspora, slavery.

Ultee, Maarten, *Alabama, Tuscaloosa*.

Umansky, Lauri, *Arkansas State*. Email: lumansky@astate.edu.

Umit, Devrim. Ankara, Turkey. Affil: Karabük. Email: devrimumit@live.com.

Unangst, Matthew, *Jacksonville*. Email: munangs@ju.edu.

Underdal, Stanley J., *San José State*.

Underwood, Aubrey N. Atlanta, GA. Affil: Clark Atlanta. Email: aunderwood@cau.edu. Research: New Right and the media, Reagan and religion.

Underwood, Grant, *Brigham Young*. Email: gru2@byu.edu.

Underwood, Kathleen, *Grand Valley State*. Email: underwok@gvsu.edu.

Underwood, Nick L. Napa, CA. Affil: Colorado, Boulder. Email: nicholas_underwood@yahoo.com. Research: antifascism, visual culture.

Unfug, Douglas A., *Emory*. Email: dunfug@emory.edu.

Unger, Irwin, *NYU*. Email: iu1@nyu.edu.

Unger, Nancy C., *Santa Clara*. Mountain View, CA. Email: nunger@scu.edu. Research: Robert M. La Follette and progressivism, women in US environmental history.

Unger, Nikolaus. Rockaway Beach, NY. Affil: Preston High Sch. Email: nikolaus.unger@alumni.warwick.ac.uk. Research: nationalism and identity construction, modern central European culture and thought.

Unowsky, Daniel L., *Memphis*. Email: dunowsky@memphis.edu.

Unsinn, Summer, *Arthur and Elizabeth Schlesinger Library*. Email: sunsinn@radcliffe.harvard.edu.

Unterman, Katherine R., *Texas A&M*. Bryan, TX. Email: krunterman@gmail.com.

Unwalla, Pheroze, *British Columbia*. Email: pheroze@mail.ubc.ca.

Upart, Anatole. Greenville, SC. Affil: Chicago. Email: upart@uchicago.edu.

Upchurch, Charles, *Florida State*. Brooklyn, NY. Email: cupchurch@fsu.edu. Research: gender and sexuality, 18th-/19th-c Britain.

Upchurch, Taylor Gray. Atlanta, GA. Email: tgu205@nyu.edu.

Upham-Bornstein, Linda L., *Plymouth State*. Email: luphambornstein@plymouth.edu.

Upton, Todd P. Littleton, CO. Affil: Metropolitan State, Denver. Email: tj_upton@comcast.net. Research: perceptions of Loca Sancta 300-1000 AD, 12th-c Latin sermons.

Ural, Susannah J., *Southern Mississippi*. Email: susannah.ural@usm.edu.

Urashima, Mary Adams. Huntington Beach, CA. Email: Mary.Adams.Urashima@gmail.com. Research: Japanese American, California.

Urban, Andrew T., *Rutgers*. Email: aturban@amerstudies.rutgers.edu.

Urban, Elizabeth, *West Chester*. Email: eurban@wcupa.edu.

Urban, Kelly L., *South Alabama*. Mobile, AL. Email: kurban@southalabama.edu. Research: tuberculosis in 20th-c Cuba.

Urban-Mead, Wendy E., *Bard*. Annandale On Hudson, NY. Email: wum@bard.edu. Research: Christian/southern Africa/gender.

Urbanski, Charity Leah, *Washington, Seattle*. Email: urbanski@uw.edu.

Urbansky, Sören, *German Hist. Inst*. Email: urbansky@ghi-dc.org.

Urbiel, Alexander, *Ramapo*. Email: aurbiel@ramapo.edu.

Urdank, Albion Mier, *UCLA*. Email: aurdank@history.ucla.edu.

Uribarri, Laura Margarita. Santa Teresa, NM. Affil: Texas, El Paso. Email: lmuribarri@utep.edu.

Uribe-Uran, Victor M., *Florida International*. Miami, FL. Email: uribev@fiu.edu. Research: 18th-/19th-c family law, comparative legal.

Urofsky, Melvin I., *Virginia Commonwealth*. Email: murofsky@vcu.edu.

Ursic, Theresa. San Pedro, CA. Affil: Los Angeles Harbor. Email: ursict@att.net.

Uryadova, Yulia, *Longwood*. Email: uryadovay@longwood.edu.

Uryga, Alexander. La Porte, IN. Affil: Michigan City Area Sch. Email: alexuryga@gmail.com.

Usbeck, Frank. Leipzig, Germany. Email: frank.usbeck@posteo.de. Research: military and new media, Native American economy and self-determination.

Ushioda, Sharlie Conroy. Swarthmore, PA. Affil: Lower Merion Sch. District. Email: sharlie.ushioda@gmail.com. Research: Japan since 1868, women.

Usilton, Larry W., *North Carolina, Wilmington*. Email: usiltonl@uncw.edu.

Usner, Daniel H., Jr., *Vanderbilt*. Email: daniel.h.usner@vanderbilt.edu.

Usselman, Steven W., *Georgia Inst. of Tech*. Email: steve.usselman@hsoc.gatech.edu.

Ussishkin, Daniel, *Wisconsin-Madison*. Chicago, IL. Email: ussishkin@wisc.edu. Research: European societies and war, government.

Usuanlele, Uyilawa, *SUNY, Oswego*. Email: uyilawa.usuanlele@oswego.edu.

Uthup, Thomas, *Baldwin Wallace*. Email: tuthup@bw.edu.

Utley, Jonathan G., *Tennessee, Knoxville*.

Utley, Philip L. New York, NY. Email: putley@pobox.com. Research: Siegfried Bernfeld 1892-1953.

Utterback, Kristine T., *Wyoming*. Email: utterbck@uwyo.edu.

Uva, Katharine, *Lehman, CUNY*. Email: katie.uva@gmail.com.

Uwaelue, Charis Chiamaka. Ojodu, Nigeria. Affil: Nigeria, Nsukka. Email: charis.uwaelue.203803@unn.edu.ng.

Uzoigwe, Godfrey N., *Mississippi State*. Email: guzoigwe@history.msstate.edu.

V v

Vacante, Jeff, *Western Ontario*. Email: jvacant2@uwo.ca.

Vacca, Alison Marie, *Tennessee, Knoxville*. Email: avacca@utk.edu.

Vacca, Carolyn Summers, *St. John Fisher*. Email: cvacca@sjfc.edu.

Vachani, Nilita. New York, NY. Affil: NYU. Email: nilita@nyu.edu.

Vacroux, Alexandra M. Cambridge, MA. Affil: Harvard. Email: vacroux@fas.harvard.edu.

Vadlamudi, Sundara. Sharjah, United Arab Emirates. Affil: American, Sharjah. Email: sundarv@utexas.edu. Research: South Asia, Indian Ocean studies.

Vail, David D., *Nebraska, Kearney*. Email: vaildd@unk.edu.

Vaillant, Derek W., *Michigan, Ann Arbor*. Ann Arbor, MI. Email: dvail@umich.edu. Research: geopolitics of media history, technology and culture.

Vaitheespara, Ravindiran, *Manitoba*. Email: ravi.vaithees@umanitoba.ca.

Vajda, Matthew. Kent, OH. Affil: Kent State. Email: mjvajda@charter.net. Research: Shays' Rebellion/Massachusetts militia, heavy metal music.

Valante, Mary A., *Appalachian State*. Email: valantema@appstate.edu.

Valderrama, Carolina. Boise, ID. Email: carolinavaldechav@gmail.com.

Vale, Catherine M. Chandler, AZ. Affil: Arizona State. Email: valecatherinem@gmail.com.

Valencia, Louie Dean, *Texas State*. San Marcos, TX. Email: lv1027@txstate.edu; lvalencia@fordham.edu. Research: fascism/youth/queer culture/HIV/AIDS, knowledge production and distribution.

Valencius, Conevery Bolton, *Boston Coll*. Chestnut Hill, MA. Email: conevery.valencius@bc.edu. Research: earthquakes and earth sciences, energy development.

Valentin, Edward, Jr. Houston, TX. Affil: Rice. Email: edward.valentin@rice.edu. Research: black soldiers in the post-Civil War era.

Valentine, Emmalee Faith. Valley View, TX. Affil: Texas, Arlington. Email: emmalee.valentine@mavs.uta.edu.

Valentine, Janet G., *US Army Command Coll*. Email: janet.g.valentine.civ@mail.mil.

Valentine, Robert T., *Lehman, CUNY*. Email: robert.valentine@lehman.cuny.edu.

Valenze, Deborah M., *Barnard, Columbia*. New York, NY. Email: dvalenze@barnard.edu. Research: food, 18th-c money and culture.

Valenzuela, Juan Pablo. Acworth, GA. Affil: Kennesaw State. Email: jpv4479@kennesaw.edu. Research: social movements, Cold War Latin America/US/hemispheric.

Valeri, Mark, *Washington, St. Louis*. Saint Louis, MO. Email: mvaleri@wustl.edu. Research: American religion/social thought/economics, Reformation theology and Calvinism political.

Valerio-Jimenez, Omar S., *Texas, San Antonio*. Email: omar.valerio-jimenez@utsa.edu.

Valiani, Arafaat A., *Oregon*. Email: valiani@uoregon.edu.

Valier, Helen, *Houston*. Email: hkvalier@uh.edu.

Valk, Anne, *Williams*. Email: av7@williams.edu.

Valley, Marc A. Gray, TN. Email: marcthedoctor@yahoo.com. Research: military, 1800s technology and naval.

Valone, Stephen J., *St. John Fisher*. Email: svalone@sjfc.edu.

Valussi, Elena, *Loyola, Chicago*. Email: evalussi@luc.edu.

Van Beurden, Sarah, *Ohio State*. Email: van-beurden.1@osu.edu.

Van Cleave, Peter D. Mesa, AZ. Affil: Arizona State. Email: pvanclea@asu.edu.

Van Cleef, Ron J. Bronx, NY. Affil: SUNY, Stony Brook. Email: ronvancleef@aol.com. Research: national and sexual identity, cultural.

van Dalen, Elaine. New York, NY. Affil: Columbia. Email: ev2423@columbia.edu.

Van Dam, Raymond H., *Michigan, Ann Arbor*. Email: rvandam@umich.edu.

Van De Mieroop, Marc, *Columbia (Hist.)*. Email: mv1@columbia.edu.

Van de Moortel, Aleydis, *Tennessee, Knoxville*. Email: advm@utk.edu.

van den Arend, Alan Russell. Baltimore, MD. Affil: Johns Hopkins. Email: alan.vandenarend@gmail.com. Research: classical reception, Latin tradition.

Van Der Meer, Arnout H.C., *Colby*. Email: arnout.van.der.meer@colby.edu.

van der Velde, Adrian. Urbana, IL. Affil: Illinois, Urbana-Champaign. Email: adrianv3@illinois.edu. Research: early modern Dutch/Germanic pamphlets, Saint Eustatius.

Van Dermark, Lisa G. Granby, MA. Affil: Asnuntuck Comm. Coll. Email: ellevandermark@gmail.com. Research: US environmental, feminist/gendered emphasis.

van Deusen, Nancy E., *Queen's, Can.* Bellingham, WA. Email: nancy.vandeusen@queensu.ca. Research: conquest/early settlement of South America.

Van Deventer, David E., *California State, Fullerton*. Email: dvandeventer@fullerton.edu.

Van Die, Marguerite, *Queen's, Can.* Email: vandiem@queensu.ca.

Van Dixhoorn, Adriaan Cornelis. Middelburg, Netherlands. Affil: Utrecht. Email: a.vandixhoorn@ucr.nl. Research: knowledge cultures, regional.

Van Dyken, Tamara, *Western Kentucky*. Email: tamara.vandyken@wku.edu.

Van Engen, John H., *Notre Dame*. Notre Dame, IN. Email: jvan@nd.edu. Research: 12th century, church.

van Erve, Wouter, *Texas Woman's*. Email: wvanerve@twu.edu.

Van Helden, Albert, *Rice*. Email: helden@rice.edu.

Van Horn, Jennifer, *Delaware*. Email: jvanhorn@udel.edu.

Van Huizen, Philip, *Western Washington*. Email: Philip.VanHuizen@wwu.edu.

Van Ingen, Linda, *Nebraska, Kearney*. Email: vaningenL1@unk.edu.

van Isschot, Luis, *Toronto*. Toronto, ON, Canada. Email: luis.vanisschot@utoronto.ca. Research: human rights, natural resource extraction.

Van Ittersum, Martine J. Dundee, Scotland, United Kingdom. Affil: Dundee. Email: ittersum@post.harvard.edu. Research: Hugo Grotius, Dutch and English East India Companies.

Van Kirk, Sylvia, *Toronto*.

Van Kley, Dale K., *Ohio State*. Email: vankley.1@osu.edu.

Van Lidth de Jeude, Peter C. P., *Principia*. Email: Peter.vanLidth@principia.edu.

van Liere, Frans A., *Calvin*. Email: fvliere@calvin.edu.

van Liere, Katherine, *Calvin*. Email: kvliere@calvin.edu.

van Meer, Elisabeth, *Charleston*. Email: vanmeerb@cofc.edu.

Van Meter, Robert, Jr., *Skidmore*. Email: rvanmeter@skidmore.edu.

Van Meter, Suzanne, *Clarion, Pa.* Email: svanmeter@clarion.edu.

Van Minnen, Peter, *Cincinnati*. Email: peter.vanminnen@uc.edu.

Van Norman, William C., Jr., *James Madison*. Harrisonburg, VA. Email: vannorwc@jmu.edu. Research: slaves and planters in 19th-c Cuba.

van Nus, **Walter**, *Concordia, Can.*

Van Raden, Travis A. Iowa City, IA. Email: travis.vanraden@gmail.com.

van Rahden, Till, *Carleton, Can.* Email: till.vanrahden@carleton.ca.

Van Sant, John E., *Alabama, Birmingham*. Birmingham, AL. Email: jvansant@uab.edu. Research: Japan-US, late Tokugawa-early Meiji philosophy.

Van Slyke, Lyman P., *Stanford*. Email: yangtze@stanford.edu.

Van Tiggelen, Brigitte, *Science History Inst.* Email: bvantiggelen@sciencehistory.org.

Van Tine, Warren R., *Ohio State*. Email: vantine.1@osu.edu.

van Tuyll, Hubert P., *Augusta*. Email: hvantuyl@augusta.edu.

Van Valen, Gary, *West Georgia*. Email: gvanvale@westga.edu.

Van Valkenburg, Cynthia Lee. Escalon, CA. Affil: Modesto Jr. Coll. Email: vanvalkenburg54@msn.com. Research: California, railroads and West.

Van Vleet, Stacey A. Berkeley, CA. Affil: Indiana. Email: vanvleet@indiana.edu. Research: Tibet, China.

Van Vranken, Erika, *State Hist. Soc. of Missouri*. Email: vanvrankene@shsmo.org.

Van Vugt, William E., *Calvin*. Email: wvanvugt@calvin.edu.

Van Wagenen, Michael Scott, *Georgia Southern*. Email: mvanwagenen@georgiasouthern.edu.

Van Young, Eric J., *California, San Diego*. San Diego, CA. Email: evanyoung@ucsd.edu. Research: Lucas Alaman 1792-1853, Mexican independence 1810-21.

Van Zandt, Cynthia J., *New Hampshire, Durham*. Email: cynthia.vanzandt@unh.edu.

Van Zee, Ben. Pennington Gap, VA. Affil: Chicago. Email: benvanzee@gmail.com.

Vanatta, Sean Harris. Princeton, NJ. Affil: Princeton. Email: svanatta@princeton.edu. Research: postwar political economy, consumer credit.

VanBurkleo, Sandra F., *Wayne State*. Detroit, MI. Email: ad5235@wayne.edu; svanbur@comcast.net. Research: American constitutional and legal, women and law.

Vance, Jonathan F. W., *Western Ontario*. Email: jvance@uwo.ca.

Vance, Katelynn. Alexandria, VA. Email: KatelynnVance@gmail.com.

Vance, Michael, *St. Mary's, Can.* Email: michael.vance@smu.ca.

Vance, Shannon H., *East Carolina*. Email: vances18@ecu.edu.

Vance-Eliany, Sharon A., *Northern Kentucky*. Email: vances1@nku.edu.

Vandenberg-Daves, Jodi Ellen. La Crosse, WI. Affil: Wisconsin, La Crosse. Email: jvandenberg-daves@uwlax.edu.

Vandepaer, Elizabeth L. West Palm Beach, FL. Affil: Nation. Email: ligeia313@hotmail.com. Research: Edwardian Jewish mothers, British height and health.

Vander Lugt, Russ. Fairbanks, AK. Affil: Alaska Fairbanks. Email: rwvanderlugt@alaska.edu. Research: Frontier, American West.

Vanderlaan, Monique Elizabeth. Tucson, AZ. Affil: Arizona State. Email: Monique.E.Vanderlaan@gmail.com.

VanderMeer, Phillip, *Arizona State*. Email: p.vander.meer@asu.edu.

Vandermeulen, David J. Dublin, OH. Email: dvandermeulen@sprynet.com.

Vanderpoel, Matthew. Providence, RI. Affil: Chicago. Email: vanderpoelensis@gmail.com.

Vanderpool, Derek Paul. Mountain View, CA. Affil: Khan Lab Scool. Email: derek@khanlabschool.org. Research: political culture in France 1934-47, memory and the French Revolution.

Vandervort, Bruce C., *Virginia Military Inst.; Soc. for Military Hist.* Email: vandervortb@vmi.edu.

VanDriel, Mark. Columbia, SC. Affil: South Carolina, Columbia. Email: vandriel@email.sc.edu.

Vang, Chia Youyee, *Wisconsin-Milwaukee*. Email: vangcy@uwm.edu.

Vang, Nengher N., *Wisconsin-Whitewater*. Email: vangn@uww.edu.

Vanger, Milton I., *Brandeis*. Cambridge, MA. Research: Jose Batlle y Ordonez, Uruguay 1915-29.

VanGorder, Megan. DeKalb, IL. Affil: Northern Illinois. Email: z1848953@students.niu.edu.

Vankeerberghen, Griet, *McGill*. Email: griet.vankeerberghen@mcgill.ca.

Vann, J. Daniel, III. Asheville, NC. Affil: Pennsylvania State System of Higher Education. Email: vann@aya.yale.edu. Research: North Carolina.

Vann, Michael G., *California State, Sacramento*. Santa Cruz, CA. Email: mikevann@csus.edu. Research: world, French colonial empires.

Vann, Richard T., *Wesleyan*. Email: rvann@wesleyan.edu.

Vannette, Jennifer. Midland, MI. Affil: Central Michigan. Email: jgvannette@gmail.com. Research: religious and racial NGOs, human rights.

VanSandt, Zoe Irene, *Austin Comm. Coll.* Email: vansandt@austincc.edu.

Vapnek, Lara, *St. John's, NY.* Jamaica, NY. Email: vapnekl@stjohns.edu. Research: women's work.

Vaporis, Constantine N., *Maryland, Baltimore County*. Email: vaporis@umbc.edu.

Vardi, Gil-li. Stanford, CA. Affil: Stanford. Email: gvardi@stanford.edu. Research: evolution of military thought, military culture.

Vardi, Liana, *SUNY, Buffalo*. Buffalo, NY. Email: vardi@buffalo.edu. Research: France, early modern Europe.

Varela-Lago, Ana M., *Northern Arizona*.

Varey, David, *Royal Military*. Email: varey-d@rmc.ca.

Varga-Harris, Christine, *Illinois State*. Email: cvargah@ilstu.edu.

Vargas, Daisy. Tucson, AZ. Affil: Arizona. Email: daisyvargas@email.arizona.edu.

Vargas, Michael, *SUNY, New Paltz*. New Paltz, NY. Email: vargasm@newpaltz.edu. Research: Dominican Order in Spain.

Vargas, Zaragosa, *North Carolina, Chapel Hill*. Email: zvargas@email.unc.edu.

Vargas-Betancourt, Margarita. Gainesville, FL. Affil: Florida. Email: margaritavargas2013@gmail.com. Research: imperialism and archives, diaspora from Latin America.

Varias, Alexander, *Chestnut Hill; Villanova*. Email: alexander.varias@villanova.edu.

Varlamos, Michael N. Grosse Pointe Woods, MI. Affil: Wayne State. Email: fmichaelnv@mac. com.

Varlik, Nühket, *Rutgers, Newark/New Jersey Inst. of Tech.; South Carolina, Columbia*. Email: varlik@rutgers.edu.

Varon, Elizabeth R., *Virginia*. Email: erv5c@ virginia.edu.

Varon, Jeremy P., *New School*. Email: varonj@ newschool.edu.

Vartanian, Pershing, *San Diego State*. Email: vartania@sdsu.edu.

Varuolo, Michael. Durham, NH. Affil: New Hampshire, Durham. Email: mv1021@ wildcats.unh.edu.

Varzally, Allison, *California State, Fullerton*. Email: avarzally@fullerton.edu.

Vascik, George S., *Miami, Ohio*. Email: vascikgs@miamioh.edu.

Vasconcellos, Colleen A., *West Georgia*. Email: cvasconc@westga.edu.

Vasile, Ronald S. Downers Grove, IL. Affil: Lockport Township High Sch. Email: ronvasile@sbcglobal.net. Research: I&M Canal, William Stimpson.

Vasquez, George L., *San José State*. Email: George.Vasquez@sjsu.edu.

Vasquez, Mel Joseph K. Jacksonville, FL. Affil: North Florida. Email: redflutter23@gmail.com.

Vassalle, Francesca. Port Washington, NY. Email: fvassalle@gradcenter.cuny.edu.

Vassar, Mark, *Arthur and Elizabeth Schlesinger Library*. Email: mark_vassar@radcliffe.harvard. edu.

Vatai, Frank L., *California State, Northridge*. Email: frank.vatai@csun.edu.

Vatter, Sherry G. Los Angeles, CA. Affil: California State, Long Beach. Email: svatter@ csulb.edu. Research: Ottoman Syria social, Ottoman painting.

Vaughan, Bryan F. Crawfordville, FL. Email: Bvaug146@hotmail.com. Research: US military/US South, maritime.

Vaughan, Mary Kay, *Maryland, Coll. Park*. Email: mkv@umd.edu.

Vaughn, James Martin, *Texas, Austin*. Austin, TX. Email: jmvaughn@austin.utexas.edu. Research: 18th-c British imperialism, origins of British Indian Empire.

Vaughn, Mark Kennedy, *US Army Command Coll*. Email: mark.k.vaughn.civ@mail.mil.

Vaughn, Sally N., *Houston*. Email: snvaughn@ sbcglobal.net.

Vaught, David J., *Texas A&M*. College Station, TX. Email: d-vaught@tamu.edu. Research: baseball in rural America.

Vaught, Seneca D., *Kennesaw State*. Email: svaught3@kennesaw.edu.

Vaum, Jillian. Washington, DC. Affil: Pennsylvania. Email: jvaum@sas.upenn.edu.

Vause, Erika, *St. John's, NY*. Email: vausee@ stjohns.edu.

Vazansky, Alexander, *Nebraska, Lincoln*. Email: avazansky2@unl.edu.

Vazquez, Josefina Zoraida. México D.F., Mexico. Affil: El Colegio de México. Email: jvazquez@ colmex.mx. Research: first Mexican federalism 1824-35, army and state in Mexico 1821-48.

Vedeler, Harold Torger, *Central Connecticut State*. Newington, CT. Email: vedelerhat@ ccsu.edu. Research: reign of Samsuiluna, Old Babylonian year names.

Vedoveli Francisco, Paula. São Paulo, Brazil. Affil: Princeton. Email: paula.vedoveli@gmail. com.

Veeder, Stacy Renee, *Charleston*. Email: veedersr@cofc.edu.

Veeser, Cyrus, *Bentley*. Email: cveeser@bentley. edu.

Vego, Milan Nikola, *Naval War Coll*. Email: vegom@usnwc.edu.

Veidlinger, Jeffrey, *Michigan, Ann Arbor*. Ann Arbor, MI. Email: jveidlin@umich.edu. Research: Jewish cultural identity in Russia, Jewish memory in eastern Europe.

Veit, Helen, *Michigan State*. Email: hveit@msu. edu.

Veit, Richard, *Monmouth*. Email: rveit@ monmouth.edu.

Vela, Nicholas Jacob. Corpus Christi, TX. Email: nicholasjvela@outlook.com.

Velasco, Alejandro, *NYU*. Email: av48@nyu.edu.

Velasquez, Daniel. Chapel Hill, NC. Affil: North Carolina, Chapel Hill. Email: Daniel. Velasquez@unc.edu. Research: Veracruz/New Orleans/Havana/Pensacola.

Veldman, Meredith, *Louisiana State*. Email: hyveld@lsu.edu.

Velez, Diana, *Houston*. Email: dvelez@uh.edu.

Velez, Karin A., *Macalester*. Saint Paul, MN. Email: kvelez@macalester.edu. Research: Catholic expansion, early modern religion.

Velikanova, Olga, *North Texas*. Email: velikanova@unt.edu.

Vellon, Peter G., *Queens, CUNY*. Email: peter. vellon@qc.cuny.edu.

Velmet, Aro, *Southern California*. Los Angeles, CA. Email: velmet@usc.edu. Research: empire and interracial marriage in interwar France, immigration in postwar France.

Veloz, Larisa, *Texas, El Paso*. Email: llveloz@utep. edu.

Vemsani, Lavanya. Portsmouth, OH. Affil: Shawnee State. Email: lvemsani@shawnee. edu. Research: Indian society/religion/ literature, South Indian historical identity.

Venables, Robert W. Ithaca, NY. Affil: Cornell. Email: rwv3@cornell.edu.

Vendell, Dominic. New York, NY. Affil: Columbia. Email: D.Vendell@exeter.ac.uk.

Venditto, Elizabeth O'Ressa. Brooklyn, NY. Affil: Minnesota, Twin Cities. Email: vendi002@ umn.edu. Research: religion and migration, migration and nation-building.

Venet, Wendy Hamand, *Georgia State*. Email: wvenet@gsu.edu.

Venit-Shelton, Tamara, *Claremont McKenna*. Email: tvenit@cmc.edu.

Venkatasubramanian, Varsha. Berkeley, CA. Affil: California, Berkeley. Email: varshanet@ gmail.com. Research: dam and hydrological development, Cold War.

Venosa, Joseph, *Salisbury*. Email: jlvenosa@ salisbury.edu.

Venters, Aglaia Maretta. Baton Rouge, LA. Email: aglaia.venters@gmail.com. Research: French concepts of Louisiana.

Venters, Louis, *Francis Marion*. Email: lventers@ fmarion.edu.

Ventura, Theresa M., *Concordia, Can*. Montreal, QC, Canada. Email: Theresa.Ventura@ concordia.ca. Research: US, Progressive Era.

Vera, Juan Camilo. Miami, FL. Affil: Miami. Email: j.vera@umiami.edu.

Verboon, Caitlin. Blacksburg, VA. Affil: Virginia Tech. Email: cverboon@vt.edu. Research: Civil War and Reconstruction, African American/US race relations.

Verbrugge, Martha H., *Bucknell*. Email: verbrgge@bucknell.edu.

Verbrugghe, Gerald P., *Rutgers, Camden*. Email: verbrugg@camden.rutgers.edu.

Vergara, Angela, *California State, Los Angeles*. Santa Monica, CA. Email: avergar@calstatela. edu. Research: labor, Chile.

Vergara, German, *Georgia Inst. of Tech*. Atlanta, GA. Email: german.vergara@hsoc.gatech.edu. Research: Latin America, environmental.

Verhoeven, Claudia, *Cornell*. Email: cv89@ cornell.edu.

Verhoff, Gwendolyn E. Chesterfield, MO. Affil: St. Louis Comm. Coll., Wildwood. Email: gverhoff1@stlcc.edu. Research: nuclear technology/health/environment.

Vermij, Rienk H., *Oklahoma (Hist. of Science)*. Email: rienk.vermij@ou.edu.

Verna, Chantalle F., *Florida International*. Email: verna@fiu.edu.

Vernal, Fiona, *Connecticut, Storrs*. Email: fiona. vernal@uconn.edu.

Vernet, Julien P. Kelowna, BC, Canada. Affil: British Columbia, Okanagan. Email: julien. vernet@ubc.ca. Research: colonial Louisiana and Quebec, US 1776-1815.

Vernon, James, *California, Berkeley*. Email: jvernon@berkeley.edu.

Verrier, Joseph. Coventry, RI. Email: joe.e.verrier@gmail.com.

Verrone, Richard B. Lubbock, TX. Affil: Texas Tech. Email: richard.verrone@ttu.edu. Research: post-1939 US-Laos-Vietnam relations, counterinsurgency.

Verskin, Alan, *Rhode Island*. Email: verskin@uri. edu.

Vest, Jacques Bert. Ann Arbor, MI. Affil: Michigan, Ann Arbor. Email: jacquesb@umich. edu. Research: media and senses, intellectual and cultural.

Vester, Katharina, *American*. Email: vester@ american.edu.

Vester, Matthew A., *West Virginia*. Email: matt. vester@mail.wvu.edu.

Vetter, Jeremy, *Arizona*. Tucson, AZ. Email: jvetter@email.arizona.edu. Research: US environmental, science.

Via, Anthony P., *SJ*, *Gonzaga*. Email: via@ gonzaga.edu.

Viator, Felicia Angeja. San Francisco, CA. Affil: San Francisco State. Email: felicia.viator@ gmail.com. Research: popular culture, California.

Vicens, Belen, *Salisbury*. Email: bxvicenssaiz@ salisbury.edu.

Vicente, Marta V., *Kansas*. Email: mvicente@ ku.edu.

Vichcales, Kevin B. San Antonio, TX. Affil: Incarnate Word. Email: vichcale@uiwtx.edu.

Vick, Brian E., *Emory*. Atlanta, GA. Email: bvick@ emory.edu. Research: Vienna Congress and political culture, German nationalism/gender/ law.

Vickery, Kenneth P., *North Carolina State*. Email: kpvicker@ncsu.edu.

Vickrey, Mark, *Kennesaw State*. Email: mvickre1@kennesaw.edu.

Vidan, Gili. Cambridge, MA. Affil: Harvard. Email: gvidan@g.harvard.edu.

Vider, **Stephen Joshua**, *Cornell*. Philadelphia, PA. Email: stephen.vider@gmail.com. Research: LGBTQ domesticity, homeless youth.

Vidmar, **John C.**, **OP**, *Providence*. Email: jvidmar@providence.edu.

Vidojkovic, **Dario**. Regensburg, Germany. Affil: Regensburg. Email: dario.vidojkovic@geschichte.uni-regensburg.de. Research: German Kaiserreich and Balkans foreign relations, 19th-/early 20th-c mass media/stereotypes.

Viehe, **Fred W.**, *Youngstown State*. Youngstown, OH. Email: fwviehe@ysu.edu. Research: women in 19th-c US underworld, Fredericaka Mandelbaum.

Vieira, **Kerry**, *World Hist. Assoc.* Email: info@thewha.org.

Viens, **Katheryn P.** Attleboro, MA. Email: kviens@mindspring.com. Research: development of early railroads, technology transfer Britain and US.

Vierick, **Robert Scott**, *Hist. Assoc.* Email: svierick@historyassociates.com.

Vieth, **Jane K.**, *Michigan State*. Email: vieth@msu.edu.

Vietoris, **John M.**, **FSC**, *Lewis*. Email: vietorjo@lewisu.edu.

Vigil, **Ralph H.**, *Nebraska, Lincoln*. Email: rvigil2@unl.edu.

Viglini, **Nicole Ellen**. San Francisco, CA. Affil: California, Berkeley. Email: nicole.viglini@berkeley.edu.

Vignone, **Joseph Leonardo**. Somerville, MA. Affil: Harvard. Email: vignone@fas.harvard.edu.

Vigus, **Robert**. Aubrey, TX. Affil: North Central Texas. Email: robert.vigus@yahoo.com.

Villagomez, **Cynthia Jan**. Winston Salem, NC. Affil: Winston-Salem State. Email: villagomezcy@wssu.edu. Research: monastic economy in late antiquity, Middle Eastern perceptions of Africans.

Villalpando, **Demmy**. San Diego, CA. Affil: Chicago. Email: villalpando@uchicago.edu.

Villani, **Stefano**, *Maryland, Coll. Park*. Email: villani@umd.edu.

Villanueva, **Capt James**, *US Military Acad.* Email: james.villanueva@usma.edu.

Villanueva, **Nicholas**, **Jr.** Broomfield, CO. Affil: Colorado, Boulder. Email: nicholas.villanueva@colorado.edu. Research: immigration, borderlands.

Villarreal, **Christina Marie**. Austin, TX. Affil: Texas, Austin. Email: christinamariev09@gmail.com. Research: Latin American borderlands, fugitive slaves.

Villegas, **Marisa Y.** Hayward, CA. Affil: Oakland Unified Sch. District. Email: mariazteca13@gmail.com.

Villegas-Ramirez, **Marisa Y.** Hayward, CA. Affil: Oakland Unified Sch. District. Email: marisa.villegas@ousd.org.

Villella, **Peter B.** Greensboro, NC. Affil: US Air Force Academy. Email: peterbvillella@gmail.com. Research: native peoples in colonial Mexico, development of Mexican Creole identity.

Vincent, **James W.**, *Charleston*. Email: vincentj@cofc.edu.

Vincent, **Jennifer**. Palm Bay, FL. Affil: Central Florida. Email: jvincent2@knights.ucf.edu.

Vincent, **K. Steven**, *North Carolina State*. Email: steven_vincent@ncsu.edu.

Vincent, **Stephanie**. Kent, OH. Affil: Kent State. Email: smvincent11@gmail.com. Research: business, consumption.

Vinikas, **Vincent A.**, *Arkansas, Little Rock*. Email: vxvinikas@ualr.edu.

Vinkovetsky, **Ilya**, *Simon Fraser*. Burnaby, BC, Canada. Email: ivink@sfu.ca. Research: Russian merchant networks in Eurasia and, Russia and making of Bulgarian nation.

Vinovskis, **Maris A.**, *Michigan, Ann Arbor*. Ann Arbor, MI. Email: vinovski@umich.edu. Research: US social, family.

Vinson, **Ben**, **III**, *Case Western Reserve*. Cleveland, OH. Email: ben.vinson@case.edu. Research: African diaspora, colonial Mexico.

Vinson, **Frank B.**, *Georgia Coll. and State*.

Vinson, **Robert Trent**, *William and Mary*. Email: rtvins@wm.edu.

Vinz, **Warren L.**, *Boise State*. Email: wvinz@aol.com.

Viola, **Lynne**, *Toronto*. Toronto, ON, Canada. Email: lynne.viola@utoronto.ca. Research: peasants/deportations, Stalinism.

Violette, **Aurele J.**, *Purdue, Fort Wayne*. Email: aviolette@verizon.net.

Vipond, **Mary**, *Concordia, Can.* Email: Mary.Vipond@concordia.ca.

Vipond Quesada, **Julie**, *Texas Southern*. Email: julie.vipond@tsu.edu.

Virani, **Shafique**, *Toronto*. Email: shafique.virani@utoronto.ca.

Virdi, **Jaipreet**, *Delaware*. Email: jvirdi@udel.edu.

Viscomi, **Joseph John**, **II**. London, United Kingdom. Affil: Birkbeck, London. Email: josephviscomi@gmail.com. Research: decolonization, displacement.

Viscusi, **Peter L.**, *Central Missouri*. Warrensburg, MO. Email: pviscusi@charter.net. Research: Domitian, monasticism.

Vise, **Melissa E.**, *Washington and Lee*. Lexington, CT. Email: visem@wlu.edu; melissavise@gmail.com.

Visser, **Thomas D.**, *Vermont*. Email: thomas.visser@uvm.edu.

Vitale, **Antonella**. Berkeley, CA. Affil: Graduate Center, CUNY. Email: antvitale74@gmail.com.

Viterbo, **Paula**, *Robert H. Smith Center*. Email: pviterbo@monticello.org.

Vitiello, **Joanna J. Carraway**, *Rockhurst*. Email: joanna.carraway@rockhurst.edu.

Vitiello, **Massimiliano**, *Missouri–Kansas City*.

Vitz, **Matthew**, *California, San Diego*. Email: mvitz@ucsd.edu.

Vitz, **Robert C.**, *Northern Kentucky*. Email: vitz@nku.edu.

Vivian, **Daniel J.**, *Kentucky*. Lexington, KY. Email: daniel.vivian@uky.edu; vivian.daniel.j@gmail.com. Research: aftermath of slavery in American culture, memory of plantation slavery 1900-40.

Vivian, **Miriam Raub**, *California State, Bakersfield*. Email: mvivian@csub.edu.

Vizdos, **Pamela**. Bay Village, OH. Email: vizdosfamily@att.net.

Vladimirov, **Katya V.**, *Kennesaw State*. Email: kvladimi@kennesaw.edu.

Vlahovich, **Brett M.** Seattle, WA. Affil: Shorecrest High Sch. Email: vlahovib@gmail.com.

Vlastos, **Stephen**, *Iowa*. Email: stephen-vlastos@uiowa.edu.

Vlossak, **Elizabeth**, *Brock*. Email: evlossak@brocku.ca.

Voegeli, **V. Jacque**, **III**, *Vanderbilt*. Email: jacque.voegeli@vanderbilt.edu.

Voekel, **Pamela**, *Dartmouth*. Hanover, NH. Email: pamela.voekel@dartmouth.edu. Research: Latin American modernity, Mexico.

Voelkel, **James R.**, *Science History Inst.* Email: jvoelkel@sciencehistory.org.

Voelker, **David J.** Green Bay, WI. Affil: Wisconsin, Green Bay. Email: voelkerd@uwgb.edu. Research: history pedagogy.

Voeltz, **Richard A.** Lawton, OK. Affil: Cameron. Email: richardhst@aol.com. Research: Edwardian England, media studies and history.

Vogel, **William F.** Minneapolis, MN. Affil: Minnesota, Twin Cities. Email: vogel322@umn.edu.

Vogt, **Albert**, *South Florida, St. Petersburg*.

Vogt, **Nicholas**, *Indiana*. Email: pnvogt@indiana.edu.

Voisey, **Paul L.**, *Alberta*. Email: pvoisey@ualberta.ca.

Volk, **Kyle G.**, *Montana*. Email: kyle.volk@umontana.edu.

Volk, **Steven S.**, *Oberlin*. Email: steven.volk@oberlin.edu.

Voll, **John**, *Georgetown*. Washington, DC. Email: vollj@georgetown.edu. Research: contemporary Islamic revivalism, world history conceptualizations.

Volmar, **Daniel**. Cambridge, MA. Affil: Harvard. Email: dvolmar@g.harvard.edu.

Volpe, **Vernon L.**, *Nebraska, Kearney*. Email: volpev@unk.edu.

Voltz, **Noel Mellick**, *Utah*. Salt Lake City, UT. Email: noel.voltz@utah.edu. Research: African American, Atlantic world.

Volz, **Stephen**, *Kenyon*. Gambier, OH. Email: volzs@kenyon.edu. Research: 19th-c Tswana evangelists, colonialism in southern Africa.

von Bothmer, **Bernard**, *San Francisco*. San Francisco, CA. Email: bvonbothmer@yahoo.com. Research: US.

von Daacke, **Kirt**. Charlottesville, VA. Affil: Virginia. Email: kv2h@virginia.edu. Research: race/community in rural antebellum south, free blacks in antebellum Virginia.

Von Dassanowsky, **Robert**. Colorado Springs, CO. Affil: Colorado, Colorado Springs. Email: rvondass@uccs.edu. Research: German, film studies.

Von Dassow, **Eva**, *Minnesota (Hist.)*. Email: vonda001@umn.edu.

Von Den Steinen, **Karl**, *California State, Sacramento*. Email: karl@csus.edu.

von der Goltz, **Anna**, *Georgetown*. Washington, DC. Email: af778@georgetown.edu. Research: 20th-c Germany, modern Europe.

von der Krone, **Kerstin**, *German Hist. Inst.* Washington, DC. Email: krone@ghi-dc.org. Research: modern Jewish/Jewish education, intellectual/book/knowledge production.

Von Eschen, **Penny M.**, *Virginia*. Charlottesville, VA. Email: pmv3c@virginia.edu. Research: post-1945 US in world, globalization and American culture.

Von Germeten, **Nicole N.** Corvallis, OR. Affil: Oregon State. Email: nvongermeten@yahoo.com. Research: Africans in Latin America, religion and society in Latin America.

von Glahn, **Richard**, *UCLA*. Email: vonglahn@history.ucla.edu.

Von Greyerz, Kaspar H. Bern, Switzerland. Affil: Basel. Email: Kaspar.vonGreyerz@unibas.ch. Research: early modern religion/knowledge/science.

von Hoffman, Alexander. Cambridge, MA. Affil: Harvard. Email: alexander_von_hoffman@harvard.edu. Research: 19th-/20th-c housing, late 20th-c inner city community development.

von Kraus, Rudiger. Boston, MA. Email: rudigervonkraus@gaiustacitus.com. Research: American-Romanian relations 1944-89, Romanian industrialist Nicolae Malaxa.

Von Sivers, Peter, *Utah.* Email: peter.vonsivers@utah.edu.

von Stackelberg, Emmet. New Brunswick, NJ. Affil: Rutgers. Email: emstack@gmail.com.

von Weissenberg, Marita, Xavier, Ohio. Cincinnati, OH. Email: vonweissenbergm@xavier.edu. Research: late medieval religious and social.

Vong, Sam C., Texas, Austin. Washington, DC. Affil: Smithsonian Inst. Email: scvong@gmail.com. Research: refugees, Asian American.

vonHaas, Marie M. Albuquerque, NM. Affil: New Mexico. Email: mvonhaas@unm.edu. Research: global, North/Central/South American West.

Voogt, Pieter G., *Kennesaw State.* Email: gvoogt@kennesaw.edu.

Voorhees, David William, NYU. Hudson, NY. Affil: Jacob Leisler Inst. Email: dwv1@nyu.edu; info@jacobleislerinstitute.org. Research: Jacob Leisler, Anglo-Dutch New York and New Jersey.

Vorenberg, Michael, Brown. Providence, RI. Email: michael_vorenberg@brown.edu. Research: 19th-c US, Civil War and Reconstruction.

Vosmeier, Matthew N. Hanover, IN. Affil: Hanover. Email: vosmeier@hanover.edu.

Voss, Robert J. Maryville, MO. Affil: Northwest Missouri State. Email: robvoss@nwmissouri.edu. Research: railroads/Indian territory/capitalism, rail/Native America.

Voss, Stuart F., *SUNY, Plattsburgh.* Email: vosssf@plattsburgh.edu.

Voss-Hubbard, Mark, *Eastern Illinois.* Email: mvosshubbard@eiu.edu.

Voßkamp, Nathalie. Borken, Germany. Affil: Köln. Email: nathalie.vosskamp@uni-koeln.de. Research: tourism, Hawaii.

Vostral, Sharra L., *Purdue.* Email: svostral@purdue.edu.

Vourlojianis, George N., *John Carroll.* Email: gvourlojianis@jcu.edu.

Vrana, Heather A., Florida. Gainesville, FL. Email: hvrana@ufl.edu. Research: disability in Central America, Central American social movements.

Vrtis, George H., Carleton Coll. Northfield, MN. Email: gvrtis@carleton.edu. Research: US environmental, environmental and technology studies.

Vsetecka, John. Lansing, MI. Affil: Michigan State. Email: vsetecka@msu.edu.

Vu, Linh Dam. Tempe, AZ. Affil: Arizona State. Email: linhdvu@gmail.com. Research: war dead in 20th-c China, terrorism.

Vuic, Kara Dixon, Texas Christian. Fort Worth, TX. Email: k.vuic@tcu.edu. Research: gender and war, war and society.

Vushko, Iryna, *Hunter, CUNY; Princeton.* Email: iv30@hunter.cuny.edu.

W w

Wabuda, Susan, Fordham. Stamford, CT. Email: wabuda@fordham.edu. Research: early modern England.

Wachendorfer, Dieter H. W., Jr. Frankfurt am Main, Germany. Email: doc.wado@t-online.de. Research: Age of Reformation in Germany, 30 Years' War in Europe 1618-48.

Waddell, Mark, *Michigan State.* Email: waddellm@msu.edu.

Waddell, Steve, *US Military Acad.* Email: steve.waddell@usma.edu.

Waddle, Joshua, *Northern Iowa.* Email: flywheel@uni.edu.

Waddy, Helena, *SUNY, Coll. Geneseo.* Email: waddy@geneseo.edu.

Wade, Alisa J., *California State, Chico.*

Wade, Bethany Marie. Pittsburgh, PA. Affil: Pittsburgh. Email: bmw73@pitt.edu.

Wade, Harry, *Texas A&M, Commerce.* Email: harry.wade@tamuc.edu.

Wade, Michael G., *Appalachian State.* Email: wademg@appstate.edu.

Wade, Rex A., *George Mason.*

Wade, Susan W., *Keene State.* Email: swade@keene.edu.

Wadelington, Flora J., *North Carolina A&T State.* Email: fjwadeli@ncat.edu.

Wadewitz, Lissa K., *Linfield.* Email: lwadewi@linfield.edu.

Wadkins, Mary Jane, *Columbus State.* Email: mjwadkins@hotmail.com.

Wagenheim, Olga J., *Rutgers, Newark/New Jersey Inst. of Tech.*

Wages, Brian. Provo, UT. Affil: Brigham Young. Email: brianwages90@gmail.com.

Waggoner Karchner, Kate. Toledo, OH. Affil: Michigan, Ann Arbor. Email: kgwag@umich.edu.

Waghelstein, John D., *Naval War Coll.* Email: john.waghelstein@usnwc.edu.

Wagle, Narendra K., *Toronto.*

Wagman, Jamie S. Granger, IN. Affil: St. Mary's, Ind. Email: jwagman@saintmarys.edu. Research: US birth control, women's voices.

Wagner, Jonathan, *Minot State.* Email: jonathan.wagner@minotstateu.edu.

Wagner, Kaleigh. Wilmington, NC. Email: kaleighmwagner@gmail.com.

Wagner, Steven. Uxbridge, United Kingdom. Affil: Brown. Email: Steven.wagner@brunel.ac.uk. Research: international security.

Wagner, Wende, *State Hist. Soc. of Missouri.* Email: wagnerwl@shsmo.org.

Wagner, William E., *Colorado Denver.* Email: william.wagner@ucdenver.edu.

Wagner, William G., *Williams.* Email: wwagner@williams.edu.

Wagner-Wright, Sandra, *Hawai'i, Hilo.* Email: sandraww@hawaii.edu.

Wagnon, William O., Jr., *Washburn.* Email: bill.wagnon@washburn.edu.

Wagstrom, Thor, *Metropolitan State.* Email: thor.wagstrom@metrostate.edu.

Waheed, Sarah F., *Davidson.* Email: sawaheed@davidson.edu.

Wailoo, Keith A., Princeton. Princeton, NJ. Email: kwailoo@princeton.edu. Research: medicine and science, US cultural and intellectual.

Wainwright, Philip, *Emory.* Email: global@emory.edu.

Waiser, William A., *Saskatchewan.* Email: bill.waiser@usask.ca.

Waite, Charles, *Texas-Rio Grande Valley.* Email: charles.waite@utrgv.edu.

Waite, Gary K., *New Brunswick.* Email: waite@unb.ca.

Waite, Kevin. Pasadena, CA. Affil: Durham. Email: kevin.a.waite@durham.ac.uk. Research: American slavery/proslavery expansion, Civil War-era West.

Waite, Peter B., *Dalhousie.*

Waits, William B. Lambertville, NJ. Email: wwaits9@comcast.net.

Wake, Naoko, Michigan State. East Lansing, MI. Email: wake@msu.edu. Research: illness/gender/sexuality, cultural and intellectual.

Wakefield, Andre, *Pitzer.* Email: andre_wakefield@pitzer.edu.

Wakefield, Zach. Morristown, NJ. Affil: Pingry Sch. Email: zwakefield@ves.org.

Wakelam, Randall, *Royal Military.* Email: randall.wakelam@rmc.ca.

Wakeman, Rosemary, *Fordham.* Email: rwakeman@fordham.edu.

Wakild, Emily L. Boise, ID. Affil: Boise State. Email: emilywakild@boisestate.edu. Research: national park creation, environmental policy.

Walch, Teresa. Modi'in, Israel. Affil: Hebrew, Jerusalem. Email: teresa.walch@gmail.com.

Walcher, Dustin, Southern Oregon. Ashland, OR. Email: walcherd@sou.edu. Research: international affairs, global capitalism.

Walden, Keith, *Trent.* Email: kwalden@trentu.ca.

Waldman, William C. Portland, OR. Email: walchef@gmail.com.

Waldman, Zoe Joelle. Ann Arbor, MI. Affil: Michigan, Ann Arbor. Email: waldmanz@umich.edu.

Waldron, Arthur N., *Pennsylvania.* Email: awaldron2@mac.com.

Waldstreicher, David L., *Graduate Center, CUNY.* Email: dwaldstreicher@gc.cuny.edu.

Walens, Susann M., *Western Connecticut State.* Email: walenss@wcsu.edu.

Wales, Jonathan, *Providence.* Email: Jonathan.Wales@providence.edu.

Waley-Cohen, Joanna, NYU. New Haven, CT. Email: jw5@nyu.edu. Research: Chinese social and cultural, China and world.

Walia, Mark K., *California State, Fullerton.* Email: mwalia@fullerton.edu.

Walicki, Andrzej, *Notre Dame.* Email: Waliki.1@nd.edu.

Walker, Anita, *Connecticut, Storrs.* Email: anita.walker@uconn.edu.

Walker, Barbara B., Nevada, Reno. Reno, NV. Email: bbwalker@unr.edu. Research: Russia and eastern Europe, cultural.

Walker, Barrington, *Queen's, Can.* Email: walkerb@queensu.ca.

Walker, Brett Laurence, Montana State, Bozeman. Belgrade, MT. Email: bwalker@montana.edu; brett.laurence.walker@gmail.com. Research: Japan, environment.

Walker, C. Michael. Waskom, TX. Affil: Bossier Parish Comm. Coll. Email: walker_michael@hotmail.com. Research: WWI, Crusades.

Walker, Carmen V., *Bowie State.* Email: cwalker@bowiestate.edu.

Walker, Charles F., California, Davis. Davis, CA. Email: cfwalker@ucdavis.edu. Research: natural disasters, earthquakes and nationalism.

Walker, **Clarence E.**, *California, Davis*. Davis, CA. Email: cewalker@ucdavis.edu. Research: American black 1450-present, 19th-c social and political.

Walker, **David A.**, *Northern Iowa*. Email: david.walker@uni.edu.

Walker, **David Mckinley**, *Boise State*. Email: davidwalker2@boisestate.edu.

Walker, **David**, *California, Santa Barbara*. Email: dwalker@religion.ucsb.edu.

Walker, **David**, *South Florida, St. Petersburg*.

Walker, **Evan**. Minneapolis, MN. Email: wevan99@gmail.com.

Walker, **Ezekiel**, *Central Florida*. Email: Ezekiel.Walker@ucf.edu.

Walker, **Gavin**, *McGill*. Email: gavin.walker@mcgill.ca.

Walker, **Helen Campbell**, *William and Mary*. Email: hcwalk@wm.edu.

Walker, **Jacqueline B.**, *James Madison*. Email: walkerjb@jmu.edu.

Walker, **James**, *Waterloo*. Email: jwwalker@uwaterloo.ca.

Walker, **Janelle**. Chicago, IL. Affil: DePaul. Email: janellelynwalker@gmail.com.

Walker, **Joel Thomas**, *Washington, Seattle*. Email: jwalker@uw.edu.

Walker, **John Thomas**. Roswell, GA. Affil: Georgia State. Email: xxxtwalker@gmail.com.

Walker, **Joshua Charles**. Lakewood, OH. Affil: 9/11 Memorial & Museum. Email: walker.809@gmail.com.

Walker, **Juliet E. K.**, *Texas, Austin*. Email: jekwalker@austin.utexas.edu.

Walker, **Louise E.**, *Northeastern*. Boston, MA. Email: l.walker@northeastern.edu; louise.e.walker@gmail.com. Research: Mexico and Latin America, economic and political.

Walker, **Lydia**. Hanover, NH. Affil: Dartmouth. Email: lydia.rose.walker@gmail.com.

Walker, **Mack**, *Johns Hopkins (Hist.)*. Email: erwalk@worldnet.att.net.

Walker, **Mark**, *Union Coll*. Email: walkerm@union.edu.

Walker, **Meredith Ancret**. Phoenix, AZ. Affil: Grand Canyon. Email: MeredithAncret@gmail.com.

Walker, **Pamela J.**, *Carleton, Can*. Email: pamela.walker@carleton.ca.

Walker, **Peter William**. Laramie, WY. Affil: Wyoming. Email: pww2104@columbia.edu. Research: British Empire, American Revolution.

Walker, **Rachel E.**, *Hartford*. West Hartford, CT. Email: racwalker@hartford.edu. Research: science, women/gender/sexuality.

Walker, **Samuel E.**, *Nebraska, Omaha*. Email: swalker@unomaha.edu.

Walker, **Stewart E.**, *III*. Monrovia, MD. Affil: Montgomery County Public Sch. Email: gwalker1732@yahoo.com. Research: Revolutionary War veterans, Civil War veterans.

Walker, **Sue Sheridan**, *Northeastern Illinois*.

Walker, **Tamara J.**, *Toronto*.

Walker, **Timothy D.** North Dartmouth, MA. Affil: Massachusetts, Dartmouth. Email: twalker@umassd.edu. Research: European/India/Atlantic colonial medicine, global slave trade.

Walker, **Vanessa**, *Amherst*. Email: vwalker@amherst.edu.

Walker, **William O.**, *III*. San Antonio, TX. Affil: Toronto. Email: walkerw52@yahoo.com.

Research: LBJ and Latin America, American century.

Walker, **William T.**, *Chestnut Hill*. Email: wwalker@chc.edu.

Walkers, **Anders**. Saint Louis, MO. Affil: St. Louis Sch. of Law. Email: anders.walker@slu.edu.

Walker-Said, **Charlotte M.** New York, NY. Affil: John Jay, CUNY. Email: cwalker-said@jjay.cuny.edu.

Walkowitz, **Daniel J.**, *NYU*. New York, NY. Email: daniel.walkowitz@nyu.edu. Research: American folk dance movement, comparative public history movements.

Walkowitz, **Judith R.**, *Johns Hopkins (Hist.)*. New York, NY. Email: jw27@nyu.edu. Research: modern European women, Victorian cultural and social.

Wall, **Barbra M.** Charlottesville, VA. Affil: Virginia. Email: bmw8y@virginia.edu. Research: hospitals and healthcare systems, nursing.

Wall, **Helena M.**, *Pomona*. Email: hwall@pomona.edu.

Wall, **Irwin M.**, *California, Riverside*. Email: irwin.wall@ucr.edu.

Wall, **James**. Augusta, GA. Affil: Augusta. Email: jbwall@uga.edu.

Wall, **Michael C.**, *Georgetown*. Email: wallm@georgetown.edu.

Wall, **Sharon**, *Winnipeg*. Email: s.wall@uwinnipeg.ca.

Wall, **Wendy L.**, *Binghamton, SUNY*. Email: wwall@binghamton.edu.

Wallace, **Andrew**, *Northern Arizona*. Prescott, AZ. Email: profawallace@cableone.net. Research: American Southwest, Arizona.

Wallace, **Brigid C**. Catonsville, MD. Affil: Towson. Email: bcwhistorian@gmail.com. Research: industrial slave labor, French and Hatiatian revolutions.

Wallace, **Christine Susan**. Manuka, Australia. Affil: Australian National. Email: chris.wallace@anu.edu.au. Research: political biography, women and golf.

Wallace, **Dawn Kaylor**. Guntersville, AL. Affil: Alabama, Tuscaloosa. Email: dawn_wallace1@yahoo.com.

Wallace, **Geoffrey H**. Washington, DC. Affil: Georgetown. Email: gwallac67@gmail.com. Research: food in colonial Latin America, environmental.

Wallace, **Jessica Lynn**, *Georgia Coll. and State*. Email: jessica.wallace@gcsu.edu.

Wallace, **Michael L.**, *Graduate Center, CUNY*. Email: mawjj@aol.com.

Wallace, **Ned F.**, *Texas-Rio Grande Valley*. Email: ef.wallace@utrgv.edu.

Wallace, **Patricia**, *Baylor*. Email: patricia_wallace@baylor.edu.

Wallace, **Peter G.**, *Hartwick*. Oneonta, NY. Email: wallacep@hartwick.edu. Research: early modern frontiers, confessionalization.

Wallace, **Rachel**, *Loyola, New Orleans*. Email: rewallla@loyno.edu.

Wallace Fuentes, **M. Ivonne**, *Roanoke*. Email: wallacefuentes@roanoke.edu.

Wallach, **Jennifer Jensen**, *North Texas*. Email: jennifer.wallach@unt.edu.

Wallenstein, **Peter**, *Virginia Tech*. Email: pwallens@vt.edu.

Waller, **Altina L.**, *Connecticut, Storrs*. Email: altina.waller@uconn.edu.

Waller, **John**, *Michigan State*. Email: wallerj1@msu.edu.

Waller, **Richard D.**, *Bucknell*. Email: rwaller@bucknell.edu.

Waller-Trupp, **Leanne**. Montgomery, AL. Email: leanne0514@yahoo.com.

Walling, **Karl F.**, *Naval War Coll*. Email: kfwallin@nps.edu.

Wallis, **Eileen V**. Pomona, CA. Affil: California State Polytechnic. Email: evwallis@cpp.edu. Research: California, gender and race in American West.

Wallis, **Faith**, *McGill*. Email: faith.wallis@mcgill.ca.

Wallner, **James Ian**. Washington, DC. Affil: R Street Inst. Email: jameswallner@gmail.com.

Wallner, **Rachel**. Evanston, IL. Affil: Northwestern. Email: rwallner@u.northwestern.edu.

Walls, **Martha**, *Dalhousie*. Email: martha.walls@msvu.ca.

Walls, **Richard**. Santa Maria, CA. Affil: California Polytechnic State. Email: rwalls@calpoly.edu.

Walsh, **David A.**, *Rochester*. Email: david.walsh@rochester.edu.

Walsh, **Harry M**. Saint Paul, MN. Email: harrywalsh375@gmail.com.

Walsh, **James P.**, *San José State*. Email: James.Walsh@sjsu.edu.

Walsh, **Jennifer**. Alexandria, VA. Email: jen@jenwalsh.com.

Walsh, **Jennifer**, *Azusa Pacific*. Email: jwalsh@apu.edu.

Walsh, **John C.**, *Carleton, Can*. Email: john.walsh@carleton.ca.

Walsh, **John**. San Marcos, CA. Affil: California State, San Marcos. Email: walsh039@cougars.csusm.edu.

Walsh, **Joseph**, *Loyola, Md*. Email: jwalsh@loyola.edu.

Walsh, **Julie A.**, *American International*. Email: julie.walsh@aic.edu.

Walsh, **Kevin**, *State Hist. Soc. of Missouri*. Email: walshkr@shsmo.org.

Walsh, **Lorena S**. Middle Haddam, CT. Email: lorenapeterwalsh@sbcglobal.net. Research: 17th-/19th-c Chesapeake agriculture, trans-Atlantic slave trade.

Walsh, **Sarah**, *Washington State, Pullman*. Email: sarah.walsh@wsu.edu.

Walshaw, **Sarah**, *Simon Fraser*. Email: sarah_walshaw@sfu.ca.

Walter, **Amanda Lauren**, *Towson*. Northville, MI. Email: awalter@towson.edu; av9699@wayne.edu. Research: clerical workers in labor movement, US politics of 1970s and 1980s.

Walter, **Katherine L.** Lincoln, NE. Affil: Nebraska, Lincoln. Email: kwalter1@unl.edu.

Walter, **Matthew John**, *Sul Ross State*. Email: mwalter@sulross.edu.

Walter, **Richard John**, *Washington, St. Louis*. Email: rjwalter@wustl.edu.

Walters, **Ashley Elizabeth**. Philadelphia, PA. Affil: Stanford. Email: awalters@stanford.edu.

Walters, **Jordan Biro**, *Wooster*. Email: jbiro@wooster.edu.

Walters, **Kevin A**. Madison, WI. Affil: Wisconsin, Madison. Email: kwalters@warf.org. Research: Cold War.

Walters, **Lindsey K**. Cambridge, United Kingdom. Affil: Cambridge. Email: lkw31@cam.ac.uk.

Walters, **Lori C.**, *Central Florida*. Email: lcwalter@ist.ucf.edu.

Walters, **Michael**. Pittsburgh, PA. Affil: Pittsburgh. Email: michael.walters81@gmail.com.

Walters, **Ronald G.**, *Johns Hopkins (Hist.)*. Baltimore, MD. Email: rgw1@jhu.edu. Research: early US, family.

Walthall, **Anne**, *California, Irvine*. Irvine, CA. Email: walthall@uci.edu. Research: Tokugawa/Meiji, gender.

Walther, **Eric H.**, *Houston*. Email: ewalther@uh.edu.

Walther, **Thomas R.**, *Pittsburg State*.

Waltner, **Ann**, *Minnesota (Hist.)*. Minneapolis, MN. Email: waltn001@umn.edu. Research: traditional China.

Walton, **Calder**. Cambridge, MA. Affil: Harvard. Email: calder_walton@hks.harvard.edu.

Walton, **Kristen P.**, *Salisbury*. Email: kpwalton@salisbury.edu.

Walton, **Leah A.** Charlotte, NC. Affil: North Carolina, Charlotte. Email: lwalton6@uncc.edu.

Walton, **Linda A.**, *Portland State*.

Walton, **Rodney Earl**. Miami, FL. Affil: Florida International. Email: rwalton@fiu.edu. Research: 1945 Okinawa artillery observation, oral.

Walton, **Steven**, *Michigan Tech*. Email: sawalton@mtu.edu.

Walton, **Whitney**, *Purdue*. West Lafayette, IN. Email: awhitney@purdue.edu. Research: study abroad in US and France 1890-1970.

Walton-Hanley, **Jennifer A**, *Western Kentucky*. Email: jennifer.walton-hanley@wku.edu.

Waltz-Chambers, **Alexandria Frances**. Layton, UT. Affil: Utah. Email: alexandriawaltz@gmail.com. Research: Youth Subcultures, Gender.

Walz, **Eric**. Rexburg, ID. Affil: Brigham Young, Idaho. Email: walze@byui.edu. Research: Japanese immigration to US, intermountain West immigration/community.

Walz, **Ralph C.**, *Seton Hall*.

Walz, **Robin R.** Juneau, AK. Affil: Alaska Southeast. Email: rwalz@alaska.edu. Research: 19th-/20th-c French popular culture.

Wamagatta, **Evanson N.**, *Biola*. Email: evanson.wamagatta@biola.edu.

Wamsley, **E. Sue**, *Kent State*. Email: ewamsley@kent.edu.

Wandel, **Lee Palmer**, *Wisconsin-Madison*. Madison, WI. Email: lpwandel@wisc.edu. Research: exile, cartography.

Wandel, **Torbjorn V.**, *Truman State*. Email: twandel@truman.edu.

Wang, **Anran**. North York, ON, Canada. Affil: Cornell. Email: wanganran0117@gmail.com.

Wang, **Chao**. Chicago, IL. Affil: Chicago. Email: alecwang@uchicago.edu.

Wang, **Chelsea Zi**, *Claremont McKenna*. Email: cwang@cmc.edu.

Wang, **Di**, *Texas A&M*. Taipa, Macau. Affil: Macau. Email: di-wang@tamu.edu; diwang@umac.mo. Research: West's Reponses to the May Fourth M., secret societies 1650-1950.

Wang, **Edward**, *Rowan*. Email: wangq@rowan.edu.

Wang, **Erik H.** Princeton, NJ. Affil: Princeton. Email: haixiaow@princeton.edu.

Wang, **Fei-Hsien**, *Indiana*. Email: feihwang@indiana.edu.

Wang, **Guanhua**, *Connecticut, Storrs*. Email: g.wang@uconn.edu.

Wang, **Gungwu**. Singapore. Affil: National, Singapore. Email: eaiwgw@nus.edu.sg. Research: diasporas, nation-building.

Wang, **Haochen**. Saint Louis, MO. Affil: Washington, St. Louis. Email: haochen@wustl.edu.

Wang, **Hongjie**, *Georgia Southern*. Email: hongjiewang@georgiasouthern.edu.

Wang, **Jessica**, *British Columbia*. Email: jessica.wang@ubc.ca.

Wang, **Jingbin**. Camden, NC. Affil: Elizabeth City State. Email: jwang4885@gmail.com. Research: Sino-American relations, ideology and diplomacy.

Wang, **Ke-wen**, *St. Michael's*. Email: kwang@smcvt.edu.

Wang, **Liping**, *Minnesota (Hist.)*. Email: lipin003@umn.edu.

Wang, **Luman**, *Massachusetts, Boston*. Email: wangluman@gmail.com.

Wang, **Ning**, *Brock*. Email: nwang@brocku.ca.

Wang, **Shuo**, *California State, Stanislaus*. Email: swang@csustan.edu.

Wang, **Sixiang**. Los Angeles, CA. Affil: UCLA. Email: sw2090@columbia.edu. Research: Korea and empire, early modern knowledge in Korea.

Wang, **Tao**, *Iowa State*. Email: twang@iastate.edu.

Wang, **Wensheng**, *Hawai'i, Manoa*. Honolulu, HI. Email: wensheng@hawaii.edu; alfwangcn@yahoo.com. Research: Qing sociopolitical, Qing cultural.

Wang, **Xi**, *Indiana, Pa*. Indiana, PA. Email: wangxi@iup.edu. Research: African American suffrage, constitutionalism.

Wang, **Xiuyu**, *Washington State, Pullman*. Vancouver, WA. Email: xiuyuwang@wsu.edu. Research: modern China-Tibet relations, Qing China statecraft and ethnohistory.

Wang, **Yeh-chien**, *Kent State*.

Wang, **Yi**, *Binghamton, SUNY*. Email: wangy@binghamton.edu.

Wang, **Yijun**, *NYU*. New York, NY. Email: yw2392@columbia.edu.

Wang, **Yiwen Yvon**, *Toronto*. Toronto, ON, Canada. Email: yyvon.wang@utoronto.ca; y.yvon.wang@gmail.com. Research: sexuality in late Qing/early Rep. China, print culture and markets in Beijing.

Wang, **Yuanchong**, *Delaware*. Email: ychwang@udel.edu.

Wang, **Zheng**, *Michigan, Ann Arbor*. Email: wangzhen@umich.edu.

Wangdi, **Yosay**, *Grand Valley State*. Email: wangdiy@gvsu.edu.

Wangerin, **Laura**, *Seton Hall*. Summit, NJ. Email: laura.wangerin@shu.edu; lwangerin@wisc.edu. Research: medieval Europe, politics and society.

Wanner, **Catherine**, *Penn State*. Email: cew10@psu.edu.

Warber, **Samantha**, *Grand Valley State*. Email: warbersa@gvsu.edu.

Ward, **Allen M.**, *Connecticut, Storrs*. Email: allen.ward@uconn.edu.

Ward, **Darrick**. Reno, NV. Affil: Nevada, Reno. Email: jedidarrick@yahoo.com.

Ward, **David Lawrence**. Williamsburg, VA. Affil: William and Mary. Email: davidlward@icloud.com. Research: Continental Army soldiers.

Ward, **Evan R.**, *Brigham Young*. Provo, UT. Email: evan_ward@byu.edu. Research: Colorado River Delta, Sunbelt water issues.

Ward, **James A., III**, *Tennessee, Chattanooga*.

Ward, **James J.** Allentown, PA. Affil: Cedar Crest. Email: jjward@cedarcrest.edu. Research: German politics/history/memory, postwar Berlin.

Ward, **James Mace**, *Rhode Island*. Email: jmward@uri.edu.

Ward, **Janet A.**, *Oklahoma (Hist.)*. Norman, OK. Email: janet.ward@ou.edu. Research: modern urban planning and architecture, Berlin.

Ward, **Jason Morgan**, *Emory*. Atlanta, GA. Email: jmward4@emory.edu. Research: racial violence and memory, 20th-c racial politics.

Ward, **Joseph P.**, *Utah State*. Logan, UT. Email: joe.ward@usu.edu. Research: Tudor-Stuart Britain.

Ward, **Kerry R.**, *Rice*. Houston, TX. Email: kward@rice.edu. Research: slavery and human trafficking, oceanic world.

Ward, **Kyle**, *Minnesota State, Mankato*. Email: kyle.ward@mnsu.edu.

Ward, **Max M.**, *Middlebury*. Email: maxwellw@middlebury.edu.

Ward, **Monica Rose**. Brick, NJ. Affil: North Carolina, Greensboro. Email: mrward2@uncg.edu. Research: 18th-c Creek Indians, Creek town of Little Tallassee.

Ward, **Walter David**, *Alabama, Birmingham*. Email: wdward@uab.edu.

Warder, **Graham D.**, *Keene State*. Email: gwarder@keene.edu.

Wardhaugh, **Robert**, *Western Ontario*. Email: rwardhau@uwo.ca.

Ware, **Susan W**. Cambridge, MA. Affil: Radcliffe Inst. for Advanced Study. Email: sdware@aol.com.

Waring, **Luke**. Columbia, MO. Affil: Princeton. Email: lwaring@princeton.edu.

Waring, **Stephen P.**, *Alabama, Huntsville*. Email: warings@uah.edu.

Wark, **Wesley K.**, *Toronto*.

Warlow, **Rebecca**, *National Library of Medicine*. Email: rebecca.warlow@nih.gov.

Warmund, **Joram**, *Long Island, Brooklyn*. Email: joram.warmund@liu.edu.

Warner, **John H.**, *Yale*. Email: john.warner@yale.edu.

Warner, **John**. Indianapolis, IN. Affil: American Public. Email: john.warner79@gmail.com.

Warner, **Jonathan**, *OAH*. Email: jonwarne@oah.org.

Warner, **Lyndan**, *St. Mary's, Can*. Email: lyndan.warner@smu.ca.

Warner, **Rick R.**, *Wabash; World Hist. Assoc.* Crawfordsville, IN. Email: warnerri@wabash.edu. Research: Latin America, world.

Warner, **Rollin M**. Manteca, CA. Affil: Town Sch. for Boys. Email: warnerrollinm1960@alumni-gsb.stanford.edu.

Warner Mettler, **Meghan M**. Oelwein, IA. Affil: Upper Iowa. Email: meghan-warner@uiowa.edu. Research: post-WWII US-Japan cultural relations, disability in American culture.

Warnicke, **Retha M.**, *Arizona State*. Email: retha.warnicke@asu.edu.

Warren, **Adam W. V.**, *Washington, Seattle*. Seattle, WA. Email: awarren2@uw.edu. Research: medicine and public health in Peru, burial practices and reforms in Peru.

Warren, Christian S., *Brooklyn, CUNY*. Email: cwarren@brooklyn.cuny.edu.

Warren, Frank A., *Queens, CUNY*. Flushing, NY. Email: frank.warren@qc.cuny.edu. Research: 20th-c US.

Warren, Jared. New York, NY. Affil: NYU. Email: jnw295@nyu.edu.

Warren, Kim D., *Kansas*. Email: kwarren@ku.edu.

Warren, Louis S., *California, Davis*. Email: lswarren@ucdavis.edu.

Warren, Richard A., *St. Joseph's*. Philadelphia, PA. Email: warren@sju.edu. Research: 19th-c political culture.

Warren, Stephen, *Iowa*. Email: stephen-warren@uiowa.edu.

Warren, Thomas Ross. Sackets Harbor, NY. Email: T.ross.warren@gmail.com.

Warren, Wendy A., *Princeton*. Email: wawarren@princeton.edu.

Warren, Wilson J., *Western Michigan*. Kalamazoo, MI. Email: wilson.warren@wmich.edu. Research: 20th-c labor politics, history education.

Warsh, Molly A., *Pittsburgh*. Pittsburgh, PA. Email: warsh@pitt.edu. Research: early modern empires, world.

Warshauer, Matthew S., *Central Connecticut State*. Email: warshauerm@ccsu.edu.

Wartell, Rebecca. Boulder, CO. Affil: Colorado, Boulder. Email: rebecca.wartell@colorado.edu.

Warwick, Jacqueline, *Dalhousie*. Email: jwarwick@dal.ca.

Wasem, Ruth E.. Austin, TX. Affil: Texas, Austin. Email: wasemruth@utexas.edu.

Washburn, Amy. Brooklyn, NY. Affil: Kingsborough Comm. Coll., CUNY. Email: amy.washburn@kbcc.cuny.edu. Research: Irish studies, women's and gender studies.

Washburn, Jeffrey D.. University, MS. Affil: Mississippi. Email: jdwashbu@go.olemiss.edu.

Washington, Angela. Bronx, NY. Affil: San Jose State. Email: washington.angela@gmail.com.

Washington, Eric M., *Calvin*. Email: emw23@calvin.edu.

Washington, Garrett L., *Massachusetts, Amherst*. Email: gwashington@history.umass.edu.

Washington, Margaret, *Cornell*. Ithaca, NY. Email: mw26@cornell.edu. Research: African American cultural/intellectual/religious, gender.

Washington, Michael H., *Northern Kentucky*. Email: washington@nku.edu.

Washington, Versalle F., *Dayton*.

Wasserman, Janek, *Alabama, Tuscaloosa*. Email: iwasserman@bama.ua.edu.

Wasserman, Mark, *Rutgers*. Highland Park, NJ. Email: wasserm@rci.rutgers.edu. Research: Mexican business.

Wasserman-Soler, Daniel I., *Alma*. Alma, MI. Email: wassermandi@alma.edu. Research: language and communication, evangelization.

Wasserstein, Bernard M. J., *Chicago*. Amsterdam, Netherlands. Email: bmjw@uchicago.edu. Research: modern Jewish/Middle East, 20th-c European politics and diplomacy.

Wasserstein, David J., *Vanderbilt*. Nashville, TN. Email: david.wasserstein@vanderbilt.edu. Research: Islamic Spain, Jews under Islam.

Wasserstrom, Jeffrey N., *California, Irvine*. Irvine, CA. Email: jwassers@uci.edu. Research: comparative urban, gender and revolution.

Wasson, Ellis A.. Radnor, PA. Affil: Delaware. Email: ewasson@udel.edu. Research: 19th-c Whig Party, 19th-c British politics.

Wasyliw, Zenon V., *Ithaca*. Email: wasyliw@ithaca.edu.

Waterhouse, Benjamin Cooper, *North Carolina, Chapel Hill*. Email: waterhou@email.unc.edu.

Waterman, G. Scott. Charlotte, VT. Affil: Vermont; Comm. Coll. of Vermont. Email: Scott.Waterman@uvm.edu. Research: Holocaust, American Communism.

Waterman, Kenneth O.. Honolulu, HI.

Waters, Amy L., *State Hist. Soc. of Missouri*. Email: watersa@shsmo.org.

Waters, Anne B.. New York, NY. Affil: Columbia. Email: Anne.waters@columbia.edu.

Waters, Brandi. Sewell, NJ. Affil: Yale. Email: brandimwaters@gmail.com. Research: slavery/medicine/law, Colombia and Brazil.

Waters, Chris, *Williams*. Williamstown, MA. Email: cwaters@williams.edu. Research: 20th-c British national identity, 20th-c psychoanalysis/homosexuality.

Waters, Leslie, *Texas, El Paso*. El Paso, TX. Email: lwaters@utep.edu; lesliewaters@gmail.com. Research: eastern Europe, migrations.

Waters, Matthew W., *Wisconsin-Eau Claire*. Email: watersmw@uwec.edu.

Waters, Neil L., *Middlebury*. Gresham, OR. Email: nwaters@middlebury.edu. Research: Taisho Japan youth groups, life and afterlives of Ninomiya Sontoku.

Waters, Robert A., Jr.. Ada, OH. Affil: Ohio Northern. Email: rawatersjr@yahoo.com. Research: US Cold War relations with Guyana, US labor's Cold War foreign policy.

Watkins, Andrea S., *Northern Kentucky*. Email: watkinsan@nku.edu.

Watkins, Daniel James, *Baylor*. Email: daniel_watkins@baylor.edu.

Watkins, Elizabeth, *California, Berkeley*. Email: watkinse@dahsm.ucsf.edu.

Watkins, Jerry T., III. Williamsburg, VA. Affil: William and Mary. Email: jayw80@gmail.com.

Watkins, Kent. Bethesda, MD. Affil: American Academy of Housing and Sustainable Communities. Email: kent.watkins@yahoo.com. Research: slavery and Tillinghasts, creation of HUD and urbanism.

Watkins, Sharon B., *Western Illinois*. Email: stw300@comcast.net.

Watkins, Thomas H., *Western Illinois*. Email: stw300@comcast.net.

Watrous, Stephen D., *Sonoma State*.

Watson, Alan D., *North Carolina, Wilmington*. Email: watsona@uncw.edu.

Watson, Andrew, *Saskatchewan*. Email: a.watson@usask.ca.

Watson, Cameron James. Elorrio, Spain. Affil: Nevada, Reno. Email: katuzarra@gmail.com.

Watson, Carole M.. Washington, DC. Affil: NEH. Email: carolemwatson@gmail.com.

Watson, Cecelia A.. London, United Kingdom. Email: cawats@gmail.com. Research: William James and art, Overstudy.

Watson, Dwight D., *Texas State*. Email: dw25@txstate.edu.

Watson, Elwood D., *East Tennessee State*. Email: watson@etsu.edu.

Watson, Griff, *Tennessee State*. Email: gwatson@mytsu.tnstate.edu.

Watson, Harry L., II, *North Carolina, Chapel Hill*. Chapel Hill, NC. Email: hwatson@email.unc.edu. Research: North Carolina, antebellum US.

Watson, Janet S. K., *Connecticut, Storrs*. Storrs Mansfield, CT. Email: janet.watson@uconn.edu. Research: 20th-c European cultural, modern Britain.

Watson, Jesse, *Oberlin*. Email: jesse.d.watson@gmail.com.

Watson, Kristen L.. Brooklyn, NY. Email: kwatson8@pratt.edu.

Watson, Samuel, *US Military Acad.* Email: samuel.watson@usma.edu.

Watson, William B., *MIT*. Email: wbwatson@mit.edu.

Watt, Jeffrey R., *Mississippi*. University, MS. Email: hswatt@olemiss.edu. Research: witchcraft and Inquisition in Italy, Consistory of Geneva.

Watt, Lori, *Washington, St. Louis*. Email: loriwatt@wustl.edu.

Watterson, Nancy, *Cabrini*. Email: nlw724@cabrini.edu.

Watts, Edward Jay, *California, San Diego*. La Jolla, CA. Email: ewatts@ucsd.edu; edward.watts@gmail.com. Research: ancient education, Christianization.

Watts, Jennifer, *Huntington Library*. Email: jwatts@huntington.org.

Watts, Jill M., *California State, San Marcos*. Email: jwatts@csusm.edu.

Watts, Steven A., *Missouri, Columbia*. Email: wattss@missouri.edu.

Watts, Sydney E., *Richmond*. Richmond, VA. Email: swatts@richmond.edu. Research: de-Christianization in 18th-c France, food.

Waugh, Daniel C., *Washington, Seattle*. Email: dwaugh@uw.edu.

Waugh, Dwana, *Sweet Briar*. Email: dwaugh@sbc.edu.

Waugh, Earle, *Alberta*. Email: earle.waugh@ualberta.ca.

Waugh, Joan, *UCLA*. Email: jwaugh@history.ucla.edu.

Waugh, Scott L., *UCLA*. Los Angeles, CA. Email: swaugh@history.ucla.edu. Research: medieval England.

Wawro, Geoffrey D. W., *North Texas*. Email: wawro@unt.edu.

Way, Albert G., *Kennesaw State*. Email: away5@kennesaw.edu.

Way, John T., *Georgia State*. Email: jway@gsu.edu.

Way, Peter, *Windsor*. Email: peterway@uwindsor.ca.

Way, Thaisa, *Washington, Seattle*. Email: tway@uw.edu.

Wayne, Beatrice Tychsen. Toronto, ON, Canada. Affil: Harvard. Email: beatrice.wayne@gmail.com.

Wayne, Michael, *Toronto*. Email: michael.wayne@utoronto.ca.

Wayno, Jeffrey M. New York, NY. Affil: Columbia. Email: jeffrey.wayno@columbia.edu. Research: medieval church institutional, communication.

Wcislo, Francis W., *Vanderbilt*. Nashville, TN. Email: francis.w.wcislo@vanderbilt.edu. Research: biography and imperial Russia, Russian women and power.

Weare, Walter B., *Wisconsin-Milwaukee*. Email: bweare@uwm.edu.

Weart, Spencer. Hastings On Hudson, NY. Email: sweart1@gmail.com.

Weatherbie Greco, Brittanie. Boston, MA. Affil: Massachusetts, Boston. Email: Brittanie. Greco@umb.edu. Research: Boston busing crisis, reading/writing/archives.

Weatherhead, Dean, *US Dept. of State*.

Weatherly, Megan S., *Stephen F. Austin State*. Email: msweatherly@sfasu.edu.

Weatherwax, Sarah, *Library Co. of Philadelphia*. Email: printroom@librarycompany.org.

Weaver, Elton, III. Memphis, TN. Affil: LeMoyne-Owen. Email: elton_weaver@loc.edu.

Weaver, Eric Beckett. Budapest, Hungary. Affil: Debrecen. Email: ericbweaver@gmail.com. Research: post-1700 south central Europe, Hungary 1800-1939.

Weaver, Frankie Nicole. Baldwinsville, NY. Affil: SUNY, Buffalo. Email: fnl@buffalo.edu. Research: American anti-apartheid activism, New York City theatre and performance.

Weaver, Jace. Athens, GA. Affil: Georgia. Email: jweaver@uga.edu.

Weaver, John C., *McMaster*. Hamilton, ON, Canada. Email: jweaver@mcmaster.ca. Research: suicide 1900-2000, post-1960 globalization.

Weaver, Karol Kimberlee, *Susquehanna*. Email: weaverk@susqu.edu.

Weaver, Michael K., *Texas-Rio Grande Valley*. Email: michael.weaver@utrgv.edu.

Weaver, Stewart A., *Rochester*. Rochester, NY. Email: stewart.weaver@rochester.edu. Research: Himalayan exploration.

Weaver Olson, Nathan Wade. Saint Paul, MN. Affil: Minnesota, Twin Cities. Email: olso6158@umn.edu. Research: afromestizos and indigenous Americans, categories of racial and social difference.

Weaver-Zercher, David L., *Messiah*. Email: dzercher@messiah.edu.

Webb, David D., *Central Oklahoma*. Email: dwebb@uco.edu.

Webb, Derek A. Washington, DC. Email: dawebb21@gmail.com.

Webb, George E., *Tennessee Tech*. Email: gwebb@tntech.edu.

Webb, Jeff A., *Memorial, Newfoundland*. Email: jeff.webb@mun.ca.

Webb, Jessica. Fort Worth, TX. Affil: Texas Christian. Email: jessica.webb@tcu.edu.

Webb, Mattie Christine. Goleta, CA. Affil: California, Santa Barbara. Email: mattie@ucsb.edu.

Webb, Samuel L., Jr., *Alabama, Birmingham*.

Webb, Silas. Owens Cross Roads, AL. Affil: Syracuse. Email: siwebb@syr.edu. Research: Punjabi diaspora, South Asians in Britain.

Webb, Stephen S., *Syracuse*. Email: sswebb@maxwell.syr.edu.

Webel, Mari K., *Pittsburgh*. Email: mwebel@pitt.edu.

Weber, Alison, *Virginia*. Email: apw@virginia.edu.

Weber, Brooke. Rochester, MN. Email: weber.brooke.a@gmail.com.

Weber, Charles W., *Wheaton, Ill.* Wheaton, IL. Email: charles.weber@wheaton.edu. Research: African and Asian nationalism, Asian church.

Weber, Devra, *California, Riverside*. Email: devra.weber@ucr.edu.

Weber, Jennifer L., *Kansas*. Email: jlweber@ku.edu.

Weber, John W., *Old Dominion*. Email: jwweber@odu.edu.

Weber, Margaret Baker, *Wisconsin-Eau Claire*. Email: webermb@uwec.edu.

Weber, Mark E. Paso Robles, CA. Affil: Cuesta. Email: mweber1776@gmail.com.

Weber, Ralph E., *Marquette*.

Weber, Ronald J., *Texas, El Paso*. Email: rweber@utep.edu.

Weber, William A., *California State, Long Beach; Soc. for Hist. Education*. Long Beach, CA. Email: william.weber@csulb.edu. Research: 18th-19th-c canons in opera world, Bourdieu's ideas historically.

Webre, Stephen, *Louisiana Tech*. Ruston, LA. Email: swebre@latech.edu. Research: colonial Central America/Guatemala, colonial frontiers.

Webster, John C. B. Mystic, CT. Email: pjwebster@worldnet.att.net. Research: Christianity in India, Dalit movement in India.

Weddle, Bonita, *New York State Archives*. Email: bonita.weddle@nysed.gov.

Weddle, Thaddeus Beamer. California, MD. Email: tbwweddle@gmail.com.

Weekly, Nancy, *SUNY, Buffalo State*.

Weeks, Daniel, *Rutgers*. Email: dweeks@monmouth.edu.

Weeks, David L., *Azusa Pacific*. Email: dweeks@apu.edu.

Weeks, Michael A. Provo, UT. Affil: Utah Valley. Email: michaelandsacha@hotmail.com.

Weeks, Patricia, *South Florida, St. Petersburg*.

Weeks, Philip, *Kent State*. Email: pweeks@kent.edu.

Weeks, Theodore R., *Southern Illinois, Carbondale*. Email: tadeusz@siu.edu.

Weeks, William Earl, Jr., *San Diego State*.

Weems, Robert E., Jr., *Wichita State*. Email: robert.weems@wichita.edu.

Wegner, Gregory, *Wisconsin-La Crosse*. Email: gwegner@uwlax.edu.

Wegner, John M., *Eastern Michigan*. Email: jwegner@emich.edu.

Wehn, Paul B. Green Village, NJ. Email: wehn@verizon.net.

Wehrle, Edmund F., *Eastern Illinois*. Email: efwehrle@eiu.edu.

Wehrle, Edmund S., *Connecticut, Storrs*.

Wehrli, Eric G., Jr. Fort Wayne, IN. Affil: Canterbury Sch. Email: ewehrli@canterburyschool.org. Research: 18th-c Scottish politics/government, Anglo-Scottish relationship.

Wehrman, Andrew M., *Central Michigan*. Mount Pleasant, MI. Email: wehrm1am@cmich.edu. Research: politics of disease and medicine, American Revolution.

Wehrman, Michael J. Frostburg, MD. Affil: Frostburg State. Email: mwehrman@gmail.com. Research: early medieval hagiography, Christianization and conversion.

Wei, William, *Colorado, Boulder*. Email: william.wei@colorado.edu.

Wei, Yang, *Colorado Colorado Springs*. Email: ywei@uccs.edu.

Weicksel, Sarah Jones. Crofton, MD. Affil: Pennsylvania. Email: sarah.weicksel@gmail.com. Research: American Civil War era, material culture/clothing/gender/race.

Weideman, Julian. Princeton, NJ. Affil: Princeton. Email: julian.weideman@gmail.com.

Weidemann, Erika. College Station, TX. Affil: Texas A&M, Coll. Station. Email: elweidemann@tamu.edu. Research: Immigration.

Weigel, Richard D., *Western Kentucky*. Email: richard.weigel@wku.edu.

Weigold, Marilyn E., *Pace*. Briarcliff Manor, NY. Email: mweigold@pace.edu. Research: environmental, regional.

Weikart, Richard C., *California State, Stanislaus*. Email: rweikart@csustan.edu.

Weil, Francois. Saint-Mandé, France. Affil: Ecole des Hautes Etudes en Sci. Sociales. Email: fweil@ehess.fr. Research: French migrations to Americas, genealogy in American culture.

Weil, Rachel J., *Cornell*. Ithaca, NY. Email: rjw5@cornell.edu. Research: 17th-/18th-c political culture, prisons.

Weiler, Peter, *Boston Coll*. Email: weiler@bc.edu.

Weiman, David F., *Columbia (Hist.)*. Email: dfw5@columbia.edu.

Weimer, Adrian Chastain, *Providence*. Email: aweimer@providence.edu.

Weimer, Daniel. Wheeling, WV. Affil: Wheeling Jesuit. Email: dweimer1914@gmail.com. Research: US foreign relations, cultural.

Weimer, Lawrence D., *NYU*. Email: lweimer@nyu.edu.

Weinberg, Bob, *Swarthmore*. Swarthmore, PA. Email: rweinbe1@swarthmore.edu. Research: Soviet Jewish.

Weinberg, Carl R., *Indiana*. Bloomington, IN. Email: crweinbe@indiana.edu. Research: anti-evolutionism.

Weinberg, David H., *Bowling Green State; Wayne State*. Email: davidweinberg@wayne.edu.

Weinberg, Eyal. Austin, TX. Affil: Texas, Austin. Email: eyalw@utexas.edu. Research: Brazilian military regime, Cold War Latin America.

Weinberg, Gerhard L., *North Carolina, Chapel Hill*. Efland, NC. Email: gweinber@email.unc.edu. Research: modern Germany, Europe.

Weinberg, Sydney S. New York, NY. Affil: Ramapo.

Weinberger, Lael. Chicago, IL. Affil: Chicago. Email: laelweinberger@gmail.com.

Weinberger, Stephen, *Dickinson*. Email: weinberg@dickinson.edu.

Weiner, Amir, *Stanford*. Email: weiner@stanford.edu.

Weiner, Benno Ryan, *Carnegie Mellon*. Email: bweiner@andrew.cmu.edu.

Weiner, Carl D., *Carleton Coll*. Saint Paul, MN. Email: cweiner@carleton.edu. Research: early modern and modern France, French Revolution.

Weiner, Dana E., *Wilfrid Laurier*. Email: dweiner@wlu.ca.

Weiner, Douglas R., *Arizona*. Email: dweiner@u.arizona.edu.

Weiner, Gordon, *Arizona State*.

Weiner, Herbert Jonathan. San Francisco, CA. Email: h.weiner@sbcglobal.net.

Weiner, Howard R., *Staten Island, CUNY*. Email: howard.weiner@csi.cuny.edu.

Weiner, Lynn, *Roosevelt*. Oak Park, IL. Email: lweiner@roosevelt.edu. Research: higher education, 20th-c women.

Weiner, **Richard**, *Purdue, Fort Wayne*. Email: weinerr@pfw.edu.

Weiner, **Robert I.**, *Lafayette*. Email: weinerr@lafayette.edu.

Weinert, **Mark**, *George Fox*. Email: mweinert@georgefox.edu.

Weinfeld, *David*. Richmond, VA. Affil: Virginia Commonwealth. Email: daweinfeld@vcu.edu. Research: US intellectual, black-Jewish relations.

Weingart, *J. Walter*, *Whitman*. Walla Walla, WA. Email: weingart@whitman.edu. Research: England, early modern Europe.

Weingartner, *James J.* Edwardsville, IL. Affil: Southern Illinois, Edwardsville. Email: jweinga@siue.edu. Research: Germany, modern Europe.

Weinreb, **Alice Autumn**, *Loyola, Chicago*. Email: aweinreb@luc.edu.

Weinrib, *Laura*. Chicago, IL. Affil: Chicago. Email: weinrib@uchicago.edu.

Weinstein, *Barbara*, *NYU*. New York, NY. Email: bw52@nyu.edu; bswein99@aol.com. Research: region and nation in Brazil, modern Latin America.

Weinstein, **Jodi L.**, *New Jersey*. Email: weinstei@tcnj.edu.

Weinstein, **Stephen**, *La Guardia and Wagner Archives*. Email: sweinstein@lagcc.cuny.edu.

Weinstein-Sears, *Alyssa Briddell*. Houston, TX. Affil: Gratz. Email: abw5053@gmail.com.

Weintraub, **Jennifer**, *Arthur and Elizabeth Schlesinger Library*. Email: jennifer_weintraub@radcliffe.harvard.edu.

Weir, *David A.* Nyack, NY. Affil: Nyack. Email: David.Weir@nyack.edu. Research: colonial New England.

Weir, **Robert M.**, *South Carolina, Columbia*. Email: ar2weir@gmail.com.

Weirich, **Sarah**, *Center for Hist. of Physics*. Email: sweirich@aip.org.

Weis, **Dan**, *Nebraska, Omaha*.

Weis, **Tracey M.**, *Millersville, Pa.* Email: tracey.weis@millersville.edu.

Weis, **W. Michael**, *Illinois Wesleyan*. Email: mweis@iwu.edu.

Weisberger, *R. William*. Butler, PA. Email: mingobill@aol.com.

Weisbrot, *Robert S.*, *Colby*. Waterville, ME. Email: rsweisbr@colby.edu. Research: postwar America.

Weise, *Constanze*. Arkadelphia, AR. Affil: Henderson State. Email: coweise@gmail.com. Research: religious/political/cultural, transnational.

Weise, **Julie**, *Oregon*. Email: jweise@uoregon.edu.

Weise, **Robert S.**, *Eastern Kentucky*. Email: rob.weise@eku.edu.

Weisenberger, **Carol A.**, *Northern Iowa*. Email: carol.weisenberger@uni.edu.

Weisensel, **Peter R.**, *Macalester*. Email: weisensel@macalester.edu.

Weiser, **Keith Ian**, *York, Can.* Email: kweiser@yorku.ca.

Weisiger, *Marsha L.*, *Oregon*. Eugene, OR. Email: weisiger@uoregon.edu. Research: western rivers and ideas of wild-ness, environment and counterculture.

Weismeyer, *Michael*. Collegedale, TN. Affil: Southern Adventist. Email: mweismeyer@ucla.edu. Research: science education, early California colleges.

Weiss, *Ben*. Austin, TX. Affil: Texas, Austin. Email: benweiss13@gmail.com.

Weiss, *Camille*, *Suffolk*. Salem, MA. Email: cweiss@suffolk.edu. Research: early modern French and Italian courts, satirical literature.

Weiss, *Gillian L.*, *Case Western Reserve*. Cleveland Heights, OH. Email: gillian.weiss@case.edu. Research: early modern France, comparative slaveries.

Weiss, *Harold J.*, *Jr.* Leander, TX. Affil: Jamestown Comm. Coll.

Weiss, **James R.**, *Salem State*. Email: jweiss@salemstate.edu.

Weiss, **Jessica**, *California State, East Bay*. Email: jessica.weiss@csueastbay.edu.

Weiss, **John H.**, *Cornell*. Email: jhw4@cornell.edu.

Weiss, **Max D.**, *Princeton*. Email: maxweiss@princeton.edu.

Weiss, *Richard*, *UCLA*. Email: rweiss@history.ucla.edu.

Weiss Muller, *Hannah*, *Brandeis*. Maynard, MA. Email: mullerh@brandeis.edu; hannahweissmuller@gmail.com. Research: 18th-c British Empire, subjecthood.

Weissbach, **Lee Shai**, *Louisville*. Email: weissbach@louisville.edu.

Weisser, **Henry G.**, *Colorado State*. Email: henry.weisser@colostate.edu.

Weisser, *Olivia A.*, *Massachusetts, Boston*. Email: olivia.weisser@umb.edu.

Weissman, **Neil**, *Dickinson*. Email: weissmne@dickinson.edu.

Weissman, *Rebecca E.* Columbia, SC. Affil: South Carolina; Columbia Coll.; Midlands Tech. Email: Rebeccaeliseweissman@gmail.com.

Weitekamp, *Margaret A.* Washington, DC. Affil: Smithsonian Inst. Email: weitekampm@si.edu. Research: collecting and collectibles, space.

Weitz, *Eric D.*, *Graduate Center, CUNY*. Princeton, NJ. Affil: City Coll., NY. Email: eweitz@ccny.cuny.edu. Research: international human rights, Germany and genocide.

Weitz, *Lev*. Washington, DC. Affil: Catholic. Email: weitz@cua.edu. Research: Middle Eastern Christian communities, family law.

Weitzberg, *Keren*. London, United Kingdom. Affil: Univ. Coll. London. Email: k.weitzberg@ucl.ac.uk. Research: modern Kenya and Somalia, Indian Ocean.

Weitzer, **William H.**, *Leo Baeck Inst.* Email: wweitzer@lbi.cjh.org.

Welborn, **James Hill**, **III**, *Georgia Coll. and State*. Email: james.welborn@gcsu.edu.

Welch, **Courtney**, *North Texas*. Email: mcwelch1897@yahoo.com.

Welch, **Deborah**, *Longwood*. Email: welchds@longwood.edu.

Welch, **Gaylynn J.**, *SUNY, Coll. Potsdam*. Email: welchgj@potsdam.edu.

Welch, *Jeanie Maxine*. Huntersville, NC. Affil: North Carolina, Charlotte. Email: jeaniemwelch@gmail.com.

Welch, **Kim M.**, *Vanderbilt*. Email: kimberly.m.welch@vanderbilt.edu.

Welch, **Todd**, *Utah State*. Email: todd.welch@usu.edu.

Welch, **William M.**, **Jr.**, *Troy*. Email: wwelch@troy.edu.

Welchans, **Katherine**, *Nebraska, Omaha*.

Weld, *Kirsten A.*, *Harvard (Hist.)*. Email: weld@fas.harvard.edu.

Weldemichael, **Awet Tewelde**, *Queen's, Can.* Email: awet.weldemichael@queensu.ca.

Weldon, **Nick**, *Hist. New Orleans*. Email: nickw@hnoc.org.

Weldon, **Stephen P.**, *Oklahoma (Hist. of Science)*. Email: spweldon@ou.edu.

Welke, *Barbara Young*, *Minnesota (Hist.)*. Minneapolis, MN. Email: welke004@umn.edu. Research: product liability socio-legal, individuality and citizenship.

Welky, **David B.**, *Central Arkansas*. Email: dwelky@uca.edu.

Welland, **Heather**, *Binghamton, SUNY*. Email: hwelland@binghamton.edu.

Wellenreuther, *Hermann*. Goettingen, Germany. Affil: Goettingen. Email: hwellen@gwdg.de. Research: early modern Atlantic.

Weller, **Cecil Edward**, **Jr.**, *Houston-Clear Lake*. Email: weller@uhcl.edu.

Weller, **Charles**, *Washington State, Pullman*. Email: rcw@world-hcrc.com.

Weller, **Grant Thomas**, *Colorado State, Pueblo*. Email: grant.weller@csupueblo.edu.

Wellman, **Darien**, *North Carolina A&T State*. Email: dmwellma@ncat.edu.

Wellman, **Judith M.**, *SUNY, Oswego*. Email: judith.wellman@oswego.edu.

Wellman, *Kathleen*, *Southern Methodist*. Dallas, TX. Email: kwellman@smu.edu. Research: 18th-c French physiology, elite women of French Renaissance.

Wells, *Allison*. Iowa City, IA. Affil: Iowa. Email: allison-wells@uiowa.edu. Research: Spanish-American War, imperialism.

Wells, *Anne S.*, *Soc. for Military Hist.* Lexington, VA. Email: awells@rockbridge.net.

Wells, *Brandy Thomas*, *Oklahoma State*. Columbus, OH. Affil: Ohio State. Email: wells.1287@osu.edu. Research: African American.

Wells, **Charlotte C.**, *Northern Iowa*. Email: charlotte.wells@uni.edu.

Wells, *Christopher W.*, *Macalester*. Saint Paul, MN. Email: wells@macalester.edu. Research: automobile and American environment, green architecture.

Wells, *Elleanor Margaret*. Annapolis, MD. Affil: Harvard Extension Sch. Email: elleanorwells@icloud.com.

Wells, *Jamin J.* Pensacola, FL. Affil: West Florida. Email: jwells2@uwf.edu. Research: coastal, tourism.

Wells, **Jeff**, *Nebraska, Kearney*. Email: wellsrjd@unk.edu.

Wells, *Jennifer C.* Washington, DC. Affil: George Washington. Email: JenniferWells@gwu.edu.

Wells, *Jonathan Daniel*, *Michigan, Ann Arbor*. Ann Arbor, MI. Email: jonwells@umich.edu. Research: 19th-c America, social and cultural.

Wells, **Robert V.**, *Union Coll.* Email: wellsr@union.edu.

Wells, *Robert Wayne*. Louisville, KY. Affil: Indiana. Email: robwells@umail.iu.edu.

Wells, **Ronald**, *Calvin*. Email: well@calvin.edu.

Wells, *Scott*, *California State, Los Angeles*. Los Angeles, CA. Email: swells2@calstatela.edu. Research: intellectual and cultural, Germany in central Middle Ages.

Wells-Oghoghomeh, **Alexis S.**, *Vanderbilt*. Email: alexis.s.wells@vanderbilt.edu.

Wellstead, **Adam**, *Michigan Tech*. Email: awellste@mtu.edu.

Wellstead, **Nikolas**. Beaverton, OR. Affil: Colorado, Boulder. Email: nikolas.wellstead@gmail.com. Research: English Reformation, Tudor-Stuart London.

Welsch, **Christina C.**, *Wooster*. Wooster, OH. Email: cwelsch@wooster.edu. Research: 18th-c South Indian military networks, British East India Company.

Welsh, **Janet Margaret**, *OP*. River Forest, IL. Affil: Dominican. Email: jwelshop@dom.edu.

Welsh, **John**. Braidwood, IL. Affil: Reed-Custer Sch. District. Email: john.welsh@rc255.net.

Welsh, **Michael E.** Greeley, CO. Affil: Northern Colorado. Email: michael.welsh@unco.edu. Research: National Park Service, education.

Welsh, **Rachel Quisqueya**. Alexandria, VA. Affil: NYU. Email: rqw203@nyu.edu.

Welsh, **W. Jeffrey**, *Scranton*. Email: william.welsh@scranton.edu.

Welte, **Heidi Nicole**. Philadelphia, PA. Email: heidiwelte@gmail.com.

Welter, **Barbara**, *Graduate Center, CUNY*. Email: bwelter@hunter.cuny.edu.

Welter, **Volker**, *California, Santa Barbara*. Email: welter@arthistory.ucsb.edu.

Welty, **Kyle**, *Texas-Rio Grande Valley*. Email: kyle.welty@utrgv.edu.

Wempe, **Sean Andrew**, *California State, Bakersfield*. Bakersfield, CA. Email: swempe@csub.edu; wempe.wolf86@gmail.com. Research: German imperialism and internationalism, global public health structures.

Wen, **Xin**, *Princeton*. Email: xinwen@princeton.edu.

Wenc, **Christine D.** Madison, WI. Affil: Greenwood Hist. Email: christinewenc@gmail.com.

Wendeln, **Maria S.** Holland, MI. Affil: Wayne State. Email: an1204@wayne.edu.

Wendt, **Bruce H.** Billings, MT. Affil: Billings West High Sch. Email: wendtb@billingsschools.org.

Wendt, **Simon**. Berlin, Germany. Affil: Frankfurt. Email: wendt@em.uni-frankfurt.de. Research: black armed resistance and civil rights, memory and gender.

Wenger, **Beth S.**, *Pennsylvania*. Philadelphia, PA. Email: bwenger@sas.upenn.edu. Research: Jewish, America.

Wenger, **Diane E.**, *Wilkes*. Email: diane.wenger@wilkes.edu.

Wennerlind, **Carl**, *Barnard, Columbia*. New York, NY. Email: cwennerl@barnard.edu. Research: economic thought.

Wennersten, **John R.** Washington, DC. Email: jrwennersten@gmail.com. Research: US environment, Chesapeake Bay.

Wentling, **Sonja P.**, *Concordia Coll*. Email: wentling@cord.edu.

Wenz, **Andrea Beth**, *Oakland*.

Wenzel, **Anna**. New York, NY. Affil: NYU. Email: aew483@nyu.edu.

Werking, **Cassandra Jane**. East Greenbush, NY. Affil: Kentucky. Email: cj.werking@uky.edu.

Werlich, **David P.**, *Southern Illinois, Carbondale*. Email: elmaximo@siu.edu.

Werlinger, **Timothy L.** Chula Vista, CA. Email: twerlinger@gmail.com.

Werner, **Hans**, *Winnipeg*. Email: h.werner@uwinnipeg.ca.

Werner, **Stephen**. Saint Louis, MO. Affil: Werner Inst. Email: swernerjr@hotmail.com.

Wert, **Justin J.** Norman, OK. Affil: Oklahoma. Email: jwert@ou.edu.

Wert, **Michael J.**, *Marquette*. Glendale, WI. Email: michael.wert@marquette.edu; michaelwert@yahoo.com. Research: memory of Meiji restoration.

Werth, **Paul W.**, *Nevada, Las Vegas*. Las Vegas, NV. Email: werthp@unlv.nevada.edu.

Wertheimer, **John**, *Davidson*. Email: jowertheimer@davidson.edu.

Wertheimer, **Laura Anne**, *Cleveland State*. Email: l.wertheimer@csuohio.edu.

Wesdock, **Ryan**. Blacksburg, VA. Affil: Virginia Tech. Email: ryan.wesdock@gmail.com. Research: free speech/censorship, oology/ornithology.

Wesley, **Timothy Leon**, *Austin Peay State*. Clarksville, TN. Email: wesleyt@apsu.edu. Research: Civil War era politics and religion, American South.

Wesser, **Robert F.**, *SUNY, Albany*.

West, **Carroll Van**, *Middle Tennessee State*. Email: Carroll.West@mtsu.edu.

West, **Elliott**, *Arkansas, Fayetteville*. Email: ewest@uark.edu.

West, **Hugh A.**, *Richmond*. Richmond, VA. Email: hwest@richmond.edu. Research: 18th-c thought, Georg Forster.

West, **Michael R.**, *Holy Cross*. Email: mwest@holycross.edu.

West, **Michael**, *Binghamton, SUNY*. Email: mwest@binghamton.edu.

West, **Sally**, *Truman State*. Kirksville, MO. Email: swest@truman.edu. Research: Russia, modern Europe.

West, **Scott**, *Dayton*. Email: scott.west@notes.udayton.edu.

Westad, **O. A.**, *Yale*.

Westbrook, **Robert B.**, *Rochester*. Email: robert.westbrook@rochester.edu.

Westcott, **Timothy C.**, *Park*. Email: tim.westcott@park.edu.

Westerfeld, **Jennifer Taylor**, *Louisville*. Email: jennifer.westerfeld@louisville.edu.

Westerkamp, **Marilyn J.**, *California, Santa Cruz*. Email: mjw@ucsc.edu.

Westerlin, **Jonathan**. Elkhorn, NE. Email: westerlin@me.com.

Westermann, **Andrea**, *German Hist. Inst.* Email: westermann@ghi-dc.org.

Westermann, **Edward B.**, *Texas A&M, San Antonio*. Email: edward.westermann@tamusa.edu.

Westervelt, **Benjamin W.**, *Lewis & Clark*. Email: bww@lclark.edu.

Westheider, **James E.**, *Cincinnati*. Batavia, OH. Email: james.westheider@uc.edu. Research: African American military, 20th-c social.

Westhoff, **Laura M.**, *Missouri–St. Louis*. Saint Louis, MO. Email: westhoffL@umsl.edu. Research: grassroots democracy 1930-70, social movements.

Westin, **R. Barry**, *Richmond*. Email: bwestin@richmond.edu.

Westkaemper, **Emily M.**, *James Madison*. Harrisonburg, VA. Email: westkaem@jmu.edu. Research: gendered depictions of past, activism of women working in media.

Westling, **Jon**, *Boston Univ*. Email: westling@bu.edu.

Westman, **Robert S.**, *California, San Diego*. Email: rwestman@ucsd.edu.

Weston, **Timothy B.**, *Colorado, Boulder*. Email: timothy.b.weston@colorado.edu.

Westover, **V. Robert**, *Brigham Young*. Email: robert_westover@byu.edu.

Westwick, **Peter J.**, *Southern California*. Email: westwick@usc.edu.

Westwood, **Lisa D.** Rocklin, CA. Affil: ECORP Consulting, Inc. Email: LWestwood@ecorpconsulting.com.

Westwood, **Sarah Davis**. Evanston, IL. Affil: Boston Univ. Email: swestwoo@bu.edu.

Wetherell, **Charles**, *California, Riverside*. Email: charles.wetherell@ucr.edu.

Wetta, **Frank J.**, *Kean*. Email: fwetta@kean.edu.

Wettemann, **Robert Paul**, *US Air Force Acad*. Email: robert.wettemann@usafa.edu.

Wetzel, **Benjamin**. Upland, IN. Affil: Taylor. Email: ben_wetzel@taylor.edu. Research: American religious and political 1860-1920, Theodore Roosevelt studies.

Wetzel, **David**. San Francisco, CA. Affil: California, Berkeley. Email: dwetzel@berkeley.edu. Research: diplomacy of Franco-Prussian War, 20th-c Germany.

Wetzell, **Richard**, *German Hist. Inst.* Washington, DC. Email: wetzell@ghi-dc.org. Research: German penal reform 1880-1945, modern German law/science/politics.

Wexler, **Victor G.**, *Maryland, Baltimore County*. Email: wexler@umbc.edu.

Weyant, **Thomas B.** Spearfish, SD. Affil: Black Hills State. Email: tbweyant@gmail.com. Research: anti-war and civil rights in Pittsburgh, student activism.

Weyeneth, **Robert**, *South Carolina, Columbia*. Email: weyeneth@mailbox.sc.edu.

Wey-Gomez, **Nicolas**, *California Inst. of Tech.* Email: nweygome@hss.caltech.edu.

Weyhing, **Richard T.**, *SUNY, Oswego*. Email: richard.weyhing@oswego.edu.

Whalen, **Brett Edward**, *North Carolina, Chapel Hill*. Email: bwhalen@email.unc.edu.

Whalen, **Carmen T.**, *Williams*. Email: cwhalen@williams.edu.

Whalen, **Emily Ingrid**. Virginia Beach, VA. Affil: Texas, Austin. Email: emilyingridwhalen@gmail.com.

Whalen, **Kathleen N.**, *Washington State, Pullman*. Pullman, WA. Email: kfry@wsu.edu. Research: Chinese in American West, Japanese American labor.

Whalen, **Kevin**. Morris, MN. Affil: Minnesota, Morris. Email: kwhalen@morris.umn.edu.

Whalen, **Philip**, *Coastal Carolina*. Email: pwhalen@coastal.edu.

Whaley, **Donald M.**, *Salisbury*.

Whaley, **Gray H.**, *Southern Illinois, Carbondale*. Email: gwhaley@siu.edu.

Whatley, **Charlotte Clare**. Houston, TX. Affil: Wisconsin, Madison. Email: cwhatley@wisc.edu.

Whayne, **Jeannie M.**, *Arkansas, Fayetteville*. Email: jwhayne@uark.edu.

Whealey, **Alice**. Athens, OH. Affil: California, Berkeley. Email: aaw216@hotmail.com. Research: Western-Byzantine-Islamic interactions, reception of antiquity.

Whealey, **Robert H.**, *Ohio*. Athens, OH. Email: whealey@ohio.edu. Research: Spanish Civil War, European diplomacy since 1914.

Whealy, **Mervin Blythe**. Bakersfield, CA. Affil: Maryland Univ. Coll. Email: mbwhealy@hotmail.com.

Wheat, *David*, *Michigan State*. Email: dwheat@ msu.edu.

Wheatland, *Thomas P.*, *Assumption*. Belmont, MA. Email: twheatland@assumption.edu. Research: German emigres in 20th-c America, critical theory.

Wheatley, *Natasha*, *Princeton*. Princeton, NJ. Email: nwheatley@princeton.edu. Research: Europe, international.

Wheatley, *Steven C.* Mountainside, NJ. Affil: American Council of Learned Societies. Email: swheatley@acls.org. Research: higher education.

Wheeler, **Arthur F.**, *CSC*, *Portland*. Email: wheeler@up.edu.

Wheeler, *Derek*, *Robert H. Smith Center*. Email: dwheeler@monticello.org.

Wheeler, **Kenneth W.**, *Rutgers*.

Wheeler, **Leigh Ann**, *Binghamton, SUNY*. Email: lwheeler@binghamton.edu.

Wheeler, *Rachel M.* Indianapolis, IN. Affil: Indiana-Purdue, Indianapolis. Email: wheelerr@iupui.edu.

Wheeler, **Robert A.**, *Cleveland State*. Email: r.wheeler@csuohio.edu.

Wheeler, **William Bruce**, *Tennessee, Knoxville*. Email: wwheele1@utk.edu.

Whelan, **Heide W.**, *Dartmouth*. Email: heide.w.whelan@dartmouth.edu.

Whelan, **Irene M.**, *Manhattanville*. Email: Irene.Whelan@mville.edu.

Whelchel, **Aaron D.**, *Washington State, Pullman*.

Whidden, *James*, *Dalhousie*. Wolfville, NS, Canada. Affil: Acadia. Email: jamie.whidden@ acadiau.ca. Research: Egypt and Middle East, British imperialism in Egypt/Middle East.

Whigham, **Thomas L.**, *Georgia*. Email: twhigham@uga.edu.

Whipple, **Amy C.**, *Xavier, Ohio*. Email: whipplea@xavier.edu.

Whisenhunt, **Donald W.**, *Western Washington*. Email: Donald.Whisenhunt@wwu.edu.

Whisnant, *Anne Mitchell*, *North Carolina, Chapel Hill*. Chapel Hill, NC. Affil: East Carolina. Email: anne_whisnant@unc.edu. Research: US national parks, public.

Whitaker, *Jan*. Northampton, MA. Email: janwhitaker@verizon.net. Research: American restaurants.

Whitaker, *Robert D.* Little Elm, TX. Affil: Louisiana Tech. Email: whitakerbob@gmail. com. Research: globalization, crime and policing.

Whitby, **Michael**, *National Defence Headquarters*. Email: michael.whitby@forces. gc.ca.

Whitcomb, **Katheryn E.**, *Gettysburg*. Email: kewhitco@gettysburg.edu.

Whitcomb, **Thomas**, *Keene State*. Email: twhitcom@keene.edu.

White, **Angela M.**, *Indiana–Purdue, Indianapolis*. Email: angwhite@iupui.edu.

White, **April**, *Nebraska, Kearney*. Email: whiteac@unk.edu.

White, **Ashli**, *Miami*. Email: acwhite@miami.edu.

White, **Bonnie**, *Memorial, Newfoundland*. Email: bjwhite@grenfell.mun.ca.

White, **Calvin**, **Jr.**, *Arkansas, Fayetteville*. Email: calvinwh@uark.edu.

White, **Carlis C.**, *Slippery Rock*. Email: carlis. white@sru.edu.

White, **Carolyn W.**, *Alabama, Huntsville*.

White, **Charles M.**, *Portland State*.

White, *Christopher*. Concord, MA. Affil: Vassar. Email: cwhite@post.harvard.edu.

White, **Christopher**, *Marshall*. Email: whitec@ marshall.edu.

White, **D. Anthony**, *Sonoma State*.

White, *Dan S.*, *SUNY, Albany*. Brookline, MA. Email: dwhite@albany.edu; danswhite@ comcast.net. Research: community in history.

White, **David H.**, **Jr.**, *Citadel*.

White, **Deborah Gray**, *Rutgers*. Email: dgw@ history.rutgers.edu.

White, *Edward George*. Oak Park, IL. Affil: Triton. Email: ewhite0640@comcast.net. Research: Vietnam War.

White, **G. Edward**, *Virginia*. Email: gew@virginia. edu.

White, **Holly N. Stevens**, *Omohundro Inst.* Email: hnstevens@wm.edu.

White, **Jason Cameron**, *Appalachian State*. Email: whitejc3@appstate.edu.

White, **John C.**, *Alabama, Huntsville*.

White, **John H.**, **Jr.**, *Miami, Ohio*.

White, **Joshua Michael**, *Virginia*. Email: jmwhite@virginia.edu.

White, *Kevin F.* West Sussex, United Kingdom. Affil: Sussex. Email: kevin_white78@ btinternet.com. Research: behavior, education.

White, *Leland J.*, *National Coalition for Hist.* Washington, DC. Email: lwhite@ historycoalition.org.

White, **Luise S.**, *Florida*. Email: lswhite@ufl.edu.

White, **M. Alison**, *US Senate Hist. Office*. Email: alison_white@sec.senate.gov.

White, *Michelle A.*, *Tennessee, Chattanooga*. Chattanooga, TN. Email: michelle-white@utc. edu. Research: early modern England and women.

White, *Owen C.*, *Delaware*. Newark, DE. Email: owhite@udel.edu. Research: modern France, French colonial empire.

White, *Richard*, *Stanford*. Stanford, CA. Email: whiter@stanford.edu. Research: US West, environmental.

White, *Samuel A.*, *Ohio State*. Columbus, OH. Email: white.2426@osu.edu. Research: Ottoman Empire environmental, Little Ice Age.

White, *Shane*. Sydney, Australia. Affil: Sydney. Email: shane.white@sydney.edu.au.

White, *Sophie K.* Notre Dame, IN. Affil: Notre Dame. Email: swhite1@nd.edu. Research: French Louisiana.

White, **Stephen D.**, *Emory*. Email: stephen.d.white@emory.edu.

White, **Stephen**, *Arkansas Tech*.

White, **Thomas**, *Duquesne*. Email: whitet@duq. edu.

White, **Timothy R.**, *New Jersey City*. Email: twhite@njcu.edu.

Whiteaker, **Larry H.**, *Tennessee Tech*. Email: lwhiteaker@tntech.edu.

Whited, **Tamara L.**, *Indiana, Pa.* Email: twhited@ iup.edu.

Whitehead, **Barbara J.**, *DePauw*. Email: whitehea@depauw.edu.

Whitehead, *James R.* Indianapolis, IN. Email: jrwhitehead19@gmail.com.

Whitehead, *Janice E.* Indianapolis, IN. Email: jkewhitehead@gmail.com.

Whitehead, *Michael J.* Gainesville, FL. Affil: American Military. Email: mjwusmcusn@ gmail.com.

Whitehurst, **G. William**, *Old Dominion*. Email: drbillodu@cox.net.

Whitehurst, *Karen Guest*. West Hartford, CT. Email: karen.whitehurst@gmail.com.

Whites, *LeeAnn*, *Missouri, Columbia*. Email: whitesl@missouri.edu.

Whiteside, **James B.**, *Colorado Denver*. Email: jamesb.whiteside@comcast.net.

Whitesides, **Greg G**, *Colorado Denver*. Email: john.whitesides@colorado.edu.

Whitfield, *Harvey Amani*, *Vermont*. Burlington, VT. Email: harvey.whitfield@uvm.edu. Research: Vermont, Atlantic provinces.

Whitford, *Andrew J.* Wellesley Island, NY. Affil: Canadian Army Command and Staff Coll. Email: andywhitford00@gmail.com. Research: refugees from Vietnam in Hong Kong 1979, post-Vietnam Anglo-American relations.

Whiting, *Ashley*. Fayetteville, AR. Affil: Arkansas, Fayetteville. Email: ashleywh@uark.edu.

Whiting, *Gloria McCahon*, *Wisconsin-Madison*. Madison, WI. Email: gwhiting@wisc.edu. Research: race and slavery in early America, women/gender/family.

Whitley, **W. Bland**, *Princeton*. Email: wwhitley@ princeton.edu.

Whitley, *W. Ralph*, *II*. Concord, NC. Email: walterwhitley@earthlink.net. Research: Kannapolis NC church.

Whitlock, **Tammy C.**, *Kentucky*. Email: hrhwhitlock@uky.edu.

Whitman, **Mark I.**, *Towson*. Email: mwhitman@ towson.edu.

Whitmer, **Kelly**, *South*. Email: kjwhitme@ sewanee.edu.

Whitmire, *Leslie*. Atlanta, GA. Affil: Georgia State. Email: lwhitmire1@student.gsu.edu.

Whitmore, *Allan R.* Westbrook, ME. Affil: Southern Maine. Email: Whitmore@Maine. edu. Research: George Washington Madox 1821-82, Jonathan Cilley-William Graves 1838 Duel.

Whitney, **Elspeth**, *Nevada, Las Vegas*. Email: elspeth@unlv.nevada.edu.

Whitney, **Jeanne E.**, *Salisbury*. Email: jxwhitney@salisbury.edu.

Whitney, **Robert**, *New Brunswick*. Email: whitney@unbsj.ca.

Whitney, **Susan**, *Carleton, Can*. Email: susan. whitney@carleton.ca.

Whitney, *Zane Allen*, *Jr*. Centereach, NY. Email: theatre.generalist10@gmail.com. Research: planning of D-Day.

Whitson, *Connor*. Collegeville, PA. Affil: American. Email: cw6139a@american.edu.

Whitt, *Jacqueline E.* Carlisle, PA. Affil: US Army War. Email: jacqueline.whitt@gmail.com. Research: narrative and American grand strategy, diversity and inclusion in US military.

Whittaker, *Thomas Edward Ian*. Somerville, MA. Affil: Harvard. Email: twhittaker@g. harvard.edu.

Whittemore, **Barry**, *North Georgia*. Email: barry. whittemore@ung.edu.

Whittenburg, *Catherine*. Williamsburg, VA. Affil: Colonial Williamsburg Foundation. Email: cwhittenburg@cwf.org.

Whittenburg, **James P.**, *William and Mary*. Email: jpwhit@wm.edu.

Whitters, **Mark**, *Eastern Michigan*. Email: mwhitters@emich.edu.

Whyman, *Susan E*. Fair Haven, NJ. Email: swhyman50@gmail.com. Research: Enlightenment and Industrial Revolution, Birmingham UK and urban culture.

Wiard, **Jennifer**, *Washburn*. Email: jennifer. wiard@washburn.edu.

Wibel, **Michael N**. Karlsruhe, Germany. Email: Michael.Wibel@t-online.de.

Wiblin, **Roger**. Rexburg, ID. Affil: Brigham Young, Idaho. Email: wiblinr@byui.edu. Research: dance, African religion.

Wicentowski, **Joseph C**., *US Dept. of State*. Arlington, VA. Email: joewiz@gmail.com. Research: modern China and Japan, public health social.

Wichhart, **Stefanie K**., *Niagara*. Lockport, NY. Email: skw@niagara.edu. Research: British policy in Egypt and Iraq WWII.

Wichman, **Wendy Jeanne**. Honolulu, HI. Affil: Hawaii, Manoa. Email: wichman@hawaii.edu.

Wick, **David Philip**. Salem, MA. Affil: Gordon, Mass. Email: dmpl.wick@verizon.net. Research: ancient Near East, Egypt.

Wicken, **William C**., *York, Can*. Email: wwicken@yorku.ca.

Wickenden, **Nicholas**. Edmonton, AB, Canada. Affil: Alberta.

Wicker, **Benjamin Ford**. Hammond, LA. Affil: Southeastern Louisiana. Email: benjamin. wicker@selu.edu. Research: effects of chemistry on Western Civ., recreating historical chemistry.

Wicker, **Natori Krystina**. Steubenville, OH. Email: natoriwicker@yahoo.com.

Wickersham, **Jane K**., *Oklahoma (Hist.)*. Email: jwickersham@ou.edu.

Wickett, **Murray R**., *Brock*. Email: mwickett@brocku.ca.

Wickman, **Thomas Michael**, *Trinity Coll., Conn*. Wethersfield, CT. Email: thomas.wickman@trincoll.edu. Research: winter encounters in early Northeast, lower Connecticut River in the 17th c.

Wicks, **Nilce Parreira**. Seal Beach, CA. Affil: UCLA. Email: nilcepwicks@ucla.edu.

Wickstrom, **John B**., *Kalamazoo; Western Michigan*. Email: john.wickstrom@kzoo.edu.

Widell, **Robert Warner, Jr.**, *Rhode Island*. Email: professorwidell@gmail.com.

Widener, **Daniel**, *California, San Diego*. Email: dwidener@ucsd.edu.

Wieben, **Corinne**. Greeley, CO. Affil: Northern Colorado. Email: corinne.wieben@unco.edu. Research: marriage litigation/medieval Italy, gender/masculinity/violence.

Wiecek, **Willam M**., *Syracuse*. Email: wmwiecek@law.syr.edu.

Wieck, **Lindsey Passenger**. San Antonio, TX. Affil: St. Mary's, Tex. Email: lpassenger@gmail. com.

Wiecki, **Stefan Wolfgang**, *Presbyterian*. Email: swwiecki@presby.edu.

Wieczynski, **Joseph L**., *Virginia Tech*.

Wiedemer, **Noelle**, *SUNY, Buffalo State*. Email: wiedemnj@buffalostate.edu.

Wiederrecht, **Ann E**. Onyx, CA. Affil: Bakersfield Coll. Email: awiederr@gmail.com.

Wieland, **Alexander R**., *US Dept. of State*.

Wiemers, **Alice**, *Davidson*. Email: alwiemers@davidson.edu.

Wien, **Peter**, *Maryland, Coll. Park*. Email: pwien@umd.edu.

Wien, **Thomas**, *Montréal*. Email: thomas.wien@umontreal.ca.

Wiener, **Ann Elizabeth**, *Science History Inst*. Email: awiener@sciencehistory.org.

Wiener, **Joel H**. Teaneck, NJ. Affil: Graduate Center, CUNY. Email: jwiener267@aol. com. Research: British and US journalism 1830-present.

Wiener, **Jon**, *California, Irvine*. Email: wiener@uci.edu.

Wiener, **Martin J**., *Rice*. Email: wiener@rice.edu.

Wiener, **Roberta**, *Soc. for Military Hist.* Email: wienerr@vmi.edu.

Wier, **Melanie**, *Herbert Hoover Presidential Library*. Email: melanie.wier@nara.gov.

Wieringa, **Jeri**. Portland, OR. Affil: George Mason. Email: jwiering@gmu.edu. Research: digital, religion in 19th-c US.

Wiersma, **Antia**. Amsterdam, Netherlands. Affil: Royal Netherlands Hist. Soc. Email: antia.wiersma@huygens.knaw.nl. Research: biographical study, feminist theory.

Wiese, **Andrew**, *San Diego State*. Email: awiese@sdsu.edu.

Wiese, **Jason**, *Hist. New Orleans*. Email: jasonw@hnoc.org.

Wiesen, **Jonathan**, *Alabama, Birmingham*. Email: jwiesen@uab.edu.

Wiesner-Hanks, **Merry E**., *Wisconsin-Milwaukee; World Hist. Assoc.* Milwaukee, WI. Email: merrywh@uwm.edu. Research: world, women/gender.

Wiest, **Andrew A**., *Southern Mississippi*. Email: andrew.wiest@usm.edu.

Wigen, **Kären E**., *Stanford*. Email: kwigen@stanford.edu.

Wigger, **John H**., *Missouri, Columbia*. Email: wiggerj@missouri.edu.

Wiggins, **Benjamin Alan**. Minneapolis, MN. Affil: Minnesota. Email: benwig@umn.edu. Research: actuarial science, race.

Wiggins, **Danielle L**., *California Inst. of Tech.* Pasadena, CA. Email: dwiggins@caltech.edu.

Wiggins, **Sarah W**., *Alabama, Tuscaloosa*. Email: swiggins@dbtech.net.

Wight, **David Michael**. Greensboro, NC. Affil: North Carolina, Greensboro. Email: wightd@uci.edu.

Wightman, **Ann M**., *Wesleyan*. Email: awightman@wesleyan.edu.

Wiker, **Gregory Daniel**. Ephrata, PA. Affil: Rochester. Email: gdwiker@gmail.com. Research: British Empire 1775-1870, Bermuda 1775-1869.

Wilburn, **Drew**, *Oberlin*. Email: Drew.Wilburn@oberlin.edu.

Wilburn, **Kenneth E**., *East Carolina*. Email: wilburnk@ecu.edu.

Wilcox, **Clifford**. Ventura, CA. Email: cliff. wilcox@gmail.com. Research: sociology and anthropology, 'Chicago School' of urban sociology.

Wilcox, **Larry D**. Toledo, OH. Affil: Toledo. Email: larry.wilcox@utoledo.edu. Research: WWII documentary films, visualization of Holocaust.

Wilcox, **Robert W**., *Northern Kentucky*. Email: wilcox@nku.edu.

Wilczewski, **Michal Janusz**, *Illinois, Chicago*. Chicago, IL. Email: mwilcz5@uic.edu. Research: interwar Poland, peasant studies.

Wild, **H. Mark**, *California State, Los Angeles*. Los Angeles, CA. Email: mwild@calstatela.edu.

Research: immigration and social, urban development.

Wildenthal, **Lora**, *Rice*. Houston, TX. Email: wildenth@rice.edu. Research: human rights, German colonialism.

Wilder, **Colin F**., *South Carolina, Columbia*. Email: wildercf@mailbox.sc.edu.

Wilder, **Craig Steven**, *MIT*. Email: cwilder@mit. edu.

Wilder, **Gary M**. Forest Hills, NY. Affil: Graduate Center, CUNY. Email: gwilder@gc.cuny.edu. Research: French empire, colonial state.

Wilding, **Nick**, *Georgia State*. Email: nwilding@gsu.edu.

Wilentz, **Sean**, *Princeton*. Email: swilentz@princeton.edu.

Wiles, **Clair K**. Eugene, OR. Affil: North Eugene High Sch. Email: clair.wiles@gmail.com.

Wilford, **F. Hugh**, *California State, Long Beach*. Email: hugh.wilford@csulb.edu.

Wilhite, **Alyssa Diane**. Tyler, TX. Email: alyssa. wilhite@yahoo.com.

Wilinski, **Jesse**. Fredericksburg, VA. Affil: National Archives. Email: jesse.wilinski@nara. gov. Research: Civil War, slavery/abolition/emancipation.

Wilk, **Gavin J**. Huntington, NY. Email: gwilk@hotmail.com. Research: Irish republican activism in US 1922-39.

Wilke, **Ekkehard-Teja P**. Riverside, IL. Affil: East-West. Email: wil3t@eastwest.edu.

Wilken, **Robert L**., *Virginia*. Email: rlw2w@virginia.edu.

Wilkerson, **Jessica**, *Mississippi*. Oxford, MS. Email: jcwilker@olemiss.edu. Research: women's activism in US South and Appalachia, War on Poverty in Appalachia.

Wilkerson-Freeman, **Sarah L**., *Arkansas State*. Email: sarahwf@astate.edu.

Wilkie, **Jacqueline S**., *Luther*. Email: wilkieja@luther.edu.

Wilkie, **James W**., *UCLA*. Email: wilkie@ucla.edu.

Wilkie, **Vanessa Jean**, *Huntington Library*. Los Angeles, CA. Email: vwilkie@huntington.org. Research: early modern England, gender and family.

Wilkins, **Charles L**., *Wake Forest*. Email: wilkincl@wfu.edu.

Wilkins, **Joe B., Jr.** Daphne, AL. Affil: Columbia Southern. Email: wilkinsbnc@gmail.com.

Wilkins, **Mira**. Miami, FL. Affil: Florida International. Email: wilkinsm@fiu.edu. Research: foreign investment in US, multinational enterprise.

Wilkinson, **A.B.**, *Nevada, Las Vegas*. Email: AB.Wilkinson@unlv.edu.

Wilkinson, **Conor**. New York, NY. Affil: Columbia. Email: conor.wilkinson1@gmail.com. Research: health/community/lifeways/death, linguistics/culture/politics/identity.

Wilkinson, **Glenn**, *Calgary*. Email: grwilkin@ucalgary.ca.

Wilkinson, **Mark**, *Virginia Military Inst.* Email: wilkinsonmf@vmi.edu.

Wilkinson, **Melissa**, *State Hist. Soc. of Missouri*. Email: wilkinsonme@shsmo.org.

Wilkinson, **Steven Ian**. New Haven, CT. Affil: Yale. Email: steven.wilkinson@yale.edu.

Wilkinson, **William J**., *Henry Ford Coll.*

Willbanks, **James H**., *US Army Command Coll.* Email: james.h.willbanks.civ@mail.mil.

Willen, *Diane*, *Georgia State*. Catonsville, MD. Email: dwillen@gsu.edu. Research: Puritanism, 17th-c religion and gender.

Willett, **Julie**, *Texas Tech*. Email: j.willett@ttu. edu.

Willhite, *Kelly Jaye*. Hurricane Mills, TN. Email: mrsnurse@live.com.

Williams, **Alan J.**, *Wake Forest*. Email: awill@wfu. edu.

Williams, **Ashley**, *Massachusetts Hist. Soc.* Email: awilliams@masshist.org.

Williams, *Austin Randall*. Kansas City, MO. Affil: Missouri, Kansas City. Email: arwadd@mail. umkc.edu. Research: HIV/AIDS and LGBTQ civil rights, oral history.

Williams, *Bernard D.*, *Scranton*. Pompano Beach, FL. Email: bernard.williams@scranton. edu. Research: modern Europe, Latin America.

Williams, *Carol J.* Lethbridge, AB, Canada. Affil: Lethbridge. Email: carol.williams@uleth.ca. Research: indigenous women's work and activism, reproductive justice transnational.

Williams, **Chad Louis**, *Brandeis*. Email: chadw@ brandeis.edu.

Williams, *Charles E.* Arlington, VA. Email: cewill627@gmail.com.

Williams, **D. Alan**, *Virginia*. Email: daw5z@ virginia.edu.

Williams, **Daniel K.**, *West Georgia*. Email: dkw@ westga.edu.

Williams, **Daryle**, *Maryland, Coll. Park*. Email: daryle@umd.edu.

Williams, *Deborah*. Goshen, IN. Affil: Southern New Hampshire. Email: debsancestors@gmail. com.

Williams, *Duncan*. Los Angeles, CA. Affil: Southern California. Email: duncanwi@usc. edu.

Williams, **Erica C.**, *Hist. Assoc.* Email: ewilliams@ historyassociates.com.

Williams, **Harry McKinley**, *Carleton Coll.* Email: hwilliam@carleton.edu.

Williams, **Hettie V.**, *Monmouth*. Email: hwilliam@monmouth.edu.

Williams, *Jakobi*, *Indiana*. Bloomington, IN. Email: jakowill@indiana.edu. Research: Illinois Black Panther Party, racial coaliton politics in Chicago.

Williams, **James B.**, *Indianapolis*. Email: williamsjb@uindy.edu.

Williams, **James M.**, *SUNY, Coll. Geneseo*. Email: williams@geneseo.edu.

Williams, *Jeffery*. Columbia, SC. Affil: South Carolina. Email: Jefferyw@email.sc.edu.

Williams, **Jeffrey C.**, *Northern Kentucky*. Email: williamsj@nku.edu.

Williams, **John A.**, *SUNY, Stony Brook*. Email: John.Williams@stonybrook.edu.

Williams, *John R.*, *Colorado Coll.* Colorado Springs, CO. Email: jwilliams@coloradocollege. edu. Research: China, popular culture.

Williams, **Kat D.**, *Marshall*. Email: williamskath@ marshall.edu.

Williams, **Kidada E.**, *Wayne State*. Email: kidada. williams@wayne.edu.

Williams, *Kyle E.* Tulsa, OK. Affil: Rutgers. Email: williams.kyle.edward@gmail.com. Research: capitalism, cultural/intellectual.

Williams, **Lance**, *Missouri Science and Tech.* Email: lancewms@mst.edu.

Williams, **Lea E.**, *Brown*. Email: Lea_Williams@ Brown.edu.

Williams, **Learotha**, **Jr.**, *Tennessee State*. Email: lwilli22@tnstate.edu.

Williams, **Lee E.**, **II**, *Alabama, Huntsville*. Email: willial@uah.edu.

Williams, **Leroy T.**, *Arkansas, Little Rock*. Email: drlee629@aol.com.

Williams, **Lou Falkner**, *Kansas State*. Email: lwill@ksu.edu.

Williams, **Louise B.**, *Central Connecticut State*. Email: williamsl@ccsu.edu.

Williams, **Mark Kenneth**, *Charleston Southern*. Email: mkwilliams@csuniv.edu.

Williams, *Mason B*. Williamstown, MA. Affil: Williams. Email: mbw2@williams.edu. Research: urban policing 1970-95.

Williams, **Max R.**, *Western Carolina*. Email: swilliams@dnet.net.

Williams, **Michael A.**, *Washington, Seattle*. Email: maw@uw.edu.

Williams, **Michael Vinson**, *Mississippi State; Texas, El Paso*. Email: mwilliams@history. msstate.edu; mvwilliams@utep.edu.

Williams, *Micheal*. Crawfordville, FL. Affil: Florida State. Email: mw18e@my.fsu.edu.

Williams, **Nadejda**, *West Georgia*. Email: nwilliam@westga.edu.

Williams, **Ogechukwu Ezekwem**, *Creighton*. Email: ogechukwuwilliams@creighton.edu.

Williams, **Owen**, *Folger Inst.* Email: owilliams@ folger.edu.

Williams, *Patrick G.*, *Arkansas, Fayetteville*. Fayetteville, AR. Email: pgwillia@uark.edu. Research: 19th-c US, American South.

Williams, *Patrick*. Orlando, FL. Affil: Central Florida. Email: patrick_rw@excite.com.

Williams, **Rebecca R.**, *South Alabama*. Email: rwilliams@southalabama.edu.

Williams, **Rhonda Y.**, *MIT; Vanderbilt*. Email: rhonda.williams@vanderbilt.edu.

Williams, **Richard S.**, *Washington State, Pullman*. Email: sarek@wsu.edu.

Williams, **Robert C.**, *Davidson; Hist. Assoc.* Email: bob03harmony@yahoo.com.

Williams, **Rosalind**, *MIT*. Email: rhwill@mit.edu.

Williams, *Scott M.* Weatherford, TX. Affil: Weatherford. Email: swilliams@wc.edu. Research: history pedagogy, introductory level courses.

Williams, **Shannen Dee**, *Tennessee, Knoxville; Villanova*. Email: swill132@utk.edu; shannen. williams@villanova.edu.

Williams, *Stephanie*. San Marcos, CA. Affil: California State, San Marcos. Email: willi337@ cougars.csusm.edu.

Williams, **Timothy**, *Oregon*. Email: timw@ uoregon.edu.

Williams, **Virginia S.**, *Winthrop*. Email: williamsv@winthrop.edu.

Williams, *Walter Franklin*. Arlington, TN. Email: wwillims@memphis.edu.

Williamson, *Angela*. Cordova, TN. Affil: Withers Collection Museum & Gallery. Email: awill713@outlook.com.

Williamson, *Arthur H.*, *California State, Sacramento*. Sacramento, CA. Email: williamsonah@csus.edu. Research: apocalypse and political thought, George Buchanan 1506-82.

Williamson, *Daniel C.*, *Hartford*. West Hartford, CT. Email: dwilliams@hartford.edu. Research: Anglo-Irish relations/Northern Ireland, Anglo-American relations after WWII.

Williamson, **George S.**, *Florida State*. Email: gwilliamson@fsu.edu.

Williamson, **Gustavus G.**, **Jr.**, *Virginia Tech*.

Williamson, *J. Franklin*. Barnesville, GA. Affil: Gordon State. Email: fwilliamson@ gordonstate.edu. Research: public mourning for wartime dead, reconsidering civil-military relations.

Williamson, **Jacquelyn C.**, *George Mason*. Email: jwilli98@gmu.edu.

Williamson, *Joel*, *North Carolina, Chapel Hill*. Chapel Hill, NC. Email: annaleoww@aol.com. Research: southern US race relations.

Williamson, **Rosco**, *Point Loma Nazarene*. Email: roscowilliamson@pointloma.edu.

Williamson, *Samuel R.*, *Jr.* Pittsboro, NC. Affil: South. Email: swilliam@sewanee.edu. Research: Austria-Hungary 1910-14, 20th-c strategic thought.

Williamson, **Savannah L.**, *Sul Ross State*. Email: savannah.williamson@sulross.edu.

Williamson, **Wilbert E.**, *Henry Ford Coll.* Email: billwilliamson3890@att.net.

Williams-Searle, **Bridgett M.**, *St. Rose*. Email: williamb@mail.strose.edu.

Williard, *David Christopher*, *St. Thomas, Minn.* Saint Paul, MN. Email: will0208@ stthomas.edu. Research: US Civil War and Reconstruction, US military.

Williard, *Hope Deejune*. Lincoln, United Kingdom. Affil: Lincoln. Email: h.williard@ gmail.com. Research: friendship in early medieval west, epistolary culture.

Williford, *Daniel J.*, *Wisconsin-Madison*. Ann Arbor, MI. Email: wildj@umich.edu.

Willig, *Timothy David*, *Indiana, South Bend*. Mishawaka, IN. Email: twillig@iusb.edu. Research: British-Indian affairs/Great Lakes, early American Republic frontier.

Willingham, **Robert A.**, *Roanoke*. Email: willingham@roanoke.edu.

Willingham, *William F.* Portland, OR. Affil: Army Engineer Div. Email: w.willingham@comcast. net.

Willis, **Alan Scot**, *Northern Michigan*. Email: awillis@nmu.edu.

Willis, **F. Roy**, *California, Davis*.

Willis, **John C.**, *South*. Email: jwillis@sewanee. edu.

Willis, **John M.**, *Colorado, Boulder*. Email: jwillis@ colorado.edu.

Willis, **John**, *Carleton, Can.* Email: john.willis@ carleton.ca.

Willis, **Kirk**, *Georgia*. Email: kw@uga.edu.

Willis, **Lee L.**, **III**, *Wisconsin-Stevens Point*. Email: lwillis@uwsp.edu.

Willis, *Thabiti*, *Carleton Coll.* Northfield, MN. Email: jcwillis@carleton.edu. Research: religious encounters, African and diaspora religions.

Willman, **Robert I.**, *Mississippi State*.

Willoughby, *Christopher D. E.* Murray, KY. Affil: Schomburg Center for Research in Black Culture. Email: cdwillou@gmail.com. Research: slavery, medical education.

Willoughby, **Larry**, *Austin Comm. Coll.* Email: jlw@austincc.edu.

Willoughby, *Urmi Engineer*, *Murray State*. Bellefonte, PA. Email: uenginee@gmail. com. Research: environmental, historical epidemiology.

Willrich, Michael, *Brandeis*. Waltham, MA. Email: willrich@brandeis.edu. Research: American social and legal.

Wills, Brian S., *Kennesaw State*. Email: bwills2@kennesaw.edu.

Wills, David W. Amherst, MA. Affil: Amherst. Email: dwwills@amherst.edu. Research: religion in early Atlantic world, blacks and early US mssionary movement.

Wills, Garry, *Northwestern*. Email: g-wills@northwestern.edu.

Wills, Jocelyn, *Brooklyn, CUNY*. Brooklyn, NY. Email: jwills@brooklyn.cuny.edu. Research: American dream and reality, Surveillance Capitalism.

Wills, Steven, *Nebraska Wesleyan*. Email: swills@nebrwesleyan.edu.

Willsky-Ciollo, Lydia E. N. Fairfield, CT. Affil: Fairfield. Email: lciollo@fairfield.edu. Research: Henry David Thoreau, women's social reform.

Wilson, Andrew D., *Keene State*. Email: awilson@keene.edu.

Wilson, Andrew R., *Naval War Coll.* Email: wilsona@usnwc.edu.

Wilson, Andrew W. Urbana, IL. Affil: Illinois, Urbana-Champaign. Email: andrew.wilson@huskers.unl.edu. Research: US and Cold War, Latin America and world.

Wilson, Andrew, *Loyola, Chicago*. Email: awilso@luc.edu.

Wilson, Benjamin, *Harvard (Hist. of Science)*. Email: btwilson@fas.harvard.edu.

Wilson, Carol E., *Washington Coll.* Email: cwilson2@washcoll.edu.

Wilson, Carrie E. Aberdeen, MD. Email: carrie.wilson1006@gmail.com.

Wilson, Catharine A., *Guelph*. Email: cawilson@uoguelph.ca.

Wilson, Catherine L. Long Beach, CA. Affil: California State, Long Beach. Email: lynnroadz@yahoo.com.

Wilson, Charles Lamone. Detroit, MI. Affil: Madonna. Email: Charlesofwilson@gmail.com.

Wilson, Charles Reagan, *Mississippi*. Email: crwilson@olemiss.edu.

Wilson, Christie Sample. Austin, TX. Affil: St. Edward's. Email: christiw@stedwards.edu. Research: early modern French social/demographic, Great Plains population and environment.

Wilson, Clyde N., Jr., *South Carolina, Columbia*. Email: cwilson@clicksouth.net.

Wilson, Daniel J. Allentown, PA. Affil: Muhlenberg. Email: dwilson@muhlenberg.edu. Research: polio in US, masculinity and disability.

Wilson, David Alexander, *Toronto*. Email: david.wilson@utoronto.ca.

Wilson, David B., *Iowa State*. Email: davidw@iastate.edu.

Wilson, David Harold. Camano Island, WA. Email: dewisant@frontier.com.

Wilson, David L., *Southern Illinois, Carbondale*. Email: dwilson@siu.edu.

Wilson, Erica. Dallas, TX. Email: eshawnwil@gmail.com.

Wilson, Evan, *Naval War Coll.* Newport, RI. Email: evan.wilson@usnwc.edu; wilson.evan@gmail.com. Research: naval and maritime, demobilization.

Wilson, Evelyn L. Baton Rouge, LA. Affil: Louisiana State, Baton Rouge. Email: ewilson@sulc.edu. Research: African Americans during Reconstruction, free persons of color.

Wilson, Francille Rusan, *Southern California*. Email: frwilson@usc.edu.

Wilson, G. Alan, *Trent*.

Wilson, Gary. Dickinson, TX. Affil: Mainland. Email: gwilson@com.edu.

Wilson, Gaye, *Robert H. Smith Center*. Email: gwilson@monticello.org.

Wilson, Gerald L., *Duke*. Email: gerald.wilson@duke.edu.

Wilson, Glee E., *Kent State*.

Wilson, Greg Stone. Pittsburgh, PA. Email: gregory.wilson1@snhu.edu.

Wilson, Harold E., *Alberta*.

Wilson, Harold S., *Old Dominion*. Email: hwilson@odu.edu.

Wilson, James A., *Texas State*. Email: jw04@txstate.edu.

Wilson, James Graham, *US Dept. of State*.

Wilson, Jamie J., *Salem State*. Email: jwilson2@salemstate.edu.

Wilson, Jeffrey K., *California State, Sacramento*. Email: jkwilson@csus.edu.

Wilson, Jeremy Burton. Lebanon, TN. Affil: Lebanon High Sch. Email: jeremyburtonwilson@gmail.com.

Wilson, John R., *Alberta*.

Wilson, Jonathan, *California Polytechnic State*. Email: jdwilson@calpoly.edu.

Wilson, Karen S. Los Angeles, CA. Email: ksw2052@gmail.com. Research: social networks/urban development, augmented reality of historic sites.

Wilson, Kathleen, *SUNY, Stony Brook*. Email: kathleen.wilson@stonybrook.edu.

Wilson, Kathryn E., *Georgia State*. Email: kewilson@gsu.edu.

Wilson, Kent. Alexandria, VA. Email: lkentwilson@gmail.com.

Wilson, Laura Merrifeld. Indianapolis, IN. Affil: Indianapolis. Email: lmwilson@uindy.edu.

Wilson, Leslie E., *Montclair State*. Email: wilsonl@mail.montclair.edu.

Wilson, Lindsay Blake, *Northern Arizona*. Email: lindsay.wilson@nau.edu.

Wilson, Louis E., *Smith*. Email: lwilson@smith.edu.

Wilson, Major L., *Memphis*.

Wilson, Mark B., *Lehman, CUNY*. Bronx, NY. Affil: Graduate Center, CUNY. Email: mark.wilson@lehman.cuny.edu; mark@markbwilson.com. Research: roman republic, ancient and medieval.

Wilson, Mark R., *North Carolina, Charlotte*. Charlotte, NC. Email: mrwilson@uncc.edu. Research: US military-industrial relations, historical methods.

Wilson, Martin W. Delaware Water Gap, PA. Affil: East Stroudsburg. Email: mwilson@po-box.esu.edu. Research: colonial America, 20th-c world.

Wilson, Mary Christina, *Massachusetts, Amherst*. Email: wilson@history.umass.edu.

Wilson, Mary Lynn, *San José State*. Email: Mary.Wilson@sjsu.edu.

Wilson, Michael L. Richardson, TX. Affil: Texas, Dallas. Email: mwilson@utdallas.edu. Research: bohemian subcultures, mass consumption.

Wilson, Noell H., *Mississippi*. Email: nrwilson@olemiss.edu.

Wilson, Norman J., *Messiah*. Mechanicsburg, PA. Email: nwilson@messiah.edu. Research: Europe 1450-1750 (Regensburg/Ratisbon), Historiography.

Wilson, R. Jackson J., *Smith*. Email: rwilson@wilson.org.

Wilson, Raymond, *Fort Hays State*.

Wilson, Robert J., III, *Georgia Coll. and State*. Email: bob.wilson@gcsu.edu.

Wilson, Roderick I., *Illinois, Urbana-Champaign*. Email: riwilson@illinois.edu.

Wilson, Steven, *Lincoln Memorial*. Email: steven.wilson@lmunet.edu.

Wilson, Theodore Allen, *Kansas*. Email: taw@ku.edu.

Wilson, Thomas A., *Hamilton*. Email: twilson@hamilton.edu.

Wilson, Tiana. Austin, TX. Affil: Texas, Austin. Email: wilsontu@utexas.edu.

Wilson, Veronica Anne, *Pittsburgh, Johnstown*. Email: vwilson@pitt.edu.

Wilt, Paul C., *Westmont*. Email: wilt@westmont.edu.

Wiltenburg, Joy, *Rowan*. Philadelphia, PA. Email: wiltenburg@rowan.edu. Research: laughter in early modern England/Germany.

Wiltse, Jeff, *Montana*. Email: jeff.wiltse@mso.umt.edu.

Wilz, Patrick. Minneapolis, MN. Affil: Minnesota, Twin Cities. Email: wilzx003@umn.edu.

Winans, Adrienne A., *Utah Valley*. Orem, UT. Email: Adrienne.winans@uvu.edu; winans.13@gmail.com. Research: Asian American, women/gender/sexuality.

Winch, Julie P., *Massachusetts, Boston*. Wells, ME. Email: julie.winch@umb.edu. Research: America and African American, maritime.

Winchell, Meghan K., *Nebraska Wesleyan*. Email: mwinchel@nebrwesleyan.edu.

Winchester, Juti A., *Fort Hays State*. Email: jawinchester@fhsu.edu.

Windel, Aaron M., *Simon Fraser*. Email: awindel@sfu.ca.

Winders, William, *Georgia Inst. of Tech.* Email: william.winders@hts.gatech.edu.

Windsor, Lee, *New Brunswick*. Email: lwindsor@unb.ca.

Wineburg, Sam S. Palo Alto, CA. Affil: Stanford. Email: wineburg@stanford.edu.

Winer, Linda Ruth. Arlington, VA. Affil: Fairfax County Public Sch. Email: llinwin@aol.com.

Winer, Rebecca Lynn, *Villanova*. Swarthmore, PA. Email: rebecca.winer@villanova.edu. Research: medieval women, Mediterranean.

Winerock, Emily. Pittsburgh, PA. Email: contact@winerock.com. Research: Puritanism in early modern England, dance.

Wines, Roger A., *Fordham*. Email: pegrogwines@optonline.net.

Winford, Brandon Kyron, *Tennessee, Knoxville*. Knoxville, TN. Email: bwinford@utk.edu. Research: black business, civil rights movement.

Wing, John T., *Staten Island, CUNY*. Staten Island, NY. Email: john.wing@csi.cuny.edu. Research: environmental, early modern Spain.

Winger, Stewart Lance, *Illinois State*. Email: swinger@ilstu.edu.

Wingerd, Mary C., *St. Cloud State*.

Wingerd, Zachary D., *Baylor*. Email: zachary_wingerd@baylor.edu.

Wingfield, **Matthew James**. Harrisonburg, VA. Affil: James Madison. Email: wingfimj@dukes. jmu.edu.

Wingfield, **Nancy M.**, *Northern Illinois*. Email: nmw@niu.edu.

Wingo, **Rebecca S.**, *Cincinnati*. Cincinnati, OH. Email: wingora@ucmail.uc.edu; rebecca. wingo@gmail.com.

Winiarski, **Douglas Leo**, *Richmond*. Midlothian, VA. Email: dwiniars@richmond.edu. Research: popular religion, 18th-c New England.

Winichakul, **Thongchai**, *Wisconsin-Madison*. Email: twinicha@wisc.edu.

Wink, **Andre**, *Wisconsin-Madison*. Email: awink@ wisc.edu.

Winkelmann, **Tessa Ong**, *Nevada, Las Vegas*. Email: tessa.winkelmann@unlv.edu.

Winkle, **Kenneth J.**, *Nebraska, Lincoln*. Email: kwinkle1@unl.edu.

Winkler, **Allan M.**, *Miami, Ohio*. Oxford, OH. Email: winkleam@muohio.edu. Research: post-WWII America, Nuclear Age.

Winkler, **Jonathan Reed**. Dayton, OH. Affil: Wright State. Email: jonathan.winkler@wright. edu. Research: 20th-c US foreign/military policy, development of communications technology.

Winkler-Morey, **Anne**, *Metropolitan State*. Email: anne.winklermorey@metrostate.edu.

Winling, **LaDale C.**, *Virginia Tech*. Email: lwinling@vt.edu.

Winn, **Robert E**, *Northwestern Coll*. Email: rewinn@nwciowa.edu.

Winn, **Thomas H.**, *Austin Peay State*.

Winnie, **Laurence H.**, *Southern Methodist*. Dallas, TX. Email: lwinnie@smu.edu. Research: French church.

Winnik, **Herbert C.**, *St. Mary's, Md*. Solomons, MD. Email: hcwinnik@smcm.edu; hcwinnik@ earthlink.net.

Winquist, **Alan H.** Upland, IN. Affil: Taylor. Email: alwinquis@taylor.edu.

Winroth, **Anders**, *Yale*. New Haven, CT. Email: anders.winroth@yale.edu. Research: medieval, legal.

Winship, **Michael P.**, *Georgia*. Email: mwinship@ uga.edu.

Winslow, **Rachel**, *Westmont*. Email: rwinslow@ westmont.edu.

Winter, **Alan A.** Bernardsville, NJ. Email: dralanwinter@hotmail.com.

Winter, **David R.**, *Brandon*. Email: winterd@ brandonu.ca.

Winter, **Emma L.**, *Columbia (Hist.)*. Email: ew2176@columbia.edu.

Winter, **Jay M.**, *Yale*. Email: jay.winter@yale.edu.

Winter, **Stefan**, *Québec, Montréal*. Email: winter. stefan@uqam.ca.

Winterer, **Caroline**, *Stanford*. Email: cwinterer@ stanford.edu.

Wintermute, **Bob**, *Queens, CUNY*. Email: b_ wintermute@hotmail.com.

Winters, **Donald L.**, *Vanderbilt*. Email: donald.l.winters@vanderbilt.edu.

Winters, **John Cresswell**. Alexandria, VA. Affil: Graduate Center, CUNY. Email: jwinters@ gradcenter.cuny.edu. Research: Iroquois, memory.

Winters, **Julia V**. Hatfield, MA. Affil: St. John's, NY. Email: jwinters889@gmail.com. Research: ocean liners, maritime.

Wintersteen, **Kristin A.**, *Houston*. Houston, TX. Email: kawinter@central.uh.edu. Research:

Latin American environmental history, Pacific World.

Wintz, **Cary D.**, *Texas Southern; US Air Force Acad*. Houston, TX. Email: wintz_cd@tsu. edu; cary.wintz@usafa.edu. Research: Harlem Renaissance, 20th-c race and culture.

Wirts, **Kristine M.**, *Texas-Rio Grande Valley*. Edinburg, TX. Email: kristine.wirts@utrgv.edu. Research: early modern European society, artisan culture.

Wirtschafter, **Elise Kimerling**. Beverly Hills, CA. Affil: California State Polytechnic. Email: ekwirtschafter@gmail.com. Research: diplomacy, intellectual.

Wirzbicki, **Peter J.**, *Princeton*. Princeton, NJ. Email: pw14@princeton.edu. Research: US intellectual.

Wise, **Benjamin E.**, *Florida*. Email: benwise@ufl. edu.

Wise, **Keith**, *Alma*. Email: kwise@edzone.net.

Wise, **M. Norton**, *UCLA*. Email: nortonw@ history.ucla.edu.

Wise, **Michael David**, *North Texas*. Email: michael.wise@unt.edu.

Wiseman, **Renee**. Las Vegas, NV. Affil: Nevada, Las Vegas. Email: ReneeMWiseman@gmail. com. Research: Romanization, slavery systems of ancient world.

Wishnia, **Judith**, *SUNY, Stony Brook*. Email: Judith.Wishnia@stonybrook.edu.

Wisniewski, **Michael**. Fulton, NY. Email: mjw7501@yahoo.com.

Wisnoski, **Alexander**, **III**, *North Georgia*. Email: alexander.wisnoski@ung.edu.

Witgen, **Michael**, *Michigan, Ann Arbor*. Email: mwitgen@umich.edu.

Witherell, **Larry L.**, *Minnesota State, Mankato*. Email: larry.witherell@mnsu.edu.

Witherspoon, **Kevin B.**, *Lander*. Email: kwitherspoon@lander.edu.

Witherspoon, **Reginald**, *Henry Ford Coll*. Email: rwitherspoon@comcast.net.

Withington, **Ann F.**, *SUNY, Albany*.

Withycombe, **Shannon**, *New Mexico*. Albuquerque, NM. Email: swithycombe@unm. edu. Research: medicine.

Witkowski, **Gregory R.**, *Indiana–Purdue, Indianapolis*. Email: gwitkows@iupui.edu.

Witmer, **Andrew**, *James Madison*. Email: witmerad@jmu.edu.

Witschorik, **Charles A**. San Jose, CA. Affil: San Francisco Univ. High Sch. Email: mexicaw12@ gmail.com.

Witt, **John Fabian**. New Haven, CT. Affil: Yale Law Sch. Email: john.witt@yale.edu. Research: American law, American politics.

Witt, **Lori Lynnette**. Pella, IA. Affil: Central. Email: wittl@central.edu.

Wittern-Keller, **Laura**, *SUNY, Albany*. Email: lwittern@albany.edu.

Wittmann, **Rebecca E.**, *Toronto*. Email: wittmann@chass.utoronto.ca.

Wittner, **David G.**, *Utica*. Email: dwittner@utica. edu.

Wittner, **Lawrence S.**, *SUNY, Albany*. Email: wittner@albany.edu.

Wladaver-Morgan, **Susan**. Portland, OR. Affil: Portland State. Email: swladamor2@gmail. com. Research: recent US social, US West.

Woehrlin, **William F.**, *Carleton Coll*. Email: wwoehrli@carleton.edu.

Woell, **Edward J.**, *Western Illinois*. Macomb, IL. Email: EJ-Woell@wiu.edu. Research: 19th-c religion, War of Vendee.

Woessner, **Martin V**. New York, NY. Affil: City Coll., NY. Email: mwoessner@ccny.cuny.edu. Research: reception of Martin Heidegger, international intellectual.

Woeste, **Victoria Saker**. West Lafayette, IN. Email: vwoeste@gmail.com. Research: antisemitism/civilrights/religion, agriculture/ regulation/environment.

Woesthoff, **Julia M.**, *DePaul*. Email: jwoestho@ depaul.edu.

Woestman, **Kelly A.**, *Pittsburg State*. Email: woestman@pittstate.edu.

Wofford, **Drewry Frye**, **III**. Miami, FL. Affil: Miami. Email: d.wofford@umiami.edu. Research: civil aviation and diplomatic relations, Concorde/ France/USA/Great Britain.

Wohl, **Anthony S.**, *Vassar*. Email: aswohl@aol. com.

Wohl, **Harold B.**, *Northern Iowa*.

Wohl, **Robert A.**, *UCLA*. Email: rwohl@ucla.edu.

Wohlford, **Corinne M**. Saint Louis, MO. Affil: Fontbonne. Email: cwohlford@fontbonne. edu.

Wokeck, **Marianne S.**, *Indiana–Purdue, Indianapolis*. Indianapolis, IN. Email: mwokeck@iupui.edu. Research: ethnicity in colonial Pennsylvania, transatlantic migration 1500-1800.

Woker, **Madeline**. New York, NY. Affil: Columbia. Email: mw2981@columbia.edu.

Wolar, **Glynn G**. North Platte, NE. Affil: North Platte Comm. Coll. Email: wolarg@mpcc.edu. Research: environment, religion.

Wolcott, **Victoria W.**, *SUNY, Buffalo*. Williamsville, NY. Email: vwwolcot@buffalo.edu. Research: urban, African American.

Wolf, **David**. Oxnard, CA. Email: wolfgroupasia@ gmail.com. Research: business and world wars, Air Transport Command in WWII.

Wolf, **Eva Sheppard**. San Francisco, CA. Affil: San Francisco State. Email: shepwolf@sfsu.edu. Research: free blacks and race in antebellum Virginia, free labor ideology and transition to capitalism.

Wolf, **Jacqueline H.**, *Ohio*. Email: wolfj1@ohio. edu.

Wolf, **Kenneth Baxter**, *Pomona*. Email: kwolf@ pomona.edu.

Wolf, **M. Montgomery**, *Georgia*. Email: mwolf@ uga.edu.

Wolfart, **Johannes C.**, *Carleton, Can*. Email: johannes.wolfart@carleton.ca.

Wolfe, **Jason M**. Baton Rouge, LA. Affil: Louisiana State, Baton Rouge. Email: wolfe1871@gmail. com. Research: European and African identity in Southwest Africa, German missionaries in Africa.

Wolfe, **Joel W.**, *Massachusetts, Amherst*. Amherst, MA. Email: jwolfe@history.umass. edu. Research: automobiles in Brazil, Brazil social and economic.

Wolfe, **Justin**, *Tulane*. Email: jwolfe@tulane.edu.

Wolfe, **Margaret Ripley**. Church Hill, TN. Email: mrwolfe47@embarqmail.com. Research: 20th-c social, American women.

Wolfe, **Michael W**., *Queens, CUNY*. Richmond Hill, NY. Email: michael.wolfe@qc.cuny. edu; wolfe.michael1@gmail.com. Research: Reformation religious culture, 16th- to 17th-c urban military.

Wolfe, *Mikael D.*, *Stanford*. Stanford, CA. Email: mikaelw@stanford.edu; mikaelwolfe@mac.com. Research: climate, revolution.

Wolfe, **Thomas Cox**, *Minnesota (Hist.)*. Email: wolfe023@umn.edu.

Wolfe-Hunnicutt, **Brandon**, *California State, Stanislaus*. Email: bwolfehunnicutt@csustan.edu.

Wolff, *Barry*. Northbrook, IL. Email: barry@barrywolffassociates.com.

Wolff, **Larry**, *NYU*. Email: lw59@nyu.edu.

Wolff, *Robert S.*, *Central Connecticut State*. New Britain, CT. Email: wolffr@ccsu.edu. Research: race/ethnicity/American nationalism, slavery and abolition in the Americas.

Wolfgang, *James Stephen*. Bolingbrook, IL. Affil: Kentucky. Email: wolf@uky.edu. Research: interaction of science and religion, religion and Civil War.

Wolfinger, *James*. Normal, IL. Affil: Illinois State. Email: jdwolfi@ilstu.edu. Research: WWII/Pacific War, Philadelphia/African American politics.

Wolfington, **Christopher**. Stroudsburg, PA. Email: WolfingtonTeaching@Gmail.com.

Wolin, **Richard**, *Graduate Center, CUNY*. Email: rwolin@gc.cuny.edu.

Woll, **Allen L.**, *Rutgers, Camden*. Email: awoll@camden.rutgers.edu.

Wollert, *Edwin*. Corvallis, OR. Affil: Oregon State. Email: editor@stoneringpress.com.

Wollons, **Roberta**, *Massachusetts, Boston*. Email: roberta.wollons@umb.edu.

Wolnisty, *Claire Marie*, *Austin Coll*. San Angelo, TX. Email: cwolnisty@austincollege.edu; cwolnisty@angelo.edu. Research: southern immigration/Confederados, slavery expansion.

Woloch, *Isser*, *Columbia (Hist.)*. New York, NY. Email: iw6@columbia.edu. Research: 18th- to mid–19th-c western Europe, French social.

Woloch, *Nancy*, *Barnard, Columbia*. New York, NY. Email: nw49@columbia.edu; nwoloch@barnard.edu. Research: American cultural, social.

Woloson, **Wendy**, *Rutgers, Camden*.

Wolper, **Ethel Sara**, *New Hampshire, Durham*. Email: ethel.wolper@unh.edu.

Wolpert, **Rembrandt**, *Arkansas, Fayetteville*. Email: wolpert@uark.edu.

Wolters, **Raymond**, *Delaware*. Email: wolters@udel.edu.

Wolters, **Timothy S.**, *Iowa State*. Email: wolters@iastate.edu.

Wolverton, **Lisa**, *Oregon*. Email: lwolvert@uoregon.edu.

Womack, **John**, **Jr.**, *Harvard (Hist.)*. Email: jwomack@fas.harvard.edu.

Wong, **Aliza Siu**, *Texas Tech*. Email: aliza.wong@ttu.edu.

Wong, *Connie Mai*. Southaven, MS. Email: conniemaiwong@gmail.com. Research: Christian Crusades, Reformation.

Wong, *Deric*. Arlington, VA. Email: dkwong00@gmail.com.

Wong, **H. T.**, *Eastern Washington*.

Wong, **K. Scott**, *Williams*. Email: kwong@williams.edu.

Wong, **R. Bin**, *UCLA*. Email: wong@history.ucla.edu.

Wong, **Young-tsu**, *Virginia Tech*. Email: ywong@vt.edu.

Wongsrichanalai, **Kanisorn**, *Massachusetts Hist. Soc.* Email: kwongsrichanalai@masshist.org.

Woo, *Hyeseon*. West Lafayette, IN. Email: woo28@purdue.edu.

Wood, **Amy Louise**, *Illinois State*. Email: alwood@ilstu.edu.

Wood, *Betty*. Cambridge, United Kingdom. Affil: Cambridge. Email: bcw11@cam.ac.uk.

Wood, *Brad A.* Dallas, TX. Affil: Duke. Email: baw22@duke.edu.

Wood, **Bradford James**, *Eastern Kentucky*. Email: brad.wood@eku.edu.

Wood, **Curtis W.**, **Jr.**, *Western Carolina*. Email: woodcw@email.wcu.edu.

Wood, **David L.**, *California State, Northridge*.

Wood, **Elizabeth A.**, *MIT*. Email: elizwood@mit.edu.

Wood, **Elizabeth J.**, *Christopher Newport*. Email: elizabeth.wood@cnu.edu.

Wood, **Gary V.**, *Andrews*. Email: gwood@andrews.edu.

Wood, *Gordon S.*, *Brown*. Providence, RI. Email: gordon_wood@brown.edu. Research: early Republic, Benjamin Franklin.

Wood, **Gregory John**, *Frostburg State*. Email: gwood@frostburg.edu.

Wood, **James A.**, *North Carolina A&T State*. Email: woodj@ncat.edu.

Wood, **James B.**, *Williams*. Email: jwood@williams.edu.

Wood, *Jon Delmas*. Washington, DC. Affil: George Washington. Email: jon.wood@alum.ptsem.edu.

Wood, *Julia Erin*, *Texas A&M*. College Station, TX. Email: erin.wood@tamu.edu. Research: Student Nonviolent Coordinating Committee, transnational civil rights.

Wood, *Kelly Elizabeth*. New York, NY. Affil: NYU. Email: kew476@nyu.edu.

Wood, *Kirsten E.*, *Florida International*. Miami, FL. Email: woodk@fiu.edu. Research: US taverns c. 1780-1850.

Wood, **Laurie**, *Florida State*.

Wood, *Matthew*. Sugar Grove, IL. Affil: Leman Middle Sch. Email: woodm@wego33.org.

Wood, *Michael Thomas*. Tuscaloosa, AL. Affil: Alabama. Email: michael.t.wood@ua.edu. Research: transnational US South and Cuba, sport studies.

Wood, **Molly M.**, *Wittenberg*. Email: mwood@wittenberg.edu.

Wood, **Nathaniel David**, *Kansas*. Email: ndwood@ku.edu.

Wood, **Patricia**, *York, Can*. Email: pwood@yorku.ca.

Wood, *Peter H.*, *Colorado, Boulder; Duke*. Longmont, CO. Email: peter.wood@colorado.edu; pwood@duke.edu. Research: colonial and revolutionary America, Native and African American.

Wood, *Richard E.* Bethany, OK. Affil: Seminole State. Email: oakwood06@yahoo.com. Research: US Quakerism since 1800, US peace churches since 1850.

Wood, *Ronnie A.* Garner, NC. Affil: North Carolina State. Email: rawood2@ncsu.edu.

Wood, *Sharon E.*, *Nebraska, Omaha*. Omaha, NE. Email: swood@unomaha.edu. Research: slave women's politics, gender and place.

Wood, *Stephanie*, *Oregon*. Eugene, OR. Email: swood@uoregon.edu. Research: gender in Mesoamerica, Mexican women.

Wood, *Tara S.*, *Ball State*. Muncie, IN. Email: tswood@bsu.edu. Research: Elizabeth I, national identity.

Wood, *Tony*. New York, NY. Affil: NYU. Email: tony.wood@nyu.edu. Research: radical transnational imaginaries, politics of nationalism in Latin America.

Wood, **William**, *Point Loma Nazarene*. Email: billwood@pointloma.edu.

Woodall, **G. Carole**, *Colorado Colorado Springs*. Email: gwoodall@uccs.edu.

Woodard, *Blair D.*, *Portland*. Portland, OR. Email: woodard@up.edu. Research: US-Cuban relations through pop culture, visual culture in foreign relations.

Woodard, *James P.*, *Montclair State*. Montclair, NJ. Email: woodardj@mail.montclair.edu. Research: Latin America.

Woodard, **Nelson E.**, *California State, Fullerton*. Email: nwoodard@fullerton.edu.

Woodbury, **Malishai**, *North Carolina A&T State*. Email: woodbury@ncat.edu.

Woodbury, **Matthew Marshall**. Ann Arbor, MI. Affil: Michigan, Ann Arbor. Email: mmwoodbury@gmail.com. Research: Humanitarianism.

Woodfin, **Warren**, *Queens, CUNY*.

Woodfork, **Jacqueline Cassandra**, *Whitman*. Email: woodfojc@whitman.edu.

Woodhouse, *Adam J.* Chicago, IL. Affil: Chicago. Email: adam.woodhouse@icloud.com.

Woodhouse, **Keith**, *Northwestern*. Email: keith.woodhouse@northwestern.edu.

Woodman, **Harold D.**, *Purdue*. Email: hwoodman@purdue.edu.

Woodroofe, **Louise Prentis**, *US Dept. of State*.

Woodruff, **Nan E.**, *Penn State*. Email: new7@psu.edu.

Woodrum, *Robert H.* Stone Mountain, GA. Affil: Georgia Perimeter. Email: robertwoodrum@bellsouth.net.

Woods, *Colleen*, *Maryland, Coll. Park*. College Park, MD. Email: woodscp@umd.edu. Research: US in world, comparative colonialisms.

Woods, **James M.**, *Georgia Southern*. Email: jmwoods@georgiasouthern.edu.

Woods, **Jeffrey**, *Arkansas Tech*. Email: jwoods@atu.edu.

Woods, **John E.**, *Chicago*. Email: j-woods@uchicago.edu.

Woods, *L. M.* Worland, WY.

Woods, **Louis L.**, *Middle Tennessee State*. Email: Louis.Woods@mtsu.edu.

Woods, **Marjorie Curry**, *Texas, Austin*. Email: marjoriewoods@austin.utexas.edu.

Woods, *Michael Eugene*, *Marshall*. Email: woodsm@marshall.edu.

Woods, **Randall Bennett**, *Arkansas, Fayetteville*. Email: rwoods@uark.edu.

Woods, **Rebecca**, *Toronto*. Email: rebecca.woods@utoronto.ca.

Woods, **Robert L.**, **Jr.**, *Pomona*. Email: rwoods@pomona.edu.

Woods, **Warren J.**, *Hist. New Orleans*. Email: warrenw@hnoc.org.

Woodson-Boulton, **Amy**, *Loyola Marymount*. Los Angeles, CA. Email: awoodson@lmu.edu. Research: art museums/cultural, 19th-c Britain and Ireland.

Woodsum, *Antonina Griecci*. Amherst, MA. Affil: Columbia. Email: agw2121@columbia.edu.

Woodward, Hobson, *Massachusetts Hist. Soc.* Email: hwoodward@masshist.org.

Woodward, James F., *California State, Fullerton.* Email: jwoodward@fullerton.edu.

Woodward, Ralph Lee, Jr., *Tulane.* Email: rwoodward@tulane.edu.

Woodward, Walter W., *Connecticut, Storrs.* Email: walter.woodward@uconn.edu.

Woodwell, Douglas, *Indianapolis.* Email: woodwelld@uindy.edu.

Woodworth, Phyllis Bannan. Vancouver, WA. Email: pmbannan@yahoo.com. Research: Hunan family life 1908-51.

Woodworth, Steven E., *Texas Christian.* Email: s.woodworth@tcu.edu.

Woodworth-Ney, Laura Ellen, *Idaho State.* Email: woodlaur@isu.edu.

Woody, Andrea, *Washington, Seattle.* Email: awoody@uw.edu.

Woodyatt, Lyle J. Fairfax, VA. Research: Chicago school in architecture, presidencies 1901-21.

Wooldridge, Chuck, *Lehman, CUNY.* New York, NY. Email: chuck.wooldridge@lehman.cuny. edu; chuckwooldridge@gmail.com. Research: iconoclasm, sovereignty and ritual.

Wooley, Deanna Gayle, *Purdue, Fort Wayne.* Email: wooleyd@pfw.edu.

Woolf, Daniel Robert, *Queen's, Can.* Email: woolfd@queensu.ca.

Woolner, Cookie, *Memphis.*

Wooster, Ralph A., *Lamar.*

Wooster, Robert, *Texas A&M, Corpus Christi.* Email: robert.wooster@tamucc.edu.

Wooten, William. Houston, TX. Affil: Lone Star, University Park. Email: wooten.history@ lonestar.edu. Research: origins of WWII, Spanish American Cuban War.

Worger, William H., *UCLA.* Email: worger@ history.ucla.edu.

Works, John A., Jr., *Missouri–St. Louis.* Email: historyworks@umsl.edu.

Worobec, Christine D., *Northern Illinois.* Washington, DC. Email: worobec@niu.edu. Research: lived orthodoxy in imperial Russia, Orthodox pilgrimages in Russia and Ukraine.

Worrall, Arthur J., *Colorado State.* Email: arthur. worrall@colostate.edu.

Worringer, Renee E., *Guelph.* Email: rworring@ uoguelph.ca.

Worsencroft, John, *Louisiana Tech.* Email: johnw@latech.edu.

Worsham, Natalie. New Orleans, LA. Affil: Louisiana State. Email: natalieworsham88@ gmail.com.

Worster, Donald E., *Kansas.* Email: dworster@ ku.edu.

Worthen, Molly C., *North Carolina, Chapel Hill.* Chapel Hill, NC. Email: mworthen@unc.edu. Research: intellectual, modern evangelicalism.

Worthen, Shana, *Arkansas, Little Rock.* Email: ssworthen@ualr.edu.

Worthing, Peter M., *Texas Christian.* Email: p.worthing@tcu.edu.

Worthington, Kim. Princeton, NJ. Affil: Princeton. Email: Kw8@Princeton.edu. Research: memory, book and social movements.

Wortley, John T., *Manitoba.*

Wortman, Richard, *Columbia (Hist.).* New York, NY. Email: rsw3@columbia.edu. Research: 19th-c Russia.

Wosh, Peter J., *NYU.* Email: pw1@nyu.edu.

Wou, Odoric Y. K., *Rutgers, Newark/New Jersey Inst. of Tech.* Email: wou@andromeda.rutgers. edu.

Woynowski, Kent, *Hist. New Orleans.* Email: kentw@hnoc.org.

Wragge-Morley, Alexander, *NYU.* Email: awm5@nyu.edu.

Wranovix, Matt P. Longmeadow, MA. Affil: New Haven. Email: mwranovix@newhaven.edu. Research: book ownership among parish clergy, game elements in history education.

Wrathall, John D. Minneapolis, MN. Email: gustavwrathall@gmail.com.

Wright, Ashley, *Washington State, Pullman.* Email: ashley.wright2@wsu.edu.

Wright, Ben. Dallas, TX. Affil: Texas, Dallas. Email: bgw@utdallas.edu. Research: religion in early America, slavery and antislavery.

Wright, Benjamin. Austin, TX. Affil: Texas, Austin. Email: b.wright@austin.utexas.edu.

Wright, Brad H. Smyrna, TN. Affil: Middle Tennessee State. Email: bradley.wright@ mtsu.edu. Research: post-1940 urban Mexico, popular politics and social movements.

Wright, Bradford W. Palm Desert, CA. Affil: Imperial Valley. Email: bwalkerwright@yahoo. com. Research: post-1945 American popular culture, 1970s.

Wright, Christopher James, *Citadel.* Email: christopher.wright@citadel.edu.

Wright, Conrad E., *Massachusetts Hist. Soc.* Watertown, MA. Email: cwright@masshist. org; cewmbw@aol.com. Research: colonial/ revolutionary America, postrevolutionary America.

Wright, Craig G., *Herbert Hoover Presidential Library.* Email: craig.wright@nara.gov.

Wright, David C., *Calgary.* Email: wrightd@ ucalgary.ca.

Wright, David, *McGill.* Email: david.wright@ mcgill.ca.

Wright, Donald P., *US Army Command Coll.* Email: donald.p.wright.civ@mail.mil.

Wright, Donald R. Beaufort, SC. Affil: SUNY, Coll. Cortland. Email: wrightd21@gmail.com. Research: globalization and Africans, Africa and Atlantic.

Wright, Emily Helen. Richmond, VA. Affil: Tulane. Email: ewright6@tulane.edu. Research: antebellum South/Protestant women, education/benevolence/slave religion.

Wright, Harrison M., *Swarthmore.*

Wright, J. Barry, *Carleton, Can.* Email: barry. wright@carleton.ca.

Wright, James E., *Dartmouth.* Email: james.e.wright@dartmouth.edu.

Wright, Johnson Kent. Phoenix, AZ. Affil: Arizona State. Email: johnson.wright@asu. edu. Research: Enlightenment, political revolutions.

Wright, Joshua K. Salisbury, MD. Affil: Maryland, Eastern Shore. Email: jkwright1492@yahoo. com. Research: masculinity and gender studies, film studies.

Wright, Kami. Scarsdale, NY. Affil: Scarsdale High Sch. Email: kwright@scarsdaleschools. org.

Wright, Marcia, *Columbia (Hist.).* Sunapee, NH. Email: mw32@columbia.edu. Research: eastern and southern Africa.

Wright, Mary. Otis Orchards, WA. Affil: Western Oregon. Email: mawright05@wou.edu.

Research: 911 emergency services, martial arts development in US.

Wright, Micah Wayne. Boise, ID. Affil: Texas A&M, Coll. Station. Email: Micah.W.Wright@ gmail.com. Research: US interventions in Caribbean, Puerto Rican military service.

Wright, Miller Shores. Mobile, AL. Affil: Rice. Email: msw6@rice.edu.

Wright, Miriam, *Windsor.* Email: mwright@ uwindsor.ca.

Wright, Parrish E. Ann Arbor, MI. Affil: Michigan, Ann Arbor. Email: pewright@umich.edu.

Wright, Robert A., *Trent.* Email: rawright@ trentu.ca.

Wright, Scott K., *St. Thomas, Minn.* Email: skwright@stthomas.edu.

Wright, Sharon Hubbs, *Saskatchewan.* Email: sharon.wright@stmcollege.ca.

Wright, Thomas C., *Nevada, Las Vegas.* Email: tom.wright@unlv.edu.

Wright, William D., *Southern Connecticut State.*

Wright, William J., *Tennessee, Chattanooga.*

Wright-Lewis, Kay. Glenn Dale, MD. Affil: Howard. Email: kay.wrightlewis@howard. edu; kaywlew@aol.com. Research: slavery and abolition/violence/trauma, racialized warfare/ women/resistance.

Wright-Rios, Edward N., *Vanderbilt.* Nashville, TN. Email: edward.wright-rios@vanderbilt. edu. Research: popular culture, Catholicism.

Wrightson, Keith, *Yale.* Email: keith.wrightson@ yale.edu.

Wrobel, David M., *Oklahoma (Hist.); Western Hist. Assoc.* Norman, OK. Email: David.Wrobel@ ou.edu. Research: American western regional identity, American western historiography.

Wrobel, Piotr, *Toronto.* Toronto, ON, Canada. Email: piotr.wrobel@utoronto.ca. Research: Poland.

Wu, Albert Monshan. Paris, France. Affil: American, Paris. Email: awu@aup.edu. Research: German missionaries in China, Christianity.

Wu, Ellen D., *Indiana.* Email: wue@indiana.edu.

Wu, Guo, *Allegheny.* Email: gwu@allegheny.edu.

Wu, Judy Tzu-Chun, *California, Irvine.* Irvine, CA. Email: j.wu@uci.edu. Research: Women, Asian American.

Wu, Justin Zhuo Jun. Chapel Hill, NC. Affil: North Carolina, Chapel Hill. Email: justinzjwu@gmail. com. Research: Hong Kong, identity.

Wu, Lan, *Mount Holyoke.* Email: lwu@mtholyoke. edu.

Wu, Shellen Xiao, *Tennessee, Knoxville.* Knoxville, TN. Email: swu5@utk.edu. Research: modern China, geography and geopolitics.

Wu, Shu-chin, *Agnes Scott.* Email: swu@ agnesscott.edu.

Wu, Shu-hui, *Mississippi State.* Email: shuwu@ history.msstate.edu.

Wu, Silas, *Boston Coll.* Email: wu@bc.edu.

Wu, Yulian. East Lansing, MI. Affil: Michigan State. Email: wuyulian@msu.edu. Research: material culture, gender.

Wujastyk, Dominik, *Alberta.* Email: wujastyk@ gmail.com.

Wulf, Karin A., *William and Mary; Omohundro Inst.* Rockville, MD. Email: kawulf@wm.edu. Research: US women, colonial America.

Wulf, Laura, *Massachusetts Hist. Soc.* Email: lwulf@masshist.org.

Wunder, **Amanda J.**, *Graduate Center, CUNY; Lehman, CUNY*. New York, NY. Email: awunder@gc.cuny.edu; ajwunder@gmail.com. Research: early modern Spain, art.

Wunder, **John R.**, *Nebraska, Lincoln*. Email: jwunder1@unl.edu.

Wunderli, **Richard M.**, *Colorado Colorado Springs*. Email: rwunderl@uccs.edu.

Wunderlin, **Clarence E.**, **Jr.**, *Kent State*. Email: cwunderl@kent.edu.

Wurtzel, **Ellen B.**, *Oberlin*. Oberlin, OH. Email: ellen.wurtzel@oberlin.edu. Research: urban, border studies.

Wussow, **Walter J.**, *Wisconsin-Eau Claire*. Email: wussowwj@uwec.edu.

Wyatt, **Don J.**, *Middlebury*. Middlebury, VT. Email: wyatt@middlebury.edu. Research: Confucianism, Chinese intellectualism and militarism.

Wylie, **Diana S.**, *Boston Univ.* Email: dwylie@bu.edu.

Wynd, **Alice Elizabeth**. Rochester, NY. Affil: Rochester. Email: awynd@ur.rochester.edu.

Wynkoop, **Mary Ann**, *Missouri–Kansas City*. Email: wynkoopm@umkc.edu.

Wynn, **Charles Taylor**, **Sr.**, *Kennesaw State*. Email: cwynn6@kennesaw.edu.

Wynn, **Charters**, *Texas, Austin*. Email: wynn@utexas.edu.

Wynn, **Kerry**, *Washburn*. Email: kerry.wynn@washburn.edu.

Wynne, **Benjamin R.**, *North Georgia*. Email: ben.wynne@ung.edu.

X x

Xia, **Qing**. Beijing, China. Affil: Tsinghua. Email: xiaqing1025@163.com.

Xia, **Yafeng**, *Long Island, Brooklyn*. Email: yafeng.xia@liu.edu.

Xia, **Yun**, *Valparaiso*. Email: yun.xia@valpo.edu.

Xiang, **Hongyan**, *Colorado State*. Email: hongyan.xiang@colostate.edu.

Xiao, **Honglin**, *Elon*. Email: hxiao@elon.edu.

Xiao, **Zhiwei**, *California State, San Marcos*. Email: zxiao@csusm.edu.

Xiong, **Victor**, *Western Michigan*. Email: victor.xiong@wmich.edu.

Xu, **Stella Yingzi**, *Roanoke*. Email: sxu@roanoke.edu.

Xu, **Xiaoqun**, *Christopher Newport*. Email: xxu@cnu.edu.

Xu, **Yamin**, *Le Moyne*. Email: xuy@lemoyne.edu.

Xu, **Yan**, *Spelman*. Email: yxu@spelman.edu.

Xue, **Yong**, *Suffolk*. Email: yxue@suffolk.edu.

Y y

Yablon, **Nick William**, *Iowa*. Email: nick-yablon@uiowa.edu.

Yacovone, **Donald**. Medford, MA. Affil: Harvard. Email: yacovone@fas.harvard.edu. Research: antislavery legacy.

Yacovone, **Mary E.**, *Massachusetts Hist. Soc.* Email: myacovone@masshist.org.

Yaghoubian, **David N.**, *California State, San Bernardino*. Email: dny@csusb.edu.

Yakubik, **Brandon Matthew**. New Castle, PA. Email: brandonmatthewyakubik@gmail.com.

Yale, **Elizabeth E.**, *Iowa*. Email: elizabeth-yale@uiowa.edu.

Yalen, **Deborah H.**, *Colorado State*. Email: deborah.yalen@colostate.edu.

Yalzadeh, **Ida**. Providence, RI. Affil: Brown. Email: Ida_Yalzadeh@brown.edu.

Yamashita, **Samuel H.**, *Pomona*. Claremont, CA. Email: syamashita@pomona.edu. Research: Pacific war, food.

Yamauchi, **Edwin M.**, *Miami, Ohio*. Email: yamauce@miamioh.edu.

Yan, **Vivian Sin Mei**. Stanford, CA. Affil: Stanford. Email: vsmyan@stanford.edu.

Yandle, **Paul**, *North Greenville*. Email: pyandle@ngu.edu.

Yang, **Alice**, *California, Santa Cruz*. Email: ayang@ucsc.edu.

Yang, **Anand A.**, *Washington, Seattle*. Seattle, WA. Email: aay@uw.edu. Research: migration, crime and law.

Yang, **Daqing**, *George Washington*. Email: yanghist@gwu.edu.

Yang, **Dominic Meng-Hsuan**, *Missouri, Columbia*. Email: yangmeng@missouri.edu.

Yang, **Guangshuo**. Pittsfield, ME. Affil: Northwestern. Email: gy@u.northwestern.edu. Research: knowledge making and transmission, knowledge and localized identity.

Yang, **Lei**. Northfield, MN. Affil: Carleton Coll. Email: lyang3@carleton.edu.

Yang, **Li Wei**, *Huntington Library*. San Marino, CA. Email: lwyang@huntington.org; lwyang31@gmail.com. Research: American West.

Yang, **Shao-yun**, *Denison*. Email: yangs@denison.edu.

Yang, **Timothy**, *Georgia*. Athens, GA. Email: timothy.yang@uga.edu; tyang23@gmail.com.

Yanikdag, **Yucel**, *Richmond*. Email: yyanikda@richmond.edu.

Yankaskas, **Lynda K.**, *Muhlenberg*. Allentown, PA. Email: lyankaskas@muhlenberg.edu. Research: library history / public space, early Republic.

Yankowitz, **Emily Anne**. Scarsdale, NY. Email: emily.yankowitz@yale.edu.

Yannakakis, **Yanna P.**, *Emory*. Atlanta, GA. Email: yanna.yannakakis@emory.edu. Research: colonial Mexico native intermediaries, colonial Mexico political culture.

Yans, **Virginia Y.**, *Rutgers*. New York, NY. Email: virginiayans@earthlink.net. Research: Margaret Mead, Supreme Court.

Yao, **Ping**, *California State, Los Angeles*. Los Angeles, CA. Email: pyao@calstatela.edu. Research: traditional Asia, China.

Yao, **Zhibin**. Melrose, MA. Email: zhibin.yao@pitt.edu.

Yap Kwai Foon, **Jaime**. Selangor Darul Ehsan, Malaysia. Affil: Sunway. Email: jaimey@sunway.edu.my. Research: Classroom Action Research/Blended Learn.

Yaqub, **Salim C.**, *California, Santa Barbara*. Goleta, CA. Email: syaqub@history.ucsb.edu. Research: post-1945 US-Arab political relations, post-1945 US political.

Yarak, **Larry W.**, *Texas A&M*. Email: yarak@tamu.edu.

Yarbrough, **Fay A.**, *Rice*. Houston, TX. Email: fyarbrough@rice.edu. Research: African American, American Indian.

Yarbrough, **John W.** Dallas, TX. Affil: North Lake. Email: jyrbro@hotmail.com.

Yarbrough, **Luke Benson**. Los Angeles, CA. Affil: UCLA. Email: lukeyarbrough@humnet.ucla.edu. Research: Ayyubid Egypt, Polemic.

Yarce, **Julio**. Medford, NY. Affil: Miami. Email: jcy13@miami.edu.

Yaremko, **Jason M.**, *Winnipeg*. Email: j.yaremko@uwinnipeg.ca.

Yarfitz, **Mir**, *Wake Forest*. Email: yarfitmh@wfu.edu.

Yarker, **Dirk Norman**. Harlingen, TX. Affil: Texas Southmost. Email: dyarker84@gmail.com. Research: Roman peace, Mediterranean world education.

Yarrington, **Douglas K.**, *Colorado State*. Email: doug.yarrington@colostate.edu.

Yasar, **Murat**, *SUNY, Oswego*. Email: murat.yasar@oswego.edu.

Yasutake, **Rumi**. Kyoto, Japan. Affil: Konan. Email: rumiyasutake@ybb.ne.jp. Research: women's civilziing mission, globalization.

Yates, **Brian J.**, *St. Joseph's*. Email: byates@sju.edu.

Yates, **Charles**, *Earlham*. Email: yatesch@earlham.edu.

Yates, **JoAnne**, *MIT*. Email: jyates@mit.edu.

Yates, **Robin D. S.**, *McGill*. Email: robin.yates@mcgill.ca.

Yavenditti, **Michael J.**, *Alma*. Email: yavendit@alma.edu.

Yaycioglu, **Ali**, *Stanford*. Email: ayayciog@stanford.edu.

Yazawa, **Melvin**, *New Mexico*. Email: yazawa@unm.edu.

Yazdani, **Mina**, *Eastern Kentucky*. Email: mina.yazdani@eku.edu.

Yeager, **Gertrude M.**, *Tulane*. Email: tyeager@tulane.edu.

Yeager, **Kevin L.** Baltimore, MD. Affil: Bryn Mawr Sch. Email: kyeager617@gmail.com. Research: 18th-c American backcountry, Scots-Irish/UlsterScots.

Yeager, **Mary A.**, *UCLA*. Email: yeager@ucla.edu.

Yeakey, **Lamont H.**, *California State, Los Angeles*. Email: lyeakey@calstatela.edu.

Yearwood, **Peter J.** Strand, Waigani, Papua New Guinea. Affil: Papua New Guinea. Email: yearwopj@upng.ac.pg. Research: origins of League of Nations, imperialism in Africa 1913-20.

Yeats, **Dylan**. Brooklyn, NY. Affil: NYU. Email: Dylan.yeats@nyu.edu.

Yeaw, **Katrina Elizabeth Anderson**, *Arkansas, Little Rock*.

Yee, **Ethan Leong**. Walnut Creek, CA. Affil: Columbia. Email: ely2105@columbia.edu.

Yee, **Michael**. San Diego, CA. Affil: California State, San Marcos. Email: michaelyee@csusm.edu.

Yee, **Shirley Jo-Ann**, *Washington, Seattle*. Seattle, WA. Email: sjyee@u.washington.edu. Research: women and occupations, race/ethnicity/gender/urban.

Yeh, **Chiou-ling**, *San Diego State*. Email: cyeh@sdsu.edu.

Yeh, **Wen-hsin**, *California, Berkeley*. Atherton, CA. Email: sha@berkeley.edu. Research: modern and contemporary China/Taiwan, ideas/cities/politics.

Yelengi, **Nkasa T.**, *Minnesota Duluth*. Email: nyelengi@d.umn.edu.

Yellen, **Bailey**. New York, NY. Email: byellen330@gmail.com.

Yellen, **Jeremy A**. Shatin, NT, Hong Kong. Affil: Chinese, Hong Kong. Email: jyellen@cuhk. edu.hk. Research: Japanese wartime empire, decolonization in Southeast Asia.

Yellin, **Eric S**., *Richmond*. Email: eyellin@ richmond.edu.

Yelton, **David K**. Rutherfordton, NC. Affil: Gardner-Webb. Email: dyelton@gardner-webb.edu. Research: WWII 1944-45, militias.

Yermakova, **Anna**. Cambridge, MA. Affil: Harvard. Email: ayermakova@fas.harvard.edu.

Yetman, **Robert C**. Cherry Hill, NJ. Affil: Catholic. Email: 84yetman@cua.edu.

Yi, **Doogab**. Seoul, South Korea. Affil: Seoul National. Email: doogab@gmail.com. Research: sciences and social sciences, science and technology and social values.

Yi, **Guolin**, *Arkansas Tech*. Email: gyi@atu.edu.

Yick, **Joseph K**., *Texas State*. Email: jy02@txstate. edu.

Yigit, **Tarik Tansu**. Watertown, MA. Affil: Harvard. Email: tariktansuyigit@gmail.com. Research: American Civil War and Ottoman geography, American Civil War veterans in Egypt.

Yildiz, **Murat Cihan**, *Skidmore*. Saratoga Springs, NY. Email: myildiz@skidmore.edu; muratcihanyildiz@gmail.com. Research: Ottoman, modern Middle East.

Yilmaz, **Hale**, *Southern Illinois, Carbondale*. Email: yilmaz@siu.edu.

Yilmaz, **Huseyin**, *George Mason*. Email: hyilmaz@gmu.edu.

Yilmaz, **Seçil**, *Franklin & Marshall*. Email: syilmaz@fandm.edu.

Yin, **Qingfei**, *Virginia Military Inst*. Lexington, VA. Email: yinq@vmi.edu. Research: Sino-Vietnamese relations, Cold War.

Yin, **Xiao-huang**, *Occidental*. Email: emyin@ oxy.edu.

Yingling, **Charlton W**., *Louisville*. Email: charlton.yingling@louisville.edu.

Yingst, **Brayden**. Friendswood, TX. Affil: Houston, Clear Lake. Email: bray.yingst@ gmail.com.

Yip, **Ka-che**, *Maryland, Baltimore County*. Email: yip@umbc.edu.

Yirga, **Felege-Selam**. Columbus, OH. Affil: Ohio State. Email: yirga.5@osu.edu.

Yirush, **Craig Bryan**, *UCLA*. Email: yirush@ history.ucla.edu.

Yocum, **Sandra A**. Dayton, OH. Affil: Dayton. Email: syocum1@udayton.edu.

Yoder, **April**. West Haven, CT. Affil: New Haven. Email: ayoder@newhaven.edu. Research: Latin America, sport.

Yoder, **Eric D**. Folsom, CA. Email: eyoder0@ hotmail.com.

Yoder, **Joel F**. Chicago, IL. Affil: Loyola, Chicago. Email: jyoder@luc.edu. Research: Herbert Spencer, religion and science.

Yohn, **Susan M**., *Hofstra*. Brooklyn, NY. Email: susan.yohn@hofstra.edu. Research: 19th-/20th-c America, women.

Yokota, **Kariann A**., *Colorado Denver*. Email: kariann.yokota@ucdenver.edu.

Yokota, **Ryan Masaaki**. Chicago, IL. Affil: DePaul. Email: rmyokota@yahoo.com. Research: Okinawan nationalism.

Yokoyama, **Hannah**. Eureka, CA. Affil: Humboldt State. Email: hky2@humboldt.edu.

Yonemoto, **Marcia A**., *Colorado, Boulder*. Boulder, CO. Email: yonemoto@colorado.edu.

Research: women and gender, early modern societies.

Yonke, **Eric J**., *Wisconsin-Stevens Point*. Email: eyonke@uwsp.edu.

Yoo, **David K**., *UCLA*. Email: dkyoo@ucla.edu.

Yoon, **Chong-kun**, *James Madison*. Email: yoonck@jmu.edu.

Yoon, **Seungjoo**, *Carleton Coll*. Email: syoon@ carleton.edu.

Yoon, **Sun-Hee**, *California State, Dominguez Hills*. Email: syoon@csudh.edu.

York, *Allen Christopher*. Conway, SC. Affil: Horry-Georgetown Tech. Email: allen.york@ hgtc.edu.

York, **Anne Marie**, *Youngstown State*. Email: ayork@ysu.edu.

York, **Neil L**., *Brigham Young*. Email: neil_york@ byu.edu.

York, **William H**., *Portland State*. Email: why@ pdx.edu.

Yoshida, **Takashi**, *Western Michigan*. Email: takashi.yoshida@wmich.edu.

Yoshii, **Midori**, *Albion*. Email: myoshii@albion. edu.

Yoshitani, **Col Gail E. S**., *US Military Acad*. Email: gail.yoshitani@usma.edu.

Yosmaoglu, **Ipek K**., *Northwestern*. Evanston, IL. Email: i-yosmaoglu@northwestern.edu. Research: Macedonian nationalism, Ottoman Empire.

Yost, *Charles*. Urbandale, IA. Affil: Notre Dame. Email: charles.yost1@gmail.com. Research: Byzantine religious, relations between Latin and Greek church.

Young, **Adrian Michael**, *Denison*. Email: younga@denison.edu.

Young, **Alden Harrington**, *Drexel*. Email: ahy24@drexel.edu.

Young, **Alfred**, *Georgia Southern*. Email: ayoung@georgiasouthern.edu.

Young, *Ashley Rose*. Hidden Valley, PA. Affil: National Museum of American Hist. Email: youngar@si.edu. Research: US southern and Atlantic foodways.

Young, **Bailey K**., *Eastern Illinois*. Email: bkyoung@eiu.edu.

Young, **Brian J**., *McGill*. Email: brian.young@ mcgill.ca.

Young, **Carl**, *Western Ontario*. Email: cyoung73@ uwo.ca.

Young, **Charles R**., *Duke*.

Young, *Charles*. Magnolia, AR. Affil: Southern Arkansas. Email: chipster@firebug.com. Research: Korean War POWs, Cold War homefront.

Young, **Christopher J**., *Indiana, Northwest*. Email: cjy@iun.edu.

Young, *Edward*, *III*. New York, NY. Affil: Xavier High Sch. Email: younge@xavierhs.org.

Young, **Elliott G**., *Lewis & Clark*. Email: eyoung@ lclark.edu.

Young, *Ernest P*., *Michigan, Ann Arbor*. Ann Arbor, MI. Email: epyoung@umich.edu. Research: early 20th-c China, nationalism/reform/revolution.

Young, **George F.W**., *St. Mary's, Can*. Email: geofw.young@smu.ca.

Young, **Glennys**, *Washington, Seattle*. Email: glennys@uw.edu.

Young, *James Alan*. Harrisburg, PA. Affil: Montgomery County Comm. Coll. Email: jyoung17102@gmail.com.

Young, **Jason R**., *Michigan, Ann Arbor*. Email: youngjr@umich.edu.

Young, **Jeffrey R**., *Georgia State*. Email: jryoung@gsu.edu.

Young, *Jeremy C*. Saint George, UT. Affil: Dixie State. Email: jeremy.young@dixie.edu. Research: charismatic social movements, emotional experience.

Young, *Julia G*. Arlington, VA. Affil: Catholic. Email: youngjg@cua.edu. Research: Mexican emigration 1926-35, Mexican emigrants and Cristero War.

Young, **Katherine A**., *Loyola, Chicago*. Email: kyoung3@luc.edu.

Young, *Kevin C*. Fair Haven, NJ. Affil: Rutgers. Email: woodyoung@verizon.net. Research: African/Nigerian postcolonial conflict, Thucydides in historical criticism.

Young, *Kevin*, *Massachusetts, Amherst*. Amherst, MA. Email: kayoung@history.umass.edu. Research: modern Bolivia, US-Latin American relations.

Young, **Louise**, *Wisconsin-Madison*. Email: louiseyoung@wisc.edu.

Young, **Mark E**., *Houston*. Email: markyoung@ uh.edu.

Young, *Mary E*., *Rochester*. Rochester, NY. Email: yngm@mail.rochester.edu. Research: Cherokee removal context/viewpoints, Indian non-violent conflict resolution.

Young, *Michael B*., *Illinois Wesleyan*. Bloomington, IL. Email: myoung@iwu.edu. Research: James VI and I and homosexuality, Charles I and Parliament.

Young, **Nancy Beck**, *Houston*. Email: nyoung2@ uh.edu.

Young, *Pearl J*. Kennesaw, GA. Affil: Kennesaw State. Email: pyoung29@kennesaw.edu. Research: American Civil War, American South.

Young, **Phoebe S. K**., *Colorado, Boulder*. Email: phoebe.young@colorado.edu.

Young, **Robert J**., *Winnipeg*. Email: r.young@ uwinnipeg.ca.

Young, *Robert*. Columbia, MD. Affil: Carroll Comm. Coll. Email: osnfeel@comcast.net.

Young, *Stephanie C*. Santa Monica, CA. Affil: RAND Corporation. Email: syoung@rand.org. Research: defense budget.

Young, **W. Evan**, *Dickinson*. Email: youngw@ dickinson.edu.

Youngblood, **Denise J**., *Vermont*. Email: denise. youngblood@uvm.edu.

Youngs, **J. William T**., **Jr**., *Eastern Washington*. Email: jyoungs@ewu.edu.

Yousef, *Hoda A*, *Denison*. Granville, OH. Email: yousefh@denison.edu. Research: literacy studies, gender studies.

Yousefi, **Najm al-Din**, *California State, Chico*. Email: nyousefi@csuchico.edu.

Ysursa, **John M**., *Boise State*. Email: johnysursa@ boisestate.edu.

Yu, **Gloria**. Berkeley, CA. Affil: California, Berkeley. Email: gloria.yu@berkeley.edu.

Yu, **Henry**, *British Columbia*. Email: henry.yu@ ubc.ca.

Yu, *Wen*. Newton Center, MA. Affil: Harvard. Email: wenyu@fas.harvard.edu. Research: modern Chinese intellectual, Confucianism since 17th century.

Yuan, *Tsing*. Plainsboro, NJ. Email: tsingyuan@ msn.com. Research: 16th-/18th-c trade, comparative migration and diaspora.

Yucesoy, Hayrettin, *Washington, St. Louis*. Email: yucesoy@wustl.edu.

Yuh, Ji-Yeon, *Northwestern*. Evanston, IL. Email: j-yuh@northwestern.edu. Research: Korean diaspora, nationalism and memory.

Yuhl, Stephanie E., *Holy Cross*. Email: syuhl@ holycross.edu.

Yuksel Muslu, Cihan, *Houston*.

Yusufjonova-Abman, Zamira, *San Diego State*.

Z z

Zabin, Serena R., *Carleton Coll.* Northfield, MN. Email: szabin@carleton.edu. Research: Boston, commercial culture.

Zacair, Philippe, *California State, Fullerton*. Email: pzacair@fullerton.edu.

Zaccarini, M. Cristina, *Adelphi*. Email: zaccarin@ adelphi.edu.

Zacek, Joseph Frederick, *SUNY, Albany*.

Zacek, Natalie A. Manchester, United Kingdom. Affil: Manchester. Email: natalie.a.zacek@ manchester.ac.uk. Research: horse racing in 19th-c US, West Indians in 18th-c London.

Zachernuk, Philip, *Dalhousie*. Email: pzachern@ dal.ca.

Zacks, Michelle H. New Haven, CT. Affil: Gilder Lehrman Center. Email: michelle.zacks@yale. edu. Research: environmental, culture and politics of fisheries.

Zadoff, Mirjam, *Indiana*. Email: mizadoff@ indiana.edu.

Zadoff, Noam, *Indiana*. Email: nzadoff@indiana. edu.

Zadzilko, Raymond J. Ebensburg, PA. Affil: Social Security Admin. Email: rayzadzilko@ hotmail.com.

Zagarri, Rosemarie, *George Mason*. Arlington, VA. Email: rzagarri@gmu.edu. Research: America and British East India 1770-1840.

Zahavi, Gerald, *SUNY, Albany*. Email: gzahavi@ albany.edu.

Zahler, Reuben C., *Oregon*. Email: rczahler@ uoregon.edu.

Zahniser, Marvin R., *Ohio State*. Email: marzahn@wideopenwest.com.

Zahra, Tara, *Chicago*. Email: tzahra@uchicago. edu.

Zaidi, Noor, *Maryland, Baltimore County*. Email: nzaidi@umbc.edu.

Zainaldin, Jamil S., *Emory*. Email: jz@ georgiahumanities.org.

Zajicek, Benjamin, *Towson*. Email: bzajicek@ towson.edu.

Zakar, Adrien. Menlo Park, CA. Affil: Stanford. Email: adrienpzakar@gmail.com.

Zakic, Mirna, *Ohio*. Athens, OH. Email: zakic@ ohio.edu. Research: ethnic Germans in WWII, National Socialism and collaboration.

Zalar, Jeffrey T., *Cincinnati*. Email: jeffrey.zalar@ uc.edu.

Zaldivar, Antonio M., *California State, San Marcos*. Email: azaldivar@csusm.edu.

Zallen, Jeremy, *Lafayette*. Email: zallenj@ lafayette.edu.

Zaller, Robert, *Drexel*. Email: zallerrm@drexel. edu.

Zalma, Adam. New York, NY. Affil: Lipper & Co. Email: azalma@history.rutgers.edu. Research: urban land/landscape/environment, Staten Island NY.

Zaman, Maheen, *Augsburg*. Email: zamanm@ augsburg.edu.

Zaman, Taymiya R., *San Francisco*. San Francisco, CA. Email: zamant@umich.edu; trzaman@usfca.edu. Research: Islamicate autobiography in Mughal India, Pakistan.

Zamindar, Vazira F.-Y., *Brown*. Email: Vazira_F-Y_Zamindar@Brown.edu.

Zammito, John H., *Rice*. Houston, TX. Email: zammito@rice.edu. Research: European Enlightenment, 18th-c science.

Zamora, Emilio, Jr., *Texas, Austin*. Email: e.zamora@austin.utexas.edu.

Zamora, Jack Edmond. Toledo, OH. Affil: Toledo. Email: jack.zamora@rockets.utoledo.edu. Research: Ohio political formation, early Republic political.

Zamora, Lois, *Houston*. Email: lzamora@uh.edu.

Zanalda, Giovanni, *Duke*.

Zanasi, Margherita, *Louisiana State*. Baton Rouge, LA. Email: mzanasi@lsu.edu. Research: nation building and national identity, economic thought.

Zangani, Federico, *Wheaton, Mass.* Email: zangani_federico@wheatoncollege.edu.

Zanoni, Amy. New Brunswick, NJ. Affil: Rutgers. Email: amy.zanoni@rutgers.edu.

Zanoni, Elizabeth Ann, *Old Dominion*. Email: ezanoni@odu.edu.

Zansitis, Richard A. Houston, TX. Affil: Rice. Email: zansitis@rice.edu.

Zappia, Charles A., *San Diego Mesa*. San Diego, CA. Email: czappia@sdccd.edu. Research: corporatization of higher education, community college historians.

Zappia, Natale, *Whittier*. Whittier, CA. Email: nzappia@whittier.edu. Research: 18th-/19th-c California borderlands, 20th-c US West environmental.

Zaremba, Frank J. Fords, NJ. Email: franzzee2002@yahoo.com.

Zaretsky, Eli, *New School*. Email: zarete@ newschool.edu.

Zaretsky, Natasha. Carbondale, IL. Affil: Southern Illinois, Carbondale. Email: zaretsky@siu.edu. Research: recent US, cultural.

Zarinebaf, Fariba, *California, Riverside*. Email: fariba.zarinebaf@ucr.edu.

Zarnow, Leandra Ruth, *Houston*. Email: lrzarnow@central.uh.edu.

Zarrow, Peter G., *Connecticut, Storrs*. Storrs Mansfield, CT. Email: peter.zarrow@uconn. edu. Research: Chinese and comparative political thought, Chinese textbooks/museum culture.

Zarrow, Sarah Ellen, *Western Washington*. Bellingham, WA. Email: sarah.zarrow@wwu. edu. Research: eastern Europe, Jewish.

Zarsadiaz, James, *San Francisco*. Email: jzarsadiaz@usfca.edu.

Zastoupil, Lynn B., *Rhodes*. Email: zastoupil@ rhodes.edu.

Zatlin, Jonathan R., *Boston Univ.* Boston, MA. Email: jzatlin@bu.edu. Research: German-Jewish, Socialism.

Zatsepine, Victor, *Connecticut, Storrs*. Email: victor.zatsepine@uconn.edu.

Zavardino, Christian Hartung. Syosset, NY. Email: czavardino@ucla.edu.

Zavelo, Kelsey Lynn. Durham, NC. Affil: Duke. Email: kelsey.zavelo@duke.edu.

Zayarnyuk, Andriy, *Winnipeg*. Email: a.zayarnyuk@uwinnipeg.ca.

Zbarskyy, Oleksandr. Oakland, CA. Email: od_alexander@yahoo.com. Research: British/ American cultural/historical interaction, British Empire.

Zdatny, Steven, *Vermont*. Burlington, VT. Email: steven.zdatny@uvm.edu. Research: French hairdressing, French fashion/social.

Zdencanovic, Ben. New Haven, CT. Affil: Yale. Email: ben.zdencanovic@yale.edu.

Zdinak, Zachariah Edward. Stratton, OH. Affil: Franciscan, Steubenville. Email: zachariahzdinak@gmail.com. Research: WWII, US presidents.

Zeichner, Noah. Seattle, WA. Affil: Ingraham High Sch. Email: nczeichner@seattleschools. org.

Zeide, Anna, *Oklahoma State*. Email: zeide@ okstate.edu.

Zeidel, Robert F. Afton, MN. Affil: Wisconsin, Stout. Email: zeidelr@uwstout.edu. Research: immigration, Progressive Era.

Zeiler, Michael. Mill Valley, CA. Email: free_ enterprise_dynamics@msn.com.

Zeiler, Thomas W., *Colorado, Boulder*. Boulder, CO. Email: thomas.zeiler@colorado.edu. Research: WWII, globalization.

Zelikow, Philip D., *Virginia*. Email: zelikow@ virginia.edu.

Zelin, Madeleine, *Columbia (Hist.)*. Email: mhz1@columbia.edu.

Zelizer, Julian E., *Princeton*. Princeton, NJ. Email: jzelizer@princeton.edu. Research: national security politics, America in 1970s.

Zelko, Frank S., *Hawai'i, Manoa*. Email: fzelko@ hawaii.edu.

Zeller, Chad Carl. Daytona Beach, FL. Email: chad3232132@aol.com.

Zeller, Neici M., *William Paterson*. Email: zellern@wpunj.edu.

Zeller, Suzanne, *Wilfrid Laurier*. Email: szeller@ wlu.ca.

Zeller, Thomas, *Maryland, Coll. Park*. Email: tzeller@umd.edu.

Zellers, Bruce L., *Oakland*. Email: zellers@ oakland.edu.

Zelner, Kyle F., *Southern Mississippi*. Email: kyle. zelner@usm.edu.

Zelnik, Eran, *California State, Chico*. Email: ezelnik@csuchico.edu.

Zeltsman, Corinna, *Georgia Southern*. Email: czeltsman@georgiasouthern.edu.

Zeman, Theodore J., *St. Joseph's*. Philadelphia, PA. Email: drcf3@comcast.net. Research: American Civil War and military.

Zeng, Peng. San Diego, CA. Affil: Illinois Inst. of Tech. Email: pzeng@iit.edu. Research: Civil War consequence on US politics, public health in Keningrad 1945-48.

Zeng, Xiaoshun. Seattle, WA. Affil: Washington, Seattle. Email: zengx672@uw.edu. Research: public health in China, national minorities in China.

Zeng, Zhaojin. Pittsburgh, PA. Affil: Pittsburgh. Email: zhaojin.zeng@pitt.edu.

Zenger, Robin, *Arizona*. Email: rzenger@email. arizona.edu.

Zens, Robert, *Le Moyne*. Email: zensrw@ lemoyne.edu.

Zepcevski, Joline, *Metropolitan State*. Email: joline.zepcevski@metrostate.edu.

Zepeda Cortes, Maria Barbara, *Lehigh*. Email: maz213@lehigh.edu.

Zeps, **Michael J.**, *Marquette*. Email: michael.zeps@marquette.edu.

Zerner, **Ruth**, *Lehman, CUNY*. Bronx, NY. Email: ruth.zerner@lehman.cuny.edu. Research: Holocaust and survivorship, human rights.

Zerubavel, **Yael**, *Rutgers*. Email: yaelzeru@jewishstudies.rutgers.edu.

Zevin, **Alexander**, *Staten Island, CUNY*. Email: alexander.zevin@csi.cuny.edu.

Zguta, **Russ**, *Missouri, Columbia*. Columbia, MO. Email: zgutar@missouri.edu. Research: early Ukrainian hospitals.

Zhai, **Jing**. Austin, TX. Affil: Texas, Austin. Email: zhaijing1988@gmail.com.

Zhai, **Zongqi**. Irvine, CA. Affil: Shenzhen Coll. of International Education. Email: zhaizongqi12@gmail.com.

Zhang, **Aihua**. Shelby, NC. Affil: Gardner-Webb. Email: aihua_22@yahoo.com. Research: women/gender/modernity, transnationalism.

Zhang, **Cong Ellen**, *Virginia*. Email: cz5h@virginia.edu.

Zhang, **Dewen**, *Maryland, Coll. Park*.

Zhang, **Elya J.**, *Rochester*. Rochester, NY. Email: elya.zhang@gmail.com; elya.zhang@rochester.edu. Research: social networks, government personnel.

Zhang, **Hong**, *Central Florida*. Email: Hong.Zhang@ucf.edu.

Zhang, **Jiayan**, *Kennesaw State*. Email: jzhang@kennesaw.edu.

Zhang, **Li**. Beijing, China. Affil: Beihang. Email: lzhague@yahoo.com. Research: globalization, transition of Chinese rural economy.

Zhang, **Ling**, *Boston Coll*. Email: ling.zhang.2@bc.edu.

Zhang, **Meng**, *Loyola Marymount*. Los Angeles, CA. Email: Meng.Zhang@lmu.edu. Research: East Asia, China.

Zhang, **Mindi**. Chicago, IL. Affil: Chicago. Email: zhangshuai0408@hotmail.com.

Zhang, **Qiong**, *Wake Forest*. Email: zhangq@wfu.edu.

Zhang, **Ting**, *Maryland, Coll. Park*.

Zhang, **Xin**, *Indiana–Purdue, Indianapolis*. Email: xzhang@iupui.edu.

Zhang, **Ying**, *Ohio State*. Email: zhang.1889@osu.edu.

Zhang, **Yunqiu**, *North Carolina A&T State*. Email: yzhang@ncat.edu.

Zhang, **Zhen**, *NYU*. Email: zz6@nyu.edu.

Zhao, **Jie**, *Southern Maine*. Email: zhaoj@maine.edu.

Zhao, **Luyue**. Chicago, IL. Email: luyue@uchicago.edu.

Zhao, **Xiaojian**, *California, Santa Barbara*. Email: xiaojian@asamst.ucsb.edu.

Zheng, **Xiaowei**, *California, Santa Barbara*. Goleta, CA. Email: zheng@history.ucsb.edu; zhengxiaowei@gmail.com. Research: comparative revolution, constitutionalism in China.

Zheng, **Yanqiu**. Dallas, PA. Affil: Misericordia. Email: jstxmaple@hotmail.com. Research: Chinese nationalism.

Zhou, **Nan**. Columbus, OH. Affil: Ohio State. Email: zn601338684@gmail.com.

Zhu, **Jing**. Berlin, Germany. Affil: Humboldt. Email: jing.zhus@hotmail.com.

Zhu, **Liping**, *Eastern Washington*. Email: lzhu@ewu.edu.

Zhu, **Pingchao**, *Idaho*. Email: pzhu@uidaho.edu.

Zhuk, **Sergei I.**, *Ball State*. Muncie, IN. Email: sizhuk@bsu.edu. Research: Brezhnev's Ukraine social, American studies in USSR.

Ziegenhorn, **William K.** Los Altos Hills, CA. Affil: Foothill. Email: ziegenhornbill@fhda.edu.

Ziegler, **Herbert F.**, *Hawai'i, Manoa*. Email: hziegler@hawaii.edu.

Ziehr, **Andrew J.** Dodgeville, WI. Affil: Wisconsin, Platteville. Email: ajziehr@gmail.com.

Zientek, **Adam Derek**, *California, Davis*. Email: azientek@ucdavis.edu.

Zieren, **Gregory R.**, *Austin Peay State*. Clarksville, TN. Email: ziereng@apsu.edu. Research: Gilded Age, US economic.

Zierler, **David**, *US Dept. of State*.

Zilberstein, **Anya**, *Concordia, Can*. Email: anya.zilberstein@concordia.ca.

Zilfi, **Madeline C.**, *Maryland, Coll. Park*. Email: mzilfi@umd.edu.

Zimansky, **Paul**, *SUNY, Stony Brook*. Email: paul.zimansky@stonybrook.edu.

Zimberoff, **Jordan C.** Geneva, IL. Email: zimjc73@yahoo.com.

Zimdars, **Benjamin**, *Mary Washington*.

Zimmer, **Kenyon W.**, *Texas, Arlington*. Arlington, TX. Email: kzimmer@uta.edu. Research: international migration and radicalism, national/ethnic/racial identity.

Zimmer, **Mary Erica**, *MIT*. Email: ezimmer@mit.edu.

Zimmer, **Thomas**. Bethesda, MD. Affil: Freiburg; Georgetown. Email: thomas.zimmer@geschichte.uni-freiburg.de.

Zimmerli, **Nadine**, *William and Mary; Omohundro Inst*. Williamsburg, VA. Email: nizimmerli@wm.edu. Research: cosmopolitanism.

Zimmerman, **Andrew**, *George Washington*. Washington, DC. Email: azimmer@gwu.edu. Research: empire, social and political theory.

Zimmerman, **Jonathan L.**, *NYU*. Philadelphia, PA. Affil: Pennsylvania. Email: jlzimm@aol.com. Research: history of college teaching, K-12 teachers and controversial issues.

Zimmerman, **Kari E.**, *St. Thomas, Minn*. Email: zimm2550@stthomas.edu.

Zimmerman, **Kenneth**. Henderson, NV. Affil: History Business. Email: kenocc12@gmail.com. Research: scientific methods, debate over why economics doesn't work.

Zimmerman, **Loretta E.**, *Portland*.

Zimmerman, **Patrick W.** San Francisco, CA. Affil: Sidelinesapp.com. Email: pkwzimm@gmail.com. Research: New Media and European Left, regionalism and nationalism.

Zimmerman, **Sarah J.**, *Western Washington*. Email: Sarah.Zimmerman@wwu.edu.

Zimmerman, **Susan C.**, *Henry Ford Coll*. Email: zimmdhsmun@yahoo.com.

Zimmermann, **T. C. Price**, *Davidson*. Email: tczimmerman@aol.com.

Zimmers, **Stefan**, *Georgetown*. Email: zimmerss@georgetown.edu.

Zimo, **Ann E.** Durham, NH. Affil: New Hampshire, Durham. Email: ann.zimo@unh.edu. Research: Muslim population of Kingdom of Jerusalem, medieval nomadic peoples.

Zimring, **Carl A.** Brooklyn, NY. Affil: Pratt Inst. Email: carl.zimring@gmail.com. Research: consumption/waste/recycling, US environmental racism.

Zimring, **David Ross**. El Cerrito, CA. Affil: Diablo Valley. Email: davidrzimring@gmail.com. Research: native northerners in Confederacy.

Zinberg, **Cecile**, *California State, Fullerton*. Email: czinberg@fullerton.edu.

Zinkle, **Austin Chase**. Lexington, KY. Affil: Kentucky. Email: austin.zinkle@uky.edu. Research: far-right extremism, black freedom struggle.

Zinoman, **Peter B.**, *California, Berkeley*. Berkeley, CA. Email: pzinoman@berkeley.edu. Research: Southeast Asia, Vietnam.

Zinsser, **Judith P.**, *Miami, Ohio*. Oxford, OH. Email: zinssejp@miamioh.edu. Research: Emilie Du Chatelet, narrative authority.

Ziobro, **Melissa**, *Monmouth*. Email: mziobro@monmouth.edu.

Ziomek, **Kirsten Laurie**, *Adelphi*. Email: kziomek@adelphi.edu.

Zipf, **Karin L.**, *East Carolina*. Email: zipfk@ecu.edu.

Zipperstein, **Steven J.**, *Stanford*. Email: szipper@stanford.edu.

Zirinsky, **Michael P.**, *Boise State*. Email: mzirins@boisestate.edu.

Zirkle, **Robert A.** Alexandria, VA. Affil: Inst. for Defense Analyses. Email: rzirkle@ida.org.

Ziskind, **Jonathan R.**, *Louisville*.

Ziskowski, **Angela**, *Coe*. Email: aziskowski@coe.edu.

Zitomersky, **Joseph G.** Montpellier, France. Affil: Paul Valery, Montpellier III. Email: zitomersky.joseph@orange.fr.

Zlatar, **Zdenko**. Sydney, Australia. Affil: Sydney. Email: zdenko.zlatar@sydney.edu.au.

Zmolek, **Michael A.**, *Iowa*. Email: michael-zmolek@uiowa.edu.

Znamenski, **Andrei A.**, *Memphis*. Email: znmenski@memphis.edu.

Zoebelein, **Jennifer**. Kansas City, MO. Affil: National WWI Museum and Memorial. Email: jzoebelein@theworldwar.org.

Zola, **Alan G.** Carol Stream, IL. Affil: Benedictine. Email: AlanZola@comcast.net.

Zolberg, **Vera**, *New School*. Email: zolbergv@newschool.edu.

Zoller, **Silke**. Austin, TX. Affil: Temple. Email: silke.zoller@temple.edu. Research: Cold War foreign policy, diplomatic.

Zolov, **Eric S.** Stony Brook, NY. Affil: Franklin & Marshall. Email: eric.zolov@stonybrook.edu. Research: US-Mexican relations 1958-73, 1960s.

Zombek, **Angela Marie**, *North Carolina, Wilmington*. Email: zombeka@uncw.edu.

Zonderman, **Andrew**. Raleigh, NC. Affil: Emory. Email: azonder@emory.edu. Research: German migrations in British Empire, 18th-c English boxing.

Zonderman, **David A.**, *North Carolina State*. Raleigh, NC. Email: david_zonderman@ncsu.edu. Research: American labor, museums/public.

Zook, **Melinda**, *Purdue*. Email: mzook@purdue.edu.

Zophy, **Jonathan W.**, *Houston-Clear Lake*. Email: zophy@uhcl.edu.

Zoumaras, **Thomas**, *Truman State*. Email: zoumaras@truman.edu.

Zschoche, **Sue**, *Kansas State*. Email: suez@ksu.edu.

AHA members in ***bold italic***; *Directory*-listed affiliations in *italic*

Zsigmond, *Zsolt*. Gödöllo, Hungary. Email: zs.zs7308@gmail.com. Research: nationalism, national identity.

Zubovich, *Gene*, *Mississippi State*. San Francisco, CA. Email: gene.zubovich@utoronto.ca. Research: religious liberalism in US, intellectual/cultural.

Zucchi, **John E**., *McGill*. Email: john.zucchi@mcgill.ca.

Zucconi, *Adam*. Colonial Heights, VA. Affil: Richard Bland, William and Mary. Email: azucconi@rbc.edu.

Zucconi, **Laura M**., *Stockton*. Email: zucconil@stockton.edu.

Zuckerman, **Michael W**., *Pennsylvania*. Email: mzuckerm@history.upenn.edu.

Zuelow, *Eric G. E*. Portland, ME. Affil: New England. Email: ezuelow@une.edu. Research: tourism, English pubs intellectual.

Zukas, *Alexander M*. La Jolla, CA. Affil: National. Email: azukas@nu.edu. Research: 20th-c unemployment, 18th-c cartography.

Zulawski, **Ann**, *Smith*. Email: azulawsk@smith.edu.

Zumoff, *Jacob A*., *New Jersey City*. Email: jzumoff@njcu.edu.

Zunz, **Olivier**, *Virginia*. Email: oz@virginia.edu.

Zuo, **Ya Leah**, *Bowdoin*. Email: lzuo@bowdoin.edu.

Zupanov, *Ines G*. Paris, France. Affil: Centre National de la Recherche Scientifique, Paris. Email: zupanov@ehess.fr. Research: South Asia, Catholic missions.

Zupko, **Ronald E**., *Marquette*. Email: ronald.zupko@marquette.edu.

Zurro, *Damian F*. Mishawaka, IN. Email: dzurro@nd.edu.

Zutshi, *Chitralekha*, *William and Mary*. Williamsburg, VA. Email: cxzuts@wm.edu. Research: religious identities in Kashmir, Kashmir and Central Asian contacts.

Zwarich, **Natasha**, *Québec, Montréal*. Email: zwarich.natasha@uqam.ca.

Zwart, *David E*., *Grand Valley State*. Allendale, MI. Email: zwartdav@gvsu.edu. Research: Dutch American ethnicity, history education.

Zweiniger-Bargielowska, **Ina**, *Illinois, Chicago*. Email: inazb@uic.edu.

Zweiri, *Mahjoob*. Doha, Qatar. Affil: Qatar. Email: mzweiri@qu.edu.qa. Research: Middle East, Iran.

Zwicker, *Lisa F*., *Indiana, South Bend*. Mishawaka, IN. Email: zwicker@iusb.edu; lisaswartout@yahoo.com. Research: Jewish women in Central Europe, gender and culture.

Zwicker, *Steven*, *Washington, St. Louis*. Email: szwicker@wustl.edu.

Zwirecki, **Paul Jason**, *OAH*. Email: pzwirecki@oah.org.